Tax Rate Schedules for 2017

Tax Rate for Corporations

Taxable Income		Pay	+	% on Excess	of the amount over
Over	But Not Over				
$0	$ 50,000	$0		15%	$0
50,000	75,000	7,500		25	50,000
75,000	100,000	13,750		34	75,000
100,000	335,000	22,250		39	100,000
335,000	10,000,000	113,900		34	335,000
10,000,000	15,000,000	3,400,000		35	10,000,000
15,000,000	18,333,333	5,150,000		38	15,000,000
18,333,333	—	0		35	0

Tax Rate for Estates and Trusts

Taxable Income		Pay	+	% on Excess	of the amount over
Over	But Not Over				
$0	$2,550	$0.00		15%	$0
2,550	6,000	382.50		25	2,550
6,000	9,150	1,245.00		28	6,000
9,150	12,500	2,127.00		33	9,150
12,500	—	3,232.50		39.6	12,500

2018

CCH FEDERAL TAXATION
Comprehensive Topics

GENERAL EDITORS

Ephraim P. Smith
California State University, Fullerton

Philip J. Harmelink
University of New Orleans

James R. Hasselback
Clarion University

CONTRIBUTING AUTHORS

Ted D. Englebrecht
Louisiana Tech University

Christopher J. Fenn
Georgia State University

Edward C. Foth
DePaul University

Philip J. Harmelink
University of New Orleans

James R. Hasselback
Clarion University

Sharon Lassar
University of Denver

Robert Ricketts
Texas Tech University

Ephraim P. Smith
California State University, Fullerton

Larry Tunnell
New Mexico State University

Wolters Kluwer

Chapters 1–13, 22, 23, and 24 also appear in *2018 CCH Federal Taxation—Basic Principles.*

Revision Author and Consultant: David L. Gibberman, J.D.
CCH® StudyMATE™ Author: David L. Gibberman, J.D.

EDITORIAL STAFF
Production: Jennifer Schencker
Cover Design: Geraldine Lally

ISBN 978-0-8080-4612-7

2700 Lake Cook Road
Riverwoods, IL 60015
800 344 3734
CCHGroup.com

Printed in the United States of America

Preface

CCH Federal Taxation—Comprehensive Topics introduces students of accounting to the complex and absorbing study of federal taxation. *Comprehensive Topics* covers a broad range of subjects from the definition of income to corporate reorganizations.

The order in which topics are introduced in this book represents a simple and clear division among the basic taxable entities. The initial chapters deal with topics affecting individual taxpayers. As the cornerstone for the foundation of federal taxation, these topics constitute an extensive outline of the basics. This book distills the major ideas and operational techniques for dealing with problems encountered in these areas. The second major focus of the book is on corporations and partnerships. Eight chapters examine the tax complexities of these entities. In addition, three chapters cover the taxation of estates, gifts, and trusts and the techniques for retirement and estate planning. The final chapter covers multijurisdictional taxation. Chapter 2, "Tax Research, Practice, and Procedure," is pertinent to all tax entities and acquaints the student with the fundamentals necessary for understanding complex tax issues. Also, it gives students an introduction to doing tax research online.

The twenty-sixth edition of *CCH Federal Taxation—Comprehensive Topics* has been prepared to ensure that all material presented is complete and reflects all tax acts, issued regulations, and case developments through March 2017. *Comprehensive Topics* is designed to be used either in a one-semester class or in a two-semester sequence. This book was not prepared as a restatement of the Internal Revenue Code and related tax law. Many such works currently exist. It was designed as a learning device to present federal tax information in a way that will stimulate thought and planning as well as mastery of the difficult, tightly interwoven intricacies of federal tax law in a sequence different from that presented in the Code. This was done so that common ideas and underlying similarities could be linked in the mind of the student and unifying characteristics could be drawn together to present a clearer and more functional picture of the whole.

This edition continues the practice of using Tax Return Problems. The problems are highlighted as such in the Problems section of the following chapters: 4-7, 10-12, 14, 19, 22, 23, and 25. For faculty teaching the course in the fall semester of 2017, draft copies of Form 1040 and accompanying schedules are usually available in September.

The contributing authors of this volume wish to thank many of their colleagues for helpful suggestions and for the time and energy they have given to improving the manuscript.

March 2017   Ephraim P. Smith

How to Use This Book

CCH Federal Taxation—Comprehensive Topics has been organized to make it easy to study the fundamental concepts of federal tax laws affecting individuals. Special features, end-of-chapter materials, an appendix, and supplementary materials are provided to further assist in the learning process.

CHAPTER OPENINGS

All chapters begin with the same elements: a list of the learning objectives and an overview. This information provides a framework for understanding the material that will be studied in the chapter.

SPECIAL FEATURES

Special features—Keystone Problems, Planning Pointers, and Tax Blunders—appear throughout the book. Their purpose is to make familiar the specific applications of the tax law, suggest tax-saving strategies, and illustrate methods of avoiding undesired tax consequences. Additionally, vivid and realistic examples to illustrate salient points are included within the chapters to show application of the law and accounting techniques.

END-OF-CHAPTER MATERIALS

Every chapter ends with a summary of the material covered. Questions and Problems follow for applying the principles learned and allowing the instructor to evaluate and recall the main ideas discussed in the chapter. The problems are sequenced in the order in which the topics are presented in the chapter. Also included are Comprehensive Problems and Research Problems. Comprehensive Problems are designed to develop computational skills, while the purpose of the Research Problems is to provide an opportunity to learn and utilize the methodology of tax research.

END-OF-BOOK MATERIALS

In addition to the Topical Index, other useful research materials are found at the end of the book. The Appendix covers various Tax Rate Schedules, and the Glossary of Tax Terms contains over 200 definitions. In addition, the Finding Lists and Table of Cases detail the textbook's citations by Internal Revenue Code Sections, Regulation Sections, Revenue Procedures, Revenue Rulings, and court cases.

SUPPLEMENTARY MATERIALS

A *Study Manual,* sold separately, outlines and highlights the in-depth textbook presentation and contains Objective Questions (and Answers) for self-evaluation. It also includes a series of Tax Return Problems designed to complement conceptual study of federal taxation and to provide exposure to various aspects of tax return preparation.

To order the *Study Manual* for this volume *(CCH Federal Tax Study Manual, 2018),* contact your bookstore or write or call: Wolters Kluwer, 2700 Lake Cook Road, Riverwoods, Illinois 60015 (800-344-3734; CCHGroup.com).

ACCESS UPDATES

CCH has created a special webpage to keep you up to date with changing tax laws and new developments. This page will also hold any revised content that may be created before the next edition is released.

Visit *CCHGroup.com/CTBP* to find information on updates to the book and latest developments!

FREE ONLINE AIDS

CCH® StudyMATE™ is an online learning center for college students. The *Study MATE Fundamental Tax Topics* library was created to supplement this textbook by providing an easy online tutor to help students with difficult concepts and test them on their knowledge. Each course contains online learning features to capture student attention and "Test Your Knowledge" questions to aid comprehension. At the end of each course, a 15-question final exam is presented. Students have the opportunity to take the exam three times. After passing the exam, students can e-mail a completion certificate to their professor.

Professors and students who use CCH textbooks have free access to the Fundamental Tax Topics library for a full year! To view the courses available, visit *www.cchstudymate.com*. To enroll, follow the instructions provided on the tear-out instruction card bound into the book and use the access code as payment.

Anyone with questions, comments, or feedback can contact us at *studymate@cch.com*.

Contents

A detailed Table of Contents for each chapter begins on page ix.

Table of Contents

CHAPTER 3 INDIVIDUAL TAXATION—AN OVERVIEW

CHAPTER 5   GROSS INCOME—EXCLUSIONS

CHAPTER 6   DEDUCTIONS: GENERAL CONCEPTS AND TRADE OR BUSINESS DEDUCTIONS

CHAPTER 7 DEDUCTIONS: BUSINESS/INVESTMENT LOSSES AND PASSIVE ACTIVITY LOSSES

TAX SHELTERS AND AT-RISK RULES

PASSIVE ACTIVITY LOSS RULES

BUSINESS AND INVESTMENT LOSSES

CHAPTER 8 DEDUCTIONS: ITEMIZED DEDUCTIONS

MEDICAL EXPENSES

CHAPTER 11 PROPERTY TRANSACTIONS: NONRECOGNITION OF GAINS AND LOSSES

EFFECT OF COMPLETE LIQUIDATION ON CORPORATIONS

EFFECT OF COMPLETE LIQUIDATION ON SHAREHOLDERS

LIQUIDATION OF SUBSIDIARIES

STOCK PURCHASES TREATED AS ASSET ACQUISITIONS

CHAPTER 17 CORPORATE REORGANIZATIONS

TYPES OF CORPORATE REORGANIZATIONS

CHAPTER 19 PARTNERSHIPS—FORMATION AND OPERATION

CHAPTER 20 PARTNERSHIPS—DISTRIBUTIONS, SALES, AND EXCHANGES

CHAPTER 21 S CORPORATIONS

CHAPTER 22 FEDERAL ESTATE TAX, FEDERAL GIFT TAX, AND GENERATION-SKIPPING TRANSFER TAX

IMPACT OF ECONOMIC GROWTH AND TAX RELIEF RECONCILIATION ACT OF 2001, TAX RELIEF ACT OF 2010, AND AMERICAN TAXPAYER RELIEF ACT OF 2012

ASSESSMENT OF THE 2010 TAX RELIEF ACT

LEGAL TERMS COMMON TO ESTATES AND TRUSTS

COMPUTATION AND PAYMENT OF ESTATE TAX

CHAPTER 23 INCOME TAXATION OF TRUSTS AND ESTATES

CCH Study**MATE**™

Your Personal Online Tax "Tutor"—24/7!

If you find taxes difficult, you're not alone!

Now you have CCH StudyMATE™, a personal online "tutor." With StudyMATE you can plug into online learning any time of day or night. CCH StudyMATE walks you through the most important concepts covered in your textbook using individual learning sessions designed to make learning as easy as possible.

CCH Study MATE is easy to use, and since you've bought our book, you have free access to our Fundamental Tax Topics Library for a full year! CCH StudyMATE courses are designed with web learning in mind, so you can navigate your way through them independently. They are relatively short, but each course covers a substantial amount of material—including the top concepts covered in your textbook. These are student-centered courses with presentations that are different than those found in the text, so they give you another voice—another opportunity for concepts to sink in.

How Many Courses Do I Take?

Your instructor may want you to access all the courses in the fundamental series, you may be asked to take selective courses on certain topics, or your instructor may leave it up to you to use StudyMATE as you choose.

Access CCH Study MATE at www.cchstudymate.com

For your records, print your User ID and Password below:

User ID: _____

Password: _____

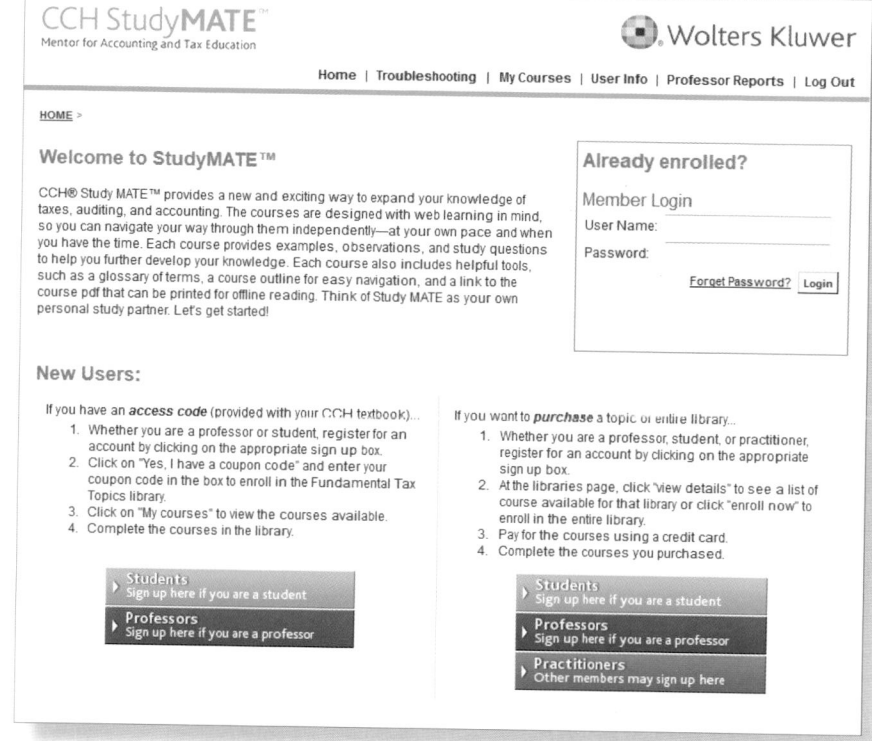

So, How Do I Get In?

Getting started is easy.

1. Go to www.cchstudymate.com and follow the instructions for New Users with an ACCESS CODE to sign up for a free account. Fill in the information on the registration page including a user ID and password of your choice.

2. Continue following the online instructions to enter your access code (provided below).

3. Click on MY COURSES to view the list of online courses, then click on the course title to begin.

ACCESS CODE:

CCHSM_18_COMP_1_154003

Technical Support: 866-798-5897 • support@learning.net

Wolters Kluwer • 2700 Lake Cook Road • Riverwoods, IL 60015

Take advantage of all the CCH StudyMATE courses offered!

The Fundamental Topics library covers the most important federal tax concepts typically covered in a one- or two-semester tax course.

- Accumulated Earnings and Personal Holding Company Taxes
- Alternative Minimum Tax
- Business Deductions
- Calculating Gain or Loss Realized from a Disposition of Property
- Characterization of Gain or Loss from a Disposition of Property
- Deductions for Losses and Bad Debts
- Deductions for an Individual's Personal and Investment Expenses
- Distributions Liquidating a C Corporation
- Distributions by C Corporations to Their Shareholders
- Education Savings Plans and Other Tax Breaks for Educational Expenses
- Estate Tax
- Federal Income Taxation—An Overview
- Federal Tax Practice and Procedure
- Generation-Skipping Transfer Tax
- Gift Tax
- Gross Income
- Gross Income—Exclusions
- Income Tax Credits
- Income Taxation of Trusts, Estates, and Their Beneficiaries
- Multijurisdictional Taxation: International and State and Local Transactions
- Nonrecognition of Gain or Loss from a Disposition of Property
- Organization and Income of C Corporations
- Partnerships-Distributions to Partners and Sales of Partnership Interests
- Partnerships—Formation and Operation
- Qualified and Nonqualified Retirement Plans (Including IRAs)
- Reorganization of a C Corporation
- S Corporations
- Tax Accounting

Chapter

1

Introduction to Federal Taxation and Understanding the Federal Tax Law

OBJECTIVES

After completing Chapter 1, you should be able to:

1. Identify types of taxes used by federal and state governments to raise revenues.
2. Understand the methods of tax collection and the trends shown by tax collection statistics.
3. Differentiate between tax avoidance and tax evasion.
4. Recall the underlying rationale of the federal income tax and its historical development.
5. Describe the route a tax bill takes until enacted into law.
6. Define the basic tax concepts and terms of federal income taxation.

INTRODUCTION

Federal taxation is the fuel by which Americans power their "Ship of State." The tax structure which supports our federal government has gone from quill and ink records of revolutionary assessments to lightning speed computers which calculate and validate millions of income tax returns submitted by individuals and corporations. Federal taxes, in addition to the income tax, include a variety of other taxes covering estates, gifts, and customs, as well as excise taxes, and other minor categories of tax. Our governments can thus select among a variety of tax alternatives to produce the revenues required to operate national programs and carry out national policies.

Taxes are big business. Unfortunately, many business decisions are made in the United States today without regard to federal tax consequences. Individuals are concerned with personal income tax decisions and gift and estate tax decisions, while corporations concern themselves with corporate taxes, personal holding company taxes, and accumulated earnings tax decisions. Further, businesspersons must concern themselves with the choice of business entity: corporation, partnership, or S corporation. Differences in tax costs can be considerable. Advantages and disadvantages are virtually unlimited. This book presents information which is required knowledge if you make business decisions.

While most businesspersons (and many advisors) think about how to make decisions in nontax terms, the tax accountant bears the burden of introducing tax considerations. The topics presented in this book must be viewed in terms of decision-making—therefore, tax planning and tax research are of the utmost importance. Tax decisions are not made in a vacuum. Lawyers, accountants, financial managers, and a host of other experts work as a team in the decision-making process. This book is intended to serve as a guide for accounting students and for MBA students interested in gaining insight into and expertise in the tax complexities of business decision-making.

OVERVIEW

This chapter presents information on the magnitude of federal taxes collected and on taxpayer obligations. Then, a brief historical account is presented of federal tax collections prior to and after the adoption of the Sixteenth Amendment to the Constitution, which enabled Congress to levy "taxes on incomes, from whatever source derived." Following this is an introductory discussion of the federal legislative process and an analysis of the social, political, and economic rationale underlying the federal tax law. Finally, basic tax concepts are explained.

Fundamental Aspects of Federal Taxation

¶1101   ## SOURCES OF REVENUE

Types of Taxes

From the very beginning, with the ratification of the Sixteenth Amendment to the Constitution, through various Revenue Acts and many court cases, a set of tax laws has evolved that raised $2.899 trillion, net of refunds, on over 243 million tax returns processed by the IRS in 2015. This was higher than the $2.69 trillion raised in 2014. The federal government uses a number of different types of taxes to generate the cash flow it needs for operating the government. The following is a listing of the various types of federal taxes:

Income taxes	Corporations, individuals, fiduciaries
Employment taxes	Old age, survivors, disability, and hospital insurance (federal insurance contributions, self-employment insurance contributions), unemployment insurance, railroad retirement
Estate and gift taxes	Estate, gift, and generation-skipping transfers
Excise and customs taxes	Alcohol, tobacco, gasoline, other

Over the years individuals have borne the burden in the arena of tax payments. Individual taxes account for approximately 49.83 percent of total tax collections. Corporate income tax collections account for approximately 11.72 percent of total tax receipts.

Historically, Americans have been staunch supporters of the federal government's tax efforts. The rate of participation and compliance is one of the highest in the world. Realistically, the impact of estimating withholding provisions and the threat of government audits have aided in the outstanding record of the Internal Revenue Service.

Individual Income Taxes

Presently the United States government taxes income, transfers, and several transaction-type items (excise, customs, etc.). The major source of revenues is the tax on individuals (see Table 2). In 2015, individuals contributed 49.83 percent of the gross internal revenue collected. Since 1943, the U.S. has been on a pay-as-you-go system. Income taxes withheld by employers increased from $1.17 trillion in 2014 to $1.24 trillion in 2015. In 2015, 119 million individual taxpayers received a tax refund which totaled almost $403.3 billion.

Corporate Income Taxes

Corporate income taxes accounted for 11.72 percent of the total revenue collected by the U.S. government in 2015. The Tax Reform Act of 1986 reduced the top corporate income tax rate from 46 percent to 34 percent. The Revenue Reconciliation Act of 1993 raised the corporate income tax rate to 35 percent. The American Jobs Creation Act of 2004 created many business incentives. The corporate tax rate has changed from 1 percent in 1913 to a high of 52 percent between 1952 and 1962. Generally, corporations are subject to tax based on net income without regard to dividends distributed to their shareholders.

Estate and Gift Taxes

Estate and gift taxes accounted for only 0.66 percent of the total revenue collected by the government in 2015. The estate tax, as we know it today, was enacted on September 8, 1916, and is levied on the transfer of property. The gift tax was originally enacted in 1924, was repealed in 1926, and then was restored in 1932.

Excise and Customs Taxes

Excise and customs taxes are levied on transactions, not on income or wealth. Examples of excise taxes are the taxes on alcohol, tobacco, and gasoline. The government collects the tax, usually at an early stage of production. In 2015, 2.64 percent of the government's revenue, or $76.5 billion, came from excise taxes.

Customs taxes are levied on certain goods entering the country. There are several reasons why the government levies this tax but by far the most important reason is the protection of U.S. industry from foreign competition.

State and Local Taxes

Just as the federal government needs an ever-increasing amount of dollars to satisfy its requirements, so do the states and local communities. State and local taxes are also big business. The major source of revenue for state governments is the income tax and the sales tax. For local communities, the property tax is a major source of revenue. State governments raised $916.5 billion in 2015, up from $875.0 billion in 2014. California collected the most in state taxes followed by New York and Texas.

Value-Added Tax

The value-added tax (VAT) is of fairly recent origin and much more popular overseas than in the United States. The concept of a VAT was first proposed by a German industrialist and government consultant, Dr. Wilhelm von Siemens, in 1918. In the next three decades much discussion took place. France was the first major country to adopt the VAT. In 1919, France instituted a general sales tax. This stayed in place until 1948, when it was replaced with a tax on production at each stage of the manufacturing process.

There are many forms of taxation, but basically all taxes can be categorized as direct taxes or indirect taxes. The federal income tax on individuals and corporations is a direct tax. Indirect taxes are those levied on producers or distributors with the expectation that these taxes will be passed on to the ultimate consumer. The VAT is an example of an indirect tax. It is merely a sales tax assessed at any or all levels of production and distribution. It is applied only on the value added to the product in an early stage of production or distribution. Notice that the VAT is a tax on products, not on business entities. The major drawback of the VAT is that it is extremely regressive.

EXAMPLE 1.1	A sweater is produced at a cost of $10. If the VAT is 5 percent, then each taxpayer, regardless of income level or ability to pay, must pay the fifty cents for VAT.

The VAT continues to be discussed as an attractive source of revenue in the United States. Each 1 percent of VAT would be expected to raise $12 billion. Even with the exclusions for food and medicine, $7.6 billion would be raised per percentage point of tax. Despite these attractions, the VAT worries many Americans. First, it is a very regressive tax. Second, there is some concern that ultimately the VAT will partially replace the personal income tax. Proponents of the VAT, however, maintain that its use would help shrink the "tax gap" (discussed at ¶1121). That is, the element of the population not currently paying taxes would have to pay a VAT tax, since it is a layered sales tax.

Flat Tax

The past several years have seen heated discussions about using a flat tax. Proponents of a flat tax point to the lower cost of administration and the ease of preparation by Americans as the major benefits. A flat tax would take an individual's total income minus an allowance for family size and apply one tax rate. This rate would apply to all individuals. There would be no deductions.

Various senators and representatives have presented proposals for consideration. A flat tax has been proposed composed of two tax forms—one for individuals and one for businesses. Their proposal would tax individuals on total income minus an allowance based on family size and then apply a 17 percent tax rate. For businesses, the tax rate would be the same 17 percent, but it would be applied against the firm's gross revenue minus costs of purchases, wages, salaries, capital equipment, structures, land, and pensions. To date, none of these proposals has been successful.

Fair Tax

The Fair Tax is a consumption tax. The proponents of the fair tax would replace the Internal Revenue Code with a consumption tax. In many respects it would resemble the sales tax that many states now collect. Proponents suggest that low income individuals would receive a rebate from the government as a way to reduce the regressive nature of the tax.

KEYSTONE PROBLEM	The federal government currently uses many forms of taxation, both direct and indirect, to raise revenue. Would it not be more effective and less burdensome just to employ a single tax? What would you consider to be a more effective and efficient system of raising revenue?

¶1101

¶1121 TAX COLLECTION AND PENALTIES

Returns

The Internal Revenue Service processed over 243 million federal tax returns and supplementary documents in 2015—a slight decrease from 2014. This is in comparison to 143 million tax returns processed in 1980. It collected $2.899 trillion in 2015, a 7.8 percent increase from 2014. Taxes and tax collections are indeed big business. Table 1, derived from the 1980 Annual Report of the Commissioner of the Internal Revenue Service and the 2015 Internal Revenue Service Data Book, details the magnitude of work required to support our government. Approximately 61.2 percent of all returns are filed by individuals. In 2015, individuals filed 148.8 million returns, for a total of approximately $1.44 trillion. In 2015, corporate collections increased to $339.8 billion.

Table 1. NUMBER OF RETURNS FILED BY PRINCIPAL TYPE OF RETURN
(Figures in Thousands)

Type of Return	1980	2014	2015	Increase or Decrease Between 1980 and 2015	
				Amount	Percent
Grand total	143,446	239,875	243,249	99,803	69.58
Income tax, total	107,827	185,540	187,730	79,903	74.10
Individual	93,143	147,445	148,841	55,698	59.80
Declaration of estimated tax	8,699	23,608	24,122	15,423	177.30
Fiduciary	1,877	3,824	3,951	2,074	110.50
Partnership	1,390	3,799	3,883	2,493	179.35
Corporation	2,718	6,864	6,933	4,215	155.08
Estate tax	148	34	36	(112)	(75.68)
Gift tax	216	335	238	22	10.19
Employment tax	26,499	30,066	30,196	3,697	13.95
Exempt organizations	444	1,467	1,580	1,136	255.86
Excise tax	909	987	1,025	116	12.76
Supplemental documents	6,064	21,446	22,445	16,381	270.14

Sources: 1980 Annual Report of the Commissioner of the Internal Revenue Service and Internal Revenue Service Data Books 2014 and 2015.

Tax Collections

Tax collections have increased dramatically between 1980 and 2015. This was due in part to the growth in the economy. Table 2 gives data on tax collections from 1980, 2014, and 2015. Obviously, the increase in tax collections from 1980 to 2015 is staggering—$2,380,029,294,000. Now, notice the detail. Corporate taxes have increased 369.5 percent between 1980 and 2015, while individual income taxes have increased 402.4 percent. Estate and gift taxes have increased 194 percent in the same period. Keep these figures in mind as you read the chapters that follow.

Just as the dollar amounts have increased in tax collections, so has the number of returns filed. From 1980 to 2015, the number of corporate income tax returns increased by 155.1 percent. During the same time period, the number of individual income tax returns increased by 59.8 percent. The number of individuals requesting an individual income tax refund decreased slightly in 2015 to 119 million.

Table 2. GROSS INTERNAL REVENUE COLLECTIONS (net of refunds)
(Figures in Thousands)

Source	Percent of 2015 Collections	1980	2014	2015	Increase or Decrease Between 1980 and 2014	
					Amount	Percent
Grand total	100.00	$519,375,273	$2,690,755,432	$2,899,404,567	$2,380,029,294	458.25
Income taxes, total	61.55	359,927,392	1,629,309,851	1,784,565,232	1,424,637,840	395.81
Corporation	11.72	72,379,610	317,827,591	339,835,905	267,456,295	369.52
Individual	49.83	287,547,782	1,311,482,260	1,444,729,327	1,157,181,545	402.43
Employment taxes, total	35.15	128,330,480	972,398,691	1,019,263,017	890,932,537	694.25
Old-age, survivors, disability, and hospital insurance	34.62	122,486,499	958,001,399	1,003,876,259	881,389,760	719.58
Unemployment insurance	0.31	3,309,000	8,463,751	8,956,148	5,647,148	170.66
Railroad retirement	0.22	2,534,981	5,933,541	6,430,610	3,895,629	153.67
Estate and gift taxes, total	0.66	6,498,381	19,275,209	19,119,016	12,620,635	194.21
Excise taxes, total	2.64	24,619,021	69,771,681	76,457,302	51,838,281	210.56

Sources: 1980 Annual Report of the Commissioner of the Internal Revenue Service and Internal Revenue Service Data Books 2014 and 2015.

Tax Audits and Penalties

The U.S. tax system is a voluntary compliance tax system. The total number of federal tax returns filed in 2015 was 243,249,000, of which 148,841,000 were filed by individual taxpayers. The IRS conducted examinations of 1,373,788 returns, and on the basis of these examinations, it recommended additional tax and penalties of $25.1 billion.

Although audits of individual returns made up the bulk of the examinations (1,228,117 returns), they resulted in only $12.3 billion of the total recommended collections, while audits of corporate returns yielded $10.4 billion. Of course, audits do not always favor the IRS, as evidenced by the fact that, of the individual returns examined, almost 40,000 resulted in additional refunds; this amount was up from 38,000 in 2014.

Until recently, there had been an upsurge in the number of taxpayers who illegally sought, either openly or covertly, to reduce or eliminate their tax obligation. However, the IRS has responded to the challenge by taking advantage of the developing computer technology. Computers already scrutinize tax returns, check errors, and perform a number of routine, repetitive tasks with speed, efficiency, and great accuracy. The IRS continues to match almost all information returns that businesses are required to submit on magnetic media to verify that correct amounts are reported on taxpayers' returns. Information returns include W-2 Forms listing salary and 1099 Forms listing other income.

In 2015, the IRS audited over 1.2 million individual income tax returns or 0.8 percent of all individual tax returns. The percentage of returns audited was slightly lower than the previous year. Table 3 presents information on the percentage of returns audited by type of return.

For years, the audit rate for individual returns had been declining. For fiscal year 2015, the audit rate for individual returns was 0.8 percent. In FY 1997 it was 1.28 percent, and in FY 1995 it was 1.67 percent.

Table 3. PERCENTAGE OF RETURNS AUDITED

Type of Return	Percentage Audited	
	2014	2015
Individual	0.9	0.8
Partnership	0.4	0.5
Corporation	1.3	1.3
Estate	8.5	7.8
Gift	0.8	0.9
Excise	1.5	1.3
Employment	0.2	0.2

Sources: Internal Revenue Service Data Books 2014 and 2015.

Because of severe budget deficits during the late 1980s and 1990s, the personnel needed to audit the growing number of returns filed have not been added. A major reason for the decline in audit rates has been staff reduction at the IRS and the movement of IRS personnel to focus on customer service. Since the late 1980's, staff in the examinations division was reduced by over 30 percent. Table 4 graphically depicts the percentage of returns audited by the Internal Revenue Service.

Table 4. PERCENTAGE OF RETURNS AUDITED—1980—2015

Sources: 1980 Annual Report of the Commissioner of the Internal Revenue Service and Internal Revenue Service Data Book 2015.

Naturally, for certain types of taxpayers and those with higher incomes, the probability of audit is much greater. Individuals with income of over $100,000 were most likely to be audited.

The Internal Revenue Service has acknowledged that the problem of tax evasion is indeed a serious one. The "tax gap," that is, the total revenue lost through tax evasion, has increased from $81 billion in 1981 to $345 billion in 2001 and to $450 billion in 2006. IRS officials estimate that enforcement activities along with late payments have recovered $65 billion of the tax gap for 2006 resulting in a net tax gap in 2006 of $385 billion. The IRS updated the study and the average annual tax gap for 2008–2010 was $458 million. Enforcement activities recovered $52 billion for a net annual tax gap of $406 billion. The IRS estimated that 61 percent of the tax gap was caused by individuals and the remainder by corporations. Today, the voluntary compliance rate is estimated by the Commissioner of Internal Revenue to be 83 to 85 percent. Each percentage point of noncompliance costs the government $26 billion in lost revenue.

The Tax Reform Act of 1986 closed many of the loopholes associated with tax shelters. Since 1988 the IRS has been using a revised audit-selection formula that is aimed at high-income returns. Further, the Tax Acts of 1986 and 1987, the Technical and Miscellaneous Revenue Act of 1988, and the Revenue Reconciliation Acts of 1989, 1990, and 1993 changed the penalties imposed on taxpayers for not complying with the tax laws.

The Improved Penalty and Compliance Act, which was incorporated into the Revenue Reconciliation Act of 1989, revamped the civil tax penalty provisions of the Internal Revenue Code. The goal was to create a fairer, less complex, and more effective penalty system. The Act made changes in the following broad areas:

1. Document and information return penalties
2. Accuracy-related penalties

3. Preparer, promoter, and protestor penalties
4. Penalties for failures to file or pay tax

¶1131   TAXPAYER OBLIGATIONS

Tax accountants, lawyers, and businesspersons, since the inception of the first federal income tax law, have concerned themselves with choosing among the various forms a transaction may take. There is an acute awareness among tax accountants that tax consequences of an action may differ depending upon procedural variations and alternative approaches to a business decision. The increasing complexity of the modern tax laws serves only to accentuate the problem.

Because of the extreme difficulty experienced in trying to differentiate between tax avoidance and tax evasion, Congress enacted, in the 1954 Internal Revenue Code, a provision which illustrates circumstances that constitute prima facie evidence of the tainted purpose. The 1986 Code contends with the problem of criminal tax evasion in Section 7201, entitled "Attempt to Evade or Defeat Tax." It reads:

> Any person who willfully attempts in any manner to evade or defeat any tax imposed by this title or the payment thereof shall, in addition to other penalties provided by law, be guilty of a felony and, upon conviction thereof, shall be fined not more than $100,000 ($500,000 in the case of a corporation), or imprisoned not more than five years, or both, together with the costs of prosecution.

The goal of every businessperson should be profit maximization. The government endorses this goal. Tax avoidance is legal and a legitimate pursuit of a business entity.

Tax Avoidance

All citizens have the prerogative to arrange their transactions and affairs in such a manner as to reduce their tax liabilities. A good businessperson is obligated to search out those transactions and to time those events which will lower the tax liability. Judge Learned Hand, in S.R. Newman, declared many years ago:

> Over and over again courts have said that there is nothing sinister in so arranging one's affairs as to keep taxes as low as possible. Everybody does so, rich or poor; and all do right, for nobody owes any public duty to pay more than the law demands: taxes are enforced extractions, not voluntary contributions. To demand more in the name of morals is mere cant. CA-2, 47-1 USTC ¶9175, 159 F.2d 848.

There is a clear demarcation between tax avoidance and tax evasion. The saving of tax dollars requires specific actions so as to avoid the tax liability prior to the time it would have occurred according to law. It requires the proper handling of affairs so that items of income are subjected to a lower tax rate than would apply if no action had been taken. In some instances, it requires the postponing of income which is subject to taxation until a time when the individual's tax bracket would be lower.

Tax Evasion

To be guilty of evading taxes, the individual must already have a tax liability. All actions must be definitely complete, and in spite of this liability, the taxpayer does not report income. The courts have ruled that it is not wrong to find a form of a transaction that does not lead to any tax liability. However, there is a legal obligation to disclose a tax liability based on completed transactions, and the refusal to report the tax liability is illegal.

The Tax Court in *Berland's Inc. of South Bend* (16 TC 182, acq., 1951-2 CB 1, Dec. 18,057) said that the purpose of tax evasion must be the "principal" purpose, and the taxpayer is not guilty of tax evasion merely because the tax consequences of the particular transaction are considered. Furthermore, the Tax Court said:

> The consideration of the tax aspects of the plan was no more than should be expected of any business bent on survival under the tax rates then current. Such consideration is only part of ordinary business prudence.

What frequently distinguishes tax avoidance from tax evasion is the intent of the taxpayer. The intent to evade tax occurs when a taxpayer knowingly misrepresents the facts. Intent is a mental process, a state of mind. A taxpayer's intent is judged by his or her actions. The taxpayer who knowingly understates income leaves evidence in the form of identifying earmarks, referred to as "badges" of fraud. Internal revenue agents are on the lookout for these badges of fraud. The more common badges are:

1. Understatement of income. The IRS considers the failure to report entire sources of income, such as tips, or specific items where similar items are included in income, such as dividends received, as an

indication that there may have been an understatement of income. Other such indications include the unexplained failure to report substantial amounts of income determined by the IRS to have been received, the concealment of bank accounts or other property, and the failure to deposit receipts to a business account contrary to normal practices.

2. Claiming of fictitious or improper deductions. To the IRS, a substantial overstatement of deductions is a badge of fraud that could warrant a further look at the taxpayer's books. Other indications of improper deductions are the inclusion of obviously unallowable items in unrelated accounts and the claiming of fictitious deductions or dependency deductions for nonexistent, deceased, or self-supporting persons.

3. Accounting irregularities. Accounting practices that are considered a badge of fraud include the keeping of two sets of books or no books, false entries, backdated or postdated documents, inadequate records, and discrepancies between book and return amounts.

4. Allocation of income. The distribution of profits to fictitious partners and the inclusion of income or deductions in the return of a related taxpayer with a lower tax rate than that of the taxpayer are indications of an intentional misstatement of taxable income.

5. Acts and conduct of the taxpayer. Aside from the improper reporting of income or deductions, a taxpayer's conduct can give the IRS reason to question the propriety of a return. For example, false statements, attempts to hinder an examination of a return, the destruction of books or records, the transfer of assets for purposes of concealment, or the consistent underreporting of income over a period of years are badges of fraud.

The presence of one or more of these badges of fraud does not in itself mean that the return is fraudulent. However, it should alert an examiner that additional probing and inquiry are necessary. Internal Revenue Manual, Sec. 4.10.

Corporate Tax Avoidance

Normally, the Commissioner and the courts accept a corporation as being distinct from its shareholders. However, if it appears that a sham transaction has taken place, then the Commissioner has grounds for taking action. Judge Learned Hand, in summarizing many cases on the subject of tax avoidance v. tax evasion, stated in *National Investors Corp. v. Hoey*:

> To be a separate jural person for purposes of taxation, a corporation must engage in some industrial, commercial, or other activity besides avoiding taxation: in other words, that the term "corporation" will be interpreted to mean a corporation which does some "business" in the ordinary meaning; and that escaping taxation is not "business" in the ordinary meaning. 44-2 USTC ¶9407, 144 F.2d 466, 467-68 (CA-2 1944).

Section 269 of the Internal Revenue Code provides the Commissioner with a very important tool in judging whether or not a corporate acquisition is tax avoidance or merely a sham. If the Commissioner feels that there is no principal purpose for the tax-free acquisition, "such deduction, credit, or other allowance" may be disallowed. The key defense by the taxpayer is to substantiate that there was indeed a "principal purpose." If there is a principal purpose, nothing stops the taxpayer from having other purposes, such as the saving of taxes. *Kershaw Mfg. Co., Inc.*, 24 TCM 228, TC Memo. 1965-44, Dec. 27,268(M).

Taxpayer's Assessment of Tax Liability

In order to decrease potential tax liability, the taxpayer must choose the action that will allow the greatest tax savings. An example of a tax savings device is investment in municipal bonds instead of corporate bonds. The interest derived from corporate bonds is taxable income, whereas the interest received from municipal bonds is tax free. In the above example, the taxpayer does not have to hide the fact that there is a lower tax liability on the profit.

When contemplating a transaction, the taxpayer makes an assessment of the tax liability. Naturally, any doubtful issues are resolved in the taxpayer's own favor. Certainly, there is nothing fraudulent about using this procedure. On the other hand, if the taxpayer knowingly overstates expenses, thereby reducing the tax liability, then the taxpayer is guilty of tax evasion.

¶1151

BRIEF HISTORY OF THE FEDERAL INCOME TAX

The origin of taxation in the United States dates back to the Constitution and, therefore, the Constitution is the ultimate source of the power to tax. Originally, the Constitution empowered Congress "to lay and collect taxes, duties, imports and excises, to pay the debts and provide for the common defense and general welfare of the United States." In granting this power, Congress also limited the power of taxation in that "all duties, imports, and excises shall be uniform throughout the United States, that direct taxes should be laid in proportion to the population." It was within these confinements that many cases tested the constitutionality of the early tax laws—a test many of the taxes did not pass. During the late 1800s, the terms "uniform" and "direct taxes" were very important concepts.

Income Tax Law of 1894

In the late 1880s, support was mounting at the state level for an income tax. In Ohio, the State Democratic Convention approved a graduated income tax in the summer of 1891. Reflecting on the mood of the country at that time, William Jennings Bryan supported an income tax as preferential to a tax on tobacco and beer which he felt would put an unfair hardship on the poor. Although this proposed tax and others like it were never passed, they encouraged others to investigate the possibilities of a federal income tax. Ultimately this led to the actual passage of the Wilson Tariff Bill of 1894. This bill was not an income tax bill; however, an amendment was attached to the bill which allowed for an income tax. The provisions of this income tax law stated that the tax would commence on January 1, 1895, and continue until January 1, 1900. It was a 2 percent tax on all "gains, profits, and income" over $4,000 "derived from any kind of property, rents, interest, dividends, or salaries, or from any profession, trade, employment, or vocation." Income was defined to include interest on all securities except federal bonds which were exempt by law of their issuance from any federal taxation. The Act also imposed a 2 percent tax on net profits of corporations but not on partnerships.

There was much criticism of this law. Concerns arose that provisions such as the $4,000 exemption made the law discriminatory against certain groups. Consequently, many cases were brought before the courts. The major point raised by opponents of the Act was whether or not such a tax on income derived from property was a "direct tax" in the sense commonly understood in the Constitution. A direct tax was held to be a tax on the land and, therefore, had to be apportioned among the states.

The Supreme Court declared the law unconstitutional in the famous *Pollock v. Farmers' Loan & Trust Co.* case, 157 U.S. 429, 15 S.Ct. 673 (1895). It characterized the income tax as a "direct tax" and stated that the Constitution provides that "no direct tax shall be laid, unless in proportion to the census or enumeration hereinbefore directed to be taken." Therefore, the Court invalidated a significant portion of the law and rendered income tax apportionment impossible. Further, the Court considered the property tax a direct tax and excise and duties taxes as indirect taxes. The Court stated, in a five-to-four decision, that a tax on real estate and on personal property is a direct tax and, therefore:

> unconstitutional and void, because not apportioned according to representation, all these sections constituting one entire scheme of taxation, are necessarily invalid.

The Court expressed, in one of its longest opinions, no opinion on whether or not the income tax provisions were unconstitutional. Thus, with this decision, the first federal income tax law since the Civil War in the United States was declared to be unconstitutional.

Corporation Excise Tax of 1909

Support for an income tax was growing even though the courts had voided all attempts made by Congress. Government was becoming more costly and new sources of revenue were essential. The Spanish American War produced a great need for funds, and many believed that an income tax was the only solution. In the Pollock decision, the Supreme Court voted five to four that the tax was unconstitutional. By late 1908, it was abundantly clear that only by passage of a constitutional amendment would the government receive the power needed to impose a federal income tax. Therefore, an amendment was passed by Congress in 1909. However, because of the length of time required to ratify a constitutional amendment, Congress simultaneously passed the Corporation Excise Tax of 1909. The Supreme Court had ruled in the Pollock case that an "excise tax" was not required to be apportioned. Further, the Court indicated in several cases that an income tax on corporations would be upheld if it were deemed an excise tax levied on corporations for the privilege of carrying on or doing business as a corporation, granted the amount of tax due was based upon the net income of the corporation.

The Tax Act of 1909 was the first Act to be upheld by the courts that taxed corporate profits. Prior to this time, corporate profits were tax free except for a short period of time during the Civil War. The 1909 Act provided that corporations would pay an annual special excise tax. This tax amounted to 1 percent on net income over $5,000 exclusive of dividends from other corporations.

As can be imagined, many influential people objected to the 1909 Act. By 1910, fifteen cases challenging the Act had reached the Supreme Court. In a unanimous decision, the Supreme Court upheld that the Tax Act of 1909 was not a direct tax, but an indirect tax and "an excise upon the particular privilege of doing business as a corporate entity."

The Revenue Act of 1909 was a tax for the privilege of doing business as a corporation, even though the assessment was on the net income of the corporation. A unanimous Supreme Court upheld the law in *Flint v. Stone Tracy Co.*, 220 U.S. 107, 31 S.Ct. 342 (1911).

When examining the differences between the 1895 law which was held to be unconstitutional and the 1909 law which was upheld as constitutional, the difference is indeed in only a few words, changing a tax upon income to a tax measured by income. Justice Day wrote the opinion for the Supreme Court and stated that the difference was "not merely nominal, but rests upon substantial difference between the mere ownership of property and the actual doing of business in a certain way."

Sixteenth Amendment and the Revenue Act of 1913

Taxation laws as we know them today derive their authority from the Sixteenth Amendment as passed by Congress on July 12, 1909. The amendment stated:

> The Congress shall have power to lay and collect taxes on incomes, from whatever source derived, without apportionment among the several States, and without regard to any census or enumeration.

Alabama became the first state to ratify the amendment in the same year that it was passed—1909. On February 25, 1913, the final vote for ratification was received.

Congress now was given the clear authority to enact a tax on income from whatever source derived. Taxes could be either direct or indirect and could be imposed without regard to any census or enumeration.

On October 3, 1913, pursuant to the power granted by the Sixteenth Amendment, Congress enacted the Revenue Act of 1913 which imposed a tax on the net income of individuals and corporations. The Revenue Act of 1913 was retroactive to March 1, 1913. This date is important for tax purposes because this is the date which is sometimes used as a basis for computing gains and losses. Simultaneous to the enactment of the Revenue Act, the Corporation Excise Tax was repealed.

The Revenue Act of 1913 serves as the basis for the income tax laws of the United States. However, it would never have been passed without its two precedents, the Income Tax Law of 1894 and the Corporation Excise Tax of 1909. These two laws laid the foundation and framework for an income tax. The Supreme Court ruling in the Pollock case made it mandatory that an amendment to the Constitution be passed to allow for a direct tax on income.

1913 to Date

Following the passage of the Sixteenth Amendment, there have been many changes in the tax law. Many of the more important changes in our federal taxing system are outlined below. Some of the data for 1916–1962 came from World Tax Series: Taxation in the United States, CCH (Commerce Clearing House), 1963, pp. 117–118.

1913   The Revenue Act of 1913—Normal tax and surtax approved. Personal exemptions established.

1916   The Revenue Act of 1916—Established the estate tax.

1917   Charitable contributions granted tax deductible status. Federal income taxes were disallowed as a tax deduction. Credit for dependents allowed for first time.

1918   Tax preferences and exemptions established. Tax credit was granted for foreign income taxes paid. Carryforward provisions adopted for net operating losses. Depletion deductions for mines and oil and gas wells were instituted. Tax-free corporate mergers and other reorganizations permitted.

1921   Capital gains rates established. Profit-sharing and pension trusts exempted from tax.

1924   Gift tax enacted to prevent avoidance of the estate tax.

1926   January 1, 1926—Gift tax repealed.

1932   Gift tax restored in more effective form.

1934   The personal exemption and exemption for dependents were made deductible in determining net income for the purpose of surtax as well as normal tax.

1935 Federal Social Security Act enacted.

1936 Mutual investment companies allowed deduction for dividends distributed by them.

1938 LIFO adopted as an acceptable inventory method.

1939 Internal Revenue Code of 1939—Set out to codify separately the Internal Revenue laws.

1942 Net operating losses were allowed to be carried back. Provisions were made or changed for medical expenses, alimony, capital gains, and a standard deduction in lieu of itemized deductions.

1943 Current Tax Payment Act—Pay-as-you-go system adopted.

1948 Marital deduction originated for estate and gift tax. Split-income treatment approved for married couples.

1950 Self-employment tax enacted.

1954 Internal Revenue Code of 1954—Successor to the 1939 Code. Completely overhauled federal tax laws. Largest piece of federal legislation enacted to date. Broad changes were made in an attempt to codify income, estate, gift, and excise tax laws along with administration and procedure rules into one document.

1962 The Revenue Act of 1962—Granted a tax credit of 7 percent for investment in Section 38 Property. Further, the concept of "depreciation recapture" was introduced.

1964 The Revenue Act of 1964—Intended to stimulate sagging economy. Largest corporate and individual tax rate reduction since the Act of 1913.

The Act extended depreciation recapture to business realty. Foreign investment income subjected to increased taxation.

1966 The Tax Adjustment Act of 1966—Suspended the 7 percent investment credit. It was reinstituted six months later.

Graduated withholding replaced flat-rate. Corporations required to pay estimated tax more quickly.

1969 The Tax Reform Act of 1969—Investments in commercial and industrial buildings were significantly affected when depreciation allowances were reduced and the recapture rules changed. Investment tax credit repealed.

1971 The Revenue Act of 1971—Restored investment credit at 7 percent.

1974 Employee Retirement Income Security Act of 1974 (ERISA)—Major changes to the entire private pension system.

1975 The Tax Reduction Act of 1975—Reduced taxes for both individuals and corporations. Changed the investment tax credit from seven to 10 percent for a two-year period.

1976 The Tax Reform Act of 1976—Established at-risk rules for tax shelters and eliminated many tax shelters. Also, the Act made extensive changes in the treatment of foreign income.

1977 The Tax Reduction and Simplification Act of 1977—Attempted to simplify the system. Established zero-bracket amount exemption deductions.

1978 The Revenue Act of 1978—Revised corporate rate structures. New structure taxes the first $100,000 of income on a graduated scale, ranging from 17 to 40 percent, and at a 46 percent rate on all taxable income over $100,000. The Act made the 10 percent investment credit permanent.

The Act also made changes to capital gains, tax shelter rules, employee benefits, and estate and gift taxes.

1978 The Energy Tax Act of 1978—Instituted a tax credit for residential energy savings.

1980 The Bankruptcy Act of 1980—Added a seventh type of tax-free reorganization, the "G" type. Clarified rules for tax treatment of bad debts.

1980 The Windfall Profit Tax Act—Excise tax levied on domestic oil.

1980 The Installment Sales Revision Act of 1980—Revised installment sales rules.

1981   Economic Recovery Tax Act (ERTA)—Largest tax cut bill ever passed. Top individual tax rates decreased from 70 to 50 percent. All property placed in service after December 31, 1980, eligible for the Accelerated Cost Recovery System (ACRS). Increased allowable contributions to Keoghs, SEPs, and other retirement systems. Permitted two-earner married couples a deduction to reduce the inequity of the "marriage penalty." Extended the investment credit to include a wider array of investments.

1982   Tax Equity and Fiscal Responsibility Act (TEFRA)—Largest revenue-raising bill ever passed. Tightened up on itemized deductions. New rules on partial liquidations and for the taxation of distributed appreciated property. Tightened up pension rules. Corporate deductions for certain tax preferences cut by 15 percent. Required that basis of depreciated property must be reduced by 50 percent of investment credit. ACRS modified for 1985 and 1986 and Federal Unemployment Tax Act (FUTA) notes increased.

1982   Technical Corrections Act of 1982—Made changes to: ACRS, the investment credit, targeted jobs credit, the credit for research costs, and incentive stock options. Made changes to the Windfall Profit Tax Act.

1982   Subchapter S Revision Act of 1982—Enacted many new provisions for S corporations.

1983   Social Security Act Amendments of 1983—Bailed out the Social Security System.

1984   Deficit Reduction Act of 1984—Composed of two parts: first, the Tax Reform Act of 1984 and second, the Spending Reduction Act of 1984. The Tax Reform Act of 1984 provided for reducing the holding period on capital gains from more than one year to more than six months, extending the ACRS recovery period for 15-year real property to 18 years, taxing interest-free loans between family members, and drastically slashing the income-averaging provisions.

1986   The Tax Reform Act of 1986—The most significant and complex tax revision in the history of this country. The scope of the changes was so comprehensive that the tax law was redesignated the Internal Revenue Code of 1986.

1987   Revenue Act of 1987—Focused primarily on business tax rules. Areas affected included accounting for long-term contracts, limitations on the use of the installment method, application of corporate tax rates to master limited partnerships, and changes in the estimated tax rules for corporations. The Act postponed for five years the reduction to 50 percent of the top estate and gift tax rate.

1988   Family Support Act of 1988—Provided for major reform in the area of modifying the principal welfare program, Aid to Families with Dependent Children (AFDC). Also included in the Act was the modification of employee business expense reimbursement rules. Beginning in 1989 additional amounts will have to be deducted as miscellaneous itemized deductions.

1988   Technical and Miscellaneous Revenue Act of 1988—TAMRA contained a number of substantive provisions. Included in the Act were the taxpayer's bill of rights, limitations on the completed-contract accounting method, and extension of the exclusions for employee-provided educational assistance and the business energy credits.

1989   P.L. 101-140. Repealed Code Sec. 89. The nondiscrimination and qualification rules for employee benefit plans were repealed. Prior law nondiscrimination rules were reinstated.

1989   Medicare Catastrophic Coverage Repeal Act of 1989—Repealed the medicare surtax retroactively.

1989   Revenue Reconciliation Act of 1989—The Act achieved a deficit reduction of about $17.8 billion and accelerated the rate of collection of withholding and payroll tax. The Act also changed the partial interest exclusion on ESOPs. Modifications were also made to the like-kind exchange rules.

1990   Revenue Reconciliation Act of 1990—The Act contained a number of significant changes, including a deficit reduction of about $40 billion in 1991. The Act also increased from two to three the number of statutory rates, 15 percent, 28 percent, and 31 percent. Also, a maximum capital gain rate of 28 percent was established.

1991 Tax Extension Act of 1991—The Act extended, for six months only, 11 tax provisions that were to expire on December 31, 1991.

1992 Energy Policy Act of 1992—The Act greatly increased the amount of employer-provided transportation benefits excludable by employees.

1993 Revenue Reconciliation Act of 1993—The Act raised the tax rates for high-income earners. Changes also were made to the AMT, passive losses, and Section 179. Corporate tax rates increased by 1 percent.

1994 Social Security Domestic Employment Reform Act of 1994—The Act raised the threshold for paying Social Security and federal unemployment taxes on domestic workers from $50 per quarter to $1,000 annually, retroactive to the beginning of 1994.

1994 General Agreement on Tariffs and Trade (GATT)—To offset the loss of revenue from the reduction in tariffs, Congress passed several tax and revenue provisions. The major revenue items were: estimated tax treatment for Code Sec. 936 and subpart F income; increased premiums for employers with underfunded pension plans; and reduced interest rates on large corporate tax refunds.

1996 Taxpayer Bill of Rights 2—The Act included more than 40 separate provisions, many of which provided useful tools for tax practitioners representing clients before the IRS.

1996 Small Business Job Protection Act—The major portion of tax law changes passed in 1996 was contained in this Act. It also contained many technical corrections. The balance of the Act was divided into four major categories: small business provisions, S corporation reform, pension simplification, and revenue-raising offsets.

1996 Health Insurance Portability and Accountability Act—The focus of this Act was on portability of health insurance. However, this Act contained tax provisions that focus on a variety of health-related issues, as well as several revenue-raising provisions unrelated to health care.

1996 Personal Responsibility and Work Opportunity Reconciliation Act—The tax impact of this Act was primarily limited to the earned income tax credit.

1997 Taxpayer Relief Act of 1997—The Act provided significant tax cuts for many taxpayers. Major features included a reduction in capital gains tax rates, expanded IRAs, educational tax incentives, estate tax relief, and a child tax credit.

1998 IRS Restructuring and Reform Act of 1998—The major intent of the Act was to rein in the Internal Revenue Service. Two of the most important provisions of the Act dealt with changing the holding period for a capital asset to be classified as long-term so as to receive the most favored capital gain rate from more than 18 months down to more than 12 months. The second important area of the Act was the "technical corrections" section, which clarified many of the key provisions in the Taxpayer Relief Act of 1997. There were over seventy technical corrections contained in the Act.

1998 Tax and Trade Relief Extension Act of 1998—This Act included extensions of several expiring tax credits through June 30, 2000. The major extensions provided for in this legislation include the research tax credit, the work opportunity credit, and the welfare-to-work credit.

1999 Tax Relief Extension Act of 1999—This Act extended the time period for which tax credits and exclusions continued to be available.

2000 FSC Repeal and Extraterritorial Income Exclusion Act of 2000; the Consolidated Appropriations Act, 2001; the Installment Tax Correction Act of 2000—The year 2000 saw the passage of three important tax bills that contain many provisions impacting taxpayers. The Community Renewal Tax Relief Act of 2000 was contained in the Consolidated Appropriations Act, 2000. This Act renewed provisions designed to enhance investment in low and moderate-income, rural and urban communities. The Act also extended for two years medical savings accounts (MSAs). Also included was a provision expanding innocent spouse relief. The Installment Tax Correction Act of 2000 reinstated the availability of the installment method of accounting for accrual basis taxpayers.

2001 Economic Growth and Tax Relief Reconciliation Act of 2001—The largest tax cut since 1981. The Economic Growth and Tax Relief Reconciliation Act of 2001 (P.L. 107-16) was estimated to provide tax savings of $1.35 trillion over the next 10 years. The Act contained over 440 Code changes and numerous phase-in and transitional rules. The wide range of changes primarily affected individuals, from cuts in marginal income tax rates to changes in contribution limits for retirement plans.

2002 The Job Creation and Worker Assistance Act of 2002 was passed in March 2002. This Act contained a number of general business incentives, special relief for New York City, individual incentives, extenders, and some technical corrections.

2003 Jobs and Growth Tax Relief Reconciliation Act of 2003—The third largest tax cut in U.S. history. The purpose of the tax bill was to jump-start the U.S. economy. The bill contained ten major provisions. Half of the provisions accelerated tax cuts originally scheduled not to take effect until 2006.

2004 Working Families Tax Relief Act of 2004—The primary focus of this $146 billion package was on offering the middle class tax relief.

2004 American Jobs Creation Act of 2004—The primary focus of this $145 billion package was on business incentives.

2005 Energy Policy Act of 2005—The $14.5 billion energy package contained incentives for oil, gas, electric, nuclear and alternative fuel industries.

2005 The Safe, Accountable, Flexible, Efficient Transportation Equity Act: A Legacy for Users—This $286.5 billion, six-year, highway and mass transit bill authorized funds for federal-aid highways, highway safety programs and transit programs.

2005 The Katrina Emergency Tax Relief Act of 2005 (KETRA)—Signed into law by President Bush on September 23, 2005. KETRA provided $6.1 billion in emergency tax relief for victims of Hurricane Katrina. Another major provision of the bill was that it provided tax incentives for charitable giving.

2005 Gulf Opportunity Zone Act of 2005—The hurricane relief act is an $8.6 billion package of tax incentives primarily aimed at the gulf region. Major provisions included creation of Gulf Opportunity (GO) Zones, fifty percent bonus depreciation related to rebuilding in the zones, expansion of Code Sec. 179 expensing for investments in the GO Zone, enhancements of low-income housing and rehabilitation credits within the zones, and expanded tax-exempt bond limits within the zones.

2006 Pension Protection Act of 2006—Provided for significant strengthening of traditional pension plans. Specific focus was on the funding rules for defined benefit plans and strengthening the reporting rules for plan administrators. Further, the Act made permanent the retirement savings enacted under the Economic Growth and Tax Relief Act of 2001.

2006 Tax Relief and Health Care Act of 2006—The Act extended a number of provisions including the higher education tuition deduction, state and local sales tax deduction, welfare to work tax credit, teacher classroom expenses and tax credits for research and development.

2007 Small Business and Work Opportunity Tax Act of 2007—Provided for incentives for small businesses together with an increase in the federal minimum wage. The Act extended the work opportunity tax credit through August 31, 2011. Further, the Act enhanced the Section 179 deduction, extending it through 2010 and indexing it for inflation.

2007 Mortgage Forgiveness Debt Relief Act of 2007—The Mortgage Forgiveness Debt Relief Act was a way of giving tax relief for debt forgiveness on mortgages and continuing the deduction for mortgage insurance payments.

2008 Economic Stimulus Act of 2008—The Act was designed to jump start the U.S. economy. The centerpiece of the Act provided for rebates to individuals reaching as high as $600 and $1,200 for married couples. Beyond the rebates to individuals, the Act also provided for $44.8 billion in business incentives. The major business incentive was the enhanced Code Section 179 expensing. It raised Code Section 179 expensing from $128,000 in 2008 to $250,000 and increased the threshold for reducing the deduction from $510,000 to $800,000.

2008 Farm and Military Acts of 2008—The Food, Conservation and Energy Act of 2008 provided benefits to farmers, ranchers and timber producers. The Military Tax Relief Bill provided benefits to members of the armed forces who are receiving combat pay, saving for retirement, or purchasing a new home.

2008 Housing Assistance Act of 2008—This Act provided first-time homebuyers with a refundable credit of 10% of the purchase of a new home up to $7,500, subject to certain phase-out rules. Furthermore, it provided taxpayers who claim the standard deduction an additional deduction up to $500 or $1,000 on a joint return for state and local property taxes. It also provided an increase for low-income housing tax credits.

2008 Emergency Economic Stabilization Act of 2008—The centerpiece of the legislation was the $700 billion which was made available to stabilize the economy. The Act also included AMT (alternative minimum tax) relief along with the extension of numerous tax provisions that were set to expire.

2009 The American Recovery and Reinvestment Act of 2009—The $789 billion new law contained nearly $300 billion in tax relief. Major provisions included: Making Work Pay Credit, enhancements to the child tax credit, a 2009 Alternative Minimum Tax (AMT) patch, many energy incentives, and extension of bonus depreciation and Section 179 expensing.

2009 Worker, Homeownership, and Business Assistance Act of 2009—The major provisions of the Act were that it extended and expanded the first-time homebuyer credit, it allowed for up to $2,400 in unemployment benefits to be tax-free in 2009, and it allowed for enhanced credits for the years 2009 and 2010 for the earned income credit and the child tax credit.

2010 The Hiring Incentives to Restore Employment Act—This bill is referred to as the HIRE Act. The HIRE Act greatly expanded Code Section 179 expensing, COBRA premium assistance extended through March 31, 2010, and an employer's payroll tax holiday and retention credit for employers hiring workers who were unemployed.

2010 Small Business Jobs Act of 2010—The bill contained several important tax provisions. The Act significantly increased the maximum expensing under Section 179 to $500,000 and increased the beginning of the phase-out range to $2 million for tax years beginning in 2010 and 2011. Also, the Act extended the 50 percent bonus first year depreciation for one year.

2010 Tax Relief, Unemployment Insurance Reauthorization, and Job Creation Act of 2010—The 2010 Tax Relief Act extended for two years the Bush-era tax cuts including the capital gains and dividend tax cuts. Further it cut payroll taxes two percentage points in 2011, placed a two-year patch on the alternative minimum tax and revived the estate tax.

2012 American Taxpayer Relief Act of 2012—The Act allows all Bush-era tax cuts to sunset after 2012 for individuals with income over $400,000 and $450,000 for couples. Also, the Act permanently patches the alternative minimum tax, increased capital gains rates to 20 percent for those individuals making over $400,000 and extended for five years the American Opportunity Tax Credit.

2014 The Tax Increase Prevention Act of 2014 was signed into law by President Obama on December 19, 2014. H.R. 5771 extends temporarily over 50 expired provisions. The law also creates Achieving a Better Life Experience (ABLE) which affords benefits for persons with disabilities.

2015 Bipartisan Budget Act of 2015—President Obama signed into law the Act on November 2, 2015. It contains several important tax provisions especially with respect to partnership audit rules. It eliminates TEFRA, after December 31, 2017, unified partnership audit rules together with protocols for electing large partnership rules. In its place will be a more streamlined audit regime. The Act also makes changes to the Patient Protection and Affordability Care Act (ACA) with respect to employers with over 200 employees automatically enrolling full-time employees into an employer health plan.

2015 Protecting Americans from Tax Hikes (PATH) Act of 2015—The PATH Act of 2015 did much more than just extend the 50-plus provisions that expired at the end of 2014. Some provisions were made permanent, others extended for five years (through 2019) and others extended for two years (through 2016). Among the more notable extensions for individuals are: the American Opportunity Tax Credit, deduction for certain expenses for elementary and secondary school teachers, increases in the earned income credit and transit benefits parity. For businesses the more notable extensions are: enhanced expensing under Section 179, and the research tax credit.

¶1161 FEDERAL TAX LEGISLATIVE PROCESS

When reviewing the tax acts since the mid to late 1970s, it becomes obvious that tax reform is a yearly event. Tax bills are passed for numerous reasons (i.e., revenue needs, incentive for economic development, or to affect the economy). Tax bills in this country have not followed a uniform path. Normally, major tax legislation originates with the President sending a message to Congress. An alternative approach is for congressional initiative on a tax bill.

The Constitution requires that revenue legislation originate in the House of Representatives. Therefore, the first step is for hearings before the House of Representatives Ways and Means Committee. Many influential bodies present recommendations to this Committee—the Secretary of the Treasury, the Office of Management and Budget, etc. After meeting with various bodies, the Committee meets in executive session, and a tax bill is transmitted by means of a Committee report to the House.

The House of Representatives debates the bill usually under a "closed rule" procedure, which permits amendments to come only if approved by the Ways and Means Committee. If the bill is defeated it may be referred back to committee; if it passes, it is sent to the Senate where it is first discussed in the Senate Finance Committee.

Hearings are held by the Finance Committee which might result in amendments to the House bill. The amendments may range from insignificant to totally changing the bill. The bill is then transmitted to the whole Senate. One significant difference between the House and the Senate is that, in the Senate, any Senator may offer amendments from the floor of the Senate. After passage, if there are any differences between the House and Senate versions of the bill, it goes to the Joint Conference Committee, which is composed of ranking members of the House Ways and Means Committee (seven members) and the Senate Finance Committee (five members) for resolution. The Conference Committee version of the bill must be accepted or rejected—it cannot be changed by either the House or the Senate. Assuming passage by the House and the Senate, the bill becomes law when approved by the President. If it is vetoed, both the Senate and the House must vote affirmatively by a two-thirds majority to override the President's veto.

Exhibit 1 illustrates the sequence of events whereby a tax bill is introduced before the House Ways and Means Committee, passes through the House of Representatives, the Senate Finance Committee, and the Senate. As indicated in the final portion of Exhibit 1, if approved by the President, the tax bill will be incorporated into the Internal Revenue Code.

Exhibit 1. THE LEGISLATIVE PROCESS

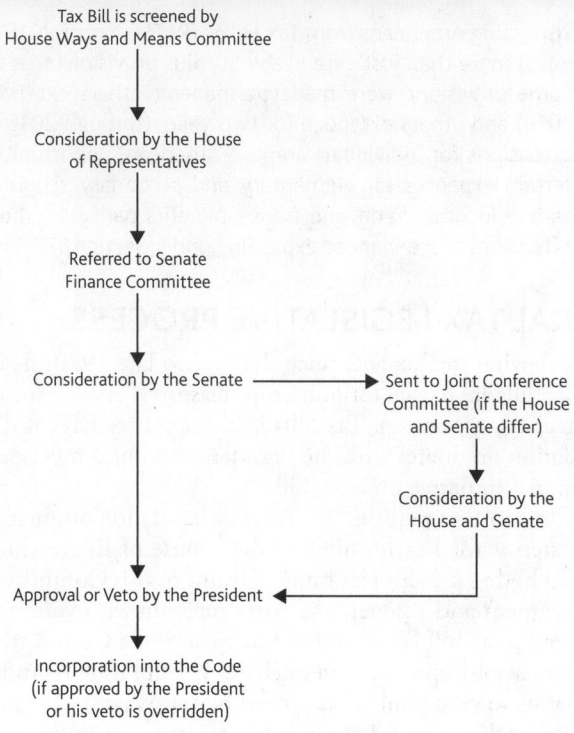

Tax Bill is screened by
House Ways and Means Committee

↓

Consideration by the House
of Representatives

↓

Referred to Senate
Finance Committee

↓

Consideration by the Senate ————→ Sent to Joint Conference
Committee (if the House
and Senate differ)

↓

Consideration by the
House and Senate

↓

Approval or Veto by the President ←————

↓

Incorporation into the Code
(if approved by the President
or his veto is overridden)

¶1165   TAX REFORM

Tax reform acts are passed by Congress and signed into law by the President quite regularly. Several tax reform acts stand out because of the magnitude of the act. The year 1986 was a most interesting year for tax legislation. Both political parties, Democrats and Republicans, were "demanding" tax reform. The Treasury Department presented to President Reagan a massive tax reform plan that would impact the tax liability of most individuals and corporations. President Reagan, in his 1986 budget, called for a tax system that would be "simpler, more neutral, and more conducive to economic growth."

Tax Reform Act of 1986

The Senate passed a bill with only two rate brackets, 15 and 27 percent (28 percent was the final figure approved). Like that of the House of Representatives, their bill called for the removal of many tax deductions. One new feature added in the Senate bill was the drastic reduction in the number of people eligible for Individual Retirement Accounts (IRAs). After much debate, compromising, and political maneuvering, the Tax Reform Act of 1986 was passed and signed into law by President Reagan on October 22, 1986. The Tax Reform Act of 1986 carries the label of the most extensive overhaul of the U.S. tax code in almost 40 years, as well as the most fundamental reform of the U.S. tax structure. The scope of the changes was so comprehensive that the tax code was renamed the Internal Revenue Code of 1986.

One of the measures adopted in the Tax Reform Act of 1986 was that inflation adjustments would be provided annually for several specific items such as the standard deduction, tax brackets, personal exemption amounts, and the earned income credit. Indexing was designed to protect individuals from "bracket creep"—that is, where an individual's income increases only by the inflationary rate but the taxpayer moves into a higher tax bracket. Table 5 presents comparative data for the inflation-indexed items for 2016 and 2017.

Table 5. 2016-2017 PARTIAL COMPARISON OF TAX CHANGES FOR INDIVIDUALS

Item

Filing requirements		2016	2017
If filing status is:		A return is required if gross income was at least:	A return is required if gross income was at least:
Single	Under 65	$10,350	$10,400
	65 or older	11,900	11,950
Head of Household	Under 65	$13,350	$13,400
	65 or older	14,900	14,950
Married Filing Jointly	Both under 65	$20,700	$20,800
	One spouse 65 or older	21,950	22,050
	Both 65 or older	23,200	23,300
	Not living with spouse at end of year (or on date spouse died)	$4,050	$4,050
Married Filing Separately	All	$4,050	$4,050
Qualifying Widow(er)	Under 65	$16,650	$16,750
	65 or older	17,900	18,000

Note: Children and other dependents should see Chapter 3 for special rules.

Table 5. 2016-2017 PARTIAL COMPARISON OF TAX CHANGES FOR INDIVIDUALS—Continued

Item

Tax rates		2016			2017	
Married filing jointly or surviving spouse	10%	0	$18,550	10%	0	$18,650
	15%	$18,550	to $75,300	15%	$18,650	to $75,900
	25%	$75,300	to $151,900	25%	$75,900	to $153,100
	28%	$151,900	to $231,450	28%	$153,100	to $233,350
	33%	$231,450	to $413,350	33%	$233,350	to $416,700
	35%	$413,350	to $466,950	35%	$416,700	to $470,700
	39.6%	Over	$466,950	39.6%	Over	$470,700
Single	10%	0	to $9,275	10%	0	to $9,325
	15%	$9,275	to $37,650	15%	$9,325	to $37,950
	25%	$37,650	to $91,150	25%	$37,950	to $91,900
	28%	$91,150	to $190,150	28%	$91,900	to $191,650
	33%	$190,150	to $413,350	33%	$191,650	to $416,700
	35%	$413,350	to $415,050	35%	$416,700	to $418,400
	39.6%	Over	$415,050	39.6%	Over	$418,400
Married filing separately	10%	0	to $9,275	10%	0	to $9,325
	15%	$9,275	to $37,650	15%	$9,325	to $37,950
	25%	$37,650	to $75,950	25%	$37,950	to $76,550
	28%	$75,950	to $115,725	28%	$76,550	to $116,675
	33%	$115,725	to $206,675	33%	$116,675	to $208,350
	35%	$206,675	to $233,475	35%	$208,350	to $235,350
	39.6%	Over	$233,475	39.6%	Over	$235,350
Head of household	10%	0	to $13,250	10%	0	to $13,350
	15%	$13,250	to $50,400	15%	$13,350	to $50,800
	25%	$50,400	to $130,150	25%	$50,800	to $131,200
	28%	$130,150	to $210,800	28%	$131,200	to $212,500
	33%	$210,800	to $413,350	33%	$212,500	to $416,700
	35%	$413,350	to $441,000	35%	$416,700	to $444,550
	39.6%	Over	$441,000	39.6%	Over	$444,550
Social Security wage base	The maximum amount for 2016 is $118,500.			The maximum amount of taxable and creditable annual earnings subject to the Social Security and self-employment income tax is $127,200.		

Table 5. 2016-2017 PARTIAL COMPARISON OF TAX CHANGES FOR INDIVIDUALS—Continued		
Item	**2016**	**2017**
Personal Exemptions	$4,050, indexed for inflation; reduced or eliminated at high income levels.	$4,050, indexed for inflation; reduced or eliminated at high income levels.
	The personal exemptions for high-income taxpayers whose adjusted gross income exceeds the threshold amount tied to filing status ($311,300—joint returns or surviving spouses; $285,350—heads of households, $259,400—single taxpayers, and $155,650—married persons filing separate return) are reduced by two percent for each $2,500 by which AGI exceeds the threshold amount.	The personal exemptions for high-income taxpayers whose adjusted gross income exceeds the threshold amount tied to filing status ($313,800—joint returns or surviving spouses; $287,650—heads of households, $261,500—single taxpayers, and $156,900—married persons filing separate return) are reduced by two percent for each $2,500 by which AGI exceeds the threshold amount.
Standard deduction		
Basic standard deduction		
Single	$6,300	$6,350
Head of household	9,300	9,350
Married filing jointly or qualifying widow(er)	12,600	12,700
Married filing separately	6,300	6,350
Additional standard deduction for blindness or 65		
Married (filing jointly or separately) or qualifying widow(er)	$1,250	$1,250
Single or head of household	$1,550	$1,550
Dependent's standard deduction	Cannot exceed the greater of (A) $1,050 or (B) earned income plus $350 (limited to $6,300).	Cannot exceed the greater of (A) $1,050 or (B) earned income plus $350 (limited to $6,350).
Nanny Tax	Wage threshold for paying Social Security and federal unemployment taxes on domestic workers is $2,000 annually.	Wage threshold for paying Social Security and federal unemployment taxes on domestic workers is $2,000 annually.

Tax Relief, Unemployment Insurance Reauthorization, and Job Creation Act of 2010

In mid-December 2010, Congress passed and President Obama signed a tax bill that will cost approximately $857 billion. It reduces individual tax rates, provides a more generous $1,000 child tax credit, tax breaks for students, a two-year alternative minimum tax patch, a two percentage point payroll tax cut, and 100 percent bonus depreciation, enhances jobless benefits for people unemployed, and revives the estate tax for decedents dying after December 31, 2009.

American Taxpayer Relief Act of 2012

The "fiscal cliff" was averted. The Act allowed the Bush-era tax cuts to sunset for taxpayers with incomes over $400,000 and for couples with income over $450,000. Many tax breaks that were to expire were extended. It permanently patches the alternative minimum tax and provides for a maximum estate tax of 40 percent with a $5 million exclusion.

Other highlights of the Act include: raising the tax on incomes over $400,000 (individuals) and $450,000 (filing jointly) to 39.6 percent; raising the maximum capital gains tax to 20 percent; five year extension on the American Opportunity Tax Credit; and a two year extension on certain business tax items.

The Act also extends all marriage penalty relief provisions. However, the Act reinstates the limitation on itemized deductions and revives the personal exemption phaseout.

Expired Tax Provisions—Tax Extenders

At the end of 2014, President Obama signed into law the Tax Increase Prevention Act of 2014 which extended 51 tax provisions. These provisions are referred to as extenders. It is the usual procedure of Congress to pass a bill that renews the expired provisions each year. On December 18, 2015, President

Obama signed into law the Protecting Americans from Tax Hikes (PATH) Act of 2015. A number of individual and business tax incentives were made permanent. Below is a listing of the most important extenders that are covered in this book.

Extenders made permanent

- Certain expenses of elementary and secondary school teachers
- Transit benefits parity for employer-provided mass transit and parking benefits
- Tax-free distributions from IRAs for charitable purposes for individuals age 70½ and older
- Reduced earnings threshold for additional child tax credit
- Earned income credit modifications
- State and local general sales tax deduction
- Special rule for qualified conservation contributions
- Enhanced Code Sec. 179 expensing
- Research tax credit
- Tax treatment of certain payments to controlling exempt organizations
- Basis adjustment to stock of S corporations making charitable contributions of property
- Employer wage credit for employees who are active duty members of the uniformed services
- 15-year straight-line cost recovery for qualified leasehold improvements, qualified restaurant buildings and improvements, and qualified retail improvements
- Treatment of certain dividends of regulated investment companies
- Exclusion of 100 percent of gain on certain small business stock
- Reduction in S corporation recognition period for built-in gains tax
- Subpart F exception for active financing income of food inventory
- Temporary minimum low-income housing tax credit rate for non-federally subsidized buildings

Extenders through 2019

- The New Markets Tax Credits
- Work Opportunity Tax Credit
- Bonus depreciation
- Look-through treatment of payments between related controlled foreign corporations

Extenders through 2016

- Exclusion from gross income of discharge of principle residence acquisition indebtedness
- Mortgage insurance premiums treated as qualified residence interest
- Deduction for qualified tuition and related expenses
- Indian employment tax credit
- Qualified zone academy bonds
- Seven-year recovery period for motorsports entertainment complexes
- Special expensing rules for certain film and television productions
- Energy efficient commercial buildings deduction
- Excise tax credits and payment provisions relating to alternative fuel
- Approximately thirty tax extenders expired on December 31, 2016. As of press time, Congress has not acted on them.

Underlying Rationale of the Federal Income Tax

¶1171   ## OBJECTIVES OF THE TAX LAW

The federal income tax is comprised of a complicated and continually evolving blend of legislative provisions, administrative pronouncements, and judicial decisions. The primary purpose of the tax law is obviously to raise revenue, but social, political, and economic objectives are also extremely important. These various objectives, which frequently work at cross-purposes with the revenue raising objective of the law, must be examined and understood to gain an appreciation of the rationale underlying the immense multipurpose body of law known as the federal income tax.

It is easy to criticize the entire tax law for being too complex. However, any time one law attempts to raise revenue and achieve a variety of social, political, and economic objectives, while simultaneously attempting to be equitable to all income levels and administratively feasible for the government to enforce, it cannot avoid being complex.

Tax loopholes are frequently attacked as being counterproductive to the revenue raising objective of the Treasury because they cost the U.S. government billions of dollars in lost revenue. However, some of these so-called loopholes can be thought of as tax incentives, enacted by Congress to encourage certain types of investment, or to achieve specified social, economic, or political objectives.

For example, the tax law provides that interest from municipal bonds is generally excluded from gross income, while interest received from all other sources, including savings accounts and corporate obligations, is subject to taxation. The municipal bond provision thus offers excellent tax benefits for individuals with available resources to invest, but these bonds typically provide a lower yield than corporate obligations.

Primarily because of this tax benefit, municipal bonds are a popular type of investment for wealthy taxpayers. To better evaluate the criticism that municipal bonds are a tax loophole, the probable tax consequences of this type of investment can be examined in the case of a taxpayer in the 39.6 percent marginal tax bracket.

EXAMPLE 1.2

Cliff, a 39.6% bracket taxpayer, has $50,000 available to invest. After evaluating the pros and cons of stocks, bonds, money market certificates, and other types of investments, his decision is limited to the following two choices:

	Freemont	Data-Search
Freemont Highway municipal bonds, rate of interest		9%
Data-Search Inc., corporate bonds, rate of interest		12%
Interest income (before taxes)	$4,500	$6,000
Income taxes	0	2,376
Yield (after taxes)	$4,500	$3,624

Result. Cliff will select the Freemont municipal bonds. Even with a lower rate of interest than the corporate obligations, Freemont provides a larger after-tax yield.

A common but simplistic criticism of this tax provision is that the wealthy individual has used a loophole to avoid $1,782 of taxes ($4,500 interest × 39.6 percent tax rate), thereby depriving the U.S. government of a corresponding amount of revenue. However, this criticism must be weighed against the underlying purpose of the municipal bond provision which is encouraging taxpayers to invest in state and local obligations and allowing the various municipalities to compete for resources in the bond market at a lower rate of interest than corporate bonds.

¶1175   ECONOMIC FACTORS

Over the years, numerous provisions of the tax law have been employed to help stimulate the economy, to encourage capital investment, or to direct resources to selected business activities. Perhaps the most well-known provision of the tax law, designed to serve as a stimulus to the economy, was the investment tax credit. This credit, which served to encourage investment in qualified property, primarily tangible personal property used in a trade or business, had been suspended for a period of time, repealed, reinstated, and again repealed.

Similar to its use of the investment credit, Congress has used depreciation write-offs as a means of controlling the economy. Viewed as a popular stimulus for business investment is the tax benefit resulting from the accelerated cost recovery methods of depreciation. Additionally, the related election to expense allows the taxpayer to deduct as much as $500,000 (in 2015) of the cost of qualifying property in the year of purchase. However, where the cost of qualified property placed in service during the year exceeds $2 million, the $500,000 ceiling is reduced by the amount of such excess. The PATH Act of 2015 makes permanent this business provision. Beginning in 2016 both amounts will be indexed for inflation. For 2017, the expense deduction is $510,000 and the $2 million cost of the property placed into service increases to $2,030,000.

Various other tax provisions have been employed to help stimulate selected industries. Thus, unique tax benefits, such as the provisions for percentage depletion, apply to the mining of natural resources. Correspondingly, farming activities benefit from special elections to expense rather than capitalize soil and water conservation expenditures under an approved conservation plan.

Small business investment has been encouraged by various provisions. For example, certain types of small businesses may elect to file as an S corporation, which essentially provides the limited liability protection of corporate status, while treating most items of income as if the entity were a partnership. Correspondingly, a special rule allows ordinary loss treatment for small business stock.

Even the tax rate structure for regular corporations encourages small business. The current corporate tax brackets are as follows:

Taxable Income					
Over	But not over:	Pay	+	%	of Excess over:
$ 0	$ 50,000	$ 0		15	$ 0
50,000	75,000	7,500		25	50,000
75,000	100,000	13,750		34	75,000
100,000	335,000	22,250		39	100,000
335,000	10,000,000	113,900		34	335,000
10,000,000	15,000,000	3,400,000		35	10,000,000
15,000,000	18,333,333	5,150,000		38	15,000,000
18,333,333	—	6,416,667		35	18,333,333

An additional 5 percent rate is incorporated into the rate schedule above in order to phase out benefits of the graduated rates up to 34 percent. Thus, the graduated rate benefits are phased out between $100,000 and $335,000 of taxable income by increasing the maximum 34 percent rate to 39 percent. Similarly, to phase out the benefit of the 34 percent bracket, the tax rate on income between $15,000,000 and $18,333,333 increases from the maximum rate of 35 percent to 38 percent.

¶1181

SOCIAL FACTORS

Numerous tax provisions can best be explained in light of their underlying social objectives. For example, premiums paid by an employer on group-term insurance plans are not treated as additional compensation to the employees. This provision encourages business investment in group-term insurance and provides benefits to the family of a deceased employee. Also, social considerations provide the rationale for excluding employer-paid premiums on accident and health plans or the premiums on medical benefit plans from an employee's gross income.

Deferred compensation plans allow an individual to defer taxation on current income until retirement. The preferential tax treatment is an attempt to encourage private retirement plans to supplement the Social Security benefits. Other socially motivated tax provisions include the deduction for charitable contributions, the child care credit for working parents, and the credit for the elderly.

Frequently, social considerations help to explain a tax provision that discourages certain types of activities. For example, even though an individual may have incurred a fine or a penalty while engaged in a regular business activity, no deduction is allowed for this type of expenditure. The basis underlying this Congressional policy is that by allowing such a deduction, the law would be implicitly condoning and encouraging such activities. Correspondingly, bribes to government officials and illegal kickbacks or rebates are not deductible, even if related to the active conduct of one's trade or business.

¶1185

POLITICAL FACTORS

Since the tax law is created by Congress, and Congress consists of several hundred elected officials, political factors play a major role in the development of tax legislation. Special interest groups frequently seek to influence tax legislation, while Congressmen themselves are often likely to introduce legislation which would be of particular benefit to their own district or, perhaps, to selected constituents. Of course, special interest legislation does invite widespread criticism if it does not also serve a useful economic or social objective.

As with the economic and social objectives, many politically inspired provisions have been designed in a negative context to discourage certain types of activities. Thus, provisions such as the alternative minimum tax, which imposes an alternative tax rate on taxable income increased by tax preference items, the limitation on investment interest expense, or the accumulated earnings restrictions on corporations can be explained on this basis.

TAX POLICY AND REFORM MEASURES

If there has been a trend through the years in tax statutes, it has been toward reform. The word "reform" itself first appeared in the popular name of the tax act entitled Tax Reform Act of 1969, but the concept of reform had begun to take shape long before and the enactment of reform measures has continued unabated through the years.

During the later part of the 1980s, various changes in the tax law, especially the passage of the Tax Reform Act of 1986, have resulted in the most dramatic tax modifications in tax policy since the enactment of the Internal Revenue Code of 1913. For the first time in 73 years, Congress attempted to address the broad public-policy implications of the entire tax law. In undertaking the revision of 1986, Congress sorted through a massive panorama of loopholes, inequities, and antiquated provisions and eliminated provisions that had lost much of their original social, political, or economic purpose.

Clearly, the tax policy implications of the 1986 revision will be under examination for some time to come. A major impact can be expected on the manner in which individuals and businesses save, invest, earn, and spend their money. For example, with the curtailment of the deduction for contributions to individual retirement accounts (IRAs), high-yield securities such as dividend-paying blue chip stocks, corporate bonds, and "municipals" might become more attractive investments than growth stocks. In fact, many wage earners may find it advantageous to pay taxes on their entire salary, rather than investing in a deferred compensation plan if they anticipate future increases in their marginal tax rates. Correspondingly, with the elimination of the consumer interest deduction, many individuals may shift to making cash purchases instead of incurring nondeductible obligations. Of course, some homeowners may be tempted to circumvent these restrictive provisions by using home equity loans to finance consumer purchases.

The Taxpayer Relief Act of 1997 cut taxes in a fashion that had not been seen since 1981. The reduction of capital gains tax rates will have a significant impact on investment strategies.

The student of tax law can anticipate frequent if not annual changes to the way individuals and businesses are taxed. The source of tax revenue to finance the operation of the federal government during the next decade will be a hotly debated issue. Some tax policymakers will promote new taxation schemes, such as a consumption tax, while others will advocate a tax policy that is revenue-neutral and neutral as to its impact on various income groups.

Basic Tax Concepts

ESSENTIAL TAX TERMS DEFINED

When studying federal income taxation, it is important to keep in mind several basic tax concepts. By understanding these basic concepts unique to federal taxation, the course will be more interesting and meaningful. Because some of the terms set out below have definitions peculiar to income taxation, it is advisable that they be carefully examined before proceeding to the discussion of specific topics. Refer to the Glossary of Tax Terms in the back of the book for a comprehensive listing of tax terms discussed throughout the text.

Accrual basis of accounting

The accrual basis is distinguished from the cash basis. On the accrual basis, income is accounted for as and when it is earned, whether or not it has been collected. Expenses are deducted when they are incurred, whether or not paid in the same period. In determining when the expenses of an accrual-basis taxpayer are incurred, the all-events test is applied. Such test provides that the expenses are deductible in the year in which all of the events have occurred that determine the fact of liability and the amount of the liability can be determined with reasonable accuracy. Generally, all of the events that establish liability for an amount, for the purpose of determining whether such amount has been incurred, are treated as not occurring any earlier than the time that economic performance occurs.

Assignment of income doctrine

The assignment of income by an individual who retains the right of ownership to the property has generally proved ineffective as a tax-shifting procedure. For the assignment to be effective, a gift of the property would be necessary. For example, Ben is preparing to attend Major State College. As a means of paying for room and board, his father assigns to Ben his salary. This is an invalid assignment of income and Ben's father would be liable for the tax. In *Lucas v. Earl*, 2 ustc ¶496, 281 U.S. 111-115, 50 S.Ct. 241 (1930), the Supreme Court ruled that the government could "tax salaries to those who earned them and provide that the tax could not be escaped by anticipatory arrangements and contracts however skillfully devised to prevent the salary when paid from vesting even for a second in the man who earned it." Also, in this case the Court stated that "no distinction can be taken according to the motives leading to the arrangement by which the fruits are attributed to a different tree from that on which they grew."

Basis

The basis of property is the cost of such property. It usually means the amount of cash paid for the property and the fair market value of other property provided in the transaction.

EXAMPLE 1.3	An individual paid cash of $20,000 for an automobile and assumed a $7,500 loan on the car; thus, the basis in the automobile is $27,500.

EXAMPLE 1.4	An individual paid $500,000 for a tract of land and a building. Purchase commissions, legal and recording fees, surveys, transfer taxes, title insurance, and charges for installation of utilities amounted to $70,000. The basis of the property would be $570,000. Any amounts owed by the seller and assumed by the buyer are included in the basis of the property.
	The definition and the determination of "basis" are of utmost importance because it is that figure which is usually used for depreciation and the determination of gain or loss. If property was acquired by gift, inheritance, or in exchange for other property, special rules for finding its basis apply.

Business purpose

When a transaction occurs it must be grounded in a business purpose other than tax avoidance. Tax avoidance is not a proper motive for being in business. The concept of business purpose was originally set forth in *Gregory v. Helvering*, 35-1 USTC ¶9043, 293 U.S. 465, 55 S.Ct. 266 (1935). In this case, the Supreme Court ruled that a transaction aiming at tax-free status had no business purpose. Further, the Court stated that merely transferring assets from one corporation to another under a plan which can be associated with neither firm was invalid. This was merely a series of legal transactions that when viewed by the Court in its entirety had no business purpose.

Capital asset

Everything owned and used for personal purposes, pleasure, or investment is a capital asset. Examples of capital assets are stocks, bonds, a residence, household furnishings, a pleasure automobile, gems and jewelry, gold, silver, etc. Capital assets do not include inventory, accounts or notes receivable, depreciable property, real property, works created by personal efforts (copyrights), and U.S. publications.

Cash basis

The cash basis is one of the two principal recognized methods of accounting. It must be used by all taxpayers who do not keep books. As to all other taxpayers (except corporations, certain partnerships, and tax-exempt trusts) it is elective, except that it may not be used if inventories are necessary in order to reflect income. On the cash basis, income is reported only as it is received, in money or other property having a fair market value, and expenses are deductible only in the year that they are paid.

Claim of right

The term claim of right asks whether cash or property received by an individual to which the individual does not have full claim and which the individual might have to return in the future must be included in income. The question here is whether the taxpayer must report the income when received or wait until the taxpayer has full right to it. In *North American Oil Consolidated v. Burnet*, 3 USTC ¶943, 286 U.S. 417 (1932), the Supreme Court resolved the question by stating that amounts received by an individual under a claim of right must be included in gross income even though the individual might have to refund the amount at a later time.

Conduits

Some entities are not tax paying. They pass through their income (loss) to owners (beneficiaries). A partnership is an example of a conduit. Partnerships do not pay taxes; they merely report the partnership's taxable income or losses. The income (loss) flows directly to the partners. However, partnerships do compute partnership taxable income. Other types of conduits are grantor trusts and S corporations.

Constructive-receipt doctrine

When a cash-basis individual receives income, or it is credited to an account the individual may draw upon, or it is set aside for the individual, the courts have ruled that the individual has constructively received the income. This concept was developed to stop taxpayers from choosing the year in which to recognize income. Once an individual has an absolute right to the income, it must be recognized. A good example of the constructive receipt doctrine is interest earned on a bank account. If interest is credited to the taxpayer's account, it is of no consequence that the taxpayer does not withdraw the money. The day the interest is credited to the account is the day the taxpayer must include the amount in income.

Entity

Generally, for tax purposes there are four types of entities: individuals, corporations, trusts, and estates. Each entity determines its own tax and files its own tax return. Each tax entity has its specific rules to follow for the determination of taxable income. Basically the concept of "entity" answers the question "Who is the taxpayer?" Note that partnerships were not in the list of entities. For tax purposes, partnerships are not tax-paying entities. The income (loss) flows directly to the partners.

Gross income

Gross income, for income tax purposes, refers to all income that is taxable. The law enumerates specific items of income that are not to be included in gross income and, therefore, are nontaxable. With these exceptions, all income is includible in gross income.

Holding period

The holding period of property is the length of time that the property has been held by the taxpayer, or the length of time that the taxpayer is treated for income tax purposes as having held it. The term is most important for income tax purposes as it relates to capital gains transactions. Whether capital gain or loss is short or long term depends on whether the asset sold or exchanged has been held by the taxpayer for more than 12 months.

Income

The fundamental concept of income is set forth in the Sixteenth Amendment—"incomes, from whatever source derived." It is the gain derived from capital, labor, or both. For tax purposes the term "income" is not used alone. The most common usages are gross income, adjusted gross income, and taxable income.

Income-shifting

Income-shifting is the transfer of income from one family member to another who is subject to a lower tax rate or the selection of a form of business that decreases the tax liability for its owners.

Pay-as-you-go tax system

The American tax system is often referred to as a pay-as-you-go tax system. Much of the federal government's tax collections come from withholdings and estimated taxes. The various types of taxpayers pay tax throughout the year, not just at year-end. The United States has been on a pay-as-you-go system since 1943.

Realized v. recognized gain or loss

A gain or loss is realized when a transaction is completed. However, not all realized gains and losses are taxed (recognized). A recognized gain or loss occurs when a taxpayer is obligated to pay tax on a completed transaction.

Substance v. form

Individuals should arrange their financial transactions in a manner that will minimize their tax liability. If a transaction is all it purports to be and not merely a transaction to avoid taxes, then it is valid. If the transaction is solely to avoid taxes and there is no business purpose to the transaction, then it is invalid. The fact that a taxpayer uses one form of transaction rather than another to minimize taxes does not invalidate the transaction. A good example of when substance v. form is a significant issue is in the area of leases. Payments under a lease are tax deductible. Payments under a purchase agreement are not tax deductible. Therefore, it is of utmost importance to determine the true "substance" of this type of transaction. Questions to be asked might include: Do any equity rights transfer to the lessee at the end of the lease period?

May the lessee buy the property at a nominal purchase price? With a lease transaction it is immaterial that the parties refer to the transaction as a lease. The true substance of the transaction controls over the form.

Tax benefit rule

A recovery is includible in income only to the extent that the deduction reduced tax in any prior year by any amount. Therefore, where a deduction reduced taxable income but did not reduce tax, the recovery amount is excludable from income. This rule applies to both corporate and noncorporate taxpayers.

Taxable income

Taxable income for a corporation is gross income minus all deductions allowable, including special deductions such as the one for dividends received. Taxable income for individuals who itemize deductions is equal to adjusted gross income minus personal exemptions, minus the greater of itemized deductions or the standard deduction amount. For taxpayers who do not itemize, taxable income is adjusted gross income minus personal exemptions minus the standard deduction.

Wherewithal to pay

The concept that the taxpayer should be taxed on a transaction when he or she has the means to pay the tax. For example, a taxpayer owns property that is increasing in value. The IRS does not tax the increased value until the taxpayer sells the property. At the time of sale, the taxpayer has the wherewithal to pay.

SUMMARY

- Taxes are indeed big business. The Internal Revenue Service collected $2,899,404,567,000 in 2015.
- Individuals contributed 49.83 percent of all taxes raised by the IRS.
- Corporations contributed approximately 11.72 percent of all taxes raised by the IRS.
- A basic understanding of tax terminology will help business leaders run their corporations.

QUESTIONS

1. Clearly, individuals are carrying a much heavier tax burden than corporations. Is this justified?

2. Some economists have argued that corporate taxes should be eliminated and only individuals should be taxed. Explain.

3. Discuss excise tax when used as a measure for social control (i.e., tax on alcohol and gasoline).

4. Why is the value-added tax (VAT) considered regressive?

5. How might the VAT be used to balance the budget?

6. What is the test which distinguishes between tax avoidance and tax evasion?

7. If your interest is in tax avoidance, name several types of investments that will lower your tax liability.

8. "The tax evader is a criminal." Support or refute this statement.

9. Discuss the badges of fraud.

10. What is meant by the term "tax gap"?

11. Why is income-shifting considered such a major tax planning concept?

12. What was the constitutional impediment to income taxation prior to the Sixteenth Amendment?

13. The federal taxing system has tried to reflect changes in society and lifestyles. Give three examples.

14. What was the purpose of the Sixteenth Amendment?

15. Of what importance is the date March 1, 1913?

16. Where must revenue legislation originate?

17. Which committees of Congress are responsible for revenue legislation?

18. What is the purpose of the Joint Conference Committee?

¶1195

PROBLEMS

19. The legislative process of a tax bill begins with the:
    a. House Ways and Means Committee
    b. President
    c. Senate Finance Committee
    d. Any of the above

20. The Sixteenth Amendment granted Congress the right to:
    a. Create progressive tax rates
    b. Create a value-added tax
    c. Tax income from whatever source derived
    d. Impose a national property tax

21. The value-added tax has great appeal to politicians because:
    a. It has the potential to raise large sums of money.
    b. It taxes the rich and not the poor.
    c. It is progressive in nature.
    d. All of the above.

22. An attractive characteristic of the personal income tax is:
    a. It does not tax the poor.
    b. It is equitable.
    c. It is free from loopholes.
    d. It has the ability to raise a considerable amount of money.

23. The Tax Reform Act of 1986:
    a. Amended the Internal Revenue Code of 1954
    b. Replaced the Internal Revenue Code of 1954 with the Internal Revenue Code of 1986
    c. Replaced the Internal Revenue Code of 1954 with the Internal Revenue Code of 1987
    d. Was found to be unconstitutional by the Supreme Court in 1987

24. The American Recovery and Reinvestment Act of 2009 did all of the following except:
    a. Enhanced the child care credit
    b. Expanded energy incentives
    c. Created a homebuyer credit
    d. Lowered personal income tax rates for the wealthy

25. When approving a tax bill and there are differences between the House and Senate versions, the differences are resolved by the:
    a. President
    b. Speaker of the House
    c. President of the Senate
    d. Joint Conference Committee

26. Net capital gains are:
    a. Taxed at a maximum rate of 31 percent.
    b. Taxed at a maximum rate of 28 percent.
    c. Taxed at a maximum rate of 20 percent
    d. Taxed at a maximum rate of 15 percent.

27. The American Taxpayer Relief Act of 2012 did all of the following except:
    a. Permanently patched the Alternative Minimum Tax
    b. Sunset the Bush-era tax cuts
    c. Installed a maximum 20 percent capital gains tax rate
    d. Extended the American Opportunity Tax Credit

28. Which item listed below is not a capital asset?
    a. Stocks
    b. Pleasure automobile
    c. Bonds
    d. Depreciable property

29. Major features of conduits are:
    a. Pass through their income to owners
    b. Need not file income tax returns
    c. Need not pay taxes
    d. Both (a) and (c) above

30. What are several major provisions of the Emergency Economic Stabilization Act of 2008?

31. **Research Problem.** The following case highlights the right of the taxpayer to select among legitimate business alternatives in order to avoid taxes. Read the case and prepare a written brief.

    Peterson & Pegau Baking Co., 2 BTA 637 (1925), Dec. 775.

Chapter

2

Tax Research, Practice, and Procedure

OBJECTIVES

After completing Chapter 2, you should be able to:

1. Identify the primary authoritative sources of the tax law and understand the relative weight of these authorities.
2. Explain the role of the court system as a forum for both the taxpayer and the government.
3. Develop a familiarity with the various forms of judicial citations.
4. Understand the general organization of a loose-leaf tax service and the importance of a citator service and other types of secondary reference materials.
5. Describe the organization of the Internal Revenue Service and selected rules relating to practice before the IRS.
6. Discuss the examination of returns, including correspondence examinations, office examinations, and field examinations.
7. Explain the appeals process, both within the IRS and through the court system.
8. Understand the possible communications between the IRS and taxpayers, including private rulings, determination letters, and technical advice.
9. Describe some of the more common penalties to which taxpayers and tax preparers might be subject.
10. Understand ethics as related to the tax practitioner.

OVERVIEW

To the general public, the tax practitioner is often viewed simply as a preparer of tax returns. However, from a broader, more professional perspective, tax practice also involves extensive research, creative tax planning, and effective representation of clients before the audit or appellate divisions of the Internal Revenue Service.

Tax research is the process whereby one systematically searches for the answer to a tax question, using the various primary and secondary sources of tax-related information. This involves reviewing and evaluating appropriate Internal Revenue Code sections, Treasury Regulations, Internal Revenue Service Rulings, and court decisions. Research into this voluminous material is typically facilitated by the use of one of the loose-leaf tax services, which are organized and cross-referenced in such a manner as to assist the researcher in the confusing trek through the overwhelming mass of authoritative data. Also, due to rapid technological advances made in computer-assisted tax research, the researcher may access the most complete and up-to-date authoritative data with online tax research services.

The tax specialist needs to understand the organizational structure of the IRS and its administrative procedures to provide fully informed tax consulting services to taxpayers involved in disputes with the IRS. Thus, this chapter includes a discussion of the internal organization of the IRS and how its various administrative groups function, the rules relating to practice before the IRS, and the procedures for examination of returns, including service center examinations, office examinations, and field examinations.

What actions can a taxpayer take if there is an adverse decision by the tax auditor or revenue agent? To provide an answer to this question, this chapter details and explains the appeals process, both within the IRS and through the court system. Another approach available to the taxpayer is the right to request advice from the IRS on the tax consequences of a particular transaction. This chapter discusses the various communications between the IRS and taxpayers, including private letter rulings, determination letters, and technical advice.

Some of the more common penalties to which taxpayers and tax preparers might be subject are also discussed. Tax practitioners should be familiar with the code of professional ethics of their profession since a violation of these standards might mean that "due care" has not been exercised and the practitioner might be subject to charges of negligence.

Tax Reference Materials

¶2001 ## CLASSIFICATION OF MATERIALS

Tax reference materials are usually classified as primary "authoritative" sources or secondary "reference" sources. Primary source materials include the Internal Revenue Code (Statutory Authority), Treasury Regulations and Internal Revenue Service Rulings (Administrative Authority), and the various decisions of the trial courts and the appellate courts (Judicial Authority).

Secondary reference materials consist primarily of the various loose-leaf tax reference services. Additional secondary materials include periodicals, textbooks and treatises, published papers from tax institutes and symposia, and newsletters.

Reminder. While the editorial opinions included in the secondary reference materials are extremely knowledgeable and comprehensive, neither the IRS nor the courts will afford any authoritative weight to these opinions. One exception is Mertens, *Law of Federal Income Taxation.* This tax service is often quoted in judicial decisions.

Both primary and secondary sources can be accessed through one of the computer-assisted research services. These electronic data bases are updated daily and contain many source documents not normally found in the traditional tax library.

Primary Source Materials

¶2021 ## STATUTORY AUTHORITY

Statutory authority is primarily the Internal Revenue Code, but it also includes the U.S. constitution and tax treaties. The authority of the U.S. government to raise revenue through a federal income tax is derived from the Sixteenth Amendment to the Constitution. Following ratification of this Amendment, the federal income tax law was enacted on October 3, 1913, and was made retroactive to March 1, 1913. Various other revenue acts were soon enacted. From these provisions, a loose and disconnected body of tax law emerged, making it virtually impossible to systematically engage in tax research. Accordingly, to facilitate a convenient form of organization, the various revenue acts that were legislated between 1913 and 1939 were codified into Title 26 of the United States Code, known as the Internal Revenue Code of 1939.

In subsequent years, with the growing complexity of the tax law, the Code was revised and rewritten as the Internal Revenue Code of 1954. During the next thirty-two years numerous tax laws were incorporated as amendments into the 1954 Code. Accordingly, the Economic Recovery Tax Act of 1981 (ERTA), the Tax Equity and Fiscal Responsibility Act of 1982 (TEFRA), and the Tax Reform Act of 1984 were included as part of the Internal Revenue Code of 1954, as amended. However, in 1986, as a result of the sweeping changes made by the Tax Reform Act of 1986, Congress changed the name of the tax law to the Internal Revenue Code of 1986.

Organization of the Code

The Internal Revenue Code of 1986 is comprised of nine subtitles (A-I), each consisting of individual, consecutively numbered chapters (1-98). The subtitles most commonly encountered by the tax practitioner that form the basis of this book are Subtitle A, "Income Taxes," including Chapters 1–6, and Subtitle B, "Estate and Gift Taxes," including Chapters 11–13. The remaining subtitles relate to topics such as employment taxes, excise taxes, alcohol and tobacco taxes, etc. Portions of Subtitle F, "Procedure and Administration," including Chapters 61–80, are also examined in this text.

The major portion of the Code dealing with federal income tax is located in Chapter 1 of Subtitle A. This extremely important Chapter, entitled "Normal Taxes and Surtaxes," is further divided into Subchapters (A–Y), and each Subchapter is then generally divided into parts and subparts, which are then divided into sections. These sections are typically referred to as "Code Sections."

The following exhibit (Exhibit 1) provides a Table of Contents for Chapter 1 of Subtitle A of the Internal Revenue Code of 1986.

Exhibit 1. INTERNAL REVENUE CODE OF 1986—SELECTED TABLE OF CONTENTS
Subtitle A—Income Taxes
Chapter 1—Normal Taxes and Surtaxes

Subchapter		Beginning Section Number
A	Determination of Tax Liability	1
B	Computation of Taxable Income	61
C	Corporate Distributions and Adjustments	301
D	Deferred Compensation, Etc.	401
E	Accounting Periods and Methods of Accounting	441
F	Exempt Organizations	501
G	Corporations Used to Avoid Income Tax on Shareholders	531
H	Banking Institutions	581
I	Natural Resources	611
J	Estates, Trusts, Beneficiaries, and Decedents	641
K	Partners and Partnerships	701
L	Insurance Companies	801
M	Regulated Investment Companies and Real Estate Investment Trusts	851
N	Tax Based on Income from Sources Within or Without the United States	861
O	Gain or Loss on Disposition of Property	1001
P	Capital Gains and Losses	1201
Q	Readjustment of Tax Between Years and Special Limitations	1301
S	Subchapter S: Tax Treatment of S Corporations and Their Shareholders	1361
T	Cooperatives and Their Patrons	1381
U	Designation and Treatment of Empowerment Zones, Enterprise Communities, and Rural Development Investment Areas	1391
V	Title 11 Cases	1398
W	District of Columbia Enterprise Zone	1400
X	Renewal Communities	1400E
Y	Short-Term Regional Benefits	1400L

Citing the Code

Code Sections, particularly those found within Chapter 1 of Subtitle A, are cited by detailed reference to section, subsection, paragraph, and subparagraph. On occasion, the reference is even broken down to inferior subdivisions, such as a clause.

For example, Section 453(e)(3)(A)(i) might serve as an illustration.

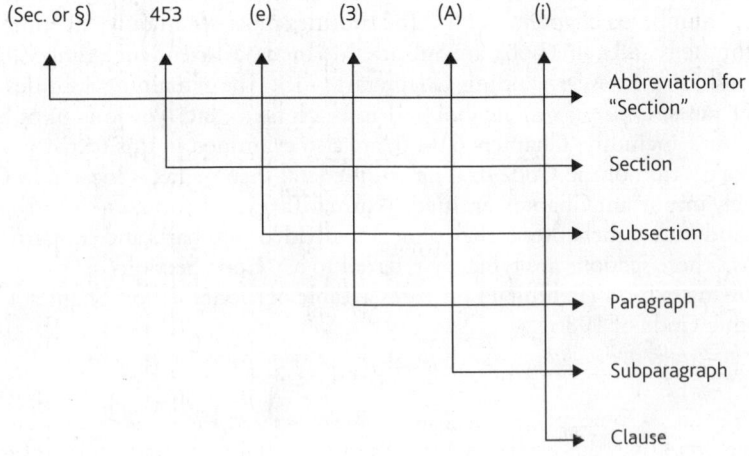

Throughout this text, references to Code Sections are in the form explained above. Unless otherwise noted, references to Code Sections relate to the Internal Revenue Code of 1986. References to the 1939 or 1954 Code are specifically noted.

Congressional Committee Reports

Congressional Committee Reports are the minutes or official statements made by members of the House Ways and Means Committee, Senate Finance Committee, and Conference Committee on their intention in passing a specific piece of legislation. Unlike Treasury Regulations, Revenue Rulings, and Revenue Procedures issued by the IRS that are not binding on the courts, congressional intent expressed in Committee Reports very often is binding as these Committee Reports are regarded as very high authority. Committee Reports are published in the *Cumulative Bulletin* and by private publishers, including Wolters Kluwer, CCH and Research Institute of America. Additionally, the *Congressional Record* reports floor debates in the House of Representatives and in the Senate.

Blue Books

As stated in the House Committee Report to the Revenue Reconciliation Act of 1989 (P.L. 101-239), "Blue Books" have been added to the list of authorities on which taxpayers may rely for interpretation of the tax law (see discussion at ¶2035). Blue Books are prepared by the Staff of the Joint Committee on Taxation for major tax acts. Although Blue Books are generally based on Committee Reports for an act, they often contain additional interpretative information. The IRS has used this interpretative information in numerous rulings as the basis for a particular position. Blue Books are published electronically by Wolters Kluwer, CCH.

¶2035   ADMINISTRATIVE AUTHORITY

As a result of congressional authority, the Secretary of the Treasury or a delegate, the Commissioner of Internal Revenue, is authorized to provide administrative interpretation of the tax law. As noted in Section 7805(a):

> Except where such authority is expressly given by this title to any person other than an officer or employee of the Treasury Department, the Secretary or his delegate shall prescribe all needful rules and regulations for the enforcement of this title, including all rules and regulations as may be necessary by reason of any alteration of law in relation to internal revenue.

Treasury Regulations

Treasury Regulations have generally been classified into three broad categories: legislative, interpretative, and procedural. Legislative regulations are those which are issued by the Treasury under a specific grant of authority by Congress to prescribe the operating rules for a statute. Generally, legislative regulations have the force and effect of law. Interpretative regulations are issued pursuant to the general rule-making power granted to the Commissioner under Code Sec. 7805(a) and provide taxpayers with guidance in order to comply with a statute. Although interpretative regulations do not have the force and effect of law, the courts customarily accord them substantial weight. Procedural regulations are considered to be directive rather than mandatory and, thus, do not have the force and effect of law. They explain the IRS's position and provide the mechanics for compliance with the various federal income tax laws, as for example the making and filing of tax elections.

The Regulations are organized in a sequential system consistent with the Code. Additionally, the Regulations are prefixed by a number which designates the applicable area of taxation to which they refer. For example, following are the more important Regulation prefixes:

Part		
Part	1.	Final income tax regulations
Part	20.	Estate Tax
Part	25.	Gift Tax
Part	31.	Withholding taxes
Part	301.	Procedure and Administration
Part	601.	Statement of Procedural Rules

Accordingly, an "Income Tax" Regulation relating to Section 453 of the Code would be cited as Reg. §1.453, followed by a dash, then the sequential number of issue, with subparts added for more detailed reference.

Proposed Regulations

New Regulations and changes to existing Regulations usually are issued in proposed form before they are finalized. During the interval between the publication of the Notice of Proposed Rulemaking and finalization of the Regulation, taxpayers and other interested parties are permitted to file objections or suggestions. Proposed Regulations do not have the same weight as Temporary Regulations. Tax law publishers such as Wolters Kluwer and Thomson Reuters provide a comprehensive listing of these Proposed Regulations, showing the date of their proposal and date of adoption and also publish the text of the Proposed Regulations.

Temporary Regulations

Sometimes Temporary Regulations are issued by the Treasury Department. Their purpose is to provide interim guidance regarding recent tax legislation until final Regulations are adopted. Temporary Regulations (issued after November 20, 1988) must also be issued as Proposed Regulations and must undergo public and administrative scrutiny during a comment period as do Proposed Regulations. Every Temporary Regulation issued after November 20, 1988, will expire three years from the date of issuance. Prior to its expiration, a Temporary Regulation has the same weight as a Final Regulation.

Final Regulations

Finalized Regulations are published in the *Federal Register* as are the Proposed Regulations and Temporary Regulations. All tax Regulations are also published in the *Internal Revenue Bulletin*. Final Regulations and Temporary Regulations are designated as Treasury Decisions (T.D.s) and are assigned a sequential number in order of issuance for the year. The effective date and date of adoption are significant.

Final Regulations as well as Proposed and Temporary Regulations are reproduced in major tax services.

Revenue Rulings and Revenue Procedures

Revenue Rulings, the official pronouncements of the IRS, are similar to Treasury Regulations in that they represent administrative interpretations of the internal revenue laws. Revenue Rulings are issued with respect to a particular issue and insure that this issue will be handled uniformly throughout the country, both in planning and in auditing. Revenue Rulings, however, do not have the same authoritative weight as regulations. Every issue of the *Internal Revenue Bulletin* includes the following statement:

> Rulings and procedures reported in the Bulletin do not have the force and effect of Treasury Department Regulations, but they may be used as precedents. Unpublished rulings will not be relied on, used, or cited as precedents by Service personnel in the disposition of other cases. In applying published rulings and procedures, the effect of subsequent legislation, regulations, court decisions, rulings, and procedures must be considered, and Service personnel and others concerned are cautioned against reaching the same conclusions in other cases unless the facts and circumstances are substantially the same.

Revenue Procedures are published official statements of procedure issued by the IRS that affect either the rights or the duties of taxpayers or other members of the public under the Internal Revenue Code and related statutes and regulations. Revenue Procedures usually reflect the contents of internal management documents. A statement of the IRS position on a substantive tax issue will not be included in a Revenue Procedure. Revenue Procedures are directive and not mandatory.

Both Revenue Rulings and Revenue Procedures are originally published in the weekly issues of the *Internal Revenue Bulletin,* printed by the U.S. Government. However, through 2008, on a semiannual basis, the bulletins were compiled, reorganized by Code section classification, and published in a bound volume designated the *Cumulative Bulletin.* Once published in the *Cumulative Bulletin,* a Revenue Ruling or Revenue Procedure received a permanent citation as shown below:

Rev. Rul. 2006-12   2006-1 CB   637

Ruling number 12 of 2006

Volume 1, 2006 *Cumulative Bulletin*

Page 637

After 2008, a Revenue Ruling, such as Rev. Rul. 2014-12, would be cited as Rev. Rul. 2014-12, 2014-15 I.R.B. 923. This is the 12th Rev. Rul. of 2014 in the 15th weekly issue of the Internal Revenue Bulletin on page 923. The citation for a Revenue Procedure is identical, except the abbreviation "Rev. Proc." is used in place of "Rev. Rul."

Other Administrative Pronouncements

In addition to substantive rulings (Revenue Rulings and Revenue Procedures) published to promote a uniform application of the tax laws, the IRS issues communications to individual taxpayers and IRS personnel in three primary ways: (1) Private Letter Rulings, (2) Determination Letters, and (3) Technical Advice Memoranda. These documents are part of the IRS rulings program, which is discussed in detail at ¶2225.

Digests of Private Letter Rulings may be found in *Private Letter Rulings* (published by Thomson Reuters), Bloomberg BNA *Daily Tax Reports,* and Tax Analysts & Advocates *Tax Notes. IRS Letter Rulings Reports* (published by Wolters Kluwer) contains both digests and the full texts of all Private Letter Rulings. These documents may also be accessed electronically through Wolters Kluwer's IntelliConnect®. Determination Letters are not published; however, the IRS is now required to make individual rulings available for public inspection. Technical Advice Memoranda are available similar to Private Letter Rulings.

IRS List of Substantial Authority for Taxpayer Reliance

The IRS has provided guidance on (1) adequate disclosure of items and positions taken on tax returns for purposes of avoiding the accuracy related penalty for understatement of tax, Rev. Proc. 94-36, 1994-1 CB 682, and (2) a listing of substantial authority that may be relied on to avoid imposition of that penalty. Reg. §1.6662-4(d)(3). In addition, the IRS issues a list of positions for which there is not substantial authority. This list must be issued by the Secretary of the Treasury (and revised not less frequently than annually) and published in the *Federal Register.* Code Sec. 6662(d)(2)(D).

The purpose of the list is to assist taxpayers in determining whether a position should be disclosed in order to avoid the substantial understatement penalty. House Committee Report, Revenue Reconciliation Act of 1989. Thus, a taxpayer could choose to disclose that position to avoid the imposition of the accuracy-related penalty. However, inclusion of a position on this list is not conclusive as to whether or not substantial authority exists with respect to that position.

Prior to 1990, the list of substantial authority was restricted to: (1) the Internal Revenue Code, (2) final and temporary regulations, (3) court cases, (4) IRS administrative pronouncements, (5) tax treaties, and (6) congressional intent reflected in committee reports accompanying legislation. Reg. §1.6661-3.

The list of substantial authority now includes (1) the Joint Committee on Taxation's General Explanation of tax legislation (i.e., the "Blue Book"); (2) proposed regulations; (3) information or press releases; (4) notices, announcements, and other similar documents published in the *Internal Revenue Bulletin;* (5) private letter rulings; (6) technical advice memoranda; (7) actions on decisions; and (8) general counsel memoranda. Reg. §1.6662-4(d)(3)(iii). "Authority" does not include conclusions reached in treatises, legal periodicals, and opinions rendered by tax professionals.

With respect to the test for "substantial authority," the IRS continues to apply the principle that there is substantial authority for the tax treatment of an item only if the weight of authorities supporting such treatment is substantial in relation to the weight of authorities supporting contrary tax treatment. The type of document providing the authority affects the weight to be accorded an authority. Reg. §1.6662-4(d)(3)(i) and (ii).

¶2055

JUDICIAL AUTHORITY

The ultimate test in the interpretation of the Code, in determining the validity of Regulations, and in applying the "law" to the facts of a given case takes place in the courts. The court system provides the taxpayer with the opportunity to test before a neutral forum both the position taken by the taxpayer and that taken by the Commissioner with respect to any issue. The courts historically have played a substantial role in the interpretation, application, and enforcement of the tax law. Exhibit 2 outlines the trial and appellate court alternatives for federal tax litigation.

Trial Court System

There are three tribunals that have original jurisdiction to hear and decide tax cases arising under the Internal Revenue Code. A taxpayer can file a petition with the United States Tax Court, in which event assessment and collection of the deficiency will be stayed until the Tax Court's decision becomes final. But the taxpayer may, if he or she prefers, pay the deficiency and then sue for a refund in a U.S. District Court or the United States Court of Federal Claims.

Exhibit 2. JUDICIAL APPEALS ALTERNATIVES

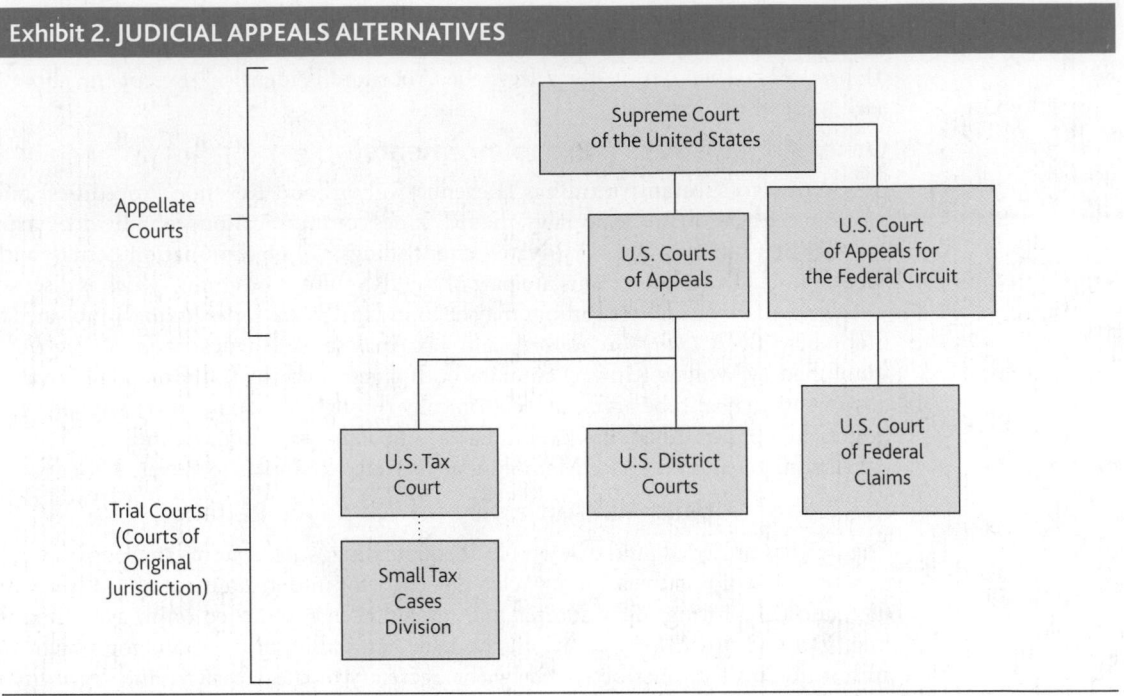

U.S. Tax Court

The United States Tax Court consists of 19 judges appointed by the President for 15-year terms. It is a special court whose jurisdiction is limited almost exclusively to litigation under the Internal Revenue Code. Prior to 1943, the Tax Court was known as the Board of Tax Appeals. Although the Tax Court is a single court located in Washington, D.C., hearings are held in several cities throughout the nation, usually with only a single judge present who submits his opinion to the chief judge. Only rarely does the chief judge decide that a full review is necessary by all 19 judges.

Decisions of the Tax Court are issued as either "regular" or "memorandum" decisions. "Regular" decisions are those which require an interpretation of the law. In theory, "memorandum" decisions concern only well-established principles of law and require only a determination of facts. However, on occasion, the courts have cited "memorandum" decisions. Hence, both kinds of Tax Court decisions should be regarded as having precedent value.

Viewing itself as a national court hearing cases from all parts of the country, for many years the Tax Court had followed a policy of deciding cases on what it thought the result should be. The Tax Court has abandoned its "national law" view, under which it applied its own rule on a nationwide basis without limitation by rules of the circuits in which tax controversies arose. The Tax Court has adopted the position that it will follow precedents of the Circuit Court of Appeals of jurisdiction (known as the *Golsen* rule). As a result, it is entirely possible that the Tax Court will rule differently on identical fact patterns for two taxpayers residing in different circuits in the event of inconsistent holdings between the various Circuit Courts.

The Tax Court is the only court to which a taxpayer may take a case without first paying the tax. Consequently, taxpayers resort to it in many instances; and because it is a court of limited jurisdiction dealing primarily with tax matters, its decisions are accorded considerable weight. This is particularly true of decisions in which the Commissioner of Internal Revenue has acquiesced.

Historically, the policy of the IRS has been to announce in the *Internal Revenue Bulletin* the determination of the Commissioner to acquiesce or not acquiesce in most of the regular decisions of the Tax Court. An announcement of acquiescence (cited Acq.) indicates that the IRS has accepted the conclusion reached in the case but not necessarily the reasons given by the court in its opinion. An announcement of nonacquiescence (cited Nonacq.) usually means that the IRS will continue to litigate the issue if it arises again. Since 1991, the IRS has indicated acquiescences or nonacquiescences for memorandum decisions of the Tax Court as well as for decisions of other courts. An announcement of acquiescence is not legally binding on the IRS and thus can be retroactively withdrawn at any time. If a case is being relied upon, it is important to determine whether it has been acquiesced in by the Commissioner, the extent of the acquiescence (if any), and whether the initial acquiescence may have been withdrawn at a later date.

Additionally, a procedure is used in the Tax Court for cases involving disputes of $50,000 or less. The taxpayer who uses the "small tax case" procedures should be aware that the decision may not be appealed. The advantage to using this procedure is the fact that the formal procedures of the Tax Court are relaxed and made informal.

Judicial Citations—Tax Court Regular Decisions. Regular and memorandum decisions of the Tax Court are reported separately. The Government Printing Office publishes bound volumes of only the regular decisions under the title *United States Tax Court Reports* (cited TC).

Permanent Citation: *Microsoft Corporation,* 115 TC 228 (2000).

Thus, the decision appears in Volume 115 of the *United States Tax Court Reports,* page 228, issued in 2000.

Because there is usually a time lag between the date a decision is rendered and the date it appears in bound form, a temporary citation is used until a permanent citation can be substituted.

Temporary Citation: *Gilda A. Petrane v. Commissioner,* 129 TC —, No. 1 (July 2007).

Thus, the temporary citation identified that the decision appeared in Volume 129 of the *United States Tax Court Reports,* page left blank, 1st regular decision issued by the Tax Court since Volume 128 was issued. Once Volume 129 was issued, the permanent citation incorporating the page was substituted and the number of the case is not used.

Permanent Citation: *Gilda A. Petrane v. Commissioner,* 129 TC 1 (2007).

Judicial Citations—Tax Court Memorandum Decisions. The government provides only photocopies of the memorandum decisions. However, memorandum decisions are published by both Wolters Kluwer and Thomson Reuters in bound volumes separate from those in which they report other tax cases. The Tax Court memorandum decisions are published by Wolters Kluwer under the title *Tax Court Memorandum Decisions* (cited TCM), while the Thomson Reuters series is called *Thomson Reuters Memorandum Decisions* (cited TC Memo).

Wolters Kluwer Citation: *Harvey D. Perry, Jr. v. Commissioner,* 84 TCM 1, T.C. Memo. 2002-165 (2002).

Thomson Reuters Citation: *Harvey D. Perry, Jr. v. Commissioner,* 2002 TC Memo ¶2002-165.

Although presented in a different way, the reference in both citations indicates that the memorandum decision was the 165th memorandum decision issued by the Tax Court in 2002.

Both regular and memorandum decisions for years prior to 1943 were published by the government under the title *United States Board of Tax Appeals Reports.*

Citation: *J.E. Burke,* 19 BTA 743 (1930).

Thus, the decision appears in Volume 19 of the *United States Board of Tax Appeals Reports,* page 743, issued in 1930.

U.S. District Courts

The U.S. District Courts were the main courts of original jurisdiction for tax cases prior to the establishment of the Board of Tax Appeals which later became the Tax Court. A taxpayer can take a case to the U.S. District Court for the district in which the taxpayer resides only if the taxpayer first pays the tax deficiency assessed by the IRS and then sues for a refund. Each state has at least one District Court in which both tax and nontax litigation are heard. Only in a District Court can one obtain a jury trial, and even there a jury can decide only questions of fact—not those of law.

Judicial Citations—U.S. District Courts Decisions. Published decisions of the U.S. District Courts, including both tax and all other types of litigation, are reported in the *Federal Supplement* (cited F.Supp.) published by West Publishing Company. In addition, the tax decisions of the District Courts are also published in the two special tax reporter series, Wolters Kluwer *United States Tax Cases* (cited USTC) and Thomson Reuters *American Federal Tax Reports* (cited AFTR).

West Citation: *Eugene B. Glick,* 96 F.Supp. 2d 850 (DC Ind., 3/14/00).

The order of citation is volume number, reporter, page number.

Wolters Kluwer Citation: *Eugene B. Glick,* 2000-1 USTC ¶50,372 (DC Ind., 3/14/00).

Paragraph reference rather than a page number gives the location of the case.

Thomson Reuters Citation: *Eugene B. Glick,* 86 AFTR 2d 2000-5083 (DC Ind., 3/14/00).

The prefix "2000" preceding the page number indicates the year the case was decided.

U.S. Court of Federal Claims

The U.S. Court of Federal Claims is a single court consisting of 16 judges appointed by the President. The court resides in Washington, D.C. and the decision to travel is made on a case-by-case basis and is heard by the trial judge to whom the case has been assigned. Prior to October 29, 1992, the court was known as the U.S. Claims Court, and prior to October 1, 1982, the court was known as the U.S. Court of Claims whose decisions were appealed directly to the Supreme Court.

In federal tax matters, the U.S. Court of Federal Claims has concurrent jurisdiction with the U.S. District Courts. The Court of Federal Claims is a constitutional court and has jurisdiction in judgment on any claim against the United States which is:

1. Based on the Constitution
2. Based on any Act of Congress
3. Based on any regulation of an executive department

Judicial Citations—U.S. Court of Federal Claims Decisions. Since 1992, decisions of the Court of Federal Claims have been reported by West Publishing Company in the *Federal Claims Reporter* (cited FedCl). The decisions of the Claims Court from October 1982 until 1992 were reported by West Publishing Company in a series designated the *U.S. Claims Court Reporter* (cited ClCt). Decisions of the predecessor Court of Claims were published by the U.S. Government Printing Office in a separate series of volumes entitled the *U.S. Court of Claims Reports* (cited CtCl). The decisions of the predecessor Court of Claims were also published by West Publishing Company from May 1960 through September 1982 in the *Federal Reporter* 2d Series (cited F.2d), while decisions between 1932 and 1960 were reported in the *Federal Supplement* (cited F.Supp.).

In addition, the tax decisions of the Court of Federal Claims (and the predecessor Claims Court and Court of Claims) are also published in the Wolters Kluwer *United States Tax Cases* (cited USTC) and Thomson Reuters *American Federal Tax Reports* (cited AFTR).

West Citation: *Katz v. U.S.,* 22 ClCt 714 (ClCt, 1991).

Scott v. U.S., 354 F.2d 292 (CtCl, 1965).

Betz v. U.S., 40 Fed Cl 286 (Fed Cl, 1998).

Wolters Kluwer Citation: *Katz v. U.S.,* 91-1 USTC ¶50,289 (ClCt, 1991).

Scott v. U.S., 66-1 USTC ¶9169 (CtCl, 1965).

Betz v. U.S., 98-1 USTC ¶50,199 (Fed Cl, 1998).

Thomson Reuters Citation: *Katz v. U.S.,* 67 AFTR2d 91-733 (ClCt, 1991).

Scott v. U.S., 16 AFTR2d 6087 (CtCl, 1965).

Betz v. U.S., 81 AFTR2d 98-611 (Fed Cl, 1998).

Appeals Court System

If either the taxpayer or the IRS is not satisfied with a trial court decision, an appellate court may be asked to review that decision. There are two levels of courts that handle appeals from the three courts of original jurisdiction. Appeals may be taken to the United States Courts of Appeals of jurisdiction or the U.S. Court of Appeals for the Federal Circuit. As a final step, the controversy may be appealed from the appellate courts to the Supreme Court.

The authority of decisions of all Courts of Appeals stands above that of the Tax Court, a District Court, or the Court of Federal Claims. The United States Supreme Court is, of course, the final authority as to what a statute means or as to any question of federal law.

U.S. Circuit Courts of Appeals

Appeals in tax cases may be taken from the U.S. District Courts or the Tax Court by either the IRS or the taxpayer to the United States Courts of Appeals of jurisdiction. Jurisdiction is based upon the location of the taxpayer's residence. There are eleven numbered circuits and additional unnumbered circuits for the District of Columbia Circuit and the Federal Circuit. See Exhibit 3.

Normally, a Circuit Court's review, made by a panel of three judges is limited to the application of law—not the determination of facts. In this process, the appellate court of any circuit is obligated to follow the findings of the Supreme Court but not those of the other Circuit Courts. When conflicts develop between circuits, District Courts of each individual circuit are required to follow any precedent set by the appellate court of their own circuit (i.e., the Circuit Court to which their decisions may be appealed). Also, as noted earlier, pursuant to the *Golsen* rule, the Tax Court follows the policy of observing precedent set by the appellate court of the circuit in which the taxpayer resides. In this way, consistency in the application of law is maintained between the Tax Court and the District Court of jurisdiction even though there may exist an inconsistency in the law's application to taxpayers residing in various circuits.

Judicial Citations—U.S. Circuit Courts of Appeals Decisions. All decisions, both tax and nontax, of the various Circuit Courts are published by West Publishing Company in the *Federal Reporter* including 2nd and 3rd Series (cited F.2d and F.3d). In addition, tax decisions of the Circuit Courts are also contained in Wolters Kluwer's *United States Tax Cases* (cited USTC) and Thomson Reuters *American Federal Tax Reports* (cited AFTR). Citations indicate not only the volume and page, but also the particular court.

West Citation: *Diane S. Blodgett v. Commissioner,* 394 F.3d 1030 (CA-8, 2005).

Wolters Kluwer Citation: *Diane S. Blodgett v. Commissioner,* 2005-1 USTC ¶50,146 (CA-8, 2005).

Thomson Reuters Citation: *Diane S. Blodgett v. Commissioner,* 95 AFTR2d 2005-448 (CA-8, 2005).

U.S. Court of Appeals for the Federal Circuit

On October 1, 1982, the seven judges of the Court of Claims and the five judges of the Court of Customs and Patent Appeals became the 12 judges of the newly created Court of Appeals for the Federal Circuit (CA-FC). The IRS and taxpayers appeal decisions from the U.S. Court of Federal Claims to this court. The court is empowered to sit in various locations around the country and can be expected to make an effort to hold sessions in the major cities where its business arises.

U.S. Supreme Court

Appeals to the U.S. Supreme Court from the Circuit Courts of Appeals and the Court of Appeals for the Federal Circuit may be made generally by a petition for certiorari. The Supreme Court may grant certiorari at its discretion; further, the Supreme Court is not required to give reasons for its refusal to review. However, past experience has shown that the Court generally grants certiorari only if:

1. The issue has resulted in conflicting decisions in the Circuit Court of Appeals or
2. The issue involved raises an important and continuing problem in the administration of the tax law.

If the Supreme Court declines to review the decision, it will formally deny the petition for certiorari.

Judicial Citations—U.S. Supreme Court Decisions. All Supreme Court decisions are published by the U.S. Government Printing Office in the *United States Supreme Court Reports* (cited U.S.), West Publishing Co. in the *Supreme Court Reporter* (cited S.Ct.), and the Lawyer's Co-Operative Publishing Co. in the *United States Reports, Lawyer's Edition* (cited L.Ed.). Like all other federal tax cases (except those rendered by the U.S. Tax Court), tax-related Supreme Court decisions are reported by Wolters Kluwer in *United States Tax Cases* (cited USTC) and Thomson Reuters in *American Federal Tax Reports* (cited AFTR).

GPO Citation: *Drye, Jr. v. U.S.,* 528 U.S. 49 (1999).

West Citation: *Drye, Jr. v. U.S.,* 120 S.Ct. 474 (1999).

Lawyer's Ed. Citation: *Drye, Jr. v. U.S.,* 145 L.Ed.2d 466 (1999).

Wolters Kluwer Citation: *Drye, Jr. v. U.S.,* 99-2 USTC ¶51,006 (1999).

Thomson Reuters Citation: *Drye, Jr. v. U.S.,* 84 AFTR2d 99-7160 (1999).

Exhibit 3. FEDERAL JUDICIAL CIRCUITS

Secondary Source Materials

¶2075

ANALYSIS OF TAX LAW SOURCES

The voluminous bulk and complexity of our tax law make it extremely difficult to systematically research all of the statutory and administrative provisions associated with a given set of tax issues. The problem is further compounded when one also attempts to analyze, evaluate, and update the leading court cases that impact on these issues. Fortunately, secondary reference materials provide a convenient cross-referenced and continuously updated road map to guide the practitioner in the complicated task of wading through a growing maze of primary tax authority.

Tax Research Services

There are various tax research services that are published with the specific purpose of providing comprehensive reference information on the ever-changing tax law and on-going developments in administrative rulings and case decisions. The use of any particular tax research service is best described in materials made available to users by the representatives of the tax research services. However, there are some general points to be made on the use of these tax research services. First, it is important to check for the latest developments on any topic, issue, or case being researched under a specific statute, regulation, or ruling. Second, editorial analysis, be it a synopsis or digest, provided by the tax research services for case decisions or administrative rulings is an interpretative commentary. Such editorial commentary, no matter how knowledgeable, is not intended to be a substitute for the authoritative primary source document.

Internet Based Research Systems

The role of electronic research systems cannot be overstated. To say that most print materials are also available online does not describe the increasingly integrated and comprehensive search capabilities of online research systems. Users can access computerized tax law data banks with their personal computers by using various tax research publisher's online internet based research systems. Whatever format the researcher uses, all data bases are now integrated with primary and secondary source materials from which the researcher can retrieve full text documents or search for key words or phrases. Publishers' computerized tax research systems can also be used to access citation information to locate all judicial decisions that have cited a particular decision or statute. These online citators are more current than was possible in print format.

Wolters Kluwer Tax Products on the Internet

As an example of an electronic tax research system, Wolters Kluwer's IntelliConnect® offers a completely integrated suite of tax research materials including primary source documents, i.e., the Internal Revenue Code, Treasury Regulations, Revenue Rulings, tax case decisions, administrative guidance and more. In addition to primary source material, Intelliconnect includes editorial analysis and content including fully searchable versions of most Wolters Kluwer products including the Standard Federal Tax Reporter. The Standard Federal Tax Reporter is a comprehensive Federal tax resource and the organization of this resource is described more fully below, following this discussion of internet based research systems.

In addition to the Standard Federal Tax Reporter, Wolters Kluwer research products online include *Practical Tax Expert*, which provides tax research, focusing on the topics that matter most to the small firm preparer, such as individual and small business taxation. It provides practical explanations of tax law, including examples, comments, planning notes and compliance notes, as well as a variety of tools and practice aids. It includes discussions of source material including the Internal Revenue Code, Treasury Regulations, Rulings and other IRS material, all properly cited and linked for further research.

Practical Tax Professional provides tax research, focusing on the topics that matter most to the small firm practitioner, such as individual and small business taxation, while also providing coverage of a full range of federal tax research issues.

Tax Research Consultant is another tax research product available on IntelliConnect®. Tax Research Consultant covers all tax topics, not just income, and it is arranged by topic rather than Code section. This service is updated weekly.

IntelliConnect® includes many other tax research resources and is organized by overall category including Federal Tax, State Tax, Financial and Estate Planning, Accounting, etc. Within each category, various resources and products are available for research and practice assistance. The electronic format of the internet-based tax research services provides an opportunity to include automated tools and calculators, which makes the tax research systems ideal not only for tax research but also to find quick answers and practice aids. IntelliConnect® includes Smart Charts on many topics as well as calculators, decision tools and more. In addition to these features, the internet-based research systems provide an opportunity for the most current information that can be updated more frequently than the print resources. IntelliConnect® includes the Wolters Kluwer daily news service, Tax Day, current journals and newsletters, the latest Wolters Kluwer briefings on major tax developments, a Case Citator that is current to date and many other electronic products including Wolters Kluwer's well-regarded Law, Explanation and Analysis books on current legislation. Subscribers to internet based tax research systems receive log in information providing access to the full array of resources anytime and virtually anyplace.

In addition to the internet-based tax research systems, new applications are being continuously developed by most tax research services. Wolters Kluwer offers tax research information specifically designed for mobile devices including iPhones and iPads. Some of these applications include CCH Mobile, eBooks, current journals, and newsletters.

It must be noted here that despite the encompassing nature of electronic research and search methods, students are well advised to have a firm understanding of the nature, basis and authority of the documents they are using to support a tax position and how the various sources of authority are interrelated and linked. Therefore, following the internet screen shots below on the Wolters Kluwer internet based system, a more detailed description of the organization of various tax research products is included with the understanding that these original research resources are still available in print format and are now also available through the electronic research systems.

Complete, current, and reliable tax information is on the Internet from Wolters Kluwer at *CCHGroup.com*. Many tax research products are also available on mobile applications.

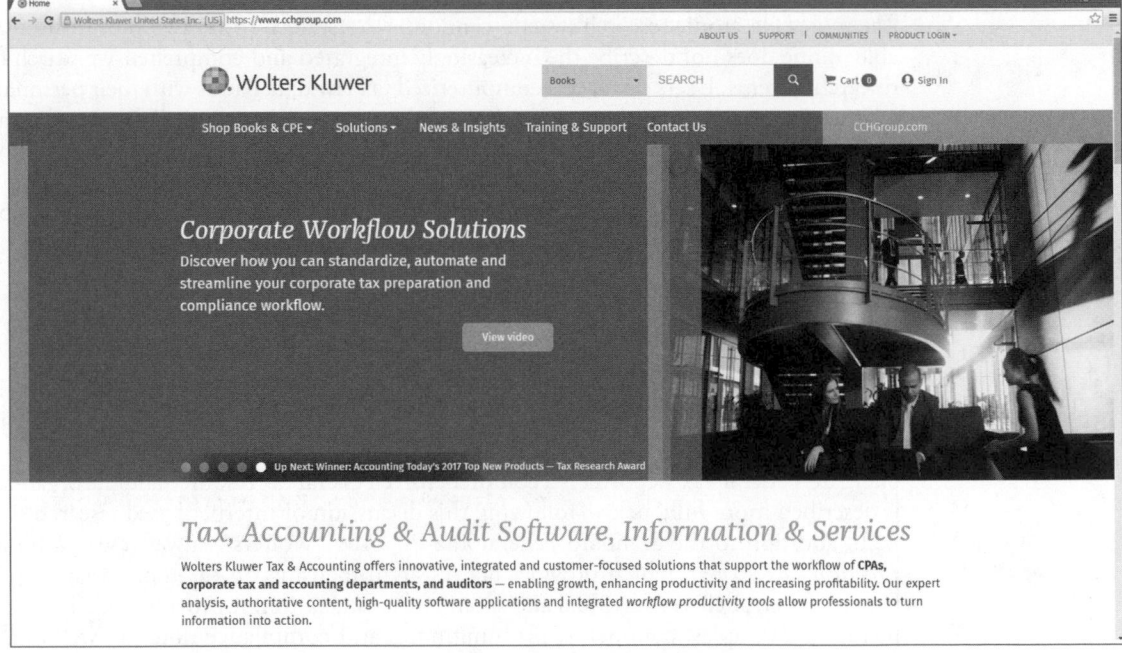

Researching a Topic

In the Internet browser's Address bar, go to *http://intelliconnect.cch.com*. You will be taken to the Log In page where you can enter your User ID and Password in order to reach the IntelliConnect® home page where you can initiate a search.

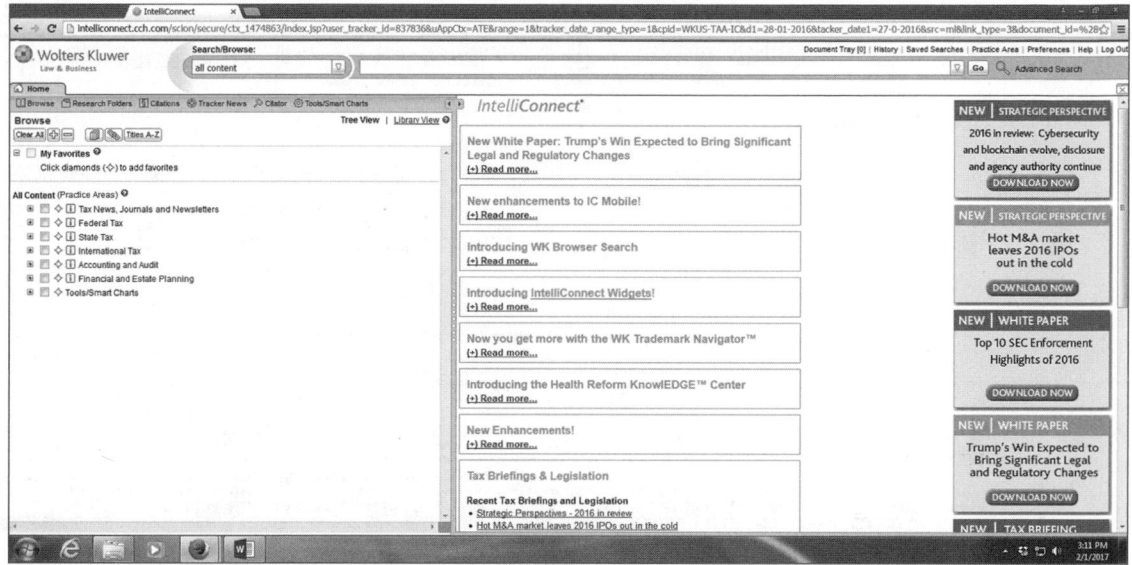

Type your search term or phrase in the navigation bar at the top of the screen. For purposes of illustration look for the "nanny tax threshold for 2017" and click Go. On the left side of the screen you can choose to Narrow Your Results. For this example click the plus next to "by Document Type" and when the list expands, click on Explanations.

This screen displays the results that best match your query. Click on the first document and the screen will split so that the document will appear at the bottom.

Review the document to see if it contains the information with respect to the nanny tax threshold for 2017. In this example the first item listed contains information on the nanny tax threshold for 2017. The nanny tax increases to $2,000 for 2017. Cash amounts paid for a nanny are not subject to FICA taxes if less than $2,000 during 2017.

Once you have found the information you were searching for you might want to email it to yourself. There are several options in the middle of the Tri-screen. Click on Save/Email and choose Email document from the drop down list. Enter the required information and click send.

The only way to become proficient at using an electronic data base is through practice and experience. The tax student is encouraged to experiment with Wolters Kluwer's online tax research system by searching for the answer to a tax question. Once the art of electronic searching is mastered, it will be obvious how much more comprehensive and efficient it is than a traditional paper search. For example, what authority can you find to justify a deduction for home office expense by a college professor? What authority can you find that would deny the deduction?

IRS Homepage

The IRS homepage on the World Wide Web (*http://www.irs.gov*) went online on January 8, 1996. During its first 24 hours of operation, close to one million "hits" were recorded. Features on the IRS homepage include the following: Tax Stats, About IRS, Careers, Freedom of Information Act (FOIA), The Newsroom, Accessibility, Site Map, Español, and Help.

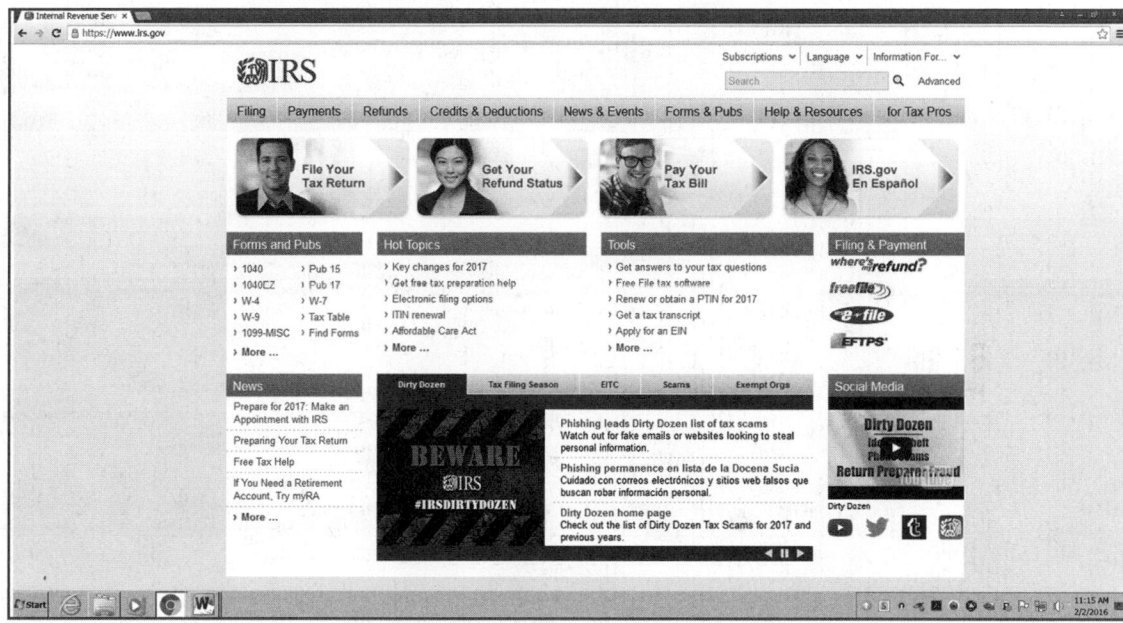

One very useful aspect of the IRS homepage is the ability to retrieve the latest in tax news. Use the IRS News & Events to access information on important topics (as shown below). From the IRS homepage, click on News & Events.

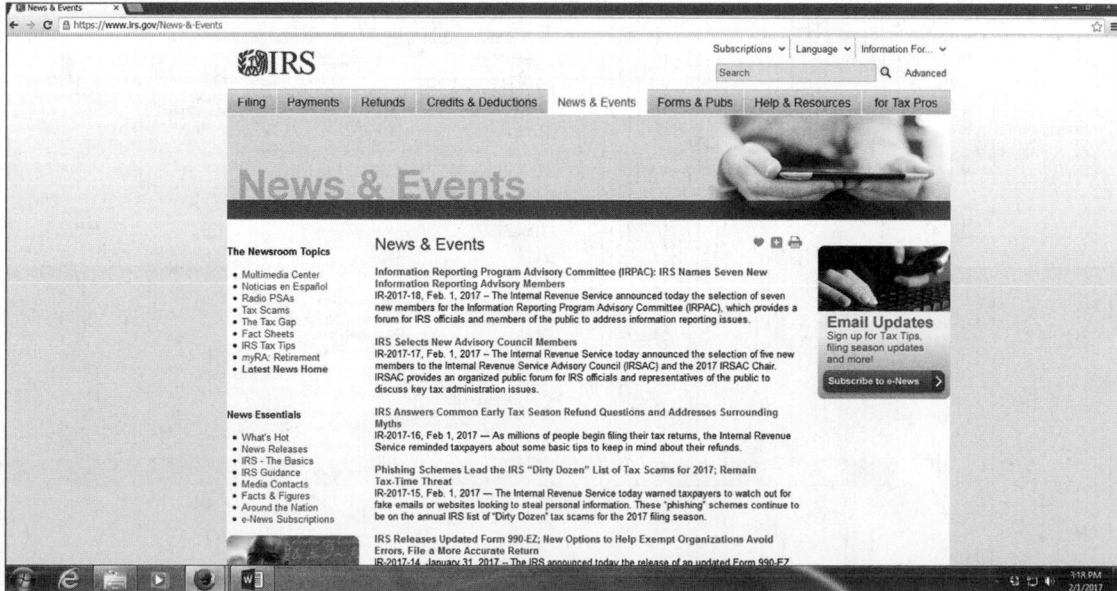

Across the top of the page the tabs provided are: Filing, Payments, Refunds, Credits & Deductions, News & Events, Forms & Pubs, Help & Resources and for Tax Pros. Besides retrieving tax news from the

IRS, tax forms and publications may be downloaded. The sixth item listed across the top of the page is Forms and Publications. By clicking on Forms and Publications, the Forms and Publications page appears. All IRS tax forms may be retrieved from this site. Please note that forms and publications from prior years are available back to 1992.

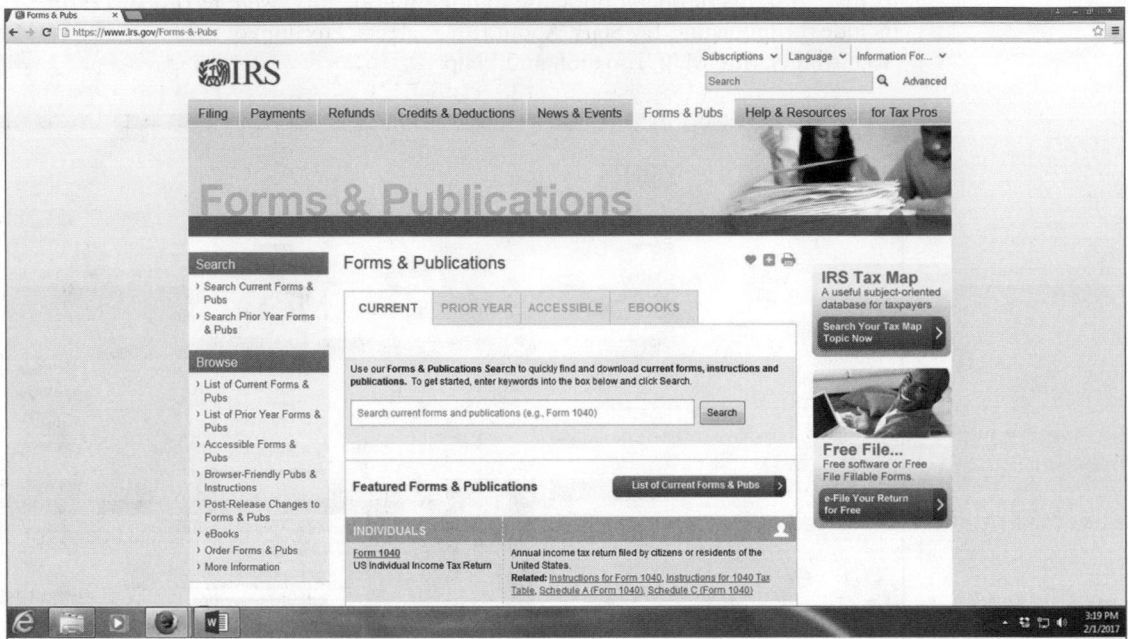

By clicking on the "List of Current Forms & Pubs" link, *http://apps.irs.gov/app/picklist/list/formsPublications.html* appears. All IRS tax forms may be retrieved from this site.

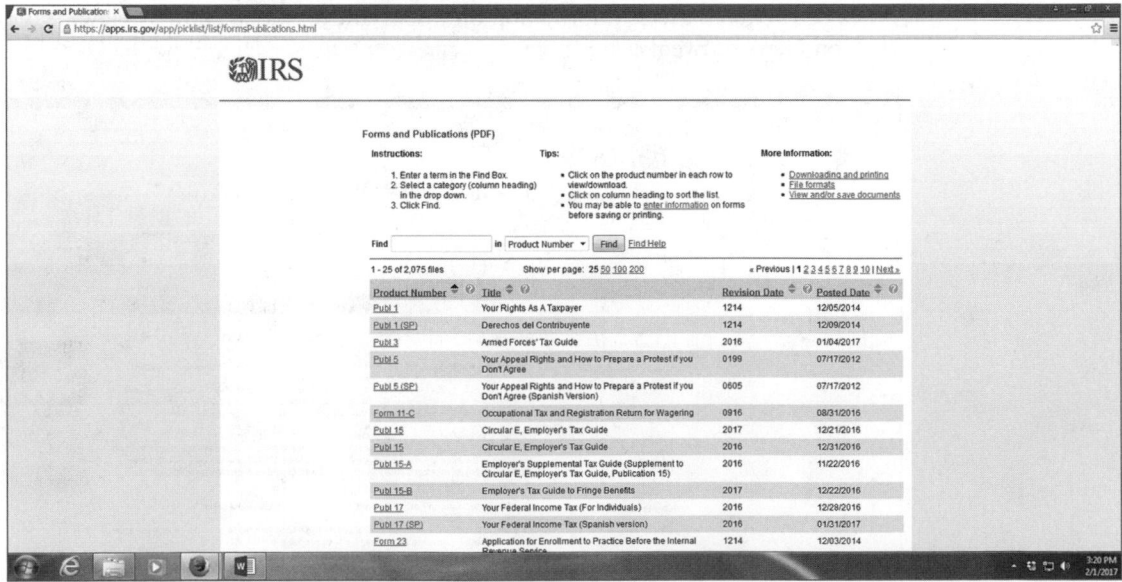

Searching the Internet

A good way to search the Internet is by using search engines. A search engine allows you to type in a term or phrase which describes your area of interest. For example, open your Internet browser's search screen and type in the phrase "tax history." Once the search is complete, all of the finds are listed and linked to millions of useful sources (sample screens shown below).

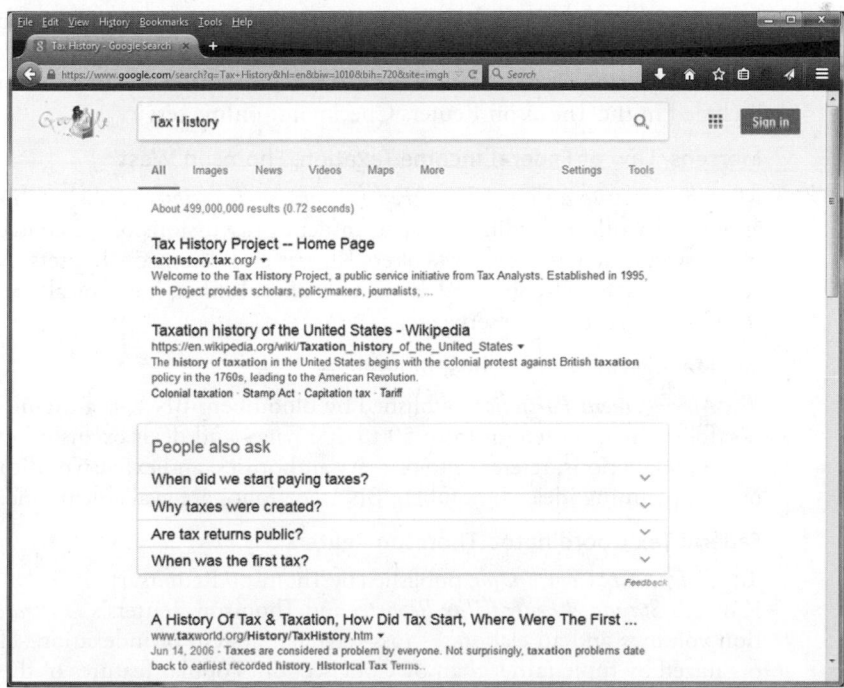

Standard Federal Tax Reporter, Wolters Kluwer

Wolters Kluwer publishes loose-leaf reporters in all major federal tax areas. These reporters are also available on Wolters Kluwer's tax research system, IntelliConnect®. The most comprehensive of these tax reference services is the *Standard Federal Tax Reporter,* frequently referred to as the *Standard* or *Fed.* Other specialized tax services include the *Federal Excise Tax Reporter* and the *Federal Estate and Gift Tax Reporter.* The *Federal Tax Guide,* also published by Wolters Kluwer, is a two-volume service covering many of the same topics that are included in the *Standard.*

The *Standard Reporter* consists of 25 coordinated and cross-referenced loose-leaf volumes that provide comprehensive coverage of the income tax law. The service also provides weekly supplements presenting current federal court decisions, new rulings, and changes in the law or regulations, digests of Tax Court decisions, as well as reviews of the significant legislative changes, and editorial comments which provide tax planning ideas related to current developments.

The major portion of the *Standard,* Volumes 1 through 18, compiles the legislative, administrative, and judicial aspects of the income tax law. The volumes are arranged in Code Section order and reflect the current income tax law and accompanying related regulatory texts (including proposed amendments to the Regulations) as well as legislative Committee Reports, followed by "Explanations" and supplemented with digests of associated administrative rulings and judicial decisions. Volume 19, "New Matters," is used to retain current developments such as digests of Tax Court decisions, full texts of rulings, current tables of decisions and rulings, and the Supreme Court Docket.

The *Standard* also includes the "U.S. Tax Cases Advance Sheets" Volume in which are reported the full texts of new income tax decisions from the federal courts, including the U.S. Supreme Court and the U.S. Court of Federal Claims. In the two Internal Revenue Code Volumes may be found the current internal revenue statutes. The two Citator Volumes access the basic Compilations by case name and document number. The Index Volume leads to the basic contents by subject through the Topical Index and also features a tax calendar, rate tables and tax rate schedules, tax planning information, checklists, and special tables.

United States Tax Reporter, Thomson Reuters

United States Tax Reporter, published by Thomson Reuters, consists of 18 coordinated loose-leaf volumes organized by Code sections and updated on a weekly basis. The service is similar to Wolters Kluwer's and also includes a two-volume Internal Revenue Code, a seven-volume Citator, a one-volume Index, a one-volume Table of Cases, Rulings, and Tax Tables, a Recent Developments volume, an Advance Sheets volume for AFTR2d cases and a volume of proposed amendments to Federal Tax Regulations. Thomson Reuters also publishes loose-leaf tax services for excise taxes and for estate and gift taxes. This service is included in the Thomson Reuters Checkpoint online service.

Mertens, Law of Federal Income Taxation, Thomson West

Merten's *Treatise on the Law of Federal Income Taxation,* published by Thomson West, is an intensive, annotated work, providing excellent in-depth discussions of general concepts of tax law. However, unlike services such as those of Wolters Kluwer and Thomson Reuters, Mertens is not generally used as a comprehensive, self-contained reference service. Rather, it is typically regarded as a useful complement to the traditional reference services.

Tax Management Portfolios, Bloomberg BNA

Tax Management Portfolios, published by Bloomberg BNA, is a useful supplement to a tax library. Each portfolio ranges in length from 50 to 200 pages and deals exclusively with a special tax topic, covering Code, Regulations, reference to primary authorities, and extensive editorial discussion, including numerous tax planning ideas. Bloomberg BNA Portfolios are available online.

Federal Tax Coordinator, Thomson Reuters

The *Federal Tax Coordinator,* published by Thomson Reuters, is somewhat similar in organization to Wolters Kluwer's *Standard Federal Tax Reporter* and Thomson Reuters's *United States Tax Reporter,* with compilation volumes and an elaborate cross-reference system of indexation. However, the 26-volume service is organized by topic rather than by Code section. Popular features of the *Tax Coordinator* are the editorial explanations, illustrations, planning ideas, and warnings of potential tax traps. This service is included in the Thomson Reuters Checkpoint online service.

The Citator

Probably the most comprehensive method for evaluating and updating case law is through the use of a citator. The *Wolters Kluwer Citator,* published annually as a two-volume loose-leaf reference service, contains an alphabetical listing of the Tax Court (formerly the Board of Tax Appeals) and federal court decisions since 1913. The Current Citator Table is updated annually in print. It is updated currently online in IntelliConnect®. Additionally, the *Wolters Kluwer Citator* indicates a paragraph reference where each case is digested in the Compilation Volumes of the *Standard Federal Tax Reporter.* More than one paragraph reference will be given if a case involves several tax issues. The *Citator* is available on IntelliConnect® and offers instant linking to the cases cited.

Each listing outlines the judicial history of a selected case beginning with the highest court to have ruled on that issue. Then, in descending order, the actions of lower courts are also cited and described. Finally, under each listing, the *Citator* refers to other court cases, which helps to evaluate a given decision as a precedent.

The *Citator 2nd,* published by Thomson Reuters, is a seven-volume service with monthly and annual cumulative supplements organized in a manner somewhat consistent with that of the *Wolters Kluwer Citator.* Essentially, Thomson Reuters provides an alphabetical list of court cases followed by a descriptive legislative history of each case. However, in those cases involving more than one issue, the Thomson Reuters citator also cross-references its descriptive system of judicial references according to the various issues. Citators are included in the online services of Wolters Kluwer and Thomson Reuters.

To illustrate the usefulness of the citator to the researcher, the Wolters Kluwer Citator will be explained in greater detail. Refer to Exhibit 4, a sample taken from the Wolters Kluwer Citator and locate the *Atlas Life Insurance Co.* case. The case name is followed by paragraph (¶) references to the Compilation Volumes in which the decision appears as an annotation to the law, regulations, and other cases in point. The black dot preceding each court action in the case permits the researcher to quickly scan the judicial history of the case. *Atlas Life Insurance Co.* was decided on appeal in the Supreme Court in 1965, which reversed the decision of the Court of Appeals for the Tenth Circuit. The Court of Appeals decision reversed the ruling of the District Court of Oklahoma.

Exhibit 4. WOLTERS KLUWER CITATOR—COURT CASES SAMPLE SECTION

Atlas, Inc.—continued
Mervis Industries, Inc., DC-Ind, 94-2 USTC ¶ 50,324, 866 FSupp 1143
TMG II, DC-DofC, 91-2 USTC ¶ 50,513, 778 FSupp 37
Newgard, Jr., Trust, L.A., DC-ND, 89-2 USTC ¶ 9395
Carter, DC-Calif, 82-1 USTC ¶ 9314
Viva Ltd., DC-Colo, 81-1 USTC ¶ 9169, 490 FSupp 1002
Vavrina v. Koch, DC-Md, 80-2 USTC ¶ 9697
Waite, Inc.,, DC-Pa, 80-1 USTC ¶ 9128, 480 FSupp 1235
Atlas Insurance Company .... ¶ 12,014.311, 12,014.3205
● **CA-5**—(aff'g unreported DC per curiam), 64-2 USTC ¶ 9828; 338 F2d 334
Atlas Leasing, Inc. (See Central De Gas De Chihuahua, S.A.)
Atlas Life Insurance Co. ...... ¶ 25,736.60, 25,913.74
● **SCt**—(rev'g CA), 65-1 USTC ¶ 9407; 381 US 233; 85 SCt 1379; Ct D 1903; 1965-2 CB 220
Bankers Life and Casualty Co., CA-7, 98-1 USTC ¶ 50,346, 142 F3d 973
American Mutual Life Ins., FedCl, 2000-1 USTC ¶ 50,314, 46 FedCl 445
Standard Life & Accident Ins. Co., SCt, 77-2 USTC ¶ 9480, 433 US 148, 97 SCt 2523, Ct D 1986, 1977-2 CB 230
Consumer Life Ins. Co., SCt, 77-1 USTC ¶ 9364, 430 US 725, 97 SCt 1440, Ct D 1985, 1977-1 CB 178
Boli, CA-FC, 87-2 USTC ¶ 9566, 831 F2d 276
Goldin, CA-2, 87-1 USTC ¶ 9128, 809 F2d 187
Reserve Life Insurance Co., CtCls, 81-1 USTC ¶ 9147, 640 F2d 368
Investors Diversified Services, Inc., CtCls, 78-1 USTC ¶ 9379, 216 CtCls 192, 575 F2d 843
Group Life & Health Ins. Co., CA-5, 70-2 USTC ¶ 9683, 434 F2d 115
Franklin Life Ins. Co., CA-7, 68-2 USTC ¶ 9459, 399 F2d 757
Northwestern Mutual Life Ins. Co., ClsCt, 85-1 USTC ¶ 9233, 7 ClsCt 501
Union Mutual Life Ins. Co., DC-Me, 76-2 USTC ¶ 9661, 420 FSupp 1181
Jefferson Standard Life Ins. Co., CA-4, 69-1 USTC ¶ 9278, 408 F2d 842
Franklin Life Ins. Co., DC-Ill, 67-2 USTC ¶ 9515
Union Central Life Ins. Co., TC, Dec. 38,339, 77 TC 845
Ball, TC, Dec. 30,153, 54 TC 1200
Allstate Fire Ins. Co., TC, Dec. 28,197, 47 TC 237
● **CA-10**—(rev'g DC), 64-2 USTC ¶ 9510; 333 F2d 389
● **DC-Okla**—63-1 USTC ¶ 9452; 216 FSupp 457

Atlas Mixed Mortar Co. .... ¶ 21,817.636
● **BTA**—Dec. 6956; 23 BTA 245
Harrold, CA-4, 52-1 USTC ¶ 9107, 192 F2d 1002
Levin, TC, Dec. 20,224, 21 TC 996
Jenkins, TC, Dec. 20,125(M), 13 TCM 61
Vincent, TC, Dec. 19,366, 19 TC 501
Patsch, TC, Dec. 19,288, 19 TC 189
Harrold, TC, Dec. 18,045, 16 TC 134
Atlas, Nicholas (See Lester, Emanuel)
Atlas Oil & Refining Corp. .... ¶ 44,432.01
● **TC**—Dec. 24,943; 36 TC 675; A. 1962-2 CB 3
Adkins-Phelps, Inc., CA-8, 68-2 USTC ¶ 9609, 400 F2d 737
Wisconsin Central Railroad Co., CtCls, 62-1 USTC ¶ 9121, 155 CtCls 781, 296 F2d 750
Atlas Oil and Refining Corp. ¶ 38,963.32, 38,963.59, 38,967.626
● **TC**—Dec. 20,387; 22 TC 552; NA. 1955-1 CB 7
Simpson Est., TC, Dec. 49,836(M), 67 TCM 2938, TC Memo. 1994-207
Union Texas International Corp., TC, Dec. 52,710, 110 TC 321
Atkinson, TC, Dec. 46,340(M), 58 TCM 1257, TC Memo. 1990-37
Woods, TC, Dec. 45,602, 92 TC 776
Century Data Systems, Inc., TC, Dec. 42,872, 86 TC 157
Reef Corp., TC, Dec. 27,309(M), 24 TCM 379, TC Memo. 1965-72
Pollack, TC, Dec. 26,693(M), 23 TCM 433, TC Memo. 1964-63
Rose, TC, Dec. 21,160, 24 TC 755
Harlan, TC, Dec. 54,209, 116 TC 31
Atlas Oil & Refining Corp. .... ¶ 20,307.20
● **TC**—Dec. 18,601; 17 TC 733; A. 1952-1 CB 1
Miles Production Co., TC, Dec. 47,265, 96 TC 595
Century Data Systems, Inc., TC, Dec. 42,872, 86 TC 157
Atlas Tool Co., TC, Dec. 35,124, 70 TC 86
Dougherty, TC, Dec. 32,138, 60 TC 917
Reef Corp., TC, Dec. 27,309(M), 24 TCM 379, TC Memo. 1965-72
Rose, TC, Dec. 21,160, 24 TC 755
Rev. Rul. 58-256
Atlas Plaster & Fuel Co. ...... ¶ 8637.681, 42,201.57
● **CA-6**—(aff'g BTA), 1932 CCH ¶ 9067; 55 F2d 802; Ct D 541; XI-2 CB 323
Tumwater Lbr. Mills Co., CA-9, 1933 CCH ¶ 9403, 65 F2d 675
Bluegrass Plant Foods, Inc., TC, Dec. 22,918(M), 17 TCM 271, TC Memo. 1958-53
● **BTA**—Dec. 5821; 18 BTA 1123
Atlas Plywood Co. .... ¶ 11,075.5135, 11,075.6044,

In addition to the historical record of the case, citations are given for the court actions taken in a particular case which show where the full text of the decision may be found. A citation to *U.S. Tax Cases* (USTC), for example, refers to an expansive series of volumes published by Wolters Kluwer that cover tax-related court opinions issued since 1913. The volumes, published twice a year, cover Supreme Court, Courts of Appeals, District Courts, and Court of Federal Claims cases. The Thomson Reuters citator would refer to the *American Federal Tax Reports* (AFTR), the comparable Thomson Reuters series of federal court cases. Memorandum decisions of the Tax Court are published by Wolters Kluwer under the title *Tax Court Memorandum Decisions* (cited TCM), while the Thomson Reuters series is called *TC Memorandum Decisions* (cited TC Memo).

The Citator typically gives even further research information than already discussed. For each case listed in the Citator there is given the "cited record" of that case. These "cited records" list the names and citations of later cases which discussed and distinguished the main case. Thus, the "cited record" permits the researcher to evaluate the judicial authority of the related case.

For the very latest developments in any case, the researcher using the Wolters Kluwer Citator should consult the Current Citator Table. Following this procedure, the researcher must be sure to check the "Case Table" (for the current year) in Volume 19, the "New Matters" volume of the *Standard*. Appeals to higher courts, IRS acquiescences or nonacquiescences, and government decisions on whether to appeal federal court cases are shown in the "Case Table" (for the current year) for all cases. (Where Supreme Court action is indicated in the Case Table, more information on the case may be obtained from the Supreme Court Docket located in the New Matters Volume.) The "Finding Lists" section of the Citator allows the researcher to determine the status of Revenue Rulings and Revenue Procedures.

Books

In addition to the loose-leaf reference services and the bound volumes of tax-related court cases published in the special reporter series *U.S. Tax Cases* (USTC) available from Wolters Kluwer or the *American Federal Tax Reports* (AFTR) available from Thomson Reuters, a well-equipped tax library should contain numerous leading tax textbooks.

Following are selected, highly recommended tax books:

Price on Contemporary Estate Planning, John R. Price and Samuel A. Donaldson (Wolters Kluwer)

Federal Tax Practitioner's Guide, Susan Flax Posner (Wolters Kluwer)

Federal Income Taxation of Corporations and Shareholders, Boris I. Bittker and James I. Eustice (Thomson/WG&L)

S Corporation Taxation, Robert W. Jamison (Wolters Kluwer)

Practical Guide to Partnerships and LLCs, Robert Ricketts and Larry Tunnell (Wolters Kluwer)

Practical Guide to U.S. Taxation of International Transactions, Robert J. Misey, Jr. and Michael S. Schadewald (Wolters Kluwer)

Partnership Taxation, Arthur B. Willis, John S. Pennell, Philip F. Postlewaite, and Richard Lipton (Thomson/WG&L)

Tax Institutes

Current tax topics are discussed and technical papers presented at the various tax institutes and symposia held annually at universities and other locations throughout the United States. The well-known tax institutes such as New York University and the National Tax Association—Tax Institute of America publish their annual proceedings. The papers of the Annual University of Chicago Federal Tax Conference are published in the March issue of *TAXES—The Tax Magazine* as are the proceedings of the Tax Council Policy Institute (TCPI) annual meeting published in the June issue. The papers from the annual UCLA Tax Controversy Institute are published each year in the December-January issue of the *Journal of Tax Practice and Procedure*.

Tax Periodicals

Several monthly and quarterly journals contain current articles dealing exclusively with technical tax matters. Some of these magazines cover a broad range of tax topics, while others specialize in a particular area of taxation.

Following are some of the more popular tax periodicals:

Corporate Taxation (Thomson/WG&L)

CPA Journal (New York State Society of Certified Public Accountants)

Estate Planning (Thomson/WG&L)

International Tax Journal (Wolters Kluwer)

Journal of the American Taxation Association (American Accounting Association)

Journal of Passthrough Entities (Wolters Kluwer)

Journal of Tax Practice and Procedure (Wolters Kluwer)

Journal of Taxation (Thomson/WG&L)

Journal of Taxation of Financial Products (Wolters Kluwer)

National Tax Journal (National Tax Association—Tax Institute of America)

Practical Tax Strategies (Thomson/WG&L)

Tax Adviser (American Institute of Certified Public Accountants)

Tax Executive (Tax Executive Institute)

Tax Law Review (New York University)

Tax Lawyer (American Bar Association)

Taxes—The Tax Magazine (Wolters Kluwer)

Trusts and Estates (Penton Media, Inc.)

Newsletters

The practitioner needs to stay on top of current developments in the tax field and for this purpose finds that weekly and even daily updates of pertinent tax law information is needed. Daily reporting is available both electronically through on-line computer legal research systems from tax publishers and through the mail. There is the daily *Tax Day News* and *Federal Tax Weekly*, published by Wolters Kluwer; the Bloomberg BNA *Daily Tax Report*, available from the Bureau of National Affairs; and Tax Analysts' *Tax Notes Today*. The most popular weekly newsletters are *Federal Tax Weekly*, published by Wolters Kluwer; the *Federal Taxes Weekly Alert*, published by Thomson Reuters; and Tax Analysts' weekly *Tax Notes*.

Research Methodology

¶2125 **TYPES OF TAX RESEARCH SITUATIONS**

Essentially, there are two types of tax research cases or situations. The "closed-fact" case, sometimes referred to as ex post facto research, involves the legal interpretation of historical events. In such cases, the taxable transactions have already occurred and can no longer be altered, although various tax elections and alternatives might still be available. Two common examples of "closed-fact" situations are preparation of a tax return after the taxable year is completed and representation of a taxpayer before the Audit Division of the IRS on the examination of a previously filed tax return.

In contrast, the "open-fact" case typically involves events that have not yet been finalized (i.e., controllable facts). Thus, this type of research relates primarily to future planning decisions. However, whether the primary focus of a research engagement is for tax compliance or tax planning, the underlying methods and techniques should be systematic, thorough, properly documented, and effectively communicated to the client.

¶2135 **RESEARCH MODEL**

The following research model presents a five-step systematic format that can be applied to a "closed-fact" or an "open-fact" case:

1. Gathering the facts and identifying the tax issues to be researched.
2. Locating and studying the primary and secondary authorities relevant to the enumerated tax issues.
3. Updating and evaluating the weight of the various authorities.
4. Reexamining various facets of the research.
5. Arriving at conclusions and communicating these conclusions to the client.

STEP 1: Gathering the Facts and Identifying the Tax Issues to Be Researched

During this difficult part of the research process it is necessary to elicit a comprehensive, unbiased report from the client. Difficulty stems from the fact that taxpayers often tend to have a simple perspective of the tax issues related to their problem. They fail to see the multiple issues that might be involved in what they perceive as a single, straightforward issue.

EXAMPLE 2.1

Mary Jones, a single taxpayer, moved from New York to Miami in 2017. Accordingly, she sold her residence in New York at a gain well in excess of $400,000. In preparation of her 2017 tax return, since the gain on the sale of this residence is quite substantial, the researcher must examine the facts and explore the tax-savings elections.

Mary is asked to provide all information related to these events, and she supplies the real estate closing statement reflecting the sale of the New York residence. As far as Mary is concerned, she has supplied "all" information necessary to resolve this issue. However, the following facts must still be ascertained:

1. What was the cost of the New York residence?
2. Should any improvements be capitalized as part of the basis of the New York residence?
3. Were there any selling costs involved with the sale?
4. Over the years, were there any property assessments that should be capitalized as part of the basis of the New York residence?
5. Was any portion of the New York residence depreciated as a home office deduction on prior tax returns?
6. Is Mary eligible for the $250,000 tax-free exclusion?

STEP 2: Locating and Studying the Secondary and Primary Authorities Relevant to the Enumerated Tax Issues

For each issue enumerated in Step 1, the research might begin with a thorough reading of the compilation materials found in the tax services whether in print format (loose-leaf and books) or electronic format. The editorial explanations and observations provide useful insights and help direct the research process. Additionally, the research should continue with a review of the applicable Code sections, Regulations, and digests of selected judicial decisions. Those cases which seem particularly appropriate to the research should be cited to facilitate reference for subsequent follow-up study. Finally, before leaving the tax services, it is imperative to refer to the "Current Developments" section to examine the impact of recent actions.

STEP 3: Updating and Evaluating the Weight of the Various Authorities

The statutory and administrative authorities selected in Step 2 must now be evaluated to determine relative weight. Additionally, the relevant court cases must be assessed in terms of their value as judicial precedent. Before relying upon a particular decision, it is essential to refer to one of the loose-leaf citator services and review the history and current status of that case.

It is not uncommon to discover conflicting interpretations of similar issues by different courts. In place of a national law policy, the Tax Court has adopted the position that better judicial administration requires it to follow a Court of Appeals decision. Nevertheless, courts at the same level of jurisdiction may issue conflicting opinions; whereas, the Internal Revenue Service is not obligated to adhere to either decision on a nationwide basis. Accordingly, a District or Circuit Court decision favorable to a taxpayer has significant precedent value only within that district or circuit.

STEP 4: Reexamining Various Facets of the Research

After studying and evaluating the various statutory, administrative, and judicial authorities, it often becomes necessary to reexamine the original tax problem. It may even become necessary to seek additional facts and modify or expand the research process.

Additionally, if there are any authorities in conflict with the projected conclusions, it is essential to study them carefully. The researcher must not only be able to support his or her own research conclusions, but also must be prepared to defend these conclusions in light of conflicting authorities.

During this phase of the research, it may sometimes be useful to clarify the meanings of unfamiliar or highly technical words or terms. A standard dictionary may provide some guidance, but if the words are not generally used in a nonlegal context, *Black's Law Dictionary* should be consulted.

STEP 5: Arriving at Conclusions and Communicating the Conclusions to the Client

Communicating the conclusions of the tax research to the client requires professional judgment. The client should be advised of the potential benefits and risks associated with the recommended actions. Since the communication will be in writing, it is essential to determine how much or how little detail should be noted. Additionally, the communication must be expressed at the client's level of sophistication. This sometimes presents a difficult task, especially when the research involves complex issues and highly technical reasoning.

Essentially, the communication should be concise, well-structured, and should follow an organized format that includes:

1. A review of the facts
2. An enumeration of the various tax issues
3. The conclusions
4. A discussion of the reasoning and authorities supporting the conclusions

While the client might be concerned only with the section dealing with conclusions, the professional substance of the communication is contained in the reasoning and authority. It is in this section of the report that the various authorities are discussed and evaluated. Finally, it is in this section that the client is supplied with authoritative support, should it ever become necessary to defend against a challenge by the Internal Revenue Service.

¶2147

RESEARCH CASES AND EXAMPLES

The following cases and examples illustrate the *step-by-step* application of selected aspects of research methodology. Additionally, details are outlined to highlight the *trial-and-error* nature of tax research and the need for patience, perseverance, and creativity.

CASE 1. (Illustrating a Code Section approach to tax research.)

TAX PROBLEM

Sue Wilson had her personal automobile stolen in 2017 and received an insurance reimbursement in 2018. In preparing her 2017 tax return, the preparer must ascertain how much of a theft loss may be claimed and in which year it should be deducted.

FACTS

The automobile was acquired in 2015 at a cost of $20,000 and was stolen on June 14, 2017. The fair market value at the time of theft was $10,000. On January 15, 2018, the insurance company paid $7,500 to Wilson as a "full reimbursement" for the theft.

ISSUES

Is the theft deductible since the vehicle is used exclusively for personal use? If deductible, how much of a loss may be claimed? In which year, 2017 or 2018, should the loss be claimed?

RESEARCH

On determining that Section 165 of the Internal Revenue Code deals with Deductions for Losses, the researcher using the *Standard* tax service (whether in print or electronic format) should refer to the Compilation Volumes where the texts of the Code sections and Regulations, both with all amendments to date, and Explanations, plus digests of applicable rulings and decisions are located. Code section reference is facilitated by referring to the backbone of the various loose-leaf volumes. Section 165(h) provides authoritative support for deducting a *personal* casualty loss or theft and outlines details of the $100 and 10 percent of adjusted gross income limitations for this deduction.

Regulation §1.165-1(d)(2)(ii), which is located in the *Standard* Compilations immediately following Section 165, is reprinted in Exhibit 5. The illustration provided in this Regulation is similar to the Wilson facts.

Accordingly, it would appear that, to the extent Sue can claim a theft loss, it will be deductible in 2017. However, a major question relates to the calculation of the loss. Is the loss measured by the $20,000 original cost of the automobile or by the $10,000 fair market value?

Reg. §1.165-7(b)(1) gives the general rule to be followed in determining the amount deductible for casualty losses:

> . . . the amount of loss to be taken into account . . . shall be the lesser of either—(i) The amount which is equal to the fair market value of the property immediately before the casualty reduced by the fair market value of the property immediately after the casualty; or (ii) The amount of the adjusted basis prescribed [by regulation] for determining the loss from the sale or other disposition of the property involved.

Exhibit 5. STANDARD FEDERAL TAX REPORTS—COMPILATION SAMPLE PAGE: Regulations

Regulations

[¶9803] §1.165-1 Losses.—* * *

(d) *Year of deduction.* (1) A loss shall be allowed as a deduction under section 165(a) only for the taxable year in which the loss is sustained. For this purpose, a loss shall be treated as sustained during the taxable year in which the loss occurs as evidenced by closed and completed transactions and as fixed by identifiable events occurring in such taxable year. For provisions relating to situations where a loss attributable to a disaster will be treated as sustained in the taxable year immediately preceding the taxable year in which the disaster actually occurred, see section 165(h) and §1.165-11.

(2)(i) If a casualty or other event occurs which may result in a loss and, in the year of such casualty or event, there exists a claim for reimbursement with respect to which there is a reasonable prospect of recovery, no portion of the loss with respect to which reimbursement may be received is sustained, for purposes of section 165, until it can be ascertained with reasonable certainty whether or not such reimbursement will be received. Whether a reasonable prospect of recovery exists with respect to a claim for reimbursement of a loss is a question of fact to be determined upon an examination of all facts and circumstances. Whether or not such reimbursement will be received may be ascertained with reasonable certainty, for example, by a settlement of the claim, by an adjudication of the claim, or by an abandonment of the claim. When a taxpayer claims that the taxable year in which a loss is sustained is fixed by his abandonment of the claim for reimbursement, he must be able to produce objective evidence of his having abandoned the claim, such as the execution of a release.

(ii) If in the year of the casualty or other event a portion of the loss is not covered by a claim for reimbursement with respect to which there is a reasonable prospect of recovery, then such portion of the loss is sustained during the taxable year in which the casualty or other event occurs. For example, if property having an adjusted basis of $10,000 is completely destroyed by fire in 1961, and if the taxpayer's only claim for reimbursement consists of an insurance claim for $8,000 which is settled in 1962, the taxpayer sustains a loss of $2,000 in 1961. However, if the taxpayer's automobile is completely destroyed in 1961 as a result of the negligence of another person and there exists a reasonable prospect of recovery on a claim for the full value of the automobile against such person, the taxpayer does not sustain any loss until the taxable year in which the claim is adjudicated or otherwise settled. If the automobile had an adjusted basis of $5,000 and the taxpayer secures a judgment of $4,000 in 1962, $1,000 is deductible for the taxable year 1962. If in 1963 it becomes reasonably certain that only $3,500 can ever be collected on such judgment, $500 is deductible for the taxable year 1963.

The Regulation further provides that if the property is used in a trade or business or is held for the production of income and is totally destroyed, the amount of loss is measured exclusively by the adjusted basis of the property.

In preparing Wilson's 2017 tax return, the theft loss will be computed as follows:

1.	Original cost	$20,000
2.	Fair market value (before theft)	10,000
3.	Fair market value (after theft)	0
4.	Loss in value, caused by theft	10,000
5.	Basis for loss: lesser of line 1 or line 4	10,000
6.	Less: Insurance recovery	7,500
7.	Sustained loss	2,500
8.	Less: Section 165(h) limitation	100
9.	Deductible amount (before 10 percent of AGI limitation)	$2,400

The $2,400 loss, calculated at line 9, should be combined with all other casualty or theft losses incurred in 2017. The aggregate will be deductible to the extent that it exceeds 10 percent of Wilson's 2017 adjusted gross income.

CASE 2. (Illustrating a topical index approach to tax research.)

TAX PROBLEM

Philip Davis, a full-time electrician employed by the Exeter Hotel, hires a preparer to prepare his 2017 tax return. Davis works exclusively at the hotel but feels that he is entitled to deduct the cost of operating his personal vehicle. Davis transports several thousand pounds of electrical parts, equipment, and tools to work each day.

FACTS

The Exeter Hotel does not provide a convenient, well-protected location for Davis to store the various electrical items. Accordingly, the van has a customized interior with appropriate shelves and cabinets for the electrical items. The van, which is also used by Davis as a personal vehicle, was purchased on April 1, 2017, at a cost of $19,000, which includes $2,000 for the customized interior.

ISSUE

Can Davis claim a full or partial transportation expense deduction even though the cost of commuting is not deductible?

RESEARCH

The subject indexes to the CCH Compilation Volumes (whether in print or electronic format) are located in a separate volume entitled the Index Volume. The researcher determines a few key topics under which the relevant references might be found.

First attempt. Locate the term "Transportation." The heading "expenses for" refers the searcher to the topic "Traveling expenses." Under this listing are numerous headings, but the entry at "automobile expenses" leading to "Automobiles: expenses" seems to be the most relevant reference.

Second attempt. Locate the topic "Automobiles" and the term "expenses." Under this listing, the following subheadings seem appropriate for additional research:

.. equipment transported   8590.04; 8590.25

.. tools transported   8590.04; 8590.25

The paragraph reference 8590.25 given in the Index leads to Code Section 162 in the CCH Compilations Volume and thereunder to a digest of the *Fausner* case (*Fausner v. Commissioner*, 73-2 USTC ¶9515), a 1973 Supreme Court decision that disallowed a transportation deduction. In examining this digest, reprinted below, it would appear that Davis cannot deduct any part of his transportation expense.

Exhibit 6. STANDARD FEDERAL TAX REPORTS—COMPILATION SAMPLE PAGE: Annotations

TRADE OR BUSINESS EXPENSES §162 [¶8590]

.25 Equipment and tool transportation.—An individual could not deduct any part of his automobile expenses where he used his car to transport bulky equipment to and from his places of employment because storage facilities were lacking where it was shown that the individual would have used his car to commute to work in any event. Under this circumstance, it was held that it was not possible to allocate the automobile expenses between nondeductible commuting expenses and deductible business expenses incurred in transporting the tools nor had the existence of any additional expense been shown, with the result that the entire cost of traveling to and from the taxpayer's work constituted commuting expenses.

D. Fausner, Sup. Ct., per curiam, 73-2 USTC ¶9515, 413 US 838, aff'g CA-5, per curiam, 73-1 USTC ¶9180, 472 F2d 561.

Code §162 ¶8590.25

However, following the *Fausner* decision, the IRS issued Rev. Rul. 75-380, 1975-2 CB 59, superseding Rev. Rul. 56-25, 1956-2 CB 152, and revoking Rev. Rul. 63-100, 1963-1 CB 34. The full text of Rev. Rul. 75-380 is given at paragraph 8540.2501. Of particular importance to Davis is the following observation in Rev. Rul. 75-380:

Therefore, in situations where a taxpayer can establish that additional expenses were incurred for transporting work implements to and from work, a reasonable and feasible method of allocation within the scope of the Supreme Court's opinion in *Fausner* would be to allow an ordinary and necessary business expense deduction for only the portion of the cost of transporting the work implements by the mode of transportation used which is in excess of cost of commuting by the same mode of transportation without the work implements. The fact that a taxpayer might have or would have used a less expensive mode of transportation if it had not been necessary to carrying the work implements is immaterial.

Based on this logic, it would seem that Davis may, at least, claim a depreciation deduction for the $2,000 that he spent to install shelves and cabinets in his van. However, he would not be entitled to claim a deduction for the cost of transportation to and from work.

Subsequently, following Rev. Rul. 75-380, the Tax Court found in *H.A. Pool*, 36 TCM 93, Dec. 34,233(M), T.C. Memo. 1977-20, that a transportation deduction was allowed for the excess cost of driving a truck rather than a car, since it was necessary to transport tools to work, and the car would not have been able to carry that weight. Following the reasoning in *Pool*, we might also be able to contend that the excess cost of acquiring a van, rather than a passenger automobile, is eligible for a transportation deduction. Of course, in this instance, we are taking a somewhat aggressive position, and our client must be advised of the inherent risk of being challenged by the Internal Revenue Service. The final decision, whether or not to claim this deduction, rests with the client.

Tax Administration

¶2211

ORGANIZATION OF THE IRS

The administration and enforcement of federal internal revenue taxes are required to be performed under the supervision of the Secretary of the Treasury. Code Sec. 7801(a). The Internal Revenue Service, a division of the Department of the Treasury, has been delegated the operational aspects of the determination, assessment, and collection of all internal revenue taxes. The Commissioner of Internal Revenue, the official in charge, is appointed by the President and serves under the Secretary of the Treasury. Code Sec. 7802.

The Internal Revenue Service (IRS) consists of a National Office, headquartered in Washington, D.C., and an extensive field organization composed of over a hundred thousand revenue agents, revenue officers, and support personnel. The main task of the National Office is to develop uniform policies for the nationwide administration of the tax law and coordinate the various operations of the IRS.

Internal Revenue Service Restructuring and Reform Act of 1998

In accordance with the Internal Revenue Service Restructuring and Reform Act of 1998, the IRS modified its entire structure. The structure divides the IRS into four operating divisions. Each operating division is responsible for serving a group of similar taxpayers. The structure is organized to reflect specific types of taxpayers and common issues associated with these taxpayers. See Exhibit 7.

Exhibit 7. IRS ORGANIZATION CHART

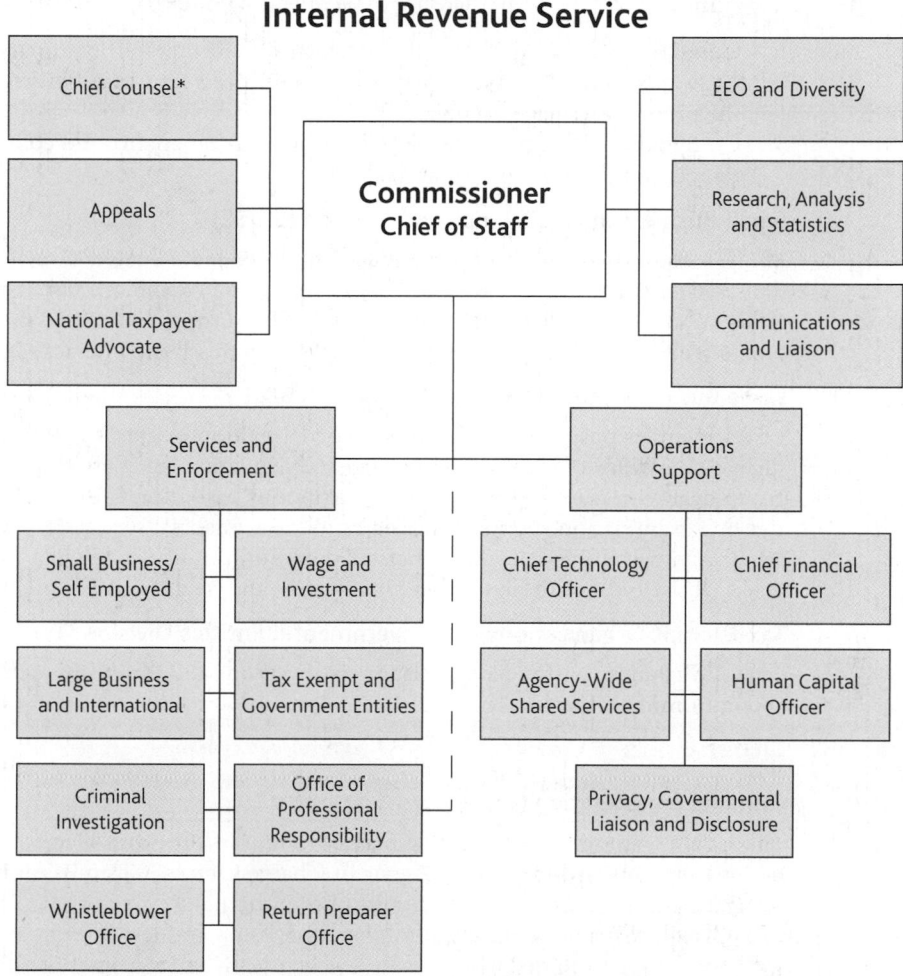

U.S. Department of Treasury

Internal Revenue Service

* With respect to tax litigation and the legal interpretation of tax law, the Chief Counsel also reports to the General Counsel of the Treasury Department. On matters solely related to tax policy, the Chief Counsel reports to the Treasury General Counsel.

The IRS's mission is to:

Provide America's taxpayers top quality service by helping them understand and meet their tax responsibilities and by applying the tax law with integrity and fairness to all.

The four operating divisions are supported by two agency-wide service organizations: (1) Information Systems; and (2) Agency-Wide Shared Services. In addition, the IRS Appeals Office, the Taxpayer Advocate Service, the Office of the Chief Counsel and Criminal Investigation are nationwide organizations that provide separate specialized services.

The Operating Divisions

Wage and Investment Income Division (W&I)

W&I covers individual taxpayers who only receive wage and/or investment income, which includes approximately 88 million filers. Most of these taxpayers only deal with the IRS when filing their tax returns each year. Compliance matters are limited to such issues as dependency exemption, credits, filing status, and deductions. Much of the income earned by W&I taxpayers is reported by third parties (such as employers, banks, brokerage firms) and the income is generally collected through third party withholding. Thus, this group is generally highly compliant. Most of these taxpayers earn under $50,000 a year.

Within the W&I group, there are three operating units:

1. Communications, Assistance, Research and Education—The primary role is education;
2. Customer Account Services—The role is to process returns submitted by taxpayers and validate that the proper taxes have been paid;
3. Compliance—The role is to address the limited compliance and collection issues that may arise with respect to this group of taxpayers.

Small Business and Self-Employed Division (SB/SE)

SB/SE is comprised of fully or partially self-employed individuals and small businesses. It includes corporations and partnerships with assets less than or equal to $10 million. Also, estate and gift taxpayers, fiduciary returns and all individuals who file international returns are examined by this group, which includes approximately 45 million filers. Typical taxpayers from this group interact with the IRS 4 to 60 times per year.

Large Business and International Division (LB&I)

LB&I includes businesses with assets over $10 million or about 210,000 filers. Many complex matters such as tax law interpretation, accounting and regulation issues are common. The largest taxpayers in this group deal with the IRS on an almost continuous basis. The LB&I is aligned by six industry groupings and one examination support function as follows: financial services; natural resources and construction; heavy manufacturing and transportation; communications, technology and media; retailers, food, pharmaceuticals, and healthcare; global high wealth; and field specialists.

Tax-Exempt Organizations and Governmental Entities Division (TE/GE)

TE/GE includes pension plans, exempt organizations and the governmental entities, and is comprised of about 24 million filers.

Other Units

Criminal Investigation (CI)

The CI unit reports directly to the Service Commissioner and Deputy Commissioner. It operates as a nationwide unit with 35 Special Agent In Charge Offices. CI's mission is to the serve the public by investigating potential criminal violations of the Internal Revenue Code and related financial crimes. The new CI will focus more on tax administration issues and less on nontax crimes (such as drug cases). It will provide a streamlined investigative review process and a geographic alignment that is more consistent with the location of the various United States Attorney's Offices.

IRS Appeals Office

The IRS Appeals Office is headquartered in Washington, D.C., but will maintain the geographic location of current offices. The field staff has been realigned to closely mirror the new operating structure. Thus, within a particular office, Appeals Officers will be designated to work on cases from a particular operating division. Three appeals operating units will manage operations for each of the taxpayer segments as follows: (1) Appeals—Large and Mid-Size Businesses; (2) Appeals—Small Business/Self-Employed and Exempt/Governmental Entities; and (3) Appeals—Wage and Investment.

National Taxpayer Advocate (NTA)

The NTA was designed to help taxpayers who have problems with the IRS, and who were not able to get them resolved through the normal administrative process. The NTA is organized around two major functions: (1) the casework function—to resolve all individual taxpayer problems; and (2) the systemic analysis and the advocacy function—to work with the operating divisions to identify systemic problems, analyze root causes, implement solutions, and proactively identify potential problems with new systems and procedures. The NTA will be physically located in geographic locations to allow contact with local taxpayers. A local NTA within each operating division will help to identify system problems in the division.

Office of Chief Counsel

Within the Office of Chief Counsel there is a Division Counsel for each operating division. The Division Counsel provides legal advice and representation, and participates in the plans and activities of the operating division management. The main focus of the Operating Division Counsel is to provide legal services to the operating divisions, take part in planning the strategic use of litigation resources and assist the operating divisions in developing compliance approaches and new taxpayer service initiatives.

Field Counsel will provide litigation services and legal advice on locally managed cases. Field Counsel will consist of attorney groups that will report to an assigned Operating Division counsel.

Office of Professional Responsibility

The Office of Professional Responsibility establishes and enforces consistent standards of competence, integrity, and conduct for tax professionals

Whistleblower Office

The IRS Whistleblower Office processes tips received from individuals who spot tax problems in their workplace, while conducting day-to-day personal business or anywhere else they may be encountered. The Whistleblower Office is responsible for assessing and analyzing the tips and after determining their degree of credibility, the case is assigned to the appropriate IRS office for further investigation.

Communications and Liaison

The Communications and Liaison Division attempts to ensure that communications with customers, Congress, and stakeholders are consistent and coordinated. The Division also attempts to ensure that there is a quality work environment that is operationally efficient and effective, including an emphasis on automating business processes. It attempts to ensure that there is appropriate collection, use, and protection of information to accomplish IRS business objectives.

Office of Privacy, Governmental Liaison and Disclosure

This Division is intended to preserve and enhance public confidence by advocating for the protection and proper use of identity information.

Return Preparer Office

This office's mission is to improve compliance by providing comprehensive oversight and support of tax professionals. Its goal is to improve the compliance and accuracy of tax returns prepared by tax return preparers.

¶2215

REPRESENTATION OF TAXPAYERS

Rules for persons representing taxpayers before the IRS are published in Treasury Department Circular No. 230. See 31 CFR Part 10. The phrase "practice before the IRS" includes all matters connected with presentation to the IRS relating to a client's rights, privileges, or liabilities under laws or regulations administered by the IRS. Circular No. 230, Sec. 10.2.

Neither the preparation of a return nor the appearance as a witness for the taxpayer is considered practice before the IRS. Attorneys or certified public accountants who are not under suspension or disbarment may practice before the IRS, as may any person enrolled as an agent. The latter individual, however, must demonstrate special competence in tax matters by written examination administered by the IRS. Treasury Department Circular No. 230, Sec. 10.4.

In certain situations, other persons may represent taxpayers. Individuals may appear on their own behalf, and, in addition, Treasury Department Circular No. 230, Sec. 10.7, states a number of situations where individuals may appear on behalf of others without enrollment:

1. An individual may represent another individual who is his or her full-time employer, a partnership of which he or she is a general partner or a full-time employee, or a family member.
2. Corporations, associations, or organized groups may be represented by bona fide officers or full-time employees.
3. Trusts, receiverships, guardianships, or estates may be represented by their trustees, receivers, guardians, administrators, or executors or full-time employees.
4. An individual who prepares the taxpayer's return as a preparer may represent the taxpayer before officers and employees of the Examination Division of the IRS.

EXAMPLE 2.2   Sam Spaulding is being audited by the IRS for tax years 2015 and 2016. He prepared his own 2015 return, but ABC Tax Return Preparation Service prepared his 2016 return. ABC could represent Sam on matters relating to the 2016 return but only at the agent or examining officer level, not at the higher level of the Appeals Division.

Circular No. 230, Secs. 10.20 to 10.30, states a number of rules relative to practice before the IRS by tax preparers:

1. They shall not neglect or refuse promptly to submit records or information requested by the IRS.
2. They shall advise the client promptly of any noncompliance, error, or omission that may have been on any return or document submitted to the IRS.
3. They shall exercise due diligence in preparing returns and documents and in determining the correctness of oral or written representations made by them to the IRS and to clients.
4. They shall not unreasonably delay the prompt disposition of any matter before the IRS.
5. They shall not in any IRS matter knowingly and directly or indirectly employ or accept assistance from any person who is under disbarment or suspension from practice before the IRS.
6. They shall not charge an unconscionable fee for representation of a client in any matter before the IRS.
7. They shall not represent clients with conflicting interests.
8. They shall not use or participate in the use of any form of public communication containing false, fraudulent, misleading, or unfair statements or claims.

¶2225   RULINGS PROGRAMS

Since passage of the first income tax laws, the IRS has engaged in major publication efforts to provide taxpayers and their advisors with the most current interpretive views of all areas of federal income tax law. The *Internal Revenue Bulletin* is the authoritative instrument of the IRS for announcing official rulings (Revenue Rulings and Revenue Procedures) and for publishing Treasury Decisions, Executive Orders, Tax Conventions, legislation, and other items of general interest. Since publication invites reliance, taxpayers must be aware of the degree of authoritative weight that may be accorded such documents. See detailed discussion at ¶2035.

In addition, Technical Information Releases (TIRs) and Announcements are periodically distributed by the IRS to advise the public of various technical matters. While these pronouncements are published weekly in the *Internal Revenue Bulletin,* they are not usually included in the *Cumulative Bulletin.*

The IRS also issues communications to individual taxpayers and IRS personnel in three primary ways: (1) letter rulings, (2) determination letters, and (3) technical advice memoranda. These documents are part of the IRS Rulings Program, which includes published rulings appearing in the *Internal Revenue Bulletin.*

Letter Rulings

A letter ruling is a "written determination issued to a taxpayer that interprets and applies the tax laws to that taxpayer's specific set of facts." Rev. Proc. 2017-1, Sec. 2.01, 2017-1 IRB. Letter rulings generally are issued on uncompleted, actual (rather than hypothetical) transactions or on transactions that have been completed before the filing of the tax return for the year in question. Thus, the emphasis of the letter rulings program is upon the questions or problems of the taxpayer, in contrast to the published rulings program, where the emphasis is centered on uniformity of interpretation of the tax law.

It is the policy of the IRS, however, not to issue letter rulings in a number of general areas:

1. Results of transactions that lack bona fide business purposes or have as their principal purpose the reduction of federal taxes.
2. Matters on which a court decision adverse to the government has been handed down and the question of following the decision or litigating further has not yet been resolved.
3. Matters involving the prospective application of the estate tax to the property or the estate of a living person.
4. Matters involving alternate plans of proposed transactions or involving hypothetical situations.
5. Matters involving the federal tax consequences of any proposed federal, state, local, or municipal legislation.
6. Whether a proposed transaction would subject the taxpayer to a criminal penalty.

Further, it is the policy of the IRS to provide revised lists of those areas of the Internal Revenue Code in which advanced rulings or determination letters will not or will "not ordinarily" be issued. ("Not ordinarily" connotes that unique and compelling reasons must be demonstrated to justify a ruling or determination letter.) Additions or deletions to the revised lists are made as needed to reflect the current policy of the IRS and are set out in several Revenue Procedures. For example, no ruling will be issued to determine whether compensation is reasonable in amount and therefore allowable as a deduction under Code Sec. 162. This is but one of over 120 areas identified by the IRS for nonissuance of letter rulings. There is also a listing of over 50 areas in which rulings will not ordinarily be issued. Rev. Proc. 2017-3, Sec. 3 and 4, 2017-1 IRB. Areas in international transactions for which rulings will not be issued are also listed. Rev. Proc. 2017-7, Sec. 3, 2017-1 IRB.

The issuance of rulings serves to reduce the number of disputes with revenue agents. A favorable ruling generally will avoid any controversy with an agent in the event of a later audit. For the taxpayer, rulings reduce the uncertainty of tax consequences of a particular action. On the other hand, a ruling request has some disadvantages. Cost is a factor since, under the IRS user fee program, a taxpayer will have to pay fees to have a request prepared. Code Sec. 7805. Rev. Proc. 2017-1, Appendix A, 2017-1 IRB. Also, there is often delay in obtaining a ruling, which could be difficult for the taxpayer if time is a significant factor.

Detailed instructions as to the information that a taxpayer should submit in requesting a ruling are given in Rev. Proc. 2017-1, *supra.*

PLANNING POINTER

Although there may be advantages to obtaining a ruling, it may not always be desirable to request a ruling. If the tax results are uncertain but the taxpayer wants to go ahead with a proposed transaction, it might be unwise to request a ruling. Also, if time is a crucial factor and the proposed transaction is so complex that a long time might pass before a response to a ruling request would be given, it might be unwise to request a ruling.

Determination Letters

The determination letter program is part of the letter rulings program. Determination Letters are not published; however, the IRS is now required to make individual rulings available for public inspection. A determination letter is a written statement issued by a Director in response to an inquiry by an individual or an organization. It applies to the particular facts involved and is based upon principles and precedents previously announced by the National Office to a specific set of facts. Rev. Proc. 2017-1, Sec. 2.03, *supra.* Determination letters are issued in response to taxpayers' requests submitted to the Director, whereas letter rulings are issued by the National Office. The most important use of determination letters in prospective transactions is in the qualification of pension plans and the determination of the tax-exempt status of an organization.

PLANNING POINTER

It is advisable for taxpayers to request a determination letter in connection with pension plans; otherwise, the taxpayer may later find out that the plan does not qualify and deductions might be disallowed.

A Director may not issue a determination letter in response to an inquiry relating to a question specifically covered by statute, regulations, rulings, etc. published in the *Internal Revenue Bulletin* where (1) it appears that the taxpayer has directed a similar inquiry to the National Office; (2) the identical issue involving the same taxpayer is pending in a case before the Appeals Office; (3) the determination letter is requested by an industry, trade, or similar group; or (4) the request involves an industry-wide problem. Reg. §601.201(c)(4). The form for a request for a determination letter is the same as that for a ruling. Rev. Proc. 2017-1, *supra.*

Technical Advice Memoranda

A technical advice memorandum is advice or guidance furnished by the National Office upon request of a District or an Appeals Office in response to any technical or procedural question that develops during the examination or appeals process. Rev. Proc. 2017-2, Sec. 3, 2017-1 IRB. Both the taxpayer and the District or Appeals Office may request technical advice. The taxpayer may request advice where there appears to be a lack of uniformity in the application of law or where the issue is unusual or complex. Technical advice adverse to the taxpayer and furnished to an Appeals Office does not preclude the possibility of settlement. Technical advice can also be advantageous from the IRS's viewpoint in that it serves to establish consistent holdings in field offices. Responses to requests for technical advice memoranda sometimes become the basis for a Revenue Ruling.

User Fee Program

The payment of user fees is required for all requests to the IRS for rulings, opinion letters, determination letters, and similar requests. The IRS issues schedules of fees and procedures for the collection of the fees along with other guidelines as prescribed by the Revenue Act of 1987. The fee schedules range from $275 to $28,300. Rev. Proc. 2017-1, Appendix A, 2017-1 IRB.

¶2245   TAXPAYER COMPLIANCE ASSISTANCE

In order to assist taxpayers, individuals, corporations, partnerships, and other legal entities to be in compliance with requirements of the Internal Revenue Code and regulations, the IRS develops and issues IRS Publications that address a variety of general and special topics of concern to taxpayers. A typical IRS Publication highlights changes in the tax law in a specific area (for example, Pub. No. 508, Educational Expenses), explains the purpose of the law, defines terminology, lists exemptions, provides several examples, and includes sample worksheets and filled-in forms. As to taxpayer reliance, the IRS warns in every IRS Publication that information provided covers only the most common tax situation and is not intended to replace the law or change its meaning. Even though IRS Publications do not bind the IRS, the information contained in IRS Publications provides essential guidance for tax law compliance, particularly in technical or specialized areas.

Tax Practice and Procedure

¶2301   EXAMINATION OF RETURNS

Selection of Returns

The selection of returns for examination begins at the service centers. Returns can be selected by computer programs or by manual selection. The IRS uses the Discriminant Inventory Function (DIF) system, which involves computer scoring using mathematical formulas to select tax returns with the highest probability of errors. Returns with the highest scores are then manually examined by district classifiers, who determine whether a return should be subject to examination. *Internal Revenue Manual,* Sec. 4.1.5.1.1. Taxpayers are divided into classes, including such classifications as business versus nonbusiness; total positive income of varying amounts for nonbusiness returns; and total gross receipts of varying amounts for business returns. Total Positive Income (TPI) is defined as the sum of positive income items on the return such as wages, interest, dividends, and other income items, with losses treated as zero.

Returns are sometimes chosen at random for the National Research Program (NRP). NRP is a program for measuring taxpayer compliance through specialized audits of individual tax returns. The principal uses of NRP data are to measure the levels of compliance and tax administration gaps necessary for formulation of the IRS's long-term enforcement policies, to determine changes in compliance levels over a period of time in order to properly direct enforcement programs, to develop and improve return selection procedures and changes in the DIF scores, to identify alternative methods of operation, and to achieve greater operating economies.

Other events that might give rise to an examination are:

1. Total positive income is above specified amounts.
2. Another IRS office or a non-IRS party might provide information (e.g., a tip from a bitter former spouse).
3. A claim for refund may result in a closer examination of the return.
4. A return of a related party (family member, partner) might be examined to determine the correctness of the taxpayer's return.

EXAMPLE 2.3	Arthur and Beverly Saunders were divorced in 2017. During their marriage, Arthur had not reported some consulting income he received beyond his regular salary. Beverly, still upset about the divorce, reports Arthur to the IRS. This may result in an audit.

EXAMPLE 2.4	In 2017, Charles Regus files an amended return with a sizeable refund claim as a result of educational expense deductions that he could have taken on his 2015 return, but which he failed to take because he was uncertain as to whether they would qualify. It is possible that close examination of his 2015 return might occur as a result of this claim for refund. However, if Charles believes he has a good case, he should file the amended return.

Correspondence Examinations

Correspondence examinations involve relatively simple problems that can generally be resolved by mail. These examinations would include mathematical errors, broadly defined in Code Sec. 6213(g)(2) to mean (1) an error in addition, subtraction, multiplication, or division shown on any return; (2) an incorrect use of any IRS table if such incorrect use is apparent from other information on the return; (3) inconsistent entries on the return; (4) an omission of information required to be supplied on the return to substantiate a return item; and (5) a deduction or credit that exceeds a statutory limit that is either a specified monetary amount or a percentage, ratio, or fraction—if the items entering into the application of such limit appear on the return.

EXAMPLE 2.5	James Judson, single, incorrectly determines his tax liability because he used the joint rate schedule rather than the single rate schedule. This correction and adjustment can be resolved by mail.

The Service Center personnel might also question specific items under the Unallowable Items Program. For example, a deduction of Social Security taxes by the taxpayer would result in notification by the Service Center. Such a contact is considered to be an examination in contrast to a mathematical/clerical error notification, which is not considered to be an examination. (If it is an examination, one is entitled to a notice of deficiency and to administrative appeal.) The IRS also matches information returns of some taxpayers with income tax returns. If there is a discrepancy, the return will be corrected, or the file might be referred for examination and possibly criminal investigation.

District Office Examinations

A District Office examination of a return is conducted by a tax auditor of the Audit Division either by correspondence or by interview. Sometimes the matters are so simple they can be handled by correspondence. Verification of particular itemized deductions such as interest, taxes, or charitable contributions might be handled by correspondence. *Internal Revenue Manual*, Sec. 4.10.2 and 3.

Returns selected for interview examinations generally require some analysis and judgment as well as verification. Examples of types of issues which lend themselves to interview examinations are income items that are not subject to withholding, deductions for travel and entertainment, items such as casualty and theft losses that involve the use of fair market value, education expenses, deductions for business-related expenses, and determination of basis of property. Also, if the taxpayer's income is low in relation to financial responsibilities as indicated on the return through the number of dependents or interest expense, or if the taxpayer's occupation is of the type that required only a limited formal education, an office interview might be deemed appropriate. Certain business activities or occupations reported may lend themselves to office interview examinations (e.g., auto repair shops, restaurants, service stations, professional persons, farmers, motels, and others).

EXAMPLE 2.6	Edward Egars, an outside salesperson, reports income of $25,000 and takes travel and entertainment deductions before application of the 50 percent limit on meals and entertainment of $15,000. Edward could be called in for an office examination to verify his travel and entertainment expenses.

EXAMPLE 2.7 Jane Judson has adjusted gross income of $15,000 and gives $7,000 in cash contributions to her church. Since her contributions exceed the norm for her bracket and approach the maximum limitation for her income level, she could be called in to verify her charitable contributions.

PLANNING POINTER In an office examination, the taxpayer or a representative should provide only information or support for items that are requested of the taxpayer by the IRS; otherwise, the tax auditor might open up other areas for investigation. Situations may vary, but some practitioners believe that it is better for the taxpayer, assuming there is a representative such as a CPA or a lawyer, not to be present because the representative can keep better control over the interview and also maintain a less emotional atmosphere.

When there is a disagreement after an office examination, if practicable, the taxpayer is given an opportunity for an interview with the tax auditor's immediate supervisor or for a conference with an Appeals Officer. Reg. §601.105(c)(1)(ii). If these actions are not feasible, the taxpayer will be sent a 30-day letter from the District Office indicating the proposed adjustments and the courses of action. If the taxpayer agrees with the adjustment, the taxpayer can sign the agreement form. If the taxpayer disagrees, an Appeals Office conference may be requested within 30 days or the taxpayer may ignore the 30-day letter and wait for the 90-day letter, which allows the taxpayer to file a petition in the Tax Court. Reg. §601.105(c)(1)(ii) and (d)(1)(iv).

Field Examinations

Field examinations are conducted by revenue agents and involve more complex issues than do office examinations. Field audits take place in the taxpayer's or the taxpayer's representative's office or home. The revenue agent must identify items that may need adjustment, gather the appropriate evidence, and apply the applicable Code provisions, Regulations, and other interpretative rulings. Techniques have been developed by the IRS to try to ensure that revenue agents consider all areas necessary for a proper calculation of the tax liability. An agent has power to subpoena all books and records and to compel the attendance of witnesses. Code Sec. 7602.

The agent completes a report called the Revenue Agent Report (RAR). In agreed cases, a copy of the RAR is sent to the taxpayer before review. If the taxpayer agrees with the revenue agent's adjustments and proposals, the taxpayer can sign Form 870 (Waiver of Restrictions on Assessment and Collection of Deficiency in Tax). In unagreed cases, the taxpayer does not receive the RAR until after review by the Review Staff.

PLANNING POINTER The revenue agent should be treated courteously and should be promptly furnished information and substantiation relating to applicable tax return items. Although the cooperation of the taxpayer (or the taxpayer's representative) is important, the taxpayer should respond only to questions asked by the agent. Disclosing unnecessary information could cause problems for the taxpayer.

There are some advantages to settling with the revenue agent. In addition to being less costly than settling at higher levels, negotiations with the revenue agent are generally more informal than negotiations at higher levels and less demanding on technical aspects. Also, if questionable issues exist but were not raised at the agent level, it may be wise to settle at that level in order to avoid the possibility of persons at higher levels raising those questionable issues. Similarly, there is an advantage to the revenue agent to have an agreed case because it involves more effort and time to write a report on an unagreed case than on an agreed case.

Audit Reconsideration

The audit reconsideration is a procedure that is used when a taxpayer has ignored a statutory notice of deficiency or where there has been a breakdown in communication between the taxpayer and the IRS. *Internal Revenue Manual,* Sec. 4.13.4.4. An audit reconsideration is permitted when a new notice was not sent to the taxpayer's new address, the taxpayer had not received any notification from the IRS on any assessment, and the taxpayer had not been given an opportunity to submit any required substantiation or necessary documentation.

¶2311 APPEALS PROCESS

Administrative Process

If the taxpayer and the agent do not agree, the taxpayer will be sent a 30-day letter that explains the appellate procedures and urges the taxpayer to reply within 30 days either by signing the waiver or by requesting a conference. If the taxpayer does not respond to the 30-day letter, a statutory notice of deficiency (90-day letter) will be sent giving the taxpayer 90 days to file a petition with the Tax Court. Thus, if the taxpayer and agent do not agree, the taxpayer has several options:

1. The taxpayer may request a conference in the IRS Appeals Office.
2. After receiving the statutory notice of deficiency, the taxpayer may file a petition in the Tax Court within the 90-day period.
3. The taxpayer could wait for the 90-day period to expire, pay the assessment, and start a refund suit in the District Court or the Court of Federal Claims.

If the IRS and the taxpayer agree, the statutory notice of deficiency issued by the IRS (90-day letter) may be rescinded. The rescinded notice voids the limitations regarding credits, refunds, and assessments, and the taxpayer will have no right to petition the Tax Court based on such notice. Rescinding the deficiency notice will allow for resolution of the controversy within the IRS.

IRS Appeals Office

If an appeal is made within the IRS, an appropriate request must be made. The request must be accompanied by a written protest unless:

1. The proposed increase or decrease in tax or claimed refund is not more than $2,500 for any of the tax periods involved in field examination cases.
2. The examination was conducted by a tax auditor (i.e., an office examination) or by correspondence. (See IRS Publication No. 5, Appeal Rights and Preparation of Protests for Unagreed Cases.)

If a protest is required, it should be sent within the 30-day period granted in the letter containing the examination report. The protest should contain:

1. A statement that the taxpayer wants to appeal the findings of the examiner to the Appeals Office
2. Taxpayer's name and address
3. The date and symbols from the letter transmitting the proposed adjustments and findings the taxpayer is protesting
4. The tax periods or years involved
5. An itemized schedule of the adjustments with which the taxpayer does not agree
6. A statement of facts supporting the taxpayer's position in any contested factual issue
7. A statement outlining the law or other authority on which the taxpayer is relying

A taxpayer may go to the Appeals Office at two different times: (1) if the protest is filed within the 30-day period as stated in the 30-day letter, or (2) if the 30-day period passes and the taxpayer files a petition in the Tax Court within 90 days after receipt of a statutory notice of deficiency.

Exhibit 8 shows graphically the income tax appeal procedures within the IRS (as described above) and through the court system (as described on the following pages).

Exhibit 8. INCOME TAX APPEAL PROCEDURE

Income Tax Appeal Procedure
Internal Revenue Service

At any stage of procedure:
You can agree and arrange to pay.
You can ask the Service to issue you a notice of deficiency so you can file a petition with the Tax Court.
You can pay the tax and file a claim for a refund.

There are a number of important factors to consider in filing a protest and going to the Appeals Office. It is less expensive than litigation and yet the taxpayer leaves open the opportunity to file a petition in the Tax Court or to sue for refund in a District Court or the Court of Federal Claims. In addition, a taxpayer is often able to gather more information about the IRS position in the event the taxpayer needs to carry the case further, and there may be a chance that the taxpayer can convince the Appeals Officer that the IRS was incorrect at the agent level. The Appeals Officer may be at some disadvantage in that the case was not personally prepared and the Appeals Officer is relying on the information presented by the revenue agent, which could be an advantage to the taxpayer.

On the other hand, there may be some disadvantages to having an Appeals Conference. New issues might be raised in an Appeals Conference, although the IRS's policy is to avoid raising an issue unless the grounds for such action are "substantial" and the potential effect upon tax liability is "material." 26 CFR Sec. 601.106(d)(1). The Appeals Officer must have a strong reason for raising an issue. The *Internal Revenue Manual,* Sec. 8.6.1.4, has given the following example in the past:

EXAMPLE 2.8	If a District Director disallowed a claimed farm loss solely on the ground that it was a hobby loss and stated nothing concerning the items making up the loss, there would not be substantial grounds for raising a new issue concerning the amount of the loss merely because the Appeals Officer suspected that the items had not been verified. On the other hand, if the examiner had indicated in the report that the items had not been verified, there would be good reason for the Appeals Officer to refer the case back to the District Director if it was believed such action was necessary. If the District Director stated that some of the items of claimed expense were personal in nature, this would constitute substantial grounds for the Appeals Officer to raise a new issue or to refer the case back to the District Director for further information and investigation.

Taxpayers may represent themselves at the Appeals Conference or be represented by an attorney, CPA, or person enrolled to practice before the IRS. The Appeals Officer, who actually handles the appeals, reports to the Regional Director of Appeals who, in turn, reports to the Regional Commissioner. Proceedings before the Appeals Officer are informal and are held in the District Office. The Appeals Officer may request that the taxpayer submit additional information, which could involve additional conferences.

The Appeals Officer may resolve controversies between the taxpayer and the IRS by considering the "hazards of litigation." The *Internal Revenue Manual,* Sec. 8.1.1.3, states that a fair and impartial resolution "reflects on an issue-by-issue basis the probable result in event of litigation, or one which reflects mutual concessions for the purpose of settlement based on the relative strength of the opposing positions where there is a substantial uncertainty of the result in event of litigation." If there is uncertainty as to the application of the law, the Appeals Officer will consider a settlement in view of the hazards that would exist if the case were litigated. Thus, the Appeals Officer, in evaluating a case for settlement, will objectively assess how a court might look at the case rather than attempt to obtain the best results for the IRS. The Appeals Officer considers the value of the evidence that would be presented, the witnesses, the uncertainty as to an issue of fact and the uncertainty as to a conclusion considering the court in which the case might be litigated or appealed.

If a satisfactory settlement of the issue is reached after consideration by the Appeals Office, the taxpayer will be requested to sign Form 870-AD. By signing Form 870-AD, the taxpayer waives restrictions on the assessment and collection of any deficiency. Form 870-AD does not stop the running of interest when filed. It is merely the taxpayer's offer to waive restrictions, and interest will run until 30 days after the IRS has accepted the offer. If the taxpayer does not agree with the decision at the Appeals level, a notice of deficiency will be issued by the Appeals Office after consideration by the Regional Counsel of the memorandum recommending a notice of deficiency.

Taxpayer's Rights

The Taxpayer Bill of Rights is a series of provisions which require the Treasury Department to outline in "simple and nontechnical terms the rights of a taxpayer and the obligations of the IRS during an audit." Additionally, the IRS is required to inform taxpayers of their administrative and appeals rights in the event of an adverse decision, as well as the procedures related to refund claims, taxpayer complaints, collection assessments, levies, and tax liens. The Treasury Department has prepared and released the required information statement, IRS Publication No. 1, Your Rights as a Taxpayer.

The Taxpayer Bill of Rights is divided into four major categories:

1. Taxpayer rights and IRS obligations
2. Levy and lien provisions
3. Proceedings by taxpayers
4. Authority of the Tax Court

Most significantly, the law requires abatement of penalties resulting from reliance on erroneous written IRS advice, authorizes recovery of damages for failure of the IRS to remove a lawful lien, permits the filing of an application for hardship relief with the IRS Taxpayer Advocate, and outlines provisions whereby a taxpayer, who substantially prevails in an administrative or court proceeding against the IRS, may recover reasonable administrative and litigation costs. Additionally, the law allows a taxpayer or an IRS representative to make an audio recording of an in-person interview regarding the determination or collection of any tax.

To ensure the effective administration of the Taxpayer Bill of Rights, an Office for Taxpayer Services has been established, under the direction of an Assistant Commissioner for Taxpayer Services. Responsibilities of this office include: telephone, walk-in and taxpayer educational services, and the design and production of tax and informational forms. Also, there is a Taxpayer Advocate, holding the rank of Assistant to the Commissioner, who may act, under the Problem Resolution Program, on behalf of the taxpayer during the audit or collection process.

Appeal Through the Court System

Within 90 days of mailing of a notice of deficiency, the taxpayer may petition the Tax Court for re-determination of the deficiency. Code Sec. 6213(a). If the 90-day deficiency notice was issued by the Appeals Office, it is possible to arrange for pretrial settlement with the Regional Counsel of the IRS even after the case has been docketed in the Tax Court. Taxpayers filing a petition with the Tax Court may have their cases handled under less formal rules applicable to "small tax cases" if the amount of the deficiency or claimed overpayment is not greater than $50,000. However, "small tax cases" are not appealable and are not to be treated as precedents for any other cases. Code Sec. 7463(a) and (b). If the taxpayer does not file a petition with the Tax Court within 90 days, the opportunity to appeal to the Tax Court is lost.

The taxpayer can pay the deficiency and file a claim for refund by filing Form 1040X (Amended U.S. Individual Income Tax Return) and mailing it to the IRS Center where the taxpayer filed the original return. A claim for refund must be filed within three years from the date the return was filed or within two years from the date the tax was paid, whichever is later. Code Sec. 6511(a). If the return was filed before the due date, the three-year period starts to run from the date the return was due.

A suit to recover may not be started until after six months from the date the taxpayer filed the claim for refund, unless a decision on the claim for refund was made before then. A suit for refund must be started before the end of two years from the date of mailing of a notice to the taxpayer disallowing part or all of the claim. Code Sec. 6532(a).

Federal Court System

There are three trial courts or courts of original jurisdiction: the U.S. Tax Court, the U.S. District Courts, and the U.S. Court of Federal Claims. Appeal from a decision of the Tax Court of the U.S. District Court may be taken by either side to the federal Court of Appeals for the circuit in which the taxpayer resides or the corporation has its principal place of business. A review of a decision of the U.S. Court of Federal Claims is taken to the U.S. Court of Appeals for the Federal Circuit. The Supreme Court has jurisdiction to hear appeals or review decisions of the federal Court of Appeals and the U.S. Court of Appeals for the Federal Circuit. (See Exhibit 9.) For a detailed discussion of the trial court system, see ¶2055.

Choice of Tax Forum

There are a number of factors to consider in deciding whether to litigate a case and where to litigate.

1. **Jurisdiction.** The Tax Court handles only income, estate, gift, and excess profits tax cases. The District Court and the Court of Federal Claims can litigate all areas of internal revenue taxes.
2. **Payment of tax.** In the Tax Court, payment of tax is not generally allowed. Section 6213(b)(4) allows the taxpayer to pay the tax after receiving a 90-day letter and still sue in the Tax Court. This feature can be used by the taxpayer to stop the accrual of interest on the deficiency while still choosing the Tax Court forum. In the District Court and the Court of Federal Claims, payment of tax is required. Thus, whether the taxpayer has the money to pay the tax may be a factor in the choice of tax forum.
3. **Jury trial.** A jury trial is available only in the District Court. Often, tax cases do not make good jury cases because of their complexity. Also, sometimes jurors may be prejudiced against a taxpayer who is wealthier than they are.
4. **Rules of evidence.** The rules of evidence are most strict in jury trials where efforts must be made to keep the jurors from hearing inappropriate evidence. The evidence rules are most lenient in the Tax Court.
5. **Expertise of judges.** Since the Tax Court hears only tax cases, the judges are all very knowledgeable in tax law. The District Court judges are generally the least technically oriented since the District Court hears many types of cases.
6. **Publicity.** There will likely be the most publicity in the District Court since such suit is brought in the district in which the taxpayer lives.
7. **Legal precedent.** The court decisions by which the particular forum will be bound may also be a consideration. The Tax Court is bound by Tax Court decisions (unless the Court of Appeals of the

circuit to which the case might be appealed held differently), by the Court of Appeals to which the case might be appealed, and by the U.S. Supreme Court. (See *J.E. Golsen*, 54 TC 757, Dec. 30,049 (1970), aff'd, 71-2 USTC ¶9497, 445 F.2d 985 (CA-10 1971), cert. denied, 404 U.S. 940, 92 S.Ct. 284.) The District Court is bound by decisions of the Court of Appeals for the circuit to which the decision would be appealed, and by the U.S. Supreme Court. The Court of Federal Claims is bound by decisions of the Court of Appeals for the Federal Circuit and by U.S. Supreme Court decisions.

8. **Factual precedent.** In certain types of cases, one court may be more favorable to the taxpayer than another court. For example, regarding the characterization of voluntary payments to employees' widows as a gift or as compensation, the Tax Court decisions have consistently been unfavorable to the taxpayer, while results in the Courts of Appeals have been more balanced. 2017 CCH Standard Federal Tax Reports ¶5507.4741.

9. **Statute of limitations.** The statute of limitations is suspended in a filing in the Tax Court whereas suit in the Court of Federal Claims and the District Court does not suspend the statute of limitations. Suspension of the statute of limitations means that the IRS can raise new issues and claims for additional taxes.

10. **Discovery.** In the District Court and the Court of Federal Claims, both parties (i.e., taxpayer and IRS) have available to them discovery tools that allow them access to the other party's evidence prior to trial. In the Tax Court, the parties are expected "to attain the objectives of discovery through informal consultation or communication" and no depositions are permitted (except in very limited circumstances). Tax Court Rule 70.

PLANNING POINTER	It is important for taxpayers to be aware of the characteristics of the courts so that an appropriate choice can be made if the taxpayer decides to go to court. A taxpayer, having made a decision to go to the District Court, for example, cannot later decide to go to the Tax Court. The taxpayer must think very seriously before taking a case to court. Not only may the economic costs be high, but the psychological and emotional costs may be high. The taxpayer must consider whether the tax savings will be worth the legal fees, time, and psychological costs. A taxpayer, in deciding to which court to take a case, should not look simply at the statistics on taxpayer winnings in the various courts. Statistics like that have some value only if winnings by taxpayers on similar issues are being examined.
KEYSTONE PROBLEM	If a taxpayer is called up for an office examination, what should the taxpayer do? If the taxpayer and the tax auditor do not agree, what steps should be taken? What factors would be considered in deciding whether or not to pursue the matter?

¶2315 SETTLEMENT AGREEMENTS

Where a taxpayer and the appeals officer have reached an agreement as to some or all of the issues in controversy, generally the appeals officer will request that the taxpayer sign a Form 870, the same agreement that is used at the district level. However, when neither party with justification is willing to concede in full the unresolved area of disagreement and a resolution of the dispute involves concessions for the purposes of settlement by both parties, a mutual concession settlement is reached, and a Form 870-AD type of agreement is to be used. Form 870 becomes effective as a waiver of restrictions and assessment when received by the Internal Revenue Service, whereas the Form 870-AD is effective upon acceptance by or on behalf of the Commissioner of Internal Revenue.

¶2325 REFUNDS

Claims for refund of individual income taxes are to be made on Form 1040X (Amended U.S. Individual Income Tax Return) and on Form 1120X for corporate income tax refunds. The claim for refund must be filed no later than three years from the date the return was filed or no later than two years from the date the tax was paid, whichever period expires later. Code Sec. 6511(a). If the return was filed before the due date, the three-year period starts to run from the date the return was due. There is a special seven-year period of limitation on a claim for refund based on a debt that became wholly worthless or on a worthless security. If the refund claim relates to a net operating loss, capital loss, or credit carryback, the refund claim may be filed within three years after the time for filing the tax return for the year of the loss (or unused credit). Code Sec. 6511(d).

Any tax deducted or withheld at the source during any calendar year shall be deemed to be paid on the 15th day of the fourth month following the close of the taxable year. Code Sec. 6513(b). Thus, a refund for taxes withheld must be filed within three years of the due date of the return (including extensions). Code Sec. 6511(b).

EXAMPLE 2.9

In 2017, Joe, a college student, worked part-time during the summer. He earned $3,000 and had income tax withheld of $400. He did not file a 2017 tax return by April 15, 2018. If he does not file his 2017 tax return by April 15, 2021, he cannot obtain the refund of $400.

¶2333   INTEREST ON UNDER/OVERPAYMENTS

The interest rate that taxpayers must pay for underpayment of taxes is equal to the federal short-term rate plus three percentage points. In the case of overpayment of taxes, the amount of interest owed by the Treasury is equal to the federal short-term rate plus three percentage points. Code Sec. 6621(a). These interest rates are adjusted quarterly, with the new rates becoming effective two months after the date of each adjustment.

Interest is also paid by the IRS on overpayments of tax. However, if any overpayment of tax is refunded within 45 days after the due date of the return (or filing date if later), no interest is allowed. If any overpayment results from a carryback (net operating loss, capital loss, or credit) through filing an amended return, interest is paid only if the overpayment is not refunded within the 45-day period. Code Sec. 6611(e) and (f).

¶2355   STATUTE OF LIMITATIONS

Assessment of any tax must be made within three years after the return was filed or after the due date for filing, whichever is later. Code Sec. 6501(a). After making an assessment of tax, the IRS has 10 years in which to initiate collection proceedings. Code Sec. 6502(a).

EXAMPLE 2.10

Fred Forbes filed his 2017 return on February 20, 2018. The government may not assess any additional tax for 2017 after April 15, 2021. If, on the other hand, he had filed his 2017 return on October 8, 2018, the statute of limitations would expire on October 8, 2021.

There are some exceptions to the general rule:

1. There is no limitation on the period for assessment in three cases: (1) false return, (2) willful attempt to evade tax, and (3) no return. Code Sec. 6501(c)(1)-(3).

EXAMPLE 2.11

Linda Lord failed to file tax returns in 2006 and 2007 when she had $20,000 gross income. If the government discovered in 2017 that the returns were not filed, it could assess 2006 and 2007 taxes against Linda.

2. If the taxpayer omits from gross income an amount that is in excess of 25 percent of the amount of gross income stated on the return, the tax may be assessed at any time within six years after the return is filed or the due date for filing, if later. In computing gross income, revenues from the sale of goods or services are not to be reduced by cost of goods sold. Code Sec. 6501(e)(1). Gross income also includes capital gains but is not reduced by capital losses.

EXAMPLE 2.12

On her 2016 return filed on March 20, 2017, Vera Vaughn reported her salary of $35,000 and taxable interest of $5,000. She failed to report a $9,000 capital gain. Since the $9,000 omission does not exceed $10,000 (25 percent of $40,000), the statute of limitations expires on April 15, 2020. If the omitted capital gain had been $11,000, the statute of limitations would expire on April 15, 2023.

EXAMPLE 2.13   As a sole proprietor, George Ganger had $50,000 sales and $20,000 cost of goods sold, which were reported on his 2016 tax return filed on March 14, 2017. Through an oversight he failed to report $8,000 interest. Since $8,000 interest does not exceed $12,500 (25 percent of $50,000), the statute of limitations expires on April 15, 2020.

3. Where both the taxpayer and the IRS agree, the statute of limitations may be extended for a specific period. The extension must be executed before the expiration of the applicable limitation period. Code Sec. 6501(c)(4).
4. Certain taxpayers may request a prompt assessment. The period of assessment may be shortened to 18 months in the case of a decedent, the estate of a decedent, or a corporation that is dissolved or contemplating dissolution. Code Sec. 6501(d). The purpose of this rule is to allow an estate or corporation to settle its affairs early without having to make contingent plans for later possible tax assessments.
5. If a personal holding company fails to file with its return a schedule regarding its status as a personal holding company, the tax may be assessed at any time within six years after the return is filed. Code Sec. 6501(f).
6. In the case of a deficiency attributable to the application of a carryback (capital loss, net operating loss, or credit), the statute of limitations runs from the year of the loss rather than the carryback year. Code Sec. 6501(h) and (j).

Sections 1311 through 1314 contain provisions to mitigate the effect of the statute of limitations where inequitable results might occur.

¶2365   PENALTIES

Penalties are treated as additions to federal internal revenue taxes and are, therefore, not deductible for federal income tax purposes.

Delinquency Penalties

The penalty for *failure to file* a return on the due date (determined with regard to any extension of time for filing) is 5 percent of the amount of tax due if the failure is for not more than one month, with an additional 5 percent for each additional month or fraction thereof, but not exceeding 25 percent in the aggregate. Code Sec. 6651(a)(1). The penalty is imposed on the net amount due—the difference between (1) the amount required to be shown on the return and (2) the amount paid on or before the due date and the amount of credit that may be claimed on the return. Effective for returns due after December 31, 1989, in case of a fraudulent failure to file a return, the failure to file penalty is increased to 15 percent if the net amount of tax due for each month the return is not filed up to a maximum of five months or 75 percent. Code Sec. 6651(f). The failure to file penalty is reduced by the 0.5 percent failure to pay penalty for any month in which both apply.

The penalty for *failure to pay* the amount of tax due on a tax return or for failure to pay an assessed tax within 10 days of the date of notice is one-half of one percent of the tax for one month or less and an additional one-half of one percent per month or part thereof until the penalty reaches 25 percent. An additional one-half of one percent per month is assessed if the taxpayer fails to pay a deficiency within 10 days after a notice is issued. Code Sec. 6651(a)(2) and (3) and (d). The penalty is imposed on the net amount due.

Either or both of the penalties can be avoided if the taxpayer can show that failure to file and/or pay was due to reasonable cause and not to willful neglect. Code Sec. 6651(a)(1), (2), and (3). The burden of establishing these facts is on the taxpayer. The *Internal Revenue Manual*, Sec. 20.1.7.9.1, gives some indication of what would be considered as reasonable cause for purposes of the delinquency penalties:

1. A return mailed in time but returned for insufficient postage.
2. A return filed within the legal period but in the wrong district.
3. Death or serious illness of the taxpayer or in the immediate family.
4. Unavoidable absence of the taxpayer.
5. Destruction of the taxpayer's business or business records by fire or other casualty.
6. Erroneous information given the taxpayer by an IRS official, or a request for proper blanks or returns not furnished by the IRS in sufficient time to permit the filing of the return by the due date.
7. The taxpayer made an effort to obtain assistance or information necessary to complete the return by a personal appearance at an IRS office but was unsuccessful because the taxpayer, through no fault, was unable to see an IRS representative.

8. The taxpayer is unable to obtain the records necessary to determine the amount of tax due for reasons beyond the taxpayer's control.
9. The taxpayer contacts a competent tax adviser, furnishes the necessary information, and then is incorrectly advised that the filing of a return is not required.

If the cause does not fall within one of the reasonable causes listed above, the District Director will decide whether the taxpayer established a reasonable cause for delinquency. *Internal Revenue Manual,* Sec. 20.1.7.9.1.

Accuracy-Related and Fraud Penalties

The penalties relating to the accuracy of tax returns are consolidated into one accuracy-related penalty equal to 20 percent of the portion of the underpayment to which the penalty applies. The penalty applies to the portion of underpayment attributable to one or more of the following five areas:

1. Negligence
2. Substantial understatement of income tax
3. Substantial valuation misstatement
4. Substantial overstatement of pension liabilities
5. Substantial estate or gift tax valuation understatement
6. Understatements resulting from listed and reportable transactions

The penalty does not apply to any portion of an underpayment attributable to a penalty for fraud. Code Sec. 6662(a) and (b).

For purposes of the consolidated penalty, "underpayment" means the amount by which any tax exceeds the excess of (1) the sum of (a) the amount shown as the tax by a taxpayer on the return, plus (b) amounts not shown as tax that were previously assessed, over (2) the amount of rebates made. Code Sec. 6664(a).

The accuracy-related penalties will not be imposed if it is shown that there was a reasonable cause for the underpayment and that the taxpayer acted in good faith with respect to the underpayment. Code Sec. 6664(c)(1).

Negligence Penalty

A 20 percent penalty is imposed for underpayment of tax due to negligence or disregard of rules and regulations. Code Sec. 6662(a).

EXAMPLE 2.14 Due to negligence, Steven Stover underpaid his taxes for 2017 by $30,000. His penalty is $6,000 (20% × $30,000).

The term "negligence" includes any failure to make a reasonable attempt to comply with the provisions of the Code, and the term "disregard" includes any careless, reckless, or intentional disregard. The definition of negligence is not limited only to the items specified. Thus, all behavior that is considered negligent under present law continues to be within the scope of the negligence penalty. Also, any behavior that is considered negligent by the courts but that is not specifically included within the definition is subject to the penalty.

In an effort to provide guidance as to the scope of the term "negligence," the *Internal Revenue Manual,* Sec. 4.10.6.2.1, states that it is "the omission to do something which a reasonable person, guided by those considerations which ordinarily regulate the conduct of human beings, would do, or doing something which a reasonable person would not do." According to the *Manual,* Sec. 4.10.6.2.1, the following are examples of cases in which negligence may exist:

1. Taxpayer continues year after year to make substantial errors in reporting income and claiming deductions even though these mistakes have been called to the taxpayer's attention in previous reports.
2. Taxpayer fails to maintain proper records after being advised through inadequate record procedures to do so and subsequent returns containing substantial errors are filed.
3. Taxpayer took careless and exaggerated deductions unsubstantiated by facts.
4. Taxpayer failed to give any explanation for the understatement of income and for failure to keep books and records.

Substantial Understatement of Tax Liability

If there is a substantial understatement of income tax, an amount equal to 20 percent of the amount of the understatement can be assessed. A substantial understatement of income tax occurs when the understatement exceeds the greater of 10 percent of the tax required to be shown on the return or $5,000. Code Sec. 6662(d)(1). In the case of a corporation (except for an S corporation or a personal holding company), the understatement must exceed the greater of 10 percent of the tax required to be shown on the return or $10,000. The amount of the understatement is equal to the excess of the tax required to be shown on the return over the amount of tax that is actually shown on the return.

The penalty can be avoided if there was substantial authority for the tax treatment; if relevant facts affecting the treatment are adequately disclosed in the return or a statement attached to the return; and in the case of tax shelter items, if the taxpayer reasonably believed that the tax treatment of such item was more likely than not the proper treatment. Code Sec. 6662(d)(2)(B) and (C). The penalty can be waived on showing of reasonable cause and that the taxpayer acted in good faith. Code Sec. 6664(c).

Substantial Valuation Misstatement Penalty

All taxpayers having an underpayment of tax attributable to a valuation misstatement are subject to this 20 percent penalty. Code Sec. 6662(e). There is a substantial valuation misstatement if the value of any property (or the adjusted basis of any property) is 150 percent or more of the amount determined to be the correct amount of the valuation or adjusted basis of the property. If the portion of the underpayment that is subject to the penalty is attributable to one or more gross valuation misstatements, the penalty will be applied at the rate of 40 percent. A gross valuation misstatement occurs if the value of the property (or the adjusted basis) was 200 percent or more of the correct amount of the valuation of the adjusted basis of the property. Code Sec. 6662(h)(2)(A). No penalty will be imposed on a taxpayer for a substantial valuation misstatement unless the portion of the underpayment attributable to substantial valuation misstatements exceeds $5,000, or $10,000 in the case of a corporation other than an S corporation or a personal holding company.

EXAMPLE 2.15 Bert Barge gives a painting he purchased three years ago to his alma mater and takes a charitable contribution deduction in the amount of $50,000, the value placed on it by his art professor friend. If the actual value was only $20,000 and if the tax underpayment is $10,000, Bert would be subject to a $4,000 valuation misstatement penalty (40 percent of $10,000). The valuation was more than 200 percent of the correct valuation.

Although valuation misstatements of charitable property resulting in understatements of tax are subject to the accuracy penalty provisions, the charitable deduction penalty waiver for qualified appraisers is still possible. No penalty will be imposed for an underpayment of tax resulting from a substantial or gross misstatement of charitable deduction property if it can be shown that there was a reasonable cause for the underpayment and that the taxpayer acted in good faith.

Substantial Overstatement of Pension Liabilities

The 20 percent penalty for substantial overstatement of pension liabilities applies only if the actuarial determination of pension liabilities is 200 percent or more of the amount determined to be correct. Code Sec. 6662(f). If a portion of the substantial overstatement to which the penalty applies is attributable to a gross valuation misstatement of 400 percent or more, the penalty is doubled to 40 percent of the underpayment. Code Sec. 6662(h). No penalty is imposed if the underpayment for the tax year attributable to substantial overstatements of pension liabilities is $1,000 or less.

Estate or Gift Tax Valuation Understatements

A 20 percent penalty is imposed for estate or gift tax valuation understatement if the value of any property claimed on an estate or gift tax return is 65 percent or less of the amount determined to be the correct amount of the valuation. Code Sec. 6662(g). If the understatement is attributable to a gross valuation misstatement of 40 percent or less of the correct amount, the penalty amount is 40 percent of the underpayment. Code Sec. 6662(h)(2)(C). This penalty applies only if the underpayment attributable to the understatement exceeds $5,000 for a tax period with respect to gift tax (or with respect to the estate in the case of estate tax).

Understatements Resulting from Listed and Reportable Transactions

An accuracy-related penalty was added by the American Jobs Creation Act of 2004 for understatements resulting from listed and reportable transactions. Code Sec. 6662A. The penalty applies to understatements attributable to (1) any listed transaction, and (2) any reportable transaction with a significant tax avoidance purpose. The penalty is generally 20 percent of the understatement if the taxpayer disclosed the transaction, and 30 percent if the transaction was not disclosed.

The listed and reportable transactions penalty is coordinated with three other penalties; (1) The Code Sec. 6662 accuracy-related penalty; (2) Code Sec. 6663 fraud penalty; and (3) The valuation misstatement penalties under Code Sec. 6662(e) and 6662 (h). There is a "reasonable cause" exception, although it is more demanding than the reasonable cause exception to the accuracy-related (Code Sec. 6662) and fraud (Code Sec. 6663) penalties.

Penalty for Aiding Understatement of Tax Liability

Any person who aids in the preparation or presentation of any tax document in connection with matters arising under the internal revenue laws with the knowledge that the document will result in the understatement of tax liability of another person is subject to a penalty of $1,000 ($10,000 for a corporation) for a taxable period. Code Sec. 6701.

Civil Fraud Penalty

If any part of an underpayment is due to fraud, the penalty imposed is 75 percent of the underpayment (the "civil fraud" penalty). Code Sec. 6663(a). Once the IRS establishes that any portion of an underpayment is due to fraud, the entire underpayment is assumed to be attributable to fraud, unless the taxpayer proves otherwise. Code Sec. 6663(b). The 20 percent accuracy-related penalty does not apply to any portion of an underpayment on which the fraud penalty is imposed. However, the accuracy-related penalty may be applied to any portion of the underpayment not attributable to fraud.

EXAMPLE 2.16   Beth Barrett owes a $50,000 deficiency, all due to civil fraud. In addition to the $50,000 tax deficiency, Beth will be liable for a $37,500 (75 percent of $50,000) civil fraud penalty.

Criminal Fraud Penalty

In addition to the civil fraud penalty, criminal fraud penalties may be imposed. Section 7201 provides that "any person who willfully attempts in any manner to evade or defeat any tax imposed by this title or the payment thereof shall, in addition to other penalties provided by law, be guilty of a felony. . . ." In order for there to be criminal fraud, the attempt to evade or defeat tax must be willful, which implies a "voluntary intentional violation of a known legal duty." *C.J. Bishop,* 73-1 USTC ¶9459, 412 U.S. 346, 93 S.Ct. 2009 (1973). Thus, an individual's behavior could not be willful if the actions are done through carelessness, or genuine misunderstanding of what the law requires.

A taxpayer convicted of criminal fraud is subject to a fine of up to $100,000 ($500,000 in the case of a corporation) or imprisonment of up to five years, or both, together with the costs of prosecution. Code Sec. 7201. The more important fraud provisions include the following:

1. Any person who willfully fails to collect or pay over withholding tax is guilty of a felony and, upon conviction, will be fined not more than $10,000, or imprisoned not more than five years, or both, together with the costs of prosecution. Code Sec. 7202.
2. Any person who willfully fails, when required, to pay estimated tax, to file a return, to keep records, or to supply information will be guilty of a misdemeanor and, upon conviction, will be fined not more than $25,000 ($100,000 in the case of a corporation) or imprisoned not more than one year, or both, together with the costs of prosecution. Code Sec. 7203.
3. Any person who willfully furnishes a false or fraudulent statement or who willfully fails to supply an employee with a statement of wages and withholdings will, if convicted, be fined not more than $1,000 or imprisoned not more than one year, or both. Code Sec. 7204.
4. Any person who willfully supplies false or fraudulent information regarding exemptions will, if convicted, be fined not more than $1,000 or imprisoned for not more than one year, or both. Code Sec. 7205.
5. Any person who is convicted under the fraud and false statement statute will be fined not more than $100,000 ($500,000 in the case of a corporation) or imprisoned not more than three years, or both, together with the costs of prosecution. Code Sec. 7206. This statute includes:

a. Making a false declaration that is made under the penalties of perjury
b. Aiding or assisting in preparation or presentation of returns, claims, or other documents that are false as to any material matter
c. Simulating or falsely executing any bond or other document required by the internal revenue laws
d. Removing, depositing, or concealing any property with intent to evade or defeat assessment or collection of any tax
e. Concealing property or withholding, falsifying, or destroying records relating to the financial condition of the taxpayer in connection with an offer in compromise or a closing agreement

6. Any person who willfully delivers or discloses any list, return, statement or other document known to that person to be fraudulent or false as to any material matter will be fined not more than $10,000 ($50,000 in the case of a corporation) or imprisoned not more than one year, or both. Code Sec. 7207.

Estimated Taxes and Underpayment Penalties

All taxpayers are generally required to make interim tax payments of substantially all of their accrued tax liability for the current year. For individuals, this is generally accomplished through withholding. Where withholding is insufficient, however, as is frequently the case with self-employed individuals, the taxpayer must file a declaration of estimated tax and may have to make quarterly estimated tax payments. The specific requirements are set forth in ¶9165.

If the total amount of tax paid through withholding and estimated tax payments is not enough, an underpayment penalty is imposed. The underpayment is computed on a quarterly basis and the interest penalty is then applied to these quarterly underpayments. Code Sec. 6654(d)(1). The charge runs until the amount is paid or until the due date of the return, whichever is earlier. An individual taxpayer can avoid the penalty for underpayment if the payments of estimated tax are at least as large as any one of the following:

1. 90 percent of the tax shown on the return or 100 percent (110 percent if adjusted gross income for 2002 and later exceeds $150,000) of the tax shown on the return for the preceding taxable year (assuming it showed a tax liability and covered a taxable year of 12 months). Code Sec. 6654(d)(1)(A) and (B).
2. An amount equal to 90 percent of the tax for the taxable year computed by annualizing the taxable income received for the months in the taxable year ending before the month in which the installment is required to be paid. Code Sec. 6654(d)(2).

The underpayment penalty can be waived if the underpayment is due to casualty, disaster, or other unusual circumstances, or occurs during the first two years after a taxpayer retired after reaching age 62, or became disabled. Code Sec. 6654(e)(3).

A penalty is also imposed on corporations by Code Sec. 6655 for any underpayment of estimated corporate tax. However, no penalty is imposed if the corporation pays estimated tax at least as large as any one of the following:

1. The tax shown on the return of the corporation for the preceding year
2. The tax based on the prior year's income but determined under the current year's rates
3. The tax shown on the return of the corporation for the current year.
4. An amount equal to at least 100 percent of the tax due on the current year's taxable income for specified cutoff periods and on an annualized basis. Code Sec. 6655(d)(1)(B)(ii) and (e).

Note: Large corporations (those with taxable income of $1 million or more in any one of the three preceding tax years) do not qualify for the first two exceptions.

Failure to Make Deposits of Taxes

Employers are liable for payment of the tax that must be withheld. Code Sec. 3402. Unless underpayment is due to reasonable cause and not due to willful neglect, a penalty of as much as 15 percent of the amount of the underpayment may be imposed. Code Sec. 6656(a) and (b).

Tax Preparer Penalties

If an income tax return preparer, in preparing a tax return with an understatement of tax liability, takes a frivolous position or one for which there is not a realistic possibility of being sustained on its merits, the penalty is the greater of $1,000 or 50 percent of the income derived by the tax return preparer with respect to the return. Code Sec. 6694(a). An "income tax return preparer" is any person who prepares for compensation or who employs one or more persons to prepare for compensation any return of tax or any claim for refund of tax. Code Sec. 7701(a)(36). No more than one individual associated with a firm will qualify as a preparer with respect to the same return or refund claim. Under the "one-preparer-per-firm" rule, should more than one member of a firm be involved in providing advice, the individual with supervisory responsibility for the matter will be subject to the penalty as a nonsigning preparer. Reg. §1.6694-1. A preparer is not subject to penalty for failure to follow a rule or regulation if the preparer in good faith and with a reasonable basis takes the position that the rule or regulation does not accurately reflect the Code.

A penalty of the greater of $5,000 or 75 percent of the income derived by the tax return preparer with respect to the return applies if any part of any understatement of liability as to a return or claim for refund is due to a willful attempt to understate the liability or to any reckless or any intentional disregard of the rules or regulations. Code Sec. 6694(b).

EXAMPLE 2.17   A guarantee of a specific amount of refund by a preparer is an example of an action that would give rise to this penalty. Or if the preparer intentionally disregards information given by the taxpayer in order to reduce the taxpayer's liability, the preparer is guilty of a willful attempt to understate tax liability.

PLANNING POINTER   This does not mean that the preparer may not rely in good faith on the information furnished by the taxpayer. However, the preparer must make reasonable inquiries if the information furnished by the taxpayer appears to be incorrect or incomplete.

A $50 penalty applies each time a preparer (1) fails to furnish a copy of the return to the taxpayer, (2) fails to sign the return, or (3) fails to furnish an identifying number. Code Sec. 6695(a)-(c). The maximum amount for each of these penalties is limited to $25,500. Any preparer who fails to retain a copy of the returns prepared or a list of the returns prepared is liable for a penalty of $50 for each such failure, with a maximum fine of $25,500 applicable to any one return period. Code Sec. 6695(d). A penalty of $50 applies for each failure to retain and make available to the IRS upon request a list of the preparers employed during a return period and $50 for each failure to set forth a required item in the information list (to a maximum of $25,500 for any single return period). Code Sec. 6695(e). Any preparer who endorses or otherwise negotiates a refund check issued to a taxpayer for a return or claim for refund prepared by the preparer is liable for a penalty of $510 with respect to each such check. Code Sec. 6695(f).

¶2370 DISCLOSURE OF A POSITION ON A RETURN

The taxpayer may avoid the substantial-understatement penalty and the tax return preparer may avoid the penalty for taking a position for which there is not a realistic possibility of being sustained on its merits by disclosing the item on Form 8275, Disclosure Statement. To avoid the accuracy-related penalty, the taxpayer must disclose any nonfrivolous position for which there is not substantial authority but which has a reasonable basis. Code Sec. 6662(d)(2)(B)(ii). Similarly, the tax return preparer may avoid the $1,000 Code Sec. 6694(a) penalty if any nonfrivolous position that does not have a realistic possibility of being sustained on its merits is disclosed on Form 8275. The "realistic possibility" standard is treated in the regulations as being identical to the "substantial authority" standard in Code Sec. 6662(d)(2)(B)(i). Reg. §1.6694-2(b)(1). Thus, the requirement for disclosure in order to avoid the accuracy-related penalty is identical for both taxpayers and tax preparers, even though the statutory language differs somewhat. Once adequate disclosure has been made, tax preparers are not subject to the penalty as long as the position taken is not frivolous (i.e., not patently improper). Reg. §1.6694-2(c)(1) and (2). For taxpayers, however, the position taken must have a "reasonable basis," in order to avoid the penalty. Code Sec. 6662(d)(2)(B)(ii)(II). The regulations treat this standard as "significantly higher than the not frivolous standard applicable to preparers." Reg. §§1.6662-3(b)(3)(ii) and 1.6662-4(e)(2)(i).

¶2375 ETHICS RULES FOR PRACTITIONERS

CPAs and attorneys must practice according to the code of professional ethics of their professions. The codes are similar to Treasury Department Circular No. 230. The Tax Committee of the American Institute of Certified Public Accountants (AICPA) also issued 10 statements on selected topics between 1964 and 1977. The first two statements were withdrawn in 1982. The eight remaining statements were revised in 1988 and in 2001. Prior to 2001, they were advisory opinions of the Committee as to what are appropriate standards of conduct in certain situations. Effective October 31, 2001, the Statements are enforceable standards for AICPA members. Effective January 1, 2010, the new sixth standard combined the previous sixth and seventh standards to give seven standards. Summaries of the current seven "Statements on Standards for Tax Services" follow.

1. With respect to tax return positions, a CPA should comply with the following standards:
   a. A CPA should not recommend to a client that a position be taken with respect to the tax treatment of any item on a return unless the CPA has a good faith belief that the position has a realistic possibility of being sustained administratively or judicially on its merits if challenged.
   b. A CPA should not prepare or sign a return if the CPA knows that the return takes a position that the CPA could not recommend under the standard expressed in paragraph 1(a).
   c. A CPA may recommend a position that the CPA concludes is not frivolous so long as the position is adequately disclosed on the return.
   d. In recommending tax return positions and in signing returns, a CPA should, where relevant, advise the client as to the potential penalty consequences of the recommended tax return position, and the opportunity, if any, to avoid such penalties through disclosure.

   The CPA should not recommend a tax return position that exploits the Internal Revenue Service audit selection process or serves as a mere "arguing" position solely to obtain leverage in the bargaining process of settlement negotiation with the Internal Revenue Service.

2. The CPA should make a reasonable effort to obtain from the client, and provide, appropriate answers to all questions on a tax return before signing as a preparer.

   Statement No. 2 indicates that reasonable grounds may exist for omitting an answer:
   a. The information is not readily available and the answer is not significant in terms of taxable income or loss or the tax liability shown on the return.
   b. Genuine uncertainty exists regarding the meaning of a question in relation to the particular return.
   c. The answer to the question is voluminous; in such cases, assurance should be given on the return that the data will be supplied upon an examination.

3. In preparing a return, the CPA may in good faith rely without verification upon information furnished by the client. The CPA should make reasonable inquiries if the information furnished appears to be incorrect, incomplete, or inconsistent either on its face or on the basis of other facts known to the CPA. The CPA should refer to the client's returns for proper years whenever feasible.

   Where the Internal Revenue Code or income tax regulations impose a condition with respect to deductibility or other tax treatment of an item, the CPA should make appropriate inquiries to determine whether such condition has been met.

4. A CPA may prepare tax returns involving the use of the taxpayer's estimates if it is impracticable to obtain exact data, and the estimated amounts are reasonable under the facts and circumstances known to the CPA. When estimates are used, they should be presented in a way that avoids the implication of greater accuracy than exists. Estimated amounts should not be presented in a manner which provides a misleading impression as to the degree of factual accuracy.

   There are unusual circumstances where disclosure that an estimate is used is necessary to avoid misleading the Internal Revenue Service regarding the degree of accuracy of the return. Some examples of unusual circumstances are as follows:
   a. The taxpayer has died or is ill at the time the return must be filed.
   b. The taxpayer has not received a K-1 for a flow-through entity at the time the return must be filed.
   c. There is litigation pending which bears on the return.
   d. Fire or computer failure destroyed relevant records.

5. The recommendation of a position to be taken concerning the tax treatment of an item in the preparation of a tax return should be based upon the facts and the law as they are evaluated at the time the return is prepared. Unless the taxpayer is bound as to tax treatment in a later year, the disposition of an item in an administrative proceeding does not govern the taxpayer in the treatment of a similar item in a later year's return. Therefore, if the CPA follows the standards of Statement No. 1, the CPA may recommend a tax return position, or prepare a tax return that departs from the treatment of an item as concluded in an administrative proceeding or a court decision regarding a prior year's return.

6. The CPA should inform the client promptly upon learning of an error in a previously filed return, an error in a return that is the subject of an administrative proceeding, or upon learning of a client's

failure to file a required return. The CPA should recommend the measures to be taken and such recommendation may be given orally. The CPA should not inform the IRS, and may not do so without the client's permission, except where required by law.

If the CPA is requested to prepare the current year's return and the client has not taken appropriate action to correct an error in a prior year's return, the CPA should consider whether to withdraw from preparing the return. If the CPA does prepare the current year's return, the CPA should take reasonable steps to ensure that the error is not repeated.

When the CPA is representing a client in an administrative proceeding with respect to a return which contains an error known to the CPA, the CPA should require the client's agreement to disclose the error to the IRS. Lacking such agreement, the CPA should consider whether to withdraw from representing the client and whether to continue a professional relationship with the client.

7. In providing tax advice to clients, the CPA should use professional judgment to ensure that the advice reflects competence and appropriately serves the client's needs. No standard format or guidelines need be followed in communicating written or oral advice to a client.

The CPA may communicate with a client when subsequent developments affect advice previously provided with respect to significant matters. However, the CPA cannot be expected to communicate later developments except while assisting a client in implementing procedures or plans associated with the advice provided or unless the CPA undertakes this obligation by specific agreement with the client.

TAX BLUNDERS

1. Laura Lerner found out that taxpayers have either partially or completely won around 50 percent of cases brought to the Tax Court. Therefore, she decides on litigation in the Tax Court, where she thinks she has a fairly good chance of being successful. However, in looking at the tax issue with which Laura is concerned, a tax researcher discovers that the taxpayer has never won a case like hers. Laura should not have relied on the overall statistics.
2. Edward Enders decides to take his case to the Tax Court because then he does not have to pay the tax before litigation. After some time has passed, someone tells him that a jury would probably have looked favorably on his case, and now he wants to go to District Court. Having gone to the Tax Court, Edward cannot now take his case to District Court.
3. Vera Vokel, known for her temper, her frugality, and her dislike for the IRS, is requested to come in to the local IRS office for an office examination. Although she had a CPA prepare her return, she decides she would like to save the fees it might cost her to have the CPA represent her and, therefore, decides to go in alone for the examination. In the course of the discussion, she becomes furious at the auditor and is disallowed her items at issue. Vera should have had her CPA represent her and she should probably not have been present herself so that the audit could be conducted in a businesslike and unemotional manner.

SUMMARY

- The primary authoritative sources of the law are statutory, administrative, and judicial.
- The taxpayer can appeal within the IRS and/or decide to go to Tax Court, the District Court, or the Court of Federal Claims, and then attempt to appeal to the Court of Appeals and the Supreme Court.
- A tax researcher can use loose-leaf tax services, a citator, other types of secondary reference materials, or electronic tax research systems and the internet in the research process.
- The Internal Revenue Service consists of the national office, and an extensive organization consisting of 4 operating divisions and other units.
- The examination of tax returns can be as simple as a correspondence examination or a more involved office examination or field examination.
- A tax practice can involve tax compliance and tax planning.
- Communications between the IRS and taxpayers can include private letter rulings, determination letters, and technical advice.
- There are numerous penalties to which taxpayers and tax preparers may be subject.
- The knowledge and use of ethics is very important for the tax practitioner.

QUESTIONS

1. Does the Internal Revenue Code of 1986 include pre-1986 tax law?

2. In which Subtitle and Chapter of the Internal Revenue Code is the majority of the income tax law found?

3. Are the federal courts bound to follow Treasury Regulations when deciding a tax case?

4. Do Regulations have higher authority in federal tax law than Revenue Rulings?

5. List the various "administrative" sources of tax law.

6. How is the manner of citing a Revenue Ruling or a Revenue Procedure affected by the passage of time?

7. In which Judicial Circuit is the District of Columbia?

8. List the three trial courts that have jurisdiction over tax cases.

9. What are the primary differences between Regular and Memorandum decisions of the U.S. Tax Court?

10. Is an announcement of acquiescence by the Commissioner of Internal Revenue legally binding upon the IRS?

11. What do the following abbreviations represent? BTA, USTC, AFTR, AFTR2d, S.Ct., CA-3, TCM.

12. Which tax service is known for its willingness to take a stand on controversial issues not covered by legislation or tax law?

13. Which tax service is frequently quoted in judicial decisions?

14. Refer to the Sue Wilson research illustration in the chapter (Case #1). Assume, at the time of filing her 2017 tax return, Sue Wilson believed she would receive a recovery on a claim for the full value of the automobile. However, in August 2018, Sue received only $8,000 from the insurance company. How much of a loss will she claim in 2017? In 2018? (Give your answer before consideration of the 10 percent of AGI limitation.)

15. Which computer-based research system contains the text of tax treaties?

16. Where can the historical record of a court case be found?

17. Describe the organization of the Internal Revenue Service.

18. Who may practice before the Internal Revenue Service?

19. Define and distinguish between a Private Letter Ruling, a Determination Letter, and a Technical Advice Memorandum.

20. Define DIF; NRP.

21. What events might cause an IRS examination?

22. What kind of taxpayer errors could be solved by mail?

23. What types of tax issues lend themselves to an interview or office examination?

24. Why might a taxpayer in a field examination want to make every effort to settle with the revenue agent?

25. Define 30-day letter; 90-day letter.

26. Describe the appeals process within the IRS.

27. Describe the trial and appellate court system for federal tax litigation.

28. What factors should a taxpayer consider in choosing a tax forum?

29. What are the two delinquency penalties?

30. What could constitute "reasonable cause" for purposes of the delinquency penalties?

31. What is the negligence penalty?

32. What two parties might be subject to the understatement of tax liability penalty?

33. Describe the valuation overstatement penalty.

34. How may an individual avoid a penalty for underpayment of tax liability?

35. Jim files his return one month after the due date and pays the remaining $8,000 of tax owed by him. What are his delinquency penalties?

36. Due to negligence, Rose underpaid her taxes by $20,000. What is her negligence penalty?

37. Olivia is being audited by the IRS. The revenue agent determines that certain expenses that were deducted on her return are not valid, and he accordingly makes adjustments to her tax liability. Upon receipt of her 30-day letter, she phones you, a CPA, for advice regarding possible future action on the matter. What options would you discuss with Olivia?

PROBLEMS

38. Based upon the organization of the Internal Revenue Code, what general topic would be covered in Code Sec. 731?
    a. Capital gains and losses
    b. Partners and partnerships
    c. Exempt organizations
    d. Insurance companies

39. Which of the following is published in the *Federal Register?*
    a. Technical Information Releases
    b. Revenue Rulings
    c. Revenue Procedures
    d. Treasury Regulations

40. To read an IRS Revenue Ruling that was issued within the past week which source should be used?
    a. Internal Revenue Code
    b. Cumulative Bulletin
    c. Federal Register
    d. Internal Revenue Bulletin

41. Which of the following publications includes the memorandum decisions of the United States Tax Court?
    a. Federal Register
    b. Cumulative Bulletin
    c. Internal Revenue Bulletin
    d. Tax Court Memorandum Decisions (TCM) (published by Wolters Kluwer)
    e. U.S. Tax Cases (USTC) (published by Wolters Kluwer)

42. Which of the following publications includes the regular decisions of the United States Tax Court?
    a. Federal Register
    b. Internal Revenue Bulletin
    c. United States Tax Court Reports
    d. Tax Court Memorandum Decisions (TCM) (published by Wolters Kluwer)
    e. U.S Tax Cases (USTC) (published by Wolters Kluwer)

43. Matthew, a sole proprietor, employs Timothy as his full-time employee. Timothy's 2016 tax return is being audited by the IRS. Because of Timothy's high regard for Matthew's knowledge and judgment, Timothy has asked Matthew to represent him in the audit. May Matthew represent Timothy?

44. Marvin filed his 2015 tax return on August 15, 2016, having obtained an automatic extension of time to file. However, not having the money to pay the tax bill at that time, he arranged with the IRS to pay his tax liability six months later. On February 15, 2017, Marvin paid the tax. Subsequently, on November 13, 2017, he discovered a deduction that he neglected to take on his 2015 return and he wishes to file a claim for a refund. May he do so?

45. Your client, Steve, is an engineer whose income has doubled over the past four years. He feels that by incorporating he could reduce his tax significantly. However, he can demonstrate no business purpose for incorporating as he is employed by an international oil company and he does no outside work. He asks you to request a ruling from the IRS regarding his proposed incorporation. Would you request a ruling for him?

46. Ron mailed his 2016 federal tax return on April 15, 2017, attaching only a first-class postage stamp. However, the postage should have been higher since the return weighed three ounces. His return is sent back to him on April 22, 2017, at which time he pays the additional postage. Will Ron be required to pay a delinquency penalty?

47. Karen engaged Joe, a CPA, to prepare her tax return. Karen received a refund check of $300 from the IRS. She endorsed the check and mailed it to Joe as payment for the preparation of her return. Joe took the check to his bank and deposited the amount in his bank account. Describe the possible consequences of this situation.

48. Jim, a retail merchant, reported the following on his 2016 return:

Sales	$200,000
Cost of goods sold	$80,000
Gross profit	$120,000

What amount must be omitted from income for the six-year statute of limitations to apply?

49. Andrea, a CPA, is representing her client, Rodney, in an administrative proceeding. In the course of this engagement, she discovers an error in the return that may result in a material understatement of tax liability. What, if anything, should Andrea do with regard to this discovery?

50. Mary, a CPA, prepared Gordon's tax return for the current year. In preparing his return, she took a deduction that is contrary to the Code. She feels that he is entitled to this deduction because of her belief that possible conflicts exist between two sections of the Internal Revenue Code. Is Mary in conflict with the AICPA "Statements on Responsibilities in Tax Practice"?

51. An individual files an income tax return for the calendar-year 2016 on September 20, 2017, and pays $1,200, which is the balance of the tax due. Disregarding interest, how much in delinquency penalties would he have to pay?

52. Tommy gives a painting to a church and takes a charitable contribution deduction in the amount of $50,000. If the actual value was only $20,000 and if the tax underpayment is $12,000, how much valuation overstatement penalty should he pay?

53. Sandy had the following items on her timely filed 2016 income tax return:

Gross receipts	$400,000
Cost of goods sold	($300,000)
Capital gain	$20,000
Capital loss	($30,000)

Sandy inadvertently omitted some income on her 2016 return. What is the statute of limitations if she omitted $100,000 of income on the return? What if she omitted $120,000 of income?

54. On February 15, 2015, Brent filed his 2014 income tax return (due April 15, 2015), and he paid a tax of $15,000 at that time. On June 10, 2016, he filed an amended 2014 return showing an additional $3,000 of tax which was then paid. In 2017, Brent found that he should claim a refund of $6,000 because he failed to take some deductions to which he was entitled. What amount can he recover if he files the claim for refund on March 14, 2018? What if he files the claim on May 15, 2018?

55. Angela filed her 2016 income tax return on February 14, 2017, showing gross income of $20,000. She mistakenly deducted a $6,000 casualty loss that in good faith she considered deductible. By what date must the IRS assert a notice of deficiency?
    a. February 14, 2020
    b. April 15, 2020
    c. February 14, 2023
    d. April 15, 2023

56. Harold and Maude filed a joint return for 2016 reporting:

Gross business income	$400,000
Net business income	80,000
Net capital gain	40,000

Maude inadvertently omitted some income from this return. The six-year statute applies only if Maude's omitted gross income exceeds:
    a. $20,000
    b. $30,000
    c. $100,000
    d. $110,000

57. Reginald filed his 2016 income tax return on January 15, 2017. On November 1, 2017, he learned that his investment of $10,000 in 1,000 shares of Ultimate Corp. had become worthless in 2016. What is the last day on which he must file an amended 2016 return to claim this loss?
    a. January 15, 2020
    b. April 15, 2020
    c. November 1, 2020
    d. April 15, 2024

58. If a practitioner who is authorized to practice before the IRS knows that a client has not complied with the revenue laws of the United States with respect to a matter administered by the IRS, the practitioner is required to:
    a. Advise the client of the noncompliance
    b. Immediately notify the IRS
    c. Do nothing
    d. Advise his client and immediately notify the IRS

59. Anna's 2015 individual tax return was examined and the IRS proposed changes resulting in additional tax. Anna wishes to bypass the IRS's appeal system and file a refund suit in the United States Court of Federal Claims on contested income tax issues. Your advice to Anna should be:
    a. Request that her return be reexamined
    b. Pay all of the additional tax and file another Form 1040 tax return
    c. Pay all of the additional tax, then file a claim for refund and request in writing that the claim be immediately rejected
    d. File a claim for refund and do nothing else

60. Peter's return was examined and the result was additional tax of $16,000 due to unreported lottery winnings. Peter has received a letter notifying him of his right to appeal the proposed changes within 30 days. Which of the following should Peter do in preparing his appeal?
    a. Call the examiner and request a conference
    b. Provide a brief written statement of the disputed issues
    c. Submit a written protest within the time limit specified
    d. Submit a written protest explaining additional expenses not previously claimed

61. Which of the following statements is not correct in respect to tax return preparer penalties?
    a. The penalty for an understatement due to the preparer's negligent or intentional disregard of one or more rules or regulations is $250; for willful understatement of liability the penalty is $1,000.
    b. If a preparer in good faith and with reasonable basis takes the position that a rule or regulation does not accurately reflect the Code, he or she is not subject to either penalty.
    c. The IRS has the burden of proof that a preparer has negligently or intentionally disregarded a rule or regulation.
    d. Many Code sections require the existence of specific facts and circumstances. In order to avoid a penalty, a preparer shall make appropriate inquiries of the taxpayer to determine that the requirements have been met incident to claiming a deduction.

62. **Research Problem.** What is the current status of Rev. Rul. 57-82?

63. **Research Problem.** Code Sec. 303(b)(2)(A)(ii) makes reference to two other Code sections. What are they?

64. **Research Problem.** Which Rev. Rul. does Rev. Rul. 76-74 supersede?

65. **Research Problem.** What is the date of IRS Letter Ruling 8302032?

66. **Research Problem.** On what date was Reg. §1.274-8 adopted?

67. **Research Problem.** What Code Section immediately follows Code Sec. 280?

68. **Research Problem.** Refer to a citator and locate the following case: *New York Life Insurance Co. v. Edwards*.
    a. What happened on appeal to the Court of Appeals?
    b. What happened on appeal to the Supreme Court?

69. **Research Problem.** What Code sections cover the standard deduction, trade or business expenses, losses, medical expenses, and moving expenses?

70. **Research Problem.** What two Code sections are referred to in Code Sec. 56(f)(2)(F)(ii)(II)?

71. **Research Problem.** Refer to the *Pennsylvania Indemnity Co.* case in a citator. What was the disposition of the case on appeal to the Supreme Court from the Court of Appeals?

72. **Research Problem.** Reg. §1.212-1(n) refers to two Code Sections. What are they?

73. **Research Problem.** Refer to *Black's Law Dictionary* or a similar legal reference book and ascertain the definition of the following words or terms: annotated, certiorari, remanded, dictum, acquiesced.

74. **Research Problem.** A taxpayer has a cellular telephone, used 45 percent for business and 55 percent for personal use. Is the MACRS depreciation method allowable?

75. **Research Problem.** What is the effective date of Code Sec. 1031(f)?

76. **Research Problem.** A borrower is personally liable on a real estate mortgage with an outstanding balance of $1.5 million. Borrower's basis in the property is $1 million and the property has a current fair market value of $1.2 million. The property is repossessed by the bank.
    a. If the borrower is insolvent both before and after the repossession, what taxable gain, if any, is recognized by borrower?
    b. Does your answer to (a) change if the borrower is not personally liable on the mortgage (i.e., a nonrecourse debt)? Why or why not?

77. **Research Problem.** Anthony Antunicci, a Massachusetts lawyer, has tired of the long, cold New England winters. He recently spent three months in Florida where he took a Florida bar review course which enabled him to successfully pass the Florida bar exam. He has since opened a second law office in Coral Gables and plans to work in that office from January through March each year. His younger brother, Joey, will operate their Boston office in his absence.

Can Anthony deduct the cost of the Florida bar review course as an education expense since he has already established himself in the profession of being a lawyer by previously passing the Massachusetts bar exam?

(**Hint:** to answer this question using CCH IntelliConnect®, use the search term: (lawyer or attorney) and (bar review course and second state).)

78. **Research Problem.** Jane was notified by the IRS that she should appear at the local IRS district office with records supporting travel expense deductions taken on her 2014 tax return. Because she had to meet with some clients, she did not appear at the IRS office, nor did she bother to make an appointment for an alternative time. To what penalty or penalties could Jane be subject?

79. **Research Problem.** A corporate client was the target of a hostile takeover by a corporate raider. In successfully thwarting the hostile takeover, the Board of Directors incurred legal fees of $100,000.
    a. What is the proper tax treatment of these fees?
    b. Assume that the takeover was friendly. Does this change your answer? If so, explain why your answer is different

80. An oil tanker collided with a ship in Tampa Bay. The resulting oil spill severely curtailed the fishing business for two months. The Franklin Fishing Boat Co. made a claim against the tanker's owner for impairment of Franklin's revenue during the two-month period. Mr. Franklin received an initial payment of $50,000 from the tanker's owner, $20,000 of which was for lost revenue and $30,000 of which was for punitive damages allowed by state law from a handler of hazardous substances. How much of the award, if any, is taxable?

Individual Taxation—An Overview

OBJECTIVES

After completing Chapter 3, you should be able to:

1. Understand the components of the tax formula.
2. Apply the standard deduction to each filing status.
3. Determine whether an individual qualifies as a personal exemption.
4. Distinguish among the five different filing statuses.
5. Apply the tax tables and the tax rate schedules to taxable income.

OVERVIEW

This chapter discusses the components of the tax formula and studies the implications of the standard deduction to the taxpayer. Additionally, the qualifications for the personal exemption are analyzed. Finally, the basic filing statuses are examined as well as the role of the tax tables and the tax rate schedules.

¶3001

COMPONENTS OF THE TAX FORMULA

Taxable income is computed using one of the two overall accounting methods, the cash method or the accrual method. It is also possible to use a combination of the two overall methods. Under the cash method, income is reported when it is received and deductions are taken when the expense is paid. The accrual method requires income to be reported when all the events necessary to fix the right to receive payment have occurred and there is reasonable certainty regarding the amount. Likewise, accrual basis taxpayers usually claim a deduction in the year in which all events that fix the liability have occurred, provided the amount of the liability is reasonably determinable.

A basic understanding of the method used to calculate the tax liability is a necessity in the study of federal income taxation. That method is as follows:

	Gross Income
–	Deductions for Adjusted Gross Income
=	Adjusted Gross Income
–	Greater of Itemized Deductions or Standard Deduction
–	Personal Exemptions
=	Taxable Income
×	Tax Rate
=	Tax Liability
–	Tax Credits and Prepayments
=	Net Tax Due or Refund

¶3011

GROSS INCOME

Gross income includes all items of income from whatever source unless specifically excluded. Examples of gross income include compensation for services, interest, rents, royalties, dividends, and annuities. An individual's income from business is included in gross income after deducting the cost of goods sold.

The receipt of income can be in different forms such as cash, property, services, or even a forgiveness of an indebtedness. However, income is not reported by a taxpayer until it is realized.

Gross income and inclusions and exclusions will be discussed in further detail in Chapters 4 and 5.

¶3015

DEDUCTIONS FOR ADJUSTED GROSS INCOME

To arrive at adjusted gross income, all deductions specifically allowed by law are subtracted from gross income. Some of the items allowed as deductions for adjusted gross income include:

1. Trade or business expenses, such as advertising, depreciation, and utilities.
2. Certain reimbursed employee expenses, such as travel, transportation, and entertainment expenses.
3. Moving expenses.
4. Losses from sale or exchange of property.

These deductions are sometimes referred to as "deductions from gross income" or, since almost all the allowable deductions in this section are business expenses, the deductions are sometimes referred to as "business deductions." These deductions are discussed in Chapter 6.

¶3025

ADJUSTED GROSS INCOME

In the tax formula there are deductions for adjusted gross income and then deductions from adjusted gross income. It is important to take these deductions in the proper categories. Adjusted gross income is an important subtotal because certain other items are based on the amount of adjusted gross income. The credit for child and dependent care expenses along with itemized deductions for medical expenses, charitable contributions, personal casualty losses, and miscellaneous expenses are all based on adjusted gross income. The phaseout of itemized deductions and personal exemptions are also based on adjusted gross income.

¶3035 ITEMIZING v. STANDARD DEDUCTION

Itemized deductions are certain expenses of a personal nature that are specifically allowed as a deduction. Items included in this group are: medical expenses, state and local income taxes, property taxes, home mortgage interest, charitable contributions, personal casualty losses, and miscellaneous employee expenses.

Taxpayers receive the benefit of a minimum amount of itemized deductions called the standard deduction. The standard deduction is a fixed amount used to simplify the computation of the tax liability. It is also designed to eliminate lower-income individuals from the tax rolls. All taxpayers subtract the larger of their itemized deductions or the standard deduction.

The standard deduction is based on the filing status of the taxpayer and is made up of the "basic standard deduction" plus any "additional standard deduction." The standard deduction is adjusted annually, if necessary, for inflation.

Filing Status	Basic Standard Deduction 2017
Single	$6,350
Married Filing Jointly	12,700
Married Filing Separately	6,350
Head of Household	9,350
Surviving Spouse	12,700

The standard deduction is of principal benefit to moderate and low income level taxpayers since the amount is usually more than the total itemized deductions, which means that such taxpayers need not report their itemized deductions. Thus, the need to audit such returns by the IRS is substantially reduced since the opportunities for error or misstatement of taxable income are lessened.

Overall Limitation on Itemized Deductions

For tax years beginning after 1990, an individual whose adjusted gross income exceeds a threshold amount is required to reduce the amount allowable for itemized deductions by 3 percent of the excess over that threshold. For 2017, the threshold amount is $313,800 for married filing jointly, $287,650 for head of household, $261,500 for single, and $156,900 for married filing separately. These thresholds are indexed for inflation. There was no phaseout for 2010 through 2012.

In no event, however, may the reduction be more than 80 percent of allowable itemized deductions, not counting the deductions for medical expenses, investment interest, casualty losses, or wagering losses to the extent of wagering gains. The reduction is applied only after first taking into account the other Code provisions that determine how much of a particular type of expense may be deducted, such as the 2 percent limitation on miscellaneous deductions.

EXAMPLE 3.1

Mark and Sylvia Ward are married taxpayers who file a joint return. In 2017, they have adjusted gross income of $363,800 and preliminary itemized deductions of $18,000. Their itemized deductions consist of medical expenses ($8,000), state and local taxes ($7,000), and charitable contributions ($3,000). Their adjusted itemized deductions on their return would be $16,500, computed as follows:

Medical expenses		$8,000
State and local taxes	$7,000	
Charitable contributions	3,000	
	$10,000	
Less: 3% of AGI in excess of $313,800	1,500	8,500
Adjusted itemized deductions		$ 16,500

Additional Standard Deduction for Age and Blindness

An additional standard deduction is allowed for aged or blind taxpayers. The additional standard deduction is the total of the additional amounts allowed for age and blindness. The dollar value of an additional amount will depend on the taxpayer's filing status. The extra standard deductions effective for 2017 are shown below. The amounts are adjusted for inflation.

Filing Status	Dollar Value of One Additional Filing Status Amount 2017
Single	$1,550
Married Filing Jointly	1,250
Married Filing Separately	1,250
Head of Household	1,550
Surviving Spouse	1,250

Taxpayers can receive an additional standard deduction for being both aged and blind. Thus, a married couple, both of whom are aged and blind, receive an additional standard deduction of $5,000 ($1,250 × 4).

EXAMPLE 3.2

Rebecca Greene, 55, qualifies as a head of household in 2017. Her basic standard deduction is $9,350. She is not entitled to an additional standard deduction.

EXAMPLE 3.3

Assume the same facts as in Example 3.2, except that Rebecca is 67 and legally blind. Her basic standard deduction for 2017 is $9,350. She is also entitled to an additional standard deduction of $3,100 ($1,550 for her age and $1,500 for her blindness). Her total standard deduction is $12,450.

EXAMPLE 3.4

Jeffrey and Donna Dirk are both 72 and file a joint return for 2017. Donna is blind. Their basic standard deduction is $12,700. They are entitled to an additional standard deduction of $3,750 ($1,250 × 2 for their age plus $1,250 for Donna's blindness). Their total standard deduction is $16,450.

To qualify for the old-age additional standard deduction, the taxpayer and/or spouse must be age 65 before the close of the year. For purposes of the old-age additional standard deduction, an individual attains the age of 65 on the day preceding the 65th birthday. Thus, an individual whose 65th birthday falls on January 1 in a given year attains the age of 65 on the last day of the calendar year immediately preceding.

A person is considered blind for the extra standard deduction if that person's central visual acuity does not exceed 20/200 in the better eye with correcting lenses, or if visual acuity is greater than 20/200 but is accompanied by a limitation in the fields of vision such that the widest diameter of the visual field subtends an angle no greater than 20 degrees.

If the taxpayer or spouse dies during the year, the number of additional standard deduction amounts for age or blindness is determined as of the date of death. Thus, the additional standard deduction for age will not be allowed for an individual who dies before attaining the age of 65 even though the individual would have been 65 before the close of the year.

The additional standard deductions for age 65 or older and blindness apply only to taxpayers and their spouses. No additional standard deduction amounts are allowed to taxpayers who claim an exemption for dependents who are aged or blind.

EXAMPLE 3.5

Darren Davidson is single and fully supports his 70-year-old father. Darren qualifies as a head of household. Darren's regular standard deduction is $9,350 for 2017. Darren may claim a dependency exemption for his father but may not claim the additional standard deduction amount for his dependent father.

Married Taxpayers Filing Separately

All taxpayers may not be able to take the larger of itemized deductions or the standard deduction. Rules require both spouses to either itemize or use the standard deduction. If one spouse takes itemized deductions the other spouse is required to also itemize even if itemized deductions are less than the standard deduction for married individuals filing separately.

EXAMPLE 3.6	Joe and Mary Bloome are married but decide to file separate returns for 2017. Joe has adjusted gross income of $30,000 and $6,450 of itemized deductions, while Mary has $25,000 of adjusted gross income and $3,300 of itemized deductions. Joe and Mary can elect not to itemize, in which case they will each use the standard deduction of $6,350. However, if they decide to itemize, Joe will have itemized deductions of $6,450 and Mary will have $3,300 of itemized deductions. Since Joe itemizes, Mary is also required to itemize.

PLANNING POINTER	In situations where total itemized deductions are approximately equal to the standard deduction, it is possible for cash basis taxpayers to obtain a deduction for itemized deductions in one year and to use the standard deduction the next year by proper timing of payments. For example, an individual may pay two years' church pledges in one year and nothing the next year. It may also be possible to pay real estate or city and state income tax estimated payments prior to the end of the year.

¶3045   PERSONAL EXEMPTIONS

The personal exemption for 2017 is $4,050. From 1979 through 1984, the personal exemption was $1,000. The application of the index for inflation raised the personal exemption to $1,040 for 1985 and $1,080 for 1986. The Tax Reform Act of 1986 raised the personal exemption to $1,900 for 1987, $1,950 for 1988, and $2,000 for 1989. The personal exemption as adjusted for inflation after 1989 was raised to $2,050 for 1990, $2,150 for 1991, $2,300 for 1992, $2,350 for 1993, $2,450 for 1994, $2,500 for 1995, $2,550 for 1996, $2,650 for 1997, $2,700 for 1998, $2,750 for 1999, $2,800 for 2000, $2,900 for 2001, $3,000 for 2002, $3,050 for 2003, $3,100 for 2004, $3,200 for 2005, $3,300 for 2006, $3,400 for 2007, $3,500 for 2008, $3,650 for 2009 and 2010, $3,700 for 2011, $3,800 for 2012, $3,900 for 2013, $3,950 for 2014, $4,000 for 2015, and $4,050 for 2016.

No personal exemption amount is allowable on the return of an individual who is eligible to be claimed as a dependent on another taxpayer's return. For example, a child will not be allowed the personal exemption on his or her own return if that child is eligible to be claimed on the parent's return.

The deduction for personal exemptions is reduced or even eliminated for certain high-income taxpayers. Taxpayers whose adjusted gross income exceeds the appropriate threshold amount (based on filing status) have to reduce exemptions by 2 percent for each $2,500 of adjusted gross income or fraction thereof in excess of the threshold amount. The phaseout of the tax benefit for personal exemptions began in 1991, and the threshold amounts are adjusted for inflation (cost-of-living index adjustment).

¶3055   TAX RATES

The tax formula implies that the "Taxable Income" figure is multiplied by the appropriate tax rate to arrive at the "Tax Liability." In reality, the "Tax Liability" is either derived from the appropriate column of the tax tables or is computed from the appropriate line in the tax rate schedules.

Prior to 1986 the maximum tax rate was 50 percent. The tax rate schedules for 1987 ranged from 11 percent to 38.5 percent. The tax rate schedules (reproduced in the Appendix) include seven tax brackets for 2017: 10 percent, 15 percent, 25 percent, 28 percent, 33 percent, 35 percent, and 39.6 percent.

¶3065   TAX CREDITS AND PREPAYMENTS

Any tax credits are applied against the income tax. It is significant to note the difference between a credit and a tax deduction. A deduction reduces income to which the rate applies and indirectly reduces the tax liability. A credit directly reduces the tax liability.

The principal credits include the earned income credit, child tax credit, credit for the elderly, general business credit, dependent care credit, education credits, and foreign tax credit. These credits will be discussed in further detail in Chapter 9.

The tax liability is further reduced by the amounts withheld on income and by any estimated payments made during the year. Income taxes may be withheld on the various sources of income that a taxpayer receives during the year. Employers are required to withhold income tax on compensation paid to their employees. In addition, estimated payments may be necessary if enough taxes have not been withheld.

¶3075 **NET TAX DUE OR REFUND**

The tax result after applying the credits and prepayments to the "Tax Liability" is the amount that must be paid to the Internal Revenue Service or the amount overpaid and to be refunded to the taxpayer.

¶3085 **CLASSIFICATION OF TAXPAYERS**

The Internal Revenue Code defines the term "taxpayer" as any person subject to any internal revenue act. The term "person" includes an individual, a trust, estate, partnership, association, company, or corporation. A "partnership" includes a syndicate, group, pool, joint venture, or other unincorporated venture, through or by means of which any business, financial operation, or venture is carried on and which is not a trust or estate or a corporation. The term "corporation" is not defined but is stated to include associations, joint-stock companies, and insurance companies.

A proper classification of taxpayers is essential in determining the type of tax return to be filed. Individuals have little trouble choosing the right tax return, but problems often arise with artificial entities such as trusts, estates, partnerships, corporations, and associations.

Taxpayers are usually classified according to the type of tax return that they are required to file. Excluding most information returns (which are not tax returns in the strict sense of the term) and returns for organizations exempt from income tax, almost all tax returns will fall into one of the following four categories:

Type Of Return	Form	Filed By
Individual	1040	Every natural person with income of statutory minimums
Corporation	1120	Corporations, including organizations taxed as corporations
Fiduciary	1041	Trusts and estates with income in excess of statutory minimums
Partnership	1065	Partnerships or joint ventures (information return only)

Personal Exemptions

In computing taxable income an individual is allowed a deduction for each personal exemption allowed. The personal exemption is $4,050 for 2017. After 1989, the personal exemption amount is indexed for inflation.

Such exemptions are (1) the exemptions for an individual taxpayer and spouse, and (2) the exemptions for dependents of the taxpayer. However, no personal exemption amount is allowed on the return of an individual who is eligible to be claimed as a dependent on another taxpayer's return.

¶3201 **TAXPAYER AND SPOUSE**

Since there are two taxpayers on a joint return, two exemptions are allowed on the return even though there may be only one individual earning income. Where a joint return is filed by the taxpayer and spouse, no other person is allowed an exemption for the spouse even if the spouse otherwise qualifies as a dependent of another person.

The taxpayer is allowed an exemption for the spouse of the taxpayer if a joint return is not filed. However, the spouse must have no income for the year and must not be the dependent of another taxpayer. Thus, a taxpayer is not entitled to an exemption for the spouse on a separate return for the year in which the spouse has any gross income even though the income is not sufficient to require the spouse to file a return.

Exemptions	6a	☐	**Yourself.** If your parent (or someone else) can claim you as a dependent on his or her tax return, **do not** check box 6a.				No. of boxes checked on 6a and 6b _____
	b	☐	**Spouse**				No. of your children on 6c who:
	c		**Dependents:**	**(2)** Dependent's social security number	**(3)** Dependent's relationship to you	**(4)** ✔ if qualifying child for child tax credit (see page 19)	• lived with you _____
			(1) First name Last name			☐	• did not live with you due to divorce or separation (see page 19) _____
If more than six dependents, see page 19.				┊ ┊		☐	
				┊ ┊		☐	Dependents on 6c not entered above _____
				┊ ┊		☐	Add numbers entered on lines above ▶ ☐
	d		Total number of exemptions claimed				

Source: Form 1040

¶3225 DEPENDENTS

Taxpayers are allowed to claim a personal exemption and receive a $4,050 deduction in 2017 for each dependent.

The statutory definition of a dependent has been rewritten to categorize each dependent as a qualifying child or a qualifying relative. The definition also creates a uniform definition of child for dependency exemption, child credit, earned income tax credit, dependent care credit, and head of household filing status.

Qualifying Child

A child is a qualifying child of a taxpayer if the child satisfies each of four tests:

Principal Abode. The child has the same principal place of abode as the taxpayer for more than one half the taxable year. Temporary absences due to special circumstances, including absences due to illness, education, business, vacation, or military service, are not treated as absences.

Relationship. The child has specified relationship to the taxpayer. The child must be the taxpayer's son, daughter, stepson, stepdaughter, brother, sister, stepbrother, stepsister, or a descendant of any such individual. An individual legally adopted by the taxpayer, or an individual who is lawfully placed with the taxpayer for adoption by the taxpayer, is treated as a child of such taxpayer by blood. A foster child who is placed with the taxpayer by an authorized placement agency or by judgment, decree, or other order of any court of competent jurisdiction is treated as the taxpayer's child.

Age. The child has not yet attained a specified age. In general, a child must be under age 19 (or 24 in the case of a full-time student) in order to be a qualifying child. In general, no age limit applies with respect to individuals who are totally and permanently disabled at any time during the calendar year. The prior-law requirements are retained that a child must be under age 13 for purposes of the dependent care credit, and under age 17 for purposes of the child tax credit.

A tie-breaking rule applies if more than one taxpayer claims a child as a qualifying child. First, if only one of the individuals claiming the child as a qualifying child is the child's parent, the child is deemed the qualifying child of the parent. Second, if both parents claim the child and the parents do not file a joint return, then the child is deemed a qualifying child first with respect to the parent with whom the child resides the longest period of time, and second with respect to the parent with the highest adjusted gross income. Third, if the child's parents do not claim the child, then the child is deemed a qualifying child with respect to the claimant with the highest adjusted gross income.

The prior-law support and gross income tests (discussed below) for determining dependency do not apply to a child who meets the requirements of the uniform definition of qualifying child.

Support. A child who provides over half of his or her own support is not considered a qualifying child of another taxpayer.

Qualifying Relative

Taxpayers generally may claim an individual who does not meet the uniform definition of qualifying child with respect to any individual who is a qualifying relative. A qualifying relative must meet all of the following tests:

1. Relationship or member of household
2. Gross income
3. Support
4. Not a qualifying child

Relationship or Member of the Household Test

The dependent must be a relative of the taxpayer or a member of the taxpayer's household. Individuals considered to be related to the taxpayer and eligible for the dependency exemption include: a child or a descendant of a child; a brother, sister, stepbrother, or stepsister; the father or mother, or an ancestor of either; a stepfather or stepmother; a son or daughter of a brother or sister of the taxpayer; a brother or sister of the father or mother of the taxpayer; and a son-in-law, daughter-in-law; father-in-law, mother-in-law, brother-in-law, or sister-in-law. A nonrelated person must be a member of the taxpayer's household for the entire year to qualify as a dependent. The taxpayer must maintain and occupy the household. An individual is not a member of the taxpayer's household if any time during the year the relationship between the individual and the taxpayer is in violation of local law.

Gross Income Test

A taxpayer is allowed an exemption for each dependent whose gross income for the year is less than the personal exemption amount ($4,050 for 2017).

EXAMPLE 3.7

> Colleen Drew, age 21, earned $4,350 working part-time while attending school full-time. Colleen's lives the entire year with her friend who pays more than one-half of Colleen's support. Colleen's friend will not be able to claim Colleen as a dependent since Colleen made more than $4,050.

The gross income amount is determined before the deduction of any expenses, such as materials, taxes, and depreciation. Thus, a taxpayer would not be able to claim his grandmother for 2017 if she received $4,150 in rental income, even though her expenses reduced the net income to less than $4,050. However, cost of goods sold is subtracted from gross receipts to determine gross income. Receipts which are excludable from gross income are not counted in applying the gross income test.

Support Test

Over one-half of the support of a dependent must be furnished by the taxpayer. In determining whether the taxpayer has provided over half of the support, the support received from the taxpayer as compared to the entire amount of support which the individual receives from all sources, including support which the individual supplies, will be taken into account.

In computing the amount which is contributed for the support of an individual, there must be included any amount which is contributed by the individual for his or her own support, including receipts which are excludable from gross income, such as benefits received under Social Security or money withdrawn from a savings account. However, it is only the amount actually spent on support which is taken into consideration, not the total amount available for support.

The term "support" includes food, shelter, clothing, medical and dental care, education, and similar items. Generally, the amount of an item of support will be the amount of expense incurred by the one furnishing the item. If the item of support furnished by an individual is in the form of property or lodging, it will be necessary to measure the amount of the item of support in terms of its fair market value. The value of personal services is not included in support determination. *F. Markarian,* 65-2 USTC ¶10,755, 352 F.2d 870 (CA-7 1965), cert. denied, 384 U.S. 988, 86 S.Ct. 1886.

Where the taxpayer owns the home in which the dependent lives, the fair rental value of the lodging furnished is part of the total support. However, this does not mean an equal allocation between taxpayers and dependents. It is recognized that an adult has certain minimum base housing costs which cannot be treated as equal to the minimum housing costs of minor children. In one case, the court allocated 60 percent of the housing costs to the mother and 40 percent to be divided equally among three children. *J.D.M. Cameron,* 33 TCM 725, Dec. 32,654(M), T.C. Memo. 1974-166. Amounts paid to others to care for children while working are included as part of support. *T. Lovett,* 18 TC 477, Dec. 19,018 (1952), Acq., 1952-2 CB 2. The amount paid may also qualify for the dependent care credit.

Some capital expenditures may qualify as items of support. The cost of an automobile is counted in determining who furnished over half of a dependent's support. A television set furnished and set apart in the child's bedroom is also an item of support. Rev. Rul. 77-282, 1977-2 CB 52.

Welfare payments made by a state agency to or on behalf of a dependent are attributable to the agency rather than the taxpayer. *H. Johnson,* 33 TCM 659, Dec. 32,630(M), T.C. Memo. 1974-150; *H.M. Lutter,* 75-1 USTC ¶10,439, 514 F.2d 1095 (CA-7 1975), cert. denied, 423 U.S. 931, 96 S.Ct. 283. This may deny a dependency exemption to the taxpayer since the agency may have provided more than half the support

¶3225

of a child. However, amounts expended by a state for training and education of handicapped children are not taken into account in determining support. This rule applies only if the institution qualifies as an "educational institution" and the residents qualify as "students." Rev. Rul. 59-379, 1959-2 CB 51, clarified by Rev. Rul. 60-190, 1960-1 CB 51. Social Security Medicare benefits are disregarded in the computation of support. Rev. Rul. 79-173, 1979-1 CB 86.

Amounts received as scholarships for study at an educational institution are not considered in determining whether the taxpayer furnishes more than one-half the support of the student. Amounts received for tuition payments and allowances by a veteran are not considered scholarships in determining the support test.

EXAMPLE 3.8	John has a cousin who lives with John and who receives a $5,000 scholarship to Academic University for one year. John contributes $4,100, which constitutes the balance of the cousin's support for that year. John may claim the cousin as a dependent, as the $5,000 scholarship is not counted in determining the support of the cousin and, therefore, John is considered as providing all the support of the cousin.

Not a Qualifying Child Test

An individual who is a qualifying child of the taxpayer or of any other taxpayer cannot be a qualifying relative.

Special Rules Applying to Dependents

The taxpayer and the dependent will be considered as occupying the household for the entire year notwithstanding temporary absences from the household due to special circumstances. A nonpermanent failure to occupy the common abode by reason of illness, education, business, vacation, military service, or a custody agreement under which the dependent is absent for less than six months in the tax year, will be considered temporary absence due to special circumstances.

The fact that the dependent dies during the year will not deprive the taxpayer of the deduction if the dependent lived in the household for the entire part of the year preceding death. Similarly, the period during the year preceding birth of an individual will not prevent the individual from qualifying as a dependent.

No exemption will be allowed for any dependent who has filed a joint return with the dependent's spouse. However, the dependency exemption will still be allowed where a joint return is filed by a dependent and spouse merely as a claim for refund and where no tax liability would exist for either spouse on the basis of separate returns. Rev. Rul. 65-34, 1965-1 CB 86.

The term "dependent" does not include an individual who is not a citizen or national of the United States unless such individual is a resident of the United States or a country contiguous to the United States. This exception does not apply to any child that has the same principal place of abode as the taxpayer and is a member of the taxpayer's household and the taxpayer is a citizen or national of the United States.

The term "student" means an individual who, during each of five calendar months during the calendar year, is a full-time student at an educational institution, or is pursuing a full-time course of instructional on-farm training. A full-time student is one who is enrolled for some part of five calendar months for the number of hours or courses which is considered to be full-time attendance. The five calendar months need not be consecutive. School attendance exclusively at night does not constitute full-time attendance. However, full-time attendance may include some attendance at night in connection with a full-time course of study.

Dependents will not be allowed to claim exemptions for dependents in any year they are themselves a dependent.

Social Security numbers are required for all individuals who are claimed as dependents. Failure to include the Social Security number or other required information can result in the loss of the exemption.

Multiple Support Agreements

Special rules allow a taxpayer to be treated as having contributed over half of the support of an individual where two or more taxpayers contributed to the support of the individual if (1) no one person contributed over half of the individual's support, (2) each member of the group which collectively contributed more than half of the support of the individual would have been entitled to claim the individual as a dependent except for the fact that they did not contribute more than one-half of the support, (3) the member of the group claiming the individual as a dependent contributed more than 10 percent of the individual's support, and (4) each other person in the group who contributed more than 10 percent of the support files a written declaration that they will not claim the individual as a dependent for the year.

EXAMPLE 3.9

Brothers Alfred, Bill, Chuck, and Don contributed the entire support of their mother in the following percentages: Alfred, 30 percent; Bill, 20 percent; Chuck, 29 percent; and Don, 21 percent. Any one of the brothers, except for the fact that he did not contribute more than half of her support, would have been entitled to claim his mother as a dependent. Consequently, any one of the brothers could claim a deduction for the exemption of the mother provided a written declaration from each of the brothers is attached to the return of the individual taking the exemption. If, on the other hand, Don were a neighbor instead of a brother, he would not qualify as a member of the group for multiple support agreement purposes. He would not be eligible to claim the mother since she was not a member of Don's household. Don would not be required to sign the multiple support agreement.

Divorced or Separated Parents

When taxpayers are divorced, legally separated, or never married, special rules apply to determine which one is entitled to exemptions for their children. These rules may result in a taxpayer who did not provide more than half of the support of the child being entitled to the exemption.

To qualify, the parents must be divorced or legally separated under a decree of divorce or separate maintenance, separated under a written separation agreement, or lived apart at all times during the last six months of the year. In addition, both parents together must provide more than one-half of the child's support. The child must be in the custody of one or both parents for more than one-half of the calendar year. Thus, a dependency exemption may not be claimed by one of the parents if a person other than the parents provides one-half or more for the support of the child during the year or has custody of the child for one half or more of the year.

As a general rule, a child will be treated as receiving over half of the support from the parent having custody for the greater number of nights for the year. If the parents of the child are divorced or separated for only a portion of a year after having joint custody for the prior portion of the year, the parent who has custody for the greater number of nights of the remainder of the year after divorce or separation will be treated as having custody for a greater portion of the year.

EXAMPLE 3.10

Bill, a child of Jim and Cathy Durell, who were divorced on June 1, received $5,000 for support during the year, of which $2,200 was provided by Jim and $1,950 by Cathy. No multiple support agreement was entered into. Prior to the divorce, Jim and Cathy jointly had custody of Bill. For the remainder of the year, Jim had custody of Bill for the months of October through December, while Cathy had custody of Bill for the months of June through September. Since Cathy had custody for four of the seven months following the divorce, she had custody for the greater number of nights and is the custodial parent for the year and is allowed the personal exemption.

Post-1984 Divorces

For divorces taking place in years after 1984, the custodial parent is entitled to the exemption in all cases unless he or she expressly waives the right to the exemption. This may be done by the custodial parent signing a written declaration that he or she will not claim the exemption. The noncustodial parent is required to attach this declaration to his or her tax return each year when claiming the exemption. Failure to attach Form 8332, Release of Claim to Exemption for Child of Divorced or Separated Parents, means that the noncustodial parent cannot claim the exemption, regardless of the amount of support furnished.

Form 8332
(Rev. February 2009)
Department of the Treasury
Internal Revenue Service

Release/Revocation of Release of Claim to Exemption for Child by Custodial Parent

▶ Attach a separate form for each child.

OMB No. 1545-0074

Attachment Sequence No. **115**

Name of noncustodial parent | Noncustodial parent's social security number (SSN) ▶

Part I   Release of Claim to Exemption for Current Year

I agree not to claim an exemption for _____
                                                        Name of child

for the tax year 20____ .

_____   _____   _____
Signature of custodial parent releasing claim to exemption   Custodial parent's SSN   Date

Note. If you choose not to claim an exemption for this child for future tax years, also complete Part II.

Part II   Release of Claim to Exemption for Future Years (If completed, see **Noncustodial parent** on page 2.)

I agree not to claim an exemption for _____
                                                        Name of child

for the tax year(s)_____ .
                          (Specify. See instructions.)

_____   _____   _____
Signature of custodial parent releasing claim to exemption   Custodial parent's SSN   Date

Part III   Revocation of Release of Claim to Exemption for Future Year(s)

I revoke the release of claim to an exemption for _____
                                                                        Name of child

for the tax year(s)_____ .
                          (Specify. See instructions.)

_____   _____   _____
Signature of custodial parent revoking the release of claim to exemption   Custodial parent's SSN   Date

---

EXAMPLE 3.11

Mike and Jennifer are divorced. Mike pays over half of the support of their child, Amanda. Amanda resides with Jennifer for the greater part of the year. Mike is unable to claim Amanda as a dependent on his return because he does not have a signed Form 8332 from Jennifer.

KEYSTONE PROBLEM

The personal exemption reduces taxable income by $4,050 in 2017. In certain situations, such as multiple support agreements and children of divorced parents, it is possible to assign the personal exemption for a dependent to one of the eligible parties. What should be taken into consideration in determining which party should receive the personal exemption?

The individual claiming the child as a dependent also qualifies for the child tax credit provided other requirements are met.

¶3227   HIGH-INCOME PHASEOUT OF EXEMPTIONS

For tax years beginning after 1990, the deduction for personal exemptions is reduced or even eliminated for certain high-income taxpayers. If a taxpayer's adjusted gross income exceeds the appropriate threshold amount (based on filing status) below, the deduction for exemptions is reduced by 2 percent for each $2,500 or fraction thereof by which the adjusted gross income exceeds the threshold amount. In the case of a married person filing separately, the exemption deduction is reduced by 2 percent for each $1,250 or fraction thereof by which such adjusted gross income exceeds the threshold amount. In no case will the deduction for exemptions be reduced by more than 100 percent.

For 2017, the threshold amounts (adjusted annually for inflation) are as follows:

Joint return or a surviving spouse	$313,800
Head of household	287,650
Single taxpayer	261,500
Married person filing a separate return	156,900

The deduction for personal exemptions will be fully eliminated when adjusted gross income exceeds the threshold amount by more than $122,500.

EXAMPLE 3.12

Assume a married couple with four personal exemptions has $357,300 in adjusted gross income. The couple's personal exemption deduction would be computed as follows:

Adjusted gross income	$357,300
Threshold for phaseout	313,800
Excess over threshold	$43,500
Each $2,500	÷ 2,500
Number of $2,500s	17.4
Number of $2,500s or fractions thereof	18
Phaseout rate	2%
Reduction in personal exemptions	36%
Personal exemption amount	$4,050
Personal exemptions (4)	× 4
Initial personal exemption deduction	$16,200
Personal exemption percent allowed	× 64%
Personal exemption deduction	$10,368

Filing Status and Requirements

The tax liability of an individual not only varies with the amount of income but also depends upon marital status. Taxpayers must determine their income tax liability from among five different filing statuses:

1. Married individuals filing jointly
2. Married individuals filing separate returns
3. Single individuals
4. Heads of households
5. Surviving spouses

Filing Status — Check only one box.

1. Single
2. Married filing joint return (even if only one had income)
3. Married filing separate return. Enter spouse's social security no. above and full name here. ▶ _____
4. Head of household (with qualifying person). (See page 18.) If the qualifying person is a child but not your dependent, enter this child's name here. ▶ _____
5. Qualifying widow(er) with dependent child (year spouse died▶ 19   ). (See page 18.)

Source: Form 1040

A married taxpayer meeting the "abandoned spouse" requirements may be considered as an unmarried person for tax purposes. These requirements are: (1) the taxpayer must file a separate return, (2) the taxpayer's spouse cannot be a member of the household during the last six months of the year, (3) the taxpayer must furnish over half the cost of maintaining the taxpayer's home, and (4) the taxpayer's home must be the principal residence of a dependent child for more than one-half of the year.

EXAMPLE 3.13

Melvin Moore left Esther and their two children on April 15, 2017, and has not been heard from since. Esther furnishes the entire cost of the household and the support of the two children for the remainder of the year. For 2017, Esther would qualify as an abandoned spouse and thus be considered as unmarried. If Melvin had left during the last half of the year, or if there were no children, Esther would not qualify as unmarried under the abandoned spouse rules. She would file as married filing separately.

An individual qualifying as an abandoned spouse will qualify for head of household status. Head of household status provides the spouse with a lower rate than the tax rate for a married person filing a separate return or a single individual.

Married persons are taxed at the lowest rate if they file jointly, and at the highest rates if they file separately. Unmarried taxpayers who are heads of households use a set of rates between those for single people and those for married couples filing jointly. Surviving spouses use the same rates as those married filing jointly. All unmarried taxpayers who do not qualify for another filing status must file as single taxpayers.

¶3301   MARRIED INDIVIDUALS FILING JOINTLY

A married couple may file a joint return including their combined incomes, or each spouse may file a separate return reflecting his or her income only. A joint return is not allowed if either the husband or wife is a nonresident alien at any time during the tax year, or if the husband and wife have different tax years. However, if at the end of a tax year one spouse is a U.S. citizen or a resident alien and the other spouse is a nonresident alien, a special election may be made to treat the nonresident spouse as a U.S. resident. If no election is made, the taxpayer's status is married filing separately unless there is a dependent which would allow head of household status to be used.

Joint returns were originally enacted to establish equity for married taxpayers in common law states since in community property states married taxpayers are able to split their income. Therefore, the progressive rates are constructed upon the assumption that income is earned equally by the two spouses. A joint return may be filed and the splitting device may be used even if one spouse has no income.

If a joint return is filed, the income and deductions of both spouses are combined. The exemptions to which either spouse is entitled are combined, and both spouses sign the return. In a joint return, the general rule is that both spouses are jointly and severally liable for any deficiency in tax, interest, and penalties.

A joint return may be made for the survivor and a deceased spouse or for both deceased spouses. The tax year of such spouses must begin on the same day and end on different days only because of the death of either or both spouses. The surviving spouse must not remarry before the close of the tax year and the spouses must have been eligible to file a joint return on the date of death.

The determination of whether an individual is married is made as of the close of the tax year, unless the spouse dies during the year, in which case the determination will be made as of the time of death. A married couple does not have to be living together on the last day of the tax year in order to file a joint return, but an individual legally separated under a decree of divorce or separate maintenance will not be considered married.

¶3315   MARRIED INDIVIDUALS FILING SEPARATELY

If a husband and wife file separate returns, they should each report only their own income and claim only their own exemptions and deductions on their individual returns.

Separate returns will result in approximately the same tax liability as a joint return where both spouses have approximately equal amounts of income. However, when the incomes are unequal, it is generally advantageous for married taxpayers in noncommunity property states to file a joint return since the combined amount of tax on separate returns is higher than the tax on a joint return.

Special circumstances may warrant the use of separate returns. Where one spouse incurs significant medical expenses, the smaller adjusted gross income of a separate return results in a larger medical deduction since medical expenses are allowed only to the extent they exceed 10 percent of adjusted gross income. It may be desirable to file separate returns to protect against a potential deficiency on the other spouse's return where there is some concern over the tax liability or there is a questionable item on the return itself.

In community property states, a married couple's income is treated as earned equally by the two spouses. Income earned on capital investment made from a spouse's separate property in most community property states remains the separate property of that spouse. There are three community property states in which income from separate property is treated as community property (Texas, Idaho, and Louisiana). See discussion of the "Texas Rule" at ¶4215. Community property income and deductions must be accounted for on the same basis. Deductions pertaining to the separate property of one spouse must be taken by that spouse. However, where the income from that property is taxable one-half to each spouse, the deductions must be divided between the husband and wife.

The Code places numerous limitations upon deductions, credits, etc., where married taxpayers file separately. If both husband and wife have income, they should generally figure their tax both jointly and separately to insure they are using the method resulting in less tax.

If an individual has filed a separate return for a year for which a joint return could have been filed and the time for filing the return has expired, a joint return by the husband and wife may still be filed. The joint return must be filed within three years of the due date of the original return for which a change is requested. All payments, credits, refunds, or other payments made or allowed on the separate return of either spouse are taken into account in determining the extent to which the tax based on the joint return has been paid.

If a joint return has been filed for a year, the spouses may not thereafter file separate returns for that year after the time for filing the return for that year has expired.

¶3325   SINGLE INDIVIDUALS

A single individual for tax purposes is an unmarried person who does not qualify as head of household. Generally, if only one of the two individuals is working, it is advantageous from a tax standpoint to enter into marriage. However, where the incomes are approximately equal, the total tax will be smaller if they are not married.

¶3345   HEADS OF HOUSEHOLDS

Unmarried individuals who maintain a household for qualifying children or dependents are entitled to use the head of household rates. The definition of a dependent for purposes of head of household status is the same as the uniform definition contained in the dependency exemption rules. The dependent must be a qualifying child or a qualified relative of the taxpayer. Over one-half of the cost of maintaining the household must be furnished by the taxpayer. The household must be the principal abode for more than one-half of the year. A qualifying relative must qualify as the taxpayer's dependent. A dependent relative who is a dependent only because of a multiple-support agreement cannot qualify a taxpayer for head of household status. A legally adopted child of a taxpayer is considered a child of the taxpayer by blood. A dependent foster child is treated like a dependent blood son or daughter, rather than as an unrelated individual. However, the foster child must be a dependent to enable the parent to use head of household status. Rev. Rul. 84-89, 1984-1 CB 5. A taxpayer with a qualifying child is not required to claim the qualifying child as a dependent in order to qualify for head of household status. A nonrelative cannot qualify an individual for head of household status.

| EXAMPLE 3.14 | Sara Shuster is unmarried and maintains a household in which she and her son reside. The son is claimed by his father as a dependent. Since Sara is not required to claim the dependency exemption on her child, she may use the head-of-household tax rate schedule. If the son is married, Sara must be able to claim him as a dependent in order to file as head of household. |

The taxpayer's dependent parents need not live with the taxpayer to enable the taxpayer to qualify as a head of household. The household maintained by the taxpayer must actually constitute the principal place of abode of the father or mother or both of them. The father or mother must occupy the household for the entire year. A rest home or home for the aged qualifies as a household for this purpose.

| EXAMPLE 3.15 | Meg Morgan, an unmarried individual living in Baltimore, maintains a household in Los Angeles for her dependent mother. Meg may use the head-of-household tax rate schedule even though her mother does not live with her. |

Although generally a married couple cannot file a joint return if one of them is a nonresident alien, the taxpayer who is a U.S. citizen will qualify as a head of household if the taxpayer is the one providing the maintenance of the household and if there is a related dependent living with the taxpayer the entire year. The law provides that, for purposes of the head of household status, the taxpayer is treated as unmarried.

A taxpayer does not qualify for head of household status if the only other person living in his household is a nonresident alien spouse because the spouse does not qualify as a dependent. However, a taxpayer having a nonresident alien spouse may qualify if an unmarried dependent or unmarried stepchild lives with the taxpayer. Rev. Rul. 55-711, 1955-2 CB 13, amplified by Rev. Rul. 74-370, 1974-2 CB 7.

A physical change in the location of a home will not prevent a taxpayer from qualifying as a head of household. The fact that the individual qualifying the taxpayer for head of household status is born or dies within the tax year will not block a claim for head of household status. The household must have been the principal place of abode of the individual for the remaining or preceding part of the year.

A nonpermanent failure to occupy the common abode by reason of illness, education, business, vacation, military service, or a custody agreement under which a child or stepchild is absent for less than six months in a year will not bar the head of household status. However, it must be reasonable to assume that the household member will return to the household and the taxpayer continues to maintain the household or a substantially equivalent household in anticipation of such return.

The costs of maintaining a household are the expenses incurred for the mutual benefit of the occupants. They include property taxes, mortgage interest, rent, utility charges, upkeep and repairs, property insurance, and food consumed on the premises. Such expenses do not include the cost of clothing, education, medical treatment, vacations, life insurance, and transportation. In addition, the cost of maintaining a household does not include any amount which represents the value of services rendered in the household by the taxpayer or by a person qualifying the taxpayer as a head of household. The taxpayer, for example, cannot impute a value for services provided by the taxpayer for cooking, cleaning, and doing laundry.

It is possible for a household to be a portion of a home. The Tax Court held that a widow and her unmarried daughter occupying one level of a four-level house and sharing two levels constituted a household. *J.F. Fleming Est.,* 33 TCM 619, Dec. 32,611(M), T.C. Memo. 1974-137. Since the widow paid more than one-half of the household maintenance expenses attributable to her and her daughter, she qualified as a head of household.

¶3355 SURVIVING SPOUSES

Special tax benefits are extended to a surviving spouse. In addition to the right to file a joint return for the year in which a spouse dies, a taxpayer whose spouse died in either of the two years preceding the tax year, and who has not remarried, may file as a surviving spouse provided the surviving spouse maintains a household for a dependent child or stepchild.

Surviving spouses use the same tax rate schedules and tax tables as married taxpayers filing joint returns. The surviving spouse provisions do not authorize the surviving spouse to file a joint return; they only make the joint return tax rates available.

The surviving spouse must provide over half the cost of maintaining the household in which both the surviving spouse and dependent live. Of course, an exemption for the deceased spouse is available in the year of death but is not available on the return of the surviving spouse in the two years following death.

EXAMPLE 3.16 Albert Olm's wife died in 2017, leaving a child who qualifies as Albert's dependent. In the year of death, Albert and his deceased wife are entitled to file a joint return and claim three exemptions—one each for Albert, his deceased spouse, and the dependent child. If the child continues to live with Albert in a household provided by him and be his dependent, Albert will be allowed to file as a surviving spouse for 2018 and 2019. Only two exemptions will be allowed in those years—one for Albert and one for the dependent child.

¶3365 TAX RETURNS OF DEPENDENTS

For 2017, the standard deduction for an individual who can be claimed as a dependent on the tax return of another taxpayer is the greater of the individual's earned income plus $350 (up to the maximum allowable standard deduction) or $1,050. However, an individual over 18 or a full-time student over 23 will not qualify as a dependent if income exceeds $4,050.

An individual may not claim a personal exemption if the individual can be claimed as a dependent on another taxpayer's return. It does not matter whether the other taxpayer actually claims the exemption.

EXAMPLE 3.17 Michael Turner, who is single, is claimed as a dependent on his parents' 2017 tax return. He receives $1,500 in interest income from a savings account. In addition, he earns $1,800 while working part-time after school. The standard deduction for a single individual for 2017 is $6,350. However, Michael is limited to a standard deduction of $2,150, the larger of his earned income of $1,800 plus $350 or $1,050.

EXAMPLE 3.18	Sonya Ross is single and claimed as a dependent on her parents' 2017 tax return. She has $1,200 in interest income and also earns $400 from part-time employment. Her standard deduction is limited to $1,050, the larger of her earned income of $400 plus $350 or $1,050.

EXAMPLE 3.19	Tom Moss, a 22-year-old, full-time college student, is claimed as a dependent on his parents' 2017 return. Tom is married and files a separate return. Tom has $1,500 in interest income and wages of $6,550. His standard deduction is $6,350, because the greater of $1,050 or his earned income ($6,550) plus $350 is $6,900, but his standard deduction cannot be more than the $6,350 maximum allowable standard deduction.

Kiddie Tax

If a dependent child is subject to the kiddie tax and has more than $2,100 of net unearned (investment) income for the year, his or her net unearned income is taxed to the child at the additional rate of tax that the parent would be required to pay if the child's net unearned income were included in the parents' taxable income. This applies regardless of the source of the assets creating the child's net unearned income as long as the child has at least one living parent as of the close of the tax year and does not file a joint return. The income of the custodial parent is used for the tax computation in the case of parents that are not married. The parent with the greater taxable income is to be used when married parents file separately.

The kiddie tax applies in the following circumstances:

1. 17-year old or younger—subject to the kiddie tax regardless of the amount of his or her earned income.
2. 18-year old—subject to the kiddie tax unless the child has earned income exceeding one-half of their support.
3. 19- to 23-year old full-time student—subject to the kiddie tax unless the child has earned income exceeding one-half of their support.

Net unearned income is unearned income (such as interest, dividends, capital gains, and certain trust income) less the sum of $1,050 (referred to as the first $1,050 clause) and the greater of: (1) $1,050 of the standard deduction or $1,050 of itemized deductions, or (2) the amount of allowable deductions which are directly connected with the production of unearned income. Thus, unearned income is reduced by $2,100 unless the child has itemized deductions connected with the production of unearned income exceeding $1,050. The amount of net unearned income cannot exceed taxable income for the year.

The child in each of the following examples is subject to the kiddie tax. In each of the examples no personal exemption is allowed since the child is a dependent of another taxpayer.

EXAMPLE 3.20	Amy Acorn has $300 of unearned income and no earned income. Amy will have no tax liability since her standard deduction of $1,050 will reduce taxable income to zero.

EXAMPLE 3.21	Bill Barnes has $1,300 of unearned income and no earned income. Bill will have $250 of taxable income ($1,300 gross income – $1,050 standard deduction). His net unearned income is reduced to zero by the first $1,050 clause and the $1,050 standard deduction. The $250 taxable income is taxed at Bill's tax rate.

EXAMPLE 3.22	Charles Clewis has $2,300 of unearned income and no earned income. His $1,050 standard deduction reduces taxable income to $1,250. The $2,300 of unearned income is reduced by (1) the first $1,050 clause and (2) the $1,050 standard deduction, leaving $200 of net unearned income. The $200 of net unearned income is taxed at the additional rate of the parents while the remaining $1,050 of taxable income is taxed at Charles's rate.

EXAMPLE 3.23	Dave Drummer has $800 of earned income and $400 of unearned income. Dave's standard deduction is $1,150 (the amount of earned income plus $350). His taxable income is $50 ($1,200 gross income – $1,150 standard deduction). Since the unearned income is less than $2,100, there is no net unearned income. The taxable income is taxed at Dave's tax rate.

EXAMPLE 3.24	Frank Fisher has $450 of earned income and $2,200 of unearned income. His taxable income is $1,600 ($2,650 gross income – $1,050 standard deduction). Frank's $2,200 unearned income is reduced by $2,100 (the first $1,050 clause + the $1,050 standard deduction), leaving $100 of net unearned income. The $100 of net unearned income is taxed at the parent's rate. Frank is taxed at his rate on the remaining $1,500 taxable income ($1,600 taxable income – $100 taxed at parent's rate).

EXAMPLE 3.25	Gene Gambol has $1,100 of earned income plus $3,000 of unearned income. He has $1,100 of itemized deductions (net of the 2 percent floor) which are directly connected with the production of the unearned income. Gene has $450 of other itemized deductions. His taxable income is $2,550 ($4,100 gross income – $1,550 of itemized deductions). Gene's net unearned income of $850 is taxed at his parents' rate. The unearned income is reduced by $2,150 (the first $1,050 clause + the entire $1,100 of deductions relating to the production of unearned income since it exceeds $1,050). Gene is taxed at his rate on $1,700 ($2,550 taxable income – $850 taxed at his parents' rate).

PLANNING POINTER	Parents can avoid having a dependent's income taxed at their rate by making gifts to children of assets that will not generate income until after the child's income no longer qualifies for the kiddie tax. The tax on the income would then be taxed at the child's tax rate. Examples of such assets include single premium ordinary life insurance policies, Series EE savings bonds, and property expected to appreciate over time.

A parent may elect to include on his or her return the unearned income of a child whose income is between $1,050 and $10,500. The child's income must consist solely of interest and dividends. The child is treated as having no gross income and does not have to file a tax return if the election is made.

The electing parent must include the gross income of the child in excess of $2,100 on the parent's tax return for the year, resulting in the taxation of that income at the parent's highest marginal rate. There is an additional tax liability equal to the lesser of (1) $105 or (2) 10 percent of the child's income exceeding $1,050. This liability reflects the child's unearned income from $1,050 to $2,100 that would otherwise be taxed to the child at the 10 percent tax rate.

¶3375   FILING REQUIREMENTS

The obligation to file a return depends on the amount of gross income, marital status during the year, and age. Only income which is taxable is included in the computation of gross income in order to determine whether or not a return must be filed.

With certain exceptions, the gross income level at which taxpayers must file returns is determined by adding the standard deduction to the personal exemptions allowed for the taxpayer. Because married individuals filing separately must both itemize or both use the standard deduction, the standard deduction amount is not added to the personal exemption to determine the gross income filing figure. The old-age additional standard deduction entitles an individual to increase the gross income level filing requirement by $1,250 or $1,550. However, no increase is permitted for blindness or for exemptions for dependents.

For 2017, Code Sec. 6012 requires a tax return to be filed if gross income for the year is at least as much as the amount shown for the categories in the following table.

Filing Status	Gross Income
Single	
Under 65 and not blind	$10,400
Under 65 and blind	10,400
65 or older	11,950
Dependent with unearned income	1,050
Dependent with no unearned income	6,350
Married Filing Joint Return	
Both spouses under 65 and neither blind	$20,800
Both spouses under 65 and one or both spouses blind	20,800
One spouse 65 or older	22,050
Both spouses 65 or older	23,300
Married Filing Separate Return	
All—whether 65 or older or blind	$4,050
Head of Household	
Under 65 and not blind	$13,400
Under 65 and blind	13,400
65 or older	14,950
Surviving Spouse	
Under 65 and not blind	$16,750
Under 65 and blind	16,750
65 or older	18,000

Even if the aforementioned gross income requirements are not met, a return nevertheless must be filed if an individual had net earnings from self-employment of $400 or more.

A return should be filed by any taxpayer eligible for the earned income credit even though the taxpayer does not meet any of the above filing requirements. A refund can result even if no income tax has been withheld.

Taxpayers must record their identifying number (Social Security number) on their returns. Returns filed by taxpayers claiming exemptions for dependents must include the dependents' Social Security numbers.

¶3385

TAX TABLES

The tables are based on taxable income. The tables apply to taxpayers with taxable income of less than $100,000. Separate tables are provided for single taxpayers, married taxpayers filing jointly and surviving spouses, married taxpayers filing separately, and heads of households.

Each line of the tax tables represents an interval of taxable incomes. Under $3,050 the intervals are $25 and above $3,050 the intervals are $50. The tax given in the tables is based on the midpoint taxable income of each interval. Thus, the tax from the tables for the interval $40,000—$40,050 is the same as the tax determined from the tax rate schedules for $40,025.

The tax tables may not be used by the following taxpayers:

1. Estates or trusts
2. Taxpayers claiming the exclusion for foreign earned income
3. Taxpayers who file a short period return
4. Taxpayers whose income exceeds the ceiling amount

It is expected that 95 percent of all individual taxpayers will be able to determine their tax liability from the tables.

To find the income tax from the tax tables, the taxpayer must (1) find the line that includes the taxable income and (2) read down the column until the taxable income line is reached. For a married couple filing jointly with taxable income of $72,623, the income tax would be $9,634.

Sample Tax Table For 2017					
At Least	But Less Than	Single	Married Filing Jointly	Married Filing Separately	Head of a Household
$72,600	$72,650	$13,895	$9,634	$13,777	$12,409
72,650	72,700	13,908	9,646	13,791	12,421
72,700	72,750	13,920	9,659	13,805	12,434
72,750	72,800	13,933	9,671	13,819	12,466

The 2016 Tax Tables are provided in the Appendix.

¶3395   TAX RATE SCHEDULES

Taxpayers using the tax rate schedules must compute their tax based on taxable income. The tax rate schedules are used by those not eligible to use the tax tables. The tax rate schedules are presented in the Appendix and inside the front cover.

¶3405   SELF-EMPLOYMENT TAX AND MEDICARE SURTAXES

The tax on net self-employment income is levied to provide the self-employed with the same benefits that employees receive through their payment of the Social Security tax (FICA). In general, the tax is levied, assessed, and collected as part of the regular income tax.

The tax is imposed for the purposes of insuring the self-employed individual for old-age, survivors, and disability benefits and for hospitalization benefits under the Social Security program. For 2017, the tax rate is 15.3 percent, made up of two parts: (1) an old-age, survivors, and disability insurance (OASDI) rate of 12.4 percent and (2) a Medicare hospital insurance (HI) rate of 2.9 percent. The self-employed individual is considered both the employer and the employee.

In general, net self-employment income equals the gross income derived by an individual from a trade or business carried on as a sole proprietor, less any allowable deductions, plus the distributive share of a partnership's net income. If a self-employed individual has more than one business, the net self-employment income is the total of the net earnings of all businesses. A loss in one business is deductible from the earnings of the other businesses.

Not all self-employment income is subject to tax. Remuneration paid for the services of a newsboy under age 18 is exempt from the tax. Dividends are included only by a dealer in stock and securities. Interest is included only if on business loans. Rental income is included only by a real estate dealer or in cases in which services are rendered to the occupants. Generally, self-employment income does not include any item that is excluded from gross income. Wages received by a child under 18 from a parent are not subject to the self-employment tax.

The self-employment tax is imposed on "net earnings from self-employment." Net earnings from self-employment is net self-employment income less a special deduction. The actual deduction, however, is not subtracted from a taxpayer's net self-employment income in computing net earnings from self-employment. Instead, a taxpayer reduces net self-employment income by an amount (termed a "deemed deduction") equal to net self-employment income multiplied by one-half of the self-employment tax rate, or 7.65 percent. This deduction is incorporated into Schedule SE by multiplying the net self-employment income by .9235. (This gives the same deduction as multiplying net self-employment income by .0765 and then subtracting the result.)

A taxpayer is allowed a deduction for the employer's portion of the self-employment tax (currently one-half) as a deduction from gross income.

EXAMPLE 3.26

In 2017, Pierre Painter, a self-employed artist, had $45,000 in self-employment income. His deductible business expenses amounted to $15,000. Pierre's self-employment tax is computed as follows:

Gross income from self-employment	$45,000
Less: Business expense deductions	15,000
Net self-employment income	$30,000
Less: Deemed deduction ($30,000 × 7.65%)	2,295
Net earnings from self-employment	$27,705
Self-employment tax ($27,705 × 15.3%)	$ 4,239

On Form 1040, Schedule SE, Pierre would simply multiply his net self-employment income of $30,000 by .9235.

The cap on wages and self-employment income that is taken into account in calculating the portion of the FICA tax applicable to old-age, survivors, and disability insurance (OASDI) is $127,200 for 2017. This also applies to wages, self-employment income, and income derived under the Railroad Retirement Act. There is no longer a cap on wages and self-employment income that is taken into account in calculating the Medicare hospital insurance (HI) portion of the self-employment tax.

EXAMPLE 3.27

Katie Adams has $150,000 in self-employment income for the year. Her net earnings from self-employment is $138,525 ($150,000 × .9235). She will be subject to an OASDI tax of $15,773 ($127,200 × 12.4%) and an HI tax of $4,017 ($138,525 × 2.9%). Thus, her total self-employment tax is $19,790.

Thus, self-employment and Social Security (FICA) tax rate parity is achieved between self-employed persons and employees. Both employees and their employers are liable for Social Security tax and the employer must contribute 6.2 cents per dollar earned by the employee up to the cap limitation ($127,200 for 2017) for OASDI and another 1.45 cents per dollar without a cap for HI.

The net earnings from self-employment subject to the OASDI portion of the self-employment tax are limited to the self-employment base ($127,200 for OASDI and unlimited for HI in 2017) less any wages from which Social Security tax was withheld during the year. Thus, the tax is applied to the lesser of (1) the self-employment base ($127,200) minus income subject to Social Security taxes or (2) the net earnings from self-employment.

EXAMPLE 3.28

In 2017, Margaret Moore has $129,200 in income from self-employment and receives $8,900 in wages that are subject to Social Security taxes. Margaret's net earnings from self-employment are $119,316 ($129,200 × .9235). Her net earnings from self-employment subject to OASDI self-employment tax for the year are $118,300 ($127,200 – $8,900, the wages on which Social Security tax was withheld), which is less than net earnings from self-employment. Her net earnings from self-employment subject to the HI self-employment tax are $119,316, the full amount of the net earnings from self-employment. Thus, her total self-employment tax is $18,129 ($118,300 × 12.4% + $119,316 × 2.9%).

The employer portion of the self-employment tax liability for the year is allowed as a deduction on the tax return. This deduction is taken as a deduction from gross income on the front of Form 1040.

EXAMPLE 3.29

Jim Jergens has $40,000 in self-employment income. His net earnings from self-employment are $36,940 ($40,000 × .9235). The self-employment tax is $5,652 ($36,940 × 15.3%). The employer portion of this amount, $2,826 ($36,940 × 7.65%), is allowed as a deduction from gross income.

If the net earnings from self-employment are less than $400, there is no self-employment tax. However, this does not mean that the first $400 of net earnings from self-employment is not subject to the self-employment tax.

EXAMPLE 3.30

Sylvia Knight's only source of income for 2017 is $433.14 from self-employment. The net earnings from self-employment are $400 ($433.14 × .9235). The self-employment tax is $61.20 ($400 × 15.3%). Sylvia has a deduction from gross income for the employer portion of the self-employment tax, or $30.60 ($400 × 7.65%). If Sylvia had managed to earn less than $433.14, there would have been no self-employment tax.

An optional method of computing self-employment income may be used by persons whose net income from a trade or business is relatively low. The details are omitted, but the method enables taxpayers to obtain greater credit for Social Security benefits than their income would normally allow.

Additional Medicare Tax on Earned Income

A 0.9% Additional Medicare Tax applies to wages and net self-employment income for tax years after 2012. The tax applies to wages exceeding $200,000 for single, head-of-household, or surviving spouse; $250,000 for married filing jointly; $125,000 for married filing separately. The applicable thresholds are not adjusted for inflation.

The tax applies to the employee's share of wages. The tax does not apply to the employer's employment taxes. Box 5 of the W-2 is used for determining the Additional Medicare Tax and withholding.

There are no special rules for nonresident aliens and U.S. citizens living abroad for purposes of the Additional Medicare Tax. Wages, other compensation, and self-employment income that are subject to Medicare tax will also be subject to the Additional Medicare Tax if in excess of the applicable threshold.

The threshold amount for the Additional Medicare Tax applies separately to the FICA and the Railroad Retirement Tax Act (RRTA). Therefore, the amount of RRTA compensation taken into account in determining the Additional Medicare Tax under the RRTA will not reduce the threshold amounts under Section 1401(b)(2)(A) for determining the Additional Medicare Tax under the SECA.

The Additional Medicare Tax on earned income is part of the employer's overall withholding. The employee reconciles the final total of any Additional Medicare Tax when they file their Form 1040 for the tax year.

Employers are required to apply the additional withholding at $200,000 of wages, including taxable fringe benefits, bonuses, tips, commissions, or other supplemental payments, the total amount of taxable Box 5. It does not matter what filing status is shown on Form W-4. The employer applies the $200,000 threshold to each spouse in applying the Additional Medicare Tax. In effect the employer disregards the amount of wages received by the other spouse in computing the Additional Medicare Tax for each spouse.

EXAMPLE 3.31

One spouse received $210,000 of wages, while the other spouse earns $35,000 of either W-2 wages or net self-employment income. The employer of the first spouse is required to withhold an additional 0.9% Additional Medicare Tax on the last $10,000 of taxable wages (i.e., $90) even though the couple will not owe the 0.9% Additional Medicare Tax when they file their 2017 Form 1040. They will receive a tax credit against any other type of tax that may be owed.

If an employer fails to withhold the 0.9% Additional Medicare tax, and the tax is subsequently paid by the employee, the IRS will *not* collect the tax from the employer. The employer will remain subject to any applicable *penalties* on additions to tax for failure to withhold the 0.9% Additional Medicare tax as required. Code Sec. 3102(f)(3). The employee is personally responsible if the employer fails to withhold the 0.9% additional Medicare tax. Code Sec. 3102(f)(2).

The self-employed does not receive an income tax deduction for one-half of the 0.9% Additional Medicare Tax on earned income. Any deduction comes from the employer's portion of employment taxes.

EXAMPLE 3.32

A husband and wife each have "Box 5 Medicare wages" of $150,000 listed on their respective W-2s. The combined $300,000 "earned income" will be shown on Form 8959 for calculating the 0.9% Additional Medicare Tax. The couple will owe a 0.9% Additional Medicare Tax of $450 (($300,000 – $250,000 threshold) x 0.9%) which will be included as "Other Taxes" on page 2 of Form 1040.

¶3405

EXAMPLE 3.33	A husband has $150,000 of "Box 5 Medicare wages" listed on his W-2. His wife has a K-1 from her law firm listing Box 14 net earnings from self-employment of $162,426 ($150,000 net self-employment income). The couple will owe $450 of Additional Medicare Tax on their collective earned income.

EXAMPLE 3.34	A husband has $150,000 of "Box 5 Medicare wages" listed on his W-2. His wife has a K-1 from her law firm with net earnings from self-employment of $150,000. The wife also has a $50,000 loss from the start-up of a new Schedule C business. Since the self-employment income of the wife would now be only $100,000, when it is added to the $150,000 in W-2 wages of the husband, the couple is not above the "applicable threshold" of $250,000 for married filing jointly. Therefore, no Additional Medicare Tax on their collective earned income would be due..

EXAMPLE 3.35	A husband and wife each have "Box 5 Medicare wages" of $150,000 listed on their respective W-2s. The wife also has a $50,000 loss from the start-up of a new Schedule C business. The couple would still owe $450 of Additional Medicare Tax. The self-employment loss is not permitted to offset W-2 wages.

EXAMPLE 3.36	The husband has $190,000 in wages subject to Medicare tax and the wife has $150,000 in compensation subject to RRTA taxes. The husband and wife do not combine their wages and RRTA compensation to determine whether they are in excess of the $250,000 threshold for a joint return. The husband and wife are not liable to pay Additional Medicare Tax because the husband's wages are not in excess of the $250,000 threshold and the wife's RRTA compensation is not in excess of the $250,000 threshold.

EXAMPLE 3.37	C, a single filer, has $130,000 in wages and $145,000 in net earnings from self-employment. C's wages are not in excess of the $200,000 threshold for single filers, so C is not liable for the Additional Medicare Tax on these wages. Before calculating the Additional Medicare Tax on self-employment income, the $200,000 threshold for single filers is reduced by C's $130,000 in wages, resulting in a reduced self-employment income threshold of $70,000. C is liable to pay the Additional Medicare Tax on $75,000 of self-employment income; $145,000 in self-employment income minus the reduced threshold of $70,000.

Net Investment Income Tax

After 2012, a 3.8% "Net Investment Income Tax" is imposed on individuals and estate and trusts. Code Sec. 1411. The Net Investment Income Tax will be calculated on Form 8960 and shown as "Other Taxes" on page 2 of Form 1040.

For individuals, the tax is imposed on the lesser of:

a.   An individual's "net investment income" for the tax year, or
b.   Any excess of "modified adjusted gross income" (MAGI) for the tax year over a threshold amount. Code Sec.1411(a)(1).

The "threshold amount" is $200,000 for single taxpayers and heads-of-households; $250,000 for married filing jointly and surviving spouses; $125,000 for married filing separately. Code Sec. 1411(b). MAGI means an individual's adjusted gross income for the tax year increased by otherwise excludable foreign earned income or foreign housing costs under Sec. 911 as reduced by any deduction, exclusion, or credits properly allocable to or chargeable against such foreign earned income. Code Sec. 1411(d).

EXAMPLE 3.38	Elmer, a single individual, earns $190,000 in wages and/or net self-employment income and also has $40,000 of "net investment income" for the year. Assuming a $230,000 MAGI, he will have to pay a 3.8% Net Investment Income Tax on the lesser of his (1) $40,000 of net investment income, or (2) $30,000 ($230,000 MAGI − $200,000 threshold). Elmer will pay a $1,140 ($30,000 × 3.8%) Net Investment Income Tax for the year.

¶3405

EXAMPLE 3.39

During the year, an unmarried taxpayer received no wages or self-employment income, but lives strictly off of her $1 million in "net investment income" from a stock and bond portfolio. Assuming a $1 million MAGI, she will have to pay a 3.8% Net Investment Income Tax on the lesser of her (1) $1 million net investment income or (2) $800,000 ($1 million – $200,000 threshold). As a result, she will pay a $30,400 ($800,000 x 3.8%) Net Investment Income Tax for the year.

The Net Investment Income Tax does not apply to a non-resident alien or to a trust "all the unexpired interests in which are devoted to charitable purposes." The tax does not apply to a trust that is exempt under Sec. 501 or a charitable remainder trust exempt from tax under Sec. 664.

"Net investment income" is defined as: [Code Sec. 1411(c)(1) and (c)(2)]

1. Gross income from interest, dividends, annuities, royalties, and rents (unless such income is "derived in the ordinary course of any trade or business");
2. Other gross income from any passive trade or business; or
3. Net gain included in computing taxable income that is attributable to the disposition of property other than property held in any trade or business that is not a "passive trade or business."

"Income derived in the ordinary course of a trade or business" does not include any trade or business that is either a passive activity of the taxpayer, or involves trading in financial instruments and commodities. The passive activity and trading in financial instruments and commodities are defined as "passive business investment income" for purposes of the 3.8% Medicare tax.

Financial Instruments include: Equity interest such as stock, Proof of indebtedness, Options, Notional principal contracts, Other derivatives, and Other evidence of an interest in one of the foregoing items.

A passive investor's share of Form 1065 or Form 1120S from Box 1 on Schedule K-1 would be "other gross income from any passive trade or business."

A Sec. 1231 gain reported on a K-1 from the sale of assets used in a trade or business that the taxpayer "materially participates" would not be treated as "net investment income" subject to the 3.8% Net Investment Income Tax. However, it would be "net investment income" to a passive investor.

"Net investment income" includes any income, gain, or loss that is attributable to an investment of working capital. Income or gain from investment in working capital is treated as not derived in the ordinary course of a trade or business. Code Sec. 1411(c)(3). For example, a business puts some of its excess working capital into an income-producing investment such as a certificate of deposit or interest-bearing account, or stocks that pay dividends or result in capital gains or losses when sold.

Net investment income does not include: Code Sec. 1411(c)(6).

1. Any distribution from qualified employee benefit plan or retirement arrangements;
2. Any distributions from a regular IRA or Roth IRA;
3. Social security benefits;
4. Any item excluded from gross income.
5. Any item taken into account in determining self-employment income for the tax year on which an individual pays self-employment tax under Sec. 1401(b).

The K-1 profits reported in Box 1 of a materially participating shareholder are not considered "unearned income" for purposes of the 3.8% Medicare tax.

EXAMPLE 3.40

John is an owner of a business that rents equipment and machinery. He also materially participates in that business. Regardless of the business being operated as an S corporation, LLC/partnership, or a sole proprietorship, any net income or loss therefrom would not be considered for purposes of the 3.8% Net Investment Income Tax calculation. However, a Schedule C sole proprietor or the K-1 recipient of "Box 1—Trades or Business Income" from an LLC/partnership would still have the potential for the 0.9% Medicare tax on earned income.

EXAMPLE 3.41

> John leases a building to his rental business. This is a self-rental situation and self-rentals are not classified as passive income. The gross rental income will be deemed to be derived in the ordinary course of a trade or business and, therefore, exempt from the Net Investment Income Tax. Gain or loss from the property will also be treated as gain or loss from the disposition of property held in a nonpassive trade or business.

If a taxpayer is a "real estate professional" and they also "materially participate" in their rental activities, then Sec. 469 passive loss rules do not apply. Any rental income or loss derived from such rental activities will not factor into the taxpayer's calculation of the 3.8% Net Investment Income Tax if they meet the definition of trades or business for Section 162. The IRS has provided a safe harbor for the trades or business definition: If a taxpayer qualifies as a real estate professional and also spends more than 500 hours participating in either a separate or grouped rental activity, the IRS will treat those rental activities as trades or businesses. Reg. §1.1411-4(g)(7)(i).

EXAMPLE 3.42

> John is a "real estate professional" for purposes of the passive loss rules. He also "materially participates" in the rental activities that he owns. The Net Investment Income Tax would not apply to the rental activities if his "rental activities" are treated as "trades or business" under Sec. 162. The income would not be subject to any self-employment tax under Sec. 1402. However, assume the rental activities are not "trades or business" for Sec. 162. As a result, any net rental income or loss would be part of his 3.8% Net Investment Income Tax calculation.

For purposes of the Net Investment Income Tax, the definition allows the reduction for any otherwise allowable deductions "properly allocable to such income or gain."

1. Deductions under Sec. 62 related to gross income
2. Itemized deductions under Sec. 63
3. Loss deductions under Sec. 165

A large capital loss in excess of any capital gain for a particular tax year can only offset up to $3,000 of other "net investment income." A large advisory fee for managing a stock portfolio can only offset "net investment income" to the extent it exceeds 2% of AGI as a miscellaneous itemized deduction. Investment interest expense can only be used to offset "net investment income" to the extent otherwise allowed on Form 4952. Any state or local tax attributable to the sources of net investment income may be deducted in computing net investment income. Any otherwise allowable deductions must also be reduced by the itemized deduction phaseout.

Employment Taxes for Household Employers

If a taxpayer hires someone to do household work and was able to control what work he or she did and how he or she did it, the taxpayer has a household employee. The taxpayer has to have an employer identification number (EIN) and pay employment taxes.

A Form W-2, Wage and Tax Statement, must be filed for each household employee paid $2,000 or more in cash wages in 2017 that are subject to social security and Medicare taxes. If the wages were not subject to these taxes but the employee wishes to have federal income taxes withheld, a W-2 must be filed for that employee. A Form W-3, Transmittal of Wage and Tax Statements, must also be filed if one or more W-2s are required to be filed.

If cash wages are paid of $1,000 or more in any calendar quarter of 2016 or 2017 to household employees for 2017, the taxpayer may also be subject to federal and state unemployment taxes.

In the case of persons performing domestic services in a private home of the employer and person performing agricultural labor, if the employer pays the employee's liability for FICA taxes or state unemployment taxes without deduction from the employee's wages, those payments are not wages for FICA purposes. Code Sec. 3121(a)(6).

TAX BLUNDERS

1. Sara Michaels and Tommy Tooks marry on December 31. Sara earned $120,000 for the year, and Tommy earned $100,000. If Sara and Tommy had waited until the beginning of the following year to marry they would have realized a significant tax savings. Each filing as single taxpayers will result in less total tax than filing jointly.
2. Assume Sara earned $95,000 and Tommy earned $5,000 because he attended school most of the year and they marry at the beginning of the next year. There would be a significant tax savings in marrying at the end of the first year and filing jointly over each filing as single taxpayers.
3. Sara and Tommy decide to file as married filing separately. Sara has $7,000 in itemized deductions and Tommy has $2,500 in itemized deductions. Since Sara itemized on her return Tommy is required to itemize. They may be better off to have both take the standard deduction since the total standard deductions would be $12,700 while itemizing only results in a $9,500 total deduction.

SUMMARY

- The standard deduction eliminates low- to moderate-level taxpayers from the tax rolls. The standard deduction is made up of two parts: the basic standard deduction and the additional standard deduction. Both of these parts are adjusted each year for inflation. The standard deduction differs depending upon filing status.

- Taxpayers are allowed a personal exemption for themselves and their spouse, plus an exemption for each qualified dependent. Taxpayers who are dependents are not allowed a personal exemption for themselves.

- Taxpayers must determine their tax liability from among five different filing statuses.

- Special taxation rules are imposed on returns filed by individuals that are dependents of other taxpayers.

- In general, filing requirements are based on a taxpayer's gross income, filing status, and age.

- Self-employed individuals are required to pay a self-employment tax that is equivalent to the Social Security taxes paid by employees.

- Taxpayers could potentially be subject to a 0.9% Additional Medicare Tax and the Net Investment Income Tax.

QUESTIONS

1. What is the purpose in knowing and understanding the components of the tax formula?

2. What is the distinction between deductions for adjusted gross income and deductions from adjusted gross income?

3. How does a tax deduction differ from a tax credit?

4. What other terms are used to describe deductions for adjusted gross income?

5. Analyze any differences between increasing the standard deduction and increasing the exemption allowed.

6. Explain the rationale behind an individual's arranging financial affairs to use the standard deduction one year and itemized deductions in another year.

7. What is the reason that some taxpayers are not entitled to the standard deduction or are entitled to only part of it? Explain.

8. How is the standard deduction computed for a dependent child with unearned income?

9. George files a separate return. His wife's only source of income is $600 in interest income. Can George claim an exemption for his wife on his separate return?

10. Are taxpayers allowed to claim the additional old-age or blindness standard deduction for dependents?

11. In determining the dependency exemption, how is the value of lodging provided a dependent computed for the support test?

12. Bill and Becky had a child born on April 15. The child died within three hours of birth. Can they claim an exemption for the child?

13. Can a student attending a class in night school qualify as a full-time student?

14. Rhoda and Mike are both full-time students who married late in the year. Rhoda had $1,800 in wages from a part-time job and Mike had $950 in dividend income. They filed a joint return and received a refund of the $175 that had been withheld on Rhoda's wages. Rhoda's parents paid over one-half of Rhoda's support. Can Rhoda's parents claim her as a dependent?

15. Explain the concept of the "multiple support agreement." What are the requirements for such an agreement?

16. During the year, Alice Johnson was supported by her four sons, Amos, Luther, Bennet, and Ivan, in the following percentages:

Amos	8%
Luther	32%
Bennet	18%
Ivan	42%

Which of the brothers is entitled to claim his mother as a dependent, providing a multiple support agreement exists?

17. Homer and Wilma received a divorce in 2008. During the year, Homer contributed $950 support for their only child in the custody of Wilma. Absent any written agreement relative to the receipt of the dependency exemption, who should be entitled to the exemption?

18. What conditions must exist in Problem 17 for Homer to take the dependency exemption?

19. Tom and Jane were legally separated during the preceding year under a written separation agreement. Jane had custody of their two children for the entire year while Tom contributed $2,000 support for each child. Absent any written agreement relative to the receipt of the dependency exemption, who should be entitled to the exemptions?

20. What form is used to grant an exemption to the noncustodial parent?

21. Calculate the number of exemptions and the standard deduction that the taxpayer is entitled to take in 2017 in each of the following independent cases:

    a. John, age 66, and his wife, age 64, file a joint return.

    b. Jack, age 62 and blind, and his wife, who became 65 on January 1 of the following year, file a joint return.

    c. Jim and Mary, both 52, contribute more than half the support for Jim's father, who lives with them. Jim's father is 72 and blind. Jim and Mary file a joint return.

    d. Harry, age 66, is a widower who maintains a home for himself and his 22-year-old son who attends college full time. Harry provided more than one half of his son's support.

    e. Jackson is 28 and his wife, Joan, is 27. They have two children, one three-year-old and the other seven years old. On March 29 of this year, Joan gave birth to a daughter, who died the next day. Jackson and Joan file a joint return.

    f. Joe, age 65, and his wife, JoAnne, age 64, maintain a home for their unmarried daughter, age 23, who earned $4,000 and attends college on a part-time basis. Joe and JoAnne contributed $6,000 toward her support. Joe and JoAnne file a joint return.

    g. William, a 42-year-old bachelor, pays $450 per month support for his 75-year-old mother who is disabled and is living in a rest home. She receives a taxable pension of $100 per month and uses the entire $550 per month for routine living expenses.

    h. Same as (g), except William's mother also receives $400 per month from dividends on stock she owns. She also uses this amount for routine living expenses.

    i. Billy Bob and his wife, Mary Sue, both 45, maintain a home for Mary Sue's friend, Jackie Jo, age 17, who came to dinner one night several years ago and has lived with them since. Jackie Jo attends school and has no income. Billy Bob and Mary Sue file a joint return.

    j. Benson, a 45-year-old widower, maintains a home for his 22-year-old son, Chester, who attends college full-time on a $4,000-per-year scholarship. Chester also works part-time while at school, earning $1,500 per year. Benson contributes $2,000, which constitutes the balance of Chester's support for the year.

    k. Same as (j), except Chester contributes the $4,000 per year from his savings account instead of receiving it from the scholarship award.

    l. Richard, a bachelor under 65, maintains a home in which a son of a deceased friend has lived the entire year. Richard furnishes over one half of the support of the young man, who attends school. The young man also works part time after school, earning $2,800 per year.

    m. Dan and his wife, Pam, maintain a household for and completely support three foster children. The children have been living in Dan and Pam's home all year. On December 31 of the tax year, Pam gives birth to a son.

22. What is meant by filing status?

23. What filing status options are available to Darlene, assuming she separated from her husband in March? Darlene is the sole support of her daughter, who lives with Darlene.

24. How do head of household expenses differ from the expenses used in the support test?

25. Are all individuals required to file an income tax return?

26. Charles has interest income of $1,100 and no other income. He is claimed as a dependent by his parents. Is he required to file an income tax return?

27. Why might an individual file an income tax return even though not required to do so?

28. Under what circumstances must a return be filed by an individual even though there is only $800 in taxable income?

29. What is the difference between the tax tables and the tax rate schedules?

30. What is the limit for self-employment tax?

PROBLEMS

31. Tom and Linda are married taxpayers who file a joint return. They have itemized deductions of $13,050 and four exemptions. Assuming an adjusted gross income of $40,000, what is their taxable income for 2017?

32. Compute Marie's taxable income for 2017, assuming she is single and claims two dependent children. Her adjusted gross income is $70,000, and she has itemized deductions of $9,500.

33. Which of the following taxpayers should itemize? Explain.
    a. Robert is a single taxpayer. He has itemized deductions of $6,550.
    b. Jane qualifies as head of household. Her itemized deductions total $8,550.
    c. Brian is married and files a separate return. He has itemized deductions of $6,550.
    d. Lisa is a surviving spouse. Her itemized deductions are $12,400.

34. Compute the taxable income for 2017 under each of the following circumstances:
    a. Jim is married and files a joint return. Jim and his wife have two dependent children. They have adjusted gross income of $30,000 and itemized deductions of $12,400.
    b. Jim is single with no dependents. His adjusted gross income is $20,000 with itemized deductions of $3,800.
    c. Jim is a full-time college student under 24 supported by his father. Jim earned $2,600 from a part-time job and had $500 of interest income. His itemized deductions were $600.
    d. Jim is married but files separately and claims two dependent children. His adjusted gross income is $65,000 and he claims $8,900 of itemized deductions. Jim's wife also itemizes on her return.
    e. Assume the same situation as in (d), but Jim's itemized deductions are only $1,500.

35. Duke and Pat Collins have adjusted gross income of $358,000. They have itemized deductions of $20,000 consisting of $8,000 in medical expenses that exceed 10% of adjusted gross income, $3,000 in property taxes, $4,000 in housing interest, and $5,000 in miscellaneous itemized deductions that exceed 2 percent of adjusted gross income. What is the amount of their itemized deductions?

36. What is Mary's taxable income for 2017, assuming she has $6,150 of earned income and $800 of unearned income and is claimed as a dependent by her parents?

37. Compute Stanley's taxable income for 2017, assuming he has $1,000 in wages from working in a grocery store and $2,200 in interest income from some bonds he owns. Stanley, age 16, is claimed as a dependent on his parents' return.

38. Bradford is 12 years old and is claimed as a dependent on his parents' return. In 2017, he received unearned income of $2,200. Bradford's itemized deductions totaled $150. Determine Bradford's taxable income.

39. What is the standard deduction and the number of exemptions that a married couple will be allowed, assuming that they are not over 65 or blind, that they fully support the husband's 82-year-old blind mother, and that they have no other dependents?

40. Has Jodi provided more than 50 percent of the support in the following situations?
    a. Jodi contributed $4,200 to her mother's support during the year. Her mother received $5,300 in Medicare payments that were used to pay her medical expenses.
    b. Jodi's daughter was a full-time student. Jodi paid $2,000 towards her daughter's living expenses. The daughter earned $1,800 from a part-time job and spent that plus $600 from her savings to help support herself.

41. Margaret is attending school full-time for the year. Her parents paid $3,000 toward her support. She earned $2,000 from a part-time job which she used toward her support. In addition, Margaret withdrew $1,500 from her savings account to help in her support. Have her parents provided over one-half of Margaret's support?

42. Myrtle is fully supported by her three children and Fred, a close friend of the family. Mark paid $4,000 toward Myrtle's support, while Nancy, Opel, and Fred paid $3,200, $800, and $2,000, respectively. Which individuals are eligible to claim Myrtle under a multiple support agreement?

43. Annie was divorced in 2002. She provided over half the cost of maintaining the home that she and her 22-year-old son lived in the entire year. Her former husband provided more than half of the son's total support, and he claims the son as a dependent. What is Annie's best filing status for the year?

44. A single taxpayer with one dependent (nonrelative) has $358,000 of adjusted gross income. What is the amount of the deduction for personal exemptions allowed this taxpayer?

45. What is the best filing status in each of the following situations?
    a. Phillip and Catherine were married on December 31, 2017.
    b. John and Sandra were married in 2016. John left Sandra in March 2017, and she has not heard from him since that time.
    c. Melody and Werner were married during the year. Werner is a resident and citizen of Germany.

46. What is the taxpayer's filing status for 2017 in each of the following situations?
    a. Bill's wife died in 2016. Bill maintained a household for his two dependent children in 2017.
    b. Bill is unmarried and lives in an apartment. He supported his aged parents, who live in a separate home. Bill provided over half of the cost of maintaining his parents' home and also provided over half of each of his parents' support.
    c. Bill is unmarried and maintains a household for his 18-year-old daughter and her husband. Bill pays over half of the support of his daughter. The daughter files a joint return with her husband.

47. Indicate the filing status and the number of exemptions allowed to Sandy for 2017, 2018, 2019, and 2020, assuming her husband died in 2017 and Sandy has been the sole support of her son since that time.

48. Mike and Ellen Evans decide to part in April. Mike moves into an apartment two blocks away. The children spend each weekend with Mike. What filing statuses are available to Mike and Ellen, assuming they are not divorced before the end of the year?

49. Which of the following individuals are required to file a tax return for 2017? Assume no tax has been withheld.
    a. Rebecca, single and with no dependents, earned $6,700 for the year.
    b. Hugh and Jane are married and file a joint return. They have four children. Their gross income is $17,000 and they have itemized deductions of $8,000.
    c. Peter has self-employment income of $450. He is a full-time college student and is claimed as a dependent on his parents' return.

50. Julian and Georgia file a joint return. They have adjusted gross income of $112,000 and itemized deductions of $12,900. Are they required to use the Tax Rate Schedules or the Tax Tables in computing their income tax?

51. Eric is single and has no dependents for 2017. He earned $30,000 and had deductions from gross income of $1,800 and itemized deductions of $6,550. Compute Eric's income tax for the year using the Tax Rate Schedules.

52. Allen has taxable income of $75,475 for 2017. Using the Tax Rate Schedules in the Appendix, compute Allen's income tax liability before tax credits and prepayments for each of the following filing statuses.
    a. Married filing jointly
    b. Married filing separately
    c. Single
    d. Head of household

53. Determine the amount of self-employment tax due for 2017, assuming that Lynette earned $30,000 in wages and also earned $20,000 from a business that she owned.

54. A husband and wife who earned Box 5 Medicare wages of $175,000 and $125,000, respectively. Determine the amount of withholding for the Additional Medicare Tax and the amount of tax that they would owe on their final Form 1040.

55. A single taxpayer has $150,000 in wages and $180,000 in net self-employment income. What is the amount of Additional Medicare Tax that would be due on Form 1040 for the year?

56. What is the amount of the net investment income tax for a single individual that has $250,000 of modified adjusted gross income and $25,000 of net investment income?

57. Melvin leases a building that he owns to his wholly-owned S corporation for $30,000 for the year. Melvin materially participates in the S corporation. What amount does Melvin have to report as net investment income for the year from the $30,000?

58. Mr. Smith died early in the year. Mrs. Smith remarried in December and, therefore, was unable to file a joint return with Mr. Smith. What is the filing status of the decedent, Mr. Smith?
    a. Single
    b. Married filing separate return
    c. Married filing joint return
    d. Head of household
    e. Surviving spouse

59. Which of the following is not considered when determining the total support test for a child?
    a. Fair rental value of lodging
    b. Medical insurance premiums
    c. Birthday presents
    d. Scholarship
    e. Recreation

60. Which relative does not have to live in the same household of the taxpayer claiming head of household filing status?
    a. Aunt
    b. Son
    c. Granddaughter
    d. Father
    e. Brother

61. To qualify for head of household rates, which of the following must be present?
    a. You must be unmarried on the last day of your tax year.
    b. You must maintain a household and contribute over 50 percent of the cost of maintaining the household.
    c. The person for whom the household is maintained has to be a relative.
    d. (a) and (b).
    e. All of the above.

62. **Comprehensive Problem.** What is the total tax due for 2017, including self-employment tax, for Stuart, assuming that he earned $20,000 in wages, earned $24,000 in self-employment income from his first business, had a loss of $10,000 from his second business, received $3,000 in interest income, and had $5,100 in nonqualified dividend income?

63. **Comprehensive Problem.** Richard and Jennifer were married in 2008. They have a five-year-old child and a son born November 15, 2017. Richard's 67-year-old father lived in a nursing home until his death on May 23, 2017. Richard and Jennifer provided all of his support until his death. Richard earned $43,000 in salary during the year. They also received $2,100 in interest from the credit union. They incurred $7,800 in itemized deductions during the year. Compute Richard and Jennifer's income tax for 2017 using the Tax Rate Schedules.

64. **Comprehensive Problem.** Scott and Glenna are married with two dependent children. They have $74,000 in wage income and $4,600 in interest income on some bonds they own. They have deductions for adjusted gross income of $4,000 and itemized deductions of $12,900. Neither of the children has any income. Determine the tax savings for the family if Scott and Glenna were to transfer the bonds to the children, both under 18.

65. **Research Problem.** Sidney and Angelene were married in 2013. During 2017, they were both employed, each earning $32,000 for the year. They discovered that there was a significant tax savings if they could file as single taxpayers and thus arranged a vacation trip and a divorce before the end of the year. Early in 2018 they remarried. What is their filing status for 2017? See Rev. Rul. 76-255.

Chapter

4

Gross Income

OBJECTIVES

After completing Chapter 4, you should be able to:

1. Define and distinguish among the various concepts of income: economic, accounting, and legal.
2. Recognize the various items included in gross income.
3. Determine when items are included in income.
4. Understand the rules governing alimony.
5. Differentiate alimony from child support.
6. Comprehend the rules for recapturing alimony.
7. Understand the rules governing the discharge of indebtedness for both solvent and insolvent taxpayers.

OVERVIEW

Gross income, according to the Internal Revenue Code, includes all income unless specifically exempted by law. This comprehensive definition requires a more probing discussion of what must be included in income. Further, we must concern ourselves with "how much" must be included in income and what portion of total income may be excluded.

The Concept of Income

A frustrating characteristic of the English language is that a single term can be used to express a variety of concepts. Take the concept of income: economists, the courts, and accountants use this term, but for each, the definition imparts a singular *view*.

¶4001   ECONOMIC INCOME

The economic concept of income is more general than the accounting definition. The most commonly accepted definition of economic income is that of J. R. Hicks. He defines economic income as being "the maximum amount a person can consume during a week and still expect to be as well-off at the end of the week as he was at the beginning." J. R. Hicks, *Value and Capital* (Oxford: Clarendon Press, 1946), p. 172. This assumes that there were no capital contributions or withdrawals during the period measured. The economist's definition is not practical for tax purposes because the concept of "well-being" is not capable of objective measurement. The economic concept of income places a heavy emphasis on the future. No objective rules exist for determining well-being at any moment in time. Economists must deal in terms of real wealth, which includes holding gains and losses rather than monetary wealth alone. H. C. Simons maintained, "The precise, objective measurement of income implies the existence of perfect markets from which one, after ascertaining quantities, may obtain the prices necessary for routine valuation of all possible inventories of commodities, services, and property rights." *Personal Income Taxation* (Chicago: University of Chicago Press, 1921), p. 50. Since no such markets exist where the necessary prices for valuation may be obtained, the economic concept is an inappropriate measure of taxable income.

¶4015   THE LEGAL/TAX CONCEPT OF INCOME

The legal concept of income is also less precise than that of the accountant. Congress has not defined income, but has specified how particular items of income are to be taxed. The concept of income has crystalized through a series of court cases. The legal concept is different from the economic and accounting concepts. Gross income includes "all income from whatever source derived" unless specifically exempted by law. Code Sec. 61(a).

Eisner v. Macomber

In the case of *Eisner v. Macomber*, 1 ustc ¶32, 252 U.S. 189, 40 S.Ct. 189 (1920), the Supreme Court dealt at great length with the problem of defining income. The Court stated:

> After examining dictionaries in common use . . . , we find little to add to the succinct definition adopted in two cases arising under the Corporation Tax Act of 1909 . . . "Income may be defined as the gain derived from capital, from labor, or from both combined," provided it be understood to include profit gained through sale or conversion of capital assets. . . .

> Here we have the essential matter: *not* a gain *accruing* to capital; not a *growth* or *increment* of value in the investment; but a gain, a profit, something of exchangeable value, *proceeding* from the property, severed from the capital, however invested or employed, and *coming in,* being "*derived* "—that is, *received* or *drawn* by the recipient (the taxpayer) for his separate use, benefit and disposal; that is income derived from property.

> The same fundamental conception is clearly set forth in the Sixteenth Amendment—"incomes, from whatever source derived"—the essential thought being expressed with a conciseness and lucidity entirely in harmony with the form and style of the Constitution.

Like the accountants' concept, the legal concept does not embrace holding gains or losses. The legal definition of income is close to the accountants', but not identical, as will be highlighted in the remainder of the chapter.

EXAMPLE 4.1   Rachel owned 300 shares of Imperial Soap which she purchased for $1,000. She sold the stock this year for $1,200. Rachel realized a gain of $200, not the $1,200 proceeds she received from the sale. Only the $200 is included in gross income. The $1,000 is Rachel's return of capital.

¶4025

ACCOUNTING INCOME

The accountant desires to measure income over a specified period of time. Income, from an accounting point of view, is the excess of revenues over the costs incurred in producing those revenues. The emphasis for the accountant is on completed transactions. Therefore, unlike the economist, the accountant does not recognize holding gains. The accountant deals exclusively with objectively measurable forms such as monetary transactions.

Realization of Income

As in financial accounting all gains must be "realized" before they are includible in income. This usually occurs at the time of an arm's-length transaction.

EXAMPLE 4.2

> Tom Spears buys a parcel of real estate for $100,000 in 2002. In 2017, he has it appraised and finds that the property's market value is $150,000. He has a paper gain of $50,000, but he has no taxable income. Also in 2017, he sells the property for $150,000, at which time the income is "realized" and "recognized."

Under the accrual method of accounting, income is recognized when a transaction is consummated. Under the cash method of accounting, income is recognized only when cash is received. The cash method and accrual method of accounting are discussed in Chapter 13. To prevent cash basis taxpayers from choosing the year in which to recognize income, the Internal Revenue Service applies the constructive receipt doctrine.

Economic Benefit, Constructive Receipt, and Assignment of Income Doctrines

This chapter discusses three doctrines: the economic benefit doctrine, the constructive receipt doctrine, and the assignment of income doctrine. The doctrines focus on the following questions: what is income, when is it taxable, and to whom is it taxable?

In determining "what" is income and "when" an item must be included in the taxable income of a cash basis taxpayer, two concepts were conceived: the economic benefit doctrine and the constructive receipt doctrine. Over time the courts have tended to blur the distinction between these two doctrines. *F. Bowden,* 61-1 USTC ¶9382, 289 F.2d 20 (CA-5 1961), reversing 32 TC 853 (1959).

¶4101

ECONOMIC BENEFIT DOCTRINE

The economic benefit doctrine addresses the "what" and the constructive receipt doctrine addresses the "when." Any amount of compensation granted or paid to the individual for services rendered, be it cash, bonus, profit sharing, compensation in kind, or any other ingenious method of payment, must be included in gross income. Gross income is defined under the broad language of Code Sec. 61(a) of the Internal Revenue Code as "all income from whatever source derived." Thus, taxable income may consist of cash, receivables, property, land, or any other form of economic benefit.

¶4125

CONSTRUCTIVE RECEIPT DOCTRINE

The second doctrine, that of constructive receipt, was defined in the case of *Ross.* In this case, the Circuit Court of Appeals stated that the doctrine of constructive receipt was conceived "in order to prevent the taxpayer from choosing the year in which to reduce it (income) to possession." *L. W. Ross,* 48-2 USTC ¶9341, 169 F.2d 483 (CA-1 1948).

The Regulations explain the doctrine of constructive receipt, based upon the fact that income is:

> credited to [the taxpayer's] account, or set apart for him, or otherwise made available so that he may draw upon it at any time. . . . However, income is not constructively received if the taxpayer's control of its receipt is subject to substantial limitations or restrictions. Reg. §1.451-2.

A distinctive feature of the constructive receipt doctrine is that it affects only cash basis taxpayers, since they are deemed to have received income prior to the time of actual receipt. Because the accrual basis taxpayer is assumed to have recognized income at the moment it is "earned," there is no need to apply the constructive receipt doctrine. It is of no consequence if an individual refuses compensation. The courts have ruled that once the individual has an "absolute right" to the compensation, the amount of the remuneration must be included in the taxpayer's income. However, where the individual has only a conditional right, the courts hold that no present income was received. Generally, any compensation granted to an individual to which the individual has an absolute right is regarded as constructively received income. The taxpayer must include in current income any amounts of compensation which the taxpayer has refused to accept.

EXAMPLE 4.3

> Leah was an employee of Loss Leaders Inc. On December 2, 2017, Loss Leaders announced a year-end bonus for all employees. Checks would be available for pickup at the cashier's desk December 29, 2017. Leah called in sick on December 29, 2017, and she did not stop by the cashier's desk until January 5, 2018. Leah must include her bonus on her 2017 tax return. She had a right to the bonus on December 29, 2017. It is immaterial that she chose not to collect her bonus on December 29, 2017.

As between the two doctrines, economic benefit and constructive receipt, logically the applicability of the economic benefit doctrine comes first. If the taxpayer has not received economic benefit, then it is not necessary to determine whether the taxpayer is in constructive receipt of income. Now that the concepts of "what" is income and "when" an item must be included in taxable income have been explained, it is necessary to determine "to whom" the income is taxable.

¶4201   ASSIGNMENT OF INCOME DOCTRINE

The assignment of income doctrine means that income is taxed to the individual who earned it, even if the right to the income has been transferred to another individual prior to recognition. Compensation, interest, rents, dividends, and other forms of income usually must be included in the gross income of the recipient. A tax problem arises when an individual attempts to limit tax liability by assigning income. For example, a taxpayer has the employer forward a portion of the salary to one of the taxpayer's creditors instead of to the taxpayer. The taxpayer would have to recognize this as income inasmuch as the taxpayer received benefit from the proceeds and had control of the income.

In *Helvering v. Horst,* 40-2 USTC ¶9787, 311 U.S. 112, 61 S.Ct. 144 (1940), the Supreme Court ruled that a father who gave his son interest coupons, detached from bonds prior to their maturity, was liable for the tax on the interest even though the interest was received by his son. The Court stated:

> Income is "realized" by the assignor because he, who owns or controls the source of income, also controls the disposition of that which he could have received himself and diverts the payment from himself to others as the means of procuring the satisfaction of his wants. The taxpayer has equally enjoyed the fruits of his labor or investment and obtained the satisfaction of his desires whether he collects and uses the income to procure those satisfactions, or whether he disposes of his right to collect it as the means of procuring them.

In the preceding case, if the father wished to avoid the tax liability, he would have had to transfer the property which produced the income.

Generally, the courts have felt that a person should not be allowed to reduce tax liability by the voluntary assignment of income. This is referred to as the "fruit-of-the-tree" doctrine. Income (fruit) is taxable to the individual who has earned it. Thus, assignment of income will be disregarded, for tax purposes, unless the source of the income (tree) is also assigned. In *Lucas v. Earl,* 2 USTC ¶496, 281 U.S. 111, 50 S.Ct. 241 (1930), the Court stated that the "fruit" may not be "attributed to a different tree from that on which it grew."

If a person only has physical possession over the income of another person, he or she has no tax liability. Regardless of whether or not the person received it as an agent or creditor, it is taxed to the owner of the property. The rules which govern the assignment of income apply both to income from property as well as to income from services.

EXAMPLE 4.4

> Jack Smith owns a warehouse complex and assigns the rents to his daughter Linda. Jack remains liable for the tax on the rental income, even though Linda is receiving the rental income.

EXAMPLE 4.5   Linda Katz, a recent college graduate, earns $350 per week. In an effort to repay a college loan to her uncle she assigns half of her pay to him. Linda is taxed on the full $350 per week.

¶4215   COMMUNITY PROPERTY INCOME

The question of tax liability for married persons filing separate returns arises frequently during discussions concerning to whom is income taxable. Various states treat this problem differently so that there is no solution which is universally applicable. The existence of community property laws in several states requires treatment of tax liability which is significantly different from those states in which there are no community property laws.

In the eight community property states (Arizona, California, Idaho, Louisiana, Nevada, New Mexico, Texas, and Washington), all property acquired by a husband and wife *after* marriage is considered as owned by them in community, and, as such, is referred to as community property. Any income from these properties is automatically considered joint or community income, and if taxpayers are filing separate tax returns, the income would be shared equally between them on their separate returns. In 1985, Wisconsin implemented a marital property act; therefore, for federal income tax purposes it is considered a community property state. In 1998, Alaska became a community property state. Alaska adopted an optional system, whereby a couple can choose to opt-in to the community property system.

Property acquired *before* marriage or inherited by one spouse during marriage is considered to be that spouse's separate property. In California, Arizona, Nevada, New Mexico, Washington, and Wisconsin, any income from these separate properties is considered separate income; thus, if the spouses are filing separately, the income would not be shared and would be reported on that spouse's separate return. This is called the "California Rule." Conversely, in Texas, Idaho, and Louisiana, income from these separate properties is considered community income; thus, if the spouses are filing separately, the income would be shared between them on their separate returns. This is called the "Texas Rule."

Section 66 of the Internal Revenue Code sets forth a specific rule for treatment of community income where the spouses live apart. Section 66 was passed by Congress in 1980 and was effective 1981 and thereafter. The need for this section arose because in community property states each spouse is liable for one-half the tax on income. Generally, when spouses are living apart, the spouse that earns the income will keep it.

If two individuals are married to each other at some time during a calendar year, but live apart for the *entire* tax year, do not file a joint return, and one or both have earned income, none of which is transferred between them, the following rules cover the reporting of income on their separate tax returns:

1. Earned income (other than trade or business income and partnership income) is treated as income of the spouse who rendered the personal services.
2. Trade or business income is treated as the husband's income unless the wife exercises substantially all of the management and control of the business.
3. Community income derived from the separate property of one spouse is treated as the income of such spouse.
4. All other community income is taxed in accordance with the applicable community property law. Code Sec. 879(a).

¶4225   TENANCY BY THE ENTIRETY

If property is held by a married couple as tenants by the entirety, all income from the property must be included by the husband in his return or must be shared equally by husband and wife, depending on state law. In states which have abolished the common law rule, such as Delaware, Florida, Indiana, Maryland, Michigan, Missouri, New York, Oregon, Pennsylvania, and the District of Columbia, one-half of the income is reported on the husband's tax return and one-half on the wife's tax return.

¶4235   JOINT TENANTS AND TENANTS IN COMMON

Parties holding property as joint tenants each report income from the property in direct proportion to their interest in the property. When one of the parties dies, the interest in the property is automatically passed to the surviving joint tenant. Upon the death of a tenant in common, the deceased's interest is automatically transferred to the heirs. Parties holding property as tenants in common are taxed on their proportionate share of income based on their contribution of ownership of the property.

Items Included in Gross Income

Having discussed the concept of income, what it is, when it is taxable, and to whom it is taxable, attention now will be focused on the types of items which are included in gross income.

¶4301 LIST OF INCOME ITEMS

As has been explained, the concept of income is broad and general. Section 61(a) of the Code simply lists fifteen items which must be included in gross income. Remember, gross income is in no way limited to these fifteen income items.

1. Compensation for services, including fees, commissions, fringe benefits, and similar items
2. Gross income derived from business
3. Gain derived from dealings in property (discussed in Chapters 10–12)
4. Interest
5. Rents
6. Royalties
7. Dividends
8. Alimony and separate maintenance payments
9. Annuities (discussed in Chapter 5)
10. Income from life insurance and endowment contracts
11. Pensions
12. Income from discharge of indebtedness
13. Distributive share of partnership gross income
14. Income in respect of a decedent
15. Income from an interest in an estate or trust

Section 61(a) clearly points out that gross income is not limited to these items, but that these are merely the most typical sources of income. It is irrelevant whether or not the above items are received in money, goods, or services. Note that items such as gifts or inheritances are not included. On the other hand, illegal gains such as gambling gains and income from swindling or extortion must be included in income. Sections 71–90 of the Internal Revenue Code concern themselves with items to be included as gross income. Obviously there are a number of items that are specifically exempted from gross income. Chapter 5 discusses these items. They can be found in Sections 101–139 of the Internal Revenue Code.

¶4315 COMPENSATION FOR SERVICES

All compensation received by the individual is included in gross income. This would include salary, bonuses, tips, commissions, director's fees, and any other amounts received for personal services. This compensation is taxed when received and not when earned unless the individual reports income under the accrual method. Generally, the individual includes as income the fair market value of property received. If the taxpayer receives corporate stock as compensation for services, the fair market value of the stock, at the time of transfer, must be included in gross income.

EXAMPLE 4.6	Charlotte Moss, a cash basis taxpayer, received a paycheck on Friday, January 2, 2018. The pay period covered is for the previous two weeks' work. This money is included on her 2018 tax return, not her 2017 return. However, if Charlotte had had the option of receiving her paycheck on December 31, 2017, by simply requesting it, then, under the constructive receipt doctrine, her salary would have been taxed in 2017.

Year-end bonuses are included in the tax return for the year they are received. Voluntary payments such as severance pay and Christmas bonuses also must be included. Meals and living quarters which an employee receives constitute gross income unless they are furnished for the convenience of the employer. Further, they must be furnished on the employer's premises. With respect to lodging, it must be a condition of employment. See ¶5185 for a complete discussion of meals and lodging as compensation.

EXAMPLE 4.7	Charlotte's employer, IBC Inc. informed employees on December 15, 2017, that a 5 percent cash bonus, based on 2017 earnings, would be paid to all employees on February 9, 2018. Charlotte would have to include her bonus in her 2018 tax return.

Bartering is becoming a more common practice in the United States today. Bartering is the exchange of your property or services for another's property or services. The fair market value of property or services received must be included in gross income.

EXAMPLE 4.8	Robert Jones, owner of Jones' Dry Cleaning, was discussing his income tax problems with one of his best customers, Sam Owen. Sam is an accountant and is self-employed. During the course of their conversation, they struck a deal. Jones would do all of Owen's cleaning and Owen would do Jones's accounts and tax returns. No money would exchange hands. In this instance, both Jones and Owen must include in their income the fair market value of services received.

Small items given by the employer to the employee, such as a turkey at Thanksgiving or a ham at Christmas, are not taxable to the employee even though the employer is allowed a deduction for the item as a business expense. However, a small cash stipend, such as a $20 bill at Christmas or a gift certificate, would be considered as taxable and includible in gross income.

¶4325   COMPENSATION v. GIFT

Section 102(a) explicitly excludes the value of property acquired by gift from being included in gross income. However, Section 102(b) does not exclude the income earned on the property after it is received.

In determining whether or not a payment or transfer is in the form of compensation or a gift, the Supreme Court has said that it is necessary to consider all the relevant surrounding circumstances and especially to determine the intent of the parties involved. *A.G. Bogardus,* 37-2 USTC ¶9534, 302 U.S. 34, 58 S.Ct. 61 (1937). The Fifth Circuit Court of Appeals said that a gift is "not intended as a return of value or made because of any intent to repay another what is his due, but bestowed only because of personal affection or regard or pity, or from general motives of philanthropy or charity." *C. Schall,* 49-1 USTC ¶9298, 174 F.2d 893 (CA-5 1949).

A payment or transfer can be considered compensation by one party and a gift by the other. However, the Supreme Court stated in *Bogardus:*

> The statute definitely distinguishes between compensation on the one hand and gifts on the other hand, the former being taxable and the latter free from taxation. The two terms are, and were meant to be, mutually exclusive; and a bestowal of money cannot, under the statute, be both a gift and a payment of compensation.

When determining if the payment was compensation or a gift, the courts look to see if the transferor took a tax deduction for the payment. If the transferor did, then it indicates that the payment was meant to be compensation. On the other hand, if the transferor did not take a tax deduction for the sum, it is not conclusive, but it is evidence that a gift was intended. The mere fact that an employer was not legally obliged to make a payment is not, in itself, evidence of a gift. Code Sec. 102(c).

In the landmark case of *Duberstein,* the Supreme Court reiterated the statement that a gift proceeds from "detached and disinterested generosity." *M. Duberstein,* 60-2 USTC ¶9519, 363 U.S. 278, 80 S.Ct. 1190 (1960). Duberstein received a Cadillac from the president of a company with whom he had done business for quite some time. Duberstein had on several occasions given business leads to this other company. Naturally, the Commissioner insisted Duberstein must include the fair market value in gross income and Duberstein insisted it was a gift. The Supreme Court stated:

> despite the characterization of the transfer of the Cadillac by the parties and the absence of any obligation, even of a moral nature, to make it, it was at bottom a recompense for Duberstein's past services, or an inducement for him to be of further service in the future.

The *Duberstein* case concludes with the general premise that corporations ordinarily just do not make gifts without receiving some economic benefit in return.

¶4331 JURY DUTY PAY

Jury duty pay must be included in gross income. However, any jury duty pay remitted to an employer in exchange for compensation for the period the employee was on jury duty is deductible from gross income. Code Sec. 62(a)(13).

¶4335 PRIZES AND AWARDS

Gross income includes amounts received as prizes and awards from radio and television give-away and quiz shows, lotteries, door prizes, and awards from contests. Where the prize or award is not made in money but in the form of property, the fair market value of such property must be included in gross income.

Scientific and Charitable Prizes and Awards

Prizes and awards in the fields of science, charity, and the arts (such as the Pulitzer Prize and the Nobel Peace Prize) are includible in gross income unless the recipient assigns the prize or award to a governmental agency or tax-exempt charitable organization. This assignment must be made prior to the recipient's using the item that is awarded. To be eligible for the exclusion the recipient (1) must have been selected without any action on the recipient's part to enter the contest and (2) must not be required to render any substantial future services as a condition to receiving the prize or award. Code Sec. 74(b). If a proper assignment is made, none of the winnings need be included in the recipient's gross income. However, the recipient is not allowed a charitable contribution deduction.

Employee Achievement Awards

Employee awards for length of service or safety achievement are excludable from gross income by the employee and are deductible by the employer if they are awarded as part of a meaningful presentation, and:

1. The awards do not exceed a total of $400 for all *nonqualified plan awards* received by any one employee during the tax year, or
2. The awards do not exceed $1,600 for all *qualified plan awards* received by any one employee during the tax year.

However, the $1,600 limitation applies in the aggregate. Thus, the $400 limitation and the $1,600 limitation cannot be added together to allow deductions exceeding $1,600. Code Sec. 274(j)(2).

A qualified plan award is one awarded as part of an established written plan or program by the employer that does not discriminate in favor of highly compensated employees. An employee achievement award will not be considered a qualified plan award if the average cost of all employee achievement awards provided by the employer during the tax year exceeds $400. The average cost does not include awards of nominal value. Code Sec. 274(j)(3)(B). The following example illustrates the tax status of employee achievement awards.

EXAMPLE 4.9 Ben Smith received three employee achievement awards during 2017. Two were qualified awards of a tennis racket valued at $200 and a television/stereo valued at $1,300. The third was a nonqualified award of a briefcase valued at $250. Ben's employer satisfies all the requirements for qualified plan awards. Inasmuch as Ben's total of awards received exceeds $1,600, he must include the excess $150 ($1,750 – $1,600) in gross income.

A length of service award does not qualify if it was received by an employee within the first five years of employment or if the recipient received a length of service award within the previous four years. Safety achievement awards cannot be given to more than 10 percent of the employees. Managers, administrators, clerical employees, and other professional employees are not eligible for safety achievement awards.

¶4345 SCHOLARSHIPS AND FELLOWSHIPS

Generally, gross income does not include any amount received as a qualified scholarship by an individual who is a degree candidate at an educational organization. A qualified scholarship is the amount received by a degree candidate that is excludable up to the aggregate amount incurred by the candidate for tuition and course-related expenses, such as books, supplies, and equipment. No exclusion is allowed for room, board, or incidental expenses. Also, no exclusion is allowed if payments received are a result of services.

Non-degree candidates must include in income scholarships and fellowships. The exclusion provision applies only to degree candidates. Under special rules the exclusion provision extends to tuition reductions provided for the education of employees of an educational institution. The rules do not affect the exclusion for employer-provided educational assistance to an employee (see ¶5201).

EXAMPLE 4.10

Mary Smart is a full-time undergraduate student at State University. Mary is an honor student and received a $3,000-per-year scholarship. The scholarship award pays for Mary's tuition ($2,000), books ($200), equipment ($300), and incidental expenses ($500). Mary would have to include in her gross income only the $500 for incidental expenses.

¶4355 GROSS INCOME DERIVED FROM BUSINESS

Gross income is defined by the Code as including gross income derived from a business. Gross income means total sales revenues less cost of goods sold, plus income from investments and any other incidental income. The Regulations state that gross income shall be determined as follows:

> without subtraction of selling expenses, losses or other items not ordinarily used in computing costs of goods sold . . . . The cost of goods sold should be determined in accordance with the method of accounting consistently used by the taxpayer. Reg. §1.61-3(a).

EXAMPLE 4.11

The income statement of ABC, a manufacturing enterprise, shows the following information:

Gross Sales		$195,000
Less: Cost of Goods Sold:		
Inventory, January 1	$30,000	
Purchases	160,000	
Goods Available for Sale	$190,000	
Less: Inventory, December 31	45,000	
Cost of Goods Sold		$145,000
Gross Profit (Gross Income)		$50,000

The taxpayer, in this example, would include $50,000 in gross income. The net profit or loss of a business is determined by subtracting from gross profit (income) all selling, as well as general and administrative, expenses. Continuing on from the previous calculations:

Gross Profit (Income)		$50,000
Less: Selling Expenses	$12,000	
General and Administrative Expenses	8,000	
Total Operating Expenses		$20,000
Net Profit (Income)		$30,000

In the determination of penalties and additional tax due to the omission of items of income, gross income is defined in Code Sec. 6501(e)(1)(A)(i) as total income received or accrued "prior to diminution by the cost of such sales."

¶4375 PARTNERSHIPS AND S CORPORATIONS

Partnerships and S corporations are not taxed, but their taxable income is taxed to the individual partners or shareholders. Each partner or shareholder absorbs a proportionate share of the firm's income, whether or not distributed. An S corporation is a small business corporation desiring not to be taxed at the corporate level. A corporation desiring S corporation status must meet various requirements, including valid stockholder approval of S status.

¶4385   INTEREST

Interest received by a taxpayer or credited to the taxpayer must be included in gross income. Interest income includes interest on bank accounts, loans, notes, corporate bonds, and U.S. savings bonds. Interest income received on obligations of states, territories, or a possession of the United States is generally wholly exempt from taxation.

EXAMPLE 4.12

> Leo Lionstone has a savings account at First National Bank that pays him interest on June 30 and December 31 of each year. In 2017, $25 of interest income was credited to his account in June and $28 of interest income on December 31. Even though Leo makes no withdrawals during the year, he must include $53 of interest income in his 2017 gross income. He had an absolute right to the money; therefore, he must recognize the income.

A cash basis taxpayer reports interest income when received. Interest earned on bank accounts is considered received, under the constructive receipt doctrine, when credited to the account. An accrual basis taxpayer reports interest income as it accrues. Interest on U.S. Series EE savings bonds may be reported each year or the taxpayer may elect to report the entire amount in the year that the bond matures. Once the taxpayer chooses a method, all of the taxpayer's Series EE savings bonds must be reported in the same manner. Code Sec. 454.

Banks and other financial institutions often hand out inexpensive gifts, such as flashlights, tote bags, or mouse pads, to attract new deposits or induce customers to add to their existing accounts. Under a IRS revenue procedure, a noncash gift is a de minimis premium, and thus taxfree, if it does not have a value of more than $10 for a deposit of less than $5,000, or $20 for a deposit of $5,000 or more. The value is based on the cost of the premium to the financial institution. The financial institution that hands out such a gift is not required to treat it as interest for information-reporting purposes. Rev. Proc. 2000-30.

Below-Market Interest Loans

A below-market interest demand loan is defined as a demand loan with an interest rate below the applicable federal short-term rate. For many years, individuals have been making use of below-market interest rate loans. This was especially popular among family members. To remedy this tax-avoidance scheme, the Tax Reform Act of 1984 imputed interest on interest-free or below-market demand and term loans. A demand loan is defined as any loan payable in full on demand of the lender. A term loan is a below-market loan if the amount loaned exceeds the present value of all payments due under the loan. Imputed interest is computed by using the statutory federal rate of interest. The federal rate is adjusted monthly and published by the IRS. In an effort to simplify the computation of forgone interest on below-market demand loans, the IRS established a "blended annual rate." For the year 2016, the blended annual rate is up to 0.73 percent compared to 0.45 percent in 2015. The IRS usually announces the blended annual rate for each year during the summer.

Section 7872(c), relating to loans with below-market interest rates, applies to:

1. Gift loans;
2. Compensation-related loans;
3. Corporation-shareholder loans;
4. "Tax-avoidance" loans (i.e., tax avoidance being the principal purpose of the loan); and
5. Other below-market loans in which the interest arrangements have a significant effect on federal tax liability.

A below-market loan is treated as a gift, dividend, contribution to capital, payment of compensation, or other payment depending on the substance of the transaction. For below-market loans that are not gift loans, "forgone interest" is deductible by the borrower and must be included in the lender's gross income. In an employer-employee relationship it is treated as additional compensation. With respect to a corporation-shareholder relationship it is treated as if the corporation paid a dividend. The forgone interest on a gift loan is treated as a taxable gift. Forgone interest may be defined as the additional interest which would have been paid had the loan been granted at "the market rate" rather than at the artificially low rate created for the below-market rate loan.

Gift, Employee, and Commercial Loans

The rules for below-market loans do not apply to:

1. Gift loans between individuals if:
   a. the aggregate outstanding amount of loans between such individuals does not exceed $10,000, and
   b. the loan is not attributable to the purchase or carrying of income-producing assets; or
2. Compensation-related or corporation-shareholder loans if:
   a. the aggregate outstanding amount of loans between the borrower and the lender does not exceed $10,000, and
   b. the avoidance of federal tax is not a principal purpose of the loan. Code Sec. 7872(c).

Special rules exist for gift loans between individuals that do not exceed $100,000. The imputed interest is limited to the borrower's net investment income for the tax year. However, if the borrower uses the proceeds for investment purposes and the borrower's investment income is in excess of $1,000, interest is imputed. If the borrower has net investment income of $1,000 or less for the year, the borrower's net investment income is deemed to be zero.

Some loans are specifically excluded from the rules for below-market loans, such as:

1. Loans made available by lenders to the general public on the same terms and conditions;
2. Loans subsidized by a federal, state, or municipal government that are made available to the general public;
3. Certain employee-relocation loans;
4. Loans to or from a foreign person, unless the interest would be effectively connected with the conduct of a U.S. trade or business and not exempt from U.S. tax under an income tax treaty; and
5. Loans on which the interest arrangement can be shown to have no significant effect on the federal tax liability of the lender or the borrower.

If a taxpayer structures a transaction to be similar to a loan not subject to the rules and one of the principal purposes of structuring the transaction is the avoidance of federal tax, the loan will be considered a tax-avoidance loan and subject to the rules for below-market loans.

Whether an interest arrangement has a significant effect on the federal tax liability (item 5, above) will be determined by all the facts and circumstances. Some factors to be considered are:

1. Whether items of income and deduction generated by the loan offset each other;
2. The amount of such items;
3. The cost of complying with the below-market loan provisions if they applied; and
4. Any reasons, other than taxes, for structuring the transaction as a below-market loan.

These rules apply to term loans made after June 6, 1984, and to demand loans outstanding after that date.

Bond Transactions

When a bond is sold between interest dates and the accrued interest is added to the selling price, the seller must recognize the interest as income. All interest earned from the date of purchase is taxable to the buyer.

EXAMPLE 4.13 Aaron Adams purchases a $1,000 bond of the Rhody Corporation from Baron Ziegler at face value. Interest is paid at a rate of 6 percent on April 1 and October 1. The bond was purchased on June 1 for $1,015 ($15 representing accrued interest). Baron, the seller, must report $15 as interest income. On October 1 Aaron will receive $30 interest of which $15 ($30 – $15) will be taxable.

"Flat" Basis Bonds

Occasionally, a taxpayer will buy a bond with defaulted interest included in the purchase price. In this case, the entire amount is considered a capital investment. However, if after the purchase date interest accrues on the bond, this would be considered interest income when received. Recovery of defaulted interest on a flat bond results in no income. All interest in excess of basis, but less than the face amount of the bonds, is taxable as a capital gain.

EXAMPLE 4.14	Aaron Adams purchases a $1,000 bond of the Rhody Corporation for $700 "flat." Interest is paid at the rate of 6 percent on April 1 and October 1. On June 1, when Adams bought the bond, there was $105 accrued interest in default. On October 1, Adams received $120 interest from Rhody Corporation. The $105 of defaulted interest is considered a return of investment and the $15 ($120–$105) is interest income. Adams's basis in the bond is now $595 ($700–$105).

¶4395   RENT AND ROYALTY INCOME

Rental income is the amount received by the owner of property for allowing someone else to use it. Rental income must be included in gross income. All expenses incurred by the landlord (i.e., depreciation, taxes, repairs, and other ordinary and necessary expenses attributable to the rental property) are deductible from gross income. If the tenant instead of paying rent pays off obligations of the landlord, then this amount must be included in the gross income of the landlord. However, the landlord may deduct these expenses if they would otherwise be deductible. For example, if the tenant pays the property taxes in lieu of rent, the landlord may deduct this sum from gross income. However, the landlord may deduct this sum from gross income in the year received, whether the taxpayer is on the cash or accrual basis, but anticipated expenses may not be deducted until actually paid. The tenant, if rent is paid in advance, is not allowed a tax deduction for rent expense until the year in which the payment is due even though the cash basis is used. Rent received in advance is always taxable when received.

Security deposits received from tenants are not included in gross income if they are to be returned to the tenant. If the security deposit is to be used as a final payment of rent, then it is advance rent and must be included in gross income when it is received.

EXAMPLE 4.15	Makayla rents an apartment for $1,000 per month. Eric, the landlord, requires Makayla to put down a $500 security deposit. If there is no damage to the apartment when Makayla moves out her security deposit will then be returned. Eric does not include the $500 in his gross income because the security deposit is to be returned.

Royalty income received for allowing someone the use of copyrights, patents, licenses, and rights to oil, gas, or other mineral properties is includible in gross income.

Lessee Improvements

Improvements made by the lessee are not income to the lessor either at the time the improvements are made or upon termination of the lease. Code Sec. 1019. Gain or loss will be recognized only at the time the property is sold.

However, where the lessee makes repairs which are the responsibility of the lessor or makes improvements in lieu of rent, the lessor has rental income to the extent of the market value of the improvements.

EXAMPLE 4.16	Robert Wolf entered into a 50-year lease with Cleveland Inc. on January 7, 1995. Wolf remodeled the building at a cost of $50,000. The building has a book value of $20,000 to Cleveland Inc. In 2017, Wolf defaulted and Cleveland Inc. took back the building. The improvements made by Wolf are not income to Cleveland Inc. in 2017. Only when the building is sold would Cleveland Inc. recognize gain on the improvements.

EXAMPLE 4.17	Robert Wolf and Cleveland Inc. agreed that Mr. Wolf would make improvements to the building amounting to $10,000. In exchange for making these improvements, Cleveland Inc. will not charge Mr. Wolf rent of $10,000 in 2017. In this case, Cleveland Inc. has $10,000 of rental income for 2017.

Lease Cancellations and Bonuses

Bonuses received for the granting of a lease are considered rental income. Also, payments received by a landlord to cancel or modify a lease must be included in gross income. However, payments made to a tenant to cancel a lease are considered as "amounts received in exchange for such lease or agreement." Code Sec.

1241. Further, Section 1241 applies to amounts received for the cancellation of a distributor's agreement if the distributor has a substantial capital investment in the distributorship. Usually, the payment received by a tenant results in capital gain income because the lease is considered a capital asset (see ¶12,155).

¶4401   DIVIDEND INCOME

The term "dividend" means "any distribution of property made by a corporation to its shareholders out of its earnings and profits." Code Sec. 316(a). In the above definition, dividends were defined in terms of "property." The term property is defined as "money, securities, and any other property." Code Sec. 317(a). Notice, it does not include stock or rights to acquire stock.

The American Taxpayer Relief Act of 2012 raised the top marginal federal tax rate on dividends to 20 percent, up from 15 percent. For 2017, the 20 percent tax rate applies to individuals whose income exceeds $418,400 (individuals), $470,700 (filing jointly) and $444,550 (heads of households). Taxpayers whose income level is below the above stated amounts will be taxed at a maximum rate of 15 percent.

For taxpayers whose ordinary income is taxed below 25 percent, dividends will be subject to a zero percent rate.

EXAMPLE 4.18   Clifford, a single taxpayer, has taxable income of $100,000. Included in this amount is $5,000 of qualified dividends. Clifford's marginal tax rate is 28 percent. However, on the dividend income of $5,000, his tax rate is 15 percent.

Distributions from a corporation in the form of a dividend only come after they have been authorized by the board of directors. The distribution may take the form of cash or other assets, but a true dividend must come from earnings accumulated after February 28, 1913. Code Sec. 316; Reg. §1.316-1. Retained earnings are the corporation's taxable income that has been retained in the business and not previously distributed. Usually, the directors, when desiring to make a distribution to the stockholders, award cash. Basically there are two common types of dividends:

1. Cash
2. Stock (dividends and rights)

Cash Dividend

When dealing with dividends, one must be cognizant of four dates:

1. Declaration
2. Record
3. Payment
4. Receipt

EXAMPLE 4.19	The board of directors of the Rhody Corporation declares on March 3, 2017, a cash dividend of $1.00 per share to be paid on May 27, 2017, to each stockholder of record as of April 28, 2017. The stockholder received the dividend on June 9, 2017. The four dates in the example were:

1. Declaration Date—March 3, 2017
2. Record Date—April 28, 2017
3. Payment Date—May 27, 2017
4. Receipt Date—June 9, 2017

Anyone who owns shares of stock of Rhody Corporation on April 28, 2017, is entitled to a $1.00 per share cash dividend. Therefore, the market value of the stock from March 3 until April 28 should reflect the $1.00 per share dividend. If a share of stock is sold on May 5, 2017, the stockholder still will receive the dividend because he or she was a shareholder on the date of record. The person receiving the cash dividend must recognize dividend income for that amount. However, corporate dividends received by individuals are taxed at a maximum rate of 15/20 percent. The shareholder having the unqualified right to demand payment must recognize taxable income. Reg. §1.301-1. The date the dividend is received by the taxpayer, not the date the dividend is declared, determines taxability. Unlike accrued interest income on bonds, no part of the purchase may be allocated to dividend income.

Although from a theoretical viewpoint in the above example, the $1.00 dividend can be identified from the purchase price, in reality this is not always the case. With interest on bonds, the interest can be readily determined at any time. A person who has a stockbroker collect the dividend is still required to pay tax on it under the rules of the constructive receipt doctrine. Also, if a dividend is declared and a person dies before the payment date, the dividend income is not included in the final income tax return, but in the estate income tax return. *M. Putnam Est.,* 57-1 USTC ¶9200, 352 U.S. 82, 77 S.Ct. 175 (1956).

Mutual Funds

Individuals holding an interest in a mutual fund may receive any combination of three types of distribution: ordinary dividends, return of capital, and capital gains dividends. Taxpayers are notified within 45 days after the close of the tax year of the distribution into the above three classes from dividends distributed during the year. For example, the stockholders will be informed of the portion of the dividends received to be treated as a long-term capital gain. Further, they will be apprised of the portion of the mutual fund's established capital gains they must report as long-term capital gains even though the company has retained them. Ordinary dividends of a mutual fund are reported as dividend income to the recipient.

Life Insurance and Annuity Contracts

Dividends on life insurance and annuity contracts are excludable from gross income and are considered a reduction in the cost of the policy. Code Sec. 301. If it is a fully paid-up life insurance policy and the dividend exceeds the net premiums paid, then the excess is fully taxable. Also, once payment of the proceeds under the contract has commenced, then any dividend received is fully taxable.

EXAMPLE 4.20	Leah Lambert and her husband receive the following dividends during 2017:

	Leah	Husband
Able Auto Parts	$300	
Get Rich REIT		$450
Canadian Exploration	$250	
Live Long Insurance		$200

For the year 2017, all of the above-listed dividends are includible in gross income except the dividend from Live Long Insurance, which is considered a reduction in premium cost. Therefore, Leah has $550 of dividend income and her husband has $450 in dividend income, for a total of $1,000. This total amount of $1,000 must be included in gross income.

EXAMPLE 4.21	Leah and her husband purchased a 10-year endowment policy. The policy commences payments on January 1, 2018. Therefore, any dividends issued by the company in 2017 would not be taxable. Any dividends issued by the company after January 1, 2018, would be fully taxable.

EXAMPLE 4.22	Assume in Example 4.21 that Leah and her husband paid $25,000 for the policy. Over the years, they had received $2,200 in dividends. Therefore, their basis in the policy is $22,800 ($25,000 – $2,200).

The above rules concerning life insurance and annuity contracts apply regardless of whether the taxpayer receives the dividend in cash or lets it accumulate to purchase additional insurance.

Stock Dividends

A stock dividend is defined as a distribution by a corporation of its own stock, including treasury stock. Reg. §1.305-1. Stock dividends usually are not included in the gross income of the recipient. However, there are certain exceptions to this rule. They are as follows:

1. Distributions in lieu of money. If the stockholder has the option of receiving stock in lieu of money, then the corporate distribution is taxable to the recipient.
2. Disproportionate distributions. If some shareholders receive property and other shareholders receive stock so as to alter the individual stockholder's proportionate interest in the corporation, then the distribution is included as gross income.
3. Distributions of common and preferred stock. If some stockholders receive common stock and other stockholders receive preferred stock, then the distribution is considered part of gross income.
4. Distributions on preferred stock. A stock dividend on preferred stock is taxable to the recipient unless it increases the conversion ratio of convertible preferred stock made specifically to take into account a stock dividend or stock split on the convertible preferred stock in which case it is tax free. Code Sec. 305(b)(4).
5. Distributions of convertible preferred stock. A distribution of convertible preferred stock is taxable to the recipient unless it can be proven to the Commissioner that the individual stockholder's equity in the corporation remains constant.

Upon receipt of a nontaxable stock dividend, the stockholder must allocate the original cost over all the shares the stockholder presently owns.

EXAMPLE 4.23	Aaron Adams owns 100 shares of Rhody Corporation common stock which he purchased for $11 per share in 2010 for a total cost of $1,100. Rhody Corporation pays a 10 percent stock dividend in June 2017, and Aaron receives 10 shares (10 percent of 100 shares) of stock. Therefore, he now owns 110 shares of stock and his basis is $1,100 or $10 per share ($1,100/110 shares). At the time any of the 110 shares is sold, its basis is $10 per share.

EXAMPLE 4.24

If, in Example 4.23, instead of receiving the common stock, Aaron received 20 shares of Rhody Corporation preferred stock as a stock dividend and it had a fair market value of $10 per share and the 100 original shares of Rhody Corporation common stock at this time had a fair market value of $2,000, then the following computations would be necessary:

Computations:

Basis of original stock	$1,100
Fair market value of original stock	$2,000
Fair market value of the new preferred stock	200
Fair market value of preferred and common	$2,200
Basis of original 100 shares after stock dividend 1,100 × 2,000/2,200	$1,000
Basis of new stock after the dividend 1,100 × 200/2,200	$100

To determine whether or not the sale should be treated as a long-term capital gain, the date when the original shares were purchased is the controlling factor. To be classified as a long-term gain, a capital asset must be held for more than one year. For 2017, the tax on capital gains is a maximum of 20 percent if held greater than 12 months (28 percent for collectibles and section 1202 gains) and the taxpayer's income is over $418,400 if single, $470,700 for joint filers.

The new shares take on the basis of the old shares. If lots of the old shares were purchased on different dates and the dividend shares cannot be identified with any particular lot, then the new shares take the basis of the earliest purchased stock. Reg. §1.1012-1(c).

Stock Rights

A stock right is defined as a distribution by a corporation to its shareholders of *rights* to purchase corporate stock. Usually, the shareholder has a right to buy the stock at less than fair market value. Therefore, the stock rights have a market value. The stockholder receiving the rights has three alternative courses of action. The stockholder may exercise, sell, or hold the stock rights.

If the market value of the stock rights is less than 15 percent of the market value of the stock with respect to which it is distributed, then the basis of the rights is zero unless the shareholder irrevocably elects to allocate the basis between the stock and the rights. Code Sec. 307(b)(1). Where the market value of the rights is 15 percent or greater, the basis must be allocated between the stock and rights according to their respective values on the date on which the rights are distributed to the stockholder, not the record date. In Chapter 10, at ¶10,125, a full discussion appears on the allocation of basis for taxable and nontaxable stock rights.

¶4451 DIVORCE AND SEPARATION

There are two sets of rules depending on when the divorce took place. The first set is for divorces occurring before 1985 and the second set is for divorces occurring after 1984.

Pre-1985 Agreements

Although this is an old law, some individuals are still covered by it. Prior to the Tax Reform Act of 1984, Code Sec. 71 defined alimony as a series of support payments received after divorce or legal separation. If the following four conditions exist, then the recipient must include the alimony payments in gross income and the person making the payments is entitled to a tax deduction for adjusted gross income. The conditions are as follows:

1. Payments are required under the terms of the decree of divorce or separate maintenance or a written separation agreement or a decree of support.
2. Payments must be to discharge the legal obligation of support.
3. Payments must be periodic.
4. Payments must not be for child support.

The following payments would not qualify:

1. Lump-sum settlements,
2. Payments not required under the decree or agreement,
3. Payments not arising out of a marital relationship (repayment of a loan), and
4. Payments made before the decree.

Determining whether or not payments are periodic or lump-sum in nature can be quite difficult. If the installments are to be paid over an indefinite period of time, or where the period of time exceeds 10 years, by the terms of the decree, then the payments will qualify. It is not necessary that the payments come in regular intervals. However, only 10 percent of the total sum specified qualifies for alimony treatment. If more than 10 percent is paid in any year, that excess is considered a property settlement.

EXAMPLE 4.25

The decree provides for the wife to receive $280,000 over 40 years at a rate of $7,000 per year. The $7,000 payment each year would qualify as alimony and the husband would receive the tax deduction. However, assume the wife received $58,800 in each of the first two years and the remaining $162,400 ($280,000 − $117,600) equally ($4,274 per year) over the following 38 years. The husband, in this situation, can deduct only $28,000 (10% of $280,000) in each of the first two years. During the remaining years, he may deduct $4,274 a year.

Alimony and separate maintenance payments received by the taxpayer are included in gross income. Further, the payer is allowed a tax deduction in the year the payment is made.

Post-1984 Agreements

Payments under instruments executed after December 31, 1984, that meet the following requirements are deductible as alimony:

1. Payments must be made in cash.
2. Payments must be made under a divorce or separation instrument.
3. Parties must live in separate households after a divorce or separation decree is entered.
4. Alimony must end at the payee's death.
5. Parties involved may not file a joint return.
6. Payments must not be for child support.

A special feature was added that the parties could designate by written agreement payments otherwise qualifying as alimony payments as excludable by the payee and nondeductible by the payer. Code Sec. 71(b)(1)(B).

The Tax Reform Act of 1986 changed only a few rules with respect to divorces. However, because of the lower tax rates and increased exemptions for dependents, tax planning for pending divorces is essential and tax planning for divorces executed after 1986 is highly recommended.

Alimony Termination on Payee's Death

Under the 1986 law, the requirement that the "instrument must state" that payments must terminate on the payee's death has been repealed. This amendment is effective for divorce or separation instruments executed after December 31, 1984.

Front-Loading Limitation

The Tax Reform Act of 1986 fixed the amount of annual payments exempt from recapture at $15,000. The front-loading requirement under the recapture rules was set at three post-separation years.

Recapture Rules

Under the revised recapture rules the tax treatment of past payments has been changed to require the inclusion of previously deducted alimony or separate maintenance payments in income. The revised recapture rules also allow the recipient spouse, who previously included the alimony in income, to deduct the recaptured amount.

Under the recapture rules adopted by the Tax Reform Act of 1986, payments will be recaptured if:

1. Payments made in the second post-separation year exceed the payments in the third post-separation year by more than $15,000, and/or
2. Payments made in the first post-separation year exceed the average of (the alimony payments of the second post-separation year and the third post-separation year less the year 2 recapture) by more than $15,000.

The excess amounts in the first and second post-separation years only may be recaptured in the third post-separation year. The following examples illustrate the alimony recapture rules.

EXAMPLE 4.26

Bob and Mary Barnsen were divorced on January 13, 2017. Mary pays Bob the following amounts of alimony under the terms of her divorce decree.

Year	Amount
2017 (1st post-separation year)	$70,000
2018 (2nd post-separation year)	40,000
2019 (3rd post-separation year)	20,000

Mary computes her amount to be recaptured as follows:

Year 2 Calculation	Amount
Payments in the second year	$40,000
Less: Payments in the third year	20,000
	20,000
Less: $15,000	15,000
Amount of second-year payments subject to recapture in 2019	$5,000

The amount of second-year payments used in computing the recapture for the first post-separation year is $35,000 ($40,000 – $5,000).

Year 1 Calculation	Amount
Payments in the first year	$70,000
Less: Average payments made in the second and third year (($35,000 + $20,000) ÷ 2)	27,500
	$42,500
Less: $15,000	15,000
Amount of first-year payments subject to recapture in 2019	$27,500

In calculating the recapture account for the first year, only $35,000, rather than $40,000, is treated as paid in the second year. This is because the average of payments made in the second and third years does not include the $5,000 payment made in the second year that is recaptured in the third year. Bob has gross income of $70,000 and $40,000 in 2017 and 2018, respectively. In 2019, the recapture of $32,500 exceeds the $20,000 alimony received; therefore, Bob has a deduction of $12,500. Mary deducts alimony of $70,000 in the first post-separation year and $40,000 in the second. In year three, she must recapture $32,500 ($5,000 + $27,500) which exceeds her third year payment of $20,000. Therefore, she has income of $12,500 in 2019.

EXAMPLE 4.27

Bill and Alice Bailey were divorced on January 6, 2017. Bill makes the following alimony payments to Alice under a divorce decree.

Year	Amount
2017 (1st post-separation year)	$50,000
2018 (2nd post-separation year)	18,000
2019 (3rd post-separation year)	0
Year 2 Calculation	
Payments in the second year	$18,000
Less: Payments in the third year	0
	$18,000
Less: $15,000	15,000
Amount of second-year payments subject to recapture in 2019	$3,000
Year 1 Calculation	
Payments in the first year	$50,000
Less: Average payments made in the second and third year (($15,000 + $0) ÷ 2)	7,500
	$42,500
Less: $15,000	15,000
Amount of first-year payments subject to recapture in 2019	$27,500

In calculating the recapture amount for the first year, only $15,000, rather than $18,000, is treated as paid in the second year. This is because the average of payments made in the second and third years does not include the $3,000 payment made in the second year that is recaptured in the third year.

Bill will show $30,500 as income on his 2019 tax return and Alice will show a tax deduction of $30,500 on her 2019 tax return.

Bill deducts as alimony $50,000 in 2017 and $18,000 in 2018 and Alice includes in her gross income $50,000 and $18,000 in those two years.

Exceptions to the Recapture Rule

There are three exceptions to the recapture rule (in addition to the $15,000 floor).

1. Payments cease by reason of death or remarriage prior to the end of the third post-separation year.
2. Payments received under a temporary support order before the divorce or separation.
3. Payments pursuant to a continuing liability to pay a fixed part of your income from a business or property or from compensation for employment or self-employment.

If the payer stops or reduces the amount of alimony or separate maintenance during any of the first three post-separation years for any other than the above listed reasons then the payments are subject to recapture.

EXAMPLE 4.28

Randy Reeves is required under the terms of a divorce decree to make payments to Candy of $50,000 in 2017, $30,000 in 2018, and $35,000 in 2019. Randy makes the first payment in 2017 and one-half the second payment when Candy remarries. Randy immediately stops making alimony payments. The recapture rule does not apply.

Exemption for Dependent Child

Under prior law, the spouse who had custody of the child was generally entitled to the personal exemption, provided the parents together furnished over half of the child's support. For years beginning after 1984, the custodial parent is entitled to the exemption unless the right to claim it is expressly waived. Code Sec. 152(e). For the custodial parent to transfer the exemption, the custodial parent must sign a written declaration transferring the exemption to the noncustodial parent. This written declaration may be made annually, for more than one year, or permanently. Even when the custodial parent transfers the exemption to the noncustodial parent, the custodial parent is still eligible for head of household filing status, the earned income credit, and the child and dependent care credit.

TAX BLUNDERS

1. Bob and Judy are in the middle of a divorce case. After the divorce Judy will be in the 28 percent tax bracket, and Bob will be in the 15 percent bracket. Judy wants to pay Bob $20,000 per year as alimony. Bob is insisting he receive $10,000 as alimony and $10,000 as child support. Bob will be the custodial parent. In this case it would benefit Judy to pay Bob's tax on the additional $10,000 alimony. She will save $1,300 by counting all $20,000 as alimony ($2,800 tax savings less $1,500 payment of Bob's tax on $10,000).
2. Same facts as above. Judy would be wise to pay Bob for the personal exemption for the child. The savings to Bob is at the 15 percent rate. Judy would benefit from the 28 percent rate.
3. The lower tax rates drastically reduce the net after-tax value for alimony payments. The payer's net after-tax cost of alimony increases as the individual's tax bracket decreases.

    Assume Frank and Robin Forkes were divorced in 1982. Frank makes annual alimony payments of $15,000. In 1987, Frank had $90,000 of taxable income, which placed him in the 38.5 percent tax bracket. Therefore, his net after-tax cost for alimony was $9,225. In 2017, with the same taxable income his after-tax cost for alimony payments increased to $11,250 because Frank is in the 25 percent tax bracket in 2017.

Just as the lower tax rates prove disadvantageous to the payer of alimony, the increased exemption for dependents ($4,050 in 2017) makes the dependency exemption all the more important. Under present law, the custodial parent is automatically entitled to the dependency exemption.

Legal Fees

If a spouse is collecting alimony, legal fees incurred to enforce the payment are deductible as an itemized deduction by that spouse. Legal fees incurred in arranging the divorce settlement are not deductible. The payer-spouse cannot deduct any legal fees for the arrangement of the divorce or for the adjustment of alimony payments.

Payment in Arrears

Payments of amounts in arrears are deductible when paid. When a lump-sum settlement occurs for payment in arrears, even this is deductible.

Medical and Dental Expenses

Payments made for medical and dental expenses of the payee-spouse by the payer-spouse must be included in the gross income of the payee-spouse if they qualify as alimony. In addition, the payee-spouse is allowed to deduct these two expenses if the payee-spouse itemizes deductions.

Payments made for medical expenses of children of divorced parents may be deducted by the spouse making the payment. In this case, the children will be treated as dependents of both parents.

Transfer of Property Between Spouses

Under prior law, property transfers between divorcing spouses were taxable when they involved the release of support or marital rights. The 1984 tax law provides that no gain or loss will be recognized for property transfers between spouses during marriage, or former spouses incident to a divorce on transfers taking effect after July 18, 1984. The basis the property will carry is the same in the hands of the receiving spouse as it was in the hands of the transmitting spouse. Incident to a divorce means the transfer must occur within one year after the marriage ceases or is related to the cessation of the marriage.

EXAMPLE 4.29   Tom and Roberta Thorne are finishing up the terms of their divorce settlement. Roberta insists Tom turn over to her stock Tom purchased three years ago at a cost of $5,000. The current fair market value of this stock is $9,000. Under the pre-1985 tax law, Tom would have a $4,000 taxable gain, but under the 1984 tax law, the transfer of property between spouses results in no tax liability. Roberta will assume the stock with a tax basis of $5,000.

Child Support

Payments made by one spouse which are specifically identified for the support of minor children are not taxable to the other spouse and are not deductible by the first spouse. The support must be for the children of the parent making the payment. The custodial parent is entitled to the exemption unless he or she signs a waiver.

EXAMPLE 4.30
> By the terms of the divorce settlement, Bob Barter is directed to pay alimony of $1,600 per month and child support of $800 per month. Assume that $800 per month is more than 50 percent of the child's support. Bob is not allowed an exemption for support of his child. The custodial parent is entitled to the exemption. The $800 is not included in income nor deductible by Bob.

When the instrument sets forth one amount for alimony and one amount for child support and a particular payment is less than the total of the two, the payment will first apply towards the child support. Child support payments, if in arrears, must be paid before any future amounts may be considered as alimony.

Where the divorce decree, for example, requires the husband to pay $1,000 a month to his divorced wife and $500 a month for the support of a minor child and the husband pays only $500, it is nevertheless considered to be payment for the support of the child. Reg. §1.71-1(e).

Reporting Requirements

The taxpayer paying alimony must furnish the payee's taxpayer identification number on the tax return. Code Sec. 215(c). A $50 penalty in a calendar year will be levied for failure to comply with the reporting requirement unless it can be shown that failure to comply was due to reasonable cause and not to willful neglect. Code Sec. 6724(d)(3).

¶4485   DISCHARGE OF DEBT

When a debt is cancelled for a consideration, in whole or in part, the debtor realizes taxable income for the amount of the debt discharged. Code Sec. 61(a)(12). For example, if the debtor performed a personal service for the creditor and the debt was fully or partially cancelled, the debtor would have to realize as income the cancelled amount as compensation for services. Reg. §1.61-12(a).

Creditor's Gifts

If a creditor gratuitously cancels a debt, then the amount forgiven is not income but a nontaxable gift. Code Sec. 102(a). The Supreme Court ruled that the cancellation of a debt by the creditor for "no consideration" is a gift and, therefore, no taxable income is involved. *Helvering v. American Dental Co.,* 43-1 USTC ¶9318, 318 U.S. 322, 63 S.Ct. 577 (1935). However, where consideration of any kind or amount is given for cancellation of the debt, it may be extremely difficult to prove the cancellation was gratuitous.

Bankruptcy and Insolvency

Generally, income from a nongratuitous discharge of indebtedness is includible in gross income unless it is excludable under Code Sec. 108. For discharges after 1986, two types of exclusions are provided in the following priority order (Code Sec. 108(a)):

1. The discharge occurs in a bankruptcy case under Title 11 of the U.S. Code.
2. The discharge occurs when the taxpayer is insolvent outside of bankruptcy. An insolvent taxpayer is one who has an excess of liabilities over the fair market value of assets immediately prior to the discharge. The exclusion is limited to the insolvent amount.

Discharge or reduction of debt in bankruptcy does not generate income. If the debt was incurred in connection with property used in a trade or business, the amount of debt that was discharged reduces certain tax attributes that could otherwise provide benefits in the future. Section 108(b)(5) allows the taxpayer to elect to apply any portion of the cancellation of debt to reduce the basis in depreciable property before reducing other tax attributes. This election by the taxpayer is available regardless of whether the debt is evidenced by a security. If the taxpayer does not elect to reduce the basis in depreciable property, then the amount excluded from gross income (the portion of the debt that was cancelled) reduces tax attributes in the order given in Code Sec. 108(b)(2):

1. Net operating losses and carryovers
2. General business credit
3. Capital loss carryovers
4. Reduction of basis of the property of the taxpayer
5. Foreign tax credit carryovers

Tax attributes other than credit carryovers are reduced one dollar for each dollar of debt discharge excluded. Code Sec. 108(b)(3)(A). Where a taxpayer excludes income from the discharge of indebtedness in a Title 11 bankruptcy case or the discharge occurs when the taxpayer is insolvent and the taxpayer is required to apply such excluded income to reduce its tax attributes, the reduction for post-1986 tax years in foreign tax credit, research credit, and the general business credit carryovers is to be made at a rate of 33 1/3 cents per dollar excluded. Code Sec. 108(b)(3)(B).

An insolvent taxpayer is allowed to exclude from gross income any discharge of indebtedness except that the amount excluded cannot exceed the amount by which the taxpayer is insolvent. Code Sec. 108(a)(3).

EXAMPLE 4.31

Mike Merchant has assets of $50,000 and liabilities of $85,000. If one of Mike's creditors forgives him of $40,000 worth of debt, then Mike must recognize $5,000 ($50,000 – ($85,000 – $40,000)) of taxable income.

Mortgage Debt Forgiveness

The Mortgage Forgiveness Debt Relief Act of 2007 offers distressed homeowners with a limited tax exclusion for debt forgiveness and mortgage insurance payments. Generally, homeowners will be able to exclude up to $2 million of mortgage debt forgiveness. This exclusion will be available from January 1, 2007 through 2014. The Emergency Economic Stabilization Act of 2008 extended this provision for three more years. A taxpayer whose principal residence has declined in market value will be able to refinance the loan without incurring a tax on the debt forgiveness. The American Taxpayer Relief Act of 2012 extended this provision through December 31, 2013. The Tax Increase Prevention Act of 2014 extended this provision through December 31, 2014. The PATH Act of 2015 extended mortgage debt forgiveness for the years 2015 and 2016. To date, Congress has not extended this provision.

Purchase Money Debts

If a debt owed to the seller for the purchase of property is reduced by the seller, then no income is recognized by the purchaser. The reduction is a purchase price adjustment, not a discharge in indebtedness. Consequently, the purchaser recognizes no income even though the obligation has been reduced. In order for this rule to apply, there must be a "pure" cancellation of indebtedness income; the only relationship between the parties must be that of debtor and creditor, and the debt forgiveness must not simply be the method by which the creditor makes a payment to the debtor for services or property. Code Sec. 108(e)(5).

Corporate Debts

A shareholder's gratuitous forgiveness of the corporation's indebtedness or cancellation of the corporation's indebtedness to the shareholder is usually considered a contribution of capital to the corporation to the extent of the principal debt. Code Sec. 108(e)(6); Reg. §1.61-12(a).

EXAMPLE 4.32

Benjamin Warren is sales manager and shareholder of Cleveland Widget Inc. The company is in bankruptcy and Benjamin has not been paid for several months. Benjamin agrees to cancel the debt for the unpaid wages. Cleveland Widget Inc. recognized no income; instead, the cancellation is treated as a contribution of capital. Benjamin, who is on the cash basis, recognizes no income from the unpaid wages.

Student Loans

A special income exclusion applies to the discharge of all or part of a student loan under a governmental agency student loan program if, pursuant to the loan agreement, the discharge is made because the individual works for a specified period of time in certain geographical areas for certain classes of employers (e.g., as a doctor or nurse in a rural area). Code Sec. 108(f). The amount of the loan that is forgiven is excluded from gross income.

KEYSTONE PROBLEM

Roy and Ann are students at one of the country's finest state universities and wish to marry in the near future. Roy has inherited a potato farm from his late grandfather. Both have scholarships and part-time jobs. They will receive as gifts, property (a small house), and some stocks and bonds. Further, both have cash from savings and investments (about $10,000). Roy is also in debt ($5,000) to his uncle for a defunct rock band he had started as a freshman. His uncle will forgive the debt if Roy marries and settles down. The young couple have come to you for advice on financial planning. What are the principal considerations you feel they would need to take into account in planning their financial future? What steps would you advise them to take in setting up their affairs? Consider such concerns as terms of property ownership, whether to file a tax return jointly or separately, whether to choose the cash or accrual basis for paying tax, how to minimize tax liability, and other factors which you feel are relevant to the problem.

Stock Option Plans

¶4601 RESTRICTED STOCK PLANS

Stock or other property that is transferred by an employer as compensation for services rendered but that, when received, is subject to certain restrictions that affect its value, is governed by the rules contained in Code Sec. 83. As a general rule, the value of any property transferred in connection with services rendered is taxable as compensation, whether the property is goods, common stock, a partnership interest, or any other property. An exception is provided for unsecured, unfunded promises to pay. Code Sec. 83(a); Reg. §1.83-3(c).

Property Substantially Vested

The property is taxable whenever the right to it is "substantially vested," which means it is either transferable or not subject to a substantial risk of forfeiture. It is to be valued without regard to any such restriction unless it is one that will never lapse. Code Sec. 83(a)(1).

EXAMPLE 4.33

A corporation, through its bonus plan, gave one of its vice-presidents 2,660 shares of common stock with a value of $76,000 at the time. There were no conditions attached. The vice-president has compensation of $76,000 with an offsetting deduction to the corporation. The result would be the same if the stock were transferred directly to a trust for the vice-president's minor children. If the vice-president had to pay $26,000 for the stock, only $50,000 is taxable. His basis is $76,000. A subsequent sale will result in a short- or long-term capital gain or loss. If the stock is subject to a substantial risk of forfeiture, *e.g.*, it is nontransferable for five years, no income results until the restriction lapses.

The general rule is that compensation results if property is transferred "in connection with" services rendered. Thus, it does not matter whether:

1. Services are rendered as an employee or independent contractor.
2. The property was transferred by the employer or another person, such as a shareholder.
3. The property was transferred to the compensated person or to anyone else, *e.g.*, a beneficiary, a trust, a corporation, or other agent. Any income received, *e.g.*, dividends, before the property is substantially vested is also treated as compensation.

If the property is sold before it is substantially vested, ordinary income results in the amount of the proceeds. But if the property is forfeited *before* it is substantially vested, no tax loss is incurred (except for amounts paid). If the property is forfeited *after* it is substantially vested and the value was reported as compensation, an ordinary loss results. Reg. §1.83-1(b)(1) and (2). This could happen if the property was transferable, but subject to a substantial risk of forfeiture.

Property Not Substantially Vested

If property transferred in connection with services rendered is not "substantially vested," *i.e.*, it is subject to a substantial risk of forfeiture, an election may nevertheless be made to include the current fair market value of the property in gross income. Code Sec. 83(b). The election is irrevocable and must be filed with the IRS within 30 days with a copy to the employer. Making the election locks in a basis equal to the fair market value included in gross income and starts the holding period running. Section 83(h) includes a matching principle: The employer's deduction is taken whenever the property is included in the employee's gross income and in the same amount.

There are two advantages of making the election:

1. Any future appreciation will qualify as a capital gain, historically taxed at rates lower than ordinary income.
2. The appreciation between the date of transfer and the date of substantial vesting is not taxed until the eventual disposition of the property in a taxable sale or exchange.
3. There will be no self-employment tax on the increase in value.

EXAMPLE 4.34	Cornelius Track received $5,000 worth of stock from his employer on condition that he worked in the same position the next four years, which he did. At the time the stock vested it was worth $12,000. Cornelius waited another six years before selling the stock for $19,000. If Cornelius did *not* make the Section 83(b) election, he would have taxable compensation of $12,000 when the stock vested (with an offsetting deduction to the employer), and an additional $7,000 of capital gain in the year of sale. Had he made the election he would have had $5,000 of compensation up front (offsetting deduction to the employer), *no* income at the time of vesting, and $14,000 of capital gain at the sale 10 years after the initial transfer.

The disadvantages of making the Section 83(b) election include the early outlay of cash to pay tax as well as the unavailability of a loss deduction should the property be forfeited before it becomes substantially vested.

The election should therefore be made only if the property has good appreciation potential *and* it is likely that any required conditions will be met.

Substantial Risk of Forfeiture

A substantial risk of forfeiture exists if a person's rights to full enjoyment of such property are conditioned upon the future performance of substantial services by an individual. Code Sec. 83(c). The following are examples of substantial risks of forfeiture:

1. The property must be returned unless earnings go up.
2. Substantial services must be rendered.
3. A successful completion of "going public" is a condition.

Conditions not constituting substantial risks include:

1. The person is being discharged for cause or for committing a crime.
2. The person accepts a job with a competitor.
3. The employer must pay the full market value upon forfeiture.

PLANNING POINTER	An executive receives $20,000 worth of restricted stock from his employer, conditional upon five years of service. Under the general rules, the executive will have no income for five years, at which time the then fair market value will be ordinary income. If the executive signs a promissory note for $20,000, he can make a Section 83(b) election without recognizing income. This will start the holding period running and lock in a basis of $20,000. Five years later, the corporation tears up the note, resulting in $20,000 of compensation to the executive and a business deduction of $20,000 to the corporation. If the stock is sold for $50,000 upon the lapse, for example, then or later, the executive will report a long-term capital gain of $30,000. In the absence of a note and the election, the full $50,000 would have been ordinary income (with an offsetting deduction to the employer).

¶4615   INCENTIVE STOCK OPTION (ISO) PLANS

Incentive stock options (ISOs) are the latest development in statutory stock option arrangements, replacing the restricted and qualified stock option provisions that previously existed. The term "incentive stock option" means an option granted by a corporation to an individual to purchase stock of the corporation if certain requirements are met. Code Sec. 422(b). The employee must have received the option for some reason connected with employment and must remain employed by the corporation (including a parent or subsidiary) issuing the option from the time of issuance until three months before it is exercised (one year in the case of a disabled employee).

Incentive stock options may be received and exercised by the employee of a corporation without recognizing any gross income. Income is reported only after a taxpayer disposes of the stock. However, for purposes of computing the alternative minimum tax, the taxpayer generally must include the amount by which the fair market value of the stock exceeds the exercise price at the time the taxpayer's rights to the stock are either freely transferable or not subject to a substantial risk of forfeiture. Code Sec. 56(b)(3).

The employee must hold the stock for a minimum of two years after the option is granted and for one year after the option is exercised. If the requisite holding period is not met, the bargain element (value less exercise price) is ordinary income to the employee in the year of sale with an offsetting deduction to the employer. The value on exercise becomes the employee's cost basis. The sale will result in short- or long-term capital gain or loss under the general rules. If the requisite holding period is met, long-term capital gain or loss on the disposition of the stock will be realized to the extent of the difference between the option price and the amount for which the stock is sold.

EXAMPLE 4.35	On April 1, Year 1, Gumballs, Inc. granted Juan an ISO to purchase 1,000 shares of its stock for $30 a share (its fair market value) for the next five years. On March 28, Year 2, Juan exercised the option and paid $30,000 when the stock sold for $42 a share. On September 17, Year 3, Juan sold the stock for $57,000. Gumballs, Inc. receives no deduction upon grant, exercise, or sale. Juan reports a long-term capital gain of $27,000. For purposes of the alternative minimum tax only, he has an adjustment item in the year of exercise of $12,000 ($42,000 – $30,000). Had Juan sold the stock for $53,000 on March 31, Year 3, the special two-year holding period would *not* have been met. As a result Juan, in Year 3, would have had $12,000 of ordinary income and $11,000 of long-term capital gain. He still would have an AMT adjustment item of $12,000. In Year 3, the year of the sale, Gumballs, Inc. would have compensation expense of $12,000 in this case.

PLANNING POINTER	Long-term capital gains generally are taxed at a maximum of 20 percent. Meeting the holding period requirements of the ISO would also be advantageous to the shareholder if the shareholder had capital losses that would otherwise not be deductible and have to be carried over. The shareholder meeting the holding period requirements would also cause the corporation to lose the compensation deduction. Therefore, the employer should, if necessary, offer a cash bonus to employees who are still in a position to violate the one- or two-year holding period, so as to secure a deduction for the employer. The bonus, after taxes, must, of course, be less than the tax savings resulting from the compensation deduction.

For options to qualify as ISOs the following requirements must be met:

1. The term of the option may not exceed 10 years.
2. The option price must be no less than the fair market value of the stock on the date of issuance.
3. The option must be transferable by inheritance only.
4. The option plan must specify the aggregate number of shares that may be issued and the employees eligible to receive the option.
5. The option must be granted within 10 years of the earlier of the date of adoption of the plan or the date it was approved by the shareholders.
6. If the employee owns more than 10 percent of the company, the option price must be at least 110 percent of the market value and its term may not exceed five years. Code Sec. 422(b) and (c).

To the extent that the aggregate fair market value of stock with respect to which ISOs are exercisable for the first time by an individual during any calendar year exceeds $100,000, such options are not considered ISOs. Code Sec. 422(d). Further, an option granted after 1986 will not be treated as an ISO if the terms of the option at the time it is granted provide that it will not be treated as an incentive stock option. Code Sec. 422(b).

¶4625 EMPLOYEE STOCK PURCHASE PLANS

An employee stock option plan is, generally, one permitting employees to buy stock in the employer corporation at a discount. Options issued under an employee stock purchase plan qualify for special tax treatment. Code Sec. 423. No income is recognized under such a plan at the time the option is granted; the recognition is deferred until stock acquired under the plan is disposed of.

If stock acquired under such a plan is disposed of after being held for the required period, the employee will realize ordinary income to the extent of the excess of the fair market value of the stock at the time the option was granted over the option price. Any further gain is a capital gain. If the stock is disposed of when its value is less than its value at the time the option was granted, the amount of ordinary income will be limited to the excess of current value over the option price.

An employee stock purchase plan must provide that only employees may be granted options and must be approved by the stockholders of the granting corporation within 12 months before or after the date the plan is adopted. Code Sec. 423(b). Other conditions that must be met either by the plan or in the stock offering are:

1. The option price may not be less than the smaller of (a) 85 percent of fair market value of the stock when the option is granted or (b) 85 percent of the fair market value at exercise.
2. The option must be exercisable within five years from the date of grant where the option price is not less than 85 percent of the fair market value of the stock at exercise. If the option price is stated in any other terms, the option must not be exercisable after 27 months from the date of the grant.
3. No options may be granted to owners of five percent or more of the value or voting power of all classes of stock of the employer or its parent or subsidiary.
4. No employee may be able to purchase more than $25,000 of stock in any one calendar year.
5. The option may not be transferable (other than by will or laws of inheritance) and may be exercisable only by the employee to whom it is granted.
6. If the exercise price was less than the value of the stock upon grant and the option was exercised, the employee may have compensation income (with an offsetting deduction by the employer) upon disposition, including a transfer at death. The compensation equals the lesser of fair market value at grant or at exercise, less the exercise price, and is added to the stock basis. There is no offsetting deduction by the employer.

EXAMPLE 4.36

Brenda Tripper was given a Section 423 option to buy 500 shares of Zoom, Inc. stock for $45 a share when it was selling for $51. She exercised the option two years later when the stock was selling for $58 and sold the stock after another three years for $71 a share. The lesser of $58 or $51, less $45 a share, or $6 a share, is compensation in the year of sale, i.e., $3,000. Brenda's basis is increased by $6 a share to $51. Thus, her long-term capital gain is $20 per share ($71 – $51), or $10,000. If Brenda had died, rather than sold the shares, her final return would show $3,000 in compensation but no capital gain. (Her basis increase of $6 a share would be irrelevant, since her death results in a fair market value basis.)

¶4655 NONSTATUTORY STOCK OPTION PLANS

The term "nonstatutory stock options" refers to those options that do not qualify for the favorable tax treatment accorded options that are covered by a specific Code provision as are qualified stock options, incentive stock options, employee stock purchase plans, and restricted stock options. Code Secs. 421-425. While statutory options generally are not taxed until the taxpayer disposes of the options and any gains on the dispositions are taxed at capital gains rates, nonstatutory stock options usually are taxed at ordinary income rates at the time they are granted, the options being considered compensation for services rendered by the employee. Generally, if an option is acquired under a nonstatutory program, the employee may be taxed when (1) the option is granted, (2) the option is exercised, (3) the option is sold, or (4) the restrictions on the disposition of the option-acquired stock lapse. Reg. §1.83-7(a).

EXAMPLE 4.37   Joseph Barkin is granted a nonmarketable, nonstatutory option to buy 10,000 shares of his employer's stock at $40 per share for five years at the time the stock is selling for $36 per share. Four years later, Joseph exercises the option when the stock is selling for $47 per share. Joseph has no income, and his employer receives no deduction at the time the option is granted. Upon exercise of the option, Joseph has ordinary compensation of $70,000, the bargain element, and his employer receives a corresponding deduction. Joseph's basis in the stock is $470,000. Upon a later sale, Joseph generates a short- or long-term capital gain or loss with the holding period starting at the time the option is exercised.

The taxation of a nonstatutory stock option will depend upon the date when the option was granted. Generally, if the nonstatutory option was granted after April 21, 1969, its taxation will be determined by Code Sec. 83 and Reg. §1.83-7. Thus, if the option has a readily ascertainable fair market value at the time it is granted in connection with the performance of services, the person who performed the services realizes compensation either (1) when the rights in the option become transferable, or (2) when the right in the option is not subject to a substantial risk of forfeiture. If the option does not have an ascertainable fair market value at the time when it is granted, taxation occurs when the right to receive the stock is unconditional. The difference between the option cost and the fair market value of the stock at the time the optionee has a right to receive it is taxed as compensation.

SUMMARY

- The economic benefit doctrine and the constructive receipt doctrine were conceived to explain what constitutes income and when an item of income is taxable.

- Under the accrual method of accounting, income is recognized when a transaction is consummated; under the cash method of accounting, income is recognized only when cash is received or constructively received.

- Section 61(a) of the Internal Revenue Code provides a list of 15 items that are includible in gross income. Gross income, however, is not limited to these items. (See checklist on the next page.)

- Several rules, including the alimony recapture rules, govern when alimony payments should be included in the recipient's gross income and when they are deductible by the payer.

- Alimony is support payment made from one spouse to the other after divorce or legal separation. Child support consists of payments made by one spouse that are specifically identified for the support of minor children. Alimony and child support payments are subject to different tax treatments.

- When a debt is cancelled for a consideration, the debtor realizes taxable income for the amount of the debt discharged. Special rules govern the discharge of indebtedness for insolvent taxpayers.

CHECKLIST

Inclusions in Gross Income

Agreement not to Compete	Gambling Winnings
Alimony	Hobby Income
Annuities	Illegal Transactions (gains from gambling, betting, lotteries, embezzlement, protection money, etc.)
Awards	Insider's Profits
Back Pay	Interest
Bad Debt Recoveries	Jury Duty Fees
Bargain Purchase from Employer	Kickbacks
Bonuses	Mileage Allowance
Breach of Contract Damages	Military Pay
Buried Treasure	Notary Fees
Business Income	Partnership Income
Cancellation of Debts	Pensions
Cancellation of Lease	Per Diem Allowance
Christmas Bonuses	Prizes
Commissions	Professional Fees
Compensation for Personal Services	Punitive Damages
Debts Forgiven	Rents
Director's Fees	Retirement Pay
Discounts	Rewards
Dividends	Royalties
Embezzlement Proceeds	Salaries
Employee Death Benefits	Severance Pay
Employee's Awards	Social Security Benefits for the
Employee's Bonuses	Well-to-Do
Estate and Trust Income	Supplemental Unemployment
Benefits	Tips and Gratuities
Executor's Fees	Travel Allowances
Fees	Unemployment Compensation
Gain from Sale of Property	U.S. Savings Bonds (interest)
Gain from Sale of Securities (including government securities)	Wages

QUESTIONS

1. Explain and differentiate between the three concepts of income: economic, legal, and accounting.

2. Compare and contrast the economic benefit doctrine and the constructive receipt doctrine.

3. Explain the fruit-of-the-tree doctrine and why it was established by the courts.

4. Ilana is short of money, so he asks his boss for an advance of $25. Is this taxable income to Ilana?

5. Mr. Chen directs his employer to deduct $50 per week from his pay for the purchase of U.S. savings bonds. Can Mr. Chen exclude this amount from his gross income? Explain.

6. Distinguish between compensation and gifts and identify the tax consequence associated with each.

7. Under what conditions will scholarships or fellowships granted by an educational institution not be included in gross income.

8. Are selling and administrative expenses of a business deducted before or after gross income?

9. In a rental agreement, when are improvements to the property made by the lessee regarded as income?

10. Describe under what terms a stock dividend would not be included in gross income.

11. An elderly woman gives stocks and bonds to her son for management and safekeeping. She keeps the stocks and bonds in her own name. He is to manage the portfolio at his choosing. To whom are the dividends and capital gains taxable at year-end?

12. Under what conditions are alimony payments from divorces included in the recipient's gross income?

13. Give some examples of payments not qualifying as alimony.

14. Describe the intent of the "front-loading" provisions with respect to alimony payments.

15. Explain the tax status of child support payments.

16. Are payments for a life insurance policy that is owned by a former spouse who is the beneficiary of the policy deductible as alimony by the payer?

17. John and Jane divorced in 2017. They have two children, ages 6 and 11. The divorce decree requires John to pay $800 a month to Jane and does *not* specify the use of the money. According to the decree, the payments will stop after the children reach 18 or graduate from high school, whichever comes first. May John deduct the payments as alimony?

18. All of the following would be *excluded* from income as a qualified scholarship by an individual who is a candidate for a degree at a qualified educational institution, except:
    a. Tuition
    b. Student fees
    c. Course books
    d. Room and board

19. On January 1, 2016, John made a loan of $6,000 to his neighbor. The loan was evidenced by a written promise to repay the principal within three years and was to bear interest at a rate of 6% per annum. John's neighbor paid interest for the first year only and then his financial condition deteriorated. In 2017, John learned that he would only be able to recover $3,000 of the loan. The loan was *not* made in the course of John's business. May John deduct $3,000 of the loan on his tax return?

20. If another person cancels or pays your debts, but not as a loan or gift, have you constructively received this amount, and generally must you include it in your gross income for the year?

PROBLEMS

21. Leah Sarah is employed at Cleveland Inc. at an annual salary of $45,000. Leah received $35,000 in salary in 2017 from Cleveland Inc., a prosperous company. They credited the unpaid salary to Leah Sarah's account. Leah only had to stop by the payroll office to receive her money. In January 2018, Leah Sarah requested and received the remaining $10,000 of her salary. How much income must Leah Sarah report on her 2017 income tax return?

22. Cal Corey and his wife are living in Las Vegas, Nevada, and own an apartment house from which they receive $20,000 a year in net rental income. Cal's wife also owns an apartment house, which she purchased as an investment while she was working before their recent marriage. The net rental income from this building is $15,000 a year. If the Coreys file separate returns what would each file for rental income on their tax returns?

23. Fred Miller, a teacher, had several additional sources of income during 2017. He received a $500 gift as a result of his helping a friend build a house, and he was assigned $300 of interest due his uncle on bonds his uncle owns. He also had the use of a van (value of $1,000) for the year from his parents who were traveling. Further, he received free, $600 of gasoline for the van because he tutored the son of the station owner free of charge. What of the additional income must be included in his income tax return?

24. Helen Troy, a student seeking a Master's degree in accounting, was awarded a 50 percent scholarship to graduate school (valued at $3,000) and a $6,000 per year teaching assistantship (not required of Master's level students). She also, because of her great beauty, won first prize in the Miss International Beauty Pageant. The prize included $14,000 in cash, a $25,000 car, a $10,000 scholarship, and travel expenses of $2,000 relating to the pageant. What must she include as gross income?

25. Billy Dent, as the owner of an apartment building, receives and makes the following payments during 2017:

Received in January 2017 rent that was due in December 2016	$5,000
Received in December 2017 rent not due until January 2018	4,000
Security deposit which is to be refunded when tenant vacates the apartment	500

How much rental income must Billy Dent include on his 2017 income tax return?

26. Abby, a cash basis taxpayer, is paid an annual salary of $250,000 plus a percentage of net profits. The additional compensation for 2017 was $50,000. This sum is payable to her on February 9, 2018 after the annual audit had been completed. However, a tentative credit of $10,000 was entered to her drawing account on December 1, 2017 and was immediately available to her. Abby comes to your office and asks you how much compensation must be included in her gross income for 2017. What will you tell her? Why?

27. Judd Harrison owns 200 shares of stock in the Widget Company for which he paid $1,600 in 1999. The board of directors of the company decided to pay a 10 percent stock dividend in April 2017, for which Judd received 20 shares of stock. Was this a taxable stock dividend? Explain.

28. Joe and Mabel, a married couple filing a joint return, have modified adjusted gross income of $385,000. Included in this sum is $100,000 of net investment income. Are Joe and Mabel subject to the 3.8 percent Net Investment Income Tax?

29. Abby is a single taxpayer with $250,000 of modified adjusted gross income which includes $80,000 of net investment income. Abby owes 3.8 percent Net Investment Income Tax on what amount of her income?

30. In January 2018, Judd Harrison decides to sell 100 shares in the Widget Company. Since April 2017, no stock dividends had been paid by the company. On the date the stock is sold the market price is $12 a share. What is the basis per share that Judd must use in computing any gains or losses? (Refers back to Problem 27.)

31. In 2017, Ollie Lingo and his wife have several endowment life insurance policies. On the first, which begins payment in 2018, but was fully paid by 2010, a dividend of $200 is declared and paid. On the second, which began payment in 2016, a $500 dividend is paid. On the third, which has two more years before it is paid up, a dividend of $100 is paid. How much of dividends received, if anything, is to be excluded from gross income? (In none of the cases cited above has the taxpayer received dividends in excess of premiums paid.)

32. For each independent situation, determine the amount, if any, that is includible in the gross income of the employee.
    a. The employee of a motel has the choice of free lodging on the premises (fair market value $400 per week) or extra cash compensation. He is not required to live on premises. He chooses the lodging.
    b. An employee arranges to have his annual bonus, $1,000, paid directly to his son. His objective is to make a wedding gift to the son.
    c. An employee earns a salary of $500 per week. Pursuant to a court order, $100 of his salary goes to his ex-wife for child support.

33. R.E. Lee entered into a 10-year lease in 2012 with Mr. Grant. In addition to the $18,000 a year rent he paid in 2017, he prepaid two months of 2018 rent totaling $3,000. Also, in 2017, Mr. Lee remodeled the kitchen at a cost of $4,500. How much rental income must Mr. Grant include in gross income in 2017? What is the tax status to Mr. Grant of the remodeling work completed by Mr. Lee?

34. Arnold and Barbara Cane were divorced in June 2017. Pursuant to the divorce decree, Arnold is obliged to perform as follows:
    a. Transfer title of their personal home to Barbara. They purchased the house in 1998 and their basis today is $400,000. The fair market value of the house is $500,000. The house is subject to a 25-year, $250,000 mortgage.
    b. Arnold is to continue making payments on the house until it is fully paid off. In 2017, Arnold made payments totaling $18,000.
    c. Arnold is to make $3,000 per month payments to Barbara. Of this amount one-half is for child support. The divorce decree further states that alimony is to cease upon the death of the wife. In 2017, he made six payments.

    How do the transactions in the divorce agreement affect Arnold's and Barbara's taxable income?

35. John and Mary Johnson were divorced in January 2017. By terms of their divorce decree John had to pay alimony to Mary at the rate of $50,000 in 2017, $25,000 in 2018, and zero in 2019. For the first three years of the agreement, determine what portions of the payments are deductible by John and includible in Mary's gross income.

36. Roy Rainer will pay his wife, Mae, alimony according to the following schedule:

Year 1	$50,000
Year 2	$40,000
Year 3–Year 8	$20,000

Roy and Mae were divorced on January 6, 2017.

For the first three years of the agreement, what portions are excludable and includible in Mae's gross income?

37. Richard and Sally Murphy were divorced in 2015. By the terms of their decree Richard pays Sally $1,000 a month for alimony and child support. When Jane, their 14-year-old daughter, reaches age 18, the payments will be reduced by $300 per month.

    Explain to Richard and Sally their tax status for 2017.

38. An individual performed special valuable services not called for by his employment, in consideration for which his employer agreed to pay him a bonus in an amount to be determined later. After due consideration, however, the firm prefers instead to cement the employee's relation to it by selling him, without any restriction, a block of its stock worth $5,000 for $1,000 cash. Has the employee thereby received any amount includible in his gross income for the year?

39. A married taxpayer, age 57, has the following receipts:

Salary	$50,000
Dividends from stock of domestic corporation	1,455
Interest on state toll road bonds	750
Gambling winnings	110
Rents	5,600

During the tax year, the taxpayer pays $2,200 in taxes on his rental property and $2,650 for its operation and maintenance. He had gambling losses of $65. He made no charitable contributions. Calculate the taxpayer's gross income, adjusted gross income, and taxable income.

40. Robert Reed, a bachelor, maintains his parents in a nursing home. They have no income of their own and are completely dependent on their son. His parents are 75 and 72 years of age. Robert has the following sources of income:

Salary	$45,000
Interest on Municipal Bonds	750
Interest on Bank Accounts	800
Dividends on Common Stock of U.S. Corporation	500

Robert has itemized deductions of $12,000. Robert owns several apartment buildings. His net rental income was $3,000 for the year. Then, on December 31 one of his best tenants brought in a check for $500. This money covers the months of December and January. Robert is confused on how to account for this rental income. It is not included in the $3,000 listed above. Compute Robert's taxable income.

41. Fran Finery's boutique has assets of $100,000 and liabilities of $140,000. Fran's major creditor cancels $50,000 in liabilities.

Discuss the tax ramifications of this forgiveness of debt. Assume the majority of Fran's assets are depreciable property. Discuss the tax ramifications facing the Finery Corporation assuming it is not in bankruptcy. Then, discuss the ramifications assuming the Finery Corporation is in bankruptcy.

42. If Mack Mudd becomes insolvent with assets of $35,000 and liabilities of $65,000 and one of his creditors cancels a debt of $10,000, what amount must Mack recognize as income?

43. Faraway Travel, Inc. granted its vice-president, Chris Best, an incentive stock option on 1,000 shares of Faraway stock at $25 a share, its fair market value, on July 22, Year 1. Chris exercised the option on October 31, Year 2, at $42 a share and sold the stock for $47 a share on December 15, Year 3.
    a. What were the tax consequences to Chris?
    b. To Faraway?
    c. What difference, if any, does it make if Chris sold the stock on October 31, Year 3?

44. **IRS Adapted Problem.** Mr. Garcia, a cash-basis taxpayer, owns an apartment building. His records reflect the following information for 2017:

Tenant G paid cost of floor repairs that were Mr. Garcia's responsibility	$950
Security deposits to be returned to tenants upon expiration of their leases in 2019	1,350
Advance rents received in December for the first six months of 2018	3,000

What is the amount of gross rental income Mr. Garcia should include in his gross income?
    a. $2,300
    b. $3,000
    c. $3,950
    d. $4,350
    e. $5,300

45. **IRS Adapted Problem.** Roger signed for a ten-year lease to rent office space from Doug. In the first year, Roger paid Doug $5,000 for the first year's rent and $5,000 as rent for the last year of the lease. How much must Doug include in income in the first year of the lease?
   a. $0
   b. $5,000
   c. $5,500
   d. $10,000

46. **IRS Adapted Problem.** Each of the following would be one of the requirements for a payment to be alimony under instruments executed after 1984 except:
   a. Payments are required by a divorce or separation instrument.
   b. Payments can be a noncash property settlement.
   c. Payments are *not* designated in the instrument as *not* alimony.
   d. Payments are *not* required after death of the recipient spouse.

47. **IRS Adapted Problem.** Robert divorced Laura in 2014. During 2017, per the divorce decree, Robert made the following payments:

The entire mortgage payment on house (jointly owned, and payments with stop after death of the recipient spouse)	$10,800
Tuition for their child	$6,000
Child support	$4,500
Life insurance policy premiums on policy owned by Laura	$3,000

What is the amount Robert can deduct as alimony on his 2017 tax return?
   a. $3,000
   b. $5,400
   c. $8,400
   d. $10,800

48. The "fruit-of-the-tree" concept is associated with which doctrine regarding income:
   a. Constructive Receipt Doctrine
   b. Assignment of Income Doctrine
   c. Economic Benefit Doctrine
   d. All of the above
   e. None of the above.

49. Which of the following item(s) must be included in an individual's return as income?
   a. Compensation for services
   b. Prizes and awards
   c. Inheritance
   d. (a) and (b)
   e. All of the above.

50. **IRS Adapted Problem.** In which of the following situations will the divorced custodial parent be entitled to the dependency exemption for the child?
   a. The noncustodial parent provides $1,500 of support for the child and the custodial parent provides $1,200.
   b. The custodial and noncustodial parent both provide $1,500 of support for the child.
   c. The custodial parent provides $1,500 of support for the child and the noncustodial parent provides $1,200.
   d. All of the above.

51. **IRS Adapted Problem.** Which of the following is not considered "constructive receipt" income in 2017?
   a. Andrew Mason was informed that his check for services rendered was available on December 15, 2017, but he waited until January 16, 2018, to pick up the check.
   b. A payment on a sale of real property placed in escrow on December 16, 2017, but not received by Benjamin Miles until January 12, 2018, when the transaction was closed.
   c. Earned income of Candice Cord was received by her agent on December 30, 2017, but was not received by her until January 5, 2018.
   d. Daniel Dryer received a check on December 30, 2017, for services rendered, but was unable to make a deposit until January 5, 2018.
   e. Ellen Elks received stock on December 30, 2017, for services rendered, but was unable to find a buyer for the stock until January 20, 2018.

52. **IRS Adapted Problem.** A distribution of stock or stock rights is generally considered a taxable dividend unless it is which of the following:
    a. A distribution in lieu of money
    b. A proportionate distribution
    c. A distribution with respect to preferred stock
    d. A distribution of convertible preferred stock

53. **Comprehensive Problem (Tax Return Problem).** David and Doris Kelley were divorced on February 3, 2017. They lived apart during 2017. The divorce decree required David to make the following payments:
    a. Transfer full title to their jointly owned family home to Doris. Fair market value of the home is $180,000, basis $150,000.
    b. $1,000 per month mortgage payments on the house, above. The mortgage has 20 years remaining before being fully paid off, but the payments would end on her death.
    c. $2,000 per month for 10 years' support payments to Doris, of which $600 per month is child support.
    d. Doris insisted that the children attend private schools. In 2017, David paid $1,500 in tuition for the children's private high school.

    David paid his lawyer $5,000 to represent him in the divorce proceedings. David and Doris agreed that Doris would maintain a home for the children. Further, Doris agreed to allow David to claim one child as a dependency exemption. This agreement was put in writing and signed by Doris.

    Besides the divorce, David has had a big year financially. He owns an apartment house and he requires each new tenant to place a $750 security deposit with him before moving into the apartment. When the tenant ultimately vacates the apartment, David will refund the deposit. In 2017, David collected $3,750 in security deposits and rental income of $15,000.

    David entered a local raffle in 2017. David won first prize, which was a new automobile with a window price of $20,000. He checked with several local car dealers and was positive that if he had purchased a similar car on his own, the price would have been $18,200.

    David loaned his sister Lois $5,000. Lois was repaying the loan at $100 per month plus interest of $40. Since Lois was about to depart on an extended vacation on December 2, 2017, she gave David $200 plus interest of $80 to cover the months of December and January.

    David has a good job that pays an annual salary of $50,000. In 2017, business was very good and in December 2017 bonuses were announced for the employees. David earned a $4,000 bonus for 2017. Bonuses would be mailed to the employees during the first week of January 2018. David has itemized deductions of $20,000.

    Determine David's 2017 taxable income.

54. **Comprehensive Problem (Tax Return Problem).** Bert and Barbara Longfelt support in nursing homes both Bert's parents and Barbara's parents. Bert's parents are 70 and 68 years of age respectively and have no income except for the $3,600 in Social Security they receive annually. Barbara's parents, both 72 years of age, have the following sources of income:

Social Security	$9,800
Interest Income (Joint Ownership)	$2,600
Dividend Income	$900

Bert's annual salary is $45,000 and his wife's annual salary is $55,000.

They have two small children who live at home. Also, they own an apartment house from which they derive $6,000 net rental income. Two items from their rental property confused them so they did not include them in their rental income:

Security deposits received and to be used against final month's rent	$500
Two tenants paid rent in advance in December 2017. The rent was due January 1, 2018	$600

Barbara owned stock prior to her marriage to Bert and received the following cash dividends:

General Corp. nonqualified common stock dividend (U.S. corporation)	$300
Live Forever Life Insurance Co. (dividends on life insurance policy)	$100

Bert and Barbara have several sources of interest income:

Interest income from savings accounts	$850
Interest income from State of Tennessee Highway Bonds	$400

Barbara entered the local area bake-off, won first place for her cherry pie, and received a $1,000 cash prize.

Bert, who is an accountant, made an arrangement with Harold the dentist. Bert would do Harold's tax work if Harold would take care of Bert and his family's dental work. During the year, Bert estimated that the value of his services to Harold was $900 and that Harold gave Bert and his family $1,800 worth of dental services. In December, Bert did a consulting assignment on a weekend and received $700. No Social Security or taxes were withheld.

During the year, they had $15,000 withheld for federal taxes.

During 2017, Bert and Barbara have $14,000 of itemized deductions. Compute Bert and Barbara's net tax due, including self-employment tax. Assume dividends are taxed at ordinary rates.

55. **Research Problem.** Robert Olsen was a very successful college basketball player. Knowing that he would be offered a multimillion dollar contract, he established a corporation assigning to it his services in professional sports in exchange for a monthly salary. Upon audit the IRS challenged this assignment of contract. Who will prevail? See *C. Johnson,* 78 TC 882, Dec. 39,069 (1982).

Chapter

5

Gross Income—Exclusions

OBJECTIVES

After completing Chapter 5, you should be able to:

1. List the items specifically excluded from gross income.
2. Distinguish between exclusions and deductions.
3. Determine the nontaxable portion of life insurance and annuities.
4. Determine the nontaxable portion of Social Security benefits.
5. Distinguish between taxable and nontaxable interest income.
6. Determine the tax status of various fringe benefits.
7. Understand the tax status of various educational assistance plans.

OVERVIEW

Section 61(a) of the Internal Revenue Code defines gross income as including "all income from whatever source derived." It includes all income unless expressly exempted by law. The exempted classes are referred to as "exclusions from gross income." This chapter discusses those items that have been specifically excluded from gross income. In addition to several cash considerations, a major portion of the chapter will be dedicated to a discussion of various types of fringe benefits. Finally, the tax status of these elements of income and their relative value to employees will be discussed.

No matter what the type of job, taxes take a significant portion of each weekly or monthly paycheck. Therefore, the proper arrangement of income to derive the greatest benefit from sources which are includible and excludable in gross income is of great importance.

Sections 101 through 139 of the Internal Revenue Code list "Items Specifically Excluded from Gross Income." Selected sections are as follows:

Sec.	Description
Sec. 101.	Certain death benefits
Sec. 102.	Gifts and inheritances
Sec. 103.	Interest on state and local bonds
Sec. 104.	Compensation for injuries or sickness
Sec. 105.	Amounts received under accident and health plans
Sec. 106.	Contributions by employer to accident and health plans
Sec. 107.	Rental value of parsonages
Sec. 108.	Income from discharge of indebtedness
Sec. 109.	Improvements by lessee on lessor's property
Sec. 110.	Qualified lessee construction allowances for short-term leases.
Sec. 111.	Recovery of tax benefit items
Sec. 112.	Certain combat zone compensation of members of the Armed Forces
Sec. 115.	Income of States, municipalities, etc.
Sec. 117.	Qualified scholarships
Sec. 118.	Contributions to the capital of a corporation
Sec. 119.	Meals or lodging furnished for the convenience of the employer
Sec. 120.	Amounts received under qualified group legal services plans
Sec. 121.	Exclusion of gain from sale of principal residence
Sec. 122.	Certain reduced uniformed services retirement pay
Sec. 123.	Amounts received under insurance contracts for certain living expenses
Sec. 125.	Cafeteria plans
Sec. 126.	Certain cost-sharing payments
Sec. 127.	Educational assistance programs
Sec. 129.	Dependent care assistance programs
Sec. 130.	Certain personal injury liability assignments
Sec. 131.	Certain foster care payments
Sec. 132.	Certain fringe benefits
Sec. 134.	Certain military benefits
Sec. 135.	Income from United States savings bonds used to pay higher education tuition and fees
Sec. 136.	Energy conservation subsidies provided by public utilities
Sec. 137.	Adoption assistance programs
Sec. 138.	Medicare Advantage MSA
Sec. 139.	Disaster relief payments
Sec. 139A.	Federal subsidies for prescription drug plans
Sec. 139B.	Benefits provided to volunteer firefighters and emergency medical responders.
Sec. 139C.	COBRA premium assistance
Sec. 139D.	Indian health care benefits
Sec. 139E.	Indian general welfare benefits
Sec. 140.	Cross references to other Acts

Note that the items listed are exclusions from gross income. Do not confuse exclusions from gross income with deductions from gross income, a subject discussed in later chapters. Basically, an exclusion does not appear on the individual's tax return, whereas deductions must appear. It should be noted that even though some income sources may be considered exclusions and are not reported on an individual's 1040 tax return, they may still be subject to tax (i.e., a gift which requires a gift tax return by the donor). This chapter provides an overview of commonly encountered exclusions. Not all types of exclusions are discussed in this chapter. For example, Sections 107 and 118 are not discussed. The exclusions from income which will be discussed more fully include cafeteria plans, life insurance, fringe benefits, and retirement plans.

Common Exclusions from Gross Income

¶5001 GIFTS AND INHERITANCES

A gift, bequest, or inheritance is excluded from gross income. Code Sec. 102(a). Therefore, it follows that the donor does not receive a tax deduction for the property transmitted. A gift transpires when there is a valid transfer of property from one individual to another for no consideration. If property received by gift or inheritance later produces income, the income is taxable. Although the recipient of a gift pays no tax on receipt of the gift, the donor may be required to pay a transfer tax, known as the gift tax.

¶5015 LIFE INSURANCE PROCEEDS

Generally, life insurance proceeds received by the beneficiary are not included in gross income if such amounts are paid by reason of death of the insured. Code Sec. 101(a)(1). Premiums on life insurance policies are not deductible by the insured; therefore, it logically follows that the proceeds from the policy would be excluded from gross income. It is immaterial who the beneficiary is or whether the policy was part of a "group" life insurance plan or was individually purchased. If, however, the payment is delayed and the total amount when received includes some interest, the interest is taxable.

When the proceeds are received for reasons other than death, such as surrender of a life insurance policy, the insured is allowed to recover tax free the amount actually paid for the contract. Code Sec. 72(e)(2)(B). If the cost of the policy exceeds the proceeds, the loss is not deductible. *London Shoe Co., Inc.*, 35-2 USTC ¶9664, 80 F.2d 230 (CA-2 1935), cert. denied, 298 U.S. 663, 56 S.Ct. 747.

In computing the premiums paid under the policy, all dividends received must be subtracted from the amounts paid in.

EXAMPLE 5.1

> Ralph Rogers surrendered an endowment policy and received $25,000 from the insurance company. Over time, Ralph had paid in $14,500 in premiums. He must recognize $10,500 ($25,000 – $14,500) of income. He may exclude from income only the amount of his total premiums paid.

Amounts received under a life insurance contract after December 31, 1996, on the life of the insured, terminally or chronically ill individual may be excluded from gross income.

¶5025 SALE OF RESIDENCE

Gross income may not include all the gain realized from the sale or exchange of a principal residence. The gain to be excluded is limited to a maximum of $500,000 ($250,000 for married individual filing a separate return). For detailed discussion, see Chapter 11.

¶5035 RECOVERY OF TAX BENEFIT ITEMS

Gross income includes amounts received that were part of an earlier year deduction or credit. This is considered a recovery and generally must be included in gross income in the year received. Common types of recoveries are refunds, such as state tax tax refunds, and reimbursements or rebates. Chapter 8, ¶8115, discusses state income tax refunds and the tax benefit rule.

¶5055   RETIREMENT INCOME

Historically, Social Security benefits, both monthly and lump-sum, had been excluded from tax. The exclusion extended to benefits received under the Railroad Retirement Act. Benefits received from retirement systems of other countries are not excluded from the federal income tax.

A portion of the Social Security benefits or railroad retirement benefits must be included in taxable income for taxpayers whose provisional income exceeds a base of $25,000 for a single taxpayer ($32,000 for a married taxpayer filing a joint return and zero for a married person filing a separate return). Provisional income equals modified adjusted gross income plus one-half the Social Security benefits received. Modified adjusted gross means adjusted gross income plus interest on tax-exempt bonds, interest on U.S. savings bonds used to pay higher education tuition and fees, employer adoption assistance, the interest deduction on higher education loans, the deduction for qualified education expenses, and the foreign income exclusion. The amount of Social Security benefits includible in taxable income is the lesser of one-half of the benefits or one half of the excess of the taxpayer's provisional income over the base.

EXAMPLE 5.2

Bill and Linda Peterson, both over age 65, have the following sources of income:

Interest Income (taxable)	$26,000
Dividend Income	4,000
Net Rental Income	6,000
Adjusted Gross Income	$36,000
Social Security Benefits	$15,000
Computations:	
Adjusted Gross Income	$36,000
1/2 of Social Security Benefits	7,500
Provisional Income	$43,500
Base Amount for Married Couple	32,000
Excess	$11,500
50 Percent of Excess	$5,750

Of the $15,000 Bill and Linda received in Social Security benefits, they must include $5,750 in their gross income. Remember, the maximum amount to be included in gross income is the lesser of 50 percent of the "excess" or 50 percent of the Social Security benefit received.

EXAMPLE 5.3

Assume the same facts as in Example 5.2, except that Bill and Linda also have $9,000 of interest income from tax-exempt bonds.

Computations:	
Adjusted Gross Income from Example 5.2	$36,000
Plus: Tax-Exempt Interest	9,000
1/2 of Social Security Benefits	7,500
Provisional Income	$52,500
Less: Base Amount for Married Couples	32,000
Excess	$20,500
50 Percent of Excess	$10,250

In this instance, Bill and Linda must include $7,500 in their gross income. This is because 50 percent of their Social Security benefits is the maximum amount that can be included in gross income.

Social Security benefits are taxable to the individual who receives the benefits. Therefore, if a child receives Social Security benefits, the benefits are taxable to the child using the same formulas that are discussed above.

The Revenue Reconciliation Act of 1993 created a second threshold for years after 1993. This second threshold applies to taxpayers with provisional income greater than $34,000 for a single taxpayer and $44,000 for a married taxpayer filing a joint return. Taxpayers with provisional income exceeding the second threshold will be taxed up to 85 percent of their Social Security benefits.

Taxpayers with provisional income exceeding these amounts will include the lesser of:

A. 85 percent of the taxpayer's Social Security benefits, or
B. the total of the following calculation:
   1. 85 percent of the amount that provisional income exceeds the new threshold amounts, plus
   2. the smaller of: (a) the amount of Social Security benefits included under prior law; or (b) $4,500 for an unmarried taxpayer, or $6,000 for married taxpayers filing jointly.

Married taxpayers filing separate returns have no base amount and must include in gross income the lesser of: (a) 85 percent of their Social Security benefits; or (b) 85 percent of their provisional income. For illustrations when provisional income exceeds the thresholds, see Examples 5.6 through 5.9.

EXAMPLE 5.4	Linda, a single taxpayer, has AGI of $26,000 and Social Security benefits of $8,000. Linda's provisional income is $30,000 and she must include in her AGI $2,500 of her Social Security benefits. Inasmuch as her provisional income is below the threshold amount ($34,000), she includes in AGI the lesser of 50 percent of her Social Security benefits or one-half the excess of combined income over the base.

EXAMPLE 5.5	Philip and Linda, a married couple filing a joint return, have AGI of $30,000 and Social Security benefits of $14,000. Therefore their provisional income is $37,000. Philip and Linda must include in their AGI $2,500 of their Social Security benefits. Inasmuch as provisional income, $37,000, does not exceed the threshold amount ($44,000), only $2,500 is included in the AGI of Philip and Linda.

EXAMPLE 5.6	Pat, a single taxpayer, has AGI of $36,000 and she received $10,000 in Social Security benefits. Pat's provisional income is therefore $41,000. Pat must include in her AGI $8,500 of her Social Security benefits. This is computed as follows: A. $10,000 × 85% = $8,500 B. [($41,000 – $34,000) × 85%] + $4,500 = $10,450

EXAMPLE 5.7	Steve and Marla, a married couple filing a joint return, have AGI of $50,000 and Social Security benefits of $14,000. Steve and Marla have provisional income of $57,000. They must include $11,900 of their Social Security benefits in their gross income. This is computed as follows: A. $14,000 × 85% = $11,900 B. [($57,000 – $44,000) × 85%] + $6,000 = $17,050

EXAMPLE 5.8	Ron, a single taxpayer, has AGI of $32,000 of income and $8,000 of Social Security benefits. Ron's provisional income is $36,000 and he must include $5,700 of his Social Security benefits in his income. This is computed as follows: A. $8,000 × 85% = $6,800 B. [($36,000 – $34,000) × 85%] + $4,000* = $5,700 *$8,000 × 50% = $4,000 maximum includible under prior law

EXAMPLE 5.9

Norm and Pat, a married couple filing a joint return, have AGI of $40,000 and Social Security benefits of $12,000. Norm and Pat have provisional income of $46,000 and they must include $7,700 of Social Security benefits in their AGI. This is computed as follows:

A. $12,000 × 85% = $10,200
B. [($46,000 – $44,000) × 85%] + $6,000* = $7,700

*$12,000 × 50% = $6,000 maximum includible under prior law

¶5075 INTEREST ON GOVERNMENT OBLIGATIONS

Savings Bonds

Interest earned on United States savings bonds is fully taxable. On Series EE bonds, no interest per se is paid each year, but the bond is issued at a discount and each year increases in value until maturity. The difference between the purchase price of the bond and the redemption value is taxable interest income. Cash basis taxpayers have the choice of reporting interest income on a yearly basis or reporting all interest income when the bonds finally mature, while accrual basis taxpayers must accrue the increase in the redemption value each year as interest. If cash basis taxpayers exercise the election to report the interest currently, all such bonds owned by them must be similarly treated for all subsequent years.

Taxpayers who elected to defer recognizing income until the bonds mature may change their method of reporting income to a yearly basis without permission from the IRS. However, in the year of change all interest accrued to date, not previously reported, must be included in gross income.

Series EE bonds were first issued in 1980. Prior to 1980, Series E bonds were issued. Series HH bonds replaced Series H bonds in 1980, as well. Series HH and Series H bonds are treated identically for tax purposes. August 2004 was the last date that Series HH bonds were issued. After that date taxpayers were no longer able to reinvest series HH bonds or exchange series EE bonds for HH bonds. These bonds are issued at face value and interest is paid twice a year by check. Cash basis taxpayers must report interest income in the year it is received.

Taxpayers who owned Series E bonds prior to 1980 and did not report interest income on a yearly basis could trade their E bonds for Series H bonds and not realize taxable income unless they received cash on the trade. The same rules hold for Series EE bonds as for Series HH bonds today. On the E/EE bonds, the taxpayer defers the recognition of income until the taxpayer disposes of the bonds or they mature. Then the taxpayer reports as interest income the difference between the redemption value and the total cost of traded bonds, plus any amount received at the time of trade.

EXAMPLE 5.10

Robert and Mary Moore had the following interest income in 2017:

1. Interest on Series EE bonds, $300
2. Interest on bank savings account, $400

Robert and Mary have taxable interest income of $700. If they elect, they can defer the recognition of income on the Series EE bonds until the bonds mature. In that case, then total interest to be included in gross income totals $400.

Educational Savings Bonds

A tax exclusion is provided for interest earned on U.S. savings bonds used to finance the higher education of the taxpayer, the taxpayer's spouse, or dependents. Code Sec. 135. The bonds must have been purchased after December 31, 1989, and the exclusion is available only to the individual who purchased the bonds. The purchaser of the bonds must have reached the age of 24 and be the sole owner of the bonds. The bonds must be redeemed during the same tax year in which the qualified educational expenses are incurred by the taxpayer, the taxpayer's spouse, or any dependents.

Qualified higher education expenses include tuition and fees, net of scholarships and other tuition reduction amounts. Qualified higher education expenses must be further reduced by expenses taken into account for the American Opportunity Tax Credit and Lifetime Learning credits. Books, supplies, room and board and expenses incurred for sports, games, or hobbies other than as part of a degree program are not covered.

The key to computing the exclusion is the amount of qualified higher education expenses that the individual incurs in the year the bonds are redeemed. If these expenses exceed the aggregate redemption amount (principal plus interest), then all of the interest may be excluded, subject to an income-linked phase-out discussed below. If the redemption amount is larger than the qualified educational expenses, however, the exclusion is reduced on a pro rata basis.

EXAMPLE 5.11	During 2017, Mary Adams, age 50, redeems Series EE bonds and receives $5,000 of principal and $2,500 of accrued interest. Mary's daughter attends college and has qualified expenses of $8,000. Mary may exclude from her gross income the entire $2,500 of interest.

EXAMPLE 5.12	Same facts as in Example 5.11, except Mary's daughter incurred only $6,000 in qualified expenses. Mary may exclude from gross income only $2,000. This is calculated as follows: $$\frac{\text{Qualified Expenses}}{\text{Series EE Proceeds}} = \text{Percentage Exclusion}$$ Percentage Exclusion × Series EE Interest = Interest Exclusion Percentage Exclusion = $6,000/$7,500 = 80% Interest Exclusion $2,500 × 80% = $2,000

The exclusion for accrued interest is subject to phaseout provisions. The phaseout ranges for 2017 are as follows:

Filing Status	Modified AGI
Married filing jointly	$117,250—$147,250
Single (including head of household)	$78,150—$93,150

Married individuals filing separately are not eligible for the exclusion.

For those falling within the phaseout range, the amount of interest otherwise excludable will be reduced (but not below zero) by multiplying that interest by a fraction that is determined by dividing the excess of modified AGI (that is, the excess of modified AGI over the bottom figure of the phaseout range) by the number of dollars in the phaseout range ($30,000 for joint returns and $15,000 for single taxpayers).

EXAMPLE 5.13	Same facts as in Example 5.11, but also assume that Mary is a single mother and that her modified AGI is $90,150. Mary may exclude from her gross income $500. This amount is computed as follows: $2,500 – ($2,500 × $12,000/$15,000) = $500 The $12,000 is the excess of modified AGI over the phaseout range.

State and Municipal Bonds

Interest received on state and local government bonds is generally excludable from gross income. Code Sec. 103(a). The term "state or local bond" means an obligation of a state or political subdivision, and the term "state" includes the District of Columbia and any possession of the U.S. Code Sec. 103(c). Tax-exempt bonds are an attractive investment for many well-to-do investors because the after-tax return on such bonds is considerably higher than taxable bonds.

EXAMPLE 5.14	Kayla, a highly paid corporate executive, was in the 39.6 percent marginal tax bracket. She was contemplating buying some bonds, but could not decide whether to buy corporate bonds, paying 12 percent interest, or a municipal bond, paying 9 percent. Since Kayla is in the 39.6 percent marginal tax bracket, the 12 percent corporate bond nets Kayla only 7.248 percent. Therefore, the 9 percent tax-free interest income from the municipal bonds is a better decision.

EXAMPLE 5.15	Sam Roberts, a well-to-do banker, has the following securities in his portfolio:

1. One $5,000, 10 percent corporate bond, annual interest income, $500
2. Ten shares of ABC Inc. stock, no dividends paid
3. One $10,000 bond issued by the Port Authority of N.Y. in 2008 at 6 percent
4. Dividend on life insurance policy, $100
5. One $10,000, 5 percent State of Ohio bond issued in 2007, annual interest, $500

Of the items listed above, the interest on the corporate bond must be included in gross income. The shares of stock paid no dividend; therefore, there is no dollar amount to be included in gross income. However, if a dividend had been paid, it would have been includible in Sam Roberts's gross income. The $600 interest on the Port Authority bond is fully tax-exempt as is the interest on the State of Ohio bond. The life insurance dividend is considered a reduction in premium and is not includible in gross income.

Interest received on state or local bonds is generally excludable from gross income when bond proceeds are used exclusively for traditional government purposes. However, interest on state and local bonds used to benefit other persons is not tax free when it is from (1) private activity bonds that are not exempt, (2) state or local bonds that have not been issued in registered form, or (3) arbitrage bonds.

Private Activity Bonds

Private activity bonds are issued by state and local governments to help finance private business. Private activity bonds that qualify for tax exemption include (1) exempt-facility bonds (e.g., proceeds used to finance airports, water facilities, waste disposal facilities, electric energy or gas facilities), (2) qualified mortgage bonds (proceeds used to finance certain owner-occupied residences), (3) qualified veteran's mortgage bond (issued only by five states), (4) qualified small issue bonds (face amount of bond issue is $1 million or less), (5) qualified student loan bonds, (6) qualified redevelopment bonds (proceeds used to redevelop blighted areas), or (7) qualified tax-exempt organization bonds. Code Sec. 141(e). Tax-exempt interests received by the taxpayer is not included for the regular tax computation but is included in the alternative minimum tax calculation.

Registered Bonds

In order to restrict the number of long-term bearer obligations and to maintain liquidity in the financial markets, certain obligations must be issued in a registered form in order to be tax-exempt. This applies to certain bonds issued after August 15, 1986. A registration-required bond means any bond other than a bond which (1) is not of a type offered to the public, (2) has a maturity (at issue) of not more than one year, or (3) is issued abroad with safeguards to ensure that the obligations are sold and resold only to persons who are not U.S. persons and that no interest or principal is payable to any U.S. person. Code Sec. 149.

Arbitrage Bonds

Arbitrage bonds are generally denied tax-exempt status unless a special tax or rebate is paid to the United States. Code Sec. 148. Arbitrage bonds are used for speculative purposes by state or local issuing authorities. A bond issue becomes an arbitrage issue if the proceeds are used to buy other obligations, frequently federal obligations, that have a higher yield than the state issue.

Employee Benefits

¶5101   ## FRINGE BENEFITS

In the United States today fringe benefits are a very significant part of the worker's compensation package. Compensation experts maintain that approximately one-third of a worker's gross compensation is composed of fringe benefits. From a tax viewpoint, there are two types of fringe benefits: statutory and nonstatutory. A statutory fringe benefit is specifically excluded by some provision of the law. An example of a statutory fringe benefit would be employees' accident and health plans, which are covered by Section 105 of the Internal Revenue Code. A nonstatutory fringe benefit is one not specifically mentioned in the law. Examples of nonstatutory fringe benefits are free parking for employees and an employer-subsidized cafeteria. In an effort to clear the air concerning fringe benefits, the Tax Reform Act of 1984 codified the tax treatment of a number of nonstatutory fringe benefits. Gross income specifically does not include:

1. No-additional-cost services
2. Qualified employee discounts
3. Working condition fringe benefits
4. De minimis fringe benefits (property or service, the value of which is so small as to make the accounting for it unreasonable or administratively impracticable)

Nondiscrimination rules, as set forth in Section 132, must be met for the above-listed fringe benefits.

No-Additional-Cost Services

The value of no-additional-cost services provided to employees or their spouses or dependent children by employers is excludable from income. This exclusion applies whether the service is provided directly for no charge, at a reduced price, or through a cash rebate of all or part of the amount paid for the service. Reg. §1.132-2. In order for the exclusion to apply, however, the employer must not incur any significant additional costs in providing the service to the employee (disregarding any amounts paid by the employee for the service) and the service provided to the employee must be one that is offered for sale to customers in the ordinary course of the line of business of the employer for which the employee is working.

For determining whether a fringe benefit qualifies as an excludable no-additional-cost service, transportation of passengers by air and transportation of cargo by air are treated as the same service. Thus, an employee performing services in the air cargo industry may receive air travel as a no-additional-cost service. This also includes passenger travel provided through reciprocal agreements with other airlines. Code Sec. 132(h)(8).

In determining the cost of a service, the employer must include revenue that is forgone because the service is provided to an employee rather than to a nonemployee.

EXAMPLE 5.16   Regional Airlines provides its employees with seats on flights it runs. Assuming Regional provides these seats only if, at the time the plane is ready to depart, there are empty seats for the employees to occupy, no cost is attributed to this service because of forgone revenue. However, if Regional permits its employees to book no-additional-cost seats in advance of a flight's departure and then does not offer these seats for sale to the public, forgone revenue would be attributed to the cost of providing this benefit.

In addition, an employer must include the cost of labor incurred in providing no-additional-cost services to employees for purposes of determining whether substantial additional costs have been incurred. However, labor cost is not included if the services are merely incidental to the primary services being provided.

The no-additional-cost services exclusion is available to employees of one employer for services provided to them by an unrelated employer (another employer not under common control) under a reciprocal arrangement between the two employers. For the services to qualify they must be: (1) of the same type, (2) under a written reciprocal agreement between employers, and (3) no substantial additional cost to either employer.

An employee working for an employer in multiple lines of business is limited to the line of business of the employer for which the employee works. For example, a company that owns both an airline and a hotel could not offer an employee of the airline a free hotel room. However, an important exception exists to employees who service more than one line of business. Therefore, the C.E.O. of the company or the V.P. for Finance could exclude fringes from both lines of business since they both render service to both businesses.

Examples of no-additional-cost services are excess capacity services such as hotel accommodations, telephone services, and transportation by aircraft, train, bus, subway, and cruise line.

Services that are not eligible for treatment as no-additional-cost services are nonexcess capacity services such as the use of a stock brokerage firm or a mutual fund to purchase stock or an interest in the mutual fund. However, if you receive nonexcess capacity services, the value of the benefit may be a qualified employee discount.

Qualified Employee Discounts

Certain employee discounts provided to employees on the selling price of qualified property or services of the employer are excludable from gross income. In order to be excludable, the discounts must be available to employees on a nondiscriminating basis. The employee discount may not exceed the gross profit percentage normally offered by the employer to customers. In the case of qualified services, the excludable amount cannot exceed 20 percent of the price offered to nonemployee customers.

EXAMPLE 5.17   Abigail's Cut-Rate had total sales of $1,000,000 for 2017. The cost of merchandise for this period was $500,000. Therefore, the gross profit percentage was 50 percent. The employees were offered a 60 percent discount on merchandise purchased from the company. In this case, the employees had to include 10 percent of the value of the merchandise they purchased in their gross income.

EXAMPLE 5.18   Mary Ray works for a computer manufacturer. She bought a portable computer from a local computer store and received the usual employee discount. Mary also received a one-year parts and labor warranty. Normally, the computer shop does not give one-year warranties on machines. Mary need not include the value of the discount in her income but she must include the value of the warranty.

The value of the discounts can be excluded from the income of officers, owners, or highly compensated employees only if these discounts are made available on substantially the same terms to each member of a group of employees which is defined under a reasonable classification set up by the employer that does not discriminate in favor of officers, owners, or highly compensated employees. Code Sec. 132(j).

Working Condition Fringe Benefits

The fair market value of any property or service provided to an employee by an employer as a working condition fringe benefit is excludable from the gross income of the employee to the extent that the employer can deduct the costs as an ordinary and necessary business expense.

The following are examples of working condition fringe benefits that would be excludable:

1. Value of use of an employer-provided car or plane for business purposes
2. Subscriptions to business periodicals by an employer for employees
3. Safety precautions provided by an employer for employees
4. Employer expenditures for on-the-job training or travel by an employee
5. Fair market value of the use of consumer products manufactured for sale to nonemployee customers but provided to employees for product testing and evaluation outside the employer's workplace

Qualified Transportation Fringe Benefits

Generally, transportation expenses of an employee are not deductible. However, transit passes provided to employees at a discount, not to exceed $255 per month for 2017, may be excluded from an employee's gross income. Further, employer-provided parking valued at up to $255 per month, even if it is chosen instead of cash, may be excluded from gross income.

De Minimis Fringe Benefits

De minimis fringes result when the value of the property or service provided to the employee is so minimal that accounting for it would be unreasonable. Examples of *de minimis* fringes include:

1. Typing of personal letters by company secretaries
2. Occasional personal use of the company copying machine
3. Occasional parties or picnics for employees

4. Traditional holiday gifts (small fair market value)
5. Tickets occasionally given out for entertainment events
6. Coffee and donuts furnished to employees
7. Occasional supper money or taxi fare due to overtime work

While many of these employee benefits are typically not included in an employee's gross income, in most circumstances, the employer is allowed a deduction for costs incurred.

Any cash benefit or its equivalent (such as the use of a company credit card) cannot be excluded as a de minimis benefit under any circumstances. In addition, season tickets to sporting or theatrical events, the commuting use of an employer-provided car or other vehicle more than once a month, membership in a private country club or athletic facility, and use of employer-owned or leased facilities, such as an apartment or hunting lodge, for a weekend are never excludable as de minimis fringe benefits.

¶5115   GROUP-TERM LIFE INSURANCE

An employee is allowed to exclude from gross income all of the cost of a group-term life insurance policy provided by an employer if the face amount of the policy does not exceed $50,000. Code Sec. 79. When over $50,000 of group-term life insurance is purchased, the cost of the premium for the amount of insurance over $50,000 must be included in compensation of the employee.

The $50,000 coverage limitation is eliminated and the total cost of group-term life insurance coverage in any amount is excluded from the gross income of the employee where (1) the employee is disabled, (2) the employer is directly or indirectly the beneficiary of the insurance, or (3) a charitable organization is the sole beneficiary. Some retired employees may also be entitled to a full exclusion.

For a group-term policy to be covered by Code Sec. 79, it must not discriminate in favor of highly compensated employees. It is perfectly acceptable to have a group plan where coverage is directly proportional to salary.

The cost of group-term life insurance provided to an employee during any taxable period for inclusion in the employee's gross income is to be determined under the uniform premium table method. Under this method the cost of group-term life insurance protection in excess of the excludable amount is determined on the basis of uniform premiums by five-year age brackets. The age of the employee for purposes of the age brackets used in the table is the employee's age on the last day of the tax year. The amount that must be included under the uniform premium table is generally less than the actual cost of the insurance. If the employee contributes an amount to purchase group-term life insurance, the amount is subtracted from what would otherwise be included in the employee's gross income.

| EXAMPLE 5.19 | Nine Lives Corp. purchased group-term life insurance for all its employees. The company pays 100 percent of the premiums for all employees, equal to twice the employee's salary. Otto Olson, age 52 and vice president of Nine Lives, earns $37,500 per year. Therefore, the company paid premiums on a $75,000 group-term policy. For an individual 50–54 years of age, the premium is assumed to be $2.76 (see Table 1) per $1,000 of coverage. |

Total coverage	$75,000
Tax-free group insurance	50,000
Insurance subject to tax	$25,000
Cost per thousand dollars per year of insurance for 52-year-old	$2.76
Taxable income to Otto (25 × $2.76)	$69

Table 1. UNIFORM PREMIUMS FOR $1,000 OF GROUP-TERM LIFE INSURANCE PROTECTION	
5-Year Age Bracket	**Cost Per $1,000 of Protection for 1-Month Period**
Under 25	$ .05
25 to 29	.06
30 to 34	.08
35 to 39	.09
40 to 44	.10
45 to 49	.15
50 to 54	.23
55 to 59	.43
60 to 64	.66
65 to 69	1.27
70 and above	2.06

Source: Table 1, Reg. §1.79-3(d)(2).

EXAMPLE 5.20   Assume in Example 5.19, that Otto contributes 50 cents per thousand dollars of protection per year. The amount includible in his gross income is $31.50 ($69 cost of $75,000 coverage less employee contribution of $37.50).

A company may have a group term life insurance plan where the employee pays the entire premium. If the employees are charged a uniform premium, it is still possible that some of the older workers will be subject to tax on coverage over $50,000.

EXAMPLE 5.21   Alfred Ajax is 62 years old and elects group-term insurance of $100,000 and there are no employer contributions. His employer established a uniform rate of $.25 per $1,000 per month. Alfred would have to include $96 in his gross income. The cost of the coverage over the $50,000 group policy is $396 ($0.66 × 12 months × 50). Alfred's annual contribution is $300 (.25 × 12 months × 100).

PLANNING POINTER   The fact that premiums on group-term insurance for coverage of over $50,000 are taxable to the employee need not mean that such compensation is not valuable. Usually group plans are far more attractive than policies that can be obtained individually, and therefore, may be extremely beneficial as part of a total employee compensation package.

¶5125   ANNUITIES

An annuity is a contract that pays a fixed income at set regular intervals for a specific period of time. The amount of income depends upon the premium paid, the life expectancy of the annuitant, and the number of years payments are to be received. When income is received as an annuity under an annuity, endowment, or life insurance contract, the amount received generally consists of two separate parts: (1) a nontaxable return of the annuitant's investment in the contract and (2) a taxable amount representing a gain on the investment (interest). Code Sec. 72(a).

Under special rules for the taxation of amounts received as an annuity and paid out for reasons other than the death of the insured, the tax-free portion of annuity income is spread evenly over the annuitant's lifetime. This annuity method is not limited to payments that are to be received during the taxpayer's lifetime. It also applies to payments that are to be made for a prescribed number of years.

Exclusion Ratio Formula

The excludable portion of an annuity payment is the annuity payment times the exclusion ratio. The exclusion ratio is the "investment in the contract" divided by the "expected return" under the contract as of the "annuity starting date." These terms are further defined below. The formula for determining the excludable portion may be stated as follows:

$$\text{Amount of exclusion} = \text{Total payment for the year} \times \frac{\text{Investment in the contract}}{\text{Expected return for life of contract}}$$

The following example illustrates the computation of the exclusion ratio.

EXAMPLE 5.22

Makayla Perez purchased an annuity contract that provided for payments of $100 per month. She paid $12,650 for the annuity. Makayla's expected return under the contract is assured to be $16,000.

Annual annuity payments	($100 × 12)	$1,200
Investment in the contract		12,650
Expected return		16,000
Exclusion ratio	$\frac{\$12,650}{\$16,000}$	79.1%
Monthly exclusion	($100 × 79.1%)	79.10
Monthly amount to be included in gross income		20.90

Once the exclusion ratio is determined, one of two sets of rules is applied depending on the taxpayer's annuity starting date.

1. **Annuity starting date before 1987.** The exclusion ratio is applied every year there is a payment, regardless of whether the annuitant lives beyond the life expectancy. If this happens, the annuitant may exclude, over the life of the contract, more than the cost. On the other hand, if the annuitant dies at an age earlier than that of the life expectancy, the total of the yearly exclusions will be less than the cost.
2. **Annuity starting date after 1986.** The exclusion ratio is applied to payments until the total exclusions equal the investment in the contract. All later payments are fully taxable. On the other hand, if the annuitant dies before the investment in the contract is fully recovered tax free through the annuity exclusion, an itemized deduction is provided for the last tax year in an amount equal to the unrecovered portion of the investment.

Annuity Starting Date Defined

The annuity starting date is the first day of the first period for which an amount is received as an annuity under the contract. The first day of the first period for which an amount is received as an annuity is the later of (1) the date upon which the obligations of the contract become fixed or (2) the first day of the period that ends on the date of the first annuity payment.

EXAMPLE 5.23

Henry Li purchased a deferred single life annuity on January 1, 2017, payable in monthly installments on the first of each month, beginning August 1 of that year for the preceding calendar month. The August 1 payment is for the period beginning July 1. The annuity starting date is July 1.

Investment in the Contract Defined

The investment in the contract is, generally, the total amount of premiums or other consideration paid for the contract less amounts, if any, received prior to the annuity starting date that are excludable from gross income. Accordingly, if a taxpayer paid premiums of $5,000 for an annuity contract and had recovered $1,000 tax free as of the annuity starting date, the investment in the contract for purposes of the exclusion ratio formula would be $4,000. Once payments have started and the tax-free amount of each annuity payment is determined then any increases in annuity payments are fully taxable.

Expected Return Under the Contract

The expected return under the contract is limited to amounts receivable as an annuity or as annuities. If no life expectancy is involved (as in the case of installment payments for a fixed number of years), the expected return is found by multiplying the total amount payable from the annuity installments by the number of payments to be received. Code Sec. 72(c)(3); Reg. §1.72-5(c) and (d).

To determine the expected return under contracts involving life expectancy, actuarial tables prescribed by the IRS must be used (see Tables 2–6 following Example 5.30). The tables provide a multiplier (based on life expectancy) that is applied to the annual payment in order to obtain the expected return under the contract. This procedure can become quite complex since annuities may be based, variously, on one life, joint lives only, joint lives and continuing to the last survivor, and for life or term certain.

Single Life Annuities

To demonstrate the general principles note the following example of a single life annuity.

EXAMPLE 5.24

Marvin Mariner retires at age 65. His annuity contract provides for him to receive $100 per month for life. His total premiums under the policy had been $14,400.

Annual annuity payment	($100 × 12 months)	$1,200
Multiple from Table 2, Age 65		20.0
Expected return	($1,200 × 20.0)	$24,000

Marvin had an investment cost of $14,400 in the annuity and an expected return of $24,000. Therefore, the exclusion ratio was $14,400/$24,000 = 60%. Since he receives $1,200 a year, he may exclude from gross income $720 ($1,200 × 60%). Where payments are made quarterly, semiannually, or annually, the applicable multiple shown in Table 5 may be used.

If Marvin received his first semiannual payment six full months after the annuity starting date, the adjusted multiple would be 19.8 (20.0 – .2). If Marvin were to receive $600 six months after his annuity starting date, his expected return would be $23,760 ($1,200 × 19.8). See Table 5.

Joint and Survivor Annuities

Under a joint and survivor annuity two individuals receive periodic payments for life. Some policies adjust the amount of the payment after the death of the first annuitant.

EXAMPLE 5.25

Robert and Betty Moss purchased a joint and survivorship annuity contract. The contract provided for the couple to receive $200 per month for life. Upon the death of one spouse, the surviving spouse would continue to receive $200 per month. Robert Moss was 69 years old and his wife was 66. The cost of the policy was $36,825.

Computations:

Annual annuity payments	($200 × 12)	$2,400
Multiple from Table 3		22.9
Expected return	($2,400 × 22.9)	$54,960
Investment in annuity contract		$36,825

Exclusion ratio $\dfrac{\$36,825}{\$54,960} = 67\%$

Annual exclusion	($2,400 × 67%)	$1,608

EXAMPLE 5.26

Assume the same facts as in Example 5.25, except that when the first spouse dies the surviving spouse will receive only $150 per month. The cost of the annuity is $29,450.

Computations:

Multiple from Table 3, Ages 69 and 66		22.9
Multiple from Table 4		13.1
Expected return after first death	($1,800 × 22.9)	$41,220
Expected return differential after first death	($600 × 13.1)	$7,860
Expected return from annuity		$49,080
Cost of annuity		$29,450

Exclusion ratio $\dfrac{\$29,450}{\$49,080}$ = 60%

Therefore, while both individuals are alive they can exclude $120 ($200 × 60%) per month. After the death of one spouse, the exclusion will be only $90 ($150 × 60%).

EXAMPLE 5.27

Assume the same facts as in Example 5.26, except that Robert purchases the annuity and the annuity contract provides that if Robert dies first, Betty will receive only $150 per month instead of $200. The cost of the annuity is $29,450.

Computations:

Multiple from Table 3		22.9
Multiple from Table 2		16.8
Multiple applicable to second annuitant		6.1
Expected return (first annuitant)	($2,400 × 16.8)	$40,320
Expected return (second annuitant)	($1,800 × 6.1)	$10,980
Expected return from annuity		$51,300

Exclusion ratio $\dfrac{\$29,450}{\$51,300}$ = 57.4%

Therefore, while both individuals are alive, they can exclude $114.80 ($200 × 57.4%) per month. After the death of Robert, the exclusion will be $86.10 ($150 × 57.4%) per month.

EXAMPLE 5.28 Assume the same facts as in Example 5.27, except that Robert purchases the annuity and the annuity contract provides that if Betty dies first, Robert will receive only $150 per month instead of $200. The cost of the annuity is $29,450.

Computations:

Multiple from Table 3		22.9
Multiple from Table 2		19.2
Multiple applicable to second annuitant		3.7
Expected return (first annuitant)	($2,400 × 19.2)	$46,080
Expected return (second annuitant)	($1,800 × 3.7)	$6,660
Expected return from annuity		$52,740

Exclusion ratio $\dfrac{\$29,450}{\$52,740} = 55.8\%$

Therefore, while both individuals are alive, they can exclude $111.60 ($200 × 55.8%) per month. After the death of Betty, the exclusion will be $83.70 ($150 × 55.8%) per month.

Employee Annuities

If the employer paid in all of the cost of the pension or annuity, the payments received by the employee are fully taxable to the employee. If the employee made contributions, the total amount that an employee may exclude from income is the total amount of the employee's contributions. The employee uses the exclusion ratio until the investment in the contract is recovered. Thereafter, all proceeds are included in income. Also, if the employee's benefits cease prior to the date the employee's total contributions have been recovered, the amount of unrecovered contributions is allowed as a deduction on the annuitant's last tax return.

The Small Business Job Protection Act of 1996 provides for a simplified method for determining the portion of an annuity distribution from a qualified retirement plan.

Refund Annuities

When payments are received under a guaranteed refund provision, the value of such payments reduces the investment in the contract. Obviously, where a refund has been received, an adjustment to the "investment in the contract" must be made so as to determine the excludable portion. The adjustment required to the "investment in the contract" is determined as follows:

1. Divide maximum amount guaranteed by the amount to be received annually and round off to the nearest whole year.
2. Refer to the actuarial table entitled "Percent Value of Refund Feature" to determine the appropriate percentage figure to be employed (see Table 6).
3. Multiply percentage found in the table by the smaller of (a) original investment in the contract, or (b) the total amount guaranteed.
4. Subtract the amount determined in Step 3 from the original "investment in the contract."

The following example illustrates the above provisions.

EXAMPLE 5.29	Joseph Jacobs, 65, purchased for $25,000 an immediate installment refund annuity, payable $100 per month for life. The contract provided that, in the event the husband did not live long enough to recover the full purchase price, payments were to be made to his wife until the total payments under the contract equaled the purchase price. Joe's investment in the contract adjusted for the purpose of determining the exclusion ratio is computed in the following manner:

Investment in Contract

Cost of the annuity contract (investment in the contract, unadjusted)	$25,000
Amount to be received annually	$1,200
Number of years for which payment guaranteed ($25,000 divided by $1,200)	20.8
Rounded to nearest whole number of years	21
Percentage located in Table 6 for age 65 (age of the annuitant as of the annuity starting date) and 21 (the number of whole years)	20%
Subtract value of the refund feature to the nearest dollar (20% of $25,000)	$5,000
Investment in the contract adjusted for the present value of the refund feature without discount for interest	$20,000

Monthly Exclusion

Adjusted investment in contract	$20,000
Annual payments	1,200
Multiple from Table 2, Age 65	20.0
Expected return ($1,200 × 20)	24,000

$$\text{Exclusion ratio} \quad \frac{\$20,000}{\$24,000} \quad = \quad 83.3\%$$

Monthly exclusion (83.3% of $100)	$83.33

IRS Actuarial Tables

Gender-neutral annuity tables used to compute that portion of an annuity that is includible in gross income have been adopted. These tables apply to amounts received as an annuity after June 30, 1986.

Table 2. ORDINARY LIFE ANNUITIES—ONE LIFE—EXPECTED RETURN MULTIPLES			
Age	Multiple	Age	Multiple
57	26.8	72	14.6
58	25.9	73	13.9
59	25.0	74	13.2
60	24.2	75	12.5
61	23.3	76	11.9
62	22.5	77	11.2
63	21.6	78	10.6
64	20.8	79	10.0
65	20.0	80	9.5
66	19.2	81	8.9
67	18.4	82	8.4
68	17.6	83	7.9
69	16.8	84	7.4
70	16.0	85	6.9
71	15.3	86	6.5

Source: Table V, Reg. §1.72-9.

Table 3. ORDINARY JOINT LIFE AND LAST SURVIVOR ANNUITIES—TWO LIVES—EXPECTED RETURN MULTIPLES

Age	65	66	67	68	69	70	71	72	73	74
65	25.0	24.6	24.2	23.8	23.4	23.1	22.8	22.5	22.2	22.0
66	24.6	24.1	23.7	23.3	22.9	22.5	22.2	21.9	21.6	21.4
67	24.2	23.7	23.2	22.8	22.4	22.0	21.7	21.3	21.0	20.8
68	23.8	23.3	22.8	22.3	21.9	21.5	21.2	20.8	20.5	20.2
69	23.4	22.9	22.4	21.9	21.5	21.1	20.7	20.3	20.0	19.6
70	23.1	22.5	22.0	21.5	21.1	20.6	20.2	19.8	19.4	19.1
71	22.8	22.2	21.7	21.2	20.7	20.2	19.8	19.4	19.0	18.6
72	22.5	21.9	21.3	20.8	20.3	19.8	19.4	18.9	18.5	18.2
73	22.2	21.6	21.0	20.5	20.0	19.4	19.0	18.5	18.1	17.7
74	22.0	21.4	20.8	20.2	19.6	19.1	18.6	18.2	17.7	17.3
75	21.8	21.1	20.5	19.9	19.3	18.8	18.3	17.8	17.3	16.9
76	21.6	20.9	20.3	19.7	19.1	18.5	18.0	17.5	17.0	16.5
77	21.4	20.7	20.1	19.4	18.8	18.3	17.7	17.2	16.7	16.2
78	21.2	20.5	19.9	19.2	18.6	18.0	17.5	16.9	16.4	15.9
79	21.1	20.4	19.7	19.0	18.4	17.8	17.2	16.7	16.1	15.6
80	21.0	20.2	19.5	18.9	18.2	17.6	17.0	16.4	15.9	15.4

Source: Table VI, Reg. §1.72-9.

Table 4. ANNUITIES FOR JOINT LIFE ONLY—TWO LIVES—EXPECTED RETURN MULTIPLES

Age	65	66	67	68	69	70	71	72	73	74
65	14.9	14.5	14.1	13.7	13.3	12.9	12.5	12.0	11.6	11.2
66	14.5	14.2	13.8	13.4	13.1	12.6	12.2	11.8	11.4	11.0
67	14.1	13.8	13.5	13.1	12.8	12.4	12.0	11.6	11.2	10.8
68	13.7	13.4	13.1	12.8	12.5	12.1	11.7	11.4	11.0	10.6
69	13.3	13.1	12.8	12.5	12.1	11.8	11.4	11.1	10.7	10.4
70	12.9	12.6	12.4	12.1	11.8	11.5	11.2	10.8	10.5	10.1
71	12.5	12.2	12.0	11.7	11.4	11.2	10.9	10.5	10.2	9.9
72	12.0	11.8	11.6	11.4	11.1	10.8	10.5	10.2	9.9	9.6
73	11.6	11.4	11.2	11.0	10.7	10.5	10.2	9.9	9.7	9.4
74	11.2	11.0	10.8	10.6	10.4	10.1	9.9	9.6	9.4	9.1
75	10.7	10.5	10.4	10.2	10.0	9.8	9.5	9.3	9.1	8.8
76	10.3	10.1	9.9	9.8	9.6	9.4	9.2	9.0	8.8	8.5
77	9.8	9.7	9.5	9.4	9.2	9.0	8.8	8.6	8.4	8.2
78	9.4	9.2	9.1	9.0	8.8	8.7	8.5	8.3	8.1	7.9
79	8.9	8.8	8.7	8.6	8.4	8.3	8.1	8.0	7.8	7.6
80	8.5	8.4	8.3	8.2	8.0	7.9	7.8	7.6	7.5	7.3

Source: Table VI A, Reg. §1.72-9.

Table 5. MULTIPLE ADJUSTMENTS

If the number of whole months from the annuity starting date to the first payment date is—

	0–1	2	3	4	5	6	7	8	9	10	11	12

And payments under the contract are to be made:

	0–1	2	3	4	5	6	7	8	9	10	11	12
Annually	+0.5	+0.4	+0.3	+0.2	+0.1	0	0	–0.1	–0.2	–0.3	–0.4	–0.5
Semi-annually	+.2	+.1	0	0	–.1	–.2	...	...	...	...	...	...
Quarterly	+.1	0	–.1	...	...	...	...	...	...	...	...	...

Source: Reg. §1.72-5(a)(2)(i).

Table 6. PERCENT VALUE OF REFUND FEATURE

Years—

Age	21	22	23	24	25	26	27	28	29	30
55	8	9	9	10	11	12	13	14	15	16
56	9	9	10	11	12	13	14	15	16	18
57	9	10	11	12	13	14	15	17	18	19
58	10	11	12	13	14	16	17	18	19	21
59	11	12	13	15	16	17	18	20	21	22
60	12	14	15	16	17	19	20	21	23	24
61	14	15	16	17	19	20	22	23	25	26
62	15	16	18	19	20	22	23	25	27	28
63	16	18	19	21	22	24	25	27	29	30
64	18	19	21	23	24	26	28	29	31	33
65	20	21	23	25	26	28	30	31	33	35
66	21	23	25	27	28	30	32	34	35	37
67	23	25	27	29	31	32	34	36	38	40
68	25	27	29	31	33	35	37	38	40	42
69	28	29	31	33	35	37	39	41	43	44
70	30	32	34	36	38	40	42	43	45	47
71	32	34	36	38	40	42	44	46	47	49
72	35	37	39	41	43	45	46	48	50	51
73	37	39	41	43	45	47	49	51	52	54
74	40	42	44	46	48	50	51	53	54	56
75	42	44	46	48	50	52	54	56	57	58
76	45	47	49	51	53	54	56	58	59	60
77	47	50	51	53	55	57	58	60	61	62
78	50	52	54	56	57	59	61	62	63	64
79	53	55	56	58	60	61	63	64	65	66
80	55	57	59	60	62	63	65	66	67	68

Source: Table VII, Reg. §1.72-9.

¶5140 ADOPTION EXPENSES

There is a limited exclusion from gross income of up to $13,570, for 2017, of adoption expenses per child, where such expenses are paid or incurred by the taxpayer's employer under a qualified adoption assistance program. This exclusion is available for all children, with or without special needs. To be eligible, the child must be under the age of 18. Qualified adoption expenses include ordinary and necessary adoption expenses, court costs, attorney fees, and other expenses incurred for the principal purpose of the legal adoption of an eligible child. This exclusion is available for tax years beginning after 1996. An exclusion for adoption expenses must be coordinated with the adoption credit. (See ¶9031.) The employer-provided adoption expenses are available to eligible taxpayers who have modified adjusted gross income below $203,540. The exclusion is phased out between an adjusted gross income of $203,540 and $243,540.

If the adoption involves a citizen or resident of the United States, then the expenses are excludable from gross income in the year incurred. If the adoption involves a non-U.S. child, then the expenses are excludable in the year the adoption is finalized.

EXAMPLE 5.30 Ron and Roberta begin adoption proceedings in 2017 for an infant through a U.S.-based agency. During 2017, they incurred $3,000 of legal fees. During 2018, they incur $2,000 of additional adoption fees, and on November 16, 2018, they finalize the adoption. The $5,000 in expenses were incurred through Ron's employer's adoption assistance program. Ron and Roberta have $80,000 of adjusted gross income in 2018. They may exclude from gross income the $3,000 in 2017 and $2,000 paid by Ron's employer in 2018.

¶5145 COMPENSATION FOR INJURIES AND SICKNESS

The law specifically excludes from gross income:

1. Amounts received under workers' compensation acts as compensation for personal injuries or sickness
2. Amount of any damages received (whether by suit or agreement and whether as lump sums or as periodic payments) on account of personal injuries or sickness
3. Amounts received for personal injuries or sickness through accident and health insurance which the worker purchased
4. Amounts received as a pension, annuity, or similar allowance for personal injuries or sickness resulting from active service in the armed forces of any country or in the Coast and Geodetic Survey or the Public Health Service, or as a disability annuity payable under the provisions of Section 808 of the Foreign Service Act of 1980
5. Amounts received as disability income attributable to injuries incurred as a direct result of violent attack which the Secretary of State determines to be a terrorist attack and which occurred while such individual was an employee of the United States engaged in the performance of official duties outside the United States (Code Sec. 104(a))

Note the above-mentioned exclusions from gross income under workers' compensation acts cover occupational injury and sickness. Nonoccupational injuries and sicknesses are *not* covered. Further, payments received in excess of applicable workers' compensation laws are *not* excludable. However, benefits received under an accident and health insurance plan due to taxpayer's contributions are excludable from gross income. "No fault" insurance disability benefits received under the owner's insurance policy are excluded from gross income as well.

EXAMPLE 5.31 Lucy Kim worked for Cleveland Inc. for many years and was covered by workers' compensation and an accident and health plan that she personally purchased. On April 15, Lucy was seriously injured when a light fixture fell and broke her neck. She collected $4,000 for medical expenses incurred and $3,000 from her insurance company for her lost wages. Lucy may exclude from her gross income both the $4,000 received for medical expenses incurred and the $3,000 from her insurance company.

Damages compensating an injured person for personal injuries or sickness are excludable from gross income. These damages are often excludable even when measured by the amount of wages that might have been earned but for the injuries. Damages received for nonphysical injuries are not excludable from gross income. However, an exclusion from gross income is allowed to the extent damages received are used to pay medical expenses attributable to emotional distress.

Punitive damages are taxable as ordinary income, regardless of whether or not they are derived from physical or nonphysical injury. This restriction is effective for amounts received after August 20, 1996, but does not apply to punitive damages awarded in wrongful death actions if applicable state law in effect on September 13, 1995, provides that only punitive damages may be awarded.

Damages received from actions based on age, injury to reputation, emotional distress, race, or sex discrimination violations are includible in gross income if the tort occurred after August 20, 1996.

EXAMPLE 5.32	Mary Castro was seriously injured in an automobile accident. The driver of the other car was charged and convicted of reckless driving. Mary received the following payments.	
	Reimbursement for medical and hospital expenses	$6,500
	Loss of income reimbursement due to accident	2,500
	Punitive damages	8,000
	Payments for pain and suffering	3,000
	Total payments received	$20,000
	From the above payments, Mary includes the $8,000 received for punitive damages in her income.	

The entire amount of damages received by the individual in connection with physical injuries or physical sickness are excludable from income. See Rev. Rul. 85-97. Where the awards by the court, or, for that matter, the damages received in an out-of-court settlement, are really for lost profits in a business, then the amounts are excluded from income if the award is received on account of a personal physical injury. When reimbursement for medical expenses incurred is received, the individual cannot take an itemized deduction for the same expenses. Further, if, for example, the taxpayer incurred medical expenses in 2017 and deducted them on the 2017 tax return and in June 2018 received reimbursement for the same expenses, the reimbursement must be included in gross income to the extent of the previous deduction.

¶5155   ACCIDENT AND HEALTH PLANS

Benefits received by an employee under an accident and health plan where premiums are paid by the employer are excludable from gross income if they come under the following conditions:

1. Permanent injury or loss of bodily function if amounts are paid on the nature of the injury and not on work time lost by employee
2. Reimbursement for medical expenses of employee, spouse, or dependents (Code Sec. 105(b) and (c))

To qualify the plan must not discriminate in favor of highly compensated executives, shareholders, or certain officers. Further, reimbursements are deductible only to the extent of actual medical expenses.

EXAMPLE 5.33	Bea Safe was seriously injured while working on the job in June 2017. During the course of the year she received the following payments on account of her injury:	
	Workers' compensation	$750
	Medical expense reimbursement	6,000
	Damages for loss of limb	10,000
	In the example, all three items are excluded from gross income.	

The premiums the employer pays to fund an accident and health plan for employees are not taxed to the employee. It is immaterial whether or not payment is for an insured plan. Further, the plan can cover the employee for personal injuries or sickness, the employee's spouse, or any dependents. Code Sec. 106; Reg. §1.106-1.

It does not matter if the employer contributions for health and accident insurance are purchased as a group policy or an individual policy. However, if the policy provides for benefits beyond health and accident insurance then only the portion of the employer's contribution associated with the health and accident insurance is excluded.

Amounts received by the employee for sickness or injury through the employer-paid health and accident plan are excluded from gross income as long as they are for medical care reimbursement. Amounts paid under the plan that are not medical care reimbursement must be included in the employee's gross income.

¶5165   QUALIFIED LONG-TERM CARE INSURANCE

After 1996, qualified long-term care insurance contracts are generally treated as accident and health insurance contracts. Amounts received as benefits under the contract may be excluded from gross income as amounts received for personal injury or sickness.

¶5185   MEALS AND LODGING

Meals furnished to an employee or the employee's family are considered compensation to the employee. However, employees may exclude the value of meals furnished by the employer if (1) the meals are furnished on the business premises of the employer, and (2) they are furnished for the convenience of the employer. Code Sec. 119(a)(1). For example, a waitress in a luncheonette works from 6 a.m. to 2 p.m. Her employer provides for her breakfast and lunch at the luncheonette free of charge. Further, she is required to have her meals on the premises. Under the circumstances, the meals are not income to the waitress. If the waitress had the right to free lunches on her days off, they would be included in her gross income.

The value of lodging may be excluded from gross income if (1) the lodging is on the employer's premises, (2) the lodging is for the convenience of the employer, and (3) the employee must accept the lodging as a condition of employment. Code Sec. 119(a)(2). Normally such lodging is provided for employees who must be available to respond to emergencies, as in the case of ambulance drivers. The required lodging must be a condition of employment to be excluded from gross income. If the above tests are not met, the value of the meals and lodging is income to the employee. Reg. §1.61-2(d)(3).

EXAMPLE 5.34   Dr. Bruce Lee works at Metro General Hospital and is required to be on the premises because he is on call from Friday at 6:00 p.m. to Monday at 8:00 a.m. Dr. Lee is not required to report the value of meals and lodging received while on duty.

Qualified campus lodging furnished by an educational institution to faculty and other employees may be eligible for exclusion from gross income where an adequate rental is charged. For rental to be considered adequate, applicable appraisal tests must be met. Code Sec. 119(d).

¶5195   CAFETERIA PLANS

Cafeteria plans are employer-sponsored benefit packages that offer employees a choice between taking cash and qualified benefits (such as accident and health coverage or group-term life insurance coverage). Code Sec. 125; Reg. §1.125-1. No amount is included in the gross income of a cafeteria plan participant solely because he or she may choose among the benefits of the plan; but, if the participant chooses cash, it would be includible in gross income as compensation. If qualified benefits are chosen, they are excludable to the extent allowed by the law.

The cafeteria plan must limit its offering of benefits only between cash and qualified benefits to employees. A qualified benefit is any benefit that is not includible in the gross income of the employee by reason of an express provision of the law. The only taxable benefit that a cafeteria plan may offer is cash. The menu of items in the plan might include such nontaxable benefits as group-term life insurance, disability benefits, and accident and health benefits. This is not meant to be an exhaustive list of benefits includible in a cafeteria plan. Other fringes which may be included are dental plans, vacation days, and qualified dependent care assistance. Unused benefits from one plan year may not be accumulated by an employee and carried over to succeeding years.

However, the following plans have been expressly prohibited from inclusion: qualified scholarships (Code Sec. 117), educational assistance programs (Code Sec. 127), or excludable fringe benefits (Code

Sec. 132). An exception is made for employer contributions to profit-sharing or stock bonus plans under a qualified cash or deferred arrangement as defined by Code Sec. 401(k)(2). The beauty of the cafeteria approach to fringe benefit management is that the employer is allowed a tax deduction for providing the fringe benefits offered in the plan while the employee participants recognize no income if they choose the nontaxable benefits. Further, the employees select fringe benefits they desire and need and not benefits of no interest to them or benefits already available to their spouses.

Participation in the cafeteria plan must be restricted to employees. The maximum number of years that can be required by the employer of the employee before allowing an employee to partake in the plan is three years. Further, the rules must be the same for all employees. The plan must not discriminate in favor of highly compensated individuals, shareholders owning more than 5 percent of the voting power or value of the stock, or certain key employees. Unless the cafeteria plan meets the above-stated anti-discrimination rules, the highly paid individuals or shareholders must include in gross income the maximum benefits they are entitled to receive. However, the plan will remain intact for the participants not included in the prohibited class. Code Sec. 125(b) and (e).

The reporting requirements for cafeteria plans are quite stringent. Employers must report to the IRS the name and address of and the amount of benefits provided to highly compensated employees. Also, they must report the number of highly compensated employees, along with a list of the number eligible to participate in the plan, the number who actually participate, and the amount of fringe benefits includible in income, and the total cost of the plan during the year.

EXAMPLE 5.35

Ralph Jones works for Lorain Inc. and earns $30,000 per year. His employer has a basic cafeteria plan. Prior to the beginning of the benefit year, the employee must select the coverage desired. Ralph may choose among the following: $2,000 in cash or medical coverage up to $2,000 for the year, group-term life insurance, and day care facilities. Any unused benefit is forfeited. Therefore, if Ralph selects medical coverage and uses only $1,200, he forfeits the remaining $800.

Why choose medical coverage over cash? If Ralph chooses to receive the $2,000 in cash, he will immediately be taxed on the amount. Then, when he purchases a medical plan, he would be using after-tax dollars. Usually, group plans are considerably less expensive than privately purchased plans. By selecting group medical coverage, Ralph recognizes no income; therefore, he is selecting a nontaxable benefit plan with before-tax dollars. Remember this risk—if Ralph does not use all of his $2,000 covered medical expenses, he loses the dollars.

PLANNING POINTER

Cafeteria plans prove quite advantageous for married couples. If both spouses work for companies having cafeteria plans, they should arrange their affairs so as to provide themselves with full coverage. Typically, married couples find themselves with two medical plans and no dental plan. Cafeteria plans correct this drawback and are of great benefit to families.

¶5201 EDUCATIONAL ASSISTANCE PLANS

Payments of up to $5,250 per year received by an employee for tuition, fees, books, and supplies under an employer's assistance program may be excluded from gross income. Code Sec. 127. Any excess is includible in the employee's gross income and is subject to employment and income tax withholding.

The Economic Growth and Tax Relief Reconciliation Act of 2001 extended the exclusion to include graduate education. The graduate education exclusion became effective after December 31, 2001. This provision applies whether or not the educational courses are work-related. The Tax Relief Act of 2010 extends these provisions through December 31, 2012. The American Taxpayer Relief Act of 2012 extends permanently the exclusion of up to $5,250.

Expenses disallowed because they exceed the $5,250 limit may be excludable if they meet the working condition fringe benefit rules under Code Sec. 132. Excludable assistance payments may not cover tools or supplies that the employee retains after completion of the course or the cost of meals, lodging, or transportation. Although the courses covered by the plan need not be job-related, courses involving sports, games, or hobbies may be covered only if they involve the employer's business. Reg. §1.127-2(c).

The plan must be written. The employer may pay the expenses directly, reimburse the employees for their expenses, or provide the education directly. The plan need not be funded and prior approval of the plan by the IRS is not required, but the plan must not discriminate in favor of highly compensated employees. Further, not more than 5 percent of the total amount paid out during the year may be paid to or for employees who are shareholders or owners who own at least 5 percent of the business. An employer who maintains an educational plan must maintain records and file a return with respect to the plan. Code Sec. 6039D.

¶5215   TUITION REDUCTION PLANS

Qualified tuition reductions (QTRs) made available to employees (and their families) of qualified educational institutions are excludable from the employee's gross income. A QTR is the amount of reduction in tuition for education that is furnished by an educational institution to an employee (or an employee's dependent children or certain other individuals) provided certain requirements are met. The tuition reduction must be for education below the graduate level. Code Sec. 117(d). However, under a special rule, tuition reduction benefits paid to graduate teaching and research assistants employed by qualified educational institutions may be excluded from gross income. Code Sec. 117(d)(5).

Qualified Tuition Program

A qualified tuition program (QTP), also known as a Code Section 529 Plan, is a program that allows an individual to purchase tuition credits or make cash contributions to an account on behalf of a beneficiary for payment of qualified higher education expenses. Generally for years after 2001, no amount is included in gross income of a beneficiary or contributor with respect to any distribution from a QTP used by qualified education expenses.

The PATH Act of 2015 expands the definition of qualified higher education expenses to include computer equipment and technology for the years beginning in 2015. To receive this tax benefit the program must be established by a state government or agency. For years after 2002, they may also be established and maintained by eligible educational institutions, such as, colleges, vocational schools or other post-secondary educational institutions.

¶5235   DEPENDENT CARE ASSISTANCE PROGRAMS

An employee receiving dependent care assistance payments provided under an employer's written non-discriminatory plan generally may exclude such payments from gross income. Code Sec. 129. The exclusion for employer-provided dependent care assistance is limited to $5,000 a year ($2,500 in the case of a separate return by a married individual). Also, the exclusion is subject to an earned income limitation. Thus, an unmarried taxpayer may not exclude from gross income more than his or her earned income for the tax year, and a married taxpayer may not exclude more than the lesser of his or her earned income or the spouse's earned income. In applying the earned income test for a married taxpayer, the earned income of an incapacitated or student spouse is deemed to be $250 per month if one qualifying dependent is involved or $500 if two or more qualifying dependents are involved.

The employer's plan must be for the exclusive use of its employees and must not discriminate in favor of employees who are officers, owners, or highly compensated employees or their dependents. The purpose of the service provided must be to enable an individual to work. An employee who excludes the value of child or dependent care services from income may not claim any income tax deduction or credit with respect to such amounts.

Qualifying expenses include amounts paid for household services and care of the qualifying person. A qualifying person is any child under age 13, a disabled spouse, or any disabled person, provided that the qualifying person is a dependent of the taxpayer. The person who provides the care may not be the taxpayer's spouse or a person claimed by the taxpayer as a dependent. Further, if the taxpayer's child provides the care, the child must be age 19 or older by the end of the tax year.

The exclusion for employer-provided dependent care assistance may not be claimed unless the taxpayer reports the dependent care provider's correct name, address, and taxpayer identification number on the tax return. The exclusion may be claimed even though the information is not provided if it can be shown that the taxpayer exercised due diligence in attempting to provide this information. Code Sec. 129(e)(9). Similar information reporting requirements also apply to employers that provide dependent care programs for their employees. The exclusion for dependent care assistance programs must be coordinated with the dependent care credit. (Chapter 9)

¶5255   MILITARY BENEFITS

Qualified military benefits are excluded from gross income. Qualified military benefits are benefits that are received either in cash or in kind by members of the armed services or their dependents by reason of military service and that, as of September 9, 1986, were excludable from gross income by law, regulation, or administrative practice. However, the personal use of a car is not excludable as a qualified military benefit. Code Sec. 134.

Military retirement pay based on years of service and/or age must be included in gross income. Code Sec. 61(a)(11). However, veterans' benefits administered by the Veterans Administration are excludable from gross income. This includes amounts paid to veterans or their families in the form of educational, training, or subsistence allowances, disability compensation and pension payments for disabilities, and veterans' pensions.

TAX BLUNDERS

1. Harry and Rachel are both retired and have $33,500 of interest income and receive social security benefits of $12,000. This year they decided to redeem two Series EE bonds with accumulated interest of $3,500 each. This transaction boosts their provisional income to $46,500. Since they passed the $44,000 threshold, the proceeds from the sales of the second bond required them to include in gross income a larger portion of their social security benefits. Harry and Rachel should cash one bond in year one and one bond in year two.
2. Robert is single and collects social security. This year his provisional income exceeded $34,000. It was composed of $32,000 of interest income and $12,000 of social security benefits. In an effort to reduce his taxes, he sold several of his taxable bonds and bought tax-exempt bonds. This did not solve his problem. In the calculation of provisional income, tax-exempt interest income is included.
3. Orange County, Inc. provided their employees with a physical fitness center on their premises. They decided in a cost cutting move to close the center and buy memberships for all their employees and their families at the local fitness club. This was cheaper for Orange County, Inc. than maintaining their own facility. By closing their facility and buying memberships in a health club, the company could no longer treat the expenditure as a de minimis fringe benefit. The employees now had income for the cost of the membership.

KEYSTONE PROBLEM

Commonwealth Medicine Company, a hospital supply firm, has had difficulty attracting new personnel, particularly at the executive level. They feel that the company is competitive in the area of salary, but that total compensation packages should be examined more carefully. Of course, many factors will determine the final list. However, you are asked to examine one consideration in developing these packages, which is to reduce the tax impact on the employee. Therefore, you wish to devise a plan that will provide benefits for employees that will not be included in their taxable income. Include in your examination the concept of cafeteria plans. Also investigate the consequences of limiting the plans to selected levels of personnel.

SUMMARY

-   Sections 101 through 139 of the Internal Revenue Code list "Items Specifically Excluded from Gross Income."
-   A portion of Social Security benefits must be included in taxable income for taxpayers who meet certain requirements described by the Revenue Reconciliation Act of 1993.
-   A tax exclusion is provided for interest earned on U.S. savings bonds used to finance the higher education of the taxpayer, the taxpayer's spouse, or the taxpayer's dependents.
-   Certain employee discounts provided to employees on the selling price of qualified property or services of the employer are excludable from gross income, provided that the discount meets certain qualifications.

- Cafeteria plans offer employees a choice between taking cash and qualified benefits, which are any benefits that are not includible in the gross income of the employee by reason of an express provision of law.
- Educational assistance plans are subject to a number of tax status rules for determining exclusion.

From Gross Income to Taxable Income—Simplified

GROSS INCOME
- Wages, Salaries
- Dividends Received
- Interest Received
- Annuities, Pensions
- State and Local Income Tax Refunds
- Alimony Received
- Gross Business Profits
- Gains on Sales or Exchanges
- Commissions, Bonuses, Tips, Fringe Benefits
- Rents and Royalties (Prizes)
- Farm Income
- Punitive Damages
- Social Security
- Unemployment Compensation

minus

DEDUCTIONS FROM GROSS INCOME
- Trade or Business Expenses
- Performing Artists' Expenses
- Sales or Exchanges or Property Losses
- Rent and Royalties Income Production Expenses
- Depreciation and Depletion—Life Tenants and Income Beneficiaries' Property
- Self-Employed Retirement Plan Contributions
- Individual Retirement Account Contributions
- Pension Plan Lump-Sum Distributions (Ordinary Income Portion)
- Time Savings Accounts Premature Withdrawls Penalties
- Alimony Paid
- Reforestation Amortization
- Jury Duty Pay Remitted to Employer
- Self-Employment Tax Credit (one-half)
- Self-Employed Health Insurance
- Moving Expenses
- Student Loan Interest

equals

ADJUSTED GROSS INCOME

minus

ITEMIZED DEDUCTIONS OR STANDARD DEDUCTION AMOUNT
- Medical and Dental Expenses
- Taxes (State and Local Income, Personal Property, and Real Estate Taxes)
- Interest (Qualified Residence Interest, Investment Interest)
- Charitable Contributions
- Casualty and Theft Losses
- Employee Unreimbursed Expenses
- Miscellaneous Itemized Deductions

minus

EXEMPTIONS
- Taxpayer
- Spouse
- Dependents

equals

TAXABLE INCOME

CHECKLIST

Exclusions from Gross Income

Accident and Health Insurance Proceeds

Annuities (amounts contributed by taxpayer)

Awards for Noncompetitive Achievements

Bequests and Devises

Car Pool Receipts

Casualty Insurance Proceeds

Child Support Payments

Cost-of-Living Allowances Paid to U.S. Employees Stationed Outside the U.S.

Damages Received for: Personal Injuries or Sickness

Disability and Death Payments

Dividends on Life Insurance

Educational Assistance Plans

Federal Employees' Compensation Act Payments

Federal Income Tax Refunds

Fringe Benefits (group plans, premiums paid by employer)

Gains: Sale of Residence (up to $500,000)

Gifts, Bequests, and Inheritances

Group-Term Life Insurance (if coverage is up to $50,000)

Inheritances

Interest on Tax-Free Securities

Lessee's Improvements

Life Insurance Proceeds

Long-Term Care Insurance

Meals and Lodging (for convenience of employer)

Military Allowances

Moving Expenses

Old Age, Disability, and Survivor's Payments (Social Security Actor Railroad Retirement Act)

Payments to Beneficiary of Deceased Employee

Political Campaign Contributions (limited)

Railroad Retirement Act Pensions

Relocation Payments

Rental Allowance of Clergymen

Scholarships (limited amount)

Social Security Payments (depending on gross income)

Tuition Paid by Employer (job-related only)

Veterans' Benefits

Workers' Compensation and Similar Payments

QUESTIONS

1. How does a tax exclusion differ from a tax deduction?

2. An individual surrenders, for $20,000, an endowment life insurance policy in which he had a $15,000 investment. How much of the $20,000 of proceeds must be included in gross income?

3. What effect does interest on tax-exempt bonds have on the taxation of social security benefits?

4. How is the amount of Social Security benefits included in taxable income calculated?

5. On Series EE U.S. savings bonds, what different tax consequences arise from the two choices in reporting interest?

6. List several social justifications for issuing private activity bonds.

7. What is an annuity, and what features determine the amount of income associated with such a contract?

8. How is the excludable portion of an annuity calculated?

9. What five categories of compensation for injuries and sickness are excluded from gross income?

10. How are employer contributions to accident and health and group legal services plans treated by employees on their own income tax returns?

11. Describe the elements of a cafeteria plan and what are the beneficial aspects of such a plan for employers and employees.

12. How does a joint and survivor annuity differ from a single person annuity? How is the computation of the exclusion different for the joint annuity?

13. Name two types of fringe benefits, discussed in this chapter, that cannot be included in a cafeteria plan?

14. Indicate whether the following income sources must be included or may be excluded from gross income:
    a. Insurance proceeds for loss of finger
    b. Prizes
    c. Embezzlement proceeds
    d. Interest on all savings deposits
    e. Child support
    f. Interest on Series HH bonds
    g. Receipt of alimony by divorced husband
    h. Income produced from property acquired by gift
    i. Gifts and inheritances
    j. Scholarship grants for tuition
    k. Compensation for injuries or sickness
    l. Interest income on bonds issued by State of Ohio
    m. Life insurance proceeds from a group plan

15. Give an example of when meals provided to an employee by an employer may be excluded form income.

16. Mindy is a candidate for a bachelor's degree at a local state university. She received a grant that covered the following expenses:

Tuition	$4,000
Books and Supplies	1,000
Payment for Research Services	2,000

Mindy's tuition this year was $8,000. She spent the entire $7,000 award on tuition. What amount must Mindy include in her gross income?

17. Abigail received $6,000 from her employer as reimbursement for her expenditures on tuition, fees, and books while attending State University. Abigail is working toward a graduate degree in business administration. Must Abigail recognize the $6,000 as income?

18. If an employee is covered by a group-term life insurance plan that pays the entire premium of the policy, must the employee include the premium coverage in income if her salary is over $50,000 per year?

PROBLEMS

19. In January 2017, Leon McLeod received a gift of a beach cottage valued at $250,000 from his great-uncle who owned a number of such buildings. The cottage was rented each year to college students who occupied it during the school year. The annual net rental income received is $20,000 per year. The 2017 tax return of McLeod would include what elements of this transaction?

20. The Hightown Council refused to increase the town budget. Robert Read was laid off from work on August 4, 2017. Earlier in the year he had been temporarily disabled from a job-related injury and had received disability benefits. At year-end Robert Read and his wife have the following sources of income:

Disability income	$ 2,500
Unemployment compensation	5,000
Salary—	
January 1—August 4, 2017	10,000
Wife's salary	9,000
Supplemental unemployment compensation—	
employer provided	3,000

What amount of Read's family income was includible in gross income?

21. In 2017, Windsor Knott, an employee of the Victoria Tie Company, was seriously injured in the factory stockroom. He was hospitalized for 30 days and lost partial use of his left hand. During his hospitalization and recovery period, he received the following:

Workers' compensation	$ 9,000
Medical expenses reimbursement	10,000
Disability insurance benefits (insurance paid by taxpayer)	4,000
Accident and health insurance benefits (company policy benefits based on the degree of permanent injury)	9,500

Determine Knott's tax liability with regard to these payments. If the medical expenses had been deducted from Knott's 2017 tax return and reimbursement was received in 2018, how would the reimbursement be reflected in the 2018 return?

22. David and Renee Kimberly, ages 75 and 65, respectively, have the following sources of income:

Private pension receipts	$20,000
Social Security	12,000
Interest on bank deposits	2,500
Dividends from domestic corporations	2,000
Interest on tax-exempt securities	700

Their itemized deductions total $11,000. Compute their taxable income.

23. Hi Tech Accounting Services changed its fringe benefit package as of the first of this year. Employees are now eligible to receive group term life insurance equal to twice their annual salary up to $100,000. Harry's salary is $90,000 per year. Prior to this year employees received group term life insurance up to $50,000. Harry is 52 years of age and has adjusted gross income of $78,000. Does Harry suffer any tax consequences because of this change in policy?

24. Charles Adams, who is single, retired on March 3, 2017, at the age of 65. For the year 2017, he receives the following income:

Salary	$14,000
Interest income	2,000
Dividend income	1,000
Tax-exempt income	1,000
Social Security benefits	5,000
Net rental income	6,000

What is Charles' modified AGI? What amount, if any, of his Social Security benefits must Charles include in his 2017 gross income? What is Charles' taxable income for 2017?

25. Felix Boots, a 35-year-old male, is vice president of the Kitty-Lit Pet Products Company and earns $50,000 per year. The company provides paid group-term life insurance of twice the officers' salaries for all officers of the company. The cost of the policy to the company for Mr. Boots is $650 per year. How much of the $650 must Felix include in his gross income? If Kitty-Lit changed its policy so as to enable all employees to be covered at twice their annual salary, what would Felix have to include in his gross income?

26. A. Fluent, an investor in stocks and bonds, wanted to increase his portfolio but wanted to minimize his tax liability on the income from the bonds. He is presented with the following alternative investments: U.S. Series EE bonds, bonds for industrial development for mass transit, and qualified veterans' mortgage bonds. Which should he choose for his investment? Why?

27. Norm and Pat, a married couple filing a joint return, have the following sources of income:

Wages	$35,000
Interest income	4,000
Dividend income	3,000
Social Security benefits	9,000

Both Norm and Pat are over 65 years of age. Determine their taxable income.

28. Ron and Gayle, both over 65 years of age, have the following sources of income:

Consulting income	$36,000
Interest income	4,000
Tax-exempt interest	4,000
Social Security benefits	12,000

Ron and Gayle have itemized deductions of $16,000. Compute their taxable income.

29. Robert Provider purchases a joint and survivor annuity providing for payments of $200 per month for his life and upon his death for his wife, Robin, for the remainder of her life. As of the annuity starting date Robert is 68 and Robin is 66. The annuity cost Robert $36,000. Determine the exclusion ratio for the annuity.

30. On September 23, 2017, Mary Jones bought an annuity contract for $22,050 that will give her $125 a month for life, beginning October 30. Mary is 61 years old. Determine the exclusion ratio and the amount of the annuity to be included in Mary Jones's 2017 gross income.

31. Don Smith's wife died in January while still employed and, as her beneficiary, he began receiving an annuity of $147 per month. There was no investment in the contract after June 30, 2013. The investment in the contract was $7,938. Don Smith, age 65, received his first monthly annuity check as of February 3, 2017. Determine the amount of his pension to be included in his gross income.

32. Assume the same facts as in Problem 31, except that in January 2018, because of a cost-of-living increase, Don's annuity payment was increased to $175 per month. Determine the amount of the 2018 annuity payment to be included in Don's gross income.

33. Philip Southerly purchases a joint and survivor annuity providing for payments of $200 per month for his life and, after his death, $100 per month for his wife's life. As of the annuity starting date he is 70 years old and his wife is 67. The annuity cost Philip $28,000. Determine the exclusion ratio for the annuity Philip purchased and the amount of the pension to be included in gross income.

34. Peter Seaman, at age 45, purchased an annuity which will pay him $250 a month for life once he reaches age 65. He paid in $25,000. At retirement, he will have quarterly payments from the annuity. Peter receives his first annuity payment three months after the starting date (January 20). Perform the calculations and determine what amount he may exclude from gross income. What was the exclusion ratio? What was the adjusted multiple used to calculate the exclusion?

35. Beth, who is single, redeems her Series EE bonds. She receives $12,000, consisting of $8,000 principal and $4,000 interest. Beth's qualified educational expenses total $16,500. Further, Beth's adjusted gross income for the year is $40,000. Determine what, if any, interest income Beth must include in her gross income.

36. Linda Sue Carr worked for a large food brokerage firm. In January of this year she was terminated. After a court battle Linda Sue was reinstated in her job and received from the firm in November $7,500 in punitive damages. Must Linda Sue include the $7,500 in punitive damages in her 2017 gross income?

37. Steven Spokesman, a high school teacher in a local school district, was fired for publicly criticizing the local school district. The court ruled that Steven's freedom of speech had been violated and the school district was required to pay $24,000 in damages. Steven paid his lawyer $8,000 to defend him. Determine: (1) whether Steven must include the $24,000 in gross income and (2) whether he can deduct the $8,000 in legal fees?

38. Actress Nola Talent sued her coworker, actor Burt Dirt, for slander, citing his speech at a press interview where he labeled her a "floozy" and an "incompetent excuse for an actress." In her suit she claimed that as a consequence of this slander she not only felt degraded but was denied further acting roles. The court awarded her $100,000 in compensatory damages for damage to her acting career and $1,000 in punitive damages for the slander of her character. How is this reflected in her income tax return?

39. Robert Careless was injured while working on the production line on July 8, 2017. He received the following payments as a result of his serious injury:

Workers' compensation	$6,000
Medical expense reimbursement	2,000
Damages for personal injury	5,000

During 2017, Robert earned $16,000 in wages. How much of the above-listed amounts must Robert include in his gross income?

40. Roger Corby, a student, was employed seven nights a week at the Campus Inn as a desk clerk. He was required to be on duty from 11 p.m. to 6 a.m. and on call at various other hours, although he was rarely called after 12 a.m. His employer also required that he live on the premises and furnished him with a room free of charge, adjacent to the desk. Roger used the room as his permanent living quarters. Roger also ate all his meals free in the Inn dining room. Roger excluded the value of all these benefits from his tax return. What was the response of the IRS examiner?

41. On May 1, 2017, Anthony was in an automobile accident while on his way to work. Following doctor's advice, Anthony stayed home for six months to recover from his injuries. While at home, Anthony filed a lawsuit against the other driver. On December 1, 2017, the lawsuit was settled and Anthony received the following amounts:

| Compensation for lost wages | $30,000 |
| Personal injury damages (none of which was for punitive damages) | 50,000 |

How much of the settlement must Anthony include in ordinary income on his 2017 tax return?

42. **IRS Adapted Problem.** Ms. Green is single and over 65 years old. She received the following income in 2017:

Interest from certificates of deposit	$3,000
Tax-exempt interest	6,000
Taxable dividends	5,000
Taxable pension	15,000
Wages from consulting work	9,000
Social Security	14,000

She did not have any adjustments to income. What is the taxable amount of Ms. Green's Social Security?
a. $7,000
b. $9,350
c. $11,000
d. $11,900
e. $13,850

43. **IRS Adapted Problem.** All of the following fringe benefits can be excluded from the employee's income except:
    a. Transportation up to $255 per month for combined commuter highway vehicle transportation and transit passes, and $255 per month for qualified parking.
    b. Holiday gifts, other than cash, with a low fair market value.
    c. Qualified employee discounts given employees on certain property and services offered to customers in the ordinary course of the line of business in which the employees perform services.
    d. Memberships to municipal athletic facilities for employees, their spouses, and their dependent children.

44. **IRS Adapted Problem.** In December 2017, Mr. Stone cashed qualified Series EE U.S. Savings Bonds, which he had purchased in January 2011. The proceeds were used for his son's college education. All of the following statements are correct concerning the exclusion of the interest received except:
    a. He cannot file as married filing separate.
    b. Eligible expenses include room and board.
    c. If the proceeds are *more* than the expenses, he will be able to exclude only part of the interest.
    d. Before he figures his interest exclusion, he must reduce his qualified higher education expenses by certain benefits.

45. On January 4, 2017, Ralph Stuart, an employee of Hard Manufacturing Inc., enrolled for the spring semester at State University where he is a candidate for an undergraduate degree in accounting. His employer reimbursed him for the following expenses: $2,000 for tuition, $600 for books and $100 for transportation to State University. What amount should Ralph exclude from his gross income in 2017?
    a. $0
    b. $2,000
    c. $2,600
    d. $2,700

46. **IRS Adapted Problem.** Mr. Hines received a $6,200 grant from a local university for the fall of 2017. Mr. Hines was a candidate for a degree, and was required to be a research assistant, for which services he received payment under the grant. The $6,200 grant provided the following:

Tuition	$3,600
Books and supplies	500
Pay for services as research assistant	2,100

Mr. Hines spent the entire $6,200 on tuition, books, and supplies. What amount must Mr. Hines include in his income for 2017?
    a. $2,100
    b. $2,600
    c. $3,200
    d. $3,600

47. **IRS Adapted Problem.** The following items were received as court awards and damages during 2017. All should be included in ordinary income for 2017 by the taxpayer who received them except:
    a. Compensation for lost wages due to slander
    b. Compensatory damages for physical injury
    c. Damages for breach of contract
    d. Interest on damages for breach of contract

48. Jose Reyes surrendered an endowment policy and received $50,000 from the ABC Insurance Company. Over time Jose had paid $35,000 in premiums. In addition, over time Jose had collected $5,000 of dividends on the policy. How much gain (loss), if any, must Jose recognize from surrendering the endowment policy?
    a. $50,000
    b. $15,000
    c. $20,000
    d. 0
    e. $10,000

49. Jacob is 69 years old and elects group-term life insurance of $200,000. The employer pays 60 percent of the cost of the life insurance plan; and employees pay at a uniform rate of $0.35 per $1,000 per month to cover the other 40 percent of the plan cost. How much, if any, would Jacob have to include in his gross income?
    a. $2,286
    b. $1,446
    c. $1,372
    d. $914
    e. $2,236

50. Ilana is a successful sole proprietor who owns a cosmetic store. She was injured in a car accident. The driver of the other car was found to be at fault for the accident. Ilana received the following payments:
    I. Hospital expenses
    II. Payments for pain and suffering
    III. Punitive damages
    IV. Loss of income from not being able to work in the cosmetic store
    V. Medical expenses

    Of the following payments, which one(s) is (are) includable in Ilana's gross income?
    a. I, and III.
    b. II and III.
    c. III.
    d. III and IV.
    e. None of the above.

51. **Comprehensive Problem (Tax Return Problem).** Rodney and Alice Jones have three small children, ranging in age from 5 to 10. One child is blind and needs special care. Rodney works as an accountant for a large CPA firm and has gross income of $45,000. Alice is a lawyer with a national law firm and earns $48,000. Rodney's parents are quite old, and he and his two brothers entirely support them according to the following percentages:

Rodney	45%
Steven	40%
Robert	15%

The brothers decide that in 2017 Rodney should be allowed to declare his parents as dependents.

Rodney's employer provides group-term life insurance at twice the employee's annual salary. Rodney is 40 years of age.

During 2017, Rodney and Alice receive the following dividends on their jointly held investments:

Dividends from Mexico Inc. (Mexican Corp.)	$700
Dividends from Widget Steel Corp.	150

They received interest income from the following investments:

Interest on State of Ohio highway bonds	$800
Interest on deposits in savings and loans	400

The Joneses have itemized deductions of $15,000. Compute their taxable income.

52. **Comprehensive Problem (Tax Return Problem).** Mr. and Mrs. Sam Morris retired on February 10, 2017, and call you in for tax advice. Both Sam and his wife Sarah have worked for many years. Sam is 65 years of age and his wife is 63.

Facts:	
Dependent child: Age 21	
Social Security Benefits	$9,900
Salaries:	
Sam (January 1—February 10)	7,000
Sarah (January 1—February 10)	5,500
Interest Income:	
Port Authority of N.Y. Bonds	300
Interest from Bank Deposits	1,400
Corporate Bonds	900
Highway Bonds of Ohio	100
Dividend Income:	
Microsoft Common Stock	4,000
General Electric Common Stock	2,000
AGA Ltd. of England	1,000
Net Rental Income	4,000

One of their tenants moved out on July 14, 2017, and Sam determines that they had damaged the stove, and therefore returned only $50 of their $150 security deposit.

The Morrises' daughter borrowed $10,000 two years ago to purchase a new automobile. She has made payments to her parents and on September 1, 2017, only $2,500 was still outstanding on the loan. On their daughter's birthday, they told her she no longer had to make payments.

Sam was Vice President of a very large corporation. As part of his fringe benefit package, the corporation purchased for him $50,000 of group-term life insurance. The corporation continues to pay for his life insurance even after retirement.

The Morrises' three children gave their parents a gala retirement party. Many friends and relatives were invited. Gifts valued at over $1,000 were received by the couple.

In October, Mrs. Morris entered a contest being run by a local bank. She submitted drawings for a bank logo. Her drawing was selected and she received $500.

Many years ago, Sam purchased an annuity policy for $9,000. Starting on March 3, 2017, he began receiving lifelong monthly payments of $60.

The Morrises' 21-year-old daughter is in college. She worked during the summer and earned $2,500. Interest on her savings accounts amounted to $500. Her parents paid for the college tuition of $4,000.

The Morrises have itemized deductions of $14,000.

Determine the Morrises' taxable income for 2017.

53. **Research Problem.** Larry Sorich, as part of his estate planning, assigned his $100,000 group-term life insurance policy to his niece. Larry's employer provided for only $50,000 of coverage; therefore, the niece paid for the premiums on the supplemental insurance. Larry did not include in gross income the premiums for the supplemental insurance. Larry's accountant challenged him on this arrangement. Who prevailed? See Rev. Rul. 71-587, 1971-2 CB 89.

Chapter

6

Deductions: General Concepts and Trade or Business Deductions

OBJECTIVES

After completing Chapter 6, you should be able to:

1. Name the four categories of deductions allowable to individual taxpayers: (1) trade or business, (2) production of income, (3) losses, and (4) personal.
2. Identify the types of losses that may be deducted in computing a taxpayer's taxable income.
3. Discuss criteria for determining whether taxpayer expenditures are deductible.
4. Explain common business deductions, such as advertising, salaries and wages, fringe benefits, bad debts, etc.
5. Identify allowable business deductions related to capital expenditures, such as depreciation, amortization, depletion, repairs, and improvements, etc.
6. Understand restricted business deductions for lobbying activities and business start-up costs.
7. Discuss allowable deductions for transportation, travel, entertainment, employee moving expenses, and student loan interest.

OVERVIEW

Deductions allowable to individual taxpayers fall into four categories: trade or business deductions (including business-related expenses of employees), production of income deductions, losses, and personal deductions. This chapter examines the general concepts of taxation underlying each of these categories of allowable deductions for individuals and includes an introduction to trade or business deductions, including allowable deductions for transportation, travel, entertainment, and employee moving expenses.

Section 162 allows as a deduction all the ordinary and necessary expenses paid or incurred during the taxable year in carrying on any trade or business. Although Code Sec. 162 appears to be all-inclusive in allowing all business expenditures as tax deductions, the requirements for the deductibility of business expenditures place well-defined limitations on business deductions. For this reason, a basic knowledge of allowable business deductions is of value to an informed businessperson.

With some notable exceptions, trade or business deductions are the same for all business taxpayers regardless of whether the business is organized as a corporation, partnership, or sole proprietorship. Although the income tax form used to report deductions is different, the allowable deductions generally are the same. This chapter is concerned mainly with business deductions as they appear on a sole proprietor's Schedule C, which is filed with the IRS as part of the taxpayer's individual income tax return.

Categories of Allowable Deductions

¶6001 ## CLASSIFICATION OF TAX DEDUCTIONS

Generally speaking, four categories of expenses may be deductible by individual taxpayers:

1. **Trade or business expenses.** Deductions applicable to trade or business including the business-related expenses of employees (Code Sec. 162).
2. **Expenses incurred for the production of income.** Deductions related to the production of investment income including those incurred: (1) for the production or collection of income; (2) for the management, conservation, or maintenance of property held for the production of income; and (3) in connection with the determination, collection, or refund of any tax (Code Sec. 212).
3. **Deductions for losses.** In addition to expenses incurred in trade or business activities, and investment (production of income) activities, taxpayers are allowed to deduct certain losses incurred on the sale or other disposition of property used in a trade or business activity or an investment activity. Losses related to property used for personal purposes are generally not deductible unless caused by theft or other casualty.
4. **Personal expenses.** Most personal expenses are not deductible. A number of exceptions, however, have been created by Congress over the years allowing taxpayers to claim itemized deductions for a variety of personal expenses. Other personal expenses are allowable as "adjustments" to gross income, which have the same effect as deductions.

¶6101 ## DEDUCTIONS "FOR" vs. "FROM" AGI

Once the deductibility of an item is established, the tax formula for individuals requires that the deduction be classified as either a deduction *for* adjusted gross income (AGI) or a deduction *from* AGI (itemized deduction). In short, the deduction process requires that two questions be asked. First, is the expense deductible? Second, is the deduction *for* or *from* adjusted gross income (AGI)?

Classification is significant for several reasons. First, itemized deductions may be deducted only to the extent they exceed the standard deduction. Thus, a taxpayer whose itemized deductions do not exceed the standard deduction receives no tax benefit from his/her itemized deductions. In contrast, deductions *for* AGI may be claimed *in addition to* the standard deduction (or itemized deductions if greater).

A second reason for properly classifying deductions concerns the treatment of certain itemized deductions. Medical expenses, for example, are deductible only to the extent they exceed 10% of the taxpayer's adjusted gross income. Similarly, miscellaneous itemized deductions are deductible only to the extent they exceed 2% of AGI. Charitable contributions are subject to a ceiling, rather than a floor, based on AGI. As discussed in Chapter 8, depending on the type of property contributed, the charitable contributions deduction cannot exceed 20, 30, or 50 percent of AGI. Thus, classification of a deduction as "above the line" (i.e., "for" AGI) reduces AGI and may indirectly affect the deductible portion of other expenses which are deducted "below the line" (i.e., "from" AGI).

EXAMPLE 6.1

Jamie Dean owns and operates a small business. During 2017, she paid property taxes of $20,000 and suffered a personal casualty loss of $10,000. She also had other itemized deductions in an amount above the standard deduction. Her adjusted gross income, before considering the above expenses, was $90,000. If the property taxes are deductible "from" AGI, she will be allowed to deduct $1,000 of her casualty loss (the amount by which the $10,000 loss exceeds 10% of her AGI). However, if she can deduct the property taxes "above the line" ("for" AGI), her adjusted gross income will be $70,000 and her deductible casualty loss will increase by $2,000 (10% of the $20,000 reduction in AGI) to $3,000. Deducting the property taxes "for" rather than "from" AGI reduced Jamie's taxable income by $2,000.

Aside from the effect on AGI, taxpayers also have an incentive to classify non-personal expenses as deductions "for" AGI rather than as miscellaneous itemized deductions in order to avoid the floor on deductibility of these expenses. If the taxpayer can properly deduct such expenses as business expenses deductible "for" AGI, the full amount of the expense will be deductible. If the taxpayer is required to deduct it instead as a miscellaneous itemized deduction, some or all of the expense will not be deductible, depending on the size of the taxpayer's AGI.

Adjusted gross income for Federal income tax purposes also serves as the tax base or the starting point for computing taxable income for many state income taxes. Several states do not allow the taxpayer to itemize deductions. Consequently, misclassification may also affect the taxpayer's state income tax liability.

Still another reason for properly classifying expenses concerns the self employment tax. Under the Social Security and Medicare programs, self employed individuals are required to make an annual contribution based on their net earnings from self employment. Net earnings from self employment include gross income from the taxpayer's trade or business less allowable trade or business deductions attributable to that income. Failure to properly classify a deduction as a deduction for AGI attributable to self employment income will increase the taxpayer's self-employment tax liability.

¶6115   DEDUCTIONS "FOR" AGI

"Above the line" deductions allowable in computing AGI (i.e., deductions "for" AGI) are governed by Code Secs. 62, 162, and 212. Deductions *for* AGI are listed in Table 1:

Table 1. DEDUCTIONS "FOR" AGI

Trade or business deductions (e.g., expenses of a sole proprietorship or self employed business person, including farmers, normally reported on Schedule C of Form 1040)

Losses from sale or exchange of business or investment property (reported on Schedule D of Form 1040, or on Form 4797)

Deductions attributable to rents or royalties (reported on Schedule E of Form 1040)

Educator expenses for books, supplies, equipment, etc. up to $250

Certain employee business expenses (reported on Form 2106):

    Expenses that are reimbursed by an employee's employer (and included in the employee's income);

    Certain business expenses of reservists;

    Expenses incurred by a qualified performing artist (see below);

    Expenses incurred by an official of a state or local government who is compensated on a fee basis

Deductions for eligible contributions to Health savings accounts (HSAs)

Moving expenses, subject to certain limitations (reported on Form 3903)

Deduction for employer portion (50%) of self employment tax paid by self employed persons

Deductions for contributions to Individual Retirement Accounts or Keogh retirement plans

Deduction for health insurance premiums for eligible self-employed taxpayers

Deductions for penalties imposed for premature withdrawal of funds from a savings account

Alimony payments

Deduction for qualified payments of student loan interest and qualified tuition and fees paid during the taxable year

Domestic production activities deduction

¶6125   DEDUCTIONS "FROM" AGI—ITEMIZED DEDUCTIONS

As seen above, relatively few non-business expenses are deductible *for* AGI. Most personal expenses are not deductible, but those that are must be deducted *from* AGI as itemized deductions. In addition, most investment expenses, as well as most job-related expenses of employees, must be deducted from AGI, typically as *miscellaneous itemized deductions*. Miscellaneous itemized deductions, which are deductible only to the extent they exceed 2% of AGI, are discussed in more depth in Chapter 8.

The miscellaneous itemized deductions category is comprised primarily of *unreimbursed* employee business expenses, investment expenses, and deductions related to taxes such as tax preparation fees. Examples of these (assuming they are not reimbursed by the employer) are listed in Table 2:

Table 2. COMMON DEDUCTIONS "FROM" AGI
Employee travel away from home (including meals and lodging)
Employee transportation expenses
Outside salesperson's expenses [except that "statutory employees" (e.g., full time life insurance salespersons, certain agent or commission drivers, and traveling salespersons) are allowed to report their income and expenses on a separate Schedule C and avoid the 2% of AGI limitation]
Employee entertainment expenses
Employee home office expenses
Union dues
Professional dues and memberships
Subscriptions to business journals
Job seeking expenses (in the same business) or employment seeking expenses
Education expenses
Investment expenses, including expenses for an investment newsletter, investment advice, and rentals of safety deposit boxes
Tax preparation fees or other tax related advice including that received from accountants or attorneys, tax seminars, and books about taxes

With respect to the last item above, the IRS allows taxpayers who own a business, farm, or rental real estate or who have royalty income to allocate a portion of the total cost of preparing their tax return to the cost of preparing Schedule C (trade or business income), Schedule E (rental and royalty income), or Schedule F (farm income) and deduct these costs "for" AGI. Rev. Rul. 92-29, 1992-1 CB 20. The same holds true for expenses incurred in resolving tax controversies, including expenses relating to IRS audits of business or rental activities.

Trade or Business Deductions

¶6201

OVERVIEW—CODE SEC. 162

Two provisions in the Internal Revenue Code provide the authority for the deduction of most expenses: Code Sec. 162 governs the deductibility of trade or business expenses and Code Sec. 212 governs the tax treatment of expenses incurred "for the production of income." Numerous other provisions of the Code also pertain to deductions. These other provisions, however, normally build on the basic rules contained in Code Secs. 162 and 212. For this reason, the importance of these two provisions cannot be overstated.

Code Sec. 162(a), which governs the deductibility of trade or business expenses reads, in part, as follows:

In General.—There shall be allowed as a deduction all the ordinary and necessary expenses paid or incurred during the taxable year in carrying on any trade or business, including—

(1) a reasonable allowance for salaries or other compensation for personal services actually rendered;
(2) traveling expenses (including amounts expended for meals and lodging other than amounts which are lavish or extravagant under the circumstances) while away from home in the pursuit of a trade or business;
(3) rentals or other payments required to be made as a condition to the continued use or possession, for purposes of the trade or business, of property to which the taxpayer has not taken or is not taking title or in which he has no equity.

Although Code Sec. 162(a) specifically enumerates three items that are deductible, the provision's primary importance lies in its general rule: all *ordinary* and *necessary* expenses of carrying on a trade or business are deductible. This is true, with some exceptions, whether the taxpayer is a sole proprietor, a partner in a partnership, or a corporation. The income tax form used to report the deductions is different, but the allowable deductions are generally the same. Typical trade or business deductions allowable to a sole proprietor and reported on Schedule C of Form 1040 are listed in Table 3.

Table 3. TYPICAL BUSINESS DEDUCTIONS ALLOWABLE TO SOLE PROPRIETOR— REPORTED ON SCHEDULE C OF FORM 1040
(Subject to various limitations)

Advertising

Bad debts from sales or services

Bank service charges

Car and truck expenses

Commissions

Cost of goods sold

Depletion

Depreciation

Dues and publications

Employee benefit programs

Freight charges

Insurance

Interest on indebtedness

Legal and professional services

License fees

Office expenses

Pension and profit-sharing plans

Rent on business property

Repairs

Supplies

Taxes

Travel, meals, and entertainment (limited)

Utilities and telephone

Wages

¶6205   GENERAL CRITERIA

An examination of the language of Code Sec. 162 indicates that an expenditure must satisfy four criteria to be properly classified as a trade or business expense:

1. It must be related to carrying on a trade or business activity;
2. It must be ordinary and necessary;
3. It must be reasonable; *and*
4. It must be paid or incurred during the taxable year.

All four of the above requirements must be satisfied or the expense is not deductible as a trade or business expense (though it might still be deductible as an itemized deduction from AGI). However, in some cases, expenses may not be deductible even where they do satisfy all of the above requirements. Other provisions in the Code often operate to prohibit or limit a deduction otherwise allowable under Code Sec. 162. For example, an expense may be ordinary, necessary, and related to carrying on a trade or business, but if it is also related to producing tax-exempt income, Code Sec. 265 prohibits a deduction. This limitation, and others, will be discussed later in this chapter.

¶6215   EXPENSE MUST BE INCURRED IN A TRADE OR BUSINESS ACTIVITY

Whether an expense is deductible depends in part on the type of activity in which it was incurred. A deduction is authorized by Code Sec. 162 only if the expenditure is paid or incurred in an activity that constitutes a trade or business. The purpose of this requirement is to deny deductions for expenses incurred in activities that are primarily personal in nature. For example, the costs incurred in pursuing "hobby" activities, such as collecting antiques or racing automobiles, normally would be considered nondeductible personal expenditures. Of course, this assumes that such activities do not constitute a trade or business. (The rules governing the deduction of "hobby" losses are discussed in more detail in Chapter 7).

The Code provides few clues as to when an activity will be considered a trade or business activity rather than a personal activity. Over the years, however, two criteria have emerged from the many court decisions addressing the issue. The first requirement that must be satisfied in order for an activity to be treated as a trade or business activity is a legitimate *profit motive*. *Doggett v. Burrett*, 3 USTC ¶1090, 12 AFTR 505, 65 F.2d 192 (CA-D.C., 1933). In other words, for the taxpayer's expenses to be deductible, they must be motivated by a genuine hope for a profit. For example, taxpayers who collect antiques or race automobiles can deduct all of their expenses related to these activities only if they are able to demonstrate that those activities were motivated primarily by the hope of producing income. If the required profit motive is lacking, expenses of the activity generally are deductible *only* to the extent of income generated by the activity.

EXAMPLE 6.2

Don Feen is an avid bowler. He is a member of several bowling leagues and often bowls in tournaments. During the past year, he won $1,200 in prize money from his tournament play. He spent $3,500 on travel, bowling supplies and entry fees for tournaments. Although he incurred a net loss of ($2,300) in his bowling activity, he does not mind. He does not bowl with the intent of making a profit. Accordingly, only $1,200 of his bowling expenses are deductible.

The second requirement imposed by the courts before an activity qualifies as a *trade or business* relates to the level of the taxpayer's involvement in the activity. Business status requires both a profit motive and a sufficient degree of taxpayer involvement in the activity to distinguish the activity from a passive investment. No clear guidelines have emerged indicating when a taxpayer's activities rise to the level of carrying on a business. The courts, however, generally have permitted business treatment where the taxpayer has devoted a major portion of time to the activities or the activities have been regular or continuous. *Grier v. U.S.*, 55-1 USTC ¶9184, 46 AFTR 1536, 218 F.2d. 603 (CA-2, 1955).

EXAMPLE 6.3

Charles Green owns multiple rental units, including several condominiums and townhouses. He manages his rental properties entirely by himself. His management activities include seeking new tenants, supplying furnishings, cleaning and preparing the units for occupancy, advertising, and bookkeeping. In this case, Charles' involvement with the rental activities is sufficiently continuous and systematic to constitute a business. *Edwin R. Curphey*, 73 TC 766 (1980). If the rental activities were of a more limited nature, they might not qualify as a trade or business. The determination ultimately depends on the facts of the particular situation.

EXAMPLE 6.4

Helen Thompson owns a sizable portfolio of stocks and bonds. Her managerial activities related to these securities consist primarily of maintaining records and collecting dividends and interest. She rarely trades in the market. Her activities are those normally associated with a passive investor, and accordingly would not constitute a trade or business under Code Sec. 162. *Higgins v. Comm.*, 41-1 USTC ¶9233, 25 AFTR 1160, 312 U.S. 212 (UCSC, 1941).

On the other hand, if Helen had a substantial volume of transactions, made personal investigations of the corporations whose stock she was interested in purchasing, and devoted virtually every day to such work, her activities could constitute a trade or business. *Samuel B. Levin v. U.S.*, 79-1 USTC ¶9331, 43 AFTR2d 79-1057, 597 F.2d 760 (Ct. Cls., 1979). Again, however, the answer depends on the specific circumstances of the taxpayer's activity.

¶6225 EXPENSE MUST BE ORDINARY AND NECESSARY

The second test for deductibility is whether the expense is ordinary and necessary. An expense is *ordinary* if it is normally incurred in the type of business in which the taxpayer is involved. *Deputy v. DuPont*, 40-1 USTC ¶9161, 23 AFTR 808, 308 U.S. 488 (USSC, 1940). This is not to say that the expense is habitual or recurring. *Dunn and McCarthy, Inc. v. Comm.*, 43-2 USTC ¶9688, 31 AFTR 1043, 139 F.2d 242 (CA-2, 1943). In fact, the expense may be incurred only once in the taxpayer's lifetime and be considered ordinary. The test is whether other taxpayers in similar businesses or income producing activities would customarily incur the same type of expense.

EXAMPLE 6.5

> Pete has been in the newspaper business for 35 years. Until this year, his paper had never been sued for libel. However, this year, the paper was sued by a citizen whose alleged crimes were covered in a front page story. To protect the reputation of the newspaper, Pete incurred substantial legal costs related to the libel suit. Although the paper has never incurred legal expenses of this nature before, the expenses are ordinary since it is common in the newspaper business to incur legal expenses to defend against such charges.

It is interesting to note that the "ordinary" criterion normally becomes an issue in circumstances that are, in fact, unusual. For example, in *Goedel*, 39 B.T.A. 1 (1939), a stock dealer paid premiums for insurance on the life of the President of the United States, fearing that his death would disrupt the stock market and his business. The Court denied the deduction on the grounds that the payment was not ordinary but unusual or extraordinary.

A deductible expense must be not only ordinary, but also *necessary*. An expense is necessary if it is appropriate, helpful, or capable of making a contribution to the taxpayer's profit seeking activities. The necessary criterion, however, is rarely applied to deny a deduction. The courts have refrained from such a practice since to do so would require overriding the judgment of the taxpayer. The courts apparently feel that it would be unfair to judge *currently* whether a previous expenditure was necessary at the time it was incurred.

It should be emphasized that not all *necessary* expenses are *ordinary* expenses. Some expenses may be appropriate and helpful to the taxpayer's business but may not be normally incurred in that particular business. In such cases, no deduction is allowed.

EXAMPLE 6.6

> James Kincaid was the sole owner of Kincaid Corporation when it went bankrupt three years ago. A number of creditors lost significant amounts of money due to the bankruptcy. This year, James set up a new business and incorporated it as the Second Time Around Corporation. In order to establish good credit, James had the new corporation pay in full all the former creditors of Kincaid Corporation who lost money in the previous bankruptcy. James had no legal obligation to make these payments. The Second Time Around Corporation deducted these payments on its tax return as ordinary and necessary business expenses. James could argue that the payments made to the former creditors of Kincaid Corporation were necessary payments in order to establish credit for the new corporation, but he probably would have difficulty establishing that the payments were ordinary since they were not typical expenditures that would be made by other taxpayers in a similar situation. Example based on facts in *Welch v. Helvering*, 3 USTC ¶1164, 290 US 111, 54 S.Ct. 8 (1933). However, see *Harold L. and Temple M. Jenkins v. Commissioner*, 47 TCM 238, TC Memo 1983-667 for a case where the deduction was allowed in similar circumstances. Although the IRS disagreed with this decision, it chose not to appeal (AOD 1984-022, March 23, 1984).

TAX BLUNDER

In Example 6.6, James Kincaid made business payments that were, in his opinion, necessary business expenditures. They were not, however, ordinary business expenditures. If James had discussed his plans with a competent tax adviser before making the payments, he may well have taken a different course of action.

¶6235

EXPENSE MUST BE REASONABLE

The third requirement for a deduction is that the expense be reasonable in amount. An examination of Code Sec. 162(a) reveals that the term "reasonable" is used only in conjunction with compensation paid for services (e.g., a reasonable allowance for salaries). The courts have held, however, that reasonableness is implied in the phrase "ordinary and necessary." *Lincoln Electric Co.*, 49-2 USTC ¶9388, 176 F.2d 815 (CA-6 1949), cert. denied, 338 U.S. 949, 70 S.Ct. 488. In practice, the reasonableness standard is most often applied in situations involving salary payments made by a closely held corporation to a shareholder who also is an employee. In these situations, if the compensation paid exceeds that ordinarily paid for similar services—that which is reasonable—the excessive payment may represent a nondeductible dividend distribution. The distinction between reasonable compensation and dividend income is critical because dividends, unlike salaries, are not deductible by the corporation, although both are taxable to the recipient.

EXAMPLE 6.7	Joann Mason is the president and sole owner of Sign Corporation. During the year, Sign Corporation paid Joann a salary of $300,000. Sign Corporation claimed a tax deduction on its tax return for the full salary payment. The Internal Revenue Service (IRS), when auditing Sign Corporation's tax return, could argue that the salary payment to Joann was unreasonable in amount and that a portion of it should be treated as a disguised dividend. The rationale behind the IRS's argument is that dividend payments are not an allowable deduction for a corporation. It may be that by paying an unreasonably high salary to Joann, Sign Corporation was attempting to get a tax deduction for a payment which, in effect, was a nondeductible dividend payment. The same logic could also apply to unreasonably large lease payments and rental payments to stockholders in closely held corporations.
EXAMPLE 6.8	Larry Gill purchased a race car which he used to advertise his closely held company. In addition to driving and maintaining his own car, he also sponsored another driver. Over a two year period, his company spent about $25,000 and $40,000, respectively, maintaining Larry's race car and another $3,000 in each year to sponsor the other driver. The Tax Court ruled that such advertising was ordinary and necessary, but that the amounts expended on his own car were not reasonable – given the relatively small cost of sponsoring another driver, the $65,000 spent on his own car constituted an excessive, and thus unreasonable, expenditure for advertising. The excess of the amounts spent on his own car over those spent to sponsor the other driver were reclassified as nondeductible dividends to Mr. Gill. *Gill v. IRS*, 67 TCM 2311, TC Memo 1994-92, aff'd CA-6, 96-1 USTC ¶50,138.
PLANNING POINTER	In order to lessen the chance of a tax deduction being considered unreasonable by the IRS, the officials of a closely held corporation should substantiate the reasonableness of deductible payments made to owners of the corporation. The reasonableness of an expenditure could be substantiated by documenting similar payments made to shareholder employees by other closely held corporations of comparable size and type. If other comparable businesses are paying similar amounts, the reasonableness of the payments would appear more evident.

¶6245   EXPENSE MUST BE PAID OR INCURRED DURING THE TAXABLE YEAR

Code Secs. 162 and 212 both indicate that an expense is allowable as a deduction only if it is "paid or incurred during the taxable year." Use of both terms, "paid" and "incurred," is necessary because the year in which deductions are allowable depends on the method of accounting used by the taxpayer. Code Sec. 461(a). The term *paid* refers to taxpayers using the cash method of accounting while the term *incurred* refers to taxpayers using the accrual method of accounting. Accordingly, the year in which a deduction is allowed usually depends on whether the cash or accrual method of accounting is used.

Determining when other expenses, such as taxes and bad debts, are incurred is dependent on the nature of the underlying transaction, and the extent to which the expense may be recoverable. Deductibility also depends on the nature of the expense itself – for example, federal income taxes are not deductible at all.

Accrual Method Taxpayers

An accrual method taxpayer deducts expenses when they are incurred. Code Sec. 461(h) provides that for this purpose, an expense is considered incurred when the *all events test* is satisfied and *economic performance* has occurred. Two requirements must be met under the all events test: (1) all events establishing the existence of a liability must have occurred (i.e., the liability is fixed); and (2) the amount of the liability can be determined with reasonable accuracy. Therefore, before the liability may be accrued and deducted it must be fixed and determinable.

EXAMPLE 6.9

In *Hughes Properties, Inc.*, 86-1 USTC ¶9440, 58 AFTR2d 86-5015, 106 S. Ct. 2092 (USSC, 1986), an accrual method corporation owned a gambling casino in Reno, Nevada. The casino operated progressive slot machines that paid a large jackpot about every four months. The increasing amount of the jackpot was maintained and shown by a meter. Under state gaming regulations, the jackpot amount could not be turned back until the amount had been paid to a winner. In addition, the corporation had to maintain a cash reserve sufficient to pay all the guaranteed amounts. At the end of each taxable year, the corporation accrued and deducted the liability for the jackpot as accrued at year end. The IRS challenged the accrual, alleging that the all events test had not been met, and that the amount should be deducted only when paid. It argued that payment of the jackpot was not fixed but contingent, since it was possible that the winning combination may never be pulled. Moreover, the Service pointed out the potential for tax avoidance: the corporation was accruing deductions for payments that may be paid far in the future, and thus—given the time value of money—was overstating the amount of the deduction. The Supreme Court rejected these arguments, stating that the probability of payment was not a remote and speculative possibility. The Court noted that not only was the liability fixed under state law, but it also was not in the interest of the taxpayer to set unreasonably high odds, since customers would refuse to play and would gamble elsewhere.

Cash Method Taxpayers

Determining when a cash method taxpayer has paid an expense is generally not difficult. A cash method taxpayer "pays" the expense when cash, check, property, or service is transferred. Neither a promise to pay nor a note evidencing such a promise is considered payment. Consequently, when a cash method taxpayer buys on credit, no deduction is allowed until the debts are paid. However, if the taxpayer borrows cash and then pays the expense, the expense is deductible when paid. For this reason, a taxpayer who charges expenses to a credit card is deemed to have borrowed cash and made payment when the charge is made. Thus, the deduction is claimed when the charge is actually made and not when the bank makes payment or when the taxpayer pays the bill. Rev. Rul. 78-39, 1978-1 CB 73. When the taxpayer pays by mail, payment is usually considered made when the payment is mailed (i.e., dropped in the post office box). Rev. Rul. 73-99, 1973-1 CB 412.

Restrictions on Use of the Cash Method

Under the general rule, a cash method taxpayer deducts expenses when paid. Without restrictions, however, aggressive taxpayers could liberally interpret this provision to authorize not only deductions for routine items, but also deductions for capital expenditures and other expenses that benefit future periods (e.g., supplies, prepaid insurance, prepaid rent, and prepaid interest). To preclude such an approach, a number of limitations have been imposed on the cash method of accounting.

Provisions of both the Code and the Regulations limit the potential for deducting capital expenditures, prepaid expenses, and the like. For example, Code Sec. 263 provides that no current deduction is allowed for a capital expenditure, such as the costs of purchasing equipment, vehicles, and buildings. These costs must be recovered over the useful life of the acquired property, through the allowance for depreciation.

The Regulations—at least broadly—deal with other expenditures that are not capital expenditures per se but that also benefit future periods. According to the Regulations, any expenditure resulting "in the creation of an asset having a useful life which extends *substantially beyond the close of the taxable year* may not be deductible when made, or may be deductible only in part." Reg. §1.446-1(a)(1). In this regard, the courts agree that "substantially beyond" means a useful life of more than one year. *Martin J. Zaninovich*, 69 TC 605, *rev'd* in 80-1 USTC ¶9342, 45 AFTR2d 80-1442, 616 F.2d 429 (CA-9, 1980). Perhaps the simplest example of this rule as so interpreted concerns payments for supplies. Assuming the supplies would be exhausted before the close of the following tax year, a deduction should be allowable when payment is made. In regard to other prepayments, however, the application of this principle has spawned a hodgepodge of special rules.

Prepaid Rent

The 9th Circuit Court of Appeals' decision in *Zaninovich* above held that a cash method taxpayer's prepayments for rents or services may be deducted in the year paid when two conditions are present: (1) the period for which the payment is made does not exceed one year following the end of the current tax year, and (2) the taxpayer is contractually obligated to prepay an amount for a period extending beyond the close of the year. *Martin J. Zaninovich, supra*. If either of these conditions is not satisfied, advanced payment of rent is not deductible until the subsequent year(s).

EXAMPLE 6.10

> Rick Hatfield, a farmer, is a cash method calendar-year taxpayer. In 2017, he leased farm land for the twenty year period December 1, 2017 to November 30, 2037. The lease agreement provides that annual rent for the period December 1 to November 30 is payable on December 20 each year. The yearly rent is $24,000. On December 20, 2017, Rick paid the $24,000 rental for the next year. The prepayment is deductible because it is for a period not exceeding a year and Rick is obligated to pay for the entire year in advance on December 20. However, if the lease agreement required only monthly rentals of $2,000 each (instead of an annual payment of $24,000), only $2,000 would be deductible (representing the rent allocable to the month of December) because the remainder of the payment was voluntary. *Bonaire Development Co.*, 82-2 USTC ¶9428, 679 F.2d 159 (CA-9, 1983), *aff'g*, 76 TC 789 (1981).

Prepaid Insurance

Prepayments of insurance premiums normally are not deductible when paid. Instead, the IRS holds that this expense must be prorated over the period actually covered by the insurance policy. Rev. Rul. 70-413, 1970-2 CB 103. However, the "one year" exception noted above with respect to prepaid rent may also apply here.

EXAMPLE 6.11

> On December 15, 2017, Thelma purchased an insurance policy covering theft of her inventory. The policy cost $3,000 and covered the period 2018-2020. Thelma may not deduct any portion of the cost of the insurance policy in 2017. The cost will be deductible $1,000 per year in each of the next three years.

Prepaid Interest

Code Sec. 461(g) expressly denies the deduction of prepaid interest. Prepaid interest must be capitalized and deducted ratably over the period of the loan. The same is true for any costs associated with obtaining the loan. The sole exception is for "points" paid for a debt incurred by the taxpayer to purchase his or her *principal* residence. "Points" are a form of prepaid interest often charged to a borrower by a mortgage lender as a condition of making the loan. For example, a mortgage lender may charge 1.5 "points," or 1.5 percent of the amount being borrowed, as a fee to extend a mortgage loan. Points paid by a taxpayer to obtain a mortgage to *purchase* his or her *principal* residence can be deducted in the year paid. This treatment does not apply to points paid on a loan incurred to refinance the taxpayer's existing mortgage. The IRS has ruled that points paid on refinancing must be capitalized and amortized over the life of the loan the same as other types of prepaid interest. Rev. Rul. 87-22, 1987-1 CB 146.

EXAMPLE 6.12

> Karen applied for a loan for the purchase of a new house costing $200,000. The bank agreed to make her a loan of 80% of the purchase price, or $160,000 (80% of $200,000) for thirty years at a cost of two points (two percentage "points" of the loan obtained). Thus, she must pay $4,000 (2% of $200,000) to obtain the loan. Assuming it is established business practice in her area to charge points in consideration of the loan, the $4,000 in points (prepaid interest) are deductible. However, if the house is not Karen's principal residence, then the points must be deducted ratably (amortized) over the 30 year loan period. Similarly, if the loan had been incurred to *refinance* the original mortgage on the home, the points would not be currently deductible, but would be amortized over the term of the loan (30 years in this case).

Other Prepayments

Perhaps the Service's current view of the proper treatment of most prepayments is best captured in a ruling concerning prepayment for animal feed. In this ruling, the taxpayer, a cattle rancher, purchased a substantial amount of feed prior to the year in which it would be used. The purchase was made in advance because the price was low due to a depressed market. The IRS granted a deduction for the prepayment because there was a business purpose for the advanced payment, the payment was not merely a deposit, and it did not materially distort income. Based on this ruling and related cases, prepayments normally should be deductible if the asset will be consumed by the close of the following year, there is a business purpose for the expenditure, and there is no material distortion of income. Rev. Rul. 79-229, 1979-2 CB 210.

Taxes

Most taxes incurred by a trade or business (with the exception of federal income taxes) are deductible for tax purposes as business expenses. Federal income taxes are not deductible on the federal income tax return since the return is being prepared to compute the amount of federal income taxes due.

Payroll taxes paid by an employer are fully deductible, but taxes withheld from employee wages such as federal, state, and local income taxes payable and F.I.C.A. taxes are not. The latter type of tax expense (withholdings from employees' wages) is not *incurred* by the employer, but by the employee. Accordingly, the employer is not allowed a deduction for these expenditures.

Similarly, while property taxes are generally deductible by the taxpayer who pays them, if business property is sold during the year, the property taxes related to the property must be allocated between the buyer and the seller based on the number of days during the tax year that each party held the property. Code Sec. 164(d). The seller is treated as paying the tax up to, but not including, the date of sale. This allocation is required regardless of which party actually pays the property tax and regardless of the method of accounting used by the two parties. The rationale is that the buyer *incurs* the property tax for the period during which he or she owns the property. To the extent that tax has previously been paid by the seller, a portion of the purchase price paid by the buyer is treated as compensation for the buyer's share of the previously paid property tax. The seller, having been reimbursed for this portion of the property taxes, is allowed to deduct only the portion attributable to the period during which he or she owned the property, and the buyer deducts the rest.

EXAMPLE 6.13

On October 1, Joe purchased a tract of land from Kelly for $138,000. Kelly had previously paid annual property taxes on the land in the amount of $8,030. Assuming a 365 day year, Joe has owned the land for 92 days (Oct. 1 through Dec. 31), and Kelly for 273 days. Thus, $2,024 of the property tax for the year of the sale is allocable to Joe (92 days/365 days). Joe, not Kelly, will be allowed to claim a deduction for this portion of the annual property taxes, and the deemed selling price of the land will be $135,976 ($138,000 - $2,024). Note that while Kelly will be allowed to deduct only $6,006 of the property taxes paid during the year (the part deemed to be "incurred" by her), she will also be deemed to have sold the land for only $135,976 (rather than the $138,000 actual selling price), reducing any gain she may recognize on the sale by an amount equal to the foregone property tax deduction.

Bad Debts

The determination of whether a bad debt loss has been incurred can be difficult. Several issues must be considered. First, the taxpayer must be able to establish that an actual debt existed. This is generally rather easy for business debts, but can be quite difficult for debts between family members, friends, or other related parties. If the nature of the underlying transaction is not a valid debt – for example, if the taxpayer did not really intend to collect the debt, or if collection was to occur only in the event that the borrower was able to repay the purported loan, the transaction will be recharacterized as a gift rather than a loan and no deduction will be allowed.

The second issue to be considered is the amount of the loss, if any, actually incurred. Generally speaking, the amount of a bad debt deduction is limited to the adjusted basis of the debt in the hands of the taxpayer. For a business taxpayer using the cash method of accounting, the adjusted basis of business accounts receivable is normally zero; the receivables have not been recognized for tax purposes because income is recorded only when cash is collected. Since the income from the receivables has yet to be realized, no loss is incurred in the event the receivables are not collected.

EXAMPLE 6.14

On September 16, 2017, Roscoe Accounting Services, a cash method taxpayer, sells $300 of accounting services to Ron Ranger on credit. One month later, Ron is declared bankrupt and cannot pay any of the $300 debt to Roscoe. Since Roscoe uses the cash method of accounting, income is not recognized for tax purposes until cash is collected and, therefore, its accounts receivable have a zero basis. Roscoe is not entitled to a bad debt deduction for the $300 bad account receivable since the receivable has a zero basis for tax purposes.

¶6245

Finally, assuming the taxpayer has a tax basis in a valid debt, the taxpayer must be able to establish that the debt is not collectible. A business bad debt deduction can be taken by proving only partial worthlessness of a debt while full worthlessness of a debt must be proven in order to claim a nonbusiness bad debt deduction. Worthlessness of a debt is established by reviewing the facts existing in each case. Reg. §1.166-2(b). The debtor's bankruptcy, death of the debtor, or unsuccessful court action against the debtor to collect the debt may be indications of the worthlessness of a debt. A taxpayer does not necessarily have to take legal action against a debtor to prove worthlessness of a debt. The facts may suggest that legal action would not have resulted in recovery of any of the debt.

Business Bad Debts

The deductibility of a bad debt further depends on the character of the underlying debt. Generally speaking, business bad debts are fully deductible by the taxpayer from gross income as an ordinary business expense in the year they become either partially or wholly worthless. (If the debt is not wholly worthless, only the amount not expected to be collected can be deducted.) Non-business bad debts, in contrast, can be deducted for tax purposes only if the debt is completely worthless. Moreover, worthlessness of a nonbusiness bad debt is always treated as a short-term capital loss and is subject to the $3,000 limitation applicable to the deduction for net capital losses (discussed in greater detail in Chapter 12). Code Sec. 166(d)(1)(B).

In contrast, when a taxpayer can demonstrate that a business debt has become wholly or partially worthless, the taxpayer can claim a deduction from *gross* income (i.e., a deduction "for" AGI) for the full amount not expected to be collected. A business debt is a debt (1) created or acquired in connection with the taxpayer's trade or business, or (2) the worthlessness of which has been incurred in the taxpayer's trade or business. Reg. §1.166-5(b). Amounts advanced to a corporation in exchange for a bond, debenture, note or other evidence of indebtedness are investments, rather than business debts. Accordingly, the partial or total worthlessness of such investments is *not* deductible as a business bad debt (although it may be deductible as a nonbusiness bad debt). Similarly, amounts advanced to a corporation by a shareholder to be used by the corporation to pay its debts are not business loans, regardless of how they are structured.

EXAMPLE 6.15	Susan Sanford owes $1,000 to the Sioto Lumber Company, an accrual method taxpayer, for lumber purchased from the company. Sioto Lumber Co. estimates that it will eventually collect from Susan only $300 of the $1,000 debt. Since the debt to Sioto is a business debt, Sioto is entitled to a $700 bad debt deduction this year for partial worthlessness of the business debt.

A cash method taxpayer can deduct a business bad debt only if an actual cash loss has been sustained or if the amount to be deducted was previously included in income. Nearly all accrual method taxpayers must use the specific charge-off method to deduct business bad debts; the reserve method for computing and deducting bad debts may be used only by small banks and thrift institutions. Under the specific charge-off method, when a specific debt, or portion thereof, becomes worthless, it is written off as an ordinary deduction for tax purposes.

Since the tax treatment accorded business bad debts and nonbusiness bad debts differs, the taxpayer must show that the dominant motivation in making the loan was business related in order to obtain the more favorable tax treatment. Specific charge-off is based on actual worthlessness and is not applicable merely because the taxpayer gives up attempts to collect. A worthless debt arising from unpaid rent, interest, or a similar item is not deductible unless the income that such item represents has been reported for income tax purposes by a taxpayer using the accrual method of accounting.

Nonbusiness Bad Debts

Nonbusiness bad debts are debts that are not created or acquired in connection with a trade or business. Loans to relatives and friends are the most common type of nonbusiness debt. Nonbusiness bad debts can be deducted for tax purposes only if full worthlessness of the debt has been determined and then only by the specific charge-off method. The deduction is allowed in the year when full worthlessness takes place, regardless of how old the debt is. In contrast to a business bad debt which is deductible as an ordinary loss in the year incurred, a nonbusiness bad debt deduction is always treated as a short-term capital loss and is subject to the $3,000 limitation applicable to the deduction for capital losses (discussed in greater detail in Chapter 12). Code Sec. 166(d)(1)(B).

EXAMPLE 6.16

Clara owes $1,000 to Mike on a personal loan. Mike estimates that he will only collect $300 of his $1,000 loan to Clara. Mike is not entitled to a $700 bad debt deduction at this time since total worthlessness must be proven before a bad debt deduction can be taken for a nonbusiness bad debt. If Clara paid $300 to Mike and the remaining $700 of debt is subsequently determined to be worthless, a $700 nonbusiness bad debt deduction can then be claimed by Mike since total worthlessness of the *remaining* debt has been established.

Expenses Incurred for the Production of Income

¶6301

CODE SEC. 212—PRODUCTION OF INCOME OR PROTECTION OF ASSETS

Prior to enactment of Code Sec. 212, many investment related expenses were not deductible because the activities did not rise to the level of a trade or business activity. Congress enacted Code Sec. 212 in 1942, allowing for the deduction of expenses related to the "production or collection of income." As a result, the question of deductibility (assuming the other requirements discussed above are met) is effectively reduced to a single important question: Is the expense related to an activity engaged in for profit?

Production of income expenses are deductible if they are incurred:

1. For the production or collection of income;
2. For the management, conservation, or maintenance of property held for the production of income; or
3. In connection with the determination, collection, or refund of any tax.

Generally speaking, expenses related to the production of income consist primarily of those expenses incurred in rental and investment activities as well as tax planning and compliance expenses. To be deductible, such expenses must be ordinary, necessary, and reasonable. Unlike trade or business expenses, expenses related to the production of income are generally deductible as miscellaneous itemized deductions with the exception of rents and royalty expenses which are deductible for AGI on Schedule E. Code Sec. 62(a)(4).

¶6315

INVESTMENT EXPENSE DEDUCTIONS

Typical investment expenses which are deductible include safe deposit box rentals, rent and royalty expenses, investment counsel fees, subscriptions to investment-related journals, newspapers, and other publications, investment custodial fees, legal and accounting fees related to investments, and investment-related clerical fees and office rent. Code Sec. 212. The Code also allows an annual investment-related interest expense deduction which is limited to net investment income. This deduction is discussed in Chapter 8. Code Sec. 163(d).

¶6325

TAX PLANNING AND COMPLIANCE EXPENSES

All expenses incurred by individual taxpayers in connection with the determination, collection, or refund of any tax are deductible under Code Sec. 212 as nonbusiness expenses. Deductions in this area apply to tax planning expenses and tax compliance expenses of individuals and are properly classified as miscellaneous itemized deductions on the tax return. Businesses classify tax planning and compliance expenses as trade or business deductions. The cost of having a tax return prepared by a CPA or tax service is deductible as well as the legal fees incurred in contesting a tax liability in court. Deductions for tax planning and compliance expenses are not limited to the income tax area but also extend to gift and estate tax returns. Fees paid for tax advice regarding estate planning as well as divorce proceedings are also deductible. Rev. Rul. 72-545, 1972-2 CB 179.

EXAMPLE 6.17

Barbara is involved in divorce proceedings. Some of the legal advice she has received regarding the divorce involves advice on minimizing her future tax liability. If the part of the legal fee related to tax advice can be separated from the total legal fee for the divorce (and if it can be substantiated) Barbara may deduct this amount on her tax return as a tax planning expense.

TAX BLUNDER

In Example 6.17, assume that Barbara receives a bill from her lawyer that states "Legal Services — $3,000." If she does not request a breakout of the portion of the legal fee relating to tax planning advice, Barbara will lose the opportunity for a tax planning advice deduction on her tax return.

Deductions for Losses

¶6401   CODE SEC. 165

Code Sec. 165 establishes the general framework governing the deductibility of losses. This statute permits a deduction for the following categories of losses so long as they are not compensated for by insurance or otherwise (for example by settlement of a lawsuit):

1. Losses incurred in a trade or business (deductible without limitation);
2. Losses incurred in transactions entered into for profit, though not connected with a trade or business (deductible as capital losses); and
3. Losses of property not connected with a trade or business if such losses arise from fire, storm, shipwreck, or other casualty, or from theft (deductible as itemized deductions, subject to certain limitations discussed in Chapter 8).

Losses cannot be deducted unless attributable to a closed and completed transaction. Mere declines in value or other unrealized losses cannot be deducted. Normally, for the loss to qualify as a deduction, the property must be sold, abandoned, or scrapped. In some cases, (e.g., stock in a bankrupt company), a taxpayer may not be able to sell property because it has become completely worthless. In such cases, if the taxpayer can demonstrate the worthlessness of the property, a deduction will be allowed for the loss. The amount of the loss for tax purposes cannot exceed the taxpayer's basis in the property.

Note that personal losses—other than those attributable to a casualty or theft—are not deductible. For example, a loss incurred on the sale of a personal residence is not deductible.

EXAMPLE 6.18

Janet owns 100 shares of Clinton Corporation stock which she purchased on January 4, 2017, for $84 per share. On December 31, 2017, Clinton Corporation stock was selling at $52 per share. Janet cannot deduct the $32 per share decline in value on her 2017 tax return since it is an unrealized loss. Janet would have to sell her stock before year end in order to recognize a loss for tax purposes.

Examples of losses that can be deducted by individual taxpayers are listed in Table 4. Tax losses are discussed in greater detail in Chapter 7.

Table 4. LOSSES DEDUCTIBLE ON AN INDIVIDUAL'S TAX RETURN (SUBJECT TO VARIOUS LIMITATIONS)

Losses deductible for AGI

Business net operating loss carryback or carryforward

Business or investment-related casualty or theft loss

Loss on sale or exchange of business property

Loss on sale or exchange of investment property

Worthless securities

Losses deductible from AGI

Gambling losses but only to extent of gambling winnings

Personal casualty or theft loss

Other Allowable Deductions "For" AGI

¶6505   BUSINESS INVESTIGATION START-UP AND ORGANIZATIONAL COSTS

Business investigation expenses are those costs of seeking and reviewing prospective businesses prior to reaching a decision to acquire or enter any business. For example, expenses incurred to analyze potential markets, products, the availability of workers, transportation facilities, etc. before entering into a new business would constitute business investigation expenses. Once the taxpayer has decided to enter the new business, additional costs may be incurred for pre-opening advertising, employee training, lining up distributors, suppliers, or potential customers, legal and accounting fees, etc. These expenses, incurred after the decision to acquire a business, but before such business actually begins operations, are called "start-up" expenses.

For many years, the deductibility of expenses of business investigation and start up turned solely on whether the taxpayer was "carrying on" a business at the time the expenditures were incurred. Notwithstanding some modifications, the basic rule still remains: when the taxpayer is in the same or similar business as the one he or she is starting or investigating, the costs of investigation and start up are wholly deductible in the year paid or incurred. *The Colorado Springs National Bank v. U.S.*, 74-2 USTC ¶9809, 34 AFTR2d 74-6166, 505 F.2d 1185 (CA-10, 1974). The deduction is allowed whether or not the taxpayer ultimately decides to expand his/her business. *York v. Comm.*, 58-2 USTC ¶9952, 2 AFTR2d 6178, 261 F.2d 421 (CA-4, 1958). However, this rule often forces taxpayers to litigate to determine whether a business existed at the time the expenses were incurred. Prior to the enactment of Code Sec. 195, if the taxpayer could not establish the existence of a business, the expenditures normally were treated as capital expenditures with indeterminable lives. *Morton Frank*, 20 TC 511 (1953). As a result, the taxpayer could only recover the expenditure if and when he or she disposed of or abandoned the business.

EXAMPLE 6.19

Selma owns and operates an ice cream shop on the north side of the city. A new shopping mall is opening on the south side of the city, and the developers have approached her about locating a second ice cream shop in their mall. Last year, Selma paid a consulting firm $1,000 for a survey of the potential market on the south side. Because Selma was in the ice cream business when the expense was incurred, the entire $1,000 is deductible whether or not she decides to open a second ice cream shop in the southside mall.

Code Sec. 195, implemented in 1980, allows taxpayers to elect to deduct up to $5,000 of start-up expenditures in the tax year in which their trade or business begins. The $5,000 amount must be reduced by the amount by which the start-up expenditures exceed $50,000. The remainder of any start-up expenditures must be amortized over a 180 month period beginning with the month in which the active trade or business begins. It is important to recognize that Code Sec. 195 is elective. Expenses for research and development, interest payments, and taxes are not considered start up expenditures. Code Sec. 195(c)(1). Consequently, these costs are not subject to Code Sec. 195 and may be deducted under normal rules.

EXAMPLE 6.20

Jerry, a calendar year, cash method taxpayer, recently graduated with a degree in restaurant, hotel and institutional management. Jerry paid an accountant $1,200 in September to review the financial situation of a small restaurant he was thinking of buying. In December, Jerry purchased the restaurant and began actively participating in its management. Jerry may deduct the full $1,200 accountant's fee on his tax return for the current year as a start-up expenditure.

EXAMPLE 6.21

Until February, Carlos Aguirre worked for a home builder in Ohio. In March, he left his job and started his own construction company. While his new offices were under construction, he set up shop in a trailer on the construction site. He hired two outside sales representatives who began establishing their customer networks, and an architect to work in the design phase of the business. He paid a printer to print brochures for the new company, and began advertising in local media. All told, he spent $45,000 on these items before the new company opened its doors to the public. Under Code Sec. 195, he can deduct the first $5,000 of these expenses, and must amortize the remaining $40,000 over 180 months beginning in the first month the company begins doing business. Assume the company began actual business operations in July. Carlos' deduction for start-up expenses in its first year of operations will be $6,333, consisting of the $5,000 first-year deduction plus $222.22 per month ($40,000 ÷ 180 months) for 6 months (July—December). Note that if Carlos had spent $52,000 in start-up expenses, rather than $45,000, the amount deductible in the current year would have been only $3,000 plus $272.22 ($49,000 ÷ 180 months) per month for 6 months. The $5,000 first year deduction would be reduced by the excess of total start-up expenses incurred over $50,000.

As suggested above, the taxpayer must enter the business to qualify for amortization. No deduction is allowed for costs incurred to investigate a *new* business that the taxpayer decides not to pursue.

Similar rules apply to "organizational" expenses incurred in forming a new corporation [Code Sec. 248] or partnership [Code Sec. 709(b)]. The first $5,000 of such expenses may be deducted on the corporation's or partnership's first tax return, with any amounts in excess of $5,000 amortized over 180 months. As with start-up expenses, the $5,000 deduction is reduced (but not below zero) by the amount by which total organizational expenditures exceed $50,000. Organizational expenditures include expenditures for legal and accounting services, filing fees paid to the state for legal recognition of the new entity, expenditures on directors' fees paid to temporary directors, and expenditures on organizational meetings of directors, shareholders or partners.

¶6515   BUSINESS GIFTS

Code Sec. 274(b) allows a deduction for business gifts in amounts up to $25 per recipient per year. The expenses are deductible "for" AGI as business expenses for self-employed taxpayers. Taxpayers working as employees can deduct such expenditures as miscellaneous itemized deductions. A business gift normally does not have to be included in the gross income of the recipient. The following items are specifically excluded from the definition of business gifts:

1. Items costing $4 or less which have the name of the taxpayer permanently imprinted on them
2. Signs, display racks, and other promotional materials to be used on the business premises of the recipient; and
3. Tangible personal property awarded to an employee by reason of length of service or safety achievement that does not exceed $400 in value (nonqualified plans) or $1,600 in value if awarded according to a qualified plan award where the average award does not exceed $400.

EXAMPLE 6.22

During the current year, the salesperson for ABC Vending Co. gave the owner of Video Games Co. a total of five bottles of high quality wine as business gifts at various times during the year. The five bottles of wine were purchased by ABC Vending Co. for a total of $150. ABC Vending Co. is entitled to a maximum deduction of $25 for the business gifts. The remaining $125 cost of the gifts is not deductible for tax purposes.

¶6535   TRANSPORTATION EXPENSES

Transportation expenses are defined for tax purposes as the costs of transporting a taxpayer from one location to another when the taxpayer is not travelling away from home overnight for business. Reg. §1.62-1(g). Transportation expenses include air fares, taxi fares, automobile expenses, parking fees, turnpike tolls, etc.

Transportation expenses of a self-employed taxpayer are deductible for AGI as trade or business expenses. Unreimbursed employee transportation expenses are deductible from AGI as miscellaneous itemized deductions subject to the 2 percent of AGI limitation (see discussion in Chapter 8). In order for transportation expenses to be deductible by an employee, however, the expenses must be paid or incurred in connection with services performed as an employee. Commuting expenses of an employee going from home to work and back have generally been held to be nondeductible expenses. The length of commute is considered a matter of personal preference and therefore irrelevant for tax purposes. If a taxpayer has a temporary work assignment beyond the general work area, however, and chooses to return home each night, the transportation expenses related to the round trip are deductible if not reimbursed by the employer. Work assignments with a duration in excess of one year are considered nontemporary and related transportation costs are nondeductible commuting expenses. Code Sec. 162.

EXAMPLE 6.23	John Rinaldo is the manager of a retail store in the city of Clyde. He drives 10 miles to and from work each day. Transportation costs associated with his drive to and from work each day would not be deductible since they are ordinary commuting expenses. In August, John's employer requested that he be the temporary manager for two weeks at the company store in Sidney while the regular manager took vacation. The Sidney store is approximately 120 miles round-trip from John's home. His employer did not reimburse him for his transportation expenses in going to the Sidney store. The transportation expenses incurred by John during his two-week assignment in Sidney are deductible on John's tax return as transportation expenses incurred in going to a temporary work assignment beyond his general work area.

Another deductible employee transportation expense is the expense of going from one job to another job during the same workday. The costs of going to the first job and home from the second job are not deductible, but the costs of traveling from the first job to the second job are deductible. *R. Paolini,* 43 TCM 513, Dec. 38,784(M), T.C. Memo. 1982-69. Where an employee incurs additional transportation expenses beyond what would normally be incurred in commuting to work because the employee has to transport heavy and bulky tools to work, these additional expenses are also deductible as transportation expenses. Rev. Rul. 75-380, 1975-2 CB 59.

Computing Automobile Expenses

Automobile expenses are deductible as transportation expenses if incurred in connection with a trade or business or by an employee in connection with employment duties to the extent not reimbursed by the employer. Two methods are available for computing automobile expenses: the taxpayer can keep records of the actual operating costs of the automobile, including an allowance for depreciation, or, in certain instances, can deduct a standard mileage rate.

If the taxpayer uses the actual operating cost method of determining deductible automobile expenses, records must be kept of the actual costs of operation of the automobile, which include gas, oil, repairs, insurance, depreciation, licenses, and other costs. The taxpayer deducts the portion of these expenses that applies to the business use of the automobile.

The other method for calculating automobile expenses is the standard mileage rate method. Under this method, the taxpayer keeps track of the number of miles driven in the car in connection with his or her business activities and claims a standard cost per mile. For 2017, the standard mileage rate is 53.5 cents per mile. Notice 2016-79, IR 2016-169, Dec. 14, 2016. Parking fees, tolls, and state and local property taxes paid on the automobile can be deducted in addition to the standard mileage rate. However, other actual expenses (gasoline, repairs, depreciation, etc.) cannot. In lieu of depreciation, taxpayers using the standard mileage rate must reduce the tax basis of the automobile by 25 cents per business mile.

Note that the standard mileage rate cannot be used if the taxpayer has previously used the actual expense method and claimed a depreciation deduction in excess of straight line in the first year the automobile was used for business. The reverse is not true, however; a taxpayer opting to use the standard mileage method in the first year the auto is used for business may change to the actual operating costs method in a subsequent year.

PLANNING POINTER	The actual cost method of calculating automobile expenses will usually result in a larger deduction for tax purposes than the standard mileage rate method. The disadvantage of the actual cost method as compared to the standard mileage rate method is the additional recordkeeping requirements that are required.

¶6545   TRAVEL EXPENSES

Code Section 162(a)(2) allows a deduction for all the ordinary and necessary expenses paid or incurred during the taxable year in carrying on any trade or business, including travel expenses incurred while the taxpayer is away from home overnight. Travel expenses consist of the costs of transportation (airfare, taxi fare, etc.), amounts spent for meals and lodging other than amounts which are lavish or extravagant under the circumstances, and other incidental expenses such as laundry and dry cleaning expenses. Self-employed taxpayers deduct travel expenses for AGI as trade or business expenses. Unreimbursed employee travel expenses are deductible from AGI as miscellaneous itemized deductions, subject to the 2% floor.

To be deductible, travel expenses must be incurred while the taxpayer is "away from home" overnight. Overnight does not mean a full 24-hour period, but a period substantially longer than a normal work day where it is reasonable to need sleep or rest to meet normal job requirements. Rev. Rul. 75-168, 1975-1 CB 58.

EXAMPLE 6.24	Linda James, a CPA, drives from Columbus, Ohio to Cincinnati, Ohio, a distance of 100 miles, on Thursday night in order to attend a business meeting in Cincinnati on Friday morning at 9 a.m. The meeting ends at 11 a.m. and Linda drives back to Columbus. Linda can deduct the travel expenses related to her trip even though it did not cover a 24-hour period.

The travel deduction is available for taxpayers who incur expenses to engage in business at locations distant from the taxpayer's "tax home." For this purpose, however, a taxpayer's tax home is deemed to be located at the location of the taxpayer's "principal place of business." If a taxpayer chooses to live in an area other than where he or she works, that choice is deemed to be a personal preference not mandated by business considerations. In such cases, no deduction is allowed for costs incurred in travel between the taxpayer's residence and his or her principal place of business.

Questions regarding the location of a taxpayer's "home" for tax purposes often arise in two situations. The first is when a taxpayer works in more than one location. In such cases, the IRS considers the following three factors in determining which of the taxpayer's multiple work locations is his or her "principal" place of business: (1) length of time spent at each location; (2) degree of business activity at each location; and (3) amount of income derived from each location. The more important location when measured against these three criteria is the taxpayer's principal place of business. No deduction is allowable for travel to that location.

EXAMPLE 6.25	Larry Robinson, a CPA and a single taxpayer, works for a CPA firm in Cleveland, Ohio, from June through October each year and works for a CPA firm in Miami, Florida, from November through May. Larry makes approximately $20,000 in salary from his work in Cleveland and approximately $35,000 in salary from his work in Miami. Which area is Larry's tax home, Cleveland or Miami? Consideration of the length of time spent at each location indicates Miami as the tax home (seven months versus five months). Amount of income derived from each location also indicates Miami as the tax home ($35,000 versus $20,000). Since Miami is Larry's tax home, living costs in the Miami area are not deductible on Larry's tax return. Travel expenses incurred when traveling to and from and working in Cleveland are deductible as temporary living expenses. Another factor to consider in this case is that the IRS might argue that Larry has two tax homes, Cleveland and Miami. This issue could be refuted, however, if Larry can demonstrate that his travel expenses in Cleveland duplicate some of the living expenses he incurs in Miami when he is living in Cleveland. Apartment or motel expenses incurred in Cleveland while, at the same time, Larry still maintains an apartment in Miami are duplicate living expenses.

Questions also arise when the taxpayer's business or employer requires that he or she work in a distant location for a lengthy period of time. A deduction for travel expenses, including duplicate living expenses (lodging, utilities, food, etc.) is available where the work away from the taxpayer's home is temporary— i.e., where it is not indefinite (the taxpayer does not know how long it will last) and it does not last for more than one year. Even if the taxpayer does not incur duplicate living expenses, he or she may take a business deduction for daily transportation expenses paid or incurred in traveling between the taxpayer's residence and a temporary work location, regardless of the distance traveled. Rev. Rul. 90-23, 1990-1 CB 28. Because the alternative work location is temporary, travel between the taxpayer's home and that location is not treated as a commuting expense, which is ordinarily nondeductible.

Where the assignment is not temporary, however, no deduction for travel from the taxpayer's residence to his or her work location is allowed. If the assignment is indefinite, or lasts more than one year, the assigned location becomes the taxpayer's principal place of business. A taxpayer cannot deduct the cost of meals and lodging while performing duties at a principal place of business, even though the taxpayer maintains a permanent residence elsewhere. Congress did not intend to allow as a business expense those outlays that are not caused by the exigencies of the business but by the action of the taxpayer in having a home, for the taxpayer's convenience, at a distance from the business. Such expenditures are not essential for the conduct of the business and were not within the contemplation of Congress, which proceeded on the assumption that a person engaged in business would live within reasonable proximity of the business. *Barnhill v. Commissioner*, 148 F.2d 913 (4th Cir. 1945), 1945 CB 96; *Commissioner v. Stidger*, 386 U.S. 237 (1967), 1967-1 CB 32.

Combining Business and Personal Travel

Travel expenses are deductible for tax purposes if a taxpayer is away from home in pursuit of a trade or business including employment activities and attending a convention. A person may, however, combine personal activities such as sightseeing with a business trip. If the primary purpose of the trip is business, travel expenses including all transportation expenses are deductible as business expenses even though some time is spent on personal activities. Any direct costs associated with the personal activity, however, are not deductible. If the primary purpose of the trip is personal, travel expenses are not deductible even though some business activities are conducted during the trip. Direct costs of any business activity conducted on a personal trip such as renting a car to attend a business meeting are deductible by the taxpayer. Costs associated with taking a spouse along on a business trip are not deductible unless it can be shown that the presence of the spouse had a business purpose and the spouse is also employed by the person paying or reimbursing the expenses. Reg. §1.162-2(c).

More restrictive travel requirements apply to travel outside of the United States. Travel expenses, including transportation expenses incurred on foreign trips, must be allocated between business and personal activities unless travel outside of the United States does not exceed seven days or time attributable to personal activities is less than 25 percent of the total travel time. Code Sec. 274(c). Additional travel restrictions apply to attendance at foreign conventions and attendance at business meetings on cruise ships. Code Sec. 274(h).

Substantiation of Travel Expenses

Taxpayers must substantiate expenditures for travel and transportation expenses by adequate records or by sufficient evidence corroborating the taxpayer's statements as to (1) amount, (2) time and place, (3) business purpose, and (4) business relationship to the taxpayer. Taxpayers must have documentary evidence for any lodging expense while traveling away from home and for any other expenditure of $75 or more, except transportation charges if documentary evidence is not readily available.

In lieu of substantiating actual travel-related meal and lodging costs, employers and employees may utilize optional IRS per diem allowances. The federal per diem rate is equal to the sum of the federal lodging expense allowance and the federal meal and incidental expense (M&IE) rate for the locality of travel. For travel occurring after October 1, 2016, the M&IE rates are $68 per day for any high-cost locality and $57 per day for other localities within the United States. The M&IE rate for travel outside the United States is equal to 40 percent of the per diem rate for the locality of travel. The maximum per diem rate is $282 for high-cost localities ($214 for lodging plus $68 for M&IE), while for all other localities the maximum per diem rate is $189 ($132 for lodging and $57 for M&IE). Notice 2016-58, IRB 2016-41, October 11, 2016. The per diem amount is subject to the 50 percent limit on meals and entertainment expenses, which is discussed in ¶6755. IRS Pub. 1542.

¶6560   MOVING EXPENSES

A deduction is allowed for moving expenses paid or incurred in connection with the commencement of work by a taxpayer as an employee or as a self-employed individual at a new principal place of work. Code Sec. 217. In order to qualify for the moving expense deduction, a taxpayer must move because of a new job location. It is not necessary that the taxpayer have a prior job location. Moving expenses incurred without changing job locations are not deductible.

Time and Distance Requirements

In order for moving expenses to be deductible, the taxpayer also must meet a time requirement and a distance requirement. The time requirement states that an employee must work full-time at the new job location for at least 39 weeks in the 12-month period following the move in order for the moving expenses to be deductible. If self-employed, the taxpayer must work in the new location for 78 weeks during the two-year period following the move for the expenses to be deductible with 39 of the weeks required to be in the first 12 months. The time requirement does not apply if a worker dies, is discharged from work, becomes disabled, or is transferred by the employer. Reg. §1.217-2(d)(1).

If a taxpayer has not completed the time requirement when filing an income tax return, the moving expense deduction can be taken in the year the expenses are paid assuming that the taxpayer will meet the time requirement in the following tax year. If the time requirement is not met in the following year, the moving expense deduction taken in the prior year normally must be recognized as income in the year the time requirement is not met. Alternatively, the taxpayer may file an amended return for the prior year to delete the moving expense deduction for that year.

The distance requirement states that the distance between the taxpayer's old residence and new job location must be at least 50 miles farther than the distance between the old residence and the old job location. If the taxpayer has no old job location (new worker, unemployed), the distance test is met if the new job location is at least 50 miles from the old residence. Code Sec. 217(c)(1).

EXAMPLE 6.26 Robert Long is transferred by his employer from Kenton to Westchester. Robert also moves his family from Kenton to Westchester. Robert's old residence was 10 miles from his old job location. Robert's new job location is 75 miles from his old residence. Robert satisfies the 50-mile distance requirement since the distance between his old residence and new job location is 65 miles farther than the distance between the old residence and the old job location.

Classification of Moving Expenses

The tax law allows a deduction for two categories of moving expenses: (1) expenses incurred to move household goods and personal effects and (2) travel and lodging expenses incurred by the taxpayer in moving the family from the old residence to the new residence. The cost of meals is not deductible. If family travel to the new residence is accomplished by automobile, the taxpayer can deduct actual car expenses or an optional allowance of 17 cents per mile.

EXAMPLE 6.27 Robert Long incurs the following moving expenses in connection with his move from Kenton to Westchester:

Expenses of moving household goods	$3,500
Travel and lodging for family in moving from old residence to new location	450
Pre-move house-hunting trips	1,400
Temporary living expenses in new location	1,200
Real estate commission on sale of old home	4,000
Total moving expenses	$10,550

The expenses of moving household goods and of moving Robert's family to the new location are deductible in full. Pre-move house-hunting trips, temporary living expenses, and selling expenses incurred in selling the taxpayer's old house are not deductible. The overall moving expense deduction is $3,950 ($3,500 + $450).

Year of Deduction

The moving expense deduction generally is taken by a cash basis taxpayer in the year the expenses are paid. The moving expense deduction is treated as a deduction from gross income to arrive at adjusted gross income. Code Sec. 62(a). Qualified moving expenses reimbursed by an employer are excludable from an employee's gross income as a qualified fringe benefit to the extent they meet the requirements for a qualified moving expense reimbursement. Qualified moving expense reimbursements include any amount received, directly or indirectly, by an employee from an employer as a payment for, or a reimbursement of, expenses that would be deductible as moving expenses under Code Sec. 217 if directly paid or incurred by the employee. Qualified moving expense reimbursements do not include payments for, or reimbursements of, expenses that were deducted by the taxpayer in a prior tax year.

¶6560

¶6570   **STUDENT LOAN INTEREST**

Interest payments on student loans are deductible "above-the-line." That means that a taxpayer can deduct the interest whether or not he or she itemizes deductions. Eligible taxpayers may deduct up to $2,500 of interest expense on a qualified education loan under Code Sec. 221. The deduction is phased out for single taxpayers with adjusted gross income between $65,000 and $80,000 and for joint filers with adjusted gross income between $135,000 and $165,000. Married taxpayers filing separately may not take the deduction. Also, an individual is not entitled to the deduction if the taxpayer can be claimed as a dependent by another taxpayer for the tax year beginning in the calendar year in which the individual's tax year begins.

EXAMPLE 6.28   In 2017, Jamie paid $1,800 interest on a qualified education loan. Her modified AGI (AGI before subtracting deductions for education expenses, domestic production activities, and the foreign earned income exclusion) was $71,000. Jamie is single, so her deduction for qualified student loan interest is phased out by the ratio of her excess AGI ($6,000), divided by $15,000. In this case, her deduction for student loan interest is reduced by 40% ($6,000/$15,000). Note that unlike other phase-out provisions of the Code, the phase-out rules for student loan interest apply to the deduction itself, rather than to the limitation on that deduction. Jamie would have been entitled to an $1,800 deduction (the lesser of the interest actually paid or $2,500). Reducing this deduction by 40%, she will be allowed a deduction of $1,080 (60% times $1,800).

To be eligible for the deduction the education loan must be used to pay for any of the following expenses: tuition, fees, room and board, books and supplies, or other related expenses.

¶6575   **HEALTH INSURANCE AND HEALTH SAVINGS ACCOUNTS**

The tax law has long allowed employers to treat costs incurred for employee health insurance as a fringe benefit, deductible by the employer but not taxable to the employee. Such beneficial treatment of employer health insurance plans is designed to make health insurance affordable and to increase the portion of the population that is covered by health insurance. To equalize the tax treatment of self-employed taxpayers and employees, Code Sec. 162(l)(6) allows *self-employed* taxpayers to deduct premiums paid for health insurance above the line, as a deduction in computing AGI. For those taxpayers who are not self-employed, health insurance premiums are deductible as part of the itemized deduction for medical expenses, discussed in chapter 8.

The Internal Revenue Code also provides incentives for taxpayers to self-insure. To this end, Code Sec. 223 allows taxpayers who are covered by so-called "high deductible" plans to establish a "Health Savings Account" (HSA). HSAs, similar to IRAs, allow taxpayers to make tax-deductible contributions to an account which will be allowed to accumulate tax-free and fund future medical expenses of the taxpayer and/or dependents. The account is designed for taxpayers who are covered only by "high-deductible" health insurance plans. The premiums on high-deductible insurance plans are much lower than for more standard insurance coverage. Eligible taxpayers (or their employers) can use the difference to fund their HSAs. These plans provide particular advantages for those taxpayers who do not expect to use the full amount in the account for medical expenses since the unspent balance remaining in the account belongs to the taxpayer.

Health insurance plans typically require the insured to pay for a portion of the cost of his or her medical care (the "deductible" amount), with the insurance company paying for costs in excess of this amount. As the name implies, a "high deductible" plan is one where these "deductible" amounts are high relative to more standard insurance plans. Note that the term "deductible" in this context refers not to the tax treatment of the insurance premiums, but to the amount of medical expenses that will not be covered by insurance (i.e., that will be "deducted" from the insurance reimbursement).

Self-employed taxpayers can claim a deduction "for" AGI for HSA contributions up to $6,750 for 2017. Rev. Proc. 2016-28, IRB 2016-20, May 16, 2016. The contribution limit is $3,400 if the taxpayer has "self-only" coverage as opposed to family coverage. Individuals who have reached the age of 55 may contribute an additional $1,000 beyond these limits each year. Taxpayers working for small employers (typically under 50 employees) may exclude a like amount of employer contributions to their HSAs as nontaxable fringe benefits. A "high deductible plan" for purposes of HSA eligibility is a plan with an annual deductible of at least $1,300 for self-only coverage or $2,600 for family coverage, and which limits the taxpayer's annual "out-of-pocket expenses" (deductibles, co-payments, but not premiums) to no more than $6,550 for self-only coverage or $13,100 for family coverage. Taxpayers whose health insurance plans do not meet these requirements may not make contributions to an HSA, nor can taxpayers who are eligible for Medicare. Likewise, taxpayers who do not have health insurance may not make contributions to an HSA.

HSA distributions are tax-free to the extent used to pay qualified medical expenses of the taxpayer or his or her dependents. Distributions for non-medical purposes are fully taxable. Moreover, in addition to the income tax, taxable distributions are also subject to a 10% penalty unless made after the beneficiary reaches the age of 65, dies, or becomes disabled. Medical expenses paid with HSA distributions cannot be deducted by the taxpayer. Note that one benefit of HSA accounts is that they can serve double duty as retirement accounts: distributions received after the taxpayer reaches age 65 are taxable, but are not subject to the 10% penalty.

¶6585 MANUFACTURING DEDUCTION

The American Jobs Creation Act of 2004 created a new deduction for manufacturers. The deduction effectively reduces the corporate income tax rate for domestic manufacturing three percentage points from a top rate of 35 percent down to 31.85 percent. Domestic manufacturers who qualify for the deduction include not only traditional manufacturers but also domestic producers in the areas of construction, engineering, energy production, computer software, films and videotape, and processing of agricultural products.

The manufacturing deduction on qualified production activities is equal to nine percent of the lesser of qualified production activities income or taxable income for the year. The deduction started at a transition percentage of three percent for 2005 and 2006 and increased to six percent for 2007 through 2009. For 2010 and later years, the deduction percentage is 9%. The deduction is limited to 50 percent of the W-2 wages paid by the taxpayer during the tax year.

Corporations, individuals, S corps, partnerships, estates, trusts, and cooperatives can take advantage of the new deduction. Taxpayers can also use the new deduction for AMT purposes. The manufacturing deduction is discussed in greater detail in Chapter 7.

Employee Business Expenses

¶6601 EMPLOYEE BUSINESS EXPENSES—IN GENERAL

The definition of *trade or business* does not include the performance of services as an employee. Code Sec. 62(a)(1). However, ordinary and necessary expenses incurred by an employee in connection with his or her employment are deductible under Code Sec. 162 as business expenses. In order to be deductible by the employee, however, an employment-related expense must be directly related to the performance of employment duties or be required by an employment agreement. Code Sec. 62; *F.M. Magill*, 4 BTA 272, Dec. 1499 (1926).

Unreimbursed employee business expenses are allowed as miscellaneous itemized deductions. Miscellaneous deductions are only deductible to the extent they exceed 2 percent of the taxpayer's adjusted gross income. Business expenses incurred by an employee under a reimbursement arrangement with the employer are normally not shown on the tax return. The reimbursement arrangement must require the employee to substantiate the expenses to the employer and must not allow the employee to keep the excess reimbursement. If full reimbursement is not made, the unreimbursed expenses are only allowable as miscellaneous itemized deductions, limited to amounts in excess of 2 percent of the taxpayer's adjusted gross income. See ¶8601 for an expanded discussion.

Commuting expenses incurred going to and from work are assumed to be personal expenses incurred by all employees and, therefore, are not deductible. Work uniforms suitable for everyday use, such as a suit and tie, are also considered to be personal expenses and not deductible since they can be used by taxpayers at other times besides work. Expenses incurred in purchasing work uniforms which are not suitable for everyday use, such as a fire fighter's uniform or a police officer's uniform, are proper tax deductions.

If an employee accounts to an employer for business-related expenses and is reimbursed by the employer, the employee does not normally have to report the expenses on the tax return.

Table 5. TYPICAL EMPLOYMENT-RELATED EXPENSES DEDUCTIBLE AS TRADE OR BUSINESS DEDUCTIONS (SUBJECT TO VARIOUS LIMITATIONS)
Expenses not shown on return
Reimbursed expenses
Expenses deductible from AGI (miscellaneous itemized deductions subject to 2% of AGI limitation)
Away-from-home travel expenses
Employment agency fees
Employment-related education
Entertainment expenses (limited)
Job-hunting expenses
Office at home (limited)
Outside salesperson's expenses
Professional society dues
Small tools and supplies
Subscriptions to professional journals
Transportation expenses
Union dues
Work clothes and uniforms

An important and often controversial issue with respect to employment-related expenses is the question of whether an individual is in fact an employee or can instead be classified as a self-employed "independent contractor." If a taxpayer is self-employed, all trade or business expenses are deductible for AGI, whereas, if the individual is an employee, any unreimbursed employment-related trade or business expenses are deductible as miscellaneous itemized deductions subject to the 2 percent limitation. In determining whether an individual is an employee or is self-employed, an analysis should be made of the individual's employment activity. Factors such as the following should be considered: (1) does the individual work for many firms or clients or just work for one firm or client, (2) are the individual's services available to the public, (3) does the individual determine work hours and schedules, and (4) does the individual receive regular payments from one firm or from a variety of firms? To determine whether an individual is an employee or is self-employed no one factor should be considered as controlling, but rather all these factors should be reviewed.

EXAMPLE 6.29   Susan is a lawyer who has practiced law for over 10 years. During this period, she has served many clients but, for the past several years, she has spent most of her time with only one client, Randall Corporation. In fact, in 2017 she did not receive fees from any client other than Randall, she moved her office into the Randall Corporation headquarters building, and she abides by the Randall Corporation full-time work schedule. Also, she no longer seeks business from other clients. Is Susan still self-employed in 2017 or is she now an employee of Randall Corporation? An analysis of the facts in this example would seem to indicate that Susan is now an employee of Randall. She receives fees from only one source (Randall), she no longer seeks business from other clients, and she spends her full time at Randall Corporation.

Limitations on the Deductibility of Expenses

¶6701   ## CERTAIN DEDUCTIONS LIMITED OR DISALLOWED

Some provisions of the Code specifically prohibit or limit the deduction of certain expenses and losses despite their apparent relationship to the taxpayer's business or profit seeking activities. These provisions operate to disallow or limit the deduction for various expenses unless such expenses are specifically authorized by the Code. As a practical matter, these provisions have been enacted to prohibit abuses identified in specific areas. Several of the more fundamental limitations are considered below.

¶6715   HOBBY EXPENSES AND LOSSES

A taxpayer must establish that he or she pursues an activity with the objective of making a profit before the expense is deductible as a business or production of income expense. When the profit motive is absent, the deduction is governed by Code Sec. 183 as an activity not engaged in for profit (i.e., a hobby). Code Sec. 183 generally provides that hobby expenses of an individual taxpayer or S corporation are deductible only to the extent of the gross income from the hobby. Thus, no deduction is allowed for net losses incurred from the conduct of activities deemed by the IRS to constitute "hobbies," where the taxpayer lacks a genuine intent to make a profit. The factors considered by the IRS and the courts in determining whether a taxpayer's activities rise to the level of a trade or business rather than a hobby are explained further in Chapter 7.

¶6725   PERSONAL DEDUCTIONS

Personal, living, and family expenses are not deductible on a tax return unless expressly permitted. Code Sec. 262. Table 6 summarizes the general types of personal expenses and how they are treated for tax purposes.

Although many personal expenditures are not deductible for tax purposes, there is some logic and rationale behind allowing a deduction or credit for certain personal expenditures on an individual's tax return. Some personal deductions are allowed as tax deductions because they are involuntary payments which place a burden on the taxpayer's finances and inhibit the ability to pay income taxes. Deductions allowed for medical and dental expenses, casualty and theft losses, and alimony fall into this category. Other personal deductions and credits are allowed in order to encourage certain types of behavior on the part of taxpayers. For example, the allowance of a charitable deduction for tax purposes encourages the giving of gifts to charity and thereby promotes the public good. Certainly the deduction for state and local income taxes lessens to some degree the problems associated with double and triple taxation of the same income.

Table 6. TYPICAL PERSONAL EXPENDITURES DEDUCTIBLE OR NOT DEDUCTIBLE ON TAX RETURN (SUBJECT TO VARIOUS LIMITATIONS)	
Expenditures deductible for AGI	
Alimony	Interest paid on qualified education loans
Individual retirement accounts (IRAs) (limited)	Penalty on early withdrawal of savings
Moving expenses	Jury duty fees paid to employer
Expenditures deductible from AGI (itemized deductions)	
Charitable contributions	Medical and dental expenses
Gambling losses (to extent of gambling winnings)	Personal casualty and theft losses
Hobby expenses (to extent of hobby income)	State and local taxes
Interest expense (limited)	
Expenditures eligible for tax credit	
Adoption expenses	Tuition, books and other course expenses
Child and disabled dependent care expenses	
Expenditures not deductible	
Commuting expenses	Household living expenses
Depreciation on property held for personal use	Life insurance premiums
Funeral expenses	Political contributions
Losses on sales of property held for personal purposes (e.g., house, car, etc.)	

The disallowance of personal expenditures by Code Sec. 262 complements the general criteria allowing a deduction. Recall that the general rules of Code Secs. 162 and 212 permit deductions for ordinary and necessary expenses incurred in a *profit seeking activity*. Where the taxpayer's motive is personal, rather than for profit, no deduction is allowed. Some of the items specifically disallowed by Code Sec. 262 are summarized in the last section of Table 6.

Legal expenses related to divorce actions and the division of income producing properties are often a source of conflict. Prior to clarification by the Supreme Court, several decisions held that divorce expenses incurred primarily to protect the taxpayer's income producing property or his or her business were deductible. The Supreme Court, however, has ruled that deductibility depends on whether the expense arises in connection with the taxpayer's profit seeking activities. That is, the origin of the expense determines deductibility. *U.S. v. Talbot Patrick et al.,* 63-1 USTC ¶9286, 372 U.S. 53, 83 S Ct. 618 (S Ct., rev'g CA-4, 1963). Under this rule, if the spouse's claim arises from the marital relationship—a personal matter—then no deduction is allowed. Division of income producing property would only be incidental to or a consequence of the marital relationship.

Legal expenses related to a divorce action may be deductible where the expense is for advice concerning the tax consequences of the divorce. Rev. Rul. 72-545, 1972-2 CB 179. The portion of the legal expense allocable to counsel on the tax consequences of a property settlement, the right to claim children as dependents, and the creation of a trust for payment of alimony are deductible.

Note that this rule applies to all legal expenses incurred by taxpayers, not just those associated with divorce proceedings. If the origin of the legal issue is inherently personal, the associated legal fees are not deductible even if they may provide the taxpayer with some economic benefit.

EXAMPLE 6.30	Gary is the president of a local bank. Last year, he was charged with driving while intoxicated. He hired a good lawyer at a cost of several thousand dollars, and the charges were dropped. Gary may well have lost his job at the local bank had the charges been made public. He certainly would have lost his job had he been convicted. Nonetheless, his legal fees are not deductible since the underlying cause of his legal difficulties was personal and not related to his trade or business of working at the bank.

PLANNING POINTER	Tax work performed for a business by a CPA and legal work performed by an attorney may be of importance to the business and, at the same time, be of personal significance to the owner of the business. To the extent possible, fees associated with the business portion of a professional service should be kept separate from the personal portion of a professional service on any billing prepared by a professional person rendering a professional service. Documentation of the business portion of a professional service versus the personal portion may be beneficial in substantiating a business tax deduction for professional services.

¶6735   PUBLIC POLICY RESTRICTIONS

Although an expense may be entirely appropriate and helpful, and may contribute to the taxpayer's profit seeking activities, it is not deductible if the allowance of a deduction would frustrate well-defined public policy. The courts established this longstanding rule on the theory that to allow a deduction for expenses such as fines and penalties would encourage violations by diluting the cost of the penalty. *Hoover Motor Express Co., Inc. v. U.S.,* 58-1 USTC ¶9367, 1 AFTR2d 1157, 356 U.S. 38 (USSC, 1958). Historically, however, the IRS and the courts were free to restrict deductions of any type of expense where, in their view, it appeared that the expenses were contrary to public policy—even if the policy had not been clearly enunciated by some governmental body. As a result, taxpayers were often forced to go to court to determine if their expense violated public policy.

Recognizing the difficulties in applying the public policy doctrine, Congress amended Code Sec. 162, adding provisions which are specifically designed to limit its use. The rules identify and disallow a deduction for specific types of expenditures considered contrary to public policy. Specifically, Code Sec. 162(f) now disallows deductions for fines, penalties, and illegal payments.

Fines and Penalties

Under Code Sec. 162(f), no deduction is allowed for any fine or similar penalty paid to a government for the violation of any law.

EXAMPLE 6.31	Taylor is a sales representative for an office supply company. While calling on customers this year, she received parking tickets totalling $100. No deduction is allowed for payment of these tickets because the violations were against the law.

EXAMPLE 6.32

> Upon audit of Murray's tax return, the IRS determined that he neglected to report $10,000 of tip income from his job as a waiter, resulting in additional tax of $3,000. Murray was also assessed a negligence penalty on his tax return for intentional disregard of the rules. The penalty—20% of the tax due—is not deductible.

Under Code Sec. 162(g), the term "fines" includes any amounts paid in settlement of the taxpayer's actual or potential liability for a fine, penalty, or related charge. For example, if a company agrees to pay a settlement to the government in order to avoid being fined or penalized, the settlement is treated as a nondeductible fine or penalty for tax purposes. This is true even if the company admits no wrongdoing. Note, however, that while payments in settlement of potential fines or penalties are not deductible, payments incurred to remedy the underlying problem that resulted in the dispute are deductible. Reg. §1.162-21(c) Example (3). For example, if a company is fined $100,000 and ordered to clean up a site following an environmental accident, the costs of cleaning up the site are deductible, while the $100,000 fine is not.

Similarly, no deduction is allowed for two thirds of treble damage payments made due to a violation of antitrust laws. Reg. §1.162-21(b). Thus, only one third of fines incurred for violation of government antitrust provisions is deductible; the remaining two-thirds is treated as a fine or penalty for which no deduction is allowed.

Illegal Kickbacks, Bribes, and Other Payments

Code Sec. 162(c) also disallows any deduction for four categories of illegal payments:

1. Kickbacks or bribes to U.S. government officials and employees if illegal;
2. Payments to governmental officials or employees of foreign countries if such payments would be considered illegal under the U.S. Foreign Corrupt Practices Act;
3. Kickbacks, bribes, or other illegal payments to any other person if illegal under generally enforced U.S. or state laws that provide a criminal penalty or loss of license or privilege to engage in business; and
4. Kickbacks, rebates, and bribes, although legal, made by any provider of items or services under Medicare and Medicaid programs.

Kickbacks or bribes not described above will be deductible if the taxpayer can demonstrate that they are ordinary and necessary.

EXAMPLE 6.33

> Randy travels all over the world, looking for unique items for his gift shop. Occasionally when going through customs in foreign countries, he is forced to "bribe" the customs official to do the necessary paperwork and get him through customs as quickly as possible. These so called grease payments to employees of foreign countries are deductible unless they violate the Foreign Corrupt Practices Act. In general, such payments are not considered to be illegal.

Expenses of Illegal Business

Expenses incurred in conducting an illegal business are generally deductible. *Max Cohen v. Comm.*, 49-2 USTC ¶9358, 176 F.2d 394 (CA-10, 1949) and *Neil Sullivan v. Comm.*, 58-1 USTC ¶9368, AFTR2d 1158, 356 U.S. 27 (USSC, 1958). Similar to the principle governing taxation of income from whatever source derived (including income illegally obtained), the tax law is not concerned with the lawfulness of the activity in which the deductions arise. No deduction is allowed, however, if the expense itself constitutes an illegal payment as discussed above. Moreover, Code Sec. 280E creates a significant exception to this policy, prohibiting the deduction of any expenses related to trafficking in controlled substances (i.e., drugs).

EXAMPLE 6.34

In a 2007 Tax Court case (*Californians Helping to Alleviate Medical Problems, Inc. v. Commissioner*, 128 TC 173, No. 14, May 15, 2007), the IRS challenged the deductions claimed by a corporation in connection with its activity of purchasing medical marijuana and distributing it to its members suffering from AIDS and other debilitating diseases. The corporation in question was formed to provide caregiving services to its members, who paid a membership fee to join the organization. A secondary purpose was to provide its members with medical marijuana and to instruct them on how to use medical marijuana to benefit their health. Members were prohibited from reselling marijuana obtained from the corporation, and violation of this prohibition resulted in expulsion of the member from the group.

The IRS initially disallowed any deduction for expenses incurred by the organization, including those incurred in purchasing the medical marijuana distributed to its members. The Service argued that such expenses were not deductible under Code Sec. 280E, as the corporation was engaged in the activity of trafficking in a controlled substance. The Service subsequently acknowledged that the company's cost of goods sold (i.e., the cost of purchasing the marijuana) was deductible, leaving as the sole issue before the court the question of whether the company's other expenses were deductible. The state of California had legalized the use of marijuana for medical purposes in 1996; such use, however, remained illegal under federal law. The court ruled that Code Sec. 280E did apply to expenses incurred in the distribution of marijuana to the corporation's members, but not to expenses incurred in performing the company's other caregiving services. An allocation of expenses between these two activities was required, and only those expenses allocable to the distribution of medical marijuana were disallowed. *See also Olive v. Commissioner*, 139 TC 2, August 2, 2012.

¶6745

LOBBYING AND POLITICAL CONTRIBUTIONS

Although expenses for lobbying and political contributions may be closely related to the taxpayer's business, Congress has traditionally limited their deduction. These restrictions usually are supported on the grounds that it is not in the public's best interest for government to subsidize efforts to influence legislative matters.

Lobbying

Lobbying expenditures are deductible only if incurred for the purpose of influencing legislation at the *local* level. Therefore, the expense of influencing national and state legislation (including the costs of hiring lobbyists to represent the taxpayer in these matters) is not deductible. This prohibition is extended to the costs of any direct communication with executive branch officials in an attempt to influence official actions or positions of such official.

Even at the local level, the taxpayer must have a direct interest in the local legislation before lobbying expenses may be deducted. Although the definitional boundaries of the term "direct" are vague, a taxpayer is considered as having satisfied the test if it is reasonable to expect that the local legislative matter affects or will affect the taxpayer's business. However, a taxpayer does not have a direct interest in the nomination, appointment, or operation of any local legislative body. Reg. §1.162-20(b).

No deduction is allowed for any expenditure incurred to influence the general public on legislative matters, elections, or referendums, whether the issue is a local, state, or national issue. Code Sec. 162(e)(2). The Internal Revenue Service has suggested the following examples of nondeductible lobbying activities aimed at influencing the public:

1. Advertising in magazines and newspapers concerning legislation of direct interest to the taxpayer. Rev. Rul. 78-112, 1978-1 CB 42. This prohibition presumably extends to radio and television as well. However, expenses for "goodwill" advertising presenting views on economic, financial, social, or similar subjects of a general nature, or encouraging behavior such as contributing to the Red Cross, are deductible. Reg. §1.162-20(a)(2).
2. Preparing and distributing to a corporation's shareholders pamphlets focusing on certain legislation affecting the corporation and urging the shareholders to contact their representatives in Congress. Rev. Rul. 74-407, 1974-2 CB 45, as amplified by Rev. Rul. 78-111, 1978-1 CB 41.

EXAMPLE 6.35	Wanda owns a restaurant in Austin, Texas. Legislation has been introduced by the City Council to impose a sales tax on food and drink sold in Austin, to be used for funding a dome stadium. Wanda placed an ad in the local newspaper stating reasons why the legislation should not be passed. She testified in front of the City Council on the proposed legislation on several occasions. She also paid dues to the Austin Association of Restaurant Owners organization, which estimates that 60% of its activities were devoted to lobbying for local legislation related to restaurant owners. Wanda may deduct the cost of travel and 60% of the dues to the Restaurant Owners' Association since the local legislation is of direct interest to her. She may not deduct amounts spent to purchase the newspaper ad since it was intended to influence the general public.

Political Contributions

No deduction is permitted for any contributions, gifts, or any other amounts paid to a political party, action committee, or group or candidate related to a candidate's campaign. Code Sec. 162(e). This rule also applies to indirect payments, such as payments for advertising in a convention program and admission to a dinner, hall, or similar affair where any of the proceeds benefit a political party or candidate. Code Sec. 276.

¶6755   MEALS AND ENTERTAINMENT EXPENSES

Under regular rules, entertainment expenses are deductible by a taxpayer if the expenditures can be substantiated and are "directly related to" or "associated with" a taxpayer's business. Code Sec. 274(a). An entertainment expenditure is directly related to a taxpayer's business if the taxpayer can show that there was some general expectation of deriving some income or specific benefit from the expenditure and business was discussed or engaged in during the entertainment. A taxpayer can also show that an entertainment expenditure is directly related to the business if it is provided in a clear business setting where the guest may recognize the business motive of the taxpayer in incurring the expenditure. An entertainment expenditure is associated with a taxpayer's business if the entertainment immediately precedes or is followed by a substantial business discussion. Reg. §1.274-2(d)(1).

EXAMPLE 6.36	Linda James, an insurance agent, takes Paul Mason, president of Mason Furniture Co., to dinner in order to discuss new types of insurance coverage. Linda pays the bill for dinner. Linda can deduct the dinner expense as an entertainment expense directly related to her business. If, after the dinner, Linda takes Paul to see a professional baseball game and pays for the tickets, the cost of the tickets is deductible by Linda as an entertainment expense associated with her business since the entertainment followed a substantial business discussion.

A business entertainment activity where substantial distractions occur such as a professional sporting event or night club entertainment usually does not qualify under the regular rules as being directly related to the taxpayer's business since the presumption is that the distractions preclude the conduct of business activity. Expenditures for activities of this type usually qualify as entertainment expense deductions only if such activities are associated with the taxpayer's business and immediately precede or follow substantial business discussions as noted in the preceding example. The "immediately preceding or following" requirement is generally met if the entertainment activity takes place on the same day as the business discussion.

Only 50 percent of the amount of otherwise allowable meals and entertainment expenses is deductible subject to certain exceptions. The exceptions allowing full deductibility include meal and entertainment expenses fully taxed as compensation to the recipient, traditional recreational expenses paid by employers for employees, and expenditures for samples and promotional items made available to the general public. Items subject to the percentage limitations are food, beverages, taxes, tips, tickets, and cover charges. Transportation expenses such as taxicab fares are 100 percent deductible. Entertainment expenses of a self-employed taxpayer are deductible for AGI as trade or business expenses subject to the 50 percent rule. Entertainment expenses incurred by the taxpayer as an employee and not reimbursed by an employer are deductible from AGI as itemized deductions subject to the 50 percent limitation and the 2 percent floor on miscellaneous itemized deductions.

Entertainment Facilities

Expenditures by a taxpayer relating to the ownership of entertainment facilities such as yachts, hunting lodges, and fishing camps are generally not deductible as entertainment expenses. Out-of-pocket costs related to the use of entertainment facilities of this type, however, if directly related to or associated with the taxpayer's business are deductible for tax purposes. In addition, deductions for club dues are no longer allowed. This restriction applies to any club, whether organized for business, pleasure, recreation, or any other social purpose. The restriction, however, does not apply to professional organizations such as bar associations, business organizations such as trade associations, and civic organizations such as Kiwanis, Lions, and Rotary.

Substantiation of Entertainment Expenses

No entertainment deduction is allowed for tax purposes unless the taxpayer substantiates by adequate records or by other sufficient evidence corroborating the taxpayer's own statements the amount of the expense, the time and place of the entertainment, the business purpose of the entertainment, and the business relationship of the persons entertained to the taxpayer. Adequate substantiation for the entertainment expense deduction includes an account book or expense statement with all pertinent information maintained by the taxpayer during the year and documentary evidence including itemized receipts, paid bills, etc., for each expenditure of $75 or more made during the year. Reg. §1.274-5.

¶6765 EXPENSES AND INTEREST RELATING TO TAX-EXEMPT INCOME

Code Sec. 265 sets forth several rules generally disallowing deductions for expenses relating to tax exempt income. These provisions prohibit taxpayers from taking advantage of the tax law to secure a double tax benefit: tax exempt income and deductions for the expenses that help to produce it. The best known rule prohibits the deduction for any *interest* expense or non-business expense related to tax exempt *interest* income. Code Sec. 265(2). Without this rule, taxpayers in high tax brackets could borrow at a higher rate of interest than could be earned and still have a profit on the transaction.

EXAMPLE 6.37	Carla, an investor in the 28% tax bracket with substantial investment income, borrows funds at 9% and invests them in tax exempt bonds yielding 7%. If the interest expense were deductible, the after tax cost of borrowing would be 6.48% [(100% - 28% = 72%) × 9%]. Since the interest income is nontaxable, the after tax yield on the bond remains 7%, or .52 percentage points higher than the effective cost of borrowing. Code Sec. 265, however, denies the deduction for the interest expense, thus eliminating the feasibility of this arrangement. It should be noted, however, that *business* expenses other than interest related to tax exempt interest income may be deductible.

If the income that is exempt is not interest, none of the related expenses are deductible. Code Sec. 265(1).

EXAMPLE 6.38	Eduardo operates a minor league baseball team. The team paid premiums for disability insurance under which the company would receive proceeds under the policy in the event a player is injured. Proceeds received under a disability policy are not taxable. Accordingly, the premiums on the policy are not deductible even though the policy is presumably an ordinary and necessary business expense. Rev. Rul. 66-262, 1966-2 CB 105.

Similar to the insurance premiums in the example above, Code Sec. 264 provides that no deduction is allowed for life insurance premiums paid on policies covering the life of any officer, employee, or any other person who may have a financial interest in the taxpayer's trade or business, if the taxpayer is the *beneficiary* of the policy. Like the disability insurance proceeds in the preceding example, life insurance proceeds are excludible from the recipient's taxable income. Thus, premiums paid by a business on a key-person life insurance policy *where the company is the beneficiary* are not deductible. In contrast, payments made by a business on group-term life insurance policies where the *employees* are the beneficiaries are deductible.

¶6775 RELATED PARTY TRANSACTIONS

Without restrictions, related taxpayers (such as husbands and wives, shareholders and their corporations, etc.) could arrange transactions creating deductions for expenses and losses that do not actually affect their economic position. For example, a husband and wife could create a deduction simply by having one spouse sell property to the other at a loss. In this case, the loss is artificial because the property remains within the family and their financial situation is unaffected. Although the form of ownership has been altered, there is no substance to the transaction. To guard against the potential abuses inherent in transactions between related taxpayers, Congress designed specific safeguards contained in Code Sec. 267.

Related Taxpayers

The transactions that are subject to restriction are only those between persons who are considered "related" as defined in Code Sec. 267(b). The following taxpayers are deemed to be related for purposes of Code Sec. 267:

1. The following family members – brothers and sisters (including half blood), spouses, ancestors (i.e., parents and grandparents), and lineal descendants (i.e., children and grandchildren);
2. An individual and a corporation if the individual owns, either directly or *indirectly*, more than 50 percent of the corporation's stock;
3. An individual and a partnership in which the partner owns more than a 50% interest;
4. A personal service corporation and an employee owner (whether or not he or she owns more than 50% of the corporation's stock): a personal service corporation is a corporation whose principal activity is the performance of personal services that are performed by the employee owners;
5. Certain other relationships involving regular corporations, S corporations, partnerships, estates, trusts, and individuals.

Disallowed Losses

The taxpayer is not allowed to deduct any loss realized on a sale or exchange of property directly or indirectly to a related taxpayer (as defined above). However, any loss disallowed on the sale may be used to offset gain (if any) realized on the subsequent sale of the property by the related taxpayer to an unrelated third party.

EXAMPLE 6.39	A father owns land that he purchased as an investment for $20,000. He sells the land to his daughter for $15,000, producing a $5,000 loss. The $5,000 loss is not deductible by the father because the transaction is between related taxpayers. Assume, however, that the daughter later sells the property for $22,000. She realizes a $7,000 gain ($22,000 sales price - $15,000 basis). She is allowed to deduct the $5,000 loss previously disallowed to her father, so that she recognizes a gain of only $2,000 ($7,000 realized gain - $5,000 previously disallowed loss).

EXAMPLE 6.40	Assume the same facts as in the previous example, except that the daughter sold the property for only $19,000, rather than $22,000. In this case, she realizes a gain on the sale of $4,000 ($19,000 - $15,000). Again, she is allowed to offset this gain with the disallowed loss previously realized by her father. This reduces her taxable gain to zero (his disallowed loss was $5,000, which is greater than her realized gain of $4,000). Note, however, that the $5,000 disallowed loss is used only to the extent of the daughter's $4,000 gain. The remaining portion of the disallowed loss ($1,000) cannot be deducted.

EXAMPLE 6.41	Susan owns 100% of Equinox Corporation. She sells stock with a basis of $100,000 to her good friend Teri for $75,000, generating a $25,000 loss for Susan. Teri, in turn, sells the stock to Equinox Corporation for $75,000, thus recouping the amount she paid Susan with no gain or loss. In effect, this transaction is between Susan and her wholly owned corporation —the sale to the corporation is indirect, passing through her friend Teri. Consequently, Susan will not be allowed to deduct her $25,000 loss on the sale.

Unpaid Expenses and Interest

Prior to enactment of Code Sec. 267, another tax avoidance device used by related taxpayers involved the use of different accounting methods by each taxpayer. In the typical scheme, a taxpayer's corporation would adopt the accrual method of accounting while the taxpayer reported on the cash method. The taxpayer could lend money, lease property, provide services, etc., to the corporation and charge the corporation for whatever was provided. As an accrual method taxpayer, the corporation would accrue the expense and create a deduction. The cash method individual, however, would report no income until the corporation's payment of the expense was actually received. As a result, the corporation could accrue large deductions without ever having to make a disbursement and, moreover, without the taxpayer recognizing any offsetting income. The Code now prohibits this practice between "related taxpayers" as defined above. Code Sec. 267(a)(2) provides that an accrual method taxpayer can deduct an accrued expense payable to a related cash method taxpayer only in the period in which the payment is included in the recipient's income. This rule effectively places all accrual method taxpayers on the cash method of accounting for purposes of deducting such expenses.

EXAMPLE 6.42	Barry owns 100% of X Corporation, which manufactures electric razors. Barry uses the cash method of accounting while the corporation uses the accrual method. Both are calendar year taxpayers. On December 27, the corporation accrues a $10,000 bonus for Barry. However, due to insufficient cash flow, X Corporation is not able to pay the bonus until January 10 of the subsequent year. The corporation may not deduct the accrued bonus this year, but must wait until next year when Barry includes the payment in his income.
EXAMPLE 6.43	Assume the same facts as above, except that X is a personal services corporation (e.g., a medical practice) in which Barry owns only 20% of the outstanding stock. The results are the same as above because Barry and X are still related parties: a personal service corporation and an employee owner.

¶6785　PAYMENT OF ANOTHER TAXPAYER'S OBLIGATION

As a general rule, a taxpayer is not permitted to deduct the payment of expenses incurred by another taxpayer. A deduction is allowed only for those expenditures satisfying the taxpayer's own obligations or arising from such obligations.

EXAMPLE 6.44	Quentin lost his job several weeks ago. This month, he received a bill from the state for property tax on his farm. Since he did not have the money to pay the taxes, his daughter, Emily, paid them. Although Emily paid the property taxes, she will not be allowed a deduction because the property taxes were the obligation of her father.
PLANNING POINTER	Note that while Emily cannot deduct the property taxes paid on her father's behalf in the above example, if her father itemizes deductions, he may be able to claim the deduction. In a 2010 Memorandum Decision, the Tax Court applied the "substance–over–form" doctrine to allow a taxpayer to claim itemized deductions for medical expenses and taxes paid by her mother on her behalf. The court ruled that although the taxpayer's mother paid the expenses directly, in substance she should be treated as having transferred the funds to the taxpayer, who then transferred them to the creditors. The court noted that there was no risk of double deductions because the mother did not claim and was not entitled to either deduction. The taxpayer, who was treated as having paid the expenses with money received from her mother, was entitled to claim the deductions. Lang, TC Memo. 2010-286.
EXAMPLE 6.45	Percy is the majority stockholder of Rancid Corporation. During the year, the corporation had financial difficulty and was unable to make an interest payment on an outstanding debt. To protect the goodwill of the corporation, Percy paid the interest. The payment is not deductible, and Percy will be treated as having made a contribution to the capital of the corporation in the amount of the payment.

An exception to the general rule is provided with respect to payment of medical expenses of a dependent. To qualify as a dependent for this purpose, the person needs only to meet the relationship, support, and citizen tests. Code Sec. 213(a)(1). If the taxpayer pays the medical expenses of a person who qualifies as a dependent under the modified tests, the expenses are treated as if they were the taxpayer's expenses and are deductible subject to limitations applicable to the taxpayer.

¶6795 CAPITAL EXPENDITURES

A capital expenditure is ordinarily defined as an expenditure providing benefits that extend beyond the close of the taxable year. It is a well established rule in case law that a business expense, though ordinary and necessary, is not deductible in the year paid or incurred if it can be considered a capital expenditure. Normally, a capital expenditure may be deducted ratably over the period for which it provides benefits. For example, the Code authorizes deductions for depreciation or cost recovery, amortization, and depletion where the asset has a determinable useful life. Code Secs. 167, 168, 169, 178, 185, 188, and 611.

Capital expenditures creating assets that do not have a determinable life, however, generally cannot be depreciated, amortized or otherwise deducted. For example, land is considered as having an indeterminable life and thus cannot be depreciated or amortized. The same is true for stocks and bonds. Expenditures for these types of assets are recovered (i.e., deducted) only when there is a disposition of the asset through sale, exchange, abandonment, or other disposition. At that point, the cost of the asset can be offset against the amount realized (if any).

As a general rule, assets with a useful life of one year or less need not be capitalized. For example, taxpayers can write off short lived assets with small costs such as supplies (e.g., stationery, pens, pencils, calculators), books (e.g., the Internal Revenue Code), and small tools (e.g., screwdrivers, rakes, and shovels).

Capital Expenditures vs. Repairs

The general rule of case law disallowing deductions for capital expenditures has been codified for expenditures relating to property. Code Sec. 263 provides that deductions are not allowed for any expenditure for new buildings or for permanent improvements or betterments made to increase the value of property. Additionally, expenditures substantially prolonging the property's useful life, adapting the property to a new or different use, or materially adding to the value of the property are not deductible. Reg. §1.263(a)-1(b). Conversely, the cost of incidental repairs that do not materially increase the value of the property nor appreciably prolong its life, but maintain it in a normal operating state, may be deducted in the current year. Reg. §1.162-4. For example, costs of painting, inside and outside, and papering are usually considered repairs. *Louis Allen*, 2 BTA 1313 (1925). However, if the painting is done in conjunction with a general reconditioning or overhaul of the property, it is treated as a capital expenditure. *Joseph M. Jones*, 57-1 USTC ¶9517, 50 AFTR 2040, 242 F.2d 616 (CA-5, 1957).

EXAMPLE 6.46

Louis operates his own limousine business. Expenses for a tune up such as the cost of spark plugs and labor would be deductible as routine repairs and maintenance since such costs do not significantly prolong the car's life. In contrast, if Louis had the transmission replaced, allowing him to drive the limousine for another few years, the cost must be capitalized.

Acquisition Costs

As a general rule, costs related to the acquisition of property must be capitalized. For example, freight paid to acquire new equipment or commissions paid to acquire land must be capitalized. In addition, Code Sec. 164 requires that state and local general sales taxes related to the purchase of property must be capitalized. The costs of demolition or removal of an old building prior to using the land in another fashion must be capitalized as part of the cost of the land. Code Sec. 280B. Costs of defending or perfecting the title to property, such as legal fees, are normally capitalized. Reg. §1.263(a)-2. Similarly, legal fees incurred for the recovery of property must be capitalized unless the recovered property is investment property or money that must be included in income if received. Reg. §1.212-1(k).

Business Deductions Related to Capital Expenditures

A capital expenditure for tax purposes is an expenditure which is expected to benefit more than one tax year. Generally, capital expenditures do not qualify as tax deductions in the year the expenditures are made but must be allocated to the tax years which will receive some benefit from the expenditures. This process of allocating the cost of a capital expenditure to various tax periods is called depreciation, amortization, or depletion depending on the type of capital expenditure involved in the allocation process. The term "depreciation" is usually connected with tangible (physical presence) property, "amortization" with intangible (no physical presence) property, and "depletion" with natural resources.

¶6801   DEPRECIATION OF TANGIBLE PROPERTY

Depreciation is the process of allocating the cost of a tangible asset to expense over its estimated useful life. To be depreciable, tangible property must have a limited life. Tangible property can be divided into two parts: real property and personal property. Real property is land, land improvements, buildings, and building improvements. Land does not have a limited life; therefore, it does not qualify for depreciation. Personal property is usually business machinery and equipment and office furniture and fixtures. The term "personal property" should not be confused with property owned by an individual for personal use.

A tax deduction for depreciation of the cost of tangible property has been allowed for tax purposes since the inception of the federal income tax in 1913. In 1981, the tax depreciation system was dramatically changed and simplified by adoption of the Accelerated Cost Recovery System (ACRS).

Accelerated Cost Recovery System (ACRS)

ACRS applies to most tangible property, new or used, placed in service for business or investment purposes after 1980 and before 1987. Property which is not eligible for ACRS includes property placed in service before 1981, property depreciated using a method not expressed in terms of years (units of production method), property which is amortized, and certain public utility property. Code Sec. 168(e). ACRS was substantially modified by the Tax Reform Act of 1986. Thus, most tangible property placed in service after 1986 must now be depreciated under the Modified Accelerated Cost Recovery System (MACRS).

Modified Accelerated Cost Recovery System (MACRS)

MACRS applies to most tangible property, new or used, placed in service for business or investment purposes after 1986. The general MACRS rules classify property based on class life for purposes of determining the applicable depreciation method, the applicable recovery period, and applicable convention. Absent an election out of MACRS, the IRS-established class lives must be used to determine the applicable MACRS recovery period even when the taxpayer may prefer a longer period. Rev. Proc. 87-56, 1987-2 CB 674, clarified and modified by Rev. Proc. 88-22, 1988-1 CB 785; IRS Letter Ruling 9015014, January 9, 1990. Salvage value is disregarded in computing the MACRS deduction. Asset recovery classifications are provided by statute. Code Sec. 168(c).

1. **3-year property.** This class includes over-the-road tractor units, dies, molds, and small tools.
2. **5-year property.** This class includes autos, light-duty trucks, computers, and office equipment, such as typewriters, or calculators.
3. **7-year property.** This class includes most manufacturing equipment, furniture, and fixtures.
4. **10-year property.** This class includes mainly public utility property.
5. **15-year property.** This class includes public utility personal property.
6. **20-year property.** This class includes public utility personal property.
7. **27.5-year property.** This class includes residential rental property.
8. **39-year property.** This class includes nonresidential real property, such as office buildings, hotels, shopping centers, warehouses, and manufacturing facilities.
9. **50-year property.** Railroad gradings or tunnel bores.

MACRS also specifies the standard cost recovery method for each of the above asset classes. The cost of property in the 3-, 5-, 7-, and 10-year classes is recovered using the 200 percent declining-balance method of depreciation. Fifteen- and 20-year assets are depreciated using the 150 percent declining-balance depreciation method. The cost of 27.5-year and 39-year real property assets is recovered using the straight-line depreciation method. For all asset classes, the cost of the property or unadjusted basis is not reduced by salvage value in making the depreciation computation. When the declining-balance method is used, a switch to the straight-line method is allowed at the appropriate time to maximize the tax deduction.

Instead of computing MACRS depreciation in the above manner, optional MACRS depreciation tables are available for taxpayer use. These tables contain annual percentage depreciation rates which can be applied to the unadjusted basis of property in each tax year. An example of a MACRS depreciation table for 3-, 5-, 7-, 10-, 15-, and 20-year life property is shown in Table 7.

Averaging Conventions for Depreciation

Under MACRS, a half-year averaging convention applies to personal property. Under this convention, property placed in service or disposed of during a taxable year is considered placed in service or disposed of at the midpoint of that year. Table 7 uses the half-year convention. A midquarter convention applies when more than 40 percent of the cost of all personal property is placed in service during the last quarter of the taxable year. Under the midquarter convention, personal property is treated as placed in service (or disposed of) in the middle of the quarter in which it was actually placed in service. An example of a MACRS depreciation table for 5-year and 7-year property under the midquarter convention is shown in Table 8. In determining whether 40 percent of the aggregate basis of MACRS property is placed in service during the last three months of a tax year, property placed in service and disposed of within the same tax year is disregarded. Code Sec. 168(d)(3). For real property, both residential and nonresidential, depreciation is based on the number of months the property is in service during the taxable year with a midmonth convention applying in the first month of service and in the last month of service. The averaging convention that is used in the year when property is placed in service must also be used in the year when the property is disposed of.

Table 7. MACRS DEPRECIATION TABLE

General Depreciation System

Applicable Depreciation Method: 200 or 150 Percent

Declining Balance Switching to Straight Line

Applicable Recovery Periods: 3, 5, 7, 10, 15, 20 years

Applicable Convention: Half-year

	and the Recovery Period is:					
	3-year	5-year	7-year	10-year	15-year	20-year
If the Recovery Year is:	the Depreciation Rate is:					
1	33.33	20.00	14.29	10.00	5.00	3.750
2	44.45	32.00	24.49	18.00	9.50	7.219
3	14.81	19.20	17.49	14.40	8.55	6.677
4	7.41	11.52	12.49	11.52	7.70	6.177
5		11.52	8.93	9.22	6.93	5.713
6		5.76	8.92	7.37	6.23	5.285
7			8.93	6.55	5.90	4.888
8			4.46	6.55	5.90	4.522
9				6.56	5.91	4.462
10				6.55	5.90	4.461
11				3.28	5.91	4.462
12					5.90	4.461
13					5.91	4.462
14					5.90	4.461
15					5.91	4.462
16					2.95	4.461
17						4.462
18						4.461
19						4.462
20						4.461
21						2.231

Source: Rev. Proc. 87-57, 1987-2 CB 117, Table 1.

Table 8. MACRS 5-YEAR AND 7-YEAR RECOVERY RATES
(Mid-Quarter Convention)

| | Placed in Service During: | | | | | | | |
| | 1st Quarter | | 2nd Quarter | | 3rd Quarter | | 4th Quarter | |
Year	5-Year	7-Year	5-Year	7-Year	5-Year	7-Year	5-Year	7-Year
1	35.00%	25.00%	25.00%	17.85%	15.00%	10.71%	5.00%	3.57%
2	26.00	21.43	30.00	23.47	34.00	25.51	38.00	27.55
3	15.60	15.31	18.00	16.76	20.40	18.22	22.80	19.68
4	11.01	10.93	11.37	11.97	12.24	13.02	13.68	14.06
5	11.01	8.75	11.37	8.87	11.30	9.30	10.94	10.04
6	1.38	8.74	4.26	8.87	7.06	8.85	9.58	8.73
7		8.75		8.87		8.86		8.73
8		1.09		3.34		5.53		7.64

EXAMPLE 6.47

In 2017, Max Book Company, a calendar year taxpayer, purchased the following assets:

1. April 10—Business equipment, cost $28,000, salvage value $3,000
2. July 7—Car, cost $14,000, salvage value $2,000
3. September 12—Office building, cost $85,000

Ignoring the Section 179 deduction and bonus depreciation, MACRS depreciation for 2017 on these assets would be:

Depreciation

1. Business equipment ($28,000 cost × 14.29% from Table 7) (7-year life, 200% DB)	$4,000
2. Car ($14,000 cost × 20% from Table 7) (5-year life, 200% DB)	2,800
3. Office building ($85,000 cost/39-year life × 3 1/2 months/12 months) (straight-line depr.)	636
Total	$7,436

EXAMPLE 6.48

Refer to Example 6.47 and assume the business equipment purchased in April 2017 was instead purchased in November 2017. Based on these facts, depreciation on all personal property purchased in 2017 would be based on the midquarter convention since more than 40 percent of all personal property placed in service was placed in service during the last quarter of the taxable year. MACRS depreciation for 2017 on the assets in Example 6.47 would now be:

Depreciation

1. Business equipment ($28,000 cost × 3.57% from Table 8) (7-year life, 200% DB) (or $28,000 × 3.57% from Table 8)	$1,000
2. Car ($14,000 × 15% from Table 8) (5-year life, 200% DB)	2,100
3. Office building (Same as Example 6.47)	636
Total	$3,736

¶6805   ALTERNATIVE MACRS SYSTEM

MACRS deductions are reduced for certain property by requiring that an alternative MACRS method, based on the Asset Depreciation Range System (ADR) class lives, be used for (1) tangible property used predominantly outside the United States, (2) tax-exempt use property, (3) tax-exempt bond-financed property, (4) property imported from a foreign country for which an Executive Order is in effect because the country maintains trade restrictions or engages in other discriminatory acts, and (5) property for which an alternative MACRS election has been made (see below). Mixed-use property (property used for both business and personal purposes) that is used 50 percent or more for personal use is also required to be depreciated under the alternative MACRS rules. Code Sec. 168(g). Under the alternative MACRS rules, the applicable depreciation method for all property is the straight-line method. The deduction is computed by applying the straight-line method (without regard to salvage value), the applicable convention, and the applicable prescribed longer recovery period for the respective class of property.

Special Election

Instead of the regular MACRS deduction, taxpayers may irrevocably elect to apply the alternative MACRS system to any class of property for any tax year and depreciate assets using the straight-line method or the 150 percent declining method of depreciation. Table 9 lists alternative MACRS system 5-year and 7-year recovery rates (half-year convention) using straight-line depreciation. If elected, the alternative system applies to all property in the MACRS class placed in service during the tax year of the election. For residential rental property and nonresidential real property, the election may be made on a property-by-property basis.

Table 9. ALTERNATIVE MACRS SYSTEM

5-Year and 7-Year Recovery Rates

(Half-Year Convention)

Straight-Line Depreciation

Recovery Year	5-Year Property	7-Year Property
1	10.00%	7.14%
2	20.00	14.29
3	20.00	14.29
4	20.00	14.28
5	20.00	14.29
6	10.00	14.28
7		14.29
8		7.14

EXAMPLE 6.49   In September, Max Cracker Co., a calendar-year taxpayer, purchased two pieces of equipment. One piece of equipment cost $25,000 and had a salvage value of $4,000. The other piece of equipment cost $20,000 and had a salvage value of $2,000. Max Cracker Co. elects to depreciate the equipment using the alternative depreciation system and to depreciate the assets over the MACRS class lives using straight-line depreciation. Both pieces of equipment are seven-year assets under MACRS. Salvage value is ignored in the depreciation computation and only one-half-year depreciation is allowed in the year of acquisition. Thus, depreciation for the two pieces of property is $3,213 ($45,000 cost × 7.14% From Table 9).

¶6815   DEPRECIATION OF REAL PROPERTY

As discussed previously, the method of depreciation used for tax purposes depends on the nature of the property being depreciated. Generally speaking, most tangible business-use property other than real estate is depreciated under MACRS using accelerated depreciation methods. Real property, in contrast, must be depreciated using the straight-line method. Realty is divided into two categories for tax purposes--residential and non-residential. Residential real estate is depreciated using the straight-line method over 27.5 years, while non-residential real estate is generally depreciated over 39 years, also using the straight-line method.

Real estate is treated as residential realty if at least 80% of the gross rental income from the building is attributable to rental income from dwelling units. Code Sec. 168(e)(2)(A). A dwelling unit is a house, apartment, etc. used to provide living accommodations on a long-term basis. Hotel or motel rooms rented on a transient basis are not dwelling units. Generally speaking, a unit is rented on a transient basis if the average rental term is less than 30 days.

As noted in ¶6801, depreciation of real property operates on a mid-month convention, meaning that the taxpayer takes a half-month's depreciation for the month placed in service (and the month of sale or other disposition). Thus, a taxpayer placing an apartment complex in service in the month of March will be allowed 10.5 months' depreciation, no matter what day of the month the property was actually acquired.

EXAMPLE 6.50	Kingsbury Corp. is developing an "extended stay" hotel on a parcel of real estate in a mid-sized city. The company expects to spend $20,000,000 on the project and is uncertain whether the property will be classified as residential or non-residential realty. If the building is residential real estate, the company will be allowed a deduction for depreciation of $727,273 (rounding up) per year for each full year of the property's 27.5-year depreciable life. If, instead, the building is classified as non-residential (because less than 80% of the rental income from the property is from customers staying 30 days or more), the allowable annual depreciation deduction will be only $512,821 (rounding up) over a 39-year depreciable life.

Special Rules for Qualified Leasehold Improvement, Retail Improvement, or Restaurant Property

The *American Jobs Creation Act of 2004* temporarily reduced the depreciable lives of 3 categories of depreciable real estate from 39 to 15 years. The reduced depreciable life, intended as economic stimulus, applied to qualified leasehold improvement property, qualified retail improvement property, and qualified restaurant property. The shorter depreciable lives were initially applicable to qualified property investments incurred between January 1, 2004 and December 31, 2007, with the expectation that the economy would have recovered from recession by 2008. When the recession unexpectedly deepened in 2008, Congress implemented the first of a series of extensions before finally making the shorter lives permanent in December 2015. Hence, qualified leasehold improvement property, retail improvement property, and restaurant property purchased after 2014 are depreciable over 15 years, using the straight-line method.

Qualified Property

There are three categories of real property that are eligible to be depreciated over 15 years. *Qualified leasehold improvement property* is any improvement to the interior of non-residential realty leased between unrelated parties if the improvements are in a portion of the building used exclusively by the lessee (i.e., the person to whom the property is being leased), and are made more than 3 years after the building was first placed in service. Code Sec. 168(k)(3). Note that the improvements may be made by either the lessee or lessor--whichever party pays for the improvements is allowed the depreciation deduction. Moreover, although the building must be at least 3 years old, the lease agreement may be brand new. Indeed, many leasehold improvements are made by the landlord to an older building in order to entice a new tenant to lease the property. In other cases, tenants will make improvements to leased property prior to moving in so that the property will fit their needs before they begin operations from that location.

The following types of improvements are not qualified for the shorter depreciable life for tax purposes:

- enlargement of the building;
- elevators or escalators;
- improvements to a structural component of the building that benefits a common area; or
- improvements to the internal structural framework of the building. Code Sec. 168(k)(3)(B).

EXAMPLE 6.51	Smith & Jones is a law firm. In July, 2017 it leased space in a multi-story building, signing a ten-year lease agreement beginning September 1, 2017. Prior to beginning operations in the mall, the company paid $2,000,000 to install hard-wood flooring, wall coverings, and new lighting in the space to be used by its partners and associates. The improvements were finished in time for the company to begin using the space on September 1. Assuming that the building was more than 3 years old when the lease was signed, and that the leased space will be used by Smith & Jones, the company's 2017 and 2018 depreciation deductions will be as follows:

Cost of leasehold improvements	$2,000,000
Depreciable life (15 years × 12 months per year)	180 months
Depreciation expense per month	$11,111/mo
Allowable deduction 2017 (3½ months)	$ 38,889
Allowable deduction 2018 (and thereafter)	$ 133,333

EXAMPLE 6.52	Assume the same facts as in Example 6.51 except that the building leased by Smith & Jones was less than 3 years old at the date that the law firm made the improvements. Because the building was new, the leasehold improvements do not qualify for the shorter 15-year depreciable life. Accordingly, the leasehold improvements must now be depreciated over 39 years, using the straight-line method. The law firm's 2017 and 2018 depreciation deductions will now be substantially smaller:

Cost of leasehold improvements	$2,000,000
Depreciable life (39 years × 12 months per year)	468 months
Depreciation expense per month	$4,274/mo
Allowable deduction 2017 (3½ months)	$ 14,957
Allowable deduction 2018 (and thereafter)	$ 51,288

Qualified retail improvement property is similarly defined as any improvement to the interior of a non-residential building that is open to the general public and is used "in the retail trade or business of selling tangible personal property to the general public." As with qualified leasehold improvement property, the building must have been placed in service more than 3 years prior to the date the improvements were made. Code Sec. 168(e)(8). Improvements may be made by the owner of the building or by a tenant; the depreciation deductions will be available to the taxpayer who pays for them. Also as above, escalators, elevators, enlargement of the building, improvements to the internal structure of the building, and improvements to "common areas" of the building (e.g., not used for retail trade) do not qualify

The final category of property eligible for 15-year straight-line depreciation is *qualified restaurant property*. Restaurant property is defined much more broadly than either of the above two categories. Qualified restaurant property includes any building or improvements to a building, if more than 50 percent of the building's square footage is devoted to the preparation of, and on-premises seating for the consumption of prepared meals. Code Sec. 168(e)(7). There are no requirements regarding the age of the building, and no restrictions on the type of expenditures that qualify for the reduced depreciable life. Thus, the entire cost of a building used as a restaurant may be depreciated over 15 years beginning with the first year in which the building is placed in service by the taxpayer.

EXAMPLE 6.53	Taste Buds Inc. opened a new restaurant in a building purchased in October, 2017. The purchase price of the building was $3,000,000, and the restaurant opened for business on November 4, 2017. Assuming this is the only qualified restaurant property purchased by the company that year, Taste Buds could claim a depreciation deduction of $25,000 on its 2017 tax return:

Cost of the building	$3,000,000
Depreciable life (15 years × 12 months per year)	180 months
Depreciation expense per month	$16,667/mo
2017 depreciation deduction (1.5 months)	$ 25,000

¶6825 CODE SEC. 179 ELECTION TO EXPENSE CERTAIN DEPRECIABLE ASSETS

Development and General Rules

Accelerated depreciation, which increases the rate at which taxpayers are allowed to "recover" the costs of business-use property against their taxable incomes, is one of the easiest and most common business incentives used by Congress. In general, the faster the recovery period, the larger the tax benefit and the lower the net cost of the newly acquired property. This is particularly true for property that is purchased with borrowed money. For example, if a taxpayer pays ten percent of the cost of a new equipment purchase in the first year, and receives a tax benefit equal to 35% of the cost of that purchase, the net out-of-pocket cost in the year of purchase is negative--the tax benefits received by the taxpayer are greater than the cash paid in the year of purchase to buy the asset. The taxpayer actually receives more money in the form of tax savings than it spent to acquire the asset (in the current year). For this reason, Congress is quite fond of provisions that allow taxpayers to deduct a significant portion of the purchase price of business-use assets in the year of purchase.

An area of particular interest to Congress is Code Sec. 179, which allows taxpayers to immediately expense a portion of the cost of newly acquired depreciable property rather than depreciating it over multiple years. When first enacted, the statute allowed taxpayers to expense up to $5,000 of depreciable equipment in the year of acquisition. The cost of purchases in excess of this amount was subject to depreciation. Between 1997 and 2003, the amount that could be expensed in the first year was gradually increased to $25,000. Beginning in 2003, the Sec. 179 amount was increased to $100,000 and indexed for inflation. In 2007, the first-year deduction was increased to $125,000, and for 2008 and 2009, it was increased further to $250,000. Beginning in 2010, Congress increased the amount that could be expensed under Code Sec. 179 to $500,000, and in 2015, Congress made the $500,000 first-year expensing deduction permanent. Thus, for all years after 2009, taxpayers can immediately expense up to $500,000 of eligible property placed in service in the current year. Any purchases in excess of the amount expensed under Sec. 179 can be depreciated under MACRS. Moreover, after 2016, this amount will be indexed for inflation. For 2017, the inflation-adjusted first-year deduction is $510,000. Rev. Proc. 2016-55, IRB 2016-45, November 7, 2016.

EXAMPLE 6.54

Bienvenida Corp purchased a business-use asset this year for $300,000. The company purchased the asset on credit, paying 10 percent down, and agreeing to pay off the balance due over the ensuing 5 years. The asset was fully deductible under Code Sec. 179. Assuming the company's marginal tax rate was 35%, the deduction will reduce its current year income tax liability by $105,000. It paid only $30,000 (10% × $300,000) this year to purchase the asset. Thus, the purchase actually *increased* the company's net cash flow this year. Of course, in future years, the additional payments against the loan will not be deductible and thus will not reduce the company's tax liability in those years.

Code Section 179 Property

The Section 179 deduction can be claimed for all purchases of "Code Section 179" property made during the taxable year. The property must be purchased (as opposed to being acquired in a nontaxable exchange), but there is no requirement that it be new. Thus, the deduction can be claimed on the purchase of new or used property as long as the purchase is from an unrelated seller.

There are two categories of Code Section 179 property. The first is tangible property that is depreciable under Code Section 1245. This category includes "off-the-shelf" computer software, equipment (machines, computers, etc.), furniture and fixtures, etc. used for business purposes. It also includes depreciable property attached to a building structure that is not a structural component of the building (e.g., air conditioning equipment, lighting, wall coverings, etc.), again so long as these items are used in the taxpayer's business operations. Finally, business-use automobiles with a gross vehicle weight in excess of 6,000 pounds can qualify for a Code Section 179 deduction under guidelines described in ¶6845.

The second category of property eligible for the Code Sec. 179 deduction is qualified leasehold improvement, retail improvement, and restaurant property (described in ¶6815). The availability of Sec. 179 for these expenditures is especially beneficial due to the relatively lengthy 15-year recovery period over which such investments would otherwise have to be depreciated.

Limitations

The Code Sec. 179 deduction is phased out as the taxpayer's equipment acquisitions exceed an overall investment limit of $2,030,000 in 2017. The phase-out is dollar-for-dollar, so that the 179 deduction is reduced to zero when total eligible purchases during the tax year reach $2,540,000. As with the $500,000 maximum deduction, the phase-out limitation is indexed for inflation for years after 2016.

The deduction is further limited to the taxpayer's taxable trade or business income for the current year. For this purpose, trade or business income is measured before the Sec. 179 deduction and includes income and expenses from *all* of the trade or business activities in which the taxpayer is engaged, rather than just the income from the trade or business in which the purchased property is used. For example, a self-employed taxpayer whose spouse is employed by another business can count both the spouse's employment earnings and the net income from the trade or business in computing the taxable income limitation (assuming the taxpayer and her spouse file a joint return). To the extent the taxpayer's Sec. 179 deduction is limited by the taxable income limitation, any unused deduction can be carried forward into subsequent tax years.

EXAMPLE 6.55

In 2017, Ginger Gilmore purchased $2,100,000 in depreciable equipment for use in her commercial nursery business. The nursery's business income before accounting for the Code Sec. 179 deduction (but *after* accounting for depreciation) was $385,000. Assume that Ginger had no other source of income. Ginger's allowable deduction under Sec. 179 for 2017 was calculated as follows:

Code Sec. 179 deduction, before limitations		$510,000
Total investment in eligible property (current year)	$2,100,000	
Overall investment limit	(2,030,000)	
Reduction in Sec. 179 deduction		(70,000)
Allowable Sec. 179 deduction before application of taxable income limit		$440,000
Taxable income before Sec. 179 deduction		385,000
Allowable Sec. 179 deduction (lesser of $385,000 or $440,000)		$385,000
Sec. 179 carryover to 2018		$ 55,000

Note that the carryover to 2018 does *not* include the $70,000 phase-out reduction. Only the portion of the otherwise allowable deduction that exceeds the net taxable income can be carried forward.

¶6835   BONUS DEPRECIATION

"Bonus" depreciation, provided for the first time in 2008, is another approach used by Congress to stimulate business activity. For 2008, 2009 and 2010, Congress allowed businesses to take a "bonus" depreciation deduction equal to 50 percent of the cost of depreciable property placed in service in those years, with the remainder of the cost being recovered under MACRS depreciation. Congress increased the rate of bonus depreciation to 100 percent of the cost of eligible property acquired after September 8, 2010, but allowed the rate to fall back to 50 percent beginning on January 1, 2012. The rate remained at 50 percent through 2014. In December, 2015 Congress extended bonus depreciation for qualified property acquired between 2015 and 2019. The rate remains at 50 percent for property purchased in 2015, 2016 or 2017. In 2018, the rate declines to 40 percent, and for purchases in 2019 the rate falls to 30 percent. Code Sec. 168(k)(7).

Bonus depreciation, like the Code Sec. 179 deduction, provides an additional incentive to increase investment in depreciable property, especially since the remaining cost of the property remains eligible for accelerated depreciation under MACRS. It is important, however, that taxpayers apply these provisions in the proper order. Under Reg. §1.168-1(d)(3) Example 2, taxpayers must deduct the Code Sec. 179 deduction first, then bonus depreciation. MACRS depreciation is then calculated on the remaining balance of the property acquisition.

EXAMPLE 6.56

Wilder Manufacturing, Inc. purchased new equipment in December 2017 at a total cost of $1,200,000. The property is 5-year depreciable property under MACRS and is eligible for both the Sec. 179 deduction and 50 percent bonus depreciation. The company opted to take both of these deductions, and to depreciate the remaining cost under MACRS. Its depreciation deductions and Sec. 179 deductions with respect to this acquisition of property for 2017 and 2018 are calculated as follows:

	2017	2018
Original cost of the property	$1,200,000	N/A
Code Sec. 179 deduction	(510,000)	N/A
Remaining cost	690,000	N/A
Bonus depreciation (50 percent)	(345,000)	N/A
Depreciable cost	$ 345,000	$345,000
MACRS depreciation rate (Table 8, mid-quarter convention)	5%	38%
MACRS depreciation	17,250	131,000
Add: Code Sec. 179 deduction (per above)	510,000	0
Bonus depreciation (per above)	345,000	0
Total deduction (MACRS, Sec. 179 and bonus depreciation)	**$872,250**	**$131,000**

Note that the previous example ignores the taxable income limitation applicable to the Code Sec. 179 deduction. However, that limitation does not limit the computation of the Sec. 179 deduction, only its deductibility. As illustrated in the following example, any portion of the deduction not allowable in 2017 can be carried to 2018.

EXAMPLE 6.57

Assume the same facts as in Example 6.56 above. Further assume that Wilder Manufacturing had net taxable income of $600,000 *before* accounting for depreciation, bonus depreciation and the Sec. 179 deduction. Its 2017 deduction under Sec. 179 would be limited to $237,750, as illustrated below:

	2017
Taxable income before depreciation, bonus depreciation and the Code Sec. 179 deduction	$600,000
Bonus depreciation	(345,000)
MACRS depreciation	(17,250)
Taxable income before Code Sec. 179 deduction	$237,750
Total Sec. 179 deduction—2017 purchases	510,000
Allowable portion (limited to taxable income per above)	(237,750)
Carryforward to 2018 (can be deducted in addition to up to $510,000 claimed for 2018 purchases, so long as total does not exceed income limitation)	**$272,250**

Eligible Property

"Eligible property" is defined somewhat more narrowly for purposes of bonus depreciation than it is for Code Sec. 179. Under Code Sec. 168(k)(2), eligible property for the bonus depreciation deduction consists of machinery, equipment or other tangible personal property with a depreciable life of 20 years or less, most computer software, and a new category of realty, "qualified improvement property." Qualified improvement property is any improvement made to the interior of a building if the improvement is placed in service after the building was placed in service. Code Sec. 168(k)(3)(A). Furthermore, property is not qualified for bonus depreciation unless the "original use" of such property begins with the taxpayer. Thus, property must be new—used property purchased by the taxpayer during the year is eligible for the Code Sec. 179 deduction, but not for bonus depreciation.

¶6845   DEPRECIATION OF AUTOMOBILES

Limitations on Depreciation of Automobiles

Calculation of depreciation expense for business-use automobiles is subject to a complex set of rules. In general, automobiles are classified as five-year property, and are eligible for both bonus depreciation and MACRS depreciation. However, the annual depreciation deductions for automobiles is subject to strict limits referred to as the "luxury automobile depreciation limitations." Under Code Sec. 280F, limitations are imposed on the amount of depreciation that may be claimed in each year of the life of a business-use automobile as indicated in Table 10.

Table 10. DEPRECIATION LIMITS FOR BUSINESS-USE AUTOMOBILES	Passenger Cars	Trucks and Vans
First year (year in which auto is first placed in service)	$11,160	$11,560
Second year	$5,100	$5,700
Third year	$3,050	$3,460
All succeeding years	$1,875	$2,075
Note: vehicles can be depreciated beyond five years if they continue to be used for business purposes and the total cost has not yet been fully recovered as of the end of the fifth year.		

Note that the first year limitation includes $8,000 for bonus depreciation for new vehicles. Also, as indicated in Table 10, the depreciation limits for trucks and vans are slightly higher than those for passenger automobiles, reflecting the generally higher cost for such vehicles than for passenger cars. It is very important to note that these limitations apply only to vehicles that are suitable for use as passenger cars. Automobiles with a gross vehicle weight (GVW) in excess of 6,000 pounds are not considered to be passenger cars, nor are ambulances, taxis or limousines. Accordingly, cars and trucks with a GVW in excess of 6,000 pounds are not subject to these limitations.

Business Use

If the automobile is used less than 100 percent for business purposes, the depreciation deduction limitations are determined by multiplying the limitation amount by the business-use percentage. If the business-use percentage of the car is less than 50 percent in any year, MACRS depreciation must be computed using the alternative MACRS method (straight-line method over a five-year life).

EXAMPLE 6.58

On January 23, 2017, Lucille purchased a new car for $35,000. The following table compares the depreciation deductions she would be allowed to deduct each year from 2017-2021 if she uses the car 100% for business purposes vs. 75% for business:

Depreciation allowed in:	Percent Used for Business	
	100%	75%
2017 (half-year)	$11,160	$8,370
2018	5,100	3,825
2019	3,050	2,288
2020	1,875	1,406
2021	1,875	1,406
Total depreciation deductions	$23,060	$17,295

Note that if Lucille continues to use the car for business in years after 2021, she will be allowed to deduct up to $1,875 in depreciation expense (reduced for non-business use) each year that she continues to use the car. .

Section 179

While Code Sec. 179 can be used to expense a portion of the cost of automobiles in the year of acquisition, the deduction is treated as depreciation expense and is generally subject to the luxury automobile depreciation limitations summarized in Table 10. Code Sec. 280(d)(1). Thus, taxpayers usually do not claim a Sec. 179 deduction with respect to autos because it does not increase the allowable deduction.

As noted above, however, the limitations of Sec. 280F do not apply to automobiles, trucks or vans with gross vehicle weights in excess of 6,000 pounds. Prior to 2004, these vehicles could be fully expensed under Sec. 179, subject only to the overall limitation on the annual Sec. 179 write-off. Thus, for example, a taxpayer purchasing an SUV with a gross vehicle weight in excess of 6,000 pounds in 2003 could write off the lesser of the cost of the vehicle or $100,000 in that year. This provision generated substantial criticism as it provided an incentive to automobile manufacturers to make SUVs bigger and heavier and thus less fuel efficient. In response to these criticisms, the *American Jobs Creation Act of 2004* implemented an additional limitation on the Code Sec. 179 deduction for passenger automobiles with GVWs between 6,000 and 14,000 pounds.

For years after 2004, the maximum amount that can be deducted under Sec. 179 with respect to the purchase of an automobile with GVW between 6,001 and 14,000 pounds is $25,000. Code Sec. 179(b)(5). Because the limitation is intended to apply only to non-commercial vehicles, it does not apply to vehicles designed to have a seating capacity of more than 9 persons behind the driver's seat (e.g., buses), vehicles with a cargo area of at least 6 feet in interior length (e.g., commercial trucks), or vehicles that have seating rearward of the driver's seat (e.g., delivery vans).

If a taxpayer purchases a qualified SUV at a cost greater than $25,000, the amount spent above $25,000 may be depreciated under the bonus and MACRS depreciation rules. Because the limitations under Code Sec. 280F apply only to vehicles with GVWs of 6,000 pounds or less, depreciation of the excess cost (over $25,000) of an eligible vehicle is not subject to the luxury auto limitations.

EXAMPLE 6.59

In 2017, Gabrielle purchased a new SUV for $70,000. The vehicle has a gross vehicle weight of 8,000 pounds and is therefore eligible for the Sec. 179 deduction. In addition, because its GVW exceeds 6,000 pounds, the SUV is not subject to the luxury auto depreciation limitations of Code Sec. 280F. Assuming the vehicle is used 100% for business, Gabrielle will be able to deduct the following amount in 2017:

Original cost of the SUV	$70,000
Code Sec. 179 deduction*	(25,000)
Remaining basis	$45,000
Bonus depreciation	(22,500)
Depreciable basis for MACRS	$22,500
MACRS 1st yr rate (Table 7)	20%
MACRS depreciation	$ 4,500
Add: Sec. 179 deduction	25,000
Bonus depreciation	22,500
Total deduction 2017	**$52,000**

* Sec. 179 deduction limited to $25,000 for SUVs regardless of overall maximum allowed under statute.

The language of Code Sec. 179(b)(5) provides that the $25,000 limitation applies to the cost of each SUV purchased and placed in service during the tax year. Thus, if a taxpayer purchases more than one qualified vehicle in a given year, a $25,000 deduction under Code Sec. 179 will be available for *each* vehicle purchased.

EXAMPLE 6.60

In 2017, Mendoza Corp purchased two new SUVs for $35,000 each (total expenditure $70,000). The vehicles each had a GVW of 8,000 pounds and were therefore eligible for the Sec. 179 deduction. As in the example above, the remaining cost of each vehicle after taking the Sec. 179 deduction is eligible for both bonus and MACRS depreciation. Assuming the vehicles are both used 100% for business, Mendoza will be able to deduct the following amount in 2017:

Original cost of the SUVs	$70,000
Code Sec. 179 deduction*	(50,000)
Remaining basis	$20,000
Bonus depreciation	(10,000)
Depreciable basis for MACRS	$10,000
MACRS 1st yr rate (Table 7)	20%
MACRS depreciation	$ 2,000
Add: Sec. 179 deduction	50,000
Bonus depreciation	10,000
Total deduction 2017	**$62,000**

* Sec. 179 deduction limited to $25,000 for SUVs regardless of overall maximum allowed under statute.

¶6855   PROPERTY CONVERTED FROM PERSONAL TO BUSINESS USE

As noted above, conversion of property from business to non-business use will create tax issues with respect to depreciation and Code Sec. 179 deductions previously claimed. However, it is also relatively common for taxpayers to convert property from personal use to business use. For example, a taxpayer may move to another city and decide to convert his or her personal residence into rental property. Similarly, a taxpayer starting her own business may convert a personal use auto to business use property in connection with the new business.

In such cases, Reg. §1.167(g)-1 provides that the tax basis of the asset for tax purposes will be equal to the lesser of the fair market value of the property at the date of conversion to business (or investment) use or its adjusted tax basis at the date of conversion. This will be the taxpayer's tax basis for purposes of computing depreciation expense and loss (if any) from a subsequent sale of the asset. If the asset is later sold for a profit, the original basis of the asset, adjusted for depreciation, will be used to calculate the taxable gain. With respect to depreciation, the asset will be treated as having first been placed in service in the year of conversion to business-use property. The appropriate convention will apply under MACRS (mid-year, mid-quarter, or mid-month). Note that in most cases, no deduction will be allowed under Code Sec. 179 for property converted from personal to business use. Unlike depreciation under MACRS, Code Sec. 179 applies to property "purchased" by the taxpayer from an unrelated seller during the taxable year for use in a trade or business. Code Sec. 179(d)(1) and (2). Since the conversion of property from personal to business use does not involve a purchase transaction, Code Sec. 179 will not be applicable.

EXAMPLE 6.61

Javier and Maria Gonzales purchased a new home in September, 2007 for $425,000. They used the home as their personal residence until July 2017, when Maria was transferred by her employer to another city. The real estate market had declined rather substantially and the Gonzales decided not to sell their home, but to place it on the rental market instead. They placed the home for rent on August 1, 2017. After a brief period of showing the home, it was rented in October, 2017. At that date, an independent appraisal estimated the value of the home to be $300,000. Allocating 5% of the value of the home to land, the Gonzales will be allowed to depreciate $285,000 of the home under MACRS. It is 27.5 year property and is depreciated using the mid-month convention. Moreover, it was converted to business use on August 1, 2017, the date it was placed on the rental market. It does not matter that the home was not rented until October of that year. For 2017, the Gonzales will be allowed to claim a depreciation deduction of $3,886 ($285,000 depreciable basis of the home ÷ 27.5 years x 4.5 months/12 months).

KEYSTONE PROBLEM	The property ledger used for tax purposes by Able Garment Co., a calendar year taxpayer, is shown below. Compute the amount of the 2017 and 2018 depreciation deductions allowable to Able Garment Co. for these assets on its tax returns based on regular MACRS depreciation percentage rates (ignore bonus depreciation and the Section 179 deduction).

Able Garment Co.

Property Ledger as of December 31, 2017

Asset	Year Purchased	Cost	Salvage Value
1. Car	2017	$19,000	$1,000
2. Cargo van (>6,000 lbs GVW)	2017	22,000	1,500
3. Office furniture	2017	14,250	1,000
4. Business equipment	2017	38,950	5,000
5. Building (Office)	Sept. 2017	95,000	—

¶6865   AMORTIZATION

In financial accounting, the term "amortization" is normally defined as the process of allocating the cost of an intangible asset to expense over its estimated useful life. The Code is not as precise in the use of the term "amortization." The Regulations actually refer to the process of allocating the cost of an intangible asset to expense as depreciation instead of amortization. Reg. §1.167(a)-3. In other sections of the Code, reference is made to amortizing the cost of tangible assets, a process which is usually referred to as depreciation in financial accounting.

Intangible Assets

Intangible assets used in a trade or business and having limited useful lives subject to reasonable estimation can be amortized over an appropriate useful life. The straight-line depreciation method is used to compute the amortization deduction. Code Sec. 197 provides for a 15-year amortization period for specified intangible assets referred to as "section 197" intangibles. A section 197 intangible includes goodwill, going concern value, licenses or permits granted by a governmental agency, covenants not to compete, franchises, trademarks, trade names, patents, and copyrights.

Other Allowable Amortization Deductions

In some instances, amortization deductions are allowed for capital expenditures which are more favorable to a taxpayer than the normal depreciation allowances applicable to the property. These amortization deductions are provided to taxpayers as tax incentives to participate in investment activities which are considered to have some public interest attached to them. For example, taxpayers may elect to amortize the cost of pollution control facilities over a 60-month period. Code Sec. 169.

¶6875   RESEARCH AND EXPERIMENTAL EXPENDITURES

The term "research and experimental" expenditures (R&E) includes all experimental and laboratory costs connected with the development of an experimental or pilot model, plant process, product, formula, invention, or similar property. It does not include expenditures for ordinary testing or inspection of materials or products for quality control or for efficiency surveys, management studies, consumer surveys, advertising, or promotion. Reg. §1.174-2(a). R&E connected with a trade or business can be treated as a current deduction for tax purposes or, if elected by the taxpayer, be deferred and amortized over a period of not less than 60 months starting in the period when benefits from the R&E are first realized. Code Sec. 174(a) and (c). Subsequent changes in treatment require approval of the IRS. Any R&E involving the purchase of property which would normally be subject to depreciation such as equipment or the purchase of land cannot be deducted immediately but must be handled in accordance with its regular treatment for tax purposes. Code Sec. 174(c).

EXAMPLE 6.62

In 2017, Jones Ribbon Co. incurs R&E for the first time. R&E included the following amounts:

R&E Salaries	$350,000
R&E Materials	150,000
Total R&E	$500,000

Jones Ribbon Co. could choose to treat all R&E incurred in 2017 as a current deduction of $500,000.

If Jones Ribbon Co. elects to capitalize and amortize 2017 R&E, the monthly amortization deduction, assuming a 60-month amortization period, would be:

$500,000/60 = $8,333.33 per month amortization in 2017 starting with the month when benefits from the R&E are first realized.

PLANNING POINTER

Generally, immediate expensing of R&E is advantageous to a taxpayer for tax purposes as compared to capitalization and amortization of R&E. This is true because immediate expensing results in larger tax deductions in earlier years and lower tax payments.

¶6885 DEPLETION OF NATURAL RESOURCES

Depletion is normally defined as the process of allocating the cost of a natural resource to expense over its estimated useful life. For tax purposes, however, it is possible that depletion deductions for a natural resource may exceed the cost of the natural resource. Some natural resources which are subject to depletion include metals such as gold, silver, and copper, and minerals like coal, clay, sand, and oil.

The owner of a natural resource is entitled to the depletion deduction. Reg. §1.611-1(b). Land on which the natural resource is located is not subject to depletion.

Two methods are available to taxpayers for computing the depletion deduction: the cost depletion method and the percentage depletion method. The taxpayer would normally compute the proper deductions using both depletion methods and then claim the higher deduction for tax purposes. Reg. §1.611-1(a).

Cost Depletion Method

The cost depletion computation involves dividing the basis of the natural resource by the estimated units to be recovered from the natural resource to determine the depletion amount per unit. The depletion amount per unit is then multiplied by the units of the natural resource sold during the year which gives the cost depletion deduction for the tax year.

EXAMPLE 6.63

In 2017, Basil Natural Resource Development Company acquires the rights to a natural resource for $5,000,000. The estimated recoverable units from the natural resource at the time of purchase amount to 250,000 units. The depletion amount per unit is $5,000,000/250,000 = $20 depletion amount per unit. If 40,000 units of the natural resource were sold during 2017, the depletion deduction using the cost depletion method would be $800,000 (40,000 units sold during year × $20 depletion amount per unit).

Percentage Depletion Method

Percentage depletion is computed by taking a specified depletion percentage and applying it to the gross income for the year derived from the sale of the natural resource. Some depletion percentages specified in the Code include 5 percent for sand and gravel, 10 percent for coal, 15 percent for gold, silver, and copper, and 22 percent for uranium. Code Sec. 613. The deduction for percentage depletion with respect to a particular property cannot exceed 50 percent of the taxpayer's net taxable income derived from the natural resource produced from that property (before accounting for the depletion deduction) for the taxable year.

EXAMPLE 6.64

Referring to the previous example, Basil Natural Resource Development Company sells 40,000 units of its natural resource during 2017 at an average price of $160 per unit. Assuming a specified depletion percentage of 15 percent stated for the natural resource and operating expenses of $115 per unit of natural resource, the percentage depletion deduction is computed as follows:

1. Gross income derived from natural resource

(40,000 units × $160)	$6,400,000
Code specified depletion percentage	15%
Percentage depletion deduction subject to limitation	$960,000

2. Taxable income limitation

Gross income	$6,400,000
Operating expenses before depletion (40,000 units × $115)	4,600,000
Taxable income before depletion deduction	$1,800,000
Limitation percentage	50%
Percentage depletion deduction limitation	$900,000
Percentage depletion deduction, lesser of (1) or (2)	$900,000

As mentioned earlier, a taxpayer should compare the computed cost depletion deduction with the computed percentage depletion deduction and deduct the higher amount. In the two examples, the cost depletion deduction was $800,000 and the percentage depletion deduction was $900,000. Thus, taxpayer would deduct the $900,000 percentage depletion deduction amount.

A taxpayer's tax basis in the natural resource is reduced, but not below zero, by the amounts of depletion deductions taken by the taxpayer. If the basis of the natural resource property is reduced to zero, after being reduced by depletion deductions, depletion can still be claimed by a taxpayer using the percentage depletion method since it is not based on the cost of the taxpayer's investment in natural resource property.

¶6901   SUBSTANTIATION OF TAX DEDUCTIONS

As noted earlier, tax deductions are allowed to taxpayers only if they are specifically authorized. In addition, taxpayers must be able to substantiate the deductions claimed on their tax returns if requested by the IRS through the audit process. Taxpayers can normally substantiate tax deductions by providing documentary evidence such as receipts, invoices, and cancelled checks. In some instances, oral testimony of the taxpayer or other persons in support of the taxpayer may be of some value. In the past, the IRS has argued in court that if a taxpayer fails to substantiate a deduction, then the entire deduction should be disallowed. In an important trend-setting case, however, the court held that if substantiation for a tax deduction was lacking but it was reasonable to assume that some amount of expense had been incurred, then it is reasonable to assume that some estimated tax deduction should be allowed. *G.M. Cohan,* 2 USTC ¶489, 39 F.2d 540 (CA-2 1930). The reasoning applied in the *Cohan* case to justify a reasonable deduction when substantiation for a deduction is lacking has become known as the *Cohan* rule for tax purposes. The *Cohan* rule applies to all tax deductions with the exception of travel and entertainment expenses, business gifts, charitable contributions, and a few other expenditures where substantiation is required before a deduction will be allowed.

EXAMPLE 6.65

Lavelle attends church each Sunday and always puts a twenty-dollar bill in the church collection basket. Lavelle does not use church envelopes and does not make a charitable contribution by check. She claims charitable contributions to her church of $1,040 on her 2017 tax return. In an audit of her 2017 tax return by the IRS, Lavelle is questioned on the amount of her charitable contributions. She has no documentary evidence to support her charitable contribution deduction of $1,040. Starting in 2007, the *Cohan* rule no longer applies to charitable contributions and Lavelle will be denied a charitable contribution deduction due to the lack of substantiation.

TAX BLUNDER

In Example 6.64, Lavelle should have used church envelopes and had the church notify her in writing of her total charitable contributions at the end of the year. Alternatively, had she paid her contributions by check, she would have the cancelled checks to substantiate her gifts.

A taxpayer must be able to substantiate tax deductions claimed on the return. If a tax return is audited by the IRS, documentary evidence such as invoices, paid receipts, and cancelled checks are very important in substantiating deductions. Oral evidence of other individuals may be of some value. Oral evidence of the taxpayer may also be of some value, but the IRS is certainly aware that many taxpayers, when questioned, merely declare that their deductions were computed correctly. The *Cohan* rule is of some use to taxpayers in that it generally provides a floor for tax deductions. The *Cohan* rule, however, will rarely result in a taxpayer's being allowed a tax deduction equal to the amount originally claimed. Also, the *Cohan* rule is no longer applicable with respect to a number of deductions, as discussed above.

SUMMARY

- Allowable tax deductions are divided into four categories: trade or business, production of income, losses and personal. Basic personal living expenses of an individual taxpayer normally are not deductible with the exception of certain personal expenditures that have been allowed by Congress for various reasons as itemized deductions.

- In order to be deductible, trade or business expenditures must (1) be ordinary and necessary, (2) be reasonable in amount, and (3) be related to an activity which is deemed to be a trade or business. Some expenditures which meet all these requirements, however, may still be disallowed if they are contrary to public policy, or were incurred to generate tax-exempt income. Other expenses may be denied if they were incurred in connection with a personal transaction. Thus, for example, legal expenses may not be deductible even if ordinary, necessary to preserve a taxpayer's business assets, and reasonable in amount if they are attributable to a dispute arising from a personal transaction, such as divorce. Finally, it is important to distinguish between expenses and capital expenditures. The latter are not currently deductible but must be capitalized and recovered over time.

- Certain employment related expenses of employees are deductible as trade or business deductions if they are directly related to the performance of the employees' duties or are required by an employment agreement.

- More common trade or business deductions allowable under the criteria discussed above include advertising, bad debts, salaries, interest payments, rental payments, insurance, and legal fees. Allowable business deductions related to capital expenditures include depreciation, amortization, and depletion. Business start-up expenditures and business gifts are restricted deductions.

- Expenses incurred to produce income must meet the same requirements as those incurred in a trade or business in order to be deductible, with the exception of the requirement that they be incurred in a trade or business activity. This category of deductions includes investment expenses and tax planning and preparation expenses.

- All expenses incurred by individual taxpayers in connection with the determination, collection, or refund of any tax are deductible.

- Individual taxpayers are allowed deductions for business losses, investment losses, and casualty or theft losses. Personal losses other than casualty and theft losses are not deductible. With the exception of some selected expenditures, basic personal living expenses of a taxpayer are not deductible.

- Some additional factors that may affect the amount of an allowable tax deduction are tax accounting method used, substantiation of deductions, and deductible amounts paid on behalf of another taxpayer.

QUESTIONS

1. Tax deductions for an individual taxpayer can be divided into what three categories?

2. What are production of income tax deductions? What allowable deductions are included in the production of income deductions category?

3. Explain the difference between a deduction for AGI and a deduction from AGI. Which type of deduction would be more advantageous for tax purposes?

4. How might an improper classification of a deduction as for or from AGI affect the itemized deductions on a taxpayer's return? How might this improper classification have an effect on a taxpayer's state income tax liability?

5. List the criteria that must be met before an expenditure can be considered as an allowable trade or business tax deduction.

6. Explain why the IRS would be interested in the reasonableness of a salary payment to an employee/owner of a closely held corporation.

7. If an activity of a taxpayer is determined to be a hobby for tax purposes, what tax deductions are available to the taxpayer? Are there any limitations on these deductions?

8. If an expenditure is part business-related and part personal, how does the taxpayer determine the business-related amount that is deductible for tax purposes?

9. What is the logical argument that supports the statutory disallowance of a deduction for any expenditure related to tax-exempt income?

10. Explain the difference between an employee and an independent contractor from a tax standpoint. What difference does it make for tax purposes if someone is characterized as an employee or independent contractor?

11. What losses are tax deductible for individual taxpayers?

12. How can a taxpayer substantiate a tax deduction if called on to do so by the IRS in an audit of the taxpayer's return?

13. What is the difference between a business and nonbusiness bad debt for tax purposes?

14. What are the basic requirements for a bad debt deduction on a tax return? Do any of these requirements differ between business and nonbusiness bad debts?

15. Can a current tax deduction for salaries and wages include payments for services performed in past years and for services to be performed in future years? Why is a sole proprietor not entitled to a tax deduction for salary payments to himself or herself?

16. Is salvage value ever considered when using MACRS depreciation? When using MACRS, is depreciation ever allowed on an asset in the year of disposal?

17. To qualify for the immediate expensing election (Code Sec. 179), an asset must meet what qualifications?

18. What is the difference between the cost depletion method and the percentage depletion method for tax purposes? Which method does a taxpayer use if the taxpayer is eligible for both methods?

19. What restrictions apply to tax deductions for business gifts?

20. Define the term "transportation expenses" as used for tax purposes. Give three examples of transportation expenses which are deductible by employees.

21. Define the term "travel expenses" as used for tax purposes. Define the term "away from home" as interpreted by the IRS.

22. In order for entertainment expenses to be deductible, the expenses must be "directly related to" or "associated with" a taxpayer's business. Define the terms "directly related to" and "associated with."

23. With regard to moving expenses paid or incurred by a taxpayer in connection with the commencement of work, what time and distance requirements must be met by the taxpayer in order to justify a moving expense deduction?

PROBLEMS

24. For the current year, Al Johnson used his personal car for both business and personal purposes. He drove 18,000 miles in the car during the year: 10,000 miles were for business-related purposes and 8,000 miles were for personal purposes. He incurred the following car expenses during the year:

Expense	Amount
Gas	$7,900
Maintenance	900
Repairs and depreciation	900
Car washes	500
Total	$10,200

Based on this information, what part of the above car expenses is deductible as business-related expenses on Al's current year income tax return?

25. Refer to the facts in Problem 24 and assume that Al's total car expenses amounted to only $4,700. What is the amount of Al's car expense deduction on his current year tax return?

26. Indicate whether the following expenditures are trade or business deductions (T), production of income deductions (PI), personal deductions (P), or are not deductible (X). Also indicate if the deductible expenditures are deductible "for" or "from" AGI.
    a. Business advertising
    b. Interest expense on home mortgage
    c. Union dues of employee
    d. Bank service charges on business checking account
    e. Entertainment expenses of employee not reimbursed by employer

27. Indicate whether the following expenditures are trade or business deductions (T), production of income deductions (PI), personal deductions (P), or are not deductible (X). Also indicate if the deductible expenditures are deductible "for" or "from" AGI.
    a. Interest expense on business loan
    b. Hobby expenses in excess of hobby income
    c. Commuting expenses of individual taxpayer
    d. Rent payments by illegal gambling business
    e. Payment to bribe government official made by a business

28. Are any of the following losses deductible on an individual's income tax return? If so, is the loss deductible "for" or "from" AGI? Explain each loss.

Loss	Amount
Loss on sale of stock by individual's business	$4,000
Hobby loss in excess of hobby gross income	3,000
Gambling losses in excess of gambling winnings	8,000
Loss on sale of stock on individual's investment portfolio	9,000
Decline in value of stock held in individual's investment portfolio	7,000
Loss on sale of personal automobile	2,000
Total	$33,000

29. Which of the following trade or business expenditures of Ajax Inc. are deductible on its current year tax return? If an expenditure is not deductible, explain why it is not a valid deduction.

Expenditure	Amount
Salaries and wages to employees	$400,000
Purchase of new office building	250,000
Payment of illegal parking fines of President	1,400
Payment of wedding expenses for President's daughter's wedding	16,000
Entertainment expenses related to company business	25,000
Interest on money borrowed to buy tax-exempt securities	9,000
Total expenditures	$700,400

30. Indicate whether the following expenditures are deductible for AGI or from AGI.
    a. Medical expenses of individual taxpayer
    b. Safe deposit box rental for business
    c. Interest expense on business loan
    d. Investment counseling fees incurred by individual investor
    e. Gambling losses to extent of gambling winnings of individual gambler not involved in gambling business

31. Indicate whether the following expenditures are deductible for AGI or from AGI.
    a. Entertainment expenses of employee not reimbursed by employer
    b. Moving expenses of employee
    c. Transportation expenses of employee not reimbursed by employer
    d. Hobby losses to extent of hobby income

32. Are any of the following expenditures deductible on an individual taxpayer's income tax return? Explain each item.

Expenditure	Amount
Cost of having income tax return prepared by a CPA	$100
Legal fee for divorce proceeding of which 20 percent related to tax planning advice	3,000
Lost wages for time missed from work while having income tax return prepared	250
Legal fee for estate planning advice of which 35 percent related to tax planning advice	900
Cost of having federal gift tax return prepared by a CPA	100
Total expenditures	$4,350

33. Two years ago, Jack Peters borrowed $150,000 from the First National Bank which he used to buy equipment used in his business. Business slowed considerably this year, and Jack was unable to make payments on the loan. To keep the bank from foreclosing on the note and putting his son out of business, Jack's father made several payments on the loan during the year. Of the total payments he made on the loan, $10,000 was attributable to interest and the remainder was applied to reduce the principal balance.

Can Jack's father deduct the $10,000 in interest expense he paid on Jack's loan? Explain.

34. For the current month, Jackson Cement Co. incurred payroll expenses as follows:

Gross salaries and wages	$675,000
Payroll taxes:	
OASDI (Social Security Tax)—employer's share	41,850
HI (Medicare tax)—employer's share	9,788
	726,638
Amounts withheld and paid to the government:	
Employee income taxes withheld	(108,990)
OASDI—employees' share	(41,850)
HI—employees' share	(9,788)

    a. What amount can Jackson claim as a tax deduction for salary and wage expense?
    b. How much can Jackson deduct as tax expense?

35. Bevis Bag Co. purchased a tract of land on August 31 of the current year, paying $225,000. Prior to the sale, the seller paid property taxes of $18,000 on the property. The taxes covered the calendar year period January 1 through December 31.
    a. Will Bevis be allowed to deduct any portion of the property taxes paid by the seller prior to the sale? If so, how much?
    b. What will be Bevis' tax basis in the land?

36. Compute MACRS depreciation for the following qualified assets for the calendar years 2017 and 2018: (Ignore bonus depreciation and the Section 179 deduction.)

Asset	Year Purchased	Cost	Salvage Value
Business equipment (7-year property)	March 2017	$85,500	$10,000
Car	May 2017	14,000	1,000
Office furniture (7-year property)	July 2017	18,050	3,000
Building (Office)	January 2017	185,000	5,000

37. Refer to the facts in Problem 36 and assume that the straight-line method under the alternative MACRS system was elected over the MACRS recovery period for all the assets listed. Based on these facts, compute the 2017 and 2018 depreciation deductions for each of the assets listed. (Ignore bonus depreciation and the Section 179 deduction.)

38. Refer to the facts in Problem 36 and assume that the office building purchased in January 2017 and the car purchased in 2017 were both sold in June 2018. How much depreciation can be claimed as a deduction on these two assets in 2018 for the portion of the year they were held by the taxpayer? Assume MACRS depreciation is used.

39. Refer to the facts in Problem 36 and assume the business equipment purchased in March was instead purchased in November. Based on these facts, compute the MACRS depreciation for the business equipment, car, and office furniture for calendar years 2017 and 2018. (Ignore bonus depreciation and the Section 179 deduction.)

40. In 2017, Jason Products Co., a calendar year taxpayer, purchased business equipment (7-year property) for $2,150,000. No other personal property was purchased during the year. Jason wants to take the largest possible tax deduction in 2017 related to this property. Compute the largest tax deduction possible in 2017 for the business equipment. (Consider bonus depreciation and the Code Sec. 179 deduction).

41. LB Corporation purchased a business car in June 2017 for $42,000. The car weighs 4,000 pounds and will be used 100 percent of the time in the business. Compute the largest depreciation deduction possible in 2017. No other property purchases were made during the year. (Consider bonus depreciation and the Section 179 deduction, if applicable.)

42. Refer to the facts in Problem 41 and assume the business car purchased is an SUV weighing 8,000 pounds. Compute the largest depreciation deduction possible in 2017. (Consider bonus depreciation and the Section 179 deduction, if applicable.)

43. LCD Corporation purchased residential real property for $385,000 (exclusive of land cost) and placed it in service on August 16, 2017. Compute MACRS depreciation on the property for 2017 and 2018.

44. Refer to the facts in Problem 43 and assume the property purchased is nonresidential rental property. Compute MACRS depreciation on the property for 2017 and 2018, assuming the property is not qualified leasehold improvement, retail improvement or restaurant property.

45. In March, Gary Parker started a new career as a real estate agent. He established Gary Parker Company, LLC on March 11 and began seeking clients. He listed his first property on March 21, and closed his first sale on April 9. Gary used his SUV, purchased three years ago and previously used for personal purposes, as his business auto. Once he began business as a real estate agent, he used the vehicle 100 percent for business purposes. Gary purchased the SUV three years ago for $42,000. At the date he started his real estate practice, it was worth approximately $28,000.
    a. What is the maximum amount Gary can claim as a first-year deduction under Code Sec. 179 this year with respect to the vehicle?
    b. What is the maximum amount of depreciation expense Gary can claim with respect to the vehicle on the current year tax return?

46. Assume the same facts as in Problem 45. Further assume that next year, Gary sells the SUV for $20,000.
    a. How much depreciation expense can Gary deduct as a business deduction with respect to the SUV on next year's tax return?
    b. How much gain or loss will Gary recognize for tax purposes in connection with the sale of the vehicle next year?

47. In the current year, James Jar Co., a calendar year taxpayer, incurred the following research and experimentation expenditures (R&E): Salaries—$150,000; and Materials—$100,000.
    a. If James Jar Co. treats R&E as a current deduction, what is the amount of the current year deduction?
    b. If James Jar Co. capitalizes R&E and amortizes it over a 60-month period, what is the amount of deduction on a monthly basis that James can take, starting with the month when benefits from the R&E are first realized?

48. At the beginning of the year, NRD Company purchased the rights to a natural resource for $10,000,000. The estimated recoverable units from the natural resource amount to 3,500,000 units. During the year, NRD sold 1,000,000 units of the natural resource for $10 per unit and incurred operating costs other than depletion of $5 per unit. Based on these facts:
    a. Compute NRD's depletion deduction using the cost depletion method.
    b. Compute the company's depletion deduction using the percentage depletion method. Assume a 15 percent specified depletion percentage.
    c. Which depletion deduction, cost or percentage, will NRD use this year?

49. In 2017, Mary Kelly drove her personal car 2,800 miles for business purposes. She also incurred $182 in parking fees and $191 in turnpike tolls connected with her business trips. None of her automobile expenses were reimbursed by her employer. Compute Mary's deduction for automobile expenses on her current year tax return, assuming all of the above expenses are valid and she elects to use the standard mileage allowance method to figure her automobile expenses.

50. Herman Welbe owns one car dealership in Ohio and one in Florida. Each year, Herman lives eight months in Ohio and four months in Florida. In the current year, Herman received $900,000 net income from his Ohio dealership and $250,000 net income from his Florida dealership. Based on these facts, is Herman entitled to any travel expenses for tax purposes in relation to his trips between his two dealerships and for living expenses incurred at either location? Explain.

51. On Monday, Harvey Leonard travels from Chicago to New York on a business trip. The trip lasts five days. Three days of the trip are spent conducting business activities and two days are spent on personal sightseeing activities. Harvey incurs $550 in airfare costs in going to and returning from New York, $50 a day in expenses for meals, and $100 a day for lodging while in New York.
    a. What amount is deductible on Harvey's tax return for travel expenses related to the above activities? Assume Harvey is self-employed.
    b. Assume Harvey is an employee and is reimbursed $700 by his employer for the trip. What amount is deductible on Harvey's tax return for unreimbursed travel expenses related to the above activities?

52. This year, Juan Sanchez incurred the following employment-related moving expenses:

Expenses related to moving household goods	$4,000
Expenses to drive from old location to new location	60
Temporary living expenses in new location	1,800
Real estate commission on sale of old home	2,200
Total expenses	$8,060

Juan received no reimbursement from his employer for his moving expenses. Based on the above facts, and assuming that Juan meets the time and distance requirements, compute Juan's moving expense deduction that would appear on his current year tax return.

53. For an individual taxpayer, expenses connected with rents and royalties are normally deducted:
    a. For AGI
    b. From AGI
    c. Either for or from AGI
    d. For AGI but limited to a maximum percentage amount

54. An ordinary trade or business expenditure is one which is:
    a. Reasonable in amount
    b. Commonly incurred by other businesses
    c. Appropriate for a particular business
    d. Not a capital expenditure

55. A necessary trade or business expenditure is one which is:
    a. Reasonable in amount
    b. Commonly incurred by other businesses
    c. Appropriate for a particular business
    d. Not a capital expenditure

56. In 2017, the maximum amount of capital expenditures eligible for immediate expensing is:
    a. $139,000
    b. $25,000
    c. $510,000
    d. $2,030,000

57. **Comprehensive Problem (Tax Return Problem).** John Stantus, single, is the sole owner of Stantus Accounting Services, Co. He started the company, which is organized as a sole proprietorship, on February 10 of the current year. For this year, Stantus Accounting Services reported the following amounts of income and expenses:

Fee revenues	$840,000
Expenses:	
Employee wages	(125,000)
Payroll taxes	(9,563)
Advertising	(3,600)
Insurance	(2,400)
Utilities	(7,200)
Rent	(10,000)
Supplies	(5,000)
Selling expenses	(35,000)

- John purchased a car on February 1 of the current year for $24,000. He uses the car for both business and personal purposes. Mileage logs indicate that John put 40,000 miles on the car this year. Of that total, 28,000 miles were business related and the remaining 12,000 were related to personal travel. John wants to deduct the maximum amount allowable for business use of his car.

- John also purchased office equipment, computers and other five-year property for use in the business. He purchased $625,000 worth of such depreciable assets in March. He wants to deduct the maximum amount allowable under Code Sec. 179 and depreciate the remaining cost (if any) using bonus and MACRS depreciation.

- Selling expenses include $6,000 spent for meals and entertainment incurred on John's sales calls during the year.

- Selling expenses also include $12,000 in illegal payments to city officials paid to secure a lucrative contract with the city. John was uncomfortable making this payment, but reasoned that the contract was important to get his business off to a good start.

- Selling expenses also include gasoline, parking fees, and other documented auto expenses totaling $2,500 attributable to John's sales calls.

Assume that John reports the revenue and expenses of Stantus Accounting Services on Schedule C, that he uses the cash method of accounting, and that he has no other taxable income, deductions or credits other than the items listed above. As noted above, he is single, with no dependents. He lives at 105 1st Street in Jackson, Mississippi (zip code = 39201). His social security number is 555-33-4444. His business address is 501 19th Street, Jackson, MS 39201. Skipping Schedule SE (on which you would ordinarily calculate the self-employment tax), prepare John's 2017 Individual Income Tax Return. (Note: you may have to use 2016 forms.)

58. **Comprehensive Problem.** Peter Nerf, a single taxpayer, is an accountant employed by a large corporation. This year, he was transferred from the company's headquarters office to an office in another state. For the year, he had the following items of income and expense:

Wages received from his employer		$75,000
Moving expenses:		
Expenses to move household furniture	$3,000	
Travel from old residence to new location	700	
Temporary living expenses in new location	2,100	
Real estate commission on sale of old home	5,000	10,800
Medical expenses		6,600
Charitable contributions		5,000
Job related expenses (subscriptions, licenses, etc.) not reimbursed by Peter's employer		2,350

Peter's moving expenses were not reimbursed by his employer. Assuming that he had no other taxable income, deductions or credits other than those listed above, calculate Peter's taxable income for the current year.

59. **Research Problem.** The following selected court cases have helped to shape the tax law in regard to allowable trade or business tax deductions. Read the following court cases and prepare a brief written abstract for each case.
   a. *New Colonial Ice Co.,* 4 USTC ¶1292, 292 U.S. 435.
   b. *T.H. Welch v. Helvering,* 3 USTC ¶1164, 290 U.S. 111.

60. **Research Problem.** Prepare a brief written abstract for each of the following additional selected court cases relating to allowable trade or business deductions.
   a. *A. Trujillo,* 68 TC 670, Dec. 34,554.
   b. *Illinois Terminal Railroad Co.,* 67-1 USTC ¶9374, 179 Ct.Cls. 674, 375 F.2d 1016 (Ct.Cls. 1967).
   c. *I.R. Wharton,* 53-2 USTC ¶9597, 207 F.2d 526 (CA-5 1953).

Chapter

7

Deductions: Business/Investment Losses and Passive Activity Losses

OBJECTIVES

After completing Chapter 7, you should be able to:

1. Determine the amount and classification of losses originating from business operations.
2. Ascertain the amount and classification of losses from investment-related activities.
3. Understand tax shelters and the rationale for at-risk rules.
4. Achieve a thorough understanding of the intricacies of the passive activity rules.
5. Identify and determine the amount of allowable business and theft losses.
6. Calculate the amount of a net operating loss and determine the amounts to be carried back and forward.
7. Understand the allowable home office expenses and determine the limitation on the deduction for such losses.
8. Achieve an understanding of the vacation home rental rules and the limitation on such losses.
9. Understand the benefits and calculations related to the new manufacturing deduction under Code Sec. 199.

OVERVIEW

Deductions are provided in the Code for losses resulting from unprofitable investment-related activities, dispositions of certain assets, and unprofitable business operations. In each of these cases certain limitations or adjustments may apply, thus limiting the amount of deductible loss. Generally, deductible losses from a business, property held for production of income, or investment property are deductible for adjusted gross income. Losses derived from personal-use property, if deductible, are usually deducted from adjusted gross income as itemized deductions.

This chapter deals with losses originating from business operations and certain investment-related activities. Tax shelters, at-risk rules, passive activity rules, business casualty and theft losses, net operating losses, hobby losses, home office expenses, and vacation homes are among the topics addressed. Casualty losses derived from personal-use properties are discussed in Chapter 8, and losses resulting from the sale of capital assets (e.g., stocks and bonds) and business-use assets (Code Sec. 1231) are discussed in Chapter 12.

Tax Shelters and At-Risk Rules

¶7001   TAX SHELTERS

A tax shelter is an activity providing deductions and/or credits to an investor which will reduce tax liability with respect to income from other sources. Prior to the Tax Reform Act of 1986, tax shelters played an unreasonably influential role in the financial planning of many individuals. A Treasury study revealed that in 1983, 21 percent of tax returns reporting total positive income greater than $250,000 paid taxes equaling *10 percent or less* of total positive income (which is composed of salary, interest, dividends, and income from profitable businesses and investments). S. Rept. No. 313, 99th Cong., 2d Sess. (1986), p. 714.

Congress recognized the undesirable consequences that tax shelters created, which included declining federal tax revenues, diverting investment capital from productive activities to tax avoidance schemes, and perhaps most importantly, the loss of faith in the federal tax system. The Senate Finance Committee went so far as to say: "Extensive shelter activity contributes to public concerns that the tax system is unfair and to the belief that tax is paid only by the naive and unsophisticated." The reason Congress had allowed tax shelters to exist in the first place was to encourage investment in certain areas in order to promote economic growth.

EXAMPLE 7.1	
	Arthur Johnson, a corporate executive, had income of $275,000 during 1983 (before passive loss rules). He took advantage of the tax laws (legally) by purchasing a shopping center in January 1983. The price was $500,000. He paid $25,000 down and financed the balance over 20 years. Rental income averaged $3,500 a month, while payment on the $475,000 note was $6,000 a month. Maintenance, taxes, and repairs averaged $1,500 a month. Initially, it appears that Mr. Johnson was losing $4,000 a month ($3,500 – $6,000 – $1,500) during his first year of ownership ($48,000 a year). But after considering his tax bracket (50 percent) and depreciation (12 percent for 1983), his net cash flow actually increased by $5,000 for the year because of preferential tax rules:

Net Cash Flow Before Tax Benefit	$(48,000)
Depreciation (12% × $500,000)	(60,000)
Principal Payment Adjustment*	2,000
Net Deductible Loss	$(106,000)
Times Tax Bracket	× .50
Tax Benefit	$53,000
Net Cash Flow Before Tax Benefit	(48,000)
Net Cash Flow	$5,000

* $2,000 of the note payments were applied to principal (i.e., not deductible), all other monthly expenses were deductible.

Notice that the tax benefit in the preceding example was treated as an immediate cash inflow. It simply reduced the taxpayer's tax liability by the tax benefit amount, which, essentially, represented taxes that would have been paid on income from other sources, such as salary, dividends, interest, etc. When coupled with the possibility that the property could increase in value, this was a popular form of investment and an easy concept for tax shelter salesmen to sell. However, most such investments never provided a net cash flow as illustrated in the example.

Practically all tax shelters were formed as limited partnerships. Limited partnerships were used because they allowed losses and credits to be passed through to the partners' individual tax returns. A limited partner is a partner who is not personally liable for the debts of the partnership. More importantly, a limited partner can utilize deductions and/or credits that "flow through" from the partnership. Some examples of the activities tax shelter limited partnerships engaged in included equipment leasing, real estate, oil and gas, movie productions, cattle breeding, cattle feeding, and farming. Even though most tax shelters never made a profit, thousands of taxpayers bought into them for the sole purpose of avoiding income taxes. Thus, genuine economic value was rarely considered in making an investment decision to acquire an interest in a tax shelter activity.

The Tax Reform Act of 1986 significantly impacted such investment decisions with the passage of the passive activity rules. Code Sec. 469. *Essentially all limited partnership investments, rental properties, and businesses in which an owner does not materially participate have been affected.* The general rule is that losses arising from a passive activity are not deductible, except against income from a passive activity. The unused portion of the loss, however, is not lost but is suspended (i.e., carried over) until offset by passive income in a future tax year or until the entire activity is disposed of in a fully taxable transaction.

EXAMPLE 7.2

Assume the same facts as in the preceding example, except that if Arthur Johnson purchased the shopping center in 2017, his investment would fall under the passive activity rules, which would allow no deduction (i.e., no tax benefit) for the loss in 2017. The entire disallowed loss would become a suspended loss until passive income is later received or he appropriately disposes of the rental property. For instance, if in 2018 the shopping center yields $25,000 in income, then the loss from 2017 would be used to offset the income and any unused balance of suspended loss would be carried over to 2019.

¶7125   AT-RISK RULES

Prior to the 1986 Act, Congress made a rather weak attempt to curb tax shelter abuse by enacting the at-risk provisions (Code Sec. 465) in 1976. The at-risk rules disallow losses that are in excess of an investor's amount at risk. In a general sense, at risk is the amount of investment that an investor could possibly lose. The rules apply to individuals as well as closely held corporations. An investor's amount at risk is computed as follows:

	Cash invested
+	Adjusted basis of other property invested
+	Borrowings for which investor is personally liable
+	Borrowings for which investor has pledged collateral
+	Allocated portion of income
–	Allocated portion of losses
–	Withdrawals
=	Amount at risk

The formula does not indicate to what extent the allocated losses are deductible for tax purposes, because the amount at risk is reduced (but not below zero) regardless of the extent to which the losses are deductible. The deductible portion of any possible losses is calculated *after* applying the at-risk rules.

An investor is not at risk for nonrecourse borrowings, stop-loss arrangements, no-loss guarantees, or borrowings in which the lender has an interest (as in seller financing). Code Sec. 465. A nonrecourse loan is a loan that is secured by the property purchased, rather than the personal assets of the borrower (i.e., the borrower is not personally liable). A recourse loan, on the other hand, is one where the borrower is personally liable for repayment.

EXAMPLE 7.3

Betty Smith gave $10,000 cash, pledged $10,000 for security of a partnership loan, and gave a computer with an adjusted basis of $5,000 for her interest in a limited partnership. Her amount at risk is $25,000. The activity allocated a $40,000 loss (passive loss) to her. Only $25,000 (the amount at risk) of the $40,000 loss can be used to offset income from other passive activities during the year. Since she is not at risk for the remaining $15,000, it is carried over into a future tax year until she becomes at risk, which would then free up this amount to be offset against passive income.

EXAMPLE 7.4

Assume Betty Smith gave $10,000 cash and signed a nonrecourse note for property that the limited partnership was acquiring. Ms. Smith would only be at risk for her $10,000 cash investment, and, consequently, only $10,000 of the $40,000 could be used to offset income from other passive activities. The remaining $30,000 is carried over until she becomes at risk.

Generally, taxpayers are not considered at risk with regard to nonrecourse loans. However, a partner is considered to be at risk for certain *qualified* nonrecourse loans on real property. A qualified nonrecourse loan is one acquired from:

1. a person who is actively and regularly engaged in the business of lending money, or
2. any federal, state, or local government (including loans guaranteed by such governments) (Code Sec. 465(b)(6)(B))

An exception to this rule applies for loans acquired from:

1. Related parties,
2. The seller of the property, or
3. A person who receives a fee due to the taxpayer's investment in the property.

A partner would not be at risk for such loans. Code Sec. 49(a)(1)(D)(iv).

Because losses reduce the amount at risk, such losses usually may be recaptured if the investor's amount at risk is less than zero at the close of a taxable year. Code Sec. 465(e). Thus, when an individual's amount at risk drops below zero, the taxpayer will include in gross income the amount of the excess. A drop in at risk, for example, can occur when a debt arrangement is changed from recourse to nonrecourse.

TAX BLUNDER

Lynn R. and Wade L. Moser et al., the taxpayers, entered into a leveraged computer leasing transaction with Finalco Inc. Finalco entered into leases with end-users, purchased the equipment, financed the purchase with a lending institution, and then resold the equipment in a sale and leaseback transaction to Lease Pro Inc., a company engaged in the purchase, sale, and leasing of computer equipment. The taxpayers then purchased the equipment from Lease Pro and leased it back to Finalco. The fixed monthly rental payment that Finalco owed to the taxpayers was the same amount as the monthly installments that the taxpayers owed to Lease Pro that, in term, was identical to the monthly installments Lease Pro owed to Finalco. As a result, in making payments, no cash was exchanged because the amount owed by each group equaled the amount each group was due. From 1981 to 1983, the taxpayers reported net losses totaling $300,937. However, these losses were disallowed because the court held that the taxpayers were not at risk under Code Sec. 465(b)(4). That is, this section suspends at-risk treatment where a transaction is structured, by whatever technique, to remove any realistic possibility that the taxpayer will suffer an economic loss if the transaction turns out to be unprofitable. *W.L. Moser*, 90-2 USTC ¶50,498, 914 F.2d 1040 (CA-8 1990). Whenever the circular nature of the taxpayers' obligations effectively shields the taxpayers from economic loss, Code Sec. 465(b)(4) will hold that the taxpayers are not at risk for any portion of the notes underlying the transaction.

Passive Activity Loss Rules

¶7201   ## APPLICATION OF RULES

The at-risk rules are still in effect and are applied before passive loss restrictions. Once the at-risk rules are satisfied, a passive loss can then be used in the following ways: offset passive income, offset other income (under certain conditions), and/or become suspended. Passive income and losses are "before AGI" items.

EXAMPLE 7.5

Bob McKeown contributed $35,000 cash and signed a $15,000 nonrecourse note to invest in Limited Partnership A (LPA). He is at risk for $35,000 in the partnership. Bob is also at risk for $50,000 in Limited Partnership B (LPB). Both activities are considered to be passive activities. During the year, LPA experienced a loss and allocated to him his portion of the loss, $65,000. LPB had a better year and allocated $25,000 of income to Bob. Because Bob is at risk for only $35,000 for LPA, only $35,000 of the $65,000 loss is considered as a passive loss. As a result, $25,000 of the $35,000 passive loss from LPA can be used to offset the $25,000 of passive income (before AGI) from LPB. Ten thousand dollars ($35,000 – $25,000) of the passive loss from LPA is suspended under the passive loss rules. At the end of the year, Bob's amount at risk for LPA will be zero ($35,000 – $35,000). The remaining $30,000 ($65,000 – $35,000) loss from LPA is carried over under the at-risk rules until Bob increases his amount at risk in LPA. Once Bob satisfies the at-risk rules, this amount will become a passive loss and may be used to offset future passive gains. Bob will be at risk for $75,000 ($50,000 + $25,000) for LPB at the end of the year.

Partnership	Initial Amount At Risk	Allocated Gain (Loss)	Loss Passive Income (Loss)	Carryover Under At-Risk Rules	Suspended Passive Loss	Ending Amount At Risk
A	$35,000	($65,000)	($35,000)	($30,000)	($10,000)	$0
B	$50,000	$25,000	$25,000	—	—	$75,000

If Bob had received $45,000 of passive income from LPB (instead of $25,000), his results would be different. He could offset the passive income with $35,000 of passive losses from LPA, resulting in $10,000 of net passive income, and have no suspended passive loss. His amount at risk for LPA is still zero and he still has a loss carryover under the at-risk rules of $30,000. His ending amount at risk for LPB would be $95,000 ($50,000 + $45,000).

Partnership	Initial Amount At Risk	Allocated Gain (Loss)	Passive Income (Loss)	Loss Carryover Under At-Risk Rules	Suspended Passive Loss	Ending Amount At Risk
A	$35,000	($65,000)	($35,000)	($30,000)	$0	$0
B	$50,000	$45,000	$45,000	—	—	$95,000

¶7205 CLASSIFICATION OF INCOME

Because of the passive activity rules, income is required to be classified as active, passive, or portfolio. Ordinarily, active income is attributable to the direct efforts of the taxpayer, such as salary, commissions, wages, etc. Passive income is income derived from a passive activity. Portfolio income is interest, dividends, annuities, and royalties not derived in the ordinary course of a trade or business. The gain from the sale of property that produces portfolio income (e.g., stocks and bonds) is also classified as portfolio income. Code Sec. 469(e). The reason for the classification is to keep separate the types of income that passive losses can offset. As previously mentioned, passive losses can only offset passive income and cannot be used as a deduction against active or portfolio income (except in certain instances). Similarly, tax credits from passive activities can only offset taxes incurred from passive income.

Portfolio income received by a limited partnership and allocated to the partners is not passive income, and the partners cannot offset the portfolio income by passive losses from this partnership or any other passive activity. Thus, limited partnerships that receive portfolio income and experience net income (or loss) from operations must separately allocate income (loss) generated from operations and portfolio income to its partners.

¶7211 DISALLOWANCE OF PASSIVE LOSSES AND CREDITS

For tax years after 1990, no passive activity losses or credits may be deducted against active and portfolio income. Interests in passive activities acquired by the taxpayer on or before October 22, 1986 (the date on which the Tax Reform Act of 1986 was enacted), were eligible for a special deduction and credit phaseout of losses for a five-year period. Code Sec. 469(m)(2). Thus, after 1990, passive losses in excess of passive gains are not deductible and must be carried forward.

¶7215 SUSPENDED LOSSES

Generally, any loss or credit from a passive activity which is disallowed by the passive loss rules is treated as a deduction or credit allocable to such activity in the next taxable year. Code Sec. 469(b). Suspended losses can become deductible against future income from passive activities or against nonpassive income upon the fully taxable disposition of an entire interest. Keeping suspended losses for each passive activity separate is necessary in order to determine the amount of an activity's deductible portion of suspended loss whenever an event qualifying for the deduction occurs (e.g., a fully taxable disposition).

EXAMPLE 7.6

Linda Helmsly owned the following passive activities during 2017 (all were acquired after 1986, and she was at risk for all losses):

Activity	Income/(Loss)	Suspended (Loss)*
ABC	$35,000	$0
XYZ	(45,000)	(20,000)
BBD	(60,000)	(80,000)
	$(70,000)	

* Suspended losses from previous years.

The amount of net loss experienced in 2017, $70,000, is not deductible but is suspended. It must be allocated, however, between all activities showing a loss for the year (XYZ and BBD):

Activity	Allocation	Suspended (Loss)	Total Suspended (Loss)
ABC	N/A	$ 0	$ 0
XYZ	$45,000/$105,000 × $70,000	(30,000)	(50,000)
BBD	$60,000/$105,000 × $70,000	(40,000)	(120,000)

APPLICATION OF THE AT-RISK AND PASSIVE LOSS RULES

Step 1. Determine the amount at risk for each passive activity (before considering gain or loss for that year).

Step 2. Determine whether each passive activity results in a gain or loss for the tax year.

Step 3. If an activity results in a gain:

(a) Increase the amount at risk for that activity.

(b) Treat gain as passive gain.

Step 4. If an activity results in a loss:

(a) Reduce the amount at risk for that activity (but not below zero) by the amount of the loss.

(b) Any excess losses are carried over under the at-risk rules.

(c) Treat losses (except for amounts carried over) as passive losses.

Step 5. Add up all passive gains.

Step 6. Add up all passive losses.

Step 7. Reduce passive gains (but not below zero) by passive losses and any passive loss credits. Include any net passive gain in gross income.

Step 8. Carry over excess passive losses as suspended passive losses.

(a) If more than one activity results in a passive loss, allocate suspended passive losses between the activities in proportion to the amount of their passive losses.

(b) In future tax years, use suspended passive losses to offset passive income.

¶7225 DISPOSITION OF A PASSIVE ACTIVITY

If a passive activity is disposed of in a fully taxable transaction, any losses (including suspended losses from prior years) may be recognized by the taxpayer in the year of disposition. Such losses can offset active and portfolio income (nonpassive income). However, losses from the sale of passive activities to related parties generally are not deductible. See Chapter 10.

The excess of the sum of Items 1 + 2 over 3 will be treated as a loss which is not from a passive activity (i.e., deductible against nonpassive income):

1. Any loss from the activity for the tax year, including suspended losses from prior years, plus
2. Any loss realized from the disposition of the activity, over
3. Net income or gain from all passive activities (determined without regard to losses from the disposition or losses from the activity). Code Sec. 469(g)(1).

Passive activity interests that are capital assets and are appropriately disposed of are subject to the capital asset rules for losses (Code Sec. 1211) after applying the passive loss rules. See Chapter 12. A limited partnership interest held as an investment is a capital asset.

EXAMPLE 7.7

Rob Williams had gross income of $125,000 in 2017 and owned the following passive activities during the year:

Activity	Gain/(Loss)	Suspended (Loss)
ZZZ	$15,000	$(50,000)
XXX	(10,000)	(28,000)
YYY	(22,500)	(45,000)

All activities were acquired after 1986, and Rob was at risk for all losses. He sold his entire interest in ZZZ in a fully taxable transaction. ZZZ was a limited partnership in which Rob was a limited partner. He acquired the limited partnership interest in 1987. The selling price was $22,000, while his basis in the interest was $55,000. The result is computed as follows:

Selling price	$22,000
Adjusted basis	(55,000)
Realized loss	$(33,000)

The $50,000 of suspended losses will first offset the $15,000 gain from ZZZ, and the balance ($35,000) will be deductible against active and portfolio income. The $33,000 realized loss resulting from the sale of the limited partnership interest will become a long-term capital loss.

Death, Gift, and Other Transfers

If an interest in a passive activity is transferred by reason of death, suspended losses are deductible on a decedent's income tax return to the extent that the excess of the stepped-up basis in the hands of the transferee over the decedent's adjusted basis is less than the amount of suspended loss.

EXAMPLE 7.8

Zeb McFarland died and left a passive activity to his nephew. Zeb's basis in the activity was $25,000, while the nephew's basis was "stepped up" to $40,000. Suspended losses amounted to $21,000. The amount of passive loss deduction that can offset nonpassive income is $6,000, the $21,000 suspended loss minus the $15,000 step-up in basis.

If an interest in a passive activity is transferred by gift, the suspended losses are not deductible but are added to the recipient's basis.

EXAMPLE 7.9

Jennie Franklin gave her daughter a limited partnership interest in a real estate activity. Suspended losses amounted to $20,000. The mother's adjusted basis at the time of the gift was $30,000. The daughter's basis would be the mother's adjusted basis plus the amount of suspended losses, or $50,000 (assuming fair market value was greater than $30,000).

¶7231   TAXPAYERS AFFECTED BY PASSIVE LOSSES

The passive loss limitations apply to individuals, estates, trusts, closely held corporations, and personal service corporations. Code Sec. 469(a)(2). This list describes taxpayers that would otherwise be entitled to the tax benefits of losses or credits from a passive activity. Partnerships and S corporations are not included. Limitations on losses or credits from activities operated by these entities are passed through and applied at the level of the partners and shareholders, respectively.

Personal Service Corporations

The application of the passive activity loss rules to personal service corporations is intended to prevent taxpayers from sheltering personal service income simply by incorporating as a personal service corporation and acquiring passive activity investments at the corporate level. In general, a corporation is a personal service corporation if (1) it is a C corporation, (2) its principal activity is the performance of personal services, (3) the services are substantially performed by employee-owners, and (4) such employee-owners own more than 10 percent of the fair market value of the corporation's outstanding stock. Whether these qualifications are satisfied is determined during a testing period for the tax year, which is generally the corporation's prior tax year. Temp. Reg. §1.469-1T(g)(2).

Closely Held Corporations

A closely held corporation's losses and credits from a passive activity may be limited if (1) it is a C corporation that is not a personal service corporation, and (2) more than 50 percent of its stock is owned directly or indirectly by (or for) not more than five individuals. Noting the distinction between taxpayers is worthwhile because closely held corporations are able to offset passive losses with net active income, but not portfolio income. Code Sec. 469(e)(2). Consequently, a closely held corporation is the only entity affected by the passive loss rules that can deduct losses from a passive activity that it owns.

EXAMPLE 7.10	Jasper Corporation, a closely held corporation, generated $150,000 of income from operations during the year. It also received passive losses of $200,000 and interest of $30,000. (Jasper Corporation was fully at risk for the amount of loss.) The corporation's taxable income is $30,000 because it can offset passive losses with active income, but not with portfolio income. The remaining $50,000 of passive losses will become suspended.

Oil and Gas Working Interests

A working interest which a taxpayer holds in oil and gas properties is not subject to the passive activity rules. Code Sec. 469(c)(3). The working interest cannot be held through any entity that limits the taxpayer's liability (e.g., limited partnership interest or stock in a corporation). A working interest is a working or operating mineral interest in any tract or parcel of land. Temp. Reg. §1.469-1T(e)(4)(iv).

¶7235   MATERIAL PARTICIPATION

A passive activity is defined as "any activity which involves the conduct of a trade or business, and in which the taxpayer does not materially participate." Code Sec. 469(c)(1). Also included in the definition are rental activities, without regard to the extent of taxpayer participation. Temp. Reg. §1.469-1T(e)(1)(ii). As a consequence, trade or business activities in which a taxpayer does materially participate are not passive activities. Nevertheless, rental of real estate properties is generally classified as a passive activity regardless of the level of participation.

"Material participation" requires a taxpayer to be involved in the operations of the activity on a regular, continuous, and substantial basis. Code Sec. 469(h)(1). When making this rule, Congress was aware that many taxpayers would accumulate suspended losses from tax shelter investments as a result of the passive loss rules. Moreover, some of these taxpayers might own profitable businesses that could be turned into passive activities (which would then be used to offset passive losses). The change from an active business to a passive activity could possibly be achieved by lowering a taxpayer's level of participation in the active business. The result of such maneuvering would impede the overall effectiveness of the passive loss provisions. Material participation, then, was devised to include virtually all "passive" business owners but at the same time exclude certain "active" business owners from being brought into the passive loss arena.

On the other hand, a business in which an individual materially participates is not a passive activity. Therefore, if the business experiences a loss, the loss will be deductible against all other types of income (passive, active, and/or portfolio) without regard to the passive loss restrictions. Additional guidance in making the determination as to who qualifies as a material participant is provided under the regulations by furnishing seven tests. Temp. Reg. §1.469-5T(a). Thus, an individual will be treated as materially participating in an activity for the tax year if any of the following tests apply:

Test 1.	The individual participates in the activity for more than 500 hours during the tax year.
Test 2.	The individual's participation in the activity constitutes substantially all of the participation in such activity of all individuals (including individuals who are not owners) for the tax year.
Test 3.	The individual participates in the activity for more than 100 hours during the tax year, and such individual's participation for the tax year is not less than the participation in the activity of any other individual (including nonowners) for the tax year.
Test 4.	The activity is a "significant participation" activity for the tax year, and the individual's aggregate participation in all significant participation activities during such year exceeds 500 hours (see below).
Test 5.	The individual materially participated in the activity for any five tax years, whether or not consecutive, during the 10 tax years that immediately preceded the tax year.
Test 6.	The activity is a personal service activity and the individual materially participated in the activity for any three tax years, whether or not consecutive, preceding the tax year.
Test 7.	Based on all of the facts and circumstances, the individual participates in the activity on a regular, continuous, and substantial basis during the tax year.

Also note that in determining whether a taxpayer materially participates, the participation of a taxpayer's spouse will be taken into account. Code Sec. 469(h)(5).

Significant Participation

An individual is treated as significantly participating in an activity for a tax year if and only if the individual participates in the activity for more than 100 hours during the year. A significant participating activity is a trade or business in which an individual significantly participates, but not to the extent of material participation as determined by the other six tests. Temp. Reg. §1.469-5T(c). In other words, an individual may have ownership interests in several businesses, but participates infrequently (less than material participation in each). If the hours of participation for each activity exceed 100, and the total number of hours in all such businesses exceeds 500, then the individual is treated as materially participating in all such businesses.

EXAMPLE 7.11

David Jones owns an interest in six businesses. His level of participation is as follows:

Activity	Hours
A	100
B	125
C	90
D	135
E	140
F	100
Total	690

David is not a material participant in any one of the activities above. In addition, he is not significantly participating in activities A, C, and F (not more than 100 hours of participation in each). The aggregate amount of participation in the significant participating activities is 400 hours from activities B, D, and E. Therefore, David is not treated as materially participating under Test 4, and all activities fall under the passive loss rules.

EXAMPLE 7.12

Assume the same facts as in Example 7.11, except that activity C had 105 hours of participation. Because the number of participation hours is in excess of 100, activity C is a significant participation activity. This brings the aggregate number of hours in significant participating activities to 505. David would now be considered to be a material participant, and therefore only activities A and F would fall under the passive loss rules.

¶7235

Limited Partners

Limited partners, by the very nature of their relationship to the partnership, are not considered to be material participants. As a general rule, limited partners are not involved in the day-to-day management of partnership affairs. However, if limited partners participate in the activity, they may become material participants in the partnership if one of the following applies:

1. The limited partner holds a general partnership interest at all times during the partnership's tax year ending with or within the individual's tax year (or the portion of the partnership's tax year during which the individual—directly or indirectly—owns such limited partnership interest).
2. The limited partner participates more than 500 hours (Test 1).
3. The limited partner participates for any five years during the 10 tax years immediately preceding the tax year at issue (Test 5).
4. For a personal service activity, the limited partner materially participated in the activity for any three years preceding the year at issue (Test 6). Temp. Reg. §1.469-5T(e).

Participation Standard

The Internal Revenue Service considers an individual to be participating when any work is done by such individual in connection with an activity in which the individual owns an interest at the time the work is done. Individuals are not considered as participating in the following situations:

1. Work not customarily done by an owner if one of the principal purposes for the work is to avoid the disallowance of any loss or credit from such activity under the passive loss rules.
2. Work done in the individual's capacity as an investor (such as studying and reviewing financial statements of the activity, preparing or compiling summaries or analyses of the finances or operations of the activity for the individual's own use, and monitoring the finances or operations in a nonmanagerial role). Temp. Reg. §1.469-5T(f).

¶7261

IDENTIFYING AN ACTIVITY

Determining the scope of a particular activity is important for identifying whether a taxpayer has two or more separate activities or one activity having two or more undertakings. Two situations in which this determination is vital occur when material participation is involved and upon disposition of the activity. For example, if an owner is involved in an activity that has two separate and distinct undertakings, such as rental property and retail sales, then a determination must be made as to whether the two undertakings will be treated as one activity or two activities. If the sales/rental business is treated as one activity, then the individual will only have to satisfy the material participation rules for one activity. A disposition of one of the undertakings, however, will not qualify as a "disposition of an entire interest" for purposes of recognizing a loss against nonpassive income. But if the sales/rental business is treated as two separate activities, then the material participation requirements must be met for each separate activity. In addition, because each undertaking is a separate activity, a disposition of an entire interest is allowed if one of the undertakings (now an activity) is sold.

Proposed Regulations were issued in 1992 which provide guidance for grouping a taxpayer's trade or business activities and rental activities under the passive activity rules. The regulations define trade or business activities as activities that:

1. Involve the conduct of a trade or business (within the meaning of Code Sec. 162);
2. Are conducted in anticipation of the commencement of a trade or business; or
3. Involve research or experimental expenditures that are deductible under Code Sec. 174 (or would be deductible if the taxpayer adopted the method described in Code Sec. 174(a)). Prop. Reg. §1.469-4(b)(1).

Rental activities are defined as activities constituting rental activities within the meaning of Temporary Regulation §1.469-1T(e)(3). They are discussed in detail in the next section of this chapter.

Under the Regulations, a taxpayer may treat one or more trade or business activities or rental activities as a single activity. To qualify for such treatment, the activities must constitute an appropriate economic unit for determining gain or loss for purposes of Code Sec. 469.

A facts and circumstances approach is used to determine whether or not various activities may be treated as a single activity. Any reasonable method of applying the relevant facts and circumstances may be used for this purpose. Certain factors are considered the most important in determining whether separate activities constitute an appropriate economic unit. However, not all factors need be present. They are:

1. Similarities and differences in types of businesses;
2. The extent of common control;
3. The extent of common ownership;
4. Geographical location; and
5. Interdependence between activities.

Interdependence between activities may exist if firms buy or sell goods to one another, have customers in common, provide products or services together, share employees, or are accounted for on the same set of books and records. Reg. §1.469-4(c)(1) and (2).

EXAMPLE 7.13	Ernie operates a bookstore and a restaurant in a shopping mall in Atlanta and a bookstore and a restaurant in Miami. Depending upon how Ernie applies the facts and circumstances test, he may end up with one to four activities for purposes of the passive activity rules. Both bookstores and restaurants could be grouped into one activity. Alternatively, he may have two separate activities, one constituting the bookstores and one constituting the restaurants. He may also have an Atlanta activity and a Miami activity. Finally, he may treat each business as a separate activity. Reg. §1.469-4(c)(3)

EXAMPLE 7.14	Ted owns a large retail business. He is the sole proprietor of a firm that provides bookkeeping services to businesses. The retail business is the primary client of the bookkeeping firm. Because the two activities are under common control, Ted could treat the retail activity and the bookkeeping activity as a single activity. Reg. §1.469-4(c)(3).

The Regulations generally prohibit the grouping of rental activities with nonrental trade or business activities. However, such groupings are permissible if the income generated by one activity is insubstantial in relation to the income generated by the other activity. No guidance is provided in the Proposed Regulations on the meaning of the word "insubstantial" in this context. Reg. §1.469-4(d). But prior temporary regulations indicate that an activity providing 20 percent or less of the total revenue of two activities may be considered insubstantial.

Two separate rental activities, one involving personal property and the other involving real property, may not be grouped into one activity. An exception to this rule arises when personal property is rented in connection with real property. Reg. §1.469-4(e).

Limited partners in partnerships are generally prohibited from grouping the limited partnership activity with other activities. However, such groupings are permitted with other activities in which the taxpayer is a limited partner and which carry on the same type of business. If the taxpayer is not a limited partner in the second activity, the grouping may still be achieved by applying the facts and circumstances test. Reg. §1.469-4(f)(1) and (2).

Activities that have been grouped under any of the above criteria may not be regrouped in subsequent taxable years unless it can be demonstrated that the original grouping was clearly inappropriate. Alternatively, a material change in the facts and circumstances (such as a change in ownership) may occur that would justify a regrouping of activities. Reg. §1.469-4(g).

The Commissioner has the authority to regroup a taxpayer's activities. This will occur if the grouping does not result in appropriate economic units under the facts and circumstances test and one of the primary purposes of the taxpayer's grouping is to avoid the passive loss rules. Reg. §1.469-4(h).

EXAMPLE 7.15	Bob and three friends each own separate retail businesses, and they invested in limited partnerships years ago that generate annual passive losses. Bob and his friends acquire limited partner interests in a partnership created to provide janitorial services to their respective retail businesses. The janitorial service is run by a general partner selected by Bob and the others. The janitorial service is set up to insure that it generates a profit. The four limited partners plan to treat the janitorial service as a separate activity and use losses from their other limited partnership to offset the net profit from the janitorial service. Applying the facts and circumstances test, each partner's interest in the janitorial service and the partner's respective business would constitute one appropriate economic activity, rather than two. In addition, it is obvious that the partners created the janitorial service and treated it as a separate activity in order to circumvent the passive loss rules. Hence, the Commissioner would likely require the partners to treat their respective interests in the janitorial service and their individual businesses as one activity instead of two. Penalties may also be levied against them under Code Sec. 6662. Reg. §1.469-4(h).

Activities carried on by a partnership or S corporation are first grouped by the partnership or S corporation by applying these rules. After the activities are grouped by the partnership or corporation, the individual partner or shareholder then groups the activities with other activities, as appropriate, in which the partner or shareholder is personally involved. Reg. §1.469-4(j).

Under certain circumstances, a taxpayer who disposes of a substantial part of an activity during a taxable year may treat the part disposed of as a separate activity. To do so, the taxpayer must establish the following with reasonable certainty:

1. The amount of disallowed deductions and credits carried over from prior years that are allocable to that part of the activity for the taxable year; and
2. The amount of gross income and any other deductions and credits allocable to that part of the activity for the taxable year. Reg. §1.469-4(k).

¶7273　RENTAL ACTIVITIES

An activity is a rental activity if during the year: (1) tangible property held in connection with the activity is used by customers or is held for use by customers, and (2) gross income attributable to the conduct of the activity represents amounts paid principally for the use of the property. Temp. Reg. §1.469-1T(e)(3). Generally, any rental activity is a passive activity, without regard to material participation. Code Sec. 469(c)(2) and (4).

The following tests and examples are exceptions to rental activity status (i.e., if any test is met, then the activity is not a rental activity);

1. The average period of customer use for rental property is seven days or less.

EXAMPLE 7.16	George Lee owns a home video movie rental store. The average period of customer use is two days. The store is not a rental activity.

2. The average period of customer use is 30 days or less, and significant personal services are provided by or on behalf of the owner in connection with making the property available for use by customers. Significant personal services include services performed by individuals. In making the determination, factors such as the frequency with which the service is provided, type and amount of labor required, and the value of the services relative to the amount charged for the use of property will be weighed.

EXAMPLE 7.17	Monica Sellers owns a computer leasing service. The average period of customer use is more than seven days but less than 30 days. Pursuant to the lease agreements, skilled technicians and programming consultants employed by her maintain and service malfunctioning equipment as well as implement programs for no additional charge. The value of the maintenance, repair, and implementation services exceeds 50 percent of the amount charged for the use of the equipment. Significant personal services are provided and the activity is not a passive activity.

3. Extraordinary personal services are provided by or on behalf of the owner in connection with making the property available for use by customers. Extraordinary personal services are services provided to customers so that use of the property is actually incidental to the receipt of such services.

EXAMPLE 7.18	The use of a hospital's boarding facilities generally is incidental to the receipt of personal services provided by the hospital's medical staff. The hospital's boarding operations are not rental activities.

4. The rental of such property is treated as incidental to a nonrental activity of the taxpayer.

EXAMPLE 7.19	Bob Townson owns 3,000 acres of unimproved land for the principal purpose of realizing gain from appreciation. In order to defray the cost of carrying the land, he leases it to a rancher who allows cattle to graze on it. If the gross rental income is less than 2 percent of the lesser of the land's fair market value or the adjusted basis (incidental to the nonrental activity), then the land is not a rental activity. Assuming that the land is worth $600,000 and his adjusted basis is $450,000, the rent must be less than $9,000 (2% × $450,000) in order for it to be incidental.

5. The taxpayer customarily makes the property available during defined business hours for nonexclusive use by various customers.

EXAMPLE 7.20	Operating a golf course that is available during prescribed business hours for nonexclusive use by various golfers is not a rental activity.

6. The taxpayer provides property for use in an activity conducted by a partnership, S corporation, or joint venture in which the taxpayer owns an interest, but the activity is not a rental activity. Temp. Reg. §1.469-1T(e)(3)(B)(ii).

EXAMPLE 7.21	Patricia Bowers is a partner in a law firm. She provides to the firm the use of expensive, sophisticated audio equipment for the purpose of analyzing a case. The equipment is unloaded in the firm's office and used for a specified period of time for a fee. The law firm is not engaged in a rental activity. None of her fees from the audio equipment will be considered as income from a rental activity.

PLANNING POINTER	Even though an activity is not classified as a rental activity, it may still fall into passive activity status if the material participation requirements are not met.

¶7281   RENTAL REAL ESTATE ACTIVITIES

An individual is allowed to avoid the passive loss limitations for all rental real estate activities in which the individual *actively participates*. A $25,000 offset against nonpassive income can be attained if the taxpayer's modified adjusted gross income (AGI computed without regard to any passive activity loss, taxable Social Security benefits, or deductions for IRA contributions) is $100,000 or less. Code Sec. 469(i). The offset is before AGI.

EXAMPLE 7.22	Alex Alexander owned three rental houses and had modified AGI of $77,500 for the year. The combined loss of the rental houses was $28,000. He was an active participant in the management of the rental properties. Alex qualifies for the $25,000 offset and will be able to reduce nonpassive income by that amount. The remaining $3,000 loss will become a suspended loss and will be allocated among all properties experiencing a loss.

Active participation, as opposed to material participation, need not be regular, continuous, and substantial. Active participation by an individual can include making some of the management decisions (such as approving prospective tenants, setting the terms of rental arrangements, and approving the costs of repairs or capital improvements). An outside property management firm, then, can be hired to provide appropriate management services on a day-to-day basis without jeopardizing active participation status. In addition, a taxpayer must hold a 10 percent or more interest in the property at all times during the year to be an active participant. Generally, a limited partner does not actively participate in a rental real estate activity that is owned through an interest in a limited partnership. As in the case of material participation, the participation of a taxpayer's spouse will be taken into account in determining whether the taxpayer actively participated.

Single individuals and married taxpayers filing jointly can qualify for the maximum $25,000 amount. Married individuals who live apart from their spouses at all times during the year can qualify for $12,500 each. Married individuals who do not live apart for the entire year and file separately cannot qualify for any part of the $25,000 offset.

The maximum level of modified AGI is $100,000 in qualifying for the full $25,000 ($12,500 for qualified married individuals filing separately) deduction. However, when modified AGI exceeds $100,000, the excess is subject to a phaseout of the full offset: For every dollar of modified AGI in excess of $100,000, the $25,000 ($12,500) offset is reduced by 50 cents (or 50 percent of the excess). Thus, the $25,000 offset is fully phased out at a modified AGI of $150,000.

EXAMPLE 7.23

Ron Reingold owned two rental properties during the year and actively participated in the management of the properties. His modified AGI was $140,000. Ron's loss from the rental activities is $10,000. Ron is entitled to a $5,000 offset. Ron's deduction is limited to the $5,000 offset, and the remaining $5,000 becomes a suspended loss, figured as follows:

Modified AGI	$140,000
Maximum level allowed	(100,000)
Excess	$40,000
Excess	$40,000
Times reduction %	× .50
Offset reduction	$20,000
Maximum offset	$25,000
Offset reduction	(20,000)
Offset after phaseout	$5,000

Revenue Reconciliation Act of 1993 Changes to Benefit Real Estate Professionals

Additional relief was provided by the Revenue Reconciliation Act of 1993 for individuals and closely held C corporations that materially participate in rental real estate activities. After 1993, provided certain requirements are met, losses and credits from rental real estate activities will not be subject to the passive loss limitations. These requirements are designed to demonstrate that the taxpayer is a material participant in the activity, and commits a minimum amount of time, on an annual basis, to the activity.

Individuals are eligible if:

1. more than one-half of the personal services performed in trades or businesses by the taxpayer during such taxable year are performed in real property trades or businesses in which the taxpayer materially participates, and
2. such taxpayer performs more than 750 hours of services during the taxable year in real property trades or businesses in which the taxpayer materially participates.

For closely held C corporations to qualify:

1. The corporation must materially participate in rental real estate activities; and
2. The corporation must derive more than 50 percent of its gross receipts for the taxable year from such activities.

The criteria for determining material participation are the same as under previous law. Furthermore, as under prior law, a limited partner in a limited partnership is generally not considered to be a material participant in the partnership.

These changes in the law were intended to benefit real estate professionals, those who commit the majority of their time to performing real estate activities. Thus, the average passive investor in such activities will not qualify for relief under these provisions.

However, a couple filing jointly could benefit from the new rules if at least one spouse satisfies the requirements. For example, one spouse may work as a real estate broker or as a real estate leasing agent and the other spouse could own rental property. Losses incurred on the rental property may be treated as losses from an activity in which the taxpayer materially participates (i.e., not as passive losses) if the real estate broker spouse satisfies the new requirements.

EXAMPLE 7.24   During 2017, Beth Miller materially participated in the following personal service activities: 800 hours as a personal estate planner, 450 hours in rental real estate activities, and 600 hours as a real estate broker. Beth devoted more than one-half of her personal services to real property trades or businesses, and her material participation in those real estate activities exceeded 750 hours. Hence, any loss incurred by Beth in either real estate activity will not be subject to the passive loss rules. She will be able to offset any losses from either real estate activity against active or portfolio income.

¶7287   CHANGE OF ACTIVITY STATUS

Under the passive activity rules, it is quite possible for an activity to change from passive to nonpassive. For example, an individual may not materially participate in a business for a previous tax year, but in later years may become a material participant. Thus, while the taxpayer was not a material participant, the business was a passive activity. Then when the taxpayer becomes a material participant, circumstances would appear to terminate the application of passive activity rules. A passive activity could become a "former passive activity" if any of the following apply:

1. The taxpayer qualifies as a material participant.
2. The activity no longer qualifies as a trade or business or rental activity.

EXAMPLE 7.25   Fred Manson's real estate activities consisted of five rental properties located on a 25-acre tract. For each rental property, an acre was carved out of the larger tract and was sold last year, leaving Fred with 20 acres of unproductive land. His real estate activities no longer qualify as a rental activity for the current year and, therefore, will be characterized as a former passive activity.

Generally, the passive loss rules do not apply to a former passive activity, except for the former passive activity's suspended losses. A former passive activity's suspended losses will continue to be suspended, but can be offset against (1) passive income from other passive activities or (2) nonpassive income from the former passive activity. Code Sec. 469(f).

EXAMPLE 7.26   Sally Dennison was not a material participant for the past few years in SSS, a partnership. The partnership was engaged in the business of selling, constructing, maintaining, and repairing fireplaces, fireplace equipment, and chimneys. Sally became a partner in the business during 2008, and her share of allocated losses for 2008–2016 was $55,000. Because she owned no other passive activities, the $55,000 was a suspended loss. In 2017, she became a material participant, and SSS significantly improved its operating position. Her share of the net income amounted to $29,500 for the year, which is now characterized as nonpassive income. The $55,000 suspended loss will offset the $29,500 of nonpassive income from SSS, while the remaining $25,500 continues to be suspended.

Business and Investment Losses

¶7301 BUSINESS CASUALTY AND THEFT LOSSES

Business and investment casualty losses which receive similar tax treatment are discussed in this section. Personal casualty losses are reviewed in greater detail at ¶8501.

The following losses can be deducted by an individual taxpayer (Code Sec. 165(c)):

1. Losses incurred in a trade or business;
2. Losses incurred in any transaction entered into for profit though not connected with a trade or business; or
3. Losses of property not connected with a trade or business, if such losses arise from fire, storm, shipwreck, or other casualty, or from theft.

Casualty losses usually are losses from fire, storm, or other catastrophe. Theft losses are losses arising from robbery, embezzlement, or larceny. Reg. §1.165-8(d). Generally, all casualty and theft losses are deductible if incurred in a trade or business or in connection with an investment with the exception of losses caused by a taxpayer's willful act or willful negligence. Reg. §1.165-7(a)(3)(i).

Proper Year of Deduction

A casualty loss is normally deductible in the year it occurs. If a casualty loss is incurred in an area designated as a disaster area by the President of the United States, the taxpayer can elect to deduct the casualty loss in the tax year preceding the year of the loss. The intent behind permitting a taxpayer to deduct a disaster area casualty loss in the tax year preceding the loss is to lessen the immediate tax burden on the taxpayer and, thereby, lessen the financial burden related to the casualty loss.

EXAMPLE 7.27

> Greenwood Paper Co. incurred a casualty loss of $10,000 in 2017. The $10,000 loss is normally deductible on Greenwood's 2017 income tax return. Because the casualty occurred in an area designated as a disaster area by the President of the United States, Greenwood may elect to deduct the casualty loss on its 2016 tax return. Since the 2016 tax return was already filed, an amended return would be filed for 2016 to claim a tax refund.

No casualty loss can be taken in the year of loss if a reasonable prospect exists that full reimbursement of the loss from insurance or other source will be received in some future tax year. Reg. §1.165-1(d)(2)(i). The casualty loss deduction is limited to the actual expected loss after expected insurance reimbursement. If the actual insurance reimbursement is less than the amount anticipated in past tax years, the difference can be deducted as a casualty loss deduction in the year the claim is settled.

A theft loss is different from a casualty loss in that a theft loss is deductible in the year the theft is discovered (which may not necessarily be the same as the year of theft). As with casualty losses, a theft loss deduction is limited to the actual expected loss after expected reimbursement. If the reimbursement is less than the amount anticipated in past tax years, the difference can be deducted in the year the claim is settled.

Computation of Deduction

A deduction resulting from the *partial destruction* of business property is limited to the lesser of the following:

1. The adjusted basis of the casualty property, or
2. The decline in fair market value of the casualty property.

Any insurance or other form of compensation will reduce the amount deductible. If such property is *completely destroyed or stolen,* the deductible loss is the adjusted basis of the property less any reimbursement (regardless of decline in the fair market value).

As a general rule, if reimbursement is less than the property's adjusted basis, then no gain can be realized. If reimbursement is less than adjusted basis but more than the amount of loss (computed using decline in FMV), then a taxpayer experiences neither a gain nor a loss.

EXAMPLE 7.28   The following casualty and theft losses occurred at Turnkey Construction Company during 2017:

		Fair Market Value		
Event	Adjusted Basis	Before Casualty	After Casualty	Insurance Reimburse
1. Stolen Equip.	$12,000	$6,000	$ 0	$6,000
2. Fire—Bldg.	$77,000	$95,000	$45,000	$35,000
3. Wreck—Truck	$21,000	$18,500	$10,000	$10,000

The loss deduction for each casualty and theft is figured as follows:

1. Stolen equipment (theft loss—treated the same way as complete casualty loss)

Adjusted basis	$12,000
Less: Insurance	6,000
Theft loss deduction	$6,000

2. Fire in building (partial business casualty—lesser of adjusted basis or decline in fair market value)

Decline in FMV	$50,000
Less: Insurance	35,000
Casualty loss deduction	$15,000

3. Wrecked truck (partial business casualty with insurance proceeds greater than amount of loss)

Decline in FMV	$8,500
Less: Insurance	10,000
Net	$(1,500)

The net amount of $1,500 is not a realized gain because the property's adjusted basis was $21,000 (the formula used to compute realized gain is insurance proceeds less adjusted basis, which would provide a $11,000 loss). On the other hand, the difference between the property's adjusted basis and insurance proceeds ($11,000 loss) is not a deductible loss because a partial casualty loss deduction requires the lesser of adjusted basis or decline in FMV in determining the amount of loss. Thus, a partial casualty where insurance proceeds are greater than the amount of loss yields neither a gain nor a loss (because the property's adjusted basis is greater than the insurance proceeds).

In some instances, however, a casualty or theft may result in a taxpayer realizing a gain. This could occur when the insurance coverage, which is normally based on fair market value, exceeds the cost basis of the property (i.e., insurance proceeds less adjusted basis equals realized gain).

Basis Adjustment

Whenever a taxpayer has a partial or complete casualty, the following items will reduce the property's adjusted basis if there was no gain realized:

1. Amount of reimbursement
2. Amount of deductible loss

EXAMPLE 7.29

Jack Caldwell's business office was partially destroyed by a tornado. His adjusted basis in the building was $210,000, and the decline in FMV was $150,000. Insurance proceeds amounted to $100,000. Mr. Caldwell's adjusted basis in the property is computed as follows:

Decline in FMV	$150,000
Less: Insurance	100,000
Deductible loss	$50,000
Adjusted basis before casualty	$210,000
Less: Insurance	100,000
Less: Deductible loss	50,000
Adjusted basis after casualty	$60,000

In determining a casualty property's decline in value, appraisals establishing the property's fair market value before the casualty as well as after the casualty are important evidence for defending the amount of a casualty loss deduction. The cost of repairs to restore the casualty property to its condition before the casualty may also be sufficient evidence to indicate the amount of the loss deduction. Reg. §1.165-1(d)(2)(ii).

¶7331   NET OPERATING LOSSES (NOLS)

Prior to the Taxpayer Relief Act of 1997, a business that had a net operating loss in one taxable year could carry the loss back to offset taxable income in the three preceding tax years or carry the loss forward to offset future taxable income for up to 15 years. Code Sec. 172.

For tax years beginning after August 5, 1997, the NOL carryback period is shortened to two years, and the NOL carryforward period is extended to 20 years. (Special carryback rules exist in relation to: (1) real estate investment trusts that do not receive carrybacks; (2) specified liability losses that are subject to a ten-year carryback; (3) excess interest losses that do not receive carrybacks; (4) farming losses that may be carried back for five years; and (5) corporate capital losses that are not affected by the changes.)

Further, the three-year carryback period is retained for the portion of the NOL that relates to casualty and theft losses of individual taxpayers and to NOLs that are attributable to Presidentially declared disasters *and* are incurred by taxpayers engaged in farming or by a small business (gross receipts of $5 million or less for a three-tax-year period).

Further, a five-year NOL carryback period applies for qualified disaster losses (Code Sec. 172(b)(1)(J), as added by the Emergency Economic Stabilization Act of 2008 (P.L. 110-343)). Also, a farming loss may be carried back for five years (Code Sec. 172(b)(1)(G) and (i)), and it does not include a qualified disaster loss.

EXAMPLE 7.30

Able Box Company has a net operating loss of $50,000 in 2017. The loss can be carried back to offset previous taxable income in 2015 and 2016. If any of the 2017 net operating loss remains after being carried back two years, the remainder can be carried forward to offset future taxable income for up to 20 years (2018–2037).

The objective of the net operating loss deduction is to increase tax fairness regarding the taxation of business income. A 12-month tax accounting period is an arbitrary period of time to tax business enterprises. Business affairs cannot be arranged into arbitrary 12-month periods. In order to alleviate the arbitrariness of a 12-month accounting period, the net operating loss deduction allows a business to offset tax losses against taxable income over a longer period of time which would normally include an entire business cycle of up and down periods.

The net operating loss deduction is available only for losses connected with a trade or business. An excess of nonbusiness and personal deductions over nonbusiness and personal income, with the exception of personal casualty and theft losses, is not eligible for NOL treatment. Personal casualty and theft losses, however, are considered to be business losses for purposes of computing the net operating loss deduction. The three-year carryback period is retained for the portion of the NOL that relates to casualty and theft losses of individual taxpayers.

Carryback and Carryforward Procedures

A business incurring a net operating loss in a taxable year can carry the loss back two years and forward 20 years. The net loss shown on a taxpayer's return usually requires adjustment in several ways before becoming a net operating loss. A business can elect to forgo the NOL carryback and carry it forward only.

PLANNING POINTER	In deciding whether to carry a net operating loss back or to just carry it forward, the taxpayer has to analyze the advantages and disadvantages of each approach. A carryback results in an immediate tax refund. Due to the time value of money, it is advantageous to forgo a carryback in favor of a carryforward only when the estimated marginal tax rate to be applied to future income is expected to be substantially higher than the tax rate which applied to the income subject to the carryback.

If a net operating loss is carried back, it must be carried back two years first. Next, if any NOL remains it is carried forward to the next year. Then if any balance remains, it is carried forward until used up or lost because of the passage of time.

EXAMPLE 7.31	Able Box Company has a net operating loss in 2017. If Able elects to carry back the NOL, it must carry back the loss to 2015. If any NOL remains, then the balance is applied against 2016 income and so on until it is used up or expires.

Taxpayers are required to file amended returns for the tax years in which they carry back net operating losses. The operating loss deduction is a deduction for adjusted gross income. Certain itemized deductions which are limited by adjusted gross income such as medical expenses and certain miscellaneous itemized deductions may have to be recomputed in the carryback year due to the change in adjusted gross income caused by the inclusion of the NOL. Charitable contributions are excluded from recomputation due to the carryback of a NOL. Code Sec. 170(b).

Computation of Net Operating Loss

The term "net operating loss" is defined as the "excess of deductions over gross income." Code Sec. 172(c). This excess of deductions over gross income is subject to modifications which limit the net operating loss to only business losses. A loss reported on a tax return by an individual taxpayer with business income is modified in the following ways in order to determine a net operating loss deduction:

Taxable Income/Loss

+   Any NOL deduction from another year

+   Deductions for personal and dependency exemptions

+   Nonbusiness capital losses exceeding nonbusiness capital gains

+   Nonbusiness deductions in excess of nonbusiness income

=   Net operating loss

Nonbusiness deductions include all itemized deductions (less personal casualty and theft losses and unreimbursed employee business expenses) plus self-employed retirement plan contributions. Nonbusiness income is all income not derived from a trade or business, such as dividends, interest, and nonbusiness capital gains. Salary and wages are considered to be trade or business income for purposes of computing an NOL.

EXAMPLE 7.32

Larry Watkins owns and operates a pizza parlor. In 2017, Larry had the following income and deductions listed on his individual tax return.

Business income	$45,000	
Salary from second job	15,000	
Interest	5,000	
Dividends	2,000	
Long-term capital gain (LTCG)	1,000	$68,000
Less:		
Business deductions	$70,000	
Personal exemption	4,050	
Itemized deductions (included $10,000 personal casualty)	19,000	93,050
Taxable income		($25,050)

Larry's net operating loss for 2017 is computed as follows:

Taxable income (negative amount)			($25,050)
Add:			
Personal exemption		$4,050	
Nonbusiness deductions in excess of nonbusiness income:			
Itemized deductions	$19,000		
Less: Personal casualty	10,000		
Nonbusiness deductions	$9,000		
Less: Nonbusiness income			
Interest	5,000		
Dividends	2,000		
LTCG	1,000	1,000	
			5,050
Net operating loss deduction			($20,000)

If only the "business-related" items were considered, then the NOL could be figured as follows:

Business income	$45,000	
Salary from second job	15,000	
Total business income		$60,000
Business deductions	$70,000	
Personal casualty loss	10,000	
Total business deductions		$80,000
Net operating loss deduction		($20,000)

Recomputation of Tax Liability in Carryback Year

After the net operating loss is computed for the tax year in which the loss is incurred, the loss is then carried back two years to the appropriate tax year unless an election is made to only carry the loss forward. As previously mentioned, adjustments may have to be made for items relying on adjusted gross income in determining their deduction.

If including the net operating loss deduction in the carryback year results in a tax loss in the carryback year, required adjustments have to be made to the tax loss to determine the amount of net operating loss deduction that can be carried forward to the next year. The required adjustments are similar to the adjustments discussed previously which were required to determine the original amount of the net operating loss.

¶7345   HOBBY LOSSES

Special rules apply to expenses and losses incurred in pursuing an activity not engaged in for profit. Hobby expenses are generally deductible only to the extent of income produced by the activity. Under Code Sec. 183, expenses that are otherwise deductible under the Code without regard to the existence of a business or profit motive (taxes, interest, casualty losses, etc.) are still deductible regardless of the amount of hobby income. However, such deductions reduce the amount of hobby income available to offset other hobby deductions. Other hobby expenses are deductible in an amount equal to the excess of hobby income over deductions otherwise allowable without regard to profit motive.

In determining whether an activity is engaged in for profit, reference is made to objective standards, taking into account the facts and circumstances of each case. Although a reasonable expectation of profit is not required, the circumstances should indicate that the taxpayer entered into, or continued, the activity with the objective of making a profit.

Among the factors considered in determining whether activities are engaged in for profit are (Reg. §1.183-2(b)):

1. The taxpayer's history of income or losses with respect to the activity.
2. The amount of occasional profits, if any, which are earned.
3. The cause of the losses.
4. The success of the taxpayer in carrying on other similar or dissimilar activities.
5. The financial status of the taxpayer.
6. The time and effort expended by the taxpayer in carrying on the activity.
7. The expertise of the taxpayer or advisors.
8. The manner in which the taxpayer carries on the activity.
9. Expectation of profit by the taxpayer.
10. Expectation that assets used in the activity may appreciate in value.
11. Elements of personal pleasure or recreation.

If any activity is not engaged in for profit, deductions are allowable in the following order and only to the following extent (Reg. §1.183-1(b)(1)):

1. Amounts deductible without regard to whether the activity giving rise to such amounts was engaged in for profit are allowable in full. Examples of these expenses include interest under Code Sec. 163 and realty taxes under Code Sec. 164.
2. Amounts deductible if the activity had been engaged in for profit, but only if the deduction does not result in an adjustment to the basis of property. Such deductions are allowed only to the extent the gross income of the activity exceeds the deduction under (1).
3. Amounts which result in an adjustment to the basis of property are deductible only to the extent that income exceeds the deductions allowed under (1) and (2). Deductions falling within this category include such items as depreciation, partial losses with respect to property, partially worthless debts, amortization, and amortizable bond premiums. If such expenses exceed the remaining hobby income, then the deductible amount (equal to remaining hobby income) is prorated among such properties in the ratio of the bases of all property. Basis of the property is reduced only by the amount actually deductible under Code Sec. 183.

The deduction for the allowed hobby expenses is an itemized deduction subject to the 2 percent floor on miscellaneous itemized deductions. For example, the feed expense incurred by a person who earns hobby income from the breeding, training, and showing of dogs is deductible only to the extent that the deduction, when aggregated with other miscellaneous deductions, exceeds 2 percent of the taxpayer's adjusted gross income. Hobby expenses that are deductible without reference to whether they are incurred in an activity designed to produce income, such as certain taxes, remain fully deductible. The gross receipts from the hobby are reported on line 21 of Form 1040.

TAX BLUNDER

Thomas O. and Carol J. Elliott, taxpayers, conducted an Amway distributorship in the evenings and on weekends from 1979 to 1983. They claimed deductions for various business expenses that were allegedly necessary to the Amway distributorship. Taxpayers submitted records to support their claimed deductions consisting of a notebook with incomplete entries and many unannotated receipts. Consequently, taxpayers conducted the Amway distributorship in an unbusinesslike fashion. As a result, the Elliotts failed to show that they engaged in the Amway distributorship with the actual and honest objective of making a profit, and, therefore, taxpayers improperly claimed deductions for business expenses. Furthermore, they are liable for additions to tax and negligent penalties for underpayment of tax. *T.O. Elliott,* 90 TC 960 (1988). A taxpayer who maintains good books and records for his/her activity is more likely to have the requisite profit intent required to escape the hobby loss rules.

EXAMPLE 7.33

Gene Allison operates a fishing boat during three months of the year and is not engaged in this activity for profit. He used the boat for his own personal use for one month and leased it to another person for two months. He has income from such operations of $3,000, taxes of $1,400, utilities of $900, maintenance expenses of $600, and depreciation of $1,200. His deductions are limited to $3,000, the amount of the income from the boat, as follows:

Category 1—Taxes	$1,400
Category 2—Two-thirds of $1,500 utilities and maintenance	1,000
Category 3—Two-thirds of $1,200 depreciation limited to excess of $3,000 boat income over $2,400 total of Category 1 and 2 deductions	600
Total deductions	$3,000

The $1,400 is itemized as part of the taxes deduction, and the $1,600 is placed in the miscellaneous itemized deduction section of Schedule A that is reduced by 2 percent of adjusted gross income.

If profit results from the activity in three out of five consecutive years ending with the tax year in question, a rebuttable presumption is created that an activity was not engaged in as a hobby. This permits the taxpayer to avoid the restrictions on the deduction of hobby losses. In the case of horse racing, breeding, and showing, a rebuttable presumption is created if profit results from the activity in two out of seven consecutive years.

A taxpayer may elect to delay a determination as to whether the presumption applies until the close of the fourth (or sixth, in the case of horse racing, breeding, or showing) tax year after the tax year in which the taxpayer first engages in the activity. A taxpayer is required to execute a waiver of the statute of limitations in order to make the election.

PLANNING POINTER

Remember the eleven factors from the regulations can work either for or against the taxpayer(s). For example, in Budin v. Comm. (T.C. Memo 1994-185), the taxpayers were engaged in horse breeding, training, and jumping activities. Significant losses were incurred by the taxpayers during the years in question. The court noted that Elbert and Shirley Budin did not conduct their horse activity in a business like manner. Specifically, the Budin's avowed purpose was horse breeding; however, they had acquired geldings, which were incapable of breeding. Therefore, the true spirit of the regulations must be adhered to for tax purposes.

¶7351 HOME OFFICE EXPENSES

If a taxpayer uses a portion of a personal residence for business-related activities, expenses allocable to the portion of the home used for business purposes may qualify as a tax deduction. For personal home expenses to be tax deductible, however, a portion of the home must be used exclusively on a regular basis as:

1. The principal place of business for any trade or business of the taxpayer;
2. A place of business which is used by patients, clients, or customers in meeting or dealing with the taxpayer in the normal course of a trade or business; or
3. In the case of a separate structure which is not attached to the dwelling unit, in connection with the taxpayer's trade or business (Code Sec. 280A(c)).

For tax years beginning after December 31, 1998, the Taxpayer Relief Act of 1997 expands the definition of a "principal place of business." A home office qualifies as a taxpayer's principal place of business under the Act if:

1.   The office is used by the taxpayer to conduct administrative or management activities of the taxpayer's trade or business; and
2.   There is no other fixed location of the trade or business where the taxpayer conducts substantial administrative or management activities of the trade or business.

If the taxpayer is an employee, the exclusive use test mentioned above must be for the convenience of the employer and not merely for the convenience of the employee. In other words, if an employee has an office on the employer's premises, then the likelihood of having a home office for the same purpose in a personal residence is greatly reduced.

The exclusive use test means that if the portion of the home used for business activities is also used for personal (nonbusiness) activities, then no deduction will be allowed. An exception to the exclusive use test applies when personal residences are used to provide day care services for children, handicapped individuals, and elderly persons. The day care facility exception applies only if the taxpayer has applied for, been granted, or is exempt from having a license, certification, registration, or approval under applicable state law. Personal family use of the day care facilities is acceptable but, in determining the allowable deduction, expenses allocable to the personal use time are not deductible. Code Sec. 280A(c). The regular basis test means that the portion of the home used for business purposes must be used for business on a regular basis, not occasionally.

EXAMPLE 7.34 Roger Blaine, a physician, uses a portion of his personal home as his principal medical office on an exclusive and regular basis. Expenses related to the portion of the home used for business purposes are deductible on Roger's tax return. If Roger occasionally meets patients in the family living room, which is also used regularly for family activities, then none of the expenses allocable to the living room are deductible since the room is not used exclusively and on a regular basis for business.

PLANNING POINTER Exclusive use of a portion of a home for business purposes is required to qualify for a business use of home deduction. Exclusive use for business purposes does not require, however, that the portion of the home used for business purposes be physically separated from the remainder of the home. A specified space within a room can qualify for the deduction as long as the exclusive use test is met. G. Weightman, 42 TCM 104, CCH Dec. 37,986(M), T.C. Memo. 1981-301.

Typical expenses deductible for a portion of a personal home used for business activities are heating, water, electricity, maintenance and repairs, depreciation, real estate taxes, and interest on a home mortgage. The portion of these expenses allocated to the business use of the home usually is based on the square feet used for business in relation to the total square feet available in the home. In no instance can the deduction for the business use of a home exceed the gross income derived from the business activities carried on at home and from the amount of income generated from rental activity of the home reduced by all related tax deductions other than the business use of home deduction. If the expenses of the business use of the home exceed the gross income derived from the business activity less related deductions, expenses normally allowable as deductions to all taxpayers (such as real estate taxes and interest on a home mortgage loan) are deducted first. If any income remains, other expenses are then deducted to the extent of the remaining income, with depreciation taken last.

Any excess expenses that are not deductible in the current year can be carried forward to offset income from the same home office business activities in succeeding years. Code Sec. 280A(c). Also, for any home office deduction related to work as an *employee,* the deduction is categorized as a miscellaneous itemized deduction subject to the 2 percent of adjusted gross income limitation which applies to miscellaneous itemized deductions (except for mortgage interest and property taxes, which are fully deductible).

EXAMPLE 7.35

Esther Simcox, a self-employed management consultant, maintains an office in her home on an exclusive and regular basis. The business office space accounts for one-fifth of the total space in her home. In 2017, Esther had gross income of $25,000 from her consulting business. Deductions related to her management consulting income, other than the business use of home deduction, amounted to $5,000. During 2017, Esther incurs the following home expenses:

Real estate taxes	$3,600	
Interest on mortgage loan	4,200	
Tax deductions normally allowable to all taxpayers		$7,800
Maintenance on home	$1,200	
Utilities (water, electricity, gas, sewer)	2,500	
Other expenses (repairs, maid service, etc.)	3,000	
Operating expenses		6,700
Total depreciation (straight-line)		2,500
Total		$17,000

Esther's home office deduction for 2017 is $3,400, determined by taking the $17,000 of home expenses times 1/5, the portion of the home used for business purposes. If Esther's gross income from the consulting business less related deductions, other than the business use of home deduction, amounted to only $2,000 in 2017, then the business use of home deduction is limited to $2,000. In calculating the business use of home deduction, tax deductions normally allowable to all taxpayers are deducted first.

Impact of Revenue Procedure 2013-13(1/15/13)

The IRS announced a simplified, optional method of claiming a home office deduction. Specifically, the new optional deduction is limited to $1,500 per year based on $5 per square foot for up to 300 square feet. Taxpayers using this new option will not be able to depreciate the portion of their home used in their trade or business. However, they can still claim allowable mortgage interest, real estate taxes, and casualty losses on their home as itemized deductions on Schedule A of Form 1040.

Comparison to Example 7.35-Above. Assume that the above office space of one-fifth amounted to 300 square feet. Under Rev. Proc. 2013-13, the deduction for the qualified business use of her home is $1,500 (300 sq.ft. × $5). Esther can deduct the real estate taxes and mortgage interest on her Schedule A and the business expenses of $5,000 on Schedule C. But she cannot deduct the depreciation of $2,500. It appears that taxpayers with large deductions should first figure the deductions out under the old method ($3,400) and then compare that figure to the new method's maximum of $1,500. Also, it should be noted that the home office deduction goes on Form 8829 and is then carried to Schedule C. In contrast, deductions that are itemized are not worth as much as Schedule C deductions. Also, since the taxpayer did not take any depreciation on her home, then her basis is higher and less gain will be reported under Sec. 1231. Naturally, these considerations are just some of the variables to guage with the client before adopting this new procedure when filing tax returns.

¶7371

VACATION HOME EXPENSES

Special rules limit the amount of rental expense deductions that may be taken by an individual taxpayer (investor) on a residence that is rented out for part of a year and used for personal purposes during other parts of the year. Code Sec. 280A. If a personal residence is rented out for less than 15 days during the year, any rental income received is excluded from gross income and no rental expense deductions are allowed. Code Sec. 280A(g). However, regular expense deductions attributable to all personal residences (such as mortgage interest, property taxes, and personal casualty losses) are still available. If a residence is rented out during the year for more than 14 days, then the property will either be a personal residence (personal-use property) or rental property (which could provide a deductible loss subject to the passive loss rules).

A vacation home becomes a personal residence when its owner uses it excessively for personal purposes. Excessive personal use is measured by the greater of 14 days or 10 percent of the number of rental days. That is, if the owner personally uses the residence *more than the greater of* (1) 14 days or (2) 10 percent of rental days, then the dwelling will be a personal residence and rental losses are not deductible. If rental expenses exceed rental income, then regular expenses (mortgage interest, property taxes, and casualty losses) are deducted first. (Any remaining regular expenses are deductible as itemized deductions.) Other rental expense deductions (maintenance, repairs, depreciation, etc.) are limited to the remaining amount of rental income (after it is reduced by the amount of regular expenses that were deducted first).

EXAMPLE 7.36

Joel Harris owned a condo in a resort area. During the year, he personally used it for 17 days, and it was rented for 100 days. Because he used the condo for more than either 14 days or 10 percent of rental days (10 days), the vacation home will be treated as a personal residence and losses will not be allowed.

However, if an individual rents out a vacation home for more than 14 days and does not use it excessively for personal purposes, then it will be treated as rental property. That is, if the taxpayer does not use it for personal purposes for the greater of 14 days or 10 percent of rental days, then losses are allowed to be deducted for AGI (subject to the passive activity rules). If an individual actively participates in the rental real estate activity, then up to $25,000 of losses can be used to offset nonpassive income.

EXAMPLE 7.37

John Henderson owns a vacation home in Palm Springs. His expenses related to the home during the year are as follows:

Mortgage interest and taxes	$20,000
Utilities, maintenance, and repairs	5,000
Depreciation	15,000
Total expenses	$40,000

Assume Mr. Henderson rents out the home for less than 15 days during the year and uses it personally for more than 14 days. He receives rental income of $4,000. None of the rental income is reported on his income tax return, and no rental expenses are deductible on his tax return. The mortgage interest and taxes of $20,000, however, are allowable.

In determining rental expense deductions, the allocation formulas used to compute rental expenses differ depending on the type of expense being allocated and interpretation of the tax law by the Tax Court and the IRS. For regular expenses allowable to all taxpayers, the Tax Court allocation formula is based on a full year (365 days). *D.D. Bolton*, 82-2 USTC ¶9699, 694 F.2d 556 (CA-9 1982). The IRS prefers to allocate regular expenses based on total usage of the residence. For other expenses, the allocation formula is based on total usage of the residence.

EXAMPLE 7.38

Assume Mr. Henderson rents out the vacation home for 25 days during the year and receives rental income of $10,000. He uses the dwelling for personal purposes for 30 days during the year. Under these assumptions, the rental income of $10,000 is included in his income because he rented the home out for more than 14 days. The dwelling will be treated as a personal residence because he used it for personal purposes for the greater of (1) 14 days, or (2) 10 percent of the rental days. The rental expense deductions are computed using both the IRS method and the Tax Court method as follows:

	Tax Court	IRS
Rental income	$10,000	$10,000
Less: Mortgage interest payments and property taxes		
($20,000 × 25 rental days/365 days a year)	1,370	
($20,000 × 25 rental days/55 total use days)		9,091
Less: Utility expenses, maintenance, and repair expenses, etc.		
($5,000 × 25 rental days/55 total use days)	2,272	
($5,000 × 25 rental days/55 total use days, but limited to $909—cannot create a loss)		909
Amount remaining for depreciation	$6,358	$0
Less: Depreciation		
($15,000 × 25 rental days/55 total use days = $6,818, but limited to $6,358)	6,358	0
Net Rental Loss	$0	$0

EXAMPLE 7.39

Assume Mr. Henderson rents out the home for 25 days during the year and receives rental income of $10,000. He uses the home for personal purposes for seven days during the year. Under these assumptions, all rental income is recognized on his income tax return since the dwelling was rented out for more than 14 days. Because the residence will be treated as rental property (personal use was less than 14 days or 10 percent of rental days), losses are allowed. His rental income and rental expenses are computed as follows:

	Tax Court	IRS
Rental income	$10,000	$10,000
Less: Mortgage interest and property taxes		
($20,000 × 25 rental days/365 days a year)	1,370	
($20,000 × 25 rental days/32 total use days)		15,625
Less: Utility expenses, maintenance, and repair expenses, etc.		
($5,000 × 25 rental days/32 total use days)	3,906	3,906
Income or loss before depreciation	$4,724	($9,531)
Less: Depreciation		
($15,000 × 25 rental days/32 total use days)	11,718	11,718
Net Rental Loss	($6,994)	($21,249)

Under either the Tax Court or the IRS approach, the loss is less than the $25,000 loss allowed for rental property in which there is active participation. In this case, the remainder of the mortgage interest is not deductible because the vacation home is not considered a second residence. Therefore, the IRS approach is more favorable to the taxpayer.

Personal use days of a vacation home by an owner generally include the following: days of personal use by the owner or by a member of the owner's family including spouse, ancestors, lineal descendants, children, brothers, and sisters; and days of use under an arrangement to exchange one residence for another for a period of time; and days of use by any individual if not rented at a fair rental. Code Sec. 280A(d)(2)(A). Time spent at a vacation home by an owner while making repairs usually does not count as days of personal use if at least two-thirds of each day, up to eight hours a day, is spent making repairs.

KEYSTONE PROBLEM

Kim Boles, single and 38 years old, owned the following passive activities during 2017:

Activity	2017 Gain/(Loss)	Acquired
XYZ	($10,000)	10/05/86
LMN	($12,500)	06/22/87
TUV	$11,000	09/01/88

She was the sole proprietor of a small business that had gross revenues of $35,000 and expenses of $72,000. She participated in the business 2,000 hours. The business had a computer stolen from its office. The computer's basis was $12,000, and its fair market value was $7,500 at the time of the theft. The amount of the theft is not included in expenses as stated above.

Kim also owned a condo in Vail, Colorado. She used it 17 days for personal purposes and rented it 150 days. Gross rentals were $1,300, while all expenses other than interest and taxes were $1,700. Interest and taxes amounted to $6,500.

Kim received $15,400 salary from a part-time job, received $1,500 in dividends, and had total itemized deductions of $3,000. Compute Kim's taxable income for 2017 and any other tax consequences that are appropriate under the IRS method.

¶7371

¶7375   MANUFACTURING DEDUCTION UNDER CODE SECTION 199

Code Sec. 199 was enacted by The American Jobs Creation Act of 2004 to help U.S. manufacturers stay competitive with their foreign rivals and to replace certain export tax benefits that were previously repealed. H. R. Conf. Rep. No. 108-755. For tax years beginning after 2004, these goals are achieved by allowing a deduction equal to a statutory percentage multiplied by the lesser of (1) a taxpayer's qualified production activities income (hereafter referred to as QPAI) for a tax year or (2) a taxpayer's taxable income for that tax year. Code Sec. 199(a)(1) and (2). When the taxpayer is an individual, the limitation noted in item (2) is adjusted gross income as derived in Code Sec. 199(d)(2). The deduction started at a transition percentage of three percent for 2005 and 2006 and rose to six percent for 2007 through 2009. By 2010, the manufacturing deduction was nine percent of the lesser of QPAI for the year or taxable income for the year. Also, the deduction may not exceed fifty percent of the W-2 wages paid by the taxpayer to the taxpayer's employees during the year. Code Sec. 199(b)(1).

In order to appreciate the above new terms and benefits, several definitions and illustrations are warranted.

Qualified Production Activities Income

Under Code Sec. 199(c)(1), QPAI means the enterprise's domestic gross receipts reduced by the sum of:

1. The costs of goods sold that are allocable to domestic production gross receipts;
2. Other deductions, expenses, or losses that are directly allocable to domestic production gross receipts (such as selling and marketing expenses); and
3. A proper share of other deductions, expenses, and losses not directly allocable to domestic production gross receipts or another class of income (such as general and administrative expenses allocable to selling and marketing expenses).

Domestic Production Gross Receipts

Domestic production gross receipts (hereafter referred to as DPGR) are defined under Code Sec. 199(c)(4) to include gross receipts from the following sources:

1. Any sale, exchange or other disposition, or any lease, rental or license, of qualifying production property that was manufactured, produced, grown or extracted by the enterprise in whole or in significant part within the United States (certain agriculture-related receipts also qualify). "Qualifying production property" generally includes any tangible personal property, computer software, or sound recordings.
2. Any sale, exchange or other disposition, or any lease, rental or license, of a qualified film produced by the enterprise. "Qualified film" includes any motion picture film or videotape (including live or delayed television programming, but not including certain sexually explicit productions) if 50% or more of the total compensation relating to the production of the film (including compensation in the form of residuals and participations) is compensation for services performed in the United States by actors, production personnel, directors, and producers.
3. Any sale, exchange or other disposition of electricity, natural gas, or potable water produced by the taxpayer in the United States.
4. Construction activities performed in the United States (including activities directly related to the construction or substantial renovation of residential and commercial buildings and infrastructure).
5. Engineering or architectural services performed in the United States for construction projects located in the United States.

Limitations. DPGR does not include the gross receipts of the taxpayer derived from:

1. The sale of food and beverages prepared by the taxpayer at a retail establishment. Code Sec. 199(c)(4)(B)(i).
2. The transmission or distribution of electricity, natural gas, or potable water. Code Sec. 199(c)(4)(B).
3. Property leased, licensed, or rented by the taxpayer for use by a related person. Code Sec. 199(c)(7)(A).

Wages-Paid Limitation

Pursuant to Code Sec. 199(b), the term wages means the wages paid for withholding tax purpose plus certain elective deferrals for retirement contributions and salary reduction arrangements. Because there is no single box on the Form W-2 that satisfies Code Sec. 199(b)(2)'s definition of wages, the IRS has provided in Notice 2005-14, Sec. 4.02(2)(b) for the following methods: (1) the unmodified box method; (2) the modified box one method; or (3) the tracking wages method. Due to the complexity of the three methods, only the unmodified box method will be illustrated. This method allows the taxpayer to use the lesser of:

1. The total entries in Box 1 (wages subject to federal income tax) of the W-2s for all employees of the taxpayer; or
2. The total entries in Box 5 (wages subject to Medicare) of the W-2s for all employees of the taxpayer.

Also, it should be noted, for purposes of Code Sec. 199(b), wages do not include any amounts paid to independent contractors or any amounts paid to partners. Consider carefully the following depiction of the new rules under Code Sec. 199.

EXAMPLE 7.40	Company X is a C corporation with three equal owners, all of whom are full-time employees. X has no other employees. It pays the owner/employees each $200,000 in salary. Assume that the salaries are considered reasonable compensation. The wage-based cap on the deduction for the manufacturing deduction is $300,000 (50% of the total wages of $600,000).

EXAMPLE 7.41	Assume the same facts as in the above example except that Company X is a limited liability company treated as a partnership for tax purposes. Under the IRS's position (Notice 2005-14), none of the $600,000 paid to the owners is wages. As a result, no manufacturing deduction would be available.

EXAMPLE 7.42	LA Drilling Company has taxable income in 2017 of $8 million, $5 million of which came from a qualified production activity. The company paid its employees wages subject to federal income tax (Box 1) of $3 million. The Medicare wages (Box 5) were $2 million. Eligible wages under the unmodified box method would be the lesser of $3 million or $2 million. The company's manufacturing deduction is the lesser of:

1. $1 million of wages ($2 million x .50), or
2. 9% of the lesser of :
   a. $8 million of taxable income
   b. $5 million of taxable income from the qualified production activities.

Thus, the manufacturing deduction is $450,000 ($5 million x .09).

Tax Policy Considerations

Because the manufacturing deduction definition is very broad, many domestic producers will qualify for the new deduction. That is, the Code Sec. 199 deduction is not limited to traditional manufacturing, but includes the following: construction, engineering, energy production, computer software, films and videotape, and processing of agricultural products. As a result, the issue of states losing money from this deduction should be considered. Specifically, times are tough for many states and giving up tax revenue via the manufacturing deduction may be something that they are unwilling to do. Therefore, it may be that a number of the states will not follow the federal statutes with respect to this deduction.

Since outsourcing has become a way of life in many businesses, will the Code Sec. 199 deduction discourage the use of independent contractors that do not qualify for wages on Form W-2?

Because sole proprietors do not pay themselves W-2 wages, then any deduction earned under Code Sec. 199 is eliminated by the W-2 wage limitation. Could this direct partnerships, sole proprietors, and single-member limited liability companies to incorporate as C or S corporations to secure the manufacturing deduction?

SUMMARY

■ Deductions arising from tax shelters are subject to the at-risk rules and the passive activity rules. The at-risk provisions are structured to deny taxpayers from deducting losses in excess of their actual economic investment in the endeavor. In general, deductions or expenses incurred by passive activities can only be deducted against passive income, and any unused passive losses are suspended and carried forward to future years to offset passive income in those years.

■ Net operating losses from business endeavors may be carried back two years and forward 20 years.

■ Hobby losses require that expenses can only be deducted up to the amount of gross income derived from the activity.

■ Business casualty or theft losses are the lesser of the decline in fair market value or the adjusted basis, but will equal adjusted basis when the property is totally destroyed. The three-year carryback period is retained for the portion of the NOL that relates to casualty and theft losses of individual taxpayers.

■ Losses from ownership of a vacation home may be deductible if the home qualifies as rental property. The excessive use test is used in making the rental property determination (i.e., the greater of 14 days or 10 percent of the rental days). Once a home is determined to be rental, the losses are subject to the passive loss rules.

QUESTIONS

1. What is a tax shelter? Generally, what two limitations apply to the deductibility of most tax shelter loss deductions?

2. Why were tax shelters popular before the Tax Reform Act of 1986? Briefly explain why tax shelter investments are not as popular today.

3. Generally, what is "at risk"?

4. What is a nonrecourse loan? Will a nonrecourse loan given by the seller of real estate to the buyer increase the amount the buyer has at risk? Explain.

5. What is the general rule for the deductibility of passive losses?

6. Briefly, how do the at-risk rules and passive activity rules function together?

7. Differentiate between the following: active income, passive income, and portfolio income.

8. On what date was the Tax Reform Act of 1986 enacted, and what significance does this date have for losses derived from passive activities in 2017?

9. What is a "suspended loss"? How can suspended losses offset nonpassive income?

10. Generally, how will a suspended loss attributable to a passive activity that is transferred by reason of death be treated for federal income tax purposes?

11. Generally, how will a suspended loss attributable to a passive activity that is transferred by gift be treated for federal income tax purposes?

12. What type of taxpayers (entities) are affected by the passive loss rules? What is the significance of a closely held corporation with regard to the deductibility of passive losses?

13. Briefly, what is "material participation"? Why is the determination of whether a taxpayer materially participates important?

14. What are the seven tests that help to establish material participation?

15. What is "significant participation," and why is it notable?

16. What is an undertaking? What is a "separate source of income production," and why is this meaningful?

17. How are both business and rental operations usually treated when carried on at the same location by the same owner? How can both undertakings be treated as one activity?

18. How can a taxpayer combine real estate undertakings?

19. How can nonrental undertakings be combined?

20. Identify the six tests concerning rental properties that help to establish a nonrental activity.

21. What relief from passive loss restrictions is provided to help taxpayers deduct losses from rental real estate activities? What are the qualifications?

22. What is "active participation"?

23. What consequences does a taxpayer face when one of several activities is no longer a passive activity?

24. Explain the tax treatment of the following business casualty losses: complete destruction of the property and partial destruction of the property.

25. How does an expected insurance reimbursement for a business casualty loss affect the amount of a casualty loss deduction? Does it make a difference whether an expected insurance reimbursement for business casualty loss differs from the actual insurance reimbursement when the claim is settled?

26. How will a business property's basis be adjusted as a result of a casualty loss?

27. Generally, are net operating losses available for personal-use expenditures? Explain.

28. What carryback and carryforward procedures apply to business net operating losses?

29. What qualifications must be met before a taxpayer is allowed a home office deduction?

30. How can a vacation home become rental property? What is the difference between "rental property" and "personal residence"?

PROBLEMS

31. Billy Bob is at risk for $10,000 in Partnership A and $22,000 in Partnership B on January 1, 2017. Both partnerships are passive activities to Billy Bob. Billy Bob's share of net income from Partnership A during 2017 was $8,000. His share of losses from Partnership B was $12,000. What are the tax consequences to Billy Bob for 2017? How much is he at risk for each activity on January 1, 2018? Does he have any loss carryovers under the at-risk rules? Does he have any suspended losses under the passive loss rules?

32. What would be your answer to Problem 31 if Billy Bob's share of net income from Partnership A was $9,000 and his loss from Partnership B was $25,000?

33. In 2017, Wilmah Lansing invested in the Triple-K Limited Partnership by paying $15,000 cash and signing a $40,000 nonrecourse note. She also pledged $25,000 worth of securities for a loan obtained by the partnership. Her basis in the securities was $10,000. What amount does Wilmah have at risk in Triple-K as of January 1, 2018, if the partnership broke even (no income or loss)?

34. Refer to the facts in Problem 33 and assume that Triple-K allocated to Wilmah net income of $10,000 from operations in 2017. What amount does Wilmah have at risk as of January 1, 2018? Would your answer be different if she also withdrew $5,000? Explain.

35. Refer to the facts in Problem 33 and assume instead that Triple-K allocated to her a loss of $60,000 in 2017. What amount does Wilmah have at risk as of January 1, 2018?

36. In 2003, Keith Jackson invested in a partnership known as Astonishing Discoveries, Ltd. He was a limited partner. Mr. Jackson paid $25,000 cash and, along with all other partners, signed a nonrecourse note with which Astonishing Discoveries acquired an office park. The loan was made by the seller, a large financial institution that customarily made such loans. Jackson's allocated portion of the note was $100,000. In 2017, he received a $45,000 allocated loss from the partnership and had net passive income of $35,000 from other passive activities for the year. His adjusted gross income for 2017 was $145,000. Compute the following items for 2017:
    a. Amount at risk
    b. Passive loss deductions (against nonpassive income)
    c. Suspended loss.

37. Tammy Faye Jones owned three passive activities in 2017 (she had no suspended losses prior to 2017):

Activity	Date Acquired	2017 Allocated Gain/(Loss)
One	7/20/93	(60,000)
Two	9/01/97	40,000
Three	3/10/98	(30,000)

How much is her passive loss deduction (against nonpassive income) and suspended loss for each activity and the manner in which it is allocated?

38. Brent Fullback owned four passive activity interests in 2017:

Activity	Date Acquired	2017 Allocated Gain/(Loss)	Pre-2017 Suspended Loss
A-1	11/22/92	14,000	(27,000)
B-2	01/25/95	(22,000)	(25,000)
C-3	07/03/97	(5,000)	(8,000)
D-4	08/01/99	(3,000)	(1,000)

On March 2, 2017, Fullback sold his entire interest in A-1 for $15,000. His basis in the activity on January 1, 2017, was $11,000. Compute the following:
    a. Gain or loss realized from the sale of A-1
    b. Passive loss deduction (against nonpassive income) and type (i.e., ordinary income (loss) or capital income (loss))
    c. Suspended losses and how they are allocated

39. Jean Kelley owned three limited partnership interests in 2017:

Partnership	Date Acquired	2017 Allocated Gain/(Loss)	Pre-2017 Suspended Loss
MNO	05/03/97	(4,000)	(14,000)
OSD	10/14/97	10,000	(3,000)
CMP	11/15/98	(6,000)	(2,000)

How much is her passive loss deduction (against nonpassive activities) and suspended loss for each activity?

40. Thomas Settleton owned an interest as a general partner in LBO partnership. Settleton was not a material participant in the activity. His basis was $25,000 on the date he gifted the LBO partnership interest to his son, Willard. Suspended losses amounted to $40,000 as of that date. What are the federal income tax consequences of the gift to the son?

41. Teri Frazier owned three businesses and rental properties in 2017. During the year, her hair salon business experienced a $32,000 net loss. She participated 200 hours in the hair salon business. All of the salon's employees worked more than 600 hours for 2017. Her second business was a coin-operated laundry. She did not participate over 100 hours in the laundry operation. It had a net loss of $14,500. The third business was a flower shop, which had net income of $45,000 for 2017. She participated well over 1,000 hours in the flower shop business. None of the activities was located within one-half mile of each other. She also received dividends of $12,000 from her IBM stock, and interest of $14,000 from her AT&T bonds. In addition, Frazier had a net loss of $18,000 from her real estate rentals (where she was an active participant). Compute her adjusted gross income.

42. Darian Basemore owned an interest in five businesses in 2017. His level of participation and percentage of ownership in each enterprise is as follows:

Activity	Hours of Participation	Ownership Percentage
Ven-Tale	180	22%
MovERent	88	17
AZ Airlines	950	33
Sadd Books	135	12
Kingdom Autos	185	25

In which activity, if any, will Darian be considered a material participant?

43. Janice Hoplin, MD, owned her own medical clinic. She also owned the office building in which the clinic was located. The medical activity generated $125,000 of net income. She managed the building, which had 15 other medical professionals (tenants), from her medical office. The office rental activity provided her with a $12,000 net loss for the year. What is Janice's adjusted gross income?

44. Dave Eichoff had adjusted gross income for 2017 of $122,000 before any passive losses or other rental activities. He owned a mountain cabin in Idaho, which he rented for 125 days and which was not used by him at all during the year. The property will experience a net loss of $12,500. He also had a limited partnership interest that was purchased in 1985 and yielded a loss of $22,000. What is Dave's adjusted gross income after considering the passive activity and rental losses?

45. Diane Parker acquired an interest in a movie theater in June 2005. The theater broke even from 2005 to 2012. Parker did not actively participate in the activity during those years. She participated in the activity for 350, 400, 450, and 420 hours during 2013, 2014, 2015, and 2016, respectively. This was well below all other employees. The theater had losses allocated to her of $21,000, $6,000, $19,000, and $12,000 for 2013, 2014, 2015, and 2016, respectively. In 2017, however, she participated 750 hours in the business, and her share of the movie theater net income was $24,000. Her income from other sources (portfolio income) was $27,500. What are the income tax consequences to Diane for 2017?

46. Mary Beth is a CPA, devoting 3,000 hours per year to her practice. She also owns an office building in which she rents out space to tenants. She devotes none of her time to the management of the office building. She has a property management firm make all management decisions for her. During 2017, she incurred a loss, for tax purposes, of $30,000 on the office building. How must Mary Beth treat this loss on her 2017 tax return?

47. Assume the same facts as in Problem 46, except that Mary Beth is a real estate agent. She works 1,000 hours per year as a real estate agent and 1,200 hours per year managing her office building. How may she treat the loss on the office building?

48. Max Computer Center incurred the following casualty and theft losses in 2017:

Event		
a.	=	Robbery-Equip.
b.	=	Fire-Truck
c.	=	Fire-Equip.

	FAIR Market Value			
Event	Adjusted Basis	Before Casualty	After Casualty	Insurance Reimburse
a.	$8,000	$9,000	$0	$7,500
b.	$4,000	$5,000	$2,000	$3,500
c.	$9,000	$6,000	$0	$6,000

Compute the casualty and theft loss for each item listed.

49. In 2017, Mary Jackson had the following income and deductions listed on her individual income tax return:

Business income	$25,150
Interest income on personal investments	2,000
Less: Business expenses	45,000
Less: Personal exemption	4,050
Less: Nonbusiness deductions	3,000
Loss shown on tax return	$(24,900)

Compute the amount of Mary's 2017 net operating loss.

50. Ralph Sample had the following income and deductions listed on his 2017 income tax return:

Salary	$25,150
Business income	65,000
Interest income on personal investments	10,000
Less: Business expenses	102,000
Less: Personal exemption	4,050
Less: Nonbusiness deductions	12,000
Loss shown on tax return	$(17,900)

Compute the amount of Ralph's 2017 net operating loss.

51. During 2017, Jane Mason incurred the following home expenses:

Real estate taxes	$4,000
Interest on home mortgage	7,000
Maintenance on home	2,000
Other home expenses including depreciation	4,000
Total	$17,000

Assume that Jane qualified for the home office deduction, all of the above expenditures qualified for the deduction as home office expenses, 8 percent of the space in the home was used for the business activity, and Jane earned $9,000 in 2017 after all deductions other than home office expenses.

a. Compute Jane's home office deduction for 2017.

b. Assume instead that Jane earned only $1,000 after all deductions other than home office expenses. What is her home office deduction?

52. In 2017, Joan Cannon incurred the following expenses relating to her vacation home:

Mortgage interest	$6,000
Property taxes	4,000
Utility expenses	4,000
Depreciation	6,000
Total expenses	$20,000

During 2017, Joan personally used the vacation home for 20 days. Determine the rental expense deduction that she is entitled to claim on her 2017 tax return in each of the following cases. Use the Tax Court method of allocating normal expenses allowable to all taxpayers.

a. Joan rents out the vacation home for 10 days during the year and receives $800 in rental income.

b. Joan rents out the vacation home for 30 days during the year and receives $1,500 in rental income.

c. Joan rents out the vacation home for 230 days during the year and receives $9,000 in rental income.

53. Refer to Problem 52, Part (c) and assume the IRS approach to allocating normal expenses allowable to all taxpayers is used. Based on these facts, what rental expense deductions are allowable in 2017?

54. Which of the following is not a passive activity?
    a. Owning a limited partnership interest in an oil and gas limited partnership
    b. Having rental residential properties
    c. Owning a business and not materially participating
    d. Being a material participant in a small-tool rental business (averaging three days use)

55. Benson Company experienced partial destruction of a warehouse from a tornado. The warehouse had a basis of $200,000 at the time of the casualty. Its fair market value before the accident was $1,000,000 and afterward, $600,000. How has this event changed the basis of the warehouse?
    a. No effect
    b. Decrease by $200,000
    c. Decrease by $400,000
    d. Decrease by $100,000 plus insurance proceeds received

56. Which of the following taxpayers would be least likely to qualify for a home office deduction?
    a. Self-employed individual
    b. Employee with an office on the employer's premises
    c. Owner of property held for production of income
    d. Employee whose home office is for the employer's convenience

57. Net operating losses can be increased by which of the following?
    a. Personal casualty losses
    b. Business casualty losses
    c. Unreimbursed employee business expenses
    d. All of the above

58. Bob White owned a cabin in the Great Smoky Mountains. He used it for 16 days and rented it out for 190 days during the year. Which of the following is true?
    a. All allocated expenses are deductible (subject to the passive loss rules).
    b. Only allocated expenses up to gross rentals are deductible.
    c. The vacation home qualifies as a principal residence.
    d. All rentals are received tax free and no expenses, other than taxes and interest, are deductible.

59. John Malley owns an S corporation wherein he is a full-time employee. The S corporation manufactures a unique part for drilling bits used in off-shore oil rigs. In 2017, he has AGI of $720,000 and QPAI of $800,000. Compute the following for 2017:
    a. Manufacturers' deduction under Code Sec. 199 (assume that the W-2 wage limit is not a problem).
    b. John's new AGI.

60. John Henderson's portable sawmill was completely destroyed by a fire and he carried no insurance on the property. The adjusted basis for depreciation of the sawmill building and equipment at the time of the fire was $65,000, and its fair market value was $50,000. The value of the equipment after the fire was only scrap value, amounting to $200. How much is Mr. Henderson's deductible casualty loss?

61. Assume that the sawmill in Problem 60 was damaged by the fire but not completely destroyed. Just before the fire the sawmill had a fair market value of $50,000 and immediately after the fire its fair market value was $3,500.
    a. Under these facts, John's loss is limited to how much?
    b. Had the fair market value of the sawmill been $80,000 just before the fire and $10,000 just afterward, how much is John's deductible casualty loss?

62. Travis Goggans grows, manufactures, and sells veneer logs and strips. In 2017, he has QPAI of $4 million and taxable income of $5 million. Because Travis uses almost exclusively independent contractors, his W-2 wage base is only $200,000. How much is Travis Goggans' manufacturing deduction under Code Sec. 199?

63. **Comprehensive Problem (Tax Return Problem).** Harvey and Betty Duran, both age 37, are married with one dependent child. Determine their taxable income from the following information for 2016, and their tax liability. Both the ABC and XYZ partnerships are passive activities. Assume dividends are taxed as ordinary income.

Harvey's salary	$45,000
Betty's salary	62,000
Dividends received from domestic corporations (nonqualified)	11,000
Interest	7,000
Itemized deductions	6,920
Net loss from ABC Partnership (acq. 1983)	(14,200)
Net loss from XYZ Partnership (acq. 1988)	(6,000)
Harvey's business income (moonlighting)	7,700
Harvey's business deductions (before home office expenses)	22,000
Harvey's home office expenses	10,500
Net loss on rental property	(31,000)
Federal Income tax withheld	9,600

64. **Comprehensive Problem.** Michael Rambo, single and calendar year taxpayer, is the sole owner of Slice-It Pizza Company, a sole proprietorship. Michael materially participated in the activity. In 2017, Slice-It Pizza reported revenues of $600,000 and deductions of $410,000, exclusive of a net operating loss deduction of $150,000.

The NOL was carried forward from 2016. For tax purposes, Michael reports revenues and expenses of Slice-It Pizza on Schedule C of Form 1040—Individual Income Tax Return. If Michael has no other taxable income, deductions or credits in 2017, other than those listed above, what tax effect does the $150,000 NOL have on his 2017 tax return? Ignore liability for self-employment taxes.

65. **Research Problem.** Clients Buddy and Debbie Jamison are considering converting their private vacation home to rental property. They have asked for advice as to the tax aspects of owning such property. The only real estate they own is their principal residence and the vacation home. Some of the following sources may prove to be helpful in preparing a report for the clients: Code Sec. 280A; Code Sec. 469; Reg. §1.165-9(b); *A.B. Wood,* (CA-5) 52-2 USTC ¶9374, 197 F.2d 859; *E.G. McKinney,* 42 TCM 468, Dec. 36,077(M), T.C. Memo. 1981-377, aff'd (CA-10) 83-2 USTC ¶9655; *T.B. Jefferson,* 50 TC 963, Dec. 29,153; *L.M. McAuley,* 35 TCM 1236, Dec. 34,005(M), T.C. Memo. 1976-276.

66. **Research Problem.** The taxpayer, Hugh Ames, has been engaged in the general practice of medicine for more than 30 years. In 1991, he took over the operation of his family farm and decided to convert the farm into a cattle farm. He employed full-time help on the farm, but he himself did much of the physical work involved in improving the farm. In formulating his plans and in carrying them out, Dr. Ames had the advice and assistance of the local farm agent, an expert cattleman, and an expert farm machinery mechanic.

Dr. Ames raised cattle as well as catfish and quarter horses. However, after encountering technical and demand problems, he discontinued the raising of catfish and horses. He was presently raising thoroughbreds and was confident that this venture would prove more profitable.

During the period from 1991 through 2017, Dr. Ames' farming operation resulted in substantial losses, averaging approximately $15,000 per year. During the taxable years of 2016 and 2017, his farm losses totaled $30,000 and $25,000 respectively. The evidence showed Dr. Ames had not made a profit, on a year-to-year basis, during this entire period, although his testimony to the IRS agent was that he always had operated and still operated his farm with a profit motive. Can Dr. Ames deduct the losses? See *Gregory, Jr. v. U.S.* (37 AFTR2d 76-785) and *Loy D. Mercer v. Comm'r,* (67-1 USTC ¶9390).

Chapter

8

Deductions: Itemized Deductions

OBJECTIVES

After completing Chapter 8, you should be able to:

1. List items making up the medical expense deduction.
2. Apply rules for the interest expense deduction.
3. Explain the requirements for the charitable contribution deduction.
4. Explain the requirements for the personal casualty and theft losses deduction.
5. Identify deductions for employee business expenses and investment expenses, as well as other miscellaneous itemized deductions.

OVERVIEW

In computing taxable income, personal, living, or family expenses are generally disallowed. However, tax rules do allow some deductions for expenses which are essentially personal in nature. These types of expenses are deductible from adjusted gross income, referred to as itemized deductions, and deducted on Schedule A of the individual tax return.

This chapter discusses those expenses that are specifically allowed as itemized deductions. These deductions include: medical expenses, taxes, interest, charitable contributions, casualty and theft losses, employee business expenses, investment expenses, and other miscellaneous itemized deductions.

While these itemized deductions are allowed by law, there is an overall limitation on the amount of itemized deductions that can be taken. High-income taxpayers whose AGI exceeds a certain threshold amount are required to reduce the allowable itemized deductions by a designated percent. This provision is detailed in Chapter 3.

Medical Expenses

¶8001   REQUIREMENTS FOR THE DEDUCTION

Individuals can deduct many types of medical expenses as itemized deductions. The deduction is allowable only to individuals and only for medical expenses actually paid during the year, regardless of when the expenses were incurred or the method of accounting used by the taxpayer. Any medical expense deduction will be reduced by the amount of any insurance reimbursement or other similar compensation. Only medical expenses in excess of 10 percent of adjusted gross income are deductible. Code Sec. 213.

EXAMPLE 8.1

Jerome Jenkins, 35, has an adjusted gross income of $20,000 and pays for the following medical expenses during the year:

Medical insurance	$1,820
Medicines and drugs	175
Other medical expenses	500

The medical deduction is computed as follows:

Medicines and drugs	$175
Medical insurance	1,820
Other medical expenses	500
Total Medical Expenses	$2,495
Less 10% of $20,000 (adjusted gross income)	2,000
Total Medical Expense Deduction	$495

For medical expenses to be deductible, they must be for the medical care of the taxpayer, the taxpayer's spouse, or a dependent of the taxpayer. A child of divorced parents is treated as the dependent of both parents for purposes of the medical expense deduction. The gross income requirement is waived for purposes of determining who is a "dependent" with respect to the medical care deduction.

EXAMPLE 8.2

Joan Farley pays medical expenses for the care of her father. Joan also pays over half of the support of her father but is unable to claim her father as a dependent because he has $5,000 of income for the year. The income ceiling for dependents in 2017 is $4,050. Joan may include the medical expenses for the care of her father in her medical expense computation even though she can not claim her father as a dependent.

¶8015   MEDICAL CARE EXPENSES

The medical expense deduction is specifically limited to amounts spent for medical care. The term "medical care" is broadly defined to include amounts paid for the diagnosis, cure, mitigation, treatment, or prevention of disease. Accordingly, payments for the following are payments for medical care: hospital services, nursing services, medical, laboratory, surgical, dental and other diagnostic and healing services, X-rays, medicines, and drugs. Amounts paid for accident or health insurance are generally deductible as medical expenses. Further, expenses paid for "medical care" include those paid for transportation primarily for and essential to medical care, such as the expense of using an ambulance. Amounts expended for illegal operations or treatments are not deductible. An expenditure which is merely beneficial to the general health of an individual, such as an expenditure for a vacation or for health club fees, is also not deductible.

Payments for unnecessary cosmetic surgery (such as facelifts or cheek implants) whose purpose is solely to improve the patient's appearance do not qualify as a medical expense deduction for tax purposes. This rule does not apply to cosmetic surgery necessary to help correct a deformity arising from a congenital abnormality, or heal an injury arising from an accident or a disfiguring disease. Any employer reimbursements for unnecessary cosmetic surgery under a medical expense reimbursement plan must be included in the gross income of the employee in the year received.

EXAMPLE 8.3

In June 2017, Jane Martin undergoes a liposuction operation solely to improve her physical appearance. None of the expenses related to this operation would be deductible for tax purposes on her 2017 income tax return.

EXAMPLE 8.4

Should the costs of changing one's sex qualify as a medical deduction? After all, the change is just cosmetic and isn't necessary, is it? Interestingly, gender identity disorder is a condition recognized by the medical community, so a strong case can be made that a sex change operation is just a means of treating that condition. Although it initially disagreed, the IRS later decided to follow this decision. Action on Decision 2011-003, Nov. 4, 2011. A 2010 Tax Court case (*O'Donnabhain*, 134 TC No. 34, Dec. 58,122 (2010)) ruled that a sex change operation was deductible as a medical expense.

¶8025 CAPITAL EXPENDITURES

Capital expenditures for home improvements and additions which are constructed primarily for the medical care of an individual generally qualify for a medical expense deduction only to the extent that the cost of the improvement or addition exceeds any increase in the value of the affected property that is due to the improvement. The entire cost of additions or improvements that do not increase the value of the home is deductible as a medical expense. Medical expense deductions have been allowed for the costs of installing elevators in the homes of persons suffering from heart disease, air conditioning devices for persons suffering from allergies, and specially built swimming pools for persons suffering from polio.

EXAMPLE 8.5

Gary Greene is advised by a physician to install an elevator in his residence so that his wife, who is afflicted with heart disease, will not be required to climb stairs. If the cost of installing the elevator is $1,500 and the increase in the value of the residence is only $1,100, the difference of $400 is deductible as a medical expense. However, if the value of the residence is not increased by the addition, the entire cost of installing the elevator qualifies as a medical expense.

Specific types of capital expenditures incurred to accommodate a personal residence to the needs of a physically handicapped individual are fully deductible medical expenses since these types of expenditures do not increase the fair market value of the residence. Examples are construction of entrance ramps, widening of doorways, or installation of railings to allow use of wheelchairs,

Capital expenditures which are related only to the sick person and not related to permanent improvement or betterment of property are deductible if such expenditures otherwise qualify as expenditures for medical care. For example, expenditures for eye glasses, handicapped service animals, dentures, artificial limbs, wheel chairs, crutches, inclinators, or air conditioners (if detachable from the property and purchased only for the use of a sick person) are deductible.

¶8035 TRANSPORTATION AND LODGING EXPENSES

Transportation expenses incurred in order to obtain medical care are deductible. However, the transportation deduction does not include the cost of any meals while away from home receiving medical treatment unless the meals are provided as part of the in-patient care at a hospital or similar facility. If a doctor prescribes an operation or other medical care, and the taxpayer chooses for purely personal considerations to travel to another locality for the medical care, neither the cost of transportation nor the cost of meals and lodging is deductible. Instead of a deduction for actual expenses incurred, a standard mileage rate of $.17 per mile for 2017 is allowed in computing the cost of driving an automobile for medical purposes. Parking fees and tolls may be deducted in addition to the mileage rate deduction.

Lodging while away from home on trips that are primarily for and essential to medical care is deductible. This deduction is not allowed for amounts paid for lodging that is lavish or extravagant. No medical deduction is allowed for any amount of lodging expenses if there is any significant element of personal pleasure, recreation, or vacation in the travel away from home.

The amount of the deduction for lodging is subject to a limitation of $50 per night for each eligible person. The deduction is allowed not only for the patient but also for a person who must travel with the patient. This means that if a parent accompanies a dependent child on a trip away from home for medical treatment, the parent could deduct up to $100 per day for lodging expenses.

EXAMPLE 8.6

Corola Combs travels out of state for special surgery for her daughter. She travels 400 miles round trip and incurs $12 in parking fees and tolls. Corola spends three nights in a hotel while her daughter is in the hospital. Her lodging expense totals $165, and she spends $90 eating out. Her meal expenses are not deductible. Her other qualifying medical expenses are:

Lodging limited to $150 ($50 per night × 3 nights)	$150
Mileage 400 miles × $.17 per mile	68
Parking fees and tolls	12
Qualifying medical expenses from trip	$230

¶8045 HOSPITAL AND OTHER INSTITUTIONAL CARE

The cost of in-patient hospital care (requiring an overnight stay), including the cost of meals and lodging, is deductible. The extent to which expenses for care in an institution other than a hospital (e.g., a nursing home, home for the aged, or therapeutic center for alcohol or drug addiction) qualify as a deduction for medical care is primarily a question of fact, and depends on the condition of the individual and the nature of the services received. If the availability of medical care in an institution is the principal reason for the patient's presence there, the entire cost of the care, including meals and lodging furnished incident to such care, is deductible. However, if an individual is placed in the institution primarily for personal or family reasons, then only that portion of the cost attributable to medical or nursing care (excluding meals and lodging) is deductible.

EXAMPLE 8.7

Alexis Amberson is 80, totally disabled, and suffers from a chronic ailment. Her family places her in a nursing home equipped to provide medical and nursing care services. The nursing home expenses are $25,000 a year. Of this amount, $8,500 is directly attributable to medical and nursing care. Since Alexis is in need of intensive medical and nursing care and has been placed in the nursing home facility for this purpose, all $25,000 is deductible (subject to the 10 percent of AGI limitation). Had Alexis been placed in the nursing home primarily for personal or family considerations, only $8,500 would be deductible.

Although education ordinarily does not qualify as medical care, special schooling for a mentally or physically handicapped individual is deductible, if the resources of the institution for alleviating the individual's mental or physical handicap are the principal reason for the individual's presence there. In such a case the cost of attending the school includes the cost of meals and lodging, if supplied, and the cost of ordinary education that is incidental to the special services furnished by the school.

¶8055 MEDICINES AND DRUGS

Only amounts paid for insulin and prescription medicines or drugs are deductible as a medical expense. Pharmaceutical items acquired without a prescription (such as over-the-counter ibuprofen or allergy medicines) do not qualify even though they are used for a particular illness, disease, or medical condition. Cosmetics and toiletries are not considered medicines and drugs.

EXAMPLE 8.8

Larry James, 28, had adjusted gross income of $22,000 in 2017. He paid a doctor $800 for medical expenses, a hospital $2,000, $200 for prescription drugs, and $150 for over-the-counter cold remedies and vitamins during 2017. His 2017 medical expense deduction is computed as follows:

Doctor	$800
Hospital	2,000
Medicine and drugs	200
Over-the-counter cold remedies and vitamins	0
Medical expenses	$3,000
Less: 10% of $22,000 (adjusted gross income)	2,200
Allowable medical expense deduction	$ 800

¶8065   MEDICAL INSURANCE PREMIUMS

A medical expense deduction is allowed for premiums paid for medical care insurance (including contact lens insurance), subject to the 10 percent limitation. If amounts are payable under an insurance contract for other than medical care (such as indemnity for loss of income or, life, limb, or sight), no amount paid for the insurance is deductible unless the medical care charge is stated separately in the contract or furnished in a separate statement. Long-term health care insurance premiums are deductible, but in 2017, the maximum deduction for prepaid long-term care insurance premiums is $410 for a taxpayer age 40 or less to $5,110 for a taxpayer more than age 70.

The basic cost of Medicare insurance (Medicare Part A) is not deductible unless voluntarily paid by the taxpayer for coverage. However, the cost of extra Medicare (Medicare Part B) is deductible. Self-employed persons are allowed to deduct 100 percent of amounts paid for health insurance for herself, her spouse, her dependents, and her under-27-year-old children as a business expense (deductible for adjusted gross income). Code Sec. 162(l). See ¶6575 for a discussion of deductions for Medical Savings Accounts. In general, this deduction is reduced by any premium tax credits the taxpayer takes.

Under the Affordable Care Act's individual mandate, taxpayers without health insurance will pay a penalty of the higher of a flat penalty of $695 per person or 2½% of income. "Income" for this purpose is generally adjusted gross income minus the standard deduction and personal exemption(s). For example, a single individual making $50,000 would have a $990 penalty for 2017. The penalty is not deductible.

Medical expenses are deductible only in the year paid. If medical expenses are reimbursed under a medical care insurance plan in the same year as paid, then the reimbursement merely reduces the amount that would otherwise be deductible. However, where reimbursement, from insurance or otherwise, for medical expenses is received in a year subsequent to a year in which a deduction was claimed, the reimbursement must be included in gross income in the year received to the extent attributable to deductions allowed in the prior year.

EXAMPLE 8.9

Morris Masters, 45, had adjusted gross income of $60,000 in 2017. He had a medical operation and, as a result, paid $5,000 in 2017 for hospitalization and $700 in doctors' bills. His transportation mileage for medical reasons totaled 200 miles. He also paid $640 for prescription medicines and drugs, $275 for contact lenses, and a $900 medical insurance premium in 2017. Under the medical insurance policy carried by the taxpayer, there is an allowance for the operation of only the first $1,000, which amount Morris received in 2017. His deduction for medical expenses is computed as follows:

Hospitalization (medical operation)	$5,000	
Less: Reimbursement from insurance company	1,000	$4,000
Premium on medical insurance policy		900
Doctors' bills		700
Prescription medicines and drugs		640
Contact lenses		275
Transportation for medical purposes (200 miles × $.17)		34
Total		$6,549
Less: 10% of $60,000 (adjusted gross income)		6,000
Total medical expenses deduction		$ 549

If Morris received the $1,000 reimbursement in 2018 rather than 2017, he would have a deduction of $1,549 ($549 + $1,000) in 2017 and income of $1,000 in 2018 (assuming he itemizes in 2017).

Taxes

¶8101   SUMMARY OF DEDUCTIBLE TAXES

The following taxes are deductible as itemized deductions (Code Sec. 164(a)):

1. State, local, or foreign real property taxes
2. State or local personal property taxes

3. State, local, or foreign income taxes
4. State and local general sales taxes

Other state, local, and foreign taxes not listed above are deductible only if they are trade or business expenses or are incurred in the production of income. The following discussion of taxes relates only to the deductibility of nonbusiness taxes by individuals.

¶8105   PROPERTY TAXES

Local, state, and foreign real property taxes are generally deductible only by the person upon whom they are imposed, and in the year in which they were paid or accrued. If they relate to nonbusiness real property, they are deductible as an itemized deduction.

A tax paid for local benefits such as street, sidewalk, and other similar improvements (also known as special assessments) is not deductible if imposed because of some direct benefit to the property against which the assessment is levied. Special assessments are not deductible, even though some incidental benefit may flow to the public welfare. Special assessments can, however, be added to the basis of the related property.

If real property is sold during the year, the real property tax deduction must be allocated between the buyer and the seller based on the number of days during the year that each party held the property. The seller is treated as paying the taxes up to, but not including, the date of sale. This allocation is required regardless of which party actually writes the check for the property tax or the method of accounting used by the taxpayers.

EXAMPLE 8.10   William Wasserman sold land to David Deere on April 1. Property taxes of $1,460 were paid by David on November 27 to cover the real property taxes for the entire calendar year. Assuming it is not a leap year, William is entitled to a $360 real property tax deduction ($1,460/365 = $4 per day × 90 days). David is entitled to a $1,100 real property tax deduction ($4 per day × 275 days).

A tenant-stockholder in a cooperative housing corporation may deduct amounts paid or accrued to the corporation to the extent that they represent the tenant-stockholder's proportional share of the real property taxes on the apartment building or houses and land on which situated. Similarly, a taxpayer who owns an apartment in a condominium apartment complex may deduct the taxes assessed on the taxpayer's interest in the property and paid by the taxpayer each year, provided the taxpayer itemizes deductions in filing a federal income tax return.

To be deductible, personal property taxes must be ad valorem (i.e., a tax that is based on the value of the personal property.) A tax which is based on criteria other than value does not qualify as ad valorem. For example, a motor vehicle tax based on weight, model year, and horsepower, or any of these characteristics, is not an ad valorem tax. However, a tax which is partly based on value and partly based on other criteria may qualify in part.

EXAMPLE 8.11   Gayla Gopher paid $135 for motor vehicle license plates. The license plate fee is based on a combination of value and weight of the automobile. If $75 of the $135 fee is based on the value of the automobile, then $75 is deductible as a tax.

Taxes imposed by some states on intangible personal property or the income therefrom are deductible.

¶8115   INCOME TAXES

State or city income taxes, including franchise taxes measured by net income, are deductible as itemized deductions by individuals. Either state and local sales taxes or state and local income taxes can be deducted, but not both. State and local income taxes on interest income that is exempt from federal income tax are also deductible. However, state and local income taxes on other exempt income are not deductible.

Taxpayers may deduct state and local income taxes withheld from their salary. They may also deduct tax payments made on prior year income in the year they were actually withheld or paid.

EXAMPLE 8.12

During 2017, Carl Castor had $1,200 in state income taxes withheld from his salary. In addition, he paid an additional $325 in 2017 when he filed his 2016 state income tax return. Carl's state income tax deduction for 2017 is $1,525, the amount he actually paid during 2017.

Any estimated state tax payments made that are in fact not required to be made are not deductible. For example, if a taxpayer made an estimated state income tax payment but the estimate of the state tax liability for the year shows that the taxpayer will receive a refund of the full amount of the estimated payment, then the taxpayer was not required to make the payment and may not deduct it as an itemized deduction.

If a taxpayer receives a refund of state, local, or foreign income taxes, all or part of the refund may need to be included in income in the year received. The tax benefit rule requires the taxpayer to include a tax refund in gross income of the year received to the extent that a tax benefit resulted from the deduction of the item in the earlier year. This includes refunds resulting from taxes that were overwithheld, not determined correctly, or redetermined as a result of an amended return. A refund of state, local, or foreign taxes may not be used to reduce the amount of taxes paid during the year to lower the deduction. The taxes paid and the refund received must be reported separately.

EXAMPLE 8.13

Paul Plymouth, a single taxpayer, received a refund of $1,000 in 2018 from his 2017 state income tax return. Paul had total itemized deductions in 2017 of $6,950, including $2,500 for state income taxes. The amount to be included in gross income for 2018 is $600. The amount included is the lesser of the refund received ($1,000) or the excess itemized deductions taken in 2017 ($600). The $1,000 refund received in 2017 will not affect the itemized deduction for state income taxes in either 2018 or 2017.

Itemized deductions for 2017	$6,950
Less: Standard deduction for 2017	6,350
Excess itemized deductions for 2017	$600

Individual taxpayers are able to deduct the greater of state and local income taxes or state and local general sales taxes as an itemized deduction on their federal income tax returns. Code Sec. 164(b)(5). The amount to be deducted for state and local general sales taxes is either (1) the total of actual general sales taxes paid as substantiated by accumulated receipts, or (2) an amount from IRS-generated tables, plus the amount of general sales taxes from the purchase of a motor vehicle, boat, or motor home.

Interest

¶8201   **REQUIREMENTS FOR DEDUCTION**

Interest is the amount which one has contracted to pay for the use of borrowed money. For tax purposes the term has the usual ordinary, everyday meaning given to it in the business world. *Old Colony R.R. Co.,* 3 USTC ¶880, 284 U.S. 552, 52 S.Ct. 211 (1932). Interest incurred in a trade or business is deductible. However, as discussed in Chapter 6, interest incurred to purchase assets on which the income is tax exempt (such as state and municipal bonds) is not deductible.

It is not necessary that the parties to a transaction label a payment made for the use of money as interest for it to be treated as interest. The method of computation also does not control its deductibility, so long as the amount in question is an ascertainable sum paid for the use of borrowed money.

The timing of a deduction for interest expense depends on whether the taxpayer is on the cash basis or the accrual basis. Taxpayers on the cash basis will deduct interest expense when the payment of the interest is actually made. Deducting the amount of the interest from the original loan amount is not considered "payment" for this purpose. Accrual basis taxpayers, on the other hand, will deduct interest as it accrues. Prepaid interest ("points") is generally amortized over the life of the loan, but is currently deductible if paid in connection with a loan made to purchase the taxpayer's principal residence. (See ¶8265 for further information.)

EXAMPLE 8.14

On November 1 Ben borrows $10,000 to be used in his business. He actually receives $9,400, but will have to pay the full $10,000 back on April 30 of the next year. If he is a cash basis taxpayer, he will deduct the entire $600 of interest in the next year, when it is paid. If he is on the accrual basis, he would deduct $200 (2/6) this year and $400 (4/6) next year.

Interest deductions for tax purposes can be separated into six types: personal (consumer) interest, qualified residence interest, investment interest, trade or business interest, passive investment interest, and qualified education loan interest. Each of these six types of interest deductions is explained in the following sections.

¶8205 PERSONAL (CONSUMER) INTEREST

Generally, interest on personal loans is not deductible by individuals. The vast majority of nondeductible personal interest consists of interest on credit card debt, automobile loans, or student loans. Of course, if the credit card or automobile are used for business purposes then the related interest is business, not personal, interest, and is deductible. Similarly, under certain circumstances student loan interest is deductible (see below). Interest on tax deficiencies (even those arising from individual business income) is also personal interest, and it is therefore not deductible.

EXAMPLE 8.15

Sara Short incurs personal interest of $1,000 on an auto loan. Sara is not allowed an itemized deduction for the auto loan interest.

¶8210 QUALIFIED EDUCATION LOAN INTEREST

Taxpayers are allowed an interest deduction *for AGI* of up to $2,500 for interest paid on qualified education loans. Qualified education loans are loans incurred to pay expenses for undergraduate and graduate tuition, room and board, and related expenses. In 2017, the deduction is phased out for single taxpayers with AGI between $65,000 and $80,000 and married taxpayers filing joint returns with AGI between $135,000 and $165,000. The deduction will be allowed in figuring adjusted gross income.

¶8215 QUALIFIED RESIDENCE INTEREST

Taxpayers may deduct interest on loans secured by first or second homes, but the homes must be "qualified residences." A home is a qualified residence if it is the taxpayer's principal residence or if it is a second residence designated for this purpose that is used for personal purposes for more than the greater of 14 days or 10 percent of the number of days it is rented (such as a vacation home). Taxpayers having more than two residences can designate each year which residence is to be considered the second residence. If the second residence is not used by the taxpayer or rented at any time during the year, the taxpayer need not meet the requirements that the residence be used for personal (nonrental) purposes for more than 14 days. Code Sec. 163(h). For 2007 through 2016, "qualified residence interest" includes premiums for qualified mortgage insurance, which are otherwise nondeductible. Code Sec. 163(h)(3)(E)(i).

Qualified residence interest on acquisition indebtedness is deductible. Acquisition indebtedness is up to $1,000,000 of debt incurred to acquire, construct, or substantially improve any qualified residence and which is secured by the residence. If a residence is refinanced, the amount qualifying as acquisition indebtedness is limited to the amount of acquisition debt existing at the time of refinancing plus any of the amount of the new loan which is used to substantially improve the residence.

A taxpayer can also deduct the interest on a limited amount of home equity loans. The limit is the lesser of $100,000 or the equity (fair market value less acquisition indebtedness) in the home. "Fair market value" for this purpose is determined on the date the last debt was secured by the home, so a later decline in fair market value will not affect the deduction. No restrictions are placed on the use of the home equity loan funds other than the purchase of tax-free investments. (However, if the proceeds are not used for home improvement, the interest is not deductible for AMT purposes.) Interest on the debt equal to or under the above limits is fully deductible while interest attributable to debt over the limits is not deductible.

The IRS has taken the position that if the initial mortgage exceeds $1,000,000, up to $100,000 of the excess will qualify as home equity interest. Rev. Rul. 2010-25.

EXAMPLE 8.16

> Shelly McGuire bought a house for $1,500,000 and paid $300,000 down on it. Her interest on the $1,200,000 initial mortgage was $72,000. The interest on $1,100,000 of her mortgage will be deductible, since $1,000,000 would be treated as acquisition indebtedness and $100,000 would qualify as a home equity loan. Her residence interest deduction will be limited to $1,100,000/$1,200,000 of $72,000, or $66,000.

TAX BLUNDER

Tim Johnson borrowed $20,000 on a car loan to finance the purchase of a new car. Tim also owns a home on which he has no mortgage. He did not consider a home equity loan when he purchased his car. The interest payments on his car do not qualify for an interest deduction on his tax return. Tim should have considered a home equity loan to finance the purchase of his car.

Taxpayers can turn nondeductible personal (consumer) interest into deductible qualified residence interest by taking out a home equity loan on their personal residence and using the proceeds to pay off personal loans, automobile loans, and credit card balances.

¶8225   INVESTMENT INTEREST

The deduction for investment interest is limited to the amount of net investment income. Investment interest in excess of this limitation is carried forward and treated as investment interest in the succeeding tax year. However, an investment interest carryover is allowed in a subsequent year only to the extent the taxpayer has net investment income in the later year.

Definition of Investment Interest

Interest that is subject to the investment interest limitation is defined as interest on debt incurred or continued to purchase or carry property held for investment. Property held for investment includes any property that produces income of the following types: interest, dividends, annuities, or royalties not derived in the ordinary course of a trade or business. The most common types of property held for investment are stocks, bonds, and raw land.

Investment income includes gross income from property held for investment such as dividends, interest, and royalties. Net short term gains are normally included in the definition of investment income, and net long term gains are not. However, a taxpayer has the option of giving up the long-term capital gain rate (0/15/20%) on the sale of long term capital assets in order to have all or a portion of the long-term capital gains included as net investment income, thereby increasing the allowable deductible investment interest expense. The taxpayers also have the option of giving up the preferential tax rate treatment for dividends in order to have the dividend income included as net investment income.

Net investment income is investment income net of investment expenses. Investment expenses are deductible expenses (other than interest) directly connected with the production of investment income, such as investment advisor fees.

EXAMPLE 8.17

> Roberta Ramsey has $17,000 of investment interest expense and $4,000 of net investment income in 2017. Her investment interest deduction for 2017 is $4,000. The other $13,000 of investment interest she paid may be carried over to 2018 and deducted in that year to the extent that it, together with 2018 investment interest and other investment interest carryovers, does not exceed the investment interest limitation.

¶8235   TRADE OR BUSINESS INTEREST

Most interest payments incurred in a trade or business are fully deductible for tax purposes. Trade or business interest payments are deductible in computing adjusted gross income and are discussed in Chapter 6.

¶8245   PASSIVE INVESTMENT INTEREST

Passive investment interest is the interest incurred on money borrowed to invest in a passive activity. The amount of passive investment interest is subtracted from any gain or added to any loss from the passive activity. Losses from passive activities are subject to the passive loss limitation rules explained beginning at ¶7201.

¶8255 PAYMENTS FOR SERVICES

Payments for specific services which the lender performs in connection with the borrower's account are not deductible as interest. For example, interest does not include the separate charges made for investigation of the prospective borrower and the borrower's collateral, closing costs of the loan and the papers drawn in connection with the closing, or fees paid to a third party for servicing and collecting the particular loan. Rev. Rul. 69-188, 1969-1 CB 54.

¶8265 PREPAID INTEREST

Taxpayers on either the accrual or cash method of accounting are generally required to deduct prepaid interest over the time period during which the prepaid interest represents the cost of using the borrowed funds. Interest subtracted in advance from the proceeds of a loan is not considered paid until the loan payments are made.

EXAMPLE 8.18

On October 1, 2017, Horace Holmes borrows $50,000 from the bank on a one-year, 10 percent loan. The bank subtracts the interest in advance and remits $45,000 to Horace. He pays the due amount of $50,000 on September 30, 2018. Horace has an interest expense deduction of $5,000 for 2018. He is not considered to have prepaid the interest in 2017. If he had received the full $50,000 from the bank and prepaid the $5,000 interest in 2017, $1,250 (3/12) would have been deductible in 2017 and $3,750 (9/12) would have been deductible in 2018.

"Points" are additional interest charges which are usually paid when a loan is closed and which are generally imposed by the lender in lieu of a higher interest rate. Where points are paid as compensation for the use of borrowed money, rather than as payment for the lender's services, the points substitute for a higher stated annual interest rate. These types of points are similar to a prepayment of interest, and are to be treated as paid over the term of the loan. An exception allows the current deduction of points paid in connection with a mortgage incurred in the purchase or improvement of the taxpayer's principal residence. This exception applies only if points are generally charged in the geographical area where the loan is made and to the extent of the number of points generally charged in that area for a home loan. Points paid on refinancing must be deducted ratably over the life of the loan. Any unamortized points are deductible when the loan is paid off.

¶8275 MORTGAGE INSURANCE PREMIUMS

Mortgage insurance premiums paid by a taxpayer in connection with acquisition indebtedness on a qualified residence are treated as qualified residence interest and are deductible as an itemized deduction through 2016. The allowable deduction is phased out ratably if the taxpayer's adjusted gross income exceeds $100,000 ($50,000 for a married taxpayer filing a separate return).

Charitable Contributions

Contributions made to "qualified domestic organizations" by individuals and corporations are deductible as charitable contributions. Code Sec. 170. Any charitable contribution actually paid during the year is allowable as a deduction regardless of the method of accounting used by the taxpayer.

Ordinarily, a contribution is deemed made at the time delivery is made. The unconditional delivery or mailing of a check which subsequently clears in due course will constitute a contribution on the date of delivery or mailing. A "pledge" by a taxpayer to make a contribution is not deductible until it is actually paid.

EXAMPLE 8.19

On December 1, 2017, Sherri Jones made a pledge to donate $1,200 to the City Museum. She mailed a check for $800 to the museum on December 30, 2017, and mailed another check for $400 on January 31, 2018. The museum did not receive the $800 check until January 5, 2018, and deposited it on January 6. The museum received and deposited the $400 check on February 3, 2018. Her pledge does not affect the timing or the deductibility of her contributions. She can deduct $800 in 2017, the year the $800 check was mailed (the time of "delivery"), and the other $400 is deductible in 2018.

¶8301   QUALIFIED ORGANIZATIONS

To qualify for the deduction, a contribution must be made to one of the following organizations:

1. The United States, a state, a possession of the United States, or any political subdivision of the foregoing
2. Corporation, trust, community chest, fund, or foundation that is created or organized in the United States and operated exclusively for religious, charitable, scientific, literary, or educational purposes
3. Veterans' organization
4. Domestic fraternal society
5. Nonprofit cemetery company

Generally, contributions made to foreign organizations are not deductible. No deduction is allowed for amounts paid to an organization which participates in any political campaign activities on behalf of or in opposition to any candidate for public office.

Gifts made to individuals generally are not deductible. For a contribution to be deductible, a donor cannot earmark it for the benefit of a specific individual.

EXAMPLE 8.20	Fred Fromm made donations to needy individuals. The payments were made by Fred from personal funds directly to the individuals after an investigation of their needs. There was no specific fund established or maintained by Fred or any other person for the purpose of distributing the money to the needy individuals. Fred is not allowed a charitable contribution deduction for his donations to the individuals.

EXAMPLE 8.21	Charlotte sets up an account with GoFundMe to raise money for her personal medical expenses. George contributes $50 to Charlotte's account. George has not made a deductible charitable contribution.

TAX BLUNDER

Referring to the facts in Example 8.20, Fred should have made donations to qualified charitable organizations who help needy individuals instead of making the contribution directly to needy individuals. In this way, Fred would have preserved a charitable contribution deduction on his federal income tax return.

An organization must meet specific requirements in order to be exempt from taxation. Code Sec. 501. However, this does not necessarily mean that a contribution to that organization is deductible by the donor. The IRS publishes a list of organizations which have applied for and received rulings or determination letters holding contributions to them to be deductible. If an organization has not received a determination letter, it is not recognized as an organization to which contributions are deductible unless it is an organization described in (1), above.

Qualified charitable organizations are divided into two categories: public charities and private charities. Public charities include:

1. Churches or a convention or association of churches
2. Educational organizations which normally maintain a regular faculty, curriculum, and a regularly enrolled body of students
3. Hospitals and medical research organizations
4. Organizations supported by the government which are organized to administer property to or for the benefit of a college or university described in (2), above
5. Governmental units
6. A corporation, trust, or community chest, fund, or foundation that is created or organized in the United States and is organized and operated exclusively for religious, charitable, scientific, literary, or educational purposes
7. Certain types of private foundations

Private foundations are organizations which do not normally receive donations from the general public. There are two types of private foundations: operating and nonoperating. A private operating foundation is generally an organization with respect to which more than 50% of its assets are devoted directly to activities for which it is organized and operated and that distributes substantially all of its income for the conduct of its charitable purposes. Private operating foundations are treated as public charities.

Most private foundations fall into the nonoperating foundation classification. Private nonoperating foundations that distribute all of their contributions to public charities are also treated as public charities. Thus, a public charity is any qualified charity except for private nonoperating foundations that do not distribute all of their income to public charities. These private nonoperating foundations not contributing all of their income are classified as private charities.

¶8315 VALUATION OF CHARITABLE DONATIONS

If a charitable contribution is made in property, the amount of the contribution is normally the fair market value of the property at the time of the contribution. The fair market value is generally the price at which the property would change hands between a willing buyer and a willing seller, with both having a reasonable knowledge of relevant facts. No charitable deduction is allowed for the contribution of services.

Where the taxpayer receives some benefit in return for payment to a charitable organization, the deduction is reduced by the value of the benefit received. Where a charitable organization sponsors charity balls, bazaars, banquets, shows, or athletic events, there is a presumption that the price of admission is not a gift, and that the payment is for an item of value. The burden is on the taxpayer to show that the amount paid exceeds the fair market value of admission. The fact that the full payment or a portion of the payment made by the taxpayer is used by the organization exclusively for charitable purposes has no bearing upon the determination to be made as to the value of the admission or the amount qualifying as a contribution. The IRS says that a benefit is "insubstantial" and won't reduce the deduction if it is not more than the lesser of 2% of the payment or $107 (for 2017).

EXAMPLE 8.22 Members of a charitable organization sell candy to raise funds for the charity. The candy is purchased at $5 per box, normally sells for $8 a box, but is sold at $10 per box. The organization promotes the sale as a "tax-deductible donation." Only $2 per box qualifies as a charitable contribution. Other instances in which a deductible contribution could be claimed for the excess paid above fair market value would be (1) purchase of a ticket (from a charitable organization) to an artist's benefit performance and (2) purchase of an item at a benefit auction for more than its fair market value.

Taxpayers who make a payment to a college or university for the right to purchase tickets to an athletic event are entitled to deduct only 80 percent of the payment as a charitable deduction regardless of whether the tickets would have been available without making the payment.

The IRS has ruled that a taxpayer could deduct a portion of its donation to a state university's foundation for which the taxpayer received the right to purchase tickets for seating at university athletic events in a special skybox. The IRS concluded that the payment for the skybox lease was made to an educational institution for the right to purchase tickets and for the tickets themselves and, thus, the taxpayer was allowed to deduct 80 percent of its payment under Code Sec. 170(l). TAM 200004001.

Unreimbursed expenditures made incident to the rendering of services to an organization may constitute a deductible contribution. These expenses include reasonable expenditures for meals and lodging while away from home in the course of performing donated services.

Automobile expenses incurred in travel or transportation to perform charitable services are deductible. A standard mileage rate of $.14 per mile (not indexed for inflation) or the actual expenses of operating the automobile may be used. Rev. Proc. 2004-64. Parking fees and tolls are added to either method of computation. General repairs or maintenance expenses, depreciation, insurance, or registration fees are not deductible. The costs of meals for the volunteers or the costs of child care for the volunteer's own children while the individual is performing services are not deductible.

TAX BLUNDER

John Adams does volunteer work for a number of charitable organizations. He uses his car in connection with his volunteer work but does not keep track of the miles driven while performing his charitable duties. Because he didn't keep track of his mileage, John has foregone a $.14 per mile charitable contribution deduction for all of the miles driven while performing his volunteer work.

¶8325   LIMITATIONS ON CHARITABLE CONTRIBUTIONS

An individual's charitable contribution deduction is subject to 20 percent, 30 percent, and 50 percent of AGI limitations. If a husband and wife file a joint return, the deduction for contributions is the aggregate of the contributions made by the spouses.

The limitation that applies generally depends on the type of property contributed and the type of charity (public or private) to which the contribution is made. Individuals are limited to a deduction of 50 percent of adjusted gross income for charitable contributions of cash and "ordinary income property" made to public charities (such as churches, Goodwill, etc.—see ¶8301). Contributions of appreciated capital gain property to public charities and contributions of cash and "ordinary income property" to private charities are limited to 30 percent of adjusted gross income. An individual may only deduct charitable contributions made to certain private charities to the extent the contributions do not exceed 20 percent of adjusted gross income. In addition, the total charitable contribution deduction is limited to 50 percent of adjusted gross income. For purposes of the charitable contribution deduction limitations, adjusted gross income is computed before any deduction for net operating loss carrybacks.

Ordinary Income Property

"Ordinary income property" means property that if sold at the time of contribution would trigger income other than long-term capital gains. For example, ordinary income property includes property held by the donor as inventory, depreciation recapture property, a work of art created by the donor, a manuscript prepared by the donor, letters and memorandums prepared by or for the donor, and capital assets held one year or less by the donor (short term capital gain property).

When ordinary income property is contributed, the amount of the deduction must be reduced by the amount that would have been recognized as ordinary income if the property had been sold by the donor at its fair market value at the time of the contribution. Essentially, the deduction for ordinary income property is limited to the basis of the property.

EXAMPLE 8.23	Donna Fairfield contributes equipment held as inventory to the Salvation Army. The equipment has a basis of $10,000 and a fair market value of $12,000. Her charitable deduction is limited to $10,000 ($12,000 fair market value – $2,000 ordinary income).

Capital Gain Property

Capital gain property is appreciated property where the sale would result in a long-term capital gain if the property were sold at fair market value at the time of the contribution. Section 1231 property (which is discussed in Chapter 12) is considered capital gain property for charitable contributions purposes. If the contributed property would have produced both ordinary income and long-term capital gain if sold, the fair market value (as used for computing the deduction) must be reduced by the amount which would have been ordinary income, typically the potential depreciation recapture on the property.

EXAMPLE 8.24	Brent Bates contributed an asset to a qualified charity. The asset has a fair market value of $1,000 and a basis to him of $400. If the sale would result in a $600 gain of which $250 would be classified as ordinary income and $350 as long-term capital gain, the asset is considered to be capital gain property. However, the charitable contribution deduction is limited to $750 ($1,000 FMV – $250 ordinary income element).

The charitable contribution deduction for capital gain property that is either (1) contributed to a private charity or (2) tangible personal property which has an "unrelated use" to the organization receiving it must be reduced by the property's unrecognized long-term capital gain. This reduced contribution amount is the basis of the property.

"Unrelated use" means a use which is unrelated to the purpose or function of the charitable organization. For example, if a painting contributed to an educational institution is used by the organization for educational purposes by being placed in its library for display and study by art students, its use is "related" to the educational purpose of the institution. However, if the painting is sold and the proceeds are used by the organization for educational purposes, the use of the property is unrelated.

EXAMPLE 8.25

> Lois Lacey contributes an antique lamp to a qualified charity. The lamp has a fair market value of $5,000 and a basis to her of $3,000. The charity intends to sell the lamp and use the proceeds for charitable purposes. Lois's charitable deduction is limited to $3,000.

Contributions of "qualified appreciated stock" to private charities are deductible at the full fair market value of the stock. "Qualified appreciated stock" is any stock of a corporation (1) for which market quotations are readily available on an established securities market, and (2) which is a long-term capital asset.

PLANNING POINTER

> If the property to be contributed has not appreciated over the taxpayer's basis, the contribution is valued at fair market value. It is not wise to contribute property that would otherwise create a deductible loss if sold. The taxpayer should sell the property and donate the proceeds to the charitable organization.

Charitable Contribution Percentage Limits

As indicated previously, charitable contributions are subject to several limitations that are based on adjusted gross income. There are 50 percent, 30 percent, and 20 percent category limits that are determined by the type of property contributed and the type of charity receiving the donated property. In addition, there is an overall limit on total charitable contributions that is 50 percent of adjusted gross income.

A carryover of any unused charitable contributions is allowed for up to five years, even if the taxpayer does not itemize for the current year. Current charitable contributions are considered first and then carryforwards are considered on a first-in, first-out basis. Any carryovers will be subject to the same percentage limitations as when they were first originated.

50 Percent Limitation Category

The deduction for contributions of cash and ordinary income property made to public charities may not exceed 50 percent of an individual's adjusted gross income for the year. The deduction for the 50 percent category is the smaller of (1) the 50 percent category contribution amount or (2) 50 percent of adjusted gross income.

EXAMPLE 8.26

> Beatrice Bold donates $10,000 to State University, a public charity. Her adjusted gross income for the year is $17,000. She would be limited to a charitable deduction of $8,500 ($17,000 × 50%). She would have a five-year carryover of $1,500, which would be subject to the 50% of AGI limitation in all future years.

30 Percent Limitation Category

The 30 percent limit category is comprised of two distinct 30 percent limits that must be kept separate. The 30 percent public category consists of contributions of capital gain property or appreciated Section 1231 (depreciable) property made to any public charitable organization. The 30 percent private category consists of contributions of cash or ordinary income property to private charities.

An individual may elect to reduce 30 percent capital gain property (contributed to a public charity) by the long-term capital gain and have the reduced contribution qualify for the 50 percent limitation category. This "reduced contribution election" applies to all contributions of 30 percent capital gain property made during the year or carried over to such year. The "reduced contribution election" is normally only tax advantageous to the taxpayer if the contributed property has appreciated only a small amount.

Neither capital assets reduced because of the "reduced contribution election" nor capital assets reduced because of "unrelated use" are considered 30 percent capital gain property, but instead are placed in the 50 percent limitation category.

EXAMPLE 8.27	Teri Rogers contributes $5,000 of common stock to the local homeless shelter, which is a public charitable organization. The stock has a basis to her of $4,800. Teri could now elect to reduce the 30 percent capital gain property by the $200 long-term capital gain on the property and classify the contribution as 50 percent limitation category property. If Teri has AGI of $10,000, a "reduced contribution election" would allow her to deduct a $4,800 charitable contribution deduction (with zero carryover) instead of a $3,000 charitable contribution deduction (with $2,000 carryover) with no election. If the basis of the stock to her was $3,400, a "reduced contribution election" would result in a deduction of $3,400 (with zero carryover) instead of a $3,000 deduction (with $2,000 carryover) with no election. Clearly, the tax advantage of the "reduced contribution election" is greater if the property has appreciated only a small amount.

20 Percent Limitation Category

An individual may deduct charitable contributions made during the year to any qualified charitable organization not considered to be a public charity (generally any "private charity"). Such contributions are limited to 20 percent of adjusted gross income. The 20 percent limitation generally applies to private charities and to certain other organizations, such as war veterans' organizations, domestic fraternal societies, and nonprofit cemeteries.

The deduction for capital gain property donated to a private charity must be reduced by the long-term capital gain inherent in the property. Donations of "qualified appreciated stock," however, are deductible at full fair market value.

EXAMPLE 8.28	Brandon Fryar has adjusted gross income for the year of $100,000. On February 1, 2017, he donates stock to a private charity. The stock has a fair market value of $25,000 and a basis to him of $10,000. He must reduce the fair market value by the long-term capital gain, leaving a charitable contribution deduction of $10,000. If the stock were qualified appreciated stock, his deduction in the current year would be $20,000. He would be allowed a deduction equal to the full fair market value but would only be able to deduct up to 20 percent of adjusted gross income this year. The other $5,000 would be carried over to the five subsequent years (subject to the 20% limitation in each year).

50 Percent Overall Limitation

There is an overall limitation placed on total deductions for all charitable contributions equal to 50 percent of adjusted gross income. This limitation is applied after the other limitations are computed. In applying the overall limitation, the 50 percent deduction, 30 percent public deduction, 30 percent private deduction, and 20 percent deduction must be taken, in that order.

Since the overall 50 percent limitation amount is the same as the specific 50 percent limitation amount, if the 50 percent contributions exceed the 50 percent limitation there will be no further deductions allowed from the other categories.

The 30 percent public deduction limit is determined by taking the smaller of (1) 30 percent of AGI or (2) 50 percent of AGI minus the 50 percent contributions.

The 30 percent private deduction limit is determined by taking the smaller of (1) 30 percent of AGI or (2) 50 percent of AGI minus all 50 percent contributions and minus the 30 percent public contributions. The 50 percent and 30 percent public *contribution* amounts are used in computing the limitations rather than the related *deduction* amounts.

The 20 percent deduction limit is determined by taking the smaller of (1) 20 percent of AGI or (2) 50 percent of AGI minus the 50 percent contributions, the 30 percent public contributions, and the 30 percent private contributions. (Further limitations on 20 percent contributions exist but are beyond the scope of this book. They can be found in Publication 526.)

EXAMPLE 8.29 Darin Drum has adjusted gross income for the year of $100,000. On March 1, 2017, he makes two charitable contributions. He makes 30 percent public charity contributions in the amount of $42,000. He also contributes $23,000 in qualified appreciated stock to a private charity. His charitable contribution deduction for the year is limited to $38,000, computed as follows. His $42,000 30 percent public charity contribution is limited to $30,000 ($100,000 × 30%). His $23,000 contribution of qualified appreciated stock to a private charity is first limited to $20,000 ($100,000 × 20%) and further limited to $8,000 ($50,000 maximum charitable deduction under the 50 percent overall limitation minus the $42,000 30 percent contribution amount). His total deduction will therefore be $30,000 + $8,000 = $38,000. Next year Darin will have a $12,000 ($42,000 - $30,000) carryover subject to the 30 percent public limit and a $15,000 ($23,000 - $8,000) carryover subject to the 20 percent limit.

Steps In Determining Individual Charitable Contributions

Step 1. Determine the contribution amounts. The contribution amount is the fair market value reduced by any ordinary income and by the long-term capital gain deduction required because of unrelated use, reduced contribution election, or contribution to a private charity.

Step 2. Place all contributions into 50 percent, 30 percent public, 30 percent private, and 20 percent limitation categories.

Property Given	Contribution Amount	Limitation Category
Cash		
Public Charity	Cash	50%
Private Charity	Cash	30% Private
Ordinary Income Property		
Public Charity	Basis	50%
Private Charity	Basis	30% Private
Capital Gain Property		
Public Charity	FMV-OI	30% Public
Public Reduced Contribution Election	Basis	50%
Private Charity	Basis	20%
Appreciated Tangible Personal Property with Unrelated Use		
Public Charity	Basis	50%
Private Charity	Basis	20%
Qualified Appreciated Stock		
Public Charity	FMV	30% Public
Private Charity	FMV	20%

Step 3. Determine each percent limit amount based on the 50 percent, 30 percent public, 30 percent private, and 20 percent limits.

Step 4. Determine each percent deduction limit. Any difference between the contribution amount and the deduction allowed in each category is carried over for five years.

Step 5. Add the respective percent deduction amounts, as limited, to arrive at the total charitable contribution deduction for the year.

EXAMPLE 8.30

Grace Goodheart has $100,000 of adjusted gross income and made charitable contributions as follows: $13,000 cash to the Red Cross, $24,000 (fair market value) in stock to the Boy Scouts, $9,000 in cash to a private charity, and $23,000 in qualified appreciated stock to a private charity. The charitable contribution deduction is computed as follows:

Limitation Category	Contribution Amounts	AGI Limit Amounts	Remaining Overall Limit (50%)	Deductible Amounts	Carryover
50%	$13,000	$50,000	$50,000	$13,000	$0
30% Public	24,000	30,000	37,000	24,000	0
30% Private	9,000	30,000	13,000	9,000	0
20%	23,000	20,000	4,000	4,000	19,000
Total Charitable Deduction				$50,000	

There are no reductions to arrive at the contribution amounts above. The AGI limit amounts are AGI times the percent (50%, 30%, or 20%) that relates to the limitation category.

The deductible amounts are determined as follows:

1. The 50 percent deduction is the smaller of the $13,000 contribution or $50,000 ($100,000 × 50 percent).
2. The 30 percent public deduction is $24,000, the smaller of (1) the $24,000 contribution amount, (2) $30,000 ($100,000 AGI × 30 percent) or (3) $37,000 [$50,000 minus $13,000 (50% contributions)].
3. The 30 percent private deduction is $9,000 because it is the lesser of (1) the $9,000 contribution, (2) $30,000 (30% of $100,000 AGI) or (3) the $50,000 limit minus the 50 percent and 30 percent public contributions ($50,000 - $13,000 - $24,000 = $13,000).
4. The 20 percent limit deduction is $4,000, the lesser of (1) the $23,000 contribution amount, (2) $20,000 ($100,000 AGI × 20 percent), or (3) $4,000, the $50,000 (50% overall) limit minus the $13,000 50 percent contribution amount, the $24,000 30 percent public contribution amount, and the $9,000 30 percent private contribution amount.

After reducing the overall 50% limit for prior 50% and 30% contributions, there is only $4,000 of 50% limit left in which to deduct the 20% contributions.

¶8355

FILING AND SUBSTANTIATION REQUIREMENTS

The deduction for contributions is an itemized deduction and is therefore made on Schedule A of Form 1040. Cash contributions of less than $250 must be substantiated by a bank record (cancelled check, bank statement, credit card statement) or a written acknowledgment from the donee organization. Any charitable contribution of $250 or more must be substantiated by a contemporaneous written acknowledgment of the contribution from the donee organization. The written acknowledgment should include the amount of cash contributed and/or a description of the property contributed. The written acknowledgment must state whether the donee provides any goods or services in consideration for the contribution.

If the contribution is made in property other than money and is over $500, the taxpayer is required to state the kind of property contributed, the method used in determining the fair market value of the property at the time the contribution was made, and whether or not the amount of the contribution was reduced.

For contributed property for which the claimed value of one item or group of similar items exceeds $5,000, the taxpayer claiming the deduction must attach an appraisal of the donated property's fair market value to the income tax return. The appraisal must be obtained from a qualified appraiser. If the donee sells the property within two years (three years for related-use tangible personal property), the donee must furnish the IRS and the donor with a statement regarding the sale.

In regard to donations of automobiles to charities, if the claimed value of the donated motor vehicle, boat or plane exceeds $500 and the item is sold by the charity, the taxpayer is limited to a charitable donation equal to the gross proceeds from the sale.

Personal Casualty and Theft Losses

¶8501 CASUALTY LOSSES

This section discusses personal casualty and theft losses. Business casualty losses are discussed in Chapter 7. Personal casualty and theft losses are deductible as itemized deductions while business casualty and theft losses are deductible from gross income.

Criteria for Deduction

Any uninsured loss arising from fire, storm, shipwreck, or other casualty is allowable as a deduction in the year in which the loss is sustained. Code Sec. 165(c)(3). The IRS position is that the loss must be the result of sudden, unexpected, identifiable, and provable events of an unusual nature, such as an accident, mishap, or sudden invasion by a hostile agency, the cause of which was unknown, or was an unusual effect of a known cause, which occurred by chance and unexpectedly.

Loss through progressive deterioration of property through a steadily operating cause or a normal process is not deductible. The following have been found not to qualify as casualty losses: destruction of trees by disease or insects (*J.A. Appleman,* 64-2 USTC ¶9860, 338 F.2d 729 (CA-7 1964); *H.F. Burns,* 59-2 USTC ¶9514, 174 F.Supp. 203 (DC Ohio 1959), aff'd pcr curiam, 61-1 USTC ¶9127, 284 F.2d 436 (CA-6 1960); Rev. Rul. 57-599, 1957-2 CB 42); death of livestock; dry rot damage; gradual damage to pilings by storms, tides, and worms; various automobile breakdowns; accumulated water damage to basement walls; freeze and thaw road damage (*H. Stacy,* 29 TCM 542, Dec. 30,132(M), T.C. Memo. 1970-127); and damage from termites (*J.A. Austra,* 25 TCM 178, Dec. 27,837(M), T.C. Memo. 1966-28).

Determination of Amount of Loss

To determine the amount of deductible loss, the fair market value of the property immediately before and immediately after the casualty generally must be ascertained by competent appraisal. This appraisal must recognize the effects of any general market decline affecting undamaged as well as damaged property, which may have occurred simultaneously with the casualty, so that any deduction will be limited to the actual loss resulting from damage to the property.

Cleanup expenses are deductible as a part of the casualty loss. Costs of photographs and appraisal fees are not deductible as part of the casualty loss, but are deductible as an itemized expense in the determination of correct tax liability. Costs incurred to protect damaged property from future losses are not deductible as part of the casualty loss. Personal living expenses, such as temporary housing, rentals, medical care, lights, fuel, food and drink, or moving expenses are also not deductible as casualty losses.

The cost of repairs of the property damaged is acceptable as evidence of the loss of value. The taxpayer must show that (1) the repairs were necessary to restore the property to its condition immediately before the casualty, (2) the amount spent for such repairs was not excessive, (3) the repairs don't repair more than the damage suffered, and (4) the value of the property after the repairs doesn't, as a result of the repairs, exceed the value of the property immediately before the casualty.

A casualty loss occurs when an automobile owned by the taxpayer is damaged due to the faulty driving of the taxpayer or other person operating the automobile. However, an automobile accident will not qualify as a casualty loss if it is due to the willful act or willful negligence of the taxpayer or of one acting on the taxpayer's behalf. Damage resulting from the faulty driving of the operator of the vehicle with which the taxpayer collides is also eligible for the casualty deduction.

The amount of loss to be taken into account is the lesser of either (1) the excess of the fair market value of the property immediately before the casualty minus the fair market value of the property immediately after the casualty, or (2) the amount of the adjusted basis of the property.

Limitations on Losses

Each personal casualty loss must be reduced by $100. The $100 reduction is applied per event, not per item damaged in an event. Where the recognized casualty losses exceed the recognized casualty gains, the annual casualty deduction is limited to the net casualty loss in excess of 10 percent of adjusted gross income. If the recognized casualty losses exceed the recognized casualty gains after reductions, all gains and losses are ordinary. Where the recognized gains exceed the recognized losses, each gain or loss is treated as a capital gain or loss. The $100 and 10 percent of adjusted gross income reductions apply separately to each individual taxpayer who sustains a loss, even though the property damaged or destroyed is owned by two or more individuals. However, a husband and wife filing a joint return are treated as one individual taxpayer. Business casualty losses are not subject to either the $100 or the 10 percent of AGI reductions.

EXAMPLE 8.31	Roberta Reynolds has $60,000 of adjusted gross income, a casualty loss of $8,500, and a casualty gain of $12,000. The casualty loss of $8,500 is reduced by $100 to $8,400 and netted against the $12,000 gain. The 10 percent of AGI reduction does not apply since a gain results from the netting. The $12,000 casualty gain is treated as a capital gain and the $8,400 casualty loss is treated as capital loss.

EXAMPLE 8.32	Ken Garrett has $40,000 of adjusted gross income, a $9,000 casualty loss after the $100 reduction, and a $3,000 casualty gain. The casualty loss deduction is limited to $2,000. The casualty loss must be reduced by the casualty gain and then reduced by 10 percent of adjusted gross income ($9,000 – $3,000 – $4,000).

If a loss is sustained in respect of property used partially for business and partially for nonbusiness purposes, the 10 percent and $100 reductions apply only to that portion of the loss properly attributable to the nonbusiness use.

Casualty losses are deductible in the year incurred. However, no portion of the casualty loss can be taken until it can be determined with reasonable certainty whether or not a reimbursement for the loss will be received. If a portion of the loss is not covered by a claim for reimbursement, then that portion of the loss is deductible in the year in which the casualty occurs.

EXAMPLE 8.33	Robert Rayer's personal use property having a basis of $20,000 and a fair market value of $23,000 is completely destroyed by fire in 2017. Robert has an insurance claim for $8,000, which is settled in 2018. He had adjusted gross income of $17,000 in 2017. Robert's 2017 loss equals $10,200 ($20,000 – $8,000 – $100 – $1,700 (10 percent of adjusted gross income)). The loss is deductible in 2017, the year incurred, because the loss can be ascertained with reasonable accuracy.

A taxpayer is not permitted to deduct a casualty loss for damage to insured property unless a timely insurance claim is filed. This rule applies to the extent that any insurance policy provides for full or partial reimbursement of the loss. The portion of the loss not covered by insurance (for example, a deductible) is not subject to this rule.

EXAMPLE 8.34	Tom Tower's automobile was damaged when Tom struck a tree during a snow storm. The damage amounted to $2,300. Rather than notify his automobile insurer because of fear of an increase in the cost of his insurance or cancellation of his policy, Tom paid for the repair costs. Except for the amount of his insurance deductible, Tom may not deduct any casualty loss because he failed to file an insurance claim.

Losses from Federally Declared Disasters

In order to accelerate tax refunds to taxpayers that have sustained a disaster loss, a taxpayer who has sustained a disaster loss may elect to deduct the loss for the tax year immediately preceding the year in which the loss actually occurred. This special provision applies only to disasters occurring in an area determined by the President of the United States to warrant assistance by the federal government. In addition, in federally declared disaster areas, taxpayers will never have to recognize gain on the receipt of insurance proceeds for personal property contained in personal residences.

If an election is made, the disaster is deemed to have occurred in the tax year immediately preceding the year in which the disaster actually occurred, and the loss deemed to have been sustained in the preceding tax year. An election to claim the disaster deduction must be made by filing a return, an amended return, or a claim for refund clearly showing that the election has been made.

¶8525   THEFT LOSSES

Any loss arising from theft is generally deductible in the year the taxpayer discovers the loss. However, if there is a reasonable prospect of reimbursement of the loss, no portion of the loss is deductible until the year in which it can be ascertained with reasonable certainty whether or not a reimbursement for the loss will be received.

The deductible amount of a theft loss is determined in the same manner as a casualty loss. The fair market value of the property immediately after the theft is considered to be zero. Theft losses of nonbusiness personal property are limited by the same $100 and 10 percent of adjusted gross income reductions that apply to casualty losses.

Miscellaneous Itemized Deductions

Miscellaneous itemized deductions include the following items: employee business expenses, job-seeking expenses, education expenses, investment expenses, wagering losses, and tax counsel and return preparer fees. Most miscellaneous itemized deductions, with some exceptions, are grouped together on a tax return and are deductible to the extent that the total of all of the miscellaneous items exceeds 2 percent of the taxpayer's adjusted gross income. All of these miscellaneous itemized deductions are discussed in more detail in the following sections.

¶8601   EMPLOYEE BUSINESS EXPENSES

The tax treatment of employee business expenses depends on whether the expenses are categorized as reimbursed expenses or nonreimbursed expenses. Business expenses incurred by an employee under a reimbursement arrangement with an employer are normally not shown on the tax return. Unreimbursed business expenses are deductible as miscellaneous itemized deductions, limited to amounts in excess of 2 percent of the taxpayer's adjusted gross income.

¶8603   REIMBURSED EMPLOYEE EXPENSES

The tax treatment of reimbursed expenses of employees depends on whether or not the employee makes an adequate accounting to the employer for the expenses. An adequate accounting by an employee to an employer would normally include filing an expense report listing time, place, and nature of an expense along with any supporting documentary evidence. Reg. §1.162-17(b)(4). Also, the reimbursement arrangement must not allow the employee to keep any excess reimbursement.

If an employee makes an adequate accounting to the employer and reimbursement equals expenses, neither the reimbursement nor the expenses have to be shown on the employee's tax return. If an employee makes an adequate accounting to the employer and expenses exceed reimbursement and the employee desires to deduct the excess expenses, all employee expenses and all reimbursement must be listed on the employee's tax return, with the excess unreimbursed expenses being deductible as miscellaneous itemized deductions subject to the 2 percent nondeductible floor.

EXAMPLE 8.35

Mary Turner incurs the following employee expenses which she submits to her employer for reimbursement under an adequate accounting reimbursement plan.

Travel expenses	$1,100
Transportation expenses	300
Entertainment expenses	600
Total expenses	$2,000

If Mary receives $2,000 in reimbursement from her employer, neither the expenses nor the reimbursement would have to be shown on her return. If Mary receives $1,400 in reimbursement from her employer, she would have to show the $2,000 of expenses and the $1,400 of reimbursement on her return in order to claim the $600 of excess employee expenses as an itemized deduction. The $600 deduction would be allocated proportionately to each type of expense incurred ($600/$2,000 = 30%). The allocation would be $330 to travel, $90 to transportation, and $180 to entertainment expenses. The $180 deduction for entertainment expenses would be subject to a 50 percent limitation, which would then put the entertainment deduction at $90. The total of the $330 travel, the $90 transportation and the $90 entertainment deductions would be subject to the 2 percent of AGI floor on miscellaneous itemized deductions.

If an employee does not make an adequate accounting to an employer, all employee expenses and any reimbursement would have to be listed on the employee's return. Reg. §1.162-17(b). Employee business expenses paid or incurred under "nonaccountable plans" are deductible by an employee only as miscellaneous itemized deductions subject to the 2 percent of AGI floor. "Nonaccountable plans" are arrangements that: (1) do not require the employee to substantiate the reimbursed expenses to the employer, or (2) permit the employee to retain amounts in excess of the substantiated expenses covered under the arrangement. Code Sec. 62(c); Temp. Reg. §1.62-1T(f).

¶8605 UNREIMBURSED EMPLOYEE EXPENSES

Unreimbursed employee expenses are allowed only as miscellaneous itemized deductions, and are only deductible to the extent they exceed 2 percent of adjusted gross income. Major categories of employee expenses, which, if unreimbursed, must be taken as itemized deductions subject to the 2 percent of AGI floor, include the following: transportation expenses, travel expenses, entertainment expenses, job-seeking expenses, and qualifying educational expenses.

Other allowable employee expenses (subject to the 2 percent of AGI limitation if the expenses are unreimbursed) include professional society dues, employment agency fees, cost of small tools and supplies needed on the job, subscriptions to professional journals, union dues, and work clothes and uniforms not suitable for everyday use. Transportation, travel, and entertainment expenses are discussed in Chapter 6. Job-seeking expenses, education expenses, and other miscellaneous itemized deductions are discussed in greater detail in the following sections of this chapter.

KEYSTONE PROBLEM

Ralph Unit incurs the following qualified employee (business) expenses:

Travel expenses (excluding meals)	$4,000
Meals	1,600
Transportation expenses	2,000
Entertainment expenses	2,400
Total expenses	$10,000

What amounts of the above employee (business) expenses are deductible for AGI on Ralph's tax return and what amounts are deductible from AGI as itemized deductions based on each of the following assumptions? (Treat each assumption independently from the other assumptions.)

Assumption 1: Ralph is self-employed.

Assumption 2: Ralph is a business executive and receives reimbursement of $8,000 from his employer for these expenses under an adequate accounting reimbursement plan.

¶8655 JOB-SEEKING EXPENSES

Job-seeking expenses incurred by an individual are deductible for tax purposes if the individual is employed in a particular trade or business and is looking for work in the same trade or business (e.g., a teacher looking for work as a teacher, an accountant looking for work as an accountant, etc.) Rev. Rul. 75-120, 1975-1 CB 55, clarified by Rev. Rul. 77-16, 1977-1 CB 37. Job-seeking expenses include travel and transportation expenses incurred while going to and from different job locations, expenses of preparing a resume, mailing expenses, and employment agency fees. If deductible, job-seeking expenses are deductible from AGI as miscellaneous itemized deductions subject to the 2 percent of AGI floor.

Job-seeking expenses are deductible by an individual looking for work in the same trade or business regardless of whether or not the individual is successful in finding a job. Job-seeking expenses are not deductible if the individual is looking for work in a new trade or business or if the expenses relate to the individual's first job. If an individual is unemployed when incurring the job seeking expenses, the expenses are deductible if the individual is looking for work in the same trade or business in which the individual was employed prior to unemployment.

EXAMPLE 8.36

Larry Kemp, a high school business teacher in Michigan, is looking for a high school teaching position in another state. He incurs travel expenses, employment agency fees, and some other miscellaneous expenses in his search for a new position. Larry eventually finds a teaching position in Iowa. Larry's job-seeking expenses are deductible since he was looking for work in the same trade or business. Even if Larry had been unsuccessful in finding a new job, the expenses would have been deductible since he was looking for work in the same trade or business.

If, instead, Larry was planning to leave the teaching profession and was looking for work as a public accountant, none of his job-seeking expenses would have been deductible since he was looking for work in a new trade or business. This is true regardless of whether Larry was successful or unsuccessful in finding a job as a public accountant.

If an individual combines job-seeking trips in the same trade or business with other personal activities, such as vacationing, the travel and transportation costs incurred on the trip are deductible only if the primary purpose of the trip was to seek new employment. Rev. Rul. 75-120, 1975-1 CB 55. If the purpose of the trip was primarily personal in nature, only the actual expenses incurred at the destination in seeking new employment are deductible for tax purposes.

¶8665 EDUCATION EXPENSES

Education expenses incurred by an individual taxpayer for continuing professional education and vocational education courses, professional development courses, and, in some instances, college degree programs are deductible for tax purposes if certain requirements are met. Education expenses are deductible by an individual taxpayer if incurred (1) to maintain or improve skills required in a present job or (2) to meet expressed requirements of an employer or applicable law to retain an employment position or rate of compensation. Reg. §1.162-5(a). However, even though either of these two requirements are met, education expenses are not deductible if they are personal expenditures. The two categories of nondeductible education expenses are those that (1) are required of the individual in order to meet the *minimum education* requirements for qualification in present employment, trade, or business or (2) qualify the individual for a *new trade or business.*

For tax years through 2016, taxpayers can claim an "above the line" deduction (a deduction for AGI for qualified education expenses. Code Sec. 222. The maximum deduction is $4,000. Single taxpayers with adjusted gross income below $65,000 ($130,000 for married filing jointly) can claim the deduction. Taxpayers whose adjusted gross income falls between $65,000 and $80,000 ($130,000 and $160,000 for joint filers) may deduct $2,000. Married individuals filing a separate return are not eligible for this deduction. The tuition deduction cannot be taken in the same year as an American Opportunity Tax Credit or Lifetime Learning Credit for the same student. See ¶9031.

Maintaining or Improving Skills

Education expenses incurred by an individual taxpayer to maintain or improve skills required in a present job such as a business executive taking a continuing education course in management techniques normally are deductible for tax purposes by the taxpayer. If education expenses incurred by an individual to maintain or improve existing skills also qualify the individual for a new trade or business, the education expenses are not deductible for tax purposes.

EXAMPLE 8.37

Joan Mackey, a business executive, takes a three-day continuing professional education management course entitled "Advanced Management Techniques" which is relevant to her current management position. The $2,400 cost of the course is paid by Joan from her personal funds and is not reimbursed by her employer. The $2,400 payment is deductible on Joan's tax return as an education expense deduction. Joan is also attending law school at the present time and plans to get a law degree since knowledge of legal affairs will be of considerable help to her in her present management position. Joan is paying the cost of law school from her personal funds. The costs associated with attending law school are not deductible by Joan as education expenses since a law degree will qualify her for a new trade or business. It does not matter that knowledge of legal affairs will help Joan in her present management position.

Employer Requirements or Minimum Standards

Education expenses incurred by an individual taxpayer to meet expressed requirements of an employer or applicable law to retain an employment position or rate of compensation normally are deductible for tax purposes. If the education expenses are incurred, however, to meet minimum education standards for qualification in the individual taxpayer's existing trade or business, the expenses are not deductible.

EXAMPLE 8.38

The Trotwood School System normally requires that all school teachers have, as a minimum, a bachelor's degree in education before they can teach in the school system. An exception to this rule is made for Jane Prim, who is hired in her senior year of college. Education expenses incurred by Jane to finish her senior year of college are not deductible on her individual income tax return since they are incurred to meet minimum education standards for qualification in Jane's trade or business which is teaching.

One year after Jane receives her bachelor's degree in education, the Trotwood school board adopts a requirement that all teachers in the school system must have a master's degree in education within six years in order to continue to teach in the system. If Jane decides to pursue her master's degree in education, the education expenses related to the degree are deductible on Jane's individual income tax return since Jane would incur the expenses in attempting to meet expressed requirements of her employer to retain her employment position.

New Trade or Business

Normally, education expenses incurred by an individual taxpayer to obtain a bachelor's degree are not deductible since the degree either is needed to meet minimum education requirements for the job the college graduate takes after graduation or qualifies the graduate for a new trade or business. Education expenses incurred by an individual relating to a master's degree may or may not be deductible depending on whether the degree qualifies the recipient for a new trade or business. For such expenses to be deductible, the individual usually has to establish a connection between the courses taken and the taxpayer's present business position. If the master's degree qualifies the individual for a new trade or business, education expenses incurred while working on the degree are not deductible even if there is a connection between the courses taken and the person's present position. Education expenses incurred when working on professional degrees such as the M.D. degree and J.D. degree normally are not deductible by an individual since, in each instance, the degree qualifies the individual for a new trade or business.

A review of all surrounding facts should be made in deciding whether certain education expenditures have qualified an individual for a new trade or business. A change in duties such as an elementary school teacher taking courses to become a high school teacher is not considered to be a new trade or business. Reg. §1.162-5(b)(3). Education expenses related to bar exam review courses and CPA review courses have been considered to be nondeductible since they prepare an individual for a new trade or business. Rev. Rul. 69-292, 1969-1 CB 84.

Classification of Education Expenses

Deductible education expenses include tuition, books, other miscellaneous education expenses, and any related travel and transportation costs. Transportation costs include the costs of going from a work location to school for a night school student. If an individual taxpayer is self-employed, all deductible education expenses are deductible for AGI. If the taxpayer is an employee, all deductible education expenses (except for qualified higher education expenses) are deductible from AGI as miscellaneous itemized deductions, subject to the 2 percent floor. Reg. §1.162-6.

¶8675   WORK CLOTHES AND UNIFORMS

Taxpayers generally may not deduct the cost and upkeep of work clothing. Taxpayers may deduct the cost and upkeep of special equipment or work clothes only if they are required as a condition of employment and are not suitable for everyday use. Both conditions must be met to qualify such expenses as miscellaneous itemized deductions, subject to the 2 percent of AGI limitation.

The cost of uniforms that must be worn by ballplayers, fire fighters, police officers, letter carriers, nurses, jockeys, and civilian faculty members of a military school is deductible. Generally, the cost of uniforms of full-time active duty personnel in the armed forces is not deductible.

¶8680

TAX COUNSEL AND RETURN PREPARER FEES

Expenses paid or incurred by an individual in connection with the determination, collection, or refund of any tax are deductible. The deduction is allowed whether the taxing authority is federal, state, or municipal, and whether the tax is income, estate, gift, property, or any other tax. Thus, expenses paid or incurred by a taxpayer for tax counsel or expenses paid or incurred in connection with the preparation of returns or in connection with any proceedings involved in determining the extent of the tax liability or in contesting a tax liability are deductible as miscellaneous itemized deductions, subject to the 2 percent floor.

Investment Expenses

Deductions for investment expenses are allowed if the expenses are incurred for the production or collection of income or for the management, conservation, or maintenance of property held for the production of income. To be deductible, investment expenses must be ordinary and necessary, must be reasonable in amount, cannot be capital expenditures, cannot relate to the generation of tax-exempt income, and cannot frustrate public policy.

Most investment expenses are categorized as miscellaneous itemized deductions and are deductible by individuals only if the aggregate amount of miscellaneous itemized deductions exceeds 2 percent of the taxpayer's adjusted gross income. Code Sec. 67(a). One exception is deductions attributable to property held for the production of rents or royalties, which are deductible for adjusted gross income. Code Sec. 62(a)(4).

In this section the following investment expense deductions are reviewed: rent and royalty expenses and miscellaneous investment expenses.

¶8701

RENT AND ROYALTY EXPENSES

Rents and royalties are closely related for tax purposes. Rents generally involve payments for the use of land, buildings, and other tangible property whereas royalties usually involve payments for copyrights, patents, and oil, gas, or mineral property. Rental income and expenses are normally treated as related to investment property if only minimal services are provided to the tenants. "Minimal service" usually means that service is limited, for instance, to providing heat, light, and trash pickup. If additional services (such as maid services) are provided to tenants, rental income and expenses may have to be considered as business income and expenses. If royalty income and expenses are derived from royalty property where the taxpayer has an operating interest or if the taxpayer is self-employed and created the royalty property, such as a writer with a copyright on a book, royalty income and expenses are trade or business income and expenses instead of investment income and expenses.

All rent and royalty expenses are deductible for AGI. Code Sec. 62(a)(4). Normal rent and royalty expenses include depreciation, depletion, repairs and maintenance expenditures, insurance, interest, taxes, and other items. If one piece of property is part rental property and part personal property, expenses must be allocated between the investment portion of the property and the personal portion with only the investment portion of the expenses being deductible for tax purposes.

¶8745

MISCELLANEOUS INVESTMENT EXPENSES

Typical investment expenses which are deductible under Code Sec. 212 were mentioned previously in Chapter 6. These included safe deposit box rentals, rent and royalty expenses, investment counseling fees, subscriptions to investment-related journals, newspapers, and other publications, investment custodial fees, legal and accounting fees related to investments, investment interest expense subject to limitations previously discussed, investment-related clerical fees, and investment-related office rents. Expenses of attending conventions, seminars, or similar meetings for investment purposes, however, are not deductible for tax purposes.

Investment-related expenses allowed under Code Sec. 212 are deductible from adjusted gross income as miscellaneous itemized deductions, subject to the 2 percent of AGI limitation. Rent and royalty expenses, however, are an exception and are deductible for adjusted gross income.

Other Miscellaneous Expenses

A small group of miscellaneous expenses is not subject to the 2% of AGI floor. These expenses include gambling losses to the extent of gambling winnings, certain casualty and theft losses related to income-producing property, federal estate tax on income in respect of a decedent, and the unrecovered investment in an annuity at the taxpayer's death.

¶8775   WAGERING LOSSES

Losses sustained during the year on wagering transactions are allowed as an itemized deduction but only to the extent of the gains during the year from wagering. In the case of a husband and wife filing a joint return, the combined wagering losses of the spouses are allowed to the extent of the combined wagering gains. Code Sec. 165(d).

The Supreme Court has ruled that a professional gambler is entitled to deduct gambling losses as a trade or business expense. The fact that the taxpayer did not offer goods or services to others did not preclude characterization of the activities as a trade or business, rather, the appropriate "business" test was that the taxpayer must be involved in the activity with continuity and regularity and the taxpayer's primary purpose for engaging in the activity must be for income or profit. *R.P. Groetzinger,* 87-1 USTC ¶9191 480 U.S. 23, 107 S.Ct. 980 (1987), aff'g 85-2 USTC ¶9622, 771 F.2d 269 (CA-7 1985).

Thus, if gambling is conducted as a business, any wagering losses are deductible as business losses, but only to the extent of wagering gains. However, the deduction of a professional gambler's non-wagering business expenses, such as transportation, meals and lodging, are not limited by wagering gains. *Mayo,* 136 TC — No. 4, Dec. 58,524 (2011); Action on Decision 2011-006. Losses of nonprofessional gamblers are nonbusiness losses and are deductible (to the extent of gains) only if itemized on Schedule A of Form 1040. They are not subject to the 2 percent floor on miscellaneous itemized deductions.

¶8785   UNRECOVERED INVESTMENT IN ANNUITY

A taxpayer who contributes after-tax amounts to the cost of an annuity can exclude from income a part of each annuity payment received as a tax-free return of the cost of the annuity. If the taxpayer dies before the entire cost of the annuity is recovered tax-free, any unrecovered cost of the annuity can be deducted as a miscellaneous deduction on the taxpayer's final tax return, not subject to the 2 percent floor.

SUMMARY

- Personal expenditures are generally disallowed as deductions on the tax return. However, certain personal expenses, as listed in the Internal Revenue Code, are specifically allowed as itemized deductions. These deductions are taken on Schedule A of Form 1040. Itemized deductions are beneficial to a taxpayer only if the total of the itemized deductions exceeds the standard deduction.

- Only medical expenses actually paid during the year are allowed as an itemized deduction. The total of the allowable medical expenses must be reduced by 10 percent of adjusted gross income. Medical expenses must be for the medical care of the taxpayer, spouse, or a dependent of the taxpayer.

- State, local, and foreign property taxes, income taxes, and sales taxes make up the taxes category of itemized deductions. Federal income, estate, gift, and Social Security taxes imposed on the taxpayer are not deductible.

- Certain interest paid or accrued on indebtedness qualifies as a deduction in computing taxable income. Prepaid interest is not deductible when paid but must be allocated to the periods for which it represents the cost of borrowing funds. Interest expense incurred to purchase tax-exempt income-producing assets is not deductible.

- Charitable contributions must be made to qualified organizations in order to qualify for the deduction. Only contributions made during the year are deductible. There are limits imposed on charitable contributions equal to 50 percent, 30 percent, and 20 percent of adjusted gross income, depending on the type of property given and the charity to which it is given.

- Certain personal casualty and theft losses may qualify as itemized deductions. Generally, the loss is equal to the smaller of the reduction in fair market value or the basis of the asset, reduced by (1) insurance proceeds, (2) $100 for each casualty, and (3) 10 percent of adjusted gross income.

- Most miscellaneous itemized deductions are deductible only to the extent they exceed 2 percent of adjusted gross income. However, some miscellaneous itemized deductions (such as wagering losses) are not subject to the 2 percent floor.

QUESTIONS

1. What limits are imposed on the medical expense deduction?

2. When are capital expenditures incurred for medical reasons deductible?

3. When is the cost of transportation deductible as a medical expense?

4. Harry and Mary Holmes had the following health expenses. Which expenses are deductible as medical expenses?
   a. Nonprescription vitamins for Harry
   b. Trip to Florida for general health reasons
   c. Trip to Hawaii for specialized surgery only performed by one doctor located in Hawaii
   d. Crutch rental for period after surgery
   e. Cost of transportation to and from doctor

5. Ron and Judy Rupert have the following health expenses. Which expenses are deductible as medical expenses?
   a. Toothpaste and dental floss for cavity prevention
   b. Acupuncture treatments for Ron
   c. Medical insurance premiums
   d. Contact lenses for Judy
   e. Cosmetic surgery (liposuction operation) for Judy

6. What criteria must be met for personal property taxes to qualify as an itemized deduction?

7. When is a refund of a state or local income tax reported as income?

8. Which of the following taxes are deductible for federal income tax purposes as an itemized deduction?
   a. Ad valorem personal property tax
   b. FICA tax imposed on employees
   c. Federal gift tax
   d. Sales taxes imposed on purchase of living room furniture

9. Which of the following taxes are deductible for federal income tax purposes as an itemized deduction?
   a. Federal income tax
   b. Federal gasoline tax
   c. State income tax
   d. Excise tax imposed on cigarettes

10. What items are included in "net investment income" for purposes of the investment interest limitation?

11. What special rules apply to prepaid interest?

12. Briefly describe the two major categories of qualified charitable organizations for tax purposes.

13. Distinguish between private operating foundations and private nonoperating foundations.

14. Dana Davenport donates eight hours of her time on a Saturday to help out a qualified charity. What is her charitable deduction?

15. If an asset is given to a charitable organization and the asset is sold, what is the effect on the charitable contribution deduction?

16. What happens to any unused charitable contributions?

17. When is the taxpayer required to attach an appraisal of a charitable contribution to his or her return?

18. What is the definition of a casualty loss?

19. When is a theft loss deductible?

20. In order for employee expenses to be deductible for tax purposes, what basic requirement(s) must be met?

21. What are nonaccountable employee reimbursement plans?

22. What conditions must be present before an individual taxpayer can deduct job seeking expenses? What types of expenditures are included in job seeking expenses for tax purposes?

23. Under what conditions would education expenses be deductible for tax purposes by an individual taxpayer?

PROBLEMS

24. Oliver Olms pays all of his father's medical expenses for the year, which total $8,800. Oliver also pays over half of his father's support but is unable to claim his father as a dependent because his father has $6,000 in gross income. Will Oliver be able to claim the $8,800 as a medical expense deduction on his individual income tax return?

25. You have a heart ailment. On the advice of your doctor, you install an elevator in your home so you will not have to climb the stairs. It costs $15,000 to install the elevator. The elevator has a 20-year life and increases the fair market value of your home by $3,000. What is the medical deduction for the elevator assuming the 10 percent limitation has been met?

26. Tom and Shannon Shores, both age 40, filed a joint return and paid the following medical expenses:

Hospital costs	$3,200
Doctor's bills	1,600
Medicine and drugs	800
Hospitalization insurance premiums	4,000

In addition, they incurred the following medical expenses for Tom's mother who is totally dependent upon and lives with Tom and Shannon:

Cosmetic surgery (face-lift operation)	$5,400
Doctor's bills	2,600
Medicines and drugs	1,000

They live 10 miles from the medical center and made 20 trips there for doctor office visits and hospital stays this year. Tom and Shannon's adjusted gross income is $85,000. What is Tom and Shannon's medical expense deduction for this year?

27. Assume the same facts as in Problem 26, except that the insurance company reimbursed Tom and Shannon $4,100 of their hospital and doctor's bills. Determine the medical expense deduction.

28. Blake sold a house to Miranda on July 1. Blake paid the entire calendar-year property taxes of $4,380 on June 1. How much will each of them be entitled to deduct for the year?

29. Carlos Diego paid the following expenses during 2017:

State sales tax	$600
Sales tax on purchase of automobile	800
License plate "tax" based on weight of vehicles	35
State income tax paid	6,000
Federal income tax paid	16,000

What is Carlos's tax expense deduction for 2017?

30. During the following years Adolpho T. (single) had (1) withheld, (2) paid (by check – presumably estimated tax payments or paid with the extension) and (3) received a refund of the following amounts for state income tax purposes:

	2017	2018
Withheld	$2,500	$3,000
Paid by check	$1,200	$1,400
Refund	$800	$1,600

The refunds were all of amounts "paid" (withheld and paid by check) in the prior year. Adolpho's total itemized deductions in 2017 were $8,100. What is Adolpho's state income tax deduction for each year, and his income from the refund in 2018? What would his income from the 2018 refund be if it was $2,000, rather than $1,600?

31. In 2017, Sally Morris, a single taxpayer, pays $3,000 of interest on qualified student loans. Her AGI is $40,000. What is her qualified student loan interest deduction in 2017?

32. Assume the same facts as in Problem 31, except that Sally has AGI of $70,000. What is her qualified student loan interest deduction in 2017?

33. The interest paid on Josephine Young's personal residence for the year 2017 totals $4,800; the interest paid on her personal credit card is $80; the interest paid on a note to the National Bank (¾ of which was used to buy state and municipal bonds, the rest to buy stock) is $1,000. If she has interest income of $2,000, what is Josephine's total interest deduction for the year?

34. Mike and Sally Card file a joint return for the 2017 tax year. Their adjusted gross income is $65,000 and they incur the following interest expenses:

Qualified education loans	$3,500
Personal loan	1,000
Home mortgage loan	4,000
Loan used to purchase a variety of stocks, bonds, and securities	15,000

Investment income and related expenses amount to $7,000 and $500, respectively. What is Mike and Sally's interest deduction for the 2017 tax year?

35. Greg Grove pays $15,000 interest in 2017 on a home equity loan with an interest rate of 10 percent and an average balance of $150,000 during the year. His equity (fair market value minus acquisition debt) in his house is $180,000. How much of this interest is deductible on Greg's tax return for 2017?

36. Matilda Moore has $21,000 of investment interest expense and $7,000 of net investment income in 2017. How much of the investment interest expense is deductible for tax purposes in 2017?

37. On December 1, Raphael Renoir borrows $20,000 from the bank on a 15 percent, one-year business loan. Raphael prepays the interest of $3,000 at the time of the loan. What is the interest deduction allowed Raphael, assuming he is a cash basis, calendar year taxpayer? What would your answer be if, instead of prepaying the $3,000 interest, it was deducted from the loan proceeds?

38. On December 1 Bernie took out a 15-year loan for $300,000. He paid 2% in "points" in order to get the loan, or $6,000. This is essentially prepaid interest. If the loan is used to purchase his principal residence, what is the maximum he can deduct in the current year? If the loan is used to purchase a home he will use as a rental property, what is the maximum he can deduct?

39. Frank Freshman mailed a check for $200 on December 30, 2017, in part payment of a $350 pledge he made to State University on November 1. The University did not deposit the check until January 3, 2018. What is the amount of the charitable contribution deduction allowed Frank for 2017?

40. Mark Moody has adjusted gross income of $50,000 for the year. During the year, he gave his church $3,000 cash and land having a fair market value of $40,000 and a basis of $20,000. The land was held long-term. A contribution of $8,000 in cash was also made to a private charity. How much may be deducted as contributions if Mark does not elect to reduce the fair market value by the appreciation in value of the land donated? How much is the charitable contributions carryover?

41. Elmore Eisner made the following contributions during the current tax year:

Cash to United Way	$5,000
Land to Boy Scouts to be used as a summer camp:	
Cost	20,000
Fair market value	30,000
Painting to a 20 percent charity for permanent display in foundation's public gallery:	
Cost	5,000
Fair market value	7,000
Cash to individual needy families around town	3,000

   a. Assuming Elmore's adjusted gross income is $80,000, what is his charitable contribution deduction for the year and carryover?
   b. What is the charitable contribution and carryover if the cost and fair market value of the painting are $25,000 and $27,000, respectively?

42. In each of the following independent cases determine the amount of charitable contributions allowed the individual before consideration of any percentage limitations.
   a. Charlie Chubbs contributed an item of inventory from his sole proprietorship to a public charity for its use. The fair market value of the asset was $800 and his basis was $600.
   b. Durwood Dodson contributed some shares of common stock that he had held long-term to a private charity. The basis of the stock was $8,000 and it had a fair market value of $7,000.
   c. Esther Ensign contributed tangible personal property that she had held long-term to a public charity. The asset had a fair market value of $10,000 and a basis of $6,000. The charity intended to sell the asset and use the proceeds for charitable purposes.

43. Ralph Reeves gave some stock that he owned to charity. The stock had a FMV of $40,000 and a basis of $32,000. His adjusted gross income is $100,000. Determine the allowed charitable contribution deduction and carryover under the following assumptions:
   a. Given to a public charity, no election
   b. Given to a public charity, elects the reduced contribution election
   c. Given to private charity
   d. Qualified appreciated stock given to private charity

44. Jackson Jumper has owned a beach house at Padre Island for the last 20 years. In 2017, while swimming in the surf at Padre one afternoon, someone stole his billfold (containing $150 cash), his wristwatch (cost $250; FMV $200) and, worst of all, his ice chest full of beer (cost = FMV = $75). As if that were not enough, later that day his beach house was completely destroyed by fire. His adjusted basis in the house was $200,000 but the FMV was $270,000 because of the resort areas developing around his property. The house was insured for only $170,000. What is Jackson's casualty and theft loss for the year assuming a $100,000 adjusted gross income?

45. Billy Pilgrim owned a car which he used two-thirds for business and one-third for personal use. The car had cost $18,000 and he had taken $6,000 depreciation on the business-use portion of the car. He was involved in a wreck for which repairs for the damage to the car amounted to $3,600. He had no insurance. What is Billy's casualty loss for the current tax year assuming a $15,000 adjusted gross income?

46. In 2017, Pablo Pacheco was involved in an auto collision which totally destroyed his new car. He sued the other driver for damages and his lawyer was confident of relief. The FMV of the car immediately before the accident was $24,000. In 2018, the other driver died penniless, but up to that date Pablo has received only $1,000 of the damage award. What is Pablo's casualty loss for each year, assuming his adjusted gross income each year is $50,000?

47. For 2017, Sam Simpson was involved in a collision while driving his automobile. The automobile, which originally cost $16,000 and was used solely for his personal use, had an appraised value of $7,200 for trade-in purposes just before the accident. After the collision, the car was traded in on a new car, but the trade-in value was only $1,300. Assuming that Sam has adjusted gross income of $30,000 and carried no collision insurance, what amount can he deduct as a net casualty loss for the year?

48. In 2017, Peter Carlson incurs the following qualified employee expenses, which he submits to his employer for reimbursement under an adequate accounting reimbursement plan.

Travel expenses	$2,400
Meal and entertainment expenses (100 percent of cost)	1,200
Total expenses	$3,600

   How would these employee expenses and reimbursement be treated on Peter's individual tax return if he receives the following reimbursement from his employer?
   a. $3,000
   b. $3,600

49. Kathleen incurs $2,000 of travel expenses looking for a job. Her AGI is $50,000. How would she treat these expenses if she is a graduating student looking for her first job? What if she is an accountant looking for a different accounting position? What if she is in sales, but would like to find a job in information systems?

50. Kearney Kramer donated to his church stock which he had held for five months. The stock had a fair market value of $1,000 at the time of the gift, but had only cost Kearney $700. What is the amount deductible as a charitable contribution?
   a. $1,000
   b. $880
   c. $700
   d. $300
   e. None of the above

51. Which of the following unreimbursed employee expenses is deductible for adjusted gross income?
   a. Transportation expenses
   b. Union dues
   c. Travel expenses
   d. None of the above

52. If an employee does not make an adequate accounting to the employer and employer reimbursement of employee expenses exceeds the expenses, the employee business expenses are:
   a. Not shown on the employee's tax return
   b. Shown as miscellaneous itemized deductions subject to the 2 percent nondeductible floor
   c. Shown as miscellaneous itemized deductions not subject to the 2 percent nondeductible floor
   d. None of the above

53. If an employee makes an adequate accounting to the employer and employer reimbursement of employee expenses is less than the expenses, the excess expenses are:
   a. Not deductible on the employee's tax return
   b. Deductible as miscellaneous itemized deductions subject to the 2 percent nondeductible floor
   c. Deductible as miscellaneous itemized deductions not subject to the 2 percent nondeductible floor
   d. None of the above

54. **Comprehensive Problem.** Andy and Marcia Tufts, both age 35, are married with two dependent children and file a joint return. Assume the children do not qualify for the child tax credit (Ch. 9). From the following information, compute their tax owed or refund due for 2017.

Andy's salary	$50,000
Federal income tax withheld	4,000
Marcia's salary	42,000
Federal income tax withheld	3,500
Andy's contribution to an IRA (assume IRA is deductible for AGI)	2,000
Dividends received from domestic corporations	950
Medical expenses for doctors and hospitals	8,200
Premiums for health insurance	2,600
Prescription drugs and medicines	800
Eyeglasses for one of the children	175
Interest on home mortgage	7,800
Interest on credit cards	300
Real property taxes on residence	2,300
State income taxes	2,800
Fee for preparation of tax returns	125
Union dues and subscriptions	480

55. **Comprehensive Problem.** Larry Johnson, 45 and single, has the following income and deductions in 2017. Using the tax rate schedules rather than the tax tables, compute Larry's tax owed or refund due for 2017. Assume dividends are not qualified.

Salary	$50,000
Interest income	3,200
Dividends	800
Medical Expenses	6,150
Property Taxes on Personal Residence	3,600
Interest on Home Mortgage	7,600
State and Local Income Taxes	2,400
State and Local Sales Taxes	2,000
Investment Interest Expense	5,000

In addition, Larry's car (value = $15,000, cost = $20,000) was stolen during the year, and the insurance reimbursement was only $7,000. He also had $2,000 of travel expenses related to his job that were not reimbursed and $3,000 of federal income tax withheld from his salary.

He elects to treat his dividends as net investment income, so they are not subject to the special long-term capital gains tax rates.

56. **Research Problem.** Mary Sage's daughter has a serious medical problem. Mary, 36, must take her daughter to a distant city to be treated. Mary and her daughter stay for seven days to receive treatment. Mary incurs $1,000 in transportation costs, $800 in motel costs, and $240 for meals. What amount is deductible as a medical expense deduction before the 10 percent limitation?

57. **Research Problem.** The following selected court cases have helped to shape the tax law in regard to travel expense deductions. Read the following cases and prepare a brief written abstract for each case.
    a. *Burns v. Gray,* 61-1 USTC ¶9294, 287 F.2d 698 (CA-6 1961).
    b. *R. Rosenspan,* 71-1 USTC ¶9241, 438 F.2d 905 (CA-2 1971), cert. denied, 404 U.S. 864, 92 S.Ct. 54.
    c. *H.A. Stidger,* 67-1 USTC ¶9309, 386 U.S. 287, 87 S.Ct. 1065 (1967).

Chapter

9

Tax Credits, Prepayments, and Alternative Minimum Tax

OBJECTIVES

After completing Chapter 9, you should be able to:

1. Understand tax credits, both nonrefundable and refundable.
2. Compute estimated tax payments.
3. Apply the alternative minimum tax rules to individual taxpayers.

OVERVIEW

After completing this chapter, a student should be able to distinguish between the various types of tax credits available to taxpayers and to determine which credits represent a reduction of the income tax, which credits represent a return of a taxpayer overpayment of other types of taxes, and which credits can be used in other years if not fully used in the present year. This chapter will also provide tax planning hints on avoiding the alternative minimum tax provisions.

Nonrefundable Tax Credits

¶9001 ## TYPES OF CREDITS

A tax credit is a direct reduction of the tax due. It differs from a deduction which is a reduction in income subject to tax. For this reason, a credit is more valuable than the same amount of deduction. For example, a tax credit of $100 saves $100 in tax; a deduction of $100 saves $25 of tax for a taxpayer in the 25 percent marginal tax bracket and $15 for a taxpayer in the 15 percent marginal tax bracket.

Credits are divided into two types: (1) nonrefundable and (2) refundable. In the case of nonrefundable credits, there have been no payments to the government and therefore a taxpayer cannot obtain a refund of a credit if the credit exceeds the gross tax. Nonrefundable credits cannot be used to offset the recapture of any other credit or to offset taxes other than the income tax.

With the exceptions of the credit for earned income and the child tax credit, refundable credits are prepayments. Refundable credits can be offset against the recapture of other credits and against other taxes.

The credits must be computed in the order in which they are presented to insure that any limitations are properly applied. The limitations are stated in terms of the gross tax reduced by previously computed credits.

¶9015 ## HOUSEHOLD AND DEPENDENT CARE CREDIT

A credit is allowed up to 35 percent of employment-related expenses for care of qualifying individuals. Job-related expenses are allowed up to $3,000 (maximum $1,050 credit) for one individual and up to $6,000 (maximum $2,100 credit) for two or more individuals. The credit is reduced by one percentage point for each $2,000 of adjusted gross income, or fraction thereof, above $15,000. Code Sec. 21(a)(2) and (c). The credit is not reduced below 20 percent. Thus, taxpayers with adjusted gross income of over $43,000 will have a credit of 20 percent.

Adjusted Gross Income		Applicable Percentage	Credit Limitation	
			One Person	Two or More Persons
$0 to	$15,000	35%	$1,050	$2,100
15,001 to	17,000	34	1,020	2,040
17,001 to	19,000	33	990	1,980
19,001 to	21,000	32	960	1,920
21,001 to	23,000	31	930	1,860
23,001 to	25,000	30	900	1,800
25,001 to	27,000	29	870	1,740
27,001 to	29,000	28	840	1,680
29,001 to	31,000	27	810	1,620
31,001 to	33,000	26	780	1,560
33,001 to	35,000	25	750	1,500
35,001 to	37,000	24	720	1,440
37,001 to	39,000	23	690	1,380
39,001 to	41,000	22	660	1,320
41,001 to	43,000	21	630	1,260
43,001 and above		20	600	1,200

Employment-related expenses are those expenses paid for household and personal care of qualifying individuals which are necessary for the taxpayer to be gainfully employed or in active search for gainful employment. Code Sec. 21(b)(2); Reg. §1.44A-1(c)(1). Gainful employment includes working for others, either full time or part time, or employment in one's own business or partnership. Volunteer work for a nominal salary does not constitute gainful employment.

If the taxpayer is not employed or actively seeking employment during any part of the year, expenses allocable to that part of the year are not considered for the credit. Thus, for example, a teacher who does not teach during the summer months could not use child care expenses incurred during the summer in computing the credit.

¶9015

The maximum expenses eligible for the credit must be reduced by amounts excludable from income under an employer-provided dependent care assistance program. The name, address, and the taxpayer identification number of the person providing the dependent care must be shown on the return of the taxpayer receiving the credit.

A "qualifying individual" is a dependent under age 13; a dependent of the taxpayer who is physically or mentally incapable of caring for himself or herself and who has the same principal place of abode as the taxpayer for more than one-half of the year; or the spouse of the taxpayer, if the spouse is physically or mentally incapable of caring for himself or herself and who has the same principal place of abode as the taxpayer for more than one-half of the year. Code Sec. 21(b)(1). The uniform definition of dependent for the dependency exemption is used for the dependent care credit. An individual is not treated as having the same principal place of abode of the taxpayer if at any time during the year the relationship between the individual and the taxpayer is in violation of local law. Code Sec. 21(e)(1).

The credit is available to a divorced or separated parent who has custody of a child who is under age 13 or who is physically or mentally incapable of self-care, even though the parent may not be entitled to a dependency exemption under the terms of a divorce decree or settlement agreement. Code Sec. 21(e)(5). The child will not be a qualifying individual for the other parent.

Only employment-related expenses qualify for the credit. These include ordinary and necessary household services to maintain a home. Any taxes required to be paid for FICA and federal unemployment or similar state payroll taxes on wages paid to an individual for providing household and personal care that constitutes employment are considered to be employment-related expenses. Disabled dependent or spouse care expenses for services performed outside the taxpayer's home are includible only if the disabled spouse or disabled dependent regularly spent at least eight hours a day in the taxpayer's home. Child care expenses are not confined to services performed within the taxpayer's home and include those for household services, day care centers, nursery school, and kindergarten. Expenditures for services provided by a dependent care center not in compliance with state or local regulations are not eligible for this credit. Expenses incurred to send a dependent to an overnight camp may not be claimed. Code Sec. 21(b)(2). No credit is allowed for any amounts paid to an individual for which the taxpayer is allowed a personal exemption deduction or who is a child of the taxpayer and has not reached the age of 19 at the close of the tax year. Code Sec. 21(e)(6).

Employment-related expenses cannot exceed the earned income of a single taxpayer. In the case of married taxpayers, expenses are limited to the earned income of the spouse with the lower income. Code Sec. 21(d)(1).

EXAMPLE 9.1

> Bob and Linda are married taxpayers filing a joint return with two dependents. They incurred $7,200 of employment-related child care expenses. Linda worked part time and had earnings of $5,400. Bob had earnings of $40,000. Since Linda's income was less than the amount of the employment-related expenses, the credit was based on her earnings. Since their adjusted gross income exceeds $43,000, the credit is reduced to 20 percent. The credit would be $1,080 ($5,400 × 20%).

In case of married taxpayers where, for any month, one spouse is either a full-time student at an educational institution or incapable of self-care, that spouse will be considered to have earned income of $250 per month if there is one qualifying individual in the household, and $500 per month if there are two or more qualifying individuals. Code Sec. 21(d)(2). If both spouses are students or are incapable of self-care, this rule applies to only one spouse for any one month. The $250 and $500 figures are used only in computing the lower income of the two spouses and are not included in the income of the taxpayers.

Married couples must file a joint return to claim the credit. The taxpayer who (1) has not lived with the other spouse for over six months at the end of the year, (2) lives with a qualifying dependent, and (3) provides over one-half of the cost of maintaining the household will be considered as single for the purpose of this credit. Code Sec. 21(e)(2) and (4). The taxpayer will not have to take the other spouse's income into consideration or file a joint return. There is no carryover of any unused household and dependent care credit.

¶9025 ELDERLY AND DISABLED PERSONS CREDIT

An important tax benefit for the elderly is the retirement income credit. This provision was added in 1954 because of concern that persons receiving Social Security benefits were favored over persons receiving comparable forms of retirement income. In 1976, changes were made to eliminate what was viewed as discrimination against those who are required to support themselves by working in their later years. Beginning in 1984, the credit was expanded to include the permanently and totally disabled. This expansion of the credit for the elderly was coupled with the repeal of the disability income exclusion effective for years after 1983.

Individuals can receive a 15 percent credit to be applied against their tax on all types of income, including earned income. To qualify for the credit for the elderly, an individual must (1) have reached age 65 before the end of the tax year or (2) have retired on disability before the close of the tax year and must have been permanently and totally disabled when he or she retired. The maximum base amount against which the 15 percent credit can be claimed is $5,000 for a single person and married persons filing jointly where only one spouse qualifies. The maximum is $7,500 when both spouses are qualified individuals and file a joint return. The figure is $3,750 when a married individual files a separate return. Code Sec. 22(a)-(c).

Where a qualified individual has not attained age 65 before the end of the tax year, the maximum base amount cannot exceed that individual's disability income for the year. Married individuals must file a joint return to receive the credit unless the spouses lived apart for the entire year. Nonresident aliens are not eligible for the credit. Code Sec. 22(c), (e)(1), and (f).

The maximum base amount must be reduced by Social Security, railroad retirement benefits, or other exempt pension benefits. Code Sec. 22(c)(3). Social Security and railroad retirement benefits also may be partially taxed under Section 86. Any amounts included in gross income will not reduce the maximum base amount. No reduction is required for pension or annuity payments from a tax-qualified pension plan, even though the amounts may be excluded from gross income. The maximum base amount is also reduced by one-half of the amount of adjusted gross income above certain income levels: $10,000 for married persons filing jointly, $5,000 for married persons filing separately, and $7,500 for single persons. Code Sec. 22(d)(1). Thus, for a single person, the credit would no longer be available when adjusted gross income reaches $17,500 ($7,500 plus two times $5,000). For the joint return the credit would be available up to an income level of $20,000 if only one spouse qualifies and up to $25,000 if both spouses qualify. On a joint return, the reduction is based on amounts received by either spouse.

The amount of the credit cannot exceed the income tax due for the year. There are no provisions for carryovers of any unused credit. Thus, if the credit exceeds the tax due, any remaining credit is lost.

EXAMPLE 9.2

Larry is single over 65 and reports $12,000 of adjusted gross income. In addition, he received Social Security benefits of $1,500 for the year. His credit for the elderly will be computed as follows:

Maximum Base Amount		$5,000
Less: Social Security	$1,500	
1/2 (AGI in excess of $7,500)	2,250	3,750
Balance available for credit		$1,250
Credit allowed ($1,275 × 15%) based on compensation		$188
Taxable income ($12,000 −$6,350−$1,550−$4,050 =$50)		
Income tax due		$5
Credit allowed		$5

¶9031 AMERICAN OPPORTUNITY TAX AND LIFETIME LEARNING CREDITS

Beginning in 1998, two new tax credits became available to low- and middle-income individuals for tuition expenses incurred by students pursing college or graduate degrees or vocational training.

The American Opportunity Tax Credit (formerly the HOPE Credit) provides a maximum nonrefundable tax credit of $2,500 per student for each of the first four years of post-secondary education. The $2,500 per year limitation is made up of 100 percent of the first $2,000 of qualified expenses plus 25 percent of next $2,000 of qualified expenses. The American Opportunity Tax Credit applies for the first four years of higher education. The credit is applicable to the taxpayer, spouse, and dependents. The student must be enrolled at least half time to qualify for the American Opportunity Tax credit. Qualified expenses include tuition, fees, books, and course materials. The American Opportunity Tax credit phases out for AGI between $80,000 and $90,000 for singles; and $160,000 and $180,000 on a joint return. Except for dependent taxpayers subject to the kiddie tax, 40% of the credit is refundable.

The Lifetime Learning Credit provides a maximum credit of $2,000 for 20 percent of qualified tuition expenses paid by the taxpayer for any year the American Opportunity Tax Credit is not claimed. The Lifetime Learning credit is 20 percent of the first $10,000 of qualified tuition, fees, and course materials paid for taxpayer, spouse, and/or dependent. It is figured on a per tax return basis. The credit applies for any number of years of higher education. The Lifetime Learning credit phases out for single taxpayers with income exceeding $56,000 and marrieds with income exceeding $112,000.

EXAMPLE 9.3

Joe and Sheila Ames have three children in college. Joni, a freshman, incurs $2,400 in tuition expenses during 2017. Mike, a junior, incurs $3,000 in tuition expenses. Sally, in graduate school, incurs $8,500 in tuition expenses. Joe and Sheila paid all of the tuition expenses, and their adjusted gross income does not exceed the limits. They will be allowed a credit on their 2017 tax return of $6,050. The American Opportunity Tax Credit applies to Joni and Mike and is limited to 100 percent of the first $2,000 of expenses and 25 percent of the next $2,000 for each of them. The Lifetime Learning Credit applies to Sally and is limited to 20 percent of the first $10,000 of expenses.

¶9032 CHILD TAX CREDIT

Taxpayers are allowed a credit for qualifying children under age 17. The credit is $1,000 per child for tax years after 2002. The credit phases out when modified adjusted gross income exceeds $75,000 for single taxpayers, $110,000 for married taxpayers filing a joint return, and $55,000 for married taxpayers filing separately. The credit is reduced by $50 for each $1,000, or fraction thereof, of modified adjusted gross income above the threshold levels. Modified adjusted gross income is determined by adding the exclusions from gross income for foreign earned income and foreign housing costs and income of residents of Guam, American Samoa, the Northern Mariana Islands, and Puerto Rico.

The child tax credit generally uses the same relationships to define an eligible child as are used in the uniform definition of a child for purposes of the dependency exemption. This means that a qualifying child for purposes of the child credit includes the taxpayer's children and their descendants, as well as the taxpayer's siblings (including half-siblings and step-siblings) and their descendants. A qualifying child must be the taxpayer's dependent, and must not provide more than one-half of his or her own support for the year. A taxpayer's child may also be the taxpayer's stepchild; a child legally adopted by the taxpayer or lawfully placed with the taxpayer for legal adoption by the taxpayer; or a foster child who has been placed with the taxpayer by an authorized placement agency or by a judgment, decree, or other order of any court of competent jurisdiction.

At least a portion of the child tax credit is refundable for all taxpayers with qualifying children, regardless of the amount of the taxpayer's regular tax or alternative minimum tax liability. The child tax credit is refundable to the extent of 15 percent of the taxpayer's earned income in excess of $3,000, up to the per child credit amount. The refundable child tax credit is referred to as the additional child tax credit.

Taxpayers with three or more children may calculate the refundable portion of the credit using the excess of their Social Security taxes (i.e., the taxpayer's share of FICA taxes and the employee's share of self-employment taxes) over the earned income credit, instead of the 15 percent amount.

The nonrefundable child tax credit allowable must be reduced by the amount of this refundable child tax credit.

EXAMPLE 9.4	Arleta Kern is single and has two qualifying children. If Arleta has gross income of $21,500, she will have a child tax credit of $2,000. Her gross income will be reduced to zero by the standard deduction for head of household and three personal exemptions. The initial nonrefundable child tax credit of $2,000 ($1,000 × 2) is unavailable since there is no income tax liability. Arleta's refundable child tax credit is $2,775, which is 15 percent of her earned income over $3,000. However, the refundable credit is limited to $2,000. If Arleta has gross income of $26,500, she would have a tax of $500. The $500 would be reduced to zero by the first $500 of the nonrefundable credit, leaving a refundable credit of $1,500. Any tax liability must first be reduced by any dependent care credit, credit for the elderly, and education credits.

EXAMPLE 9.5	John and Barbara Hassen have three children. Their adjusted gross income would have to exceed $32,950 before they could qualify for the nonrefundable child tax credit. The standard deduction for a married couple plus five personal exemptions will reduce their taxable income to zero. They will not qualify for a nonrefundable child tax credit. They will qualify for a refundable child tax credit of $3,000 (($32,950 – $3,000) × .15 = $4,493 limited to $3,000 ($1,000 × 3)). If the entire $32,950 were subject to FICA taxes, the Hassens would have paid $2,521 in FICA taxes. Assuming they qualify for the maximum earned income credit, their earned income credit would be $4,410. Thus, until the FICA taxes exceed the earned income credit, the second method of computing the refundable child tax credit will create no refundable child tax credit. However, when using a $3,000 reduction, the 15 percent computation will always give a higher refundable credit than the excess of FICA taxes over the earned income credit.

¶9033 CREDIT FOR QUALIFIED RETIREMENT SAVINGS

A nonrefundable tax credit is allowed for elective contributions made by eligible taxpayers to a qualified retirement plan. The maximum annual contribution eligible for the credit is $2,000. The credit rate depends on the adjusted gross income of the taxpayer. Only joint returns with adjusted gross income of $62,000 or less, head of household returns of $46,500 or less, and single returns of $31,000 or less are eligible for the credit.

The credit is in addition to any deduction or exclusion that would otherwise apply with respect to the contributions. The credit is available to individuals who are 18 or over, other than individuals who are full-time students or claimed as a dependent on another taxpayer's return.

The credit rates based on adjusted gross income are as follows:

Adjusted Gross Income						Applicable percentage
Joint Return		Head of a household		All other cases		
Over	Not over	Over	Not over	Over	Not over	
$0	$37,000	$0	$27,750	$0	$18,500	50
37,000	40,000	27,750	30,000	18,500	20,000	20
40,000	62,000	30,000	46,500	20,000	31,000	10
62,000	—	46,500	—	31,000	—	0

¶9034 ADOPTION ASSISTANCE CREDIT

A nonrefundable tax credit of up to $13,570 of qualified adoption expenses per child has been provided for 2017. Qualified expenses include adoption fees, court costs, attorney fees, and other expenses related to the legal adoption of an eligible child. Also, employees are entitled to exclude from income up to $13,570 of adoption expenses per adopted child where such amounts are paid or incurred by their employers under a qualified adoption assistance program. In the case of a special needs child, $13,570 is allowed as an adoption credit and as an exclusion from income, regardless of whether the taxpayer has qualified adoption expenses. The credit and exclusion are phased out beginning at modified adjusted gross income levels between $203,540 and $243,540. No credit is allowed for any expenses reimbursed by the employer or by a federal, state, or local program.

Expenses may include the cost of construction, renovations, alterations, or purchases specifically required by the state to meet the needs of the child. The increase in basis of the property that would result from such an expenditure must be reduced by the amount of credit allowed. Expenses incurred in carrying out a surrogate parenting arrangement or in adopting a spouse's child do not qualify for the credit. The child must be under age 18 or incapable of self-care in order to qualify for the credit.

The credit is taken in the year of adoption and includes expenses incurred in previous years. The adoption credit for the special needs child is allowed for the tax year in which the adoption becomes final. A carryforward period of five years is allowed for any credit disallowed because of limitation based on tax liability. Code Sec. 23.

EXAMPLE 9.6

In 2017, a married couple incurs $14,000 in adoption expenses for a child. Their modified adjusted gross income is $207,540. They would be allowed a credit of $12,213 ($13,570 – (($207,540 – $203,540)/$40,000 × $13,570).

EXAMPLE 9.7

A married couple incurs $12,000 in adoption expenses for a child. The employer reimburses the couple for $8,000 of the expenses under a qualified adoption assistance program. The couple will be eligible for an adoption credit of $4,000 ($12,000 expenses incured minus $8,000 exclusion from employer plan). However, taxpayers should always choose the adoption credit for the first $13,570 of adoption expenses before using any exclusion.

¶9035   FOREIGN TAX CREDIT

Both individuals and corporations may claim a credit against the United States tax for certain income taxes of foreign countries and possessions of the United States. Code Sec. 27(a). The foreign tax credit is the method employed by the United States and many other economically developed countries to deal with the problem of double taxation that arises whenever two taxing jurisdictions have a reasonable claim to impose a tax on the same income.

For example, a United States citizen is subject to tax on his or her worldwide income simply because of his or her citizenship. But if he or she were employed in Canada, the Canadian government has at least an equal right to tax the income. To avoid the possibility that combined taxes may exceed 100 percent, the usual rule is that "home yields to source." Thus, the U.S. citizen would be required to include and pay tax to Canada. To avoid double taxation, a credit is allowed for the Canadian tax against the U.S. liability.

As an alternative to the credit, a deduction of foreign income taxes may be taken under Code Sec. 164. A credit against the tax ordinarily results in a greater tax benefit than a deduction from gross income. However, in a few instances the limitation on the allowable credit will cause the deduction to be of greater benefit. All foreign taxes must be treated the same way—they must all be deducted or all claimed as a credit. The credit does not apply to payment of royalties made in the guise of a tax, such as under an oil production sharing agreement made after 1977. Code Sec. 901(e).

The credit is equal to the lesser of the actual tax paid to the foreign country or a limitation. Taxpayers are required to compute the limitation on the amount of foreign tax that can be used to reduce U.S. tax under the overall limitation. A taxpayer totals the taxes paid to all foreign countries and possessions. This total is then subjected to a limitation computed by multiplying the U.S. tax liability by a fraction consisting of taxable income from foreign sources over the worldwide taxable income. Code Sec. 904(a). For individuals, worldwide taxable income is computed as adjusted gross income less total itemized deductions or standard deduction (personal exemptions are not deducted). Thus, the credit cannot exceed that proportion of the U.S. tax which U.S. taxable income from sources within that country bear to the entire U.S. taxable income for the same year.

EXAMPLE 9.8

Anco, a domestic corporation, had worldwide taxable income of $500,000 and a tentative U.S. tax liability of $170,000. From its operations in a foreign country, Anco had $100,000 of taxable income on which a $45,000 tax was imposed. Anco's foreign tax credit is limited to $34,000 (($100,000/$500,000) × $170,000 = $34,000). If the actual tax paid the foreign country was less than the computed limitation, the credit would be the actual tax paid.

EXAMPLE 9.9

Allen Armstrong has worldwide taxable income (after the standard deduction) of $385,000 for 2017 and a tentative U.S. tax liability of $110,449. Included in his worldwide income was $100,000 taxable income from a foreign country on which a $38,000 tax was imposed. Allen's foreign tax credit is limited to $28,688 (($100,000/$385,000) × $110,449). The personal exemption is totally phased out.

Unused foreign taxes may be carried back one year and then forward ten years. The credit is first carried to the earliest year and then to the next earliest year. There is no carryover to the year the foreign tax is deducted.

After 1997, an individual with $300 or less ($600 on a joint return) of creditable foreign taxes is exempt from the foreign tax credit limitation. Taxpayers can take a credit for the full amount of the foreign taxes provided all of their gross foreign-source income is from interest and dividends and all of that income and the foreign tax paid on it is reported to them on Form 1099-INT or Form 1099-DIV (or substitute statement).

TAX BLUNDER

John Jones worked part of the year in a foreign country. He paid $20,000 in income taxes to the foreign country. On his tax return he took an itemized deduction for the income taxes paid. Unless the limitation reduced the credit significantly, it is very likely that taking a credit for the foreign income taxes paid will provide a much larger tax benefit to John than will an itemized deduction.

¶9042 RESIDENTIAL CREDITS

Individual taxpayers are allowed a residential energy property credit of up to $500 for nonbusiness energy property, such as residential exterior doors and windows, insulation, heat pumps, furnaces, central air conditioners, and water heaters. Code Sec. 25C. The credit applies to qualified energy efficiency improvements and qualified energy property placed in service in 2011 through 2016.

A credit is allowed individuals for solar and fuel cell equipment installed on a personal residence. The tax credit is available to help individual taxpayers pay for residential alternative energy equipment. Code Sec. 25D. The credit is 30 percent of the cost of eligible solar water heaters, solar electricity equipment (photovoltaics), and fuel cell plants. The credit is available for equipment placed in service during 2011 through 2016.

¶9045 GENERAL BUSINESS CREDIT

In order to provide a uniform limitation on the amounts of business credits that may be offset against tax liability and uniform rules for carrybacks and carryforwards, there are over 30 business credits that have been combined into a single credit called the general business credit. The amount of the current year business credit is the sum of those credits determined for the tax year. Some of the more important credits are listed:

1. Investment credit
2. Work opportunity credit
3. Alcohol fuels credit
4. Increasing research credit
5. Low-income housing credit
6. Disabled persons access credit
7. Renewable electricity production credit
8. Empowerment zone credit
9. Indian employment credit
10. Employer Social Security credit from employee tips
11. Orphan drug credit
12. New markets tax credit
13. Small employer pension plan startup cost credit
14. Employer-provided child care credit
15. New hire retention credit

The ceiling limitations, carryover, and recapture provisions apply to the total of the general business credits.

Investment Credit

Taxpayers purchasing "qualified investments" are allowed a credit against the tax liability for a portion of the amount of their investment for the year the property is placed in service. Under Section 46(a) the investment credit is the sum of:

1. Rehabilitation credit
2. Energy credit

Rehabilitation Credit

A two-tier investment credit for qualified rehabilitated buildings makes up the rehabilitation credit. The credit is (1) 20 percent for rehabilitations of certified historic structures and (2) 10 percent for rehabilitations of other buildings originally placed in service before 1936. The 20 percent credit applies to both residential and nonresidential buildings and the 10 percent credit applies to nonresidential property. Code Sec. 47(a).

Certain expenditures do not qualify for the credit. The costs of acquiring a building or an interest in a building, such as a leasehold interest, are not considered as qualifying expenditures. The costs of facilities related to an existing building, such as a parking lot, also are not considered as qualifying expenditures. Expenditures incurred by a lessee do not qualify for the credit unless the remaining lease term on the date the rehabilitation is completed is at least as long as the applicable recovery period under the general depreciation rules (generally, 27.5 years for residential property and 39 years for nonresidential property). Straight-line depreciation must be used to qualify for the rehabilitation credit.

In addition, the cost of constructing a new building, or of completing a new building after it has been placed in service, will not qualify. Construction costs are considered to be for rehabilitation and not for new construction if (1) at least 50 percent of the existing external walls are retained as external walls, (2) at least 75 percent of existing external walls are retained as internal or external walls, and (3) at least 75 percent of the existing internal structure framework is retained in place. These tests do not apply to certified historic structures. Code Sec. 47(c).

The basis of a rehabilitated building must be reduced for the full rehabilitation credit.

Energy Credit

An energy credit is available for a taxpayer's investment in energy property. The eligible property and rates are shown in the table below.

Qualified fuel cell property	30%
Solar energy property	30%
Geothermal property	10%

The energy property must be depreciable property built or acquired by the taxpayer and must be either depreciable or amortizable. The energy property basis must be reduced by 50 percent of the credit taken. Code Sec. 48(a).

Recapture of Credit

If qualified property is disposed of by sale or exchange, gift, or involuntary conversion before the close of the recapture period, the investment credit may be recaptured. For recovery property, the amount of increase in tax is determined by applying the recapture percentage to the amount of investment credit taken on the asset. Code Sec. 50.

If Property Ceases To Be Investment Credit Property Within	Recapture Percentage
First Year	100
Second Year	80
Third Year	60
Fourth Year	40
Fifth Year	20

EXAMPLE 9.10

> Billingsly Corporation purchased qualified business energy investment property with a MACRS life of five years for $30,000. Billingsly claimed an investment credit of $3,000 ($30,000 × 10%). If Billingsly sold the asset after four years of useful service, 20 percent of the $3,000, or $600, would be the increase in tax due because of the recapture.

If property with a basis reduced is disposed of in a transaction that triggers the recapture of an investment credit, then the basis "immediately before the event resulting in such recapture" is increased by 50 or 100 percent of the recaptured amount. Code Sec. 50(c)(3). The basis adjustment will affect gain or loss on disposition of the asset and also depreciation recapture.

EXAMPLE 9.11

> Jerome Jackson purchased five-year Section 38 depreciable property for $30,000. After holding the asset for more than four years, Jerome sells it. A 10 percent investment credit of $3,000 was taken in the year of purchase and the asset basis was reduced by 50 percent of the credit taken. On disposition, investment credit would be recaptured in the amount of $600. The basis of the asset would be increased by one-half of this amount, or $300, for purposes of determining gain or loss and depreciation recapture.

Any increase in income tax because of recapture is treated as income tax imposed on the taxpayer even though the taxpayer has no income tax liability, has a net operating loss for the year, or no income tax return is otherwise required for the year. The investment credit recapture is not reduced by other nonrefundable tax credits.

If the investment credit allowable has not been used as a tax reduction, but is reflected in an unused carryover, the recapture will result in an adjustment of the carryover.

In determining the actual useful life of qualified property, the property is treated as placed in service on the first day of the month in which the property is placed in service. If property ceases to be qualified property, the cessation is treated as occurring on the actual date of the disqualification (i.e., sale, transfer, retirement). When the cessation is for any reason other than the occurrence of an event of a specific date, the cessation is treated as occurring on the first day of the tax year.

EXAMPLE 9.12

> Bare Corporation purchases energy equipment with a life of five years on June 15, 2012, for $12,000. On June 7, 2017, the equipment is sold. Even though the asset was held for less than five years, for investment credit purposes, the asset was held more than five years (considered placed in service June 1, 2012, and sold June 7, 2017). None of the investment credit taken will be recaptured.

Taxpayers using an averaging convention in computing depreciation for qualified property may use the assumed dates of additions and retirements in determining the actual useful life of the property. This election must be used consistently and may not result in a substantial distortion of investment credit.

The death of a taxpayer does not trigger investment tax credit recapture. Moreover, recapture does not apply to the transfer caused by death of a partner's interest in a partnership, a beneficiary's interest in an estate or trust, or a shareholder's shares of stock in an S corporation. The property is treated as if it had actually been held for the entire useful life.

EXAMPLE 9.13

> Benjamin Burr purchased $9,000 worth of energy equipment for his sole proprietorship, taking a $900 investment tax credit. He died four years later, leaving the equipment to his daughter. There is no recapture of the credit and the daughter can dispose of the equipment immediately without recapture.

Recapture does not occur when property is transferred in a tax-free transfer by a corporation pursuant to a reorganization or a liquidation of a controlled subsidiary. Also, recapture does not occur when property is transferred in connection with a mere change in the form of carrying on a trade or business, provided that the taxpayer maintains a substantial interest in the business. Recapture will still occur if an early disposition occurs in a subsequent transaction that is not exempt.

TAX BLUNDER

Alvin Armend purchased energy equipment for $20,000 on June 1, 2012, taking the investment credit of $2,000. He sold the equipment on May 18, 2017. Since he sold the equipment before the five-year holding period, he must recapture $400 of the investment credit. Had Alvin held on to the asset for two more weeks he would have saved $400 in taxes.

At-Risk Limitations

The Economic Recovery Tax Act of 1981 contained an investment credit at-risk limitation which applies to businesses which are subject to loss limitations under Section 465. Generally, the taxpayer is allowed an investment credit for only that portion of an investment for which the taxpayer is at risk. A taxpayer is generally not at risk for nonrecourse debt. Where the taxpayer's at-risk amount increases, additional investment credit is allowed on the increase. If the taxpayer's at-risk amount decreases, the investment credit may be subject to recapture.

The investment credit at-risk rules do not apply to amounts borrowed for qualified energy property. In order to qualify under the exception, the taxpayer must have an investment in the property that is at risk in an amount that is at least 25 percent of the unadjusted basis of the property. In addition, any nonrecourse financing for the property must be a level payment loan. A level payment loan is a loan repaid in substantially equal installments including both principal and interest. Code Sec. 49.

Work Opportunity Credit

The work opportunity tax credit may be elected by employers who hire individuals for certain target groups suffering from unusually high unemployment. The credit is taken with respect to first-year wages paid to eligible individuals who begin work after September 30, 1997, and before January 1, 2020. The work opportunity credit equals 40 percent of the first $6,000 of wages for the first year of employment. The $6,000 limit is computed on each eligible employee for wages attributable to services rendered during the one-year period beginning with the day the individual begins work for the employer (maximum credit of $2,400 per employee). Code Sec. 51(a) and (b). The employee must complete a minimum of 120 hours of service for the credit to apply. If the employee completes at least 120 hours of service but less than 400 hours of service, the employer is entitled to a credit of 25 percent rather than the 40 percent.

EXAMPLE 9.14

Astabula Corp. hires Maxine Brown, a certified targeted group member, on December 1, 2016. The company pays $1,200 of wages to Maxine in December 2016 and $14,000 in 2017. The work opportunity credit for 2016 is $480 ($1,200 × 40%). The first $4,800 of wages paid in 2017 are also eligible for the credit of $1,920.

The Vow to Hire Heroes Act provides for an expanded Work Opportunity Credit (WOC) of up to $5,600 for employers that hire veterans who have been looking for employment for more than six months. Employers that hire veterans who have been unemployed for more than four weeks but less than six months are eligible for a maximum tax credit of $2,400. A $9,600 tax credit is available to employers that hire veterans with service-connected disabilities who have been looking for employment for more than six months. The credit applies for eligible veterans starting work after November 21, 2011, and before January 1, 2020. The credit is 40% of first-year wages. Tax exempt groups can take the credit as an offset against payroll taxes.

An employer's deduction for wages is reduced by the amount of the work opportunity credit. Also, wages taken into account in computing the work opportunity credit are not taken into account in computing any empowerment zone employment credit allowed by Code Sec. 1396.

The following individuals are members of targeted groups eligible for the work opportunity credit: (1) a qualified IV-A (Aid to Families with Dependent Children (AFDC)) recipient, (2) a qualified veteran, (3) a qualified ex-felon, (4) a designated community resident, (5) a vocational rehabilitation referral, (6) a qualified summer youth employee, (7) a qualified food stamp recipient, (8) a qualified SSI recipient, or (9) long-term family assistance recipients.

An employer must obtain certification from a state employment security agency that an individual is a member of a targeted group. An individual may not be treated as a member of a targeted group unless an employer either obtains written certification from the designated local agency on or before the day the individual begins work indicating that the individual is a member of a targeted group or completes a prescreening notice on or before the day employment is offered.

The work opportunity credit is elective with the taxpayer. If the credit is elected, the employer's deduction for wages is reduced by the amount of the tentative credit before application of the various limitations. Therefore, the employer has the option of taking the credit or the deduction.

EXAMPLE 9.15

> Bertram Ross hired a qualified work opportunity credit employee. The employee begins work on March 2, 2017, and is paid $8,800 during the year. The work opportunity credit allowed is $2,400 ($6,000 maximum amount × 40%). The taxpayer's tax deduction for wages is $6,400 ($8,800 wages paid – $2,400 work opportunity credit).

For long-term family assistance recipients the amount of the credit for a tax year is 40 percent of the qualified first-year wages plus 50 percent of the qualified second-year wages. The credit applies only to the first $10,000 of wages in each year with respect to any individual. Thus, the maximum total credit per qualified employee is $9,000 for the two years.

EXAMPLE 9.16

> Dewey Corporation hires Nina Alexis on June 5, 2017. Dewey pays Nina $7,000 in wages in 2017. Dewey Corporation can take a credit of $2,800 ($7,000 × 40%) in 2017. Dewey will also be eligible for a 40 percent credit on any wages paid Nina before June 5, 2018, but limited to $1,200 ($3,000 × 40%). The first $10,000 of wages paid Nina during the period of June 5, 2018, and June 4, 2019, will be eligible for a 50 percent credit.

Alcohol Fuels Credit

To foster the production of gasohol, an income tax credit for alcohol and alcohol blended rules applies to fuel sales and uses. There is a 60-cent-per-gallon credit for alcohol of at least 190 proof and a 40-cent-per-gallon credit for alcohol of at least 150 but less than 190 proof for persons producing alcohol fuels or using them in a trade or business. Further, the amount of the allowable tax credit must be reduced to the extent that the alcohol is used in gasohol and other alcohol fuels for which there is an excise tax exemption for fuel taxes. Code Sec. 40.

The alcohol fuels credit is claimed as one of the components of the general business credit. Thus, it is subject to the maximum tax liability rules and the carryback and carryforward rules.

Taxpayers may elect to have the alcohol fuels credit not apply for any tax year. The election may be made or revoked at any time before the three-year period beginning on the last date for filing a return for such tax year, without regard to extensions.

Research Credit

A tax credit is allowed for qualifying research and development expenditures paid or incurred after June 30, 1996. The research credit is equal to the sum of (1) 20 percent of the excess (if any) of the *qualified research expenses* for the tax year over the base amount and (2) 20 percent of the *basic research payments*. Code Sec. 41(a). Thus, the research activities credit has two components: an incremental credit and a basic research credit.

Incremental Research Activities Credit

The credit for increasing research activities applies only to research expenditures incurred in carrying on a trade or business in which a taxable entity is already engaged. Expenditures incurred, for example, in developing or improving a product, a formula, an invention, a plant process, or an experimental model are eligible for the credit. No credit is available for expenses relating to a potential trade or business. Thus, new businesses conducting research for future production that undertake research geared to the development of a new business activity may not claim the credit.

Qualified research expenses are the same as those costs eligible for a deduction under Code Sec. 174 (see ¶6435) other than expenses for foreign research, research in the social sciences, arts or humanities, or subsidized research. Credit-eligible research is limited to research undertaken to discover information that is (1) technological in nature and (2) intended to be useful in the development of a new or improved business component. Further, the research must be elements of a process of experimentation for a functional purpose (i.e., it must relate to a new or improved function, performance, reliability, or quality). Qualified research expenses cover in-house expenses for the taxpayer's own research (wages for substantially engaging in or directly supervising or supporting research activities, supplies, and computer use charges) and 65 percent of amounts paid or incurred for qualified research done by a person other than an employee of the taxpayer. Prepaid contract research expenses are to be taken into account over the period in which the research is conducted.

Basic Research Credit

The second element of the research credit computation is 20 percent of the basic research payments. This is sometimes referred to as the university research credit because the credit is available to corporations for basic research to be performed by universities, colleges, and other qualified organizations (scientific research organizations, organizations promoting scientific research, and organizations that make basic research grants). The amount of basic research payments taken into account is the excess of such basic research expenditures over the qualified organization base period amount. Those expenses that do not exceed such base period amount are treated as contract research expenses and are subject to the 65-percent rule.

Any business deduction for qualified research expenses or basic research payments must be reduced by 100 percent of the research credit. An election permits a taxpayer to avoid reducing the deduction by electing to reduce the research credit by the product of (1) 50 percent of the credit and (2) the maximum corporate tax rate. The election is made for each tax year. It is irrevocable and must be made no later than the time for filing the taxpayer's return for the year of the election.

Beginning in 2016, eligible small businesses ($50 million or less in gross receipts) may claim the credit against alternative minimum tax liability and the credit can be utilized by certain small businesses against the employer's payroll tax liability.

Low-Income Housing Credit

A nonrefundable income tax credit applies to newly constructed or substantially rehabilitated qualified low-income housing projects placed in service after 1986. The credit is claimed over a credit period which is the 10 tax years beginning with the tax year in which the building is placed in service. First-year credits must be prorated to reflect a partial year of qualification. If the credit is prorated, the balance of the first year's credit is available in the eleventh year. The basis for purposes of depreciation is not reduced by the amount of low-income credit claimed. Code Sec. 42(a).

The applicable credit rate is the appropriate percentage issued by the IRS for the month in which the building is placed in service. For newly constructed units or rehabilitation expenditures exceeding specified minimum amounts per low-income unit that are not federally subsidized, the credit rate is computed so that the present value of the 10 annual credit amounts at the beginning of the credit period equals 70 percent of the qualified basis of the low-income units. For qualified federally subsidized units the rate is such that the present value equals 30 percent.

The credit rate equal to the 30 percent present value also applies to the cost of acquisition of certain existing low-income units. The credit for acquisition cost may be claimed only if the property was placed in service more than 10 years before the acquisition and there is substantial rehabilitation. Rehabilitation expenditures during any 24-month period must constitute a qualified basis equaling the greater of $3,000 per low-income unit or 10 percent of the unadjusted basis of the building. Rehabilitation expenses for any building are treated as a separate new building. If such test is satisfied and the substantial rehabilitation expenditures are not federally subsidized, such expenditures are eligible for the credit determined under the 70 percent present value applicable credit rate. A 30 percent present value applicable credit rate would apply to the existing portion of such building.

EXAMPLE 9.17   Mildred Meridian incurs $100,000 in qualifying costs to rehabilitate low-income property on January 1, 2017. The expenditures are not federally subsidized. Assume that the applicable credit rate is 9 percent. Mildred is eligible for a $9,000 credit for each year from 2017 through 2026.

The amount of the credit is the product of the applicable credit rate and the taxpayer's share of the qualified basis of the property allocable to the units occupied by low-income tenants. A separate calculation to compute the qualified basis must be made for property qualifying for each of the credits. Each qualified basis amount is equal to the total basis of the low-income property multiplied by the percentage of units occupied by tenants with the appropriate income level.

A low-income housing project qualifies for the credit if it is residential rental property, if the units are used on a nontransient basis, and if a minimum occupancy requirement is met. Hotels, dormitories, nursing homes, hospitals, life-care facilities, and retirement homes do not qualify for the credit. At least 20 percent of a project's units must be occupied by individuals having incomes of 50 percent or less of the area median income (adjusted for family size) or at least 40 percent of the units must be occupied by individuals having incomes of 60 percent or less of area median income (again adjusted for family size). The taxpayer must irrevocably elect which of the two requirements (the 20 percent or the 40 percent test) will apply to the project. The gross rent paid by families in units qualifying for the credit cannot exceed 30 percent of the income limitation applicable to the tenants, based on family size.

Qualified low-income housing projects must maintain their qualification for a minimum of 15 years from the beginning of the year in which the project first qualifies for the credit. If not, a portion of the credits must be recaptured with interest. The allowable credits are reduced to two-thirds per year prior to recapture in determining the recapture amount.

The credit receives special treatment under the passive activity loss limitations. Qualifying projects are considered "active real estate rentals" regardless of the form of ownership or the investor's actual participation in the operations. The "active" status covers only the credit and does not extend to any income or loss from the project. There is no phaseout of the credit benefits as adjusted gross income exceeds $100,000. The credit is subject to the general business credit limitation and is subject to the carryback and carryforward rules.

Disabled Persons Access Credit

A tax credit is available to an eligible small business for expenditures incurred to make the business accessible to disabled individuals. An eligible small business is defined as any person (including any predecessor) that either (1) had gross receipts for the preceding tax year that did not exceed $1 million or (2) had no more than 30 full-time employees during the preceding tax year. The amount of the credit is equal to 50 percent of the amount of the eligible access expenditures for that year that exceed $250 but that do not exceed $10,250. The amount of the credit must reduce the expenditures otherwise eligible for deduction or basis increase. Code Sec. 44.

EXAMPLE 9.18

Dana Corporation, an eligible small business, spends $8,750 to install ramps to its building to make the building accessible to handicapped individuals. Dana is allowed a credit of $4,250 (($8,750 – $250) × 50%). Only $4,500 is eligible for depreciation as the $8,750 expenditure must be reduced by the $4,250 credit.

A taxpayer may elect to currently deduct up to $15,000 annually of barrier removal expenses. Code Sec. 190. A deduction is not allowed to the extent that a credit is taken for these expenditures.

Renewable Electricity Production Credit

The renewable electricity production credit is an amount determined by the kilowatt hours of electricity produced by the taxpayer from qualified energy resources. The production must take place at a qualified facility during the 10-year period beginning on the date the facility was originally placed in service. The electricity production must be sold to an unrelated person during the year. Code Sec. 45.

Empowerment Zone Employment Credit

The general business credit includes an empowerment zone employment credit for employers. The credit is generally equal to 20 percent of the first $15,000 of wages paid during the year to each employee who is a resident of a designated empowerment zone and who performs substantially all employment services within the zone in a taxpayer's trade or business. Code Sec. 1396. The deduction that the employer would normally be allowed for wages is reduced by the amount of the empowerment zone credit claimed for the tax year. Several empowerment zones have been designated by the Secretary of Housing and Urban Development and the Secretary of Agriculture from urban and rural areas nominated by state and local governments.

Indian Employment Credit

The amount of the Indian employment credit is an amount equal to 20 percent of the excess of qualified wages paid or incurred during the year plus qualified employee health insurance costs paid or incurred over the sum of the qualified wages and qualified employee health insurance costs paid or incurred during the calendar year 2017. Code Sec. 45A. A qualified employee must be a member of an Indian tribe or the spouse of an enrolled member of an Indian tribe. Substantially all of the services performed must be performed within an Indian reservation. The principal place of abode of the employee while performing the services must be on or near the reservation in which the services are performed.

Employer Social Security Credit

A business credit is allowed to food and beverage establishments for the amount equal to the employer's Federal Insurance Contribution Act (FICA) obligation (7.65 percent) attributable to tips in excess of those treated as wages for purposes of satisfying the minimum wage provisions of the Fair Labor Standards Act. To prevent a double benefit, no deduction is allowed for any amount taken into account in determining the credit.

Orphan Drug Credit

The orphan drug tax credit is available for amounts paid or incurred after June 30, 1996. The credit is an amount equal to 50 percent of the qualified clinical testing expenses for the taxable year. Code Sec. 45C(a). Basically, the term "clinical testing" means any human clinical testing that is carried out under an exemption for a drug being tested for a rare disease.

New Markets Tax Credit

A tax credit was created in 2000 to spur investment in low-income or economically disadvantaged areas. The new markets tax credit is five percent of a qualified equity investment in a qualified community development entity (CDE). The five-percent rates for the first three allowance dates and increases to six percent for each of the four remaining dates. The allowance dates are the initial offering date and the first six anniversary dates of the initial offering date. The total credit is, therefore, 39 percent and is claimed over seven allowance dates.

A qualified equity investment is the cost of any stock in a corporation or any capital interest in a partnership that is a qualified CDE if:

1. The investment is acquired on the original issue date solely in exchange for cash,
2. Substantially all of the cash is used to make qualified low-income community investments, and
3. The investment is designated by the qualified CDE for new markets credit purposes.

If, during the seven years from the original issue date of the qualified equity investment, a recapture event occurs with respect to the investment, then the new markets tax credit must be recaptured. The recaptured credit will increase the tax for the year in an amount equal to the amount of credits claimed plus interest for the resulting underpayment. The interest will not be deductible, nor may any other credits be taken against the addition to tax caused by the credit recapture.

Credit for Plan Startup Costs of Small Employers

Small employers with no more than 100 employees will receive a tax credit for some of the costs of establishing new retirement plans. The credit equals 50 percent of the startup costs incurred to create or maintain a new employee retirement plan. The credit is limited to $500 in any tax year, and it may be claimed for qualified costs incurred in each of the three years beginning with the tax year in which the plan becomes effective. The employer must not have established or maintained a qualified employer plan during the three-tax-year period immediately preceding the first tax year in which the new plan is effective. Deductible expenses must be offset by the amount of the credit taken. At an employer's election, the credit may be claimed in the year immediately preceding the first year in which the new plan is effective.

Credit for Employer-Provided Child Care Expenses

A tax credit for child care expenses acts as an incentive for businesses to provide child care for their employees. The credit is equal to the sum of 25 percent of the qualified child care expenses plus 10 percent of the qualified child care resources and referral expenditures. The total credit amount claimed for any given tax year cannot exceed $150,000. Double benefit for child care expenses is prevented by a reduction in the basis of the qualified property for the expenses claimed as a credit and the barring of the use of the same expenses to claim any other deductions or credits. If an employer terminates its interest in providing child care, all or part of the claimed credit must be recaptured as an increase in tax.

Other Credits

Congress added a number of new credits during 2005 with the Energy Act and the Hurricane Relief Act.

A homebuilder's credit for new energy-efficient homes is available during 2006 through 2016. An eligible contractor may claim a tax credit of $1,000 or $2,000 for a qualified new energy-efficient home that a person acquires from the contractor during 2006 through 2016 for use as a residence during the tax year. An eligible contractor is a person who constructs a new energy-efficient home, or a manufacturer that produces a qualified new energy-efficient manufactured home. A $2,000 credit per dwelling is allowed where consumption of energy is at least 50 percent below that of a comparable dwelling unit sold for use as a residence. A $1,000 credit is allowed for a manufactured home that meets a 30 percent energy efficiency standard.

Limitation on General Business Credit

The general business credit may not exceed "net income tax" minus the greater of (1) the tentative minimum tax or (2) 25 percent of "net regular tax liability" above $25,000. Code Sec. 38(c). The term "net income tax" means the sum of the regular tax plus the alternative minimum tax and minus all other nonrefundable credits, except the credit for prior year minimum tax. "Net regular tax" is the regular tax liability reduced by such credits.

EXAMPLE 9.19 Lindy Corporation has purchases that entitle it to $62,000 in general business credits. Its tax liability before the deduction of the general business credit is $45,000. Except for the ceiling, Lindy's credit for the year would be $62,000. However, the ceiling on the credit yields a maximum credit of $40,000 ($45,000 – 25% × ($45,000 – $25,000)).

Where a husband and wife file separately, the $25,000 amount becomes $12,500. However, this reduction will not apply if the spouse of the taxpayer has no qualified investment for the tax year and no carryback or carryover to the tax year. The $25,000 is apportioned among component members of a controlled corporation. Each partner in a partnership takes the $25,000 figure into account separately, as do beneficiaries of estates and trusts and shareholders in S corporations.

Carryback and Carryforward of Unused Credits

When the general business credit exceeds the above limitation in any year, the excess or unused credit may be carried back for one year and forward for 20 years. The entire amount of the unused credit must be carried back and then forward to each of the 20 remaining carryover years in order. Credits carried over are used first and then credits earned currently; after that, any carryback credits are applied. Unused credits from two or more years are used up in the order they occurred—the oldest first. The credit for investment in the current year, plus any carryover credits, cannot exceed the general limitations in effect for that year.

The first-in, first-out method of general business credit carryover reduces the potential loss of general business credits from the expiration of credit carryovers, since the earliest years are used before the credit for the current year. Code Sec. 39.

Refundable Tax Credits

Since refundable credits generally represent payments that have been made to the government, fewer difficulties are encountered in carryback and carryover, recapture, limitations, and sequencing.

¶9105 WITHHOLDING OF TAX ON WAGES CREDIT

The tax deducted and withheld on wages is allowable as a credit against the tax. If the tax has actually been withheld, a credit or refund will be made even though the tax has not been paid to the government by the employer. However, the IRS may credit any overpayment against any outstanding tax, interest, or penalty owed by the taxpayer. Code Sec. 31(a).

¶9115 SOCIAL SECURITY TAX REFUNDS CREDIT

Where an employee receives wages from more than one employer during the year, amounts may be deducted and withheld as employee Social Security tax on amounts exceeding $127,200 for 2017. A special refund of the excess amount may be obtained only by claiming credit for the amount in the same manner as if such special refunds were an amount deducted and withheld as income tax at the source. The present rate is 6.2 percent on $127,200. The credit is computed separately for each spouse on a joint return. Code Sec. 31(b).

EXAMPLE 9.20

Lorence Larsen works for two different employers during 2017. He earned $58,000 from the first employer and $71,800 from the second. Each employer withheld Social Security taxes. Lorence is allowed a credit for the excess Social Security taxes paid in of $161.20 (($129,800 – $127,200) × 6.2%).

Where an employer withholds Social Security taxes on more than the maximum amount, a credit may not be claimed for the excess. The employer should adjust the overcollection with the employee.

¶9125 EARNED INCOME CREDIT

A refundable tax credit is provided for low-income workers. The credit is based on "earned income," which is explained below. The earned income credit may be characterized as a form of negative income tax since the credit is refundable to the taxpayer even if no tax liability exists. This credit does not represent a refund of a previous payment made by the taxpayer.

Taxpayers entitled to exclude income under the foreign earned income exclusion are not allowed the credit. The earned income credit is reduced by any alternative minimum tax imposed for the tax year.

Basic Earned Income Credit

For 2017, the maximum credit is 34 percent of earned income up to $10,000, or a credit of $3,400 for one child. The maximum credit of $3,400 is reduced by an amount equal to 15.98 percent of the excess of the greater of the adjusted gross income or earned income over $18,340. Code Sec. 32. For two children, the credit percentage is 40 percent of earned income up to $14,040, with a maximum credit of $5,616 and a phaseout percentage of 21.06 percent. For three children, the credit is 45 percent of earned income up to $14,040, with a maximum credit of $6,318 and a phaseout of 21.06 percent.

Eligible taxpayers with no children may receive a credit of 7.65 percent of the first $6,670 of earned income, for a maximum of $510. The phaseout percentage is also 7.65 percent on income exceeding $8,340. The phaseout amounts are increased by $5,550 for married filing jointly.

The definition of a qualifying child for purposes of the earned income credit is generally the same as the uniform definition of a child contained in the dependency exemption rules. A qualifying child must be the taxpayer's son, daughter, step-son, step-daughter, brother, sister, stepbrother, stepsister, or a descendant of any such individual. An adopted child is treated as a child by blood if the child was legally adopted by the taxpayer, or was lawfully placed with the taxpayer for legal adoption by the taxpayer. A foster child is also treated as the taxpayer's child if the child was placed with the taxpayer by an authorized placement agency or by judgment, decree, or other order of any court of competent jurisdiction. A child providing more than one-half of his/her own support can still be a qualifying child for the earned income credit. The custodial parent qualifies for the earned income credit when the exemption is granted to the noncustodial parent. The child must have the same principal place of abode as the taxpayer for more than one-half of the tax year. The child must be under 19 (or under age 24 in the case of a full-time student) in order to be a qualifying child. No age limit applies to individuals who are totally and permanently disabled at any time during the tax year. Married individuals must file a joint return in order to receive the benefits of the credit.

Taxpayers without qualifying children must meet three requirements: (1) the individual has a principal residence in the United States for more than one-half of the taxable year, (2) the individual (or, if married, either the individual or the individual's spouse) is at least 25 years old and not more than 64 years old at the end of the taxable year, and (3) the individual cannot be claimed as a dependent for any taxable year beginning in the same calendar year as the taxable year for which the credit is claimed.

Earned income includes wages, salaries, tips, and employee compensation. In addition, net earnings from self-employment are included in earned income. Earned income is to be reduced by any loss in earnings from self-employment. Earned income is to be computed without regard to any community property laws which may otherwise be applicable. Pension and annuity income is not considered earned income for the purpose of the credit. Taxpayers may choose to include combat pay in earned income for purposes of computing the earned income credit.

The earned income credit is denied to individuals where the aggregate amount of disqualified income exceeds $3,450 for 2017. Disqualified income includes both taxable and nontaxable interest, dividends, net rental and royalty income, net capital gain income, and net passive income.

EXAMPLE 9.21	Malcolm Meyers maintains a household for himself and his 12-year-old son. For the year, he received $18,840 in wages and $300 in interest income. His earned income credit for the year is computed as follows:		
	Maximum credit: 34% of $18,840, limited to $3,400		$3,400
	Reduction: Greater of AGI or earned income	$19,140	
	Less phaseout amount	18,340	
	Excess	$800	
	15.98% of excess		128
	Allowable earned income credit		$3,272

When a taxpayer who claims the EIC reports net earnings from self-employment with little or no reported expenses and the Service determines that the taxpayer has additional allowable expenses, the Service must subtract these additional expenses to determine the taxpayer's correct net earnings from self- employment. If the Service determines that the taxpayer has additional allowable expenses but is unable to determine the amount of these expenses because of the taxpayer's failure to substantiate them as required by Code Sec. 6001 and Reg. §1.6001-1(a), the Service may disregard the claimed "net" earnings from self- employment when determining the taxpayer's eligibility for the EIC and liability for self-employment tax. If the Service determines the business does not exist, the Service must disregard the claimed net-earnings from self-employment. If such a determination is made, the Service should consider imposition of penalties, up to and including the fraud penalty imposed under Code Sec. 6663. [CCA 200022051]

The credit is refundable. Thus, taxpayers with a credit exceeding their liability can claim the difference as a refund. Even if a return is not required because of an individual's low income, a return should be filed to obtain the credit.

EXAMPLE 9.22	Nancy Pearson maintains a household for herself and her dependent daughter. Nancy's only income is $7,000 from wages. Under the filing requirement rules, she is not required to file a return. However, to receive the $2,380 ($7,000 × 34%) earned income credit, a return must be filed.

¶9135   WITHHOLDING OF TAX AT SOURCE CREDIT

Taxpayers are allowed a credit for income taxes withheld on nonresident aliens, foreign corporations, and tax-free covenant bonds. Code Sec. 33.

¶9155   GASOLINE AND SPECIAL FUELS TAX CREDIT

Generally, the taxpayer can claim a credit for federal excise taxes on the nonhighway use of gasoline and special fuels. These include gasoline or special fuels used for farming purposes and special fuels used in local transit systems and for aviation purposes. Code Sec. 34.

Gasoline and lubricating oil must be used in a trade or business or in an income-producing activity. The credit for gasoline must be included in income where the cost of the product was deducted as a business expense.

¶9165   ESTIMATED TAX PAYMENTS CREDIT

A credit is permitted for quarterly estimated payments made by taxpayers. Individuals whose tax liability is not substantially covered by withholding may have to pay estimated taxes. All individuals must file a declaration of estimated tax for the year if the estimated tax, including self-employment tax, exceeds the tax to be withheld by $1,000 or more.

The estimated tax for the current year is computed by (1) estimating the taxpayer's gross income for the year, (2) subtracting estimated deductions and exemptions, and (3) computing the income tax on the balance. The estimated self-employment tax, alternative minimum tax, and medicare surtaxes are added to the resulting income tax. The tax to be withheld from wages during the year and other expected credits are subtracted. The result is the "estimated tax," and if it is less than $1,000 no estimated payments need be made.

Where estimated returns are required for the current tax year, they must be filed by April 15, June 15, September 15, and January 15 (following year). The taxpayer may elect to credit a preceding year's overpayment against the current year's estimated tax.

In filing a declaration of estimated tax, the taxpayer is required to take into account the then existing facts and circumstances, as well as those reasonably to be anticipated. In the absence of contrary indications, current employment, salary rate, and regularly paid dividends may be presumed to continue throughout the year. Amended or revised declarations may be made in any case in which the estimates differ from those reflected in the previous declaration.

No penalty is imposed for failure to file an estimated tax declaration, or for errors in the declaration, but there is a penalty for underpayment of estimated tax. The amount of the penalty is the amount of the underpayment times the underpayment interest rate for the period of the underpayment.

An "underpayment," for other than high-income individuals, is determined by adding the amount of income taxes paid and the excess Social Security credit and then subtracting the lesser of (1) 90 percent of the actual amount of tax due on the return or (2) the previous year's tax. The underpayment is computed as of each of the four quarterly filing dates. Thus, a taxpayer making uneven payments throughout the year could have an underpayment for some quarters and not others. The penalty applies despite any reasonable cause and is not deductible as an expense.

After 2002, high-income individuals must use 110 percent of the previous year's tax liability. A high-income individual is one who had more than $150,000 in adjusted gross income for the preceding year ($75,000 for married individuals filing separately).

An equal part of tax withheld from wages is considered as tax paid on each of the four quarterly filing dates, unless the taxpayer proves otherwise.

PLANNING POINTER

Generally, a taxpayer cannot avoid a penalty on underpayments in early quarters of the year by increasing estimated payments in the later quarters. However, if an employee realizes that he or she has underpaid for the earlier quarters, the employee could have a larger amount of income taxes withheld late in the year. Since any withholding is considered to be equally withheld throughout the year, the extra year-end withholding will increase the amount considered to have been paid in the earlier quarters and help lessen or eliminate any underpayment penalty.

KEYSTONE PROBLEM

There are two kinds of tax credits, nonrefundable and refundable, that basically must be taken in the proper order. Since some of the credits have no carryover provisions and are lost if not used in a particular year, what effect could an increase in a credit, such as the investment credit, have on the other credits?

Alternative Minimum Tax

¶9401   ## IMPOSITION OF TAX

The minimum tax is a special form of tax imposed on certain taxpayers in addition to the regular federal income tax. The objective of the tax is to recapture tax reductions resulting from the use of special tax relief or "tax shelter" provisions of the tax law.

"Alternative minimum taxable income" (AMTI) means the taxable income of the taxpayer for the year determined with adjustments and increased by tax preferences. Alternative minimum taxable income is reduced by an exemption amount to arrive at net alternative minimum taxable income which is then multiplied by a 26 or 28 percent alternative minimum tax rate. The first $187,800 of AMTI is taxed at 26 percent and AMTI in excess of $187,800 is taxed at 28 percent. However, dividends taxed at 15 percent and long-term capital gains taxed at 15, 25, and 28 percent for regular tax purposes are also taxed at those rates in the alternative minimum tax computation. The foreign tax credit and the nonrefundable personal credits are the only nonrefundable credits allowed against the tax in arriving at the tentative minimum tax. The alternative minimum tax is the amount resulting after deducting the regular tax (reduced by all nonrefundable credits) from the tentative minimum tax. Code Sec. 55(b).

Alternative Minimum Tax Formula

	Taxable Income
+ or –	Adjustments to Taxable Income
+	Tax Preferences
=	Alternative Minimum Taxable Income (AMTI)
–	Exemption Amount
=	Net Alternative Minimum Taxable Income
×	26 or 28% Tax Rate
=	Tax
–	Alternative Minimum Tax Foreign Tax Credit
=	Tentative Minimum Tax (TMT)
–	Regular Tax for the Year
=	Alternative Minimum Tax (AMT)

The alternative minimum tax (AMT) requires additional recordkeeping and separate basis computations. The AMT adds substantial complexity to the tax system.

¶9415   ADJUSTMENTS TO TAXABLE INCOME

In determining AMTI, taxable income must be computed with the following adjustments. Code Sec. 56(a). Adjustments to taxable income can increase or decrease alternative minimum taxable income.

Depreciation

Taxpayers who, in calculating regular tax liability, depreciate real property under MACRS must use the alternative depreciation system in calculating AMTI. The real property alternative depreciation system calls for a 40-year straight line depreciation. The alternative depreciation system is not required for real property acquired after 1998.

Depreciation deductions for personal property and property which is not subject to straight-line depreciation must be recomputed under the 150 percent declining-balance method under the alternative depreciation system. Taxpayers must switch from the declining-balance method to the straight-line method in the first tax year that maximizes the deduction. Thus, the excess of AMT depreciation over MACRS depreciation in the later years of an asset can be used to offset the excess of accelerated depreciation over straight line in the early years of other assets.

EXAMPLE 9.23

A corporation purchases a $10,000 five-year machine for use in business in 2016. The depreciation methods for regular tax and alternative minimum tax purposes along with the adjustment are as follows:

Year	200% Declining Balance	150% Declining Balance		Adjustment
2016	$2,000	$1,500	+	$500
2017	3,200	2,550	+	650
2018	1,920	1,785	+	135
2019	1,152	1,666	–	514
2020	1,152	1,666	–	514
2021	576	833	–	257

In the first three years an amount must be added to taxable income, while a deduction is taken in the last three years.

Mining Exploration, Circulation, Research and Development Expenditures

Circulation expenditures of periodicals must be amortized ratably over three years. Mining exploration and development expenditures must be amortized ratably over 10 years. Research and experimentation expenditures must be amortized ratably over 10 years. For tax years after 1990, individuals who materially participate in an activity are not required to capitalize and amortize research and experimental expenditures generated by such activity that are otherwise allowed as a business expense deduction under Code Sec. 174(a).

The basis for gain or loss upon disposition is determined using the AMTI basis.

Pollution Control Facilities

For property placed in service after 1986, the five-year amortization method for depreciating pollution control facilities must be replaced by the alternative depreciation system. The adjusted basis used in AMTI calculations (but not for regular tax calculations) to determine the gain or loss on the sale of property for which depreciation has been adjusted must reflect the depreciation adjustment rather than the costs that were deductible in regular tax computations.

Long-Term Contracts

The percentage-of-completion method of accounting to determine gain or loss from long-term contracts must be substituted for any other method of accounting, such as the completed-contract method or the cash basis method, for both regular tax purposes and for AMT purposes. This change will directly affect those taxpayers who were using a form of completed-contract method of accounting for AMT purposes.

The adjustment is the excess of income from use of the percentage-of-completion method over the long-term contract method used on long-term contracts. For example, if the deferred income from a three-year contract is $750,000, no income is reported under the completed-contract method of reporting until the third year. Assuming the costs on the contract are incurred in equal proportions, $250,000 is included in AMTI for each of the three years.

Passive Farming Losses

No deduction is allowed for losses from any farming syndicate or any other farming activity in which the taxpayer does not materially participate. A loss from one farm activity may not be used to offset income from another farm activity. Disallowed losses are carried forward indefinitely and used for AMTI purposes to offset future income from the farming activity. Suspended losses are deductible when the activity is disposed of. Code Sec. 58(a).

Incentive Stock Options

An adjustment must be made to taxable income when incentive stock options are exercised. The excess (if any) of the stock's fair market value at the time of exercise over the amount paid by the employee for the stock is an adjustment that in figuring AMT taxable income is added to the taxable income shown on the tax return. This adjustment is made in the first year in which the rights in the stock are freely transferable or are not subject to a substantial risk of forfeiture.

EXAMPLE 9.24   Arthur Aster pays an exercise price of $15 to purchase stock having a fair market value of $20. The adjustment in the year of exercise is $5, and the stock has a basis of $15 for determining gain or loss for regular tax purposes and $20 for alternative minimum tax purposes. If, in a subsequent year, Arthur sells the stock for $45, the gain recognized is $30 for regular tax purposes and $25 for alternative minimum tax purposes.

Net Operating Losses

The net operating loss (NOL) must be calculated under special rules and cannot offset more than 100 percent of AMT income. The AMT rules generally require that the regular tax NOL must be adjusted for AMTI adjustments and tax preferences.

Gains and Losses on Sale or Exchange of Property

AMTI must be adjusted for any difference between gain or loss reported for the regular tax and that figured for the AMT. For AMT purposes, a property's basis is reduced only by the amount of depreciation allowed in computing AMTI. Therefore, the adjusted basis of the property may differ for regular and minimum tax purposes. The gain or loss for AMTI upon disposition of the asset is determined by the AMTI basis. Similar adjustments must be made to gains and losses on the sale of assets involving mining exploration and development costs, circulation expenditures, research and development expenditures, pollution control facilities, long-term contracts, and incentive stock options.

Personal Exemption

No deduction for personal exemptions may be claimed against alternative minimum taxable income. Code Sec. 56(b)(1)(E). Accordingly, the personal exemption taken in computing taxable income must be added back as an adjustment.

Itemized Deductions

The standard deduction is not allowed for the alternative minimum taxable income computation. Code Sec. 56(b). Only an individual's actual itemized deductions are allowed in computing AMTI and then only those itemized deductions not limited by the discussion below. In some situations it may be better to itemize even when the standard deduction is larger than the itemized deductions because only certain itemized deductions are added back for AMT purposes.

In computing taxable income, total itemized deductions for 2017 must be reduced for high income taxpayers by 3 percent of adjusted gross income exceeding $313,800 for married filing jointly, $287,650 for head of household, $261,500 for single, and $156,900 for married filing separately. This reduction does not apply to the alternative minimum tax. Consequently, itemized deductions included in the alternative minimum taxable income computation do not have to be reduced. The alternative minimum tax form reduces adjusted gross income by the disallowed itemized deduction.

Miscellaneous Itemized Deductions

No deduction is allowed for AMTI computation for any allowable miscellaneous itemized deductions except:

1. Wagering losses
2. Any deduction for impairment-related work expenses
3. The deduction for estate tax in case of income in respect of a decedent
4. Any deduction in connection with personal property used in a short sale
5. The deduction where a taxpayer restores substantial amount held under claim of right
6. The deduction where annuity payments cease before investment is recovered
7. The deduction for amortizable bond premium
8. The deduction in connection with cooperative housing corporations

Thus, the disallowed miscellaneous itemized deductions are added back to taxable income in arriving at AMTI.

Medical Expenses

Medical expenses are deductible for AMTI only to the extent that they exceed 10 percent of adjusted gross income.

Taxes

State, local, and foreign *real property* taxes, state and local *personal property* taxes, and state, local and foreign *income,* war profits, or excess profits taxes allowed as itemized deductions for regular tax purposes are not allowed in the AMTI computation. Thus, the only taxes deductible for AMTI purposes are the windfall profit tax (on oil removed before August 23, 1988) and the generation-skipping tax imposed on income distributions. A refund of state and local taxes paid, for which no alternative minimum tax deduction was allowed, is not included in alternative minimum taxable income.

Interest

The amount deductible for regular tax purposes for home mortgage interest may be greater than the permitted AMT deduction. For minimum tax purposes, upon refinancing a loan that gives rise to qualified housing interest, interest paid on the new loan is treated as qualified housing interest to the extent that (1) it so qualified under the prior loan, and (2) the amount of the loan was not increased. Thus, the home-equity loan exception to the regular tax rules does not apply to AMT.

EXAMPLE 9.25

Jane Juniper owes $80,000 on a mortgage on a principal residence purchased for $100,000 and with a current fair market value of $125,000. June takes out a second mortgage for $25,000. The interest on the additional $25,000 principal in excess of the prior $80,000 loan cannot be deducted for AMT purposes.

¶9415

¶9425 TAX PREFERENCE ITEMS

The following tax preferences must be added back to taxable income in arriving at alternative minimum taxable income. Code Sec. 57.

Depletion

The depletion preference is the excess of the percentage depletion deduction over the adjusted basis of the property at the end of the year. The preference applies to percentage depletion for all minerals, not just oil and gas.

Intangible Drilling Costs

The tax preference for intangible drilling costs on oil, gas, and geothermal wells is the amount by which the excess intangible drilling costs are greater than 65 percent of net income from the resource properties. Excess intangible drilling costs are the amount by which the intangible drilling deduction for regular tax purposes exceeds the amount which would have been allowable if the costs had been capitalized and amortized over 120 months.

Tax-Exempt Interest

A tax preference has been added for tax-exempt interest on private activity bonds issued after August 7, 1986. This preference does not apply to bonds issued for the benefit of tax-exempt charitable or educational institutions or to bonds issued for public purposes such as schools and municipally owned public utilities. Tax-exempt interest on private activity bonds issued in 2009 and 2010 is not an item of tax preference.

Accelerated Depreciation or Amortization

There is a tax preference for excess depreciation and amortization taken on certain properties acquired before 1987. (However, any properties acquired in 1986 that use the cost recovery rules are not subject to this tax preference.) Pre-1987 tax preference items include:

1. Depreciation on real property acquired before 1987 that is in excess of straight-line depreciation over the useful life
2. Amortization of certified pollution control facilities (the excess of 60-month amortization over depreciation otherwise allowable)

¶9435 EXEMPTION AMOUNT

The allowable exemption amounts for 2017 are $84,500 for married persons filing joint returns and surviving spouses, $54,300 for single individuals, and $42,250 for married individuals filing separate returns or estates or trusts. The exemption amounts are reduced by 25 cents for each $1 by which alternative minimum taxable income exceeds $160,900 for married taxpayers filing jointly, $120,700 for single individuals, and $80,450 for married taxpayers filing separately. Code Sec. 55(d).

EXAMPLE 9.26	A married couple with AMTI of $300,000 is allowed an exemption amount of $49,725 ($84,500 – .25 × ($300,000 – $160,900)). If their AMTI were to exceed $498,900, there would be no deduction for the exemption amount.

The exemption phaseout level for married taxpayers filing separately has been made equal to the phaseout level for married taxpayers filing jointly. In the case of taxpayers filing separately whose AMTI exceeds $249,450, a special computation is necessary. The taxpayer must increase the AMT taxable income by 25 percent of the amount it exceeds $249,450. However, the increase cannot be more than $42,250.

The AMT exemption amount for minor children is limited to the greater of the child's earned income for the year plus $1,050 or the child's share of the unused parental minimum tax exemption (the excess of the Code Sec. 55(d) amount over the parent's AMTI) for tax years beginning in 1991.

¶9445 TAX CREDITS

Only the personal nonrefundable credits plus the foreign tax credit reduce AMT liability for noncorporate taxpayers. Thus, the general business credit is unavailable against the AMT for individuals even if it is allowable for regular tax purposes arising from qualified purchases or as a carryover. Taxpayers remaining in an AMT position for a number of years may lose allowable general business credits because the carryovers will have expired before they can be used. Even if the credits are used before expiring, the passage of time will erode the value of the credits. Code Sec. 59.

Individuals paying foreign taxes are permitted to use a portion of the specially calculated foreign tax credit against the tentative minimum tax. The foreign tax credit is allowed to the extent of the foreign tax on the taxpayer's foreign-source alternative minimum taxable income.

In computing the income tax on taxable income, the general business credit is taken only to the extent that it reduces the regular tax for the year to the tentative minimum tax. Thus, we cannot have a situation where the general business credit reduces the regular tax and then the alternative minimum tax is increased to offset the general business credit taken.

EXAMPLE 9.27	Matches Corporation has a regular tax before the general business credit of $50,000, general business credits of $22,000, and a tentative minimum tax of $40,000. Only $10,000 of the general business credit is taken, reducing the regular tax to $40,000. Since the regular tax is equal to the tentative minimum tax, no alternative minimum tax is imposed.

¶9455   CARRYOVER OF CREDIT

The alternative minimum tax paid in one year may be carried forward indefinitely as a credit against the regular tax liability. The credit may not be used, however, to offset any future minimum tax liability. A taxpayer is not allowed to take a credit larger than the amount necessary to reduce the regular tax to the amount of the tentative minimum tax. Code Sec. 53.

EXAMPLE 9.28	Andrew Ames has a tentative minimum tax of $100,000, a regular tax before the AMT credit of $120,000, and an AMT credit of $35,000 from previous years. Without the AMT credit, the taxpayer would have no alternative minimum tax because the regular tax exceeds the tentative minimum tax. Since the full AMT credit would reduce the regular tax below the tentative minimum tax, only $20,000 of the AMT credit carryforward may be used to reduce the regular tax.

The AMT credit for any tax year is the excess of the adjusted net minimum tax imposed for all tax years beginning after 1986 over the amount allowable as a credit in previous years. The adjusted net minimum tax is the amount of net minimum tax (alternative minimum tax) for a year reduced by the amount which would be the net minimum tax (alternative minimum tax) for that year if only certain adjustments and tax preferences were taken into account. The adjustments and tax preferences taken into account for this computation include:

1. The same itemized deduction adjustments discussed under the AMTI adjustments
2. The following tax preferences: depletion, tax-exempt interest, and gain exclusion allowed on small business stock.

The purpose of the minimum tax credit is to prevent the double taxation of deferral preferences and adjustments. These deferral preferences and adjustments are subject to the alternative minimum tax in a tax year earlier than the year they are subject to the regular tax. For example, accelerated depreciation taken in a year creates a tax adjustment or tax preference. This adjustment or preference may cause an additional tax because of the alternative minimum tax. In later years, taxable income will be higher because of the smaller depreciation deductions under accelerated depreciation, thus causing a higher income tax. Thus, the total depreciation deductions will not be received without the benefit of the alternative minimum tax credit. Therefore, the amount of the minimum tax credit to be carried forward is the excess of the AMT paid over the AMT that would be paid if AMTI included only "exclusion" preferences and adjustments (those items that result in a permanent reduction of regular tax liability).

TAX BLUNDER

Tommy Rose, who is subject to the alternative minimum tax, each year purchases some private activity bonds. The interest on these bonds will be free from income tax but will be taxed at 26 or 28 percent under the alternative minimum tax.

¶9475   ## ALTERNATIVE MINIMUM TAX PLANNING

Individuals subject to the alternative minimum tax generally benefit by accelerating income into an AMT year. Income recognized in an AMT year will generally be taxed at 26 or 28 percent rather than at the higher regular tax rate.

Ways to accelerate income into an AMT year include:

1. Taking capital gains before year-end
2. Receiving bonuses, commissions, and other income before year-end
3. Redeeming Treasury bills and U.S. savings bonds before year-end
4. Exchanging tax-exempt municipal bonds for taxable bonds paying a higher interest rate

Individuals may also benefit by delaying expenses until a regular tax year. Payment of allowed itemized deductions, such as charitable contributions, provides a tax benefit in an AMT of only 26 or 28 percent, while delaying the payment to a regular tax year may allow a deduction at greater than 28 percent. Any payment in an AMT year of an itemized deduction not allowed for AMT purposes, such as property taxes, will produce no tax savings, since reducing the regular tax merely increases the AMT by an equal amount.

Care must be taken not to accelerate too much income into an AMT year or to defer too many expenses into a regular tax year. Only accelerate receipt of income or defer expenses up to the point where the tax due under the tentative minimum tax equals the regular tax.

Taxpayers may be able to improve their AMT position by finding investments that produce passive income to offset passive tax-shelter losses. Since tax-shelter losses are not deductible for AMT purposes, the alternative minimum tax will not be increased to the extent that the passive income offset passive losses. Income-producing limited partnerships and rental properties generating passive income may be appropriate investments.

Interest on private-activity municipal bonds is a tax preference for the AMT. Thus, taxpayers holding private-activity municipal bonds in AMT years will find this income taxable. These taxpayers may be better off to trade these bonds for regular municipal bonds or higher paying taxable bonds.

EXAMPLE 9.29	Mark and Samantha Mandell, the parents of two children, had the following tax facts:

Income

Wages	$241,198
Business Income	89,500
1202 Capital Gain	50,000
Collectibles Capital Gain	25,000
Dividend Income	7,000
Interest Income	8,500

Expenses

1/2 Self-Employment Tax	1,198
Moving Expenses	10,000
Medical Expenses	42,000
Casualty Loss	39,100
Housing Interest	8,000
Investment Interest	28,000
Personal Interest	2,000
Charitable Contributions	27,000
Real Estate Taxes	10,500
Other Nonbusiness Deductions	23,000

Other Tax Preferences

Private Purpose Municipal Bond Income	12,050
Excess of Accelerated Depreciation	20,000
General Business Credit	10,000

The computation of their income is as follows:

Gross Income

Wages	$241,198	
Business Income	89,500	
1202 Capital Gain	0	
Collectibles Capital Gain	25,000	
Dividend Income	7,000	
Interest Income	8,500	
Total Gross Income		$371,198

Deductions from Gross Income

1/2 Self-Employment Tax		$ 1,198
Moving Expenses		$10,000
Adjusted Gross Income		$360,000

Itemized Deductions

Medical Expenses ($42,000 – 10% AGI)	$ 6,000	
Real Estate Taxes	10,500	
Housing Interest	8,000	
Investment Interest	8,500	
Personal Interest ($2,000 × 0%)	0	
Charitable Contributions	27,000	
Casualty Loss ($39,100 – $100 – 10% AGI)	3,000	
Other Itemized Deductions ($23,000 – 2% AGI)	15,800	
Less: 3% ($360,000 – $311,300)	– 1,386	
Total Itemized Deductions		– 77,414
Personal Exemptions ($4,050 × 4) × .8		– 10,044
Taxable Income		$272,542
Income Tax		$62,646
General Business Credit		0
Regular Tax for the Year		$62,646

EXAMPLE 9.29 CONTINUED

Alternative Minimum Tax Computation

Taxable Income		$272,542
Itemized Deduction Adjustment		– 1,386
Personal Exemptions ($4,050 × 4) × .6	$10,044	
Medical Expenses	0	
Real Estate Taxes	10,500	
Other Itemized Deductions	15,800	
Total Adjustments to Taxable Income		+ 36,344
Tax Preferences		
Private Purpose Municipal Bond Income	12,050	
Excess Depreciation	20,000	
Total Tax Preferences		32,050
Alternative Minimum Taxable Income		$339,550
Alternative Minimum Tax Exemption		– 39,837
Net Alternative Minimum Taxable Income		$299,713
Tax Rate		× 26/28%
Tentative Alternative Minimum Tax		$79,254
Regular Tax for the Year		62,646
Alternative Minimum Tax		$16,608

The gain on the Code Sec. 1202 stock is reduced by 100 percent.

The personal exemptions of $16,200 was reduced to $10,044 because of adjusted gross income. The adjusted gross income caused the itemized deductions to be reduced.

The collectibles capital gain is taxed at the 28 percent collectibles rate. The dividends are taxed at the 15 percent rate. These special rates are used for both the regular tax and AMT computations.

The investment interest expense is limited to the $8,500 investment income. The capital gains and dividend income are taxed at 15% dividend rate and thus are not investment income.

$54,596	Tax on $240,542 ($272,542 – $25,000 collectibles gain – $7,000 dividends)
7,000	Tax on collectibles gain ($25,000 × 28%)
1,050	Tax on dividends ($7,000 × 15%)
$62,646	Income Tax

The alternative minimum tax computation begins with taxable income and adds back certain adjustments and tax preferences.

The itemized deduction reduction reduces taxable income.

The personal exemption is added back.

The medical expenses are reduced by an additional 2.5 percent of adjusted gross income only for taxpayers over 65.

Taxes are not allowed as an alternative minimum tax itemized deduction. Other itemized deductions are also not allowed in the alternative minimum tax computation.

The housing interest, charitable contributions, and casualty losses are not adjusted as they are allowed in AMT computation.

The alternative minimum tax exemption of $84,500 is reduced by $44,663 because the taxpayers' alternative minimum taxable income exceeds $160,900. The reduction is 25 percent of any excess over $160,900.

The taxpayers are unable to use the $10,000 general business credit because of the alternative minimum tax. They are able to carry the unused general business credit back one year and forward 20 years.

EXAMPLE 9.29 CONTINUED

The AMT credit carryforward is computed as follows:

Taxable Income		$272,542
Itemized Deduction Adjustment		– 1,386
Personal Exemptions	$10,044	
Medical Expenses ($360,000 × 2.5%)	0	
Real Estate Taxes	10,500	
Other Itemized Deductions	15,800	
Total Adjustments to Taxable Income		+ 36,344
Tax Preferences for AMT Credit		
Private Purpose Municipal Bond Income	12,050	
Total Tax Preferences for AMT Credit		+ 12,050
AMTI for AMT Credit		$319,550
Alternative Minimum Tax Exemption		– 44,837
Net AMTI for AMT Credit		$274,713
Tax Rate		× 26/28%
Tentative AMT for Credit Purposes		$72,754
Regular Tax for the Year		– 62,646
Alternative Minimum Tax for AMT Credit		$9,608
Alternative Minimum Tax		$16,608
Alternative Minimum Tax for AMT Credit		– 9,608
Alternative Minimum Tax Credit		$7,000

The alternative minimum tax exemption is $44,837. Since AMTI exceeded $160,900, there was a $39,663 reduction in the exemption amount.

A comparison of the computation of the alternative minimum tax and the alternative minimum tax for AMT credit reveals two differences: (1) the $20,000 depreciation tax preference is not included in the AMT credit computation because it is not an exclusion item and (2) the alternative minimum tax exemption is $44,837 instead of $39,837. These two differences, $25,000, at a 28 percent rate results in a $7,000 alternative minimum tax credit.

SUMMARY

- A tax credit is a direct reduction in the tax due. A tax credit is more valuable than a deduction of the same amount.
- Credits are divided into two types: nonrefundable and refundable.
- In nonrefundable credits, there have been no payments to the government, so the taxpayer is not entitled to a refund even of the credit exceeds the gross tax. Nonrefundable credits must be taken in the proper order.
- Refundable credits allow the taxpayer to reduce the tax liability below zero. With the exception of the earned income credit and the child tax credit, the refundable credits represent a return of money paid into the government.
- The alternative minimum tax is a tax imposed in addition to the regular income tax to recapture the reductions resulting from the use of special tax relief provisions of the tax law. Certain adjustments and preferences are added back to taxable income and then an exemption amount is subtracted before applying the alternative minimum tax rates.

QUESTIONS

1. Explain the difference between a tax credit and a tax deduction. Which would help a 28 percent tax bracket taxpayer most, a $2,000 deduction or a $400 credit? A 15 percent tax bracket taxpayer?

2. Explain what is meant by the terms "refundable" and "nonrefundable" credits. How might these classifications affect the tax liability of a taxpayer?

3. Why is the household and dependent care credit sometimes only 20 percent and other times as high as 35 percent?

4. Can a taxpayer qualify for the household and dependent care credit if he or she is not employed?

5. Is the dependency exemption required for the household and dependent care credit?

6. What limits are placed on employment-related expenses for the household and dependent care credit?

7. Must married taxpayers file a joint return in all cases to qualify for the household and dependent care credit?

8. How does an individual qualify for the credit for the elderly?

9. What effect does the receipt of Social Security benefits have on the credit for the elderly?

10. What is the amount of the child tax credit for 2017?

11. What is the maximum child tax credit a taxpayer may receive for an 18-year-old full-time college student in 2017?

12. Can the child tax credit for taxpayers result in a refundable personal credit?

13. What expenses are eligible for the Hope Scholarship Credit?

14. How many years of post-secondary education expenses are eligible for the Hope tuition credit?

15. What expenses are eligible for the Lifetime Learning Credit?

16. What is the purpose of the foreign tax credit?

17. When would a taxpayer choose to itemize foreign taxes rather than take the foreign tax credit?

18. How are the various business credits reported on the tax return?

19. What buildings qualify for the rehabilitation credit?

20. How does the rehabilitation credit differ from the investment credit?

21. How does an investment credit affect the basis of an item purchased?

22. How will a premature disposal of investment credit property affect a taxpayer?

23. What happens to the basis of an asset that has a recapture of an investment credit?

24. Are taxpayers allowed a credit on the total expenditure for research?

25. What is the ceiling limitation for the general business credit?

26. When several years of general business credits are carried over to the present year which also has a general business credit, in what order are the credits taken?

27. What basic group of employees qualifies for the work opportunity credit?

28. Which nonrefundable credits if not used in the present year can be carried over to other years?

29. Is it possible for a taxpayer to have a credit for excess Social Security if the taxpayer worked for more than one employer and the total wages came to $38,000?

30. Describe the earned income credit.

31. Sara's only source of income was wages of $6,000. She and her daughter live with her parents. The daughter is claimed as a dependent by the father. Is Sara eligible for the earned income credit?

32. Discuss the declaration of estimated tax filing requirements of individuals.

33. If a taxpayer does not file estimated taxes and is underpaid for the year, what penalty may be imposed?

34. What is the purpose of the alternative minimum tax?

35. What is a tax preference item?

36. When is it possible to have a tax preference for the alternative minimum tax if the taxpayer is using straight-line depreciation?

37. List the itemized deductions that are not allowed in the computation of alternative minimum taxable income.

38. When is interest deductible as an itemized deduction for income tax purposes but not allowed as an itemized deduction for the alternative minimum tax.

39. What items create the alternative minimum tax credit?

PROBLEMS

40. Compute the child and dependent care credit in each of the following independent cases:
    a. Jack and Jill Jones are married and file a joint return. Jill worked full time earning $20,000, while Jack attended law school the entire year. They incurred $6,500 of child care expenses during the year for their two children, ages eight and six.
    b. Mary Morgan is a widow who worked full time the entire year earning $23,000. She incurred the following child care expenses for her six-year-old daughter in order to be employed during the year:

Kindergarten	$400
Babysitters	600
Private school (first grade)	600

    c. Bill and Debra Page are divorced and have one dependent child, Betty, age nine. Bill had custody of Betty for five months this year and claimed Betty as an exemption on his tax return. Debra had custody of Betty for the remainder of the year. Debra incurred $3,600 of employment-related expenses during the year, while Bill incurred $2,500 of employment-related expenses. Both were employed for the entire year and each earned $20,000 in wages this year.

41. Frank and Emma Browne are both over 65 and file a joint return. Emma received $800 from Social Security benefits and Frank received $1,200 from railroad retirement benefits. In addition to the benefits, they reported income of $18,000 from their antique shop.
    a. Compute Frank and Emma's tax credit for the elderly.
    b. Assume that only Emma was over 65 and compute the tax credit for the elderly.

42. A married couple with two children has $16,000 of earned income. There is no taxable income after deducting the standard deduction and personal exemptions. What is the amount of their child tax credit?

43. Fannie, a widow, lives in an apartment with her two minor children (ages 4 and 6) whom she supports. Fannie earns $35,000 during 2017. She uses the standard deduction. Calculate the amount, if any, of Fannie's earned income credit.

44. A married couple with two children has earned income of $30,000 with no withholding. Assume they have a taxable income of $100, they paid $2,295 in FICA taxes, and they will receive an earned income credit of $3,582. Their tax on $100 is $10. What is the amount of their income tax liability?

45. A married couple with three children has earned income of $15,000 and adjusted gross income of $50,000 with no withholding. Assume a standard deduction of $12,700 and personal exemptions of $20,250. Their tax on $17,050 is $1,705. They have no earned income credit. They paid $1,148 in FICA taxes. What is the amount of their income tax due?

46. Walt is single, age 67, and retired. His taxable income for 2017 is $1,320, and the tax on this amount is $132. Walt's tax credit for the elderly is $225. What is the amount of the credit for the elderly that Walt can claim on his tax return?

47. Philip and Susan Moyer have two children who are both in the first four years of college. They incur $4,500 in tuition expenses for each of the two children. What is the maximum amount of American Opportunity Tax Credit?

48. Cathy Thomas, a single mother, has modified AGI of $82,000. In 2017, her daughter begins work on her bachelors degree at an accredited institution. Cathy pays $6,000 in qualified tuition for the daughter's first semester. What is the amount of American Opportunity Tax Credit Cathy is allowed on her return?

49. Michael is divorced and the exemption for his daughter is claimed by his ex-wife. What is the amount of American Opportunity Tax Credit allowed Michael when he pays $2,500 in tuition for his daughter to attend her first year at an accredited four-year college?

50. What is the amount of Lifetime Learning Credit allowed a taxpayer assuming that he or she incurred $3,000 in tuition and fees and $8,000 in room and board for an eligible college student?

51. In 2017, Lenny Traveler had adjusted gross income of $26,350 from investments in the U.S., while earning $40,000 from foreign sources. Lenny's potential U.S. tax liability is $9,389, and he had to pay $9,000 in foreign income taxes. What amount can Lenny, a U.S. citizen, claim as a foreign tax credit?

52. ABC Corporation has international earnings of $500,000 and a U.S. tax liability of $170,000. From foreign operations ABC generated $120,000 of income on which a $55,000 tax was imposed. What is ABC's foreign tax credit and total tax liability?

53. Mark has a tentative general business credit of $120,000 for the current year. His net regular tax liability before the general business credit is $135,000, and his tentative minimum tax is $100,000. Compute Mark's allowable general business credit for the year.

54. Zap Industries had a tentative general business credit in 2017 of $60,000. Its tax liability in 2016 was $20,000. Its tax liability before the general business credit in 2017 is $50,000.
    a. What is Zap Industries' 2017 tax liability?
    b. Are there any effects on the tax liabilities of the previous year?
    c. If so, what are they?

55. Yoyo Corporation bought $42,000 worth of energy equipment in November 2012, taking an investment credit of $4,200. In March 2017, the firm sells the equipment for $30,000. What is the investment credit recapture?

56. Martha and Marty Mertens are married and file a joint return. Marty started his own business at the beginning of the current tax year and reported net income of $14,000 for the year. Martha worked full time as a waitress earning $8,000, excluding tips of $3,000. Marty and Martha maintained a home for their 11-year-old son. What is their earned income credit for 2017?

57. What is the adjustment that must be made to taxable income in computing alternative minimum taxable income for 2017, assuming that an individual purchased an office building on January 8 for $400,000?

58. What is the amount of tax preference for alternative minimum tax purposes assuming that an individual sells some qualified small business stock held more than five years at a $20,000 gain.

59. What is the allowable exemption for the alternative minimum tax assuming that a married couple has alternative minimum taxable income of $200,000?

60. Calculate the exemption amount for the following cases for 2017 for a single taxpayer, married taxpayer filing jointly, and a married taxpayer filing separately when AMTI is $300,000.

61. Tamara and Tony Mapp, a married couple, report the following items for the year:

Taxable income	$80,000
AMT adjustments	30,000
Tax preferences	40,000
Regular tax liability	16,000

What is their alternative minimum tax for the year?

62. Donna, an unmarried individual who is age 66, has taxable income of $245,000. She has AMT positive adjustment of $68,000 and tax preferences of $6,000.
    a. What is Donna's AMT?
    b. What is the total amount of Donna's tax liability?

63. Alex and Alicia Andrews file a joint tax return. On the return they show Alex's salary of $110,000, interest income from corporate bonds of $3,000, dividends from domestic corporations of $1,000, and a net long-term capital gain of $60,000. They also had the following expenses for itemized deductions: $18,000 medical expenses, $8,000 home mortgage interest, $5,000 in consumer interest, $4,000 in deductible taxes, $2,000 charitable contributions, and $1,200 in miscellaneous deductions not subject to the 2 percent limitation. The Andrews claim five exemptions on their return. Determine their net alternative minimum taxable income.

64. What is the amount of AMT credit carryforward for 2017, assuming that an individual had an alternative minimum tax of $20,000 and an alternative minimum tax for AMT credit of $12,000?

65. Which of the following are tax adjustments or preference items for purposes of the alternative minimum tax?
    a. $20,000 net long-term capital gain over net short-term capital losses
    b. $3,000 net short-term capital gain
    c. $10,000 straight-line depreciation on building acquired in 1989
    d. $1,500 interest from City of Buffalo bonds

66. Which of the following qualify as "employment-related" expenses for the credit for child care?
    a. Nursery school fees
    b. Transportation to nursery school
    c. Housekeeper's salary
    d. Housekeeper's meals
    e. Gardener's salary

67. What is the amount of dependent care credit before any income tax limitation for a couple with two children where they spend $6,500 for dependent care and the husband earns $25,000 for the year and the wife earns $4,500?
    a. $1,755
    b. $1,215
    c. $60
    d. $0

68. Which of the following items is not an adjustment for the alternative minimum tax?
    a. Taxes
    b. Wagering losses
    c. Personal exemption
    d. Standard deduction

69. **Comprehensive Problem.** Determine the tax due, including the alternative minimum tax, for Patty Perkins, assuming she is single using the following tax information:

Adjusted Gross Income	$100,000
Itemized Deductions	20,000
Alternative Minimum Tax Itemized Deductions	12,000
Tax Preference Items	40,000
General Business Credit	17,000

70. **Comprehensive Problem.** From the following information determine the total 2017 tax due for Charlene and Dick Storm, assuming they file a joint return, have three dependents, and are not members of a qualified retirement plan.

Dick's Wages	$33,000
Charlene's Wages	41,000
Dick's Contribution to an IRA	2,000
Charlene's Contribution to an IRA	800
Charlene's Self-Employment Income	12,000
Tax Preference Items	40,000
General Business Credit	7,000
Housing Interest	8,000
Consumer Interest	2,000
Property Taxes	3,000

71. **Research Problem.** An asset is purchased on May 15, 2013, for $100,000. The full 10 percent investment credit of $10,000 is taken on the asset. On June 23, 2017, a Code Sec. 108 election is made to exclude gain arising from the discharge of business indebtedness in the amount of $7,000. What is the amount of investment credit recapture? See *Panhandle Eastern Pipe Line Co. & Affiliates,* 81-2 USTC ¶9496, 654 F.2d 35 (Ct Cls 1981).

Chapter

10

Property Transactions: Determination of Basis and Gains and Losses

OBJECTIVES

After completing Chapter 10, you should be able to:

1. Understand the factors in determining realized and recognized gain or loss.
2. Determine the basis in various types of asset purchases and the allocation of basis.
3. Determine the basis of property acquired by gift and from a decedent.
4. Determine the basis in stock transactions, including stock dividends, stock rights, and wash sales.
5. Compute gains and losses in related party transactions and the income recognized in installment sales.

OVERVIEW

Chapters 10 through 12 contain discussions of topics related to the income tax consequences of property transactions including sale, exchange, or other disposition of property. By the end of the three chapters on property transactions, the student should gain familiarity with the following broad topics: (1) determination of basis; (2) realized gain or loss; (3) recognized gain or loss; (4) situations where gain or loss is not recognized or only partially recognized; and (5) classification of recognized gain or loss as ordinary or capital.

Chapters 10 and 11 discuss the first four broad topics while Chapter 12 focuses on the classification of recognized gain or loss as ordinary or capital. More specifically, Chapter 10 is concerned with the realization and recognition of gain or loss and with the determination of basis under varying circumstances including: an ordinary purchase, a bargain purchase, acquisition through gift, acquisition through inheritance, conversion of property from personal use to business use, nontaxable and taxable stock dividends and stock rights, and wash sales.

Factors in Determining Gain or Loss

¶10,001 DEFINITION OF REALIZED GAIN OR LOSS

Realized gain or loss is the difference between the amount realized (see ¶10,015) from the sale or other disposition of property and the adjusted basis (see ¶10,025) at the time of sale or disposition. If the amount realized exceeds the adjusted basis, there is a realized gain. On the other hand, if the adjusted basis exceeds the amount realized, there is a realized loss. Code Sec. 1001(a); Reg. §1.1001-1(a).

The term "other disposition" is interpreted broadly and includes transactions such as trade-ins, casualties, thefts, and condemnations. The term does not include a fluctuation in market value of an asset because the possibility for the taxpayer to gain or lose value of an asset still exists and no identifiable event has occurred to "fix" the gain or loss realized. Reg. §1.1001-1(c)(1).

EXAMPLE 10.1

> Adam Acres sells property with an adjusted basis of $20,000 for $30,000 and has a realized gain of $10,000. If he had sold the property for $15,000, he would have had a $5,000 realized loss. If Adam exchanged Beach Corporation stock with an adjusted basis of $4,000 for Clark Corporation stock with a fair market value of $7,000, he has a realized gain of $3,000. If, however, Adam had Danville Corporation stock with an adjusted basis of $5,000 that has appreciated in value to $8,000, there is no realized gain because there is no sale or other disposition of the property.

The recovery of cost doctrine allows the taxpayer to recover the cost of property before being taxed on the sale proceeds. While owning the asset, the taxpayer may recover the cost through depreciation deductions, providing it is depreciable property. Basis is reduced for the depreciation deductions and at the time of sale or other disposition the remaining amount of cost is recovered through a comparison of the amount realized with the adjusted basis to determine whether there is a realized gain or loss.

¶10,015 AMOUNT REALIZED

The amount realized from the sale or other disposition of property is the sum of any money received plus the fair market value of other property received. It does not include any amount received from the purchaser as reimbursement for real property taxes which are treated as imposed on the purchaser, but it does include amounts representing real property taxes which are treated as imposed on the seller, if they are paid by the purchaser. Code Sec. 1001(b). The amount realized from a sale or other disposition of property also includes the amount of liabilities from which the transferor is relieved as a result of the sale or disposition. The amount realized is reduced by selling expenses.

EXAMPLE 10.2

> Darlene Brown owns land worth $40,000 which is subject to a $16,000 mortgage. She sells it to Edward Greene who pays $24,000 cash and also assumes the mortgage. She incurs $2,000 selling expenses. Darlene's amount realized is $38,000 ($24,000 + $16,000 – $2,000).

The "fair market value" of the property is the price a willing buyer and a willing seller would reach after bargaining where neither party is acting under compulsion. Various sources can provide evidence of value. Stock exchange quotations generally provide evidence of the fair market value of stock except for unusually large blocks of stock. Sales of similar property on the open market are also evidence of value, and the opinion of appraisers or experts is generally given significant weight.

To summarize:

	Cash Received
+	Fair Market Value of Property and Services Received
+	Liabilities of Seller Assumed by Buyer
–	Selling Expenses
	Amount Realized

¶10,025 ADJUSTED BASIS

The concept of basis is important in federal income taxation. In effect, it measures the amount of the taxpayer's investment in the property, which the taxpayer is able to have returned without tax consequences. The taxpayer's original basis of property purchased is generally cost, but in some situations it may be fair market value, or a substituted basis. To figure the adjusted basis, the original cost or other basis is adjusted in various ways to reflect additions and reductions in investment.

The basis of property must be increased by capital expenditures and decreased by capital returns. These adjustments are made to all types of property for all events occurring after acquisition whether original basis is cost, fair market value, or a substituted basis. Code Secs. 1011 and 1016. Increases in basis have the effect of reducing the amount of gain realized or increasing the amount of realized loss as well as depreciation or cost recovery. Decreases in basis have the effect of increasing the amount of realized gain or decreasing the amount of loss and depreciation or cost recovery.

To summarize:

	Original Basis
+	Capital Expenditures
–	Capital Returns
	Adjusted Basis

Capital *expenditures* are costs chargeable to the capital account. Routine repair and maintenance expenses are not capital expenditures. However, improvements, betterments, acquisition costs, purchase commissions, and legal costs for defending title are all capital expenditures. Capital *returns* include depreciation, depletion, amortization, tax-free dividends, compensation or awards for involuntary conversions, deductible casualty losses, insurance reimbursements, and cash rebates received by a purchaser. Code Sec. 1016(a).

The basis reduction for ACRS or MACRS cost recovery, depreciation, amortization, or depletion is no less than that allowable under the law. If the taxpayer claimed a higher deduction than was allowable and that deduction was allowed for tax purposes (i.e., actually deducted on the taxpayer's return), the basis reduction is that higher allowed amount. If a taxpayer takes no depreciation, then the amount allowable is the amount allowable under the straight-line method. Code Sec. 1016; Reg. §1.1016-3(a)(2)(i). (Basis, of course, is not reduced for depreciation on assets where it is not allowable, such as on personal use assets as a residence or personal automobile.)

EXAMPLE 10.3   Judy Jergens purchased a business building in January 2004 for $390,000 to be depreciated straight-line over 39 years. She took depreciation of $10,000 a year from 2004 through 2014 and none for 2015 and 2016. She sold the asset on January 2, 2017, for $450,000 and reported a $170,000 gain ($450,000 – ($390,000 – $110,000)). She was incorrect, however, because she should have reduced the basis by the greater of the allowed or allowable depreciation, and $10,000 depreciation was also allowable for 2015 and 2016. Thus, her gain should have been $190,000 ($450,000 – ($390,000 – $130,000)).

Basis may also be reduced by the amortization of a premium on taxable bonds at the taxpayer's election, and a reduction in interest income in computing taxable income is then allowed. The basis is reduced because it is a recovery of the cost. If no election to amortize premium on taxable bonds is made, then the taxpayer recognizes a smaller capital gain or a larger capital loss upon ultimate sale or disposition. The premiums on tax-exempt bonds must be amortized for purposes of reducing basis, but no reduction in interest income in computing taxable income is allowable because the interest income is not included in taxable income. Reg. §1.171-1(b).

EXAMPLE 10.4   On January 2, 2017, Vernon Vaughn paid $1,200 for a $1,000 face value taxable bond which will mature on January 1, 2027, and he elects to amortize the premium. For 2017, he is allowed a $20 reduction in interest income, and the adjusted basis of the bond at December 31, 2017, is $1,180. If the bond is tax-exempt, the basis is reduced to $1,180, but no reduction in interest income is allowed in computing taxable income.

¶10,030

HOLDING PERIOD

Property has to be held for longer than one year to be long-term. Code. Sec. 1222. In figuring the holding period, the day the property was acquired is excluded, but the day it was disposed of is included. Holding period will be discussed in detail in Chapter 12.

¶10,035

RECOGNITION AND NONRECOGNITION OF GAIN OR LOSS

If a realized gain or loss is recognized, the gain is includible and the loss is deductible in determining taxable income. Thus, "recognition" means that the result of a particular transaction is considered to be taxable income or a deductible loss. Generally, recognition occurs at the time of sale or exchange.

There are certain situations where the realized gain or loss is not recognized. In the case of like-kind exchanges, part or all of the gain or loss may not be recognized. Also, in the case of involuntary conversions and sales of residences, part or all of the realized gain may not be recognized (Chapter 11).

There are also situations where a realized gain may be recognized, but realized losses are not recognized. For example, a sale of a personal-use asset, such as an automobile, results in gain recognition but not loss recognition. (An exception to the latter rule is that losses resulting from casualty and theft of personal-use assets are deductible, provided they exceed certain limits, but the condemnation loss on a personal-use asset is not deductible.) Similarly, sales between related taxpayers may result in gain recognition but no loss recognition. Code Sec. 267(a)(1).

Exhibit 1. Gain or Loss Summary

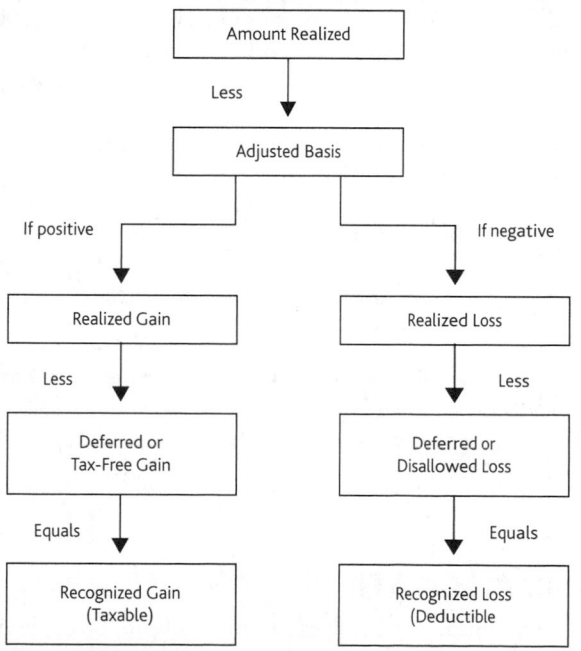

The following examples and Exhibit 1 illustrate the above rules.

EXAMPLE 10.5	Albert Austin sold for $14,000 stock with an adjusted basis of $10,000. His realized and recognized gain is $4,000. If he sells the stock for $7,000, his realized and recognized loss is $3,000.

EXAMPLE 10.6	Ellen Eagle trades in a business machine with an adjusted basis of $10,000 for another like-kind business machine with a fair market value of $15,000. Although she realizes a gain of $5,000, this gain is not recognized because of the like-kind provisions of Code Sec. 1031.

EXAMPLE 10.7	Patrick Power has land with an adjusted basis of $50,000 that was condemned, and the authorities gave him a $75,000 award. Although Patrick has a $25,000 realized gain, he does not have to recognize this gain if the land were replaced with land costing $75,000 or more.

EXAMPLE 10.8	Karen Kohl sells her personal use automobile that cost her $10,000 for $12,000. She has a $2,000 realized gain which must be recognized. If she sells it for $7,000, she has a $3,000 realized loss but none of it is recognized.

EXAMPLE 10.9	Joyce Johnson sells stock costing $8,000 to her brother, Fred, for $12,000. The $4,000 realized gain must be recognized by Joyce. If Joyce sells the stock to Fred for $5,000, the $3,000 realized loss is not recognized because the stock was sold to a related party.

Determination of Basis

Basis is important in computing (1) gain or loss on sale or disposition of property and (2) MACRS or depreciation deductions, cost depletion, and amortization.

¶10,101   COST

The original basis for property is its cost, except as otherwise provided in the law. The cost is the amount paid for such property in cash or other property. Code Sec. 1012; Reg. §1.1012-1(a). Basis includes acquisition costs such as commissions, legal fees, recording fees, sales taxes, as well as installation and delivery costs. The cost of property includes not only the amount of money or other property paid but also the amount of mortgage or liability incurred in connection with the purchase. It makes no difference whether the taxpayer assumes the liability or merely takes the property subject to the liability. When the property is disposed, any remaining amount of mortgage or liability of which the seller is relieved is treated as part of the amount realized. Real estate taxes are included as part of the property's basis if the buyer assumes the seller's obligation to pay them. In some cases, a taxpayer may elect to deduct certain expenditures (such as interest) currently or capitalize them. Code Sec. 266; Reg. §1.266-1(b).

EXAMPLE 10.10	Rodney Reeves purchased a new machine to be used in his business. He paid $20,000 in cash and signed a note payable in the amount of $40,000. In addition, he paid $3,000 in state sales tax, installation charges of $2,000, and delivery charges of $1,000. Rodney's cost basis of the machine is $66,000 ($20,000 + $40,000 + $3,000 + $2,000 + $1,000).

¶10,115   BASIS ALLOCATION

If a single transaction involves a number of properties, in order to establish their basis, the total cost must be allocated among the separate properties according to their relative fair market value. The basis that each property takes as a result of this allocation is the original unadjusted basis for tax purposes. This rule applies in determining basis for gain or loss and depreciation purposes. Reg. §§1.61-6(a) and 1.167(a)-5.

EXAMPLE 10.11	Cathy Camper purchases a tract of land for $2,500,000 with an office building on it. The contract does not specify the amount for each piece of property, so relative fair market value is used to allocate the basis. If the fair market value of the building is $1,800,000 and the fair market value of the land is $1,200,000, the building basis is $1,500,000 and the remaining $1,000,000 is allocated to the basis of the land.

Allocation is necessary for several reasons. Some of the property may be depreciable (buildings) and other property not depreciable (land). Different treatment may be necessary for the assets—such as Section 1231 assets compared to capital asset treatment. (See Chapter 12.) Or it may be that only some of the assets purchased are sold. If only one item is involved, allocation may be required because of different treatment such as in the case where part of the asset is used for business and part for personal use. Or the initial one asset may be sold in separate transactions, such as when a piece of land is divided into two parcels and sold. If a business is purchased, goodwill is assigned to the excess of the purchase price over the fair market value of the assets. Code Sec. 1060.

PLANNING POINTER	The purchaser will likely want an allocation to depreciable assets as high as possible so as to obtain larger depreciation in the future. From a seller's viewpoint, it may be preferable to have a larger amount allocated to nondepreciable assets, so as to get potentially more capital gain treatment (Chapter 12). Purchasers and sellers are required to specify the values of individual assets where multiple assets are acquired in a single transaction (Form 8594).

¶10,125   STOCK DIVIDENDS

Allocation of basis may also be necessary in the case of nontaxable stock dividends and nontaxable stock rights. For nontaxable stock dividends, the basis of the original stock is allocated to the old and new shares. Code Secs. 305(a) and 307; Reg. §§1.305-1–1.305-7. See ¶4401 for further discussion on the determination of whether or not stock dividends and stock rights are taxable. In the case of identical stock (common on common), the basis of the original common shares is allocated among the total number of shares owned. The holding period begins on the day following the date of the original acquisition. To be held long-term, an asset must be held more than one year. For a discussion of holding period, see ¶12,201–¶12,215.

If the stock is not identical (e.g., preferred shares received on common), then the basis of the common stock is allocated between the common and preferred stock according to the relative fair market value.

EXAMPLE 10.12	Curt Coleman owns 1,000 shares of Brockwood Corp. common stock and receives a nontaxable 20 percent common stock dividend. He paid $12,000 for the stock originally ($12 per share). His basis per share on both the old and new shares is $10 ($12,000/1,200).

EXAMPLE 10.13	Assume instead that Curt received a nontaxable preferred stock dividend of 100 shares of Brockwood Corp. preferred shares when the fair market value (FMV) of the preferred was $80 per share and the fair market value of the common was $16 per share. Then the basis of the preferred shares is $4,000 as follows:

$$\left[\frac{\text{FMV of Preferred Stock}}{\text{FMV of Preferred Stock} + \text{FMV of Common Stock}} \times \text{Basis of Common Stock} \right]$$

$$\left[\frac{\$8,000}{\$8,000 + \$16,000} \times \$12,000 \right]$$

and the basis of the common shares is $8,000 ($12,000 – $4,000).

In the case of taxable stock dividends, the amount of income is the stock's fair market value at the date of distribution. The basis of the new stock is its fair market value at the time of the receipt of the stock dividend and the basis of the old stock remains the same. The holding period of the new stock begins on the day following the date of the receipt of the stock dividend.

EXAMPLE 10.14   Jim Juniper owns 1,000 shares of Brown Corp. common stock with a basis of $5,000. He receives a 20 percent taxable stock dividend when the fair market value of each share of stock is $8. Jim reports $1,600 of income (200 shares at $8) and his basis for the new shares is $8 per share. The holding period of the new shares begins on the day following the date of receipt of the stock dividend. His basis in the old stock remains the same.

¶10,130   STOCK RIGHTS

If nontaxable stock rights are received, whether or not any part of the basis of the stock is allocated to the rights depends on the fair market value of the rights as compared with the fair market value of the stock. If the fair market value of the rights at the time of the distribution is less than 15 percent of the fair market value of the old stock at that time, the basis of such rights is zero unless the taxpayer elects to allocate. If the value is 15 percent or more, a basis must be allocated to the rights, but only if the rights are exercised or sold. The stock basis is allocated between the stock and the rights according to the relative fair market value at their distribution date.

If nontaxable rights are sold, the holding period begins on the day following the date the original stock was acquired. Code Sec. 1223(5); Reg. §1.1223-1(e). If the rights are exercised, the new stock's holding period starts on the day following the date of exercise. Reg. §1.1223-1(f).

EXAMPLE 10.15   On January 19, 2016, Florence Frost purchased 100 shares of Duke Corporation common stock for $88 per share. On July 22, 2017, she received 100 nontaxable rights to subscribe to 100 additional shares at $90 per share. The fair market value of each right was $10 and the fair market value of each share of stock is $100 on the date of issuance of the rights. Since the relative fair market value is less than 15 percent, Florence need not allocate any of her basis in the stock to the rights. Any proceeds from the sale of the rights are long-term capital gain and the basis of the new shares that may be purchased through exercise of the rights is the subscription price of $90.

EXAMPLE 10.16   If Florence in the preceding example elected to allocate part of the basis of the stock to the rights, she would allocate $800 to the 100 rights, or $8 per right as follows:

$$\left[\frac{\text{FMV of Rights}}{\text{FMV of Rights} \;+\; \text{FMV of Stock}} \times \text{Basis of Stock}\right]$$

$$\left[\frac{\$1{,}000}{\$10{,}000 \;+\; \$1{,}000} \times \$8{,}800\right]$$

If one-half or 50 of the rights are sold for $1,000, there is $600 long-term capital gain ($1,000 – $400). If 50 rights are exercised, the basis of each share obtained through exercise of the rights is $98 ($90 + $8) and the holding period for the new shares begins on the day following the date of exercise of the rights.

Note: The property must be held more than 12 months to be long-term and to be eligible for the lowest capital gains rate (i.e., a maximum rate of 15 percent or 20 percent for those in the 39.6 percent tax bracket). Property is held short-term if it is held 12 months or less. (See Chapter 12 for more discussion.).

PLANNING POINTER

With the opportunity to elect to allocate part of the basis of the stock to the rights, the taxpayer has the opportunity to control income to a limited extent. In Example 10.16 above where Florence sold 50 rights for $1,000, she has either $1,000 long-term capital gain if she did not allocate any of the basis of the stock to the rights or $600 long-term capital gain if she did allocate basis to the rights. The latter might be preferable if she already had capital gains from other transactions. If, on the other hand, she had capital losses, she might prefer not to allocate basis to the rights so as to offset a larger $1,000 capital gain against her losses.

In the case of taxable stock rights, the amount of income and the basis of the rights constitute the fair market value of the rights at the date of distribution, and the holding period of the rights begins on the day following the date of distribution. If the rights are exercised, the basis of the new shares is the subscription price plus the basis of the rights, and the holding period of the new shares begins on the day following the date of exercise. The basis and holding period of the old stock remain the same.

EXAMPLE 10.17

Betty Blue owns 100 shares of King Corp. stock purchased in January 2015 for $1,300. On January 20, 2017, she receives 100 taxable stock rights valued at $300 with the right to purchase additional shares at $15. Betty reports $300 income as a result of receipt of the stock rights, which is also the basis of the rights. The holding period of the rights begins on January 21, 2017. On February 23, 2018, she exercises 50 rights and sells the remaining 50 rights for $4 each. The basis of each new share is $18 ($15 + $3) and the holding period begins on the day following the date of exercise. She has long-term capital gain of $50 (50 × ($4 − $3)) on the sale of the rights, and since the rights were held longer than 12 months the gain will be taxed at a maximum rate of 15 percent (assuming her taxable income is less than $418,400).

¶10,135 FAIR MARKET VALUE

If property is received in exchange for services, there is a taxable transaction. If property is acquired in a taxable exchange, the basis of the property received is generally its fair market value at the time of exchange. See ¶10,015 for definition of fair market value.

EXAMPLE 10.18

Wilbur Wilson gives up inventory with a basis of $2,000 in exchange for a machine with a fair market value of $3,000. He has a realized and recognized gain of $1,000. His basis in the machine is the fair market value of $3,000.

EXAMPLE 10.19

Diane Davis does accounting work for Wanda Wales, and, in exchange for the services rendered, she receives a ring with a fair market value of $500. Diane reports $500 of income and has a basis of $500 for the ring (i.e., the fair market value).

Other situations may require the use of fair market value as basis. If the price paid is a bargain purchase, then the basis of the property is its fair market value. Reg. §§1.61-2(d)(2)(i) and 1.301-1(j). For example, assume an employee pays only $4,000 for an asset purchased from his employer when the fair market value is $7,000. The employee reports $3,000 as income and has a basis in the asset of $7,000, its fair market value. On the other hand, if the price paid for property includes payments made for reasons other than the acquisition of the asset (such as making a capital contribution or helping out a family member), then the amount in excess of the fair market value is not included in the buyer's cost or basis.

¶10,145 PROPERTY ACQUIRED BY GIFT

A taxpayer's original basis for property acquired by gift is the same as the property's adjusted basis in the hands of the donor or the last preceding owner by whom it was not acquired by gift. If, however, the property's fair market value at the time of the gift is less than the adjusted basis to the donor, then the basis for determining *loss* is the fair market value at the time of the gift. Code Sec. 1015(a). A selling price of gift property between the basis for determining gain and a lesser fair market value will result in neither gain nor loss. If the property was depreciable property to the donor, the gain basis is used by the donee to calculate depreciation, cost recovery, or amortization. Reg. §1.167(g)-1.

The holding period of gift property begins on the day following the date the property was acquired by the donor. If, however, the fair market value of the property at the date of the gift was less than the donor's adjusted basis and the property is sold at a loss, the holding period begins on the day following the date of the gift. Code Sec. 1223(2); Reg. §1.1223-1(b).

EXAMPLE 10.20	On June 3, 2015, Mary Marvel buys stock for $25,000, and, on January 21, 2017, she gives the stock to her daughter Irene when its fair market value is $28,000. 1. If Irene sells the property for $32,000 on June 7, 2017, her gain is $7,000 ($32,000 – $25,000). The gain will be a long-term capital gain since Irene includes in her holding period the time the stock was held by Mary. 2. If Irene sells the property for $24,000, she will have a long-term capital loss of $1,000 ($24,000 – $25,000).
EXAMPLE 10.21	Assume that the fair market value of the stock in Example 10.20 on the date of the gift is $22,000 instead of $28,000. 1. If Irene sells the property for $20,000, the loss is $2,000 ($20,000 – $22,000) and it will be short-term capital loss since the holding period begins on the day following the date of the gift when fair market value is used as the basis. 2. If Irene sells the property for $23,000, she will have neither gain nor loss. In other words, in this example, any selling price between $22,000 and $25,000 results in no gain or loss.
PLANNING POINTER	Taxpayers should avoid making gifts of property that have a fair market value less than basis because neither the donor nor the donee is able to take a deduction for the unrealized loss that occurred between the original acquisition and the gift by the donor. The donee is not able to take the deduction for the unrealized loss because of the loss rules for gift property. A better alternative is for the donor to sell the property that has declined in value, take the loss deduction (assuming it is deductible), and then give the proceeds to the donee. If, however, there is the expectation that the donee will keep it until the value exceeds the adjusted basis in the hands of the donor, then the donor may still wish to consider giving property that has declined in value.
EXAMPLE 10.22	Allen Armstrong has 300 shares of Pierce Corporation stock that he purchased five years ago for $30,000. Allen would like to give the property to his son Michael, but the total fair market value is now only $20,000. If the gift is made and Michael sells the stock for $20,000, neither Allen nor Michael will be able to take advantage of the $10,000 loss deduction for the decline in value. Allen should sell the stock, take the loss deduction (subject to the capital loss rules), and then give the proceeds to Michael. If, however, Michael wants to keep the stock, and it is expected that the stock will increase in value to above the $30,000 basis for determining gain, Allen should feel free to give the stock to Michael.

Increase in Basis for Gift Taxes Paid

The basis of gift property may be increased if gift taxes were paid by the donor. If the property's fair market value at the date of the gift is greater than the donor's adjusted basis, then the donee's basis is increased by all or a portion of the gift tax paid by the donor.

For gifts made after December 31, 1976, the basis is increased by the portion of gift tax that is attributable to the net appreciation in value of the gift. Net appreciation in value is defined as the amount by which the fair market value of the gift exceeds the donor's adjusted basis immediately before the gift. Code Sec. 1015(d)(6). The amount of basis increase is as follows:

$$\frac{\text{Net appreciation}}{\text{Taxable amount of gift}} \times \text{Gift tax paid}$$

This adjustment plus the donor's adjusted basis becomes the basis for asset write-offs and for gain or loss determination.

EXAMPLE 10.23	In 2017, Todd Tromb gave property with an adjusted basis of $34,000 to Stephen Strom when the fair market value was $74,000. After the exclusion, gift taxes paid on the property were $7,500. Since the net appreciation is $40,000 and the taxable amount of the gift after the $14,000 gift tax exclusion is $60,000, two-thirds of the gift taxes, or $5,000, is added to $34,000 to obtain a $39,000 basis.

EXAMPLE 10.24	If the adjusted basis to Todd in Example 10.23 is $80,000, there is no appreciation and none of the $7,500 gift tax is added to determine the donee's basis. In this case, Stephen's gain basis is $80,000; his basis for determining loss is $74,000, the fair market value at the time of the gift.

If a gift consists of several items, then the taxpayer must allocate the gift tax paid with respect to each item. Also, a special allocation of gift taxes must be made where a taxpayer receives a gift of property from a donor who has made gifts to more than one person during the year the gift taxes were paid. Code Sec. 1015(d)(2).

For gifts made prior to 1977, the full amount of the gift tax is added to the donor's adjusted basis, but the basis may not be increased above the fair market value at the date of the gift. Code Sec. 1015(d)(1).

EXAMPLE 10.25	Assume that in 1976 Todd gave Stephen property with an adjusted basis of $50,000 when its fair market value was $60,000. Gift taxes paid on the property were $7,500. Then Stephen's basis is $57,500. If the fair market value was $55,000 at the time of gift, then the basis increase would have been limited to $55,000 since the addition of gift taxes paid cannot cause the donee's basis to go above the fair market value at the time of the gift.

PLANNING POINTER	The donor is able to avoid recognition of gain on any appreciated property by giving away the property. Assuming that the donee sells the property and that the donee is in a lower tax bracket, there could be benefits from making the gift. Also, since the basis of appreciated property would be increased for at least a portion of gift taxes paid, this would provide a "step-up" in basis. Even if the low tax bracket donee keeps the property for some time, there may be an advantage to making the gift.

¶10,175   PROPERTY ACQUIRED FROM DECEDENT

The general rule is that the basis of property acquired from a decedent is the fair market value of the property at the date of the decedent's death. Code Sec. 1014(a). This is often referred to as a "step-up" in basis since the fair market value of property of the decedent is generally more than the adjusted basis. The effect of this rule is that any appreciation while the decedent owned the property escapes income taxation. However, there could, of course, be a "step-down" in basis if the fair market value of the property at the date of the decedent's death were lower than the adjusted basis. In this case, the decline in value while the decedent owned the property is not recognized for income tax purposes.

EXAMPLE 10.26	If Sally Sparrow purchased land parcel A for $5,000 in 1977 and it appreciated in value to $100,000 by 2017, when she died, her daughter Jane, the heir, will have $100,000 as her basis in the land. Thus, the $95,000 increase in value is never subject to income taxation. If Sally owned land parcel B costing $50,000 in 2007 that declined in value to $30,000 by 2017, when she died, Jane would have $30,000 as the basis in land. Here, the $20,000 decline in value while Sally owned the land is not deductible for tax purposes.
	Note: The basis of the property is the same as the value placed on the property for estate tax purposes. There is no basis adjustment for any estate tax that may have been paid on the property. (Contrast this with the gift tax adjustment for the basis of gift property.)

Under the 2001 Act, the step-up in basis at death did not apply to decedents dying during 2010 and electing not to be subject to the estate tax. In general, the property passing out of an estate was subject to the gift tax rules governing basis. Code Sec. 1022(a). Basis was the lesser of the decedent's adjusted basis in the property or the fair market value of the property at the decedent's death. However, the decedent's spouse could receive $3 million of basis increase allocated to property that the spouse was to receive directly or in a qualifying marital trust. Code Sec. 1022(d)(4)(B)(iii). Also, an executor could allocate an aggregate basis increase of up to $1.3 million regardless of the beneficiary of the property. Code Sec. 1022(d)(4)(B)(i). Congress reinstated the step-up basis rules for 2011 and the step-up basis rules are used throughout the chapter.

PLANNING POINTER	As a general rule, appreciated property should be retained until death. Selling it causes gain to be recognized. Giving it away results in the donee taking the donor's low carryover basis. Conversely, property that has declined in value should be sold in order to take any available deductions for recognized losses.

EXAMPLE 10.27	Assuming the same facts as in the preceding example, if Sally had sold land parcel A, she would have recognized $95,000 gain. If she had given the property to Jane, Jane would use $5,000 as the carryover basis. If Sally had sold parcel B for $30,000, she would have had a loss of $20,000. Giving it to Jane would have been a poor choice since Jane would have taken as her basis the fair market value at the date of the gift if she sold it for less than $30,000 and none of the $20,000 decline in value would have been recognized by either party.

Alternate Valuation

If the executor elects for estate tax purposes to value the decedent's gross estate as of six months after death, the basis of the property is the fair market value at that time. Code Sec. 1014(a)(2). If the property is distributed before the alternate valuation date, the basis is the fair market value at the date of distribution or other disposition. The alternate valuation may be used only where the election will reduce both the value of the decedent's gross estate and the federal estate tax liability. Code Sec. 2032(a)(2) and (c).

EXAMPLE 10.28	Edward Eggard died during the year, and property he owned with an adjusted basis of $50,000 and a fair market value of $150,000 went to his beneficiary, Larry Larsen. The executor elected to value the property at the alternate valuation date when the value was $140,000. In this case, $140,000 is the basis to Larry even if the property is distributed later. If, however, the property was distributed three months after Edward's death when the fair market value was $145,000 and the executor chose the alternate valuation date, the basis to Larry is $145,000.

Exception

Where appreciated property was acquired by the decedent by gift during the one-year period before death and the property is acquired from the decedent by the original donor, the adjusted basis to the recipient is the adjusted basis in the hands of the decedent immediately before death. Code Sec. 1014(e).

EXAMPLE 10.29	Ken Kooms gave property to Wesley, his father, when the adjusted basis of the property was $5,000 and the fair market value was $75,000. Wesley died six months after the gift (when the property was valued at $80,000) and he left the property to Ken. Ken's basis in the property will be $5,000, the basis to Wesley at the time of his death. If Wesley had lived more than a year, then Ken's basis would have been the fair market value at the date of Wesley's death.

Survivor's Basis

For property that is jointly owned, the part of the property included in the estate of the decedent is considered to be acquired from the decedent by the survivor. In noncommunity property states, the survivor's basis in the part of the property included in the decedent's estate is the fair market value on the date of death (or alternate valuation date). The basis of the property not included in the decedent's estate is cost or other basis. Code Sec. 2040.

| EXAMPLE 10.30 | William and Nancy North live in a noncommunity property state and bought property jointly for $100,000. When William died, the total property value was $150,000 and $75,000 was included in his estate. Nancy's basis in the property after William's death is $125,000 (her $50,000 plus the $75,000 value of William's portion). |

Property which represents both the surviving spouse's share of community property and the decedent's share of community property will have a basis equal to its fair market value on the date of the decedent's death. Code Sec. 1014(b)(6).

| EXAMPLE 10.31 | Edwin and Dawn Durham live in a community property state and own community property acquired for $200,000. If Edwin dies when the fair market value is $500,000, one-half or $250,000 is included in Edwin's estate. If Dawn inherits Edwin's share of community property, the total basis of the property is $500,000 ($250,000, or Dawn's share of the community property, plus $250,000, the value of Edwin's property at the date of his death). |

Holding Period

The holding period of property acquired from a decedent is long-term. This is the case regardless of how long the beneficiary or decedent held the property and regardless of whether the property is disposed of at a gain or at a loss.

| EXAMPLE 10.32 | Norton Newbert purchases property on December 16, 2016, and dies on January 17, 2017. The property is distributed on February 17, 2017, to Perry Portman, who sells it on May 17, 2017. Even though Perry held the property only three months and the total time from acquisition by Norton to sale by Perry was only five months, the gain or loss will be deemed to be long-term. |

¶10,201   STOCK TRANSACTIONS

Identification of Shares

When a seller can identify the shares of stock sold or transferred, the basis is the basis of the stock so identified. Shares of stock are adequately identified if it can be shown that shares which were delivered to the buyer were from a lot acquired on a certain date or for a certain price. Reg. §1.1012-1(c)(2). If the shares of stock were purchased at different dates or at different prices and the lot from which the stock was sold or transferred cannot be adequately identified, the stock sold is charged against the earliest of the stock purchases (i.e., the FIFO rule). Reg. §1.1012-1(c)(1).

| EXAMPLE 10.33 | Violet Vernon acquires 100 shares of Wilson Corp. stock in 2014 at $15 a share and 200 shares of Wilson stock in 2015 at $25 a share. If she sells 200 shares in 2017 for $35 a share and can specifically identify the shares sold as those from the 2015 purchase, she has a $2,000 gain (($35 – $25) × 200). If she cannot specifically identify the shares, she must assume that 100 shares were from the 2014 purchase and the remaining 100 were from the 2015 purchase. Her gain in that case is $3,000 (($35 – $15) × 100) + (($35 – $25) × 100). |

| PLANNING POINTER | Specific identification of shares makes it easier to control income. If a lower income is desired, higher cost shares may be specifically identified as being sold. If, on the other hand, a higher income from sale of stock is preferable (perhaps because other income is low this year but expected to be high in future years), lower cost shares may be specifically identified as being sold. |

If stock is held by a broker or agent, an adequate identification is made if the taxpayer specifies to the broker the particular shares to be sold and within a reasonable time receives a written confirmation of the transfer instruction. If a single stock certificate represents stock from different lots, where such certificate is held by the taxpayer and where the taxpayer sells a part of the stock represented by such a certificate through a broker an adequate identification is made if the taxpayer specifies to the broker the particular shares to be sold and within a reasonable time receives a written confirmation of transfer instruction. Reg. §1.1012-1(c)(3).

Wash Sales

Wash sales occur when substantially identical stock is bought within 30 days before or after the sale. No deduction for losses is allowed on the sale of stock or securities if, within a period beginning 30 days before the date of the sale and ending 30 days after the date of sale, substantially identical stock or securities are acquired. Code Sec. 1091(a). Substantially identical stock or securities means the same in all important particulars such as earning power, interest rate, value of assets, preference, etc. Rev. Rul. 58-210, 1958-1 CB 523. Also, no deduction is allowed if the taxpayer has during that 61-day period entered into a contract or option to acquire substantially identical stock or securities. Reg. §1.1091-1(a).

The purpose of the wash sale rules is to prevent a tax avoidance scheme. Without the rules, taxpayers would be able to sell securities on which they could show a loss and then buy back substantially identical securities. With the wash sale rules, the realized loss is disallowed; however, the disallowed loss is not "lost" but is added to the basis of the newly acquired stock. Code Sec. 1091(d); Reg. §1.1091-2. In adding the disallowed loss to the cost of the new acquired stock, the taxpayer ultimately will be able to recover the cost of the new stock and the unrecovered cost of the old stock. The holding period of the new securities purchased in a wash sale includes the period the old securities were held. Code Sec. 1223(4).

EXAMPLE 10.34

Simon Sugarman has the following transactions:

September 12, 2016:   Purchases 100 shares of Winston Corp. stock for $20 a share.

February 24, 2017:   Sells 75 shares of stock purchased on September 12, 2016, for $14 per share.

March 7, 2017:   Purchases 50 shares of Winston Corp. stock for $15 per share.

November 17, 2017:   Sells the remaining 75 shares for $12 a share.

The results of the above transactions are as follows:

1.   On the February 24, 2017 sale, the realized loss is $450, but $300 of it is disallowed and $150 is short-term loss (stock held less than 12 months). Only two-thirds of the realized loss is disallowed because only two-thirds (50 out of 75) is considered to be a wash sale (i.e., because 50 shares are later purchased on March 7).
2.   The basis of the 50 shares acquired on March 7, 2017, is $1,050 ($750 + $300).
3.   The loss realized on November 17, 2017, is $650, computed as follows:

Selling price		$900
Basis: $20 × 25 shares	$500	
March 7 stock	1,050	1,550
Loss		$(650)

It is considered long-term loss since the holding period of the stock acquired on March 7, 2017, includes the holding period from September 12, 2016, to February 24, 2017.

¶10,215   PERSONAL-USE PROPERTY CONVERSION

When property purchased for personal use is converted to business or income-producing use, the basis for determining loss is the lesser of (1) the fair market value of the property at the time of the conversion, or (2) the adjusted basis for loss at the time of the conversion. Reg. §1.165-9(b)(2). This rule is to prevent the taxpayer from converting a nondeductible personal loss into a deductible business loss. The basis for gain is the adjusted basis on the date of conversion. The basis for determining depreciation is the basis for determining loss. Reg. §1.167(g)-1. No gain or loss results on sale of converted personal-use property if the amount realized is between the basis for gain and the basis for loss.

EXAMPLE 10.35

Terry Trudman has a residence that had an adjusted basis of $150,000 but a fair market value of $100,000 at the time of conversion to rental property. The basis for determining loss is $100,000. The basis for determining gain is $150,000, the adjusted basis at the time of the conversion. If $10,000 depreciation (computed on the basis for determining loss) is taken between the time of conversion and sale, the results under the following assumptions are:

1. In a sale for $85,000, the loss is $5,000 or $85,000 – $90,000 ($100,000 –$10,000).
2. In a sale for $175,000, the gain is $35,000 or $175,000 – $140,000 ($150,000 – $10,000).
3. In a sale for $130,000, there is neither gain nor loss because by using the basis for gain one gets a loss of $10,000 ($130,000 – $140,000) and by using the basis for loss, one gets a gain of $40,000 ($130,000 – $90,000).

KEYSTONE PROBLEM

Determine what the initial basis of an asset would be in the following situations:

1. Purchase of asset
2. Bargain purchase
3. Lump-sum purchase of several assets
4. Property acquired by gift
5. Property acquired from a decedent
6. Property converted from personal use to business or income-producing use
7. Property acquired in a wash sale
8. Nontaxable stock dividends and stock rights

¶10,225 RELATED PARTIES

No loss deduction is allowed on sales or exchanges of property, directly or indirectly, between certain related parties. Without this provision, related taxpayers might enter transactions solely for the purpose of obtaining loss deductions and reducing their tax liabilities when the property still remained in the family. With the provision, the Internal Revenue Service does not have to be concerned about the reasonableness of the selling price. Any losses disallowed, however, may be used to offset the gain realized by the related purchaser on a later sale of the property. Code Sec. 267(a) and (d). This offset possibility is available only to the original transferee. The buyer's holding period includes only the time the buyer has held the property and does not include the period held by the seller. Reg. §1.267(d)-1(c)(3).

Related parties under Code Sec. 267(b) and (c) include the following:

1. Members of a family including brothers and sisters (including by the half blood), spouse, ancestors, and lineal descendants
2. A corporation where the taxpayer owns directly or indirectly more than 50 percent in value of the outstanding stock
3. Two corporations where more than 50 percent in value is owned, directly or indirectly, by the taxpayer if either corporation is a personal holding company or a foreign personal holding company during the taxable year
4. A grantor and a fiduciary of any trust
5. A taxpayer and an exempt organization controlled by the taxpayer

EXAMPLE 10.36

Norman Norseman owned stock costing $15,000 which he sold to his son Wayne for $12,000. Norman's $3,000 loss is disallowed. If Wayne later sells the stock for $17,000, he will have a gain of $2,000. His $5,000 realized gain is reduced by Norman's disallowed loss of $3,000. If Wayne sells the stock for $14,000, he does not recognize any gain. The $2,000 realized gain is wiped out by Norman's disallowed loss. If Wayne sells the stock for $10,000, he has a $2,000 recognized loss ($10,000 less $12,000). Norman's disallowed loss does not increase Wayne's loss, but can only reduce the amount of gain recognized. If the property sold was a personal use asset (rather than stock) and sold at $10,000, even the $2,000 loss would not be deductible by Wayne.

In case of a sale or exchange of property, directly or indirectly, between related taxpayers, any gain realized is ordinary income if the property is depreciable property in the hands of the transferee. Related parties for this purpose are (1) a taxpayer and an entity that is controlled by the taxpayer, and (2) a taxpayer and any trust of which such taxpayer is a beneficiary. Code Sec. 1239(a)-(c). This provision keeps a taxpayer, for example, from getting capital gain treatment on a sale of property to a controlled entity and the entity from then getting ordinary depreciation deductions on the amount paid for the property.

¶10,245   INSTALLMENT REPORTING

An installment sale is a disposition of property where at least one payment is to be received after the close of the taxable year in which the disposition occurs. The installment method allows gain to be spread over more than one year. The amount of income recognized is the proportion of the payments received in the year which the gross profit bears to the total contract price. Code Sec. 453(b) and (c). Installment reporting is discussed in more detail in Chapter 13.

EXAMPLE 10.37

On October 21, 2017, Brenda Brewster sells property with an adjusted basis of $30,000 for $100,000. The buyer pays Brenda $20,000 cash at the time of the sale transaction with the remaining $80,000 to be paid in five annual installments of $16,000 beginning in October 2018 with interest at 12 percent. During 2017, Brenda reports $14,000 ($20,000 × 70% gross profit rate), and in each of the following five years she would report $11,200 ($16,000 × 70% gross profit rate) in addition to the interest.

TAX BLUNDERS

1. Harriet Harrison has investment property with an adjusted basis of $50,000 that has declined in value to $30,000 and she gives it to Jane Juniper. Needing cash, Jane sells the property a few months later for $31,000. Jane recognizes no gain or loss because the selling price is between the basis for determining gain ($50,000) and the basis for determining loss ($30,000). Harriet should have sold the property and then given the proceeds to Jane. Then Harriet could have had a $20,000 loss.

2. Paul Paget, age 85, has investment property that he has owned for 40 years with an adjusted basis of $20,000 that has appreciated to $400,000. He gives the property to his son, Tim, who will take $20,000 as his basis. Paul should have kept the property until his death so that Tim would be able to use a stepped-up basis of fair market value at the date of death. (Gift and estate tax considerations could alter the conclusions relating to this hypothetical situation.)

3. George Gainer, age 80, has rental property with an adjusted basis of $100,000 and a fair market value of $40,000. He has taxable income of $90,000. George has made a decision to keep the property because it has been in the family since he was a child. For best results, George should have sold the property and taken the loss deduction. If he gives it away, no one can take a deduction for the decline in value. If he keeps it until his death, the heir takes the fair market value at the date of death as the basis (a step-down in basis, assuming the fair market value remains around $40,000 until his death).

SUMMARY

- Realized gain or loss is the difference between the fair market value of the property received and the adjusted basis of property given up.

- Recognized gain or loss is the amount that appears on the tax return as an included income item or a deductible loss.

- The original basis for property acquired by purchase is its cost.

- Allocation of basis may be necessary in the case of nontaxable stock dividends and nontaxable stock rights.

- A taxpayer's original basis for property acquired by gift is generally the same as the property's adjusted basis in the hands of the donor.

- For inherited property, the general rule is that the basis of the property is the fair market value of the property at the date of the decedent's death.

- If a seller of stock wishes to identify the shares of stock sold, the basis is the basis of the stock so identified; otherwise, a taxpayer should use the FIFO rule.

- No loss deduction is allowed on sales or exchanges of property, directly or indirectly, between certain related parties.

- The installment method allows gain to be spread over more than one year.

QUESTIONS

1. Distinguish between realized gains and losses and recognized gains and losses.

2. How is the adjusted basis of property determined?

3. List three capital additions or expenditures and three capital returns or recoveries and discuss the treatment of each category for tax purposes.

4. Why is allocation of basis necessary?

5. Are gains and losses from the sale or exchange of personal use assets recognized for tax purposes?

6. When is fair market value of an asset used as the basis for an asset?

7. What is the basis and holding period of nontaxable stock dividends?

8. What is the basis and holding period of taxable stock dividends?

9. What is the basis and holding period of nontaxable stock rights?

10. What is the basis and holding period of taxable stock rights and the basis and holding period of the shares of stock if the rights are exercised?

11. What is the basis of gift property?

12. What adjustment, if any, must be made to the basis of property acquired by gift if the gift was made prior to 1977? After 1976?

13. What is the basis of an asset acquired from a decedent?

14. What is the alternate valuation of assets acquired from a decedent?

15. Distinguish the holding period of assets acquired by gift with that of assets acquired from a decedent.

16. How is basis computed when a sale of shares of stock occurs?

17. When is the sale or exchange of stock or securities considered a wash sale? How is any loss treated?

18. What is the basis of a personal use asset that is converted to business or income-producing use?

19. What are the special rules for gains or losses on sales to related parties?

20. What are the benefits of installment reporting?

PROBLEMS

21. Frank Fleming recently purchased some new equipment that he plans to use in his business. He paid $43,000 for the equipment. He also paid $2,500 in delivery and installation costs, $1,600 in legal fees, and $3,800 in sales taxes. What is Frank's basis in this equipment?

22. Martha McDonald purchased an office building in 1997 for $630,000. In 2017, she sells the building for $950,000. Over the years, she had replaced the windows and doors at a cost of $60,000, repainted the exterior at a cost of $15,000, and installed an elevator at a cost of $90,000. Martha had taken straight line depreciation on the building for 20 years, for a total of $400,000.
    a. What is Martha's basis in the building at the time of the sale?
    b. What is her realized gain?
    c. What is her recognized gain?

23. Albert Armstrong sells for $800,000 a business building, which he purchased 14 years ago for $570,000. During the 14 years of ownership, he painted the building at a cost of $7,500, installed an air conditioning system for $60,000, cleaned the carpeting for $3,000, repaired the fence for $5,000, installed permanent bookcases for $40,000, replaced the electrical wiring system at a cost of $150,000, and partitioned off some of the rooms at a cost of $50,000. Albert has taken straight-line depreciation on the building for a total of $420,000. What is his basis in the building at time of sale? What is his realized and recognized gain on the sale of the building?

24. Rex Redd purchased a business building on January 1, 2003, for $975,000 and used the straight-line depreciation over 39 years. He took $25,000 depreciation for 2003 through 2014 and none for 2015 and 2016. He sold the building on January 2, 2017. What is Rex's adjusted basis in the building on January 2, 2017?

25. On January 1, 2016, Rodney Rapp paid $110,000 for taxable bonds with a face value of $100,000 which mature on January 1, 2026. He sold them on December 31, 2017 for $104,000. What is Rodney's gain or loss? What if the bonds were tax exempt?

26. Lance Lang received 50 shares of $10 par value stock from Randy Rainey in return for performing legal services. The fair market value of the 50 shares was $750. What is Lance's basis in the stock and what amount, if any, is included in his taxable income?

27. Which of the following results in a recognized gain or loss?
    a. Sale of stock, which has an adjusted basis of $5,000, for $7,000.
    b. Sale of a personal auto with an adjusted basis of $10,000 for $12,000.
    c. Sale of a personal residence with an adjusted basis of $75,000 for $65,000.

28. Gail Gumm purchased a piece of land, a building, and two trucks for a lump sum of $630,000. On the date of purchase, the land had a fair market value of $125,000, the fair market value of the building was $500,000, one truck is valued at $25,000, and the other at $50,000. What is Gail's basis in the land, the building, and each truck?

29. Gordon Gladstone owns 120 shares of Jones Corp. common stock which he purchased on June 10, 2016, for $1,800. One year later, he received a 25 percent nontaxable common stock dividend. On December 16, 2017, he sold 85 shares at $20 a share. What is the basis of the shares sold and what is Gordon's gain upon sale?

30. On August 2, 2016, Henry Hughes paid $30,000 for 500 shares of Young Corp. common stock. On July 28, 2017, he received a nontaxable 20 percent common stock dividend. On December 23, 2017, he sold the 100 shares received in July for $4,400. What is the basis of the 100 shares sold? What is the gain or loss on the sale? Is it short-term or long-term?

31. Naomi owns 1,000 shares of Nordstrom Corp. common stock which she purchased for $40,000 and later receives a nontaxable preferred stock dividend of 200 shares of Nordstrom preferred stock when the FMV of the preferred was $75 per share and the FMV of the common was $60 per share. What is the basis of the common and preferred shares after the dividend?

32. Jamie owns 1,000 shares of Jasper Corp. common stock with a basis of $20,000. She receives a 10 percent taxable stock dividend when the FMV of each share of stock is $12. How much income does she have? What is the basis in the new shares? When does the holding period of the new shares begin? What is the basis in the old stock?

33. Whitney Wells owns 600 shares of Fargo Company stock. She purchased these shares in 2015 for $30 each. In 2017, she received 600 nontaxable stock rights to subscribe to 600 additional shares at $35/share. The fair market value of each right was $4 and the fair market value of each share of stock is $40. Assume that Whitney exercises 300 of the rights and sells the rest for $4,500.
    a. What is Whitney's basis in the old stock? What is the basis in the new stock?
    b. What is Whitney's basis in the old stock if the fair market value of each right was $8 instead of $4? What is the basis in the new stock?
    c. What is the amount of gain under the assumption in part (b) if Whitney sells the 300 rights for $4,500?

34. Kevin Klein owns 900 shares of Palmer Corp. stock which he purchased three years ago for $65 each. He receives one nontaxable right for each share of stock owned. The rights entitle Kevin to receive one share of stock for every three rights plus the payment of $50 per share. On the date of distribution, the market value of the stock was $75 and the market value of the rights was $12. If Kevin exercises 600 of the rights and sells the remaining rights for $3,000, what is his basis in the old stock, the rights, the newly purchased stock, and what is his gain or loss on the sale?

35. Brian owns 200 shares of Bell Corp. stock purchased in January 2015 for $2,400. On January 30, 2017, he receives 200 taxable stock rights valued at $5 with the right to purchase additional shares at $25.

    a. How much income does Brian have? What is the basis in the rights? When does the holding period of the rights begin?

    b. On February 20, 2018, Brian exercises 100 rights and sells the remaining 100 rights for $7 each. What is the basis of each new share? When does the holding period begin? How much and what kind of gain does he have on the sale of the rights?

36. Bradley Brownstone acquired depreciable gift property from Chester Craine. On the date of the gift, Chester's adjusted basis in the property was $17,000 and the fair market value was $12,000. What is Bradley's basis for purposes of determining a gain? For purposes of determining a loss?

37. Sarah Shore bought 500 shares of stock on October 22, 2016, for $30,000. On March 25, 2017, she gave half the shares to her sister Cindy when the fair market value of the shares was $55 per share. If Cindy sells the property for $14,000, what is her gain or loss?

38. Maria Mann gives Peggy property worth $15,000. Maria's basis in the property is $10,000.
    a. If Peggy sells the property for $17,000, what is her gain or loss on the sale?
    b. If Peggy sells the property for $5,500, what is her gain or loss?
    c. If the fair market value on the date of the gift is $7,500 and Peggy sells the property for $5,500, what is the gain or loss?
    d. If the fair market value is $7,500 and Peggy sells the property for $8,000, what is the gain or loss?

39. In 2017, Paula Pierce receives gift property with a fair market value of $94,000 (adjusted basis to the donor of $34,000). Assume the donor purchased the property in 2007 and paid gift tax of $12,000 on the transfer.
    a. What is Paula's basis for gain and loss?
    b. What is the holding period?

40. In February 2017, Judy Judd gave her son Steven a Mercedes for his graduation gift. The automobile had a basis of $54,000 to Judy but was worth $84,000 at the time of the gift. Judy paid $21,000 gift taxes on the gift. The taxable gift is $70,000 after the $14,000 exclusion. Assume that Steven used the car for business purposes.
    a. What is Steven's gain or loss if the automobile is sold in April 2017 for $86,000?
    b. What is the gain or loss recognized if the car is sold for $55,000?
    c. What is the gain or loss recognized if the fair market value at the time of the gift had been $45,000 instead of $84,000 and Steven sold the car for $86,000?
    d. What is the answer to (c) if the selling price is $44,000?
    e. What is the answer to (c) if the selling price is $47,000?

41. Marsha Moore gave property with an adjusted basis of $28,000 to Alfred when the fair market value of the property was $25,000. Gift taxes paid on the property were $3,000. What is Alfred's basis for gain? What is his basis for loss?

42. Callie Cooper purchased two pieces of property in 1987: Property Q cost $15,000 and Property R cost $30,000. In 2017, when Callie died, she left the property to her daughter, Christy. At that time Property Q had appreciated in value to $80,000 while Property R had declined in value, now worth only $10,000.
    a. What is Christy's basis in each piece of property?
    b. What are the tax consequences of the changes in value of the properties from the time of original purchase to the death of Callie?

43. Beverly Bergman purchased land for $30,000 in 2007. The land was valued at $180,000 on April 15, 2017, when Beverly died. Her son Jack inherited the land. Six months later, on October 15, 2017, the property was valued at $170,000.
    a. What is Jack's basis in the land?
    b. If the executor of Beverly's estate elected the alternate valuation date, what is Jack's basis?
    c. If the executor elected the alternate valuation date but distributed the property on July 21, 2017, what would be Jack's basis?
    d. If the executor elected the alternate valuation date but distributed the property on November 19, 2017, what would be Jack's basis?
    e. If Jack sells the property on December 22, 2017, will he have short-term or long-term gain or loss?

44. Evelyn Everest gave property to her mother Sharon when the adjusted basis of the property was $12,000 and the fair market value was $80,000. Sharon died eight months later when the property was valued at $85,000 and she left the property to Evelyn.
    a. What is Evelyn's basis?
    b. If Sharon had died more than a year after receiving the gift when the fair market value was $85,000, what would the basis have been to Evelyn?

45. Sam Spurr gave property to Robert Reddy when its fair market value was $70,000 and the adjusted basis was $50,000. Robert died two years later when the fair market value of the property was $75,000, and he left the property to Sam. What is Sam's basis in the property?

46. Brothers Andrew and Vincent Vaughn jointly acquired property for $200,000 with rights of survivorship, paying three-fourths and one-fourth, respectively. Andrew died; the property was valued at $300,000 and $225,000 was added to his estate. What is Vincent's basis in the property after Andrew's death?

47. On April 18, 2017, Jane Juniper purchased 30 shares of Bryan Corp. stock for $210, and on September 29, 2017, she purchased 90 additional shares for $900. On November 28, 2017, she sold 48 shares, which could not be specifically identified, for $576 and on December 8, 2017, she sold another 25 shares for $188. What is her recognized gain or loss?

48. Harold Haas owns 100 shares of Spartan Corp. common stock with an adjusted basis of $10,000. On July 28, 2017, he sold all 100 shares for $9,000. On August 18, 2017, he purchased 80 shares of Spartan common stock for $7,500 and 20 shares of Spartan preferred stock for $3,000. What is Harold's recognized gain or loss on the sale and what is his basis per share in the new stock?

49. Ashley Adams owns stock in C Corp costing $25,000. She sells the stock to her daughter, Brittany, for $18,000. Two years later, Brittany sells the stock for $27,000.
    a. What is Ashley's gain or loss on the transaction?
    b. What is Brittany's gain or loss on the transaction?
    c. What is Brittany's gain or loss if she sold the stock for $24,000?
    d. What is Brittany's gain or loss if she sold the stock for $16,000?

50. Brenda Brewster owned stock costing $12,000 which she sold to her daughter, Rita, for $8,000. Rita sold the stock later for $14,000.
    a. What is Brenda's gain or loss?
    b. What is Rita's gain or loss?
    c. If Rita had sold the stock for $10,000, how much gain or loss would she recognize?
    d. If Rita had sold the stock for $6,000, how much gain or loss would she recognize?

51. Emily Eagels owned stock with a basis of $50,000 which she sold to her sister, Janet, for $42,000. Three months later, Janet sold the stock through a broker for $52,000. What is the gain or loss to Emily? What is the gain or loss to Janet?

52. Sheryl Sugarman owned 60 percent of the outstanding stock of Octavian Corp. The corporation sold stock (cost $5,000) to her for $2,500. Sheryl sold the stock for $7,000. What is the corporation's allowed loss? What is Sheryl's gain?

53. On September 16, 2017, Donald Dunn sold for $80,000 property with an adjusted basis of $20,000. The buyer paid $20,000 down with the remaining $60,000 to be paid in four equal annual installments of $15,000 beginning in September 2018 with interest at 12 percent. How much income does Donald report in 2017 and the following four years? Ignore interest.

54. In 2017, Cathy Cummings, single, 66 years of age, and legally blind, had wages and net rental income (after depreciation) of $20,000 and received $500 in interest income. She had $11,000 of allowable itemized deductions. In addition, she had the following transactions during 2017:
    a. She sold stock for $2,800. She had inherited the stock from her father, who had an adjusted basis in the stock of $1,200. The fair market value at the date of his death was $1,800.
    b. During 2016, Cathy had purchased some Almond Corp. stock. On January 22, 2016, she paid $5 a share for 20 shares, and on May 13, 2016, she paid $8 a share for 10 shares. She sold 15 shares during 2017 for $10 a share. Those shares most recently purchased were identified as being sold.
    c. Cathy sold to her sister Janice stock in Bass Corp. for $800. She had an adjusted basis of $950 in this stock.
    d. Cathy built a new house in 2017 and converted her former residence into rental property. At the time of the conversion, the adjusted basis of the old house was $144,000 with a fair market value of $140,000. She sold the rental house for $141,000 in October 2017, four months after its conversion to rental property, and took depreciation of $1,000 for the four months.

    Compute Cathy's taxable income for 2017. Treat all income as ordinary income.

55. During 2017, Peter Patel sold a piece of land he had purchased for $40,000. The buyer paid cash of $50,000 and transferred to Peter a piece of farm equipment having a fair market value of $30,000. The buyer also assumed Peter's $10,000 loan on the land. Peter paid selling expenses of $5,000. What is Peter's recognized gain on this sale?
    a. $25,000
    b. $45,000
    c. $80,000
    d. $90,000

56. During 2007, John Johnson purchased 50 shares of common stock in Corporation DEF for $4,500. In 2013, DEF declared a stock dividend of 20 percent. The new stock received by John in the stock dividend was identical to the old stock. In 2017, DEF's stock split 3 for 1 at a time when the fair market value was $120 per share. What is John's basis in each of his shares of DEF's stock if both distributions were nontaxable?
    a. $120 per share
    b. $90 for 50 shares and zero for all additional shares
    c. $75 for 60 shares and $142.50 for 120 shares
    d. $25 per share

57. During 2017, Mary Maloney received a gift of property from her aunt. At the time of the gift, the property had a fair market value of $164,000, the taxable gift was $150,000, and the adjusted basis to her aunt was $104,000. Mary's aunt paid a gift tax on the property of $45,000. What is the amount of Mary's basis in the property?
    a. $104,000
    b. $122,000
    c. $150,000
    d. $164,000

58. Kenneth King inherited 100 shares of Corporation ABC stock from his father, who died on March 4, 2017. His father paid $17 per share for the stock on May 3, 1997. The fair market value of the stock on the date of death was $63 per share. On September 4, 2017, the fair market value of the stock was $55 per share. Kenneth sold the stock for $68 per share on December 5, 2017. The executor of the estate did not elect the alternate valuation date for valuing the father's estate. An estate tax return was filed. What was Kenneth's basis in the stock on the date of the sale?
    a. $1,700
    b. $4,600
    c. $5,500
    d. $6,300

59. **Comprehensive Problem (Tax Return Problem).** Kevin Korda, age 35, married Emily, age 30, during 2017. Kevin pays alimony of $1,000 a month and provides $7,200 a year in support for his son from a previous marriage. The son lives with Kevin's ex-wife, who provides $3,000 a year in support. During 2017, Kevin earned $45,000 and Emily earned $30,000 at her regular job and $8,000 in self-employment income from selling cleaning products out of her home. Kevin and Emily paid $3,800 state income taxes, $2,500 property taxes on their home, $2,300 charitable contributions, $4,400 interest on their home mortgage, and $3,000 medical expenses. In addition, they had the following transactions during 2017:
    a. Kevin sold for $34,000 property which he had received from his father. His father's basis in the property at the time of the gift was $35,000 and the fair market value was $30,000.
    b. Kevin sold his personal use automobile (adjusted basis of $25,000) for $15,000 and purchased a new car for $28,500.
    c. Emily received $300 in dividends from the 50 shares of $10 par Webster Corp. common stock which she owns. The stock has an adjusted basis of $1,400 to Emily and was purchased on April 28, 2017. On July 19, 2017, she also received 50 nontaxable stock rights with a fair market value of $5 when the fair market value of the stock was $30 per share. Five rights plus $20 entitle her to one share of common stock. On October 24, 2017, she exercised 30 of the rights and sold the other 20 for $100.

d. Kevin and Emily purchased 50 shares of Waverly Corp. stock for $35 a share on April 18, 2017. On May 19, 2017, they purchased 30 more shares for $45 each and on June 16, 2017, they purchased 20 shares for $50 each. On August 11, 2017, they sold 75 shares for $4,500.

Compute Kevin and Emily's taxable income. Treat any gain as ordinary income. Ignore the self-employment tax considerations.

60. **Comprehensive Problem (Tax Return Problem).** Carl Chubbs, age 64, earned $55,000 during 2017. His wife, Dawn, age 66, is blind. During 2017, Carl and Dawn received $1,000 in dividends. They sold their personal use automobile which they had owned for two years (adjusted basis of $18,500) for $19,000. They sold to their son 50 shares of Riverdale Corp. stock for $500. Their basis was $12 per share; fair market value was $20 per share. Carl and Dawn sold property Carl had inherited from his sister for $12,500. At the time of Carl's sister's death the basis of the property was $7,500 and the fair market value was $10,000; six months after death the fair market value was $9,000. The alternate valuation date was elected by the executor in valuation of the estate of Carl's sister. In addition, Carl and Dawn paid $8,500 interest on their home, made a cash contribution to their college alumni foundation in the amount of $5,000, paid state sales taxes of $500, paid state income taxes of $2,500, paid federal income taxes of $8,000, and had medical expenses of $800. Compute Carl and Dawn's taxable income. Treat all income as ordinary income.

61. **Research Problem.** Brian Bradley, a calendar year taxpayer, purchased 1,000 shares of Newton Corp. stock on October 23, 2016, for $15,000. He sold these shares on January 13, 2017, for $7,000. On each of the four days from January 16 through January 19, 2017, Brian purchased 500 shares of substantially identical stock for $3,000. What is the tax effect for Brian and what will be the basis of each of the four batches of new stock?

Chapter

11

Property Transactions: Nonrecognition of Gains and Losses

OBJECTIVES

After completing Chapter 11, you should be able to:

1. Describe the rules for exclusion of gain on the sale of a personal residence.
2. Discuss the nonrecognition of gain or loss in transactions involving like-kind exchanges and involuntary conversions.
3. Explain the holding period rules for property acquired in a nontaxable exchange.
4. Describe the mandatory rules for recognition and basis of new property and elective rules for nonrecognition and basis of new property in involuntary conversions.
5. Discuss other transactions in which gain or loss may be postponed or deferred, including exchange of property for stock or a partnership interest, exchanges of insurance policies, and exchange of stock in the same corporation by a shareholder.

OVERVIEW

As discussed in the previous chapter, a taxpayer has a realized gain when the fair market value of the property received is greater than the basis of the property given up. On the other hand, there is a realized loss when the fair market value of the property received is less than the basis of the property given up. The realized gain or loss upon a sale or other disposition of property is recognized unless there is a provision for nonrecognition.

This chapter deals with situations where there may be nonrecognition of gain or loss. Sometimes the gain or loss may be permanently excluded, meaning that the gain or loss will never be included in taxable income.

EXAMPLE 11.1

> Mary Mertson, single, sold her personal residence for $275,000 so that she could move into a small apartment in a retirement home. Her basis in the residence was $60,000. Mary may exclude the $215,000 realized gain since single taxpayers may exclude up $250,000 of gain on a sale of a personal residence. This is a permanent exclusion.

At other times, however, nonrecognition is temporary in that there is deferral of recognition. This is because the basis of the replacement property will be adjusted to reflect the deferred gain or loss. A deferred or postponed gain is subtracted from the cost of the replacement property while a deferred or postponed loss is added to the cost to determine the basis of the new property.

EXAMPLE 11.2

> Sam Sorges exchanged a business machine with an adjusted basis of $40,000 for another business machine with a fair market value of $90,000. The $50,000 realized gain is deferred because it is a like-kind exchange under Code Sec. 1031 and the basis of the new machine is $40,000 (fair market value of replacement property of $90,000 less deferred gain of $50,000). If the replacement property is sold for $95,000 shortly after the exchange, the recognized gain is $55,000. Thus, the original deferred gain of $50,000 and the $5,000 excess of the $95,000 over the $90,000 fair market value of the replacement property ultimately is recognized at the time of sale of the replacement property.

Deferral of gain or loss occurs in certain situations because the economic position of the taxpayer has not really changed in substance. Thus, the taxpayer, for example, by making an exchange of one business machine for another business machine is considered to have a continuation of the original investment. Another reason for nonrecognition of gain is that the transaction frequently results in no increase in resources to pay the tax. This reason is consistent with the wherewithal to pay concept, which recognizes that if a taxpayer lacks the resources coming from the transaction, he or she should not have to pay tax as a result of a transaction.

In this chapter, sales of residence, like-kind exchanges, and involuntary conversions will be discussed in detail, with less attention being devoted to exchanges of property for stock or partnership interests, exchanges of life insurance policies, exchanges of stock in the same corporation by a shareholder, exchanges of U.S. obligations, and reacquisition of real property.

Sale of a Personal Residence

The Taxpayer Relief Act of 1997 repealed Code Sec. 1034 (deferral of gain on sale of residence) and amended Sec. 121 (the once-in-a-lifetime exclusion of gain). Prior law under Code Sec. 1034 allowed taxpayers to defer the gain on the sale of a principal residence if a replacement residence was purchased within two years equal to or exceeding the adjusted selling price of the former residence. The current law under Code Sec. 121 is considerably more generous than the old law.

¶11,001   THE GENERAL RULES

For sales or exchanges of residences after May 6, 1997, married taxpayers may exclude up to $500,000 of gain upon the sale of their residence and single taxpayers may exclude up to $250,000 of their gain. Code Sec. 121(b)(1) and (2). Taxpayers must have owned and occupied the residence as their principal residence for two out of the last five years prior to the sale. Code Sec. 121(b)(3)(A). The exclusion applies to only one sale or exchange every two years. Code Sec. 121(b)(3)(B). For married taxpayers, the exclusion is allowed if (1) either spouse meets the ownership test, (2) both spouses meet the use test, and (3) neither spouse is ineligible for exclusion because of a sale or exchange of a residence within the last two years. Code Sec. 121(b)(2)(B), (C), and (D). Because this exclusion replaces the deferral of gain provision of Code Sec. 1034 and the one-time $125,000 exclusion for taxpayers age 55 or older, application of the exclusion does not result in a reduction of the basis of a replacement residence as was the case under prior law.

EXAMPLE 11.3   Jack and Jill Jackson sold their residence that they had purchased for $175,000 in September 2007. During the time of their ownership, they made improvements totaling $25,000 and then sold the home in September 2017 for a selling price of $600,000. Their realized gain is $400,000 ($600,000 less $200,000). They can exclude the whole gain since it is less than $500,000.

EXAMPLE 11.4   Suppose that Jack and Jill in Example 11.3 sold their residence for $800,000. Their realized gain is $600,000, but they can exclude $500,000 and will recognize $100,000. The $100,000 will be taxed at a maximum rate of 15/20 percent since they had held the residence more than 12 months. See Code Sec. 1(h)(1)(E) and Chapter 12. However, if Jack and Jill sold their residence for only $150,000, they have a realized loss of $50,000 that they will not be able to deduct.

Taxpayers may elect out of this exclusion provision for any sale or exchange. Code Sec. 121(f). Thus, for example, taxpayers who plan to sell within two years two properties that meet the exclusion eligibility requirements and who first sell the property with the lesser gain may choose to elect out of the exclusion to reserve its use for the second sale where the gain is larger.

The fact that the use of the provision is limited to once every two years does not prevent a husband and wife from filing a joint tax return and each excluding up to $250,000 of gain from the sale of each spouse's principal residence. The rule still applies as long as each spouse would have been eligible to exclude up to $250,000 of gain if the couple had filed separate returns. Further, if a single taxpayer eligible for the exclusion marries someone who has used the exclusion within two years before the marriage, that individual may still use the $250,000 exclusion.

The American Jobs Creation Act of 2004 does not allow an exclusion if the taxpayer sells a principal residence within five years of acquiring the property through a like-kind exchange.

¶11,005   PRINCIPAL RESIDENCE

In order to obtain exclusion of gain, the home must be the principal residence for two of the five years before the sale. A principal residence is the home in which the taxpayer lives. Whether or not a home is the taxpayer's principal residence depends upon all the facts and circumstances in each case. A principal residence can be a houseboat, a house trailer, or stock held by a tenant-stockholder in a cooperative housing corporation or a condominium. Reg. §1.1034-1(c)(3); Rev. Rul. 64-31, 1964-1 CB 300.

In December 2002, Regulations were issued clarifying some controversial areas relating to sale of residence. Taxpayers do not need to allocate gain between the business and residential use if the business use occurred within the same dwelling unit as the residential use. While they may exclude gain on the residence up to the allowed amount, they must pay tax at a maximum rate of 25 percent on any gain attributed to the total depreciation they took after May 6, 1997.

EXAMPLE 11.5	Rose Rambler bought a home in 2012 for $120,000 and used one-third of it as an office in her accounting practice. In 2017, she sells the home for $210,000 (realizing a gain of $90,000). Rose can exclude all of the gain except for the depreciation taken, which would be taxed at a maximum rate of 25 percent.

The Housing Assistance Tax Act of 2008 provides that gain from the sale of a principal residence that is allocable to periods of "nonqualified use" is not excluded from the taxpayer's income. Certain usage is not treated as nonqualified, including leaving the home vacant and temporary absences because of a change in employment, health, or unforeseen circumstances. The new rules apply to periods starting in 2009, but pre-2009 periods are grandfathered in and are considered qualified use. Gain is allocated to periods of nonqualified use based on the ratio of the aggregate periods of nonqualified use during the period the property was owned by the taxpayer to the total period of time the property was owned by the taxpayer. Thus, if a taxpayer bought a home on January 1, 2017, and rented it out until January 1, 2023, when the taxpayer moved into the home, then sold the home on January 1, 2025, the two-out-of-five year ownership and use requirements are met. However, six years out of the eight-year ownership period is nonqualified use, and therefore six eighths of the gain would not be eligible for exclusion.

¶11,015   SPECIAL PROVISIONS

Special provisions are included to consider other types of transactions or events or to take into consideration various types of taxpayers. In keeping with the main provisions of the law, the special provisions also often are more generous to particular taxpayers.

Proration of Exclusion

The $250,000 or $500,000 exclusion can still be prorated if the sale is due to a change in place of employment, a change in health, or unforeseen circumstances, even if a taxpayer does not meet the ownership, usage, or sale within two years requirement. The December 2002 Regulations clarified what could qualify as "unforeseen circumstances." The following must involve the taxpayer, spouse, co-owner, or a member of the taxpayer's household to qualify: death; divorce or legal separation; becoming eligible for unemployment compensation; a change in employment that leaves the taxpayer unable to pay the mortgage or reasonable basic living expenses; and multiple births resulting from the same pregnancy. Damage to the residence resulting from a natural or man-made disaster or an act or war or terrorism, and condemnation, seizure or other involuntary conversion of the property, and other circumstances at the discretion of the IRS Commissioner could also qualify as "unforeseen."

The amount of the exclusion is $250,000 or $500,000 multiplied by the portion that is the shorter of (1) the aggregate periods during which the ownership and use requirements were met during the five-year period ending on the date of the sale or (2) the period after the date of the most recent sale bears to two years. Code Sec. 121(c).

EXAMPLE 11.6	Wilbur and Wanda Windsor purchased a home in San Francisco for $300,000 on August 1, 2016. Wilbur obtains a job in Memphis, and on December 1, 2017, the Windsors sell their home in San Francisco for $750,000. The Windsors realized a $450,000 gain, but because they owned and resided in their home for less than two years (16 months), their exclusion is limited to $333,333 ($500,000 × 16 months divided by 24 months = $333,333), and they would have to recognize $116,667.

EXAMPLE 11.7

Assume that as a result of a job switch, Wilbur and Wanda, who purchased the San Francisco home (#2) on August 1, 2016, did not sell their prior residence (#1) until September 1, 2016. If they sell residence #2 for $750,000 on December 1, 2017 for health reasons, with a $450,000 realized gain, the time between the sale of residence #1 and the sale of residence #2 (9/1/16 to 12/1/17) is shorter than the ownership and use period (8/1/16 to 12/1/17) of residence #2. The proration is based on the shorter period of 15 months and the excluded gain is $312,500 ($500,000 × 15 months divided by 24 months = $312,500), and they would recognize $137,500.

Widowed Taxpayers

A widowed taxpayer's period of ownership of a residence includes the period the deceased spouse owned and used the property before death. Code Sec. 121(d)(2). The Mortgage Forgiveness Debt Relief Act of 2007 allows a surviving spouse to exclude from gross income up to $500,000 of the gain from the sale of a principal residence owned jointly with a deceased spouse if the sale occurs within two years of the death of the spouse and other ownership and use requirements have been met.

EXAMPLE 11.8

If Edwin Edwards dies, his spouse Elaine can sell the home they both occupied and be eligible for the exclusion during the two-year period following his death, provided the two-year ownership requirement was met prior to Ed's death. Elaine would be eligible for the $500,000 exclusion during the two years after his death, but would only be eligible for the $250,000 exclusion in subsequent years as a single taxpayer.

Divorced Taxpayers

In the case of a residence that is transferred to a taxpayer incident to a divorce, the time during which the taxpayer's spouse or former spouse owned the residence is added to the taxpayer's period of ownership. A taxpayer who owns a residence is considered to have used it as a principal residence while the taxpayer's spouse or former spouse is granted use of the residence under the terms of the divorce or separation instrument. Code Sec. 121(d)(3).

EXAMPLE 11.9

Rex and Robin Reed purchased a home for $150,000 on August 11, 2015. On March 26, 2016, they were divorced, and as part of the divorce agreement, the home was transferred to Robin, who sold the home on September 16, 2017, for $250,000. Robin can exclude the $100,000 gain since she owned and used the residence for more than two years.

EXAMPLE 11.10

Assume that in the preceding example, as part of the divorce agreement, Rex retained ownership of the residence but the use of the home was granted to Robin as long as Rex owns the residence. If Rex sells the residence on September 16, 2017, for $250,000, he can exclude the $100,000 gain since he can count the time that Robin used the residence as part of the divorce agreement.

PLANNING POINTER

If taxpayers are contemplating divorce and own a highly appreciated home (over $250,000 of appreciation), it may be preferable to sell the residence before the divorce. Prior to divorce, the full $500,000 exclusion applies, whereas after the divorce if only one of the taxpayers remains the owner, that spouse would be entitled to an exclusion of only $250,000.

Taxpayers should exercise caution in divorce planning. Traditionally, wives have received custody of the children and have often obtained ownership of the home. Now with the gain on the sale of residence eligible for a sizeable amount of exclusion, potential divorcees will need to consider this in their divorce agreement and in their negotiations. For some taxpayers, it may be preferable to sell the home prior to divorce to obtain the full $500,000 exclusion.

Incapacitated Taxpayers

If a taxpayer becomes physically or mentally incapable of self-care, the taxpayer is deemed to use a residence as a principal residence during the time in which the taxpayer owns the residence and resides in a care facility licensed by a State or political subdivision such as in a nursing home. The taxpayer must have owned and used the residence as a principal residence for a period of at least one year during the five years preceding the sale in order to use this provision. Code Sec. 121(d)(7).

EXAMPLE 11.11	Alice Adams purchased a residence for $150,000 on October 7, 2015. In November 2016 she became ill and was confined to a nursing home. On October 21, 2017, she sells her residence for $250,000. Alice can exclude the gain of $100,000 because she has used the residence at least one year during the preceding five years.

Involuntary Conversions

The exclusion is available in cases of involuntary conversion of a residence, such as destruction, theft, seizure, requisition, or condemnation of property, that are treated as a sale or exchange of a residence. Code Sec. 121(d)(5). The amount realized from the sale or exchange of property is reduced by the amount of gain excluded from gross income. If the basis of the property sold or exchanged was determined under the involuntary conversion rules of Code Sec. 1033(b), then the holding and use by the taxpayer of the converted property shall be treated as holding and use by the taxpayer of the property sold or exchanged.

EXAMPLE 11.12	Marvin and Mildred Matson purchased a residence on March 25, 2015, for $160,000. On September 3, 2017, a hurricane completely destroyed their home. The home was insured for its replacement value and homes in the Matsons' area had appreciated greatly. They received insurance proceeds of $460,000. The Matsons do not recognize any of the $300,000 realized gain on the involuntary conversion of their home by the hurricane because it is less than the $500,000 exclusion allowed under Code Sec. 121. If, however, the Matsons had received $725,000 of insurance proceeds (i.e., a realized gain of $565,000), the $725,000 would be reduced by the $500,000 gain excluded, leaving $225,000 of proceeds to be used when applying the gain deferral provision of Code Sec. 1033. In this case, a replacement residence would be required to defer the gain in excess of the exclusion. Thus, a replacement cost of $225,000 or more would be necessary to defer the remaining $65,000 of realized gain.

Co-ops

In the case of a tenant-stockholder of cooperative housing corporation (as defined in Code Sec. 216), the ownership requirement applies to the ownership of the stock of the corporation and the use requirement applies to the house or apartment that the taxpayer is entitled to occupy as a stockholder. Code Sec. 121(d)(4).

EXAMPLE 11.13	Carl Carlson is part owner of Red River Estates, a cooperative housing corporation that owns and manages a 15-unit complex. Carl may exclude gain on the sale of his interest if he owned the stock for at least two of the five years prior to the sale and if he occupied a unit in the complex for at least two of the five years prior to the sale.

PLANNING POINTER

Taxpayers should keep records of capital improvements since there always is the possibility that income might ultimately be recognized in the event they have extraordinarily large profits due to rapid appreciation and/or they keep their residence for a long period of time. If taxpayers personally make a number of capital improvements because they are skilled at making improvements or if they wish to claim a depreciation deduction for a home office or rental use of the residence, good records are also important. Further, if the residence is involved in a divorce settlement or tied up in an estate, accurate records could be critical.

Taxpayers who have large gains (over $500,000 for couples and over $250,000 for single taxpayers) may want to consider retaining the property the remainder of their lives, since the heirs will still get the step up in basis under Code Sec. 1014(a). Assume that Howard and Hilda Haley purchased a home in New York City for $200,000 in 1987 and are considering its sale in 2017. The expected selling price, however, is $2 million, which would require them to recognize gain of $1.3 million ($1,800,000 realized gain less excluded gain of $500,000). Even at a 20 percent maximum tax rate, this would still result in a tax of $260,000. Since the Haleys are in their seventies, they should consider retaining the property until their death since the appreciation will then not be taxed at all. The heirs will have a step-up in basis equal to the fair market value at the date of death. The value of the property, of course, will be included in the decedent's estate for estate tax purposes.

¶11,025   DEFINITIONS RELATED TO RESIDENCE

The following are the major terms encountered in sales of residences.

Amount realized is the selling price reduced by the selling expenses. The selling price includes not only the cash received but also the liability that might be assumed by the buyer. Reg. §1.1034-1(b)(4).

Adjusted basis of the residence is its cost and commissions, plus any capital improvements, less insurance reimbursements and deductible casualty losses, and less any nontaxable gain on the sale of the previous residence under prior law.

Gain realized is the excess, if any, of the amount realized over the adjusted basis of the residence.

Selling expenses include advertising costs, broker commissions, legal fees in connection with the sale, and "points" paid by the seller to obtain a mortgage for the buyer. Reg. §1.1034-1(b)(4); Rev. Rul. 68-650, 1968-2 CB 78.

Like-Kind Exchanges

¶11,201   DEFINITION

Exchanges involving like-kind property held for investment or business purposes can qualify for nonrecognition of gain or loss. The reason for nonrecognition is that the taxpayer is considered to be in the same economic position after the exchange has occurred and so is, in effect, continuing the old investment. Also, unless the taxpayer has received cash or other property, the taxpayer does not have the wherewithal to pay the tax on the realized gain as a result of the exchange transaction.

Section 1031(a) states that "no gain or loss shall be recognized on the exchange of property held for productive use in a trade or business or for investment if such property is exchanged solely for property of like kind which is to be held either for productive use in a trade or business or for investment." The word "solely" is important. If the property received also consists of other non-like-kind property or cash (known as "boot"), gain may be recognized. Code Sec. 1031(b). The nonrecognition rule for like-kind exchanges is mandatory—if one has a like-kind exchange, one must have nonrecognition of gain or loss.

EXAMPLE 11.14

Brad Burns exchanged an office building with an adjusted basis of $75,000 (fair market value $250,000) for another office building with a fair market value of $250,000. Although Brad has realized a gain of $175,000 ($250,000 fair market value received less the adjusted basis of $75,000), he does not recognize any gain under the Section 1031 like-kind exchange provision.

¶11,215   QUALIFYING PROPERTY

Property qualifying for like-kind exchange treatment must be held either for productive use in a trade or business or for investment. However, business property may be exchanged for investment property and vice versa. Property held for personal use does not qualify for nonrecognition but if held for both business and personal use, the business part qualifies. Certain properties are excluded from like-kind exchange treatment. Stock in trade or other property held primarily for sale, stock, bonds, notes, or other securities are not considered properties held for productive use in a trade or business or for investment. The transfer of partnership interests does not fall under the tax-free exchange provisions. Also, livestock of different sexes is not like-kind property. Code Sec. 1031(a) and (e); Reg. §1.1031(a)-1(a).

The words "like-kind" refer to the nature or character of the property and not to its grade or quality. Reg. §1.1031(a)-1(b). The exchange of real property for real property generally qualifies for like-kind exchange treatment. Examples include improved real estate for unimproved real estate, city real estate for a farm, and a lease of real property with 30 years or more to run for real estate. Like-kind treatment also applies to the exchange of personalty for personalty. However, not all exchanges of personalty used for investment or business purposes qualify for nonrecognition. The exchanged property must be of a like class. That is, the property must be within the same general "asset class" as indicated by Rev. Proc. 87-56, 1987-2 CB 674. Some of the business asset classes include:

1. Office furniture, fixtures, and equipment
2. Information systems such as computers and their peripheral equipment
3. Airplanes
4. Automobiles
5. Light general purpose trucks
6. Heavy general purpose trucks

Thus, an exchange of office equipment for a computer would not qualify as a like-kind exchange, nor would a business car for a light general purpose truck. Further, like-kind treatment does not apply to the exchange of realty for personalty. Thus, the exchange of a building (realty) for a machine (personalty) is not a like-kind exchange.

EXAMPLE 11.15

Eugene Eckbert made the following exchanges:

1. Office building for an apartment building
2. Apartment building for a personal residence
3. Land for an office building
4. Jewelry for a new personal automobile
5. Stock held as an investment for a business building
6. Inventory for a business automobile
7. Apartment building for a business truck

Only exchanges (1) and (3) qualify as like-kind exchanges. Exchange (2) is not a like-kind exchange because a personal residence is received; (4) involves personal use items; (5) involves stock; (6) has an exchange of inventory; and (7) involves an exchange of realty for personalty.

PLANNING POINTER

Taxpayers may prefer to avoid the nonrecognition rules. Since the rules are mandatory, taxpayers have to structure the transaction in such a way that the disposal of the old asset is a sale rather than a like-kind exchange. If a gain will be realized, taxpayers may prefer to sell the asset if they are in a low tax bracket in the year of sale, which would mean that the tax would be relatively low, especially if there were some opportunity for special capital gain treatment. In such a case, the basis of the newly purchased asset may be higher than the basis of the new asset if the transaction were a like-kind exchange. The high basis may be preferable especially if the taxpayer expected to be in higher tax brackets in future years.

If a loss will be realized on disposal of an asset, it may be preferable to recognize it through a sale transaction rather than through a like-kind exchange. This could be especially important if the taxpayer were in a high bracket in the year of sale and in lower brackets in future years when the asset would be depreciated.

There must be a genuine sale and purchase in order to avoid the Section 1031 nonrecognition rules. If the transaction involves a sale of an asset to one party and a purchase of another similar asset from the same party, the IRS could treat the two transactions as a like-kind exchange. Thus, it is advisable to have the sale and purchase be with different parties.

Trade-in of Property Used Partly for Business

Where there is an exchange of property used partly for business and partly for personal purposes, as in the case of trade-in of an automobile, only the gain or loss allocable to the business portion of the traded-in property affects the nonrecognition of gain or loss. The asset must be used more than 50% for business use to qualify for like-kind exchange.

Commissions and Expenses

Brokerage commission expenses paid in connection with tax-free exchanges are applied in three different ways in determining the tax consequences that result from such exchanges. The Internal Revenue Service has ruled (1) that commission expenses can be deducted or offset in computing the amount of gain or loss that is realized in a like-kind exchange; (2) that commission expenses paid can be offset against cash payments received in determining the amount of gain that may be recognized in such exchanges; or (3) that commission expenses may also be included in the basis of the property received. Rev. Rul. 72-456, 1972-2 CB 468.

¶11,225 RECEIPT OF BOOT

As mentioned earlier, no gain or loss is recognized when like-kind property is exchanged. When property that is not like-kind (i.e., cash or other property, known as "boot") is received, then any realized gain is recognized to the extent of the boot received, but not to exceed realized gain. If there is a realized loss in a boot received situation, such loss is not recognized. Code Sec. 1031(b) and (c).

EXAMPLE 11.16

Kent Powers exchanged a business machine with an adjusted basis of $28,000 and a fair market value of $40,000 for a similar machine worth $35,000 and $5,000 cash. Kent's realized gain is $12,000 and because he received $5,000 cash, the recognized gain will be $5,000.

EXAMPLE 11.17

Assume the same facts as in Example 11.16, except that Kent's adjusted basis in his old machine was $36,000 instead of $28,000. The realized gain is $4,000 and the recognized gain is also $4,000 even though he received boot in the amount of $5,000. Recognized gain would not exceed the realized gain.

EXAMPLE 11.18

Assume the same facts as in Example 11.16, except that Kent's adjusted basis in the old machine was $44,000. He would have realized a loss of $4,000 which would not be recognized even though there was boot received.

¶11,235   GIVING BOOT

If boot is given, generally no gain or loss is recognized.

| EXAMPLE 11.19 | Greg exchanges a business machine with an adjusted basis of $12,000 and a fair market value of $18,000 for a similar machine with a fair market value of $26,000. He also gives $8,000 cash. Although Greg realizes $6,000 gain, he recognizes no gain. |

| EXAMPLE 11.20 | Assume the same facts as in Example 11.19, except that Greg's old machine had a basis of $28,000. He would have realized a loss of $10,000 which would not be recognized. |

If, however, the boot given is property that has a difference between its basis and fair market value, then gain or loss will be recognized on the boot given. Reg. §1.1031(d)-1(e). It is as if the boot property was sold separately from the like-kind property. Although this rule for recognition in a boot given situation is a special case, it can produce strange results. The taxpayer can have a recognized gain greater than realized gain or a realized gain and a recognized loss.

| EXAMPLE 11.21 | Becky Barrows exchanges real estate with a basis of $150,000 (fair market value of $165,000) for other real estate with a fair market value of $230,000. She also gives up shares of Ridgeway Corporation stock worth $65,000 with a basis of $30,000. Becky's realized gain is $50,000 ($230,000 – $150,000 – $30,000) and she must recognize a gain of $35,000 ($65,000 – $30,000). |

| EXAMPLE 11.22 | Assume the same facts as in Example 11.21, except that the fair market value of the Ridgeway Corporation stock was $95,000 and the fair market value of Becky's real estate is $135,000. Becky then has a realized gain of $50,000 but a recognized gain of $65,000 ($95,000 – $30,000). |

| EXAMPLE 11.23 | Assume the same facts as in Example 11.21, except that Becky's stock in Ridgeway Corporation had a fair market value of only $20,000 and the fair market value of Becky's real estate is $210,000. She then has a realized gain of $50,000 and a recognized loss of $10,000. |

¶11,245   ASSUMPTION OF LIABILITIES

If a liability is assumed by the transferee, such assumption is treated like boot received by the taxpayer-transferor. Code Sec. 1031(d). Accordingly, the transferor will recognize gain under the same rules as in a boot received situation outlined above. It is treated as if the transferor received cash and then paid off the liability.

| EXAMPLE 11.24 | Judy Murryhill exchanged a business machine with an adjusted basis of $20,000 and worth $38,000 for another machine worth $28,000. Judy still owed $10,000 on the machine and the liability was assumed by the transferee. Judy realized a gain of $18,000 and recognized a gain of $10,000 since the liability assumed by the transferee is like boot received. |

If the taxpayer as transferor also assumes a liability, then, in determining the amount of boot received, consideration given in the form of an assumption of liabilities by the transferor may be offset against consideration received in the form of an assumption of liabilities by the transferee. Reg. §1.1031(d)-2. The amount of boot given in the form of money or liabilities assumed by the transferor reduces the amount of liabilities treated as boot received.

EXAMPLE 11.25   Martin Merchant exchanges a farm with an adjusted basis of $100,000 and a fair market value of $170,000 for Richard Richmond's farm with a fair market value of $150,000. Martin's mortgage of $30,000 is assumed by Richard whose mortgage of $10,000 is assumed by Martin. Martin realizes a gain of $70,000, but since the mortgages can be offset, he recognizes only $20,000 gain ($30,000 – $10,000).

Fair market value of property received	$150,000
Plus: Mortgage assumed by transferee (Richard)	30,000
Less: Mortgage assumed by transferor (Martin)	10,000
Net consideration received	$170,000
Less: Adjusted basis	100,000
Gain realized	$70,000
Gain recognized	$20,000

EXAMPLE 11.26   Assume the same facts as in Example 11.25, except that Martin's farm had a fair market value of $140,000 and the mortgage assumed by him was $40,000. Martin has a realized gain of $40,000 but recognizes no gain since the mortgage assumed by Richard does not exceed that assumed by Martin.

Fair market value of property received	$150,000
Plus: Mortgage assumed by transferee (Richard)	30,000
Less: Mortgage assumed by transferor (Martin)	40,000
Net consideration received	$140,000
Less: Adjusted basis	100,000
Gain realized	$40,000
Gain recognized	$0

If the transferor assumes a liability in excess of the amount of liability assumed by the transferee, the excess does not reduce any cash received by the transferor in determining how much gain is recognized. Consideration given in the form of cash or a mortgage assumed by the transferor, however, is offset against consideration received in the form of an assumption of a mortgage by the transferee. Reg. §1.1031(d)-2.

EXAMPLE 11.27   Rose Rand exchanges an apartment building with an adjusted basis of $140,000 and a fair market value of $190,000 for Sylvia Simon's apartment building with a fair market value of $180,000 and cash of $45,000 from Sylvia. Rose's mortgage of $40,000 is assumed by Sylvia, whose mortgage of $75,000 is assumed by Rose. Rose realizes gain of $50,000, but recognizes a gain of $45,000, to the extent of the cash received. Only the mortgages can be offset; the cash received may not be offset against the excess mortgage assumed by Rose.

Fair market value of property received		$180,000
Plus: Cash		45,000
Mortgage assumed by transferee (Sylvia)	$40,000	
Less: Mortgage assumed by transferor (Rose)	75,000	
Net consideration received		$190,000
Less: Adjusted basis		140,000
Gain realized		$50,000
Gain recognized		$45,000

Exhibit 1. CALCULATION OF BASIS OF NEW PROPERTY IN LIKE-KIND EXCHANGE

Method 1	General Rule	Boot Received			Boot Given					Liability Assumption	Offset Liabilities		Liability and Cash	
Adjusted basis of property given	$75,000	$28,000	$36,000	$44,000	$12,000	$28,000	$150,000	$150,000	$150,000	$20,000	$100,000	$100,000	$140,000	$140,000
+ Boot Given					+8,000	+8,000	+30,000	+30,000	+30,000		+20,000		+20,000	
+ Gain recognized		+5,000	+4,000				+35,000	+65,000					+45,000	+10,000
+ Liability assumed by transferor										+10,000	+10,000	+40,000	+75,000	+10,000
– Boot received		–5,000	–5,000	–5,000									–45,000	
– Loss recognized									–10,000					
– Liability assumed by transferee										–10,000	–30,000	–30,000	–40,000	–40,000
= Basis of acquired property	$75,000	$28,000	$35,000	$39,000	$20,000	$36,000	$215,000	$245,000	$170,000	$20,000	$100,000	$110,000	$175,000	$140,000

Method 2	General Rule	Boot Received			Boot Given					Liability Assumption	Offset Liabilities		Liability and Cash	
FMV received	$250,000	$35,000	$35,000		$26,000	$230,000	$230,000			$28,000	$150,000	$150,000	$180,000	$180,000
– Deferred gain	–175,000	–7,000			–6,000	–15,000	–50,000			–8,000	–50,000	–40,000	–5,000	–40,000
+ Deferred loss		+4,000			+10,000	+15,000*	–10,000**							
= Basis of acquired property	$75,000	$28,000	$35,000	$39,000	$36,000	$215,000	$245,000	$170,000	$20,000	$20,000	$100,000	$110,000	$175,000	$140,000

* This is a special situation where because of the difference between the fair market value and the basis of boot given, there was recognized gain of $65,000 and a realized gain of $50,000. The $15,000 excess of recognized gain over realized gain has to be added to the fair market value of the new property.

** This is a special situation where because of the difference between the fair market value and the basis of the boot given, there was a recognized loss of $10,000 and a realized gain of $50,000. The gain is deferred and subtracted from the fair market value of the new property as is the $10,000 recognized loss.

PLANNING POINTER	Relative to Example 11.27, before the transfer Sylvia should have paid off $30,000 of the mortgage with cash received by Rose as $15,000 and the mortgage assumed by Rose $45,000 (instead of $75,000). The realized gain would still have been $50,000, but the recognized gain would have been only $15,000.

EXAMPLE 11.28	Assume the same facts as in Example 11.27, except that Sylvia's mortgage assumed by Rose is $10,000 and the cash given by Rose is $20,000 (instead of Rose's receipt of cash from Sylvia). Rose's realized gain is $50,000 but her recognized gain is only $10,000. Both the mortgage assumed by Rose and the cash given by Rose may be offset against Rose's liability assumed by Sylvia.

Fair market value of property received		$180,000
Plus: Mortgage assumed by transferee (Sylvia)		$40,000
Less: Mortgage assumed by transferor (Rose)		10,000
Net consideration received		$210,000
Less: Adjusted basis	$140,000	
Cash	20,000	160,000
Gain realized		$50,000
Gain recognized		$10,000

¶11,255   BASIS OF ACQUIRED PROPERTY

There are two ways of figuring the basis of the newly acquired property in a like-kind exchange.

1. One method starts with the adjusted basis of the property given up (Code Sec. 1031(d)) as follows:

    Adjusted basis of the like-kind property given

    +   Boot given
    +   Gain recognized
    +   Liability assumed by the transferor
    −   Boot received
    −   Loss recognized
    −   Liability assumed by the transferee
    =   Basis of the property acquired

2. The second method starts with the fair market value of the property received as follows:

    Fair market value of the like-kind property received

    −   Deferred gain
    +   Deferred loss
    =   Basis of the acquired property

Exhibit 1 summarizes what the basis would be for each of the situations in the example at ¶11,201 and the examples at ¶11,225–¶11,245 under the two methods of figuring the basis of newly acquired property in a like-kind exchange.

¶11,265   HOLDING PERIOD

The holding period for property acquired in a nontaxable exchange includes the holding period of the property given in exchange if the property was a capital asset or property used in a taxpayer's trade or business. Code Sec. 1223(1); Reg. §1.1223-1(a). However, the holding period of property received as boot in a like-kind exchange transaction begins on the day following the date of its receipt. This holding period rule also applies to property acquired through an involuntary conversion under Code Sec. 1033 (see ¶11,301).

EXAMPLE 11.29	Linda Lane traded in a machine purchased in 2014 for another machine during 2017. The holding period of the new machine begins on the day following the date of the 2014 purchase. If, in addition, Linda received shares of stock as boot, the holding period of the stock begins on the day following the date of the receipt of the stock in 2017.

¶11,275   THREE-PARTY EXCHANGES

Sometimes a taxpayer is unable to find a party with whom to have a like-kind exchange because the party whose property the taxpayer seeks wants to sell for cash rather than trade. The three-party exchange is a device that is designed to solve this dilemma. If the taxpayer can find a purchaser who is willing to pay cash and arrange a triangular exchange, the taxpayer can effect a tax-free exchange and a cash sale can be obtained by the party who holds the desired property. Generally, a transaction will be a nontaxable exchange to the taxpayer if the taxpayer intends to and does exchange the property, and does not receive or have control over the cash flowing to the seller. There is a 45-day deadline on identifying the substitute like-kind property and a 180-day deadline on receipt of the exchange property after the taxpayer transfers the property relinquished in the exchange. Code Sec. 1031(a)(3).

An acceptable arrangement to the taxpayer can take different forms. In each of the following examples it is assumed that the taxpayer wishes to exchange business property for like-kind property owned by a taxpayer who wants to sell rather than have an exchange.

EXAMPLE 11.30	Alice Amber transfers her property to Betty Beryl, who transfers cash to Carla Crystal, who then transfers her property to Alice. For Alice, this would be considered to be a nontaxable exchange even though she transferred her property to someone other than the person from whom she received the property. Rev. Rul. 57-244, 1957-1 CB 247; *W.H. Haden Co.*, 48-1 USTC ¶9147, 165 F.2d 588 (CA-5 1948).

EXAMPLE 11.31	Alice and Carla exchange their properties and Betty then purchases Alice's former property from Carla. The courts have maintained that this transaction will qualify as an exchange for Alice even though IRS might attempt to argue that Carla would be acting as Alice's agent for a sale. *L.Q. Coupe*, 52 TC 394, CCH Dec. 29,610 (1969), Acq. 1970-2 CB XIX; *J.H. Baird Publishing Co.*, 39 TC 608, CCH Dec. 25,816 (1962), Acq. 1963-2 CB 4. It would be an exchange for Alice because she has received property in exchange for property without receiving or controlling cash.

EXAMPLE 11.32	Betty could purchase the property from Carla and then immediately exchange the property for the property owned by Alice. The transaction would be an exchange for Alice if it could be shown that Alice intended to make an exchange, and if Betty used her own funds to acquire Carla's property. Rev. Rul. 77-297, 1977-2 CB 304; *J. Alderson*, 63-2 USTC ¶9499, 317 F.2d 790 (CA-9 1963).

If arrangements more complicated than the above examples are made, there could potentially be difficulties in obtaining exchange treatment for the taxpayer. The regulations, however, allow for the use of an intermediary if the intermediary takes three steps: (1) acquires the seller's property; (2) acquires the replacement property; and (3) transfers the replacement property to the seller. Reg. §1.1031(a)-3(g)(4)(ii).

Involuntary Conversions

Gain may be deferred in an involuntary conversion through an election, providing the replacement occurs with qualified property within a specified time period and of a sufficient magnitude. An involuntary conversion occurs through a casualty, theft, or condemnation. The reason for possible deferral is to assist those who have sustained financial difficulties through one of the above events and because the taxpayer's economic position has not changed if replacement property is acquired. Also, the wherewithal to pay concept is another justification for this provision in that the taxpayer frequently does not have the financial resources to pay taxes on any realized gain.

¶11,301   DEFINITION OF AN INVOLUNTARY CONVERSION

An involuntary conversion is the compulsory or involuntary conversion of property resulting from "its destruction, in whole or in part, theft, seizure, or requisition or condemnation or threat or imminence thereof." Code Sec. 1033(a).

A condemnation generally occurs when a governmental body takes private property for public use and pays a reasonable price for it. A property transfer due to threat or imminence of condemnation also qualifies as an involuntary conversion. A news report that property is being considered for condemnation is not a threat or imminence. There must be confirmation that the property is going to be acquired for public purposes and the taxpayer has reasonable grounds to believe the property will be taken. Rev. Rul. 74-8, 1974-1 CB 200, modifying Rev. Rul. 63-221, 1963-2 CB 332. Sales to third parties (as opposed to the condemning authority) also qualify as involuntary if made under the threat or imminence of condemnation. Rev. Rul. 81-180, 1981-2 CB 161. The later sale of the property by the third party to the condemning authority also qualifies for involuntary conversion treatment if the proceeds are reinvested in qualified property even if the third party knew that the threat existed before he acquired the property. A "condemnation" does not include a notice that property will be condemned because it is unfit for human use. Rev. Rul. 57-314, 1957-2 CB 523.

EXAMPLE 11.33   Joseph Jordon, who owned a lot, learned that the City Council had just approved the condemnation of the lot for use as a city parking garage to be built in two or three years. Joseph decides to sell the property to Judy Garnet at a gain. The sale is an involuntary conversion and Joseph may elect deferral of the gain recognition.

If livestock is destroyed by or sold or exchanged on account of disease or because of drought, such events are involuntary conversions. Also, if it is not feasible because of soil contamination or other environmental conditions to replace the livestock with other livestock, other farm property (including real property) qualifies as replacement property. Code Sec. 1033(d)-(f).

¶11,305   INVOLUNTARY CONVERSION RULES FOR PROPERTY DAMAGED IN DISASTER

For purposes of the nonrecognition-of-gain rule regarding involuntarily converted property that is replaced with similar property, any tangible property that is acquired and held for productive use in a business is treated as similar or related to business or investment property that was involuntarily converted as a result of a Presidentially declared disaster. Code Sec. 1033(h)(2).

This provision is intended to afford relief to businesses forced to suspend operations for a substantial time because of the property damage. If valuable markets and customers are lost during the suspension and the business fails, the owner may want to reinvest the capital in a new business venture.

EXAMPLE 11.34   Ena ran a small retail store on the beaches of Florida. The area was hit by a hurricane and her business was destroyed. The President declared the area a disaster area. Ena used the insurance proceeds from her business to purchase equipment to enter into a consulting business. Ena may elect not to recognize gain with respect to the involuntarily converted beach business.

¶11,315   REPLACEMENT PROPERTY— MANDATORY RULES

There are two mandatory rules for recognition of gain or loss in case of an involuntary conversion.

1. If there is a direct conversion of property into other property similar or related in service or use instead of into a money award, no gain will be recognized. The basis of the replacement property is the same as the adjusted basis of the old property. Code Sec. 1033(a)(1) and (b).

EXAMPLE 11.35   Sandra Storm owned land which had an adjusted basis of $25,000. The land was condemned by the state and she received other land to replace her condemned property. The replacement land had a fair market value of $40,000. Sandra will recognize no gain and the basis in the new land is also $25,000.

2. If there is a realized loss, the loss must be recognized (assuming the loss is allowed). The basis of the replacement property acquired is its cost.

EXAMPLE 11.36

Wade Wilson's factory building having an adjusted basis of $600,000 was destroyed by fire, and he received insurance proceeds in the amount of $500,000. He purchased another factory for $800,000. Wade recognizes his realized loss of $100,000, and the basis of the new factory is $800,000.

Losses realized from involuntary conversions of income-producing or business property are recognized. Casualty and theft losses of personal use assets are also recognized (subject to limits discussed in Chapter 8); however, condemnation losses of personal use assets are not recognized.

EXAMPLE 11.37

Sara Sheridan's personal residence with an adjusted basis of $80,000 is destroyed by fire and she receives insurance proceeds of $60,000. The $20,000 realized loss is recognized subject to the limitations for personal casualty loss deductions. If Sara's residence is condemned instead of destroyed by fire, the $20,000 realized loss is not recognized.

¶11,325   REPLACEMENT PROPERTY—ELECTIVE RULES

If the cost of the replacement property exceeds the proceeds or amount realized, the taxpayer may make an election to recognize none of the realized gain. The basis of the replacement property is the cost of the replacement property less deferred gain. Code Sec. 1033(a)(2) and (b). The holding period of the replacement property, if an election to defer gain is made, includes the holding period of the old converted property. Code Sec. 1223(1)(A).

EXAMPLE 11.38

Jim Johnson's office building with an adjusted basis of $175,000 is destroyed by fire, and he receives insurance proceeds of $250,000. He buys a replacement office building for $280,000. Jim realized a gain of $75,000, but he can make an election to recognize no gain since the replacement cost is greater than the insurance proceeds. The basis of the replacement property is $205,000 ($280,000 less $75,000 deferred gain) and the holding period of the replacement property begins with the holding period of the old property.

PLANNING POINTER

There may be times when it is better not to make the election for nonrecognition of gain. This may be the case if the taxpayer is in a relatively low tax bracket in the current year or because an expiring net operating loss carryover may be offset against the gain. Also, the election may not be desirable if the basis of the replacement asset would be a cost that would result in a higher basis than if the gain had not been recognized.

If the amount realized exceeds the cost of the replacement property, the taxpayer may make the election to recognize gain only to the extent of that excess. The basis of the replacement property is the cost of the replacement property less any deferred gain. Code Sec. 1033(a)(2) and (b).

EXAMPLE 11.39

Thomas Thompson owned land with an adjusted basis of $100,000 that was condemned by the state. He received an award of $140,000, and he purchased other land for $125,000. Thomas realizes gain of $40,000 and (assuming he makes the election to defer recognition) recognizes gain of $15,000, the extent to which the amount realized ($140,000) exceeds the cost of the replacement property ($125,000). His basis in the replacement land is $100,000 ($125,000 less $25,000 deferred gain).

If more than one property is purchased, the basis is allocated among the properties according to their relative costs. Rev. Rul. 73-18, 1973-1 CB 368.

EXAMPLE 11.40	Assume the same facts as in the preceding example, except that the replacement property consisted of three parcels of land costing $60,000, $40,000, and $25,000. The basis of $100,000 would be allocated among the three parcels as follows:

$$\text{Parcel 1:} \quad \frac{\$60,000}{\$125,000} \times \$100,000 = \$48,000$$

$$\text{Parcel 2:} \quad \frac{\$40,000}{\$125,000} \times \$100,000 = \$32,000$$

$$\text{Parcel 3:} \quad \frac{\$25,000}{\$125,000} \times \$100,000 = \$20,000$$

The acquisition of involuntary conversion replacement property from related parties is not allowed. However, a de minimis exception applies if the realized gain on the involuntary conversion is $100,000 or less.

¶11,335 SEVERANCE DAMAGES

Severance damages may be paid to a taxpayer when part of the taxpayer's property is condemned and the value of the remaining property is decreased by the condemnation. Severance damages reduce the basis of the damaged property and any excess received above the basis of the property is recognized gain. Rev. Rul. 68-37, 1968-1 CB 359. An award received from a condemning authority may be considered as severance damages only where such designation has been stipulated by both contracting parties. When it is not clearly shown that the award includes a specific amount as severance damages, it is assumed that the proceeds were given in consideration of the property taken by the condemning authority (i.e., the condemnation award). Rev. Rul. 59-173, 1959-1 CB 201.

EXAMPLE 11.41	Margaret Moore receives severance damages of $100 per acre for 40 acres because of the decline in value resulting from an earlier condemnation of an adjacent parcel of Margaret's land. The $4,000 received in severance damages reduces the basis of the 40 acres of land. If the damages exceed the basis of the land, any excess is recognized gain.

¶11,345 QUALIFYING REPLACEMENT PROPERTY

With some exceptions, the rules for replacement property for involuntary conversions under Code Sec. 1033 are more strict than for like-kind exchanges under Code Sec. 1031. The Code provides that the replacement property in an involuntary conversion must be similar or related in service or use to the property converted. Code Sec. 1033(a)(1).

Functional-Use Test

It sometimes is difficult to determine just what qualifies as "similar or related in service or use"; however, two tests have generally been applied depending on whether the taxpayer is an owner-user or an owner-investor. If the taxpayer owned and used the property that was converted, the replacement property must be used in the same way as the converted property. This is known as the functional-use test. Rev. Rul. 64-237, 1964-2 CB 319.

EXAMPLE 11.42	Assume that the taxpayers make the following replacements as a result of a casualty: 1. Personal residence is replaced by a rental apartment house. 2. Manufacturing plant is replaced by a retail store. 3. Bowling alley is replaced with a billiard center. Rev. Rul. 76-319, 1976-2 CB 242. 4. Business car is replaced with a delivery truck. 5. Farm with one residence is replaced by a farm with two residences, one of which is leased. Rev. Rul. 54-569, 1954-2 CB 144. The first four replacements do not meet the functional-use test and any gain realized would have to be recognized.

Taxpayer-Use Test

If the taxpayer is an owner-investor, the replacement property must have the same relationship of service or use to the taxpayer as the converted property had. This is known as the taxpayer-use test. Rev. Rul. 64-237, 1964-2 CB 319. The taxpayer decides this by determining (1) whether the properties are of similar service; (2) the nature of the business risks connected with the properties; and (3) what the properties demand in the way of management, service, and relations to tenants. IRS Publication No. 334, Tax Guide for Small Business.

EXAMPLE 11.43	Assume that the taxpayers make the following replacements as a result of a casualty: 1. Rental manufacturing plant is replaced by a building rented out as a warehouse. 2. Rental apartment house is replaced by a personal residence. The first replacement qualifies as replacement property, but the second replacement does not.

Exchanges of Stock

A taxpayer can also elect nonrecognition of gain in an involuntary conversion by purchasing 80 percent or more of the stock of a corporation owning similar property. The purchase of the stock qualifies as replacement property, and the gain would be recognized under Code Sec. 1033 to the extent the amount realized exceeds the cost of the stock. Code Sec. 1033(a)(2). The basis of the corporation's assets must be reduced by the amount which the taxpayer must reduce the basis of the stock.

¶11,355   CONDEMNATION OF REAL PROPERTY—SPECIAL RULE

A more liberal replacement rule applies for a condemnation of real property. If real property held for productive use in a trade or business or for investment purposes is involuntarily converted, property of a like kind qualifies as property similar or related in service or use.

EXAMPLE 11.44	Malcolm Moore's factory building was condemned. He purchases a rental apartment building, which qualifies as "like-kind," thus meeting the test for proper replacement property for condemnation of real property.

A taxpayer may elect to treat outdoor advertising displays as real property for purposes of the involuntary conversion rules providing the taxpayer has not elected to write off part of the cost under Code Sec. 179. Code Sec. 1033(g)(3)(A).

¶11,365   TIME LIMIT

The allowed period for replacement with qualified property begins on the earlier of the date of disposition of the converted property or the earliest date of the threat or imminence of the condemnation of the converted property. The taxpayer has until two years after the close of the first taxable year in which any part of the gain is realized from the involuntary conversion to replace with qualified property. For Presidentially declared disaster areas, the time limit for a principal residence is increased to four years. Code Sec. 1033(h)(1)(B). The taxpayer has three years after the close of the first taxable year in which gain is first realized in the case of condemnations of real property. Code Sec. 1033(a)(2)(B) and (g)(4).

EXAMPLE 11.45	Arthur King's office building (adjusted basis of $200,000) is destroyed by fire on October 18, 2016, and he receives insurance proceeds on January 22, 2017, in the amount of $350,000. Assuming Arthur is a calendar year taxpayer, he has until December 31, 2019, to replace the property. He has until two years after the end of the tax year in which gain is realized (realization occurred on January 22, 2017). The date the fire occurred was not the date from which to count.

¶11,355

EXAMPLE 11.46	If Arthur's office building had been condemned, he would have until December 31, 2020, to replace the property, which is three years after the end of the year in which the gain was first realized.

¶11,385   REPORTING REQUIREMENTS

If the taxpayer elects to defer gain in an involuntary conversion because of either replacement or intended replacement, the taxpayer should include supporting details in the return for the taxable year in which any of the gain is realized. If the taxpayer later finds that property will not be replaced at all or does not purchase new replacement property costing a sufficient amount, the taxpayer will have to file an amended return recomputing the tax liability for the year the election was made. If the taxpayer did not make an election when the property was involuntarily converted, and the replacement time period has not expired, the taxpayer can still file a claim for credit or refund. Reg. §1.1033(a)-2(c)(2).

EXAMPLE 11.47	In 2017, Jim Jacobs receives a $200,000 award for the condemnation of his office building that has a basis of $120,000. He elects to defer recognition of the $80,000 gain, expecting to pay at least $200,000 for the new building. In 2018, he purchases another office building for $175,000. Jim must file an amended return for 2017 and recognize the $25,000 gain ($200,000 award less $175,000 replacement cost).

KEYSTONE PROBLEM	Are there times when a taxpayer might prefer the following? 1. To have a sale rather than a like-kind exchange 2. To recognize the realized gain rather than make the nonrecognition of gain election in an involuntary conversion

PLANNING POINTER	It is often advisable to take advantage of the nonrecognition of gain provision for like-kind exchanges and involuntary conversions under Code Secs. 1031 and 1033. This is true even though the basis of the new assets will be reduced. The time value of money is relevant here in that the present value of current tax reductions will be greater than the present value of future reduced depreciation deductions.

¶11,395   DEPRECIATION RULES

Taxpayers who exchange modified accelerated cost recovery system (MACRS) property through either a Section 1031 like-kind exchange or a Section 1033 involuntary conversion, are required to treat the excess basis of the acquired MACRS property as newly purchased. The new asset will now be treated as two separate properties for depreciation purposes.

Generally, exchanged basis (carryover basis from the exchange property) is depreciated over the remaining recovery period of the relinquished MACRS property, using the same depreciation method and convention. This general rule applies if the replacement property has the same or shorter recovery period, or the same or more accelerated depreciation method, than the relinquished property. If the replacement property MACRS property has a longer recovery period, or less-accelerated depreciation method, the replacement property is treated as placed in service when the relinquished property was placed in service.

Excess basis, the additional basis in the replacement property over and above the amount of exchanged basis, will be placed in a separate asset with a new depreciation schedule.

Taxpayers may elect not to apply the new rules if the rules are too burdensome or depreciation components are too difficult to track. However, if a taxpayer elects not to apply the new rules, the taxpayer must treat the entire basis (both the exchanged and excess basis) of the replacement MACRS property as being placed in service by the acquiring taxpayer at the time of replacement.

Other Transactions Involving Nonrecognition

This focus of this chapter is on residence sales, like-kind exchanges, and involuntary conversions. Additional provisions resulting in nonrecognition of gain or loss are discussed only briefly.

¶11,401   CORPORATE AND PARTNERSHIP EXCHANGES

No gain or loss is recognized by shareholders if property is transferred to a controlled corporation by one or more persons in exchange for stock in the corporation. Code Sec. 351. Moreover, no gain or loss is recognized to a corporation upon the receipt of money or other property in exchange for the stock of such corporation. Code Sec. 1032. Similarly, no gain or loss is recognized to either a partnership or its partners when property is contributed to the partnership in exchange for a partnership interest. Code Sec. 721. These corporate and partnership provisions are examined more closely in other chapters.

¶11,405   STOCK-FOR-STOCK EXCHANGES

No gain or loss is recognized if common stock (in a corporation) is exchanged solely for common stock in the same corporation, or if preferred stock is exchanged solely for preferred stock in the same corporation. Nonrecognition applies even though voting stock is exchanged for nonvoting stock or nonvoting stock is exchanged for voting stock. Code Sec. 1036(a); Reg. §1.1036-1(a). This nonrecognition provision applies to an exchange between two individuals and to transactions between a stockholder and the corporation. This nonrecognition provision does not apply if stock is exchanged for bonds, or preferred stock is exchanged for common stock (or vice versa), or if common stock in one corporation is exchanged for common stock in another corporation. However, exercising the right to convert bonds into the obligor corporation's stock or converting preferred stock for common stock in the same corporation under a conversion privilege in the preferred stock is nontaxable. Rev. Rul. 72-265, 1972-1 CB 222.

¶11,415   INSURANCE CONTRACT EXCHANGES

No gain or loss is recognized on the exchange of the following:

1. Life insurance contract for a life insurance contract, endowment contract, or annuity contract
2. Endowment contract for another endowment contract providing for regular payments beginning at a date not later than the date payments would have begun under the contract exchanged, or for an annuity contract
3. Annuity contract for an annuity contract (Code Sec. 1035(a))

EXAMPLE 11.48	Michelle Millard exchanges a life insurance contract for an endowment contract. She recognizes no gain or loss on the exchange.

¶11,435   U.S. OBLIGATIONS EXCHANGES

No gain or loss is recognized upon the surrender of U.S. obligations to the United States if they were issued under chapter 31 (Public Debt) of Title 31 (Money and Finance) in exchange solely for other such obligations. Code Sec. 1037(a).

¶11,455   REACQUISITIONS OF REAL PROPERTY

Where a sale of real property gives rise to indebtedness to the seller which is secured by the real property sold and such property is repossessed by the seller to satisfy the purchase obligation, no loss is recognized on repossession. Gain is recognized only to the extent of the cash (or other property) received less the gain on the original sale already included in income. The amount of the gain is limited to the gain on the original sale less repossession costs and gain previously reported. Code Sec. 1038; Reg. §1.1038-1.

TAX BLUNDERS

1. Henry and Hillary Houseman purchased a home in September 2013 in Boom City for $75,000. Henry is an excellent carpenter and spent a great deal of time fixing up and renovating the home. The Housemans spent $150,000 on materials and capital improvements during 2014. Considerable new business came to Boom City so that the city grew rapidly over a three-year time period, and there was a heavy demand for housing. In 2017, the Housemans sold their home for $720,000. The Housemans maintained no records so they would have a $645,000 gain of which $500,000 would be excluded, leaving $145,000 to be recognized. If, however, they had maintained records of their improvements, they would have had a gain of $495,000, all of which could be excluded.

2. Gordon Gimbel had an office building that he wanted to dispose of but he could not decide whether to sell it or try to exchange it. His building had an adjusted basis of $50,000 and a fair market value of $150,000. He located another office building with an equivalent fair market value and made the exchange. Gordon is in a low tax bracket in the year of the exchange but, because of expansion of his business, he expects high income in future years.

   Gordon will recognize no gain in the year of the exchange and he will carry over the $50,000 low basis. Thus, when he has low income he has no gain from the exchange and he will have low depreciation deductions in high income years. It would probably have been preferable to sell the property, recognize the gain while he is in a low tax bracket and then buy another asset which would have a high basis and for which he would be able to take higher depreciation deductions in years in which he has high income.

3. Irene Wildwood had a rental building which she wanted to dispose of, but could not decide whether to sell it or try to exchange it. The building had a fair market value of $250,000 and a basis of $50,000. She decided to sell the building and purchased another apartment building in another part of the city for $275,000. Irene is in a high tax bracket this year, but expects to have significantly lower income in future years. Irene should have attempted, if at all possible, to have a like-kind exchange so that she would have had no income recognized in the current year when she is in a high tax bracket and then she would have a lower basis (and low depreciation) in the future years when she would be in a low tax bracket. With a sale, she has high income in the current year and a high basis in the new building on which high depreciation deductions will be taken in years when she has low income.

4. Lorraine Larsen has an office building in a declining neighborhood which has an adjusted basis of $500,000 and a fair market value of $300,000. She would like to dispose of the building but cannot decide whether to sell or exchange it. Lorraine is in a high tax bracket this year and expects to be in lower tax brackets in the future years. She ends up exchanging it for a building in another part of the city. It has a fair market value of $250,000, and she receives boot of $50,000. No loss is recognized even though she realized a $200,000 loss and she will have a high basis ($450,000) on which she will take high depreciation in low income years. Lorraine should have sold the old building so that she could have recognized the loss when she is in a high tax bracket. If she had bought a new building for comparable fair market value, she would have had a lower basis on which to take depreciation in the future years, when her income would be low anyway.

SUMMARY

- Married taxpayers may exclude up to $500,000 of gain upon the sale of their residence and single taxpayers may exclude up to $250,000 of their gain.

- No gain or loss is recognized on the exchange of property held for productive use in a trade or business or for investment if such property is exchanged solely for property of like kind that is held either for productive use in a trade or business or for investment.

- In a like-kind exchange, when property that is not like-kind is received, then any realized gain is recognized to the extent of the boot received. If there is a realized loss in a boot received situation, such loss will not be recognized. If boot is given, generally no gain or loss is recognized. If a liability is assumed by the transferee, such assumption is treated like boot received by the taxpayer transferor.

- There are two ways of determining the basis of the newly acquired property in a like-kind exchange.

- There are two mandatory rules for recognition of gain or loss in the case of an involuntary conversion, relating to a direct conversion of property and a realized loss.

- There are elective rules in involuntary conversions that allow the taxpayer to elect to recognize gain realized only to the extent that the proceeds exceed the cost of the replacement property.

QUESTIONS

1. Describe the current tax law for sale of residence.

2. Why might a taxpayer wish to elect out of the new exclusion on the sale of residence?

3. Is it possible to defer gain through the purchase of a new residence?

4. Why would the exclusion on sale of residence be prorated?

5. What special rules affect three types of taxpayers?

6. What residence-related matter did the Housing Assistance Tax Act of 2008 address?

7. Why are certain exchanges permitted to be nontaxable?

8. When might a taxpayer prefer a sale over a like-kind exchange that would result in nonrecognition of gain under Section 1031?

9. What are two acceptable methods of calculating the basis of new property acquired in a like-kind exchange?

10. What are four broad types of like-kind exchanges?

11. Define the following relative to like-kind exchanges:
    a. Boot
    b. Postponed gain or loss
    c. Gain or loss realized
    d. Gain or loss recognized

12. Discuss the tax consequences if a personal residence is involuntarily converted.

13. What are the broad types of involuntary conversions?

14. Explain the rules for nonrecognition of gain in an involuntary conversion.

15. What is necessary for a "threat or imminence of condemnation" to qualify property for involuntary conversion treatment?

16. What is the time limitation for replacing involuntarily converted property?

17. How are losses from involuntary conversions treated?

18. Explain the difference between the taxpayer-use test and the functional-use test, and give an example as to when each applies.

19. What exchanges of insurance policies, endowment contracts, or annuities qualify for nonrecognition?

20. How is adjusted basis of a residence computed?

PROBLEMS

21. Leonard and Linda Lindsay sold for $350,000 in October 2017 their residence that they had purchased in 2007 for $100,000. They made major capital improvements during their 10-year ownership totaling $30,000.
    a. What is their excluded gain? How much must they recognize?

    b. Suppose instead that the Lindsays sold their home for $700,000. They moved into a smaller home costing $200,000. What is their excluded gain? How much must they recognize?
    c. Assume instead that the Lindsays resided in a very depressed neighborhood and the home was sold for only $80,000. How much gain or loss is recognized?

22. John Johnson, single, sold his home that he had owned for 20 years for $650,000. He purchased it for $125,000 and made $50,000 of capital improvements on the home during his time of ownership.
    a. How much gain is excluded? How much is recognized?
    b. If John purchased another home for $425,000, how much is excluded and recognized?

23. Milton and Maxine Miller purchased a home in New York City for $350,000 on October 1, 2016. Milton obtained a job in Richmond, Virginia, and on December 1, 2017, the Millers sold their home in New York for $550,000.
    a. How much gain can the Millers exclude and how much is recognized?
    b. Assume that the Millers instead sold their home on December 1, 2017, for $750,000. How much gain can the Millers then exclude and how much is recognized?

24. Tina and Tom Talley purchased a home in 2002 for $450,000. Over the years, they made substantial improvements, totaling $100,000. In 2016, the couple was divorced. As part of the settlement, the house was transferred to Tina. In 2017, Tina sold the house for $850,000.
    a. What is Tina's realized gain on the transaction?
    b. What is her recognized gain?

25. Thomas and Tonya Taylor purchased a home for $125,000 on September 15, 2015. On October 8, 2016, they were divorced, and as part of the divorce agreement, the home was transferred to Thomas, who sold it on October 16, 2017, for $245,000.
    a. How much can Thomas exclude and how much is recognized?
    b. Assume instead that, as part of the divorce agreement, Tonya retained ownership of the residence but the use of the home was granted to Thomas as long as Tonya owns the residence. If Tonya sells the residence on October 16, 2017, for $245,000, how much can Tonya exclude?

26. Arnold Atkins purchased a residence for $160,000 on September 26, 2015. In October 2016 he became ill and was confined to a nursing home. On October 8, 2017, he sold the residence for $245,000. How much gain can Arnold exclude?

27. Oscar Olson, single, purchased a residence on February 19, 2015, for $170,000. On September 7, 2017, a tornado completely destroyed his home. The home was insured for its replacement value, and homes in Oscar's area had appreciated greatly. He received proceeds of $400,000.
    a. How much does Oscar exclude and recognize?
    b. If Oscar instead had received proceeds of $525,000, how much gain would be excluded and recognized? How much of a replacement residence would have to be purchased in order to exclude or defer all gain realized?

28. Carl Carter had purchased a residence on January 12, 2016, for $165,000 and then sold it on April 12, 2017, for $440,000 because of severe health problems.
    a. How much gain can Carl exclude and how much must he recognize?
    b. If Carl instead sold the home for $300,000, how much could Carl exclude and how much must he recognize?

29. Which of the following exchanges qualify as like-kind exchanges?
    a. Unimproved land for warehouse
    b. Factory for apartment building
    c. Computer for small building
    d. Inventory for business machine
    e. Computer for a printer

30. Lewis Lamont owns a yacht (personal use) that has a fair market value of $220,000 and an adjusted basis of $310,000. His AGI in the current year is $150,000. Calculate Lewis's realized and recognized gain or loss on the yacht if:
    a. Lewis sells the yacht for $220,000.
    b. Lewis exchanges the yacht for another worth $220,000.
    c. The yacht burns and is completely destroyed and Lewis receives insurance proceeds of $200,000.

31. Sheila Sprinkle transferred business property with a fair market value of $50,000 and an adjusted basis of $25,000 for business property worth $40,000 and $10,000 cash.
    a. What is Sheila's recognized and realized gain on the transaction and the basis in the new property?
    b. What is the answer to (a) if Sheila's adjusted basis in her old property was $45,000?
    c. What is the answer to (a) if Sheila's adjusted basis in her old property was $55,000?

32. Ben Bonn and Lester Lambert exchange business machines. Ben's adjusted basis in his property is $3,200, and the fair market value is $4,500. Lester's property has an adjusted basis of $1,700 and a fair market value of $2,000. Lester also gives Ben $2,500 cash. What is Ben's realized and recognized gain and basis in the new property? What is Lester's realized and recognized gain and basis in the new property?

33. Lily Landry and Emma Erickson exchange equipment in a like-kind exchange. Emma gives up equipment with a fair market value of $30,000 (adjusted basis $25,000) and Lily transfers equipment with a fair market value of $23,000 (adjusted basis $20,000) plus $7,000 in cash.
    a. What is Emma's realized and recognized gain or loss and basis in the new property?
    b. What is Lily's realized and recognized gain or loss and basis in the new property?

34. Betsy Banks owns a car which she uses exclusively for business. The car's fair market value is $22,000 and the adjusted basis is $25,000. Betsy exchanges the car for another car worth $28,000 to be used exclusively in business and gives $6,000 cash.
    a. What is her realized and recognized gain or loss and basis in the new car?
    b. How would your answers to (a) change if she used the car for personal use?

35. Wayne Wyatt exchanges land with an adjusted basis of $300,000 and a fair market value of $600,000 for Fred Forbes's office building, worth $500,000, and $100,000 cash. Fred had an adjusted basis of $350,000 in the building.
    a. What is Wayne's realized and recognized gain or loss and the basis in the office building?
    b. What is Fred's realized and recognized gain or loss and the basis in the land?
    c. Assume no cash was received by Wayne and the office building was worth $600,000. What is Wayne's realized and recognized gain or loss and the basis in the office building?

36. Joe Jenner exchanges property with an adjusted basis of $120,000 (fair market value $150,000) for property worth $200,000. As part of the exchange, he gave up stock in Riveris Corporation worth $50,000 with a basis of $30,000.
    a. What is Joe's recognized gain and basis in the new property?
    b. If the fair market value of the stock is $90,000 and the fair market value of Joe's property is $110,000, what is Joe's recognized gain and basis in the new property?
    c. If the fair market value of the stock is $20,000 and the fair market value of Joe's property is $180,000, what is Joe's recognized gain or loss and basis in the new property?

37. Susan Sundry exchanges her small office building (adjusted basis of $127,000 and fair market value of $154,000) for Tina Thompson's warehouse (adjusted basis of $112,000 and fair market value of $123,000). Tina assumes Susan's mortgage of $31,000. What is Susan's recognized gain on the exchange and her basis in the warehouse?

38. Allen Aubrey exchanges his factory (adjusted basis of $339,000 and fair market value of $525,000) for an apartment building with a fair market value of $360,000. He also receives $165,000 in cash. What is his realized and recognized gain or loss? Determine the basis of his apartment building using two different methods.

39. Charlotte Citron exchanged business machines with Darlene Darbey. Charlotte's machine had an adjusted basis of $10,500 and a fair market value of $9,000. Darlene's machine had an adjusted basis of $8,500 and a fair market value of $6,000 and Darlene gave Charlotte $3,000 cash. What is Charlotte's realized gain or loss, recognized gain or loss, and the basis of the new property? Answer the same questions for Darlene.

40. Debbie Davis and Elizabeth Engels exchanged like-kind property. Debbie had an adjusted basis of $12,000 in her property (fair market value is $15,000). Elizabeth's property had an adjusted basis of $9,000 and a fair market value of $10,500, and Elizabeth gave Debbie $4,500 in cash. Determine Debbie's and Elizabeth's realized gain or loss, recognized gain or loss, and the basis in their new property.

41. Bruce Baxter exchanges an office building worth $1,025,000 for a warehouse owned by Dan Denton. Bruce's adjusted basis in the office building is $750,000 and Dan's basis is $800,000. The fair market value of Dan's warehouse is $825,000. Bruce's office building is subject to a $200,000 mortgage which Dan assumes.
    a. What is Bruce's realized and recognized gain or loss and his basis in the warehouse?
    b. What is Dan's realized and recognized gain or loss and his basis in the office building?

42. Emmett Embers exchanges a business building with an adjusted basis of $207,000 and a fair market value of $300,000 for George Gunn's land (to be held as investment) with an adjusted basis of $165,000 and a fair market value of $390,000. Emmett assumes George's $90,000 mortgage on the land. Determine Emmett's and George's realized gain or loss, recognized gain or loss, and the basis in the new property.

43. Linda Loren transfers an apartment building with an adjusted basis of $150,000 and a fair market value of $240,000 for Carol Comb's apartment building (adjusted basis $140,000) with a fair market value of $200,000. Linda's mortgage of $60,000 is assumed by Carol whose mortgage of $20,000 is assumed by Linda. What is the realized and recognized gain or loss for Linda and Carol and what are their bases in their acquired buildings?

44. Peter Paterson transfers an apartment building with an adjusted basis of $160,000 and a fair market value of $235,000 for Charlie Claussen's apartment building (adjusted basis $120,000) with a fair market value of $220,000 and cash of $55,000 from Charlie. Peter's mortgage of $45,000 is assumed by Charlie whose mortgage of $85,000 is assumed by Peter. What is the realized and recognized gain or loss for Peter and Charlie and what are their bases in their acquired buildings?

45. Chad Carter exchanged land with an adjusted basis of $100,000 and a fair market value of $150,000 for Nash Nunn's land worth $140,000 (basis $120,000) and $15,000 cash. Chad's mortgage of $35,000 is assumed by Nash and Nash's mortgage of $40,000 is assumed by Chad.
    a. What is Chad's realized and recognized gain or loss and the basis in his new land?
    b. What is Nash's realized and recognized gain or loss and the basis in his new land?

46. Sidney Southern owned a restaurant which was condemned on November 20, 2016. On January 15, 2017, he received a condemnation award of $280,000. The adjusted basis of his restaurant was $120,000. He purchased another restaurant on March 17, 2017, for $300,000.
    a. What is Sidney's lowest recognized gain or loss? What is his basis in the restaurant?
    b. What would be the answer to (a) if the replacement cost was $240,000?
    c. What is the last possible date on which Sidney could have purchased qualified replacement property?
    d. What is the answer to (c) if the restaurant had been destroyed by fire instead of being condemned?

47. Gerald Gold's property is condemned by the local authorities. The property has an adjusted basis of $135,000 and a fair market value of $225,000. The local authorities replace Gerald's property with other property with a fair market value of $160,000. What is Gerald's realized gain, recognized gain, and the basis in the new property?

48. The government condemns and seizes Gary Greene's business property in order to widen the interstate. His adjusted basis in the property is $160,000. Gary receives $50,000 from the government.
    a. What is the amount of Gary's realized and recognized gain or loss in this transaction?
    b. What if the property is Gary's personal home?

49. Herbert Harrison's business property with an adjusted basis of $170,000 is condemned by the local authorities. He receives a $250,000 condemnation award.
    a. What is Herbert's realized and recognized gain or loss?
    b. What is Herbert's realized and recognized gain or loss if he purchases qualified replacement property for $220,000?

    What is Herbert's basis in the new property?

    c. What is Herbert's realized and recognized gain or loss if he purchases replacement property for $280,000?

    What is Herbert's basis in the new property?

    d. What is Herbert's realized and recognized gain or loss and the basis in the new property if the condemnation award is $150,000 and the replacement property costs $220,000?

50. Steven Seller owned and managed a clothing store that was destroyed by a hurricane. He received an insurance award of $200,000 for the store, which had an adjusted basis of $120,000. A year later he replaced the clothing store with another one for $225,000.
    a. What is Seller's realized and recognized gain or loss, and the basis of the replacement clothing store?
    b. What is Seller's realized and recognized gain or loss and the basis if he replaced the clothing store with a car repair shop which he managed?

51. John and Amy Turner, married filing jointly, are both 36 years of age. They have two sons and a daughter. John and Amy have earned income of $93,500 and $58,300 respectively, and their allowable itemized deductions are $14,400. They had the following transactions during 2017:
    a. On March 31, 2017, they sold their personal residence for $160,000. Their basis in the residence was $108,000. Six months later, they purchased a new residence for $130,000. They had incurred $6,000 of selling expenses.
    b. Amy exchanged land obtained before the marriage for an office building. She had a basis in the land, which was worth $100,000, of $50,000. The office building was worth $105,000.
    c. John sold property for $45,000. He had inherited the property from an aunt who had an adjusted basis of $10,000 in the property. The property was worth $30,000 at the time of the aunt's death.
    d. John and Amy sold stock which they had received as a wedding present. The donor had an adjusted basis of $8,000 in the stock. The stock was worth $12,000 at the time of the gift. John and Amy received $10,000 for the stock.

    Compute John and Amy's lowest taxable income. Treat all income as ordinary income.

52. Jim Loner, a self-employed individual, owned a truck driven exclusively for business use. The truck had an original cost of $32,000 and an adjusted basis on December 31, 2016, of $14,400. On January 2, 2017, he traded it in for a new truck costing $40,000 and was given a trade-in allowance of $8,000. The new truck will also be used exclusively for business purposes and will be depreciated with no salvage value. What is the basis of the new truck?
    a. $32,000
    b. $33,600
    c. $40,000
    d. $46,400

53. For purposes of determining like-kind property for nontaxable exchanges, which of the following items held for business or investment purposes are not like-kind property?
    a. Improved real estate for unimproved real estate
    b. Store building for farm buildings
    c. Machine for truck
    d. Dairy herd for farm acreage
    e. Tractor for combine

54. Which of the following statements is true regarding the exchange of like-kind property?
    a. If like-kind property is exchanged and money is paid, a taxable gain or deductible loss must be recognized by the payer of the cash.
    b. If like-kind and unlike property are given up, a taxable gain or deductible loss must be recognized only on the unlike property given up.
    c. The realized gain or loss in (a) (above) is recognized to the extent of the cash payment. The liability assumed does not limit the recognized gain.
    d. The gain or loss in (b) (above) is equal to the difference between the fair market value of the like-kind property and that property's adjusted basis.

55. Fred Frisby sells his personal residence for $178,000 (adjusted basis of $156,000) and within three months moves into a new residence he purchased for $250,000. What is his basis in the new residence?
    a. $250,000
    b. $228,000
    c. $178,000
    d. $156,000

56. Within a 30-day time period, Martha Meyer transfers her property to Michelle Mann, who transfers cash to William Woolsey, and William transfers his like-kind property to Martha. Which of the following statements is true?
    a. This constitutes a nontaxable exchange to Martha.
    b. The transaction will be taxable to all parties involved.
    c. The transaction is nontaxable to William and Martha.
    d. This exchange is a transaction that is taxable to Martha.

57. **Comprehensive Problem (Tax Return Problem).** Adam Armstrong, age 60 and single, earned $51,000 during 2017. He contributed $3,000 to the United Fund, paid $16,000 in federal income taxes, $2,750 in state income tax, $400 in state sales tax, and $2,300 in mortgage interest charges. Adam also had the following transactions:

   a. Sold for $50,000 stock that he had received as a gift which had an adjusted basis of $26,000 to the donor and a fair market value of $46,000 on the date of the gift and the taxable gift was $35,000. The donor had held the stock for two years and paid a gift tax of $14,000.

   b. Exchanged land held for five years as an investment for an apartment building and $25,000 cash. On the date of exchange, the land had an adjusted basis of $135,000. The apartment building had a fair market value of $335,000.

   c. An office building Adam owned was condemned by the state to make room for a state building. The building had an adjusted basis of $70,000 and a fair market value of $172,000. Adam received another building from the state and it had a fair market value of $150,000.

   d. Adam sold his personal residence for $145,000. He incurred $2,500 in selling expenses. The residence had an adjusted basis of $56,000. He moved into an apartment.

   Calculate Adam's lowest taxable income. Treat all income as ordinary income.

58. **Comprehensive Problem (Tax Return Problem).** Barry and Connie Rawles, husband and wife, are both age 34 and have two sons. Barry earned $51,000 and Connie earned $45,000 during 2017. Barry and Connie paid $3,200 state income taxes, $12,000 federal income taxes, $3,500 property taxes, $4,600 to First Presbyterian Church, $600 to needy families, $6,400 interest on their home mortgage, and $6,800 medical expenses. In addition, they had the following transactions:

   a. They sold their personal residence for $170,000. Their basis in the residence was $104,000. They incurred $7,000 in selling expenses. They purchased a new residence six months later for $220,000.

   b. Connie sold for $40,000 property she had inherited from her father in 2012. Her father's basis in the property was $15,000 and the fair market value on the date of death was $30,000.

   c. They sold for $6,000 business property which they had acquired as a gift in 2014. The basis to the donor was $7,500 and the fair market value on the date of the gift was $7,000.

   d. They exchanged 100 shares of Conway Corp. common stock, with a basis of $3,000, for 75 shares of Conway Corp. nonvoting common stock with a fair market value of $10,000.

   Determine Barry and Connie's lowest taxable income. Treat all income as ordinary income.

59. **Research Problem.** Carl Cushman, a college professor, age 58, purchased and moved into a house on August 1, 2015. He used the house continuously until September 1, 2016, on which date he went abroad for a one-year sabbatical leave. During part of the period of leave, the property was unoccupied and it was leased during the remainder of the period. On October 1, 2017, one month after returning from such leave, he sold the house. Can Carl use the exclusion for the sale of residence?

Chapter

12

Property Transactions: Treatment of Capital and Section 1231 Assets

OBJECTIVES

After completing Chapter 12, you should be able to:

1. Discuss the special rules and limitations on transactions involving capital gains and losses.
2. Compute capital gains and losses for individuals and corporate taxpayers.
3. Define capital assets.
4. Describe the rules for holding periods, including special rules where property is stock or is acquired through involuntary conversions, exchanges, or gifts, or from decedents.
5. Describe the rules for reporting an individual taxpayer's capital gains and losses.
6. Define Section 1231 assets and describe the netting procedures.
7. Give the reasons for Section 1231, 1245, and 1250 as well as the definition and operations of the provisions.
8. Describe the nature of the recapture rules for Section 1245 and 1250 property.
9. Discuss the special recapture rules for gifts and inheritances, like-kind exchanges, involuntary conversions, charitable contributions, and installment sales.

OVERVIEW

The previous two chapters dealt with the determination of realized and recognized gain or loss and with basis as well as situations where there might be nonrecognition of gain or loss. Up to this point, recognized gains and losses have been treated as if they were ordinary gains and losses, which means they are includible or deductible in full respectively. This chapter focuses on transactions involving capital gains and losses which are subject to some special rules and limitations.

Some of the significant items excluded from the definition of capital asset are land and depreciable property used in a trade or business. These items, however, may receive capital gain treatment through Section 1231. This chapter examines the definition of Section 1231 assets and the netting procedures. Also included in the chapter is a discussion of the rules for recapture of depreciation under Sections 1245 and 1250. The recapture rules mean that some of the realized gain on disposition of certain Section 1231 assets may be recognized as ordinary income. In the Section 1250 asset area, the recapture rules vary with the type of property and, because they have undergone changes over the years, they are somewhat involved for the beginning tax student.

Special Rules and Limitations on Transactions

¶12,001   **BACKGROUND**

The Taxpayer Relief Act of 1997 significantly changed the taxation of capital gains. Prior to 1997, capital gains were divided into two categories: short-term capital gains and long-term capital gains. From 1991 until the 1997 changes, short-term capital gains ended up being taxed at ordinary income tax rates, which could be as high as 39.6 percent, while long-term capital gains were taxed at a maximum of 28 percent. To qualify as long-term capital gain or loss, a taxpayer must have held the capital asset for more than one year; if the asset was held one year or less, the capital gain or loss was short-term.

Congress wished to lower the maximum long-term capital gains tax rate to 20 percent in the 1997 Act. However, Congress did not wish to make the lower rate available to all long-term capital gains, and the 1997 rules divided long-term capital gains into three categories: long-term capital gains taxed at a maximum rate of 28 percent, long-term capital gains taxed at a maximum rate of 25 percent, and long-term capital gains taxed at a maximum rate of 20 percent.

To qualify for the 20 percent long-term capital gain tax rate, the capital asset had to be held for more than 12 months. For taxpayers in the 15 percent tax bracket, this long-term capital gains tax rate became 10 percent. Prior to the Taxpayer Relief Act of 1997, there was no special long-term capital gains tax rate available to the lower tax bracket taxpayers.

The 2003 Tax Act included a reduction in rates for long-term capital gains and qualified dividends to 15 percent for the four highest tax brackets and 5 percent for the two lower brackets. The lower rates applied to sales and dispositions of capital assets after May 5, 2003. The 15 percent rate on dividends applied to all qualified dividends received in 2003 and later years. For 2008 through 2012, the long-term capital gain and qualified dividend tax rate was 0 percent for taxpayers in the two lower tax brackets.

The American Taxpayer Relief Act of 2012 raised the top rate for capital gains and dividends to 20 percent effective in 2013. In 2017, that rate applies to the extent that a taxpayer's income exceeds the thresholds set for the 39.6 percent rate ($418,400 for single filers; $470,700 for joint filers and $444,550 for heads of households). All other taxpayers will continue to be allowed a capital gains and dividends tax at a maximum rate of 15 percent. A zero percent rate also will continue to apply to capital gains and dividends for those taxpayers in the 10 and 15 percent tax brackets.

EXAMPLE 12.1

In calculating the tax on net capital gain in 2017, the results are as follows under two assumptions, for taxpayers with married filing jointly status:

(1) assuming $500,000 net capital gains and $100,000 ordinary taxable income;
(2) assuming $420,000 ordinary income and $100,000 capital gains.

Given the $470,700 threshold for both the 39.6 percent ordinary income rate and the 20 percent maximum rate on capital gain set under the American Taxpayer Relief Act of 2012, the following rates would apply:

For (1), $100,000 ordinary income will be taxed under the regular income tax tables, up through the 25 percent marginal rate that starts at $75,900; $370,700 of the capital gain will be taxed at the 15 percent rate ($470,700 threshold less $100,000 ordinary income); and the remaining $129,300 capital gain is taxed at 20 percent.

For (2), $420,000 ordinary income will be taxed under the regular income tax tables, up through the 35 percent marginal rate that starts at $416,700; $50,700 of the capital gain will be taxed at the 15 percent rate ($470,700 threshold less $420,000 ordinary income); and the remaining $49,300 capital gain is taxed at 20 percent.

The 28 percent long-term capital gains tax rate applies to collectibles and Section 1202 gains. Generally, collectibles (as defined in Code Sec. 408(m)) include works of art, rugs, antiques, metal, gems, stamps, coins, and alcoholic beverages. However, certain newly minted gold and silver coins issued by the federal government and coins issued under state laws are subject to the 15 percent tax rate even though such coins generally qualify as "collectibles." Section 1202 stock is certain small business stock that meets very specific criteria. Gain on the disposition of Section 1202 stock held at least 5 years qualifies for a 50, 75, or 100 percent exclusion, depending on the date the qualified stock was purchased. If the Section 1202 stock was purchased after September 27, 201, and was held 5 years, the gain qualifies for a 100 percent exclusion. Specifically, if the stock was purchased from August 11, 1993 through February 17, 2009, the exclusion is 50%. If purchased from February 18, 2009 through September 27, 2010, the exclusion is 75%, and if purchased after September 27, 2010, the exclusion is 100%.

The 25 percent long-term capital gains tax rate applies to what is referred to as "unrecaptured Section 1250 gain." Unrecaptured Section 1250 gain is the amount of the long-term capital gain that would be treated as ordinary income if a Section 1250 asset were classified as a Section 1245 asset. (See a later part of the chapter for a discussion of Section 1245 and 1250 assets, depreciation recapture, and the determination of the amount of "unrecaptured Section 1250 gain.") Under the old rules, the unrecaptured Section 1250 gain was taxed at a maximum tax rate of 28 percent. Congress did not wish for this amount to be taxed at the then new lower 20 percent tax rate.

Because of the potential benefit of long-term capital gains, the capital loss limitations, and the continuation of Section 1231 assets (as discussed at ¶12,601), the study of the tax structure applicable to capital gains continues to be of importance to the student. Indeed, a tax rate increase occurred in 1993, when the top ordinary rate increased to 39.6 percent, thereby creating a potential differential of 19.6 percent over the capital gain rate of 20 percent. Similarly, in 2017, the top ordinary rate of 39.6 percent exceeds the 20 percent capital gain rate by 19.6 percent.

¶12,025   CAPITAL ASSET DEFINITION

Capital assets are not actually defined in the Internal Revenue Code. Instead, Code Sec. 1221 defines a capital asset as any property held by the taxpayer *except*:

1. Stock in trade or other inventory property or property held by the taxpayer primarily for sale to customers in the ordinary course of a trade or business
2. Depreciable property used in a trade or business
3. Real property used in a trade or business
4. Copyright, literary, musical, or artistic composition, letter or memorandum, or similar property held by (1) a taxpayer whose personal efforts created such property, (2) a taxpayer for whom such property was prepared or produced, or (3) a taxpayer in whose hands the basis of the property is determined by reference to the basis of the property held by a taxpayer described in (1) or (2)
5. Accounts or notes receivable acquired in the ordinary course of a trade or business for services rendered or from the sale of property
6. U.S. government publications (1) received by the taxpayer from the government other than by purchase at the price at which they are offered for sale to the public, or (2) held by a taxpayer whose basis in such publications is determined by reference to a taxpayer described in (1)

As seen from the above definition, the Code defines a capital asset by listing the assets that are not capital assets. The major items excluded from capital assets are inventory and business fixed assets such as land, buildings, machinery, and equipment. Because these assets are excluded from capital assets, the conclusion might be drawn that they are subject to ordinary income treatment. This, however, is not the case. Depreciable property and land used in a trade or business receive special treatment. Under Code Sec. 1231, if the net result from sales of such properties is a gain, it may be subject to capital gain treatment and, if the net result is a loss, it is subject to ordinary loss treatment.

The primary capital assets are investment property such as stocks and bonds and personal-use assets such as a residence or personal automobile. Gains and losses from the sale of investment property are recognized as capital gains and losses. Gains from the sale or exchange of personal-use assets are capital gains, but losses from transactions in personal-use assets are never deductible, unless a casualty or theft is involved.

EXAMPLE 12.2   Caroline Collector sold at a loss some jewelry she used for two years. She is not able to deduct the loss, since jewelry is a personal-use asset. If she sold the jewelry at a gain, she would have a capital gain. If, on the other hand, Caroline held the jewelry as an investment in her safe deposit box and never wore the jewelry, any gain or loss would be a capital gain or loss.

PLANNING POINTER

The classification of an asset as capital or ordinary can be important. Not only is there potential special tax treatment for long-term capital gains and losses, but there may be advantages if capital gain property is given as a charitable contribution. In that case, the amount of the charitable contribution is the fair market value of the donated property which, if it were sold, would result in a long-term capital gain. If it is ordinary income property, the charitable contribution is limited to the basis of the property.

Special Situations in Capital v. Ordinary Treatment

¶12,101 INVENTORY

Taxpayers may no longer avoid capital asset treatment by proving that property, which otherwise fits within the definition of a capital asset, was acquired for business rather than investment purposes. The U.S. Supreme Court has held that a taxpayer's motivation in purchasing an asset is irrelevant to a determination of whether the asset falls within the broad statutory definition of a "capital asset." *Arkansas Best Co.,* 88-1 USTC ¶9210, 485 U.S. 212, 108 S.Ct. 971 (1988), aff'g 86-2 USTC ¶9671, 800 F.2d 215 (CA-8 1986). Thus, losses incurred by a diversified holding company from the sale of bank stock that had been purchased in order to supply new capital to the financially troubled institution were capital in nature.

¶12,115 SALE OF A BUSINESS

When a business that has operated as a sole proprietorship is sold, the sale is not treated as the sale of one asset. Instead, it is treated as the sale of the individual assets of the business. *E.A. Watson,* 53-1 USTC ¶9391, 345 U.S. 544, 73 S.Ct. 848 (1953); *Williams v. McGowan,* 46-1 USTC ¶9120, 152 F.2d 570 (CA-2 1945); Rev. Rul. 55-79, 1955-1 CB 370. The proceeds received are allocated to the assets according to their relative fair market values. The gain or loss on some of the assets will be ordinary gain or loss and on other assets there will be capital gain or loss.

The sale of a partnership interest is the sale of a capital asset and results in capital gain or loss to the partners except that the part of the gain or loss that is related to unrealized receivables or substantially appreciated inventory items is treated as ordinary gain or loss. Code Secs. 741 and 751(a). The sale of corporate stock results in a capital gain or loss if the stock was a capital asset in the hands of the seller.

¶12,125 PATENTS

Certain transfers of patents may result in capital gain treatment. Code Sec. 1235. The reason for this provision is to encourage invention, although the same tax treatment is not available to authors and artists. In the latter cases, their works (writings and art) are specifically excluded from capital assets. However, a taxpayer can elect to treat the sale or exchange of a musical composition or copyright in musical works by the taxpayer's personal efforts as a sale of a capital asset.

If an inventor transfers (other than by gift, inheritance, or devise) property consisting of all substantial rights to a patent, or an undivided interest therein, the transfer is considered the sale or exchange of a capital asset held the requisite time period to meet the long-term holding period rules. This rule holds even if payments are payable periodically over a period ending when the purchaser's use of the patent ends or if payments are contingent on the productivity, use, or disposition of the property transferred. Code Sec. 1235(a).

EXAMPLE 12.3

Bennett Burrow, an inventor, sold his patent to Smith Corporation for a lump-sum payment of $100,000 plus $6 per unit sold. He had a zero basis in the patent. Bennett has a long-term capital gain of $100,000 and the $6 per unit royalty will also receive long-term capital gain treatment regardless of how long the patent was held.

"All substantial rights" means all rights which are of value at the time the rights to the patent are transferred. It does not include a grant of rights to a patent (1) which is limited geographically within the country of issuance; (2) which is limited in duration by the terms of the agreement to a period less than the remaining life of the patent; (3) which grants rights to the grantee in fields of use within trades or industries, which are less than all the valuable rights at the time of the grant; or (4) which grants to the grantee less than all the claims or inventions covered by the patent at the time of the grant. Reg. §1.1235-2(b).

EXAMPLE 12.4	Vance Vox sells patent rights to his invention, but the rights limit the use of the invention to the state of California. Vance's sale of patent rights does not qualify for capital gain treatment since the rights are limited within the United States.

The transferor must be a holder which refers to the creator of the property or any individual who has purchased an interest in the property from such creator if such individual is neither the employer of the creator nor related to the creator. Code Sec. 1235(b).

¶12,135   FRANCHISES

A franchise includes an agreement which gives one of the parties (the transferee) the right to distribute, sell, or provide goods, services, or facilities, within a specified area. Rules are provided for the treatment to the transferee and transferor of a franchise, trademark, or trade name. Code Sec. 1253. Specifically, a transfer of a franchise, trademark, or trade name is not treated as a sale or exchange of a capital asset if the transferor retains any significant power, right, or continuing interest with respect to the property. Amounts received on account of a transfer, sale, or disposition which are contingent on the productivity, use, or disposition of the property are also not treated as a sale or disposition of a capital asset. Code Sec. 1253(a)-(c).

The term "significant power, right, or continuing interest" includes but is not limited to the following rights with respect to the transferred interest:

1. To disapprove any assignment of such an interest
2. To terminate the franchise at will
3. To prescribe the standards of quality of products
4. To require that the transferee sell or advertise only products or services of the transferor
5. To require the transferee to purchase substantially all supplies or equipment from the transferor
6. To require payments contingent on the productivity, use, or sale of the property (Code Sec. 1253(b)(2))

Since most franchises involve the transferor retaining at least some of these rights, the transferor is going to have ordinary income upon the transfer of a franchise.

Amounts paid by the transferee which are contingent on the productivity, use, or disposition of the property transferred are allowed as business deductions. Other payments are generally amortized over 15 years. Code Sec. 197(g).

EXAMPLE 12.5	Farmers Corporation grants Grace Gobbler a franchise to sell fried chicken for a period of 20 years with renewals. Farmers Corporation retains the powers and rights described above. Grace is required to pay $100,000 initially and then three percent of sales. The $100,000 payment and the percentage payments are ordinary income to Farmers. Grace may deduct the percentage payments as ordinary business expenses. The initial payment of $100,000 is amortized over 15 years beginning in the year the payment is made.

EXAMPLE 12.6	Denny Doone, a transferee of a franchise, sells the franchise to a third party, transferring all significant powers and rights. Payments to Denny are not contingent. Any reportable gain will be capital gain to him.

¶12,155   LEASE CANCELLATION PAYMENTS

Amounts received by a lessee (tenant) for the cancellation of a lease are considered as amounts received for the exchange of such lease or agreement. Code Sec. 1241. The type of gain or loss will depend on the character of the lease. A nondepreciable leasehold (for example, for a personal-use asset as a residence) is a capital asset. A depreciable lease used in a trade or business is either an ordinary asset or a Section 1231 asset. Amounts received by the landlord for canceling a lease are ordinary income. *W.M. Hort,* 41-1 USTC ¶9534, 313 U.S. 28, 61 S.Ct. 757 (1941).

EXAMPLE 12.7	Terry Thomson pays Lydia Lancer, the owner of his apartment, $500 in order to cancel his lease. Lydia treats the $500 as ordinary income.

EXAMPLE 12.8	Lydia pays Tony Terrace, a tenant of one of her apartments, $900 to cancel the lease. Tony would report $900 capital gain since the lease was a nondepreciable leasehold and thus a capital asset.

¶12,165 OPTIONS

Gain or loss from the sale or exchange of an option to buy or sell property or from failure to exercise such option is of the same character as the property to which the option relates. If loss is attributable to failure to exercise an option, the option is deemed to have been sold or exchanged on the day it expired. Code Sec. 1234(a).

EXAMPLE 12.9	Jerrold Jackson had an option on 1,000 shares of King Corporation stock. Although the stock increased in value, Jerrold did not purchase the stock. Instead, he sold the option at a gain. Jerrold would report a capital gain since the King Corporation stock would have been a capital asset to him if he had purchased it.

Holding Period

¶12,201 COMPUTATION OF HOLDING PERIOD

Holding period continues to be important in 2017 because of the reduced rate at which net capital gains are taxed and because the basic structure for capital gains and losses has been retained in the Code. Additionally, the definition of Section 1231 assets includes those assets used in a trade or business and held long-term. Gains and losses on these Section 1231 assets continue to be separately computed.

Property has to be held for longer than one year to be long-term. Code Sec. 1222. Note, as discussed in a later section, the tax advantages on the gain side occur when property is held greater than 12 months (where the maximum rate is generally 15 percent). In figuring the holding period, the day the property was acquired is excluded, but the day it was disposed of is included. Since the day after acquisition is the start of the holding period, this same date in each of the following months is the start of the new month. It does not matter how many days are in each month. Property acquired on the last day of the month must be held on or after the first day of the thirteenth succeeding month to be held long-term. Rev. Rul. 66-7, 1966-1 CB 188.

EXAMPLE 12.10	Cindy Crier purchased shares of stock on February 17, 2016. If she sells the stock on February 18, 2017, or later, she will have long-term capital gain or loss in the 15/20 percent basket. If she sells the stock on February 17, 2017, or earlier, she will have short-term capital gain or loss.

EXAMPLE 12.11	If Jack Jeffrey purchases shares of stock on January 31, 2016, and sells the stock on February 1, 2017, or later, he will have long-term capital gain or loss in the 15/20 percent basket. If he sells the stock on January 31, 2017, or earlier, he will have short-term capital gain or loss.

¶12,215   SPECIAL RULES FOR HOLDING PERIOD

The general rule is that the holding period runs from the day following the date of acquisition to the date of disposition, but there are special rules in certain circumstances.

Property Acquired Through Exchanges and Conversions

The holding period of property received in an exchange includes the holding period of the property given in the exchange if the basis of the acquired property has the same basis in whole or in part as the property exchanged. Code Sec. 1223(1). The property exchanged must be a capital asset or Section 1231 assets (i.e., property used in a trade or business). Property acquired as a result of an involuntary conversion is also considered an exchange for this purpose.

EXAMPLE 12.12   On July 9, 2017, George Grundy exchanged 100 shares of Jones Corporation Class A stock (bought on July 14, 2013, for $1,500) for Jones Corporation Class B stock in a nontaxable exchange. George sells the Class B shares on December 16, 2017, for $1,200. Since the holding period of the Class B shares began on July 15, 2013, and the basis is $1,500, George has a long-term capital loss of $300.

EXAMPLE 12.13   Kathy Krupp sold her office building on November 15 at a gain. She had purchased this building only four months earlier upon receiving insurance proceeds after a fire destroyed her old building, on which she had deferred all the realized gain and which she had owned for five years. Kathy's sale of her building on November 15 results in a long-term capital gain since she would have a holding period of five years, four months on the building. That is, she counts the five years she owned the former building in her holding period.

Property Acquired by a Gift and from a Decedent

The holding period of property acquired by gift includes the holding period of the donor if the basis of the property is the same in whole or in part as it had been in the hands of the donor. Code Sec. 1223(2); Reg. §1.1223-1(b). If at the date of the gift the property has a fair market value that is less than the donor's adjusted basis and the property is sold at a loss, the holding period begins on the day following the date of the gift.

EXAMPLE 12.14   On March 17, 2017, Justin Jaeger received shares of stock as a gift from his father, who had owned it for four years and who had an adjusted basis of $5,000 in the stock. The stock had a fair market value of $8,000. Justin sold the stock on June 17, 2017, for $9,000. Although Justin has owned it only three months, he has a $4,000 long-term capital gain since he includes the period that his father owned it.

EXAMPLE 12.15   Assume the facts in the preceding example, except that the fair market value at the date of the gift was $3,000 and he sold it for $2,500. Justin has a short-term capital loss of $500 since his holding period begins on the day following the date of the gift which means he held the stock three months. When the asset has declined in value from the donor's basis, Justin will have carryover basis for gain computations and fair market value for loss computations.

Gains and losses from the sale or exchange of inherited property are treated as long-term (greater than 12 months and subject to the capital gains rates) regardless of how long the property was held. Code Sec. 1223(11).

EXAMPLE 12.16

On April 23, 2017, Alice Amberson inherited stock from her aunt, who had owned the stock for three months. On June 23, 2017, Alice sells the stock at a gain. Alice has long-term capital gain even though she owned the property only two months and even though the total ownership by Alice and her aunt was only five months.

Individual Taxpayers

¶12,301   ## DETERMINATION OF TAXABLE INCOME

An individual's capital gains and losses are reported on Form 8949 and carried to Schedule D. The process is not specifically described in the Code but is necessary under the definitions in Code Sec. 1222.

For sales and exchanges after 1998, it is necessary to hold assets more than 12 months in order for the lowest long-term capital gains rates to apply, in which case the maximum rate is 15 percent (0 percent for individuals in the 10 and 15 percent tax bracket) or 20 percent for those taxpayers in the 39.6% bracket. Further, the 15 and 20 percent (0 percent for 10 and 15 percent bracket taxpayers) rates applies only to adjusted net capital gains, which are net capital gains (i.e., the excess of net long-term capital gains over the net short-term capital losses) without regard to:

1. **Collectibles Gain.** Generally, collectibles (as defined in Sec. 408(m)) do not qualify for the lowest rates. Thus, stamps, antiques, gems, and most coins would still be taxed at the maximum rate of 28 percent. (Taxpayers will only be taxed at the maximum 28 percent rate if they are in the 28 percent or higher marginal tax bracket.) Certain newly minted gold and silver coins issued by the federal government and coins issued under state law, however, are subject to the lower capital gains rate, even though such coins generally qualify as "collectibles."

2. **Section 1202 Gains.** When a taxpayer sells or exchanges Sec. 1202 stock (i.e., certain small business stock) that the taxpayer has held for more than five years, 50 percent of the gain is excluded from the taxpayer's gross income. If the taxpayer qualifies for this 50 percent exclusion, any recognized gains from the sale or exchange of this stock would be taxed at the maximum rate of 28 percent. (Taxpayers will only be taxed at the maximum 28 percent rate if they are in the 28 percent or higher marginal tax bracket.)

3. **Unrecaptured Section 1250 Gain.** Unrecaptured Sec. 1250 gain is the amount of the long-term capital gain that would be treated as ordinary income if Sec. 1250(b)(1) included all depreciation with an applicable percentage of 100 percent, and only gains from Sec. 1250 property held for more than 12 months were taken into account. This gain is taxed at a maximum rate of 25 percent. (Taxpayers will only be taxed at the maximum 25 percent rate if they are in the 25 percent or higher marginal tax bracket.) See ¶12,815.

The steps for determining taxable income are as follows:

1. Group all gains or losses into four "baskets" and determine a net figure for each basket. The *short-term basket* contains short-term capital gains and losses and short-term capital loss carryovers. The *28 percent basket* contains collectibles gains and losses, Section 1202 gains, and long-term capital loss carryovers. The *25 percent basket* contains any Section 1250 gain (up to total depreciation taken but not to exceed the recognized gain) that exceeds the portion of gain recaptured at the taxpayer's ordinary marginal tax rate (see ¶12,801 to ¶12,935 to see how this is calculated). The *15/20 percent basket* contains long-term capital gains and losses, not included in the other brackets, and unrecaptured Section 1231 long-term gains.

2. A net loss from the 28% group is used
   a. To reduce gain from the 25% basket
   b. Then to reduce net gain from the 15/20% basket

3. A net loss from the 15/20% group is used
   a. To reduce gain from the 28% basket
   b. Then to reduce gain from the 25% basket

4. Net short-term capital losses are applied
   a. To reduce net long-term gains from the 28% basket
   b. Then to reduce gain from the 25% basket
   c. Finally to reduce net gain from the 15/20% basket

5. Net short-term capital gains are applied to reduce net losses from either the 15/20% or 28% baskets.
6. Any resulting net capital gain that is attributable to a particular rate basket is taxed at the basket's marginal tax rate.
7. Any excess loss is deductible up to $3,000 ($1,500 for married filing separately) as under prior law, and the remainder is carried over.

EXAMPLE 12.17	On May 26, 2017, Nancy Northfield sold for $4,000 shares of stock acquired on December 23, 2016, for $3,200. She has a short-term capital gain of $800. On July 22, 2017, she sold for $8,000 shares of stock purchased for $8,300 on March 21, 2017. She has a short-term capital loss of $300. Nancy's net short-term capital gain is $500. If these are the only capital transactions, the $500 is taxed at an ordinary rate up to 39.6 percent.
EXAMPLE 12.18	On June 16, 2017, John Jennings sold for $3,000 shares of stock he had acquired for $2,400 on January 24, 2017. He has a short-term capital gain of $600. On August 19, 2017, he sold for $7,000 shares of stock he purchased for $8,300 on April 15, 2017. He has a short-term capital loss of $1,300 on this sale. John's net short-term capital loss is $700. If these are the only capital transactions, John receives a $700 deduction.
EXAMPLE 12.19	On December 15, 2017, Nancy sold for $6,200 shares of stock she had acquired for $10,000 on November 18, 2016. She has a long-term capital loss of $3,800. On November 14, 2017, she sold for $14,000 shares of stock she had acquired for $12,000 on October 14, 2016. This is a $2,000 long-term capital gain. Nancy's net long-term capital loss is $1,800. If these are the only capital transactions, Nancy has a deductible loss of $1,800.
EXAMPLE 12.20	On November 10, 2017, John sold for $11,000 stock that he had acquired for $8,000 on October 14, 2016. He has a long-term capital gain of $3,000 on this transaction. On December 12, 2017, he sold for $6,000 stock he had acquired for $7,800 on November 11, 2016. He has a long-term capital loss of $1,800 on this transaction. John has a net long-term capital gain of $1,200. If these are the only capital transactions, John would be taxed at a maximum rate of 15/20 percent.
EXAMPLE 12.21	On December 2, 2017, Brian Boyd sold for $12,000 collectibles he had purchased on October 29, 2016, for $7,000. He also sold on the same day for $14,000 stock he had purchased on July 29, 2016, for $8,000. Brian is taxed at a maximum rate of 28 percent on the collectibles gain of $5,000 and at a maximum rate of 15/20 percent on the $6,000 gain.
EXAMPLE 12.22	If Nancy has the net short-term capital gain of $500 from Example 12.17 and the net long-term capital loss of $1,800 from Example 12.19, she has a net overall loss of $1,300, which is deductible.
EXAMPLE 12.23	If John has the net short-term capital loss of $700 in Example 12.18 and the net long-term capital gain of $1,200 in Example 12.20, John has an overall gain of $500 taxed at a maximum rate of 15/20 percent.
EXAMPLE 12.24	Edwin Edwards, a 33 percent bracket taxpayer, had three stock transactions that gave the following results during 2017: STCG $6,000, LTCG $8,000, collectibles gain $10,000. His overall net gain is $24,000, and he will be taxed at 15 percent on the $8,000, 28 percent on the $10,000, and 33 percent on the $6,000.
EXAMPLE 12.25	During 2017, Tim Turner had a net LTCG of $7,500 and a net STCL of $10,500. Tim's net overall loss is $3,000, and he may take a $3,000 deduction.

EXAMPLE 12.26	During 2017, Joan Janner had a net STCG of $5,000 and a net LTCL of $7,000. The net overall loss is $2,000 and Joan receives a deduction for $2,000.

EXAMPLE 12.27	Beth, a single 33 percent taxpayer, had 2017 capital gains and losses as follows: a short-term capital loss of $12,000 and a short-term capital gain of $5,000, a 28 percent collectibles gain of $4,000, $1,000 unrecaptured Section 1250 gain (losses are not possible here), and a 15 percent long-term capital gain of $1,000. Beth has an initial net short-term capital loss of $7,000. The $7,000 net loss is used to offset the $4,000 in the 28 percent basket, then the $1,000 in the 25% basket, and finally the $1,000 in the 15 percent basket. The remaining short-term loss is $1,000. This loss is deductible by Beth in 2017.

EXAMPLE 12.28	If Beth's figures were the same as in the previous example but she did not have the short-term capital loss of $12,000 then her short-term netting would result in a $5,000 net gain, since it is the only item in her short-term basket. The remaining nettings would all be net gains. Beth's $5,000 net short-term capital gain would be taxed at 33 percent, her net collectibles gain of $4,000 would be taxed at 28 percent, the $1,000 unrecaptured Section 1250 gain would be taxed at 25 percent, and her long-term capital gain of $1,000 would be taxed at 15 percent.

EXAMPLE 12.29	If Beth's figures from Example 12.28 were as follows: a short-term capital loss of $12,000 and a short-term capital gain of $5,000, a collectible gain of $4,000, $1,000 of unrecaptured Section 1250 gain, and a 15 percent long-term capital gain of $5,000. Beth has a net short-term capital loss of $7,000. The $7,000 net short-term capital loss is first used to offset the $4,000 in the 28 percent basket, then the $1,000 in the 25 percent basket, and finally the $5,000 in the 15 percent basket. This leaves $3,000 to be taxed at the 15 percent long-term capital gains rate.

¶12,315   CAPITAL LOSS CARRYOVERS

If the capital losses exceed the limits described above, the excess may be carried over indefinitely. The amounts carried over are offset against capital gains in the subsequent years. The carryforward losses will be treated as if they occurred in the subsequent years. For example, a capital loss is carried over to the following year and is offset against capital gains according to the regular steps for computation of net overall capital gain or loss. If the taxpayer has both short-term and long-term losses in total exceeding the limit allowed as a deduction, short-term losses are applied to the limit first even if they were incurred after the long-term losses. Any long-term carryovers are placed in the 28 percent basket in the following year.

EXAMPLE 12.30	Greg Grove has a net STCL of $2,000 and a net LTCL of $5,500 during 2017. The net STCL is used up first dollar for dollar to give a $2,000 deduction. Then the net LTCL is used up to get the remaining $1,000 deduction for a total $3,000 deduction. This leaves $4,500 LTCL to be carried over to 2018. In 2018, this $4,500 LTCL carryover is treated as if it were a LTCL incurred during 2018 and is placed in the 28 percent basket.

EXAMPLE 12.31	Michelle Martin has a net STCL of $4,000 and a net LTCL of $2,000 in 2017. The STCL is used up first for a $3,000 deduction and $1,000 STCL is carried over to 2018. The net LTCL of $2,000 is also carried over to 2018. In 2018, she has a STCG of $600 and a LTCG of $1,200. In 2018, the STCL carryover of $1,000 is offset against the STCG of $600 to get a net STCL of $400. The LTCL carryover of $2,000 is offset against the LTCG of $1,200 for a net LTCL of $800. For 2018, Michelle is allowed a deduction of $1,200 ($400 + $800).

¶12,401 CORPORATE TAXPAYERS DISTINGUISHED

The capital gain and loss treatment of corporate taxpayers differs from that of individual taxpayers in four ways.

1. The corporation is not allowed any special advantage for net capital gains (i.e., the excess of net LTCG over net STCL). Instead, corporate capital gains are taxed at regular corporate tax rates, with the maximum tax rate of 35 percent.
2. The corporation is not allowed a deduction in the current year for a net overall capital loss position. Capital losses for corporations are allowed only to the extent of the capital gains.
3. A net overall capital loss can still be used by a corporation. It is carried back three years and carried forward five years against capital gains.
4. Corporate carrybacks and carryovers are treated as short-term.

Special Provisions for Certain Investments

¶12,501 NONBUSINESS BAD DEBTS

Nonbusiness bad debts are debts that are not related to the taxpayer's trade or business. They are treated as a short-term capital loss in the year of worthlessness, regardless of how long they were outstanding. The debts must be completely worthless. Code Sec. 166(d)(1); Reg. §1.166-5(a)(2). However, a taxpayer has a totally worthless bad debt when none of what is still owed can be collected, even though the taxpayer may have collected some of the debt in the past. Only a bona fide debt qualifies for deduction as a bad debt. A bona fide debt is a debt that arises from a debtor-creditor relationship based on a valid and enforceable obligation to pay a sum of money. Reg. §1.166-1(c).

EXAMPLE 12.32 In 2015, Beth Burrow loaned $7,000 to her friend Nancy Newburg. In 2017, Nancy declared bankruptcy, with the result that the debt is totally worthless. Beth may deduct the $7,000 loss as a short-term capital loss. If she has no other capital gains or losses, she deducts $3,000 in 2017 and carries the remaining $4,000 to 2018.

PLANNING POINTER Since nonbusiness bad debts result in short-term capital losses, the taxpayer is subject to the regular capital loss limitation of $3,000. Taxpayers should be cautious in making large nonbusiness loans that may become worthless (unless they have capital gains to offset the losses) since it might take a long time to receive the tax deduction given the limitation on the capital loss deduction in a particular year.

¶12,515 WORTHLESS SECURITIES

If a security that is a capital asset becomes worthless, the loss is a capital loss on the last day of the taxable year in which the security becomes worthless. Code Sec. 165(g)(1). Thus, worthless stock that may have been held short-term may result in a long-term capital loss.

EXAMPLE 12.33 Donna Drummond, a calendar-year taxpayer, purchased stock for $4,000 on May 31, 2016. On January 31, 2017, the stock became worthless. She is considered to have held the stock from May 31, 2016, to December 31, 2017 (more than 12 months). Donna has a long-term capital loss even though the stock was worthless after she held it only eight months.

¶12,525 SMALL BUSINESS STOCK

Individual taxpayers are allowed ordinary loss deductions for losses from the sale or exchange, or from worthlessness of certain small business stock (known as "Section 1244 stock"). Code Sec. 1244(a). The maximum deduction for any taxable year is limited to $50,000. Code Sec. 1244(b). On a joint return, the limit is $100,000 whether the stock is owned by one spouse or both spouses. Reg. §1.1244(b)-1. Any excess above these limits is capital loss. The ordinary loss deduction not used in the year sustained is treated as attributable to a trade or business and increases the net operating loss of the shareholder and becomes part of the shareholder's net operating loss carryback and carryover. Code Sec. 1244(d)(3).

The term "Section 1244 stock" refers to stock issued by a small business corporation for money or other property. Code Sec. 1244(c)(1). Section 1244 stock must not be convertible into other securities of the corporation. Reg. §1.1244(c)-1(b). A corporation is considered a small business corporation if the aggregate amount of money and other property received by the corporation for stock as a contribution to capital and as paid-in surplus does not exceed $1 million at the time of stock issuance. Code Sec. 1244(c)(3).

The amount of the "other property" is the adjusted basis to the corporation of such property reduced by any liability to which the property was subject or which was assumed by the corporation. In addition, for the period of five years ending before the loss the corporation must have derived more than 50 percent of its gross receipts from sources other than royalties, rents, dividends, interest, annuities, and sales or exchanges of stocks or securities. If the corporation has been in existence for less than five years, the relevant time period is the time it has been in existence. Special rules also apply for corporations where deductions exceed gross income. Code Sec. 1244(c)(1)-(3).

| EXAMPLE 12.34 | Elaine Eggelston, single, acquires 1,000 shares of Section 1244 stock in 2011 for $150,000 and sells all of it in 2017 for $80,000. She has a $50,000 ordinary loss and a $20,000 long-term capital loss. If she had been married and filed a joint return, she would have had a $70,000 ordinary loss. This assumes that the five-year, 50 percent test is met. |

| PLANNING POINTER | The taxpayer should consider selling stock in two or more taxable years in order to take advantage of the loss limits. Thus, in this example, if Elaine had sold 500 shares in 2017 for $40,000 and the other 500 shares for $40,000 in 2018, she would have had a $35,000 ordinary loss deduction in both years. |

The allowance of an ordinary loss deduction on Section 1244 stock is permitted only to an individual who must be the original owner, or to an individual who is a partner in a partnership at the time of original acquisition. Code Sec. 1244(a); Reg. §1.1244(a)-1(b). The partner's share of the ordinary loss is the partner's share of the partnership's loss on sale of the stock. An individual acquiring stock from a shareholder by purchase, gift, or inheritance is not entitled to ordinary loss deductions under Section 1244.

If a shareholder receives Section 1244 stock as a result of contributing property that had a fair market value less than its adjusted basis immediately before the exchange, the basis of the stock is reduced to the fair market value of the property in computing the amount of the ordinary loss.

| EXAMPLE 12.35 | In 2011, Walter Winston, single, transfers property with an adjusted basis of $160,000 and a fair market value of $120,000 in exchange for 100 percent of the Section 1244 stock of Thompson Corporation. In 2017, he sells the stock for $85,000. Although he has a recognized loss of $75,000, Walter may recognize only $35,000 ordinary loss and the remaining $40,000 loss is long-term capital loss. |

If a taxpayer makes additional contributions to capital after acquiring Section 1244 stock causing the basis in the stock to increase, a loss on the stock is treated as allocated partly to Section 1244 stock and partly to stock which is not Section 1244 stock. Code Sec. 1244(d)(1).

| EXAMPLE 12.36 | Joe Jamestown purchased Section 1244 stock costing $50,000 in 2010 and made an additional capital contribution in 2011 in the amount of $20,000. In 2017, Joe sells the stock for $28,000. Of the $42,000 loss, five-sevenths ($50,000/$70,000) or $30,000 is ordinary loss and the remaining $12,000 is a capital loss. |

| PLANNING POINTER | Instead of just making an additional capital contribution of $20,000, Joe should have received additional stock for his $20,000 investment. With the additional investment qualifying as Section 1244 stock, the entire $42,000 loss would be an ordinary loss. |

¶12,525

¶12,530

GAINS ON SMALL BUSINESS STOCK

Noncorporate investors who were the original holders of qualified small business stock acquired after August 10, 1993, and who held it for at least five years are eligible to exclude 50 percent of the gain from the sale of the stock from their gross income. The American Recovery and Reinvestment Act of 2009 increased the exclusion to 75 percent for stock acquired after the date of enactment (February 17, 2009) and before January 1, 2011. The remaining portion of the gain would be taxed as long-term capital gain at a maximum rate of 28 percent. Taxpayers subject to the alternative minimum tax, however, would have to include 7 percent of the excluded gain as a tax preference item. The Small Business Jobs Act of 2010 raised the exclusion for stock purchased after September 27, 2010 and before January 1, 2011, to 100%. The excluded gain was not an AMT preference. The Tax Relief, Unemployment Insurance Reauthorization, and Job Creation Act of 2010 extended the provisions through 2011. The American Taxpayer Relief Act extended the provisions through 2013 and in 2014. Code Sec. 1202. The PATH Act of 2015 made the 100% exclusion permanent.

Purchase Date	Exclusion
8-11-1993 thru 2-17-2009	50%
2-18-2009 thru 9-27-2010	75%
After 9-27-2010	100%

The exclusion is limited to $10 million of the gain from the sale of the stock by an investor in the same corporation or, if greater, 10 times the adjusted basis of the stock in the corporation that the investor sold during the year.

Other major requirements for the exclusion are:

1. The stock must be issued by a C corporation in exchange for money, property other than stock, or compensation for services rendered to the corporation.
2. The corporation must use at least 80 percent by value of its assets in the active conduct of one or more trades or businesses and can have no more than $50 million in gross assets when it issues the stock.
3. The corporation cannot engage in certain types of businesses, such as businesses that provide personal services (e.g., health, law, or accounting); banking, insurance, financing, leasing, or investing; the extraction or production of natural resources eligible for percentage depletion; farming; and the operation of hotels, motels, and restaurants.
4. Gain from the sale of stock of a DISC (or former DISC), regulated investment company, real estate investment trust, real estate mortgage investment conduit, cooperative, or corporation claiming the possessions tax credit does not qualify for the exclusion.

¶12,535

DEALERS IN SECURITIES

Generally, securities held by a dealer are ordinary assets because they are considered to be inventory. The gains or losses from sale of these securities are considered ordinary gains or losses. However, under special circumstances, it is possible for a dealer to classify securities as capital assets and receive capital gain or loss treatment on the sale or exchange.

Gain from the sale or exchange of a security is not considered as a capital gain unless the security was clearly identified in the dealer's records as a security held for investment before the close of the day on which it was acquired. Also, it may not be held by the dealer as primarily for sale to customers in the ordinary course of a trade or business at any time after the day of acquisition. Losses are not considered ordinary if the security was clearly identified in the dealer's records as a security held for investment. Code Sec. 1236(a) and (b).

For purposes of these rules, the term "security" means any share of stock in any corporation, note, bond, debenture, or evidence of indebtedness, or any evidence of an interest in or right to subscribe to or purchase any of the foregoing. "Floor specialists" have until the seventh business day after acquisition to make their identification. A floor specialist is a person who is a member of a national securities exchange, is registered as a specialist with the exchange, and meets the requirements for specialists established by the Securities and Exchange Commission. Code Sec. 1236(c) and (d).

EXAMPLE 12.37	Wilbur Washburn, a dealer in securities, purchases XYZ Corporation stock on January 14, 2017. On that date, he identifies the stock as assets held for investment. On November 21, 2017, he sells the stock. Any resulting gain or loss is capital gain or loss.

EXAMPLE 12.38	If Wilbur, in the preceding example, withdrew the stock from the investment account and held it as inventory, then the sale at a gain results in ordinary gain, but the sale at a loss results in a capital loss.

¶12,545 SUBDIVIDED REAL ESTATE

Taxpayers who sell developed real estate that has been subdivided can be considered to be dealers and may have to report gain as ordinary income. However, some relief is provided to investors in real estate. Code Sec. 1237. Any lot or parcel which is a part of a noncorporate taxpayer's or S corporation's real property is not considered to be held primarily for sale to customers solely because of subdivision activities. The property may not previously have been held primarily for sale to customers and no substantial improvements may have been made to the lots. Code Sec. 1237(a)(1) and (2).

Substantial means that the improvements have increased the value of a lot by more than 10 percent. Shopping centers, other commercial or residential buildings, and the installation of hard surface roads or utilities such as sewers, water, gas, or electric lines are considered substantial improvements. Surveying, filling, draining, leveling and clearing operations, and the construction of minimum all-weather access roads are not considered substantial improvements. Reg. §1.1237-1(c)(3) and (4). The lots also must have been held, except in case of inheritance, for a period of five years.

If the above conditions are met and the taxpayer has not sold more than five lots or parcels from a single tract through the end of the tax year, capital gain treatment results. If more than five lots or parcels are sold or exchanged, gain from any sale or exchange of any lot occurring in or after the taxable year in which the sixth lot or parcel is sold is recognized as ordinary income up to five percent of the selling price. The remaining gain is capital gain. Selling expenses first offset the amount taxed as ordinary income and then offset the capital gain. Code Sec. 1237(b)(1) and (2). Section 1237 does not apply to losses realized upon the sale of subdivided property. Reg. §1.1237-1(a)(4)(i).

EXAMPLE 12.39	Jerry Johnson, who meets all requirements of Code Sec. 1237, sells five lots during 2016 at a gain of $20,000. During 2017, he sells the sixth lot (basis $4,000) at a selling price of $15,000 and incurs $500 of selling expense. Jerry recognizes long-term capital gain of $20,000 in 2016. In 2017, he has $250 ordinary income and $10,250 capital gain computed as follows:

Selling price		$15,000
Less: Basis	$4,000	
Selling expenses	500	4,500
Gain on sale of lot		$10,500
5% of selling price	$750	
Less: Selling expense	500	
Amount reported as ordinary income		250
Capital gain		$10,250

If the selling expenses had been $750 or more, the total amount of gain would have been capital gain.

PLANNING POINTER	Taxpayers may wish to have investor status because there may be a significant difference in tax on the gain side. If there is a loss situation, however, the taxpayer will be better off by having dealer status so that the taxpayer's losses will be ordinary without limits, instead of capital losses with limits.

Section 1231 Assets and Procedure

¶12,601

BACKGROUND

Prior to 1938, business property was included as a capital asset. However, this meant that taxpayers selling such assets at a loss were subject to the capital loss limitations. This resulted in taxpayers' retaining their business property as long as possible rather than selling it. Therefore, in the Revenue Act of 1938, depreciable property used in a trade or business was excluded as a capital asset. Although this meant that there would not be a capital loss limitation, it also meant that gains would be ordinary income rather than the more favorable capital gains. In 1942, Congress responded by allowing taxpayers to treat net gains from the sale of business property as capital gains and net losses as ordinary losses.

¶12,615

DEFINITION OF SECTION 1231 ASSETS

Section 1231 assets include depreciable property and land used in a trade or business and held long-term. Code Sec. 1231(b). (Long-term means more than 12 months.) Such assets consist mainly of machinery and equipment, business cars and trucks, buildings, and land. They also include a number of items not specifically related to a trade or business:

1. Timber, coal, or domestic iron ore to which Code Sec. 631 applies
2. Livestock including:
   a. Cattle and horses held for draft, breeding, dairy, or sporting purposes for 24 months or more.
   b. Livestock (other than cattle, horses, and poultry) held for draft, breeding, dairy, or sporting purposes for 12 months or more.
3. Unharvested crops on land used in a trade or business and held long-term if the crop and the land are sold or exchanged at the same time and to the same person.
4. The involuntary conversion of business property and capital assets held long-term.

   Note. Gains and losses from casualties and thefts are treated separately, as will be seen later.

Certain items are specifically excluded from the definition of Section 1231 assets:

1. Inventory on hand at the close of the tax year and property held primarily for sale to customers in the ordinary course of the trade or business.
2. A copyright, a literary, musical, or artistic composition, a letter, or memorandum, or similar property held by a taxpayer whose personal efforts created such property. A taxpayer can elect to treat the sale or exchange of a musical composition or copyright in musical works created by the taxpayer's personal efforts as a sale of a capital asset.
3. A publication of the United States government received from the government other than by purchase at the price offered for sale to the public.

It should be noted that to be Section 1231 property, property must be held more than 12 months (24 months or more for cattle and horses). If a business asset is held short-term, the income from sale will be ordinary. In the case of involuntary conversions resulting from a business casualty or theft, Section 1231 does not apply where recognized losses exceed the recognized gains from such conversions. In this case, the net casualty and theft loss is treated as ordinary loss. This is what is often referred to as the first netting (to be discussed later). Although capital assets that are involuntarily converted were included above as Section 1231 assets, for personal-use assets this provision applies only to condemnation gains since losses on condemnations of personal-use assets are not deductible. Personal-use casualty and theft gains and losses are not part of Section 1231, but are subject to a separate netting.

EXAMPLE 12.40   Maria Martina is an artist who owns an art gallery where she sells paintings she has painted. The building is a Section 1231 asset as is the furniture in the gallery. The paintings, however, are ordinary assets since they were created by her own personal efforts.

¶12,645 ## COMPUTATIONAL PROCEDURES

In working with Section 1231 transactions, the taxpayer must take into account three steps after the determination of the realized gain or loss. The realized gain or loss, of course, is the difference between the fair market value of the property received and the adjusted basis of the property given up.

Step 1. Determine the amount of the gain to be recaptured as ordinary income. There is no recapture if there is a realized loss. The determination of the amount to be recaptured as ordinary income is more complicated under the law for Section 1250 property that is sold or exchanged and which has depreciation that has not been recaptured (see later section).

Step 2. Nonpersonal casualty or theft gains and losses from assets held more than 12 months must be netted (sometimes referred to as the first netting). Condemnation gains and losses do not enter into this netting. Casualty and theft gains and losses are the difference between (1) the insurance proceeds, if any, and (2) the adjusted basis of the property for complete destruction of business property (or the lesser of the adjusted basis or the sustained loss for partial destruction of business property).

a. If the casualty or theft gains exceed the casualty or theft losses, then a further netting is made with the Section 1231 gains or losses (see Step 3) for the taxable year.

b. If the casualty or theft losses exceed the casualty or theft gains, the casualty or theft gains and losses are separately treated as ordinary. The gains are ordinary income and the losses are deducted for adjusted gross income.

Note. With the special netting for casualty and theft gains and losses, especially for Section 1231 assets, such events will be given the same treatment as if the assets were disposed of through sale or exchange.

EXAMPLE 12.41	Betty Blue has a casualty gain of $5,000 resulting from an insurance recovery from an accident with her business car, and a fire loss after insurance recovery to her office building in the amount of $6,000. Betty has adjusted gross income of $35,000 before considering these items. After netting the above, Betty has a loss of $1,000, meaning that the casualty and theft gains and losses will be ordinary. The $5,000 is ordinary income and the $6,000 is an ordinary deduction for adjusted gross income. After considering the $5,000 income and the $6,000 deduction, Betty has final adjusted gross income of $34,000. (Examples 12.41 and 12.42 ignore recapture potential.)

EXAMPLE 12.42	If Betty's casualty gain from the accident of her business car in Example 12.41 was $10,000 instead of $5,000, she has a net gain of $4,000 ($10,000 – $6,000) which means that the $4,000 will be further netted with the Section 1231 gains or losses (in Step 3).

PLANNING POINTER	If the taxpayer has a business casualty loss and a business casualty gain (of approximately the same magnitude) in the same year, the taxpayer may wish to attempt to postpone recognition of the casualty gain under the involuntary conversion nonrecognition rules of Code Sec. 1033. In this way, the taxpayer can receive an ordinary deduction for the casualty loss. Otherwise the casualty loss and casualty gain cancel each other out.

Step 3. Section 1231 gains and losses and any net casualty gains from Step 2 (the first netting) are netted. Gains and losses from condemnations of business property held more than 12 months are included in this netting. For personal-use assets, condemnation gains are included; condemnation losses from personal-use assets are not deductible and thus are not considered.

a. If the gains exceed the losses, the excess of gains over losses is treated as ordinary income to the extent of Section 1231 net losses for the previous five years that have not been recaptured. Any remaining Section 1231 gain in excess of these prior losses is a long-term capital gain. Code Sec. 1231(a) and (c). If a portion of a taxpayer's net Section 1231 gain is recharacterized as ordinary income under Section 1231(c), that portion will consist first of any net Section 1231 gain in the 28 percent basket, then any Section 1231 gain in the 25 percent basket, and finally any net Section 1231 gain in the 15/20 percent basket.

b. If the losses exceed the gains, all the gains and losses are ordinary. The losses are deducted for adjusted gross income.

¶12,645

EXAMPLE 12.43   Bill Bradley had sales of assets held long-term with results as follows:

Office equipment loss	($20,000)
Office equipment gain (in addition to recapture)	$45,000

Bill has a net gain of $25,000 ($45,000 – $20,000) on his Section 1231 transactions assuming no prior years' Section 1231 net losses. His net gain of $25,000 will be treated as a long-term capital gain and can be used to offset other capital losses.

EXAMPLE 12.44   Anne Arkady has a Section 1231 net gain of $20,000 during 2017. In the past, the net Section 1231 transactions were as follows:

Year	Net Sec. 1231 Transactions
2016	($4,000)
2015	($8,000)
2014	$25,000
2013	($5,000)
2012	($1,000)

In 2014, Anne had $6,000 ordinary income and $19,000 long-term capital gain after recapturing the losses from 2012 and 2013. In 2017, Anne has ordinary income of $12,000 (recapture of the $8,000 2015 loss plus the $4,000 2016 loss) and long-term capital gain of $8,000 ($20,000 gain less $12,000 losses recaptured). If her 2017 net gain were $10,000 instead of $20,000, all of it would be ordinary and $2,000 of the 2016 net loss would remain to offset Section 1231 net gain in post-2017 years.

EXAMPLE 12.45   Carl Collins had sales of assets held long-term with results as follows:

Machinery gain (in addition to recapture)	$14,000
Factory building loss	($35,000)

Carl has a net loss of $21,000 ($35,000 – $14,000) on his Section 1231 transactions and each item will be treated as ordinary. The $21,000 net loss is an ordinary loss *for* adjusted gross income.

EXAMPLE 12.46   Assume that Betty Brewer had a $10,000 casualty gain, a $6,000 casualty loss, a Section 1231 gain of $9,500 on the sale of business equipment and a Section 1231 loss of $6,500 on the sale of a business truck. With the $4,000 gain ($10,000 casualty gain – $6,000 casualty loss) carried from the first netting, Betty has a net gain in the second netting of $7,000 ($4,000 + $9,500 – $6,500), which will be considered as a long-term capital gain assuming no prior years' Section 1231 net losses.

EXAMPLE 12.47

If Betty in Example 12.46 had only the Section 1231 loss of $6,500 (and no Section 1231 gain of $9,500) along with the net casualty gain of $4,000 ($10,000 casualty gain – $6,000 casualty loss) carried over from the first netting, she has a net loss of $2,500 on the second netting. All gains and losses are ordinary. Thus, Betty has the following:

Ordinary income from the casualty gain	$10,000
Ordinary loss deduction for adjusted gross income	(6,000)
Ordinary loss deduction for adjusted gross income	(6,500)
Net effect on adjusted gross income	($2,500)

If Betty had adjusted gross income of $15,000 without the transactions in these examples, she would have a final adjusted gross income of $12,500.

¶12,655   PERSONAL CASUALTY AND THEFT GAINS AND LOSSES

Personal-use casualty and theft gains and losses are separately netted and do not enter into the business casualty netting or the Section 1231 netting. If the gains exceed the losses, then all such gains and losses are treated as capital gains and losses. Personal-use casualty and theft losses are determined after the $100 per occurrence reduction. If the personal-use casualty and theft losses exceed the gains, the gains and losses are ordinary. Losses are deducted in full to the extent of gains. Losses in excess of gains are subject to the 10 percent adjusted gross income floor. Code Sec. 165(h).

EXAMPLE 12.48

Jim Jannings had the following gains and losses:

1. Gain from office equipment held four months	$500
2. Loss from theft of watch held two years (after $100 reduction)	($600)
3. Gain from insurance recovery on accident of business car owned three years in addition to recapture	$6,000
4. Loss from hurricane damage to office building owned five years (after insurance recovery)	($8,000)
5. Loss from sale of business equipment held more than one year	($5,000)
6. Gain from sale of warehouse held two years (in addition to recapture)	$8,000
7. Net LTCG	$6,000
8. Net STCL	($2,000)

Jim's adjusted gross income before the above transactions was $50,000. Ignoring recapture of depreciation (discussed at ¶12,701) and assuming no prior years' Section 1231 net losses, the tax treatment is as follows: Item (1) is an ordinary gain since the property was not held more than 12 months. Item (2) is a potential casualty deduction but does not enter the first netting because it is a personal theft. Items (3) and (4) are considered in the netting of casualty gains and losses, giving a net loss of $2,000 and making the items ordinary. This net loss is a deduction for adjusted gross income. Items (5) and (6) are considered in the Section 1231 netting, resulting in a net gain of $3,000. This will be treated as a long-term capital gain and will be combined with the Net LTCG of $6,000 to give $9,000. The overall net capital gain is $7,000 ($9,000 – $2,000), which would be taxed at a maximum rate of 15 percent.

Initial adjusted gross income	$50,000
Add: Item (1)	500
Less: Items (3) and (4)	(2,000)
Add: Items (5), (6), (7), and (8)	7,000
Adjusted gross income	$55,500

Since the personal casualty loss of $600 on the stolen watch (Item (2)) is less than $5,550 (10% of $55,500), there is no casualty or theft itemized deduction allowable for that item.

EXAMPLE 12.49	Assume the facts of Example 12.48, except that Item (2) was a fire damage loss to a personal residence of $10,000 after the $100 per occurrence reduction instead of the theft loss of the watch. Since the personal casualty loss of $10,000 is greater than $5,550 (10% of $55,500), there is an itemized deduction of $4,450 ($10,000 – $5,550) from adjusted gross income.

Depreciation Recapture—Section 1245

¶12,701   ## PURPOSE OF RULES

The purpose of Section 1245 is to prevent taxpayers from taking ordinary depreciation deductions and then receiving long-term capital gain treatment through Section 1231 at the time of sale of the property. The following example illustrates how the law worked *before* 1962.

EXAMPLE 12.50	Lloyd Lewis purchased equipment for $10,000 in January 1956 and took depreciation of $6,250 under the straight-line method through December 1960. On December 31, 1960, he sold the equipment with a basis of $3,750 for $9,000 resulting in a realized and recognized gain of $5,250, which was Section 1231 gain. Assuming that Lloyd had no other Section 1231 transactions, this gain would be treated as long-term capital gain. Thus, Lloyd was able to take $6,250 ordinary depreciation deductions while owning the equipment from 1956-1960 and then obtain long-term capital gain treatment at the time of sale. Long-term capital gains had significant tax advantages at that time.

Congress believed that this was too much of a benefit to taxpayers; therefore, in 1962, it enacted Section 1245 which significantly changed the effect of Section 1231 for many assets. The idea in Section 1245 is that there should be recapture of depreciation as ordinary income in realized gain situations. There is no recapture of depreciation, however, when losses are realized. Calculation of the recapture is necessary to determine how much of the realized gain is ordinary income and how much is Section 1231 gain.

¶12,715   ## DEFINITION OF SECTION 1245 PROPERTY

Section 1245 property is really a subcategory of depreciable Section 1231 property. Section 1245 property is personal property (in the legal sense—not personal-use property) which is subject to depreciation or amortization. Code Sec. 1245(a)(3). It includes:

1. Property (not including a building or its structural components) if such property is tangible and was used as an integral part of specified business activities
2. Amortizable property such as patents and leaseholds of Section 1245 property
3. Single purpose agricultural or horticultural structures
4. Storage facilities (not including a building or its structural components) used in connection with the distribution of petroleum or any primary product of petroleum
5. Railroad gradings or tunnel bores (as defined in Code Sec. 168(e)(4))

Section 1245 property includes personal property such as machinery, equipment, cars, and trucks, all used in a trade or business. Depreciable property which is expensed under Section 179 is also Section 1245 property. Expenditures to remove architectural and transportation barriers to the handicapped which are deductible under Section 190 are Section 1245 property as are properties subject to accelerated amortization under Section 169 for pollution control facilities, and Section 188 for child care facilities. In addition, Section 1245 provisions apply to nonresidential real property if the recovery of cost is under the statutory percentage method of the accelerated cost recovery system (ACRS) rather than the straight-line method. Such property is technically not Section 1245 property, but it receives Section 1245 treatment on recapture.

EXAMPLE 12.51

Peter Paulson owns the following assets:

1. Machinery used in his auto repair shop
2. Truck used in his business
3. Furniture in the office of the shop
4. Furniture in his home
5. Oil and inventory items used in his business

Items (1), (2), and (3) are Section 1245 assets. Item (4) consists of capital assets and item (5) consists of inventory or ordinary assets.

¶12,725 COMPUTATIONAL PROCEDURES

On the disposition of Section 1245 property, ordinary income is recognized to the extent of the total depreciation taken (including immediate expensing under Code Sec. 179), but not to exceed the recognized gain. Any excess recognized gain over the amount recaptured as ordinary income is treated as Section 1231 gain (in the second netting). In a casualty gain, any excess gain over the amount recaptured as ordinary income is a casualty gain. There is no recapture as ordinary income where there is a recognized loss. All the recognized loss on the sale or disposition of Section 1245 property (a subcategory of Section 1231 property) is treated as a Section 1231 loss.

EXAMPLE 12.52

Jack Jumper purchased business equipment for $20,000 on January 1, 2013, and took depreciation of $13,752 up to January 1, 2017, when he sold it for $11,248. Jack's adjusted basis is $6,248 and he has a realized and recognized gain of $5,000. He has recapture potential of $13,752, the amount of the depreciation taken, but he will recapture only $5,000 as ordinary income since the amount recaptured as ordinary income does not exceed the recognized gain.

EXAMPLE 12.53

Assume the facts of Example 12.52, except that the equipment was sold for $21,248 on January 1, 2017. Jack has realized and recognized gain of $15,000 ($21,248 – $6,248), of which $13,752 is recaptured as ordinary income and the remaining $1,248 is Section 1231 gain.

EXAMPLE 12.54

Assume the same facts as in Example 12.52, except that the equipment was sold for $2,000 on January 1, 2017. There is no recapture when there is a recognized loss, so the $4,248 is a Section 1231 loss.

¶12,735 DEPRECIATION METHODS

Prior to 1981, a number of methods of depreciation were available including both accelerated and straight-line methods. Useful lives were estimated and played an important part in depreciation, as did salvage value. For property placed in service after 1980, the accelerated cost recovery system (ACRS) applies and is required for most properties. Under this system, salvage value and useful lives are not important as they were formerly. ACRS was substantially modified by the Tax Reform Act of 1986. Most tangible property placed in service after 1986 must now be depreciated under the Modified Accelerated Cost Recovery System (MACRS). Under MACRS, different types of property are placed in specific categories. See Chapter 6, ¶6401, for further discussion on depreciation.

¶12,745 ACRS OR MACRS PROPERTY

The same general rule on Section 1245 recapture that applied to pre-ACRS property applies to ACRS or MACRS property. However, there is one difference. Although there are specific recapture rules under Section 1250 for real property, nonresidential real property purchased under ACRS receives Section 1245 recapture treatment if the accelerated method of cost recovery (depreciation) is used. (See ¶12,835.)

¶12,755   **SUMMARY: SECTION 1245 RECAPTURE**

1. Section 1245 property held long-term is a subcategory of depreciable Section 1231 property.
2. All gains or losses on property held short-term are recognized as ordinary income or loss since property held for that time period is not Section 1231 property.
3. The amount of recapture potential is the *total* depreciation taken after 1961. This will frequently mean that all the recognized gain on Section 1245 property is recognized as ordinary income since the total depreciation taken is usually higher than the recognized gain.
4. There is no recapture when losses are recognized on Section 1245 assets. Such losses are Section 1231 losses.
5. The recapture rules for Section 1245 property acquired before 1981 and under ACRS or MACRS are the same.
6. Although Section 1245 includes depreciable personal property, nonresidential real property can receive Section 1245 recapture treatment if the accelerated method is used under ACRS.

Depreciation Recapture—Section 1250

¶12,801   **DEFINITION OF SECTION 1250 PROPERTY**

Section 1250 property is depreciable real property that is not Section 1245 property. It, like Section 1245 property, is a subcategory of depreciable Section 1231 property. It consists mainly of buildings and their structural components as well as other depreciable real property. It also includes intangible real property such as leaseholds of land or Section 1250 property. Code Sec. 1250(c); Reg. §1.1250-1(e)(3).

EXAMPLE 12.55   Charles Cobb owns the following assets:

1. Office building
2. Apartment building containing 10 apartments rented to tenants
3. Personal residence

Items (1) and (2) are Section 1250 assets, but item (3) is a capital asset.

¶12,815   **PURPOSE OF RULES**

The purpose of Section 1250 is to prevent taxpayers from receiving the full benefits of accelerated depreciation and long-term capital gain treatment through Section 1231 at the time of sale of the property. Section 1250 was originally enacted in 1964 but has undergone several changes since that time. Therefore, it is important to keep track of the time periods involved as well as the types of property.

The recapture potential under Section 1250 differs from that under Section 1245 in at least one very important respect. Section 1250 deals with excess depreciation (the excess of accelerated depreciation over straight-line), whereas Section 1245 deals with total depreciation. Thus, the recapture potential under Section 1250 is less severe than that under Section 1245. Under Section 1250, the taxpayer has ordinary income to the extent of the lesser of (1) the gain recognized or (2) additional (excess) depreciation. Any gain not recaptured as ordinary income is Section 1231 gain. Recapture as ordinary income is not applicable to Section 1250 property disposed of at a recognized loss, just as with Section 1245 property; such losses are Section 1231 losses.

Additional depreciation for real property held more than one year is the excess of the amount of depreciation deducted over the amount of depreciation that would have been taken if straight-line depreciation had been used. Code Sec. 1250(a)(1) and (b)(1). The additional (or excess) depreciation has a specified percentage applied to it depending on the time period the property was held and the type of property held. If property is held for less than one year, the entire gain upon sale will be ordinary.

Under the Taxpayer Relief Act of 1997, unrecaptured Sec. 1250 gain is long-term capital gain taxed at a rate of 25 percent and is the amount of the long-term capital gain that would be treated as ordinary income if Section 1250(b)(1) included all depreciation taken with an applicable percentage of 100 percent. For property sold after July 28, 1998, only gain from Section 1250 property held for more than 12 months is taken into account. In less complex language, all or a portion of the recognized gain from the sale or exchange of depreciable real property is to be recaptured. This is determined by treating the property as if it were depreciable personal property (i.e., Section 1245 property) and is taxed at a maximum rate of 25 percent. The remaining gain would be Section 1231 gain and would be considered in the Section 1231 netting and ultimately taxed at a maximum rate of 15/20 percent, assuming that it was not offset by losses in the Section 1231 and capital nettings.

¶12,825   NONRESIDENTIAL REAL PROPERTY— PRE-1981 ACQUISITIONS

For property acquired before 1981, taxpayers could use various depreciation methods subject to limitations and were required to estimate useful lives and salvage values. Taxpayers who acquired the property prior to 1981 are required to continue using the old methods as long as that property is held. Basically, the most liberal depreciation methods available for various types of property were as follows:

New nonresidential real property	150% declining balance
Used nonresidential real property	Straight-line
New residential real property	200% declining balance
Used residential real property with an estimated useful life of at least 20 years	125% declining balance

For nonresidential real property, the recapture potential is 100 percent of the amount of the excess depreciation taken after December 31, 1969. Code Sec. 1250(a). The amount to be recaptured as ordinary income cannot exceed the recognized gain. If there is excess recognized gain above the amount recaptured as ordinary income as a result of the "excess depreciation" calculation, any unrecaptured depreciation will be taxed at the maximum rate of 25 percent. If there is then still any excess recognized gain, it is a 15/20 percent gain. If straight-line depreciation was used, the 1997 Act requires that there is recapture to the extent of total depreciation taken (taxed at the maximum rate of 25 percent) but not to exceed recognized gain.

EXAMPLE 12.56	Paul Prentice purchased an office building on January 1, 1975, for $400,000 and used the 150 percent declining balance depreciation method for the first 40 years he owned the asset. The estimated useful life was 40 years with no salvage. On January 1, 2017, Paul sells the property for $500,000. His depreciation is as follows:

Year(s)	150% Declining Balance	Straight-Line Depreciation	Excess Depreciation
1975	$15,000	$10,000	$5,000
1976-2014	385,000	390,000	(5,000)
2015-2016	0	0	0
	$400,000	$400,000	$ 0

Paul has a realized and recognized gain of $500,000 ($500,000 – $0 adjusted basis). He has $0 (($400,000 – $400,000) × 100%) recaptured as ordinary income, $400,000 is taxed at 25 percent, and the remaining $100,000 is taxed at a maximum of 15/20 percent.

EXAMPLE 12.57	If Paul in the preceding example had sold the property on January 1, 2017, for $8,000, none of the recognized gain of $8,000 ($8,000 – $0) would have been recaptured as ordinary income and there would have been $8,000 taxed at 25 percent, and none taxed at the 15/20 percent rate.

¶12,835   NONRESIDENTIAL REAL PROPERTY—ACRS

Under ACRS (1981–86 acquisitions), nonresidential real property may be depreciated using the prescribed (accelerated) method or the optional straight-line method. The taxpayer may select one of various recovery periods if the optional straight-line method is used. If the taxpayer uses the accelerated method, gain is treated as ordinary income to the extent of *total* depreciation taken. Code Sec. 1245(a). Thus, by using accelerated cost recovery or depreciation, the taxpayer is subject to the more severe recapture rules of Section 1245. With the 1997 Act, even if the optional straight-line depreciation method was used, there is a recapture of total depreciation (but not to exceed recognized gain), which is taxed at a maximum rate of 25 percent. Any excess recognized gain is 15/20 percent gain.

EXAMPLE 12.58	Mary Murphy purchased an office building on January 1, 1984, for $150,000. She used the statutory percentage (accelerated) method in computing cost recovery under ACRS. On January 1, 2017, she sold the building for $170,000. She took cost recovery allowances (depreciation) of $150,000, which gives her an adjusted basis of $0 and a realized and recognized gain of $170,000. She has $150,000 of ordinary income, and the remaining $20,000 is a 15/20 percent gain.
	Because Mary used the accelerated method rather than the straight-line method, she must recapture as ordinary income to the extent of the *total* depreciation taken rather than the excess depreciation, as would have been the case for real nonresidential property acquired prior to 1981 or for real residential rental property both before 1981 and after 1980 (see ¶12,845).

EXAMPLE 12.59	If Mary in Example 12.58 had used the optional straight-line method over 15 years, she would have had depreciation each year of $10,000 ($150,000 divided by 15) or $150,000 total for the 15 years. In this case, Mary would have no recapture as ordinary income and the total recognized gain of $170,000 ($170,000 selling price less $0 adjusted basis ($150,000 – $150,000)) would consist of $150,000 unrecaptured Section 1250 gain subject to the 25 percent tax rate and $20,000 taxed at a maximum of 15/20 percent.

¶12,841   NONRESIDENTIAL REAL PROPERTY—MACRS

Nonresidential real property acquired after 1986 (and before May 13, 1993) is depreciated under a straight-line method over a 31.5-year period. For nonresidential real property placed in service on or after May 13, 1993, the recovery period is 39 years. Starting with the 1997 Act, dispositions of this type of property result in recapture to the extent of total depreciation taken (and taxed at a maximum rate of 25 percent), but not to exceed recognized gain. Any excess recognized gain is 15/20 percent gain.

EXAMPLE 12.60	On December 19, 2017, Jane Judd, a 35 percent bracket taxpayer, sold for $500,000 an office building she had acquired on January 4, 2012, for $390,000. During her time of ownership, she took straight-line depreciation over a 39-year time period, mid-month convention, in the amount of $59,166. She has a realized and recognized gain of $169,166 ($500,000 less adjusted basis of $330,834), of which $59,166 is Section 1231 gain, and which will be netted with other Section 1231 gains and losses. (If this is the only Section 1231 transaction for Jane, it would be taxed at a rate of 25 percent on $59,166 and at a maximum of 15/20 percent on $110,000.)

¶12,845   RESIDENTIAL REAL PROPERTY—PRE-1981 ACQUISITIONS

As with taxpayers who acquired personal or nonresidential real property prior to 1981, taxpayers who acquired residential rental real property prior to 1981 are required to continue using the old depreciation methods as long as that property is held.

For residential real property, the recapture potential is 100 percent of the amount of the excess depreciation taken after December 31, 1975. The 1970 through 1975 recapture potential percentage is 100 percent minus one percentage point for each full month the property was held over 100 months. Code Sec. 1250(a). In other words, the percentage for the 1970-1975 period is 200 minus the total number of months held. This is the only difference between the recapture rules of nonresidential real property and residential rental housing for property acquired prior to 1981.

Because of this difference, the following steps are necessary for recapture on residential rental housing:

1. Determine the excess depreciation for the period after 1975.
2. Multiply the lesser of the recognized gain or the excess depreciation in (1) by 100 percent.
3. Subtract the post-1975 excess depreciation from the recognized gain to get the "unabsorbed gain."

4. Determine the excess depreciation for the 1970-1975 time period.
5. Multiply the lesser of the unabsorbed gain in (3) or the excess depreciation in (4) by (200 less the total of months held, but not less than zero).
6. Add the amounts obtained from steps (2) and (5). This is the amount recaptured as ordinary income.
7. If there is excess recognized gain above the amount recaptured as ordinary income as a result of the "excess depreciation" calculation, any unrecaptured depreciation is taxed at the maximum rate of 25 percent under the Taxpayer Relief Act of 1997. The amount to be recaptured as ordinary income cannot, of course, exceed the recognized gain. Any excess of recognized gain over the amount recaptured as ordinary income in step (6) and over the amount recaptured subject to the 25 percent rate is subject to the 15/20 percent rate.

EXAMPLE 12.61

Assume the same facts as in Example 12.56 at ¶12,825, except that the building was residential rental housing and Paul used the 200 percent declining-balance method for the first 40 years he owned the asset rather than the 150 percent declining-balance method. His depreciation is as follows:

Year(s)	200% Declining Balance	Straight-Line Depreciation	Excess Depreciation
1975	$20,000	$10,000	$10,000
1976-2014	380,000	390,000	(10,000)
2015-2016	0	0	0
	$400,000	$400,000	$ 0

If Paul sells the building for $500,000, he has a realized and recognized gain of $500,000. This is the difference between the selling price of $500,000 and the adjusted basis of $0 ($400,000 – $400,000). Following the steps outlined above for residential rental housing, the following computations result:

1. The excess depreciation for the period 1976 through 2016 is $0 ($380,000 – $390,000).
2. Step (1) is less than the recognized gain, so $0 is multiplied by 100 percent.
3. The unabsorbed gain is $500,000 ($500,000 – $0).
4. The excess depreciation for 1975 is $10,000 ($20,000 – $10,000).
5. The lesser of (3) or (4) is $10,000, which is multiplied by zero percent (200 less 504 months held, but not less than zero percent) to give $0.
6. The total amount recaptured as ordinary income is $0 ($0 from Step (2) and $0 from Step (5)).
7. The remaining depreciation taken of $400,000 ($400,000 less $0 from Step (6)) is taxed at the maximum rate of 25 percent. The remaining gain of $100,000 is taxed at the 15/20 percent rate.

EXAMPLE 12.62

Assume the same facts as in Example 12.61, except that the selling price was $835 instead of $500,000. This would give a realized and recognized gain of $835 ($835 – $0). The unabsorbed gain in Step (3) is then $835 ($835 – $0) and it would then be $835 (the lesser of the unabsorbed gain in Step (3) or the excess depreciation in Step (4)) that would be multiplied by zero percent to give $0 (Step (5)). Then the amount recaptured as ordinary income is $0 (Step (6)) and the remaining $835 is taxed at the maximum rate of 25% (Step (7)).

¶12,855 RESIDENTIAL REAL PROPERTY—ACRS

The tax treatment of residential real property under ACRS (1981-86 acquisitions) is the same as that for such property acquired prior to 1981 (i.e., the post-1975 period). Gain is recaptured as ordinary income to the extent of 100 percent of excess depreciation, but not to exceed recognized gain. Excess depreciation is the excess of accelerated depreciation over the straight-line method over the relevant time period (15-year period for property placed in service before March 16, 1984). With the 1997 Act, even if the optional straight-line depreciation method was used, there is recapture of total depreciation (but not to exceed realized gain), which is taxed at a minimum rate of 25 percent. Any remaining recognized gain is then 15/20 percent gain.

EXAMPLE 12.63	Assume the same facts as in Example 12.58 at ¶12,835, except that Mary purchased an apartment building instead of an office building. Mary still has a realized and recognized gain of $170,000. This is the difference between the selling price of $170,000 and the adjusted basis of the building of $0 ($150,000 – $150,000). Since straight-line depreciation would have been $150,000 (15 × $10,000 per year ($150,000/15)), her excess depreciation to be recognized as ordinary income is $0. There is $150,000 that is taxed at the maximum rate of 25 percent and the remaining $20,000 is subject to 15 percent. This is less severe than the recapture for nonresidential real property in Example 12.60 at ¶12,841.

¶12,861 RESIDENTIAL REAL PROPERTY—MACRS

Residential real property acquired after 1986 is depreciated under a straight-line method over a 27.5-year period. With the 1997 Act, even if the optional straight-line depreciation method was used, there is recapture of total depreciation, which is taxed at a maximum rate of 25 percent, but not to exceed recognized gain. Any excess recognized gain after depreciation has been recaptured is subject to 15/20 percent.

EXAMPLE 12.64	On December 19, 2017, Jane Judd, a 33 percent bracket taxpayer, sold for $500,000 an apartment building she had acquired on January 4, 2012, for $275,000. During her time of ownership, she took straight-line depreciation over a 27.5-year time period, mid-month convention, in the amount of $59,166. She has a realized and recognized gain of $284,166 ($500,000 less adjusted basis of $215,834), of which $59,166 is taxed at the maximum rate of 25 percent, and the remaining $225,000 is taxed at a maximum rate of 15/20 percent.

¶12,865 LOW-INCOME HOUSING—PRE-1987 ACQUISITIONS

For periods after 1969, the applicable recapture percentage as ordinary income for low-income housing is 100 percent minus one percentage point for each full month the property was held over 100 months. Code Sec. 1250(a)(1)(B)(iii). (This is 200 – the total number of months held.) This rule applies for sale of federally assisted housing projects and low-income housing depreciated under Code Sec. 167(k). With the 1997 Act, the remaining depreciation taken is recaptured and taxed at a maximum rate of 25 percent, but not to exceed recognized gain. Any excess gain after depreciation has been recaptured is 15/20 percent gain.

EXAMPLE 12.65	On January 1, 1986, Fred Frombly purchased for $2 million an apartment building that qualified as low-income housing. On January 1, 2017, he sold the building for $2.1 million. Accelerated depreciation has been taken in the amount of $900,000. Straight-line depreciation would have been $600,000. Realized and recognized gain is $1 million ($2,100,000 – $1,100,000), of which $0 is ordinary income (0% (200 – 372 months) × $300,000 ($900,000 – $600,000)), $900,000 is taxed at a maximum rate of 25 percent, and the remaining $100,000 is taxed at a maximum of 15/20 percent.

¶12,875 SUMMARY: SECTION 1250 RECAPTURE

1. Section 1250 property held long-term is a sub-category of depreciable Section 1231 property.
2. Section 1250 property is real property, but if accelerated depreciation is used for nonresidential real property under ACRS, the recapture rules of Section 1245 apply.
3. All gains or losses on property held one year or less are recognized as ordinary income or loss since property so held is not Section 1231 property.
4. The amount of recapture potential as ordinary income is based on excess depreciation in Section 1250 rather than total depreciation as in Section 1245.
5. There is no recapture when losses are recognized on Section 1250 assets. Such losses are Section 1231 losses.

6. There are differences between types of real property—nonresidential, residential rental, and low-income housing.
7. There are differences in the recapture rules for property acquired before 1981, after 1980 but before 1987, and after 1986.
8. The Taxpayer Relief Act of 1997 requires any unrecaptured Section 1250 gain to be taxed at a maximum capital gains rate of 25 percent, although total recaptured depreciation is not to exceed recognized gain.

KEYSTONE PROBLEM

An asset was purchased on January 1, 1975, for $500,000. Depreciation taken on the asset up to the time of sale on January 1, 1987, was $480,000. The selling price was $300,000. Straight-line depreciation would have been $360,000. Depreciation taken during 1975 was $50,000.

1. How is the recognized gain treated for tax purposes for the following assets?
   a. Business machine
   b. Factory building
   c. Apartment building
2. How is the recognized gain treated if the acquisition date is January 1, 1986, the asset is depreciated under the same assumptions, but is fully depreciated when it is disposed of 31 years later on January 1, 2017?
   a. Factory building
   b. Apartment building

Recapture Rules in Other Events

There are special rules with respect to the recapture rules for different types of events.

¶12,901   GIFTS AND INHERITANCES

Gifts do not trigger recapture to the donor, but the recapture potential carries over to the donee. Code Secs. 1245(b)(1) and 1250(d)(1); Reg. §§1.1245-4(a) and 1.1250-3(a). Thus, when the donee disposes of the property, the donee must take into account the donor's depreciation deductions that are subject to recapture in addition to his or her own depreciation if it is depreciable property to the donee. If it is not depreciable property to the donee (e.g., personal-use property), the recapture potential from the donor still carries over.

EXAMPLE 12.66

Clara Cranberry gives a gift of Section 1245 property to her son David. The adjusted basis of the property at the time of the gift is $5,000 and the amount of recapture potential is $6,000. David takes $2,000 depreciation on the property before he sells it for $12,000. There is no recapture for Clara, the donor. The gain realized and recognized by David is $9,000 ($12,000 less $3,000 basis), of which $8,000 is recaptured as ordinary income ($6,000 recapture from Clara and $2,000 recapture from the time that David owned it). The remaining $1,000 is Section 1231 gain.

When property is transferred at death, both the decedent and the heir escape recapture. Code Secs. 1245(b)(2) and 1250(d)(2).

¶12,915   LIKE-KIND EXCHANGES AND INVOLUNTARY CONVERSIONS

Generally, a like-kind exchange does not result in income recognition under Section 1031. However, gain may be recognized if boot is received. Such gain is ordinary income if subject to recapture under Sections 1245 and 1250 and the 25 percent rate recapture under the 1997 Act.

EXAMPLE 12.67	Herbert Hughes has a machine (Section 1245 property) with an adjusted basis of $6,000 (fair market value of $10,000), originally costing $15,000 when purchased in 2011. In 2017, he exchanges it for another machine with a fair market value of $8,000 and receives cash of $2,000. Herbert's realized gain is $4,000 (amount realized of $10,000 ($8,000 + $2,000) less basis of $6,000). The recapture potential is $9,000, to the extent of the total depreciation taken, but since the recognized gain is $2,000 (to the extent of boot received), only $2,000 is recognized and it will be ordinary income. The remaining $7,000 recapture potential carries over to the new machine.

EXAMPLE 12.68	If Herbert in Example 12.67 had received a machine with a fair market value of $10,000 and no cash, he would still have a realized gain of $4,000, but he would have no recognition of gain because no boot was received. The total $9,000 recapture potential carries over to the new machine.

In the case of involuntary conversions, the taxpayer has an election under Code Sec. 1033 to recognize gain only to the extent that the proceeds exceed the cost of the replacement property. The recognized gain is subject to ordinary income recapture and the 25 percent rate recapture under the 1997 Act. Code Secs. 1245(b)(4) and 1250(d)(4).

¶12,925   CHARITABLE CONTRIBUTIONS

If charitable contributions of Section 1245 or Section 1250 property are made, the contribution deduction is reduced by the amount of income recaptured as ordinary income if the property had been sold. Code Sec. 170(e)(1)(A).

EXAMPLE 12.69	In 2017, Mark Matches donated a small apartment building (acquired in 1986) to a qualified charity when the adjusted basis was $160,000 and the fair market value was $300,000. Mark had taken depreciation deductions in excess of straight line of $60,000. His charitable contribution deduction is $240,000 ($300,000 less the $60,000 recapture potential as ordinary income) subject to the limitations on charitable deductions for individuals in any given year.

¶12,935   INSTALLMENT SALES

For installment sales of depreciated property, the full amount of any depreciation recapture as ordinary income is to be reported in the year of sale even if no payments are received in that year. Code Sec. 453(i). The remaining gain, if any, is Section 1231 gain.

EXAMPLE 12.70	In February 2017, Helen Humphrey sells equipment used in her business for $40,000 to be paid in five annual installments of $8,000 plus interest beginning in 2018. The equipment was acquired in 2012 for $30,000 and its adjusted basis was $12,000 at the time of the sale. The realized gain is $28,000 ($40,000 – $12,000) and a total of $18,000 is to be recaptured as ordinary income (i.e., the total depreciation taken) in 2017. The basis is increased by the amount recaptured to $30,000, and the remaining gross profit is then $10,000 resulting in a 25 percent gross profit rate. Of each annual payment of $8,000, $2,000 (25 percent of $8,000) is taxed at the 15/20 percent rate.
	If a portion of the capital gain from an installment sale is 25 percent gain and a portion is 15/20 percent or 0 percent gain, the taxpayer is required to take the 25 percent gain into account before the 15/20 percent or 0 percent gain, as payments are received.

COMPREHENSIVE EXAMPLE

Alan B. Arrow, single, age 40, had the following sales and casualty and theft items during 2017:

1. On January 1, he sold for $11,000 business equipment with an adjusted basis of $4,000. Alan had paid $10,000 for the equipment on January 1, 2013, and had taken $6,000 depreciation.
2. On January 1, he sold for $325,000 an apartment building with an adjusted basis of $175,000. He had paid $275,000 for the building on January 1, 2007, and had taken $100,000 straight-line depreciation.
3. On January 1, he sold for $3,000 a business car with an adjusted basis of $5,000 (cost $22,000 and depreciation taken of $17,000), and acquired on January 1, 2013.
4. Alan's Rolex watch that cost $4,000 in 2006 was stolen in July. The insurance company paid him $4,500.
5. A fire damaged his personal residence (owned three years) in Florida in the amount of $8,000 over his insurance coverage and the $100 per occurrence reduction.
6. A fire damaged Alan's warehouse (owned two years) in the amount of $10,000 above his insurance coverage.

(Assume that there are no prior years' Section 1231 net losses to recapture.)

Alan's adjusted gross income before considering the above items was $60,000. Item (1) results in a realized gain of $7,000 ($11,000 –$4,000) of which $6,000 is recaptured as ordinary income to the extent of total depreciation taken and the remaining $1,000 is Section 1231 gain. Item (2) results in a realized gain of $150,000 ($325,000 – $175,000) of which $100,000 is unrecaptured Section 1250 gain taxed at the top rate of 25 percent and the remaining $50,000 is Section 1231 gain. Item (3) results in a Section 1231 loss of $2,000 ($3,000 – $5,000). Item (4) is a personal theft gain of $500, Item (5) is a personal casualty loss of $8,000, and Item (6) is a business casualty loss of $10,000. The personal casualty and theft netting of Items (4) and (5) is a loss of $7,500, and the $7,500 is deducted as an itemized deduction only to the extent it exceeds 10 percent of adjusted gross income. The first netting of the business casualty and theft gains and losses is a loss of $10,000 (Item (6)) which means that the item will be ordinary.

There is $6,000 depreciation recaptured as ordinary income. The second netting of Section 1231 gains and losses yields a $149,000 gain ($1,000 gain + $50,000 gain – $2,000 loss + $100,000 Section 1250 gain). $100,000 is taxed at the 25 percent rate and $49,000 will be taxed at a maximum rate of 15 percent.

Alan's income would be computed as follows:

Initial adjusted gross income	$60,000
Ordinary income recapture	6,000
Unrecaptured Section 1250 gain (taxed at 25 percent rate)	100,000
Casualty loss on warehouse (ordinary)	(10,000)
Long-term capital gain	49,000
Adjusted gross income	$205,000

Alan does not get itemized deduction for the personal casualty loss, ($7,500 is less than 10% of $205,000). The $100,000 recaptured depreciation in item (2) is taxed at a maximum rate of 25 percent.

TAX BLUNDERS

1. Homer Holmes made a loan of $100,000 to his supplier, the Harris Company, because he was a friend of the major shareholder, George Harris, and because he wanted his supply of reasonably priced inventory to continue. Harris Company goes bankrupt and is unable to repay the loan. Because he was not in the business of making loans, Homer thought he was entitled only to a nonbusiness bad debt deduction, which would be treated as a short-term capital loss, and he treated it as such on his tax return. However, Homer could probably argue successfully that his loan was a business loan since it was made in order to assure a supply of inventory for his business.

2. Bruce Bradley, a 39.6 percent marginal bracket taxpayer, has a casualty loss on one of his office buildings held more than one year in the amount of $50,000 during 2017. He also incurred during 2017 a casualty gain on another office building held more than one year in the amount of $195,000 (including $140,000 unrecaptured Section 1250 gain taxed at 25 percent) which he chose to recognize. He replaced the latter building with another similar office building within a few months at a cost exceeding his proceeds from the insurance on his old building. Bruce has a casualty gain of $145,000 which will be carried over to the second netting. Assuming he has no Section 1231 gains and losses and no capital gains or losses, Bruce will have taxes on that in the amount of $35,750 (15 percent × $5,000 plus 25 percent × $140,000). Bruce should have elected to defer the casualty gain under the Section 1033 rules for nonrecognition of gain in an involuntary conversion. In that way, he could have taken a $50,000 ordinary loss deduction giving him a tax benefit or reduction of $19,800 (39.6 percent of $50,000).

SUMMARY

- The Code defines a capital asset by listing the assets that are not capital assets.
- There are short-term and long-term capital gains and losses that have to be considered.
- There are special rules for holding periods where property is acquired through involuntary conversions, exchanges, gifts, or from decedents.
- Working with capital gains and losses involves following a sequence of steps.
- Section 1231 assets include depreciable property and land used in a trade or business and held long-term, as well as several other items not specifically related to a trade or business.
- Working with Section 1231 transactions involves a sequence of steps, including the calculation of the amount of income to be recaptured as ordinary income, which depends on the type of property and the time period in which the property is acquired.
- There are special recapture rules for the disposal of property received through gifts, inheritances, and involuntary conversions, and for disposal through charitable contributions and installment sales.

QUESTIONS

1. How are capital assets defined?

2. When a sole proprietorship is sold, how is it treated for tax purposes?

3. What determines whether or not a transfer of a patent is considered to be a sale or exchange of a capital asset resulting in long-term capital gain treatment?

4. What determines whether or not a transfer of a franchise is to be considered as a sale or exchange of a capital asset?

5. How are lease cancellation payments treated by a lessee and a lessor?

6. When does the holding period begin for property acquired through the following transactions?
   a. Nontaxable exchange
   b. Involuntary conversion

7. How is the holding period determined for property acquired by a gift and from a decedent?

8. What potential advantage is there for a net overall capital gain situation?

9. How are net overall capital losses treated?

10. What happens to capital losses in excess of the allowed current year deduction?

11. How does the capital gain and loss treatment of corporate taxpayers differ from that of individuals?

12. How are nonbusiness bad debts treated?

13. What is the tax treatment of worthless securities?

14. What is Section 1244 stock? What are its advantages?

15. What special tax treatment is available for subdividers of real estate?

16. Why did Congress enact Section 1231?

17. What is included in Section 1231 property?

18. What is not included in Section 1231 property?

19. Describe what is meant by the "first netting."

20. Describe what is meant by the "second netting."

21. What was the purpose of enacting Section 1245?

22. What is Section 1245 property? What is the Section 1245 recapture rule?

23. What is Section 1250 property?

24. When is recapture on nonresidential real property governed by Section 1245 rules and when is it governed by Section 1250 recapture rules?

25. Describe the recapture provisions for both the donor and the donee when Section 1245 and Section 1250 property are given away.

26. What are the recapture rules in the event of death of the Section 1245 or Section 1250 property owner?

27. Is there recapture of depreciation when like-kind exchanges of Section 1245 and Section 1250 property occur? Explain.

28. What are the recapture rules when an involuntary conversion occurs with nonrecognition of some of the gain?

29. What effect does giving away property with recapture potential have upon a charitable contribution?

PROBLEMS

Note. In the problems below, assume there are no prior years' Section 1231 losses to recapture unless stated otherwise.

30. Which of the following is a capital asset? Explain.
    a. Gold ring received as a gift
    b. Personal automobile
    c. Accounts receivable obtained in the ordinary course of business
    d. Shares of stock in the Riviera Corporation
    e. Building owned and used by the Riviera Corporation
    f. Business cars and trucks owned and used by the Riviera Corporation
    g. Home in Florida used for only four months during the winter
    h. Copyright on a book written and owned by the author

31. Explain the difference between the following situations:
    a. Lois sells a letter written to her by President Ronald Reagan in 1982 to a collector for $5,000.
    b. Lois sells a signed copy of the book *To Kill a Mockingbird*, which she purchased in 1980 for $5 to a collector for $5,000.

32. Byron Bright, an inventor, sells the patent rights on his latest invention to Wilson Corporation. Wilson intends to manufacture and sell Byron's invention. Byron will receive $50 per unit Wilson sells plus a lump-sum payment of $500,000. What is the tax treatment of each type of payment for Byron? If Wilson Corporation is limited to producing and selling Byron's invention in the western section of the United States, what is the tax treatment of each type of payment?

33. Cathy Crafts grants Dan Deputy a franchise to sell cards and gifts. Dan pays Cathy a fee of $1,000 per month plus a percentage of the monthly profits. Dan must purchase his supplies from Cathy and Cathy retains the right to terminate Dan's franchise. What are the tax consequences of this arrangement to Cathy and Dan?

34. Jim Junction purchased a truck for business on November 17, 2016, for $40,000. On July 21, 2017, he exchanged the truck for another truck in a like-kind exchange. The new truck had a fair market value of $42,000. When does the holding period on the new truck begin and what is its basis?

35. Boyd Bayer acquired 100 shares of Evans Corporation stock for $3,000 on January 8, 2016. He gave the stock to his daughter Susan on January 8, 2017, when the fair market value was $2,400. On March 22, 2017, Susan sold the stock for $1,500. What is the nature and the amount of the gain or loss for Susan in 2017?

36. Alice Almond purchased Smith Corporation stock on February 23, 2016, and on November 15, 2016, she gave the stock to her son Dennis. She paid $10,000 for the stock and the value at the time of the gift was $12,000. On April 19, 2017, Dennis sold the stock for $13,000.
    a. Does Dennis have short-term or long-term gain or loss and how much?
    b. If the value of the stock at the time of the gift was $9,500, and Dennis sold it on April 19, 2017, for $8,000, does he have short-term or long-term gain or loss and how much?

37. Ed Elsewhere has the following capital gains and losses during 2017 as a result of sales of shares of stock. What is the net effect of the gains and losses on Ed's tax return in each of the following cases?

   a. STCG $1,500
       STCL   ($2,250)
       LTCG $5,500
       LTCL   ($2,500)
   b. STCG $6,000
       STCL   ($4,500)
       LTCG $0
       LTCL   ($750)
   c. LTCL   ($4,000)
       LTCG $8,500
       STCL   ($2,250)
       STCG $3,000
   d. LTCG $750
       LTCL   ($2,250)
       STCG $900
       STCL   ($800)
   e. LTCG $3,500
       LTCL   ($3,000)
       STCG $2,000
       STCL   ($6,500)
   f. LTCL   ($4,250)
       LTCG $250
       STCL   ($2,500)
       STCG $500

38. Ted Thomas, a single taxpayer with no dependents, has the following transactions in 2017:

AGI (before capital gains and losses)	$500,000
Long-term capital gain	18,000
Long-term capital loss	(4,000)
Short-term capital gain	6,000
Short-term capital loss	(8,000)

   a. What is Ted's net capital gain or loss?
   b. If your answer to (a) was a net capital gain, what is the maximum rate at which it would be taxed?
   c. If his AGI were $25,000, what is the maximum rate at which it would be taxed?

39. Gordon Grumps is married and files separately. During 2017, he had the following capital gains and losses:

STCL	($1,000)
STCG	1,900
STCL carryover from 2016	(200)
LTCG	600
LTCL	(10,000)

   Gordon's taxable income is $6,000. What is Gordon's capital loss deduction for 2017 and his carryover?

40. Bert Baker had $50,000 salary during 2017 and had the following capital gains and losses:

STCL carryover from 2016	($4,000)
STCL	(2,000)
STCG	1,000
LTCL carryover from 2016	(5,000)
LTCL	(3,000)
LTCG	6,000

   How should Bert treat the above on his 2017 tax return?

41. Cannon Corporation had a net long-term capital gain of $50,000 and a net short-term capital loss of $75,000 in 2017. What are the tax consequences to Cannon as a result of its capital transactions?

42. On April 22, 2017, Al Aikens, a calendar year taxpayer, purchased stock in Webster Corp. for $15,000. What is the nature of Al's loss if Webster Corp. files for bankruptcy and Al's stock becomes worthless on the following dates?
   a. December 20, 2017
   b. January 17, 2018
   c. September 19, 2018

43. Charlotte and Carl Conner purchased 1,000 shares of qualifying Sec. 1244 stock in 2013 for $125,000. In 2017, they sold the stock for $15,000.
    a. What is the amount of their loss?
    b. What is the tax treatment of the loss?

44. Compute the taxpayer's losses for the following situations.
    a. Arthur Angler, single, acquires 500 shares of Section 1244 stock in 2014 for $100,000 and sells all of it for $40,000 in 2017. How is the loss treated by Arthur?
    b. Assume in the preceding part that Arthur made an additional capital contribution of $50,000 in 2015 and then sold all of the stock for $90,000 in 2017. How is the loss treated by Arthur?

45. Shirley Swift transferred property with an adjusted basis of $24,000 and a fair market value of $18,000 to Alex Corporation in exchange for 100 shares of its Section 1244 stock. Three years later, in 2017, Shirley sold 50 shares of the stock for $7,200. What is the nature and the amount of gain or loss for Shirley?

46. Kirk Kelley, a single taxpayer, was engaged in the following transactions in 2017:
    ■ Kirk lent a friend $2,500; that person did not pay the loan when it was due and then declared bankruptcy. The loan was deemed totally uncollectible.
    ■ Kirk was notified on July 20, 2017 by his stock broker that some corporate bonds he owned have become worthless. He had purchased the bonds for $12,000 on August 22, 2016.
    ■ Kirk had a $40,000 loss on the disposition of Sec. 1244 stock purchased several years ago.
    a. What are the nature and amount of the losses on Kirk's transactions?
    b. What is his AGI for 2017 assuming gross income before the transactions was $700,000?

47. Terry Thompson, who meets all the requirements of Section 1237, sells five lots during 2016 at a gain of $30,000. During 2017, he sells the sixth lot (basis $5,000) at a selling price of $20,000 and incurs $300 in selling expenses. What is the nature of Terry's 2017 income from this transaction?

48. Which of the following are Section 1231 assets? Explain. Assume all the items have been held long-term.
    a. Machinery used in the business
    b. Personal home
    c. Factory building
    d. Land held as an investment
    e. Land used in a business
    f. Shares of stock in Jones Corporation
    g. Inventory
    h. Musical composition held by the composer

49. Andrew Graham had the following recognized gains and losses during 2017:

Personal use casualty loss (watch owned 2 years)	($ 400)
Section 1231 gain	$ 500
Section 1231 loss	($ 750)
Net LTCG	$3,000
Net STCL	($2,000)

What are the net tax consequences of these gains and losses to Andrew?

Andrew's adjusted gross income is $40,000 without considering the above items.

50. Barbara Bliss had the following recognized gains and losses during 2017:

Casualty items:

Business casualty gain (property held 5 months)	$100
Business casualty loss (property held 19 months)	($200)
Business casualty gain (property held 21 months)	$500
Section 1231 gain	$750
Section 1231 loss	($600)
LTCL	($4,000)
STCL	($250)

What are the net tax consequences of these gains and losses for Barbara?
Barbara's adjusted gross income is $30,000 without considering the above items.

51. Steven Stronghold had a Section 1231 net gain of $25,000 in 2017. His previous net Section 1231 items were $12,000 in 2010, ($8,000) in 2011, ($6,000) in 2012, ($3,000) in 2013, ($1,000) in 2014, ($4,000) in 2015, and ($1,000) in 2016.
    a. How is Steven's $25,000 net Section 1231 gain treated in 2017?
    b. If Steven's 2017 net Section 1231 gain was $12,000 instead of $25,000, how would it be treated?

52. Jackie Jaguar had a fur coat that cost $12,000 when purchased in 2007 and that was worth $14,000 when it was stolen on April 15, 2017. Her television, which cost $800 in 2011 and was worth $600, was also stolen. She received $10,000 from her insurance company for the theft of the two items. On July 20, 2017, her summer cottage with a basis of $50,000 and a fair market value of $62,000 was completely destroyed by a tornado. The insurance proceeds were $65,000. What gain or loss would Jackie recognize and how is it treated? Jackie's adjusted gross income for 2017 is $25,000.

53. What type of asset is each of the following?
    a. Machinery used in the taxpayer's business
    b. Personal-use automobile
    c. Business-use automobile
    d. Office furniture in taxpayer's business
    e. Furniture in the taxpayer's home
    f. Business inventory

54. Indicate whether the following items are Section 1245 or Section 1250 property or, if neither, indicate what type of property they are considered to be (e.g., capital asset, Section 1231 asset). (Remember that Section 1245 and Section 1250 properties are sub-categories of depreciable Section 1231 property.) Assume all the items have been held long-term.
    a. Equipment used in the business
    b. Personal automobile
    c. Truck used in the business
    d. Escalator used in the business
    e. Inventory
    f. Residential rental housing
    g. Nonresidential real property depreciated under the straight-line method
    h. Leasehold of Section 1245 property

55. In 2017, Dan Dunne sold a business machine for $75,000. He had purchased the machine in 2013 for $90,000, had depreciated it on the straight-line basis using a life of five years, and had taken a total of $63,000 depreciation.
    a. How should Dan treat the recognized gain or loss on the sale?
    b. How should Dan treat the gain or loss if he had used an accelerated depreciation method with a total of $71,100 taken in the four years?

56. In 2017, Emma Evans sold a piece of equipment from her business for $80,000. The equipment was purchased in 2013 for $72,000, had a useful life of five years, and was depreciated on a straight-line basis. A total of $50,400 depreciation was taken.
    a. How will the gain or loss on the sale be treated?
    b. How would Emma have treated the gain or loss if she had sold the property for $15,000?

57. Harold Hunch purchased Section 1250 commercial property on January 1, 1980, and sold it on January 1, 2017, at a gain of $250,000. Depreciation taken was $500,000; straight-line depreciation would have been $400,000.
    a. How should Harold treat the gain or loss?
    b. What would your answer have been in (a) if the property had been residential rental housing?

58. Determine the taxpayer's income and the treatment of the income.
    a. On January 1, 1975, Glen Gopher purchased an office building for his business for $1,000,000. He sold the building on January 1, 2017, for $1,250,000. Glen used the accelerated depreciation method over a 40-year life and his total depreciation deductions amounted to $1,000,000, of which $37,500 was depreciation taken before January 1, 1976. Straight-line depreciation would have been $25,000 a year. How much income does Glen recognize and how will it be treated?
    b. Assume the facts of (a), except that the building was an apartment building rented to tenants. How much income does Glen recognize and how will it be treated?

59. On January 1, 1985, Ivan Innkeeper purchased an office building for $900,000. He used the ACRS statutory (accelerated) depreciation method and took $900,000 depreciation before he sold the building for $950,000 on January 1, 2017. Straight-line depreciation would have been $900,000.
    a. How much income does Ivan recognize and how will it be treated?
    b. What would your answer be to (a) if he had used the optional straight-line method?

60. Assume the facts of the preceding problem except that the building was an apartment building.
    a. How much income does Ivan recognize and how will it be treated?
    b. What would your answer be to (a) if he had used the optional straight-line method?

61. Irene Irwin gave her son James a Section 1245 machine. The machine has an adjusted basis of $25,000 and Irene had taken $10,000 in depreciation. James used the machine for 15 months and took $5,000 in depreciation before selling the machine for $30,000. What is the amount of depreciation Irene must recapture as ordinary income? What is James's gain on the sale and how is it treated?

62. Karen Klaus has a machine (Section 1245 property) with an adjusted basis of $4,000 and a fair market value of $16,000. The machine originally cost $17,000 when purchased in 2013. In 2017, she exchanged it for another machine with a fair market value of $12,000 and received $4,000 cash.
    a. What are the tax consequences of the exchange for Karen?
    b. What would the tax consequences be if the new machine had a fair market value of $16,000 and no cash was received?

63. Larry Lyons donated a small office building to a qualified charity when the adjusted basis was $90,000 and the fair market value was $160,000. Larry had taken depreciation deductions in excess of straight-line depreciation of $50,000. What is Larry's charitable contribution before application of limits?

64. In March 2017, Mary Marionette sold equipment used in her business for $80,000, to be paid in eight annual installments of $10,000 plus interest beginning in 2018. The equipment was acquired in 2013 for $48,000, and its adjusted basis was $20,000 at the time of the sale. How is the income from this sale recognized and how will it be treated?

65. Ivan Investor sold a parcel of land during 2017 realizing a $50,000 gain. Ivan has used this parcel for a parking lot during the 120 months that he has owned the land. The amount and tax classification of the gain recognized by Ivan on this sale is:
    a. Ordinary income of $50,000
    b. A Section 1231 gain of $50,000
    c. A Section 1245 ordinary income item of $50,000
    d. A Section 1250 ordinary income item of $50,000

66. Mary Martin owns a custom curtain/drapery business. In 2017, she purchased three new sewing machines and in a separate transaction, sold her three old machines for $6,000. She had bought the old machines for $5,000 and had properly claimed depreciation of $3,000. What is the amount and character of Mary's gain?
    a. $0 ordinary gain and $4,000 Section 1231 gain
    b. $2,000 ordinary gain and $4,000 Section 1231 gain
    c. $3,000 ordinary gain and $1,000 Section 1231 gain
    d. $4,000 ordinary gain and $0 Section 1231 gain

67. In 2017, Gordon Grant sold an office building for $180,000. He had purchased the building in 1986 for $150,000 and had properly deducted $100,000 of depreciation, which included $15,000 in additional (excess) depreciation. How will Gordon treat the gain on the sale of this office building?
    a. $15,000 ordinary income; $115,000 Section 1231 gain
    b. $30,000 ordinary income; $100,000 Section 1231 gain
    c. $100,000 ordinary income; $30,000 Section 1231 gain
    d. $0 ordinary income; $130,000 Section 1231 gain

68. Which of the following property is not Section 1231 property?
    a. Unharvested crop on land held for more than one year and used for farming
    b. Dairy cattle held more than two years
    c. Musical instruments in a music store
    d. Music store building

69. Section 1250 recapture provisions apply to all of the following except:
    a. Residential real property
    b. Government-financed housing
    c. Low-income housing
    d. ACRS nonresidential real property depreciated under the statutory (accelerated) method

70. **Comprehensive Problem.** Terry Trooper, a single taxpayer, had the following transactions during 2017:
    a. Sold 60 shares of Troy Corporation common stock on March 22, 2017, for $660. The stock was purchased on January 31, 2017, for $7 per share.
    b. Sold family gemstones held for three years for $10,000. The gemstones had a cost and basis of $7,800.
    c. Three-year note from his brother became worthless. The note was $750.
    d. Stock in Tyler Corporation became worthless on December 20, 2017, when the corporation filed for bankruptcy. The stock was purchased for $250 on June 30, 2017.
    e. Received $200 from a renter to cancel a lease held on rental property.

    What is Terry's taxable income if his only other income was salary, net rental income and interest totaling $40,000? He has itemized deductions of $7,000 and no dependents.

71. **Comprehensive Problem (Tax Return Problem).** Bill and Alice Savage, husband and wife and both age 42, have the following transactions during 2017:
    a. They sold their old residence on January 28, 2017, for $380,000. The basis of their old residence, purchased in 2007, was $70,000. The selling expenses were $20,000. On May 17, 2017, they purchased and moved into another residence costing $150,000.
    b. On April 28, 2017, they sold for $8,000 stock that Alice had received as a gift from her mother, who had purchased the stock for $10,000 in 2012. Her mother gave Alice the stock on November 15, 2016, when the fair market value was $9,400.
    c. On May 24, 2017, Bill sold for $21,000 stock inherited from his father. His father died on June 14, 2016, when the fair market value of the stock was $9,000. Bill's father paid $7,000 for the stock in 2010.
    d. On August 11, 2017, they sold a personal automobile for $8,000; basis of the automobile was $20,000 and it was purchased in 2014.
    e. They had a carryover and other stock transactions as follows:

LTCL carryover from 2016	($7,000)
STCG	$2,000
LTCG	$3,500

    Bill had salary of $40,000 and Alice had salary of $28,000. They have no children. They paid state income taxes of $3,200, sales tax of $400, federal income taxes of $15,000, and property taxes of $1,800. In addition, they contributed $5,600 to their church and paid $4,000 interest on their home mortgage.

    Compute Bill and Alice's taxable income for 2017.

72. **Comprehensive Problem.** Kate King had the following transactions or involuntary conversions during 2017:

    a. Her uninsured diamond ring that cost $3,500 in 2011 was stolen.

    b. Her vacation home purchased in 2011 for $70,000 was destroyed by a tornado. Insurance recovery was $85,000.

    c. Machinery purchased in 2013 for $12,000 with a basis at the time of sale of $3,000 was sold on January 1 for $13,000.

    d. A business car purchased in 2012 for $20,000 with a basis of $8,700 at the time of sale was sold on January 1 for $6,700.

    e. Land owned for six years was condemned by the state. The award was $100,000 and the land had cost $65,000. No replacement of the property was made.

    f. 100 shares of Atlas Corporation stock were sold for $8,000 on July 17. The stock was originally purchased in 2007 for $3,000.

    g. 200 shares of Brown Corporation stock were sold for $4,000 on April 19, 2017. The stock was originally purchased on December 23, 2016, for $10,000.

    Kate, single and age 34 with no dependents, has adjusted gross income of $44,000 and itemized deductions of $7,000 without considering the above items. What is her taxable income for 2017?

73. **Comprehensive Problem.** Mark Mullins had the following transactions or involuntary conversions during 2017:

    a. His diamond gemstones costing $4,000 in 2011 were sold for $5,000.

    b. His office building owned for four years was damaged by fire. The loss after insurance recovery was $12,000.

    c. Equipment purchased in 2012 for $18,000 with a basis at the time of sale of $6,000 was sold for $11,000 on January 1, 2017.

    d. An apartment building purchased on January 1, 1986, for $300,000 was sold for $124,000 on January 1, 2017. Mark took accelerated depreciation of $236,000. Straight-line depreciation would have been $200,000.

    e. Land used in his business for four years was condemned by the state. The award was $60,000. Cost of the land was $74,000. No replacement of the property was made.

    f. 200 shares of Carter Corporation stock were sold for $19,000 on August 25, 2017. The stock was originally purchased in 2012 for $15,000.

    g. 100 shares of Dalton Corporation stock were sold for $8,000 on July 23, 2017. The stock was originally purchased on February 10, 2017, for $2,000.

    Mark, single and age 42 with no dependents, has adjusted gross income of $56,000 and itemized deductions of $8,000 without considering the above items. What is Mark's taxable income for 2017?

74. **Research Problem.** In 2016, Allen Appleton sells his business to David, but he sells the claim against Fred that arose during the course of his business to George, who is not in a business. The claim becomes worthless in George's hands in 2017. Can George take a business loss for the bad debt since it originally arose in the course of a business?

75. **Research Problem.** Harlan Huston had a net Section 1231 gain in 2017 of $40,000. His net Section 1231 gains and losses were as follows:

Year	Net Sec. 1231 Gains/(Losses)
2016	($15,000)
2015	($6,000)
2014	($16,000)
2013	$5,000
2012	($20,000)

How is the $40,000 net Section 1231 gain treated by Harlan in 2017?

Chapter

13

Tax Accounting

OBJECTIVES

After completing Chapter 13, you should be able to:

1. List what are permissible tax years.
2. Explain the requirements for changing a tax year.
3. Identify the available accounting methods.
4. Understand the rules for accounting method changes.
5. Account for the capitalization of inventory costs.
6. Describe long-term contract reporting.
7. Define the installment method of accounting.

OVERVIEW

The first 12 chapters are presented primarily from the individual taxpayer's point of view (including self-employed taxpayers). This chapter provides a general discussion of the previous material as it applies to other entities and provides a discussion of accounting periods and accounting methods as they apply to all entities. Discussions of specific provisions as they apply to other entities (e.g., corporations, partnerships, etc.) are contained in subsequent chapters.

The term "financial accounting" refers to the reporting of the financial data of an enterprise through financial statements prepared in accordance with generally accepted accounting principles.

Income tax accounting, hereafter referred to as "tax accounting," is concerned with the reporting of financial data to satisfy the requirements of the Internal Revenue Code, the Regulations which interpret the Code, rulings by the IRS which further interpret the Code and Regulations, and the decisions of the courts on litigated issues.

Tax accounting is statutory. It is concerned with the determination of taxable income as the base to which tax rates are applied to establish the tax liability for a period, usually one year. Basically, taxable income or taxable loss is the net result of summarizing revenues, gains, expenses, and losses. This result is determined in considerable degree in accordance with accepted accounting principles and conventions. At every step in the process, however, there are differences, based on tax statutes and interpretations thereof, which distinguish taxable income from financial income. These differences are numerous and may prove substantial in amount.

The variations between taxable income and financial income are so great as to require specialization in taxation as distinguished from financial accounting. The two disciplines, however, are fundamentally related, and tax issues are usually resolved concurrently with the financial accounting issues.

The basic approach of the income tax is to impose a tax on the net result of financial transactions occurring during a fixed period of time called the tax year. The time for reporting income and deductions thus becomes of vital importance in determining taxable income. Therefore, the Internal Revenue Code provides that taxable income must be computed on the basis of the taxpayer's tax year and permissible method of accounting.

There are some differences between financial and tax accounting, differences that are attributable to a number of factors. Financial accounting is designed to reflect the income position of a profit-seeking taxpayer; the rules of tax accounting not only must have regard for this but also must reflect the need to raise revenue equitably. Further, the general thrust and purpose of the tax law, to prescribe detailed rules in the interest of certainty, is bound to create conflicts with tailor-made systems designed for particular taxpayers in many instances. Experience has indicated that certain tax rules are necessary in order to control tax avoidance. Thus, the Internal Revenue Service has been provided with Code Sec. 482, under which it may reallocate items of income, deduction, credit, or allowance in order to prevent tax avoidance when two or more organizations are controlled by the same interest. Further, if the taxpayer's method of accounting does not clearly reflect income, Code Sec. 446 authorizes the IRS to require the use of a method that will do so. Additionally, the Supreme Court has indicated that the use of generally accepted accounting principles (GAAP), which apply to financial accounting and are considered to be the "best" accounting practices, does not necessarily clearly reflect income and does not shift the burden of proof to the IRS to show otherwise. *Thor Power Tool Co.*, 79-1 USTC ¶9139, 439 U.S. 522 (1979).

Once the questions of what items are includible in gross income and what items are deductible in computing taxable income are answered, a second set of questions must be faced. These relate to when such qualifying items are to be utilized in that computation. In other words, in what tax year is an item of income actually to be included in gross income? In what tax year is a deduction to be subtracted from gross income?

The general answers to most of these "when" questions are furnished in terms of the method of accounting regularly employed by the taxpayer in his or her business and recordkeeping. That record, however, must "clearly reflect income." Various accounting methods are available in computing taxable income, but the significant effect of the selection of one method of reporting over another is that of timing. Total income and total deductions over the long run will generally be the same regardless of the method used. However, yearly determinations of taxable income may differ materially depending on the method selected.

Taxable Income and Tax Liability for Various Entities

¶ 13,001   ## RECAPITULATION OF TAXABLE INCOME AND TAX LIABILITY

Table 1 contains a general outline of the computation of taxable income for various entities. A comparison of each provides an indication of some similarities and differences. All entities subtract exclusions to determine gross income. However, the types of exclusions are different; some apply to all entities (e.g., the exclusion for municipal bond interest income), and some apply to particular entities (e.g., the exclusion for qualified fringe benefits, which applies to individuals). Additionally, Code Sec. 61 applies to all entities in computing gross income.

Each entity also is permitted to reduce gross income by qualified deductions. However, the type, classification, and computation of deductions can vary. Only individuals dichotomize their deductions into "for adjusted gross income" and "from adjusted gross income," the latter being deductions for personal expenses such as personal exemptions and itemized deductions that do not apply to other entities. Corporations have routine deductions and several "special" deductions such as the dividends-received deduction. This deduction applies only to corporations. Some items are not deductible by conduit entities (e.g., S corporations) but instead pass through to the owners, while some have different constraints. For example, the charitable contribution deduction is constrained by adjusted gross income for individuals, but is constrained by "modified" taxable income for corporations; yet both entities must go through the same general process of classifying the contributions as cash, ordinary income assets, and long-term capital assets.

To the extent that each entity (including self-employed taxpayers) has business activities, Code Sec. 162 applies to trade or business expenses, and the general criteria for a deduction apply (e.g., ordinary, necessary, reasonable, etc.). Code Sec. 212 applies to an entity's nonbusiness expenses and is most applicable to individuals. Similarly, the "hobby loss" rules of Code Sec. 183 apply to individuals and S corporations. Thus, while each entity is entitled to deductions in the computation of its taxable (or ordinary) income, the nature of these deductions can vary. In subsequent chapters, significant differences are explained further.

Table 1. COMPUTATION OF TAXABLE INCOME	
Individuals	
Income Broadly Conceived	XXXXX
Less: Exclusions	− XXX
Gross Income	XXXXX
Less: Deductions for Adjusted Gross Income	− XX
Adjusted Gross Income	XXXXX
Less: Deductions from Adjusted Gross Income	− XX
Taxable Income	XXXXX
C Corporations	
Income Broadly Conceived	XXXXX
Less: Exclusions	− XXX
Gross Income	XXXXX
Less: Deductions	
Routine	− XX
Special	− XX
Taxable Income	XXXXX
S Corporations	
Income Broadly Conceived	XXXXX
Less: Exclusions	− XXX
Gross Income	XXXXX
Less: Deductions	− XX
Ordinary Income	XXXXX
Partnerships	
Income Broadly Conceived	XXXXX
Less: Exclusions	− XXX
Gross Income	XXXXX
Less: Deductions	− XX
Ordinary Income	XXXXX
Estates and Trusts	
Income Broadly Conceived	XXXXX
Less: Exclusions	− XXX
Gross Income	XXXXX
Less: Deductions	− XX
Taxable Income	XXXXX

Table 2 contains a general outline of each entity's computation of net tax due or refund due. Pure conduits do not pay an income tax; rather, various components such as income, certain deductions, and credits pass through to the owners or beneficiaries. Those entities that do pay a tax utilize taxable income to determine gross tax liability, which is then reduced by the credits and prepayments to which they are entitled. However, the type and/or computation varies (e.g., only individuals are entitled to the earned income credit).

Table 2. NET TAX LIABILITY	
Individuals	
Gross Tax Liability	yyyyy
Less: Credits	– yy
Net Tax Liability	yyyyy
Less: Prepayments	– yy
Net Tax or Refund Due	yyyyy
C Corporations	
Gross Tax Liability	yyyyy
Less: Credits	– yy
Net Tax Liability	yyyyy
Less: Prepayments	– yy
Net Tax or Refund Due	yyyyy
Estates and Trusts (assuming not completely a conduit)	
Gross Tax Liability	yyyyy
Less: Credits	– yy
Net Tax Liability	yyyyy
Less: Prepayments	– yy
Net Tax or Refund Due	yyyyy

In summary, many of the concepts that you learned in the first 12 chapters apply to all entities. However, there are numerous and substantial differences that require additional explanation. The remainder of this chapter deals with accounting periods and accounting methods as they pertain to all entities, but the focus begins to shift to business entities. Subsequent chapters deal with the specific entities.

Accounting Periods

The basic approach of income taxation is to impose a tax on the net result of financial transactions occurring during a fixed period of time, otherwise called the "tax year." The time for reporting income and deductions is of vital importance in determining taxable income. Therefore, Code Sec. 441 requires that taxable income must be computed on the basis of the taxpayer's tax year. This annual accounting period may be either a calendar year or a fiscal year.

¶13,007

THE TAX YEAR

"Tax year" means the calendar year or the fiscal year on the basis of which the taxable income is computed. The tax year may not exceed 12 calendar months, except where a 52-53-week tax year is adopted. (No further mention of this option is made in this text because of the relative infrequency with which this taxable period is encountered in practice.) The term "calendar year" means a period of 12 months ending on December 31. A taxpayer who has not established a fiscal year must file a tax return on the basis of a calendar year.

A "fiscal year" is defined as a period of 12 months ending on the last day of any month other than December. A fiscal year will be recognized by the IRS only if it is established as the annual accounting period for the taxpayer and the taxpayer's books are kept on the same basis. Therefore, to establish and maintain a fiscal year as the tax year, the taxpayer must correlate accounting, financial, and business practices with the fiscal year used for tax returns.

The keeping of books does not require that the records be bound. Records that are sufficient to reflect income adequately and clearly on the basis of an annual accounting period are normally regarded as the keeping of books. Informal records consisting of check stubs, rent receipts, and dividend statements are not considered regular books of account.

When a return is required for a fractional part of a year, the "tax year" means the period for which such return is filed. This fractional period is referred to as a "short tax year." A short tax year is any period for which a return has been filed that contains less than 12 months. Frequently, the first or the final tax period of a particular tax entity is a short tax year. Additionally, when a tax year is changed, the period between the end of the old tax year and the beginning of the new tax year is a short tax year for which a return must be filed.

¶13,015   ELECTION OF THE TAX YEAR

Taxpayers, other than most C corporations, generally must use a "required taxable year". Reg §1.441-1. There are a few exceptions. For example, a partnership, S corporation, or Personal Service Corporation may use a taxable year other than its required taxable year if it so elects under Code Sec. 444 or establishes a business purpose to the satisfaction of the IRS under Code Sec. 442.

A new taxpayer may adopt any tax year that satisfies the requirements of Code Sec. 441 and the regulations thereunder without obtaining prior approval of the IRS. A taxable year of a new taxpayer is adopted by filing its first Federal income tax return using that taxable year. An extension of time for filing the return does not extend the time for adoption of a tax year. Reg. §1.441-1.

Individuals

Since most individual taxpayers keep no books and records prior to filing a first tax return, the calendar year is the default tax year. The establishment and maintenance of adequate books of account may not be delayed beyond the end of the first accounting period if the taxpayer selects a fiscal year. Informal records do not meet this requirement, even if they become part of a formal system of accounting after the close of the fiscal year.

Income Averaging for Farming and Fishing Businesses

The above rules regarding tax periods apply to farmers. However, Code Sec. 1301 allows individual farmers and fisherman to elect to use income averaging over a three-year period when determining tax liability. The irrevocable election applies to farm income or fishing income attributable to a farm or fishing business. The tax liability in any tax year is equal to the tax on the taxpayer's taxable income reduced by that year's elected farm or fishing income to be averaged over the three preceding years and increased by the tax due on the increase in taxable income of the three prior years due to the one-third farm or fishing income averaged over the three preceding years.

Sole Proprietors

Sole proprietors of a business must use the same period for business tax reporting purposes that they use for their personal books.

EXAMPLE 13.1	Evelyn Aldo establishes a tax year when she files her first return. She begins business in a later year as a sole proprietor. Evelyn must use the same tax year for the business unless permission from the IRS to change is obtained.

Partnerships

Except for partnerships that qualify under the business purpose exception or make an election under Code Sec. 444, a partnership must use the same tax year as that of its partners who have a majority interest (an aggregate interest of greater than 50 percent) in partnership profits and capital. If partners owning a majority interest have different tax years, the partnership must adopt the same tax year as that of its principal partners. When neither condition is met, a partnership is required to adopt a year that results in the least aggregate deferral of income to the partners. Reg. §1.706-1. A principal partner is a partner having an interest of 5 percent or more in partnership profits or capital. Partnership income is considered to be earned by the partners on the last day of the partnership's tax year. The least aggregate deferral method requires the partnership to calculate the income that would be deferred by the partners based on the partners' tax years (and therefore the number of months from the partnership's tax year-end to the partner's tax year-end). The calculation is based on each partner's ownership percentage and tax year-end. For each possible year-end, each partner's ownership percentage is multiplied by the number of months the partner would defer income. The result for each partner is totaled, and the totals for all possible tax years are compared. The partnership tax year is the one with the smallest total. These tax year requirements are designed to reduce the partners' income deferral opportunities via tax year selection.

The partnership must adopt the tax year of its majority interest partner or partners if that interest has a common tax year on the first day of the partnership's existing tax year. Further, if a change in the tax year is required under this rule, no additional change is required in the next two years following the year of change.

EXAMPLE 13.2	A partnership is formed by an individual and a corporation, each owning a 50 percent interest. The individual has a calendar year as its tax year, and the corporation has a tax year that ends on August 31. The partnership must determine its tax year using the least aggregate deferral method because neither the majority interest rule nor the principal partnership rule applies. If the corporation owned more than a 50 percent interest in the partnership, the partnership would have to adopt a tax year ending on August 31.

EXAMPLE 13.3	A partnership is owned by numerous individuals and corporations. All of the individuals have calendar years and none of the individuals are principal partners. One corporation owns 45 percent and has a fiscal year ending on May 31. The other corporations have various other fiscal years and none are principal partners. If the individuals together own more than 50 percent of the partnership, the partnership must adopt the calendar year because the majority partners have a calendar year. If the individuals do not own more than 50 percent, the partnership must adopt a fiscal year ending on May 31 because the principal partners have a fiscal year ending May 31.

EXAMPLE 13.4	The BPT partnership has three owners, Barry, Pete, and Tom. Barry and Pete each own 30 percent, and Tom owns 40 percent. Their tax years end on March 31, September 30, and December 31, respectively. In this situation neither the majority interest nor the principal partner methods can be used to determine BPT's tax year; thus, the least aggregate deferral method must be used, and it is determined as follows.

| | | | Possible Tax Year-Ends | | | | | |
| | | | **3/31** | | **9/30** | | **12/31** | |
Partner	Interest	Tax Year	Months Deferred	Total	Months Deferred	Total	Months Deferred	Total
Barry	30%	3/31	0	0	6	1.8	3	0.9
Pete	30%	9/30	6	1.8	0	0	9	2.7
Tom	40%	12/31	9	3.6	3	1.2	0	0
				5.4		3.0		3.6

Note: Months deferred equals the months from the possible partnership tax year-end to the partner's tax year-end. Total equals the months deferred multiplied by the partner's ownership interest.

Thus, the BPT partnership must use a September 30 tax year-end because it has the lowest total amount (3.0) and, therefore, the least aggregate deferral.

A newly-formed partnership that wants to adopt a taxable year other than its required taxable year or a tax year elected under Code Sec. 444 must establish a business purpose and obtain the approval of the IRS. A partnership's selection of a tax year to coincide with a natural business year would constitute sufficient business purpose.

The natural business year is established by the partnership showing that it received at least 25 percent of its gross receipts in the last two months ending on the proposed year's end and for the corresponding time period of each of its two preceding years. See discussion of Business Year below.

Corporations

A corporation may select a fiscal year or a calendar year as its tax year. The tax year of a corporation may differ from that of its shareholders.

A corporation in existence during any portion of a tax year must file a return. If a corporation is not in existence throughout an entire accounting period, the corporation must file a return for that fractional part of a year during which it is in existence. A new corporation comes into existence on the date of its incorporation. This may cause problems for a corporation that is inactive for a period of time after incorporation. Unless the corporation files a return selecting a tax year during the initial period, the time period may pass for electing a tax year, and the corporation may be forced to file a calendar-year return. This will happen if the first tax year ends more than 12 months after incorporation.

S Corporations

The tax year of an S corporation is generally required to be a calendar year. However, a tax year other than a calendar year may be used if the S corporation can satisfy the IRS that there is a legitimate business purpose for such use. Code Sec. 1378(b).

Estates

An estate is a new taxpayer, and it may adopt any tax year without obtaining prior approval. The ability to select a fiscal period enables the executor to do two things: (1) control the number of months in the first and final returns of the estate, thereby controlling the amount of income taxable to the estate during this period, and (2) postpone the time of realization of income by the beneficiaries due to the timing of distributions.

Trusts

Trusts, other than charitable and tax-exempt trusts, must use the calendar year. Code Sec. 644.

Business Year

The intent of an entity to make its tax year coincide with its natural business year constitutes a valid business purpose. Where a business has a nonpeak and a peak period, the natural business year usually ends at, or soon after, the close of the peak period. A business with a steady monthly income does not have a natural business year.

A natural general business year generally exists if, in the last two months of the selected tax year, a taxpayer receives at least 25 percent of its gross receipts and has done so for three consecutive 12-month periods.

Approval to adopt or change to a natural business year is secured by automatic consent procedures under Rev. Proc. 2006-46, 2006-2 CB 859 by filing Form 1128 (Application To Adopt, Change, or Retain a Tax Year).

Election of Tax Year Other Than Required Tax Year

Code Sec. 444 allows certain partnerships, S corporations, and personal service corporations to elect a tax year that is different from their required tax year. The deferral period that is created by adopting the tax year must be the lesser of the deferral period currently in use or three months. Taxpayers making this election are required to follow procedures and make enhanced estimated tax payments to the IRS that are intended to represent the value of the tax deferral obtained by the partners and shareholders through the use of a tax year different from the required tax year. A Code Sec. 444 election is made by filing Form 8716 (Election to Have a Tax Year Other Than a Required Tax Year) with the IRS by the earlier of: (1) the 15th day of the fifth month after the month that includes the first day of the tax year for which the election is first effective, or (2) the due date (without extensions) of the income tax return resulting from the Code Sec. 444 election. A copy of the Form 8716 must also be attached to the income tax return for the first tax year for which the election is made. Willful failure to make enhanced estimated tax payments results in the cancellation of the election by the entity.

Change of Accounting Periods

Required tax years are defined by regulation for most types of business entities. If a taxpayer changes its annual accounting period, the new accounting period shall become the taxpayer's taxable year only if the change is approved by the IRS. Code Sec. 442. A change in accounting period may be approved if there are substantial business reasons for the change. While the IRS has authority to grant a taxpayer's request to adopt, change, or retain an annual accounting period under a facts and circumstances test, it is expected to be applied only in "rare and unusual circumstances." Deferral of income to owners will not be treated as a business purpose. In addition, administrative and convenience business reasons such as the following are not sufficient to establish a business purpose: (1) the use of a particular year for regulatory purposes; (2) the hiring patterns of a particular business; (3) the use of a particular year for administrative purposes, such as promotion, compensation or retirement arrangements with staff, partners, or shareholders; and (4) the fact that a particular business involves the use of price lists, model years, or other items that change on an annual basis. Rev. Proc. 2002-39, 2002-1 CB 1046.

If a taxpayer's records are inadequate or there is an accounting period that does not meet the requirements for a fiscal year, the tax year must be the calendar year. In this instance, the adoption of a fiscal year is treated as a change in the annual accounting period and prior approval from the IRS is required.

A change in accounting period usually involves a short-period tax year. This period begins with the first day after the close of the former accounting period and ends at the close of the day preceding the beginning of the new accounting period.

EXAMPLE 13.5	Mita Corporation wishes to change its tax year from a calendar year to a tax year ending on May 31, 2017. Mita Corporation will have a short tax year for the period January 1 to May 31, 2017.

¶13,101   IRS PERMISSION OR CONSENT

In order to secure IRS approval to change accounting period, the taxpayer must file Form 1128 (Application To Adopt, Change, or Retain a Tax Year) by the due date (not including extensions) of the Federal income tax return for the first effective year. In the case of a change in tax year, the first effective year is the short period required to effect the change. Part II of Form 1128 is completed by those seeking automatic IRS approval for a change in tax year under various Revenue Procedures. Part III of Form 1128 is a ruling request that requires payment of the appropriate user fee and is used by those seeing to change to a tax year for which no automatic consent procedures apply. For example, if a taxpayer wishes to establish a business year under the annual business cycle test or seasonal business cycle test it would file a ruling request. Rev. Proc. 2002-39, 2002-1 CB 1046.

To prevent substantial distortion of income that may result from a change in tax period, an agreement between the taxpayer and the IRS is required. This agreement must provide the terms, conditions, and adjustments necessary to implement the change. The following examples of income distortion are given in Reg. §1.442-1(b):

1. Deferring a substantial portion of income, or shifting a substantial portion of deductions, from one year to another so as to reduce the tax liability
2. Causing a similar deferral in the case of a related taxpayer, such as a partner, a beneficiary, or a shareholder in an S corporation
3. Creating a short period in which there is a substantial amount of income to offset an expiring net operating or capital loss

If approval is granted, the taxpayer must file an income tax return for the short period. There are special rules for computing the tax for a short year caused by a change in the accounting period. These are discussed later in the chapter.

¶13,115   EXCEPTIONS TO PERMISSION REQUIREMENTS

However, despite the prior approval requirements, there are some instances when a tax year may be changed without receiving advance approval.

Individuals

A newly married husband or wife can obtain automatic approval to change his or her tax year in order to use the tax year of the other spouse so that a joint return can be filed for the first or second tax year of that spouse ending after the date of marriage. Reg. §1.442-1(d)(1). Also, individuals who file income tax returns on a fiscal year basis may obtain automatic IRS approval to change their annual accounting period to a calendar year. Rev. Proc. 2003-62, 2003-2 CB 299.

EXAMPLE 13.6

> Larry Raser and Donna Chilton marry on September 24, 2017. Donna is on a fiscal year ending June 30, and Larry is on a calendar year. Donna wishes to change to a calendar year in order to file a joint return with Larry. Donna may not change to a calendar year for 2017 since she would have to file a return for the short period from July 1 to December 31, 2016, by April 15, 2017. Since the date of marriage occurred after this due date, the return could not be filed under the special rule for newly married couples.
>
> Donna, however, may change to the calendar year for 2018 by filing a return by April 15, 2018, for the short period from July 1 to December 31, 2017. If Donna files such a return, Larry and Donna may file a joint return for calendar-year 2018, which is Larry's second tax year ending after the date of marriage. Of course, Donna could request and receive permission to change to the calendar year before the marriage and thus be allowed to file a joint return for the calendar-year 2017.

Any other husband and wife wishing to change to the accounting period of the other spouse so that they may file a joint return must make proper application. Permission may be granted for this reason in appropriate cases, even though no substantial business purpose for requesting the change is established.

Partnerships, S Corporations, and Personal Service Corporations

All partnerships, S corporations, and personal service corporations generally must conform their tax years to the tax year of their owners, unless such entities can establish a business purpose for having a different year. An entity that must change its tax year to match that of its owner is required to file a return for the resulting short tax year.

Corporations

Rev. Proc. 2006-45, 2006-2 CB 851, provides procedures for a corporation (other than an S corporation) to obtain automatic approval to change its annual accounting period. The automatic approval rules generally do not apply to the following classes of corporations, although there are exceptions under each category.

- A corporation that has changed its annual accounting period within the most recent 48-month period ending with the last month of the requested taxable year;
- A corporation that has an interest in a pass-through entity;
- A corporation that is a shareholder of a foreign sales corporation (FSC) or interest charge domestic international sales corporation (IC-DISC), as of the end of the short period (although there are exceptions);
- A corporation that is a FSC or an IC-DISC;
- A corporation that is a personal service corporation. (Rev. Proc. 2006-46 2006-2 CB 859 contains procedures for certain automatic changes);
- A corporation that is a controlled foreign corporation;
- A corporation that is a tax-exempt organization (other procedures apply to tax-exempt organizations);
- A corporation that is one of several other types listed in Rev. Proc. 2006-45 such as a cooperative association, a REIT, a Qualified Settlement Fund or Designated Settlement Fund, a Code Sec. 936 possessions corporation, a corporation exiting a consolidated group, and certain members of consolidated groups.

If the corporation has an NOL or capital loss (CL) in the short period resulting from the change then the NOL or CL may not be carried back but must be carried forward beginning with the first taxable year after the short period. However, the NOL or CL may be carried back if it is $50,000 or less or results from a short period of nine months or longer and is less than the NOL or CL for a full 12-month period beginning with the first day of the short period.

EXAMPLE 13.7	In 2017, Jeffco changed its accounting period from a September year end to a December year end. It had a $100,000 NOL for the three-month short period ending December 31, 2017. Jeffco cannot carry back the NOL. It must carry it forward to the new accounting period (calendar-year 2018).
	If Jeffco is changing from a March 31 year end to a December 31, it might be able to carry back the NOL. Jeffco's short period would start on April 1 and end on December 31, a period of 9 months. If its results from operations for April 1, 2017 to March 31, 2018 produce an NOL that is less than $100,000, then Jeffco may carryback the NOL. Alternatively, if Jeffco's NOL had been $45,000, then it would be able to carry back its NOL.

A statement on behalf of the corporation must be filed on or before the time for filing the return for the short period. The statement must indicate that the corporation is changing its annual accounting period under Reg. §1.442-1(b) and must contain information indicating that all the above conditions have been met.

¶13,165 SHORT TAX YEARS

When a change in an accounting period is instituted, a separate return is filed for the short period beginning with the day following the close of the old tax year and ending with the day preceding the first day of the new tax year. The return is filed within the time prescribed for filing a return for a tax year of 12 months ending on the last day of the short period.

General Rule

The general rule calls for the tax to be computed for the short period by placing the short period's taxable income on an annual basis. This is accomplished by multiplying the modified taxable income by 12 and dividing the result by the number of months in the short period. The tax for the short period is the same as the tax computed on an annual basis. Without this provision, taxpayers would be able to avoid a large tax liability by having a portion of the income taxed for a shorter period. Tax preferences must be annualized to determine the applicability of the alternative minimum tax. Code Sec. 443(d).

A change in accounting period could result in tax savings due to the progressive tax rate structures. Some income would be "sheltered" by avoiding a higher tax rate. To prevent this from happening, the tax for the short period is based on annualized income. The procedures are as follows:

1. Annualize the short-period income

$$\text{Annualized income} = \text{Short-period income} \times \left[\frac{12}{\text{No. months in short period}} \right]$$

2. Determine the tax on the annualized income
3. Determine the short-period tax

$$\text{Short-period tax} = \text{Tax on annualized income} \times \left[\frac{\text{No. months in short period}}{12} \right]$$

EXAMPLE 13.8	Xeno Corporation files a return, because of a change in its accounting period, for the three-month short period ending June 30, 2017. It has taxable income of $20,000 during the short period. Its tax liability is computed as follows:

1.	Taxable Income Annualized ($20,000 × 12/3)	$80,000.00
2.	$50,000 × 15%	$7,500
	$25,000 × 25%	6,250
	$5,000 × 34%	1,700
	Tax on Annualized Income	15,450.00
3.	Tax for Short Period ($15,450 × 3/12)	$3,862.50

Individuals must use the tax rate schedules to compute their tax liabilities for the short period. Also, they cannot use the standard deduction; instead they must reflect the itemized deductions incurred in the short period. Personal exemptions must be prorated to the short period. Very few individuals change their accounting period.

Alternative Method

Because annualization of the short-period income may result in inequities to the taxpayer, there is an exception to the general rule which may result in less tax. Code Sec. 443(b)(2). The procedures are as follows:

1. Determine taxable income for the 12-month period beginning on the first day of the short period.
2. Determine the tax on the taxable income for this 12-month period.

3. $$\text{Short-period tax} = \text{Tax on 12-month period} \times \left[\frac{\text{Taxable income for short period}}{\text{Taxable income for 12-month period}} \right]$$

4. The short-period tax computed in Step 3 cannot be less than it would have been if it had been computed on short-period taxable income without placing it on an annualized basis.

EXAMPLE 13.9

Referring to Example 13.8, assume that Xeno's taxable income for the 12-month period beginning April 1, 2016, is $30,000. The tax on $30,000 is $4,500. The short-period tax would be $3,000 ($4,500 × $20,000/$30,000). This amount is not less than the tax on the short-period income without being annualized ($3,000 = ($20,000 × 15%)). The $3,000 short-period tax determined via the alternative method is compared to the short-period tax computed under the regular method ($3,862.50) and, if less, will be used. In this example, the alternative method produces a tax savings of $862.50 and Xeno Corporation would file a claim for a refund.

The short tax year which results from a change in accounting period is treated as a full tax year for other purposes of the tax rules such as carrybacks and carryforwards. Tax planners must be careful that the creation of a short tax year return does not reduce the benefits a taxpayer would obtain from loss and credit carrybacks and carryforwards which could otherwise be obtained without the short tax year.

¶13,175   ACCOUNTING PERIOD TAX PLANNING

A taxpayer should consider the various factors influencing the choice of accounting period and select the accounting period as soon as possible after beginning operations. The significant factor in selecting an accounting period is timing. Most frequently, total income and total deductions over the long run will generally be the same regardless of the period used. However, yearly determinations of taxable income may differ materially depending on the accounting period selected.

Business Factors

The choice of an annual accounting period depends on several business factors, such as a slack season when personnel are available, or a date when inventories and bank loans are low, which in turn presents a favorable balance sheet for credit purposes. Because income tax rates are on a graduated basis, the lowest taxes over a period of years will be achieved if income can be kept as level as possible over this period of time. Generally, this objective can be obtained if the expenses incurred in earning income are charged off in the same year the income is earned.

Natural Business Year

It is desirable that the accounting period chosen be in agreement with the natural business year. That is, the tax period should include both the income earned and the expenses incurred in generating that income. For example, if a business earns most of its income in the fall while most of the expenses are incurred or paid in the following spring, the calendar year should not be selected as the accounting period, since income would be perpetually distorted. Some advantages of closing a tax period at the end of the natural business year are: (1) inventories are at their lowest point and may be inspected and tabulated more quickly and valued more accurately, (2) receivables are at their minimum and bad debt adjustments can be determined more accurately, and (3) bank loans usually have been liquidated or reduced to their minimum for the tax period. Additionally, financial statements prepared at the end of a natural business year more accurately reflect the results of activities over one complete cycle of operations.

The accounting method adopted by the taxpayer may well be an important factor. Since income and expenses generally accrue before they are received or paid, it may be possible to close the accounting period earlier if the accrual method is used rather than the cash receipts and disbursements method, thereby reflecting a more accurate picture of the income for the period.

Special Circumstances

A corporate taxpayer can select its year based on the particular circumstances of the initial period, rather than any adherence to the concept of the natural business year. The objective is usually to defer tax. Accordingly, a corporation may close its first year at the time it reaches a taxable income of $75,000 and thus avoid the 34 percent rate. If the corporation is an S corporation, where income is passed through to its shareholders who report on the calendar year, adoption of a year ending on the last day of January or a subsequent month, instead of the preceding December 31, serves to defer taxation of the income to the shareholders. However, new S corporations are required to adopt a calendar year unless the taxpayer can show a business reason for electing a fiscal year.

Affiliated Groups

In the case where a new corporation is a subsidiary or a parent of an affiliated group, the accounting period selected should conform to that of the existing members of the group. The consolidated return regulations require that the tax year of all members of an affiliated group be the same as that of the common parent corporation. Accordingly, recognition of this possibility may avoid the trouble of changing the accounting period for the new corporation, the subsidiary, or the entire group, if the new corporation is the parent.

¶13,180   SPECIAL RULES—THE TAX YEAR

Among the most important tax principles supplementing or providing relief from the integrity of the taxable year are the following:

Carrybacks and Carryforwards. Net operating losses generally are carried back two years and forward 20, with an election to forego the carryback. Capital losses of corporations are carried back three years and forward five years. Charitable contributions in excess of annual limits are carried forward five years. Unused credits also are carried back and forward.

Installment Method. Certain taxpayers may defer tax payments until sales proceeds are collected.

Ten-Year Forward Averaging. A special averaging formula, independent of other income, is available for lump-sum distributions from qualified pension and profit-sharing plans for taxpayers born before 1936.

Mitigation Provisions. To prevent double taxation or double deductions, special rules are provided. Code Secs. 1311-1314.

Arrowsmith Doctrine. A judicially developed rule allows the character of an item in the current year to be determined by looking back to a related transaction in a prior year.

Claim-of-Right Doctrine. If a taxpayer must pay back an amount in the current year which was included in income in a previous year, a deduction in the current or previous year is permitted. Code Sec. 1341.

Tax Benefit Rule. If a taxpayer recovers an amount deducted in a previous year, then this amount is included in income in the year recovered to the extent a deduction was allowed in the previous year. Code Sec. 111.

Cost recovery. Capital expenditures may have to be written off over a number of years through amortization (intangibles), depletion (natural resources), or depreciation or cost recovery (tangibles). Upon disposition, previous write-offs may have to be taken into ordinary income, in full or in part ("recapture").

Accounting Methods

¶13,201   OVERALL METHODS

In computing taxable income, taxpayers for expediency purposes or out of ignorance frequently follow those general tax accounting procedures that are well publicized. Unfortunately, this often results in lost opportunities to improve cash flow and/or minimize tax liability.

In addition to selecting one general method of accounting, a taxpayer must select many specific accounting procedures and conventions to be utilized in implementing a single method of accounting. Once a taxpayer knows that a choice exists, the alternative most appropriate to the particular set of circumstances may then be selected. Each election may have a significant impact on the tax liability ultimately reported for any taxpayer.

Section 446 specifies that taxable income is to be computed in accordance with the accounting method regularly used in keeping books. A "method of accounting" includes not only the overall system of accounting of the taxpayer but also the accounting treatment of any item. No uniform method of accounting can be prescribed for all taxpayers. A taxpayer may adopt the forms and systems of accounting that are best suited to the taxpayer's purpose. Informal records are not sufficient; regular books of account are necessary.

A taxpayer whose sole source of income is wages need not keep formal books in order to have an accounting method. Tax returns or other records may be sufficient to establish the use of the method of accounting utilized in the preparation of the taxpayer's tax returns.

If the accounting method regularly used by the taxpayer in keeping books for tax purposes clearly reflects income, that method must be used in the annual return. However, no method of accounting will be regarded as clearly reflecting income unless all items of gross profit and deductions are treated with consistency from year to year.

Approved standard methods of accounting ordinarily will be regarded as clearly reflecting income. Where the method used by the taxpayer does not clearly reflect income, or if no method of accounting has been regularly used by the taxpayer, then the tax computation is to be made under a method that the IRS agrees will clearly reflect income. "Clearly reflects income" means that income should be reflected with as much accuracy as standard methods of accounting practice permit, not merely that the taxpayer's books should be kept fairly and honestly.

The two most commonly used overall methods that are specifically authorized are (1) the cash method and (2) the accrual method. Code Sec. 446. Other permissible methods of accounting for income and expenses are the long-term contract method and the crop method for farmers.

Special treatment is accorded various types of revenue (e.g., installment sales, prepaid subscription income, and obligations issued at a discount) and many types of expenses (e.g., bad debts, real estate taxes, redemption of trading stamps, and expenses whose benefits are received over a period of years). In addition, any combination of permissible methods may be authorized under the regulations.

Subject to the limitations on the cash method of accounting discussed below, a taxpayer filing a first return is allowed to adopt any permissible method of accounting in computing taxable income for the tax year covered by such return. These requirements are sufficiently flexible to permit every taxpayer a maximum opportunity to select the most favorable method of accounting. Except for an occasional refusal to authorize a change in accounting method, the statutory requirements have been interpreted rather liberally.

¶13,215   CASH METHOD

The vast majority of individuals and many businesses use the cash method, primarily because of its simplicity. It generally is used by taxpayers whose principal income is derived from the performance of a service. Unless other restrictions apply, the cash method must be used if the taxpayer keeps no regular books or has inadequate books for the accrual method. Income is recognized in the tax year when cash and/or cash equivalents are actually or constructively received. Expenses generally are deductible in the year paid unless they are attributable to more than one year.

Income may be received in the form of cash, a check, or cash equivalents. Reg. §1.446-1(a)(3). The fair market value of the property is the measure of income. Thus, if a taxpayer receives stock in return for the performance of a service, then the taxpayer's income is equal to the fair market value of the stock, regardless of accounting method. Similarly, the receipt of a negotiable promissory note produces taxable income in the year of receipt equal to the note's fair market value. Mere promises to pay, not represented by notes or secured, are not regarded as income when received. *A.M. Bedell*, 1 USTC ¶359, 30 F.2d 662 (CA-2 1929).

Income also may be received in other forms. A taxpayer may receive the right to use another's property; that is, the taxpayer does not receive the property outright but is allowed to use the property. In this situation the taxpayer recognizes income equal to the fair rental value of the property. Alternatively, a taxpayer may receive services from another taxpayer. Instead of receiving cash or property, the taxpayer enters into a bartering agreement whereby the form of payment is the rendering of services to the taxpayer. In this situation the taxpayer recognizes income equal to the fair market value of the services received. Finally, the form of income may be the discharge of indebtedness; the taxpayer does not receive cash directly but instead has debt forgiven. Depending on the circumstances, all, some or none of the forgiven debt may be included in income. Code Sec. 61. Thus, cash equivalents may take many different forms.

Cash or cash equivalents are income in the year actually or constructively received. Reg. §1.446-1(c)(1)(i). Income is constructively received in the tax year in which it is credited to the taxpayer's account, set apart for the taxpayer, or made available to the taxpayer to draw upon if the taxpayer's control of its receipt is not subject to substantial limitations or restrictions. Reg. §1.451-2(a). The payer must have the ability to pay, must set aside funds for payments, and must not place substantial restrictions on the taxpayer's ability to access the funds (or property). If these conditions are met, then the taxpayer cannot deliberately turn his or her back on income and thus select the year of reporting. *Hamilton National Bank of Chattanooga*, 29 BTA 63, Dec. 8240 (1933).

EXAMPLE 13.10	In 2017, Fry Company credits its employees with bonus stock, but the stock is not available to them until 2020. The employees have not constructively received the stock in 2017.

EXAMPLE 13.11	Sally James received a $700 dividend check from Astin Company on December 26, 2017. Sally did not cash the check until January 4, 2018. Sally must include the $700 in her gross income for 2017. If Astin Company had mailed the check on December 29, 2017, and it was not received until January 2018, then Sally would not include it in her gross income for 2017 because she has no constructive or actual receipt until 2018.

The deductibility of expenses does not coincide with the recognition of income under the cash method. There is no such thing as constructive payment. Expenses are recognized in the year they are paid. However, special rules can apply to an expenditure attributable to more than one tax year. If an expenditure results in the creation of an asset having a useful life that extends substantially beyond the close of the tax year, the expenditure may not be deductible, or may be deductible only in part, for the tax year in which made. A special rule requires prepaid interest to be capitalized (treated as an asset) and recognized as an expense over the time period to which it relates. Code Sec. 461(g). Regulations on expenditures to acquire or create intangible assets include a 12-month rule that applies to many prepaid expenses. Reg. §1.263(a)-4(f). Under the regulations, a taxpayer does not have to capitalize amounts paid to create or facilitate the creation of any right or benefit for the taxpayer that does not extend beyond the earlier of: (1) 12 months after the first date on which the taxpayer realizes the right or benefit; or (2) the end of the tax year following the tax year in which payment is made.

EXAMPLE 13.12	Umbrella Corporation purchases casualty insurance from Weather Inc. at a monthly rate of $2,000. On August 1, 2017, Umbrella prepays its insurance expense for the first six months of 2018 in the amount of $12,000. The 12-month rule applies to the $12,000 payment because the rights or benefits attributable to Umbrella's prepayment of its insurance do not extend beyond December 31, 2018. Accordingly, Umbrella is not required to capitalize its prepaid insurance.

An expense may be "paid" in cash or in property but not by the note of the taxpayer even if secured by collateral. Generally, unconditional delivery of a check has the same consequences as delivery of cash. Delivery means actual delivery of the check to the payee or an agent. However, one court has held that a check is considered delivered when it is put in the mail on the theory that the postal service is acting as the agent for both the sender and receiver. *Estate of E.B. Witt v. Fahs*, 56-1 USTC ¶9534, 160 F.Supp. 521 (DC Fla. 1956).

If a cash-basis taxpayer borrows funds with which to pay deductible expenses (as opposed to directly giving the creditor a note for repayment)—whether the funds are paid to the taxpayer first or directly to the creditor (subject to an understanding that the taxpayer will make repayment to the lender)—the payments are deductible in the year made, not in the later year when the taxpayer makes repayment to the person who advanced the funds to the taxpayer or paid the expenses on the taxpayer's behalf.

Rev. Proc. 2000-22, 2000 CB 1008, as modified by Rev. Proc. 2001-10, 2001-1 CB 272, allows taxpayers with inventories, whose average annual gross receipts (averaged over three years) do not exceed $1 million, to use the cash method of accounting. Inventories on hand must be accounted for under Reg. §1.162-3 as supplies that are not incidental. The taxpayer must not regularly use any method other than the cash method to ascertain income as reported to shareholders, partners, or other owners or beneficiaries.

Rev. Proc. 2002-28, 2002-1 CB 815 allows certain taxpayers (whose principal business activity is providing services or is custom manufacturing) with average gross receipts between $1 million and $10 million to use the cash method of accounting. However, manufacturing, wholesale trade, retail trade, mining activities, and information industries do not generally qualify.

¶13,215

¶13,225 LIMITATIONS ON USE OF CASH METHOD

Three types of taxpayers cannot use the cash method of accounting for tax purposes. (Code Sec. 448). These three types of taxpayers include:

1. C corporations
2. Partnerships which have a C corporation as a partner
3. Tax shelters

The prohibition on use of the cash method does not apply to farming and timber businesses, qualified personal service corporations, and entities with gross receipts of not more than $5 million. The $5 million exemption does not apply to any tax shelter. Individuals, partnerships that do not have a C corporation as a partner, and S corporations are not prohibited from using the cash method. Code Sec. 448.

A tax shelter is defined as: (1) any enterprise, other than a C corporation, for which, at any time, interests in such enterprise have been offered for sale in any offering required to be registered with any federal or state securities agency; (2) any partnership or other entity if more than 35 percent of the losses of such entity during the tax year are allocable to limited partners or limited partnerships; or (3) any partnership, investment plan, or other plan or arrangement the principal purpose of which is the avoidance of federal income tax. Reg. §1.448-1T(b).

Small businesses that can use or continue to use the cash method of accounting are those businesses with average annual gross receipts of $5 million or less over the past three years. The three-year period does not include the current tax year in which the determination is being made. The enterprise is required to change to the accrual method in the year following the year it fails to meet the small business test. A business may not change back to the cash method when its average receipts later fall below $5 million.

Average annual gross receipts are computed by dividing the sum of the gross receipts for so many of the previous three years as the taxpayer conducted business by the number of such tax years. The change to the accrual method must be made in the tax year following this three-year period. In those cases where the enterprise has not been in existence for the entire three-year period, the test will be based on the number of tax years the enterprise was in existence.

Gross receipts are computed by deducting sales returns and allowances from gross receipts. Gross receipts, as defined in the Form 1120 instructions, include gross receipts or sales from business operations with the exception of dividends, interest, gross rents, other income, and net gains and losses from sales of capital and business assets. Gross receipts for a short tax year of less than 12 months are annualized for purposes of the $5 million test. This annualization is computed by multiplying the gross receipts by 12 and dividing the result by the number of months in the short tax year. Code Sec. 448(c).

A qualified personal service corporation may use the cash method of accounting. A corporation is treated as a qualified service corporation only if it meets both a function test and an ownership test. The function test is met if substantially all of the corporation's activities involve the performance of services in the fields of health, law, engineering, architecture, accounting, actuarial science, performing arts, or consulting. The ownership test in general limits stock ownership in the corporation to certain types of persons. Specifically, this test requires that "substantially all" of the value of the corporation's stock must be owned by (1) current or retired employees, (2) the estates of current or retired employees, or (3) persons who acquired the stock by reason of the death of such employees within the prior 24 months. For purposes of applying the ownership test, community property laws are disregarded, and stock owned by an ESOP or a pension plan is considered to be owned by the beneficiaries of the plan. At least 95 percent of the value of the stock must be held directly or indirectly by the required individuals in order for the "substantially all" requirement to be met. Reg. §1.448-1T(e).

¶13,230 SPECIAL RULES—CASH METHOD

Among the most important tax rules interacting with the cash method of accounting are:

Exchanges of Property. In the absence of a nonrecognition provision, both parties recognize gain or loss even if no cash changes hands. The gain or loss equals value received less the adjusted basis of property relinquished. Code Sec. 1001.

Exchanges of Services. If a CPA renders accounting services to a dentist who settles the account with "free" dental services then each party has income equal to the fair market value of the service received.

Constructive Receipt. Actual receipt is not required. Thus, a paycheck is taxable on receipt even if not cashed until the next tax year and interest credited to a savings account is taxed immediately, even if not withdrawn until the next tax year.

Prepayments of Services. Generally, no deduction is allowed until services have been rendered, except for *de minimis* amounts.

Capital Expenditures. Cash and accrual method taxpayers alike must amortize, deplete, depreciate and cost recover assets with a life extending "substantially beyond" the current tax year. Reg. §1.461-1(a)(1).

Farmers. Farmers generally may use the cash method even if inventories are substantial. Reg. §1.471-6(a). Limitations are imposed on farming "tax shelters." Code Secs. 447, 448, and 464.

Checks. A deductible payment made by check is deductible in the year the check is mailed or delivered, even if not cashed until the next tax year.

¶13,235   ACCRUAL METHOD

In general, two tests (the all-events test and economic-performance test) must be met before income or an expense is recognized under the accrual method. Under the accrual method, income is reported when the right to receive income comes into being, that is, when all the events which determine the right to receive income have occurred and the amount can be determined with reasonable accuracy. Reg. §1.451-1(a). Deductions are taken in the year when the legal obligation to make payments comes into existence and all the events have occurred that determine the fact of the liability and the amount can be determined with reasonable accuracy, unless properly allocable to another year. Reg. §1.461-2. The all events test is not met until economic performance with respect to the item has occurred. Code Sec. 461(h).

If the liability arises because a service or property is provided to the taxpayer, then economic performance occurs when the other party provides such service, such property, or the use of such property. If the liability requires the taxpayer to provide a service or property, then economic performance occurs when said service or property is provided. However, Code Sec. 461(h)(3) provides an exception for recurring items if the all events test is met. In such situations the item is deductible during the year if economic performance occurs within eight and one-half months after the close of the tax year.

The accrual basis has not been allowed where the taxpayer has not kept any books or has kept inadequate ones. Also, the accrual method cannot be used where, due to the nature of the business, the amounts accrued—constituting the bulk of reported income—represent only a tentative estimate which cannot be verified from the records until subsequent years.

If the income has not been reduced to possession or constructively received, it becomes taxable under the accrual method when three circumstances are present: (1) there is an unconditional right to receive it, (2) the amount is determinable with reasonable accuracy, and (3) the amount is collectible.

Thus, in order that income be accruable, existence of the right to the income, subject to no contingencies, is the primary essential. If a taxpayer's right to receive is dependent upon future events, there is no accrual until those contingencies occur or lapse.

Second, it also is essential to first provide the general formula (or rules for determining the amount of the income) even if the precise amount has not been determined at this time. The taxpayer may make his or her own determination and accrue the amount so determined, even though the actual determination for payment purposes may show it to be in error or even though some portion of the money received by the taxpayer might have to be refunded in some future year.

The third and final condition is that the amount must be collectible. Even though notes or other receivables may not be marketable, they may be collectible. If the right to receive arises from a sale of real property, an accrual-basis seller should report such right at its fair market value. However, if the sale is of personal property, the full face value of the right must be reported as income.

EXAMPLE 13.13

Darryl Harris sells a building for $200,000, receiving $50,000 in cash and a $150,000 mortgage note due in five years with a 10 percent interest rate. The mortgage note has a $135,000 fair market value. The basis of the building is $95,000. Darryl will report a gain of $90,000 ($50,000 cash + $135,000 fair market value of the mortgage note = $185,000 selling price minus $95,000 basis). If the full $200,000 is collected, $15,000 will be reported as interest income. If the asset sold were personal property rather than the building, the selling price would be $200,000.

Only if there is clear and convincing evidence that real doubt and uncertainty exist as to whether the amount due will ever be collected can there be postponement of reporting income. The possibility of default is not sufficient. The courts have held that year-end is the time to test collectibility on unpaid items. An event occurring subsequent to that time has no effect on the accountability.

An accrual-basis taxpayer need not accrue as income any portion of amounts billed for the performance of services which, on the basis of experience, it will not collect. However, the income must be accrued if the taxpayer charges any interest or penalty for failure to make timely payments in connection with the amount billed. The offering of a discount for early payment of an amount billed will require the reporting of income as long as the full amount of the bill is otherwise accrued as income and the discount for early payment treated as an adjustment to income in the year such payment is made.

The amount of billings that, on the basis of experience, will not be collected is equal to the total amount billed, multiplied by a fraction whose numerator is the total amount of such receivables that were billed and determined not to be collectible within the most recent five tax years of the taxpayer and whose denominator is the total of such amounts billed within the same five-year period. If the taxpayer has not been in existence for the prior five tax years, the portion of such five-year period that the taxpayer has been in existence is to be used.

EXAMPLE 13.14	Assume that an accrual-basis taxpayer has $150,000 of receivables that have been created during the most recent five tax years. Of the $150,000 of accounts receivable, $3,000 has been determined to be uncollectible. The amount, based on experience, which is not expected to be collected is equal to 2 percent ($3,000 divided by $150,000) of any receivables arising from the provision of services that are outstanding at the close of the tax year.

If a taxpayer is contesting a liability of a claimed amount, the deduction cannot be taken until the contest is settled by court decision, compromise, or otherwise. However, if the taxpayer pays the disputed amount or places it beyond its control (e.g., in an escrow account) then the taxpayer can claim a deduction when payment is made. Any difference between what was placed in escrow and the actual settlement amount is either deducted (if settlement was greater than escrow payment) or included in income (if settlement was less than escrow payment) in the year of settlement.

A taxpayer who has not recognized income on amounts not expected to be collected must recognize additional income in any tax year in which payments on amounts not recognized are received. If a receivable is determined to be partially or wholly uncollectible, no portion of the loss arising as a result of such determination that was not recognized as income at the time the receivable was created is allowed as a deduction.

The main disadvantage of the accrual method of accounting is a reduction in the taxpayer's control over the timing of both gross income and tax deductions. Under accrual accounting, a taxpayer may have to recognize income prior to the receipt of cash with which the taxpayer can pay the tax liability.

Prepaid Income and Expenses

The treatment of payments received in advance by an accrual-basis taxpayer for services to be rendered or goods to be delivered in a subsequent tax year has been the subject of litigation for many years. Generally, prepaid income has been held to be taxable in the year received. The treatment varies from financial accounting conventions consistently used by many accrual-method taxpayers in the treatment of payments received in one tax year for services to be performed by them in succeeding tax years. The Supreme Court has supported the IRS position that the deferral of prepayments under financial accounting rules does not clearly reflect taxable income because the seller has already received payment. See *American Automobile Assn.*, 61-2 USTC ¶9517, 367 U.S. 687 (1961). The contingent liability to refund part of the income received does not postpone income recognition.

A taxpayer is generally allowed a deduction in the tax year which is the proper tax year under the method of accounting used in computing taxable income. If, however, the taxpayer's method of accounting does not clearly reflect income, the computation of taxable income must be made under the method which, in the opinion of the IRS, clearly reflects income.

EXAMPLE 13.15	Smith Co. uses the cash basis of accounting. On July 1, 2017, Smith Co. prepaid insurance premiums for the next two years. The annual premium amount was $2,400. Smith Co. deducted $4,800 as insurance expense for 2017 since the cash was paid on July 1 of that year. Even though Smith Co. uses the cash basis of accounting, the IRS will conclude that the deduction does not create a clear reflection of income. It will require Smith Co. to recognize insurance expense over the life of the policy ($4,800/24 = $200 per month; $1,200 insurance expense in 2017).

Other areas that under certain circumstances and within certain limits that receive special treatment include:

(1) prepaid subscription income—the taxpayer may elect to recognize income over the subscription period;

(2) prepaid membership dues—the taxpayer may elect to recognize income ratably over the time period it is liable (if not more than 36 months);

(3) prepaid service income—if the taxpayer will perform the services by the close of the next tax year then it may elect to recognize income as earned over that time period;

(4) certain advanced payments for future sales of inventories—under very specific rules, the taxpayer may elect to defer income until properly earned;

(5) prepaid interest expense—the expense is deductible in the periods in which the use of money occurs (e.g., over the life of the debt); and

(6) bad debts—most taxpayers cannot use the reserve method of accounting for bad debts.

EXAMPLE 13.16	On November 1, 2017, a calendar-year, accrual-basis membership organization sells a two-year membership for $2,400 payable in advance. It elects to recognize income over the life of the membership; so it recognizes $200 ($2,400 × 2/24) in gross income in 2017, $1,200 ($2,400 × 12/24) in 2018 and $1,000 ($2,400 × 10/24) in 2019.

EXAMPLE 13.17	On October 1, 2017, Maria Juarez, a calendar-year, accrual-basis taxpayer who runs a dance school, receives a $1,200 payment for a one-year contract beginning on that date to provide 48 dance lessons. Ten lessons were provided in 2017 and 38 are provided in 2018. Maria elects to recognize income as earned; so she recognizes $250 ($1,200/48 × 10) in 2017 and $950 in 2018. Even if Maria only provided 25 lessons in 2018 she still would recognize $950 because the maximum deferral is to the next tax year.

TAX BLUNDER

Bob Mumper is an accrual-basis, calendar-year taxpayer who performs a service. In 2017, he received prepayments of $200,000 for services he will perform in 2018. Mumper is in the 39.6% tax bracket in 2017, and he is uncertain about future years' tax brackets. Mumper assumed that under the claim of right doctrine he had to include the $200,000 in gross income in 2017 and did so accordingly.

Mumper could have and should have used the prepaid service income method. This would have deferred income recognition until 2018, which would have reduced his tax liability by at least $79,200 (39.6% × $200,000) in 2017. Even if Mumper is in the 39.6% bracket in 2018, the time value of money would have worked in his favor and would have increased the present value of his after-tax cash flows.

¶13,240   ## ACCRUAL METHOD TAX PLANNING

Tax planning by accrual method taxpayers can affect the amount of taxable income being reported for the year. Listed below are various techniques that taxpayers may use to increase or decrease taxable income for the tax year.

Income may be *deferred* by the following techniques:

1. Delays in shipping goods sold (if shipping time is accrual time)
2. Shipping F.O.B. destination, delaying the title change (if title change is accrual point)
3. If allowed, switching from accrual to installment reporting
4. Sales and leasebacks at a loss (e.g., Section 1231 property)
5. Lease with option to buy or just sales of options
6. Using an independent escrow account beyond year end
7. Deferring December billings for services until January (if billing is accrual point)
8. Advanced payments may be structured as conditional prepayments or as loans.

Income may be *accelerated* by the following techniques:

1. The reverse of the above reduction techniques
2. The sale of installment notes

3. Sales and leasebacks of appreciated assets
4. Increased year-end orders through payment deferrals, next year discounts, and special promotions
5. Electing out of the installment method for casual sales.

Deductions may be *increased* by the following techniques:

1. Paying bonuses to officers and/or shareholder-employees
2. Prepaying nonrefundable commissions
3. Increasing deferred compensation contributions, such as to an ESOP or a Code Sec. 401(k) plan
4. Incurring expenses before the end of the year, such as charitable contributions, advertising, accelerating repairs, settling disputed amounts
5. Purchasing business equipment and autos at year-end. The depreciation deduction generally is the same as if the property were purchased at the beginning of the year (if the mid-quarter rules do not apply)
6. Making use of all travel and entertainment expenses.

Deductions generally will be decreased if the reverse of the above is done. If a deduction will be more beneficial next year then its incurrence should be deferred.

¶13,245   SEPARATE SOURCES OF INCOME

Where a taxpayer has two or more separate and distinct businesses, a different method may be used for each business, provided separate books and records are maintained clearly reflecting the income of each. But the taxpayer may not shift profits and losses between businesses through inventory adjustments, sales, purchases, or expenses. Reg. §1.446-1(d).

EXAMPLE 13.18	Olivia Lee operates a beauty shop and a record store as separate sole proprietorships. The income and deductions of the beauty shop can be accounted for under the cash method of accounting, while those of the record store must be under the accrual method of accounting because inventories are an income-producing factor (see ¶13,265).

In a situation where there are overlapping costs, expenditures on behalf of each activity are to be taken up in the books or tax return for that activity in accordance with the applicable method of accounting. As to any business for which separate records are maintained, the rule of consistency would continue to apply.

This principle has been extended to situations where the taxpayer uses one method for business income and another for personal income. The Regulations state that a taxpayer using one method of accounting in computing items of income and deductions for trade or business may compute other items of income and deductions not connected with the trade or business under a different method of accounting.

¶13,265   HYBRID METHODS

Many combinations of permissible accounting methods may be used. For example, the accrual method, which must be used for purchases and sales of inventory, may be combined with the cash method for other items of income and expense. But a taxpayer's choice is not unlimited. If the cash method is used for income, it must also be used for expenses. And if the accrual method is used for expenses, it must also be used for income.

The accrual method is required if inventories are an income-producing factor. Reg. §1.446-1(c)(2)(i). If this were not mandatory, a cash-basis taxpayer could very easily reduce reported net income by increasing stock of inventory and could increase reported net income by depleting normal inventory. The effect of this required adjustment is to change only the computation of the tax deduction for the cost of inventory sold from a strict cash basis to an accrual basis of accounting.

The fact that inventories are essential does not necessarily mean that an accrual method of accounting is needed on an overall basis, especially if the business is one in which inventories are comparatively small, with little change from year to year, and little of the business (purchase or sales) is done on a credit basis. In such cases, a taxpayer may keep books and prepare returns almost entirely on a cash basis, making adjustments only for the variations in opening and closing inventories.

¶13,275   **TANGIBLE PROPERTY REGULATIONS**

The regulations apply to costs incurred throughout the entire life cycle of the taxpayer's tangible property, from the time the taxpayer (1) first begins considering whether (and which) property to acquire, (2) through maintaining and improving the property during its operational life, and (3) finally to the treatment of the property's remaining basis when the taxpayer disposes of the property. The final regulations seek to provide guidance for each of these three phases of expenditures.

Section 263(a) generally requires the capitalization of amounts paid to acquire, produce, or improve tangible property. Section 162 allows a deduction for all the ordinary and necessary expenses paid or incurred during the taxable year in carrying on any trade or business, including the costs of certain supplies, repairs, and maintenance.

The regulations provide criteria for determining the unit of property, which is the first step for determining whether expenditures to improve tangible property must be capitalized or can be currently expensed.

Change of Accounting Methods

¶13,301   **IRS PERMISSION OR CONSENT**

While there is no prohibition against changing the method of accounting, Code Secs. 446 and 481 require that permission be obtained from the IRS before adopting the new method for income tax purposes. The purpose of the prior consent provision is to promote consistency in accounting practices from year to year, thereby securing uniformity in the collection of revenue. Rev. Proc. 2015-13, 2015-5 IRB 419 as modified provides general procedures to obtain the consent of the IRS to change a method of accounting. The revenue procedure provides the procedures to obtain advance (non-automatic) consent of the IRS to change a method of accounting and provides the procedures to obtain the automatic consent of the IRS to change a method of accounting described in Rev. Proc. 2015–14, 2015–5 I.R.B. 450 as modified. The list of the accounting method changes for which automatic consent is available is frequently updated. For most voluntary accounting method changes, taxpayers use the automatic consent procedures. There are several advantages to making a voluntary accounting method change under the automatic consent procedures as opposed to the advance consent procedures. There is no user fee, notice of IRS approval of the change is not required, and Form 3115 (Application for Change in Accounting Method) can be submitted up to the extended filing date of the tax return for the year of change.

An advance consent accounting method change is a change that cannot be made under the automatic consent procedures. Permission to change the method of tax accounting will not be granted unless the taxpayer and the IRS agree to the terms and conditions under which the change will be effected. Where two methods clearly reflect income, the IRS has considerable discretion in prescribing the conditions under which it will consent to a change from one to the other.

Change in Overall Plan or Material Items

A change of accounting method includes a change in the overall plan of accounting as well as a change in the treatment of any material item used in the plan. In most instances, a method of accounting is not established for an item unless there is a pattern of consistent treatment. Major changes in accounting method include:

1. Change to or from the cash-basis method
2. Change in the method of valuing inventory
3. Change from the accrual method to a long-term contract method or vice versa
4. Change involving the adoption, use, or discontinuance of any other specialized method of computing income, such as the crop method by farmers
5. Certain changes in computing depreciation or amortization
6. Change for which the Code or Regulations specifically require that the consent of the IRS be obtained (Reg. §1.446-1(e)).

A material item is any item that involves the timing of inclusion or deduction. According to the Tax Court, the term means a "material item of gross income or deductions," not "a material item of net income" or "a material difference in income" resulting from the computation under two different methods of accounting. *Connors, Inc.,* 71 TC 913, Dec. 35,900 (1979).

Correction of Mathematical Errors

A change in method does not include correction of mathematical and posting errors, or of errors in the computation of tax liability. For example, corrections of items that were deducted as interest or salary, but which are in fact payments of dividends, and of items that were deducted as business expenses, but which are personal expenses, are not changes in method. An adjustment to the useful life of a depreciable asset also is not an accounting method change. Although such adjustments may involve the question of the proper timing of a deduction, these items are traditionally corrected by adjustments in the current and future years.

Change in Underlying Facts

An accounting change does not include a change in treatment resulting from a change in underlying facts. On the other hand, a correction to require depreciation in lieu of a deduction for the cost of a class of depreciable assets which had been consistently treated as an expense in the year of purchase involves the question of the proper timing of an item and is to be treated as a change in method of accounting. Reg. §1.446-1(e).

IRS-Directed Changes

Although taxable income is to be computed according to a taxpayer's regular accounting method used in keeping the books, if that method does not clearly reflect income, then the IRS may prescribe a method which does.

The IRS's authority to require a taxpayer to adopt an overall or specific change in accounting method necessary to clearly reflect income does not justify an arbitrary requirement of change. If a taxpayer's accounting method clearly reflects income, the IRS may not determine income by another method which would also clearly reflect income. Presumably, this rule would also apply to the method of treating a particular item of income or expense, such as depreciation. A taxpayer may, of course, conform books or returns to a suggestion by an Internal Revenue agent, for convenience, to cooperate with the local office of the Internal Revenue Service and facilitate audits of returns, or to avoid the expense of an appeal or refund proceedings, but the taxpayer cannot be required to make the change.

The IRS can change an incorrect method, but the change must be to a correct method. If the IRS has directed a taxpayer to change the method of accounting and the taxpayer has complied, the IRS cannot later argue that the change was improper because the taxpayer had not obtained formal permission to make it. And where an unusual method of accruing expenses on construction contracts was proposed by the IRS and the taxpayer followed that method, the IRS was not allowed to object in later years that the method did not clearly reflect income.

The Fifth Circuit has held that, where a taxpayer changed the accounting method and not the basis of the tax returns, the IRS may not require the returns to be filed on the new basis if both methods clearly reflect income despite the Code requirement that the book method must be used in computing income. *J.C. Patchen,* 58-2 USTC ¶9733, 258 F.2d 544 (CA-5 1958).

Combination of Methods

A combination of acceptable methods of accounting will be permitted if such combination clearly reflects income and is consistently used. However, if the taxpayer uses a hybrid method that is not authorized by the Regulations, the IRS may make adjustments to conform to either the cash or accrual basis, whichever more closely resembles the taxpayer's method of keeping books. The burden is on the taxpayer to show errors in determining which method predominates for book purposes, or to show that the hybrid method is acceptable. The fact that a taxpayer has filed returns on a hybrid basis for a number of years, without objection, does not bar the IRS from requiring a change.

Cash to Accrual Method

Taxpayers desiring to change their overall method of accounting from the cash receipts and disbursements method of accounting to the accrual method may do so by filing a timely Form 3115 (Application for Change in Accounting Method) under the automatic consent procedures.

Net operating losses and tax credit carryforwards can reduce the amounts of any positive adjustment. For purposes of determining estimated payments, adjustments are recognized as occurring ratably throughout the year.

Denial of Change

Refusal to consent to a change in accounting method is ordinarily within the IRS's administrative discretion and cannot be reversed unless the taxpayer can prove the IRS abused its discretion. The IRS is not required to permit a change of accounting method for tax purposes just because the taxpayer is ordered to change the accounting method by another administrative agency. The Tax Court stated "that a taxpayer may be required to account one way for one government agency and another way for a different government agency may well be a hardship, and we have no doubt it is, but we are certain that the remedy does not lie with us as a judicial byproduct of a tax determination." *National Airlines, Inc.,* 9 TC 159, Dec. 15,940 (1947).

¶13,325   ADJUSTMENT—VOLUNTARY/REQUIRED CHANGE

When a taxpayer computes taxable income under a different accounting method than that used in the preceding year, adjustments must be made in order to prevent items from being duplicated or entirely omitted. The general intent is that no item may be omitted and no item may be duplicated as a result of a change. These adjustments apply not only when the taxpayer voluntarily changes the accounting method with the consent of the IRS, but also when a change in method is required by the IRS.

The term "adjustments" is defined as the net amount of all adjustments, taking only the net dollar balance into account. The net amount of the adjustments would be the result of the consolidation of adjustments (both plus and minus) for the various accounts, such as inventory, accounts receivable, and accounts payable at the beginning of the tax year. In the case of a change in the treatment of a single material item, the amount of the adjustment is determined by the net dollar balance of that particular item. Reg. §1.481-1(c).

EXAMPLE 13.19

Jones Co. is on the calendar year and uses the cash method of accounting. Jones Co. changed to the accrual method in 2017. Net income for 2017 under the accrual method was $60,000, computed as follows:

Sales	$200,000
Cost of goods sold	120,000
Gross profit	$80,000
Expenses	20,000
Net income	$60,000

In December 2016, there was $10,000 inventory on hand. Also, accounts receivable and accounts payable were $6,000 and $4,000, respectively.

The $60,000 net income must be adjusted for amounts which would be duplicated or be omitted because of the change in accounting methods. The net adjustment is $12,000; therefore, adjusted net income for 2017 would be $72,000. The adjustments are as follows:

Positive adjustment for the ending inventory balance because this amount was deducted when acquired	$10,000
Positive adjustment for the ending accounts receivable because this amount has never been included in income	6,000
Negative adjustment for the ending accounts payable because this amount has never been deducted	(4,000)
Net adjustment	$12,000

Rev. Proc. 2015-13 provides a single adjustment period for positive and negative adjustments. In general, the adjustment period for taxpayer-initiated changes that result in a positive adjustment is four years of which the tax year is the first year. However, if the adjustment is less than $50,000, the taxpayer may elect a one-year adjustment period. If the taxpayer ceases business operations (e.g., the firm liquidates) prior to the end of the four-year period, then any remaining adjustment is taken into consideration in the year of cessation. The adjustment period is one year for negative adjustments. Finally, a positive adjustment due to a change initiated by the IRS generally is recognized over the four-year period as noted above. However, the IRS can require that it be recognized over a shorter time period. Under Rev. Proc. 2002-18, 2002-1 CB 678, a negative adjustment due to an IRS-initiated change can be recognized in the year of the change.

EXAMPLE 13.20	In Example 13.18, Jones Co. has two options regarding the $12,000 adjustment. It can spread the $12,000 over four years, increasing net income for 2017 to $63,000 and increasing net income by $3,000 in 2018, 2019, and 2020. Alternatively, since the adjustment is less than $50,000, Jones could elect to use a one-year adjustment period and add the $12,000 to its $60,000 in 2017. If Jones has losses from other activities or a net operating loss carryover, then it might want to select this option.

EXAMPLE 13.21	Harry Co. changed its method of accounting in 2017. The net adjustment due to the change was $60,000. Since this amount exceeds the less-than-$50,000 threshold, Harry Co. is not eligible to elect the one-year adjustment period. Thus, Harry Co. must use the four-year adjustment period, and one-fourth of the $60,000 will be included in income in 2017, 2018, 2019, and 2020.

If a taxpayer has claimed insufficient depreciation in prior years, the taxpayer may change his or her depreciation method to claim allowable depreciation. This is considered to be a change in accounting method, and the omitted depreciation from previous years is considered to be an adjustment which the taxpayer may elect to use the one-year adjustment period. The taxpayer is required to own the asset on the first day of the tax year in which the change of accounting method applies. Rev. Proc. 2008-52.

¶13,355   TIME AND FORM OF APPLICATION

A taxpayer requesting to change a method of accounting under the automatic change procedures must file a Form 3115 (Application for Change in Accounting Method) in duplicate, as follows: (1) the original completed Form 3115 must be attached to the taxpayer's timely filed (including any extension) original tax return implementing the requested change for the year of change; and (2) a signed copy must be filed with the IRS in Covington, KY no earlier than the first day of the year of change and no later than the date the taxpayer files the original Form 3115. A taxpayer requesting to change a method of accounting under the non-automatic change procedures must file a Form 3115 with the appropriate user fee during the requested year of change, except as specifically provided in published guidance. If the taxpayer is under examination, before an Appeals office, or before a federal court with respect to any income tax issue, the taxpayer must provide additional signed copies to relevant officials.

The taxpayer should, to the extent applicable, furnish (1) all information requested on the form, disclosing in detail all classes of items which would be treated differently under the new method and showing all amounts which would be duplicated or omitted as a result of the proposed change, and (2) the computation of the adjustments to take into account such duplications and omissions.

It should also be stated in the application that the taxpayer proposes to take the adjustment into account over the appropriate period as required by the IRS in accordance with rules that have been discussed previously. Code Sec. 481; Rev. Proc. 2015-13. Permission will not be granted unless the taxpayer and the IRS agree to the terms, conditions, and adjustments under which the change will be effected.

There is no requirement that, once the IRS has approved the change, the taxpayer must use the new accounting method in filing returns thereafter. However, the IRS, in its letter granting the change of accounting method, states that if the taxpayer does not wish to make the change, the IRS should be advised within 30 days of the date of the letter. The taxpayer who decides not to change a method of accounting after the 30-day period is not precluded from keeping the present method in effect.

¶13,365   ACCOUNTING METHOD TAX PLANNING

Keeping income levels near average from year to year is a major tax saver. The desire to balance income stems from the graduated scale of tax rates. Two persons having the same total taxable income over a number of years may pay widely different taxes because of the progressive rate structure. A taxpayer should choose accounting methods and procedures that will stabilize taxable income over the years so as to produce minimum taxes. Of course, where there are greater ups and downs in taxable income at higher rates, the tax savings become greater as taxable income is leveled out. The cash-basis taxpayer may time the receipt of income either by accelerating it to boost an otherwise poor year or by postponing it so as not to overburden the current year. There is nothing in income tax law that requires a creditor to press or decline to press for payment of an obligation in a particular tax year.

Income from sales arises when title to the goods passes to the customer; that is, in the case of most regular sales, at the time of delivery to a common carrier. By withholding shipment until after the end of the accounting period, a taxpayer may keep the amount of sales for the year down and thereby reduce income. In other instances, the seller may defer income by shipping goods on approval or on consignment subject to acceptance or sale in the following year.

A taxpayer may also reduce taxable income by accelerating business expenses for replenishment of supplies that are not part of inventory, performance of repairs, advertising, or business trips. Remember, however, that only ordinary and necessary expenses are deductible.

For an individual who engages in investment activities in occasional "business" ventures, the cash basis of accounting may offer substantial tax advantages through its ability to control year-end expenditures and receipts. For a business activity, the accrual method of accounting may offer advantages by its tendency to level out income, thus avoiding high-bracket peak income periods. There is no rule that would preclude a taxpayer from using the cash basis for nonbusiness items and salary and the accrual method for business income.

The number of alternative accounting procedures and conventions is substantially greater than the number of alternative general methods of accounting. The Code authorizes a number of accounting procedures to determine the cost allocation available for depreciation. The cost-of-goods-sold determination can be made under any of several alternative inventory costing conventions. Each of these accounting conventions or procedures will yield a different taxable income for a given tax year.

TAX BLUNDER

Dean Chips operated a successful garage as a sole proprietorship on the cash basis. He obtained IRS permission to change to the accrual method, which resulted in a net increase in income under Code Sec. 481(a). Pursuant to Code Sec. 481(c), he spread the adjustment over 10 years (the adjustment period used at that time—it now is four years), starting with the year of change. Two years later, he incorporated his business in a "tax-free" Code Sec. 351 transaction. The IRS argued that the remaining 70 percent of the adjustment was accelerated upon incorporation, resulting in taxable income to Dean immediately. The Ninth Circuit agreed with the IRS that Code Sec. 481 requires continuity of the *taxpayer,* rather than the *business. D.R. Shore,* 80-2 USTC ¶9759, 631 F.2d 524 (CA-9 1980); Rev. Rul. 77-264, 1977-1 CB 238. Furthermore, the exception under Code Sec. 381 does not apply to corporate *organization,* only to corporate *reorganization.* Thus, even if Dean was the sole shareholder and even though the incorporation did not result in gain, it did accelerate income (so much for tax-free incorporations).

¶13,375   TIMELINESS

Making an accounting election usually requires some overt act on the part of a taxpayer. Proper timing is critical to making a valid election. Failure to make a timely election precludes a consideration of procedural compliance since the election will not be effective. To this extent, then, timing should be deemed of paramount importance.

The Code contains many elections that pertain to newly organized businesses. Failure to make the election on a timely basis may result in higher immediate taxes.

Inventories

¶13,401   USE OF INVENTORIES

If inventories are an income-producing factor, not only must inventories be kept, but the taxpayer must use the accrual method of accounting for purchases and sales. Reg. §§1.446-1(a)(4)(i) and 1.471-1. The result is that a major deduction, cost of goods sold, is deferred until the inventory is sold. Because cost of goods sold equals opening inventory, plus inventory purchased or produced, less ending inventory, an incentive exists to value ending inventories as low as possible. A low valuation results in an immediate tax benefit through a higher cost of goods sold deduction. Although the benefit is theoretically a mere deferral, the deferral is of indefinite duration. Also, as inventories grow with the expansion of the business, more and more profits are deferred. The value of ending inventory is a function of (1) what costs are included and (2) the cost flow assumptions made. The details are discussed below.

¶13,415   VALUATION OF INVENTORY

An inventory is an itemized list, with valuations, of goods held for sale or consumption in a manufacturing or merchandising business. The inventory should include all finished or partly finished goods, and only those raw materials and supplies that have been acquired for sale or that will physically become a part of merchandise intended for sale. Goods in transit to which the taxpayer has title should be included in inventory, and goods on hand in which title has passed to the buyer should not be included in inventory. Reg. §1.471-1.

There are two fundamental requirements for valuation of inventory: (1) it must conform as nearly as possible to the best accounting practice in the trade or business and (2) it must clearly reflect income. Code Sec. 471. In determining whether income is clearly reflected, great weight is given to consistency in inventory practice. Reg. §1.471-2. Nevertheless, a legitimate accounting system will be disallowed where it distorts income.

Inventory may be valued at cost or lower-of-cost-or-market. Reg. §1.471-2. However, if the LIFO method (discussed later) is used, then the taxpayer cannot use lower-of-cost-or-market. Also, lower-of-cost-or-market must be applied to each item in inventory; a taxpayer cannot value the entire inventory at cost and at market and then select the lower amount.

¶13,425   COST METHODS

The cost of merchandise on hand at the beginning of the period (beginning inventory) is its inventory price as of the last day of the previous year. The cost of merchandise purchased is the invoice price, less trade discounts, plus incidental costs incurred to acquire the goods (such as transportation and other handling costs). Reg. §1.471-3. Additionally, the following indirect costs must be capitalized unless the taxpayer's average annual gross receipts for the preceding three taxable years do not exceed $10 million: storage and warehousing; purchasing; handling, processing, assembly, and repacking; and administrative costs. Code Sec. 263A(b).

The cost of merchandise produced by the taxpayer includes the cost of direct materials, direct labor, and indirect costs. Reg. §1.471-3. Manufacturers must use absorption costing (full costing) to value inventories; they cannot use direct costing or prime costing. Indirect costs that must be capitalized include repairs, maintenance, utilities, rent, and indirect labor and materials. Indirect costs do not include marketing expenses, advertising and selling expenses, and research and experimentation costs. Reg. §1.471-11. Additionally, Code Sec. 263A expanded the definition of includible costs by requiring most entities (especially manufacturers) to use the uniform capitalization (UNICAP) rules. This expanded list requires the capitalization of more items than does financial accounting.

¶13,435   UNIFORM CAPITALIZATION RULES

UNICAP generally applies to real or personal property produced by the taxpayer and real or personal property acquired by the taxpayer for resale. Code Sec. 263A(b). Costs to be capitalized include direct costs and an expanded list of indirect costs. Reg. §1.263A-1(b)(2). Under UNICAP, indirect costs include:

1. Factory repairs and maintenance; utilities; rent; depreciation, amortization, and depletion; small tools; and insurance;
2. Indirect labor and production supervisory labor; administrative costs; indirect materials and supplies; rework, scrap, and spoilage; storage and warehousing costs; purchasing costs; handling, processing, assembly, and repacking costs; and quality control and inspection costs;
3. Taxes (other than income taxes);
4. Deductible contributions to pension, profit-sharing, stock bonus, or annuity plans; and
5. Interest, but only for real property, long-lived property, or property requiring more than two years to produce (one year for property costing more than $1 million).

Costs not required to be capitalized include nonmanufacturing costs such as marketing, selling, advertising and distribution expenses, and research and experimentation costs.

Cost Allocation Procedures

After identifying all costs that are required to be capitalized (known as total additional Code Sec. 263A costs), the next step in costing inventory is to allocate these costs. The Regulations provide allocation methods for direct labor, direct materials, and indirect costs. The allocation method should result in the capitalization of all costs that directly benefit or are incurred because of production or resale activities. Reg. §1.263A-1(b)(3).

All direct labor costs must be capitalized. The costs should be associated with specific production activities and products, and allocated to them accordingly (using specific identification or tracing). All direct material costs also should be capitalized. These costs should be allocated to products using the taxpayer's method of accounting for inventories that contain the direct materials (e.g., FIFO, LIFO, specific identification). The above mentioned allocation methods are not mandatory; the taxpayer may use any other method which reasonably allocates such costs.

Indirect costs are allocated to activities and products using one of three methods: specific identification (in which the costs are specifically identified with activities or products that directly benefit from the costs), standard costing (in which the costs are allocated to products based upon established standards), or burden rates (in which the costs are allocated based on direct labor hours, direct labor costs, and similar expenses).

Simplified Retail Method

Taxpayers who acquire property for resale and are required to capitalize costs under Code Sec. 263A may elect to use the simplified retail method to allocate costs. Under this method, costs for off-site storage and warehousing; purchasing; and handling, processing, assembly, and repacking are fully capitalized. Determining the amount of mixed service costs (general and administrative costs) to be allocated requires two steps. First determine the amount of mixed service costs that are additional Code Sec. 263A costs, then allocate this amount to ending inventory.

The amount of mixed service costs included under Code Sec. 263A is determined by multiplying such costs by the ratio of

1. Total labor costs included in off-site, storage, purchasing, and handling cost, to
2. Total labor costs incurred in the taxpayer's business, excluding the labor included in the mixed service costs.

Once this amount is determined, then it is allocated to ending inventory by multiplying the amount in ending inventory that was purchased during the year by the ratio of

1. Total additional Code Sec. 263A costs, to
2. Taxpayer's total purchases during the year.

EXAMPLE 13.22

Kimby Co. uses the first-in, first-out (FIFO) method of accounting for its inventory. During the year it incurred $200,000 of storage costs, $300,000 of purchasing costs, $100,000 in handling and processing costs. The labor costs included in these amounts were $180,000. The company also incurred $250,000 of mixed service costs. Kimby Co.'s total labor costs, excluding amounts included in mixed service costs, were $2,000,000. Kimby's beginning inventory (excluding additional Code Sec. 263A costs) was $1,000,000. Total purchases during the year were $7,000,000 and ending inventory was $1,500,000 (excluding additional Code Sec. 263A costs). Since Kimby Co. uses the FIFO method, the full $1,500,000 of ending inventory is considered purchased during the year.

Kimby Co.'s ending inventory is $1,633,350, consisting of the original cost of $1,500,000, increased by capitalized additional Code Sec. 263A resale costs of $133,350. This is determined as follows. First, determine the amount of mixed service costs that are considered to be additional Code Sec. 263A costs using the labor ratios:

Labor ratio	=	$180,000/$2,000,000 = 9%
Mixed service costs considered additional Code 263A costs	=	9% × $250,000 = $22,500.

Next, determine total additional Code Sec. 263A and allocate this amount to ending inventory using the additional Code Sec. 263A costs to purchases ratio.

Costs to purchase ratio	=	$622,500/$7,000,000 = 8.89%
Additional Code Sec. 263A costs allocated to ending inventory	=	8.89% × $1,500,000 = $133,350.

Simplified Production Method

Taxpayers may elect to use the simplified production method to allocate capitalized costs for property produced. This method can only be used for property that is the taxpayer's stock in trade or includible in inventory, or for property held by the taxpayer primarily for sale to customers in the ordinary course of business. The method cannot be used for property acquired for resale and for property produced by the taxpayer for use in its business. Reg. §1.263A-1(b)(5). Under this method, additional Code Sec. 263A costs are allocated based on an absorption ratio and the allocation requires two steps. First, compute the absorption ratio. This is the ratio of

1. total additional Code Sec. 263A costs incurred during the year, to
2. total Code Sec. 471 costs incurred during the year.

(Code Sec. 471 costs are those costs that otherwise would be capitalized under absorption costing.) Once this ratio is determined, then the amount of additional Code Sec. 263A costs required to be capitalized is determined by multiplying the absorption ratio times the amount of Code Sec. 471 costs incurred during the year which, under the taxpayer's method of accounting for inventory (e.g., FIFO or LIFO), are included in the taxpayer's ending inventory.

If the taxpayer uses FIFO, then the absorption ratio is applied to the Code Sec. 471 costs included in ending inventory. However, if the taxpayer uses LIFO, then the absorption ratio is applied to the Code Sec. 471 costs included in this year's increase in inventory (the incremental layer).

EXAMPLE 13.23

Nifo Co. produces widgets. It began operations this year. It uses the FIFO method to account for its inventories. During the year it incurred $15,000,000 of Code Sec. 471 costs and $2,000,000 of additional Code Sec. 263A costs. Ending inventory consisted of $1,000,000 of Code Sec. 471 costs.

Nifo Co.'s ending inventory is $1,133,333, consisting of $1,000,000 of Code Sec. 471 costs, increased by capitalized additional Code Sec 263A costs of $133,333. This is determined as follows:

Absorption ratio	=	$2,000,000/$15,000,000 = 13.33%
Additional Code Sec. 263A costs allocated to ending inventory	=	13.33% × $1,000,000 = $133,333.

¶13,445   LOWER-OF-COST-OR-MARKET (LCM) METHOD

Unless the taxpayer is using LIFO, the ending inventory may be written down to a lower market value (e.g., replacement cost). Reg. §1.472-4. In addition, damaged or obsolete goods may be written down to realizable prices less costs of disposition. Reg. §1.471-2(c). The determination of lower cost or market must be applied to each *item* of inventory. Reg. §1.471-4(c).

EXAMPLE 13.24

A lumber dealer has three grades of lumber at the end of the tax year. They are valued as follows:

Grade	Cost	Market	LCM
1	$3,000	$5,000	$3,000
2	2,000	1,500	1,500
3	5,000	4,000	4,000
	$10,000	$10,500	$8,500

The ending inventory is $8,500, written *down* from $10,000, even though the inventory as a whole has *increased* in value.

¶13,453   VALUATION OF INVENTORY ITEMS

Taxpayers may use one of four cost flow assumptions to value their inventories: specific identification; first-in, first-out (FIFO); last-in, first-out (LIFO); or weighted average. The accounting method selected does not have to agree with the actual physical flow of goods. Specific identification usually is impractical because each item in inventory must be tracked very carefully. Generally, it is used for large items, such as appliances, which are more easily tracked. It is more convenient in many instances to use one of the other cost flow assumptions.

The FIFO method assumes that goods on hand in beginning inventory and the first goods purchased are the first goods sold to customers. Thus, ending inventory is valued at the price of most recent purchases. Cost of goods sold is based upon the cost of beginning inventory and the prices of goods purchased earlier in the year. Taxpayers using FIFO also may use the lower-of-cost-or-market method.

The LIFO method assumes that the goods most recently purchased are the first goods sold to customers. Thus, ending inventory is valued at beginning inventory amounts and at the price of goods acquired earlier in the year. Cost of goods sold is based upon the prices of the most recent purchases.

The LIFO method can be adopted in the taxpayer's first year of business or in the initial year that inventories are maintained by using it on that year's tax return. Code Sec. 472. The taxpayer can change to the LIFO method by attaching Form 970 (Application to Use LIFO Inventory Method) with the tax year for the year of change. If LIFO is used for tax purposes then it also must be used for financial reporting purposes. LIFO produces a smaller taxable income when prices are rising, so there is an incentive (tax savings) to select this method. However, because of the conformity requirements for tax and financial reporting purposes, some firms do not select LIFO because it also produces a smaller net income on the financial statements. However, those taxpayers using LIFO are permitted to use other methods in the footnotes, appendices or supplements to the financial statements. Reg. §1.472-2(e)(3). Also, taxpayers using LIFO may not use the lower-of-cost-or-market method.

The weighted average method values ending inventory (and cost of goods sold) based on the weighted average price of all goods available for sale during the year. The value of ending inventory generally is between those amounts obtained under the FIFO and LIFO methods.

EXAMPLE 13.25

James Co. sells desks. Inventory on January 1 consisted of 300 desks valued at $400 per desk ($120,000). It purchased 700 desks on April 3 at $425 per desk ($297,500) and 900 desks on September 3 at $500 per desk ($450,000). During the year it sold 1,500 desks at a total sales price of $1,050,000. Ending inventory, cost of goods sold and gross profit using FIFO, LIFO and weighted average are as follows:

	FIFO	LIFO	Weighted Average
Sales	$1,050,000	$1,050,000	$1,050,000
Beginning inventory	$120,000	$120,000	$120,000
Purchases	747,500	747,500	747,500
Cost of goods available for sale	$867,500	$867,500	$867,500
Ending inventory			
FIFO (400 $500)	200,000		
LIFO (300 $400; 100 $425)		162,500	
Weighted average			
($867,500/1,900 = $457/unit)			
(400 $457)			182,800
Cost of goods sold	$667,500	$705,000	$684,700
Gross profit	$382,500	$345,000	$365,300

If a taxpayer changes his or her inventory method, an adjustment is needed to account for the differences at date of conversion. The change could be from LIFO to FIFO, FIFO to LIFO, lower-of-cost-or-market to LIFO, etc. In such a situation, the adjustment is spread over four years (unless the adjustment is less than $50,000, in which case the taxpayer may elect to use the one-year adjustment period).

KEYSTONE
PROBLEM

Financial management has traditionally been opposed to adopting LIFO because it would result in reporting lower earnings in the financial statements to shareholders.

1.   Are they correct in the short run? Why?
2.   Are they correct in the long run? Why?

¶13,473   DOLLAR-VALUE LIFO METHOD

Instead of determining quantity increases of each item in the inventory and then pricing each item, as is required under regular LIFO, the dollar-value LIFO method may be used. The increase in LIFO value is determined by comparing the total dollar value of the beginning and ending inventories at base-year (first LIFO year) prices and then converting any dollar-value increase to current prices by means of an index. Taxpayers are allowed, under the dollar-value LIFO method, to determine base-year dollars through the use of government indexes. Code Sec. 472(f). The Regulations permit the use of several price index methods. Reg. §1.472-8. The "double extension method," the most frequently used, works as follows:

1.   Determine opening inventory at base-year prices (the prices in effect when LIFO was adopted).
2.   Determine ending inventory at base-year prices.
3.   Compute the difference. The result is either an increase (increment) or a decrease (decrement).
4.   Determine a price index to value the increment, if any. The index equals ending inventory at current prices/ending inventory at base-year prices.
5.   Adjust the inventory "layers" for any increment or decrement. Every increment represents a new layer. Any decrement uses up the most recently added layer or layers first.

The following example is adapted from Reg. §1.472-8(e)(2)(v), Examples (1) and (2).

EXAMPLE 13.26

Skylark Inc. adopts LIFO in Year 1. Opening inventory was $14,000, which became the base period price. Ending inventory was $24,250 at actual prices, $20,000 at base-year prices. Thus, keeping prices constant, the increment was $6,000. The index was:

$$\frac{\$24,250}{\$20,000} = 1.2125$$

The increment is therefore $6,000 × 1.2125, or $7,275, and the ending inventory is $21,275, as opposed to $24,250 under FIFO, resulting in an increased cost of goods sold of $2,975. To summarize:

	1/1/Year 1	Index	12/31/Year 1
Opening inventory	$14,000	1.0	$14,000
Increment	6,000	1.2125	7,275
Ending LIFO inventory	$20,000		$21,275

If, at the end of Year 2, ending inventory was $18,000 at base period prices and $27,000 at current prices, there was a decrement with the following result:

	1/1/Year 1	Index	12/31/Year 2
1/1/Year 1 inventory	$14,000	1.0	$14,000
Remaining Year 1 increase	4,000	1.2125	4,850
LIFO inventory	$18,000		$18,850

At the end of Year 3, ending inventory was $25,000 at base period prices and $30,000 at current prices (30/25 = 1.2). The Year 3 year-end inventory consists of three "layers" as follows:

	1/1/Year 1	Index	12/31/Year 3
1/1/Year 1 inventory	$14,000	1.0	$14,000
Year 1 increase	4,000	1.2125	4,850
Year 3 increase	7,000	1.2	8,400
LIFO inventory	$25,000		$27,250

The computations above assume that only one "pool" was used. If substantially heterogeneous products exist, more than one pool must be used. Since each pool generates its own index and each pool may have numerous layers, the feasibility of dollar-value LIFO techniques depends on the availability of computers.

¶13,481   SIMPLIFIED DOLLAR-VALUE LIFO METHOD

Taxpayers may elect to use the simplified dollar-value LIFO method, but it then must be used to value all LIFO inventories. The simplified dollar-value LIFO method is designed to enable small businesses to use the LIFO method but avoid the extra costs and burden of maintaining records needed for the other LIFO methods. A taxpayer may elect the method for any year in which its average annual gross receipts for the preceding three years do not exceed $5 million. Code Sec. 474(c).

Using the method is relatively easy and straightforward. The taxpayer groups its inventory into pools for each major category in the applicable government price index provided by the Bureau of Labor Statistics (11 categories for retailers and 15 categories for all other taxpayers). Each pool then is separately adjusted using the appropriate government index. Retailers use the Consumer Price Index, and all other taxpayers use the Producer Price Index.

The taxpayer does not compute base period prices. Instead, the taxpayer uses year-end inventory values and determines an assumed base period value by applying the government price index. If the resulting base period value exceeds the opening inventory value at base period prices, then the increment is valued using the same index.

EXAMPLE 13.27	Susan Co. adopted the simplified dollar-value LIFO method. Inventory at actual prices in Year 1 and Year 2 was $200,000 and $300,000, respectively. The Consumer Price Index for Years 1 and 2 was 115 percent and 125 percent, respectively. Susan Co.'s ending inventory for Year 2 would be valued at $282,609, consisting of $200,000 from Year 1 plus the Year 2 increment of $82,609. The Year 2 increment is determined as follows:

Year 2 ending inventory at assumed base-year prices	=	$300,000 × 1.15/1.25 = $276,000
The increment at Year 1 base price	=	$276,000 – $200,000 = $76,000
The increment at Year 2 base price	=	$76,000 × 1.25/1.15 = $82,609

¶13,485   ESTIMATES OF INVENTORY SHRINKAGE

Code Sec. 471 permits a business to determine its year-end closing inventory by using estimates for shrinkage (e.g., loss due to theft). A year-end physical count is not necessary if the business: (1) normally takes a physical count of its inventories at each business location on a regular and consistent basis and (2) makes proper adjustments to its inventories and to its estimating methods to the extent its estimates differ from actual shrinkage.

Using this method results in a change in accounting method, but IRS permission is not required to make the change. Also, any adjustments to income due to this change are taken into account over a four-year period.

EXAMPLE 13.28	SQ Co., a calendar-year taxpayer, generally takes a physical count of inventory every three months. In 2017, it claimed a $30,000 deduction for inventory shrinkage based on an estimate of shrinkage on December 31, 2017. Since it takes a physical count on a regular basis, it is permitted to use an estimate for inventory shrinkage.

PLANNING POINTER	A widely-held view is that a major potential cost in changing from the "lower-of-cost-or-market" method of valuing inventories to LIFO is that opening inventory must be written back up to cost and the write-up taken into income. This adverse tax aspect may be avoided or may be nonexistent in the following situations: No inventory on hand at the end of the year prior to the year of change was written down from cost. The portion of the inventory written down may be (any of the following): 1. Sold before year-end at a discount or disposed of as giveaways, prizes, or bonuses to customers 2. Given to employees as deductible compensation 3. Contributed to charity, resulting in nonrecognition of income as well as a deduction (prior to year-end) 4. Abandoned (i.e., "dumped") Thus, with proper tax planning, no income will have to be recognized.

TAX BLUNDER

Hind Co. uses the FIFO inventory method because this method reflects the true physical flow of inventory. Ending inventory under FIFO was $400,000 in 2017. Had Hind Co. used LIFO, ending inventory would have been $240,0000. Hind Co. has been in the 34% tax bracket and believes it will continue to be in the 34% tax bracket.

Actual physical flow of inventory is irrelevant for costing purposes. The cost flow used (assumed) is artificial and does not need to coincide with the actual physical flow. Had Hind Co. used LIFO, it would have increased cost of goods sold by $160,000, and taxable income would have decreased by $160,000, producing a tax savings of $54,400 (34% × $160,000). Again, given the time value of money, this would be preferable.

Long-Term Contracts

¶13,501   ALTERNATIVE ACCOUNTING METHODS

The term long-term contract means any contract for the manufacture, building, installation, or construction of property if such property is not completed within the taxable year into which the contract is entered. A contract for the manufacture of property will not be treated as a long-term contract unless it involves the manufacture of any unique item which is not normally included in finished goods inventory or requires more than 12 calendar months to complete. Code Sec. 460(f). A taxpayer generally has two alternatives to account for long-term contracts: the percentage-of-completion method (or modified percentage-of-completion method in some cases) and the completed-contract method (in limited circumstances). The accounting method selected must be used for all long-term contracts in the same trade or business. Reg. §1.451-3(a).

Under the percentage-of-completion method taxpayers report income under the contract annually based on estimated progress. The percentage of completion is determined by comparing allocated costs to the contract and direct costs incurred by the close of the year to the estimated total contract costs. Code Sec. 460(b). The total contract price is multiplied by the percentage to determine the amount of income reported in that year.

Under the percentage-of-completion method the taxpayer must use a look-back method in the year the contract is completed. This method requires the taxpayer to compare the actual completion level to the claimed level (to reflect the actual profit for each year of the contract) and to redetermine taxable income and tax liability accordingly. Interest is charged on any underpayment and is received for any overpayment. However, long-term contracts completed within two years of contract commencement are exempt from the look-back method if the gross contract price does not exceed the lesser of $1,000,000 or 1 percent of the taxpayer's average gross receipts for the last three years preceding the year in which the contract was entered. Code Sec. 460(b).

Code Sec. 460 permits taxpayers to elect not to apply the look-back method for long-term contracts completed during the year and in all subsequent years if the actual contract taxable income is within 10 percent of estimated taxable income under the percentage-of-completion method (using estimated contract price and costs).

EXAMPLE 13.29   Jones Co. enters into a three-year construction contract in 2017. Jones Co. estimated (reported) net income using the percentage-of-completion method was $100,000, $200,000, and $300,000 for 2017, 2018, and 2019 respectively. In 2019, when the contract is completed, Jones Co. determines that actual net income for each year was $108,000, $210,000, and $282,000, respectively, for the three years. Ten percent of $108,000 is $10,800, and 10% of $318,000 is $31,800. Since the $100,000 claimed in 2017 and the $300,000 cumulative income in 2018 ($200,000 in 2018 and $100,000 in 2017) are within the 10 percent range, Jones can elect not to apply the look-back method.

The modified percentage-of-completion method is available for contracts that are less than 10 percent complete at the end of the year. If this condition is met, then taxpayers may elect to defer reporting any income from the contract until at least 10 percent of the work is completed. Code Sec. 460(b)(5). In the year that 10 percent is completed, the taxpayer will report income on all the work completed in that year using the "regular" percentage-of-completion method described above. The rationale for this election is that it often is difficult to estimate the total costs of a long-term project at its beginning; the modified method gives the taxpayer some time and experience to provide a "better" estimate.

Under the completed-contract method taxpayers report no income until final completion of the contract, regardless of when the funds are collected. All costs are accumulated and recognized at completion. The use of this method provides substantial opportunity to defer income, and as such is severely restricted. Only small construction contractors and home construction contractors can use this method. Small contractors are those whose average gross receipts for the three preceding tax years do not exceed $10,000,000. Contracts of small construction must be expected to be completed within two years of the commencement date. Code Sec. 460(e).

Final completion of the contract is based on an analysis of all the facts and circumstances. However, a taxpayer may not delay completion of a contract for the principal purpose of deferring federal income taxes. Reg. §1.460-1(c)(3). Additionally, if the buyer reasonably disputes the work, then income or deduction with respect to said dispute is recognized in the year the dispute is resolved. If the amount reasonably in dispute is extensive and so affects the contract price that it is not possible to determine whether a gain or loss will result from the contract, then no gain or loss is recognized until the dispute is settled. Reg. §1.460-4(d)(4).

¶13,515   COMPARISON OF THE METHODS

The following, simplified example illustrates the difference between the percentage-of-completion and completed-contract methods:

EXAMPLE 13.30

In 2017, Building Construction Co. entered into a contract to build a small warehouse for $2,500,000. Total estimated costs to complete are $2,000,000, and the project is expected to be completed in 2018. Actual costs incurred in 2017 and 2018 were $800,000 and $900,000, respectively. Results for 2017 and 2018 are shown below.

Percentage-of-Completion Method	2017	2018
Gross Revenue	$1,000,000[a]	$1,500,000[b]
Actual Costs	(800,000)	(900,000)
Gross Profit Reported	$200,000	$600,000

    a. ($800,000/$2,000,000) × $2,500,000

    b. $2,500,000 – $1,000,000

Completed-Contract Method	2017	2018
Gross Revenue	$0	$2,500,000
Actual Costs	0	(1,700,000)
Gross Profit Reported	$0	$800,000

¶13,535   CAPITALIZATION OF EXPENSES

All costs associated with the contract are capitalized and are deducted as profits are recognized. This principle applies to direct costs, such as material and direct labor costs, as well as to overhead, such as repairs and maintenance, utilities, rent, cost recovery, shipping costs, general and administrative expenses, scrap and spoilage costs, etc. Construction period interest must always be capitalized. The following expenses must be capitalized; they may not be expensed if the percentage-of-completion method is used:

1. Cost recovery of assets employed for work on specific contracts
2. Pension costs representing current service costs
3. General and administrative expenses relating to specific contracts
4. Research and development expenses with respect to specific contracts
5. Scrap and spoilage costs

In any event, bidding expenses, indirect research and development expenses, and marketing, advertising, and selling expenses may be deducted currently.

¶13,540   SPECIAL RULES

The Regulations provide guidance in those situations where a long-term contract is either being disputed in amount or is delayed beyond its scheduled date of completion.

Disputed Amounts

Generally, the disputed amount, if any, simply reduces gain or increases a loss in the year of completion. However, if the disputed amount is "substantial" then no gain or loss is recognized until the controversy is settled. Reg. §1.460-4(d)(4).

Unreasonable Delays

The completion of a contract may not be delayed (e.g., by deferring the formal acceptance of the project) for the principal purpose of tax postponement. Reg. §1.460-4(d)(4). Because of the time value of money, a deferral of the income from the last month of one year until the first month of the next year may be quite valuable, even with no change in the marginal tax rate.

Installment Sales

¶13,601 ## USE OF INSTALLMENT METHOD

An installment sale is a disposition of property where at least one payment is received after the close of the taxable year in which the disposition occurs. Code Sec. 453(b). Thus, there is no requirement for numerous payments over several years; one payment in a subsequent year would qualify as an installment sale. The installment method may be used by cash-basis taxpayers as a means to defer gain recognition or to spread gain recognition over several tax periods. The method may not be used if the property is disposed of at a loss. Additionally, the installment method only affects when the gain is recognized, it does not change the character of the gain (capital or ordinary). How this gain is taxed is determined by the applicable laws in the year the installment payment is received, not in the year of sale. The seller reports gains under the installment method on Form 6252 (Installment Sale Income).

Any depreciation recapture coming under Sections 1245 and 1250 must be taken into income in the year of sale. If a portion of the capital gain from an installment sale is 25 percent gain and a portion is 15 percent or 0 percent gain, the taxpayer is required to take the 25 percent gain into account before the 15 percent or 0 percent gain, as payments are received.

The installment method is not available to all taxpayers. It cannot be used: by dealers in real and personal property; for any sale of personal property under a revolving credit plan; for sales of depreciable property to a controlled entity (e.g., to a corporation in which the taxpayer owns directly and indirectly more than 50 percent of the value of the outstanding stock), unless the taxpayer can establish that tax avoidance was not a principal purpose of the disposition; and for sales of stock or securities which are traded on an established securities market (or to the extent provided in the regulations for property other than stock or securities regularly traded on an established market). Code Sec. 453.

Although nondealers may use the installment method, Code Sec. 453A imposes a special interest charge if the sale price of the real or personal property (other than personal-use and farm property) exceeds $150,000. This interest charge is on the tax liability deferred on the property sold. However, the interest charge only applies if the installment obligation is outstanding at year-end and if the face amount of all installment obligations which arose during the year and are outstanding at year end exceeds $5 million.

The taxpayer must use the installment method for tax purposes if the taxpayer disposes of property under an installment contract and the disposition qualifies for the installment method. However, the taxpayer may make an irrevocable election not to use the installment method. Code Sec. 453(d). In such a case, the gain would be recognized in the year of disposition. Finally, all depreciation recapture occurs in the year of sale, regardless of the fact that the taxpayer uses the installment method.

EXAMPLE 13.31

James Hoffman sold a truck in 2017 for $36,000. The truck's adjusted basis was $15,000 at the time of sale, and $9,000 had been claimed in depreciation. James collected $12,000 in 2017 and will receive $12,000 in 2018 and 2019. James uses the installment method for this sale.

Amount realized	$36,000
Adjusted basis	15,000
Realized gain	21,000
Code Sec. 1245 gain	$9,000
Gross profit percentage = 33.33% ($12,000/$36,000)	

In 2017, James will recognize a $9,000 Code Sec. 1245 gain and a $4,000 Code Sec. 1231 gain ($12,000 x 33.33%). James also will recognize a $4,000 Code Sec. 1231 gain ($12,000 x 33.33%) in 2018 and in 2019.

¶13,655   COMPUTATION OF GAIN

The installment method recognizes income as payments are received. There are several steps to follow.

Step 1.	Determine the gross profit from the sale. Gross profit equals the selling price minus the property's adjusted basis, selling expenses, and depreciation recapture (if any).
Step 2.	Determine the contract price. The contract price generally equals the amount the seller will receive. If there are no liabilities on the property, then contract price equals selling price. If there are liabilities on the property which the buyer assumes, then the contract price equals all payments to be received by the seller (i.e., the selling price reduced by the mortgage assumption). If the liabilities exceed the property's adjusted basis (increased by selling expenses for this comparison only), then such excess increases the contract price (it equals all payments to be received by the seller plus the excess). The contract price can never be less than the gross profit.
Step 3.	Compute the gross profit percentage (which can never be greater than 100 percent). Gross profit percentage = Gross profit/Contract price.
Step 4.	Determine the amount of gain to be recognized in the year of sale. Recognized gain = Payments received × Gross profit percentage.

EXAMPLE 13.32

Ann Rogers, 45 years old, sold property for $125,000. Her selling expenses were $5,000 and her basis was $40,000. She received $25,000 down and will receive $20,000 in each of the following five years. Ann's gross profit is $80,000 ($125,000 − ($5,000 + $40,000)). The contract price is $125,000, and the gross profit percentage is 64 percent ($80,000/$125,000). She will recognize a gain of $16,000 in the year of sale (64% × $25,000) and $12,800 in each of the following five years (64% × $20,000). Thus, total gain recognized over the six years is $80,000 ($16,000 + (5 × $12,800)). Ann also will recognize income for the interest she receives over this period.

EXAMPLE 13.33

Assume the same facts as in Example 13.31 except that the property was depreciable property subject to $15,000 of depreciation recapture under Code Sec. 1245. Ann's gross profit is $65,000 ($125,000 − ($5,000 + $40,000 + $15,000)). The contract price is still $125,000. The gross profit percentage is 52 percent ($65,000/$125,000). She will recognize a $13,000 gain in the year of sale (52% × $25,000) and $15,000 ordinary income from the depreciation recapture. In each of the following five years she will recognize a gain of $10,400 (52% × $20,000). Total gain recognized over the six years also is $80,000 ($13,000 + $15,000 + (5 × $10,400)). Ann also will recognize income for the interest she receives over this period.

EXAMPLE 13.34

Assume the same facts as in Example 13.31 except that there is a $5,000 mortgage on the property which the buyer assumes. Additionally, Ann will receive $20,000 in the year of sale and $20,000 in each of the following five years. In this case, Ann's gross profit is $80,000 ($125,000 − ($5,000 + $40,000)). The contract price is $120,000 ($125,000 − $5,000); Ann will receive $120,000 in cash payments from the buyer. The gross profit percentage is 66.67 percent ($80,000 ÷ $120,000). She will recognize a gain of $13,333 ($20,000 × 66.67%) in the year of sale and in each of the following five years. Total gain recognized over the six years is $80,000 ($13,333 × 6), allowing for a $2 roundoff. Ann also will recognize income for the interest she received over this period.

EXAMPLE 13.35

Assume the same facts as in Example 13.31 except the property is subject to a $50,000 mortgage which the buyer assumes. Additionally, Ann will receive $15,000 in the year of sale and $12,000 in each of the following five years. In this case the liability exceeds the adjusted basis by $5,000 ($50,000 − ($40,000 + $5,000 selling expenses)). Whenever the liability exceeds the adjusted basis (increased by selling expenses), the gross profit percentage is 100 percent. Also, the excess is treated as a payment in the year of sale. Thus, Ann recognizes a gain of $20,000 (100% × ($15,000 + $5,000)) in the year of sale and $12,000 (100% × $12,000) in each of the following five years. Total gain recognized over the six years is $80,000 ($20,000 + (5 × $12,000)). Ann also will recognize income for the interest she received over this period.

EXAMPLE 13.36

Sal Weintraub sold $20 million of nondealer real estate during the year under the installment method. At year-end $15 million is outstanding. Deferred gross profit on the outstanding obligations is $4 million. The maximum tax rate in effect during the year was 35 percent. Code Sec. 453A applies in this situation, and Sal must pay the special interest charge. Assume that the federal short-term interest rate in December was 8 percent. The interest due is $102,672, computed as follows:

1. Determine the portion of installment obligations outstanding at year-end in excess of $5 million and divide this by the total amount of installment obligations outstanding at year-end.

    ($15,000,000 – $5,000,000) ÷ $15,000,000 = 66.67%

2. Determine the tax liability deferred on all installment obligations outstanding at year-end by multiplying the deferred gross profit on such obligations by the maximum tax rate in effect for the tax year.

    ($4,000,000 × 35%) = $1,400,000

3. Determine the applicable interest rate, which is equal to the federal short-term interest rate for the last month of the tax year, increased by 3 percentage points.

    (8% + 3%) = 11%

4. Determine the interest due (which is considered personal interest expense).

    (66.67% × $1,400,000 × 11%) = $102,672

¶13,675   ELECTING OUT OF INSTALLMENT REPORTING

As noted earlier, a taxpayer may elect not to use the installment method. This election must be made by the due date (including extensions) for filing the tax return for the year of the installment sale. Reg. §15A.453-1(d)(3). However, there are potential drawbacks to such an election. For example, if a capital asset or a Section 1231 asset is sold at a gain on the installment plan and the seller elects not to use installment reporting, there are at least two obvious drawbacks:

1. The gain is accelerated and the tax is due in the year of sale before the proceeds are received.
2. If the value of the note is less than its face value, a cash-basis taxpayer will limit the capital gain and may convert the discount into ordinary income on collection if the collection of a note does not qualify as a "sale or exchange." (This problem does not affect accrual-method sellers since they accrue the face value.) Under Code Sec. 1271(a)(1) and (b)(1), retiring a debt instrument is a sale or exchange, unless issued by a natural person.

EXAMPLE 13.37

Rita Brown sells a painting held for five years as an investment. The painting was purchased for $5,000 and sold to Joe Smith for $15,000, $6,000 down and a $9,000 face value note worth $7,000 due in three years together with 10 percent interest. If she opts for installment reporting, her gross profit percentage is 66 2/3:

$$\frac{(\$15,000 - \$5,000)}{\$15,000}$$

resulting in a capital gain of $4,000 in the year of sale and $6,000 upon collection of the note (plus interest).

If Rita elects *not* to use installment reporting, the result is as follows:

Year of Sale:

Amount realized	
Cash	$6,000
Fair market value of note	7,000
	$13,000
Less adjusted basis	5,000
Long-term capital gain	$8,000
Year of Collection:	
Collection of principal	$9,000
Less basis in note	7,000
Ordinary income	$2,000

Which action is preferable depends on Rita's tax bracket (and the rate applicable to her capital gain).

The Regulations are flexible enough to permit installment reporting even if the selling price and, therefore, gross profit percentage are unknown at the initial sale. Reg. §15A.453-1(c). Three main situations can be identified:

1. **Maximum selling price.** If payments are contingent, but subject to a ceiling, the ceiling is presumed to be the selling price. The gross profit percentage is initially based on this maximum and is subsequently modified as more facts become available.
2. **Given payment period.** Here the seller's basis is prorated over the term. The result may be gains in some years, losses in others.
3. **No maximum price, no given term.** Here the seller recovers basis over 15 years, which may also lead to gain or loss in any given year, presumably of the same character.

In view of this expansion of the scope of the installment reporting provisions, the cost recovery method (the "open transaction" approach) is likely to have even less applicability than before.

PLANNING POINTER

The taxpayer's current and expected future tax rates should be carefully considered when deciding to use the installment method of reporting. If the taxpayer's future tax rates are expected to decline, then using the installment method could produce significant tax savings. Conversely, if the taxpayer expects to be in higher tax brackets in the future, then the installment method could result in significant increases in taxes. Remember, the time value of money also must be considered.

EXAMPLE 13.38

Jennifer Lynn sold a short-term capital asset in 2017. She has no capital loss carryovers and sold no other capital assets during the year. She does not plan to sell any capital assets during the next four years. The amount realized from the sale was $40,000, and the property's adjusted basis was $20,000. Her realized and recognized gain is $20,000. Jennifer will receive $8,000 at the date of sale and $8,000 (plus interest) per year for the four years after the year of sale. The value of the note is equal to its face value. The gross profit percentage is 50 percent ($20,000/$40,000). If she uses the installment method of reporting, then she will recognize a $4,000 ($8,000 x 50%) short-term capital gain (plus interest income) in each of the five years. If she elects out of the installment method of reporting, then she will recognize a $20,000 short-term capital gain (which will be taxed as ordinary income since she has no other capital asset transactions) in 2017, plus interest income as received.

If Jennifer is in the 33 percent bracket in 2017 but expects to be in the 15 percent bracket in 2018 through 2021, then she would save $2,400 in taxes by using the installment method (ignoring the time value of money).

Tax on $20,000 if recognized in 2017 ($20,000 x 33%)		$6,600
Tax on $4,000 in 2017 ($4,000 x 33%)	$1,320	
Tax on $4,000 in 2018 through 2021 ($4,000 x 15% = $600 x 4)	2,400	3,720
Tax savings from using the installment method of reporting		$2,880

If Jennifer is in the 15 percent bracket in 2017 but expects to be in the 28 percent bracket in 2018 and 2019 and the 25 percent bracket in 2020 and 2021, then she would save $2,320 in taxes by electing out of the installment method (ignoring the time value of money).

Tax on $20,000 if recognized in 2017 ($20,000 x 15%)		$3,000
Tax on $4,000 in 2017 ($4,000 x 15%)	$600	
Tax on $4,000 in 2018 through 2019 ($4,000 x 28% = $1,120 x 2)	2,240	
Tax on $4,000 in 2020 and 2021 ($4,000 x 25% =$1,000 x 2)	2,000	4,840
Tax savings from electing out of the installment method of reporting		$1,840

¶13,685   DISPOSITIONS OF INSTALLMENT OBLIGATIONS

There are times when a taxpayer who sold property on the installment method needs or wants to dispose of the installment obligation prior to maturity. In this instance, the taxpayer must determine the obligation's adjusted basis and determine the gain or loss on the disposition. The adjusted basis of the installment obligation is equal to the face amount of the obligation in excess of the income that would have been reported if the obligation had been paid in full. To determine gain or loss, the adjusted basis is compared to the amount realized if the obligation is sold and to the obligation's fair market value if it is disposed of other than by sale. The character of the gain or loss is based upon the property which was sold under the installment method. Code Sec. 453B(a).

EXAMPLE 13.39

In 2017, Katherine Beales sold a piece of art for $50,000. She received $10,000 in 2017 and in 2018. She purchased the piece in 2007 for $8,000; thus, her gross profit was $42,000 and the contract price was $50,000. The gross profit percentage was 84 percent ($42,000/$50,000). In 2019, she sold the installment obligation for $28,000. Her basis in the obligation is $4,800 (unpaid balance of $30,000 minus amount of income reported if unpaid balance paid in full (84% × $30,000)). Thus, Katherine's gain on the sale of the installment obligations is $23,200 ($28,000 – $4,800). The gain is a long-term capital gain since the art piece was a long-term capital asset when it was sold in 2017. Katherine also will recognize income for the interest she received while the obligation was outstanding.

In addition to a sale, there are several other situations where a disposition of an installment obligation results in a recognized gain or loss, primarily to prevent income-shifting among taxpayers. In each of these, the fair market value of the obligation is used as the amount realized. Code Sec. 453B(a).

The following lead to income recognition at the time the installment obligation is transferred: gifts or forgiveness of payments, especially if the obligee and obligor are related; taxable exchanges; and corporate distributions. Additionally, gain recognition occurs on "second dispositions," whereby the taxpayer sells the property to a related party and within two years of the sale and before the taxpayer receives all payments with respect to such sale, the related party disposes of the property (i.e., the "second" disposition). At the time of the second disposition, the amount realized from the second distribution is treated as being received by the original taxpayer. Code Sec. 453(e).

Gain or loss is not recognized in the following situations: transfers to a controlled corporation under Code Sec. 351; transfers in certain corporate reorganizations and liquidations; certain transfers to and from partnerships; transfers upon the death of a taxpayer; transfers incident to a divorce; and transfers to a spouse.

EXAMPLE 13.40	Jack Moore purchased land in 2009 for $40,000. Jack sold the land to his daughter in 2016. The terms of the sale call for Jack to receive $20,000 in 2016 and $15,000 in 2017, 2018, 2019, and 2020, plus interest. The gross profit is $40,000, the contract price is $80,000 and the gross profit percentage is 50 percent. Jack received payments in 2016 and 2017, recognizing $10,000 and $7,500, plus interest, respectively, in 2016 and 2017. In 2018, Jack forgave the remaining payments. The forgiveness is a taxable disposition. Jack is considered to have received the remaining payments ($45,000) and his recognized gain in 2018 is $22,500 (50% × $45,000).

¶13,695   REPOSSESSIONS

The repossession of personal property sold under the installment method is a taxable event. Gain or loss is recognized equal to the difference between the fair market value of the property repossessed and the adjusted basis of the installment obligation. Any costs incurred during the repossession increase the adjusted basis of the installment obligation. The character of the gain or loss recognized is the same as the character of the gain or loss recognized on the original sale of the property. The basis of the repossessed property is its fair market value. Code Sec. 453B.

Loss is not recognized and no bad debt deduction is allowed on the repossession of real property. Gain is recognized to a limited extent. Code Sec. 1038 limits gain recognition to the lesser of (1) the cash and fair market value of property received from the buyer in excess of gain previously recognized by the holder of the installment obligation or (2) the gain not yet recognized by the holder of the installment obligation (deferred gross profit), reduced by the costs incurred during the repossession. The character of the gain is the same as that recognized under the original sale of the property. The basis of the repossessed real property is the adjusted basis of the installment obligation, increased by costs incurred during the repossession and by any gain recognized from the repossession.

EXAMPLE 13.41	John Wells sold a car in January 2017 for $20,000. He received $4,000 down and $16,000 was due in 2018 His basis in the car at the time of sale was $12,000. John made numerous attempts to collect the $16,000 and in December he repossessed the car. He incurred $700 in repossession costs and the car's fair market value at time of repossession was $15,000. In 2017, John reported a capital gain of $1,600 (40% × $4,000). The adjusted basis of the installment obligation at the time of repossession was $9,600 ($16,000 – (40% × $16,000)). To determine John's gain on the repossession, this basis is increased by the repossession costs. Thus, John recognizes a $4,700 capital gain in December 2018 ($15,000 – ($9,600 + $700)). John's basis in the repossessed car is $15,000, its fair market value.

EXAMPLE 13.42	Tom O'Brien sold land in January 2017 for $50,000. He received $20,000 down and $30,000 was due in January 2018. Tom acquired the land in 2010 for $10,000. The gross profit percentage is 80 percent. Tom recognized a $16,000 long-term capital gain in 2017. Tom was unable to collect the $30,000 and repossessed the land in October 2018, incurring $1,000 in the process. The land's fair market value in October 2018 was $52,000. Tom's recognized long-term gain is $4,000, equal to the lesser of $4,000 ($20,000 received – $16,000 gain previously recognized) or $23,000 ($24,000 gain not yet recognized – $1,000 repossession costs). His basis in the repossessed land is $11,000 (the basis of the installment obligation ($30,000 – (80% × $30,000)) plus the gain recognized on repossession ($4,000) plus the costs incurred to repossess ($1,000).

¶13,699 INTEREST ON DEFERRED PAYMENT SALES

A seller of capital assets historically had an incentive to charge little or no interest while inflating the selling price, thus converting ordinary interest income into capital gains or a reduced capital loss. Section 483 limits the taxpayer's opportunity to do so, but does not eliminate it altogether. Unless the seller charges at least a rate equal to the "applicable federal rate" the IRS will impute interest at such a rate compounded semiannually, resulting in additional interest income to the buyer and a lower selling price (and a lower gross profit), but also providing the buyer with higher interest deductions (and a lower basis). Interest will not be imputed to a sale where all the payments are due within six months. Additionally, there are several special rules, including:

1. Unlike installment reporting, Code Sec. 483 applies to sales at a loss.
2. No interest is imputed unless the selling price is in excess of $3,000.
3. Sales of patents where the selling price is contingent on the use, production, or disposition of such patents, and private annuity sales are excluded.
4. Only 6 percent interest need be charged for sales of up to $500,000 of real property to a family member, including siblings, spouses, an ancestor, or a lineal descendant.

EXAMPLE 13.43   Antoinette Clerici sold land in 2017 for $40,000. The adjusted basis of the property was $50,000. Antoinette received $12,000 in 2017 and will receive $28,000 in 2018. No interest was charged. Antoinette has a $10,000 loss and cannot use the installment method to report it. However, since it is a deferred contract she must charge interest; thus, the IRS will impute interest and reduce the selling price accordingly. This increases her loss, causes her to recognize interest income, reduces the buyer's basis in the land, and causes interest expense for the buyer which may or may not be deductible.

Since the statutory rate may be below the market rate for second mortgages and unsecured personal loans, some flexibility of designing a price/terms combination that is attractive for tax purposes still exists.

¶13,710 ADVANTAGES AND DISADVANTAGES OF INSTALLMENT METHOD

There are several advantages and disadvantages associated with the installment method of reporting.

Advantages of engaging installment sales and reporting profits when collections are made include:

1. Tax liabilities are deferred until the proceeds from the sales are available
2. Marginal tax rates may decline in future years
3. Interest income, to some extent, may be converted to capital gains by charging a lower interest rate and a higher price (but the imputed interest rules affect this)
4. Since the seller finances the purchase, sales are more easily made.

Disadvantages of installment sales include:

1. There is a default risk and potential collection costs
2. In periods of inflation there is a loss of purchasing power
3. Although taxes are deferred, so are collections. Because the after-tax proceeds are likely to far exceed the taxes payable, an installment sale is unlikely to be made merely for tax purposes
4. Marginal tax rates may increase during the collection years
5. Although the *holding period* in the year of sale determines whether the transaction is short-term or long-term, the *character* of the gain is determined in the year of collection. In one case, the taxpayer sold a capital asset but wound up with ordinary income, in part, in the years of collection. *Z. Klien,* 42 TC 1000, Dec. 26,947.
6. All depreciation recapture takes place in the year of sale.

PLANNING POINTER

Olga Lopez purchased some land years ago as an investment for $40,000. She owns it free and clear, wishes to sell it for its value of $100,000 and would like as much cash up front as possible while deferring the tax as long as possible. Any potential buyer would most likely wish to finance the acquisition. If Olga sells the land on the installment plan, her gross profit of 60 percent will apply to payments in the year of sale as well as to future collections. After competent tax advice, she did the following:

1. She borrowed $40,000 with the property as collateral. The receipt of the loan proceeds is tax free.
2. After a reasonable time, she sold the property for $100,000 by letting the buyer take over the $40,000 loan and taking back a second mortgage below the market rate.
3. Even though her gross profit is now 100 percent, she received $40,000 tax free and converted interest income and favorable terms into an additional long-term capital gain on a tax-deferred basis.

SUMMARY

- Taxable income must be computed on the basis of the taxpayer's tax year.
- The annual accounting period may be either a calendar year or a fiscal year.
- The tax year cannot exceed 12 months except where a 52-53-week tax year is adopted.
- A fiscal year is a period of 12 months ending on the last day of any month other than December or a 52-53-week annual accounting period.
- A fiscal year is permitted only if the taxpayer's books are kept on the same basis.
- Usually the taxpayer needs a business purpose for approval of a change in tax periods.
- Prior approval must be obtained before changing to a new tax year.
- A return required for a fractional part of the year (due to a change in accounting periods) is known as a short-period return.
- To obtain IRS approval to change accounting periods, Form 1128 must be filed by the due date of the Federal income tax return for the first effective year.
- The taxpayer's method of accounting must "clearly reflect income."
- A taxpayer may change accounting methods voluntarily or may be required to change.
- To obtain advance IRS permission to change accounting methods, Form 3115 must be filed anytime during the year in which the change is desired.
- The taxpayer faced with a substantial tax due to a change of accounting methods generally has a four-year adjustment period.
- An understanding of accounting periods and methods is crucial to understanding the taxation of any entity.
- Many accounting methods used for financial accounting are similar to those used for tax accounting, but there are many differences too.
- Several inventory methods are available to the taxpayer: specific identification, FIFO, and LIFO, and variations thereto.
- Certain costs with respect to inventory must be capitalized.
- The percentage-of-completion method must be used for long-term contracts.
- The installment method of accounting is used when proceeds from the sale of certain property are received in a year other than the year of sale.
- A taxpayer may elect not to use the installment method.
- Accrual-basis taxpayers may not use the installment method.

QUESTIONS

1. How does financial accounting differ from tax accounting?

2. Jason is single and uses the calendar year for his tax year. He died on May 15, 2017. When is his final income tax return due?

3. If a taxpayer is on the fiscal year, what is the requirement regarding the taxpayer's books?

4. Pam recently married Henry. When she was single she used a calendar tax year. For a variety of reasons she is considering changing her tax year. When would she not need IRS permission to change her tax year?

5. Can a sole proprietor use a fiscal tax year for a business if the individual is on a calendar tax year?

6. What tax year options are available to a partnership?

7. Small Company wants to elect a tax year that follows its business cycle, which ends July 20. Is it permitted to do this?

8. If a corporation begins business on June 12, 2017, when may it close its first tax year?

9. What tax year options are available to an S corporation?

10. Must an estate use the calendar year only for its tax year?

11. What is the latest time that an application for a change in accounting period may be filed?

12. Big Co. changed its tax year at midyear. It must annualize its short year to determine its tax liability. What does annualizing a short year mean?

13. In which of the following cases must the taxpayer annualize its income for a period of less than 12 months?
    a. Alpha Corporation was formed on August 17 and decided to report on the calendar year.
    b. Beta Corporation was formed on March 8 and decided to use the fiscal year ending July 31.
    c. Gamma Corporation has been using a fiscal year ending April 30 and changed to a calendar year.
    d. Zeta Corporation, a calendar-year corporation, was liquidated on September 23.

14. What is the definition of "method of accounting"?

15. Code Sec. 446 requires the taxpayer's method of accounting clearly reflects income. What does "clearly reflects income" mean?

16. Name the two most commonly used overall methods of accounting.

17. Thomas is a sole proprietor who uses the cash method of accounting. As such, the constructive receipt rule applies to him. What is the purpose of the constructive receipt rule?

18. When considering the cash versus the accrual method of accounting:
    a. Is there any type of business that must be on the cash method?
    b. Is there any type of business that must be on the accrual method?
    c. What kind of business has a choice?

19. A cash-basis taxpayer generally is allowed a deduction upon payment of business expenses. May it deduct all payments when paid?

20. May the same taxpayer use several different methods of recognizing income simultaneously?

21. Can the IRS require Bill Inc. to change its method of accounting in all circumstances?

22. Generally, what additional indirect production costs incurred in the manufacture of inventory must be capitalized under the uniform capitalization rules that were not required to be capitalized under the full absorption method?

23. Rock Inc. is a manufacturer. It incurred numerous overhead costs this year. How should it treat the costs in determining its inventory?

24. Char Co.'s uses financial accounting practices/methods for tax purposes. Is this practice an automatic defense against a challenge by the IRS that some (all) such practices do not clearly reflect income?

25. Why should an individual not use an installment sale as opposed to a cash sale?

26. Spancer Co. is in the construction business. Can it use the completed contract method to account for its long-term contracts?

27. How are liabilities in excess of basis treated in an installment sale?

PROBLEMS

28 Which entities utilize deductions for adjusted gross income and deductions from adjusted gross income? Why do only these entities use said deductions?

29. A partnership is owned 62 percent by a corporation and 38 percent by an individual. The corporation has a fiscal year ending on September 30. The individual is a calendar-year taxpayer. What is the tax year of the partnership, assuming it does not qualify under the business purpose exception?

30. An S corporation wishes to adopt a fiscal year ending on August 31 because that is the end of its model year. Will the S corporation be given permission to adopt the fiscal year?

31. What are the accounting period options for the following businesses?
    a. C corporation starting business on March 11
    b. Sole proprietorship starting business on May 27 with a proprietor on the calendar-year basis and a natural business year ending January 31
    c. Partnership owned by three calendar-year individuals and a natural business year ending April 30
    d. S corporation with a natural business year ending March 31

32. A partnership has two equal calendar-year partners and is switching from a fiscal year ending on June 30 to a calendar year. If the partnership has $40,000 in net income resulting from the short period, how will each partner report the short period income?

33. Hal is single and in 2017 he obtained IRS permission to change from the calendar year to a fiscal year ended August 31, 2017. Hal earned $70,000 through August 31, 2017 and had $6,000 in itemized deductions during January 1 through August 31, 2017. What is Hal's gross tax liability for the short period?

34. The Light Record Corporation has been on the calendar year since its inception five years ago. It wishes to change to an April 30 natural business year. For 2017, the calendar year of proposed change, Light had a taxable income of $200,000, of which $50,000 was earned from January through April.
    a. What must Light Corporation do to obtain the change in period? When must it do it?
    b. What is the tax liability for the short year?

35. Lyle Inc. is a cash-basis, calendar-year taxpayer. In 2017, it changes to the accrual method of accounting. Its 2017 income computed under the accrual method is $75,000. The following information also is available:

	December 31, 2016	December 31, 2017
Accounts receivable	$27,000	$34,000
Accounts payable	19,000	23,500

What is Lyle's required adjustment to income for 2017 and how should Lyle report it?

36. X Corporation was formed and began operations on September 1, 2017. X Corporation expects to have taxable income of $25,000 each quarter of operations for the first two years. X Corporation is indifferent with respect to its accounting period. What would you suggest regarding initial selection of an accounting period?

37. Wagner Co. is a cash-basis, calendar-year taxpayer. On August 1, 2017, it paid an insurance premium of $4,800 for coverage from August 1, 2017 to July 31, 2018. What is the largest deduction Wagner Co. can take in 2017?

38. Assume the same facts as the problem above except the premium is for coverage from August 1, 2017 to July 31, 2019. What is the largest deduction Wagner Co. can take in 2017?

39. Jennifer uses the cash method. Which of the following transactions result in gross income in the current year?
    a. Car, worth $7,000, received as a consulting fee
    b. $500 of interest credited to his checking account, but not withdrawn
    c. Wages payable from a corporation with ample funds, in which he is a 12 percent shareholder, unpaid at year-end
    d. Stock, worth $20,000, for services rendered, fully vested if Jennifer still works for the corporation in three years
    e. $700 of dental services (bill cancelled upon Jennifer's estate planning advice to the dentist's mother-in-law)
    f. Sale of a used car for a note due in one year, face value $3,000, fair market value $2,500. No elections were made

40. Jen Company decided to change its method of accounting from the cash basis to the accrual basis in 2017 because sale of inventories had become a material income-producing item. Its taxable income for 2017 under the accrual basis was $250,000. It determined that the balances of accounts receivable, inventory, and accounts payable as of December 2016 were:

Accounts receivable	$18,000
Inventory	14,000
Accounts payable	11,000

    a. What is Jen Company's required adjustment due to the change in accounting methods?
    b. What can Jen Company do with the adjustment?

41. Berry Co. started business in 2016. Its ending inventory at actual prices was $150,000 at base-period prices. It uses the simplified dollar-value LIFO inventory method and the price index was 130% in 2016. Its ending inventory at actual prices in 2017 is $180,000 and the price index is 140%. What is Berry Co.'s 2017 ending inventory?

42. Ludlow Inc. started business in 2016. It uses the simplified dollar-value LIFO inventory method. Ending inventories at actual prices are as follows:

Year	Amount
2016	$200,000
2017	220,000
2018	225,000

The price index in 2016, 2017 and 2018 is 120%, 125%, and 130%, respectively. What are the dollar values of its ending inventory in 2017 and 2018?

43. Smith Inc. discovered it had made several math errors during 2017. It wants to correct the errors and is unsure as to whether this would qualify as a major change in accounting method requiring IRS approval. Advise Smith Inc.

44. Wash Company sells washing machines. On January 1, 2017, it had 20 units in inventory, valued at $400 per unit. During 2017, it sold 200 units at $700 per machine. Wash Company purchased 190 units during 2017 at a cost of $420 per unit. Determine Wash Company's gross profit under the FIFO and LIFO methods.

45. Mill Co., a calendar-year manufacturer, which uses the FIFO inventory method, previously allocated production costs to inventory by use of a burden rate based on the ratios of total indirect production costs incurred during the year compared to total direct labor costs during the year. Mill Co. incurred the following costs during the year:

Direct material	$500,000
Direct labor	1,500,000
Indirect costs inventoried under pre-1986 TRA law	1,500,000
Additional costs inventoried under Code Sec. 263A	750,000
Ending inventory prior to the capitalization of additional Code Sec. 263A costs	700,000

Mill Co. had an inventory turnover rate of five times.

Compute the total amount of additional Code Sec. 263A costs to capitalize for FIFO inventory under the simplified production method.

46. Sugarcane Company incurs handling costs totaling $15 million and purchasing costs of $4 million. Inventoriable general and administrative costs related to handling and purchasing totals $1 million. Purchases for the year are $100 million. Sugarcane Company uses FIFO. Its purchases in ending inventory total $40 million. Compute the total resale costs to be capitalized to ending inventory using the simplified resale method.

47. X Company has four inventory items at year end. Inventory information (based on FIFO) is as follows:

Item	Cost	Market
1	$6,000	$8,000
2	3,000	2,400
3	10,000	9,000
4	4,000	7,000

Determine X Company's ending inventory using the lower-of-cost-or-market method.

48. Sam Co. sells a product whose cost (and sales price) has risen continually. This has produced increases in Sam Co.'s gross receipts and Sam Co. would like to use an inventory method that would minimize its tax liability. Would you recommend specific identification, FIFO, or LIFO? Why?

49. Falzone Inc. uses the dollar-value LIFO method to account for its inventory. Inventory on January 1, 2017, was $30,000 at base-year prices. Inventory on December 31, 2017, was $63,000 at actual prices and $50,000 at base-year prices. Determine Falzone's ending inventory using dollar-value LIFO.

50. Mar Co. is a construction company. In 2017, it entered into a two-year contract to construct a building for $3,000,000. It estimated that actual costs will be $2,500,000. Actual costs in 2017 are $1,500,000. In 2018, actual costs are $800,000. What income does Mar Co. report in 2017 and 2018 under the completed contract and percentage-of-completion methods?

51. Steve sold for $200,000 his undivided one-third interest in an apartment building in which he had a $30,000 adjusted basis. The buyer put $40,000 down, assumed Steve's share of the mortgage, and signed an installment obligation with a face value of $120,000. $20,000 of the principal was paid at the end of the year of sale. Compute the following:
    a. Contract price
    b. Gross profit and gross profit percentage
    c. Payment in year of sale
    d. Gain in the year of sale

52. Do either of the transactions below qualify for installment reporting? If not, why not?
    a. Credit sales of dealer inventory
    b. Credit sales of property not held as inventory

53. $20 million of nondealer real estate obligations arose in and are outstanding at the end of calendar-year 2017. Deferred gross profit on such installment obligations equals $5 million. Assume that the highest tax rate applicable in 2017 is 28 percent and the interest rate for December 2017 is 7 percent. Compute the amount of interest to be paid for 2017 on the amount of deferred gross profit, assuming the property was used in a trade or business.

54. Brice sells a piece of raw land with a basis of $10,000 which he has owned for years as an investment. What are the tax consequences to Brice, a cash-basis taxpayer, for the following consideration received:
    a. Cash of $30,000
    b. Motel worth $50,000, subject to $20,000 of liabilities
    c. Installment note due in one year without interest with a face value of $30,000 and a fair market value of $27,000
    d. Same as (c), but Brice elects out of installment reporting

55. Joe England sold equipment on May 10, 2016 for $100,000. He bought the equipment on November 7, 2014 for $140,000, and accumulated depreciation at the date of sale was $60,000. Joe collected $50,000 in 2016 and will collect $50,000 in 2017. Joe used the installment method for the sale. What is Joe's recognized gain in 2016 and 2017?

56. Assume the same facts as the problem above except the selling price is $180,000 and Joe will collect $90,000 in 2016 and 2017.
    a. What is Joe's recognized gain in 2016 and 2017?
    b. Go to irs.gov and print the most-recent form 6252. Complete form 6252 for 2016's income tax filing purposes.

57. Adjustments due to a change in accounting method do not include which of the following:
    a. Taken into account in the year of change
    b. Spread over four years starting with the year of change
    c. Spread over four years starting in the year of change only if a negative adjustment
    d. None of the above

58. In 2017, Bob will sell land that he bought in 2007 for $50,000 to Tom. The selling price is $250,000. Tom has given Bob two options for the sale. Under option 1, Bob would receive the $250,000 at the date of sale. Under option 2, Bob would receive $125,000 at sale date and $125,000 one year later (in 2018). Tom also would pay Bob $8,750 interest in 2018 (at the time he pays the remaining $125,000 to Bob). Bob's overall tax rate is 35% and the land is a capital asset to Bob. Bob uses a 5% after-tax discount rate for all his investment decisions. Which option should Bob take?
    a. Option 1
    b. Option 2
    c. Neither, Bob is indifferent

59. Jessica sold an apartment building, in which she had a $400,000 adjusted basis, for $1,100,000. The buyer paid $150,000 down, assumed Jessica's mortgage, and signed an installment obligation with a face value of $500,000. $50,000 of principal was paid at the end of the year of sale. Jessica's contract price, gross profit percentage, and payment in the year of sale are:
    a. $550,000, 100 percent, and $200,000
    b. $700,000, 100 percent, and $200,000
    c. $700,000, 100 percent, and $250,000
    d. $1,100,000, 60 percent, and $200,000

60. In 2017, Chris sold a painting to Bernie for $40,000. Chris received $10,000 in 2017 and will receive $30,000 in 2018. Chris's bought the painting in 2013 for $15,000. Bernie did not pay Chris $30,000 when it was due, and after numerous attempts to collect (and $1,000 in expenses), Chris repossessed the paining in 2018. The painting was worth $45,000 when repossessed.

    What is Chris's recognized gain in 2017?
    a. $25,000
    b. $10,000
    c. $6,250

    What are the results of the repossession to Chris?
    a. $45,000 LTCG; basis = $45,000
    b. $33,750 LTCG; basis = $45,000
    c. $33,750 LTCG; basis = $44,000
    d. $32,750 LTCG; basis = $45,000

61. Which of the following is not considered "constructive receipt" of income?
    a. X was informed its check for services rendered was available on December 20, 2017, but it waited until January 21, 2018, to pick up the check.
    b. Earned income of X was received by its agent on December 30, 2017, but not received by X until January 6, 2018.
    c. X received a check on December 30, 2017, for services rendered, but was unable to make a deposit until January 3, 2018.
    d. A payment on the sale of real property was placed in an escrow account on December 20, 2017, but not received by X until January 13, 2018, when the transaction closed.

62. Xeno Corporation purchased supplies from Kimbo Company in 2017. The total invoice was for $20,000, but Xeno claimed that only one-half of the order was received and paid only $10,000 in 2017. Both parties honestly disputed the bill and Xeno refused to pay the contested amount. They went to court and a judgment requiring Xeno to pay an additional $5,000 was issued in 2018. How should Xeno report this expense?
    a. $10,000 in 2017 and $5,000 in 2018
    b. $15,000 in 2017
    c. $15,000 in 2018
    d. $20,000 in 2017 and $5,000 of income in 2018
    e. None of the above

63. Bevin Inc. uses the FIFO method for valuing inventory. Its inventory purchases in 2017 totaled $5,000,000 and its ending inventory on December 31, 2017 is $2,000,000 (before the Code Sec. 263A cost allocation). It incurred the following costs in 2017:

Item	Amount
Storage	$190,000
Purchasing	200,000
Handling	80,000
Labor costs for the above items	150,000
Mixed services	220,000

    Total labor costs excluding amounts in the mixed service costs are $4,000,000. What is the value of Bevin Inc.'s ending inventory?
    a. $2,470,000
    b. $2,191,300
    c. $2,008,250
    d. $2,000,000

64. X uses the LIFO method in computing its inventory. It had 1,000 units on hand at the end of 2017. Based on the following information, what is the value of its ending inventory on December 31, 2017?

Beginning inventory: 500 units with a per-unit cost of $2.00 and a per-unit market value of $3.00

Purchases: September 25, 2017, 1,500 units with a per-unit cost of $3.00 and a per-unit market value of $3.00. November 12, 2017, 1,000 units with a per-unit cost of $4.00 and a per-unit value of $4.00.
   a. $2,500
   b. $3,000
   c. $4,000
   d. $5,000

65. Y uses the FIFO method in computing its inventory. On January 1, 2017, its beginning inventory of 3,500 units consisted of the following:

1,000 purchased April 10, 2016, at $1.00 per unit

2,000 purchased June 23, 2016, at $2.00 per unit

500 purchase July 11, 2016, at $3.00 per unit

During 2017, Y purchased the following units:

3,000 purchased September 1, 2017, at $4.00 per unit

1,000 purchased December 16, 2017, at $5.00 per unit

During 2017, it sold 2,300 units. What is the value of its ending inventory?
   a. $13,300
   b. $15,300
   c. $19,900
   d. $22,900
   e. None of the above

66. Richard sold a rare automobile he had held as an investment in 2016. Richard purchased the automobile in 1990; its adjusted basis at the time of the sale was $70,000, and the selling price was $250,000. Richard received $50,000 in 2016 and was to receive $50,000 per year plus interest in each of the four succeeding years. On January 5, 2018, Richard sold the installment obligation (he did not receive an installment payment in 2017) for $145,000. Richard's gain on the sale of the installment obligation in 2018 is:
   a. $42,000
   b. $72,000
   c. $103,000
   d. $108,000
   e. $150,000

67. John sold a painting in February 2017 for $40,000. He received $10,000 in February and was to receive $15,000 in 2018 and 2019, plus interest. He purchased the painting in 2006 for $15,000, and its basis at time of sale was $15,000. The buyer defaulted on the obligation on January 1, 2018, and John repossessed the painting. He incurred no costs to repossess the painting, and its fair market value at repossession date was $39,000. John's recognized gain on the repossession is:
   a. $6,250
   b. $11,250
   c. $25,000
   d. $27,750
   e. $39,000

68. John's basis in the painting in problem 67 is:
   a. $0
   b. $25,000
   c. $30,000
   d. $39,000
   e. $42,250

69. **Comprehensive Problem.** Bill is a cash-basis, calendar-year taxpayer. Which of the following December items result in gross income or deductions for the current year?

    a. Check received for December rent, $700, not deposited until January 4

    b. Check for $1,100 to pay Bill's state income taxes mailed December 28, cashed January 7

    c. Cash received in the amount of $500 for services to be rendered the following year

    d. Interest of $800 credited to his savings account, added to Bill's account balance

    e. Check received on December 29 for January rent, $700, deposited on January 9

    f. Charitable contribution of $300, charged on Bill's MasterCard

    g. Bills totaling $2,000 sent for services rendered during the year, uncollected as of year-end

70. **Comprehensive Problem.** Do any of the transactions below qualify for installment reporting? If not, why not?

    a. Sale of property in December, with payment received in full the following January at a gain

    b. Sale of property at a loss, payments to be received in equal annual installments over seven years

    c. Exchange of like-kind investment property where the transfer took place in two different years

    d. Sale in one year at a gain, 90 percent of the proceeds received immediately, the remaining 10 percent in year two

    e. Sale of securities at a gain, the proceeds being 13 percent a year of current fair market value to be received over the life of the seller

    f. Sale of stock with zero basis for 10 percent of the gross life of the gross sales of a business for 11 years

71. **Research Problem.** A manufacturer of pollution control facilities reported its profits on the completed-contract method. To value its raw materials and work in process, the taxpayer used the LIFO method, thus "having it both ways" (i.e., deferring profits and maximizing the cost of goods sold). The IRS claimed that the two methods are mutually exclusive and that the costs of materials, labor, supplies, etc. are to be treated as deferred expenditures, deductible only when the contracts are completed. Is the IRS correct? (See *Peninsular Steel Products & Equipment Co., Inc.,* 78 TC 1029, Dec. 39,113 (1982).)

72. **Research Problem.** John Smythe has a margin account with Investit Investment Company. The stocks and bonds in the account earned dividends and interest of $10,000 in 2017. The $10,000 was paid directly to the margin account and used for reinvestment purposes only. Smythe received a substitute Form 1099-DIV which indicated the composition of the $10,000. However, Smythe did not report the $10,000 as income in 2017. He reported it as income in 2018 when he closed the margin account. The IRS has indicated that Smythe must include the $10,000 in 2017, and in addition to taxes has assessed interest and penalties. Smythe seeks your advice. (See, for example, *A.L. Christoffersen,* 84-2 USTC ¶9990, 749 F.2d 513 (CA-8 1984).)

Chapter

14

Taxation of Corporations—Basic Concepts

OBJECTIVES

After completing Chapter 14, you should be able to:

1. Identify which entities are classified as corporations.
2. Discuss tax-free organizations and transfers to controlled corporations.
3. Understand the use of debt in the corporate capital structure.
4. Apply the ordinary loss deduction rules of Code Sec. 1244 on dispositions of stock.
5. Use the gain exclusion of Code Sec. 1202 on dispositions of stock.
6. Determine corporate taxable income, including special deductions available to corporations.
7. Compute corporate income tax, including the regular tax and the alternative minimum tax.
8. Describe controlled and affiliated groups and the filing of consolidated returns.
9. Know corporate income tax return requirements.
10. Understand how corporations account for differences between book income and taxable income.

OVERVIEW

Corporate taxation is divided into six areas. They are (1) formation, (2) operation, (3) distributions, (4) redemptions, (5) liquidations, and (6) reorganizations. In this chapter, the formation and operation of corporations are discussed. Chapter 15 describes distributions and redemptions, Chapter 16 presents liquidations, and Chapter 17 details reorganizations. Chapter 18 discusses the penalty taxes, such as the accumulated earnings tax and the personal holding company tax, that may be imposed on corporations.

Chapters 14 through 18 limit their discussion to regular corporations taxed under Subchapter C of the Internal Revenue Code. Special corporations taxed under Subchapter S are discussed in Chapter 21. These S corporations have features closer to the partnership form of organization than the corporate form of organization.

Special rules allow assets and liabilities to be transferred to corporations tax free. There is a carryover of basis and tacking of holding periods in these tax-free exchanges.

Code Sec. 1244 allows the original shareholders of small business stock to obtain an ordinary deduction for a loss on dispositions of the stock rather than receive capital loss treatment. Gain on the sale still remains capital gain. Code Sec. 1202 also enables noncorporate taxpayers to exclude 50, 75, or 100 percent on any gain from the sale or exchange of qualified small business stock held for more than five years which was originally issued after August 10, 1993.

A corporation is a separate legal entity and taxpayer. A corporation computes its taxable income in much the same manner as an individual. However, there are special deductions available to corporations. Dividends received by a corporation from other domestic corporations are deductible to the extent of 70 to 100 percent. The first $5,000 of organizational expenditures may be expensed in the first year and the remaining expenditures may be deducted ratably over a period of 180 months. Charitable contributions are limited to 10 percent of taxable income. Corporations may claim capital losses only against capital gains. Disallowed capital losses are carried back three years and forward five years. Net operating losses are normally carried back two years and forward 20 years.

Corporate income tax rates vary from 15 to 39 percent of taxable income. Corporations may be subject to a 20 percent tax on net alternative minimum taxable income, which is taxable income with certain adjustments and tax preferences. If the alternative minimum tax exceeds the regular tax, the excess is added to the regular tax. Dividends must be paid out of after-tax income and included in taxable income of the shareholders receiving the dividends.

Affiliated groups may elect to file consolidated returns rather than separate returns. Members of controlled groups must share certain tax benefits. Corporations use Form 1120 in filing their annual income tax returns.

Entity Choice

Many issues must be addressed when forming a business. A major concern is the type of entity. The three major types are sole proprietorships, partnerships, and corporations. Each entity has certain tax and nontax advantages and disadvantages; therefore, a decision must be made regarding which entity is most beneficial. The initial choice of entity is very important. However, under certain circumstances, the entity structure can be changed at a later date. Following is a brief discussion of each entity.

¶14,001 SPECIFIC ENTITIES

Sole Proprietorships

A sole proprietorship is a form of business in which one person owns all the assets and is fully responsible for all the liabilities. While this entity is treated as a separate entity for accounting purposes, it is not a separate legal entity. As such, a separate tax return is not filed for a sole proprietorship. Instead, its results from operations are reported on Schedule C (Profit or Loss From Business (Sole Proprietorship)) of Form 1040 (U.S. Individual Income Tax Return). The net income or loss is included with the taxpayer's other income, losses, and deductions for the year and is subject to a tax rate from 10 percent to 39.6 percent.

Partnerships

A partnership is a form of business in which two or more persons or entities own all the assets and are responsible for the liabilities. It is based on a voluntary contract between these parties. The partnership is formed with the intent that the owners (partners) will contribute assets and/or labor in return for a share of the profits. Most states have adopted the Uniform Partnership Act which governs partnership activities.

A partnership is similar to a sole proprietorship in that it is not a separate entity. However, for accounting and tax-reporting purposes, it is treated as a separate entity. Thus, a tax return, Form 1065 (U.S. Partnership Return of Income), is filed for the partnership. Although a tax return is filed, a partnership is not a taxpaying entity; rather, the income, expenses, gains, losses, credits, etc. pass through to its owners. Schedule K-1 (Partner's Share of Income, Credits, Deductions, etc.) of Form 1065 contains an indication of each partner's share of such items. The partner includes these items with the personal activities reported on Form 1040.

Corporations

A corporation is a legal entity created by the authority of state law. It is separate and distinct from its owners (shareholders). A corporation may be owned by one or more persons or entities. However, some states require at least two owners. For income tax purposes, there are two business types of corporations: regular corporations (C corporations) and electing corporations (S corporations). Both corporations are separate legal entities. The distinction between them is for income tax purposes only.

A C corporation is a separate taxpaying entity. It files Form 1120 (U.S. Corporation Income Tax Return). All its income and expenses are reported in this return and it pays a tax that ranges from 15 percent to 39 percent. The shareholders are not liable for a tax based on the corporation's income. However, shareholders must include dividend distributions in their taxable income.

An S corporation is not a separate taxpaying entity. It files Form 1120S (U.S. Income Tax Return for an S Corporation), but in general does not pay an income tax. Like a partnership, the income, expenses, gains, losses, credits, etc. pass through to the shareholders. Schedule K-1 (Shareholders' Share of Income, Credits, Deductions, etc.) contains each shareholder's share of these items.

Limited Liability Companies

In 1977, Wyoming passed the first limited liability company (LLC) legislation. In 1988, the IRS issued Rev. Rul. 88-76, 1988-2 CB 360, holding that a Wyoming LLC would be treated as a partnership for federal income tax purposes. All 50 states now recognize LLCs. However, the legislation is not similar across all jurisdictions, and technical requirements vary. Regardless, the number of LLCs in the United States continues to grow at a very fast pace.

The LLC has corporate and partnership characteristics. From a nontax perspective, LLCs provide flexibility to a firm's structure and operations, and they also provide their owners (members) with limited liability with respect to firm debts and obligations. For tax purposes, the LLC is treated as a conduit entity whereby its income passes through to its owners, thereby eliminating the double taxation associated with corporations other than S corporations; however, it may elect to be taxed as a corporation. See ¶14,015 for a discussion.

Limited Liability Partnerships

A limited liability partnership (LLP) is similar to an LLC and is organized under each state's statutes. These statutes generally apply to service organizations that are organized as partnerships and are most beneficial to large partnerships such as large public accounting firms. LLP status enables the firm to achieve limited liability benefits but be taxed as a partnership.

Comparative Advantages and Disadvantages

Each entity has certain tax and nontax attributes associated with it. Knowledge of these attributes enables taxpayers to select an entity which is most appropriate for them. Some of these attributes are briefly discussed below.

Limited Liability

Limited liability is one of the major advantages of a corporation. The shareholders' personal assets are not subject to claims of the corporation's creditors; only their investment in the corporation is subject to these claims. However, certain professional corporations do not have limited liability. Similarly, owners of small corporations usually have to guarantee the loans of their corporations. Partners and sole proprietors have unlimited liability unless the partners are limited partners in a limited partnership or unless the firm is organized as a limited liability partnership (LLP) or a limited liability company (LLC).

Employee Status

Sole proprietors and partners are not considered employees of their firms. This is a disadvantage because certain tax-exempt fringe benefits are not available to them and the firm cannot deduct the costs of these benefits. Similarly, their shares of self-employment income are subject to the self-employment tax of 15.3 percent on a maximum of $127,200, plus 2.90 percent on amounts over $127,200. The 15.3% is composed as follows: 12.4% for old age, survivors, and disability insurance (OASDI) and 2.9% for Medicare. Once the taxpayer reaches the $127,200, only Medicare is due on subsequent earnings. However, one-half of this amount qualifies as a deduction for adjusted gross income in computing taxable income. Shareholders employed by their corporation have employee status, although there are restrictions on shareholders who also are employees of their S corporation. Code Sec. 1372(a).

Additionally, starting in 2013, all taxpayers are subject to an additional 0.9% Medicare tax (so effectively the Medicare tax for these taxpayers is 3.80% (2.90% + 0.9%)). The additional Medicare tax applies once a taxpayer's income exceeds a threshold. After 2012, the threshold is $200,000 for single and head of houshould taxpayers and $250,000 for married taxpayers filing a joint return and surviving spouses.

Double Taxation

A disadvantage of C corporations is that they are subject to a form of double taxation. An income tax is imposed on the taxable income of the corporation, and no deduction is allowed for distributions to shareholders. When after-tax profits are distributed to shareholders as dividends, the shareholders generally must include the amounts in their taxable income. However, the tax rate applied to dividends received by shareholders is as follows: 0% for taxpayers in the 10 percent or 15 percent bracket and 15% for taxpayers in all other brackets except the rate is 20% for those in the 39.6 percent bracket. Partnerships, S corporations, and sole proprietorships are not subject to this because they are conduits. Their income passes through to the owners and is taxed at that level only.

Pass-Through Benefits

Corporate losses cannot pass through to shareholders. Also, dividend distributions to shareholders are taxed at capital gains rates, regardless of the type of income (tax-exempt, capital gains, etc.) that generated the earnings and profits from which the dividends came. Since sole proprietorships, partnerships, and S corporations are conduits, all income, gains, losses, credits, etc. pass through to their owners. These items retain their identity when they pass through. Thus, the firms' net losses can be used to offset personal income. Also, tax-exempt income passes through as such and is not taxable to the sole proprietor or partner. Additionally, the owners can use their shares of capital losses to offset their personal capital gains. Conversely, their shares of capital gains could be offset by their personal capital losses (or carryovers). Regular corporations do not provide these benefits.

Capital Formation

Corporations are better able to raise funds via owner-financing because of the comparative ease to expand ownership. The issuance of stock does not change the entity. A proprietor is solely responsible for owner-financing. The issuance of ownership interest in return for funds terminates the sole proprietorship. A partnership is better able to owner-finance than is a sole proprietorship because it has more owners.

Fiscal Period

A regular corporation can elect a fiscal period different from that of its owners. A sole proprietorship must have the same fiscal period as its owner. A partnership must have the same fiscal period as its partners who have a majority interest. In general, an S corporation must use a calendar year as its tax year unless it can establish a business purpose for using another tax year.

¶14,015 DEFINITION OF A CORPORATION

If the corporate form of business is selected, the owners must be certain that their entity is treated as a corporation for federal income tax purposes. A corporation is a legal entity owing its existence to the laws of the state in which it is incorporated. The state laws define all legal relationships of the corporation. Prior to 1997, a legal corporation was not guaranteed corporate status for federal tax purposes unless it had a majority of corporate characteristics (centralized management, continuity of life, free transferability of interests, and limited liability). Similarly, noncorporate entities sometimes could and would be taxed as corporations if they had a majority of these characteristics. This created much uncertainty for many organizations.

Regulations to Code Sec. 7701 have simplified the entity classification issue. Under the "check-the-box" system, certain business entities (entities other than trusts or those subject to special rules) automatically will be treated as corporations for federal tax purposes. These entities are: firms incorporated under federal or state law, associations, joint-stock companies, or joint-stock associations (as organized under a state statute), insurance companies, banks, business entities wholly owned by a state or political subdivision of the state, business entities that are taxed as corporations under another Code section, and certain foreign entities. Eligible entities (entities other than trusts or those subject to special rules) that are not automatically treated as a corporation may elect ("check-the-box") to be treated as a corporation for federal tax purposes.

If an entity has one owner, it may elect to be treated as a corporation or by default it will be treated as an entity not separate from its owner (sole proprietorship). If an entity has two or more owners, it can elect to be taxed as a corporation for federal tax purposes, otherwise it will be taxed as a partnership.

An eligible entity makes its election to change its default classification by filing Form 8832 (Entity Classification Election). The entity also indicates the effective date of the election. The effective date cannot be more than 75 days prior to the date Form 8832 is filed nor more than 12 months after it is filed. Also, a copy of Form 8832 must be attached to the entity's tax return for the year of election. Finally, once the election is made, the election cannot generally be changed for five years.

EXAMPLE 14.1	Gary, Richard, and Tom formed GRT partnership on February 1, 2017. GRT is an eligible entity; thus, if it wants to be taxed as a corporation for federal tax purposes, it must file Form 8832 within 75 days.

Organization of and Transfers to a Corporation

¶14,101 USE OF CORPORATE FORM

If the corporate form is desired, the owners must be certain that they meet all filing requirements of the state in which the company is organized. After completing this, the owners must decide what type of property to transfer to the corporation and how this property should be transferred. For example, should the owners transfer cash to purchase stock or make loans to the corporation? Similarly, should land or other assets be sold to the corporation, contributed in return for its stock, or leased to the corporation? The answers to these questions have significant tax implications.

In general, taxpayers who exchange property other than cash for other property recognize a gain or loss. The difference between the value of the property received and the adjusted basis of the property given up produces a realized gain or loss. Under Code Sec. 1001 this gain or loss is recognized by the taxpayer unless another section of the Internal Revenue Code provides for nonrecognition of the gain or loss.

There are several reasons why nonrecognition treatment is preferable with respect to corporate formation and transfers to corporations. The owners who receive stock in return for their property are not cashing in on their investment. There has been no change in their wherewithal to pay taxes, rather the stock represents a continuation of their investment in a different form. There is no substantive change in the owners' investments. Additionally, the government does not want to discourage corporate formation and subsequent transfers to corporations. Taxing such transfers when there has been no change in wherewithal to pay would act as a deterrent. Thus, under certain conditions Code Sec. 351 provides for nonrecognition of gain or loss upon transfer of property to a corporation in return for its stock.

¶14,105   GENERAL REQUIREMENTS

The rule under Code Sec. 351 is mandatory and provides that no gain or loss is recognized upon the transfer of property to a corporation solely in exchange for its stock if the taxpayer transferring the property (the transferor) is in control of the corporation immediately after the exchange. The basis rules provided in Code Secs. 358 and 362 assure that the nonrecognition is deferred and not permanent. These sections generally apply a carryover basis to the stock received by the transferor and to the property received by the transferee corporation. Code Sec. 1223 also enables both parties to tack on the holding period of the property transferred to the stock and the property, respectively, if they constitute capital assets or Section 1231 assets.

There are three major requirements of Code Sec. 351: (1) the transfer must consist of property, (2) the transfer must be solely in exchange for stock, and (3) the transferors must be in control immediately after the exchange. Each requirement is discussed separately.

TAX BLUNDER

Susan Jones is in the 35 percent tax bracket. She transfers property with an adjusted basis of $50,000 and a fair market value of $30,000 to X Co. in a transaction that qualifies under Code Sec. 351. Under Code Sec. 351, Jones will not recognize a loss on the transfer. Jones should not have transferred the property. She would have been better off selling the property to the corporation (assuming the related-party loss rules of Code Sec. 267 do not apply) and recognizing the $20,000 loss this year. Both the time value of money and her tax bracket favor such action.

¶14,111   TRANSFERS OF PROPERTY

Code Sec. 351 does not define property. However, it does indicate what is not property. Services, certain debt of the transferee corporation, and certain accrued interest on the transferee's debt are not treated as property. Code Sec. 351(d). Other than these exceptions, the definition of property is very comprehensive and includes all types of property such as cash, accounts receivables, inventories, patents, installment obligations, equipment, and buildings.

EXAMPLE 14.2   Jerome Smith transfers land to North Corporation in return for 90 percent of its stock. The adjusted basis of the land is $40,000. The fair market value of the stock is $90,000. Jerome has a realized gain of $50,000 ($90,000 – $40,000) and no recognized gain. Jay Jones performs accounting services for North Corporation in return for 10 percent of its stock (fair market value is $10,000). Jay has $10,000 of ordinary income. The receipt of the stock is treated as compensation for services rendered. Jay's basis in the stock is its fair market value, $10,000.

¶14,115   TRANSFERS FOR STOCK

Code Sec. 351 requires that the transferor receive the corporation's stock. The receipt of securities in exchange for property does not qualify as a Section 351 transfer. If the transferor receives stock and securities, (assuming other conditions are met) the exchange qualifies under Code Sec. 351, but the securities are treated as boot, regardless of the life of the securities. Also, receipt of anything else constitutes boot and may cause gain recognition. Common and preferred stock and voting and nonvoting stock are acceptable.

However, "nonqualified preferred stock" is considered boot. Nonqualified preferred stock is preferred stock that: (1) the holder has the right to require the issuer or a related party to redeem or purchase; (2) the issuer or a related party is required to redeem or purchase; (3) the issuer or a related party has the right to redeem or purchase, and, as of the issue, it is more likely than not that such right will be exercised; or

(4) the dividend rate varies in whole or in part with reference to interest rates, commodity prices, or other similar indices. There are a few exceptions to this definition (and exceptions to these exceptions), such as the right cannot be exercised for 20 years or the right only may be exercised upon the death, disability, or mental incompetence of the holder. Finally, for Code Sec. 351 purposes, stock rights and stock warrants are not considered stock. Reg. §1.351-1(a)(1)(i) and (ii).

Stock that enables the shareholder to participate in corporate growth to a significant extent avoids being classified as preferred stock for Code Section 351 purposes, and therefore qualifies as stock for nonrecognition purposes. Such stock is not treated as participating in corporate growth unless there is a real and meaningful likelihood of the shareholder participating in the earnings and growth of the corporation. Code Sec. 351(g).

EXAMPLE 14.3	Jay Smith transfers land to Hext Corporation in exchange for 100 percent of its stock and four 10-year bonds. The exchange qualifies under Code Sec. 351, but the receipt of the four bonds constitutes boot.

EXAMPLE 14.4	Gina West contributes property to Franken Inc. in a transaction that qualifies as a Code Sec. 351 transfer. In return for the property, she received common stock worth $20,000 and nonqualified preferred stock worth $15,000. The nonqualified stock is considered boot; thus, Gina has received $15,000 boot in the exchange and may be required to recognize a gain. (See ¶14,135 for the treatment of boot.)

¶14,125   CONTROL OF THE CORPORATION

For purposes of Code Sec. 351, control is defined in Code Sec. 368(c). The transferors must be in control immediately after the transfer, regardless of whether they were in control prior to the transfer. Further, the transferors must possess at least 80 percent of the total combined voting power of all classes of stock entitled to vote and at least 80 percent of the total number of shares of all other classes of stock of the corporation. With respect to the nonvoting stock, the IRS has indicated that control requires the ownership of at least 80 percent of the total number of shares of each class of outstanding nonvoting stock. Rev. Rul. 59-259, 1959-2 CB 115.

Control can apply to one person or a group of people. If more than one person transfers property, the aggregate ownership of the group is used to determine if control exists immediately after the exchange. "Persons" is defined as including individuals, trusts, estates, partnerships, associations, companies, or corporations. Reg. §1.351-1(a)(1). This Regulation also indicates that the term "immediately after the exchange" does not require simultaneous exchanges by two or more persons as long as the rights of each party have been previously defined. The execution of this prearranged plan also must proceed in an expeditious and orderly manner.

EXAMPLE 14.5	Roger Caldwell and Charles Mann transfer property to Bond Corporation in return for 60 percent and 40 percent of its stock, respectively. Although neither has control individually, together they own 100 percent of the stock and meet the control requirements.

The stock received by the transferors does not have to be in proportion to the value of the property transferred. However, if the stocks received are disproportionate to the value of properties transferred, the transaction will be closely scrutinized to determine the true nature of the transaction. If the disproportionality is suspect, the transaction may be treated as if the stock had first been received in proportion and then been used to make gifts, to pay compensation, or to satisfy liabilities among the transferors. Reg. §1.351-1(b)(1).

EXAMPLE 14.6	Mark Smith and Ralph Jones transfer property worth $150,000 and $50,000, respectively, to Best Corporation in return for 100 percent of its stock. Mark and Ralph each receive 100 shares of stock. The exchanges qualify under Code Sec. 351 because together Mark and Ralph are in control immediately after the exchange. However, the IRS may tax the transaction as if Mark had received 150 shares and then transferred 50 shares to Ralph. This subsequent transfer to Ralph might be treated as a compensation payment to Ralph, in which case Ralph would have ordinary income of $50,000. Mark would have income (loss) if the value of the stock ($50,000) is different from Mark's adjusted basis. Also, Ralph's basis in the 50 shares would be $50,000. Recasting the transaction as, in part, a gift or loan repayment also would impact income and/or basis computations.

If stock is received for property and services rendered, all of the stock received by the transferor is used in determining whether the transferors are in control immediately after the exchange. However, stock issued for property which is of relatively small value in comparison to the value of the stock already owned (or to be received for services) by the person who transferred such property will not be counted in determining whether the transaction meets the 80 percent control tests. Reg. §1.351-1(b)(1).

EXAMPLE 14.7	Bill Roe transfers property to a new corporation for 70 percent of the stock. Joe Brown receives 30 percent of the stock in the corporation for his work in organizing the corporation. Joe must recognize income upon receipt of his stock and the stock does not qualify for the 80 percent control test. Bill's transfer is a taxable event since he does not have at least 80 percent control after the transfer.

EXAMPLE 14.8	Sebastian Corporation has 100 shares of stock outstanding. Jan Kruger contributes an asset with a basis of $10,000 and a fair market value of $19,000 along with services worth $1,000 to the corporation for 400 shares of the corporation's stock. The transfer would qualify under Code Sec. 351 since, as the transferor, she has 80 percent of the stock in the corporation. Jan would have to recognize $1,000 of income from the services but would not recognize the $9,000 gain on the asset. If the property were worth only $1,000 and the services $19,000, the transfer would not qualify under Code Sec. 351.

A loss of control shortly after the transfer could cause the transaction to fail to qualify under Code Sec. 351. If the loss of control was due to the disposition of stock according to a prearranged plan, the transferors will not, in most cases, have control immediately after the exchange.

EXAMPLE 14.9	Bill Bradley and Joe Crawford each receive 50 percent of the stock of Block Corporation upon incorporation. Unknown to Bill, Joe has committed himself to sell more than 40 percent of his stock (bringing Joe's and Bill's control under 80 percent) to Max even before the transfer. Section 351 treatment will be denied to both parties.

PLANNING POINTER	Once the stock is received, the transferor may, of course, do whatever is desired with it, after a reasonable time. A highly recommended device is to set the stage for future capital gains by giving some stock, say 10 or 20 percent, to a spouse and/or children. After more than 10 years, the corporation may purchase back this stock (a redemption), resulting in capital gains to the family members upon the termination of their interest. Code Sec. 302(b)(3). Alternatively, property may be gifted so as to qualify donees as transferors.

¶14,135   RECEIPT OF BOOT

If all the requirements of Code Sec. 351 are met, the transferors recognize no gain or loss. Also, their basis in stock received is equal to the adjusted basis of property surrendered.

EXAMPLE 14.10

Larry Lewis and Lance Thompson decide to form Sands Corporation. Larry transfers $10,000 in cash and property with an adjusted basis of $25,000 and a fair market value of $90,000 in return for 100 shares of stock. Lance transfers $20,000 in cash and property with an adjusted basis of $110,000 and a fair market value of $80,000. Lance also receives 100 shares of stock. Since they own 100 percent of the stock, they are in control and the transaction qualifies under Code Sec. 351. Larry has a realized gain of $65,000 ($100,000 – $35,000) and no recognized gain. His basis in the 100 shares of Sands Corporation is $35,000 ($10,000 + $25,000). Lance has a realized loss of $30,000 ($100,000 – $130,000), of which none is recognized. His basis in the 100 shares of Sands Corporation is $130,000 ($20,000 + $110,000).

Property other than stock is considered boot. (Although, as noted earlier, nonqualified preferred stock is considered to be boot.) The receipt of limited amounts of boot does not disqualify a transfer from Code Sec. 351. However, gain must be recognized to the extent of the lesser of the realized gain or the fair market value of the boot received. Code Sec. 351(b). The character of the gain depends on the property transferred. Losses are never recognized under Code Sec. 351.

EXAMPLE 14.11

Max Murphy and Jake Jones form Small Corporation. Max transfers land with an adjusted basis of $10,000 for stock worth $15,000 and $5,000 cash. Jake transfers equipment with an adjusted basis of $25,000 for stock worth $10,000 and $7,000 cash. Max has a realized gain of $10,000, but only $5,000 is recognized. Jones has a realized loss of $8,000 and none of it is recognized.

EXAMPLE 14.12

Same as Example 14.11, except that Max's land has an adjusted basis of $16,000. Max has a realized gain of $4,000 which is fully recognized. Jake has an unrecognized $8,000 loss because Code Sec. 351 still applies to the exchange.

If more than one asset is transferred, the boot must be allocated among the assets. The IRS endorses the view that the boot is to be allocated in accordance with fair market values. Reg. §1.358-2(b). This is necessary because gain or loss must be computed on each asset. Rev. Rul. 68-55, 1968-1 CB 140. Since no losses are recognized in a Section 351 transaction, and there are assets transferred with realized losses, less gain will be recognized on the appreciated assets because boot is allocated to loss assets as well. In addition to affecting the amount of gain recognized, the allocation also impacts the character of gain (e.g., ordinary income, capital gain, Section 1231 gain) because the character depends on the asset transferred.

EXAMPLE 14.13

George Anderson transfers land and inventory to Candle Corporation in return for 100 percent of its stock. The land has a fair market value of $120,000 and an adjusted basis of $40,000. The inventory has a fair market value of $80,000 and an adjusted basis of $90,000. George receives stock worth $150,000 and $50,000 in cash. The effects of this transfer are illustrated below.

	Land	Inventory	Total
Fair market value	$120,000	$80,000	$200,000
Adjusted basis	40,000	90,000	130,000
Realized gain (loss)	$80,000	$(10,000)	$70,000
Boot allocation	$30,000	$20,000	$50,000
	(60%)	(40%)	
Recognized gain (loss)	$30,000	$None	$30,000

Thus, if the land is a capital asset to George, he would recognize a $30,000 capital gain.

¶14,141   TRANSFERS OF LIABILITIES

There are many instances when property transferred to a corporation is subject to a liability. The corporation usually assumes the liability as part of the transaction. Because transfers to controlled corporations usually involve transfers of liabilities, especially when existing businesses such as sole proprietorships or partnerships incorporate, taxing the transfer could be a deterrent to corporate formation. Code Sec. 357 provides relief in this situation by not treating the transfer of liabilities as boot if the transaction qualifies under Code Sec. 351. The assumption of a liability by the transferee corporation will not be treated as boot for gain recognition purposes and will not disqualify Code Sec. 351 treatment. Code Sec. 357(a). (As discussed later, the assumption of the liability will affect basis considerations).

EXAMPLE 14.14	Sally Flowers transfers a building with an adjusted basis of $100,000 and a fair market value of $140,000 to Inter Corporation in return for all of its stock worth $60,000. The building is subject to a mortgage of $80,000 which Inter Corporation assumes. The transaction qualifies as a Code Sec. 351 transfer. Sally has a realized gain of $40,000 ($60,000 + $80,000 – $100,000). None of the gain is recognized.

There are two exceptions to the general rule under Code Sec. 357(a). These exceptions result if the transfer of liabilities had a tax avoidance purpose or if the sum of liabilities assumed exceeds the adjusted basis of all properties transferred by the transferor.

Tax Avoidance or No Business Purpose

All liabilities transferred to the corporation will be treated as boot if the principal purpose of the liability assumption was to avoid federal income tax or if there was no bona fide business purpose for the transfer. Code Sec. 357(b). The taxpayer must overcome these appearances by the clear preponderance of the evidence.

Tax avoidance generally is not a problem. The lack of a bona fide business purpose also is not a problem if the liabilities were incurred in the normal course of business. The time between when the funds are borrowed and when the transfer to the corporation occurs is an important factor.

If funds were borrowed just prior to the transfer, it will be difficult to overcome the lack of a business purpose, especially if the proceeds were used for personal benefit. In such instances, the transferor should be prepared to provide clear evidence to verify the business purpose for the loan and its transfer.

EXAMPLE 14.15	George Small transfers land with an adjusted basis of $40,000 and a fair market value of $95,000 to Giant Corporation in return for all of its stock. The stock is worth $65,000. Two days prior to the transfer, George borrowed $30,000 against the land. The $30,000 liability was assumed by Giant Corporation as part of the exchange. George has a realized gain of $55,000 (($65,000 + $30,000) – $40,000). George has a recognized gain of $30,000 because it appears that there was no business purpose for the loan or its transfer.

Liability in Excess of Basis

If the sum of the liabilities assumed exceeds the total adjusted basis of all properties transferred, the transferor must recognize gain on the exchange to the extent of such excess. Code Sec. 357(c). Without the recognition of gain, the stock received by the transferor would have a negative basis. With the application of this provision and related basis rules, the transferor's basis in the stock is zero.

EXAMPLE 14.16	Sara Topper transfers a building with an adjusted basis of $30,000 and a fair market value of $100,000 to Sunny Corporation in return for 100 percent of its stock. The building is subject to a $50,000 mortgage which Sunny Corporation assumes. Sara must recognize a gain of $20,000 equal to the excess of the mortgage over the adjusted basis of the building.

If there is more than one transferor, gains should be recognized on a person-by-person basis.

EXAMPLE 14.17	Fred Smart transfers property with an adjusted basis of $45,000, a fair market value of $80,000, and a mortgage of $59,000 to a new corporation. Ginger Snow simultaneously invests $14,000 in cash. Fred must recognize a gain of $14,000 because the liability exceeds his basis in the asset. He is not allowed to count Ginger's investment in the total basis contribution.

PLANNING POINTER

An individual wishes to incorporate by transferring an asset to the corporation for all of the corporation's stock. The asset has a fair market value of $200,000 and a basis of $50,000. The asset has a liability attached in the amount of $80,000. This transfer would result in a $30,000 recognition of income because the liability exceeds the basis of the asset. The individual would be well advised to include other assets in the transfer with a net basis of at least $30,000 to avoid any income recognition.

If the transferor transfers more than one asset and fewer than all of them are encumbered, but liabilities exceed aggregate basis, gain is recognized on all assets. The recognized gain is to be allocated among the assets in accordance with fair market values.

EXAMPLE 14.18

Mary Meyers transfers inventory worth $20,000 with an adjusted basis of $10,000 and a building worth $100,000 with an adjusted basis of $50,000 and a mortgage of $90,000 in return for 100 percent of Sage Corporation's stock. Sage Corporation also assumes the mortgage. Mary's recognized gain is $30,000 ($90,000 – ($50,000 + $10,000)). $5,000 is recognized on the inventory ($30,000 × 20/120) and $25,000 is recognized on the building ($30,000 × 100/120). Without the transfer of inventory, Mary would have recognized a $40,000 gain on the building ($90,000 – $50,000).

Code Sec. 357(c) presents potential problems for taxpayers who incorporate their cash-basis businesses. Usually, these firms have a large amount of unrealized accounts receivables (zero basis). They also have unrealized accounts payable, which are treated as liabilities, and could create a liability in excess of basis problem. However, liabilities that would give rise to a deduction when paid (i.e., accounts payable of a cash-basis taxpayer) and amounts payable under Code Sec. 736 (i.e., payments to a retiring partner or to liquidate a deceased partner's interest) are excluded in determining the amount of liabilities assumed by the corporation. Code Sec. 357(c)(3).

EXAMPLE 14.19

Matilda Worth incorporates her sole proprietorship operated on the cash method of accounting. She transfers equipment with an adjusted basis of $10,000 and zero basis accounts receivable and accounts payable. The accounts payable have an outstanding balance of $17,000 but no basis because of the cash method of accounting. Without the relief provision, an automatic gain of $7,000 would result (liabilities in excess of basis). Under Code Sec. 357(c), Matilda will recognize no gain. The corporation succeeds to her zero basis in the accounts receivables and accounts payable. Upon payment, the corporation will deduct the accounts payable as a business expense.

PLANNING POINTER

Transfer of zero basis receivables will result in double taxation of the receivables. A tax will be imposed when the corporation collects the receivables and there will be a second tax imposed on the shareholders when dividends are paid by the corporation. It would be better not to transfer the zero base receivables to the corporation. The shareholder will then report the income upon collection, and the receivables are taxed only once.

Recourse vs. Nonrecourse Debt

Code Sec. 357(d) addresses recourse and nonrecourse liabilities. Recourse liabilities are considered to be assumed if the transferee-corporation has agreed (and is expected) to satisfy the obligation, regardless of whether the transferor-shareholder has been relieved of such liability. In general, nonrecourse liabilities also are treated as having been assumed by the corporation for property subject to the liability. However, if the nonrecourse liability is on multiple assets and some of those assets were not transferred to the corporation then the amount of liability considered assumed is reduced by the amount that the shareholder and corporation agree will be satisfied by the shareholder. This reduction is limited to the fair market value of the assets not transferred.

EXAMPLE 14.20	Jessica owns four assets (A, B, C and D). Each asset's adjusted basis and fair market value is as follows:

Asset	Adjusted Basis	Fair Market Value
A	$300,000	$500,000
B	400,000	700,000
C	600,000	900,000
D	200,000	300,000
Total	$1,500,000	$2,400,000

The assets are encumbered with a $1,000,000 nonrecourse debt. Jessica transferred assets A, B, and C to Mumper Corporation in a transaction that qualified under Code Sec. 351. Jessica and Mumper agree that she will satisfy $150,000 of the nonrecourse debt; as such, Mumper is treated as having assumed $850,000 of the nonrecourse debt. The most that Mumper will be considered as assuming is $700,000, regardless of what Jessica and it agree to because the amount assumed cannot be reduced by more than asset D's fair market value.

¶14,155   BASIS DETERMINATION

Shareholder's Basis

Code Sec. 358 provides that the shareholder's basis in stock received in a Section 351 transfer is equal to the adjusted basis of property exchanged, increased by the amount of gain recognized on the exchange, and decreased by the fair market value of boot received. Code Sec. 358. The basis of the boot received is its fair market value. Also, the assumption of a liability is considered boot for basis purposes even though it was not for gain purposes under Code Sec. 357. If more than one class of stock is received, the property basis must be allocated to the classes of stock in proportion to their fair market value.

EXAMPLE 14.21	Bob Ripon transfers land with an adjusted basis of $5,000 and a fair market value of $14,000 to Wendy Corporation in return for all its stock. Bob has a realized gain of $9,000, but no gain is recognized. Bob's basis in the stock is $5,000.

EXAMPLE 14.22	Same as Example 14.21, except that Bob also receives a $1,000 short-term note (boot). Bob has a realized gain of $9,000 and a recognized gain of $1,000 (the lesser of the realized gain or the fair market value of the boot received). Bob's basis in the stock is $5,000 ($5,000 + $1,000 – $1,000). Bob's basis in the short-term note is $1,000, its fair market value.

EXAMPLE 14.23	Jane Seaman transfers land with an adjusted basis of $7,000 and a fair market value of $5,000 to Wall Corporation. Jane receives $800 in cash and all of Wall Corporation's stock. Jane has a realized loss of $2,000, and none of the loss is recognized. Jane's basis in the stock is $6,200 ($7,000 – $800).

EXAMPLE 14.24	Harry Bold transfers land with an adjusted basis of $40,000 and a fair market value of $50,000 to Handy Corporation in return for all its stock and $12,000 in cash. Harry has a realized gain of $10,000. Even though he received $12,000 in cash, Harry's recognized gain is limited to the realized gain; thus, he has a recognized gain of $10,000. Harry's basis in the stock is $38,000 ($40,000 + $10,000 – $12,000).

EXAMPLE 14.25	Hal Lamb transfers property with a fair market value of $90,000 and an adjusted basis of $50,000 to X Corporation for all its stock. The land is subject to a $30,000 mortgage. Hal has a realized gain of $40,000 but no recognized gain. His basis in the stock is $20,000 ($50,000 – $30,000).

¶14,155

EXAMPLE 14.26	Assume the same facts as Example 14.25, except that the mortgage is $70,000. Hal's realized gain is $40,000 and his recognized gain is $20,000 (liability in excess of basis). Hal's basis in the stock is zero ($50,000 + $20,000 – $70,000).

EXAMPLE 14.27	Susan Anders transferred assets with a fair market value of $100,000 and an adjusted basis of $60,000 to a corporation in return for 100 shares of its Class A stock (100 percent) and 100 shares of its Class B stock (100 percent). The fair market value of the Class A stock was $80,000. The fair market value of the Class B stock was $20,000. Susan had a realized gain of $40,000 (($80,000 + $20,000) – $60,000) but no recognized gain. Her basis in both classes of stock was $60,000. This was allocated to the classes in accordance with their relative fair market values. Thus,

$$\text{Basis of Class A stock} = \$60,000 \times \frac{\$80,000}{(\$80,000 + \$20,000)} = \$48,000$$

$$\text{Basis of Class B stock} = \$60,000 \times \frac{\$20,000}{(\$80,000 + \$20,000)} = \$12,000$$

EXAMPLE 14.28	Assume the same facts as in Example 14.27, except that Susan received five 10-year bonds instead of Class B stock. Susan's realized gain still is $40,000. However, her recognized gain is $20,000, the lesser of the $40,000 realized gain or the fair market value of boot received ($20,000 bonds). Her basis in the bonds is $20,000 (fair market value) and her basis in the stock is $60,000 ($60,000 + $20,000 – $20,000).

Stockholder's Holding Period

The shareholder's holding period in stock received in a Section 351 transfer includes the holding period of property transferred if the assets were capital assets or Section 1231 assets (recapture potential is irrelevant). Code Sec. 1223(1). If both ordinary income property and capital or Section 1231 assets are transferred, the shareholder winds up with two holding periods in the stock since the holding period of stock issued for ordinary income property begins on the day following receipt. Tacking is permitted even if realized gains are recognized in full or in part because of the receipt of boot. The holding period for boot received begins on the next day of the transaction.

EXAMPLE 14.29	Kerry Brooks transfers a capital asset to a corporation under Code Sec. 351. Kerry held the capital asset long term before the transfer. The stock received from the transfer is considered held long term regardless of the length of time held before any sale of the stock. The holding period of the capital asset tacks on to the holding period of the stock.

Corporation's Basis

The corporation's basis in property received is equal to the transferor's adjusted basis increased by any gain recognized by the transferor. Code Sec. 362. Liabilities assumed by a corporation do not affect the basis of the assets received from shareholders in Section 351 transfers. If the liability exceeds the basis of the asset transferred, gain equal to the excess liability will be recognized by the transferor and cause the property's basis to increase.

EXAMPLE 14.30	Peter Rhone transfers property with an adjusted basis of $3,000 and a fair market value of $5,000 to Pest Corporation in a Section 351 transfer. Peter's realized gain is $2,000, of which none is recognized. His basis in the stock is $3,000. Pest Corporation's basis in the property is $3,000.

EXAMPLE 14.31	Assume the same facts as Example 14.30, except that the property is subject to a $1,000 liability which Pest Corporation assumes. Peter has a realized gain of $2,000. None of the gain is recognized. His basis in the stock is $2,000 ($3,000 – $1,000). Pest Corporation's basis in the property is $3,000.

EXAMPLE 14.32	Assume the same facts as Example 14.31, except that the property is subject to a liability of $3,500. Peter has a realized gain of $2,000 and a recognized gain of $500 (liability in excess of basis). Peter's basis in the stock is zero ($3,000 + $500 – $3,500). Pest Corporation's basis in the property is $3,500 ($3,000 + $500).

Transfers of Property with Built-In Losses

Sometimes property whose adjusted basis exceeds its fair market value is transferred to a corporation (a built-in loss at the time of transfer). The normal basis rules would give the corporation a basis in such property that is greater than its fair market value, effectively creating a built-in loss for the corporation. Code Sec 362(e) prohibits this by requiring the corporation to reduce its basis in such property. If the corporation's aggregate adjusted basis of property received exceeds the fair market value of such property then the corporation's basis in such property is limited to the property's fair market value. If more than one asset is transferred in the transaction then the corporation's basis in each asset is reduced in proportion to each property's built-in loss. However, the corporation does not have to make this basis reduction if both it and the transferor-shareholder elect to reduce the shareholder's basis in the corporation's stock (to the fair market value of the property transferred).

EXAMPLE 14.33	Jacob transfers a machine with an adjusted basis of $150,000 and a fair market value of $100,000 to Jules Corporation in return for its stock. The transfer qualified under Code Sec. 351. Under the general basis rules of Code Sec. 362, Jules Corporation's basis in the machine would be $150,000 (the shareholder's adjusted basis at the time of transfer); however, since the property's adjusted basis exceeds its fair market value, Jules's basis is limited to $100,000 (the property's fair market value). Alternatively, Jacob may take a basis in his Jules Corporation stock of $100,000 (instead of $150,000) and Jules Corporation will take a $150,000 basis in the machine if both Jules and he elect this treatment.

EXAMPLE 14.34	Kristin transferred three machines (A, B and C) to Shull Corporation in a transfer that qualified under Code Sec. 351. Each asset's adjusted basis and fair market value is as follows:

Asset	Adjusted Basis	Fair Market Value	Built-In Gain (Loss)
A	$200,000	$150,000	($50,000)
B	250,000	180,000	(70,000)
C	350,000	410,000	60,000
Total	$800,000	$740,000	($60,000)

The $60,000 built-in loss is distributed to assets A and B according to their relative built-in losses, so $25,000 ($60,000 x ($50,000/$120,000)) is allocated to A and $35,000 ($60,000 x ($70,000/$120,000)) is allocated to B. Accordingly, Shull Corporation's basis in each asset is as follows:

Asset	Basis		
A	$200,000 – $25,000	=	$175,000
B	$250,000 – $35,000	=	215,000
C	$350,000 – 0	=	350,000
Total			$740,000

Again, if Kristin and Shull Corporation elect, Shull Corporation will take a basis in each asset equal to its adjusted basis at the time of transfer ($200,000, $250,000 and $350,000 in A, B and C, respectively, if Kristin takes a $740,000 basis in the Shull Corporation's stock).

Corporation's Holding Period

The corporation tacks on the shareholder's holding period in assets transferred. The transferor may transfer ordinary income property to a corporation, in whose hands it becomes a capital asset or vice versa.

¶14,165   RECAPTURE RULES

Depreciation Recapture

In a Section 351 transfer in which no boot is received and, therefore, no gain is recognized, there is no recapture of depreciation. Code Secs. 1245(b)(3) and 1250(d)(3). The recapture potential shifts to the corporation. If gain is recognized on the exchange because boot is received, it is characterized as ordinary income to the extent of depreciation recapture. If only part of the depreciation is recaptured, the remaining portion is shifted to the corporation.

EXAMPLE 14.35   Larry Bloom purchased a truck for $40,000 and took $23,000 in depreciation prior to transferring it to Vail Corporation in a Section 351 exchange. The truck had a fair market value of $20,000 at the time of the exchange. Larry has a realized gain of $3,000 but no recognized gain ($20,000 – $17,000). His basis in the stock is $17,000. Vail Corporation's basis in the truck is $17,000. It also inherits the $23,000 recapture potential.

EXAMPLE 14.36   Assume the same facts as Example 14.35, except that in addition to receiving stock, Larry also receives $2,000 in cash. Total value received still is $20,000. Larry has a realized gain of $3,000 and a recognized gain of $2,000 as ordinary income. His basis in the stock is $17,000 ($17,000 + $2,000 – $2,000). Vail Corporation's basis in the truck is $19,000 ($17,000 + $2,000). Vail Corporation also inherits the remaining depreciation recapture potential of $21,000.

EXAMPLE 14.37   Assume the same facts as in Example 14.35 except that the fair market value of the truck is $22,000, and Larry received stock worth $15,000 and $7,000 in cash. Larry's realized gain is $5,000 ($22,000 – $17,000). Although he received $7,000 boot, his recognized gain is limited to the realized gain. Thus, Larry's recognized gain is $5,000 of ordinary income. His basis in the stock is $15,000 ($17,000 – $7,000 + $5,000). Vail Corporation's basis in the truck is $22,000 ($17,000 + $5,000), and it inherits $18,000 recapture potential.

General Business Credit Recapture

A premature disposition of business property in which the general business tax credit has been taken (i.e., Section 38 property) generally triggers recapture of the portion not earned. (See ¶9045 for a discussion of the credit.) Unlike depreciation recapture, the recapture of the general business tax credit occurs regardless of whether any gain was realized or recognized on the transaction. However, no recapture is triggered if the taxpayer changes only "the form of conducting the trade or business as Section 38 property and the taxpayer retains a substantial interest in such trade or business." Code Sec. 50(a)(1).

What constitutes a substantial interest is not defined in the Internal Revenue Code and has been a source of contention and controversy. For example, exchanging a 50 percent interest in a partnership for a 35 percent interest in a corporation probably would qualify for exemption from recapture. However, in one case the Tax Court has held that exchanging a 48 percent partnership interest for a 7.22 percent stock interest did not qualify. *J. Soares*, 50 TC 909, CCH Dec. 29,138 (1968).

If no general business tax credit recapture is triggered on the transfer, the recapture potential stays with the shareholder. Future recapture is triggered when the corporation disposes of the property or when the shareholder disposes of a substantial interest in the business.

EXAMPLE 14.38	In 2017, Bill and Joe incorporated their equally-owned partnership and each received 50 percent of the stock in the new corporation, Fecowycz Incorporated. On January 2, 2015, the partnership had purchased energy property for $50,000 (five-year property) and had claimed a general business credit of $5,000. No general business credit was recaptured upon incorporation.
	On January 3, 2018, Fecowycz Incorporated sold the energy property. The sale triggers a $2,000 recapture of the general business credit. Both Bill and Joe must recapture $1,000 of the credit in 2018.

TAX BLUNDER

Susan transferred equipment to ABC Co. in a Code Sec. 351 transfer. Susan purchased the equipment for $60,000. The adjusted basis of the equipment was $40,000 and its fair market value was $50,000. Susan had a choice; she could receive 100 shares of ABC Co. or 90 shares of ABC Co. and $5,000. She chose the stock plus cash option. Susan has a realized gain of $10,000 ($50,000-$40,000) and a recognized gain of $5,000 (boot received). Additionally, the recognized gain is all Code Sec 1245 gain (ordinary income) because of the depreciation recapture rules. Susan should have chosen the stock only option. This option would have shifted the depreciation recapture potential to ABC Co.

¶14,175   SECTION 351 TRANSFER OR TAXABLE EXCHANGE

Code Sec. 351 is a mandatory provision. Gain or loss is not recognized on a transfer which qualifies under Code Sec. 351. The corporation's basis in the property is a carryover basis equal to the shareholder's adjusted basis in the property. Also, the shareholder's basis in the stock received is equal to the adjusted basis of property transferred.

There may be times when taxpayers want recognition on the exchange. If taxpayers have property whose fair market value is less than the adjusted basis, they may want to recognize this loss. Code Sec. 351 must be avoided to accomplish this. An arm's-length sale or an exchange for short-term debt would be a transaction outside the purview of Code Sec. 351. The loss will not be recognized if the shareholder and corporation are related parties as defined in Code Sec. 267 (i.e., if the shareholder owns directly or indirectly more than 50 percent in value of the corporation's outstanding stock).

The shareholder might want to recognize gain on the transaction because this provides the corporation with a stepped-up basis (fair market value), especially if the shareholder is in a lower tax bracket than the corporation. However, under Code Sec. 1239 capital gain treatment will be denied the shareholder if the property is depreciable property in the hands of the corporation and the shareholder and corporation are related parties. Thus, the ordinary income treatment under Code Sec. 1239 will apply if the shareholder directly or indirectly owns more than 50 percent of the value of the corporation's stock.

EXAMPLE 14.39	Jim Jones, who owns 70 percent of Best Corporation, sells Section 1231 property to Best Corporation for $100,000 (the property's fair market value). The adjusted basis of the property is $60,000. Jim has a realized and recognized gain of $40,000 ($100,000 – $60,000). The gain will be a Section 1231 gain. However, if the property is depreciable property for the corporation (e.g., a building), the $40,000 gain is ordinary income.

Shareholders must determine whether a Section 351 transfer is most advantageous for them. The transaction must be structured properly so that either it falls under Code Sec. 351 or is beyond its control, depending upon which result is desired.

KEYSTONE PROBLEM

The sole proprietor of a printing shop is in the fortunate position of having greatly appreciated assets (the land and building where the business is located) as well as an exceedingly competent business manager. The manager is in fact so good that another position elsewhere has been offered. The owner persuades the manager to stay by giving 25 percent of the business. This is accomplished by incorporating the business and signing over 25 percent of the common stock to the manager. No tax advice is sought and the tax consequences are rather severe:

1. Code Sec. 351 has not been met, so the owner has "sold" the assets to the corporation. The gain will equal the value of the full 100 percent stock interest less the basis in the assets on a item-by-item basis.
2. The manager has taxable compensation in the amount of the value of the 25 percent stock interest since property received for services is taxable under Code Sec. 83. (However, an offsetting deduction is available.)

The two main requirements for incorporating tax free are that the transferors of property must be in at least 80 percent control after the transfer and that they received only stock for their property. In accordance with these two requirements, there are several alternative ways to handle this transaction so as to limit taxes or avoid them completely. Explain.

¶14,185   REPORTING REQUIREMENTS

Shareholders and corporations who are parties to a Section 351 exchange must attach statements to their income tax returns for the period in which the exchange occurred. Reg. §1.351-3(a) and (b). The shareholder's statement must include the following:

1. A description of the property transferred and its adjusted basis
2. A description of the type and number of shares of stock received, including its fair market value
3. A description of the securities received, including principal, terms, and fair market value
4. An indication of the amount of money received
5. A description of any other property received (i.e., boot), including its fair market value
6. A description of the liabilities assumed by the corporation, including when and why they were created and the business reason for the assumption

The statement of the controlled corporation must include:

1. A description of all property received from transferors
2. An indication of the transferor's adjusted basis in the property
3. An indication of the number and type of stock issued, including its fair market value
4. A description of the stock issued and outstanding prior to and immediately after the exchange
5. A description of the securities issued, including fair market value
6. A description of all securities outstanding prior to and immediately after the exchange
7. An indication of the amount of money distributed to the transferors
8. A description of any other property distributed, including its fair market value
9. A description of liabilities assumed by the corporation, including when and why they were created and the business reason for the assumption

Corporate Capital Structure

A corporation's capital structure consists of the stock and debt it issues. Capital is raised from shareholders by issuing stock. Different classes of stock (i.e., common, preferred, voting, nonvoting) can be issued. Capital is raised from nonshareholders by issuing debt, in which case a formal debtor-creditor relationship is established. Additionally, shareholders and/or nonshareholders may contribute assets to the corporation not in return for stock or debt. These contributions to capital are motivated for different reasons. For example, a city might donate land to a corporation so that it may build a factory. The city will benefit from increased employment opportunities and tax revenues. Each method of raising capital can have significant consequences to the transferor and the corporation.

¶14,201   EQUITY IN THE CAPITAL STRUCTURE

Shareholder Contributions

A corporation does not recognize a gain or loss on the receipt of money or other property in exchange for its stock. Code Sec. 1032. Also, it does not recognize income when it receives money or other property as a contribution to capital (i.e., the corporation does not issue stock, debt, money, or property in return for the contributed property). Code Sec. 118. However, the exclusion does not apply to any money or property transferred to the corporation in consideration for goods or services rendered, or to subsidies paid for the purpose of inducing the corporation to limit production.

The corporation's basis in the property depends upon the nature of the transaction. If stock is issued in return for the property and Code Sec. 351 applies to the transaction, the corporation's basis equals the transferor's adjusted basis increased by any gain recognized by said transferor. If the transaction is a taxable exchange (i.e., the corporation purchases land by issuing its stock), the corporation's basis is the fair market value of the stock.

The shareholder's basis in the stock is equal to the adjusted basis of the property transferred, increased by any recognized gain and decreased by the fair market value of boot received if it is a Section 351 transfer. The shareholder's basis in stock received in a taxable exchange is equal to the fair market value of the property transferred.

The corporation's basis of property received from a shareholder as a contribution to capital equals the shareholder's adjusted basis increased by any gain recognized by the shareholder. Code Sec. 362. Since the shareholder receives no stock, the shareholder's basis in the stock owned prior to the contribution is increased by the amount of cash and adjusted basis of the property transferred plus any gain recognized by the shareholder on the transfer. Usually shareholders do not recognize a gain or loss when they transfer property as a contribution to capital.

Similarly, amounts received from voluntary pro rata payments from shareholders are not income to the corporation even though no stock is issued. The payments represent an addition to the price paid for the shares of stock held by the shareholders. Reg. §1.118-1.

EXAMPLE 14.40	Cindy Blair, a sole shareholder in Alpha Inc., contributed land to be used by the corporation as a parking lot. She receives no additional stock in the corporation. The land has a fair market value of $100,000 and an adjusted basis of $40,000. Cindy has a $60,000 realized gain but no recognized gain. Her basis in Alpha stock is increased by $40,000. Alpha Inc. recognizes no gain or loss. The corporation's basis in the land is $40,000.

EXAMPLE 14.41	Dancing Shoes Corporation requires additional funds for conducting its business and obtains such funds through voluntary pro rata payments by its shareholders. The payments are credited to a special paid-in capital account and no additional shares are issued. The amounts received from the shareholders do not constitute income to the corporation. The payments are in the nature of assessments upon the shareholders and represent an additional price paid for the shares of stock held by the individual shareholders.

Special rules apply to the forgiveness of corporate debts by shareholders. As a general rule, when a debt is cancelled, the debtor must recognize income. However, if a shareholder in a corporation which is indebted to the shareholder gratuitously forgives the debt, the transaction amounts to a contribution to the capital of the corporation to the extent of the principal of the debt.

EXAMPLE 14.42	Mary Sullivan owns stock in Dogette Corporation and also lent the corporation $10,000. Mary gratuitously cancels the $10,000 debt. The forgiveness of the debt is a nontaxable contribution to capital. The corporation recognizes no income and Mary increases her stock basis by $10,000.

Nonshareholder Contributions

Contributions by nonshareholders also are excluded from gross income of the corporation as long as the transfer is not for goods and services. Nonshareholder contributions are usually prompted by expectation of some indirect benefit. Cities often provide corporations with land or other property as an inducement to locate in their area.

The basis to the corporation of property received from a nonshareholder is zero. Where the corporation receives a cash contribution from a nonshareholder, the corporation is required to reduce the basis of any property acquired during the next 12-month period by the amount of cash received. When all of the money has not been spent in the 12-month period, the basis of other property must be reduced by the amount not spent. Property subject to depreciation must be reduced first, then property subject to amortization, then property subject to depletion, and finally any other remaining property. The reduction of the basis of each of the properties within each category is to be made in proportion to the relative basis of such properties. Code Sec. 362(c)(1) and (2); Reg. §1.362-2.

EXAMPLE 14.43	Calumet City donates land to Wilder Corporation as an inducement for the corporation to expand operations. The land has a basis of $10,000 and a fair market value of $25,000. Wilder recognizes no income and will have a zero basis in the land.

EXAMPLE 14.44	Hamilton City donates $50,000 in cash and land with a fair market value of $75,000 to Miler Corporation as an inducement to locate there. Within the next 12 months, it purchased property for $40,000 with the donated cash. Miler Corporation has no income. Its basis in the land and property purchased for $40,000 is zero. Additionally, starting with depreciable assets, the basis of Miler's other properties must be reduced by the $10,000 not spent.

The corporation recognizes no income from nonshareholder contributions. However, since any basis in the property received or acquired is zero, the normal benefits of depreciation, amortization, or depletion are denied. Thus in the long run, the corporation recognizes income when the asset is sold.

¶14,215 DEBT IN THE CAPITAL STRUCTURE

In addition to issuing stock during corporate formation, the corporation also should issue long-term debt because debt has certain advantages over equity. Interest payments on the debt are deductible by the corporation while dividends are not deductible. Additionally, debt repayment is an acceptable reason for accumulating income and, therefore, avoiding the accumulated earnings tax under Code Sec. 531. Most redemptions of stock are not acceptable reasons. Repayment of the principal is tax free to the creditor, whereas payments made to shareholders for their stock may be considered dividends or taxable redemptions. Finally, should the debt instrument become worthless, then the loss may be an ordinary loss if the debt is business related (if nonbusiness bad debt, then it is treated as a short-term capital loss).

There are some disadvantages to debt. Interest payments are income to the debtholder. Similarly, the debtholder will have income for amounts received in excess of basis. Additionally, if the debtholder is a corporation, it is not entitled to the dividends-received deduction when it receives interest payments. Finally, the corporation issuing the debt must make timely payments of interest and principal in accordance with the terms of the debt instrument. Stock does not have this constraint; that is, dividends usually are voluntary distributions.

EXAMPLE 14.45	John Jones invests cash in Adams Corporation in return for stock and long-term debt in a Section 351 transfer. During the year, John receives a dividend of $5,000 and interest payments of $6,000. Jones has $11,000 of gross income. Adam Corporation has a $6,000 deduction for the interest payment. No deduction is allowed for the dividend payment. Assuming Adams Corporation's tax rate is 34 percent, the after-tax cost of the interest payment is $3,960 ($6,000 × (1.00 − .34)); the deduction saved it taxes of $2,040 ($6,000 × .34). The after-tax cost of the dividend was $5,000 because it was not deductible.
	However, the interest income is taxed at Jones' regular tax rate, whereas the dividend income is taxed at a reduced rate. Assuming that Jones is in the 35 percent tax bracket, the interest income is taxed at 35%, or $2,100 ($6,000 × .35) and the dividend income is taxed at 15 %, or $750 ($5,000 × .15). Thus, the debt still is preferable but the benefit of interest versus dividends is not as great as it used to be because the difference in treatment at the individual shareholder level offsets some of the benefits at the corporate level.

Because of the advantages of debt financing, there are instances when taxpayers attempt to treat equity instruments as debt. Usually these instruments are debt in legal form but in substance are equity. Using the doctrine of substance over form, the IRS will attempt to reclassify this debt as equity. Code Sec. 385 provides guidance in classifying an instrument as debt or equity. The section lists five factors that may be considered:

1. Does the instrument contain an unconditional promise to pay on demand or on a specified date a definite amount for adequate consideration and at a fixed rate of interest?
2. Is the debt preferred over or subordinated to other debts?
3. How high is the corporation's debt to equity ratio (is the corporation thinly capitalized)?
4. Is the debt convertible into stock?
5. What is the relationship between stock and debt ownership (is it proportionate)?

Also, the classification of a corporate instrument issued after October 24, 1992, as stock or debt by the corporate issuer is binding on the issuer and all holders. Code Sec. 385(c). This classification is not binding on the IRS.

On October 13, 2016, the IRS released final and temporary regulations under Section 385. The Section 385 regulations are generally applicable to tax years ending on or after January 19, 2017. The regulations treat certain related-party interests that otherwise would be treated as indebtedness as stock for federal tax purposes and set threshold documentation requirements that must be met for certain related-party interests in a corporation issued or deemed issued on or after January 1, 2018, to be treated as indebtedness.

EXAMPLE 14.46   Maurice Severs starts a new corporation with $50,000 and receives $45,000 of 12-year notes and $5,000 of stock. The full $50,000 will most likely be viewed as equity by the IRS because of the debt-to-equity ratio (9-to-1). If Maurice issued $25,000 of debt and $25,000 of equity, the arrangement would probably be respected. Thus, the corporation may deduct interest on the notes and Maurice may receive $25,000 tax free as repayment of principal.

¶14,235   SECTION 1244 STOCK

Although debt can be more advantageous than equity, certain stock issuances receive special treatment which makes them favorable. Shareholders are permitted to deduct losses on the worthlessness or sale (including redemptions and liquidations) of Section 1244 stock as ordinary. Gains on the disposition of such stock are capital gains. Thus, the shareholders receive the best of both situations, ordinary loss treatment (up to a statutory limit) if the corporation fails and capital gain treatment if the corporation is successful.

The reason for this treatment is to place shareholders of small corporations on a more nearly equal basis with sole proprietors and partners and to encourage the flow of funds into small corporations. Certain restrictions apply to ensure that the provision benefits small corporations.

Eligible Shareholders

Only individuals and partnerships are eligible for ordinary loss treatment if they were original holders of the stock. The stock loses its Section 1244 status when it is transferred. If a partnership is an original holder, the subsequent loss is passed through to those partners who were partners when the stock was issued. Reg. §1.1244(a)-1(b)(2).

Loss Limitation

Ordinary loss treatment is limited to an annual $50,000 per shareholder and $100,000 on a joint return regardless of which spouse owns the stock. If the loss is greater than these limits ($50,000 or $100,000), the excess is treated as a capital loss. Section 1244 losses are treated as attributable to the taxpayer's trade or business. As such, they have business status for net operating loss purposes. Thus, if the Section 1244 loss exceeds the shareholder's taxable income, the excess is carried over under the net operating loss provisions.

EXAMPLE 14.47   Marge Summers, a single taxpayer, has a basis of $120,000 in Section 1244 stock when it becomes worthless. She incurs a $50,000 ordinary loss and a $70,000 capital loss. If she is married by year-end, even if the loss had been sustained months earlier, a $100,000 ordinary loss and a $20,000 capital loss would result on a joint return.

Corporate Requirements

Only a domestic small business corporation can issue Section 1244 stock. The stock can be common or preferred and voting or nonvoting. The corporation must qualify as a small business at the time the stock is issued. The total dollar amount of money and property received by the corporation for its stock, as a contribution to capital and as paid-in capital, cannot exceed $1,000,000 at the time the stock is issued. The property's fair market value is not used in determining the $1,000,000 limit. Property received by the corporation is valued at its adjusted basis, reduced by any liabilities that were assumed by the corporation. Stock issued for services rendered does not qualify as Section 1244 stock.

The issuing corporation does not need to adopt a plan to issue Section 1244 stock. Determination of Section 1244 stock is made at the time of issuance. All stock issued qualifies as Section 1244 stock as long as the firm has not issued more than $1,000,000 of stock. Regulation 1.1244-(c)-2 provides special rules for determining which shares of stock are eligible for Section 1244 treatment if the firm has issued more than $1,000,000 of stock (however, this is beyond the scope of this text).

If the adjusted basis of the property transferred in return for Section 1244 stock exceeds its fair market value, the adjusted basis of such stock for the sole purpose of computing the Section 1244 loss is reduced by the amount of such excess. This treatment prevents the conversion of a capital loss on the property into an ordinary loss on the Section 1244 stock. Increases in basis through contributions to capital or otherwise are not counted for ordinary loss computation purposes. Code Sec. 1244(d)(1)(B).

EXAMPLE 14.48	Roy Ready incorporated a truck with a basis of $20,000 and a fair market value of $13,000. He subsequently contributed another $11,000 in the business before his stock became worthless. Since his basis in the stock was $31,000 ($20,000 + $11,000), his loss also is $31,000; only $13,000 is an ordinary loss under Code Sec. 1244. The remaining loss of $18,000, consisting of the paper loss at the time of incorporation plus capital contributions, is capital in nature.

PLANNING POINTER	In Example 14.48, the taxpayer could have maintained the $11,000 capital contributions as a Section 1244 deduction by purchasing stock in the corporation for $11,000 instead of contributing the $11,000 and adjusting the basis of the stockholdings. The purchase price of the stock would have been its adjusted basis for gain or loss purposes and for determining the Code Sec. 1244 loss.

The corporation must be an operating company at the time the loss is sustained. The corporation's gross receipts from sources other than dividends, interest, royalties, rents, annuities, and sales or exchanges from stock or securities must exceed 50 percent of the corporation's gross receipts for the five most recent tax years. The operating company requirement need not be satisfied if the total deductions allowed the corporation—other than the dividends-received deduction and the net operating loss deduction—exceeds the total gross income for the five-year period.

Reporting Requirements

Taxpayers must substantiate their claims of a Section 1244 loss. The taxpayer is required to maintain records sufficient to distinguish Section 1244 stock from any other stock the taxpayer may own in the corporation. The corporation also should maintain records showing all of the following:

1. The persons to whom stock was issued, the date of issuance to these persons, and a description of the amount and type of consideration received from each person.
2. The basis to the shareholder of any property received by the corporation and the fair market value of the property at the time it is received by the corporation.
3. The amount of money and the basis to the corporation of other property received for its stock as a contribution to capital and as paid-in capital.
4. Financial statements of the corporation, such as its income tax returns, that identify the sources of the gross receipts of the corporation for the period consisting of the five most recent tax years.
5. Information relating to any tax-free stock dividends made with respect to Section 1244 stock and any reorganization in which stock is transferred by the corporation in exchange for Section 1244 stock.

¶14,245   SECTION 1202 STOCK

Code Sec. 1202 is designed to aid small business capital formation. Within limits, Code Sec. 1202 enables noncorporate taxpayers to exclude 100 percent of the gain from the sale or exchange on qualified small business stock held for more than five years. The exclusion is 75 percent for investors who acquired the stock after February 17, 2009 and before September 28, 2010. The exclusion was increased to 100 percent for stock acquired after September 27, 2010. The exclusion is 50 percent for stock issued before February 18, 2009. The definition of small business stock is not the same as that used in Code Sec. 1244. Assuming all requirements are met, the stock effectively is identified as Code Sec. 1202 stock when issued.

Eligible Shareholders

Only individuals are eligible for the 50 (75/100) percent exclusion if they were the original holders of the stock and the stock was issued in exchange for money, property other than stock, or compensation for services rendered to the corporation. If a conduit entity was an original holder, the subsequent gain is passed through to those owners who were owners when the stock was issued. Conduits can be holders of Section 1202 stock. Partnerships, S corporations, regulated investment companies, and common trust funds qualify as conduits for purposes of Code Sec. 1202. The gain and share of the stock's adjusted basis pass through proportionately to the owners (e.g., partners) of the conduit. Code Sec. 1202 applies only to stock originally issued after August 10, 1993, which is held for more than five years by the taxpayer. The stock generally loses its Section 1202 status when it is transferred unless the transfer is tax free and by gift, by death, from a partnership to a partner, or a stock-for-stock transfer.

Gain Limitation

Only gain from the sale or exchange of qualified small business stock is eligible for the 50 (75/100) percent exclusion. Exclusion treatment is subject to per-issuer cumulative limitations. The amount of eligible gain is limited to the greater of:

1. $10,000,000 reduced by the aggregate of eligible gain recognized from the sale of the corporation's stock which has been taken into account by the taxpayer in prior years, or
2. 10 times the aggregate adjusted basis of qualified small business stock issued by the corporation and disposed of by the taxpayer during the taxable year. For this purpose only, the adjusted basis of the stock is not increased for additions to basis which took place after the date of original issuance.

In determining the taxpayer's eligible gain, if the stock was acquired in exchange for property (other than money or stock), then for Code Sec. 1202 purposes only, the basis of the stock shall be no less than the property's fair market value at the time of transfer. The basis adjustment for any subsequent contribution to capital also shall be no less than the property's fair market value at the time of the transfer. This prevents taxpayers from converting gain on the contributed property to Code Sec. 1202 gain eligible for the 50, 75, or 100 percent exclusion. Assuming all requirements are met, the stock effectively is identified as Code Sec. 1202 stock when issued.

EXAMPLE 14.49   On January 10, 2011, Sara Shertzer acquired stock in Snave Co. for $300,000. Snave Co. is a qualified small business for Code Sec. 1202 purposes. On December 18, 2017, Sara sold the stock for $600,000. Sara's realized gain is $300,000, and her recognized gain is $0. One-hundred percent of the $300,000 capital gain is excluded since it is within the limits of (1) $10,000,000 or (2) 10 × $300,000 = $3,000,000.

EXAMPLE 14.50   On February 20, 2011 Sam Ellsworth transferred property to Maxo Co. in return for 100 percent of its common stock. The corporation is a qualified small business for Code Sec. 1202 purposes. Sam's adjusted basis in the property was $500,000, and it had a fair market value of $2,000,000. On February 25, 2017, Sam sold one-fourth of his shares for $800,000. Sam's realized gain is $675,000 ($800,000 – ($500,000 × .25)). His recognized gain is $375,000 ($675,000 – $300,000 excludable gain). In this situation the fair market value of the property will be used to determine the excluded gain. One-fourth of $2,000,000 is $500,000, so the gain for Code Sec. 1202 purposes is $300,000 ($800,000 – $500,000). One-hundred percent of the $300,000 is the excluded gain. The $300,000 excluded gain is within the limits of (1) $10,000,000 of (2) 10 × ($2,000,000 × .25) = $5,000,000.

Corporate Requirements

Only a domestic C corporation can issue Section 1202 stock. The stock can be common or preferred and voting or nonvoting. The corporation must qualify as a small business at the time the stock is issued. The corporation's aggregate gross assets cannot exceed $50,000,000 anytime before the issuance of the stock and immediately after the issuance. Aggregate basis is equal to cash and the aggregate adjusted basis of property held. For this test only, the adjusted basis of contributed property is equal to its fair market value at the time of transfer. If aggregate gross assets subsequently exceed $50,000,000, the corporation no longer can issue Section 1202 stock; however, previously issued Section 1202 stock is not disqualified.

The corporation must be an operating company which is actively engaged in a trade or business during substantially all of the time the taxpayer held its stock. A corporation meets this requirement if at least 80 percent of its assets are used in the active conduct of one or more qualified trades or businesses as defined in Code Sec. 1202(e)(3). Most services and financing businesses would not qualify. If more than 10 percent of the total value of its assets consists of real estate not used in the active conduct of a qualified trade or business, then the corporation fails the active business test.

Code Sec. 1045 enables a taxpayer other than a corporation to roll over tax-free gains on the sale of qualified small business stock held for more than six months if the proceeds from the sale are used to purchase other qualified small business stock within 60 days of the sale. The taxpayer's basis in the newly acquired stock is reduced by the amount of capital gain not recognized. Also, the holding period of the stock sold is tacked on to the holding period of the newly acquired stock.

EXAMPLE 14.51   Justin Wells invests $300,000 in Shapot Corporation on September 1, 2015. Shapot Corporation qualifies as a small business corporation. On August 14, 2017, Justin sells his Shapot Corporation stock for $550,000. He then buys stock in Clerici Inc., also a small business corporation, for $525,000. Since Justin did not reinvest all $550,000, he must recognize a $25,000 gain.

Code Sec. 1044 Rollovers

Code Sec. 1044 allows individual and corporate (not an S corporation) taxpayers to roll over their gains on the sale of publicly traded securities into a Specialized Small Business Investment Company (SSBIC). An SSBIC is any partnership or corporation which is licensed under Section 301(d) of the Small Business Investment Act of 1958. The taxpayer must make the rollover into the SSBIC within 60 days of the sale of the publicly traded securities, and the taxpayer will only recognize his or her gains to the extent that the sale amount exceeds the cost of the SSBIC interest.

The amount of gain that can be rolled over in any one year is limited. For individuals it cannot exceed the lesser of (a) $50,000 or (b) $500,000, reduced by the amount of gain from prior years that has already been deferred due to this rollover provision. The rollover limit for C corporations is the lesser of (a) $250,000 or (b) $1,000,000, reduced by the amount of gain from prior years that has already been deferred due to this rollover provision. The deferred gain is a basis adjustment (reduction) to the newly acquired SSBIC interest.

Stock or Debt

Whether stock or debt is preferable depends on many considerations. Individual shareholders are entitled to the benefits of Code Secs. 1202 and 1244, which make stock advantageous to them. Corporate shareholders are not entitled to the benefits of Code Secs. 1244 and 1202, but they are entitled to the dividends-received deduction (discussed at ¶14,385), which also makes stock advantageous to them.

A major advantage of debt to the issuing corporation is that the corporation is entitled to a deduction for interest payments but not for dividend payments. The recipient shareholder has gross income regardless of whether it is interest or dividends (except for corporate shareholders entitled to the dividends-received deduction), although dividends are taxed at a reduced rate for individual shareholders. A disadvantage of debt is that a loss upon its sale or worthlessness usually results in a nonbusiness bad debt (which is treated as a short-term capital loss by individuals) or a capital loss. Corporate shareholders might be able to claim a business bad debt deduction.

Thus, whether stock or debt is preferred depends in part on the type of shareholders, the marginal tax rates of the shareholders and the corporation, and the possibility of a Section 531 tax imposition (discussed in Chapter 18). Nontax factors also are important.

PLANNING POINTER

Toni Travels invested $50,000 cash in a wholly-owned corporation. Since she was aware of the advantages of debt in the capital structure, she received $25,000 in stock and $25,000 in debt. A few years later, the corporation became worthless. Only the $25,000 basis in the stock is eligible for ordinary loss treatment under Code Sec. 1244. The worthless debt is deductible only as a capital loss. Toni may have been better advised to have taken only stock in the original transfer to the corporation.

TAX BLUNDER

Sally Rogers owns 100 shares of Dino Co. She acquired the shares on December 20, 2012, for $100,000. Dino Co. qualifies as a small business corporation for Code Sec. 1202 purposes. Sally believed she would have a very large estimated tax payment due on January 15, 2017, so she sold the shares on January 2, 2017, for $250,000. Sally's estimated tax payment was much less than she expected. Sally was uncertain of (and somewhat indifferent about) what to do with the proceeds from the sale of the Dino Co. shares, so she put the proceeds into a three-month certificate of deposit. The result of these events is that Sally must recognize the $150,000 fully in 2017. Sally did not hold the stock for more than five years, so the sale does not qualify for the 100 percent exclusion. However, she still could have deferred gain recognition by reinvesting in shares of a small business corporation. Had she not been indifferent regarding her investment choice, she might have made a much better decision.

Determination of Corporate Taxable Income

¶14,301

GENERAL RULES

There are many similarities between the rules used to determine taxable income for corporations and those used for individuals. Gross income is determined in the same manner for corporations and individuals. That is, Code Sec. 61, which defines gross income, applies to both types of taxpayers, although some deductions, such as alimony, apply only to individuals. Corporations also are entitled to exclusions from gross income. Thus, corporations can exclude interest income on municipal bonds. However, most of the statutory exclusions in Code Secs. 101 to 139 pertain to individuals only.

All corporate deductions are business deductions. Ordinary and necessary expenses incurred to carry on a trade or business are deductible. Code Sec. 162. These are similar to some of the *for adjusted gross income deductions* (*for AGI*) allowed to individuals. However, some of the *for AGI* deductions, such as alimony payments and contributions to IRAs, apply only to individuals. Corporations do not have *from adjusted gross income deductions (from AGI)*. They are not entitled to deductions for personal expenses. Also, they do not have itemized deductions, a standard deduction, or deductions for personal exemptions. However, there are some deductions that apply to corporations only, such as the dividends-received deduction under Code Sec. 243.

Because corporations do not have itemized deductions, the limitations and reductions used to compute deductions are different. For example, corporations do not reduce a casualty loss by $100 or a net casualty loss by 10 percent of adjusted gross income. Interest expense is not classified as personal interest under Code Sec. 163 if incurred by corporations and, therefore, is fully deductible.

Property transactions are taxed similarly. The determination of realized gain or loss and the classification of this gain or loss as capital, ordinary, or Code Sec. 1231 is similar. Both corporations and individuals are subject to depreciation recapture rules under Code Secs. 1245 and 1250. The deferral provisions for like-kind exchanges under Code Sec. 1031 and involuntary conversions under Code Sec. 1033 apply to corporations and individuals.

¶14,305

ACCOUNTING PERIODS

One of the elections a new corporation must make is its choice of an accounting period. In general, corporations have the same choices as do individuals. They may choose a calendar year or a fiscal year. However, a corporation has more flexibility in choosing its accounting period. It may choose any calendar or fiscal tax year regardless of the tax years of its owners. This ability to have a tax year different from that of its owners can produce tax savings, especially in the year of incorporation.

Other entities do not have this freedom. For example, S corporations are required to adopt the calendar year unless they can establish a business purpose for a fiscal year. Deferral of income to shareholders is not a business purpose. Code Sec. 1378(b). Partnerships must have the same tax year as their partners who have a majority interest. If there is no majority interest, the partnership uses the tax year of all its principal partners. If there are no principal partners, the least aggregate deferral method must be used unless the partnership can establish a business purpose for using a fiscal year. Code Sec. 706(b).

Personal service corporations are corporations whose primary activity is the performance of personal services. These services are primarily performed by employee-owners. Personal-service corporations must use a calendar year for their tax year unless they can establish a business purpose for a fiscal year. Code Sec. 441(i).

¶14,311 ACCOUNTING METHODS

The corporation must select an accounting method in its initial tax year. Generally, the cash basis, accrual basis, or a hybrid basis which contains elements of the cash and accrual methods may be elected. Most corporations, however, must use the accrual method. However, this constraint does not apply to S corporations, qualified farming businesses, qualified personal service corporations, and corporations with average annual receipts of $5 million or less for the three prior tax years.

A corporation that meets the exception above (e.g., an S corporation) may use any of the three methods. However, corporations that maintain inventory for sale to customers are required to use the accrual method of accounting for determining sales and cost of goods sold.

¶14,315 CAPITAL GAINS AND LOSSES

The process used to determine a corporation's capital gains and losses is similar to that used by individuals. Gains and losses resulting from the taxable sale or exchange of capital assets must be reclassified as short-term or long-term. Next, the net short-term and the net long-term positions must be computed. If the short-term gains exceed the short-term losses, a net short-term gain results. If the short-term losses exceed the short-term gains, a net short-term loss results. Long-term gains and losses are netted in similar manner to determine the net long-term gain or loss.

The next step is to determine the corporation's overall capital asset position. This is dependent upon the two net positions. If they are opposite (i.e., a net loss and a net gain), then they are combined. If they are similar (i.e., both net gains or net losses), then they are kept separate. Thus, there are six possible combinations:

1. Net long-term capital gain greater than net short-term capital loss. These are combined to produce a net capital gain.
2. Net long-term capital gain less than net short-term capital loss. These are combined to produce a net capital loss.
3. Net short-term capital gain greater than net long-term capital loss. These are combined to produce capital gain net income.
4. Net short-term capital gain less than net long-term capital loss. These are combined to produce a net capital loss.
5. Net long-term capital gain and net short-term capital gain. These are not combined. The net long-term capital gain is treated as a net capital gain, and the net short-term capital gain is treated as capital gain net income.
6. Net long-term capital loss and net short-term capital loss. These are not combined.

The taxation of corporate capital gains and losses depends on the net position (i.e., combinations one to six above).

Net Capital Gain

Corporations do not receive preferential treatment of net long-term capital gains. Net capital gains (combinations 1, 3, and 5, above) must be included in the corporation's gross income and are taxed at the same rate as ordinary income, a flat 35 percent in the case of many corporations.

EXAMPLE 14.52	Hands Corporation has gross receipts from sales of $230,000, deductible expenses of $75,000, and a net capital gain of $48,000. Hands' gross income is $278,000 ($230,000 + $48,000). Its taxable income is $203,000 ($278,000 – $75,000). Its tax liability will be computed on the $203,000; the $48,000 net capital gain does not receive preferential treatment.

Net Capital Losses

Unlike individuals, corporations may not take a deduction for net capital losses in the year in which they occur. The net capital loss can never be used to reduce ordinary income. Corporate taxpayers may claim capital losses only against capital gains.

Net capital losses (combinations 2, 4, and 6, above) of a corporation are carried back to the three preceding tax years to offset net capital gains claimed in those years. If some net capital loss remains, it is carried forward for a period of five tax years. The carryovers must be taken back to the third, second, and first preceding tax years in that order, and any remaining losses carried forward to the five succeeding tax years in order. Unused losses at the end of the five-year carryforward period are lost forever. Also, all net capital losses carried back or forward become short-term capital losses regardless of their original status.

EXAMPLE 14.53	Civic Corporation incurred a net long-term capital loss of $15,000 in 2017. It also had gross receipts from sales of $120,000 and deductible expenses of $70,000 in 2017. Civic's gross income is $120,000, and its taxable income is $50,000 ($120,000 – $70,000). The $15,000 net capital loss does not affect taxable income in 2017. Civic Corporation carries the loss back to 2014, 2015, and 2016, in that order, to offset any net capital gains of those years. If the loss is not exhausted, the remainder is carried, in order, forward to 2018, 2019, 2020, 2021, and 2022. The $15,000 is treated as a short-term capital loss in any of the carryback or carryforward years.

EXAMPLE 14.54	Assume the same facts as in Example 14.53, except that Civic Corporation had a net short-term capital gain of $7,000 in 2014, a net short-term capital gain of $2,000 and a net long-term capital gain of $3,000 in 2015, and no capital gains or losses in 2016. The $15,000 net capital loss incurred in 2017 first is carried back to 2014 and offsets the $7,000 net short-term capital gain. Civic will receive a refund of taxes paid on that gain. The remaining $8,000 loss ($15,000 – $7,000) is carried to 2015 where it offsets the $2,000 net short-term capital gain and then the $3,000 net long-term capital gain. Civic will receive a refund of taxes paid on both gains. The remaining loss of $3,000 ($8,000 – ($2,000 + $3,000)) is carried to 2016. Since there were no net capital gains in that year, the $3,000 loss will be carried to 2018.

¶14,325   DEPRECIATION RECAPTURE

Corporations generally compute the ordinary income recapture on Section 1245 and Section 1250 assets in the same manner as individuals. Section 1245 assets are generally subject to ordinary income recapture to the extent of the full depreciation taken on the asset. Section 1250 assets acquired before 1981 are generally subject to ordinary income recapture to the extent of the cumulative excess of the depreciation taken over the amount allowed using straight-line depreciation. Nonresidential real property placed in service in years 1981 through 1986 is subject to depreciation recapture to the extent of the full depreciation taken if an accelerated depreciation method was used. Residential real estate continues to use the pre-1981 recapture rules. Post-1986 acquisitions of buildings are depreciated on a straight-line basis.

However, corporations have special recapture rules under Code Sec. 291. Application of these rules may result in a greater amount of ordinary income than the Section 1250 recapture rules for other business organizations. Code Sec. 291 requires that 20 percent of the excess of any amount that would be treated as ordinary income under Code Sec. 1245 over the amount treated as ordinary income under Code Sec. 1250 is additional depreciation recapture, and thus, ordinary income. Similar rules apply to amortization of pollution control facilities and intangible drilling costs incurred by corporate taxpayers. The computation of Section 291 gain is shown below.

Amount that would have been ordinary income if Section 1245 property	$XXX
Less: Amount of ordinary income under Section 1250	(XX)
Excess of Section 1245 gain over Section 1250 gain	$XXX
Section 291 applicable percentage	× 20%
Section 291 gain (ordinary income)	$XXX

If the gain recognized on the transaction exceeds the ordinary income recognized under Code Sec. 1245, 1250, or 291, then such excess is a Section 1231 gain. The effect of Section 291 is to reduce the amount of capital gain available to offset capital losses.

EXAMPLE 14.55	Computer Services Corporation acquired an office building for $1,170,000. The building was depreciated under the straight-line method. The building was sold nine years later for $960,000. Depreciation taken on the building up to the time of sale was $270,000 ($30,000 per year for nine years). The adjusted basis at the time of sale was $900,000 ($1,170,000 – $270,000). Computer Services Corporation has a $60,000 gain on the sale (amount realized of $960,000 less adjusted basis of $900,000). Since straight-line depreciation was used, there is no depreciation recapture under Code Sec. 1245 or 1250. However, ordinary income of $12,000 recognized under Code Sec. 291 is computed as follows:

Ordinary income if Section 1245 gain	$60,000
Less: Ordinary income under Section 1250	0
Excess Section 1245 gain	$60,000
Section 291 percentage	× 20%
Section 291 gain (ordinary income)	$12,000

The remaining $48,000 gain ($60,000 – $12,000) is Section 1231 gain.

¶14,335   NET OPERATING LOSS

A corporation is allowed to carry its net operating loss (NOL) back two years and forward 20 years. An election may be made to forego the carryback and to carry the NOL forward only. The election must be made by the due date (including extensions) of the tax return for the year in which the NOL occurred. Code Sec. 172(b). However, any unused NOL at the end of the carryforward period is lost forever. Thus, the carryover rules for NOLs are the same for corporations and individuals.

The election to not carry the loss back to the two preceding years may be advantageous if the prior years' taxable incomes were in a lower tax bracket than the tax rate expected in the future. Also, the corporation would not want to carry back a NOL to a tax year in which the corporation had utilized a credit that is due to expire or that has expired.

EXAMPLE 14.56	NIFCO incurs a net operating loss of $20,000 in 2017. Normally, the corporation would carry the loss back to 2015. However, during 2015 the corporation had only $25,000 of taxable income. The corporation incurred a tax liability of $3,750 ($25,000 × 15%). It is expected that the corporation will be in the 34 percent tax bracket in the future. By carrying back the $20,000 loss to 2015, the corporation will receive a refund of $3,000 ($20,000 × 15%). By carrying the loss forward, the corporation expects to receive a tax benefit of $6,800 ($20,000 × 34%).

Unlike individuals, corporations are not required to make adjustments to the NOL for capital gains and losses, nonbusiness expenses, or personal exemptions since they are not allowed deductions for these items in the computation of taxable income. Also, corporations are permitted the full dividends-received deduction (see ¶14,385) in computing their NOLs. Similar to individuals, NOL deductions for each year are considered separately. Thus, NOL carryovers from other years are omitted in computing the NOL for the present year, as is the domestic production activities deduction.

EXAMPLE 14.57

In 2017, Mighty Corporation has $200,000 of gross income from operations and operating deductions of $300,000. The corporation also received $50,000 in dividends from a 30-percent owned domestic corporation. The corporation has a net operating loss for the year of $90,000, computed as follows:

Gross Income		
Operations	$200,000	
Dividends	50,000	
Total Gross Income		$250,000
Deductions		
Operations	$300,000	
Dividends-received deduction ($50,000 × 80%)	40,000	
Total Deductions		340,000
Net Operating Loss		$90,000

Mighty Corporation may carry the $90,000 NOL back to 2015, and then 2016 if still not used, or may elect not to carry back and instead carry the NOL forward.

EXAMPLE 14.58

Assume the same facts as in Example 14.57. In addition, Mighty Corporation had taxable income of $40,000 in 2015. Mighty could carry back the $90,000 NOL to offset 2015 taxable income. It would receive a refund of taxes paid in 2015. The 2015 taxable income would use $40,000 of the NOL, leaving $50,000 to be carried to 2016.

The ability of corporations to carry back NOLs to claim a refund is restricted if the NOL is due to interest expense arising from debt used in corporate equity reduction transactions (CERTs). Code Sec. 172(b)(1)(D). A CERT is a transaction where either (1) the corporation acquires at least 50 percent (by value or vote) of the stock of another corporation—a major acquisition—or (2) the corporation makes an excess distribution. An excess distribution occurs if a corporation's total distributions and redemptions exceed the lesser of (1) 150 percent of the corporation's average annual distributions or redemptions for the preceding three years or (2) 10 percent of the fair market value of the stock at the beginning of the tax year.

The amount disallowed as a carryback is equal to the excess of the NOL for the tax year over the NOL reduced by the interest deductions incurred in a CERT. Code Sec. 172(b). The amount disallowed as a carryback is not lost forever; it is carried forward. However, to the extent that this carryover creates or adds to an NOL in the carryforward years, restrictions are placed on the corporation's ability to carry back those NOLs.

EXAMPLE 14.59

Worldwide Corporation had an $8,000,000 NOL for the year. Included in the NOL were interest deductions of $5,000,000 on debt used in a CERT. The NOL without this deduction would have been $3,000,000. Worldwide can carry back only $3,000,000 of the NOL.

¶14,345   CHARITABLE CONTRIBUTIONS

The deductibility of charitable contributions is dependent upon (1) what type of property is donated, (2) when the property is donated, and (3) to whom the property is donated, as well as the corporation's adjusted taxable income. In order to receive a deduction, the property must be donated to a qualified charitable organization. Code Sec. 170(c). A deduction is allowed only in the year of transfer or payment (i.e., when the contribution occurs). However, an accrual-basis corporation may claim a deduction in the year preceding payment if its board of directors authorized a charitable contribution during the year and payment of the contribution is made by the 15th day of the third month of the next tax year. Code Sec. 170(a).

| EXAMPLE 14.60 | The board of directors of Willis Corporation authorized a $3,000 cash donation to a qualified charitable organization on December 13, 2017. The payment was not made until February 25, 2018. Willis Corporation is a calendar-year corporation. If the corporation is on the accrual method of accounting, the charitable deduction will be allowed for 2017. Under the cash method, the deduction would not be allowed until 2018, the year paid. |

The amount deductible is dependent upon the type of property contributed and the corporation's adjusted taxable income. Property type determines the initial dollar measure of the contribution. The overall deduction for contributions by a corporation is limited to 10 percent of adjusted taxable income (as described below).

Ten Percent Limitation

The maximum amount deductible by a corporation for charitable contributions is 10 percent of its adjusted taxable income. Thus, the deduction is limited to the lesser of 10 percent of adjusted taxable income or the sum of the initial measures of all property donated during the tax year. Adjusted taxable income is equal to taxable income without regard to the charitable contribution deduction, the dividends-received deduction, any net operating loss carryback, any capital loss carryback, and the domestic production activities deduction. Code Sec. 170(b)(2). If the charitable contributions for the tax year exceed the 10 percent limitation, the excess can be carried forward for five years. Carryovers are used on a first-in, first-out basis after first deducting the current year's contributions. Code Sec. 170(b) and (d).

| EXAMPLE 14.61 | Block Inc. reports the following items: |

Gross income from sales	$310,000
Deductible expenses	220,000
Domestic dividends received (10 percent owned)	15,000
Net operating loss carryover	20,000
Charitable contributions	11,000

Taxable income is computed as follows:

Gross income from sales		$310,000
Domestic dividends		15,000
Gross income		$325,000
Deductible expenses	$220,000	
Net operating loss carryover	20,000	
Charitable contributions	8,500	
Dividends-received deduction	10,500	259,000
Taxable income		$66,000

For charitable contribution purposes, adjusted taxable income equals $85,000; i.e., taxable income before the charitable contribution deduction and the dividends-received deduction ($325,000 – ($220,000 + $20,000). (No adjustment is made for the NOL carryover. An adjustment would have been made if it were a carryback.) Thus, the charitable contribution deduction is limited to $8,500 ($85,000 × 10 percent). The remaining $2,500 ($11,000 – $8,500) is carried forward to the following tax year.

For dividends-received deduction purposes, adjusted taxable income equals $96,500; i.e., taxable income before the dividends-received deduction and the NOL deduction ($325,000 – ($220,000 + $8,500). Thus, the dividends-received deduction is equal to 70% times the lesser of $15,000 or $96,500.

| PLANNING POINTER | A number of corporations have set up their own private foundations so as to make contributions of up to 10 percent in good years. |

Initial Measure of Contribution

The initial dollar measure of the contribution depends upon the property contributed to the charity. The initial measure of cash contributions is the amount of cash contributed. The initial measure of property contributions is their fair market value. However, under certain conditions fair market value is not allowed. Additionally, in order to receive a deduction for noncash contributions, the corporation must meet the qualified appraisal and documentation rules of Code Sec. 170(f)(11). These rules require special substantiation of deductions for contributions of more than $500, $5,000 and $500,000 (the requirements are greater as the amount increases).

Long-Term Capital Gain Property

If the corporation contributes property whose sale would have resulted in a long-term capital gain, the initial measure of the contribution is its fair market value (i.e., the appreciation also is deductible). However, if the property is tangible personal property not related to the charity's tax-exempt purpose (e.g., donating a painting to a hospital), the appreciated property is donated to certain private nonoperating foundations (as defined in Code Sec. 509(a)), or the property is any patent, copyright, trademark, trade name, trade secret, know-how, software (with some exceptions), or similar property, or applications or registrations of such property then the initial measure is fair market value minus the amount of long-term capital gain that would have been recognized if the property had been sold. Code Sec. 170(e)(1).

EXAMPLE 14.62   Blake Corporation donates a painting that it bought several years ago for $30,000 to Orleans City Museum. At the time of the contribution the painting had a fair market value of $75,000. The initial measure of the contribution is $75,000.

EXAMPLE 14.63   Assume the same facts as in Example 14.62, except that Blake Corporation donates the painting to Orleans City Hospital. The initial measure of the contribution is $30,000 ($75,000 fair market value less the $45,000 long-term capital gain that would have been recognized if Blake Corporation had sold the painting).

Section 1231 property would be considered as long-term capital gain property unless it has depreciation recapture potential under Code Secs. 1245, 1250, and 291. To the extent of the recapture potential it is considered ordinary income property.

Corporations also are permitted an additional deduction equal to a percentage of the qualified donee income received or accrued by a charity on the corporation's contribution of any patent, copyright, trademark, trade name, trade secret, know-how, software (with some exceptions), or similar property, or applications or registrations of such property. The amount of any additional charitable contribution deduction is based on a sliding scale and equals 100 percent in the first and second years following the date of the contribution, 90 percent in the third year and reduced by 10 percent each year such that it is 10 percent in the eleventh and twelfth years following the date of the contribution. This additional charitable deduction is allowed only to the extent that that aggregate of the amounts that are calculated with these percentages exceed the amount of the deduction claimed on the contribution of the patent or other qualified intellectual property. Code Sec. 170(m)(4).

EXAMPLE 14.64   On March 10, 2017, Hines Company contributed a patent to a qualified charity. The patent's fair market value was $1,000,000 and its adjusted basis was $100,000. Hines Company obtained all the required documentation to substantiate the deduction. The charity did not receive any income from the patent in 2017, but in 2018, it received $150,000. Hines Company is entitled to a $100,000 charitable contribution deduction in 2017. In 2018, it is entitled to a $50,000 charitable contribution deduction computed as follows: 100% x $150,000 = $150,000 but the aggregate amount under the percentages only exceeds the claimed amount of the deduction ($100,000) by $50,000, thus the qualified donee income deduction is limited to $50,000.

Ordinary Income Property

Ordinary income property is property that, if sold, would produce ordinary income to the seller. Examples of such property are inventories, short-term capital assets, and property subject to recapture under Code

Sec. 1245, 1250, or 291. The initial measure of these contributions is equal to the fair market value reduced by any ordinary income that would have been recognized if the property had been sold. Usually this is equal to the lesser of the property's fair market value or adjusted basis. If the property is tangible personal property not related to the charity's tax-exempt function, then the initial measure of the contribution is fair market value minus the gain that would have been recognized if the property were sold.

EXAMPLE 14.65	Best Co. donated inventory to a public charity. At the time of donation, the inventory had a basis of $10,000 and a fair market value of $12,000. The initial measure of the contribution is $10,000 ($12,000 – $2,000).

EXAMPLE 14.66	Assume the same facts as in Example 14.65, except that the inventory's fair market value is $8,000. In this case, the initial measure of the contribution is $8,000.

EXAMPLE 14.67	Sandy Corporation donated an automobile to a public charity. The charity will use the automobile in its operations. The automobile was acquired for $10,000. At the time of donation the automobile had a fair market value of $12,000 and an adjusted basis of $4,000. The initial measure of the contribution is $6,000 ($12,000 – $6,000 ordinary income recognized if property sold).

EXAMPLE 14.68	Assume the same facts as in Example 14.67, except that the automobile will not be used by the charity. In this case, the initial measure of the contribution is $4,000 ($12,000 – $8,000 gain recognized if property sold).

Inventory

Corporations contributing qualified inventory property to public charities can deduct the adjusted basis of the property plus one-half of the appreciation, not to exceed twice the amount of the adjusted basis. Code Sec. 170(e)(3) and (4). Qualified inventory must have use related to the function or purpose of the charitable organization. The inventory must be used for the care of the ill, the needy, or infants. The charitable organization cannot receive any money, property, or services for the transfer or the use of the qualified inventory.

EXAMPLE 14.69	Block Inc. donated inventory to a charity. The fair market value of the inventory was $15,000 and its adjusted basis was $4,000. The initial measure of the contribution is $4,000 ($15,000 fair market value minus $11,000 ordinary income recognized if it had been sold).

EXAMPLE 14.70	Assume the same facts as Example 14.69, except that the property donated was qualified inventory to be used for the ill, the needy, or infants. In this case, the initial measure of the contribution is $8,000 ($4,000 + one-half of the appreciation (1/2 of $11,000) = $9,500, but this is limited to twice the adjusted basis (2 × $4,000)).

If the inventory contributed is "apparently wholesome" food, the fair market value is the amount for which the quantity of property contributed would have been sold by the donor at the time of the contribution. The fair market value of food that cannot or will not be sold solely by reason of the taxpayer's internal standards, lack of market, or similar circumstances is determined without regard to the internal standards, lack of market, or other circumstances. The same valuation rules apply if the taxpayer produces the food exclusively for purposes of transferring it to a public charity; the fact that the item was produced for transfer is disregarded.

Contributions of food inventory is subject to a limitation of 15 percent of adjusted taxable income. Also, the general 10 percent limitation applicable to other contributions is reduced by the amount of these contributions.

| EXAMPLE 14.71 | HRB Inc. has adjusted taxable income of $300,000 and contributes bread to a homeless shelter during the year. It also contributes $6,000 cash to a school in the neighborhood where its bakery is located. The bread would otherwise have been sold for $40,000 and has a basis of $30,000. The initial measure of the contribution of bread is $35,000 ($30,000 + one-half of the appreciation (1/2 of $10,000)). Since this amount is less than 15 percent of adjusted taxable income, it is fully deductible. However, HBR's general 10 percent of adjusted taxable income limit on its charitable deduction is reduced to zero, so that HBR may not deduct its $6,000 contribution of cash to the school. |

TAX BLUNDER

X Company made a contribution of ordinary income property to a qualified charity. The adjusted basis of the property was $70,000, and its fair market value was $30,000. X Company received a charitable deduction of $30,000 (its fair market value, reduced by any gain recognized had it been sold). X Company should not have given this property to the charity. It never will recognize the $40,000 loss on the property. X Company would have been better off to have sold the property, recognize the $40,000 loss, and then make a $30,000 cash contribution to the charity. Under this scenario, X Company still would have had a $30,000 charitable contribution, and it also would have had a $40,000 recognized ordinary loss.

¶14,355   RELATED TAXPAYERS—LOSSES AND EXPENSES

A special rule applicable to related taxpayers may cause (1) the disallowance of deductions for losses on sales or exchange, directly or indirectly, of property between related taxpayers, and (2) the deferral of deductions for accrued business and interest expenses of the taxpayer which remain unpaid at the end of the taxpayer's tax year and which are payable to a related cash-basis taxpayer. Code Sec. 267. Related taxpayers are viewed as consisting of a single economic unit. Thus, related parties are unable to artificially recognize losses and create deductions for tax purposes where no losses or deductions have been sustained within the economic unit.

In addition to certain family members, related persons include: (1) a corporation and an individual with direct and/or indirect ownership of more than 50 percent, (2) two corporations if the same persons own more than 50 percent in value of the outstanding stock in each corporation, and (3) a fiduciary of a trust and a corporation if the trust or grantor owns more than 50 percent of the stock. The constructive ownership rules apply in determining ownership. Code Sec. 267(b).

The loss disallowance rules apply to any sale at a loss even if no tax avoidance motive exists and the selling price is at fair market value. The disallowance of any loss is permanent for the seller. The buyer's initial basis in the property is the purchase price (fair market value). However, the buyer is permitted to reduce any gain recognized on a subsequent sale by the amount of the previously disallowed loss.

| EXAMPLE 14.72 | A corporation sells an asset to Barry Winslow, its sole shareholder, at its fair market value of $10,000. The corporation has an adjusted basis in the asset of $12,000. The corporation will not be allowed a deduction for its $2,000 loss incurred on the sale. Barry sells the asset several years later for $15,000. Barry has a realized gain of $5,000 ($15,000 − $10,000); however, his recognized gain is $3,000 ($5,000 realized gain − $2,000 loss previously unrecognized by the corporation). |

Expenses commonly disallowed under the related taxpayer rule are interest and compensation payable by an accrual-basis corporation to its cash-basis shareholders. Persons who are related are required to use the same accounting method with respect to transactions between themselves in order to prevent a deduction without the corresponding inclusion in income. The accrual-basis taxpayer is allowed the deduction for expenses incurred to cash-basis taxpayers when the payment is made.

| EXAMPLE 14.73 | Nation Corporation, using the accrual method of accounting, incurs a $2,000 salary expense due to its cash-basis sole shareholder at the end of 2017. The amount is paid on January 15, 2018. The corporation will not be allowed a deduction for the salary expense until 2018, when the salary is paid. |

¶14,365 ORGANIZATIONAL EXPENDITURES

Expenditures related to the organization process are incurred when a corporation is formed. Some of these expenditures benefit the corporation over its entire corporate life and are capitalized as organizational expenditures. Organizational expenditures are an intangible asset which have an indefinite life.

Generally, assets with indefinite lives may not be amortized for federal income tax purposes. However, the corporation may elect to expense organizational expenses in the year it begins business. The deduction is limited to the lesser of: (1) the actual organizational expenses or (2) $5,000. The $5,000 is reduced dollar-for-dollar by the amount that total organizational expenses exceed $50,000 (thus, at $55,000 there would be no deduction). The remaining organizational expenses may be amortized in a 180-month period beginning with the month the corporation begins business. Code Sec. 248(a). Only those expenditures incurred before the end of the tax year in which the corporation begins business are eligible for amortization. The corporation is deemed to have made an election for the taxable year in which it begins business. It can forego the election by capitalizing the organizational expenses on the tax return for its first taxable year. Organizational expenses that are capitalized are deductible upon corporate dissolution. If the election is made and the business is dissolved prior to the end of amortization period, then the remaining organizational expenditures are deductible in the year of dissolution.

Organizational expenditures are any expenditures which are (1) incident to the creation of the corporation, (2) chargeable to a capital account, and (3) of a character that if expended incident to the creation of a corporation having a limited life would be amortizable over such life. Typical organizational expenditures include legal and accounting fees, incorporation fees, and organizational meetings expenses. Note that expenses in connection with underwriting securities (e.g., commissions, printing costs, etc.) are not eligible. Expenses of transferring assets to the corporation also are not organizational expenditures. Reg. §1.248-1(a) and (b).

EXAMPLE 14.74

Petit Corporation begins business on August 1, 2017, and adopts the calendar year. Petit incurs the following expenses in 2017:

Expenses of organization meetings	$6,000
Fee paid for incorporation	3,200
Legal services in setting up corporation	3,000
Expenses of printing and sale of stock certificates	2,500
Accounting fees for monthly statements	2,000

Petit uses the cash method of accounting and paid all expenses in February 2018. Petit's total organizational costs are $12,200 ($6,000 + $3,200 + $3,000). The expenses of printing and sale of stock certificates and the accounting fees do not qualify as organizational expenditures. If Petit does not elect out of the deemed election then its first year deduction equals $5,200 ($5,000 + $200 ($7,200/180 = $40/month x 5 months = $200)).

¶14,375 START-UP EXPENDITURES

Start-up expenditures are different from organizational expenditures. Start-up expenditures are business expenses paid or incurred in connection with investigating the creation or acquisition of an active trade or business, creating an active trade or business, or conducting an activity engaged in for profit and for the production of income before the time in which the active trade or business begins. Code Sec. 195(c). Start-up expenditures must be capitalized. However, the corporation may elect to expense start-up expenses in the year it begins business. The deduction is limited to the lesser of: (1) the actual start-up expenses or (2) $5,000. The $5,000 is reduced dollar-for-dollar by the amount that total start-up expenses exceed $50,000 (thus, at $55,000 there would be no deduction). The remaining start-up expenses may be amortized a 180-month period beginning with the month the corporation begins business. Code Sec. 195(b). If the business is disposed of prior to the end of the amortization period, then any remaining start-up expenditures are deductible in the year of disposition. Code Sec. 195(b).

The election to amortize start-up expenditures must be made by the due date of the return, including extensions, for the first tax year in which the trade or business begins. Reg. §1.195-1. The expenditures must be such that if incurred in connection with the operation of an existing active trade or business would be deductible in the tax year paid or incurred. Code Sec. 195(c)(1)(B). Examples of start-up expenditures are market surveys, fees incurred for consultants, travel costs, legal fees, and advertising expenses. Where the taxpayer incurs investigation expenses for expanding a present trade or business, a deduction is allowed whether the decision is made to acquire or not acquire the business. The expenditures are not for the investigation of a "new" business.

¶14,385   DIVIDENDS-RECEIVED DEDUCTION

Corporation income is subject to double taxation, once at the corporate level and again at the shareholder level at the time of distribution of after-tax earnings. Triple taxation may occur if a corporation receives dividends out of after-tax earnings of another corporation. Without a special provision, the corporation earning the income would be subject to taxation and the income would be taxed a second time when paid as dividends to a recipient corporation. The income would be taxed a third time when the recipient corporation pays dividends to its shareholders. To provide some relief, a dividends-received deduction is allowed. Code Sec. 243.

The dividends qualifying for the dividends-received deduction are those dividends paid by domestic corporations subject to the corporate income tax. Only dividends paid out of a corporation's earnings and profits qualify for the dividends-received deduction. Distributions received from S corporations are not eligible for the dividends-received deduction. The S corporation is exempt from the corporate income tax and distributions are not income to the recipients; thus, there is no need for the dividends-received deduction.

The deduction allowed is a percentage of the dividend received. This percentage is based upon the percentage of ownership by the corporate shareholder. Corporations owning less than 20 percent of the distributing corporation may deduct 70 percent of the dividend received. If the corporate shareholder owns 20 percent or more but less than 80 percent of the distributing corporation, then the corporate shareholder is entitled to deduct 80 percent of the dividend received. Finally, if the corporate shareholder owns 80 percent or more of the distributing corporation and both corporations are members of an affiliated group, then a 100 percent deduction is permitted.

The firm's dividends-received deduction is equal to the relevant percent (70% or 80%, depending on ownership) times the lesser of: (1) dividends received from taxable, unaffiliated domestic corporations or (2) the firm's taxable income, as adjusted (described below). Taxable income, as adjusted, is not used if the firm has a current net operating loss or if the full dividends-received deduction (the relevant percent times the amount of dividends received) creates a net operating loss. In these situations, the firm takes the full dividends-received deduction (based on the amount of the dividend and not constrained by taxable income, as adjusted).

The limitations on the aggregate amount of dividends-received deductions are first determined for dividends received from 20 percent or more owned corporations and then separately determined for dividends received from under 20 percent owned corporations after taxable income is reduced by the former.

EXAMPLE 14.75

Dade Corporation has the following income and expenses:

Gross income from operations	$200,000
Expenses from operations	(150,000)
Dividends received from a 15%-owned domestic corporations	100,000
Taxable income before the dividends-received deduction	$150,000

The dividends-received deduction is $70,000 ($100,000 × 70%).

Taxable income, as adjusted, equals the corporation's taxable income computed without regard to:

1. The dividends-received deduction
2. Any net operating loss carryback and carryforward deduction
3. Any capital loss carryback
4. Domestic production activities deduction (Code Sec. 246(b))

EXAMPLE 14.76

Assume the same facts as in Example 14.75, except that the gross income is only $140,000 instead of $200,000. Taxable income before the dividends-received deduction is $90,000. Instead of a $70,000 deduction, the dividends-received deduction is limited to $63,000 (70% × $90,000).

EXAMPLE 14.77

Assume the same facts as in Example 14.75, except that the gross income from operations is $110,000. Taxable income before the dividends-received deduction is $60,000 ($110,000 + $100,000 – $150,000). If the corporation received the full dividends-received deduction of $70,000 (70% × $100,000), then it would have an NOL of $10,000 ($60,000 – $70,000); thus, it is permitted the full deduction and is not limited to a $42,000 deduction (70% × $60,000).

In summary, the full dividends-received deduction is available if the corporation has an NOL or would have an NOL if it received the full deduction. Also, if taxable income, as adjusted, is greater than the dividend received, a full deduction is available. The full dividends-received deduction is not available if taxable income is less than the dividend received but large enough such that a full dividend-received deduction not make it negative. In this case, the deduction is limited to a percentage of taxable income, as adjusted.

EXAMPLE 14.78

Continuing Example 14.75, as long as the gross income from operations is $120,000 or more but less than $150,000, there will be taxable income not including the dividends-received deduction of $70,000 or more. The net loss from operations will be $30,000 or less. The dividends-received deduction will be limited to 70 percent of taxable income before the dividends-received deduction.

Gross income from operations	$120,000
Expenses from operations	(150,000)
Dividends received	100,000
Taxable income before dividends-received deduction	$70,000
Dividends-received deduction ($70,000 × 70%)	49,000
Taxable income	$21,000

Since the full dividends-received deduction ($70,000) would make taxable income zero (not negative), the deduction is limited to $49,000 (70% × $70,000).

PLANNING POINTER

If there is any doubt prior to year-end whether the full dividends-received deduction is available, steps should be taken to defer income and accelerate deductions to ensure a net operating loss after the full deduction. Typical strategies include deferred payment sales, delaying shipping, stepping up acquisitions of cost recovery property, sales and leaseback at a loss, the use of escrow accounts, the payment of bonuses, stepping up repairs and maintenance, etc.

EXAMPLE 14.79

Continuing with Example 14.78, if gross income from operations decreased by $1 or operating expenses increased by $1, the corporation would be allowed the full dividends-received deduction of $70,000.

Gross income from operations	$120,000
Expenses from operations	(150,001)
Dividends received	100,000
Taxable income before dividends-received deduction	$69,999
Dividends-received deduction	70,000
Taxable income	($1)

Stock must have been held for more than 45 days to be eligible for the dividends-received deduction. The stock also must be held without being protected by an offsetting short sale or option. Code Sec. 246(b) and (c). This restriction prevents corporations from purchasing dividend-paying stock shortly before the declaration of dividends and selling the stock immediately after receiving the right to the dividend. For example, without this requirement a corporation would pay tax of only $102 on $1,000 of dividend income ($1,000 × 30% dividend inclusion rate × 34% corporate tax rate) while generating a tax savings of $340 ($1,000 loss × 34%) if the stock were to decline by the amount of the dividend payment.

Debt-Financed Portfolio Stock

A restriction applies to the dividends-received deduction when a corporation has issued debt to finance its purchase of the stock. This reduction is equal to the ratio of the amount of portfolio indebtedness to the adjusted basis of the portfolio stock. Portfolio indebtedness means any debt directly attributable to the taxpayer corporation's investment in portfolio stock. Without such a restriction, a corporation would be able to fully deduct interest paid to finance its investment in dividend-paying stock and be taxed on only 20 or 30 percent (100 percent minus dividends-received deduction) of the related dividend income.

EXAMPLE 14.80	A corporation purchases 25 percent of the stock in another corporation for $300,000, of which $120,000 or 40 percent is borrowed. The corporation receives dividends of $24,000 from the investment. The allowable dividends-received deduction is limited to $11,520 ($24,000 × 80% × (100% – 40%)).

Extraordinary Dividends

The basis of stock held by a corporation must be reduced by the nontaxed portion of any extraordinary dividend received by the corporation with respect to stock. Code Sec. 1059. Stock basis is not reduced if the stock was held for more than two years before the earliest date that the dividend is declared, agreed to, or announced. The nontaxed portion of a cash distribution is the amount that is offset by the dividends-received deduction. The nontaxed portion of a property distribution is the fair market value of the property reduced by any liabilities assumed by the shareholder that is offset by the dividends-received deduction.

Generally, a dividend is deemed extraordinary when it exceeds 10 percent of a corporate taxpayer's adjusted basis in a share of stock. The 10 percent becomes 5 percent in the case of preferred stock for purposes of determining whether the dividend is extraordinary. In determining whether the dividend is extraordinary, an alternative permits the taxpayer to substitute the fair market value of the share of stock on the day before the ex-dividend date for its adjusted basis. This is intended to mitigate the effect of basis reduction where a shareholder can demonstrate that the stock has appreciated significantly since the shareholder's original investment.

The nontaxed portion of dividends on certain "disqualified" preferred stock issued after July 10, 1989, is treated as an extraordinary dividend (and therefore would be subject to basis reduction). The preferred stock is considered to be disqualified if (1) the preferred stock at the time it is issued has a dividend rate that declines, or can reasonably be expected to decline, in the future; (2) the issue price of the preferred stock exceeds its liquidation rights or its stated redemption price; or (3) the preferred stock is structured so as to avoid other provisions of Code Sec. 1059 and to enable corporate shareholders to reduce tax through a combination of dividends-received deductions and loss on the disposition of the stock. Code Sec. 1059(f).

The reduction in basis is treated as occurring at the beginning of the ex-dividend date.

EXAMPLE 14.81	Matter Corporation purchases 100 shares of Fact Corporation stock for $3,000, or $30 per share, on February 2, 2016. On November 3, 2017, Matter Corporation receives a dividend of $4 per share. Matter deducts 70 percent of the $400 in dividends, or $280, on its tax return for the year. The dividend is considered to be extraordinary because it exceeds 10 percent of Matter's adjusted basis in the shares. Matter will reduce its basis by $280 (the nontaxed portion of the distribution) for purposes of determining gain or loss. If Matter can show that the fair market value of the stock is at least $40 on the day before the ex-dividend date, the dividend would not be extraordinary because it would not exceed 10 percent of the fair market value. Thus, Matter would not have to reduce the basis of its stock.

Any basis adjustment may not reduce the corporation's basis in the stock below zero. However, nontaxed portions of extraordinary dividends that otherwise would reduce basis below zero in the absence of this limitation are treated as gain from a sale or exchange of the stock in the year in which the extraordinary dividend is received.

An extraordinary dividend basis reduction will not apply if the stock was held by the taxpayer for the entire period the distributing corporation and any predecessor has been in existence. Also, dividends qualifying for the 100 percent dividend deduction are not subject to the extraordinary dividend rule.

Dividends Received from Affiliated Corporations

Where dividends are received from an affiliated corporation and the corporation group is not filing a consolidated return, a 100 percent dividends-received deduction may be elected by the group. An affiliated group exists where a corporation owns 80 percent or more of the outstanding voting stock and 80 percent or more of the value of all outstanding stock of another corporation.

The election to deduct the entire dividend is made by the parent corporation for its tax year. Each member of the group must consent to the election. Members of the affiliated group must share one corporate tax rate schedule, one accumulated earnings credit, and one alternative minimum tax exemption.

EXAMPLE 14.82	Parent Corporation owns 90 percent of the stock in Subsidiary Corporation. Subsidiary Corporation pays a $54,000 dividend to Parent Corporation. Parent Corporation can elect to deduct the full 100 percent of the dividend ($54,000) in the computation of taxable income. Subsidiary Corporation must consent to the election because it must also agree on the sharing of the corporate tax rate schedule, accumulated earnings credit, and the alternative minimum tax exemption.

¶14,391   EXECUTIVE COMPENSATION

In general, a corporation and its executives attempt to design a compensation package that maximizes the executives' after-tax cash flows at the least cost and cash outflow to the corporation. Thus, the compensation package usually includes a combination of cash payments (salary and bonus), fringe benefits (nontaxable and taxable), and deferred compensation. However, in developing the package, the corporation is constrained in that the compensation package must be reasonable in amount Reg. §1.162-7(a). The Internal Revenue Service can use the substance over form doctrine to find that some of the compensation is unreasonable and in substance is a dividend (not deductible by the corporation) and not compensation.

Code Section 162(m) also limits the deductibility of executive compensation of publicly-traded corporations to $1 million. The restriction applies to the corporation's five highest-paid executives (including the chief executive officer). Compensation in excess of this amount is not deductible unless it is based on a performance-based compensation plan.

¶14,395   DOMESTIC PRODUCTION ACTIVITIES DEDUCTION

Because the United States taxes worldwide income and has relatively high corporate income tax rates, Congress has passed various tax provisions that provide incentives to firms that export their products. Congress's objective, in part, has been to make U.S. firms more competitive in international markets. The World Trade Organization has declared many of these provisions to be illegal subsidies and has required the United States to repeal them. In response, Congress repealed the most recent tax provisions (incentives) dealing with extraterritorial income and replaced it with the domestic production activities deduction. This deduction is available to a wide-range of businesses and is not only an international activity deduction; it does not require exporting or any activity outside the United States. The property must be manufactured, produced, grown or extracted in whole or in significant part in the United States (significant part means a firm would qualify if its direct labor and overhead costs incurred to manufacture or produce the product equal at least 20 percent of the product's total cost. Reg. §1.199-3.).

Code Sec. 199 gives domestic manufacturers a deduction equal to a percentage of their taxable income (computed without regard to the deduction). The purpose of the deduction is to reduce the effective tax rates for these firms. The deduction equals nine percent times the lesser of: (1) taxable income (before this deduction) for the taxable year or (2) qualified production activities income for the taxable year. The deduction cannot exceed 50 percent of the firm's W-2 wages for the taxable year that are allocable to qualified production activities. This provision (restriction) is designed to encourage firms to keep jobs in the USA.

Under Code Sec. 199, qualified production activities income is broadly defined and equals the excess (if any) of the taxpayer's domestic production gross receipts for the taxable year over the sum of (1) the cost of goods sold that are allocable to such receipts, and (2) other direct and indirect expenses, losses, or deductions properly allocable to such receipts.

Domestic production gross receipts equals the taxpayer's gross receipts derived from (1) any lease, rental, license, sale, exchange, or other disposition of qualifying production property that was manufactured, produced, grown, or extracted by the taxpayer in whole or in significant part within the United States, (2) any qualified film produced by the taxpayer, (3) electricity, natural gas, or potable water produced by the taxpayer in the United States, (4) construction of real property performed in the United States by the taxpayer in the ordinary course of such trade or business, or (5) engineering or architectural services performed in the United States by the taxpayer in the ordinary course of such trade or business with respect to the construction of real property in the United States.

Since taxable income is an upper bound, the maximum tax savings in dollars equals nine percent times taxable income times the firm's marginal tax rate, and since the deduction does not require any additional expenditures (unlike most other expense deductions), the tax savings also is the net cash flow associated with the deduction. Looking at the firm's tax rate, the deduction effectively reduces the rate by an amount equal to the firm's marginal tax rate times nine percent.

EXAMPLE 14.83	Fry Corporation's taxable income for 2017 before the domestic manufacturers' deduction was $10,000,000. Its income from qualified production activities in 2017 was $8,000,000. Fry Corporation's W-2 wages for 2017 were $3,000,000. Its domestic production activities deduction is $720,000 (9% × lesser of: (1) $10,000,000 or (2) $8,000,000; and this amount does not exceed 50% × W-2 wages (50% × $3,000,000 = $1,500,000)).

EXAMPLE 14.84	Julia, Inc.'s 2017 taxable income is $15,000,000, and this is the lesser of all three constraints. The after-tax cash flow from the domestic production activities deduction equals $472,500 ($15,000,000 × 35% × .09). The reduction to its overall tax rate equals 3.15% (35% × .09).

Determination of Corporate Income Tax Liability

¶14,401   COMPUTATION OF TAX LIABILITY

After determining its taxable income, a corporation then must compute its income tax liability. This is a multiple-step process. The corporation first computes its regular tax liability. This amount is reduced by any tax credits to which it is entitled, such as the foreign tax credit (Code Sec. 27) and the general business credit (Code Sec. 38). Additionally, the corporation must compute an alternative minimum tax to which it may be subject. Any recapture of previously claimed tax credits is added to the resultant amount to produce the corporation's income tax liability.

¶14,405   CORPORATE REGULAR INCOME TAX RATES

The marginal federal tax rate for corporations and associations taxed as corporations ranges from 15 to 39 percent (Code Sec. 11(b)) as follows:

Taxable income	Rate
$0 to $50,000	15%
$50,001 to $75,000	25%
$75,001 to $100,000	34%
$100,001 to $335,000	39%
$335,001 to $10,000,000	34%
$10,000,001 to $15,000,000	35%
$15,000,001 to $18,333,333	38%
Over $18,333,333	35%

To discourage corporations from taking advantage of the lower brackets, certain affiliated corporations must share the lower brackets. Code Sec. 1563.

Corporations with over $100,000 in taxable income are subject to a 5 percent tax on such excess between $100,000 and $335,000. The maximum additional tax is $11,250 (($335,000 − $100,000) × 5%). This figure represents the savings from being in a tax bracket below 34 percent on the first $75,000. At $335,000 of taxable income, the result is the equivalent of a "flat tax" of 34 percent. The 34 percent "flat tax" is imposed on corporations whose taxable income ranges from $335,001 to $10,000,000. At $10,000,001, the tax rate increases to 35 percent. Corporations with over $15,000,000 in taxable income are subject to a 3 percent tax on the excess between $15,000,001 and $18,333,333. The maximum additional tax is $100,000 (($18,333,333 − $15,000,000) × 3%). This figure represents the savings from being in the 34 percent bracket on the first $10,000,000. At $18,333,333 of taxable income, the result is the equivalent of a "flat tax" of 35 percent. These tax rates are shown in the above tax rate schedule, and in the corporate tax rate schedule on the inside back cover of this book.

EXAMPLE 14.85

Alpha Corporation has taxable income of $85,000. The tax incurred would be $17,150, computed as follows:

$50,000 × 15%	$7,500
25,000 × 25%	6,250
10,000 × 34%	3,400
	$17,150

EXAMPLE 14.86

Assuming a taxable income of $100,000, the tax would be $22,250, computed as follows:

$50,000 × 15%	$7,500
25,000 × 25%	6,250
25,000 × 34%	8,500
	$22,250

EXAMPLE 14.87

Assuming a taxable income of $180,000, the tax would be $53,450, computed as follows:

$50,000 × 15%	$7,500
25,000 × 25%	6,250
25,000 × 34%	8,500
80,000 × 39%	31,200
	$53,450

EXAMPLE 14.88

Assuming a taxable income of $335,000, the tax would be $113,900, computed as follows:

$50,000 × 15%	$7,500
25,000 × 25%	6,250
25,000 × 34%	8,500
235,000 × 39%	91,650
	$113,900

This is equivalent to $335,000 × 34%.

EXAMPLE 14.89

Assuming a taxable income of $5,000,000, the tax would be $1,700,000, computed as follows:

$5,000,000   ×   34%

EXAMPLE 14.90	Assuming a taxable income of $14,000,000, the tax would be $4,800,000, computed as follows:

$10,000,000 × 34% $3,400,000
4,000,000 × 35%   1,400,000
                         $4,800,000

EXAMPLE 14.91	Assuming a taxable income of $17,000,000, the tax would be $5,910,000, computed as follows:

$10,000,000 × 34% $3,400,000
5,000,000 × 35%   1,750,000
2,000,000 × 38%   760,000
                         $5,910,000

EXAMPLE 14.92	Assuming a taxable income of $18,333,333, the tax would be $6,416,666, computed as follows:

$10,000,000 × 34% $3,400,000
5,000,000 × 35%   1,750,000
3,333,333 × 38%   1,266,666
                         $6,416,666

This is equivalent to $18,333,333 × 35%.

EXAMPLE 14.93	Assuming a taxable income of $20,000,000, the tax would be $7,000,000, computed as follows:

$20,000,000   ×   35%

The computations in Examples 14.84 through 14.92 are designed to explain how the corporate rate structure works. In computing gross tax liability, a corporation would use the corporate rate schedule on the inside back cover of this book. Thus, for example, using the information in Example 14.84, gross tax liability would be determined as follows: $13,750 + .34($85,000 − $75,000), which equals $17,150 ($13,750 + $3,400).

These rates are low enough to encourage incorporation for businesses that intend to retain their earnings. There is double taxation only if dividends are paid. Thus, if the corporation's taxable income is $50,000 a year or less, a tax of 15 percent may be viewed as a reasonable price to pay for the indefinite deferral of the second tax at the shareholder level.

Personal service corporations are taxed at a flat tax rate of 35 percent. They are not given the benefit of the tax savings of the lower brackets. A personal service corporation is one in which substantially all of the activities involve the performance of services in the fields of health, law, engineering, architecture, accounting, actuarial science, performing arts, or consulting. Substantially all of the stock (95 percent) must be held by employees, retired employees, or their estates.

¶14,415   CORPORATE ALTERNATIVE MINIMUM TAX

Alternative minimum tax rules have been devised to ensure that no taxpayers with substantial economic income can avoid significant tax liability by using exclusions, deductions, and credits. The underlying purpose was that Congress had concluded that both the perception and the reality of fairness in taxation had been harmed by instances in which corporations paid little or no tax in years when they reported substantial earnings, and may even have paid substantial dividends to shareholders.

The alternative minimum tax (AMT) assessed on corporations is similar to the AMT that individuals must pay. The AMT is payable to the extent that it exceeds the corporation's regular income tax and must be taken into consideration in the corporate quarterly tax payments. Code Secs. 55-59. The starting point for computing the AMT is the corporation's taxable income. Taxable income is modified for certain items such as tax preferences and reduced by an exemption amount. The resultant amount, the net alternative minimum taxable income, is multiplied by 20 percent to yield a tentative minimum tax (TMT). If TMT is greater than the corporation's regular income tax, then the excess is the corporation's AMT liability and must be added to its regular tax liability to determine the total tax due. If TMT is less than the corporation's regular tax, then it has no AMT liability. In summary, the tax is computed as follows:

	Taxable Income
(+ or –)	Adjustments to Taxable Income
+	Tax Preference Items
(+ or –)	Adjusted Current Earnings Adjustment
–	AMT-NOL Deduction (limited to 90 percent)
=	Gross Alternative Minimum Taxable Income (AMTI)
–	Exemption Amount
=	Net Alternative Minimum Taxable Income
×	20% Tax Rate
=	Gross Alternative Minimum Tax
–	AMT Foreign Tax Credit
=	Tentative Minimum Tax (TMT)
–	Regular Income Tax (before credits but minus the regular Foreign Tax Credit and Possessions Tax Credit)
=	Alternative Minimum Tax (AMT)

Small corporations are not liable for the corporate AMT. A corporation qualifies as a small corporation if it had average gross receipts of $5,000,000 or less for its first three-year period ending before the tax year for which the AMT exemption is being claimed. Once the corporation qualifies as a small corporation under the $5,000,000 test then it will continue to be exempt from the AMT as long as its average gross receipts for the prior three years do not exceed $7,500,000. A new corporation coming into existence generally is considered to be an exempt corporation in its first year regardless of the size of its gross receipts for the year. To qualify as a small corporation for its second year, its average gross receipts for the first year must be $5,000,000 or less. Once it meets this test then the limit for subsequent years is $7,500,000; thus, to qualify as a small corporation for its third year its average gross receipts for the first two years must not exceed $7,500,000.

If a corporation loses its small corporation status because it has average gross receipts for the prior three-year period in excess of $7,500,000, it becomes liable for the AMT. However, the AMT liability is based only on certain preferences and adjustments that pertain to transactions that were entered into after the corporation lost its small corporation status.

EXAMPLE 14.94   James Co. is a small corporation for AMT purposes. In 2017, it determined that its average gross receipts for 2014, 2015, and 2016 was $7,900,000. James Co. is subject to the AMT for 2017. Its AMT will only be based on preferences and adjustments for transactions on or after January 1, 2017.

Adjustments to Taxable Income

The AMT is aimed at recovering some of the tax savings generated by a variety of other deductions and methods for computing tax liability. Thus, in determining AMTI, the taxpayer is required to make special adjustments to certain tax items that have been used to calculate regular taxable income. The adjustments may either increase or decrease alternative minimum taxable income. These adjustments reflect timing differences between the reporting methods for regular tax purposes and the alternative minimum tax. These adjustments are positive initially but reverse themselves in later years. The adjustments to taxable income are (Code Sec. 56):

1. Depreciation on post-1986 acquisitions and 1986 acquisitions using MACRS depreciation
2. Mining and exploration costs
3. Long-term contracts
4. Net operating losses
5. Pollution control facilities
6. Installment sales
7. Circulation expenses
8. Capital construction funds
9. Insurance companies deduction
10. Farming losses

Depreciation

The depreciation deduction for real property placed in service after 1986 and property placed in service in 1986 for which the MACRS depreciation rules are adopted must be recomputed for AMT purposes under the alternative depreciation system (ADS), generally the straight-line method, over 40 years. However, no adjustment is needed for real property placed in service after December 31, 1998.

Personal property placed in service after 1986 must be depreciated using the 150 percent declining-balance method under the ADS, switching to straight-line in the year that maximizes the deduction.

Thus, two separate depreciation schedules must be computed: (1) depreciation for regular income tax purposes and (2) depreciation for AMT purposes. In the early years of an asset's life, regular tax depreciation will exceed AMT depreciation and the difference will be a positive adjustment to taxable income in the AMT computation. In later years, AMT depreciation will exceed regular tax depreciation and cause a negative adjustment to taxable income.

In determining AMTI, the taxpayer computes the allowable depreciation deduction for tangible property placed in service after 1998 using the 150% declining balance method. The method switches to the straight-line as of the beginning of the year that applying that method to the property's adjusted basis will yield a higher allowance.

EXAMPLE 14.95

A corporation purchases a $10,000 machine for use in business in 2014. Assuming the machine is a 5-year asset for both MACRS and ADS, the depreciation methods for regular tax and alternative minimum tax purposes along with the adjustment are as follows:

Year	200% Declining Balance	150% Declining Balance	Adjustment
2014	$2,000	$1,500	+ $500
2015	3,200	2,550	+ 650
2016	1,920	1,785	+ 135
2017	1,152	1,666	− 514
2018	1,152	1,666	− 514
2019	576	833	− 257

In the first three years, the adjustment involves an amount that must be added to taxable income, while in the last three years the adjustment entails an amount that must be subtracted from taxable income. Thus, the corporation will make a $514 negative adjustment in 2017.

For AMT purposes, a property's basis is only reduced by the amount of depreciation allowed in computing AMTI. Therefore, the adjusted basis of the property may differ for regular and minimum tax purposes. The gain or loss for AMTI upon disposition of the asset is determined by the AMTI basis.

Mining Exploration and Development Costs

Mining exploration and development costs that are generally deductible in the current year are required to be computed under the 10-year straight-line amortization for AMT purposes. The adjusted basis of property for which mining exploration and development costs are incurred may differ for regular tax and AMT purposes, giving rise to different amounts of gain or loss between the two systems upon the disposition of such property. The tax preference adjustment for mining exploration and development costs may be avoided if the taxpayer makes a regular tax election to deduct such expenditures over a 10-year period.

EXAMPLE 14.96

Douglas Corporation's taxable income for 2016 is $13,750,000. Included in its expenses was a $600,000 deduction for mining exploration costs incurred in 2016. Douglas Corporation had no other tax preferences (or adjustment items). Its AMTI for 2016 is $14,290,000, computed as follows:

Taxable income	$13,750,000
Adjustment	
Excess mining exploration costs (amount expensed minus amount allowed over a 10-year amortization period; $600,000 minus $60,000)	540,000
AMTI	$14,290,000

Long-Term Contracts

Taxpayers must use the percentage-of-completion method for long contracts entered into after March 1, 1986, to determine income for purposes of calculating the AMTI. In the case of small construction contracts (other than home construction contracts) entered into after June 21, 1988, the percentage of completion is determined under the simplified cost allocation method. Home construction contracts entered into in tax years beginning after September 30, 1990, are not required to use the percentage-of-completion method.

Net Operating Losses

The regular NOL deduction is replaced by the AMTI-NOL deduction. The regular NOL must be modified to take into account the same adjustments and tax preferences made to determine AMTI. The AMTI-NOL deduction cannot offset more than 90 percent of AMTI determined before the NOL deduction. The purpose of the limitation is to assure that corporations at least pay a minimum amount of taxes, 2 percent of AMTI each year (remaining AMTI (10%) × 20% tax rate). However, the exemption and credits might reduce this to zero.

Pollution Control Facilities

The five-year amortization method for depreciating pollution control facilities must be replaced by the alternative depreciation system. The adjusted basis used in AMTI calculations to determine the gain or loss on the sale of property for which depreciation has been adjusted must reflect the depreciation adjustments rather than the costs that were deductible in regular tax computations. Effective for property placed in service after December 31, 1998, the recovery periods used for AMT purposes conform with the recovery periods used under MACRS using the straight-line method.

Installment Sales

Generally, the installment method is not available for dealer dispositions of stock in trade and other property held by the taxpayer primarily for sale to customers in the ordinary course of business. The realized gain is recognized in the year of sale. Thus, no AMT adjustments will generally be required for such dealer sales. The installment method may be used in determining AMTI for all nondealer dispositions of property.

Circulation Expenditures

The amount of circulation expenditures (i.e., the costs of establishing, maintaining, or increasing the circulation of newspapers, magazines, or other periodicals) allowed as a current deduction for regular tax purposes must be amortized over a three-year period for AMT purposes. This tax preference applies to personal holding companies. However, under the AMT rules, corporate taxpayers are free to capitalize or deduct their circulation expenditures. Thus, for most C corporations there is no AMT adjustment for circulation expenditures.

Capital Construction Funds

Contributions made by shipping companies to capital construction funds (established under Section 607 of the Merchant Marine Act of 1936) may not be deducted from AMTI and a fund's earnings (including gains or losses) may not be excluded from AMTI. No reduction in the basis of a vessel, barge, or container need be made to reflect amounts withdrawn from a fund, if the amounts have been included in AMTI.

Insurance Companies Deduction

The special deduction from regular tax allowed to Blue Cross and Blue Shield organizations for one-fourth of their annual claims and administrative expenses (less the prior tax year's adjusted surplus) may not be claimed against AMTI.

Farming Losses

No deduction is allowed for losses from any farming syndicate or any other farming activity in which the taxpayer does not materially participate. A loss from one farming activity may not be used to offset income from another farming activity. Disallowed losses are carried forward indefinitely and used for AMTI purposes to offset future income from the farming activity. Suspended losses are deductible when the activity is disposed. These provisions apply to personal service corporations.

Tax Preference Items

Tax preferences must be added back to the corporation's taxable income to compute AMTI. These preferences are usually the result of some tax benefit received in the computation of taxable income. Unlike AMT adjustments which can either increase or decrease AMTI, tax preference items only increase AMTI. The tax preference items are (Code Sec. 57(a)):

1. Depletion
2. Intangible drilling costs
3. Private activity bonds interest
4. Accelerated depreciation and amortization on pre-1987 property

Depletion

The depletion preference for corporate taxpayers is the excess of the allowable percentage depletion deduction over the adjusted basis of the property at the end of the year. The preference applies to percentage depletion for all minerals, not just oil and gas. However, the preference does not apply to most oil and gas companies.

Intangible Drilling Costs

The amount of excess intangible drilling costs for the year is treated as a tax preference to the extent that it exceeds 65 percent of the corporate taxpayer's net income for the tax year from oil, gas, and geothermal properties. The amount of excess intangible drilling costs, for this purpose, is the excess of the deduction for the current cost of drilling productive wells over the deduction that would have been allowable if such costs had been capitalized and either (1) amortized over a 10-year period or (2) deducted, at the election of the taxpayer, as cost depletion, whichever is more favorable. The intangible drilling costs preference is computed separately for geothermal properties and for oil and gas properties.

Private Activity Bonds Interest

A tax preference has been added for tax-exempt interest on private activity bonds issued after August 7, 1986. This preference does not apply to bonds issued for the benefit of tax-exempt charitable or educational institutions under Code Sec. 501(c)(3) or to bonds issued for public purposes such as schools and municipally owned public utilities.

Accelerated Depreciation and Amortization on Pre-1987 Property

There is a tax preference for excess depreciation and amortization taken on certain properties acquired before 1987. A taxpayer is not likely to have excess depreciation on an asset acquired thirty years ago.

EXAMPLE 14.97

Hoover Inc. has taxable income of $12,300,000. Included in its expenses was a $500,000 deduction for percentage depletion. The $500,000 was in excess of the depletable property's adjusted basis (i.e., the property has a zero adjusted basis). No other tax preferences or adjustments were needed. AMTI for Hoover Inc. is $12,800,000, computed as follows:

Taxable income	$12,300,000
Tax Preferences	
Percentage depletion in excess of adjusted basis	500,000
AMTI	$12,800,000

Adjusted Current Earnings

Corporations are required to make an adjustment based on adjusted current earnings. The adjustment equals 75 percent of adjusted current earnings (ACE) less AMTI.

The adjusted current earnings adjustment may be either an increase or a decrease in taxable income when computing AMTI. The negative adjustment is limited to the aggregate positive adjustment for ACE in prior tax years, minus negative adjustments previously claimed. Code Sec. 56(g)(2). Any unused negative adjustment is lost forever.

| EXAMPLE 14.98 | A corporation has the following AMTI (before ACE adjustments and alternative tax NOL deductions) and ACE for 2015 to 2018. |

	2015	2016	2017	2018
AMTI	$5,000,000	$4,000,000	$7,000,000	$9,200,000
ACE	7,000,000	4,000,000	6,000,000	8,000,000

A positive ACE adjustment of $1,500,000 (75% × ($7,000,000 – $5,000,000)) is made in 2015. No adjustment is needed in 2016 since ACE and unadjusted AMTI are equal. A negative ACE adjustment of $750,000 (75% × ($6,000,000 – $7,000,000)) is made in 2017. Finally, a negative ACE adjustment of $750,000 is made in 2018 because of the limitation on negative ACE adjustments. The computed adjustment is $900,000 (75% × ($8,000,000 – $9,200,000)) but this is constrained to $750,000, the aggregate positive adjustment ($1,500,000) reduced by the aggregate negative adjustment ($750,000). The remaining $150,000 is lost forever.

The determination of ACE is complicated and Reg. §1.56(g)-1 provides further guidance on its calculation. The starting point in determining ACE is AMTI, determined without regard to the alternative tax NOL deduction and the ACE adjustment, adjusted for several items. Many of these adjustments are similar to those required to compute corporate earnings and profits (E&P) under Code Sec. 312. However, ACE is not the same as E&P because not all items affect both similarly (for example, federal income taxes are deductible in computing E&P but are not deductible in computing ACE).

The adjustments to AMTI for purposes of computing ACE are as follows. AMTI is increased by items excluded from gross income in computing AMTI if the items increase a corporation's earnings and profits (E&P). Examples of this adjustment are tax-exempt interest and key-person life insurance proceeds. These amounts are reduced by the nondeductible expenses incurred to produce them.

Deductions taken to compute AMTI that are not deductions for purposes of computing E&P must be eliminated (i.e., AMTI is increased). An example of this adjustment is the dividends-received deduction. However, although the dividends-received deduction (DRD) is not permitted for E&P purposes, the deduction is permitted for ACE purposes with respect to dividends received from 20 percent owned corporations (80 percent DRD) and for 100 percent dividends (100 percent DRD) to the extent that the dividend is attributable to taxable income of the paying corporation. The 70 percent DRD is not permitted for ACE purposes.

No adjustment is made to ACE related to the E&P effect of charitable contributions. Code Sec. 56(g)(4)(I). Thus, the excess of fair market value deduction allowed for tax purposes over the basis deduction for book purposes is not included in the ACE adjustment.

Adjustments also must be made so that ACE is computed as if the corporation did not use the installment method; ACE adjustments must reflect use of cost depletion, capitalized and amortized intangible drilling costs, use of the alternative depreciation system under Code Sec. 168(g) for assets placed in service after 1989, and straight-line depreciation for property depreciated under MACRS. However, ACE adjustments are not required for intangible drilling, and for percentage depletion for oil and gas. Finally, other E&P-type adjustments include adjustments for circulation and organizational expenditures that are not amortizable for ACE purposes, mineral exploration and development costs that must be amortized for ACE purposes, and LIFO inventory adjustments.

Exemption Amount

Before the 20 percent tax rate is applied, corporations may be able to reduce AMTI by the exemption amount. Code Sec. 55(d). The allowed exemption amount is $40,000. The exemption amount is reduced by 25 cents for each $1 by which alternative minimum taxable income exceeds $150,000. Consequently, the exemption is completely eliminated for AMTI of $310,000 or more.

EXAMPLE 14.99	A corporation with AMTI of $300,000 is allowed an exemption amount of $2,500 ($40,000 – .25 × ($300,000 – $150,000)). If the AMTI were $310,000 or more, there would be no deduction for the exemption amount.

Tentative Minimum Tax

AMTI is reduced by the allowable exemption amount resulting in the corporation's net alternative minimum taxable income (the tax base for AMT purposes). This base is multiplied by the AMT tax rate of 20 percent to determine the gross alternative minimum tax. The tentative minimum tax is calculated by subtracting AMT foreign tax credits from the gross alternative minimum tax. Credits not allowed in the current year are carried over under the foreign tax carryover rules. Code Sec. 59.

Net AMT Liability

The corporate taxpayer's AMT for a tax year is the excess of the tentative minimum tax over the regular tax. Following the computation of the tentative minimum tax (20% × (AMTI – exemption amount) – AMT foreign tax credit = tentative minimum tax), a comparison must be made between the tentative AMT liability and the corporation's regular tax liability. The regular tax figure to which the tentative minimum tax is compared is the regular tax on corporate income reduced by the foreign tax credit and the possessions tax credit. Furthermore, for comparative purposes, certain adjustments to the regular tax liability must be made.

The regular income tax does not include the tax on accumulated distributions of trusts. Nonrefundable credits (i.e., general business credit) generally cannot be used to reduce the regular tax liability to less than the tentative minimum tax. Credits that cannot be used by the taxpayer due to the effect of the alternative minimum tax can be carried over to other tax years under rules generally applicable to credit carryovers. The following rules summarize the comparison process:

1. If the tentative AMT liability *exceeds* the regular tax liability (as modified by only the nonrefundable foreign tax credit and the possessions tax credit), then the corporate taxpayer pays the tentative AMT (which is comprised of the regular tax and the excess of the tentative AMT or net AMT liability).
2. If the tentative AMT liability is less than the regular tax liability, then all nonrefundable credits will be allowed to reduce the corporation's regular tax liability to the extent of the tentative AMT liability but not below it. Thus, the corporate taxpayer must pay at least the tentative AMT liability.

EXAMPLE 14.100	Williams Inc. has taxable income of $400,000. Williams has alternative minimum tax adjustments and tax preferences of $300,000. The regular tax is a flat 34 percent of $400,000, or $136,000. The tentative minimum tax equals 20 percent of $700,000, or $140,000. The alternative minimum tax becomes $4,000. (No exemption was allowed since AMTI was $310,000 or more).

EXAMPLE 14.101	A corporation has taxable income of $500,000 along with a general business credit of $22,000. The corporation has adjustments and preferences of $300,000. The income tax before credits is $170,000 ($500,000 × 34%). The tentative minimum tax is $160,000 (($500,000 + $300,000) × 20%). The corporation is allowed only $10,000 of the general business credit. A $10,000 general business credit reduces the regular income tax to the tentative minimum tax, thus no alternative minimum tax is incurred. The remaining general business credit of $12,000 is carried over to other tax years.

Minimum Tax Credit

Adjustments and tax preferences used to modify taxable income to compute AMTI consist of items that are timing differences and permanent differences. Timing differences defer tax liability and permanent differences produce a permanent reduction in taxable income. The entire amount of the AMT liability is available for the minimum tax credit in tax years beginning after 1989.

The purpose of the minimum tax credit is to prevent the double taxation of deferral preferences and adjustments. These deferral preferences and adjustments are subject to the alternative minimum tax in a tax year earlier than the year they are subject to the regular tax.

The extent to which deferral preference items cause tentative minimum tax to exceed the regular tax may be carried forward and used as an offsetting credit against regular tax to which the corporation may be subject in future years. A taxpayer is not allowed to take a credit larger than an amount necessary to reduce the regular tax to the amount of the tentative minimum tax.

EXAMPLE 14.102	In 2017, Heit Corporation had taxable income of $350,000. For AMTI purposes it had $150,000 of deferral adjustments and $300,000 of exclusion preferences. Its regular tax was $119,000 ($350,000 × .34). Its net alternative minimum taxable income was $800,000 ($350,000 + $150,000 + $300,000; since AMTI was greater than $310,000 there is no exemption). The AMT was $41,000 ((20% × $800,000) – $119,000). The entire amount of the AMT liability ($41,000) may be carried forward as a credit.

EXAMPLE 14.103	A corporation has a tentative minimum tax of $100,000, a regular tax before the AMT credit of $120,000, and a minimum tax credit of $35,000. Without the minimum tax credit, the corporation would not have an alternative minimum tax because the regular tax exceeds the tentative minimum tax. Since the full minimum tax credit would reduce the regular tax below the tentative minimum tax, only $20,000 of the minimum tax credit carryforward may be used to reduce the regular tax.

The AMT credit is limited for small corporations currently not subject to the AMT. The credit is limited to the amount by which the corporation's regular tax liability (reduced by other credits) exceeds 25 percent of the excess, if any, of the corporation's regular tax liability (reduced by other credits) over $25,000.

EXAMPLE 14.104	Niffo Company is a small corporation for 2017 and does not have an AMT liability. It has a large AMT carryover from previous years. Niffo's regular tax liability (after other credits) in 2017 is $80,000. Its allowable credit for 2017 is $66,250, computed as follows: $80,000 – 25% ($80,000 – $25,000) = $66,250.

EXAMPLE 14.105

SQ Corporation is a calendar-year taxpayer. For its tax year ended December 31, 2017, it had the following income and expenses.

Gross sales	$13,800,000
Interest income	140,000
Dividend income from 30% owned domestic corporation	90,000
Short-term capital gain	25,000
Cost of goods sold	11,800,000
Wage expense	300,000
Interest expense	40,000
Depreciation expense	145,000
Charitable contributions	26,000
Other expenses	1,400,000

Included in the interest income is $100,000 from municipal bonds. Depreciation for book purposes is $110,000 and for AMT purposes is $128,000. The $26,000 charitable contribution is for a donation of long-term capital gain property whose adjusted basis is $12,000. Other expenses do not include the federal income tax. SQ's alternative minimum tax is computed as follows.

Income	Taxable Income
Gross sales	$13,800,000
Cost of goods sold	11,800,000
Gross profit	2,000,000
Interest income	40,000
Dividend income	90,000
Short-term capital gain	25,000
Total Income	$2,155,000
Expenses	
Wages expense	300,000
Interest expense	40,000
Depreciation expense	145,000
Other expenses	1,400,000
Total Expenses	$1,885,000
	$270,000
Charitable contribution deduction	26,000
Dividends-received deduction	72,000
Taxable income	$172,000
Tax Liability	$50,330
Alternative Minimum Tax Computation	
Taxable Income	$172,000
Tax Preferences	
Excess depreciation	17,000
AMTI before ACE adjustment	$189,000
ACE adjustment (.75 × (ACE − AMTI)), (.75 × ($307,000* − $189,000))	88,500
Alternative Minimum Taxable Income	$277,500
Alternative Minimum Tax Exemption ($40,000 − .25 × ($277,500 − $150,000))	8,125
Net AMTI	$269,375
20% Tax Rate	× .20
Gross AMT	$53,875
AMT Foreign Tax Credit	0
Tentative Minimum Tax	$53,875
Regular Income Tax	50,330
Alternative Minimum Tax	$3,545

* ACE = $189,000 (AMTI before ACE) + $100,000 (tax-exempt interest) + $18,000 (excess of depreciation for books over depreciation for AMT) = $307,000. The ACE adjustment does not include the 80 percent dividends-received deduction nor the $14,000 excess of charitable deduction for tax purposes over the deduction for book purposes.

PLANNING POINTER	Corporations subject to the alternative minimum tax generally benefit by accelerating income into an AMT year and delaying expenses until a regular tax year. Payment of allowable deductions, such as charitable contributions, provides a tax benefit in an AMT year of only 20 percent, while delaying the payment to a regular tax year may allow a deduction at 34 percent. Also, income recognized in an AMT year will generally be taxed at 20 percent rather than at the higher regular tax rate.

¶14,433 CONTROLLED GROUPS OF CORPORATIONS

The corporate tax rate varies from 15 percent on the first $50,000 of taxable income to a flat rate of 35 percent on taxable income in excess of $18,333,333. Instead of forming one corporation, shareholders could form several corporations in an attempt to distribute the income-generating property so as to assure that each corporation's taxable income did not exceed $50,000. This would result in significant tax savings.

EXAMPLE 14.106	A corporation with taxable income of $350,000 has a tax liability of $119,000 ($350,000 × 34%). If seven corporations were formed and the property distributed such that each corporation had $50,000 of taxable income, then the total tax liability of the corporations would be $52,500 (($50,000 × 15%) × 7). The result is a tax savings of $66,500 ($119,000 – $52,500).

Code Sec. 1561 was enacted to limit the benefits that taxpayers might receive by using multiple corporations. Multiple corporations that are members of a controlled group must share certain tax benefits as if they were one corporation. These benefits include the lower tax brackets, the alternative minimum tax exemption of $40,000, the Section 179 election to expense certain depreciable property, and the $250,000 accumulated earnings credit. The impact of Code Sec. 1561 may be illustrated as follows.

EXAMPLE 14.107	If, in Example 14.106, the seven corporations are members of a controlled group, then they must share the tax brackets equally unless all the members agree to an unequal allocation of the brackets. Thus, each of the seven corporations will have $7,143 ($50,000 ÷ 7) taxed at 15 percent and $3,571 ($25,000 ÷ 7) taxed at 25 percent. Additionally, the 5 percent surtax on taxable income in excess of $100,000 is allocated. Thus, if the total taxable income for the group of corporations exceeds $335,000, then each member will have a tax rate of 34 percent.

Parent-subsidiary corporations, brother-sister corporations, combined groups, and certain insurance companies are controlled groups. Code Sec. 1563(a). Affiliated groups and controlled groups are not synonymous. An affiliated group always involves a parent-subsidiary relationship. Thus, parent-subsidiary corporations are both controlled groups and affiliated groups. However, two corporations owned by the same individual (brother-sister corporations) are a controlled group but not an affiliated group.

Parent-Subsidiary Corporations

A parent-subsidiary controlled group consists of one or more chains of corporations connected through stock ownership with a common parent corporation. Code Sec. 1563(a)(1). The parent corporation must own at least 80 percent of the total voting power of all classes of voting stock or at least 80 percent of the total value of shares of all classes of stock of at least one corporation (the subsidiary). Once this initial parent-subsidiary relationship is established, then another corporation can be included in the group if the parent corporation, the subsidiary corporation, or any other corporation in the group individually owns or collectively own at least 80 percent of the total voting power of all of its classes of voting stock or at least 80 percent of the total value of shares of all of its classes of stock.

EXAMPLE 14.108	

Alpha and Beta are members of a parent-subsidiary controlled group. Alpha is the parent.

EXAMPLE 14.109

Alpha, Beta, and Chi are members of a parent-subsidiary controlled group. Alpha is the parent.

EXAMPLE 14.110

Alpha, Beta, Chi, and Delta are members of a controlled parent-subsidiary. Alpha is the parent.

The controlled parent-subsidiary group is subject to the restrictions of tax benefits mentioned earlier. However, a benefit of this controlled group is that it may elect to file a consolidated return.

Brother-Sister Corporations

In general, a brother-sister controlled group consists of two or more corporations owned by five or fewer individuals, estates, or trusts who (1) own at least 80 percent of the combined voting power of all voting stock or at least 80 percent of the total value of shares of all classes of stock of each corporation and (2) own more than 50 percent of total combined voting power of all voting stock or more than 50 percent of the total value of all classes of stock of each corporation. In calculating the 50 percent test, ownership of each person is included only to the extent that such ownership is identical with respect to each corporation. Thus, only the smallest percentage owned in any of the corporations is counted. Stock owned by family members or certain entities may be attributed to a taxpayer under the attribution rules. Code Sec. 1563(d)(2).

However, under Code Sec. 1563(a)(2) the 80 percent test is not used for purposes of Code Sec. 1561 rules only regarding sharing of lower tax brackets, the alternative minimum tax exemption, the Section 179 expenses, and the accumulated earnings credit. Thus, for Code Sec. 1561 purposes only, only the 50 percent test is used. Thus, a group could be a brother-sister controlled group for Code Sec. 1561 purposes but not be a brother-sister controlled group for all other purposes. Brother-sister controlled groups also may not file a consolidated tax return.

EXAMPLE 14.111

Alpha, Beta, and Chi Corporations each have only one class of stock outstanding. The ownership of this stock is as follows:

Shareholders	Corporations			Identical Ownership
	Alpha	Beta	Chi	
Jones	25%	20%	55%	20%
Smith	25%	30%	35%	25%
Nelson	50%	50%	10%	10%
	100%	100%	100%	55%

Alpha, Beta, and Chi are members of a controlled brother-sister group because both ownership tests are met. Five or fewer individuals own at least 80 percent of each corporation (they own 100 percent of each) and they have greater than a 50 percent common ownership (55 percent identical ownership).

EXAMPLE 14.112 Same as Example 14.111, except for the following ownership:

Shareholders	Corporations			Identical Ownership
	Alpha	Beta	Chi	
Jones	5%	30%	45%	5%
Smith	65%	10%	35%	10%
Nelson	30%	60%	20%	20%
	100%	100%	100%	35%

Alpha, Beta, and Chi are not members of a controlled brother-sister group. Although the 80 percent test is met, the identical ownership test of greater than 50 percent is not met. (In determining identical ownership, include the minimum ownership in each row.) Both tests must be met in order to have a brother-sister controlled group.

In determining ownership for the 80 percent test, only individuals who own stock in each and every corporation of the controlled group are counted. Reg. §1.1563-1(a)(3).

EXAMPLE 14.113 Alpha and Beta each have one class of stock outstanding. Ownership is as follows:

Shareholders	Corporations		Identical Ownership
	Alpha	Beta	
Boggs	55%	100%	55%
Lyle	45%	0%	0%
	100%	100%	55%

At first glance it appears that both the 80 percent and greater than 50 percent tests are met. However, since Lyle does not own stock in Beta Corporation, his ownership is not counted in calculating the 80 percent test. Thus, the 80 percent test is not met and there is not a brother-sister controlled group. (See *Vogel Fertilizer Co.*, 1982-1 USTC ¶9134, 455 U.S. 16, 102 S.Ct. 821 (1982).)

EXAMPLE 14.114 Alpha, Beta and Chi Corporations each have only one class of stock outstanding. The ownership of the stock is as follows:

Shareholders	Corporations			Identical Ownership
	Alpha	Beta	Chi	
Jones	20%	15%	15%	15%
Smith	20%	20%	20%	20%
Nelson	20%	35%	18%	18%
Delta Corporation	40%	30%	47%	N/A
	100%	100%	100%	53%

Although the 80 percent test is not met, the 50 percent test is met. Thus, Alpha, Beta and Chi are a brother-sister controlled group for Code Sec. 1561 purposes and must share tax brackets, the alternative minimum tax exemption, the Section 179 expenses, and the accumulated earnings credit.

Combined Groups

A combined group consists of three or more corporations of which each is a member of a parent-subsidiary controlled group or a brother-sister controlled group and one of the corporations is a common parent in the parent-subsidiary controlled group and also is a member of the brother-sister controlled group. Code Sec. 1563(a)(3).

| EXAMPLE 14.115 | Delta, Gamma, and Sigma Corporations each have only one class of stock outstanding. The ownership of their stock is as follows: |

| | Corporations | | |
Shareholders	Delta	Gamma	Sigma
Jones	60%	40%	—
Hill	40%	60%	—
Gamma Corp.	—	—	80%
	100%	100%	80%

Delta and Gamma are members of a brother-sister controlled group. Gamma and Sigma are members of a parent-subsidiary group. Since Gamma also is a member of the brother-sister group, Delta, Gamma, and Sigma are members of a combined group.

Allocations of Income, Deductions, and Credit

In addition to restrictions placed on controlled groups by Code Sec. 1561, Code Sec. 482 has the potential to effect further constraints. Members of controlled groups may attempt to minimize tax liability by shifting income, deductions, or credits in an advantageous fashion. Code Sec. 482 gives the IRS the power to rearrange the distribution, thereby reducing the controlled group's ability to manipulate tax liabilities. Specifically, the IRS has the right to reallocate gross income, deductions, and credits between two or more corporations owned or controlled by the same interests if such reallocation is necessary to prevent the evasion of taxes or to clearly reflect income.

¶14,445   CONSOLIDATED RETURNS

For tax planning purposes, a parent-subsidiary controlled group has three alternatives: (1) file separate returns, (2) file a consolidated return, or (3) file separate returns with a Code Sec. 243 election of a 100 percent dividends-received deduction. The parent-subsidiary group may make an irrevocable election to file a consolidated tax return. Code Sec. 1501. Each member must consent and each subsidiary must conform its tax year and accounting methods to those of the parent. Consolidated returns must continue to be filed until the IRS grants permission to stop or the group no longer qualifies. For example, if the parent's stock ownership in the subsidiary falls below 80 percent, then the group no longer qualifies to file a consolidated return.

Certain corporations are precluded from being included in a consolidated return. Tax-exempt corporations, life and mutual insurance companies, foreign corporations, U.S. possessions corporations, regulated investment companies and real estate investment trusts, and foreign sales corporations are not eligible to be included in a consolidated return. Code Sec. 1504(b).

There are certain advantages in filing consolidated returns. Income from one member is offset by losses generated by other members. Also, capital losses of a member corporation that otherwise would not be deductible can be used to offset other members' capital gains. Additionally, income from intercompany transactions is not included in the determination of consolidated income. Finally, the group does not have any allocation problems under Code Sec. 482.

There are certain disadvantages in filing a consolidated return. The election is irrevocable and is binding on all subsequent years unless the group is terminated or the IRS grants the group permission to discontinue filing consolidated returns. Also, losses on intercompany transactions are not deductible. Additionally, the recordkeeping needed to file a consolidated return can be significant and, therefore, more costly than if separate returns are filed.

Although the filing of a consolidated tax return has certain advantages, there are several limitations that affect the members' ability to offset income by using the losses or deductions of other members. A loss corporation's net operating loss carryover may be applied against the consolidated income of the group on consolidated returns. However, tax losses of other group members cannot offset the income of another member corporation to the extent that said income is paid out as dividends on certain nonvoting, nonconvertible preferred stock issued after November 17, 1989. Code Sec. 1503(f). Also, if the loss year was a separate return limitation year (SRLY), then the loss may be carried over only against income of the loss corporation. An SRLY is any year in which a member of the group filed a separate tax return. A separate return year is not an SRLY if the corporation was a member of the affiliated group for each day of that year. Under certain conditions, a loss corporation can acquire a profitable subsidiary and apply its loss carryover against the profits of that corporation.

An additional limitation is the inability to offset a built-in deduction of a subsidiary against consolidated income. Built-in deductions can arise if the subsidiary had an SRLY. Any built-in deductions are deducted only against income of the subsidiary that sustained the deductions. The built-in deduction rules do not apply if the group acquired the assets more than 10 years prior to the tax year or the total adjusted basis of all assets (other than cash, marketable securities, and goodwill) of the acquired subsidiary did not exceed the fair market value of all such assets by more than 15 percent. Reg. §1.1502-15.

EXAMPLE 14.116	Maryland Corporation purchases all of the stock of Baltimore Corporation at the end of the year. Baltimore Corporation owns an asset with a basis of $50,000 and a fair market value of $30,000. The asset is sold in the following year for $22,000 and a consolidated return is filed. Of the $28,000 loss, $20,000 is treated as a built-in loss and can be deducted only against the separate income of Baltimore Corporation.

EXAMPLE 14.117	Assume the asset from Example 14.116 is depreciable property. Depreciation deductions attributable to the $20,000 difference between basis and fair market value are treated as built-in deductions and limited to deductions against the separate income of Baltimore.

The rules and regulations pertaining to consolidated income tax returns are very complex. Several treatises, each consisting of several volumes, exist on the subject.

¶14,465 CORPORATE TAX RETURNS

All corporations, with certain exceptions, are required to file a corporate tax return each year. A return must be filed even if the corporation has no taxable income. Code Sec. 6012(a)(2). A corporation that is in existence for only a portion of a tax year is required to file a tax return covering that partial tax year.

A corporation also is required to make estimated tax payments throughout the year unless its estimated tax for the year is less than $500. The corporation must make these payments by the 15th day of the 4th, 6th, 9th, and 12th month of its tax year. Code Sec. 6655(c). Corporations on a calendar year must make the payments by April 15, June 15, September 15, and December 15. In the aggregate these payments must be equal to the lesser of 100 percent of the corporation's actual tax liability (including any alternative minimum tax) or 100 percent of the tax liability for the preceding tax year. The 100 percent test applies only if the preceding tax year was for 12 months and the corporation filed a tax return showing a tax liability. Code Sec. 6655(d). Large corporations (with taxable income of $1,000,000 or more in any one of the three preceding tax years) may use the preceding year's tax liability to estimate the first quarterly payment only; subsequent quarterly payment must be based on this year's expected taxable income. With few exceptions, the corporation will be assessed a nondeductible penalty if it does not make the required payments.

A corporation is required to file Form 1120 by the 15th day of the fourth month following the end of its tax year. Thus, a calendar-year corporation is required to file its return by April 15. However, corporations with a fiscal year ending June 30 must file Form 1120 by September 15. A corporation may receive an automatic extension of six months from the original due date if it files for an extension by the due date of the return. Code Sec. 6081. Form 1120 and related schedules (e.g., Schedule M-1, M-2 and M-3) are available at *www.irs.gov* (the IRS's website).

Form 1120 generally reports taxable income according to various tax rules. The corporation is required to report, on Schedule L, its beginning and ending balance sheets. The balance sheets are taken from the corporation's basic financial accounting records.

Also included in Form 1120 are Schedule M-1 (Reconciliation of Income (Loss) per Books With Income per Return) and Schedule M-2 (Analysis of Unappropriated Retained Earnings per Books). Schedule M-3 (Net Income (Loss) Reconciliation for Corporations With Total Assets of $10 Million or More) is required of large and midsize firms in lieu of Schedule M-1. The net income on the financial books of a corporation may differ from the taxable income on its return. This is caused by differences in accounting methods between financial and taxable income. For example, accelerated depreciation may be used for taxable income computations while straight-line depreciation may be used for financial accounting purposes. Schedule M-1 is used to reconcile these differences.

The reconciling elements of Schedule M-1 fall into four categories:

1. Expenses taken on the books but not taken on the tax return (e.g., federal income taxes)
2. Expenses not taken on the books but taken on the tax return (e.g., charitable contribution carryovers from earlier tax years)
3. Income reported on the books but not reported on the tax return (e.g., tax-exempt municipal bond interest)
4. Income not reported on the books but reported on the tax return (e.g., prepayments recognized as income because of the claim of right doctrine)

These differences are either permanent differences or temporary differences. Permanent differences are income, deduction, gain, or loss items which affect either taxable income or book income, but not both. An example of a permanent difference would be nontaxable municipal bond interest that is included in book income but excluded from taxable income determination. Temporary differences are income, deduction, gain, or loss items that affect both taxable income and book income, but not in the same tax year. Temporary differences affect (create, increase or decrease) a deferred tax asset or liability for book purposes. A temporary difference exists where accelerated depreciation is taken for tax purposes but straight-line depreciation is used for book purposes. Temporary differences reverse themselves over the life of the business.

Schedule M-1 has two columns. In the left column, entries are made for book income, federal income tax, excess of capital losses over capital gains, income items in the return not included in the books (e.g., prepaid rent) and expenses deducted on the books but not on the return (e.g., gifts costing over $25). In the right hand column, entries are made for income reported on the books and not included in the return (e.g., tax-exempt interest) and expenses deducted on the return but not on the books (e.g., excess of accelerated depreciation used for tax purposes over straight-line used for book purposes). The difference between the right hand column and the left hand column should equal the corporation's taxable income before the net operating loss deduction and special deductions.

EXAMPLE 14.118

Harris Corporation had the following results from operations during 2017:

Net income per books, after taxes	$77,000
Taxable income	75,000
Federal income taxes	13,750
Tax-exempt interest on municipal bonds	3,000
Net capital loss (capital losses in excess of capital gains)	1,250
Premiums paid on life insurance for key employees	1,000
Life insurance proceeds received because of death of key employee	10,000
MACRS depreciation in excess of straight-line depreciation used for book purposes	5,000

Harris Corporation's Schedule M-1 is as follows:

Schedule M-1	Reconciliation of Income (Loss) per Books With Income per Return (See page 20 of instructions.)		
1 Net income (loss) per books	77,000	7 Income recorded on books this year not included on this return (itemize):	
2 Federal income tax per books	13,750		
3 Excess of capital losses over capital gains	1,250	Tax-exempt interest $	
4 Income subject to tax not recorded on books this year (itemize):		....	13,000
		8 Deductions on this return not charged against book income this year (itemize):	
5 Expenses recorded on books this year not deducted on this return (itemize):		a Depreciation . . . . $.............	
a Depreciation . . . . $...................		b Charitable contributions $.............	
b Charitable contributions $...................		....	
c Travel and entertainment $...................		....	
....		....	5,000
	1,000	9 Add lines 7 and 8	18,000
6 Add lines 1 through 5	93,000	10 Income (line 28, page 1)—line 6 less line 9	75,000

Schedule M-2, which serves as a bridge of the two balance sheets, also has two columns. The left column is for opening retained earnings, book income for the year, and any increases in retained earnings. The right hand column is for distributions and other items that decrease retained earnings. For example, an adjustment to decrease revenues in a previous period would affect the right hand column. The difference between these two columns is the ending retained earnings. This figure should equal the corporation's unappropriated retained earnings at the end of the tax year entered in the Schedule L balance sheet on Form 1120.

The reconciliation of retained earnings serves to disclose unusual transactions which have a bearing on the corporation or its shareholders. Where the reconciliation of retained earnings shows distributions to the corporate shareholders, the IRS should establish that the shareholders have reported the relevant income.

EXAMPLE 14.119

Assume the same facts in Example 14.118 and the following additional facts. Harris Corporation's beginning balance of unappropriated retained earnings is $160,000. During the year it distributed a cash dividend of $25,000 to its shareholders.

Harris Corporation's Schedule M-2 is as follows:

Schedule M-2	Analysis of Unappropriated Retained Earnings per Books (Line 25, Schedule L)				
1	Balance at beginning of year	160,000	5 Distributions: a Cash	25,000
2	Net income (loss) per books	77,000	b Stock	
3	Other increases (itemize):		c Property	
			6 Other decreases (itemize):	
			7 Add lines 5 and 6	25,000
4	Add lines 1, 2, and 3	237,000	8 Balance at end of year (line 4 less line 7)	212,000

Large and midsize corporations (those with total assets of $10 million or more) must file Schedule M-3 (Net Income (Loss) Reconciliation for Corporations with Total Assets of $10 Million or More) in lieu of Schedule M-1. Schedule M-3 requires more information than Schedule M-1. Its purpose is to make the differences between financial accounting net income (book income) and taxable income more transparent. It requires separate reconciliations of book income and taxable income and of book and tax expense/deduction items. It also requires that firms distinguish between permanent and timing differences.

Schedule M-3 provides the IRS information that will help identify firms that have engaged in aggressive transactions and therefore improve the audit process of corporations. However, completion of Schedule M-3 is quite complex, so coverage in this book is limited to basic examples of adjustments. (It would be helpful if you download Schedule M-3 from the IRS website and refer to it as you read the remainder of this section.)

Part I of Schedule M-3 requests financial information, e.g., the source of the financial information (audited financial statements, SEC Form 10-K, etc.), any restatements of the firm's income statement items for the year and previous five years, and any required adjustments to the firm's net income (loss) due to restatements. Additionally, corporations must indicate the accounting standard used for book purposes. Many corporations use U.S. GAAP; however, the convergence efforts between U.S. accounting standards setters (FASB and SEC) and the International Accounting Standards Board have led to greater use of International Financial Reporting Standards (IFRS). Eventually U.S. corporations may be required to use IFRS and some currently may voluntarily use IFRS. Since U.S. GAAP and IFRS do not fully align, the IRS needs to know which accounting method is used for book purposes so it can better follow book-to-tax adjustments.

In Part I, corporations must convert worldwide consolidated book net income (loss) to adjusted net income (loss) for includible corporations only. Some corporations included in the corporation's worldwide consolidated book income might not be included in its consolidated group for tax purposes. Adjustments must be made to eliminate any nonincludible entities' incomes (losses). The adjusted net income (loss) must then be reconciled to the firm's taxable income reported on Form 1120. Examples 14.120 through 14.122 are based on the examples in the instructions to Schedule M-3.

EXAMPLE 14.120

Mump Inc. is a Detroit-based corporation with stores in the Detroit metropolitan area. It has assets of $500 million. In 2016, it bought 100% of Can Co., a Canadian firm based in Windsor, Canada. Mump Inc. issues consolidated statements for financial accounting purposes; however, Can Co. is not part of its tax consolidated group. In 2017, Mump Inc. reported $80 million of consolidated net income on its audited financial statements. Can Co.'s net loss of $10 million was included in the $80 million. Since Can Co. is not an includible corporation for tax purposes, Mump Inc. makes a $10 million positive adjustment to the $80 million.

Part II requires the reconciliation of net income (loss) items of includible corporations. It contains 25 income/loss items whereby the firm must reconcile book income (loss) to taxable income (loss) by identifying each difference as a temporary or permanent difference. Items included are unearned/deferred revenue, capital loss limitation and carryforward used, and hedging transactions. Column a contains book income (loss) amounts, column b contains temporary differences, column c contains permanent differences, and column d contains income (loss) per tax return.

EXAMPLE 14.121

In 2017, Wing Company's book income was $20 million and it had assets of $300 million. It earned $20,000 interest income on Ohio municipal bonds, which was included in its book income and received $70,000 in prepaid income from customers, which it recorded as unearned revenue for book purposes. It also reported $100,000 in book income from its distributive share of income in Slow Co. (a partnership). The Schedule K-1 Wing Company received from Slow Co. reported the following: $50,000 ordinary income; $70,000 long-term capital gain; $40,000 charitable contribution; and $2,000 Code Section 179 expense. Wing Company treats the difference between book income and taxable income from its investment in Slow Co. as a permanent difference.

Wing Company must make the following adjustments on Part II of Schedule M-3:

Line	Column a	Column b	Column c	Column d
9	$20,000		($20,000)	$-0-
13	$-0-	$70,000		$70,000
20	$100,000		($22,000)	$78,000

Part III requires the reconciliation of expense claimed for book income to the deduction claimed for tax purposes of includible corporations. It contains 37 items where the firm again must identify the temporary and permanent differences. Items included are: bad debt expense, depreciation, depletion, domestic production activities deduction, and fines and penalties. Column a contains book income (loss) amounts, column b contains temporary differences, column c contains permanent differences, and column d contains income (loss) per tax return. Lines 1 and 2 of Part III require a corporation to indicate its current income tax expense (taxes paid/payable this year based on the corporation's taxable income) and deferred income tax expense (which is the net change in deferred tax liability due to temporary differences between book income and taxable income).

EXAMPLE 14.122

Continuing with the Example 14.121, for tax purposes Wing Co. claimed a $300,000 domestic production activities deduction on its tax return. Included in Wing Company's assets are goodwill from previous acquisitions and intellectual property. The goodwill is not deductible for tax purposes but is deductible for book purposes if subject to impairment. In 2017, $120,000 was impaired. The intellectual property is amortizable for both book and tax purposes; book amortization expense was $25,000 and was $40,000 for tax purposes.

Wing Company must make the following adjustments on Part II of Schedule M-3:

Line	Column a	Column b	Column c	Column d
22			$300,000	$300,000
26	$120,000		($120,000)	$-0-
28	$25,000	$15,000		$40,000

Corporations with at least $10,000,000 but less than $50,000,000 in total assets at the end of the tax year may file Schedule M-1 in place of Schedule M-3, Parts II and III. The objectives of the IRS policy are to reduce corporate filing burden and simplify corporate reporting.

As noted earlier, Schedule M-3 is designed to help the IRS better audit corporations. The IRS also developed Schedule UTP (uncertain tax positions statement), which also is designed to increase the IRS's audit effectiveness and efficiency. Corporations with assets of at least $10 million that issued audited financial statements and have one or more tax positions must file form UTP. (A tax position taken on a tax return is one that would result in an adjustment on that tax return if the position is not sustained.) The new form in part evolved from what firms must report for financial accounting purposes; thus, it is discussed further at the end of the next section.

¶14,470 INCOME TAXES AND FINANCIAL ACCOUNTING

Book Income (Loss) and Taxable Income (Loss) Differences

The Financial Accounting Standards Board (FASB) also is concerned about the effects of permanent and temporary differences between book income and taxable income, and the effect these have on financial statement transparency and usefulness. Accounting Standards Codification (ASC) 740 (Income Taxes, ASC Topic 740) provides how firms should determine and account for current income tax expense and deferred income taxes arising from temporary differences. In general, it does not address permanent differences. Deferred income taxes can produce either an asset or a liability.

A firm's income tax provision is its tax expense for financial accounting purposes. It has two components (is the sum of these components): current tax expense (or benefit) and deferred tax expense (or benefit). Current tax expense is the amount of taxes paid or payable (or refundable) based on the corporation's taxable income and existing tax law. Deferred tax expense (or benefit) represents the net change during the year in the corporation's deferred tax liabilities and assets. Deferred tax assets are due to deductible temporary differences and carryforwards. If, based on available evidence, it appears more likely than not that some or all of the deferred tax asset will not be realized then it must be reduced by a valuation allowance. Deferred tax liabilities are due to taxable temporary differences.

A deferred tax asset is recognized when taxable income is greater than book income, and can occur for a variety of reasons: revenues or gains are recognized for tax purposes earlier than for book purposes, expenses or losses are deductible earlier for book purposes than for tax purposes, the book basis of an asset is less than its tax basis, etc. The firm records the deferred tax asset only if it is more likely than not (greater than 50% likelihood) to materialize. A deferred tax liability is recognized when taxable income is less than book income and generally occurs when the opposite timing relationship exists between book and tax recognition; e.g., revenue or gains are recognized for book purposes earlier than for tax purposes, expenses or losses are deductible later for book purposes than for tax purposes, the book basis of an asset is greater than its tax basis.

Once recorded, deferred tax assets and deferred tax liabilities appear on the balance sheet and must be classified as current or noncurrent. If the deferral is due to a related asset or liability then its classification is based on this specific asset or liability; for example, a deferred tax asset or tax liability due to depreciation is noncurrent since property, plant and equipment is a noncurrent asset. If the deferral is not due to a specific asset or liability then it is classified based upon its expected reversal date (current if this period and noncurrent if some future period).

Deferred tax assets and deferred tax liabilities are unusual in that they do not fit the normal scheme where assets are beneficial and liabilities are not. The deferred tax asset is due to book income being less than taxable income, which means that the firm paid more in taxes than it recorded as an income tax expense for book purposes. Effectively, the firm has "prepaid" some expected future taxes, and this prepayment acts as a non-interest bearing receivable from the U.S. government. However, when (if ever) the prepayment will occur is not known with certainty. Similarly, deferred tax liability arises because the firm's taxable income is less than its book income, which means that the firm paid less in taxes than it recorded as an income tax expense for book purposes. The firm has some future tax liability it expects to (might) incur when the timing differences reverse. In the interim, it has full use of the cash it would have used to pay the taxes and the actual liability may never occur.

EXAMPLE 14.123

Tomco's pretax book income and taxable income differ because of one item, prepaid income received from its customers. Its income before the prepaid income was $900,000 in 2017 and $1,200,000 in 2018. Assume that corporate tax rates are a constant 35%. Tomco received $100,000 in prepaid income in 2017 and it earned the $100,000 in 2018. For book purposes Tomco recognizes the $100,000 income in 2018 but for tax purposes it recognizes the $100,000 income in 2017. Its current and deferred tax position is as follows:

	2017		2018	
	Book	**Tax**	**Book**	**Tax**
Income before prepaid income	$900,000	$900,000	$1,200,000	$1,200,000
Prepaid income	-0-	100,000	100,000	-0-
Income after prepaid income	$900,000	$1,000,000	$1,300,000	$1,200,000
Tax rate	x 35%	x 35%	x 35%	x 35%
Income tax expense	$315,000	$350,000	$455,000	$420,000
Current tax expense (payable)		$350,000		$420,000
Deferred tax expense 2017:	$35,000 [($900,000 – $1,000,000) x 35%] increase in deferred tax asset			
Deferred tax expense 2018:	$35,000 [($1,300,000 – $1,200,000) x 35%] decrease in deferred tax asset			

In this example the temporary difference reverses in one year. In 2017 income tax expense was less than current tax expense, and the difference of $35,000 is a deferred tax asset. In 2018 when the temporary difference reverses, income tax expense is $35,000 more than current tax expense and the deferred tax asset is reduced. The journal entries follow:

2017:

Income tax expense	$315,000	
Deferred tax asset	35,000	
Income taxes payable		$350,000

2018:

Income tax expense	$455,000	
Deferred tax asset		35,000
Income taxes payable		$420,000

EXAMPLE 14.124 Smith Company's pretax book income and taxable income differ because of one item, depreciation expense. Its income before depreciation expense was $900,000 in 2017 and $1,200,000 in 2018. Assume that corporate tax rates are a constant 35%. Book depreciation expense in 2017 and 2018 was $100,000 per year. Tax depreciation expense was $150,000 in 2017 and $50,000 in 2018. Its current and deferred tax position is as follows:

	2017		2018	
	Book	Tax	Book	Tax
Income before depreciation expense	$900,000	$900,000	$1,200,000	$1,200,000
Depreciation expense	100,000	150,000	100,000	50,000
Income after depreciation expense	$800,000	$750,000	$1,100,000	$1,150,000
Tax rate	x 35%	x 35%	x 35%	x 35%
Income tax expense	$280,000	$262,500	$385,000	$402,500
Current tax expense (payable)		$262,500		$402,500

Deferred tax expense 2017: $17,500 [($800,000 – $750,000) x 35%] increase in deferred tax liability

Deferred tax expense 2018: $17,500 [($1,100,000 – $1,150,000) x 35%] decrease in deferred tax liability

In this example the temporary difference reversed in one year. In 2017 income tax expense was greater than current tax expense, and the difference of $17,500 is a deferred tax liability. In 2018 when the temporary difference reverses, income tax expense is $17,500 less than current tax expense and the deferred tax liability is reduced. The journal entries follow:

2017:

Income tax expense	$280,000	
Income taxes payable		$262,500
Deferred tax liability		17,500

2018:

Income tax expense	$385,000	
Deferred tax liability	17,500	
Income taxes payable		$402,500

Theoretically, deferred tax assets represent future tax benefits that will reduce future income taxes payable. However, if events indicate that some of the future tax benefit will more likely than not be realized then the firm must use a valuation allowance account (a contra-asset) to revalue the net deferred tax asset. According to ASC 740, both positive and negative evidence must be evaluated in determining whether a valuation adjustment is needed. Past and current information about the firm's current financial position and results of operations should be used. Expectations about future reversals of existing taxable temporary differences, future taxable income, expected future tax rates, and tax planning strategies that might/would be implemented also should be evaluated. If the weight of all evidence indicates that a valuation allowance is needed then the firm is required to do so.

EXAMPLE 14.125 Sueco's NOL carryover for 2017 is $500,000. Assuming a 35% tax rate, the expected future tax benefit is $175,000 ($500,000 x 35%), which would result in a deferred tax asset of $175,000. However, evidence suggests that Sueco will only be able to use $400,000 of the NOL, which gives rise to a $35,000 ($100,000 x 35%) allowance adjustment. The journal entry follows:

Deferred tax asset	$175,000	
Deferred tax asset valuation allowance		$35,000
Income tax expense		140,000

EXAMPLE 14.126

Kimco's taxable income in 2017 was $30,000,000. Its book income was $28,000,000. There is a $2,000,000 temporary difference (item is currently deductible for book purposes but not for tax purposes). In 2018, after careful analysis of all relevant factors, Kimco determines that it is more likely than not that $300,000 of the deferred tax asset will never be realized. Tax rates are a constant 35%. Kimco makes the following journal entries in 2017 and 2018:

2017:

Income tax expense	$9,800,000	
Deferred tax asset	700,000	
Income taxes payable		$10,500,000

2018:

Income tax expense	$105,000	
Deferred tax asset valuation allowance		$105,000

Kimco's net deferred tax asset at the end of 2018 is $595,000 ($700,000 - $105,000). Each year Kimco will evaluate all relevant factors to determine if adjustments are needed to increase or decrease the valuation allowance account.

Again, the intent behind these financial accounting requirements is to provide additional information and transparency about a firm's financial position, cash flows and results of operations to financial statement users.

Uncertain Tax Positions

ASC 740 provides acceptable accounting methods for firms' uncertain tax provisions. It also requires additional disclosure about the unrecognized tax benefits associated with these positions.

Per ASC 740, a tax position can result in a permanent reduction of income taxes payable, a deferral of income taxes otherwise currently payable to future years, or a change in the expected realizability of deferred tax assets. The tax position contains, but is not limited to, a decision not to file a tax return; shift of income between jurisdictions; characterization of income or decision to exclude reporting taxable income in a tax return; a decision to classify a transaction, entity or other position in a tax return as tax exempt; or an entity's status (e.g., pass-through, tax-exempt).

An uncertain tax position must be recognized if it has a more-likely-than-not chance (greater than 50%) of being sustained if contested by the IRS. Being sustained sets a high threshold because it presumes an audit will occur, the IRS has full knowledge of the transactions and events, and all administrative and judicial appeals will occur. It also requires significant judgment and substantial documentation.

If the position does not meet the more-likely-than-not threshold then the firm cannot recognize the tax benefit until it does meet the threshold, the firm settles the position with the IRS or through litigation, or the statute of limitations on the transaction expires. If the position does meet the more-likely-than-not threshold then the firm must measure the amount of benefit recognized for financial accounting purposes. The measure equals the largest amount of benefit that has a greater than 50% chance of being realized upon settlement. The measurement process is quite complex and beyond the scope of this text.

Since the firm in all likelihood takes the tax position in determining its taxable income, its income tax expense for book purposes will be greater than it income taxes payable. Since this difference is due to the uncertain position, the firm must recognize a liability for the unrecognized tax benefit because theoretically at some point the IRS might challenge the position, deny it (or some part of it) and the firm would owe additional taxes.

EXAMPLE 14.127

Vlade Company has two uncertain tax positions. Position A provides a $300,000 tax benefit and position B provides a $500,000 tax benefit. Position B does not meet the more-likely-than not threshold, so for financial accounting purposes it cannot be recognized this year. Position A does meet the threshold, so Vlade Company must measure the benefit before recording it for financial accounting purposes. Based on probability analysis, it determines that $160,000 has a greater than 50% chance of being realized upon settlement with the IRS, so for financial accounting purposes it will record a benefit of $160,000.

EXAMPLE 14.128	In 2017, Sunny Company's tax rate is 35%. Its pretax book income and taxable income are $30,000,000 before considering an uncertain tax position that produces a $2,000,000 deduction for federal income tax purposes. Since the position fails the greater than 50% chance of being realized requirement, Sunny Company cannot record it for book purposes; thus, book income will be $2,000,000 greater than taxable income. So, it makes the following journal entry:

Income tax expense	$10,500,000	
Income taxes payable		$9,800,000
Liability for unrecognized tax benefits		700,000

EXAMPLE 14.129	Continuing with example 14.128, the IRS challenged Sunny Company's position in 2019 and ultimately allowed a $900,000 deduction. Sunny Company makes the following journal entry:

Liability for uncertain income tax benefits	$700,000	
Income taxes payable		$385,000
Income tax expense		315,000

Schedule UTP (Uncertain Tax Position Statement)

The financial accounting treatment of uncertain tax positions hopefully improves firm transparency and financial statement quality. However, it also provides the IRS with additional information to investigate aggressive firm behavior. In an effort to obtain more transparency and information, the IRS issued Schedule UTP. The IRS spends about 25% of its time auditing large corporations by searching for issues. Schedule UTP is expected to enable the IRS to prioritize its selection of taxpayers and issues that pose the greatest compliance risk, reduce the time needed to identify issues and complete audits, ensure that the taxpayer and IRS spend more time discussing the law, and, overall, improve audit effectiveness and efficiency.

Schedule UTP requires firms with assets of $10 million or more to report each U.S. federal income tax position taken on its federal income tax return if (1) the corporation has taken a tax position on its U.S. tax return for the current tax year or a prior tax year and (2) either the corporation or a related party has recorded a reserve with respect to that tax position in audited financial statements, or the corporation or related party did not record a reserve for that tax position because the corporation expects to litigate the position. A reserve is considered recorded for federal income tax purposes when a reserve for federal income tax with respect to a tax position is recorded in the audited financial statements of the corporation or related party. These positions must be reported regardless of the accounting standards used (U.S. GAAP, IFRS or country-specific standards). Additionally, under certain conditions, a tax position for which a reserve was not recorded for financial accounting purposes still must be reported on Schedule UTP. A tax position for which a reserve was not recorded in the audited financial statements, of which the probability of settling with the IRS is less than 50% and for which the corporation intends to litigate the tax position and believes it is more likely then not to prevail in the litigation must be reported on Schedule UTP. Schedule UTP is attached to the firm's Form 1120. (It would be helpful if you download Schedule UTP from the IRS website and refer to it as you read the remainder of this section.)

A tax position taken on a tax return is a tax position that would result in an adjustment to a line item on that return if the position is not sustained. If multiple tax positions affect a single line item then each tax position must be reported separately. The corporation is required to report a concise description of each uncertain tax position. Schedule UTP specifically indicates that the financial accounting treatment of the tax position should be used as a guide. So, if for financial accounting purposes no reserve was required for a tax position taken on the tax return because the amount was immaterial or the tax position was sufficiently certain so that no reserve was required then the corporation does not have to report the tax position on Schedule UTP.

Schedule UTP requires significant disclosure. Part I and Part II addresses the current and prior tax years, respectively. Per the instructions to Schedule UTP, each uncertain tax position (UTP) must be disclosed along with: the primary Code Section relating to the UTP; whether the UTP creates a temporary or permanent difference; and the employer identification number (EIN) of the pass-through entity to which the UTP relates (if it is related to a pass-through entity). Additionally, the corporation must determine if the

UTP is a major tax position (not including expected-to-litigate positions) based on its relative size to the sum of all UTPs taken on the tax return. If the size of the UTP divided by the sum of the sizes of all UTPs taken on the tax return is at least ten percent then it is a major tax position. If it is a major position then this must be indicated on Schedule UTP. Since multinational corporations sometimes use transfer prices to shift income, each UTP also must be identified as either a transfer pricing position (T) or other UTP (G). Finally, the corporation must rank each UTP based on its size, whereby the largest UTP is ranked 1.

Part III of Schedule UTP requires the corporation to give a concise description (no more than a few sentences) of each UTP listed in Part I or Part II. The description must include all relevant facts affecting the tax treatment of the UTP and information that can be expected to apprise the IRS of the identity of the UTP and the nature of the issue. Neither the hazards of the UTP nor an analysis of support for or against the UTP should be included.

SUMMARY

- Taxpayers have a choice of selecting a sole proprietorship, partnership, or corporation as the form to do business.
- Partnerships and sole proprietors may select to be taxed as a corporation for federal tax purposes by using the "check-the-box" system.
- The transfer of property solely for stock of a corporation that is at least 80 percent controlled by the transferor group is tax free.
- Realized gains are recognized on said transfers to the extent of boot received.
- Boot includes property other than stock (although nonqualified preferred stock is boot) as well as liabilities in excess of basis.
- Property basis carries over to the stock and to the corporation.
- Debt is favored over equity because interest is deductible by the corporation and dividends are not deductible.
- High debt-equity ratios are subject to IRS investigation and could lead to debt being classified as equity.
- If debt is reclassified as equity, the interest deduction is lost and interest and principal payments may be classified as dividends.
- Corporations with $1,000,000 or less in equity capital that issue stock for property generally qualify for Code Sec. 1244.
- Losses (except for built-in losses) on the sale of Code Sec. 1244 stock are ordinary up to $50,000 ($100,000 on a joint return), but gains are capital gains.
- Code Sec. 1202 also enables noncorporate taxpayers to exclude 100 percent (75 percent for stock acquired after 2/17/09 and before 9/28/10; 50 percent for stock acquired after 8/10/93 and before 2/18/09) of any gain from the sale or exchange of qualified small business stock held for more than five years which was originally issued.
- Taxpayers may rollover the gain from sale of Code Sec. 1202 stock if they invest the proceeds in a qualified small business corporation within 60 days of sale.
- Corporate tax rates vary from 15 to 39 percent.
- Very large corporations generally pay a flat 35 percent.
- Corporations also may be subject to the alternative minimum tax, although qualified small companies are exempt from it.
- Special features of corporate taxation include: (a) organization expenses are amortized over 180 months; (b) dividends received from U.S. corporations are subject to a dividends-received deduction of 70, 80, or 100 percent; (c) charitable deductions of up to 10 percent of taxable income (as adjusted) are allowed; and (d) capital losses in excess of capital gains must be carried back three years and then forward five years.
- Multiple corporations that are members of a controlled group (brother-sister, parent-subsidiary, or combined group) must share certain tax benefits as if they were one corporation (e.g., tax brackets, Code Sec. 179 election to expense).
- Parent-subsidiary controlled groups may file a consolidated return.

- The corporate annual tax return is due by the 15th day of the fourth month following the close of the tax year, except for those with a June 30 year end.
- Form 1120 is used and requires the computation of taxable income, the reporting of balance (analyzing sheets), and the completion of Schedules M-1 or M-3 (reconciling book income to taxable income) and M-2 (analyzing unappropriated retained earnings per books).
- Some corporations also must file Schedule UTP, which provides the IRS with information about the corporation's uncertain tax positions.
- Schedule UTP evolved from the financial accounting treatment of timing differences and uncertain tax positions as stipulated in ASC 740. ASC 740 provides guidance regarding the financial accounting treatment and disclosure of timing differences, the valuation of deferred tax benefits, and the treatment of uncertain tax positions. Its purpose is to make financial statements more transparent and useful.

QUESTIONS

1. Chris is starting a new business called Church Company. What entity structure may he use?

2. Can a corporation elect to be taxed as a partnership?

3. What is the main tax advantage of the corporate form of organization?

4. What is the purpose of Code Sec. 351 in regard to transfers to corporations?

5. Sam is a sole proprietor and is a cash-basis taxpayer. He is forming Mark Co. One of the assets he will contribute as par of a Code Sec. 351 transfer is accounts receivable. What basis will Mark Co. take in the accounts receivable?

6. Bill, Charlie, and Tom form a corporation. Each receives 100 shares of stock. Bill and Charlie transfer property and Tom performs services for the stock. Does the exchange qualify under Code Sec. 351?

7. Susie and Marilyn transfer property in exchange for all of Falco stock. Susie transfers land and building worth $200,000 in exchange for 150 shares and Marilyn transfers equipment worth $200,000 for 50 shares of stock. Does this exchange qualify as nontaxable under Code Sec. 351?

8. Kim transfers two assets to Jen Co. in a Code Sec. 351 exchange: land bought seven years ago and inventory. What is Kim's holding period in the stock?

9. Anne received stock and boot in a transfer that qualified under Code Sec. 351. She has a realized gain on the transaction. How does boot affect any gain realized under Code Sec. 351?

10. Jennifer transfers properties to Mump Co. in an exchange that meets all the requirements of Code Sec. 351. Several of the properties have liabilities, which also are transferred to the corporation. Will the transfer of the liabilities cause gain recognition for Jennifer?

11. What is the basis in a shareholder's stock after a Code Sec. 351 exchange?

12. What is the corporation's basis in property received under Code Sec. 351?

13. Mara transferred assets to Con Co. on May 15, 2017. Mara acquired the assets on June 15, 2014. What is Con Co.'s holding period for the assets?

14. Is there any depreciation recapture under a Code Sec. 351 exchange?

15. What are the tax consequences of a cash contribution to capital by a nonshare-holder?

16. Why do taxpayers constantly try to increase the debt-equity ratio of a corporation?

17. What requirements must be met for stock to qualify as Code Sec. 1244 stock? What are the tax consequences of meeting these requirements?

18. James, who is single, owns Iper Company stock that became worthless this year. If the stock is Code Sec. 1244 stock then what type of loss does James have for tax purposes?

19. What is the "built-in loss" rule of Code Sec. 1244? What is the purpose of the rule?

20. Rhia Co. began operations in 2017. Are there restrictions on the tax year it may use?

21. When is the cash method of accounting not available to corporations?

22. Are net capital gains and losses treated similarly for individuals and corporations?

23. What is the special depreciation recapture rule that applies to corporations?

24. What is the purpose of the dividends-received deduction? What corporations are entitled to claim this deduction? What dividends qualify for this deduction?

25. Under what circumstances is the dividends-received deduction on a given dividend received not available?

26. Just Corporation owns 11 percent of Shap Co.'s stock. What is the divdends-received deduction it will use?

27. What restrictions apply to the dividends-received deduction of dividends received from debt-financed stock purchases?

28. What happens to the basis of stock on which an "extraordinary" dividend has been received?

29. What are the main differences between net operating losses of individuals and corporations?

30. Milroy Inc. had a $250,000 net operating loss (NOL) this year. In which years can Milroy Inc. use this NOL?

31. In the absence of Code Sec. 248, how would organizational expenditures be treated?

32. What is the amortization period for organizational expenditures?

33. How do corporations treat start-up expenditures?

34. What is the maximum charitable contribution allowance for corporations? Is there a carryover to other years?

35. What is the corporate contribution base for charitable deductions?

36. When is the full fair market value deduction not available on a transfer of property to charity?

37. Describe the disallowed deductions and losses of corporations.

38. When may it be a tax advantage to incorporate even though the income may be double taxed?

39. What is the purpose of the additional 5 percent tax on corporate income between $100,000 and $335,000? The additional 3 percent tax on corporate income between $15,000,000 and $18,333,333?

40. Distinguish between adjustments to taxable income and tax preferences under the alternative minimum tax.

41. How does an asset's regular tax basis differ from its AMT basis?

42. What is the adjusted current earnings adjustment in the computation of the alternative minimum tax?

43. Describe the appreciated property charitable deduction tax preference.

44. What is the purpose of the minimum tax credit?

45. Frumer Inc. is the parent corporation of a parent-subsidiary controlled group. The subsidiaries were acquired this year. It is considering filing a consolidated tax return. What are the advantages and disadvantages of this?

46. Are all affiliated corporations eligible to file consolidated returns?

47. What is a built-in deduction on a consolidated return?

48. Parent Corporation owns all the stock in Subsidiary Corporation and is on the calendar-year tax year. Subsidiary Corporation has a fiscal year ending on August 31. Are they allowed to file a consolidated tax return?

49. Must corporations make estimated tax payments? If so, when?

50. What are the four general categories of Schedule M-1 adjustments needed to reconcile book income and taxable income?

51. What is the purpose of the reconciliation of taxable income with book income?

52. What is the purpose of Schedule UTP?

53. Sevish Co.'s taxable income is greater than its book income. What is the result of this situation?

PROBLEMS

54. Bob, Sam, and Tom formed IU Inc. in 2017. Bob contributed equipment (Code Sec. 1231 property) he acquired in 2014 for $190,000. On the date of transfer, the equipment's adjusted basis and fair market value were $100,000 and $150,000, respectively. Bob received 150 shares of IU Inc. Sam transferred land (capital asset) which he acquired in 2011. The land's adjusted basis and fair market value on the date of transfer were $50,000 and $250,000, respectively. Bob received 250 shares of IU Inc. Tom contributed inventory with an adjusted basis of $35,000 and a fair market value of $50,000 in return for 50 shares of IU Inc.
    a. What are the tax consequences to Bob?
    b. What are the tax consequences to Sam?
    c. What are the tax consequences to Tom?

55. Olivia and Tatiana form Jen Co. in 2017. Olivia contributed services worth $24,000 and property worth $1,000 and Tatiana contributed property worth $25,000. Each received 25 shares of Jen Co. Is the transaction nontaxable under Code Sec. 351?

56. Assume the same facts in 55 except Olivia received 40 shares and the fair market value of the property she contributed was $16,000. Is the transaction nontaxable under Code Sec. 351?

57. In 2017, Thomas transferred land he bought in 2008 worth $100,000 to Andy Co. in return for 50 shares of stock. The land has an adjusted basis of $30,000 and is subject to a $50,000 mortgage. The transfer is part of a qualified Code Sec. 351 transfer (Thomas is one of several transferors). What are the tax consequences to Thomas?

58. Yager and Boggs formed Y&B Company in 2017. Yager contributed a building with a fair market value of $97,000, a mortgage of $75,000 and an adjusted basis of $50,000 in return for 22 shares of Y&B Company stock. (Y&B assumed the mortgage.) Boggs contributed land with a fair market value of $22,000 and an adjusted basis of $40,000 in return for 12 shares of Y&B Company stock and 10 $1,000 bonds. Lyle performed legal and accounting work during the incorporation process in return for six shares of stock. Determine the tax consequences of the transfers to *all* parties.

59. Bill decided to incorporate his printing business and to give his manager, Charlie, a share in the business. Bill's sole proprietorship transferred the following to Tom Co.:

	Basis	Value
Accounts payable	$0	$7,000
Accounts receivable	0	8,000
Printing press	6,000	10,000
Truck	24,000	20,000
Cash	2,000	2,000

Bill received 70 shares of the stock, worth $29,000. Charlie invested $2,000 in cash and received the remaining 30 shares of the stock.

What are the tax consequences to Bill, Charlie, and Tom Co.?

60. Susan Sweets is a 40 percent shareholder in Acclaim Inc., a theatrical supplies company. She transfers a fully depreciated car with a value of $12,000 to the corporation, but does not receive any consideration for it.
    a. What are the tax consequences to Susan?
    b. What are the tax consequences to the corporation?
    c. What, if any, changes if Susan received another 10 percent stock interest for the car?

61. The municipality of Viewpoint, Kansas, wishes to attract local businesses. As part of a development program, it donated a building with a basis of $50,000 and a value of $200,000 plus $75,000 in cash to Sound & Fury Drums Inc. What are the tax consequences to Sound & Fury?

62. In each of the following situations, determine if there is any depreciation or general business credit recapture.
    a. Joe incorporates his sole proprietorship and subsequently gifts the stock to his two children.
    b. Joe and nine others put their businesses in one corporation in return for five to 15 percent of the stock. Joe's share is 8 percent.
    c. Joe incorporates his sole proprietorship. Soon thereafter, the corporation sells some of the assets.
    d. Same as (c), but the corporation abandons some of the assets.
    e. Joe gifts his car, used only for business, to his son, who transfers it to his 100 percent owned corporation.

63. Zebra Corporation received a gift of a tract of land from a nonshareholder to encourage Zebra Corporation to build a plant on the land. The value of the land was $20,000. Zebra Corporation also received cash of $25,000 from nonshareholders, which was used to buy machinery costing $25,000.
    a. How much income does Zebra Corporation report as a result of these transactions?
    b. What is the basis of the assets to Zebra Corporation?

64. Gary and Tom own 100 shares of Rosa Co. stock. Gary acquired the stock for $60,000 from Rosa Co. three years ago when it was formed. Tom acquired the stock two years ago from Julie for $$45,000. Gary and Tom are single. Rosa Co. meets all the requirements of Code Sec. 1244. Rosa Co. just went through bankruptcy this year and its stock is completely worthless. What are the tax consequences to Gary and Tom?

65. In 2015, Susan Christian transferred a machine with a fair market value of $30,000 and an adjusted basis of $40,000 to JPC Corporation in return for 60 shares of stock. The stock qualified as Code Sec. 1244 stock and the transfer qualified under Code Sec. 351. In 2017, JPC Corporation liquidated due to bankruptcy and Susan's stock became worthless. What is Susan's tax position in 2017?

66. Niffy Corporation, a domestic C corporation, issued 100 shares of Code Sec. 1202 stock on November 1, 2012, to Jennifer. This was the first time it issued such stock. Jennifer sold the shares on November 15, 2017. She had a $20,000 recognized gain on the sale. How much of the gain can Jennifer exclude, assuming Niffy Corporation always has been actively engaged in a trade or business and always has qualified as a small business corporation?

67. A corporation has income of $80,000 from operations, a $12,000 short-term capital gain, and a $16,000 long-term capital loss. What is the corporation's taxable income for the year?

68. Baginski Corporation purchased a residential building and depreciated it using straight-line depreciation. Determine the amount of ordinary income and Code Sec. 1231 income to be recognized assuming:

Selling price	$480,000
Cost	500,000
Depreciation taken	270,000

69. Cablephones Inc., which is not a member of an affiliated group, had gross income from operations of $390,000 and deductible expenses of $420,000. Dividends of $300,000 were received from more than 20 percent owned U.S. corporations.
    a. What is the dividends-received deduction?
    b. What would the dividends-received deduction be if the deductible expenses were $451,000?

70. What is the dividends-received deduction allowed a corporation that receives $170,000 in dividends from a 45 percent owned domestic corporation if 37 percent of the cost of the investment is borrowed to make the purchase?

71. McIntyre Corporation purchases 1,000 shares of a 10 percent owned domestic corporation at $100 per share. McIntyre receives a $25 per share dividend within the first year after the purchase. What is the amount by which McIntyre must reduce the basis of the acquired stock?

72. Lyle Co. had an $800,000 net operating loss (NOL) in 2017. Its taxable income in 2015 and 2016 was $100,000 and $900,000, respectively. 2017 was an unusual year and Lyle Co. expects to be profitable in 2018 and all subsequent years. It estimates that its taxable income (before a deduction for an NOL carryover) will be $335,000 in 2018 and $4,000,000 in 2019. Lyle Co. uses 6% as its after-tax discount rate. Should Lyle Co. carry back the NOL or carry it forward?

73. Bevin Inc. had the following in 2017:

Gross income from operation	$450,000
Dividends from 22%-owned corporation	150,000
Operating expenses	310,000
Charitable contributions	30,000
NOL deduction from 2015	20,000
Domestic production activities deduction*	11,000
*based on all limits	

   a. What is Bevin Inc.'s taxable income in 2017?
   b. What carrybacks or carryovers does it have from 2017?

74. Susco had the following items this year:

Gross receipts	$700,000
Operating expenses	500,000
Long-term capital gain	40,000
Long-term capital loss	(20,000)
Short-term capital gain	16,000
Short-term capital loss	(44,000)

What is Susco's taxable income and does it have any carrybacks/carryovers?

75. In problem 74 above, what would be Susco's taxable income if the long-term capital gain were $70,000 (instead of $40,000)?

76. Caskets Inc. was incorporated on June 1, but did not start business until September 1. It adopted a fiscal year ending March 31, coinciding with the end of its natural business cycle. In connection with organizing the business, Caskets Inc. incurred the following expenses:

Legal fees for incorporating	$8,000
Accounting fees for opening corporate books	400
Tax planning advice	300
Printing and issuing stock certificates	50
Incorporation fee to state	100
Temporary directors' fees	2,000
Legal fees for the transfer of assets to the corporation	500
	$11,350

   a. What is the amount of the organizational expenditures?
   b. How much of the amount is deductible in the corporation's first taxable year?

77. Ludlow Corporation has excess inventory that it no longer wants. In order to clear out its warehouse to make room for shipments of new inventory, it has decided to donate the inventory (bedding equipment) to several hospitals. The basis of the inventory is $170,000 and its fair market value is $220,000. The corporation made no other contributions this year. Determine its charitable contribution deduction assuming that its taxable income before the dividends-received deduction and charitable contributions deduction is $1,000,000 and included in gross income is $100,000 in dividends received from a 35-percent-owned domestic corporation.

78. Donor Corporation had the following income and deductions for last year:

Sales	$5,000,000
Cost of sales	3,500,000
Other operating expenses	800,000
Dividends (from 5 percent owned domestic corporations)	100,000

Donor Corporation also made contributions (not included above) to qualifying charitable organizations of $175,000. Determine Donor Corporation's taxable income for the year.

79. Barbara sells an asset to her wholly-owned corporation. The asset has a basis of $32,000 and a fair market value at the time of the sale of $27,000. What is the corporation's recognized gain or loss if it sells the asset for $30,000 several years later?

80. On April 4, 2017, Mexco sold stock it held as an investment. It had a $300,000 short-term capital loss on the sale. It also sold a building, equipment, and the land under the building on July 1, 2017. Information about each asset is presented below. Mexco used MACRS depreciation on the equipment and straight-line depreciation on the building. Additionally, Mexco had a $75,000 Code Sec. 1231 loss last year (and it has no Code Sec. 1231 gains or losses in previous years). Mexco did not sell any other assets this year. What are the tax results of the sale?

	Building	Equipment	Land
Cost	$700,000	$200,000	$100,000
Accumulated depreciation to sale date	400,000	130,000	
Amount realized on the sale	500,000	90,000	300,000

81. Red Paint Corporation generated $100,000 of taxable income from operations last year, plus a $70,000 gain from the sale of land used as a parking lot for six years. What is the amount of federal income tax payable?

82. A & G Drug Store Inc. has been in operation for six years. The first four years it accumulated operating loss carryovers of $65,000. The fifth year it earned $25,000 in operating income and had $8,000 of dividend income. In its sixth year it had $54,000 in operating income and $11,000 of dividend income from X Corporation (A & G owns 10% of X Corporation, and did so in year 5). Compute A & G Drug's tax liability for its sixth year.

83. Determine the amount of adjustments and tax preferences for the alternative minimum tax in each of the following situations:
    a. Equipment acquired in this year was depreciated under MACRS. Depreciation claimed for the year was $40,000; depreciation would have been $30,000 under the 150% declining balance method.
    b. An asset was sold for $180,000 using the installment method of accounting. Only $20,000 of the $60,000 gain on the sale was reported this year since the asset constituted nondealer property.
    c. The corporation owned some Leon County school bonds on which it received $15,000 of tax-exempt interest.
    d. The corporation purchased $100,000 of Section 1245 five-year property during the year on which it used 200 percent declining-balance depreciation.

84. Determine the alternative minimum tax assuming a corporation has the following information:

Taxable income	$600,000
Adjustments to income	300,000
Tax preferences	200,000
General business credit	30,000

85. Assume the same information as in the previous problem, except that the adjustments to income are $100,000. What is the alternative minimum tax?

86. Presented below is Argo Company's adjusted current earnings and preadjustment alternative minimum taxable income for 2016 through 2019:

Year	Preadjustment AMTI	ACE
2016	$400,000	$350,000
2017	400,000	800,000
2018	700,000	600,000
2019	650,000	300,000

Determine the ACE adjustment (positive or negative) for each of the years.

87. Determine the alternative minimum tax assuming a corporation has the following:

Taxable income	$500,000
Adjustments to income (other than the ACE adjustments)	200,000
Tax preferences	100,000
Adjusted current earnings (ACE)	900,000

88. Windy Company had the following AMTI and ACE for 2016, 2017, and 2018. Indicate the ACE adjustment for each year.

	2016	2017	2018
AMTI	$500,000	$500,000	$500,000
ACE	400,000	300,000	800,000

89. The four Ames brothers own 25 percent each of two corporations, Unicycles Inc. and Tandem Inc. Last year, the two corporations generated $50,000 and $100,000 in taxable income, respectively. What is the total corporate tax liability?

90. The matrix below shows the stock ownership in four corporations by four unrelated individuals:

Shareholder	Percentages of Stock Owned in Corporations			
	A	B	C	D
1	10	5	10	20
2	30	40	30	10
3	30	15	10	20
4	30	40	50	50

Which of the above corporations, if any, are members of a brother-sister controlled group? Explain why each corporation is included or not.

91. Tiller Corporation's net income per books (after taxes) was $68,450. During the year, it had the following transactions:

Federal income taxes	$13,750
Net capital loss	4,000
Premiums paid on key person life insurance policy	2,800
Interest paid on a loan to acquire tax-exempt bonds	2,000
MACRS depreciation (for financial accounting purposes, Tiller claimed $4,000 of straight-line depreciation)	11,000
Tax-exempt interest on municipal bonds	9,000

Determine Tiller Corporation's taxable income assuming it does not have an NOL deduction or special deductions. Reconcile the difference between book income and taxable income.

92. Crates Corporation's financial income before income taxes for the year was $250,000. Organization costs of $90,000 are being written off over a 10-year period for financial statement purposes. For tax purposes, these costs are being written off over the minimum allowable period. For the year, Crates' taxable income was:
    a. $235,000
    b. $247,600
    c. $250,000
    d. $253,000

93. A corporation with $300,000 in taxable income has a tax liability of:
    a. 34 percent of $300,000
    b. $22,250 + 34 percent of $200,000
    c. $22,250 + 34 percent of $200,000 + 5 percent of $200,000
    d. 15 percent of $50,000 + 25 percent of $25,000 + 34 percent of $225,000

94. Cybele formed a corporation and transferred a building with a basis of $50,000, subject to a $70,000 mortgage, and cash of $15,000 to it for stock. Cybele's basis in her stock and the corporation's basis in the building are:

	Stock	Building
a.	Zero	$50,000
b.	$15,000	50,000
c.	Zero	40,000
d.	Zero	55,000

95. The following statements about the dividends-received deduction are true, except:
    a. The stock on which dividends are received must be held for at least 46 days.
    b. The deduction is not available if the long position is offset by a similar short position.
    c. The deduction is limited to a percentage of taxable income prior to charitable contribution, net operating loss, and capital loss deductions.
    d. Even if a consolidated return is *not* filed, a 100 percent dividends-received deduction is available for payments between members of the same affiliated group.

96. Excluding extensions, which one of the following Form 1120 tax returns is filed late?

	Tax Year Ended	Date Filed
a.	January 31, 2018	May 15, 2018
b.	August 31, 2017	December 2, 2017
c.	July 31, 2017	November 29, 2017
d.	December 31, 2018	April 15, 2019

97. During 2017, Jones transferred $15,000 cash and a building with an adjusted basis of $50,000 and a fair market value of $90,000 to Malibu Gardens Corporation in return for 90 percent of its only class of stock. In addition, for a bona fide business purpose, Malibu Gardens assumed the $65,000 outstanding mortgage on the building. What is the amount of Jones's recognized gain on the transfer?
    a. $0
    b. $5,000
    c. $15,000
    d. $25,000
    e. None of the above

98. In 2017, Sally transferred a building with an adjusted basis of $40,000 and a fair market value of $45,000 to Sandy Corporation. In exchange, she received the following:
    1. 80 percent of Sandy Corporation's only class of stock, fair market value of $25,000
    2. Equipment with a fair market value of $25,000 and an adjusted basis of $10,000

    What is Sandy Corporation's basis in the building received in the transfer?
    a. $5,000
    b. $25,000
    c. $50,000
    d. $45,000
    e. None of the above

99. Indo Corporation was organized on January 4, 2017, and began active business on January 5, 2017. Indo incurred the following expenses in connection with creating its business.

Professional fees for stock issuance	$400
State incorporation fees	200
Printing costs for stock certificates	150
Broker's commissions on sale of stock	700
Legal fees for drafting the charter	600
Expenses for temporary directors	500

    What is the maximum amount of organizational expenses which may be deducted by Indo on its 2017 tax return?
    a. $1,300
    b. $1,700
    c. $1,850
    d. $2,550
    e. None of the above

100. Sinco Company had $300,000 of income from business operations and $700,000 of allowable expenses. It also received $20,000 in dividends from a domestic corporation in which it owns 22 percent of the stock. What is Sinco Company's net operating loss?
    a. $380,000
    b. $396,000
    c. $397,000
    d. $400,000
    e. None of the above

101. Jones is a sole proprietorship. He would like to be taxed as a corporation for federal tax purposes. Jones may become a corporation by:
    a. Filing a corporate return for this year
    b. Timely filing Form 7701 and attaching it to this year's return
    c. Timely filing Form 8832 and attaching it to this year's return
    d. He cannot be taxed as a corporation

102. XYZ is a corporation. It needs to raise some capital and is uncertain whether to issue debt or equity. Which of the following statements is true?
    a. Both interest payments and dividend payments are deductible as expenses
    b. Interest payments are deductible but dividend payments are not deductible as expenses
    c. Principal repayment and stock retirement are deductible expenses
    d. The shareholders (noncorporate and corporate) are indifferent as to whether they receive interest or dividends
    e. All of the above are true
    f. None of the above are true

103. In the year of formation, a corporation:
    a. May elect a tax period other than those of its major shareholders
    b. Must elect the same tax period as its major shareholders
    c. Must use the cash basis for its accounting method
    d. None of the above

104. Smith Co. sells a machine during the year for $100,000. Smith acquired the machine for $140,000. At the time of sale, the machine's adjusted basis was $47,200. Smith Co.'s recognized gain on the sale is:
    a. $52,800 Code Sec. 1231 gain
    b. $52,800 Code Sec. 1245 gain
    c. $10,560 Code Sec. 291 gain and $42,240 Code Sec. 1231 gain
    d. $52,800 long-term capital gain
    e. None of the above

105. Bevco incurred start-up expenditures while investigating the acquisition of a business. With respect to such expenditures, Bevco:
    a. Can expense them in the year incurred
    b. Must capitalize them and deduct them in the year of liquidation
    c. Can expense the first $5,000 in the year incurred and elect to amortize the remaining costs over 180 months
    d. Must capitalize them but may elect to amortize them over 50 months

106. Which of the following corporate groups may file a consolidated tax return?
    a. Brother-sister group
    b. Parent-subsidiary group
    c. Both brother-sister and parent-subsidiary groups
    d. None of the above corporate groups may file a consolidated tax return.

107. Shock Inc. has several uncertain tax positions this year. It should do which of the following:
    a. Determine if the probability of the position being sustained upon IRS challenge is greater than 50%.
    b. Determine the largest dollar amount of benefit of the position that has a greater than 50% chance of being realized upon settlement.
    c. For financial accounting purposes, record the benefit calculated in b.
    d. All of the above

108. Feld Corporation's taxable income for 2017 before the domestic production activities deduction was $5,000,000. Its income from qualified production activities in 2017 was $6,000,000. Feld Corporation's W-2 wages allocable to qualified production activities for 2017 were $2,000,000. What is Feld Corporation's domestic production activities deduction?

109. A, B and V Corporations each have only one class of stock outstanding. The ownership of the stock is as follows:

Shareholders	Corporations			Identical Ownership
	A	J	V	
James	15%	20%	15%	15%
Jennifer	15%	20%	20%	15%
Kimberly	15%	25%	15%	15%
Susan	15%	10%	20%	10%
Tom Corporation	40%	25%	30%	N/A
	100%	100%	100%	55%

Are any of the corporations part of a brother-siser controlled group for Code Sec. 1561 purposes?

110. Tatco's pretax book income and taxable income differ because of one item, warranty expense. Tatco reports a $200,000 warranty expense and a related estimated liability for warranties for book-income purposes in 2017. It does not recognize an expense for tax purposes based on the estimate. In 2018, Tatco paid the $200,000 expense (settled customer claims) for tax purposes. Its income before warranty expense was $900,000 in 2017 and $1,200,000 in 2018. Assume that corporate tax rates are a constant 35%. What is its current and deferred tax position in 2017 and 2018?

111. **Comprehensive Problem.** Last year, Intrepid Corporation's tax return revealed the following items:

Dividends from 20 percent owned domestic corporations	$60,000
Gross income from services rendered	300,000
Miscellaneous expenses	250,000
Long-term capital gains	30,000
Net operating loss carryforward	15,000
Charitable contributions	20,000

a. What is Intrepid's dividends-received deduction?
b. What is the charitable contribution deduction?
c. What is the taxable income for the year?

112. **Comprehensive Problem.** Mr. Trent transferred three apartment buildings to a new corporation in exchange for all its stock. The facts pertaining to the buildings were:

Building	Basis	Value	Mortgage	Recapture Potential
1	$10,000	$100,000	$60,000	$0
2	15,000	80,000	0	5,000
3	20,000	30,000	0	4,000

a. What gains are realized and recognized on each building? What is the character of the gains?
b. What is the corporation's basis in each building?
c. What is Mr. Trent's basis in his stock?

113. **Comprehensive Problem.** Jones, Able, and Smith want to form Shriver Corporation. They want to accomplish this in the most tax efficient (least costly) way possible. They have asked for advice. The counselor will receive $10,000 (in stocks and bonds). The relevant information follows. Each bond has a face value of $2500.

PARTY	GIVES		RECEIVES
Jones	**Fair Market Value**	**Adjusted Basis**	
Machine	$100,000	$70,000*	
Land	40,000	20,000	(1) 25 shares of stock
Building	65,000	45,000**	(2) $20,000

* Acquired for $85,000; straight-line depreciation taken.
** Acquired for $70,000; straight-line depreciation taken; liability of $60,000 is assumed by Shriver Corporation.

PARTY	GIVES		RECEIVES
Able	**Fair Market Value**	**Adjusted Basis**	
Machine	$70,000	$80,000*	(1) Eight shares of stock
Building	50,000	65,000**	(2) Two 10-year bonds
			(3) $5,000

* Acquired for $95,000; straight-line depreciation taken.
** Acquired for $75,000; straight-line depreciation taken; liability of $70,000 is on the property.

PARTY	GIVES		RECEIVES
Smith	**Fair Market Value**	**Adjusted Basis**	
Machine	$80,000	$80,000	
Automobile	15,000	10,000*	(1) 23 shares of stock
Truck	40,000	30,000**	(2) Eight 10-year bonds

* Acquired for $15,000; straight-line depreciation taken.
** Acquired for $40,000; straight-line depreciation taken.

PARTY	GIVES	
Counselor	Services	$10,000	(1) One share of stock
			(2) Two 10-year bonds

Determine all tax consequences for Jones, Able, Smith, the counselor, and Shriver Corporation assuming the transfer occurred in 2017. Also assume that Jones, Able, and Smith are unrelated parties.

114. **Research Problem.** In 2015, Salt Lake Resorts Inc. generated a capital gain of $300,000 and no other taxable income or loss. In 2017, the corporation suffered a net operating loss of $50,000, which was carried back to 2015. Salt Lake Resorts Inc. did not make an election to carry forward only. The corporation has large tax preferences. The IRS claims that (1) no tax benefit results from the carryback, and (2) the NOL is nevertheless used up. Salt Lake Resorts Inc. believes that either a tax benefit results or it can carry forward the $50,000 net operating loss to 2018. Is the IRS right? Why?

(See *Foster Lumber Co., Inc.,* 76-2 USTC ¶9740, 429 U.S. 32, 97 S.Ct. 204 (1976).)

115. **Research Problem.** Cambo Corporation, a calendar-year taxpayer, was formed in 2014 and incurred $60,000 in organizational expenditures. Had the corporation made a proper election under Code Sec. 248, it would have been entitled to a $7,000 deduction in 2014. However, on its 2014 tax return it erroneously claimed a $60,000 current deduction (i.e., it expensed the full amount in the year it was organized). Upon audit in 2017, the IRS disallowed the $60,000 deduction and also did not allow Cambo a $7,000 deduction. Cambo Corporation seeks your advice on this issue.

(See Reg. §1.248-1(c); *Bay Sound Transportation Co.,* 1967-2 USTC ¶9641 (DC Texas 1967), aff'd in part and rev'd in part on other issues, 1969-1 USTC ¶9371, 410 F.2d 505 (CA-5 1969).)

116. **Tax Return Problem.** KJJ Corp. was formed on October 10, 2001 by Kimberly Jen (123-45-6789), Jennifer James (234-56-7890) and James Kim (345-67-8901). It is a hardware store and is located at 175 Clerk Road, Newtown, OH 45105. KJJ's employer identification number is 10-1010101 and its business code is 444130. KJJ's telephone number is 513-525-1234 and its e-mail address is *KJJCorp@kjj.com.*

KJJ Corp. uses the calendar year and the accrual basis. It uses straight-line depreciation for tax and book purposes and FIFO and lower-of-cost-or-market for inventory purposes.

Kimberly, Jennifer and James each received 200 shares of KJJ Corp.'s common stock on October 10, 2001. No other stock has been issued or is outstanding. Each is a full-time employee of the firm and each is paid $200,000.

KJJ Corp. made a $105,000 ($35,000 to each owner) cash distribution in 2016.

During 2016, KJJ Corp. made estimated federal tax payments of $55,000 each quarter.

Financial information for 2016 follows:

Income Statement

Income

Sales		$5,400,000
Sales returns and allowances		20,000
Net sales		5,380,000
Cost of goods sold		3,120,000
Gross profit		2,260,000
Interest income		
Corporate bonds	$20,000	
State bonds	60,000	80,000
Dividend income		100,000
Total income		$2,440,000

Expenses

Salaries—officers	$600,000	
Salaries and wages—other	510,000	
Life insurance premiums on three owners/officers KJJ Corp. is the beneficiary	20,000	
Repairs and maintenance	30,000	
Taxes (state, local, payroll)	249,000	
Interest expense		
Loans to acquire state bonds	$25,000	
Other	47,000	72,000
Advertising		36,000
Charitable contribution		25,000
Depreciation		120,000
Employee benefits program		63,000
Total expenses		1,725,000
Net income before taxes		$715,000
Federal income taxes		(214,200)
Net income per books		$500,800

Balance Sheet

	12/31/15	12/31/16
Assets		
Cash	$400,000	$550,000
Trade and accounts receivables	600,000	623,000
Inventories	1,500,000	1,330,000
Corporate bonds	250,000	260,000
State bonds	800,000	851,000
Stock (< 20%-owned, domestic corporations)	900,000	1,000,000
Prepaid federal income taxes	0	5,800
Property, plant and equipment	3,000,000	3,030,000
Accumulated depreciation	(1,100,000)	(1,220,000)
Land	50,000	50,000
Other assets	6,000	3,000
Total Assets	$6,406,000	$6,482,800
Liabilities and Owners' Equity		
Accounts payable	$301,000	$257,000
Other current liabilities	405,000	430,000
Mortgages	1,500,000	1,200,000
Capital stock	3,000,000	3,000,000
Retained earnings	1,200,000	1,595,800
Total Liabilities and Owners' Equity	$6,406,000	$6,482,800

Prepare KJJ Corp.'s From 1120 and related schedules/forms: Forms 1125-A and 1125-E, and Schedules C, J, K, L, M-1, and M-2. (Do not complete Form 4562 [depreciation calculation] since you do not have all the information). Go to *www.irs.gov* and download the necessary forms.

Chapter

15

Corporate Nonliquidating Distributions

OBJECTIVES

After completing Chapter 15, you should be able to:

1. Understand the computation of earnings and profits (E&P), the role of current and accumulated E&P, and the sources of a distribution.
2. Recognize the tax consequences to the distributing corporation and the shareholder distributee.
3. Judge the tax aspects of property distributions to corporate and noncorporate distributees.
4. Describe why dividends paid in stock are generally tax free and why there are several exceptions.
5. Recall when stock redemptions are treated as dividends v. sales or exchanges and how indirect ownership is ascertained.
6. Define death tax redemptions.
7. Explain the tax consequences to a corporation purchasing its own stock.

OVERVIEW

Corporations make distributions to shareholders for many reasons and in many ways. Distributions to shareholders because of their shareholder status (as opposed to employee or creditor) may be in cash, property, or the distributing corporation's own stock or stock rights. The tax status of these distributions determines whether the shareholder and/or the corporation have income, as well as the type of income. The tax status of the distribution depends upon what was distributed, why it was distributed, and the surrounding circumstances of the distribution.

Distributions can be broadly classified as distributions where the shareholder does not surrender stock and those where the shareholder does surrender stock. The former are treated as dividends to the extent that they are made out of the corporation's earnings and profits. However, distributions of stock and/or stock rights may or may not be treated as dividends. Distributions in exchange for the shareholder's stock may be classified as dividends, stock redemptions, or a liquidation of the corporation.

This chapter discusses distributions of cash or property that appear to be dividends, distributions of a corporation's stock and/or stock rights, and stock redemptions. This classification can have significant tax effects on the shareholder and the distributing corporation. Distributions in complete liquidations are discussed in Chapter 16.

Distributions with Respect to Stock

¶15,001   **DIVIDEND DISTRIBUTIONS**

Most corporations pay dividends on both common and preferred stock. Dividends on preferred stock generally must be paid before dividends on the common stock. Preferred shareholders also take precedence over common shareholders in the event of liquidation.

The more profitable a corporation is, the more likely it is to make distributions. This is due partly to the ability to pay and partly to the imposition of an accumulated earnings tax on corporations that allow their earnings to accumulate above certain levels. Code Sec. 531. Since dividends are nondeductible to the corporation, but taxed to the shareholders at reduced rates (often called "double taxation"), Congress has found this penalty tax necessary to encourage dividend distributions.

The tax status of a cash or property distribution to shareholders is affected by the distributing corporation's earnings and profits (E&P). Such a distribution is considered a dividend to the extent that it is made from the distributing corporation's E&P for the current tax year or E&P accumulated since March 1, 1913. Code Sec. 316(a). Dividends are included in gross income and taxed at reduced rates. Code Sec. 301(c). However, a corporate distributee is entitled to the dividends-received deduction provided by Code Sec. 243.

Distributions in excess of the corporation's E&P are considered to be a return of capital. The excess is applied against the shareholder's adjusted basis in the stock. As such, it is nontaxable and reduces the adjusted basis. If the distribution is greater than the shareholder's adjusted basis, then the excess is treated as a gain from the sale or exchange of the stock. Code Sec. 301(c). It is a capital gain if the stock is a capital asset. Normal holding period rules are used to determine whether the gain is long-term or short-term.

EXAMPLE 15.1	Ace Corporation distributes $30,000 to each of its two equal shareholders, Barbara Bates and Elmer Platt. Ace Corporation's E&P is $40,000. Barbara's adjusted basis in her stock is $15,000. Elmer's adjusted basis in his stock is $7,000. Barbara and Elmer each have a taxable dividend of $20,000. In addition, Barbara has a $10,000 return of capital which is nontaxable and reduces her adjusted basis in the stock to $5,000 ($15,000 − $10,000). Elmer has a $7,000 return of capital which is nontaxable and reduces his adjusted basis in the stock to zero. He also must recognize a $3,000 gain for the amount in excess of his adjusted basis.

¶15,011   **EARNINGS AND PROFITS (E&P)**

Although earnings and profits (E&P) have a significant impact in determining the tax status of distributions, the term is not defined in the Internal Revenue Code. Code Sec. 312 provides an indication of how certain transactions affect E&P, but it does not specifically define it. E&P is a tax term. It has some similarities to retained earnings, but it is not equal to it. E&P is a measure of the corporation's economic capacity to pay a dividend. Its main purpose is to measure the amount of a distribution which represents a taxable dividend to the shareholder. Thus, certain transactions that reduce or increase retained earnings may not have a similar effect on E&P. For example, a stock dividend reduces retained earnings but does not reduce E&P.

EXAMPLE 15.2	The Camping Corporation pays a 20 percent stock dividend, consisting of 10,000 shares with a $1 par value and a fair market value of $5. The accounting entries would be a debit (a reduction) to retained earnings of $50,000, a credit to capital stock of $10,000, and a credit to paid in capital of $40,000. For tax purposes, the stock dividend is irrelevant. E&P stays the same since the stock transaction in no way has reduced the corporation's capacity to pay a dividend in cash or property.

E&P is used up on a LIFO basis; that is, distributions are considered to come from current E&P first and then from accumulated E&P since March 1, 1913. A new corporation begins with no E&P. Current E&P is determined annually. Each year a corporation adds to accumulated E&P to the extent that it does not distribute current E&P. If a corporation distributes more than its current E&P, then the accumulated E&P is reduced by such excess, but never below zero. If current E&P is negative, then the deficit also reduces accumulated E&P. Finally, for distributions in excess of E&P: (1) current E&P is allocated on a pro rata basis and (2) accumulated E&P is allocated on a chronological basis.

| EXAMPLE 15.3 | Jasmine Company was formed in 2015. It had negative current E&P of $30,000 in that year. In 2016, its current E&P was $70,000. In 2017, current E&P was a negative $65,000. In 2018, Jasmine's current E&P was $40,000 and it distributed $10,000 in cash to its shareholders. The effects on E&P are as follows: |

Year	Current E&P	Accumulated E&P	Distributions
2015	($30,000)	($30,000)	$0
2016	70,000	40,000	0
2017	(65,000)	(25,000)	0
2018	40,000	5,000	10,000

Accumulated E&P in 2015 equals the deficit in current E&P. Accumulated E&P in 2016 equals its beginning balance (– $30,000) plus current E&P ($70,000), or $40,000. Accumulated E&P in 2017 equals its beginning balance ($40,000) plus current E&P (– $65,000), or – $25,000. Finally, accumulated E&P at the end of 2018 equals its beginning balance (– $25,000) plus current E&P less the distribution ($40,000 minus $10,000), or (– $25,000 plus $30,000 = $5,000).

Determination of Current Earnings and Profits

The starting point in the computation of current E&P is taxable income or loss for the current year. The method of accounting (cash or accrual) used to compute taxable income also must be used to compute E&P. Reg. §1.312-6(a). The main adjustments, which primarily are found in Code Sec. 312, may be categorized as follows:

A. Items That Are Excluded from Both Taxable Income and E&P

(no adjustments to taxable income)
1. Gifts and bequests
2. Contributions to capital
3. Realized, but not recognized, gains and losses
   a. Like-kind exchanges (Code Sec. 1031)
   b. Involuntary conversions (Code Sec. 1033)
   c. Transfers to controlled corporations (Code Sec. 351)
   d. Transfers pursuant to a reorganization (Code Sec. 361)
   e. Disallowed wash sale losses (Code Sec. 1091)

B. Items That Are Nondeductible, but That Reduce E&P

(negative adjustments to taxable income)
1. Federal income taxes
2. Capital losses
3. Life insurance premiums (where the beneficiary is the corporation)
4. Disallowed losses from related party transactions (Code Sec. 267)
5. Charitable contributions in excess of the 10 percent limit
6. Unreasonable compensation
7. Interest and expenses attributable to tax-free income (Code Sec. 265)
8. Nondeductible penalties and fines
9. Miscellaneous nondeductible items that reduce capital

C. Items That Are Exempt from Income, but That Increase E&P

(positive adjustments to taxable income)
1. Tax-exempt municipal bond interest (Reg. §1.312-6(b))
2. Life insurance proceeds
3. Compensation for certain injuries
4. Recovery of losses which generated no tax savings
5. Federal income tax refunds from previous tax years
6. Other tax-free income which increased capital

D. Items That Are Deductible from Taxable Income, but Not from E&P
(positive adjustments to taxable income)
1. Accelerated depreciation or cost recovery in excess of straight-line (no adjustment is needed if the method used was not based upon time (e.g., the units-of-production method))
2. Percentage depletion in excess of cost depletion (Reg. §1.312-6(c)(1))
3. Capital loss carryovers
4. Net operating loss carryovers
5. Charitable contributions carryovers
6. Dividends-received deduction
7. Domestic production activities deduction
8. Other deductions which do not reduce capital

E. Items That Are Deferred to Later Tax Years, but That Increase E&P
(positive adjustments to taxable income)
1. Deferred gain on installment sales (all gain increases E&P in year of sale)
2. Long-term contract reported on completed-contract method (use percentage-of-completion method)

Component items lose their identity at the time they become part of E&P. Thus, when income items enter the E&P account and serve as the basis for corporate distributions, they automatically create taxable income to the shareholder recipients. This is so even for items which were nontaxable to the corporation in the first place. Also, these adjustments may lead to other adjustments. For example, if a corporation sells an asset for which accelerated depreciation was used, then not only is the excess depreciation added to E&P, but also in the year of sale the gain or loss on that asset must be adjusted. Such gain or loss is included in taxable income and must be adjusted because the adjusted basis of that property for E&P purposes is based on straight-line depreciation, not accelerated depreciation.

The adjustments required for depreciation are more involved than many of the other adjustments because of the many changes made in the tax law with respect to depreciation. The impact on E&P from depreciation and cost recovery is as follows:

1. If a "facts and circumstances" useful life is employed and depreciation is computed on the basis of time, any accelerated portion in excess of straight-line does not reduce E&P. The excess is added to taxable income. Code Sec. 312(k)(1).
2. When the Modified Accelerated Cost Recovery System (MACRS) is used, straight-line cost recovery must still be used for E&P purposes. Thus, for MACRS property placed in service after 1986, E&P must be computed under "the alternative depreciation system." Code Sec. 312(k)(3). Personal property with a class life is depreciated for E&P purposes over such life (if there is no class life, 12 years is used) while real property is depreciated over 40 years, and amounts expensed under Code Sec. 179 are written off over five years.
3. If a method *not* based on time is used (e.g., the "units of production" method or the "income forecast method"), E&P is reduced in full by the deduction.
4. When the asset is sold, the E&P basis is used to determine gain or loss for E&P purposes. Such gain or loss must not exceed that recognized for income tax purposes. Code Sec. 312(f)(1).

EXAMPLE 15.4	Halan Corporation exchanges land, held for investment, with a fair market value of $50,000 and adjusted basis of $20,000, for land with a fair market value of $50,000. The exchange qualifies under Code Sec. 1031 as a like-kind exchange. Halan Corporation has a realized gain of $30,000 and no recognized gain. The $30,000 gain is not included in taxable income, nor is it included in E&P. This is an example of Category A items which do not require adjustments to taxable income to compute current E&P.

EXAMPLE 15.5	Lands Corporation sold property with a fair market value of $16,000 and an adjusted basis of $20,000 to its sole shareholder. Lands Corporation has a realized loss of $4,000. However, Lands Corporation is disallowed the loss deduction because this is a related party transaction under Code Sec. 267. The loss is not deductible in computing taxable income but is deducted from taxable income in computing current E&P. This is an example of Category B adjustments.

EXAMPLE 15.6	Globe Corporation receives $5,000 in tax-exempt municipal interest. The $5,000 does not enter into the computation of corporate taxable income and thus is not subject to corporate taxation. However, the $5,000 is added to taxable income to compute current E&P. This is an example of Category C adjustments.

EXAMPLE 15.7	On January 2, 2016, Jasper Company purchased a machine for $12,000 and depreciated it under MACRS over five years. Straight-line over 12 years is allowed for E&P purposes. Cost recovery in 2016 was $2,400 ($12,000 × 20%). Depreciation for E&P purposes in 2016 was $500 (($12,000/12) × ½). The adjustment in 2016 for E&P purposes was $1,900 ($2,400 − $500). Cost recovery in 2017 was $3,840 ($12,000 × 32%). Depreciation for E&P purposes in 2017 was $1,000 ($12,000/12), thus an adjustment of $2,840 ($3,840 − $1,000). The positive adjustments to taxable income to compute current E&P in 2016 and 2017 are examples of Category D adjustments.

EXAMPLE 15.8	Assume the same facts as Example 15.7, except that the machine is sold on March 3, 2018, for $11,000. The adjusted basis of the property at the date of sale is $4,608 ($12,000 − ($2,400 + $3,840 + $1,152)). The realized and recognized gain on the sale is $6,392 ($11,000 − $4,608) and is included in the determination of taxable income. The adjusted basis of the property for E&P purposes is $10,000 ($12,000 − depreciation for 2016 ($500), 2017 ($1,000) and 2018 ($500)). Thus, the gain for E&P purposes is $1,000 ($11,000 − $10,000). As such, a negative adjustment of $5,392 ($6,392 − $1,000) is made to taxable income in 2018 to compute current E&P.

EXAMPLE 15.9	In 2017, Peter Corporation sells land with an adjusted basis of $60,000 for $80,000 to Campbell Company, an unrelated taxpayer. Campbell Company agrees to make two annual payments of $40,000 plus interest at 12 percent of the unpaid balance. The first payment occurs in 2018. Peter Corporation does not elect out of the installment method. Peter Corporation has a realized gain of $20,000 ($80,000 − $60,000) but does not recognize any gain in 2017. However, in computing current E&P in 2017, the $20,000 gain must be added to taxable income. This is an example of Category E adjustments.

Current E&P and Accumulated E&P

The taxability of a distribution is affected by the distributing corporation's current and accumulated E&P. Distributions are deemed to be made from current E&P first and then from accumulated E&P since March 1, 1913. Code Sec. 316(a). There are several possible situations with respect to the amount of the distribution and E&P.

1. The corporation's current E&P is positive. The distributions are less than current E&P. In this case the distributions are fully taxable as dividends, even if the corporation's accumulated E&P is negative.

EXAMPLE 15.10	Hock Company has current E&P of $16,000 for the year. During the year, it distributed $10,000 in cash to its shareholders. The $10,000 is deemed to be distributed from current E&P and is fully taxable as a dividend.

2. The corporation's current and accumulated E&P are positive. The distributions are greater than current E&P but not greater than the sum of current and accumulated E&P. The current E&P is allocated to each distribution in relative proportion of the current E&P to the total of all distributions. The accumulated E&P is allocated to each distribution on a FIFO basis (i.e., in chronological order of the distributions). Also, distributions can reduce E&P to zero but never make it negative.

EXAMPLE 15.11

Hindle Corporation has current E&P of $15,000 and accumulated E&P of $10,000. It made a cash distribution of $8,000 on March 1, 2017, and a cash distribution of $12,000 on October 11, 2017. Current E&P is allocated as follows:

$$\frac{\text{Current E\&P}}{\text{Total distributions}} = \text{Percent of each distribution out of current E\&P}$$

$$\frac{\$15,000}{20,000} = \frac{3}{4} \quad \text{and thus}$$

Distribution	Total Distributed	Current E&P	Allocation Accumulated E&P	Taxable Amount
March 1, 2017	$8,000	$6,000	$2,000	$8,000
October 11, 2017	12,000	9,000	3,000	12,000
Total	$20,000	$15,000	$5,000	$20,000

3. The corporation's current and accumulated E&P are positive. The distributions are greater than current E&P and the sum of current and accumulated E&P. Current and accumulated E&P are allocated as in Situation 2, above. However, in this case, part of the distributions will be a return of capital.

EXAMPLE 15.12

Assume the same facts as Example 15.11, except that Hindle's accumulated E&P on January 1, 2017, is $3,000.

Distribution	Total Distributed	Current E&P	Allocation Accumulated E&P	Taxable Amount	Return of Capital
March 1, 2017	$8,000	$6,000	$2,000	$8,000	$0
October 11, 2017	12,000	9,000	1,000	10,000	2,000
Total	$20,000	$15,000	$3,000	$18,000	$2,000

4. The corporation's current E&P is positive and its accumulated E&P is negative and the distributions are greater than current E&P. Current E&P is allocated to each distribution as noted in Situation 2, above. Accumulated E&P remains negative and the excess of each distribution over its share of current E&P is a return of capital.

EXAMPLE 15.13

Coats Inc. has current E&P of $30,000 in 2017. Its accumulated E&P on January 1, 2017, was a negative $21,000. It made cash distributions of $20,000 on April 1 and $30,000 on October 1. The distribution is taxed as follows:

Distribution	Total Distributed	Current E&P	Allocation Taxable Amount	Return of Capital
April 1, 2017	$20,000	$12,000	$12,000	$8,000
October 1, 2017	30,000	18,000	18,000	12,000
Total	$50,000	$30,000	$30,000	$20,000

5. The corporation's current E&P and its accumulated E&P are negative. In this case, the distributions are a return of capital.

EXAMPLE 15.14

Salz Company made a cash distribution of $25,000 on June 3, 2017. Its accumulated E&P on January 1, 2017, was a negative $10,000 and its current E&P for 2017 was a negative $17,000. The $25,000 is not treated as a dividend. It is a return of capital.

¶15,011

6. The corporation's current E&P is negative but its accumulated E&P is positive. Since accumulated E&P is used up on a chronological basis, the accumulated E&P is netted with current E&P at the date of the distribution. The negative current E&P is allocated ratably during the year; thus, it is prorated to each distribution based on the number of days in the tax year to the date of the distribution. This procedure assumes that the negative E&P occurred evenly throughout the tax year. If the corporation can show when the actual deficit occurred, then it may use that date for allocating the negative current E&P.

EXAMPLE 15.15

On January 1, 2017, Cote's Corporation has accumulated E&P of $15,000. Its current E&P for 2017 was a negative $10,950. It made two cash distributions of $6,000 each on April 1 and July 1. The status of these distributions is as follows. The negative current E&P is allocated on a daily basis of $30 ($10,950/365).

Distd.	Total Distr.	Pro rata Portion of Current E&P	Accumulated E&P on Distribution Date	Taxable Amount	Return of Capital
Apr. 1	$6,000	($2,700)	$15,000 – $2,700 = $12,300	$6,000	$0
July 1	$6,000	($5,430)	$15,000 – $6,000 – $5,430 = $3,570	$3,570	$2,430

On April 1 the pro rata portion of current E&P is a negative $2,700 ($30 × 90 days). Since accumulated E&P minus current E&P is greater than the distribution, the distribution is taxable. On July 1, the pro rata portion of current E&P is a negative $5,430 ($30 × 181 days). Only $3,570 is left in accumulated E&P after subtracting the April 1 dividend and the current E&P on July 1 from beginning accumulated E&P.

At this point, accumulated E&P is zero and any other distributions in 2017 would be returns of capital. If no other distributions are made in 2017, then accumulated E&P on January 1, 2018, would be a negative $5,520 (the zero balance in accumulated E&P at July 1, 2017, plus the remaining deficit of $5,520 in current E&P). If there is more than one shareholder, then E&P is allocated to each shareholder.

EXAMPLE 15.16

Newman Corporation has accumulated E&P of $10,000 on January 1, 2017. Its current E&P for 2017 is $50,000. It made cash distributions of $40,000 each on May 1 and November 1. On January 1, 2017, Newman had two shareholders, Lisa and Reece. Each owned 100 shares which they acquired in 2010. Lisa's adjusted basis of her stock was $35,000 and Reece's was $19,000. On October 15, 2017, Susan bought 50 shares from Reece for $18,000. The results of these events are as follows:

$$\frac{\text{Current E\&P}}{\text{Total distributions}} = \frac{\$50,000}{\$80,000} = \frac{5}{8} = \text{Portion of each distribution from current E\&P}$$

$$\text{May 1 distribution:} \quad \$40,000 \times \frac{5}{8} = \$25,000 \text{ from current E\&P}$$

$$\text{November 1 distribution:} \quad \$40,000 \times \frac{5}{8} = \$25,000 \text{ from current E\&P}$$

The $10,000 accumulated E&P is used up by the May 1 distribution; thus, $35,000 ($25,000 + $10,000) of the May 1 distribution is a dividend and $25,000 of the November 1 distribution is a dividend.

EXAMPLE 15.16 CONTINUED	The effects on each shareholder are:			

May 1 Distribution

Lisa: 100 shares; 100/200 = 1/2 of E&P allocated to Lisa
Reece: 100 shares; 100/200 = 1/2 of E&P allocated to Reece
Total 200 shares

Lisa:
$17,500 dividend (1/2 × $35,000)
2,500 return of capital (new basis in 100 shares is $32,500)
$20,000 total

Reece:
$17,500 dividend (1/2 × $35,000)
2,500 return of capital (new basis in 100 shares is $16,500)
$20,000 total

October 15 Sale

Reece:
Amount Realized $18,000
Adjusted Basis (8,250) (1/2 × $16,500)
Realized and Recognized Gain $ 9,750

November 1 Distribution

Lisa: 100 shares; 100/200 = 1/2 of E&P allocated to Lisa
Reece: 50 shares; 50/200 = 1/4 of E&P allocated to Reece
Susan: 50 shares; 50/200 = 1/4 of E&P allocated to Susan
Total 200 shares

Lisa:
$12,500 dividend (1/2 × $25,000)
7,500 return of capital (new basis in 100 shares is $25,000)
$20,000 total

Reece:
$6,250 dividend (1/4 × $25,000)
3,750 return of capital (new basis in 50 shares is $4,500)
$10,000 total

Susan:
$6,250 dividend (1/4 × $25,000)
3,750 return of capital (new basis in 50 shares is $14,250)
$10,000 total

PLANNING POINTER

The timing of distributions can significantly affect the shareholders' tax consequences. If a corporation has no current and accumulated E&P but has the funds to make a distribution, then making a distribution, as opposed to waiting for next year when the corporation will be very profitable, will produce tax savings to the shareholders.

Preferred Stock Dividends

Current E&P must be allocated first to distributions on stock on which dividends must be paid before dividends are paid on other classes of stock. Rev. Rul. 69-440, 1969-2 CB 46. Thus, where a corporation has both preferred stock and common stock, any current E&P will be allocated to the preferred stock first and then to common stock.

EXAMPLE 15.17

Carriage Corporation has both preferred and common shareholders. The corporation has a deficit in accumulated E&P at the beginning of the year. The current E&P is $10,000. The corporation makes a dividend distribution of $8,000 to the preferred shareholders and $5,000 to the common shareholders. The preferred shareholders will report the full $8,000 as dividend income, while the common shareholders will report only $2,000 as dividend income and $3,000 as return of capital. Since the preferred shareholders receive their dividends first, only $2,000 of current E&P is left for the common shareholder distribution.

Dividend Reinvestment Plans

Many corporations give shareholders the opportunity to agree to automatically reinvest all or some of their dividends in more shares on which dividends are paid. The participation in such a plan does not make such distributions any less taxable. To encourage reinvestment of dividends, it is customary to grant a discount from the current market price. The IRS takes the position that a discount, if any, is in the nature of an additional dividend and taxable as such. Reg. §1.301-1(j). If this happens, the discount is added to the cost basis in the stock purchased, resulting in a cost equal to the market value. Reg. §1.301-1(h); Rev. Rul. 76-53, 1976-1 CB 87. (In IRS Letter Ruling 9406012, the IRS held that a discount was not dividend income. However, the ruling dealt with cooperatives and special circumstances. It is unlikely that it would apply to corporate shareholders.)

EXAMPLE 15.18	Jessica owns 2,000 shares of Jake Company. During 2017, Jake Company declared a dividend and Jessica was entitled to $3,000. She participates in the firm's dividend reinvestment plan, so she did not receive cash; instead, she received 100 shares when the selling price of the shares was $33 per share. Her dividend income for 2017 is $3,300 ($3,000 plus the $300 discount). Her per share basis in the 100 shares is $33 ($3,300/100).

Tax-Free Distributions

If a corporation makes partially or wholly tax-free distributions, it must file Form 5452 (Corporate Report of Nondividend Distributions) with the corporation's income tax return for the tax year. The distributing corporation also will normally inform its shareholders of the tax status of distributions to them.

¶15,015   CASH DISTRIBUTIONS

The measure of a cash distribution is easy to obtain; it is the amount of cash distributed. It is considered to be a dividend to the extent of current and accumulated E&P as explained at ¶15,011. (The discussion there assumed all distributions were in the form of cash.) The shareholder recognizes income to this extent and the distributing corporation reduces current E&P and then accumulated E&P accordingly. Also, the distributing corporation does not recognize a gain or a loss on the distribution.

EXAMPLE 15.19	James Corporation has current E&P of $30,000 for 2017. It distributed $10,000 to Kimberly, its sole shareholder. Kimberly has $10,000 of dividend income. James Corporation recognizes no gain or loss on the distribution and reduces current E&P by $10,000.

¶15,021   PROPERTY DISTRIBUTIONS

Property distributions are more complex than cash distributions. Several questions arise:

1. With respect to the recipient shareholder, what is the measure of the distribution and how much is dividend income? What is the shareholder's basis in property received? When does the holding period for the property begin?
2. With respect to the distributing corporation, is gain or loss recognized on the distribution, and if so, what is its character? What is the effect of the distribution on the corporation's E&P?

Tax Consequences to Shareholders

Determination of Dividend Income

If a corporation distributes property rather than cash, then the amount of the distribution is the property's fair market value determined on the date of the distribution. Code Sec. 301(b). If the property is encumbered with a liability and the shareholder assumes the liability, then the measure of the distribution is the property's fair market value reduced by the liability (but never below zero). Code Sec. 301(b)(2). The distribution is considered to be a dividend to the extent of the distributing corporation's current and accumulated E&P. Amounts in excess of E&P are treated as returns of capital and reduce the shareholder's adjusted basis in the stock, but never below zero. Once the adjusted basis is zero, additional amounts distributed are treated as gain from the sale or exchange of the stock.

Basis in Property Received

The shareholder's basis in the property received is its fair market value on the date of distribution. Code Sec. 301(d). The assumption of a liability by the shareholder does not affect the basis in the property. Also, the status of the distribution (i.e., dividend or return of capital) does not affect the basis. Independent of the shareholder's method of accounting, the dividend is not taxable until received. Reg. §1.301-1(b). The shareholder's holding period begins on the day following the date of receipt; the shareholder does not receive the distributing corporation's holding period in the property. Code Sec. 1223.

EXAMPLE 15.20	Swimwear Inc. has E&P of $10,000 at the end of the current year, during which it distributed securities with a basis of $3,000 and a value of $8,000, to a shareholder, Abigail Flynn. Abigail must recognize $8,000 of dividend income, she receives an $8,000 basis in the securities, and the holding period starts the day following receipt.

EXAMPLE 15.21	Same as Example 15.20, except E&P (as computed at the end of the year without any reduction for the distribution but including the $5,000 gain on distribution) is only $6,000. Abigail must recognize only $6,000 of dividend income. Her basis in the securities received is still $8,000 and she must reduce her basis in her Swimwear stock by $2,000, the excess of the distribution over E&P. If the $2,000 exceeds her basis, to that extent she has a capital gain.

EXAMPLE 15.22	Cashing Corporation has current E&P of $75,000. On November 4, 2017, it distributes land with a fair market value of $48,000 and an adjusted basis of $30,000 to Melonie Craig, its sole shareholder. The property is subject to an $11,000 liability, which Melonie assumes. The amount of the distribution is $37,000 ($48,000 – $11,000). Since E&P is greater than $37,000, the full amount is treated as a dividend. Melonie's basis in the land is $48,000 (fair market value). Her holding period begins on November 5, 2017, the day following receipt.

TAX BLUNDER

Arrow Inc. distributes securities with a value of $20,000 and a basis of $27,000 to its shareholders, the Sunny Corporation. Arrow realizes, but cannot recognize, the $7,000 loss, and E&P is reduced by $27,000. Sunny has dividend income of $20,000, assuming sufficient E&P. In any event, the distributee's basis equals $20,000. The holding period starts on the day following the distribution. The dividends-received deduction, if available, is computed on the value of $20,000. Arrow would have been well advised to have sold the securities for $20,000, recognizing a $7,000 loss that reduces taxable income and E&P, and then to have distributed the proceeds to Sunny Corporation.

Property that has declined in value should not be distributed by a corporation. The shareholder's basis in the property is its fair market value, not the corporation's adjusted basis. Thus, the loss due to decline in value will never be recognized. The distributing corporation would be better advised to sell the property, recognize the loss, and distribute the proceeds (plus tax savings, if desired).

A corporate shareholder that receives an extraordinary dividend must reduce its basis in the stock at the beginning of the ex-dividend date by the untaxed portion of such dividend. Code Sec. 1059. An extraordinary dividend is a distribution amounting to more than 10 percent of the greater of the stock basis or stock value the day before the ex-dividend date (5 percent for preferred stock). Dividends declared within 85 days are aggregated, as are dividends declared within a year if they exceed 20 percent. The rule does not apply if the stock was held since the corporation's inception and no dividends were paid previously. Also, the nontaxed portion of dividends on certain "disqualified" preferred stock issued after July 10, 1989, is treated as an extraordinary dividend.

EXAMPLE 15.23	Pearls Jewelry Inc. purchased 1,000 shares of Long Shot Inc. for $20,000, 16 months ago. Long Shot declared a dividend of $3 per share. Pearls' taxable dividend was $900 ($3,000 less the 70 percent dividends-received deduction). Accordingly, Pearls' basis in the stock is reduced by $2,100 ($3,000 – $900). If the fair market value of the stock was $30,000 or more the day before the ex-dividend date, no basis reduction would be required (10 percent of $30,000 is $3,000, thus there would not be an extraordinary dividend).

Tax Consequences to Distributing Corporation

Gain or Loss Recognition

A corporation that distributes property that has appreciated in value must recognize a gain at the time of distribution. The corporation is treated as if it had sold the property. The gain equals the property's fair market value less its adjusted basis. Code Sec. 311(b). However, the corporation does not recognize a loss if the property had declined in value. Also, the corporation recognizes no gain or loss if it distributes its own stock or stock rights to its shareholders. Code Sec. 311(a).

The character of the recognized gain depends on the property distributed; thus, it may be ordinary income, capital gain, or Section 1231 gain.

EXAMPLE 15.24	Jasper Corporation distributes land to Harold Cooper, its sole shareholder. The adjusted basis of the land is $25,000 and its fair market value is $47,000. Jasper Corporation must recognize a gain of $22,000 (presumably a capital gain). Harold's basis in the land is $47,000.

EXAMPLE 15.25	Assume the same facts in Example 15.24, except that the land's adjusted basis is $60,000. Jasper Corporation cannot recognize the $13,000 loss and Harold's basis in the land is only $47,000.

Depreciation Recapture

To the extent any gain would have been ordinary income because of depreciation recapture if the property had been sold for its fair market value, rather than distributed, ordinary income is recognized on a distribution. Code Secs. 291, 1245(a), and 1250(a). This also is true for property expensed under Code Sec. 179.

EXAMPLE 15.26	Arrow Inc. distributes an auto originally purchased for $20,000, but fully depreciated, to a shareholder when it is worth $2,500. Arrow will recognize $2,500 of ordinary income on the distribution. This result is independent of E&P (i.e., it does not matter how much, if any, of the distribution represents a dividend). The result would be the same if the auto were a bonus (compensation).

General Business Credit Recapture

A corporation also generally has to recognize gain where the distribution includes property on which the general business tax credit has been taken and property on which deductions subject to recapture have been taken. A distribution of property on which a general business tax credit was taken is considered a disposition of the property, subject to general business credit recapture. The amount of credit recaptured is based on the amount of time that asset has been held by the corporation. Code Sec. 50.

Installment Obligations

If the corporation sells property on a deferred payment plan, is using the installment method to report gain, and distributes the installment obligation while one or more installments are still unpaid, gain is accelerated. Code Sec. 453B(a). The gain equals the fair market value of the unpaid installments less their basis, and the character follows the property originally sold.

EXAMPLE 15.27	Arrow Inc. sold land held as an investment for $100,000 to an individual, payable $20,000 at the time of sale plus eight equal installments of $10,000 each, starting a year after closing, together with 11 percent interest on the loan balance. Since the basis in the land was $40,000 (40 percent of the selling price), the gross profit percentage is 60 percent. After collecting three annual installments, Arrow distributed the mortgage to its two shareholders as tenants in common when the fair market value of the note was $43,000.

Amount realized	$43,000
Basis in note (40% of $50,000)	20,000
Gain recognized	$23,000

The gain is a long-term capital gain since the land originally sold was a capital asset held long term at the time of the closing. The shareholders' basis in the note equals $43,000, its fair market value. If the note is collected in full, the shareholders will have to recognize $7,000 of ordinary income since the face value is $50,000 and collecting a note from an individual is not a sale or exchange. Code Sec. 1271(a)(1) and (b)(1).

Liabilities in Excess of Fair Market Value

A corporation might distribute property encumbered with a liability. If the distributed property is subject to a liability or the shareholders assume the liability, then the property's fair market value is treated as being not less than the amount of the liability. Code Sec. 311(b)(2). Thus, if the fair market value is less than the amount of the liability, then the liability is considered to be the property's fair market value.

EXAMPLE 15.28	Arrow Inc. distributes a building with a basis of $15,000 and a value of $40,000, but subject to a nonrecourse liability of $60,000, to an individual shareholder. The corporation is deemed to have sold the property for the greater of $60,000 or $40,000, thus recognizing a gain of $45,000 ($60,000 – $15,000) of the same character as the building, for example, a Section 1231 gain, except for the portion, if any, representing depreciation recapture. The shareholder, however, has no dividend since the value does not exceed the liability. Nevertheless, the shareholder has a basis in the building of $60,000.
	If the value of the building is $60,000, the shareholder still has no dividend, the corporation picks up $45,000 of gain, and the shareholder's basis is $60,000. If the value of the building is $80,000, the shareholder receives a dividend of $20,000 ($80,000 – $60,000) and a basis of $80,000, and the corporate gain is $65,000 ($80,000 – $15,000).

E&P Adjustments

The general rule is that E&P is reduced by the adjusted basis of the distributed property. Code Sec. 312(a). If the corporation distributes appreciated property, then E&P is increased by the appreciation in value and decreased by the property's fair market value. Code Sec. 312(b). (The appreciation produces a realized and recognized gain as noted previously. This gain is included in taxable income and subject to federal income taxes.) If the distributed property is subject to a liability or the shareholder assumes the liability, then this amount is subtracted from the amount used to decrease E&P (i.e., either fair market value or adjusted basis).

EXAMPLE 15.29	Land with a basis of $20,000 and a value of $50,000 is distributed to an individual shareholder. The $30,000 gain is recognized by the corporation. Current E&P is increased by the gain of $30,000 and decreased by the fair market value, $50,000. The net decrease in current and accumulated E&P is simply equal to $20,000, the basis in the property prior to the distribution, but the distribution caused $30,000 of current income and E&P to be created.

EXAMPLE 15.30	Same as Example 15.29, except the land is subject to a mortgage liability of $35,000. Current E&P is still increased by $30,000, the realized gain, but the decrease in E&P is reduced from $50,000 to $15,000 by the transferred liability. (The result would be the same if the shareholder had paid $35,000 in cash.)

EXAMPLE 15.31	Same as Example 15.29, except the land has a basis of $50,000 and a value of $20,000. No loss is recognized, and E&P is reduced by the basis of $50,000.

If the corporation distributes its own debt obligation, E&P is reduced by the lesser of the principal amount or the "issue price" (fair market value). Code Sec. 312(a)(2).

EXAMPLE 15.32	Julia Inc. distributed an IOU with a face value of $20,000 and a fair market value of $15,000 to an individual shareholder. There is a dividend of $15,000 and an E&P reduction of $15,000. In addition, the shareholder has original issue discount of $5,000.

¶15,025 CONSTRUCTIVE DIVIDENDS

A constructive dividend is any tangible benefit in cash or property received by a shareholder in his or her capacity as such from the corporation where E&P exists. Dividends usually occur because the board of directors declared that they should be paid. However, this is not a necessary condition. A dividend can result from a variety of transactions. Sometimes this is due to shareholder and/or corporate ignorance (i.e., the shareholders were not attempting to circumvent dividend status) and on other occasions it is due to the direct efforts of the shareholder and/or corporation to disguise the dividends as something else. (The latter is done either to exclude income for the shareholder or provide deductions for the corporation or shareholder.) Regardless, in either situation (unintentional or intentional), the economic substance of the transaction will take precedence over its form, and if deemed so, will be treated as a dividend to the extent of current and accumulated E&P. This is a constructive dividend since no formal (actual) cash or property dividend has been declared or paid.

Examples of the most frequently encountered constructive dividends are:

1. **Unreasonable compensation and disallowed expenses.** If salaries or bonuses are paid in excess of "fair value," such excess may be disallowed as a compensation expense and taxed as a dividend to the shareholder-employee. This is true even though dividends are paid as well. The problem may be reduced by a repayment contract between the corporation and the shareholder. Similarly, if the corporation reimburses the employee-shareholder for travel and entertainment expenses found to be personal in nature, a dividend may result. The corporation is denied a deduction for the excess portion.
2. **Corporate satisfaction of shareholder liabilities.** If a corporation makes a third-party payment to the creditor of a shareholder, a dividend may result.
3. **Shareholder loans.** A loan to a shareholder may be treated as a dividend unless it appears to be a loan to an independent third party. Thus, the loan should be evidenced by a note, be secured, carry a fair interest rate, and have a repayment schedule. Demand loans that stay on the books are automatically suspect.
4. **Corporate loans.** A loan from a shareholder might be reclassified as equity. If so, any "interest" payments will be reclassified as dividends.
5. **Free personal use of corporate property.** Obvious examples include the use of corporate autos, living quarters, recreational facilities, and the like. Dividend income is equal to the fair rental value of the property.
6. **Bargain sales and rentals to the shareholder or persons related to the shareholder.** Sometimes a corporation may sell property to a shareholder for an amount that is less than the fair market value or may rent property to a shareholder for less than its fair rental value. The difference between the price or rent paid and fair market or rental value may be treated as a dividend.
7. **Premium sales and rentals to the corporation.** If a corporation purchases property from a shareholder at a price greater than the property's fair market value, then the excess may be treated as a dividend. Similarly, if a corporation leases property from a shareholder at an excessive rental rate, then the excess over the fair market value may be treated as a dividend.

EXAMPLE 15.33	Jim Simms borrows $20,000 without interest from his wholly-owned corporation, VIP Inc. If VIP has ample E&P and the formalities of an arm's-length loan transaction are not carried out, a dividend of $20,000 will result. Even if treated as a bona fide debt, interest must be imputed at the "applicable federal rate" under Code Sec. 7872 with the following results:

1. VIP has interest income and has constructively paid a nondeductible dividend (E&P goes up and down by the same amount, with the net effect being a reduction for taxes paid on the imputed interest income).

2. Jim has dividend income equal to the imputed interest he did not pay. The interest expense may be deductible in whole or in part. If it is personal interest, then it is not deductible.

¶15,032   DISTRIBUTIONS OF STOCK DIVIDENDS

In general, if shareholders receive stock in proportion to their ownership interest, then they are not taxable because the shareholders are in the same economic position after the distribution as they were prior to it. Thus, a 10 percent shareholder still owns 10 percent of a corporation after a distribution in which all shareholders have received pro rata stock dividends. The nontaxability of pro rata distributions based on this logic was established by the Supreme Court. *Eisner v. Macomber,* 1 USTC ¶32,252, 252 U.S. 189, 40 S.Ct. 189 (1920).

Following *Eisner v. Macomber,* the proportionate test was added to the Internal Revenue Code and it still applies. The general rule is that gross income does not include stock distributions made by a corporation to its shareholders with respect to its stock. Code Sec. 305. However, there are several exceptions:

1. Distributions which, at the option of the shareholders, are payable in either stock or property.
2. Disproportionate distributions whereby some shareholders receive property and other shareholders receive an increase in their proportionate share in the assets or E&P of the corporation.
3. Distributions whereby some common stock shareholders receive preferred stock and other common stock shareholders receive common stock.
4. Distributions on preferred stock, other than an increase in the conversion ratio of convertible preferred stock made solely to take account of a stock dividend or stock split with respect to stock into which the preferred stock is convertible.
5. Distributions of convertible preferred stock, unless it can be shown that such distributions will not produce disproportionate distributions as described in (2), above.

Tax-Free Stock Distributions

If the stock dividend is not taxable, then the total basis of the old stock is allocated between the old and the new stock. Code Sec. 307(a). The holding period of the new stock takes on the holding period of the old stock. Code Sec. 1223(5). Note that a nontaxable stock dividend is the same as a stock split. Thus, a six-for-five split is the same as a 20 percent stock dividend because an additional share is received for each five held.

If the old shares and the new shares are not identical, then the total basis of the old shares is allocated to the old and new shares based on their relative fair market values. The holding period for the old and new shares still will refer back to the original (old) shares.

EXAMPLE 15.34	Jack Jones purchased 100 common shares in Motherlode Inc. for $1,200. His basis is $12 a share. Five years later, he received a tax-free stock dividend of 20 percent (i.e., 20 additional shares). His $1,200 basis is unchanged, but his basis per share equals $10 ($1,200/120). The holding period of the new shares refers back to the original purchase.

EXAMPLE 15.35

Same as Example 15.34, but Jack received 20 shares of preferred stock worth $700 tax free at a time when his 100 shares of common stock were worth $1,400. His $1,200 basis must now be allocated between the common and the preferred stock based on relative fair market values.

Common: ($1,400/$2,100) × $1,200 = $800
Preferred: ($ 700/$2,100) × $1,200 = $400

The holding period of the common stock tacks on to that of the preferred stock.

A nontaxable stock dividend does not affect the distributing corporation's E&P. Since "nothing is distributed," E&P is not reduced.

Taxable Stock Dividends

If a shareholder receives a taxable stock dividend, then the amount of the distribution is equal to the stock's fair market value at the date of the distribution. The shareholder has income to the extent of the corporation's current and accumulated E&P. The shareholder's basis in the stock is its fair market value on the distribution date and the holding period begins on the day following receipt.

The distributing corporation reduces E&P by the fair market value of the stock and does not recognize a gain or loss on the distribution.

EXAMPLE 15.36

Derek Stewart owns 100 shares of Speer Corporation which he acquired on January 17, 2012, for $10,000. On March 1, 2017, Derek received 10 shares of Speer Corporation stock in a taxable distribution. The fair market value of the stock on March 1, 2017, was $150 per share. Speer Corporation's current E&P for 2017 was $45,000. Derek has taxable income of $1,500 ($150 × 10). His basis in the original shares remains at $10,000. His basis in the new shares is $1,500. His holding period in the new shares begins on March 2, 2017. Speer Corporation's E&P is decreased by $1,500.

Distributions Payable in Stock or Money

Any time any shareholder has an option to elect whether to receive a stock dividend or a property dividend, such as cash, then the distribution of stock or stock rights is taxable to all shareholders under Code Sec. 301. Section 305(b)(1) brings the distribution within Code Sec. 301 for all shareholders regardless of (1) whether all or none of the shareholders exercise the option or are entitled to the election, (2) whether the election is exercised or exercisable before or after the board of directors declares the dividend, and (3) whether the source of the election arises from the corporate charter, director declaration, or other circumstances.

EXAMPLE 15.37

General Corporation declares a dividend payable in shares of stock at the rate of one additional share for each common share presently held. The dividend is not taxable.

EXAMPLE 15.38

Suppose in Example 15.37, one shareholder persuades the board of directors to allow an election of taking either the one additional share for each common share held or a $12 dividend. If no election is made, the shareholder also receives stock. The dividend is taxable to all the shareholders.

Disproportionate Distributions

A proportionate distribution is one where the shareholders' ownership interest does not change; e.g., if the shareholder owned 20% of a firm before the distribution then the shareholder would have to own 20% of the firm after the distribution. A disproportionate distribution occurs if the shareholders' ownership interest in the firm is different after the distribution; e.g., if the shareholder owned 20% of the firm before the distribution but owned 25% after the distribution. A distribution that changes the interest of some shareholders because they receive the firm's stock while other shareholders receive cash or other property is a disproportionate distribution. Code Sec. 305(b)(2) causes this distribution to be taxable under Code Sec. 301 with the possible exception of cash in lieu of fractional shares.

EXAMPLE 15.39	Corporation C has ten shares each of class A and class B common stock authorized and issued. It declares a 100 percent stock dividend on the class A stock and a cash dividend on class B stock. Prior to the distributions, the ratio of class A to class B was 1 to 1. After the distributions, the ratio is 2 to 1. Since the proportionate owner-ship of class A stock has gone from 1/2 to 2/3, the additional shares of class A stock are taxable as ordinary income to the shareholders of the corporation when they are received or accrued by them.

Class A and class B stock distributions do not have to be paid at the same time in order for the class A stock dividend to be taxable. One class might be paid quarterly and the other annually, resulting in a taxable event for all. In order to guarantee that the class A stock dividends are nontaxable, Reg. §1.305-3(b)(4) provides that no cash dividends can be paid for at least 36 months before and after the stock dividend and no preconceived plan can exist. Otherwise, the cash dividends and stock dividends will be linked together under the step transaction doctrine as a "series distribution" and all will be taxable.

EXAMPLE 15.40	Tindine Corporation paid cash dividends to some of its shareholders on February 15, 2016. On April 5, 2017, Tindine distributed its stock to other shareholders, resulting in an increase in their proportionate interests. The stock dividend will be taxable to the shareholders. If the cash distributions occurred on February 15, 2014, then the 36-month rule would not affect the stock distribution because it occurred more than 37 months later.

Sometimes a corporation will find that issuing and transferring of fractional shares is troublesome, expensive, and inconvenient. A corporation may declare a dividend payable in stock and distribute cash in lieu of fractional shares. Under Reg. §1.305-3(c), such a distribution does not violate Code Sec. 305(b)(2), providing the total amount of cash distributed is 5 percent or less of the fair market value of the stock dis-tributed. Cash received for a fractional share represents the sale of the fractional shares and gain or loss must be reported. If cash is received in lieu of fractional shares, the amount received in cash is dividend income.

EXAMPLE 15.41	Corporation R issues a stock dividend of one additional common share for every five shares. The total of outstanding shares is 250, of which Jake owns 103, Mike owns 106, and Jane owns 41. Fifty new shares could be distributed (250/5), with Jake receiving 20 3/5, Mike 21 1/5, and Jane 8 1/5. The value of the new shares is $10 per share. The corporation can give Jake $6, Mike $2, and Jane $2 in lieu of 3/5, 1/5, and 1/5 of a share, respectively, and still guarantee that the distribution is not taxable to the shareholders. The total value of the distribution is $500 (50 × 10), and 5 percent of $500 is $25. Since the total cash to be paid is $10, the distribu-tion of the shares is nontaxable under Reg. §1.305-3(c)(2). Jake, Mike, and Jane should report the $6, $2, and $2 as dividend income.

Distributions of Common and Preferred Stock

When some common shareholders receive preferred stock and the other shareholders receive common stock, the distribution falls under Code Sec. 305(b)(3) and is taxable. The same result arises when a situ-ation is created where the end product may have both preferred and common stock in the distribution. The "series of distribution" rules previously discussed also apply to Code Sec. 305(b)(3).

EXAMPLE 15.42	Valley Corporation has only common stock. A dividend of newly created preferred stock is declared. The newly created preferred stock can be converted into common stock within six months. This transaction falls within Code Sec. 305(b)(3) since it is reasonable to anticipate that, within a short period of time, some shareholders will be exercising this conversion right and others will not (i.e., the end product may have both preferred and common stock in the distribution).

Distributions on Preferred Stock

Section 305(b)(4) treats a distribution on preferred stock as a taxable event under Code Sec. 301 unless the distribution is made in regard to convertible preferred stock in order to take into account a stock dividend that would otherwise result in the dilution of the conversion of rights.

EXAMPLE 15.43	The shareholders in Sun Corporation may convert their preferred stock into common stock in a one-for-one swap. The common stockholders received a two-for-one stock split. Can the corporation issue convertible preferred stock to the shareholders without being taxable under Code Sec. 305(b)(4)? Yes, if the preferred stock is also split two for one so that no dilution of the conversion right occurs.

According to Reg. §1.305-5, the distinguishing feature of "preferred stock" for Code Sec. 305(b)(4) purposes is not its privileged position in relation to other classes of stock, but that such privileged position is limited and that such stock does not participate in corporate growth to any significant extent.

Distributions of Convertible Preferred Stock

Under Code Sec. 305(b)(5), distributions of convertible preferred stock are taxable unless the corporation shows that no disproportionate distribution has occurred. A disproportionate distribution is not likely to occur when (1) the conversion rights run for many years, (2) the dividend rate is consistent with market conditions at the time of the distribution, and (3) predictions as to the time and extent of any stock conversion cannot be made. Reg. §1.305-6(a)(2).

EXAMPLE 15.44	Sky Corporation issues newly authorized convertible preferred stock and distributes the stock as a dividend. The preferred stock has a normal dividend rate of 5 percent at issuance and could be converted into common stock any time in the next 20 years. The distribution is not taxable.

A disproportionate distribution is likely to occur when (1) the conversion right must be exercised shortly after the date of the distribution of stock, and (2) factors such as dividend rates, redemption provisions, and marketability of conversion stock and of convertible stock indicate that some shareholders will exercise their rights. Reg. §1.305-6(a)(2).

EXAMPLE 15.45	On February 8, Land Corporation declared a dividend on convertible preferred stock that a shareholder could convert into common stock before July 8. An investment company has agreed to purchase any preferred stock from any shareholders who do not wish to convert their shares to common stock. This dividend is taxable. A reasonable assumption is that part of the shareholders will convert and some will not. This situation results in a receipt of property by some shareholders and an increase in the proportionate interest of the rest.

¶15,035   STOCK RIGHTS

The holder of stock rights has the option of acquiring new shares of stock in a corporation within a defined period and at a specific price which is usually below the stock's fair market value when the rights were issued. The same rules and regulations that govern stock dividends also govern stock rights. Thus, distributions of stock rights are nontaxable if they are proportionate. The distributions are taxable if disproportionate or if they fall under the exceptions in Code Sec. 305(b).

Tax-Free Distributions of Stock Rights

Tax-free rights are treated the same as tax-free stock splits and stock dividends. The holding period refers back to the time the old stock was acquired, and the basis is equal to an allocated basis. The basis in the rights equals the cost basis of the old stock times the proportion of the fair market value of the rights at the time of the distribution over the total fair market value of the old stock and the rights at that time. However, unlike the case of stock dividends, the shareholder may choose to give the rights a zero basis if their value constitutes less than 15 percent of the value of the old stock at the time of the distribution. Code Sec. 307(b)(1).

If the rights are allocated a basis, then a subsequent sale of the rights will produce a realized gain or loss equal to the selling price minus the allocated basis. The holding period is equal to the holding period of the stock. Alternatively, if the rights are exercised, then the basis of the acquired stock is equal to its cost plus the basis allocated to the rights. The holding period of the acquired stock (regardless of whether the rights were taxable or nontaxable) begins on the day following the date the rights are exercised. Finally, if the rights elapse (i.e., they are not sold or exercised), then the allocated basis is added back to the basis of the original shares of stock.

Distributions of nontaxable stock rights do not affect the corporation's E&P. Also, the corporation does not recognize a gain or loss on the distribution.

EXAMPLE 15.46

A shareholder owns 100 shares of stock with a basis of $1,200 and a value of $2,100. The shareholder receives 50 tax-free rights worth $700. The value of the rights is not less than 15 percent of the stock ($700 ÷ $2,100 = 33 1/3 percent); thus, a basis must be allocated to the rights. The basis in the rights equals ($1,200 × (700 ÷ $2,800)), or $300. Thus, the basis in the stock is reduced to $900. The holding period of the rights dates back to that of the stock. If the shareholder sells the rights for $500, then a gain of $200 ($500 – $300) results. If the selling price is $140, then a $160 loss ($140 – $300) results.

EXAMPLE 15.47

The shareholder owns a block of stock purchased for $5,000, but worth $6,000. A nontaxable distribution of rights worth $100 is received, and promptly sold. Since the value of the rights is less than 15 percent of the value of the stock ($100 ÷ $6,000 = 1.67 percent), no allocation is required. If the shareholder elects to allocate basis to the rights, the basis is ($5,000 × ($100 ÷ $6,100)), or $82. By making the election, the shareholder's gain becomes only $18, rather than the full $100. The shareholder's basis in the stock is reduced correspondingly to $4,918.

If the rights expire without being exercised, any basis assigned to the rights are added back to the basis of the stock.

Taxable Distributions of Stock Rights

If the distribution of stock rights is taxable, for example, because of a choice of cash or rights, then the amount of the distribution is equal to the fair market value of the rights. Dividend income results to the extent of the corporation's current and accumulated E&P. The shareholder's basis in the rights equals their fair market value and the holding period for the rights begins on the day following the date of the distribution. The distributing corporation reduces E&P by the fair market value of the stock rights at the date of the distribution.

KEYSTONE PROBLEM

Lyle Corporation began operations in 2015. Current E&P in 2015 was a negative $80,000. In 2016, current E&P was a negative $40,000. Lyle Corporation expects to be profitable in 2017 and all subsequent years, and it projects current E&P to be a positive $40,000 in 2017, $50,000 in 2018, and $60,000 in 2019. Lyle Corporation estimates that starting in 2017 it will have $40,000 in cash each year available for dividend distributions. Lyle Corporation is considering three alternative distribution patterns: (1) $40,000 in each of the three years; (2) zero in 2017, $80,000 in 2018, and $40,000 in 2019; and (3) zero in 2017 and 2018 and $120,000 in 2019. Which distribution pattern should be elected? Why?

Stock Redemptions

¶15,101 CLASSIFICATIONS FOR TAX TREATMENT

A stock redemption occurs when a corporation acquires its stock from its shareholders in return for cash or property. The surrender of stock may be treated as a sale or exchange, in which case the shareholders will recognize a gain or loss equal to the difference between the fair market value of the property received minus the stock's adjusted basis. Alternatively, the surrender of stock may be classified as a dividend and be taxable as ordinary income to the extent of the redeeming corporation's current and accumulated E&P.

There are numerous reasons why stock redemptions occur. For example, the shareholder may want to terminate all interest in a corporation. Instead of selling the stock to outsiders or current shareholders, it may be easier to sell the stock to the corporation. This would enable the current shareholders to retain complete control of the corporation without using their own funds. Similarly, the shareholder may not be able to find an outside buyer (especially, if the corporation is small and/or closely held). If a shareholder dies, it might be easier for the estate to sell the stock to the corporation or the corporation might be required to buy the stock under a buy-sell agreement. Finally, the corporation might believe that its best investment choice is to "invest in itself" and will buy its own stock and hold this stock in treasury for future needs.

Whether the redemption is treated as a sale or exchange or as a dividend depends on numerous factors. The rationale underlying the statute dealing with stock redemptions is to prevent the shareholders from converting ordinary income (dividends) into capital gains (from the sale or exchange of stock). The statute enables shareholders to determine the amount and type of income derived as a result of the redemption, their basis and holding period in the property received in the redemption, and their basis in the stock still owned. The redeeming corporation must determine whether it recognizes a gain or loss on the property transferred to shareholders in the redemption and how E&P is affected by the redemption.

¶15,103   SALE OR EXCHANGE TREATMENT

Code Sec. 317(b) indicates that a redemption occurs if the corporation acquires its stock from a shareholder in exchange for the property, regardless of whether the stock is cancelled, retired, or held as treasury stock. Code Secs. 302 and 303 govern the tax treatment of most redemptions. A redemption may be treated as an exchange of the stock or as a dividend. Since a sale or exchange of stock for payment would result in tax-free return of basis plus capital gain treatment of any gain realized if all conditions are met, it is clearly to the advantage of most taxpayers to have the redemption treated as an exchange. In addition to producing lower income, the capital gain could be used to offset capital losses. The following major types of stock redemptions qualify for exchange treatment:

1. The redemption must not be essentially equivalent to a dividend. Code Sec. 302(b)(1).
2. The redemption must be substantially disproportionate with respect to the shareholder. Code Sec. 302(b)(2).
3. The redemption must be in complete termination of the shareholder's interest in the corporation. Code Sec. 302(b)(3).
4. The redemption must be made to noncorporate shareholders in partial liquidation. Code Sec. 302(b)(4).
5. The redemption must be for the purpose of paying shareholder death taxes. Code Sec. 303.

If any of these conditions is met, then the redemption escapes the ordinary income treatment of dividends. Where a redemption is treated as a dividend, the shareholder's basis in the stock redeemed attaches to the remaining stock. This basis attaches to other stock held by the taxpayer or to any stock the taxpayer is considered to own constructively. Reg. §1.302-2(c).

EXAMPLE 15.48   Jenny Park owns 100 shares of Xanadu Corporation which she acquired in 2012 for $10,000. On March 20, 2017, Xanadu redeemed 80 of her shares in return for $12,000. If the redemption is treated as an exchange, then Jenny has a $4,000 long-term capital gain ($12,000 – $8,000). If Jenny had received property worth $12,000 instead of cash, then she still would have a $4,000 long-term capital gain. In addition, her basis in the property would be $12,000, its fair market value, and the holding period would begin on March 21, 2017.

EXAMPLE 15.49   Assume the same facts as Example 15.48, except that the redemption does not qualify as an exchange and that Xanadu's current E&P is $35,000. Jenny would have dividend income of $12,000. Her basis in the remaining 20 shares would be equal to $10,000, their original basis of $2,000 (20 shares × $100 per share) plus the $8,000 basis of the 80 shares surrendered in the redemption. If Jenny had received property worth $12,000 instead of cash, then she still would have $12,000 of dividend income. Her basis in the property would be $12,000, and the holding period would begin on March 21, 2017.

PLANNING POINTER   A corporate shareholder normally prefers that a distribution be treated as a dividend, rather than a redemption. The corporation normally can reduce dividend income by the dividends-received deduction.

EXAMPLE 15.50	Nibble Corporation owns 5 percent (200 shares) of Smackers Company which it acquired several years ago for $10,000 ($50 per share). Smackers redeems 160 of Nibble's shares in exchange for $32,000 ($200 per share). Smackers' current E&P is $50,000. If the redemption is treated as an exchange, then Nibble has a $24,000 long-term capital gain ($32,000 − $8,000). However, if the redemption is treated as a dividend, then Nibble has received a $32,000 dividend but also is allowed a 70 percent dividends-received deduction. Assuming the taxable income constraint does not apply, this deduction is $22,400, producing a net increase in taxable income of $9,600, which is much less than the $24,000 long-term capital gain.

¶15,105   CONSTRUCTIVE OWNERSHIP RULES

The main tool in preventing sale or exchange treatment when a redemption is made is to require a "real" reduction in stock ownership, counting both actual and constructive ownership. The status of redemptions is controlled under Code Sec. 302(b)(1), (2), (3), and (4), which provide tests which look at ownership interest before and after the redemption. Ownership is defined as shares actually owned and those constructively owned (i.e., one shareholder's shares may be attributed to another shareholder for purposes of determining ownership interest).

The attribution rules are found in Code Sec. 318 and are summarized below:

1. An individual is deemed to own stock held by the individual's family, defined as a spouse, children, grandchildren, and parents. Brothers, sisters, and grandparents are not considered family members for Code Sec. 318 attribution purposes.
2. Partners and beneficiaries are deemed to own stock held by partnerships, estates, and trusts in proportion to their interests and vice versa. Thus, there is attribution to and from entities.
3. There is attribution to and from corporations, but only if the shareholder owns at least 50 percent of the value of the corporate stock.
4. Stock constructively owned is deemed to be directly owned for purposes of reattribution, with two exceptions:
   a. Stock owned indirectly by an individual because of family attribution cannot be reattributed to another family member.
   b. Stock constructively owned by entities and held by owners and beneficiaries will not be reattributed to other owners or beneficiaries.
5. The owner of an option to buy stock is deemed to own such stock.

EXAMPLE 15.51	A corporation is owned by two parents and five children who are all married. Each parent owns 100 percent of the corporation, directly or indirectly. However, each child's spouse indirectly owns only what the child owns since family attribution does not go indirect twice, and each child indirectly owns only what the parents own.

EXAMPLE 15.52	A corporation is owned 40 percent by a father and 60 percent by an irrevocable trust with his two children as equal beneficiaries. The children are deemed to own the 60 percent the trust owns *and* the 40 percent the father owns. Thus, each child is deemed to own 70 percent of the corporation, the 30 percent owned by the trust and the 40 percent owned by the father. A child is *not* deemed to own stock directly or indirectly owned by a sibling. The father is deemed to own 100 percent of the stock, his 40 percent, and the 60 percent owned constructively by his children. The trust owns 60 percent directly and 40 percent indirectly for a total of 100 percent.

¶15,111   REDEMPTIONS NOT EQUIVALENT TO DIVIDENDS

Section 302(b)(1) provides for exchange treatment if the redemption is not essentially equivalent to a dividend. There is no specific test to determine whether a redemption meets this requirement and this has led to substantial litigation. It remains an imprecise test depending on the facts and circumstances of each case.

The imprecision in this test is intentional. Congress did not want these requirements to be too restrictive and this test was added to enable redemptions of preferred stock to qualify as exchanges. See S. Rep. No. 1622, 83rd Cong., 2d Sess., at 44.

Several court cases have been instrumental in establishing criteria to determine whether the redemption is not essentially equivalent to a dividend. The Supreme Court has indicated that there must be a meaningful reduction of the shareholder's proportionate interest. It further established that the constructive ownership rules of Code Sec. 318 will apply in determining ownership prior to and after the distribution. Finally, it indicated that a business purpose for the redemption does not make the redemption not essentially equivalent to a dividend—the key test is whether a meaningful reduction in the shareholder's proportionate interest occurred. *M.P. Davis,* 70-1 ustc ¶9289, 397 U.S. 301, 90 S.Ct. 1041 (1970). What constitutes a meaningful reduction was not defined.

The Tax Court has indicated that redemptions leading to a loss of control by the redeeming shareholder will qualify as meaningful reductions under Code Sec. 302(b)(1). *J. Paparo,* 71 TC 692, Dec. 35,856 (1979). Thus, a reduction in stock ownership from 57 percent to 50 percent was considered a meaningful reduction since the shareholder no longer had control. Rev. Rul. 75-502, 1975-2 CB 111. Additionally, redemptions of minority shareholders' interests may fall under this test. The IRS has ruled that a reduction from 27 percent to 22 percent was a meaningful reduction. Rev. Rul. 76-364, 1976-2 CB 91. In Rev. Rul. 76-385, 1976-2 CB 92, the IRS held that a reduction in minority shareholders' interest as small as 0.0000037 percentage points also was meaningful for Code Sec. 302(b)(1) purposes.

EXAMPLE 15.53	Mr. and Mrs. Jones each own 25 percent of Daniels Corporation. Each of their two children also own 25 percent of Daniels Corporation. In 2017, most of Mr. Jones's shares are redeemed by the corporation for business reasons. Mr. Jones directly and indirectly owned 100 percent of Daniels Corporation before and after the redemption. Thus, no meaningful reduction in ownership interest has occurred.

EXAMPLE 15.54	On June 5, 2017, Julie Greene owns 60 percent of Cagy Corporation. Cagy redeems some of Julie's stock on June 6, 2017, thereby bringing her interest to 47 percent. Since Julie has lost a controlling interest in the corporation, this redemption qualifies under Code Sec. 302(b)(1). A meaningful reduction in ownership interest has occurred; the redemption is not essentially equivalent to a dividend.

Much uncertainty remains under Code Sec. 302(b)(1). If shareholders want exchange treatment, then they are best advised to try to qualify under another test (e.g., Code Sec. 302(b)(2)). Code Sec. 302(b)(1) remains an option in redemptions of preferred stock (Reg. §1.302-2(a)) or in situations where a controlling interest is lost.

¶15,115   SUBSTANTIALLY DISPROPORTIONATE REDEMPTIONS

Code Sec. 302(b)(2) provides three mechanical tests to determine if a redemption is substantially disproportionate. If these tests are met, then the redemption is treated as an exchange. Thus, it is relatively clear and easy to determine if a redemption qualifies for exchange treatment under Code Sec. 302(b)(2). As with Code Sec. 302(b)(1), these tests are applied on a shareholder-by-shareholder basis and the constructive ownership rules under Code Sec. 318 apply. The three tests are:

1. After the redemption, the shareholder must hold less than 50 percent of the outstanding voting stock.
2. The shareholder's proportionate interest in the outstanding voting stock after the redemption must be less than 80 percent of what it was prior to the redemption.
3. After the redemption, the stockholder's proportionate interest in the outstanding common stock must be less than 80 percent of what it was prior to the redemption. The 80 percent determination is made using fair market value if there is more than one class of stock. If there is only one class of stock, then tests 2 and 3 are the same.

Calculation of the first test is relatively straightforward. The second test can be met by calculating two ratios:

1. Voting stock owned by stockholder divided by the total voting stock of the corporation equals percent (before redemption)
2. Voting stock owned by stockholder divided by the total voting stock of the corporation equals percent (after redemption)

If ratio (2) is less than 80 percent of ratio (1), the distribution is substantially disproportionate and is eligible for capital gain treatment. The third test is handled similarly, except that common stock is substituted for the voting stock.

EXAMPLE 15.55

Leonard Corporation has four unrelated shareholders, Lynn, David, Sara, and Karen. Each shareholder owns 100 shares of common stock. On June 15, 2017, Leonard redeemed 55 shares from Lynn, 25 shares from David, and 20 shares from Sara. This redemption is substantially disproportionate with respect to Lynn only. David and Sara have dividend distributions.

Owner	Ownership Before Redemption		Ownership After Redemption		Less than 80 Percent
	Shares	Percentage	Shares	Percentage	Ownership Test
Lynn	100	25%	45	15%	15/25 = 60%
David	100	25%	75	25%	25/25 = 100%
Sara	100	25%	80	27%	27/25 = 108%
Karen	100	25%	100	33%	33/25 = 132%
Total	400	100%	300	100%	

All shareholders meet this first test (less than 50 percent ownership of the outstanding voting stock after the redemption). However, only Lynn meets the less than 80 percent ownership test. Her percent ownership after the redemption divided by her percent ownership before the distribution is 60 percent. David's percent is 100 and Sara's is 108 percent.

EXAMPLE 15.56

Assume the same facts as in Example 15.55, except that Lynn and David are husband and wife. In this case, the redemption is not substantially disproportionate with respect to Lynn, David, or Sara.

Owner	Ownership Before Redemption		Ownership After Redemption		Less than 80 Percent
	Shares	Percentage	Shares	Percentage	Ownership Test
Lynn	200	50%	120	40%	40/50 = 80%
David	200	50%	120	40%	40/50 = 80%
Sara	100	25%	80	27%	27/25 = 108%
Karen	100	25%	100	33%	33/25 = 132%
Total	400*	100%	300*	100%	

* Although there is attribution between Lynn and David, the total number of shares outstanding remains at 400 before the redemption and 300 after it.

All shareholders meet the first test (less than 50 percent ownership after the redemption). However, none meet the less than 80 percent ownership test. Lynn's and David's ownership percentages are exactly 80 percent, not less than 80 percent.

If a disproportionate redemption is one in a series of redemptions which, in the aggregate, will not be disproportionate to any shareholder, then the requirements of Code Sec. 302(b)(2) will not be met. The IRS can use the step transaction doctrine to collapse a series of redemptions into one and evaluate it accordingly.

EXAMPLE 15.57   Assume the same facts as in Example 15.55, except that in 2018 Leonard Corporation redeemed 20 shares from Sara and 55 shares from Karen. If these redemptions are collapsed with the redemptions in 2017 then not only are the redemptions in 2018 not substantially disproportionate but the 2017 redemptions are reevaluated and also will not qualify as substantially disproportionate.

Owner	Ownership Before Redemption		Ownership After Redemption		Less than 80 Percent Ownership Test
	Shares	Percentage	Shares	Percentage	
Lynn	100	25%	45	20%	20/25 = 80%
David	100	25%	75	33%	33/25 = 132%
Sara	100	25%	60	27%	27/25 = 108%
Karen	100	25%	45	20%	20/25 = 80%
Total	400	100%	300*	100%	

¶15,121   COMPLETE TERMINATION OF SHAREHOLDER'S INTEREST

A shareholder receives sale or exchange treatment under Code Sec. 302(b)(3) if the shareholder's interest in a corporation is completely terminated. As with redemptions under Code Sec. 302(b)(1) and (2), this test is at the shareholder level and is done on a shareholder-by-shareholder basis. At first glance, it appears that a complete termination of an interest also satisfies the three mechanical tests under Code Sec. 302(b)(2) and, therefore, qualifies as a substantially disproportionate redemption. If all shareholders are unrelated (under Code Sec. 318), then, in fact, this is the result (i.e., it meets the requirements of Code Sec. 302(b)(2) and (3)).

EXAMPLE 15.58   Pat and Cooper are unrelated and each owns 50 shares in a corporation. The corporation redeems all of Pat's shares. This is a complete redemption of all of Pat's shares and qualifies for sale or exchange treatment. Pat will be allowed to reduce the proceeds from the sale by her basis in the shares, with the difference being capital gain or loss. Of course, this redemption would also qualify under the disproportionate rules of Code Sec. 302(b)(2).

If the shareholders are related then the constructive ownership rules of Code Sec. 318 may preclude sale or exchange treatment. A major difference between redemptions under Code Sec. 302(b)(2) and Code Sec. 302(b)(3) is that under certain circumstances the family attribution rules are waived if the redemption is a complete termination of a shareholder's interest. Code Sec. 302(c)(2). Thus, family attribution may disqualify the redemption from being substantially disproportionate but will not cause it to fail the test for a complete termination of a shareholder's interest.

EXAMPLE 15.59   A family corporation is owned 60 percent by the father, 30 percent by the mother, and 10 percent by their only child. Each shareholder is deemed to own 100 percent of the corporation because of the attribution rules. The redemption of any shareholder's stock by the corporation would still leave that shareholder with deemed ownership of 100 percent of the stock, and thus the disproportionate redemption rules of Code Sec. 302(b)(2) would not apply. However, if, for example, the child's interest is completely terminated and the conditions below are met, then family attribution will be waived. As such, the redemption will receive sale or exchange treatment because it qualifies under Code Sec. 302(b)(3).

The family attribution rules under Code Sec. 318(a)(1) are waived if an agreement is filed in which the terminating shareholder agrees to sever almost every connection with the corporation for 10 years. The agreement also constitutes authority to keep the statute of limitations open so that the IRS can, if the contract is broken, go back and assess the tax, plus interest, and penalties on the retroactive dividend. The agreement is attached to the tax return for the year in which the redemption occurred. The shareholder also must agree to notify the IRS if an interest in acquired within the 10-year period.

Here is a checklist of what the redeemed shareholder can or cannot do during the 10-year period following the complete redemption:

1. *Cannot* retain an ownership interest in the corporation.
2. *Cannot* be or become an officer, director, or employee of the corporation.
3. *Can* be a creditor of the corporation, for example, to facilitate a deferred payment sale of the stock to the corporation, but the stock cannot be pledged as security for the loan.
4. *Can* inherit stock in the corporation any time and keep it.
5. *Cannot* be a "consultant" if the shareholder retains effective direction and control.
6. *Can* be an independent contractor, but even here there is a danger, particularly if the corporation is the shareholder's only client and/or the fee is not "fair."
7. *Cannot* do directly what cannot be done indirectly, for example, through a controlled partnership or corporation.
8. *Cannot* acquire a prohibited interest in the parent, subsidiary, or successor of the redeeming corporation.
9. *Can* be a trustee of the corporate pension plan, unless the shareholder is a plan beneficiary.
10. *Can* have free office space unless it is for future services.

The bottom line is that the redeemed shareholder is limited to being a creditor, an infrequent bona fide independent contractor, or an uncompensated advisor. If a shareholder's interest is completely terminated and the redemption is invalid, then the basis of the redeemed stock is added to the basis of the stock of the shareholders who caused the redemption to be invalid (i.e., the related parties).

EXAMPLE 15.60

Fred Frome owns 40 percent of the only class of stock in Fred and Sons Cooling Co. His three sons, Sam, Steve, and Seth, own 20 percent each. Fred acquired his stock in 2010 for $10,000. The three sons acquired their interests in 2010 for $5,000 each. The corporation buys Fred's stock for $50,000, amply covered by earnings and profits. If Fred does not file the 10-year agreement, he still owns 100 percent of the stock after applying the constructive ownership rules in Code Sec. 318. He will, therefore, have a dividend of $50,000 and his basis in the stock will disappear as to him, regardless of amount, since there is no direct ownership of stock to which it can attach. It will, however, be added to the sons' bases. Reg. §1.302-2(c). Thus, each son's basis in his stock will be $8,333 ($5,000 + $3,333). The same result will follow retroactively if Fred files the 10-year agreement but becomes a shareholder, officer, director, or employee before its expiration.

However, if the 10-year agreement is filed *and* not violated, a sale or exchange of stock has taken place. He will recognize a long-term capital gain of $40,000 ($50,000 – $10,000).

Entities, such as estates and trusts, may also waive family attribution. Both the entity and the beneficiaries must meet the complete redemption and the 10-year restriction rules and agree to be jointly and severally liable for any tax, plus additions to the tax, resulting from a breach. Code Sec. 302(c)(2)(C).

Family attribution rules will not be waived in two circumstances. Code Sec. 302(c)(2)(B). First, the family attribution rules will not be waived if any portion of the redeemed stock was acquired directly or indirectly within the 10-year period ending on the date of the distribution by the redeemed shareholder from a person whose stock would be attributable to that shareholder under Code Sec. 318(a). This provision is designed to prevent a shareholder from transferring stock to a related party followed by the corporation redeeming the stock from the related party in a complete termination of interest, and, therefore, producing capital gain.

EXAMPLE 15.61

Assume that a father owns 100 percent (100 shares) of a corporation and transfers 20 shares to his daughter. Her 20 shares are subsequently redeemed by the corporation. If this rule did not apply, the father will have converted ordinary income (dividends) into capital gains (sale or exchange treatment on the redemption).

The second circumstance where the family attribution rules will not be waived occurs if a related party (under Code Sec. 318(a)) owns stock that was acquired from the redeeming shareholder within the 10 previous years unless such stock also is redeemed in the same transaction. This provision is designed to prevent shareholders from receiving sale or exchange treatment by transferring some of their stock to a related party, and following this with a redemption of their remaining shares, (i.e., the shares not transferred).

EXAMPLE 15.62	Mother owns 100 shares of Dungy Corporation and transfers 60 shares to her daughter; subsequently, mother's 40 shares are redeemed by Dungy. The family attribution rules will not be waived; therefore, mother does not receive sale or exchange treatment.

PLANNING POINTER	When incorporating a sole proprietorship tax free under Code Sec. 351, the foresighted owner should keep Code Sec. 302(b)(3) in mind. As a result, the owner's spouse and/or children should be given stock in the corporation, at least a minority interest. If the business is successful, the spouse and/or children may be redeemed out by the corporation under sale or exchange rules if a 10-year agreement is filed. It should be noted that there is a 10-year waiting period before the redemption can take place with the desired result. Code Sec. 302(c)(2)(B).

TAX BLUNDER

One shareholder purchased all or most of the other outstanding shares and then had the corporation redeem the purchased shares. The redemption would then be pro rata with respect to the redeeming shareholder and thus taxable as a dividend. If the shareholder wanting a larger interest in the corporation had the corporation redeem the shares of the other shareholders, the shareholders would have received capital gain treatment under Code Sec. 302(b)(3) and the controlling shareholder would not have been taxed on the redemption, which was treated as a dividend.

¶15,125   **REDEMPTIONS IN PARTIAL LIQUIDATION**

The previously discussed redemptions are tested at the shareholder level and are applied on a shareholder-by-shareholder basis. Code Sec. 302(b)(4) provides for redemptions that are tested at the corporate level. If the distribution is considered a partial liquidation under Code Sec. 302(e), then noncorporate shareholders will receive sale or exchange treatment. The effects of the redemption on the shareholders' interests (e.g., complete termination of interest, meaningful reduction in interest, etc.) do not affect the redemption's status. Also, constructive ownership rules do not affect the results. Finally, exchange treatment results whether the redemption is proportional or disproportional. Code Sec. 302(b)(4) does not apply to corporations. Thus, unless the distribution qualifies as a redemption under Code Sec. 302(b)(1), (2), or (3), the corporation will have dividend treatment.

A partial liquidation results (1) if the distribution is not essentially equivalent to a dividend (determined at the corporate level and not the shareholder level) or (2) if the distribution is due to the corporation's ceasing to conduct a qualified trade or business. In addition, the distribution must be pursuant to a plan and must occur within the tax year in which the plan is adopted or within the succeeding tax year.

The courts have interpreted the term "not essentially equivalent to a dividend" to mean a genuine contraction of business. See *J. W. Imler*, 11 TC 836, Dec. 16,691 (1948), Acq. 1949-1 CB 2. Typical cases held *not* to qualify as partial liquidations include the sale of excess inventory, the reduction of working capital, the distribution of a small portion of business assets, and the distribution of unwanted assets. On the other hand, the discontinuance of a significant product line leading to a bulk sale of inventory has qualified as a partial liquidation, as has the distribution of insurance proceeds received because of a fire destroying a significant part of the corporate premises.

The first test is vague and subjective. The second test, the distribution occurs because the corporation ceases to conduct or distributes the assets of a qualified trade or business, is very objective. After the distribution, the corporation must continue to actively conduct a qualified trade or business. Thus, if the corporation has been engaged in two or more trades or businesses for the last five years and ceases to conduct one of these businesses, then the cessation and subsequent distribution qualifies as a partial liquidation.

The qualified trade or business must have been actively conducted for five years prior to the distribution and cannot have been acquired during such period in a taxable transaction. Code Sec. 302(e)(3). There are a few miscellaneous considerations:

1. In a closely-held setting, it is irrelevant whether the shareholder physically turns in stock certificates or whether such certificates are formally cancelled.
2. The IRS position is that the percentage of stock redeemed is the same percentage of total stock as the distribution is of the fair market value of net assets prior to the distribution. Rev. Rul. 56-513, 1956-2 CB 191.

3. Noncorporate shareholders include partnerships, estates, and trusts to the extent the partners and beneficiaries are not corporations. Code Sec. 302(e)(5).

EXAMPLE 15.63	Hardy Company has experienced financial difficulties in 2016 and 2017. In December 2017, it sells excess inventory and machinery it no longer uses and distributes the proceeds to its shareholders in redemption of some of their stock. This does not qualify as a partial liquidation.

EXAMPLE 15.64	Stanton Corporation has two shareholders, Wayne Jones and Sandy Corporation. Wayne owns 250 shares that he acquired in 2004 at $45 per share. Sandy Corporation owns 250 shares that it acquired in 2014 at $30 per share. Stanton Corporation's current E&P for 2017 was $70,000. In August 2017, it distributed $8,000 to each shareholder in return for 100 shares of each shareholder's stock. The distribution qualified as a partial liquidation. Wayne has a $3,500 long-term capital gain ($8,000 minus $4,500 ($45 × 100)). However, since there has been no change in Sandy Corporation's interest (50 percent before and after the redemption), it will not receive sale or exchange treatment. Instead, it has $8,000 dividend income on which it can claim a dividends-received deduction of 80 percent ($6,400). Also, its basis in the 100 shares redeemed ($3,000) is added to the basis in its remaining 150 shares ($4,500), producing an overall basis of $7,500 for the 150 shares.

¶15,131   REDEMPTIONS TO PAY DEATH TAXES

Sometimes the stock of a deceased shareholder is redeemed by a closely-held corporation because the estate or heirs need funds to pay death taxes and funeral expenses. Constructive ownership rules under Code Sec. 318 usually preclude sale or exchange treatment under Code Sec. 302 because closely-held corporations usually are owned by related parties (e.g., family members). Under certain conditions, Code Sec. 303 provides relief in this situation by providing sale or exchange treatment on the redemption for an amount equal to the sum of federal and state death taxes and funeral and administrative expenses.

The intent of Code Sec. 303 is to provide relief because stock in closely-held corporations generally is not very marketable; as such, the heirs or estate cannot easily sell the stock to raise the needed funds. However, they can have the corporation redeem the shares; thus, Code Sec. 303 treats the heirs or estate as if they sold the stock. This benefit can be quite substantial because the basis in inherited property is its fair market value at the decedent's date of death (assuming no alternative elections are made). Code Sec. 1014. This stepped-up basis results in little, if any, realized gain. However, if the redemption receives dividend treatment, then the full amount of the distribution (to the extent of current and accumulated E&P) is taxable as ordinary income.

EXAMPLE 15.65	Jackson Corporation has three shareholders. George owns 40 shares which he acquired in 2010 for $10,000. Sally and Susan each own 30 shares which they acquired in 2014 for $60,000 each. George died on June 1, 2017, when the fair market value per share was $3,000. On December 16, 2017, Jackson Corporation redeems George's 40 shares from Adrian, George's beneficiary, and distributes $120,000 to Adrian. Adrian's basis in the 40 shares is $120,000. Jackson's current E&P in 2017 is $200,000. If the redemption qualifies for sale or exchange treatment under Code Sec. 303, then there is no realized gain and no recognized gain ($120,000 – $120,000 = zero). However, if the redemption is treated as a dividend, then Adrian has $120,000 of ordinary income. Clearly, Code Sec. 303 has a significant impact on Adrian's 2017 tax position.

PLANNING POINTER	An option can be created giving the administrator for the decedent's estate the right to require the corporation to redeem from the estate an amount of stock to provide the necessary liquid assets to pay death taxes and funeral and administrative expenses under Code Sec. 303. Such an option can be placed in a written agreement between the stockholder and the corporation and should be designed so as to meet the requirements of Code Sec. 303.

Requirements and Limitations

A number of requirements and limitations must be satisfied in order to obtain sale or redemption treatment under Code Sec. 303.

1. There must be a distribution of property to a stockholder by a corporation in redemption of part or all of the stock of such corporation.
2. Such stock must be included in determining the gross estate of a decedent for purposes of the federal estate tax. However, stock possessing a substituted basis acquired from stock which was included in the gross estate also qualifies. For example, stock may have been included in the decedent's gross estate and later exchanged for other stock in a nontaxable reorganization. The latter stock can qualify under Code Sec. 303.
3. The value of the stock included in the decedent's estate must be greater than 35 percent of the adjusted gross estate.
4. The proceeds under Code Sec. 303 are limited to the sum of estate, inheritance, legacy, or succession taxes imposed (including interest) and the funeral and administrative expenses allowable under Code Sec. 2053 or 2106.
5. Qualifying redemptions are limited to those shareholders whose interests in the estate are reduced directly (or through a binding obligation to contribute) by any payment of death taxes or funeral and administrative expenses.
6. Any distributions made more than four years after the decedent's death are subject to additional limitations.

Gross Estate Adjustments

The requirement listed in (3), above, in part, limits the benefits of Code Sec. 303 to situations where the stock is a substantial portion of the decedent's total assets. The redeemed stock must be included in the gross estate of a decedent for federal estate tax purposes. Such included stock must have a federal estate tax value of more than 35 percent of the value of the adjusted gross estate. Adjusted gross estate (AGE) is the gross estate less the sum of the deductions allowable under Code Sec. 2053 or 2054. Code Sec. 303(b)(2)(A). These allowable deductions include:

1. Funeral expenses
2. Administrative expenses
3. Claims against the estate
4. Unpaid mortgages and other indebtedness
5. Losses incurred by the estate

EXAMPLE 15.66   The gross estate of a decedent, Ed Smythe, has a fair market value of $3,000,000, consisting of $2,200,000 in cash and $800,000 in stock of Silver Corporation. Funeral and administrative expenses amounted to $450,000; thus, the adjusted gross estate is $2,550,000 ($3,000,000 – $450,000). Thirty-five percent of the adjusted gross estate is $892,500 (35% × $2,550,000). Since the value of the stock does not exceed $892,500, the 35 percent test is not met. Thus, a redemption of any of the stock would need to qualify under Code Sec. 302 for sale or exchange treatment.

EXAMPLE 15.67   Assume that in example 15.66, the $3,000,000 estate consisted of $1,600,000 in cash and $1,400,000 in stock of Silver Corporation. A redemption of the stock would qualify under Code Sec. 303 since its value exceeds $892,500 and, therefore, the 35 percent test is met.

A special rule applies to an estate which includes stock of two or more corporations. Under Code Sec. 303(b)(2)(B), the stock of two or more corporations may be aggregated to satisfy the 35 percent test if 20 percent or more of the value of each corporation's outstanding stock is included in the decedent's gross estate. For purposes of the 20 percent requirement, stock which, at the decedent's death, represents the surviving spouse's interest in property held by the decedent and the surviving spouse as community property, or as joint tenants, tenants by the entirety, or tenants in common is treated as having been included in determining the value of the decedent's gross estate.

EXAMPLE 15.68

The gross estate of a decedent, Pete Brown, has a fair market value of $1 million, and the Code Secs. 2053 and 2054 expenses are $225,000. Included in the gross estate is stock of three corporations:

	Value of Shares Held	Value of Corporation
Alpha	$175,000	$500,000
Beta	125,000	400,000
Gamma	75,000	600,000

None of the three corporations meet the 35 percent of AGE test (35% × $775,000 = $271,250). However, since Alpha and Beta meet the 20 percent test, the stock of both corporations can be treated as stock of a single corporation valued at $300,000. Clearly, $300,000 is greater than $271,250. Gamma does not meet the 20 percent test and cannot be included in the 35 percent test. Thus, redemptions of Alpha and/or Beta stock will qualify for sale or exchange treatment (within dollar limitations) under Code Sec. 303.

PLANNING POINTER

The 35 percent test is critical to the use of a Code Sec. 303 redemption. If the stockholdings do not satisfy this test, certain steps may be taken to insure qualification. The value of a stockholder's interest in a corporation may be increased, the stockholder's adjusted gross estate may be decreased, or a combination of both can be employed in order to qualify for Code Sec. 303 treatment. For example, a stockholder could purchase more shares in the corporation. Further, assets other than closely-held stock may be given away before death in order to help satisfy the 35 percent test.

Limitation on Redemption Amount

The limitation mentioned in (4), above, is imposed because the purpose of this special redemption is to help pay estate taxes and related expenses. However, the redeemed shareholders are not required to use the proceeds to pay these taxes and expenses. If the estate has cash sufficient to pay such expenses and uses this cash to pay the expenses, then the redeemed shareholders still will receive sale or exchange treatment under Code Sec. 303.

If the proceeds from a redemption exceed the Code Sec. 303 limitation amount, such excess is treated under the general rule in Code Sec. 302. The fact of the excess does not destroy the favorable treatment of the remainder of the proceeds under Code Sec. 303.

When there is more than one redemption distribution during the prescribed time period, the distribution is applied against the total amount that qualifies for exchange treatment in the order in which the distributions are made. All distributions are considered, including distributions that fall under a different Code provision. Reg. §1.303-2(g)(1).

EXAMPLE 15.69

Decedent's gross estate is $800,000 and the sum of the death taxes and funeral and administrative expenses is $225,000. Included in determining the gross estate is stock of a corporation valued at $450,000 for estate tax purposes. In the first year of administration, one-third of the stock is distributed to a legatee, and shortly thereafter the corporation redeems it for $150,000. In the second year, another one-third of the stock includible in the estate is redeemed for $150,000. The first distribution is applied against the $225,000 that qualifies for Code Sec. 303 treatment as payment in exchange for stock under Code Sec. 303(a). Of the second distribution, only $75,000 is treated as in full payment in exchange for stock under Code Sec. 303.

Time Limitation

Code Sec. 303 benefits only are available to distributions made in redemption of such stock within one of the following time periods:

1. The permissible time period is between the decedent's death and the 90th day after the expiration of the period of limitation in Code Sec. 6501(a) (i.e., three years). Since the federal estate tax return is due nine months after the decedent's death under Code Sec. 6075(a), the qualified time limitation is approximately four years.

2. In the case of Tax Court litigation, the permissible time period is extended until 60 days after the Tax Court's decision becomes final.

3. If an election is made under Code Sec. 6166, relating to the extension of time to pay the estate tax attributable to a farm or closely-held business, the Code Sec. 303 period is identical with these extension periods. However, any amounts distributed after the four-year period are still limited to the sum of the death taxes and funeral and administrative expenses. Code Sec. 303(b)(1).

EXAMPLE 15.70

When Eben Stone died, his gross estate was valued at $3,000,000. Included in that amount was 500 of the 1,000 outstanding shares of Suba Corporation which were worth $1,800,000. The deductible expenses under Code Secs. 2053 and 2054 were $300,000 and estate taxes were $400,000. Suba Corporation redeemed 250 shares from Eben's estate in return for $1,000,000. Because of Code Sec. 318, the redemption does not meet the requirements of Code Sec. 302. The consequences of the redemption are as follows. Since the value of the stock is more than 35 percent of the adjusted gross estate ($1,800,000/$2,700,000 is 66.67 percent), the requirements are met for sale or exchange treatment under Code Sec. 303. The estate is responsible for the expenses and taxes and the maximum that qualifies under Code Sec. 303 is $700,000 ($300,000 + $400,000). The estate has a long-term capital gain of $70,000 ($700,000 – $630,000). The $630,000 ($1,800,000 × (175 ÷ 500)) is the basis in the number of shares qualifying for the redemption ($700,000 ÷ $1,000,000 = 70% of 250 shares = 175 shares). The remaining $300,000 distributed is a dividend (assuming sufficient E&P).

¶15,135   REDEEMING CORPORATION'S TAX CONSEQUENCES

There are three main concerns that the redeeming corporation must address. Can the corporation deduct expenses related to the redemption of its own stock? Does the corporation recognize a gain or loss on property it distributes to shareholders in exchange for its own stock? What is the effect of the redemption on the corporation's E&P?

Expenses Deduction

In general the costs incurred by a corporation in the redemption of its stock are not deductible. These costs, such as transfer fees and legal and accounting fees, must be capitalized and they are not amortizable because they are not ordinary and necessary business expenses; they are part of the purchase price of the stock. Rev. Rul. 69-561, 1969-2 CB 25. However, in some instances the courts have allowed a deduction (for example, see *Foster*, TC Memo. 1966-273, and *General Pencil Co.*, 3 TCM 603 (1944)).

Gain or Loss Recognition

If a corporation distributes property as part of the redemption then, under Code Sec. 311, no loss is recognized. However, gains are recognized if the property has appreciated in value. The realized and recognized gain is equal to the property's fair market value minus its adjusted basis. The type of gain depends upon the property distributed. Since losses are not recognized, it is best to sell property whose adjusted basis is greater than its fair market value. The corporation has a recognized loss and can distribute cash (the proceeds) to its shareholders.

EXAMPLE 15.71

Fieldstone Corporation uses an asset with a basis of $40,000 and a fair market value of $55,000 to redeem some of a shareholder's stock. Fieldstone must recognize a gain of $15,000 ($55,000 – $40,000) as a result of the redemption. This gain will be recognized even though the shareholder may have dividend income because the requirements of Code Sec. 302 or 303 were not met.

E&P Effects

The effects of the distribution on the corporation's E&P depend upon whether the redemption is treated as a dividend or as a sale or exchange. If the redemption is treated as a dividend, then E&P is reduced by the amount of the distribution. E&P also is increased by any gain recognized on the distribution (i.e., if the corporation distributed appreciated property) because the gain is in gross income.

If the redemption is treated as a redemption (i.e., sale or exchange) then E&P is increased by any gain recognized on the distribution. Additionally, E&P is decreased by the same percentage as the redeemed stock bears to the corporation's total stock outstanding. If the amount of the distribution exceeds this value, then such excess reduces the corporation's capital account. Code Sec. 312(n)(7).

EXAMPLE 15.72

Campbell Company has 100 shares of stock outstanding. Its E&P is $200,000 and its paid-in-capital is $130,000. It redeems for $60,000 all the stock of Mr. Roberts (25 shares) in a Code Sec. 302(b)(3) redemption. E&P is reduced by 25 percent (25 shares redeemed ÷ 100 shares outstanding) because Campbell Company redeemed 25 percent of its stock. Thus, E&P is reduced by $50,000 (25% × $200,000). The remainder of the distribution, $10,000 ($60,000 – $50,000) reduces the paid-in-capital account. After the redemption, Campbell Company's E&P is $150,000 and its paid-in-capital is $120,000.

¶15,141   REDEMPTIONS THROUGH RELATED CORPORATIONS

There are certain instances when an apparent sale of stock must be recast as a redemption. The sale is recast as a redemption because the shareholders are attempting to receive distributions of corporate earnings while avoiding dividend income.

Code Sec. 304 applies to a corporation's acquisition of a shareholder's stock in another corporation in exchange for property when the shareholder has control of both corporations. Property includes money, securities, and any other property but does not include stock (or rights to acquire such stock) in the corporation making the distribution. Code Sec. 317(a).

Control for the purposes of Code Sec. 304 is defined as the ownership of stock possessing at least 50 percent of the total combined voting power of all classes of stock entitled to vote, or at least 50 percent of the total value of all classes of stock. Code Sec. 304 also applies if an individual has a 50 percent interest in a corporation which, in turn, has control of another corporation. For purposes of determining the 50 percent control, the constructive ownership rules of Code Sec. 318(a) apply.

EXAMPLE 15.73

Roberta Rogers owned two corporations, Alpha and Beta. She sold some of her stock in Alpha to Beta. Roberta received capital gain treatment because the transaction was a sale and therefore the redemption tests of Code Secs. 302 and 303 were avoided. After the sale, Roberta had the same control of Alpha as she had before the sale. Code Sec. 304 was enacted to prevent the avoidance of Code Secs. 302 and 303 from happening by requiring that the sale be treated as a redemption subject to the requirements of Code Secs. 302 and 303. Code Sec. 304 applies to sales of stock involving two brother-sister corporations and to sales of a parent corporation's stock to one of its subsidiaries.

Brother-Sister Corporation Transactions

If an individual is in control (as defined under Code Sec. 304) of two corporations and transfers stock to one corporation in exchange for property, then the exchange generally is treated as a redemption by the acquiring corporation. However, if the distribution is treated as a dividend, then the acquiring corporation is considered to have received the stock as a contribution to its capital. In return, the acquiring corporation is considered to have issued some of its stock to the shareholder and then to have immediately redeemed such stock for the amount distributed in the exchange.

In applying the provisions of Code Sec. 302(b) to the exchange, reference is made to the shareholder's ownership of stock in the issuing corporation and not to the shareholder's ownership of stock in the acquiring corporation. The amount of dividend income is determined as if the property were distributed by the acquiring corporation to the extent of its E&P and then by the issuing corporation to the extent of its E&P.

Since the stock received by the acquiring corporation is treated as a contribution to its capital, its basis in the stock is equal to the shareholder's basis in the stock. The shareholder's basis in the acquiring corporation's stock is increased by the basis of the stock sold by the shareholder.

EXAMPLE 15.74　Cindy Baron owns 100 percent of Baruck Corporation and 70 percent of Mimi Company. Each corporation has 100 shares of stock outstanding. Cindy acquired the Baruck stock in 2014 for $15,000. She acquired the Mimi stock in 2011 for $20,000. In 2017, Cindy sells 20 shares of Baruck to Mimi for $35,000. The E&P of Baruck and Mimi is $50,000 and $25,000, respectively. If the sale receives sale or exchange treatment under Code Sec. 302(b), then Cindy has a long-term capital gain of $32,000 ($35,000 – $3,000; her basis in the 20 shares is $3,000 (20 × $150 per share)). Mimi's basis in the 20 shares of Baruck would be $35,000, the purchase price. However, the sale does not meet any of the redemption requirements under Code Sec. 302(b); it is not substantially disproportionate, there has not been a meaningful reduction in Cindy's interest, and there has not been a complete termination of her interest. Thus, Cindy will have dividend income up to $75,000 (the combined E&P of Baruck and Mimi). Since the amount of the distribution is $35,000, all of it is treated as a dividend. Cindy's basis in the 20 shares of Baruck is added to her basis of shares in Mimi. Thus, her basis in the 70 shares is $23,000 ($20,000 + $3,000). Mimi's basis in the 20 shares of Baruck is $3,000, equal to Cindy's basis in the stock. Finally, the $35,000 distribution is treated as coming out of Mimi's E&P first. Thus, Mimi's E&P is reduced to zero ($25,000 – $25,000) and Baruck's E&P is reduced to $40,000 ($50,000 – $10,000).

Parent-Subsidiary Corporation Transactions

If a subsidiary corporation acquires stock in its parent from a shareholder owning at least 50 percent of the parent corporation, Code Sec. 304 applies to the transaction. The transaction is construed as a distribution from the subsidiary to the parent and a subsequent distribution from the parent to the individual shareholder. The acquisition is treated as though the parent had redeemed its own stock.

If the redemption does not qualify for sale or exchange treatment under Code Sec. 302(b) or 303, then the amount of dividend income is determined as if the property were distributed by the acquiring corporation (subsidiary) to the extent of its E&P and then by the issuing corporation (parent) to the extent of its E&P. The subsidiary's basis in the parent corporation stock it acquired is equal to the amount it paid for the stock. The shareholder's basis in the stock in the parent corporation is increased by the basis of the parent stock the shareholder sold to the subsidiary.

EXAMPLE 15.75　James Jergens owns 85 shares of Parent Corporation. James acquired the shares in 2008 for $85,000. Parent Corporation owns 65 shares in Sub Corporation. Each corporation has 100 shares of stock outstanding. The E&P of Parent and Sub is $20,000 and $35,000, respectively. In 2017, James sells 15 shares of Parent to Sub for $25,000. If the sale receives sale or exchange treatment, then James has a long-term capital gain of $10,000 ($25,000 – $15,000, his basis in the 15 shares (15 × $1,000)). Sub's basis in the 15 shares is $25,000, the purchase price. However, the redemption does not meet any of the provisions of Code Secs. 302 and 303 and, therefore, is treated as a dividend. James has dividend income of $25,000 which is treated as a distribution of Sub's E&P. James's basis in his remaining 70 shares of Parent are increased by $15,000 (the basis of the 15 shares to be sold to Sub) to $85,000. Sub's E&P is reduced by $25,000. After the redemption, the Sub's E&P is $10,000 and Parent's E&P is $20,000. Finally, Sub's basis in the 15 shares of Parent stock is $25,000, the purchase price.

To the extent that a Code Sec. 304 transaction between two corporations is deemed a dividend, the transferor and the acquiring corporations are treated as if (1) the transferor had transferred the stock involved in the transaction to the acquiring corporation in exchange for stock in the acquiring corporation in a Code Sec. 351 transfer, and (2) the acquiring corporation then had redeemed the stock it is treated as having issued. If Code Sec. 304 applies to a distribution treated as a dividend, then regardless of how long the stock has been held, the amount treated as a dividend is deemed an extraordinary dividend for Code Sec. 1059 purposes. As such, the transferor must reduce its basis in its remaining shares by the amount of the distribution qualifying for the dividends-received deduction, and if this amount exceeds the basis, then such excess is treated as gain on the sale or exchange of the stock in the year the extraordinary dividend was received.

EXAMPLE 15.76	X Co. owns 100% of W Co. and 70% of Y Co. Y Co. owns 100% (100 shares) of Z Co. Y Co.'s adjusted basis of its Z Co. shares is $1,000. Y Co. sells 80 shares of its Z Co. stock to W Co. for $950. The redemption falls under Code Sec. 304 and will result in Y Co. recognizing a $950 dividend. Y Co.'s dividends-received deduction is $665 (70% × $950), leaving $285 taxable. Since this also is considered an extraordinary dividend, Y Co.'s basis in its remaining 20 shares of Z Co. is reduced to $335 ($1,000 – $665).

¶15,145   PREFERRED STOCK BAILOUTS

The use of related corporations to circumvent the redemption requirements of Code Secs. 302 and 303 is severely restricted by Code Sec. 304. Another way shareholders attempted to bail out corporate earnings was with preferred stock. The transactions were structured as follows.

1. The corporation issued nonvoting preferred stock in a nontaxable stock dividend distribution with respect to common stock.
2. The shareholder assigned a portion of the common stock's basis to the preferred stock. In addition, the preferred stock received the holding period of the common stock.
3. The shareholder sold the preferred stock to an unrelated third party for the stock's fair market value. This produced a capital gain, usually long-term, equal to the difference between the fair market value and the allocated basis in the preferred stock.
4. The corporation redeemed the preferred stock from the unrelated third party in a redemption that qualified as a complete termination of the interest. The third party received sale or exchange treatment and usually had a nominal gain (i.e., "payment" for helping the shareholder bail out the earnings).

Code Sec. 306 was enacted to prevent shareholders from using the above plan to circumvent the redemption requirements of Code Secs. 302 and 303. Effectively, certain stock are "tainted" when received in a nontaxable stock dividend and the sale of such stock produces ordinary income rather than capital gain. However, proceeds from the sale (not redemption) of this "tainted" stock qualify for the reduced tax rate applicable to dividend income (i.e., either 0%, 15% or 20%) depending on the taxpayer's tax bracket.

Definition of Section 306 Stock

The distributing corporation must have E&P at the time of the distribution in order for the preferred stock to receive the taint of Code Sec. 306. Code Sec. 306(c)(2). If the corporation had no current or accumulated E&P at the time of distribution, then any and all distributions (cash, property, or preferred stock) would not be taxable as dividends; thus, the effect of the E&P requirement is to put the non-common stock distribution on equal footing with other distributions. However, the amount of E&P is immaterial; even a small amount of E&P will cause the taint of Code Sec. 306. Also, since the distribution is not taxable (i.e., the recipient shareholder does not recognize income when the stock is issued), there is no reduction to the distributing corporation's E&P.

There are three categories in which Section 306 stock can occur when there is corporate E&P (Code Sec. 306(c)):

1. Non-common stock is distributed to a stockholder and any part of the distribution is not included in the gross income of the stockholder.
2. Non-common stock is received in a reorganization or divisive transaction in which the gain is not recognized and the effect of the transaction is substantially the same as the receipt of a stock dividend.
3. Stock (other than stock in Category 2, above) which has a substituted basis is determined with reference to the basis of Section 306 stock.

Stock Distributed to Seller

The first situation where stock may be classified as Section 306 stock occurs when a shareholder sells or disposes non-common stock that was received in a distribution that was not fully included in gross income. Thus, a completely taxable stock dividend would fall outside the scope of Code Sec. 306. However, stock rights distributed to stockholders tax free, and any stock received through the exercise of such rights, may be Section 306 stock. Similarly, common stock with a privilege of converting into non-common stock or property (whether or not the conversion privilege is contained in such stock) is not treated as common stock.

Stock Received in Corporate Reorganization or Separation

Stock received in exchange for Section 306 stock also is tainted. Non-common stock received in a reorganization or divisive transaction is tainted if cash received in lieu of such stock would have been treated as a dividend under Code Sec. 302(d); Reg. §1.306-3(d).

EXAMPLE 15.77	Acqa Corporation has only common stock outstanding. In a statutory merger under Code Sec. 368(a), Acqa merges with Garber Corporation. The stockholders of Acqa Corporation receive both common and preferred stock in Garber Corporation. The preferred stock received by these stockholders is Section 306 stock.

EXAMPLE 15.78	Sam Barns and Barbara Meyers each own one-half of the 2,000 outstanding shares of preferred stock and one-half of the 2,000 outstanding shares of common stock of Peanut Corporation. In a recapitalization under Code Sec. 368(a)(1)(E), each stockholder exchanges the preferred stock for a new issue of preferred stock (which is not substantially different). Unless the exchanged preferred stock was not Section 306 stock, the new issue of preferred stock is Section 306 stock.

Stock Having Transferred or Substituted Basis

This definition, of course, overlaps with Category 2 and in such cases, Category 2 controls. The three major areas where this category is applicable are (1) corporate organizations under Code Sec. 351, (2) exchanges of stock for similar stock in the same corporation under Code Sec. 1036, and (3) transference by gift of Section 306 stock. Note that inherited stock is not Section 306 stock because the basis of inherited property is fair market value at the date of decedent's death (or alternative date if elected). Thus, there is no substituted basis. Reg. §1.306-3(e).

EXAMPLE 15.79	Harvey Black owns Section 306 stock in Briscoe Corporation. He transfers this tainted stock to Hill Corporation (in exchange for Hill common stock) in a transaction falling within Code Sec. 351. The Hill common stock received by Harvey Black would be Section 306 stock. Furthermore, the Briscoe Section 306 stock now in the hands of Hill Corporation (the transferee) is still Section 306 stock. Thus, a single block of tainted stock has turned into two blocks of tainted stock.

PLANNING POINTER	For planning purposes, a taxpayer should realize that if both common stock and preferred stock are issued to the stockholders at the time of organization of the corporation, the preferred stock is not Section 306 stock. Also, a dividend of common treasury stock to common stockholders is not Section 306 stock, if the treasury stock is the same in all respects as the common stock on which it is declared. Rev. Rul. 55-746, 1955-2 CB 224.

Dispositions of Section 306 Stock

The tax consequences of Section 306 stock occur when the stockholder disposes of the tainted stock. These taxable dispositions are divided into two categories: (1) sale or other disposition (other than redemption) and (2) redemption.

As to a disposition other than a redemption, any amount realized by the stockholder is ordinary income to the extent of the amount that would have been a taxable dividend if cash had been distributed rather than Section 306 stock. The ordinary income is not limited to the realized gain on the sale, but may be as great as the amount realized on the sale. There are two limitations on the amount of ordinary income. The recognized ordinary income is limited to the smaller of (1) the corporate current and accumulated earnings and profits at the time of the distribution, and (2) the fair market value of the Section 306 stock on the date of distribution by the corporation. Again, the ordinary income from the non-redemption sale is treated as a dividend that is subject to the reduced rates of 0%, 15% or 20%, depending on the shareholder's tax bracket. Any excess of the amount realized over the sum of the ordinary income and the adjusted basis of the stock is treated as a capital gain. Code Sec. 306(a)(1). If the amount received is less than the shareholder's basis, then the unused basis is added to the shareholder's basis in the common stock.

EXAMPLE 15.80	On December 15, Apple and Banana owned equally all of the stock of Fruity Corporation (which files on a calendar-year basis). On this date, Fruity Corporation distributed pro rata 100 shares of preferred stock as a nontaxable dividend on its common stock. On December 15, the preferred stock had a fair market value of $10,000, and the company had no E&P. The 50 shares of preferred stock distributed to Apple had an allocated basis to him of $10 per share (or a total of $500 for the 50 shares). Apple sells the 50 shares of preferred stock on July 1 nine years later for $6,000 at a time when Fruity's E&P was $14,000. Since there was no E&P on the date of distribution, the preferred stock is not Section 306 stock. Apple would recognize a $5,500 capital gain ($6,000 – $500).

EXAMPLE 15.81	Assume the same facts as in Example 15.80, except that E&P on December 15 was $20,000. Ordinary income is recognized to the extent of $10,000 (Apple's share of E&P on December 15) or $5,000 (the fair market value of the 50 shares Apple received). Thus, Apple has $5,000 of ordinary income. Apple also has a capital gain of $500 ($6,000 – $5,500 ($5,000 ordinary income + $500 adjusted basis)).

EXAMPLE 15.82	Barry owns all the common stock (100 shares) of Sky Corporation. He acquired the shares in 2010 for $15,000. In 2014, Sky Corporation distributed 40 shares of preferred stock to Barry in a nontaxable distribution. At that time the corporation's E&P was $60,000 and the per-share fair market values of the common and preferred stock were $200 and $125, respectively. Barry must allocate a basis of $3,000 to the preferred stock ($15,000 × ($5,000 ÷ $25,000)). In 2017, Barry sold the preferred stock for $5,000. Although his realized gain is $2,000 ($5,000 – $3,000), Barry has ordinary income of $5,000 (the fair market value of the preferred stock when distributed since this was less than the E&P of $60,000). The unrecovered basis of $3,000 in the preferred stock is added to his basis in the common stock, bringing it to $15,000 ($12,000 + $3,000).

Losses are not recognized on the sale of Section 306 stock. In order to avoid double taxation on the common stock when loss on the disposition of the Code Sec. 306 is disallowed, the unused basis of the preferred stock is added back to the stock retained by the stockholder. Reg. §1.306-1(b)(2).

EXAMPLE 15.83	Assume the same facts as in Example 15.80, except that Apple sells his 50 shares of preferred stock for $5,100. Of this amount, $5,000 is treated as ordinary income and no loss is allowed. $400 is added back to the basis of the Fruity common stock (the allocated basis of $500 reduced by the $100 received).

An ordinary dividend in cash may be less harmful than a sale of Section 306 stock. A dividend reduces the company's E&P and qualifies for a dividends-received deduction, whereas a disposition of Section 306 stock does not reduce E&P and does not qualify for the dividends-received deduction. Reg. §1.306-1(b)(1).

A taxpayer might try to issue preferred stock that has many constraints so as to reduce its fair market value at date of distribution, and, therefore, limit the taint. Subsequently, the constraints or conditions would be lifted with the result that the preferred stock's fair market value would increase. To stop such a practice, Code Sec. 306(g)(1) indicates that where substantial changes are made in the conditions of the stock, the fair market value is the greater of the value on the distribution date or the value at the time of the change in conditions. Also, the amount of the E&P will be the greater of the amount at the time of distributions or the amount at the time of substantial change.

If Section 306 stock is redeemed, a different set of rules is applicable. The ordinary income in a redemption is the smaller of (1) the amount received on redemption, or (2) the E&P on the date of the redemption. The amount of the E&P on the date of distribution is immaterial. Any amount of the proceeds in excess of the ordinary income is a return of capital (until the basis is gone), and any remainder is treated as a capital gain. In essence, a redemption of Section 306 stock is covered by Code Secs. 301(a) and 302(d).

EXAMPLE 15.84

In December, Blake Inc. distributes a nontaxable preferred stock dividend of 10,000 shares on its common stock. At this time, the accumulated E&P is $500,000 and the fair market value of the preferred stock is $100,000. Carl Combs owns 200 shares of the common stock, with a cost of $10,000. He receives 500 shares of the Blake preferred stock, which is worth $5,000. At the time of distribution, his common stock was worth $15,000. Thus, $2,500 would be allocated to the preferred stock ($10,000 × ($5,000 ÷ $20,000)) and $7,500 would remain with his common stock ($10,000 × ($15,000 ÷ $20,000)). Carl sells all of his preferred stock to Donald for $6,000. His share of the E&P is $25,000 ((500/10,000) × $500,000). Carl would recognize ordinary income of $5,000 and the basis of his common stock would return to $9,000 ($7,500 + ($2,500 − $1,000)).

EXAMPLE 15.85

Assume the same facts as in Example 15.84, except that Carl's preferred stock is redeemed by Blake Inc. for $6,000. Carl would recognize ordinary income of $6,000, and the basis in his common stock would return to $10,000 ($7,500 + $2,500). The $6,000 ordinary income would be treated as dividend income.

Exceptions to Section 306 Treatment

Code Sec. 306(b) provides four exceptions to the ordinary income treatment. In the case of a sale or other disposition of the stock (other than a redemption), no ordinary income is recognized where the entire stock interest of the stockholder is terminated (stock attribution rules of Code Sec. 318(a) apply) and the stock is not transferred directly or indirectly to a person whose stock ownership would be attributable to the stockholder. Code Sec. 306(b)(1)(A). Only the stock interest need be terminated. The reasoning for this exception: the stockholder could have obtained the same results by selling shares of stock before the Code Sec. 306 distribution.

Where there is a redemption of the Section 306 stock and Code Sec. 302(b)(3) applies (a complete termination of interest), ordinary dividend treatment is avoided. The constructive ownership rules of Code Sec. 318 apply, but the waiver of the attribution rule of Code Sec. 302(c) is available. The punitive rules likewise do not apply if the tainted stock is redeemed in a partial or complete liquidation.

EXAMPLE 15.86

Fred Bass desires to retire from the business and to terminate all stock and other interests in Runner Corporation. To accomplish this objective, Fred proposes to sell 30 shares of common stock and 18 shares of preferred stock to his daughter Jane, sell 25 shares of common stock to key employees of Runner who are not related to Fred or Jane, and to have the remaining common and preferred stock redeemed by Runner. Fred's reasons for selling some of the preferred stock to Jane rather than having all of the preferred stock redeemed are to leave Jane with voting control of Runner for a smaller investment than would otherwise be necessary while giving the key employees other than Jane a greater participation in the growth of Runner than they would have if Jane owned more than half of the common stock. These goals will be accomplished because the preferred stock is worth only one-tenth as much per share as the common stock but entitles its holder to one vote per share, the same as the common stock.

The redemption of the common stock and the Section 306 stock coupled with the sale of the remaining common stock and Section 306 stock to Jane, and other key employees qualifies as a complete termination of interest under Code Sec. 302(b)(3). Furthermore, the dispositions of the Section 306 stock are excepted from the ordinary income treatment of Code Sec. 306(a) by Code Sec. 306(b)(4)(B). See Rev. Rul. 77-455, 1977-2 CB 93.

No ordinary income is recognized in a tax-free exchange under Code Secs. 351 and 1036. This exception is only a temporary escape route since the non-common stock received in the exchange becomes Section 306 stock under Code Sec. 306(c)(1)(C). Where the transferor of tainted stock receives boot, the fair market value of the boot becomes subject to Code Sec. 306(a).

Another exception to Code Sec. 306(a) treatment occurs where, in the opinion of the IRS, a transaction is not in pursuance of a plan having as one of its principal purposes the avoidance of federal income tax. Code Sec. 306(b)(4). This exception would apply to the case of dividends and isolated dispositions of Section 306 stock by minority stockholders. Reg. §1.306-2(b)(3). A taxpayer should ask for an advance ruling from the IRS before relying on this exception.

¶15,205   DISTRIBUTIONS BY CLOSELY-HELD CORPORATIONS

The tax treatment of distributions to shareholders provides several opportunities to minimize the impact of federal income taxes and to maximize the after-tax wealth of the overall economic unit (consisting of the corporation and its shareholders). Usually the shareholders are related (i.e., family corporation) but this is not always the case.

Paying a dividend is frequently regarded as undesirable because it is nondeductible to the corporation, but taxable to the shareholder (although at a reduced rate for individual shareholders). As a result, numerous alternatives are often considered first when profits exist, particularly in a closely-held setting where shareholders and management are one and the same. Here is a brief list of the main ways to get the funds out of a profitable corporation, ranging from the most to the least desirable for tax purposes. The ranking is tentative and may vary with facts and circumstances:

1. Payments that produce current, tax-free benefits to the shareholder-employees and are deductible by the corporation. Examples include medical plans, legal plans, and group-term life insurance.
2. Payments that produce future, taxable benefits to the shareholder-employees and are currently deductible by the corporation. The typical example is qualified deferred compensation plans (e.g., pension and profit-sharing plans and thrift plans).
3. Payments that produce current, taxable benefits to the shareholder-employees and are deductible by the corporation. Examples include salaries, bonuses, and taxable fringe benefits.
4. Payments that produce current benefits to the shareholder-employees, result in capital gains or losses, do not have to be repaid, but are nondeductible by the corporation. Included here are stock redemptions not taxed as dividends and shareholder sales of property to the corporation.
5. Payments that produce current, nontaxable benefits to the shareholder-employees, but which have to be repaid and are nondeductible to the corporation. Shareholder loans fall under this heading. Unless appropriate formalities are observed, dividend treatment may result.
6. Payments that produce current, taxable benefits to the shareholder-employee and are nondeductible to the corporation. These payments are dividends and in the last place. (Chapter 18 discusses two penalty taxes that may be applicable if earnings are accumulated.)

PLANNING POINTER

Annie Gall is the sole shareholder of Beach Blankets Inc. She wishes to give $20,000 to her favorite charity, Last Chance College. If she were to have Beach Blankets redeem some of her shares to raise the $20,000, Annie would have to report $20,000 in dividend income. Annie decides to give $20,000 of her stock in Beach Blankets to Last Chance College. Seeing that there is no market for the stock, Last Chance sells the stock to Beach Blanket for $20,000 of notes, payable over 10 years with interest. Here are the tax results:

1. Annie receives a $20,000 charitable contribution deduction currently.
2. Annie has no dividend income.
3. Annie owns 100 percent of the corporation before and after the redemption.
4. The corporation recognizes no gain or loss but reduces its E&P account by 50 percent.
5. The corporation pays the $20,000 later but receives no deductions (except for interest).

As long as the charity is not obligated to sell the stock, this is accepted by the courts and the IRS. *D.D. Palmer*, 75-2 USTC ¶9726, 523 F.2d 1308 (CA-8 1975); Rev. Rul. 78-197, 1978-1 CB 83.

TAX BLUNDER

A businessman owned 100 percent of the stock in a corporation, directly or indirectly, using attribution rules. Needing a loan, he approached the Small Business Administration (SBA). His loan application was approved with one condition: He had to invest an additional $25,000 in the corporation. As a way of complying, he issued $25,000 of par value preferred stock and purchased the whole issue for $25,000 in cash. The SBA loan was granted, the business prospered, and eventually he no longer needed SBA support. At that time, he turned in his preferred stock to the corporation (which cancelled it) in exchange for $25,000. He reported no gain or loss on the transaction.

Result. $25,000 of dividends. The amount was covered by E&P, and he owned 100 percent of the corporation, directly or indirectly, before and after the redemption. Having a good business reason for the transaction is irrelevant.

SUMMARY

- Earnings and profits (E&P) represents a corporation's ability to make a dividend.
- E&P has some similarities to retained earnings.
- E&P affects the taxability of corporate distributions and redemptions.
- Current E&P is computed annually.
- Accumulated E&P consists of undistributed prior years' E&P.
- Current E&P and accumulated E&P can be negative.
- Distributions first come out of current E&P, then out of accumulated E&P.
- A distribution never can make E&P negative; it only can bring them to zero.
- If a distribution exceeds current E&P, then current E&P is reduced proportionally and accumulated E&P is reduced chronologically.
- A distribution that is not a dividend is treated as a return of capital and is applied against the shareholder's stock basis; once basis is zero then all additional amounts are treated as gain from sale of the stock.
- In general, a redemption receives sale or exchange treatment; however, there are exceptions to this.
- A redemption must meet Code Sec. 302 or Code Sec. 303 to receive sale or exchange treatment.
- Other redemptions receive dividend treatment to the extent of corporate E&P.
- Code Secs. 304 and 306 restrict the use of controlled corporations and preferred stock to circumvent Code Secs. 302 and 303, respectively.

QUESTIONS

1. What is E&P and what is its significance?

2. Distinguish between current and accumulated E&P.

3. What are the broad categories of adjustments made to determine current E&P?

4. Mar Company made a dividend distribution of property to its shareholders. Mar Company's adjusted basis in the property is less than its fair market value. What is the shareholders' basis in the property?

5. Zest Company distributes property to its shareholders throughout the year. Some of the distributions are dividends and a few qualified as redemptions. The adjusted basis of all property was different from the fair market value. Does it recognize a gain or loss when it distributes property as a dividend or in a redemption?

6. Nap Co. distributes appreciated property subject to a small liability to Susan. Susan assumes the liability. Nap Co. has large E&P. What is the measure of the distribution, the amount of Susan's dividend income, her basis in the property, and her date basis in the land?

7. Wake Company distributed appreciated property as its dividend to shareholders. What are the tax effects of the distribution to Wake Company?

8. Clemco has current and accumulated E&P. It makes a distribution to its shareholders. How is the distribution sourced (i.e., from which category of E&P does it first come)?

9. Perfect Co. is a closely-held corporation. It has very large E&P so its majority owner asked the firm's accountant what options were available to the firm to distribute some of the E&P and if the IRS might question the distributions. Advise the accountant.

10. Ann owns ten percent of Phil Co. She received 200 shares of Phil Co. this year as a stock dividend and was told it was a taxable stock dividend. When is a stock dividend taxable?

11. Olivia owns 1000 shares of Westfield Inc. She received stock rights from Westfield Inc. Olivia is uncertain if the distribution is taxable or nontaxable. When are distributions of stock rights taxable?

12. What is a stock redemption?

13. How is the E&P account affected in a redemption?

14. Sal's shares in Fin Inc. were redeemed by Fin Inc. in a transaction that qualifies under Code Sec. 303. Sal inherited the shares from Rita shortly after her death and the redemption occurred the next day. Rita acquired the shares several years ago and they had significantly appreciated in value prior to her death. Will Sal have a large gain on the redemption?

15. East Co. redeemed Oscar's stock. Oscar received $20,000 for all the shares he owned. His adjusted basis in the shares was $14,000. Can either party recognize a loss on the redemption?

16. What is a substantially disproportionate redemption?

17. What does a 10-year agreement entail?

18. Berk Company has several lines of business. It decided that one line was a drag on earnings so it sold it. Proceeds from the sale of the line of business were distributed to its shareholders in return for some of the shareholders' stock. Will the distribution qualify as a redemption in partial liquidation?

19. First Inc. redeemed some shares from its shareholders. Several of the shareholders are related. Do the constructive ownership rules possibly affect the tax status of the redemption?

20. What is the treatment of a sale of stock among related corporations?

21. What is a preferred stock bailout?

22. What is Section 306 stock?

23. How much dividend income is recognized by a seller of Section 306 stock?

24. Following are four "income and expense" items of Flor Inc.: dividend income (an 80% dividends-received deduction was claimed); tax-exempt municipal bond interest income; domestic production activities deduction; federal income taxes. In computing its current E&P, what adjustments to taxable income would Flor Inc. make?

PROBLEMS

25. Given the following information, determine the taxable portion and return of capital in each situation, as well as accumulated E&P on January 1, 2018.

	2017 Current E&P	January 1, 2017 Accumulated E&P	July 1, 2017 Distribution
a.	$75,000	$20,000	$65,000
b.	75,000	20,000	85,000
c.	75,000	(14,000)	65,000
d.	75,000	20,000	105,000
e.	75,000	(15,000)	85,000

26. Genesis Inc. was formed in 2014. Its current E&P and distributions to shareholders made each year are listed below.

Year	Current E&P	Distribution
2014	($10,000)	$0
2015	($6,000)	9,000
2016	$11,000	7,000
2017	$15,000	19,000

What is Genesis Inc.'s year-end accumulated E&P (after the distributions) at the end of each year and what is the tax status of each distribution?

27. Door Co.'s taxable income was $1,000,000 this year and it paid $340,000 in federal income taxes. Related information for the year follows:
    - $4,000 fines (not deducted to compute taxable income)
    - $7,000 NOL carryover (deducted to compute taxable income)
    - $10,000 municipal bond interest income
    - $15,000 net long-term capital loss
    - $20,000 depreciation (deducted to compute taxable income) in excess of E&P allowance
    - $30,000 domestic production activities deduction (deducted to compute taxable income)
    - $50,000 dividend income from a 21%-owned domestic corporation (included in taxable income)

    What is Door Co's current E&P for the year?

28. The following information is taken from Lynnso Corporation's records for 2017:

Gross receipts from operations	$500,000
Dividends received from a 40 percent owned domestic corporation	100,000
Interest on State of Ohio bonds	30,000
Life insurance proceeds received due to death of a key employee	40,000
Cost of goods sold	200,000
NOL carryover from 2016	13,000
MACRS depreciation (straight-line would have been $30,000) on equipment	43,000
Straight-line depreciation on building	15,870
Charitable contributions	45,000
Wages expense	50,000
Life insurance premiums on key-man insurance	10,000

    a. Determine Lynnso Corporation's taxable income for 2017.
    b. Compute Lynnso Corporation's current E&P for 2017.

29. Flash Co. distributed $40,000 to Skip Inc., a 25 percent shareholder. Flash Co.'s E&P applicable to Skip Inc.'s distribution is $20,000 and Skip Inc. had a basis in its stock of $14,000.
    a. How much dividend income does Skip Inc. have?
    b. How much and what kind of taxable income does Skip Inc. have because of the distribution?
    c. What is Skip Inc.'s basis in its stock immediately after the distribution?

30. Special Motors Inc. has E&P of $53,000. It distributes a building to the individual sole shareholder. The building has a basis of $17,000 and a value of $54,000, is subject to a mortgage of $31,000, and has $6,000 of depreciation recapture potential.
    a. What is the character and amount of any gain or loss recognized by Special Motors?
    b. What is the amount of the dividend?
    c. What is E&P after the distribution?
    d. What is the shareholder's basis in the building?

31. Smith Co. has no E&P, current or accumulated, prior to the following independent transactions with its sole shareholder, Chris:

    Distribution of LIFO inventory with a basis of $7,000, a FIFO value of $11,000, and a market value of $13,000.

    Distribution of land with a basis of $21,000, a mortgage of $34,000, and a value of $58,000.

    Sale of property to Chris for $20,000 (basis $5,000, value $25,000).
    a. Does Chris have to recognize any income?
    b. Does Smith Co. have any gains or losses?
    c. What are the required adjustments to E&P?

32. Tara Corporation had current E&P of $320,000 in 2017. During 2017, it distributed numerous items to its sole shareholder, Anne. Indicate the effects of the distribution to Anne and Tara Corporation for each item distributed.
    a. Inventory with a fair market value of $30,000 and an adjusted basis of $20,000.
    b. Truck used in business with a fair market value of $17,000 and an adjusted basis of $9,100. The truck's original cost was $22,000.
    c. Land with a fair market value of $210,000 that was held as an investment and was acquired in 2012 for $150,000.
    d. Land with a fair market value of $105,000 that was used in the business. The land was acquired in 2012 for $50,000 and had an outstanding mortgage of $30,000.
    e. Installment obligation having a face amount of $43,000 and an adjusted basis of $29,000. The installment obligation was obtained when Tara sold ordinary income property.

33. Sopra Company is a closely-held corporation. Tony owns 60%, Carmella owns 20% and Meadow owns 20%, and all are related. Sopra Company has very large E&P. It was audited this year by the IRS and several issues were identified. Indicate the potential tax consequences of each issue.
    a. Tony sold property held as a capital asset to Sopra Company for $400,000 when its FMV was $300,000.
    b. Sopra Company paid Meadow a salary of $200,000 but the IRS determines that $60,000 was unreasonable.
    c. Sopra Company lent Carmella $100,000 four years ago. Carmella has not paid any interest nor has she repaid any part of the loan.
    d. Tony leases property to Sopra Company for $400,000 per year. Normal rental value is $200,000 per year.

34. Combat Toys Inc. has an accumulated deficit and current E&P of $20,000. Joe Gunn, a 60 percent shareholder, withdrew $35,000 from the corporation. Joe reported no income from the transaction, and upon audit he claimed it was a loan. No note had been executed, but on the eve of the audit, Joe signed a demand note for $35,000, payable to Combat Toys. The IRS claims Joe has a dividend of $35,000. What is the most likely result if the case goes to court?

35. Karl Stick is president of Stock Company. He also owns 100 percent of its stock. Karl's salary is $120,000. At the end of the year, Karl was paid a bonus of $100,000 because the firm had a good year. Stock Company deducted $220,000 as compensation expense for the year. Upon audit, $80,000 of the deduction was disallowed. How could this happen? How would you advise Stock Company?

36. Refer to Problem 35 and assume that Karl's tax bracket is 31 percent and Stock Company's is 34 percent. What is the dollar impact of the IRS reclassification?

37. Bill incorporated his business four years ago and owns 100 percent of its stock. The corporation distributes a piece of land, used as a parking lot for the customers, to Bill. Bill's basis in his stock is $21,000, the land has a basis of $7,000 and a value of $24,000, and E&P is $5,000.
    a. What are the tax consequences to the corporation?
    b. To Bill?

38. Charlie received one warrant (right) to purchase a share of common stock for each ten shares she owned in Ludlow Inc. as a "dividend." The exercise price was $70, the price of the stock was $54, and the value of the warrant was $7. Charlie makes no elections. What are the tax consequences to Charlie and Ludlow if:
    a. Charlie's warrants expire worthless?
    b. Charlie exercised the warrants when the stock price was $85?
    c. Charlie sold the warrants for $12 a share?

39. Super Xtra Inc. is publicly held. One of its shareholders, Fred, owns 100 shares of common stock with a basis of $5,000 and a value of $12,000. On October 17 of this year, Fred receives 25 rights (to buy 25 new shares of stock). Each right is worth $12.
    a. Does Fred have any gross income?
    b. What is Fred's basis in his rights?
    c. When does the rights' holding period start?
    d. What difference would it make if Fred could have taken a $300 debenture in lieu of the rights, but did not?

40. Antoinette owns 400 shares of common stock of Gertz Incorporated which she acquired on May 28, 2012, for $50,000. On April 14, 2017, Antoinette received 40 shares of Gertz's common stock. The fair market value of the 40 shares on April 14, 2017, was $15,200. Gertz's current E&P for 2017 was $30,000.
    a. Assuming that the stock dividend was a proportionate dividend and no other distribution options were available, determine Antoinette's taxable income and Antoinette's basis in the 400 shares and the 40 shares, as well as each group's holding period. If she sold the 40 shares for $16,000 on October 17, 2017, then what is her gain or loss and what is its character?
    b. Compute Antoinette's taxable income, basis in the shares and their holding periods assuming that the stock dividend was disproportionate. If she sold the 40 shares on October 17, 2017, for $14,000, then what is her gain or loss and what is its character?

41. Gary owns 100 shares of common stock (class A) in Justine Inc. which he acquired on October 10, 2007, for $5,000. On July 8, 2017, Gary received 20 shares of class B common stock in a proportionate distribution. At the time of the distribution the fair market values of the class A and class B stock were $75 and $45 per share, respectively. Justine's current E&P for 2017 was $60,000. On August 18, 2017, Gary sold the 20 shares of class B stock for $1,000.
    a. What are the tax consequences of the distribution on July 8, 2017, to Gary?
    b. What are the tax consequences of the sale on August 18, 2017, for Gary?

42. Hendricks Corporation has very large E&P. On May 15, 2017, it declared a 15% stock dividend payable to all shareholders. On September 15, 2017, when each share was worth $500, it distributed the shares. Jimmy owns 200 shares of Hendricks Corporation. He acquired the shares five years ago for $23,000. Jimmy sold 100 shares of Hendricks Corporation on December 15, 2017 at $600 per share after all transaction costs.
    a. What are the tax consequences of the distribution to Jimmy?
    b. How much, if any, gain or loss does Jimmy recognize on the sale of the 100 shares and what is its character?

43. Beatles Inc. has 1,000 shares issued and outstanding. The shares are owned as follows:

Name	Shares
Paul	250
John Corp. (Paul owns 70% of John Corp.)	250
George Inc. (Paul owns 25% of George Inc.)	250
Ringo Partnership (Paul is a 40% partner of Ringo Partnership)	250

How many shares is Paul consider to own for redemption purposes?

44. Salkey Company has two owners, Gus and Jack, who are father and son. Gus owns 100 shares which he acquired in 2012 for $15,000. Jack owns 100 shares which he acquired in 2014 for $21,000. Salkey's current E&P in 2017 is $70,000. On March 18, 2017, Salkey redeemed 35 shares from Gus in return for land worth $50,000 and an adjusted basis of $10,000.
    a. Does the redemption qualify as a sale?
    b. What are the income tax consequences to Gus, Jack, and Salkey Company?
    c. Would your answers to (a) and (b) differ if Gus and Jack were brothers? If so, how?

45. Monica is a preferred stockholder with a basis of $9,000 in her 100 shares in Small Appliances Inc. She has one-half her stock redeemed for $6,000 in a transaction that qualifies as a sale. Small Appliances's balance sheet prior to the redemption reads in part:

Common stock, authorized, issued and outstanding, 10,000 shares, par $1	$10,000
Paid-in-capital, common stock	40,000
Preferred stock, authorized, issued and outstanding, 1,000 shares, par $5	5,000
Paid-in-capital, preferred stock	20,000
Earnings and profits	76,000

   a. What is Monica's gain and its character?
   b. What is her basis in the remaining shares?
   c. What adjustments are to be made to the equity accounts?
   d. What difference does it make if, instead of cash, Monica receives property with a basis of $4,000?

46. Samson Corporation has 1,000 shares of common stock outstanding. Sal owns 560 shares, Rita owns 250 shares, and Susan owns 190 shares. None of the owners are related. On August 14, 2017, Samson redeemed 150 shares from Sal. Sal's adjusted basis in the 560 shares was $28,000. In return for the 150 shares, Sal received $17,000. Samson's current E&P for 2017 was $45,000. Sal prefers to receive sale or exchange treatment.
   a. Indicate if Sal might be able to receive sale or exchange treatment.
   b. Indicate the tax consequences to Sal if the redemption is treated as a dividend or if it is treated as a sale or exchange.

47. Staton Inc. has four unrelated shareholders, Wayne, Judy, Erica, and Josh. Their respective bases in the shares are $15,000, $17,000, $19,000, and $21,000. Each shareholder owns 100 shares of Staton. On November 8, 2017, Staton Inc. redeemed 50 shares of Wayne's stock for $10,000 and 20 shares of Judy's stock for $4,000. Staton's current E&P for 2017 was $30,000. What are the tax consequences to Wayne and Judy?

48. Foxrun Company has three equal shareholders, Thomas, Kimberly, and Jennifer. Kimberly and Jennifer are Thomas's daughters. On September 2, 2017, Foxrun redeemed all of Thomas's stock in return for $250,000. Thomas had acquired the stock in 2010 for $190,000. Foxrun's current E&P for 2017 was $325,000. Thomas would like to minimize his federal income tax liability in 2017. Explain the alternatives available to him and how they would impact his 2017 taxable income.

49. The AB Corp. has been owned equally by individuals A and B for over five years. AB operates two qualified businesses, Q and R. The XYZ Corp. wishes to acquire Division Q, worth $500,000 (asset basis $300,000), and AB wants to sell. AB Corp. distributes the assets of Q to A and B, who thereafter sell them to XYZ. What are the tax consequences to all parties if:
   a. The distribution does qualify as a partial liquidation?
   b. The distribution does not qualify under Code Sec. 302(b)(4)?

50. Falzone Company has two shareholders, Rita and Sal Corporation. Rita acquired her 300 shares in 2009 for $30,000 and Sal Corporation acquired its 200 shares in 2005 for $15,000. On August 2, 2017, Falzone Company sold one of its businesses that it had held since 2005. Due to this sale, Falzone Company redeemed 50 shares from each shareholder in exchange for $20,000 each. Falzone's E&P at the time of the redemption was $250,000. What are the tax consequences of this transaction to Rita and Sal Corporation?

51. Jim Lester was the sole shareholder of Lester Resorts Inc. His basis was $10,000 in the stock. Jim died when his stock was worth $500,000. His gross estate, including the stock, was $1,400,000, funeral and administration expenses amounted to $100,000, and estate and inheritance taxes totalled $200,000. Lester Resorts redeemed 80 percent of the stock from the estate for $500,000 when its E&P was $50,000. What are the tax consequences to Lester's estate and Lester Resorts?

52. Larry owns 90 of the 100 outstanding shares of EDP Corporation. Larry acquired the 90 shares in 2006 for $15,000. He also owns 70 of the 100 outstanding shares of EDT Corporation. Larry acquired the 70 shares in 2009 for $21,000. On October 18, 2017, Larry sold 25 shares of EDT stock to EDP Corporation for $43,000. EDT and EDP have current E&P in 2017 of $22,000 and $31,000, respectively.
    a. How will the sale be treated for federal income tax purposes?
    b. How much income, and what type, does Larry recognize?
    c. What is his basis in his stock?
    d. What is the effect of the transaction on EDP and EDT?

53. James owns 100 shares of Price Company which are Section 306 stock. He also owns 300 shares of its common stock. He wants to dispose of these shares in 2017 and is considering several options. Indicate the tax consequences of each option.
    a. Making a gift of the stock to his son.
    b. Selling all his stock (common and preferred) to an unrelated third party.
    c. Selling all his stock (common and preferred) to Price Company in a Code Sec. 302(b)(3) redemption.
    d. Selling the 100 shares to Robert Thomas, assuming that Price will have no E&P in 2017.
    e. Same as (d), except Price will have E&P in 2017.
    f. Having Price redeem the 100 shares in 2017, assuming that Price will have no E&P in 2017.
    g. Same as (f), except Price will have E&P in 2017.

54. Marcus owned 200 shares (100 percent) of Sterling Company's common stock. His basis in the shares was $12,000. In 2014, Sterling issued a preferred stock dividend to Marcus. The 50 shares he received had a fair market value of $10,000. Sterling's E&P in 2014 was $8,000. The fair market value of the common stock was $20,000 immediately after the dividend. In 2017, when Sterling's E&P was $15,000, Marcus sold the 50 shares of preferred stock to an unrelated party for $9,000. What are the tax consequences of these transactions to Marcus?

55. Bob owns 100 shares of Dylan Company. Dylan Company's other 400 outstanding shares are owned by unrelated parties. Bob bought the shares on December 14, 2007 for $20,000 ($200 per share). On August 10, 2017, Dylan Company redeemed 60 shares from Bob. Bob received $50,000 for the shares. Dylan Company's paid-in-capital balance was $120,000 and its E&P was $400,000 in 2017.
    a. What is the effect of the transaction on Bob and Dylan Company if the redemption is treated as a dividend?
    b. What is the effect of the transaction on Bob and Dylan Company if the redemption qualifies for redemption status?

56. First Co. had a deficit in E&P of $90,000 on December 31 last year. Its taxable income was $180,000 for this year. Cash dividends on common stock totaling $80,000 were paid in December this year. Modern should report the distribution to its shareholders as:
    a. Return of capital 100 percent
    b. Dividends 80/90, return of capital 10/90
    c. Dividends 50 percent, return of capital 50 percent
    d. Dividend

57. Sell Corporation has 400 shares of its only class of stock outstanding. Mr. Church owns 60 shares, his wife owns 80 shares, his son owns 200 shares, and his son's daughter owns 60 shares. Under the constructive ownership rules for stock redemptions, how many shares of Sell Corporation's stock is the son's daughter considered to own?
    a. 60
    b. 200
    c. 260
    d. 400
    e. None of the above

58. During 2017, Kay Co. made the following distributions to an individual shareholder who owns 455 shares of its only class of stock.

Cash	$20,000
Equipment:	
Adjusted basis	75,000
Fair market value	85,000
Liability	15,000

The shareholder assumed the mortgage on the property. Kay Co's earnings and profits prior to the distribution were $70,000. Assuming a 40 percent corporate tax rate, what is the net adjustment to be made to the earnings and profits account due to the distribution?
   a. $10,000 increase
   b. $70,000 decrease
   c. $74,000 decrease
   d. $80,000 decrease
   e. None of the above

59. In 2017, a corporation distributed property with an adjusted basis of $100,000 and a fair market value of $140,000 to its shareholders. Its earnings and profits for 2017 were $170,000, and accumulated earnings and profits on January 1, 2017, were $370,000. What is the amount of gain recognized by the corporation on the distribution?
   a. $0
   b. $40,000
   c. $70,000
   d. $140,000
   e. None of the above

60. During 2017, Hero Co. distributed equipment having a fair market value of $300,000 and an adjusted basis of $150,000 to James in exchange for 85 percent of his interest in Hero. The distribution was under a plan of partial liquidation that resulted in a contraction of the business. James's adjusted basis in the stock exchanged was $180,000. Hero's earnings and profits were $500,000 prior to the distribution. What is the character and amount of James's recognized gain on the distribution?
   a. $120,000 capital gain
   b. $150,000 capital gain
   c. $150,000 capital loss
   d. $300,000 dividend income
   e. None of the above

61. Monty Company distributed $70,000 to Susan in redemption of all her stock. Susan's basis in the stock is $20,000 and her pro rata share of earnings and profits is $30,000. Assuming all the requirements for a redemption are met, how should Susan treat the distribution for federal income tax purposes?
   a. $0
   b. $20,000 dividend income
   c. $30,000 dividend income and $20,000 capital gain
   d. $50,000 capital gain
   e. None of the above

62. **Comprehensive Problem.** For each of the following independent distributions to shareholders, determine the impact on E&P; recognized gain, if any, to the distributing corporation; the amount of the dividend; and the basis in the property to the distributee, assuming ample E&P to start with:
   a. A cash distribution of $50,000.
   b. The distribution of an IOU with a face value of $50,000 and a market value of $45,000.
   c. The distribution of inventory with a basis of $2,000 and a value of $5,000 to an individual shareholder.
   d. The distribution of land with a basis of $25,000, a mortgage of $40,000, and a value of $100,000 to an individual shareholder.

63. **Comprehensive Problem.** Manuel Mesa is a 50 percent shareholder in a landscaping corporation, Mo Lo Inc. He has just incorporated his own wholly-owned landscaping business, Trim Inc. The other (unrelated) shareholder in Mo Lo wishes to buy Manuel out with one-half the assets of Mo Lo, consisting of tractors, tools, and equipment, all written down below current value. Manuel wishes to transfer these assets to Trim. What are the tax consequences of the following transaction alternatives, and which one, if any, is preferable?
   a. Mo Lo redeems Manuel's stock with the property and Manuel contributes the assets to the capital of Trim.
   b. Manuel contributes his Mo Lo stock to Trim and Mo Lo redeems its stock from Trim for the assets.
   c. Same as (a), except Manuel sells the assets to Trim for an installment obligation.
   d. Same as (b), but Manuel sells his stock to Trim on the installment plan.

64. **Research Problem.** Hobbies and Games Inc. has had taxable income the last three years, but is breaking even this year. Sondra, the sole shareholder, has a $25,000 basis in her stock. After consulting with a local CPA, the corporation does the following:

    a. Sets up an Employee Stock Ownership Plan (ESOP).

    b. Contributes $40,000 to the ESOP, borrowed for the occasion from a local bank.

    c. Deducts the $40,000 as a contribution to a qualified plan, thus creating a net operating loss of $40,000. The loss is carried back, resulting in a refund of taxes paid the last three years.

    d. Permits the ESOP to purchase 49 percent of Sondra's stock; she reports a long-term capital gain of $27,750. (See IRS Letter Rulings 8147187 and 8222026.)

    Can all these transactions be executed under the rules applicable to employee stock ownership plans?

65. **Research Problem.** Joe Tucker is the sole shareholder of Tucker Parts Inc. The corporation is cash rich, and Joe wishes to sell his stock to Bill Corker, who has limited funds. The parties proceed as follows:

    a. Joe sells 40 percent of his stock to Bill for $50,000, payable over 10 years.

    b. Tucker Parts redeems the remaining 60 percent of Joe's stock for $75,000 in cash.

    What are the tax consequences to Joe?

    Does it make any difference if the two steps are reversed?

    (See *Zenz v. Quinlivan,* 54-2 USTC ¶9445, 213 F.2d 914 (CA-6 1954); Rev. Rul. 55-745, 1955-2 CB 223.)

66. **Research Problem.** Constant Corporation is a family-owned corporation. In 2016, Constant redeemed stock from some of its owners. Because of the attribution rules of Code Sec. 318, the redemptions did not qualify for sale or exchange treatment. However, none of the family members like each other, and they believe that family attribution should be waived because the "bad blood" between them makes them "unrelated." Advise them about this assertion. (See Rev. Rul. 80-26, 1980-1 CB 66; *D. Metzger Trust,* 76 TC 42, Dec. 37,614 (1981), aff'd 82-2 USTC ¶9718, 693 F.2d 459 (CA-6 1982); *R.F. Haft Trust,* 75-1 USTC ¶9209, 510 F.2d 43 (CA-1 1975); and *B.E. Niedermeyer,* 62 TC 280, Dec. 32,621 (1974), aff'd, 76-1 USTC ¶9417, 535 F.2d 500 (CA-9 1976), cert. denied, 492 U.S. 1000, 97 S.Ct. 528.)

Chapter

16

Corporate Distributions in Complete Liquidations

OBJECTIVES

After completing Chapter 16, you should be able to:

1. Determine the tax treatment of the liquidating corporation, including the recognition of gain or loss.
2. Determine the tax treatment of shareholders upon a complete liquidation, including the computation of gain or loss and the basis of property received.
3. Understand the effects of a parent corporation's election to treat a stock purchase as an asset purchase.

OVERVIEW

Chapter 15 discussed ordinary corporate distributions, including distributions of property and stock, as well as stock redemptions and partial liquidations. After those distributions, the corporation continued to exist as an operating entity. This chapter discusses the winding up of a corporation's business affairs followed by a complete liquidation of the corporation.

The tax consequences of a complete liquidation of a corporation are examined from the standpoint of the effect on the liquidating corporation and its shareholders. Special rules apply to the liquidation of a controlled subsidiary.

Complete Liquidations

At some point in the life of a corporation it may be determined that the corporation should be liquidated. In that event, the corporation's shareholders will surrender all of their stock in the corporation and receive their pro rata shares of any remaining assets after all creditors have been paid.

¶16,001   REASONS FOR LIQUIDATION

The shareholders of a corporation may wish to liquidate a corporation for any number of reasons. The reasons for liquidation may be based on economics, or a liquidation may be necessary because the corporate form of organization is no longer beneficial, or it may be necessary to liquidate because of a desire to sell the business. Included among the reasons for a corporate liquidation are:

1. Lack of business profitability
2. Avoidance of double taxation of corporate earnings
3. Avoidance of corporate penalty taxes such as the personal holding company tax or the accumulated earnings tax
4. Recognition of losses at the shareholder level
5. Conversion of assets into cash for alternative purposes
6. A potential buyer's unwillingness to purchase stock in the corporation

There are several advantages to liquidating a corporation. Amounts distributed in complete liquidation of a corporation are treated as in full payment in exchange for the stock. Code Sec. 331(a). Thus, if the stock is held as a capital asset, liquidating distributions are subject to capital gain treatment and can be used to offset capital losses from other sources. Such capital gain treatment applies even though part of the distribution consists of accumulated E&P. If these same amounts had been distributed in a nonliquidating distribution, they would be taxed as ordinary dividends.

Another benefit of a liquidation is that depreciable assets may obtain a stepped-up tax basis that will result in larger depreciation deductions and a smaller gain or larger loss in the event of a future sale or exchange. Other benefits of a liquidation may be summarized as follows:

1. A new corporation has the opportunity to issue preferred stock without the taint of Code Sec. 306. However, care must be taken that the IRS does not treat a liquidation followed by a reincorporation as a reorganization.
2. Shareholders may be able to recognize a capital loss (ordinary loss if Code Sec. 1244 is applicable) if the basis of their stock is greater than the fair market value of the assets distributed.
3. If a corporation is a personal holding company because it derives most of its income from passive investment income sources, a liquidation will prevent the continued application of the personal holding company tax.

¶16,021   LIQUIDATION STATUS REQUIREMENTS

In order for the liquidation rules to apply to a liquidating corporation and its shareholders, a corporation must be in a status of liquidation. Under Reg. §1.332-2(c), a status of liquidation exists when a "corporation ceases to be a going concern and its activities are merely for the purpose of winding up its affairs, paying its debts, and distributing any remaining balance to its shareholders." A liquidation may be completed prior to the actual dissolution of the liquidating corporation. In fact, legal dissolution of the corporation (i.e., termination of a corporate entity's legal existence under state law) is not required. Furthermore, the mere retention of a nominal amount of assets for the sole purpose of preserving the corporation's charter will not invalidate a complete liquidation.

To constitute a distribution in complete liquidation, the distribution must be (1) made by the liquidating corporation in complete cancellation or redemption of all of its stock in accordance with a plan of liquidation, or (2) one of a series of distributions in complete cancellation or redemption of all of its stock in accordance with a plan of liquidation.

It is not necessary that there be a formal plan of liquidation. According to the Tax Court, there are three basic tests that must be met to qualify for liquidation status. *W.G. Maguire Est.,* 50 TC 130, Dec. 28,932 (1968).

1. There must be a manifest intention to liquidate.
2. There must be a continuing purpose to terminate corporate affairs.
3. The corporation's activities must be directed toward such termination.

¶16,061   SUMMARY OF LIQUIDATION RULES

In general, gain or loss is recognized by a corporation upon the distribution of property to its shareholders in a complete liquidation. Code Sec. 336. The corporation's earnings and profits are generally eliminated along with the corporation's basis in any property distributed in the liquidation. Section 331 provides that a shareholder treat the property received in liquidation of a corporation as proceeds obtained from the exchange of stock. The shareholder's gain or loss is determined by deducting the adjusted basis of the shareholder's stock from the fair market value of the property received. The gain or loss is generally a capital gain or loss since the shareholder's stock is usually a capital asset. The shareholders will have a fair market value basis in any property received. Code Sec. 334(a).

No gain or loss is recognized by a parent corporation upon the receipt of assets in the complete liquidation of a controlled subsidiary. Code Sec. 332. Additionally, no gain or loss is recognized by the liquidating subsidiary, and its tax attributes and basis for assets carryover to its parent. This provision allows a controlled group of corporations to eliminate unwanted subsidiaries without the recognition of gain, and is based on the premise that there has been no real change in the economic investment of the shareholders of the parent corporation.

Effect of Complete Liquidation on Corporations

A corporation must generally recognize gain or loss on the distribution of property in complete liquidation.

¶16,101   GAIN OR LOSS RECOGNITION

Generally, a corporation must recognize gain or loss upon a distribution of property in liquidation, computed as if the property were sold to the distributee shareholder at its fair market value. Code Sec. 336(a). The type of gain or loss recognized (e.g., ordinary, capital, Section 1231) depends on the nature of the property to the corporation, as well as the property's holding period.

EXAMPLE 16.1	Groll Inc. adopts a plan of complete liquidation and subsequently distributes an auto to a shareholder that was originally purchased for $38,000, with an adjusted basis of $22,000 and a fair market value of $25,000. Groll must recognize $3,000 ($25,000 FMV – $22,000 basis) of gain. The entire gain is ordinary income because of depreciation recapture under Code Sec. 1245.

¶16,121   LIABILITIES

If a liquidating corporation distributes property and a shareholder assumes a liability on the property or takes the property subject to a liability, the fair market value of the property is treated as being not less than the amount of the liability. Thus, if the amount of liability exceeds the fair market value of the property, gain must be recognized to the extent that the liability exceeds the property's adjusted basis.

EXAMPLE 16.2	Mall Inc. distributes cash of $40,000 and a building with a fair market value of $100,000 and a basis of $20,000 (subject to a mortgage of $130,000) to its sole shareholder. Since the building and mortgage are distributed at a time when the mortgage exceeds the fair market value of the building, Mall recognizes a gain of $110,000 ($130,000 mortgage – $20,000 basis).

EXAMPLE 16.3	Same as Example 16.2, except that the amount of mortgage is only $60,000. Mall recognizes a gain of $80,000 ($100,000 FMV – $20,000 basis).

If the liquidating corporation does not pay the income tax resulting from the gains recognized on liquidating distributions, the shareholders must pay the tax because they are the transferees of the assets on which the gains were recognized. In such case, the amount of the distribution is reduced by the amount of tax liability, thus reducing the shareholders' gain or increasing their loss.

EXAMPLE 16.4	Orchards Corp. adopts a plan of complete liquidation and distributes an asset with a basis of $20,000 and a fair market value of $50,000. Assuming a 34 percent tax rate, the corporation's recognized gain of $30,000 results in an income tax liability of $10,200. If the liability is not paid by the corporation, it becomes a liability of the transferee shareholder and reduces the shareholder's liquidating distribution to $39,800 ($50,000 FMV – $10,200 tax liability).

¶16,131   LOSS RECOGNITION

Under Code Sec. 336(a), losses as well as gains are recognized on the distribution of property in complete liquidation. If the losses are sufficiently large, they may result in a net operating loss that can be carried back to the corporation's two preceding taxable years to obtain a refund of income tax paid in those years. However, if the losses are capital losses, or if the corporation has had little taxable income in recent years, the losses may provide little, if any, tax benefit to the liquidating corporation.

Additionally, Code Sec. 336(d) provides special limitations on the recognition of losses. These limitations are generally designed to prevent the contribution of built-in loss property to a corporation prior to its liquidation in order to generate a recognized loss at the corporate level to offset recognized gains.

The first limitation is found in Code Sec. 336(d)(1) which provides that no loss can be recognized on a distribution of property to a more than 50 percent shareholder (including both direct and constructive ownership under Code Sec. 267(d)) if the distribution is (1) not pro rata or (2) the distributed property is "disqualified property." Disqualified property is property acquired by the corporation in a Code Sec. 351 transfer (i.e., a nontaxable transfer to a controlled corporation in exchange for stock) or as a contribution to capital during the five-year period ending on the date of the distribution. Disqualified property also includes property whose basis is determined (in whole or in part) by reference to the adjusted basis of disqualified property (e.g., property acquired in a like-kind exchange involving disqualified property).

EXAMPLE 16.5	Ping Corporation's stock is held equally by two brothers. Four years prior to its liquidation, the shareholders made a capital contribution of property (basis of $90,000 and FMV of $100,000) to Ping Corporation. In liquidation, Ping Corporation transfers the property (now worth $75,000) to the brothers. Because each brother owns directly and constructively more than 50 percent of the stock and the property is disqualified property, none of the $15,000 realized loss can be recognized by Ping Corporation.

EXAMPLE 16.6	Pong Corporation is owned 60 percent by Eldon Purry and 40 percent by Frank Fox. Pursuant to a plan of complete liquidation, Pong distributes securities that it had purchased to Purry. The securities (which are not disqualified property) have a basis of $40,000 and a FMV of $10,000. Because the securities are distributed to a more than 50 percent shareholder in a non-pro rata distribution, Pong's realized loss of $30,000 cannot be recognized.
	If the securities had instead been distributed 60 percent to Purry and 40 percent to Fox, the $30,000 loss would be recognized by Pong. Similarly, if Purry and Fox were not related and the securities were distributed only to Fox, the loss would have been recognized.

Note that the above rules prohibit contributions of property with built-in losses followed by distributions of the property to related persons. Absent additional restrictions, a corporation could sell the contributed property or distribute the property to a 50 percent or less shareholder and recognize the loss. To prevent this potential abuse, a second limitation is provided in Code Sec. 336(d)(2). The limitation applies to the computation of a liquidating corporation's loss on the sale, exchange, or distribution of property that was acquired in a Code Sec. 351 transfer or as a contribution to capital. The adjusted basis of the property must be reduced (but not below zero) by the excess of the adjusted basis of the property on the date of its contribution over its fair market value at such time, if a principal purpose of the acquisition was to generate a loss in connection with the liquidation.

EXAMPLE 16.7

> A shareholder makes a capital contribution of Gainacre with a basis of $8,000 and a FMV of $20,000 and Lossacre with a basis of $15,000 and a FMV of $10,000 on August 1, 2016. During April 2017, a plan of liquidation is adopted and Lossacre is sold for $8,000. If the purpose of contributing Lossacre was to recognize the loss in the liquidation, Lossacre's basis of $15,000 must be reduced by the $5,000 of built-in loss. Then the liquidating corporation's recognized loss is limited to $2,000 ($10,000 basis – $8,000 selling price); the $5,000 of built-in loss at the time of contribution is disallowed.

Generally, any property acquired in the above manner within two years before the corporation adopts a plan of liquidation is presumed to be part of a loss recognition plan. However, Regulations are expected to provide that this rule will be disregarded unless there is no clear and substantial relationship between the contributed property and the conduct of the corporation's current or future business. Thus, if contributed property is actually used in the corporation's business, this rule should not apply if there is a business purpose for placing the property in the corporation. On the other hand, if Code Sec. 336(d)(2) does apply, its effect is to limit the amount of recognized loss to the decline in value that occurs while the property is in the hands of the corporation; any built-in loss at time of contribution is disallowed.

The importance of Code Sec. 336(d)(2) may be diminished over time since the inbound loss limitation rule of Code Sec. 362(e)(2) effectively disallows most precontribution losses by stepping down the basis of transferred property to fair market value when it is acquired by a corporation. Code Sec. 362(e)(2), which is discussed in Chapter 14, applies to capital contributions and Code Sec. 351 transfers, but does not apply in Example 16.7 because there was overall net appreciation in the contributed properties.

If a plan of liquidation is adopted and disallows a built-in loss that was deducted in a previous tax year, the liquidating corporation must recapture the loss by including it in gross income, or can file an amended return for the preceding year in which the loss was deducted.

EXAMPLE 16.8

> Assume the same facts as in Example 16.7, except that the property is sold in 2016, and the plan of liquidation is adopted in 2017. Assuming Code Sec. 336(d)(2) disallows the loss that was deducted in 2016, the corporation must recapture the loss by including it in gross income for 2017, or the corporation can file an amended return for 2016 in order to remove the loss as a deduction.

TAX BLUNDER

On January 2 of the current year, Whiteford Corporation adopted a plan of complete liquidation. Pursuant to the plan it will distribute a parcel of land, Lossacre, to Flo who owns 55 percent of Whiteford's outstanding stock. Lossacre was purchased four years ago for $400,000, but is worth only $325,000 at the time of the liquidating distribution.

Because Lossacre is being distributed in a non prorata liquidating distribution to a more than 50 percent shareholder, the realized loss of $400,000 - $325,000 = $75,000 cannot be recognized. Additionally, since Lossacre's basis to Flo will be $325,000, the land's basis will be reduced by $75,000 without the benefit of a loss deduction. Instead, Whiteford should have distributed Lossacre to a shareholder whose stock ownership does not exceed 50 percent, or should have sold Lossacre to an unrelated taxpayer. Under either alternative, Whiteford would be allowed to recognize the $75,000 loss.

¶16,141   EXPENSES OF LIQUIDATION

The treatment of expenses incurred in conjunction with a liquidation can be summarized as follows:

1. Expenses of adopting a plan of liquidation and terminating the business (e.g., accountants' and lawyers' fees, etc.) are deductible as ordinary and necessary business expenses under Code Sec. 162.
2. Expenses incurred in selling assets can not be deducted, but instead must be offset against the amounts realized from sales.
3. If some of the expenses are attributable to a tax-free reorganization, such portion is nondeductible.
4. Organizational expenditures that have been capitalized may be deducted upon liquidation.
5. Expenses incurred by shareholders are nondeductible, but reduce the amount realized from the liquidating distribution.

¶16,161   REPORTING REQUIREMENTS

Form 966 (Corporate Dissolution or Liquidation) must be filed with the IRS within 30 days of the adoption of the plan of liquidation. The corporation must also file a separate Form 1099-DIV (U.S. Information Return for Recipients of Dividends and Distributions) for each shareholder that receives a liquidating distribution of $600 or more during a calendar year. When the liquidation is completed (all substantial assets have been distributed), the corporation's final tax year ends. The final tax return must include a copy of the corporate resolution to liquidate, a list of the properties sold, sale dates, realized gains and losses, as well as the date of final distribution and the amount of retained assets, if any.

Failure to file Form 966 or to file it on time will not invalidate a complete liquidation. Rev. Rul. 65-80, 1965-1 CB 154. However, it is possible that penalties may result under Code Sec. 7203.

Effect of Complete Liquidation on Shareholders

In a typical liquidation, shareholders are deemed to have exchanged their stock, whether or not the certificates are formally cancelled, for the cash and property received in the liquidating distribution. Code Sec. 331. As a result, gain or loss is recognized, and a fair market value basis results for property received. Code Sec. 334(a). Special rules under Code Sec. 332, discussed at ¶16,301, govern liquidations of controlled subsidiaries.

¶16,201   DISTRIBUTIONS OF PROPERTY

When a corporation is liquidated, the corporation distributes its property to the shareholders and/or sells the property and distributes the proceeds. In any event, the shareholders are deemed to have exchanged their stock for the property and cash received. Code Sec. 331. This approach generally results in capital gain or loss treatment to the shareholders, assuming their stock is held as a capital asset. Note that the character of the shareholders' gain or loss is determined by the nature of the stock, not by the character of the property distributed. The amount of a shareholder's gain or loss is computed by subtracting the shareholder's stock basis from the fair market value of the property received. A fair market value basis results for the assets received. Code Sec. 334(a).

There are several exceptions to the general rule that a shareholder recognizes capital gain or loss from a complete liquidation.

1. If the stock was Section 1244 stock, the shareholder's loss is an ordinary loss to the extent of $50,000 per year ($100,000 on a joint return).
2. If the shareholder is a dealer in securities, any gain or loss on liquidation is an ordinary gain or loss if the stock was held primarily for resale in the ordinary course of business.
3. No gain or loss is recognized to a parent corporation liquidating its at least 80-percent-owned subsidiary. Code Sec. 332.

Liabilities to Shareholders

If a shareholder assumes a liability of the liquidating corporation, or receives property that is subject to a liability, then the liability reduces the amount realized by the shareholder, thus reducing the shareholder's gain or increasing the shareholder's loss.

EXAMPLE 16.9

In complete liquidation of a corporation, Alvin receives a building with a fair market value of $80,000 and assumes a mortgage of $30,000 on the building. If the basis of Alvin's stock is $15,000, Alvin's gain from the liquidation is $35,000 (($80,000 FMV – $30,000 liability) – $15,000 basis). Alvin's basis for the building is the building's FMV of $80,000.

Series of Distributions

If a series of liquidating distributions are made, the shareholder may use the cost recovery method for recognition of gain or loss. Rev. Rul. 85-48, 1985-1 CB 126. Each payment received is first applied against the basis of stock. As soon as basis is exceeded, gain must be recognized. However, no loss can be recognized until the final distribution is received.

EXAMPLE 16.10	Everett owns 1,000 shares of Imperial Corporation purchased at a cost of $10,000. During 2015, 2016, and 2017, Everett receives the following distributions in a series of distributions in complete liquidation of the corporation:

December 6, 2015	$6,000
May 15, 2016	3,000
March 31, 2017	2,500

Since the liquidating distributions are made over more than one year, the cost recovery method is used to determine gain or loss. The 2015 distribution of $6,000 is nontaxable and reduces Everett's stock basis to $4,000. The $3,000 distribution in 2016 is also nontaxable and reduces Everett's basis to $1,000. The $2,500 2017 distribution first reduces stock basis to zero, with the remaining $1,500 in excess of stock basis treated as capital gain.

EXAMPLE 16.11	Assume the same facts as in Example 16.10, except that the 2016 distribution was the final distribution. Again the cost recovery method would apply the 2015 distribution against Everett's stock basis. The 2016 distribution would reduce stock basis to $1,000. However, since the 2016 distribution is now the final distribution, the $1,000 of unrecovered stock basis would be recognized as a capital loss in 2016.

Multiple Blocks of Stock

Often a shareholder has acquired more than one block of stock. If the stock was acquired at different times and for different amounts, the proceeds must be divided by the number of shares so that gain or loss can be computed on each block of stock. Reg. §1.331-1(e).

EXAMPLE 16.12	A shareholder acquired 1,000 shares in the liquidating corporation; 500 shares three years ago for $7,000 and 500 shares five months ago for $4,000. If the shareholder's liquidating distribution is worth $12,000, the amount realized is allocated equally to each block of shares, resulting in a long-term capital loss of $1,000 and a short-term capital gain of $2,000.

Disproportionate Distributions

In some situations, shareholders receive distributions in complete liquidation of a corporation that are disproportionate to their shareholdings (e.g., a shareholder owns 10% of a corporation's stock but receives only 5% of the corporation's net assets). If a shareholder receives less than a proportionate share, the excess of the proportionate share over the amount actually received is treated as if it had been used in a separate transaction by the shareholder to make gifts, pay compensation, satisfy obligations, etc. depending on the particular facts and circumstances. If a shareholder receives more than a proportionate share, the excess is treated as a payment received that is attributable to those shareholders who receive less than their proportionate share. Rev. Rul. 79-10, 1979-1 CB 140.

¶16,221   BASIS OF PROPERTY RECEIVED IN LIQUIDATION

If the liquidation is taxable to the shareholder under Code Sec. 331, the shareholder's basis for the property received in the liquidation is the property's fair market value on date of distribution. If more than one item of property is received, each item of property receives a fair market value basis, regardless of the nature of the item in the hands of the liquidating corporation or the distributee shareholder. Thus, a shareholder is treated as if the shareholder had purchased the property for its fair market value in a taxable exchange using stock as the consideration for the purchase. The shareholder's holding period for the property begins on the day after the day the property is received, the same as for any purchased property.

¶16,241   DISTRIBUTIONS OF INSTALLMENT OBLIGATIONS

The general rule that the liquidating corporation recognizes gain or loss on the distribution of property also applies to the distribution of installment obligations. However, the *shareholder* who receives the installment obligation may defer the tax on any stock gain attributable to the installment obligation until collections on the installment obligation are made if:

1. The obligation was received from the sale or exchange of property by the corporation during the 12-month period beginning on the date the liquidation plan was adopted,
2. The liquidation is completed by the close of this 12-month period, and
3. The obligation is not attributable to the sale of inventory, stock in trade, or property held for sale to customers, unless it was a bulk sale of substantially all such property to one person. Code Sec. 453(h)(1).

A special computation of a shareholder's gain must be made if the shareholder receives a liquidating distribution that includes an installment obligation that meets the above requirements. In this case, part of the shareholder's stock is treated as having been exchanged for the installment obligation, with the remaining stock exchanged for any other property received. To determine the gain on each part, the shareholder's stock basis is allocated between the installment obligation and the other property received based on their relative fair market values. The stock gain resulting from the other property received in the liquidation is immediately recognized, while the stock gain attributable to the installment obligation is recognized as the installment payments are received.

EXAMPLE 16.13

Cabins Inc. adopted a plan of liquidation and made an installment sale of its only asset (a motel) to an unrelated individual. The installment note calls for payment of $20,000 (plus interest) in each of the next six years. Cabins distributes the $120,000 note to its sole shareholder, Ben Baker, who has a stock basis of $24,000. Assuming the installment sale and liquidation were completed within 12 months of the date the plan of liquidation was adopted, Ben's gain of $120,000 – $24,000 = $96,000 will be reported as the installment payments are received. Since the gross profit ratio is $96,000/$120,000, 80 percent of each $20,000 installment payment will be recognized as gain.

EXAMPLE 16.14

Same as Example 16.13, except that the motel is sold for a down payment of $30,000, with $30,000 (plus interest) to be received in each of the next three years. If Cabins distributes the cash of $30,000 and the $90,000 installment note in liquidation, Ben's $24,000 stock basis must be allocated between the cash and the installment note as follows:

Property	FMV	Percent	Allocated Stock Basis	Realized Gain
Cash	$30,000	25%	$6,000	$24,000
Installment Note	90,000	75%	18,000	72,000
Total	$120,000	100%	$24,000	$96,000

Ben must recognize $24,000 of gain in the year of liquidation. One-third of the remaining $72,000 of gain will be recognized in each of the next three years as each installment payment of $30,000 is received.

PLANNING POINTER

If a corporation sells property in the process of liquidation, it should consider making some of these sales on the installment method. Since the installment method is available only for sales at a gain, and the corporate seller must recognize this gain upon making a liquidating distribution of the installment obligation, the ideal installment sale meets the following requirements:

1. The fair market value is slightly higher than the asset's basis.
2. The shareholder to whom the obligation is distributed has a low stock basis.

This will result in maximum deferral of the shareholder's gain without causing significant corporate tax to be incurred.

¶16,253   CONTINGENT LIABILITIES

In some cases, after a liquidation is completed, shareholders are required to pay a contingent liability of the corporation, or a liability that was unknown at the time the corporation was liquidated. This shareholder payment does not change the shareholders' original reporting of their liquidating distributions. Instead, the shareholders' payment results in a deduction, the nature of which depends upon the character of the original gain or loss that the shareholders reported. The type of deduction or loss that would have been available to the corporation if it had paid the liability before liquidation is not relevant. Thus, if the liquidation resulted in a shareholder reporting a capital gain or loss, the shareholder's subsequent payment of a contingent corporate liability results in a capital loss. *F.D. Arrowsmith,* 52-2 USTC ¶9527, 334 U.S. 6, 73 S.Ct. 71 (1952).

EXAMPLE 16.15

Mark Dollmaker liquidated his wholly owned corporation and recognized a long-term capital gain of $30,000 in 2015. In 2017, he finally settled a state income tax issue resulting from an audit of the liquidated corporation's tax returns and paid $4,000 in his capacity as a transferee of the corporation's assets. Mark must deduct his $4,000 payment as a long-term capital loss in 2017 because the 2015 liquidation had resulted in a capital gain. Note that Mark must deduct his payment as a capital loss even though the corporation would have had an ordinary deduction if the corporation had paid the state taxes before liquidation.

¶16,261   CORPORATE DEBTS TO SHAREHOLDERS

Section 331 has no application to a distribution in satisfaction of corporate indebtedness to a shareholder, assuming the debt is a bona fide debt. However, if the "debt" is in substance an equity investment, the shareholder's stock basis is increased, resulting in a smaller gain or larger loss under Code Sec. 331. If the debt obligation is treated as debt, no gain or loss will be recognized to the holder unless the amount of cash and the fair market value of the property received differs from the holder's basis in the obligation.

If the corporation becomes insolvent, the type of loss recognized by the holder depends upon the nature of the debt obligation. If the debt obligation that becomes worthless is a capital asset and constitutes a security, the loss is generally treated as a capital loss on the last day of the taxable year in which the security becomes worthless. The term "security" not only includes stock, but also a bond, note, or other evidence of indebtedness issued by a corporation with interest coupons or in registered form. Code Sec. 165(g)(2).

In some cases, a security may result in an ordinary loss if the security is not a capital asset when it becomes worthless. For example, a worthless security that was held as inventory by a securities dealer would result in an ordinary loss deduction. Additionally, a special provision permits a parent corporation to deduct an ordinary loss on the worthlessness of the securities of a subsidiary corporation that is at least 80 percent owned. To qualify, at least 90 percent of the gross receipts of the subsidiary for all taxable years must be derived from sources other than passive income. Code Sec. 165(g)(3).

If the debt obligation that becomes worthless is not classified as a security, the resulting loss may be deducted as either a nonbusiness or business bad debt. Generally, loans made by a shareholder to a corporation are investment related and result in a nonbusiness bad debt that is deductible as a short-term capital loss. However, if the loan is made to protect the shareholder's employment with the corporation (i.e., the shareholder's trade or business), the loss is treated as a business bad debt deductible as an ordinary loss. Whether a loan results in a business or nonbusiness bad debt depends upon the dominant motive for making the loan.

PLANNING POINTER

An individual shareholder can transfer capital gain to low-bracket family members (e.g., children or grandchildren not subject to the kiddie tax) by gifting a corporation's stock prior to liquidation. The transfer should take place well ahead of the adoption of the plan of liquidation to avoid the anticipatory assignment of income doctrine.

KEYSTONE PROBLEM

The corporation proposed to be liquidated has considerable operating income. It also has assets with fair market values lower than their basis.

1. Does it matter whether the corporation is liquidated at the beginning or the end of its tax year?
2. Does it make sense to defer the liquidation until the shareholder dies if the stock has appreciated in value? What if the stock has decreased in value?

¶16,275   LIQUIDATION-REINCORPORATION

A typical liquidation-reincorporation transaction involves an attempt by shareholders to liquidate an existing corporation, realize capital gain on the distribution of appreciated assets, obtain a stepped-up fair market value basis for such assets, and then reincorporate some (or all) of the assets in a new corporation that continues the business of the old corporation. In an alternative form of the transaction, an existing corporation sells some (or all) of its assets to a newly formed corporation that is controlled by the existing corporation's shareholders and then liquidates.

Prior to 1987, if the liquidation was respected as an independent transaction, the shareholders' gain was taxed at preferential capital gains rates, the appreciated assets received a stepped-up basis without any corporate level tax (except for depreciation recapture and similar items), and the earnings and profits of the old corporation were eliminated. With the repeal of the nonrecognition rules that applied to liquidations, the potential tax advantages of a liquidation-reincorporation are diminished. However, a liquidation-reincorporation might still be attempted if the potential tax benefits of a complete liquidation outweigh the costs of a corporate-level tax because the corporation's built-in gain is minimal, the liquidating corporation has net operating losses or built-in losses that can offset the gains, or the shareholders have a high stock basis in the liquidating corporation and can utilize the resulting capital losses.

The IRS often attacks these transactions, arguing that the liquidation is not an independent transaction and that a liquidation-reincorporation is in substance a reorganization under Code Sec. 368(a)(1)(D). As a reorganization, the assets in the new corporation have a transferred basis, there is a carryover of the liquidated corporation's earnings and profits and other tax attributes to the new corporation, and the shareholders receive dividend treatment for any retained assets.

Generally, a liquidation-reincorporation is treated as a Type D reorganization if the shareholders of the liquidated corporation own 50 percent or more of the new corporation. Additionally, in order to obtain a favorable advance ruling on a corporate liquidation, no assets of the liquidating corporation can be transferred to another corporation where more than 20 percent of the stock of both corporations is owned by the same shareholders. Rev. Proc. 90-3, 1990-1 CB 402.

Liquidation of Subsidiaries

¶16,301   SPECIAL RULES

There are special rules that apply only to the liquidation of controlled subsidiaries. Under Code Sec. 332, no gain or loss is recognized by a parent corporation on the receipt of property distributed in complete liquidation of a subsidiary. This provision reflects the theory that a liquidation of a subsidiary represents only a change of form, since there has been no real change in the economic investment of the shareholders of the parent corporation. The subsidiary's basis for assets carries over to the parent corporation so that any deferred gain or loss at the time of liquidation is recognized if the parent subsequently sells the liquidated subsidiary's former assets.

If Code Sec. 332 applies, the parent corporation inherits all of the subsidiary's tax accounting attributes at the time of liquidation (e.g., earnings and profits, capital loss carryforwards, NOL carryforward, potential for depreciation recapture, etc.). Additionally, the parent's basis for its subsidiary's stock disappears, so that the parent's realized gain or loss resulting from the liquidation will never be recognized.

EXAMPLE 16.16   Parent Corporation owns 100 percent of the stock of Subsidiary Corporation and has a basis of $100,000 for its Subsidiary shares. Subsidiary is liquidated and its assets having a basis of $80,000 and a FMV of $150,000 are distributed to Parent. Parent's realized gain of $50,000 ($150,000 FMV–$100,000 stock basis) is not recognized. Parent's basis for the assets it receives is $80,000, the same basis as Subsidiary had for the assets before liquidation.

¶16,309   NONRECOGNITION RULES OF SECTION 332

Section 332 applies only if three requirements are met.

First Requirement: 80 Percent Ownership

The parent corporation must own at least 80 percent of the combined voting power and at least 80 percent of the total value of all the stock of the subsidiary corporation (except nonvoting, nonparticipating preferred stock) on the date that the plan of liquidation is adopted and at all times until the subsidiary's liquidation is completed. The parent corporation must satisfy this ownership requirement directly; no constructive ownership rules apply.

PLANNING POINTER	Although Code Sec. 332 is not an elective provision, the 80 percent ownership requirement can be used for tax planning. A parent corporation that wishes to avoid the nonrecognition rules under Code Sec. 332 (i.e., to recognize a loss on its subsidiary's stock) can sell some of the subsidiary's stock to reduce its ownership below 80 percent before or during the liquidation process. Then the general rule of Code Sec. 331 will apply and the loss will be recognized. On the other hand, a parent corporation owning less than 80 percent of a subsidiary may wish to increase its ownership to at least 80 percent before the plan of liquidation is adopted so that Code Sec. 332 will apply to the liquidating distributions and the recognition of gains will be deferred.

Second Requirement: Cancellation of Stock

There must be a distribution in complete cancellation or redemption of all of the subsidiary's stock pursuant to a plan of complete liquidation. Legal dissolution of the subsidiary is not required. A minimal amount of assets may be retained by the subsidiary in order to protect its legal existence and preserve its corporate charter.

Third Requirement: Timing

There are two alternative time periods during which the liquidating distributions must take place:

1. If all liquidating distributions are made within one taxable year of the subsidiary, no formal plan of liquidation need be adopted. A shareholders' resolution authorizing the distributions will suffice even though no time limit for completing the transfers is specified. Furthermore, the year in which the liquidation occurs does not have to be the same year in which the shareholders' resolution or plan of liquidation is adopted.

2. If the liquidating distributions extend beyond one taxable year, a formal plan of liquidation must be adopted and all liquidating distributions must be made within three taxable years of the close of the taxable year in which the first distribution is made. If the liquidation is not completed within the specified time period, Code Sec. 332 will not apply to any of the liquidating distributions.

If any of the above three requirements are not satisfied, Code Sec. 332 will not apply, and the liquidating distributions will be taxed to the parent corporation under Code Sec. 331.

¶16,315   PARENT'S INDEBTEDNESS TO SUBSIDIARY

If a parent corporation is indebted to its subsidiary, and the subsidiary distributes its parent's debt obligations to the parent as part of a complete liquidation of the subsidiary, a question arises as to whether the parent corporation will recognize gain resulting from this discharge of indebtedness. In such case, no gain is recognized because the parent's notes are considered "property" and, under Code Sec. 332, no gain is recognized by a parent corporation when it receives property in complete liquidation of its controlled subsidiary.

¶16,335   INSOLVENT SUBSIDIARY

Section 332 does not apply if the subsidiary is insolvent since the parent corporation does not receive any distribution in exchange for its subsidiary's stock. A subsidiary is insolvent if its liabilities exceed the fair market value of its assets. In this case, the parent corporation's loss on its subsidiary's securities is treated as a loss from worthless securities under Code Sec. 165(g). Although the resulting loss is generally a capital loss, the parent instead receives ordinary loss treatment if (1) the parent corporation owns at least 80 percent of the voting power and at least 80 percent of each class of non-voting stock (except non-voting stock which is limited and preferred as to dividends), and (2) more than 90 percent of the subsidiary's gross receipts for all taxable years were derived from sources other than royalties, rents, dividends, interest, annuities, and gains from sales or exchanges of stocks and securities. Any subsidiary debt obligation not qualifying as a security under Code Sec. 165(g)(2) is deductible by the parent corporation as a business bad debt.

EXAMPLE 16.17	Subsidiary Corporation, a wholly owned subsidiary of Parent Corporation, has assets with a total FMV of $100,000 and total liabilities of $130,000. Parent's basis in its Subsidiary stock is $90,000. A plan of liquidation for Subsidiary is adopted and Subsidiary distributes all of its assets and liabilities to Parent. Since Subsidiary is insolvent, Code Sec. 332 does not apply to Subsidiary's liquidation because none of Subsidiary's assets are considered to have been distributed in cancellation of its stock. Parent's $90,000 loss on its Subsidiary stock is a loss from worthless securities, which is deductible as an ordinary loss if the 90 percent gross receipts test of Code Sec. 165(g)(3) is met.

¶16,345 MINORITY SHAREHOLDERS

The nonrecognition of gain or loss rule under Code Sec. 332 only applies to the parent corporation. When a subsidiary is liquidated, any minority shareholders must recognize their gain or loss under Code Sec. 331. The basis of property received by the minority shareholders is equal to the property's fair market value. Code Sec. 334(a).

¶16,353 PARENT'S BASIS FOR PROPERTY

If a controlled subsidiary is liquidated by its parent corporation under Code Sec. 332, the basis for the subsidiary's property (as well as the holding period) carries over to the parent corporation under Code Sec. 334(b)(1). This rule applies to all of the subsidiary's property that is transferred to the parent corporation, including property that is transferred in cancellation of the subsidiary's debt obligations to the parent.

TAX BLUNDER

Rock Corp. has a basis of $300,000 for its ownership of 85% of the outstanding stock of Stone Corp. Stone is liquidated and Rock receives a distribution of assets from Stone with a basis of $90,000 and a fair market value of $100,000. Although Rock realizes a loss on the liquidation of $200,000 ($300,000 basis - $100,000 FMV), the loss cannot be recognized, and Rock's basis for the assets received totals $90,000. Rock's loss cannot be recognized because it owns at least 80% of Stone Corp. and the liquidation qualifies as a Code Sec. 332 liquidation.

Instead, Rock should have sold enough of its Stone Corp. stock to reduce its ownership to below 80% before the liquidation of Stone. Then Stone Corp's liquidation would no longer qualify for Code Sec. 332 treatment, and Rock would be able to recognize its loss of $200,000. Additionally, Rock would have a fair market value basis of $100,000 for the assets it received.

¶16,365 NONRECOGNITION RULES OF SECTION 337

Under Code Sec. 337, no gain or loss is recognized by a liquidating subsidiary corporation on the distribution of its property to its parent corporation in a complete liquidation to which Code Sec. 332 applies. This special nonrecognition rule applies only to distributions to the parent corporation (i.e., the corporation meeting the 80 percent stock ownership requirements of Code Sec. 332(b)). This is to be expected since it is only the parent corporation that takes a transferred basis for the subsidiary's assets and succeeds to the subsidiary's tax attributes. Thus, the depreciation recapture rules of Code Secs. 1245, 1250, and 291 do not apply when the subsidiary distributes depreciable property to its parent in liquidation. Instead, the subsidiary's basis for depreciable property as well as the potential for depreciation recapture carries over to the parent corporation.

The nonrecognition rules of Code Sec. 337 generally do not apply to the liquidation of a subsidiary if its parent corporation is a tax-exempt distributee or a foreign corporation. This exception is based on the concern that these distributees are not subject to tax on a subsequent disposition of the property.

¶16,371 DISTRIBUTIONS TO MINORITY SHAREHOLDERS

The nonrecognition rules of Code Sec. 337 apply only to distributions to a parent corporation in a Code Sec. 332 liquidation. Distributions to minority shareholders are governed by the general rule of Code Sec. 336 which requires that gain be recognized if appreciated property is distributed in complete liquidation of a corporation. However, it is important to note that Code Sec. 336(d)(3) prevents the recognition of loss on the distribution of property to minority shareholders in a Code Sec. 332 liquidation. These recognition of gain (but not loss) rules for distributions to minority shareholders are based on how the property is actually distributed, rather than on a hypothetical pro rata liquidating distribution to all shareholders.

EXAMPLE 16.18

Parent Corporation is the owner of 80 percent of Subsidiary Corporation's stock with a basis of $40,000. The remaining 20 percent is owned by Mandy Moore, who has a basis for her Subsidiary stock of $15,000. Subsidiary is liquidated under Code Sec. 332 and distributes property with a FMV of $90,000 and a basis of $30,000 to Parent, and distributes property with a FMV of $25,000 and a basis of $20,000 to Mandy.

Subsidiary's realized gain of $60,000 ($90,000 − $30,000) on the distribution of property to Parent is not recognized. Parent's realized gain of $50,000 ($90,000 − $40,000) on the receipt of the property is not recognized, and Parent has a transferred basis of $30,000 for the property received.

Subsidiary's $5,000 gain ($25,000 − $20,000) on the distribution of property to Mandy is recognized. Mandy's realized gain of $10,000 ($25,000 − $15,000) is recognized, and Mandy has a FMV basis of $25,000 for the property received.

PLANNING POINTER

To take advantage of these liquidation rules, the subsidiary's appreciated property should be distributed to only the parent corporation in order to avoid the recognition of gain, while only money should be distributed to minority shareholders. On the other hand, property that has declined in value should be sold to an unrelated taxpayer to permit the recognition of loss. Otherwise, the realized loss will not be allowed as a deduction if the property is distributed to a minority shareholder, or the loss will be deferred if the property is distributed to the parent corporation.

¶16,385   SUBSIDIARY'S INDEBTEDNESS TO PARENT

A taxpayer must generally recognize gain or loss if the indebted taxpayer transfers property to satisfy its debt obligation. However, Code Sec. 337(b) provides an exception to this general rule. Specifically, if a subsidiary corporation is indebted to its parent and the subsidiary is liquidated under Code Sec. 332, then no gain or loss is recognized by the subsidiary when it transfers its property to the parent to satisfy the debt. This is because Code Sec. 337(b)(1) treats the property as a liquidating distribution to the parent corporation. Thus, the parent corporation takes a carryover basis for all property received in liquidation of its subsidiary, regardless of whether the property is received in exchange for stock, or in satisfaction of the subsidiary's debt. Note, that this nonrecognition rule does not apply to property that is distributed in satisfaction of indebtedness to minority shareholders. In that case, the subsidiary's gain or loss is recognized.

EXAMPLE 16.19

Parent Corporation owns 100 percent of the stock of Subsidiary Corporation, and also owns Subsidiary Corporation bonds with a face amount (and basis) of $100,000. A plan of liquidation is adopted and Subsidiary is liquidated under Code Sec. 332. Pursuant to the liquidation, Subsidiary distributes property with a FMV of $100,000 and a basis of $30,000 in cancellation of the bonds. Subsidiary does not recognize any gain on the transfer of its property in cancellation of the bonds. Parent recognizes no gain or loss on its Subsidiary bonds because their basis equals the FMV of the property received. Parent has a carryover basis of $30,000 for the property received from Subsidiary.

TAX BLUNDER

Parent Corporation owns 80% of the single class of stock of Subsidiary Corporation, with the remaining 20% of Subsidiary stock owned by Rachel. A plan of liquidation is adopted for Subsidiary Corporation and a parcel of land that it owns, but Parent Corporation does not want, is distributed to Rachel in cancellation of her stock. The land, which had been acquired by purchase 6 years ago, had a basis of $90,000 and a fair marker of $40,000 at time of liquidation.

¶16,385

Because Subsidiary is being liquidated in a Code Sec. 332 liquidation, the realized loss of $50,000 on the distribution of land to Rachel can not be recognized by Subsidiary, and its basis to Rachel will be its fair market value of $40,000. As a result, the land's basis has been reduced by $50,000 without the benefit of a loss deduction. Instead, Subsidiary Corporation should have sold the land to a third party in order to recognize the loss, and then the proceeds of sale could have been distributed to Rachel.

Stock Purchases Treated as Asset Acquisitions

¶16,401   **PURPOSE OF ELECTION**

In many cases, a controlling interest in a corporation's stock is purchased in order to acquire the target corporation's assets. When a purchase of stock was promptly followed by a liquidation of the target corporation into the parent, some courts held that the transitory ownership of the stock should be disregarded, and the purchase price of the stock should be allocated to the assets. This view became known as the *Kimbell-Diamond* doctrine after a leading case, *Kimbell-Diamond Milling Co.*, 51-1 USTC ¶9201, 187 F.2d 718 (CA-5 1951). This approach was codified in Code Sec. 334(b)(2). Under this provision, the parent received an asset basis equal to its stock basis if at least 80 percent control of the target corporation was acquired by purchase within a 12-month period and a plan of liquidation of the target corporation was adopted within two years after the purchase of control was completed. Congress subsequently removed the necessity to physically liquidate the subsidiary to achieve an asset basis equal to the stock basis by repealing Code Sec. 334(b)(2) and substituting a Code Sec. 338 election.

As under prior law, Code Sec. 338 requires that at least 80 percent control be acquired by purchase within a 12-month period. Code Sec. 338(a). This is termed a "qualified stock purchase." The election to utilize Code Sec. 338 must then be made on or before the fifteenth day of the ninth month beginning after the month during which the 80 percent control requirement is met. Code Sec. 338(g).

¶16,417   **STOCK PURCHASE REQUIREMENT**

Section 338 applies only to a qualified stock purchase. A *qualified stock purchase* is the purchase of 80 percent or more of the voting power and 80 percent or more of the value of all classes of stock (except for nonvoting, nonparticipating preferred stock) during a 12-month acquisition period. Code Sec. 338(d)(3). A *purchase* is generally defined as a taxable stock acquisition from an unrelated party. Thus, a purchase does not include stock acquired by gift, inheritance, contribution to capital, tax-free reorganization, and a Code Sec. 351 transfer to a controlled corporation.

The *12-month acquisition period* begins with the date of the first acquisition by purchase of stock included in a qualified stock purchase. The *acquisition date* is the first day on which there is a qualified stock purchase (i.e., purchase of 80 percent within a 12-month period). Purchases of stock of the target corporation by affiliates of the purchasing corporation are attributed to the purchasing corporation. The 80 percent stock purchase requirement can be met through a combination of stock purchases and redemptions of the target corporation's stock.

EXAMPLE 16.20   Parent Corporation purchases 40 percent of Target Corporation's stock on April 3, 2017. Subsidiary (Parent's 100-percent-owned subsidiary) purchases 40 percent of Target's stock on August 2, 2017. Since Parent and Subsidiary are affiliated corporations, Parent has made a qualified stock purchase of Target's stock and the acquisition date is August 2, 2017.

EXAMPLE 16.21   Parent Corporation purchases 75 percent of Target Corporation's stock on May 3, 2017. Target redeems the 25 percent minority interest on October 2, 2017. Parent has made a qualified stock purchase of Target's stock. The acquisition date is October 2, 2017, the first day on which Parent has acquired by purchase at least 80 percent of Target's stock.

EXAMPLE 16.22	Parent Corporation purchases 20 percent of Target Corporation's stock on November 2, 2015, 20 percent on June 3, 2016, 40 percent on December 1, 2016, and 20 percent on May 2, 2017. Parent has made a qualified stock purchase of the Target stock since during a 12-month period beginning June 3, 2016, Parent has purchased at least 80 percent of Target's stock. The acquisition date is May 2, 2017.

¶16,425   REQUIREMENTS FOR ELECTION

Generally a Code Sec. 338 election must be made on or before the fifteenth day of the ninth month beginning after the month in which the acquisition date occurs. The election is irrevocable and is made by the purchasing corporation on Form 8023 (Corporate Qualified Stock Purchase Elections) which is filed with the IRS service center applicable to the purchasing corporation.

EXAMPLE 16.23	Parent Corporation purchases 35 percent of Target Corporation's stock on March 1, 2017, and an additional 50 percent of Target's stock on September 10, 2017. The acquisition date is September 10, 2017, and the Code Sec. 338 election must be made on or before June 15, 2018.

¶16,435   OLD TARGET CORPORATION

A target corporation is any corporation whose stock is acquired by another corporation in a qualified stock purchase. A Code Sec. 338 election will cause the target corporation to be treated as two distinctly different corporations—*old target* and *new target*. If a Code Sec. 338 election is made, the old target is treated as having sold all of its assets for their fair market value as of the close of the acquisition date. This fictional sale of assets results in the old target's recognition of any realized gains and losses. The assets are then treated as having been purchased by the new target corporation as of the beginning of the day following the acquisition date.

The old target corporation does not become part of the purchasing corporation's affiliated group. If the old target corporation is similarly not includible in a consolidated return of the seller, the target corporation's final tax return must reflect any income earned through the acquisition date, as well as the gains and losses resulting from the Code Sec. 338 deemed sale of assets. Generally, any tax attributes of the old target corporation (e.g., NOL and capital loss carryforwards) can be used to offset the income recognized on this final return. Any unused tax attributes of the old target corporation are extinguished and do not carry over to the new target corporation.

If the old target corporation is a subsidiary member of an affiliated group filing a consolidated return, a separate deemed sale return for the old target corporation is required. The selling group's consolidated return includes the old target's items of income and deduction through the acquisition date, excluding the deemed sale items. The old target's deemed sale return stands alone and does not include any operating income or loss.

¶16,443   ADVANTAGES OF ELECTION

Since a target corporation must recognize all of its gains on the deemed sale of its assets, a Code Sec. 338 election may prove undesirable because of the significant up-front tax costs associated with the basis step-up. However, there are still several situations in which a Code Sec. 338 election can be beneficial.

If the target corporation has NOLs that are expiring or subject to limitation under Code Sec. 382, the election can be beneficial because the NOLs can offset the recognized gains on the deemed sale, thereby giving the purchaser a stepped-up basis in the assets with little or no tax cost.

There also are significant planning possibilities under Code Sec. 338(h)(10). If a target corporation is a subsidiary in a consolidated group and its stock is sold, an election pursuant to Code Sec. 338(h)(10) allows the sellers to treat the transaction as if the target made a taxable sale of its assets and then was liquidated into its parent under Code Sec. 332. The effect of this rule is that the selling consolidated group recognizes the gain from the deemed sale of assets in its consolidated return, but no gain or loss is recognized on the sale of the target's stock. Furthermore, the seller's consolidated tax attributes are available to shelter the fully taxable deemed asset sale. If the old target has any remaining tax attributes (e.g., NOLs, tax credits), they remain in the selling group. The election is made on Form 8023 and effectively is a joint election because the seller can make this election only if the buyer makes a Code Sec. 338 election.

¶16,451 NEW TARGET CORPORATION

The new target corporation becomes a member of the purchasing corporation's affiliated group as of the day after the acquisition date. It is treated as a new corporation and does not inherit any of the old target's tax attributes. The new target is also treated as having purchased the assets of the old target for a price that equals the adjusted grossed-up basis of the target's stock which includes:

1. The grossed-up basis of the purchasing corporation's recently purchased stock (i.e., stock of the target corporation purchased during the 12-month acquisition period), plus
2. The basis of the purchasing corporation's nonrecently purchased stock (i.e., stock of the target corporation purchased prior to the 12-month acquisition period), plus
3. Liabilities of the target corporation (including the tax liability resulting from the Code Sec. 338 election) and other relevant items.

The basis of nonrecently purchased target corporation stock is the purchasing corporation's historic basis for the stock. The grossed-up basis of recently purchased stock will equal the purchasing corporation's basis in its recently purchased stock multiplied by a fraction—the numerator of which is 100 percent minus the percentage (by value) of nonrecently purchased stock, and the denominator of which is the percentage (by value) of recently purchased stock. Code Sec. 338(b)(4).

$$\text{Grossed-up basis} = \text{Basis of recently purchased stock} \times \frac{100\% - \%\text{ of nonrecently purchased stock}}{\%\text{ of recently purchased stock}}$$

The basis of nonrecently purchased stock may be increased to its market value if the purchasing corporation makes an election to recognize gain as if the nonrecently purchased stock were sold on the acquisition date. Code Sec. 338 (b)(3). If the election is made, the basis of nonrecently purchased stock will generally equal the average price per share of the recently purchased stock.

EXAMPLE 16.24

Parent Corporation purchases 10 percent of Target Corporation's stock for $50,000 in 2015. On July 3, 2017, Parent purchases an additional 80 percent of Target's stock for $1 million. The stock acquired in 2015 is nonrecently purchased stock; the stock acquired in 2017 is recently purchased stock. If Parent makes a Code Sec. 338 election, the grossed-up basis for Parent's recently purchased stock is $1,125,000 (($1,000,000 × (90%/80%)).

Assuming Parent does not elect to increase the basis of the nonrecently purchased Target stock, and if Target has no liabilities, Parent's adjusted grossed-up basis for the Target stock is $1,125,000 + $50,000 = $1,175,000.

¶16,465 ALLOCATION OF BASIS

The Regulations provide rules for allocating the purchase price of the target corporation's stock if a Code Sec. 338 election is made. The basis for assets is determined by use of the residual value method. Under this method, the amount allocated is the adjusted grossed-up basis of the stock. This amount is determined as of the beginning of the day following the acquisition date and must be allocated to four categories of assets in the following order:

1. Class I—Cash, demand deposits, and other cash equivalents
2. Class II—Certificates of deposit, U.S. government securities, readily marketable securities, and similar items
3. Class III—All assets (both tangible and intangible) other than those in Classes I, II, and IV such as receivables, inventory, machinery, and equipment
4. Class IV—Intangible assets in the nature of goodwill and going concern value

The basis assigned to Class I assets is their face value. The remaining aggregate grossed-up basis is then assigned to Class II assets based on their relative fair market values. Any excess is then assigned to the Class III assets, again according to relative fair market values. In making the allocation to the Class II and III assets, the amount allocated as basis can never exceed an asset's fair market value. The fair market value of an asset is the asset's gross value computed without regard to any mortgage, liens, or other liabilities related to the asset. When the purchase price has been allocated to the first three categories of assets, any remaining purchase price represents a premium that exceeds the value of identifiable assets. This premium is then assigned to Class IV assets and results in goodwill.

EXAMPLE 16.25

Parent Corporation purchases 80 percent of the stock of Target Corporation for $400,000 on July 3, 2017, and makes a Code Sec. 338 election. On the acquisition date, Target has assets with a FMV of $475,000 and $25,000 of liabilities. Old Target is deemed to have sold its assets, and new Target is deemed to have purchased them for $475,000. Assume no income tax liability was incurred on the deemed sale because of old Target's NOL carryovers. Parent's adjusted grossed-up basis for the Target stock is $525,000 (($400,000 × (100%/80%)) + $25,000 of liabilities). Assume that Target's assets have the following fair market values on the day after the acquisition date:

Asset Class	Asset	FMV
I	Cash	$50,000
II	Marketable securities	75,000
III	Inventory	150,000
III	Equipment	200,000
		$475,000

The allocation of the $525,000 of adjusted grossed-up basis is as follows:

(Class I):	Allocate $50,000 to cash.
(Class II):	Allocate $75,000 to marketable securities.
(Class III):	Allocate $350,000 to the Class III assets. The inventory and equipment have a basis equal to fair market value.
(Class IV):	Allocate the remaining $50,000 to goodwill.

If the value of the identifiable assets is greater than the adjusted grossed-up basis of the stock, there has been a bargain purchase. If the value of the Class III assets exceeds the adjusted grossed-up basis remaining to be allocated, the remaining basis is allocated to the Class III assets in proportion to their relative fair market values. This results in a potential step-down in basis for receivables and inventory and will result in the recognition of income when the inventory is sold and the receivables are collected.

¶16,485   **CONSEQUENCES OF NO ELECTION**

If Code Sec. 338 is not elected, the purchasing corporation has a basis for the target corporation's stock equal to its purchase price. The basis for the target's assets remains unchanged, and all of the target's tax attributes remain, subject to any applicable limitation rules. If the target is subsequently liquidated under Code Sec. 332, no gain or loss is recognized by the purchasing and target corporations, there is a transferred basis for all of the target's assets, and a carryover of all of target's tax attributes. However, Code Sec. 269 provides that if the principal purpose for a liquidation of the target corporation within two years of acquisition is the avoidance of tax, the benefit of any deductions resulting from the liquidation may be denied.

¶16,493   **SPECIAL RULE**

Regulations are to be issued under Code Sec. 336(e) that will allow a parent corporation that owns at least 80 percent of a subsidiary's stock, and sells, exchanges, or distributes all of the subsidiary's stock, to elect to be taxed as if it had sold all of the subsidiary's assets instead of the subsidiary's stock. The parent corporation is effectively treated as if it had first liquidated the controlled subsidiary under Code Sec. 332 and then sold all of the subsidiary's assets.

This election is similar to the Code Sec. 338(h)(10) election except that the purchaser does not have to be a corporation. In addition to a sale or exchange, the Code Sec. 336(e) election can apply when the parent corporation distributes all of its subsidiary's stock in a taxable distribution.

TAX BLUNDER

A self-made businessman started a business on a shoestring many years ago that was worth $1 million when he wanted to retire. He then went to a lawyer and adopted a plan of liquidation. On the way home, he died of a heart attack. His wife, wishing to carry out his intent, went ahead with the liquidation.

Result. $1 million of capital gain to the estate and an income tax of $200,000 since he had "realized" the gain under Code Sec. 331 before he died (income in respect of a decedent). What his wife should have done was to cancel the liquidation. The estate would have had a stepped-up basis in the stock of $1 million. Subsequently, a plan of liquidation could have again been adopted, and the liquidation could take place tax free to the estate.

SUMMARY

- The tax treatment of complete liquidations is determined by Code Secs. 331 through 338.

- A shareholder generally recognizes gain or loss on the exchange of stock in a complete liquidation under Code Sec. 331 and will have a fair market value basis for property received.

- A parent corporation does not recognize gain or loss on the liquidation of an 80 percent of more controlled subsidiary under Code Sec. 332 and will have a transferred basis for property received.

- A liquidating corporation generally recognizes gain or loss on liquidating distributions made to shareholders, except that no gain or loss is recognized on liquidating distributions made to the parent corporation in a Code Sec. 332 liquidation.

- A Sec. 338 election has the effect of treating a qualified stock purchase as a purchase of the target corporation's assets.

SUMMARY OF RELEVANT CODE SECTIONS

Corporate Liquidation	
Subpart A.	**Effects on Recipients**
Section 331	Gain or Loss to Shareholders in Corporate Liquidations
Section 332	Complete Liquidations of Subsidiaries
Section 334	Basis of Property Received in Liquidations
Subpart B.	**Effects on Corporations**
Section 336	Gain or Loss Recognized on Property Distributed in Complete Liquidation
Section 337	Nonrecognition for Property Distributed to Parent in Complete Liquidation of Subsidiary
Section 338	Certain Stock Purchases Treated as Asset Acquisitions

QUESTIONS

1. What is meant by a "status of liquidation"?

2. Contrast a complete liquidation with the legal dissolution of a corporation.

3. What happens to a corporation's tax attributes (e.g., earnings and profits, NOL carryforwards) in a complete liquidation?

4. Contrast the tax treatment of a shareholder in a redemption under Code Sec. 302 with a shareholder's tax treatment in a liquidation under Code Sec. 331.

5. In what situations will a shareholder recognize an ordinary loss as a result of a complete liquidation of a corporation?

6. How does the assumption of corporate liabilities affect the amount realized by a shareholder in a complete liquidation? How does the assumption of liabilities affect the basis for assets received in a complete liquidation?

7. Discuss the concept of transferred basis as it relates to a complete liquidation.

8. When is "double taxation" on a corporate liquidation an advantage over nonrecognition at the corporate level?

9. What problem is encountered on a liquidation that is followed by a reincorporation?

10. Discuss the tax treatment of liquidating distributions of installment obligations.

11. In what situations will a liquidating corporation be allowed to recognize loss in a non-pro rata liquidating distribution?

12. Sec. 336(a) provides that "gain or loss shall be recognized to a liquidating corporation on the distribution of property in complete liquidation as if such property were sold to the distributee at its fair market value." Explain five exceptions to this rule.

13. Explain the circumstances that permit a shareholder, who receives an installment obligation from a liquidating corporation, to defer recognition of gain until the shareholder receives the payments on the obligation.

14. When will a shareholder's realized gain or loss be recognized if the cost recovery method is applied to a series of liquidating distributions received by the shareholder?

15. Under what circumstances must a subsidiary recognize gain or loss upon liquidating into its parent?

16. In what situation will a corporate shareholder receive non recognition treatment in a complete liquidation?

17. When might a parent corporation want to avoid a Code Sec. 332 liquidation? How could this be accomplished?

18. In a Code Sec. 332 liquidation, what is the tax effect of the distribution of property by a subsidiary in satisfaction of its indebtedness to its parent corporation?

19. Discuss a parent corporation's tax treatment if the securities that it owns in a subsidiary corporation become worthless.

20. Discuss the tax treatment of expenses incurred by a corporation in conjunction with a complete liquidation.

21. How does an acquiring corporation make a Code Sec. 338 election?

22. Why is Code Sec. 338 of limited interest today?

23. What is the benefit of a Code Sec. 338(h) (10) election?

24. What is meant by a parent corporation's "grossed-up" basis in the subsidiary's stock under Code Sec. 338(b)?

25. Describe the residual method for allocating basis to assets following a Code Sec. 338 election.

26. Why is the tax cost of incorporating an existing business generally low, while the tax cost of liquidating a business conducted in corporate form generally high?

PROBLEMS

27. Baretta Corp. owns 100 percent of the stock of PPK Corp., and also owns PPK Corp. debentures with a face amount (and basis) of $200,000. A plan of liquidation is adopted and PPK is liquidated under Code Sec. 332.

    Pursuant to the liquidation, PPK distributes inventory with a FMV of $200,000 and a basis of $220,000 in cancellation of the debentures.
    a. How much loss can be recognized by PPK Corp. on the distribution of the inventory to Baretta?
    b. What is Baretta Corp.'s tax basis for the inventory received from PPK?

28. Ellen received a liquidating distribution from Lopas Corp. as part of a redemption of all of its stock. Ellen's basis for her Lopas stock was $13,000. In exchange for her stock, Ellen received property with a $10,000 basis and a $35,000 fair market value that is subject to a $18,000 mortgage, and also received cash of $15,000.
    a. What is Ellen's realized and recognized gain from this complete liquidation?
    b. What is Ellen's tax basis for the non-cash property he received?

29. Brenda owns 100 percent of Walker Corp. She has a basis for her stock of $20,000. The corporation's only assets are cash of $20,000 and land with a basis of $75,000 and a value of $95,000. Earnings and profits are $125,000. Walker Corp. liquidates and distributes its assets to Brenda, whose stock is cancelled.
    a. What is the gain recognized by Walker Corp.?
    b. What happens to Walker's earnings and profits?
    c. What gain is recognized by Brenda?
    d. What is Brenda's basis for the land?

30. A cash-method corporation adopts a plan of complete liquidation and distributes the following assets to its shareholders:
    - A truck that was purchased for $25,000, is worth $18,000, and has a basis of $11,000.
    - An installment note receivable with a remaining face amount of $20,000, resulting from a sale of a warehouse for $75,000 seven years ago in which the warehouse's basis at the time of sale was $25,000.
    - Accounts receivable of $7,000.
    - Supplies and small tools previously expensed, worth $350.

    What gains are recognized by the liquidating corporation on the distributions in complete liquidation?

31. The stock of Richmond Corp. is owned 60 percent by Sid and 40 percent by Mark, who are unrelated individuals. During 2016, Sid transferred land (basis of $300,000; FMV of $260,000) as a contribution to the capital of Richmond Corp. During March 2017, Richmond Corp. adopted a plan of liquidation and subsequently made a non pro rata distribution of the land to Mark. At the time of the liquidating distribution, the land had a FMV of $230,000.
    a. What amount of loss can be recognized by Richmond Corp. on the distribution of land to Mark?
    b. What is Mark's tax basis for the land that he received?

32. Alex purchased one thousand shares of Ambrose Corporation stock on March 10, 2016, for $95,000. On August 1, 2017, Alex received the following as a distribution in cancellation of his stock in a complete liquidation of Ambrose:

Fair Market Value	
Cash	$5,000
Equipment	10,000
Land	30,000
Building	120,000
Liabilities	(20,000)
	$145,000

a. What is the amount and character of Alex's recognized gain?

b. What is Alex's basis for each of the items of property received?

c. When does the holding period for each of the items of property begin?

d. How would your answer to (a) change if Alex had purchased 500 shares of Ambrose stock 15 months ago for $10,000, and the remaining 500 shares six months ago for $80,000?

33. Ted purchased all of the stock of Fontana Manufacturing Corporation in 2015 for $170,000. Under Ted's leadership, Fontana Manufacturing soon became unprofitable, and Ted decided to liquidate Fontana as of the close of business on June 30, 2017. All of Fontana's assets were needed to pay third-party creditors, and Ted received nothing for his $170,000 investment.

a. Describe the amount and character of Ted's loss.

b. How would your answer to (a) change if Fontana Manufacturing were instead owned by TED Corporation?

34. Marcia is a 50 percent shareholder of Chevez Corp., which is in the process of liquidation. Marcia's basis for her stock is $25,000. Chevez's balance sheet on the date of liquidation is as follows:

Assets	Basis	Value
Cash	$32,000	$32,000
100 shares of Public Co.	20,000	6,000
Accounts receivable	200,000	170,000
Land	50,000	300,000
Building (depreciated straight line)	246,000	500,000
Totals	$548,000	$1,008,000

Equities	Value
Mortgage on real estate	$310,000
Unsecured liabilities	182,000
Capital stock	10,000
Paid-in capital	30,000
Earnings and profits	16,000
Total	$548,000

If Marcia receives her 50 percent share of all assets and liabilities, determine her gain and her basis in each asset received as a result of the liquidation. Assume that Chevez's marginal tax rate is 30 percent but that no tax was paid by Chevez.

35. Martin Corporation adopts a plan of complete liquidation. Two months later Martin sells its main asset, a motel, in which it has a basis of $300,000, for $800,000 to an unrelated partnership. Martin received a $200,000 down payment and a mortgage note payable in installments of $10,000 a month for 5 years plus 6 percent interest on the remaining balance. Martin Corporation uses its existing cash to pay the tax and distributes the $200,000 cash from the sale, and the note to its only shareholder, Laura, who has a basis of $30,000 for her stock. If there is no recapture, what are the tax consequences to Martin Corporation and to Laura?

36. Ray owns 400 shares of stock in of Fisher Corporation. He had inherited 300 shares (estate tax value $15,000) seven months ago and had purchased 100 shares for $2,000 five months ago. Fisher completely liquidates, and Ray receives a building worth $50,000, that is subject to a mortgage of $38,000, in cancellation of his 400 shares.
    a. What gain and/or loss does Ray recognize?
    b. What is his basis in the building?

37. Shennel owns 65 percent of Tower Corporation. In 2016, Shennel contributed property with an adjusted basis of $25,000 and a fair market value of $10,000 to Tower as a contribution to capital. In 2017, Tower adopted a plan of complete liquidation and distributed this same property back to Shennel in exchange for her stock. At the time of distribution, the property had a basis of $10,000 and a fair market value of $5,000. What amount of loss is recognized by Tower Corporation on the distribution and what is Shennel's basis for the property she receives?

38. The Dicken Corp. has two unrelated shareholders, Dick and Ken, each owning 50 percent of the stock. Dicken has only one asset, a tract of land with a value of $130,000 that was purchased for $150,000. What are the tax consequences of the following alternative liquidations?
    a. Dicken distributes the land to the shareholders as equal tenants in common.
    b. Dicken sells the land to Ken's mother-in-law for a note that is distributed to Dick and Ken as equal tenants in common.
    c. Same as part a. except that Dick is Ken's father.

39. Fraser Corp., a 75 percent owned subsidiary of McCoy Corp., made a pro rata distribution of a parcel of land that had been used in its business in redemption of its stock in a complete liquidation. The parcel of land had a basis of $300,000 and a fair market value of $410,000. What amount and character of gain (if any) must be recognized by Fraser Corp. as a result of the distribution?

40. Parent Corporation purchased 80 percent of the stock of Subsidiary Corporation in one transaction for $200,000. The remaining 20 percent is owned by the MAC partnership. Subsidiary's only asset is an office building depreciated on the straight-line method, with an adjusted basis of $50,000 and a value of $400,000. It is subject to a mortgage of $140,000.
    a. If Parent makes a Code Sec. 338 election, what are the tax consequences to Parent, Subsidiary and MAC?
    b. If Parent does not make a Code Sec. 338 election and liquidates Subsidiary under Code Sec. 332, what are the tax consequences to Parent, Subsidiary, and MAC?

41. Perry Corporation purchased 10 percent of Target Corporation's stock for $35,000 in 2014. On March 1, 2017, Perry purchased an additional 80 percent of Target's stock for $200,000. At that time, Target's identifiable assets had a fair market value of $300,000 and an adjusted basis of $240,000. Target also had liabilities of $60,000.
    a. What is the acquisition date for purposes of making a Code Sec. 338 election? By what date must Perry file a Code Sec. 338 election?
    b. Assuming that a Code Sec. 338 election is made, what is the deemed sale price of Target's assets?
    c. What is the amount of the adjusted grossed-up basis that is allocated to Target's assets, assuming that a tax liability of $15,000 resulted from the deemed sale of assets?
    d. What amount of goodwill results from the allocation of basis to Target's assets?

42. Palm Corporation is owned 60 percent by Jay and 40 percent by Scott. Jay and Scott are unrelated individuals. Palm's two principal assets are cash of $140,000 and a building that Palm purchased 10 years ago and that now has an adjusted basis of $80,000 and a fair market value of $60,000. What amount of loss is recognized by Palm Corporation if it makes the following alternative distributions in complete liquidation?
    a. Palm distributes the building plus $60,000 in cash to Jay and $80,000 in cash to Scott.
    b. Palm distributes $120,000 in cash to Jay and the building plus $20,000 in cash to Scott.
    c. Palm distributes 60 percent of the cash and a 60 percent interest in the building to Jay and 40 percent of the cash and a 40 percent interest in the building to Scott.
    d. Same as (c), except that the building had been contributed to Palm Corporation by Scott as a contribution to capital during 2016, when the building's basis was $90,000 and its fair market value was $65,000.
    e. Same as (c), except that the building had been contributed to Palm Corporation by Jay as a contribution to capital four years ago (during 2013), when the building's basis was $120,000 and its fair market value was $110,000.

43. Panashe Corporation purchased 20 percent of Servco Corporation's stock on each of the following dates: January 4, 2016; April 3, 2016; July 14, 2016; December 15, 2016; and January 5, 2017. Can Panashe make a Sec. 338 election to have the Servco stock purchases treated as an acquisition of assets? By what date must the election be made?
    a. How would your answers change if the purchase dates were instead January 4, 2015; April 3, 2016; July 14, 2016; December 15, 2016; and January 5, 2017?
    b. How would your answers change if the purchase dates were instead January 4, 2016; April 3, 2016; July 14, 2016; January 4, 2017; and April 15, 2017?

44. Doug and Sally (unrelated individuals) own 60 percent and 40 percent respectively of the outstanding stock of Platt Corporation. Platt's assets consist of land (Sec. 1231 property) that was purchased in 2013 for $90,000 and now has current fair market value of $60,000 and other property that has a basis of $20,000 and a fair market value of $40,000. Pursuant to a plan of complete liquidation, Platt Corporation distributes the land to Doug and the other property to Sally on July 23, 2017.
    a. How much gain and loss does Platt Corporation recognize on the liquidating distributions? Can you offer any suggestions that will improve the tax consequences of the liquidating distributions?
    b. How would your answers to part a. change if the land had instead been contributed as a capital contribution by Doug in 2013 when the land had a basis of $90,000 and a fair value of $95,000?

45. Elm Corporation has 100 shares of stock outstanding of which Oak Corporation owns 75 shares with a basis of $10,000, and Sherman Forest owns 25 shares with a basis of $30,000. Elm Corporation has a $50,000 net operating loss carryover and the following assets (all held long-term):

	Basis	Fair Market Value
Cash	$20,000	$20,000
Installment Note	10,000	40,000
Land	1,000	10,000
Equipment (all Sec. 1245 recapture)	5,000	10,000
	$36,000	$80,000

    a. What are the tax consequences if Elm Corporation adopts a plan of complete liquidation and distributes the $20,000 cash to Sherman and all its remaining assets to Oak Corporation?
    b. As an alternative, what are the tax consequences if Elm Corporation distributes $20,000 cash to Sherman in redemption of his 25 shares, and 10 days later, Elm adopts a plan of complete liquidation and distributes its remaining assets to Oak Corporation? What are Elm and Oak trying to accomplish through the redemption of Sherman's shares?

46. Giles Corporation adopted a plan of liquidation during September 2017 and subsequently sold its only asset, land, that had a basis of $480,000 to Pat (an unrelated taxpayer) for $500,000. Under the terms of the sale, Giles received $100,000 cash and Pat's note in the amount of $400,000. The note is payable on January 3, 2018 and carries an adequate rate of interest. Immediately after the sale, Giles distributed the $100,000 cash and note (with a fair market value of $400,000) in complete liquidation to Carlos, the sole shareholder of Giles Corporation. Carlos has a basis of $200,000 for his Giles stock.
    a. What amount of gain must Giles Corporation recognize on the distribution of the note to Carlos?
    b. Assuming Carlos wants to defer gain recognition, what amount of gain must be recognized by Carlos for 2017?
    c. What amount of gain will be recognized by Carlos when he collects the $400,000 payment on the note in 2018?

47. Mann Corp. owns 80 percent of Tomlin Corp.'s stock and Vicky owns the remaining 20 percent of Tomlin's stock. Mann Corp.'s basis for its Tomlin stock is $405,000 and Vicky's Tomlin stock has a basis of $65,000. Pursuant to a plan of complete liquidation of Tomlin Corp., Mann Corp. receives property with a $550,000 adjusted basis and a $680,000 fair market value, and Vicky receives property with a $190,000 adjusted basis and a $170,000 fair market value.
    a. What amount of gain or loss is recognized by Tomlin Corp. as a result of the liquidating distributions?
    b. What amount of gain or loss is recognized by Mann and Vicky as a result of the liquidating distributions?
    c. What tax basis will Mann Corp. and Vicky have for the property they receive in the liquidation?

48. Felicia owns stock of Huff Corporation that she purchased several years ago for $10,000. Huff has $250,000 of accumulated earnings and profits. What are the tax consequences to Felicia on the liquidation of Huff Corporation in the following alternative situations:

    a. Huff distributes $5,000 in 2016 and $15,000 in 2017 to Felicia in exchange for all of her stock?
    b. Huff distributes $8,000 cash and an installment obligation with a face amount and fair market value of $12,000, payable $4,000 per year for three years with market rate of interest. The installment obligation was received by Huff four months ago after the adoption of the plan of liquidation, on the sale of a capital asset.
    c. Would the result in part b. be any different if the stock of Huff were publicly traded?

49. Pearl owns 60 percent of Gorman Corp.'s stock. During 2013, Pearl contributed property with an adjusted basis of $20,000 and a fair market value of $15,000 to Gorman Corp. in a transaction qualifying under Code Sec. 351. During the current year, Gorman adopted a plan of complete liquidation and distributed this same property back to Pearl. At the time of distribution the property had an adjusted basis of $15,000 and a fair market value of $7,000.
    a. How much loss will be recognized by Gorman Corp. as a result of the liquidating distribution?
    b. How will your answer to Part a. change if Gorman Corp. makes a proportionate liquidating distribution of the property with a 60 percent interest in the property to Pearl?

50. Reina owned stock in Kane Corp. During the current year, Kane Corp. completely liquidated and distributed the following to Reina:

Cash	$50,000
Warehouse	
Fair market value	550,000
Subject to a mortgage of	100,000

Reina's basis for her Kane Corp. stock was $275,000 and she will take title to the warehouse subject to the mortgage. What is Reina's recognized gain resulting from the liquidation and her basis for the warehouse?

51. Judy owned two blocks of Burr Corp. stock which she had purchased as investments:

Shares	Acquired	Basis
50	1/2/16	$10,000
200	11/8/16	30,000

Judy's stock represented 30 percent of Burr Corp's outstanding stock. Pursuant to the complete liquidation of Burr Corp., Judy received a $60,000 cash distribution on October 20, 2017, in exchange for her 250 shares. Burr Corp's accumulated earnings and profits immediately before the liquidation totaled $100,000. What is the amount and character of Judy's income that must be recognized as a result of the liquidation?

52. Swob Corp. purchased 20 percent of Park Corp's stock on each of the following dates: January 2, 2015; July 1, 2016; August 15, 2016; March 15, 2017; and June 2, 2017. If Swob Corp. wants to apply the provisions of Sec. 338 to its acquisition of Park Corp., by what date must an election be made?

53. Blaho Corp. has a $300,000 basis in its 100 percent ownership of the stock of Fraser Corp. What are the tax consequences to Blaho Corp. and Fraser Corp. of the following alternative liquidating distributions made by Fraser to Blaho?
    a. Assets having a basis of $175,000 and a fair market value of $350,000 are distributed to Blaho?
    b. Assets having a basis of $350,000 and a fair market value of $275,000 are distributed to Blaho?

54. The stock of Broward Corporation is owned by Ted (65%) and Fred (35%) who are father and son. Pursuant to a plan of complete liquidation, Broward distributes land with a fair market value of $400,000 to Fred in exchange for his stock. Broward had purchased the land four years ago for $500,000, and the land is distributed to Fred along with a mortgage liability of $150,000 which Fred assumes. Fred's basis for his Broward stock at the time of liquidation was $75,000.
    a. How much loss is recognized by Broward Corporation as a result of the liquidating distribution to Fred?
    b. How much gain or loss is recognized by Fred as a result of the liquidation?
    c. What is Fred tax basis for the land that he received?

55. Pace Corp. owns 100% of the stock of Strom Corp. Pace's basis for the Strom Corp. stock is $225,000. Pursuant to a plan of complete liquidation, Strom distributes to Pace assets with a fair market value of $800,000 and an adjusted basis of $300,000, along with liabilities of $100,000. At the time of liquidation, Strom has accumulated earnings and profits of $600,000.
    a. How much gain is recognized by Strom Corp. on the liquidating distribution to Pace Corp.?
    b. How much gain is recognized by Pace as a result of the liquidation?
    c. What tax basis does Pace Corp. have for the assets it receives from Strom Corp.?
    d. What happens to Pace's $225,000 basis for its Strom stock?
    e. What happens to Strom's $600,000 of accumulated earnings and profits?

56. **Comprehensive Problem.** Parent Corporation purchased 75 percent of Subsidiary Corporation seven years ago. The remaining 25 percent is owned by Roy. Subsidiary's current balance sheet shows the following figures:

	Basis	Value
Demand deposit	$20,000	$20,000
IBM stock	30,000	50,000
Parking lot	5,000	30,000
Building	0	100,000
Mortgage	(15,000)	(15,000)

Subsidiary has a net operating loss carryover of $7,000 and earnings and profits of $22,000.

Subsidiary redeems Roy's 25 percent stock interest in exchange for the IBM stock. Subsidiary then adopts a plan of complete liquidation and distributes its assets to Parent in complete liquidation.

a. What is the tax result to Roy?
b. Does Subsidiary recognize any gain on the redemption or the liquidation?
c. What are Parent's bases for the assets received?
d. What happens to Subsidiary's NOL and E&P?

57. **Comprehensive Problem.** Merten Corp. is 100% owned by Carmen. Merten owns one asset, a building worth $550,000 with a $90,000 basis. Carmen's stock basis is $150,000. A plan of complete liquidation is adopted. What are the tax consequences to both parties in each of the following independent cases?

a. The building is deeded to Carmen, who is taxed under Code Sec. 331.
b. The building is sold for an installment note that is distributed to Carmen.
c. Merten sells the building and presents a cashier's check for $100,000 to Carmen.
d. The building is deeded to Carmen Corp., in a Code Sec. 332 liquidation.

58. **Research Problem.** Anaconda Ltd. has substantial earnings and profits and appreciated assets. It adopts a plan of complete liquidation and distributes its assets to its shareholders. Soon thereafter, the shareholders transfer the assets to a new corporation, King Cobra Inc., in return for King Cobra stock, but retain cash and marketable securities.

What are the shareholders trying to accomplish?

How will the IRS most likely treat the transactions?

(See, e.g., Reg. §§1.301-1(1) and 1.331-1(c); Rev. Rul. 61-156, 1961-2 CB 62.)

Chapter

17

Corporate Reorganizations

OBJECTIVES

After completing Chapter 17, you should be able to:

1. Identify the characteristics of the seven basic types of reorganization.
2. Understand the tax consequences to shareholders and security holders, including basis computations and the effect of the receipt of boot.
3. Describe the tax consequences to corporations that are a party to the reorganization, including nonrecognition of gain or loss, basis for acquired property, carryover of tax attributes, and the use of subsidiaries to facilitate a reorganization.
4. Discuss the types of consideration that may be used in different reorganizations.

OVERVIEW

Gain or loss is generally recognized for tax purposes on a sale or exchange of property that has increased or decreased in value. Corporate reorganizations are a major exception to this rule. There are provisions that permit nonrecognition of gain or loss in various types of corporate reorganizations to ensure that the tax laws do not impede corporate realignments. Reorganizations are generally nontaxable because the new enterprise, the new corporate structure, and the new property are substantially continuations of the old investment.

A corporate reorganization may have the attributes of a corporate formation, distribution, redemption, and liquidation all in the same transaction. The Code recognizes *seven* types of tax-free reorganization, some of which overlap. Most reorganizations involve two corporations and their shareholders. However, in a recapitalization, only one corporation is involved, while in other types of reorganization three or more corporations may participate.

The basic thrust of the reorganization provisions, Code Secs. 354-368, is to provide tax-free treatment to *all* parties to a reorganization when the legislative and judicial requirements have been met. Thus, shareholders may swap "old" for "new" securities tax free, and property may be transferred from one corporation to another, also tax free. As in other types of tax-free transactions, basis carries over and holding periods tack on.

There are three basic categories of reorganization:

1. *Acquisitive reorganizations,* where one corporation acquires the stock or assets of another corporation. Examples include the Type A, B, C, and acquisitive Type D reorganizations.
2. *Divisive reorganizations,* where one corporation divides itself into two or more corporations and distributes stock to its shareholders. This is the divisive Type D.
3. Mere changes in the capital structure or the identity, form, or state of incorporation of a single corporation. These are the Type E and F reorganizations.

The Type G, which facilitates the reorganization of a bankrupt corporation, fits best under divisive reorganizations, but is arguably a unique fourth type.

A tax-free reorganization is concerned with a change in ownership of a corporation's assets or its stock by other than purchase. The word "tax free" is really a misnomer, as the tax effects of a transaction are merely postponed until some time in the future. Thus, a corporate reorganization generally results in tax deferral.

The possible advantages of a reorganization over a purchase include both economic as well as tax considerations. For example, one major economic advantage of a merger is that it may be accomplished without the use of cash. A major tax consideration of a reorganization involves the possible retention of the tax attributes of one or more of the participating corporations, with the continued use of a net operating loss deduction often of most importance.

Many business considerations will impact the choice of a particular type of reorganization. Additionally, a determination must be made as to whether a proposed acquisition violates federal and state antitrust laws. In some cases, shareholder approvals must be obtained and the registration requirements of federal and state laws must be met.

Types of Corporate Reorganizations

¶17,001 STATUTORY DEFINITIONS

For tax purposes, there are seven basic types of corporate reorganization. The concept of a "reorganization" is broader than the accounting and legal terms of "mergers," "consolidations," and "business combinations," but, at the same time, each type of reorganization is narrowly defined with many specific requirements. Code Sec. 368 defines the different types of reorganization. The types of reorganization are commonly referred to by the subparagraph in which they are defined. Code Sec. 368(a)(1)(A) defines a Type A reorganization; Code Sec. 368(a)(1)(B) defines a Type B reorganization and so forth.

Seven Types of Corporate Reorganizations

A. A statutory merger or consolidation.
B. The acquisition by one corporation of the stock of another corporation. The acquiring corporation must exchange solely all or part of its voting stock, or all or part of the voting stock of a corporation that is in control of the acquiring corporation. The acquiring corporation must have control of the acquired corporation immediately after the acquisition, whether or not the acquiring corporation had control immediately before the acquisition. This is a "stock-for-stock" reorganization.
C. The acquisition by one corporation of substantially all of the properties of another corporation. The acquiring corporation must exchange solely all or part of its voting stock, or all or part of the voting stock of a corporation that is in control of the acquiring corporation. In determining whether the exchange is solely for stock, the assumption by the acquiring corporation of a liability of the acquired corporation or of property subject to a liability is disregarded. This is a "stock-for-assets" reorganization.
D. A transfer by a corporation of all or part of its assets to another corporation. Immediately after the transfer, the transferor or one or more of its shareholders must be in control of the corporation to which the assets are transferred. Also, in pursuance of the plan, stock or securities of the corporation to which the assets are transferred must be distributed in a transaction that qualifies under Code Sec. 354, 355, or 356.
E. A recapitalization.
F. A mere change in identity, form, or place of organization of one corporation, however effected.
G. A transfer by a corporation of all or part of its assets to another corporation in a bankruptcy or receivership proceeding; but only if, in pursuance of the plan, stock or securities of the corporation to which the assets are transferred are distributed in a transaction that qualifies under Code Sec. 354, 355, or 356.

To understand the tax consequences of corporate reorganizations, it is necessary to have a basic understanding of corporate formations (Code Sec. 351), distributions (Code Sec. 301), stock redemptions (Code Secs. 302–304), and complete liquidations. (Code Secs. 331–337). This material is covered in Chapters 14–16 and should be reviewed if needed.

¶17,005 GENERAL REQUIREMENTS

No gain or loss is recognized if stock or securities in a corporation that is a party to a reorganization are exchanged solely for stock or securities of the same corporation or another corporation that is a party to the reorganization. Code Sec. 354(a). In this context, the term "securities" means long-term debt.

In order to receive nonrecognition treatment, the stock or securities that are exchanged must be those of a party to the reorganization. The parties to a reorganization include:

1. A corporation resulting from the reorganization.
2. Both corporations in the case of a reorganization involving one corporation acquiring the stock or assets of another corporation.

Additionally, in some reorganizations, the corporation controlling the acquiring corporation qualifies as a party to the reorganization. Code Sec. 368(b).

Some types of reorganization permit the transfer of property other than stock or securities of a party to the reorganization. The receipt of such property (termed "boot") results in the recognition of gain to the extent of the lesser of (1) the realized gain or (2) the amount of money plus the fair market value of any other property received. For this purpose, boot also includes the fair market value of an excess principal (face) amount of securities received over the principal amount of securities surrendered. A shareholder's recognized gain is treated as dividend income if the receipt of boot has the same effect as a dividend distribution. Otherwise, the shareholder's gain will be generally treated as a capital gain.

In order to achieve reorganization treatment, the transactions must be pursuant to a "plan of reorganization." This plan should be written since Reg. §1.368-3 calls for the adoption of a plan by each of the parties to the reorganization and also requires that a copy of the plan be filed with each corporation's tax return for the year of occurrence. However, a failure to strictly comply with the plan requirements does not negate the reorganization. In many cases, corporations planning a corporate reorganization obtain an advance letter ruling from the IRS ensuring that the proposed transactions qualify as a corporate reorganization.

Reorganization treatment requires that there be a "continuity of proprietary interest." This means that the former shareholders of the acquired corporation must receive stock in the acquiring corporation. Although the amount of stock that is needed to meet this requirement is not specified in the Code, Regulations require that stock of the acquiring corporation be at least 40 percent of the total consideration to be received by the shareholders of the acquired corporation. Reg. §1.368-1(e)(3). However, not all of the shareholders of the acquired corporation need to receive a proprietary interest in the acquiring corporation. The requirement is applied to the total consideration given to the shareholders of the acquired corporation and must be met in the aggregate.

There must also be a "continuity of business enterprise." This means that the acquiring corporation must either continue the acquired corporation's historic business, or use a significant portion of the acquired corporation's historic business assets in a business.

Finally, there must be a bona fide "business purpose" for a transaction to qualify as a corporate reorganization. In this context, the potential tax savings inherent in a corporate reorganization is not a valid business purpose. On the other hand, a valid business purpose includes an acquisition that is made to assure the continued availability of materials that are used in the acquiring corporation's production process.

Note that a tax-free reorganization is not always desirable. For example, the acquiring corporation may prefer to purchase assets so that the acquired assets will have a basis equal to fair market value, rather than a carryover basis that would result from a reorganization. Additionally, a reorganization may not be desirable if the target corporation or its shareholders have substantial unrealized losses that they wish to recognize.

¶17,009   TYPE A REORGANIZATIONS

Basic Form of Transaction

A Type A reorganization includes a merger or a consolidation meeting state law requirements. Reg. §1.368-2(b).

In a statutory merger, shown in Figure 1 (see following page), Parent Corporation (acquiring corporation) acquires the assets and assumes the liabilities of Target Corporation by operation of law. Target Corporation's shareholders receive Parent stock, and Target Corporation is dissolved under state law. Even though Parent may issue its stock (and other consideration) directly to Target's shareholders, the transaction is treated as if the consideration was transferred to Target Corporation and then distributed to its shareholders. Afterwards, Parent's original shareholders and Target's former shareholders own all the stock of Parent Corporation.

In a consolidation, shown in Figure 2 (below), a new corporation is formed (Newco) to acquire all the assets and liabilities of two or more consolidating corporations, Target 1 (T1) and Target 2 (T2). The shareholders of both consolidating corporations exchange their stock for Newco stock, and T1 and T2 are dissolved under state law. Afterwards, the former shareholders of T1 and T2 own all the stock of Newco.

EXAMPLE 17.1	Fast-Food Corporation acquires all the properties of Taco Corporation in exchange for 3,000 shares of stock in Fast-Food Corporation. The Fast-Food Corporation stock is distributed to Taco's shareholders in complete liquidation of Taco Corporation. This transaction qualifies as a Type A reorganization (assuming the requirements of state law are met). It is a statutory merger.

Figure 1. MERGER

Figure 2. CONSOLIDATION

EXAMPLE 17.2

Steel Corporation and Wool Corporation transfer their assets to a new corporation, Steel Wool, in exchange for the stock of Steel Wool. Steel and Wool then transfer the Steel Wool stock to their respective stockholders in exchange for the Steel and Wool stock. Steel and Wool are then liquidated and the two businesses are carried on by Steel Wool as one business. This is a Type A reorganization, a consolidation.

Because a corporate reorganization normally results in a continuation of the business activities of the previous corporations, the acquiring corporation will generally either assume liabilities of the acquired organization or take property subject to liabilities. In a statutory merger or consolidation, the acquiring corporation acquires *all* of the assets and liabilities of the target corporation, including any contingent or unknown liabilities.

Care must be taken prior to the reorganization to determine the existence of unknown and contingent liabilities since these liabilities may affect the amount of consideration that the acquiring corporation is willing to pay. Contingent or escrowed stock arrangements can be used to adjust the amount of consideration to properly reflect the outcome of the contingencies relating to the liabilities.

Consideration Allowed

The Type A reorganization is the most flexible type of reorganization as far as the type of consideration that can be given to the target corporation's shareholders. At least 40 percent of the consideration must be stock of the acquiring corporation (either voting or nonvoting) to satisfy the continuity of proprietary interest requirement, but other consideration such as cash, options, debt obligations, or other property can also be paid without disqualifying the acquisition as a reorganization.

Advantages and Disadvantages of a Type A Reorganization

The main advantages of a Type A reorganization include:

1. The consideration that can be paid to the target's shareholders is flexible. Nonvoting stock can be used, as well as convertible securities, warrants, cash, or other property.
2. In contrast to other types of reorganizations, a straight Type A reorganization does not require that "substantially all" of the target's assets be acquired in the transaction. This means that, subject to the continuity of business enterprise requirement, the target corporation can spin off or sell unwanted assets prior to its acquisition without disqualifying the acquisition as a reorganization.

The main disadvantages of a Type A reorganization include:

1. All liabilities of the acquired corporation (including unknown and contingent liabilities) must be assumed by the acquiring corporation.
2. A majority of the shareholders (two-thirds in some states) of both corporations must approve the reorganization. Having the shareholders vote could prove costly and time-consuming.
3. Dissenting shareholders of the target corporation normally have appraisal rights (i.e., the right to have their shares valued and purchased for cash). A substantial number of dissenting shareholders could necessitate a large cash outlay.
4. The acquired corporation may have contracts, rights, or privileges that are not transferable. These contracts, rights, or privileges expire when the acquired corporation dissolves.

Tax Consequences of a Type A Reorganization

Acquired Corporation's Shareholders

The exchange of stock or securities is tax free, provided the principal amount of securities received does not exceed the principal amount of securities surrendered. Code Sec. 354(a)(1). Cash, an excess principal amount of securities, or other boot received causes the recognition of a realized gain. Code Sec. 356(a). The basis of the stock and securities received by the acquired corporation's shareholders is the same as the basis of the stock and securities surrendered, increased by any gain recognized (including any amount treated as a dividend), and decreased by the amount of money and the fair market value of any other property received. Code Sec. 358(a)(1). Any boot property received has a basis equal to fair market value. Code Sec. 358(a)(2).

EXAMPLE 17.3

Pursuant to a Type A reorganization, Target Corporation is merged into Parent Corporation. As part of the transaction, Irene Greene exchanges her Target stock that has a basis of $10,000 for Parent stock with a fair market value of $15,000.

1. If she receives Parent stock only, no gain is recognized, her basis in the Parent stock received is $10,000, and the holding period of her Parent stock includes the holding period of her Target stock.
2. If Irene receives $3,000 of cash and Parent stock worth $12,000, her realized gain of $5,000 ($15,000 – $10,000) is recognized to the extent of the $3,000 boot, and Irene must report a capital gain of $3,000. Her basis for the Parent stock is $10,000 (Target stock basis of $10,000 less boot of $3,000 plus gain recognized of $3,000).
3. If the cash in (2) has the effect of a dividend, Irene's recognized gain must be reported as $3,000 of dividend income. Her stock basis is $10,000 as determined in (2).
4. If Irene receives Parent stock worth $12,000 and Parent's bond with a principal amount and fair market value of $3,000, her realized gain of $5,000 is again recognized to the extent of $3,000. Even though it is Parent's bond, the fair market value of the bond is treated as boot received because Irene did not surrender any bonds. Her basis for the bond is its fair market value of $3,000. Her basis for the Parent stock is $10,000 ($10,000 Target stock basis, less the $3,000 FMV of the bond, plus the recognized gain of $3,000).

Acquiring Corporation

No gain or loss is recognized by the acquiring corporation on the issuance of its stock. Code Sec. 1032(a). The acquiring corporation receives a carryover basis for the transferor's assets, increased by any gain recognized to the transferor. Code Sec. 362(b). Since no gain or loss is generally recognized by the target corporation, the acquired assets generally have a transferred basis.

Note that the shareholders of the target corporation are not the "transferor" of the assets, and gain recognized by them because of the receipt of boot does not increase the basis of the assets that are acquired. Similarly, any gain recognized by the acquiring corporation because of the payment of boot property to the target's shareholders does not increase the basis of the acquired assets.

The holding period for the acquired assets includes the period of time they were held by the target. The acquiring corporation also succeeds to all of the target's tax attributes, although some carryovers (e.g., NOL carryover) may be limited in their deductibility.

EXAMPLE 17.4

Parent Corporation transfers $400,000 of its common stock and $200,000 of cash to acquire Target Corporation's assets and liabilities in a statutory merger. Target's assets have a fair market value of $700,000 and a basis of $500,000, and Target has $100,000 of liabilities. Parent recognizes no gain or loss on the transfer of its stock. The $500,000 basis for Target's assets carries over to Parent, along with all of Target's tax attributes.

Acquired Corporation

No gain or loss is recognized by the target corporation upon the transfer of its assets solely in exchange for stock or securities of the acquiring corporation. Code Sec. 361(a). Similarly, the *receipt* of money or other boot property does not cause the recognition of gain to the target corporation. Generally, neither the acquiring corporation's assumption of the target's liabilities, nor the acquisition of the target's assets subject to liabilities, causes the recognition of gain to the acquired target corporation. Code Sec. 357(a).

The gain and loss recognition rules that apply to ordinary distributions and complete liquidations do not apply to distributions pursuant to a plan of reorganization. Code Sec. 361(c)(4). Thus, no gain or loss is recognized by the target corporation when it distributes the acquiring corporation's stock and securities that were received in the reorganization. However, the target corporation recognizes gain (but not loss) on the distribution of appreciated boot property pursuant to the plan of reorganization. Ordinarily, there is little gain (if any) recognized because the boot property's basis is its fair market value on date of receipt, and it normally is distributed shortly thereafter. Code Sec. 358(a)(2).

EXAMPLE 17.5

Assume the same facts as in Example 17.4. No gain or loss is recognized to Target Corporation on the receipt and distribution of the Parent Corporation stock and cash to its shareholders. The shareholders recognize gain to the extent of boot received.

Acquiring Corporation's Shareholders

In a merger where the acquiring corporation survives, there is no change in the tax status of the acquiring corporation's shareholders. They simply own a smaller percentage of a larger corporation.

¶17,015   RECEIPT OF BOOT

If a shareholder or security holder receives cash or other property (i.e., boot) in addition to the stock or securities that are permitted to be received without the recognition of gain under Code Sec. 354 or 355, then a realized gain must be recognized to the extent of the lesser of (1) the realized gain or (2) the fair market value of the boot received. Code Sec. 356(a)(1). No loss can be recognized as a result of the receipt of boot. Code Sec. 356(c). The distributee's basis for boot property is the property's fair market value. Code Sec. 358(a)(2).

EXAMPLE 17.6

Pursuant to a plan of reorganization, Allan Luden received the following consideration from Cherry Corporation in exchange for Lime Corporation stock having a basis of $85:

Cherry Corp. stock (FMV)	$100
Cash	25
Other property (FMV)	50
Total FMV of consideration received	$175
Basis of Lime Corp. stock surrendered	85
Realized gain	$90

In this case, the amount of gain recognized by Allan is limited to the amount of cash plus the FMV of other property received, which totals $75. Allan's basis for the other property received equals its FMV of $50.

EXAMPLE 17.7

If, in Example 17.6, Allan's Lime Corporation stock had a basis to him of $125, he would realize and recognize a gain of $50.

EXAMPLE 17.8

If, in Example 17.6, Allan's Lime Corporation stock had a basis to him of $200, he would realize a loss of $25 on the exchange, but the loss would not be recognized.

The definition of boot also includes the fair market value of an excess principal (face) amount of securities received over the principal amount of securities surrendered. If securities are received but no securities are surrendered, the fair market value of all securities received are treated as boot.

EXAMPLE 17.9

Pursuant to a plan of reorganization, Sharon Baker received the following consideration from Red Corporation in exchange for Blue Corporation stock with a basis of $7,000:

Red Corp. stock (FMV)	$8,000
Red Corp. securities (FMV)	2,000
Total consideration received	$10,000
Less: Basis of Blue Corp. stock surrendered	7,000
Realized gain	$3,000

In this case, Baker's realized gain would be recognized to the extent of the fair market value of the excess securities received, $2,000.

If a shareholder or security holder surrenders securities, but a greater principal amount of securities is received, the fair market value of the excess principal amount of securities received is treated as boot. Code Sec. 356(d)(2)(B).

EXAMPLE 17.10

Pursuant to a plan of reorganization, George Carter exchanged a Zim Corporation security with a basis of $700 and a principal amount of $1,000, for a new Zim Corporation security in the principal amount of $1,200 with a fair market value of $1,080.

Zim Corp. security received (FMV)	$1,080
Basis of Zim Corp. security surrendered	700
Realized gain	$380

Carter's realized gain is recognized to the extent of the fair market value of the excess principal amount of security received, $180, computed as follows:

Principal amount of securities received	$1,200
Principal amount of securities surrendered	1,000
Excess principal amount received	$200

$$\frac{\$200\ \text{(excess principal received)}}{\$1,200\ \text{(total principal received)}} \times \underset{\text{(FMV of security received)}}{\$1,080} = \underset{\text{(FMV of excess principal amount received)}}{\$180}$$

¶17,025   CHARACTER OF RECOGNIZED GAIN

After the amount of recognized gain is computed, its character must be determined. If an exchange has the effect of a dividend, then a shareholder's recognized gain must be treated as a dividend to the extent of the shareholder's ratable share of earnings and profits. Code Sec. 356(a)(2). Any amount of recognized gain in excess of the amount to be treated as a dividend will be treated as capital gain.

Whether the receipt of boot has the effect of a dividend has been an issue of much controversy. Generally, whether a dividend has been received is determined in a manner consistent with the stock redemption rules that are found in Code Sec. 302. Under this approach, which applies the constructive stock ownership rules of Code Sec. 318, an exchange that is deemed to be either a substantially disproportionate redemption under Code Sec. 302(b)(2) or a redemption not essentially equivalent to a dividend under Code Sec. 302(b)(1) would not have the effect of a dividend and would instead be treated as capital gain.

The Supreme Court ended the controversy in this area by permitting a shareholder to obtain capital gain treatment by applying the Code Sec. 302 tests to the shareholder's stock ownership in the acquiring corporation that resulted from the reorganization. *D.E. Clark,* 89-1 USTC ¶9230, 489 U.S. 726, 109 S.Ct. 1455 (1989). In *Clark,* the taxpayer owned all of the stock of the target corporation that was merged into the acquiring corporation in a corporate reorganization. The taxpayer received acquiring corporation stock and cash as a result of the merger. Following the merger, the taxpayer owned less than 50 percent of the acquiring corporation's stock and less than 80 percent of the amount of stock that the taxpayer would have owned if the taxpayer had instead received only stock in the acquiring corporation and no boot.

The Court's analysis requires one to imagine a pure stock-for-stock exchange, followed immediately by a postreorganization redemption of a portion of the shareholder's shares in the acquiring corporation in return for a payment in an amount equal to the amount of boot received in the reorganization. As a result of the Supreme Court's analysis, boot received by a shareholder in a corporate reorganization will generally result in capital gain treatment so long as the shareholder, as a result of the reorganization, owns (directly and constructively under Code Sec. 318) less than 50 percent of the acquiring corporation's stock.

EXAMPLE 17.11

Juniper Corporation has 100 shares outstanding and is wholly owned by David Worth. Berry Corporation has 100 shares outstanding and is wholly owned by Eric Embers. David and Eric are not related. Pursuant to a plan of reorganization, Juniper is merged into Berry, with David receiving 60 shares of Berry Corporation and cash of $40,000.

If David had received no cash, he would have received 100 Berry Corporation shares.

As a result of the reorganization, David owns 60 of the 160 outstanding Berry Corporation shares (37.5 percent). Had David received no boot, he would have owned 100 out of 200 outstanding Berry Corporation shares (50 percent). Using the Supreme Court's approach, the cash of $40,000 is deemed to have been received in redemption of the 40 shares of Berry Corporation that David did not receive. Applying the Code Sec. 302(b)(2) tests, David's resulting 37.5 percent (60/160) ownership of Berry Corporation, is less than 50 percent, and less than 80 percent of the ownership that David would have had (100/200) if he had received no boot (37.5% is less than (80% × 50%)). Thus, since the receipt of the $40,000 of cash would qualify for exchange treatment under Code Sec. 302(b)(2), David's recognized gain will be treated as capital gain.

EXAMPLE 17.12

Assume the same facts as in Example 17.11 except that David and Eric are father and son. Since David constructively owns all of Eric's stock under Code Sec. 318, David directly and constructively owns all of Berry Corporation's outstanding stock after the merger. Thus, none of the Code Sec. 302 tests can be met and the receipt of the cash of $40,000 will be treated as a dividend (assuming Berry Corporation has at least $40,000 of earnings and profits).

¶17,053   TYPE B REORGANIZATIONS

Basic Form of Transaction

In contrast to the Type A and C reorganizations that are used to acquire a target corporation's assets, the Type B reorganization is used to acquire the target's stock. In a Type B reorganization, the acquiring corporation must exchange solely voting stock to acquire control of the target corporation. A Type B reorganization usually takes the form of a tender offer to the target's shareholders, and often does not involve the target corporation itself.

As shown in Figure 3 below, Parent Corporation (acquiring corporation) exchanges solely voting stock of Parent with the shareholders of Target Corporation to obtain control of Target. After the exchange, Parent's original shareholders together with Target's former shareholders own all of the stock of Parent Corporation, which in turn, is in control of Target Corporation.

It is important to note that the "solely voting stock" requirement applies only to the consideration that is used to acquire the target corporation's stock. Other consideration (e.g., nonvoting stock, cash, debentures) can be used to acquire the outstanding debt securities of the target corporation, or other assets owned by shareholders of the target corporation.

Figure 3. TYPE B REORGANIZATION

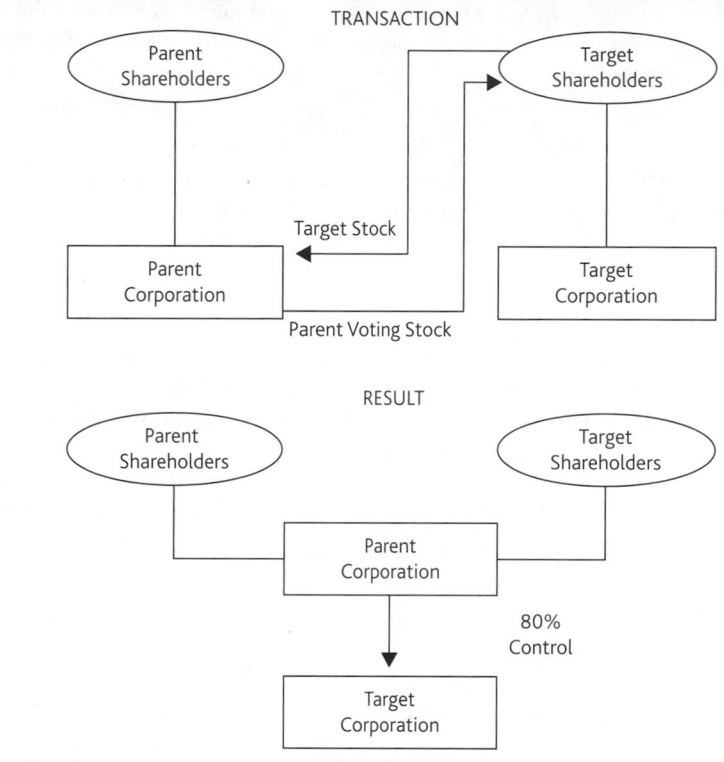

80-Percent-Control Requirement

The acquiring corporation must "control" the acquired corporation immediately after the transaction. "Control" is defined as the ownership of at least 80 percent of the total combined voting power *and* 80 percent of each class of nonvoting stock. Rev. Rul. 59-259, 1959-2 CB 115.

EXAMPLE 17.13

Carnival Inc. acquires 800 shares of Masks Inc.'s 1,000 outstanding shares from Masks' shareholders by giving them 500 shares of newly issued voting shares in Carnival. This is a Type B reorganization.

The requirement that the acquiring corporation be in control immediately after the exchange does not limit the reorganization to a single transaction. If the acquisition of stock occurs over a relatively short period of time (i.e., 12 months), Reg. §1.368-2(c) permits the transactions to qualify as a Type B reorganization. However, a problem arises if a corporation acquires some stock for cash and then at a later date issues solely voting stock to acquire an additional amount of stock sufficient to meet the 80-percent-control requirement. The question to be resolved is whether the two acquisitions are related. If they are, then the voting-stock-for-stock exchange is taxable because the overall acquisition of the target's stock was not made solely for voting stock of the acquiring corporation. If the two acquisitions are not related, then the exchange of the acquiring corporation's voting stock for the target's stock is viewed as a separate transaction, and qualifies as a Type B reorganization. The longer the period of time between a cash purchase and the acquisition for voting stock, the greater the probability that they will be treated as unrelated.

EXAMPLE 17.14

Parent Corporation purchased 25 percent of Target Corporation's stock five years ago. Parent currently acquires an additional 60 percent of Target's stock solely in exchange for Parent voting stock. The exchange of Parent voting stock for Target stock qualifies as a Type B reorganization because the acquisitions for cash and stock are treated as unrelated.

EXAMPLE 17.15

Alternatively, assume Parent Corporation purchased 10 percent of Target Corporation's stock for cash during March 2017. During September 2017, Parent made a tender offer and acquired an additional 75 percent of Target's stock solely in exchange for Parent voting stock. When the March and September acquisitions are combined, Target's stock has not been acquired solely for Parent's voting stock. Thus, the exchange of Parent stock for Target stock fails to qualify as a Type B reorganization and is treated as a taxable exchange.

If a Type B reorganization is desired after the acquiring corporation has already purchased some target stock, the acquiring corporation can make an unconditional sale of the purchased stock to an unrelated third party. Then the IRS will allow a subsequent voting-stock-for-stock exchange to qualify as a Type B reorganization. Rev. Rul. 72-354, 1972-2 CB 216.

Consideration Allowed

The acquiring corporation must acquire the target corporation's stock solely with its voting stock. The voting stock may be either common or preferred stock, as long as "normal" voting rights are conferred. Convertible preferred voting stock may be used, but not convertible bonds, even if convertible at all times into voting stock. Rev. Rul. 69-91, 1969-1 CB 105. Options to purchase voting stock, such as rights and warrants, do *not* qualify as voting stock. *Southwest Consolidated Corp.,* 42-2 USTC ¶9248, 315 U.S. 194, 62 S.Ct. 546 (1942). Cash is strictly prohibited, except for the following:

1. Cash may be paid in lieu of issuing fractional shares that the acquired corporation's shareholders are entitled to receive. Rev. Rul. 66-365, 1966-2 CB 116.
2. The acquiring corporation may pay the acquired corporation's legal, accounting, and appraisal fees and other expenses directly related to the stock acquisition in cash, but not any expenses incurred by the acquired corporation's shareholders. Rev. Rul. 73-54, 1973-1 CB 187. The acquired corporation may, however, redeem the stock of dissenting, minority shareholders for cash or property, in a separate transaction. Rev. Rul. 68-285, 1968-1 CB 142.

EXAMPLE 17.16

Boatcraft Inc. wishes to acquire the stock of Canoes Inc., but shareholders owning 25 percent of Canoes' stock insist on cash. Canoes then uses its cash and redeems the stock of those shareholders wanting cash. Boatcraft subsequently exchanges its voting stock and obtains all of Canoes' remaining outstanding shares. Since Boatcraft used solely voting stock to acquire control of Canoes, its exchange of Boatcraft voting stock for Canoes stock qualifies as a Type B reorganization.

Advantages and Disadvantages of a Type B Reorganization

The main advantages of a Type B reorganization are:

1. The acquired corporation remains in existence as a subsidiary of the acquiring corporation, which can be an important consideration if it has an established identity. Any nonassignable contracts, leases, franchises, and licenses, as well as all of its tax attributes remain unaffected.
2. In contrast to a Type A reorganization, a Type B does not depend on meeting the requirements of local law. No formal shareholder vote is required. The acquisition normally takes the form of a tender offer to the target's shareholders, even if the target's management does not approve.
3. The assets of the acquiring corporation are protected from the target's liabilities because of the continued separate corporate existence of the target.
4. In contrast to a Type C reorganization, a Type B reorganization does not require that the target corporation retain substantially all of its assets.
5. Some of the problems that may be applicable to asset acquisitions (e.g., transfer fees, state and local income taxes, substantial recordkeeping) are avoided when only stock is acquired.

The main disadvantages of a Type B reorganization are:

1. Only voting stock can be used to acquire the target's stock. This may have a dilutive effect on the control exercised by the acquiring corporation's original shareholders.
2. Acquisition of less than 100 percent of the target's stock results in a dissenting minority interest that may create problems at shareholder meetings.

3. Even if a consolidated tax return is filed, the desirable tax attributes of the acquired corporation (e.g., NOL and tax credit carryforwards) remain segregated and generally cannot be used to benefit the acquiring corporation.

Tax Consequences of a Type B Reorganization

Acquired Corporation's Shareholders

No gain or loss is recognized by the target's shareholders on the exchange of their target stock for voting stock of the acquiring corporation. Code Sec. 354(a)(1). As a result, their basis and holding period for the target stock carries over to the acquiring corporation's stock received in the exchange. Code Sec. 358(a)(1).

Acquiring Corporation

No gain or loss is recognized to the acquiring corporation on the issuance of its voting stock. Code Sec. 1032. The basis and holding period of the acquired corporation's stock is a carryover basis and holding period from the former shareholders of the target corporation. Code Sec. 362(b).

Acquired Corporation

The acquired corporation remains in existence and retains all of its tax attributes.

Acquiring Corporation's Stock Basis

The acquiring corporation will need to know what its basis is for the acquired target corporation stock in the event of a later sale, exchange, or other disposition of the stock. Of course, its basis for the target stock will be the same as it was in the hands of the former target shareholders. Determining what this basis is can be a practical problem if the target corporation was publicly held since the former target shareholders would have purchased the stock at various times, or may have received it by gift or inheritance. Fortunately, the IRS has approved the use of estimating and sampling procedures so that the aggregate basis may be determined statistically. Rev. Proc. 81-70, 1981-2 CB 729.

EXAMPLE 17.17	Target Corporation's only class of stock is 100 percent owned by Kelly Morgan, who has a basis of $300,000 for her stock. Pursuant to a plan of reorganization, Kelly exchanges her Target stock for $500,000 of Parent Corporation's voting stock. Although Kelly realizes a $200,000 gain, no gain is recognized, and Kelly's basis for the Parent stock is $300,000. Parent recognizes no gain or loss when it issues its voting stock and has a $300,000 basis for the Target stock acquired from Kelly.

¶17,105   TYPE C REORGANIZATIONS

Basic Form of Transaction

The acquiring corporation issues its voting stock to acquire substantially all the assets of the target corporation. If the target corporation is liquidated immediately after the exchange, then the effect of the acquisition is much the same as a statutory merger and is often referred to as a "practical merger."

Figure 4. TYPE C REORGANIZATION

In a Type C reorganization, the acquired corporation must distribute the stock, securities, and other property that it received from the acquiring corporation in the reorganization, together with any property that it retained and did not transfer to the acquiring corporation, to its shareholders as part of the plan of reorganization. Because of this distribution requirement, the target corporation is effectively liquidated as part of the plan of reorganization.

As shown in Figure 4, Parent Corporation (acquiring corporation) transfers its voting stock in exchange for substantially all of the assets and liabilities of Target Corporation (acquired corporation). Target then distributes the Parent stock, together with any assets not transferred to Parent, to its shareholders in cancellation of their Target stock.

Meaning of "Substantially All" Assets

What constitutes "substantially all" of the acquired corporation's assets is not specifically defined in the Code. For advance ruling purposes, the IRS requires that at least 70 percent of the gross assets *and* at least 90 percent of the net assets must be acquired. Rev. Proc. 77-37, 1977-2 CB 568.

EXAMPLE 17.18	Target Corporation has assets with a total fair market value of $600,000 and has liabilities of $100,000. Seventy percent of Target's gross assets equals $420,000 (70% × $600,000), and 90 percent of Target's net assets equals $450,000 (90% × ($600,000 – $100,000)). To obtain an advance ruling regarding a proposed Type C reorganization, at least $450,000 of Target's assets must be acquired.

Revenue Rulings issued by the IRS and various courts have been more flexible in interpreting the "substantially all" test and have indicated that the test is satisfied if all significant operating assets are transferred to the acquiring corporation. Rev. Rul. 78-47, 1978-1 CB 113.

Consideration Allowed

The consideration used to acquire substantially all of the acquired corporation's assets must consist *solely* of the acquiring corporation's voting stock. Code Sec. 368(a)(1)(C). For purposes of this solely voting stock requirement, the assumption of a liability of the acquired corporation or the acquisition of property subject to a liability is completely disregarded. This is understandable because creditors ordinarily would not permit the transfer of assets without the transfer of related debt for fear that the transferor would be unable to repay the debt with its remaining assets.

Additionally, there is a boot relaxation rule under which consideration other than voting stock can be used provided that at least 80 percent of the total fair market value of all of the target's assets is acquired for voting stock. Code Sec. 368(a)(2)(B). Technically, this rule permits up to 20 percent of the target's assets to be acquired for boot. However, for purposes of applying this rule, liabilities assumed or taken subject to by the acquiring corporation are included in the computation of the 20 percent limit. The practical effect of this rule is that boot cannot be used in a Type C reorganization because the target corporation's liabilities, which must be assumed, ordinarily exceed 20 percent of the total fair market value of its assets.

EXAMPLE 17.19

The following example illustrates the 80 percent rule of Code Sec. 368(a)(2)(B).

	Case 1	Case 2	Case 3
Total FMV of Target Corp. assets	$100,000	$100,000	$100,000
Liabilities assumed by Parent Corp.	(30,000)	(18,000)	(19,000)
Cash paid by Parent Corp.	0	(2,000)	(2,000)
Parent voting stock transferred	$70,000	$80,000	$79,000

In Case 1, no boot was paid so Target Corporation's liabilities are disregarded in determining whether solely voting stock was used, and it qualifies as a Type C reorganization. In Case 2, even though boot was paid it nevertheless qualifies as a Type C reorganization because the voting stock that was transferred equals at least 80 percent of the total FMV of Target's assets. Case 3 fails to qualify as a Type C reorganization because boot was paid and the Parent Corporation voting stock transferred was less than 80 percent of the total FMV of Target's assets.

The IRS has ruled that if the acquiring corporation assumes the acquired corporation's liability to pay cash to dissenting shareholders, the cash payment to shareholders is treated as a transfer of cash to the acquired corporation and causes the boot relaxation rule of Code Sec. 368(a)(2)(B) to apply. Rev. Rul. 73-102, 1973-1 CB 186.

Distribution Requirement

In order to qualify as a Type C reorganization, the acquired corporation must distribute the stock, securities, and other properties that it receives from the acquiring corporation, as well as any of its properties that were not transferred to the acquiring corporation, in pursuance of the plan of reorganization. If the acquired corporation is liquidated, any distribution to its creditors in connection with the liquidation will be treated as pursuant to the plan of reorganization.

The time period during which the distribution must be completed is not specified in Code Sec. 368(a)(2)(G). However, the distribution should be made promptly and the acquired corporation should not engage in the active conduct of a business after the reorganization transaction.

Finally, Code Sec. 368(a)(2)(G)(ii) authorizes the IRS to waive the distribution requirement if an actual distribution would result in a substantial hardship and the acquired corporation and its shareholders agree to be treated as if the undistributed assets had been distributed and then contributed to the capital of a new corporation.

Advantages and Disadvantages of a Type C Reorganization

The main advantages of a Type C reorganization are:

1. Not all liabilities of the target need be assumed or acquired, as is the case in a Type A reorganization where all liabilities (including unknown and contingent liabilities) must be assumed.
2. Not all assets need be acquired. As long as substantially all assets are acquired, unwanted assets can remain with the target corporation and be distributed to its shareholders.

3. Only the target corporation's shareholders have to approve the acquisition and liquidation that typically are a part of a Type C reorganization. This saves the time and expense of having the acquiring corporation's shareholders approve the reorganization transaction.

Disadvantages of a Type C reorganization:

1. Because the target's assets are not transferred by operation of law (as in a Type A), substantial transfer costs are ordinarily incurred in acquiring the assets. The transfer of assets will generally be taxable for state income tax purposes even though tax free at the federal level.
2. Substantially all of the target's assets must be acquired. This generally precludes a spin-off of an unwanted business before the reorganization, or a sale of unwanted assets immediately after the acquisition.
3. Generally, the boot relaxation rule cannot be used. Solely voting stock must be used to make the acquisition because the target corporation's liabilities exceed 20 percent of the total fair market value of its assets.

Tax Consequences of a Type C Reorganization

Acquired Corporation's Shareholders

No gain or loss is recognized by the target's shareholders if they receive only stock of the acquiring corporation. Their old stock basis and holding period carry over to their new stock. If boot is received (including an excess principal amount of securities), the lesser of the realized gain or the fair market value of the boot is recognized as gain. The basis for the stock received is equal to the basis of the stock given up, reduced by the boot received, and increased by the gain recognized. The boot property has a basis equal to fair market value.

EXAMPLE 17.20

Pursuant to a Type C reorganization, Parent Corporation acquires all of Target Corporation's assets and liabilities in exchange for Parent voting stock worth $800,000 and stock in Whitecliff Corporation (not a party to the reorganization) with a value of $50,000, and a basis of $20,000. Target's assets have a fair market value of $1,000,000 and a basis of $600,000, while its liabilities total $150,000.

Upon the liquidation of Target, Fred Marker exchanges Target stock with a basis of $9,000 and a value of $10,000 for Parent stock worth $8,000 and Whitecliff Corporation stock worth $2,000. Fred recognizes a gain of $1,000 (lesser of boot of $2,000, or realized gain of $1,000). Fred's basis for his Parent stock equals $8,000 (old basis of $9,000, less boot of $2,000, plus $1,000 of recognized gain). Fred's basis for the Whitecliff Corporation stock is its fair market value of $2,000, and its holding period begins on the day after receipt. Fred's holding period for his Parent stock includes the holding period of his Target stock.

Acquired Corporation

No gain or loss is recognized by the target corporation on the exchange of its assets for stock and securities of the acquiring corporation, nor on the distribution of that stock or securities to its shareholders. However, gain is recognized on the distribution of any appreciated property that was not transferred to the acquiring corporation. The target corporation's tax year ends on the date of the asset transfer. Code Sec. 381(b)(1).

Acquiring Corporation

The acquiring corporation does not recognize any gain when it issues its own stock. The basis for the acquired assets is the same as the target's basis for the assets, increased by any gain recognized to the target corporation. All of the target's tax attributes carry over to the acquiring corporation.

EXAMPLE 17.21

Assume the same facts as in Example 17.20. Parent Corporation recognizes no gain on the issuance of its stock but does recognize gain of $30,000 on the transfer of the Whitecliff Corporation stock. Since no gain is recognized to Target Corporation, Parent's basis for the acquired assets is $600,000.

Type B Reorganization Followed by Liquidation

If a Type B reorganization is closely followed by a liquidation of the acquired subsidiary, the overall acquisition of assets is tested as a Type C reorganization under the step transaction doctrine. This could prove fatal to the reorganization because of the substantially all test that is found in a Type C (but not in a Type B) reorganization. For example, a distribution or spin-off of some of the target's assets just prior to the acquisition might cause the acquisition to fail the substantially all test, and therefore the acquisition does not qualify as a Type C reorganization, even though the acquisition of the target's stock would have qualified as a Type B reorganization if the target had not been liquidated.

KEYSTONE PROBLEM	Ark Inc. wishes to acquire the assets of Bark Inc., all of which are appreciated. What are the tax consequences to the corporations and Bark's shareholders if the acquisition is handled in the following alternative ways? 1. Ark acquires the assets of Bark for consideration consisting of 80 percent voting stock in Ark (7 percent of Ark's stock) and 20 percent cash. Bark liquidates, and the Ark stock and cash received by Bark are distributed to Bark's shareholders, who turn in all their Bark stock. 2. Bark Inc. adopts a plan of complete liquidation and transfers all its assets to Ark Inc. for 30 percent cash and 70 percent Ark voting stock. Bark distributes the consideration received to its shareholders in complete liquidation.

¶17,157   TYPE D REORGANIZATIONS

Basic Forms of Transactions

There are two distinct types of Type D reorganizations, "divisive" and "acquisitive." Common in both types is the transfer of assets from one corporation to another in exchange for stock or securities, which are then distributed to the transferor's shareholders.

If "substantially all" assets are transferred, a Type D reorganization may also meet the definition of a Type C, but it is nevertheless treated as a Type D reorganization. An acquisitive Type D reorganization results if the transferor corporation receives at least 50 percent control (voting power or value) of the transferee, while 80 percent control is required in a divisive Type D reorganization. Code Sec. 368(c).

Whereas Type A, B, and C reorganizations are used to combine corporations, the Type D reorganization is generally used to divide a corporation. If the transferor survives as an operating entity, a divisive Type D reorganization takes place, tax free only if the requirements of Code Sec. 355 are met. This means that the transferor obtains and distributes control in the transferee corporation to its shareholders. Divisive Type D reorganizations are known as "spin-offs, split-offs, and split-ups."

A *spin-off* occurs when part of the assets of a corporation are transferred to a new corporation controlled by the transferor and the stock or securities in the latter are distributed to the shareholders of the original corporation without a surrender by the shareholders of stock or securities in the distributing corporation. A *split-off* is similar to a spin-off, except that the shareholders surrender a part of their stock in the distributing corporation for the stock in the controlled corporation. In a *split-up*, the distributing corporation transfers its assets to two or more newly created corporations in exchange for their stock and then effects a complete liquidation, the shareholders of the distributing corporation receiving stock in the new corporations in exchange for their stock in the distributing corporation.

EXAMPLE 17.22	Money Corporation, a bank, owns an 11-story office building where it occupies the ground floor in the conduct of its banking business, and the remaining 10 floors are rented to various tenants. The 10 rented floors are managed and maintained by the corporation's real estate department. The bank forms a new corporation, to which it transfers the building, and distributes all of the stock of the new corporation to the bank's shareholders. This is a spin-off.

EXAMPLE 17.23	Assume the same facts as in Example 17.22, except that the bank shareholders are required to surrender 30 percent of their stock and receive pro rata distributions of all of the stock in the new corporation. This is a split-off.

EXAMPLE 17.24

Money Corporation transfers its banking business to new Coins Corporation and transfers the building to new Dollars Corporation, in exchange for all of the stock of Coins and Dollars. It then transfers the Coins and Dollars stock to its shareholders in exchange for all of their Money stock. Money Corporation is then liquidated. This is a split-up.

The distributing corporation must distribute (1) all of the stock and securities of the controlled corporation or (2) at least 80 percent of the voting stock and 80 percent of all other classes of stock (but all or part of the securities may be retained). Moreover, the distributing corporation cannot retain any part of the stock or securities of the controlled corporation for the purpose of avoiding federal income taxes.

The principle of nonrecognition of gain or loss on receipt of a distribution applies where the distribution is pro rata among all the shareholders of the distributing corporation and whether the shareholders surrender stock in the distributing corporation. However, for full nonrecognition of gain, no stock in the controlled corporation can have been acquired by the distributing corporation within five years prior to the distribution in a transaction in which gain or loss was recognized in whole or in part. Code Sec. 355(a)(3)(B). If stock was so acquired, it is treated as "other property."

Spin-Offs

In a spin-off, a corporation transfers one of its businesses, typically the assets of a division, to a newly formed subsidiary in exchange for its stock, in what, in isolation, would simply be a Code Sec. 351 transfer. Promptly thereafter, the parent's stock in the new subsidiary is distributed to the parent's shareholders. A spin-off also includes the distribution of a preexisting subsidiary's stock to the shareholders of the parent.

As can be seen from Figure 5, A's shareholders end up owning stock in two different corporations, A Corporation and D Corporation.

Figure 5. SPIN-OFF

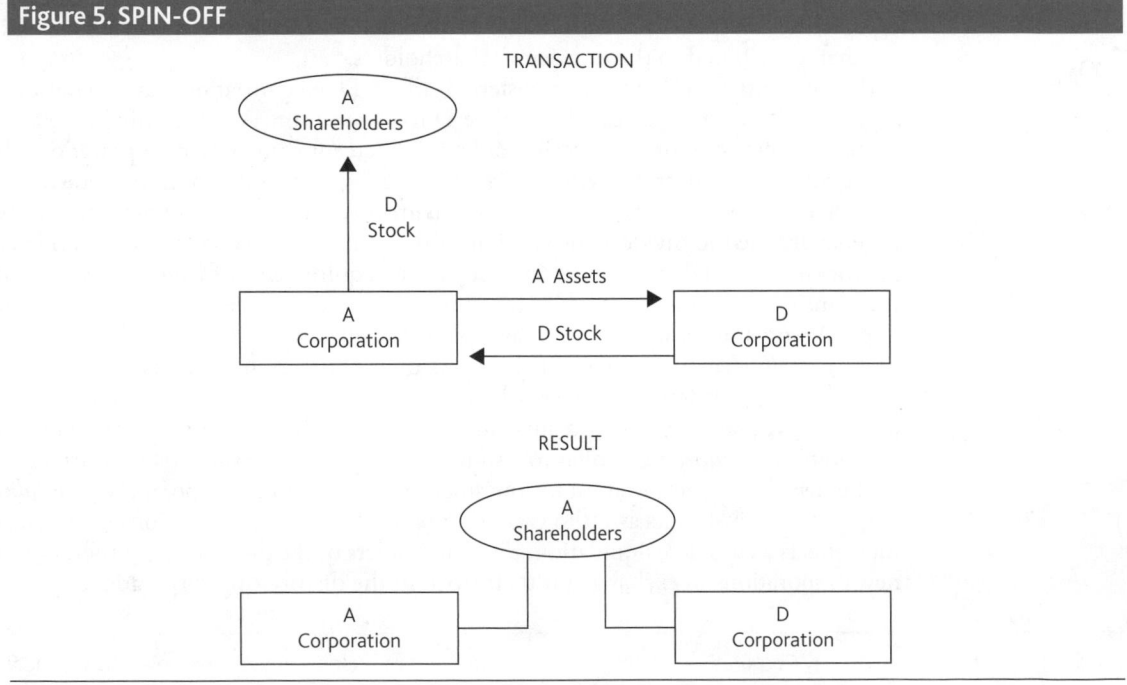

Split-Offs

A split-off is similar to a spin-off, except that one or more shareholders in the parent must give up all or part of their stock in the parent to receive stock in the subsidiary.

After the transaction is completed, A's shareholders end up with shares in both A Corporation and D Corporation. If shareholders give up only a portion of their shares in A Corporation for shares in D Corporation, all shareholders will own shares in both A Corporation and D Corporation. This is the same result as in a spin-off. However, if some of the original A shareholders give up all of their shares in A for D shares, different shareholders will own shares in A Corporation from those shareholders owning stock in D Corporation. If A's shareholders exchange their A shares in differing proportions for D shares, the transaction might result with some shareholders holding shares only in A Corporation, some shareholders owning shares only in D Corporation, and some shareholders owning shares in both A Corporation and D Corporation.

Figure 6. SPLIT-OFF

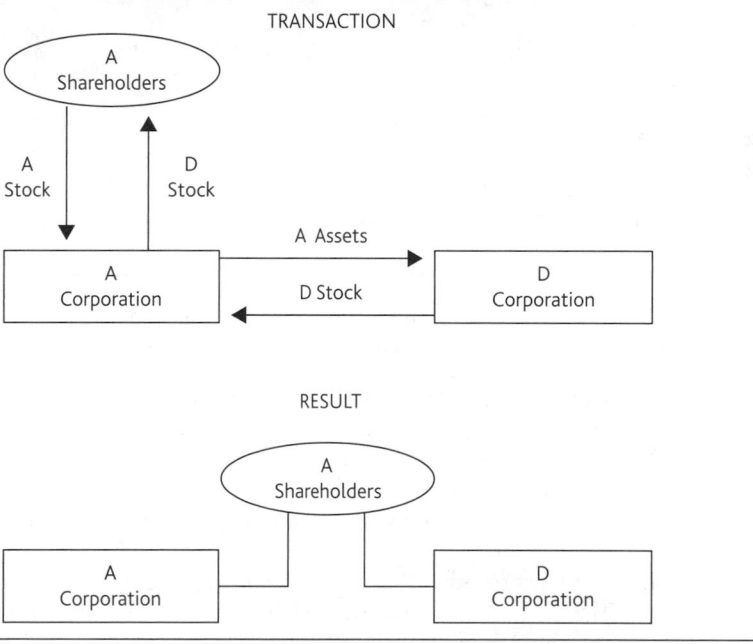

Split-Ups

In a split-up, a corporation transfers *all* its assets to two or more new corporations, whereupon the shareholders in the transferor give up *all* their stock in the transferor for those of the transferee corporations.

In a split-up, two new corporations are formed, with the original corporation going out of existence. The former shareholders of A Corporation own stock in D1 Corporation and D2 Corporation. More likely than not, the purpose of the split-up is to have one group of former A shareholders own D1 Corporation and a different group of former A shareholders own D2 Corporation, though that is not required.

Figure 7. SPLIT-UP

A divisive transaction is quite similar to a partial liquidation in that both provisions may be used in contracting or breaking up a corporation. Either approach may be appropriate in the following situations:

1. There may be a desire to discontinue and transfer one or more of the operations of the business, or its assets.
2. There may be a desire to protect the corporation from possible liabilities arising from present or future business ventures.
3. State law or business considerations may require separate branches of the business to be separately incorporated.
4. Antitrust or other decrees may require the corporation to divest itself of a business.
5. There may be a desire to split the corporate operations among some but not all members of the shareholder group.
6. There may be a desire to eliminate some of the shareholders because of a divergence of opinion as to corporate policies, or to provide for a complete retirement from the business of elderly shareholders.

PLANNING POINTER

A Type D reorganization can be a particularly appropriate tool if there is a need to segregate the ownership interests in a corporation. For example, a corporation is composed of two business operations, each of equivalent value, and the corporation is owned equally by two shareholders. If one of the shareholders has a particular interest in one of the corporation's operations and is in disagreement with the other owner over the direction of the business, a division of the corporation can be effected under Code Sec. 368(a)(1)(D) which can end the dispute. Each shareholder could become the sole owner of a corporation, with the respective corporations owning one of the operations of the predecessor corporation. The stock ownership need not necessarily be equal and the two business operations do not have to be of equivalent value. The stockholders can decide in what proportions to split the corporation.

Tax Consequences of a Type D Reorganization

Transferor Corporation

If the stock in the transferee corporation is *not* distributed, no gain or loss is recognized on the transfer of property under Code Sec. 351(a). However, if the stock or securities in the transferee are distributed to the stockholders of the transferor, the requirements of Code Sec. 355 must be met to provide nonrecognition on the transfer of property under Code Sec. 361. In any event, a realized gain must be recognized if liabilities in excess of basis are transferred. Code Sec. 357(c). Gain is recognized on any "boot" property distributed. Code Sec. 361(c).

Transferor Corporation's Shareholders

If the requirements of Code Sec. 355 are met, stock and security holders in the transferor recognize no gain or loss when they receive stock in the transferee corporation or swap securities in the transferor for those in the transferee. Code Sec. 355(a)(1). There are three main exceptions:

1. Excess principal amounts of debt securities received over principal surrendered are taxed to the extent of their fair market value. Code Secs. 355(a)(3)(A) and 356(d)(2)(C). This results in a dividend in a spin-off, and a possible capital gain in split-offs and split-ups.
2. If the transaction was principally a device to distribute earnings and profits of the transferor or transferee corporation, the transaction is taxable. Code Sec. 355(a)(1)(B).
3. If boot is received (i.e., property other than stock or securities), it may be taxed as a dividend, if it has the effect of a dividend, or as a gain on the exchange of securities to the extent a gain is realized. Generally, a dividend results in a spin-off since there is no exchange, and a capital gain results in an exchange, be it a split-off or a split-up. Whether or not there is boot, no *loss* can be recognized if Code Sec. 355 applies. Code Sec. 356(c).

EXAMPLE 17.25	Magicworld Inc. incorporates a domestic branch and distributes 100 percent of the new subsidiary to its shareholder, who must give up two shares in Magicworld for each 10 shares in Dragonrider Inc., the new corporation. This is a split-off, a divisive Type D reorganization, resulting from a Code Sec. 351 transfer, followed by meeting the Code Sec. 355 requirements.
	Magicworld recognizes no gain or loss under Code Sec. 361; the shareholder has no gain or loss under Code Sec. 355. The shareholder's basis in the old stock carries over and the holding period tacks on.

General Requirements

The general requirements to be satisfied before Code Sec. 355 will apply may be summarized as follows:

1. **Business purpose.** The transferor (the "old" corporation) must have a substantial business purpose for the transaction.
2. **Continuity of interest.** The pretransaction shareholders need a continuing equity interest in the post-transaction corporation(s).
3. **No "device."** The distribution cannot be primarily a device to avoid dividend treatment to the shareholders.
4. **Corporate control.** The distributor corporation must have Code Sec. 368(c) control (the 80 percent test) of the corporation whose securities it distributes, measured immediately prior to the distribution.
5. **Shareholder control.** Sufficient stock must be distributed to constitute 80 percent control in the hands of the distributees.
6. **Active trade or business.** After the distribution, all surviving corporations must be actively engaged in a trade or business. Also each trade or business must be at least five years old at the time of distribution.

Trade or Business Requirement

The trade or business requirement in a divisive Type D reorganization consists of a two-part test:

1. Both the distributing and the controlled corporation must be engaged in the active conduct of a trade or business immediately after the distribution.
2. These trades or businesses must have been conducted for at least five years. Code Sec. 355(b)(1)(A).

An "active trade or business" does *not* include passive investments, whether in securities or real estate, or the mere ownership or leasing of property (unless significant services are rendered). Reg. §1.355-3(b)(2)(iv). On the other hand, a holding corporation is considered to be conducting the trade or business of its subsidiary if it holds few or no assets other than the stock or securities of its controlled subsidiary. One trade or business can be split in two if both, considered separately, constitute a trade or business. Rev. Rul. 64-147, 1964-1 CB 136.

To constitute an active trade or business, the Regulations contemplate:

1. A specific group of activities
2. A profit motive
3. Management and operational functions
4. The collection of income and the payment of expenses (Reg. §1.355-3(b)(2)(iv)).

The *same* trade or business must have been conducted for at least five years, with two exceptions:

1. A new trade or business can be acquired in a tax-free transaction, such as a reorganization.
2. Control of a corporation, other than by purchase, can be acquired during the five-year period. Code Sec. 355(b)(2).

Applications of Divisive Type D Reorganizations

Under Code Sec. 355, there is no requirement that the shareholders hold on to their new stock. Nor is there a requirement that the distribution be pro rata. The shareholders need not surrender any stock in a spin-off. The distributing corporation may become a minority shareholder in the transferee since it need only distribute 80 percent of the stock in the subsidiary.

Note that if the shareholders sell their new stock or securities soon after receipt, the transaction may fail as a "device" if the sales are pursuant to a predistribution commitment. Code Sec. 355(a)(1)(B) and (2)(A).

The objectives to be accomplished through the means of Code Sec. 355 include the following:

1. **Shareholder Disagreements.** If two shareholders or groups of shareholders have a falling out, the business may be split in two. Two new corporations are formed, and each shareholder or group of shareholders receives all the stock in one of the corporations in return for the stock in the transferor. This can qualify as a split-up.
2. **Antitrust Divestiture.** One of the remedies granted the government in a successful antitrust suit against a private corporation is a divestiture of the prohibited assets. One way to dispose of the division is to incorporate it, then spin it off to the shareholders.
3. **Estate Planning.** A split-up or spin-off involving shareholders of different generations might serve estate planning objectives, such as being part of a gift program, as well as teaching the younger generation the company's operations.

A business purpose must exist. Saving taxes alone does not qualify as a business purpose, but is permissible as *one* purpose.

PLANNING POINTER

A divisive Type D reorganization is an interesting alternative to a redemption or a partial liquidation. If two shareholders wish to split a business in two, it could be done as a split-off or as a redemption. In either case, the assets of one division would be transferred to a new corporation and its stock distributed to one shareholder in redemption of the original stock. If the requirements of Code Sec. 355 are met, the transaction is tax free and the stock and asset bases carry over. In a redemption under Code Sec. 302(b)(3), the corporation pays tax on the increase in value of the distributed assets, and the shareholder pays tax on the gain but receives a fair market value basis for the assets.

¶17,165

GAIN RECOGNIZED IN DIVISIVE TRANSACTIONS

Concerns developed that a purchaser of less than 80 percent of the stock of a parent corporation might attempt to utilize Code Sec. 355 to acquire a subsidiary (or a division incorporated for this purpose) from the parent corporation without the parent incurring any corporate-level tax. For example, the purchaser might acquire stock of the parent equal in value to the value of the desired subsidiary, and later surrender that stock in exchange for stock of the subsidiary in a transaction intended to qualify as a non-pro rata, tax-free split-off. Such a disguised sale of a subsidiary by the parent corporation would not only avoid the recognition of gain to the parent corporation, but would also provide the purchaser with a stepped-up fair market value basis in the subsidiary's stock, possibly enabling the purchaser to make a subsequent disposition of the subsidiary tax free.

EXAMPLE 17.26

Parent owns 100 percent of the stock of Subsidiary. Subsidiary stock has a FMV of $5 million and an adjusted basis of $2 million. Mason Corporation offers to purchase Subsidiary from Parent. If Parent were to sell its Subsidiary stock, Parent would recognize a gain of $3 million. Alternatively, if Mason Corporation purchases $5 million of Parent stock, and Parent subsequently distributes its Subsidiary stock in exchange for Mason's Parent stock, the transaction would qualify as a tax-free split-off. Parent would recognize no gain on the distribution of its Subsidiary stock, and Mason would have a basis of $5 million in the acquired Subsidiary stock.

Legislation sought to prevent such disguised sales by requiring the recognition of corporate-level gain on a distribution of subsidiary stock otherwise qualifying under Code Sec. 355 if, immediately after the distribution, a shareholder holds a 50-percent-or-greater interest in a distributed subsidiary (or the distributing corporation) that is attributable to stock that was acquired by purchase within the five-year period ending on the date of the distribution. Code Sec. 355(d). In such case, the distributing corporation will recognize gain just as if it had sold the distributed stock to the distributee for its fair market value. Thus, in Example 17.26 above, Parent will now recognize $3 million of gain on the distribution of its Subsidiary stock, if Mason Corporation had purchased the Parent stock within the five-year period ending on the date of distribution.

More specifically, a distributing corporation must recognize gain in the case of a *disqualified distribution* of stock or securities in a controlled corporation. For this purpose, a disqualified distribution is any Code Sec. 355 distribution if, immediately after the distribution, any person holds disqualified stock in either the distributing corporation or any distributed controlled corporation constituting a 50-percent-or-greater interest in such corporation. Code Sec. 355(d)(2).

Disqualified stock includes stock in the distributing corporation or any controlled corporation acquired by purchase during the five-year period ending on date of the distribution. Code Sec. 355(d)(3). Additionally, disqualified stock includes stock in any controlled corporation received in the distribution, to the extent that it is attributable to distributions on stock in the distributing corporation acquired by purchase during the five-year period ending on the date of the distribution.

EXAMPLE 17.27

During 2017, Larsen Corporation purchases a 20 percent interest in the stock of Brewing Corporation and a 10 percent interest in the stock of its controlled subsidiary, Spirits Corporation. Subsequently, Brewing distributes 40 percent of the stock of Spirits to Larsen in exchange for Larsen's 20 percent interest in Brewing. Brewing must recognize gain on the distribution of its Spirits stock to Larsen because all 50 percent of the stock of Spirits held by Larsen is disqualified stock.

In determining whether a person holds a 50-percent-or-greater interest, related persons are treated as one person. For example, a corporation and its more-than-50-percent-owned subsidiary (or a husband and wife) are treated as one person. The related party rules that are applied for this purpose are the rules of Code Secs. 267(b), 318(a)(2), and 707(b)(1), substituting 10 percent for 50 percent.

There are additional restrictions on certain spin-offs that are designed to limit the ability of a corporation to follow the structure of *Morris Trust* (66-2 USTC ¶9718 (Code Sec. 355(e)) and, in effect, dispose of a portion of its business to new shareholders without the recognition of gain. If either the controlled or distributing corporation is acquired pursuant to a plan or arrangement in existence on the date of distribution, gain is generally recognized to the distributing corporation as of the date of distribution. Recognition can be avoided if more than 50 percent of the historical shareholders retain ownership in the distributing and acquiring corporations. Acquisitions occurring within the four-year period beginning two years before the date of distribution are presumed to have occurred pursuant to a plan or arrangement. The application of this provision is not restricted to stock acquired by *purchase* but may apply to stock acquired by other means as well.

TAX BLUNDER

Pharmaceuticals Corporation, in an attempt to diversify, purchased all of the stock of Computer Corporation which had been in operation for 10 years. Although profitable, Computer never attained the income targets that had been established for it, and as a result, Pharmaceuticals believed it could maximize shareholder stock value by spinning off the stock of Computer to its shareholders four years after acquisition. Such a transaction would be nontaxable to both Pharmaceuticals as well as its shareholders.

Of course the distribution of the Computer stock fails as a spin-off because the stock had been acquired by Pharmaceuticals in a taxable transaction within the last five years. On the distribution, Pharmaceuticals would be taxed on the stock's appreciation in value, and the fair market value of the Computer stock would be taxed as a dividend to Pharmaceuticals' shareholders. Instead, if Pharmaceuticals had waited one more year and had held the Computer stock for at least five years, the desired tax-free spin-off to shareholders would have been attained.

¶17,217   TYPE E REORGANIZATIONS

Basic Form of Transaction

The Type E reorganization is a recapitalization and the only one of the seven types of reorganizations that always involves only one and the same corporation. Thus, a Type E reorganization has been defined as "the reshuffling of the capital structure within the framework of an existing corporation." *Southwest Consolidated Corp.*, 42-2 USTC ¶9248, 315 U.S. 194, 62 S.Ct. 546 (1942). In a typical situation, one class of securities is exchanged for another (e.g., stock for stock and/or bonds, or bonds for stock and/or bonds). Below are some examples of recapitalizations.

Stock-for-Stock Exchanges

If common stock is exchanged for common stock or preferred stock is exchanged for preferred stock, no gain or loss is recognized. Code Sec. 1036. A shareholder may go from voting to nonvoting stock or vice versa. This is true without regard to the reorganization provisions.

When preferred stock is exchanged for common stock or vice versa, the reorganization provisions come into play. The exchange is tax free *if* the fair market values are equal. Code Sec. 354(a)(1). If there is an excess, the difference will be labeled whatever the facts indicate, such as a gift or compensation for services. Rev. Rul. 77-109, 1977-1 CB 87. As part of an estate plan, a business owner will frequently swap old common stock for a combination of preferred stock with voting rights and a stated redemption price and new common stock, then gift the new common stock to his or her children. This is a tax-free Type E reorganization, but the gift of stock may be subject to federal gift tax.

The conversion of convertible preferred stock into the common stock of the same corporation qualifies as a Type E reorganization. Thus, the conversion is generally tax free, the shareholder's basis carries over, and the holding period tacks on. Part of the stock received may be a dividend, but only if either:

1. Dividend arrearages on the preferred stock are, in effect, paid off with extra common stock or
2. The conversion is part of a plan to increase the proportional ownership interest of a class of shareholders.

TAX BLUNDER

Coral Corp. has 100 shares of Class A common stock outstanding. Frank Juarez owns 50 shares, while his son, Matt, owns 25 shares and his daughter, Megan, owns the remaining 25 shares. In preparation for Frank's retirement, the corporation distributes 50 nonconvertible preferred shares to Frank, and 50 additional shares of common stock to Matt and Megan. Subsequently, Frank gifts his 50 shares of common stock to Matt and Megan. Unfortunately, the stock distributions to Frank, Matt, and Megan will be taxed as a dividend because the stock distributions have resulted in the receipt of preferred stock by some common shareholders while other common shareholders received common stock (see ¶15,032).

Instead, the change in stock ownership to prepare for Frank's retirement could have been accomplished tax free if the transaction had been structured as a corporate reorganization (i.e., a recapitalization). For example, a plan of recapitalization could have been adopted under which each share of Class A common stock was exchanged for either one share of nonconvertible preferred stock, or three shares of new Class B common stock. Then Frank could have exchanged his Class A common stock for preferred stock, and Matt and Megan could have exchanged their Class A common stock for Class B common stock, the exchanges accomplished in a nontaxable transaction.

Debt-for-Stock Exchanges

Somewhat surprisingly, a creditor does not recognize gain or loss when exchanging bonds for stock, be it common or preferred. Reg. §1.368-2(e)(1). This general rule applies to convertible bonds if converted into stock of the debtor corporation but not to the conversion into stock of another corporation. The latter exchange is taxable to both the corporation and the bondholders. Rev. Rul. 69-135, 1969-1 CB 198. A corporation is not taxed when retiring its debt with stock under the general rules (e.g., no gain or loss is recognized when treasury stock is issued for "property"). Code Sec. 1032. However, unless the corporation is insolvent or in bankruptcy, it generally has ordinary income from discharge of indebtedness if stock worth less than the principal of the debt is issued to creditors. Code Sec. 108(e)(10).

Any original issue discount on bonds retired as part of a recapitalization evaporates since the creditors only realize, but do not actually recognize, gain on the receipt of the stock. Rev. Rul. 75-35, 1975-2 CB 272.

PLANNING POINTER

When a creditor of a corporation receives stock with a value that is less than the basis of the debt, the creditor does *not* wish to have a tax-free exchange. In an isolated case, where there is no plan of reorganization, the creditor receives a bad debt deduction. However, any subsequently recognized gain on the stock is ordinary income to the extent of the bad debt deduction under Code Sec. 108(e)(7).

Debt-for-Debt Exchanges

If the principal amount of debt received in a reorganization exceeds the principal amount of debt surrendered, the fair market value of the excess is boot and is taxed accordingly. Code Sec. 356(a)(2).

EXAMPLE 17.28

A bondholder exchanges 10 percent coupon bonds with a principal amount of $10,000 and a basis of $8,000 for 12 percent coupon bonds with a principal value of $10,000 and a fair market value of $9,500. No gain is recognized, despite the realized gain, since there is no excess principal amount of bonds received. Thus, the basis of the old bond carries over to the new bond and the holding period tacks on.

EXAMPLE 17.29

Same as Example 17.28, except the principal amount received is $11,000. Now the realized gain of $1,500 ($9,500 − $8,000) is recognized to the extent of the fair market value of the excess principal amount of bonds received. This fair market value can be determined by multiplying the excess principal amount by the ratio of total fair market value to total principal. In this example, the fair market value of the excess is $864 ($1,000 × ($9,500 ÷ $11,000)). The basis of the new bond is increased by the recognized gain and the holding period of the old bond tacks on.

Stock-for-Debt Exchanges

A shareholder who surrenders stock solely in return for debt instruments has a taxable exchange. There is *no* protection in the reorganization rules. At least two different approaches to taxation exist, depending on the circumstances:

1. If the shareholder surrenders all of the shareholder's stock for debt in the issuing corporation, a complete termination of interest may result. Code Sec. 302(b)(3). Then a capital gain or loss results, computed as the fair market value of the debt received less the adjusted basis in the stock.
2. If the distribution of debt is pro rata and does not reduce a shareholder's interest, the distribution of debt has the effect of a dividend and will be taxed as a dividend to the extent of the shareholder's ratable share of earnings and profits of the distributing corporation. Code Sec. 356(a)(2).

¶17,277 TYPE F REORGANIZATIONS

A Type F reorganization consists of a "mere change in identity, form, or place of organization of one corporation, however effected." Code Sec. 368(a)(1)(F). A Type F reorganization may also meet the definition of a Type A, C, or D reorganization as well, but it will still be treated as a Type F reorganization. Rev. Rul. 57-276, 1957-1 CB 126. Because the "old" corporation continues without change of ownership, the taxable year does not end (Code Sec. 381(b)), net operating losses may be carried back as well as forward (Code Sec. 381(b)), and neither Code Sec. 1244 nor S corporation status will be endangered. Reg. §1.1244(d)-3(d)(1); Rev. Rul. 64-250, 1964-2 CB 333.

EXAMPLE 17.30

Pewter Inc. changes its name to Silverworks Inc. As a result, the shareholders turn in their old stock certificates for new stock certificates with the new name. This is the simplest possible Type F reorganization.

EXAMPLE 17.31	Regal Inc., incorporated in Illinois, wishes to change its state of incorporation to Florida and its name to Kingswood Inc. Regal transfers all its assets to the newly formed Kingswood in exchange for its stock. Regal liquidates by transferring its Kingswood stock to its shareholders and the Regal stock is cancelled. Technically, this transaction may meet the definition of a Type A, C, and an acquisitive Type D reorganization. It is, however, treated as a Type F reorganization.

EXAMPLE 17.32	Five hot dog restaurants transfer all their assets to a new corporation in exchange for stock in order to become the beginning of a national chain. This does *not* qualify as a Type F reorganization since more than one operating corporation is involved. The transaction may be treated as a Code Sec. 351 transaction or an acquisitive Type D reorganization, but no Type F reorganization has occurred.

¶17,285   TYPE G REORGANIZATIONS

The Bankruptcy Tax Act of 1980 added a seventh type of tax-free reorganization, Type G. Requirements are as follows:

1. A debtor corporation must be involved in a receivership, foreclosure, or similar proceeding under state law or a proceeding under Chapter X of the Bankruptcy Act under federal law.
2. The debtor transfers all or part of its assets to another corporation solely in return for stock or securities in such corporation.
3. The stock or securities received must be distributed in a transaction qualifying under Code Sec. 354, 355, or 356.
4. The creditors of the debtor corporation must receive voting stock in the transferee corporation valued at least 80 percent of the debts of the debtor corporation.

If the debtor corporation receives boot, it recognizes a gain to the extent of the lesser of realized gain or value of the boot, unless it is distributed pursuant to the plan of reorganization. Code Sec. 361(b)(1)(A) and (B).

Considerations for Nonrecognition Treatment

¶17,321   REORGANIZATION AS AN ALTERNATIVE TO LIQUIDATION

With a few exceptions, double taxation is the result of a liquidation of a corporation. Double taxation can sometimes be avoided if it is feasible to effect a corporate reorganization. For example, if the shareholders merely wish to change the location of the business, a Type F reorganization may be all that is required. Thus, instead of a liquidation-reincorporation situation, a merger treated as a tax-free reorganization is effected.

EXAMPLE 17.33	An Illinois corporation wants to become a Nevada corporation. There is no need to adopt a plan of liquidation, distribute the assets, and then reincorporate them. Rather, a Nevada corporation is formed by the shareholders, who then merge the Illinois corporation into the new Nevada corporation.

¶17,351   USE OF SUBSIDIARIES IN REORGANIZATIONS

Type A Reorganizations

Rather than acquiring a corporation directly, an acquisition-minded corporation may form a subsidiary to do the acquiring for it. Using a subsidiary provides the following advantages:

1. The parent is not liable for the liabilities of the acquired corporation, all of which must be assumed in a statutory merger since legally the subsidiary is the acquiring corporation.
2. Since the parent is the only shareholder in the subsidiary, no formal consent to the acquisition is needed from the parent corporation's shareholders.

The steps in a typical subsidiary merger are as follows:

Step 1.	The parent transfers the consideration to be paid for the target corporation (e.g., stock in the parent, cash, or other property) to the subsidiary, in exchange for all the stock in the subsidiary.
Step 2.	The subsidiary transfers the consideration to the target corporation in exchange for the target's assets and liabilities.
Step 3.	The target corporation liquidates, and its shareholders receive stock in the parent and other consideration when the target's stock is cancelled.

This is a *triangular* merger and qualifies as a Type A reorganization if three requirements are met:

1. Only parent stock is used (no subsidiary stock is allowed).
2. The transaction would have qualified as a Type A reorganization if the parent had acquired the target directly. Code Sec. 368(a)(2)(D).
3. "Substantially all" of the target corporation's assets are acquired. The IRS's position is that this means at least 90 percent of the value of net assets *and* at least 70 percent of the value of gross assets. Rev. Proc. 79-14, 1979-1 CB 496.

A *reverse* triangular merger is similar to a triangular merger except that the subsidiary is merged into the target. The subsidiary's assets are transferred to the target, and the target corporation's shareholders receive stock in the parent for their stock in the target. The parent receives the stock in the target when the subsidiary's stock is cancelled.

To qualify a *reverse* merger as a Type A reorganization, two additional requirements apply:

1. The target must hold substantially all of the subsidiary's assets, as well as its own, after the merger.
2. The target corporation's former shareholders must give up at least 80 percent control in exchange for voting stock in the parent. Code Sec. 368(a)(2)(E).

Thus, far less flexibility is permitted in comparison to a regular Type A reorganization.

Type B Reorganizations

A Type B reorganization may be effected through the use of a subsidiary if two conditions are met:

1. The parent corporation is in control of the subsidiary, using the standard 80 percent test. Code Sec. 368(c).
2. The subsidiary acquires control of the acquired corporation using solely voting stock of its parent. Code Sec. 368(a)(1)(B). The subsidiary may, or may not, be formed for the purpose of the acquisition.

EXAMPLE 17.34	Furniture Inc. wishes to acquire the stock of Oak Inc. Mahogany Inc. is a wholly owned subsidiary of Furniture. Furniture contributes its voting stock to the capital of Mahogany, which Mahogany then uses to acquire the stock of Oak. After the transaction, Oak is a second-tier subsidiary of Furniture. A Type B reorganization has taken place.

EXAMPLE 17.35	Candymakers Inc. forms a new corporation, Chocolate Inc., and transfers voting convertible preferred stock in Candymakers to Chocolate in exchange for all the stock in Chocolate. Chocolate thereafter acquires control of Vanilla Inc. using the voting stock of Candymakers. Again, a Type B reorganization results.

EXAMPLE 17.36	Vans Inc. is a wholly owned operating subsidiary of Autoworks Inc. Solely for Vans voting stock, Vans acquires control of Wagons Inc. This is *not* a triangular Type B reorganization but a regular Type B reorganization because Vans (as the acquiring corporation) is using its own voting stock. The acquiring corporation may always be a subsidiary or a parent of another corporation.

Type C Reorganizations

As in a Type A or B reorganization, a parent corporation may use a controlled subsidiary to act as the acquiring corporation in a Type C reorganization. The requirements are:

1. The assumption of liabilities and the 20 percent "boot relaxation" rules apply. See ¶17,105.
2. Stock in the subsidiary cannot be used; voting stock of the parent must be used. Code Sec. 368(a)(1)(B).

¶17,351

¶17,375

POSTREORGANIZATION TRANSFERS TO SUBSIDIARIES

Once an acquiring corporation has acquired assets or stock in a reorganization that qualifies as a Type A, B, C, or G reorganization, it may subsequently transfer all or part of the assets or stock to a new or existing controlled subsidiary. Code Sec. 368(a)(2)(C). No waiting period is required.

The transfer is treated as a Code Sec. 351 transfer, rather than as part of the reorganization which is over and done with. This rule provides flexibility in arranging the desired corporate and capital structure of an acquiring corporation subsequent to the acquisition.

Carryover of Tax Attributes

¶17,457

INTRODUCTION

When a corporation acquires the stock of another corporation, such as in a Type B reorganization or in a purchase of stock, the acquired corporation's shareholders change, but the tax status of the acquired corporation generally stays the same. A different situation exists when the acquired corporation is liquidated and the acquiring corporation becomes the owner of the assets. Specific rules govern which tax attributes of the acquired corporation follow the assets, and place limitations on the carryover of beneficial tax attributes. These rules are found in Code Sec. 269 and Code Secs. 381 through 384.

¶17,465

ATTRIBUTE CARRYOVER TRANSACTIONS

The following asset acquisitions result in the carryover of the tax attributes of the acquired corporation:

1. Liquidations of a controlled subsidiary under Code Sec. 332, if the asset bases carry over under Code Sec. 334(b)(1)
2. Type A, C, acquisitive D, F, and G reorganizations (Code Sec. 381(a))

    Note that the following transactions are *not* covered by mandatory carryover:

1. Type B reorganizations because the acquired corporation remains in existence.
2. Divisive Type D reorganizations because one corporation divides into two or more entities. No "new" business is acquired.
3. Type E reorganizations because only one corporation is involved.
4. Transfers to a controlled corporation under Code Sec. 351 because no new business is acquired.

    Under (2) and (4), however, earnings and profits may have to be allocated among the resulting corporations. Code Sec. 312(h); Reg. §§1.312-10 and 1.312-11.

¶17,473

LIMITATIONS ON CARRYOVERS

There are 22 tax attributes or classes of tax attributes listed in Code Sec. 381(c), all of which *must* be carried over (subject to some limitations, discussed below). The most important ones are:

1. Earnings and profits (see ¶17,497)
2. Net operating loss carryovers (see ¶17,481)
3. Accounting methods, including inventory methods, depreciation methods, and installment reporting
4. Tax credit carryovers, notably foreign tax credits and work opportunity credits
5. Capital loss carryovers
6. Excess charitable contributions
7. Items potentially subject to the tax benefit doctrine.

Thus, if the transaction is eligible, *all* attributes must be carried over, whether favorable (e.g., net operating losses) or unfavorable (e.g., earnings and profits).

¶17,481

NET OPERATING LOSS LIMITATION

The taxable year of the acquired corporation, except for Type F reorganizations, ends on the date of the transfer of assets. Code Sec. 381(b). As a result, its net operating loss carryover winds up in the acquiring corporation sometime during the latter's taxable year. The deduction allowed for the acquiring corporation's taxable year during which the reorganization occurred is limited to the acquiring corporation's taxable income allocable to the days after the acquisition date.

EXAMPLE 17.37	Fur Stuffs Inc. acquired Sable Inc.'s assets in a Type C reorganization on October 19, 2017. Both corporations are on the calendar year. If Sable has a net operating loss carryover, only one-fifth (73/365) of Fur Stuff's taxable income can be offset by Sable's NOL carryover. Any unused carryovers are suspended until the following year.

¶17,485 OWNERSHIP CHANGES—ANNUAL LIMITATION

Uniform limitations on NOL carryforwards apply to "new" loss corporations if there has been a more-than-50-percentage-point ownership change as compared to the "old" loss corporation. The limitation rules (which also cover capital loss carryforwards and credits) apply to taxable and nontaxable transactions, including corporate organizations, distributions, redemptions, liquidations, and taxable and tax-free reorganizations (other than Type F). Once an ownership change (ownership and/or equity shift) has occurred, the NOL carryover that may be utilized each year is limited to the long-term tax-exempt rate multiplied by the stock value of the loss corporation immediately prior to the ownership change. Code Sec. 382. For the year of acquisition, the Code Sec. 382 limitation is available only to the extent allocable to days after the acquisition date.

EXAMPLE 17.38	When Mutt Inc. merged into Jeff Inc., Mutt shareholders received 40 percent of Jeff stock in exchange for 100 percent of Mutt stock. An ownership change occurred. Had they received 50 percent or more of the Jeff stock there would have been no ownership change.

EXAMPLE 17.39	Locks Inc. has a stock value of $800,000 and has $2 million of NOLs. At this point, it redeems 60 percent of its outstanding stock that is owned by Jane for $480,000. As a result, the other shareholder, Joe, becomes the sole shareholder. Since Joe's ownership interest is increased by 60 percentage points, from 40 to 100 percent, there has been an ownership change. Therefore, the NOL available to offset income of Locks Inc. in the future is limited annually to $320,000 (the value of the "old" loss corporation is reduced by redemption proceeds in the ownership change transaction) times the long-term tax-exempt rate (published monthly and based on the yield on a diversified pool of general obligation municipal bonds with maturity more than nine years), in this case, 3 percent. Since $320,000 × .03 is $9,600, this becomes the annual limitation.

Continuity of Business Enterprise

Once a more-than-50-percent ownership change occurs, NOL and other carryforwards are completely disallowed, unless there is a "continuity of business enterprise." This requirement may be met in two ways:

1. The "old" loss corporation's historic business is continued for at least two years following the ownership change, or
2. The "old" loss corporation's assets, or at least a significant portion of them, are utilized in a business for at least two years. Code Sec. 382(c).

Changes in location or in key employees are permitted.

Reason for Limitation

By limiting the annual utilization of an NOL carryover to the stock value of the loss corporation times the yield on municipals, the purchaser of tax losses is unable to derive a benefit in excess of the income available by simply selling the stock in the loss corporation and investing the proceeds in municipal bonds. Thus, without reducing the NOL in the aggregate, the spreading out of the carryover is likely to limit abuses and trafficking in tax attributes.

Testing Period

The amount of ownership change is measured during a three-year period known as the "testing" period. The testing period is generally the three-year period preceding an ownership change. However, the testing period does not start until the first day of the first year from which there is a carryover, nor can it start prior to a previous ownership change in excess of 50 percent. Code Sec. 382(i).

Attribution Rules

To determine whether an ownership change has occurred, the following attribution rules apply:

1. Spouses, an individual's parents, grandparents, and children are treated as one shareholder.
2. Stock held by an entity, such as a corporation, partnership, estate, or trust, is treated as owned proportionately by shareholders, partners, and beneficiaries.
3. No attribution is made to entities from owners.
4. Options count as stock if an ownership change would result. Code Sec. 382(l)(3).

Built-In Gains and Losses

If the old loss corporation has a net unrealized built-in gain, the Code Sec. 382 limitation for any recognition period taxable year is increased by the new loss corporation's recognized built-in gain for that taxable year. If the old loss corporation had a net unrealized built-in loss, the recognized built-in loss for any recognition period taxable year is subject to the Sec. 382 limitation just as if it were a prechange NOL.

The amount of net unrealized built-in gain (or loss) is the amount by which the fair market value of the assets of the old loss corporation immediately before an ownership change exceeds (or is less than) the aggregate adjusted basis of those assets at that time. The term "recognition period" means the five-year period beginning on the change date. A loss corporation's net unrealized built-in gain or loss will be treated as zero unless it exceeds the lesser of (1) $10 million, or (2) 15 percent of the fair market value of the loss corporation's assets immediately before the ownership change.

Miscellaneous Provisions

Here is a summary of relevant provisions not previously discussed:

1. If a corporation has both prechange and postchange loss carryforwards, it is allowed to use prechange losses first.
2. Publicly held corporations are protected by a 5 percent shareholder rule applied to public trading. Thus, despite the fact that 60 percent of the shareholders, consisting of under-5-percent owners, sold their stock during a three-year period, the limitations are inapplicable.
3. Ownership transfers due to death, gifts, divorce, or separation, as well as acquisitions by employee stock ownership plans, are not counted as ownership shifts.
4. The loss corporation's value is reduced by any capital contribution made if a principal purpose was to avoid the limitations discussed above. If a capital contribution is made within two years of the change date, the value is automatically reduced.
5. The loss corporation's value is reduced by liquid nonbusiness assets, if in excess of one-third of the value of total assets.
6. Special relief provisions apply to corporations involved in bankruptcy proceedings. Code Sec. 382(l)(5).

¶17,497   EARNINGS AND PROFITS

The acquiring corporation succeeds to the acquired corporation's earnings and profits as of the date of the transfer of assets. This is so whether the balance is positive or negative. However, an acquired deficit can only serve to reduce earnings and profits generated *after* the acquisition. To determine the offset in the year of acquisition, only the pro rata share of earnings allocable to the acquiring corporation's remaining year is relevant. Code Sec. 381(c)(2)(A) and (c)(2)(B).

EXAMPLE 17.40	Hardware Inc. acquires Nuts & Bolts Inc. in a Type A reorganization when 73 days remain in its 365-day taxable year. Nuts & Bolts has a deficit in E&P of $82,000 and Hardware has current E&P of $60,000. Nuts & Bolts' deficit can be used to offset 73/365 × $60,000 of Hardware's current E&P, or $12,000. The remaining deficit is carried forward to offset future earnings of Hardware.

PLANNING POINTER	In a Type A reorganization, there are several limitations on net operating losses and other desirable tax attributes but none on earnings and profits. If E&P are eliminated in a liquidation, other desirable tax attributes are generally eliminated as well. E&P may be an important consideration in structuring a transaction as a liquidation or a reorganization.

Judicial Requirements

¶17,517   ## INTRODUCTION

Whenever a significant nonrecognition provision exists (e.g., like-kind exchange, tax-free incorporation, or tax-free distribution) from a partnership, taxpayers often attempt to structure a transaction that would otherwise result in a taxable gain so that the nonrecognition provision applies. On the other hand, when a loss is realized, an attempt may be made to avoid the nonrecognition provision so as to recognize the loss.

Over the years, the IRS has successfully imposed several judicial requirements on tax-free reorganizations that must be met in addition to the literal compliance with the bare definitions in Code Sec. 368. The main judicially developed doctrines are:

1. Business purpose
2. Continuity of proprietary interest
3. Continuity of the business enterprise
4. Step transactions
5. Liquidation and reincorporation

¶17,525   ## BUSINESS PURPOSE

The business purpose doctrine dates back to a classic Supreme Court case in 1935. *Gregory v. Helvering*, 35-1 USTC ¶9043, 293 U.S. 465, 55 S.Ct. 266 (1935). Mrs. Gregory went through a literal reorganization for the sole purpose of converting a dividend into capital gains. She was successful in the Board of Tax Appeals (now the Tax Court), but lost an appeal, affirmed by the Supreme Court, on the grounds that there was no "real" business purpose. Forming a corporation, issuing stock, transferring assets, etc. may all be disregarded, even if the literal definition of a reorganization is met, if there is no business purpose.

The business purpose requirement is reflected in the Regulations that say in part: "A scheme . . . such as a mere device that puts on the form of a corporate reorganization as a disguise . . . having no business or corporate purpose, is not a plan of reorganization." Reg. §1.368-1(c).

EXAMPLE 17.41   Mr. Gumm runs a highly successful sole proprietorship. He is approached by Spearmint Inc., a publicly owned corporation that wishes to purchase his business for $2 million worth of listed common stock in Spearmint. Since Mr. Gumm's basis in the assets of the business amounts to only $300,000, he would have to recognize $1,700,000 of gain if he sold his business assets. To defer the gain, Mr. Gumm instead incorporates his business under Code Sec. 351, becoming Gumm Inc., whereupon Spearmint acquires the stock in Gumm Inc. in a Type B reorganization. Most likely, the incorporation and the reorganization will be disregarded as having no business purpose, and Mr. Gumm will be treated as having made a taxable sale of the business assets.

The smaller the corporation, the more difficult it is to distinguish between the business purpose of the shareholders and that of the corporation. See *H.S.W. Lewis*, 49-2 USTC ¶9377, 176 F.2d 646 (CA-1 1949). A leading Supreme Court case, however, requires a direct and substantial benefit to the *corporation. J.R. Bazley*, 47-2 USTC ¶9373, 332 U.S. 752, 67 S.Ct. 1489 (1947).

¶17,533   ## CONTINUITY OF PROPRIETARY INTEREST

There is no statutory requirement that the "old" shareholders in the acquired corporation, individually or in the aggregate, receive equity in the acquiring corporation, or that they retain a proprietary interest for any length of time subsequent to the reorganization.

However, over the years, the courts have developed and defined the continuity of proprietary interest doctrine. The main argument is that if the shareholders primarily receive cash and short-term notes, the transaction is in substance a sale, rather than a reorganization. This was articulated by the Supreme Court in two early cases. *Pinellas Ice & Cold Storage Co.*, 3 USTC ¶1023, 287 U.S. 462, 53 S.Ct. 257 (1933); *V.L. LeTulle*, 40-1 USTC ¶9150, 308 U.S. 415, 60 S.Ct. 313 (1940). Even long-term mortgage bonds are considered proceeds from a sale if no equity interest is retained.

Based on these and similar cases, the Regulations refer to the continuity of proprietary interest requirement in this manner: "Requisite to a reorganization . . . a continuity of interest therein on the part of . . .

the owners of the enterprise prior to the reorganization . . . there is not a reorganization if the holders of the stock and securities of the old corporation are merely the holders of short-term notes in the new corporation." Reg. §1.368-1(b).

It may be recalled that the consideration in a Type B reorganization is limited to voting stock, while in a Type C reorganization cash, notes, and other property are subject to a 20 percent limitation. Thus, the continuity of proprietary interest problem exists primarily in Type A statutory mergers and consolidations.

Regulations require a minimum equity participation in the acquiring corporation equal to 40 percent of the fair market value of the stock in the acquired corporation. Reg. §1.368-1(e)(3). The test is an aggregate one. Not every shareholder must remain, nor do the remaining shareholders have to receive equity in the same proportion. The continuity of proprietary interest requirement does not apply to Type E and Type F reorganizations.

¶17,541   CONTINUITY OF THE BUSINESS ENTERPRISE

The Regulations require "a continuity of the business enterprise under modified corporate form." Reg. §1.368-1(b). This requirement does *not* require (1) the retention of assets for any given length of time nor (2) the new corporation to engage in the identical business of its predecessor. To meet the continuity of business enterprise rules, the Regulations require that one of two tests be met:

1. The acquiring corporation must continue the historic business of the acquired corporation or
2. The acquiring corporation must use a significant part of the acquired corporation's assets in its business. Reg. §1.368-1(d).

Note that the continuity of business enterprise requirement may be important in the context of Code Sec. 355 spin-offs, split-offs, and split-ups; in the carryover of tax attributes; and in the liquidation-reincorporation areas, in addition to the reorganization area. However, the continuity of business enterprise requirement is not applicable to Type E and Type F reorganizations.

¶17,549   STEP TRANSACTIONS

The step transaction doctrine means that two or more transactions are mutually dependent so that only the overall end result is significant for tax purposes. Thus, two or more steps, significant in themselves, if viewed in isolation, may be disregarded altogether or consolidated into one transaction. The Supreme Court has stated that "if one transaction is to be characterized as a 'first step,' there must be a binding commitment to take the later steps." *I. Gordon,* 68-1 USTC ¶9383, 391 U.S. 83, 88 S.Ct. 1517 (1968).

The step transaction doctrine is invariably invoked against the taxpayer and is a special case of the general "substance over form" argument. It can be asserted in all areas of taxation. Some examples of its use in the reorganization area are set out below.

| EXAMPLE 17.42 | In a Type C reorganization, the acquiring corporation refuses to acquire certain assets. The unwanted assets are therefore sold or transferred to a new corporation prior to the reorganization. Combining the two transactions into one makes the acquisition taxable for failure to meet the "substantially all" assets requirement. The leading case is *Helvering v. Elkhorn Coal Co.,* 38-1 USTC ¶9238, 95 F.2d 732 (CA-4 1938), cert. denied, 305 U.S. 605, 59 S.Ct. 65. |

| EXAMPLE 17.43 | A Type A reorganization may be reclassified as a purchase of assets, or a Type B reorganization as a purchase of stock, if the acquired corporation's shareholders promptly sell their new stock after the reorganization. |

| EXAMPLE 17.44 | The acquiring corporation purchases stock in the acquired corporation for cash and later acquires the rest of the stock for its own voting stock in an attempted Type B reorganization. If both acquisitions are part of the same plan, the cash is boot and the attempted Type B reorganization fails. |

¶17,557

LIQUIDATION AND REINCORPORATION

Liquidations are taxable, reorganizations are not, in the absence of boot. Earnings and profits generally survive a reorganization but are eliminated in a liquidation. A classic tax avoidance device is to do the following:

1. A corporation distributes its assets in complete liquidation, a transaction that may be largely tax free to the corporation because of loss carryforwards that offset the gains recognized on liquidation and result in capital gains to the shareholders.
2. The corporation is dissolved and its E&P disappears with it, while the shareholders have a fair market value basis in the property.
3. The shareholders retain liquid assets, then start the old business anew in a new or existing corporation, perhaps transferring operating assets to it under Code Sec. 351 or Code Sec. 118 (contribution to capital).

The IRS attacks this type of scheme by:

1. Characterizing the liquidation-reincorporation as a reorganization,
2. Treating the retained assets as boot received in a Type D reorganization, or
3. Disallowing or disregarding the transactions as having no "business purpose," having no substance, being a sham, etc.

¶17,569

ACQUISITIONS MADE TO EVADE OR AVOID INCOME TAX

The IRS is authorized to deny any tax benefit (e.g., deduction, credit, built-in loss, etc.) under the following conditions:

1. A person acquires at least 50 percent control of a corporation, directly or indirectly.
2. A corporation acquires the property of another corporation, receiving a carried-over basis, and neither the corporation nor its shareholders controlled the transferee just before the acquisition.
3. The principal purpose of the acquisition was the evasion and/or avoidance of federal income tax.

Deductions, allowances, or credits may be disallowed in whole or in part. Code Sec. 269(b). Thus, even if a tax benefit, such as a net operating loss, is carried over under Code Sec. 381 and its use restricted under Code Sec. 382(b), it may be disallowed altogether if Code Sec. 269 is applied.

EXAMPLE 17.45

Classic Figurines Inc. acquires the much larger corporation Marble Inc. primarily for the latter's huge net operating loss carryover. The acquisition complies with the state merger law and is technically a Type A reorganization. As soon as practicable, Classic Figurines disposes of the assets of Marble, thus phasing out its business. The NOL will most likely be disallowed altogether under Code Sec. 269. In addition, if Marble's assets are sold for substantially less than their carryover basis, the losses may be disallowed as well, also under Code Sec. 269.

TAX BLUNDER

A service corporation was quite successful. After a few years, the corporation had $500,000 in assets, of which $425,000 were liquid assets not needed in the business. The two owners wanted the funds but did not want dividend income. After some consideration, they did the following:

1. The corporation adopted a plan of complete liquidation.
2. Another corporation was formed.
3. The assets needed in the business were sold for their adjusted basis to the new corporation, which also hired the employees of the old corporation.
4. All liquid assets plus proceeds from the sale were distributed to the shareholders.
5. The shareholders reported capital gain under Code Sec. 331; the "old" corporation reported *no* gain or loss.

The IRS balked and the court decided as follows:

1. Since all necessary operating assets were transferred to another corporation controlled by the shareholders of the transferor, the transaction was an acquisitive Type D reorganization.

2. Therefore, all funds distributed to shareholders were boot and treated as dividends to the extent of E&P in the transferor.
3. Basis of assets carried over to the new corporation
4. The net effect was as if the original corporation had simply paid a dividend. See *J. Smothers*, 81-1 USTC ¶9368, 642 F.2d 894 (CA-5 1981).

Note that there is sometimes a fine line between a liquidation and a reorganization.

SUMMARY

- The purpose of the reorganization provisions is to facilitate changes and adjustments in what remains as a modified corporate structure.
- A reorganization must serve a business purpose, the acquired corporation's shareholders must receive a continuing equity interest in the surviving entity, and the acquiring corporation must continue to use the acquired business assets.
- A corporate reorganization includes the acquisition of stock or assets of one corporation by another, mergers and consolidations under state law, and recapitalizations and divisions of a single corporation.
- Generally no gain or loss is recognized on the exchange of stock or securities in parties to the reorganization.
- The receipt of boot by shareholders may be taxed as a capital gain or as a dividend.
- No gain or loss is recognized to a corporation that transfers its property solely in exchange for stock or securities pursuant to the plan or reorganization.
- Generally all tax attributes of the acquired corporation carry over to the acquiring corporation.

SUMMARY OF RELEVANT CODE SECTIONS

Code Sec. 368 Definitions

Provides the requirements for the seven different types of corporate reorganization.

Code Sec. 354 Nonrecognition to shareholders and security holders

No gain or loss is recognized if stock or securities in a party to a reorganization is exchanged solely for stock or securities in such corporation or in another corporation a party to the reorganization.

Code Sec. 355 Receipt of stock or securities of controlled corporation

No gain or loss is recognized on the receipt of stock or securities if the distribution meets the requirements of a spin-off, split-off, or split-up.

Code Sec. 356 Receipt of additional consideration

A shareholder's or security holder's gain is recognized to the extent of the lesser of the (1) realized gain, or (2) FMV of other property (including the FMV of an excess principal amount of security received). A recognized gain is treated as a dividend if the receipt of boot has the effect of a dividend.

Code Sec. 357 Assumption of corporation's liabilities

The assumption of a corporation's liabilities is generally not treated as money or other property received. Gain is recognized in a Type D reorganization to the extent that total liabilities exceed the total basis of property transferred.

Code Sec. 358 Basis to shareholders and security holders

The basis for stock and securities received equals the basis of stock and securities exchanged, plus gain recognized, and minus boot received.

Code Sec. 361 Nonrecognition of gain or loss to corporations

No gain or loss is recognized if a corporation that is a party to the reorganization exchanges its property solely in exchange for stock or securities in another corporation that is a party to the reorganization.

Code Sec. 362 Basis to corporations

The basis of property acquired in a reorganization equals the transferor's basis increased by any gain recognized to the transferor.

Code Secs. 381-384 Carryovers

A corporation's tax attributes carryover to the acquiring corporation in an acquisitive reorganization, but may be limited in use by Code Secs. 382, 383, and 384.

Code Sec. 269 Denial of tax benefits

Tax benefits may be disallowed if the principal purpose of an acquisition is the evasion or avoidance of federal income tax.

Code Sec. 1032 Issuance of stock

No gain or loss is recognized to a corporation on the receipt of money or other property in exchange for its stock.

QUESTIONS

1. Identify and briefly describe the seven types of corporate reorganization.

2. Which of the types of statutory reorganization are "acquisitive"?

3. Explain the doctrines of "continuity of business enterprise" and "continuity of proprietary interest."

4. Will the continuity of proprietary interest requirement be met if the shareholders of the acquired corporation sell their stock soon after the reorganization?

5. Will an acquiring corporation recognize gain or loss when it issues its stock to acquire the assets or stock of a target corporation in a reorganization?

6. Explain the concept of exchanged basis as it relates to shareholders who exchange stock in corporations that are a party to a reorganization.

7. How do exchanging shareholders and security holders determine their basis for the stock and securities received in a corporate reorganization?

8. When will an exchange of securities of parties to a reorganization result in the receipt of boot? When will a corporate note be treated as a security?

9. When will boot received in a corporate reorganization be treated as a dividend?

10. Define a Type A reorganization, and differentiate between a statutory merger and a consolidation.

11. What are the relative advantages and disadvantages of a Type A reorganization?

12. Can nonvoting stock and securities be used in a Type A reorganization? Is there any limit on the use of boot?

13. What is the definition of control for purposes of a Type B reorganization?

14. What are the relative advantages and disadvantages of a Type B reorganization?

15. How may dissenting minority shareholders of the acquired corporation be bought out for cash in a Type B reorganization?

16. Is there any transfer of the acquired corporation's tax attributes to the acquiring corporation in a Type B reorganization?

17. Define a Type C reorganization and explain its unique requirements.

18. Explain the concept of *substantially all* assets as it applies in the context of a Type C reorganization.

19. Explain the boot relaxation rule of a Type C reorganization.

20. If an acquiring corporation is widely held, how can it avoid obtaining the consent of its shareholders in a Type A reorganization?

21. In what types of reorganization may subsidiaries of the acquiring corporation be used?

22. Prior to being acquired, a transferor corporation spins off its unwanted assets to shareholders. It subsequently transfers its remaining assets to the acquiring corporation solely for voting stock of the acquiring corporation. Could the acquisition qualify as a Type C reorganization? Could the transaction qualify as a Type A reorganization?

23. Define a Type D reorganization and identify its unique requirements.

24. Define and differentiate a spin-off, split-off, and split-up.

25. Explain the difference between a *triangular merger* and a *reverse triangular merger*.

26. Discuss the limitations that may apply to the use of a net operating loss that is acquired in a corporate reorganization.

PROBLEMS

27. Pursuant to a corporate reorganization, Katie exchanged 1,000 shares in Burton Corp. with a basis of $12,000 and a value of $9,500, for stock in Mead Corp. worth $9,000 and cash of $500.
    a. What is Katie's realized and recognized gain or loss from the reorganization?
    b. What is Katie's tax basis for her Mead Corp. stock?

28. Leno Hardware is owned and operated as a sole proprietorship by Larry Leno. The location is excellent, and he is approached by a buyer, Hard Bargains Inc., a national chain of hardware stores. What are the tax consequences in the following situations?
    a. Larry sells the store for cash.
    b. Larry sells the store for marketable stock in Hard Bargains.
    c. Larry incorporates the store and exchanges the stock for shares in Hard Bargains.
    d. Same as (c), but Larry incorporated his hardware store two years earlier.

29. Maxco Inc. wishes to acquire Minnow Inc. The latter has 500,000 shares of common stock outstanding with voting rights and 100,000 shares of nonvoting preferred stock.
    a. How many shares of each class of stock must Maxco acquire to qualify the acquisition as a Type B reorganization?
    b. If Maxco uses its treasury stock to make the acquisition, does it matter how much Maxco paid for the shares?
    c. If Maxco liquidates Minnow soon after the reorganization and acquires Minnow's assets, are the reorganization rules still met?
    d. If Minnow purchased the stock of some minority shareholders for cash just before the reorganization, does Maxco's acquisition still qualify as a Type B reorganization?
    e. If Maxco uses only its voting, convertible preferred stock, is the "solely for voting stock" requirement met?
    f. How can Maxco determine its basis in Minnow's stock if Minnow was publicly held?

30. Reynolds Corp. acquired the assets of Putvan Corp. in a nontaxable merger transaction on December 1, 2017. On the date of acquisition, Putvan had a net operating loss carryover of $500,000. Reynolds had taxable income of $480,000 for its 2017 calendar year without regard to the acquired net operating loss. Assuming Sec. 382 does not apply, how much of the acquired loss can Reynolds use to offset its taxable income for 2017?

31. Choice Corp. decides to incorporate one of its divisions. As a result, assets with a basis of $200,000, but worth $800,000, and liabilities of $325,000 are transferred to a new corporation, Prime Inc., in exchange for all its stock. The stock in Prime is then distributed to the shareholders of Choice.
    a. What gain is realized by Choice Corp.?
    b. What gain is recognized by Choice Corp.?
    c. What is Prime's basis for the assets received from Choice?
    d. What is Choice Corp.'s basis for the stock in Prime?
    e. A shareholder who owns Choice stock with a basis of $4,500 and a fair market value of $7,000, receives stock in Prime worth $2,000. What is her basis and holding period for the Prime stock she received?

32. As part of a Type A reorganization, Hall Corp. transferred property with a value of $15 million and a basis of $8 million, in exchange for $13 million worth of stock in Gate Corp. and $2 million worth of two-year Gate Corp. notes. Hall immediately distributed the Gate stock and Gate notes to its shareholders pursuant to the plan of reorganization. How much income must Hall Corp. recognize as a result of its distribution of the Gate stock and Gate notes to its shareholders?

33. Builders Inc. purchased 40 percent of the stock of Stairways Inc. for cash and acquired the remaining 60 percent for its own voting stock pursuant to a single plan. As soon as practicable, Stairways Inc. liquidates and Builders acquires all of its assets.
    a. Could the acquisition qualify as a Type B reorganization?
    b. Could the acquisition qualify as a Type C reorganization?
    c. Does the liquidation qualify as a Code Sec. 332 liquidation of a subsidiary?

34. Auto Supplies Inc. has earnings and profits of $200,000 and a stock portfolio. It transfers appreciated stock worth $150,000 with a basis of $80,000 to a newly created corporation, Peak Enterprises Inc., for 100 percent of Peak's stock. Auto Supplies distributes the Peak stock equally to its three shareholders who promptly liquidate Peak. What are the tax consequences of the above if the stock portfolio is seven years old?

35. Compute the realized and recognized gain or loss and the new basis in the following transactions, all of which took place pursuant to a plan of recapitalization.
    a. A shareholder exchanged 100 shares of $5 par value preferred stock with a basis of $1,000 for 200 shares of $4 par value common stock worth $800.
    b. A bond holder exchanged a bond with a basis of $800 and a par value of $1,000 and received 50 shares of common stock worth $1,050.
    c. A shareholder exchanged stock with a basis of $2,000 for bonds worth $5,500 and a par value of $4,000.
    d. A bondholder exchanged a bond with a basis of $900 and a par value of $1,000 for another bond with a value of $1,500 and a par value of $1,500.

36. Kelly owns all the stock in Duncan Corp. Her Duncan stock has a basis of $120,000 and a fair market value of $150,000. Duncan Corp. is merged into Munro Corp. Pursuant to the reorganization, Kelly receives Munro preferred stock worth $50,000 and Munro common stock worth $100,000 in exchange for her Duncan Corp. stock.
    a. What is the amount and character of Kelly's realized and recognized gain?
    b. What is Kelly's tax basis for her Munro Corp. preferred stock and common stock?

37. Northwestern Ltd. (NW) acquires the only class of stock of Southeastern Ltd. (SE) from the latter's shareholders. Which of the following independent transactions qualify as a Type B reorganization?
    a. NW issues its voting convertible preferred stock for all of SE's stock.
    b. NW, which has owned 60 percent of SE's stock for eight years, acquires the remaining 40 percent for its voting common treasury stock.
    c. SE redeems the stock of 15 percent of its shareholders with cash, whereupon NW issues its voting common stock for the remaining 85 percent.
    d. NW acquires 80 percent of SE's stock, 78 percent for its voting stock and 2 percent for cash (in lieu of fractional shares).
    e. NW acquires all of SE's stock for its voting common stock plus options to buy more voting common stock.
    f. Same as (a), but NW promptly liquidates SE and acquires its assets.
    g. As part of the same plan, NW acquires 30 percent of the SE stock for cash and the remaining 70 percent for voting stock six months later.

38. Carson Corporation has a basis of $10 million in the stock of its 100-percent-owned subsidiary, Griffen Corporation. Both Carson and Griffen have been actively conducting business for more than five years. In July 2014, Hall Corporation purchased 4 percent of Carson's stock for $50 million. In May 2017, Carson distributed all of its Griffen stock to Hall in redemption of the Carson stock owned by Hall. At the time of the distribution, the Griffen stock was worth $60 million. What are the tax effects of the redemption to Carson Corporation and Hall Corporation?

39. Rose Inc. is an accrual-basis, calendar-year corporation with only voting common stock outstanding. On October 19, 2017, it acquired the assets of Nagg Inc. by issuing 3,000 of its voting common shares in a Type A reorganization. Nagg has a $300,000 net operating loss carryover and the value of its stock is $2 million. Rose's taxable income for the year of acquisition is $280,000. Assume the long-term tax-exempt rate is 3 percent.
    a. What is Rose's net operating loss deduction for the year of acquisition assuming that the Sec. 382 limitation does not apply? For the following year?
    b. What is Rose's net operating loss deduction for the year of acquisition if the Sec. 382 limitation does apply to the acquisition? For the following year?

40. Nardine Corporation acquired Tabor Corporation pursuant to a statutory merger under state law. As a result of the merger, Tabor Corporation's former shareholders received common stock in Nardine having a value of $300,000, long-term bonds of Nardine with a principal amount (and fair market value) of $400,000, and cash of $300,000. What type of reorganization has taken place? Describe the tax consequences to Tabor Corporation, its former shareholders, and Nardine Corporation.

41. Mountain Corporation forms Hill Corporation, and acquires Mound Corporation by merging Mound into Hill Corporation, with the former Mound Corporation shareholders receiving solely voting stock of Mountain Corporation.
    a. What type of reorganization has taken place? Describe the tax consequences to Mound Corporation, its former shareholders, and Mountain Corporation.
    b. How would your answers change if the former Mound shareholders instead received only nonvoting stock of Mountain Corporation?

42. Pursuant to a corporate reorganization, Marcia exchanged stock she owned in Casey Corp. for stock in Mills Corp. valued at $70,000, plus a Mills Corp. bond worth $9,000 (face amount of $10,000). Marcia had paid $71,000 for her stock in Casey 18 months ago.
    a. What is the amount and character of Marcia's recognized gain?
    b. What is Marcia's basis for her Mills Corp. bond?
    c. What is Marcia's basis for her Mills Corp. stock?

43. Green Corporation purchased 100 percent of the outstanding stock of White Corporation during 2015. During 2017, Green Corporation distributes all of its White Corporation stock to Green shareholders. Both Green and White corporations have been in business for more than 10 years.
    a. Describe the tax consequences to Green Corporation and its shareholders.
    b. How would your answer change if Green Corporation had acquired the White Corporation stock in 2015 in a Type B reorganization?

44. Holly, the sole shareholder of Peach Corporation, has a basis for her Peach stock of $500,000. As part of a statutory merger of Peach Corporation into Pear Corporation, Holly exchanges her Peach stock for Pear stock with a fair market value of $1,000,000 and $200,000 in cash. Holly owns a 40 percent interest in Pear Corporation as a result of the merger transaction. Both Peach Corporation and Pear Corporation have accumulated earnings and profits in excess of $2 million.
    a. What is the amount and character of Holly's recognized gain resulting from the merger and the basis for her new Pear stock?
    b. Assume the same facts except that the Pear stock received in the merger gives Holly a 60 percent interest in Pear Corporation. What is the amount and character of Holly's recognized gain resulting from the merger and the basis for her new Pear stock?

45. Wood Corporation is owned equally by two individuals—Allan and Baker. Wood Corporation has two operating divisions, Oak and Pine, that have been conducting business for more than five years. Allan and Baker can no longer agree on the management of Wood Corporation's activities and decide to separate. Baker agrees to a plan whereby the assets of the Pine division worth $800,000 (adjusted basis of $300,000) and liabilities of $100,000 will be transferred to newly formed Nuwood Corporation in exchange for all of Nuwood's stock. The Nuwood stock (having a value of $700,000) will then be distributed to Baker in exchange for all of his Wood Corporation stock having a basis of $200,000.

    a. Will the plan qualify as a corporate reorganization? What type?

    b. What would be the amount of Wood Corporation's recognized gain on the transfer of the Pine division assets to Nuwood? On the distribution of the Nuwood stock to Baker?

    c. What would be the amount and character of Baker's recognized gain on the receipt of the Nuwood stock?

    d. What is the basis of Baker's Nuwood stock?

46. Parent Corporation and its wholly owned Subsidiary Corporation wish to acquire the stock of Target Corporation. Target has outstanding 100,000 shares of common stock and $300,000 of convertible debentures owned by several unrelated individuals. The market price of the Target stock and the conversion ratio of the debentures make it unlikely that any debentures will be converted in the near future.

    a. Parent proposes to acquire the Target stock in exchange for Parent voting stock, and to purchase the Target convertible debentures for cash. Will the cash payment for the Target convertible debentures violate "the solely for voting stock" requirement of Code Sec. 368(a)(1)(B)? Will the "control" requirement be met if Parent purchases only $200,000 of the Target debentures?

    b. What are the tax consequences to the Target debenture holders if they exchange their debentures for Parent corporation debentures instead of cash? Would your answer change if the Target debenture holders exchanged their debentures for Parent voting stock instead of Parent corporation debentures?

    c. Will the transaction qualify as a Type B reorganization if Parent acquires the Target stock solely in exchange for Parent voting stock and then immediately transfers the Target stock to Subsidiary Corporation?

    d. Would the transaction qualify as a Type B reorganization if Parent transferred Parent voting stock to Subsidiary Corporation, and then Subsidiary acquired the Target stock in exchange for Parent voting stock? Would the transaction qualify if Subsidiary acquired the Target stock for a combination of Parent voting stock and Subsidiary voting stock?

47. Metal Corporation owns all of the stock of Iron Corporation, and owns 100 shares of Steel Corporation, which has 1,000 shares of stock outstanding. The 100 shares of Steel were purchased by Metal in 2005. In 2017, Metal merges Iron Corporation into Steel Corporation, with Steel Corporation surviving after the merger. As a result of the merger, Steel's shareholders (other than Metal) exchange 900 shares of Steel stock for Metal Corporation voting stock.

    a. Does the merger of Iron into Steel qualify as a reverse merger under Code Sec. 368(a)(2)(E)?

    b. Assume that Iron had been an operating company and that it transferred 35 percent of its total assets to Metal immediately before being merged into Steel. Will the merger qualify as a reverse merger under Code Sec. 368(a)(2)(E)?

    c. Assume that Metal had purchased 300 shares of Steel during 2005. Would the acquisition of the remaining 700 shares of Steel by merger of Iron into Steel qualify under Code Sec. 368(a)(2)(E)?

    d. Assume that Metal had not purchased any shares of Steel during 2005. Further assume that 25 percent of Steel's shareholders dissent to the merger and wish to receive cash instead of Metal Corporation stock. Can the merger of Iron into Steel still qualify under Code Sec. 368(a)(2)(E) if Metal transfers sufficient cash to buy out the dissenting shareholders?

48. Pursuant to a Type D corporate reorganization, Cheng Corp. transferred some of its assets to newly formed Racine Corp. The assets transferred had a basis of $60,000 and a value of $90,000, and were subject to a liability of $67,000. In exchange for the assets, Cheng Corp. received 100 percent of the stock in Racine which it then distributed to its shareholders in a qualifying spin-off under Section 355. What amount of income must Cheng Corp. recognize as a result of the reorganization?

49. Shipyard Corp. acquired Boatworks Corp. in a Type A reorganization on July 1, 2017. On the date of acquisition, Boatworks had a deficit in its earnings and profits of $30,000. Although Shipyard had no accumulated earnings and profits, its current earnings and profits from its calendar-year 2017 operations totalled $40,000. What amount of the acquired earnings and profits deficit of $30,000 can be used to offset Shipyard's current earnings and profits for 2017?

50. Gate Corp. acquired all of Way Corp's assets in a Type C reorganization on October 19, 2017. On the date of acquisition, Way Corp. had an unused net capital loss of $70,000. Gate Corp. had a net capital gain (computed without regard to any capital loss carryover) of $40,000 for calendar-year 2017. What amount of the acquired net capital loss of $70,000 can be used to offset Gate Corp's net capital gain for 2017?

51. Diamond Corp. acquired all of Emerald Corp's assets in a Type A reorganization on December 31, 2016. On the date of acquisition, Diamond had accumulated earnings and profits of $400,000, and Emerald had an accumulated earnings and profits deficit of $450,000. For calendar-year 2017, Diamond had current earnings and profits of $100,000 and made cash distributions totaling $300,000 to its shareholders. What amount of the $300,000 received by Diamond's shareholders must be reported as dividend income for 2017?

52. Maples Corp., whose outstanding stock is worth $4 million, has a net operating loss carryforward of $1 million. Maples is owned 45 percent by Alan and 55 percent by Cline, who are otherwise unrelated. Because of their managerial differences, it has been decided that Maples will redeem all of Cline's stock in exchange for $2.2 million of cash on December 31, 2016. Assuming the long-term tax-exempt rate is 3 percent, what amount of the net operating loss may Maples Corp. use to offset its taxable income for calendar-year 2017?

53. Tiburon Corp. proposes to acquire Target Corp. in a tax-deferred triangular merger using its 100%-owned Subsidiary Corp. The sole shareholder of Target will receive $350,000 of Tiburon Corp. voting stock and $200,000 cash as a result of the merger.
    a. Can the proposed transaction qualify as a Type A forward triangular merger? Explain.
    b. Can the proposed transaction qualify as a Type A reverse triangular merger? Explain.

54. Denise owns Gal Corp. stock which she purchased ten years ago for $370,000. Pursuant to a plan of corporate reorganization, Gal Corp. will be merged into Lewis Corp. As a result of the merger, Denise receives Lewis Corp. stock valued at $300,000 plus Lewis Corp. bonds valued at $100,000, in exchange for her Gal Corp. stock.
    a. What is Denise's realized gain and recognized gain resulting from the merger?
    b. What is Denise's tax basis for the Lewis Corp. bonds?
    c. What is Denise's tax basis for the Lewis Corp. stock that she received?

55. **Comprehensive Problem.** Determine whether the following transactions qualify as Type C reorganizations:
    a. The acquisition of all assets and liabilities of Bark Inc. by Ark Inc. for 20 percent of Ark's voting preferred stock.
    b. Same as (a), but Ark sells 30 percent of Bark's assets within a week because they are not needed.
    c. The acquisition of all assets of Bark Inc. for $10 million of voting common stock, plus the assumption by Ark Inc. of $15 million of Bark's liabilities.
    d. The acquisition of Bark's assets for $8 million of Ark's voting common, the assumption of $2 million of liabilities, and the payment by Ark of $100,000 cash.
    e. The acquisition of Bark's assets for $50 million of voting, cumulative convertible preferred stock.
    f. Same as (e), except that the consideration consists of bonds convertible at any time into voting common stock.

56. **Comprehensive Problem.** Label the following transactions:
    a. A Nevada corporation formed a corporation in Florida and transferred all assets to it for 100 percent of its stock. It then distributed the stock to its shareholders in cancellation of their Nevada corporation stock and was dissolved.
    b. ABC Corp. acquired all the stock of MNO Corp. for its convertible bonds. All MNO assets were transferred to ABC, whereupon MNO was dissolved.
    c. A corporation issues $30,000 worth of its own voting stock to retire some of its outstanding bonds with a principal amount of $40,000.
    d. Convertible preferred stock is converted into common stock of the issuing corporation.
    e. A corporation incorporates a division and distributes the shares received pro rata to its shareholders.
    f. A corporation distributes preferred stock to common shareholders for each 10 shares of common stock outstanding.

57. **Research Problem.** Mr. Aslak owns all the stock in Shoes Inc., which owns 85 percent of Skiing Inc. Ms. Quinn, the manager of Skiing, wishes to share in the profits of the prosperous firm by buying 5 percent of its stock. Shoes Inc. then distributes its stock interest in Skiing to Mr. Aslak, who then sells a 5 percent interest in Skiing to Ms. Quinn for $15,000. Assume the sale of stock to a key employee has a valid business and corporate purpose.

How would the IRS view the above transaction?

(See Rev. Rul. 69-460, 1969-2 CB 51; Reg. §1.355-2(c).)

58. **Research Problem.** In practice, the number of shares paid for an acquired corporation may be contingent on its future performance (e.g., sales and/or earnings). Perhaps 500,000 shares are "paid" up front, while another 250,000 are placed in escrow, pending certain future events. If such contingent consideration is used in a purported reorganization:

a. Is it still possible to have a tax-free reorganization?

b. Does it matter whether negotiable "certificates of contingent interest" are issued?

c. Does it matter what the motivation is for the deferred arrangement?

(See, e.g., Rev. Rul. 66-112, 1966-1 CB 68; Rev. Proc. 77-37, 1977-2 CB 568.)

18

Accumulated Earnings and Personal Holding Company Taxes

OBJECTIVES

After completing Chapter 18, you should be able to:

1. Explain why the accumulated earnings and personal holding company taxes were enacted.
2. Identify the circumstances under which the two taxes are imposed.
3. Discuss the nature and effect of the two taxes.
4. Compute the amount of the accumulated earnings and personal holding company taxes.
5. Apply planning devices available to avoid, reduce, or defer the incidence of taxation.
6. Explain the similarity of, and differences between, the two taxes.
7. Work with research problems and cases involving the two taxes.

OVERVIEW

The accumulated earnings and personal holding company taxes are penalty taxes enacted to compel C corporations to distribute their taxable income to their shareholders rather than accumulate the income and shelter their shareholders from the individual income tax that they would have to pay if the income were distributed to the shareholders as dividends. Under the Code, the income of a C corporation (unlike the income of a pass-through entity such as a partnership, S corporation, or limited liability company) is taxed twice—once when received by the corporation and a second time when distributed to shareholders as dividends. Without the accumulated earnings and personal holding company taxes, C corporations would have an incentive to retain their income instead of distributing them to shareholders as dividends.

The accumulated earnings tax is imposed on taxable income accumulated by a C corporation in excess of the reasonable needs of the business. What the reasonable needs of a business are varies depending on the facts and circumstance.

The personal holding company tax is imposed on personal holding companies that have undistributed personal holding company income. "Undistributed personal holding company income" is a personal holding company's taxable income, with certain adjustments, reduced by the amount of dividends paid by the corporation.

The two taxes, which are mutually exclusive, are imposed in addition to a corporation's regular income tax. Corporations know when they are subject to the personal holding company tax and what they can do to avoid imposition of the tax because the tax is mechanically applied. By contrast, corporations cannot be certain whether they are subject to the accumulated earnings tax because imposition of that tax depends upon the particular facts and circumstances.

Accumulated Earnings Tax

¶18,001   ## RATE AND NATURE OF TAX

A C corporation's earnings are taxed twice—once when earned by the corporation and a second time when distributed to the corporation's shareholders as dividends. Since one tax is preferable to two, there is obviously an incentive to let the earnings remain in the corporation.

The tax rates applicable to a corporation's taxable income are as follows:

15 percent on the first	$50,000
25 percent on the next	25,000
34 percent on the next	25,000
39 percent on the next	235,000
34 percent on the next	9,665,000
35 percent on the next	5,000,000
38 percent on the next	3,333,333
35 percent on excess over	18,333,333

Thus, if the corporation has $75,000 of taxable income, the average tax rate is only 18.33 percent. This, in itself, is a reason to incorporate a venture if the earnings are not needed currently by the shareholders. Thus, the corporate tax may be viewed as the price to be paid for the indefinite deferral of the second tax on the shareholders. The corporation is then used as a tax shelter.

EXAMPLE 18.1

> Cassandra Glass owns and operates an unincorporated gift shop. This year the store has taxable income of $40,000. Based on that income and her other income, Cassandra is in the 28 percent marginal tax bracket. She has to pay $11,200 in taxes (28% × $40,000 = $11,200) on her income from the gift shop. If she had incorporated her gift shop, she would have had to pay $6,000 in taxes (15% × $40,000 = $6,000) on her income from the gift shop and could have reinvested the $5,200 ($11,200 - $6,000 = $5,200) in tax savings in her business. However, when her business' earnings are distributed to her as dividends, she will have to pay tax on those dividends.

To prevent C corporations from accumulating an excess amount of earnings, Congress enacted the accumulated earnings tax. The accumulated earnings tax is 20 percent of a corporation's accumulated taxable income, which is a corporation's taxable income, with certain adjustments, minus the amount of dividends paid by the corporation and the accumulated earnings credit. Code Secs. 531 and 535.

The accumulated earnings tax is imposed only if a corporation accumulates earnings in excess of the reasonable needs of the business. What the reasonable needs of a business are varies depending on the particular facts and circumstances. The accumulated earnings tax is imposed in addition to other taxes that a corporation must pay, but a corporation may not be subject to both the accumulated earnings tax and the personal holding company tax for the same year. Corporations may avoid imposition of the accumulated earnings tax by distributing their earnings to their shareholders as dividends.

¶18,015   ## BASIS FOR LIABILITY

A C corporation will be subject to the accumulated earnings tax if it satisfies all of the following requirements: Code Secs. 532, 535.

1. It was formed or availed of for the purpose of avoiding income tax being imposed on its shareholders, or the shareholders of another corporation, by permitting earnings and profits to accumulate instead of being distributed.
2. It has accumulated earnings and profits in excess of the reasonable needs of its business.
3. It is not exempt from the tax.

Although the accumulated earnings tax usually is imposed on closely held corporations with few shareholders, it may be imposed on corporations with many shareholders, including publicly held corporations.

Whether or not the accumulated earnings tax applies to a corporation does not depend on the number of the corporation's shareholders. Code Sec. 532(c).

Exempt Corporations

The following types of corporations are not subject to the accumulated earnings tax: Code Sec. 532(b).

1. S corporations. Code Sec. 1363(a).
2. Personal holding companies (as defined by Code Sec. 542, discussed in ¶18,225).
3. Tax-exempt corporations.
4. Passive foreign investment companies (as defined by Code Sec. 1297).

¶18,025   TAX-AVOIDANCE PURPOSE

One of the requirements for a corporation to be subject to the accumulated earnings tax is that the corporation be formed or availed of for the purpose of avoiding income tax being imposed on its shareholders or the shareholders of another corporation. Code Sec. 532(a). Does the tax-avoidance motive have to be the principal purpose for a corporation accumulating earnings and profits in excess of its reasonable business needs? No - the U.S. Supreme Court has held that tax avoidance need only be one of a corporation's purposes in accumulating earnings and profits in excess of its reasonable business needs. *The Donruss Company*, SCt, 69-1 ustc ¶9167, 393 U.S. 297, 89 S.Ct. 501 (1969).

Rebuttable Presumption of Tax Avoidance

A corporation is rebuttably presumed to have been formed or availed of for a tax-avoidance purpose if either of the following is true:

1. The corporation has accumulated earnings and profits in excess of the reasonable needs of its business. Code Sec. 533(a).
2. The corporation is a mere holding or investment company. Code Sec. 533(b).

A corporation is a "holding company" if it has practically no activities except for the holding of property, the collection of income from property, and the investment of income from property. If the corporation's activities include, or consist substantially of, the buying or selling of investment property, the corporation will be considered an "investment company." Reg. §1.533-1(c).

For purposes of determining whether a corporation has accumulated earnings and profits in excess of the reasonable needs of its business, a corporation's liquid assets are valued at their fair market value, less the cost of converting them into cash, not their original cost to the corporation. *Ivan Allen Co.*, 75-2 ustc ¶9557, 422 U.S. 617, 95 S.Ct. 2501 (1975).

Other Evidence of Tax Avoidance

The existence of a tax avoidance purpose for a corporation may be indicated by a variety of circumstances, such as: Reg. §1.533-1(a)(2).

1. Dealings between the corporation and its shareholders, such as personal loans by a corporation to a shareholder or corporate expenditures for the personal benefit of a shareholder.
2. A corporation's investment of its undistributed earnings in assets that have no reasonable connection with the corporation's business.
3. The amount of a corporation's undistributed earnings and profits.

¶18,035   REASONABLE NEEDS OF THE BUSINESS

In order to justify an accumulation of income, there must be a reasonable business need for the accumulation and a definite plan for its use. Since a corporation is given a credit for its reasonable business needs (including reasonably anticipated needs) in figuring the accumulated earnings tax, the resolution of most disputes hinges on this issue.

The statute does not contain a comprehensive definition of reasonable business needs. However, a number of acceptable and unacceptable grounds for accumulating income are listed in the Regulations. Reg. §1.537-2. Acceptable grounds are:

1. Product liability loss reserves
2. Distributions in redemption of stock
3. Business expansion and plant replacement

4. Acquisition of a business through purchase of stock or assets
5. Debt retirement
6. Working capital
7. Investments or loans to suppliers or customers necessary to the maintenance of the corporation's business

The acceptable grounds for accumulating earnings are not limited to those listed in the Regulations. Every business and every industry many have its own reasons for accumulating earnings. Some of these reasons may be extraordinary expenses, self-insurance, lawsuits pending, key-person life insurance, etc.

| EXAMPLE 18.2 | The Glass Gift Shop, Inc. accumulated $200,000 to open a new gift shop. The $200,000 is an accumulation for the reasonable needs of the business. |

Examples of unacceptable reasons for a corporation to accumulate earnings and profits include: Reg. §1.537-1(f).

1. To make personal loans to shareholders or their relatives or friends
2. To expend funds for the personal benefit of the corporation's shareholders
3. To loan money to another corporation in a different business if the same shareholders control both corporations
4. To make investments unrelated to the corporation's business.
5. To provide against unrealistic hazards.

| EXAMPLE 18.3 | Brenda Glass, the sole owner of the Glass Gift Shop, Inc., accumulated $100,000 of the corporation's earnings to pay for her daughter's college education. The $100,000 is not an accumulation for the reasonable needs of the *business*. |

To justify an accumulation for the reasonably anticipated needs of a business, there must be an indication that the future needs of the business require the accumulation, and the corporation must have specific, definite, and feasible plans to use the amount accumulated. Reg. §1.537-1(b)(1).

| EXAMPLE 18.4 | The owners of Birdie Golf Shop, Inc. accumulated $500,000 in earnings. When their accumulation was challenged by the IRS, they justified it by saying that they were saving the money so that they could expand their business whenever they wanted. Although accumulations for the expansion of a business are for the reasonable business needs of a corporation, this accumulation is not because there were no specific, definite, and feasible plans to use the $500,000 to expand the business. |

Working Capital Needs

Corporations may accumulate earnings to meet their need for working capital (i.e., the amount of cash and assets readily convertible into cash needed to meet current expenses and satisfy typical contingencies). Working capital typically is defined as a corporation's current assets minus current liabilities. Courts often use an operating-cycle approach to determine the amount of working capital a corporation needs. An operating cycle consists of the period required to convert cash into raw materials, raw materials into an inventory of marketable products, and the inventory into sales and accounts receivable and, finally, to collect outstanding accounts.

To obtain a crude measure of the working capital needs of a corporation, the Tax Court in the 1960s designed a measure now known as the *Bardahl* formula. *Bardahl Mfg. Corp.,* 24 TCM 1030, CCH Dec. 27,494(M), TC Memo 1965-200; *Bardahl International Corp.,* 25 TCM 935, CCH Dec. 28,064(M), TC Memo 1966-182. This frequently used formula adds inventory and receivables turnover, subtracts payables turnover, and multiplies the result by a corporation's total operating costs for the year. This formula can be expressed mathematically as:

(Inventory Turnover + Accounts Receivable Turnover – Accounts Payable Turnover) × Operating Expenses = Working Capital Portion of Reasonable Business Needs.

The liquidity requirement thus computed qualifies as a reasonable business need.

The formula has been revised and adapted to different industries and to take into account seasonal peaks.

EXAMPLE 18.5

1. If cost of goods sold equals $500,000 and average inventory equals $50,000, inventory turnover in days equals ($50,000 ÷ $500,000) × 360 = 36.
2. If sales equal $800,000 and average receivables equal $200,000, receivables turnover in days equals ($200,000 ÷ $800,000) × 360 = 90.
3. If purchases equal $300,000 and average payables equal $50,000, payables turnover in days equals ($50,000 ÷ $300,000) × 360 = 60.
4. 36 + 90 – 60 = 66.
   The operating cycle expressed as a percentage of a year equals 66 ÷ 360, or 18.33 percent.
5. If other expenses equal $150,000, the working capital need equals ($500,000 + $150,000) × .1833, or $119,145. If actual working capital is less than this, the shortage qualifies as a reasonable business need. Any excess holdings do not qualify under the formula, but may qualify on other grounds.

PLANNING POINTER

Even though excessive inventories and slow receivables collections reduce the accumulated earnings tax, this is hardly a good reason to be in this situation on purpose. Inventory levels should be kept to the minimum attainable level, and receivables should be collected as soon as practicable. The liquid funds resulting therefrom then should be invested productively in the business, and not in passive investments, to the extent possible. The absence of nonbusiness assets defeats the tax regardless of the level of accumulated earnings.

¶18,045   COMPUTING THE AMOUNT OF THE ACCUMULATED EARNINGS TAX

The amount of accumulated earnings tax imposed on a corporation subject to the tax is computed by multiplying the corporation's accumulated taxable income by 20 percent. Code Sec. 531. Interest accrues on the amount of tax owed from the due date (not including extensions) of the corporation's income tax return for the year until the tax is paid. Code Sec. 6601(a), (b)(4).

A corporation's accumulated taxable income for a tax year is computed as follows: Code Sec. 535.

Step 1: Determine the corporation's taxable income for the tax year.

Step 2: Add the following amounts to the corporation's taxable income:

+ Dividends-received deduction.

+ Net operating loss deduction.

+ Any capital loss carryover or carryback.

Step 3: Subtract the following amounts:

– Federal income taxes (not including the accumulated earnings tax or personal holding company tax), to the extent that they exceed the corporation's foreign tax credit for the tax year.

– Foreign income taxes that the corporation could not deduct because a foreign tax credit was taken with respect to the taxes.

– The portion of the corporation's charitable deduction disallowed because it exceeded the percentage limitation.

– The amount of the corporation's capital loss that could not be deducted because it exceeded the corporation's capital gains, reduced by the lesser of nonrecaptured capital gains deductions or the corporation's accumulated earnings and profits at the close of the preceding tax year (unless the corporation is a mere holding or investment company). "Nonrecaptured capital gains deductions" means the difference between the aggregate amount of capital gains deducted by the corporation when computing its accumulated taxable income for tax years beginning after July 18, 1984 and the aggregate amount of the corporation's capital gains recovered for preceding tax years.

– The corporation's net capital gain for the tax year, reduced by the amount of taxes attributable to that net capital gain. The amount of taxes attributable to that net capital gain is the difference between the corporation's federal income taxes (not including the accumulated earnings tax) for the year and what the corporation's federal income taxes would have been if the net capital gain had not been included in the corporation's taxable income for the tax year.

Step 4: Subtract the accumulated earnings credit (defined in ¶18,055).

Step 5: Subtract the dividends-paid deduction (defined in ¶18, 065). The result is the corporation's accumulated taxable income for the tax year.

These adjustments are made to a corporation's taxable income to more accurately reflect the amount actually available to the corporation for business purposes. *Ivan Allen Co.*, 75-2 USTC ¶9557, 422 U.S. 617, 95 S.Ct. 2501 (1975).

EXAMPLE 18.6

Thin Ice, Ltd. had $300,000 of taxable income and paid $100,250 in federal income tax on that taxable income. It had a dividends-received deduction of $10,000 and a net operating loss deduction of $40,000. Its accumulated income credit was $50,000. Its accumulated earnings tax would be calculated as follows:

Taxable income:		$300,000
+	Dividends-received deduction:	$10,000
+	Net operating loss deduction:	$40,000
		$350,000
−	Federal income tax:	$100,250
		$249,750
−	Accumulated income credit:	$50,000
Accumulated taxable income:		$199,750

Accumulated earnings tax = $199,750 × 20% = $39,950

¶18,055   ACCUMULATED EARNINGS CREDIT

Corporations are allowed an accumulated earnings credit against their accumulated taxable income. Code Sec. 535(c). Although denoted as a credit, the accumulated earnings credit actually is a deduction that is subtracted when calculating a corporation's accumulated taxable income.

For corporations other than mere holding and investment companies, the accumulated earnings credit is the greater of the statutory minimum or the amount retained by the corporation for the reasonable needs of its business, minus the deduction allowed corporations for net capital gains. For a mere holding or investment company, the accumulated earnings credit is the amount by which $250,000 exceeds the corporation's accumulated earnings and profits at the close of the preceding tax year.

A minimum amount of $250,000 ($150,000 for personal service corporations in health, law, engineering, architecture, accounting, actuarial science, performing arts, and consulting) may be accumulated by all corporations. This statutory minimum is reduced by accumulated earnings and profits at the end of the previous taxable year.

EXAMPLE 18.7

Toyworld Inc., a chain of toy stores, had accumulated earnings of $190,000 at the end of last year. This year, its accumulated taxable income (prior to the accumualted earnings credit) is $150,000.

If no reasonable needs of the business can be established for the current year, the accumulated earnings credit equals $60,000 ($250,000 – $190,000). Thus, the tax base would be $90,000 ($150,000 – $60,000).

If reasonable needs of the business can be established for the year of $310,000, the credit is the greater of (1) $310,000 – $190,000 or (2) $250,000 – $190,000, or $120,000. Thus, the tax base would be reduced to $30,000 ($150,000 – $120,000). Note that reasonable needs cannot be added to the flat credit of $250,000. To avoid the tax, Toyworld Inc. would have to show a need for $340,000.

Note that once accumulated earnings exceed $250,000, it is necessary to show a business need for every dollar of the excess plus the amount of current earnings to avoid the tax.

¶18,065   DIVIDENDS-PAID DEDUCTION

The purpose of the accumulated earnings tax is to discourage the retention of after-tax income beyond the reasonable needs of the business. Only amounts that could have been distributed as dividends are taxed. As a result, a deduction is granted for the following dividends:

1. Dividends actually paid during the taxable year that are taxable as ordinary income to the shareholders. Code Secs. 561(a) and 562(a).

2. Dividends taxable as ordinary income distributed within 2 1/2 months after the end of the taxable year. Code Sec. Secs. 561(a)(1), 562(a) and 563(a).
3. Amounts labeled *consent dividends* in the corporate tax return for the taxable year. Code Secs. 561(a)(2) and 565(a). A consent dividend is an amount on which the shareholder agrees to be taxed as a dividend although it is *not* actually distributed. As a result, the shareholder is deemed to have received the dividend, then to have contributed it to the capital of the corporation. The shareholder's stock basis is increased accordingly. Consent dividends are appropriate when the corporation has limited liquid assets.

EXAMPLE 18.8 Myra Greene agrees to a consent dividend from Myra's Food Shop Inc. on a timely filed corporate tax return for the previous year in the amount of $10,000. The corporation's accumulated taxable income is reduced by $10,000, Myra reports $10,000 in ordinary dividend income, and her basis in her stock is increased by $10,000. To pay the tax, Myra must provide funds from other sources, since no cash was received from the corporation.

Personal Holding Company Tax

¶18,201 RATE AND NATURE OF TAX

If a C corporation in any given year meets the definition of a personal holding company (PHC), a flat 20 percent tax is imposed on its undistributed personal holding company income. Code Sec. 541.

Unlike the accumulated earnings tax, the personal holding company tax is self-assessed (i.e., payable at the same time that a corporation files its regular corporate income tax return) —on Schedule PH (U.S. Personal Holding Company (PHC) Tax) for IRS Form 1120 (U.S. Corporation Income Tax Return). Like the accumulated earnings tax, the personal holding company tax is imposed in addition to the regular corporate income tax. Unlike the accumulated earnings tax, there is no credit reducing the tax base on which the tax is imposed. The personal holding company tax is imposed on the personal holding company's first dollar of undistributed personal holding company income.

To be vulnerable to the tax, the corporation must be controlled by five or fewer individuals and have predominantly investment-type income (other than capital gains). The tax will never have to be paid if sufficient dividends are paid, are deemed to be paid, or are paid retroactively.

EXAMPLE 18.9 Extra Fun Party Supplies Inc. is a personal holding company with undistributed personal holding company income of $20,000. A personal holding company tax of 20 percent, or $4,000, is payable in addition to the regular corporate tax.

¶18,215 REASON FOR THE TAX

If a high tax bracket individual incorporates a stock portfolio and reinvests all dividends, in the absence of the personal holding company tax rules, many tax-avoiding results may be accomplished. For example, seventy percent of dividends received from domestic corporations are tax free. Code Sec. 243. The remaining 30 percent are taxed at rates starting at 15 percent on the first $50,000. Thus, the tax on $100,000 of dividends would be $100,000 × .30 × .15, or $4,500, a rate of 4.5 percent. Eventually, the corporation can liquidate, resulting in a capital gains tax at the shareholder level. Code Sec. 331. Alternatively, the shareholder dies and the shareholder's heirs receive a stock basis equal to fair market value, thus escaping the capital gains tax altogether. Code Sec. 1014.

The congressional answer to this potential abuse was to impose a tax on the corporation's undistributed personal holding company income, effectively forcing the corporation to distribute the dividends to the shareholder. Thus, the personal holding company tax, will represent a direct, out-of-pocket loss to the shareholders.

EXAMPLE 18.10 Excel Ltd. is a personal holding company and has undistributed personal holding company income of $100 this year. Excel must file Form 1120, Schedule PH and pay $15 in personal holding company tax without prompting by the IRS. This is in addition to the regular corporate tax.

¶18,225   PERSONAL HOLDING COMPANY DEFINED

To be classified as a personal holding company, a corporation must meet the following two tests for for the tax year (and not qualify as a corporation exempt from the personal holding company tax):

1. The *stock ownership test.* Five or fewer individuals must own more than 50 percent of the value of the outstanding stock, actually or constructively, at any time during the second half of the taxable year. Code Sec. 542(a)(2). Rules for determining stock ownership are discussed in ¶18,235.
2. The personal holding company *income test.* At least 60 percent of the corporation's adjusted ordinary gross income (defined in ¶18,255) for the tax year must be personal holding company income (defined in ¶18,265). Code Sec. 542(a)(1).

A corporation may meet these tests one year and not another. It is important to recognize that meeting the definition of a personal holding company does *not* mean that any additional tax is due. Classification is merely a condition for the tax to be imposed. The personal holding company tax is based on *undistributed personal holding company income.* To a corporation distributing all of its earnings, both the personal holding company tax and the accumulated earnings tax are irrelevant.

EXAMPLE 18.11	Comfort Bedding Inc. is owned equally by eight family members. The stock ownership test is met. Eighty percent of adjusted ordinary gross income is comprised of dividends from other corporations. Comfort Bedding meets the definition of a personal holding company. However, no personal holding company tax is payable, unless Comfort Bedding has "*undistributed* personal holding income" during a year it meets the definition of a personal holding company.

Excepted Corporations

The following types of corporations are excepted from the definition of personal holding company: Code Sec. 542(c).

1. Tax-exempt corporations.
2. Banks and domestic building and loan associations.
3. Life insurance companies.
4. Surety companies.
5. Foreign corporations.
6. Certain lending and finance companies.
7. Certain small business investment companies operating under the Small Business Investment Act of 1958.
8. Corporations subject to the jurisdiction of a bankruptcy court in a bankruptcy case (unless a major purpose of instituting or continuing the bankruptcy case is to avoid the personal holding company tax).

Although not excepted from the definition of personal holding company, S corporations are excepted from the personal holidng company tax. Code Sec. 1363(a).

EXAMPLE 18.12	Cordelia Crafts opened a craft store. She incorporated the store and made an S elecion. Because her corporation is an S corporation, it is not subject to the personal holding company tax.

¶18,235   STOCK OWNERSHIP TEST

As previously discussed, one of the requirements for a corporation to qualify as a personal holding company for a tax year is that more than 50 percent of the value of the corporation's outstanding stock must have been owned, directly or indirectly, by no more than five individuals at any time during the last half of the tax year. Code Sec. 542(a)(2).

PLANNING POINTER	If 10 or more unrelated individuals own an equal number of shares, the stock ownership test cannot be met, by definition (because no five individuals would own more than 50 percent of the value of the corporation's outstanding stock).

For purposes of the stock ownership requirement, the following organizations are considered individuals:

1. Qualified pension, profit-sharing, and stock bonus plans described in Code Sec. 401(a).
2. Trusts described in Code Sec. 501(c)(17) that provide for payment of supplemental unemployment compensation under certain conditions.
3. Private foundations [defined in Code Sec. 509(a)].
4. The portion of a trust permanently set aside or used exclusively for charitable purposes.

Constructive ownership rules are applied to determine what stock is owned indirectly by an individual. Code Sec. 544. Indirect ownership does not apply if the shareholders are unrelated, but this is unlikely in a closely held corporation. The constructive ownership rules are as follows:

1. Stock owned directly or indirectly by or for members of an individual's family (brothers, sisters, spouse, ancestors, and lineal descendants) is considered owned by such individual.
2. Stock owned directly or indirectly by or for a corporation, partnership, estate, or trust is considered owned proportionately by the shareholders, partners, or beneficiaries.
3. An individual is considered to own stock owned, directly or indirectly, by or for the individual's partner.
4. If a person has an option to acquire stock, the stock subject to the option will be considered owned by that person.
5. Stock considered constructively owned by a person under Rule 2 or Rule 4 is treated as actually owned by that person for purposes of applying Rules 1, 2, and 3. However, stock treated as constructively owned by an individual under Rules 2 and 3 will not be treated as owned by that individual for purposes of applying those rules to make someone else the constructive owner of that stock.
6. If stock can be considered owned by an individual under Rule 4 or under Rule 2 or Rule 3, it will be considered owned by the individual under Rule 4.

For purposes of determining what stock of a corporation is outstanding, outstanding securities convertible into the corporation's stock (whether or not the securities can be converted into stock during the tax year) are considered outstanding stock of the corporation. If some of the outstanding securities can be converted at a later date than others, the securities having the earlier conversion date may be treated as outstanding stock even though others are not so treated, but no convertible securities may be treated as outstanding stock unless all outstanding convertible securities with a prior conversion date also are treated as outstanding stock. Code Sec. 544(b).

EXAMPLE 18.13

Two parents and their children own all of the stock in a corporation. Each individual is deemed to own 300 percent of the stock.

¶18,245   PERSONAL HOLDING COMPANY INCOME TEST

To meet the personal holding company income test, 60 percent or more of the corporation's adjusted ordinary gross income (AOGI) must constitute personal holding company income (PHCI). Thus, if:

$$\frac{\text{PHCI}}{\text{AOGI}} \geq .60, \text{ the personal holding company income test is met.}$$

What constitutes PHC income is discussed in ¶18,265. What constitutes adjusted ordinary gross income is discussed in ¶18,255.

EXAMPLE 18.14

Auto Stereo Inc. has $100,000 of adjusted ordinary gross income and $59,000 of personal holding company income. Because the corporation's personal holding company income represents $59,000 ÷ $100,000 = 59% of its adjusted ordinary gross income, the corporation is not a PHC and cannot be subject to the PHC tax. This is true even though the only income after expenses may be from personal holding company income. Another $2,500 in income that constitutes both adjusted ordinary gross income and personal holding company income, however, would make Auto Stereo Inc. a PHC ($61,500 ÷ $102,500 = .60).

¶18,255   ORDINARY GROSS INCOME AND ADJUSTED ORDINARY GROSS INCOME

Corporations must calculate the amount of their ordinary gross income to determine their adjusted ordinary gross income and to determine whether certain items of income can be excluded from their personal holding company (PHC) income. Corporations must calculate the amount of their adjusted ordinary gross income to determine whether they satisfy the PHC income requirement (one of the tests for determining whether a corporation is a personal holding company) and whether certain items of income may be excluded from their PHC income.

Ordinary Gross Income

A corporation's ordinary gross income is its gross income minus the following amounts: Code Sec. 543(b)(1).

1. Gains from the sale or other disposition of capital assets.
2. Gains from the sale or other disposition of Section 1231(b) property.

Adjusted Ordinary Gross Income

A corporation's adjusted ordinary gross income is its ordinary gross income minus the following amounts: Code Sec. 543(b)(2).

1. *Deductions allocable to rents.* Deductions allocable to a corporation's gross income from rents for depreciation and amortization of property (other than tangible personal property not customarily retained by any one lessee for more than three years), property taxes, interest, and rent.
2. *Deductions allocable to certain royalties and working interests in oil and gas wells.* Deductions allocable to a corporation's gross income from mineral, oil, and gas royalties, and from gross income from working interests in an oil or gas well, for depreciation, amortization, depletion, property and severance taxes, interest, and rent.
3. *Interest.* Interest on direct obligations of the U.S. held for sale to customers in the ordinary course of trade or business if the corporation is a dealer making a primary market for such obligations and interest on condemnation awards, judgments, and tax refunds.
4. *Deductions allocable to certain amounts not counted as rent.* Deductions allocable to compensation for the use of, or the right to use, any tangible personal property manufactured or produced by a corporation engaged in substantial manufacturing or production of that type of tangible personal property if the deductions are for depreciation or amortization of property (other than tangible personal property not customarily retained by any one lessee for more than three years), property taxes, interest, or rent.

¶18,265   PERSONAL HOLDING COMPANY INCOME

Corporations must calculate the amount of their personal holding company (PHC) income for the tax year to determine whether they satisfy the personal holding company income test (discussed in ¶18,245), one of two tests used to determine whether a corporation should be classified as a personal holding company. Code Sec. 542(a)(1).

A corporation's PHC income is the portion of its adjusted ordinary gross income (defined in ¶18,255) that consists of the following amounts: Code Sec. 543(a).

Dividends. Dividends must be included in a corporation's PHC income.

Interest. Interest must be included in a corporation's PHC income unless it constitutes any of the following:

1. Rent.
2. Interest on amounts set aside in a reserve fund under Section 511 or 607 of the Merchant Marine Act of 1936.
3. Interest received by a broker or dealer in connection with (a) any securities or money market instruments held as property held primarily for sale to customers in the ordinary course of business, (b) margin accounts, or (c) any financing for a customer secured by securities or money market instruments.

Royalties. Royalties (other than mineral, oil, or gas royalties or copyright royalties - for which there are special rules) must be included in a corporation's PHC income.

Mineral, oil, and gas royalties. Adjusted income from mineral, oil, and gas royalties must be included in a corporation's PHC income unless all three of the following tests are satisfied:

1. *Test 1.* The corporation's adjusted income from mineral, oil, and gas royalties is 50 percent or more of its adjusted ordinary gross income.
2. *Test 2.* The corporation's PHC income does not exceed 10 percent of its ordinary gross income. For this purpose, PHC income includes copyright royalties and adjusted income from rents but does not include adjusted mineral, oil, and gas royalties.
3. *Test 3.* The sum of the corporation's deduction for trade or business expenses (other than deductions for compensation for personal services rendered shareholders and deductions specifically allowable under provisions other than Code Sec. 162) equals or exceeds 15 percent of the corporation's adjusted ordinary gross income.

"Adjusted income from mineral, oil, and gas royalties" means gross income from mineral, oil, and gas royalties (including production payments and overriding royalties), reduced by depreciation, amortization, depletion, property and severance taxes, interest, and rent with respect to such royalties. Code Sec. 543(b)(4).

Copyright royalties. Copyright royalties must be included in a corporation's PHC income unless all three of the following tests are satisfied:

1. *Test 1.* The corporation's income from copyright royalties is at least 50 percent of its ordinary gross income. For purposes of this test, copyright royalties do not include royalties received for the use of, or right to use, copyrights or interests in copyrights on works created in whole or in part by any shareholder.
2. *Test 2.* The corporation's PHC income does not exceed 10 percent of its ordinary gross income. For purposes of this test, PHC income includes adjusted income from rents, adjusted income from mineral, oil, and gas royalties, and copyright royalties for the use of, or right to use, copyrights on works created in whole or in part by any shareholder owning more than 10 percent of the corporation's stock. PHC income does not include other copyright royalties or dividends from a corporation if the corporation paying the dividends meets Test 1 and Test 3 and the corporation owns at least 50 percent (by vote and value) the stock of the corporation paying the dividends.
3. *Test 3.* The sum of the corporation's deductions that are allocable to such royalties and that are allowable under Code Sec. 162 as trade or business expenses (other than deductions for compensation for personal services rendered by shareholders, deductions for royalties paid or accrued, and deductions specifically allowable under Code sections other than Code Sec. 162) equals or exceeds 25 percent of the amount by which the corporation's ordinary gross income exceeds the sum of the royalties paid or accrued and depreciation deductions allowable with respect to copyright royalties.

Computer software royalties. Royalties received in connection with the licensing of computer software must be included in PHC income unless all four of the following tests are satisfied: Code Sec. 543(d).

1. *Test 1.* The corporation is engaged in the active business of developing, manufacturing, or producing computer software.
2. *Test 2.* The royalties constitute 50 percent or more of the corporation's ordinary gross income for the tax year.
3. *Test 3.* Either (a) the corporation's total allowable deductions under Code Secs. 162 (for trade or business expenses), 174 (for research expenditures), and 195 (for start-up expenditures) allocable to the computer software business are 25 percent or more of its ordinary gross income or (b) the corporation's average of such deductions for the five tax years ending with the current tax year is 25 percent or more of its average ordinary gross income for that period.
4. *Test 4.* The sum of the corporation's taxable distributions and deduction for dividends paid after the end of the tax year is at least equal to the difference between its PHC income and 10 percent of its ordinary gross income. For purposes of this test, "PHC income" has a special definition provided by Code Sec. 543(d)(5)(B).

Annuities. Amounts received as annuities must be included in a corporation's PHC income.

Rents. Adjusted income from rents must be included in a corporation's PHC income unless both of the following tests are met:

1. The corporation's adjusted income from rents is at least 50 percent of its adjusted ordinary gross income.
2. The sum of the dividends paid during the tax year, the dividends considered paid on the last day of the tax year, and consent dividends for the tax year equals or exceeds the amount by which the

corporation's PHC income exceeds 10 percent of the corporation's ordinary gross income. For this purpose, PHC income includes copyright royalties and adjusted income from mineral, oil, and gas royalties but does include adjusted income from rents or compensation received for use of corporation property by a 25 percent or more shareholder.

"Adjusted income from rents" means gross income from rents, reduced by depreciation, amortization, property taxes, interest, and rent allocable to the gross income. Code Sec. 543(b)(3).

Use of corporate property by shareholders. A corporation's PHC income includes compensation received for the use of, or right to use, tangible property of the corporation by or for an individual who at any time during the tax year directly or indirectly owned at least 25 percent in value of the corporation's outstanding stock unless the corporation's PHC income does not exceed 10 percent of its ordinary gross income. For purposes of this limitation, PHC income has a special definition provided by Code Sec. 543(a)(6)(C).

Personal service contracts. PHC income includes amounts received under a contract that requires the corporation to furnish personal services if any person other than the corporation has the right to designate the individual who is to perform the services, or if the individual who is to perform the services is designated in the contract, and the individual who has performed, is to perform, or may be designated to perform such services directly or indirectly owned 25 percent or more in value of the corporation's outstanding stock at any time during the tax year. Also included in PHC income are amounts received from the sale or other disposition of such a contract.

EXAMPLE 18.15   Joseph Sennetti is a professor of electrical engineering. He incorporates his consulting practice and owns all of the stock. If Joseph's corporation enters into a contract with Alpha Corporation, Inc. and the contract designates Joseph as the person who will perform consulting services or gives Alpha Corporation the right to designate who will perform consulting services, amounts paid pursuant to the contract will be PHC income. However, if the contract between Joseph's corporation and Alpha Corporation does not designate Joseph as the person to perform consulting services or give Alpha Corporation the right to decide who shall perform consulting services, none of the amounts paid pursuant to the contract will be treated as PHC income, even though Joseph is the only person employed by his corporation to perform consulting services. Rev. Rul. 75-250, 1975-1 CB 172.

Produced film rents. Produced film rents must be included in PHC income unless the rents constitute at least 50 percent of the corporation's ordinary gross income.

Income from Estates and Trusts. A corporation's PHC income includes amounts that have to be included in a corporation's taxable income as the beneficiary of an estate or the beneficiary or grantor of a trust.

Note that the effect of the definition of personal holding company income is to prevent companies engaged in certain types of activities from being classified as personal holding companies. For example:

1.   Companies whos principal source of income is rental income.
2.   Companies actively engaged in developing, manufacturing, or producing computer software.
3.   Publishers whose principal source of income is copyright royalties.
4.   Companies whose principal source of income is mineral, oil, and gas royalties.
5.   Movie production companies.

PLANNING
POINTER If the stock ownership test is met and dividends are not to be paid, the income ratio test becomes crucial. To decrease the income ratio, the numerator must be decreased and/or the denominator increased. The following observations may be made:

1. Capital gains, Section 1231 gains, and tax-exempt interest *do* improve the ratio since they are excluded from both the numerator and the denominator. For example, if

$$\frac{PHCI}{ADGI} = \frac{100}{150} = .667$$

Then, instead of taxable interest, $50 is tax exempt and the ratio becomes

$$\frac{50}{100} = .50$$

2. Growth stock paying little or no dividends but with appreciation potential will improve the ratio.
3. If personal services are rendered, no one outside the corporation should be able to designate the individual to render the service, thus improving the ratio.

¶18,275   REAL ESTATE COMPANIES

An important escape hatch from the definition of a personal holding company is provided for real estate companies. Corporations that rent real property can exclude their adjusted income from rents from their personal holding company (PHC) income (and thus avoid classification as a personal holding company) if both of the following tests are satisfied: Code Sec. 542(a)(2).

1. Test 1. Their adjusted income from rents constitutes 50 percent or more of their adjusted ordinary gross income.
2. Test 2. The sum of the dividends paid during the tax year, dividends considered paid on the last day of the year, and consent dividends for the tax year equals or exceeds the amount by which their PHC income for the year exceeds 10 percent of their ordinary gross income. For purposes of this test, PHC income is computed without regard to adjusted income from rents and amounts received as compensation for use of corporate property by shareholders but includes copyright royalties and adjusted income from mineral, oil, and gas royalties.

This rule can be illustrated by the following example:

EXAMPLE 18.16   Office Space Ltd. generated the following items of income and deductions last year:

Rent income	$40,000
Depreciation	15,000
Property taxes	4,000
Mortgage interest	12,000
Other business expenses	7,000
Dividends received	8,000
Long-term capital gain	5,000
Dividends paid	4,000

Ordinary gross income equals $48,000 ($40,000 + $8,000). Adjusted ordinary gross income equals $17,000 ($48,000 – $15,000 – $4,000 – $12,000). Adjusted income from rents equals $9,000 ($40,000 – $15,000 – $4,000 – $12,000). To determine whether the corporation can exclude its $9,000 adjusted income from rents from its PHC income, two tests must be satisfied. To satisfy the first test, the corporation's adjusted income from rents ($9,000) must constitute 50 percent or more of the corporation's adjusted ordinary gross income ($17,000). Because $9,000 ÷ $17,000

= 53%, the first test is satisfied. To satisfy the second test, the dividends paid by the corporation ($4,000) must exceed the difference between the corporation's PHC income for the year (computed without regard to adjusted income from rents), $17,000 - $9,000 = $8,000, and 10 percent of the corporation's ordinary gross income ($48,000), 10% × $48,000 = $4,800. Because the amount of dividends paid ($4,000) exceeds $8,000 - $4,800 = $3,200, the second test is satisfied. Therefore, the corporation may exclude its adjusted income from rents from its PHC income. Because the ratio between the corporation's PHC income ($8,000) and adjusted ordinary gross income ($17,000), $8,000 ÷ $17,000 = 47%, is less than 60 percent, the corporation fails the PHC income requirement and does not qualify as a personal holding company.

¶18,285   CALCULATING THE AMOUNT OF THE PERSONAL HOLDING COMPANY TAX

Once a corporation meets the ownership and income tests and is classified as a personal holding company, a 20 percent tax is due on "undistributed personal holding company income," if any. Code Sec. 545. Corporations use Schedule PH (U.S. Personal Holding Company (PHC) Tax) for IRS Form 1120 (U.S. Corporation Income Tax Return) to compute the amount of personal holding company tax that they owe for the tax year.

A corporation's undistributed personal holding company (PHC) income for a tax year is computed as follows: Code Sec. 545.

Step 1:	**Determine the amount of the corporation's taxable income.**
Step 2:	**Add the following amounts:**
+	Net operating loss deduction.
+	Dividends-received deduction.
+	Excess expenses and depreciation. The amount (if any) by which the trade or business expenses and depreciation allocable to the operation and maintenance of property that the corporation owned or operated exceeded the rent or other compensation received by the corporation for the use of, or the right to use, the property, unless the corporation establishes that the rent or other compensation received was the highest obtainable (or, if none was received, that none was obtainable), the property was held in the course of a business carried on bona fide for profit, and either there was reasonable expectation that the operation of the property would result in a profit or that the property was necessary to conduct the corporation's business.
Step 3:	**Subtract the following amounts:**
–	Federal income taxes accrued during the tax year (not including the accumulated earnings or personal holding company taxes).
–	Income, war profits, and excess profits taxes accrued (or deemed paid) during the tax year to foreign countries and U.S. possessions (even though a foreign tax credit was claimed for such taxes).
–	Charitable contributions that could not be deducted because of the 10 percent limitation on contributions by corporations (but not in excess of the percentage limitations on contributions by individuals).
–	Net operating loss for the preceding year (calculated without taking the dividends-received deduction).
–	Net capital gain, minus the amount of income taxes attributable to that net capital gain. The amount of income taxes attributable to that net capital gain is the difference between the amount of income taxes (other than the personal holding company tax) imposed for the tax year minus the amount of such taxes computed without including the net capital gain in taxable income.
Step 4:	**Subtract the dividends-paid deduction (discussed in ¶18,295). The result is a corporation's undistributed PHC income.**

| EXAMPLE 18.17 | Stett Ltd., a PHC, paid $50,000 in taxes on $150,000 in taxable income. Taxable income included $40,000 in domestic dividends and a Section 1231 gain of $15,000 (on which $5,000 of tax was paid). Dividends paid for the year amounted to $60,000. |

The computation of the PHC tax is as follows:

	Taxable income	$150,000
−	Taxes payable	50,000
−	Net capital gains after tax	10,000
+	Dividends-received deduction (70% of $40,000)	28,000
=	Adjusted taxable income	$118,000
−	Dividends-paid deduction	60,000
=	Undistributed personal holding company income	$58,000
	PHC tax 20% × $58,000 =	$11,600

| KEYSTONE PROBLEM | Consider the most likely effect on the accumulated earnings tax and personal holding company tax, as well as corporate shareholder transactions, under the following circumstances:

1. E&P is abolished and all distributions to shareholders are taxed as long-term capital gain.
2. Same as (1), except distributions are taxed as ordinary income. |

¶18,295   DIVIDENDS-PAID DEDUCTION

The tax on undistributed personal holding company income is rarely paid since five kinds of dividends are deductible to arrive at the tax base.

Dividends Paid During the Tax Year

The dividends-paid deduction includes dividends paid during the tax year. Code Sec. 561(a)(1). There are several caveats here. If only property is distributed, the corporation's adjusted basis at the time of distribution is deductible, even if a higher value is taxed to the shareholder. Reg. §1.562-1(a). The dividends must be proportional to the number of shares held and not favor one class of stock over another. Code Sec. 562(c). If the distribution is disproportional, none of the distribution qualifies, not just the disproportional excess.

Dividends Paid Within 2½ Months After the Taxable Year

Another category of deductible dividends is dividends paid within 2½ months after the tax year. Code Sec. 563(b). The corporation may elect to treat such payments as dividends paid during the previous year to the extent of the lesser of: (1) 20 percent of dividends actually paid during the tax year, or (2) undistributed personal holding company income for the year.

Consent Dividends

Another element in the dividends-paid deduction is consent dividends. Code Secs. 561(a)(2) and 565(a). The shareholder may elect (by the due date of the corporate return) to pretend that the shareholder received a dividend and reinvested the amount in the corporation with the following effects. The shareholder has dividend income and the corporation has a dividends-paid deduction on the last day of the corporation's taxable year. The shareholder receives an increase in the stock basis for the amount deemed contributed to capital. Since the consent dividend reduces earnings and profits, the possibility of tax-free dividends (return of capital) is increased.

| EXAMPLE 18.18 | Minerva Most is the sole owner of Personal Defense Inc. With the corporate tax return for last year, she exhibited her intent to make a consent dividend in the amount of $15,000. Result: No money changes hands. Personal Defense receives a dividend paid deduction of $15,000, Personal Defense's earnings and profits decline by $15,000, Minerva must report $15,000 of dividend income, and Minerva's adjusted basis in Personal Defense stock is increased by $15,000. |

Deficiency Dividends

The fourth member of the group of dividend deductions is deficiency dividends. Code Sec. 547. Unlike the consent dividend, a deficiency dividend is *actually* paid, perhaps several years later, but with retroactive effect. It cannot be paid before a deficiency in the personal holding company tax has been determined, nor can it be paid more than 90 days thereafter. A "determination" means a decision by the Tax Court, or a judgment, decree, or other order by any court of competent jurisdiction, that has become final; a closing agreement; or an agreement between the IRS and corporation relating to the corporation's liability for the personal holding company tax. Code Sec. 547(c). If the requirements are met and a proportional dividend is paid, the dividends-received deduction is available for the prior year. However, the retroactive effect is limited to the tax itself. Interest and penalties must still be paid. Code Sec. 547(a).

Dividend Carryovers

Dividend carryovers represents the final component of the dividends-paid deduction. Code Secs. 561(a)(3) and 564. Dividends paid may be carried over and deducted the next two years to the extent they exceed "adjusted taxable income." Adjusted taxable income is basically undistributed personal holding company income prior to the dividends-paid deduction. The corporation can carry forward dividends paid even if paid in a year the corporation was not classified as a personal holding company.

¶18,301   MISCELLANEOUS TAX CONSEQUENCES OF PHC CLASSIFICATION

There are two tax consequences of classification as a personal holding company (in addition to becoming subject to the personal holding company tax). First, the accumulated earnings tax cannot be imposed in the year or years that a corporation is a personal holding company. Code Sec. 532(b)(1). Second, a personal holding company is not entitled to a research credit for basic research payments. Code Sec. 41(c).

SUMMARY

- Both the accumulated earnings tax and the personal holding company tax seek the same objective: To encourage the distribution of dividends by taxing undistributed earnings, thus enforcing the double taxation of C corporations.

- Both taxes are imposed on the corporation, not on the shareholders, and are based on some measure of retained earnings.

- Dividends-paid deductions are allowed for both taxes, including a deduction for dividends paid within 2 ½ months after the end of the taxable year, as well as for consent dividends.

- Net capital gains are excluded for both taxes.

- Both taxes are imposed at a flat 20 percent rate.

- The personal holding company tax is self-assessed, while the accumulated earnings tax is initiated by the IRS.

- The personal holding company tax is computed mechanically, while the intent, plans, and history of the corporation play an important role when determining whether, and to what extent, the accumulated earnings tax is applicable.

- The personal holding company tax is imposed only on closely held corporations controlled by individual shareholders. The accumulated earnings tax can be imposed on publicly held corporations, at least if there is considerable control in the hands of a few.

QUESTIONS

1. Identify three items of nontaxable receipts which nevertheless increase earnings and profits.

2. Give the acceptable reasons to accumulate earnings as specified in the Code.

3. What is the *Bardahl* formula and how is it computed?

4. What factors tend to indicate that excess accumulations exist?

5. Why are public corporations less likely to be subject to the accumulated earnings tax?

6. John Ferret is the sole shareholder of two corporations.

   Unusual Pets Inc. is a pet shop with $240,000 in current and accumulated earnings, all invested in certificates of deposit and none of which is needed in the business.

   Shadow Inc. is a private investigations service specializing in divorces. Shadow has only $190,000 in current and accumulated earnings, $150,000 of which is needed in the business and all of which is invested in extremely illiquid assets.

   Which of the two corporations is more vulnerable to the accumulated earnings tax?

7. How are short- and long-term capital gains and losses treated in computing accumulated taxable income?

8. How is the accumulated earnings credit determined?

9. How are assets to be valued for the purpose of the accumulated earnings tax?

10. Identify four types of corporations excluded from PHC status.

11. What is the definition of a personal holding company? If the definition is met, is any additional tax necessarily due?

12. Why is a corporation more likely to be subject to the personal holding company tax in a "bad" year?

13. What unique personal holding company problems may confront a small personal service corporation?

14. When is rent excluded from PHCI?

15. Distinguish between a consent dividend and a deficiency dividend.

16. How do capital gains and Section 1231 gains enter into the computation of undistributed PHCI?

17. What are the similarities between the accumulated earnings tax and the personal holding company tax?

18. May the personal holding company tax and the accumulated earnings tax be imposed on the following corporations?
    a. The same corporation in the same taxable year
    b. The same corporation in two different taxable years
    c. An S corporation

19. What is the tax rate on undistributed personal holding company income? On accumulated taxable income?

20. What is the impact of accelerated cost recovery on the personal holding company tax? On the accumulated earnings tax?

PROBLEMS

21. The Loophole Tax Service Inc. has accumulated earnings of $135,000 and current earnings of $60,000. If the dividends-paid deduction is $8,500 and reasonable business needs amount to $160,000, what is the accumulated earnings credit?

22. A manufacturer of billiard and bowling equipment paid an accumulated earnings tax of $45,000, relating to the previous taxable year. What is the impact on the tax situation of the corporation and its two individual shareholders?

23. Mr. Wilson incorporated his bookstore, Occult Books Unlimited, five years ago. Accumulated earnings are $230,000, current earnings are $80,000, and he can show a need for $150,000 of inventory. What is the amount of accumulated taxable income? If the tax is paid, what are the accumulated earnings at the end of the current year?

24. Margo's Cookies Inc. has working capital of $210,000. Selected operating figures include:

Average inventory	$150,000
Average accounts receivable	80,000
Average accounts payable	50,000
Purchases	300,000
Net sales	960,000
Cost of goods sold	600,000
Other expenses (including depreciation of $50,000 and taxes of $90,000)	440,000

According to the *Bardahl* formula, what is Margo's working capital need in total?

25. War Games Inc. breaks even on its operations one year, but has dividend income of $2,000. Could it be a personal holding company?
    a. The following year, War Games has a net operating loss of $50,000 and dividend income of $3,000. Could it be a personal holding company?
    b. Ultra-Vision Inc. is owned only by entities (e.g., a trust, a partnership, and a corporation). Can it be a personal holding company?

26. Party Supplies Inc. is owned 60 percent by Sylvester and 40 percent by an unrelated corporation. How much stock is Sylvester deemed to own after he makes the following independent transactions?
    a. Transfer of half his stock to an irrevocable trust for his grandchildren.
    b. Transfer of half his stock as a divorce settlement to his ex-wife, Chastity.
    c. Sale of half his stock to his independent partner.
    d. Sale of half his stock to a corporation in which he is a 60 percent shareholder and the other shareholders are unrelated to him.
    e. Gift of half his stock to his niece.

27. Parkview West Inc. has gross income of $50,000, consisting of $37,000 of rent receipts and $13,000 of U.S. dividends. Rental deductions of $20,000 are claimed (interest, taxes, and cost recovery). $9,000 of dividends are paid to Susie and Sally, the only shareholders.
    a. Is the 50 percent rental test met?
    b. Is the 10 percent dividend test met?
    c. Is Parkview a personal holding company?

28. Ray Cutter, M.D., incorporated his medical practice. Soon thereafter, he transferred his stock portfolio to the corporation. Since Dr. Cutter is the only surgeon in the corporation, all patients automatically expect his services. One year, professional fees were $200,000 and dividends received were $100,000. Is Ray Cutter, M.D., Ltd. a personal holding company?

29. B-Flat Music Supplies Ltd. earned dividends of $30,000, interest of $12,000, adjusted rent of $50,000, and gross income from its primary business of $63,000 in one taxable year.
    a. Is B-Flat a personal holding company?
    b. If the dividend income was $35,000, is B-Flat a personal holding company?

30. Lark Enterprises Inc. is a personal holding company. From the information below, compute its maximum dividends-paid deduction.
   a. Land with a basis of $10,000 and a value of $50,000 was distributed during the taxable year ending December 31 to its two 50 percent shareholders as equal tenants in common.
   b. Two months later, cash of $5,000 was distributed to one shareholder and three months later property worth $5,000 to the other.
   c. On February 10 of the following year, $3,000 was distributed to each shareholder and an election was made to treat the dividends as paid the previous year.
   d. A timely election was made to treat $5,000 each as consent dividends.

31. Parking Unlimited Ltd.'s financial situation last year may be summarized as follows:

Rental income	$75,000
Depreciation on real property	20,000
Property taxes	7,000
Mortgage interest	19,000
Miscellaneous expenses	12,000
Dividend revenue	11,000
Interest income	4,000
Section 1231 gain	200,000

   a. Is Parking Unlimited a PHC?
   b. Is the 50 percent test met?
   c. How much must be paid in dividends, if any, to avoid PHC tax?

32. David Roberts runs a one-person corporation, a management consulting firm. For the first few years, he paid himself a minuscule salary, no dividends, and no fringe benefits, paying only the regular corporate tax. At the point when accumulated earnings had reached $150,000, all invested in listed stocks, he started paying himself a comfortable but reasonable salary and established a qualified pension plan for himself. From this point on, the corporation had no taxable income. Is it possible that the accumulated earnings tax will be imposed? The personal holding company tax?

33. Gary's Garage Inc. never paid a dividend and invested its after-tax earnings in tire company stock. It has no plans to expand and its working capital is ample. Gary owns 100 percent of the stock.
   a. May Gary's Garage be a PHC?
   b. If Gary's is a PHC *not* liable for the PHC tax (since there is no UPHCI), may the accumulated earnings tax be imposed?
   c. If Gary's accumulated earnings are $250,000 and current after-tax earnings are distributed, may the accumulated earnings tax be imposed?
   d. Same as (c), except accumulated earnings are $200,000, but the marketable stocks purchased with them are worth $700,000.

34. Nestor Corp., which is not a mere holding or investment company, derives its income from retail sales. Nestor had accumulated earnings and profits of $145,000 on December 31, Year 1. For the year ended December 31, Year 2, it had earnings and profits of $115,000 and a dividends-paid deduction of $15,000. It had been determined that $20,000 of the accumulated earnings and profits for Year 1 is required for the reasonable needs of the business. How much is the allowable accumulated earnings credit on December 31, Year 2?
   a. $105,000
   b. $125,000
   c. $150,000
   d. $250,000

35. To compute the accumulated taxable income, all of the items below are deductible, except:
   a. Federal income taxes
   b. After-tax net capital gains
   c. Current dividends
   d. Deficiency dividends

36. Engineering Valuations Inc. has accumulated earnings of $190,000 and current earnings of $250,000. The corporation can show a need to expand the business to the tune of $220,000. The amount of the accumulated earnings credit is:
   a. $220,000
   b. $30,000
   c. $0
   d. $60,000

37. To arrive at adjusted ordinary gross income from gross income, the following subtractions are made, except:
    a. Rent and royalty expenses
    b. Section 1231 gains
    c. Ordinary and necessary business expenses
    d. Short-term capital losses

38. **Comprehensive Problem.** Scandinavian Furniture Inc., a calendar-year corporation, is worried about the accumulated earnings tax. In February, the following facts are available for the preceding year:

Accumulated earnings and profits as of 12/31	$220,000
Taxable income (exclusive of capital gains)	110,000
Charitable contributions in excess of limit	3,000
Long-term capital gain, taxable at 34 percent	10,000
Dividends from Canadian corporations	7,000
Dividends from U.S. corporations (25 percent owned)	8,000
Total income tax liability	60,000
Demonstrable business needs	235,000

If the consent dividend route is to be used, which amount must be reported to avoid the accumulated earnings tax?

39. **Comprehensive Problem.** Marital Aids Inc. reported the following results last year:

Gross income from sales	$50,000
Salaries	20,000
Overhead	25,000
Capital gains	200,000
Net operating loss from previous year	30,000
Dividends from U.S. sources	40,000
Tax-exempt interest	10,000
Taxable interest	35,000
Income tax paid (including $59,650 on capital gains)	62,050

If the corporation has only four individual shareholders, compute the following:
a. Adjusted ordinary gross income.
b. Personal holding company income.
c. Undistributed personal holding company income.
d. Current dividend required to avoid personal holding company tax.
e. What impact would it have if taxable interest was only $12,000 and there was no NOL carryover?

40. **Research Problem.** To what extent may a corporation accumulate earnings for the reasonable needs of a related corporation?

To what extent does it matter that the following conditions prevail?
a. A parent-subsidiary relationship exists.
b. A brother-sister controlled group exists.
c. The two corporations are in different businesses.
d. The degree of common ownership or control is less than 80 percent.

(See Reg. §§1. 537-2(c)(3), 1.537-3(b); H. Rept. No. 1337, 83d Cong., 2d Sess., p. 53 (1954); S. Rept. No. 1622, 83d Cong., 2d Sess., p. 70 (1954).)

41. **Research Problem.** A corporation is resisting the personal holding company tax, but the Tax Court sides with the IRS. Within 90 days after the adverse decision, one shareholder transfers his stock and $10,000 in cash to a controlled corporation in a Code Sec. 351 transaction, while another gifts his stock to an irrevocable trust with his minor children as beneficiaries. Deficiency dividends are actually paid to the corporation and the trust. Are the shareholders able to shift the dividend income to the new entities?

    (See Rev. Rul. 60-331, 1960-2 CB 189; and *T.E.G. Smith Estate,* 61-2 USTC ¶9543, 292 F.2d 478 (CA-3 1961).)

Partnerships—Formation and Operation

OBJECTIVES

After completing Chapter 19, you should be able to:

1. Understand the characteristics of a partnership for federal tax purposes and general law purposes.
2. Determine the tax consequences of the formation of a partnership.
3. Describe the income tax reporting process for a partnership.
4. Describe the income tax reporting of partnership income by a partner.
5. Determine the basis of an interest in a partnership.

OVERVIEW

The partnership form is probably the most common type of business organization involving more than one owner. There are generally no formal requirements to be met at the time of organization because the partnership's existence is based on the business relationship of the participants and their carrying on a business as co-owners with the intention of making a profit.

The federal income tax consequences of partnerships are found in Subchapter K of the Internal Revenue Code. The Code takes significantly different approaches with respect to different aspects of the taxation of income of partnerships. In some instances, the partnership is treated as if it were an entity separate from its partners, somewhat like a corporation. In other instances the partnership is treated as an aggregation of its owners, as if they were joint tenants with undivided ownership interests. Under this aggregate concept, the partnership itself is ignored, and the focus is on the partners.

Partnership items of income and expense are usually passed through unchanged to the partners. Partnership income and expense items are reported by partners for their year with or within which the partnership year ends. The items may be allocated among the partners as specified in the partnership agreement so long as the allocation has a "real" economic effect. However, the tax law may require other means of allocation if the original tax allocations do not affect partners substantially in an economic sense.

Definition of a Partnership

¶19,001   ## CHARACTERISTICS OF A PARTNERSHIP

To the business world in general, a partnership is "an association of two or more persons to carry on as co-owners a business for profit." Uniform Partnership Act, Section 101. There does not need to be an express agreement, oral or written, in order for a partnership to exist. If the venture satisfies the definition of a partnership, it is one. The term "partnership," for tax purposes, is not confined to a partnership as defined under local law. In income tax law the term is much broader and operates almost as a catch-all. It includes any unincorporated organization with more than one owner which carries on any business, financial operation, or venture, unless the Internal Revenue Code defines such an organization as a trust, estate, or corporation. Code Secs. 761(a) and 7701(a)(2); Reg. §1.761-1(a).

Partner Defined

Obviously, for there to be a partnership, there have to be partners. For tax purposes a "partner" is "a member of a partnership," including members of joint ventures, syndicates, pools, and like groups classified for tax purposes as partnerships. Code Sec. 761(b). A partner does not have to be a natural person. Trusts, estates, corporations, and other partnerships all have been recognized as partners in appropriate circumstances.

EXAMPLE 19.1

The Eclectic Partnership was formed with the following parties each owning equal interests: Acme Corporation (its state of incorporation and charter permitted participation), the Estate of Jasper Winebringer, Halloluya Trust for the Sacred Heart Church, the Futures Unlimited Partnership, and Willie Jones. The partnership will be recognized for tax purposes.

There are two types of partners, a general partner and a limited partner. A general partner has unlimited liability for the debts of and claims against the partnership. A limited partner's liability is limited to what the partner has invested and promised to invest in the partnership. A limited partner may not participate in the management of the partnership. If a limited partner should exercise managerial authority, he or she might be treated as a general partner.

Types of Partnerships

Four types of entities are taxed as partnerships: general partnerships, limited liability partnerships, limited partnerships, and limited liability companies.

General Partnerships

A general partnership has two or more general partners who are personally liable for partnership debts, and no limited partners. A general partner can be bankrupted by a judgment brought against the partnership, even though the general partner was not personally involved in the action the judgment was based on.

Limited Liability Partnerships

A limited liability partnership (LLP) is a general partnership in which the general partners are not liable for any malpractice or torts committed by other partners. General partnerships and limited liability partnerships are often the preferred entity choice for service providers such as accountants, architects, attorneys, and physicians.

EXAMPLE 19.2

Enron used to be ranked seventh among U.S. companies with $101 billion in revenue and 19,000 employees. On December 2, 2002, it filed for bankruptcy, the largest in U.S. history, after reversing almost $600 million in profits. The reversal resulted from the discovery of losses from investments and loans collateralized by Enron stock that had been hidden in off-balance sheet entities. The fallout included the layoff of thousands of employees, stock losses in the billions by investors and employees, the resignation of senior Enron officers, the suicide of a former vice chairman, the firing by Andersen LLP of certain senior employees assigned to the audit engagement and the eventual disintegration of Andersen LLP. Class action suits by investors sought billions in damage awards from Enron and Andersen. Recall that an LLP partner is not liable for any malpractice committed by other partners. Thus, if any Andersen partner were found to be guilty of malpractice, the other partners worldwide would have no personal liability. Had Andersen been a general partnership, a partner found guilty of malpractice could cause every partner to be personally liable for any successful damage claims.

Limited Partnerships

A limited partnership is composed of at least one general partner and at least one limited partner. Limited partners may not participate in the management of the partnership, and their risks of loss are restricted to their equity investments in the limited partnership. A limited partnership is often the preferred entity choice for real estate ventures requiring significant capital contributions by owners who do not wish to participate in the management of the venture. A relatively new type of limited partnership that real estate ventures are also taking advantage of is the limited liability limited partnership (LLLP). An LLLP is a limited partnership in which the general partner(s) are not liable for the negligence or misconduct of the other general partners.

Limited Liability Companies (LLCs)

A limited liability company (LLC) is a state-registered association generally taxed as a partnership if it makes the appropriate election ("checks the box"). Its owners are called "members." Like corporate share-holders, members are not personally liable for debts of the LLC. Unlike limited partners, LLC members may participate in management without risking personal liability. However, guaranteed payments from LLCs are subject to self-employment tax, along with the members' share of ordinary income or loss from the LLC (Prop. Reg. §1.1402(a)-2, if finalized, would change this treatment). In most states the LLC ownership structure is available to both capital-intensive companies and nonprofessional service providers.

Advantages of LLCs include a single level of taxation, limited liability of members, and the inclusion of the members' share of LLC debt in the members' outside basis. Many of the LLC's advantages are available to S corporations, with three notable exceptions: (1) S corporations have more rigid owner-eligibility requirements, (2) corporate debt does not increase the outside basis of S corporation shareholders, and (3) the taxation of shareholder contributions and corporate distributions tend to follow the accounting rules for C corporations rather than partnerships. (Chapter 21 discusses the taxation of S corporations.)

Existing businesses organized as partnerships or corporations have to change their legal business form to become LLCs. For partnerships, the conversion to an LLC is generally free of any tax consequences. Rev. Rul. 95-37, 1995-1 CB 130. However, corporations have to liquidate before organizing as an LLC, and liquidation-related income taxes may be generated to the corporation under Section 336 and to the shareholders under Section 331. For these reasons, existing corporations often find it too expensive to change their entity form to the LLC.

Meaning of "Partnership Agreement"

The partnership form enables owners to make special allocations of certain income, gain, loss, deductions, or credits that are not possible under the C or S corporation forms. A partner's distributive share of these items is determined by the partnership agreement. Code Sec. 704(a). A partnership agreement includes the original agreement and any modifications to it agreed to by all the partners or adopted in any other manner provided by the partnership agreement. Code Sec. 761(c). Such agreement or modifications can be oral or written. Reg. §1.761-1(c). See *R. W. James,* 21 TCM 953, CCH Dec. 25,579(M), T.C. Memo. 1962-173. A partnership agreement may be modified with respect to a particular taxable year subsequent to the close of such taxable year, but not later than the date (not including any extension of time) prescribed by law for the filing of the partnership return.

"Check-the-Box" Classification as a Partnership

The Treasury Department's "check-the-box" regulations permit most unincorporated entities, such as general partnerships, limited partnerships, LLPs, and LLCs, to be taxed as either a partnership (with two or more owners) or a C corporation. Reg. §301.7701-1 to 301.7701-4, and -7. Eligible entities make the election as to tax status by filing Form 8832 (Entity Classification Election).

The "check-the-box" regulations are designed to provide eligible entities with a simple, certain means of choosing an entity for tax purposes. Entities with more than one owner can elect to be taxed as either a partnership or a corporation. An entity with only one owner can elect to be taxed as a corporation or a sole proprietorship. In the event of default (i.e., no election is made), entities with more than one owner are taxed as partnerships and single-owner businesses are taxed as sole proprietorships.

The election is not available to entities that are actually incorporated under state law or to entities that are required to be corporations under Federal law (e.g., certain publicly traded partnerships).

Since organizations incorporated under state law will be taxed as corporations, entities that want to be taxed as partnerships but still want to have certain corporate characteristics will often organize as limited liability companies. However, there may be tax consequences for an entity that has been taxed as a corporation and elects different future tax treatment. For example, if an association previously taxed as a corporation elects to be taxed as a partnership, the election would be treated as a liquidation of the corporation, which could trigger taxable income to the corporation and its shareholders.

Exclusion From Partnership: Co-ownership of Property

The mere co-ownership of business property does not create a partnership for tax purposes. The parties must be involved in the active conduct of a trade or business. What is an active conduct of a business is a question of fact. A partnership usually is found to exist, for example, where co-owners of an apartment building lease space and provide substantial services to tenants. On the other hand, where no substantial services are provided, the mere co-ownership of property that is maintained, kept in repair, and rented or leased does not constitute a partnership.

EXAMPLE 19.3	George and Henry Houck are brothers who inherited equal ownership interests as tenants in common in unimproved real estate located in a rural part of the county. They presently rent this land to a farmer to pasture his cattle. They merely receive the pasturage fees and pay the real estate tax on the land. Their joint ownership does not constitute a partnership.

EXAMPLE 19.4	If the inherited property in Example 19.3 had been an office building that the brothers, or either one of them, manage to the extent of locating tenants, collecting rentals, and providing janitorial services, supplies, and repairs, the co-tenancy could rise to the level of a partnership under tax law.

Exclusion From Partnership: Sharing Profits

The mere right to share in the venture's profits does not necessarily make the recipient a partner. An employee may be paid a share of the profits of a business as compensation, or a creditor may receive a percentage of the business income as interest on a loan, but such arrangements do not cause either recipient to be a partner under local law or under tax law because there is no ownership in the partnership. Also, a partnership is not created simply because the joint undertaking requires the participants to share in the expenses of the enterprise.

Anti-abuse Regulations

While the tax law allows partners a great deal of flexibility in how they wish to structure their partnership and share items of income and loss, this flexibility also creates opportunities for abuse. That is, partners may structure transactions to secure tax benefits that were never intended when the statute was created. To prevent such abuse, regulations provide the IRS with very broad anti-abuse rules that allow the IRS to disregard the form of a partnership transaction if it believes that the transaction is abusive.

The regulations require that:

1. The partnership must be bona fide, and each partnership transaction or series of related transactions must be entered into for a substantial business purpose,
2. The form of each partnership transaction must be respected under substance-over-form principles, and
3. The tax consequences under Subchapter K to each partner of partnership operations and of transactions between the partner and the partnership must, subject to certain exceptions, accurately reflect the partners' economic agreement and clearly reflect the partners' income.

The evidence of abusive intent is determined based on all the relevant facts and circumstances. Of course, the language used in these regulations is quite subjective. Therefore, practitioners are very concerned about how the IRS will apply these regulations, and disagreements over its application are inevitable. Reg. §1.701-2.

Partnership Reporting

¶19,005   ## PARTNERSHIP TAX FILING

Every partnership must file an annual return regardless of the amount of its net income or its net loss in its operations. Code Sec. 701; Reg. §1.701-1; Code Sec. 6031. Since the partnership itself is not taxable with respect to any income, the return is fundamentally an information return. For calendar-year partnerships, Form 1065 for a taxable year must be filed on or before March 15 (April 15 for tax years beginning before January 1, 2016) of the following year. A fiscal-year partnership must file by the 15th day of the third month following the close of its fiscal year. Code Sec. 6072. The partnership must report its gross income, deductions, ordinary net income, names and addresses of partners, their distributive shares of income, special credits, deductions, and other information as required. Code Secs. 6031 and 6072. Each partner's tax information must be furnished to that partner on or before the day on which the return for the taxable year is due. Code Sec. 6031(b). The return must be signed by one of the partners. The fact that a partner's name is signed to the return is prima facie evidence that the partner is authorized to sign the return on behalf of the partnership. Code Sec. 6063.

The ordinary income and expense items generated by the partnership's trade or business activities ("Code Sec. 702(a)(8) income or loss") are netted to produce a single income or loss amount. The partnership reports this amount on Form 1065 (U.S. Partnership Return of Income) page 1. Schedule K (page 4 of Form 1065) accumulates all items that must be separately reported to the partners, including Code Sec. 702(a)(8) income (from page 1). The amounts on Schedule K are allocated to all the partners based on their profit and loss sharing ratios. The partnership sends each partner a Schedule K-1, which shows that partner's share of partnership items.

The filing of Form 1065 does not start the running of the statute of limitations for the individual partner who failed to file a personal return, even though there is no fraud and the individual had no income other than that reported on the partnership return. *M. Durovic,* 73-2 USTC ¶9728, 487 F.2d 36 (CA-7 1973), cert. denied, 417 U.S. 919, 94 S.Ct. 2625 (1973). But the filing of Form 1065 is relevant in determining the question of criminal willfulness in failing to file the individual return. *H.W. Harrison,* 73-1 USTC ¶9295 (CA-2 1972), cert. denied, 411 U.S. 965, 93 S.Ct. 2144 (1973). Any disclosure on the partnership return that provides a "clue" to the IRS of reportable income is sufficient to put the IRS on notice so that the six-year statute of limitations (25 percent omission of income) will not apply. *W.W. Myers,* 72-2 USTC ¶9669 (DC Cal. 1972); *G.E. Quick Tr.,* 54 TC 1336, Dec. 30,187 (1970), aff'd per curiam, 71-1 USTC ¶9489, 444 F.2d 90 (CA-8 1971).

EXAMPLE 19.5   Jack West and Quick Martin were equal partners in Engineering, a cash-basis partnership. Quick died and Quick's estate erroneously claimed a step-up in basis for the estate's share of the partnership's accounts receivable. On the partnership return, there was disclosed only the amount of the collections in excess of their "basis." The income allocated to the estate was much less than that allocated to Jack. The partnership balance sheet showed a reduction in the accounts receivable's basis and the Schedule M reconciliation showed large tax-free distributions to the estate. While the omission from the estate's income was more than 25 percent, the partnership's disclosure provided sufficient clues that there was no omission in reporting so as to prevent the IRS from asserting the six-year statute of limitations.

If the partnership needs more time to file its return, it can obtain an automatic extension to file of six months by filing Form 7004, Application for Automatic Extension to File Certain Business Income Tax, Information, and Other Returns. Code Sec. 6081. If a partnership fails to file its return on time or fails to file a return that shows all the information required, it is subject to a penalty of $200 per month (or part of a month) for the time that the partnership return is late or incomplete, up to a maximum of twelve months. This amount is then multiplied by the total number of partners in the partnership to arrive at the penalty due. Code Sec. 6698. This penalty is not imposed if the partnership can show that failure to file a complete or timely return was due to reasonable cause. Code Sec. 6698.

Taxation of Partners

For income tax purposes, partnerships are generally treated as pass-through entities, i.e., the partnership pays no taxes, and partnership income (loss) and separately stated items are allocated to each partner at the end of the partnership's tax year according to the partnership agreement. Code Sec. 702. Each Schedule K-1 reports the partner's share of the partnership net profit (loss) and separately reported income and expense items. Partners report these items on their tax returns, even if no distributions from the partnership have been made.

EXAMPLE 19.6

A partnership is composed of two individuals sharing profits and losses equally. In the tax year the income of the partnership is $400,000. Of this amount, half is distributed to the partners and the remainder is retained in the business. Although each partner receives only $100,000 from the partnership for the year, each must report his or her entire $200,000 (50% × $400,000) share of the partnership income on his or her own individual income tax return.

The regulations require separate treatment of a partner's share of any partnership item that could affect any two partners' tax liabilities in different ways. Code Sec. 702(a) and Reg. 1.702-1(a). See ¶19,335 for a detailed listing of these separately reported income and deduction items. Calculation of earned income from operations generally follows the same rules as for individuals (i.e., all income from whatever source derived, unless specifically excluded). It is offset by cost of goods sold and operating expenses, including guaranteed payments to partners and amortization of organizational expenses, to produce a single reporting item, "Code Sec. 702(a)(8) income or loss."

EXAMPLE 19.7

Ceci is a 20 percent partner in XYZ, a cash-basis, calendar year partnership. During the current year, XYZ collected sales income of $100,000 and incurred $30,000 in business expenses. In addition, it sold machinery resulting in a $10,000 Code Sec. 1231 gain and $5,000 of Code Sec. 1245 depreciation recapture. Finally, XYZ contributed $4,000 to a qualifying charity. For the current year, Ceci is allocated Code Sec. 702(a)(8) ordinary taxable income of $15,000 [20% × ($100,000 – $30,000 + $5,000)] from XYZ. She also receives a separate allocation of a $2,000 Code Sec. 1231 gain (20% × $10,000) and an $800 charitable contribution (20% × $4,000). The gross income of the partnership increases Ceci's gross income, and the partnership's ordinary income increases Ceci's ordinary income. The Code Sec. 1231 gain and charitable contribution are separately stated because they could be treated differently on her tax return from the way they are treated on the tax returns of the other partners. For example, Ceci may have Code Sec. 1231 losses or capital losses to offset the Code Sec. 1231 gain or may be subject to a percentage limitation on charitable contribution deductions for the current year. Other partners may have no capital losses or different percentage limitations on charitable contribution deductions.

The partner's character of the items of income and expense is the same as the character of the items in the hands of the partnership. Thus, where the partnership receives tax-exempt interest the partner's share of that income is likewise tax-exempt.

Partnership Accounting Concepts

An understanding of the meaning of "outside basis," "inside basis," "capital interest," and "profit or loss interest" is essential to grasping the mechanics of partnership accounting.

¶19,025

OUTSIDE BASIS

Initial Outside Basis of Partner

Outside basis generally refers to a partner's tax basis in their partnership interest. It is used mainly in the computation of gain or loss from (1) partnership distributions (explained in Chapter 20) and (2) the sale of a partnership interest (explained beginning at ¶20,070). It is also used in determining the deductibility of partnership losses to the partner (explained at ¶19,551). In keeping with the general pattern of most nonrecognition provisions, Code Sec. 722 requires that the partner take as its initial outside basis an "exchanged basis" in the partnership interest. Code Sec. 7701(a)(44). After the formation of a partnership this amount usually equals the sum of the following:

1. the adjusted basis of any property contributed by an incoming partner to the partnership,
2. any ordinary income recognized by incoming partners who contribute services in exchange for a partnership interest, and
3. the incoming partner's share of partnership liabilities.

The holding period of a partner's partnership interest will carry over from capital and Code Sec. 1231 assets contributed by the partner. On the other hand, the holding period of any partnership interest received in exchange for the contribution of money or other types of property (such as inventory) starts the day after it is received. This means that a partnership interest will have a split holding period if, for instance, it is received in exchange for the contribution of capital assets and inventory.

Acquisition by Purchase, Gift, or Inheritance

If the partnership interest is acquired other than by contribution, the usual basis rules apply. Code Sec. 742. Thus, the initial basis of a purchased interest is its cost. If the interest is inherited, its basis is its fair market value at the time of the decedent's death or at the optional valuation date. Code Sec. 1014.

EXAMPLE 19.8	Father owned an interest in the Acme Partnership. His basis for the interest was $10,000, but its fair market value was $5,000 on the date of his death when his son inherited the partnership interest. The son's basis for the interest is $5,000, the date of death value.

If the interest is acquired by gift and the donor's basis in the interest exceeds its value at the time of the gift, the donee's basis for determining loss is the value of the interest at the time of the gift. In all other cases the donee's basis equals the donor's basis. Code Sec. 1015.

EXAMPLE 19.9	If the father in Example 19.8 had made an inter vivos gift of the partnership interest to his son, the interest would have a basis of $5,000 for purposes of determining loss and a $10,000 basis for determining gain. Any sale of the interest for amounts between $5,000 and $10,000 would result in neither gain nor loss recognition by the son.

If a partnership interest, or an addition to such an interest, is acquired as compensation for services, the amount of the resultant taxable income determines the recipient's basis in the interest. Reg. §§1.721-1(b)(1) and 1.722-1.

Adjustments to Outside Basis

After the partner's initial outside basis has been determined, this amount is adjusted upward or downward to reflect subsequent operating results or structural events. Outside basis is increased by the partner's share of:

- additional contributions to the partnership;
- the partnership's accumulated taxable income (including separately stated taxable income as discussed at ¶19,335);
- the partnership's accumulated tax-exempt income;
- the excess of the partnership deductions for depletion over the partnership's adjusted basis ("inside basis") in the depletable property;
- increases in partnership liabilities. Code Sec. 752(a).

A partner's outside basis is decreased by:

- the amount of money and the partnership's adjusted basis ("inside basis") in property other than money distributed to the partner (Code Secs. 705(a) and 733; Reg. §1.733-1);
- the partner's share of partnership losses, including capital losses;
- the partner's share of partnership expenditures that are neither deductible nor chargeable to capital (such as charitable contributions and life insurance premiums);
- the amount of the partner's percentage depletion with respect to oil and gas wells to the extent that it does not exceed the proportionate share of the properties' inside bases allocated to the partner;

- the partner's share of any Code Sec. 179 expenses (an election may be made to deduct up to $510,000 of certain tangible property in 2017 (including certain qualified real property), even if the partner cannot deduct the entire amount on the individual income tax return); and
- the partner's share of any reduction in partnership liabilities. Code Secs. 705 and 752.

EXAMPLE 19.10	Ron Barden purchases a partnership interest for $10,000 in cash. During the first tax year, his share of the partnership's ordinary income from business operations is $3,700, his share of the partnership's interest income is $300, and his share of income received by the partnership from tax-exempt municipal bonds is $300. The partnership distributes $4,000 to him during the year and retains, under the partnership agreement, the $300 tax-exempt income for future business needs. The basis of Barden's interest is increased by $4,300 (his share of both ordinary income and total interest income) and decreased by $4,000 (the amount of the distribution). His outside basis at the end of the first tax year is $10,300.

EXAMPLE 19.11	Assume that this partnership made a charitable contribution in cash and $300 was allocable to each partner. The partnership may not take the deduction for the charitable contribution since it is a separately stated item (see ¶19,335). However, the partnership reflects the contribution on Schedules K and K-1 and the partners report their individual shares on their personal tax returns. In essence, the situation is viewed as if the partners withdrew $300 from their individual partnership capital account and gave the money to the charitable organization. Thus, each partner's outside basis is decreased by $300 to reflect the charitable contribution.

Any increase (or decrease) in a partner's share of the liabilities of a partnership, whether assumed directly or indirectly by the partner, is treated as a contribution (or distribution) of money and increases (or decreases) the partner's outside basis in the partnership interest. Code Secs. 752(a) and (b).

EXAMPLE 19.12	Mo Petty contributes $18,000 cash to the Smith Partnership in exchange for a 25 percent interest in the partnership's capital and profits and losses. The Smith Partnership has $16,000 of liabilities of which Mo's 25 percent share is $4,000. Mo's outside basis in his partnership interest is $22,000 ($18,000 + $4,000).

EXAMPLE 19.13	Continuing with Example 19.12 above, during the year, Smith Partnership borrows $40,000 and Mo's outside basis increases by $10,000 [(25%)($40,000)]. If Smith Partnership had no other activities during the year, Mo's outside basis would be $32,000 ($22,000 from Example 19.12 above + $10,000) at the end of the year.

EXAMPLE 19.14	Continuing with Example 19.13, assume Smith Partnership pays down its liabilities in the amount of $8,000 at the end of the next year. Mo's outside basis decreases by $2,000 [(25%)($8,000)]. If Smith Partnership had no other activities during the year, Mo's outside basis would be $30,000 ($32,000 from Example 19.13 above - $2,000).

Adjustments to outside basis are usually made annually at the end of the partnership's tax year. Code Sec. 705(a). Actual distributions of money or other property and deemed distributions resulting from decreases in a partner's share of partnership liabilities are to be taken into account before losses in adjusting the partner's outside basis. Rev. Rul. 66-94, 1966-1 CB 166.

A partner's outside basis can never be reduced below zero. In the case where a distributee partner's outside basis is inadequate to absorb the partnership's basis in distributed property (other than money), the partner must take a basis in the distributed property equal to the outside basis in the partnership interest. (See ¶20,021 and ¶20,042 for a detailed discussion of this rule.) If the partner's distributive share of a partnership loss exceeds the partner's outside basis, the excess must be suspended (rather than deducted) until additional outside basis is obtained or created (through, for example, contributions or recognition of partnership income).

EXAMPLE 19.15

> Jane Muchner purchases a partnership interest for $5,000. During the tax year, Muchner receives a $3,000 cash distribution from the partnership. At the end of the tax year, Muchner's distributive share of partnership losses is $6,000. The distribution reduces Muchner's outside basis to $2,000. Muchner's share of losses reduces her outside basis to zero. Thus, only $2,000 of Muchner's share of partnership losses is deductible. The remaining $4,000 is suspended until she obtains additional outside basis.
>
> For a detailed discussion of loss limitations, refer to ¶19,551.

A partner's outside basis is not reported on the K-1. Instead, each partner is required to maintain a personal record of adjustments to basis. Schedule K-1 does reconcile a partner's capital account (explained later in this section), but the ending capital account balance is rarely the same as the partner's outside basis. Differences between the two amounts include the partner's share of partnership liabilities. These liabilities are not included in a partner's capital account as reported on the K-1 but are included in Item K on the partner's K-1.

¶19,035   INSIDE BASIS

While *outside basis*, as explained in the previous section, refers to the adjusted basis of a partner's interest in a partnership, *inside basis* refers to the adjusted basis of the assets of the partnership. An inequality in total outside and inside basis often results from certain transactions, such as purchase of a partnership interest by a new or existing partner, transfer of a partnership interest upon the death of a partner, buyout of a retiring partner's interest by the partnership, gift of a partnership interest, and certain partnership distributions. In many of these cases the partnership is permitted to adjust the inside basis of its assets by filing a Code Sec. 754 election. This has the result of preserving equality between outside and inside basis. See ¶20,080—¶20,083 for a discussion of the Code Sec. 754 election.

EXAMPLE 19.16

> A partnership owns a warehouse with an adjusted basis of $300,000 and a fair market value of $600,000. Cindy buys a one-third interest in the partnership for $200,000 (an amount equal to one-third of the warehouse's value.) Cindy's *outside basis* in her partnership interest is $200,000, i.e., the price she paid for her partnership interest. The *inside basis* of her share of the warehouse is $100,000 (1/3 x $300,00). Although Cindy's purchase price was based on fair market value, the warehouse's depreciation continues to be determined on the partnership's related inside basis of $300,000, of which Cindy's share is only $100,000. However, if the partnership makes a Code Sec. 754 election, the basis of the warehouse can be increased by $100,000, and all of the increase would be allocated to Cindy's "share" of the warehouse's basis.

¶19,055   PARTNER'S INTEREST IN A PARTNERSHIP

A partner usually owns both a capital interest and a *profits or loss interest* in the partnership. While a capital interest ratio reflects a partner's percentage ownership in the capital of a partnership, a profit or loss sharing ratio represents a partner's percentage allocation of the partnership's ordinary taxable income or loss and separately stated items. Code Sec. 704(a).

Each partner's capital, profit, and loss sharing ratios may appear on the partner's Schedule K-1. Often the three ratios are equal, particularly when profit and loss allocations for each year of the partnership's existence are in the same proportion as the partner's initial contributions to the partnership. However, the partnership agreement may stipulate a special allocation of certain items to specified partners, or it may allocate items in a different proportion from general profit and loss sharing ratios. These items are separately reported to the partner receiving the allocation.

For a special allocation to be recognized for tax purposes, it must have substantial economic effect to the partners receiving the special allocation. Code Sec. 704(b). An allocation has substantial economic effect if (1) there is a reasonable possibility that the allocation will substantially affect the dollar amount the partners will receive from the partnership, independent of tax consequences and (2) the partner to whom an allocation is made actually receives the economic benefit or bears the economic burden corresponding to the allocation. Reg. §1.704-1(b)(2)(ii)(a) and (iii)(a). For a detailed discussion of the allocation rules see ¶19,345.

EXAMPLE 19.17	A partnership transfers a 20 percent capital interest to Stuart Bondurant in exchange for his contribution of municipal bonds that he held for investment purposes. The partnership agreement allocates all of the tax-exempt bond interest to Bondurant as an inducement for him to join the partnership. Bondurant's capital account, and the amount that Bondurant would receive on the liquidation of the partnership, is increased by the amount of the tax-exempt income allocated to him. The allocation has substantial economic effect since the amount that Bondurant will eventually receive is affected by the allocation, and he receives the economic benefit from the allocation.

EXAMPLE 19.18	A partnership owned equally by Hugh High and Lance Low purchases tax-exempt municipal bonds. The partnership agreement allocates all of the tax-exempt bond interest to High and an equal amount of taxable income to Low since High is in a higher tax bracket than Low. This allocation would be unacceptable for tax purposes since its primary motive is tax avoidance and the capital accounts and amounts the partners will eventually receive are not affected by the allocation.

Formation of a Partnership— Contributions Requiring Special Consideration

¶19,105 CONTRIBUTIONS IN GENERAL

At the inception of a partnership, the organizers do not purchase an interest; they contribute assets and receive in exchange an interest in the partnership's capital and future income. Contributions of property in exchange for partnership interests are generally treated as nontaxable exchanges with no gain or loss recognized either to the partnership or to its partners. This tax-free treatment applies whether the contribution is made to a partnership at formation or to a partnership that already is formed and operating. Code Sec. 721; Reg. §1.721-1(a).

EXAMPLE 19.19	Ida Frank and James Stein form their partnership by transferring the following property in exchange for equal partnership interests: Ida contributes $10,000 cash, and James contributes unimproved real estate with a fair market value of $10,000 and a basis to him of $5,000. Because he has received value of $10,000 in exchange for property with a basis of $5,000, James realizes a gain of $5,000 on the transfer, but he does not currently recognize it.
	Contributions that require special tax treatment include:
	1. Property with precontribution gain/loss (¶19,115)
	2. Accounts receivable (¶19,125)
	3. Inventory (¶19,135)
	4. Capital loss property (¶19,145)
	5. Depreciable property (¶19,155)
	6. Personal-use property conversions (¶19,170)

¶19,115 TRANSFERS OF PROPERTY WITH PRECONTRIBUTION GAIN /LOSS

Precontribution gain/loss refers to the amount and character of potential gain or loss on property contributed by a partner to a partnership. It is the fair market value of contributed property less the partner's adjusted basis in the property at the time of contribution. In general, any precontribution gain or loss recognized when the partnership sells the asset must be allocated to the contributing partner. Any excess gains and losses on the sale are allocated according to the profit and loss sharing ratios in the partnership agreement. Code Sec. 704(c). Extensive regulations prevent taxpayers from disguising sales to the partnership as tax-free property contributions coupled with concurrent or subsequent tax-free distributions (disguised sales). See ¶19,235 et seq. for a discussion of disguised sales between partners and partnerships.

EXAMPLE 19.20

Greg Maxwell contributed land (fair market value = $50,000, basis = $30,000) to a partnership in exchange for a 25% partnership interest. Three years later the partnership sells the land for $75,000. Because of the sale Greg will have to recognize the $20,000 precontribution gain plus his 25% share of the other $25,000 of gain ($6,250), for a total gain of $26,250.

¶19,125   TRANSFERS OF ACCOUNTS RECEIVABLE FOR PARTNERSHIP INTEREST

Code Sec. 724 provides rules that require the partnership to recognize income or loss on any disposition of certain types of contributed property. These rules are aimed at preventing the conversion of capital losses to ordinary losses or the conversion of ordinary income to capital gains.

If property contributed to a partnership was an unrealized receivable in the hands of the contributing partner (as defined in Code Sec. 751(c)) immediately before the contribution, any gain or loss recognized by the partnership on the disposition of the property will be treated as ordinary income or loss. This rule for unrealized receivables applies regardless of the date of disposition.

The partnership will report ordinary income if its collections of these receivables exceed their transferred basis. Code Sec. 724(a). The partnership must allocate this income to the contributor to the extent the value of the accounts receivable exceeded their basis at the time of contribution. Code Sec. 704(c). Any excess of collections over the value of the accounts receivable at the date of contribution may be allocated according to the partnership agreement. However, any income from the accounts receivable allocated to other partners must be reflected in their capital accounts and ultimately distributed to them upon liquidation. The contributor need not report all the income from the receivables. Their value at contribution will often be less than their face amount. The partnership agreement can allocate any amount collected above the initial value of the receivables to any contributing partner or noncontributing partner. This allocation will increase a partner's share of taxable income but will also increase the partner's capital account and share of the partnership's assets.

EXAMPLE 19.21

Lynn Jones and Bert Richards form the JR partnership. The partnership agreement provides that Jones and Richards share equally in the capital, profits, and losses of JR. Their partnership contributions are as follows:

Nature of property	From Lynn Jones: Accounts receivable	From Bert Richards: Cash
Fair market value	$50,000 (face amount of $60,000 less estimated uncollectibles of $10,000)	$50,000
Adjusted basis	0	50,000

Later that year, JR collects the $60,000 face amount of the receivables. JR should allocate $55,000 ordinary income to Jones (100% of $50,000 precontribution gain plus 50% of $10,000 post-contribution gain) and $5,000 ordinary income to Richards (50% of post-contribution gain).

	Description:	Collection Analysis:	Pre-contribution Gain (100% allocated to Jones)	Post-contribution Gain (Shared equally between Jones and Richards)
(a)	Amount collected/FMV	$60,000	$50,000	
(b)	Lynn Jones pre-contribution basis in the receivables	0	0	
(c) = (a) – (b)	Ordinary income reported	60,000	50,000	10,000

¶19,135   TRANSFERS OF INVENTORY FOR PARTNERSHIP INTEREST

If property contributed to a partnership was inventory in the hands of the contributing partner immediately before its contribution, any gain or loss recognized by the partnership on the disposition of the property will be treated as ordinary income or loss. This rule applies only if the disposition takes place *within five years of the date the property was contributed* to the partnership. *Any* gain or loss recognized by the partnership on the disposition of property that was inventory property in the hands of a partner immediately before it was contributed will be treated as ordinary income or loss during the five-year period. Code Sec. 724(b). This rule is particularly important in keeping real estate developers from turning ordinary income from real estate "inventory" into capital gains by contributing the real estate to a non-developer partnership before sale.

EXAMPLE 19.22	Martha and Stuart Smith form MS, an equal partnership, with Martha contributing land lots held as inventory with a fair market value of $100,000, and an adjusted basis to her of $48,000. Stuart contributes $100,000 cash. MS holds the land for investment and, within 5 years from contribution, sells the land for $200,000. MS reports a $152,000 gain ($200,000 sales price − $48,000 inside basis). Martha receives an ordinary income allocation of $102,000 ($52,000 "built-in" gain plus $50,000, one-half of the balance of the gain). Stuart must report $50,000 of gain as ordinary income. If the land had been held more than 5 years from contribution, the character of the gain allocated to Martha and Stuart would have been capital instead of ordinary.

Code Sec. 724(d)(2) defines "inventory items" to include those which, if sold, generate ordinary income rather than capital gain. But land or depreciable property used by a partner in a trade or business prior to its contribution to the partnership is excluded from the definition of "inventory items." For this purpose there is no requirement that this type of property (generally Section 1231 property) must be held for more than 12 months prior to its contribution to the partnership.

EXAMPLE 19.23	Mr. Kostock owned a desk which he had used entirely in his sole proprietorship for 11 months when he contributed it to his newly formed partnership as a part of his capital contribution. If Mr. Kostock had sold the desk, any gain or loss would be ordinary since the desk would not qualify as Section 1231 property. However, if the partnership continues the business use of the desk for more than one more month and then sells it at more than its original cost to Mr. Kostock, the gain in excess of the depreciation recapture will qualify as a Section 1231 gain.

¶19,145 TRANSFERS OF CAPITAL LOSS PROPERTY FOR A PARTNERSHIP INTEREST

Code Sec. 724 provides a special rule for property contributed to a partnership that was a capital asset in the hands of the partner immediately before the contribution. If the contributing partner had an unrecognized capital loss on the property, any loss recognized by the partnership on the disposition of the property will be treated as a loss from the sale of a capital asset to the extent of the partner's unrecognized precontribution loss. This rule applies to dispositions *within five years of the date that the property was contributed.* Code Sec. 724(c). The purpose of this rule is to prevent the conversion of capital losses to ordinary losses by contributing the property to a partnership in which the property would be inventory. Note the contrast with the rule for inventory contributions. With capital loss property sold within 5 years of contribution, the amount of partnership loss characterized as capital loss is limited to the contributor's precontribution loss. With inventory sold within 5 years of contribution, both precontribution gain and post-contribution gain is characterized as ordinary income.

EXAMPLE 19.24	Todd Harke and David Combs form HC, an equal partnership, with Harke contributing marketable securities held for investment with a fair market value of $100,000, and an adjusted basis to him of $148,000. Combs contributes $100,000 cash. The partnership operates as a dealer in securities and holds Harke's contribution as inventory. Within 5 years from contribution, HC sells the securities for $30,000. MS reports a $118,000 loss ($30,000 sales price - $148,000 inside basis). Harke receives a capital loss allocation of $48,000 (his "built-in" loss). In addition, Harke and Combs each receive a $35,000 ordinary loss allocation (one-half of the $70,000 post-contribution loss). If the securities had been held more than 5 years from contribution, the character of the precontribution loss allocated to Harke would have been ordinary instead of capital.

¶19,155   TRANSFERS OF DEPRECIABLE PROPERTY FOR A PARTNERSHIP INTEREST

When a partner contributes depreciable property to a partnership in exchange for a partnership interest, the depreciable property's basis and the depreciation method and recovery period carry over to the partnership. In addition, the partnership may not elect under Code Sec. 179 to immediately expense any part of the basis of depreciable property it receives from the contributing partner. When the partnership eventually disposes of the contributed property, it may be required to recapture depreciation deductions claimed by the partner before the contribution and by the partnership after the contribution. Reg. §§1.1245-2(c)(2) and 1.1250-3(c)(3). However, to the extent the gain on a subsequent sale represents precontribution gain, that gain (including the precontribution recapture) will be allocated to the contributing partner under Code Sec. 704(c).

EXAMPLE 19.25

In year 1, Stan Ragan purchases $100,000 of 7-year business equipment for his proprietorship and claims $14,000 MACRS depreciation that year. At the beginning of year 2, he contributes the business equipment to a partnership in exchange for a 30% capital interest. At the time of contribution, the property is valued at $105,000. Ragan's $86,000 adjusted tax basis in the equipment carries over to the partnership ($100,000 cost less $14,000 year 1 depreciation). In year 2, the partnership claims $25,000 MACRS depreciation on the business equipment, resulting in an adjusted tax basis to the partnership of $61,000. At the beginning of year 3, the partnership sells the business equipment for $110,000, resulting in a $49,000 realized gain. Stan receives an allocation of 100% of the precontribution gain ($14,000 Code Sec. 1245 recapture and $5,000 Code Sec. 1231 gain). In addition, he receives 30% of the post-contribution gain, i.e., $7,500 Code Sec. 1245 recapture (30% x $25,000), and $1,500 Code Sec. 1231 gain (30% x $5,000). The remaining partners are allocated 70% of the post-contribution gain. Refer to the computations below.

	Description:	Sale Analysis	Pre-contribution Gain (100% allocated to Ragan)	Post-contribution Gain (Allocated 30% to Ragan; 70% to other partners)
(a)	Sales price/FMV of property	$110,000	$105,000	
(b)	Original cost	100,000	100,000	
(c)	Precontribution depreciation claimed by Ragan	(14,000)	(14,000)	
(d)	Post-contribution depreciation claimed by the partnership	(25,000)	N/A	
(e) = (b) – (c) – (d)	Adjusted tax basis in business equipment	61,000	86,000	
(f) = (a) – (e)	Realized gain	49,000	19,000	
(g) = lesser of: [(c) + (d)] or (f)	Code Sec. 1245 recapture (ordinary income)	39,000	14,000	25,000
(h) = (f) – (g)	Code Sec. 1231 gain	10,000	5,000	5,000

When a partnership has depreciation attributable to property with built-in precontribution gains or losses (depreciable "Code Sec. 704(c) property"), it must make appropriate depreciation allocations to the partners to avoid shifting the tax consequences of the built-in gain or loss. If the partnership sells the Code Sec. 704(c) property and recognizes gain or loss, built-in gain or loss on the property is allocated to the contributing partner. The tax basis allocation of depreciation deductions to the noncontributing partners must, to the extent possible, equal book allocations (i.e., depreciation computed using the fair market value of the contributed property) to those partners. Reg. §1.704-3(b)(1). This allocation of the tax depreciation deduction to the noncontributing partners will eliminate any inequities among the capital accounts of the contributing and noncontributing partners.

EXAMPLE 19.26

Charles and David Taylor form CD, an equal partnership. Charles contributes a machine with a fair market value of $100,000 and an adjusted basis to him of $50,000. David contributes $100,000 cash. The two-year remaining recovery period amount of depreciation is $25,000 each year for tax purposes, and $50,000 each year for book purposes. The "built-in" gain is attributed to Charles and the tax depreciation allowable is allocated to David, since the tax depreciation is allocated to the noncontributing partner (David) up to the amount of his book depreciation.. Charles's capital account is credited $100,000; David's account is credited $100,000 for his cash contribution. Assuming no other income or expense for the year, at the end of the year, CD shows a tax loss of $25,000, all attributable to the MACRS write-off. Thus, for tax purposes Charles shows neither gain nor loss; David shows a loss of $25,000 because all of the tax depreciation will be allocated to him. However, for book purposes they will share the book loss of $50,000. Their respective capital account balances show Charles, $75,000 ($100,000 - $25,000 book depreciation); David, $75,000 (same as Charles'). David's basis in CD will be $75,000 ($100,000 - $25,000 tax depreciation), and Charles' will remain at $50,000 (carryover basis from the property contributed).

EXAMPLE 19.27

Assume in Example 19.26 that, at the beginning of the second year, CD sells the machine at its depreciated fair market value of $50,000 ($100,000 – $50,000 book depreciation) and distributes the proceeds. CD has a taxable gain of $25,000 ($50,000 – $25,000 basis), all of which is precontribution gain and is therefore taxable to Charles. Assume further that CD is immediately liquidated and the $150,000 cash is distributed to Charles and David:

	Charles	David
Capital Account January 1, year 1	$100,000	$100,000
Book Loss, year 1	(25,000)	(25,000)
Capital Account January 1, year 2	$75,000	$75,000
Book Gain on sale of machinery	$0	$0
Proceeds on liquidation	$75,000	$75,000

	Charles	David
Original Basis	$50,000	$100,000
Tax Loss, year 1		(25,000)
Tax Gain, year 2	$25,000	
Ending Tax Basis (before liquidation)	$75,000	$75,000

Note that Charles' benefit of deferring the precontribution gain of $50,000 in the property he contributed has in effect been partially offset by the $25,000 tax depreciation deduction that David was allocated and got the benefit of. That leaves only $25,000 of precontribution gain to be allocated to Charles.

¶19,170   PERSONAL-USE PROPERTY CONVERSIONS

Personal (nonbusiness) property which is converted into business property by contribution to the partnership has as its inside basis different amounts for purposes of computing depreciation and any subsequent gain or loss on disposition. A partnership's "depreciable basis" is the lower of (1) the partner's basis in the property at the time of contribution or (2) the property's fair market value at the time of contribution. A partnership's "gain basis" (basis used if sold for a gain) is the partner's basis in the property at the time of contribution adjusted for any capital improvements made and depreciation incurred by the partnership during the partnership's holding period. "Loss basis" is the lower of (1) gain basis (above) or (2) the property's fair market value at the time of contribution. *L.Y.S. Au,* 40 TC 264, CCH Dec. 26,110 (1963), aff'd per curiam, 64-1 USTC ¶9447, 330 F.2d 1008 (CA-9 1964), cert. denied, 379 U.S. 960, 85 S.Ct. 648 (1965). If the amount realized is between the basis for gain and basis for loss, no gain or loss is recognized. (For a general discussion of personal-use property conversions, see Chapter 10, ¶10,215.) The partnership's holding period of the contributed property includes that of the contributing partner. Reg. §1.723-1; Code Sec. 1223(2).

EXAMPLE 19.28	Archie Drew contributes to his partnership his hunting lodge, a capital asset, which cost him $60,000 a year ago. As the lodge was used solely for personal purposes, no depreciation deduction has been taken. At the time of his contribution, the fair market value of the property is $40,000. If the partnership holds the lodge for business purposes, the partnership's depreciable basis in the lodge is $40,000, the lower of (1) $60,000, the partner's basis in the property at the time of contribution, or (2) $40,000, the property's fair market value at the time of contribution. Assuming the partnership had claimed $10,000 depreciation on the lodge during its holding period and then sold it, gain basis would be $50,000 (i.e., the partner's $60,000 basis in the property at the time of contribution reduced by the partnership's $10,000 depreciation adjustment). The partnership's loss basis would be $30,000 (i.e., the lower of (1) the $50,000 gain basis from above or (2) $30,000, the original basis for loss of $40,000 minus the $10,000 depreciation).

Formation of a Partnership—Recognition of Gain or Loss

Transfers unprotected by the nonrecognition rules of Code Sec. 721 include:

- Transfers to an investment company partnership (at ¶19,205);
- Transfers of services for a partnership capital interest (at ¶19,215);
- Transfers of services for an ascertainable partnership income interest (at ¶19,225);
- Property contributions treated as disguised sales between a *non-partner* and the partnership under a *two-year rule* (at ¶19,235);
- Property contributions treated as disguised sales between a *partner* and the partnership under a *seven-year rule* (at ¶19,240);
- Contributions of encumbered property (at ¶19,245).

The recognition rules for these transfers are discussed in the sections that follow.

¶19,205 TRANSFERS TO AN INVESTMENT COMPANY PARTNERSHIP

In order to diversify their portfolio and reduce their investment risk, some investors might try to pool their securities in common ownership if they can do it without recognizing any gain for tax purposes. Formation of a partnership for this purpose will not be tax-free if the result is the creation of an "investment company" partnership. Code Sec. 721(b). An investment company partnership will be found to exist if after the transfer (1) over 80 percent of the partnership assets (excluding cash and nonconvertible debt obligations) are held for investment, and (2) those assets are readily marketable stocks or securities (or interests in regulated investment companies or real estate investment trusts). Reg. §1.351-1(c)(1). If the assets meet these two tests and the transfer results, directly or indirectly, in diversification of the partners' interests upon their contribution to the partnership, all the realized gain, but not loss, on all the contributed assets (not merely the appreciated stock and securities, etc.) is recognized by the transferors.

Diversification Test

For the investment company rule to come into play, diversification must result from partner contributions rather than from later partnership transactions. In addition, if all contributing partners contribute diversified portfolios of stock and securities, Code Sec. 721(b) should not apply. This is because diversification is already present before the contributions. Reg. §1.351-1(c)(6).

EXAMPLE 19.29

Kelly Washburn, Marsha Curth, and Nelson Manning form an equal partnership, and they transfer to the new partnership the following marketable securities, land, and cash:

		Basis to Transferor	Fair Market Value
Kelly	I.P.M. stock	$10,000	$49,000
Marsha	R.R.S. stock	5,000	30,000
	P.D.Q. stock	20,000	10,000
Nelson	Cash	10,000	10,000
	Land	20,000	21,000
		$65,000	$120,000

Excluding the cash of $10,000, $89,000 of the remaining $110,000 of the fair market value of the transferred assets consists of marketable securities. All the parties have received diversification of their investments. Code Sec. 721(b) causes Kelly to recognize the $39,000 of gain on the I.P.M. stock, Marsha to recognize the $25,000 of gain on the R.R.S. stock, and Nelson to recognize the $1,000 of gain on the land. The loss of $10,000 realized by Marsha on the P.D.Q. stock is not recognized.

As with most statutes which are strictly drawn, careful planning, particularly in structuring the asset mix, will permit the avoidance of investment company classification. For example, tax-free treatment is available if each transferor transfers a diversified portfolio of securities to a partnership. Reg. §1.351-1(c)(6). Thus, if Kelly, Marsha, and Nelson in the above example had each owned a portfolio of securities representing ownership in a number of different publicly traded companies, the combination of these portfolios in an equal partnership would avoid recognition of gain.

¶19,215 TRANSFER OF SERVICES FOR PARTNERSHIP CAPITAL INTEREST

When a partner contributes services in exchange for an interest in the capital of the partnership, the non-recognition provision under Code Sec. 721 does not apply. The capital interest (as distinguished from a share in partnership profits) is taxed to the partner as compensation, and it is ordinary income to the extent of the fair market value of the transferred interest. Code Sec. 83(a). The value is determined at the time ownership is vested. Usually this is either at the time the transfer is made for past services, or at the time the services are rendered, where the transfer is conditioned on the completion of the transferee's future services. The basis of the partnership interest to the service partner (exclusive of the effect of partnership liabilities) is the amount of income recognized from the services.

¶19,225 TRANSFER OF SERVICES FOR ASCERTAINABLE PARTNERSHIP INCOME INTEREST

An interest in the future income of a partnership is generally not taxable to the recipient of the interest until the income of the partnership is realized and recognized. The reason for deferring the recognition of income is because of the difficulty in determining a market value of the speculative future profits. Usually, difficulty in determining fair market value is an inadequate reason for not reporting the fair market value of property received in connection with services. In an early Tax Court case, the fair market value of a profits interest received for services was required to be included in the service partner's income. Fair market value was measured easily because the interest was sold within three weeks after it was received. *S. Diamond,* 56 TC 930, Dec. 30,838 (1971), aff'd, 74-1 USTC ¶9306, 492 F.2d 286 (CA-7, 1974). A later decision used liquidation value, that is, the amount the partner would receive were the partnership terminated, to measure the amount to be included in the service partner's income. *D. St. John,* 84-1 USTC ¶9158 (CD Ill., 1983). In a more recent decision, an appellate court admitted the difficulty of measuring the amount to include in income. On the basis of the facts in the case, the court overturned the Tax Court by holding that the receipt of a profits interest for services was not taxable. *W. Campbell,* 91-2 USTC ¶50,420 (CA-8, 1991), aff'g and rev'g 59 TCM 236, Dec. 46,493(M), T.C. Memo. 1990-162. In order to reduce litigation on this issue, the Internal Revenue Service announced that it will not treat the receipt of an interest in the future income of a partnership as a taxable event for a partner unless: (1) the interest relates to a certain and predictable stream of income from partnership assets, (2) the partner disposes of the interest within two years of its receipt, or (3) the interest is a limited partnership interest in a "publicly traded partnership." Rev. Proc. 93-27, 1993-2 CB 343.

Deferral of Recognition of Income

If the capital interest, or the right to the future income, has a readily ascertainable value but it is subject to substantial restrictions which could effect a forfeiture or the interest or right is not transferable, the partner can delay recognition of the income until those restrictions lapse, or the interest or right is transferable, whichever occurs earlier.

Effect on the Partnership of a Transfer for Services

The tax consequences of a contribution of services to the partnership must be understood not only for the partner, but also for the partnership. The partnership interest may be transferred by a present holder or holders of the interest, or the interest may be created in the partnership itself.

The transferor of the partnership interest is generally entitled to a deduction or a basis adjustment for payment made to the partner in the form of the partnership interest. If the payment qualifies as an ordinary and necessary expense, e.g., compensation for services rendered to the partnership (or to the partner if he or she is the transferor), it is currently deductible. Code Secs. 707(c) and 162. If the payment is for a capital expenditure, it must be capitalized and written off over the appropriate cost recovery period for the asset. Code Sec. 263.

The transfer of the partnership interest can result in recognition of income by the existing partners and an adjustment of their bases in their partnership interests. This is because the transfer of a capital interest for services will be treated as if the partnership transferred a portion (equal to the new partner's percentage share) of the partnership's assets to the partner in exchange for the services, and the service partner then contributed this property back to the partnership. The deemed exchange of property for services will result in gain or loss to the partnership (and the partners) equal to the appreciation or depreciation in the assets deemed exchanged. This gain/loss will flow through to the original partners and increase/decrease their bases in their partnership interests. The property deemed distributed will be deemed to have a basis equal to its fair market value in the hands of the service partner, and it will retain that basis when it is deemed to be contributed back to the partnership. As indicated previously, the partnership will typically be entitled to a deduction equal to the fair market value of the services rendered, and the deduction will be split among the original partners. The basis of the partnership interest to the contributing partner (before considering partnership liabilities) will be the amount of ordinary income recognized.

EXAMPLE 19.30

Barko is a cash-basis partnership having assets with a combined basis of $270,000 and comprised of three equal partners. Each partner's outside basis in the partnership is $90,000, the same as their share of the inside basis of the partnership assets. Barko admits Harold Jackson into the partnership, giving him a one-fourth interest in the capital of the partnership. This interest is in payment of $135,000 worth of services previously rendered by Harold to the Barko Partnership.

	Share of Inside Basis—Before	Before F.M.V.	Share of Inside Basis—After	After F.M.V.
Partner 1	$90,000	$180,000	$67,500	$135,000
Partner 2	$90,000	$180,000	$67,500	$135,000
Partner 3	$90,000	$180,000	$67,500	$135,000
Harold Jackson			$135,000	$135,000

Harold has ordinary income of $135,000, the fair market value of his one-fourth capital interest. If the transfer were contingent upon Harold's performance of future services, the transfer would be deemed to take place when those services were rendered and the income would be reportable by him at that time.

The partnership is treated as if it exchanged ¼ of the partnership property to Harold for his services, after which Harold recontributed the property back to the partnership. Partners 1, 2, and 3 each have a new basis of $67,500 ($90,000 + $22,500 gain – $45,000 deduction) because they each recognize a gain of $22,500 (¼ times $90,000) in transferring partnership assets with a basis of $22,500 and a fair market value of $45,000, but they each have a reduction of $45,000 in basis for their share of the compensation deduction.

The above example covers the transfer of a capital interest in connection with services. Recall that when the transfer is one of a future partnership income interest, the transaction may or may not be taxable (due to conflicting court decisions) and the difficulty of measuring the value of the future interest should result in no income recognition at transfer.

It should be noted that under Proposed Regulations both capital and profit interests received in exchange for services would fall under Code Sec. 83, and an election could be made to immediately recognize income applicable to a nonvested interest. A safe harbor rule under the Proposed Regulations would generally allow the recipient of a profits interest to escape taxation completely on its receipt. Any taxable interest would be treated as guaranteed payment to the service partner, and the partnership would get a deduction for it. Prop. Reg. § 1.721-1.

¶19,235 DISGUISED SALES

Disguised Sales in General

As has been stated earlier, when there is a contribution of property to the partnership in exchange for a partnership interest, neither gain nor loss is generally recognized by the contributing partner. Also, when there is deemed to be a current distribution of money, the partner recognizes neither gain nor loss unless the deemed money distribution exceeds the partner's basis. This traditional method of tax accounting for property contributions and distributions would allow sellers of property to disguise a sale to a partnership as a contribution of property coupled with a subsequent distribution of money. The sellers and buyers could take the position that a bona fide contribution and an unrelated distribution had occurred and report the transaction in that manner rather than as a sale.

The sale could also be made in exchange for other property. For example, a taxpayer could contribute property "A" to a partnership and receive property "B" as a distribution in liquidation of the taxpayer's interest (*a transfer that is directly reciprocal*). Or, a partnership could be formed by partners "A" and "B" contributing properties "A" and "B," respectively, and later, property "A" would be distributed to partner "B" in liquidation of partner "B's" interest, leaving the partnership with only property "B" as its principal asset and partner "A" as its principal partner (*a transfer that is indirectly reciprocal*). Under the traditional contribution and distribution rules of partnership taxation, the "sales" would be tax-free.

Congress enacted three provisions designed to curb these abuses:

1. Two-year rule for contributions and distributions that are *directly* reciprocal. Code Sec. 707(a)(2)(B).
2. Seven-year rule for contributions and distributions that are *directly* reciprocal. Code Sec. 737.
3. Seven-year rule for contributions and distributions that are *indirectly* reciprocal. Code Sec. 704(c)(1)(B).

Two-Year Rule for Contributions and Distributions that Are Directly Reciprocal

If property is contributed to a partnership and within two years the partnership transfers money or other property to the contributing partner, then all or part of the transfer is presumed to be a sale of the property to the partnership. If the contribution and distribution are more than two years apart, then there is a presumption that a "sale" did *not* take place. Reg. §§1.707-3(c) and (d). Both presumptions are rebuttable if the taxpayer can clearly establish that the transaction is (or is not) a disguised sale. Exceptions to the two-year disguised sale presumption include *guaranteed payments for capital, reasonable preferred returns,* and *operating cash flow distributions.*

If a contribution and distribution are treated as a disguised sale, then, under the two-year rule, the "sale" part of the contribution (equal in value to the later distribution) is treated as if it occurred between the partnership and a nonpartner. Reg. §1.707-3. The part of the property not treated as being "sold" is treated as being contributed to the partnership. The partner's adjusted basis in the transferred property should be prorated between the portion of the property deemed "sold" and the portion of the property deemed contributed. Thus, the contributing partner would only be able to increase their outside basis in the partnership interest by the original basis of the part of the property that was not "sold", but instead was treated as contributed. The partnership determines its initial inside basis in the contributed property by the sum of (1) the portion of the partner's precontribution basis in the property deemed to be a "contribution" and (2) the partnership's deemed purchase price of the contributed property.

EXAMPLE 19.31

Conor transfers land to a partnership in exchange for a $10,000 capital interest and $30,000 cash. Conor had held the land for a long-term period. At the time of contribution, the land's fair market value (FMV) is $40,000 and its adjusted basis is $12,000. Seventy-five percent ($30,000 cash received/$40,000 value of the land) of the contribution is deemed to be a Code Sec. 707(a)(2)(B) disguised sale. The remaining 25 percent of the capital interest received represents a Code Sec. 721 contribution. Conor should report a $21,000 long-term capital gain ($28,000 total gain times 75%) on the disguised sale and a $3,000 outside basis ($12,000 original basis times 25%) in the partnership. The partnership should report a $33,000 inside basis ($30,000 "sale" price plus $3,000 contributed basis) in the land.

	Total	Disguised Sale [75% ($30,000/$40,000)]	Contribution [25% ($10,000/$40,000)]
FMV of capital interest	$10,000	$7,500	$2,500
Cash	30,000	22,500	7,500
Amount realized	$40,000	$30,000	$10,000
Basis in land	12,000	9,000	3,000
Realized gain	$28,000	$21,000	$7,000
Recognized gain		$21,000	$0
Character of gain		Long-term capital gain	Not recognized
Reason for tax treatment		Reg. §1.707-3(a) (recognition of realized gain from disguised sale)	Code Sec. 721 (nonrecognition on transfer of property for a partnership interest)
Conor's basis in the partnership interest =		$3,000 (25% of the basis of land is attributable to a "contribution")	
Partnership's basis in the land =		$33,000 (Conor's $3,000 basis of land "contributed" + $30,000 "sale" price)	

Even if Conor had received the $30,000 cash more than two years after receipt of a partnership interest, the IRS may still maintain that Conor's contribution was partially a disguised sale as above. However, since there would be a presumption that there was not a "sale", the IRS would have the burden of proving otherwise.

If the property contribution and the related distribution are not simultaneous, then the partner is treated as if she received an obligation to receive money (a note) on the date of the contribution. Later distributions are deemed to be payments on the hypothetical note, and gain (if any) can be recognized under the installment method if the transaction otherwise qualifies for installment sale treatment. Liabilities incurred by a partner in anticipation of the transfer are treated as part of a sale to the extent that the liability is assumed by the partnership. Again, presumptions are established. Debt incurred more than two years before the transfer is not deemed to be in anticipation of the transfer, while debt incurred within the two-year period generally is considered to be in anticipation of the transfer.

The IRS requires that disclosure be made for transactions which could be covered by these disguised sale rules. In this regard, disclosure on Form 8275 (Disclosure Statement) or an attachment to the return of a partner receiving property generally is required for (1) contribution/distribution transfers within the two-year period, and (2) certain liabilities incurred within two years prior to a transfer of property securing the debt.

¶19,240   DISGUISED SALES UNDER THE SEVEN YEAR RULE

Seven-Year Rule for Transfers That Are Directly Reciprocal

Special rules were enacted in order to prohibit the shifting of a partner's precontribution gain from a contributed property to a noncontributed property distributed to such partner. If a partner contributes appreciated property to a partnership and receives a distribution of any property other than *cash* or the *originally contributed property* within **seven years** of such contribution, the partner (or successor) recognizes the lesser of:

    i.   the excess of the fair market value of the distributed property over the partner's outside basis in the partnership before distribution, reduced (but not below zero) by any money received in the distribution; or

    ii.   the remaining net precontribution (built-in) gain. Code Sec. 737.

EXAMPLE 19.32	Assume from the preceding example that Conor receives the $30,000 distribution of cash three years after his contribution of the land. The two-year disguised sale rule would presumably not apply since the transfers did not occur within a two-year period. Also, the seven-year rule for disguised sales would not apply since he received a cash distribution. However, if his outside basis in the partnership were below $30,000 immediately before the $30,000 cash distribution, he would still be required to recognize capital gain based on the excess amount of cash received over his outside basis in the partnership. (See ¶20,022 for a discussion on excess cash distributions.)

The amount of gain recognized by a partner under Code Sec. 737 increases the partner's outside basis in the partnership interest. Code Sec. 737(c)(1). The partnership's inside basis in the property originally contributed by the distributee partner is increased by the same amount. Code Sec. 737(c)(2). The character of the gain or loss is determined by the character of the property when originally held by the contributing partner. Note that if the originally contributed property is distributed back to the contributing partner within seven years, that partner assumes the partnership's inside basis, recognizing no precontribution gain.

EXAMPLE 19.33	From the preceding example, assume that, instead of receiving a $30,000 cash distribution at the time of his land contribution, Conor receives a painting from the partnership three years after the contribution. The fair market value and inside basis of the painting are the same, $30,000. Also assume that his outside basis in his partnership interest is still $12,000 immediately before the distribution. The seven-year rule for disguised sales would apply and Conor would recognize an $18,000 gain [the lesser of (1) $18,000, i.e., $30,000 fair market value of the painting minus $12,000 outside basis in his partnership interest; or (2) his $28,000 precontribution gain, i.e., $40,000 land value minus $12,000 precontribution basis in the land]. Conor's $18,000 gain would be added to the partnership's inside (tax) basis in the land Conor originally contributed, resulting in a $30,000 adjusted inside basis ($12,000 + $18,000). Conor's outside basis in his partnership interest would also increase by the $18,000 gain to $30,000. His remaining precontribution gain attributable to the land would be only $10,000 ($40,000 fair market value at the time of contribution minus $30,000 adjusted inside basis to the partnership).

Although the values presented in the facts of Examples 19.31 and 19.33 are similar, the tax consequences are quite different as can be seen in the table below.

Comparison of Examples Illustrating the Two-Year and Seven-Year Rules		
	Example 19.31	**Example 19.33**
Timing rule	Two-year rule	Seven-year rule
Recognized gain from the disguised sale	$21,000	$18,000
Partnership's inside basis in the land after the disguised sale	$33,000	$30,000
Conor's outside basis in the partnership interest after the disguised sale	$3,000	$30,000
Conor's precontribution gain after the disguised sale	$7,000	$10,000

Because the timing and magnitude of the gain recognition under the two-year and seven-year rules likely will differ, and because the IRS's opportunity to successfully apply the disguised sale recharacterization will vary greatly depending upon the particular facts of each case, the IRS can be expected frequently to assert both theories of recognition independently (assuming the suspect distribution is within the prescribed seven-year period). The two provisions should not, however, overlap. Once the IRS is successful in recharacterizing a suspect contribution to a partnership as a disguised sale under the two-year rule, the contributing partner would already be characterized as having engaged in a taxable exchange of the appreciated property with the partnership at the outset and having triggered a recognition of built-in gain.

PLANNING POINTER	The seven-year reciprocal transfer rule under Code Sec. 737 requires that the contributing partner recognize gain if the fair market value of the property distributed exceeds the distributee partner's outside basis in the partnership interest. Thus, for example, a contribution of property to increase that partner's outside basis in his partnership interest in order to avoid recognition of gain under Code Sec. 737 will be respected. Also, Code Sec. 737 provides that the contributing partner's recognized gain is limited to the remaining net precontribution (built-in) gain. Thus a partner may be able to contribute built-in loss property, immediately prior to a partnership distribution, in order to reduce the net precontribution gain inherent in that partner's contributed properties. These strategies, however, would still need to avoid the two-year disguised sale rules under Code Sec. 707(a)(2)(B). The partnership could consider also obtaining loans which increase the partners' outside bases in their partnership interest.

Seven-Year Rule for Transfers That Are Indirectly Reciprocal

Before October 4, 1989, it was relatively simple for a seller of property to avoid gain by contributing it to a partnership that distributed it to another partner (the buyer) leaving the partnership with the property the buyer had contributed (the purchase price).

EXAMPLE 19.34	A owns land that has a $98,000 fair market value and a $10,000 adjusted basis. The BCD partnership wishes to buy and develop the land, but A does not want to recognize gain on the property's sale. A new ABCD limited partnership is formed with A contributing the land, B contributing $98,000, and C and D contributing $1,000 each. The land is then distributed to B in liquidation of B's interest. B recognizes no gain, takes a $98,000 basis in the land, and develops the land. The ACD partnership continues as an investment partnership with A as the general partner holding a 98% interest. Its sole asset is $100,000 cash.

Congress enacted provisions to prevent property owners from avoiding taxation on the disposition of their property through partnership arrangements such as that above. If the contributed appreciated property is distributed to *another* partner or a third party within **seven years** of the contribution date, the contributing partner (or successor) recognizes any remaining net precontribution gain or loss on the property. The amount of gain (or loss) recognized increases (decreases) both the contributing partner's outside basis in the partnership and any distributee partner's basis in the property received. Code Sec. 704(c)(1)(B).

EXAMPLE 19.35	In the preceding example, A's precontribution gain is $88,000 ($98,000 fair market value less $10,000 adjusted basis). A distribution of the land to B within seven years of the contribution date results in gain recognition to A in the amount of $88,000.

EXAMPLE 19.36	In year 1, CP contributes land ($10,000 basis, $40,000 fair market value) to a partnership in exchange for a 1/3 interest in capital and profits. In year 6, the partnership distributes the land to DP, also a 1/3 partner, when the land's fair market value is $50,000. CP has a taxable gain of $30,000 (i.e., $40,000 - $10,000) and gets a $30,000 increase in outside basis. DP's basis in the land is $40,000 (the partnership's $10,000 inside basis plus $30,000, the amount of CP's taxable gain).

The character of the contributing partner's gain or loss is determined as if the property had been sold by the partnership to the distributee partner. Thus, if the distributee partner holds more than a 50 percent capital or profits interest in the partnership, any gain recognized by the contributing partner is ordinary income if the property is not a capital asset in the hands of the distributee partner. Reg. §1.704-4(b)(2); Code Sec. 707(b)(2). In addition, because the property is treated as having been sold by the partnership to the distributee partner, any loss that would have been disallowed under the related party rules (see ¶19,501) had the distributed property actually been sold to the distributee partner will be disallowed.

¶19,245 CONTRIBUTION OF ENCUMBERED PROPERTY

When encumbered property is contributed to a partnership, the liability creates a dual adjustment to the outside basis of the contributing partner and the other partners. The contributing partner is relieved of a part of the total obligation to repay the loan, and the other partners are deemed to have accepted individual responsibility to repay their pro rata share of the debt. Thus, if the contributed property is subject to a liability, or if liabilities of the contributing partner are assumed by the partnership, the basis of the contributing partner's interest is reduced by the portion of the indebtedness deemed transferred to the other partners (some of the debt will be "retained" by the contributing partner through his or her ownership in the partnership). This deemed transfer of indebtedness is treated as a distribution of cash to the contributing partner, and will reduce the contributing partner's basis, but not below zero. The assumption of the contributing partner's liabilities is treated by the other partners as a contribution of money by them to the partnership and will increase their bases. Reg. §§1.722-1 and 1.752-1.

A partner's basis cannot be reduced below zero, and when the deemed distribution of money exceeds the basis of the partnership interest of the contributing partner, that excess is given capital gain treatment. Code Sec. 731(a).

| EXAMPLE 19.37 | Archie Drew acquired a 20 percent interest in a partnership in exchange for contributing property to the partnership. At the time of Archie's contribution, the property had a fair market value of $10,000 and an adjusted basis to Archie of $4,000, and it was encumbered by a mortgage of $2,000. The mortgage was assumed by the partnership. Archie's basis in his partnership interest is $2,400, computed as follows: |

Adjusted basis of property		$4,000
Liability effect:		
Deemed distribution (100% × $2,000)	$(2,000)	
Deemed contribution (20% × $2,000)	400	
Net deemed distribution		(1,600)
Archie's basis in his partnership interest		$2,400

See Reg. §1.722-1, Example (1). Notice that the net deemed distribution, that is, the net liability relief to the contributing partner, generally is calculated as follows: amount of liabilities transferred × (1 – contributing partner's interest in the partnership).

| EXAMPLE 19.38 | If, in the preceding example, the property contributed by Archie was encumbered by a mortgage of $6,000, the analysis of the transaction would be the same. However, because of the larger debt, the basis of Archie's interest would be zero. Archie's adjusted basis of $4,000 in the contributed property is reduced by the net deemed distribution of $4,800 [$6,000 × (1 – 20%)]. Since his basis cannot be less than zero, Archie reports a capital gain of $800 ($4,800 – $4,000) upon his contribution. |

| PLANNING POINTER | If a partner recognizes gain on the contribution of appreciated property that is encumbered by a liability, the partnership can increase the basis of that property by making an election under Code Sec. 754. See ¶20,080– ¶20,083. |

¶19,250 LIABILITIES ASSUMED BY PARTNERSHIP

When the partnership assumes a liability (for example, agrees to pay the debt if the collateral should be insufficient on foreclosure), the entire liability is added to the partners' bases. But where the partnership merely takes property subject to a liability (the partnership is not liable for any deficiency), the debt is reflected in the partners' bases only to the extent of the lower of (1) the amount of the debt, or (2) the fair market value of the property which is subject to the debt. Code Sec. 752(c).

EXAMPLE 19.39	Mary and Anne King each own a 50 percent interest in the MaryAnne Partnership. The partnership is owed $1,000 by a customer who is unable to pay. The customer owns an asset which has a fair market value of $70,000 but which is encumbered by an $80,000 mortgage. Hoping that the property will increase in value, the MaryAnne Partnership accepts the property in satisfaction of the $1,000, taking it subject to the mortgage but not assuming personal liability. The bases of the partners' interests in the MaryAnne Partnership are increased by $70,000. The basis of the property to the partnership is $81,000. (See ¶19,551 for the at-risk limitation on passthrough losses where the creditor has no recourse against the individual partners upon default in payment of the debt.)

Recourse and Nonrecourse Liabilities

Although the term "assumption" was used above with respect to the transfer of encumbered assets, so long as the value of the transferred property is at least as great as the encumbrance, the same treatment is given (for purposes of computing partner basis) those debts which are legally assumed and those debts where the property is merely taken subject to the encumbrance. From a practical standpoint, in both situations the partnership intends to retire the outstanding debt.

A borrower may wish to obtain funds but not be personally liable for the repayment of the debt. If a lender agrees to look for repayment only to the activity being financed, the debt is said to be a "nonrecourse debt." Otherwise, the debt is "recourse debt." Both types of debt increase the basis of a partner in the partnership interest. When the partner sells the interest in the partnership, the partner's share of the debt is added to the amount realized *and* added to the basis of the partnership interest, causing the amount of the debt to, in effect, wash out in the transaction. For nonrecourse debt, however, as the partner has no personal risk of loss if the debt is not repaid, such debt may not be available to offset partnership passthrough losses. See ¶19,551 for further discussion.

Accounts Payable of Cash-Basis Contributors

Code Sec. 704(c)(3) addresses the problem of accounts payable and accrued expense items contributed by a cash-basis taxpayer to a partnership. Generally, the contributing partner is allocated the deduction generated by payment of these items by the partnership. However, these items are not considered "liabilities" for purposes of determining a partner's basis for a partnership interest under Code Sec. 752.

Exhibit 1 summarizes the general rules for gain or loss recognition when a partner contributes property to a partnership in exchange for a partnership interest.

Exhibit 1. FORMATION: EFFECT ON CONTRIBUTING PARTNER

Any control requirement for tax-free treatment?	No control requirement. Code Sec. 721.
How is an owner's recognized gain or loss on a partnership formation determined?	Recognized gain may arise from: • contributions to an investment company partnership; • service contributions for a capital interest; • service contributions for an ascertainable income interest; • disguised sales under a two-year rule; • disguised sales under a seven-year rule; • excess net debt relief from encumbered property contributions. Realized losses are • never recognized in any exchange of property for a partnership interest; • never recognized in a disguised sale by partners owning more-than 50%; • always recognized in a disguised sale under the two-year rule by partners owning 50% or less.
Under what conditions is gain recognized from contributions to investment company partnerships?	If, after the transfer, (1) over 80% of the partnership assets (other than cash and nonconvertible debt obligations) consist of readily marketable stocks or securities held for investment; and (2) the transfer results in diversification of the partners' interests, all realized gain (but not loss) on all contributed assets is recognized.

How is gain or loss from a disguised sale under the two-year rule determined?	Recognized gain or loss =
	[a – c] x [b ÷ a], where,
	a = FMV of the property contributed;
	b = FMV of other property received within two years of new ownership;
	c = Basis of property contributed.
	[Note that: "[a – c]" (above) = realized gain; and,
	         "[b ÷ a]" (above) = % of the transaction
	            deemed a disguised sale.
	Exception: losses from disguised sales are not recognized if the distribution is to a partner owning 50% or more.

How do you determine a partner's outside basis increase from contributions involving a disguised sale under the two-year rule?	Increase in a partner's outside basis in a partnership interest = (c) x [(a – b) ÷ a], where a, b, and c are defined immediately above.
What is excess net debt relief?	Excess net debt relief = (a) – (b) – (c), where, (a) = debt relief from encumbered property contribution; (b) = debt assumption (i.e., share of partnership debt from encumbered property contribution); (c) = basis of all property contributed.
What is a partner's outside basis in a newly acquired partnership interest?	The following formula applies to both tax-free and taxable exchanges: A partner's initial outside basis in a partnership interest is generally determined as follows: + Basis in contributed property; + Any share of partnership debt assumption; – Debt relief; + Any recognized gain from excess net debt relief.

Taxable Year of Partner and Partnership

¶19,275 PARTNER'S YEAR OF INCLUSION

The partners must report their distributive share of income and losses of their partnership in the partner's taxable year in which or with which the partnership year ends. Code Sec. 706(a); Reg. §1.706-1(a). This rule, unless restricted, provides an opportunity for a perpetual deferral of substantial amounts of income.

EXAMPLE 19.40

Betty and John Jones each own a 50 percent interest in the BJ Partnership, which has a fiscal year ending September 30. During fiscal year 2017-2018 the partnership has taxable income of $120,000, which it earned ratably during the 12-month period. Thus, $30,000 was earned in 2017, and $90,000 was earned in 2018. Betty and John will report $60,000 of this partnership income on their (calendar-year) 2018 individual tax returns, although economically they each, through the partnership, earned $45,000 of it during calendar-year 2018. Notice that the taxation of the $30,000 earned by the partnership in 2017 is deferred until 2018 because the partners and the partnership have different year-ends.

The items includible and deductible on the partner's individual return are determined with reference to the partnership's method of accounting, without regard to whether the partner reports on the cash or the accrual basis. Guaranteed payments made to a partner for services or for the use of capital are includible in the partner's income at the same time as the partner's distributive share of partnership income and losses. (For a discussion of guaranteed payments see ¶19,515.)

EXAMPLE 19.41

Frank Flanagan and Max McCann are equal partners in the FM Partnership. Frank and Max both report their income on the calendar year using the cash method. For good business reasons, the partnership was permitted to use a June 30 fiscal year and the accrual method. For the fiscal year ending June 30, 2017, FM reports partnership ordinary income of $20,000 for each partner. Payment of all sums to Frank and Max was actually delayed until January 2018. Frank and Max must each report $20,000 as their 2017 income—the income earned by the partnership under its method of accounting for its fiscal year ending June 30, 2017.

Varying Interest Rule

The varying interest rule controls the allocation of partnership income to any partner whose interest in a partnership changes, whether because of the sale or purchase of a partnership interest, partial liquidation of a partner's interest, gift of an interest, or otherwise. It also applies to an incoming partner. Code Sec. 706(d)(1). In essence, the partnership may comply with either of two methods of prorating items of income and expense of the partnership. It may prorate such items on a day-by-day basis through the year in which the change of ownership occurred, or it may treat its books as having been closed for this purpose, thus segmenting the tax year into that period of time prior to the change and that period of time following. It may also use any other reasonable method to prorate income and expense items. Reg. §1.706-1(c)(2)(ii). Accordingly, an agreement cannot be modified to assign a full year's income to a partner who acquires an interest at midyear. Certain cash-basis items are, in effect, placed on the accrual basis to prevent year-end incoming partners from benefiting from deductions incurred by the partnership prior to their admission.

Allocation of Cash-Basis Items

A partnership that uses the cash basis of accounting for interest, taxes, payment for services or for the use of property, and any other item specified in the regulations, must allocate those items to the incoming and selling partners on a daily basis in proportion to their interests in the partnership at the end of each day.

Further, if any portion of such payment is for these "allocable cash-basis items" incurred in a prior tax period (but paid in the current period), it must be treated as paid on the first day of the period in which the payment is made and allocated to the partners as of that date. If a partner during the accrual period is not a partner on such first day, the partner's portion is capitalized. If any portion of the payment of an "allocable cash-basis item" is attributable to a following tax period (even though paid in the current period), it must be treated as paid on the last day of the period in which the payment is made and allocated to the partners as of such last day. Code Sec. 706(d)(2). Prepayment rules prohibit much distortion in this situation.

EXAMPLE 19.42

Four equal partners of a calendar-year, cash-basis partnership, Zemmox, admit Willie Yen to a 20 percent partnership interest on December 2, 2017. Zemmox borrowed on a demand note $100,000 on April 30, 2017. The holder had not demanded payment, but Zemmox paid $8,000 (eight months' interest) on December 31, 2017. Willie Yen's attributed share is $200 (20% of 1/8 of $8,000). The remainder, $7,800, is attributable to the other four partners holding the 80 percent interest.

EXAMPLE 19.43	If, in the preceding example, Zemmox delayed the payment until January 31, 2018, and then paid $9,000 (nine months' interest), Willie Yen's portion of the deduction is $400 (20% of 2/9 of $9,000). The remainder, $8,600, is attributable to the other four partners holding the 80 percent interest.

EXAMPLE 19.44	Assume, in the foregoing examples, that Willie Yen purchased on December 1, 2017, his 20 percent interest from Adam Dee, one of the five equal original partners of Zemmox, and the interest payment of $9,000 was made January 31, 2018. Willie Yen claims the same amount of interest, $400, his 20 percent of the December and January accruals. The $7,000 attributable to April 30–November 30, 2017, is accruable to the then five partners, of whom Adam Dee was one. His share is therefore $1,400 (1/5 × $7,000), but as he is not a partner of Zemmox on January 1, 2018, that amount is not currently deductible by the partnership and must be capitalized.

¶19,280 TAXABLE YEAR OF THE PARTNERSHIP

Required Taxable Year—Majority Interest Year

Partnerships are generally required to elect the same taxable year as their partners to prevent the deferral of income, as shown above. Code Sec. 706(b). The general rule is that the partnership must use its "majority interest taxable year," which is the common tax year, if any, used by one or more partners owning a majority interest (greater than 50%) in the partnership's capital and profits on the first day (called the "testing day") of the partnership's existing tax year. Notice that the ownership requirement is conjunctive, capital *and* profits. If the partnership changes its tax year under the majority interest rule, the IRS cannot require another change for two tax years following the year of change, unless tax avoidance can be shown.

EXAMPLE 19.45	Alice Ames and Barbara McCarthy joined Acme Corporation in forming a partnership. Alice and Barbara each received a 26 percent interest in the partnership's income and capital. They report on the calendar year. Acme Corporation received a 48 percent interest in the partnership's income and capital and it reports on a June 30 taxable year. The partnership is required to adopt the calendar year, the year of Alice and Barbara, who own a majority interest.

EXAMPLE 19.46	Same facts as in the preceding example, except the ownership interests of Alice and Barbara were each 24 percent and the corporation's interest was 52 percent. The partnership is required to adopt a June 30 taxable year, the year of the corporate partner, as it holds the majority interest.

Principal Partners' Common Tax Year

If there is no majority interest taxable year, the partnership must use the same year as that of the principal partners (i.e., those owning 5 percent or more interest in either the profits or capital of the partnership). Notice that the connecting word is disjunctive, profits *or* capital. If all the principal partners have the same tax year, then that is the required tax year for the partnership. If the principal partners do not all have the same tax year, the least aggregate deferral method should be used.

Least Aggregate Deferral Method

If there is no majority interest taxable year and all of the principal partners do not have the same taxable year, the regulations prescribe that the tax year will be the one which results in the least aggregate deferral of income by the partners. Reg. §1.706-1T(a)(2). In computing the deferral, each partner's percentage of profit is multiplied by the number of months that income would be deferred for that partner if the tax year in question were used by the partnership. Deferral to each partner is measured in terms of months from the end of the partnership's taxable year forward to the end of the partner's taxable year. For example, if the partnership year ends on July 31 and the partner's year ends on December 31, the deferral is five months because the partner's share of the partnership income from August through December is being deferred until the partner's next taxable year. The sums of these computations are compared, and the tax year producing the lowest number is the one to be used. If there are two or more months with the lowest deferral, the partnership may choose whichever one of these year-ends it wishes.

EXAMPLE 19.47

Amanda and Bob are partners in the Fruit Partnership. Amanda reports her income on the fiscal year ending June 30, and Bob reports his income on the fiscal year ending July 31. They each own a 50 percent interest in capital and profits of the partnership. There is no majority interest year since the partners have different year-ends and neither owns more than a 50 percent interest. Both partners are principal partners, but they do not have the same year-end. Therefore, the least aggregate deferral method must be used. The two test years are years ending June 30 and July 31.

Test #1 6/30 FY

Partner's	Year End	Interest in Profits	Months of Deferral	Interest X Months Deferred
Amanda	6/30	.50	0	.0
Bob	7/31	.50	1	.5
				.5

Test #2 7/31 FY

Partner's	Year End	Interest in Profits	Months of Deferral	Interest X Months Deferred
Amanda	6/30	.50	11	5.5
Bob	7/31	.50	0	.0
				5.5

The required tax year for the partnership is the June 30 fiscal year.

Natural Business Year-End

A partnership that can establish that it has a business purpose for another year may elect to use that fiscal year for reporting purposes if they apply for and are granted the permission of the Commissioner to use that fiscal year. Code Sec. 706(b)(1)(C); Reg. §1.706-1(b); Rev. Proc. 2002-39, 2002-1 CB 1046.

The "business purpose" test is met if the date selected as the end of the partnership's fiscal year conforms to the end of its natural business year. A partnership is deemed to have a natural business year-end if the partnership receives at least 25 percent of its gross receipts during the last two months of the proposed fiscal year for three consecutive years. Reg. §1.442-2(c)(2).

EXAMPLE 19.48

Partnership Unicorn has, since its inception, gross receipts from its sales or services evenly spread over its tax year. All of its partners are individuals with a calendar tax year. It has no natural business year and must adopt the calendar year.

EXAMPLE 19.49

Partnership Dragon had 30 percent of its gross receipts during the months of February and March 2017. It also experienced the same percentage of its annual receipts during February and March 2015 and 2016. Dragon has established a March 31 natural business year.

Although the 25 percent test is generally preferred because it is less subjective, a partnership can also show that it has a natural business year using an annual business cycle test (where there is a peak period of business) or a seasonal business test (where the business is only operational for part of the year).

Section 444 Election

Code Sec. 444 permits a partnership to adopt or change to a fiscal year other than the taxable year required by Code Sec. 706(b) so long as the deferral period is no greater than the shorter of the deferral period in use or three months. In either case, the partnership is required to make an advance deposit that approximates the amount of tax being deferred by the partners over the deferral period. This toll charge on the amount of deferred income is computed at the highest individual tax rate plus 1 percent. Code Sec. 7519. The complexity of the annual computation and the required advance deposit of the tax make this deferral choice unacceptable to most taxpayers.

¶19,285   **ELECTIONS BY PARTNER OR PARTNERSHIP**

Most of the elections available to partnerships are made at the partnership level. However, a partner may elect on an individual income tax return to treat foreign income taxes paid or accrued by the partnership as a deduction or as a credit. The total amount deducted or taken as a credit by a partner includes the distributive share of any such taxes paid or accrued by the partnership. Elections also made at the partner level relate to the treatment of mining and exploration expenditures and reduction of basis of property upon forgiveness of indebtedness.

All elections (other than those above) affecting the computation of income derived from a partnership are made by the partnership. Thus, elections as to methods of accounting, methods of computing depreciation, the use of the installment method, and the option to expense intangible drilling and development costs, as well as other permissible elections, must be made by the partnership. All these elections apply to all partners equally, but no election made by a partnership has any force or effect with respect to any partner's nonpartnership interests. Code Sec. 703(b); Reg. §1.703-1(b).

EXAMPLE 19.50   Abner French is a partner in Banjo Partnership, which reports the income from sales of its inventory on the installment method and utilizes the most rapid MACRS lives in depreciating its assets. Abner also operates a sole proprietorship which competes with Banjo Partnership. Abner is not bound in the sole proprietorship by either of the elections made on his behalf by Banjo Partnership.

¶19,290   **INITIAL COSTS OF A PARTNERSHIP**

Organization and Syndication Costs

The concept of matching income with the expense of generating that income would require that partnership organization costs be capitalized and amortized over the life of the partnership. Examples of partnership organization costs are legal fees for drafting the partnership agreement, accounting fees to organize the partnership, and state and local filing fees. Reg. §1.709-2(a). Expenses of selling partnership interests or transferring title of property to the partnership do not qualify as organizational costs. Up to $5,000 of organization costs can be currently deducted. Any remaining organization costs can be amortized over 180 months. The $5,000 deduction amount is reduced by the excess of cumulative organization costs over $50,000. Any amortization must begin with the first month of the partnership's commencement of business. Code Sec. 709. If the partnership is liquidated within the 180-month period, the unamortized balance may be deducted as a loss. Code Sec. 165 and 709.

EXAMPLE 19.51   In 2017, a calendar-year partnership incurred the following costs related to its formation:

Attorneys' fees—drafting partnership agreement	$5,500
Recording costs—filing the legal documents	500
Accounting fees—setting up books	4,000

The partnership commenced business April 1, 2018. In 2018, it may deduct $5,000 of the above expenses and amortize $250 ($5,000/180 x 9 months) of the remaining costs.

More restrictive rules apply to the expenses of selling partnership interests. For example, the costs of issuing and marketing interests in a partnership syndication, such as commissions, professional fees, and printing costs, must be capitalized and are not subject to amortization under the 180-month provision. Reg. §1.709-2(b).

EXAMPLE 19.52

Assume the partnership formed in the preceding example incurred the following costs:

Commissions for sale of partnership interests	$40,000
Printing marketing brochures	20,000

The above costs would have to be capitalized. They could not be charged off against income. They could only be deducted upon the termination of the partnership.

Start-up Expenditures

Closely akin to organization costs are start-up costs which are statutorily defined as (1) costs paid or incurred in connection with the investigation or acquisition of an active trade or business, (2) costs paid or incurred in the creation of such a trade or business, or (3) preactivity costs. The expenditures must be of a character which would qualify as ordinary and necessary expenses if the trade or business were active. Up to $5,000 of start-up costs (reduced for the excess of total costs over $50,000) can be deducted. Any remaining costs may be amortizable over 180 months, beginning with the month in which the active trade or business begins. Code Sec. 195.

Operation of the Partnership

¶19,301   LIABILITY FOR TAX

A partnership as such is not subject to the income tax. Persons carrying on business as partners are liable for income tax only in their separate or individual capacities, including, of course, any tax attributable to their respective shares of partnership income.

¶19,335   GROSS INCOME OF PARTNER

The words "distributive share" are sometimes confusing to newcomers in the partnership tax field. For purposes of tax returns, the partner must report the portion of the income and deduction items which are allocable to the partner, whether or not any distribution of them was actually received. This portion of the income and deduction items is that partner's "distributive share."

If there is a need to determine an individual partner's share of the partnership's gross income, each partner will include a ratable portion of the gross income used to calculate partnership ordinary income or loss, plus a ratable portion of the gross amount of any specially reported items. Code Sec. 702(c); Reg. §1.702-1(c)(1). For example, a partner is required to include the distributive share of the partnership gross income in order to determine the necessity of filing an individual return or to compute the amount of gross income received from U.S. possessions., or to determine whether there is an extension of the statute of limitations from three to six years because a partner has understated gross income by more than 25 percent.

The fraction of the partner's share of the partnership gross income that the partner is "deemed" to have reported is the same as the fraction of the partner's distributive share of any item of partnership income, gain, loss, deduction, or credit that the partner actually did report.

EXAMPLE 19.53

Abdul Maruk is entitled to one-fourth of the profits of the Abdul-Carter Partnership. The partnership has $1,000,000 of gross income and $200,000 of taxable income. Abdul reports only $30,000 as his distributive share of partnership profits. He should have shown $50,000 (1/4 of $200,000) as his distributive share of profits, and the share of the partnership gross income related to the $50,000 of income was $250,000 (1/4 of $1,000,000). However, since Abdul included only $30,000 on his return without explaining in the return the difference of $20,000, he is regarded as having stated in his return only $150,000 ($30,000/$50,000 of $250,000) as gross income from the partnership. Reg. §1.702-1(c)(2).

Ordinary Business Income of the Partnership

All income and deductions that are allowed, and that are not required to be separately stated, are netted to produce the "ordinary business income of the partnership". Usually this can be thought of as the partnership's operating income, and is reported on page 1 of Form 1065. Each partner is required to include in their individual tax return their distributive share of the ordinary business income or loss of the partnership. Code Sec. 702(a)(8); Reg. §1.702-1(a)(9). The partnership income is determined in the same manner as that of an individual, but the partnership is not allowed the following deductions in computing the ordinary income/loss of the partnership:

1. Personal exemptions deduction,
2. Foreign taxes deduction,
3. Charitable contributions deduction,
4. Net operating loss deduction,
5. Itemized nonbusiness deductions for individuals (medical and dental expenses, expenses incurred in the production or collection of income or for the management, conservation, or maintenance of property held for the production of income, or in connection with the determination, collection, or refund of any tax, child care expenses, alimony, and taxes and interest paid to a cooperative housing corporation),
6. Depletion deduction for oil and gas wells, and
7. Capital loss carryover (Code Sec. 703(a); Reg. §1.703-1(a)).

Separately Reportable Items on Partnership Return

Any item that *may* have to be treated differently by each partner must be separately stated. For example, some partners may be able to deduct charitable contributions that flow through from the partnership, but those that have already met the 50 percent of AGI limit for contributions will have to carry over those contributions. Each partner's share of these items is identified on the partner's separate Schedule K-1. The following items are separately stated:

1. Short-term capital gains and losses,
2. Long-term capital gains and losses,
3. Section 1231 gains and losses,
4. Charitable contributions,
5. All portfolio items (i.e., dividends and interest income),
6. Taxes paid or accrued to foreign countries and to possessions of the United States,
7. Recoveries of bad debts, prior taxes, and delinquency amounts,
8. Gains and losses from wagering transactions,
9. Soil and water conservation expenditures,
10. Nonbusiness expenses such as alimony payments,
11. Medical and dental expenses of partners, their spouses, and dependents (Items (10), (11), and (12) may not be taken as partnership deductions under Code Sec. 703(a)),
12. Credit for the care of certain dependents,
13. Amounts representing taxes and interest paid cooperative housing corporations,
14. Intangible drilling and development costs,
15. Pre-1970 exploration expenditures,
16. Certain mining exploration expenditures,
17. Income, gain, or loss to the partnership upon the distribution of property involving unrealized receivables and substantially appreciated inventory items,
18. Any items or class of items of income, gain, loss, deduction, or credit subject to a special allocation under the partnership agreement differing from the allocation of partnership income or loss generally (Items (7) through (18) are prescribed by Regulations pursuant to Code Sec. 702(a)(7)),
19. Expensing of certain depreciable assets (Code Sec. 179),
20. Tax-preference items (Code Sec. 702(a); Reg. §1.702-1(a)),
21. Business credits,
22. All items from separate passive activities, including real estate,
23. Qualified production activities income, and
24. Form W-2 wages.

Partners in Community Property States

In a community property state, some of the partnership income may have to be reported by the spouse who is not a partner. If separate returns are filed by a husband and wife domiciled in a community property state and only one spouse is a member of a partnership, the part of the distributive share of the partnership

¶19,335

taxable income which is community property or which is derived from community property should be reported by the husband and wife in equal proportions. Reg. §1.702-1(d).

Cash-Basis Reporting

The privilege of reporting on the cash basis has been severely restricted for larger partnerships. Any partnership (except for farming and timber partnerships) whose three year average of gross receipts for the periods ending with each of the prior three years equals or exceeds $10,000,000 is not allowed to use the cash basis. In addition, any partnership which has a C corporation as a partner may not use the cash-basis method if it had, for any preceding three tax year period, average annual gross receipts in excess of $5 million dollars. Code Sec. 448. Once the partnership three-year average exceeds the test limit, it must thereafter report on the accrual basis.

EXAMPLE 19.54 Extrap Partnership, which has a C corporation among its partners, has the following gross receipts for the indicated years:

2013	$4,500,000	2016	$5,000,000
2014	4,750,000	2017	4,000,000
2015	5,800,000	2018	3,000,000

The partnership could have reported on the cash basis for 2013–2015. It had to report on the accrual basis in 2016 because its average annual earnings for the prior three years (2013–2015) was $5,016,667. For 2017, that average is $5,183,333. For 2018, the average is only $4,933,333; yet the partnership must continue to use the accrual method.

Generally even cash basis taxpayers have to use the accrual basis to account for purchases and sales if the levels of inventories in their business are significant. For tax years ending after December 16, 2000, qualifying taxpayers may use the cash method of accounting, even for purchases and sales of inventory. To be able to avoid accounting for inventory, the taxpayer's three-year average of gross receipts for the periods ending with each of the prior three years must not exceed $1 million. Qualifying taxpayers treat inventory the same as supplies.

Character of Items Determined at Partnership Level

Generally, the determination of the character of all types of partnership income is made at the partnership level and that character carries over to the partner. The purpose of requiring items to be separately stated on the partnership return and to be separately taken into account by each partner is to facilitate the operation of the "character rule." The character of any item of income, gain, loss, deduction, or credit for the partner is to be determined "as if such item were realized directly from the source from which realized by the partnership, or incurred in the same manner as incurred by the partnership." Code Sec. 702(b); Reg. §1.702-1(b). Two exceptions to this rule are:

1. A partnership's sale of a capital asset within five years of its contribution receives ordinary treatment (for all of the gain or loss) if the asset had been previously held by the contributing partner as inventory. Code Sec. 724. Also, refer to ¶19,135.
2. If any property with a built-in capital loss is sold by the partnership within five years of its contribution to the partnership, any loss recognized by the partnership on the sale (to the extent of the built-in loss) will be a capital loss. Code Sec. 724(c).

In addition, a partner's sale of a capital asset held more than five years after its distribution receives capital treatment despite the asset having been previously held by the distributing partnership as inventory. Code Sec. 735(a)(2); Reg. §1.735-1(a)(2).

The fact that the character of the income is determined at the partnership level on occasion may produce apparently conflicting results.

EXAMPLE 19.55 Partnership Gamble sold a capital asset for which it obtained long-term capital gain treatment. Partner Hannibal, who has held his partnership interest only five months, will nevertheless report his distributable share of this gain as long-term capital gain. Rev. Rul. 68-79, 1968-1 CB 310.

Income Reporting for Large Partnerships

Electing large partnerships, defined as partnerships with 100 or more partners in the preceding year, may elect to report using simplified rules. Code Sec. 775. This election is binding for all future years and is irrevocable without the consent of the IRS. The large partnership rules allow the partnership to aggregate more items at the partnership level, which simplifies the reporting to the partners. For example, the netting of capital gains and losses is at the partnership level. If the net capital gains or losses are long-term, they are passed through as such to the partners. If the net capital gains and losses are short-term, they are combined with other partnership taxable income and will not be separately reported. An electing large partnership computes its charitable contribution deduction using a 10 percent limitation similar to how a corporation computes its charitable contribution deduction. The following items are separately reportable on the returns of electing large partnerships:

1. Taxable income or loss from passive activities,
2. Taxable income or loss from other activities,
3. Net capital gain or loss allocable to passive loss activities,
4. Net capital gain or loss allocable to other activities,
5. Tax-exempt interest,
6. Applicable net alternative minimum tax adjustment separately computed for the passive loss limitation activities and the other activities,
7. General credits,
8. Low-income housing credits,
9. Rehabilitation credits,
10. Foreign income taxes,
11. Credit for producing fuel from nonconventional sources,
12. Qualified production activities income,
13. Form W-2 wages, and
14. Other items to the extent that the IRS determines that separate treatment is appropriate.

¶19,345 ALLOCATION OF ITEMS

In addition to the requirement to report items separately because of their character, there are other situations where items must be separately reported because either the statute or the partnership agreement requires a disproportionate (or "special") allocation of income or expense items among the partners. Special allocations are required by statute for precontribution built-in gains or losses when there is a contribution of property with a fair market value different from its basis. (See ¶19,115.) Other special allocations may be provided for in the partnership agreement, but, in order to be recognized, these allocations must have a substantial economic effect on the potential future cash flows to the partners.

Special Allocations

A partner's distributive share of any item or class of items of income, gain, loss, deduction, or credit of the partnership is ordinarily determined by the partnership agreement. If the agreement does not make an allocation, or if the allocation in the agreement does not have "substantial economic effect," the partner's distributive share is determined (taking into account all facts and circumstances) in accordance with the partner's interest in the partnership. In order to have substantial economic effect, an allocation must have "economic effect" and be "substantial." Code Sec. 704(b).

An allocation has economic effect if (1) the allocation is reflected by an appropriate increase or decrease in the partner's capital account and the capital accounts are maintained according to Treasury Regulation rules, (2) liquidation proceeds (if any) are to be distributed in accordance with the partners' capital account balances, and (3) any partner with a deficit in the capital account following the distribution of liquidation proceeds is required to restore the amount of the deficit to the partnership. Reg. §1.704-1(b)(2). The intent of these rules is to have the capital account track a partner's economic interest, and to have the partner's "share" of partnership assets depend on the partner's capital account. Any special allocation is required to have an effect on the partner's capital accounts, and therefore their eventual share of partnership assets.

EXAMPLE 19.56

Albert May and Bobby Dickson form the AB Partnership with each contributing $100,000 cash. The AB Partnership promptly purchases a depreciable asset for $200,000 cash. The asset is classified as seven-year recovery property. The partnership does not elect the Section 179 expensing deduction, but it allocates the entire cost recovery amount of $28,580 to Albert. The expense is charged against his capital account, but the partnership agreement provides that upon liquidation, the partners will share equally the net proceeds of all assets. In addition, the partnership agreement does not provide for restoration of deficit balances in the partners' capital accounts. Assume that the depreciable asset is sold for its depreciated basis of $171,420, resulting in no gain or loss to the partnership, and that the partnership immediately liquidates. Albert and Bobby will each receive one-half of the proceeds upon liquidation of the partnership. After these events, the capital accounts would be as follows:

	Albert	Bobby
Contribution (capital balance)	$100,000	$100,000
MACRS deduction	(28,580)	0
Capital balance	$71,420	$100,000
Liquidating distribution proceeds	(85,710)	(85,710)
Capital balance after distribution	$(14,290)	$14,290

Since liquidation proceeds are shared equally, rather than distributed according to capital account balances, the allocation does not have economic effect. In addition, since Albert does not have any obligation to restore a deficit in his capital account if one exists (which would be distributed to Bobby in an amount equal to his positive capital account balance), Albert will not bear the burden of the allocation of Bobby's one-half share of the cost recovery deductions which have been allocated to him. Consequently, there is no economic effect to the allocation of the entire amount of cost recovery deductions to Albert, this special allocation of depreciation to Albert will be ignored, and these deductions will be charged equally to each of the partners.

For the agreement of an allocation to be valid, the economic effect of the allocation must be substantial in relation to its tax effect. Thus, an allocation of one type of income (capital gains) to one partner and another type of income (ordinary) to another partner where there is a strong probability at the time of the allocation that there will be a significant difference in the two amounts will have economic effect, but it may not be substantial in relation to the tax impact of the reported partnership income on the partner's nonpartnership income. These rules are difficult to apply even with reference to the multitude of examples included in Reg. §1.704-1(b)(5).

EXAMPLE 19.57

At the beginning of the tax year, it is anticipated that Charles Cox will have substantial individual capital losses and that David James will have substantial individual ordinary business income. Accordingly, the partners agree for the ensuing year to allocate all the partnership's ordinary income to David and all of the capital gains to Charles, the two amounts anticipated to be essentially equal in amount. Here, the economic effect is minor—both parties receive about the same amount of income—but the tax effect is major. Although the dollar amount of income derived from the partnership is equal, the allocation would allow Charles to claim substantial capital losses not otherwise currently deductible by him. As the economic effect is not substantial except for the tax effect, the allocation will not be allowed.

TAX BLUNDER

Oil Inc. and Lotta Bucks enter into a joint operating agreement to drill for oil in the Boomtown oil field. Oil Inc. contributes the mineral rights to the property, and Lotta agrees to pay the drilling costs. Since the participants are entering into an agreement for the joint extraction of oil and gas, they file a partnership return for the first year and elect to be excluded from the partnership provisions of the Internal Revenue Code.

Result. By electing out of the partnership provisions, Lotta, who pays all of the intangible drilling costs, can deduct only one-half of the intangible drilling costs. The remaining half of the costs must be capitalized. Had they not elected out of the partnership provisions, the partnership could have made a special allocation of the intangible drilling costs, and Lotta could have deducted all of the intangible drilling costs.

KEYSTONE PROBLEM

Acey and Deucy formed the Acey-Deucy Partnership on January 1, 2013, with cash investments of $120,000 and $80,000 for 60 percent and 40 percent respective interests in both the partnership's capital and income. The partnership operates a retail sales business, reports on the calendar year and uses the accrual method. From the data below, compute the partnership's 2017 ordinary business income and list the items which will be separately reportable by the partners on their individual returns.

1. All sales were made on account, $250,000.
2. Sales of $4,800 were returned for allowances; $235,000 was received as payments on account.
3. Inventory on January 1, 2017, was $64,500; purchases for 2017 were $82,500; ending inventory, $37,000.
4. The partnership uses the specific write-off method of accounting for bad debts. $1,500 in uncollectible accounts was written off.
5. The depreciable assets held by the partnership were as follows:
a. Building—cost $131,689; acquired in 2013; 2017 cost recovery, $3,377.
b. Machinery—cost $20,000; seven-year recovery property; placed in service December 31, 2017; $20,000 immediately expensed under Code Sec. 179.
6. Dividends received: $1,000 from Domestic Corp.; $750 from Foreign Corp. on which 30 percent tax was withheld at source.
7. Sold on November 29, 2017, 600 shares Domestic Corp. common stock for $8,500; 1,000 shares were purchased on December 2, 2013, for $10,000.
8. Sold on November 11, 2017, 300 shares Foreign Corp. preferred stock for $2,200; 800 shares were purchased on December 12, 2016, for $3,000.
9. Sold on January 1, 2017, for $6,325, equipment which was purchased in 2013 for $3,200 on which cost recovery of $1,801 had been previously taken.
10. Organization costs of $3,000 are being amortized for financial purposes over a 10-year period. Acey-Deucy did not deduct any of these expenses, but amortized them over the shortest possible period for tax purposes.
11. $10,000 principal and $6,000 interest were paid on the partnership's mortgage.
12. A $400 cash contribution was made to the American Red Cross.
13. Salary expense for employees was $50,000. All $50,000 was W-2 wages.
14. Rent was $12,000; real estate taxes, $2,500.
15. During 2017, Acey and Deucy made cash withdrawals of $50,000 and $25,000, respectively.

Partner-Partnership Transactions

¶19,425   ## INDIRECT OWNERSHIP

The related party rules between partners and partnerships need to be understood before transactions between these parties can be discussed. There are several Code sections concerning attribution of ownership, e.g., Code Sec. 318 (for corporations in general), Code Sec. 542 (for personal holding companies), and Code Sec. 267 (applicable to disallowance of losses between related parties in general). Code Sec. 707, specifically concerned with losses and gains in the partnership context, refers to Code Sec. 267, which has the least complex rules. The relationships creating indirect ownership for partnership purposes are:

1. A partnership interest owned, directly or indirectly, by or for a corporation, partnership, estate, or trust is considered as being owned proportionately by or for its shareholders, partners, or beneficiaries.
2. An individual is considered as owning the partnership interest owned, directly or indirectly, by or for family members.

The family of an individual (for these purposes) includes only brothers and sisters (whether by whole or half blood), spouse, ancestors, and lineal descendants. For the purpose of determining ownership, property deemed owned by a person by reason of Rule (1) (entity attribution) is treated as being actually held by that person to whom ownership is attributed, which means that the ownership could be attributed again to an entity or person related to that person. Rule (2) (family attribution) is applied only once.

EXAMPLE 19.58

Apex Partnership is owned by the following:

25% by Corporation Yahoo (100% owned by Ann Plece);

36% by Partnership Bucko (25% owned by Ann Plece; 25% owned by Jack Spratt; 25% owned by Jill Spratt; and 25% owned by Robert Plece (Jill Spratt is Ann Plece's sister and Robert Plece is their father, Jill Spratt is Jack Spratt's wife));

33% by Rabe Plece (Robert Plece's grandson, Ann's son); and

6% by Walter Washington (unrelated to any of the above).

Ann owns directly:		0	
Through her corporation		25	
Through the partnership by herself	9		
by her father	9		
by her sister	9	27	
By her son		33	85
Jill owns directly:		0	
Through the partnership by herself	9		
by her husband	9		
by her sister	9		
by her father	9	36	
By her sister (corporation)		25	61
Jack owns directly:		0	
Through the partnership by himself	9		
by his wife	9		18
Robert owns directly:		0	
Through the partnership by himself	9		
by his daughters	18	27	
By his daughter (corporation)		25	
By his grandson		33	85
Rabe owns directly:		33	
Through the partnership by his mother	9		
by his grandfather	9	18	
By his mother (corporation)		25	76
Bucko owns directly:		0	
Through the partnership by the partners		36	
By Ann (corporation)		25	61
Yahoo owns directly		25	
Through shareholder Ann		9	34

¶19,445 TRANSACTIONS BETWEEN PARTNER AND PARTNERSHIP

The Code adopts the "entity" approach to transactions between a partner and the partnership when the partner is not acting in the capacity of a partner. The transaction in these circumstances is considered as taking place between the partnership and a stranger. Code Sec. 707(a); Reg. §1.707-1(a). These transactions include, for example, loans of money or property by the partnership to the partner, the sale of property by the partner to the partnership, the purchase of property by the partner from the partnership, and the rendering of services by the partner to or for the partnership.

EXAMPLE 19.59

Partner Eager, holding a 20 percent interest in Eager & Fast Partnership, sells to the partnership land he has held for investment for more than a year, realizing a gain of $10,000. The partnership intended to use the land as a factory site but changed its plans. Within six months the partnership resells the same land to Eager at a price $1,000 in excess of that paid to Eager. Eager has a long-term capital gain of $10,000 on his sale to the partnership and a long-term capital gain of $200 distributed to him as a 20 percent partner, reflecting Eager's share of the partnership's $1,000 gain on resale.

Each situation is determined in view of all of the facts. If the person is determined to be in fact a partner, then the following factors are among those to be used in determining whether the partner is receiving the allocation and distribution in the capacity of a partner.

1. Is the payment subject to an appreciable risk as to amount, or is there a strong likelihood the payment will be made as anticipated without regard to the success or failure of the venture?
2. Is the partner status of the recipient transitory, or does the partner contemplate a continuing relationship with the partnership?
3. Is the allocation close in time to the rendition of services or the transfer of the property to the partnership? It is immaterial whether the payment is before or after the rendition or transfer.

¶19,501   GAIN OR LOSS ON TRANSACTIONS BETWEEN PARTNER AND PARTNERSHIP

As in other situations involving transactions between related taxpayers, Congress and the Treasury Department have provided rules to prevent tax avoidance through partner/partnership transactions. The disguised sale rules are covered in ¶19,235 et seq. Other rules are designed to deny the deduction of certain losses and the acquisition of a stepped-up basis at capital gain rates where the same parties are in control of both sides of the transaction. The rules are somewhat similar to those applicable in the case of sales of property between corporations and controlling stockholders.

Denial of Loss Deduction

No deduction is allowed for a loss on a sale or exchange of property (other than an interest in the partnership) taking place, directly or indirectly, between a partnership and a person who owns, directly or indirectly, more than a 50 percent interest in the capital or profits of the partnership. Similarly, no loss deduction is allowed on a sale or exchange taking place, directly or indirectly, between two partnerships in which the same persons own, directly or indirectly, more than a 50 percent interest in the capital or profits of each partnership. Code Sec. 707(b)(1); Reg. §1.707-1(b)(1).

If there is a sale or exchange between a partnership and a person who is related to a partner who owns 50 percent or less of the partnership, the sale or exchange is considered to take place between the person and the members of the partnership separately. Therefore, if there is a loss on the sale or exchange, the part of the loss from the hypothetical sale between the person and the related partner will be disallowed. Reg. §1.267(b)-1(b).

EXAMPLE 19.60

The wife of a 20 percent partner sells equipment to the partnership. She sustains a $10,000 tax loss on the sale. With respect to her loss, $2,000 will not be recognized for federal income tax purposes.

Recoupment of Disallowed Loss by Related Purchaser

If, however, the purchaser of property in a transaction with respect to which a loss was disallowed later sells the property for a gain, the amount of the loss previously disallowed is treated as a part of the purchaser's basis. In effect, this allows the related purchaser to use the disallowed loss to offset any later gain on the sale of the asset.

EXAMPLE 19.61	George Avis is a 60 percent partner in the Beegood partnership. The partnership sells George an old truck for $2,000 (its basis to the partnership was $2,500). George will use the truck for personal purposes. The partnership is not allowed to deduct its $500 loss on the transaction. If, however, George later sells the truck for $3,250, he may reduce his actual gain of $1,250 ($3,250 - $2,000) by the amount of loss previously disallowed to the partnership, $500, and thus report a gain on the transaction of only $750.

EXAMPLE 19.62	If, in the preceding example, George sold the truck for $1,750, he would recognize only a $250 ($1,750 - $2,000) loss. The previously disallowed loss of $500 cannot be used to increase a later loss.

Sale of Capital Assets to or from Controlled Partnerships

In the sale or exchange of property between a person and a partnership in which the person owns, directly or indirectly, an interest of more than 50 percent in capital or profits, any gain recognized is treated as ordinary gain unless the property is a capital asset in the hands of the transferee immediately after the transfer. The same rule applies to sales and exchanges between partnerships in which the same persons own, directly or indirectly, an interest in capital or profits greater than 50 percent. Code Sec. 707(b)(2); Reg. §1.707-1(b)(2).

EXAMPLE 19.63	Joe Michie and his son Jay each own a 40 percent interest in the Michie partnership. Beverly, Joe's wife, holds no interest in the partnership. Beverly sells for $40,000 to the Michie partnership a parcel of land with a basis to her of $30,000 which she has held as an investment. The partnership builds a factory on the site, so the land is not a capital asset to the partnership. Beverly, who has indirect control of the partnership, recognizes $10,000 ordinary income on the sale, rather than the $10,000 of capital gain she would have recognized if she had sold the land to an unrelated party.

EXAMPLE 19.64	In the preceding example, if the Michie partnership held the land for investment, the land would be a capital asset to the partnership. In that case, Beverly's gain would be a capital gain.

The rule is applicable even though a transaction falling within the scope of the rule is actually the result of arm's-length bargaining.

EXAMPLE 19.65	Fruit Growers Partnership, owned entirely by James and Johnson, sold one of its citrus groves to Orchards Partnership, owned entirely by their children. The children operated Orchards Partnership entirely independently of their parents. James and Johnson owned no direct interest in Orchards Partnership. Neither did the children own any direct interest in the Fruit Growers Partnership. The IRS deemed this a transfer between controlled partnerships; thus, the gain on the sale of the citrus trees was ordinary income to the selling partnership. See Rev. Rul. 67-105, 1967-1 CB 167.

Code Sec. 1239 expands the reach of the rule which treats recognized gain as ordinary income by treating recognized gain as ordinary income if the transferred property is depreciable by the transferee. So, even though the property may be a capital asset in the hands of the transferee immediately after the transfer (thereby escaping the rule of Code Sec. 707(b)(2)), if it is depreciable by the transferee, the seller's recognized gain is ordinary income.

EXAMPLE 19.66	Milton Freidburg owns a 60 percent interest in the Ajax partnership. His wife, Marla, sells a duplex to the partnership. Marla has rented the duplex, holding it as an investment. The Ajax partnership will rent and hold the duplex in the same manner. Marla recognizes a $50,000 gain on the sale. The gain is reported by Marla as ordinary income, despite the fact that the duplex was a capital asset to her and the partnership.

Installment Sales

Deferred payment sales of depreciable property between related parties are governed by Code Sec. 453(g), which prohibits use of the installment method and requires that all payments be deemed received in the year of disposition if tax avoidance is a principal purpose of the sale. If tax avoidance is not a principal purpose, the installment method of reporting is available between a partner and the controlled partnership, but a subsequent sale of the property within two years of the purchase will accelerate any unpaid installments at the time of the second sale. If the selling partner does not have, directly or indirectly, control of the partnership, the installment sale is treated as any other such transaction between strangers would be.

EXAMPLE 19.67	In the current year, partner Bernie Winston, who owns 55 percent of the Wimpy Partnership, sells to Wimpy land with a basis to Bernie of $40,000 for a sales price of $200,000 (its fair market value). The partnership is to pay $40,000 at the time of the purchase, and $40,000 (plus reasonable interest) in annual installments during each of the next four years. The partnership will hold the land as an investment (a capital asset). Since it is an installment sale, Bernie will report the gross profit percentage of 80% [($200,000 - $40,000)/$200,000] times the cash received during the year as capital gain. Bernie will report capital gain of $32,000 (80% × $40,000) in the current year. If the Wimpy Partnership sells the land the next year, Bernie will have to report the remaining $128,000 ($160,000 total gain - $32,000 recognized in the first year) of capital gain that year. If Bernie owned less than 50 percent of the partnership, he would continue to report his gain ratably as he collected the sales price from the Wimpy Partnership, whether Wimpy sold the land or not.

Concurrent Reporting of Items

The income and the deduction of payments between related parties must be reported in the same year where the payee is on the cash basis and the payer is on the accrual basis. Both the deduction and the income are reportable when the payee reports the item. Code Sec. 267(a)(2). The rule applies to the payments between a partnership and any partner who owns (directly or indirectly) any interest in the capital or income of a partnership. Code Sec. 267(e). This rule, however, does not apply to certain qualified expenses of partnerships owning low-income housing or to guaranteed payments made to a partner.

¶19,515   GUARANTEED PAYMENTS

Partnership agreements often provide for the payment of salaries to partners and for the allowance of interest on their capital. After deducting amounts credited to the members of the partnership under these headings, the balance of the profits for the period is allocated among the partners in accordance with their general profit and loss ratios.

"Guaranteed payments" of this sort are treated, within limitations, as if made to a nonpartner. They are deductible by the partnership as a business expense for the taxable year in which paid or accrued in accordance with its usual accounting method. The partner will likewise include in income the amount the partnership deducts, and will include it in income on the last day of the partnership's tax year. But to be currently deductible, the payment must be for an expense item, not a capitalizable charge, such as fees for supervised construction of a capital asset. Code Sec. 707(c); *J.E. Cagle*, 63 TC 86, Dec. 32,828 (1974), aff'd, 76-2 USTC ¶9672, 539 F.2d 409 (CA-5 1976).

EXAMPLE 19.68	Edgar Dickens reports on the calendar year and cash basis. The Edgar, Franklin, and George Partnership of which he is a member files its returns on the accrual basis for the year ending April 30, 2017. Edgar is entitled to a salary of $48,000 per year from the partnership. Edgar's salary for the months of May, June, and July 2016, totals $12,000 and is paid to him on time, but he receives nothing more from the partnership during the balance of its fiscal year. The partnership will deduct the full $48,000 salary to which Edgar was entitled on its return for the year ending April 30, 2017. Edgar must report as income the entire $48,000 on his 2017 calendar-year individual return although he has actually received only $12,000, and that in 2016. But if the partnership were on the cash basis, Edgar's salary would be deductible by the partnership only as paid. Edgar would include in his income for the year within which the partnership year ends the amount actually paid to him during that partnership tax year, since that is the amount the partnership would deduct.

Insufficient Income to Cover Guaranteed Payments

If the aggregate partnership ordinary income is insufficient to cover guaranteed payments, the partners' distributive shares may be income to some partners and losses to others.

EXAMPLE 19.69	The Harry, Isadore, and Jacob Partnership earned only $1,000 of ordinary income before deduction of Harry Portugal's $10,000 salary. The partnership's deduction of the $10,000 guaranteed payment to Harry would produce a $9,000 loss. Harry, whose profit and loss ratio is 10 percent, reports his $10,000 salary as income and is entitled to an ordinary deduction of $900 for his distributive share of the loss. Isadore and Jacob, each possessing a 45 percent interest in profit and loss, are each entitled to an ordinary deduction of $4,050 (45 percent of $9,000). Rev. Rul. 56-675, 1956-2 CB 459.

Guaranteed payments are not applied to reduce a partner's distributive share of income items required to be reported separately (such as interest income or capital gains), even where there is insufficient ordinary income to cover the guaranteed payments. Reg. §1.707-1(c), Example (4).

EXAMPLE 19.70	Suppose, in the preceding example, that the $1,000 partnership income is derived solely from long-term capital gains and the partnership's only expense is Harry's salary. Harry should report his salary of $10,000 as ordinary income and $100 as his 10 percent share of the long-term capital gain, $1,000. The partnership's ordinary loss, due solely to the deduction of Harry's salary, is $10,000, and Harry will deduct $1,000 as his 10 percent share of this ordinary loss. Isadore's and Jacob's distributive shares consist of $450 (45% × $1,000) of long-term capital gain and $4,500 (45% × $10,000) of ordinary loss.

Partner Not an "Employee" of the Partnership

Individual taxpayers who are general partners are subject to self-employment tax on their shares of partnership income or loss as well as guaranteed payments that they receive if the partnership is engaged in a trade or business. Limited partners are subject to self-employment tax solely on guaranteed payments for services. Code Sec. 1402. The guaranteed payments provision is applicable only for purposes of determining the partner's income and the partnership's business deduction. Thus, a partner who receives guaranteed payments is not regarded as an employee of the partnership for purposes of income tax withholding, or qualified pension or profit-sharing plans. However, the partner may be considered an employee for purposes of excluding compensation earned outside of the United States under Code Sec. 911. *A.O. Miller*, 52 TC 752, Dec. 29,690 (1969), Acq. 1972-2 CB 2.

Deductibility of Losses

¶19,551   ## LOSS—LIMITATIONS

Since partnership losses pass through to the partners, a partnership does not carry over losses to other years. Code Sec. 703(a)(2)(D). However, a partner's distributive share of a partnership operating loss may pass through to the partner, become a component of the partner's individual net operating loss, and give rise to a carryback or carryover deduction on the partner's individual tax return.

Reporting Rules

To determine the partner's personal net operating loss deduction, the partner must take into account the distributive share of items of income, gain, loss, deduction, or credit of the partnership. The character of any such item is determined as if it were realized directly from the source of the item or incurred in the same manner as incurred by the partnership. Similarly, when a partner computes his or her nonbusiness deductions, the partner must separately take into account his or her share of the nonbusiness deductions of the partnership and combine these amounts with deductions from nonpartnership sources. In the same way, the partner must separately take into account his or her share of the nonbusiness gross income of the partnership and combine this amount with nonpartnership income from nonbusiness sources. Reg. §1.702-2.

Losses in Excess of Partner's Basis

A partner's distributive share of partnership loss (including capital loss) is allowed as a deduction only up to the adjusted basis of the partner's interest in the partnership at the end of the partnership year in which the loss occurs. Any partner's loss that is disallowed due to the lack of basis will be deductible by the partner up to the partner's basis increases in a future year (through contributions, partnership income, etc.). Code Sec. 704(d); Reg. §1.704-1(d).

EXAMPLE 19.71

At the end of year 1, partnership AB has a loss of $20,000. Partner Boyce's distributive share of this loss is $10,000. At the end of the year, Boyce's adjusted basis for his interest in the partnership (not taking into account his distributive share of the loss) is $6,000. Boyce's distributive share of partnership loss is allowed to him as a deduction (in his taxable year within or with which the partnership taxable year ends) only to the extent of his adjusted basis of $6,000. The $6,000 loss allowed decreases the adjusted basis of his interest to zero. Assume that, at the end of year 2, the adjusted basis of Boyce's interest in the partnership has increased to $3,000 (not taking into account the $4,000 loss disallowed in year 1). $3,000 of the $4,000 loss disallowed for year 1 is carried over and allowed to Boyce for year 2, thus again decreasing the adjusted basis of his interest to zero. If, at the end of year 3, Boyce has an adjusted basis for his interest of at least $1,000 (not taking into account the remaining disallowed loss of $1,000), he will be allowed to deduct the $1,000 loss previously disallowed. Reg. §1.704-1(d), Example (1).

PLANNING POINTER

For any year in which a partner's distributive share of losses exceeds the basis of the partner's interest (including the partner's share of partnership liabilities), the loss deduction may be obtained by having the partnership buy property on credit or borrow money. The resultant increase in each partner's share of the liability incurred is treated as a contribution of cash, thus increasing the basis of the partner's interest. Code Secs. 722 and 752(a). This makes it possible for the partner, to some extent, to control the year in which a loss deduction will be taken.

Classification of Loss Pass-Through

As discussed earlier, certain items of partnership income or loss are required to be separately stated. Included are short-term capital gains or losses, long-term capital gains or losses, and gains or losses from the sale or exchange of Section 1231 assets. If any one (or more) of these separately stated items is a loss and if the partner's distributive share of the aggregate of these losses (as well as ordinary losses) exceeds the partner's basis of the partnership interest, the allowed portion of each type of loss is equal to the partner's share of the particular type of loss multiplied by the ratio of the partner's total allowed loss to the partner's total of all losses, both allowed and disallowed. Reg. §1.704-1(d)(2).

For the purpose of limitation, the total of the losses for the year includes the losses disallowed in prior years and carried forward to the current year. Neither any gains among these separately stated items nor any net ordinary income is offset against the losses in arriving at a partner's share of the losses. Instead, these latter items are reported in the ordinary manner and increase the basis of the partner's interest in determining how much of the partner's share of the losses is deductible.

EXAMPLE 19.72

At the end of the partnership taxable year, partner David Izaak has the following distributive share of partnership items: long-term capital loss, $4,000; short-term capital loss, $2,000; nonseparately stated income, $4,000. Partner David's adjusted basis for his partnership interest at the end of the year, before adjustments for any of the above items, is $1,000. As adjusted under Code Sec. 705(a)(1)(A), David's basis is increased from $1,000 to $5,000 at the end of the year because of the addition of the $4,000 of nonseparately stated income. David's total distributive share of partnership loss is $6,000. Since, without regard to losses, David has a basis of only $5,000, he is allowed to deduct only 5/6 of each loss; that is, $3,333 (5/6 × $4,000) of his long-term capital loss and $1,667 (5/6 × $2,000) of his short-term capital loss. David must carry forward to succeeding taxable years $667 as a long-term capital loss and $333 as a short-term capital loss. Reg. §1.704-1(d)(4), Example (3).

EXAMPLE 19.73	Assume that in the preceding example David has nonpartnership capital gains of $6,000 (long-term, $3,000; short-term, $3,000) during the year. The partnership capital losses of $3,333 (long-term) and $1,667 (short-term) are offset against these nonpartnership capital gains.

PLANNING POINTER	Occasionally a partner might consider selling a partnership interest for which the partner has a loss carryover due to the basis limitation. If the partner contemplates selling the interest under these circumstances, the partner should make a contribution of money or property with sufficient basis to increase the basis to accommodate the loss prior to the sale. Otherwise, due to a quirk in the tax law the loss carryover due to lack of basis will never be deductible.

Allocation of Recourse Liabilities to the Partners' Bases

A partner's share of a recourse partnership liability is the amount of the liability for which the partner bears the economic risk of loss. Reg. §1.752-2(a). In general, recourse liabilities are allocated to the partners using a hypothetical liquidation scenario. Reg. §1.752-2(b). Under this hypothetical scenario, all of the following are deemed to occur:

1. All of the partnership liabilities become payable in full,
2. All of the partnership assets (including cash but excluding property contributed to secure a partnership liability) become worthless,
3. The partnership disposes of its assets for no consideration in a fully taxable transaction,
4. All items of income, gain, loss, or deduction are allocated to the partners, and
5. The partnership liquidates.

Hypothetically, partners with deficit capital accounts after the allocation of losses on the sale will be required to contribute cash to the partnership to the extent of the deficit in their capital accounts. Recourse liabilities are allocated to the partners to the extent they would be required to contribute cash to restore deficit capital accounts.

EXAMPLE 19.74	Bob Anderson and Ted Carr each contributed $500 to the BT Partnership. The partnership purchased machinery for $3,000, using $500 cash and a note payable of $2,500. Bob is allocated 60 percent of the losses, while Ted is allocated 40 percent of the losses. The partnership agreement requires that, upon liquidation, partners with deficit capital accounts must contribute cash of that amount to the partnership. The books of the partnership reflect the following.

	Basis	Fair Market Value
Cash	$500	$500
Machinery	3,000	3,000
	$3,500	$3,500
Recourse liability	$2,500	$2,500
Bob, capital	500	500
Ted, capital	500	500
	$3,500	$3,500

The debt is allocated using the hypothetical liquidation scenario. Therefore, cash and machinery are deemed worthless and are sold for zero, generating a loss of $3,500. The loss is allocated 60 percent to Bob and 40 percent to Ted. After closing the losses to the partners' capital accounts, Bob has a deficit of $1,600 [$500 − (.6 × $3,500)] and Ted has a deficit of $900 [$500 − (.4 × $3,500)]. Therefore, $1,600 of the debt is allocated to Bob, and $900 of the debt is allocated to Ted. Notice that this allocation does not follow their profit and loss sharing ratios.

Allocation of Nonrecourse Liabilities to Partners' Bases

A partner's share of nonrecourse liabilities is the sum of the partner's share of (1) minimum gain, (2) precontribution gain that would be recognized if the partnership "sold" the property for the nonrecourse debt, and (3) excess nonrecourse liabilities. Reg. §1.752-3(a). The minimum gain is the excess of the amount of the nonrecourse debt over the adjusted tax basis (or book value, if different) of the property it encumbers. In other words, minimum gain is the gain that would be recognized if the debtholder were to take the property in satisfaction of the debt. Reg. §1.704-2(b). The partnership agreement should address how the minimum gain will be allocated.

The second part of the nonrecourse debt formula requires allocation of nonrecourse liabilities equal to the precontribution gain to the partner who contributed the property subject to a nonrecourse liability.

EXAMPLE 19.75   Joe White contributed a property with a tax basis of $75,000 and a fair market value of $150,000 subject to a nonrecourse debt of $100,000. Minimum gain is zero because the book value ($150,000) is greater than the nonrecourse debt. However, if the debtholder were to take the property in satisfaction of the debt, a $25,000 precontribution gain would arise. This would all be allocable to Joe since he contributed the property to the partnership, and this amount of nonrecourse debt would therefore be allocated to Joe.

Finally, the remainder of the nonrecourse liabilities is allocated to the partners based on their profit-sharing ratios. If in the preceding example, Joe had a 50 percent interest in the profits of the partnership, he would be allocated 50 percent of the remaining $75,000 of the nonrecourse liability. His total nonrecourse liabilities would be $62,500 ($25,000 + .5 × $75,000).

Limitations on Losses—At-Risk Rules

Even if there is sufficient basis to deduct a loss, the amount of loss deductible on the partner's return is limited to the partner's at-risk amount. In general, a partner's at-risk amount is equal to their basis in the partnership, except that a partner's share of nonrecourse debt will increase a partner's basis, but not their at-risk amount. A taxpayer's loss is not at-risk (and can not be deducted) to the extent that the loss is avoided through a stop-loss agreement, an indemnity agreement or like agreement, a nonrecourse loan, or a loan with recourse limited to certain nonactivity assets for security.

Nonrecourse loans are *not* generally included in the at-risk amount. Any deduction for partnership losses is limited to the partner's basis in the capital account and the proportion of any loan of the partnership for which the partner has personal exposure. Thus, limited partners, since they are not at-risk for the debts of the partnership, are generally only permitted to deduct their share of partnership losses up to their capital investment.

EXAMPLE 19.76   The Washington, Madison, and Monroe Partnership is a three-person limited partnership with Washington and Madison as general partners and Monroe as the limited partner. The capital structure of the partnership is as follows:

	Washington	Madison	Monroe
Ratio of profit and loss	40%	40%	20%
Capital account basis	$200,000	$200,000	$200,000
Share of recourse debt ($100,000)	50,000	50,000	0
"At-risk" amount for pass-through loss purposes	$250,000	$250,000	$200,000
Share of nonrecourse debt ($200,000)	80,000	80,000	40,000
Basis for purpose of sale of partnership interest	$330,000	$330,000	$240,000

However, an exception to the at-risk rules allows "qualified nonrecourse financing" incurred to hold real property to be included in the amount at-risk. "Qualified nonrecourse financing" is generally nonrecourse financing provided by organizations (banks, savings and loan associations, credit unions, regulated insurance companies, pension funds) and nonrecourse loans made or guaranteed by governmental units and their political subdivisions. The circumstances under which qualified nonrecourse financing is deemed to be "incurred to hold real property" are fairly broad in nature, and include owning real estate that is used in a trade or business.

EXAMPLE 19.77	In the preceding example, if the $200,000 debt were a "qualified nonrecourse financing" on real estate, the at-risk amount for each partner would be the same as the basis in the partnership interest.

Corporate taxpayers (other than S corporations and certain closely held C corporations) are not affected by the at-risk provisions discussed above. Thus, a corporate partner may, for purposes of partnership loss pass-through, include in its basis any partnership liability for any activity listed as "at risk" above.

Any losses that are suspended because of the at-risk rules can be deducted when the partner acquires more amounts at-risk, either by making contributions, earning income from the activity, or assuming the risk for more debt with respect to the activity. If the activity is sold or otherwise disposed of, any suspended at-risk losses become deductible.

TAX BLUNDER

Tom Mack and Ted Simon, equal partners in the T Square Partnership, are in low individual income tax brackets this year. They anticipate increased partnership earnings next year which will move them into the highest individual income tax bracket. Both partners have $20,000 of suspended losses from the partnership due to the at-risk limitations. During the current year, they replace their nonrecourse debt with recourse debt that qualifies as being at-risk.

Result. The partners have replaced nonrecourse debt with recourse debt, thus subjecting them to personal liability for the debt. They also committed an avoidable tax planning mistake because the additional at-risk amount allows them to deduct the losses in a year when they are in low individual income tax brackets instead of saving the loss deductions for the next year when they anticipate being in much higher individual income tax brackets.

Passive Activity Losses

Passive activities are those trades or businesses in which taxpayers do not materially participate. Losses from passive activities, in general, may be deducted only against passive income, and not against active or portfolio income. Any currently nondeductible amount is suspended and may be deducted against future passive income or against the proceeds from the ultimate sale of the activity or as a loss upon its abandonment. Code Sec. 469. For a more complete explanation of the passive loss rules, see Chapter 7 beginning at ¶7201.

Any rental activity is generally a passive activity regardless of whether the taxpayer materially participates (qualified real estate professionals who materially participate in rental real estate activities are exempted from this rule). However, a taxpayer may deduct losses of up to $25,000 from real estate rentals in which the taxpayer is an active participant. This deduction is phased out as the taxpayer's adjusted gross income exceeds $100,000. Active participation in rental real estate activities requires actually making management decisions involving the exercise of independent discretion concerning the rental property. Active participation includes hiring repairmen, approving new tenants, and deciding on rental terms. If the taxpayer does not actively participate in the rental real estate activities, then rental losses are treated under the usual rules for passive losses.

An individual is treated as not having actively participated in a rental real estate activity if the individual and a spouse own less than 10 percent in value of all interests in the activity. Limited partners (and to the extent of their limited partnership interests where they are also general partners) do not meet the active participation test. Limited partnership interests are treated as interests in a passive activity without regard to whether the taxpayer materially participates in the activity, unless low-income housing credits or commercial revitalization deductions are included. Under proposed regulations, limited liability company members are generally not treated as limited partners under the passive loss rules. Prop. Reg. §1.469-5(e)(3).

Whether the activity is passive or not is a question which each partner must determine independently. Even in a general partnership (where there are no limited partners), a partner who does not materially participate in the enterprise has that portion of the loss treated as being from a passive activity while the partners who materially participate are able to deduct their losses currently. The loss limitation rules (basis, at-risk, passive activity) are applied together to minimize the current deductibility of losses.

EXAMPLE 19.78	Archie, Baldy, and Chester Thompson are equal partners in a grocery store partnership. Archie and Baldy are involved full-time in the operation of the store. Chester, an attorney, takes no active part in the day-by-day operations of the enterprise. Chester is involved in no other passive activities. At the beginning of the current year each partner had a basis for his partnership interest of $50,000. Because of nonrecourse debt, their respective at-risk bases were $15,000. During the current year, the partnership incurred a loss of $60,000. Both Archie and Baldy may deduct only $15,000 of their $20,000 loss currently. As Chester's $20,000 loss is from an activity that is passive with respect to him, he can deduct nothing currently; his entire loss is suspended until he has passive income from the partnership or some other passive activity.

Where there are suspended losses under the passive loss rules, they may be recouped when the taxpayer recognizes subsequent income from passive activities or, failing that, upon the disposition by the holder of the entire interest in the passive activity. If a general or limited partnership conducts two or more separate activities and the entity disposes of all the assets used or created in one activity, such disposition is a disposition of the entire interest of the partner in that activity. Similarly, if a partner recognizes gain under Code Sec. 731(a) due to a distribution of money from the partnership in excess of the adjusted basis of the partner's interest, a ratable portion of the gain is treated as gain from the disposition of the partner's interest in each separate activity conducted by the partnership. Rev. Rul. 95-5, 1995-1 CB 100.

Termination of Partnership

¶19,615   ## CLOSING OF TAXABLE YEAR

The taxable year of a partnership does not close prior to its normal closing unless there is a "termination" of the partnership. In such an event, the partnership year is terminated as to all partners. Each partner must report, on their return for the taxable year with or within which the partnership terminates, the distributive share of profit or loss for the taxable year of the partnership closed by the termination. The taxable year of a partnership may be closed as to one or more partners, however, without a termination of the partnership. Thus, if one partner disposes (either by sale, death, liquidation, or otherwise) of an entire interest in the partnership during the partnership's taxable year, the partnership year closes with respect to that partner at that time. Assuming that the disposition does not terminate the partnership (as discussed in the next section), the taxable year of the partnership continues to its normal closing as to the remaining partners. Code Sec. 706(c); Reg. §1.706-1(c).

The termination of a partnership for federal income tax purposes is not governed by the rules for "dissolution" or "liquidation" of a partnership under state or local law. Reg. §1.706-1(c)(1). For tax purposes, a partnership is considered as terminated *only* if:

1. No part of any business, financial operation, or venture of the partnership continues to be carried on by any of its partners in a partnership, or
2. Within a 12-month period, there is a sale or exchange of 50 percent or more of the total interest in partnership capital and profits. Code Sec. 708(b)(1); Reg. §1.708-1(b)(1).

EXAMPLE 19.79	Hannibal Partnership was engaged in real estate development and also, incidentally, in farming some of its vacant land. On sale by one of the general partners of his interest (less than 50 percent), all real estate development activity ceased. This did not result in termination of the partnership because it continued to carry on its incidental farming activities. M.R. Ginsberg Est., 68-1 ustc ¶9429, 396 F.2d 989 (Ct.Cl. 1968).

EXAMPLE 19.80	On November 20 of the current year, Sarah and Bud Golden, who were both 20 percent partners in Whambo Partnership, sold their interests to Al Hall, who was a 60 percent partner. Since there was only one owner remaining, the Whambo partnership was terminated as of November 20 of the current year.

EXAMPLE 19.81	Partners Mary, Ted, and Peck Hillinger agree on April 30 of the current year to dissolve their partnership, but carry on the business through a winding-up period ending on September 30 of the current year. At that time all remaining assets, consisting only of cash, are distributed to the partners. In this case, termination of the partnership because of the cessation of business is not until September 30 of the current year.

Sales or Exchanges

For purposes of determining whether or not there has been a sale or exchange of 50 percent or more of the total interest in partnership capital and profits, a disposition of a partnership interest by gift (including assignment to a successor in interest), bequest, or inheritance or the liquidation of a partnership interest is not considered a sale or exchange. Nor does the contribution of property to the partnership constitute a sale or exchange. Reg. §1.708-1(b)(1)(ii).

"Fifty percent or more of the total interest in partnership capital and profits" means 50 percent or more of the total interest in partnership capital plus 50 percent or more of the total interest in partnership profits. Thus, the sale of a 30 percent interest in partnership profits and a 60 percent interest in partnership capital is not the sale or exchange of 50 percent or more of the interest in both partnership capital and profits. The sale or exchange of 50 percent or more of the total interest in both partnership capital and profits may result from the sale or exchange of different interests aggregating this much or more by two or more partners within a period of 12 consecutive months. Percentages are determined under this rule as of the date of each sale.

EXAMPLE 19.82	On April 12 of the current year, Tony Beyer sold his 30 percent interest in the capital and profits of Ton-Don-Son Partnership to Bill Peters and on March 27 of the subsequent year, Don Owens sells his 30 percent interest in capital and profits to Ellen. Since the two interests aggregate 60 percent of the total interest in capital and 60 percent of the total interest in profits, the partnership is considered as terminated on March 27 of the subsequent year.

Close of Taxable Year

The partnership taxable year is considered to be closed as of the first date on which there occurs either a winding-up of partnership affairs or a sale or exchange of 50 percent or more of the total interest in the partnership capital and profits within 12 months. If a partnership is considered to be terminated, the partnership is treated as contributing all of its assets to a new partnership in exchange for an interest in the new partnership, and immediately thereafter, the new partnership distributes interests in the new partnership to the purchasing partners and continuing partners in proportion to their interests in the terminated partnership. Reg. §1.708-1(b)(1)(iii) and (iv).

Withdrawal of Partner

A partnership taxable year closes with respect to a partner who disposes of an entire interest in a partnership and with respect to a partner whose entire interest is liquidated. Code Sec. 706(c)(2)(A); Reg. §1.706-1(c)(2)(i). If a partner sells or exchanges a part of the interest in the partnership or if the interest of a partner is reduced, the partnership taxable year continues to its normal conclusion, unless the partial sale or reduction terminates the partnership. If there is no termination, the partner's distributive share is determined by taking into account the partner's varying interest in the partnership during the partnership taxable year in which the sale or exchange or reduction of interest occurred. Code Sec. 706(d).

This varying interest rule applies to any partner who sells or exchanges less than an entire interest in the partnership or with respect to a partner whose interest is reduced (whether by entry of a new partner, partial liquidation of a partner's interest, gift, or otherwise). Code Sec. 706(d).

In the case of a disposition of a partner's entire interest, the partner must include in income the distributive share for the period ending with the date of the disposition, and it must be recognized in the partner's taxable year in which the disposition occurred. Code Sec. 706(c)(2)(A). In order to avoid an interim closing of the partnership's books, the withdrawing partner's share may by agreement among the partners be estimated by taking the pro rata part of the distributive share the partner would have included in taxable income had the partner remained a partner until the end of the partnership year. If this method of computing the transferor partner's share is used, any partner who is the transferee of such partner's interest must include in taxable income, as the distributive share, the pro rata part of the amount the partner would have included had he or she been a partner from the beginning of the taxable year of the partnership. Reg. §1.706-1(c)(2)(ii).

EXAMPLE 19.83	Assume that a partner is selling a 30 percent partnership interest on June 30, 2016 for $20,000. The partner has an adjusted basis for the interest of $5,000, and total income of the partnership is $100,000. The partner's pro rata share of partnership income up to June 30 is $15,000 (6/12 × $30,000), the $15,000 is includible in partner's income as the distributive share, and the basis of the partnership interest is accordingly increased to $20,000. Therefore, no gain is recognized on the sale of the partnership interest. The purchaser of this partnership interest must include in income only the distributive share of partnership income for the remainder of the partnership taxable year (6/12).

If the partnership reported under the cash receipts and disbursements method of tax accounting, the rules governing "allocation of cash-basis items" discussed at ¶19,275 come into play to prevent the incoming partner from benefiting from the items that accrued prior to the change. Code Sec. 706(d).

Death of a Partner

The tax year closes with respect to a deceased partner at the date of death. Code Sec. 706(c)(2). As with other dispositions, the tax year continues for the remaining partners. The deceased partner's final income tax return includes the partner's share of partnership income up to the date of the partner's death. The estate or other successor to the partnership interest will include its share of the partnership income for the remainder of the partnership's tax year.

EXAMPLE 19.84	Hank Brown owns a 50 percent interest in both the capital and profits of the Hank-Mate Partnership, which reports on a June 30 fiscal year. The partnership year ends with respect to Hank at his death on October 31, 2017. Hank's distributable share of the partnership's income for the partnership's June 30, 2017, fiscal year (assume $50,000) and his distributable share of the income for the short period, July 1–October 31, 2017 (assume $30,000) must be reported on Hank's final return for 2017. The income for the decedent's final year may be included in a joint return.

Even upon the death of one partner in a two-member partnership, the partnership business is not considered as terminated if the estate or other successor in interest of the deceased partner continues to share in the profits or losses of the partnership business. Probate courts in many states, however, are extremely reluctant to permit a partner's estate to continue as a member of the firm in the absence of an express direction in the will or a binding agreement between the parties.

Continuation of Partnership After Merger, Consolidation, or Division

If two or more partnerships merge or consolidate into a single partnership, the resulting partnership is considered as a continuation of the merging or consolidating partnership whose members own an interest of more than 50 percent in the capital and profits of the resulting partnership. The other merging or consolidating partnerships are considered as terminated. If more than one partnership can be considered as the continuing partnership under this rule, the one credited with contributing the greatest dollar value of assets will be so considered unless the IRS permits otherwise. But, if two partnerships merge and the members of each former partnership collectively own exactly 50 percent of the total capital and profits interests in the resulting partnership, both predecessor partnerships are considered to have been terminated and a new partnership results. Code Sec. 708(b)(2)(A); Reg. §1.708-1(b)(2)(i).

Any partnership considered to have been terminated by merger or consolidation must file a return for a taxable year ending on the date of the merger or consolidation. The resulting partnership must file a return for the taxable year of the partnership that is considered as continuing. This return must state that the resulting partnership is a continuation of such merging or consolidating partnership and must include the names and addresses of the merged or consolidated partnerships. The respective distributive shares of the partners for the periods prior to and subsequent to the date of merger or consolidation must be shown as a part of the return.

Upon the division of a partnership into two or more partnerships, any resulting partnership or partnerships is considered a continuation of the prior partnership only if its members had an interest of more than 50 percent in the capital and profits of the prior partnership. Any other resulting partnership is not considered a continuation of the prior partnership, but is considered a new partnership. Where members of a partnership which has been divided into two or more partnerships do not become members of a resulting partnership which is considered a continuation of the prior partnership, such partners' interests are considered to have been liquidated as of the date of the division. The resulting partnership that is regarded as continuing must file a return for the taxable year of its predecessor. The return must state that the partnership is a continuation of the divided partnership and must set forth separately the respective distributive shares of the partners for the period prior to and subsequent to the date of division. Code Sec. 708(b)(2)(B); Reg. §1.708-1(b)(2)(ii).

Family Partnerships

The family partnership has long been a standard tax-minimizing device. By bringing a spouse, children, parents, or other dependent relatives into the family business as partners, family income can be spread among more taxpayers and thus have more of it taxed in the dependents' lower tax brackets and less in the taxpayer's higher tax bracket. The IRS has consistently scrutinized with care all such arrangements and has carried to the courts its objections to literally hundreds of family partnerships. Acknowledging as an isolated proposition that a valid partnership may exist between related taxpayers, the IRS has not felt bound by state law in determining the validity of a partnership for tax purposes. As the federal income tax law contains its own concept of a partnership, a family partnership may be ignored for tax purposes even though it is perfectly valid in all other respects.

¶19,655   BONA FIDE PARTNERSHIP RELATIONSHIP

The tax treatment of family partnerships depends on whether capital is a material income-producing factor for the partnership or not. If it is, then a partner with a bona fide ownership of a capital interest will be recognized for income tax purposes, even if the interest was acquired by purchase or gift from a related person. Code Sec. 704(e)(1). In the case of a gift of an interest in a partnership in which capital is a material income-producing factor, if the donor has not actually relinquished control over the partnership interest, the Treasury Department will consider the partnership interest to be a sham, and the partner will not be treated as a partner for income tax purposes. *M. J. Speisman*, 58-2 USTC ¶9890, 260 F.2d 940 (CA-9 1958). Thus, there will be no shift in the incidence of taxation where a parent purportedly assigns a part of the partnership interest to a child, but the child receives no interest in the partnership assets, or any control over the business, and in fact is not accepted as a partner by the other partners.

With respect to family partnerships in which capital is not a material income-producing factor, the Supreme Court has ruled that a partnership interest is bona fide if the partners genuinely intended to join together for the purpose of carrying on the business and sharing in the profits and losses. Under this test, the performance of services and contribution of capital by the donee partner are important factors to be evaluated, but the lack of these factors does not necessarily indicate the lack of intent to create a bona fide partnership. *W. O. Culbertson*, 49-1 USTC ¶9323, 337 US 733, 69 SCt. 1210 (1949). However, over the years since Culbertson, the courts have been reluctant to uphold any donated interests in family partnerships in which capital is not a material income- producing factor and in which the donee partner performed no substantial services. Under those circumstances, the courts have only rarely found the requisite intent to form a bona fide partnership. *M. Lizzie*, TC Memo 1983-138 , 45 TCM 981, (1983); *C. Payton*, 425 F2d 1324, 70-1 USTC ¶9379 (1970).

¶19,665   ALLOCATION OF INCOME

Even after the hurdle of obtaining income tax recognition of the partnership has been crossed, the allocation of income between donor and donee must be justified. The donee's distributive share must be determined after due allowance has been made for the services contributed by the donor, and the portion of the donee's distributive share attributable to the donee's capital may not be proportionately greater than that attributable to the donor's capital. To the extent that the allocation under the agreement does not satisfy these criteria, the partnership income will be reallocated by the IRS. Code Sec. 704(e)(2); Reg. §1.704-1(e)(3); *R.C. Gorrill*, 22 TCM 804, CCH Dec. 26,183(M), T.C. Memo. 1963-168.

EXAMPLE 19.85	Father gave his son a one-half interest in a service partnership. During the year, the partnership earned $100,000, entirely due to the efforts of the father. If any part of the income is allocated to the son, the IRS will reallocate it to the father.

EXAMPLE 19.86	Father gave his son $50,000 which was contributed with an additional $50,000 by the father in the formation of a merchandising partnership. The partnership earned $50,000 net from the sale of goods. If the father's efforts had a fair market value of $20,000, a division of the partnership profits of $35,000 ($20,000 + 1/2 of ($50,000 – $20,000)) to the father and $15,000 to the son would probably withstand challenge from the IRS.

In general, an interest purchased by one member of the family from another member of the family is considered to be created by gift regardless of the consideration actually paid. For this purpose the IRS includes in "the family" the spouse, ancestors, lineal descendants, and any trusts for the primary benefit of such persons. Brothers and sisters are not included. Code Sec. 704(e)(2). However, the regulations provide that a purchase from a family member will be recognized as bona fide if (1) the terms have the usual characteristics of an arm's-length transaction, or (2) the purchase was genuinely intended to promote the success of the business. Reg. §1.704-1(e)(4)(ii).

PLANNING POINTER	While there is no reduction in the gross income reportable by a husband and wife acting as partners, there is the opportunity for both parties to have a retirement plan. There are no great problems if the wife truly renders services sufficient to generate earned income. On the other hand, if the earnings related to the wife are small, it may be advisable to merely have the husband hire his wife in his sole proprietorship (rather than form a partnership). He can have his Keogh plan, and both of them can have their IRAs.

TAX BLUNDER

James Jones Sr. inherited 500 acres of mountain land from his father in the mid-1930s when the value of the property was extremely low because of the Great Depression. The land had a basis to him of $10 per acre. James Sr. had made a gift of this property to his son, James Jr., in 1960 when the property then had a value of $100 per acre. James Sr. and his wife elected gift-splitting and used their lifetime exemptions, so there was no tax paid on the transfer. Located in a remote area of the state, the land lay idle. James Jr. considered it his retirement investment. In the current year, Harry Wright Inc., a developer, approached James Jr., convinced him that the land was worth $1,000 an acre as a potential ski resort area, and offered to manage the development and sale of the property in lots for "45 percent of the action." Wright estimated that after clearing, etc., the lots would sell for approximately $1 million. They formed a partnership, "Skiland." James Jr. invested $100,000 for 55 percent of the capital and profits; Wright Inc. invested its "know-how" for the remaining 45 percent interest. Skiland borrowed $500,000 from a local bank and purchased the mountain land from James Jr.

Result. The land had a carryover basis to James Jr. of $10 per acre, the basis for gain to his donor father. As James Jr. held the property as an investment, it qualified as a capital asset and, upon the sale of that asset, James Jr. expected long-term capital gain of $495,000. However, since the form of business selected was a partnership, James Jr. owned more than 50 percent of its capital, and the property in the hands of the partnership will be held primarily for sale to customers in the ordinary course of business, Code Sec. 707(b)(2) converted the gain into ordinary income.

Planning. If James Jr. had been willing to accept 50 percent or less of the capital and profits of the partnership or if he had selected the corporate form as the development vehicle, he might have preserved his long-term capital gain on the sale.

¶19,665

SUMMARY

- The check-the-box regulations allow an unincorporated entity with more than one owner the opportunity to elect whether it wants to be taxed as a partnership or a corporation.
- With the exception of investment partnerships, contributions of property to a partnership are generally nontaxable to the partner and to the partnership.
- The transfer of a capital interest in a partnership in exchange for services is usually a taxable event.
- The initial basis to a partner for the partnership interest is determined in the same manner as are other acquired assets (e.g., nontaxable exchange, purchase, gift, or inheritance).
- The basis of each partner's interest in the partnership includes the partner's share of the partnership liabilities (recourse and nonrecourse).
- The partner's basis in the partnership is increased for income items (taxable and nontaxable) and decreased by losses (deductible and nondeductible) and distributions.
- The partnership's required tax year is determined in a manner that minimizes deferral of income to the partners. Alternatively, the partnership may establish a natural business year or select a year with no more than three months' deferral and prepay tax on the deferred income.
- Most elections are made at the partnership level.
- The partnership does not pay tax on its income but instead files an information return that allocates its income to the partners.
- The income from the partnership retains its character when it passes through to the partners.
- The partnership may specially allocate income and deductions in accordance with the partnership agreement as long as the special allocations have substantial economic effect.
- Some items of income and deductions are required to be specially allocated to the contributing partner.
- No loss is allowed on a sale of property between a partner and a controlled partnership.
- Guaranteed payments are deductible by the partnership and includible in income by the recipient partner.
- A partner's share of losses from a partnership may be limited by the partnership basis rules, the at-risk rules, and the passive activity loss rules.
- A partnership terminates if no part of its business is continued to be carried on by any of its partners in a partnership or if there is a sale of 50 percent or more of the total interest in partnership capital and profits within a 12-month period.
- A partnership year ends with respect to a partner (but not necessarily the partnership) if the partner disposes of the entire interest in the partnership by death, sale, exchange, or otherwise.
- Family partnerships may be used to split income among family members, however, special care should be used to ensure that minors' income will not be reallocated to other partners.

QUESTIONS

1. Give illustrations of the application of the "entity" and the "aggregate" theories as applied to the treatment of partnerships.

2. Will a partnership under state law be taxed as a partnership under the Internal Revenue Code?

3. List at least three items which will increase a partner's basis in a partnership and at least three items which will decrease a partner's basis.

4. What income tax effect does a partnership's receipt of tax-exempt interest and the proceeds of key-person life insurance payable on account of the death of the insured have upon the partnership taxable income? Upon the basis of the surviving partners' interests in the partnership?

5. Discuss the partnership's treatment of contributed (1) accounts receivable of a cash-basis taxpayer, (2) inventory and (3) capital assets with a "built-in loss" at the time of the contribution.

6. Identify and discuss three situations in which a partner recognizes gain (income) or loss on the receipt of an interest in partnership capital and profits.

7. What is the difference in treatment when an incoming partner purchases an interest by agreeing to perform services for the partnership and the partnership (1) gives a 25 percent interest in the capital of the partnership, (2) gives a 25 percent interest in the future income of the partnership, or (3) gives a 25 percent interest in the partnership's future income which the incoming partner must forfeit if the partnership, as reconstituted after the incoming partner's admission, is unable to earn an average of $100,000 profit for the ensuing five years?

8. On February 19 of the current year, Bobby Morley contributes property with a $75,000 fair market value and a $40,000 basis to the Morley Partnership, in which Bobby has a 40 percent interest. On August 7 of the same year, the Morley Partnership distributes $75,000 cash to Bobby. What are two possible ways in which these transactions could be interpreted? What is the manner in which the IRS will interpret the transactions? Why?

9. Discuss the "varying interest rule," particularly as it applies to "allocable cash-basis items."

10. Discuss the consequences to a partnership that elects a fiscal year under Code Sec. 444 to avoid a required tax year of December 31.

11. Eli Kalbach, a calendar-year taxpayer, is a partner in a partnership which for many years has reported its income on a January 31 fiscal year. Explain why Kalbach claims that he is permanently deferring 11 months of partnership income by using this reporting method.

12. (a) Various elections must be made to compute a partnership's taxable income. For example, the partnership's tax year and accounting method must be chosen. Elections regarding depreciation and Code Sec. 179 expensing of assets also may have to be made. Who makes these elections?

(b) A calendar-year partnership is organized in April of the current year. It begins business in October of the current year. The partnership incurs and pays the following expenses during the last six months of the current year: $53,000 for legal and accounting fees in connection with forming the partnership and $45,000 for brokerage and registration fees in connection with issuing and marketing interests in the partnership. What options are available with respect to the $98,000 in partnership expenditures?

13. Why is it necessary for a partnership to list as separate items of expense payments to partners for meals and lodging incurred by them while away from home on partnership business?

14. Explain the probable income tax treatment of a family member's sale of property to a family partnership. Address both the problem of a sale at a loss and a sale at a gain.

15. Explain why it is that even when a partnership's only income is tax-exempt income and gains from the sales of long-term capital assets, a partner receiving a guaranteed payment must still classify the payment as ordinary income.

16. What difference does it make that a partner receiving a guaranteed salary from the partnership is not treated as an employee of the partnership?

17. Explain under what circumstances a net operating loss of a partnership can be carried over and applied against income of a partner even after the 20-year carryover period provided for net operating loss carryovers has expired.

18. Explain why a partner may have sufficient basis in a partnership interest to absorb a distributable share of a partnership loss but will not currently be permitted to deduct that loss because of the debt structure of the partnership or the activity generating the loss.

19. Discuss whether or not there is a closing of the partnership year for tax purposes when there is a sale by a partner of a 49 percent interest in the partnership. What would happen if within a 12-month period of the sale by the 49 percent partner there is a sale by another partner of a 10 percent interest in the same partnership?

20. If the partnership agreement contains no provision governing the event, what is the effect of a partner's death on the income tax reporting of the partnership? The deceased partner? The deceased partner's successor in interest?

21. Under what circumstances will the Internal Revenue Service recognize a minor child as a partner in a service partnership? In a partnership where capital is a major income-producing item?

22. In a bona fide, arm's-length transaction, a son, age 42, purchased from his father a 40 percent interest in the father's partnership, paying the full fair market value. The partnership is a manufacturing concern. The partnership's ordinary income, before partners' salaries, was $100,000. The father and son were allocated guaranteed payments of $60,000 and $40,000, respectively. The salary paid to the father is reasonably equivalent to comparable services performed for similar companies. The son rendered no services to the partnership. What will be the likely approach of the IRS on such payments?

PROBLEMS

23. Joe Quick and Jane Reddy are equal partners in the Quick and Reddy partnership. On the first day of the current taxable year, Joe's adjusted basis in his partnership interest is $10,000 and Jane's adjusted basis is $2,000. During the year, Joe had withdrawals of $25,000 and Jane had withdrawals of $20,000. Given the following partnership activity for the year, determine each partner's adjusted basis in Quick and Reddy at the end of the taxable year.

Ordinary income	$60,000
Section 1231 gains	1,000
Interest income from municipal bonds	500
Short-term capital losses	2,000
Charitable contributions	3,000

24. Diane Barnes has a 25 percent interest and Ester Newton has a 75 percent interest in the income and capital of D&E Partnership. The partnership reports ordinary income of $25,000, tax-exempt interest of $1,000, and long-term capital gains of $5,000 for the current year. Ester's basis for her partnership interest as of the beginning of the year was $60,000. She made withdrawals of $5,000 during the year. What is her basis for her interest in the partnership as of the end of the year?

25. Paul Stanley transfers $20,000 in cash, Joe Sweitzer transfers machinery with an adjusted basis of $5,000 and a fair market value of $20,000, and David Raines transfers land with an adjusted basis of $10,000, a fair market value of $26,000, and subject to a mortgage of $6,000 in exchange for equal interests in the newly formed PJD partnership. What are the partners' initial adjusted bases in their partnership interests? What is the PJD partnership's basis in its assets?

26. On September 1, 2012, Leonard contributed land held for investment with a fair market value of $200,000 and an adjusted basis to him of $120,000 for a 20 percent interest in the income and capital of Office Complex Partnership. The land was intended for use as a building site for the partnership. The partnership opted to rent facilities and on September 2, 2017, sold the contributed land for $500,000. Assuming the partnership agreement was silent with respect to this particular asset, how much gain must Leonard report for this partnership sale?

27. Elder Attorney had practiced law for several years and had accumulated $50,000 in accounts receivable. He reported his income for tax purposes under the cash receipts and disbursements method. Elder formed an equal partnership with Senior Counsel, Lawyers Unlimited, a cash-basis law partnership, and transferred his $50,000 accounts receivable to the partnership for their admitted FMV of $50,000. In the first year of the partnership, its cash-basis income was $100,000, $50,000 of which was the collection of the transferred receivables. When is the income of the partnership reported and by whom?

28. On January 17 of the current year, the Bamber Partnership was formed by Bob Miller, Carl Penn, and Don Allen. Each partner has an equal interest in the capital and profits of the partnership. The Bamber partnership will report on the basis of a calendar year. The following contributions were made when the partnership was formed.

Partner	Property	Basis to Partner	FMV
Bob	Cash	$15,000	$15,000
Carl	Inventory	9,000	15,000
Don	Capital Asset	35,000	15,000

Both the inventory and capital asset are inventory to the Bamber partnership. On May 22 the partnership sells the inventory for $27,000. On July 19 the partnership sells the capital asset which Don contributed for $9,000. The partnership agreement is silent regarding the property contributed by the partners. Without regard to the sale of the contributed properties, the Bamber partnership reports $60,000 of ordinary income for its current tax year. As a result of partnership transactions, what does each partner report on his individual tax return for the current year?

29. On January 1, 2017, Kelley became a 10 percent partner of the Realty Partnership upon contributing land he had held as an investment for five years. The basis of the land to Kelley was $200,000, but its fair market value at the time of the contribution was only $100,000. Assume that after much advertising, Realty Partnership was able to sell the property for $120,000 on December 31, 2017. How much, if any, loss is recognized by Realty Partnership on the sale and what is its character? Would your answer be different if the sale took place on January 2, 2022?

30. Marvin Bridges is a 25 percent partner in the Munson partnership. On November 23, 2016, Marvin contributes property with an adjusted basis of $75,000 and a fair market value of $250,000 to the Munson partnership. On March 15, 2017, Marvin receives a $187,500 cash distribution from the partnership.

a. Why would the IRS seek to classify the transactions as a disguised sale?

b. Assume that the IRS is successful in classifying the transactions as a disguised sale. Outline the income tax consequences to Marvin.

31. Jeff Able is a partner in the Willing and Able partnership. On June 1, 2017, Jeff transfers property to the partnership that has a fair market value of $60,000 and an adjusted basis to Jeff of $10,000. Three weeks later, the Willing and Able partnership transfers $40,000 cash to Jeff. Willing and Able would not have transferred the cash to Jeff if he hadn't first transferred the property. What are the tax consequences of the transactions to Jeff?

32. Susan Moore contributed land with an adjusted basis of $500,000 and a fair market value of $800,000 to the Whirligig partnership in exchange for a 20 percent interest in the partnership. Susan held the land as a capital asset, and Whirligig also held the land as a capital asset. Three years after Susan transferred the land, Whirligig distributes the land to another partner when the land's FMV is $1,000,000. What is Whirligig's gain on the distribution, and what is Susan's gain?

33. Jed Castanza transfers $90,000 of cash to the JN partnership for a 60 percent interest in the JN partnership. Ned transfers a building with an adjusted basis of $30,000 and a fair market value of $100,000, subject to a debt of $40,000 that the partnership assumes, in exchange for a 40 percent interest in the JN partnership. Determine each partner's adjusted basis in his partnership interest. Does either partner recognize any gain on the transfer to the partnership? What is JN's basis in the assets?

34. Assume the same facts as in problem 33 except that Ned's basis in the building is only $20,000. Determine each partner's adjusted basis in his partnership interest. Does either partner recognize any gain on the transfer to the partnership? What is JN's basis in the assets?

35. James Michaels invested $25,000 for a one-third interest in the Jabo Partnership on January 1 of the current year. The partnership purchased a building site on February 5 at a cost of $200,000, paying $50,000 as a down payment and obtaining a mortgage of $150,000 at 12 percent annual interest for only three years, then full payment of principal. Because of an unexpected rezoning of the property, it substantially increased in value. Jabo Partnership broke exactly even for the current year since their income was exactly the same as their expenses. On December 31 James sold his one-third interest to Joe Hammer, receiving $62,500 in cash. What was James's basis for his interest in the partnership immediately prior to the sale? What was the sales price of the interest? What is the character of James's gain upon the sale of his interest?

36. Ruben and Albert are both calendar-year taxpayers, and are equal partners in the RA Partnership, which has a fiscal year ending on October 31. During the 2017-2018 fiscal year the partnership earns $15,000 each month, and during the 2018-2019 fiscal year the partnership earns $20,000 each month. The partnership distributes $30,000 cash to Ruben in January 2018 and $40,000 cash to Albert in December 2018. How much income will each partner have to recognize from the partnership for 2018?

37. The Nelson partnership begins business on July 17, 2017. It is not able to use business purpose to support a tax year. The four partners, their interests in partnership capital and profits, and their tax years are as follows:

Partner	Partnership Interest (%)	Tax Year
Individual A	4	1/1-12/31
Individual B	45	1/1-12/31
Corporation C	21	7/1-6/30
Corporation D	30	10/1-9/30

What tax year must the Nelson partnership adopt?

38. In 2017 the XYZ Partnership incurred the following expenses:

Expenses of selling partnership interests	$10,000
Attorney's fees for drafting partnership agreement	30,000
Expenses of transferring title of property to partnership	8,000
Accounting fees to organize partnership	22,000

If XYZ began business on August 1, 2017, how much in total of these expenses could XYZ deduct (including amortization)?

39. Ozone Partnership constructed an office building which has a projected annual income of $100,000 for several years. Archie Edwards, the architect for the building, whose normal fee is $50,000, contributes cash for a 25 percent interest in the partnership. The partnership agreement provides Archie will receive (1) 25 percent of the earnings from the partnership and (2) an allocation and distribution of $25,000 of partnership gross income for its first two years of operation after the building is fully leased. The leasing prospects and cash flow projections are excellent. Assuming the annual gross income for the first two years is $100,000 in each year and that depreciation and cash expense items, exclusive of Archie's arrangement, total $60,000, compute the effect of the above items on the income of the partnership and of Archie. Indicate how the income would be classified.

40. Henry Hawkins owns a 20 percent interest in the HI Partnership. On July 1 he sold 100 shares of stock of IPR Corporation to the partnership for $10,000, its fair market value. The stock had cost him $5,000 10 months prior to the sale. How much and what character of profit must Henry report on this sale currently?

41. Assume that the HI Partnership in the preceding problem held the IPR stock for three months and on October 1 sold it for $15,000 to Isaac Stanley, the 80 percent partner and a real estate broker. How much profit must Henry report on this partnership sale currently? What is the character of the reported profit? How would your answer be different if Isaac were a dealer in securities?

42. Elaine is a 30% partner in the DEF Partnership. She sells some land to the partnership for $50,000, incurring a $30,000 loss on the sale. How much of the loss can she deduct? What happens if DEF later sells the property for $90,000? What would your answer be to the above questions if her ownership was 60% rather than 30%?

43. Baker, a cash-basis, calendar-year taxpayer, is a partner in an accrual-basis partnership that reports its taxable income on an October 31 fiscal year. Baker has been provided the following information:

	FY 16-17	FY 17-18
Baker's distributive share of partnership ordinary income	$30,000	$40,000
Baker's "salary"		
$1,000 per month	12,000	
$1,500 per month		18,000

The partnership was short of cash and paid none of the above to Baker until January 3, 2019. Compute Baker's income from the partnership for 2017.

44. Because it was anticipated that Bob Short would devote more time to the partnership than would his equal partner Jack Long, it was agreed that Bob would receive a "salary" of $12,000 per year. Bob and Jack agreed to divide the remaining partnership income equally. For the current year, prior to consideration of Bob's salary, the partnership income was composed of $6,000 long-term capital gain, $2,000 tax-exempt interest, and $8,000 loss from operations. Determine the amount and character of income (loss) reportable by Bob and Jack for the current year.

45. On January 1, 2014, Martha Carnes, fresh out of college, contributed $10,000 for a 30 percent interest in an accounting partnership. The senior partner was not attentive to the work, and the first year they were sued for malpractice and a judgment of $100,000 was entered against the firm. The firm borrowed $50,000 in 2014 to assist in its payment. The debt was repaid in 2016. The following shows the results of the partnership operations:

Year	Income/(Loss)
2014	($100,000)
2015	10,000
2016	50,000
2017	100,000

Compute Martha's reportable income (loss) for each year and the basis of her partnership interest at the end of each year.

46. Jack Dillon and Jake Johnson each own 50 percent of the capital interests in the JJ partnership. They share profits equally, but they agree to allocate 60 percent of the losses to Jack and 40 percent to Jake. The note payable is a recourse liability. The tax-basis balance sheet at the end of the year is as follows:

Cash	$50,000
Equipment	100,000
Total assets	$150,000
Note Payable	$90,000
Capital, Jack Dillon	30,000
Capital, Jake Johnson	30,000
Total liabilities and capital	$150,000

Determine how much of the liability is allocable to each partner.

47. Frank Caster and George Wilson were equal partners of the F&G partnership, which reported its income on a fiscal year ending September 30. For fiscal year 2016–2017, the partnership's ordinary income was $30,000. Its ordinary income for the months of October–December 2017 was $9,000. The partnership was terminated on December 31, 2017, and each partner was repaid his capital account as of September 30, 2017, plus his earnings since that date. Frank did not receive his check until January 1, 2018. What income will Frank report from the partnership on his 2017 personal return?

48. William Nest operated a consulting business as a sole proprietor in 2016, generating fees of $50,000. On January 1, 2017, he decided to set up a consulting partnership with his son Wilhelm. William transferred a used computer with an adjusted basis of $10,200 and a fair market value of $11,000 and other office equipment with an adjusted basis of $12,250 and a fair market value of $14,000. William also felt that he had generated goodwill with a value of $30,000 that was supported by a recent bona fide offer for his consulting business. On January 1, 2017, William gave his son Wilhelm $55,000, which he contributed to the new partnership, Will and Wile, for a one-half interest. The gross earnings of the new partnership for 2017 totalled $75,000—$50,000 from William's contacts and $25,000 from Wilhelm's contacts. The net income was $60,000. In anticipation of Wilhelm's growing contribution to future earnings, the agreement provides for equal division of profit. What is Wilhelm's basis for his interest immediately after his cash contribution to the partnership? How will the IRS probably require that the partnership earnings be divided?

49. For federal income tax purposes a partnership may be composed of:
    a. Two or more individuals
    b. An individual and a corporation
    c. A trust, an estate, and an individual
    d. Two or more partnerships
    e. All of the above

50. The basis of a partner's interest in a partnership is increased by:
    a. Decreases in partnership liabilities
    b. Receipt by the partnership of an item of income that is excluded from the definition of gross income
    c. Gain recognized by another partner when the other partner sells an interest in the partnership at a gain
    d. Payment by the partnership of nondeductible expense
    e. Issuance of a promissory note to the partnership to pay for an additional interest in the partnership.

51. In which of the following situations does the partnership's tax year close with respect to all partners in the partnership?
    a. An equal partner in a two-partner partnership dies. The deceased partner's interest is sold to the remaining partner.
    b. An equal partner in a four-partner partnership sells his entire interest to an unrelated third party.
    c. A 60 percent partner in a three-partner partnership gives her interest to her grandson.
    d. A 55 percent partner in a five-partner partnership has her interest liquidated through an immediate lump-sum payment from the partnership.

52. If the partnership agreement is silent regarding the matter:
    a. The partnership year ends upon the death of one partner in a two-person partnership.
    b. All items of income, deductions, and credits must be shared by the partners in proportion to their profit and loss ratios.
    c. The partnership year ends with respect to a selling partner only if the partner's sales (plus other sales) total 50 percent or more of the partnership interest.
    d. A partner who renders a disproportionate amount of time or capital to the partnership is entitled to a guaranteed payment.
    e. None of the above.

53. **Comprehensive Problem.** Hazel Patrick owns a building in which she practices dentistry. She also owns substantial amounts of equipment used in her practice. The building cost her $100,000 and its adjusted basis is $60,000; its present fair market value is $200,000. Had she used straight-line depreciation, her adjusted basis would be $75,000. Her equipment, which originally cost her $20,000 three years ago, has an adjusted basis of $5,000 and a present fair market value of $7,500. She also has cash-basis accounts receivable with a face amount of $20,000 and accounts payable in the amount of $15,000. She has $5,000 in fair market value of dental gold, which she had expensed upon purchase.

Hazel has been approached to enter into an equal partnership with another dental practitioner. They would prefer that their contributions to the partnership have substantially equal value. It has been suggested that Hazel either retain her building and rent it to the partnership at $25,000 net rent per year or place a mortgage of $100,000 against it and contribute it to the new partnership subject to the mortgage.

Compute Hazel's basis in the partnership under the alternative propositions.

Determine what and how much, if any, are the recaptures.

54. **Comprehensive Problem.** Barbara Thompson and Colleen Tiller are equal partners in the Boteq partnership. Barbara is age 72 and Colleen age 58. Both are unmarried and the partnership is their sole source of income. During the current year, Boteq's records show the following items of income and expense. In a columnar form, list those items which must be reported as partnership ordinary income and those which must be reported separately by the partnership.

(1)	Gross profit on sale of goods	$40,000
(2)	Selling and administrative expenses	30,000

Other items not included in above:

(1)	Dividends from domestic corporations	1,000
(2)	Charitable contributions to church	500
(3)	Long-term capital gains	2,000
(4)	Short-term capital losses	500
(5)	Section 1245 gain on office equipment which had an adjusted basis at sale of $400	800
(6)	Theft of day's receipts	1,200
(7)	Theft of Barbara's fur coat in the pocket of which were the receipts. Original cost $2,500, FMV at date of theft	$1,000
(8)	Royalty check for Boteq's $10,000 investment this year in a widget mining venture	400
(9)	Notice of Boteq's coal percentage depletion allowance of $1,000 (the property has been fully depleted for several years)	
(10)	Expensing of seven-year property under Code Sec. 179, purchased during the year	2,000
(11)	Social Security benefit checks payable to Barbara which were regularly deposited to Boteq's account	4,500

55. **Practice Problem—Tax Return Issues.**
Adam, Barbara, and Charlotte formed the equal ABC Partnership; Adam and Barbara each contributed cash of $100,000, and Charlotte contributed land worth $130,000 with a basis of $120,000 and subject to a mortgage of $30,000. In the first year (using the cash basis for tax purposes) they had the following for tax purposes:

Sales	$400,000
Purchases of inventory	180,000
Ending inventory	40,000
Depreciation	30,000
Section 179 expense	25,000
Salaries	40,000
Guaranteed payment to Adam	15,000
Purchases of equipment	150,000
Rent expense	20,000
Interest income	6,000
Mortgage interest expense	1,500
Ending accounts receivable	35,000

Depreciation for book purposes was $20,000, and they had a bad debt accrued expense of $4,000 for book purposes, but no actual charge-offs during the year. Interest income comes from earnings on the cash balance.

a. What is ABC's ordinary business income (for tax purposes – p. 1, line 22, Form 1065) for the year?

b. What are its separately stated items (those that go on Sch. K)?

c. Compute total tax net income, including separately stated items, and reconcile it with book net income (the M-1 reconciliation would be the reverse).

d. What are its beginning and ending balance sheets for book purposes (as would go on Sch. L, Form 1065)?

56. **Research Problem.** Mary Black, Nell Brown, and Louise Gray each has her own computer equipment and service retail store. In an effort to potentially reduce their costs and increase their control over supply channels, they buy a plant which manufactures selected computer supplies and equipment. Each makes an equal cash contribution toward the purchase of the plant, each has an equal capital and profits interest in the plant, and they agree to share all losses equally. They own the plant as tenants in common. The co-owners have a written operating agreement specifying that each has an equal interest in the plant's production, each is responsible for her equal share of expenses, and each owns a proportionate, undivided part of the plant's equipment. The agreement also provides that the plant, as such, does not have the right to market the manufactured computer supplies and equipment. In lieu of the plant's selling the manufactured computer supplies and equipment to other purchasers, Mary, Nell, and Louise agree that each will take one-third of the plant's annual output. Each takes her share of the output, commingles it with other computer equipment and supplies in their respective computer equipment and service retail stores, and sells it to customers.

With regard to the plant, research and answer the following questions:

1. Is the plant a partnership for federal income tax purposes?

2. If the plant is a partnership for federal income tax purposes, may it make an election not to be subject to the partnership provisions of Subchapter K of the Internal Revenue Code?

3. Without regard to your answer to question two, assume that the plant may elect out of Subchapter K. Are Mary, Nell, and Louise subject to the self-employment tax on their distributive shares of the plant's earnings, assuming the output was purchased by Mary, Nell, and Louise, rather than being distributed to each?

Chapter

20

Partnerships—Distributions, Sales, and Exchanges

OBJECTIVES

After completing Chapter 20, you should be able to:

1. Understand the differences in the tax treatment of current and liquidating distributions.
2. Determine the tax consequences associated with liquidating vs. non-liquidating distributions of cash from a partnership.
3. Determine the tax consequences associated with liquidating and non-liquidating distributions of property other than cash from a partnership.
4. Determine the tax consequences when a partner receives a distribution of both cash and property from a partnership.
5. Compute a partner's tax basis in property when (s)he receives multiple assets in a single distribution.
6. Identify those situations when a partner recognizes gain or loss in connection with the receipt of a partnership distribution.
7. Understand the effects that liabilities have on the measurement of tax basis in connection with partnership distributions.
8. Compute the amount of ordinary income to be recognized by a partner or partnership when the partnership makes a disproportionate distribution to a partner.
9. Measure a partner's recognized gain or loss from sale of his/her interest in a partnership.
10. Determine what portion of a partner's gain on sale of his/her partnership interest will be treated as ordinary income vs. capital gain.
11. Identify situations when a partnership will be allowed or required to make adjustments to the basis of its assets and allocate those adjustments among the partnership's assets.

OVERVIEW

The tax treatment of distributions received by a partner from a partnership differs substantially from that accorded corporate distributions. Unlike corporate distributions, partnership distributions are generally nontaxable to both the partner and the partnership. The specific tax consequences of a partnership distribution depend on whether the distribution is a liquidating distribution (liquidating the partner's interest in the partnership) or a current distribution (one that does not liquidate the partner's interest in the partnership).

Generally speaking, a current or non-liquidating distribution will trigger recognition of taxable income to a partner only if the partner receives cash in an amount greater than his or her tax basis in the partnership interest. If the partner does not receive such an "excess" cash distribution, he/she will generally recognize no taxable gain and will take a carryover basis in any property received from the partnership (i.e., will take the same tax basis in such property as the partnership had just prior to the distribution). The partner will reduce the tax basis of the partnership interest in an amount equal to the basis assigned to the distributed property. Of course, for this mechanism to work, the partner's basis in the distributed property cannot exceed his/her tax basis in the partnership interest before receipt of the distribution.

Similar rules apply to distributions received in complete liquidation of a partner's interest in the partnership. However, in such cases, the partner takes a basis in the distributed property equal to his or her tax basis in the partnership interest just prior to the distribution (i.e., a "substitute" basis). Because the distribution is in liquidation of the entire partnership interest, it would not make sense for the partner to have any remaining tax basis in the partnership interest. As with current distributions, a partner receiving a liquidating distribution from a partnership will recognize gain on receipt of the distribution only if he or she receives cash in excess of the tax basis of the partnership interest. Unlike with current distributions, however, the recipient of a liquidating distribution may also recognize a deductible loss on receipt of a distribution if the distribution consists solely of cash and/or ordinary income property with an aggregate fair market value (including cash) that is less than the partner's basis in the partnership interest.

The principle exception to these rules applies when a distribution alters the recipient partner's economic share of partnership ordinary income assets (referred to as "hot" assets). In such cases, the partner (or the partnership) will recognize ordinary income as if a portion of those hot assets had been sold. The rationale for this provision is to prevent the partnership from using distributions to allow one or more partners to avoid recognition of their shares of partnership ordinary income.

Different consequences apply when a partner sells his or her interest in a partnership. Sale of a partnership interest is a fully taxable transaction, in which the selling partner will recognize gain (or loss) to the extent the proceeds from sale exceed the tax basis of the partnership interest. Although any gain or loss recognized on the sale is generally classified as capital in nature, some (or all) of it will be characterized as ordinary income to the extent it is attributable to partnership ordinary income assets such as unrealized receivables or inventory.

Although the partnership framework is generally more tax friendly to partners, the flexibility associated with partnership distributions comes at the cost of increased complexity. Deferring the recognition of gain or loss on receipt of a distribution of cash or property requires a sophisticated system of accounting for the tax basis of the property received and the remaining interest in the partnership. Within this accounting system, the aggregate basis of the partnership's property ("inside" basis) will generally equal the aggregate basis of the partners in their partnership interests ("outside" basis). In some cases, however, this equilibrium will be violated. In such cases, the law allows partnerships to *elect* to adjust their ("inside") basis in partnership property to maintain the equivalence of inside and outside basis. The resulting process is cumbersome, but it generally works to minimize the tax costs to the partners of investing in the partnership. As a result, partnerships and limited liability companies are often the entity of choice for taxpayers organizing new companies.

Partnership Distributions

¶20,001   INTRODUCTION

One of the most significant differences between the taxation of partnerships and corporations is the treatment of distributions from the entity to its owners. In contrast to the corporate distribution scheme, in which the distribution of profits is taxable as a dividend, partnership profit distributions are nontaxable. Moreover, most property distributions from a partnership to its partners are nontaxable as well. Gains can be triggered by cash distributions, but only if the amount of cash received exceeds the partner's basis in his/her partnership interest. Thus, unlike in the corporate tax framework, the "exit" cost of leaving a partnership is generally quite low from a tax perspective.

There are exceptions, of course. So-called "**disproportionate distributions**," which alter a partner's share of partnership ordinary income property relative to his/her share of capital gain property, will often trigger gain or loss to both the partner and the partnership. These rules are designed to prohibit a partner from leaving a partnership before it has fully disposed of its inventory or other ordinary income assets, thereby avoiding a share of the resulting ordinary income (and indirectly shifting that share to the other partners). They add complexity to the distribution framework, and can result in sizable tax costs to unwary partners. This is the price partners pay, however, for the otherwise benign treatment accorded distributions generally.

¶20,011   CURRENT v. LIQUIDATING DISTRIBUTIONS

The tax consequences of partnership distributions are dependent on the nature of the distribution. For tax purposes, distributions are classified as either "current" or "liquidating" distributions. A **liquidating distribution** is one which completely liquidates a partner's entire interest in a partnership. All other distributions are classified as **current distributions**.

EXAMPLE 20.1   Jill is one of three partners in the JFK Partnership. This year, Jill encountered serious financial difficulties, and was forced to make a cash withdrawal from the partnership. In December, she withdrew half of her share of partnership capital, in the process reducing her interest in partnership profit and loss from one-third to one-fifth. This withdrawal was analogous to a stock redemption in corporate tax. Although the distribution reduced her interest in the partnership from one-third to one-fifth, it was not a liquidating distribution because Jill remained a partner. The tax consequences will be determined under the rules applicable to current distributions.

Partnership Current Distributions

¶20,020   CURRENT DISTRIBUTIONS—CASH

As noted above, a current distribution is one which does not liquidate the partner's entire interest in the partnership. Under Code Secs. 731 and 733, such distributions are generally not taxable, but instead are applied against the partner's basis in his/her partnership interest. This treatment is consistent with the premise that the distribution to a partner of some or all of his/her portion of partnership profits should not be a taxable event since the partner has already been taxed on those profits.

EXAMPLE 20.2   Shirley is a one-half partner in the ST Partnership. Her tax basis in her partnership interest at the beginning of the year was $25,000. This year, the partnership reported net profits of $56,000, of which Shirley's share was $28,000. The partnership distributed half, or $14,000, of Shirley's share of income to her on December 31. The distribution will not be taxable, but will instead be accounted for as a nontaxable reduction in Shirley's basis in the partnership interest. At the end of the year, Shirley's remaining basis in her partnership interest will be $39,000 (her $25,000 initial basis in the interest, increased by her $28,000 share of partnership income, and reduced by the $14,000 distribution).

A current distribution does not have to consist of a partner's share of partnership profits to be nontaxable. To the extent a partner receives a distribution in excess of his/her share of partnership profits, the distribution is treated as a return of capital under the above framework. As a result, under Code Sec. 731(a)(1), a cash distribution will not be taxable to the recipient partner unless it exceeds the partner's basis in his/her partnership interest. In such cases, the partner cannot treat the entire distribution as a reduction in his/her basis in the partnership interest because that basis is insufficient to absorb the entire distribution. Thus, the partner's basis in the partnership interest is reduced to zero, and he/she must recognize a taxable gain in the amount of the remaining, or "excess," cash. Under Code Sec. 741, this gain will be treated as a capital gain.

EXAMPLE 20.3

Fred's tax basis in his interest in Bedrock Partners was $12,000. He received a $16,000 cash distribution. Under Code Sec. 731(a)(1), Fred must recognize a $4,000 capital gain on receipt of the distribution. His remaining tax basis in the partnership interest under Code Sec. 733 will be zero.

Draws Against Earnings

One potential problem, particularly for partners in professional partnerships (e.g., doctors, accountants, lawyers, etc.), is that the partners often need to use their shares of partnership profits to pay monthly living expenses. Rather than wait until year-end to distribute their shares of partnership profits, many partnerships allow the partners to make monthly withdrawals against their anticipated shares of profits. These monthly payments, called "**draws**," are treated for tax purposes as if they were withdrawn on the last day of the partnership's taxable year, thus allowing the partners to add their shares of the partnership's actual income to the tax basis of their partnership interest before determining whether they received "excess" distributions during the year.

EXAMPLE 20.4

Millard is a ten percent partner in an accounting partnership. At the beginning of the year, Millard's tax basis in his partnership interest was $10,000. During the year, he received distributions from the partnership of $3,000 per month. His share of the partnership's net profits for the year totaled $30,000. Although by April Millard's cumulative distributions from the partnership exceeded his beginning tax basis in the partnership interest, none of the distributions are taxable to Millard. The monthly draws are treated as if they were all received on December 31 rather than periodically throughout the year. At that date, Millard's basis in his partnership interest was $40,000, consisting of his initial $10,000 tax basis plus his $30,000 share of partnership profits. The total amount of distributions received was only $36,000. Thus, Millard recognizes no gain as a result of the distributions. He reports his $30,000 share of partnership income on his individual tax return, and reduces his tax basis in the partnership interest to $4,000 ($40,000 year-end basis less $36,000 total distributions).

It can sometimes be difficult to determine whether a payment to a partner constitutes a draw against his or her share of partnership earnings. Generally speaking, the issue will turn on how the partnership accounts for the transaction. A "draw" should not affect the partner's interest in the partnership's capital, profits or losses. In most cases, draws are paid periodically to all partners in the partnership, paying out some or all of their anticipated shares of partnership profit. At the end of the year, any differences between anticipated profits during the year and the partnership's actual profits are reconciled, and excess "draws" will be reclassified as current distributions or as loans to the partners (to be either repaid or offset against next year's earnings). In contrast, a distribution to a partner should be accounted for by the partnership as a capital transaction—his or her interest in partnership capital, and in future profits and losses, should be reduced to reflect that the partner has withdrawn a portion of his or her investment in the partnership.

Distributions in Reduction of a Partner's Interest in Capital

Note that in applying the provisions of Code Secs. 731 and 733, a partner recognizes no gain upon receipt of a cash distribution unless the amount of cash received exceeds the partner's *total* basis in the partnership interest. This is true whether the distribution consists of some or all of the partner's share of profits, or whether it instead represents a partial liquidation of his/her interest in the partnership interest. These provisions contrast sharply with those applicable to corporate redemptions in which gain or loss is determined by comparing the proceeds received with the shareholder's basis in the portion of his/her stock holdings surrendered to the corporation.

EXAMPLE 20.5	Until December 31, Charles was a forty percent partner in Cajun Products Partners. His basis in his partnership interest was $60,000, including his share of profits for the current year. On December 31, the partnership distributed $50,000 cash to Charles in redemption of *half* his interest in the partnership. Although the distribution was in liquidation of half of Charles' interest in the partnership, for purposes of determining whether he must recognize any gain on the transaction, he must compare the amount received against his entire $60,000 basis in the partnership interest (rather than against only half that amount). Thus, the distribution is not taxable to Charles. His remaining basis in his partnership interest is $10,000 ($60,000 initial basis less $50,000 distribution).

¶20,021 CURRENT DISTRIBUTIONS—PROPERTY

The receipt of property other than cash in a current, or nonliquidating, distribution is generally nontaxable to both the partner and the partnership. The partnership simply writes the property off its books and charges the carrying value of the property against the partner's capital account. This is in sharp contrast to the corporate tax framework under which the corporation recognizes gain on the distribution of appreciated property as if the property had been sold for its fair market value, and the proceeds distributed to the shareholder(s).

EXAMPLE 20.6	Albert Partners, a real estate partnership, distributed one of its properties to Steve in a nonliquidating distribution. The partnership's tax basis in the property prior to the distribution was $75,000. The fair market value of the property was $135,000. Although the property's value exceeded its tax basis by $60,000, the partnership will recognize no gain on the distribution. It will merely write the property off its books and reduce Steve's capital account accordingly.

Consequences to Partner

Property distributions are also generally tax-free to the recipient partners. The partner takes a **carryover** basis in the property received, and reduces his/her basis in the partnership interest by a like amount. Gain will generally not be recognized by the partner until (s)he sells or otherwise disposes of the distributed property.

EXAMPLE 20.7	Quinn received a nonliquidating distribution of land from a family partnership valued at $188,000. The partnership's tax basis in the land was $106,000. Quinn's tax basis in his partnership interest prior to receipt of the distribution was $125,000. Although the value of the land exceeded Quinn's basis in his partnership interest by $63,000 ($188,000 - $125,000), Quinn will recognize no gain on the distribution. He will take a $106,000 basis in the land, and reduce his basis in his partnership interest to $19,000 ($125,000 - $106,000).

In some cases, the partnership's tax basis in distributed property may exceed the partner's basis in his/her partnership interest. In such cases, the partner cannot take a full carryover basis in the distributed property because (s)he does not have sufficient basis in the partnership interest to absorb the entire carryover amount. Under Code Sec. 732(a)(2), the partner's basis in distributed property cannot exceed his/her basis in the partnership interest. Where the partnership's basis in distributed property exceeds the partner's basis in his/her partnership interest, the tax basis of the property in the partner's hands must be "stepped down" to the lower amount.

EXAMPLE 20.8	Wendy is a thirty percent partner in White Enterprises. Her basis in her partnership interest at October 1 was $22,000. On that date, she received a nonliquidating distribution of land from the partnership valued at $68,000. The partnership's tax basis in the land was $29,000. Under Code Sec. 731(a), Wendy will recognize no gain on receipt of the distribution because she did not receive cash in excess of her basis in her partnership interest. (Indeed, she received no cash at all). Her basis in the land received from the partnership will be equal to the *lesser* of the partnership's (carryover) basis in the land, or her basis in her partnership interest. In this case, Wendy's basis in her partnership interest is lower than the partnership's basis in the distributed land. Accordingly, Wendy will take a $22,000 tax basis in the land, and her basis in her partnership interest will be reduced to zero.

¶20,022   CURRENT DISTRIBUTIONS OF CASH AND PROPERTY

As a general rule, a partner recognizes gain upon receipt of a distribution *only* to the extent that the cash portion of the distribution exceeds the partner's basis in his/her partnership interest. Where the partner receives a distribution of both cash and property, (s)he accounts for the cash portion of the distribution first. If the cash portion of the distribution does not exceed the partner's basis in the partnership interest, then no gain is recognized even if the basis of the property received as part of the same distribution exceeds the partner's remaining basis in the partnership interest.

EXAMPLE 20.9

Marion's basis in her twenty percent interest in the Robin Hood Partnership is $35,000. The partnership is planning to distribute $20,000 cash and real estate with a fair market value of $80,000, and a tax basis of $25,000, to Marion in partial liquidation of her interest. After the distribution, Marion will have only a ten percent interest in the partnership. Upon receipt of the distributions from the partnership, Marion will recognize no gain or loss. She will reduce her basis in the partnership interest from $35,000 to $15,000 to record the cash portion of the distribution. Her tax basis in the real estate received will be equal to the lesser of her remaining basis in the partnership interest ($15,000) or the partnership's carryover basis in such property just prior to the distribution ($25,000). In this case, she will take a $15,000 basis in the real estate, and reduce her remaining basis in the partnership interest to zero.

Note that marketable securities are treated as cash in applying the provisions of Code Secs. 731–733. Thus, subject to certain exceptions, a distribution of marketable securities with a *market value* in excess of a partner's basis in his/her partnership interest will trigger recognition of gain in the amount of such excess, just as if cash, rather than marketable securities, had been distributed (Code Sec. 731(c)).

PLANNING POINTER

One implication of these rules is that where a partnership plans to make separate (rather than simultaneous) distributions of cash and property, care should be exercised to make the cash distribution first. Note that no gain is recognized by a partner upon receipt of property with a tax basis in excess of the partner's basis in his/her partnership interest; the partner simply reduces the basis of the property to avoid recognition of gain. However, where cash is received in excess of basis, no such decrease in basis is possible. If the partner's basis in the partnership interest has previously been reduced to reflect the property distribution, the cash distribution may well exceed the remaining basis in the partnership interest, thus triggering gain recognition.

EXAMPLE 20.10

At the beginning of the year, Sue's basis in her partnership interest was $18,000. In April, she received a distribution from the partnership of property valued at $50,000, with a tax basis of $14,000. She recognizes no gain on receipt of the distribution, but takes a $14,000 tax basis in the property and reduces her basis in her partnership interest by a like amount. In September, she receives a cash distribution of $10,000. Because the first distribution reduced Sue's tax basis in her partnership interest to $4,000 ($18,000 beginning basis less $14,000 basis in property received), receipt of a $10,000 cash distribution will trigger recognition of a $6,000 capital gain to Sue. Her remaining basis in her partnership interest will be zero.

TAX BLUNDER

In Example 20.10 above, Sue could have avoided recognition of gain if she had asked the partnership to reverse the order of the two distributions. Had the partnership distributed the $10,000 cash in April, she would have had sufficient basis in her partnership interest to absorb the entire distribution and no gain would have been triggered. A subsequent distribution of the property would also have remained nontaxable, although her tax basis in the property would have been only $8,000 (her tax basis in the partnership interest after accounting for the cash distribution), rather than $14,000 as in the above example.

Note that the adverse consequences in the above example are not prevented by application of the general rule that the cash portion of a distribution is accounted for before the property portion of that same distribution. In the above example, the cash and property were distributed in *separate* transactions. Since they were not part of a single distribution, the cash cannot be accounted for first.

¶20,030 DISTRIBUTION OF MULTIPLE PROPERTIES

The same basic framework discussed above applies when a partner receives a distribution consisting of more than one property. The partner takes a carryover basis in each property received, subject to the restriction that the aggregate basis taken in all properties received cannot exceed the partner's outside basis in the partnership interest. The difficulty arises when basis is restricted under Code Sec. 732(a)(2); the reduction in basis required under that provision must be allocated among all the properties received by the partner.

¶20,031 THE ORDERING RULES—PROPERTIES FROM DIFFERENT CLASSES

The ordering rules under which a reduction in basis is allocated among multiple properties are located in Code Sec. 732(c). These rules require that the partner's outside basis be reduced first by any cash received in the distribution. Remaining basis is then allocated to any ordinary income property received as part of the distribution *to the extent of the basis of such property in the partnership's hands* prior to the distribution. The partner cannot take a tax basis in ordinary income assets that is greater than the partnership's basis in those assets prior to the distribution (i.e., the partner cannot increase the basis of these assets). Any remaining basis is then allocated to capital gain and Code Sec. 1231 assets.

| EXAMPLE 20.11 | Vicki is a fifty percent partner in the Arnold-Sutton Partnership. In September, when her basis in her partnership interest was $30,000, she received a nonliquidating distribution consisting of the following assets: |

	Tax Basis	FMV
Cash	$10,000	$10,000
Inventory	$18,000	$36,000
Capital gain property	$23,000	$42,000
Totals	$51,000	$88,000

Because she did not receive cash in excess of her basis in her partnership interest, Vicki will recognize no gain on the transaction. However, since her outside basis in her partnership interest prior to the distribution was less than the aggregate basis of the properties received from the partnership, she cannot take a carryover basis in each asset received. In this case, she must reduce the aggregate basis of the properties received by $21,000 (from their $51,000 basis in the partnership's hands to her $30,000 basis in the partnership interest). Under Code Sec. 732(c), she accounts for receipt of the cash first, recognizing no gain, but reducing her outside basis in her partnership interest to $20,000. She next accounts for the ordinary income property received, taking a carryover basis of $18,000 in the inventory and further reducing her outside basis in the partnership interest to $2,000 ($20,000 - $18,000). Finally, she accounts for the capital gain property. Again, she recognizes no gain, but her basis in the property is limited to the lesser of the carryover basis of such property (i.e., the partnership's basis in such property) or her remaining basis in her partnership interest. She will take a $2,000 basis in the capital gain property, reducing her basis in her remaining partnership interest to zero. Note the result of the ordering rules of Code Sec. 732(c) in this case: the entire basis reduction is applied to the capital gain property.

¶20,032 ALLOCATING BASIS REDUCTIONS—MULTIPLE ASSETS FROM SAME CLASS

When a partner receives multiple properties of the same character, the process for allocating basis reductions is somewhat more complicated. In this case, the law requires that any reduction in basis be allocated among two or more properties in the same "class" (e.g., two or more capital gain properties) as follows:

1. The reduction is allocated to those properties whose value is less than their basis to the extent of such differences;
2. If the reduction in basis is less than the "**built-in**" loss inherent in the distributed properties, it is allocated between those properties with built-in losses in proportion to their built-in losses; and
3. If the reduction in basis exceeds the built-in loss inherent in the distributed properties, the excess reduction is allocated among all properties received in proportion to their remaining bases.

Thus, to the extent a partner must reduce ("step down") the basis of distributed property, (s)he first decreases the basis of properties that have declined in value, in effect reducing future losses to be realized when those properties are sold.

| EXAMPLE 20.12 | Jeff is a partner in HamBone Partnership. This year, he received a nonliquidating distribution of the following properties from the partnership: |

	Basis	FMV	Difference
Capital Asset 1	15,000	35,000	20,000
Capital Asset 2	28,000	17,000	(11,000)
Totals	43,000	52,000	9,000

Jeff's basis in his partnership interest prior to the distribution was $38,000. He received no cash, so he recognizes no gain on the distribution. Instead, he reduces his basis in the partnership interest by the basis he takes in the distributed properties, thereby deferring gain recognition until he subsequently sells or otherwise disposes of the properties. Under Code Sec. 732(c), his basis in the distributed properties is equal to the lesser of their carryover bases ($43,000) or his basis in his partnership interest ($38,000). In this case, he will take a $38,000 aggregate basis in the two properties, requiring that he reduce their bases by $5,000. The basis reduction is first allocated to those properties which have declined in value. Only Capital Asset 2 has declined in value: its cost basis is $28,000 and its value is only $17,000. Thus, the entire $5,000 basis reduction is allocated to this asset. Jeff will take a carryover basis of $15,000 in Capital Asset 1. His basis in Capital Asset 2 will be limited to his $23,000 remaining basis in the partnership interest.

| EXAMPLE 20.13 | Rick is a partner in TFA partners. This month, he received a nonliquidating distribution from the partnership consisting of the following properties: |

	Basis	FMV	Difference
Capital Asset 1	14,000	4,000	(10,000)
Capital Asset 2	14,000	8,000	(6,000)
Totals	28,000	12,000	(16,000)

Assume that Rick's basis in his partnership interest prior to the distribution was $20,000. Again, he received no cash, and will recognize no gain. However, his basis in the distributed properties is limited to his $20,000 basis in the partnership interest prior to receipt of the distribution. This amount is $8,000 less than the aggregate basis of the two properties to the partnership. Since both properties have declined in value, Rick must allocate the ($8,000) basis reduction to both properties. Property 1 has declined in value by $10,000. Property 2 has declined in value by $6,000. Thus, 5/8ths of the basis reduction (10,000/16,000) is allocated to Property 1 and 3/8ths (6,000/16,000) to Property 2. Rick's basis in Capital Asset 1 will be reduced by $5,000, and will now be $9,000. His basis in Capital Asset 2 will be reduced by $3,000 to $11,000.

If the partner does not receive any properties that have declined in value, or if the necessary basis reduction exceeds the decline in value inherent in distributed properties, the basis reduction is then allocated among the properties received in proportion to their bases to the partnership prior to the distribution (i.e., in proportion to their carryover bases).

EXAMPLE 20.14

Gary is a partner in Wyoming High, a general partnership. He received a nonliquidating distribution of two properties from the partnership:

	Basis	FMV	Difference
Capital Asset 1	12,000	24,000	12,000
Capital Asset 2	24,000	38,000	14,000
Totals	36,000	62,000	26,000

Gary's basis in his partnership interest prior to the distribution was $30,000. He received no cash in the distribution and therefore recognizes no gain. His basis in the properties received in the distribution is equal to the lesser of their carryover bases ($36,000) or his basis in his partnership interest ($30,000). Thus, he must reduce the aggregate basis of the two properties by $6,000. Neither property has declined in value, so the basis reduction must be allocated between the two properties in proportion to their carryover bases. One-third (12,000/36,000) of the reduction must be applied to Capital Asset 1 and 2/3rds (24,000/36,000) to Capital Asset 2. Gary's basis in Capital Asset 1 will be $10,000 (12,000 carryover basis less 1/3 of 6,000 reduction). His basis in Capital Asset 2 will be $20,000 (24,000 carryover basis less 2/3 of 6,000 reduction).

Partnership Liquidating Distributions

¶20,040 OVERVIEW

A slightly different framework applies to liquidating distributions. As with current distributions, the partnership generally does not recognize either gain or loss upon making a distribution to a partner in liquidation of such partner's interest in the partnership. Also as with current distributions, a partner receiving a liquidating distribution recognizes gain only if (s)he receives cash in an amount in excess of his/her basis in the partnership interest (as is the case with current distributions, marketable securities are treated as cash for this purpose). However, it is also possible for a partner to recognize a loss on receipt of a liquidating distribution. This is in marked contrast to the rules applicable to current distributions, under which a partner never recognizes loss as long as (s)he continues to have some continuing interest in the partnership. Moreover, the determination of the partner's basis in distributed property is quite different when that property is received in a liquidating versus a current distribution.

¶20,041 LIQUIDATING DISTRIBUTIONS—RECOGNITION OF GAIN OR LOSS

As discussed above, a partner recognizes gain on receipt of a distribution from a partnership only if he or she receives cash in an amount that exceeds his/her basis in the partnership interest. This gain recognition rule applies whether or not the distribution liquidates the partner's entire interest in the partnership. In contrast, loss can be recognized by a partner upon receipt of a distribution from the partnership only if the following three circumstances are satisfied:

1. The distribution is in complete liquidation of the partner's entire interest in the partnership;
2. The distribution received by the partner consists entirely of cash (including marketable securities), and/or ordinary income assets (inventory, accounts receivable, etc.); and
3. The amount of cash, plus the carryover basis of the ordinary income assets received, is less than the partner's basis in his/her partnership interest.

These requirements reflect the accounting constraints faced by the partner in recording the liquidating distribution. First, the partner's interest in the partnership is being terminated; he or she therefore must write off the entire tax basis of the partnership interest. Second, for practical and policy reasons, the partner cannot take a basis in cash that differs from its face value, and (s)he is prohibited from taking a basis in ordinary income assets greater than the partnership's basis in those assets. That is, although the partner can decrease the basis of ordinary income assets to defer recognition of gain, (s)he cannot increase the basis of these assets. Thus, where a partner receives a liquidating distribution consisting solely of cash and/or ordinary income assets, and his/her basis in the partnership interest exceeds the basis of the assets received (including cash), (s)he must recognize loss in the amount of the excess.

EXAMPLE 20.15

Until March, Joey was a partner in a large downtown law firm. Upon discovering that he was also doing legal work outside the firm, his partners expelled him from the partnership. Joey's basis in his partnership interest prior to being expelled was $125,000. In liquidation of that interest, Joey received $100,000 cash and accounts receivable with a face value of $100,000, and a tax basis of zero. Although he received $200,000 worth of assets, Joey must take a zero basis in the accounts receivable (because that was the partnership's basis and he cannot increase it). Thus, to offset the write-off of his $125,000 basis in the partnership interest, Joey will record the cash at $100,000 and the accounts receivable at zero. He must recognize a ($25,000) capital loss. The determination of the long- or short-term nature of this loss will be based on Joey's holding period for the partnership interest. If he has been a partner for more than 12 months, the loss will be a long-term capital loss. Otherwise, it will be short-term.

Note that there is no prohibition against reducing the basis of ordinary income assets (or any other kind for that matter). If a partner receives a liquidating distribution of property with a basis in excess of his/her basis in the partnership interest, the partner reduces the basis of the property rather than recognizing gain. In this case, the rules are essentially the same for both liquidating and non-liquidating (current) distributions.

EXAMPLE 20.16

Until this year, Kathleen was a partner in a medical partnership. She decided to leave the partnership to start her own practice. In liquidation of her entire interest in the partnership, she received a distribution consisting of the following assets:

	Basis	FMV
Cash	$100,000	$100,000
Accounts Receivable	0	$75,000
Inventory	$50,000	$125,000
	$150,000	$300,000

Assume that Kathleen's tax basis in her partnership interest just prior to receipt of the distribution was $135,000. Since the amount of cash received was less than her basis, she will recognize no gain. Moreover, since her basis in her partnership interest was less than the aggregate basis of the assets received in the distribution, she must reduce the basis of those assets by $15,000 (partnership basis of $150,000 versus her basis of $135,000). Since there is no basis in the accounts receivable, and she cannot reduce the basis of cash, Kathleen will take a $35,000 basis in the inventory (her $135,000 basis in the partnership interest less the $100,000 applied to the cash received and the zero applied to the receivables).

¶20,042   LIQUIDATING DISTRIBUTIONS—BASIS OF PROPERTY RECEIVED

The determination of a partner's basis in distributed property differs when the property is received in a liquidating distribution versus a current distribution. Since the partner in receipt of a liquidating distribution has no continuing interest in the partnership, (s)he must write off the entire investment in the partnership. There can be no remaining basis in the partnership interest after the distribution because there is no longer a partnership interest. Thus, where the partner receives property other than cash or ordinary income assets in the distribution, his/her basis in such property is equal to the remaining basis of the partnership interest (after accounting for the amount of cash and ordinary income property received, if any). In essence, the partner "substitutes" the distributed property(ies) for the investment in the partnership in his/her tax accounting records.

EXAMPLE 20.17	Melanie was a partner in BearPaws Partnership until January of this year. In January, the partnership distributed a tract of real estate to her in complete liquidation of her interest in the partnership. The partnership's tax basis in the real estate was $27,000. Its fair market value was $135,000. Melanie's tax basis in her partnership interest was $40,000. Although the value of the real estate is far larger than her tax basis in the partnership interest, she will recognize no gain or loss on the transaction. Moreover, because the distribution is in complete liquidation of her interest in the partnership, she will take a $40,000 tax basis in the real estate (substituting this asset for the partnership interest in her records), even though the basis of the real estate in the partnership's hands was only $27,000. Note that had Melanie taken a carryover basis in the property from the partnership, she would still have $13,000 basis in the partnership interest. Since she is no longer a partner, this would make no sense. Thus, to write off the entire investment in the partnership, Melanie must either take a higher tax basis in the real estate than the partnership had or recognize a loss. Since the real estate is not ordinary income property, she is not prohibited from increasing its basis, and no loss can therefore be deducted.

¶20,043   LIQUIDATING DISTRIBUTIONS—RECEIPT OF MULTIPLE PROPERTIES

When the liquidating distribution consists of multiple assets, the ordering rules of Code Sec. 732(c) provide that basis is applied first to the cash portion (if any) of the distribution, then to ordinary income assets *to the extent of their basis to the partnership*, and finally to other assets. As with current distributions, any decrease in basis required when the partner records the distributed assets in his/her records is allocated first to capital gain assets. Only if the necessary decrease exceeds the carryover basis of these assets will the basis of ordinary income assets be decreased. To the extent the basis determination rules require an increase in the basis of distributed property, this increase is applied *wholly* to capital gain assets. No increase to the basis of ordinary income assets is allowed.

EXAMPLE 20.18	Elena was a partner in TresVentre Partnership until October, when she decided to strike out on her own. In liquidation of her interest in the partnership, Elena received the following assets:

	Basis	FMV
Cash	100,000	100,000
Inventory	50,000	125,000
Capital Asset 1	75,000	160,000
	$225,000	$385,000

Assume that Elena's basis in her partnership interest prior to the distribution was $190,000. Since she did not receive cash in excess of her basis in the partnership interest, she will recognize no gain on the distribution. She will take an aggregate basis of $190,000 in the properties received. This basis will be applied first to cash in the amount of $100,000 (its face value). Her remaining basis will next be applied to ordinary income assets received (inventory) to the extent of their carryover basis from the partnership ($50,000 in this case). The remaining basis of $40,000 will then be applied to the capital asset received. Thus, the required decrease in basis of $35,000 (the difference between the $225,000 carryover basis of the assets received from the partnership and her $190,000 basis in her partnership interest) is applied entirely to the capital asset.

¶20,044   ALLOCATING A BASIS INCREASE AMONG MULTIPLE PROPERTIES

Finally, when a partner receives multiple assets of the same class and an increase or decrease in basis is required, that increase or decrease must be allocated among the assets of that class under Code Sec. 732(c) as well. The procedure for allocating a basis decrease among assets of the same class is discussed above in connection with current distributions of multiple properties. A similar procedure must be followed to allocate a basis *increase* among multiple properties:

1. The basis increase is first allocated to those properties which have appreciated in value to the extent of the unrealized appreciation inherent in those properties;

2. If the required basis increase is less than the aggregate unrealized appreciation inherent in the distributed assets, the increase is allocated among all appreciated assets in proportion to the unrealized appreciation inherent therein.
3. If the required basis increase exceeds the aggregate unrealized appreciation inherent in the distributed assets, the excess is allocated among assets received in proportion to their adjusted bases (adjusted for increases in steps 1 and 2 above).

These rules are intended to apply any required basis increase first to those assets which have appreciated in value. Only if the required basis increase exceeds the aggregate appreciation inherent in the properties received will the basis of any asset be increased above fair market value. Further, note that under the ordering rules of Code Sec. 732(c)(1), basis increases will be applied only to capital gain assets. The basis of ordinary income assets cannot be increased above the carryover basis those assets had in the partnership's hands.

EXAMPLE 20.19

Erika was a twenty percent partner in EKG Partners until November 15 when she decided to withdraw from the partnership. Prior to her withdrawal, Erika's basis in her partnership interest was $150,000. In complete liquidation of that interest, Erika received a distribution consisting of the following assets:

	Basis	FMV	Difference
Inventory	50,000	125,000	75,000
Capital Asset 1	40,000	80,000	40,000
Capital Asset 2	50,000	110,000	60,000
	$140,000	$315,000	$175,000

Because the amount of cash received in connection with the distribution was less than her basis in the partnership interest, Erika will recognize no gain on the distribution. Her aggregate basis in the assets received will be equal to her $150,000 basis in her partnership interest prior to the distribution. This basis will be applied first to the inventory (ordinary income asset) to the extent of its $50,000 carryover basis from the partnership. The remaining $100,000 will be applied to Capital Assets 1 and 2, requiring a $10,000 basis increase in these assets. This basis increase will be allocated between the two assets in proportion to the unrealized appreciation inherent in each. Capital Asset 1 has appreciated in value by $40,000 and Capital Asset 2 by $60,000. Thus, 40% of the $10,000 basis increase, or $4,000, will be allocated to Capital Asset 1. Sixty percent of the increase, or $6,000, will be applied to Capital Asset 2. Erika's tax basis in each of the assets received in the liquidating distribution will be as follows:

Inventory	$50,000
Capital Asset 1	$44,000
Capital Asset 2	$56,000
Total	$150,000

Effect of Liabilities

¶20,050   ## OVERVIEW

Partnership liabilities affect the tax consequences of partnership distributions in two ways. First, to the extent the partner is relieved of a share of partnership liabilities, this relief is treated as a cash distribution from the partnership to the partner. The amount of the partner's distribution must be increased accordingly. Alternatively, when the property distributed to a partner is encumbered by a mortgage or other liability, the distribution may actually *increase* the partner's share of partnership debt. In such cases, the increase is treated as a cash contribution from the partner to the partnership. Note that such a contribution directly affects the partner's basis in his/her partnership interest, rather than the basis of the property received in the distribution. Any effect on the basis of the distributed property will be indirect.

¶20,051   REDUCTIONS IN THE DISTRIBUTEE-PARTNER'S SHARE OF PARTNERSHIP DEBT

Many distributions, other than of the partners' shares of partnership profits, will change the partners' continuing interests in the partnership. For example, if one partner withdraws a portion of his/her invested capital, his/her remaining investment in the partnership is reduced relative to that of the other partners. In effect, the distributee-partner has reduced his/her investment in future partnership operations, and will generally be entitled to a smaller share of future profits and losses from the partnership.

EXAMPLE 20.20

Last year, Wilson, Tim and Jill each invested $100,000 in a new partnership. Each partner received a one-third interest in partnership profits, losses and capital. In the partnership's first year of operations, it generated a 12 percent return on equity, reporting net income of $36,000 ($300,000 capital invested by the partners times 12 percent). At the beginning of the second year, Wilson decided to withdraw half of his net capital investment, or $56,000 (his net capital investment prior to the withdrawal was $112,000, consisting of his $100,000 initial contribution, plus his one-third share of the partnership's $36,000 Year 1 income). If the partnership continues to earn a 12 percent return on equity, its Year 2 income will be $33,600 (remaining capital of $280,000 times 12 percent). Recall that at the beginning of Year 2, Wilson reduced his capital investment in the partnership by half, to $56,000. In contrast, Tim and Jill left their entire $112,000 investment in the partnership. Thus, Wilson is now only a twenty percent partner ($56,000 divided by total capital of $280,000). Accordingly, his share of the partnership's Year 2 income should be only one-fifth, or $6,720, rather than one third. Note that this share gives Wilson a 12 percent return on his reduced capital investment in the partnership ($56,000 times .12 equals $6,720).

Reflecting the distributee-partner's reduced share of future partnership profits and losses, his/her share of partnership liabilities should be similarly reduced. Under Code Sec. 752(b), a reduction in the partner's share of partnership liabilities is treated as a cash distribution, and must be accounted for in addition to the rest of the distribution. In some cases, the liability relief will trigger recognition of gain by the partner. In most cases, however, it will simply result in a smaller basis in either the distributed property or in the partner's remaining interest in the partnership.

EXAMPLE 20.21

Prior to January, Jody was a one-third partner in the JFK Partnership. Her basis in her partnership interest was $45,000, consisting of her $15,000 contribution to partnership capital and her $30,000 (one-third) share of partnership liabilities. In January, the partnership distributed $30,000 cash to Jody in complete liquidation of her interest in the partnership. Because Jody must account for both the $30,000 direct cash distribution, and the $30,000 decrease in her share of partnership liabilities, her total distribution is effectively $60,000. Moreover, the entire amount is treated as a cash distribution. As this amount exceeds her basis in the partnership interest by $15,000, she must recognize a $15,000 gain on receipt of the distribution.

EXAMPLE 20.22

Assume the same facts as in Example 20.21, except that, rather than cash, Jody received real property with a fair market value of $30,000 in complete liquidation of her interest in the partnership. The partnership's tax basis in the real property was $25,000. As in Example 20.21, Jody must account for both the direct distribution of the real estate and the relief of her $30,000 share of partnership liabilities. The latter distribution is treated as a cash distribution. However, since it does not exceed her $45,000 basis in her partnership interest, she will recognize no gain. The deemed cash distribution is accounted for first, reducing Jody's basis in her partnership interest to $15,000. This basis is applied to the real estate received from the partnership, reducing her basis in the partnership interest to zero. She will take a $15,000 basis in the real property.

EXAMPLE 20.23

Jorge was a one-third partner in Borderline Partners until January, when he received a distribution of real property reducing his interest in the partnership from one-third to one-fifth. His tax basis in the partnership interest, prior to receipt of the distribution, was $60,000, consisting of his $40,000 investment in partnership capital and his $20,000 (one-third) share of the partnership's $60,000 outstanding debt. In a partial liquidation of his interest analogous to a stock redemption, Jorge received real property from the partnership with a tax basis of $20,000 and a fair market value of $50,000. Again, Jorge must account for the reduction in his share of partnership debt first, treating it as a cash distribution. As a one-third partner, his share of partnership debt was $20,000. As a one-fifth partner, his share of partnership debt will be $12,000 (1/5th of $60,000). Thus, the deemed $8,000 distribution reduces his basis in his partnership interest to $32,000. Since he remains a partner after the distribution, he takes a carryover, rather than a substitute, basis in the distributed property equal to the partnership's basis of $20,000. Thus, after the distribution, Jorge's basis in the distributed property is equal to its $20,000 carryover basis from the partnership, and his remaining basis in his partnership interest is $12,000 ($40,000 initial basis, less $8,000 relief of partnership debt, less $20,000 basis in distributed property).

TAX BLUNDER

Partners sometimes overlook the effect of seemingly routine partnership transactions on the partnership's debt sharing ratios. For example, admission of a new partner to the partnership will generally reduce the existing partners' shares of partnership liabilities. Allocation of a portion of partnership debt to the newly admitted partner will be treated as a cash distribution to the remaining partners. If one of those partners has a zero basis in his or her partnership interest, this deemed cash distribution will trigger the recognition of unexpected gain to that partner. It is very important that all partners recognize how partnership transactions that affect their shares of partnership liabilities will affect them for tax purposes so they are not surprised at year end when they sit down to prepare their own tax returns.

¶20,052   ## DISTRIBUTIONS OF PROPERTY ENCUMBERED BY LIABILITIES

Different consequences result when the partner receives property subject to liabilities in a partnership distribution. Under Code Sec. 752(a), the transfer of a partnership debt to a partner is treated as a cash contribution by the partner to the partnership, as is an increase in the partner's share of partnership liabilities. Thus, in many cases, the distribution of debt-encumbered property to a partner actually increases his/her basis in the partnership interest (but not necessarily in the distributed property). Care must be taken not to overlook the debt transfer when accounting for the transaction.

EXAMPLE 20.24

Larry was a twenty-five percent partner in Tunnell Enterprises until March, when his interest in the partnership was liquidated. Prior to the liquidation, his basis in the partnership interest was $50,000, consisting of his $12,000 share of partnership capital and his $38,000 share of partnership liabilities. In liquidation of this interest, Larry received property with a fair market value of $150,000, and a tax basis of $42,000. The property was encumbered by a $60,000 mortgage, for which Larry assumed personal responsibility. Accounting for this distribution requires three steps. First, Larry must account for the deemed cash contribution associated with assumption of the partnership's $60,000 liability. This deemed contribution increases his basis in the partnership interest to $110,000 (initial basis of $50,000 plus $60,000 deemed contribution). Next, he is relieved of his $38,000 share of partnership liabilities, and must treat such relief as a cash distribution from the partnership. He has sufficient basis in the interest to absorb this deemed distribution, so he recognizes no gain. However, his basis in the partnership interest is reduced to $72,000. Finally, he accounts for the property distribution. Since this is a liquidating distribution, he takes a $72,000 basis in the property, reducing his basis in the partnership interest to zero. These results can be summarized as follows:

Initial basis in partnership interest	$50,000
add: Assumption of mortgage encumbering property received in distribution	60,000
less: Reduction in share of partnership debt (from $38,000 to zero)	(38,000)
subtotal, becomes basis of property received in liquidating distribution	$72,000

Disproportionate Distributions —Distribution of "Hot" Assets

¶20,060 **OVERVIEW**

Although partnership property distributions are generally tax-free as described above, Code Sec. 751(b) carves out a significant exception for certain distributions which alter the partners' relative interests in partnership ordinary income property. Code Sec. 751(b) is necessary to prevent partners from manipulating the distribution rules to allow one or more partners to shift their shares of partnership ordinary income onto another partner(s). For example, a partner receiving a liquidating distribution consisting solely of cash and capital assets would not be a member of the partnership when it subsequently sells its inventory or other ordinary income assets. As a result, (s)he would not be allocated a share of the income resulting from the subsequent sale.

EXAMPLE 20.25

Craig is a one-third partner in the Brookline Partnership. At December 31, the partnership had the following assets:

	Tax Basis	FMV
Cash	$15,000	$15,000
Accounts Receivable	0	45,000
Land	21,000	30,000
Total	$36,000	$90,000

If the partnership were to sell all its assets for the above values, it would recognize $45,000 ordinary income and $9,000 capital gain. Craig would report his $15,000 share of the ordinary income and $3,000 share of the capital gain on his individual tax return ($18,000 total income). However, assume Craig decided to leave the partnership before any of the assets were sold. Assume further that the partnership distributed the land to Craig in complete liquidation of his partnership interest. If Craig's basis in the partnership interest was $12,000, he would recognize no gain on the distribution and would take a $12,000 basis in the land. When he subsequently sold the land, he would recognize an $18,000 capital gain. Although the amount of his total gain is the same as if he remained a member of the partnership, the character of this gain is very different. Whereas the majority of the income he would have recognized had he remained in the partnership was ordinary income (taxable at a maximum rate of 39.6 percent), all of the gain will now be taxed as capital gain (taxable at a maximum rate of 20 percent). Code Sec. 751(b) exists to prevent this kind of manipulation.

¶20,061 **TRIGGERING CODE SEC. 751(b)**

Code Sec. 751(b) is triggered when a distribution reduces any partner's share of net section 751(b) income or increases any partner's share of net section 751(b) loss. A partner's share of net section 751(b) income or loss is equal to the amount of net gain or loss that would have been allocated to the partner if the partnership sold all its assets for cash immediately before the distribution occurred. Prop. Reg. §1.751-1. The partners compare this amount to the amount of section 751(b) gain or loss that each would recognize if all the partnership's assets, including those now in the hands of the distributee-partner, were sold immediately after the distribution. If the two amounts are different, Code Sec. 751(b) will be triggered.

EXAMPLE 20.26

Arliss is a one-third partner in the ABC partnership. The partnership's book and tax balance sheets are as follows:

	Tax Basis	FMV
Cash	$30,000	$30,000
Accounts Receivable	0	60,000
Total Assets	$30,000	$90,000
Capital, Arliss	$10,000	$30,000
Capital, Betty	10,000	30,000
Capital, Carl	10,000	30,000
Total Capital	$30,000	$90,000

Assume the partnership distributes $30,000 worth of the accounts receivable to Arliss in complete liquidation of his interest in the partnership. To determine whether Code Sec. 751(b) will be triggered, the partnership must compare the partners' shares of Code Sec. 751 gain (ordinary income) before and after the distribution. Here, the only ordinary income asset is the accounts receivable. A comparison of each partner's share of gain from collection or disposition of the accounts receivable before and after the distribution is as follows:

	Pre-Distribution	Post-Distribution	Change
Partners' shares of ordinary income:			
Arliss	$20,000	$30,000	$10,000
Betty	$20,000	$15,000	($5,000)
Carl	$20,000	$15,000	($5,000)

The distribution of $30,000 of accounts receivable (basis = 0) to Arliss, shifts $10,000 of ordinary income from the eventual disposition or collection of those receivables to Arliss. The remaining partners each have a 50% interest in the receivables remaining with the partnership because Arliss is no longer a partner. Their shares each fall from one-third of $60,000 to one-half of $30,000. Thus, the distribution would shift ordinary income from Betty and Carl to Arliss. Section 751(b) therefore applies to the distribution.

Assets that generate Sec. 751(b) gain or loss, frequently referred to as "hot" assets, consist of "**unrealized receivables**" and "**substantially appreciated inventory.**" Code Sec. 751(c) and (d). Unrealized receivables consist principally of cash basis accounts receivable and depreciation recapture. Substantially appreciated inventory is defined as inventory with a fair market value which exceeds its cost basis by more than 20 percent.

EXAMPLE 20.27

Flashman Partners has the following assets:

	Basis	FMV
Cash	$10,000	$10,000
Inventory	100,000	144,000
Nondepreciable Realty	45,000	80,000
Total Assets	155,000	234,000

The partnership's inventory is substantially appreciated, with a fair market value 44% above its tax basis, well above the 20% appreciation threshold. The nondepreciable realty has also appreciated substantially in value. However, it is not inventory. Moreover, because the realty is nondepreciable, it is not subject to depreciation recapture. Thus, it is neither inventory nor an unrealized receivable. Accordingly, the realty is not a partnership hot asset.

¶20,062   THE MECHANICS OF CODE SEC. 751(b)

To the extent a distribution reduces a partner's interest in partnership ordinary income assets, the transaction is *partially* recharacterized as a sale. The partner is deemed to have received a distribution of his/her share of the partnership's ordinary income assets, and then traded them back to the partnership, *in a fully taxable transaction*, for the assets actually received. Thus, the partner recognizes ordinary income in an amount equal to the difference between the basis and fair market value of the asset(s) deemed to be involved in the transaction.

Alternatively, where a distribution increases the partner's share of ordinary income assets, it is the *partnership*, rather than the partner, that recognizes ordinary income on the transaction. As above, the partnership is deemed to have traded a portion of its ordinary income assets to the partner in exchange for a portion of the partner's share of capital gain assets. Code Sec. 751(b) is triggered either way.

EXAMPLE 20.28

Last month, Lloyd, a twenty-five percent partner in Carlton Enterprises, received a $50,000 cash distribution in complete liquidation of his interest in the partnership. Just prior to the distribution, the partnership had the following assets:

	Basis	FMV
Cash	$50,000	$50,000
Accounts Receivable	0	100,000
Nondepreciable Realty	40,000	50,000
Totals	90,000	200,000

The partnership had no liabilities. Assume that Lloyd's basis in his partnership interest prior to receipt of the liquidating distribution was $22,500. Lloyd's interests in the partnership's ordinary and capital assets just before and just after the distribution were as follows (remember, these are calculated by reference to the value, rather than the basis, of the partnership's assets):

	Pre-Distribution	Post-Distribution	Change
Ordinary Income Assets:			
Accounts Receivable	$25,000	$0	($25,000)
Other Assets:			
Cash	$12,500	$50,000	$37,500
Realty	$12,500	$0	($12,500)
			$25,000

Thus, under Code Sec. 751(b), Lloyd is treated as having exchanged his one-fourth share of the unrealized accounts receivable for $25,000 cash. In effect, he is treated as having first received a distribution of his $25,000 share of the partnership's accounts receivable, which he then sold back to the partnership in exchange for $25,000 cash. Lloyd's basis in the accounts receivable was zero (in effect, his share of the partnership's basis in these assets). Therefore, he must recognize $25,000 ordinary income on the transaction.

The remainder of the cash received is treated as a "regular" liquidating distribution. That is, he treats the remaining $25,000 cash portion of the distribution under the general rules applicable to liquidating distributions. (The reduction in his economic interest in the partnership's real estate is ignored, since it is in the same category of assets as the cash, and thus is not subject to Code Sec. 751(b).)His basis in his partnership interest was $22,500. Thus, this portion of the distribution triggers recognition of an additional $2,500 *capital* gain. In total, he recognizes $27,500 income on the transaction, just as he would have in the absence of Code Sec. 751(b). However, because Code Sec. 751(b) applies, a large portion of this gain is taxable as ordinary income, rather than as capital gain.

The net effect of Code Sec. 751(b) in situations like the one above is to recharacterize a portion of the distributee-partner's gain as ordinary income rather than capital gain. In other cases, the effect of Code Sec. 751(b) can be more severe. In particular, because the statute recasts a transaction as part distribution, part taxable exchange, it can convert an otherwise nontaxable distribution into a (partially) taxable one.

EXAMPLE 20.29

Assume in the example above that Lloyd had received the nondepreciable realty, rather than the cash, in liquidation of his interest in the partnership (each is worth $50,000). Now, under the regular rules applicable to liquidating distributions, Lloyd would recognize no gain, since he did not receive cash in excess of his basis in his partnership interest. However, under Code Sec. 751(b), a portion of the transaction is recast as a taxable exchange, rather than as a partnership distribution. Lloyd's pre- and post-distribution interests in the partnership's assets are as follows:

	Pre-Distribution	Post-Distribution	Change
Ordinary Income Assets:			
Accounts Receivable	$25,000	$0	($25,000)
Other Assets:			
Cash	$12,500	$0	($12,500)
Realty	$12,500	$50,000	$37,500
			$25,000

Again, under Code Sec. 751(b), Lloyd is treated as having first received a distribution of $25,000 worth of the partnership's accounts receivable. He is then deemed to have transferred these receivables back to the partnership in exchange for $25,000 worth of the realty. As before, his basis in the accounts receivable is zero (his twenty-five percent share of the partnership's zero basis in the receivables). Thus, he again recognizes $25,000 ordinary income. However, in this case, he has no additional income under the general rules applicable to liquidating distributions: since he received no cash, he recognizes no gain on this portion of the transaction and takes a "substitute" basis ($22,500) in the portion of the realty received in this part of the transaction. Lloyd's total basis in the realty will be $47,500 ($25,000 "cost" basis in the portion of the realty received in the deemed exchange for his interest in the receivables, plus $22,500 "substitute" basis in the portion of the distribution not governed by Code Sec. 751(b)).

PRACTICE POINTER

New proposed regulations published in November 2014 allow a partnership to use a simplified approach to calculate the income or loss triggered when Code Sec. 751(b) applies to a distribution. Under the simplified approach, partners whose shares of the partnership's Code Sec. 751 income are reduced as a result of the distribution would recognize ordinary income (or loss) in the amount of the reduction. This income or loss would increase both the partners' tax basis in their partnership interest(s) and the partnership's tax basis in the hot assets remaining on its balance sheet. All of this is deemed to occur immediately prior to the distribution and would prevent the distribution from shifting income between partners. As discussed in Chapter 2 of this text, these proposed rules will not go into effect until the proposed regulations are finalized. Until then, the approach illustrated in Examples 20.28 and 20.29 is the only approach countenanced by the regulations.

Sale of a Partner's Interest in the Partnership

¶20,070

OVERVIEW–SALE v. DISTRIBUTION

Partnerships often wish to restrict the partners' abilities to sell their partnership interests to outside parties. For example, in a professional services partnership, such as an accounting firm, a partner wanting to dispose of his/her interest in the partnership often has no alternative but to "sell" that interest back to the partnership, in exchange for a liquidating distribution. In other cases, however, partners are free to sell their interests to buyers outside the partnership. The buyer may be another existing partner, or someone completely unrelated to the partnership. In any event, the transaction is the economic equivalent of a cash distribution from the partnership, and the tax consequences are generally the same.

¶20,071 GENERAL CONSEQUENCES

When a partner sells his/her partnership interest, the consequences are generally straightforward. The partner recognizes gain in an amount equal to the difference between the amount realized on the sale and his/her basis in the partnership interest. The amount realized is equal to the amount of cash and/or the fair market value of any non-cash property received, plus the selling partner's share of partnership indebtedness (if any) which is being assumed by the buyer.

EXAMPLE 20.30

Jeri's basis in her one-third interest in Sunshine Partners is $18,000, consisting of her $10,000 share of partnership capital, plus her $8,000 share of partnership liabilities. She has recently been approached by another partner with an offer to purchase her interest for $25,000 cash. The buyer would also assume Jeri's responsibility for partnership liabilities. If Jeri decides to sell, her amount realized will be equal to $33,000: the $25,000 cash price, plus her $8,000 share of partnership debts which will be assumed by the buyer. Her tax basis in the partnership interest is $18,000, as noted above. Thus, Jeri would recognize a taxable gain of $15,000 should she decide to sell.

Note that the consequences to Jeri in the above example are exactly the same as if she had received a $25,000 cash distribution from the partnership in liquidation of her interest. To the extent that the amount of cash received, plus relief of her share of partnership debt, exceeds her tax basis in the partnership interest, she must recognize taxable gain. The only differences between a partnership liquidating distribution and sale of the interest to an outside buyer arise when either the partner exchanges the partnership interest for property other than cash, or when (s)he sells only part, rather than all, of the partnership interest.

¶20,072 EXCHANGE OF PARTNERSHIP INTERESTS OUTSIDE THE PARTNERSHIP FOR PROPERTY

Recall that when the partnership distributes property other than cash to a partner, the partner only recognizes taxable gain if Code Sec. 751(b) applies. For distributions not involving hot assets, the general distribution rules trigger recognition of gain to the partner only when cash is received in excess of basis. Where a partner exchanges his/her partnership interest with an outside buyer for property other than cash, however, gain or loss will be recognized. Because this transaction is not a distribution, the distribution rules do not apply and the exchange will be fully taxable. Note that gain recognition cannot be avoided under Code Sec. 1031; a partnership interest cannot be exchanged in a like-kind exchange.

EXAMPLE 20.31

Earl, a one-third partner in a real estate partnership, exchanged his interest in the partnership with Sheila, an unrelated "buyer," for a one-half interest in an apartment complex. Earl's tax basis in his partnership interest was $54,000, consisting of his $20,000 net contribution to partnership capital, plus his $34,000 share of partnership debt. The net value of the fifty percent interest in the apartment complex received by Earl was $82,000. He received no cash from Sheila in the exchange. Nonetheless, Earl must recognize a taxable gain of $62,000, computed as follows:

Value of interest in apartment complex	$82,000
Relief from one-third of partnership debt	34,000
Total amount realized	116,000
Tax basis in partnership interest	(54,000)
Taxable gain on exchange	$62,000

Note that had Earl received an interest in real property from the partnership as a distribution, he would have recognized no taxable gain, instead deferring the realized gain by taking a *substitute basis* in the property received.

¶20,073 PARTIAL SALE OF PARTNERSHIP INTEREST

A second case in which the tax consequences associated with sale of the partnership interest outside the partnership differ from those associated with a partnership distribution is when the partner sells only part of his/her interest, rather than all of it. In such cases, the partner will recognize taxable gain to the extent the selling price exceeds his/her tax basis *in the portion of the partnership interest which is sold.* Note the contrast with the distribution framework, in which a partial (as opposed to complete) liquidating distribution is treated as a current distribution, and triggers gain only to the extent that the partner receives cash in an amount exceeding his/her basis in the entire partnership interest.

EXAMPLE 20.32

Becky is a one-third partner in Conner Partners. Her tax basis in her partnership interest is $22,000, including her $14,000 share of partnership debt. She is considering the sale of *half* of her interest in the partnership to her brother, BJ, for $28,000 cash (plus assumption of half her share of partnership debt). If she sells half her interest for this price, her recognized taxable gain will be $24,000, computed as follows:

Cash	$28,000
Relief of debt	7,000
Total amount realized	$35,000
Tax basis in one-half interest sold	(11,000)
Recognized taxable gain	$24,000

Becky's remaining tax basis in her partnership interest will be $11,000.

Compare the above results to those which would occur if the partnership, rather than BJ, had distributed $28,000 to Becky in redemption (or partial liquidation) of half her interest in the partnership.

EXAMPLE 20.33

Assume the same facts as in Example 20.32, except that the partnership distributes $28,000 cash to Becky in liquidation of half her interest therein. Accounting for her reduced share of partnership debt, the total distribution to Becky will be $35,000, same as above. However, because this is a current distribution, this distribution to Becky will trigger taxable gain only to the extent it exceeds her $22,000 basis in her partnership interest. Thus, Becky will recognize only $13,000 taxable gain in this case (and her remaining basis in her partnership interest will be reduced to zero).

¶20,074   SALE OF AN INTEREST IN A PARTNERSHIP WITH HOT ASSETS

Under Code Sec. 741, a partner's recognized gain on the sale of all or part of his/her interest in a partnership is generally treated as a capital gain. Where the partnership has ordinary income assets, however, some or all of this gain will be treated as ordinary income under Code Sec. 751(a). The consequences are very similar to those associated with a distribution which alters a partner's interest in partnership hot assets. Note that, while inventory must be appreciated by at least 20 percent to trigger the provisions of Code Sec. 751(b) (substantially disproportionate distributions), there is no minimum appreciation threshold for triggering the provisions of Code Sec. 751(a). Sale of an interest in a partnership will generate ordinary income to the selling partner if the partnership owns appreciated inventory, even if it has appreciated by only one percent. The partner must recognize ordinary income to the extent of his or her share of ordinary income inherent in partnership ordinary income property. The remainder, if any, of the partner's gain on the sale is characterized as capital gain.

EXAMPLE 20.34	Kim is a twenty percent partner in Boucher Realty. Boucher has the following assets:

	Basis	FMV
Cash	15,000	15,000
Accounts (Rents) Receivable	0	30,000
Real Estate	80,000	120,000
Totals	95,000	165,000

The partnership has no debt. Kim's basis in her partnership interest is $19,000. She is considering selling her partnership interest to an unrelated buyer for $33,000 cash. Assume that the partnership's real estate is not subject to depreciation recapture, so that the partnership's only "hot" assets are the receivables. Kim's share of the income inherent in these receivables is $6,000 (twenty percent of $30,000).

If Kim sells her partnership interest for $33,000, her total gain will be $14,000 ($33,000 - $19,000 basis in the partnership interest). Under Code Sec. 751(a), $6,000 of this gain will be characterized as ordinary income. The remainder of her gain, $8,000, will be characterized as capital gain.

Note that in some cases, the partner's ordinary income on the deemed sale of ordinary income assets may exceed the total gain recognized. In such cases, the partner must recognize a capital loss to the extent of the excess.

EXAMPLE 20.35	Assume in Example 20.34 above that the FMV of the real estate is only $60,000, rather than $120,000. The FMV of the partnership's total assets would now be $105,000, rather than $165,000. Further assume that Kim sells her interest for $21,000 (20% of $105,000), rather than $33,000. Her total gain on the sale would be only $2,000. However, she would still be required to recognize $6,000 ordinary income under Sec. 751(a). Since this exceeds her total gain of $2,000, she would also recognize a $4,000 capital loss. Note that this capital loss is equal in amount to her share of the decline in value of the partnership's real estate (20% of the $20,000 excess of the basis of the real estate over its fair market value).

Partnership Basis Adjustments

¶20,080   OVERVIEW—BASIS ADJUSTMENTS IN GENERAL

The partnership tax framework generally assumes an equality of "inside" and "outside" basis. That is, the partnership's aggregate (inside) tax basis in its assets is generally equal to the sum of the partners' (outside) bases in their partnership interests. This equality provides an important safeguard against abusive tax manipulation schemes because the partners generally recognize the same amount and character of taxable income from selling their partnership interests as they would recognize if the partnership sold all its assets.

EXAMPLE 20.36

Nancy is a one-third partner in BrookHaven Partners. Her basis in her partnership interest is $25,000. The partnership has the following assets (and no liabilities):

	Basis	FMV
Cash	15,000	15,000
Accounts Receivable	0	45,000
Capital Assets	60,000	90,000
Totals	75,000	150,000

Since there are no debts, the value of Nancy's partnership interest is equal to her one-third share of the value of the partnership's assets, or $50,000. If she sells her partnership interest for $50,000, she will recognize a $25,000 taxable gain, of which $15,000 will be ordinary under Code Sec. 751(a) and $10,000 will be capital gain. Likewise, because Nancy's basis in her one-third partnership interest is equal to one-third of the partnership's aggregate basis in its assets, a sale by the partnership of its assets would generate a $75,000 gain, of which one-third would be allocated to Nancy. Again, $15,000 of this gain would be ordinary (one-third of the $45,000 gain on the accounts receivable) and $10,000 would be capital gain (one-third of the $30,000 gain on the capital assets).

Two types of transactions can create imbalances between the partnership's **inside basis** in its assets, and the partners' **outside bases** in their partnership interests. Perhaps the most common is the sale of a partnership interest. In the above example, if Nancy decides to sell her partnership interest for $50,000, the buyer will take a $50,000 cost basis in that interest after acquisition. Yet, the buyer's share of the partnership's inside basis in its assets remains $25,000, resulting in an inequality between inside and outside basis.

Imbalances between outside and inside basis can also be created following a distribution to a partner. Upon receipt of a liquidating distribution, the partner takes a substitute basis in the distributed property equal to his/her basis in the partnership interest, regardless of the partnership's basis in the property prior to the distribution. Similarly, in certain current distributions, the partner's basis in the distributed property is limited to his/her basis in the partnership interest even though the partnership's basis in that property was greater. Finally, when the partnership distributes cash to a partner in excess of his/her basis in the partnership interest, the partner cannot decrease his/her outside basis below zero. Accordingly, the partnership's inside basis in its assets, which will decline by the entire amount of the cash distributed, will fall below the partners' aggregate outside basis in their partnership interests.

Where outside and inside basis are not equal, the partnership can elect to adjust its inside basis in its assets to bring them into balance with the partners' outside basis. The election is claimed under Code Sec. 754 of the Internal Revenue Code, and the adjustments are made under Code Secs. 743(b) (for adjustments arising from the sale or transfer of a partner's interest) and 734(b) (for adjustments arising from partnership distributions). These adjustments are described more fully below.

¶20,081 CODE SEC. 743(b) ADJUSTMENTS–SALE OR TRANSFER OF A PARTNERSHIP INTEREST

When a partner purchases or inherits an interest in a partnership, (s)he takes a tax basis in that interest equal to its value at the date of the acquisition. However, since the acquisition transaction is between the buying and selling partners, and the partnership is not directly involved, the partnership's basis in its assets is not ordinarily affected. Therefore, the acquiring partner's basis in his/her partnership interest will generally not be equal to his/her share of the partnership's basis in its assets.

Under Code Sec. 743(b), if the partnership makes an election under Code Sec. 754, it adjusts its basis in its assets to reflect the difference between the "new" partner's basis in the newly acquired partnership interest and such partner's share of the partnership's inside basis in its assets. Typically, this means that the partnership must adjust its inside basis by the amount of gain or loss recognized by the selling partner or by the amount of the step-up in basis of the partnership interest under the estate tax provisions. (Under Sec. 1014, taxpayers take a tax basis in inherited property equal to such property's fair market value at the decedent's date of death.)

EXAMPLE 20.37

Susan sold her one-third interest in the Arnold Partnership to Carmen for $42,000. At the date of the sale, the partnership had the following assets (and no debt):

	Basis	FMV
Cash	15,000	15,000
Investment Securities	9,000	45,000
Real Estate	45,000	66,000
Totals	69,000	126,000

Susan's basis in her partnership interest prior to the sale was $23,000. She will recognize a $19,000 gain on the sale, and Carmen will take a $42,000 tax basis in the newly acquired interest. As a one-third partner, Carmen's share of the partnership's inside basis in its assets is $23,000. Thus, if the partnership makes a Code Sec. 754 election (or if one is already in effect), it must increase its inside basis in its assets by $19,000, the difference between Carmen's outside basis in her partnership interest ($42,000) and her share of the partnership's inside basis in its assets ($23,000). Note that this is equal to the gain Susan recognized on the sale.

Absent an election under Code Sec. 754, the new partner would be allocated future gain on the partnership's sale of its assets that the selling partner already recognized. Consider the example above. Susan's $19,000 gain on the sale of her partnership interest is attributable to her one-third share of the $57,000 inherent gain built into the partnership's assets. Thus, the basis adjustment under Code Sec. 743(b) is designed to prohibit the recognition of the same gain by both the seller and buyer.

TAX BLUNDER

A partner purchasing an interest in an existing partnership should be very careful to review the partnership agreement before closing the transaction. If a partner acquires an interest in a partnership that has a substantial amount of uncollected accounts receivable, substantially appreciated inventory, or other appreciated assets that are likely to be sold or collected within a short period of time, (s)he should attempt to convince the partnership to make the election under Code Sec. 754. Because these assets are likely to be sold (inventory) or collected (receivables) within the coming year, the new partner will be allocated a share of partnership ordinary income in the first year of his or her investment that was economically attributable to the departing partner from whom the interest was acquired. The election under Code Sec. 754 can be made after the new partner's acquisition of the partnership interest, so long as it is made before or concurrently with the filing of the partnership's tax return for the year of the acquisition. Failure to make the election will cause the new partner to recognize ordinary income for which (s)he receives no economic benefit. Although the income will increase his or her tax basis in the partnership interest, no tax benefit will result from the increase until the partner sells or otherwise disposes of the partnership interest in a subsequent year.

Because the Code Sec. 743(b) adjustment is intended to protect the incoming partner from recognizing income that (s)he has not economically realized, the basis adjustment is made for his/her benefit only. It is allocated among the partnership's assets in accordance with the requirements of Code Sec. 755, which essentially requires that the adjustment be made in proportion to the differences between the basis and fair market values of the partnership's assets.

EXAMPLE 20.38

Assume the same facts as in Example 20.37 above. Carmen purchased Susan's interest in the Arnold partnership for $42,000, and is entitled to a $19,000 basis adjustment under Code Sec. 743(b). This adjustment will be allocated among the partnership's assets as follows:

	Basis	FMV	Difference	Percent	Adjustment
Cash	15,000	15,000	-0-	-0-	-0-
Securities	9,000	45,000	36,000	63.16%	12,000
Real Estate	45,000	66,000	21,000	36.84%	7,000

The adjustment to the basis of the investment securities is equal to 63.16% ($36,000/($36,000 + $21,000)) of the $19,000 adjustment. The adjustment to the basis of the real estate is 36.84% ($21,000/($36,000 + $21,000)) of the total $19,000 adjustment. Note that Carmen's share of the basis of the investment securities is now $15,000 (her one-third share of the partnership's $9,000 basis plus the $12,000 basis adjustment). If the partnership sells these assets for their $45,000 fair market value, Carmen will recognize no gain (her share of the proceeds is $15,000 as is her share of the basis of these assets).

¶20,082   TRANSFEREE PARTNER'S ELECTIVE SPECIAL BASIS ADJUSTMENT

As discussed above, basis adjustments are generally allowed only if the partnership chooses to make (or has previously made) an election under Code Sec. 754. In the special case, however, in which a person purchases an interest in a partnership from an existing partner and within two years of acquisition receives a distribution of appreciated property from the partnership, Code Sec. 732(d) treats the partner as if a Sec. 754 election had been in effect at the date of purchase, whether or not such an election was actually made by the partnership. As a result, the partner determines his or her basis in the distributed property as if a Code Sec. 754 election had been in effect at the time (s)he acquired the interest in the partnership. The size of the adjustment is not diminished by any depletion or depreciation which would have been available on the stepped up basis of the property because no such depletion or depreciation was actually claimed (since no basis adjustment was made prior to receipt of the distribution). Reg. §1.732-1(d)(1)(iv).

EXAMPLE 20.39

Kate Teichman purchased a one-fourth interest in a partnership one year ago for $17,000. The partnership did not have a Code Sec. 754 election in effect and chose not to make one. At the date of her acquisition of the interest in the partnership, the partnership owned inventory with a tax basis of $14,000 and a fair market value of $16,000. Had the partnership had a Code Sec. 754 election in effect, it would have been entitled to adjust the basis of the inventory by $500 reflecting Kate's 25% share of the appreciation inherent in the inventory. This year, the partnership distributed the inventory equally to its four partners. The other partners will each take a tax basis in the inventory distributed to them of $3,500 (one-fourth of the partnership's tax basis in such inventory), assuming they have tax bases in their partnership interests of $3,500 or more. Kate's basis in the inventory distributed to her, however, will be $4,000, reflecting the $500 basis adjustment which would have been made to the inventory had the partnership had the necessary election in effect (or had chosen to make it).

¶20,083   CODE SEC. 734(b)–ADJUSTMENTS TRIGGERED BY PARTNERSHIP DISTRIBUTIONS

Differences between inside and outside basis can also be created by partnership distributions. For example, in a liquidating distribution, the partner's basis in distributed property is equal to his/her basis in the partnership interest, regardless of the original basis of such property to the partnership. In other cases, a partner will take a basis in property received in a current distribution which differs from the partnership's basis in such property. Any time a partner takes a different basis in distributed property than the partnership had, a discrepancy will develop between inside and outside basis. Code Sec. 734(b) allows the partnership to adjust the basis of its remaining assets to correct this discrepancy.

EXAMPLE 20.40

The ABC Partnership has the following assets (and no debt):

	Basis	FMV
Cash	10,000	10,000
Property 1	50,000	70,000
Property 2	150,000	270,000
	210,000	350,000

Celia, a twenty percent partner, has a $42,000 tax basis in her partnership interest. The partnership distributes Property 1 to Celia in complete liquidation of her interest in the partnership. Since she received no cash, she recognizes no gain on the distribution (assuming that neither Property 1 or 2 is a hot asset). She takes a $42,000 substitute basis in the property. Note that the partnership's basis in Property 1 was $50,000. Thus, the partnership has distributed property with an inside basis of $50,000 to liquidate outside basis of only $42,000. If it has a Code Sec. 754 election in effect, it will be allowed under Code Sec. 734(b) to increase its basis in Property 2 by $8,000 to bring its inside and outside bases back into balance. (Note that remaining outside basis will presumably be $168,000: four remaining partners with $42,000 bases each.)

Basis adjustments are also allowed under Code Sec. 734(b) when a partner recognizes gain (or loss) on receipt of a cash distribution in excess of his/her basis in the partnership interest. Note that this situation is analogous to that in Example 20.39 above. Because more basis is being removed from the partnership's balance sheet than is being absorbed outside the partnership, this situation, like the one above, results in a discrepancy between inside and outside basis.

EXAMPLE 20.41

Cleveland Partners has total assets with a tax basis of $75,000 and a fair market value of $135,000. It has no debt. George is a one-third partner in the partnership with a tax basis in his partnership interest of $25,000. Assume he receives a distribution of $45,000 cash in complete liquidation of his interest in the partnership. Under Code Sec. 731(a), George will recognize a taxable gain equal to the excess of the cash received over his tax basis in the partnership interest, or $20,000. Similar to the consequences of Example 20.39 above, the partnership has distributed property with an inside basis of $45,000 to liquidate outside basis of only $25,000. If it has a Code Sec. 754 election in effect, the partnership will be allowed under Code Sec. 734(b) to increase its basis in its remaining assets by this $20,000 excess.

In contrast to adjustments under Code Sec. 743(b), which are designed to protect the incoming partner, adjustments under Code Sec. 734(b) are designed to protect the remaining partners. Consider the facts in Example 20.41 above. Prior to the distribution, the partnership had assets with an aggregate tax basis of $75,000 and an aggregate fair market value of $135,000. Inherent in its balance sheet was a built-in gain of $60,000. George's share of this gain was one-third, or $20,000, and he recognized this amount of gain on receipt of the liquidating distribution. However, absent the basis adjustment under Code Sec. 734(b), the partnership will have remaining assets with an aggregate tax basis of $30,000 ($75,000 less $45,000 cash) and an aggregate fair market value of $90,000 ($135,000 less $45,000 cash). Thus, a $60,000 built-in gain remains inherent in the partnership's balance sheet; the remaining partners' share of this gain has increased from $40,000 (two-thirds) to $60,000. The basis adjustment corrects this potential inequity, allowing the remaining partners' share of partnership built-in (i.e., future) gain to remain at $40,000.

Retirement or Death of a Partner

¶20,090   **PAYMENTS FOR RETIRED PARTNER'S INTEREST**

Special rules apply when a partner retires from a partnership or dies. In many cases, the partnership agreement prohibits the retiring partner from selling his or her interest outside the partnership. For example, a partner in a law firm cannot simply sell her interest in the firm to another lawyer when she decides to retire. Similarly, when a partner dies, his heirs often will be prohibited from either assuming his place as a partner or selling his partnership interest to another. For example, assume that the name partner in a public accounting firm dies, leaving his entire estate to his son. In most cases, the son cannot simply inherit the deceased partner's role in the accounting firm. He may not even be an accountant, but even if he is, the other partners may not wish to admit him as a partner in the firm.

Most partnership agreements contain a provision obligating the partnership to essentially purchase the interest of a deceased or retiring partner upon termination of his or her continuing interest in the partnership (either through death or retirement). Generally, the agreement will provide a formula for determining the price and structure of the buyout payment or payments. For example, a common agreement may require the partnership to pay the retiring partner or the deceased partner's heirs a share of partnership income for a specified number of years following termination of the partnership interest, or it may require the partnership to make a payment to the retiree/decedent equal to the amount in his/her capital account, plus some pre-determined amount as compensation for the partner's share of the appreciation in partnership assets, or for clients brought to the partnership by the retiring or deceased partner.

The tax treatment of these payments is governed by Code Sec. 736. Under Code Sec. 736(b), to the extent the payments compensate the retiring/deceased partner for his/her interest in partnership "property," they are treated as distributions, governed by the rules discussed previously in this chapter. To the extent that they exceed the partner's interest in partnership "property," however, Code Sec. 736(a) treats them as either a distributive share of partnership income (if determined by reference to partnership income), or as a guaranteed payment (if determined without regard to partnership income).

EXAMPLE 20.42

After 32 years, Becca retired from a professional services partnership. The partnership paid her $450,000 cash in exchange for her agreement to relinquish all claims against current or future partnership assets. Becca's tax basis in her partnership interest was $260,000. Of the total payment, assume that $350,000 was in exchange for her interest in partnership property; the remaining $100,000 was received in exchange for her agreement to relinquish all claims against future income. It was negotiated as a fixed amount, and is not dependent on the magnitude of current or future income in any way. This amount, therefore, is taxable to Becca as a guaranteed payment, and will be classified as ordinary income. The remaining $350,000 is treated as a distribution. Since the cash distribution exceeded her tax basis by $90,000 ($350,000 received - $260,000 basis), she will recognize a long-term capital gain in this amount.

¶20,091   DETERMINING THE PARTNER'S INTEREST IN PARTNERSHIP PROPERTY

The retiring or deceased partner's interest in partnership property is equal to such partner's share of the *fair market value* of partnership assets. This is a relatively straightforward determination assuming the partnership has a current balance sheet and the partners agree on the value of all the assets. Two assets often not apparent on the partnership balance sheet, however, are partnership unrealized receivables (such as uncollected accounts receivable, depreciation recapture inherent in real estate or machinery, etc.) and partnership goodwill. Unrealized receivables, especially those associated with depreciation recapture potential, are often not separately stated on the balance sheet, and goodwill is generally not reported on the balance sheet at all (unless it is purchased goodwill from the acquisition of another business). However, in most cases the departing partner will demand to be compensated for his or her share of both unrealized receivables and unreported goodwill arising when the value of the partnership's business exceeds the value of its assets.

For many partnerships, unrealized receivables and goodwill, like other partnership assets, are included when measuring partnership "property." However, where *capital is not a material income-producing factor* (e.g., accounting, law, and other professional services partnerships), and the retiring or deceased partner was a *general* partner, unrealized receivables are never treated as partnership property and goodwill is treated as property *only* if the partnership agreement specifically provides for departing partners to be compensated for their shares of such goodwill. Thus, payments received by a general partner in a professional services partnership for his/her share of unrealized receivables will be treated as guaranteed payments under Code Sec. 736(a), as will payments for goodwill unless required by the partnership agreement. This is an important distinction as guaranteed payments are taxed to the recipient as ordinary income and are deductible by the partnership.

EXAMPLE 20.43

Bernard was a 25 percent general partner in Tall Grass Partners, a professional services firm. Upon his retirement, he received a cash payment of $160,000 for his partnership interest, in which his tax basis was $85,000. The partnership agreement was silent regarding partnership goodwill, and the balance sheet of the partnership immediately prior to his retirement was as follows:

	Basis	FMV
Cash	$80,000	$80,000
Investments	120,000	180,000
Code Sec. 1231 assets	140,000	140,000
Unrealized receivables	0	120,000
Partnership goodwill (agreed upon by partners)	0	120,000
	$340,000	$640,000

Since Bernard was a general partner in a professional services partnership (in which capital is not a material income-producing factor), the unrealized receivables do not constitute partnership property for purposes of Code Sec. 736. Moreover, because the partnership does not require that Bernard be compensated for his share of partnership goodwill, it will not be treated as partnership property either. Thus, Bernard's share of Tall Grass Partners' property is $100,000 (25 percent of the value of the cash, investments and Code Sec. 1231 assets). This portion of his retirement payment will be treated as a distribution under Code Sec. 736(b). Since his tax basis in the partnership interest is only $85,000, this distribution will trigger a $15,000 long-term capital gain. The partnership will not be entitled to deduct any portion of this payment.

Under Code Sec. 736(a), the remainder of Bernard's payment, $60,000, will be treated as a guaranteed payment, governed by the principles of Code Sec. 707(c). (Note that this is equal to his 25% share of the value of the partnership's unrealized receivables and goodwill). This portion of his retirement payment will be taxable as ordinary income to Bernard, and will be fully deductible by the partnership on its tax return for the year of the retirement.

Finally, note that if the partnership had had outstanding liabilities, Bernard would be deemed to have received a cash payment equal to his share of those liabilities in addition to any actual cash payment received. If the partnership had outstanding liabilities, and still paid him $160,000 upon retirement, the value of partnership goodwill on the above balance sheet would have to be restated to reflect the deemed payment associated with release from his share of partnership debt.

¶20,092

INCOME IN RESPECT OF A DECEASED PARTNER

The rules discussed above apply equally to payments made in liquidation of the interest of a retired or deceased partner. However, under the provisions of Code Sec. 1014, when a partner dies, his or her beneficiaries receive a stepped-up basis in the partnership interest equal to its fair market value at the date of death (or the alternate valuation date if applicable). Thus, the beneficiary of a decedent partner generally will not recognize gain on receipt of a distribution in liquidation of the inherited interest. There is one significant exception to this rule – under Code Sec. 753, payments received by the decedent's beneficiaries in excess of the value of the decedent's interest in partnership property are treated as income in respect of a decedent. Under Code Sec. 691, beneficiaries are not entitled to step-up the basis of items of income in respect of a decedent. Thus, payments governed by Sec. 736(a) (e.g., payments for the deceased partner's share of unrealized receivables and payments for goodwill if not required by the partnership agreement) will be taxable as ordinary income to the beneficiaries just as they would have been if received by the decedent before he or she died. Note that the beneficiaries will be allowed a deduction for any estate taxes attributable to the inclusion of these rights in the estate of the deceased partner.

¶20,093

DECEASED PARTNER'S FINAL INCOME TAX RETURN

The partnership's taxable year closes with respect to a deceased partner at the date of such partner's death. Code Sec. 706(c)(2). The decedent's final federal income tax return includes the partner's share of partnership income up to the date of his or her death. The estate or other successor to the partnership interest will include its share of partnership income for the remainder of the partnership's tax year. Therefore, it is possible for a partner in a fiscal-year partnership to have a bunching of income on the partner's final individual income tax return.

EXAMPLE 20.44 Hal Jordan owns a 50 percent interest in both the capital and profits of the HalMart Partnership, which has a January 31 fiscal year. The partnership year ends at Hal's death on October 31, 2017. Hal's distributable share of the partnership's income for the tax year ended on January 31, 2017 (assume $50,000) and his distributable share of the partnership's income for the short year February 1 – October 31, 2017 (assume $40,000), must both be reported on Hal's final tax return filed for 2017.

SUMMARY

- The tax consequences of a distribution depend on whether the distribution is a liquidating or non-liquidating distribution, and on whether it affects the distributee-partner's interest in partnership hot assets.

- A non-liquidating distribution does not liquidate the partner's interest in the partnership, while a liquidating distribution does.

- Unless Code Sec. 751(b) applies, a non-liquidating distribution will generally be nontaxable unless cash is received by the partner in excess of his or her basis in the partnership interest. Loss is generally not recognized on receipt of a non-liquidating distribution.

- Unless Code Sec. 751(b) applies, gain is not generally recognized on receipt of a liquidating distribution unless the partner receives cash in excess of the basis of his or her interest in the partnership. Unlike with non-liquidating distributions, however, loss may be recognized on receipt of a liquidating distribution but only if the partner receives no property other than cash or ordinary income assets and the amount of cash received, plus the tax basis of the ordinary income property is less than the partner's tax basis in the partnership interest.

- If the partnership has Code Sec. 751 assets, and the distribution changes the distributee-partner's interest in those assets, the distribution may trigger recognition of income or gain to the partner and/or the partnership.

- If the partnership makes an election under Code Sec. 754, or an earlier such election remains in effect, the partnership will be required to step up (or down) the tax basis of partnership assets to reflect the gain or loss recognized by the distributee partner, if any, on the distribution. Similarly, if the distributee partner takes a different basis in distributed property than the partnership had in such property, the partnership will be required to adjust its basis in its remaining assets to reflect this difference.

- Gains recognized on the sale of a partnership interest are generally characterized as capital gains unless the partnership has Code Sec. 751 property ("hot assets"). Where the partnership has hot assets, the partner's gain on sale of an interest in the partnership is recharacterized as ordinary income to the extent of his or share of the appreciate inherent in such assets.

- Hot assets include partnership unrealized receivables and substantially appreciated inventory. For this purpose, inventory is substantially appreciated if its fair market value exceeds 120 percent of its adjusted basis to the partnership.

- When measuring the fair market value and tax basis of partnership inventory, the term "inventory" includes *all partnership property other than cash, capital assets and Code Sec. 1231 assets*. Thus, inventory includes partnership unrealized receivables.

- Payments to retiring partners are divided into payments for partnership property and other payments. Payments for partnership property generally trigger capital gain or loss, while "other" payments are generally taxed to the recipient as ordinary income and reduce the income reported by remaining partners.

- Payments made to liquidate a deceased partner's interest that are attributable to unrealized receivables are income in respect of a decedent, not subject to the basis step-up rules of Code Sec. 1014.

QUESTIONS

1. What is the difference between a current distribution and a liquidating distribution?

2. Assume a partner agrees to leave a partnership in exchange for a distribution of land and cash. Due to a temporary cash shortage, the partnership distributes the land now, and agrees to distribute the cash in three installments. Will the distributions be treated as current or liquidating distributions?

3. Why can't a partner recognize loss upon receipt of a current distribution?

4. In what circumstances may a partner recognize loss upon receipt of a distribution from a partnership?

5. What is a partner's basis in property received from the partnership in a current distribution?

6. Why is the partner's basis in distributed property generally limited to his/her basis in the partnership interest prior to the distribution?

7. What basis will a partner take in property received in a liquidating distribution from a partnership?

8. Explain the difference between the basis rules applicable to liquidating vs. current distributions. Why do the rules differ for these two classes of partnership distributions?

9. In what circumstances does a partner recognize gain on receipt of a proportionate distribution from a partnership?

10. Explain how the basis rules work to *defer* rather than *exclude* a partner's recognition of gain associated with a partnership distribution.

11. Why can't a partner defer recognition of gain when (s)he receives a distribution of cash in excess of his/her basis in the partnership interest?

12. What are "hot" assets, and how do they affect the consequences of a partnership distribution?

13. In what circumstances will a distribution of hot assets *not* require recognition of ordinary income under Section 751(b)?

14. Assume a partner receives a disproportionate distribution consisting of hot assets from a partnership. Explain who will recognize ordinary income and why.

15. In some cases, a disproportionate distribution in liquidation of a partner's interest in the partnership can result in the partner recognizing both ordinary income and a capital loss. Explain how such a seeming anomaly could occur.

16. What are unrealized receivables of a partnership?

17. What is substantially appreciated inventory?

18. What tax basis will a partner take in hot assets received from a partnership in a disproportionate distribution?

19. When a partner sells his/her interest in a partnership, what items are included in the amount realized?

20. In general, gain or loss recognized on sale of an interest in a partnership is classified as capital gain or loss. Why?

21. How does the sale of a partnership interest compare to a liquidating distribution from a partnership? How do the tax consequences of the two transactions differ?

22. What is a "Section 754 election?" What does it allow the partnership to do?

23. Explain the difference between a basis adjustment under Section 743(b) and one under Section 734(b). Who benefits from each type of adjustment?

24. What is a partner's tax basis in a newly purchased partnership interest?

25. Assume a partnership does *not* have a Section 754 election in effect, and does not make one. If a new partner purchases his/her partnership interest from another partner, what will be his/her share of the partnership's inside basis in its assets?

26. How is a partnership affected for tax purposes when a partner sells his/her interest in the partnership to another person? Assume the partnership does not have a Section 754 election in effect and chooses not to make one.

27. Could a partner recognize a deductible loss for tax purposes on sale of his/her partnership interest to an unrelated buyer? What about on the receipt of a liquidating distribution from the partnership?

28. When does Section 736 apply to a liquidating distribution made to a partner?

29. Why is the application of Section 736 different for partnerships where capital is a material income-producing factor than for those where capital is not a material income-producing factor?

30. Who benefits when Section 736 is applied to a liquidating distribution, the partner or the partnership? Explain.

PROBLEMS

31. Mark, Pete and Mickey are equal partners in the 2MP Partnership. At the beginning of the year, Mark's basis in his partnership interest was $15,000, Pete's basis was $10,000, and Mickey's basis was $20,000. The partnership reported taxable income of $30,000 (allocated equally among the partners). At year-end, the partnership made a non-liquidating distribution of $25,000 cash to Pete.
    a. How much gain must Pete recognize on receipt of the cash distribution?
    b. What will be his remaining basis in his partnership interest?
    c. How would your answers change if the distribution had been received by Mickey, rather than Pete?

32. Wilma, Clay and Nathan are equal partners in the Cousins Partnership. At the end of the year, Wilma's tax basis in her partnership interest was $14,000, Clay's basis was $25,000 and Nathan's basis $8,000. In a non-liquidating distribution, the partnership distributed investment property to Clay with a tax basis of $18,000 and a fair market value of $45,000.
    a. How much gain must Clay recognize on receipt of the distribution?
    b. What basis will he take in the property received from the partnership?
    c. What will be his remaining basis in the partnership interest?

33. Susan was a one-third partner in Anders Mountain Partners until last month. Last month, she received a cash distribution of $25,000 in "redemption" (i.e., partial liquidation) of *half* her interest in the partnership. Her basis in her partnership interest prior to the distribution was $30,000. The distribution was *not* a disproportionate distribution and did not trigger the provisions of Section 751(b). The partnership had no liabilities.
    a. How much gain or loss will Susan recognize on receipt of the distribution?
    b. What will be her remaining basis in her partnership interest?
    c. What will be her remaining interest in the partnership in percentage terms? (Note: she was a 33% partner prior to receipt of the distribution).

34. Craig received a *cash* distribution of $50,000 in liquidation of *half* of his one-fourth interest in White Family Partners. His tax basis in his partnership interest prior to the distribution was $35,000. The distribution was not a disproportionate distribution and the partnership had no liabilities.
    a. How much gain or loss must Craig recognize on receipt of the distribution?
    b. What will be his remaining basis in his partnership interest?

35. Wayne, a one-third partner in the Count'em Partnership, received *investment property* worth $100,000 in redemption (i.e., partial liquidation) of half his interest. The partnership's tax basis in the investment property was $48,000. Wayne's tax basis in his partnership interest prior to the distribution was $40,000.
    a. Will Wayne be required to recognize any gain or loss on receipt of the distribution from the partnership?
    b. What will be his tax basis in the property received?
    c. What will be his remaining basis in his partnership interest?

36. Jonna is a one-fourth partner in Andersen Partners. At the end of the year, her tax basis in her partnership interest was $25,000. At that time, she received a non-liquidating distribution from the partnership of property with a tax basis of $22,000 and a fair market value of $38,000. The distribution was not a disproportionate distribution.
    a. How much gain must Jonna recognize on receipt of the distribution from the partnership?
    b. What basis will she take in the property received?
    c. How would your answers change if the tax basis of the property had been $38,000 and its fair market value had been $50,000?

37. Rick is a partner in the Ten Hicks Partnership. This year, he received a distribution consisting of two properties. Property 1 was worth $40,000 at the date of the distribution and had a tax basis to the partnership of $28,000. Property 2 was worth $60,000 and had a tax basis of $12,000. Rick's tax basis in his partnership interest was $30,000 prior to the distribution. The partnership did not have any hot assets either before or after the distribution.
    a. Will Rick recognize any gain or loss on receipt of the distribution?
    b. What will be Rick's tax basis in each of the properties received?
    c. What will be his remaining tax basis in his partnership interest?

38. Amy is a partner in Xiowa Partners. Her basis in her partnership interest is $69,000. In a non-liquidating distribution, Amy received three properties. Property 1 was worth $20,000 and had a tax basis of $30,000. Property 2, valued at $18,000 had a tax basis of $23,000. Property 3 was worth $32,000 and had a tax basis of $22,000. Assume all three properties are capital assets.
    a. Will Amy recognize any taxable gain or loss on receipt of the non-liquidating distribution?
    b. What basis will Amy take in properties 1, 2 and 3?
    c. What will be Amy's remaining tax basis in her partnership interest?
    d. Would your answers above be different if the distribution had been in complete liquidation of Amy's partnership interest?

39. Reconsider the facts in problem 38 above. Assume Amy's tax basis in her partnership interest had been $45,000, rather than $69,000. How would your answers change?

40. Edna was a one-third partner in OldGrad Partners until December 31, when her interest in the partnership was liquidated. Prior to the liquidation, her basis in her partnership interest was $45,000. She received $15,000 cash and property with a tax basis (to the partnership) of $50,000 and a fair market value of $64,000 in complete liquidation of her interest. The distribution was not a disproportionate distribution under Section 751(b).
    a. How much gain or loss will Edna recognize upon receipt of the distribution?
    b. What basis will she take in the property received from the partnership?

41. Kevin recently decided to leave the Jackson Partnership. His tax basis in his one-fifth interest in the partnership was $50,000. In complete liquidation of that interest, he received cash of $20,000 and property with a tax basis of $18,000 and a fair market value of $60,000. The distribution was not a disproportionate distribution subject to Section 751(b).
    a. How much gain or loss will Kevin recognize on receipt of the liquidating distribution?
    b. What will be his tax basis in the property received in the distribution?

42. In complete liquidation of her interest in the Buyers Partnership, Sarah received a cash distribution of $40,000. Her basis in the partnership interest prior to receipt of the liquidating distribution was $48,000.
    a. How much gain or loss must Sarah recognize on receipt of the liquidating distribution?
    b. Assume that Sarah received cash of only $25,000, and property worth $15,000 in complete liquidation of her interest in the partnership. How much gain or loss would she recognize? What would be her basis in the property received?

43. In complete liquidation of his interest in the KD Partnership, Scott received a distribution consisting of $38,000 cash and property valued at $62,000. The partnership's tax basis in the property, which was not inventory or unrealized receivables, was $22,000. Scott's basis in his partnership interest prior to receipt of the liquidating distribution was $35,000. The distribution was not a disproportionate distribution.
    a. Will Scott be required to recognize any gain or loss for tax purposes upon receipt of the liquidating distribution?
    b. What will be his tax basis in the property received from the partnership?

44. Stacy is a one-third partner in Tyknot Partners. Her basis in her partnership interest is $85,000, consisting of her $25,000 contribution to capital and her $60,000 share of the partnership's $180,000 outstanding liabilities. She receives a non-liquidating distribution consisting of property valued at $125,000 (tax basis $40,000). The distribution reduces her interest in the partnership from one-third to one-fifth. It is not a disproportionate distribution.
    a. Will Stacy recognize any gain or loss on receipt of the distribution?
    b. What basis will Stacy take in the property received from the partnership?
    c. What will be Stacy's remaining basis in her partnership interest?

45. Reconsider the facts of problem 44. Assume the property received by Stacy was encumbered by a mortgage of $50,000, which Stacy assumed in connection with the distribution. Assume the distribution still reduces Stacy's interest in the partnership from one-third to one-fifth. How would your answers change?

46. Williams Brothers Partnership had the following balance sheets at December 31:

	Basis	FMV
Cash	30,000	30,000
Property 1	103,000	151,000
Property 2	114,000	120,000
Property 3	32,000	50,000
TOTAL ASSETS	279,000	351,000
Liabilities	126,000	126,000
Capital, Matt	51,000	75,000
Capital, Justin	51,000	75,000
Capital, Jeff	51,000	75,000
TOTAL LIABILITIES & CAPITAL	279,000	351,000

All three properties owned by the partnership are investment properties. On December 31, the partnership distributed property 3 to Matt, reducing his interest in the partnership from one-third to one-seventh.
    a. Will Matt recognize any gain or loss in connection with this distribution?
    b. What will be Matt's tax basis in property 3 received from the partnership?
    c. What will be Matt's remaining tax basis in his partnership interest?

47. Assume in problem 46 above that Matt had received property 2, subject to a $70,000 mortgage, rather than property 3. Matt assumed responsibility for the mortgage in connection with the distribution. As before, the distribution reduced Matt's interest in the partnership from one-third to one-seventh.
    a. Will Matt recognize any gain or loss in connection with this distribution?
    b. What basis will Matt take in property 2?
    c. What will be Matt's remaining tax basis in his partnership interest?

48. Reconsider the facts of problem 46 above. Assume that Matt received neither properties 2 or 3 from the partnership. Instead, he received property 1, subject to the entire $126,000 partnership mortgage. He assumed responsibility for the mortgage in connection with the distribution.
    a. What will be Matt's interest in the partnership after the distribution (i.e., the distribution will change Matt's interest from one-third to what?)
    b. What will be Matt's tax basis in the distributed property?
    c. What will be Matt's remaining tax basis in his partnership interest?

49. Challenge Partners had the following balance sheets at December 31:

	Basis	FMV
Cash	30,000	30,000
Accounts Receivable	0	45,000
Property 1	54,000	60,000
Property 2	36,000	45,000
TOTAL ASSETS	120,000	180,000
Capital, Tina	40,000	60,000
Capital, Jane	40,000	60,000
Capital, Karen	40,000	60,000
TOTAL CAPITAL	120,000	180,000

On that date, it distributed Property 1 to Karen in complete liquidation of her interest in the partnership.
    a. Will Section 751(b) apply to this distribution?
    b. Will Karen recognize any income or gain in connection with the distribution?
    c. What will be Karen's tax basis in Property 1?

50. Consider the facts of problem 49. Assume that rather than property 1, Karen had received the accounts receivable and $15,000 cash in complete liquidation of her interest in the partnership.
    a. Would Section 751(b) apply to the distribution?
    b. How much gain will the partnership recognize in connection with the distribution?
    c. What would be the character of the partnership's gain (i.e., ordinary income or capital gain)?

51. Reconsider the facts in problem 49. Assume the partnership distributed one-third of the accounts receivable and property 2 to Karen in complete liquidation of his interest in the partnership.
    a. Will Section 751(b) apply to the distribution?
    b. How much gain will Karen recognize and what will be its character?

52. Woody is a one-third partner in Boyd Partners. His basis in his partnership interest is $28,000, consisting of his $15,000 capital interest and his $13,000 (one-third) share of partnership liabilities. He is considering selling his interest to Susan. Susan would pay Woody $47,000 cash and step into his shoes as a partner. The partnership has no hot assets.
    a. How much gain must Woody recognize on the sale, and what will be its character?
    b. What will be Susan's tax basis in the newly acquired partnership interest?

53. Assume the same facts as in problem 52, except that rather than sell his partnership interest to Susan, Woody receives a $47,000 cash distribution from the partnership in complete liquidation of his interest. How would the tax consequences for Woody differ from those associated with the sale to Susan?

54. Hucklebee Partners had the following balance sheets at December 31:

	Basis	FMV
Cash	30,000	30,000
Property 1	115,000	125,000
Property 2	125,000	170,000
Property 3	130,000	50,000
TOTAL ASSETS	400,000	375,000
Liabilities	150,000	150,000
Capital, Marci	100,000	90,000
Capital, Amy	75,000	67,500
Capital, Angela	75,000	67,500
TOTAL LIABILITIES & CAPITAL	400,000	375,000

Marci is a 40 partner in the partnership. None of the partnership's assets constitute inventory or unrealized receivables. She is considering selling her interest in the partnership to Carla, an unrelated partner.
a. What is an appropriate selling price for Marci's interest in the partnership?
b. Assume Marci and Carla agree on a selling price of $90,000. How much gain or loss will Marci recognize?
c. What will be Carla's basis in her partnership interest?

55. Sowder Partners has the following balance sheets:

	Basis	FMV
Cash	12,000	12,000
Accounts Receivable	0	70,000
Inventory	84,000	120,000
Sec. 1231 Property	24,000	38,000
TOTAL ASSETS	120,000	240,000
Capital, Teri	45,000	80,000
Capital, Brandi	15,000	40,000
Capital, Chris	60,000	120,000
TOTAL CAPITAL	120,000	240,000

Chris has been approached by an unrelated third party with an offer to purchase his interest in the partnership.
a. What is the appropriate selling price for Chris's interest?
b. Assume he agrees to sell his interest for $120,000 cash. How much gain will he recognize on the sale, and what will be its character?

56. Consider the facts in problem 55 above. Assume that rather than selling his partnership interest to an outsider, Chris receives a $120,000 cash distribution from the partnership in complete liquidation of his interest therein. How will the consequences differ from those associated with the sale?

57. Bust-out Partners had the following balance sheets at year-end:

	Basis	FMV
Cash	30,000	30,000
Property 1	33,000	51,000
Property 2	42,000	60,000
Property 3	27,000	45,000
TOTAL ASSETS	132,000	186,000
Capital, Sam	33,000	46,500
Capital, Maggie	33,000	46,500
Capital, Jack	66,000	93,000
TOTAL LIABILITIES & CAPITAL	132,000	186,000

On December 31, Jack sold his fifty percent interest in the partnership to an unrelated buyer for $93,000. None of the partnership's properties constitute inventory or unrealized receivables.
a. How much gain must Jack recognize on the sale?
b. What will be the buyer's tax basis in the newly acquired partnership interest?
c. Assume the partnership has a Section 754 election in effect. Determine the amount of the partnership's basis adjustment under Section 743(b), and allocate the adjustment among the partnership's assets.

58. Consider the facts in problem 57 above. Assume the partnership does not have a Section 754 election in effect, and decides not to make one. Shortly after the new buyer's acquisition of Jack's interest in the partnership, the partnership sells property 1 for its $51,000 fair market value.

    a. How much gain will the partnership recognize on the sale, and how much of this gain will be allocated to the new partner for tax purposes?

    b. If the partnership did have a Section 754 election in effect, how much gain would be allocated to the new partner in connection with the partnership's sale of property 1?

    c. Assume the partnership had a Section 754 election in effect when the new partner acquired Jack's fifty percent partnership interest. Assume that the partnership later sold property 1 for $69,000 (it appreciated in value after the new partner's entry). How much gain would the partnership recognize for tax purposes, and how much of this gain would be allocated to the new partner?

59. Elbegone Partnership had the following assets when one of its partners sold her interest in the partnership:

	Basis	FMV
Asset 1	26,000	50,000
Asset 2	45,000	31,000
Asset 3	36,000	48,000

    As a result of the sale of one of the partnership interests, Elbegone is required to make a $21,000 adjustment to the basis of its assets under Section 743(b).

    a. Determine the appropriate allocation of the basis adjustment among the partnership's assets.

    b. How would your answer change if the value of asset 2 had been $57,000, rather than $31,000?

60. RT Ranches is a general partnership with the following balance sheets:

	Basis	FMV
Cash	30,000	30,000
Property 1	63,000	93,000
Property 2	18,000	43,000
Property 3	24,000	53,000
TOTAL ASSETS	135,000	219,000
Capital, Larry	45,000	73,000
Capital, Robert	45,000	73,000
Capital, Clay	45,000	73,000
TOTAL CAPITAL	135,000	219,000

    On December 31, in complete liquidation of his interest, the partnership distributed property 2 and $30,000 cash to Clay. None of the partnership's properties constitute inventory or unrealized receivables.

    a. How much gain will Clay recognize in connection with the distribution?

    b. Assume the partnership did not have a Section 754 election in effect and chose not to make one. Compare the amount of taxable gain which will be reported by Larry and Robert if the partnership sells properties 1 and 3 after Clay's departure to the amount of gain they would have recognized had the partnership sold all three of its properties just prior to Clay's departure from the partnership.

    c. What explains the difference you identify in part b above? Is there a remedy available to Larry and Robert?

61. Assume the same facts as in problem 60, except that the partnership agrees to distribute property 2 and $75,000 cash to Clay in liquidation of his interest. (To fund the distribution, the partnership borrowed money from a local bank). Further assume that capital *is* a material income-producing factor for this partnership.

    a. How much gain will Clay recognize in connection with the distribution now, and what will be its character?

    b. What will be Clay's tax basis in the property received?

    c. How will the distribution affect the partnership for tax purposes?

62. How would your answers to problem 61 change if capital was *not* a material income-producing factor for the partnership?

63. Arthur Lybrand, LLP is a large law firm with the following balance sheets at September 30:

	Basis	FMV
Cash & equivalents	$400,000	$400,000
Accounts receivable	-0-	300,000
Office, furniture & fixtures	350,000	780,000
Total Assets	$750,000	$1,480,000
Liabilities	$240,000	$240,000
Partner capital	$510,000	$1,240,000
Total Liabilities & Capital	$750,000	$1,480,000

On September 30, Ernest Cooper retired from the firm. Prior to his retirement, he owned a twenty percent interest in partnership capital, profits and losses. His tax basis in the partnership interest was $150,000.

a. What is the minimum amount Ernest should accept in liquidation of his interest in the partnership?

b. Assume Ernest receives a cash payment in the amount you determined in part a. What portion, if any, of that payment will be treated as a Section 736(a) payment rather than as a distribution? Assume capital is *not* a material income-producing factor for the partnership.

c. Assume that Ernest receives a total cash payment of $500,000 from the partnership in complete liquidation of his interest therein. If the partnership agreement is silent with respect to goodwill, what portion of the payment will be taxed as ordinary income and what portion as capital gain?

d. How would your answer to question change if the partnership agreement requires that retiring partners be compensated for their shares of partnership goodwill?

64. Juanita Gordon received a total cash buyout of $300,000 in liquidation of her one-third interest in Carmeggon Partners. Her tax basis in the liquidated interest was $125,000. Of the total amount received, $100,000 was attributable her share of the partnership's unrealized accounts receivable and $50,000 to her share of partnership goodwill. Capital is *not* a material income-producing factor for the partnership, and the partnership agreement does *not* require that partners be compensated for their shares of partnership goodwill upon retiring from the partnership.

a. How much ordinary income will Juanita recognize on receipt of the buyout?

b. How much capital gain will Juanita recognize?

c. Assume that Juanita received the buyout payments over 5 years. If she received $60,000 this year (the year of her retirement), how much (if any) of that distribution will be taxable as ordinary income and how much as capital gain?

65. **Case Study.** FDR Partners is a large regional partnership. This year, Rusty acquired an interest in the firm by purchasing it from an existing partner. The firm's balance sheet just prior to Rusty's acquisition was as follows:

	Basis	FMV
Cash	30,000	30,000
Accounts Receivable	0	151,000
Building	150,000	200,000
Land	32,000	50,000
TOTAL ASSETS	212,000	431,000
Liabilities	125,000	125,000
Partners' capital	87,000	306,000
TOTAL LIABILITIES & CAPITAL	212,000	431,000

Rusty paid $50,000 for the newly purchased interest, which represented a ten percent interest in the firm. The partnership does not currently have a Section 754 election in effect. Our firm has advised Rusty that the partnership should make a Section 754 election for his benefit. Review Reg. §1.754-1 and prepare a memorandum explaining how the Section 754 election is made and when it must be made in order to benefit Rusty. Also illustrate to Rusty the different tax consequences for him if the election is made vs. if it is not made.

66. **Research Problem.** Smith Properties is a real estate partnership that focuses on the acquisition and management of commercial and residential real estate in the Southwestern United States. Edna Zapata has been a partner in the partnership for the past 15 years. This year, she decided to sell her partnership interest and focus on other interests. The partnership has the following balance sheets as of the date she sold her interest:

	Tax Basis	FMV
Cash and equivalents	$250,000	$250,000
Real estate portfolio (includes multiple properties)	2,400,000	6,000,000
Other tangible assets	500,000	500,000
Total Assets	$3,150,000	$6,750,000

	Tax Basis	FMV
Liabilities (principally mortgage liabilities on the partnership's real estate portfolio)	$1,350,000	$1,350,000
Partner capital	1,800,000	5,400,000
Total liabilities & capital	$3,150,000	$6,750,000

Edna owned a one-third interest in partnership capital and profits. As such, the fair market value of her interest in the partnership was $1,800,000. However, the partnership has a reputation for wise investment and management of properties. The buyer of Edna's interest in the partnership was willing to pay a premium for this expertise. Thus, Edna sold her interest in the partnership for $2,000,000. The buyer also assumed responsibility for Edna's one-third share of the partnership's liabilities. The partnership has a Section 754 election in effect. Determine the amount of the partnership's basis adjustment under Section 743(b), and allocate this adjustment among the partnership's assets. Assume that all of the partnership's real estate properties are business-use assets which will generate capital gain upon disposition under Code Section 1231. Explain how the excess of the purchase price over the fair market value of the partnership's tangible assets will affect the partnership's post-adjustment balance sheet.

Research Aid: Reg. §1.755.

67. **Research Problem.** Alvin Conley has been a partner in a large accounting partnership for twenty-five years. This year, he decided to retire. Although Alvin's share of partnership capital is only $100,000, the partnership agreed to pay Alvin a total of $500,000 to liquidate his interest in the partnership. The payments will be made over ten years, $50,000 per year. The partnership agreement only requires the partnership to pay Alvin his $100,000 share of partnership capital, so the terms agreed to by Alvin and the remaining partners represent a very generous severance package. The remaining partners are comfortable with the payments, however, because Alvin brought in a large percentage of the firm's clients over the years, and thus is responsible for a large part of the firm's revenues, even after he retires. How will the payments be treated for tax purposes by both Alvin and the partnership?

Research Aid: Code Sec. 736.

Chapter

21

S Corporations

OBJECTIVES

After completing Chapter 21, you should be able to:

1. Understand the requirements that organizations must meet to be eligible for S corporation status.
2. Work with the election procedures that are necessary to meet the eligibility requirements.
3. Recognize the taxes imposed on S corporations.
4. Determine how shareholders report income items passed through the corporation.
5. Distinguish between taxable and tax-free distributions of the corporation.
6. Determine when the status of an S corporation terminates.

OVERVIEW

Subchapter S was added to the Internal Revenue Code in 1958 as a means to permit small businesses "to select the form of business organization desired, without the necessity of taking into account major differences in tax consequences." Sen. Rept. No. 193, 85th Cong., 2nd Sess. 87 (1958). The objective was to permit the use of the corporate form with federal income tax consequences essentially like those of a partnership. The Subchapter S Revision Act of 1982 (P.L. 97-354) made comprehensive revisions that enhanced the utility of the election. A corporation that elects the special tax treatment under Subchapter S is specifically designated as an S corporation.

The existence of S corporations raises a number of interesting questions concerning corporate elections and tax consequences both for the corporation and for the shareholder. The answers to these questions are to be found by reading this chapter. What types of corporations are eligible to receive S corporation status? What types of shareholders are eligible to hold stock in the corporation? How is a Subchapter S election accomplished? What calendar considerations are important in regard to the election? When may a built-in gain tax be imposed on an S corporation? What additional taxes may be imposed on an S corporation? How are income, deductions, and credits computed for an S corporation? How are corporate distributions treated? How may an election be terminated? These and other issues are discussed at length in this chapter.

Selecting the Subchapter S Form

¶21,001   INTRODUCTION

In an S corporation, the corporation in general will pay no tax, whereas the shareholders must include in gross income their proportionate share of corporate income whether or not the corporate earnings are distributed to them.

The S corporation is a viable alternative that small businesses should seriously consider. The S corporation election may be beneficial to those shareholders whose marginal tax rate is lower than the corporate rate. With individual rates on a graduated basis, the S corporation provides a shelter for income earned by a corporation that would otherwise be taxed as high as 35 percent. An S election may be advantageous for a corporation even if its taxable income is less than $75,000 because its shareholders are subject to an additional tax upon the distribution of retained earnings if the S election is not made. It is beneficial also where business losses are anticipated, since these losses pass through to the shareholders, who may treat them as trade or business expenses deductible under Code Sec. 162.

The S election affects only the federal income tax consequences of the electing corporation. In eight states and the District of Columbia, the S election is not recognized, and the corporation is subject to any state taxes imposed on the corporation.

Under the passive loss rules, an S corporation in which the taxpayer does not materially participate is treated as a passive activity. The corporation's losses are deductible on the shareholder's return only against passive income. If the shareholder has no passive income, no deduction is allowed for the losses. However, the passive loss rules can work to the taxpayer's advantage when an S corporation has income. If the shareholder does not materially participate in the S corporation, the income can be used to offset tax-shelter losses since the income from the S corporation is considered passive.

TAX BLUNDER

Kathleen Parker has a regular corporation in which she does not materially participate. She decides to convert the corporation to an S corporation. The corporation has $40,000 of investment income and an operating loss of $40,000 for the year. Kathleen's only other income is wages of $75,000. She has no other investment income or expenses and no other passive investments. The $40,000 of investment income from the S corporation is passed through and included in Kathleen's gross income. The $40,000 operating loss is also passed through but is not deductible by Kathleen since it is deductible only against passive income. If Kathleen had not converted the corporation to an S corporation, she would have been able to offset the $40,000 net operating loss with the $40,000 of investment income, would have incurred no corporate income tax, and would not have to include the $40,000 investment income on her personal return.

¶21,009   ELIGIBILITY

In order to qualify under Subchapter S, a corporation must be a small business corporation. The following additional requirements must be met in order to be a small business corporation:

1. Must be a domestic corporation
2. Must have no more than 100 shareholders
3. Must include only eligible shareholders
4. Must have only one class of stock
5. Must not be an ineligible corporation

Domestic Corporation

The corporation must be a domestic corporation. The term "domestic" when applied to a corporation or partnership means created or organized in the United States or under the laws of the United States or any state. Code Secs. 1361(b)(1) and 7701(a)(4).

Not More Than 100 Shareholders

The corporation may not have more than 100 shareholders. Prior to 2005, S corporations were limited to 75 shareholders. All members of a family will be treated as one shareholder for purposes of the rules limiting the number of permissible shareholders in an S corporation. The term "members of a family" includes the common ancestor and all lineal descendants of the common ancestor, plus spouses (or former spouses) of these individuals. The common ancestor cannot be more than six generations removed from the youngest generation of shareholders at the time the S election is made. A spouse or former spouse will be treated as being of the same generation as the individual to which he or she is or was married. If one spouse dies while the couple is still married, there is only one shareholder as long as the stock remains in the deceased shareholder's estate. Code Sec. 1361(b)(1)(A) and (c)(1).

The limit on the number of shareholders has been increased from 10 to 100 over the years and may allow S corporations to be more broadly used in connection with various syndicated ventures. The increased number of shareholders will give shareholders more flexibility in estate planning.

Eligible Shareholders

Individuals (other than nonresident aliens), estates, and certain trusts are eligible to hold stock in the S corporation. Code Sec. 1361(b)(1). There are various trusts that are permissible holders of stock in an S corporation. All trusts that are included in Subpart E of the Internal Revenue Code are so permitted, provided that there is one person who is deemed to be the owner in each of the trusts. Foreign trusts, like foreign corporations and nonresident aliens, are not eligible shareholders. The IRS has specifically ruled that a corporation cannot qualify for an S corporation election if it has a partnership as a shareholder. Rev. Rul. 59-235, 1959-2 CB 192.

After 1997, tax-exempt organizations are eligible S corporation shareholders. This means that qualified pension plans, public charities, and private foundations are able to hold stock in S corporations. However, individual retirement accounts continue to be ineligible shareholders. Trade associations and benevolent associations are also not eligible shareholders of S corporation stock.

TAX BLUNDER

Fred Smyth uses funds in his self-directed individual retirement account to purchase shares in an S corporation. The corporation would no longer be an eligible S corporation as it has an ineligible shareholder. Fred should have purchased the shares with his own funds.

In the case of a Qualified Subchapter S Trust (QSST), the terms of the trust instrument need only require that there be a single income beneficiary during the life of the current income beneficiary. Thus, the possibility of multiple beneficiaries after the death of the current beneficiary will not disqualify the trust during the current beneficiary's lifetime. A QSST is required to distribute all of its income to a citizen or resident of the United States. Code Sec. 1361(d)(3)(B). If a QSST ceases to qualify on the death of an income beneficiary because of multiple beneficiaries, the trust will continue to be an eligible shareholder for the two-year period following the death of the current beneficiary. The corporation will therefore have an opportunity to continue the election by requalification of the trust or by transfer of the stock to a qualified shareholder. If the trust continues to qualify after the death of the first income beneficiary, any subsequent income beneficiary will be deemed to have made the election to be taxed under Code Sec. 678 unless the beneficiary affirmatively refuses to consent to the election. Code Sec. 1361(d)(2)(B).

PLANNING POINTER

A Qualified Terminable Interest Property (QTIP) marital deduction trust qualifies as a permitted shareholder since there is only one income beneficiary during the spouse's lifetime and any principal distributions during the spouse's lifetime must be to the spouse.

A trust may be used when the grantor wishes to avoid direct ownership of the stock by persons who are not appropriate to manage the investment. The investment responsibility is given to the trustee.

Stock in an S corporation may be held by certain electing small business trusts (ESBT). Any portion of such a trust that consists of S corporation stock will be treated as a separate trust and will be taxed at the highest rate of tax for estate and trusts (currently 39.6 percent on ordinary income and at the 28 percent long-term capital gains rate) with limited deductions and credits and no exemption amount for alternative minimum tax purposes. The ESBT lends itself to the more typical gift or testamentary pattern that employs a single trust with multiple potential beneficiaries, such as the grantor's children and spouse or other relatives. Current distribution of all income is not required. The remainder beneficiaries can be different from the income beneficiaries and can include charities.

The trust can have no beneficiaries other than individuals, estates, and certain charities. Even though a nonresident alien cannot hold S corporation stock outright, nonresident aliens can be income beneficiaries since the income will be taxed to the trust rather than to the beneficiary.

Charitable remainder unitrusts and charitable remainder annuity trusts cannot qualify as electing small business trusts. Code Sec. 1361(e)(1)(B)(iii). All beneficiaries of an electing small business trust must be individuals or estates eligible to be S corporation shareholders. While charitable remainder unitrusts and charitable remainder annuity trusts may provide income to individual beneficiaries for a term of years, they must also provide a remainder interest to a charitable organization.

One Class of Stock

There must not be more than one class of stock. Code Sec. 1361(b)(1)(D). The outstanding shares of the corporation must be identical as to the rights of the holders in the profits and in the assets of the corporation. However, differences in voting rights among shares of common stock are permitted. An instrument that is straight debt is not treated as a second class of stock. A straight debt instrument means a written unconditional promise to pay on demand or on a specified date a sum certain in money so long as the interest rate and payment dates are fixed. They are fixed if they are not contingent on the profits of the corporation, the discretion of the corporation, or other similar factors. However, the fact that the interest rate is dependent upon the prime rate or a similar factor not related to the debtor corporation will not disqualify the instrument from being treated under the safe-harbor rule. In order for the safe harbor to apply, the instrument must not be convertible into stock and must be held by a person eligible to hold S corporation stock. Code Sec. 1361(c)(4) and (5)(B). However, straight debt may nevertheless be treated as stock for other tax purposes. Sen. Rept. No. 640, 97th Cong., 2nd Sess. (1982).

PLANNING POINTER	The use of different classes of voting stock may be an effective tool in structuring management control between different business factions or in shifting ownership for estate planning purposes without relinquishing voting control.

Ineligible Corporations

Financial institutions that are allowed a deduction for bad debts under Code Sec. 585 or 593 and insurance companies subject to tax under Subchapter L do not qualify for the election. U.S. possessions corporations, DISCs, and former DISCs are also ineligible to elect Subchapter S. Code Sec. 1361(b)(2). Subchapter S casualty insurance companies can continue as S corporations by meeting certain requirements. Rev. Rul. 74-437, 1974-2 CB 274.

Prior to 1997, an S corporation could not be a member of an affiliated group. However, new rules permit an S corporation to own any percentage of the stock of a C corporation. These new rules allow S corporations to restructure their business operations by dropping separate business operations into corporate subsidiaries.

Where the parent S corporation owns 100 percent of the stock of the subsidiary corporation and elects to treat the subsidiary as a Qualified Subchapter S Subsidiary (QSSS), the subsidiary can then qualify as a QSSS. The subsidiary must also be a domestic corporation, not an ineligible corporation. Technically, the subsidiary must be a C corporation because a corporation owns all of the subsidiary's stock. A foreign subsidiary cannot qualify as a QSSS. The IRS now refers to a QSSS as a Q Sub.

The QSSS will not be treated as a separate corporation for federal income tax purposes. It will be treated as combined with the parent S corporation. Its assets, liabilities, items of income, deduction, and credit will be treated as belonging to the parent.

¶21,077   **ELECTION**

S corporation status must be elected by all of the shareholders of the corporation. Code Sec. 1362(a)(2). An election made on or before the fifteenth day of the third month of a corporation's tax year is effective beginning with the year when made. Code Sec. 1362(b)(1). For a newly created corporation, the first tax year begins at the earliest occurrence of any of the following events: (1) when the corporation has shareholders, (2) when it acquires assets, or (3) when it begins doing business.

EXAMPLE 21.1

Melba Corporation begins its first taxable year on March 13, 2017. For an election to be effective beginning with the corporation's first tax year, the election must be made within the period beginning after March 12, 2017, and ending before May 28, 2017.

The corporation must meet all the eligibility requirements (including shareholder eligibility requirements) for the pre-election portion of the tax year. All persons who held stock in the corporation at any time during the portion of the year before the election was made must consent to the election. Reg. §1.1362-2(b)(1). However, a person who becomes a shareholder after the corporation is an S corporation does not have to consent to the election. A new shareholder does not have the power to terminate the election unless that shareholder owns more than 50 percent of the stock and elects to terminate the election.

A shareholder's consent to an election must be made either on Form 2553 (Election by a Small Business Corporation) or on a separate statement signed by the shareholder in which the shareholder consents to the election of the corporation. The consent form must contain the name, address, and taxpayer identification number of the corporation and of the shareholder, the number of shares of stock or percentage of ownership owned by the shareholder, and the date (or dates) on which the stock was acquired. The shareholder's consent is binding and may not be withdrawn after a valid election is made by the corporation.

Form **2553** (Rev. December 2013) Department of the Treasury Internal Revenue Service	**Election by a Small Business Corporation** (Under section 1362 of the Internal Revenue Code) ▶ See Parts II and III on page 3. ▶ You can fax this form to the IRS (see separate instructions). ▶ Information about Form 2553 and its separate instructions is at *www.irs.gov/form2553*.	OMB No. 1545-0123

Note. This election to be an S corporation can be accepted only if all the tests are met under *Who May Elect* in the instructions, all shareholders have signed the consent statement, an officer has signed below, and the exact name and address of the corporation (entity) and other required form information have been provided.

Part I	**Election Information**	
Type or Print	Name (see instructions)	**A** Employer identification number
	Number, street, and room or suite no. (If a P.O. box, see instructions.)	**B** Date incorporated
	City or town, state, and ZIP code	**C** State of incorporation

D Check the applicable box(es) if the corporation (entity), after applying for the EIN shown in **A** above, changed its ☐ name or ☐ address

E Election is to be effective for tax year beginning (month, day, year) (see instructions) . . . . . . ▶ _____
Caution. A corporation (entity) making the election for its first tax year in existence will usually enter the beginning date of a short tax year that begins on a date other than January 1.

F Selected tax year:
   (1) ☐ Calendar year
   (2) ☐ Fiscal year ending (month and day) ▶ _____
   (3) ☐ 52-53-week year ending with reference to the month of December
   (4) ☐ 52-53-week year ending with reference to the month of ▶ _____
   If box (2) or (4) is checked, complete Part II.

G If more than 100 shareholders are listed for item J (see page 2), check this box if treating members of a family as one shareholder results in no more than 100 shareholders (see test 2 under *Who May Elect* in the instructions) ▶ ☐

H Name and title of officer or legal representative who the IRS may call for more information | **I** Telephone number of officer or legal representative

---

The election will not become effective until the following tax year if: (1) the eligibility requirements are not met for the entire pre-election portion of the year for which the election is made, (2) consents of all shareholders who had disposed of their stock prior to the making of the election are not obtained, or (3) the election is made after the fifteenth day of the third month of the year. Reg. §1.1362-1(a), (b). This rule prevents any allocation of income or loss to pre-election stockholders who either were ineligible to hold S corporation stock or did not consent to the election.

EXAMPLE 21.2

At the beginning of 2017, the stock of Essex Corporation is held equally by Tom Cox and Mary Hendrix. On February 24, Tom sells his shares to Wilbur Williams. On March 10, Wilbur and Mary make the S election by filing Form 2553. The corporation cannot become an S corporation until January 1, 2018. Although the election was timely filed, Tom did not consent to the election. Had he signed Form 2553, S status would have taken effect as of January 1, 2017.

Where stock is owned, for example, by a husband and wife as community property, or is owned by tenants in common, joint tenants, or tenants by the entirety, each person having a community interest and each tenant in common, joint tenant, and tenant by the entirety must consent to the election. Further, where stock is held by a minor, consent must be made by the minor or guardian. Stock held by a custodian for a minor under the Uniform Transfers to Minors Act is treated as owned by the minor and not by a trust.

The consent of an estate must be made by an executor or administrator of the estate. Where the stock of the corporation is held by an eligible trust, each deemed owner who is considered to be a shareholder must consent to the election. Where stock is held by a trust to which the stock was transferred pursuant to the terms of a will, the estate of the testator that is considered to be the shareholder must consent to the election. Temp. Reg. §18.1362-2(b)(2).

Generally, the IRS will give notification of acceptance of an S corporation election within 60 days after Form 2553 has been filed. Form 1120S (U.S. Income Tax Return for an S Corporation) is not to be filed until notification of acceptance is received.

The IRS has provided procedures whereby companies can obtain relief from the late filing of an S election. Revenue Procedure 2013-30 establishes broader relief provisions than previous procedures. An entity and its shareholders must meet three requirements: (1) on the first day that the entity desired to be an S corporation, it fails to qualify as an S corporation solely because of the failure to file Form 2553 on a timely basis; (2) the entity has reasonable cause for its failure to make the timely S election; and (3) the entity must file the application for relief within prescribed time limits and the shareholders have reported their share of the corporation's income consistent with the S election on all affected returns.

Extension of Time for Filing Consents

An extension of time for filing consents is permitted if there is reasonable cause for the failure to file the consent on time and the interests of the government will not be jeopardized. The extension applies only to shareholders' consents; the S election for the tax year must have been timely filed. New consents must be filed within such extended period of time as may be granted by the Internal Revenue Service by all persons who were shareholders of the corporation at any time during the tax year and by all persons who were shareholders of the corporation within the period beginning after such tax year and ending before the date on which an extension of time is granted. Temp. Reg. §18.1362-2(c).

For example, an extension may be required where the corporation does not yet have shareholders when it is first required to make the election and an extension is needed until shareholders are obtained. See *Q.A. Calhoun,* 74-1 USTC ¶9104, 370 F.Supp. 434 (DC Va. 1973).

While S corporation status is limited to small business corporations, the size is measured not in gross receipts, net income, or number of employees, but in the number of shareholders.

¶21,085   CONTRIBUTIONS TO THE CORPORATION

Section 351 allows contributions to the S corporation to be tax free to the contributing shareholder provided three conditions are met: (1) property is transferred to the corporation, (2) stock is received by the contributing shareholder, and (3) contributing shareholders receive 80 percent control of the corporation.

Just as in the case of a C corporation, there are three exceptions to the nontaxability of Section 351. Where services are provided by an individual for stock in the S corporation, the individual must report ordinary income to the extent of the fair market value of the stock received. For example, if Mary receives stock with a fair market value of $10,000 for services she performed in organizing and setting up the corporation, she would be required to report $10,000 of ordinary income and have a basis in the stock received of $10,000. Stock issued in exchange for services rendered cannot be included in satisfying the control requirement. Code Sec. 351(d).

Although the service-providing shareholder will always be taxed on the receipt of stock for services, Reg. §1.351-1(a)(1)(ii) provides that a contemporaneous transfer of a relatively significant amount of property in addition to services will allow the service-providing shareholder's entire stock interest to be counted for control purposes. Rev. Proc. 77-37, 1977-2 CB 568 requires that the value of the qualifying property be at least 10% of the value of the accompanying services.

Liabilities transferred to a corporation in a Section 351 exchange are not considered boot and thus will not cause gain to be recognized on the transfer. However, if the liabilities exceed the basis of all the assets that a shareholder transfers, income is recognized to the extent of the excess liabilities. For example, if an individual transfers an asset with a $10,000 fair market value, $4,000 basis, and a $5,500 liability attached to the corporation for all of the stock in the corporation, the individual will have to recognize a

$1,500 gain—the excess of the liability over the basis of the asset. This income recognition is necessary to prevent the shareholder from having a negative basis in the stock received.

If tax avoidance or lack of business purpose is present in connection with the assumption of the liabilities by the corporation, income also may need to be recognized. Where an individual borrows against an asset prior to transferring the asset along with the liability to the corporation, income may be recognized. No income would be recognized if the individual used the proceeds of the loan for business purposes, such as purchasing inventory or plant and equipment. However, if the individual withdrew the loan proceeds for personal use prior to transferring the asset and liability to the corporation, the IRS would call for income to be recognized to the extent of the smaller of the loan proceeds or the realized gain from the asset transfer.

The S corporation has a carryover basis in the property received from the shareholder, increased by any gain recognized by the transferor. The shareholder's basis in the stock received is the basis of the property transferred plus any gain recognized on the transfer minus any liability transferred.

¶21,105   TAX YEAR OF THE CORPORATION

The tax year of an S corporation is required to be either a year ending December 31, or any other tax year for which it establishes a business purpose to the satisfaction of the Internal Revenue Service. Code Sec. 1378(b). Partnerships are allowed to utilize a fiscal year where it is the tax year of all the partners owning a majority interest in partnership profits and capital. This exception is not available to S corporations.

An S corporation that elects to use a tax year other than the tax year required under Code Sec. 1378(b) must generally make a "required payment" for any tax year for which such an election is in effect. The required payment is intended to represent the value of the tax deferral that the owners on the S corporation receive through the use of a tax year other than the required tax year. The required payment is due on or before May 15 of the calendar year following the calendar year in which the election year begins. Generally, any required payment is assessed and collected as if it were an employment tax. Neither the S corporation nor the shareholders are entitled to a deduction with respect to a required payment. If an S corporation willfully fails to comply with the required payment rules, the entity's election under Code Sec. 444 is cancelled, effective from the year in which the willful failure occurred.

Business Purpose Exception

An S corporation may adopt a fiscal tax year if it can convince the IRS that a business purpose exists for such a tax year. The intent of an entity to make its tax year coincide with its natural business year constitutes a valid business purpose. Where a business has a nonpeak and a peak period, the natural business year usually ends at, or soon after, the close of the peak period. A business with a steady monthly income does not have a natural business year.

A business purpose generally exists if, in the last two months of the selected tax year, a taxpayer receives at least 25 percent of its gross receipts and has done so for three consecutive 12-month periods. The following factors are ordinarily insufficient to establish a business purpose with respect to a particular fiscal tax year: (1) the use of a particular year for regulatory or financial accounting purposes; (2) the hiring patterns of a particular business; (3) the use of a particular year for administrative purposes, such as the promotion of staff and the compensation or retirement arrangement with staff, partners, or shareholders; and (4) the fact that a particular business involves the use of price lists, model year, or other items that change on an annual basis.

In order to use a fiscal tax year, an S corporation must obtain the IRS's consent. An S corporation that receives permission to use a fiscal year under Rev. Proc. 2002-39 can continue to use such year without seeking approval from the IRS. However, the continuation of a fiscal year granted under Rev. Proc. 2002-39 does not apply to fiscal years granted under the three-month-or-less deferral of income under Sec. 444.

S Corporation Taxation

¶21,147   INTRODUCTION

An S corporation is not subject to the corporate tax, except for a tax on built-in gains, a tax on excessive passive investment income, LIFO recapture tax, and a tax imposed on early disposition of property on which general business credit was claimed by the corporation when it was a C corporation. For any of the four taxes to be imposed on an S corporation, the S corporation must have converted from a C corporation or have merged with a C corporation. Every S corporation must file a return on Form 1120S each tax year even though the corporation may not be subject to tax.

¶21,155   TAX ON BUILT-IN GAINS

A tax is imposed on an S corporation that has "recognized built-in gain" in order to prevent the avoidance of tax through the conversion of a C corporation to an S corporation. The tax is imposed if, for any tax year within the 5-year period (7 years for recognized built-in gains in tax years beginning in 2009 and 2010 and 10 years for tax years before 2009) beginning with the first day of the first tax year for which the S election was effective, the corporation has a recognized built-in gain. This tax does not apply to a corporation that has been an S corporation for all of its tax years.

Maximum Amount of Gain

The maximum amount of built-in gain that can be taken into account for purposes of the built-in gains tax is the amount by which the "net unrealized built-in gain" exceeds the "recognized built-in gain" for prior years beginning in the recognition period. "Net unrealized built-in gain" is the excess of the fair market value of the S corporation's assets when its S election became effective over the aggregate bases of those assets at that time. Generally, "recognized built-in gain" means any gain recognized on the disposition of any asset during the recognition period. However, it does not include gain from the disposition of an asset if the corporation establishes that: (1) the asset was not held by the S corporation when its S election became effective, or (2) the gain is attributable to appreciation that occurred after the S election became effective.

These built-in gains include not only profits from the disposition of capital assets and business-use assets, but also profits realized on the sale of inventory items, collection of accounts receivable with a zero basis because of the cash method of accounting, and other cash-basis accrued income. The completion of a long-term contract performed by a taxpayer using the completed-contract method of accounting is considered a disposition.

In cases where an asset with a built-in gain or loss is exchanged for another asset in a transaction in which the new asset's basis is determined in whole or in part by reference to the basis of the old asset, the new asset is subject to the tax on built-in gains. Specifically, the new asset will be treated as if held on the first day of S corporation status and as having the same built-in gain or loss as the old asset on that day.

Regulations will provide that the inventory method used by the taxpayer for tax purposes (i.e., FIFO, LIFO, etc.) will also be used to identify whether goods disposed of following conversion to S corporation status were held by the corporation at the time of conversion. Thus, a corporation using the LIFO inventory method will not be subject to the built-in gains tax with respect to sales of inventory except to the extent that a LIFO layer in existence prior to the beginning of the first tax year as an S corporation was invaded after the beginning of the first year.

Computation of the Tax

The amount of the tax is computed by applying the highest corporate rate to the net recognized built-in gain. The amount of the net recognized built-in gain taken into account for any tax year cannot exceed the taxable income. Any net recognized built-in gains exceeding taxable income must be carried to the succeeding year and treated as a built-in gain for that year. This carryover continues until 5 years (7 years for recognized built-in gains in tax years beginning in 2009 and 2010 and 10 years before 2009) after the effective date of the S status election. The corporate rate to be applied is the highest corporate tax rate imposed by Code Sec. 11 (currently 35 percent) or the alternative corporate tax rate on capital gains if such a rate is in effect.

Taxable income is computed with the Code Sec. 172 net operating loss (NOL) deduction and without the deductions of Code Secs. 241-250, other than the organizational expense deduction of Code Sec. 248. However, any NOL carryforward or capital loss carryforward arising in a tax year in which the corporation was a C corporation offsets recognized built-in gain to the extent otherwise permitted. No credit except for the general business credit carryforwards and the minimum tax credit from years in which the corporation was a C corporation is allowable in the computation of the tax.

The amount of any tax paid on the recognized built-in gain must be passed on to S corporation shareholders in a pro rata fashion as a loss. The character of the loss is determined by allocating the loss proportionately among the recognized built-in gains giving rise to the tax.

EXAMPLE 21.3	Samson Corporation elects S corporation status at the beginning of 2017. The corporation has an asset with a basis of $40,000 and a fair market value of $85,000 on January 1, 2017. The asset is sold during 2017 for $95,000. The corporation incurs a recognized gain of $55,000, of which $45,000 is subject to the built-in gains tax. Samson Corporation would incur a $15,750 ($45,000 × 35%) built-in gains tax. The shareholders will report $39,250 ($55,000 minus the $15,750 built-in gains tax).

¶21,161　TAX ON LIFO RECAPTURE

Any C corporation using the LIFO method that converts to S corporation status is required to recapture the excess of the FIFO inventory value over its LIFO value as of the close of the last year as a C corporation. Any amount included because of the LIFO adjustment may be reflected in the value of the inventory carried over to the S corporation by making the appropriate adjustment to basis.

The tax attributable to the LIFO inclusion in income is payable in four equal installments. The first installment must be paid on or before the due date of the C corporation's last tax return (without extensions), and the three remaining installments are due on the due dates of the S corporation's tax returns for the three succeeding tax years. If the installments are paid on their respective due dates, no interest will be charged.

EXAMPLE 21.4	Java Corporation, a C corporation, wishes to switch to an S corporation at the beginning of 2018. Java has $20,000 that must be recaptured under the LIFO recapture rules. The tax on the $20,000 will be $6,800. Java must include an additional tax of $1,700 ($6,800 ÷ 4) on its 2017 return, Java's last C corporation income tax return. In addition, Java must pay $1,700 with the filing of its 2018, 2019, and 2020 S corporation tax returns. Java's inventory account is increased by $20,000.

¶21,163　TAX ON PASSIVE INVESTMENT INCOME

A tax is imposed on the S corporation where it has (1) Subchapter C earnings and profits at the close of the tax year and (2) gross receipts for the tax year of which more than 25 percent is passive investment income. The tax is computed by multiplying the excess net passive income by the highest corporate tax rate—currently 35 percent. The only credit allowed against the tax is the credit for special fuels under Code Sec. 34. Code Sec. 1375(a) and (c)(1).

The tax on passive income prevents a holding company with accumulated earnings from electing S corporation status and avoiding the personal holding company and accumulated earnings taxes. Subchapter S imposes a corporate level tax on passive investment income that is essentially designed to counteract the holding company problem without necessarily terminating an S election. An S corporation that has never been a C corporation can enjoy an unlimited amount of passive income with no adverse tax consequences.

"Subchapter C earnings and profits" means earnings and profits of any corporation for any tax year with respect to which an election under Subchapter S was not in effect. Code Sec. 1362(d)(3).

"Excess net passive income" is that portion of net passive income for the tax year multiplied by a fraction comprised of (1) the amount by which the passive investment income for the tax year exceeds 25 percent of the gross receipts for the tax year, divided by (2) the passive investment income for the tax year. The amount of the excess net passive income for any tax year cannot exceed the corporation's taxable income. Code Sec. 1375(b)(1).

Expressed as a formula, excess net passive income (ENPI) for a tax year equals:

$$\text{ENPI} = \text{Net Passive Income} \times \frac{\text{Passive Investment Income} - 25\% \text{ Gross Receipts}}{\text{Passive Investment Income}}$$

"Net passive income" means passive investment income reduced by the allowable deductions directly connected with the production of such income. However, the net operating loss deduction under Code Sec. 172 and the special deductions allowed under Code Secs. 241-250 (e.g., dividends-received deduction, amortization of organizational expenditures) are not allowed. Code Sec. 1375(b)(2). The excess net passive income cannot exceed the corporate taxable income for the year before considering any net operating loss deduction or the special deductions of Code Secs. 241-250.

"Passive investment income" means gross receipts derived from royalties, rents, dividends, interest, and annuities. Interest includes tax-exempt interest. The passive income test is modified to exclude interest on deferred payment sales of property held for sale to customers made by the corporation and income from the conduct of a lending or finance business. Only the net gain from the disposition of capital assets (other than stock and securities) is taken into account in computing gross receipts. Code Sec. 1362(d)(3). This prevents a corporation from "churning" assets as a means of increasing gross receipts.

PLANNING POINTER	It is still possible for the corporation to escape the tax by "churning" Section 1231 assets. The sale of some of the assets used in the business could sufficiently increase gross receipts to avoid the 25 percent threshold test. Investment in rental property producing an operating loss through large depreciation and interest deductions can be used to reduce net passive income. Rental income may be removed from the passive category if the corporation provides significant services to the lessees.

EXAMPLE 21.5	S corporation has gross receipts of $300,000 for the year, of which $100,000 is passive investment income. Expenses directly connected with the production of this passive investment income are $30,000. Thus, S corporation has net passive income of $70,000 ($100,000 of passive investment income less $30,000 in expenses), and the amount by which its passive investment income for the tax year exceeds 25 percent of its gross receipts is $25,000 ($100,000 of passive investment income less $75,000 ($300,000 × 25 percent)). The excess net passive income is $17,500 ($70,000 of net passive income × ($25,000 of passive investment income in excess of 25 percent of gross receipts for the year ÷ $100,000 of passive investment income for the year)). The passive investment income tax is $6,125 ($17,500 × 35%).

Any built-in gain subject to the passive investment income tax is not subject to the S corporation built-in gains tax. Thus, any gain subject to the built-in gains tax must be reduced by that portion of the "excess net passive income" that is attributable on a pro rata basis to the gain. Code Sec. 1375(d)(4). The passive investment income tax also reduces each item of passive income by the amount of extra tax attributable to it, thereby reducing the amount of passive investment income that each shareholder must take into account in computing individual gross income. Code Sec. 1366(f)(3).

TAX BLUNDER

Dally Corporation operated as a C corporation for many years before changing to an S corporation. At the time of the S election, there was a small amount of earnings and profits. During 2017, Dally has a large gain from the sale of stock that it held, causing a passive investment income tax of $12,000. The corporation could have avoided the tax if they had distributed the earnings and profits before the end of 2017.

PLANNING POINTER	Consent dividends may be paid to eliminate accumulated earnings and profits when cash is not available for regular dividends.

Section 1375(d) gives the IRS authority to waive the tax on excess net passive income if the corporation determined in good faith that it had no C corporation earnings and profits at the close of the tax year. Also, the tax may be waived if such earnings and profits are distributed within a reasonable period of time after it is determined that the corporation did have C corporation earnings and profits.

¶21,171   GENERAL BUSINESS CREDIT RECAPTURE

A corporation's S election will not trigger imposition of the tax for early disposition of property for which a general business credit was taken. The election is regarded as a mere change in form and not a disposition of property. However, if the S corporation makes an early disposition of any property for which a credit was taken by the corporation prior to the effective date of its election, the S corporation remains liable for the general business credit recapture. Code Sec. 1371(d)(1) and (2).

The recapture of the general business tax credit claimed in years prior to S corporation status is to be made at the corporate level. An S corporation's accumulated earnings and profits will be reduced by the amount of general business credit recapture tax imposed on the corporation with respect to these credits since the earnings and profits were not previously reduced by the amount of tax savings attributable to the credit. Moreover, the basis of stock in an S corporation is to be adjusted to reflect the change in the basis of corporation property when general business credits are allowed or recaptured, with corresponding adjustments made to the accumulated adjustments account.

EXAMPLE 21.6

Donal Corporation, a C corporation, receives a general business credit on the purchase of an asset. Two years later, Donal Corporation switches to an S corporation. The following year the corporation disposes of the asset. Donal Corporation will be responsible for the recapture of the general business credit. However, if the asset was purchased after the switch to an S corporation, any recapture of the general business credit would be passed through to the shareholders.

¶21,175   ESTIMATED TAX

S corporations are required to make estimated tax payments for tax liability attributable to the built-in gains tax, excessive passive investment income tax, and tax due by reason of general business credit recapture. The corporate estimated tax provisions are generally applicable to S corporations. The required annual estimated tax payment is the lesser of: (1) 100 percent of the tax shown on the return for the tax year or (2) the sum of 100 percent of the tax liability incurred by virtue of the built-in gains tax and tax due because of general business credit recapture, plus 100 percent of the tax due on the passive investment income reported by the S corporation in the preceding year. Code Sec. 6655(g).

An S corporation cannot utilize the exception that allows estimated tax payments to be based on the corporation's prior tax year when computing tax payments attributable to built-in gains and the general business tax credit recapture. The prior year's tax exception is, however, available to all S corporations with respect to the portion of required estimated tax payments attributable to excessive passive income, even if there was no tax attributable to excess passive income in the prior year. In all cases, an S corporation can use the annualized exception.

¶21,185   PENALTIES FOR FAILURE TO FILE

There is a monthly penalty for any failure to timely file an S corporation return or any failure to provide the information required to be shown on such a return, effective or returns required to be filed after December 20, 2007. The penalty, assessed against the S corporation, is $200 times the number of shareholders in the S corporation during any portion of the tax year for which the return was required, for each month (or fraction of a month) during which the failure continues, up to a maximum of 12 months. The penalty is $195 for returns filed before 2017. Code Sec. 6699. The penalty was $89 for tax years before 2009.

An electing S corporation that neglects to file an information return by the due date, including extensions, may be liable for a 5 percent penalty for each month the return has not been filed with a maximum of 25 percent. The penalty is computed based on the net amount due. Moreover, a similar penalty of 1/2 of 1 percent per month may be imposed against a corporation that fails to pay the tax when due up to a maximum of 25 percent. If a corporation can establish that failure to file or pay tax was due to reasonable cause and not to willful neglect, it may be relieved of such penalties.

In addition, a penalty may be imposed on a corporation for failure to furnish a statement (Schedule K-1, Form 1120S, Shareholders' Shares of Income, Credits, Deductions, etc.) as required under Code Sec. 6037(b) unless such failure was due to reasonable cause and not to willful neglect. The amount of the penalty is $260 for each schedule not provided, but the total penalty cannot exceed $3,218,500 for any single year. Rev. Proc. 2016-55.

The fact that a corporation elects to operate as a tax-free S corporation does not relieve it of responsibility for filing other information returns required under the law. For instance, the corporation is still required to file an information return on Form 1099 for "fixed or determinable" gains, profits, or income paid to any person during the calendar year if total annual payments other than dividends exceed $600.

An S corporation that is created as a tax shelter, that is involved in promoting tax shelter activity, or that is a conduit for tax shelter benefits is required to provide additional reporting information on behalf of the corporation and its shareholders under Code Sec. 6111.

Treatment of Income, Deductions, and Credits

¶21,221   CORPORATE TREATMENT

The S corporation's income will be computed under the same rules presently applicable to partnerships under Code Sec. 703, except that the amortization of organization expenditures under Section 248 is an allowable deduction. As in the case of partnerships, deductions generally allowable to individuals are allowed to S corporations. However, the Code provisions governing the computation of income that are applicable only to corporations, such as the dividends-received deduction (Code Sec. 243) or the special rules relating to corporate tax preferences (Code Sec. 291), do not apply to S corporations. Items eligible for separate treatment which could affect any shareholder's liability (such as investment interest) are treated separately. Elections generally are made at the corporate level, except for those elections which the partners of a partnership may make separately. Code Sec. 1363(b) and (c)(1).

Examples of elections to be made at the corporate level include selection or change of an accounting method, inventory valuation, selection of tax year, method of depreciation and claiming general business credits, eligibility for nonrecognition of gain on an involuntary conversion, and election out of the installment sales provisions. The shareholder elections include income from discharge of indebtedness (Code Sec. 108(b)(5) and (d)(4)), the limitation on investment indebtedness (Code Sec. 163(d)), the deduction and recapture of certain mining exploration expenditures (Code Sec. 617), and taxes of foreign countries and possessions of the United States (Code Sec. 901). Code Sec. 1363(c)(2).

Generally, C corporation tax rules apply, except that an S corporation is treated in the same manner as an individual in transactions, such as the treatment of dividends received under Code Sec. 301, where the corporation is a shareholder in a regular corporation. Code Sec. 1371(a). In transactions by an S corporation with respect to its own stock, the S corporation is treated as a regular corporation. However, S corporation rules do not apply where the result is inconsistent with the purpose of the Subchapter S rules that treat the corporation as a pass-through entity.

Property distributed as a dividend to an S corporation is includible in gross income at fair market value. The distribution of appreciated property by an S corporation generally results in gain recognition to the distributing corporation in the same manner as if the property had been sold to the shareholder at its fair market value. This gain will pass through to the shareholders.

EXAMPLE 21.7

A corporation distributes an asset to its sole shareholder. The asset has a fair market value of $250,000 and a basis of $150,000. The corporation reports a gain of $100,000 which is passed through to the shareholder. The shareholder reports no further income upon the distribution unless the distribution exceeds shareholder basis and has a basis in the asset of $250,000.

If the corporation were a regular corporation, the corporation would report a gain of $100,000 on the payment of the dividend. The shareholder would have to report $250,000 of dividend income (assuming adequate earnings and profits).

Certain limitations resembling the partnership rules apply at both the corporate level and the shareholder level. The current expense limitation on certain depreciable business assets applies at both levels. Code Sec. 179(d)(8).

Separately Reported Items

The items that must be reported separately by an S corporation are the same as those that partners are required to take into account under Code Sec. 702(a). Code Sec. 1366(a)(1). These include (but are not limited to):

1. **Capital gains and losses.** Gains or losses from sales or exchanges of capital assets pass through to the shareholders as capital gains or losses.
2. **Section 1231 gains and losses.** The gains and losses on certain property used in a trade or business are passed through separately and aggregated with the shareholder's other Section 1231 gains and losses.
3. **Charitable contributions.** The corporate 10 percent limitation does not apply to the S corporation. As in the case of partnerships, the contributions pass through to the shareholders, at which level they will be subject to the individual limitations on deductibility.
4. **Interest.** Interest received by the S corporation must be separately stated as they comprise portfolio income to the shareholder in determining the investment interest limitation.
5. **Dividends.** Dividends pass through to the shareholders and qualified dividends are subject to the long-term capital gains rate.
6. **Tax-exempt interest.** Tax-exempt interest passes through to the shareholders as such and increases the shareholders' bases in their S corporation stock. Subsequent distributions by a corporation will not result in taxation of the tax-exempt income.
7. **Foreign tax credit.** Foreign taxes paid by the corporation pass through as such to the shareholders, who claim the taxes either as deductions or as credits subject to the applicable limitation. An S corporation is not eligible for the foreign tax credit with respect to taxes paid by a foreign corporation in which the S corporation is a shareholder; therefore, these taxes do not pass through to its shareholders.
8. **Credits.** As with partnerships, items involved in the determination of credits, such as the basis of Section 38 property for purposes of computing the amount of qualified investment eligible for the general business credit, pass through to the S corporation's shareholders.
9. **Depletion.** The rules governing depletion with regard to partnership interest in minerals apply to depletion of properties of an S corporation.
10. **Foreign income and loss.** Domestic losses and foreign losses pass through separately. If a corporation has foreign losses and domestic income, or vice versa, each passes through separately to shareholders without aggregation at the corporate level.
11. **Other items.** The expensing of certain depreciable business assets (Code Sec. 179) and the amortization of reforestation expenditures (Code Sec. 194) apply at both the corporate level and the shareholder level, as in the case of a partnership. Passive gains and losses and tax preferences must also be segregated and reported separately to the shareholders.

The above listing is not intended to be exhaustive. In order to determine the treatment of items, a basic principle must be kept in mind: If the item can affect the computation of a shareholder's tax liability, it must be stated separately by the corporation. Any items not reported separately comprise the S corporation's "nonseparately computed income or loss."

EXAMPLE 21.8

Ada Corporation, an S corporation, has the following tax items for the year:

Gross income	$50,000
Advertising expense	10,000
Wage expense	25,000
Long-term capital gain	5,000
Short-term capital loss	2,000
Charitable contributions	3,000

Any items having special tax significance must be reported separately, with the remaining items combined to arrive at ordinary income. Ada Corporation must report the following to its shareholders:

Ordinary income	$15,000
Long-term capital gain	5,000
Short-term capital loss	2,000
Charitable contributions	3,000

Treatment of Fringe Benefits

The statutory exemptions for fringe benefits applicable to shareholder-employees of regular corporations include the following:

1. The exclusion from income of amounts paid for an accident and health plan (Code Sec. 105(b), (c), and (d))
2. The exclusion from income of amounts paid by an employer to the accident and health plan (Code Sec. 106)
3. The exclusion of the cost of up to $50,000 of group-term insurance on an employee's life (Code Sec. 79)
4. The exclusion from income of the value of meals or lodging furnished for the convenience of the employer (Code Sec. 119)
5. The exclusion from income for benefits under a cafeteria plan (Code Sec. 125)
6. The exclusion from income for qualified transportation benefits (Code Sec. 132(a)(5))

Fringe benefits of any person owning more than 2 percent of the stock of the corporation are treated in the same manner as fringe benefits of a partner in a partnership. Code Sec. 1372(a)(2). Thus, for example, amounts paid for the medical care of a shareholder-employee are to be classified as wages to the employee and includible in the shareholder's W-2. Rev. Rul. 91-26, 1991-1 CB 184. The premiums are excludable for social security and Medicare if the payments are made under a "qualified plan" described in Code Sec. 3121(a). The shareholder is considered a self-employed individual for purposes of the deduction for medical insurance under Code Sec. 162(l)(1). However, similar amounts paid by the corporation on behalf of shareholders owning 2 percent or less of the corporation are deductible as a business expense and tax free to the employee. Any person who owns, on any day during the tax year of the S corporation, more than 2 percent of the outstanding stock of the corporation, or stock possessing more than 2 percent of the total combined voting power of all stock of the corporation, is subject to the fringe benefit limitation. The attribution rules of Code Sec. 318 apply in determining if more than 2 percent of the outstanding stock of the S corporation is owned by an individual. Code Sec. 1372(b).

EXAMPLE 21.9

S corporation has 100 shares of stock outstanding and three shareholder-employees. Mark Peters owns two shares, Nan Olds owns 40 shares, and Opel Raser owns the remaining 58 shares. The corporation pays employee accident and health insurance. In computing its taxable income for the year, S corporation must include any expenditures attributable to the accident and health insurance for shareholder-employees Nan and Opel in their wages. Nan and Opel must include the amounts paid in gross income and may deduct 100 percent for 2017 of the amount included in income as a deduction from gross income. However, the corporation is allowed a business deduction for the accident and health insurance for Mark or any other employees. Mark is allowed to exclude the premiums from gross income.

Certain fringe benefits can be provided tax-free to 2% shareholders. The following fringe benefits are tax-free if they do not discriminate in favor of the owners:

1. Dependent care assistance program (Code Sec. 129)
2. Educational assistance program (Code Sec. 127)
3. Compensation for injury and sickness (Code Sec. 104)
4. Adoption assistance program (Code Sec. 137)
5. Employment achievement award (Code Sec. 74(c))
6. No additional-cost service (Code Sec. 132(a)(1))
7. Qualified employee discount (Code Sec. 132(a)(2))
8. Working condition fringe (Code Sec. 132(a)(3))
9. *De minimis* fringe (Code Sec. 132(a)(4))
10. On-premise athletic facilities (Code Sec. 132)

Treatment of Expenses and Interest Owed to Shareholders

An S corporation is placed on the cash method of accounting for purposes of deducting business expenses and interest owed to a related-party, cash-basis taxpayer, including a shareholder who owns directly or indirectly any Code Sec. 267(e) stock in the corporation. This rule applies only where the recipient is on the cash basis and, therefore, would not apply if the recipient uses the accrual basis or the completed contract method of accounting. By treating the corporation as a cash-basis taxpayer, the corporation will take its deduction in the same year in which the shareholder takes the item into income. The deduction is not lost by the corporation if payment is made after the 2 ½ month period expires, as would be the case under prior operation of Code Sec. 267.

The usual loss disallowance rules of Code Sec. 267(a)(1) apply to transactions between two S corporations or between an S corporation and a partnership, if both entities are more than 50 percent owned by the same person. Also, an S corporation and a regular operation are treated as related if the same individual owns more than 50 percent of the value of the outstanding stock in each corporation.

Corporate Tax Preference Rules

Code Sec. 291, which deals with corporate tax preference items, applies to S corporations if the corporation or its predecessor was a C corporation for any of the three immediately preceding tax years. The purpose of the measure is to prevent C corporations from avoiding the corporate preference rules by making an S corporation election. The corporate tax preference rules, however, do not apply to any corporation that has been an S corporation since its incorporation.

C Corporation Carryovers

Carryovers from years in which the corporation was not an S corporation are not allowed to the corporation while in S corporation status. However, the intervening years count as tax years for purposes of determining the number of years to which a particular item (i.e., deductions, credits, etc.) may be carried forward or back. Code Sec. 1371(a).

EXAMPLE 21.10	C corporation has a $50,000 net operating loss for 2017 after using its carryback provisions. The corporation elects S corporation status at the beginning of 2018. The loss carryforward is not available as an offset against S corporation income and will be lost if the S election is not terminated within 20 years.

TAX BLUNDER

The S corporation has ordinary income of $40,000 for 2018. The shareholders would have to report the $40,000 on their personal returns. If the corporation had not elected S status, the C corporation would have been able to offset the $40,000 against the net operating loss carryforward and incur no tax liability.

¶21,281 SHAREHOLDER TREATMENT OF INCOME ITEMS

As with the partners of a partnership, each shareholder of an S corporation takes into account separately his or her pro rata share of each separately stated item of income, deduction, credit, etc., of the corporation and his or her share of "nonseparately computed income or loss." These rules parallel the partnership rules under Code Sec. 702.

EXAMPLE 21.11	A calendar-year S corporation has a net long-term capital gain of $75,000 and three equal shareholders. Assuming no changes in ownership during the year, each shareholder takes into account $25,000 of long-term capital gain.

Each shareholder's share of the items is taken into account in the shareholder's tax year in which the corporation's year ends. In the case of the death of a shareholder, the shareholder's portion of S corporation items is taken into account on the shareholder's final income tax return. Items from the portion of the corporation's tax year after the shareholder's death are taken into account by the estate or other person acquiring the stock.

EXAMPLE 21.12	A shareholder owing 20 percent of an S corporation dies at the midpoint of the tax year. The estate of the shareholder holds the stock for the remainder of the year. The corporation has $100,000 of taxable income for the year. The shareholder reports income of $10,000 ($100,000 × 20% × 1/2) for one-half year of ownership and the estate reports income of $10,000 for its one-half year of ownership.

A shareholder's pro rata share of an S corporation item is generally made on a per-share, per-day basis. Code Sec. 1377(a)(1). Allocations are made with respect to stock ownership, regardless of whether such shares are voting or nonvoting. Shareholders acquiring stock count the day following the day of acquisition and shareholders disposing stock count the day of disposition. In years in which there is no change in shareholders or in the relative interests of those shareholders, a shareholder's pro rata share of an item is simply the annual amount of that item multiplied by the shareholder's percentage of total stock outstanding.

EXAMPLE 21.13

One of the shareholders holding a one-third interest in an S corporation sells all of his stock on March 14. The selling shareholder's share of a $75,000 net income is $5,000 ($75,000 × 1/3 × 73/365). The purchasing shareholder's share is $20,000 ($75,000 × 1/3 × 292/365).

If a shareholder terminates an interest in a corporation during the tax year, the corporation, with the consent of all of the affected shareholders, may elect to allocate according to its permanent records (including work papers). Code Sec. 1377(a)(2).

EXAMPLE 21.14

An S corporation has $50,000 net income for the first half of the year and $200,000 for the second half of the year. A shareholder terminates his 30 percent interest in the corporation at the end of the first half of the year. Only $15,000 ($50,000 × 30%) is allocated to the terminating shareholder using the permanent records method, rather than $37,500 ($250,000 × 30% × 1/2) using the per-share, per-day method.

Character of Items

A "conduit" rule for determining the character of items realized by the corporation and included in the shareholder's pro rata share is the same as the partnership rule. Code Sec. 702(b). The character of any item included in a shareholder's pro rata share is determined as if such item were realized directly from the source from which it was realized by the corporation or incurred in the same manner as incurred by the corporation. Thus, tax-exempt interest passes through as tax-exempt interest to the shareholder. However, discharged debt excluded from an S corporation's income is expressly not treated as an item of income by a shareholder. Consequently, the shareholder's basis is not increased. Also, the "gross income" determinations made by a shareholder parallel those made using the partnership rule (Code Sec. 702(c)). The shareholder's gross income includes the shareholder's pro rata share of the gross income of the corporation. Code Sec. 1366(b) and (c). Earnings of S corporations which are required to be included in each shareholder's gross income are not self-employment income to the shareholders. Rev. Rul. 59-221, 1959-1 CB 225.

Where an S corporation has a tax imposed on built-in gains, the amount of the gain is passed through to the shareholder. Code Sec. 1366(f)(2). The tax imposed is treated as a loss sustained by the S corporation and the character of the loss is determined by allocating the loss proportionately among the recognized built-in gains.

The tax on passive income also reduces the amount of the items of passive investment income that passes through to shareholders. Allocation of the reduction is made on the basis of the ratio of each item of passive investment income to total passive investment income. Code Sec. 1366(f)(3).

If an individual who is a member of the family of one or more shareholders of an S corporation renders services to the corporation or furnishes capital to the corporation without receiving reasonable compensation, the IRS may make such adjustments in the items taken into account by such individual and shareholders as are necessary to reflect the value of the services or capital. Code Sec. 1366(e). This rule is designed to prevent a high tax bracket family member from working for little or no salary so that undistributed income may be allocated to other, low tax bracket members of the family. Both the amount of compensation and the timing of the compensation can be so adjusted.

EXAMPLE 21.15 Both parents and child each own one-third of an S corporation. Both parents devote full time to the business, with the child working infrequently. Neither parent receives a salary for the year in which the net income is $120,000. The IRS can require that reasonable compensation be paid to the parents to prevent the full one-third of the $120,000 net income from being taxed to the child.

A shareholder's allowable pro rata share of the corporation's loss is limited to the sum of the shareholder's adjusted basis in the stock of the corporation and the shareholder's adjusted basis in any indebtedness of the corporation owed to the shareholder. Disallowed losses may be carried forward or allowed in any subsequent year in which the shareholder has adequate basis in such stock or debt. Code Sec. 1366(d)(1) and (2). A shareholder's allowable loss may be limited by the passive activity rules discussed below.

Debt at the corporate level does not add to a shareholder's basis; thus, larger corporate losses arising from the leverage provided by corporate debt and allocated to a shareholder (but exceeding the shareholder's investment in stock plus any loans made by the shareholder to the corporation) may not be used by the shareholder to offset other sources of income.

EXAMPLE 21.16 John Irving has a stock basis of $8,000 in an S corporation. He has loaned the corporation $3,000 and has personally guaranteed another $5,000 bank loan made to the corporation. John's share of the corporation's operating loss for the year is $12,500. John may deduct only $11,000 of the loss on his individual return ($8,000 basis in the stock plus $3,000 loan to the corporation). The unused loss of $1,500 ($12,500 − $11,000) may be carried forward until John has an adequate basis against which the loss may be deducted.

PLANNING POINTER It may be possible to increase a shareholder's basis against which corporate losses can be deducted by substituting shareholder notes for the debt of the corporation to a third-party creditor. In Rev. Rul. 71-288, investors were allowed to increase the basis against which corporate losses could be deducted by converting corporation debt to its third-party creditors to a debt of the shareholders.

For purposes of computing the amount of foreign losses that must be recaptured under the foreign tax credit rules (Code Sec. 904(f)), the making or termination of an S corporation election is treated as the disposition of a business. Accordingly, when an S election is made, the corporation is treated as having disposed of its foreign property and will include in income the amount of any foreign losses not previously recaptured. Likewise, when an S election is terminated, the shareholders are treated as if the corporation disposed of its foreign assets, and the shareholders will include in income the amount of any foreign losses of the corporation previously passed through to them and not previously recaptured.

Subsequent to a termination of an S corporation election, any unused losses and deductions are allowed if the shareholder's basis in the stock (but not debt) of the corporation is restored by the later of the following dates:

1. One year after the effective date of the termination, or the due date for the last S corporation return, whichever is later.
2. 120 days after a determination that the S corporation election had terminated for a previous year. (A determination is defined as a court decision that becomes final, a closing agreement, or an agreement between the corporation and the IRS that the corporation failed to qualify.) Code Sec. 1377(b).

EXAMPLE 21.17 A calendar-year S corporation revokes its election effective January 1, 2018. If there is sufficient basis in the shareholder's stock on December 31, 2018, the shareholder may treat a share of any unused loss or deduction of the S corporation as having been incurred on December 31, 2017, and may deduct it for the tax year that includes that date.

The post-termination rules apply only to stock basis and not to debt. The planners should consider converting shareholder debt into stock during the post-termination transition period if a higher basis is needed to absorb any unused losses.

Any corporate items occurring during the year must be taken into account in determining basis of stock before computing a loss on worthless stock.

¶21,285 ACCUMULATED ADJUSTMENTS ACCOUNT

The accumulated adjustments account (AAA) consists of post-1982 accumulated gross income less deductible expenses and prior distributions allocable to the account. Any distributions from AAA are tax-free to a shareholder and reduce shareholder basis. The AAA is not increased for tax-exempt income or decreased for expenses related to tax-exempt income and federal taxes attributable to a C corporation. The AAA is decreased proportionately with the percentage of stock redeemed under Code Sec. 302(a) or 303(a). Code Sec. 1368(e)(1).

The other adjustments account (OAA) is a balance sheet account in the capital section that is increased for tax-exempt income or decreased for nondeductible expenditures not properly chargeable to the AAA. It represents another form of AAA in that any distributions from OAA are accounted for in the same manner as distributions from AAA, and thus are tax free.

Previously taxed income (PTI) is income that was earned and taxed to an S corporation shareholder before 1983. Any distributions are treated as a reduction of basis and are nontaxable to the shareholder. PTI is specific to the shareholder and does not carryover to the new shareholder when stock is transferred.

PLANNING POINTER
Tax-exempt income is ordinarily not a good investment for an S corporation with accumulated earnings and profits. The exempt income cannot be distributed tax free to shareholders until after all accumulated earnings and profits are paid out.

Treatment of Corporate Distributions

¶21,339 TAX CONSEQUENCES

The tax consequences to shareholders receiving distributions from an S corporation are generally designed to be comparable to those of partners under Subchapter K. However, several important differences exist.

1. Distributions of property from an S corporation are reported by shareholders at fair market value, whereas "adjusted basis" is used to measure partnership distributions.
2. Gain is recognized by an S corporation on a distribution of appreciated property in the same manner as if the property had been sold to the shareholder at its fair market value. Code Sec. 1363(d). Like other corporate gain, it passes through to the shareholders. The distribution will trigger depreciation and general business credit recapture.

   Without this rule, assets could be distributed tax free (except for recapture in certain instances) and subsequently sold without income recognition to the selling shareholder because of the stepped-up fair market value basis.

EXAMPLE 21.18
Saundra Corporation, an S corporation for its entire existence, distributes some property held as an investment to its sole shareholder. The property was purchased several years ago for $15,000 and has a fair market value of $40,000. Saundra Corporation recognizes a long-term capital gain of $25,000 upon the distribution.

3. Partners are permitted to utilize their respective shares of partnership debt in the computation of basis. Shareholders of S corporations are prohibited from including corporate borrowing in stock basis. The determination of basis has important consequences in determining the character of distributions, in establishing the amount of potential losses and other deductions that may be currently reported, and

in computing the amount for which an S shareholder is considered to be at risk under Code Sec. 465. However, any loans made by the shareholder to the corporation are included in basis computation.

4. Distributions must be made on a per-share basis. If disproportionate distributions or special allocations are made, there is a risk of creating a second class of stock which would cause loss of S corporation status.

¶21,341   DISTRIBUTIONS WITHOUT ACCUMULATED EARNINGS AND PROFITS

There is a two-tier system in effect for S corporations without accumulated earnings and profits. First, the distribution is tax free to the extent of adjusted basis of each shareholder's stock. Second, gain from a sale or exchange is reported to the extent the distribution exceeds adjusted basis of each shareholder's stock.

The exact nature of a corporate distribution may not be known until the end of the S corporation's tax year. Distributions made by an S corporation during a tax year are taken into account before applying the loss limitation for the year. Thus, distributions during a year reduce the adjusted basis for purposes of determining the allowable loss for the year, but the loss for the year does not reduce the adjusted basis for purposes of determining the tax status of the distributions made during that year. The computation of basis is determined as follows:

	Beginning of Year Basis
+	Income and Gains
	Recomputed Basis
–	Distributions
	Recomputed Basis
–	Deductions and Losses
	Ending Basis

EXAMPLE 21.19

Max Tassler is the sole shareholder whose adjusted basis at the beginning of the year is $1,000. S corporation distributes $700 to Max. S corporation has a capital gain for the year of $200 and an operating loss for the year of $900.

$1,000	Basis, Beginning of Year
+200	Add Gain
$1,200	Recomputed Basis
–700	Distribution
$500	Recomputed Basis
–500	Loss Deductions, Limited
$0	Ending Basis
$400	Loss Carried Forward

Before 1997, the beginning basis was adjusted for both the gains and losses for the year before determining the status of the distribution. The Small Business Job Protection Act of 1996 allows broader tax-free treatment of a distribution in loss years. Under prior law, the shareholder would have reported a $400 gain on the distribution.

¶21,343   DISTRIBUTIONS WITH ACCUMULATED EARNINGS AND PROFITS

S corporations with accumulated earnings and profits (AE&P) have a four-tier system for determining status of distributions: (1) tax free to the extent of the accumulated adjustment account (AAA), (2) dividend income to the extent of any AE&P, (3) tax free to the extent of OAA, and (4) gain to the extent the distribution exceeds basis. In addition, the placement of distributions in computing basis is determined by the relationship of gains and losses for the year. S corporations can acquire AE&P from earnings and profits prior to becoming an S corporation or from a C corporation acquisition.

EXAMPLE 21.20

Ernie Blake's stock basis as the sole shareholder in an S corporation is $1,000. The S corporation has $500 of AE&P and $200 of AAA. The corporation has a gain of $300 and a loss of $100. The corporation distributes $600.

$200	Beginning AAA		$500	Beginning AE&P
+300	Gain		−100	Distribution
$500	AAA		$400	Ending AE&P
−500	Distribution			
$0	AAA			
−100	Loss			
$ (100)	Ending AAA			
$1,000	Beginning Stock Basis			
+300	Gain			
−500	Distribution			
−100	Loss			
$700	Ending Basis			

For S corporations having accumulated earnings and profits, net negative adjustments (i.e., the excess of losses and deductions over income) for that year are disregarded in determining the amount in the accumulated adjustments account for purposes of determining the tax treatment of distributions made during the year.

EXAMPLE 21.21

Ernie Blake's stock basis as the sole shareholder in an S corporation is $1,000. The S corporation has $500 of AE&P and $200 of AAA. The corporation has an ordinary loss of $900 and a capital gain of $300. The corporation distributes $600.

$200	Beginning AAA		$500	Beginning AE&P
−200	Distribution		−400	Distribution
$0	AAA		$100	Ending AE&P
+300	Gain			
$300	AAA			
−900	Loss			
$ (600)	Ending AAA			
$1,000	Beginning Stock Basis			
−200	AAA Distribution			
−600	Ending AAA			
$200	Ending Basis			

Ernie's basis can also be computed by taking the $1,000 beginning basis plus the $300 capital gain, resulting in a $1,300 adjusted basis, minus the $200 distribution from AAA, reducing the adjusted basis to $1,100, minus the $900 ordinary loss, reducing the adjusted basis to $200.

An S corporation can elect to treat distributions as coming first from AE&P and then from the AAA. If such an election is made, the corporation is not required to distribute its entire AAA at the end of the year before it pays a dividend. All the affected shareholders must consent to the election. Code Sec. 1368(e)(3).

PLANNING POINTER

Corporations with potential excessive passive investment income can take advantage of the rule to avoid the special tax under Code Sec. 1375 by disposing of AE&P prior to the end of the year with a dividend distribution.

A potential trap is created for S corporations investing in tax-exempt bonds. Since the tax-exempt income does not increase the AAA, an attempt to withdraw this income could result in a taxable distribution from AE&P if there is no AAA from other sources. This could result even if the withdrawal is only in the amount of tax-exempt interest from the current year.

Distributions are free only to the extent of stock basis. For example, if a shareholder has a stock basis of $15,000 and a debt basis of $10,000 and receives a $20,000 distribution, the shareholder would have to report a $5,000 gain. The distribution cannot offset the debt basis.

¶21,351   BASIS ADJUSTMENT

Both taxable and nontaxable income and deductible and nondeductible expenses serve, respectively, to increase and decrease a shareholder's basis in the stock of the S corporation. These rules generally are analogous to those provided for partnerships under Code Sec. 705. A shareholder's stock basis in an S corporation is increased for the following: (1) separately stated items of income, (2) nonseparately computed income, and (3) the excess of the deduction for depletion over the basis of property subject to depletion. Stock basis is decreased by: (1) nontaxable distributions of capital, (2) separately stated items of loss and deduction, (3) nonseparately computed loss, (4) nondeductible expenses of the corporation that are not chargeable to capital, and (5) the amount of the shareholder's deduction for depletion with respect to oil and gas wells. If there are net deductions, the basis of stock is decreased before the basis of debt. Stock basis cannot be reduced below zero. Any excess net deductions are applied to reduce the shareholder's basis in any indebtedness of the S corporation to the shareholders, thus reducing the amount of the shareholder's basis in the debt, which will in turn reduce the amount of the shareholder's short-term capital loss deduction for the worthless debt. The basis in this indebtedness cannot be reduced below zero. Any nontaxable distributions to capital do not reduce the basis of indebtedness.

Net income items generally increase stock basis. However, if the basis of a shareholder's debt has previously been reduced because of net deductions, the debt basis is restored before there is any increase in the shareholder's stock basis.

EXAMPLE 21.22

A sole shareholder has a $7,000 stock basis and a $2,000 basis in a loan that he made to the S corporation. Ordinary income for the year was $8,200. The corporation incurred a capital loss of $2,300 and received $2,000 of tax-exempt interest. Cash distributions for the year were $15,000.

$7,000	Beginning stock basis	$2,000	Beginning loan basis
+8,200	Ordinary income		
+2,000	Tax-exempt interest		
$17,200	Recomputed basis		
−15,000	Distribution		
$2,200	Recomputed basis		
−2,200	Loss	−100	Loss
$0	Year-end basis in stock	$1,900	Year-end basis in debt

If in the following year there was $5,000 of undistributed ordinary income, the loan basis would be increased by $100 first.

If the corporation's stock becomes worthless in any tax year of the corporation or shareholder, the corporate items for that year are taken into account by the shareholders and the adjustments to the stock's basis are made before the stock's worthlessness is taken into account under Code Sec. 165(g). Code Sec. 1367(a) and (b)(2) and (3).

No increase in basis may be made for any pass-through item of corporate gross income required to be included in a shareholder's gross income unless that increase is reported on the shareholder's income tax return. An exception allows the shareholder to increase basis for tax-exempt items of income. Thus, a shareholder may not report less than his or her share of the S corporation's income and then, after the assessment period has expired, increase the basis of the stock to reflect an amount that should have been, but was not, included in income. The shareholder must increase or decrease basis for later adjustments of his or her share of a pass-through item of income, deduction, or loss.

Termination of Election

¶21,401 METHODS

There are three ways that an S corporation's status can be terminated:

1. Revocation of the election by the corporation
2. Failure to satisfy the continuing requirements of a small business corporation
3. Receipt of excessive passive investment income under certain circumstances

¶21,405 REVOCATION OF ELECTION

An S corporation election may be revoked by the corporation for any tax year of the corporation. A revocation can be made only with the consent of shareholders holding more than one-half of the number of outstanding shares of stock (including non-voting stock) of the corporation. A revocation filed up to and including the fifteenth day of the third month of the tax year is effective for the entire tax year, unless a prospective effective date is specified. The period during which a retroactive revocation can be filed thus corresponds to the time period in which a retroactive election may be made. Revocations made after the fifteenth day of the third month of the tax year are effective on the first day of the following tax year unless the revocation states some other prospective date, in which case it is effective as of the specified date. Code Sec. 1362(d)(1). Retroactive revocations are not allowed if made after the first two and one-half months of the tax year.

EXAMPLE 21.23	A calendar-year S corporation has three shareholders—Alvin Bren, who owns 55 shares; Broward McCoy, who owns 30 shares; and Clay Thor, who owns 15 shares. Alvin, acting alone, can cause the corporation to revoke its election. Either of the other two shareholders would need to act with Alvin to revoke the election. A revocation stating no date, made on or before March 15, 2017, is effective as of January 1, 2017. A revocation made after March 15, 2017, and stating no date is effective January 1, 2018. If the revocation is made on June 7, 2017, and specifies a revocation date of June 30, 2017, the S corporation election ceases on June 30, 2017.

Revocations that designate a prospective effective date result in the splitting of the year into short S corporation and C corporation tax years, with the tax consequences discussed below in connection with the tax treatment of terminations.

A person becoming a shareholder of an S corporation after the initial election does not have the power to terminate the election by affirmatively refusing to consent to the election (unless that person owns more than one-half of the stock). The shareholder is bound by the initial election.

¶21,413 CEASING TO BE A SMALL BUSINESS CORPORATION

Generally, a specific event during the tax year that causes a corporation to fail to meet the definition of a small business corporation results in a termination of the election as of the date on which the event occurred. Code Sec. 1362(d)(2). The events causing disqualification include: (1) exceeding the maximum allowable number of shareholders; (2) transfer of stock to a corporation, partnership, ineligible trust, or nonresident alien; and (3) creation of a class of stock other than the voting and non-voting common stock allowed.

PLANNING POINTER	Shareholders of S corporations should enter into agreements restricting the transferability of their shares, so as to prevent an inadvertent termination of the S election against the wishes of the majority of the shareholders.

¶21,421 EXCESSIVE PASSIVE INVESTMENT INCOME

For S corporations with accumulated earnings and profits from years in which the corporation was a C corporation, excessive passive investment income can also cause a termination of the election. If an S corporation with these earnings and profits has passive investment income that exceeds 25 percent of gross receipts for three consecutive tax years, the election is terminated beginning with the tax year following the third consecutive tax year of excess passive income. Code Sec. 1362(d)(3).

EXAMPLE 21.24

Billings Corporation, a calendar-year S corporation, has passive income in excess of 25 percent of its gross receipts for 2015, 2016, and 2017. Billings has accumulated earnings and profits from years prior to an S election. The S election is terminated as of January 1, 2018.

The terms "Subchapter C earnings and profits," "excessive net passive income," "net passive income," "passive investment income," and "gross receipts" have the same respective meanings used in discussing the tax on passive investment income.

C corporations switching to S corporation status may have major problems because of the difficulty in accurately computing accumulated earnings and profits. The statute establishes no minimum rule for accumulated earnings and profits. This fact, coupled with no statute of limitations in determining the existence of accumulated earnings and profits, could lead to a termination of S corporation status.

It is important to recognize that a corporation may have a disqualifying year for termination purposes even though it pays no tax on its excess passive investment income. No tax is imposed on the corporation where the losses from current operations exceed the passive income. If the passive income exceeds 25 percent of gross income for the year, that year counts in meeting the three-consecutive-year termination rule.

PLANNING POINTER

To avoid the termination, a corporation could distribute any accumulated earnings and profits prior to the end of the third consecutive S corporation year in which more than 25 percent of its gross receipts are in the form of passive investment income. Difficulty in determining the presence or the amount of accumulated earnings and profits, however, hinders this safety valve procedure.

¶21,429   TAX TREATMENT OF TERMINATIONS

The day before the day on which the terminating event occurs is treated as the last day of a short S corporation tax year, and the day on which the terminating event occurs is treated as the first day of a short C corporation tax year. There is no requirement that the books of a corporation be closed as of the termination date. Instead, the corporation allocates the income or loss for the entire year (i.e., both short years) on a prorated basis.

EXAMPLE 21.25

A nonresident alien purchases stock in a calendar-year S corporation on August 21, 2017. The S corporation tax year ends on August 20, 2017, and the C corporation tax year begins on August 21, 2017.

The corporation can elect, with the consent of all persons who were shareholders at any time during the S termination year and all persons who are shareholders on the first day of the C short year, to report the taxable income or loss on each return (S corporation and C corporation) on the basis of income or loss shown on the corporation's permanent records (including work papers). Under this method, items are attributed to the short S corporation and C corporation years according to the time they were incurred or realized, as reflected in such records. Code Sec. 1362(e)(1)-(3). An S corporation is *required* to use its accounting records to allocate income and deductions if there was a sale of 50 percent or more of the S corporation's stock during the termination year.

The short S corporation and C corporation tax years are treated as one year for purposes of carrying over previous C corporation losses. The income allocated to the C corporation tax year is subject to annualization for purposes of applying the corporate rate brackets. The return for the short S corporation year is due on the same date as the return for the short C corporation year. Code Sec. 1362(e)(5) and (6).

EXAMPLE 21.26

From Example 21.25, the C corporation has a short tax year consisting of 133 days and must annualize its taxable income. The tax returns for the S corporation is due on March 15, 2018 and the C corporation is due on April 15, 2018.

The choice between using the permanent records and the pro rata allocation can have a dramatic impact if there are shareholders who have terminated their interests during the year. The annualization requirement applicable to the C corporation short tax year can compound the impact of the allocation decision.

EXAMPLE 21.27

An S corporation reports its income on a calendar-year basis. On May 27, 2017, a corporation purchases stock in the S corporation, thereby terminating the S corporation's status. For the year ended December 31, 2017, the corporation's accounting records show income of $200,000, deductions of $140,000, and tax credits of $6,000. Through May 26, 2017 the corporation's records show that the corporation has earned $65,000 in income, has $47,000 in deductions, and is eligible for $2,500 in tax credits.

If the corporation does not make an election to use its own records in determining the amount of income attributable to each tax year, then it must report 146/365, or two-fifths, of its income, deductions, and tax credits for 2017 on the return for the S corporation short year, ending May 26, 2017. The C corporation would report income of $120,000 ($200,000 × 219/365), deductions of $84,000 ($180,000 × 219/365), and tax credits of $3,600 ($6,000 × 219/365). The C corporation's taxable income is $60,000 (($120,000 – $84,000) × 365/219 for annualizing). The tax for the C corporation on the annualized income is $10,000 ($50,000 × 15% + $10,000 × 25%). The tax owed by the C corporation for the short year is $2,400 ($10,000 × 219/365 – $3,600 tax credits ($6,000 × 219/365)).

If the corporation makes a valid election to use its records in determining income for the two short tax years, the S corporation must report $65,000 in income, $47,000 of deductions, and $2,500 of tax credits for the S corporation short year ending May 26, 2017. The C corporation must report income of $135,000 ($200,000 – $65,000), deductions of $93,000 ($140,000 – $47,000), and tax credits of $2,500 ($5,000 – $2,500). The C corporation's annualized income is $70,000 (($135,000 – $93,000) × 365/219). The tax for the C corporation on the annualized income is $12,500 ($50,000 × 15% + $20,000 × 25%). The tax owed by the C corporation for the short year is $5,000 ($12,500 × 219/365 – $2,500 tax credits).

The tax returns for the S corporation short year ending on May 26, 2017 is due on March 15, 2018, and the C corporation short year ending on December 31, 2017, is due on or before April 15, 2018.

Where the election is terminated because of the excessive passive investment income rule, there is no split between an S corporation short year and a C corporation short year since the termination is not effective until the beginning of the next tax year after the disqualification.

These termination rules deny a corporation the option of waiting until near the end of its tax year, when the corporation's profits or losses may be easier to estimate, to determine whether the corporation and its shareholders are better off taxed as a C corporation or as an S corporation for the entire tax year.

Section 338 provides that a purchasing corporation may elect to treat the acquisition of stock of a target corporation as a purchase of the target corporation's assets. This essentially means that, if a corporation makes a qualified purchase of the stock of an S corporation and makes an election under Code Sec. 338, all of the recapture income resulting from the election will be reported on the purchasing corporation's subchapter C return. As a result, the selling shareholders will not take this recapture income into account on their individual returns, saving shareholders who sell 80 percent or more of an S corporation's stock to another corporation from paying tax resulting from the recapture of depreciation or other tax benefits taken by the corporation when they were owners. This would occur if the buyer elected under Code Sec. 338 to step up the acquired assets' book value to the price paid for the stock of the corporation. This result is consistent with that which would ensue if a C corporation acquired the stock of another C corporation. In that case, any recapture income of the target C corporation is not included in any consolidated return of the acquiring corporation. Instead, recapture items of the target corporation normally are associated with the final return of the target corporation as selling corporation for the period ending on the date of acquisition.

The rule that allows pro rata allocations of income and losses to S and C short tax years caused by termination of an S corporation election does not apply to an S termination year if there is a sale or exchange of 50 percent or more of the corporation's stock during the termination year.

¶21,437   INADVERTENT TERMINATIONS

If the Internal Revenue Service determines that an S corporation's election is inadvertently terminated, the Service can waive the effect of the terminating event for any period, provided the corporation timely corrects the event and the corporation and the shareholders agree to be treated as if the election had been in effect for such period. Code Sec. 1362(f).

For example, a corporation determined in good faith that it had no earnings and profits. It is later determined on audit that its election terminated by reason of violating the passive income test for three consecutive years because the corporation in fact did have accumulated earnings and profits. If the shareholders were to agree to treat the earnings as distributed and include the dividends in income, it may be appropriate to waive the terminating events, so that the election is treated as never terminated. Likewise, it may be appropriate to waive the terminating event when the one class of stock requirement was inadvertently breached, but no tax avoidance resulted.

Instead of treating the corporation as having never terminated its election throughout the period of the inadvertent termination, the IRS may treat the corporation as having terminated its election only for the period when it was ineligible to be an S corporation, even though it did not re-elect S corporation status.

TAX BLUNDER

Allen, an owner of an S corporation, gave some of his shares to a trust that he set up to benefit his children. Since most trusts are not permitted to be qualified owners of an S corporation, the S status is terminated. However, if the transfer to the trust is inadvertent and the mistake is corrected as soon as it is discovered, the IRS may allow the company to retain its S status. Private Letter Ruling 8701006, September 30, 1986.

¶21,445   RE-ELECTION AFTER TERMINATION

If an election is terminated, a new election cannot be made for five tax years without the consent of the Internal Revenue Service. Code Sec. 1362(g).

¶21,453   POST-TERMINATION DISTRIBUTIONS

What happens to the income that was previously taxed to shareholders when the S corporation loses its status? The corporation has the opportunity for a limited period of time to unfreeze that previously taxed income. Specifically, any cash distributions by the corporation with respect to its stock during the post-termination transition period are applied against and reduce stock basis to the extent of the accumulated adjustments account. Code Sec. 1371(e). If the AAA is not exhausted by the end of the post-termination transition period, it becomes part of accumulated earnings and profits. Any distributions thereafter are taxed under the usual C corporation rules. The grace period applies only to cash distributions. Non-cash distributions are taxed under the usual C corporation rules. The definition of "post-termination transition period" is the same as that given at ¶21,281.

EXAMPLE 21.28	Bleyer Corporation decides to terminate its S status at the end of 2017. At that time, the corporation has $15,000 of AAA. The corporation may make up to $15,000 in cash distributions before the end of 2018 and have the distributions apply against AAA. These distributions are nontaxable to the shareholders and reduce investment basis. If less than $15,000 is distributed during 2018, the remaining AAA balance becomes part of accumulated earnings and profits and results in taxable dividends upon distributions to the shareholders.

Operational Rules

¶21,501   CASH METHOD OF ACCOUNTING

A significant advantage of an S corporation over a C corporation is that the S corporation is eligible to use the cash method of accounting. C corporations with gross receipts of more than $5 million are prohibited from using the cash method of accounting.

¶21,505   TAX ADMINISTRATION PROVISIONS

The tax treatment of items of S corporation income, loss, deductions, and credits generally is determined at the corporate level in a unified proceeding rather than in separate proceedings with shareholders. Shareholders are given notice of any administrative or judicial proceeding at which the tax treatment such items will be determined. Further, each shareholder is given the opportunity to participate in these proceedings. Shareholders are required to file returns consistent with the corporate return or to notify the Internal Revenue Service of any inconsistency. Code Secs. 6241 and 6242.

¶21,575   TAX PLANNING

The S corporation may be an advantageous tool where an enterprise is expected to incur losses during the earliest stages of its activities. The losses can be passed through to the shareholders to the extent of their bases. Where the corporation begins accumulating taxable profits, the conversion to a regular corporation could prove to be of further advantage if the income is taxed to the corporation at a lower rate than it would be taxed to the individual owners.

An S corporation sometimes can be used effectively to shift income from high to low tax bracket taxpayers. This must occur by transfers at the shareholder level. For example, family member shareholders in a high tax bracket can effectively shift the income from the high tax bracket to relatively lower tax bracket taxpayers by transferring stock to their children.

A stock transfer made to effect a shift of income must be a bona fide transfer by gift, sale, or other disposition. The court will ignore the transfer and tax all the income to the donor if the donor retains control over the stock and uses the distributions paid on the stock as if they belong to the donor.

While a primary method of shifting S corporation income to lower tax bracket taxpayers involves a shifting of equity, it may be possible to shift income of the S corporation by capitalizing with both debt and equity. The objective would be to shift income, through deductible interest payments, to lower tax bracket taxpayers, with higher tax bracket taxpayers retaining potential appreciation. However, the S corporation runs the risk of reclassification of the debt as equity, with possible termination of Subchapter S status.

The S corporation may be a replacement for the limited partnership in those circumstances where the economic results will be essentially the same when conducting the business or investment through either form of ownership. S corporation form of ownership would provide full limited liability that is not available to the general partner in a partnership. Greater control can be achieved through the use of non-voting stock than may be possible with the limited partnership. Centralization of management, continuity of life, and free transferability of interests issues would no longer create potential association problems, resulting possibly in the partnership being taxed as a regular corporation.

SUMMARY

- Certain requirements must be met for a corporation to qualify as an S corporation. These requirements must also be met in order to continue as an S corporation.

- In order for contributions to an S corporation to qualify as tax-free exchanges for stock, the same requirements of Section 351 must be met that apply to C corporations.

- Generally, the S corporation tax year is limited to a calendar year except when permission is received to adopt a fiscal year based on business purpose.

- The S corporation is not subject to the corporate income tax. However, S corporations with accumulated earnings and profits may be subject to certain other taxes based on income.

- The shareholders of S corporations are treated as partners and the corporation as a partnership for purposes of taxing the income, deducting the losses, and allocating other tax items attributable to the corporation.

- All items are allocated to the shareholders on a per-share, per-day basis. A partnership, however, may allocate those items by agreement among the partners, provided the special allocations have substantial economic effect.

- An important tax advantage that an S corporation has over a regular corporation is that only one tax is imposed on its earnings, and that tax is imposed at the shareholder level. Regular corporations are subject to a double tax—once at the corporate level, and again at the shareholder level when the after-tax corporate earnings are distributed to the shareholders.

- Generally, dispositions from S corporations are tax-free returns of basis. Distributions in excess of the accumulated adjustments account and basis may be taxable as dividend income or capital gain.

QUESTIONS

1. What is the official name given to corporations qualifying under Subchapter S of the Internal Revenue Code?

2. What are the eligibility requirements that a corporation must meet in order to qualify under Subchapter S?

3. What is a domestic corporation?

4. Is a corporation incorporated in Great Britain eligible for S corporation status?

5. An S corporation is formed by 100 shareholders, including a husband and wife holding stock jointly. They divorce, with each taking title to one-half of the jointly held stock. Will the corporation still qualify as an S corporation?

6. What shareholders will prevent a corporation from qualifying as an S corporation?

7. What requirements must be met in regard to the stock in an S corporation? What differences are allowed?

8. What is the definition of "straight debt" under Subchapter S, and what is its importance to an S corporation?

9. Which corporations are specifically excluded from S corporation status?

10. Can a corporation make a retroactive election under Subchapter S?

11. Under what circumstances can a new shareholder terminate an S corporation election?

12. May a corporation receive an extension of the 2 1/2-month period for a retroactive S corporation election?

13. What limits are placed on the selection of a tax year of an S corporation? How do these limits differ from those applicable to C corporations and partnerships?

14. George has a service business and wishes to create an S corporation with a June 30 fiscal year. What problems might George encounter in his fiscal-year selection?

15. Is an S corporation with a financial statement fiscal year ending on July 31 allowed the same fiscal year for tax purposes?

16. How do partnership tax years differ from those available to S corporations?

17. When does a business purpose exist for selecting a non-calendar tax year for an S corporation?

18. Under what circumstances may an S corporation switch to a tax year ending on December 31?

19. When may an S corporation be subject to the built-in gains tax?

20. When the built-in gains tax is imposed on an S corporation, how is the tax passed through to the shareholders?

21. What taxes may be imposed on an S corporation?

22. What conditions must be met for an S corporation to be subject to a tax on passive investment income?

23. What is the only credit available as a reduction in the tax on built-in gain and the tax on excess net passive income for an S corporation?

24. Distinguish between "net passive income" and "passive investment income" in the computation of the tax on excess net passive income of an S corporation.

25. An S corporation may be subject to both the tax on built-in gains and the tax on excess passive income. Which tax is imposed first, and what effect does the imposition have on the other tax?

26. Durrabusiness is organized as a regular C corporation in 1986. At the beginning of the present year, Durrabusiness elects to be an S corporation. Will the election cause a recapture of the general business investment credit taken on any property purchased while a C corporation?

27. If an S corporation makes an early disposition of general business credit property, who is responsible for the recapture?

28. Is an S corporation allowed the dividends-received deduction available to regular corporations?

29. In computing taxable income of an S corporation, which elections are made at the corporate level and which are made at the shareholder level?

30. Describe the treatment of a dividend distribution of appreciated property by an S corporation.

31. An S corporation is solely owned by a shareholder. During the year, the corporation receives $4,000 in tax-exempt interest. What effect does this tax-exempt interest have on the taxable income of the S corporation and the basis of the stock of the sole shareholder?

32. Differentiate the treatment of fringe benefits of a corporation, partnership, and S corporation.

33. What is the special treatment of S corporation expenses owed to shareholders? How does this treatment differ from that of a C corporation?

34. A C corporation has an unused net operating loss carryover at the end of 2017. The corporation elects S corporation status at the beginning of 2018. What happens to the unused net operating loss carryover?

35. In an S corporation, how are items of income, deductions, and credits divided among the shareholders?

36. An S corporation has both voting and non-voting stock. What effect does this differentiation in voting rights have on S corporation eligibility and on shareholder pro rata share of corporate tax items?

37. Where a shareholder terminates his or her interest during the tax year, a pro rata allocation of shareholder items can be made according to the corporation's permanent records. How may this allocation differ from the per-share, per-day allocation?

38. How may debt of the corporation affect a shareholder's basis in an S corporation?

39. From what sources can an S corporation receive accumulated earnings and profits?

40. Under what circumstances might an S corporation choose to distribute accumulated earnings and profits before distributing from the accumulated adjustments account?

41. How may an S corporation revoke its election?

42. What is the latest date in the calendar year in which an S corporation can file for a revocation of S election status and still have it effective as of the beginning of the year?

43. How can passive investment income cause an S corporation to lose its status?

44. When an S corporation has its status terminated during the year, what is the effect on the S corporation tax year and the tax year of the resulting C corporation?

45. Describe the short tax year computation necessary when an S corporation's status is terminated because of excessive passive investment income.

46. What is an "inadvertent termination" of an S corporation?

47. A corporation terminates its status as an S corporation. Describe the requirements for re-electing S corporation status.

48. What kinds of distributions are available to reduce the accumulated adjustments account after a termination of an S corporation election?

49. What is "previously taxed income" of an S corporation?

50. Why is the S corporation preferred over regular corporation status in the early years of operation?

PROBLEMS

51. Damion Corporation begins its first tax year on June 23, 2017. What is the latest date that Damion may apply for S corporation status to qualify as of the beginning of operations?

52. Alpha Corporation began business at the beginning of the year. On February 15, George sold his stock to Danny. Alpha files for S corporation status on March 10, but George refuses to consent to the election. Will S corporation status be granted?

53. Several individuals form Lang Corporation on May 1, 2017. The corporation begins acquiring assets on June 1, 2017, and begins business on August 1, 2017. What is the latest date that Lang can file Form 2553 requesting S corporation status?

54. Gamma Corporation, an S corporation, has a fiscal year ending March 31. It is required to switch to a calendar-year tax year. How many months of income would a calendar-year taxpayer be required to report in the year of change?

55. What is the built-in gains tax on an S corporation, assuming the exceptions do not apply and the corporation has taxable income of $100,000, including a built-in gain of $60,000?

56. Doom Corporation changed from a C corporation to an S corporation in 2014. For 2017, the corporation has built-in gain of $40,000 and taxable income of $30,000. Determine the built-in gains tax imposed on the corporation.

57. What is the passive investment income tax on an S corporation that has gross receipts of $200,000, passive investment income of $80,000, and expenses of $10,000 directly connected to the production of the passive income?

58. Ziad Corporation, an S corporation, distributes land held as an investment to its sole shareholder. The land was purchased for $17,000 and has a fair market value of $28,000 on the date of distribution. What are the tax implications of this distribution?

59. Donald owns 39 percent of the shares of an S corporation. The corporation pays $450 for a group-term life insurance policy. How is this payment reported by the S corporation and Donald?

60. Delta Corporation, an S corporation, has $30,000 of taxable income before charitable contributions. The corporation has $5,000 in charitable contributions for the year. What is Delta's charitable contribution deduction?

61. An S corporation is on the accrual basis and the sole shareholder is on the cash basis. For the pay period ending December 27, 2017, the shareholder earns a salary of $400. He is paid on January 3, 2018. What is the amount allowable as a deduction for 2017?

62. S corporation has $90,000 of taxable income for the year and three equal shareholders. One of the shareholders dies on March 14. His estate continues to hold the stock for the remainder of the year. Determine the amounts includible on the last return of the decedent-shareholder and on the estate's income tax return.

63. A shareholder purchases 30 percent of the stock of an S corporation two-thirds of the way through the year for $20,000. The S corporation incurs an operating loss of $300,000 for the year. What is the amount that the shareholder may deduct on his personal income tax return, assuming the at-risk and passive activity rules do not apply?

64. Germaine, the sole shareholder in Nomad Corporation, has a basis in his stock of $18,000 at the beginning of the year. The corporation has taxable income of $9,000 for the year. In addition, the corporation has a short-term capital loss of $1,200 and tax-exempt income of $800. What is Germaine's basis in his stock at the end of the year?

65. Malcolm is the sole shareholder in an S corporation. At the beginning of the year, his basis in this stock is $7,000. For the year, the corporation incurs a $4,500 loss. By the end of the year, the corporation's stock is worthless. What is the amount of loss from the worthless stock that Malcolm is allowed to take on his return?

66. Alpha Corporation, a calendar-year S corporation, has no accumulated earnings and profits at the end of the year. An individual shareholder receives a cash distribution of $10,000 during the year. How will this distribution be recognized, assuming the shareholder has an $8,200 basis in his stock?

67. Delta Corporation, a calendar-year S corporation, has an accumulated adjustments account of $8,000. It also has accumulated earnings and profits from pre-1983 years of $12,000. The sole shareholder receives a $27,000 cash distribution from the corporation. How will this distribution be treated if the shareholder's basis in the stock is $12,200?

68. An S corporation has an accumulated adjustments account balance of $50,000 at the beginning of the year and accumulated earnings and profits of $20,000. The corporation earns $40,000 for the year. The corporation makes a distribution of $120,000. What would the sole shareholder's stock basis have to be at the beginning of the year to avoid any capital gain reporting?

69. An S corporation's only transaction for the year was the receipt of $10,000 in tax-exempt interest. How would a $6,000 distribution be taxed to the sole shareholder if the S corporation has an accumulated adjustments account of a negative $6,500 at the beginning of the year?

70. Some stock in a calendar-year S corporation is sold to a nonresident alien on February 13, 2017. On what date is the corporation's status as an S corporation terminated?

71. Beta Corporation terminates its S election at the end of 2017. At that time, the corporation has an accumulated adjustments account of $2,500. How would a distribution made during 2018 qualify as nontaxable?

72. How is a taxpayer able to remove income previously taxed from an S corporation that has terminated its status without incurring any additional tax?

73. Which of the following will not prevent a corporation from qualifying for the special tax rules under Subchapter S?
    a. The corporation has more than 100 shareholders.
    b. A nonresident alien owns shares in the corporation.
    c. The corporation has both common and preferred stock.
    d. An individual retirement account owns shares in the corporation.
    e. All the shareholders are individuals or decedent estates.

74. A shareholder purchased 20 percent of the stock of an S corporation three-quarters of the way through the year for $10,000. The S corporation incurred a net operating loss of $320,000. What is the amount the shareholder may deduct on his personal income tax return, assuming the at-risk and passive activity rules do not apply?
    a. A loss of $64,000
    b. A loss of $16,000
    c. A loss of $10,000
    d. A loss of $2,000
    e. None of the above

75. An S corporation has an accumulated adjustments account of $30,000 at the beginning of the year and accumulated earnings and profits of $10,000. The corporation earns $20,000 for the year. Melvin, a 30 percent owner who paid $8,000 for his stock, receives $17,000 from the corporation. What is the amount of dividend income he must report?
    a. $10,000
    b. $2,000
    c. $3,000
    d. $0
    e. None of the above

76. John owns stock in an S corporation. John's share of the corporation's loss for the year is $5,000. His adjusted basis in the corporation stock is $1,000. In addition, John has a loan outstanding to the corporation in the amount of $2,000. What amount, if any, is John entitled to deduct with respect to the loss, assuming he meets the at-risk and passive activity requirements?
    a. $5,000
    b. $3,000
    c. $2,000
    d. $1,000
    e. None of the above

77. Acme Corporation, a calendar year S corporation, has $100,000 of Accumulated Earnings and Profits. Larry, the sole shareholder, has adjusted basis of $80,000 in stock basis with a $20,000 in Accumulated Adjustments Account. Determine the tax aspects if a $50,000 distribution is made to Larry.

78. From the previous problem determine the remaining balance in the Accumulated Earnings and Profits and the Accumulated Adjustments Account.

79. **Comprehensive Problem.** An S corporation has the following information:

Sales	$100,000
Dividend income	1,500
Tax-exempt interest	2,500
Long-term capital gain	4,000
Short-term capital gain	1,800
Cost of goods sold	50,000
Advertising expense	3,000
Charitable contributions	1,000
Interest expense	2,000
Salary expense	25,000
Other operating expenses	8,000

Compute the S corporation's taxable income for the year.

80. **Comprehensive Problem.** Aubrey Corporation changes from a regular C corporation in 2016 to an S corporation as of the beginning of 2017. For 2017, the corporation has $40,000 of built-in gain and $45,000 in accounting income. Determine any corporate tax that may be imposed on Aubrey Corporation, and the amount to be reported by the sole shareholder.

81. **Research Problem.** A C corporation acquired a machine for $100,000 and placed it in service on August 15, 2012. The corporation elected S corporation status at the beginning of 2016. On February 13, 2017, the property was sold for $40,000, payable in four yearly installments of $10,000 plus interest. What is the amount of ordinary income to be reported from the sale?

82. **Research Problem.** An S corporation's election terminated because a shareholder transferred stock to a trust not qualifying as an eligible shareholder. Is it possible for the corporation to retain its S corporation status through the "inadvertent termination" procedures? See Letter Ruling 8523097, March 15, 1985.

Chapter

22

Federal Estate Tax, Federal Gift Tax, and Generation-Skipping Transfer Tax

OBJECTIVES

After completing Chapter 22, you should be able to:

1. Recognize legal terms used in connection with wills, trusts, and estates, as well as partial interests in property, such as life estates, remainders, and reversions.
2. Understand the elements in the estate tax formula—gross estate, allowable deductions, adjusted taxable gifts, and available tax credits.
3. Determine the tax aspects of transferred property, in particular inclusion of the property in the gross estate due to the grantor's retention of an interest, such as a life estate, a reversion, or a power to revoke.
4. Discuss the special tax aspects of jointly held property, life insurance, annuities, and gifts within three years of death.
5. Understand the valuation of assets at both the date of death and the alternate valuation date.
6. Calculate the taxation of involuntary deductions, such as funeral and administration expenses and debts, and deductions under testator's control, notably the marital and charitable deductions.
7. Determine the interplay between the gift and estate tax, the two being two sides of the same coin.
8. Describe the nature of the gift tax, the gift tax formula, and transactions subject to the gift tax.
9. Identify present-interest gifts, the marital and charitable deductions, and the applicable credit amount.
10. Explain the generation-skipping transfer tax, how and when it applies, and its relationship to gift and estate taxes.

OVERVIEW

In this chapter, estate, gift, and generation-skipping transfer taxes are surveyed. All three taxes may be viewed as aspects of one comprehensive excise tax on gratuitous transfers of property by individuals to anyone, be it during life or at death. In fact, all three taxes are computed using the same multipurpose tax table.

The estate tax is a wealth transfer tax, a tax on the transfer of property at death, not on the property itself. The estate tax base equals the gross estate, consisting of all property in which the decedent had an interest, less debts and expenses and marital and charitable bequests plus taxable lifetime gifts made after 1976. For 2017, up to $5.49 million is tax free; the rest is subject to tax at rates up to 40 percent. A tax credit is allowed for gift taxes paid and for state and foreign estate taxes. The gift tax discussed in this chapter is but one part of the same overall unified wealth transfer tax system.

Special, unique rules determine the inclusion in the gross estate of life insurance, annuities, jointly held properties, and property subject to powers of appointment. These concepts are largely unrelated to the income tax treatment and require special study. Valuation problems and income tax basis aspects of estates are also discussed in this chapter.

The gross estate may include properties previously transferred in which the decedent retained an interest or power, such as a life income interest, a reversion, or a power to revoke or appoint, as well as properties passing by operation of law, such as jointly held property and life insurance payable to a named beneficiary. A comprehensive list of legal property terms is provided to increase the understanding of estate administration and the law of property.

Gross gifts generally include all gratuitous transfers. Taxable gifts are computed after exclusions and deductions, notably the marital and charitable deductions.

The applicable credit amount may defer any tax until death, but gift taxes are payable when the tax on cumulative lifetime gifts exceeds it. Cumulative taxable gifts are included in the estate tax base, with a credit for gift taxes paid. The applicable credit amount is available to the estate since its only effect during life is to defer the actual payment of gift taxes until death, within limits.

The generation-skipping transfer tax is levied on individuals with a power or an interest in a generation-skipping trust and is a toll charge on skipping a generation.

Impact of Economic Growth and Tax Relief Reconciliation Act of 2001, Tax Relief Act of 2010, and American Taxpayer Relief Act of 2012

The 2001 Act made extensive changes to the estate and gift tax rules. However, the most dramatic alteration is the repeal of estate and generation-skipping transfer (GST) taxes, but this change was effective in 2010. The 2010 Tax Relief Act reinstates the estate and generation-skipping taxes for 2011. On the other hand, most changes, including lower tax rates, increased exemptions, and the replacement of the state death tax credit with a deduction are effective for earlier years. A summary of the major changes incorporating the **2010 Act**, and the **2012 Act** is shown in Table 1 below.

Table 1. SUMMARY OF MAJOR CHANGES MADE BY THE ECONOMIC GROWTH AND TAX RELIEF RECONCILIATION ACT OF 2001, THE TAX RELIEF ACT OF 2010, AND AMERICAN TAXPAYER RELIEF ACT OF 2012 AFFECTING ESTATE, GST, AND GIFT TAXES					
Calendar Year	Estate Tax Exemption	GST Tax Exemption	Gift Tax Exemption	Highest Tax Rates	State Death Tax Credit Limitation
2001	$675,000	$1,060,000	$675,000	55%	Unlimited
2002	$1 million	$1,100,000	$1 million	50%	75%
2003	$1 million	$1,120,000	$1 million	49%	50%
2004	$1.5 million	$1.5 million	$1 million	48%	25%
2005	$1.5 million	$1.5 million	$1 million	47%	N/A (Credit repealed; deduction allowed)
2006	$2 million	$2 million	$1 million	46%	Deduction only
2007	$2 million	$2 million	$1 million	45%	Deduction only
2008	$2 million	$2 million	$1 million	45%	Deduction only
2009	$3.5 million	$3.5 million	$1 million	45%	Deduction only
2010	Repealed carryover basis	Repealed carryover basis	$1 million	Top individual rate under the Act	Deduction only
2011	Reinstated [35%] rate and $5 million	Reinstated [35%] rate and $5 million	$5 million	35%	Deduction only
2012	$5.12 million	$5.12 million	$5.12 million	35%	Deduction only
2013	$5.25 million	$5.25 million	$5.25 million	40%	Deduction only
2014	$5.34 million	$5.34 million	$5.34 million	40%	Deduction only
2015	$5.43 million	$5.43 million	$5.43 million	40%	Deduction only
2016	$5.45 million	$5.45 million	$5.45 million	40%	Deduction only
2017	$5.49 million	$5.49 million	$5.49 million	40%	Deduction only

Assessment of the 2010 Tax Relief Act

ESTATE TAXES

The law provided for a maximum tax rate of 35% and an exemption of $5 million for 2011. Also, this exemption is adjusted for inflation beginning in 2012 at $5.12 million.

In 2010, carryover basis was required to be used with a limited increase in basis of $1.3 million coupled with a basis increase of $3 million to a surviving spouse. However, the **Act** gives estates of decedents dying after December 31, 2009 and before January 1, 2011 the option to elect to apply the 2011 rules and receive a stepped-up basis.

The 2010 Tax Relief Act provides for "portability" between spouses of the unused estate tax exemption amount. Specially, portability would be available to the estate of decedents dying after December 31, 2010 and before 2013.

Example: Sam Williams dies in 2012 with a taxable estate of $4.12 million. An election is made on Sam's estate tax return for Sam's wife, Bertha, to use Sam's unused applicable exemption of $1 million; as a result, if Bertha were to die in 2017, her available exemption is $6.49 million.

GENERATION SKIPPING TAX

The generation skipping tax is reinstated at the maximum estate tax rate of 35% and an exemption of $5 million beginning in 2011 and $5.49 million in 2017.

GIFT TAXES

For gifts made after December 31, 2009 and before January 1, 2011, the gift tax is computed using a rate schedule having a top rate of 35% and an applicable exemption of $1 million. For gift made after December 31, 2010, the gift tax is reunified with the estate tax for a top tax rate of 35% and an applicable exemption of $5 million in 2011 and $5.49 million in 2017.

ASSESSMENT OF AMERICAN TAXPAYER RELIEF ACT OF 2012

The American Taxpayer Relief Act permanently provides for a maximum federal estate, gift, and GST tax rate of 40 percent with an annually inflation-adjusted $5 million exclusion for estates, gifts, and GST transfers after December 31, 2012. As a result, in 2017, the exclusion is $5,490,000.

Also, the **American Taxpayer Relief Act** makes permanent **portability** between spouses. Consider the following illustration under the new law.

Example: Sam Williams dies in 2017 with a taxable estate of $4.49 million. An election is made on Sam's estate tax return for Sam's wife, Bertha, to utilize Sam's unused exemption of $1 million; accordingly, Bertha receives a total exemption of $6.49 million.

The new unified rate schedule is reproduced below in Table 2.

Table 2. Unified Tax Rate Schedule 2013 under American Taxpayer Relief Act of 2012			
(A)	**(B)**	**(C)**	**(D)**
Amount subject to tax equal to or more than-	**Amount subject to tax less than-**	**Tax on amount in column (A)**	**Rate of tax on excess over amount in column (A) Percent**
.....	$10,000	.....	18
$10,000	20,000	$1,800	20
20,000	40,000	3,800	22
40,000	60,000	8,200	24
60,000	80,000	13,000	26
80,000	100,000	18,200	28
100,000	150,000	28,800	30
150,000	250,000	38,800	32
250,000	500,000	70,800	34
500,000	750,000	155,800	37
750,000	1,000,000	248,300	39
1,000,000		345,800	40

Legal Terms Common To Estates and Trusts

Administrator. Similar to an executor. The manager of an estate of a person who dies intestate or where the named executor fails to act as executor.

Bequest. A disposition of personal property by will; a legacy.

Conservator. A guardian; a protector; a preserver. The term conservator is usually used to designate the guardian of an incompetent person.

Devise. A disposition of land or real estate by will.

Devisee. The person to whom land or other real property is devised or given by will.

Donor. One who makes a gift. One who creates a trust.

Estate Tax. A tax levied on the *transfer* of property from a decedent.

Executor. A person appointed by a will to carry out the testator's direction and to dispose of property according to the will. The one who manages an estate. (Female=executrix).

Grantor. The person making a grant. One who creates a trust.

Guardian. One who has the care and management of the person (guardian of the person) or of the estate (guardian of the estate) or both, or of an individual during minority or incompetency.

Guardian ad litem. A guardian (usually an attorney) appointed by the court to protect and defend a minor's or incompetent's interest in the estate.

Heir. One who would receive the decedent's estate under the laws of descent and distribution where the decedent did not leave a will.

Inheritance tax. A tax levied on the receipt of property from a decedent.

Insurance trust. An agreement between the insured and a trustee whereby the proceeds of the life insurance will be payable directly to the trustee, who will hold the proceeds for investment and distribution according to the trust agreement.

Insured. The person who is insured under the life insurance policy in question.

Inter vivos trust. A trust created during the lifetime of the person setting up the trust. A testamentary trust is one set up under the will of the decedent.

Intestate. One not having a will; a person who dies without a will is said to die intestate.

Intestate laws. Statutes ("laws of intestate succession") that provide descent of estates of persons who die intestate (without a will).

Joint tenancy. Where property is held in the names of two or more persons with the title passing from the first joint tenant to die to the other joint tenant (or joint tenants) upon death.

Legacy. A disposition of personal property by will.

Legatee. The recipient of personal property by will.

Per capita. This term is used frequently in the area of the descent and distribution of a decedent's property. In effect, it means that the property should be divided equally among a group designated by the trust instrument or the will. In other words, if the decedent left two surviving children and a third child who predeceased the decedent but left two children (grandchildren of the decedent) and if the per capita method is applied, each person would receive 25 percent.

Per stirpes. This term is used frequently in the area of the descent and distribution of a decedent's property. It denotes that method of dividing an estate where a class or group of distributees takes the share to which their deceased representative would have been entitled had the deceased lived. In other words, they take according to their right of representing such deceased ancestor, and not as so many individuals. For example: If a decedent passed away leaving two surviving and one child who predeceased the decedent but left two children (the decedent's grandchildren), the two grandchildren would take the share of their deceased representative, namely, their parent. Therefore, the two grandchildren would share their parent's 1/3 and each would receive 1/6 of the total estate. The two surviving children of the deceased would each receive 1/3.

Power of appointment. A power or authority conferred by a trust or will upon another person to select or nominate the person or persons who are to receive and enjoy the property of the estate or trust or the income therefrom at a specific time.

Probate. A local law process for admitting the decedent's will, if any, and distributing the decedent's property pursuant to it or according to the laws governing the intestate's assets.

Remainderman. One who is entitled to the remainder of an estate after a particular life estate, which has been carved out of the overall estate, has expired.

Residuary clause. That provision in a will that disposes of that which remains after satisfying all debts, administration expenses, legacies, and devises.

Residuary estate. That portion of the estate that remains after the payment of debts, expenses of administration, legacies and devises. It consists of that part of the estate that has not been legally disposed of by the will prior to carrying out the residuary clause of said will.

Settlor. One who creates a trust.

Share on renunciation. When a surviving spouse renounces the will of a spouse, the surviving spouse is usually entitled to a one-third interest in all personal and real property if the decedent left a descendant. If the decedent did not leave a descendant, the surviving spouse is usually entitled to one-half of real and personal property in the estate (net of debts).

Surviving spouse's award (widow's award). The special allowance (usually money) given to the surviving spouse to cover the cost of support during the administration of the estate, which is usually limited to nine months.

Tenancy by the entirety. Generally speaking, this is a joint tenancy between husband and wife. A tenancy by the entirety cannot be terminated except by the joint action of the husband and wife during their lives. In the case of a joint tenancy, however, it may be terminated by either tenant merely by conveying the interest to another party.

Tenancy in common. Title is held by two or more persons, each owning a fractional interest in the undivided property. Upon the death of one tenant in common, the interest does not pass to the surviving tenant in common but becomes part of the probate estate and is distributed according to the deceased tenant's will.

Testamentary trust. A trust that is set up under the will of the decedent. Conversely, an inter vivos trust is one set up during the lifetime of the person setting up the trust.

Testamentary trustee. One who is appointed trustee to carry out a trust created by a will.

Testate. One having a will; a person who dies with a will is said to die testate.

Testator. One who makes or has made a will; one who dies leaving a will. (Female=testatrix).

Totten trust. A trust created by the deposit of a person's own money in his or her own name as trustee for another person. This is considered a revocable trust at the will of the trustee until the depositor dies or otherwise completes the gift during lifetime.

Trust. A fiduciary relationship with respect to property whereby the property is held by one party (called trustee) for the benefit of another party (called beneficiary). A trust is usually set up and governed by a written document.

Trust estate. Usually refers to the corpus or property of the trust.

Trustee. That person who is responsible for administering a trust agreement according to its terms. This party holds legal title to all the property in the trust for the benefit of the beneficiaries.

Computation and Payment of Estate Tax

¶ 22,001   ## ESTATE TAX COMPUTATION—SUMMARY

Here is a capsule version of the federal estate tax return filed on Form 706 (United States Estate (and Generation-Skipping Transfer) Tax Return):

Step 1.	Compile the *gross estate*, consisting of all property in which the decedent had an interest.
Step 2.	Subtract debts, funeral, and administration expenses. (The result is the *adjusted gross estate*.)
Step 3.	Subtract property passing to the surviving spouse (*the marital deduction*) and charitable transfers.
Step 4.	The result is the *taxable estate*.
Step 5.	Add *adjusted taxable gifts* (gifts, less exclusions and deductions) made after 1976.
Step 6.	The result is the estate tax base.
Step 7.	Find the *tentative estate tax* from the tax table. Code Sec. 2001. (See Table in the Appendix.)
Step 8.	Subtract gift taxes payable on gifts includible in the estate tax base.
Step 9.	Subtract the *applicable credit amount*.
Step 10.	If a tax is still payable, subtract other possible credits, such as the state tax credit, the credit for prior transfers, and the foreign tax credit.
Step 11.	The tax payable, if any, is due with the estate tax return.

For a graphic description of the estate tax elements, see Table 3.

Table 3. ESTATE TAX COMPUTATION

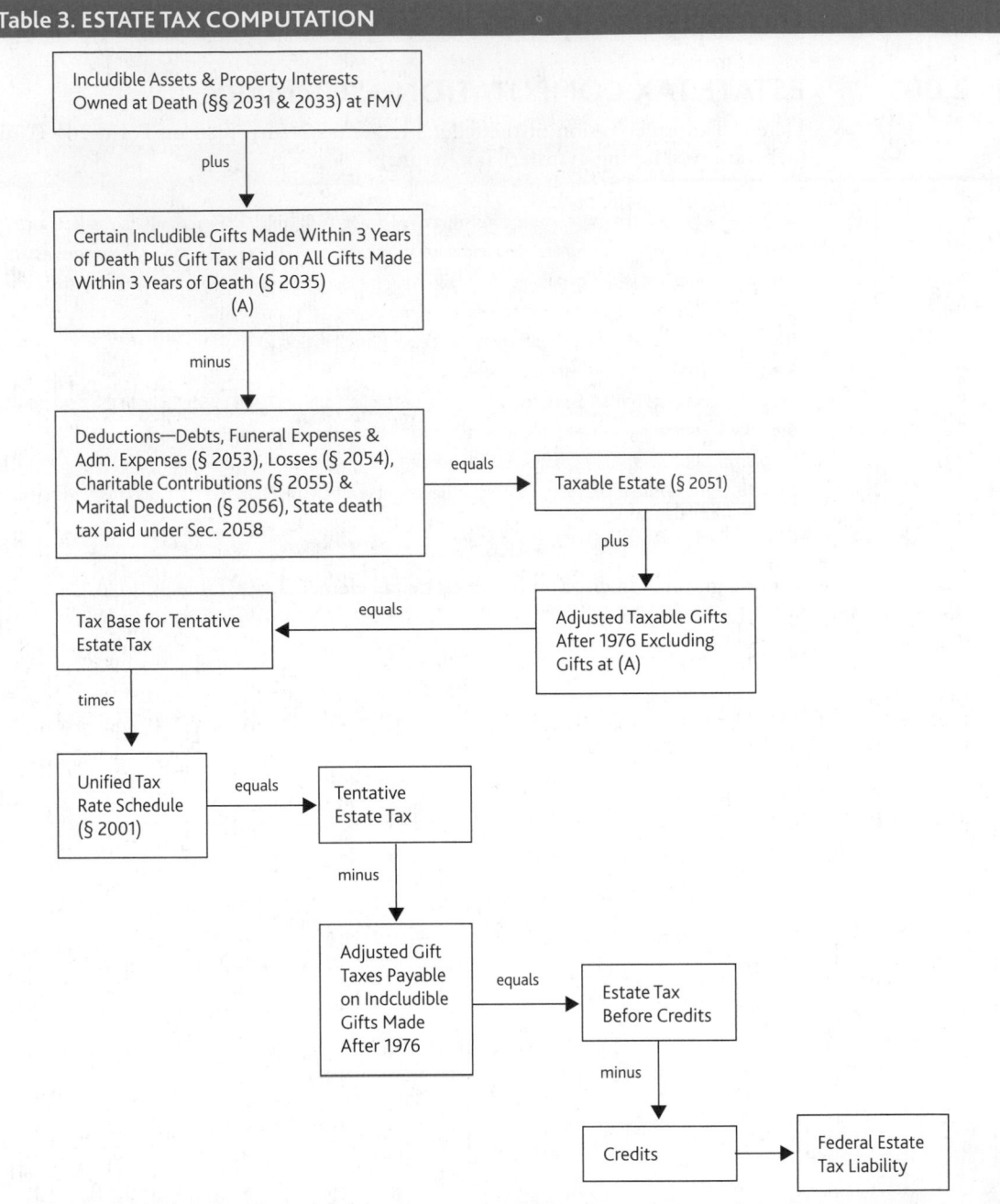

¶22,009   APPLICABLE CREDIT AMOUNT

An applicable credit amount is allowed against estate and gift taxes. Code Secs. 2010 and 2505. The applicable credit amount is a credit that is equal to the amount the government wishes to exclude from gift and estate taxation. This credit was first introduced as the "unified credit" in the Tax Reform Act of 1976. The credit eliminates the first portion of the gift and estate tax rate schedule. The amount eliminated has increased over the years since it was first introduced. The excluded amount is called the "applicable exclusion amount," and the unified credit was renamed the "applicable credit amount" by the Taxpayer Relief Act of 1997.

The applicable credit amount for estates of decedents dying after 1986 and prior to 1998 was $192,800. Any part of the credit used to offset gift taxes is still available to offset estate taxes. This is because adjusted taxable gifts are included in the estate tax base. Further, although the applicable credit amount applies for both estate and gift taxes, the computation of the credit for gift tax purposes is governed by special rules.

The applicable credit amount is subtracted from the taxpayer's estate and gift tax liability. However, the amount of the applicable credit amount available at death is not reduced, even if any portion of the credit is used to offset gift taxes on lifetime transfers. Further, the amount of the applicable credit amount is reduced by 20 percent of any portion of the $30,000 specific gift tax exemption allowable under pre-1977 law that was used with respect to gifts made after September 8, 1976, but before January 1, 1977. Thus, under this rule, the maximum reduction of the applicable credit amount is $6,000 (20 percent of $30,000).

For estates of decedents dying after 1981, the applicable credit amount has been phased in as follows:

	Unified Credit	Exemption Equivalent
1982	$62,800	$225,000
1983	79,300	275,000
1984	96,300	325,000
1985	121,800	400,000
1986	155,800	500,000
1987–1997	192,800	600,000
	Applicable Unified Credit Amount	**Applicable Exclusion Amount**
1998	$202,050	$625,000
1999	211,300	650,000
2000–2001	220,550	675,000
2002–2003	345,800	1,000,000
2004–2005	555,800	1,500,000
2006–2008	780,800	2,000,000
2009	1,455,800	3,500,000
2010	1,455,800	3,500,000
2011	1,730,800	5,000,000
2012	1,772,800	5,120,000
2013	2,045,800	5,250,000
2014	2,081,800	5,340,000
2015	2,117,800	5,430,000
2016	2,125,800	5,450,000
2017	2,141,800	5,490,000

EXAMPLE 22.1

In 2017, Kathy Kelly gives away $1 million and dies broke several years later. Due to the applicable credit amount, no gift tax was due. The $1 million gift, assuming no exclusions or deductions, is an adjusted taxable gift and becomes her estate tax base. As in the case of the gift, the transfer tax amounts to $345,000 but is offset by the applicable credit amount. Thus, the same applicable credit amount serves a dual function, both during life and in the estate.

¶22,015 UNIFIED RATE SCHEDULE

A single unified transfer tax applies to estate and gift taxes effective for the estates of decedents dying and gifts made after 1976. The rates are progressive on the basis of cumulative lifetime and at-death transfers.

For the estates of decedents dying after 1988, gift and estate tax rates presently applicable to U.S. citizens are applicable to the estates of nonresident aliens. Where permitted by treaty, the estate of a nonresident alien is allowed the applicable credit amount available to a U.S. citizen multiplied by a proportion of the total gross estate situated in the United States. In other cases, an applicable credit amount of $14,000 is allowed.

¶22,025 PAYMENT OF TAX AND RETURNS

The estate tax return filing requirements are geared to the exemption so that a return is required if the gross estate exceeds the exemption equivalent of the applicable credit amount. Code Sec. 6018(a)(1) and

(3). For 2017, the applicable credit amount is $2,141,800, which represents an exemption equivalent of $5.49 million. Thus, for estates of decedents dying currently, an executor must file a return if a gross estate exceeds $5.49 million, reduced by the decedent's adjusted taxable gifts made after 1976 and the reduction in the decedent's applicable credit amount because of taxable gifts made after September 8, 1976, and before January 1, 1977.

EXAMPLE 22.2	John Tripper died in 2017. If his gross estate exceeds $5.49 million, a return is due, even if no estate tax may be due. His estate tax return reveals the following:

Gross estate	$5,550,000
Deductions	60,000
Taxable estate	$5,490,000
Tentative tax	$2,141,800
Less: Applicable credit amount	2,141,800
Tax payable	$0

Thus, it may be worthwhile to note that for 2017 estates of decedents owning $5.49 million or less are not subject to estate taxes and need not even file a return. As a result, the estate tax is applicable to a very small percentage of total estates, perhaps less than one percent. Because of the marital deduction, the estate tax, even when applicable, is often deferred for the lifetime of the surviving spouse.

In those cases where applicable, the estate tax must be paid at the time the return is filed. Code Sec. 6161. The estate tax return, Form 706, is due nine months after death when required, together with the tax, if applicable. Code Sec. 6075(a). However, the executor of an estate can obtain an extension of time for the payment of the estate tax for a period not to exceed 12 months from the date fixed for payment of the estate tax. Code Sec. 6161(a). This extension will be granted whenever there is reasonable cause to do so. The executor (or administrator) is generally liable for the payment of the estate tax. Code Sec. 2002. If there is no executor or administrator, persons in actual or constructive possession of any of the property in the decedent's estate are required to pay the tax.

If more than 35 percent of a decedent's adjusted gross estate consists of an interest in a farm or other closely held business (sole proprietorship, a partnership interest, or stock in a closely held corporation), an executor may elect, on a timely filed estate tax return, to defer all payment of tax for five years (paying interest only) and thereafter pay the tax in equal installments over the next 10 years. Code Sec. 6166. The maximum deferral period, however, is 14 rather than 15 years because the due date for the last payment of interest coincides with the due date for the first installment of tax. Interest is payable at a special two percent rate on the estate tax attributable to the first $1 million (indexed, $1,490,000 for 2017) of qualifying property. However, the interest rate on the remaining deferred amount is reduced to 45 percent of the rate charged for underpayment of taxes, and the estate tax deduction is eliminated for interest paid on these installments. Code Sec. 6601(j). A disposition of more than half the qualifying property will accelerate the tax, as may a default. Code Sec. 6166(g).

¶22,035   CREDITS AGAINST TAX

Foreign Death Taxes

A foreign death tax credit is provided for United States citizens and residents. The credit applies to property that is subject to both federal and foreign death taxes in order to prevent double taxation. Taxes paid to possessions of the United States are regarded as foreign death taxes. Code Sec. 2014. The foreign estate tax credit allowed against the estate tax is, however, limited by apportionment. Only taxes attributable to property taxed in both countries may be allowed as a credit. In addition, the credit cannot exceed the portion of United States taxes attributed to such property.

Death Taxes on Prior Transfers

A credit is allowed against the estate tax for all or a part of the estate tax paid with respect to the transfer of property to the present decedent by a prior decedent who died within 10 years before, or within two years after, the present decedent's death. Reg. §20.2013-1. This credit can never be larger than it would be if the present decedent had not received the property. Since the purpose of this provision is to prevent the diminution of an estate by the imposition of successive taxes on the same property within a brief period, no credit is available for any gift tax that may have been paid with respect to the transfer of property to the decedent.

EXAMPLE 22.3	Sam Spade died in 2014 leaving his entire estate to his son, Adam. Two years later Adam dies. In computing Adam's estate tax, a credit is allowed on Adam's estate tax return for the assets included in Adam's estate that were inherited from Sam. The credit is the lower of the estate tax paid by Sam or the marginal estate tax that Adam is assessed on the inherited assets. The credit is reduced by the length of time between Sam's death and Adam's death:

KEYSTONE PROBLEM	The applicable credit amount of $2,141,800 is available to estates of decedents who die in 2017. It has been referred to as the "exemption equivalent" of $5.49 million. Considering both small and large estates, is a credit of $2,141,800 really equivalent to an exemption of $5.49 million?

Gross Estate

¶22,101   PROPERTY INCLUDIBLE IN GROSS ESTATE

The gross estate of a decedent includes "the value of all property to the extent of the interest therein of the decedent at the time of death." Code Sec. 2033. This is a catch-all provision, serving the same purpose as Code Sec. 61 does for income tax purposes. The *gross* estate may be far in excess of the *probate* estate since the gross estate includes jointly held property and insurance payable to a named beneficiary although passing outside the will. No property is excluded, however small, be it real or personal, tangible or intangible, U.S. or foreign. Since the tax is levied on the *transfer* of property, not the property itself, even tax-free municipal bonds are included in the tax base. Citizens and nonresident aliens are subject to the U.S. estate tax on U.S. property. Code Sec. 2103(a). Most property owned outright by the decedent in his or her own name presents no problems as to inclusion. Property held merely as a fiduciary (e.g., as trustee), however, is *not* included.

Over the years, special rules have been designed to deal with *unique properties*, such as life insurance and pensions; *split interests*, such as life estates, remainders, and reversions; and *special situations*, such as powers of appointment and other retained powers. These problem areas, among others, are discussed below. In addition, any asset may present valuation problems.

Conservation Easement

¶22,105   CODE SECTION 2031(c) EXCLUSION

The enactment of Code Sec. 2031(c) by the Taxpayer Relief Act of 1997 (P.L. 105-34) has now made conservation easements more attractive. Specifically, Section 2031(c) provides another tax advantage by allowing a reduction in estate taxes for property that is encumbered with a conservation easement. The highlights of the provision are as follows.

1. An additional estate tax deduction is provided for property containing an easement that was placed on the property before death.
2. If a conservation easement is placed on the property after death and on or before the due date (including extensions) for the estate tax return, a deduction will be allowed to the estate as long as no income tax charitable deduction is allowed to any person with respect to the easement.
3. If all requirements are met, then an estate will be able to generate tax savings of up to $200,000 ($500,000 × .40) in 2017.

In general, under Code Sec. 2031(c), when the executor makes the election, the amount excluded from the estate will be the lesser of:

A. "the applicable percentage of the value of land subject to a qualified conservation easement, reduced by the amount of any deduction under Section 2055(f) with respect to such land;" or

B. the exclusion limitation.

The applicable percentage means that the excluded amount is 40% of the FMV of the property that is encumbered with an easement if the easement reduces the value of the property by 30% or more. However, this value cannot exceed the maximum exclusion for the year at issue. Specifically, the amount that may be excluded for the gross estate is limited as follows: $100,000 in 1998; $200,000 in 1999; $300,000 in 2000; $400,000 in 2001, and $500,000 in 2002 or thereafter. If the easement does not reduce the value of the property by at least 30%, then the applicable percentage will be reduced below 40% by two percentage points for each percentage point by which the value of the conservation easement is less than 30% of the value of the property (Code Sec. 2031(c)(2)).

EXAMPLE 22.4

Jack Ames died owning land, on the Chesapeake Bay in Accomack County Virginia, subject to a qualified conservation easement. He did not retain any development rights in the property. The fair market value of the real property on the date of his death was $1 million without the conservation easement and $800,000 with the easement. Since the value of the conservation easement is $200,000, or 20% of the value of the real property without the easement, then the applicable percentage for the estate is 20% (40% reduced by twice the difference between 30% and 20%). Consequently, the exclusion amount is $160,000 (20% of $800,000).

¶22,109   PRESENT AND FUTURE INTERESTS IN PROPERTY

Anyone who owns property outright, whether personal or real, can divide up this ownership. The ways in which this can be done and the identification of these interests are crucial to the understanding of estate and gift taxes. *Life estates, remainders,* and *reversions* are such property interests and can best be illustrated through examples.

Case 1

The grantor (G) transfers (the income interest in) property to A for life. A has a *life estate;* A is a *life tenant.* A can sell the interest to B, but B still has a life estate for the life of A. G has a *reversion* because the property will revert back to G or G's heirs when A dies.

Estate tax consequences. Nothing will be taxed in A's estate because the only interest A owned, the life estate (the income interest), is extinguished upon A's death. But the whole property will be included in G's estate, less the actuarially determined value of A's life estate if A survives G.

Case 2

G transfers the property to A, but retains the income and/or possession of it for life. Here G retains a life estate and A receives a *remainder.*

Estate tax consequences. G never gave up the present enjoyment of the property; therefore, the full value of it will be included in G's estate. A's estate will also be taxed. If G outlives A, the remainder will be taxed; if not, A dies owning the property outright.

Case 3

G transfers the property to A for life, then to B. A has a life estate; B has a vested remainder. G has divested all interests. Even if B predeceases A, B's heirs will receive ownership.

Estate tax consequences. Nothing is included in G's estate, but B owns either the remainder or the property, depending on whether or not B predeceases A. Note the following:

1. All transfers of property, even partial, are subject to gift tax.
2. All adjusted taxable gifts are included in the estate tax computation even if not part of the gross estate.

Case 4

G transfers the property to A for life, and if B survives A, then to B. A has a life estate and B has a contingent remainder because B must survive A to take anything. In addition, G has a reversion because G or G's heirs will receive the property if B predeceases A.

Estate tax consequences. A's estate is unaffected. B's estate has nothing if B predeceases A. If B survives A, B's estate will include the full value of the property. G's estate has nothing if B survives A prior to G's death. G's estate will include the property, less A's life estate if G predeceases A and B, but multiplied by the probability that B will predecease A.

Case 5

G transfers the property to A for life, then to B if B survives A, otherwise to C. A has a life estate, B has a contingent remainder, and C has an *executory interest,* a remainder of sorts.

Estate tax consequences. G can never get anything back, so G's gross estate includes nothing. A's estate is unaffected. B's estate will include the property if B survives A, otherwise nothing. C's estate problem is more complex:

1.   If A predeceases B, nothing will be included.
2.   If C predeceases A and B, there is still a possibility that B will predecease A. Therefore, the property will be included in C's estate, times the probability of this happening, but the value is reduced by A's life estate.

The above transactions are generally done for family members in trust (e.g., life estate to wife, remainder to children). Annuities, term interests, life estates, reversions, and remainders are valued actuarially, using unisex Treasury tables. The tables use an interest rate equal to 120 percent of the applicable federal midterm rate compounded annually (rounded to the nearest two-tenths of one percent), adjusted monthly. Code Sec. 7520.

¶22,117   GIFTS WITHIN THREE YEARS OF DEATH

The general rule is that outright gifts made prior to death are *not* brought back into the gross estate, even if made on the deathbed. Code Sec. 2035(a). However, the taxable portion of the gift is added to the estate tax base as an "adjusted taxable gift." There are several exceptions for gifts made within three years of death.

Any gift tax paid by the decedent or the decedent's estate within three years of death is includible in the gross estate. Code Sec. 2035(b). If the gift tax is to be paid by the estate, an offsetting debt deduction is allowed. Also, a gift tax credit is allowed since the adjusted taxable gift is included in the estate tax base.

Gifts made at any time with strings attached are includible if the strings were broken within the three-year period and they would have been includible if no action had been taken. Code Sec. 2035(a)(2). This affects the following transactions:

1.   Giving up a retained life estate that would otherwise have resulted in inclusion under Code Sec. 2036.
2.   Giving up a reversion that otherwise would have brought the property back under Code Sec. 2037.
3.   Giving up a power to revoke a transfer that would have resulted in inclusion under Code Sec. 2038.
4.   Giving up an incident of ownership in a life insurance policy that would have led to the proceeds being includible in the gross estate or transferring the policy itself.

With respect to the estates of decedents dying after August 5, 1997, the value of property transferred to a donee from a decedent's revocable trust (within three years of the decedent's death) and the value of property in such a trust (with respect to which the decedent's power to revoke is relinquished during the three years before death) is not includible in the decedent's gross estate. Transfers from a revocable trust are treated as if made directly by the decedent for purposes of Code Sec. 2035 and Code Sec. 2038. Accordingly, an annual exclusion gift from a revocable trust is not included in the decedent's gross estate.

For purposes of qualifying for special estate tax benefits dependent on the amount of the adjusted gross estate and solely for testing purposes, *all* gifts within three years of death are brought back, except gifts of present interests of $14,000 or less per donee for 2017 (the exclusion is indexed annually for inflation). Code Sec. 2035(c)(3). Examples of items qualifying for special estate tax benefits include qualifying for death tax redemptions (Code Sec. 303), special use valuation for farms and closely held businesses (Code Sec. 2032A), and installment payments of the estate tax (Code Sec. 6166).

Gifts of Life Insurance

The general rule that outright gifts made prior to death are not includible in the donor's gross estate does not apply to transfers of life insurance policies on the life of the decedent made within three years of death. Code Sec. 2035(c)(3). The following situations are possible:

1. If the transfer took place *more than* three years before death and the insured did *not* pay the premiums the last three years of life, no amount is includible in the gross estate.
2. If the situation is the same as under (1), except that the insured paid the premiums within three years of death, the premiums are includible in the gross estate.
3. If the policy was transferred *within* three years of death *and* the premiums were paid by the insured, the proceeds, but not the premiums, are includible in the gross estate.
4. If the situation is the same as (3), except that some of the last three years' premiums were paid by someone other than the insured, only the proceeds allocable to the premiums paid by the insured are includible.

EXAMPLE 22.5   Ten years before his death, John Hunter purchased a $100,000 term insurance policy. Two years before his death, he irrevocably transferred the policy and all incidents of ownership to a trust which paid the last two years' premiums. John's gross estate includes $80,000 of proceeds since John paid 80 percent of the premiums.

Even if the proceeds are not includible in the gross estate, the adjusted taxable gift is includible in the estate tax base. The value of an unmatured policy, however, is next to zero for a term policy and close to the cash surrender value for ordinary life policies (the "interpolated terminal reserve," i.e., the replacement value).

¶22,125   RETAINED LIFE ESTATES

Under the provisions of Code Sec. 2036, a decedent's gross estate includes the value of any interest in property transferred by the decedent prior to death (whether in trust or otherwise) for less than full or adequate and full consideration, if the decedent retained for life, or for any period that does not, in fact, end before death:

1. The use, possession, right to the income, or other enjoyment of the transferred property; or
2. The right, either alone or in conjunction with any person, to designate the person who may possess or enjoy the property, or the related income. Code Sec. 2036; Reg. §20.2036-1(a).

The use, possession, right to the income, or other enjoyment of the property is considered retained by the decedent to the extent that it is to be utilized to discharge a legal obligation of the decedent. A legal obligation includes one to support a dependent during the decedent's lifetime. Reg. §20.2036-1(b)(2). The right to designate includes a "reserved power" to designate the person or persons to receive the income, or to possess or enjoy nonincome-producing property during the decedent's life.

The most common example of transfers includible in the gross estate through the operation of Code Sec. 2036 is a transfer by trust, with a retained life estate. This may be illustrated as follows.

EXAMPLE 22.6   Bart Henderson transfers income-producing property into trust for his son, but retains the income from the property for his lifetime. Upon Bart's death, the total fair market value of the property will be included in his gross estate under Code Sec. 2036. (Incidentally, the transfer by Bart would be subject to federal gift taxes. The amount of the gross gift would be the fair market value of the property at the date of the gift, less the portion assignable to the value of the retained life estate.)

An illustration of reserving "the use or possession" of transferred property is an implied agreement or understanding between the transferor and the recipients. In many family situations, a father or mother may give the parents' residence to a son or daughter but continue to live there for life. As a result, the house will be fully includible in the parents' gross estate. Of course, legal title to the property is irrelevant in warding off the inclusion scenario. Naturally, if the parent (transferor) occupied only one-third of the house, then only that portion would be included in the gross estate. Also, it is significant to note that the decedent must be the transferor of the life estate in order for the property to be includible in the estate.

EXAMPLE 22.7   Jack Goodwin transfers income-producing property into trust for his son, Charlie, but retains a life estate for his wife, Ellen. The trust indenture provides that if Ellen predeceases Jack, the life estate will revert to Jack. If Jack predeceases Ellen, then the life estate enjoyed by Ellen would not be includible in Jack's gross estate under Code Sec. 2036. If Ellen predeceases Jack, none of the property will be included in Ellen's estate. Although Ellen held a life estate at the time of her death, she is not the transferor of the property. Therefore, Code Sec. 2036 is not operative.

Family Partnerships

A family partnership is a typical device to shift income and appreciation to other family members and is specifically sanctioned. Code Sec. 704(e). The grantor-partner should be careful not to run afoul of the retained life estate problem by retaining too much control. If the grantor retains a power to control income distributions after the transfer, the rule could apply. The exercise of traditional managerial powers by the grantor should not invoke the rule. Thus, the scope of powers customary in recognized business relationships should not be exceeded. Here are some key factors the IRS looks at:

1. Was the partnership created for business purposes or principally to carry out a desired estate plan?
2. Did the other partners contribute any capital?
3. Did the grantor-partner have the power to accumulate or distribute income?
4. What percentage of profits was in fact distributed to the grantor-partner?

Buy/sell agreements serve a business purpose and should not be a negative factor.

Family Transfers

Set out below are examples of lifetime transfers of property in the setting of family transfers and the tax consequences for each situation.

1. H transfers property to his wife (W) for life, then to himself for life, remainder to his children. Even if H predeceases W, the property (less W's outstanding life estate) is included in his estate.
2. G transfers securities to his wife for life, then to his son, but the trustee has discretion to distribute the income to G in whole or in part. Whether or not the trustee does so, Code Sec. 2036 has no application since the *decedent* retained no interest or right.
3. G makes a transfer in trust but retains the right to use the income for support of his minor children. If he dies before the youngest child reaches majority, he dies with a retained life estate, otherwise not.
4. G makes a transfer to A for life, then to B, retaining the right to designate C as income beneficiary, but only with A's consent. Even though G's power is illusory (i.e., G can exercise his power to substitute C for A only with the consent of A, the adverse party), G still has a retained life estate.
5. G transfers property to his son for life, leaving the remainder to his grandson. G has not retained a life estate and neither has his son since the son is not the transferor. (The son's death, however, causes a taxable termination and may be subject to the generation-skipping tax, discussed later in this chapter.)
6. Upon H's death, W, his widow, has the right to receive $200,000 of life insurance. However, she instructs the insurance company to pay her the interest only for life, then to pay the proceeds to her grandchildren in equal shares. Upon W's death, Code Sec. 2036 applies.
7. G transfers property to his brother, T, for life, then to T's children. T, in return, transfers property to G for life, then to G's children. Technically, neither party retained a life estate. However, the economic effect is the same as if they both did. The *reciprocal trust* doctrine creates a retained life estate in both. *J.P. Grace Est.,* 69-1 USTC ¶12,609, 395 U.S. 316, 89 S.Ct. 1730 (1969). If the trusts are of unequal value, only the smallest value is deemed to be reciprocal.
8. G has a retained life estate in a $1 million trust. At the age of 85, when the fair market value of his interest is $50,000, G sells it to his grandson and dies. Literally, Code Sec. 2036 does not apply since G did not die with a retained life interest.

Furthermore, even if he died the next day, there is no gift in contemplation of death because the consideration was adequate. Nevertheless, $950,000 may be included in G's estate if the transaction is viewed as involving the property which otherwise would have been included. *C. Allen,* 61-2 USTC ¶12,032, 293 F.2d 916 (CA-10 1961).

¶22,133 REVERSIONS

Code Sec. 2037 also addresses the inclusion in the gross estate of the value of lifetime transfers by the decedent. This section refers to transfers "in trust or otherwise" except for an "adequate and full consideration," as does Code Sec. 2036. However, there are three conditions that must be satisfied for Code Sec. 2037 to become operative.

1. Possession or enjoyment of the property can be obtained, through ownership of such interest, only by surviving the decedent;
2. The decedent had retained a reversionary interest in the property at the time of the transfer; and
3. The value of the reversionary interest immediately before the decedent's death exceeded five percent of the value of the entire property.

The condition of survivorship cited in 1 above means that the subject property is not included in the decedent's gross estate if, immediately before the decedent's death, possession or enjoyment of the property could be obtained by a beneficiary either by surviving the decedent, or through another event such as the expiration of a term of years. The reversionary interest referred to in 2 above is, in effect, a remainder interest retained by the original transferor. The term "reversionary interest" does not include rights to income only, such as the right to receive the income from a trust after the death of another person. Reg. §20.2037-1(c)(2). To determine whether the decedent retained a reversionary interest in the property valued in excess of five percent, as referred to in 3 above, the value of the reversionary interest is compared to the value of the property transferred. This valuation does not include interests therein that are not dependent upon survivorship of the decedent. Application of the Code Sec. 2037 provisions discussed above are presented in the following examples.

EXAMPLE 22.8	John Henry transferred property into trust, giving his wife, Donna, a life estate and the remainder interest to John's then-surviving children. In the event there were no surviving children, the remainder would go to John or his estate. Each beneficiary can possess or enjoy the property without surviving John. Therefore, no part of the property is includible in John's gross estate under Code Sec. 2037, regardless of the value of John's reversionary interest.

EXAMPLE 22.9	John Henry transferred property into trust retaining a life estate, with the remainder interest to his surviving children. In the event there were no surviving children, the remainder would go to his brother or to his brother's estate. The decedent did not retain a reversionary interest. Therefore, no part of the property is includible in the decedent's gross estate under Code Sec. 2037, even though possession or enjoyment of the property could be obtained by the children only if they survived John Henry.

EXAMPLE 22.10	A transferred property into trust giving a life estate to B with the remainder to C if A predeceases B. However, if B predeceases A, the remainder would go to A. If, in fact, A predeceases B, the value of A's reversionary interest immediately before death is compared with the value of the trust corpus, without deduction for the value of B's outstanding life estate, in applying the five percent rule. Conceivably, a fractional remainder interest could be retained by the decedent. Referring to the above situation, if A had retained a reversionary interest in only one-half of the trust corpus, the value of the reversionary interest would be compared with the value of one-half of the trust corpus, without deduction for any part of the value of B's outstanding life estate.

In applying Code Sec. 2037, the value of the decedent's reversionary interest is computed in accordance with the Special Use Valuation Method.

¶22,141 REVOCABLE TRANSFERS

As did Code Secs. 2036 and 2037, Code Sec. 2038 also relates to the inclusion in the gross estate of the value of lifetime transfers by the decedent. This section also refers to transfers "in trust or otherwise" except for an "adequate and full consideration," as do Code Secs. 2036 and 2037. Under Code Sec. 2038, however, the value of property interests transferred by the decedent are includible in the gross estate if the enjoyment of the property transferred was subject, at the date of the decedent's death, to any power of the decedent to alter, amend, revoke, or terminate the transfer. Reg. §20.2038-1(a).

It is immaterial in what capacity the power was exercisable by the decedent or by another person, or persons, in conjunction with the decedent. Also, the time of exercise and the source of the power are of no importance. If the decedent transferred property by trust during life and was named as trustee with the power to revoke the trusts, the entire property would be includible in the gross estate under the operation of Code Sec. 2038. Likewise, if the decedent created a trust during life, named another person as trustee, but reserved the power to be named as a replacement trustee, Code Sec. 2038 would apply.

In order to preclude inclusion of the transferred property in the gross estate under Code Sec. 2038, the power to alter, amend, revoke, or terminate a trust must be held at all times "solely by a person other than the decedent." Further, the decedent must not have reserved any right to assume these powers. The amount includible in the gross estate under Code Sec. 2038 is "only" that portion of the property transferred that is subject, at death, to the "decedent's" power to alter, amend, revoke, or terminate. Reg. §20.2038-1(a)(3).

A revocable lifetime trust is the typical tool employed by the decedent to provide flexibility for changing personal and economic conditions. With respect to the estates of decedents dying after August 5, 1997, the value of property transferred to a donee from a decedent's revocable trust (within three years of the decedent's death) and the value of property in such a trust (with respect to which the decedent's power to revoke is relinquished during the three years before death) is not includible in the decedent's gross estate. Transfers from a revocable trust are treated as if made directly by the decedent for purposes of Code Sec. 2035 and Code Sec. 2038. Accordingly, an annual exclusion gift from a revocable trust is not included in the decedent's gross estate.

It should be obvious at this juncture that there may be considerable overlap between Code Secs. 2036, 2037, and 2038. A previous lifetime transfer by the decedent may subject the property to inclusion in the gross estate under one or more of these sections. Of course, the property is included only once, but perhaps for one or more reasons.

¶22,149 ANNUITIES

Commercial Annuities

By far, most annuities are of the commercial kind and are issued by insurance companies. Commercial annuities are valued on the basis of comparable sales. In other words, the issuer is asked: How much would a 60-year-old person have to pay to receive $3,000 a year for life? The answer is the value.

Most commercial annuities, including retirement annuities, can be divided into four groups:

1. *Straight-life annuities,* which are simply paid for the life of one person.
2. *Joint and survivor annuities,* whereby payments are made, typically to a married couple, as long as at least one of them lives.
3. *Self and survivor annuities,* whereby payments continue to be made to a beneficiary after the death of the buyer.
4. *Minimum guarantee annuities,* whereby a refund feature provides for a lump-sum payment, unless the annuitant survives a minimum period of time.

To qualify as an annuity, it is immaterial whether the payments are periodic or sporadic, equal or unequal, conditional or unconditional.

A straight-life annuity will never result in estate taxation, but once a survivor feature exists, the present value of the payments due after death will be included in the estate *if the decedent or an employer contributed to the purchase price.* This is similar to the tracing rule that applies to unmarried joint tenants (see below) and also applies to both private and commercial annuities. Code Sec. 2039(b).

EXAMPLE 22.11	H paid $500,000 to an insurance company for a joint and survivorship annuity, whereby $3,000 a month would be paid as long as he and/or his wife, W, survive. If H dies first, the full present value of W's expected payments, based on actuarial tables, will be included in his estate. If W dies first, nothing will be included in her estate.

EXAMPLE 22.12	Same as Example 22.11, except H and W pay half each. Whenever the first one dies, one-half of the full present value of the survivor's expected payments based on actuarial tables will be included in the deceased's estate.

EXAMPLE 22.13	Same as Example 22.12 except that H and W each buy separate annuities for $250,000. Since neither one contributed to the other's annuity, nothing is included in either estate.

Private Annuities

Private annuities are usually employed when there is an "estate planning sale" by an older person (the annuitant) to a younger family member (the obligor). If the annuity is simply paid to the annuitant for life with no survivor feature, nothing will be includible in the annuitant's estate since nothing passes from the decedent. Should the annuity continue to the surviving spouse or other beneficiary, the estate will include the present value of the future payments, based on the survivor's life expectancy times the fractional consideration paid by the decedent. Code Sec. 2039(b).

EXAMPLE 22.14	Several years ago, G and W sold their securities to their child for a private annuity of $5,000 a year for as long as both live, plus $3,000 a year for the life of the survivor. G had put up 80 percent of the purchase price of the securities and died first. Based on W's age at G's death, assume that according to the IRS tables prescribed under Code Sec. 7520, one dollar a year for life is worth $10.5376. As a result, G's estate will include $25,290 ($3,000 × 10.5376 × .80).

PLANNING POINTER	New proposed regulations have been issued that will tax gain on the exchange of highly appreciated property for the issuance of annuity contracts (effective date is April 18, 2007 for estate and succession planning).

Pension and Profit-Sharing Plans

No estate exclusion is allowed regardless of how annuity payments are made, even if there is a named beneficiary. Code Sec. 2039(a) and (b). Even IRAs and Keogh plans are fully includible. (All or part of a retirement annuity in "pay status" before 1985, however, may be excluded.)

¶22,157   CO-OWNERSHIPS OF PROPERTY

Tenancies in Common

Since there is no survivorship feature in a tenancy in common, the decedent's undivided interest in the property is included in the decedent's gross estate (and in the decedent's probate estate). Thus, if the decedent owned a 23 percent interest in a tract of land, 23 percent of its value is includible in the decedent's estate.

Joint Tenancies and Tenancies by the Entirety

Married Joint Tenants

If the decedent owned property as a joint tenant with a spouse with right of survivorship, including a tenancy by the entirety, a "qualified joint tenancy" exists. One-half of its value is included in the estate of the first spouse to die without regard to who paid for it. The surviving spouse becomes the sole owner by operation of law resulting in full inclusion in the surviving spouse's estate.

Unmarried Joint Tenants

Any two or more individuals may be joint tenants (e.g., parent and child, siblings, and unmarried couples). When the first joint tenant dies, the *full* value of the property is included in the estate, unless and to the extent the surviving joint tenant can show contributions in money toward the purchase price. Code Sec. 2040(a).

EXAMPLE 22.15 Fernanda and her daughter Fern own, as joint tenants, a condominium apartment, which Fernanda paid for. If Fernanda dies first, the full value is included in her estate, but if Fern predeceases her mother, *nothing* is includible in Fern's estate. If Fernanda contributed X percent of the original cost, X percent of the *value* at the time of her death would be includible in her estate if Fern survived her. If the surviving joint tenant receives the property subject to an unpaid mortgage, the mortgage balance counts as an original contribution to the extent the owner is personally liable. Rev. Rul. 79-302, 1979-2 CB 328.

Community Property

There are only 10 community property states (Alaska, Arizona, California, Idaho, Louisiana, Nevada, New Mexico, Texas, Washington, and Wisconsin). In these states, property acquired by married persons is community property, and such property retains its character once established even after a change of domicile. One-half of the value of community property owned by a husband and wife is includible in the gross estate of the first spouse to die. Community property is like an equal tenancy in common between spouses enforced by state law. That is, one-half of the community interest goes into the estate of the first to die. However, unlike joint tenancies with the right of survivorship between husbands and wives in common law states, both halves of community property receive a step-up in basis to fair market value. Code Sec. 1014(b)(6).

¶22,165   POWERS OF APPOINTMENT

If property is transferred in trust by gift or inheritance, a beneficiary may use and enjoy that property to a great extent *without that property being includible in the estate*. The beneficiary may have all the following rights and powers. Code Sec. 2041(b)(1) and (2).

1. The right to receive all the income from the property for life (i.e., a life estate).
2. The power to draw funds from the trust (invade corpus), as long as it is subject to an *ascertainable standard* relating to the beneficiary's health, education, support, or maintenance.
3. The power to withdraw the greater of five percent of the value of the trust property or, $5,000, each year.
4. The power to appoint all or part of the property to anyone the beneficiary wishes during life or by will, except to oneself, the estate, or the creditors of either.
5. The right to be the trustee of the trust.

None of the above will subject the property to estate tax in the beneficiary's estate, but there may be generation-skipping transfer tax consequences.

Definitions

If the decedent had transferred property as a gift and retained certain powers of control, they can be extremely limited and still cause the property to be included under the retained life estate, reversion, or revocable transfer rules discussed above. Once the decedent as a beneficiary simply has been given a power by someone else over property the beneficiary never owned, the power must be a *general power of appointment* to cause inclusion. The expression "general power" does not have to be stated as such.

Appointee. The person in whose favor the power is exercised.

Donee of the power. The person who has the right to appoint the property, let the power lapse, or release it.

Donor of the power. The grantor and transferor of the property subject to the power.

Taker in default. The person who winds up with the property if the power is released or lapses. This person will often be the remainderman.

General v. Special Powers

For the decedent to be deemed to have a general power of appointment, the decedent must have had the power to appoint the property to oneself, the estate, or the creditors of either by will and/or during life. Code Sec. 2041(b)(1) and (2).

The following are *not* general powers:

1. The power to appoint the property to anyone in the world, such as a child or grandchild, except to oneself, the estate, or the creditors of either.
2. The power to appoint the property to anyone, including oneself, but only with the consent of the grantor or an adverse party, such as the remainderman or an income beneficiary whose interest would be extinguished in the process.
3. The power to make use of capital up to five percent of value or $5,000, whichever is greater, once a year on a noncumulative basis.
4. The power to make use of capital for the beneficiary's health, education, support, or maintenance, but not for emergencies, welfare, or happiness.

Powers that fall short of general powers are called *special* or *limited* powers.

Once a general power exists, the release, lapse, or exercise of it during life creates a taxable gift. Code Sec. 2514. If the decedent exercises a general power in a will or lets it lapse or releases it, the property is includible in the decedent's estate.

If the donee of the power exercises it, but retains a life estate, reversion, or the power to alter, amend, or revoke, the property will be included in the donee's estate under Code Secs. 2035-2038.

General powers granted before October 22, 1942, lead to estate inclusion only if exercised, by will or during life. But a post-October 21, 1942, power is taxable whether it lapses, is released, or is exercised.

EXAMPLE 22.16	Max Mertens transfers property in trust to his son for life. The son has the power to give the property to any or all of his children *and* has the right to use whatever he needs for his own support. The property will not be included in the son's estate. If the son's power is worded as a power to consume for his happiness, welfare, and the like, chances are the power will be considered general for lack of an ascertainable standard.
EXAMPLE 22.17	B left property in trust to A for life, then to B. C has the power to appoint the property to himself. The property is includible in C's estate.
EXAMPLE 22.18	Same as Example 22.17, but C needs A's consent. Since A is the income beneficiary, A is an adverse party, and C does *not* have a general power. Therefore, none of the property would be includible in C's estate.
EXAMPLE 22.19	Same as Example 22.17, but C needs B's consent. As a remainderman, B is also an adverse party and there are no estate tax consequences to C.
EXAMPLE 22.20	G left property in trust to his wife, W, for life, then to his son, S. W has the power to appoint the property to anyone in the world but only with the consent of her daughter. Since the daughter is a permissible appointee, only one-half of the property would be includible in W's estate.
EXAMPLE 22.21	Same as Example 22.20, except that W needs the consent of both her daughters. Only one-third would be includible in W's estate.
EXAMPLE 22.22	A received a general power of appointment over a trust fund. A exercised one-half in favor of himself and the other half in favor of his grandson. Upon A's death, his estate includes one-half of the property itself to the extent he still has it. The one-half exercised in favor of his grandson is subject to gift tax.

TAX BLUNDER

The decedent was also both the trustee and the beneficiary of a trust that granted him the power to invade the trust for "proper support, maintenance, welfare, health and general happiness in the manner to which he was accustomed." Of course, the offending term is "general happiness." The estate argued that the term "happiness" was limited to support items, but the court disagreed. The court reasoned that if they were to resolve a conflict between the income and the remainder beneficiary, they would not take a "grudging and narrow interpretation." They concluded that there are several things, such as travel, that fall within the ambit of general happiness, which are not considered as necessary for health, education, support or maintenance. *Estate of Little*, 87 TC 599.

Note: Travel can be part of an ascertainable standard if the travel is part of an educational program or if it is part of the beneficiary's accustomed lifestyle.

¶22,173   ## LIFE INSURANCE

The proceeds of life insurance on the life of the decedent are includible in the decedent's gross estate under three sets of circumstances. Code Sec. 2042.

First, if the proceeds are payable to the decedent's estate, they are clearly includible in the gross estate. This could happen by choice, e.g., the estate is named as a beneficiary, or it could occur inadvertently, e.g., the named beneficiary predeceased the insured and no provision was made for a secondary beneficiary. Also, if the proceeds are payable to a trustee who is obligated to use the proceeds for the benefit of the estate, such as to pay debts and taxes, the proceeds are deemed payable to the estate. If the trustee has discretion as to whether the proceeds are to be used for the benefit of the estate, they are includible to the extent so used.

Second, if the decedent possessed at least one incident of ownership in the policy, the life insurance proceeds are includible in the gross estate. This means either that the decedent owned the policy until death or transferred the policy, but retained the right to:

1. Change the beneficiary
2. Borrow on the policy
3. Use it as collateral for a loan
4. Cancel the policy
5. Veto any of the above or retained a reversionary interest in excess of five percent

Third, if the policy was transferred irrevocably within three years of the insured's death, the proceeds are includible in the gross estate.

The standard procedure employed to completely transfer all incidents of ownership is to assign the policy to an irrevocable insurance trust. Note that the power to exercise any incident of ownership in conjunction with any other party, or the power to veto any incident of ownership, is still an incident of ownership resulting in estate inclusion. Since life insurance is a unique asset in that it can increase dramatically in value from one instant to the next, it makes sense to relinquish all incidents of ownership and make it payable to a named beneficiary. The transfer must take place more than three years prior to death to accomplish the estate exclusion. Code Sec. 2035(a)(2).

EXAMPLE 22.23   Mark Martin purchased flight insurance at the airport, handed the policy over to his son, embarked, and died one-half hour later in a plane crash. Since Mark possessed an incident of ownership in the policy, even though no opportunity existed for exercise, the full proceeds would nevertheless be included in his gross estate. *M.L. Noel Est.*, 65-1 USTC ¶12,311, 380 U.S. 678, 85 S.Ct. 1238 (1965). *Thus*, it is the *existence* of the *incident* that matters.

The rules under Code Sec. 2042 apply only to insurance on the life of the decedent. If the decedent owned "spouse insurance" or any policy on the life of another when the decedent died, only its *value*, not the proceeds, is includible in the decedent's gross estate under Code Sec. 2033. The value is the amount for which the individual insurance company would sell an identical policy at the time of death on a paid-up basis (i.e., the replacement cost, known as the "interpolated terminal reserve").

PLANNING POINTER	Here is a technique that can have favorable income, gift, and estate tax consequences: grantor transfers a life insurance policy on the grantor's own life to an irrevocable trust, whereupon the trust borrows to pay the premiums. The tax consequences are: **Gift tax.** No gift tax is incurred if the cash value does not exceed available exclusions. If the cash value is high, the grantor may borrow against the policy and transfer it subject to the loan. **Income tax.** If the trust income may be used to pay the premiums on the policy, the trust is a grantor trust and any available deductions belong to the grantor. Code Sec. 677(a)(3). **Estate tax.** If all incidents of ownership in the policy are transferred more than three years prior to the grantor's death, the proceeds are excluded from the insured's gross estate. Because of all these tax advantages, such a grantor-insurance trust is known in the profession as the "supertrust."

¶22,175   PART-SALE, PART-GIFT TRANSFERS

Sometimes a transfer is part sale and part gift. Whenever a transfer is for less than fair value (i.e., not a bona fide sale), the property is includible at full value in the estate, less consideration paid. Code Sec. 2043.

EXAMPLE 22.24	G transferred property to one of his sons, S, keeping a life estate for himself. When it is explained to him that the full value of the property will be included in his estate because of a retained life interest, he gets an idea. He sells his life interest to his other son for $5,000. Nevertheless, the full value of the property is included in his estate, less $5,000, assuming he dies within three years. Note that he did not sell the property itself, merely the *life estate*. This result follows even if the $5,000 was all the *life estate* was worth, which is all G had. The purpose of the rule is to avoid deathbed transfers of a retained life estate, powers of appointment, or a reversion. Otherwise, sales for a modest sum could remove sizeable amounts from the estate.

Valuation of Gross Estate

¶22,181   GENERAL PRINCIPLES

Valuing the gross estate is the paramount estate tax problem since the value determines the amount that will be subject to estate tax and, as a result, the estate's liquidity needs. The executor will value all property included in the gross estate either at its fair market value at the decedent's date of death or the alternate valuation date. Code Secs. 2031 and 2032.

Fair Market Value

In general, fair market value of property includible in a decedent's estate is the price at which it would change hands between a willing buyer and a willing seller, both having reasonable knowledge of relevant facts. Reg. §20.2031-1(b). Despite the brevity of the rule, valuation controversies make up a large share of audit and litigation issues.

If an item is generally available to the public in a particular market, the fair market value of the property is the price obtainable on the market in which it is most commonly sold to the public. If the item of property is generally obtainable by the public on the retail market, fair market value of the item is the price at which that item or a comparable one will sell at retail in a particular geographic market. Reg. §20.2031-1(b).

EXAMPLE 22.25	The fair market value of decedent Ginger Graham's car (property generally obtained by the public on the retail market) is the price at which a car of the same make, model, age, and condition could be purchased by members of the public. Fair market value would not be the price that a used-car dealer would pay for Ginger's car.

Alternate Valuation Date

Whenever the executor chooses the alternate valuation method, all property is valued six months after death or on the date of disposition if this date occurs first. Code Sec. 2032(a). It should be noted that whichever valuation date is selected, the election is all inclusive. That is, each asset included in the gross estate must be valued as of the elected date. Consequently, the executor may not value some items at date of death and others at the alternate date.

| EXAMPLE 22.26 | John Henry's gross estate consists of the following assets: |

	FMV at Date of Death	FMV at Alternate Date
1,000 shares of Ed's Barbecue	$700,000	$690,000
House	480,000	470,000
Farm	600,000	590,000
Georgia Power bonds	300,000	298,000
Total	$2,080,000	$2,048,000

If the executor elects the date of death value, then the estate is valued at $2,080,000, and if the alternate valuation date is selected, the estate's value is $2,048,000. Note that no mixing of values is permissible.

The election to use the alternate valuation date must reduce the value of the decedent's gross estate and the sum of the decedent's estate tax and generation-skipping transfer tax liabilities. Code Sec. 2032(c). Even property that was transferred some time before death, but which is included in the gross estate because of the retention of certain rights or for other reasons, is valued as of the date of death or six months after death.

Basis of Property

Most properties receive a basis for income tax purposes equal to the estate tax value, be it the date of death value, the value on the alternate valuation date, or the special use value. Code Sec. 1014(a). The decedent's basis is irrelevant, and a step-up or a step-down may result. An instant long-term holding period is also given by statute. Code Sec. 1223(11). The fair market value basis rule applies without regard to whether estate or inheritance taxes are paid or whether an estate tax return is due.

Under the 2001 Act, the step-up in basis at death will not apply to decedents dying during 2010 that elected not to have the estate tax apply. In general, the property passing out of an estate will be subject to the gift tax rules governing basis. Code Sec. 1022(a). Basis will be the lesser of the decedent's adjusted basis in the property or the fair market value of the property at the decedent's death. However, the decedent's spouse may receive $3 million of basis increase allocated to property that the spouse is to receive directly or in a qualifying marital trust. Code Sec. 1022(d)(4)(B)(iii). Also, an executor may allocate an aggregate basis increase of up to $1.3 million regardless of the beneficiary of the property. Code Sec. 1022(d)(4)(B)(i). However, Congress did reinstate step-up basis for 2010 as an option.

¶22,185   SPECIFIC PROPERTIES

Even though all property included in the gross estate is valued as of the same date—that is, the date of death or the alternate valuation date—special problems arise in valuing particular types of property. For this reason, special rules apply in valuing the various kinds of property or interests in property that might be included in the gross estate and these are treated in the following paragraphs.

Real Estate

The valuation of real estate is not set out in the Regulations pursuant to any formula or other precise mechanism. Reg. §20.2031-1(b). Since each piece of real estate is unique, it is not surprising for the Regulations to take this approach. However, the following methods can be used to establish the estate tax value of real estate: expert testimony, comparable sales, market assessments, recent mortgages, capitalization of earnings, and reproduction costs.

Household and Personal Effects

Household and personal effects must be valued at the price that a willing buyer would pay a willing seller for such goods. Reg. §20.2031-6(a). If the household and personal effects exceed a total value of $3,000, then there must be an appraisal and an itemized list of the jewelry, furs, silverware, paintings, antiques, oriental rugs, stamps, coin collection, and books attached to the return.

Life Insurance

The value of life insurance for estate tax purposes will be either the proceeds of the policy or its replacement value. That is, where insurance is taxed to the estate of the insured because the insurance becomes due and payable on death, then the estate tax value will be the proceeds of the policy. On the other hand, life insurance may be taxed in the estate of a person other than the insured. When this happens, the policy has not matured. As a result, the estate tax value is the replacement cost and not its face value. Reg. §20.2031-8.

Life Estates, Remainder Interests, Term Certain Interests, and Reversionary Interests

Because an individual may have an interest less than the entire fee simple ownership in property, special IRS tables must be used to value these life estates, remainders, term certain interests, and reversions. Code Sec. 7520. This actuarial valuation system requires that the interest rate to be used in valuing limited interests be updated using an interest rate derived from the federal midterm rate for the month in which the valuation is required. The method prescribes that the interest rate will be at 120 percent of the applicable federal midterm rate (AFR) compounded annually (rounded to the nearest two-tenths of one percent).

Mutual Funds

Mutual fund shares can be sold back only to the issuer and by shareholders at a fixed price under federal laws governing mutual funds. This fixed price is called the redemption or bid price and is based on the net values of the assets held by the fund on a given date. Because of this fact, the U.S. Supreme Court has ruled that mutual fund shares owned by decedents must be valued for estate tax purposes by using the redemption or bid price at the date of death or on the alternate valuation date. *D.B. Cartwright,* 73-1 USTC ¶12,926, 411 U.S. 546, 93 S.Ct. 1713 (1973); Reg. §20.2031-8(b).

¶22,187   LISTED SECURITIES

Stocks and bonds owned by a decedent are includible in the gross estate and are valued for estate tax purposes on the date of death, or on a date six months after death if the estate representative so elects. Code Sec. 2033. When the valuation is made as of six months after death, if any of the securities have been distributed in the interval, the value on the date of distribution will control. Reg. §20.2032-1(c)(2). Similarly, the valuation date, in the case of a sale during the six-month period after death, is the date of sale.

The estate tax value of stocks and bonds is the fair market value per share or bond on the applicable valuation date. In the case of listed stocks and bonds, if there were actual sales of the securities on a stock exchange or in an over-the-counter market on the valuation date, then the mean between the highest and lowest quoted selling prices on that date is taken as the fair market value per share or bond. Reg. §20.2031-2(b).

EXAMPLE 22.27	John Hughes died on September 1, 2017, and he owned 1,000 shares of IBM stock that was traded on the New York Stock Exchange. IBM traded at a high of $116 and a low of $114 on September 1. As a result, Mr. Hughes's estate tax return will reflect a value for the IBM stock of $115 per share (average of $116 and $114) and a total value of the stock of $115,000.

If there were no actual sales on the valuation date, but there were sales on trading dates within a reasonable period both before and after the valuation date, the fair market value is derived by taking (1) the mean between the highest and lowest sales on the nearest trading date before and (2) the mean between the highest and lowest sales on the nearest trading date after the valuation date, and taking a weighted average of these two means. However, it should be noted that the average is weighted inversely by the respective number of trading days separating the selling dates and the date of death. Reg. §§20.2031-2(b) and 25.2512-2(b).

EXAMPLE 22.28	Sam Lett died on November 5, 2017, and owned 1,000 shares of Zebra Corporation stock, which is traded on an over-the-counter market. On November 5 there were no sales of Zebra stock. The sales of Zebra stock nearest the valuation date of November 5 took place two trading days before (November 3) and three trading days after (November 10). On November 3, 2017, the mean sales price was $50, and on November 10, 2017, the mean sales price was $40. As a result, the date of death value is as follows: $((3 \times \$50) + (2 \times \$40))/5 = \$46$.

In certain instances, securities may be actively traded on the date of death, but that is not the value that will be utilized for estate tax purposes. Specifically, the taxpayer may own a large block of securities, and the valuer must consider the depressing effect that the sale of such a large number of shares would have on the market. This situation is referred to as "blockage" and requires that the price per share be lowered to reflect the effect of marketing such a large block of securities. Reg. §§20.2031-2(e) and 25.2512-2(e); Rev. Rul. 59-60, 1959-1 CB 237.

¶22,191   CLOSELY HELD STOCK

One of the most vexing problems in the area of estate taxation is how to value the stock of a closely held corporation. The valuation of close corporation stock differs from that of listed and active corporate stock that passes freely on the market and has its value reflected on the stock exchange or over-the-counter listings. Closely held stock rarely finds its way to the market place and its value at any particular time is determined only by reference to various factors. Numerous courts, professional journals, and government publications have discussed this valuation question. Despite this wealth of information, few areas of taxation are as unresolved and misunderstood as the valuation of closely held stock. And, since there are several million closely held corporations in the United States, valuation represents an area of critical concern confronting taxing authorities and practitioners.

Obviously, a sale of stock occurring within a reasonable time of the valuation date can provide a good indication of the stock's value. Reg. §20.2031-2. However, the fair market value of a particular item of property is not to be determined by a forced sale price. Nor is the fair market value to be determined by the sale price of the item in a market other than that in which such item is most commonly sold to the public. Reg. §20.2031-1(b). If there is no sale (as is the usual case with closely held stock), an independent expert appraiser should be consulted.

In the case of corporate stock and securities that are not listed on an exchange and whose value thus cannot be determined on the basis of sales or bid and asked prices, the value must be determined by taking into consideration, in addition to other factors, the value of stock or securities of corporations engaged in the same or a similar line of business that are listed on an exchange. Code Sec. 2031(b). Thus, in the absence of an active market, consideration may be given in the case of bonds to such factors as the soundness of the security, the interest yield, and the date of maturity. In the case of stocks, consideration may be given to the company's net worth, prospective earning power, dividend-paying capacity, and other relevant factors, including a fair appraisal of the tangible and intangible business assets (including goodwill) as of the appropriate valuation date and the demonstrated earnings capacity of the business. Reg. §§20.2031-2(f), 20.2031-3, and 20.2031-6(b).

The IRS emphasizes the following factors to be considered as valuation guides in addition to all available financial data. Rev. Rul. 59-60, 1959-1 CB 237.

1. The nature of the business and the history of the enterprise from its inception.
2. The economic outlook in general and the condition and outlook of the specific industry in particular.
3. The book value of the stock and the financial condition of the business.
4. The earning capacity of the company.
5. The dividend-paying capacity.
6. Whether or not the enterprise has goodwill or other intangible value.
7. Sales of the stock and the size of the block of stock to be valued.
8. The market price of stock of corporations engaged in the same or a similar line of business having their stocks actively traded in a free and open market, either on an exchange or over the counter.

¶22,193   BUY-SELL AGREEMENTS

In a buy-sell agreement one business owner (partner or shareholder) is obligated to sell an interest on death, retirement, or disability to the owners (cross-purchase agreement) or to the business (redemption agreement). Such agreements may be used to ease the problems of liquidity and estate valuation. Buy-sell agreements have at least three advantages. First, if the buy-sell agreement is legally binding on both parties and fair when made, the price (fixed or based on a formula) is also helpful in establishing value for estate, gift, and income tax purposes, limiting the estate tax value. The agreement must not be merely an option or right of first refusal. Second, a guaranteed price will provide the estate with instant liquidity, rather than an unmarketable ownership interest. Third, an orderly continuity of business ownership is provided. Buy-sell agreements are often funded by insurance policies.

EXAMPLE 22.29   Paul Jones and Mary Wells are equal shareholders in Quincy Corporation. When either party dies, retires, or becomes totally disabled, the other shareholder is to purchase the shares, thus becoming the sole shareholder. This is an example of a cross-purchase agreement. It should be noted that the purchasing shareholder's basis in the stock is increased by the purchase price. If the corporation is the buyer, the remaining shareholder still becomes the sole owner of the business, but there will be no basis increase.

¶22,195   SPECIAL USE VALUATION FOR FARMLAND AND CLOSELY HELD BUSINESS REALTY

When a person dies, property generally passes to that person's heirs at its fair market value as of the date of death. Code Sec. 1014(a)(1). Alternately, the executor or executrix of the estate may elect to value such property at its fair market value on a date six months after the death of the decedent (or the date of distribution to beneficiaries, if sooner). Code Sec. 2032(a)(2). This election is permissible only if it will result in a lower value for the gross estate and a lower estate tax liability. Code Sec. 2032(c).

Even with the relief provided under the alternative valuation date option, many estates holding farmland and closely held businesses have been burdened with substantial estate tax liabilities. A major factor was the requirement that such property is valued at its "highest or best" use rather than at its current use. This requirement often resulted in sale of the family farm or business to raise cash to pay the estate taxes.

Congress enacted legislation providing for special use valuation, under Code Sec. 2032A, for real property used in farms and closely-held businesses. The intent of the legislation was to lessen the estate tax burden by permitting such property to be valued at its current use, rather than its highest and best use. A related goal was to encourage heirs to continue operating family farms or closely held businesses.

Real property included in the estate of the decedent may qualify for special use valuation if:

1. The decedent was a resident of the United States at the time of death.
2. The property is qualified real property.
3. The executor elects special use valuation on the estate tax return.
4. A written recapture agreement is filed with the estate tax return. Code Sec. 2032A(a)(1).

The aggregate decrease in value of the qualifying property may not exceed $1,120,000 for 2017. Code Sec. 2032A(a)(2) and Rev. Proc. 2016-55.

EXAMPLE 22.30   Pat McMullen dies in 2017 and his estate elects special use valuation with respect to his farm under Sec. 2032A. The estate would be entitled to a maximum reduction in estate value of $1,120,000.

Qualification Requirements

"Qualified real property" is property located in the United States. It must be acquired from, or pass from, the decedent to a qualified heir of the decedent. The property must also have been used, on the date of the decedent's death, for qualified use by the decedent or a member of the decedent's family. Code Sec. 2032A(b)(1).

The adjusted value of the qualified real or personal property used in farming or another business must make up 50 percent or more of the adjusted value of the gross estate of the decedent. Furthermore, 25 percent or more of the adjusted value of the gross estate must consist of qualified real property. Code Sec. 2032A(b)(1)(A) and (B). For purposes of the 50 percent test, personal property used in farming or another business is taken into account even though personal property does not qualify for special use valuation. The adjusted value of the property is its fair market value (FMV) for estate tax purposes (without considering its special use value), reduced by mortgages and other indebtedness on the property. Code Secs. 2032A(b)(3) and 2053(a)(4).

Qualified Heir

The term "qualified heir" refers to a member of the decedent's family who acquired the real property from the decedent or to whom the property has passed. If a qualified heir disposes of any interest in qualified real property to any member of his or her family, that person becomes the qualified heir of the property. Code Sec. 2032A(e)(1).

The term "member of the family" means an individual's spouse, ancestors, and lineal descendants. Also included are lineal descendants of the spouse, parents of the individual or of the spouse, and the spouse of any lineal descendant. A legally adopted child of a person is treated as that person's child by blood. Code Sec. 2032A(e)(2).

Qualified Use

The qualified use requirement is met if the property is used as a farm for farming purposes, or in a trade or business other than farming. Code Sec. 2032A(b)(2). The property must have been used for the qualified use for at least five of the eight years ending on the date of the decedent's death. Also, the decedent, or a member of the decedent's family, must have materially participated in the operation of the farm or business during the required period of time. Code Sec. 2032A(b)(1)(C).

EXAMPLE 22.31

Rachel Pitt died leaving a gross estate valued at $6.2 million to her daughter. The estate included the family farm, which was valued at $3.2 million. The value of the farm consisted of machinery and other personal property with a fair market value of $400,000 and real property with a highest and best use value of $1,000,000. At the time of Rachel's death, the real property was subject to a $40,000 mortgage on which she was personally liable. Rachel materially participated in the operation of the farm for the last 20 years prior to her death. The computation of the 50 percent and 25 percent tests are as follows:

Calculation of Adjusted Estate:

Gross estate (fair market value)	$6,200,000	
Secured debts	40,000	
Adjusted estate		$6,160,000

Calculation of Adjusted Value of Real Property:

Real property (fair market value)	$3,200,000	
Secured debts	40,000	
Adjusted value of real property		$3,160,000

Calculation of Adjusted Value of Real Property and Personal Property Used for Farming:

Personal property (fair market value)	$400,000	
Secured debts	0	
Adjusted value of personal property		$400,000
Adjusted value of real property		3,160,000
Adjusted value of real and personal property		$3,560,000

Computation of 50% Test:

$$\frac{3,560,000}{6,160,000} = 58\%$$

Computation of 25% Test:

$$\frac{3,160,000}{6,160,000} = 51\%$$

Under the above circumstances, the requirements of both tests have been fulfilled. The 50 percent test is met because the $3,560,000 adjusted value of the qualifying use real and personal property, which is determined by subtracting the $40,000 mortgage from the $3,600,000 fair market value of such property, is at least 50 percent of the $6,160,000 adjusted value of the gross estate, determined by subtracting the $40,000 mortgage from the $6,200,000 fair market value of the gross estate. The 25 percent test is also met. The $3,160,000 adjusted value of the real property, which is determined by subtracting the $40,000 mortgage from the $3,200,000 fair market value of the real property, is at least 25 percent of the adjusted estate. Consequently, rather than valuing the farm real property at $3,200,000, the property will be valued based on its actual use as a farm. However, it must be remembered that the value cannot be reduced by an amount greater than $1,120,000 for 2017.

The term "farm" includes stock, dairy, poultry, fruit, fur-bearing animal, and truck farms; plantations; ranches; nurseries; ranges; greenhouses or other similar structures used primarily for the raising of agricultural or horticultural commodities; and orchards and woodlands. Code Sec. 2032A(e)(4).

"Farming purposes" means cultivating the soil or raising or harvesting any agricultural or horticultural commodity, including the raising, shearing, feeding, caring for, training, and management of animals, on a farm. Also included in farming is:

1. The handling, drying, packing, grading, or storing on a farm of any agricultural or horticultural commodity in its unmanufactured state.
2. The planting, cultivating, caring for, or cutting of trees.
3. The preparation of trees for market. Code Sec. 2032A(e).

Valuation Methods

There are two different methods of arriving at a special use value for qualified real property in an estate. They are the farm value method and the multiple-factor method, and they must be used exclusively. That is, if any property is to be valued under the farm value method, all farm property eligible for special use valuation must be valued accordingly. The same is true for the multiple-factor approach, which often produces a valuation considerably higher than the farm method. Obviously, the farm value method should be used if at all possible.

Farm Value Method

The special use value of a farm is determined under the farm value method as follows:

1. The average annual gross cash rental or average annual net-share rental for comparable land used for farming purposes in the locality of such farm minus
2. The average annual state and local real estate taxes for such comparable land, divided by
3. The average annual effective interest rate for all new Farm Credit Bank loans in the district. Code Sec. 2032A(e)(7).

This may be expressed mathematically as follows:

$$\text{Special Use Value} = \frac{\begin{array}{c}\text{Average Annual Gross Cash Rental for Comparable Land in Locality Used for Farming}\end{array} - \begin{array}{c}\text{Average Real Estate Taxes in the Locality for the Comparable Land}\end{array}}{\begin{array}{c}\text{Average Annual Effective Interest Rate for All New Farm Credit Bank Loans in the District}\end{array}}$$

EXAMPLE 22.32 Abigail MacDonald wishes to use the farm value method to determine the special use value of a qualified 300-acre farm. MacDonald knows that the fair market value of the land is $3,200 per acre and that the cash-rental value of comparable property is $100 per acre. She also has ascertained that state and local tax on comparable property is $19 per acre and that the average annual effective interest rate established by the Farm Credit Bank for new loans in the district is 5 percent. MacDonald uses the above formula as follows:

(1) MacDonald determines the special use value of one acre of farmland:

$$\frac{\$100 - \$19}{.05} = \$1,620$$

(2) Jones determines the special use value of the entire 300-acre farm:

$$300 \times \$1,620 = \$486,000$$

The computation of each average annual amount is to be based on the five most recent calendar years ending before the date of the decedent's death.

Multiple-Factor Method

The special use valuation of qualifying nonfarm real property and of qualifying farm real property where the farm value method is not used must be determined by applying the following factors:

1. The capitalization of income that the property can be expected to yield for farming or closely held business purposes over a reasonable period of time under prudent management.
2. The capitalization of the fair rental value of the land for farmland or closely held business purposes.
3. Assessed land values in a state that provides a differential or use value assessment law for farmland or closely held business.
4. Comparable sales of other farm or closely held business land in the same geographical area far enough removed from a metropolitan or resort area so that nonagricultural use is not a significant factor in the sales price.
5. Any other factor that fairly values the farm or closely held business value of the property. Code Sec. 2032A(e)(8)(A)-(E).

Naturally, the multiple-factor method is very subjective. Questions about acceptable capitalization rates, fair rental values, and how to weight factors can produce taxpayer and IRS controversies. The multiple-factor method does not have the safe-harbor technique of the farm value method.

Electing Special Use Valuation

The estate must elect special use valuation for the qualifying property on the initial estate tax return. Once made, the election is irrevocable, and the following information must be provided in the election notice pursuant to Reg. §20.2032A-8(a)(3):

1. The name and taxpayer identification number of the decedent as they appear on the estate tax return.
2. The relevant qualified use of the property to be specially valued.
3. A listing of the real property to be specially valued.
4. The fair market value of the real property to be specially valued, and its value based on its qualified use (both values are determined taking into account outstanding mortgages or other debt to which the property is subject).
5. The adjusted value of all real property that is used in a qualified use and that passes from the decedent to a qualified heir and the adjusted value of all real property to be specially valued.
6. Items of personal property, including their adjusted value, listed on the estate tax return that pass from the decedent to a qualified heir and are used in a qualified use.
7. The adjusted value of the gross estate (as defined in Code Sec. 2032A(b)(3)(A)).
8. The method used to determine the special value based on use.
9. Copies of written appraisals of the fair market value of the real property.
10. A statement that the decedent and/or a member of the decedent's family has owned all specially valued real property for at least five of the eight years immediately preceding the date of the decedent's death.
11. A statement listing periods during the eight-year period preceding the date of the decedent's death during which the decedent or a member of his or her family did not own the property, use it in a qualified use, or materially participate in the operation of the farm or other business (within the meaning of Code Sec. 2032A(e)(6)).
12. The name, address, taxpayer identification number, and relationship to the decedent of each person taking an interest in each item of specially valued property. The value of the property interests, based on both fair market value and qualified use, passing to each of these individuals is also required.
13. Affidavits identifying the material participant or participants and describing their activities constituting material participation.
14. A legal description of the specially valued property.

The special use valuation agreement must be executed by all parties who have an interest in the property being valued. Code Sec. 2032A(d)(2).

Recapture

The Code refers to the recapture tax as an additional estate tax. Code Sec. 2032A(c)(1). It is imposed if the qualified heir disposes of any interest in the specially valued property (other than to another qualified heir) or ceases to use it for a qualified use within 10 years after the decedent's death. However, a two-year grace period is permitted immediately following the date of the decedent's death. Code Sec. 2032A(c)(7). During this period, failure to begin the qualified use of the property will not cause recapture. The 10-year recapture period is extended by a period equal to the actual time between the date of decedent's death and the date the qualified heir commences to use the property in the qualified use. Like-kind exchanges under Code Sec. 1031 and involuntary conversions under Code Sec. 1033 will not cause recapture if the replacement property is used for the same qualified use as the original qualified property. If the original election was not to treat timber as a crop, disposition or severance of standing timber does trigger recapture. Moreover, recapture refers to the tax difference between what the estate tax liability was and what it would have been but for the special use valuation.

Deductions from the Gross Estate

¶22,201   ## EXPENSES, DEBTS, AND LOSSES

All deductions are subtracted from the gross estate. The marital and charitable deductions are unique and are discussed separately below. The main "expense" deductions are funeral and administration expenses, debts (including unpaid taxes and interest), and casualty losses.

Funeral Expenses

Funeral expenses are never deductible for income tax purposes. However, they are deductible from the gross estate to the extent allowable under local law even if they go beyond "necessary." The expenses may be incurred in the U.S. or abroad. Reg. §20.2053-1(a)(1).

Administration Expenses

Administration expenses, such as fees paid to the executor, lawyer, accountant, and appraisers, and certain interest expenses must meet two tests to be deductible:

1. The expenses must be "allowable by the law of the jurisdiction."
2. The expenses must be "actually and necessarily incurred in the administration of the decedent's estate; that is, in the collection of assets, payment of debts, and distribution of property to the persons entitled to it." Reg. §20.2053-3(a).

Thus, the expenses must be allowable and necessary. Expenses incurred for the convenience of a beneficiary are disallowed, e.g., selling expenses when a house could have been deeded to a beneficiary rather than sold.

Debts

All enforceable claims against the estate are deductible if paid. This includes accrued interest up to the date of death and unpaid taxes of all kinds, such as income, property, and gift taxes, but not the estate tax itself. Reg. §20.2053-6. The property tax is deductible to the extent the real property is includible in the gross estate. Nonrecourse debts and mortgages are deductible only to the extent of estate tax value. Liabilities must have been incurred for full consideration to avoid collusion between family members, e.g., IOUs given as presents to friends and relatives are *not* deductible even if enforceable and paid.

EXAMPLE 22.33	When Gertrude London died, she owed unpaid federal, state, and local income taxes, gift taxes on deathbed gifts, and property taxes on her home. In addition, substantial estate taxes were due, as well as excise taxes on excess retirement accumulation. Except for the estate taxes, all of the other unpaid taxes are deductible as debts of the estate, be they federal, state, or local.

Claims Against the Estate

Probate Estate Assets

Expenses and debts relating to assets subject to claims are deductible regardless of how late they are paid. A deduction is allowed prior to payment as long as the amount "is ascertainable, with reasonable certainty, and will be paid." However, the sum of the deductions may not exceed the estate value of the probate estate unless paid by the due date of the estate tax return. Code Sec. 2053(c)(1) and (2); Reg. §20.2053-1(b)(3).

Nonprobate Assets

Deductions that relate to nonprobate assets (i.e., assets included in the gross estate solely for tax purposes) are allowable as long as they are paid within the statute of limitations (i.e., within three years after the due date of the return). There is no limitation as to amount, and estimates may be used. If actual expenses differ from the estimated deduction used, an amended estate tax return must be filed.

Casualty Losses

Losses from sudden casualties, such as fire, flood, shipwreck, or theft, are deductible if sustained by the estate. Code Sec. 2054. If sustained prior to death, they are deductible on the decedent's final Form 1040 and, if sustained after distribution, they are deductible by the beneficiary. Unlike the income tax treatment, the casualty deduction is not limited by a percentage or dollar floor, and the deduction is based on the estate tax value. As is the case for income tax purposes, any loss must be reduced to the extent compensated for by insurance or otherwise. If alternate valuation is used and a casualty loss has been incurred, no deduction is allowed if the reduced value is reported as the estate value.

Allocation of Deductions on Returns

Administration expenses and casualty losses may be deducted either on Form 1041, the fiduciary income tax return of the estate or trust, *or* on Form 706, the estate tax return. The decision may be made on an item-by-item basis or an allocation may be made for individual items. Reg. §1.642(g)-2.

Theoretically, expenses should be shifted until the marginal estate tax rate equals that of the income tax. Due to the increased applicable credit amount and the unlimited marital deduction, the trend is toward using administration expenses and losses as income tax deductions, thus reducing "distributable net income" (DNI). Section 265, which bars income tax deductions for expenses incurred to purchase or carry tax-exempt municipal bonds, does not apply to the estate deduction.

The decision as to where to deduct will have ripple effects on the charitable and marital deductions, and on the trust income beneficiaries and remaindermen, and may affect the applicability of death tax redemptions, installment payments of estate tax, and special use valuation.

¶22,217   ## MARITAL DEDUCTION

The marital deduction is available in computing the taxable estate of a citizen or resident of the United States. It is allowed where any part of a deceased person's estate passes or has passed to the surviving spouse. The property so passing is deductible in computing the taxable estate to the extent that it is includible in the gross estate. Code Sec. 2056.

The marital deduction is not available for estates of nonresident noncitizens unless the individual was a resident of a country that had entered into a treaty with the United States permitting the deduction. However, although property passing to a surviving spouse who is not a U.S. citizen is generally ineligible for the estate tax marital deduction, the marital deduction will be allowed for estate and gift tax purposes with respect to a nonresident alien whose spouse is a U.S. citizen.

There is no monetary ceiling on the estate tax marital deduction. Thus, unlimited amounts of property, except for certain terminable interests (such as life estates, terms for years, annuities, etc.), can be transferred between spouses free of estate taxes.

Passing of Property to Surviving Spouse

The person receiving the decedent's property for which a marital deduction is claimed must qualify as a surviving spouse at the date of the decedent's death. A legal separation that has not terminated the marriage at the time of death does not change the status of the surviving spouse. If an interest in property passes from the decedent to a person who was a spouse but is not married to the decedent at the time of death, the interest is not considered as passing to the surviving spouse.

For purposes of the marital deduction, an interest in property is considered as *passing* from the decedent to a spouse only if the surviving spouse can receive or has received the property interest in the following circumstances:

1. Heir, devisee, or legatee
2. Surviving joint tenant
3. Beneficiary of life insurance
4. Certain gifts within three years of death
5. Widow's support allowance during probate
6. Election against the will (the statutory share in lieu of dower)
7. Beneficiary of a lapse, release, or exercise of a general power of appointment, etc. (Code Sec. 2056(c))

Disclaimers by other beneficiaries will often lead to additional amounts passing to the surviving spouse. Only the net value of the property after deducting any encumbrance thereon qualifies.

Terminable Interests

To qualify for the marital deduction, it is not sufficient that property passes to the surviving spouse. The interest must also be nonterminable. A "terminable" interest is one that meets three requirements:

1. It may lapse, expire, or terminate with the passage of time or upon the happening or nonhappening of a contingency. However, the bequest may be conditional on survival for up to six months.
2. An interest passes or has passed by gift to a third party.
3. Such third party may possess or enjoy any part of the property after the surviving spouse's interest terminates.

Property interests meeting these tests, and therefore failing to qualify for the marital deduction, include term interests, life estates, and certain annuities. The rules make it more likely that the property does not escape estate taxation in both estates. Code Sec. 2056(b)(1) and (3).

EXAMPLE 22.34	G dies, leaving his wife, W, the income from property for life, whereupon the property itself passes to the grandchildren. The life interest does *not* qualify for the marital deduction.

EXAMPLE 22.35	G leaves the property to his mother for life, then to W. The remainder does qualify for the deduction.

EXAMPLE 22.36	G leaves real estate to W and son as tenants in common. W's interest is deductible, since even if W dies before the son, her individual half passes from her by will or the laws of intestate succession.

EXAMPLE 22.37	G dies, leaving W a life interest in his stock portfolio, but it goes to his children should she remarry. If she does not remarry, she can will the stocks to anyone. No marital deduction is available, due to the condition.

EXAMPLE 22.38	G purchased a joint and survivorship annuity providing for monthly payments to G for life, and then to W should she survive. Upon G's death, the value of W's annuity is included in his estate and a marital deduction is allowed. Although W's interest expires upon her death, G left her all he had and no other person may possess or enjoy the property after W's death. Code Sec. 2056(b)(6).

Minimum Required Interest of Surviving Spouse

The spouse does not have to be given outright ownership of property to qualify for the marital deduction. A life interest plus a general power of appointment will suffice, or specifically:

1. The surviving spouse must be entitled to all income from the property for life to be paid at least annually.
2. The surviving spouse must have a general power of appointment over the whole property to be exercised alone and in all events. Such power can be exercisable either during life and/or by will. The holder of a general power is treated as the owner of the property so that the gift or estate tax cannot be avoided. Code Sec. 2056(b)(5).

The marital bequest is a function of taxes, propensity to consume, love and affection, degree of confidence in the spouse, their relative ages and health, their respective wealth, number of children, and so on.

Qualified Terminable Interest Property (QTIP)

An election exists to convert a terminable interest, a life estate, into nonterminable property eligible for the marital deduction for either gift or estate tax purposes. Code Secs. 2056(b)(7) and 2523(f). The election is made by the donor for lifetime transfers and by the executor for testamentary transfers. To qualify as "qualified terminable interest property," known in the trade as a QTIP trust, two main requirements must be met:

1. *All* income must be distributed at least annually to the donee spouse (the trust must be *simple*).
2. No one can have a power to appoint any portion of the principal or income to anyone other than the spouse during the spouse's lifetime.

The result of the election is that the marital deduction is allowed to the donor or the donor's estate for the full market value of the property in the trust, regardless of to whom the remainder goes (e.g., the children, charity, etc.). This benefit carries a price tag; the full value at the death of the spouse is included in the gross estate (or is subject to gift tax if any portion of the spouse's interest is disposed of earlier). Code Secs. 2044 and 2519.

EXAMPLE 22.39

When Frederick died, he left $1 million in trust to his wife, Cynthia, all income (except capital gains) to be distributed to her annually for her life, the remainder to the local state university. If his executor did not make the QTIP election, no marital deduction is allowed, but the trust is not subject to transfer taxes in Cynthia's estate. If the QTIP election is made:

1. Frederick's estate receives a $1 million marital deduction, but no charitable deduction.
2. If, on Cynthia's death, there is $2 million in the trust, the full value is includible in her estate, but an offsetting charitable deduction is available.

The QTIP election is perhaps most useful when a wealthy individual wishes to provide for a second spouse for life, but wishes to ensure that the children from the previous marriage will receive the principal. It should be noted that the spouse may be granted any number of powers over the principal. The income interest is merely a minimum. Also, a surviving spouse never has to accept an income interest, but may insist on a statutory share, typically one-third of the net probate estate.

For the estates of decedents dying after August 5, 1997, Code Sec. 2056(b)(7)(C) clarifies that a nonparticipant spouse's survivorship interest in a participant spouse's qualified plan, IRA, or SEP that is attributable to community property laws may qualify for qualified terminable interest property treatment if the nonparticipant spouse predeceases the participant spouse.

¶22,225   CHARITABLE CONTRIBUTIONS

The income tax aspects of charitable gifts are outside the scope of this discussion. In comparison, the estate tax rules are more liberal because:

1. The estate tax value of *all* charitable gifts included in the gross estate is deductible in full without percentage limitations.
2. Whether the testator wills property to a private foundation or a public charity, 100 percent of the value is deductible for estate tax purposes. (The income tax deduction is often limited to basis and to 30 or 50 percent of adjusted gross income.)
3. Charitable contributions made before death do double duty. They are deductible for income tax purposes. They are not includible in the gross estate.

The combined tax savings may approach 90 percent of the value gifted.

Charitable Remainder Trusts

A donor may wish to make a charitable contribution now, but:

1. The donor may be unwilling to give up current income and/or control.
2. The donor may want a spouse and/or children to enjoy the property after the donor's death.
3. The donor may wish to obtain a current income tax deduction as well as an estate tax deduction.

The solution is a gift of a *remainder* to charity. A life estate plus a remainder equals 100 percent of the property. Thus, a gift of a remainder constitutes a transfer of property subject to the retention of the life estate. In other words, there is a *present* gift, but of a *future* interest.

If the transfer is done right, the donor receives a current deduction for the value of the remainder. The deduction equals the value of the property, less the present value of the interest retained, based on mortality tables. Upon the donor's death, the full value is included because of the retained life estate, but the full value is then subtracted out as a charitable deduction.

The retained interest can take several forms: (1) term of years (e.g., 20 years, the maximum), (2) life estate for the life of the donor, (3) life estate for the joint lives of the donor and spouse, or (4) one or more life estates for the life or lives of any other person (e.g., the donor's parents or children).

There are three types of eligible charitable remainder trusts: (1) pooled income funds, (2) charitable remainder annuity trusts, and (3) charitable remainder unitrusts. Code Sec. 2055(e)(2)(A).

Pooled Income Funds

The principal difference between a pooled income fund and a charitable remainder unitrust or annuity trust is that the donor or other beneficiary of a pooled income fund is entitled only to the income actually earned by the fund, rather than to a fixed amount or fixed percentage of its value. Code Sec. 642(c)(5). Pooled income funds can be described as follows:

1. Many donors irrevocably transfer remainder interests for the use of charity, retaining a life interest for one or more beneficiaries.
2. The properties are "pooled" (i.e., commingled).
3. No tax-exempt bonds are allowed.
4. The fund is managed by the charitable organization itself, and no grantor or beneficiary can be a trustee.
5. The trust fund owns only properties transferred under (1).
6. Each beneficiary receives a share of the income earned by the trust.

For purposes of determining the amount of any charitable contribution allowable by reason of a transfer of property to a pooled fund, the value of the income interest is determined using the highest rate of return earned by the fund for any of the three taxable years immediately preceding the taxable year of the fund in which the transfer is made and the applicable mortality table (or six percent per year in the case of a fund in existence less than three taxable years).

Charitable Remainder Annuity Trusts (CRATs)

A charitable remainder annuity trust is a trust from which a specified sum or percentage (not less than five percent of the initial fair market value of all the assets actually placed in trust) is to be paid annually to one or more named individuals as income beneficiaries. For transfers in trust occurring after June 18, 1997, the annual payout cannot exceed 50 percent of the initial fair market value of the trust's assets. For transfers in trust occurring after July 28, 1997, the value of the remainder interest must be a least 10 percent of the initial fair market value of all property placed in the trust. (However, under a special rule, the minimum 10 percent rule will not apply to transfers in trust under the terms of a will or other testamentary instrument executed on or before July 28, 1997, if the decedent (1) dies before January 1, 2000, without having republished the will or amending it by codicil or otherwise or (2) was on July 28, 1997, under a mental disability to change the disposition of the property and did not regain competency before dying.) Each one of these beneficiaries must be living at the creation of the trust and payments to them must terminate not later than 20 years after creation or at their deaths. When payments terminate, the remainder goes to the charitable organization. Code Sec. 664.

EXAMPLE 22.40	Clive Barker died, leaving $100,000 in trust. If his surviving spouse, Anna, were to receive $6,000 a year for 15 years ($90,000), with the remainder to go to charity, this would be a charitable remainder annuity trust.

The beneficiary is taxed under the trust conduit rules (i.e., the beneficiary has ordinary income, capital gains, tax-free income, and return of capital) as the case may be. The trustee will furnish information on the tax status of the receipts.

Charitable Remainder Unitrusts (CRUTs)

A charitable remainder unitrust is similar to an annuity trust, except that, rather than receiving a fixed amount each year, the beneficiaries receive a fixed percentage, not less than five percent (for the beneficiaries as a group) of the net fair market value of the assets valued annually. Thus, the amount received will fluctuate from year to year.

In the case of charitable remainder unitrusts, the annual payout cannot exceed 50 percent of the fair market value of the trust assets determined annually. Also, the 10 percent rule applies with respect to each contribution of property to the trust (note that additional deductible gifts may be made to a charitable remainder unitrust under Reg. §1.664-3(b)).

EXAMPLE 22.41	Decedent left $100,000 in trust for his children for life, with the remainder going to charity. The remainder does *not* qualify for a charitable deduction unless the trust is a unitrust or an annuity trust.

EXAMPLE 22.42	Decedent left $100,000 in trust for his son for life with a minimum guarantee of five percent of the value of corpus per year, with the remainder going to charity. A deduction is available for the remainder since the trust is a charitable remainder unitrust.

EXAMPLE 22.43	Same as Example 22.42, except that the son has the power to invade corpus for his "welfare." No deduction is allowed since the son may easily deplete the principal, cutting off the charitable interest.

EXAMPLE 22.44	Same as Example 22.43, except that the son dies after three months. A deduction is permitted the grantor's estate because the charity receives the full $100,000. The son's estate includes the property since he had a general power of appointment, but an offsetting charitable deduction is allowed in his estate as well. Code Sec. 2055(a) and (b).

According to the Senate Committee Report, trusts failing to meet the requirements of the 50 percent test will be treated as complex trusts rather than charitable remainder trusts, and, as a result, all of their income will be taxed to the beneficiaries of the trust. However, there are several special provisions designed to provide relief for trusts that fail to meet the 10 percent test.

| PLANNING POINTER | Here is a planning device for the dying and the aged: If a taxable estate is likely to exist and the individual's income tax bracket is high, prepay all charitable bequests mentioned in the will. The estate will not include them, and this has the same effect as a deduction, even if made on the deathbed. In addition, an income tax deduction (subject to some limitations) will result. If the income and estate tax brackets are 40 and 40 percent respectively, 80 percent of the value of the property can be saved in taxes.

In fact, if taxation is the only consideration, a lifetime charitable transfer is always preferable to a testamentary bequest. |
|---|---|

A charitable contributions deduction is allowed for the fair market value of a charitable remainder interest in an annuity trust *or* a unitrust. The fair market value of the remainder interest of a charitable remainder annuity trust is the net fair market value of the property placed in trust less the present value of the annuity as computed by using special IRS valuation tables prescribed under Code Sec. 7520. Two actuarial factors are generally used in determining present value—a mortality component and an interest rate component. The mortality component is based on the life expectancy of a designated individual (or individuals). The interest rate component represents an assumed rate of return. The interest rate component of the IRS valuation tables is based on a rate that is 120 percent of the applicable federal midterm rate (AFR) compounded annually (rounded to the nearest two-tenths of one percent), adjusted monthly. Valuation of any interest for term of years or life, any annuity, or any remainder or reversionary interest as of May 1, 1989, requires the use of these IRS tables. The AFR is announced by the IRS monthly in a news release and published in a revenue ruling.

¶22,230   STATE DEATH TAXES

For estates of decedents dying after 2004, a deduction is allowed for death taxes paid to any state or the District of Columbia, in respect of property included in the gross estate of the decedent. Code Sec. 2058, added by P.L. 107-16. For years prior to 2005, state death taxes were creditable against the federal state tax (subject to limitations). Code Sec. 2011.

¶22,255   DISCLAIMERS

No one has to accept an unwanted gift or bequest. A qualified disclaimer within nine months leads to the property being treated as if it were never transferred. Sometimes substantial savings can result from a disclaimer. Following are some examples:

1. If the surviving spouse is left property, he or she may wish to disclaim part of the property. This could save estate taxes in the estate and the disclaimed portion would pass directly to the other beneficiaries, typically children or grandchildren. The disclaimer should be made only if the surviving spouse would not consume the excess for living expenses in any event.

| EXAMPLE 22.45 | John Jamieson leaves his entire estate of $6.49 million to his spouse who has no assets. There is no estate tax because of the marital deduction. However, when his wife dies, the $6.49 million will be included in her estate and the excess above $5.49 million will be taxed. If the wife were to disclaim $1 million, there would still be no tax to John's estate and his wife would only include $5.49 million in her estate upon death. There will be no estate tax on her death, saving $400,000 in estate taxes. |

2.   A third party, such as a child, may wish to disclaim a bequest to favor the surviving parent so as to increase the marital deduction and save estate taxes immediately. The disclaimer may also be prompted by a concern for the parent's financial needs and the hope that the property will eventually pass to the child anyway, either through a systematic gift program or by will.

3.   A beneficiary may be financially secure and disclaim to benefit the residuary legatee without any gift tax liability.

4.   If someone is given a general power of appointment and does not intend to exercise it, it makes sense for the donee to disclaim it to avoid estate tax in the donee's own estate if the donee dies possessing the power.

5.   Someone receiving an income interest may wish to disclaim it to favor a lower tax bracket family member.

6.   If a disclaimed interest will go to charity and the charity is one of the beneficiary's favorites, the beneficiary may disclaim the interest and reduce estate taxes. But the estate tax savings must be compared with the income tax savings resulting from acceptance plus contribution.

To qualify:

1.   The disclaimer must be made in writing.

2.   The disclaimer must be made within nine months of the initial transfer, including the creation of a joint tenancy, or nine months after the beneficiary reaches age 21.

3.   The disclaimer must be irrevocable and unqualified.

4.   The disclaimant must not have accepted the bequest or any benefits from it initially.

5.   The disclaimant cannot direct to whom the disclaimed property will pass. Code Secs. 2046 and 2518.

| EXAMPLE 22.46 | Many years before he died, William Stone purchased numerous securities and put them in a joint tenancy with his wife, Wilma. As soon as William died, Wilma disclaimed the one-half undivided interest in the securities (William's half) that she acquired upon William's death. Since the disclaimer was made more than nine months after the initial transfer (the creation of the joint tenancy), it is too late to be a "qualified" disclaimer. Thus, the property is still treated as if transferred to Wilma upon William's death. In addition, Wilma has made a gift for gift tax purposes to the new recipient if the disclaimer is effective to make a transfer to the residuary legatee or devisee. |

TAX BLUNDER

Oscar purchased a $250,000 life insurance policy on his own life. To save estate taxes in his estate, he transferred all rights in the policy to Sylvia, his wife. Many years later, Sylvia predeceased him, leaving him "everything she owned." Since this included the policy, Oscar was back to square one. Older, but wiser, he transferred the policy to an irrevocable trust with his children and grandchildren as beneficiaries. However, Oscar died two years later and the full proceeds of $250,000 were added to his gross estate. Also, no marital deduction was available, leading to a sizable estate tax. The proceeds of the insurance were not available to pay the tax, being held in trust with income to the children and a remainder to the grandchildren.

The above problem could have been easily avoided by using an insurance trust initially, bypassing both Sylvia's and Oscar's estates.

Federal Gift Tax

¶22,301   ## DEFINITION OF TRANSFERS BY GIFT

A federal gift tax is imposed on the right to transfer property from one person to another for less than full and adequate consideration. The transferor is called the donor and the transferee the donee. Any gift tax due as a result of a taxable gift is a liability of the donor. Code Sec. 2502(c). In the event the donor fails to pay the tax when it is due, the donee can be held liable for the tax to the extent of the value of the property received. Code Sec. 6324(b). The gift tax is an excise tax on the transfer, and is not a tax on the subject of the gift. Transfers by gift are defined in Reg. §25.2511-1(a) as follows:

> The gift tax applies to a transfer by way of gift whether the transfer is in trust or otherwise, whether the gift is direct or indirect, and whether the property is real or personal, tangible or intangible. For example, a taxable transfer may be effected by the creation of a trust, the forgiving of a debt, the assignment of a judgment, the assignment of the benefits of an insurance policy, or the transfer of cash, certificates of deposit, or federal, state, or municipal bonds.

In accordance with the above definition, all transactions whereby property or property rights or interests are gratuitously passed or conferred upon another constitute a transfer subject to the gift tax, regardless of the method or device employed to effect the transfer. The gift tax is imposed on the transfer of property, not on the performance of services. Code Sec. 2501(a)(1). Accordingly, a person who renders services for another without being compensated has not made a gift subject to the gift tax.

Time of Gift

A gift is complete as to property in which the donor has ceased to have dominion and control and has no power to change disposition of the property for the donor's own benefit or for the benefit of another, as previously cited. Reg. §25.2511-2(b). The effective date occurs at the time the donor can no longer revoke the gift, or revert the beneficial title to the property to the donor, or change the interest of the designated beneficiaries. Rev. Rul. 67-396, 1967-2 CB 351. Several examples of completed transfers are listed below:

1. The donor completes a legal check or note which constitutes a promise to pay. The gift is not complete until a check or note is paid or negotiated for value to a third person. Rev. Rul. 67-396.
2. The donor delivers a stock certificate, properly endorsed, either to the donee or to the donee's agent; the gift is complete for federal gift tax purposes on the date of delivery. Reg. §25.2511-2(h). If, however, the donor delivers a stock certificate, properly endorsed, to either his broker or the issuing corporation with directions for transfer to a donee, the gift is not complete until the stock is transferred on the corporation's books. Rev. Rul. 54-135, 1954-1 CB 205.
3. The donor transfers property, in trust, to himself as trustee for the benefit of specific named beneficiaries. The donor has made a complete gift at the time of delivery if he has retained fiduciary powers only. Reg. §25.2511-2(g).
4. The donor delivers his interest in a U.S. Savings Bond (Series E) to the registered co-owner. The gift is not complete until the bond is reissued in the donee co-owner's name alone. *E.G. Chandler,* 73-1 USTC ¶12,902, 410 U.S. 257, 93 S.Ct. 880 (1973).

¶22,315   ## BASIS OF PROPERTY TRANSFERRED BY GIFT

Generally, the income tax basis of property transferred by a gift is the same as the basis in the hands of the transferor. In certain instances, however, the basis of property acquired by gift may depend on whether the donee sells the property for a gain or loss and when the gift was made.

1. If the gift was made prior to 1921, the donee's basis for gain or loss is the fair market value of the property on the date of the gift. Code Sec. 1015(c).
2. If the gift was made after 1920 and prior to 1977, the donee's basis for gain is the donor's adjusted basis plus any gift tax paid on the transfer (but not to exceed fair market value on date of the gift). The basis for loss is the lower of the basis for gain or the fair market value of the property on the date of the gift. Code Sec. 1015(a) and (d)(1).

3. If the gift was made after 1976, the donee's basis for gain is the donor's adjusted basis plus only the gift tax attributable to the appreciation of the property to the point of the gift (but not to exceed the fair market value of the property on the date of the gift). Under Code Sec. 2503(b), to determine the amount of gift tax on the appreciation to be added to the donor's basis, the fair market value of the gift is reduced by the donor's basis and divided by the fair market value of the gift reduced by the annual exclusion. The basis for loss is the lower of the basis for gain or the fair market value of the property on the date of the gift. Code Sec. 1015(a) and (d)(6).

How to Apply the Basis Rules

The above rules are illustrated in the following examples:

EXAMPLE 22.47   In 1920, A transferred realty by a gift to create an irrevocable inter vivos trust. The property cost A $10,000 and was worth $25,000 on the date of the gift. The income tax basis to the trust for gain or loss is $25,000.

EXAMPLE 22.48   In 1975, B transferred realty by a gift to create an irrevocable inter vivos trust. The stock cost B $15,000 and had a fair market value of $60,000 on the date of the gift. B paid a gift tax of $8,000 on the transfer. As a result the trust's basis for gain or loss is $23,000 ($15,000 (B's basis) + $8,000 (gift tax paid by B)). The trust does not have a different basis for loss since the fair market value of the property on the date of the gift (i.e., $60,000) is not lower than the basis for gain (i.e., $23,000).

EXAMPLE 22.49   Assume the same facts as in Example 22.48, except that the gift occurred in 2017 (instead of 1975). The trust's income tax basis for gain is $22,826, determined as follows:

B's adjusted basis on the date of the gift	$15,000
Gift tax attributable to the $45,000 appreciation (($45,000/$46,000) × $8,000)	7,826
Trust's income tax basis for gain	$22,826

The trust's basis for loss would be $22,826, based on the same reasoning set forth in Example 22.46.

The effect of the rule provided in the Tax Reform Act of 1976 (as illustrated in Example 22.47) is to deny the donee (the trust) any increase in basis for gift tax attributable to the donor's adjusted basis. Incidentally, unless property with a fair market value of less than the donor's basis is expected to appreciate above the donor's basis prior to sale by the donee (the trust), it should not be used as gift property. In this case, to maximize the tax benefits, the donor should sell the property, recognize the tax loss, and transfer the proceeds by gift to the trust.

¶22,325   PRESENT v. FUTURE INTERESTS

An unrestricted right to the immediate use, possession, or enjoyment of property or the related income from the property (such as a life estate or term certain) is a present interest in the property. Reg. §25.2503-3(b). A future interest may be defined as one which will come into being (i.e., the use, possession, or enjoyment) at some future date. As defined in the Regulations:

> Future interests is a legal term, and includes reversions, remainder, and other interests or estates, whether vested or contingent, and whether or not supported by a particular interest or estate, which are limited to commence in use, possession, or enjoyment at some future date or time. The term has no reference to such contractual rights as exist in a bond, note, (though bearing no interest until maturity), or in a policy of life insurance, the obligations of which are to be discharged by payments in the future. But a future interest or interests in such contractual obligations may be created by the limitations contained in a trust to other instrument to transfer used in effecting a gift. Reg. §25.2503-3(a).

Consider carefully the following illustrations of present versus future interests.

EXAMPLE 22.50	During the year, Ed O'Brien makes an outright cash gift of $10,000 to Dana Flanigan. This gift qualifies as a present interest.

EXAMPLE 22.51	During the year, Ed transfers property in a trust with a life estate to Dana with income to be paid annually. The trust provides that upon Dana's death the remainder interest goes to Sara Flanigan. Ed has made two gifts: one to Dana of a life estate and one to Sara of a remainder interest. The life estate is a present interest, and the remainder is a future interest.

EXAMPLE 22.52	Assume the same facts as in Example 22.51 except that the income from the trust does not have to be paid annually to Dana. At the trustee's discretion the income may be accumulated and added to the corpus. In this case the life estate does not qualify as a present interest. The mere possibility of the trustee accumulating the income renders the life estate a future interest. Reg. §25.2503-3(c).

Concerning Example 22.51, if the life estate beneficiary's right to current income is contingent on obtaining the permission of a third party other than the trustee (including other beneficiaries), the life estate interest is deemed to be a future interest. *J. W. Blasdel,* 58 TC 1014, Dec. 31,548 (1972), aff'd, 73-1 USTC ¶12,929, 478 F.2d 226 (CA-5 1973).

Notable Exceptions

There are some exceptions to the present versus future interest rules as set forth in this section. For example, the gift of a note, or bond, that yields no interest until maturity is a gift of a present interest, although the maturity and benefits are in the future. The same would be true for the gift of a life insurance policy or other similar contract right. T.D. 7238, 1973-1 CB 544. A major exception to the general rule relates to gifts to minors utilizing various vehicles so that the gifts will be deemed to be present interests. Excellent examples are *Crummey* trusts and gifts to minors, each of which is discussed below.

Crummey Trusts

A gift of the right to demand a portion of a trust corpus is a gift of a present interest, Rev. Rul. 80-261, 1980-2 CB 219, as long as the donee-beneficiary is aware of his or her right to make the demand. Rev. Rul. 81-7, 1981-1 CB 474. Typically, the beneficiary of such a trust (known as a *Crummey* trust, *D.C. Crummey* 68-2 USTC ¶12,541, 397 F.2d 82 (CA-9 1968)) is given the right to demand an amount of corpus equal to the annual gift tax exclusion. Because donors might not want the beneficiaries to be able to withdraw trust corpus up to the $10,000, $11,000, $12,000, $13,000, and $14,000 annual exclusions available after 1981, the Economic Recovery Tax Act of 1981 provided a special transitional rule to limit the power to the old $3,000 exclusion in certain instances.

Gifts to Minors

No part of a transfer for the benefit of a minor will be considered future interest (which would not qualify for the annual exclusion) if the terms of the transfer meet the following conditions:

1. Both the property and its income may be expended by, or for the benefit of, the minor donee prior to the donee attaining the age of 21. To the extent not so expended, it will pass to the donee at that time.
2. In the event of the donee's death prior to reaching 21 years of age, the property and the income not expended will pass to the donee's estate or to persons appointed by the donee under the exercise of a general power of appointment.

A gift to a minor under a trust that confers on its beneficiary upon reaching age 21 the right to compel immediate distribution of the corpus by written notice to the trustee that is either (a) a continuing right or permits the trust to remain on its own terms or (b) a right for a limited period that, if not exercised, will permit the trust to continue on its own terms is not a gift of a future interest and qualifies for the annual gift tax exclusion under condition (1), above. Rev. Rul. 74-43, 1974-1 CB 285.

Contributions to Qualified State Tuition Programs

Any contribution to a qualified tuition program (QTP) is handled as a completed gift of a present interest from the donor to the donee at the time of the contribution. As a result, the $14,000 annual exclusion ($10,000 indexed) or $28,000 for split giving would apply to contributions to qualified state tuition programs. A donor that makes a contribution in excess of the annual exclusion may treat the gift as if it were made ratably over five years. Code Sec. 529(c)(2)(B). However, a gift tax return is required for a contribution exceeding the annual gift exclusion.

Exclusions

¶22,341   ## GENERAL CONSIDERATIONS

Annual Exclusion

For 2017, the first $14,000 given to any person during a calendar year is excluded in computing taxable gifts, if the gift constitutes a "present interest" in the gifted property. The exclusion for gifts is indexed annually for inflation.

A distinction must be made between a present and future interest to assure the availability of the annual donee exclusion. The ostensible reason for denying the annual exclusion for gifts of future interests was the difficulty associated with the determining the number of eventual donees and the value of their respective gifts. H.R. Rep. No. 708, 72d Cong., 1st Sess. 29 (1932), reprinted in 1939-1 CB (Part 2) 457, 478; S. Rep. No. 665, 72d Cong., 1st Sess. 41 (1932), reprinted in 1939-1 CB (Part 2) 496, 526.

Unlimited Donee Opportunities

There is no limit on the number of donees. The donor can claim a $14,000 annual exclusion for each present interest. Only the first $14,000 ($28,000 if splitting is elected as discussed in the next section of this chapter) given to each donee may be excluded. If the donor's gifts of present interests to each donee during a calendar year do not exceed $14,000, the gifts do not have to be reported on a gift tax return. Code Sec. 6019(a). Gifts exempted from taxation under the $14,000 annual donee exclusion are not included in the tax base for the purposes of computing estate taxes. Only adjusted taxable gifts are includible in the computation, and adjusted taxable gifts are limited to taxable gifts.

Gift-Splitting

A donor's spouse may consent to treatment as the donor of one-half of any taxable gift made to a third person. Such a consent to "gift-split" allows a married couple to use two annual per-donee exclusions and two unified credits with respect to a single gift.

EXAMPLE 22.53

In 2017, John Smith gives $5,504,000 in cash to his daughter. He gets one $14,000 annual exclusion, and so he makes a $5,490,000 taxable gift. He uses up his previously unused applicable credit amount and owes no gift tax. However, if Sara Smith (John's wife) consents to gift-split, John and Sara will get two $14,000 annual exclusions, or $28,000, and can use two applicable credit amounts.

A donor can gift-split only if he or she is a United States person (a citizen or a resident alien) and is married to a United States person at the time the gift is made. Individuals are married for gift-splitting purposes, only if they are married at the time the gift is made.

EXAMPLE 22.54

H makes a taxable gift to his son, S, on January 1, 2017. On February 17, 2017, his divorce from W is final. H and W may gift-split as long as neither remarry during the calendar year. Code Sec. 2513(a)(1).

Both the donor and the donor's spouse must consent to gift-split. The consent applies to all gifts either spouse makes during the calendar year in which they make the consent. Code Sec. 2513(a)(2). The consent does not apply, however, to any taxable gifts made by either spouse when they were not married to each other or when they were not both U.S. citizens or resident aliens. Reg. §25.2513-1(b).

The consent to split gifts applies to all gifts made during the calendar year by either spouse individually and by both spouses jointly. For example, Henry and Velma Holt consent to gift-split on a gift Velma made in January 2017. This consent also applies to any gifts Henry or Velma made during 2017 alone or jointly. Reg. §25.2513-1(b)(5).

In summary, gift-splitting has the following advantages:

1. Two annual exclusions are available instead of one.
2. Any gap between the sizes of the spouses' estates can be narrowed because only one-half of the gifts will come back as "adjusted taxable gifts" in the estate tax return of the contributing spouse.
3. The noncontributing spouse may be in a lower gift tax bracket or have an unused applicable credit amount. Because two sets of applicable credit amounts are available, no gift tax may be presently payable.

Unlimited Educational and Medical Expense Exclusion

An unlimited gift tax exclusion is available for amounts paid on behalf of a donee directly to an educational organization, provided that such amounts constitute tuition payments. In addition, amounts paid to health care providers for medical services on behalf of a donee qualify for an unlimited exclusion under this section. The exclusions for qualifying educational expenses and medical expenses are available without regard to the relationship between the donor and the donee and are available in addition to the annual exclusion Code Sec. 2503(e).

Qualifying medical expenses, for the purposes of this exclusion, are defined by reference to Code Sec. 213 (an income tax provision). The exclusion is not available to the extent the amounts paid are reimbursed by insurance.

¶22,345

MARITAL DEDUCTION

Beginning in 1982, a donor is allowed an unlimited marital deduction for lifetime gifts of separate and/ or community property to his or her spouse. Code Sec. 2523(a). But the gift tax marital deduction is not permitted for a gift of a life estate or other terminable interest. An exception to the terminable interest rule for the gift tax marital deduction is qualified terminable interest property (QTIP). Code Sec. 2523(c).

QTIP Provisions

As previously mentioned, the QTIP provisions are an exception to the terminable interest rule. Pursuant to Code Sec. 2523(e), a property interest, whether or not in trust, qualifies for the marital deduction when the following requirements are adhered to:

1. The donee spouse is entitled for life to all of the income from the property interest.
2. Such income is payable annually or at more frequent intervals.
3. The donee spouse has the power, exercisable in favor of the donee or the donee's estate, to appoint the property interest.
4. Such power is exercisable by the donee spouse alone and (whether exercisable by will or during life) is exercisable in all events.
5. No part of the property interest is subject to a power in any other person to appoint any part to any person other than the surviving spouse.

Also, to have a qualifying terminable interest under Code Sec. 2523(e), the donee spouse must be entitled to receive all the income from the property at least annually. Furthermore, no person may be able to appoint the property during the spouse's lifetime to anyone other than the spouse. When the QTIP election is made by the donor, there will not be any gift tax at that juncture. However, when the donee spouse disposes of his or her QTIP interest, either during his or her lifetime or at death, the property will be subject to gift or estate tax.

EXAMPLE 22.55	In 2017, Tony Owens creates a trust which is funded with $500,000 of Georgia Power bonds. Pursuant to the trust instrument, Donna Owens is to receive the income from the trust on an annual basis for her life. Upon Donna's death, the principal of the trust is to pass to their children. If Tony elects QTIP treatment, the interest passing to Donna will qualify for the marital deduction. The election is made on the gift tax return (Form 709, United States Gift (and Generation-Skipping Transfer) Tax Return) filed for the calendar year in which the donor transferred the interest. It should be noted that the fair market value of the QTIP property will be included in the gross estate of Donna when she dies.

Alien Spouses

An alien spouse of a U.S. citizen is generally not eligible for the unlimited gift tax marital deduction. However, the first $149,000 (for 2017) of gifts per year to an alien spouse will not be taxed. Code Sec. 2523(i). Also, it should be emphasized that the $149,000 annual exclusion for transfers by gift to a non-citizen spouse is only allowed for transfers that would meet the marital deduction test if the donee were a U.S. citizen. Therefore, a gift in trust would have to meet the exceptions to the terminable interest rule in order to qualify for the annual exclusion.

Divorce and Separation

Transfers to a spouse pursuant to a written agreement in connection with divorce are free of gift tax if the transfers are for the transferee's marital or property rights or for child support. Code Sec. 2516. This provision goes beyond the marital deduction since it covers terminable transfers and transfers after the parties are no longer married.

This special provision has no application to prenuptial agreements. When the parties transfer property pursuant to an agreement signed prior to marriage, the marital deduction is available under the general rule. Generally, divorce settlements are not treated as sales for income tax purposes, but are tax free. Code Sec. 1041.

¶22,355   CHARITABLE DEDUCTION

In the case of a donor who was a resident or a citizen of the United States at the time the gifts were made, there is an allowable charitable deduction for gifts included in the "total amount of gifts" made by the donor during the calendar year to or for the use of:

1. The United States, any State, Territory, or any political subdivision thereof, or the District of Columbia, for exclusively public purposes.
2. Any corporation, trust, community chest, fund or foundation organized and operated exclusively for religious, charitable, scientific, literary, or educational purposes, including the encouragement of art and the prevention of cruelty to children and animals, if no part of the net earnings of the organization inures to the benefit of any private shareholder or individual, if no substantial part of its activities is engaging in propaganda, or otherwise attempting to influence legislation, and if it does not participate in, or intervene in (including the publishing or distributing of statements), any political campaign on behalf of any candidate for public office.
3. A fraternal society, order, or association, operating under the lodge system, provided the gifts are to be used by the society, order, or association exclusively for one or more of the purposes set forth in subparagraph (2) of this paragraph.
4. Any post or organization of war veterans or auxiliary unit or society thereof, if organized in the United States or any of its possessions, and if no part of its net earnings inures to the benefit of any private shareholder or individual. Reg. §25.2522(a)-1(a).

The charitable deduction is not limited to gifts for use within the United States, or to gifts to or for the use of domestic corporations, trusts, community chests, funds, or foundations, or fraternal societies, orders, or associations operating under the lodge system.

Nonresident aliens are allowed a charitable deduction for gifts that relate primarily to domestic charities and for gifts to be used in the United States. Code Sec. 2522(b).

A donor who makes a gift to charity in excess of the annual gift tax exclusion is not required to file a gift tax return if the entire value of the donated property qualifies for a gift tax charitable deduction. This treatment extends to contributions of qualified conservation easements under Code Sec. 2522(d). The amount of the charitable deduction will first be reduced by the annual exclusion (if the interest is a present interest) and the remainder will be deducted as a charitable deduction. Also, charitable deductions are allowed for split interests when they qualify as annuity trusts, unitrusts, or pooled income funds.

EXAMPLE 22.56

On March 4, 2017, John Agor transferred Home Depot stock with a basis of $10,000 and market value of $30,000 to Louisiana Tech University. John had held the stock for two years at the time of the transfer. The full $30,000 is allowed to be taken on the gift tax return, but for income tax purposes, the deduction is limited to 30 percent of AGI subject to a five-year carryover. There is no taxable gift, computed as follows:

Gross gift		$30,000
Less: Annual exclusion	$14,000	
Charitable deduction	16,000	30,000
Taxable gift		$0

¶22,365   VALUATION OF GIFTS

Valuing gross gifts is the major gift tax problem since the value determines the amount that will be subject to gift tax. The gift tax regulations differ in no substantial respect from the corresponding estate tax regulations. All property is valued at fair market value at the time the gift is considered completed. Fair market value of property is the price at which such property would change hands between a willing buyer and a willing seller, neither being under any compulsion to buy or to sell, and both having reasonable knowledge of relevant facts.

Most of the concepts discussed earlier in this chapter concerning estate tax are also applicable to gift taxes. However, there is no alternative valuation date for gift tax as there is for estate taxes. Also, the special valuation methods are only available to estates.

¶22,375   NONTAXABLE TRANSFERS

Gratuitous transfers *not* subject to gift tax include:

1. Transfers to political organizations (Code Sec. 2501(a)(5)), but any appreciation is gross income to the donor (Code Sec. 84).
2. Transfers made for a business purpose (e.g., contributions to the capital of a corporation or partnership).
3. Revocable transfers, including the creation of revocable trusts, joint bank and brokerage accounts, and joint U.S. savings bonds.
4. Bargain purchases, if in arm's-length transactions.
5. Donation of services.
6. Support payments within the standard of living of the family. (Note: the support obligation to a child generally ceases on age 18 or earlier emancipation.)
7. Qualified disclaimers (in writing, within nine months). Code Sec. 2518.
8. Employment-related "gifts," such as a year-end bonus, but these are gross income items.

EXAMPLE 22.57

Two months before his death, Marvin Rose donated $5 million to a political campaign for mayor, an office sought by his best friend as candidate. The donation is not a gift for gift tax purposes. Furthermore, since there is no gift, there can be no adjusted taxable gift. Thus, the $5 million permanently escapes both gift and estate taxes. (However, no charitable deduction is allowed.)

¶22,385   CO-OWNERSHIPS OF PROPERTY

As a general rule, if property is purchased by co-tenants, any disproportional contribution results in a gift from the high to the low contributor.

EXAMPLE 22.58 Mother and daughter purchase a building as equal joint tenants for $200,000. If the daughter pays only $40,000, $60,000 is received by gift since this is her "discount" on her half. If the building is financed so that only $40,000 is put down, $8,000 by the daughter, only $12,000 is a gift. As the mother pays off the mortgage, additional gifts are made to the extent of principal payments, but they would not exceed the annual exclusion.

Revocable joint tenancies do not result in a gift until one joint tenant withdraws in excess of the contribution. Examples include joint bank accounts and U.S. savings bonds.

¶22,395 POWERS OF APPOINTMENT

General powers of appointment were discussed earlier in this chapter. If someone possesses a general power of appointment and the power is exercised, released, or simply lapses during the holder's lifetime, there is a gift. Code Sec. 2514. Special powers are not taxable.

EXAMPLE 22.59 G transfers property in trust to his wife, W, for life. W is also given the power to appoint the property to anyone in the world by gift or will. If W exercises the power in favor of anyone except herself, even an unrelated party, a taxable gift results.

EXAMPLE 22.60 Same as Example 22.59, except W has the power to appoint the property to anyone *except* herself, her estate, or the creditors of either. She exercises the power in favor of her children and grandchildren. There is no gift.

EXAMPLE 22.61 Same facts as Example 22.59, except that W needs G's consent to exercise the power. No gift tax will result because the power is reduced to a special power when the creator's consent is needed.

EXAMPLE 22.62 Same facts as Example 22.59, except that W needs G's consent to exercise the power. No gift tax will result be G transfers property to W for life, the remainder to his children. W can appoint the property to anyone, but only with the consent of the children. An exercise of power is not taxable because the consent of an adverse party is required. ause the power is reduced to a special power when the creator's consent is needed.

EXAMPLE 22.63 G transfers an insurance policy on his life to W. If their child is the beneficiary, W has completed a gift of the proceeds to such child when G dies. At that time, W's powers over the policy lapses.

Powers limited to an ascertainable standard (e.g., for the health, education, maintenance, and support of the powerholder) and powers to appoint up to $5,000 or five percent of the property (whichever is greater) each year are only special powers. Code Sec. 2514(c)(1) and (3).

¶22,405 LIABILITY FOR TAX

The gift tax is levied on the gratuitous transfer of property during life. It may not be intuitively obvious, but an individual who gives away property may have to pay an excise tax for the privilege. Thus, the gift tax is payable by *the donor* as a toll charge for the fact that the property transferred will not be subject to estate taxes (in most cases). Small gifts are disregarded and marital and charitable deductions are available. If the gift tax remains unpaid, the donee is liable to the extent of the value of the gifted property. Code Sec. 6324(b). U.S. residents and citizens are liable for gift taxes on worldwide transfers, while nonresident aliens are liable only for taxes on transfers of U.S. property, such as U.S. real estate. Code Secs. 2501(a)(1) and 2511(a).

Only individuals are subject to gift tax. The identity of the transferee is irrelevant; it could be an individual, estate, trust, or corporation, U.S. or foreign.

EXAMPLE 22.64	Richard O'Hara, U.S. citizen, sends $50,000 to the Irish government. Even though the donee is a foreign government the transfer reduces Richard's estate and is subject to gift tax, he being a U.S. citizen or resident. (No charitable contribution deduction is available for donations to foreign entities, either.)

The donor may gift the property subject to the condition that the donee pays the gift tax ("a net gift"). This has several consequences:

1. Since the donee assumes the donor's liability, the transaction becomes a part-sale part-gift, so that if the tax is in excess of the donor's basis, the donor must recognize gain.
2. The gift is reduced so that the gift tax is payable on the value of the property less the gift tax, requiring computations.
3. The donor is still primarily liable to the IRS for the tax; the donee simply owes the donor the amount of the tax.

EXAMPLE 22.65	Gustav Mueller gives away securities to his daughter, Agnes, worth $148,000, on the condition that she pays the gift tax. If the $14,000 exclusion is applicable and Gustav is in the 40 percent gift tax bracket, the gift tax is not $53,600, as it would have been if Gustav paid the gift tax. The gift tax would be $32,160 since the taxable gift of $134,000 is reduced by the donee's obligation to pay $53,600 in gift tax. Since the actual gift is only $80,400 ($148,000 – $14,000-$53,600), the gift tax is 40 percent of that, or $32,160.

Tax Return

The gift tax return, Form 709, is an annual return due April 15 under the following three circumstances. (Note: After August 5, 1997, a donor who makes a gift in excess of the annual gift tax exclusion is not required to file a gift tax return if the entire value of the donated property qualifies for a gift tax charitable deduction. Also, after 1998, the annual exclusion for gifts is indexed annually for inflation.)

1. Donor made at least one gift of a present interest in excess of $14,000 to one or more donees.
2. Donor made any gift at all of a future interest (i.e., a remainder).
3. Donor and spouse wish to elect gift-splitting, thus doubling available exclusions and credits. Code Secs. 6019(a) and 6075(b).

Gross gifts, less exclusions and deductions, are "adjusted taxable gifts." Because of the applicable credit amount ($2,141,800 in 2017), no gift tax may be due with the return. However, the *return* is still due and adjusted taxable gifts are brought back into the gross estate with a credit for gift taxes paid, if any. Note that the applicable credit amount is never "used up" for estate tax purposes and has but *one* effect during life: to defer the transfer tax until after the donor's death. (Some *states* also levy gift taxes.)

¶22,415   GIFT TAX COMPUTATION—SUMMARY

The gift tax complements the estate tax by taxing transfers depleting the estate.

Step 1.	Return required by April 15 following the calendar year in which taxable gifts were made.
Step 2.	List all gifts made during the calendar year, except gifts of nonterminable interests to spouse.
Step 3.	Husband and wife may elect to treat all gifts to third parties as made one-half by each (i.e., gift-splitting).
Step 4.	Exclude for each donee the lesser of $14,000 or amount of gifts of present interests.
Step 5.	Deduct gifts to charities in excess of exclusion.
Step 6.	Result is taxable gifts for period (A).
Step 7.	Add (A) to total lifetime prior taxable gifts (B) to get new lifetime total (C).
Step 8.	Compute from the tables the tentative tax on (C).
Step 9.	Compute from the tables the tentative tax on (B).
Step 10.	Difference is tax imposed on gifts for period.
Step 11.	Reduce tax by applicable credit amount of $2,141,800 (for 2017) or by the amount of credit previously allowable and 20 percent of the amount of the specific exemption claimed for gifts made after September 8, 1976, and before January 1, 1977 (prior law).

Generation-Skipping Transfer (GST) Tax

¶22,501   ## NATURE AND PURPOSE OF TAX

In 1976, Congress passed the original "generation-skipping transfer tax." The purpose was to supplement the federal gift and estate tax system to assure that the transfer of wealth from one generation to the next would bear substantially the same transfer tax burden, whether the transfer was outright to each succeeding generation or in trust, where it would skip a generation for federal estate tax purposes.

Prior to the 1976 legislation, a common planning device was the generation-skipping trust, which would pay income to one's child for the child's life and then distribute the trust property to his or her grandchildren at the child's death. If properly structured, there would be no federal estate tax payable at the child's death, even though the child had received the economic benefits of the trust for life. The 1976 legislation changed this and imposed a generation-skipping transfer tax on the trust at the child's death in an amount similar to what the federal estate tax would have been if the child had owned the trust property outright.

The present law, created by the Tax Reform Act of 1986, is based to a large extent on the prior law, but is described by the House Ways and Means Committee as a "simplified tax." In reality, the 1986 Act was a disappointment to those who had hoped for simplification, and the current generation-skipping rules certainly remain very complex. Although the 1986 law created an entire class of potentially taxable transfers, many additional planning opportunities are still available.

Under the 2001 Act, the generation-skipping tax was repealed for 2010. Beginning in 2011, the generation-skipping transfer exemption will equal the applicable exclusion amount. Refer to Table 1 for amounts. Code Sec. 2631(c).

¶22,515   ## OVERVIEW

The current generation-skipping transfer rules became effective under Sec. 1433(a) of the 1986 Act on October 22, 1986. The provisions also apply to all existing revocable trusts, current wills (assuming the person did not die before December 31, 1986) and inter vivos transfers made after September 25, 1985. However, a trust that was irrevocable on September 25, 1985, is exempt under Act Sec. 1433(b)(2)(A), except for transfers to the trust after that date.

The generation-skipping transfer tax is imposed on property transferred to what Code Sec. 2613(a) defines as a "skip person." A skip person is an individual or entity that is assigned to a generation that is two or more generations below that of the transferor. For example, one's grandchild would be considered a skip person. So would a partnership or corporation in which a grandchild had an interest (entity generation assignments are made based on the relationship of the person having a beneficial interest in the entity to the transferor).

Generation assignment is based on the lineal relationship of family members. A spouse is assigned to the transferor's generation, regardless of age. Code Sec. 2651(c)(1). For nonlineal descendants, generation assignment is determined by the ages of the individuals involved in relation to the age of the transferor.

A person born 12½ years or less after the transfer is assigned to the same generation as the transferor. There is a new generation for each additional 25 years thereafter from the transferor's birthdate. Code Sec. 2651(d). Thus, a person who is more than 37½ years younger than the transferor will be treated as a grandchild.

¶22,525   ## TAXABLE EVENTS

Under the law, three events will give rise to a generation-skipping transfer tax: a taxable termination, a taxable distribution, and a direct skip.

Taxable Termination

A taxable termination is defined as the termination of a nonskip person's interest in property held in trust, after which only a skip person has an interest in the trust property. Code Sec. 2612(a)(1). In general, a person has an interest in the trust if he or she obtains a *present* right to receive principal or income from the trust. Code Sec. 2652(c)(1).

EXAMPLE 22.66	A father creates a trust for the benefit of his son, with the remainder passing to his grandson. Upon the death of the son, a taxable termination occurs. Had the trust been for the benefit of his wife, with the remainder going to the son, the death of the wife would not have resulted in a taxable transfer because a nonskip person maintained the interest in the trust.

There are certain exclusions that keep a termination from being labeled a "*taxable*" termination." A transfer to a person one generation below the transferor that is subject to federal estate or gift taxation is not a taxable termination, nor is a termination that is a transfer which qualifies for the Code Sec. 2503(e) medical or tuition exclusion. Code Sec. 2611(b)(1) and (2).

Taxable Distribution

A taxable distribution is a distribution from a trust to a skip person. Code Sec. 2612(b). The 1986 Tax Act repealed the exemption for income distributions so that now both corpus and income payments may fall into the category of a taxable distribution. The addition of this provision is one of the more significant changes made by the law and has profound ramifications for discretionary trusts.

EXAMPLE 22.67	A trust is established which provides for the discretionary payment of income and corpus to the transferor's child and grandchild. In the first year, each beneficiary receives $25,000 of the trust's income. The income payment to the grandchild is a taxable distribution.

The burden of this taxable distribution is eased somewhat by an income tax deduction allowed under Code Sec. 164(a)(5) to the distributee for any generation-skipping transfer tax paid on income distributions.

Direct Skip

The potential taxation of a direct skip is arguably the most important change made by the 1986 tax law in the generation-skipping area. Under prior law, transfers to a skip person (e.g., a grandchild) that circumvented the use of a trust were not taxable transfers. However, the current law dictates that a transfer of an interest in property to a skip person qualifies as a generation-skipping transfer if it is subject to federal estate or gift tax. Code Sec. 2612(c)(1).

EXAMPLE 22.68	A wealthy grandparent transfers $1 million directly to his granddaughter. This transaction is a generation-skipping transfer.

Special rules are applicable when the transfer is to a grandchild whose parent is deceased. The child of a predeceased child is not considered a skip person to which generation-skipping transfer would apply because this grandchild of the transferor is treated as if he were the transferor's child. Code Sec. 2612(c)(2). For terminations, distributions, and transfers occurring after December 31, 1997, the predeceased parent exception to the generation-skipping transfer tax is expanded to include collateral heirs, provided that the transferor had no living lineal descendants at the time of the transfer. (The exception is also expanded to taxable terminations and distributions.)

EXAMPLE 22.69	A grandparent transfers $100,000 to his grandchild, whose father (the son of the grandparent) had passed away one year earlier. The grandchild is deemed to be in the child's generation, and thus is treated as a nonskip person. Accordingly, the transfer is not a direct skip.

¶22,535   EXEMPTIONS FROM TAX

For purposes of determining the taxable amount of a generation-skipping transfer, the following exemptions from the tax are provided:

General Exemption

An exemption of $5,490,000 for 2017 is provided for each person making generation-skipping transfers ($10.98 million if gift-splitting is elected by the transferor's spouse). Code Sec. 2631. The exemption can be allocated by a transferor to property transferred at any time, but once it is made, it is irrevocable. Code Sec. 2631.

Annual Gift Tax Exclusion

The annual $14,000 gift tax exclusion per donee for gifts of present interests is also available when computing the generation-skipping transfer tax on such gifts.

Unused Exemption

Any unused generation-skipping transfer tax exemption is first allocated to inter vivos direct skips, then to testamentary direct skips, and finally to generation-skipping trusts from which taxable transfers may be made after death. Code Sec. 2632.

Incompetency Exemption

The generation-skipping transfer tax applies to transfers under a trust to the extent that the trust consists of property included in the gross estate of an incompetent decedent or to transfers that are direct skips that occur by reason of the death of the incompetent decedent after August 3, 1990. Under prior law there was an exclusion for incompetent decedents' property.

¶22,545   RATE OF TAX

All generation-skipping transfers are subject to tax at a flat rate equal to the product of the maximum estate and gift tax rate (i.e., 40 percent) and the "inclusion ratio" with respect to the transfer.

Inclusion Ratio

The inclusion ratio is the excess (if any) of one over the "applicable fraction" determined for the trust from which such a transfer is made or, in the case of a direct skip, the applicable fraction determined for such a skip. Stated differently, 1 − (applicable fraction) = inclusion ratio.

Applicable Fraction

The applicable fraction is determined as follows: the numerator is the amount of the GST exemption allocated to the trust or property transferred in the direct skip. Its denominator is the value of the property transferred to the trust (or involved in the direct skip) reduced by the sum of any federal or state death tax attributable to the property that was recovered from the trust and any charitable deduction allowed under Code Sec. 2055 or 2522.

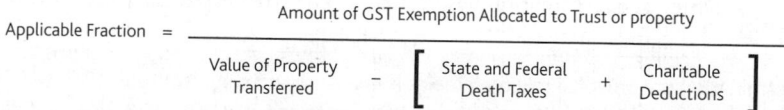

The effect of using the inclusion ratio is to exempt the appreciation allocable to the GST exemption from the GST tax when ultimately imposed. Code Secs. 2641 and 2642.

EXAMPLE 22.70	Grandpa transfers $4 million in trust for his daughter for life, remainder to Grandson, and allocates $1 million of his $5.49 million exemption to the transfer. At the time the daughter dies, the trust fund is worth $8 million. Assuming there are no estate/death taxes and charitable deductions, the calculation of the generation-skipping transfer tax would be as follows:

1. Determination of the applicable fraction: ($1 million exemption divided by $4 million in property equals an applicable fraction of .25).

2. Determination of the inclusion ratio: Subtract the applicable fraction from 1. Thus, the inclusion ratio is 1 minus .25, or .75.

The generation-skipping tax rate is the product of the inclusion ratio—in this case .75—and the maximum federal estate tax rate at the time of the transfer (i.e., 40 percent). Thus, the rate of tax on this transfer is .30 percent. The GST tax is $2,400,000 ($8 million × .30 percent).

¶22,555   TAX COMPUTATIONS

In general, the method of computing the tax base of the generation-skipping transfer tax parallels the method applicable to the most closely analogous transfer subject to estate and gift tax. The method of computing the taxable amount depends on whether a taxable distribution, a taxable termination, or a direct skip is involved. Unless otherwise directed by a trust instrument specifically referring to the generation-skipping transfer tax, the tax imposed on a generation-skipping transfer is to be charged to the property being transferred.

Taxable Distributions

In the case of a taxable distribution, the amount subject to the generation-skipping transfer tax is the amount received by the transferee, reduced by any expenses included in connection with the determination, collection, or refund of the generation-skipping transfer tax. The transferee pays the tax on the taxable distribution. If the trustee pays any amount of the tax, the trustee is treated as having made an additional taxable distribution of that amount.

Note that all of the examples that follow assume that exemptions are exhausted and that the tax rate is 40 percent in 2017.

EXAMPLE 22.71	A taxable distribution of $1 million is made to Grandson in 2017. Grandson must pay $400,000 in GST taxes, retaining $600,000.

Taxable Terminations

In the case of a taxable termination, the amount subject to tax is the value of the property in which the interest terminates. A deduction is allowed for expenses, indebtedness, and taxes attributable to the property with respect to which the termination has occurred. The trustee pays any tax due on a taxable termination.

EXAMPLE 22.72	Upon termination of a trust, $1 million remains in the trust and is subject to the GST tax. The trustee pays the tax of $400,000 in 2016 (40 percent × $1 million), remitting $600,000 in 2017 to the skip person, Grandson.

Direct Skips

In the case of a testamentary direct skip, the amount subject to tax is the value of the property received by the transferee. The person making the transfer pays the tax liability incurred from a direct skip.

EXAMPLE 22.73	Grandpa had a residual estate of $2,333,333 before taxes in 2017. He had already used up his $5.49 million estate exemption and his $5.49 million GST exemption. He left $1,000,000 to his grandson. After estate taxes, $1,400,000 remained. The GST tax is levied on the amount received by the distributee in a direct skip. Thus, $1,000,000 is distributed to Grandson and the trustee or executor pays a GST tax of $400,000 in 2017.

In the case of an inter vivos direct skip, the amount subject to the GST tax is the value of the property received by the transferee. In addition, the gift tax is computed on the combined value of the gift and the generation-skipping transfer tax.

EXAMPLE 22.74	Grandpa made a gift of $1 million to Grandson in 2017. The GST tax is $400,000. For gift tax purposes, a gift of $1.40 million was made. Thus, a gift tax of $560,000 is payable as well. Note, however, that it took only $1,960,000 to transfer $1 million to the Grandson, as opposed to $2,333,333 in a testamentary transfer to get the Grandson, $1 million.

¶22,565 PAYMENT OF TAX

The GST tax is paid by the transferor or trustee except that the distributee pays the tax on taxable distributions. The GST tax return is due by the 15th day of the fourth month after the taxable year of the person who pays the tax and during which the transfer takes place, except in the case of a direct skip, other than from a trust, where the return is due at the same time the estate or gift tax return is due with respect to the transfer. Code Secs. 2603 and 2662.

¶22,575 CREDITS AND DEDUCTIONS

If a generation-skipping transfer (other than a direct skip) occurs at the same time as, and as a result of, the death of an individual, a credit against the generation-skipping transfer tax paid to any state is permitted. However, the credit is limited to five percent of the amount of federal generation-skipping transfer tax imposed on the transfer. Expenses, debts, and taxes are deductible under the same principles as those used for estate tax purposes. Code Secs. 2604 and 2622(b).

TAX BLUNDER

Olive Harus had given her son a power of attorney seven years prior to becoming incompetent to handle her own affairs. Olive remained incompetent for nine years until death. The son's power of attorney was silent as to gifts. During the period of incompetency, the son used his power of attorney to make gifts of cash and real estate to the taxpayer's heirs. Under Virginia law, at the time of the gifts, a power of attorney did not enable the holder of the power to have gifting powers. Even though the purpose of these gifts was to reduce the estate's size by taking advantage of annual $10,000 gift tax exclusions, the IRS determined that the gifts were voidable under state law. Since the son was not legally authorized to make gifts of his mother's property, the gifts were includible in the mother's gross estate under Code Sec. 2038 as incomplete gifts. *O.D. Casey Est.,* CA-4, 91-2 USTC ¶60,091, 948 F.2d 895. The practitioner should always review the instrument creating the power of attorney and state law to ascertain gifting powers under a power of attorney authorization.

SUMMARY

- The federal estate, gift, and generation-skipping taxes are transfer taxes either at death or during life.

- The estate and gift transfer taxes are unified and subject to the same rate schedule. On the other hand, the generation-skipping tax is a flat tax at the highest estate tax rate (currently 40%).

- To understand the estate tax, one should start with the estate tax formula as depicted in Table 2. The formula begins with the gross estate less allowable deductions which yields the taxable estate. At this point, all taxable gifts after 1976 are added, and the tentative estate tax is determined. From the tentative estate tax, gift taxes payable on includible gifts after 1976 are subtracted, and, lastly, the estate tax credits are subtracted yielding the estate tax liability.

- The federal estate tax return (Form 706) must be filed within nine months of death, and the property on the return must be valued at date of death or the alternate valuation date (generally six months after death).

- The federal gift tax return (Form 709) is due April 15 following the year of the gift.

- Gifts of a present interest qualify for an annual exclusion of $14,000 per donee. However, a married couple may gift-split and thereby give $28,000 to a donee.

- The applicable credit amount for 2017 allows an estate of $5.49 million in value to not be subject to tax or a required filing. Also, an individual could give a present interest of $5,504,000 ($14,000 annual exclusion plus the $5.49 million exemption amount) in 2017 and not be subject to tax.

QUESTIONS

1. Distinguish between an estate tax and an inheritance tax.

2. What is the estate tax base?

3. What is the applicable credit amount?

4. Why is the gross estate different from the probate estate?

5. Greta Cook died in 2017. Her gross estate was $5,580,000, administration expenses were $60,000, and adjusted taxable gifts were $20,000. Compute the estate tax liability.

6. Why are certain gift taxes includible in the gross estate?

7. Why may the 50 percent "qualified joint tenancy" rule have adverse income tax effects?

8. What are the interests in, and powers over, property that may be given to a donee without estate tax consequences to the donee's estate?

9. Distinguish between a mere testamentary power to appoint property to the creditors of one's estate and a power to appoint property to anyone in the world, except oneself, one's estate, or the creditors of either.

10. Which transfers of life insurance policies prior to death are includible in the transferor's gross estate?

11. Which expenses may be deducted for income tax purposes or for estate tax purposes by election?

12. What are the requirements for a marital deduction?

13. What types of property passing to a spouse are considered terminable interests that would not qualify for the marital deduction?

14. Is it possible that a transfer made to a future spouse may later qualify for the estate tax marital deduction?

15. What is a QTIP trust, and what is the "price paid" for its use?

16. What are the main differences between the income tax and the estate tax charitable deduction?

17. What are the main differences between a unitrust and an annuity trust?

18. What are the tax advantages of a disclaimer?

19. What is the significance of a disclaimant reaching age 21?

20. Which transfers are subject to the gift tax?

21. What is a net gift?

22. What are the advantages of gift-splitting?

23. Why must the donor disclose his income tax basis in gifted property on the gift tax return?

24. What is a direct skip?

PROBLEMS

25. If Doria Oliva dies this year (2017), what estate tax is payable if the facts are:

Adjusted gross estate	$5,800,000
Adjusted taxable gifts after 1976	100,000
Gift tax paid	6,000

26. Melinda transferred $500,000 to an irrevocable, inter vivos trust, leaving the income to Elmo, her husband, for his life, and the remainder to their daughter, Ingrid, if she survives her mother. What are the estate tax consequences to Melinda's estate if:
    a. Melinda predeceased Elmo and Ingrid.
    b. Ingrid predeceased Melinda.
    c. Melinda survived Elmo, but predeceased Ingrid.

27. Janet Smith transferred, in trust, $500,000 of Georgia Power Bonds to her younger sister, Bertha Jones. These bonds pay interest quarterly, and Janet reserved the income for her life. Janet was age 60 at the time of the gift. Assume the remainder interest is 0.25509.
    a. What is the value of Janet's gift?
    b. Does the annual exclusion apply?

28. In each of the following cases, determine the amount includible in David's gross estate:
    a. An account balance of $200,000 in an IRA that the beneficiary immediately withdrew.
    b. A commercial annuity with a present value of $60,000, payable to David's wife, Selma, who contributed 40 percent of the purchase price.
    c. A qualified pension annuity with a present value of $180,000, one-third of which is attributable to David's own contributions, payable to Selma.
    d. A lump-sum distribution from a qualified profit-sharing plan of $30,000, payable to David's son, Kyle, who used five-year averaging.

29. Martha and Ludwig own their home in equal shares. Ludwig purchased the home with funds inherited from his grandfather, but Martha died first, leaving her half to Ludwig.

    What is includible in Martha's estate, and what is Ludwig's basis in the home if:
    a. They were married and owned the home as:
       1. Tenants in common
       2. Joint tenants
       3. Tenants by the entirety
       4. Community property
    b. They were brother and sister and owned the house as:
       1. Tenants in common
       2. Joint tenants

30. Identify the following property interests, powers, and events:
    a. Gus buys a piece of land with his brother, Jack. Gus's interest is 60 percent; Jack's is 40 percent.
    b. Bruce died, leaving his wife, Nancy, "30 percent of his adjusted gross estate, free and clear, in cash."
    c. Henry purchased a home "together with my wife, Ann, as co-owners with the right of survivorship."
    d. George transfers $10 million in trust to his wife, Wanda, for life, then to his son, Luke, for life, then to his daughter, Adele, if she survives Wanda, her mother. Adele also has the power to invade corpus to the extent needed to support her in her accustomed life style.
    e. Wendy owns half of all income and assets acquired by Harold during their marriage.
    f. Grandpa Jones died, still living rent free on a portion of the farm he deeded to Jack, his grandson, 11 years earlier.

31. Evelyn gave a Flymore sailplane to her husband who is an enthusiast of this sport for their wedding anniversary. Purchase cost was $37,000. She used her own funds from a separate checking account.
    a. What is the value of the gift?
    b. Does the gift have to be reported?
    c. What is the limit on a gift between spouses?

32. John and Janet Smith (husband and wife) purchased 1,000 shares of ABC Company common stock (NYSE) for $56,000 and immediately had it titled in the names of "Hugh and Donna Smith as joint tenants with rights of survivorship" (son and daughter-in-law). Assume gift-splitting in 2017.
    a. How much is the gift?
    b. What is the total of John's exclusions?
    c. What is the total of Janet's annual exclusions?

33. Joseph Grant's will provided that $1 million was to be placed in trust for his son, Steven, for life, with a remainder to Steven's children per stirpes.

    What are the estate tax consequences to Steven's estate if the trust instrument provides the following:
    a. All trust income must be distributed to Steven quarterly.
    b. Steven is to be trustee.
    c. Steven may appoint the trust property to anyone he chooses during life and by will, except to himself, his estate, or the creditors of either.
    d. Steven may invade corpus to whatever extent necessary for his support and maintenance in his accustomed mode of living, as well as for his health and education.
    e. Steven may withdraw from the principal the greater of $5,000 or five percent of the trust each year on a noncumulative basis.
    f. Is any transfer tax possible upon Steven's death?

34. In which of the following cases will the insurance proceeds be includible in Bertram's estate?
    a. Bertram purchased the policy on his life 11 years ago and transferred all rights to it to Donna, his daughter, five years before he died.
    b. Same as (a), but the transfer took place two years before Bertram's death.
    c. Two years before he died, Bertram talked his wife into buying a policy on his life. The only available funds during the marriage came from Bertram's salary.
    d. Unknown to Bertram, because Donna was concerned about his health, she bought a term policy on his life seven months before he died.

35. On June 28, 1996, Bart Richards married Martha Joiner in Atlanta, Georgia. Because Bart was so happy that Martha became his wife, he purchased a home in Atlanta for $500,000 out of his own separate funds. He immediately titled the home in their joint names with right of survivorship. Bart died on June 28, 2017. The house was worth $800,000 on Bart's date of death. The executor elects to value the home at the date of death. What value will be placed on Bart's joint interest in his estate tax return?

36. Assume the same facts as in Problem 35. What is Martha's income tax basis in the house?

37. Assume the same facts as in Problem 35, except that Bart and Martha resided in Dallas, Texas. What is Martha's income tax basis in the house?

38. Kermit Ames died on January 15, 2017. The fair market value of his house was $150,000 on his date of death. On July 15, 2017, the house was worth $130,000. Assume the alternate valuation date is selected by the executor. What value is used by the executor in the estate tax return?

39. Assume the same facts as in Problem 38, except that the executor sold the house on May 2, 2017, for $138,000. What value is used by the executor in the estate tax return?

40. Assume the same facts as in Problem 38. What is the due date of the estate tax return?

41. Tom Parks died on March 15, 2017. The values of Tom's assets on March 15 and September 15, 2017, are as indicated below:

Asset	VALUES	
	Mar. 15	Sept. 15
Land	$5,400,000	$5,350,000
Stocks	300,000	300,000
Bonds	400,000	350,000

The marginal federal estate tax bracket applicable to Tom's estate is 40 percent for property over $5.49 million. All of Tom's property, which consists of the above capital assets, will go to his children, Ted and Jason. Neither Ted nor Jason is a dealer in real estate. Should the executor elect alternate valuation under Code Sec. 2032? In deciding whether to elect the alternate valuation date, calculate both the estate tax consequences and the income tax consequences for the parties involved.

42. Mr. John Henderson died on February 17, 2017. For each of the following items indicate the amount to be included in John's gross estate. Unless stated to the contrary, assume that the items are valued as of John's death.
    a. John owned a 2006 Lincoln Town Car. At his date of death, the car's retail price was $11,750, and its wholesale price was $10,150.
    b. Same as (a), except that the executor sold the car on April 17, 2017, for $11,000 to a buyer who saw it advertised on the home shopping network on a local TV station.
    c. John owned 1,000 shares of I.B.M. On February 17, 2017, the stock sold at a high of 100 and low of 98. It closed at 99 1/4.

43. Which of the following items are deductible to the estate?
    a. Property taxes accrued at death on decedent's home, held in a qualified joint tenancy.
    b. Interest accrued during estate administration on decedent's debts for which he was personally liable.
    c. Administration expenses in excess of value of property subject to claims, if paid one year after death.
    d. Same as (c), except that the property was not subject to claims.
    e. Estimated accountants' fees to be paid when practicable.
    f. Decedent's medical expenses paid 11 months after death.

44. Because John was so happy that Dana had agreed to become his fiancee, on February 2, 2017, he gave Dana's mother, Ethel, $15,000 in cash.
    a. Does this gift qualify for gift-splitting?
    b. Does this gift qualify for gift-splitting if John and Dana marry by December 31, 2017?

45. Mortimer Piper transferred $5 million in trust to his wife, Mona, for life, then to their children in equal shares. After Mortimer died, Mona sold her income interest, then died 17 years later.
    a. What are the transfer tax consequences to Mortimer, his estate, Mona, and her estate if a QTIP election is made?
    b. Same as (a), but without a QTIP election?

46. When Harry died, he left his surviving wife, Clare, the following:
    a. A remainder in a summer house, with a life estate left to his mother.
    b. A life estate and a general power of appointment in closely held stock, which, in the last 17 years, paid no dividends.
    c. An insurance policy on her own life.
    d. An annuity payable from a qualified, noncontributory pension plan.
    e. A patent with three years to run.
    f. Income from a mutual fund for life, with a remainder to their two daughters.

Which of the above bequests qualify for the marital deduction?

47. In 2017, Mr. Colburn created a trust for the benefit of his five adult children and transferred $300,000 to it. The trustee may decide how much income to pay to each child each year. The trust will terminate at the end of 40 years, and the assets will be divided equally among the children or their estates. Does Mr. Colburn receive a gift tax exclusion of $70,000? Explain.

48. John Henry Harris was left a 1962 Impala convertible by his uncle, Billy Bob Harris. After receiving the car, John determined that five cars in his family were too many. As a result, he disclaimed the property with direction that the car go to his brother, Lee Roy Harris. Is this a valid disclaimer for estate tax purposes?

49. Stanley Rosen's cumulative lifetime taxable gifts amount to $250,000. The following year, he gives his favorite nephew $164,000 to open a liquor store.
    a. What is the taxable gift?
    b. What is the tax on the gift (prior to credits)?
    c. What is the gift tax payable?

50. The $14,000 exclusion would be available in which of the following transfers?
    a. Revocable transfer in trust to W for life, then to S.
    b. Irrevocable transfer in trust to W for life, then to S.
    c. Irrevocable transfer of a life insurance policy to a trust with two income beneficiaries.
    d. Transfer in trust to A and/or B for life, then to L, and the grantor makes the distribution decisions.
    e. Same as (d), but the independent trustee makes the distribution decisions.
    f. Nonbusiness transfer to a corporation owned 50 percent by the donor's three children.
    g. Transfer in trust to a minor, all income to be accumulated.

51. In the following independent cases explain whether the exclusion, the marital deduction, the charitable deduction, and gift-splitting are available.
    a. To mother for life, then to spouse
    b. To spouse for life, then to child
    c. To charity for five years, then to spouse
    d. To spouse for life, then to charity
    e. To child A and/or child B for life, then to grandchild

52. During the year your client, Big Jim Smith, gave $9,000 to 70 different donees. Has Big Jim made any taxable gifts during the year?

53. Isaac Binder purchased 1,000 shares of Deep-Freeze Inc. five years ago for $15,000. Two years before he died, he gave his son, Edward, 500 shares worth $6,000. He died during a bull market and willed Edward the other 500 shares, then worth $12,000.
    a. What is Edward's basis for gain or loss in the stock received by inter vivos gift?
    b. What is Edward's basis in the testamentary gift?
    c. What is Edward's holding period in the two blocks of stock?

54. John Henry paid $60,000 in 2017 in medical bills to a doctor and a hospital for his invalid father. Has John Henry made any taxable gifts in 2017?

55. Under the annuity rules, all the following are includible in the decedent's estate, except:
    a. A lump-sum distribution from a qualified profit-sharing plan to a named beneficiary who waived forward averaging.
    b. A commercial joint and survivorship annuity payable to the decedent and the spouse where the spouse furnished the purchase price.
    c. The first $100,000 of an individual retirement account payable to the decedent's grandchildren.
    d. One-half of a joint and survivorship annuity payable to the decedent and the spouse. The latter's aunt had purchased the annuity for them as a golden anniversary gift.

56. As a rule, general powers of appointment are taxable, while special powers are not. The following powers are all special powers, except:

    a. The power to appoint property to any person or entity in the world except to the oneself, the estate, or creditors.

    b. The power to invade corpus to the extent necessary to maintain one's present mode of living (which includes $1 million a year for servants, trips, jewelry, and a yacht).

    c. The power to appoint the property to the holder's children and to anyone else, but with the remainderman's consent.

    d. The mere testamentary power to appoint the property to the creditors of the holder's estate.

57. During the current year, Dana makes the following cash gifts: $5,000 to her daughter, $9,000 to her brother, and $16,000 to a business partner. Does Dana need to file a gift tax return?

58. Which one of the following is not a deduction from the gross estate of a decedent?

    a. Unpaid income taxes on income received by the decedent during life.

    b. Interest payable on a loan incurred to pay estate taxes.

    c. Selling expenses for selling estate property if these sales are necessary to settle the estate.

    d. Interest payable after a decedent's death attributable to an installment obligation incurred by decedent.

    e. Casualty loss (uninsured) incurred during settlement of the estate.

59. In the typical gift situation, the donor pays the gift tax. When a "net gift" is made, however, the donee promises the donor to pay any gift tax due. The following statements relating to net gifts are all false, except:

    a. The donor may realize a gain or loss on the transfer.

    b. The donor becomes secondarily liable for the gift tax.

    c. The donee's basis will not include an adjustment for the gift tax paid by the donee.

    d. The amount of the gift is reduced by gift taxes actually paid by the donee, but not by any reduction in the donor's unified credit.

60. Hugh Colburn's financially destitute brother, Big Al, has a daughter named Violet. Hugh offers to pay for Violet's college education. In 2017, Hugh pays Columbia University's annual tuition of $50,000 and he also gives Violet an annual allotment of $16,000. Determine Hugh's taxable gifts for 2017.

61. The generation-skipping transfer tax supplements the estate and gift taxes. The following statements about this tax are all true, except:

    a. The generation-skipping trust is liable for any transfer tax due, but the distributee has transferee liability.

    b. A generation-skipping trust must have at least two beneficiaries in different generations below that of the grantor.

    c. The same top marginal tax rate applies to estate, gift, and generation-skipping transfer taxes.

    d. A person cannot be a beneficiary if the person has no present interest in the trust.

62. **Comprehensive Problem.** During 2017, Dale Davison made the following gifts:

    a. $30,000 to the political action group to re-elect Sam Nunn for the U.S. Senate.

    b. $25,000 to Scientific Atlanta Corporation (because he believed in their research objectives). Dale was not a shareholder in Scientific Atlanta Corp.

    c. $22,000 to Mount Paran Church of God.

    d. $100,000 was put in a joint tenants account. The joint tenants were Dale and his brother Sam.

    e. $45,000 was paid to Vassar University in tuition for his daughter Sara.

    f. $100,000 was placed in trust for his son, Ralph, for life, then the remainder will go to the Southern Methodist Foundation. Ralph's life estate is valued at $40,000.

    g. A gift of real estate (basis of $60,000 and fair market value of $310,000 to his sister, Karen).

    h. A gift of a life insurance policy on Dale's life to Sara (the beneficiary). The policy was worth $8,000 but had a face value of $50,000.

    What are Dale's taxable gifts for the year?

63. **Comprehensive Problem.** When Howard Foth died in the current year, in addition to his $5.0 million of certificates of deposit and investment property worth $200,000, the following facts were disclosed by the executor:

   a. In 1979, Howard Foth decided to see what kind of fiduciary the Bank of Georgia would be for his assets. However, he did not want to establish an irrevocable trust because the fiduciary might not perform up to expectations and he might need the property later for his own retirement needs. Consequently, Howard established a revocable trust funded at $300,000, but the fair market value at death was $700,000.

   b. In 1989, Howard made a taxable gift of $90,000 to his daughter, Bertha. Due to the unified credit, Howard did not incur any gift tax.

   c. In 1987, Howard purchased a paid-up life insurance policy with a face value of $300,000 payable at death to the executor of the estate to use against any estate taxes that might be due.

   d. In 1975, Howard's mother had left him a general power of appointment over a trust valued at $215,000. This power was subject to the standard of comfort.

   e. Funeral expenses were $30,000, and administration expenses of $70,000 are considered necessary for Howard's estate.

   f. Howard left his wife, Bella, $600,000 outright in certificates of deposit.

   g. The executor paid $40,000 in state death taxes to the state of Georgia.

   Compute the net estate tax payable.

64. **Comprehensive Problem.** Dave L. Jones, a calendar-year taxpayer using the cash method of accounting, was scared to death on Halloween night, October 31, 2017. Under the terms of the will, Dave devised and bequeathed all of the property he owned to his wife, Hildegard, except for a cash gift of $100,000 to the School of Accountancy at Louisiana Tech University, a condominium in Cancun, Mexico, to his beloved son, Billy Bob, a condominium in West Palm Beach, Florida, to Lee Ray Brown, and a $20,000 cash gift to Peggy Sue Elmore (who befriended him late in life).

A review of the executor's files and discussions with Mr. Jones's attorney reveal the following facts:

a. Mr. Jones's assets at (1) date of death and (2) six months later are as follows:

	Fair Market Value	
Real Estate	10/31/17	4/30/18
Personal residence	$ 500,000	$ 500,000
Cancun condominium	3,500,000	3,450,000
West Palm Beach condominium	3,000,000	3,525,000
Stocks and Bonds		
Ford Motor Co. bonds, 60 10% bonds, face value, $1,000 each. Interest payable semiannually on July 1 and January 1	72,000	75,000
Interest accrued on Ford Motor Co. bonds from July 1, 2017, to October 31, 2017	2,000	2,000
Littleton Telephone Co., common stock, 1,000 shares traded over the counter $10 per share on October 31, 2017, and $20 on April 30, 2018	10,000	20,000
West Lumber Co., traded NYSE, 5,000 shares common stock $100 per share on October 31, 2017, and $50 per share on April 30, 2018	500,000	250,000
Cash		
Checking Account No. 23-000, First National Bank of Greenville	15,000	15,000
Money Market Savings Account No. 1-23456, Beaver Run Savings & Loan	275,000	275,000
Life Insurance		
Policy No. 1 provided for $100,000 payable to wife with no incidents of ownership	100,000	100,000
Policy No. 2 provided for $100,000 to wife, listed as owner under state law, but Dave retained the power to change the beneficiary	100,000	100,000
Other Assets		
1959 White Cadillac El Dorado Convertible, red interior with bobbing dog in rear window	20,000	20,000
Civil war memorabilia	10,000	10,000
5 carat diamond ring, blue-white perfect	50,000	50,000
Miscellaneous personal effects (clothing and shoes)	6,800	6,800
Miscellaneous household goods (dishes, pots and pans, plants, silverware, and tools)	5,000	5,000
Furniture	25,000	25,000
Oriental rugs	18,000	18,000

b. On November 7, 1976, Mr. Jones, pursuant to the legal firm's suggestion of utilizing the annual exclusion and the specific exemption, gave $33,000 to his son Billy Bob. (Note that a $6,000 adjustment to the unified credit is required because of this transaction.)

c. Mr. Jones has made annual gifts of the exact annual exclusion amount to his son and each of his grandchildren each year (including 2017) since 1977. Other than these gifts and the one above, he made no gifts during his life.

d. Dividends of $2 per share were declared on the West Lumber Co. stock on October 1, 2017, but were not paid until November 15, 2017. Assume Mr. Jones was alive on the date of record.

e. Interest of $6,500 accrued on the savings account at date of death.

f. Fees:

Funeral expenses	$12,000
Attorney's fees	30,000
Accounting fees	30,000
Executor's fees	40,000
Appraisal fees	2,300

g. Mortgage on personal residence, United Financial Mortgage Corp., 10 percent, $50,000.

h. Debts:

Accrued property taxes on personal residence	$2,000
Accrued property taxes on West Palm Beach condo	3,000

i. Taxes:

North Carolina Inheritance Tax	$45,000
Mexico Estate Tax	12,000

j. A proviso in the will provided that the marital deduction for property passing to the wife shall not be reduced for death taxes, foreign death taxes, and funeral and administrative expenses.

k. The executor has decided to take all administrative expenses on the estate return.

l. Assume the executor elected to value the assets in the gross estate at their date of death values.

Required: Compute the net estate tax payable (note that the amount paid to Mexico is the amount of the foreign tax credit).

65. **Comprehensive Problem.** Mr. B died in 2017 at the age of 72. In his will, Mr. B made several bequests to the members of his family. The executor of B's estate wants to know which of the following bequests constitute generation-skipping transfers.

a. A testamentary trust to pay the income among Mr. B's four sons in such shares as the trustee determines. The trust agreement provides that, upon the death of the first son to die, one-fourth of the trust shall be paid to his descendants *per stirpes*.

b. A trust under which the trustee may distribute income among Mr. B's descendants or apply the income for the benefit of any one of them. The trustee decides to pay the college tuition and medical school tuition for Mr. B's grandchildren.

c. Mr. B's bequeathal of the ABC Widget Company to his son, M. M decides to disclaim the property in compliance with Code Sec. 2518 because the company would interfere with his acting career. As a result, the ABC Company passes to M's son.

d. A trust to be created under which the trustee may distribute income or corpus to any of Mr. B's children or his remote descendants. The trustee makes several distributions to Mr. B's grandchildren because they really loved their grandfather.

66. **Comprehensive Problem.** Assume that the farm property shown below has been physically farmed by the decedent for the last thirty years. He willed it to his favorite son, who will continue to farm it.

    a. In each of the independent cases, indicate whether or not special use valuation is available. The values shown for the farm assets are their fair market values as computed under the highest and best use concept.

    b. Assume in each of the cases that the real estate consists of 1,000 acres, the average gross cash rent is $30 per acre, and the average real estate taxes are $5 per acre. Further assume that 10 percent is the average annual effective interest rate charged by the Farm Credit Bank. At what amount would the parcels be valued per Section 2032A for 2017?

    c. Refer to case 1. Five years after the farmer's death, his son sold the entire farm realty to a land speculator for $2,000,000. Assume that the farmer-decedent was not survived by a spouse and died in 2017. What are the tax consequences five years after the farmer's death? Who pays the tax cost? Use only the unified credit in your calculations.

    d. Same as part c, except that the sale occurs twelve years after the farmer's death.

	CASES		
	(1)	**(2)**	**(3)**
Bonds	2,200,000	2,000,000	2,200,000
Stocks	200,000	400,000	300,000
Farm real estate	3,000,000	750,000	2,900,000
Farm equipment	600,000	2,550,000	300,000
	6,000,000	**5,700,000**	**5,700,000**
Mortgage against farm realty	(50,000)	(80,000)	(20,000)
Accounting fees	(25,000)	(30,000)	(25,000)
Appraisers' fees	(25,000)	(40,000)	(25,000)
Adjusted gross estate & Taxable estate	**$5,900,000**	**$5,550,000**	**$5,630,000**

67. **Research Problem.** On May 20, 1978, decedent's husband, Hugh P. Hughes, executed a will which contained the following paragraph:

    Third: I give, devise and bequeath the 300-acre farm which I own near Macon, Georgia, to my wife, Bertha O. Hughes, for and during the term of her natural life with remainder to my children, Vince Hughes, Hedy Henderson, and Chester Hughes, in equal shares. However, with the right reserved to my wife in case of necessity, that she may sell the land if that need arises. But it is my wish that the land be preserved for the benefit of my three children.

    Hugh P. Hughes died on April 15, 2000, and decedent, Bertha O. Hughes, died on June 2, 2017. At the time of Bertha's death, the farm was worth $4 million.

    Is the farm excluded from Bertha's estate?

    In your answer, address the power of appointment of issue, and read the case of *Bette J. Berg,* 81-2 USTC ¶13,428 (DC Minn 1981).

68. **Research Problem.** John and Mary Larsson purchased a joint and survivorship annuity from the Life and Death Insurance Co. John paid for the annuity and died 11 years later, at which time Mary's survivorship interest had a value of $50,000. Mary was killed in a car crash four months later, having collected $2,000 since her husband's death.

    a. Must the date of death value be used, even though it is known that the asset is worthless prior to the due date of the return?

    b. Does it make a difference that the alternate valuation date is elected? (See *Estate of John A. Hance,* 18 TC 499, Dec. 19,025 (1952), Acq. 1953-1 CB 4, and Code Sec. 2039(a) and (b).)

69. **Research Problem.** Greene Corporation, a closely held corporation, is owned by Al Manx with 6,000 shares, Bob Barnes with 2,500 shares, and Cora Crowley with 1,500 shares. In the current year, Cora passed away. As a result of Cora's death, the executor contacts you about valuing Cora's closely held stock. In your analysis, you discover that Greene Corporation has average earnings over the representative period of $80 per share. Also, over the same period, it has paid $20 of dividends per share. The book value of Greene Corporation is $50 per share. Since the stock is not very marketable and Cora had a minority interest, you have concluded that a discount of 25 percent is appropriate for lack of marketability and minority interest.

    Required: Value Cora's closely held stock interest for estate tax purposes. In your research, review the case of *Central Trust Co. v. U.S.*, 62-2 ustc ¶12,092, 305 F.2d 393 (Ct Cl 1962) for the applicable weights to be assigned to the valuation factors of earnings, dividends, and book value.

70. **Research Problem.** In 2017, Bert Richards transferred a $100,000 savings account to his wife in trust. The terms of the trust are that income is to be distributed annually to his wife, Mary Beth, the remainder to his two children, Oscar and Bertha, in equal shares or to their estate. The value of Mary Beth's income interest is $50,000.
    a. Is this a taxable gift to Mary Beth? (See Code Sec. 2523(b)(1) and (e).)
    b. Have taxable gifts been made for Oscar and Bertha?
    c. How many annual exclusions are available? (See Code Sec. 2503(b).)

71. **Gift Tax Return Problem.** Based on the facts summarized below, use two gift Tax Forms 709 to complete the appropriate gift tax returns for Mr. and Mrs. Smith for calendar year 2016 for which each is required to file. They want to keep any gift tax liability as low as possible as a family group for the current and future years. "NYSE" means the stock is traded on the New York Stock Exchange.

John F. Smith
a. 6/29/16: John and Janet purchased $30,000 of MNO Company common stock (NYSE) and immediately had it recorded in their joint names as "John and Janet as joint tenants, with right of survivorship." John furnished $10,000 from his separate funds and Janet furnished $20,000 from her separate funds.
b. 7/10/16: Transferred 200 shares of XYZ Company common stock (NYSE) to son James. Fair market value was $30,000. It was purchased 5/1/74 for $9,000. It was previously registered in John's name only.
c. 8/1/16: Purchased 1,000 shares of ABC Company common stock (NYSE) for $52,000 and immediately had it titled in the names of "Joseph and Barbara Smith, as joint tenants with right of survivorship" (son and daughter-in-law).
d. 9/14/16: Deposited $15,000 as a birthday gift in savings account of nephew Richard Osco, account titled in Richard's mother's name as custodian under his state's Uniform gifts to Minor Act.
e. Taxable gifts made in prior years: In 1970, gave away 1,000 shares of DEF Company common stock (closely held company). Fair market value at date of gift was $93,000. John inherited these from his father who died 3/31/60 when they were worth $29,000. John claimed one exclusion, used his lifetime (specific) exemption, and paid $7,125 in gift tax (no marital gift splitting elected).

Janet B. Smith

a. 4/30/16: Gave a Flymore sailplane to her husband, who is an enthusiast of this sport, for their wedding anniversary. Purchase cost was $37,000. She used her own funds from a separate checking account.

b. 6/29/16: See John's Item A.

c. 7/15/16: Gave check for $20,000 made payable to "William and Barbara Zuck" (son-in-law and daughter).

d. 2/10/16: Janet transferred, in trust, $500,000 of Georgia Power Bonds to her younger sister, Bertha Jones. These bonds pay interest quarterly, and Janet reserved the income for her life. Janet was age 60 at the time of the gift. Assume the remainder interest is .25509.

e. Taxable gifts made in prior years: On 12/1/76, gave away 250 shares of STU Company common stock (NYSE). Fair market value date of gift was $32,000. Janet received these as a gift from her uncle in 1960. The fair market value then was $40,000. Uncle paid no gift tax. He had purchased them in 1955 for $36,000. Janet claimed one exclusion and used her lifetime (specific) exemption to avoid paying any gift tax (no marital gift splitting elected).

COMPREHENSIVE PROBLEM

Facts

Esther and Simon Ames, ages 51 and 50, respectively, have been married for 30 years and have lived in Texas where she was employed as a vice president of advertising of Eighth-note, Inc., a Texas corporation engaged in the manufacture and sale of musical instruments. However, last year there was a takeover of the corporation, and Esther lost her job. She received $250,000 in separation payments in 2016, twice her annual salary. She decided that she wanted to own her own business.

Her third cousin, Billy Ray, approached her. He wanted to know if Esther knew anyone who was interested in buying his small but profitable business located in Virginia. After some negotiations, Esther decided that she was interested and bought all the stock of Burglar Beware Lock Company.

Burglar Beware has a narrow but profitable field of business in selling heavy-duty locks for fences at junkyards, police compounds, and lots at hardware stores. Its balance sheet is attached at the end of this section. Last year, it earned $150,000 on sales of $1,000,000, including a $125,000 per annum salary for Esther. Its liabilities are comparatively small, and its net worth is about $800,000.

Burglar Beware has health insurance policies but no disability insurance coverage for its workers. It also has no pension plan. Of Burglar Beware's 12 employees, only Esther and her son, Bob, would be regarded as managers. There is really no middle management. Burglar Beware has no record of dividend payments and elected S corporation status in December of 1986.

Simon is a skilled and experienced college professor. When they moved from Texas to Virginia, he determined that he would look for a teaching position. He found a post at a salary of $40,000 per year plus hospital and major medical insurance benefits. He expects a pension of 50 percent of salary (plus Social Security) at age 67. He has in his own name approximately $40,000 in bank accounts.

When Esther and Simon moved to Virginia, they sold their Dallas home in September 2017; for $500,000 (which cost them $125,000). Currently they are renting an apartment, but are looking for a new home. They are interested in the tax ramifications of this move and spend a good deal of their time on weekends going out with realtors on the Eastern Shore of Virginia.

Esther has a $25,000 ordinary life insurance policy on her life that she has held for some time and that currently has a cash value of $15,000. She acquired the life insurance policy while in Texas. She also has $10,000 of National Service Life Insurance and a term policy of $25,000 not convertible to ordinary life for another five years. Both of these policies were acquired before marriage. She and Simon are in good health. There is no group insurance program at Burglars Beware and Esther thinks it should be considered. Esther would also like to know about a pension plan. She has heard about a simplified employee pension plan and wants your opinion on it (See Chapter 24).

Simon and Esther have two children. The elder, Bob, is a college graduate and left a job with a major insurance company to join Burglar Beware primarily as a salesman. He is 26 years old and has worked with his mother at Burglar Beware for the last six months. He also has some distinct ideas with respect to a new hydraulic lock for which he hopes he can obtain a license from the patent owner. He believes this lock could permit Burglar Beware to double its gross sales in four years. Bob is divorced and has no current plans for remarriage.

Esther and Simon's younger child, Lucille, age 23, graduated from college last May. She is a substitute teacher and is looking for a permanent job. While living with her parents, she is dating a local farmer.

Esther has regularly contributed $2,000 per year to an IRA that currently has a value of about $18,000, including accumulated earnings. Simon has a similar IRA, but his has appreciated only to $12,000.

Esther and Simon have in their joint names listed stocks valued at $70,000, with a basis of approximately $30,000. Esther also has in her own name Series H Savings Bonds worth approximately $13,000. She paid approximately $5,000 for these bonds.

Esther (an only child) has a mother, Winona, age 80, who also lives in Virginia. She owns a home with a value of approximately $480,000 and a portfolio of listed stocks, mostly inherited from her husband, valued at $250,000. The home was worth $300,000 at her husband's death and had been jointly owned since 1957. She has a trust from her husband, who died in 1998, which will not be included in her estate because she has all of the income and only a limited power of appointment currently valued at $200,000. But Winona has been diagnosed as having a terminal malignancy. The doctors estimate that she has about three years to live.

Simon has very few relatives, but he does have an uncle. Uncle Harry is age 90 and lives nearby. He worked for a number of years and currently lives on a pension, Social Security, and interest. He lives in a small home that he owns outright. The home is worth about $80,000, but he has no other substantial assets except $5,000 in the bank. Simon's concern is that Uncle Harry is now becoming forgetful and less and less able to take care of himself. Simon believes he would never consent to going into a nursing home and could not afford it in any event. Simon feels a moral obligation to take in Uncle Harry to live with their family. Uncle Harry has one other relative, a nephew who lives in Idaho and whom he seldom sees.

Burglar Beware, Inc.
Balance Sheet
September 30, 2017

Assets

Cash			$100,000
Inventory			402,000
Equipment, furniture and fixtures		$140,000	
Less: Reserve for depreciation		(15,000)	
Net			$125,000
Automobile		$16,000	
Less: Accumulated depreciation		(8,000)	
Net			$8,000
Land		$150,000	
Building	$185,000		
Less: Accumulated Depreciation	30,000	155,000	$305,000
Total			$940,000

Liabilities & Owners' Equity

Accounts payable	$140,000
Capital Stock	$800,000
Total	$940,000

Suggested Items for Group Discussion Only:

1. Statement of objectives
2. Review of facts
3. Retirement planning
4. Disability planning
5. Community property status
6. Buy-sell agreements
7. AB trust setup
8. Sale of home and diversification of investments
9. Planning recommendations for Hugh's mother
10. Planning recommendations for Donna's uncle
11. Special use valuation
12. Paying estate tax in installments

Chapter

23

Income Taxation of Trusts and Estates

OBJECTIVES

After completing Chapter 23, you should be able to:

1. Understand the intricacies and planning opportunities in a decedent's final federal income tax return.
2. Determine when 1041 returns for an estate or trust are required and how they are prepared.
3. Depict the duties and responsibilities of a fiduciary in the preparation of a federal income tax return for an estate or trust.
4. Achieve an understanding of fiduciary accounting income and distributable net income.
5. Recognize how beneficiaries are taxed on distributions from estates or trusts.
6. Calculate the alternative minimum tax for estates and trusts.
7. Identify the impact of special tax rules affecting only estates and trusts.
8. Depict tax planning strategies for estates, trusts, and beneficiaries.

OVERVIEW

What happens to a taxpayer's taxpaying responsibilities when the taxpayer dies? Is the taxpayer relieved of future tax obligations? What date does the estate take over as a tax-paying entity? What happens when property is placed in a trust by a parent for the benefit of a child? Who is the taxpayer: the parent, the child, or the trust? What happens if an estate or trust distributes income to a beneficiary? Are there federal income tax implications? Answers to these questions and to many other related questions are discussed in this chapter.

The chapter deals first with the taxation aspects of estates, focusing on a decedent's final federal income tax return and how the return might differ from a regular return if the decedent was still living. The term decedent refers to a person who is deceased.

Next, the chapter discusses the federal income tax return of an estate. An estate comes into existence on the date of a decedent's death and continues in existence until all of the decedent's property is distributed to heirs (beneficiaries) and the estate is dissolved by law.

The second part of the chapter reviews the federal income tax return of a trust. A trust is a legal entity set up to hold property. A trustee administers the property according to the dictates of a trust agreement.

Intertwined in the discussion of estate and trust income tax returns is a discussion of the duties and responsibilities of fiduciaries. A fiduciary is a person such as an administrator, trustee, or executor who has been given a special confidence and responsibility to manage property in a trust or estate according to some legal agreement (will or trust agreement) and in the best interests of the beneficiaries of the trust or estate.

Next, the tax scheme of estates, trusts, and beneficiaries are discussed in this chapter. It is possible that some of the income earned by a trust or estate will not be taxable to the trust or estate but, instead, will be picked up as income on the income tax return of a beneficiary. In some instances, a decedent's income might also be required to be reported as income on the income tax return of a beneficiary.

Also, the chapter highlights tax planning techniques that have proven useful in regard to a decedent's final return, estate and trust income tax returns, and the tax status of beneficiaries. Also discussed are the tax planning options available in return preparation of the decedent's final Form 1040, the estate or trust Form 1041 (U.S. Fiduciary Income Tax Return), and the estate's Form 706 (United States Estate (and Generation-Skipping Transfer) Tax Return).

Taxation of Estates

¶23,001   DECEDENT'S FINAL INCOME TAX RETURN

In the year a person dies (decedent), a federal income tax return is due for the period from the beginning of the decedent's tax year up to the date of death. Reg. §1.6012-3(b)(1). Death does not speed up the due date of the return. The tax return is due on the regular due date as if the decedent had continued to live for the entire tax year. Reg. §1.6072-1(b). An illustration of due dates for a decedent's final return is provided below.

EXAMPLE 23.1   A calendar-year taxpayer died on February 18, 2017. A tax return for the calendar year 2016 must be filed on or before April 15, 2017, and the tax return for the fractional part of 2017, that is, January 1 to February 18, 2017, must be filed on or before April 15, 2018.

If the decedent's gross income is below the required filing level, then no return need be filed. A return should be filed, however, if it would result in the refund of tax previously paid in or withheld. Code Sec. 6012(a)(1). Death does not change the filing status of the decedent. A joint return can still be filed with a surviving spouse if it is advantageous for tax purposes to do so. Income of the surviving spouse is included on the tax return for the entire tax year, but income of the decedent is included only up to the date of death. However, a joint return that includes a decedent may not be filed if the surviving spouse remarries before the end of the tax year in which the decedent dies or if the surviving spouse files a return for only part of the tax year because of a change in accounting period.

A fiduciary (executor or administrator of an estate) who has the responsibility of concluding the decedent's affairs has the responsibility of filing and signing the decedent's final return. If there is no executor or administrator of the decedent's estate and a joint return is to be filed, the surviving spouse can sign and file the return and indicate the date of the decedent's death on the return. A fiduciary, if appointed at a later date, has the power to change the decedent's filing status from married filing a joint return to married filing separately if there is a justifiable reason. Code Sec. 6013(a); Reg. §1.6013-1(d).

¶23,015   INCOME AND DEDUCTIONS ON FINAL RETURN

The method of accounting used by the decedent while alive determines what income and deductions are recognized on the decedent's final return. If the decedent was on the accrual basis of accounting for tax purposes, then only income accrued up to the date of death is included on the final return. Deductions that accrued up to the date of death are also shown on the final return. Income or deductions accruable only because of death are not included on the final return. Code Sec. 451(b); Reg. §1.451-1(b).

EXAMPLE 23.2   Sam Lett, a businessman, keeps his records on the accrual basis of accounting. Sam dies on September 30, 2017. Income earned by Sam through September 30, 2017, is included on his final return.

If the decedent was on the cash basis of accounting, as are most individuals, only income actually or constructively received up to the date of death is included on the final return. Income earned by a cash-basis decedent but not received prior to death is not included on the decedent's final return. Instead, the income is included on the income tax return of the estate or beneficiary who is entitled to the payment and actually receives it (income in respect of the decedent, which is discussed later).

EXAMPLE 23.3   Dave Jones, a cash-basis taxpayer who is an accountant and works for a local CPA firm, receives his salary payment on the fifteenth of the month for work completed the prior month. Dave dies on December 8. The December 15 salary payment for work completed in November is not included on his final return. The income is taxable to the estate or beneficiary who is entitled to the payment and actually receives it.

All valid tax deductible expenses paid by a cash-basis decedent before death can be deducted on a final return. Valid tax deductible expenses, which are not paid by the date of death, are normally deductible by the estate or the beneficiary who has the responsibility of discharging the obligation. Reg. §1.691(b)-1.

There is an exception to this rule for medical expenses incurred for a decedent's medical care and paid by the estate. The decedent's medical expenses paid by the estate are treated as paid at the time they are incurred and deducted on the return for the year incurred as long as they are paid within one year of the decedent's death. Code Sec. 213(c); Reg. §1.213-1(d). The purpose of this exception is that significant medical expenses might be incurred by a decedent just prior to death and, without the exception, not be deductible on any tax return. Also, if medical expenses of the decedent are paid by a surviving spouse, they are deductible in the year paid. Rev. Rul. 57-310, 1957-2 CB 206. Additionally, medical expenses paid by the executor within one year of the decedent's death may be taken either as a deduction on the estate tax return (Form 706) or the decedent's return for the year incurred (Form 1040). Moreover, it should be taken into consideration in this planning analysis that if the entire medical expense deduction is taken on the decedent's final return, the deduction is subject to the statutory limitation of 10 percent while the limitation is not applicable if the entire deduction is taken on the estate tax return (Form 706).

EXAMPLE 23.4	Medical expenses associated with the final illness of the decedent were $10,000. These expenses were paid by the estate within one year of the decedent's death. On the decedent's final return these expenses will exceed the statutory limitation by $9,000. Assume the marginal tax rate on the decedent's final return is 39.6 percent and the marginal tax rate on the decedent's estate tax return is 40 percent for 2017.

PLANNING POINTER	Deduction of the entire allowable medical expense on the final return will produce a tax savings of $3,564 ($9,000 × 39.6 percent), while deduction of the entire allowable expense on the estate tax return will produce a tax savings of $4,000 ($10,000 × 40 percent).

The decedent taxpayer is entitled to a full standard deduction on a final income tax return regardless of date of death. The standard deduction does not have to be reduced because the decedent did not live for a full 12-month period. Also, the additional amounts to the standard deduction because of blindness or old age are allowed in full regardless of the date of death during the tax year. The same is true for personal exemptions on the final return. That is, the decedent is allowed full personal exemptions on the final return, regardless of date of death.

Income in Respect of the Decedent

If the decedent was entitled to receive income at the date of death but the income was not properly includible on the decedent's final return, normally because the decedent was on the cash basis of accounting, this income is considered to be income in respect of the decedent (IRD). Income in respect of the decedent is included on the income tax return of the estate or beneficiary who is entitled to the payment and actually receives it. Code Sec. 691(a); Reg. §1.691(a)-2. Income in respect of the decedent includes but is not limited to the following items: (1) accrued income of a cash-basis decedent that was not included on the decedent's final return, (2) interest on U.S. savings bonds that has accrued but has not been reported by a cash-basis decedent, (3) dividends on stock declared before the decedent's death but payable after the date of death, (4) interest on savings accounts for cash-basis taxpayers from the last interest payment date up to the date of death, and (5) income that arises solely by reason of death of the decedent. Rev. Rul. 79-340, 1979-2 CB 320. The following examples help to clarify the above items of income in respect of the decedent.

EXAMPLE 23.5	Susan Lewis, a cash-basis taxpayer, dies on November 18. Susan normally receives a paycheck at the end of the month for a full month's work. The paycheck received on November 30 covering the period November 1 to November 18 is income in respect of the decedent and is includible as income by the party receiving it.

EXAMPLE 23.6	Bob Burl purchased U.S. savings bonds in 1989 and still held the bonds at the date of his death. Bob had not previously recognized any interest income on the bonds. The unreported interest income on the bonds is income in respect of the decedent. The estate or beneficiary that receives the bonds can elect to report all prior unreported interest income on its tax return or wait until the bonds mature or are disposed of and report the interest income at that time. If desired, an election can be made by a fiduciary to have the unreported interest income up to the date of the decedent's death included on the decedent's final income tax return. Rev. Rul. 68-145, 1968-1 CB 203. Naturally, this election can be quite valuable if the decedent's income in the final tax year is nominal.

EXAMPLE 23.7	Joan Furrow owned 1,000 shares of Sonic Corporation stock at the date of her death. Sonic declared a dividend on its common stock on November 5 with a record date on November 15 and payment date on November 30. Joan died on November 18. Since she was alive on the date of record but deceased by date of payment, the dividend payment is IRD to the successor in interest. The same result is achieved for either cash-basis or accrual-basis taxpayer.

EXAMPLE 23.8	Patrick Ralls, a cash-basis taxpayer, has a savings account at a local bank that pays and credits interest to accounts on a quarterly basis. Patrick dies on December 12. Interest income from October 1 to December 12, when credited to the account on December 31, is income in respect of the decedent to the estate or beneficiary holding the property at December 31.

EXAMPLE 23.9	Helen Troy, who dies on January 12, has an agreement with her employer that a payment of $20,000 will be made to her estate or designated beneficiary upon Helen's death in lieu of claims to future bonuses, sales commissions, etc. This payment, which arises solely by reason of death of the decedent, is income in respect of the decedent when received by the estate or beneficiary.

The character of income in respect of the decedent is the same to the estate or beneficiary reporting the income as it would have been to the decedent if the decedent had continued to live and report the income on the tax return. Code Sec. 691(a)(3); Reg. §1.691(a)-3.

If an estate or beneficiary includes income in respect of the decedent as income on a tax return, the estate or beneficiary is entitled to an itemized deduction for any federal estate tax paid because the income was also included on the decedent's federal estate tax return. Code Sec. 691(c). This itemized deduction is not subject to the two percent floor that applies to miscellaneous itemized deductions.

Deductions in Respect of the Decedent (DRD)

If a decedent incurred tax deductible expenses before death that were not deductible on the decedent's final return because they were not paid and the decedent was on the cash basis, these expenses are deductible in the year paid by either the estate or the beneficiary. If the estate pays the expenses, they are deductible by the estate in the tax year paid. If a beneficiary has an obligation to pay an expense and pays it, the expense is a proper deduction on the tax return of the beneficiary in the year of payment. Reg. §1.691(b)-1. Also, it is important to note that DRD items are deductible twice. That is, on both the Form 706 return and the Form 1041 return.

Business losses or capital losses incurred by a decedent prior to death end with the decedent's final return. The losses cannot be carried over to years subsequent to the final return. Business losses on the decedent's final return, however, are eligible for the net operating loss carryback and can be carried back to tax returns of prior years. Rev. Rul. 74-175, 1974-1 CB 52. In a community property state only 50 percent of the business or capital losses are nondeductible.

¶23,025   FEDERAL INCOME TAX CONCERNS OF AN ESTATE

The estate of a decedent is a separate taxable entity that comes into existence automatically at the death of an individual. The decedent's tax year ends on the date of death so that the tax year of the estate commences on the following day. Reg. §1.443-1(a)(2). An estate is a separate taxable entity for federal income tax purposes and retains this status until the final distribution of assets held in the estate of the beneficiaries.

The duration of an estate is the period actually required by the fiduciary to perform the ordinary duties of administration (i.e., collection of assets and the payment of debts, taxes, legacies and bequests). Because the estate is a taxable entity separate from the beneficiaries, the fiduciary may attempt to prolong its existence in order to take advantage of the lower tax bracket. That is, whenever beneficiaries of an estate are in higher tax brackets than the estate, substantial tax savings can be achieved by accumulating the estate's income in one year.

¶23,035   FIDUCIARY RESPONSIBILITIES

A fiduciary is a person such as an administrator, trustee, or executor who has been given a special confidence and responsibility to manage property in a trust or estate according to some legal agreement (will, trust agreement) and in the best interests of the beneficiaries of the trust or estate. The main responsibility of a fiduciary of an estate is to wind up the affairs of the decedent, specifically to gather the decedent's assets together, to pay claims against the assets, and to distribute the balance of the assets to the beneficiaries of the estate. A fiduciary of an estate is called an executor if named in the decedent's will, or an administrator if named by a court to settle the decedent's affairs. In some instances, a personal representative of the decedent may assume some fiduciary responsibilities with regard to an estate although not named as an executor or appointed as an administrator.

Payment of Decedent's Tax Liabilities

Included among the duties and responsibilities of a fiduciary of an estate (hereafter referred to as executor) is the responsibility to file any required tax returns and pay any tax liabilities of the decedent or the decedent's estate. Although the executor is required to file tax returns and pay taxes due, the executor ordinarily is not personally liable for the tax payments. The tax payments are made from the assets of the estate. Code Sec. 6903; Reg. §301.6903-1. If, however, the executor is negligent in handling claims against the estate and taxes are not paid, the liability for payment of the taxes extends to the executor. Reg. §1.641(b)-2.

An executor can obtain protection from personal liability for a decedent's taxes by filing Form 4810 (Request for Prompt Assessment) with the IRS after all tax returns have been filed. The request will reduce the normal three-year period within which the IRS must audit a return to eighteen months from the time the request is filed. Code Sec. 6501(d).

PLANNING POINTER	Filing of the request by the executor results in a shorter period for determining the final liability of the estate and can speed up the distribution of estate assets to the beneficiaries. Filing of the request also lessens the chance of an executor inadvertently distributing estate assets to beneficiaries that should have been used to pay the estate's tax liabilities.

¶23,045   ESTATE FEDERAL INCOME TAX RETURN

Each estate that has gross income of $600 or more during a tax year must file an estate income tax return. The appropriate IRS form for the return is Form 1041 (U.S. Fiduciary Income Tax Return). If one or more beneficiaries of an estate are nonresident aliens, a Form 1041 must be filed even if gross income is below $600. Code Sec. 6012(a); Reg. §1.6012-3.

Filing Period

Form 1041 must be filed on or before the fifteenth day of the fourth month following the close of the tax year of the estate. The executor is free to choose the end of an estate's first tax year. The executor is free to choose the same tax year as the decedent or any other year-end. The estate's first income tax return can cover a period less than 12 months. Once an executor chooses an estate's tax year-end on the first tax return, however, all subsequent returns must use the same year-end unless permission is received from the IRS for a change in accounting period.

Exemption

An estate is entitled to a $600 personal exemption on each income tax return except the final income tax return when no personal exemption is allowed. Code Sec. 642(b); Reg. §1.642(b)-1. An executor should carefully consider the choice of an estate's first tax year-end. Careful planning of the estate's tax year-end can result in maximum tax advantage.

| EXAMPLE 23.10 | The estate of James Johnson was in existence for the period February 1, 2017, through December 31, 2017. The executor chose an estate tax year-end of December 31, 2017. The first return of the estate was also the final return and no $600 exemption was allowed. In order to maximize tax advantage, the executor, in this case, could have chosen an estate tax year-end for the first return of any month-end from February 28, 2017, through November 30, 2017. A $600 personal exemption would then have been available on the first return. The estate's final income tax return would have covered the period from the end of the first return through December 31, 2017. Careful planning of the estate's tax year-end in the second case would have resulted in $600 of the estate's income being free from taxation. A disadvantage of the second case, however, is that two estate income tax returns need to be filed instead of one income tax return as in the first case. On the other hand, the advantage of filing two estate income tax returns instead of one is that the estate income is spread over two returns, thereby possibly lowering the effective marginal tax rate on the income. |

Accounting Method

An executor is also free to choose an accounting method (cash or accrual) for an estate on the first income tax return. Subsequent income tax returns must use the same accounting method unless permission is received from the IRS to make a change. An executor should consider very carefully the initial choice of accounting method for an estate since later IRS permission to change the method of accounting may be difficult to obtain.

Estimated Tax

Normally, an executor of an estate is not required to pay estimated taxes. Instead, the full amount of tax liability is due with the tax return. If an estate stays in existence for more than two taxable years, however, it must start to pay estimated tax payments in the third year.

Extension of Time to File Return

An extension of time to file a Form 1041 may be granted to an executor for a justifiable reason. An extension of time to file a return, if granted, does not extend the time for payment of the tax. The tax liability must still be estimated and payments made by the regular due dates.

Tax Rates for Estates

Regular income tax rates for federal estate income tax returns are shown in the Appendix. In addition to regular income tax rates, an estate may also be subject to the alternative minimum tax that was discussed previously in individual income taxes. If the alternative minimum tax computation results in a larger tax due than the regular tax computation, the difference is added to the estate's income tax liability.

Taxation of Trusts

¶23,209

NATURE OF TRUSTS

A trust is a legal entity created to hold property. A trustee administers the property according to the dictates of a trust agreement. For income tax purposes, a trust is a separate taxable entity which, like an estate, is entitled to a deduction for income distributions to beneficiaries. The income distributions, in turn, are subject to taxation on the beneficiaries' income tax returns.

Creation of Trusts

As noted earlier, an estate is created automatically. On the other hand, a trust must be specifically created. There are many legal or tax definitions of trusts. That is, trusts may be inter vivos or testamentary, simple or complex. Also, there are trusts that are formed for a specific function, such as alimony trusts, insurance trusts, or charitable trusts. A breakdown of the common working trust terminology follows.

Inter Vivos Trust

An inter vivos trust is a trust created during the lifetime of the grantor.

Testamentary Trust

A testamentary trust is a trust created by the will of a decedent.

Simple Trust

Pursuant to the terms of its governing instrument, a simple trust must: (1) distribute all of its state law income currently, (2) have no charitable beneficiary, and (3) make no distribution from corpus. Code Sec. 651(a)(1) and (2); Reg. §1.651(a)-1.

Complex Trust

A complex trust is a trust that is not a simple trust. The term includes trusts with a charitable beneficiary and trusts that distribute corpus or accumulated income.

Categories of Beneficiaries

Beneficiaries of trusts are divided into two categories: income beneficiaries and remainder beneficiaries. An income beneficiary has an interest in the income of the trust. A remainder beneficiary has an interest in the trust property after an income interest expires. It is possible for one person to be both an income beneficiary and a remainder beneficiary.

EXAMPLE 23.11 John Burlington establishes a trust to provide income to care for his aged mother. Upon death of the mother, the trust agreement provides that the trust corpus will be distributed to James Burlington, John's son. In this trust, John Burlington is the grantor, the aged mother is an income beneficiary, and James Burlington is a remainder beneficiary.

Tax and Nontax Reasons for Creating Trusts

There are a number of tax and nontax reasons an individual might consider creating a trust. Nontax reasons for creating a trust include the following:

1. A trust can be created to protect and conserve property and to provide competent investment management for beneficiaries such as children who are not yet competent to handle their own affairs.
2. A trust can be created to protect and conserve property and to provide competent investment management for beneficiaries who are not interested or inclined to manage the property themselves.
3. A grantor can create a trust and give explicit instructions in a trust agreement as to how the trust property is to be invested and managed. The grantor thereby can have some control over the management of the trust property even though deceased.

EXAMPLE 23.12 John Creek creates a trust and names his aged grandmother as the income beneficiary of the trust for her remaining lifetime. The purpose of the trust is to provide the grandmother with a means of support for the rest of her life. The trustee has the responsibility to manage the affairs of the trust in the best interests of the grandmother according to the dictates of the trust agreement.

Tax reasons for creating a trust include the following:

1. By creating a properly constituted trust for tax purposes, a grantor has created a new tax entity. A separate tax return is prepared for the new tax entity and a new tax rate schedule is used in computing the tax due on the trust income. Trust income is subject to taxation starting at the bottom of a new tax rate schedule. Two taxpayers now exist, the grantor and the trust, and, considering the progressive nature of the federal income tax system, overall income may be subject to a lower effective tax rate.
2. By creating a properly constituted trust for tax purposes, a grantor can effectively shift income from the grantor's tax return to the income tax return of a beneficiary who may be in a lower income tax bracket, thereby lowering the overall effective income tax rate on the income of a family unit.

In some instances, a trust can be created that qualifies as a separate legal entity but that is not a properly constituted trust for federal income tax purposes. The income from a trust of this type is taxable to the grantor instead of to the trust or beneficiaries. For qualification as a properly constituted trust for tax purposes, effective control of the property placed in trust must be relinquished by the grantor. Trusts that do not qualify for recognition as trusts for federal income tax purposes are called grantor trusts.

TAX BLUNDER

A couple had established the trust to operate their farming business and to hold family personal assets. Although they had signed a closing agreement for two prior tax years agreeing that (1) the trust was their alter ego, (2) all assets held in the name of the trust were actually their assets, and (3) all of their income, expenses, deductions and credits would be reported on their individual returns for the years at issue and all subsequent years, they continued to use the trust with fraudulent intent. The taxpayers failed to establish any reasonable cause for their failure to file the returns, and the addition to tax under Code Sec. 6651(a) was sustained.

Additionally, the government established by clear and convincing evidence that the taxpayers understated their federal income tax for two consecutive years with the intent to commit fraud and that the husband failed to file his returns for three other years with the same intent. Therefore, the husband was liable for the Code Sec. 6651(f) addition to tax, and both taxpayers were liable for the fraud penalty under Code Sec. 6663. *J. M. Smoll*, 92 TCM 84.

¶23,215   TRUST FEDERAL INCOME TAX RETURN

Each trust that has gross income of $600 or more during a tax year must file a federal income tax return. The appropriate form for the return is Form 1041 (U.S. Fiduciary Income Tax Return). If one or more beneficiaries of a trust are nonresident aliens or if the trust has taxable income, an income tax return must be filed even if gross income is below $600. Code Sec. 6012(a).

Filing Period

A trust income tax return must be filed on or before the fifteenth day of the fourth month following the close of the tax year of the trust. All trusts, with some minor exceptions, must report income on a calendar-year basis.

Exemption

A simple trust is entitled to a $300 personal-exemption deduction while a complex trust is entitled to a $100 personal-exemption deduction. A full personal exemption can be taken on the first income tax return of a trust even if it covers a period of less than twelve months. No personal exemption is allowed on the final return of a trust.

Accounting Method

A trustee is free to choose an accounting method (cash or accrual) for a trust on the first income tax return. Subsequent income tax returns must use the same accounting method unless permission is received from the IRS to make a change.

PLANNING POINTER   A trustee should consider very carefully the initial choice of accounting method for a trust since later IRS permission to change the method of accounting may be difficult to obtain.

Estimated Tax

A trustee of a trust is required to pay estimated taxes. An extension of time to file a return may be granted to a trustee for a justifiable reason.

Extension of Time to File Return

An extension of time to file a return, if granted, does not extend the time for payment of the tax. The tax liability must still be estimated and payments made by the regular due date.

Tax Rates for Trusts

Regular tax rates for trust income tax returns are shown in the Appendix. In addition to regular income taxes, a trust may also be subject to the alternative minimum tax. If the alternative minimum tax computation results in a larger tax due than the regular tax computation, the difference is added to the trust's income tax liability.

Federal Income Taxation Scheme— Estates and Trusts

¶23,301   ## DISTRIBUTABLE NET INCOME (DNI) SYSTEM

Because an estate or trust is a tax-paying entity, double taxation would be imposed if the income previously taxed to the fiduciary was again taxed when distributed to beneficiaries. In order to avoid double taxation, a system was needed to measure the amount and character of income distributed to beneficiaries or retained by an estate or trust. As a result, the concept of distributable net income (DNI) was brought into the Internal Revenue Code.

DNI Concept

In order to make the conduit principle work, a device was required to measure the *amount* of income distributed to beneficiaries or retained by the estate. Also, a measure was needed to determine the *character* of amounts distributed to beneficiaries or retained by the estate or trust. Furthermore, a true conduit approach must identify the items of estate income that are given special treatment elsewhere in the Code, such as capital gains and interest on municipal bonds, and must keep these items separate as they pass out to the estate's or trust's beneficiaries.

An analytical method or technique was required to measure the amount of income distributed and determine the character of amounts distributed. Such a method is supplied in the concept of distributable net income. DNI has three basic functions:

1. It limits the amount of the distribution deduction of the estate and trust.
2. It limits the amount on which beneficiaries can be taxed.
3. It is used to determine the character of amounts retained by an estate or trust and the character of amounts distributed to the beneficiaries. Reg. §1.643(a)-0.

Thus, DNI has been termed the yardstick or measuring rod to be employed in determining, on one hand, the maximum deduction for distributions which may be allowed to the estate or trust and for gauging, on the other hand, the extent to which beneficiaries may be taxable on the distributions.

DNI—Modification of Taxable Income

In order to serve as a measure of the maximum deduction to be allowed to trusts or estates for distributions to beneficiaries (and conversely to determine the amounts includible in the beneficiaries' gross income), taxable income must be modified in several important respects. Code Sec. 643(a) sets out the modifications to taxable income and labels this modified income "distributable net income." DNI is defined as the taxable income of the estate or trust computed with six modifications. (At this juncture, it should be noted that the taxable income of an estate or trust is generally the same as taxable income of an individual, with several exceptions. That is, the main component parts of taxable income are gross income, deductions, charitable contributions, income distribution deduction, and the personal exemption.) The modifications to taxable income for DNI are as follows:

1. No deduction is allowed for amounts distributed or distributable to beneficiaries.
2. No deduction is allowed for personal exemptions—$600 for estates, $300 for simple trusts, and $100 for complex trusts.
3. Gains from the sale or exchange of capital assets are excluded to the extent that they are allocated to corpus and are not paid, credited, or required to be distributed to any beneficiary, or paid or set aside for charities. Capital losses are excluded except to the extent that such losses are taken into account in determining the amount of capital gain to be paid, credited, or required to be distributed to any beneficiary during the taxable year.
4. With respect only to simple trusts, extraordinary dividends and taxable stock dividends are excluded if properly allocated by the trustee in good faith to corpus.
5. Interest that is fully tax-exempt (less nondeductible disbursements allocated to such interest) is included.
6. In the case of foreign trusts, income from sources without the U.S. (less nondeductible disbursements allocable to such income) is included.

¶23,325   DNI COMPUTATIONS—SIMPLE TRUSTS

The rules applicable to a trust required to distribute all of its income currently and to its beneficiaries (that is, a simple trust falling under Code Secs. 651 and 652) may be illustrated in the following manner. Reg. §1.652(c)-4.

EXAMPLE 23.13

Pursuant to the terms of a simple trust all of the income is to be distributed equally to beneficiaries X and Y and capital gains are to be allocated to corpus. The trust and both beneficiaries file returns on the calendar-year basis. No provision is made for depreciation in the governing instrument. Therefore, it will follow income. During the taxable year, the trust had the following items of income and expenses:

Rents	$25,000
Dividends of domestic corporations	50,000
Tax-exempt interest on municipal bonds	25,000
Long-term capital gains	15,000
Taxes and expenses directly attributable to rents	5,000
Trustee's commissions allocable to income account	2,600
Trustee's commissions allocable to principal account	1,300
Depreciation	5,000

Step 1—State Law Income. The state law income (also, called trust accounting income) of the trust for fiduciary accounting purposes is $92,400, computed as follows:

Rents		$25,000
Dividends		50,000
Tax-exempt interest		25,000
		$100,000
Deductions:		
Expenses directly attributable to rent income	$5,000	
Trustee's commissions allocable to income account	2,600	7,600
State law income computed under Code Sec. 643(b)		$92,400

One-half ($46,200) of the income of $92,400 is currently distributable to each beneficiary.

Step 2—Code Sec. 643(a) Ceiling. The distributable net income (income ceiling) of the trust computed under Code Sec. 643(a) is $91,100 determined as follows (cents are disregarded in the computation):

Rents		$25,000
Dividends		50,000
Tax-exempt interest	$25,000	
Less: Expenses allocable thereto ($25,000/$100,000 × $3,900)	975	24,025
Total		$99,025
Deductions:		
Expenses directly attributable to rental income	$5,000	
Trustee's commissions ($3,900 – $975 allocable to tax-exempt interest)	2,925	7,925
Distributable net income as the income ceiling		$91,100

In computing the distributable net income of $91,100, the taxable income of the trust was computed with the following modifications. No deductions were allowed for distributions to the beneficiaries and for a personal exemption of the trust. Code Sec. 643(a)(1) and (2). Capital gains were excluded. Code Sec. 643(a)(3). The tax-exempt interest was included. Code Sec. 643(a)(5).

EXAMPLE 23.13
CONTINUED

Step 3—Code Sec. 651(a) Ceiling. The deduction ceiling allowable to the trust under Sec. Code 651(a) for distributions to the beneficiaries is $67,075 computed as follows:

Distributable net income computed under Code Sec. 643(a)	$91,100
Less: Tax-exempt interest as adjusted	24,025
Distributable net income (deduction ceiling) as determined under Code Sec. 651(b)	$67,075

Since the amount of the income ($92,400) required to be distributed currently by the trust exceeds the distributable net income ($67,075) as computed under Code Sec. 651(b), the deduction allowable under Code Sec. 651(a) is limited to the distributable net income of $67,075.

Step 4—Trust's Income. The taxable income of the trust is $14,700 computed as follows:

Rents		$25,000
Dividends		50,000
Long-term capital gains		15,000
Gross income		$90,000
Deductions: Rental expenses	$5,000	
Trustee's commissions	2,925	
Distributions to beneficiaries	67,075	
Personal exemption for a simple trust	300	75,300
Taxable income		$14,700

The trust is not allowed a deduction for the portion ($975) of the trustee's commissions allocable to tax-exempt interest in computing its taxable income.

Also, it should be noted that a simple trust which is allocating capital gains to corpus can perform a supplemental calculation to check its taxable income. For example, in the above calculation the trust's taxable income was $14,700; this could have been figured as follows:

Capital gains	$15,000
Less: Personal exemption	300
Taxable income	$14,700

Step 5—Inclusion and Characterization to Beneficiaries. In determining the character of the amounts includible in the gross income of X and Y, it is assumed that the trustee elects to allocate to rents the expenses not directly attributable to a specific item of income, other than the portion ($975) of such expenses allocated to tax-exempt interest.

The allocation of expenses among the items of income, as required by Sec. 652(b), is shown below:

	Rents	Dividends	Tax-exempt Interest	Total
Income for trust accounting purposes	$25,000	$50,000	$25,000	$100,000
Less:				
Rental expenses	5,000	0	0	5,000
Trustee's commissions	2,925	0	975	3,900
Total deductions	7,925	0	975	8,900
Character of amounts in the hands of the beneficiaries	$17,075	$50,000	$24,025	$91,100

Inasmuch as the income of the trust is to be distributed equally to X and Y, each is deemed to have received one-half of each item of income: that is, rents of $8,537.50, dividends of $25,000; and tax-exempt interest of $12,012.50. The dividends of $25,000 allocated to each beneficiary are to be aggregated with the beneficiary's other dividends.

Additionally, each beneficiary is allowed a deduction of $2,500 for depreciation of rental property attributable to the portion (one-half) of the income of the trust distributed to each beneficiary. If depreciation had been a charge against income and consequently required a reserve, then it should have appeared at Step 1 reducing state law or trust accounting income, Step 2 reducing DNI as an income ceiling, Step 4 as a deduction to the trust in computing its taxable income, and at Step 5 as a reduction to rental income. Note, of course, that the beneficiaries are responsible for only $91,100 of DNI while, in fact, $92,400 has been distributed to them.

¶23,331   DEPRECIATION AND DEPLETION DEDUCTIONS

Either an estate or trust may be entitled to depreciation and depletion deductions if it holds qualified property.

Rules for Estates

Even though an estate may be allowed a depreciation or depletion deduction, it must be recognized that this is a residual claim to these deductions. For an estate, the allowable deduction for depreciation and/or depletion must be apportioned between the estate and the heirs, legatees, and devisees on the basis of income of the estate which is allocable to each. Reg. §§1.167(h)-1(c) and 1.611-1(c)(5).

Rules for Trusts

Trusts are permitted greater flexibility than estates in receiving depreciation and depletion deductions. For instance, if property is held in trust, the depreciation or depletion deductions are to be apportioned between the income beneficiaries and the trust on the basis of the trust income allocable to each. However, if the governing instrument (or local law) requires or permits the trustee to maintain a reserve for depreciation in any amounts, then the deduction is first allocated to the trust to the extent that income is set aside for a depreciation reserve. Any part of the deduction in excess of this amount set aside for the reserve is apportioned between the income beneficiaries and the trust on the basis of the trust income allocable to each. Reg. §§1.167(h)-1(b) and 1.611-1(c)(4).

EXAMPLE 23.14

> Melford Brock creates a trust, with his son, Bob, and his daughter, Nina, as income beneficiaries, by the transfer of income producing depreciable property. Pursuant to the terms of the trust instrument, the income from the trust is to be distributed annually on a 70 percent basis to Bob and 30 percent to Nina. Additionally, the trustee is permitted to set aside income as a depreciation reserve. In the current year, depreciation on the trust property amounts to $10,000, and the trustee allocates $5,000 of trust income as a depreciation reserve. As a result, the trust can claim $5,000 as a depreciation deduction, Bob can claim $3,500 ($10,000 – $5,000 × 70%)) and Nina can claim $1,500 ($10,000 – $5,000 × 30%)).

¶23,345   DNI COMPUTATIONS—COMPLEX TRUSTS AND ESTATES

In the case of a simple trust, the basic issue was the allocation of income between the trust and the beneficiaries. However, the problem of allocation among the beneficiaries will become more prominent with the complex trust and estate. Even though the complex trust and estate are taxed in substantially the same manner as a simple trust, nonetheless, some complications arise from the tier system and charitable contributions.

Tier System

There is a two-tier system of priorities (affecting DNI) that characterize the amounts distributed to beneficiaries as either income or corpus. This system provides: (1) *first tier*—income required to be distributed currently including annuity payments out of income, and (2) *second tier*—all other amounts properly paid, credited, or required to be distributed. Code Secs. 662(a)(1) and (2). This includes (a) current income that the trustee was not required to distribute; (b) accumulated income; and (c) corpus.

As a result of the system's hierarchy, the first tier has a priority on using up DNI. If the first-tier payments do not exhaust the ceiling amount of DNI, then any balance of DNI will affect the taxability of all other distributions that fall into the second tier.

EXAMPLE 23.15

> In 2017, a trust is required to pay $20,000 out of income each year to Fred. Also, the trustee in his discretion may distribute to Joe an amount for his well being. This year the trust pays Joe $15,000. The DNI of the trust is $30,000. Thus, the tier system allocates $20,000 taxable income to Fred as a first-tier beneficiary, and $10,000 taxable income to Joe as a second-tier beneficiary. The other $5,000 distributed to Joe would be a tax-free return of corpus.

First-Tier Distributions in Excess of DNI

Whenever the amount of income required to be distributed currently to all beneficiaries (first tier) exceeds DNI, the amount includible in the beneficiary's gross income is computed as follows. Reg. §1.662(a)-2.

$$\frac{\text{Amount of income required to be distributed currently to first-tier beneficiary}}{\text{Amount of income required to be distributed currently to all first-tier beneficiaries}} \times \text{Distributable net income (computed without deduction for charitable contributions)} = \text{Amount beneficiary includes in gross income}$$

EXAMPLE 23.16 A trust has $50,000 of DNI in the current year. The trustee is required by the instrument to distribute $30,000 each year to both the wife and daughter of the deceased. By utilizing the above formula, the wife and daughter would each have $25,000 from DNI and $5,000 from corpus ($30,000/$60,000 × $50,000 = $25,000).

First- and Second-Tier Distributions in Excess of DNI

In the event that first-tier distributions do not exhaust DNI, then beneficiaries may be taxed as second-tier distributions. Furthermore, if both first- and second-tier distributions exceed DNI, then another allocation formula is necessary to determine the amount that a beneficiary will be taxed on. This formula is as follows (Reg. §1.662(a)-3):

$$\frac{\text{Second-tier distributions to the beneficiary}}{\text{Second-tier distributions to all beneficiaries}} \times \text{Distributable net income (less first-tier distributions and charitable contributions)} = \text{Beneficiary's share of distributable net income}$$

EXAMPLE 23.17 A trust has $60,000 of DNI in 2017. The fiduciary is required to distribute $40,000 each year to Mary, the surviving spouse. However, at the fiduciary's discretion, amounts may be distributed to Bob and Donna, the son and daughter of the deceased, based on their health and education needs.

During the current year, the trustee distributed $40,000 to Mary, $20,000 to Bob, and $20,000 to Donna. The beneficiaries' taxable amounts are computed as follows:

Step 1—DNI	$60,000
Less: First tier	40,000
Available for second tier	$20,000
Step 2—$20,000/$40,000 × $20,000	$10,000

Thus, Mary is taxed on $40,000, and Bob and Donna are taxed on $10,000 each. However, the other $10,000 is tax free to Bob and Donna.

Planning for Types of Distributed Income

The character of distributed income in the hands of the estate or trust is the same as its character in the hands of the beneficiaries. Tax-exempt income to the estate or trust is also tax-exempt income to the beneficiaries when distributed. Capital gains and losses and ordinary income items to the estate or trust retain the same character when distributed to the beneficiaries. If a decedent's will directs that certain types of estate income be distributed to certain beneficiaries (e.g., "My son receives tax-exempt income, my daughter receives taxable income, etc."), the dictates of the will are followed in determining the taxability of estate income distributions to the beneficiaries. Code Secs. 652(b) and 662(b). If a will does not direct that income be distributed in specified ways, then all the beneficiaries share in the different types of income in proportion to the total estate income.

EXAMPLE 23.18	The executor of an estate distributes $10,000 of estate income to two beneficiaries. The distributed income consists of $6,000 of tax-exempt interest and $4,000 of taxable income. One beneficiary is entitled to 75 percent of the income; the other beneficiary is entitled to 25 percent of the income. The decedent's will does not specify the type of income to be distributed to either beneficiary. Accordingly, the 75 percent beneficiary is assumed to have received 75 percent of both types of income ($4,500 tax-exempt interest and $3,000 taxable income) while the 25 percent beneficiary is assumed to have received 25 percent of both types of income ($1,500 tax-exempt interest and $1,000 taxable income).

PLANNING POINTER	In drafting a will or trust instrument consideration should be given to the possible tax advantages of directing distributions of certain types of income to specified beneficiaries based on the character of the income. Thus, directing distributions of tax-exempt income to high tax bracket beneficiaries while directing distributions of taxable income to low tax bracket beneficiaries could result in an overall tax advantage to a family unit.

¶23,357   CHARITABLE CONTRIBUTIONS—COMPLEX TRUSTS AND ESTATES

Charitable contributions are deductible on an estate or complex trust income tax return and are not limited to a percentage of income as applicable to individuals. The instrument must indicate, however, that contributions are payable out of income before a charitable contribution can be taken. If a trust makes a charitable contribution, it is, by definition, a complex trust since simple trusts are required to distribute all income currently and cannot set aside any amount for charitable contributions. Any charitable contribution made out of tax-exempt income is not deductible on a trust or estate income tax return. If a trust or estate has both taxable and tax-exempt income and there is no designation in the will or trust agreement regarding which income was used for the contribution, the contribution is assumed to have come from all classes of income in relative proportion to the size of the contribution.

TAX BLUNDER

Taxpayers have found that whether amounts will be allowed to be claimed as charitable contributions by an estate or trust under Code Sec. 642(c) depends upon the wording of the will or trust instrument. In this respect, the courts have been strict in interpreting an intent to pay or set aside income for charitable contributions.

The taxpayer, an estate, was not allowed to deduct undistributed corporate income as a charitable contribution. Specifically, the income in question never really vested in the residuary estate so it was not permanently set aside or properly designated to be used for charitable purposes. *S.W. Richardson Foundation*, CA-5, 70-2 USTC ¶9483, 430 F.2d 710; *Riggs National Bank of Washington, D.C.*, 65-2 USTC ¶9728, 173 CtCls 479. Always check the governing instrument to see if an estate or trust is permitted to make charitable contributions.

EXAMPLE 23.19	A charitable contribution of $10,000 is made by a trust to Middleburg University. The trust agreement does not designate the specific income that should be used for the contribution. The trust has $20,000 of taxable income and $30,000 of tax-exempt income. A charitable contribution of $4,000 ($10,000 × $20,000/$50,000) is considered to have come from taxable income. The remaining charitable contribution of $6,000 ($10,000 × $30,000/$50,000) is considered to have come from tax-exempt income and is not deductible.

PLANNING POINTER	In structuring a trust agreement, consideration should be given to indicating that planned charitable contributions come from specific types of taxable income, thereby increasing the size of the charitable contribution deduction allowable to the estate or trust on the Form 1041 income tax return.

The computational rules of charitable deductions may be exemplified by the following fact situation. Reg. §1.662(c)-4.

EXAMPLE 23.20

Under the terms of a testamentary trust, one-half of the trust income is to be distributed currently to W, the decedent's wife, for life. The remaining trust income may, in the trustee's discretion, either be paid to D, the grantor's daughter, paid to designated charities, or accumulated. The trust is to terminate at the death of W and the principal will then be payable to D.

No provision is made in the trust instrument or under local law with respect to depreciation of rental property. Therefore, depreciation will follow income. Capital gains are allocable to corpus under the applicable local law. The trust and both beneficiaries file returns on the calendar-year basis.

The records of the fiduciary show the following items of income and deduction for the taxable year:

Rents	$50,000
Dividends of domestic corporations	50,000
Tax-exempt interest	20,000
Taxable interest	10,000
Capital gains (long-term)	20,000
Depreciation of rental property	10,000
Expenses attributable to rental income	15,400
Trustee's commissions allocable to income account	2,800
Trustee's commissions allocable to principal account	1,100

Step 1—State Law Income. The state law income of the trust for fiduciary accounting purposes is $111,800, computed as follows:

Rents		$50,000
Dividends		50,000
Tax-exempt interest		20,000
Taxable interest		10,000
Total		$130,000
Deductions:		
Rental expenses	$15,400	
Trustee's commissions allocable to income account	2,800	18,200
Income as computed under Code Sec. 643(b)		$111,800

(Note that depreciation and long-term capital gain are not included.)

The trustee distributed one-half of the state law income ($55,900) to W and, in his discretion, makes a contribution of one-quarter ($27,950) to charity X and distributes the remaining one-quarter ($27,950) to D. The total of the distributions to beneficiaries is $83,850, consisting of (1) income required to be distributed currently to W of $55,900 and (2) other amounts properly paid or credited to D of $27,950.

Step 2—Code Sec. 643(a) Ceiling. The distributable net income of the trust as computed under Code Sec. 643(a) is $82,750, determined as follows:

Rents			$50,000
Dividends			50,000
Taxable interest			10,000
Tax-exempt interest		$20,000	
Less: Trustee's commissions allocable to tax-exempt interest ($20,000/$130,000 of $3,900)	$600		
Charitable contributions allocable to tax-exempt interest ($20,000/$130,000 of $27,950)	4,300	4,900	15,100
Total			$125,100

EXAMPLE 23.20 CONTINUED

Deductions:		
Rental expenses	$15,400	
Trustee's commissions	3,300	
($3,900 – $600 allocated to tax-exempt interest)		
Charitable deduction	23,650	42,350
($27,950 – $4,300 attributable to tax-exempt interest)		
Distributable net income		$82,750

In computing the distributable net income of $82,750, the taxable income of the trust was computed with the following modifications. No deductions were allowed for distributions to beneficiaries and for the personal exemption of the trust. Code Sec. 643(a)(1) and (2). Capital gains were excluded. Code Sec. 643(a)(3). The tax-exempt interest (as adjusted for expenses and charitable contributions) was included. Code Sec. 643(a)(5).

Step 3—Code Sec. 661(a) Ceiling. The distributable net income of $82,750, as determined under Code Sec. 643(a), is less than the sum of the amounts distributed to W and D of $83,850. Therefore, the deduction allowable to the trust under Code Sec. 661(a) is such distributable net income as modified under Code Sec. 661(c) to exclude therefrom the items of income not included in gross income of the trust. The following computation shows the effects:

Distributable net income	$82,750
Less: Tax-exempt interest (as adjusted for expenses and the charitable contributions)	15,100
Deduction allowable under Code Sec. 661(a)	$67,650

Step 4—Trust's Income. The taxable income of the trust is $19,900, determined as follows:

Rent income		$ 50,000
Dividends		50,000
Taxable interest		10,000
Capital gains		20,000
Gross income		$130,000
Deductions:		
Rental expenses	$15,400	
Trustee's commissions	3,300	
Charitable contributions	23,650	
Distributions to beneficiaries	67,650	
Personal exemption	100	$110,100
Taxable Income		$19,900

Step 5—Inclusion and Characterization to Beneficiaries. For the purpose of determining the character of the amounts deductible under Code Secs. 642(c) and 661(a), the trustee elected to offset the trustee's commissions (other than the portion required to be allocated to tax-exempt interest) against the rental income. The determination of the character of the amounts deemed distributed to beneficiaries and contributed to charity is made as follows:

Character of Amounts Distributed to Beneficiaries and Contributed to Charity Under Code Sec. 661(a)

	Rents	Taxable Dividends	Tax-Exempt Interest	Taxable Interest	Total
Trust income	$50,000	$50,000	$20,000	$10,000	$130,000
Less:					
Charitable contributions	10,750	10,750	4,300	2,150	27,950
Rental expenses	15,400				15,400
Trustee's commissions	3,300		600		3,900
Total deductions	$29,450	$10,750	$4,900	$2,150	$47,250
Amounts distributable to beneficiaries	$20,550	$39,250	$15,100	$7,850	$82,750

EXAMPLE 23.20 CONTINUED

The character of the charitable contribution is determined by multiplying the total charitable contribution ($27,950) by a fraction consisting of each item of trust income, respectively, over the total trust income, except that no part of the dividends excluded from gross income is deemed included in the charitable contribution. For example, the charitable contribution is deemed to consist of rents of $10,750 ($50,000/$130,000 × $27,950).

Because the wife is a first-tier beneficiary and DNI is $82,750, the whole $55,900 is fully includible in her income. Thus, the character of the $55,900 is determined as follows:

$$\frac{\text{Total each class}}{\text{Total DNI}} \times \text{Includible amount}$$

					K-1 Amounts
Rents	$\dfrac{\$20,550}{\$82,750}$	×	$55,900	=	$13,882
Dividends	$\dfrac{\$39,250}{\$82,750}$	×	$55,900	=	26,515
Taxable interest	$\dfrac{\$7,850}{\$82,750}$	×	$55,900	=	5,303
Tax-exempt interest	$\dfrac{\$15,100}{\$82,750}$	×	$55,900	=	10,200
Total					$55,900

Additionally, she may deduct a share of the depreciation deduction proportionate to the trust income allocable to her; that is, one-half of the total depreciation deduction, or $5,000.

Since the sum of the amount of income required to be distributed currently to W ($55,900) and the other amounts properly paid, credited, or required to be distributed to D ($27,950) exceeds the distributable net income ($82,750) of the trust as determined under Code Sec. 643(a), D is deemed to have received $26,850 ($82,750 – $55,900) for income tax purposes. The character of the amounts deemed distributed to her is determined as follows:

					K-1 Amounts
Rents	$\dfrac{\$20,550}{\$82,750}$	×	$26,850	=	$6,668
Dividends	$\dfrac{\$39,250}{\$82,750}$	×	$26,850	=	12,735
Taxable interest	$\dfrac{\$7,850}{\$82,750}$	×	$26,850	=	2,547
Tax-exempt interest	$\dfrac{\$15,100}{\$82,750}$	×	$26,850	=	4,900
Total					$26,850

Also, D may deduct a share of the depreciation deduction proportionate to the trust income allocable to her; that is, one-fourth of the total depreciation deduction, or $2,500.

PLANNING POINTER

If no provision is made in the trust instrument with respect to depreciation, the depreciation deduction may be allocated to the amount distributed to the designated charity, and, as a result, be nondeductible by the trust or beneficiaries. Thus, tax planners would be well-advised to make sure that depreciation does not follow income. This can be easily accomplished by a trust because the trust instrument can create a reserve for depreciation and depletion deductions to the remainder beneficiaries and avoid any wastage problem.

¶23,365 TAX RETURN SPECIAL RULES

Tax Return Schedules

A fiduciary is required to file a Schedule K-1, Form 1041, trust or estate income tax return, for each beneficiary who receives an income distribution during the trust's or estate's tax year. Schedule K-1 gives information applicable to beneficiaries on how trust or estate income distributions affect their individual income tax returns. The fiduciary should furnish a copy of Schedule K-1 to each beneficiary who received a distribution during the year from an estate or trust. Beneficiaries of an estate or trust must file their returns in a manner consistent with the manner reported on the trust or estate's return or must file a notice of inconsistent treatment with the Secretary of the Treasury that identifies the inconsistent items.

Tax Credits

With some exceptions, estates and trusts are allowed the same tax credits as individual taxpayers. Tax credits of an estate or trust are allocated between the fiduciary and beneficiaries based on the amount of income distributed in relation to total state law income. Estates or trusts are not allowed to take the credit for the elderly or the earned income credit. Code Sec. 642(a) and (b).

Miscellaneous Deductions

The two percent floor imposed on miscellaneous itemized deductions for individuals also applies to estates and trusts with some exceptions. The two percent floor does not apply to the income distribution deductions.

Administration Fees

Reasonable expenditures for administering the estate, including executor fees, are deductible; but if these expenditures are deducted on the estate's estate tax return (Form 706), they cannot also be deducted on the estate's income tax return (Form 1041). If the executor of the estate claims administrative expenses as an income tax deduction, a waiver of right to an estate tax deduction must be filed with the income tax return. Code Sec. 642(g); Reg. §1.642(g)-1.

TAX BLUNDER

The Rudkin testamentary trust was established in 1967. The trustee engaged Warfield Associates, Inc., to provide investment management services for the trust. During the tax year 2000, Warfield Associates was paid $22,241 for its services. A Form 1041, U.S. Income Tax Return for Estates and Trusts, for 2000 was filed by the trust in which it reported that it had $624,816 in total income. The Form 1041 also reported a deduction of $22,241 on the line in the form for "other deductions not subject to the 2 percent floor." The trust reported that as investment management fees. The IRS issued a deficiency notice in the amount of $4,448 for 2000, disallowing in full the deduction of $22,241 in investment fees. Instead, the IRS allowed a deduction subject to the 2 percent floor.

In the instant case, the Tax Court sided with the positions taken by both the Federal and Fourth Circuits. *Rudkin Testamentary Trust*, 124 TC 304 (2005). Also, the Supreme Court on January 16, 2008 affirmed the Tax Court decision in *Rudkin*, 2008-1 USTC ¶50,132.

Caveat: Advisory fees paid by a trust are deductible only to the extent that they exceed 2 percent of the trust's adjusted gross income.

PLANNING POINTER The executor of the estate has to make an appropriate decision as to where the administrative expenses deduction has the greatest tax advantage to the estate, on the income tax return or on the estate tax return.

¶23,371 ALTERNATIVE MINIMUM TAX

For estates and trusts, the alternative minimum tax (AMT) may apply as an addition to the regular tax for a taxable year. That is, the alternative minimum taxable income (AMTI) of the entity and any beneficiary is determined by applying Subchapter J with modifications. Code Sec. 59(c). Specifically, these modifications are termed adjustments and preferences. Common adjustments to the AMTI are miscellaneous itemized deductions, state and local income taxes, real property taxes, accelerated depreciation for property placed in service after 1986, and passive activity losses. In addition to the adjustments, preferences will also affect the AMTI. Common preferences are tax-exempt interest from private activity bonds, depletion in excess of basis, accelerated depreciation of property placed in service before 1987, and intangible drilling costs.

After calculating the alternative minimum taxable income, there still remains one final adjustment. That is, the Code provides an exemption of $24,100 for estates and trusts. Code Sec. 55(d)(1)(C)(ii). The exemption will be reduced by 25 cents per $1.00 of AMTI exceeding $80,450. Estates and trusts are subject to a two-tiered graduated rate schedule. That is, a 26 percent rate applies for the first $187,800 of AMTI in excess of the exemption amount and 28 percent for the balance of AMTI.

EXAMPLE 23.21

The income tax return of John Henry's estate showed no regular tax liability. However, the estate did generate AMTI of $20,000. The use of the exemption will prevent the AMT from generating a tax liability.

EXAMPLE 23.22

Assume that John Henry's fiduciary return shows AMTI of $102,850. Because the AMTI exceeds $80,450, the exemption is reduced to $18,150 ($24,100 − (($102,850 − $80,450) × .25)).

The estate or trust must pay the higher of the tentative minimum tax or the regular tax. The following illustration describes in detail an application of the AMT.

EXAMPLE 23.23

In 2017, the John Henry estate had rental income of $200,000 and $40,000 of bonus income related to the deceased, John Henry. The estate had a MACRS depreciation deduction of $24,000, while depreciation for AMT purposes was $12,000. The trust incurred fiduciary fees of $18,000 and state fiduciary income taxes of $25,000. Also, the estate had a Code Sec. 691(c) trust tax deduction of $7,000. The fiduciary distributed $28,000 to the income beneficiary, Vivian Elmore, in 2017. For 2017, the trust's federal tax liability is calculated as follows:

	Regular Tax	AMT
Rental income	$200,000	$200,000
Bonus IRD	40,000	40,000
Depreciation	(24,000)	(12,000)
Fiduciary fees	(18,000)	(18,000)
State income tax	(25,000)	0
Code Sec. 691(c) trust tax deduction	(7,000)	(7,000)
Income distribution	(28,000)	(28,000)
Tax exemption	(600)	0
Regular taxable income	$137,400	
AMTI		$175,000
AMT exemption: $24,100 − ($175,000 − $80,450) × .25)		462
Taxable amount	$137,400	$174,538
Income tax liability	$ 52,693	
Tentative Minimum Tax		$45,380

The estate must pay $52,693 in taxes, which is the greater of the regular tax or the tentative minimum tax.

¶23,373 GIFTS, LEGACIES, AND BEQUESTS

In general, any distribution to a beneficiary by an estate or trust is treated as made out of income to the extent that the trust or estate has distributable net income. However, if amounts are properly paid or credited as gifts or bequests under the terms of the governing instrument and thus fall within the protection of Code Sec. 663(a), the distribution will not be taxed as a distribution under Code Sec. 661(a) or 662(a). That is, the amount will not be deductible by the trust nor will it be includible by the recipient. Such amounts will be received tax free under the gift exemption of Code Sec. 102.

Prior to the 1954 Code, the executor or trustee could designate the source of distribution as principal and thereby immunize the distribution. But, under the distributable net income approach adopted in the 1954 Code and continued in the 1986 Code, the distribution is taxed as income up to the extent of distributable net income regardless of the trustee's or executor's designation.

EXAMPLE 23.24	Assume that a will left equal one-third shares to a husband and two children. The estate contains $1,800,000 in securities and a house. In the first year, the estate has income of $240,000 and makes a partial distribution of the house, worth $360,000, to the widower. Under these facts, the widower has taxable income of $240,000, and, as a consequence, he is bearing a substantially disproportionate tax burden in relation to the other heirs.

Lump-Sum or Installment Payouts

In order to alleviate the inordinate tax problem (as illustrated above), that an ordinary estate distribution of corpus could cause, the Code embodies exemptions for specific legacies. The Code provision is based on the standard gift exclusion reasoning that distinguishes between gifts of corpus and gifts of income. It is, of course, traditional to say that a gift of corpus should be nontaxable to the recipient. However, this concept was redefined to require, in addition, that the gift be specific and practically lump-sum in payout (only three installments are permitted). Code Sec. 663(a).

Sixty-Five Day Rule

A fiduciary of a complex trust may elect to treat any amount or portion thereof that is properly paid or credited to a beneficiary within the first 65 days following the close of the taxable year as an amount that was properly paid or credited on the last day of that taxable year. Code Sec. 663(b). A decedent's estate may elect to treat distributions made within 65 days after the close of its tax year as if they were made on the last day of the tax year. Thus, the same income tax rule applicable to trusts is now applicable to estates.

Under the 65-day rule, distributions cannot exceed the greater of the trust accounting income for the year of election, or the trust's distributable net income for the year. Also, the limitation is reduced by distributions in the election year except those amounts for which the election was claimed in the prior tax year. Reg. §1.663(b)-1(a)(2)(i).

Separate Share Rule

Solely for the purposes of determining the amount of DNI of a trust that is allocable to a particular beneficiary, substantially separate shares of different beneficiaries in the trust are treated as separate trusts. Code Sec. 663(c). The separate share rule is a very beneficial exception to the normal taxing rules of a trust. That is, when determining the amount taxable to beneficiaries, allocation by tiers may work an injustice when a trust is administered in substantially separate shares. Consider carefully the following illustration.

EXAMPLE 23.25	Assume that a trust has two beneficiaries, Bob and Sally, and DNI of $50,000. The trustee makes a mandatory distribution of one-half this amount, or $25,000 to Bob. The trustee accumulates the other $25,000, for future distribution to Sally. Also, the fiduciary made a discretionary distribution of $20,000 from corpus to Bob. Under the tier system, Bob would be taxed on the entire $45,000 of DNI. Is this result reasonable or equitable? That is, Bob's tax is measured, in part, by $20,000 of income that can only go to Sally and will never be available for Bob.

In order to alleviate the tax problem depicted in the example above, the separate share rule was brought into the Internal Revenue Code. Therefore, in the above example, only $25,000 of DNI would be allocated to Bob and the rest would stay with the trust (Sally's share). However, the separate share rule is only allowed when the fiduciary has no discretion to allocate between beneficiaries. With respect to decedents dying after August 5, 1997, if under a decedent's will and applicable state law, separate economic interests are created in one beneficiary or class of beneficiaries that are not affected by economic interests accruing to other beneficiaries or classes of beneficiaries, the separate share rule will apply to the decedent's estate. According to the House Committee Report, application of the separate share rule to an estate is not elective (such treatment is mandatory if separate shares exist).

¶23,381   PROPERTY DISTRIBUTIONS

In-kind distributions require, at the fiduciary's election, either recognition of gain or a carryover basis. Code Sec. 643(e). The beneficiary's basis in property received in an in-kind distribution is the adjusted basis of the property in the hands of the estate or trust, increased by any gain and decreased by any loss recognized on the distribution. If no election is made, no gain or loss is recognized, but the amount deductible by the fiduciary and taken into income by the beneficiary as a distribution of DNI is limited to the lesser of the basis or the fair market value of the property. Code Sec. 643(e)(2). As a result, the beneficiary receives a carryover basis.

EXAMPLE 23.26	A trust distributes an asset with a fair market value of $20,000 and a basis of $14,000. That year it has $20,000 of DNI. Under the old rules, the distributee would have $20,000 of ordinary income and a basis of $20,000 in the asset. Under the present rules, the distribution would carry out only $14,000 of ordinary income to the beneficiary, leaving $6,000 of ordinary income to be taxed to the fiduciary, and the beneficiary would only receive a basis of $14,000.

When the fiduciary elects, the estate or trust may treat gain property as if it were sold to the distributee at its fair market value. Code Sec. 643(e)(3)(A)(iii). Nevertheless, a loss may not be recognized by a trust because recognition of losses on sales between a trust and its beneficiary are disallowed. Code Sec. 267(b)(6). An estate and a beneficiary of an estate are treated as related persons for purposes of the disallowance of a loss on the sale of an asset to a related person under Code Sec. 267 and the disallowance of capital gain treatment on the sale of depreciable property to a related person under Code Sec. 1239.

¶23,387   TERMINATION OF ESTATE OR TRUST

The termination of an estate or trust is marked by the end of the period of administration by the fiduciary and the distribution of assets to beneficiaries. At this juncture, even an insolvent estate or trust can pass out valuable tax attributes to beneficiaries. That is, in the year of termination, net operating losses, capital losses, and excess deductions of an estate or trust may be utilized by beneficiaries on their own tax returns.

PLANNING POINTER	It should be noted that net operating losses and capital losses that flow out to the beneficiaries may be carried forward by beneficiaries when they are not used in the year of receipt. However, excess deductions may only be used in the year of receipt with no carryforward. Also, excess deductions are subject to the two percent of AGI floor. As a result, it is important to plan for the year of termination in order to have enough AGI to absorb the deductions.

KEYSTONE PROBLEM

Jason Argonaut died on October 16, 2017. His widow, Rita, is a personal friend of yours and knows that you are taking a college taxation course. She is seeking tax advice on the tax problems associated with Jason's death. In the past, Jason and Rita filed a joint return on the cash basis of accounting with a calendar year-end. Jason left a will and a substantial estate. Rita and Jason had no children, and Rita is the sole beneficiary of the estate. Rita has listed the following tax concerns about which she is seeking advice from you and another friend, Robert, a lawyer, who has been named executor of the estate. Rita has a substantial current yearly income of her own and is very concerned about high rates of taxation. What tax advice would you give Rita on the following questions?

1. Jason received a paycheck on October 21, 2017, covering the work period September 16–October 16, 2017. The executor of the estate cashed the check and the proceeds are currently in the estate. How will this income be recognized for tax purposes?
2. What filing status will Rita use when preparing her 2017 income tax return? What about personal exemptions, standard deduction, tax forms, etc.?
3. Rita received a dividend check on October 31, 2017, made out in Jason's name on stock he held in his own name. The dividend had been declared on September 11, 2017 to be paid on October 30, 2017 to shareholders of record on September 30, 2017. How will this dividend income be recognized for tax purposes?
4. It is anticipated that the estate will receive significant amounts of income. Who will pay tax on this income? What are some tax planning ideas that can be used by the estate to lessen the overall income tax burden on the estate and, ultimately, on Rita, the only beneficiary of the estate?

Taxation of Trusts—Special Rules

As stated previously, the scheme of federal income taxation of a trust is to have trust income taxed once, either directly to the trust or to trust beneficiaries who have received distributions from the trust. This scheme of income taxation for trusts is simple in theory but, in practice, has resulted in the development of some tax avoidance techniques involving multiple trusts, grantor trusts, and accumulation distributions. These tax avoidance techniques, along with tax legislation and IRS regulations adopted to counteract them, are discussed in this section.

¶23,503   ## MULTIPLE TRUSTS

A person may create more than one trust for the same or different beneficiaries. If the multiple trusts are recognized as valid for tax purposes, each trust is allowed a separate personal exemption and is taxed on its separate income. Whether multiple trusts have been created is a question of grantor intent as determined from the trust agreement. Tax avoidance motives could enter into the establishment of multiple trusts. Instead of having one trust taxed on a specified amount of income, why not create 10 trusts and have one-tenth of the income taxed to each trust? The obvious tax advantages of having 10 trusts would be 10 personal exemptions plus each trust starting over at the bottom of the tax rate schedule with its income and thereby mitigating the effects of a progressive tax system. However, multiple trusts are treated as a single trust for tax purposes if the trusts have the same grantor and similar beneficiaries, if there is no independent purpose for each trust, and if avoidance of the progressive rate of income tax or the alternative minimum tax appears to be the main reason why the multiple trusts were created. Code Sec. 643(e).

¶23,525   ## GRANTOR TRUSTS

In some instances, a trust can be created that qualifies as a separate legal entity but that is not a properly constituted trust for federal income tax purposes. The income from a trust of this type is taxable to the grantor instead of to the trust or beneficiaries. For qualification as a properly constituted trust for tax purposes, control of the property placed in trust must be relinquished by the grantor. Trusts that do not qualify for recognition as trusts for federal income tax purposes are called grantor trusts. A trust is usually classified as a grantor trust if the grantor or grantor's spouse owns an interest in the trust at any time or has certain proscribed powers over the trust.

Reversionary Interest

The grantor is taxed on the income from property placed in trust if it reasonably is expected that the trust property will revert to the grantor or grantor's spouse at anytime. This rule does not apply if the trust assets revert to the grantor or grantor's spouse only after the death of an income beneficiary of the trust who is a lineal descendant of the grantor or the grantor retains less than a five percent reversionary interest in the trust corpus.

Revocable Trust

If a grantor creates a trust and retains the right to revoke the trust, the trust income is taxable to the grantor. Code Sec. 676(a).

Income for Benefit of Grantor

If, at the discretion of the grantor, trust income can be distributed to the grantor or held for future distribution to the grantor, the trust income is taxable to the grantor. Code Sec. 677.

Beneficial Enjoyment

If, in certain instances, the grantor has the power to control the beneficial enjoyment of the trust income, the trust income is taxable to the grantor. Power to control beneficial enjoyment includes the power to change beneficiaries. Code Sec. 674(b).

Administrative Powers

If the grantor has administrative control over the trust property that can be exercised to the grantor's benefit, the trust income is taxable to the grantor. Code Sec. 675. Administrative control that could work to the grantor's benefit includes the right to borrow the trust property at a below-market interest rate.

TAX BLUNDER

In response to a summons by the IRS for records of a trust, the trustee, U.S. Bank, was ordered to have a representative appear before the court and produce records of the transactions of the Northwest Enterprise Trust. Springer, the "Executive Trustee," filed a motion to quash the summons. The IRS moved to dismiss the petition because Springer, as a non-lawyer, would not be legally empowered to pursue the action as trustee on behalf of the trust. Springer filed no response. The court ruled that, except for extraordinary occasions, corporations and other unincorporated associations must appear in court through an attorney. *Springer*, 83 AFTR 2d 99-541.

   Caveat: A non-attorney may appear on his or her own behalf, but only an attorney may represent a corporation or **trust**.

SUMMARY

- Estates come into being automatically at the death of the taxpayer. The executor or administrator distributes the assets and satisfies the liabilities of the decedent either pursuant to the will or via the state's intestate succession statutes.

- Trusts must be specifically created either during the grantor's life (inter vivos) or at death (testamentary). Trusts are classified for tax purposes as either simple (distributes all trust accounting income) or complex (does not have to distribute all of its trust accounting income).

- Estate and trusts can either act as conduits or retain the income and be taxed on it.

- Estate and trusts are governed (1) by either the will or trust instrument and (2) by state law in its operations.

- To understand fiduciary taxation, an appreciation of state law income and distributable net income is required.

- Estates and trusts are subject to the alternative minimum tax (AMT) and are faced with numerous preferences and adjustments. However, estates and trusts are allowed a $24,100 exemption from the AMT.

QUESTIONS

1. On what date is a decedent's final income tax return due?

2. What income is included on a final income tax return for a cash-basis decedent? How would your answer change if the decedent was on the accrual basis of accounting?

3. What is "income in respect of the decedent"? On whose return is "income in respect of the decedent" recognized?

4. What are "expenses in respect of the decedent"? On whose return are "expenses in respect of the decedent" deducted?

5. Unreported interest income on U.S. government bonds owned by a decedent at the date of death can be handled in various ways for tax purposes. List and discuss the various ways.

6. What are the duties and responsibilities of an executor of an estate in regard to the income tax returns required by an estate?

7. Do all estates have to file federal estate income tax returns? If not, what are the requirements for filing estate income tax returns?

8. What requirements exist for determining the first tax year-end of an estate for income tax purposes?

9. When is a federal estate income tax return due? What options are available to an estate executor in paying the estate's income tax liability?

10. What exemption amounts are allowed to an estate, simple trust, and complex trust?

11. What is the difference between an inter vivos trust and a testamentary trust?

12. Define the following terms:
    a. Reversionary interest
    b. Income beneficiary
    c. Remainder beneficiary
    d. Simple trust
    e. Complex trust

13. List and discuss two nontax reasons why an individual might consider creating a trust.

14. When is a trust required to file a federal income tax return? What tax form is used for a trust's federal income tax return?

15. Why is it important for the trustee of a trust to carefully consider the choice of an accounting method for a trust?

16. Will a trust be entitled to deduct the full value of all charitable contributions made by the trust in all situations on the trust's federal income tax return?

17. What tax benefits are embodied in specific legacies and bequests?

18. What three functions does distributable net income serve in fiduciary taxation?

19. What problem does the separate share rule alleviate?

20. Beneficiaries of estates and complex trusts are subject to the tier system of taxation. Explain what is meant by a first- and second-tier beneficiary.

21. When depreciation follows income of an estate or complex trust, explain the situation where wastage could occur.

22. In relation to trust distributions to beneficiaries, explain the 65-day rule.

23. What is a Schedule K-1? When is a trustee of a trust required to file a Schedule K-1 with the trust's federal income tax return?

24. Explain when loss carryovers can be taken from a trust's federal income tax return and be used on the trust beneficiaries' individual income tax returns.

25. Explain some tax avoidance techniques that could arise in regard to multiple trusts.

PROBLEMS

26. Hershel Barker was the president and majority shareholder in Bulldog Inc. He was a cash-basis taxpayer who reported his income on a calendar-year basis. On March 1, 2017, Hershel was killed in a skiing accident. The estate has elected to report its income on a calendar-year basis.

    Required: Give the tax consequences for the parties involved in the following situations:
    a. Dividends of $10,000 had been declared by Bulldog Inc. on February 3, 2017, payable March 4, 2017, to shareholders of record on February 17, 2017. Hershel's executor received the dividends.
    b. What if the record date was March 10, 2017?

27. The trust instrument requires the trustee to distribute $40,000 annually to Carl Smith, the grantor's son. Any residual income may be distributed or accumulated for Bob Jones, Sam Smith, Earl Litt, and Carl Smith in the trustee's discretion. In the current year, the trust has distributable net income of $100,000 in domestic dividends. The trustee distributes $40,000 of income to Carl Smith. Next, he distributes $30,000 to Bob Jones, $20,000 each to Sam Smith and Earl Litt, and an additional $15,000 to Carl Smith. The trust does not have any undistributed net income from previous years.

    Required: How much of the distributions are taxable income to Carl Smith, Bob Jones, Sam Smith, and Earl Litt?

28. John Jefferson dies on November 10, 2017. John is on the cash basis of accounting for tax purposes. On November 29, 2017, a $4,000 paycheck covering the period November 1–November 8, 2017, is mailed to John's home. Who recognizes this paycheck as income? Would your answer to this question change if John was on the accrual basis of accounting at the date of his death?

29. Jane Jaffe dies on October 12, 2017. On the date of death, Jane has a bank account that pays interest on a quarterly basis. On December 31, 2017, $3,000 of interest income is credited to the bank account.
    a. If Jane was on the cash basis of accounting at the date of her death, is any of the income included on Jane's final income tax return?
    b. Would your answer to (a) change if Jane was on the accrual basis of accounting at the date of her death?
    c. If Jane does not recognize all of the interest income on her final income tax return in (a) and (b), who does recognize the interest income?

30. Richard Johnson held $50,000 of U.S. government savings bonds on the date of his death, December 11, 2017. The bonds mature in 2018. Unreported interest income on these bonds at the date of Richard's death amounted to $14,700. It is anticipated that Richard will be in the 28 percent marginal income tax bracket on his final income tax return. The one beneficiary to Richard's estate is expected to have a 15 percent marginal tax bracket in 2017 and a 28 percent marginal tax bracket in 2018. List and discuss some tax planning options that are available to the executor of Richard's estate and to the beneficiary of Richard's estate in regard to the recognition as income of the unreported interest income on the U.S. Government bonds.

31. An estate receives the following items of income and has the following deductions during the tax year 2017:

Income	
Dividends	$5,000
Taxable interest	5,000
Tax-exempt interest	5,000
Total income	$15,000
Deduction	
Fiduciary fee	$2,000

The estate files an income tax return for the calendar year 2017. No distributions were made during the year to beneficiaries. Based on these facts, what is the 2017 federal income tax liability of the estate?

32. Refer to the facts in Problem 31. If a $10,000 distribution of income was made to a beneficiary during the 2017 tax year, what is the 2017 federal income tax liability of the estate? Assume that the decedent's will does not specify that the distribution is to be paid out of any specific type of income.

33. Refer to the facts in Problem 32. How much of the $10,000 income distribution will be taxable to the beneficiary?

34. Mr. Hughes died in 2017. Pursuant to his will a testamentary trust was established. The trust instrument requires that 60 percent of the trust income be distributed currently to his wife Donna, for her life and 40 percent of the trust income be distributed to his daughter, Holly, for her life. Also, the trustee is permitted to set aside income as a depreciation reserve. In the current year, depreciation on the trust property amounts to $30,000, and the trustee allocates $10,000 of trust income as a depreciation reserve.
    a. What is the amount of the depreciation deduction allowed to the trust?
    b. What is the amount of the depreciation deduction allowed to Donna?
    c. What is the amount of the depreciation deduction allowed to Holly?

35. In 2017, a trust has $2,000 of trust accounting income and $1,600 of distributable net income. The trust properly pays $1,100 to John Smith, a beneficiary, on February 3, 2017, which the trustee elects to treat under Code Sec. 663(b) (65-day rule) as paid on December 31, 2016. The trust also properly pays to John Smith $1,200 on August 1, 2017, and $900 on January 21, 2018. For 2017, how much may be elected under the 65-day rule as properly paid or credited on the last day of 2017?

36. John Henderson's will provides for the creation of a trust for the benefit of Holly Jones. Under the specific terms, the trust is required to distribute to Holly $50,000 cash and 1,000 shares of IBM stock when she reaches 25 years of age, $60,000 cash and 1,200 shares of Xerox when she reaches 30 years of age, $30,000 cash and 2,000 shares of General Motors stock when she reaches 35 years of age, and $100,000 cash and 500 shares of DuPont stock when she reaches 40 years of age. Which if any of these items qualify for exclusion as a specific legacy or bequest?

37. The trustee of the Astro trust makes a $15,000 charitable contribution to PennOhio University. The trust agreement is silent as to the specific type of income that should be used to pay the contribution. The trust had $15,000 of taxable income and $10,000 of tax-exempt income during the year.

    How much of the $15,000 charitable contribution is deductible on the trust's federal income tax return?

38. The trustee of the James trust makes a $30,000 charitable contribution to the United Way. The trust had $20,000 of taxable income and $30,000 of tax-exempt income during the year. The trust agreement states that all charitable contributions, to the extent possible, should be paid out of taxable income. How much of the $30,000 charitable contribution is deductible on the trust's federal income tax return?

39. A trustee distributes $10,000 of income to each of nine beneficiaries of the trust. The trust had $40,000 of tax-exempt interest income during the year and $80,000 of taxable income. The trust agreement does not specify the type of income to be distributed to any beneficiary.
    a. How much of the $10,000 distribution to each beneficiary is taxable income to each beneficiary?
    b. Would your answer to (a) change if the trust agreement specifies that tax-exempt income should be distributed to beneficiaries 1-4 and taxable income should be distributed to beneficiaries 5-9?

40. The trustee of the Peterson trust is required by the trust agreement to distribute $5,000 yearly to Peter Peterson, $4,000 yearly to John Peterson, and $3,000 yearly to Sally Peterson. The trustee has the authority per the trust agreement to make additional distributions to the beneficiaries at his discretion. During 2017, the trustee actually distributes $10,000 to Peter, $15,000 to John, and $20,000 to Sally. The trust has DNI of $30,000 in 2017.

    What is the taxable amount of the distributions to Peter, John, and Sally?

41. An estate with distributable net income of $100,000 distributes the following assets to a beneficiary in December of 2017:

	Basis to Estate	Value at Date of Distribution
Cash	$40,000	$40,000
General Motors Stock	90,000	140,000
Real Estate	100,000	250,000
Mucho Taco Stock	70,000	50,000
	$300,000	$480,000

    a. What is the beneficiary's basis in the distributed assets?
    b. What would be the beneficiary's basis in the distributed assets if the election is made by the fiduciary under Code Sec. 643(e)(3)?

42. John and Ralph, two brothers who are over the age of 21, are beneficiaries of a trust created in 1982 by their father, Jim. At that time, Jim transferred securities and an apartment building to a corporate trustee. All of the income is to be distributed annually to John and Ralph for 40 years. Depreciation follows income, and at the end of 40 years, the trust will terminate and the corpus will be distributed to John and Ralph. During 2017, the trust has the following items of income and expense.

Rental income	$50,000
Taxable interest	40,000
Tax-exempt interest	30,000
Long-term capital gain (allocable to corpus)	15,000
Expenses attributable to rent	20,000
Trustee's commission (allocable to income)	4,000
Trustee's commission (allocable to principal)	1,000
Depreciation	8,000

    Required:
    a. Compute state law income.
    b. Compute DNI as an income ceiling.
    c. Compute DNI as a deduction ceiling.
    d. Compute the trust's taxable income.
    e. Compute DNI as a qualitative yardstick.

43. Which of the following items affects the charitable deduction of an estate or complex trust?
    a. Rental income
    b. Dividends
    c. Interest
    d. Tax-exempt interest

44. Which of the following deductions does not affect trust accounting income?
    a. Rental expenses
    b. Trustee's commissions allocable to income
    c. Interest expense
    d. Taxes
    e. Trustee's commissions allocable to corpus

45. Which of the following items does not normally enter into the computation of distributable net income?
    a. Charitable deduction
    b. Capital gains
    c. Trustee's commissions
    d. Rental income

46. An estate with depreciable property may not do one of the following:
    a. Pay income to first-tier beneficiaries
    b. Pay income to second-tier beneficiaries
    c. Distribute capital losses on termination
    d. Set up a reserve for depreciation

47. A trust can have the following taxable year-end:
    a. September 30
    b. June 30
    c. December 31
    d. March 31

48. John Doe had earned commissions on life insurance sold prior to his death. The commissions of $20,000 were to be paid in five annual installments. The executor of his estate collected the first installment of $4,000 and distributed the right to the remaining installments to his son, a beneficiary of the estate. How will the remaining four installments be reported for income tax purposes?

49. John Henry died on May 1, 2017. When does his final 1040 have to be filed?

50. In problem 49, when does the estate's taxable year begin?

51. In problem 49, when does the estate's taxable year end?

52. John and Mary Hughes file their income tax return on a calendar year basis. John dies on May 15, 2017. Mary remarries on July 4, 2017. Can Mary file a joint return with John for the taxable year 2017?

53. **Comprehensive Problem.** Thomas Able, a cash method, calendar-year taxpayer, died December 1, 2017. He is survived by his spouse, Nan. Tom was age 65 at the time of his death and Nan is age 66. They have no dependents, and Nan is the sole beneficiary of Tom's estate. Nan has been blind from cataracts since taking a tax course at Louisiana Tech University in 1983. The executor of the estate is the First Wachovia Corp., Winston-Salem, North Carolina. Nan and the executor elected to file a joint return for 2017. During 2017, the following cash receipts, disbursements, and expenses were recorded by the Ables and the estate of Tom Able:

    a. Cash dividends of $25,000 from Safflower Oil Corporation were received on November 28, 2017. These dividends were declared on November 3, 2017, and payable to shareholders of record on November 14, 2017. Tom Able was the stockholder in Safflower Oil Corporation.

    b. Tom was an executive in the Kane & Able Trucking Company in Winston-Salem, North Carolina, and for the two months preceding his death, Tom was not paid his monthly salary of $5,000 because of a moratorium on wages. On January 5, 2018, the trucking company paid the $10,000 to the executor of the Tom Able Estate. Tom had received all his other monthly salary payments at the end of each month.

    c. Interest of $1,800 was credited to Tom and Nan's savings accounts on August 1, 2017.

    d. Real estate taxes of $1,000 were paid by the estate on December 31, 2017, for the calendar year.

    e. Medical expenses of $5,700 related to Tom's last illness were paid by his estate on January 20, 2018. The executor has elected not to deduct these medical expenses on the estate tax return. Health insurance premiums of $500 were paid by Tom during 2017.

    f. A bonus of $4,500 from the Kane & Able Trucking Company was paid to Tom's estate on January 16, 2018.

    g. Charitable contributions of $1,200 were paid to the Ventura County Humane Society by Tom during 2017.

    h. Interest on the Ables' home mortgage amounted to $1,600 in 2017.

i.   On May 29, 2017, Tom received $25,000 in life insurance proceeds paid by reason of the death of his mother.

j.   Tom has always attended Saturday night cockfights. During 2017, he won $500 and lost $800.

k.   On June 9, 2017, Tom submitted his entry in a Fairview Books Publishing Company contest. On August 1, 2017, it was announced that Tom had won $3,000 cash and a year's worth of free computer research time worth $900. Tom accepted the $3,000 but refused the computer research time because he had heard the system was difficult to use.

l.   Nan and Tom sold stock that they had purchased on December 27, 2016, at $1,000 for $1,200 on June 24, 2017.

m.   Tom also owned a farm that produced total annual revenue of $1,000 and expenses of $100 for utilities, $200 for fertilizer and lime, $100 for miscellaneous expenses, $100 for repairs and maintenance, and depreciation expense of $200 in 2017 prior to Tom's death. The farm has been idle since Tom's death.

n.   Tom and Nan kept meticulous records verifying the $1,500 they paid in sales tax in 2017.

o.   Federal and state income taxes of $9,900 and $2,000, respectively, were withheld from Tom's salary in 2017.

p.   Tom and Nan had a $500 balance due on their 2016 North Carolina return that was paid on April 12, 2017.

Required: Compute the amount of taxable income that will go on the decedent's final return.

54. **Comprehensive Problem.** In 2017, Cabell Mapp passed away in Belle Haven, Virginia. Pursuant to his will, a testamentary trust was established. The trust instrument requires that $10,000 a year be paid to the University of Virginia. The balance of the income may, in the trustee's discretion, be accumulated or distributed to Sarah Mapp. Expenses are allocable against income and the trust instrument requires a reserve for depreciation. During the taxable year, the trustee contributes $10,000 to the University of Virginia, and in his discretion distributes $15,000 of income to Sarah Mapp. The trust has the following items of income and expenses for the taxable year.

Dividends	$10,000
Interest	10,000
Fully tax-exempt interest	10,000
Rents	20,000
Rental expenses	2,000
Depreciation of rental property	3,000
Trustee's commissions	5,000

a.   Determine trust accounting income.

b.   Determine DNI as an income ceiling.

c.   Determine DNI as a deduction ceiling.

d.   Determine the trust taxable income.

e.   Determine DNI as a qualitative yardstick.

f.   Determine Sarah Mapp's Schedule K-1 amounts.

g.   Has any wastage occurred in connection with the charitable deduction? Could this wastage have been prevented?

55. **Comprehensive Problem (Estate Tax Return Problem).**

FACTS

Howard Hayes was killed in a freak barbecuing accident at a local eatery called P.K.'s Barbecue Shack on October 28, 2015, in Wilson, North Carolina. He was survived by his wife, Helen (age 56), and two children, Isaac (34) and Heidi (32). Howard's will provided that Helen would receive one half of the residuary estate and the balance of the residue would be divided equally between the children. The will provided that any direct obligations be paid out of the principal of the residuary estate.

The post-mortem tax plan instituted by the executor requires payment of commissions in the year of termination of the estate (no deductions for commissions on this return). All expenses are first allocable to farm income and, if farm income is exhausted, then to other ordinary income. Unattached or floating deductions will all be allocated against income on a pro rata basis. At the time of Mr. Hayes' death, he owned a small farm. In 2016, fertilizer expenses totaled $5,000, seed costs were $2,500, and proceeds from the sale of crops were $68,000.

At the time of his death, Howard wanted $10,000 to be paid out of estate income to East Carolina University. The executor, after ascertaining the status of this obligation, paid the pledge on December 10, 2016.

The executor elected to report income on a calendar-year basis. The following information pertains to 2016 income:

Farm Income	$68,000
Domestic Dividends	30,000
Interest from CD	10,000
Real Estate Taxes (related to the farm)	2,000
Other Farm Expenses: Insurance	2,000
Repairs & Maintenance	4,000
Filing Fees (Clerk of Superior Court)	600
Depreciation on Farm Building (straight line)	3,000

The executor was instructed via the will to distribute income during the period of administration as follows:

Helen:	One-half of State Law Income
Isaac:	One-eighth of State Law Income
Heidi:	One-eighth of State Law Income

Reidsville Bank & Trust Co., N.A., was named executor of Howard Hayes' estate and their trust department is responsible for preparing all of the 1041 returns. The address is 1454 Scales Street, Reidsville, NC 27390. The estate's identification number is 56-1053613; the return is filed on April 5, 2017; and the officer signing the return is Tom Phillips.

The following items are required:
(1) State Law Income under Code Sec. 643(b)
(2) DNI as an income ceiling
(3) DNI as a deduction ceiling
(4) Estate's taxable income
(5) DNI as a qualitative yard stick
(6) K-1 allocations
(7) U.S. Fiduciary Income Tax Return (Form 1041)
(8) Form 4562
(9) Schedule F
(10) Schedule K-1 for Helen Hayes
(11) Schedule K-1 for Isaac Hayes
(12) Schedule K-1 for Heidi Hayes

56. **Research Problem.** When a trust terminates, there are, in most instances, terminating commissions that are charged by the fiduciary. These commissions may generate excess deductions that can be passed out to beneficiaries as itemized deductions subject to the two percent of adjusted gross income rule. Nonetheless, the allocation of such expenses with respect to character of the income has spawned litigation as to the proper allocation base.

Read the following cases and prepare a brief written summary of the allowable allocation method for terminating commissions.
   a. *C.L. Whittemore, Jr. v. U.S.,* 67-2 USTC ¶9670, 383 F.2d 824 (CA-8 1967).
   b. *A.J. Fabens,* 75-2 USTC ¶9572, 519 F.2d 1310 (CA-1 1975).

57. **Research Problem.** The following court cases have helped to clarify the rightful recipient of depreciation of property held by an estate or trust.

Read the following judicial decisions and prepare a brief written summary for each case.
   a. *Sue Carol,* 30 BTA 443, Dec. 8520 (1934), Acq. XIII-2 CB 4.
   b. *R.J. Dusek,* 67-1 USTC ¶9418, 376 F.2d 410 (CA-10 1967).
   c. *W.H. Lamkin, Executor,* 76-2 USTC ¶9485, 533 F.2d 303 (CA-5 1976).

24

Deferred Compensation and Education Savings Plans

OBJECTIVES

After completing Chapter 24, you should be able to:

1. Identify the key differences between qualified and nonqualified deferred compensation plans.
2. Explain the hurdles that must be cleared in order to achieve tax deferral status for qualified deferred compensation plans.
3. Explain the specific rules governing the timing and amount of distributions from qualified deferred compensation plans.
4. Explain how contributions to qualified deferred compensation plans are taxed.
5. Explain how distributions from qualified deferred compensation plans are taxed.
6. Identify the basic types of qualified deferred compensation plans that employers can sponsor and describe their features.
7. Identify the deferred compensation plans available to self-employed taxpayers and describe their features.
8. Distinguish between traditional and Roth IRAs and explain how they operate and are taxed.
9. Understand how nonqualified deferred compensation plans are set up to achieve tax advantages similar to those offered by qualified deferred compensation plans.
10. Identify vehicles available for educational savings and describe their features.

OVERVIEW

Investing For The Future: The Grocery Store Analogy.

An analogy can be drawn between grocery shopping and investing for future consumption.

Identifying The "Goods" To Buy. The starting point might be to select the "goods/investments" to buy such as the sample listed in the table below:

	Fruit:	Vegetables:	Cereal:	Coffee:	Soup:	Bread:
Identify the Food to Buy →	Apples, Oranges, etc,	Carrots, Celery, etc.	Fiber, Frosted, etc.	Freeze-dried, Instant, etc.	Vegetable, Tomato, etc.	Rye, Wheat, etc.

	Stocks:	Treasury Securities:	Corporate Bonds:	Real Estate:	Commodities:	Highly Liquid Cash Equivalents:
Identify the Investments to Buy → (this is a mere glimpse into the thousands of possibilities)	S&P 500, Russell 3000, Industry-specific (e.g., consumer staples, utilities), Geographic-specific (e.g., Pacific rim, Latin America), Risk specific (e.g., aggressive growth stocks, "blue chips"), Dividend specific (e.g., high yield stocks) Market-size specific (e.g., emerging markets), etc.	T-Bills, T-Notes, T-Bonds, I-Bonds, EE- Bonds, TIPS etc.	Risk Specific, Term Specific, etc.	Equity REITS, Mortgage REITS, Hybrid REITS	Foreign Currencies, Natural Resources, Industrial Metals Precious Metals, Grains, etc.	Interest-Bearing Time Deposits, Interest-Bearing Demand Deposits, etc.

Selecting The "Store." Once the goods/investments are identified, a specific "store" might be selected. Any brokerage company, bank, mutual fund management company, savings and loan association, or insurance company that is IRS-approved may be selected. Code Sec. 408(a) & (b). A short list of possible "stores" (grocers & financial institutions) is shown below.

Select the grocery store →	Kroger	Whole Foods	Costco	Farmers Market	Wal-Mart	7-Eleven
Select the financial institution →	Fidelity	Bank of America	Vanguard	1st Federal S&L	E-Trade	Prudential

Choosing The Best "Store-Shelf Packaging." When buying the "goods" identified above, the manner in which the goods are "packaged" is often an important consideration. Investment "packaging" alternatives include *mutual funds, exchange-traded funds (ETFs), money market funds, bank certificates of deposit (bank CDs), savings accounts* and *annuity contracts.* Mutual funds and ETFs are "bundles" of targeted investments such as publicly-traded stocks, corporate bonds, treasury securities, commodities and Real Estate Investment Trusts (REITs). A sample of "packaging" types is shown below:

Choose the Type of Food Packaging →	Cans	Plastic wrappers	Cartons	Jugs	Jars	Rubber bands
Choose the Type of Investment "Packaging" →	Mutual Funds	Exchange-Traded Funds	Money Market Funds	Bank Certificates of Deposit	Savings Accounts	Annuity Contracts

Choosing The Best "Check-Out Carrier." The manner in which the food packages will be carried to the car may be another important consideration. The cashier at a check-out line might ask, "Paper or plastic?" For example, corn purchased at, say, Krogers, whether packaged in pressurized cans, frozen boxes or banded bundles, might be carried out in *paper bags, plastic bags,* or *boxes.* Similarly, investments such as S&P 500 stocks, purchased at, say, Schwab, whether "packaged" in mutual funds or ETFs, might be carried in *tax-deferred, tax-free,* or *taxable* accounts:

Choose the Best "Check-Out Carrier" ➡	Paper		Plastic	Box
	Tax Deferred Accounts		**Tax-Free Accounts**	**Taxable Accounts**
Choose the Best Investment "Carrier" ➡	**Employer-Sponsored Plans:**	**Educational Savings Plans:**		
	401(k) plan, 403(b) plan, Employee stock ownership plan (ESOP), Solo 401(k) plan (for self-employed taxpayers or single-employee entities) Keogh plan, Simplified employee pension (SEP) IRA, Savings incentive match plan ("SIMPLE") Nonqualified employer-sponsored plans	529 Plans Coverdell Savings Account	Traditional IRA Roth IRA Roth 401(k) Roth 403(b)	Any account maintained at a financial institution that generates interest income, dividend income and/or capital gains that are currently taxable

Buying The "Goods." Both grocery store purchases and direct contributions into retirement or educational plans for the purpose of investment purchases must be made in U.S. dollars (using cash, check, credit card, or debit card).

The focus of this chapter is directed mainly toward the advantages of *tax-deferred* and *tax-free* accounts and the rules for holding investments in these two broad types of "investment carriers." Qualified and nonqualified retirement plans for employees and the self-employed are discussed, as well as individual retirement accounts (IRAs), including Roth IRAs. While education savings plans are not forms of deferred compensation, they are treated in this chapter of the book because they also provide tax-favored treatment for the earnings from the contributions.

Employer-Sponsored Deferred Compensation Plans: "Qualified" and "Nonqualified"

¶24,001   **QUALIFIED EMPLOYER-SPONSORED PLANS**

Qualified deferred compensation plans (QPs) are employer-sponsored plans that satisfy certain requirements in order to qualify for special tax benefits.

Qualifying Requirements

An employer-sponsored qualified plan must satisfy certain types of requirements including:

1. *Nondiscrimination.* The plan cannot discriminate in favor of highly compensated employees. Code Sec. 401(a)(4).
2. *Limitation on annual contributions.* Specified limits may apply to how much employees and employers can contribute to defined contribution plans. Code Sec. 415.
3. *Distribution rules.* Distributions made too soon may be subject to a 10 percent penalty. If made too late and/or too little in amount, a 50 percent penalty may be imposed on the recipient.
4. *Vesting.* An employee's nonforfeitable right to receive future benefits must take effect within a prescribed time frame. Code Sec. 411.
5. *Exclusive benefit of employees.* The plan must be created and operated for the exclusive benefit of the employee/participants and isolated from potential misfortunes of the employer.

Tax Benefits of Qualified Plans

The tax law encourages QPs by providing several tax benefits including the following:

1. *Contributions may be tax deferred.* Taxation of contribution amounts are generally postponed until they are distributed to participants.

2. *Deductions are immediately available to employers.* Corporate employers, self-employed taxpayers, or individuals (for IRAs) may deduct contributions even though income tax is deferred. For all plans except IRA's, the contribution may create an NOL.

3. *Income may be tax deferred.* Interest, dividends, and other income can accumulate tax free until benefits are paid. (With Roth 401(k) plans, accumulated income can be tax-free forever.)

4. *Future payouts may be subject to lower tax rates.* Tax benefits are typically paid out after retirement when the employee's effective tax rate is often lower.

5. *Payroll tax exemption may apply.* Employer contributions (but not employee contributions) are exempt from FICA and FUTA taxes when paid in and paid out of a QP.

6. *Portability option may be available.* Generally, transfers between QPs and from QPs to traditional IRAs are tax-free, thereby permitting extended tax deferral.

7. *Credit to employers for startup costs may be available.* Small employers may be entitled to receive a credit for some of the costs of establishing new QPs (see Chapter 9 ¶9045).

8. *Credit to employees for contributions to a QP may be available.* Low to middle income employees may be entitled to receive a saver's credit for elective contributions to a QP (see Chapter 9 ¶9033).

Nontax Benefits of Qualified Plans

Most QPs also have the following nontax features:

1. *Bankruptcy protection.* Plan assets are protected from the employer, employer creditors, and employee creditors. *(O.J. Simpson receives $25,000 monthly from his pension plan despite losing a $36 million judgment to the Goldman family.)*

2. *Employment incentive.* QPs can be used to attract and retain employees;

3. *Loan option available to employees.* Participants may be permitted to borrow up to $50,000 from their QPs.

¶24,015   NONQUALIFIED EMPLOYER-SPONSORED PLANS

Nonqualified Employer-Sponsored Plans (NPs) may be useful as part of an employee compensation package designed to provide executives and middle management employees with special incentives in excess of those allowed under the QP rules. According to the ERISA Industry Committee, approximately 92 percent of Fortune 1000 companies maintain NPs. Some of the more common types of NPs discussed in this chapter are listed below.

- Rabbi Trusts,
- Incentive stock options,
- Nonqualified stock options.

NPs share the same fundamental goal as QPs: the deferral of tax. However, certain features of NPs are generally regarded as favorable or unfavorable as they relate to QPs.

Favorable Features of Nonqualifed Plans

Nonqualified plans have the following favorable features:

- *More flexibility in choosing who participates.* NPs are not subject to the same minimum coverage and nondiscrimination requirements as QPs. Therefore, an NP can be designed to cover a limited group of employees.
- *Unlimited benefits.* An NP can provide benefits in excess of those permitted under QP limits.

Unfavorable Features of Nonqualifed Plans

Nonqualified plans have the following unfavorable features:

- *Limited deferral of NP benefits.* For most NPs, tax deferral on employee compensation can be achieved only under either of two conditions: (1) the employer's obligation to pay the benefits remains merely an unfunded and unsecured promise to pay; or (2) the employer's obligation is funded or secured but the employee must bear a substantial risk of losing amounts contributed to the plan.
- *No immediate tax deduction.* An employer is not entitled to a tax deduction until such time as the benefits are actually paid to the employee. As previously explained, employer contributions into most QPs are currently deductible by the employer.
- *Payroll tax on employer contributions.* Unlike QPs, for NPs, employer contributions are generally subject to Social Security and Medicare taxes when services are performed or, if later, when a person's right to receive the compensation no longer is subject to a substantial risk of forfeiture. Code Sec. 3121(v).

Qualified Plan Requirements

¶24,205 **NONDISCRIMINATION REQUIREMENTS**

Contributions and benefits provided under a qualified deferred compensation plan must not discriminate in favor of highly compensated employees. Code Sec. 401(a)(4).

An employee is a "highly compensated employee" if the employee satisfies either of the following tests (Code Sec. 414(q)):

1. The employee was a five-percent owner at any time during the year or the preceding year. If the employer is a corporation, a five-percent owner is any person who owns (or is considered as owning under the constructive ownership rules of Code Sec. 318) more than five percent of the outstanding stock of the corporation or stock possessing more than five percent of the total combined voting power of all of the corporation's stock. If the employer is not a corporation, a five-percent owner is any person who owns more than five percent of the capital or profits interest in the employer.
2. For the preceding year, the employee had compensation in excess of $120,000 (for 2017). At the employer's election, the employee also may be required to be among the top 20 percent of employees in compensation for that preceding year.

EXAMPLE 24.1   Audrey Jackson's annual compensation at Art Classics, Inc. was $160,000, but she was not among the top 20 percent of employees in terms of compensation. Even though Audrey is relatively highly paid, she may, at her employer's election, be excluded from the group of highly compensated employees.

For a plan to satisfy the nondiscrimination requirements, it must satisfy each of the following requirements (Reg. §1.401(a)(4)-1(b)):

1. Either the contributions or benefits provided under the plan must be nondiscriminatory in amount. It need not be shown that both the contributions and benefits provided are nondiscriminatory in amount.
2. All benefits, rights, and features provided under the plan must be available in a nondiscriminatory manner.
3. The timing of plan amendments must not have the effect of discriminating significantly in favor of highly compensated employees.

A plan will not be considered discriminatory merely because the contributions or benefits of, or on behalf of, the employees under the plan bear a uniform relationship to the compensation of the employees.

EXAMPLE 24.2   AJR Inc.'s qualified plan provides for the allocation of employer contributions based upon a flat rate of four percent of each employee's compensation. Nathaniel and Micaela's annual compensation is equal to $20,000 and $200,000, respectively. The plan would not be discriminatory even though Micaela's trust account would receive an $8,000 employer contribution (4% × $200,000) while Nathaniel's would receive only $800 (4% × $20,000).

Moreover, a qualified plan will not be considered discriminatory merely because the plan takes the employer's share of the Social Security tax or employer-derived Social Security benefits into account in determining its contribution or benefits formula. Such an arrangement is called social security integration.

¶24,215 **LIMITATIONS ON CONTRIBUTIONS TO A DEFINED CONTRIBUTION PLAN**

The annual additions to a defined contribution plan cannot exceed the lesser of the following amounts (Code Secs. 401(a)(16), 415(a), and (c)):

1. $54,000 (for 2017); or
2. 100 percent of the participant's compensation (earned income in the case of a self-employed individual). The annual compensation of each employee taken into account under the plan for any year may not exceed $270,000 (for 2017).

EXAMPLE 24.3

Bert Richards participates in his employer's qualified retirement plan, which provides a 10 percent employer contribution formula. Bert's annual compensation is equal to $1,080,000. The employer may contribute only 2.5 percent of this compensation into Bert's retirement plan account due to the $270,000 annual compensation limit [2.5% = (10% × $270,000) ÷ $1,080,000].

The "annual addition" is the sum for any year of the following amounts:

1. Employer contributions.
2. Employee contributions. Employee contributions do not include rollover contributions or employee contributions to a simplified employee pension that are excludable from gross income.
3. Forfeitures.

Elective Deferrals

Employees are subject to special limits for elective deferrals on contributions to the following plans:

1. 401(k) plan (at ¶24,401).
2. simplified employee pension (SEP) plan (at ¶24,535).
3. Saving Incentive Match Plan for Employees (SIMPLE) plan (at ¶24,545).

¶24,235 REQUIRED MINIMUM DISTRIBUTION RULES

Code Sec. 401 contains provisions which relate to the commencement of the payment of benefits and the minimum amounts and timing of distributions.

Early Retirement Option

Many qualified retirement plans provide for an early retirement option. In order to qualify for early retirement, participants must usually reach a certain age and have a certain number of years of service, for example, age 55 and 20 years of service. In such a plan, if a participant satisfies the service requirements for early retirement benefits, but separates from service prior to reaching the early retirement age, the plan must provide that the participant will be ineligible to receive the early retirement benefit until the attainment of the required age. Code Sec. 401(a)(14). The minimum age that must be attained in order to qualify for the early retirement option is 55. Code Sec. 72(t)(2)(A)(v). The early retirement option is not available to 5-percent owners (taxpayers owning five percent or more of the business at any time during the five plan years preceding the current plan year). Code Sec. 72(m)(5).

Mandatory Cash-outs

A qualified plan may pay out the balance of a participant's account without the participant's consent if the present value of the benefit does not exceed $5,000. Code Sec. 411(a)(11)(A). This eases the administrative burden and cost of maintaining relatively small amounts. If the present value of the benefit exceeds $1,000, and the participant does not elect otherwise, a mandatory distribution must be transferred directly to an IRA established by the plan for the benefit of the participant. Code Sec. 401(a)(31)(B), Notice 2005-5.

Required Minimum Distribution Deadlines

Code Sec. 401(a)(9) contains provisions that govern the commencement and longevity of benefit payments to a participant and to the participant beneficiary after the death of the participant. Failure to meet the minimum distributions required under this section can result in a 50 percent penalty assessment on the shortfall under Code Sec. 4974. However, "after-tax" balances are not subject to this 50 percent penalty. (The concepts "after-tax" and "before-tax" amounts are explained at ¶24,301.) The minimum distribution rules apply to qualified employer-sponsored plans (except to the extent of any Roth 401(k) amounts), certain nonqualified employer-sponsored plans (e.g., governmental 457(b) plans), and traditional Individual Retirement Accounts (IRAs).

Required Beginning Date for "Before-death" Distributions

The "required beginning date" generally is April 1 of the calendar year following the later of (1) the calendar year in which the employee attains age 70½ or (2) the calendar year in which the employee retires.

Special Timing Rule for Owners of Traditional IRAs

For owners of traditional IRAs, the required beginning date is April 1 of the calendar year following the calendar year in which the employee attains age 70½. Code Sec. 401(a)(9)(C)(ii).

EXAMPLE 24.4	Dick Ragan, age 70, works full-time at Mary's Luggage and Gifts where he participates in a qualified employer-sponsored plan. He also owns a traditional IRA. Dick would be able to delay distributions from his employer-sponsored plan until after he retires. However, distributions from the traditional IRA must begin no later than April 1 following the year he attains age 70½.

EXAMPLE 24.5	Doc Reeves and Kitty Pitts attain age 70 in Year 1. Doc's birthday is February 14 and Kitty's is September 18. Each owns separate traditional IRAs. The deadline for their required minimum distributions (RMDs) is shown in the table below.

	Doc	Kitty
Birthday:	Feb. 14, Yr. 1	Sep. 18, Yr. 1
Part of year when age 70 is attained:	1st half, Yr. 1	2nd half, Yr. 1
Year when age 70½ is attained:	Yr. 1 (Aug. 14, Yr. 1)	Yr. 2 (Mar. 18, Yr. 2)
Deadline for 1st RMD:	April 1, Yr. 2	April 1, Yr. 3
Deadline for 2nd RMD:	December 31, Yr. 2	December 31, Yr. 3
Deadline for 3rd RMD:	December 31, Yr. 3	December 31, Yr. 4

(Subsequent RMDs are due by December 31 of subsequent years.)

Satisfying the RMD Requirement with Qualified Charitable Distributions

A qualified charitable distribution (QCD) is a taxpayer-directed transfer of traditional IRA funds from the institution maintaining the IRA to a qualified charity. Only taxpayers age 70½ or older are eligible for QCDs and the aggregate annual QCD amount cannot exceed $100,000. The contribution counts toward the RMD requirement and is neither included in gross income nor deductible as an itemized deduction. Code Sec. 408(d)(8).

Required Beginning Date for "After-death" Distributions

If a participant/owner of a qualified employer-sponsored plan or IRA dies, the balance of the account can be rolled over to the qualified plan or IRA of a surviving spouse and treated as if the spouse were the participant/owner. If not rolled over to the spouse's account, distributions to the surviving spouse do not need to begin until the date the deceased participant/owner would have attained age 70½. Code Sec. 401(a)(9)(B)(iv).

An IRA inherited by a nonspouse beneficiary may not be rolled over. Code Sec. 408(d)(3)(C). However, a direct trustee-to-trustee transfer can be made by a nonspouse beneficiary from an employer-sponsored plan of a deceased participant/owner into an IRA. The following treatment applies to such transfers:

■ The transfer is treated as a tax-free rollover.
■ The transferee IRA is treated as an inherited account titled in the name of the deceased participant but payable to the beneficiary; thus, the assets once transferred may not be further rolled over.
■ The amount rolled into a transferee IRA must be distributed to the designated nonspouse beneficiary at least as rapidly as under the distribution method used before the participant/owner died. If the participant/owner dies before required minimum distributions have begun, the entire rolled-over interest must (1) be distributed within five years after the participant/owner's death, or (2) begin by the end of the year following the participant/owner's death and be paid out over the beneficiary's life or life expectancy. Code Sec. 401(a)(9)(B).

A nonspouse beneficiary who does not elect to make a qualified rollover into an inherited IRA is subject to the same five-year-or-lifetime distribution rule that applies to qualified rollovers into inherited IRAs (see above).

PLANNING POINTER

> The main benefit of the rollover rule for non-spouse beneficiaries relates to plans that require such persons to receive only the lump sum distributions (whether shortly after the participant's death or within the five-year rule). The non-spouse beneficiary rollover could enable a beneficiary under a lump-sum-only plan to reduce taxes by taking several IRA payments spread over the five years following the participant's death, or to defer taxes for as long as possible by arranging for immediate installment distributions from the IRA over the beneficiary's life or life expectancy.

TAX BLUNDER

If a check is issued directly by the trustee of a deceased participant/owner's plan to the non-spouse beneficiary, the entire amount of the distribution will be immediately taxable, even though the entire amount may be redirected to an "inherited" IRA within 60 days (the time limit for completing a qualified indirect rollover—see ¶24,345). A similar result will occur if a trustee-to-trustee transfer is made to a transferee IRA titled in the name of the non-spouse beneficiary instead of the name of the deceased participant. The transferee IRA should be titled in a manner similar to the following: "Betty Participant, deceased, IRA f/b/o Wilma Participant (beneficiary)."

Required Minimum Distribution Amounts

The RMD amount for a year is generally equal to the participant's *account balance* (for defined contribution plans) as of the end of the prior year, divided by the appropriate distribution period. Reg. §1.401(a)(9)-5, Q&A-1; Reg. §1.401(a)(9)-6, Q&A-1.

Before-death Distributions

If RMDs begin while the participant is alive, the distribution period used in determining the RMD amount is generally determined from the Uniform Lifetime Table (see below). The Uniform Lifetime Table provides the joint life expectancy of a participant and a hypothetical beneficiary whose age would be exactly ten years younger than the participant's. This table is used for all calculations, regardless of the designated beneficiary (if any), with one exception—if the sole designated beneficiary is the participant's spouse and the spouse is more than ten years younger than the participant, the applicable distribution period is determined from the Joint and Last Survivor Table at Reg. §1.401(a)(9)-9. With this table the joint life expectancies of the participant and the younger spouse are based on their actual ages. For purposes of calculating a required minimum distribution, marital status is determined as of January 1 of each year. In either case, the required minimum distribution is redetermined annually based on age at year end. Prop. Reg. §1.401(a)(9)-5, Q&A-4.

Exhibit 2. CALCULATING RMDS USING THE UNIFORM LIFETIME TABLE

Minimum amount of first distribution = (a) ÷ (b), where:

(a) = Accrued benefit or account balance as of December 31 of the year preceding the year in which the taxpayer attains the age of 70½, or retires, if applicable.

(b) = Hypothetical joint life expectancy provided in the Uniform Lifetime table below, that is based on:

(i) the taxpayer's age on December 31 of the year in which the taxpayer attains the age of 70½, (or retires, if applicable,) and

(ii) a hypothetical beneficiary whose age is exactly ten years younger than the taxpayer's.

Minimum amount of subsequent distributions = (c) ÷ (d), where:

[c] = Accrued benefit or account balance as of December 31 of the year preceding the year in which a distribution must be made (e.g., use the balance as of December 31, Year 1 if a second distribution is due by December 31, Year 2).

(d) = Redetermined joint life expectancy provided in the Uniform Lifetime table below.

EXAMPLE 24.6

Earl and Betty maintain traditional IRAs. The account balances at the beginning and end of Year 1 are $400,000 and $500,000, respectively, for Earl; $800,000 and $900,000, respectively, for Betty. Each reaches age 70 in Year 1—Earl on April 10 and Betty on November 2. Earl's first RMD deadline will be April 1, Year 2 while Betty's will occur on April 1, Year 3 (as previously discussed). In order to compute the first RMD amounts, the joint life expectancy of each individual (and a hypothetical beneficiary 10 years younger) must be determined from the Uniform Lifetime Table. The age on December 31 of the year in which age 70½ is attained must be used—age 70 for Earl (as of December 31, Year 1) and age 71 for Betty (as of December 31, Year 2). Earl's first RMD amount will be $14,599 ($400,000 Yr. 1 beginning balance ÷ 27.4 years). Betty's first RMD amount will be $33,962 ($900,000 Yr. 1 ending balance ÷ 26.5 years).

Exhibit 3. UNIFORM LIFETIME TABLE

Age of IRA Owner / Distribution Period									
Age	Life Exp.	Age	Life Exp.	Age	Life Exp.	Age	Life Exp.	Age	Life Exp.
70	27.4	80	18.7	90	11.4	100	6.3	110	3.1
71	26.5	81	17.9	91	10.8	101	5.9	111	2.9
72	25.6	82	17.1	92	10.2	102	5.5	112	2.6
73	24.7	83	16.3	93	9.6	103	5.2	113	2.4
74	23.8	84	15.5	94	9.1	104	4.9	114	2.1
75	22.9	85	14.8	95	8.6	105	4.5	115	1.9
76	22.0	86	14.1	96	8.1	106	4.2	(or older)	
77	21.2	87	13.4	97	7.6	107	3.9		
78	20.3	88	12.7	98	7.1	108	3.7		
79	19.5	89	12.0	99	6.7	109	3.4		

The hypothetical joint life expectancies used in computing subsequent RMD amounts must be predetermined as of December 31 of each subsequent year.

EXAMPLE 24.7

Roger Jennings is the owner of a traditional IRA. Roger will attain age 75 in the current year. The before-tax account balance as of the end of the prior year was $100,000. The distribution period for someone who will attain age 75 in the current is 22.9. Therefore, the minimum amount that Roger must withdraw from the IRA by the end of the current year is $4,367 ($100,000 ÷ 22.9 = $4,367).

Computing the 2nd RMD Amount

If the first RMD amount had been received between January 1 and April 1 of the year following the year the taxpayer became 70½, it must be subtracted from the prior year account balance (at (c) in Exhibit 2 above) in order to compute the second RMD amount.

EXAMPLE 24.8

Eve's traditional IRA account balances for five years are shown below:

Date	Account Balance
December 31, Year 1	$274,000
December 31, Year 2	$296,200
December 31, Year 3	$320,000
December 31, Year 4	$345,800
December 31, Year 5	$340,500

Eve becomes age 70 on June 1, Year 2, and retires at the end of Year 3. Since Eve's plan is not employer-sponsored, the retirement date is irrelevant in determining her RMD. The initial RMD (deadline and amount) is based on the year in which she becomes 70½ (Year 2). The deadlines and amounts associated with the first four RMDs are shown below.

Computation of RMD Deadlines and Amounts

No.	RMD Date	Relevant Acct. Bal. Date (12/31)	Relevant Age on Dec. 31 of:	(refer to the Uniform Lifetime Table above)	RMD Amount
1st	4/1, Yr 3	Yr 1	Yr 2: 70	$274,000 ÷ 27.4	$10,000
2nd	12/31, Yr 3	Yr 2	Yr 3: 71	[$296,200 − $10,000] ÷ 26.5	$10,800
3rd	12/31, Yr 4	Yr 3	Yr 4: 72	$320,000 ÷ 25.6	$12,500
4th	12/31, Yr 5	Yr 4	Yr 5: 73	$345,800 ÷ 24.7	$14,000

EXAMPLE 24.9

Refer to the preceding example above. If, instead of maintaining a traditional IRA, Eve maintained an employer-sponsored account such as a 401(k) plan, the retirement date is relevant in determining her RMD and the required RMD dates and amounts would be as shown below.

Computation of RMD Deadlines and Amounts

No.	RMD Date	Relevant Acct. Bal. Date (12/31)	Relevant Age on Dec. 31 of:	(refer to the Uniform Lifetime Table above)	RMD Amount
1st	4/1, Yr 4	Yr 2	71	$296,200 ÷ 26.5	$11,177
2nd	12/31, Yr 4	Yr 3	72	[$320,000 − $11,177] ÷ 25.6	$12,063
3rd	12/31, Yr 5	Yr 4	73	$345,800 ÷ 24.7	$14,000
4th	12/31, Yr 6	Yr 5	74	$340,500 ÷ 23.8	$14,307

For the third and subsequent distributions, if the participant receives more than the minimum RMD amount, the participant will not receive credit for such excess in determining the RMD amount in a future year.

If an IRA owner has more than one traditional IRA, the RMD must be determined separately with respect to each traditional IRA. However, the RMD can be taken from any or all of the traditional IRAs. Amounts required to be distributed cannot be rolled over into another traditional IRA or into an employer-sponsored plan.

After-death Distributions: Death Before RMDs Begin

If the qualified plan participant died before the distributions began, and an individual (other than the participant's surviving spouse) is designated as the beneficiary of the account, the RMD for a year after the year of the decedent-owner's death is determined by dividing the account balance at the end of the preceding calendar year by a figure calculated by determining the beneficiary's life expectancy (determined from the following Single Life Table) as of the beneficiary's birthday in the year following the year of the participant's death and reducing that figure by one for each year since the year following the participant's death.

If the sole designated beneficiary is the decedent's surviving spouse and the surviving spouse has not elected to treat the qualified plan account as his or her own, no distribution has to be made to the surviving spouse until the year in which the decedent would have reached age 70½. Once required minimum distributions have to be made, they are calculated by dividing the account balance at the end of the preceding calendar year by the surviving spouse's life expectancy (determined using the following Single Life Table) as of the surviving spouse's birthday during the year distributions must be made. A surviving spouse's life expectancy is redetermined each year (not merely reduced by one each year).

If the designated beneficiary is not an individual, the entire account balance must be distributed by the end of the fifth year following the year of the participant's death. No distribution is required for any year before the end of that fifth year.

Exhibit 4. SINGLE LIFE TABLE—AGE LIFE EXPECTANCY

Age	Life Exp.	Age	Life Exp.	Age	Life Exp.	Age	Life Exp.	Age	Life Exp.
0	82.4	25	58.2	50	34.2	75	13.4	100	2.9
1	81.6	26	57.2	51	33.3	76	12.7	101	2.7
2	80.6	27	56.2	52	32.3	77	12.1	102	2.5
3	79.7	28	55.3	53	31.4	78	11.4	103	2.3
4	78.7	29	54.3	54	30.5	79	10.8	104	2.1
5	77.7	30	53.3	55	29.6	80	10.2	105	1.9
6	76.7	31	52.4	56	28.7	81	9.7	106	1.7
7	75.8	32	51.4	57	27.9	82	9.1	107	1.5
8	74.8	33	50.4	58	27.0	83	8.6	108	1.4
9	73.8	34	49.4	59	26.1	84	8.1	109	1.2
10	72.8	35	48.5	60	25.2	85	7.6	110	1.1
11	71.8	36	47.5	61	24.4	86	7.1	111	1.0
12	70.8	37	46.5	62	23.5	87	6.7	(or older)	
13	69.9	38	45.6	63	22.7	88	6.3		
14	68.9	39	44.6	64	21.8	89	5.9		
15	67.9	40	43.6	65	21.0	90	5.5		
16	66.9	41	42.7	66	20.2	91	5.2		
17	66.0	42	41.7	67	19.4	92	4.9		
18	65.0	43	40.7	68	18.6	93	4.6		
19	64.0	44	39.8	69	17.8	94	4.3		
20	63.0	45	38.8	70	17.0	95	4.1		
21	62.1	46	37.9	71	16.3	96	3.8		
22	61.1	47	37.0	72	15.5	97	3.6		
23	60.1	48	36.0	73	14.8	98	3.4		
24	59.1	49	35.1	74	14.1	99	3.1		

EXAMPLE 24.10

Lawson Coop's mother died in Year 1. Lawson Coop, who will attain age 53 in Year 2, was designated as the sole beneficiary of his mother's traditional IRA. If the account balance at the end of Year 1 was $100,000, the minimum required distribution for Year 2 is calculated by dividing $100,000 by Lawson's life expectancy as of his birthday in Year 2 (31.4 years): $100,000 ÷ 31.4 = $3,185. If the account balance at the end of Year 2 again is $100,000, the minimum required distribution for Year 3 is calculated by dividing $100,000 by Lawson's life expectancy for the previous year (31.4 years) and subtracting one (31.4 -1.0 = 30.4): $100,000 ÷ 30.4 = $3,289.

After-death Distributions: Death On or After RMDs Begin

If the qualified plan participant died on or after the required beginning date and an individual has been designated as the beneficiary of the plan account, the required minimum distribution for a year after the year of the participant's death is determined by dividing the account balance at the end of the preceding calendar year by a figure calculated by determining the beneficiary's life expectancy (determined from the Single Life Table) as of the beneficiary's birthday in the year following the year of the participant's death and reducing that figure by one for each year since the year following the participant's death.

If the designated beneficiary is the deceased participant's surviving spouse and the surviving spouse has not elected to treat the plan account as his or her own, the amount of the minimum required distribution for a year is calculated by dividing the account balance at the end of the preceding calendar year by the surviving spouse's life expectancy (determined from the Single Life Table) as of the surviving spouse's birthday during the year distributions must be made.

If the designated beneficiary is not an individual, the amount of a required minimum distribution for a year is calculated by dividing the account balance at the end of the preceding year by the life expectancy (determined using the Single Life Table) for the participant as of the participant's birthday in the year of death and subtracting one for each year since the year of the participant's death.

Designated Beneficiary

If more than one individual has been designated as a beneficiary of a traditional IRA, the beneficiary with the shortest life expectancy is treated as the designated beneficiary. A trust cannot be a designated beneficiary. However, the beneficiaries of a trust will be treated as having been designated as beneficiaries if the following requirements are satisfied:

1. The trust is a valid trust under state law (or would be except that there is no trust principal).
2. The trust is irrevocable or will, by its terms, become irrevocable when the owner dies.
3. The trust beneficiaries are identifiable from the trust instrument.
4. The IRA trustee, custodian, or issuer has been given a copy of the trust agreement or a list of the trust beneficiaries.

Penalty for Not Making Required Minimum Distributions

If a minimum required distribution is not made, a 50 percent excise tax has to be paid on the amount not distributed as required. Code Sec. 4974(a). The penalty is reported on Form 5329 Additional Taxes on Qualified Plans (Including IRAs) and Other Tax Favored Accounts. If the individual believes the tax should not apply due to reasonable error, the tax should be paid and a letter of explanation attached to Form 5329. If the IRS waives the tax, it will issue a refund.

¶24,245   EARLY WITHDRAWAL RESTRICTIONS

If a taxable distribution is made before an employee attains age 59 ½, a 10-percent additional tax will be imposed on amounts distributed unless one of the exceptions applies. Code Sec. 72(t).

No additional tax will be imposed under the following circumstances:

1. **Distributions after the employee's death.** The distribution is made to a beneficiary or the employee's estate after the employee's death.
2. **Distributions on account of disability.** The distribution is attributable to the employee's being disabled. An employee is considered to be disabled if the employee is unable to engage in any substantial gainful activity by reason of any medically determinable physical or mental impairment that can be expected to result in death or to be of long-continued and indefinite duration.
3. **Substantially equal periodic payments.** The distribution is part of a series of substantially equal periodic payments (not less frequently than annually) made for the life (or life expectancies) of the employee or the joint lives (or joint life expectancies) of the employee and his or her designated beneficiary.
4. **Separation from service.** The distribution is made to an employee after separation from service after attainment of age 55. This early retirement exception does not apply to a distribution from a traditional IRA. Code Sec. 72(t)(3)(A).
5. **Dividends on employer securities.** The distribution consists of dividends paid with respect to employer securities.
6. **Levy.** The distribution is made on account of a levy on the qualified retirement plan.
7. **Medical expenses.** To the extent that the distribution does not exceed the amount of medical expenses allowable as a deduction for the year to the employee (determined without regard to whether the employee itemizes deductions for the tax year).
8. **Alternate payees.** Distributions to an alternate payee pursuant to a qualified domestic relations order (discussed in ¶24,345).
9. **Military call-up reservists.** Distributions to individuals called to active duty for a period in excess of 179 days.

Additional Exceptions for IRAs

In addition to the general exceptions listed above, the following exceptions apply to premature taxable distributions from IRAs:

1. **Medical insurance premiums.** Early distributions from a *traditional IRA*, as well as a *SEP* or *SIMPLE IRA*, are not subject to the 10 percent penalty if applied toward medical insurance of the individual, spouse, or dependents (without regard to the 10 percent of adjusted gross income medical expense limitation). In order to qualify, the individual must have received federal or state unemployment compensation for at least 12 weeks, and the distribution must have been made in the year such unemployment compensation had been received or the following year.

2. **Education expenses.** Early distributions from *traditional* and *Roth IRAs* to cover "qualified higher education expenses" may not be subject to the 10 percent penalty. In order to avoid the penalty, the expenses must have been incurred by the individual, the individual's spouse or child, or a grandchild of the individual or individual's spouse. Qualified expenses include tuition at a post-secondary educational institution, books, fees, supplies, and equipment. Code Sec. 72(t)(2)(E). Such expenses are reduced by amounts excluded from gross income that are used for education.

3. **"First-Time" Homebuyer Expenses.** Premature withdrawals from *traditional IRAs*, and *Roth IRAs* may not be subject to the 10 percent penalty if used to pay up to $10,000 (lifetime limit) of first-time homebuyer expenses. The funds must be used within 120 days of distribution to acquire, construct, or reconstruct a home that is the principal residence of taxpayer, spouse, child, grandchild or ancestor of taxpayer or spouse. "Acquisition costs" include any usual or reasonable settlement, financing, or other closing costs.

   An individual is a "first-time homebuyer" if the individual (and, if married, the individual's spouse) had no present ownership interest in a principal residence during the two-year period ending on the date that the principal residence was acquired. Thus, as long as the taxpayer (and spouse, if married) had not owned a home in the two years immediately preceding the closing date (not contract date), distributions can be made from an IRA to help pay for the "new" home even though it may not actually be the taxpayer's first home. Code Sec. 72(t)(2)(F).

TAX BLUNDER

Don and Sharon Bacek, both in their late 40's, sell their house after occupying it for 20 years and rent a flat. After three years in the flat, they decide to return to home ownership. They find a house to purchase, however, in order to complete the transaction, they need $10,000 for a down payment. Their only sources of funds are Sharon's traditional IRA and Don's employer-sponsored retirement account. If the funds are withdrawn from Sharon's traditional IRA, they will not be subject to the penalty, provided the funds are applied toward the purchase of the new house within 120 days of the closing date. If, on the other hand, the funds are withdrawn from Don's employer-sponsored account, they will be subject to the 10 percent early withdrawal penalty, even though they are applied toward the new home purchase within the 120-day statutory period.

SIMPLE Plan Penalty

For employees who withdraw any amount from a SIMPLE plan during the first two years of participation, the 10 percent penalty is increased to 25 percent. Code Sec. 72(t)(6).

¶24,275 VESTING REQUIREMENTS

"Vesting" refers to the process by which an employee's right to receive benefits provided by a qualified retirement plan becomes nonforfeitable. For a trust that is part of a retirement plan to be a qualified trust, the plan must give participants certain nonforfeitable rights to amounts contributed to the plan and earnings on those contributions. Code Secs. 401(a)(7), 411. These rights are the minimum rights that an employer must give an employee. Employers may give employees a faster vesting schedule.

If an employee leaves an employer before his or her right to benefits provided by the plan becomes nonforfeitable, the employee will forfeit the nonvested portion of his or her benefits.

Employee Contributions

Employees must have a nonforfeitable right to the accrued benefit derived from their own contributions (i.e., elective deferrals) to a qualified retirement plan. Code Sec. 411(a)(1). In the case of a defined contribution plan, "accrued benefit" means the balance in the employee's account.

Employer Contributions

Employees must have a nonforfeitable right to their accrued benefit derived from employer contributions to a defined contribution plan under either of the following vesting schedules (Code Sec. 411(a)(2)(B)):

1. **Three-Year ("Cliff") Vesting.** A plan satisfies three-year vesting if an employee has a nonforfeitable right to 100 percent of the employee's accrued benefit derived from employer contributions after the employee has completed at least three years of service.
2. **Two-to-Six-Year ("Graded") Vesting.** A plan satisfies two-to-six-year vesting if an employee has a nonforfeitable right to the percentage of the employee's accrued benefit derived from employer contributions determined from the following table:

Years of Service	Nonforfeitable Percentage
2	20
3	40
4	60
5	80
6 or more	100

A "year of service" means a calendar year, plan year, or other 12-consecutive-month period designated by the plan during which the participant completed 1,000 hours of service. Code Sec. 411(a)(5). A "one-year break in service" is a calendar year, plan year, or other 12-consecutive-month period designated by the plan during which the participant did not complete more than 500 hours of service. Code Sec. 411(a)(6).

¶24,285   "EXCLUSIVE BENEFIT OF THE EMPLOYEE" REQUIREMENT

General Investment Requirements

No specific limitations are provided in Code Sec. 401(a) with respect to investments that may be made by the trustees of a qualified trust. Reg. §1.401-1(b)(5). However, Rev. Rul. 69-494 (1969-2 CB 88) provides general requirements that must be met:

1. **Cost of plan assets.** The cost of fund assets must not exceed their market value at the time of purchase.
2. **Liquidity.** The plan must maintain sufficient liquidity to permit distributions.
3. **Return.** The plan must provide a fair return commensurate with market yield.
4. **Safeguards.** Prudent safeguards and diversification must be met.

With regard to *employee contributions* and elective deferrals invested in employer securities, an individual must be allowed to elect to direct the plan to divest employer securities into other investment options. Code Sec. 401(a)(35)(B). An individual who is a participant in the plan with at least three years of service or is a beneficiary of such a participant must be able to elect to divest the portion of the account invested in employer securities that is attributable to *employer contributions* in other investment options. Code Sec. 401(a)(35)(C).

TAX BLUNDER

Despite the collapses of General Motors and Lehman Brothers, which highlighted the dangers of investing in the stock of an employer, company stock still constitutes too large a portion of most 401(k) balances, experts say. In plans that offer company stock, about one in four employees have half or more of their total 401(k) balance invested in it, according to Hewitt Associates, a human resources outsourcing and consulting firm.

Tax Consequences to Employer and Employee

¶24,301   ## CONTRIBUTIONS AND DISTRIBUTIONS: BASIC TERMINOLOGY

Lump-sum v. Partial Distributions

A lump-sum distribution is a distribution of a participant's entire interest in a qualified plan within a single tax year. Any distribution of an amount constituting less than an entire interest is a partial distribution.

A participant other than a self-employed taxpayer, may qualify for a lump-sum distribution if any of the following events occurs:

- the participant's death,
- separation from the service of the employer, or
- attainment of age 59 ½.

In the case of a self-employed person, the distribution must be made because of the individual's death, disability, or attainment of age 59 ½. Code Sec. 402(e)(4)(D)(i). Unlike common law employees, self-employed persons cannot qualify for a lump-sum distribution on account of separation from service.

"Before-tax" v. "After-tax Contributions

Grasping the distinction between "before-tax" and "after-tax" contributions is essential to understanding the contribution and distribution rules governing qualified deferred compensation plans. If contributions made to qualified plans such as traditional IRAs or 401(k) plans are *deductible*, then the subsequent withdrawal of these contributions is *taxable*.

If an account balance includes *nondeductible* (i.e., after-tax*) contributions*, the owner would have a *cost basis* in the account. An individual's cost basis in distributions received from a retirement account is the sum of all nondeductible contributions minus prior distributions of nondeductible contributions (if any). Notice 87-16. The recovery of this cost basis is never recognized as taxable income.

The rules governing the deductibility of contributions are explained later in this chapter. For now, it's important to understand why deductible contributions are "before-tax" and why nondeductible contributions are "after-tax." This distinction is illustrated in Example 24.11 below.

EXAMPLE 24.11   Jonathan Ruppel earns a $100,000 salary and contributes $10,000 into a qualified retirement account. He makes no additional contributions and the account has no accumulated income. Years later, Jonathan receives a $10,000 distribution representing the original contribution amount. Assuming a 30 percent tax rate, if the original contribution had been deductible, a $3,000 federal income tax would be imposed on the distribution amount. If, on the other hand, the original contribution had not been deductible, the distribution amount would be tax-free. The relationship between deductibility and taxability is illustrated in Exhibit 5 below.

Exhibit 5. TAX EFFECT FROM BEFORE- AND AFTER-TAX CONTRIBUTIONS

Formula:	Description:	If the contribution is before tax:	If the contribution is after tax:
(a) = Given	Contribution amount	$10,000	$10,000
(b) = "Yes" or "No"	Deductible? (The rules for qualifying for a deduction are explained later in this chapter.)	Assume Yes	Assume No
(c) = Given	Gross income	$100,000	$100,000
(d) = (a) if (b) ="yes"	Deduction	(10,000)	0
(e) = (c) − (d)	Taxable income (ignoring other deductions)	90,000	100,000
(f) = Given	Tax rate	30%	30%
(g) = (e) × (f)	Tax	27,000	30,000
(h) = (d) × (f)	Immediate tax savings from the $10,000 deduction	3,000	0
(i) = (d) × tax rate in effect in the year of dist'n	Estimated future taxes payable when the $10,000 is subsequently distributed	3.000 (assuming a 30% future tax rate; however, if the future tax rate is lower (or higher), the tax burden will be less (more) than $3,000)	0
(j) = (a) [if (b) ="yes"] (j) = (a) ÷ [1 − (f)] [if (b) ="no"]	Gross income needed to fund the $10,000 contribution	10,000 (Same as the contribution amount. This explains why the contribution is "before-tax".)	14,286 (To fund a $10,000 contribution, the taxpayer needs to earn at least $14,286, which, taxed at 30%, would result in $10,000 cash after-tax. This explains why the nondeductible contribution is considered to be "after-tax." Proof: 70% × $14,286 = $10,000)

Any portion of a distribution representing accumulated income is taxable unless the plan from which the distribution is made is a Roth IRA or a Roth 401(k). These plans are discussed later in this chapter.

¶24,305 CONTRIBUTIONS AND DEDUCTIONS—GENERAL RULES

Contributions to a qualified retirement plan on behalf of an employee are excluded from the employee's gross income. Code Sec. 402. Elective deferrals also are excluded from an employee's gross income. However, elective deferrals are subject to Social Security, Medicare, and federal unemployment (FUTA) taxes.

Deduction Limit for Employers

Employers are entitled to a current deduction for contributions made to a qualified retirement plan even though the contributions are not currently includible in their employees' gross income. Code Sec. 404. For defined contribution plans, 25 percent of the compensation paid or accrued to eligible employees participating in such plans may be deducted. For purposes of applying this limit, the maximum compensation that can be taken into account for each employee is $270,000 (for 2017). Elective deferrals are included in compensation but not subject to the limit.

Year for Which Contributions May Be Deducted

Employers may deduct contributions for the tax year with or within which the calendar year for which the contributions were made. Contributions can be deducted for a tax year if they are made by the due date (including extensions) for filing a federal income tax return for that year.

Deduction Limit for Self-Employed Individuals

The deduction limit for self-employed individuals is based on the individual's net earnings from self-employment (reduced by half of the individual's self-employment tax). The maximum percentage of those earnings that can be deducted is determined by dividing the plan contribution rate by that rate plus 1.0. For example, a plan that deducts 25 percent of the compensation of plan participants may not deduct more than 20 percent [0.25/(1.0 + 0.25) = .20] of the owner's net earnings from self-employment (reduced by half of the owner's self-employment tax).

¶24,325　PARTIAL DISTRIBUTIONS—COMPUTING TAX LIABILITY

The three possible forms of partial distribution (defined at ¶24,301) include:

1. distributions made *before* an annuity starting date;
2. annuities;
3. nonannuity distributions made *on or after* the starting date of an annuity (if any).

The rules for each form of distribution are explained below.

Distributions Made Before an Annuity Starting Date

If a distribution is made before an annuity starting date (if any), it is treated in much the same way as an annuity distribution. Code Sec. 72(e)(2)(B). That is, the amount of income that is excluded from income is equal to:

(a) × [(b) ÷ (c)], where

(a) = the distribution amount
(b) = the individual's cost basis in the distribution (explained above) and
(c) = the value of the nonforfeitable portion of the taxpayer's total account balance.

EXAMPLE 24.12　Nora Lyons, age 60 and retired, receives a $10,000 partial distribution from her 401(k) plan. The plan does not pay out an annuity. Immediately before the distribution, her account balance is $100,000, including $25,000 in nondeductible contributions. Nora will exclude $2,500 from gross income ($10,000 × [$25,000 ÷ $100,000]).

The amounts at (b) and (c) above are to be determined as of the date of distribution. Alternatively, the amount at (b) may be determined as of December 31 of the calendar year immediately preceding the calendar year of the distribution and the amount at (c) may be determined as of the last valuation date in the calendar year preceding the calendar year of the distribution if such date is used on a reasonable and consistent basis in determining the cost basis and value for all nonannuity distributions under the plan.

Distributions That Are Annuities

If the annuity option is available, a qualified plan must allow married parties to choose between a joint and survivorship ("J&S") annuity and a single life ("SL") annuity. A J&S annuity stops being paid when both spouses are deceased. It is designed to provide the surviving spouse with some financial security. However, the amount of this annuity is lower, since it is based on the combined life expectancy of both spouses jointly, which, actuarially, is longer than that of either spouse.

A SL annuity, on the other hand, stops being paid when the employee dies. A surviving spouse therefore receives no benefits after the death of the participating spouse. However, the amount of a SL annuity is larger than a J&S annuity, since it's based only on the employee's life expectancy. With most plans, an employee's spouse must provide written consent for the single life annuity election. Code Sec. 401(a)(11). Annuity payments are taxed using the Sec. 72 exclusion ratio (explained at ¶5,125).

Nonannuity Distributions Made On or After an Annuity Starting Date

A nonannuity distribution made on or after an annuity starting date is generally included in full in gross income. Code Sec. 72(e)(2)(A).

EXAMPLE 24.13　Molly Darden has been receiving a $100 monthly annuity from her qualified plan account over several years. At the end of the current year, her account balance is $100,000, including a $25,000 cost basis. In order to satisfy a personal obligation, she withdraws an extra $10,000 from her account in the current year. If the withdrawal does not affect the amount of her subsequent annuity payments, the entire $10,000 is taxable in the current year. Since the distribution occurred on or after the annuity starting date, the Sec. 72 annuity rules do not apply.

¶24,345   **ROLLOVERS**

Direct Rollovers

Any amount transferred between eligible retirement plans in a direct trustee-to-trustee transfer is not includible in gross income for the tax year of the transfer. Code Sec. 402(e)(6). Such direct rollovers are not subject to the 20 percent mandatory income tax withholding that applies to indirect rollovers.

Indirect Rollovers

If any portion of the balance to the credit of an employee in a qualified employer-sponsored retirement plan is paid to the employee in an eligible rollover distribution and the distributee transfers any portion of the property received in the distribution to an eligible retirement plan within 60 days following receipt, the amount distributed will not be included in the employee's gross income for the tax year in which it was paid. Code Sec. 402(c). However, such indirect rollovers are subject to 20 percent mandatory income tax withholding.

The IRS may waive the 60-day rule for tax-free rollovers in hardship cases and in cases where taxpayers make good faith efforts to comply with the rule but fail through no fault of their own. Mitigating events include: casualty, disaster, hospitalization, incarceration, death, disability, restrictions imposed by a foreign government, and error by the financial institution. Rev. Proc. 2003-16.

Eligible Retirement Plans

The benefits accrued under a retirement plan are *portable* if they can be rolled over to another retirement plan without losing tax-advantaged status. An "eligible retirement plan" includes (Code Sec. 402(c)(8)(B)):

1. A qualified trust such as a 401(k) plan.
2. A 403(a) plan.
3. A 403(b) plan.
4. A governmental 457(b) plan.
5. A traditional IRA.

Refer to Exhibit 6 for a chart on the portability of common retirement plans. 403(a), 403(b) and 457(b) plans are omitted from this text except for the limited coverage provided at Exhibits 5, 6 and 7.

Election by alternate payee under a QDRO

If the spouse or former spouse of a plan participant receives a distribution as the alternate payee under a qualified domestic relations order, the alternate payee will be taxed on the distribution unless the alternate payee makes an eligible rollover contribution. Code Sec. 402(e).

Ineligible rollovers

An "ineligible rollover" is any distribution of all or any portion of the balance to the credit of an employee in a qualified retirement plan that is:

1. one of a series of substantially equal periodic payments (not less frequently than annually) made for the life expectancy of the employee or the joint life expectancies of the employee and the employee's designated beneficiary or for a specified period of 10 years or more;
2. required to be made from the trust under the required minimum distribution rules—see ¶24,235; or,
3. made on account of the employee's hardship.

Prohibited Rollovers

A qualified plan is under no obligation to accept rollovers. It may limit the circumstances under which it will accept rollovers or limit the type of assets it will accept. Reg. §1.401(a)(31)-1, Q&A 13. A taxpayer should make appropriate inquiries before initiating a rollover from a qualified plan account.

TAX BLUNDER

If a qualified plan participant arranges an indirect rollover into another eligible plan account, the participant would lose the earning power of 20% of the rollover amount for a period of time because the plan's trustee is required to withhold 20 percent of the rollover amount. If the participant fails to transfer 100 percent of the rollover amount into another eligible plan account within 60 days following receipt, the shortfall will be subject to a 10 percent penalty plus regular income tax.

Exhibit 6. PORTABILITY CHART									
ELIGIBLE ROLLOVER TO RECIPIENT PLAN? (Yes v. No)									
TO:	401(k)	Roth 401(k)/ 403(b)	403(b) Plan	Gov't. 457(b)	Keogh Plan	SEP IRA	SIMPLE IRA	Trad'l IRA	Roth IRA
FROM:									
401(k) – Other Than Roth 401(k)	Y[d]	N	Y[c]	Y[c]	Y[d]	Y	Y[b]	Y	Y
403(b) – Other Than Roth 403(b)	Y	N	Y	Y	Y	Y	Y[b]	Y	Y
Roth 401(k)/ 403(b) by Direct Rollover	N	Y	N	N	N	N	N	N	Y
Governmental 457(b)	Y	N	Y	Y	Y	Y	Y[b]	Y	Y
Keogh	Y[d]	N	Y[c]	Y[c]	Y[d]	Y	N	Y	Y
SEP IRA	Y[a]	N	Y[a]	Y[a]	Y[a]	Y	N	Y	Y
SIMPLE IRA [b]	Y	N	Y	Y	Y	Y	Y[e]	Y	Y
Traditional IRA	Y[a]	N	Y[a]	Y[a]	Y[a]	Y	N	Y	Y
Roth IRA	N	N	N	N	N	N	N	N	Y

Superscript Notes:
a   Only pretax amounts from a traditional IRA or SEP IRA may be rolled to these plans.
b   Rollovers to or from SIMPLE IRAs are prohibited until after 2 years of participation.
c   Pretax amounts only.
d   After-tax amounts may be received only by direct transfer or direct rollover.
e   Only one rollover allowed in any 12-month period.

¶24,355   LOANS

General Rules

As a general rule, any amount received as a loan from a qualified employer plan will be treated as a taxable distribution. Any pledge or assignment of a portion of an interest in a qualified employer plan also will be treated as a taxable distribution. Code Sec. 72(p).

An exception is made under Code Sec. 72(p)(2) and (4) for loans from most qualified employer plans (excluding IRAs) and nonqualified governmental 457(b) plans that satisfy the following requirements:

1. The amount of the loan, when added to the outstanding balance of all other loans made from the plan, does not exceed the lesser of (1) $50,000, reduced by the excess (if any) of the highest outstanding balance of loans from the plan during the one-year period ending on the day before the date on which the loan was made over the outstanding balance of loans from the plan on the date on which the loan was made, or (2) the greater of one-half of the employee's nonforfeitable accrued benefit under the plan or $10,000.
2. The terms of the loan must require that the loan be repaid within five years (unless the loan is used to acquire a participant's principal residence).
3. Required repayments must be substantially equal in amount and payable not less frequently than quarterly.

Owner-employees

Self-employed taxpayers who are owner-employees (which include sole proprietors and more-than-ten-percent partners) are eligible to borrow against a qualified retirement plan that is not an IRA. Code Sec. 4975(f)(6)(B)(iii).

Common Retirement Plans For Large Businesses

The most common types of qualified employer-sponsored retirement plans offered by businesses with more than 100 employees include:

- 401(k) plans (at ¶24,401) and
- Roth 401(k) supplemental plans (at ¶24,405).

This section provides a summary and a comparison of the most important features of these plans.

¶24,401   401(k) PLANS

A 401(k) plan is a defined contribution plan that provides a cash or deferred arrangement (CODA) within a qualified profit-sharing, stock bonus, or pre-ERISA (i.e., established before 1974) money purchase plan. The 401(k) plan has become the dominant retirement vehicle for many Americans. More than 95% of U.S. companies offer a Sec. 401(k) plan, compared to only 36% in 1984. More than 75% of the employees of these firms participate in the Sec. 401(k) plan. The main reason for the popularity of Sec. 401(k) plans is that, unlike other qualified retirements plans, a 401(k) plan participant can elect either to receive current cash compensation or have the employer contribute like amounts on a pre-tax basis to the qualified plan. The arrangement typically contains a salary reduction agreement under which employer contributions are made only if the participant elects to reduce the amount of compensation or not to take a pay increase.

Three types of contributions may be made to 401(k) CODA plans:

1. Nonelective employer contributions which are essentially treated the same way for tax purposes as employer contributions to other qualified plans (i.e., they are excludable to the participant);
2. Elective deferral contributions made by employees under a salary reduction plan. They are also excludable for income tax purposes when contributed but are subject to social security tax (FICA) and federal unemployment tax (FUTA) under Code Secs. 3121(v)(1) and 3306(r)(1).
3. Employer matching contributions equal to the amount or a certain percentage of the employees' elective contributions.

Limit on Employee Elective Deferral Contributions

Employee elective contributions are regular-tax deferred. The amount may not exceed the lesser of:

- **Percentage limit:** 100% of compensation; or
- **Amount limit:** $18,000 in 2017, indexed for inflation.

The employee elective deferral limitation is subject to the following rules:

- **Reduction in $18,000 limit.** The maximum employee annual elective contribution limit is reduced dollar-for-dollar by additional salary reduction contributions to 403(b) plans, and to other Sec. 401(k) plans (but not to governmental 457(b) plans).
- **Age 50+ catch-up contributions.** Any plan participant who is at least or will become age 50 before the end of the year can make additional elective deferral contributions of $6,000 in 2017. The age 50+ catch-up contribution does not count towards the maximum total contribution limit of $54,000.

Aggregate Limit on Employer and Employee Contributions

An aggregate limit applies to the employer contributions made on behalf of a participating employee. This sum may not exceed the lesser of:

1. **Percentage Limit** = 100% of compensation; or
2. **Amount Limit** = $54,000 in 2017, indexed for inflation. Code Sec. 415(c)(1).

EXAMPLE 24.24

Connor Corbett participates in his employer's 401(k) plan. Under the plan, employees may elect to reduce their salary by a certain percentage and have it paid into the plan's trust. In 2017, Connor elects to defer $18,000 as a CODA contribution from his $200,000 salary. The plan provides that the employer will match the employee contribution up to 5.0 percent of compensation ($10,000). Under the general definition of compensation, the employer and employee contributions are within the Code Sec. 415(c) limit. See recap below.

(a) = Given	Compensation before reduction	200,000
(b) = Given	Employee elective deferral contribution	18,000
(c) = Given	Employer matching contribution	10,000
(d) = (b) + (c)	Total employer/employee contributions	28,000
(e) = lesser of (a) or $18,000	Employee contribution limit in 2017	18,000
(f) = the lesser of: [100% × (a)] or $54,000	Aggregate contribution limit in 2017	54,000

Employer and employee contributions are not subject to regular tax until the distribution year. Employee contributions are subject to FICA and FUTA tax in the contribution year while employer contributions are permanently exempt from FICA and FUTA tax.

EXAMPLE 24.15	Referring to the preceding example, the tax consequences to Connor Corbett are summarized below.
	Amount. of salary subject to employee FICA: $200,000 *(i.e., elective employee contributions, but not employer contributions, are subject to FICA tax.)*
	Amount of salary currently subject to federal income tax: $182,000 *($200,000 – $18,000)*
	Amount of income currently not subject to federal income tax: $28,000 *($18,000 employee contribution + $10,000 employer contribution)*

¶24,405   ROTH 401(k) PLANS

Annual Contribution Limits

A 401(k) (or a 403(b)) plan may be amended to incorporate a qualified Roth contribution program. Under such a program, participants can elect to have all or a portion of their regular elective deferrals treated as Roth contributions. Catch-up contributions may also be made as Roth contributions. For participants under age 50, the maximum contribution amount is $18,000 in 2017 ($24,000 for participants age 50 or older). Unlike regular elective deferrals, Roth contributions are included in the participant's current income; however, as explained below, qualified distributions from a designated Roth account are not included in income. Code. Sec. 402(A).

Qualified Distributions

A qualified Roth 401(k) distribution must meet essentially the same criteria as one from a Roth IRA account (see ¶24,635). The portion of a distribution consisting of direct or rollover contributions is never included in a participant's income since such contributions were funded by after-tax earnings. The earnings portion of a distribution is not included in the distributee's income if the qualifying criteria have been met.

Qualified Rollovers

Qualified distributions from a Roth 401(k) account may be rolled over to either (a) another designated Roth 401(k) for the participant (if the new plan allows for rollovers), or (b) the participant's Roth IRA only to the extent permitted under Code Sec. 402(c). Such rollovers are not taken into account for purposes of the annual limits on elective deferrals. Code Sec. 402(A)(c)(3).

Plan Requirements

Because qualified distributions are not included in an employee's income, the plan must establish and maintain a separate "designated Roth account" for designated Roth contributions and attributed earnings for each employee. Failure to maintain this separate account and recordkeeping will disqualify the program. An employer may not offer a Roth 401(k)-only plan. If a 401(k) (or 403(b)) plan is offered, pre-tax elective deferrals must also be permitted.

Ideal Participants

One major advantage of a qualifed Roth contribution program is that it allows 401(k) (or 403(b)) plan participants to avoid income tax entirely on the earnings associated with designated Roth contributions. This feature may be especially advantageous to younger, lower-paid participants who have a longer retirement horizon and for whom the benefit of tax-free distribution will significantly outweigh the tax cost. Another major advantage is that the Roth 401(k) program permits contributions that are substantially greater than the Roth IRA contribution limits. In addition, income limitations are not applicable to contributions made to a qualified Roth 401(k) program. These features may be particularly appealing to higher-paid executives who do not qualify for Roth IRA contributions because their income exceeds a statutory limitation.

Exhibit 7. COMMON RETIREMENT PLANS FOR LARGE EMPLOYERS—ELIGIBLE EMPLOYERS

Characteristics:	401(k)	403(b)* ("Tax Sheltered Annuity" Plan)	457(b)* (Governmental)	457(b)* (Nongovernmental)
Description of Eligible Employers:	Taxable entities	Tax-exempt organizations that are: (a) charitable, (b) educational, (c) religious, or (d) scientific Public school systems	State and local governments	Tax-exempt organizations that are: (a) charitable, (b) educational, (c) religious, or (d) scientific
Examples of eligible employers:				
For-profit employer formed as a C or S corporation, partnership, LLC, or proprietorship	Yes	No	No	No
Federal government (refer to a discussion later in the chapter)	No	No	No	No
State and local governments	No	No (unless it's an educational institution)	Yes	No
Schools (K to university level)	No (unless it's a for-profit business)	Yes for both governmental (state & local) or 501(c)(3) tax exempt organizations	Yes for governmental (state & local) employers	Yes for 501(c)(3) organizations
Hospitals	No (unless it's a for-profit business)	Yes for 501(c)(3) organizations	Yes for governmental (state & local) employers	Yes for 501(c)(3) organizations
Museums that are tax-exempt	No	Yes for 501(c)(3) organizations	Yes for governmental (state & local) employers	Yes for 501(c)(3) organizations
Libraries that are tax-exempt	No	Yes for 501(c)(3) organizations	Yes for governmental (state & local) employers	Yes for 501(c)(3) organizations
Private research foundations	No	Yes	No	Yes
Labor unions	No	Yes	No	Yes
Private clubs	No	Yes	No	Yes

* The rules for 403(b) and 457(b) plans are complex and intentionally omitted from this text.

Exhibit 8. COMMON RETIREMENT PLANS FOR LARGE EMPLOYERS—BASIC FEATURES

Features:	401(k)	403(b) ("Tax Sheltered Annuity" Plan)	457(b) (Governmental)	457(b) (Nongovernmental)
Plan type	Qualified	Qualified	Nonqualified	Nonqualified
Able to discriminate?	No	No	Yes	Yes
Loans up to $50,000 OK?	Yes	Yes	Yes	No
Subject to 10% penalty on premature withdrawals?	Yes	Yes	No (unless the distribution consists of an amount previously rolled over from another type of plan)	No
Subject to 50% penalty on late RMDs?	Yes	Yes	Yes	No
Subject to $5,000 mandatory cash-out rules?	Yes	Yes	Yes	No
Portable with other employer-sponsored plans and IRAs?	Yes	Yes	Yes	No
Subject to statutory vesting rules for employer contributions?	Yes	Yes	No	No
Must be for exclusive benefit of employees?	Yes	Yes for retirement income accounts; No for annuity contracts and custodial accounts.	Yes	No
Protection from creditors of employer?	Yes	Yes	Yes	No

Exhibit 9. COMMON RETIREMENT PLANS FOR LARGE EMPLOYERS—CONTRIBUTION LIMITS

Limits:	401(k)	403(b)* ("Tax Sheltered Annuity" Plan)	457(b)* (Governmental)	457(b)* Non-governmental
Are employee elective deferral contributions allowed? ("GC" is defined below)	Yes, limited to the lesser of: (1) = 18,000; (2) = 100% GC + $6,000 if age 50+	Yes, limited to the lesser of: (1) = 18,000; (2) = 100% GC + $6,000 if age 50+ + $3,000 (max.) if completed 15 years of service	Yes, limited to the lesser of: (1) = 18,000; (2) = 100% GC + $6,000 if age 50+ OR + $18,000 (max.) if within 3 years of retirement	Yes, limited to the lesser of: (1) = 18,000; (2) = 100% GC + $18,000 (max.) if within 3 years of retirement (The 50 + catch-up contribution is not permitted.)
Aggregate Limit on Employer and Employee Contributions	Lesser of: (1) = $54,000 or (2) = 100% GC plus catch-up contributions	Lesser of: (1) = $54,000 or (2) = 100% GC plus catch-up contributions	Same as employee elective deferral contribution limit above.	Same as employee elective deferral contribution limit above.
Are contributions subject to FICA or FUTA?	No for employer contributions; Yes for employee contributions.	Same as 401(k)	Same as 401(k)	Yes
Are employee supplemental after-tax contributions allowed?	Yes if written into the plan	Same as 401(k)	No	No

"GC:" Gross compensation is equal to the employee's salary plus any qualified benefits such as medical insurance premiums under a cafeteria plan.

* The rules for 403(b) and 457(b) plans are complex and intentionally omitted from this text.

Common Retirement Plans For Small Businesses

The most common types of qualified employer-sponsored retirement plans among incorporated employers and self-employed persons with not more than 100 employees include:

- Solo (or "individual") 401(k) plans (at ¶24,515),
- Keogh plans (at ¶24,525),
- Simplified Employer Plans ("SEPs") (at ¶24,535), and
- Savings Incentive Match Plan for Employees ("SIMPLEs") (at ¶24,545).

The following sections provide a summary and a comparison of some of the most important features of these plans.

¶24,501   PLANS FOR SMALL BUSINESSES—BASIC CONCEPTS

Classification of Plans

No distinction is generally made between pension, profit-sharing, and other retirement plans (e.g., a 401(k) plan or SEP IRA) established by corporations and those established by individual proprietors and partnerships. In the past, the terms "Keogh Plan," or "H.R. 10 Plan" were used to distinguish a retirement plan established by a self-employed individual from a plan established by a corporation or other entity. However, retirement plans for self-employed persons are now generally referred to by the name that is used for the particular type of plan (e.g., solo 401(k), SEP IRA, or SIMPLE IRA). Keogh plans include money purchase plans and profit-sharing plans. See ¶24,525.

Most retirement plans covering self-employed persons are defined contribution plans. There are basically two types: profit-sharing plans and money purchase pension plans. Typically, contributions to a profit-sharing plan are made out of profits, although there is no requirement that a qualified profit-sharing plan contain a definite predetermined formula for determining the amount of profits to be shared. Rev. Rul. 56-366, 1956-2 CB 976.

In a money purchase pension plan, contributions are not based on profits. Reg. §1.401-1(b)(1)(i). Typically, contributions to a money purchase pension plan are expressed as a percentage of compensation and must be made regardless of whether or not the enterprise has profits. If a plan provides that contributions on behalf of participants are a fixed percentage of compensation and defines the compensation of a self-employed person as his earned income, the plan apparently will be classified as a money purchase pension plan, even though no contributions will be made on behalf of self-employed participants in a year when the enterprise has no profits. Reg. §1.401-11(b)(1).

Comparison of Plan Features

In choosing the right qualified plan for a small business, the plan features should be carefully considered to insure that owner objectives will be met. Ten important considerations are discussed below.

1. *Self as trustee.* With a solo 401(k) plan or a Keogh plan, a taxpayer may achieve maximum investment flexibility by electing to serve as trustee and manage the trust funds. This election is not available for SEP or SIMPLE IRAs.
2. *Legal entity.* Keogh and SEP IRA plans are available only to self-employed taxpayers (e.g., proprietors, partners, and members of LLCs) as well as their employees. Shareholders in C and S corporations are viewed as common-law employees rather than self-employed taxpayers. Thus, C and S corporations are not eligible to establish Keogh or SEP IRA plans.
3. *Multiple employees.* A business with more than one full-time employee (other than the taxpayer's spouse) is not eligible to maintain a solo 401(k) plan. If a sole owner-employee participating in a solo 401(k) plan hires one or more full-time employee (other than a spouse) at any time during the year, the solo 401(k) plan must revert to a corporate-styled traditional 401(k) plan with potentially cumbersome reporting requirements.
4. *IRS reporting requirements.* Taxpayers with SEP or SIMPLE IRA plans are not required to file annual reports with the IRS (except for W-2 reporting). Taxpayers with solo 401(k) plans and Keogh plans may be required to file annual IRS reports, depending on the size of the plan assets. If a solo 401(k) or a Keogh plan does not provide benefits to anyone except the owner and owner's spouse, or in the case of a partnership, one or more partners and their spouses, and total plan assets are $250,000 or

less, there are no IRS reporting requirements. However, once the amount of plan assets rises above $250,000, Form 5500-EZ must be filed by the last day of the 7th month after the plan year ends (July 31 for calendar-year plans). If any plan benefits are provided by an insurance company or insurance service, or, in the case of solo 401(k) plans, if the plan has more than one participant (other than the taxpayer's spouse), Form 5500 and appropriate schedules are required by the same deadline.

5. *Statutory deadlines.* The SEP IRA offers the most flexibility with respect to deadlines. The deadline for establishing a SEP IRA and making a contribution for the current year is the automatic six-month extension due date for the taxpayer's return (October 15 of the following year in the case of an individual taxpayer). The SIMPLE IRA plan must be established by October 1 of the current year. However, once established, contributions for the current year can be made as late as October 15 of the following year (the six-month extension due date of an individual taxpayer's return). Solo 401(k) plans and Keogh plans must be established, and contributions must be made, no later than December 31 of the current year. (Some institutions may require earlier cutoff dates.) The deadline for deemed employee elective deferral contributions under a solo 401(k) is October 15 of the following year (the six-month extension due date of an individual taxpayer's return).

6. *Vesting.* Another unique feature of a Keogh plan is that accrued employee benefits from employer contributions generally are subject to the regular vesting rules of Code Sec. 411 (previously discussed at ¶24,265). From an employer perspective, this feature may be viewed favorably because it may discourage unexpected terminations by employee-participants. Accrued employee benefits under SEP or SIMPLE plans must be free of vesting requirements and nonforfeitable at all times.

7. *Plan loans.* A taxpayer participating in a solo 401(k) or Keogh is permitted to borrow against the plan, subject to the limits described at ¶24,355. Taxpayers participating in any form of IRA (e.g., SEP, SIMPLE, traditional, or Roth), are prohibited from borrowing against the plan.

8. *Participation requirements.* Participation requirements warrant a discussion by plan.

   ▪ **Solo 401(k).** The solo 401(k) plan may be adopted only by businesses whose only eligible persons to participate in the plan are the business owner and spouse. If the business has non-owner employees who are eligible to participate in the plan, the business is not eligible to adopt the solo 401(k) plan. However, a business with non-owner employees may still be eligible to adopt a solo 401(k) only if the non-owner employees are not eligible to participate in the plan. The determination of whether other employees are eligible depends on the eligibility requirements stated in the plan. However, the requirements must remain within the following limitations for employees who:
      a. attained age 21, or
      b. have worked 1,000 hours in any 12-consecutive-month period.
      When determining the eligibility requirements for a solo 401(k) plan, the plan may exclude from participation employees who are non-resident aliens and/or those who receive benefits under a collective bargaining agreement.

   ▪ **Keogh.** A Keogh plan cannot exclude any employee from participation on account of age or years of service, except for the exclusion of employees who:
      a. are under age 21, or
      b. have less than one "year of service," i.e., less than 1,000 hours in any 12-consecutive-month period. (However, a plan that provides for 100 percent vesting after no more than two years of service may require a two-year period of service for eligibility to participate.)

   ▪ **SEP.** The SEP participation rules are most favorable from an employer perspective because they permit stricter employee-eligibility requirements than Keogh or SIMPLE plans. Under a SEP arrangement, the employer is required to contribute to the IRA of each employee who:
      a. has attained the age of 21,
      b. has performed services for the employer during at least three out of the immediately preceding five calendar years, and
      c. has received at least a specified dollar amount of compensation ($600 in 2017) from the employer for the year. Code Sec. 408(k)(2).

   ▪ **SIMPLE.** For SIMPLE IRA plans, there are no age limits. All employees who received at least $5,000 in compensation from the employer during any two preceding calendar years and who are reasonably expected to receive $5,000 in compensation during the current year must be eligible to participate. SIMPLE 401(k) plans on the other hand, generally follow the same participation requirements as traditional 401(k) plans. (The 401(k) requirements also apply to Keogh plans—see above).

Less restrictive participation requirements may be imposed than the statutory limits described above. Notice 98-4, 1998-1 CB 269, Q&As C-1 and C-2; Code Sec. 408(p)(4).

9. *Rollovers.* The rollover rules governing SIMPLE IRA plans are the most restrictive among qualified plans. A SIMPLE IRA account is not permitted to receive rollover funds from another qualified account unless the originating account is also a qualified SIMPLE IRA account. An employee is permitted to execute a SIMPLE-to-SIMPLE rollover at any time after inception of the employee's participation in the plan. Code Sec. 408(d)(3)(G). However, rollovers from SIMPLE IRAs into SEP or traditional IRAs are permitted after two years from the inception of the employee's participation. See ¶24,345 for a general discussion of rollovers to and from other qualified plans.

10. *Contribution and deduction limits.* At different levels of employee compensation ("net SEI" in the case of owner-employees as defined below) different plans may produce the largest contribution and deduction for the owner-employee. Specific formulas for the solo 401(k), Keogh plan, SEP IRA and SIMPLE IRA are explained later in this chapter.

EXAMPLE 24.16	J. P. Zack, Inc. is a calendar year corporation. A few years ago, the corporation established a SEP for its eligible employees. In order to be eligible for a current-year deduction, contributions to the separate SEP IRAs of each employee must generally be made by the due date of the corporate tax return (i.e., March 15, of the following year). However, if it has requested a six-month filing extension, the contributions may be made up to September 15 of the following year. If the employer had been a proprietor, the deadline for contributions would have been April 15 of the following year, or October 15 of that year if an automatic six-month extension had been filed. The same deadlines would apply to a Keogh or SIMPLE plan.

PLANNING POINTER	1. Taxpayers participating in a SEP, SIMPLE, or traditional IRA cannot borrow from the IRA. However, for SEP and traditional IRAs (but not SIMPLE IRAs), the account funds can be rolled into a qualified employer-sponsored plan (e.g., a solo 401(k) or a Keogh plan) that is not an IRA and then borrowed.
	2. Loans from SIMPLE 401(k) (unlike SIMPLE IRAs) are permitted. An employer may wish to establish a SIMPLE 401(k) rather than a SIMPLE IRA in order to include loans as a feature of the plan. For employees who need to tap into their retirement assets when they are ineligible to receive distributions from the plan, loans can be an attractive plan feature.

Taxation—Exposure and Timing

Employer and employee contributions generally are subject to the same rules that govern retirement plans for large, multiemployer employers. Employer contributions are permanently exempt from FICA and FUTA tax under Code Secs. 3121(v)(1) and 3306(r)(1); however, employee elective deferral contributions (to solo 401(k) and SIMPLE plans, for example) are subject to FICA and FUTA taxes in the contribution year. In most cases, employer contributions and employee elective deferral contributions (if eligible) are tax-deferred in the contribution year and taxable in the distribution year.

Concepts Related To Plans For Self-Employed Persons

The following definitions relate specifically to plans established by an unincorporated trade or business, i.e., a sole proprietorship or a partnership. These definitions are all found in Code Sec. 401(c).

"Employer"

In the qualified plan provisions, when reference is made to the term "employer," a sole proprietor is treated as the proprietor's own employer (thus, the proprietor serves two roles: that of *employer* and of *employee*). However, a partnership is considered to be the employer of each partner. Code Sec. 401(c)(4). As a result, while sole proprietors may establish their own retirement plans, only a partnership may establish a retirement plan for its partners.

Owner-employee

If a qualified retirement plan provides contributions for an owner-employee, contributions on behalf of the owner-employee may be made only with respect to earned income of the owner-employee that is derived from the trade or business with respect to which the plan is established. Code Sec. 401(a)(10)(A), (D). An "owner-employee" is any of the following (Code Sec. 401(c)(3)):

1. An employee who owns the entire interest in an unincorporated trade or business (i.e., a sole proprietor).
2. In the case of a partnership, a partner who owns more than 10 percent of either the capital interest or profits interest in the partnership. (Note that all owner-employees are also self-employed individuals. However, the reverse is not true, since a five-percent partner would be considered a self-employed individual, but not an owner-employee.

Computing the Contribution and Deduction Amounts

Contributions and deductions for a self-employed participant covered by a qualified plan are subject to the same basic rules that apply to participants who are common law employees (see 401(k) plan contribution limits at ¶24,401). However, special computations pertaining to the earned income of the self-employed individual must be made in order to determine the contribution and deduction amounts.

As a starting point, references to "compensation," in the case of a proprietor or partner, are to the "earned income" of that person from the business for which the plan is established. "Earned income" is defined as net earnings from self-employment ("net SEI"). Code Sec. 401(c)(2)(A).

In determining the amount of net SEI upon which contributions and deductions are based, the net profit from a business activity (Schedule C in the case of a proprietorship) is reduced by the following two adjustments:

1. The deduction from gross income that is allowed under Code Sec. 164(f) for 50% of the self-employment tax paid by the self-employed participant. Code Sec. 401(c)(2)(A)(vi). After this adjustment, but before the second adjustment below, the resulting amount is gross self-employment income ("gross SEI").
2. The deduction allowed for contributions made on behalf of the self-employed participant. Code Sec. 401(c)(2)(A)(v). When the entire contribution is deductible, the amount of the deduction is determined by multiplying a converted plan contribution rate by gross SEI. The plan rate is converted by dividing the *nominal plan rate* by the *integer one, plus that rate*.

EXAMPLE 24.17	If a self-employed taxpayer's plan calls for a contribution rate equal to 10 percent of the participant's compensation, the converted contribution rate is 9.0909% (determined by dividing 10% by 1.10).

EXAMPLE 24.18	Continuing from the example above, a self-employed participant who reports a Form 1040, Schedule C net profit of $100,000 and pays $10,000 self-employment tax for the same year, will be permitted a contribution (and deduction) in the amount of $8,636. (Refer to the calculation and proof below.)

(a) = Given	Schedule C net profit	100,000
(b) = ½ × $10,000	½ SE tax	5,000
(c) = (a) – (b)	Gross SEI	95,000
(d) – 10% ÷ 1.10	Converted plan rate	9.0909%
(e) = (c) × (d)	Contribution & deduction	8,636
(f) = (c) – (e)	Net SEI	86,364
(g) = plan rate × (f)	Proof ($86,364 × 10%)	8,636

The short-cut formula above is a practical necessity. Otherwise, computing the contribution and deduction amount by multiplying a nominal plan rate times net SEI, would pose an algebraic dilemma: net SEI would have to be known in order to compute the deduction amount; and, conversely, the deduction amount would have to be known in order to compute net SEI.

"Contribution" Not a Business Expense

A deduction for a contribution to a qualified plan for the benefit of a self-employed individual is not a business expense of that individual. *D.L. Gale*, 91-2 USTC ¶50,356. Therefore, it cannot be used in calculating self-employment tax. Also, it is limited to income and cannot create or increase an NOL. Code Sec. 172(d)(4)(D).

For self-employed taxpayers (proprietors and partners), a deduction is reported as an adjustment to gross income on page 1 of Form 1040 rather than on Schedule C of Form 1040 (for proprietorships) or on page 1 of Form 1065 (for partnerships). A partnership's deduction for contributions on behalf of a partner must be allocated solely to that partner. Reg. §1.404(e)-1A(f). It cannot be allocated among all of the partners pursuant to a partnership agreement.

Distributions

A self-employed taxpayer or a beneficiary will qualify for a lump-sum distribution (discussed ¶24,301) only on account of death, disability, or attainment of age 59½. A common-law employee or a beneficiary on the other hand, will qualify for a lump-sum distribution prior to age 59 ½ only on account of death or separation from service. A common-law employee's disability is treated as separation from service.

¶24,515　SOLO 401(k) PLANS

The Solo 401(k) plan is referred to by various other names including: uni-401(k), one-man 401(k), mini-401(k), self-employed 401(k), and individual 401(k) plans. Since 2002, the Economic Growth and Tax Relief Reconciliation Act of 2001 has permitted any business that employs only the owner—including C corporations, S corporations, single member LLCs, partnerships, and sole proprietorships—to participate in this plan. The employment of an owner's spouse is also permitted.

In general, the same rules that apply to traditional 401(k) plans established by multiemployee entities apply to solo 401(k) plans. Reg. §1.401(k)-1(a)(6)(i). Employer and employee contributions into the plan and income generated from these contributions are tax-deferred until the year(s) retirement benefits are received. Also, participants in Solo 401(k), unlike participants in SEP or SIMPLE IRAs, may be eligible to borrow against the plan under the same rules that apply to traditional 401(k) plans (see ¶24,355).

Solo 401(k) Plan for the Self-Employed

The self-employed taxpayer can contribute and deduct both "deemed employer" and "deemed employee" contributions (subject to the general limit for additions to defined contributions plans explained at ¶24,501).

TAX BLUNDER

Taxpayers should consider their long-term business horizons before establishing a solo 401(k) plan. Once a solo 401(k) has been established, if one or more full-time employees are hired (other than the taxpayer's spouse), the employer must revert to a traditional 401(k) and may be required to perform certain non-discrimination and top-heavy testing to ensure that the plan operates in compliance with regulatory requirements. Generally, such testing is done by professionals who specialize in that area and can be quite costly. If employees elect not to make a deferral contribution, the employer may not be eligible to contribute into the plan. If the expanded rules are violated, the IRS could disqualify the plan, forcing the employer to pay taxes and penalties on the tax-deferred amounts that had accumulated in the account.

Limit on Employee Elective Deferral Contributions

Employee contributions ("deemed employee" contributions if self-employed) are regular-tax deferred. The contribution amount may not exceed the lesser of:

1. **Amount Limit:** $18,000 in 2017; or
2. **Percentage Limit:** Up to 100% of compensation for employees (or 100% of gross SEI for proprietors and partners).

Aggregate Limit on Employer and Employee Contributions

The amount of employer contributions ("deemed employer" contributions if self-employed) may not exceed the lesser of:

1. **Amount Limit:** $54,000 in 2017; or
2. **Percentage Limit:** Up to 25% of compensation for employees (or 20% of gross SEI for proprietors and partners).

"Gross SEI" and "net SEI" are explained in the preceding section.

EXAMPLE 24.19

Ethan Robinson, age 45, is planning to start a new business through a proprietorship and is considering establishing a solo 401(k). He would like to know the maximum amount of contributions and deductions he could expect based on gross SEI projections of $5,000, $50,000, and $500,000. (Refer to computations below.)

Gross SEI Projections	Limit on Deemed Employee Contribution	Limit on Deemed Employer Contributions	Aggregate Limit on Contributions & Deductions
(a) = Sched. C Net Profit Less ½ Self-Employment Tax Deduction	(b) = Lesser of: • $18,000 or • 100% × (a)	(c) = Lesser of: • $54,000 or • 20% × (a)	(d) = Least of: • (a) or • [(b) + (c)] or • $54,000
$5,000	$5,000	$1,000	$5,000 (the gross SEI amount at "(a)")
$50,000	$18,000	$10,000	$28,000
$500,000	$18,000	$54,000	$54,000

Reduction in $18,000 Limit

The maximum employee or "deemed employee" annual elective contribution limit is reduced dollar-for-dollar by contributions to other Solo 401(k) plans but not by contributions to regular 401(k) or other multiemployee qualified retirement plans. Thus, an employee participating in an employer's 401(k) plan, who also owns a separate business (i.e., "moonlights"), may make the maximum contributions to both the corporate 401(k) plan and a solo 401(k) plan. However, the aggregate $18,000 limit would apply if a self-employed taxpayer had more than one business, with each business offering a separate Solo 401(k) plan.

Age 50+ Catch-up Contributions

Any plan participant who is at least or will become age 50 before the end of the year can make additional elective deferral contributions of $6,000 in 2017. The age 50+ catch-up contribution does not count toward the $54,000 aggregate limit on employer and employee contributions.

PLANNING POINTER

A growing number of mutual fund sponsors and retirement plan providers are offering solo 401(k) programs (e.g., Charles Schwabb, Fidelity, Merrill Lynch, Scudder, Waddell & Reed, and over 100 others.). The Solo 401(k) has more flexible investment restrictions than many IRAs and employer-sponsored plans. For example, participants can invest their contributions in any mutual fund, or individual stocks, bonds, treasury securities, or other investment securities.

¶24,525 KEOGH PLANS

Keogh plans were established in 1983 to create parity between self-employed taxpayers and corporate employees with regard to deferred compensation benefits. There are three basic forms of Keogh plans:

1. **Money purchase pensions plan.** A Keogh can be set up as a money purchase pension plan in which contributions are mandatory each year at a predetermined percentage and not based on profits. This type of plan may be best suited for businesses that have stable income and can assure the ability to make the same contribution percentage each year.
2. **Unpaired profit-sharing plan.** Alternatively, the Keogh plan can be an unpaired profit-sharing plan in which business profits are shared with employees. The profit sharing does not need to provide a definite formula for computing profits to be shared. The contribution rates can vary from year to year or can be skipped all together. However, the plan must be maintained with the intention of making regular contributions, and such contributions must be "systematic and substantial." This type of plan may be suitable for businesses where income fluctuates year to year.
3. **Paired profit-sharing plan.** A third alternative, the paired profit-sharing plan, is a profit-sharing Keogh plan that is paired with a fixed money purchase arrangement. The money purchase arrangement often involves a mutual fund, funded by the employer, to supplement the basic plan. Often, the employee

can pick among several mutual funds. In this paired situation, employer contributions are based on two formulas, one tied in to profits, and the other, a fixed percentage similar to a money purchase pension. The contribution limitation is spread between the profit-sharing Keogh and the money purchase pension (see below). The paired plan may be best suited for an employer who wants a low mandatory contribution percentage as well as discretion over making larger contributions.

Contribution Limits

For money purchase pension plans and paired profit sharing plans, the amount of employer contributions ("deemed employer" contributions if self-employed) may not exceed the lesser of:

1. **Amount Limit:** $54,000 in 2017; or
2. **Percentage Limit:** 100% of compensation for employees (or 100% of net SEI for proprietors and partners).

Most money purchase and paired profit Keogh plans provide a nominal plan rate that does not exceed 25% of employee compensation, due to the 25% deduction limitation discussed below under "deduction limits."

For unpaired single profit-sharing plans, the amount of employer contributions ("deemed employer" if self-employed) may not exceed the lesser of:

1. **Amount Limit:** $54,000 in 2017; or
2. **Percentage Limit:** 25% of compensation for employees (or 20% of gross SEI for proprietors and partners).

(See ¶24,501 for an explanation of "gross SEI" and "net SEI.")

The 50+ catch-up contribution feature available under most qualified plans is not available to Keogh participants.

Deduction Limits

Deduction limit for all Keogh plans are the lesser of:

1. Contribution amount based on actual plan rate; or
2. 25% of compensation paid or accrued on behalf of employees (or 20% of gross SEI for contributions made by, and on behalf of, proprietors and partners who are owner-employees—defined at ¶24,501).

EXAMPLE 24.20

Will Feldman, age 46, a sole proprietor with no employees, is considering establishing for himself a pension Keogh or a paired or unpaired profit-sharing Keogh. He would like to know the maximum amount of contributions and deductions he should anticipate based on gross SEI projections of $5,000, $50,000, and $500,000. Referring to the table below, at any level of gross SEI, the deduction amounts for the three types of Keoghs will always be the same. However, the pension and paired Keogh plans will provide the largest contributions at gross SEI levels below $270,000 (proof: the $54,000 statutory limit divided by the 20 percent statutory rate equivalent for contributions). At or above $270,000, the contribution limits are the same.

Gross SEI Projections	Pension and Paired Keoghs Limits		Single Profit-Sharing Keogh Limits	
(a) = Sched. C Net Profit Less ½ Self-Employment Tax Deduction	Contribution Lesser of • $54k or • 100% net SEI	Deduction Lesser of • $54k or • 20% gross SEI	Contribution Lesser of • $54k or • 25% net SEI	Deduction Lesser of • $54k or • 20% gross SEI
$5,000	$4,000 (net SEI is equal to $5,000 gross SEI minus $1,000 deduction)	$1,000	$1,000	$1,000
$50,000	$40,000 (net SEI is equal to $50,000 gross SEI minus $10,000 deduction)	$10,000	$10,000	$10,000
$270,000	$54,000	$54,000	$54,000	$54,000
$500,000	$54,000	$54,000	$54,000	$54,000

PLANNING POINTER

A Keogh plan may take the form of one of several funding vehicles, including mutual funds, annuities, real estate shares, certificates of deposit, debt instruments, commodities, securities and personal properties. The plan may be either self-managed or managed by a financial institution. Most Keogh plans are defined contribution plans since they are easier to maintain than defined benefit plans.

EXAMPLE 24.21

Hank Spearman reports the following information from his proprietorship for the year:

Gross Income = $300,000
Business Deductions = $192,000
Self-Employment tax = $16,000

Hank maintains a Keogh plan with a 30 percent nominal contribution rate (as applied to net SEI—discussed at ¶24,501). If the plan is a pension (or paired) Keogh, Hank will be able to contribute $24,000 into the plan and claim a $24,000 deduction on his return. If the plan is a profit-sharing Keogh, Hank will be able to contribute and deduct $24,000 and $20,000, respectively. The deduction can be claimed on Hank's current return even if the contributions are made as late as October 15 of the following year (the six-month extension due date of an individual taxpayer's return).

Formula:	Description:	Pension/ Paired Keogh	Profit-Sharing Keogh
(a)	Gross Income	300,000	300,000
(b)	Business Deductions	192,000	192,000
(c)	SET Deduction: SET × ½ = $16,000 × ½ = $8m	8,000	8,000
(d) = (a) − (b) − (c)	Gross SEI (i.e., SEI before the Keogh deduction)	100,000	100,000
(e) = $265,000	Statutory limit on compensation [Sec. 401(a)(17)]	270,000	270,000
(f) = Lesser of (d) or (e)	Allowable income amount for deduction formula	100,000	100,000
(g) = (f) × [plan rate ÷ (1 + rate)]	Deduction limit—based on 30% nominal plan rate for contributions	23,077	23,077
(h) = (f) × [25% ÷ (1.25)]	Deduction limit—based on 25% statutory rate	20,000	20,000
(i) = Lesser of (g) or (h)	Deduction allowed	20,000	20,000
(j) = (d) − (i)	Net SEI (i.e., gross SEI minus Keogh deduction)	80,000	80,000
(k) = Lesser of: [(e) − (i)][or (j)]	Allowable income amount for contribution formula	80,000	80,000
(l) = (k) × plan rate	Contribution limit—based on nominal plan rate	24,000	24,000
(m) = (k) × 100% (for pension plans / (m) = (k) × 25% (for profit-sharing plans)	Contribution limit—based on statutory rate of 100% (pension plan) or 25% (profit-sharing plan)	80,000	20,000
(n) = $53,000	Contribution limit—based on statutory amount	54,000	54,000
(o) = Lesser of (l), (m), or (n)	Maximum allowable contribution	24,000	20,000

¶24,535   SIMPLIFIED EMPLOYEE PENSION (SEP) PLANS

A simplified employee pension (SEP) is a written arrangement that allows an employer to make deductible contributions to a traditional IRA (a SEP IRA) set up for employees to receive such contributions. Generally, distributions from SEP IRAs are subject to the withdrawal and tax rules that apply to traditional IRAs (see ¶24,625). Code Sec. 402(h)(3) and Code Sec. 408(d).

Adopting the Plan

SEP IRAs are simpler to adopt than most other plans. An employer need only fill out the one-page IRS Form 5305-SEP by the extension due date of the employer return. The form is not filed with the IRS but is distributed to each participant. The only report containing the amount of employer contributions that the employer must file with the IRS is the employee's W-2 form.

Contribution and Deduction Limits

Contribution and deduction limits for all SEP IRAs are the lesser of:

1. $54,000; or
2. 25% of compensation paid or accrued on behalf of employees (or 20% of gross SEI for contributions made by, and on behalf of, proprietors and partners).

EXAMPLE 24.22

Peggy Warner, a sole proprietor, is considering establishing a SEP IRA for herself. She would like to know the maximum contribution and deduction limits available to her, based on gross SEI projections of $5,000, $50,000, and $500,000. (Refer to computations below.)

Gross SEI Projections:	Statutory Contribution & Deduction Limits:
Schedule C Net Profit Less ½ SE Taxes Actually Paid for the Year	The lesser of: (1) $54,000 or (2) 20% gross SEI
$5,000	$1,000
$50,000	$10,000
$500,000	$54,000

EXAMPLE 24.23

CKS partnership maintains three separate SEP accounts for each of its eligible employees, Ashley, Kathy and Mary. If the annual compensation of each employee is $5,000, $50,000, and $500,000, respectively, the maximum contribution and deduction limits available to CKS will be $1,250, $12,500, and $54,000, as shown below.

Employees	Annual Compensation	Statutory Contribution & Deduction Limits:
		The lesser of: (1) $54,000 or (2) 25% compensation
Ashley	$5,000	$1,250
Kathy	$50,000	$12,500
Mary	$500,000	$54,000

Age 50+ Catch-up Contributions

As with a solo 401(k) participant, a SEP IRA participant who has attained age 50 before the end of the plan year can make elective deferral contributions of $6,000 in 2017. (See ¶24,501 for a discussion of the tax treatment for elective deferral contributions.) The age 50+ catch-up contribution does not count towards the statutory contribution limit of $54,000 for these plans.

EXAMPLE 24.24

Referring to the preceding example above, if Mary had attained age 50 by the end of the year, she would be permitted to make a $6,000 elective deferral contribution to her SEP account. The total contributions to her SEP account for the year would be $60,000, i.e., $54,000 employer deductible contributions plus $6,000 employee deferral contributions.

No Minimum Contribution Requirements

Employers with SEPs are not subject to minimum contribution requirements. This feature compares favorably with Keogh and SIMPLE plans, which have annual minimum contribution requirements from 1 to 3 percent of employee gross compensation annually, depending on the plan type.

Deemed IRA

A SEP IRA cannot offer CODAs (cash or deferred arrangements) to employees as can Solo 401(k) and SIMPLE plans. However, it may allow employees to make voluntary contributions to a separate account in lieu of contributing to a traditional IRA or a Roth IRA. Code Sec. 408(q). The aggregate limit on contributions to a traditional IRA, a Roth IRA, and a deemed IRA (employee contributions) is $5,500 ($6,500 if age 50 or over (see ¶24,601).

Salary Reduction SEPs (SARSEPs)

In plan years beginning before 1997, an employer could establish a salary reduction (cash or deferred) arrangement as part of a SEP. Such an arrangement—commonly known as a SARSEP —may not be established in plan years beginning after 1996. However, SARSEPs established before 1997 may continue to operate, subject to the same conditions and requirements that have always applied (Sec. 1421(c) of P.L. 104-188).

¶24,545 SIMPLE PLANS

Employers with 100 or fewer employees may establish a Savings Incentive Match Plan for Employees ("SIMPLE" plan). LLCs, partnerships, sole proprietorships, and C or S corporations may be eligible to establish SIMPLE plans. Also, 501(c) tax-exempt organizations and state and local governmental entities may also be eligible.

The plan can be in the form of a 401(k) plan or an IRA. The SIMPLE 401(K) participation rules are more favorable from an employer perspective because they provide stricter employee-eligibility requirements than SIMPLE IRAs (see ¶24,501). Under either form of plan, the employer must contribute a matching contribution to the account of each eligible employee on whose behalf elective contributions were made for the plan year. Code Sec. 408(p)(2)(A)(iii). These contributions must be 100 percent nonforfeitable at all times. Neither form of SIMPLE is subject to discrimination testing.

Adopting the Plan

To adopt a SIMPLE IRA an employer need fill out only the two-page IRS Form 5305-SIMPLE (employer selects the financial institution) or 5304-SIMPLE (employer permits employees to select their own financial institution) by October 1 of the employer's current tax year. The form is not filed with the IRS but is distributed to each participant. The SIMPLE IRA trustee must file Form 5498 annually with the IRS. This form contains employer and employee contribution amounts and the fair market value of the account at year-end.

Generally, an employer must permit an employee to select the financial institution for the SIMPLE to which the employer will make all contributions on behalf of the employee. If an eligible employee who is entitled to a contribution under a SIMPLE is unwilling or unable to establish a SIMPLE account with any financial institution prior to the date on which the contribution is required to be made, an employer may execute the necessary documents to establish the SIMPLE account with a financial institution selected by the employer.

Cash or Deferred Arrangement (CODA)

Both types of SIMPLE plans, the *401(k)* type and the *IRA* type, are cash or deferred arrangements in which employees (or "deemed employees" described in ¶24,501) may elect to either:

1. be taxed on all of their compensation and receive it, net of withholdings, in the form of cash,
2. defer all or a portion of their salary (up to $12,500, or $15,500 if age 50 or older) by directing their employer to contribute it into the SIMPLE plan. The amounts contributed by employee-participants is tax deferred.

Limit on Employee Elective Deferral Contributions

Employee contributions ("deemed employee" contributions if self-employed) are regular-tax deferred. For both SIMPLE 401(k) and SIMPLE IRA plans, the contribution amount may not exceed the lesser of:

1. **Amount Limit:** $12,500 in 2017; or
2. **Percentage Limit:** Up to 100% of compensation for employees (or 100% of gross SEI for proprietors and partners).

Limit on Employer Contributions

The amount of employer contributions ("deemed employer" contributions if self-employed) may not exceed the lesser of:

1. **Amount Limit:** $12,500 in 2017; or
2. **Percentage Limit:** Up to 3% of compensation for employees (or 3% of gross SEI for proprietors and partners).

Statutory Compensation Limit

For SIMPLE 401(k) plans, *all* employer contributions are subject to the statutory compensation limit under Sec. 401(a)(17) ($270,000 in 2017). For SIMPLE IRAs, only *non-elective* employer contributions are subject to this limit.

EXAMPLE 24.25	An eligible employee with $100,000 compensation in 2017 could elect to have up to 100% of that compensation, subject to the $12,500 limitation, contributed to a SIMPLE 401(k) or IRA plan on a pre-tax basis. If the nominal plan rate for employee contributions were, say, 2%, then the contribution amount would be $2,000; if 5%, then $5,000; if 15% then $12,500 (given the $12,500 limitation); if 100%, then still $12,500. The employee contribution, while regular tax-deferred, is nevertheless subject to FICA and FUTA tax.

EXAMPLE 24.26	Eugenia Hobbs earns a $300,000 salary and participates in DT Inc.'s SIMPLE IRA. The plan provides for a 100 percent nominal rate for elective employee contributions. Eugenia could contribute $12,500 into her SIMPLE IRA account (i.e., the lesser of $12,500, the statutory limit or 100% × $300,000). DT's matching contribution could be as much as $9,000 (i.e., the lesser of $12,500, or 3% × $300,000). If the plan had been a SIMPLE 401(k), DT's matching contribution could be as much as $8,100 instead of $9,000 because, under a SIMPLE 401(k) plan, employer contributions are subject to the statutory compensation limit discussed above (i.e., $8,100 is equal to the lesser of $12,500, or 3% × $270,000).

EXAMPLE 24.27	Same facts as in the preceding example except that the plan provides for a 2 percent nominal rate for elective employee contributions. Eugenia's contribution would be limited to $6,000 (i.e., the lesser of $12,500 or 2% × $300,000). The employer's matching contribution to the SIMPLE IRA could be as much as $6,000 (the lesser of the $6,000 employee contribution or 3% × $300,000).

Computing Gross SEI

"Gross SEI" and "net SEI" are explained at ¶24,501. For SIMPLE plans, gross SEI refers to (a) – (b) – (c) where

(a) = self-employed taxpayer's gross income from the business;
(b) = business deductions; and
(c) = [(a) – (b)] × 0.9235.

For Keogh and SEP IRAs, gross SEI is determined under a similar formula except that "(c)" is equal to ½ the self-employment taxes *actually* paid.)

EXAMPLE 24.28	Richard Fenner maintains a SIMPLE IRA and reports $500,000 Schedule C net earnings. The nominal plan rate for "deemed employee" contributions is 100%, (which is limited to the $12,500 statutory amount). Richard may contribute and deduct up to $25,000 into his SIMPLE IRA account. On his tax return, he will report a $25,000 deduction on Form 1040 p. 1. *[Computations: $25,000 = $12,500 "deemed employee" limit + $12,000 "deemed employer" limit. The $12,500 deemed employer limit is based on the following computation: 3% × ($500,000 × 0.9235) = $13,853, limited to the $12,500 statutory limit for employer contributions.]*

EXAMPLE 24.29	Same facts as in the preceding example, except that Richard reports Schedule C net earnings of $12,500 instead of $500,000. He may contribute and deduct a total of $12,846. [Computations: $12,846 = $12,500 "deemed employee" limit, + $346 "deemed employer" limit. The $346 deemed employer limit is based on the following computation: 3% × (12,500 × 0.9235) = $346].

Age 50+ Catch-up Contributions

Any plan participant who is at least or will become age 50 before the end of the year can make additional elective deferral contributions of $3,000 in 2017. The age 50+ catch-up contribution does not count towards the statutory contribution limit of $12,500 for these plans.

Reducing Matching Contributions

For the SIMPLE IRA, an employer who elects to make matching contributions may choose to reduce the amount to one that is less than 3 percent but not less than 1 percent for two out of every five years. This option is not available for the SIMPLE 401(k).

Alternative Employer "Nonelective" Contributions

As an alternative to making matching contributions under a SIMPLE 401(k) or SIMPLE IRA plan on behalf of all participating employees, an employer may make "nonelective" nonmatching contributions on behalf of all eligible employees, regardless of whether they participate in the plan. (The term "non-elective" may seem to be somewhat misleading since the employer can "elect" this alternative. The label, "nonelective" refers to the fact that employers who make this election *must* contribute on behalf of all eligible employees, even those who choose not to participate in the SIMPLE plan.) Employer nonelective contributions are limited to the lesser of:

1. 2% of every eligible employee's compensation (subject to a $270,000 statutory compensation limit under Code Sec. 401(a)(17) for both SIMPLE 401(k) and SIMPLE IRA plans), or
2. $12,500 (effectively limited to $5,400, given that the $270,000 compensation limit applies to alternative employer nonelective contributions).

EXAMPLE 24.30 — ABC has ten employees, each receiving a $300,000 salary. Although all ten employees are eligible to participate in ABC's SIMPLE IRA plan, only seven choose to do so. Each of these seven participants contributes the maximum amount of $12,500 into the plan. If ABC's contributions are "matching," then ABC could contribute as much as $9,000 (i.e., 3% × $300,000) on behalf of each *participating* employee. The employer contributions would total $63,000, (i.e., 7 × $9,000). If ABC's contributions are "nonelective," then ABC could contribute a maximum $5,400 (i.e., 2% × $270,000, the statutory income limitation amount) on behalf of each *eligible* employee. The employer contributions could total no more than $54,000 (i.e., 10 × $5,400).

Deemed IRA

A SIMPLE IRA may allow employees to make voluntary contributions to a separate account in lieu of contributing to a traditional IRA. Code Sec. 408(q). The aggregate limit on contributions to a traditional IRA, a Roth IRA, and a deemed IRA (i.e., employee contributions that are not CODA contributions) is $5,500 ($6,500 if age 50 or over (see ¶24,601).

Penalty for Premature Distributions

Generally, distributions received by a participant before attaining age 59 ½ are subject to a ten-percent penalty tax in addition to the regular income tax (see ¶24,235). However, for SIMPLE IRA plans, a penalty of 25 percent (rather than 10 percent) is applicable during the two-year period beginning on the date the participant first participated in the SIMPLE IRA plan. Code Sec. 72(t)(6).

PLANNING POINTER — Because 100 percent of earnings can be contributed to a SIMPLE, SIMPLEs are well suited to employed individuals with side businesses who want to contribute as much of their self-employment earnings as possible toward retirement. However, if a taxpayer participates in a 401(k) plan as an employee, and a SIMPLE as a self-employed person, the sum of the SIMPLE and 401(k) deferrals cannot exceed the statutory limit ($18,000 in 2016). If the taxpayer is already making an employee elective deferral contribution of $18,000 into a 401(k) plan, then the taxpayer should consider either a Keogh (see ¶24,525) or a SEP (see ¶24,535) rather than a SIMPLE, in order to achieve maximum deferral.

Exhibit 10. COMMON RETIREMENT PLANS FOR SMALL BUSINESSES—BASIC FEATURES

Features	Solo 401(k)	Keogh	SEP	SIMPLE
Form of plan:	401(k)	Pension, profit-sharing, or both	IRA	IRA or 401(k)
Self as trustee OK?	Yes	Yes	No	No
Permitted legal entity type:	LLC Partnership Sole proprietorship C or S corporation	LLC Partnership Sole proprietorship	LLC Partnership Sole proprietorship	LLC Partnership Sole proprietorship C or S corporation
Limit on number of employees:	Must not exceed 1 owner-employee (except for spouse)	No limit	No limit	Must not exceed 100 employees
Annual filing requirements:	Annual IRS Form 5500-EZ or Form 5500 once balance exceeds $250,000 (by last day of 7th month after year-end)	Annual IRS Form 5500-EZ or Form 5500 once balance exceeds $100,000, or $250,000 for a one-participant plan (by last day of 7th month after year-end)	None (although certain W-2 reporting is required)	None (although certain W-2 reporting is required)
Statutory establishment deadline (financial institutions may set earlier deadlines):	By December 31 of the current year	By December 31 of the current year	By extension due date of employer return	By October 1 of current year
Statutory contribution deadline:	Employee: By Dec. 31 of current year Employer: By extension due date	By extension due date of employer return	By extension due date of employer return	By extension due date of employer return
Vesting requirements:	None (since no employee other than spouse may be employed)	Regular vesting rules (e.g., 3-yr. cliff or 6-yr. graded) apply	None (Employer contributions are always nonforfeitable)	None (Employer contributions are always nonforfeitable)
Plan loans ok?	Yes, up to $50,000	Yes, up to $50,000	No	No
Participation requirements:	Only owner-employee (and spouse) may participate	Each employee: age 21 or over & with 1 year of service (2 years with 2-year vesting)	Each employee: age 21 or over who performed services in current year and in 3 out of past 5 years who earned at least $600 for current year	SIMPLE IRA: Each employee: Any age limit Earn at least $5k for any past 2 years and be expected to do so in current year SIMPLE 401(k): (same as Keogh)
Rollovers permitted?	Yes	Yes	Yes	Yes, but rules are very restrictive for SIMPLE IRAs

Exhibit 11. COMMON RETIREMENT PLANS FOR SMALL BUSINESSES—CONTRIBUTION AND DEDUCTION LIMITS				
Features	**Solo 401(k)**	**Keogh**	**SEP**	**SIMPLE**
Contribution limits for employees (or "deemed employees") (see "Terms" below):	Lesser of: (1) = 18,000; (2) = 100% GC or gross SEI	N/A	N/A	Lesser of: (1) = 100% GC (or gross SEI), or (2) = $12,500
Contribution limits for employers (or "deemed employers")	(See aggregate contribution limit below.)	(See aggregate contribution limit below.)	(See aggregate contribution limit below.)	Elective contributions: Lesser of (a) or (b): (a) = Employee (or "deemed" employee) contributions (from above), or (b) = 3% GC (or gross SEI) for each participating employee. Nonelective contributions: 2% GC for each eligible employee
Aggregate contribution limit for employers and employees	Lesser of: (1) = $54,000 or (2) = 25% GC (or 20% *gross* SEI)	Lesser of: (1) = $54,000 or (2) = 100% GC or *net* SEI (25% for single- profit sharing plans)	Lesser of: (1) = $54,000 or (2) = 25% GC (or 20% *gross* SEI)	(Separate employee and employer limits apply—see above)
$270,000 (of GC or net SEI) limit in contribution formula?	Yes	Yes	Yes	For SIMPLE 401(k)s: Yes For SIMPLE IRAs: No, except for nonelective contributions
Age 50+ catch-up contributions:	Yes, $6,000 for 2017. *(This is in addition to the $54,000 aggregate limit.)*	No	Yes, $6,000 for 2017. *(This is in addition to the $54,000 maximum limit.)*	Yes, $3,000 for 2017
Minimum contribution limits	None	1% to 3%, depending on the form of Keogh	None	The 3% employer contribution percentage shown above may be reduced to 1% in any 2 out of 5 years.
Deduction limit for owner-employees	Same as aggregate contribution limit (see above)	Lesser of: (1) = $54,000 or (2) = 25% GC or *net* SEI	Same as aggregate contribution limit (see above)	For corporate employers: Same as employer limit above. For owner-employees: Sum of the separate contribution limits for deemed employees and deemed employers

Terms:
"GC" means gross compensation, i.e., salary paid or accrued to employees.
"Gross SEI" refers to (a) – (b) – (c) where
   (a) = self-employed taxpayer's gross income from the business;
   (b) = business deductions;
   (c) = ½ × self-employment tax actually paid (for Keoghs and SEP IRAs); or, [(a) – (b)] × .9235 (for solo 401(k)s & SIMPLE IRAs).
"Net SEI" is equal to gross SEI – the actual retirement plan deduction.

KEYSTONE PROBLEM

Joanie Jones, age 49, has recently started a consulting business in the form of a sole proprietorship. Currently, the business has no full-time employees and generates $5,000 gross self-employment income. Joanie anticipates that her gross self-employment income will increase to $100,000 within the next two years and eventually level off at $300,000. She seeks your advice on selecting a qualified retirement plan that meets her primary objective. Each objective listed below should be viewed independently and treated as Joanie's primary objective.

1. To achieve the largest contribution and deduction amounts available by law.
2. To have the ability to continue with the same type of plan in the event the business becomes incorporated.
3. To have the freedom to manage the plan's investment funds.
4. To be able to impose vesting restrictions on employer contributions in the event full-time employees are later hired.
5. To have the flexibility to vary contributions from year to year or even to skip a year altogether.
6. To be permitted to establish the plan and make contributions after the current tax year has ended and still be able to claim deductions retroactively on the current-year tax return.
7. To have the flexibility to allow voluntary employee salary deferral contributions in the event employees are later hired.
8. To minimize the cost and effort associated with setting up and maintaining the plan.
9. To have the ability to roll account funds into a Roth IRA.
10. To be permitted to make age 50+ catch-up contributions.

Personal Retirement Plans for Working Individuals

Individuals with taxable compensation who either are not covered by a qualified employer-sponsored plan (such as a 401(k) plan) or who desire to provide for additional retirement income may choose between two tax-favored arrangements to meet their retirement planning needs: the traditional individual retirement account (IRA) and the Roth IRA. A review and comparison of these arrangements is provided in the sections that follow.

¶24,601   ## COMMON RULES FOR TRADITIONAL AND ROTH IRAS

The rules governing traditional and Roth IRAs are the same with respect to:

- contribution limits,
- minimum compensation requirements,
- investment alternatives,
- establishment and funding deadlines,
- spousal IRAs,
- saver's credit for IRA contributions, and,
- tax treatment for IRA losses.

These rules are explained below. The rules that are specific for each type of IRA are covered at ¶24,625 (traditional IRAs) and ¶24,635 (Roth IRAs).

Annual Dollar Limit

In 2017, contributions to a traditional or Roth IRA are subject to an annual dollar limit that generally is the lesser of:

1. $5,500 per individual ($11,000 if married); or
2. 100% of the compensation of the taxpayer's (and taxpayer's spouse if married) taxable compensation.

For individuals who are age 50 or older at the end of the year, the annual dollar limit is increased by $1,000 in 2017. Code Sec. 219(b). Contributions to a Roth IRA may be subject to income phase-out rules (see ¶24,635).

If an individual has more than one IRA, the annual dollar limit applies to the total amount of contributions made by the individual to all of the traditional, Roth, and "deemed" (see ¶24,535 and ¶24,545) IRAs. If an individual contributes less than the annual dollar limit, the individual cannot make up the difference in subsequent years.

Brokers' commissions paid by an IRA owner on transactions involving IRA assets count toward the annual dollar limit on contributions. However, trust administration fees paid by an IRA owner are not subject to the annual contribution limit. Rev. Rul. 86-142, 1986-2 CB 60.

The rules for deducting contributions to traditional IRAs are discussed at ¶24,625. The income phase-out rules specific to Roth IRAs are explained at ¶24,635.

Minimum Compensation Requirements

Individuals with qualified compensation may establish and contribute money to a traditional or Roth IRA to provide retirement income or to supplement employer-provided retirement income. Code Sec. 408. Qualified compensation includes taxable salary, wages, professional fees, net earnings from self-employment (including an active partner's distributive share of income from a service partnership) and any alimony included in gross income. Qualified compensation does not include the following amounts (Code Secs. 219(f) and 401(c)(2)):

1. Any amount received as a pension or annuity.
2. Any amount received as deferred compensation.
3. Interest.
4. Dividend income.
5. Income from a partnership if services that are a material income-producing factor are not provided
6. Unemployment compensation.

EXAMPLE 24.31

Nancy does not work, but during the current year, she receives $40,000 in taxable alimony from her ex-husband. Nancy has sufficient qualified compensation to contribute to an IRA for the current year.

EXAMPLE 24.32

Bobby was laid off from his job and has not been able to find work. During the current year, he received $6,000 in unemployment compensation and $50,000 from the proceeds of stock held for investment (resulting in a $30,000 gain). Bobby cannot contribute to an IRA in the current year since he has no qualified compensation for the year.

Investment Alternatives

A traditional IRA or a Roth IRA may be established at any time with a bank, savings and loan association, brokerage company, mutual fund, insurance company, or other IRS-approved institution. Code Sec. 408(a), (b). Contributions, other than rollover contributions, must be made in cash. With a self-directed IRA, an IRS-approved custodian agrees to allow the taxpayer to exercise greater control over investment decisions. Self-directed IRAs can be invested in real estate (including single-family homes, urban loft developments, and farms), mortgage notes, options on real estate, private placements, investment partnerships, and operating businesses. However, the assets must be purchased by the custodian (as directed by the taxpayer) in an arm's-length transaction. Under Sec. 4975(c)(1), the asset is not permitted to be titled in the taxpayer's name. Also, under Sec. 4975(e)(2), the taxpayer cannot have owned the property, live in the property, or be involved in the investment of the asset. This stipulation also applies to the taxpayer's spouse, parents, children, fiduciaries, business associates, and persons providing services to the plan. In order for the plan to be truly self-directed, the custodian handling cash transferred in and out of the IRA cannot give the taxpayer advice about investments. Thus, it is often advisable for the taxpayer to seek investment advice from an outside professional experienced in the type of investment held in the self-directed IRA.

TAX BLUNDER

Taxpayers should exercise caution when choosing investments for a traditional IRA account. The taxable amount of an IRA distribution is subject to ordinary income treatment regardless of the nature of the investment. Thus, capital assets that are normally subject to tax-favored treatment, e.g., stocks or tax-exempt municipal bonds, are treated as ordinary income property upon distribution.

Establishment and Funding Deadlines

Individuals may establish a traditional or Roth IRA and make contributions for a year at any time during that year or by the due date (not including extensions such as the six-month automatic extension) for filing their income tax return for that year. Code Sec. 219(f)(3). A contribution may be made for a year by the due date even though the contribution is made after a tax return is filed for the year (so long as the contribution is made on or before the due date for the return). Rev. Rul. 84-18, 1984-1 CB 88.

EXAMPLE 24.33

Kate Marani is eligible to make a deductible contribution to a traditional IRA in the current year but does not have sufficient money to make a contribution. However, if she could make a $1,500 contribution, she would be eligible for an income tax refund of $1,500. If Kate files her tax return after January 1 of the following year, and claims a $1,500 deduction for a contribution to a traditional IRA, she can use her $1,500 tax refund to make the contribution by the April 15 filing deadline.

Spousal IRAs

An individual ("contributing spouse") may establish and make contributions to a traditional or Roth IRA on behalf of a spouse with little or no income ("contributee spouse"). Code Sec. 219(c).

To be eligible to establish and fund a spousal IRA, a contributee spouse must satisfy the following requirements:

1.   A joint income tax return must be filed for the tax year.
2.   The amount of the contributee spouse's taxable compensation must be less than the taxable compensation of the contributing spouse.

Each year, a contributing spouse can fund a spousal IRA up to $5,500 in 2017, (plus a catch-up contribution of up to $1,000 in 2017 if the spouse is age 50 or older) by the end of the year. However, the amount contributed cannot exceed the sum of the following (Code Sec. 219(c)):

1.   The contributing spouse's taxable compensation.
2.   The taxable income of the contributee spouse, reduced by the amount of any deductible and nondeductible contributions made on behalf of the contributee spouse to a traditional or Roth IRA.

EXAMPLE 24.34

Conor and Sara Adelaide file a joint income tax return for 2017 and report a modified adjusted gross income of $65,000. Sara is 37, and Conor is 36. All of the income is earned by Conor. Sara stays at home and cares for their three children. Conor may contribute to a traditional IRA, a Roth IRA, or both, subject to an aggregate limit of $5,500. He also may also contribute up to $5,500 to either or both types of IRAs on behalf of Sara. Sara may not make any contributions on her own behalf because she has no taxable compensation.

Saver's Credit for Contributions

Individuals who have attained age 18 as of the close of the tax year are allowed an income tax credit equal to the applicable percentage of so much of their contributions to a traditional or Roth IRA (plus other qualified retirement savings contributions) that do not exceed $2,000. See ¶9033 for a further discussion of this credit.

Tax Treatment for IRA Losses

For traditional and Roth IRAs, loss recognition is permitted only if:

1.   all of the amounts in all of the taxpayer's traditional IRAs *or* Roth IRAs have been distributed, and,
2.   total distributions are less than the unrecovered basis.

The loss rule applies separately to each type of IRA. Thus, to claim a loss on a traditional IRA, all the traditional IRAs (but not Roth IRAs) owned by the individual have to be liquidated; and to report a loss on a Roth IRA, all the Roth IRAs (but not traditional IRAs) have to be liquidated.

The unrecovered basis is the portion of the account balance consisting of nondeductible contributions. Deductible traditional IRA contributions are not part of unrecovered basis because they have a zero basis (i.e., the compensation amount needed to contribute to a traditional IRA, minus an equal amount claimed as an IRA deduction).

Traditional and Roth IRA losses are reported on Schedule A as miscellaneous itemized deductions, subject to the 2%-of-adjusted-gross-income limit.

¶24,625   SPECIFIC RULES FOR TRADITIONAL IRAS

The rules that are common to both traditional and Roth IRAs are covered in the previous section (at ¶24,601). The rules that are specific for traditional IRAs are explained in this section.

Eligible Individual

Any individual with taxable compensation (described at ¶24,601) may be eligible to contribute to a traditional IRA. In the taxable year an individual turns 70½, no further contributions to a traditional IRA can be made by that individual. Secs. 219(d)(1) and 408(o). However, the individual may establish a new traditional IRA and fund it with funds transferred from another traditional IRA or employer-sponsored qualified retirement plan.

EXAMPLE 24.35	On November 8, Year 1, Baxter will turn 70. Since Baxter will turn 70½ on May 8, Year 2, he can continue to contribute to a traditional IRA through Year 1, provided he has compensation in those years, but not in Year 2.

EXAMPLE 24.36	Margaret will turn 70 on April 2, Year 1. Since Margaret will turn 70½ in Year 1, i.e., on October 2, Year 1, she can no longer contribute to a traditional IRA beginning on January 1, Year 1.

Deduction Limit

Individuals may deduct the full amount of their contributions to a traditional IRA (subject to the annual dollar limit discussed at ¶24,601) unless they or their spouse are active participants in a pension, profit-sharing, or stock bonus plan that is a qualified retirement plan, a Section 403(a) annuity plan, a tax-deferred Section 403(b) annuity plan, an SEP, a SIMPLE plan, or a plan established for its employees by the United States, any state or political subdivision of a state, or any agency or instrumentality of any of the foregoing. Code Sec. 219(g). No deduction is allowed for amounts transferred from another traditional IRA or employer-sponsored qualified retirement plan. Code Sec. 219(d)(2). The deduction is an above-the-line deduction. Code Sec. 62(a)(7).

Deduction Limit for Nonparticipants

If *neither* taxpayer nor taxpayer's spouse (if married) participates in a qualified employer-sponsored retirement plan, then each individual's traditional IRA contribution is fully deductible (within the limits discussed at ¶24,601), regardless of modified adjusted gross income (MAGI). For purposes of the IRA deduction limitation rules, MAGI is the taxpayer's AGI (and that of the taxpayer's spouse, if applicable) determined without taking into account the IRA deduction amount (if any), the foreign earned income exclusion, the foreign housing exclusion, Series EE bond interest that is excludable because the bonds are used to pay the costs of higher education and the manufacturing deduction allowed under Code Sec. 199.

EXAMPLE 24.37	Mr. and Mrs. Harralson's 2017 joint income exceeds $1 million. Neither spouse participates in an employer-sponsored qualified retirement plan. If each spouse contributes $5,500 into separate traditional IRAs, they may report an $11,000 IRA deduction on their 2017 joint return. The Income phase-out rules (explained below) do not apply if neither spouse participates in an employer-sponsored retirement plan.

Deduction Limit for Active Participants

If a taxpayer is an active participant in an employer-sponsored qualified retirement plan, the general limit for traditional IRA deductions is phased out proportionately according to the MAGI figures listed at Exhibit 12.

Exhibit 12. PHASE-OUT RANGES FOR TRADITIONAL IRA DEDUCTIONS OF ACTIVE PARTICIPANTS IN 2017		
Filing Status:	Beginning MAGI Amount:	Ending MAGI Amount:
Single and head of household	$62,000	$72,000
Married filing jointly	$99,000	$119,000
Married filing separately	0	$10,000

An individual's modified adjusted gross income (MAGI) is the individual's adjusted gross income, including any Social Security and tier 1 Railroad Retirement Act benefits that have to be included in gross income and applying the passive loss limitations. Modified adjusted gross income also includes interest from U.S. savings bonds used to pay college expenses, employer-provided adoption assistance, interest paid on education loans, foreign earned income, the foreign housing cost exclusion or deduction, the deduction for qualified tuition and related expenses, and contributions to traditional IRAs.

The amount of the reduction is determined by multiplying the annual limitation by a fraction whose numerator is the excess of the taxpayer's modified adjusted gross income for the year over the applicable dollar amount and whose denominator is $10,000 ($20,000 if the taxpayer is a qualifying widow(er) or the taxpayer is married and filing a joint return, unless the taxpayer is not an active participant but his or her spouse is). The annual dollar limitation cannot be reduced below $200 until the amount of the reduction exceeds the annual limitation. Any reduction that is not a multiple of $10 is rounded to the next lowest $10.

The IRS Form W-2 that an individual receives from an employer will indicate whether the individual is an active participant in an employer's retirement plan. If an individual and the individual's spouse is an active participant, the deductible amount may be reduced (but not below zero). The amount of the reduction depends on the individual's tax filing status and modified adjusted gross income. Although the amount of deductible contributions that an individual can make to a traditional IRA may be reduced, the nondeductible amount nevertheless can be contributed to a traditional IRA as a nondeductible contribution. IRS Form 8606, Nondeductible IRAs, must be filed with the contributor's tax return for the year a nondeductible contribution is made.

EXAMPLE 24.38

Mr. & Mrs. Smith, both age 25, report $116,000 joint MAGI in 2017. Each spouse is an active participant in a qualified employer-sponsored retirement plan. If each spouse contributes $5,500 into separate traditional IRAs ($11,000 total), they may report only a $3,300 deduction ($1,650 attributable to each spouse) on their 2016 joint return. The deductible amount must be phased out because (a) each spouse is an active participant and (b) joint MAGI is within the $99,000-to-$119,000 phase-out range for active participants. The $1,650 deductible amount attributable to each spouse is computed as follows:

$1,650 deduction = $5,500 contribution − $5,500 × [($116,000 − $99,000) ÷ ($119,000 − $99,000)]

Deduction Limit for Non-Active Spouses of Active Participants

If the spouse of an active participant does not participate in an employer plan, the $5,500 ($6,500 if age 50 or older) maximum traditional IRA deduction attributable to the non-participating spouse (but not the active-participant spouse), is phased out at MAGI levels between *$186,000 and $196,000*, jointly computed. Code Sec. 219(g)(7). This range is favorable relative to the *$99,000-to-$119,000* phase-out range that applies to active-participant spouses.

EXAMPLE 24.39	Referring to the preceding example above, if Mr. Smith had not been an active participant in a qualified employer-sponsored plan, the deduction attributable to him would have been the same as his $5,500 contribution since the Smiths' $116,000 joint MAGI did not exceed the $186,000 MAGI phase-out threshold for nonparticipants. The deduction attributable to Mrs. Smith remains at $1,650 as explained in the preceding problem.

EXAMPLE 24.40	Mr. & Mrs. Jones, both in their 40's, report $195,000 joint MAGI for 2017. Only Mrs. Jones was an active participant in a qualified employer-sponsored retirement plan. Each may contribute $5,500 into a traditional IRA, regardless of MAGI or active participation in a qualified employer plan. However, only a $550 deduction attributable to Mr. Jones may be reported on the joint return since (a) Mr. Jones is a nonparticipant and (b) joint MAGI is within the $186,000-to-$196,000 MAGI phase-out range for nonparticipants. The $550 deductible amount attributable to Mr. Jones is computed as follows:

$550 deduction = $5,500 contribution – $5,500 × [($195,000 – $186,000) ÷ ($196,000 – $186,000)]

PLANNING POINTER	Any income generated from a nondeductible contribution to a traditional IRA is tax deferred. However, a better avenue may be to contribute a nondeductible amount into a Roth IRA where the income generally accumulates tax-free.

Borrowing to Fund a Traditional IRA

The money needed to fund a traditional IRA may be borrowed without disallowance of the interest deduction. The interest deduction however, cannot exceed net investment income. (See ¶8,680 for a discussion on investment expense limitations).

Taxation of Distributions

If a distribution is made to the IRA owner or a beneficiary and no nondeductible contributions were made to the traditional IRA, the entire amount received by the IRA owner or beneficiary has to be included in the recipient's gross income (unless the amount received is rolled over into another traditional IRA or employer-sponsored qualified retirement plan that can accept rollover contributions). The amount of the distribution has to be included in gross income as ordinary income even though earnings consisted, in part, of capital gains. Code Sec. 408(d).

If nondeductible contributions were made to the traditional IRA, the beneficiary has basis in the IRA, and distributions are treated as partly taxable and partly as a return of capital under the rules (Code Sec. 72) for taxing annuities.

When applying these annuity rules, Code Secs. 408(d)(1) and (2) require:

1. all traditional IRAs of an individual (including SEPs described at ¶24,535 and SIMPLEs described at ¶24,545) to be treated as one contract;
2. all distributions during the individual's tax year to be treated as one distribution; and
3. the value of the contract, income on the contract, and investment in the contract to be calculated (after adding back distributions made during the year) as of the close of the calendar year in which the taxable year begins.

EXAMPLE 24.41   Ted Ransopher, age 60, maintains separate IRA accounts at three banks, Tau, Alpha, and Chi. For each bank, the type of IRA, form of investment, and annual return is shown below.

Investment Information:	Tau Bank	Alpha Bank	Chi Bank
Type of IRA	Traditional	Traditional	SEP
Type of investment	Mutual Fund	CD	CD
Annual Return	0%	6%	6%
	(underperforming)		

Ted's tax accountant reports the following IRA information pertaining to each bank as of year-end (after adding basic distributions made during the year):

Year-End IRA Information:	Tau Bank		Alpha Bank		Chi Bank	
	Amount	%	Amount	%	Amount	%
After-tax contributions	600,000	100%	0	0%	0	0%
Before-tax contributions	0	0%	100,000	50%	100,000	50%
Income accumulation	0	0%	100,000	50%	100,000	50%
Balance	$600,000	100%	$200,000	100%	$200,000	100%

During the current year, Ted withdrew $100,000 from the under-performing IRA account at Tau Bank. Even though the $600,000 adjusted account balance at Tau Bank consisted entirely of after-tax contributions, only 60 percent of the withdrawal ($60,000) is tax-free while 40 percent ($40,000) is taxable. The reason: in determining how much of the $100,000 distribution tax-free, the IRA balances at all three banks must be combined and viewed as one account. The analysis is shown below.

Tau, Alpha, and Chi Bank Accounts Viewed as One Account:

Components of Account Balance	Three Banks Combined	%
After-tax amounts:		
Nondeductible contributions	600,000	60%
Before-tax amounts		
Deductible contributions	200,000	20%
Income accumulation	200,000	20%
Total before-tax amounts	400,000	40%
IRA account balance	$1,000,000	100%

Required Minimum Distributions (RMDs)

The owner of a traditional IRA must withdraw at least a minimum amount of assets from the traditional IRA each year starting April 1 of the year following the year the owner attains age 70½. If the required minimum distribution is not made, a 50 percent excise tax has to be paid on the amount not distributed as required. Code Sec. 4974(a). The penalty is calculated using IRS Form 5329, Additional Taxes on Qualified Plans (Including IRAs) and Other Tax-Favored Accounts. These rules are similar to the rules governing qualified employer-sponsored plans and governmental 457(b) plans (see ¶24,235).

If an individual maintaining more than one traditional IRA in a calendar year is required to receive a minimum distribution, the RMD amount from each IRA must be computed separately and the separate amounts totaled. The total amount may be withdrawn from one or more of the IRAs in any amount the individual chooses. Reg. §1.408-8, Q&A-9.

Rollovers of IRA Assets

Assets in a traditional IRA may be transferred to or from another IRA, a qualified employer-sponsored plan, or a governmental 457(b) plan. The rules that apply to rollovers are explained at ¶24,345.

Death of IRA Owner

How the required minimum distributions are calculated after the death of an IRA owner depends on who is the designated beneficiary of the traditional IRA and whether the IRA owner died before or after the required beginning date. The rules governing after-death distributions are covered at ¶24,235.

Penalty for Premature Distributions

A non-qualified distribution prior to age 59 ½ is fully taxable and subject to a 10% nondeductible penalty. A premature distribution of the full account balance may be deemed to occur if the participant borrows from the IRA or pledges it as loan collateral. However, a *60-day* grace period is allowed if treated as a rollover from or to another qualified retirement plan. These rules are explained at ¶24,235.

¶24,635

RULES SPECIFIC FOR ROTH IRAS

This section addresses the rules that apply only to Roth IRAs. The rules that are common to both traditional and Roth IRAs were previously explained at ¶24,601.

Comparison of Features Between Traditional and Roth IRAs

The differences between a traditional IRA and a Roth IRA include the following:

- Individuals may contribute to a Roth IRA without age restrictions. Individuals may contribute to a traditional IRA until the year in which they attain the age of 70½.
- Contributions to a Roth IRA are never tax deductible; contributions to a traditional IRA may be tax deductible.
- Earnings from a Roth IRA may be exempt from income tax. Earnings from a traditional IRA are taxed when withdrawn.
- The owner of a Roth IRA has penalty-free access to direct contributions and to nontaxable rollover contributions (but not to taxable rollover contributions and accumulated earnings), at anytime.
- AGI restrictions affect the amount of Roth IRA contributions; different AGI restrictions affect the amount of traditional IRA deductions.
  See Exhibit 13 for a side-by-side comparison of the major features of these two plans.

Contribution Limits

The annual dollar limit on Roth contributions, explained at ¶24,601, is reduced to the extent that an individual's modified adjusted gross income exceeds the applicable dollar amount. The amount of the reduction is determined by multiplying the annual dollar limit by a fraction whose numerator is the excess of the taxpayer's modified adjusted gross income for the year over the applicable dollar amount and whose denominator is $15,000 ($10,000 if the taxpayer is filing a joint return or is married but filing a separate return or is a qualifying widow(er)). The annual dollar limit cannot be reduced below $200 until the amount of the reduction exceeds the annual limitation. Any reduction that is not a multiple of $10 is rounded to the next lowest $10.

An individual's modified adjusted gross income (MAGI) is the same term that is used in applying the phase-out rules for traditional IRA deductions (see ¶24,625).

The table at Exhibit 13 summarizes the limits on the amount that can be contributed to a Roth IRA for 2017.

Exhibit 13. PHASE-OUT RANGES FOR ROTH IRA CONTRIBUTIONS IN 2017		
Filing Status:	**Beginning MAGI Amount:**	**Ending MAGI Amount:**
Single and head of household	$118,000	$133,000
Married filing jointly	$186,000	$196,000
Married filing separately	0	$10,000

EXAMPLE 24.42	Conor Finn, age 25, files as a single individual. In 2017, he reports MAGI in the amount of $121,750, all from a salary. He has not yet made any traditional, Roth, or deemed IRA contributions for the year. Conor is eligible to contribute up to $4,125 to a Roth IRA. $4,125 is the least of (a), (b) or (c), where,

(a) = $4,125, i.e., $5,500 annual dollar limit − $1,375 phase-out amount, where the $1,375 phase-out amount = $5,500 × [($121,750 − $117,000) ÷ ($133,000 − $118,000)];

(b) = $5,500, i.e., $5,500 annual dollar limit − $0 previous IRA contributions for 2017; and

(c) = $121,750, i.e., $121,750 qualified compensation − $0 previous IRA contributions for 2017.

EXAMPLE 24.43	Referring to the preceding example, assume that Conor has already contributed $3,000 to a traditional IRA in 2017. Conor is eligible to contribute up to $2,500 to a Roth IRA in 2017. The amount represents the least of (a), (b) or (c), where,

(a) = $4,125, i.e., $5,500 annual dollar limit − $1,375 phase-out amount, (as computed Example 24.42);

(b) = $2,500, i.e., $5,500 annual dollar limit − $3,000 previous traditional IRA contribution for 2017; and

(c) = $118,750, i.e., $121,750 earned income − $3,000 previous traditional IRA contribution for 2017.

EXAMPLE 24.44	Joe Ragner, age 25, lives with his parents and files as a single individual. In 2017, he reports AGI in the amount of $5,000, which consists of: (1) $2,000 self-employment income after the deduction for ½ self-employment taxes, and (2) $3,000 taxable unemployment compensation. Joe has not yet made any IRA contributions for the year. Joe could contribute up to $2,000 to a Roth IRA. This contribution limit is the least of (a), (b), or (c), where,

(a) = $5,500, i.e., $5,500 annual dollar limit − $0 phase-out amount;

(b) = $5,500, i.e., $5,500 annual dollar limit − $0 previous IRA contributions for 2017; and

(c) = $2,000, i.e., $2,000 qualified compensation − $0 previous IRA contributions for 2017.

The $3,000 taxable unemployment income does not qualify as compensation for purposes of determining the annual dollar limit.

Conversion of a Traditional, SEP or SIMPLE IRA to a Roth IRA

Individuals and married couples filing jointly may be able to convert amounts in a traditional IRA (or in a SEP or SIMPLE IRA treated as a "deemed" traditional IRA—see ¶24,535 and ¶24,545) into a Roth IRA by directing the trustee to transfer the amounts from the traditional IRA to a Roth IRA or by withdrawing the amounts from the traditional IRA and redepositing the amounts in a Roth IRA as a qualified rollover contribution. There is a "qualified rollover contribution" if an amount received is paid into a Roth IRA no later than 60 days after the date on which the amount was received. Unlike the rule for indirect transfers between traditional IRAs, there is no one-year waiting period between rollover contributions.

Taxpayers making rollovers must recognize the entire amount of the taxable distribution amount as income in the tax year the distribution takes place. Amounts transferred are not subject to the 10% early-withdrawal penalty; however, the "pre-tax" portion of the transferred amount (i.e., accumulated earnings plus deductible contributions) must be included in the taxpayer's gross income.

EXAMPLE 24.45	Cindy Ragan maintains a traditional IRA that was created with deductible contributions. Her account balance as of March 4 is $60,000, consisting of (1) $10,000 deductible contributions, (2) $20,000 after-tax contributions, and (3) $30,000 accumulated earnings. If Cindy decides to rollover her $60,000 traditional IRA balance into a Roth IRA on this date, she must include $40,000 in gross income for the year.

¶24,635

PLANNING POINTER

1. A taxpayer who wishes to convert a traditional IRA into a Roth IRA should consider the advantages associated with staggering partial rollovers over more than one year. A full conversion within one year may force the taxpayer into a higher tax bracket (a "bunching" effect). An increase from, say, the 33% bracket to the 35% bracket may not be consequential. However, an increase from, say, the 15% bracket to the 25% or higher bracket could create a severe tax burden for the taxpayer. Another advantage associated with staggered rollovers is that a taxpayer may have cash available to pay tax on a partial conversion but not enough to pay tax on a full conversion.
2. If a traditional IRA contains different types of assets, the taxpayer may indicate which ones to move. For example, if a traditional IRA is split between two mutual funds, the taxpayer may choose to move one fund or the other to the Roth IRA, or move part of each.

Roth-to-Traditional IRA Reconversions

A taxpayer may wish to "undo" a traditional-to-Roth IRA conversion. The two most common reasons for reconversions are (a) *market-driven motivation*, and (b) the need for *corrective action*.

Market-driven Motivation

A taxpayer would be motivated to reconvert a Roth IRA back to a traditional IRA if the taxable amount transferred to a Roth declined in value. Without the reconversion, the taxpayer might have to pay taxes on income that had disappeared in a market decline.

EXAMPLE 24.46

Will Feldman maintains a $100,000 taxable balance in his traditional IRA. In February of the current year, he converts the $100,000 balance into a Roth IRA. Several months later, the Roth IRA loses 40% of its value. Without a reconversion, Will would have to pay ordinary income tax on $100,000 by April 15 of the following year, even though only $60,000 of that amount remained in his Roth IRA account.

Corrective Action

If, after a direct contribution to a Roth IRA, the taxpayer determined that MAGI (as defined at ¶24,625) for the year exceeded the income limit for direct Roth contributions ($118,000-$133,000 range for single filers; $186,000-$196,000 range for joint filers), a corrective reconversion would be necessary. Otherwise the Roth earnings since inception would be subject to income taxes and penalties.

Reconversion Deadline

The deadline for "undoing" a traditional-to-Roth IRA conversion depends on whether the taxpayer's motivation for reconversion is *market-driven* or *corrective*. If market driven, the reconversion can be made as late as October 15 of the year following the conversion year, provided the automatic six-month extension has been timely filed.

Corrective reconversions can also be made as late as October 15 of the year following a traditional-to-Roth conversion year. However, unlike the deadline for market-driven conversions, filing an automatic six-month extension is not required to meet this deadline. However, a timely return must have been filed for the conversion tax year and an amended return must be filed to reflect the reconversion.

EXAMPLE 24.47

In January of the current year, Sally made a $5,500 contribution to a Roth IRA. Sally was certain her MAGI would be low enough to enable her to qualify for a full $5,500 Roth IRA contribution. However, later in the year, her employer gave her a very large and unexpected bonus, which caused her MAGI to exceed the allowed limit for any Roth IRA contribution. Her Roth IRA, because of some wise investments, had grown to $12,000 during the year. If Sally transfers the $5,500 from the Roth IRA back into her personal checking account, the entire pre-tax portion of her Roth IRA balance, $6,500, will be subject to taxation and the 10-percent early withdrawal penalty. Sally can avoid this unfavorable result by transferring the entire balance of the Roth IRA to a traditional IRA. Sally has until October 15 of the following year to make the corrective reconversion. This favorable treatment is subject to three requirements: 1. a timely return filed for the original conversion year; 2. a reconversion transfer made by October 15 of the year following the conversion year; and 3. an amended return to reflect the reconversion.

Roth Distributions

Code Sec. 408A(d)(4) imposes strict aggregation rules for multiple Roth IRA accounts and ordering rules for distributions of Roth contributions, conversions, and earnings for tax purposes. These rules are discussed below.

Aggregation Rules for Multiple Roth IRAs

In order to determine the tax effect of a Roth distribution, Roth IRAs, whether or not maintained in separate accounts, will be considered a single Roth IRA. (Code Sec. 408A(d)(4)(A). The rules for aggregating multiple Roth IRA accounts must follow the rules under Code Sec. 408(d)(2) for combining multiple traditional IRAs (see ¶24,625).

Ordering Rules for Distributions

Once the Roth IRA accounts have been aggregated (if necessary), the ordering rules require the Roth IRA holder to treat any amounts distributed as coming from the following sources in the order listed (Code Sec. 408(A)(d)(4)(B)):

1. Direct contributions (e.g., payments by check) to Roth IRA accounts are deemed to be withdrawn first;
2. Then, the taxable amount of rollover contributions, on a first-in-first-out basis;
3. Next, the nontaxable amount of rollover contributions, on a first-in-first-out basis;
4. Finally, earnings from the Roth IRA are treated as withdrawn.

Tax Consequences

In determining the taxability of Roth IRA distributions, it is first necessary to determine if the distribution is a qualified distribution or a non-qualified distribution. *Qualified* Roth distributions are not subject to income tax or the additional 10 percent penalty. *Nonqualified* Roth distributions are taxable only to the extent of the earnings portion of the Roth IRA included in the distribution. A 10 percent penalty is imposed on nonqualified distributions only to the extent of *taxable rollover contributions* and *accumulated earnings*. Nonqualified distributions consisting of *direct contributions* or *nontaxable rollover contributions* are not subject to the 10 percent penalty.

Qualified Distributions

A payment or distribution is a "qualified distribution" if two tests have been satisfied:

1. **Five-year holding period.** A qualified distribution must be made after the five-tax-year period beginning with the first tax year for which the individual made a contribution to a Roth IRA (or the individual's spouse made a contribution to a Roth IRA) established for that individual. (Code Sec. 408A(d)(2)(B). The date of a five-year holding period begins on January 1 of the contribution year. For *direct contributions*, once the five-year holding period requirement has been satisfied for the initial contribution, this requirement is deemed to be satisfied for all subsequent direct contributions, even if made into different Roth IRAs. For *rollover contributions*, a separate five-year holding period applies to each rollover.
2. **Qualifying event.** Code Sec. 408A(d)(A) identifies a qualifying event as a distribution made
   a. on or after the date on which the individual attains age 59 ½;
   b. to a beneficiary (or to the individual's estate) on or after the individual's death;
   c. because the individual is disabled (an individual is considered to be disabled if he or she is unable to engage in any substantial gainful activity by reason of any medically determinable physical or mental impairment that can be expected to result in death or to be of long-continued and indefinite duration); or
   d. for a "first home" purchase, not to exceed $10,000 (lifetime aggregate limit). (See ¶24,245 for a further discussion of this qualifying event.)

Nonqualified Distributions

A distribution that is not a qualified distribution (and neither is contributed to another Roth IRA in a qualified rollover contribution nor constitutes a corrective distribution) is includible in the owner's gross income to the extent that the amount of the distribution, when added to the amount of all prior distributions from the owner's Roth IRAs (whether or not they were qualified distributions) and reduced by the amount of those prior distributions previously includible in gross income, exceeds the owner's contributions to all of the owner's Roth IRAs. Any amount distributed as a corrective distribution (described earlier) is treated as if it never had been contributed. Reg. §1.408A-6, Q&A-4.

Returns of taxable rollover contributions that were not held in the IRA account for five years and taxable earnings are subject to the 10 percent early distribution penalty. Reg. §1.408A-6, Q&A-5. Determining the 10 percent penalty requires knowledge of extensive information, including the amount of the distribution, basis in contributions, basis in conversions, years in which conversions were made, and the amount of earnings. This requires diligent tracking of amounts contributed, amounts converted, and amounts previously distributed.

The tax consequences associated with qualified and nonqualified Roth distributions are summarized at Exhibit 14.

Exhibit 14. APPLYING THE TWO QUALIFYING TESTS TO ROTH DISTRIBUTIONS

Tests:	1st Direct Contributions	2nd Taxable Portion of Rollover Contributions	3rd Nontaxable Portion of Rollover Contribution	4th Accumulated Earnings
(1) Has the five-year holding period requirement been met?				
If yes: →	Penalty-free	Penalty-free	Penalty-free	Penalty-free only if (2) below is also met
If no: →	Penalty-free	10% Penalty	Penalty-free	10% Penalty
(2) Has the age 59 ½, death, disability, higher education, or 1st time home buying requirement been met?				
If yes: →	Tax-free	Tax-free	Tax-free	Tax-free
If no: →	Tax-free	Tax-free	Tax-free	Taxable

For direct contributions, once the five-year holding period requirement has been satisfied for the initial contribution, this requirement is deemed to be satisfied for all subsequent direct contributions, even if made into different Roth IRAs.

EXAMPLE 24.48

John-Paul, age 30, begins making direct contributions to a Roth IRA in Year 1. He contributes $2,000 per year from Year 1 to Year 7, resulting in a $14,000 Roth direct contribution basis. If, in Year 8, John-Paul takes a Roth distribution of $14,000 or less, none of the distribution would be subject to income tax (since it represents a return of basis), and none of the distribution would be subject to the 10 percent early distribution penalty. *Note: If John-Paul had taken a distribution in excess of $14,000, the amount distributed in excess of $14,000 (i.e., accumulated earnings) would have been subject to both income tax and the 10% early distribution penalty.*

PLANNING POINTER

An individual who would not reach age 59 ½ (or satisfy any other qualifying event) in five years can nonetheless convert a traditional IRA or employer-provided account (e.g., 401(k)) to a Roth IRA, and receive a distribution of the rollover contribution after five years, without being subject to the 10 percent penalty. In contrast, the same distribution from a traditional IRA or employer-provided account would be subject to the 10 percent penalty.

EXAMPLE 24.49

Conor, age 25, rolled over a $14,000 deductible traditional IRA to a Roth IRA in Year 1. Thus the entire rollover amount was taxed in Year 1, creating a $14,000 Roth rollover contribution basis. Conor made no additional contributions to the Roth IRA, and did not convert any other amounts. If, in Year 6, Conor takes a Roth distribution of $14,000 or less, none of the distribution would be subject to income tax (since it represents a return of basis), and none of the distribution would be subject to the 10 percent early distribution penalty (since separate 5-year holding period requirements had been met for each of the five rollover contributions). *Note: If Conor had taken the distribution from a traditional IRA instead of a Roth IRA, the entire distribution would have been subject to the 10% early distribution penalty since he had not reached age 59 ½ on the distribution date (or satisfied any other qualifying events).*

After-death Distributions

The minimum distribution and incidental death benefit rules that apply to traditional IRAs do not apply to Roth IRAs prior to the owner's death. Code Secs. 401(a)(9) and 408A. Thus, no distributions from a Roth IRA have to be made after the owner turns 70½. However, after the death of the owner of a Roth IRA, the minimum required distribution rules applicable to traditional IRAs following the owner's death apply to Roth IRAs. These rules are covered at ¶24,235.

Reporting Roth IRA Distributions

Distributions from Roth IRAs are reported on Part III of Form 8606 (Nondeductible IRAs). If the 10% early distribution tax applies, it is reported on Form 5329 (Additional Taxes on Qualified Plans (Including IRAs) and Other Tax-Favored Accounts).

Exhibit 15. Personal Retirement Plans for Working Individuals

Features:	Traditional IRA	Roth IRA
Ideal Investor Time Frame	Shorter time horizon	Longer time horizon
Age of Contributor	Must not be 70½ or older	No age restrictions
Minimum Compensation Requirement?	Yes	Yes
Establishment Deadline	By filing due date (April 15 of following year)	Same deadline
Contribution Deadline	By filing due date (April 15 of following year)	Same deadline
Maximum Contribution Amount	$5,500 ($6,500 if age 50+) aggregate limit for traditional IRAs, deemed IRAs (SEP or SIMPLE), and Roth IRAs	Same limit
Contribution Phase-Out (MAGI Limits)	None	MFJ: $186,000 – 196,000 Single: $118,000 – $133,000
Deduction Phase-Out (MAGI Limits)	For active participants: MFJ: $99,000 – $119,000 Single: $62,000 – $72,000 For nonparticipant spouses of active participants: $186,000 – $196,000 For nonparticipants (including married taxpayers who are both nonparticipants): Contributions are fully deductible	Never deductible
IRA Earnings	Taxed when withdrawn	Tax exempt if conditions are met
Penalty for Early Withdrawals	10%	10%
Penalty for Late Withdrawals	50% (distributions to begin no later than April 1 after the year in which the participant becomes age 70½)	None (no minimum distribution rules apply while participant is living)

Nonqualified Deferred Compensation Plans

The most common types of nonqualified deferred compensation plans include:

■ Rabbi Trusts (at ¶24,705),
■ Incentive stock options (at ¶24,725),
■ Nonqualified stock options (at ¶24,735).

General concepts common to nonqualified plans and features associated with specific plans are explained in the sections that follow.

¶24,701   NONQUALIFIED PLANS—BASIC CONCEPTS

Common Characteristics

Nonqualified deferred compensation arrangements provide employees or independent contractors with future compensation for work performed currently. Being "nonqualified" means these plans need not meet the rules for funding, distributions, vesting, nondiscrimination, and other criteria imposed on qualified plans (discussed at ¶24,201 to ¶24,285). However, under a nonqualified plan, an employer generally is not entitled to deduct contributions paid for the benefit of an employee (or independent contractor) until the beneficiary reports taxable compensation from the contributions.

Tax Effect to Employees

Compensation payable in the future (deferred events) is not taxed currently if:

- the plan is neither funded nor secured by a negotiable and freely transferable promissory note (i.e., the *economic benefit doctrine*—see ¶4101—is not met if the employee relies on the employer's mere promise to pay); or
- the employee's right to compensation amounts is subject to a substantial risk of forfeiture (i.e., the *constructive receipt doctrine*—see ¶4125— is not met if the employee lacks complete dominion and control over the amounts earned).

The courts have ruled that substantial risk of forfeiture does not mean the likelihood of a forfeiture-triggering event, rather, the likelihood of forfeiture once a triggering event occurs. For example, in *Robinson*, 86-2 USTC ¶ 9790 (1ˢᵗ Cir. 1986), an employee received restricted stock options that carried a risk of forfeiture one year beyond the exercise date. The triggering event that would cause forfeiture, a sale by the employee of the stock within one year of the exercise date, was highly improbable. Nevertheless, the court allowed deferral until one year later, when the restriction was lifted. It reasoned that, despite the improbability of the employee selling the stock during the one-year period, forfeiture was highly likely if this improbable event had occurred.

EXAMPLE 24.50

Ernie Larkins, age 22, is to receive a $1 million bonus in year 1, for signing a professional football contract. Realizing that his quarterbacking days may be numbered, he wishes to defer the bonus for 10 years, beginning in the year he attains age 32. The employer offers to establish an escrow account in which the $1 million would be transferred to an escrow agent. The escrow agent, at her sole discretion, would invest the funds in securities, which may act as a hedge against inflation. After ten years, the bonus becomes payable in equal amounts over years 11 through 20. With this arrangement the $1 million bonus would be taxable in full in year 1 since it would be both funded and nonforfeitable. The employer would be entitled to a $1 million deduction in year 1.

EXAMPLE 24.51

Referring to the preceding example above, Ernie's bonus could be structured in one of two ways to achieve tax deferral:

1. Avoiding the economic benefits doctrine. If the employer gives a mere promise to pay the $1 million plus accrued interest beginning in year 11 through 20, rather than actually funding an escrow account, the bonus would be tax deferred. This arrangement may be appropriate with a financially secure employer.
2. Avoiding the constructive receipts doctrine. Had there been a substantial risk of forfeiture (i.e., payment conditioned upon performance, attendance, gate receipts, etc.), the $1 million signing bonus could have been tax deferred until the earlier of:
   a. The date the risk of forfeiture disappears, or
   b. The dates of receipt, i.e., years 11 through 20.

Conditioning a substantial risk of forfeiture upon the achievement of specific performance by an employee may not be appealing, particularly when the employee is a professional athlete whose success or failure depends in part upon a team effort. However, as explained at ¶24,705, the Rabbi Trust has become a popular devise for creating the requisite substantial risk of forfeiture without future payment being conditioned upon the employee's performance.

Applicability of Payroll Taxes

Nonqualified deferred compensation is part of the taxable wage base for both FICA and FUTA tax purposes. Under Code Secs. 3121(v) and 3306(r), amounts deferred under a "nonqualified deferred compensation plan" are included as wages for FICA and FUTA tax purposes in the later of:

1. the year in which the services are performed; or
2. the year in which there is no substantial risk of forfeiture of the amounts.

The amount included in the wage base generally is the principal amount credited to the employee for the period plus any income attributable to that amount through the date the amount is taken into account for FICA and FUTA tax purposes. Reg. §31.3121(v)(2)-1(c).

¶24,705   RABBI TRUSTS

A Rabbi Trust is an arrangement under which the employer places assets into an irrevocable trust to secure the payment of promised deferred compensation to selected employees. Rabbi Trusts have four common characteristics:

1. **Unsecured promise.** Employees earn compensation currently and receives an unsecured promise from the employer to pay at a future date.
2. **Employer creditors.** Trust assets are subject to claims of employer creditors, not employee creditors; employees must have no vested ownership rights (similar to beneficiaries of grantor trusts).
3. **Non-employee trustee.** No employee/beneficiary may serve as trustee.
4. **Trustee powers.** The trustee has full investment discretion.

Tax Effect on Employee

Employees may defer employer contributions to a Rabbi Trust for either of two reasons:

1. The *economic benefit doctrine* does not apply because the contributions are not unconditionally and irrevocably for the employees' benefit. This lack of immediate benefit to employees is the result of the trust's exposure to employer assets.
2. The *constructive receipt doctrine* does not apply because the employee cannot receive the deferred compensation until some future time such as the termination of employment or retirement.

Tax Effect on Employer

Employer contributions to the plan are not deductible until the year in which the employee reports taxable compensation. However, income earned by the trust is taxable to the employer if it is subject to the same restriction as the contributed amounts. If, on the other hand, employees have unrestricted access to the income earned by the trust, it is taxable to the employees, even if unpaid. The character of income earned depends on the character of the assets.

Origin of Rabbi Trust

The Rabbi Trust dates back to 1980, when IRS issued a favorable ruling on a trust funded by a congregation for the benefit of a rabbi. Trustees managed and invested the trust funds; income was distributed to the rabbi quarterly; and upon the rabbi's death, disability or retirement, the trust fund, including accumulated income, would be disbursed to the rabbi or his beneficiaries. During its existence, the trust's assets were available to the creditors of the grantors, but not those of the rabbi. IRS ruled that unpaid contributions provided no economic benefit to the rabbi since they were subject to the claims of the grantor's creditors. IRS also ruled that the constructive receipt doctrine should not apply because the employee could not receive the deferred compensation until some future time. *The IRS has issued guidance setting forth model Rabbi Trust provisions.* Rev. Proc. 92-64, 1992-2 C.B. 422, *modified in part by* Notice 2000-56, 2000-2 C.B. 393.

¶24,725   INCENTIVE STOCK OPTIONS (ISOS)

Tax Effect on Employees with ISOs

An ISO is a right granted by an employer corporation that allows an employee to purchase the employer's stock at a fixed price for a stated period of time. The employee thus benefits from the potential appreciation in the value of the underlying stock from the grant date to the exercise date of the option. ISOs have become very popular in recent years because of the favorable tax treatment afforded employees under Code Sec. 422. ISOs do not trigger ordinary income at the grant date or the exercise date. Instead, all of the potential income is treated as capital gain and is not recognized until the ultimate disposition of the stock by the employee.

Qualifying Dispositions

Holding Period Requirements

ISOs must satisfy a "one-two-three" holding period rule: the employee must hold onto the stock for at least *one* year after the exercise date and *two* years after the grant date. In addition, the exercise date must not occur more than *three* months after "employee" status has terminated. Code Sec. 422(a).

Other Qualifying Conditions

The option must also meet all of the following requirements under Code Sec. 422(b) in order to qualify for special tax treatment:

1. The plan must be approved by shareholders within 12 months of adoption;
2. The grant date must be within 10 years of plan adoption;
3. The exercisable date must be within 10 years of the grant date;
4. The option price must not be less than the fair market value at grant date;
5. The option must be nontransferable to third parties (except in death);
6. The employee-grantee must not own more than 10% of the company's stock immediately before grant date.

EXAMPLE 24.52

ABC Corp. grants George Willingham 1,000 ISOs on January 1, Year 1 (the "grant" date). On this date, the stock's fair market value is $10 per share and each ISO entitles the holder to buy one share of ABC stock for $10 (the exercise price). George can exercise the ISO after one year of employment but not more than 10 years after the grant date and not more than three months after the effective severance date in the event his employment is terminated. George exercises the ISOs on December 31, Year 2 (the "exercise" date) when the stock is worth $200 per share. He sells the stock on January 1, Year 4 (the "sale" date) for $250 per share. Neither the granting nor exercising of the stock will have regular tax consequences to George in a qualifying disposition (but see discussion on AMT below). In the year of sale, George will report a $240 per share long-term capital gain. ABC is not allowed any deduction in connection with the ISOs, since no ordinary income was recognized by George. See per share computations below.

Key Dates	Qualifying Disposition
Jan. 1, Year 1 (ISO is granted.)	No ordinary income (OI); ISO's tax basis = $0 per ISO ISO tax basis = $0 cost + $0 ordinary income
Dec. 31, Year 2 (ISO is exercised.)	No ordinary income (OI); stock basis = $10 per share Stock basis = $10 cost + $0 ordinary income
Jan. 1, Year 4 (Stock is sold.)	$240 per share long-term capital gain (LTCG) $240 LTCG = $250 sale price – $10 stock basis The holding period begins on January 1, Year 3, the day after the exercise date; therefore, the holding period is long-term.

Disqualifying Dispositions

If the employee fails to satisfy any part of the "one-two-three" rule above, the gain, up to the spread at the exercise date, will be treated as compensation income. Any excess will be treated as capital gain. Thus, an early disposition disqualifies the ISO and treats the transaction as if it were a nonqualified ISO, with the exception of the date of income recognition. The example below illustrates the effects of a disqualifying disposition.

EXAMPLE 24.53	Referring to the foregoing example, suppose that George Willingham sold his shares on June 30, Year 3. Because the stock was not held for one year from the exercise date, December 31, Year 3, George made a disqualifying disposition of the stock. As before, George will recognize no income on the grant date or on the exercise date. On June 30, Year 3 (the sale date) however, George will recognize $190 per share in ordinary income ($200 - $10) and $50 per share short-term capital gain ($250 - $200). The holding period of a disqualified ISO begins on the day after the exercise date; thus, George's holding period is short-term (from January 1, Year 3, the day after the exercise date, to June 30, Year 3, the sale date). ABC is allowed a corresponding deduction of $190 per share for its tax year which includes December 31, Year 3, George's year-end.

Key Dates	Disqualifying Disposition
Jan. 1, Year 1 (ISO is granted.)	No ordinary income (OI); ISO's tax basis = $0 per ISO ISO tax basis = $0 cost + $0 ordinary income
December 31, Year 2 (ISO is exercised.)	No tax effect; stock basis = $10 per share Stock basis = $10 cost + $0 ordinary income
June 30, Year 3 (Stock is sold.)	(a) $190 per share ordinary income (OI) $190 OI = $200 exercise price − $10 stock basis (b) $50 per share short-term capital gain (STCG) $50 STCG = $250 sale price − $200 FMV at exercise date The holding period begins on January 1, Year 3, the day after the exercise date; therefore, the holding period is short-term.

Alternative Minimum Tax

For alternative minimum tax (AMT) purposes, the spread between the ISO exercise price and the fair market value of the stock on the exercise date (or on the date a substantial risk of forfeiture has been lifted) is treated as a tax prefernce for AMT. The stock's AMT basis is increased by the income recognized. The disposition of the stock triggers a negative AMT adjustment, since the AMT basis includes the tax preference income.

¶24,735   NONQUALIFIED STOCK OPTIONS (NSOs)

Tax Effect on Employees with NSOs

Nonqualified stock options (NSOs) are currently the most popular method of stock acquisition plans. These options are sometimes labeled, "nonstatutory options," because they are not described anywhere in the Code. Thus, they are not afforded any favorable tax treatment; rather, they are taxed under Code Sec. 83(a).

NSO Taxation Upon Grant Date

A nonqualified stock option is taxed when it is granted if the NSO has a "readily ascertainable fair market value" at the grant date. Reg. §1.83-1(a) and Reg. §1.83-7(a). If an NSO has a readily ascertainable fair market value, the employee must recognize compensation in the amount of that fair market value in the year the NSO is granted. Reg. §1.83-1(a). If the employee paid for the NSO, he recognizes the value of the NSO minus its cost. The employee is not taxed again when he exercises the NSO and buys corporate stock. However, the employee is taxed when he sells the stock. The employee's basis in the stock is the fair market value of the NSO on which he paid taxes, plus the amount he paid for the stock. Capital gain or loss is recognized when the stock is sold.

An NSO that is not actively traded on an established market may still have a readily ascertainable fair market value only if all of the following requirements are met:

1. the option must be transferable,
2. the option must be exercisable immediately and in full when it is granted,
3. there can be no condition or restriction on the option that would have a significant effect on its fair market value, and
4. the fair market value of the option privilege must be readily ascertainable.

Because these requirements are seldom satisfied, most nonqualified options that are not traded on an established market do not have a readily ascertainable fair market value.

NSO Taxation upon Exercise Date

If the nonqualified option does not have a readily ascertainable fair market value, it is the exercise of the option, and not the grant, that triggers the taxable event. Reg. §1.83-7(a). When the employee exercises the NSO, the employee recognizes compensation in the amount of the fair market value of the stock purchased minus any amount paid for the stock. Later, when the employee sells the stock, any gain or loss recognized is treated as capital gain or loss. The employee's holding period of the stock begins the day after the NSO was exercised.

Holding Period

The holding period of stock acquired through an NSO begins on the date after the option is granted or exercised, depending on which event triggers compensation. If an NSO has a readily ascertainable fair market value (triggering compensation recognition at the grant date), the holding period of the stock begins on the day after the grant date. If the NSO has no readily ascertainable value and compensation is not recognized until the NSO is exercised, the holding period of the stock begins on the day after the exercise date.

Lapse of NSOs

When an employee allows an NSO with a readily ascertainable fair market value to lapse, the employee's capital loss is determined by the employee's basis in the NSO (i.e., the value of the NSO that was taxed). Code Sec. 1234(a)(2). The NSO is treated as if it were sold or exchanged on the date that it lapsed. Reg. §1.1234-1(b).

Tax Effect on Employer

An employer may deduct the value of an NSO as a business expense for the tax year in which the option is included in the gross income of the employee. When the NSO has a readily ascertainable value, the employer is allowed the deduction for the year in which the option is granted. When the NSO does not have a readily ascertainable value, the employer is allowed the deduction for the year in which the option is exercised. The employer's deduction equals the amount of compensation recognized by the employee. When the employer and the employee have different tax years, the employer claims the deduction in the tax year in which or with which the employee's tax year ends. Code Sec. 83(h).

EXAMPLE 24.54

XYZ Corp. grants Wesley Bloeme 1,000 NSOs on January 1, Year 1 (the "grant" date). Each NSO grants the holder the right to buy 1 share of XYZ stock for $10. Wesley can exercise the NSO after one year of employment. The NSO's readily ascertainable fair market value on the grant date is $50 per share. (Note that with NSOs, the exercise price may be below the market value of the stock since the Code Sec. 422(b)(4) pricing rules do not apply as they do for incentive stock options.) Wesley exercises the NSO on December 31, Year 2 (the "exercise" date) when the stock is worth $200 per share. He sells the stock on January 1, Year 4 (the "sale" date) for $250 per share. Wesley must recognize $50 per share compensation on the grant date and XYZ is allowed a corresponding deduction of $50 per share for its tax year which includes December 31, Year 1, Wesley's year-end. Wesley must also report a $190 per share long-term capital gain in the year of sale. See per share computations below.

Key Dates	Readily Ascertainable Value at Grant Date
Jan. 1, Year 1 (NSO is granted.)	Compensation (OI) = $50 per share $50 OI = $50 NSO market value – $0 cost] NSO tax basis = $50 per NSO $50 NSO tax basis = $0 cost + $50 OI
Dec. 31, Year 2 (NSO is exercised.)	No compensation (OI); stock basis = $60 $60 stock basis = $10 cost + $0 OI + $50 NSO basis
Jan. 1, Year 4 (Stock is sold.)	$190 per share long-term capital gain (LTCG) $190 LTCG = $250 selling price – $60 stock basis The holding period begins on January 2, Year 1, the day after grant date; therefore, the holding period is long-term.

EXAMPLE 24.55

Referring to the foregoing example, suppose that the XYZ NSO had no readily ascertainable value on the grant date. Wesley recognizes no compensation on the grant date. He recognizes $190 per share of ordinary compensation income on December 31, Year 2, when he exercises the NSO. XYZ will be allowed a deduction of the same $190 per share for its taxable year which contains December 31, Year 2, Wesley's year-end. Wesley will also recognize a $50 per share long-term gain upon the sale of the stock on January 1, Year 4, since his holding period was more than twelve months (January 1, Year 3 – January 1, Year 4.

Key Dates	No Readily Ascertainable Value at Grant Date
Jan. 1, Year 1 (NSO is granted.)	No compensation (OI); NSO tax basis = $0 per NSO NSO tax basis = $0 cost + $0 ordinary income
Dec. 31, Year 2 (NSO is exercised.)	Compensation (OI) = $190 per share $190 OI = $200 stock value – $10 cost] Stock basis = $200 per share $200 stock basis = $10 cost + $190 OI
Jan. 1, Year 4 (Stock is sold.)	$50 per share long-term capital gain (LTCG) $50 LTCG = $250 selling price – $200 stock basis The holding period begins on January 1, Year 3, the day after exercise date; therefore, the holding period is long-term.

Education Savings Vehicles

¶24,801   COVERDELL EDUCATION SAVINGS ACCOUNTS

A Coverdell education savings account ("Coverdell ESA") is a tax-favored vehicle that can be used to pay the qualified education expenses for the elementary, secondary, and college education of a designated beneficiary. Contributions to a Coverdell ESA are not deductible, but earnings on contributions grow tax-free and are not taxed if used to pay qualified education expenses. Code Sec. 530.

Establishing a Coverdell ESA

A Coverdell ESA is a trust or custodial account created or organized in the United States for a designated beneficiary who is under age 18 (or a special-needs beneficiary). It may be opened at any bank or other IRS-approved entity that offers Coverdell ESAs. A special-needs beneficiary is an individual who, due to a physical, mental, or emotional condition (including a learning disability), requires additional time to complete his or her education.

Qualified Education Expenses

"Qualified education expenses" means "qualified higher education expenses" and "qualified elementary and secondary expenses." The term also includes contributions to a 529 plan on behalf of the designated beneficiary.

"Qualified higher education expenses" means tuition, fees, books, supplies, and equipment required to attend college and expenses for special-needs services incurred in connection with the enrollment or attendance of a designated beneficiary who has special needs. "Qualified higher education expenses" includes room and board for students attending college at least half-time.

"Qualified elementary and secondary education expenses" means expenses for tuition, fees, academic tutoring, special-needs services in the case of a special-needs beneficiary, books, supplies, and other equipment that are incurred in connection with the enrollment or attendance of the designated beneficiary as an elementary or secondary school student at a public, private, or religious school. "Qualified elementary and secondary education expenses" also includes expenses for room and board, uniforms, transportation, and supplementary items and services (including extended day programs) that are required or provided by a public, private, or religious school in connection with enrollment or attendance and expenses for the purchase of any computer technology or equipment or Internet access and related services, if such technology, equipment, or services are to be used by the designated beneficiary and the designated beneficiary's family during any of the years that the beneficiary is in school. Expenses for computer software designed for sports, games, or hobbies cannot be "qualified elementary and secondary education expenses" unless the software is predominantly educational in nature.

Contributions

Contributions may be made to a Coverdell ESA by any individual (including the designated beneficiary) whose modified adjusted gross income for the year is less than $110,000 ($220,000 if the individual is married and filing a joint income tax return or a qualifying widow(er)). Contributions also can be made by organizations, such as corporations and trusts, regardless of income. Contributions to a Coverdell ESA must be in cash and may not be made after the designated beneficiary attains age 18 (unless the designated beneficiary has special needs).

The maximum amount that may be contributed each tax year to all Coverdell ESAs for the benefit of a particular designated beneficiary is $2,000. This limit applies to contributions by all persons for the benefit of a particular designated beneficiary.

EXAMPLE 24.56	Michael Crocket, his parents, and his wife's parents all want to contribute to a Coverdell ESA for Michael's daughter, Rosie. If Michael contributes $800 to a Coverdell ESA for Rosie's benefit, the most that the others can contribute for that year is $1,200.

The amount that an individual may contribute for a tax year has to be reduced if the contributor's modified adjusted gross income exceeds $95,000 ($190,000 if the taxpayer is married and filing a joint return or a qualifying widow(er)). The amount of the reduction is determined by multiplying $2,000 by a fraction whose numerator is the difference between the individual's modified adjusted gross income and $95,000 ($190,000 if the taxpayer is married and filing a joint return or a qualifying widow(er)) and whose denominator is $15,000 ($30,000 if the individual is married and filing a joint return or a qualifying widow(er)).

EXAMPLE 24.57	Rufus Lynch would like to make a contribution to a Coverdell ESA that he established for his son, Steven. In the current year, Rufus's modified adjusted gross income is $104,000. Rufus is unmarried. The maximum amount that he can contribute to the Coverdell ESA is $800 [$2,000 − ($2,000 × [($104,000 − $95,000)/$15,000]) = $2,000 − ($2,000 × 0.60) = $2,000 − $1,200 = $800].

A taxpayer's "modified adjusted gross income" is the taxpayer's adjusted gross income increased by the following amounts:

1. Any foreign earned income excluded from gross income under Code Sec. 911.
2. Any foreign housing costs excluded or deducted from gross income under Code Sec. 911.
3. Income excluded from gross income under Code Sec. 931 because it was derived by a bona fide resident of American Samoa from sources within, or effectively connected with the conduct of a trade or business within, American Samoa.
4. Income excluded from gross income under Code Sec. 933 because it was derived by a bona fide resident of Puerto Rico from sources within Puerto Rico.

If excess contributions are made to a Coverdell ESA for a particular designated beneficiary, the beneficiary must pay a six percent penalty tax on the excess contributions. Excess contributions are the sum of the following amounts (Code Sec. 4973):

1. Contributions to a designated beneficiary's Coverdell ESAs for the year that exceed $2,000 (or, if less, the total of each contributor's limit for the year).
2. Excess contributions for the preceding year, reduced by distributions (other than those rolled over) during the year and the contribution limit for the current year minus the amount contributed for the current year.

No excise tax has to be paid on excess contributions made for one year if the contributions, plus any earnings on the contributions, are distributed before the first day of the sixth month of the following tax year.

A contribution for a tax year may be made at any time during the year and up to the due date (not including extensions) for filing a federal tax return for that year. Contributions are eligible for the gift tax annual exclusion.

Rollovers and Other Transfers

Assets in a Coverdell ESA may be rolled over tax-free from one Coverdell ESA to another Coverdell ESA if the amount withdrawn is deposited into the second Coverdell ESA within 60 days after the distribution and the second Coverdell ESA benefits the same designated beneficiary or a member of that beneficiary's family who has not attained age 30. Members of a beneficiary's family include the beneficiary's spouse, a son or daughter of the beneficiary or a descendant of either, a stepson or stepdaughter, a brother, sister, stepbrother or stepsister, the father or mother of the beneficiary or an ancestor of either, a stepfather or stepmother, a niece or nephew, an uncle or aunt, a son-in-law, daughter-in-law, father-in-law, mother-in-law, brother-in-law or sister-in-law, the spouse of any of the foregoing, or any first cousin of the beneficiary. A rollover contribution may be made only once every 12 months.

If an individual's interest in a Coverdell ESA is transferred to the individual's spouse or former spouse under a decree of divorce or separate maintenance or a written instrument incident to such a decree, the transfer will not be treated as a taxable distribution. Following the transfer, the spouse or former spouse can treat the Coverdell ESA as his or her own.

Change in Designated Beneficiary

Any change in the beneficiary of a Coverdell ESA will not be treated as a taxable distribution if the new beneficiary is a member of the family of the old beneficiary and has not attained age 30 as of the time of the change.

Distributions

The designated beneficiary of a Coverdell ESA may take a distribution at any time. No amount distributed from a Coverdell ESA has to be included in the beneficiary's gross income if it does not exceed the designated beneficiary's adjusted qualified education expenses for the year. A beneficiary's adjusted qualified education expenses are the beneficiary's qualified education expenses reduced by tax-free educational assistance, such as tax-free scholarships and fellowships, veterans' educational assistance, Pell grants, employer-provided educational assistance, and any other nontaxable payments (other than gifts or inheritances) received as educational assistance.

If the amount of a beneficiary's distributions for a year exceeds the beneficiary's adjusted qualified education expenses, the amount that has to be included in the beneficiary's gross income is calculated as follows:

1. Multiply the amount distributed by a fraction whose numerator is the amount of contributions not distributed at the end of the prior year plus the total contributions made during the year and whose denominator is the value of the account at the end of the current year plus the amount distributed during the year. This is the basis portion of the distribution.
2. Subtract the amount determined in (1) from the total amount of distributions made during the current year. This is the amount of earnings included in the distributions.
3. Multiply the amount of earnings calculated in (2) by a fraction whose numerator is the adjusted qualified education expenses paid during the current year and whose denominator is the total amount distributed during the current year. This is the amount of tax-free earnings.
4. Subtract the amount determined in (3) from the amount determined in (2). This is the amount of earnings that has to be included in the beneficiary's gross income.

If a beneficiary receives a taxable distribution, the beneficiary generally has to pay a 10-percent additional tax on the amount included in the beneficiary's gross income. However, the additional tax will not apply to distributions paid to a beneficiary (or to the estate of the designated beneficiary) on or after the death of the designated beneficiary, made because the designated beneficiary is disabled, included in gross income because the designated beneficiary received a tax-free scholarship or fellowship, veterans' educational assistance, employer-provided educational assistance, or any other nontaxable payments (other than gifts or inheritances) received as educational assistance, included in gross income only because qualified education expenses were taken into account in determining a Hope or lifetime learning credit, made on account of attendance at a U.S. military academy, or constituting a timely distribution of excess contributions.

Any balance to the credit of a designated beneficiary on the date on which the beneficiary attains age 30 must be distributed within 30 days after that date to the designated beneficiary, unless the designated beneficiary has special needs. If the design ated beneficiary dies before attaining age 30, any balance to the credit of the designated beneficiary must be distributed within 30 days after the date of the designated beneficiary's death.

Coordination with Hope and Lifetime Learning Credits

The Hope or lifetime learning credit can be claimed in the same year that a beneficiary takes a tax-free distribution from a Coverdell ESA. However, the same expenses cannot be used for both benefits. A beneficiary must reduce adjusted qualified education expenses by any expenses taken into account in determining a Hope or lifetime learning credit.

¶24,815   **529 PLANS**

A "529 plan" is a tax-favored plan that permits persons to prepay a designated beneficiary's qualified higher education expenses at a discount ("prepaid tuition plan") or contribute money to an account that earns money that is tax-free if used to pay a student's qualified higher education expenses ("college savings plan"). Such plans are sometimes collectively referred to as "qualified tuition plans." Code Sec. 529.

A wide variety of such plans are offered. For a summary of such plans and links to more details, see www.savingforcollege.com.

Prepaid Tuition Plan

A prepaid tuition plan, which may be offered by a state or college, permits persons to purchase tuition credits or certificates at a discount on behalf of a designated beneficiary. The credits or certificates entitle the designated beneficiary to the waiver or payment of the designated beneficiary's qualified higher education expenses.

College Savings Plan

A college savings plan, which may be established only by a state, permits persons to make contributions to an account established to pay the qualified higher education expenses of the designated beneficiary of the account.

Qualified Higher Education Expenses

"Qualified higher education expenses" means tuition, fees, books, supplies, and small equipment such as calculators and microscopes required for the enrollment or attendance of a designated beneficiary at a college. "Qualified higher education expenses" includes room and board for a student attending college at least half-time. The American Recovery and Reinvestment Act of 2009 allows 529 plan beneficiaries to use tax-free distributions to pay for computers and computer technology such as internet access. Expenses for special-needs services incurred in connection with enrollment or attendance of a special-needs beneficiary are "qualified higher education expenses." A special-needs beneficiary is an individual who, due to a physical, mental, or emotional condition (including a learning disability) requires additional time to complete his or her education.

Contributions

Only cash may be contributed to a 529 plan, and no deduction is allowed for contributions. The amount that may be contributed to a 529 plan on behalf of a beneficiary cannot exceed the amount needed to pay the beneficiary's qualified higher education expenses. There are no income restrictions on who can contribute to a 529 plan.

Contributions can be made to a 529 plan and Coverdell ESA for the same beneficiary. Contributions are eligible for the gift tax annual exclusion.

Rollovers and Other Transfers

No tax has to be paid when assets from one 529 plan are withdrawn and deposited in a second 529 plan for the benefit of the same beneficiary or for the benefit of a member of the beneficiary's family if the rollover is completed within 60 days after the date of the distribution. Members of a beneficiary's family include the beneficiary's spouse, a son or daughter of the beneficiary or a descendant of either, a stepson or stepdaughter, a brother, sister, stepbrother or stepsister, the father or mother of the beneficiary or an ancestor of either, a stepfather or stepmother, a niece or nephew, an uncle or aunt, a son-in-law, daughter-in-law, father-in-law, mother-in-law, brother-in-law or sister-in-law, the spouse of any of the foregoing, or any first cousin of the beneficiary. A rollover may be made only once every 12 months.

Change in Designated Beneficiary

Any change in the beneficiary of a 529 plan will not be treated as a taxable distribution if the new beneficiary is a member of the family of the old beneficiary.

Distributions

No tax has to be paid on a distribution from a 529 plan unless the amount distributed exceeds the beneficiary's adjusted qualified education expenses. A beneficiary's adjusted qualified education expenses are the beneficiary's qualified education expenses reduced by tax-free educational assistance, such as tax-free scholarships and fellowships, veterans' educational assistance, Pell grants, employer-provided educational assistance, and any other nontaxable payments (other than gifts or inheritances) received as educational assistance.

If the amount of a beneficiary's distributions for a year exceeds the beneficiary's adjusted qualified education expenses, the amount that has to be included in the beneficiary's gross income is calculated as follows:

1. Multiply the total distributed earnings shown in Box 2 of IRS Form 1099-Q, Payments From Qualified Education Programs (Under Sections 529 and 530), by a fraction whose numerator is the adjusted qualified education expenses paid during the year and whose denominator is the total amount distributed during the year.

2. Subtract the amount determined in (1) from the total distributed earnings. This is the amount that the beneficiary must include in his or her gross income.

If a beneficiary receives a taxable distribution, the beneficiary generally has to pay a 10-percent additional tax on the amount included in the beneficiary's gross income. However, the additional tax will not apply to distributions paid to a beneficiary (or to the estate of the designated beneficiary) on or after the death of the designated beneficiary, made because the designated beneficiary is disabled, included in gross income because the designated beneficiary received a tax-free scholarship or fellowship, veterans' educational assistance, employer-provided educational assistance, or any other nontaxable payments (other than gifts or inheritances) received as educational assistance, included in gross income only because qualified education expenses were taken into account in determining a Hope or lifetime learning credit, made on account of attendance at a U.S. military academy, or constituting a timely distribution of excess contributions.

Coordination with Hope and Lifetime Learning Credits

A Hope or lifetime learning credit may be claimed for the same year that a beneficiary takes a tax-free distribution from a 529 plan. However, the same expenses cannot be used to qualify for both benefits.

Exhibit 16. SAVINGS PLANS FOR EDUCATION

Item	Coverdell ESA	529 Prepaid Tuition Plan	529 Savings Plan
Purpose:	Tax-exempt accumulation of income to pay for the qualified kindergarten through postsecondary education expenses of a beneficiary under age 30.	Tax-exempt accumulation of income to pay for the qualified postsecondary education expenses of a beneficiary at any age.	Tax-exempt accumulation of income to pay for the qualified postsecondary education expenses of a beneficiary at any age.
Age Restrictions:	For qualified contributions: the beneficiary must not be over age 18 at the end of the contribution year. For qualified distributions: the beneficiary must not be more than age 30 at the end of the distribution year.	None	None
Establishment Deadline:	By December 31 of current year.	Depends on the plan	Depends on the plan
Contribution Deadline:	By filing due date (April 15 of following year).	Depends on the plan	Depends on the plan
Maximum Contribution Amount:	$2,000 per beneficiary (not per contributor) per year	Determined by each state	Determined by each state
Contribution Phase-Out (MAGI Limits):	MFJ: $190k- $220k Other: $95k - $110k	None	None
Control of the Account:	In most states, account assets become property of the beneficiary at age 18.	In most states, control of the account will always remain with the contributor.	In most states, control of the account will always remain with the contributor.
Assignability to Other Relatives:	Immediate family of beneficiary, including cousins, step-relatives, and in-laws	Same as CESA	Same as CESA
Earnings:	Tax exempt if conditions are met.	Same as CESA	Same as CESA
Penalty for Non-Qualified Withdrawals:	Earnings are taxed as ordinary income to contributor, plus a 10% penalty.	Same as CESA	Same as CESA
Effect on Financial Aid Calculation:	Considered to be an asset of the beneficiary, which means a large portion of the assets will be considered in the financial aid calculation.	Considered to be the student's resource and thus reduces financial aid dollar-for-dollar.	Assets are considered to be property of the account owner, which—unless the owner is also the beneficiary—means only a small portion of the assets will be considered in the financial aid calculation.

SUMMARY

- A qualified employer-sponsored deferred compensation plan is a plan providing for retirement benefits that satisfies strict requirements of the Code and the Employee Retirement Income Security Act of 1974 (ERISA).

- Qualified plan requirements include nondiscrimination in favor of highly-compensated employees, limitations on contributions to a defined contributions plan, limitations on benefits provided by a defined benefit plan, required minimum distributions, early withdrawal restrictions, participation requirements, coverage requirements, vesting requirements, and the "exclusive benefit of employee" requirement.

- Employees generally are not taxed on contributions made to a qualified employer-sponsored retirement plan until they are withdrawn and may be entitled to a saver's credit for contributions. Earnings on contributions accumulate tax-deferred until they are withdrawn.

- Employers are entitled to a current deduction for contributions made to a qualified retirement plan and may claim a credit for a portion of their startup costs.

- Common retirement plans for large businesses (more than 100 employees) include 401(k) plans and supplemental Roth 401(k) plans.

- Common retirement plans for small business (100 or fewer employees) include the Solo (Individual) 401(k), Keogh plan, Simplified Employee Pension (SEP) plan, and Savings Incentive Match Plan for Employees (SIMPLE).

- Individuals with taxable compensation may accumulate money for their retirement by making contributions to a traditional or Roth IRA. Contributions to a traditional IRA may be deducted unless the contributor's modified adjusted gross income exceeds a specified amount. However, deductible contributions and earnings on all contributions are taxed when withdrawn from the traditional IRA. Contributions to a Roth IRA cannot be deducted, but earnings on contributions may be withdrawn tax-free on or after age 59½.

- Nonqualified retirement plans are used to benefit key employees because they do not have to satisfy the same nondiscrimination, participation, and coverage requirements imposed on qualified retirement plans. If properly structured, contributions are not taxed to employees until withdrawn. An employer is not entitled to a deduction for contributions until they are included in the employee's gross income.

- Common nonqualfied deferred compensation plans include Rabbi Trusts, Incentive Stock Options (ISOs), and Nonqualified Stock Options (NSOs).

- Contributions can be made to a Coverdell ESA to accumulate funds on a tax-favored basis to pay for elementary, secondary, and college education expenses. Contributions may be made only if the contributor's modified adjusted gross income is less than $110,000 ($220,000 if the individual files a joint income tax return).

- 529 prepaid tuition and college savings plans can be used by any person, regardless of income, to accumulate funds for college on a tax-favored basis.

QUESTIONS

1. What are the major requirements of qualified employer-sponsored plans?

2. What are the tax advantages associated with a qualified employer-sponsored plan?

3. What are the major nontax advantages associated with qualified employer-sponsored plans?

4. What are the major similarities and differences between qualified plans and nonqualified plans?

5. What options are available to a qualified plan's trustee after a participant severs employment?

6. When are plan participants required to begin withdrawing taxable distributions from their qualified retirement accounts?

7. What penalty is imposed on taxpayers who fail to make a required minimum distribution?

¶24,815

8. How early can amounts be distributed from a qualified plan penalty-free?

9. Define the term "vesting" and identify the two vesting methods that are available to employer-sponsored qualified plans.

10. What distinguishes a direct rollover from an indirect rollover?

11. What is a Section 401(k) plan?

12. What is a Roth 401(k) plan and what are its advantages?

13. What are the most common types of qualified plans for small businesses?

14. Explain how the features listed below affect the choice of a qualified plan for a small business.
    a. Investment flexibility.
    b. Eligible legal entities.
    c. Permitted number of employees.
    d. Minimal IRS reporting requirements.
    e. Flexible IRS deadlines.
    f. Optional vesting.
    g. Plan loans.
    h. Discretion regarding employee participation.
    i. Rollover eligibility.
    j. Allowable contribution and deduction amounts.

15. How much may be contributed annually to a defined contribution Keogh plan?

16. What is the penalty for early withdrawals from SIMPLE?

17. What rules do traditional IRAs and Roth IRAs have in common?

18. How much may be contributed to an IRA on an annual basis?

19. Under what circumstances is loss recognition for traditional or Roth IRAs permitted?

20. What are the major differences between a traditional IRA and a Roth IRA?

21. Under what circumstances can employees defer compensation under a nonqualified plan?

22. Explain when payroll taxes are applied to deferred compensation under a nonqualified plan.

23. What is a Rabbi Trust?

24. What is a Coverdell Education Savings Account?

25. What is a 529 plan?

PROBLEMS

26. AJR Inc.'s qualified plan provides for the allocation of employer contributions based upon a flat rate of four percent of each employee's compensation. Nathaniel's annual compensation is equal to $20,000 and his trust account receives $800 (4% × $20,000). Micaela's annual compensation is equal to $200,000 and her trust account receives an $8,000 employer contribution (4% × $200,000). Is the plan discriminatory?

27. Tom Couch participates in his employer's qualified retirement plan, which provides a 5 percent employer contribution formula. Tom's annual compensation is equal to $450,000. What employer contribution rate can be applied to Tom's compensation?

28. Fred and Ginger attain age 70 in Year 1. Fred's birthday is June 30 and Ginger's is July 1. Each owns separate traditional IRAs. What is the deadline for Fred and Ginger's first required minimum distribution payment?

29. Bob Carnick is the owner of a traditional IRA. Bob will attain age 76 in the current year. The before-tax account balance as of the end of the prior year was $1,000,000. What is the minimum amount that Bob must withdraw from the IRA by the end of the current year?

30. Ceci becomes age 70 on June 22, Year 2, and retires at the end of Year 3. Her traditional IRA account balances for four years are shown below:

Date	Account Balance
Dec. 31, Year 1	$ 822,000
Dec. 31, Year 2	$ 888,600
Dec. 31, Year 3	$ 960,000
Dec. 31, Year 4	$1,037,400

What are the deadlines and amounts associated with Ceci's first three RMDs? (*Hint: refer to the Uniform Lifetime Table at Exhibit 3 for life expectancy information.*)

31. Refer to the previous problem. If, instead of maintaining a traditional IRA, Ceci maintains a 401(k) account, what are the deadlines and amounts associated with Ceci's first two RMDs?

32. Thomas Andrews' mother died in Year 1. Thomas, who will attain age 27 in Year 2, was designated as the sole beneficiary of his mother's traditional IRA. If the account balance at the end of Year 1 was $1,000,000, and Thomas elected to receive a lifetime annuity, what will be the deadline and amount of the first required minimum distribution?

33. Hadir earns a $150,000 salary and contributes $15,000 into a 401(k) account. He makes no additional contributions and the account has no accumulated income. Years later, Hadir receives a $9,000 distribution representing a portion of the original contribution amount. Assuming a 25 percent tax rate, what amount of federal income tax would be imposed if the original contribution had been:
a. deductible?
b. nondeductible?

34. Kathy Runde, age 66 and retired, receives a $20,000 partial distribution from her 401(k) plan. The plan does not pay out an annuity. Immediately before the distribution, her account balance is $50,000, including $10,000 in nondeductible contributions. How much of the $20,000 distribution must Kathy include in gross income?

35. Bonnie Sparks has been receiving a $200 monthly annuity from her qualified plan account over several years. At the end of the current year, her account balance is $50,000, including a $10,000 cost basis. In order to satisfy a personal obligation, she withdraws an extra $20,000 from her account in the current year. The withdrawal does not affect the amount of her subsequent annuity payments. How much of the $20,000 distribution must Bonnie include in gross income?

36. Harrison Bernhardt participates in his employer's 401(k) plan. Under the plan, employees may elect to reduce their salary by a certain percentage and have it paid into the plan's trust. In the current year, Harrison elects to defer $15,000 as a cash or deferred arrangement (CODA) contribution from his $80,000 salary. The plan provides that the employer will match the employee contribution up to 5 percent of compensation ($4,000).
   a. What amount is subject to employee FICA tax?
   b. What amount is subject to federal income tax?
   c. What amount is currently not subject to federal income tax?

37. Viva Yeboah's 401(k) plan provides a supplemental Roth 401(k) arrangement. If Viva's compensation is $500,000, will she be eligible to contribute to a Roth 401(k) account? Explain why or why not.

38. Answer the following questions about IRAs:
    a. What is the maximum amount that may be contributed annually to the separate IRA of a nonworking spouse?
    b. Is it possible to contribute the maximum annual amount to an IRA by making just one deposit every other year?
    c. What are the tax consequences of transferring an IRA to the spouse as a divorce property settlement?
    d. When is it possible to fund a million dollar balance in a newly established IRA?

39. Assuming adequate security and interest, how much may the qualified plan participant borrow from the plan in the following independent cases:
    a. The account balance is $100,000 and the participant is 60 percent vested.
    b. The account balance is $150,000 and the participant is fully vested.
    c. Same as (b), but the participant is an owner-employee and the plan is a Keogh plan.
    d. The plan is a SEP IRA with a $12,000 account balance.
    e. Assuming a loan is made, when must it be repaid?

40. During 2017, Alec Meachin earned a net profit of $80,000 from his sole proprietorship (as reported on Schedule C). He paid $10,000 self-employment taxes during the year. What is the maximum contribution and deduction amount available to Alec if he maintains a
    a. Solo 401(k) plan?
    b. SEP IRA?

41. An employee with $200,000 compensation participates in her company's SIMPLE 401(k) plan. If the employee elects to contribute the maximum allowable amount into the plan what amount should she contribute if the nominal plan rate is:
    a. 5%?
    b. 10%?

42. An employee with $400,000 compensation participates in her company's retirement plan. The plan provides for a 100 percent nominal rate for elective employee contributions. What is the maximum allowable employee and matching employer matching contribution if the plan is a:
    a. SIMPLE IRA?
    b. SIMPLE 401(k)?

43. Same facts as in the preceding problem except that the plan provides for a 2.5% nominal rate for elective employee contributions. What is the maximum allowable employee and matching employer matching contribution if the plan is a:
    a. SIMPLE IRA?
    b. SIMPLE 401(k)?

44. **Comprehensive Problem.** Spencer Strank reports the following items of income for the current year on a joint return:

Employee salary	$24,000
Interest income	2,000
Net income from consulting	20,000
Self-employment tax paid	2,800

He is a participant in his employer's qualified defined contribution retirement plan and has a nonworking spouse.
    a. How much, if anything, may Spencer deduct if he contributes the maximum amount on behalf of himself and his wife to a traditional IRA?
    b. Same as (a), but AGI is $115,000.
    c. What are the maximum contribution and deduction amounts available to Spencer if he maintains a solo 401(k) plan?
    d. What are the maximum contribution and deduction amounts available to Spencer if he maintains a money purchase Keogh plan?
    e. What are the maximum contribution and deduction amounts available to Spencer if he maintains a SEP IRA?
    f. What are the maximum contribution and deduction amounts available to Spencer if he maintains a SIMPLE 401(k)?

45. Norman Stonewell reports a salary of $60,000 this year on a joint return. He also reports $8,000 in royalty income from two books he wrote. Norman is age 48, and his wife Betty is 50.
    a. Is Norman eligible to maintain both a traditional IRA and a Keogh plan?
    b. If Betty is a nonworking spouse, what is the maximum traditional IRA contribution allowable?
    c. When must the traditional IRA accounts be opened and the contribution made?
    d. What are the maximum contribution and deduction amounts available to Norman if he maintains a profit-sharing Keogh plan?
    e. When must the Keogh plan be opened and the contribution made?

46. In 2017, Hunter and Monda (both under age 50) had compensation income of $1,000,000 and $200,000, respectively. Adjusted gross income on their joint return was $1,200,000, and neither taxpayer was a participant in a qualified retirement plan. How much may each contribute to a traditional IRA account and deduct from taxable income?

47. Jasper Fern, age 62, works full time and maintains two traditional IRA accounts. On March 23 of the current year, he withdraws $6,500 from one of his IRA accounts. The account is funded only with $6,500 nondeductible contributions. Its balance is $2,333 immediately after the withdrawal and $2,525 at year-end. The other IRA account is funded only with deductible contributions. Its balance is $40,177 as of March 23, and $43,500 balance as of December 31, the same year. What portion of Jasper's distribution constitutes gross income?

48. Abraham is single, age 48, has no employer-sponsored plan, and has a MAGI of $124,000 for 2017. What is the maximum contribution that he may make to a Roth IRA?

49. During the period Years 1 through 3, Martha made direct contributions to her Roth IRA totaling $10,000. By the end of Year 7, the IRA balance, including earnings, had grown to $30,000. At the beginning of Year 8, before Martha turned 59 1/2, she withdrew $25,000 from her Roth IRA to buy a new car. What is the tax result for Martha?

50. Orange Computer Inc. grants Steve Werks 10,000 incentive stock options (ISOs) on January 1, Year 1 (the "grant" date). On this date, the stock's fair market value is $100 per share and each ISO entitles the holder to buy one share of Orange stock for $100 (the exercise price). Steve exercises the ISOs on December 31, Year 5 (the "exercise" date) when the stock is worth $300 per share. What are the tax consequences if, in Year 7, Steve sells the stock in a qualifying disposition for $500 per share?

51. Moonbacks Inc. grants Howard Schmidt 10,000 NSOs on January 1, Year 1 (the "grant" date). Each NSO grants the holder the right to buy 1 share of Moonbacks stock for $100 over the next 10 years. The NSO's readily ascertainable fair market value on the grant date is $100 per share. Howard exercises the NSOs on December 31, Year 5 (the "exercise" date) when the stock is worth $300 per share. What are the tax consequences if, in Year 7, Howard sells the stock for $500 per share?

52. Referring to the foregoing example, if Moonbacks' NSOs had no readily ascertainable value on the grant date, how would the tax consequences be different for Howard?

53. In the current year, a taxpayer contributes $1,500 to a Coverdell ESA account on behalf of a beneficiary. If the income phase-out rules do not apply, what is the maximum allowable amount that others may contribute to the same beneficiary's account in the current year?

54. An unmarried taxpayer reports modified AGI of $98,000. What is the maximum allowable amount the taxpayer can contribute to a beneficiary's Coverdell ESA if no other contributions are being made by others?

55. In the current year, a beneficiary receives a distribution from a 529 Savings Plan in the amount of $50,000. $12,000 of the $50,000 represents distributed earnings. If the beneficiary's qualified education expense paid during the current year equal $40,000, what portion of the distribution is taxable?

56. **Research Problem.** Locate a copy of IRS Publication 590 either on the Internet or in a tax or government documents library. Prepare a chart comparing distributions from various individual retirement arrangements.

Chapter

25

Multijurisdictional Taxation: International and State and Local Transactions

OBJECTIVES

After completing Chapter 25, you should be able to:

1. Discuss the limits on the power of states and local governments to impose taxes.
2. Explain the different types of state and local taxes.
3. Explain when a state has authority to tax a nonresident individual or business.
4. Identify what activities by a nonresident business or individual will subject the business or individual to a state's taxes.
5. Discuss how states tax the income of a business operating in more than one state.
6. Discuss how a business' income is apportioned and allocated among states.
7. Explain when a country has authority to tax a nonresident individual or business.
8. Discuss how a tax treaty can affect the way a country taxes nonresidents.
9. Explain why it is important whether income is U.S.-source or foreign-source and what rules are used to make that distinction.
10. Discuss how foreign persons are taxed by the United States.
11. Explain how foreign income earned by U.S. citizens and residents is taxed by the United States.
12. Define what a *corporate inversion* is and explain when it will be disregarded for U.S. tax purposes.

OVERVIEW

This chapter discusses how individuals and businesses are taxed by states. It also discusses how U.S. citizens and residents and businesses are taxed on their foreign income and how nonresident alien individuals and business entities are taxed on their U.S.-source income.

Individuals who live in one state but work in another or own property in more than one state and companies that do business or own property in multiple states or countries are subject to a different tax system in each jurisdiction. For example, a U.S. business operating in ten states and three foreign countries may incur state income, sales, property, and payroll taxes under ten different state systems, each utilizing its own set of rules (as well as local taxes in cities in which the business operates), and three different sets of rules for each type of tax imposed on the business by the foreign countries (e.g., income, sales, export, franchise, and excise taxes). In this simple example, the "multijurisdictional" business is subject to more than 50 sets of tax rules, and that assumes that the business is conducting its operations as the same legal entity in each of these jurisdictions. The effects are increased exponentially if the business is consolidated (e.g., multiple corporations are operating under the umbrella of a parent corporation). Multistate businesses may have to file hundreds of tax returns annually.

State and Local Taxation (SALT)

Limitations on the Power of States and Local Authorities to Impose Taxes

¶25,001   ## STATE CONSTITUTIONS AND STATUTES

States impose taxes through statutes (referred to as *imposition statutes*). The amount of activity in or in connection with a state that a taxpayer must have before the taxpayer will be subject to the state's taxes is defined by the state's imposition statute, regulations, and case law and varies from state to state. Usually a state's imposition statute is written broadly and will make a taxpayer subject to state taxes if the taxpayer is an individual residing or domiciled in the state, is incorporated under state law, is "doing business" within the state, or is "earning or receiving income" from sources within the state.

Notwithstanding what a state's imposition statute says, whether or not a state has the power to tax someone is limited by the state's constitution, the U.S. Constitution, Public Law 86-272, and the Internet Tax Freedom Act. A state's constitution may limit what types of taxes may be imposed, what types of property may be taxed, how property is valued, and what rates may be imposed.

¶25,005   ## U.S. CONSTITUTION

The U.S. Constitution includes several provisions restricting the power of a state to impose taxes:

- Commerce Clause.
- Due Process Clause.
- Equal Protection Clause.
- Privileges and Immunities Clause.
- Import-Export Clause.
- Duty-of-Tonnage Prohibition.
- Supremacy Clause.
- First Amendment.

Commerce Clause

The Commerce Clause (U.S. Const., art. I, §8, cl. 3), which gives Congress the power to regulate commerce, has been the principal constitutional limitation on a state's power to tax interstate business. The clause prohibits states from burdening interstate commerce with a tax not borne by local commerce. *Western Live Stock v. Bureau of Revenue*, 303 U.S. 250 (1938). However, a state may tax interstate businesses for their fair share of state costs for the benefits interstate businesses derive within the state. *Northwestern States Portland Cement Co. v. Minnesota*, 358 U.S. 450 (1959). A state tax will pass constitutional muster if (1) it is applied to an activity that has a substantial nexus with the taxing state, (2) it is fairly apportioned, (3) it does not discriminate against interstate commerce, and (4) it is fairly related to services provided by the state. *Complete Auto Transit Inc. v. Brady*, 430 U.S. 274 (1977). A state tax affecting foreign commerce must satisfy two additional tests: (1) it must not create multiple international taxation, and (2) it must not impair federal uniformity in an area where federal uniformity is essential. *Japan Line, Ltd. v. County of Los Angeles*, 441 U.S. 434 (1979).

Due Process Clause

The Due Process Clause (U.S. Const., amend. XIV, §1) limits the territorial reach of a state's taxing powers by placing two restrictions on a state's power to tax income generated by the activities of an interstate business. *Moorman Mfg. Co. v. Bair*, 437 U.S. 267 (1978). First, no tax may be imposed on income generated by the activities of an interstate business unless there is some minimal connection between those activities and the taxing state. Second, income attributed to a state must be rationally related to values connected with the taxing state. As the U.S. Supreme Court has said, "The simple but controlling question is whether the state has given anything for which it can ask return." *State of Wisconsin v. J.C. Penney Co.*, 311 U.S. 435 (1940).

Equal Protection Clause

States have large leeway in making classifications that in their judgment produce reasonable systems of taxation. *Lehnhausen v. Lake Shore Auto Parts Co.*, 410 U.S. 356 (1973). However, the Equal Protection Clause (U.S. Const., amend. XIV, §1) prohibits states from making unreasonable classifications for tax purposes. *Allied Stores of Ohio, Inc. v. Bowers*, 358 U.S. 522 (1959). A state tax classification will not violate the Equal Protection clause if the tax has a legitimate purpose and it was reasonable for lawmakers to believe that use of the challenged classification would promote that purpose. *Western & Southern Life Insurance Co. v. State Board of Equalization*, 451 U.S. 648 (1981).

Privileges and Immunities Clause

The Privileges and Immunities Clause (U.S. Const., art. IV, §2) prevents a state from discriminating between residents and nonresidents when imposing a tax unless there is substantial reason for the difference in treatment and the discrimination practiced against nonresidents bears a substantial relationship to the state's objective. *Supreme Court of New Hampshire v. Piper*, 470 U.S. 274 (1985). Corporations are not protected by this provision because they are not "citizens" within the meaning of the clause. *Paul v. Virginia*, 75 U.S. (8 Wall.) 168 (1868).

Import-Export Clause

The Import-Export Clause (U.S. Const., art. I, §10, cl. 2) prohibits a state from taxing goods in transit through the state or from imposing taxes that discriminate against imported goods or in favor of exported goods. *Michelin Tire Corp. v. Wages*, 423 U.S. 276 (1976); *Department of Revenue v. Association of Washington Stevedoring Companies*, 435 U.S. 734 (1978).

Duty-of-Tonnage Prohibition

The Duty-of-Tonnage Prohibition (U.S. Const. art. I, §10, cl. 3) bars a state from imposing a tax or other charge on vessels for the privilege of entering, trading in, or lying in a port. *Clyde Mallory Lines v. Alabama*, 296 U.S. 261 (1935).

Supremacy Clause

The Supremacy Clause (U.S. Cont., art. VI, cl. 2) limits the power of state and local governments to tax the federal government. *M'Culloch v. Maryland*, 17 U.S. (4 Wheat.) 316 (1819). It protects not only the United States itself but also any agency or instrumentality so closely connected to the United States that the two cannot realistically be viewed as separate entities, at least insofar as the activity being taxed. *United States v. New Mexico*, 455 U.S. 720 (1982). The principle that the federal government is immune from state and local taxation is referred to as the "Doctrine of Intergovernmental Tax Immunity."

First Amendment

The First Amendment bars states from enacting taxes that burden rights protected by the First Amendment unless the burden is necessary to achieve an overriding government interest. *Minneapolis Star and Tribune Co. v. Minnesota Commissioner of Revenue*, 460 U.S. 575 (1983).

¶25,015   FEDERAL STATUTES—INTERSTATE INCOME LAW (P.L. 86-272)

Federal statutes limit the power of state and local governments to impose taxes. The limitations imposed by the federal government must be based on constitutional grounds, such as the Commerce or Supremacy clause.

In 1959, the United States Supreme Court held that the Commerce Clause does not bar a state from taxing a nondomiciliary corporation engaged exclusively in interstate commerce. *Northwestern States Portland Cement Co. v. Minnesota*, 358 U.S. 450 (1959). That same year, in response to that court decision, Congress enacted the Interstate Income Law, P.L. 86-272 (15 U.S.C. §§381-384), which limits a state's power to tax the income of an interstate business. Note that the law does not limit a state's power to tax gross receipts, net worth, capital, or property or to require a business to collect sales or use taxes.

Under that law, states (and their political subdivisions) may not impose an income tax on the income derived within the state by any person from interstate commerce if all of the following requirements are satisfied: 15 U.S.C. §381(a).

1. The only business activities within the state by or on behalf of that person during the tax year consist of the solicitation of orders by that person (or that person's representative) in the state for sales of

tangible personal property and/or the solicitation of orders by that person (or that person's representative) in the state in the name of or for the benefit of a prospective customer.

De minimis exception. A business will not necessarily forfeit its tax immunity by performing some in-state activities that go beyond "solicitation of orders." However, the de minimis exception will apply only if the non-immune activities constitute a nontrivial connection with the state. *Wisconsin Department of Revenue v. William Wrigley, Jr., Co.*, 505 U.S. 214 (1992). An activity conducted within a state on a regular or systematic basis or pursuant to company policy will usually not be considered trivial.

2. Any orders are sent outside the state for approval or rejection.
3. Any orders approved are filled by shipment or delivery from a point outside the state. Some states have taken the position that the protection afforded by P.L. 86-272 is forfeited if a seller delivers goods into a state using its own or leased vehicles.

Note that this law does not protect any of the following:

1. A taxpayer against imposition of a gross receipts tax or the obligation to collect sales tax on sales to in-state residents.
2. Any corporation incorporated in a state imposing an income tax. 15 U.S.C. §381(b). It is not clear whether P.L. 86-272 also does not protect a corporation that has qualified or registered to do business within a state. The Statement of Information Concerning Practices of Multistate Tax Commission and Signatory States under Pub. L. No. 86-272 (VII.C) takes the position that registration or qualification to do business within a state by itself will not cause a company to lose the protection of P.L. 86-272.
3. Any individual who, under state law, is domiciled in, or a resident of, a state imposing an income tax. 15 U.S.C. §381(b).
4. Any business that sells property other than tangible personal property (such as services, real property, or intangible property) in a state imposing an income tax, even though it also sells tangible personal property. *Amway Corp., Inc. v. Director of Revenue*, 794 S.W.2d 666 (Mo. 1990).
5. The leasing or licensing of tangible personal property, intangible property, or real property in a state imposing an income tax.
6. Nonsolicitation activities, such as technical assistance, repairs, or customer training, in a state imposing an income tax.

Observation: The Business Activity Tax Simplification Act of 2015 (H.R. 2584) would expand the prohibition against state taxation of interstate commerce to include out-of-state transactions involving all types of property (including intangible personal property and services) and prohibit state taxation of an out-of-state business unless it has physical presence within the taxing state.

Sales made into a state precluded by Pub. Law 86-272 from taxing the income of the seller remain subject to throwback to a state that can tax the income derived from those sales.

Sales and Solicitation of Orders

A person will not be considered to have engaged in business activities within a state merely by reason of sales in the state, or the solicitation of orders for sales in the state, of tangible personal property on behalf of that person by one or more independent contractors, or by reason of the maintenance of an office in the state by one or more independent contractors whose activities on behalf of the person in the state consist solely of making sales, or soliciting orders for sales, of tangible personal property 15 U.S.C. §381(c). An "independent contractor" means a commission agent, broker, or other independent contractor who is engaged in selling, or soliciting orders for the sale of, tangible personal property for more than one principal who holds himself or herself out as such in the regular course of his or her business activities. 15 U.S.C. §381(d)(1).

Although "solicitation of orders" is not defined by the statute, it has been interpreted as including not only explicit verbal requests for orders but also any speech or conduct that implicitly invites an order. Thus, for example, a sales representative who extols the virtues of his or her company's product is engaged in solicitation even though he or she does not come right out and ask someone to buy the product. *Wisconsin Department of Revenue v. William Wrigley, Jr., Co.*, 505 U.S. 214 (1992).

"Solicitation of orders" covers more than what is strictly essential to requesting a purchase. It also includes the entire process associated with inviting an order. "Solicitation of orders" includes activities that are entirely ancillary to requests for purchases. "Ancillary activities" are those activities that serve no independent business function for the seller apart from their connection to the solicitation of orders. Activities that a seller would engage in apart from soliciting orders are not considered ancillary to the solicitation of orders. For example, providing a car and a stock of free samples to a sales representative is part of the "solicitation of orders" because the only reason to do so is to facilitate requests for purchases. By contrast, employing a sales representative to repair or service a company's products does not constitute "solicitation of orders"; repair and servicing may help to increase purchases, but they are not ancillary to requesting purchases. *Wisconsin Department of Revenue v. William Wrigley, Jr., Co.*, 505 U.S. 214 (1992).

Section 381(c) of Title 15 to the United States Code makes an exception to these principles for an office. Maintenance of an office within a state, even though the office is used exclusively to facilitate requests for purchases, will cause a business to lose its immunity under 15 U.S.C. §381 because it does not constitute "solicitation of orders." Although activities that take place after a sale ordinarily will not constitute "solicitation of orders" because they are not entirely ancillary, there is no bright line rule prohibiting such activities from qualifying as solicitation of orders. Activities that promote a product do not qualify as "solicitation of orders." *Wisconsin Department of Revenue v. William Wrigley, Jr., Co.*, 505 U.S. 214 (1992).

Multistate Tax Commission List of Protected and Unprotected Activities

In 1986, the Multistate Tax Commission (*www.mtc.gov*), in which most states and the District of Columbia participate, adopted a "Statement of Information Concerning Practices of Multistate Tax Commission and Signatory States Under Public Law 86-272" to promote uniformity among the states in applying Public Law 86-272 by listing both protected and unprotected activities.

The following in-state activities will not cause the loss of protection for otherwise protected sales: Statement of Information Concerning Practices of Multistate Tax Commission and Signatory States Under Public Law 86-272, Section IV.B.

1. Soliciting orders for sales by any type of advertising
2. Soliciting of orders by an in-state resident employee or representative of the company if that person does not maintain or use any office or other place of business in the state other than an in-home office.
3. Carrying samples and promotional materials only for display or distribution without charge or other consideration.
4. Furnishing and setting up display racks and advising customers on the display of the company's products without charge or other consideration.
5. Providing automobiles to sales personnel for their use in conducting protected activities.
6. Passing orders, inquiries, and complaints on to the home office.
7. Missionary sales activities (i.e., solicitation of indirect customers for the company's goods).
8. Coordinating shipment or delivery without payment or other consideration and providing related information either prior or subsequent to the placement of an order.
9. Checking customers' inventories without a charge (for reorder, but not for other purposes, such as quality control).
10. Maintaining a sample or display room for two weeks (14 days) or less at any one location within the state during the tax year.
11. Recruiting, training, or evaluating sales personnel, including occasionally using homes, hotels, or similar places for meetings with sales personnel.
12. Mediating direct customer complaints when the purpose is solely for ingratiating the sales personnel with the customer and facilitating requests for orders.
13. Owning, leasing, using, or maintaining personal property for use in the employee's or representative's in-home office or automobile if that property's use is limited to the conduct of protected activities (e.g., use of a cellular telephone or personal computer to carry on protected solicitation activities).

Unprotected Activities

The following in-state activities (unless they are de minimis) are not protected by P.L. 86-272 because they are not considered either solicitation of orders or ancillary activities. Statement of Information Concerning Practices of Multistate Tax Commission and Signatory States Under Public Law 86-72, Section IV.A.

1. Making repairs or providing maintenance or service to the property sold or to be sold.
2. Collecting current or delinquent accounts, whether directly or by third parties, through assignment or otherwise.
3. Investigating credit worthiness.
4. Installation or supervision of installation at or after shipment or delivery.
5. Conducting training courses, seminars, or lectures for personnel other than personnel involved only in solicitation.

6. Providing any kind of technical assistance or service including, but not limited to, engineering assistance or design service, when one of the purposes thereof is other than the facilitation of the solicitation of orders.
7. Investigating, handling, or otherwise assisting in resolving customer complaints, other than mediating direct customer complaints when the sole purpose of such mediation is to ingratiate the sales personnel with the customer.
8. Approving or accepting orders.
9. Repossessing property.
10. Securing deposits on sales.
11. Picking up or replacing damaged or returned property.
12. Hiring, training, or supervising personnel, other than personnel involved only in solicitation.
13. Using agency stock checks or any other instrument or process by which sales are made within the state by sales personnel.
14. Maintaining a sample or display room in excess of two weeks (14 days) at any one location within the state during the tax year.
15. Carrying samples for sale, exchange, or distribution in any manner for consideration or other value.
16. Owning, leasing, using, or maintaining any of the following facilities or property in-state:
    a. Repair shop
    b. Parts department
    c. Any kind of office other than an in-home office
    d. Warehouse
    e. Meeting place for directors, officers, or employees
    f. Stock of goods other than samples for sales personnel or that are used entirely ancillary to solicitation
    g. Telephone answering service that is publicly attributed to the company or to employees or agents of the company in their representative status
    h. Mobile stores (vehicles with drivers who are sale personnel making sales from the vehicles)
    i. Real property or fixtures to real property of any kind
17. Consigning stock of goods or other tangible personal property to any person, including an independent contractor, for sale.
18. Maintaining, by any employee or other representative, an office or place of business of any kind, other than a home office that is not publicly attributed to the company or to the employee or representative in an employee or representative capacity, but only so long as the use of the office is limited to soliciting and receiving orders from customers, for transmitting such orders outside the state for acceptance or rejection by the company, or for other protected activities. A telephone or other public listing within the state for the company or for an employee or representative in that capacity or other indications through advertising that the company or its employee or representative can be contacted at a specific address within the state normally will be treated as the company maintaining an office or place of business attributable to the employee or to its employee or representative in a representative capacity. However, the normal distribution and use of business cards and stationery identifying the employee's or representative's name, address, telephone and fax numbers, and affiliation with the company by itself will not be considered as publicly attributing an office to the company or to its employee or representative.
19. Entering into franchising or licensing agreements; selling or otherwise disposing of franchises and licenses; or selling or otherwise transferring tangible personal property pursuant to a franchise or license by the franchiser or licenser to its franchisee or licensee within the state.
20. Conducting any activity not listed in protected activities that is not entirely ancillary to requests for orders, even if such activity helps to increase purchases.

The Joyce Rule is applied to determine whether a company has conducted unprotected activities within a state. Statement of Information Concerning Practices of Multistate Tax Commission and Signatory States under Pub. L. No. 86-272 (VII.E). Under the Joyce Rule, activities conducted by a person other than a company will not be attributed to the company (even though the person is affiliated with the company) unless that other person was acting in a representative capacity on behalf of the company.

¶25,020 FEDERAL STATUTES—INTERNET TAX FREEDOM ACT

Out of concern that state taxation would limit Internet use, the Internet Tax Freedom Act (§1100 et seq. of P.L. 105-277) was enacted on October 21, 1998. That act imposed a moratorium (from October 1, 1998 through October 21, 2001) barring state and local governments from taxing Internet access and imposing multiple or discriminatory state and local taxes on e-commerce. The moratorium has been extended a number of times over the years and has been made permanent by Section 922 of the Trade Facilitation and Trade Enforcement Act of 2015 (P.L. 114-125). A grandfathering provision allows states that imposed and actually enforced a tax on internet access prior to October 1, 1998 to continue doing so until June 30, 2020.

These acts have not prevented state and local governments from collecting sales and use taxes on e-commerce. A domiciliary retailer who makes an Internet sale to a resident is required to collect sales tax from that resident, and residents who make an out-of-state purchase are required to pay use tax on their purchase.

Determining Whether a Nonresident Is Subject to a State's Taxes

¶25,025 NEXUS

A state's power to tax a nonresident or require a nonresident to collect and remit taxes to the state is limited by the U.S. Constitution, federal law (such as Public Law 86-272 and the Internet Tax Freedom Act), and applicable state law. The Due Process (part of the 14th Amendment) and Commerce (Art. I, 8, cl. 3) clauses of the U.S. Constitution prohibit a state from taxing a nonresident unless the nonresident has sufficient connection to the state. The presence or activity required within a state before the state may tax a nonresident is referred to as "nexus."

> **Observation:** The broad inquiry subsumed in both constitutional requirements is whether the taxing power exerted by the state bears fiscal relation to protection, opportunities, and benefits provided by the state (i.e., whether the state has given anything for which it can ask something in return). *MeadWestvaco Corp. v. Illinois Department of Revenue*, 128 S. Ct. 1498, 170 L. Ed.2d 404 (2008).

The Due Process Clause, which bars states from depriving any person of property without due process of law, demands that there be some definite link, some minimum connection, between a state and the person, property, or transaction that it seeks to tax as well as a rational relationship between the tax and the values connected with the taxing state. *MeadWestvaco Corp. v. Illinois Department of Revenue*, 128 S. Ct. 1498, 170 L. Ed.2d 404 (U.S. 2008). Due process is satisfied when a nonresident purposefully avails itself of the benefits of an economic market in a taxing state, the nonresident's contacts with the state are not so minimal that subjecting it to tax would offend traditional notions of fair play and substantial justice, and the tax is related to the benefits that the nonresident receives from access to the state. Physical presence within a state is not required. *Quill Corporation v. North Dakota*, 504 U.S. 298 (1992).

The Commerce Clause, which gives Congress the power to regulate commerce among the states, forbids states from levying a tax that discriminates against interstate commerce or burdens interstate commerce by subjecting activities to multiple or unfairly apportioned taxation. *MeadWestvaco Corp. v. Illinois Department of Revenue*, 128 S. Ct. 1498, 170 L. Ed.2d 404 (2008). A state tax will not violate the Commerce Clause if it satisfies the following four-part test: (1) it is applied to an activity with a substantial nexus with the taxing state; (2) it is fairly apportioned; (3) it does not discriminate against interstate commerce; and (4) it is fairly related to the services provided by the state. *Complete Auto Transit, Inc. v. Brady*, 430 U.S. 285 (1977). The second and third parts of this test prohibit taxes that pass an unfair share of the tax burden onto interstate commerce. The first and fourth parts of this test limit the reach of a taxing authority to ensure that state taxation does not unduly burden interstate commerce. *Quill Corporation v. North Dakota*, 504 U.S. 298 (1992).

Despite a similarity in phrasing, the nexus requirements of the Due Process ("minimum connection") and Commerce ("substantial nexus") clauses are not identical. A taxpayer may have the minimum contacts with a taxing state required by the Due Process Clause and yet lack the substantial nexus with that state required by the Commerce Clause. The "substantial nexus" requirement is not, like the Due Process "minimum contacts" requirement, a proxy for notice, but rather a means for limiting state burdens on interstate commerce. The Due Process nexus analysis requires that a taxpayer's connections with a state be substantial enough to legitimate the state's exercise of power over the taxpayer. By contrast, the Commerce Clause's nexus requirement is informed not so much by concerns about fairness for the taxpayer as by structural concerns about the effect of a state's tax on the national economy. *Quill Corporation v. North Dakota*, 504 U.S. 298 (1992).

Physical Presence Standard

Traditionally, physical presence within a state has been required before a state can be considered to have nexus. Although physical presence is not required to satisfy the Due Process Clause, it has been required to satisfy the Commerce Clause, at least with respect to sales and use taxes. *Quill Corporation v. North Dakota*, 504 U.S. 298 (1992).

This rule has frustrated state governments. They considered the physical presence limitation on their power to tax an anachronism at the time that *Quill* was decided, and their frustration with that rule has grown as Internet commerce has grown and increased the number of out-of-state vendors able to avoid state income taxation and the number of sales to state residents for which neither sales nor use tax is collected.

Attributional Nexus

States have attempted to establish nexus with persons having no physical presence (e.g., no office, property, or employees) within a state by attributing the physical presence of others to those persons.

The U.S. Supreme Court has upheld attributional nexus when a person performs activities within a state on behalf of a person with no physical presence within the state if the activities performed are significantly associated with the out-of-state person's ability to establish and maintain a market in the state. *Tyler Pipe Industries v. Washington State Department of Revenue*, 483 U.S. 232 (1987).

It is uncertain what type and quantity of in-state activities are required for attributional nexus. Activities can be performed by independent contractors as well as employees because the distinction between independent contractors and employees is without constitutional significance. *Tyler Pipe Industries v. Washington State Department of Revenue*, 483 U.S. 232 (1987).

Affiliate Nexus

Affiliate nexus attributes one person's physical presence within a state to someone with no physical presence within the state if the two persons are affiliated.

Affiliate nexus sometimes is treated as a form of attributional nexus, but the two are distinct. Although they may overlap, there may be affiliate nexus without attributional nexus and attributional nexus without affiliate nexus. For example, agency is required for affiliate nexus but is relevant, but not required, for attributional nexus.

State law (e.g., Michigan and Nevada) may rebuttably presume that a seller has nexus with the state if an affiliated person with physical presence in the state engages in any of the following activities relating to the seller's ability to make sales to state residents:

- Sells a similar line of products or services under a business name that is the same or similar to the seller's.
- Uses its employees, agents, independent contractors, or representatives to promote sales by the seller in the state.
- Maintains an office, distribution facility, warehouse, storage place, or similar place of business in the state to facilitate the delivery of tangible personal property sold by the seller to customers in the state.
- Uses, with the seller's knowledge or consent, trademarks, service marks, or trade names in the state that are the same or substantially similar to those that the seller uses.
- Delivers, installs, assembles, or performs maintenance service for the seller's customers.
- Shares management, business systems, business practices, or employees with the seller or engages in intercompany transactions related to activities occurring with the seller to establish or maintain the seller's market in the state.
- Conducts any other activities in the state that are significantly associated the seller's ability to establish and maintain a market in the state for the seller's products or services.

A seller may rebut this presumption by providing proof that the affiliated person did not engage in any activity in the state that was significantly associated with the seller's ability to establish or maintain a market in the state for the seller's products or services.

This type of nexus has not been approved by the U.S. Supreme Court. Other courts have been reluctant to attribute one person's physical presence to another absent factors allowing courts to pierce the veil of a corporation (e.g., commingling of funds, nonobservance of corporate formalities, insufficient funds to cover liabilities). See, e.g., *SFA Folio Collections, Inc. v. Bannon*, 585 A.2d 666 (Conn. 1991).

Click-Through Nexus (Amazon Laws)

States have been enacting click-through nexus laws (often referred to as "Amazon laws" because they are aimed at Amazon.com) to permit states to require e-retailers with no physical presence within a state to collect sales tax from sales to in-state residents or to notify customers of their obligation to pay use tax to the state (and sometimes notify a state's department of revenue about such sales).

Such laws presume that there is nexus between an out-of-state e-retailer and the state if the e-retailer has entered into agreements with state residents to pay the state residents a commission or other consideration for referring potential customers to the out-of-state e-retailer and the amount of sales generated by the referrals exceeds a specified amount (such as $10,000) during the year.

Most such laws allow this presumption to be rebutted by proof that the state resident did not solicit business within the state on behalf of the out-of-state e-retailer but merely advertised a link to the e-retailer's website).

Amazon laws can be challenged on a variety of grounds. They may be challenged as unconstitutional if they make the presumption irrebuttable. They also may be found to violate the federal Internet Tax Freedom Act by discriminating between e-retailers with in-state affiliates who refer Internet sales and e-retailers with in-state affiliates who refer non-Internet-related business. Amazon laws have been held preempted by the federal Internet Tax Freedom Act. See, e.g., P*erformance Marketing Association, Inc. v. Hamer*, 2013 WL 5674845 (Ill. 2013).

Economic Nexus

Unable so far to convince Congress to reverse the physical presence requirement legislatively, states have increasingly argued that a business' economic presence within a state (such as a business' licensing of trademarks for use within a state) gives the state the requisite substantial nexus to impose taxes other than sales and use taxes on the business.

Most courts have held that economic presence can establish substantial nexus with respect to taxes other than sales and use taxes. See, e.g., *Geoffrey, Inc. v. South Carolina Tax Commission*, 313 S.C. 15, 437 S.E. 2d 13 (S.C. 1993); *Lanco, Inc. v. Director, Division of Taxation*, 188 N.J. 380, 908 A.2d 176 (N.J. 2006); *Tax Commissioner of State v. MBNA America Bank, N.A.*, 220 W. Va. 163, 640 S.E.2d 226 (W. Va. 2006); *Geoffrey, Inc. v. Commissioner of Revenue*, 453 Mass. 17 (2009); *Classics Chicago, Inc. v. Comptroller of Treasury*, 189 Md. App. 695, 985 A.2d 593 (M. App. 2010); *KFC Corp. v. Iowa Dept. of Revenue*, 792 N.W.2d 308 (Iowa 2010). Contra: *J.C. Penney National Bank v. Johnson*, 19 S.W.3d 831 (Tenn. Ct. App. 1999); *Rylander v. Bandag Licensing Corp.*, 18 S.W.3d 296 (Tex. App. 2000).

The extent of economic activity required to satisfy both the Commerce and Due Process Clauses is not clear. For example, it has been held that a foreign licensor with no physical presence in a state did not have sufficient economic activity when all products bearing the licensor's trademarks and trade names were manufactured solely by unrelated or affiliated licensees of the foreign licensor outside the state, the foreign licensor did not direct or dictate how its licensees distributed the products, and the licensees, operating no retail stores in the state, sold the products only to wholesalers and retailers in the state. *Griffith v. ConAgra Brands, Inc.*, 229 W. Va. 190, 728 S.E.2d 74 (W. Va. 2012).

Factor Presence Nexus

The Multistate Tax Commission (MTC) has proposed a factor presence nexus standard (Factor Presence Nexus Standard for Business Activity Taxes) to provide what it refers to as a "simple, certain and equitable standard" for determining when a business has substantial nexus to a state. Under this standard, a business may have substantial nexus with a state if it has a specified amount of economic activity or a reasonable amount of physical presence in the state. A business has substantial nexus to a state if it has at least $50,000 in property, $50,000 in payroll, or $500,000 in sales in the state or at least 25 percent of its total property, total payroll, or total sales are in the state. Alabama, California, Colorado, Connecticut, Michigan, Ohio, Oklahoma, Tennessee, Washington, and Wisconsin have adopted this or a similar standard.

Trailing Nexus

Most states assert that they have the power to tax nonresidents for a period of time after activities creating nexus with the state have ceased (e.g., because a business no longer has any physical presence within the state) by asserting *trailing nexus*. The doctrine is applied mainly to sales and use taxes but also has been applied with respect to income and gross receipts taxes.

In Washington, a taxpayer who has established substantial nexus with the state for purposes of its business and occupations tax will be deemed to have substantial nexus with the state for the following tax year even though the taxpayer has ended the activities creating that substantial nexus. Wash. Rev. Code §82.04.220(2). The same trailing nexus rule applies to the retail sales tax. Wash. Admin. Code §458-20-193(104).

It is not clear whether trailing nexus is constitutional. The argument that it is constitutional is stronger with respect to income taxes than with respect to sales and use taxes, where a bright-line physical presence standard is applied.

Nexus With an Individual

A state may tax all of a resident's income, whether its source is within or outside the state. *Shaffer v. Carter*, 252 U.S. 37 (1920); *New York ex rel. Cohen v. Graves*, 300 U.S. 308 (1937). A state also may tax a nonresident's income, but only to the extent that it is derived from property located within the state or attributable to transactions or activities subject to the state's regulation and entitled to receive protection or benefits from the state. *International Harvester Co. v. Wisconsin Department of Taxation*, 322 U.S. 435 (1944).

States differ as to how they define "resident." Most states will characterize an individual as a resident if the individual satisfies any of the following tests:

- The individual is domiciled within the state. An individual's "domicile" is the individual's permanent place of residence. An individual may have only one domicile at a time.
- The individual is present in the state for other than a temporary or transitory purpose.
- The individual maintains a permanent place of abode within the state.

Federal statutes may affect the determination of nexus with respect to an individual. For example:

Special rule regarding retirement income. A state is prohibited from imposing its income tax on an individual's retirement income if the individual is not a resident or domiciliary of the state (4 U.S.C. §114(a)). Prior to the enactment of this federal statute, states argued that they had substantial nexus to a nonresident's retirement income if that income was earned while the individual was a resident.

Special rules for U.S. servicemembers and their spouses. A U.S. servicemember does not lose or acquire residence or domicile for tax purposes by reason of being absent or present in any state solely in compliance with military orders (50 U.S.C. App. §571(a)(1)). Neither does a servicemember's spouse if his or her residence or domicile is the same as the servicemember (50 U.S.C. App. §571(a)(2)). Compensation that a servicemember receives will not be deemed to be income for services performed or from sources within a state if the servicemember is not a resident or domiciliary of the state in which the servicemember is serving in compliance with military orders (50 U.S.C. App. §571(b)). Neither will income for services performed by a servicemember's spouse if the spouse is in the jurisdiction solely to be with the servicemember and the servicemember is serving in compliance with military orders. (50 U.S.C. App. §571(c)).

Nexus With a Business

A state can tax a business located in another state only if that business' contacts with the state are sufficient to create nexus.

A business has to pay income tax to the state in which it was organized and to any other states in which it has an office or facilities or property, employees, or agents physically present on a regular and systematic basis. The use of independent sales representatives can also create nexus. *Scripto, Inc. v. Carson*, 362 U.S. 207 (1960)(the distinction between employees and independent contractors is "without constitutional significance"); *Tyler Pipe Industries, Inc. v. Washington Department of Revenue*, 483 U.S. 232 (1987)(the activities of a single independent contractor residing in a state was sufficient to create nexus with that state).

> **Observation:** A corporation's ownership of an interest in a partnership doing business in a state usually is sufficient to create nexus for the corporation with the state. However, some states will not find nexus when the corporation's interest is that of a limited partner.

A state may say that it has the power to tax an out-of-state business that has no physical presence within the state if an entity related to the out-of-state business does have physical presence within the state or the out-of-state business has an economic presence within the state.

Some states by statute or administrative rule provide that certain activities that otherwise would create constitutional nexus will not be treated as doing so. For example, a state statute or administrative rule may provide that nexus is not established with the state if an out-of-state business owns or utilizes a distribution facility within the state, temporarily (e.g., for 60 or fewer days) stores goods in an in-state warehouse, permits equipment that it owns to be used by an in-state manufacturer, stores inventory with an in-state business that accepts and ships orders, or has employees attend a trade show or convention within the state. These exceptions are made to support in-state businesses.

With proper planning, a business can choose the states with which it has nexus. For example, if a business manufactures its products in one state but makes most of its sales to another state, it may want to move its manufacturing facilities to that other state. If multiple entities owned by a business are involved, the entities with the greatest profit should be located in the lower-tax states, and income should be shifted to those entities in those lower-tax states.

EXAMPLE 25.1	McDenny's Corporation operates in two states: State1 is a low-tax jurisdiction, and State2 is a high-tax state. If the manufacturing facilities are located in State2 and the only transactions that occur in State1 are sales, McDenny's should plan to shift as much taxable income to State1 as possible. If McDenny's does not have any nexus with State1, a sales office should be established.

TAX BLUNDER

Trebleclef Corporation is domiciled in State1 and has never made a sale in State2. Trebleclef has agreed to sell 100 widgets to a customer in State2. Trebleclef's CEO flies to State2 to finalize the terms of the contract. Because the CEO's presence in State2 exceeds the scope of solicitation, nexus is established, and State2 can tax the transaction.

¶25,035　E-COMMERCE

The advent of the Internet and e-commerce has raised many state tax issues, such as:

1. Should states be permitted to tax Internet access? Or should such taxes be prohibited because they will discourage people from using the Internet?
2. Should states be permitted to require out-of-state retailers to collect sales and use taxes from purchasers?
3. Should states be permitted to tax income from e-commerce? Or will such taxes stifle growth of this new form of commerce?
4. How should the nexus rules be applied to e-commerce businesses?

It is important to understand the competing interests of those affected by e-commerce:

- *Federal Government.* The federal government wants to encourage e-commerce and access to the Internet.
- *State and Local Governments.* State and local governments want to collect sales taxes on Web sales made to state residents and want to collect income taxes from e-businesses that derive income from transactions with state residents. State and local governments are concerned that they are losing sales and income tax revenue because they cannot identify all of the e-businesses doing business with residents of their state. States believe that they should be compensated for the benefits that they provide out-of-state retailers (such as a market for sales and an infrastructure and protection for deliveries).
- *Brick-and-Mortar (and Click-and-Brick) Retailers.* Retailers with a physical presence within a state are at a competitive disadvantage to e-retailers with no physical presence within the state because they have to pay the cost to collect sales tax and have to add the sales tax to the cost of their products.
- *E- retailers.* E-retailers do not believe that they should have to pay the same rate of income tax as brick-and-mortar (and click-and-brick) retailers because they do not receive the same financial benefits from state and local governments (e.g., police and fire protection) as retailers with a physical presence within the state. E-retailers are concerned about what could be overwhelming costs of tax compliance. If they sell all over the United States (and even worldwide), they may have to file returns and pay taxes in each of the thousands of taxing jurisdictions. To have to keep track of and apply different tax rates and different rules regarding which items are subject or exempt from sales taxes would impose a great financial burden on e-retailers. Compliance may be impossible if an e-retailer cannot identify where a customer resides (e.g., because the product is digitized and payment is with electronic money).

Nexus Issues

Sourcing income and sales to the appropriate state and municipal locality is complex, as demonstrated in the graphic below.

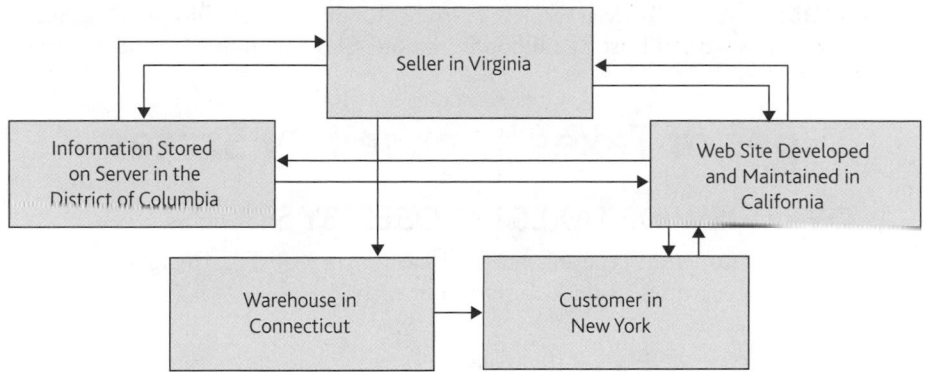

Does Virginia, where the seller's business is located, have jurisdiction over the transaction? Does California, where the Web Site is maintained, have jurisdiction? Does the District of Columbia have authority to tax the transaction because the information and processing of the order technically occurred at that location? Because the inventory is located in Connecticut, is nexus with that state established? If the customer resides in New York, at a minimum, should a sales or use tax be paid to New York? Who should collect that tax? Does New York have nexus with the seller?

There are additional complications if the residence of the customer cannot be determined (e.g., because digitized products are sold and electronic money is used to pay for the products), sales are through a Web site affiliated with the seller, digitized products are sold, or the seller has employees in multiple states (or countries).

Uncertainty about the nature of certain goods and services sold on the Internet and other items distributed through the Internet complicates nexus and other tax issues. For example, can electronic transmissions provide the physical presence within a state required to satisfy nexus? Can electronic transmissions be characterized as tangible personal property? Can cookies placed on computers within a state establish physical presence?

Sales Tax Issues

One challenge for state and local governments is to collect sales and use taxes on Internet purchases made by their residents. The U.S. Supreme Court in *Quill Corporation v. North Dakota*, 504 U.S. 298 (1992) prohibited states from requiring out-of-state sellers from collecting sales tax unless the seller has a physical presence within the state. As previously discussed, states have become increasingly aggressive in attributing to out-of-state e-businesses the physical presence of agents and affiliates physically present within a state. The constitutionality of such laws is unclear.

On November 12, 2002, 33 states and the District of Columbia approved the Streamlined Sales and Use Tax Agreement (the Agreement can be found at *www.streamlinedsalestax.org*), which makes it easier for retailers to collect sales tax by establishing one uniform system for administering and collecting sales taxes. The system reduces the number of sales tax rates, standardizes the definition of items subject to sales tax, significantly reduces the paperwork required from retailers, and uses new technology to modernize many administrative procedures. The ultimate goal of the states is to encourage Congress to require out-of-state retailers to collect use tax on purchases sent to a state even though the retailer has no physical presence in the state. Currently out-of-state retailers have no such legal obligation.

The Agreement took effect on October 1, 2005. Businesses that have not been collecting sales and use taxes in the states that comply with the Agreement can register with those states and receive amnesty for previously uncollected taxes. Collection by sellers on out-of-state sales remains voluntary. Action by Congress is required to make collection on such sales mandatory. Retailers who wish to collect sales and use taxes pursuant to the Agreement and receive amnesty for uncollected sales and use taxes must register at *https://www.sstregister.org/sellers*. A retailer who registers is required to collect sales and use taxes for each state that is in full compliance with the requirements of the Agreement. Retailers may, but are not required (unless they already are legally required to collect sales and use taxes for the state), to collect sales and use taxes for states that do not currently comply with the requirements of the Agreement but will be required to collect sales and use taxes for those states once they comply with the requirements of the Agreement.

Observation: The Marketplace Fairness Act of 2015 (S. 698) permits (Section 2) states to require retailers with at least $1 million in remote sales to collect sales and use taxes.

Types of Taxes Imposed By States

¶25,045   ## OVERVIEW OF TAXES IMPOSED BY STATES

There are numerous types of state and local taxes (SALTs). The following exhibit lists the basic types of SALTs and provides a brief description of each.

Type of Tax	Description of Tax
Individual Income Tax	Tax imposed on the taxable income of state residents from all sources and on the taxable income of nonresidents received from sources within the state
Corporate Income Tax	Tax imposed on the taxable income of corporations conducting business in the state
Gross Receipts Tax	Tax levied on a business' gross receipts from sources within the state
Sales Tax	Tax levied on retail sales
Use Tax	Tax on property purchased at retail outside a state but used within the state
Franchise Tax	Tax on the right to conduct business in the state; usually based on the company's paid-in capital allocable to the state
Real Property Tax	Tax on the assessed value of land and improvements
Personal Property Tax	Tax on the assessed value of personalty located or used in the taxing jurisdiction
Unemployment Insurance Tax	Tax on an employee's wages; designed to fund state unemployment benefits
Excise Tax	Tax typically imposed on sales of alcohol, tobacco, and gasoline
Transfer Tax	Included in this category of taxes are gift, estate, and inheritance taxes and taxes imposed on sales of real property
Severance Tax	Tax imposed on the removal or severance of natural resources

Each state controls the taxation of persons within its jurisdiction. Although different rules apply in each state, the types of taxes are generally similar. The following chart summarizes the range of rates for various types of taxes in each of the states (as of January 1, 2017, unless otherwise specified).

State	State Individual Income Tax	State Corporate Income Tax	State Unemployment Insurance Contribution Rates[1]	State Sales and Use Tax[2]	State Inheritance Tax	State Estate Tax
Alabama	2%–5%	6.5%[3]	0.59%–6.74%	4%	None	None
Alaska	None	0%–9.4%	1.0%–5.4%	None	None	None
Arizona	2.59%–4.54%	4.9%	0.03%–8.91%	5.6%	None	None
Arkansas	0.9%–6.9%	1%–6.5%	0.5%–6.4%	6.5%	None	None
California	1%–13.3%	8.84%	1.5%–6.2%	7.25%	None	None
Colorado	4.63%	4.63%[4]	0.62%–8.15%	2.9%	None	None
Connecticut	3%–6.99%	7.5%[5]	1.9%–6.8%	6.35%	None	7.2%–12%
Delaware	0%–6.6%	8.7%	0.1%–8%	None	None	0.8%–16%
D.C.	4%–8.95%	9%	1.6%–7%	5.75%	None	0.8%–16%
Florida	None	5.5%	0.1%–5.4%	6%	None	None
Georgia	1%–6%	6%	0.025%–5.4%	4%	None	None
Hawaii	1.4%–8.25%	4.4%–6.4%[6]	0%–5.6%	4%	None	10%–15.7%
Idaho	1.6%–7.4%	7.4%[7]	0.425%–5.4%	6%	None	None
Illinois	3.75%[8]	7.75%[9]	0.55%–7.75%	6.25%	None	0.8%–16%
Indiana	3.23%	6%[27]	0.505%–7.474%	7%	None	None
Iowa	0.36%–8.98%	6%–12%	0%–8%	6%	5%–15%	None

State	State Individual Income Tax	State Corporate Income Tax	State Unemployment Insurance Contribution Rates[1]	State Sales and Use Tax[2]	State Inheritance Tax	State Estate Tax
Kansas	0%–4.6%	4%–7%	0.20%–7.6%	6.5%	None	None
Kentucky	2%–6%	4%–6%	1%–10%	6%	2%–16%	None
Louisiana	2%–6%	4%–8%	0.1%–6.2%	5%	None	None
Maine	5.8%–10.15%	3.5%–8.93%	0.57%–5.4%	5.5%	None	8%–12%
Maryland	2%–5.75%	8.25%	0.3%–7.5%	6%	10%	16%
Massachusetts	5.10%[10]	8%[11]	0.73%–11.13%	6.25%	None	0.8%–16%
Michigan	4.25%	6%	0.6%–10.3%	6%	None	None
Minnesota	5.35%–9.85%	9.8%	0.2%–9.1%	6.875%	None	9%–16%
Mississippi	3%–5%	3%–5%	0.36%–5.56%	7%	None	None
Missouri	0%–6%[12]	6.25%	0%–9.75%	4.225%	None	None
Montana	1%–6.9%	6.75%[13]	0%–6.12%	None	None	None
Nebraska	2.46%–6.84%	5.58%–7.81%	0%–5.4%	5.5%	1%–18%	None
Nevada	None	None	0.25%–5.4%	6.85%	None	None
New Hampshire	5%[14]	8.5%[15]	0.05%–7%	None	None	None
New Jersey	1.4%–8.97%	6.5%–9%	1.2%–7%	6.875%[16]	11%–16%	0%–16%
New Mexico	1.7%–4.9%	4.8%–6.2%[17]	0.33%–5.4%	5.125%	None	None
New York	4%–8.82%	6.5%[18]	1.1%–8.5%	4%	None	3.06–16%
North Carolina	5.499%	3%[19]	0.06%–5.76%	4.75%	None	None
North Dakota	1.10%–2.90%	1.41%–4.31%[20]	0.28%–10.72%	5%	None	None
Ohio	0.495%–4.997%	None[21]	0.3%–8.7%	5.75%	None	None
Oklahoma	0.5%–5%[22]	6%	0.1%–5.5%	4.5%	None	None
Oregon	5%–9.9%	6.6%–7.6%[23]	1.11%–5.4%	None	None	0.8%–16%
Pennsylvania	3.07%	9.99%	2.801%–10.8937%	6%	4.5%–15%	None
Rhode Island	3.75%–5.99%[24]	7%	1.69%–9.79%	7%	None	0.8%–16%
South Carolina	0%–7%	5%	0.06%–5.46%	6%	None	None
South Dakota	None	None	0%–9.5%	4.5%	None	None
Tennessee	5%[14]	6.5%	2.3%–10%	7%	None	None
Texas	None	None[25]	0.45%–7.47%	6.25%	None	None
Utah	5%	5%	0.2%–7.2%	5.95%	None	None
Vermont	3.55%–8.95%	6%–8.5%	1.3%–8.4%	6%	None	0.8%–16%
Virginia	2%–5.75%	6%	0.17%–6.27%	5.3%	None	None
Washington	None	None[26]	0.13%–7.73%	6.5%	None	10%–20%
West Virginia	3%–6.5%	6.5%	1.5%–7.5%	6%	None	None
Wisconsin	4%–7.65%	7.9%	0.05%–12%	5%	None	None
Wyoming	None	None	0.27%–8.77%	4%	None	None

[1] These rates are effective through June 30, 2017 for New Jersey, Tennessee, and Vermont; for other states, these rates are effective for 2016.

[2] This is the general sales and use tax rate imposed by the state. This rate does not include local sales taxes that vary by locality but does include mandatory, statewide, local sales taxes added by California (1%), Utah (1.25%), and Virginia (1%).

[3] In lieu of paying the general corporation income tax on its net income, a corporation deriving income from business activities both within and outside Alabama may elect to pay a tax equal to 0.25% of its gross sales receipts derived in Alabama if its only activities in Alabama consisted of sales, it did not own or rent property in Alabama, and the dollar volume of its in-state sales did not exceed $100,000.

4   In lieu of paying the income tax, a corporation deriving income from business activities both within and outside Colorado may elect to pay a tax equal to 0.50% of its annual gross receipts derived from sales in or into Colorado if its only activities in Colorado consisted of making sales, it did not own or rent real estate within Colorado, and its gross sales in or into Colorado did not amount to more than $100,000.

5   Connecticut requires corporations to pay a tax equal to the greater of 7.5% of their taxable income, a 0.31% tax on capital stock and surplus (a maximum tax of $1 million), or $250. A 20% surcharge is imposed on corporations with at least $100 million in gross income and a tax liability exceeding $250. The surcharge is scheduled to drop to 10% starting January 1, 2018.

6   In lieu of the income tax, a corporation deriving income from business activities both within and without Hawaii may elect to pay a tax equal to 0.5% of its annual gross sales in or into Hawaii if the corporation's only activities in the state consisted of sales, it did not own or rent real estate or tangible personal property in Hawaii, and its annual gross sales in or into Hawaii during the tax year did not exceed $100,000.

7   In lieu of the income tax, a corporation with business activities both within and outside Idaho may elect to pay a tax equal to 1% of its gross sales within Idaho if its only activities within Idaho consisted of sales, it did not own or rent real estate or tangible personal property in Idaho, and its gross sales within Idaho did not exceed $100,000.

8   Illinois' individual income tax rate will be 3.25% for a tax year beginning on or after January 1, 2025.

9   Illinois' corporate income tax rate will be 7.3% for tax years beginning on or after January 1, 2025.

10 Massachusetts taxes short-term capital gain at a 12% tax rate. Taxpayers may voluntarily pay a 5.85% tax on income otherwise subject to the 5.25% tax rate.

11 In Massachusetts corporations have to pay an excise tax equal to the greater of $456 or the sum of (1) $2.60 per $1,000 of the value of its tangible property, if it is a tangible property corporation, or its net worth, if it is an intangible property corporation, plus (2) 8% of its net income.

12 Missouri's top personal income tax rate will be reduced by 0.1% for each year that the net general revenue collected during the previous fiscal year exceeds the highest amount of net general revenue in any one of the three previous fiscal years by at least $150 million. The top rate cannot be reduced below 5.5%.

13 In lieu of paying the income tax, a corporation deriving income within and without Montana may elect to pay a tax equal to 0.50% of its annual gross receipts derived from sales in or into Montana if its only activities in Montana consisted of making sales, it did not own or rent real estate or tangible personal property within Montana, and its gross sales in or into Montana did not amount to more than $100,000.

14 State income tax is levied on interest and dividends only.

15 Businesses with gross receipts not exceeding $50,000 for a tax year do not have to file a business profits tax return. Enterprises with more than $208,000 in gross receipts or an enterprise value tax base exceeding $104,000 for a tax year have to pay a business enterprise tax equal to 0.72% of the enterprise's value tax base (i.e., the sum of all compensation paid or accrued, interest paid or accrued, and dividends paid by the business enterprise, with certain adjustments, apportioned to New Hampshire).

16 The New Jersey sales and use tax rate will be 6.625% effective January 1, 2018.

17 In lieu of paying the income tax, a corporation whose annual gross sales in or into New Mexico amount to no more than $100,000 during the tax year may elect to pay a tax equal to 0.75% of its gross receipts from sales in or into New Mexico if the corporation's only activities in New Mexico consist of making sales and the corporation does not own or rent real estate within New Mexico.

18 Greater of 6.5% of net income, 0.085% of capital (0.056% for 2018, 0.038% for 2019, 0.019% for 2020, and 0% thereafter), or the fixed dollar minimum (which ranges from $25 for businesses with no more than $100,000 of New York income to $200,000 for businesses with more than $1 billion of New York income).

19 The North Carolina tax rate will be 3% if the amount of net general fund tax collected in a fiscal year exceeds $20.975 billion.

20 In lieu of the income tax, corporations with no more than $100,000 in North Dakota sales may elect to pay the alternative gross receipts tax, which is 0.6% of the first $20,000 of gross sales in North Dakota, 0.8% of gross sales in North Dakota exceeding $20,000 but not more than $55,000, and 1.0% of gross sales in North Dakota exceeding $55,000 but not exceeding $100,000.

21 The corporate income tax has been replaced with a commercial activity tax (CAT). For gross receipts greater than $150,000 but no more than $1 million, the CAT is $150. For gross receipts in excess of $1 million, the tax is 0.26%.

22 Contingent on income tax revenue, Oklahoma's top rate can be reduced to 4.85%.

23   In Oregon, a corporation may elect to pay as its income tax 0.25% of its gross sales in Oregon (0.125% of its gross sales in Oregon if its return on sales is less than 5%) if its only activities within Oregon consist of sales, it does not own or rent real estate or tangible personal property in Oregon, and its gross sales made within Oregon during the tax year did not exceed $100,000. C corporations have to pay a minimum tax based on their sales in Oregon. The minimum tax for a C corporation is $150 if its Oregon sales are less than $500,000, $500 if its Oregon sales are at least $500,000 but less than $1 million, $1,000 if its Oregon sales are at least $1 million but less than $2 million, $1,500 if its Oregon sales are at least $2 million but less than $3 million, $2,000 if its Oregon sales are at least $3 million but less than $5 million, $4,000 if its Oregon sales are at least $5 million but less than $7 million, $7,500 if its Oregon sales are at least $7 million but less than $10 million, $15,000 if its Oregon sales are at least $10 million but less than $25 million, $30,000 if its Oregon sales are at least $25 million but less than $50 million, $50,000 if its Oregon sales are at least $50 million but less than $75 million, $75,000 if its Oregon sales are at least $75 million but less than $100 million, and $100,000 if its Oregon sales are $100 million or more.

24   Rhode Island taxpayers may elect to pay a flat tax rate on federal adjusted gross income with limited deductions and adjustments to income. The flat tax rate is 5.5%.

25   Texas imposes a business margin tax equal to 0.75% (0.375% for those primarily engaged in retail or wholesale trade) of taxable margin. A corporation's margin is the lesser of (1) the lesser of 70% of the corporation's total revenue from its entire business or its total revenue from its entire business minus $1 million or (2) the corporation's total revenue from its entire business minus the greater of $1 million or an amount equal to the sum of, at the corporation's election, either the cost of goods sold or compensation, plus any compensation paid to a Texas resident during the period that the individual is serving on active duty as a member of the U.S. Armed Forces and the cost of training a replacement for the individual. A corporation's taxable margin is its margin apportioned to the state minus allowable deductions. Corporations with no more than $20 million in total revenue may elect to pay the E-Z tax rate of 0.331% on their total revenue apportioned to the state.

26   Washington has no income tax but imposes a gross receipts tax (referred to as a "business and occupation" tax).

27   6.25% before July 1, 2017; 6% after June 30, 2017 and before July 1, 2018; 5.75% after June 30, 2018 and before July 1, 2019; 5.5% after June 30, 2019 and before July 1, 2020; 5.25% after June 30, 2020 and before July 1, 2021; and 4.9% after June 30, 2021.

¶25,055   PROPERTY TAXES

For many local governments, most of their income comes from taxes on various types of property.

Real Property Taxes

Historically, local governments have derived most of their revenue by taxing the value of real property within their borders. A tax on real property tends to be regressive, meaning that it imposes a greater burden on lower-income individuals than on higher-income individuals. Only the state in which real property is situated may tax the property. Senior v. Braden, 295 U.S. 422 (1935).

Local governments tax most types of real property. School property, church property, state and municipal property, libraries, and cemeteries typically are not taxed. The U.S. Constitution prohibits states from taxing real property owned by the federal government. Van Brocklin v. State of Tennessee, 117 U.S. 151 (1886). However, federally owned property that is leased to a private party for use in a business conducted for profit can be taxed by a state. United States v. City of Detroit, 355 U.S. 466 (1958).

The amount of tax depends on the assessed value of the real property and the tax rate. The assessed value of real property is determined by local assessors and is reviewable by special boards and courts. The assessed value of real property may be its fair market value or a percentage of its fair market value. The percentage may vary depending on what type of property is involved (i.e., business or personal). To mitigate the regressive nature of the tax, local governments may give individuals a homestead exemption and may limit (even freeze) increases in assessments for certain types of individuals (e.g., lower-income seniors, long-time residents with lower income).

> **Observation:** Sometimes the tax rate is expressed as a mill rate (i.e., one tenth of one cent). For example, if the mill rate is 2, then $2 per $1,000 of assessed value will be collected.

The rate of tax is the sum of levies by municipalities, counties, townships, school districts, park districts, and other taxing authorities. States often limit the amount by which a levy may be increased each year.

Tangible Personal Property Taxes

Most states tax certain types of tangible personal property. States may tax tangible personal property only if it is situated within their borders. Frick v. Commonwealth of Pennsylvania, 268 U.S. 473 (1925). Property owned by the federal government cannot be taxed by a state. United States v. Allegheny County, Pennsylvania, 322 U.S. 174 (1944).

Tangible personal property. "Tangible personal property" is any personal property that has physical form, such as a motor vehicle or watch.

Because there are administrative difficulties in collecting this type of tax (e.g., personal property can be hidden or moved, it can be difficult to value personal property, and effective enforcement would involve serious violations of privacy), the tax may be imposed only on personal property that has to be registered (such as motor vehicles) or only on personal property that is used in a business.

Intangible Property Taxes

Some states tax certain types of intangible property (such as stocks, bonds, bank accounts, patents, trademarks, and copyrights). "Intangible property" is property that has no physical form. Such property is usually represented by a document (such as a stock certificate).

Usually licenses, franchises, and other privileges are not subject to an intangible property tax. Shares of domestic corporations also usually are exempt from taxation. The U.S. Constitution bars states from taxing direct obligations of the United States. *Home Savings Bank v. City of Des Moines*, 205 U.S. 503 (1907).

As a general rule, intangible property is taxed by the state where its legal owner is domiciled. However, intangible property also may be taxed by the state in which it is actually present and controlled. *Safe Deposit & Trust Co. of Baltimore, Maryland v. Commonwealth of Virginia*, 280 U.S. 83 (1929). More than one state may tax the same intangible property. *Curry v. McCanless*, 307 U.S. 357 (1939).

¶25,065   FRANCHISE TAXES

Many states impose an annual tax (referred to as a "franchise tax," "business privilege tax," or "capital stock tax") on domestic and foreign corporations for the privilege of existing in the state as a corporation and/or the privilege of doing business in the state. Some states (e.g., California, Florida, and New York) refer to their corporate income tax as a franchise tax.

Franchise taxes usually are measured by the value of a corporation's capital stock. Some states measure the tax based on a corporation's capital stock, surplus, long-term indebtedness, and assets. The tax may be a fixed percentage of the measure, or the measure may be divided into brackets and different rates or fixed amounts imposed on the different brackets.

A state may tax a domestic corporation's entire capital stock, surplus, long-term indebtedness, and/or assets even though the corporation does business in a foreign state. *Cream of Wheat Co. v. Grand Forks County, N.D.*, 253 U.S. 325 (1920). However, a state may measure the franchise tax imposed on a foreign corporation only by capital stock, surplus, long-term indebtedness, and/or assets employed within the state. *Cudahy Packing Co. v. Hinkle*, 278 U.S. 460 (1929). States may measure the tax on domestic corporations differently than the tax on foreign corporations, but only if the tax burdens are roughly approximate and similar in substance. *South Central Bell Telephone Co. v. Alabama*, 526 U.S. 160 (1999).

¶25,075   SALES AND USE TAXES (SUTs)

Sales and use taxes (SUTs) are imposed by most state and local governments on in-state retail sales of tangible personal property (and sometimes on sales of services). Retail sales should be distinguished from wholesale sales. Retail sales are sales directly to consumers; wholesale sales are sales of goods or services to someone expected to resell the goods or services to consumers.

State and local governments may exempt or impose a lower sales tax rate on sales of certain types of property, such as food, drugs, or fuel for residential customers. The retailer typically collects the tax from the consumer and remits it to the state. Half of the states give retailers a discount (up to 5%) for collecting sales tax. The amount of the discount usually is capped. An additional discount may be available for retailers who pay early or file and pay electronically.

States that impose a sales tax also levy a complementary use tax on tangible personal property purchased outside the state but used, stored, or consumed within the state. For example, someone who purchases a computer on-line from an out-of-state retailer does not have to pay sales tax on the purchase but does have to pay use tax to the purchaser's state of residence.

The purpose of the use tax is to eliminate sales tax evasion by subjecting property purchased in a no- or low-tax jurisdiction to the tax rate in effect in the purchaser's state of residence. However, compliance with the use tax has been significantly less than compliance with the sales tax because purchasers, not sellers, are responsible for reporting their out-of-state purchases and remitting the use tax they owe to the government. States have estimated that they lose billions of dollar each year through noncompliance.

¶25,085   STATE INCOME TAXES

There are thousands of state and local taxing jurisdictions in the United States. Currently, 46 states and the District of Columbia tax a corporation's income or gross receipts. Four states, Nevada, South Dakota, Washington, and Wyoming, have no corporate income tax. Forty-three states and the District of Columbia levy an income tax on individual taxpayers.

An individual who is a resident of a state and maintains a home in the state is generally subject to a state income tax on income earned both within and without the state. Counties and municipalities levy income taxes at minimal rates, if at all. Nonresident taxpayers typically pay income taxes only on income earned within the state or city. Allocation and apportionment of income within and without the various jurisdictions may be necessary. When multiple states tax the same income, state income tax credits may relieve the burden. For example, an individual may work in two adjacent states and reside in a third state. All three states can tax the individual. However, allocation of the income among the states and tax credits is likely to ameliorate the potential double (or triple) taxation.

Most states require employers to withhold state income taxes from wages paid to both residents and nonresidents. Some states (i.e., the District of Columbia, Illinois, Indiana, Iowa, Kentucky, Maryland, Michigan, Minnesota, Montana, New Jersey, North Dakota, Ohio, Pennsylvania, Virginia, West Virginia, and Wisconsin) have entered into reciprocal personal income tax agreements with one or more neighboring states. Under such agreements, income earned by a nonresident is taxed by that person's state of residence if both states are a party to the agreement. States enter into such agreements when they anticipate that the revenue lost will match the revenue gained.

EXAMPLE 25.2   Winona Corporation, a North Dakota employer, employs several workers who are residents of Montana. Under the reciprocal agreement between Montana and North Dakota, wages that Winona Corporation pays the Montana workers for work in North Dakota are taxed by Montana, not North Dakota. Winona Corporation must withhold Montana income tax from wages paid a Montana resident unless the Montana resident has given Winona Corporation a reciprocity exemption from withholding.

If a nonresident performs services partly within and without the state, the employer may withhold on the basis of apportionment and make necessary adjustments during the year so that the proper amount of tax is withheld.

EXAMPLE 25.3   Bob Rice is a traveling sales representative who receives commissions based on the volume of business transacted by him. The amount of income attributable to services within Nebraska is that portion of the compensation received that the volume of business transacted by Bob within Nebraska bears to the total volume of business transacted by him both within and without Nebraska (i.e., compensation × (Nebraska volume/Total volume)).

Volume of Business Transacted in Nebraska	$1,000,000
Total Volume of Business Transacted	$5,000,000
Nebraska Attribution = $1,000,000/$5,000,000 = 20%	

If the Nebraska withholding tables require that $1,000 be withheld for the pay period, then the prorated amount is $200 (20% × $1,000).

Alternative Minimum Tax

Some states impose an alternative minimum tax (AMT) in addition to the regular income tax. The AMT is imposed to prevent high income taxpayers from taking advantage of exclusions, deductions, and credits to pay a lower percentage of their income in tax than other taxpayers.

States imposing an AMT in addition to the personal income tax: California, Colorado, Connecticut, Iowa, Maryland, Minnesota, Vermont, and Wisconsin.

States imposing an AMT in addition to the corporate income tax: Alaska, California, Florida, Iowa, Maine, Minnesota, and New Jersey).

The AMT for some states is calculated similarly to the federal AMT. Other states have their own special rules or set a flat amount as the a minimum amount of tax owed.

¶25,095   COMPUTING STATE INCOME TAX

Most states have adopted all or a portion of the Internal Revenue Code ("Code") and Treasury Regulations pertaining to the Code as part of their tax laws. In those states, it is necessary to determine whether state law automatically incorporates changes in the Code or Treasury Regulations or whether the state has adopted the Code and Treasury Regulations as of a specific date and periodically updates that reference. It also is necessary to check for situations where state law diverges from the Code and Treasury Regulations.

Out of concern for their finances, states have increasingly been decoupling their income tax laws from the Code. For example, when Congress extends or expands a tax break, states may decide that they do not want (or cannot afford) to give state taxpayers the same break under state tax law. Other times decoupling occurs because states want to treat certain activities within their borders differently than they are treated by the Code.

Some of the areas where states have decoupled their tax law from federal law include:

- Depreciation. Many states do not allow bonus or other types of accelerated depreciation.
- The domestic production activities deduction under Code Sec. 199. Many states do not allow this deduction.
- Code Sec. 482, which authorizes the IRS to reallocate income, deductions, and credits among related taxpayers to prevent tax evasion and clearly reflect the taxpayers' income. Instead of adopting the guidance provided by the Treasury regulations, many states have adopted alternative rules for allocating the income of related taxpayers.

In most states the starting point for computing an individual's state income tax liability is the individual's federal adjusted gross income or federal taxable income. The starting point for calculating a C corporation's state income tax usually is the corporation's taxable income, either before or after the dividends received and net operating loss deductions. Using amounts reported on a taxpayer's federal tax return as a starting point reduces compliance and audit costs.

Regardless of whether the starting point in computing a state's corporate income tax is federal taxable income, federal taxable income before the NOL and dividends received deductions, or the state's own taxable income formula, the outcome is similar. For example, if one state uses federal taxable income and another uses federal taxable income before the NOL and dividends received deductions, the first state would require an adjustment for the NOL and the dividends received deductions. The typical formula used by states for determining a multistate corporation's state tax liability is illustrated in Table 1.

Table 1. Corporate State Income Tax Formula for Multistate Corporation	
	Federal income tax base
+	State adjustments (such as interest on state and local bonds)
–	State adjustments (such as interest on federal obligations)
	Income tax base to be allocated and apportioned
–	Allocable income (income specifically allocated to particular states)
	Total income eligible for apportionment
×	State apportionment percentage
	State apportioned income
+	Income allocated to the state
	State income tax base
×	State's income tax rate
	Tentative state income tax
–	Tax credits
	State income tax liability

EXAMPLE 25.4

A small corporation operates two retail stores in two states, each apportioning income based on gross sales. Assume the corporation's federal taxable income amounts to $200,000 (with positive adjustments to each state's tax base equal to $30,000), that tax rates imposed at the state level are 8% and 7% for States A and B, respectively, and that there is no income clearly allocable to either state. If sales were $400,000 and $300,000 in States A and B, respectively, then income is apportioned based on 4/7 and 3/7 ratios. Of course, this example is simplified because it is unusual for both states to utilize the same apportionment formula. The income tax liability for the corporation, based on these facts, is computed as:

State A Apportionment

	Federal income tax base	$200,000
+	State adjustments	30,000
	Income tax base to be apportioned and allocated	$230,000
−	Allocable income	0
	Total income eligible for apportionment	$230,000
×	State apportionment percentage ($400,000/$700,000)	.5714
	State apportioned income	$131,422
+	Income allocated to the state	0
	State income tax base	$131,422
×	State's income tax rates	8%
	Tentative state income tax	$10,514
−	Tax credits	0
	State income tax liability	$10,514

State B Apportionment

	Federal income tax base	$200,000
+	State adjustments	30,000
	Income tax base to be allocated and apportioned	$230,000
−	Allocable income	0
	Total income eligible for apportionment	$230,000
×	State apportionment percentage ($300,000/$700,000)	.4286
	State apportioned income	$98,578
+	Income allocated to the state	0
	State income tax base	$98,578
×	State's income tax rates	7%
	Tentative state income tax	$6,900
−	Tax credits	0
	State income tax liability	$6,900

States that use federal taxable income as the starting point for computing state tax liability make three types of adjustments to that federal taxable income: (1) certain items included in federal taxable income are subtracted; (2) certain items not reflected in federal taxable income are added or subtracted; and (3) certain items included in federal taxable income are measured differently for state tax purposes. Examples of these three types of adjustments include, respectively: (1) refunds of state income taxes; (2) municipal bond interest income; and (3) adjustment for the difference between MACRS used on the federal return and straight-line depreciation required on a state return. The following adjustments to federal taxable income represent the common changes necessary to convert federal to state taxable income.

Adjustments to Federal Taxable Income

1. Interest Income on Federal Obligations
2. Interest Income on State Obligations
3. Expenses Related to Generating Interest on Federal or State Obligations
4. Depreciation Adjustments (e.g., some states prohibit bonus depreciation and certain other accelerated depreciation methods)
5. Gain/Loss Adjustments Attributable to Differences between State and Federal Cost Recovery Methods
6. State Income Taxes
7. Federal Income Taxes (some states allow a deduction for such taxes)
8. Foreign Income Taxes
9. Election Adjustments (e.g., differences between state and federal installment sales rules)
10. NOL Adjustments (many states limit the use of NOLs)
11. Income Tax Refunds of State Taxes (to the extent included in federal taxable income)
12. Capital Gain and Loss Treatment
13. Mortgage Interest vs. Renters' Deductions
14. Non-business Interest Expense
15. Dividends Received Deduction (the percentage of dividends, or the nature of dividends, deductible may be limited)
16. Charitable Contributions (many states have different percentage limitations on deductible amount)
17. Domestic production activities deduction under Code Sec. 199 (some states do not allow this deduction)

EXAMPLE 25.5

Donut Hole Corporation conducts business in State1, where interest on state obligations is taxed but interest on federal obligations is not subject to state tax, and the starting point for computing state taxable income is federal taxable income. Donut Hole's income and expenses for the year are:

Sales		$990,000
+	Interest income on federal obligations	10,000
–	Expenses related to federal obligations	2,000
+	Interest income on state bonds	5,000
–	Expenses related to state obligations	1,000
–	State taxes	15,000
–	$300,000 MACRS on federal return (for financial statement and state income tax purposes, straight-line depreciation amounts to $200,000)	200,000
–	Cost of sales	500,000
–	Other business expenses	100,000
	Financial income before federal taxes	$187,000

Donut Hole's taxable income for federal tax purposes is:

Sales		$990,000
+	Interest on federal obligations	10,000
		$1,000,000
–	Cost of sales	500,000
–	Expenses related to federal obligations	2,000
–	State taxes paid	15,000
–	MACRS	300,000
–	Other business expenses	100,000
	Federal Taxable Income	$83,000

Donut Hole's taxable income for state tax purposes is:

Federal taxable income		$83,000
Modifications:		
–	Interest on federal obligations	10,000
+	Expenses related to federal obligations	2,000
+	Interest on state obligations	5,000
–	Expenses related to state obligations	1,000
+	Excess of MACRS over straight-line depreciation	100,000
+	State income taxes paid	15,000
	State Taxable Income	$194,000

¶25,105   **GROSS RECEIPTS TAX**

Ohio and Washington have a gross receipts tax (also referred to as a "turnover tax") in lieu of a corporate income tax. Delaware, New Mexico, and Virginia have a gross receipts tax in addition to a corporate income tax. As its name implies, a gross receipts tax is a tax on the total amount of a business' gross receipts.

Observation: The Interstate Income Law (P.L. 86-272), which prohibits states from taxing an out-of-state business' net income if its only business activities within the state consist of solicitation of orders for sales of tangible personal property, orders are sent outside the state for approval or rejection, and delivery is made from a point outside the state, does not apply to a gross receipts tax unless such a tax can be characterized as a tax on income. The same is true for Financial Accounting Standards Board (FASB) Statement No. 109, Accounting for Income Taxes.

States have been adopting a gross receipts tax to expand their tax base and increase their tax revenue. The tax is imposed regardless of the profitability of a business and often is imposed on all types of business entities, including flow-through entities not subject to income tax. The tax is easier to administer than an income tax, which involves complex determinations of profit.

Because the tax is imposed at each stage of production (e.g., when supplies, raw materials, and equipment are purchased) and every time that a product changes hands (e.g., when a product is sold by a manufacturer to a distributor and then to a customer), the same dollar of receipts can be taxed multiple times (this is referred to as "pyramiding"). By contrast, a sales tax is imposed only when a product is sold to a consumer.

The gross receipts tax encourages businesses to vertically integrate so that they can avoid a layer of tax. It also creates different effective tax rates for businesses in different industries. Industries involving more stages of production are taxed more than other types of industries.

How the term "gross receipts" is defined varies from state to state. Usually only a limited number of deductions and exemptions are allowed. A business usually is allowed to deduct returns, trade-ins, cash discounts, and bad debts but not the cost of goods sold, compensation, depreciation, and other operating expenses. A specified dollar amount may be exempt from the tax, and certain types of receipts may be exempted (e.g., tobacco and fuel taxes collected and dividend income).

The tax rate is lower than for income taxes because the tax base is so much larger. However, to reduce tax pyramiding, the tax rate may vary by business activity. For example, a retailer may pay a higher rate than a wholesaler, and a wholesaler may pay a higher rate than a manufacturer. The rate also may vary depending on the amount of a taxpayer's receipts.

A state may require that an out-of-state business have a minimum amount of property, payroll, or receipts within the state before it will be subject to the state's gross receipts tax.

¶25,115 ALLOCATION AND APPORTIONMENT OF INCOME AMONG STATES

When a business can be taxed by more than one state, it becomes necessary to determine what income can be taxed by each state. A similar question arises when an individual receives income from sources in more than one state. To make this determination, states have developed rules that allocate particular types of income (such as a business' nonbusiness income or an individual's wages, interest, and dividends) to specific states and apportion other income (such as business income) among the states that can tax it.

A state's tax on a nonresident's business income will be upheld as constitutional under the Commerce Clause only if the tax is fairly apportioned to income that arises from the nonresident's activities within the state. The purpose of this requirement is to ensure that a state taxes only its fair share of a taxpayer's income. *Oklahoma Tax Commission v. Jefferson Lines*, 514 U.S. 175 (1995). Without such a requirement, a taxpayer could be taxed multiple times (by multiple taxing jurisdictions) on the same income.

States can require taxpayers to apportion their business income using separate accounting or a formula. Under the separate accounting approach, standard accounting methods are used to trace income to the jurisdiction where it was earned. Because separate accounting is costly, difficult to perform, and subject to manipulation, all states use a formula to apportion income.

¶25,125 ALLOCATING INCOME TO A STATE

Each state has rules for determining whether any of a nonresident's income should be allocated to the state and become subject to the state's income tax.

Typically the following types of income will be allocated to a state:

- Wages, salaries, commissions, and other compensation paid in the state for personal services.
- Capital gains from sales or exchanges of real property located in the state.
- Capital gain from the sale or exchange of tangible personal property whose situs was in the state at the time of the sale or exchange.
- Rents and royalties from real property located in the state.
- Rents and royalties from tangible personal property utilized in the state.
- Patent and copyright royalties if the patent or copyright was utilized in the state by the payer.
- Lottery prizes awarded by the state's lottery.
- Estate or trust income from state sources.

¶25,135   SPECIAL RULES FOR ALLOCATING AND APPORTIONING A BUSINESS' INCOME

There are special rules for allocating and apportioning a business' income among the states from which it derives the income. Different rules are applied to a business' nonbusiness and business income.

To provide a uniform method for allocating and apportioning a business' business and non-business income among states and foreign countries and prevent businesses from paying tax on more than their net income, the Uniform Division of Income for Tax Purposes Act (UDITPA) was adopted by the National Conference of Commissioners on Uniform State Laws and the American Bar Association in 1957. Twenty-three states (Alabama, Alaska, Arizona, Arkansas, California, Colorado, Hawaii, Idaho, Kansas, Kentucky, Maine, Michigan, Minnesota, Missouri, Montana, New Mexico, North Dakota, Oregon, Pennsylvania, South Dakota, Texas, Utah, and Washington) and the District of Columbia have adopted UDITPA.

The Multistate Tax Commission (MTC), which was created in 1967 to promote uniformity in state tax laws, has adopted model regulations that interpret UDITPA provisions. Many states have adopted all or substantially all of the regulations or have generally consistent provisions. The MTC has recommended revisions of UDITPA, which has been incorporated nearly verbatim as Article 4 of the MTC's Multistate Tax Compact.

Allocation of Nonbusiness Income

Nonbusiness income usually is defined in the negative—as any income other than business income. See, e.g., Section 1(e) of UDITPA. Nonbusiness income includes portfolio income, such as dividends, interest, rents, patent and copyright royalties, and capital gains.

Under UDITPA, nonbusiness income is allocated as follows (UDITPA §§5-8):

1. Net rents and royalties from real property are allocated to the jurisdiction where the real property is located.
2. Net rents and royalties from tangible personal property are allocated to a particular jurisdiction to the extent that the property is utilized in that jurisdiction. All of the net rents and royalties are allocated to a particular jurisdiction if that jurisdiction is the taxpayer's commercial domicile and the taxpayer is not organized under the laws of or taxable in the jurisdiction where the property is utilized.
3. Capital gains and losses from sales of real property are allocated to the jurisdiction where the property is located.
4. Capital gains and losses from sales of tangible personal property are allocated to a particular jurisdiction if the property was situated in that jurisdiction at the time of the sale or the taxpayer's commercial domicile is in that jurisdiction and the taxpayer is not taxable in the jurisdiction where the property had a situs.
5. Capital gains and losses from sales of intangible personal property are allocated to a particular jurisdiction if the taxpayer's commercial domicile is in that jurisdiction.
6. Interest and dividends are allocated to the jurisdiction of the taxpayer's commercial domicile.
7. Patent and copyright royalties are allocated to a particular jurisdiction to the extent that the patent or copyright is utilized by the payer in that jurisdiction or, if the taxpayer's commercial domicile is in that jurisdiction, to the extent that the patent or copyright is utilized by the payer in a jurisdiction in which the taxpayer is not taxable.

Commercial domicile. "Commercial domicile" is the principal place from which a trade or business is directed or managed. UDITPA §1(b). According to the comment to UDITPA §1(b), the phrase "directed or managed" is not intended to permit the state where a company's board of directors meets and the state where a company is managed to each claim it is the company's commercial domicile.

Apportionment of Business Income

Income usually is classified as business income if it satisfies either of the following tests: See, e.g., Section 1(a) of UDITPA.

1. *Transactional test.* Income is business income if it arises from transactions and activity in the regular course of a taxpayer's trade or business.
2. *Functional test.* Income from tangible and intangible property is business income if the acquisition, management, and disposition of the property constitute an integral part of a taxpayer's regular trade or business operations.

Some courts have interpreted UDITPA as defining *business income* as income that satisfies the transactional test. Under this view, income satisfying the functional test is business income only if it also satisfies the transactional test (e.g., income from the sale of machinery used in a taxpayer's business is business income only if the business sells that type of machinery on a regular basis).

A recommended revision of UDITPA by the MTC would redefine business income (which it redefines as *apportionable income*) as any income apportionable under the U.S. Constitution (including income that satisfies either the transactional or functional test). In recent years the trend has been for states to define *business income* as all income apportionable to a state under the U.S. Constitution.

The MTC's recommended revision expands the functional test to include income arising from tangible and intangible property if the acquisition, management, employment, development, or disposition of the property is or was related to the operation of the taxpayer's trade or business.

States use various types of formulas to apportion a taxpayer's business income derived from more than one state. The United States Supreme Court has given states wide latitude in selecting an apportionment formula and has held that a formula-produced assessment will be disturbed only when a taxpayer has proved by clear and cogent evidence that the income attributed to the state is in fact out of all appropriate proportion to the business transacted in the state or has led to a grossly distorted result. *Moorman Manufacturing Co. v. G.D. Bair*, 437 U.S. 267 (1978) (a single-factor formula based on sales is presumptively constitutional).

No two states use exactly the same formula. Most states use a formula involving three factors: the total amount of property a taxpayer owns within the state (the property factor), the total amount of compensation paid by a taxpayer for services within the state (the payroll factor), and the total amount of sales made by a taxpayer within the state (the sales factor). California, Colorado, the District of Columbia, Georgia, Illinois, Indiana, Iowa, Louisiana (for most taxpayers), Maine, Michigan, Minnesota, Nebraska, New Jersey, New York, Oregon, Pennsylvania, Rhode Island, Texas, Utah (for taxpayers who generate more than 50% of their total sales by economic activities they perform that are classified in an NAICS code) and Wisconsin use only one factor (sales or gross receipts).

How a state using multiple factors weighs the factors varies from state to state. UDITPA (§9) recommends that equal weight be given to each of the three factors. A state using the three-factor formula and giving equal weight to each factor would use the following formula to apportion an enterprise's business income to the state:

$$\text{Income Apportioned to a Jurisdiction} = \frac{\text{Property Factor} + \text{Payroll Factor} + \text{Sales Factor}}{3}$$

Most states using the three-factor formula give double weight to the sales factor. The proposed revision of UDIPTA by MTC recommends that the sales factor be given double weight. Some states have special formulas for particular types of industries.

When a state gives additional weight to one factor, that additional weight increases the denominator of the formula. For example, if a state uses the three-factor formula but gives double weight to the sales factor, the formula used to apportion income to the state is:

$$\frac{\text{Property Factor} + \text{Payroll Factor} + (2 \times \text{Sales Factor})}{4}$$

If a state gives more weight to the sales factor than to the property or payroll factor, the percentage of an out-of-state corporation's income that is subject to the state's income tax increases because the corporation's principal activity in the state, sales, is weighted more heavily than its payroll and property. Giving more weight to the sales factor reduces the tax on in-state corporations that make sales nationwide but have significant property and payroll in the state.

Observation: The apportionment rules are intended to prevent corporations from having their income taxed more than once. However, because no two states use exactly the same formula to apportion a company's business income, more or less than all of a company's business income usually will be apportioned among the states. These formulas present an opportunity for tax professionals to maximize the amount of business income apportioned to states that do not tax such income (such income is referred to as "nowhere income").

EXAMPLE 25.6	Assume Morgan Corporation's business income is $500,000, the property factor is 33%, the payroll factor is 58%, and the sales factor is 43%. The apportionment factor for Morgan is 44.67% ((33% + 58% + 43%)/3), and the business apportioned to the state is $223,350 (.4467 x $500,000).

Property Factor

The property factor is a fraction that is intended to represent the extent of property usage in the state during the year. In states that follow UDITPA, the numerator is the average value of the taxpayer's real and tangible personal property owned or rented and used in the state during the tax period. The denominator is the average value (determined by averaging beginning and ending values) of all of the taxpayer's real and tangible personal property owned or rented and used during the tax period. See, e.g., UDITPA §§10, 12. Only property producing the net income to be apportioned is included in the fraction. Property producing nonbusiness income is excluded from the fraction.

EXAMPLE 25.7	Shannon Manufacturing, Inc. has total property values of $2,000,000 at the beginning of the year and $2,200,000 at year-end. Shannon Manufacturing has property located in more than one state; however, for purposes of apportioning its business income to State1, its property values are $500,000 at the beginning of the year and $490,000 at the end of the year. Shannon Manufacturing has a property factor in State1 of 23.57% ((($500,000 + $490,000)/2)/(($2,000,000 + $2,200,000)/2))).

Under UDITPA, property owned by the taxpayer is valued at its original cost plus any improvements, but not adjusted for depreciation. Leased property is valued at eight times the net annual rent rate (annual rent paid by the taxpayer less rents received from sub-rentals). UDITPA §11.

EXAMPLE 25.8	Inca, Inc. conducts business in several states. Inca owns property in a number of states; however, in State2 Inca rents its business property. The average total property values for Inca, excluding State2, amount to $1,000,000. Inca's annual rents in State2 amount to $20,000. Inca's property factor for State2 is 13.79% ((State2 Rents $20,000 × 8)/($1,000,000 Average value of other property + $160,000 from State2)).

EXAMPLE 25.9	Assume, in the above example, that Inca, Inc., has property in two states, which both use the prescribed UDITPA formula.

Property Located in:	Historical Cost: Beginning/End of Year	Lease Expenses in State
State1	$850,000/$750,000	$25,000
State2	$375,000/$425,000	$75,000
Total	$1,225,000/$1,175,000	$100,000

Total average historical cost = ($1,225,000 + $1,175,000)/2 = $1,200,000

Value of Leased Property = 8 x $100,000 = $800,000

Average Value of All Property = $1,200,000 + $800,000 = $2,000,000

State1's Property Factor:

Average historical cost = ($850,000 + $750,000)/2 = $800,000

Value of Leased Property = 8 x $25,000 = $200,000

State1's property factor = ($800,000 + $200,000)/$2,000,000 = 50%

State2's Property Factor:

Average historical cost = ($375,000 + $425,000)/2 = $400,000

Value of Leased Property = 8 x $75,000 = $600,000

State2's property factor = ($400,000 + $600,000)/$2,000,000 = 50%

The property factor is the most difficult factor to manipulate because the historical cost of assets remains relatively stable across time. Disposing obsolete inventory and fixed assets can reduce the amount of business income apportioned to a state. Warehousing inventory in a no-tax state reduces the property factor for a higher income tax state.

Payroll Factor

Under UDITPA, the payroll factor is the following fraction (UDITPA §13):

$$\frac{\text{Total Amount of Compensation Paid in the Taxing Jurisdiction}}{\text{Total Amount of Compensation Paid Everywhere}}$$

Compensation allocable to nonbusiness income is excluded from the fraction. When payroll is considered "paid" is determined using the normal accounting methods of the business. If a business is required for unemployment compensation purposes to report compensation using the cash method, the business may elect to use that same method when determining the amount of compensation to include in its payroll factor.

Generally, compensation that constitutes taxable income to the employee is included. For example, if meals and lodging are paid for an employee and they are treated as taxable income to that employee, then those payments are treated as compensation and included in the payroll factor. Some states deviate from this definition to include both taxable and nontaxable compensation, such as deferred compensation.

The term "employee" means any officer of a corporation or any individual who has the status of an employee under the common-law rules used to determine whether there is an employer-employee relationship. Payments made to an independent contractor or any other person not properly characterized as an employee are excluded from compensation for purposes of determining the payroll factor.

Under UDITPA, an employee's compensation is allocated to a single state, regardless of the number of states in which the employee works. Compensation is considered paid in a state if (1) the individual's service is performed entirely within the state, (2) the individual's service is performed both within and without the state but the service performed without the state is incidental to the individual's service within the state, or (3) some of the service is performed in the state and either the base of operations (or if there is no base of operations, the place from which the service is directed or controlled) is in the state or the base of operations or place from which the service is directed or controlled is not in any state in which some part of the service is performed, but the individual's residence is in the state. UDITPA §14.

EXAMPLE 25.10	A Corporation operates in two states. State1 imposes an 8% state income tax, and State2 levies a 5% tax. A's total payroll amounts to $3,000,000. If $2,000,000 is attributable to State1, the payroll factor for State1 is 66.67% ($2,000,000/$3,000,000) and 33.33% for State2 ($1,000,000/$3,000,000).
EXAMPLE 25.11	If A Corporation in the above example shifts $500,000 of its State1 payroll to independent contractors, then State2's payroll factor becomes 40% and State1's payroll factor is reduced to 60% (($2,000,000 – $500,000)/($3,000,000 – $500,000)).
EXAMPLE 25.12	If A Corporation instead shifts $500,000 of its payroll to the lower-tax jurisdiction, State2, considerable savings still result. State1's payroll factor decreases to 50%, as in the previous example, and State2's factor increases to 50% (($1,000,000 + $500,000)/$3,000,000). Tax savings result from the shift to a 5% state income rate from State1's 8%.
EXAMPLE 25.13	See Corporation is a multistate company, with its main offices in State1. Company payroll amounts to $300,000 for the year, and State3 compensation is $120,000, which includes $40,000 allocable to nonbusiness income. See's payroll factor for State3 is 26.67% ($80,000/$300,000).

Sales Factor

Under UDITPA, the numerator of the sales factor is the total sales of the taxpayer producing business income in the taxing jurisdiction during the tax period, and the denominator is the total sales of the taxpayer everywhere for the taxing period. UDITPA §15. Carrying charges, including interest and service charges on sales accounts, are included in the definition of sales. Typically, sales taxes are also included in the computation if the taxes are passed on to the buyer, either directly or indirectly.

As a general rule, the destination rule is used to determine where sales of tangible personal property were made. Under that rule, sales of tangible personal property are considered made within a taxing jurisdiction if the property is delivered or shipped to a purchaser (other than the United States government) within the taxing jurisdiction (regardless of the f.o.b. point or other conditions of the sale). However, if the property is shipped from an office, store, warehouse, factory, or other place of storage in the taxing jurisdiction and either the purchaser is the United States government or the taxpayer is not taxable in the jurisdiction where the property was delivered, the throwback rule discussed below applies to source the sale to the place where the property was shipped. UDITPA §16. Sales of other types of property are considered made within a taxing jurisdiction if the income-producing activity is performed in the taxing jurisdiction or the income-producing activity is performed both in and outside the taxing jurisdiction and a greater portion (based on costs of performance) of the income-producing activity is performed in the taxing jurisdiction than in any other jurisdiction. UDITPA §17.

The MTC has recommended that the market-based sourcing method (rather than the costs of performance method) be used for sales of property other than tangible personal property. Under the MTC's recommended revision of UDIPTA, sales of services and intangible property are sourced to a state if the taxpayer's market for such sales is in the state.

The following rules are used to determine whether a taxpayer's market for sales is in a state:

- In the case of the sale, rental, lease, or license of real property, the taxpayer's market is in a state to the extent that the property is located in the state.
- In the case of the rental, lease, or license of tangible personal property, the taxpayer's market is in a state to the extent that the property is located in the state.
- In the case of the sale of a service, the taxpayer's market is in a state to the extent that the service is delivered to a location in the state.
- In the case of intangible property that is rented, leased, or licensed, the taxpayer's market is in a state to the extent that the property is used in the state. Intangible property utilized in marketing a good or service to consumers is used in a state if that good or service is purchased by a consumer who is in the state.
- In the case of intangible property that is sold, the taxpayer's market is in a state to the extent that the property is used in the state.

EXAMPLE 25.14

Trekstar, Inc., conducts business in three states, with relevant information as follows:

	Total	State1	State2	State3
Net sales	$3,000,000	$2,000,000	$750,000	$250,000
Property values	$1,800,000	$900,000	$500,000	$400,000
Compensation	$1,000,000	$700,000	$200,000	$100,000
State income and tax rates	$400,000	6%	8%	9%

State1 uses the UDITPA apportionment formula to compute state taxable income. State1's sales factor is 66.67% ($2,000,000/$3,000,000), its property factor is 50% ($900,000/$1,800,000), and its payroll factor is 70% ($700,000/$1,000,000). State1 has an apportionment factor of 62.22% ((66.67% + 50% + 70%)/3) and a state income tax liability amounting to $14,933 (6% × ($400,000 × .6222)).

State2 also uses the UDITPA formula. Its apportionment factor is 24.26% (divide by 3 the sum of the sales factor 25% ($750,000/$3,000,000) plus the property factor 27.78% ($500,000/$1,800,000) plus the payroll factor 20% ($200,000/$1,000,000)) and has a state tax liability amounting to $7,763 (8% × (24.26% × $400,000)).

State3 deviates from the UDITPA formula by doubling the sales factor in its apportionment formula. The factors for sales, property, and payroll for State3 are 16.67% [2 × ($250,000/$3,000,000)], 22.22% ($400,000/$1,800,000), and 10% ($100,000/$1,000,000), respectively. Thus, State3's apportionment factor is 12.22% ((16.67% + 22.22% + 10%)/4). State3's income tax revenue from Trekstar is $4,399 (9% × (12.22% × $400,000)).

The apportionment formula results in less than 100% of Trekstar's total income subject to tax due to the apportionment formula used by State3: State1 taxes 62.22% of total income, State2 taxes 24.26% of total income, and State3 taxes 12.22% of total income, meaning that 98.7% of Trekstar's total income is subject to state taxation. If, however, the sales factor in State3 had been greater than its other factors, then Trekstar would have been subject to state income tax on more than $400,000 of its income.

EXAMPLE 25.15

Assume the same facts above except that State1 uses a single factor sales formula. Then Trekstar owes State1 $16,001 (6% × $400,000 × .6667), and 103.15% (66.67% + 24.26% + 12.22%) of its income is subject to state income tax.

Throwback and Throwout Rules

States use the throwback and throwout rules to manipulate the apportionment formula so that more corporate income is apportioned to the state.

A principle underlying the taxation of a taxpayer deriving income from more than one state is that the income should be apportioned to states where the income will be subject to income taxation. To prevent taxpayers from having "nowhere income" (i.e., income that is not apportionable to any jurisdiction that will tax the income), many states have a throwback rule, which makes a sale taxable in the state it was made if the state where the goods were delivered does not tax the taxpayer. UDITPA applies a throwback rule to the sales factor. Although sales of tangible property usually are allocated to the state where the property was shipped, if the taxpayer is not taxable in the destination state the sale will be treated as made in the state from which the property was shipped. UDITPA §14.

Most states that have a throwback rule apply it when goods are sold outside the United States, as well as within the United States. Many states have a double throwback rule applying to drop shipments (i.e., sales made by an in-state enterprise that are filled by a related out-of-state corporation and delivered to an out-of-state customer). Under a double throwback rule, the state where an order was taken may tax the sale if the sale otherwise would not be taxed by the state from which the goods were shipped or the state where the goods were delivered.

Throwout Rule. Some states (e.g., Colorado, Idaho, Illinois, Maine, Massachusetts, Oregon, and West Virginia) have a throwout rule, which excludes from the numerator and denominator of the sales factor any sales in a state in which the taxpayer is not subject to tax. This rule, which hurts taxpayers with nowhere income, would seem to violate the U.S. Supreme Court's requirement that any apportionment formula not attribute to a state an amount of income out of proportion to the business transacted in the state. However, the New Jersey Supreme Court has held that New Jersey's throwout rule (which has been repealed) is constitutional when applied to receipts that are not taxed because a state lacks jurisdiction to tax the taxpayer but not to receipts that are not taxed because the state does not have an income or similar business activity tax. *Whirlpool Properties, Inc. v. Director, Div. of Taxation*, 208 N.J. 141, 26 A.3d 446 (N.J. 2011).

PLANNING POINTER	Most of the planning opportunities in multistate taxation arise from the sales factor. One of the most straight-forward planning ideas uses the "ultimate destination concept." If a corporation changes its delivery location to a state in which nexus is insufficient or in which no state tax is levied (or in which the state income tax rate is lower), those sales are subject to less taxation than afforded by the origination state. However, this planning opportunity can be negated by the "throwback rule." The following examples illustrate the effects of this planning approach.
EXAMPLE 25.16	Madison Corporation operates in two states, with 80% of its sales made in State1 and the remaining 20% attributable to State2. Both states levy an 8% tax on state income and apportion state income based on a percentage of sales. If Madison has nexus with both states and net state taxable income is $500,000, then Madison pays $25,600 to State1 (80% × $400,000 x 8%) and $6,400 to State2 (20% × $400,000 x 8%), for a total of $32,000 in state taxes.
EXAMPLE 25.17	Assume the same facts as in the previous example except that State2's income tax rate is 4% on corporate taxable income. Then, Madison pays $25,600 to State1, but pays only $3,200 to State2 (20% x $400,000 x 4%), for a total of $28,800.
EXAMPLE 25.18	Continuing with the above example, if State1 sales are shifted to State2 through delivery strategies, then the state tax burden can be reduced. If the apportionment percentages are shifted to 50% each, then the state income tax can be reduced by $4,800 or a 17% reduction (State1 tax is 50% × $400,000 x 8% = 16,000 and State2 tax amounts to 50% × $400,000 x 4% = $8,000, for a total tax of $24,000).
EXAMPLE 25.19	If State2 is a no-tax state, the results are even more dramatic, saving half of the tax liability. The tax imposed on the amount allocable to State1, $16,000, is the sole state income tax liability.
EXAMPLE 25.20	The same result can be achieved if nexus is not established with State2.
EXAMPLE 25.21	If the throwback rule applies to State1 in Example 25.19, the planning strategy fails. All of the income not taxed in State2 is "pulled back" to State1, subjecting all of the state taxable income to tax in State1, resulting in a total tax burden of $32,000 (100% × $400,000 x 8%).
EXAMPLE 25.22	KT, Inc., operates in State1 (a double-throwback state), where an order was taken for the delivery of inventory manufactured and located at KT's supplier in State2. The goods were shipped directly from the supplier in State2 to the customer in State3. If neither State1 nor State3 taxes the sale, State1 taxes that sale under the double-throwback provision.

Apportioning a Corporate Partner's Share of Partnership Income

When a corporation is a partner in a partnership doing business in a state and the state has nexus with that partnership, it is necessary to determine whether the state apportions a partnership's income at the partnership level or the partner level. Most states require partner-level apportionment if the corporation and partnership constitute a unitary business (discussed in ¶25,145) and require partnership-level apportionment if the corporation and partnership are engaged in separate trades or businesses. However, some states require either partner-level apportionment or partnership-level apportionment regardless whether the corporation and partnership constitute a unitary business.

If a state uses partner-level apportionment, the corporate partner combines its distributive share of the partnership's income with its other income to determine the total amount of apportionable income. The corporation's apportionment percentage is calculated by taking the corporate partner's apportionment factors (e.g., sales, payroll, and property) within the state, adding the corporation's share of the partnership's apportionment factors within the state, and dividing by the sum of the corporation's apportionment factors everywhere plus the corporation's share of the partnership's apportionment factors everywhere.

If a state uses partnership-level apportionment, the corporate partner's distributive share of partnership income is apportioned based solely on the apportionment factors of the partnership within the state. The corporate partner's distributive share of partnership income is not combined with the corporation's other apportionable income, and the corporation's apportionment factors are not combined with the partnership's apportionment factors. Instead, the corporation's distributive share of partnership income is apportioned to the state by multiplying the partnership's apportionment percentage.

TAX BLUNDER

Wodgets, Inc., which had been doing business solely in State1, a state with no income tax, decided to expand its business to State2. In the year before the expansion, Wodgets' taxable income was $1,000,000, its net sales were $5,000,000, the average value of the property it owned and rented was $10,000,000, and its payroll (for purposes of the payroll factor) was $2,000,000. For various non-tax reasons, Wodgets moved its manufacturing facilities and most of its employees to State2, which taxed corporate income at a 10 percent rate. In the first year of the expansion, Wodgets' taxable income was $1,200,000, its net sales were $6,000,000 ($5,000,000 from State1 and $1,000,000 from State2), the average value of the property it owned and rented was $11,000,000 ($500,000 in State1 and $10,500,000 in State2), and its payroll was $3,000,000 ($250,000 in State1 and $2,750,000 in State2). State1 and State2 each used the UDITPA formula to apportion income. Under that formula 32 percent [(.05 + .08 + .83)/3] of its taxable income is apportioned to State1, and 68 percent [(.95 + .92 + .17)/3] of its taxable income is apportioned to State2. $1,200,000 x .32 = $384,000 of Wodgets' taxable income is apportioned to State1, and $1,200,000 x .68 = $816,000 of Wodgets' taxable income is apportioned to State2. Wodgets owes no income tax on the $384,000 apportioned to State1, which has no corporate income tax, but owes $816,000 x 10% = $81,600 in income tax in State2. If Wodgets had considered the tax consequences of its expansion and not moved its manufacturing facilities and employees to State2, 5.6 percent [(0 + 0 + .17)/3] of its taxable income would have been apportioned to State2, and its tax would have been 5.6% x $1,200,000 x 10% = $6,720.

¶25,145   UNITARY BUSINESS PRINCIPLE

When a business operates in more than one state (and/or country) as a number of activities (which may be separate legal entities), a state may treat the activities as a unitary business and tax the unitary business on the state's share of the unitary business' income from all of its separate activities. To exclude certain income from the apportionment formula, a business must prove that the income was earned in the course of activities unrelated to those carried on in the taxing state. *Allied-Signal, Inc. v. Director, Division of Taxation*, 504 US 768 (1992).

> **Observation:** The unitary business principles is applied to determine what out-of-state income a state may tax; it does not confer nexus. *Allied-Signal*, U.S., 504 U.S. 768, 112 S. Ct. 2251 (1992). A state cannot directly tax a subsidiary merely because the parent company can be taxed by the state. *Gore Enterprise Holdings, Inc.*, 437 Md. 492, 87 A.3d 1263 (Md. 2014).

Unitary Business

Under the Multistate Tax Commission's Principles for Determining the Existence of a Unitary Business (Reg. IV.1.(b)(1)), a "unitary business" is defined as "a single economic enterprise that is made up either of separate parts of a single business entity or of a commonly controlled group of business entities that are sufficiently interdependent, integrated and interrelated through their activities so as to provide a synergy and mutual benefit that produces a sharing or exchange of value among them and a significant flow of value to the separate parts."

The flow of value to a business entity that comes from being part of a unitary business conducted both within and outside a state provides the constitutional due process definite link and minimum connection giving the state power to apportion income arising from activities conducted outside the state. *Container Corp. of America v. Franchise Tax Board*, 463 U.S. 159 (1983); Multistate Tax Commission's Principles for Determining the existence of a Unitary Business (Reg. IV.1(b)).

The unitary business principle recognizes the states' authority to devise formulas to accurately assess a corporation's intrastate value or income. The principal virtue of the unitary business principle of taxation is that it does a better job of accounting for the many subtle and largely unquantifiable transfers of value that take place among components of a single enterprise than, for example, geographical or transactional accounting. *Allied-Signal, Inc. v. Director, Division of Taxation*, 504 US 768 (1992).

Courts give states great latitude in deciding whether a particular set of activities constitutes a unitary business and will overturn a state's judgment only if there is clear and cogent evidence that extraterritorial value is being taxed. *Container Corp. of America v. Franchise Tax Board*, 463 U.S. 159 (1983).

There is no objective way to determine whether business activities constitute a unitary business. Nor is there one test. The most common tests are:

- Three Unities Test.
- Contribution or Dependency Test.
- Factors-of-Profitability Test.
- Flow-of-Value Test.

Observation: References to "operational function" in the U.S. Supreme Court's *Container Corp.* and *Allied-Signal* decisions did not announce a new ground for apportioning extrastate values absent a unitary business. *MeadWestvaco Corp. v. Illinois Department of Revenue*, 128 S. Ct. 1498, 170 L. Ed.2d 404 (2008).

Three Unities Test

Under the Three Unities Test, derived from *Butler Brothers v. McColgan*, 315 U.S. 501 (1942), business activities will be treated as a unitary business if there is unity of ownership, unity of operation, and unity of use.

Unity of Ownership. There is unity of ownership if one business entity directly or indirectly owns more than 50 percent of the voting interests of another business entity or otherwise has the right to control who manages the business.

Unity of Operation. The sharing of staff functions (e.g., centralized accounting, purchasing, marketing, human resources, and professional services) is evidence that two businesses have a unity of operations.

Unity of Use. Line functions are examined to determine whether there is unity of use. Centralized management, intercompany financing, and intercompany transfers of products and know-how are evidence of unity of use.

Contribution or Dependency Test

Under the Contribution or Dependency Test, derived from *Edison California Stores, Inc. v. McColgan*, 176 P.2d 697 (Cal. 1947), business activities within a state and business activities outside the state will be treated as a unitary business if the operation of business activities within the state are dependent upon or contribute to the operation of business activities outside the state. Factors suggesting that business activities within a state are dependent or contribute to the operation of business activities outside the state include intercompany sales of goods or services, intercompany loans, the sharing of products or expertise, and the sharing of staff. Unity of ownership implicitly is required.

Factors-of-Profitability Test

Under the Factors-of-Profitability Test, derived from *Mobil Oil Corp. v. Commissioner of Taxes of Vermont*, 445 U.S. 425 (1980), business activities will be treated as a unitary business if they are functionally integrated, centralized managed, and show economies of scale.

Functional integration. Two businesses are functionally integrated if they share products, services, personnel, purchasing, marketing, distribution systems, and/or technical information.

Centralization of management. There is centralization of management if day-to-day decisions affecting two or more businesses are made by the same individuals.

Economies of scale. There are economies of scale when businesses save money by centralizing business functions, using the same workers, and taking advantage of the size of their combined operations to save money on purchases.

The Multistate Tax Commission uses the Factors-of-Profitability test to determine whether business activities constitute a unitary business. See Multistate Tax Commission Principles for Determining the Existence of a Unitary Business (Reg. IV.1(b)(2)). The presence of any one of the following factors creates a strong (but rebuttable) presumption that the taxpayer's activities constitute a single business (Reg. IV.1(b)(3)):

- Same type of business. Business activities in the same general line of business (e.g., a grocery chain) generally will be treated as a unitary business.
- Vertical integration. Business activities that are part of different steps in a vertically structured business almost always will be treated as a unitary business..
- Strong centralized management. Business activities may constitute a unitary business if there is a strong central management, coupled with centralized departments for such functions as financing, purchasing, advertising, or research.

Flow-of-Value Test

Under the Flow-of-Value Test, derived from *Container Corp. of America v. Franchise Tax Board*, 463 U.S. 159 (1983), business activities will be treated as a unitary business if "there [is] some sharing or exchange of value not capable of precise identification or measurement, beyond mere flow of funds arising out of passive investment or distinct business operation." There may be a flow of value if loans and loan guarantees are made from one business to another, other than at arm's length, or one business manages the others.

Once it is determined which business activities constitute a unitary business, the next question is which of those activities have nexus to the state. Most states have adopted the *Joyce* rule (derived from *In re Joyce, Inc.*, 66-SBE-070 (Cal. St. Bd. Of Equal. 1966)), which permits a state to consider only a member's in-state activities conducted on behalf of a unitary business for purposes of determining whether the member has nexus to the state. Other states have adopted the *Finnigan* rule (derived from *In re Finnigan Corp.*, 88-SBE-022-A (Cal. St. Bd. of Equal. 1988)), which provides that if one member of a unitary business has nexus with a state, then all members of the unitary business will be deemed to have nexus with the state.

> **Observation:** Section 4 of the Business Activity Tax Simplification Act of 2015 (H.R. 2584) would require states to apply the *Joyce* rule.

Some states apply the unitary business principle on a worldwide basis. Others permit taxpayers to make a water's-edge election to include only income earned within the United States in their apportionable income. States may require U.S. corporations that make up a unitary business to file a combined return on a worldwide basis. *Container Corp. v. Franchise Tax Board*, 463 U.S. 159 (1983). They also may require unitary businesses consisting of both U.S. and non-U.S. corporations to file combined returns. *Barclay's Bank PLC v. Franchise Tax Board of California*, 512 U.S. 298 (1994).

> **Observation:** When the unitary business principle is applied on a worldwide basis, the property and payroll factors can be affected by lower wage rates and property values in developing countries. It may be difficult for a business to comply with worldwide reporting requirements because records prepared using foreign accounting principles have to be converted to a form acceptable to a state.

EXAMPLE 25.23	Container Corp. is a vertically integrated corporation that manufactures custom-ordered paperboard packaging. California seeks to tax the income Container Corp. received from its wholly owned out-of-state subsidiaries, each of which is in the same business as the parent. The subsidiaries were relatively autonomous with respect to personnel matters and day-to-day management. However, in certain respects the relationship between Container Corp. and its subsidiaries was decidedly close. Approximately half of the subsidiaries' long-term debt either was held directly or guaranteed by Container Corp. Container Corp. provided advice and consultation regarding manufacturing techniques, engineering, design, architecture, insurance, and cost accounting to its subsidiaries. Container Corp. helped its subsidiaries to procure equipment, either by selling them used equipment it owned or by employing its own purchasing department to act as an agent for the subsidiaries. It also filled personnel needs that could not be met locally. Based on these facts, California was entitled to treat Container Corp. and its subsidiaries as a functionally integrated enterprise and therefore taxable as a unitary business. *Container Corp. of America v. Franchise Tax Board*, 463 U.S. 159 (1983).

EXAMPLE 25.24	A plastics manufacturer, Vacray Corporation, is organized with the parent performing only the financial and administrative functions. The controlled subsidiaries perform all other business functions, including production, distribution, and marketing functions. Vacray is a unitary business.

¶25,155   ESTATE, INHERITANCE, GIFT, AND GENERATION-SKIPPING TRANSFER TAXES

States often tax gratuitous transfers made by individuals during their lifetime by gift or at their death to relatives and others.

Estate Tax

The estate tax is a tax imposed on the value of an individual's property at death. It is imposed on an individual's right to transfer property at death and has to be paid by the individual's estate. Decedents who resided in a state at the time of their death typically are subject to the estate tax on the value of all property owned, within and without the state; individuals who did not reside in the state at the time of their death are taxed, by most states, only on the value of real and tangible personal property located within the state.

> **Observation:** Fourteen states (Connecticut, Delaware, Hawaii, Illinois, Maine, Maryland, Massachusetts, Minnesota, New Jersey, New York, Oregon, Rhode Island, Vermont, and Washington) and the District of Columbia impose an estate tax.

In calculating the estate tax, states exempt a certain dollar amount from tax. For example, New Jersey exempts $675,000 from its estate tax, Illinois exempts $4,000,000, and Delaware exempts an amount equal to the federal applicable exclusion amount. They also permit deductions (e.g., for funeral expenses, transfers to the decedent's surviving spouse, debts, charitable contributions, and administration expenses) and credits (e.g., for estate tax payments made to other states).

Inheritance Tax

The inheritance tax is a tax imposed on the value of property received by an individual from a decedent's estate. Unlike the estate tax, it has to be paid by each person receiving property from a decedent, not the decedent's estate.

> **Observation:** Six states (Iowa, Kentucky, Maryland, Nebraska, New Jersey, and Pennsylvania) impose an inheritance tax. Two states (Maryland and New Jersey) have both an inheritance tax and an estate tax.

The amount of inheritance tax imposed by a state usually varies depending on the relationship of the beneficiary to the decedent. Property received by a spouse usually is exempt from a state's inheritance tax. Property received by lineal ascendants and lineal descendants may be entirely exempt from a state's inheritance tax or exempt to the extent that its value does not exceed a specified amount. Those who are unrelated or distantly related to a decedent usually have to pay the greatest amount of inheritance tax.

Gift Tax

The gift tax is a tax imposed when property or an interest in property is transferred for less than adequate consideration. Connecticut is the only state that still imposes a gift tax.

As a general rule, a transfer will be treated as a gift under Connecticut law if it is treated as a gift for federal gift tax purposes. However, some transfers treated as gifts for federal gift tax purposes are not treated as gifts for Connecticut gift tax purposes. For example, transfers of tangible personal property and real property located outside Connecticut are not subject to the gift tax. Nonresidents are taxed only on gifts of real estate and tangible personal property located within the state.

No gift tax has to be paid until the amount of all Connecticut taxable gifts exceeds $2,000,000. The tax itself ranges from 7.2% (on taxable gifts in excess of $2,000,000 but not in excess of $3,600,000) to 12% (on taxable gifts in excess of $10,100,000).

Generation-Skipping Transfer Tax

The generation-skipping transfer tax is imposed on the value of lifetime and testamentary transfers made by an individual that skip one or more generations (e.g., a gift or bequest from a grandparent to a grandchild or great-grandchild). This type of tax is designed to prevent people from avoiding a round of gift or estate taxes by skipping a generation.

Observation: Hawaii, Illinois, Massachusetts, and Vermont impose a generation-skipping transfer tax.

States differ as to how the amount of the tax is calculated. In Hawaii, the amount of a state's generation-skipping transfer tax is the portion of the federal generation-skipping transfer tax attributable to state property that is transferred. In Illinois, Massachusetts, and Vermont, the amount of the tax is tied to the amount of the state tax credit that the would have been allowed by the federal generation-skipping transfer tax before the state tax credit was repealed.

¶25,165   SEVERANCE TAX

A severance tax (sometimes referred to as a "conservation" or "privilege" tax) is a tax imposed for the privilege of removing a natural resource from the soil or water. States imposing severance taxes say that such taxes are needed to reimburse the states for the loss of a public resource and the public costs of exploiting natural resources (e.g., increased demand for roads, schools, and other infrastructure). Resource-rich states use severance taxes to shift the tax burden to nonresidents.

Usually only certain types of businesses (such as mining or timber companies or producers of oil or gas) are subject to a severance tax.

Examples of severance taxes include:

- A tax on gross sales of coal, oil, and other minerals extracted from the soil
- A stumpage tax on timber
- A tax on fish, clams, and oysters.

The tax usually is a percentage of the value of the item severed. Value may be defined as market value, net value, or net proceeds. The tax rate may or may not be graduated.

The tax usually has to be paid by the person doing the severing, but sometimes the first purchaser is liable for the tax (unless the product is not sold within a specified period of time following its severance). When a producer is liable for the tax, sometimes there is a question as to what constitutes severance. For example, refining may or may not be considered part of the severance process.

Because a severance tax usually is treated as an excise tax rather than as a property tax, a severance tax is not subject to state constitutional restrictions relating to property taxes and may be imposed in addition to ad valorem taxes without being treated as prohibited double taxation.

¶25,175   UNEMPLOYMENT INSURANCE TAX

Each state requires employers to pay an unemployment insurance tax to provide funds to pay unemployment benefits to individuals who become unemployed through no fault of their own. The federal government also imposes its own unemployment insurance tax, equal to 6.2% of the first $7,000 of a worker's gross earnings, but gives employers a 5.4% credit (reducing the tax to 0.8%) if required payments to the state are timely made.

The state UI tax is imposed on a specified amount of wages ("taxable wage base"), which varies from state to state. A tax rate (referred to as the "contribution rate") is computed for each individual employer. The contribution rate depends on how much money the state needs to fund unemployment benefits and the employer's experience rating (i.e., how much money it has cost the state's unemployment insurance program). New employers are assigned a new employer rate.

¶25,185   EXCISE TAX

An excise tax is a tax imposed on the purchase of certain types of goods (such as cigarettes, alcoholic beverages, sweetened and diet drinks, and motor fuels) and activities (such as gambling, air travel, and fishing). Although the tax is paid by the seller, it is expected that it will be passed on to the purchaser and increase the cost of the good or activity.

Such taxes are designed to protect individuals by deterring them from engaging in certain activities that can be harmful to them (such as smoking cigarettes, drinking alcoholic beverages, and gambling). Excise taxes also are designed to protect society by deterring certain conduct (such as activities that hurt the environment) and compensate society for the additional costs incurred when individuals engage in certain activities (such as increased health costs caused by smoking cigarettes and damage to roads caused by driving).

¶25,195   TAXATION OF PARTNERSHIPS, S CORPORATIONS, AND LIMITED LIABILITY COMPANIES

States have special tax rules for S corporations, partnerships, and limited liability companies that have nexus to the state.

S Corporations

Most states recognize a corporation's S status under federal tax law for state tax purposes. However, S corporations are taxed the same as C corporations by the District of Columbia, Louisiana, New Hampshire, Tennessee, and Texas.

In most states that recognize S corporations, the federal S election is automatically effective for state tax purposes. However, some states require corporations to file a copy of their federal S election with the state or make a separate state election (e.g., Arkansas, New Jersey, and New York). Some states require nonresident shareholders to consent to the S election and agree to report and pay state income tax on their pro rata share of the corporation's income. A nonresident shareholder's failure to pay state income tax may revoke the corporation's S election for state income tax purposes.

Taxation of the Corporation Itself

When a state treats a corporation as an S corporation, the corporation's taxable income is usually taxed to the corporation's shareholders, not the corporation itself. However, some states will exempt an S corporation from state income tax only if all of the corporation's shareholders reside in the state or if all nonresident shareholders agree to report and pay state income tax on their distributive share of corporate income allocated and apportioned to the state. Other states (e.g., California, Illinois, Kentucky, Massachusetts, and New Hampshire) require S corporations to pay income tax on their income but at a lower rate than that applied to C corporations.

When a state does not recognize a corporation as an S corporation, the corporation is taxed like a C corporation. The corporation pays income tax on its taxable income, and shareholders do not recognize income until corporate earnings are actually or constructively distributed to them.

Although a corporation is exempt from state income tax because of its S status, it nevertheless will have to pay other types of state taxes (e.g., property, excise, and franchise taxes). States that recognize S corporations may follow the federal rules and tax corporations that convert from C to S corporations on their built-in gains, passive investment income, and LIFO recapture.

Taxation of Resident Shareholders

Shareholders of an S corporation who reside in a state usually are taxed on their pro rata share of their corporation's income, whether or not that income is distributed to them and regardless whether that income is allocated and apportioned to the state. However, some states tax resident shareholders only on their pro rata share of income allocated and apportioned to the state.

If a portion of an S corporation's income is derived from another state, resident shareholders usually receive a credit for tax paid to that other state. In lieu of a credit, some states permit resident shareholders to include in their taxable income only their share of income allocated and apportioned to the state.

Resident shareholders usually are allowed a credit for taxes paid by the corporation to another state.

Taxation of Nonresident Shareholders

Most states tax nonresidents on their pro rata share of income derived from the corporation's business activities allocated and apportioned to the state. If a nonresident shareholder merely owns stock and does not engage in the corporation's business within the state, most states source the nonresident shareholder's share of the corporation's income outside the state.

Some states allow nonresident shareholders a credit for taxes paid to the nonresident shareholder's home state on income allocated and apportioned to the nonresident shareholders' home state if the home state does not allow a credit for taxes paid to another state or the home state reciprocates with a similar credit.

Some states require S corporations to pay income tax on behalf of their nonresident shareholders unless the nonresident shareholders consent in writing to be taxed by the state. Others require or permit S corporations to withhold state income tax (usually at the highest tax rate) from their nonresident shareholders. A corporation's obligation to pay or withhold tax may be triggered only if the nonresident shareholder fails to consent to state taxation or fails to file a required state income tax return.

Partnerships

Most states will treat a business characterized as a partnership for federal income tax purposes as a partnership for state income tax purposes. However, a business characterized as a partnership for federal income tax purposes will not necessarily be characterized as a partnership for state income tax purposes, and a business characterized as a partnership for state income tax purposes will not necessarily be characterized as a partnership for federal income tax purposes.

Taxation of the Partnership Itself

Most states treat partnerships as flow-through entities and do not tax them on their taxable income. However, some states will tax partnerships on their taxable income (usually at a lower rate than that imposed on C corporations). States that do not tax partnerships on their taxable income will impose other state taxes (e.g., property, excise, and franchise taxes) on partnerships.

Taxation of Resident Partners

Partners who reside in a state generally are taxed on their entire distributive share of their partnership's income, regardless of where the income is earned. Some states tax resident partners only on their share of income allocated and apportioned to the state. If any partnership income is derived from another state, the resident partner usually is allowed a credit for taxes actually paid to the other state. Some states allow resident partners a credit for any income taxes paid to the state by the partnership.

Taxation of Nonresident Partners

Nonresident partners generally are taxed on their distributive share of partnership income allocated and apportioned to the state. Many states require partnerships to withhold tax (usually at the highest withholding tax rate) with respect to their nonresident partners' distributive share of partnership income. States argue that nonresident partners have nexus with the state because nonresidents are constructively present in the state through their partnership's presence or actions on their behalf by the general partner.

Some states allow nonresident partners a credit for taxes paid to the nonresident partner's home state on income allocated and apportioned to the home state if the home state does not allow a credit for taxes paid to other states or the home state reciprocates with a similar credit. Some states allow nonresident partners a credit for any income taxes paid to the state by the partnership.

Limited Liability Companies

How a state taxes a limited liability company (LLC) depends on whether the LLC is treated as a partnership or corporation for tax purposes. In most states, an LLC taxed as a partnership for federal income tax purposes also will be taxed as a partnership for state tax purposes.

Taxation of the LLC Itself

Most states treat an LLC classified as a partnership as a flow-through entity and do not tax the LLC on its taxable income. However, some states do tax LLCs on their taxable income (usually at a lower rate than that imposed on C corporation). Even though a state does not tax LLCs on their taxable income, it will impose other types of state taxes on LLCs.

Taxation of Resident Members

Members who reside in the state are taxed on their entire share of LLC income if the LLC is taxed like a partnership. If any of that income is derived from another state, the member usually is allowed a credit for taxes actually paid to that other state. Some states give resident members a credit for any income taxes paid by their LLC.

Taxation of Nonresident Members

Nonresident members usually are taxed on their distributive share of business income apportioned to the state and nonbusiness income allocated to the state.

Some states allow a credit for taxes paid to a nonresident member's home state on income derived within the state of nonresidence if the home state does not allow a credit for taxes paid to another state or the home state reciprocates with a similar credit. Some states give nonresident members a credit for any income taxes paid by their LLC. Many states require LLCs to withhold income tax from distributions to nonresident members.

¶25,205   STATE INCOME TAX FILING REQUIREMENTS FOR BUSINESSES

Rules for reporting and filing state income tax returns vary by state.

C Corporations

C corporations have to file a particular state's income tax return if they are subject to the state's income tax (i.e., if they do business in the state, derive income from sources within the state, or are incorporated in the state).

About half of the states permit an affiliated group of corporations to file a consolidated return. However, the prerequisites for filing a state consolidated return are not the same as the prerequisites for filing a federal consolidated return. Most states have the same ownership requirement but may require that a federal consolidated return be filed as a prerequisite for filing a state consolidated return and may require that the parent and/or each affiliate have nexus to the state. The advantages of filing a state consolidated return are that losses from affiliates can be offset against profits from other affiliates, intercorporate dividends are eliminated, gains on intercompany transactions can be deferred, and credits otherwise limited because of lack of income can be utilized. A disadvantage of filing a state consolidated return is that doing so may prevent the affiliated corporations from shifting income from high-tax to lower-tax states.

If the unitary business principle applies to a group of affiliated corporations, the corporations may be required or permitted to file a combined tax return. Some states apply the unitary business principle when apportioning income to members of the unitary group but require each member to file a separate return.

EXAMPLE 25.25

Jerry and Ben's is domiciled in State1. Jerry and Ben's owns 70% of the outstanding stock in two corporations that manage Jerry and Ben's selling operations in two other states, State2 and State3. For the current period, the three corporations have nexus with their own state and report the following:

Corporation	State Taxable Income	UDITPA Factor	State Tax Rate
Jerry and Ben's	$500,000	30%	9%
State2 Corp.	$1,000,000	30%	8%
State3 Corp.	$2,000,000	40%	6%
Total	$3,500,000	100%	

This group cannot file a consolidated return with any of the three states because it is not eligible to file a federal consolidated return (Jerry and Ben's does not own at least 80% of one of the affiliated corporations). The group, however, is eligible to file a nexus consolidated return or a unitary combination return. The total state taxable income is apportioned based on the relevant UDITPA factor for each state. The state tax liabilities are computed as follows:

Jerry and Ben's State1 Tax = $3,500,000 × 30% × 9% = $94,500

State2 Tax = $3,500,000 × 30% x 8% = $84,000

State3 Tax = $3,500,000 × 40% x 6% = $84,000

Total amount of tax paid: $94,500 + $84,000 + $84,000 = $262,500

EXAMPLE 25.26

In the previous example, assume instead that the states require separate filing. The state tax liabilities amount to:

Jerry and Ben's in State1 = $500,000 × 9% = $45,000

State2 Tax = $1,000,000 × 8% = $80,000

State3 Tax = $2,000,000 × 6% = $120,000

Total amount of tax paid: $45,000 + $80,000 + $120,000 = $245,000

EXAMPLE 25.27

JG Corporation is domiciled in State1. JG Corporation manufactures widgets in State1. The widgets are sold by a wholly owned subsidiary, ABC Corporation, which is domiciled in State2. If State1 permits unitary business groups to file a combined return, JG Corporation and ABC Corporation can file a combined return in State1.

S Corporations

Most states require S corporations to file an informational return with the state if the corporation does business or derives income from sources within the state. Some states also require S corporations to file a return if any shareholder resides in the state, even though the S corporation does not do business or derive income from sources within the state.

Shareholders residing in a state are required to file a return and pay tax on their income from all sources, including the S corporation. Shareholders who are not a resident of a state nevertheless must file a return if their S corporation has nexus with the state.

The requirement that nonresident shareholders file a return and pay taxes to every state in which their S corporation does business can be burdensome if the S corporation does business in multiple states. To encourage tax compliance, most states require or permit S corporation shareholders or their corporation to file a composite return.

A composite return lists each nonresident shareholder's pro rata share of the corporation's income, deductions, losses, and credits. The amount of tax owed by each nonresident shareholder is calculated using the maximum tax rate applicable to each shareholder and is paid by the S corporation on behalf of each shareholder.

Before a composite return can be filed, certain requirements may have to be satisfied. For example, each participating shareholder usually must have been a nonresident for the entire year, a participating shareholder's S corporation income must be the only income that the shareholder received from sources within the state, and a minimum number of shareholders must participate in the filing.

Some states require S corporations to withhold tax from corporate income owed nonresident shareholders. The amount withheld is calculated by multiplying each nonresident shareholder's pro rata share of income allocated and apportioned to the state by the highest marginal tax rate applicable to the shareholder.

Partnerships

Most states require a partnership to file an annual information return if the partnership does business or derives income from sources within the state. Some states also require a partnership to file an information return if it has any partners who are residents of the state, even though the partnership does not do business within the state.

Most states permit or require partnerships to file a composite income tax return on behalf of all or some of their nonresident partners (sometimes including nonresident corporations and pass-through entities). A composite income tax return is similar to the federal Schedule K-1. Partnerships that file a composite return pay the state income tax owed by each nonresident partner whose only source of state income is his or her distributive share of the partnership's income. By filing a composite return, a partnership relieves its nonresident partners of the need to file a separate state income tax return.

Some states require partnerships to withhold tax from distributions to nonresident partners or from a nonresident partner's distributive share of income. Withholding may be required only if a nonresident partner fails to consent to file an income tax return and pay tax on income sourced to the state or the nonresident partner refuses to be included in a composite return filed by the partnership. The amount required to be withheld is calculated by multiplying the state's highest marginal tax rate on income received by a nonresident partner by the nonresident partner's distributive share of income allocated and apportioned to the state.

Limited Liability Companies

Most states require LLCs taxed as partnerships to file an informational income tax return if they do business in the state or they have a member who is a resident of the state.

Most states permit or require LLCs taxed as partnerships to file a composite income tax return on behalf of all or some of their nonresident members. A composite income tax return is similar to the federal Schedule K-1. LLCs that file a composite return pay the state income tax owed by each nonresident member whose only source of state income is his or her distributive share of the LLC's income.

International Taxation

¶25,301   ## WORLDWIDE VS. TERRITORIAL SYSTEM OF TAXATION

Most countries (including Australia, Canada, France, Germany, Japan, and the United Kingdom) have a territorial system of taxation. Countries with a territorial system of taxation tax income from sources within the country but not foreign-source income.

EXAMPLE 25.28   Zhongguo Corporation is incorporated in a country that uses the territorial system of taxation. Zhongguo Corporation received $1 million from sources within its country of incorporation and $3 million from other sources. The corporation will be taxed by its country of incorporation on the $1 million it received but not on the $3 million that it received.

The United States and a few other countries (such as Mexico and South Korea) have a worldwide system of taxation. Under the worldwide system of taxation, a country taxes its citizens and residents on all of their income, including income received from both domestic and foreign sources. Nonresidents are taxed on income sourced to the country with a worldwide system of taxation but not on their income from other sources.

EXAMPLE 25.29   Havelton Manufacturing is a U.S. corporation. It earns $2 million from U.S. sources and $4 million from foreign sources. Havelton Manufacturing will have to include all $6 million in gross income subject to U.S. taxation.

The United States permits corporations to defer income tax on many types of foreign-source income until that income is brought back ("repatriated") to the United States. Other income (such as "passive income," which includes many types of investment income) is immediately taxed.

Taxpayers in countries using the worldwide system of taxation may have their foreign-source income taxed twice—once by the United States and a second time by the foreign country.

To alleviate double taxation of the same earnings, the United States and other countries using the worldwide system of taxation allow a tax credit for income taxes paid on foreign income. The United States limits the amount of the foreign tax credit to make sure that foreign-source income is subject to at least the same tax rate as U.S.-source income.

EXAMPLE 25.30

Johnson Toys, Inc. operates in two countries. It has $100,000 of foreign income and $500,000 of worldwide income. The tax rate in the foreign country is 15%, and the tax rate in the domestic country is 35%.

If Johnson Toys resides in a country using the territorial system of taxation, its tax will be:

$$\$400,000 \times 35\% = \$140,000$$
$$\$100,000 \times 15\% = \underline{\$ 15,000}$$
$$\$155,000$$

If Johnson Toys resides in a country using the worldwide system of taxation and not offering any credit for foreign taxes paid, its tax will be:

$$\$500,000 \times 35\% = \$175,000$$
$$\$100,000 \times 15\% = \underline{\$ 15,000}$$
$$\$190,000$$

If Johnson Toys' country of residence uses the worldwide system of taxation and offers a dollar-for-dollar credit for foreign taxes paid, its tax will be $190,000 – $15,000 = $175,000.

¶25,315   PERSONS TAXED BY THE U.S.

In the United States, U.S. persons are subject to federal income taxation on all income from whatever source derived. A *U.S. person* includes: (1) a U.S. citizen or resident; a domestic partnership; a domestic corporation; an estate (other than a foreign estate); and a trust if a U.S. court can exercise primary supervision over trust administration and one or more U.S. persons have the authority to control all substantial decisions of the trust. Code Sec. 7701(a)(30). The United States offers a foreign tax credit and permits the deduction and exclusion of certain types of foreign income to ameliorate double taxation. U.S. activities and property of foreign persons that generate U.S. income are subject to taxation by the United States.

¶25,325   TREATIES

Income tax treaties greatly affect the tax treatment of economic transactions in a country by a foreign person. For example, the United States imposes a 30 percent tax on interest, dividends, rents, salaries, wages, and annuities received from sources within the U.S. by nonresident alien individuals. Code Sec. 871(a)(1). However, many treaties reduce this tax on investment income. Some even exempt certain types of investment income (such as interest) from any income tax. Capital gains, other than gains attributable to the sale or exchange of U.S. realty, are exempt from U.S. income tax under most treaties. Compensation for personal services performed within the United States (usually for a limited period of time) is exempt from U.S. income tax under many treaties.

Currently, the United States is a partner to more than 50 income tax treaties with foreign countries. Under the Supremacy Clause of the U.S. Constitution (Art. VI, cl. 2), treaties have authority equal to federal law in the United States. If there is inconsistency between a treaty and a statute, the one most recently enacted prevails. The chart below lists countries with which the United States has income tax treaties:

Income Tax Treaty Partners		
Australia[1]	India	Poland
Austria	Indonesia	Portugal
Bangladesh	Ireland	Romania
Barbados	Israel	Russia
Belgium	Italy	Slovak Republic
Bulgaria	Jamaica	Slovenia
Canada	Japan	South Africa
China, People's Republic of[2]	Kazakstan	Spain
Commonwealth of Independent States[3]	Korea, Republic of	Sri Lanka
Cyprus	Latvia	Sweden
Czech Republic	Lithuania	Switzerland
Denmark	Luxembourg	Thailand
Egypt	Malta	Trinidad and Tobago
Estonia	Mexico	Tunisia
Finland	Morocco	Turkey
France[4]	Netherlands	Ukraine
Germany	New Zealand	United Kingdom
Greece	Norway	Venezuela
Hungary	Pakistan	Vietnam
Iceland	Philippines	

[1] This treaty covers Ashmore and Carrier Islands, Christmas Island, the Cocos Islands, the Coral Sea Islands Territory, and Norfolk Island.

[2] This treaty does not apply to Hong Kong.

[3] This treaty covers Armenia, Azerbaijan, Belarus, Georgia, Kyrgyzstan, Moldova, Tajikistan, Turkmenistan, and Uzbekistan.

[4] This treaty covers French Guiana, Guadaloupe, Martinique, and Reunion.

EXAMPLE 25.31 Marie Kenz is a U.S. citizen working abroad in a treaty-partner country. Marie is subject to income taxation in the foreign jurisdiction under the foreign country's tax laws, subject to the treaty provisions. In addition, as a U.S. citizen, Marie must file a U.S. income tax return, even though she pays income taxes in the foreign country.

The 2016 Model Income Tax Convention, released February 17, 2016, is used to facilitate negotiation of a treaty between the United States and another country by helping negotiators identify differences between the income tax policies of the two countries.

The following table lists which country's income tax applies to various types of income under the Model Income Tax Convention. For purposes of this Convention, the term "resident of a country party to the treaty" means any person who, under the laws of that country, is liable to that country's tax by reason of that person's domicile, residence, citizenship, place of management, place of incorporation, or any other criterion of a similar nature.

Treaty Provisions	
Income Category	**Treaty Treatment**
Wages and Salaries	Salaries and wages derived by a resident of one country that is party to a treaty may be taxed only by that country unless the employment is exercised in the other country that is party to the treaty. However, remuneration derived by a resident of one country with respect to employment exercised in the other country may be taxed only by the country of residence if the recipient is present in the country where employment is exercised for no more than 183 days in any 12-month period commencing or ending in the tax year, the remuneration is paid by or on behalf of an employer who is not a resident of the country where employment is exercised, and the remuneration is not borne by a permanent establishment that the employer has in the country where employment is exercised.
Interest	Interest arising in one country that is a party to the treaty but beneficially owned by a resident of the other country that is party to the treaty is taxed by that other country.
Dividends	Dividends paid by a company that is a resident of one country that is party to the treaty to a resident of the other country that is party to the treaty may be taxed by both countries. However, the tax imposed by the payor's country may not exceed 15% (5% if the beneficial owner is a company that directly owns at least 10% of the aggregate vote and value of the stock of the company paying the dividends).
Income from Real Property	Income from real property is taxed by the country where the property is situated.
Gains from Real Property	Gains derived by a resident of one country that is party to the treaty from the disposition of real property situated in the other country that is party to the treaty are taxed by the country where the property is situated.
Royalties	Royalties arising in one country that is party to the treaty but beneficially owned by a resident of the other country that is party to the treaty are taxed by that other country.
Pensions	Pensions are taxed by the country where the recipient resides. However, if the pension would be exempt from taxation in the other party to the treaty if the beneficial owner were a resident of that country, it will also be exempt from taxation in the country where the individual resides
Social Security	Social Security payments made by a country that is party to a treaty to a resident of the other country that is a party to the treaty or to a U.S. citizen are taxed only by the country making the payments.
Annuities	Annuities derived and beneficially owned by an individual who is a resident of a country that is party to a treaty are taxed only by that country.
Alimony	Alimony paid by a resident of a country that is party to a treaty to a resident of the other country that is party to the treaty are taxed only by that other country.
Child Support	Child support is exempt from tax in both countries that are parties to a treaty.
Business Profits	Business profits of an enterprise of one country is taxed by that country. However, if the enterprise carries on business in the other country that is party to the treaty through a permanent establishment situated in that country, profits attributable to that permanent establishment are taxed by that other country.
Directors' Fees	Directors' fees and similar payments derived by a resident of a country that is party to a treaty for services rendered in the other country that is party to the treaty in the individual's capacity as a member of the board of directors of a company that is a resident of the other country may be taxed by that other country.
Profits from the Operation of Ships or Aircraft in International Traffic	Profits derived by an enterprise of one country that is party to a treaty from the operation of ships or aircraft in international traffic are taxed by that country.

Different countries impose different income tax rates. Many countries levy different rates on different types of income, just as the United States taxes capital gains at varying, lower rates than other categories of income. Most treaty countries impose reduced, flat-rate withholding taxes on alien residents and foreign payees who receive interest, dividends, and royalties because it can be difficult to collect taxes from persons in another country. The following table demonstrates the diversity of tax rates imposed and the effect of treaty provisions on withholding rates.

Individual Income and Withholding Tax Rates of Selected Treaty Countries[1]

Country	Income Tax Rates on Residents (at Federal Level)	Treaty Tax Rates on Interest	Treaty Tax Rates on Dividends
Australia	0-45%	10%	5-15%
Canada	0-33%	10%	5-15%
France	0-45%	0%	5-15%
Germany	0-45%	0%	5-15%
Japan	5-45%	10%	5-10%
Mexico	1.92-35%	15%	5-10%
New Zealand	10.5-33%	10%	15%
Russia	13%	0%	5-10%
Switzerland	0-11.5%	0%	5-15%
United Kingdom	20-45%	0%	5-15%

[1] As of January 1, 2017.

¶25,335 SOURCING RULES

The sourcing rules are used to classify income as from a source within the United States, a source without the United States, or a source partly within and partly without the United States. The sourcing rules determine which income of nonresident foreign persons is subject to U.S. taxation. The rules are not as important for U.S. persons because U.S. persons are taxed on their worldwide income. However, the sourcing rules do affect the limit on a person's foreign tax credit. The *United States* includes the 50 states and the District of Columbia. Code Sec. 7701(a)(9).

The sourcing rules are categorized by the type of income. The two steps involved in sourcing income are: (1) source the income into the appropriate statutory category; and (2) classify the income as domestic or foreign. The general categories of income include personal services income, rents and royalties, interest, dividends, and various types of gains. Classification of U.S.- or foreign-source generally follows the location of the underlying income-producing activity or property, as illustrated in the following chart of sourcing rules for specific categories of income. Domestic income is generated only in the 50 states and the District of Columbia.

General Sourcing Rules

Income Category	U.S.-Source	Foreign-Source
Personal Services	Services performed in U.S.	Services performed abroad
Rents and Royalties	Property is located or used in the U.S.	Property is located or used abroad
Interest	Debtor is U.S. resident or domestic corporation	Debtor is foreign resident or foreign corporation
Dividends	Payer is U.S. corporation or foreign corporation conducting business in U.S.	Payer is foreign corporation (other than foreign corporation conducting business in U.S.)
Disposition of Realty	Property is located in U.S.	Property is located abroad
Disposition of Personal Property		
Depreciable Personal Property	Portion of gain (not in excess of depreciation adjustments) equal to portion of depreciation adjustments that are U.S. depreciation adjustments, plus remaining gain if property is disposed of in U.S.	Portion of gain (not in excess of depreciation adjustments) equal to portion of depreciation adjustments that are not U.S. depreciation adjustments, plus remaining gain if property is disposed of outside the U.S.
Inventory purchased for resale	Disposed of within U.S.	Disposed of outside U.S.
Inventory produced by taxpayer	Income from production activity within U.S. Sales activity income from sale within U.S.	Income from production activity outside U.S. Sales activity income from sale outside U.S.

Intangibles (other than goodwill)	If intangible is depreciable, portion of gain equal to portion of depreciation adjustments attributable to U.S. depreciation adjustments	If intangible is depreciable, portion of gain equal to portion of depreciation adjustments not attributable to U.S. depreciation adjustments
	To the extent that payments are contingent, property is located or used in U.S.	To the extent that payments are contingent, property is located or used outside U.S.
	To the extent that payments are not contingent, seller is U.S. resident	To the extent that payments are not contingent, seller is nonresident
Goodwill	Goodwill generated in U.S.	Goodwill generated outside U.S.
All Other	Seller is a U.S. resident	Seller is a foreign resident
Guarantee of Debt	Noncorporate resident or domestic corporation or foreign person if payment is connected with foreign person's income effectively connected with conduct of U.S. trade or business	Foreign person, unless payment is connected with foreign person's income effectively connected with conduct of U.S. trade or business
International Communications Income	50% of income of U.S. person	50% of income of U.S. person
	Income attributable to U.S. business of foreign person	All income of foreign person (except for income attributable to U.S. business)
Transportation	Transportation begins and ends in U.S.	Transportation begins and ends outside U.S.
	50% of income from transportation beginning or ending abroad	50% of income from transportation beginning or ending abroad
Space and Ocean Activity	Derived by U.S. person (except to extent income is attributable to functions performed, resources employed, or risks assumed in a foreign country	Derived by foreign person (other than CFC or foreign person engaged in U.S. business)

Sourcing Income

¶25,345   ## PERSONAL SERVICES INCOME

The source of compensation from personal services generally depends on where the personal services were performed. Services performed in the United States result in U.S.-source compensation. Services performed abroad constitute foreign-source income (Code Secs. 861(a)(3) and 862(a)(3)). *Personal services income* includes salaries, wages, fees, bonuses, commissions, and fringe benefits.

There are two major exceptions to the general rule. Under the first exception, compensation paid to a nonresident alien with only a temporary presence in the United States as a regular member of a foreign vessel engaged in transportation between the United States and a foreign country is treated as foreign-source income. The second exception provides a de minimis rule for nonresident aliens. Domestic-source income is recharacterized as foreign-source income if the conditions of Code Sec. 861(a)(3) are satisfied. This allows nonresident aliens to avoid U.S. taxation when visiting the United States on short business trips. Compensation for labor or personal services performed in the United States is not income from U.S. sources if all of the following requirements are satisfied:

1. The labor or services are performed by a nonresident alien individual temporarily present in the United States for a period(s) not exceeding a total of 90 days during the tax year.
2. The compensation does not exceed $3,000 in the aggregate.
3. The compensation is for labor or services performed as an employee of (a) a nonresident alien or foreign business not engaged in trade or business in the United States or (b) a U.S. citizen or resident or domestic business if the services are performed for an office or place of business maintained in a foreign country or U.S. possession by that individual or business.

As a general rule, when labor or personal services are performed partly within and partly without the United States, the part of the compensation that is attributable to labor or personal services performed within the United States is determined on the basis that most correctly reflects the proper source of the income under the facts and circumstances of the particular case. In many cases, the facts and circumstances will be such that an apportionment on a time basis will be acceptable. The allocation formula is: total compensation x (number of days of service in the United States/total number of days of performance of labor or services for which the payment is made). Reg. §1.861-4(b).

There are special rules for sourcing certain types of fringe benefits received as compensation for labor or personal services performed partly within and partly without the United States by an individual as an employee: Reg. §1.861-4(b)(2).

1. *Housing fringe benefit*. The source of compensation in the form of a housing fringe benefit is determined based on the location of the individual's principal place of work.
2. *Education fringe benefit*. The source of compensation in the form of an education fringe benefit for the educational expenses of an individual's dependents is determined based on the location of the individual's principal place of work.
3. *Local transportation fringe benefit*. The source of compensation in the form of a local transportation fringe benefit is determined based on the location of the individual's principal place of work.
4. *Tax reimbursement fringe benefit*. The source of compensation in the form of a foreign tax reimbursement fringe benefit is determined based on the location of the jurisdiction that imposed the tax for which the individual is reimbursed.
5. *Hazardous or hardship duty pay fringe benefit*. The source of compensation in the form of a hazardous or hardship duty pay fringe benefit is determined based on the location of the hazardous or hardship duty zone for which the hazardous or hardship duty pay fringe benefit is paid.
6. *Moving expense reimbursement fringe benefit*. The source of compensation in the form of a moving expense reimbursement generally is determined based on the location of the employee's new principal place of work. However, the source of such compensation is determined based on the location of the employee's former principal place of work if the individual provides sufficient evidence that such determination of source is more appropriate under the facts and circumstances of the particular case.

The source of multi-year compensation generally is determined on a time basis over the period to which such compensation is attributable. In the case of stock options, the facts and circumstances generally will be such that the applicable period to which the compensation is attributable is the period between the grant of the option and the date on which all employment-related conditions for its exercise have been satisfied.

An individual may determine the source of his or her compensation as an employee for labor or personal services performed partly within and partly without the United States under an alternative basis if the individual establishes to the IRS' satisfaction that, under the facts and circumstances of the particular case, the alternative basis more properly determines the source of the compensation.

EXAMPLE 25.32

Bea, a nonresident alien individual, was employed by Francais Corporation from March 1 to June 12, a total of 104 days. Bea received compensation amounting to $12,240 for that period. During the period of employment, she was present in the United States for 59 days. Her contract stipulated a 7-day-per-week call basis, and the salary was unchanged for overtime. Under these circumstances, the U.S.-source income amounts to $6,944 ($12,240 × (59/104)).

EXAMPLE 25.33

Jay, a citizen of the United States, resides in a foreign country. He is employed by a domestic corporation and paid a salary of $67,600. His contract requires him to work 5 days each week, Monday through Friday. During the year, Jay was in the United States for 6 weeks and performed services for 30 workdays during that period. During the year, he worked 240 days for which payment was made. The amount of compensation for personal services performed in the United States, and therefore U.S.-source income, is $8,450 ($67,600 × (30/240)).

EXAMPLE 25.34

Kay is a U.S. citizen and resident. She worked in the United States for the entire tax year except for a five-week foreign business trip. She worked a total of 250 days, including 24 workdays abroad, for an annual salary of $80,000. Kay's foreign-source income amounts to $7,680 ($80,000 × (24/250)), and her U.S.-source income equals $72,320 ($80,000 × (226/250) or $80,000 less $7,680).

¶25,355   RENTS AND ROYALTIES

The source of rentals and royalties from tangible property depends on the location of the property. If it is located in the United States, it is U.S.-source income. Code Sec. 861(a)(4); Reg. §1.861-5. If it is located outside the United States, it is foreign-source income. Code Sec. 862(a)(4).

The source of rentals and royalties from intangible property, such as patents, copyrights, goodwill, trademarks, and franchises, depends on where the property is used. Rentals and royalties for the use of, or for the privilege of using, intangible property in the United States is U.S.-source income. Code Sec. 861(a)(4); Reg. §1.861-5. Rentals and royalties for the use of, or for the privilege of using, intangible property outside the United States is foreign-source income. Code Sec. 862(a)(4).

EXAMPLE 25.35   A domestic motion picture company produces a U.S. movie, which it licenses and distributes in the United States as well as in English-speaking foreign locales, including Canada and Great Britain. The income generated in Canada and Great Britain is foreign-source income.

EXAMPLE 25.36   Eaty's Corporation leases a fleet of vehicles for $150,000 per year to a lessee who drives the vehicles a total of 600,000 miles. The lessee operates those vehicles 400,000 miles in the United States and 200,000 miles in foreign countries. Eaty's, the lessor, has U.S.-source income amounting to $100,000 ($150,000 × (400,000/600,000)) and $50,000 in foreign-source income ($150,000 × (200,000/600,000)) for the year.

¶25,365   INTEREST

As a general rule, interest from the United States, a state, or the District of Columbia and interest on bonds, notes, and other interest-bearing obligations of noncorporate U.S. residents and domestic corporations is U.S.-source income. Code Sec. 861(a)(1); Reg. §1.861-2(a). Interest other than that derived from sources within the United States is from sources without the United States. Code Sec. 862(a)(1).

There are three exceptions to this general rule:

1. Interest on deposits with a foreign branch of a domestic corporation or a domestic partnership is foreign-source income if the branch is engaged in the commercial banking business.
2. Interest on deposits with a foreign branch of a savings and loan association that is a domestic corporation or domestic partnership is foreign-source income.
3. In the case of a foreign partnership that is predominantly engaged in the active conduct of a trade or business outside the United States, any interest not paid by a trade or business engaged in by the partnership in the United States and not allocable to income that is effectively connected (or treated as effectively connected) with the conduct of a trade or business in the United States is foreign-source income.

EXAMPLE 25.37   Neighborly Corporation is a domestic retail business. Neighborly also sells merchandise and offers customer financing in a foreign country. Under this arrangement, the interest income realized by Neighborly in the foreign jurisdiction is foreign-source income because the debtor resides in the foreign country.

EXAMPLE 25.38   Dagen's is a foreign partnership operating in the United States. Dagen's borrows from a U.S. bank and makes periodic interest payments. The U.S. bank has foreign.-source income because Dagen's is a foreign person.

¶25,375   DIVIDENDS

As a general rule, the source of dividend income depends on the nationality or place of incorporation of the payor. Dividends paid by U.S. corporations usually are considered U.S.-source income, and dividends paid by foreign corporations usually are considered foreign-source income.

The following dividends are treated as U.S.-source income: Code Sec. 861(a)(2).

1. Dividends from a domestic corporation (unless the corporation elects the U.S. possession tax credit of Code Sec. 936).
2. If at least 25 percent of a foreign corporation's gross income from all sources for the three-year period ending with the close of its tax year preceding the declaration of dividends was effectively connected with the conduct of a trade or business within the United States, then the portion of dividends equal to the ratio between its effectively connected income and gross income from all sources during the testing period is U.S.-source income. For purposes of the foreign tax credit, dividends from a foreign corporation (other than dividends received from a wholly owned foreign subsidiary) are treated as foreign-source income to the extent that they exceed 100/70 (100/80 if the dividend is from a 20-percent or greater owned corporation) of the amount allowable as a dividends-received deduction with respect to the dividends.
3. Dividends from a foreign corporation are U.S.-source income to the extent that they are treated by Code Sec. 243(e) as dividends from a domestic corporation (because the dividends were from earnings and profits accumulated by a domestic corporation).

Other dividends are treated as foreign-source income. Code Sec. 862(a)(2).

EXAMPLE 25.39   During the year, Dogiva, Inc., pays dividends to its shareholders. If Dogiva is a domestic corporation, the dividends are U.S.-source. If Dogiva is a foreign corporation not conducting business in the U.S., the dividend payments are foreign-source.

EXAMPLE 25.40   Ice Creamery, a foreign corporation operating in the United States, earns $1,000,000 in profits during the year. Sixty percent of its sales are attributed to U.S. sources. Ice Creamery distributes $400,000 in dividends during the year. Since 25% or more of its income is derived from U.S. sources, allocation of dividends between U.S.- and foreign-source income is necessary. This results in foreign-source dividends amounting to $160,000 (40% × $400,000) and $240,000 of U.S.-source income (60% × $400,000).

¶25,385   SALE OR EXCHANGE OF REAL PROPERTY

Gain from the disposition of a United States real property interest is U.S.-source income. Code Sec. 861(a)(5). Gain from the sale or exchange of real property located outside the United States is foreign-source income. Code Sec. 862(a)(5).

A *United States real property interest* includes the following: Code Sec. 897(c)(1).

1. An interest in real property (including an interest in a mine, well, or other natural deposit) located in the United States or the Virgin Islands.
2. Any interest (other than an interest solely as a creditor) in any domestic corporation unless the taxpayer establishes that the corporation was not a United States real property holding corporation during the five-year period ending on the date that the interest was disposed. A corporation is a *United States real property holding corporation* if the fair market value of its United States real property interests equals or exceeds 50 percent of the fair market value of its United States real property interests, its interests in real property located outside the United States, plus any other of its assets that are used or held for use in a trade or business.

The following are excepted from *United States real property interest*:

1. An interest in a corporation if the corporation did not hold any United States real property interests as of the date the interest was disposed and all of the United States real property interests held by the corporation at any time during the five-year period ending on the date that the interest was disposed either were disposed of in transactions in which all gain was recognized or ceased to be United States real property interests by reason of the application of this rule to one or more other corporations.
2. If any class of a corporation's stock is regularly traded on an established securities market, stock of that class may be treated as a United States real property interest only in the case of a person who held more than five percent of that class of stock at some time during the five-year period ending on the date that the interest was disposed.

EXAMPLE 25.41	Newport Dairy, a domestic corporation, sells some of its U.S. production facilities to a foreign corporation following negotiations in the foreign country. The settlement occurs on foreign soil. The gain recognized by Newport Dairy is U.S-source income because the sold property is located in the United States.

EXAMPLE 25.42	Assume the same facts as above except that the real property is located in the foreign country and title passes in the United States. Despite the fact that settlement occurs in the United States and Newport Dairy is a domestic corporation, the location of the property sold controls the sourcing. The gain on the sale of the production facilities located in the foreign country is foreign-source income.

¶25,395   SALE OR EXCHANGE OF PERSONAL PROPERTY

Generally, the residence of the seller controls the sourcing of gain from the sale of personal property. Gain from the sale of personal property by a United States resident is U.S.-source income, and gain from the sale of personal property by a nonresident is foreign-source income. Code Sec. 865(a). There are, however, special rules for certain types of personal property, including depreciable personal property (discussed in ¶25,400), inventory (discussed in ¶25,405), and intangibles (discussed in ¶25,415). The result of these exceptions is that the general rule typically applies to a business' sale of personal property only when it sells securities because most business personalty is either inventory or depreciable assets.

The following taxpayers are United States residents: Code Sec. 865(g).

1. Any United States citizen or resident alien who does not have a tax home in a foreign country.
2. Any nonresident alien who has a tax home in the United States.
3. Any corporation, trust, or estate that is a United States person within the meaning of Code Sec. 7701(a)(30).

A nonresident is any person other than a United States resident. However, a United States citizen or resident alien will not be treated as a nonresident with respect to any sale of personal property unless an income tax equal to at least 10 percent of the gain derived from the sale is actually paid to a foreign country with respect to that gain.

¶25,400   DEPRECIABLE PERSONAL PROPERTY

Gain (not in excess of depreciation adjustments to the property) from the sale or exchange of depreciable personal property must be allocated between sources in the United States and sources outside the United States. Gain in excess of the depreciation adjustments from the sale of depreciable personal property is sourced as if the property were inventory property (discussed in ¶25,405). Code Sec. 865(c).

The portion of the gain (not in excess of the depreciation adjustments) sourced to the United States is determined by dividing the United States depreciation adjustments with respect to the property by the total depreciation adjustments and multiplying that fraction by the amount of gain (not in excess of depreciation adjustments).

Depreciation adjustments are adjustments reflected in the adjusted basis of property on account of depreciation deductions (whether allowed with respect to that property or other property and whether allowed to the taxpayer or to any other person). United States depreciation adjustments are adjustments to the adjusted basis of the property that are attributable to depreciation deductions allowable in computing taxable income from sources in the United States.

EXAMPLE 25.43	A domestic corporation sold depreciable personal property, consisting of equipment, to a foreign company for $300,000. All prior income on the equipment was attributable to U.S.-source income. The equipment was purchased three years earlier for $250,000, and $180,000 of depreciation deductions had been taken. Title passes in the foreign country upon delivery. The corporation's gain of $230,000 is allocated to U.S.- and foreign-source income as follows: depreciation recapture amounts to $180,000 attributable to U.S. sources, and gain due to appreciation results in $50,000 of foreign-source income ($230,000 gain less $180,000 U.S.-source income).

¶25,395

¶25,405   INVENTORY

There are different rules for sourcing income from sales and exchanges of inventory purchased for resale and sales and exchanges of inventory produced by a taxpayer. Code Secs. 861(a)(6), 862(a)(6). *Inventory* is defined as stock in trade of the taxpayer or other personal property of a kind that properly would be included in the taxpayer's inventory if on hand at the close of the tax year and personal property held by a taxpayer primarily for sale to customers in the ordinary course of the taxpayer's trade or business. Code Sec. 865(i)(1).

Gain from the sale of inventory that a taxpayer purchased for resale generally is sourced according to the place where it was sold. Code Sec. 861(a)(6), 862(a)(6). The place of sale is the place where the rights, title, and interest of the seller are transferred to the buyer. Reg. §1.861-7(c). If the seller retains bare legal title, the sale is deemed to have occurred at the time and place when beneficial ownership and risk of loss passed to the buyer. Reg. §1.861-7(c).

> **Observation:** If a sale is arranged in a particular manner for the primary purpose of tax avoidance, all factors of the transaction, such as negotiations, the execution of the agreement, the location of the property, and the place of payment will be considered, and the sale will be treated as having taken place where the substance of the sale occurred.

Gain from the sale or exchange of inventory that was produced (in whole or in part) by the taxpayer within the United States and sold or exchanged without the United States, or produced (in whole or in part) by the taxpayer without the United States and sold or exchanged within the United States has to be apportioned between U.S.-source income and foreign-source income. Code Sec. 863(b)(2).

The rules for apportioning gain from the sale or exchange of inventory produced by a taxpayer are set forth in Reg. §1.863-3. Under these rules, taxpayers must divide their gross income from sales and exchanges of inventory they produced between production activity and sales activity and then apply the rules for determining the source of income from production and sales activities. *Production activity* means an activity that creates, fabricates, manufactures, extracts, processes, cures, or ages inventory.

Taxpayers must divide gross income between production activity and sales activity using any of the following methods: Reg. §1.863-3(b).

1. The 50/50 method. Under the 50/50 method, half of the taxpayer's gross income is considered income attributable to production activity, and the remaining half is considered income attributable to sales activity.

2. The independent factory price (IFP) method. Under the IFP method, the amount of the gross sales price equal to the IFP will be treated as attributable to production activity, and the excess of the gross sales price over the IFP will be treated as attributable to sales activity. A taxpayer may elect to use the IFP method if the taxpayer can fairly establish an IFP. An IFP is fairly established if a taxpayer regularly sells part of its output to wholly independent distributors or other selling concerns in such a way as to reasonably reflect the income earned from production activity. A sale will not be considered to fairly establish an IFP if sales activity by the taxpayer with respect to that sale is significant in relation to all of the activities with respect to that product.

3. Books and records method. Taxpayers may elect to allocate the amount of their gross income from a sale of inventory between production and sales activities based on their books of account if they have received advance permission from the IRS. A taxpayer's books of account must make a detailed allocation of receipts and expenditures that clearly reflects the amount of the taxpayer's income from production and sales activities.

Once taxpayers have allocated their gross income between production and sales activities, they must apply the rules for determining the source of income from production and sales activities: Reg. §1.863-3(c).

1. *Income attributable to production activity.* If the taxpayer's production assets are located only within the United States or only outside the United States, its income from a production activity is sourced where the taxpayer's production assets are located. If a taxpayer's production assets are located both within and without the United States, income from sources without the United States is determined by multiplying income from production activity by a fraction whose numerator is the average adjusted basis of production assets located outside the United States and whose denominator is the average adjusted basis of all production assets within and without the United States. The remaining income is treated as from sources within the United States.

2. *Income attributable to sales activity.* The source of a taxpayer's income attributable to its sales activity is determined by the place of the sale. Income from sales within the United States is U.S.-source income, and income from sales outside the United States is foreign-source income.

EXAMPLE 25.44

A domestic corporation manufactures all of its products in the United States and sells some of its products to foreign distributors, passing title abroad. If an unrelated foreign distributor buys $10,000 worth of goods and the domestic corporation's cost of goods sold is $4,000, then gross income amounts to $6,000. Using the 50-50 method, one-half of the income is production activity, and one-half is attributable to sales activities. $3,000 of income is allocable to each activity. The $3,000 of income allocable to production activity is U.S.-source income, and the $3,000 of income allocable to sales activity is foreign-source income.

EXAMPLE 25.45

A domestic corporation produces cloth and sells the cloth to an unrelated foreign clothing manufacturer for $100. All of the corporation's production assets are located within the United States. The cost of the cloth sold, $80, is entirely attributable to production activity. The corporation does not engage in significant sales activities, in relation to its other activities, in its sales to the clothing manufacturer. Therefore, the sale to the clothing manufacturer establishes an IFP of $100. $100 of the gross sales price is treated as attributable to production activity, and no amount of income from the sale is attributable to sales activity. After reducing the gross sales price ($100) by the cost of goods sold ($80), the corporation's $20 of gross income is treated as attributable to production activity and is U.S.-source income. The domestic corporation also sells cloth to an unrelated foreign retail outlet for $110. If the corporation has elected the IFP method and the cloth is substantially similar to the cloth sold to the clothing manufacturer, the $100 gross sales price will be treated as attributable to production activity, and $10 ($110 - $100 = $10) will be treated as attributable to sales activity. After reducing the gross sales price ($110) by the cost of goods sold ($80), $20 of the gross income is treated as attributable to production activity, and $10 is treated as attributable to sales activity. The $20 is U.S.-source income, and the $10 is foreign-source income.

¶25,415   GAINS ON THE SALE OF INTANGIBLES

An *intangible* is any patent, copyright, secret process or formula, goodwill, trademark, trade brand, franchise, or other like property. How gain from the sale or exchange of an intangible is sourced depends on whether or not payments in consideration of the sale or exchange are contingent on the productivity, use, or disposition of the intangible and whether or not there have been any depreciation adjustments (discussed in ¶25,400) with respect to the intangible. Code Sec. 865(d).

To the extent that any gain from the sale or exchange of an intangible does not exceed the depreciation adjustments with respect to the intangible, the portion of the gain that is U.S.-source income is determined by multiplying the gain by a fraction whose numerator is the amount of United States depreciation adjustments with respect to the property and whose denominator is the total amount of depreciation adjustments.

To the extent that payments in consideration of the sale or exchange of an intangible are contingent on the productivity, use, or disposition of the intangible, the source of the payments is determined as if the payments were royalties. If the property is located or used within the United States, the gain is U.S.-source income. If the property is located or used outside the United States, the gain is foreign-source income.

To the extent that payments in consideration of the sale or exchange of an intangible are not contingent on the productivity, use, or disposition of the intangible, gain will be treated as U.S.-source income if the seller is a United States resident. Gain will be treated as foreign-source income if the seller is a nonresident.

There is a special rule for sales and exchanges of goodwill. Payments in consideration of the sale or exchange of goodwill are sourced based on the country in which the goodwill was generated. If the goodwill was generated in the United States, payments are U.S.-source income. If the goodwill was generated outside the United States, payments are foreign-source income.

EXAMPLE 25.46

Tall's Dairy, a domestic corporation, sells its secret ice cream formulas in foreign countries, with no portion of the sale contingent on future sales. The income related to these sales is U.S.-source income.

¶25,420 **GUARANTEE OF DEBT**

Amounts received, directly or indirectly, from the following persons will be considered U.S.-source income: Code Sec. 861(a)(9).

- A noncorporate resident or domestic corporation for the guarantee of the resident's or corporation's indebtedness.
- A foreign person for the guarantee of the foreign person's indebtedness if the amount is connected with income that is effectively connected (or treated as effectively connected) with the conduct of a U.S. trade or business.

All other amounts received from a foreign person for the guarantee of the foreign person's indebtedness will be treated as from a foreign source. Code Sec. 862(a)(9).

¶25,425 **COMMUNICATION INCOME**

In the case of a U.S. person, 50 percent of international communications income is sourced in the United States, and the other 50 percent constitutes foreign-source income. A foreign person having international communications income is deemed to have foreign-source income except when that person maintains a place of business in the United States; then, the income attributable to the U.S. business location is U.S.-source income. Code Sec. 863(e).

International communications income includes all income derived from the transmission of communications or data from the United States to any foreign country (or U.S. possession) or from any foreign country (or U.S. possession) to the United States.

| EXAMPLE 25.47 | ED&D has telecommunications operations in the United States and abroad. If ED&D is a domestic corporation, one-half of the income is foreign-source, and one-half is U.S.-source. If ED&D were a foreign corporation with no place of business in the United States, all of the income would be foreign-sourced. |

¶25,430 **TRANSPORTATION INCOME**

All transportation income attributable to transportation that begins *and* ends in the United States is treated as derived from sources with the United States. Income attributable to transportation that begins *and* ends outside the United States is foreign-source income. Code Sec. 863(c).

For other transportation having a U.S. connection, income attributable to transportation that begins *or* ends in the United States is treated as 50 percent foreign-source and 50 percent U.S.-source. This rule applies to both U.S. and foreign persons.

Transportation income means any income derived from, or in connection with, the use (or hiring or leasing for use) of a vessel or aircraft or the performance of services directly related to the use of a vessel or aircraft. Vessel or aircraft includes any container used in connection with a vessel or aircraft (e.g., containers in which automobiles are shipped overseas). The definition of *transportation income* generally does not include personal services of the taxpayer unless the transportation begins and ends in the United States or a U.S. possession. Income attributable to personal services excluded from transportation income is U.S.-source income if it is performed in the United States or within U.S. territorial waters.

¶25,435 **SPACE AND OCEAN ACTIVITY INCOME**

Space and ocean activity income derived by a United States person is U.S.-source income except to the extent that the income, based on all of the facts and circumstances, is attributable to functions performed, resources employed, or risks assumed in a foreign country or countries. Code Sec. 863(d)(1)(A); Reg. §1.863-8(b)(1).

Space and ocean activity derived by someone other than a United States person is foreign-source income, with the following exceptions: Code Sec. 863(d)(1)(B); Reg. §1.863-8(b)(2).

- *Space and ocean income derived by a controlled foreign corporation (CFC).* Space and ocean income derived by a CFC is U.S.-source income except to the extent that the income, based on all of the facts and circumstances, is attributable to functions performed, resources employed, or risks assumed in a foreign country or countries.

■ *Space and ocean income derived by foreign persons engaged in a trade or business within the United States.* Space and ocean income derived by a foreign person (other than a CFC) engaged in a trade or business within the United States is U.S.-source income to the extent that the income, based on all of the facts and circumstances, is attributable to functions performed, resources employed, or risks assumed within the United States.

Sourcing Deductions

¶25,445   ALLOCATION AND APPORTIONMENT OF DEDUCTIONS

Once gross income has been allocated between U.S. and foreign sources, deductions are allocated to the class of gross income to which they are directly related. Code Sec. 861(b); Reg. §1.861-8(a)(2).

A class of gross income may consist of one or more items of gross income enumerated in Code Sec. 61, namely: Reg. §1.861-1(a)(3).

1. Compensation for services.
2. Gross income derived from businesses.
3. Gains from dealings in property.
4. Interest.
5. Rents.
6. Royalties.
7. Dividends.
8. Alimony and separate maintenance payments.
9. Annuities.
10. Income from life insurance and endowment contracts.
11. Income from discharge of indebtedness.
12. Distributive shares of partnership income.
13. Pensions.
14. Income in respect of a decedent (IRD).
15. Income from an interest in an estate or trust.

A deduction will be considered definitely related to a class of gross income if it is incurred as a result of, or incident to, an activity or in connection with property from which that class of gross income is derived. Reg. §1.861-1(b)(2). If a deduction is incurred as a result of, or incident to, an activity or in connection with property, which activity or property generates, has generated, or could reasonably have been expected to generate gross income, the deduction will be considered definitely related to that gross income as a class, whether or not there is any item of gross income in the class that is received or accrued during the tax year and whether or not the amount of deductions exceeds the amount of the gross income in the class.

Although most deductions will be definitely related to some class of a taxpayer's gross income, some deductions are ratably apportioned to all gross income because they are related to all gross income or are treated as not definitely related to any gross income. Reg. §1.861-1(b)(1). Deductions that are ratably apportioned include: Reg. §1.861-8(e)(9).

■ Certain interest expense.
■ Real estate taxes on a personal residence or sales tax on items purchased for personal use.
■ Medical expenses.
■ Charitable contributions.
■ Alimony.

Deductions that are supportive in nature (e.g., overhead, general and administrative expenses, and supervisory expenses) may be allocated and apportioned along with the deductions to which they relate. Temp. Reg. §1.861-8(b)(3). However, it is equally acceptable to attribute supportive deductions directly to the activities or property that generate the gross income.

Sometimes, for purposes of a Code provision (e.g., for purposes of determining effectively connected taxable income or applying the foreign tax credit limitations), deductions have to be apportioned within a class of gross income between the statutory grouping of gross income (or among the statutory groupings) and the residual grouping of gross income. Reg. §1.861-8(a)(2).

If a class of gross income to which a deduction has been allocated consists entirely of a single statutory grouping or the residual grouping, there is no need to apportion that deduction. Temp. Reg. §1.861-1T(c)(1). However, if a deduction is allocated to a class of gross income included in one or more statutory groupings, it must be apportioned among the statutory groupings and, if necessary, the residual grouping. Examples of bases and factors that should be considered in apportioning a specific deduction include, but are not limited to, a comparison of units sold; the amount of gross sales or receipts; the cost of goods sold; profit contribution; expenses incurred, assets used, salaries paid, space utilized, and time spent that are attributable to the activities or properties giving rise to the class of gross income; and the amount of gross income.

The taxable income of each member of an affiliated group within each statutory grouping is determined by allocating and apportioning the expenses of each member according to apportionment fractions that are computed as if all members of the affiliated group were a single corporation. Temp. Reg. §1.861-14T(c).

Specifically, such expenses must be allocated to a class of gross income that takes into account gross income that is generated, has been generated, or could reasonably have been expected to have been generated by the members of the affiliated group. If the expenses relate to the gross income of fewer than all members of an affiliated group, then those expenses must be apportioned as if those fewer members were a single corporation.

EXAMPLE 25.48

Palmer, Inc. owns all of the stock of both Cooper Co. and Schneider, Inc. Each one is a domestic corporation. Palmer, Inc. incurred general training program expenses of $100,000 in 2016. Employees of all three companies participated in the programs. In 2016 Palmer, Inc. had U.S. source gross income of $2,000,000 and foreign source general limitation income of $500,000. Cooper Co. had U.S. source gross income of $1,500,000 and foreign source general limitation income of $800,000.Schneider, Inc. had U.S. source gross income of $3,000,000 and foreign source general limitation income of $400,000. The training expenses incurred by Palmer, Inc. are not definitely related solely to specific income-producing activities or property of Palmer, Inc. Therefore, the training expenses are allocable to all of the gross income, both foreign and domestic.

The amount allocable to foreign source general limitation income is $20,732 ($100,000 × ($500,000 + $800,000 + $400,000)/($2,500,000 + $2,300,000 + $3,400,000)).

The amount allocable to U.S. source income is $79,268 ($100,000 × ($2,000,000 + $1,500,000 + $3,000,000)/($2,500,000 + $2,300,000 + $3,400,000)).

¶25,455 SPECIAL ALLOCATION RULES FOR DEDUCTIONS

The Code contains no reference to special allocations of deductions. However, the Code authorizes the Treasury Department to determine taxable income "by processes or formulas of general apportionment." Code Sec. 863(b).

The Treasury Department has promulgated special allocation rules for the following expenses and deductions:

- Research and development expenses (R&D).
- Stewardship expenses.
- Legal and accounting fees.
- Income taxes.
- Losses on sales or exchanges of property.
- Net operating losses (NOLs).
- Interest expenses.
- Charitable contributions.

R&D Expenses

The regulations governing the allocating and apportioning of research and development expenses (R&D) incorporate the belief that research and experimentation is an inherently speculative activity, that findings may contribute unexpected benefits, and that the gross income derived from successful research and experimentation must bear the cost of unsuccessful research and experimentation. Reg. §1.861-17(a)(1). Expenditures for R&D ordinarily are considered deductions that are definitely related to all income reasonably connected with the relevant broad product category or categories of the taxpayer. Therefore, the expenses are allocable to all items of gross income as a class related to that product category. Reg. §1.861-17(a)(1).

Legally mandated R&D is allocated differently. If there is not a reasonable expectation that more than a *de minimis* gross income will be generated outside of a single geographic source, the R&D is allocated exclusively to the jurisdiction imposing the requirement. Reg. §1.861-17(a)(4).

There are two permissible methods for apportioning R&D that is not legally mandated R&D: the sales method and the optional gross income method.

- **Sales method**—An amount equal to 50 percent of the R&D is apportioned exclusively to the statutory grouping of gross income (or the residual grouping of gross income) that arises from the geographic source where the R&D expenditures that account for more than 50 percent of the amount of such deduction were performed. Reg. §1.861-17(b)(1)(i).

- **Optional gross income method**—An amount equal to 25 percent of the R&D is apportioned exclusively to the statutory grouping of gross income (or the residual grouping of gross income) that arises from the geographic source where the R&D expenditures that account for more than 50 percent of the amount of such deduction were performed. Reg. §1.861-17(b)(1)(ii).

Under the sales-based apportionment method, the research expenses remaining after the 50 percent exclusive apportionment is made are apportioned between U.S. and foreign source income in the proportion that the sales from the product category that resulted in the income bears to the total sales from the product category. Reg. §1.861-17(c)(1).

Taxpayers have two options for apportioning remaining research expenses under the gross income method. Reg. §1.861-17(d). Under Option 1, taxpayers may apportion research expenses remaining after the optional gross income method has been used ratably on the basis of gross income between the statutory groupings (or among the statutory groupings) of gross income and the residual grouping of gross income in the same proportions that the amount of gross income in the statutory grouping (or groupings) and the amount of gross income in the residual grouping bear, respectively, to the total amount of gross income, if the amount of research expenses ratably apportioned to the statutory grouping (or groupings in the aggregate) is not less than 50 percent of the amount that would have been so apportioned if the taxpayer had used the sales method and the amount of research expenses ratably apportioned to the residual grouping is not less than 50 percent of the amount that would have been so apportioned if the taxpayer had used the sales method.

Taxpayers who cannot use Option 1 can do either of the following:

- If the amount of research expenses ratably apportioned to the statutory grouping (or groupings) is less than 50 percent of the amount that would have been apportioned if the taxpayer had used the sales method, the taxpayer may apportion 50 percent of the amount of research and experimental expense that would have been apportioned to the statutory grouping (or groupings in the aggregate) under the sales method to such statutory grouping (or to such statutory groupings in the aggregate and then among such groupings on the basis of gross income within each grouping) and apportion the balance of the amount of research and experimental expenses to the residual grouping.

- If the amount of research expenses ratably apportioned to the residual grouping is less than 50 percent of the amount that would have been so apportioned if the taxpayer had used this sales method, the taxpayer may apportion 50 percent of the amount of research expenses that would have been apportioned to the residual grouping under the sales method to such residual grouping and apportion the balance of the amount of research expenses to the statutory grouping (or to the statutory groupings in the aggregate and then among such groupings ratably on the basis of gross income within each grouping).

Taxpayers may choose to use either the sales method or the optional gross income method for their original return for their first tax year to which they need to make an apportionment. Reg. §1.861-17(e). Use of either of the methods constitutes a binding election to use the method chosen for that year and for four tax years thereafter. A taxpayer may not revoke an election of a method without the IRS' prior consent.

EXAMPLE 25.49

Moss & Owen, Inc. manufactures and distributes small gasoline engines. M&O, Ltd. is a wholly owned foreign subsidiary. It also manufactures and sells the engines. During 2017 M&O incurred research expenditures of $600,000 to invent and patent a new gasoline engine. All of the research was done in the U.S. Domestic sales of the new engine totaled $50 million in 2017. Foreign sales by M&O of the engine were $30 million. Moss & Owen had gross income in 2017 of $16 million, of which $14 million was U.S.-source income from domestic sales of gasoline engines, $1 million was foreign source royalties from M&O, and $1 million was U.S.-source interest income.

Because the research expenditures were incurred in connection with small gasoline engines and were definitely related to the items of gross income to which the research gives rise (i.e., gross income from the sale of small gasoline engines in the United States), the expenses are allocable to this class of gross income. Because U.S.-source interest income is not within this class of gross income, it is not taken into account.

For purposes of applying the foreign tax credit limitation, the statutory grouping is general limitation gross income from sources without the United States, and the residual grouping is gross income from sources within the United States. The apportionment is to be based on sales. Because more than 50 percent of the R&D was performed in the United States, 50 percent of the $600,000 deduction, or $300,000, is apportioned exclusively to gross income from U.S. sources. Of the remaining $300,000, $112,500 ($300,000 × ($30 million/ ($30 million + $50 million)) is apportioned to the statutory grouping (sources within the foreign country). The amount apportioned to the residual grouping is $187,500 ($300,000 × ($50 million/($30 million + $50 million))). The total amount apportioned to the residual grouping is $487,500 ($300,000 + $187,500).

EXAMPLE 25.50

Assume the facts as in the previous example except that the apportionment is made using the optional gross income method. The exclusive apportionment to the residual grouping of gross income equals $150,000 ($600,000 × .25). The amount apportioned to the statutory grouping (sources within the foreign country) is $30,000 ($450,000 × ($1 million/($14 million + 1 million))). The amount apportioned to the residual grouping is $420,000 ($450,000 × ($14 million/($14 million + $1 million))). The total amount apportioned to the residual grouping is $570,000 ($150,000 + $420,000).

Stewardship Expenses

Stewardship expenses, which result from overseeing functions undertaken for a corporation's own benefit as an investor in a related corporation, are considered definitely related and allocable to dividends received, or to be received, from the related corporation. Reg. §1.861-8(e)(4)(ii). Stewardship expenses may result from either duplicative activities or shareholder activities. *Duplicative activities* are activities that duplicate an activity to be performed or that may reasonably be expected to be performed by a controlled corporation. *Shareholder activities* are activities whose sole effect is either to protect the renderer's capital investment in the recipient or to facilitate compliance by the renderer with legal, reporting, or regulatory requirements applicable to the renderer or to both.

If a corporation has a foreign or international department that exercises overseeing functions with respect to related foreign corporations and, in addition, the department performs other functions that generate other foreign-source income (such as fees for services rendered outside of the United States for the benefit of foreign related corporations, foreign-source royalties, and gross income of foreign branches), some part of the deductions with respect to that department are considered definitely related to the other foreign-source income. In some instances, the operations of a foreign or international department will also generate United States source income (such as fees for services performed in the United States). Permissible methods of apportionment with respect to stewardship expenses include comparisons of time spent by employees weighted to take into account differences in compensation, or comparisons of each related corporation's gross receipts, gross income, or unit sales volume, assuming that stewardship activities are not substantially disproportionate to such factors.

Legal and Accounting Fees

Fees for legal and accounting services are ordinarily considered to be definitely related and allocable to specific classes of gross income or to all of a taxpayer's gross income, depending on the nature of the services rendered. Reg. §1.861-8(e)(5). For example, accounting fees for the preparation of a study of costs to manufacture a specific product will ordinarily be definitely related to the class of income derived from (or that could reasonably have been expected to be derived from) that specific product.

Income Taxes

Generally the deduction for state; local and foreign income; war profits; and excess profit taxes is considered to be definitely related and allocable to the gross income on which the state income taxes are imposed. Reg. §1.861-8(e)(6). In allocating and apportioning the deduction, the income upon which the state income tax is imposed is determined by reference to the laws of the state. For example, if the state imposes tax on income that includes foreign source income, the portion of the state income tax attributable to such foreign source income is definitely related and allocable to foreign source income.

EXAMPLE 25.51	Mathis, Inc. is a domestic corporation with branches in three states. In 2017 the company earned $500 million, of which $100 million was foreign-source general limitation income and $400 million was U.S.-source income. The three branches determine the taxable income in their state by making adjustments to Mathis' federal taxable income. They then apportion the adjusted taxable income on the basis of the relative amount of Mathis' payroll, property, and sales within each state compared to the worldwide payroll, property, and sales. Mathis is determined to have taxable income of $225 million in State A, $200 million in State B, and $25 million in State C. The tax rates are four percent in State A, six percent in State B, and 10 percent in State C. Hence, Mathis owes $9 million to State A, $12 million to State B, and $2.5 million to State C, for a total of $23.5 million. Because none of the states exempt foreign-source income in making the calculations, the state income tax must be apportioned between foreign-source general limitation gross income and U.S.-source income. The three states together tax $450 million ($225 + 200 + 25). However, that amount exceeds Mathis' U.S.-source income of $400 million. Therefore, the state income taxes are deemed to be imposed on $400 million of U.S.-source income and $50 million of foreign-source general limitation income. Of the total state income tax of $23.5 million, $2,611,111 ($23.5 million × ($50 million/$450 million) is apportioned to foreign-source income. The remaining $20,888,889 is apportioned to U.S.-source income.

EXAMPLE 25.52	Assume the same facts as in the previous example except that State A specifically exempts foreign-source income from taxation. All of State A's taxes are therefore allocable to U.S.-source income. States B and C tax $225 million of Mathis' income, of which $175 million ($400 million - 225 million is deemed to be from U.S. sources. Therefore, the amount of state income taxes apportioned to foreign-source income is $3,222,222 (($12 million + $2.5 million) × ($50 million/225 million)). The remaining $11,277,778 is apportioned to U.S.-source income.

Losses on Sales or Exchanges of Property

The source rules for losses on the sale or exchange of property depend on whether the property is realty, personal property other than stock, or stock.

Losses on the Sale of Realty

Nonresident aliens and foreign corporations who dispose of U.S. realty are taxed as if they were engaged in a U.S. trade or business and as if the losses were effectively connected to a U.S. trade or business. Code Sec. 897(a)(1). Partnership assets are considered to be owned proportionately by its partners and used or held by the partners in the same trade or business as the partnership. Code Sec. 897(c)(4)(B).

Losses on Sales or Exchanges of Personal Property Other Than Stock

Generally, losses on the sale of personal property other than stock are allocated to the class of gross income to which gain from a sale of such property would give rise in the hands of a seller. Therefore, loss recognized by a U.S. person on the sale of a bond generally is allocated to U.S.-source income. These sourcing rules also apply to bad debts and to losses on property that is marked to market. Reg. §1.865-1(a)(1).

Losses of a U.S. person on sales of property that is attributable to an office or other fixed place of business in a foreign country generally are allocated to reduce foreign-source income if gains on such sales are taxed by the foreign country and the highest marginal rate of tax on such gains in the foreign country is at least 10 percent. Reg. §1.865-1(a)(2). Such losses will be foreign-source losses regardless if any gain would have been sourced under the depreciation recapture rules of Code Sec. 865(c), the intangible source rules for contingent payments under Code Sec. 965(d)(1)(B), or the goodwill rules of Code Sec. 865(d)(3). Reg. §1.865-1(b)(2).

EXAMPLE 25.53

On January 1, 2017, Singleton, Inc. a domestic corporation, paid $500,000 for computer chip-making equipment for use in its plant in Thailand. The computer chips produced were sold both in the U.S. and foreign countries. On April 4, 2019, Singleton sold the equipment for $140,000. Depreciation for the time period up through the date of sale amounted to $308,000, of which $200,000 was allocated to U.S.-source income and $108,000 to foreign-source general limitation income. Because gain attributable to depreciation recapture would have been general foreign-source income had the equipment been sold at a gain, all of the loss is allocated against foreign-source general limitation income.

If a U.S. citizen or resident alien has a foreign tax home, a loss on the sale of personal property will be allocated to foreign-source income if a gain on the sale of such property would have been taxable by a foreign country and the highest marginal rate of tax on such gains in the foreign country is at least 10 percent. Reg. §1.865-1(a)(3).

A partner's distributive share of loss recognized by a partnership with respect to personal property is allocated as if the partner recognized the loss. Reg. §1.865-1(a)(5). If the losses are attributable to a partnership's office or fixed place of business, the office or fixed place of business is considered to be an office of the partner.

Loss with respect to a contingent debt instrument is generally allocated to the class of gross income with respect to which interest income from the instrument would give rise. Reg. §1.865-1(b)(2).

Exceptions to the Personal Property Loss Rules

The loss rules with respect to personal property other than stock do not apply to the following: Reg. §1.865-1(c)(1)-(5).

- Foreign currency transactions.
- Inventory.
- Interest equivalents and trade receivables.
- Unamortized bond premium.
- Accrued but unpaid interest.

Rules for Stock Losses

In general, losses from the sale of stock are allocated in the same manner as are gains from the sale of stock (reciprocal-to-gain rule). Reg. §1.865-2(a)(1). For example, loss recognized by a resident of the United States on the sale of stock generally is allocated to reduce U.S.-source income. However, a loss on the sale of stock by a U.S. resident that is attributable to an office or other fixed place of business in a foreign country is allocated to reduce foreign-source income, if both of the following requirements are satisfied: Reg. §1.865-2(a)(2).

- A gain on the sale of the stock would have been taxed by the foreign country.
- The highest marginal income tax rate in the foreign country on such gains is at least 10 percent.

If a U.S. citizen or resident alien has a foreign tax home, the loss reduces foreign source income provided that the above two requirements are met. Reg. §1.865-2(a)(3). Special rules apply to bona fide residents of Puerto Rico.

Exceptions to the General Rules for Stock Losses

There are three exceptions to the stock loss rules: Reg. §1.865-2(b).

- The rules do not apply to losses from stock that constitutes inventory.
- The rules do not apply to losses from stock in an S corporation.
- The taxpayer included in income a dividend recapture amount with respect to the stock at any time during the recapture period.
  A *dividend recapture amount* includes all of the following: Reg. §1.865-2(d)(2).
- Actual dividends.
- Certain dividends that are foreign personal holding company dividends.
- Earnings from certain investments in U.S. property by controlled foreign corporations that result in an inclusion of Subpart F income.

The *recapture period* is the 24-month period preceding the date that a taxpayer recognizes loss with respect to the stock. Reg. §1.865-2(d)(3). The recapture period is increased by any period of time in which the taxpayer has diminished its risk of loss from holding the stock through the use of options or other positions or by hedging the assets of the corporation. Reg. §1.865-2(d)(3). These risks are described in Code Sec. 246(c)(4).

If the dividend recapture rule applies, the loss from the sale of stock is allocated and apportioned on a proportionate basis to the same class of income or the statutory or residual grouping to which the dividend recapture amount was assigned. This required allocation may reduce the foreign tax credit.

EXAMPLE 25.54	Barnes, Inc. is a domestic corporation. It is a shareholder of Maldonado Co., a foreign corporation. Maldonado has never owned any property in the U.S. that would give rise to Subpart F income. On July 6, 2016, it distributed $5 million in dividends to Barnes, Inc. The dividend resulted in a $250,000 foreign withholding tax, and Barnes, Inc. was deemed to have paid an additional $1.25 million of foreign income tax with respect to the dividend. On April 10, 2018, Barnes, Inc. sells its shares of Maldonado Co., and recognizes an $8 million loss. In 2018 Barnes, Inc. has $20 million of foreign-source income that is general limitation income. Barnes, Inc. also has $25 million of foreign source capital gain income that is passive income and $18 million of U.S.-source income. The $5 million dividend paid in 2016 is a dividend recapture amount. Therefore, $5 million of the $8 million loss must be allocated to the foreign-source general limitation income. The remaining $3 million loss is allocated to U.S.-source income. After the allocation, Barnes, Inc. has $15 million of general limitation foreign-source income and $25 million of foreign-source passive income. Note that because the loss reduces the foreign-source income, the fraction of income from foreign sources is reduced and the limitation on the foreign tax credit will be lower than otherwise.

Exceptions to the dividend recapture rules exist for de minimis amounts (dividend recaptures of less than 10 percent of the recognized loss). Reg. §1.865-2(b)(1)(ii).In addition, the passive-basket dividend exception generally exempts dividend recapture of amounts that would be treated as passive income. Reg. §1.865-2(b)(1)(iii). Passive income of a nonresident alien individual that is not connected with a U.S. trade or business but is received from U.S. sources is generally taxed at a flat 30 percent rate or, if lower, the applicable treaty rate. Code Sec. 871(a)(1).

Net Operating Losses

Net operating losses (NOLs) are subject to special ordering rules. Reg. § 1.904(g)-3. The NOLs must be allocated between foreign-source losses and domestic losses using a seven-step approach. Discussion of these detailed rules is outside the scope of this text

Interest Expense

Money is a fungible asset (i.e. one dollar is equally as good as another dollar). Therefore, for allocation purposes, interest expense is generally considered to relate to all activities and property rather than to any specific reason for borrowing the money. However, there are three exceptions to this rule.

Interest expense is allocated on the basis of assets. Under the asset method, interest expense is apportioned to the various statutory groupings based on the average total value of assets within each grouping for the tax year in question. Temp. Reg. §1.861-9T(g). Assets are characterized according to the source and type of income the assets generate. The value of assets within the statutory grouping and the residual grouping at the beginning and end of the tax year is determined by dividing the assets into the following three groups:

- Single category assets (these assets generate income exclusively within a single category grouping or the residual grouping).
- Multiple category assets (these assets generate income within more than one grouping).
- Assets that produce no identifiable yield or that contribute equally to the generation of all of the taxpayer's income (e.g., assets used in general or administrative functions).

There are three permissible ways to value assets for this purpose: the tax book value method (the adjusted basis of the assets) the fair market value method; and an alternate tax book value method that uses straight-line depreciation and longer depreciable lives.

EXAMPLE 25.55	Pena Co. incurred interest expense in 2017 of $2 million. The company uses the tax value method to value its assets for purposes of apportioning its interest expense. The adjusted basis of its assets is $5 million, $4 million of which generates U.S.-source income. The remaining assets of $1 million generate foreign-source general limitation income. The interest apportioned to U.S.-source income is $1.6 million ($2 million × ($4 million/$5 million)). The interest apportioned to foreign-source general limitation income is $400,000 ($2 million × ($1 million/$5 million)).

Exceptions to the Interest Apportionment Rules

The preceding interest apportionment rules are not applied to the following: Temp. Reg. §1.861-10T(b), (c), and (e).

- Qualified nonrecourse indebtedness. If the proceeds are used to purchase, construct, or improve property, the interest expense is directly allocated.
- Integrated financial transactions. Interest is allocated to the income that generates the transaction.
- Excess related person indebtedness. Interest received on the excess related person indebtedness is allocated in proportion to the relative aggregate amount of related controlled foreign corporation obligations held by the related United States shareholder.

U.S. Taxation of Foreign Persons

¶25,465   U.S. TAX ON NONRESIDENT ALIEN INDIVIDUALS

Nonresident alien individuals are subject to U.S. tax on their U.S.-source income. Code Sec. 871. How that income is taxed varies depending on whether or not the income is effectively connected with a U.S. business (when income is effectively connected with a U.S. business is discussed in ¶25,495). The rate of tax imposed may be reduced if there is a treaty between the United States and the country where the nonresident alien resides.

PLANNING POINTER	A nonresident alien individual married to a U.S. citizen or resident may elect to be taxed as a U.S. resident. Code Sec. 6013(g).

Income Not Connected With a U.S. Business

A flat 30 percent tax is imposed on a nonresident alien individual's U.S.-source gross income received as:

1. Fixed or determinable annual or periodical income, such as compensation for personal services, dividends, interest (other than original issue discount), pensions and annuities, alimony, rent, royalties, taxable scholarships and fellowship grants, commissions, and prizes. Eighty-five percent of any Social Security benefits is treated as fixed or determinable annual or periodical income.
2. In the case of a payment on an original issue discount obligation, an amount equal to the original issue discount that has accrued while held by the nonresident alien individual (and not previously taken into account). In the case of a sale or exchange of an original issue discount obligation, the amount of original issue discount that accrued while the obligation was held by the nonresident alien individual (and previously has not been taken into account).
3. Gains from the sale or exchange of patents, copyrights, secret processes and formulas, goodwill, trademarks, trade brands, franchises, and like property, or any interest in such property, to the extent that such gains are from payments that are contingent on the productivity, use, or disposition of the property or interest sold or exchanged.
4. Gains described in Code Sec. 631(b) and (c) from the disposal of timber or coal or domestic iron ore.

The tax is imposed on such amounts received only to the extent that they are not effectively connected with the conduct of a trade or business within the United States.

Certain income is excepted from the 30-percent tax:

1. Portfolio interest. Code Sec. 871(h).
2. Interest on deposits with banks and savings and loan associations if it is not effectively connected with the conduct of a trade or business within the United States. Code Sec. 871(i).
3. Interest on amounts held by an insurance company under an agreement to pay interest if it is not effectively connected with the conduct of a trade or business within the United States. Code Sec. 871(i).
4. The active foreign business percentage of any dividend and any interest paid by an existing 80/20 company.
5. Dividends paid by a foreign corporation that are treated as income from sources within the United States. Code Sec. 871(i).
6. Certain dividends received from a regulated investment company. Code Sec. 871(k).
7. Any amount received as an annuity from a Code Sec. 401(a) qualified trust or Code Sec. 403(a)(1) qualified annuity plan if (1) all of the personal services by reason of which the annuity is payable either were personal services performed outside the United States by an individual who was a nonresident alien at the time the services were performed or were personal services for a foreign employer by a nonresident alien individual temporarily present in the United States for no more than 90 days during the tax year and receiving no more than $3,000 in compensation for such services during the tax year and (2) at the time the first amount is paid 90 percent or more of the employees for whom contributions or benefits are provided under the plan or trust are U.S. citizens or residents. Code Sec. 871(f)(1).
8. Gambling winnings from blackjack, baccarat, craps, roulette, or bit-6 wheel. Code Sec. 871(j).

With respect to obligations issued on or before March 18, 2012, *portfolio interest* includes interest (including original issue discount) on certain obligations in registered and unregistered form (Code Sec. 871(h)(2)):

■ Interest paid on an obligation not in registered form if the interest is payable only outside the United States and its possessions and the face of the obligation includes a statement that any United States person who holds the obligation will be subject to limitations under the U.S. income tax laws.
■ Interest paid on an obligation in registered form if a United States person is not required by Code Sec. 1441(a) to withhold tax from the interest payments because the United States person has received a statement that the beneficial owner of the obligation is not a United States person.

With respect to obligations issued after March 18, 2012, *portfolio interest* does not include interest paid on an unregistered obligation, and interest paid on a registered obligation can qualify as *portfolio interest* even though the United States person does not receive a statement that the beneficial owner of the obligation is not a United States person if the IRS has determined that such a statement is not required.

Portfolio interest does not include:

1. Any interest on an obligation issued by a corporation that is received by a person who owns 10 percent or more of the total combined voting power of all classes of the corporation's voting stock.
2. Any interest on an obligation issued by a partnership that is received by any person who owns 10 percent or more of the capital or profits interest in the partnership.
3. Any interest whose amount is determined by reference to any receipts, sales, or other cash flow of the debtor or a related person, any income or profits of the debtor or a related person, any change in value of any property of the debtor or a related person, any dividend, partnership distribution, or similar payments made by the debtor or a related person, or any other type of contingent interest identified by the IRS, where denial of the portfolio interest exemption is necessary or appropriate to prevent the avoidance of federal income tax.

Capital Gains

If a nonresident alien individual is present in the United States for a period or periods aggregating 183 days or more during the tax year, a 30 percent tax is imposed on the amount by which the individual's capital gains from U.S. sources (other than capital gains previously described) during the tax year exceeds the individual's capital losses allocable to U.S. sources. Gains and losses may be taken into account only if, and to the extent that, they would be recognized and taken into account if they were effectively connected with the conduct of a trade or business within the United States.

Transportation Income

A four percent tax is imposed on a nonresident alien individual's U.S.-source gross transportation income for the tax year, unless the income is effectively connected with a U.S. business. Code Sec. 887.

Income Connected With a U.S. Business

A nonresident alien individual engaged in a trade or business within the United States during the tax year generally is taxed on taxable income effectively connected with the conduct of a trade or business in the United States at the same graduated income tax rates that apply to U.S. citizens and residents. Code Sec. 871(b).

Election to Treat Real Property Income as Income Connected With a U.S. Business. A nonresident alien individual who derives any income from U.S. real property held for the production of income may elect to treat all such income as income that is effectively connected with the conduct of a U.S. trade or business. Code Sec. 871(d)(1). Once an election is made, it will remain in effect for subsequent tax years until revoked with the IRS's consent. Code Sec. 871(d)(1). Once an election has been revoked, a new election may not be made before the fifth tax year beginning after the first tax year for which the revocation is effective unless the IRS consents to an earlier election. Code Sec. 871(d)(2).

Participants in Certain Exchange or Training Programs. A nonresident alien individual will be treated as being engaged in a U.S. trade or business if the individual is temporarily present in the U.S. on an "F," "J," "M," or "Q" visa. Code Sec. 871(c). Any taxable scholarship or grant received by the individual from a U.S. source will be treated as effectively connected with the conduct of a U.S. trade or business and subject to a 14 percent withholding tax. Code Secs. 871(c), 1441(a).

Deductions generally are allowed only to the extent that they are connected with income that is effectively connected with the conduct of a trade or business within the United States. Code Sec. 873(a). However, the following deductions are allowed whether or not they are connected with income that is effectively connected with the conduct of a trade or business within the United States: Code Sec. 873(b).

1. *Casualty and theft losses.* A deduction for casualty or theft losses is allowed if the loss is of property located within the United States.
2. *Charitable contributions.* A deduction is allowed for charitable contributions.
3. *Personal exemption.* Only one personal exemption is allowed unless the taxpayer is a resident of Mexico or Canada or a U.S. national. There is no limit on the number of personal exemptions that a resident of Mexico or Canada or a U.S. national is allowed. A *U.S. national* is an individual who, although not a U.S. citizen, owes permanent allegiance to the United States (such as someone from American Samoa or the Northern Mariana Islands who chose to become a U.S. national instead of a U.S. citizen). 8 U.S.C. §1101(a)(22).

Withholding of Tax

The tax required to be paid by a nonresident alien individual on income not connected with a United States business has to be withheld from payments to the individual. Code Sec. 1441(a), (b). However, no withholding is required from payments of income (other than compensation for personal services) effectively connected with the conduct of a trade or business within the United States if it is includible in the beneficial owner's gross income for the tax year. Code Sec. 1441(c); Reg. §1.1441-4(a)(1). The tax to be withheld is computed based on the gross amount (not reduced by any deductions) paid to the individual.

IRS Form W-8BEN, Certificate of Foreign Status of Beneficial Owner for United States Tax Withholding and Reporting (Individuals), is filed by a nonresident alien individual to claim a reduced rate of, or exemption from, withholding under an income tax treaty. IRS Form W-8ECI, Certificate of Foreign Person's Claim That Income Is Effectively Connected With the Conduct of a Trade or Business in the United States, is filed to claim that income is effectively connected with the conduct of a trade or business in the United States and thus not subject to withholding.

EXAMPLE 25.56 New Frontier, a domestic corporation, distributes dividends to its shareholders. Among the recipients are two shareholders with foreign addresses, one of whom has filed a written statement with New Frontier indicating U.S. citizenship. New Frontier must withhold 30% of the dividend amount paid to the foreign citizen. If the U.S. citizen had not filed the statement, New Frontier would have been obligated to withhold taxes from the dividend payment. If New Frontier has two additional shareholders who are U.S. residents, one of whom is not a U.S. citizen, no withholding is required for either taxpayer.

¶25,475   U.S. TAX ON FOREIGN CORPORATIONS

Foreign corporations are subject to U.S. tax on their U.S.-source income. Code Secs. 881, 882, 884. How that income is taxed varies depending on whether or not the income is effectively connected with a U.S. business (when income is effectively connected with a business is discussed in ¶25,495). The rate of tax imposed may be reduced by a treaty between the United States and the country where the corporation resides.

Income Not Connected With a U.S. Business

A 30 percent tax is imposed on the amount a foreign corporation receives from U.S. sources as: Code Sec. 881(a).

1. Fixed or determinable annual or periodical income, such as compensation for services, dividends, interest (other than original issue discount), annuities, rent, and royalties.
2. In the case of a payment on an original issue discount obligation, an amount equal to the original issue discount that has accrued while held by the foreign corporation (and previously not taken into account). In the case of a sale or exchange of an original issue discount obligation, the amount of original issue discount that accrued while the obligation was held by the foreign corporation (and previously has not been taken into account).
3. Gains from the sale or exchange of patents, copyrights, secret processes and formulas, goodwill, trademarks, trade brands, franchises, and like property, or any interest in such property, to the extent that such gains are from payments that are contingent on the productivity, use, or disposition of the property or interest sold or exchanged.
4. Gains described in Code Sec. 631(b) and (c) from the disposal of timber or coal or domestic iron ore.

The tax is imposed on such amounts received only to the extent that they are not effectively connected with the conduct of a trade or business within the United States.

Certain income is excepted from the 30-percent tax:

1. Portfolio interest. Code Sec. 881(c).
2. Interest on deposits with banks and savings and loan associations if it is not effectively connected with the conduct of a trade or business within the United States. Code Sec. 881(d).
3. Interest on amounts held by an insurance company under an agreement to pay interest if it is not effectively connected with the conduct of a trade or business within the United States. Code Sec. 881(d).
4. The active foreign business percentage of any dividend and any interest paid by an existing 80/20 company.
5. Dividends paid by a foreign corporation that are treated under Code Sec. 861(a)(2)(B) as income from U.S. sources.
6. Certain dividends received from a regulated investment company. Code Sec. 881(e).

Portfolio interest is excepted from the 30-percent tax. Code Sec. 881(c). With respect to obligations issued on or before March 18, 2012, *portfolio interest* includes interest (including original issue discount) on certain obligations issued in registered and unregistered form (Code Sec. 881(c)(2)):

■ Interest paid on an obligation not in registered form if the interest is payable only outside the United States and its possessions and the face of the obligation includes a statement that any United States person who holds the obligation will be subject to limitations under the U.S. income tax laws.
■ Interest paid on an obligation in registered form if a United States person is not required by Code Sec. 1441(a) to withhold tax from the interest payments because the United States person has received a statement that the beneficial owner of the obligation is not a United States person.

With respect to obligations issued after March 18, 2012, *portfolio interest* does not include interest paid on an unregistered obligation, and interest paid on a registered obligation can qualify as *portfolio interest* even though the United States person does not receive a statement that the beneficial owner of the obligation is not a United States person if the IRS has determined that such a statement is not required.

Portfolio interest does not include:

1. Any interest on an obligation issued by a corporation that is received by a person who owns 10 percent or more of the total combined voting power of all classes of the corporation's voting stock.
2. Any interest on an obligation issued by a partnership that is received by any person who owns 10 percent or more of the capital or profits interest in the partnership.

3. Any interest whose amount is determined by reference to any receipts, sales, or other cash flow of the debtor or a related person, any income or profits of the debtor or a related person, any change in value of any property of the debtor or a related person, any dividend, partnership distribution, or similar payments made by the debtor or a related person, or any other type of contingent interest identified by the IRS, where denial of the portfolio interest exemption is necessary or appropriate to prevent the avoidance of federal income tax.

Transportation income. A four percent tax is imposed on a foreign corporation's U.S.-source gross transportation income for the tax year, unless the income is effectively connected with a U.S. business. Code Sec. 887.

Income Effectively Connected With a U.S. Business

A foreign corporation engaged in a trade or business within the United States is taxed like a U.S. corporation on its taxable income that is effectively connected with the conduct of the trade or business within the United States. Code Sec. 882(a)(1).

There are special rules for certain deductions and credits: Code Sec. 882(c).

1. *Charitable contributions.* A deduction for charitable contributions is allowed whether or not connected with income that is effectively connected with the conduct of a trade or business within the United States.
2. *Foreign tax credit.* Foreign corporations are allowed a foreign tax credit only with respect to taxes paid to a foreign country or U.S. possession with respect to income effectively connected with the conduct of a trade or business within the United States.

A foreign corporation that derives any income from real property located in the United States may elect to treat it as income effectively connected with the conduct of a trade or business within the United States. Code Sec. 882(d). Once an election is made, it will remain in effect for subsequent tax years until revoked with the IRS's consent. Code Sec. 882(d)(1). Once an election has been revoked, a new election may not be made before the fifth tax year beginning after the first tax year for which the revocation is effective unless the IRS consents to an earlier election. Code Sec. 882(d)(2).

Branch Profits and Branch-Level Interest Taxes

Foreign corporations engaged in a trade or business within the United States may be liable for the branch profits and branch-level interest taxes in addition to the tax imposed on their taxable income that is effectively connected with the conduct of a trade or business within the United States. Code Sec. 884. These taxes were enacted to reduce the disparity between the taxation of foreign corporations operating in the United States through a subsidiary and foreign corporations operating in the United States through a branch.

Branch Profits Tax

The branch profits tax is 30 percent of the dividend equivalent amount for the tax year. The tax rate may be reduced by an income tax treaty between the United States and the corporation's country of residence.

A corporation's *dividend equivalent amount* is the corporation's effectively connected earnings and profits for the tax year with the following adjustments:

1. *Reduction for increase in U.S. net equity.* If the U.S. net equity (i.e., U.S. assets minus U.S. liabilities) of the corporation as of the close of the tax year exceeds the corporation's U.S. net equity as of the close of the preceding tax year, the corporation's effectively connected earnings and profits for the tax year are reduced (but not below zero) by the amount of the excess.
2. *Increase for decrease in U.S. net equity.* If the U.S. net equity of the corporation as of the close of the preceding tax year exceeds the corporation's U.S. net equity as of the close of the current tax year, the corporation's effectively connected earnings and profits for the tax year are increased by the amount of the excess. However, the increase may not exceed the corporation's accumulated effectively connected earnings and profits as of the close of the preceding tax year.

EXAMPLE 25.57	Excalibur, a foreign corporation, operates a branch office in the United States. During the year, Excalibur has $500,000 of effectively connected earnings and profits. Its U.S. assets at the end of the tax year were $1,200,000, and its U.S. liabilities at the end of the tax year were $650,000. Its U.S. assets at the beginning of the tax year were $1,000,000, and its U.S. liabilities at the beginning of the tax year were $550,000. Excalibur's branch profits tax is calculated as follows:

Effectively connected earnings and profits:		$500,000
U.S. net equity at the end of the tax year ($1,200,000 - $650,000) =	$550,000	
U.S. net equity at the beginning of the tax year ($1,000,000 - $550,000) =	$450,000	
Increase in U.S. net equity:		$100,000
Dividend equivalent amount:		$400,000
Branch profits tax (30% x $400,000) =		$120,000

Branch-Level Interest Tax

To the extent that the allocable interest paid by a U.S. trade or business of a foreign corporation (i.e., interest allocable to income that is effectively connected with the conduct of a trade or business in the United States) exceeds the interest paid by the trade or business in the United States, the excess is treated as though it had been paid to the foreign corporation on the last day of the foreign corporation's tax year and is subject to the 30 percent U.S. withholding tax (unless the rate of tax is reduced or eliminated by a treaty provision). Code Sec. 884(f).

Withholding of Tax

The tax required to be paid by a foreign corporation on income not connected with a United States business has to be withheld from payments to the corporation. However, no withholding is required from payments of income that is effectively connected with the conduct of a trade or business within the United States if it is includible in the beneficial owner's gross income for the tax year. The tax to be withheld is computed based on the gross amount (not reduced by any deductions) paid to the corporation. Code Sec. 1442(a).

IRS Form W-8BEN, Certificate of Foreign Status of Beneficial Owner for United States Tax Withholding and Reporting (Individuals), is filed by a foreign corporation to claim a reduced rate of, or exemption from, withholding under an income tax treaty. IRS Form W-8ECI, Certificate of Foreign Person's Claim That Income Is Effectively Connected With the Conduct of a Trade or Business in the United States, is filed to claim that income is effectively connected with the conduct of a trade or business in the United States and thus not subject to withholding.

¶25,485   WHAT CONSTITUTES A U.S. TRADE OR BUSINESS

Whether a person is engaged in a trade or business in the United States depends on the nature of the person's activities. A person who owns and operates a business in the United States selling services or products generally is considered engaged in a trade or business in the United States.

Performance of Personal Services

The term *trade or business within the United States* usually includes the performance of personal services within the United States at any time during the tax year. However, it does not include personal services by a nonresident alien individual if both of the following requirements are satisfied: Code Sec. 864(b).

1. The performance of personal services is for a nonresident alien individual, foreign partnership, or foreign corporation not engaged in a trade or business within the United States or for an office or place of business maintained in a foreign country or in a U.S. possession by an individual who is a U.S. citizen or resident or by a domestic partnership or domestic corporation.
2. The nonresident alien individual is temporarily present in the United States for a period or periods not exceeding a total of 90 days during the tax year, and the individual's compensation for the services does not exceed $3,000.

Partnerships

If a nonresident alien individual or foreign corporation is a partner in a partnership engaged in a trade or business within the United States, the individual or corporation will be treated as being engaged in that trade or business within the United States. Code Sec. 875.

Trusts and Estates

If a nonresident alien individual or foreign corporation is a beneficiary of an estate or trust engaged in any trade or business within the United States, the individual or corporation will be treated as engaged in that business within the United States. Code Sec. 875.

Trading in Stocks, Securities, and Commodities

The term *trade or business* does not include trading in stocks, securities, or commodities through a resident broker, commission agent, custodian, or other independent agent or for one's own account. Code Sec. 864(b)(2).

¶25,495   INCOME EFFECTIVELY CONNECTED WITH A U.S. BUSINESS

If a person was engaged in a U.S. trade or business (as defined in ¶25,485) during the tax year, all income, gain, and loss (other than certain investment income) for the tax year that is realized from U.S. sources is treated as effectively connected with the U.S. trade or business. Income, gain, and loss from foreign sources, with limited exceptions, will not be treated as effectively connected with the conduct of a trade or business within the United States. Code Sec. 864(c).

Business Profits and Losses

Profits and losses from U.S. sources that are from the operation of a business in the United States (such as profit from the sale in the United States of inventory that was purchased in the U.S. or abroad) are considered effectively connected with a trade or business in the United States.

Personal Services

Personal service income received during a tax year in which a person was engaged in a U.S. trade or business is considered effectively connected with a U.S. trade or business. Income received in a year other than the year that services were performed also is considered effectively connected with a U.S. trade or business if it would have been effectively connected if it had been received during the year that the services were performed. Income and gains from assets, and gains and losses from the sale or exchange of capital assets, generally are not considered effectively connected with a trade or business unless there is a direct economic relationship between holding the asset and the trade or business of performing personal services. Reg. §1.864-4(c)(6).

Investment Income

Investment income from U.S. sources that may or may not be treated as effectively connected with a U.S. trade or business generally falls within the following categories: Reg. §1.864-4(a).

1. Fixed or determinable income (such as interest, dividends, rents, royalties, premiums, and annuities).
2. Original issue discount recognized from the sale or exchange of an original issue discount obligation.
3. Gains from the sale or exchange of patents, copyrights, secret processes and formulas, goodwill, trademarks, trade brands, franchises, and like property, or any interest in such property, to the extent that such gains are from payments that are contingent on the productivity, use, or disposition of the property or interest sold or exchanged.
4. Gains described in Code Sec. 631(b) and (c) from the disposal of timber or coal or domestic iron ore.
5. Capital gains and losses.

Two tests are used to determine whether an item of U.S.-source income falling into one of the preceding categories is effectively connected with a U.S. trade or business. Code Sec. 864(c)(2); Reg. §1.864-4(c).

1. *Asset-use test.* Under this test, which usually applies to income that is not directly produced by trade or business activities, an item of income derived from assets used in, or held for use in, a trade or business in the United States is considered effectively connected with that business. An asset is used in, or held for use in, a trade or business in the United States if the asset is held for the principal purpose of promoting the conduct of a trade or business in the United States; acquired and held in the ordinary course of the trade or business conducted in the United States (e.g., an account receivable arising from that trade or business); or otherwise held to meet the present needs of the trade or business in the United States and not its anticipated future needs.

2. *Business-activities test.* Under this test, which usually applies when income, gain, or loss comes from the active conduct of the trade or business, income is considered effectively connected with a U. S. trade or business if the activities of a trade or business conducted in the United States were a material factor in the realization of the income. This test is most important when dividends or interest are received by a dealer in stocks or securities; royalties are received in the trade or business of licensing patents or similar property; or fees are earned by a servicing business.

Pensions

If a pension attributable to personal services performed in the United States is received, pension payments are considered effectively connected with a U.S. trade or business in each year that they are received, whether or not the recipient is engaged in a U.S. trade or business during the year that the payments are received.

Real Property Gains and Losses

Gains and losses from the sale or exchange of U.S. real property interests (whether or not they are capital assets) are treated as effectively connected with a trade or business in the United States. Code Sec. 897.

A *U.S. real property interest* includes:

1. An interest in real property (including an interest in a mine, well, or other natural deposit) located in the United States or the Virgin Islands.
2. An interest (other than an interest solely as a creditor) in a domestic corporation unless the taxpayer establishes that the corporation was at no time a United States real property holding corporation during the five-year period ending on the date that the interest was disposed.

A *United States real property interest* does not include an interest in a corporation if:

1. The corporation did not hold any United States real property interests as of the date that the interest was disposed.
2. All of the United States real property interests held by the corporation at any time during the five-year period ending on the date that the interest was disposed were disposed of in transactions in which the full amount of any gain was recognized or ceased to be United States real property interests because of dispositions by one or more other corporations.

If any class of a corporation's stock is regularly traded on an established securities market, that class of stock will be treated as a United States real property interest only in the case of a person who held more than five percent of that class of stock during the five-year period ending on the date that the interest was disposed.

A corporation is a *U.S. real property holding company* if the fair market value of the corporation's U.S. real property interests is at least 50 percent of the fair market value of its U.S. real property interests, its interests in real property located outside the United States, plus any other assets that are used in, or held for use in, a trade or business.

Nonresident alien individuals and foreign corporations may elect to treat income derived during the tax year from real property held for the production of income and located in the United States, or from any interest in such real property [including gains from the sale or exchange of such real property or an interest therein; rents or royalties from mines, wells, or other natural deposits; and gains described in Code Sec. 631(b) and (c) from the disposal of timber, coal, or iron ore], as income that is effectively connected with the conduct of a trade or business within the United States. Code Secs. 871(d) and 882(d).

Taxpayers are allowed an election so that they can avoid uncertainty in determining whether a rental activity constitutes a trade or business. Taxpayers can make an election by filing with their income tax return a statement to the effect that an election is being made and including information about the property and any prior election. Reg. §§1.871-10(d)(1)(ii), 1.882-2(a).

An election is effective for the year it is made and all subsequent years until revoked with the IRS' consent. Code Secs. 871(d)(1), 882(d)(1). If an election has been revoked, a new election may not be made without the IRS' consent before the fifth tax year beginning after the first tax year for which the revocation is effective. Code Secs. 871(d)(2), 882(d)(2). No election may be made for a tax year in which the taxpayer does not derive income from the U.S. real property. Rev. Rul. 91-7, 1991-1 CB 110.

Transportation Income

Transportation income is considered effectively connected with a U.S. trade or business if the recipient had a fixed place of business in the United States involved in earning the income and at least 90 percent of the recipient's U.S.-source transportation income is attributable to regularly scheduled transportation (or, in the case of income from the leasing of a vessel or aircraft, is attributable to a fixed place of business in the United States). Code Sec. 887(b)(4); Rev. Proc. 91-12, 1991-1 CB 473.

Foreign-Source Income Effectively Connected with a U.S. Business

As a general rule, no income, gain, or loss from foreign sources will be treated as effectively connected with the conduct of a trade or business within the United States. Code Sec. 864(c)(4). However, three types of foreign-source income will be treated as effectively connected with a trade or business in the United States if the following requirements are satisfied:

1. The person has an office or other fixed place of business in the United States to which the income can be attributed.
2. The office or place of business is a material factor in the production of such income. An office or other place of business is a material factor in producing income if it significantly contributes to, and is an essential economic element in, the earning of the income.
3. The office or place of business regularly carries on activities of a type from which the income is derived.

The three types of foreign-source income that may be treated as effectively connected with a trade or business in the United States include:

1. Rents and royalties for the use of, or for the privilege of using outside the United States, patents, copyrights, secret processes and formulas, goodwill, trademarks, trade brands, franchises, and similar property, if the rents or royalties are derived in the active conduct of the trade or business that has an office or other fixed place of business within the United States.
2. Interest, dividends, and amounts received for the provision of guarantees of indebtedness that either were derived from the active conduct of a banking, financing, or similar business within the United States or were received by a corporation whose principal business is trading in stocks or securities for its own account.
3. Income, gain, or loss from the sale or exchange (outside the United States) through a U.S. office or fixed place of business, of stock in trade, property that would have been included in inventory if on hand at the close of the tax year, or property held primarily for sale to customers in the ordinary course of business. Not included is property sold or exchanged for use, consumption, or disposition outside the United States if an office or other fixed place of business of the taxpayer in a foreign country participated materially in the sale or exchange.

¶25,505   FILING REQUIREMENTS FOR NONRESIDENT ALIEN INDIVIDUALS

Nonresident alien individuals must file a U.S. federal income tax return if any of the following applies to them: Reg. §1.6012-1(b).

1. They engaged, or are considered to have engaged, in a trade or business within the United States at any time during the tax year. They must file a return even though their income did not come from a trade or business conducted in the United States, they have no U.S.-source income, or their income is tax-exempt. However, no return has to be filed by a nonresident alien individual who earns less than the amount of one personal exemption as United States source wages effectively connected with a United States business. This exception applies even though the individual also has United States source fixed or determinable annual or periodical gains, profits, or income, provided that the individual's U.S. tax liability for that income is fully satisfied by the withholding of tax at source. IRS Notice 2005-77, 2005-2 CB 951.
2. Insufficient tax was withheld from U.S.-source income that they received.
3. They want to claim a refund for overwithheld or overpaid tax.
4. They want to claim the benefit of any deductions or credits.

Nonresident alien individuals who are required to file a federal income tax return should file IRS Form 1040-NR, U.S. Nonresident Alien Income Tax Return, or, if they qualify, IRS Form 1040-NR-EZ, U.S. Income Tax Return for Certain Nonresident Aliens With No Dependents.

Time for Filing Income Tax Return

Employees who receive wages subject to U.S. income tax withholding have until the 15th day of the fourth month following the end of their tax year. Reg. §1.6072-1(c). Other nonresident alien individuals must file their tax return by the 15th day of the sixth month after their tax year ends. Code Sec. 6072(c). To obtain the benefits of any allowable deductions or credits (not including the credit for withheld taxes), a nonresident alien individual must file a return within 16 months after the due date for filing a return. Reg. §1.874-1(b)(1).

Extension of Time to File. Taxpayers can receive an automatic six-month extension of time to file by filing IRS Form 4868, Application for Automatic Extension of Time to File U.S. Individual Income Tax Return, by the regular due date for a return. Reg. §1.6081-4(a). The extension of time to file does not extend the time to pay any tax due.

Protective return. Nonresident alien individuals may file a protective return to protect their right to receive the benefit of deductions and credits if it is later determined that some or all of their income is effectively connected with a U.S. trade or business. Reg. §1.874-1(b)(6).

¶25,515   FILING REQUIREMENTS FOR FOREIGN CORPORATIONS

Foreign corporations must file a U.S. income tax return if any of the following applies to them: Reg. §1.6012-2(g).

1. They engaged in a trade or business in the United States at any time during the tax year. They must file a return even though they did not have any income effectively connected with the conduct of a trade or business in the United States, they have no U.S.-source income, or their income is tax-exempt.
2. They had income, gains, or losses treated as if they were effectively connected with a U.S. trade or business.
3. They had any U.S.-source income (even though it is tax-exempt).
4. They seek a refund of income tax that they overpaid.

A foreign corporation does not have to file a U.S. income tax return if any of the following applies to it:

1. It did not engage in a U.S. trade or business during the tax year and all U.S. tax required to be withheld at source was so withheld.
2. Its only income is interest and dividends not subject to U.S. income taxation under Code Sec. 881(d).
3. It is a beneficiary of an estate or trust engaged in a U.S. trade or business but itself is not required to file a U.S. income tax return.

A foreign corporation required to file a U.S. income tax must file IRS Form 1120-F, U.S. Income Tax Return of a Foreign Corporation. A foreign corporation that does not owe any U.S. income tax because it is claiming a treaty exemption nevertheless must file IRS Form 1120-F to show that its income was exempted by treaty.

Time for Filing Income Tax Return

Foreign corporations (other than those who have an office or place of business in the United States) have to file any required U.S. income tax return on or before the 15th of the sixth month following the end of their tax year. Code Sec. 6072(c); Reg. §1.6072-2(b). Foreign corporations that have an office or place of business in the United States must file any required income tax return on or before the 15th day of the third month following the close of their tax year. Reg. §1.6072-2(a).

Extension of Time to File. A foreign corporation that does not maintain an office or place of business in the United States can obtain an automatic six-month extension of time to file by filing IRS Form 7004, Application for Automatic Extension of Time To File Certain Business Income Tax, Information, and Other Returns, by the due date for its income tax return. A foreign corporation that maintains an office or place of business in the United States is entitled to a three-month extension without having to file a form and can obtain an additional three-month extension by filing IRS Form 7004 by the 15th day of the third month following the end of its tax year.

Information Returns

Foreign corporations engaged in a trade or business within the United States and U.S. corporations that have at least one foreign shareholder who owns, directly or indirectly, at least 25 percent of either the total voting power of all classes of stock entitled to vote, or the total value of all classes of stock, of the corporation must complete IRS Form 5472, Information Return of a 25% Foreign-Owned U.S. Corporation or a Foreign Corporation Engaged in a U.S. Trade or Business (Under Sections 6038A and 6038C of the Internal Revenue Code), and attach it to their income tax return to report certain transactions with a related party. Code Secs. 6038A and 6038C.

Certain U.S. citizens and residents who are officers, directors, or shareholders of certain foreign corporations must complete IRS Form 5471, Information Return of U.S. Persons With Respect to Certain Foreign Corporations, and attach it to their income tax return to satisfy reporting requirements under Code Secs. 6035, 6038, and 6046.

¶25,525 FILING REQUIREMENTS FOR FOREIGN PARTNERSHIPS

Foreign partnerships must file IRS Form 1065, U.S. Return of Partnership Income, if they have gross income effectively connected with the conduct of a trade or business within the United States or have gross income derived from U.S. sources, even though their principal place of business is outside the United States or all of their partners are foreign persons. Code Sec. 6031(e); Reg. §1.6031(a)-1(b).

A foreign partnership with U.S.-source income is not required to file IRS Form 1065 if it qualifies for either of the following exceptions:

1. *Exception for foreign partnerships with de minimis U.S.-source income and de minimis U.S. partners.* No return is required if a partnership had no effectively connected income during its tax year, it had U.S.-source income of $20,000 or less during its tax year, less than one percent of any partnership item of income, gain, loss, deduction, or credit was allocable in the aggregate to direct U.S. partners at any time during its tax year, and the partnership is not a withholding foreign partnership (as defined in Reg. §1.1441-5(c)(2)(i)).

2. *Exception for foreign partnerships with no U.S. partners.* No return is required if the partnership had no effectively connected income during its tax year, it had no U.S. partners at any time during its tax year, all required IRS Forms 1042, Annual Withholding Tax Return for U.S. Source Income of Foreign Persons, and 1042-S, Foreign Person's U.S. Source Income Subject to Withholding, were filed by the partnership or another withholding agent as required by Reg. §1.1446-1(b) and (c)], the tax liability of each partner for amounts reportable under Reg. §1.1461-1(b) and (c) has been fully satisfied by the withholding of tax at the source, and the partnership is not a withholding foreign partnership as defined by Reg. §1.1441-5(c)(2)(i).

Time for Filing Form 1065

IRS Form 1065 must be filed on or before the 15th day of the third month following the close of the partnership's U.S. tax year. Code Sec. 6072(b). For partnerships that keep their records and books of account outside the United States, an extension of time to file and pay is granted to the 15th day of the sixth month following the close of their tax year. Reg. §1.6081-5(a).

Extension of Time to File. Partnerships can file IRS Form 7004, Application for Automatic Extension of Time To File Certain Business Income Tax, Information, and Other Returns, to request an automatic five-month (three-month in the case of a partnership that keeps its records and books of account outside the United States) extension of time to file.

Withholding Tax

All partnerships with effectively connected gross income allocable to a foreign partner in any tax year must file IRS Form 8804, Annual Return for Partnership Withholding Tax (Section 1446), IRS Form 8805, Foreign Partner's Information Statement of Section 1446 Withholding Tax, and IRS Form 8813, Partnership Withholding Tax Payment Voucher (Section 1446). Reg. §1.446-1(a).

Foreign partnerships must file IRS Form 8804 to report their total liability for withholding taxes for the tax year. IRS Form 8804 also is used as a transmittal form for IRS Form 8805. Foreign partnerships generally must file IRS Form 8804 on or before the 15th day of the third month (sixth month if the partnership keeps its records and books of account outside the United States and Puerto Rico) following the close of their tax year. Reg. §1.446-3(d)(1)(iii). IRS Form 8804 must be filed separately from a partnership's IRS Form 1065.

Foreign partnerships must file IRS Form 8805 to report the amount of their effectively connected taxable income and the total tax credit allocable to a foreign partner for the partnership's tax year. A separate IRS Form 8805 must be filed for each foreign partner. Foreign partnerships generally must file IRS Form 8805 on or before the 15th day of the third month (sixth month if the partnership keeps its records and books of account outside the United States and Puerto Rico) following the close of their tax year. Reg. §1.446-3(d)(1)(iii). Copy A of each IRS Form 8805 filed has to be attached to IRS Form 8804. Foreign partners must attach IRS Form 8805 to their U.S. income tax return to claim a credit for the tax withheld by their partnership.

IRS Form 8813 is used to pay the withholding tax. IRS Form 8813 must be filed on or before the 15th day of the fourth, sixth, ninth, and 12th months of the partnership's U.S. tax year. Reg. §1.446-3(d)(1)(ii).

Taxation of U.S. Shareholders Who Own Foreign Corporation Stock

¶25,535 U.S. SHAREHOLDERS OF CONTROLLED FOREIGN CORPORATIONS

Foreign business profits earned by a foreign subsidiary are not typically taxed in the United States until they are repatriated through a dividend. However, to prevent U.S. persons from avoiding U.S. tax by operating a business as a foreign corporation, the income of a controlled foreign corporation (CFC) is taxed directly to its controlling U.S. shareholders, even though the income is not distributed during the year.

If a foreign corporation is a CFC for an uninterrupted period of 30 days or more during the year, every person who is a U.S. shareholder on the last day of the tax year includes in gross income a deemed dividend equal to the sum of the shareholder's pro rata share of each of the following items: Code Sec. 951(a).

1. The corporation's subpart F income.
2. Previously excluded subpart F income withdrawn from investment in less developed countries.
3. Previously excluded subpart F income withdrawn from foreign base company shipping operations.
4. The increase in earnings invested in U.S. property.

EXAMPLE 25.58 A U.S. shareholder owns 100% of the only class of stock of a foreign corporation throughout 2017. Both parties use the calendar year. For 2017, the CFC derives $100 of subpart F income, has $100 of earnings and profits, and makes no distributions to its shareholders. The U.S. shareholder must include $100 in gross income.

Controlled Foreign Corporation Defined

A foreign corporation is a *controlled foreign corporation* (CFC) if more than 50 percent of the total combined voting power of all classes of stock, or the total value of the stock, is owned directly, indirectly, or constructively by U.S. shareholders on any day during the tax year. Code Sec. 957(a).

A *United States shareholder* is a *United States person* (defined in ¶25,315) who owns or is considered to own 10 percent or more of the total combined voting power of all classes of stock entitled to vote. Code Sec. 951(b). Stock owned directly or indirectly by or for a foreign corporation, foreign partnership, or foreign trust is considered actually owned proportionately by its shareholders, partners, or beneficiaries. Code Sec. 958(a). The constructive ownership rules of Code Sec. 318(a) are applied to the extent that a United States person is treated as a United States shareholder. Code Sec. 958(b).

EXAMPLE 25.59 U.S. persons, Morgan Karbey, Katie Wu, and Madison Corporation, own 9%, 32%, and 10%, respectively, of the one class of stock in a foreign corporation, Raji. Morgan also owns 10% of the one class of stock of Madison Corporation. For purposes of determining whether Morgan is a U.S. shareholder with respect to Raji, 10% of the 10% interest of Madison in Raji is considered as owned by Morgan. Thus, Morgan owns 10% of the stock in Raji (9% + (10% x 10%)) and is considered a U.S. shareholder of Raji. Katie and Madison Corporation are also considered U.S. shareholders because they each own 10% or more of Raji stock. The total amount of stock in Raji Corporation owned by U.S. shareholders is 51%, determined as follows:

Morgan	9%
Katie	32%
Madison Corporation	10%
Total ownership	51%

Note that the one percent of stock constructively owned by Morgan through Madison Corporation is counted for purposes of determining whether Morgan is a U.S. shareholder but is not counted for purposes of determining the percentage of stock owned by U.S. shareholders.

Subpart F Income Defined

A CFC's *subpart F income* for any taxable year consists of the sum of (Code Sec.952(a)):

1. Insurance income.
2. Foreign base company income.
3. An amount equal to the product of (1) the corporation's income [other than income that is attributable to earnings and profits included in the gross income of a United States person under Code Sec. 951 or United States income excluded from Subpart F income by Code Sec. 952(b)] and (2) the international boycott factor (as determined under Code Sec. 999).
4. The sum of the amounts of any illegal bribes, kickbacks, or other payments within the meaning of Code Sec. 162(c) paid by or on behalf of the corporation during the tax year directly or indirectly to an official, employee, or agent in fact of a government.
5. Income derived from any foreign country during any period during which Code Sec. 901(j) applies to the foreign country because the U.S. does not recognize the country, has severed diplomatic relations with the country, or has designated the country as a supporter of terrorism.

Insurance Income Defined

Insurance income is any income that is attributable to the issuing (or reinsuring) of an insurance or annuity contract and that would be taxed under Subchapter L (Code Sec. 801 et. seq.) of the Code (taxing insurance companies) if the income were income of a domestic insurance company. Code Sec. 953.

Foreign Base Company Income Defined

Foreign base company income is the sum of the following amounts: Code Sec. 954(a).

1. Foreign personal holding company income. *Foreign personal holding company income* includes dividends, interest, royalties, rents, and annuities; net gains from the sale or exchange of certain types of property (i.e., property giving rise to the previously described types of income, interests in a trust, partnership, or REMIC, or property that does not give rise to any income); net gains from commodities transactions; net foreign currency gains; income equivalent to interest; net income from notional principal contracts; and payments in lieu of dividends. Code Sec. 954(c).
2. Foreign base company sales income. *Foreign base company sales income* is income (whether in the form of profits, commissions, fees, or otherwise) derived in connection with the purchase of personal property from a related person and its sale to any person, the sale of personal property to any person on behalf of a related person, the purchase of personal property from any person and its sale to a related person, or the purchase of personal property from any person on behalf of a related person if the property that is purchased (or in the case of property sold on behalf of a related person, the property which is sold) is manufactured, produced, grown, or extracted outside the country under the laws of which the CFC is created or organized and the property is sold for use, consumption, or disposition outside that foreign country (or, in the case of property purchased on behalf of a related person, is purchased for use, consumption, or disposition outside that foreign country). Code Sec. 954(d).
3. Foreign base company services income. *Foreign base company services income* is income (whether in the form of compensation, commissions, fees, or otherwise) derived in connection with the performance of technical, managerial, engineering, architectural, scientific, skilled, industrial, commercial, or like services that are performed for or on behalf of any related person and are performed outside the country under the laws of which the CFC is created or organized. Code Sec. 954(e).
4. Foreign base company oil-related income. *Foreign base company oil-related income* is foreign oil-related income, other than income derived from a source within a foreign country in connection with oil or gas that was extracted from an oil or gas well located in that foreign country or oil, gas, or a primary product of oil or gas that is sold by the foreign corporation or a related person for use or consumption within that country or is loaded in that country on a vessel or aircraft as fuel for such vessel or aircraft. Code Sec. 954(g).

Each type of income is reduced by deductions (including taxes) properly allocable to such income. Code Sec. 954(b)(5).

De Minimis Rule

If the sum of foreign base company income and gross insurance income is less than five percent of gross income or, if less, $1,000,000, no portion of a CFC's gross income for the tax year will be treated as foreign base company income or insurance income. Code Sec. 954(b)(3).

¶25,535

Full Inclusion Rule

If the sum of a CFC's foreign base company income and gross insurance income for the tax year exceeds 70 percent of the CFC's gross income, the CFC's entire gross income for the tax year will be treated as foreign base company income or insurance income (whichever is appropriate).

Exception for Income Subject to High Foreign Taxes

Foreign base company income and insurance income do not include any item of income received by a CFC if the taxpayer establishes to the IRS' satisfaction that the income was subject to an effective rate of income tax imposed by a foreign country greater than 90 percent of the maximum tax rate imposed on U.S. corporations. This rule does not apply to foreign base company oil-related income. Code Sec. 954(b)(4).

¶25,545   TRANSFERS OF PROPERTY TO FOREIGN CORPORATIONS

Code Sec. 367 treats as taxable what otherwise would be a nontaxable transfer by a U.S. person of property to a foreign corporation as part of a corporate organization, reorganization, or liquidation. It does this by disregarding the foreign corporation's corporate status. The provision was adopted to prevent U.S. persons from avoiding or deferring tax by transferring appreciated property to a foreign corporation as part of a tax-free organization, reorganization, or liquidation and then selling the appreciated property outside the United States, where it is not subject to U.S. taxation.

This "outbound toll" applies only to gains, not to losses. No loss can be recognized by reason of Code Sec. 367. The amount of gain recognized cannot exceed the amount of gain that would have been recognized if the property transferred had been sold individually. Individual losses cannot be offset against individual gains. Temp. Reg. §1.367(a)-1T(b)(3)(i).

Certain types of transfers are excepted from this rule. For example:

- The transfer of property to a foreign corporation for use by that corporation in the active conduct of a trade or business outside the United States.
- The transfer of stock or securities of a foreign corporation that is party to an exchange or reorganization to a foreign corporation if the U.S. person owns, directly or indirectly, less than five percent of both the total voting power and total value of the stock of the transferee foreign corporation immediately after the transfer or the U.S. person enters into a five-year gain recognition agreement with respect to the transferred stock or securities. Reg. §1.367(a)-3(b)(1)(ii).

U.S. citizens and residents, domestic corporations, domestic trusts, and domestic estates that make a transfer of property to a foreign corporation that is described in Code Sec. 6038B(a)(1)(A)(such as a transfer in complete liquidation of a subsidiary, a transfer to a corporation controlled by the transferor, or a transfer as part of a corporate reorganization) must attach IRS Form 926, Return by a U.S. Transferor of Property to a Foreign Corporation, to their income tax return for the year of the transfer. If a foreign or domestic partnership makes the transfer, its domestic partners must file IRS Form 926. Reg. §1.6038B-1(b)(1).

U.S. Taxation of Foreign Income

¶25,555   GENERAL PRINCIPLES

The U.S. taxes its citizens and resident aliens on their worldwide income. However, tax relief is provided for individuals who meet certain requirements. For example, taxpayers can:

1. Exclude a certain amount of foreign earned income from their gross income. See ¶25,565.
2. Exclude or take a deduction for a certain amount of their foreign housing expenses for the year. See ¶25,575.
3. Take a credit or deduction for foreign income taxes paid. See ¶25,585.

Taxpayers cannot take a credit or deduction for foreign income taxes paid on foreign earned income that they have excluded from their gross income. Code Sec. 911(d)(6). Taxpayers can benefit by taking a credit for foreign income taxes paid on foreign earned income instead of excluding such income from their gross income when the amount of foreign income taxes that they paid exceeds the amount of U.S. income taxes that they would have to pay on such income.

¶25,565 — FOREIGN EARNED INCOME EXCLUSION

U.S. citizens and residents living abroad may elect to exclude up to $102,100 (for a tax year beginning in 2017) of their foreign earned income from their gross income if they are qualified individuals. Code Sec. 911; Rev. Proc. 2016-55, 2016-45 IRB 707.

Qualified Individual Defined

A *qualified individual* is an individual (1) who is either a U.S. citizen who has been a bona fide resident of a foreign country or countries for an uninterrupted period that includes an entire tax year or a U.S. citizen or resident who is present in a foreign country or countries during at least 330 full days during any period of 12 consecutive months and (2) whose tax home is in a foreign country or countries throughout the period of bona fide residence or 330 full days of presence. Code Sec. 911(d); Reg. §1.911-2(a).

Once a taxpayer has established bona fide foreign residence for an uninterrupted period that includes an entire tax year, the taxpayer will be treated as a qualified individual for any portion of a tax year during which the period of bona fide residence began or ended.

EXAMPLE 25.60 — Mable Freeman is a U.S. citizen using the calendar year as her tax year. She became a bona fide resident of Italy on November 3, 2016 and moved back to the United States on February 2, 2018. While she was in Italy, she made that country her tax home. Because Paulette was a bona fide resident of Italy for all of 2017, she will be treated as a qualified individual not only for 2017 but also for the portions of 2016 and 2018 that she was a bona fide resident of Italy.

Once a taxpayer has satisfied the physical presence test, the taxpayer will be treated as a qualified individual for any portion of a tax year during which the physical presence was measured.

EXAMPLE 25.61 — Brian Edwards is a U.S. citizen using the calendar year as his tax year. He moved to India on December 7, 2016 and remained there until December 15, 2018. While he was in India, he made that country his tax home. If Brian selects December 8, 2016 through December 7, 2017 as the 12-month period for determining whether he has satisfied the physical presence test, he will be considered a qualified individual from December 8, 2016 through December 31, 2016 and from January 1, 2017 through December 7, 2017.

Waiver of Period of Stay Requirement. If an individual who is a bona fide resident of, or is present in, a foreign country for any period is required to leave the country before satisfying either the bona fide residence or physical presence test because of war, civil unrest, or similar adverse conditions that prevent the normal conduct of business by the individual and the individual establishes to the IRS' satisfaction that the individual would have satisfied either the bona fide resident or physical presence test but for those conditions, the individual will be treated as a qualified resident for the period that he or she was in the foreign country. Code Sec. 911(d)(4). The IRS periodically lists the countries for which the eligibility requirements are waived.

Bona Fide Resident Defined

Whether an individual has been a bona fide resident of a foreign country is determined by applying, to the extent practical, the principles of Code Sec. 871 (relating to the determination of the residence of aliens). Reg. §1.911-2(c). Bona fide residence may be established even if temporary visits are made to the United States or elsewhere on vacation or business, but an individual with earned income from sources within a foreign country is not a bona fide resident of that country if the individual claims to be a nonresident in a statement submitted to the country's authorities and the individual's earned income is not subject to that country's income tax because of that nonresidency. Reg. §1.911-2(c).

Among the factors considered by the courts in determining whether a U.S. citizen has established bona fide residency are the following: *H. J. Sochurek*, CA-7, 62-1 USTC ¶9293, 300 F2d 34; *D. P. Lansdown*, CA-10, 96-1 USTC ¶50,025,

- Whether the taxpayer intended to remain indefinitely in the foreign country or intended to stay for a fixed period of time for a specific purpose.
- Whether the taxpayer has established a home in the foreign country for an indefinite period.

- Whether the taxpayer has assimilated into the foreign life and society (e.g., participation in the community's social and cultural activities and identification with the daily lives of the people).
- Whether the taxpayer's spouse and family also lived in the foreign country.
- Whether the taxpayer's physical presence in the foreign country was consistent with the taxpayer's employment.
- The nature, extent, and reasons for temporary absences from the taxpayer's temporary foreign home.
- Whether the taxpayer assumed economic burdens and paid taxes to the foreign country.
- Whether the taxpayer's status is that of a resident or transient or sojourner.
- How the taxpayer's employer treated the taxpayer's income tax status.
- The nature and duration of the taxpayer's employment and whether the taxpayer's assignment abroad could be promptly accomplished within a definite or specified time.
- Whether wages were paid in the foreign country or to a U.S. bank.
- Whether the taxpayer made the trip abroad in good faith or whether the purpose of the trip was tax evasion.

Physical Presence Test

In determining whether an individual has been physically present in a foreign country for at least 330 full days during any period of 12 consecutive months, the 12-month-period may begin on any day but must end on the day before the corresponding day in the twelfth succeeding month. Reg. §1.911-2(d)(1).

EXAMPLE 25.62	If April 30, 2017 is selected as the start of a 12-month period, the 12-month period must end on April 29, 2018.

A full day is a continuous period of 24 hours beginning at midnight and ending the following midnight. Reg. §1.911-2(d)(2).

EXAMPLE 25.63	Patsy Stokes, a U.S. citizen, was transferred by her employer to Venezuela. She arrived there at noon on April 24, 2017. She moved back to the United States at 2 p.m. on March 20, 2018. Because she was not physically present in Venezuela on April 24, 2017 or March 20, 1018 for a continuous period of 24 hours beginning at midnight and ending the following midnight, she cannot include either of those days as part of the 12-consecutive-months period.

The 12-month period may begin before or after an individual has arrived in a foreign country and may end before or after the individual departs the foreign country. Reg. §1.911-2(d)(1).

The 330 full days need not be consecutive; they may be interrupted by periods during which an individual is not present in a foreign country. Reg. §1.911-2(d)(2). When computing whether an individual has satisfied the physical presence test, all separate periods of presence during the 12-month period are added together. Reg. §1.911-2(d)(2).

An individual present in a foreign country who travels outside a foreign country for fewer than 24 hours will not be deemed outside a foreign country during the period of travel. Reg. §1.911-2(d)(2). If an individual in transit between two points outside the United States is physically present in the United States for fewer than 24 hours, the individuals will not be treated as present in the United States during that transit but instead will be treated as traveling over areas not within any foreign country. Reg. §1.911-2(d)(2).

Tax Home Defined

An individual's *tax home* is considered located at the individual's regular or principal place of business. If the individual has no regular or principal place of business because of the nature of the business, then the individual's regular place of abode constitutes the tax home. Neither temporary presence in the United States nor the existence of a dwelling in the U.S. necessarily constitutes the individual's place of abode. The physical presence test requires that only full days count as physical presence in the foreign country. All separate periods of presence during the period of twelve consecutive months are aggregated. A full day is a continuous period of twenty-four hours beginning with midnight and ending with the following midnight. Reg. §1.911-2(b).

Foreign Earned Income Defined

Foreign earned income is earned income attributable to services performed by an individual in a foreign country. Reg. §1.911-3(a). Where earned income is received is immaterial in determining whether earned income is attributable to services performed in a foreign county. Reg. §1.911-3(a). Income earned over waters not subject to any foreign country's jurisdiction is not income earned in a foreign country. *W.D. Rogers*, CA-DC, ¶2015-1 USTC 50,273 (a flight attendant could not exclude income earned over international waters).

Earned income includes wages, salaries, professional fees, and other amounts received as compensation for personal services actually rendered and includes the fair market value of compensation paid in a medium other than cash. Reg. §1.911-3(b)(1). Professional fees constitute earned income even though the individual employs assistants to perform part or all of the services, provided that the patients or clients are those of the professional and look to the professional as the person responsible for the services rendered. Reg. §1.911-3(b)(3).

Specifically excluded from *earned income* is the value of any meals or lodging furnished for the convenience of the employer, pensions and annuities (including Social Security benefits), and amounts received after the close of the first tax year following the tax year in which the services giving rise to the amount were performed. Reg. §1.911-3(c).

Earned income does not include any amount paid by a corporation out of its earnings and profits, other than as reasonable compensation for personal services actually rendered to the corporation. Reg. §1.911-3(b)(1). If an individual is engaged in a trade or business (other than a corporation) in which both personal services and capital are material income producing factors, a reasonable allowance for personal services actually rendered will be treated as earned income (but only to the extent that it does not exceed 30 percent of the individual's share of the trade or business' net profits. Reg. §1.911-3(b)(2).

Limitation on the Amount That Can Be Excluded

The amount of foreign earned income that may be excluded for any tax year may not exceed the lesser of (1) the qualified individual's foreign earned income for the tax year in excess of any housing cost amount (discussed in ¶25,575) or (2) the annual exclusion amount ($102,100 for a tax year beginning in 2017) multiplied by a fraction whose numerator is the number of qualifying days in the tax year and whose denominator is the number of days in the tax year (usually 365). The number of qualifying days is defined as the number of days during which the individual met the tax home requirement and either the bona fide residence requirement or the physical presence requirement. Reg. §1.911-3(d)(2).

EXAMPLE 25.64	Helen Garrett, a calendar year taxpayer, established a tax home and residence in a foreign country as of November 1, 2015, and maintained that tax home through March 30, 2017. Her uninterrupted period of bona fide residence includes fractional parts of the years 2015 and 2017 and all of 2016. The number of her qualifying days is 61 in 2015, 366 in 2016, and 90 in 2017. An individual satisfies the physical presence test for any 12-consecutive-month period during which the individual is physically present in a foreign country for 330 days and the individual's tax home is in that foreign country during each day of the physical presence. Helen is eligible for the foreign earned income exclusion for 61 days in 2015, 366 days in 2016, and 90 days in 2017 based on the physical presence test.
EXAMPLE 25.65	Darren Christensen satisfied the requirements for claiming a foreign earned income exclusion for 2017. He has 299 qualifying days for the tax year. Darren's limitation for the year is $83,638 ($102,100 X 299/365 days).
EXAMPLE 25.66	Lucy Figueroa satisfied the requirements for claiming a foreign earned income exclusion for all of 2016 and all of 2017. In 2016, when the exclusion was limited to $101,300, she received $92,000 of foreign earned income. In 2017, she received $102,000 of foreign earned income ($90,000 for services performed in 2017 and $12,000 for services performed in 2016). Lucy can exclude all of the $90,000 that she received for services performed in 2017. The portion of the $12,000 that she can exclude is the amount that she could have excluded for the year that she performed the services (2016), which is $101,300 (the 2016 limit) - $92,000 (the amount of foreign earned income already excluded for 2016) = $9,300.

TAX BLUNDER

On February 1, 2017, Earl Malloy's employer sent Earl to work at its headquarters in France. His time in France was scheduled to end on December 31, 2017, but Earl had some remaining vacation days and decided to spend them back home with his family in the United States. Earl returned to the United States on December 15, 2017. Because Earl did not remain in France for at least 330 days, he is not entitled to any foreign earned income exclusion.

Claiming the Foreign Income Exclusion

Taxpayers should file IRS Form 2555, Foreign Earned Income, to claim the foreign earned income exclusion. Taxpayers who do not claim the foreign housing exclusion and do not have self-employment income or business/moving expenses may be able to file a simplified form, IRS Form 2555-EZ, Foreign Earned Income Exclusion.

An election to take the foreign earned income exclusion applies to the tax year for which it was made and to all subsequent tax years unless revoked. A taxpayer who revokes an election cannot make another election for five year except with the IRS' consent. Code Sec. 911(e).

The amount excluded from a taxpayer's gross income is taken into account for purposes of determining the taxpayer's regular and alternative minimum tax liability with respect to income included in the taxpayer's gross income: Code Sec. 911(f).

- If the taxpayer has taxable income for the tax year, the amount of regular tax that a taxpayer has to pay is the difference between the amount of tax that the taxpayer would owe if the excluded amounts were included in the taxpayer's taxable income and the amount of tax that the taxpayer would owe if the taxpayer's taxable income equaled the amount excluded.
- If a taxpayer has a taxable excess (i.e., the taxpayer's alternative minimum taxable income for the tax year exceeds the exemption amount), the taxpayer's tentative minimum tax equals the difference between the amount of tentative minimum tax the taxpayer would owe if the amount excluded were included in the taxpayer's taxable excess and the amount of tentative minimum tax that the taxpayer would owe if the taxpayer's taxable excess equaled the amount excluded from gross income.

The amount excluded is reduced by any deductions or exclusions disallowed with respect to the excluded amount.

¶25,575   HOUSING COST EXCLUSION OR DEDUCTION

Individuals who qualify for the foreign earned income exclusion may also claim an exclusion or deduction (an above-the-line deduction) from their gross income for their housing cost amount if they have high housing costs for the year. Code Sec. 911(a).

The housing exclusion applies to amounts considered paid for with employer-provided amounts (including not only an individual's salary but also any amounts paid by an employer as reimbursement for housing expenses). Code Sec. 911(c). If an employee has no self-employment income, all of the employee's housing expenses will be considered paid for with employer-provided amounts. The housing deduction is available for amounts considered paid for from self-employment earnings. An individual with self-employment income and earnings from employment can take both an exclusion and a deduction for housing expenses. The sum of the housing exclusion and/or housing deduction and foreign earned income exclusion cannot exceed a taxpayer's foreign earned income for the year. Code Sec. 911(d)(7).

Qualifying for the Exclusion or Deduction

To qualify for the housing exclusion and/or housing deduction an individual must satisfy the following requirements: Code Sec. 911(d); Reg. §1.911-2(a).

1. The individual must be either a U.S. citizen who has been a bona fide resident of a foreign country or countries for an uninterrupted period that includes an entire tax year or a U.S. citizen or resident who is present in a foreign country or countries during at least 330 full days during any period of 12 consecutive months.
2. The individual's tax home must be in a foreign country or countries throughout the period of bona fide residence or 330 full days of presence.

Housing Cost Amount Defined

The term *housing cost amount* means the difference between the following amounts: Code Sec. 911(c)(1).

- The housing expenses of an individual for the tax year. The amount of housing expenses that a taxpayer can take into account cannot exceed 30 percent of the exclusion amount in effect for the calendar year in which the tax year begins ($102,100 for 2017) multiplied by a fraction whose numerator is the number of qualifying days during the tax year and whose denominator is the number of days in the year. If an individual qualifies for the housing cost exclusion or deduction for all of 2017, this amount would be $30,630 (30% × $102,100).
- 16 percent of the exclusion amount (computed on a daily basis) in effect for the calendar year in which the tax year begins ($44.76 per day in 2017) multiplied by the number of qualifying days during the tax year. If an individual qualifies for the housing cost deduction or exclusion for all of 2017, this amount would be $16,336 (16% × $102,100).

The maximum housing cost amount that a taxpayer can deduct or exclude from gross income for 2017 generally cannot exceed $14,294 ($30,630 – $16,336). However, the IRS increases this annual limit for countries with high housing costs. No housing cost deduction or exclusion is available if an individual qualifies for the deduction or exclusion for all of 2017 and the individual's housing expenses do not exceed $16,336.

Housing Expenses Defined

Housing expenses include rent, the fair rental value of housing provided in kind by the employer, utilities (other than telephone charges), real and personal property insurance, nondeductible occupancy taxes, lease fees, furniture rental, household repairs, and residential parking. Items specifically excluded from qualified housing expenses are: Reg. §1.911-4(b).

1. Cost of house purchase, improvements, and other capital expenditures
2. Cost of purchased furniture or accessories
3. Cost of domestic labor, including maids, gardeners, etc.
4. Amortized principal payments on home mortgage
5. Depreciation of taxpayer-owned housing
6. Deductible interest and taxes
7. Expenses of more than one foreign household (unless the second household outside the U.S. is maintained for the individual's spouse and dependents who do not live with the individual because of living conditions that are dangerous, unhealthful, or otherwise adverse)
8. Moving expenses
9. Cost of pay television subscription
10. Meals and lodging furnished for the convenience of the employer and otherwise excludible.

Claiming the Exclusion or Deduction

Individuals with employer-provided amounts may claim the foreign housing exclusion, which is the lesser of (1) that portion of an individual's housing cost amount that is paid for with employer-provided amounts or (2) the individual's foreign earned income. Individuals cannot claim less than the full amount of the housing exclusion to which they are entitled. Reg. §1.911-4(d)(1). Employer-provided amounts in excess of the exclusion must be included in gross income.

A foreign housing cost deduction is available if a qualifying individual has self-employment income. If all of an individual's income is from self-employment, the individual can deduct the housing cost amount, but not to the extent that it exceeds the difference between the individual's foreign earned income for the year minus the sum of the individual's foreign earned income exclusion and foreign housing cost exclusion for the year.

An individual who is both an employee and a self-employed individual during the year can deduct a portion of the housing cost amount and exclude the remainder. The portion that can be excluded is determined by multiplying the housing cost amount by the employer-provided amounts and dividing the result by the individual's foreign earned income. The remainder of the housing cost amount may be deducted (except to the extent it exceeds the difference between the individual's foreign earned income for the year minus the sum of the individual's foreign earned income exclusion and foreign housing cost exclusion for the year). Any portion of the foreign housing cost deduction that is not allowed because of the limit may be carried over to the next tax year (and only to that next tax year). Code Sec. 911(c)(4).

Taxpayers can claim the housing cost exclusion and/or deduction by filing IRS Form 2555, Foreign Earned Income. An election to take the housing cost exclusion and/or deduction applies to the tax year for which it was made and to all subsequent tax years unless revoked. A taxpayer who revokes an election cannot make another election for five years except with the IRS' consent. Code Sec. 911(e).

The amount excluded from a taxpayer's gross income is taken into account for purposes of determining the taxpayer's regular and alternative minimum tax liability with respect to income included in the taxpayer's gross income: Code Sec. 911(f).

- The amount of regular tax that a taxpayer has to pay is the difference between the amount of tax that the taxpayer would owe if the excluded amounts were included in the taxpayer's taxable income and the amount of tax that the taxpayer would owe if the taxpayer's taxable income equaled the amount excluded.
- The taxpayer's tentative minimum tax equals the difference between the amount of tentative minimum tax the taxpayer would owe if the amount excluded were included in the taxpayer's taxable excess and the amount of tentative minimum tax that the taxpayer would owe if the taxpayer's taxable excess equaled the amount excluded from gross income.

The amount excluded is reduced by any deductions or exclusions disallowed with respect to the excluded amount.

EXAMPLE 25.67

Eileen Mathis, a U.S. citizen, resided in a foreign country for 335 days during 2017. Her housing expenses (all reimbursed by her employer) were $24,000. This is less than the amount of housing expenses the she can take into account for the year ($30,630 × 335/365) = $28,112. Because her actual housing expenses exceeded the base amount for the year, $16,336 × 335/365 =$14,993, she may exclude $24,000 - $14,993 = $9,007 from her gross income. She must include in her gross income the remaining portion ($24,000 - $9,007 = $14,993) of her housing expenses that her employer reimbursed.

EXAMPLE 25.68

William Lyons is a U.S. citizen and calendar-year taxpayer. During all of 2017, he was a bona fide resident of the Netherlands and had his tax home there. William received $70,000 in wages for services performed in the Netherlands. He incurred no business expenses but received housing provided by his employer. The fair rental value of that housing was $15,000. He also incurred an additional $10,000 in housing expenses. William's foreign earned income for 2017 was $70,000 + $15,000 = $85,000. William elected the foreign earned income exclusion and the housing cost amount exclusion. Because he did not live in a high cost area, he may exclude $8,664 ($25,000 - $16,336) in housing expenses from his gross income. His foreign earned income exclusion is $76,336, the lesser of the exclusion amount ($102,100) or $76,336, the difference between his foreign earned income, $85,000, and his housing cost amount, $8,664. The total amount that William may exclude for 2017 is $85,000.

EXAMPLE 25.69

Assume the same facts as in the previous example except that William's only housing expenses were those provided by his employer and he received $80,000 in wages. His foreign earned income for 2017 was $95,000 ($80,000 + $15,000). He cannot exclude any of his $15,000 in housing expenses from his gross income because the amount of his housing expenses did not exceed the base housing amount for 2017 ($16,336).

¶25,585   FOREIGN TAX CREDIT

Taxpayers may take a credit or deduction for income, war profits, and excess profits taxes (collectively referred to as "income tax") that they paid to a foreign country or U.S. possession. Code Sec. 901(a). As a general rule, it is to a taxpayer's advantage to take a credit because each dollar of the credit reduces the taxpayer's tax liability by one dollar. However, under certain circumstances, taxpayers may benefit more by taking a deduction for foreign taxes paid instead of a credit (e.g., if the rate of tax on foreign income was high and the taxpayer's foreign income was a small proportion of the taxpayer's U.S. income). The foreign tax credit prevents taxpayers from being taxed twice on income earned abroad.

Who Is Eligible for the Credit

The following taxpayers are eligible for the foreign tax credit: Code Sec. 901(b).

1. U.S. citizens and residents and domestic corporations are allowed a credit for the amount of foreign income tax paid or accrued during the tax year to any foreign country or U.S. possession.
2. Nonresident aliens and foreign corporations engaged in a trade or business within the United States are allowed a credit for foreign income tax paid or accrued (or deemed paid or accrued under Code Sec. 902) to any foreign country or U.S. possession with respect to income effectively connected with the conduct of their trade or business within the United States. Code Sec. 906(a).
3. Partners, S corporation shareholders, and beneficiaries of a trust or estate are allowed a credit for their proportionate share of foreign income tax paid by their partnership, corporation, estate, or trust to a foreign country or U.S. possession.

Tax Payments Eligible for the Credit or Deduction

The foreign tax credit or deduction is allowed for income, war profits, and excess profits taxes (collectively referred to as *income tax*) paid or accrued (or deemed paid) during the tax year to a foreign country or U.S. possession. Code Sec. 901(b). A credit or deduction also is allowed for a tax paid in lieu of a tax on income, war profits, or excess profits otherwise generally imposed by any foreign country or U.S. possession. Code Sec. 903.

A foreign levy is an income tax if and only if (1) it is a tax and (2) its predominant character is that of an income tax in a U.S. sense. Reg. §1.901-2(a). A foreign levy is a tax in lieu of an income tax if and only if (1) it is a tax and (2) it meets the substitution requirement. Reg. §1.903-1(a).

A foreign levy is a tax if it requires a compulsory payment pursuant to the authority of a foreign country to levy taxes. Whether a foreign levy requires a compulsory payment pursuant to a foreign country's authority to levy taxes is determined by principles of U.S. law, not by principles of law of the foreign country.

A foreign levy is not a tax to the extent that a person subject to the levy receives (or will receive), directly or indirectly, a specific economic benefit from the foreign country in exchange for payment pursuant to the levy. A specific economic benefit is an economic benefit that is not made available on substantially the same terms to substantially all persons who are subject to the income tax generally imposed by the foreign country or, if there is no such generally imposed income tax, an economic benefit that is not made available on substantially the same terms to the population of the country in general. A person who receives a specific economic benefit is referred to as a *dual capacity taxpayer*. Dual capacity taxpayers are not allowed a credit unless they establish the portion of the levy paid that is a tax.

The predominant character of a foreign tax is that of an income tax in the U.S. sense if the foreign tax is likely to reach net gain in the normal circumstances in which it applies, but only to the extent that liability for the tax is not dependent on the availability of a credit for the tax against income tax liabilities to another country. Reg. §1.901-2(a). A foreign tax is likely to reach net gain n the normal circumstances in which it applies if and only if the tax, judged on the basis of its predominant character, satisfies each of the following requirements: Reg. §1.901-2(b).

1. *Realization requirement.* A foreign tax satisfies the realization requirement if, judged on the basis of its predominant character, it is imposed (1) upon or subsequent to the occurrence of events ("realization events") that would result in the realization of income under the income tax provisions of the Code; (2) upon the occurrence of an event prior to a realization event (a "prerealization event"), provided that the consequence of that event is the recapture (in whole or part) of a tax deduction, tax credit or other tax allowance previously accorded to the taxpayer; or (3) upon the occurrence of a prerealization event, other than one previously described, but only if the foreign country does not, upon the occurrence of a later event (other than a distribution or a deemed distribution of the income), impose a second tax with respect to the income on which tax is imposed by reason of the prerealization event (or, if it does impose a second tax, a credit or other comparable relief is available against the liability for such a second tax for tax paid on the occurrence of the prerealization event) and either the imposition of the tax upon the prerealization event is based on the difference in the values of property at the beginning and end of a period or the prerealization event is the physical transfer, processing, or export of readily marketable property.
2. *Gross receipts requirement.* A foreign tax satisfies the gross receipts requirement if, judged on the basis of its predominant character, it is imposed on the basis of gross receipts or gross receipts computed under a method that is likely to produce an amount that is not greater than fair market value.

3. *Net income requirement.* A foreign tax satisfies the net income requirement if, judged on the basis of its predominant character, the base of the tax is computed by reducing gross receipts to permit (1) recovery of the significant costs and expenses (including significant capital expenditures) attributable, under reasonable principles, to such gross receipts or (2) recovery of such significant costs and expenses computed under a method that is likely to produce an amount that approximates, or is greater than, recovery of such significant costs and expenses.

A foreign tax satisfies the substitution requirement if the tax in fact operates as a tax imposed in substitution for, and not in addition to, an income tax or a series of income taxes otherwise generally imposed. A foreign tax satisfies the substitution requirement only to the extent that liability for the foreign tax is not dependent (by its terms or otherwise) on the availability of a credit for the foreign tax against income tax liability to another country. Reg. §1.903-1(b).

Some foreign countries levy a "soak-up" tax, disguising a levy on inbound investments as an income tax, which is designed to transfer the tax burden to the United States. That is, the foreign tax is levied expecting the business to claim the foreign tax credit in the United States while the U.S. government loses revenue and the business pays taxes equal to the amount that would have been paid to the United States. Such a tax fails to qualify as a tax paid in lieu of an income tax. Reg. §1.903-1(b)(2).

Examples of the types of payments not eligible for the foreign income tax credit or deduction include: Reg. §1.901-2.

1. Penalties.
2. Fines.
3. Interest.
4. Customs duties.
5. Payments that result in economic benefits to the taxpayer.
6. Pension fund payments.
7. Unemployment fund payments.
8. Disability fund payments.
9. Soak-up taxes.

No credit or deduction may be taken for foreign income taxes paid on earnings excluded from a taxpayer's gross income by the foreign earned income exclusion or foreign housing exclusion. Code Sec. 911(d)(6).

Nor may a credit or deduction be taken with respect to taxes paid to a government that the United States does not recognize (unless it is eligible to purchase defense articles or services), with respect to which the United States has severed diplomatic relations (or does not conduct such relations), or that has been designated by the Secretary of State as supporting international terrorism. Code Sec. 901(j).

If a person participates in or cooperates with an international boycott during the tax year, the amount of the credit allowable to that person (or to United States shareholders of that person) for foreign taxes paid during the tax year is reduced by the product of the amount of the credit otherwise allowable and the international boycott factor (i.e., the fraction whose numerator reflects the person's operations in or related to a group of countries associated in carrying out an international boycott in or with which that person has participated or cooperated and whose denominator reflects that person's operations in or related to countries other than the United States. Code Secs. 908(a) and 999.

Tax payments generated by a transaction lacking economic substance are not eligible for the credit. *Salem Financial, Inc.,* Fed Cir, 2015-1 USTC ¶50,304; *The Bank of New York Mellon Corporation,* CA-2, 2015-2 USTC ¶50,473.

Denial of credit or deduction with respect to covered asset acquisitions.

Disqualified foreign income tax with respect to income or gain attributable to foreign assets in a covered asset acquisition is not eligible for the credit or deduction. Code Sec. 901(m).

Covered asset acquisition. A covered asset acquisition includes a qualified stock purchase to which Code Sec. 338(a) applies, any transaction that is treated as an acquisition of assets for U.S. tax purposes but as an acquisition of stock (or is disregarded) for foreign income tax purposes, and any acquisition of an interest in a partnership that has a basis adjustment election in effect under Code Sec. 754.

Foreign income tax is disqualified to prevent a taxpayer from claiming a foreign tax credit or deduction for taxes paid on income not subject to U.S. tax because of differences in tax basis.

Foreign Tax Credit Splitting Event

If income related to foreign income tax paid or accrued by a taxpayer is or will be taken into account by a covered person (this is referred to as a *foreign tax credit splitting event*), the taxpayer cannot take a credit for the tax until the tax year in which the taxpayer takes the related income into account for U.S. federal income tax purposes. Code Sec. 909; Reg. §1.909-2.

A *covered person* with respect to any person who pays or accrues foreign income tax is (1) any entity in which the payor directly or indirectly holds at least a 10 percent ownership interest (determined by vote or value), (2) any person who directly or indirectly holds at least a 10 percent ownership interest (determined by vote or value) in the payor, and (3) any person who is related to the taxpayer under Code Sec. 267(b) or 707(b).

Deemed Payments of Tax

A domestic corporation that owns at least 10 percent of the voting stock of a foreign corporation from which it receives dividends in any tax year is deemed to have paid a portion of the foreign corporation's post-1986 foreign income taxes (to the extent that those taxes were not attributable to dividends distributed by the foreign corporation in prior tax years). The portion is determined by dividing the amount of the dividends by the foreign corporation's post-1986 undistributed earnings (as of the close of the tax year during which the dividends are distributed and not reduced by the amount of the dividends). Code Sec. 902.

EXAMPLE 25.70

> DS1, a domestic corporation, owns all of the stock of DS9, a foreign corporation. During the year, DS9 distributes an $80,000 dividend to DS1. DS9 has $400,000 in post-1986 undistributed earnings and has paid $80,000 in post-1986 foreign income taxes. $8,000 in foreign income tax is withheld from the dividend paid to DS1. DS1 can claim a foreign credit equal to the sum of the $8,000 in foreign income tax that it actually paid plus the $20,000 in foreign income tax that it is deemed to have paid.

If a domestic corporation must include certain income of a controlled foreign corporation (CFC) in its gross income, the amount included that is attributable to the CFC's earnings and profits is deemed to be a dividend paid by the CFC to the domestic corporation and eligible for the deemed-paid credit of Code Sec. 902. Code Sec. 960. This deemed-paid credit is available to U.S. shareholders who are individuals if they have elected to be taxed at U.S. corporate tax rates on amounts included in their gross income under the Subpart F provisions. Code Sec. 962(a).

An amount equal to the foreign income taxes deemed paid by the domestic corporation is treated as a dividend received by the domestic corporation from the foreign corporation (but is not eligible for the dividends-received deduction for the U.S.-source portion of such a dividend). Code Sec. 78.

Limitation on the Amount of the Credit

A taxpayer's foreign tax credit cannot exceed the lesser of the following amounts:

- The amount of foreign income taxes actually paid or accrued
- Overall limitation
- Sum of the separate limitations

Overall Limitation on the Amount of the Credit

To prevent taxpayers from using foreign tax payments to reduce their U.S. tax liability on U.S.-source income, an overall limitation is imposed on the amount of a taxpayer's foreign tax credit. The amount of a taxpayer's foreign tax credit cannot exceed the amount determined from the following formula: Code Sec. 904(a).

$$\text{Pre-Credit U.S. Tax} \quad \times \quad \frac{\text{Taxable Income From Foreign Sources}}{\text{Total Taxable Income}}$$

A taxpayer's taxable income from foreign sources cannot exceed the taxpayer's entire taxable income.

EXAMPLE 25.71	Espanola Corporation, a domestic corporation operating abroad, has $1,000,000 of worldwide taxable income, which includes $600,000 of foreign-source income. Espanola paid $300,000 in foreign creditable taxes and has U.S. potential tax liability on worldwide income amounting to $340,000. In the absence of the foreign tax credit limitation, Espanola could offset its U.S. tax liability of $340,000 by its foreign tax payments of $300,000 and pay only $40,000 to the U.S. government. Instead, Espanola has a foreign tax credit amounting to $204,000 ($340,000 × ($600,000/$1,000,000)). Espanola's U.S. tax liability, therefore, equals $136,000 ($340,000 less $204,000 foreign tax credit). Espanola's excess credit of $96,000 can be carried back one year and forward for 10 years.

Separate Limitations

Separate limitations on the permissible foreign tax credit with respect to particular categories of income have to be calculated to prevent taxpayers from averaging foreign tax rates applied to certain types of income to reduce their U.S. tax on other categories of income. Averaging can benefit taxpayers because foreign income tax in excess of the U.S. rate does not reduce a taxpayer's U.S. tax liability. A separate limitation is applied to a category of income because the income's source (foreign or U.S.) can be manipulated, the income typically bears little or no foreign tax, or the income often bears a rate of foreign tax that is abnormally high or in excess of rates on other types of income.

Prior to the American Jobs Creation Act of 2004, taxpayers were required to calculate the foreign tax credit limitation separately with respect to 10 categories of foreign source income. Now taxpayers are required to calculate the foreign tax credit limitation separately with respect to each of the following categories of foreign source income: Code Sec. 904(d).

1. Passive category income. *Passive category income* means passive income and specified passive category income. "Passive income" generally means any income of a kind that would be foreign personal holding company income (such as dividends, interest, royalties, rents, and annuities). "Specified passive category income" includes dividends from a DISC or former DISC that are treated as income from sources without the United States, taxable income attributable to foreign trade income, and distributions from an FSC or former FSC out of earnings and profits attributable to foreign trade income.
2. Income treated as foreign-source income under an income tax treaty but treated as U.S.-source income under the Code, if the taxpayer chooses the benefits of the treaty. Code Sec. 904(d)(6).
3. Income attributable to sources within a country with respect to which no foreign tax credit is allowed (because the U.S. does not recognize the country's government, the U.S. has severed diplomatic relations with the country, or the U.S. has designated the country as supportive of international terrorism). Code Sec. 901(j).
4. General category income. *General category income* means income other than passive category income.

Congress reduced the number of separate limitations out of concern that requiring taxpayers to separate income and tax credits into the previous categories had created some of the most complex tax reporting and compliance issues for the Code. Congress believed that reducing the number of separate limitations would simplify the Code, reduce double taxation, make U.S. businesses more competitive, and create jobs in the United States.

Each separate limitation for a taxpayer is the lesser of the amount of foreign taxes paid or accrued for a particular category of income or the amount calculated using the following formula:

$$\text{Pre-Credit U.S. Tax} \quad \times \quad \frac{\text{Taxable Income for a Category of Income}}{\text{Total Taxable Income}}$$

In calculating taxable income for each category, a taxpayer must take into account only the amount included in income on the taxpayer's income tax return. Expenses and losses that are definitely related to that income are deducted. Expenses that are not definitely related to specific items of income must be apportioned to the foreign income in each category by multiplying them by a fraction whose numerator is the taxpayer's gross foreign income in the separate limit category and whose denominator is the taxpayer's gross income from all sources. Personal exemptions cannot be deducted for purposes of calculating taxable income.

EXAMPLE 25.72	ASU Corporation has $2,000,000 of worldwide income, of which $1,500,000 is foreign-source income. The foreign-source income consists of $1,000,000 of passive category income and $500,000 of general category income, on which ASU paid foreign taxes amounting to $300,000 and $200,000, respectively. If ASU's domestic tax rate is 34%, the overall foreign tax credit limitation is the lesser of taxes paid ($500,000) or the formula limit, $510,000 ($680,000 U.S. tentative tax × ($1,500,000/$2,000,000)). Under the separate income limits, the total foreign tax credit is limited to $470,000:

Passive Category Income Basket Limitation

Lesser of taxes paid, $300,000, or the formulaic limit, $340,000 ($680,000 × ($1,000,000/$2,000,000)), equals $300,000.

General Category Income Basket Limitation

Lesser of taxes paid, $200,000, or the pro rata limit, $170,000 ($680,000 × ($500,000/$2,000,000)), or $170,000.

Total Foreign Tax Credit Limitation

Passive Category Income basket limit of $300,000 plus General Category Income basket limit of $170,000, which amounts to $470,000. Note that this amount is less than the overall limitation.

EXAMPLE 25.73	Pi Corporation has foreign-source income amounting to $1,000,000 and a U.S.-source loss of $200,000. Pi's worldwide income is reduced to $800,000. If Pi's foreign-source income consists of $700,000 in the general category income basket and $300,000 in the passive category income basket, then the $200,000 loss is allocated 70% to the general category income basket and 30% to the passive category income basket.

The amount of tax paid or accrued with respect to a separate category of income includes only those taxes related to income in that separate category. Taxes are related to income if the income is included in the base upon which the tax is imposed. If a tax is related to more than one separate category of income, the tax must be apportioned among the separate categories on the basis of the following formula: Reg. §1.904-6(a).

$$\text{Foreign Tax Related to More Than One Separate Category} \times \frac{\text{Net Income Subject to Foreign Tax Included in a Separate Category}}{\text{Net Income Subject to That Foreign Tax}}$$

For purposes of apportioning foreign taxes among separate categories of income, gross income is determined under the law of the foreign country or U.S. possession. Gross income in each separate category is reduced by deducting any expenses, losses, and other amounts deductible under foreign law that are specifically allocable to the gross amount of that income under the laws of that foreign country or U.S. possession. If expenses are not specifically allocated under foreign law, the expenses are apportioned under the principles of foreign law. If foreign law does not provide for the direct allocation or apportionment of expenses, losses, or other deductions to a particular category of income, then the principles of Reg. §§1.861-8 through 1.861-14T and Code Sec. 954(b)(5) are applied.

Exception to the Limits

The overall and separate income limits do not apply to an individual taxpayer (not including an estate or trust) for a tax year if all of the following requirements are satisfied: Code Sec. 904(k).

1. The entire amount of the individual's gross income for the tax year from foreign sources consists of qualified passive income. An item of gross income is qualified passive income if the item is passive income and is shown on a payee statement furnished to the individual (such as an IRS Form 1099-DIV or Form 1099-INT). Passive income is any item of a kind that would be foreign personal holding company income (such as dividends, interest, royalties, rents, and annuities).
2. The amount of creditable foreign taxes paid or accrued by the individual during the tax year does not exceed $300 ($600 in the case of a joint return). Creditable foreign taxes do not include a tax unless the tax is shown on a payee statement furnished to the individual.
3. The individual elects to be exempt from the foreign income tax credit limitation.

Foreign Tax Credit Carryback and Carryover

The amount of foreign income tax not allowed as a credit because of the limit can be carried back one year and carried forward 10 years. Code Sec. 904(c). If an individual has elected not to be subject to the foreign income tax limitation for a tax year, the individual may not carry back or carry over any unused foreign tax to or from the tax year. Code Sec. 904(k).

Forms to File to Claim the Credit

Individuals, estates, and trusts must complete IRS Form 1116, Foreign Tax Credit (Individual, Estate, or Trust), and attach it to their income tax return to claim the credit. A separate form must be completed for each separate category of income against which the limit is applied.

Corporations must complete IRS Form 1118, Foreign Tax Credit - Corporations, and attach it to their income tax return. A separate form must be completed for each separate category of income against which the limit is applied.

PLANNING POINTER

When the amount of foreign income taxes that a taxpayer is expected to pay or accrue will exceed the limitations on the taxpayer's foreign tax credit, the taxpayer can pursue several strategies to reduce the excess. One way to reduce the excess is to decrease the amount of foreign income taxes (e.g., by taking advantages of deductions and credits, deferring the recognition of income, accelerating deductions, and realizing income in a form that is taxed at a lower rate, such as capital gains). Each dollar saved reduces the taxpayer's total tax by a dollar (up to the amount of the excess). A second way to reduce the excess is to increase the proportion of income characterized as foreign-source. For example, the rule providing that income from sales of inventory is sourced to the country where title passes can be used to generate foreign-source income. A third way to reduce the excess is to recharacterize deductions as U.S.-source. Taxpayers with a foreign tax credit in excess of the limitations receive the full benefit of deductions allocated to U.S.-source income but no benefit from deductions allocated to foreign-source income. One way for taxpayers to reduce the amount of deductions allocated to foreign-source income is to use alternative apportionment bases for sourcing administrative, selling, and other expenses. Before taxpayers re-source income and deductions, they should consider the consequences carefully. If the re-sourcing increases foreign-source income not only for U.S. tax purposes but also for foreign tax purposes and the foreign tax rate is higher than the U.S. tax rate, re-sourcing will increase the taxpayer's total taxes. A fourth way to reduce an excess credit is to shift income to a foreign country that taxes such income at a lower rate (this is referred to as *cross-crediting*).

EXAMPLE 25.74

Voyager Corporation, a domestic corporation, has $1,000,000 and $2,000,000 of U.S.- and foreign-source taxable income, respectively. If the U.S. tax rate is 35% and the foreign rate is 50%, the foreign tax credit limitation results in an excess credit of $300,000, computed as follows:

U.S. tax on worldwide taxable income $1,050,000 ($3,000,000 × 35%)

Foreign taxes paid $1,000,000 ($2,000,000 × 50%)

Foreign tax credit limitation: lesser of foreign taxes paid, $1,000,000, or overall limitation, $700,000 ($1,050,000 × ($2,000,000/$3,000,000))

Excess foreign tax credit $300,000 (foreign taxes paid $1,000,000 less limit $700,000)

If Voyager recharacterizes a portion of its U.S.-source income as foreign-source income (for U.S. tax purposes but not for foreign tax purposes), then it can increase its foreign tax credit limitation. Assume that Voyager is able to shift $500,000 of its U.S.-source income to foreign-source income using the appropriate sourcing rules. The result is to increase Voyager's foreign tax credit to $875,000, without increasing the actual foreign taxes paid, and to reduce its excess credit by $175,000, as computed below:

U.S. tax and foreign taxes paid remain unchanged

Foreign tax credit limitation: lesser of taxes paid $1,000,000 or the overall limit, $875,000 ($1,050,000 × ($2,500,000/$3,000,000))

Excess foreign tax credit $125,000 ($1,000,000 – $875,000)

¶25,601 **DOMESTIC PRODUCTION DEDUCTION**

Over the years, the United States has enacted a number of tax benefits for U.S. companies that export U.S. products. These tax benefits have been intended to help U.S. companies compete against foreign corporations that were exempt from tax, or subject to reduced tax, on their earnings from exports. In 1971, tax benefits were enacted for Domestic International Sales Corporations (DISCs). In 1984, in response to objections that tax benefits provided for DISCs constituted an export subsidy that violated U.S. commitments under the General Agreement on Tariffs and Trade (GATT), the United States enacted tax benefits for foreign sales corporations (FSCs). In February 2000, the World Trade Organization (WTO) declared the FSC regime a prohibited export subsidy. In response, the United States repealed the FSC regime and enacted the extraterritorial income (ETI) regime. In January 2002, the WTO ruled that the ETI also was a prohibited export subsidy. In response, the United States enacted the domestic production deduction, which benefits all domestic manufacturers, regardless whether they export any items.

The domestic production deduction permits taxpayers to deduct nine percent of the lesser of their qualified production activities income for the tax year, their taxable income for the tax year, or 50 percent of their W-2 wages attributable to domestic production activities for the tax year. *Qualified production activities income* is the difference between a taxpayer's domestic production gross receipts for the tax year and the sum of the cost of goods sold that are allocable to such receipts, other deductions, expenses, and losses directly allocable to such receipts, and a ratable portion of other deductions, expenses, and losses that are not directly allocable to such receipts or another class of income. Code Sec. 199.

¶25,605 **TRANSFER PRICING**

When businesses operating in various countries but owned or controlled by the same interests sell products or services or make loans among themselves, they have the opportunity to affect each other's taxable income and reduce the overall amount of taxes paid by the group. They can reduce the overall amount of taxes paid by the group by shifting taxable income from a high-tax country to a lower-tax country.

The IRS is authorized to reallocate income, deductions, credits, allowances, basis, and other items affecting taxable income among businesses owned or controlled by the same interests to prevent evasion of taxes. Code Sec. 482; Reg. §1.482-1(a)(2). In determining the true taxable income of a controlled taxpayer, the standard to be applied in every case is that of a taxpayer dealing at arm's length with an uncontrolled taxpayer. Reg. §1.482-1(b)(1).

Because it can be difficult for a taxpayer to determine what price would be used by uncontrolled taxpayers dealing at arm's length, the IRS permits taxpayers to enter into an Advance Pricing Agreement (APA) with the IRS on the best method for determining arm's-length prices for transfers among businesses owned or controlled by the taxpayer. Pursuant to an APA, a taxpayer agrees to a Transfer Pricing Method for all of the taxpayer's transfer pricing arrangements or specified transactions. Many of the United States' treaty partners also use APAs.

EXAMPLE 25.75 | A domestic corporation, Domes, manufactures windows for sale in the United States and abroad. Foreign sales are made by a wholly owned foreign subsidiary. The windows cost $60 to manufacture and $10 to market, and they sell for $100 abroad. The combined income, therefore, is $30 ($100 − $60 − $10). The tax rate is 35% in the United States and the foreign rate is 50%. If Domes uses a high transfer price, then little or no foreign tax may be incurred. For example, if the transfer price is the actual cost of the window, $60, all of the profit will be taxed in the foreign jurisdiction (i.e., $100 sales − $60 transfer price − $10 marketing). On the other hand, if the transfer price is set at $90, then Domes recognizes $30 of profit (i.e., $90 transfer price − $60 cost) and the foreign subsidiary recognizes none (i.e., $100 sales − $90 transfer price − $10 marketing), saving $4.50 per window in taxes ($30 profit × (50% − 35%)).

¶25,610 **FOREIGN CURRENCY**

U.S. companies that operate foreign subsidiaries and branches must address the issues related to foreign currency transactions. Business in a foreign country is conducted in that country's currency, and, because the exchange rate is constantly fluctuating, the actual transaction may not occur simultaneously with the translation into U.S. dollar figures. For example, if debt is issued in a foreign country, repayment is made with currency not equal to the currency of the original debt, even if the original borrowing is immediately translated into U.S. dollars.

A domestic taxpayer is responsible for denominating its taxable income in its functional currency, generally the U.S. dollar. However, if a corporation is a qualified business unit (QBU), conducts a significant share of its economic activities in a foreign country, and maintains its accounting records using that foreign currency, the QBU may adopt that country's currency. Code Sec. 985(b). A QBU is a foreign subsidiary or a foreign branch that is a separate unit of the trade or business, but never an individual. Code Sec. 989(a); Reg. §1.989(a)-1(b).

EXAMPLE 25.76   Lopo, a foreign corporation organized in a foreign country, is wholly owned by a domestic corporation, PAG. Lopo's sole function is acting as a financing vehicle for PAG and other domestic corporations that are affiliated with PAG. All borrowing and lending transactions between Lopo, PAG, and its domestic affiliates occur in U.S. dollars. Lopo's only foreign currency transactions involve paying taxes, employee wages, and other local expenses, such as rent and electricity. Lopo keeps its books and records in the foreign currency. Although Lopo keeps its books and records in the foreign currency, it primarily conducts its activities in U.S. dollars. Lopo's functional currency, therefore, is the U.S. dollar.

For purposes of determining the amount of the foreign tax credit (which is based on foreign taxes paid in the foreign currency), an accrual basis taxpayer translates the foreign income taxes using the average exchange rate for the year. Several exceptions to this general rule exist: (1) foreign income taxes that are paid more than two years after the close of the tax year to which the taxes relate; (2) foreign income taxes paid before the beginning of the relevant tax year; and (3) foreign income taxes denominated in an inflationary currency. In the case of any foreign income taxes to which the general rule does not apply, taxes are translated into dollars using the exchange rates as of the time the taxes were paid. Code Sec. 986(a).

EXAMPLE 25.77   Tilton is a cash basis, calendar-year domestic corporation that has branches in several foreign countries. During the year, Tilton remits foreign taxes amounting to 200,000LC (local currency) each of the first three quarters of the year and estimates an additional 250,000LC is owed for the year. The LC exchange rate was $.48 on March 31, $.51 on June 30, $.50 on September 30, and $.55 on December 31. Tilton's creditable foreign taxes for the year amount to:

March 31	$96,000	(200,000LC × $.48/LC)
June 30	$102,000	(200,000LC × $.51/LC)
September 30	$100,000	(200,000LC × $.50/LC)
December 31	$137,500	(250,000LC × $.55/LC)
Total foreign taxes	$435,500	

If a domestic taxpayer has a QBU with a functional currency other than the dollar, the QBU is required to compute its income or loss in its functional currency and then convert that income or loss into U.S. dollars at the average exchange rate for the tax year. Taxpayers must recognize exchange gain or loss on any remittance of property (not just currency) to the extent that the value of the currency at the time of the remittance differs from the value when earned. Post-1986 remittances from a QBU are treated as made on a pro rata basis out of post-1986 accumulated earnings. The gain or loss is treated as ordinary income or loss and is sourced by reference to the source of the income giving rise to the accumulated earnings. Code Secs. 987 and 989(b).

EXAMPLE 25.78   Heraton is a domestic corporation with a foreign branch that qualifies as a QBU and has a foreign currency, LC, as its functional currency. The LC had an average daily value during the year of $.18. The branch's taxable income for the year amounts to 6,000,000LC. Heraton translates its branch income into US$1,080,000 (6,000,000LC × $.18/LC).

With few exceptions, any foreign currency gain or loss attributable to a Code Sec. 988 transaction is computed separately and treated as ordinary income or loss.

A Code Sec. 988 transaction is any of the following transactions: Reg. §1.988-1(a).

1. A disposition of nonfunctional currency.
2. Any of the following transactions if any amount that the taxpayer is entitled to receive or is required to pay by reason of the transaction is denominated in terms of a nonfunctional currency or is determined by reference to the value of one or more nonfunctional currencies:
   - Acquiring a debt instrument or becoming an obligor under a debt instrument.
   - Accruing, or otherwise taking into account, for purposes of Subtitle A of the Code, any item of expense or gross income or receipts that is to be paid or received after the date on which so accrued or taken into account. A payable relating to cost of goods sold, or a payable or receivable relating to a capital expenditure or receipt, is within the meaning of this provision.
   - Entering into or acquiring any forward contract, futures contract, option, warrant, or similar financial instrument.

EXAMPLE 25.79	Barriot is a domestic corporation using the accrual method of accounting and a calendar year. Barriot's functional currency is the U.S. dollar. On January 15, Barriot acquires 10,000LC to purchase inventory from a foreign supplier. Payment of the purchase price of the inventory is a Code Sec. 988 transaction. On May 1, Barriot borrows 200,000LC for a period of 10 years and issues a note to the foreign lender with annual interest and principal payments. When Barriot becomes an obligor under the note, it constitutes a Code Sec. 988 transaction. Similarly, the accrual of interest expense is a Code Sec. 988 transaction.

EXAMPLE 25.80	Lyatt is a domestic corporation using the accrual method of accounting with the U.S. dollar as its functional currency. On January 2, Lyatt acquires 1,500LC for $2,250 (i.e., 1LC = $1.50). On January 5, when the spot rate is 1LC = $1.49, Lyatt deposits the 1,500LC with a foreign financial institution in a demand account. On February 1, when the spot rate is 1LC = $1.45, Lyatt withdraws the 1,500LC to purchase inventory on February 3, when the spot rate is 1LC = $1.42. No exchange gain or loss is realized until February 3 when Lyatt disposes of the 1,500LC for inventory. At that time, Lyatt realizes a currency exchange loss of $120 (1,500LC × ($1.50 – $1.42)).

¶25,615 TAX HAVENS

Tax havens offer many tax benefits for individuals and businesses. The prime characteristic of a tax haven is that it imposes taxes at a low rate or not at all. However, the term often is used as a pejorative to describe a country that helps a person evade taxes owed to the person's country of residence by secreting personal financial information from foreign tax authorities. The Organisation for Economic Co-Operation and Development (OECD) has had success in persuading countries to make their tax administration more transparent and more freely exchange tax information with foreign tax authorities.

The following are popular tax haven countries:

Anguilla	Jersey
Antigua and Barbuda	Labuan
Aruba	Liechtenstein
Bahamas	Luxembourg
Bahrain	Malta
Barbados	Marshall Islands
Belize	Mauritius
Bermuda	Monaco
British Virgin Islands	Montserrat

Brunei	Netherland Antilles
Cayman Islands	New Zealand
Channel Islands	Nevis
Cook Islands	Panama
Costa Rica	Samoa
Dominica	Seychelles
Dubai	Singapore
Gibraltar	St. Kitts
Grenada	St. Vincent
Guernsey	Switzerland
Hong Kong	Turks and Caicos Islands
Ireland	Virgin Islands (U.S.)
Isle of Man	

KEYSTONE PROBLEM

Halfnote, Inc., a domestic corporation, is planning to build a new production facility in either a high- or a low-tax foreign jurisdiction. Halfnote seeks tax advice on where it should build its new production facility.

Corporate Inversions

¶25,625 ## WHAT A CORPORATE INVERSION IS AND WHY IT IS POPULAR

There is a *corporate inversion* when a corporation changes its place of residence from one country to another (often without making a material change in its business operations). Usually the corporation changes its place of residence from a country using the worldwide system of taxation to a country using the territorial system of taxation. The transaction is referred to as an *inversion* because a smaller holding company often ends up owning a larger operating company.

There may be non-tax benefits when a corporation undertakes a corporate inversion (e.g., an inversion can give a corporation better access to international capital markets, greater operational flexibility, and better cash management).

However, the primary reason that a corporation undertakes a corporate inversion is to save taxes and reduce compliance costs. Multinational U.S. corporations can reduce their taxes by escaping the United States' worldwide system of taxation and moving to a country with a territorial system of taxation. Additional taxes can be saved if, as usually is the case, the foreign country has a lower tax rate on income than the United States. Moving their residence outside the United States can help corporations avoid the need to comply with the complicated subpart F rules for controlled foreign corporations.

There are several ways for a U.S. corporation to become a legal resident of a foreign country:

- *Stock transaction.* Shareholders of a U.S. corporation can exchange their shares for shares in a foreign corporation.
- *Merger with a foreign corporation.* A U.S. corporation can merge into a foreign corporation (leaving the foreign corporation as the survivor).
- *Spin-off.* A U.S. corporation can spin-off one or more of its businesses to a foreign subsidiary in return for stock in the foreign subsidiary.
- *Drop-down transaction.* A corporation can transfer its assets to a foreign corporation (and then have the foreign corporation transfer some or all of those assets to a newly formed U.S. subsidiary).

¶25,635   U.S. EFFORTS TO CURTAIL CORPORATE INVERSIONS

Efforts have been made to curtail corporate inversions because such inversions cause a loss of tax revenue and often the loss of jobs for U.S. citizens and residents.

Over the years, U.S. tax law has been revised to discourage corporate inversions. For example:

- Code Sec. 1248(i) requires recognition of gain when a shareholder of a U.S. corporation owning at least 10 percent of the stock of a foreign corporation exchanges stock of the U.S. corporation for stock of the foreign corporation.

- Code Sec. 163(j) was meant to deter interest stripping (whereby a foreign company or related party loans money to a U.S. corporation, the U.S. corporation deducts the interest, and the foreign company or related party pays little or no tax on its interest income). Code Sec. 163(j) limits a corporation's ability to deduct interest expense. However, it has done little to deter interest stripping because it applies only when a corporation has a debt-to-equity ratio of at least 1.5 to 1.

- Regulations under Code Sec. 367(a) make transfers of shares in domestic corporations to foreign corporations taxable if, in the aggregate, U.S. transferors own at least 50% of the foreign parent's stock by vote or value immediately after the exchange.

- Code Sec. 7874 is designed to remove the tax benefits of an inversion. Code Sec. 7874 applies if a foreign corporation acquires substantially all of the property of a U.S. corporation or partnership and after the acquisition at least 60% of the stock of the foreign corporation (by vote or value) is held by former shareholders of the U.S. corporation or former partners of the U.S. partnership. If former shareholders or partners own less than 80% of the foreign corporation's stock, the taxable income of the U.S. operating company must be at least as much as its inversion gain. If former shareholders or partners own at least 80% of the foreign corporation's stock, the foreign parent will be considered a U.S. corporation subject to U.S. taxation on all of its income. The IRS has issued regulations addressing transactions structured to avoid the purposes of Code Secs. 7874 and 367 and certain post-inversion tax avoidance transactions. See T.D. 9761, April 4, 2016.

SUMMARY

- Forty-six states and the District of Columbia tax a corporation's income or gross receipts. Most states utilize federal taxable income or taxable income before NOLs and special deductions as the starting point of determining taxable income and then make adjustments.

- Forty-three states and the District of Columbia impose an individual state income tax. Most states use a taxpayer's federal taxable income or federal adjusted gross income as the starting point for computing state taxable income and then make adjustments.

- A state's power to impose taxes on a nonresident or require a nonresident to collect and remit taxes to the state is limited by the United States Constitution. The Due Process and Commerce clauses of the United States Constitution prohibit a state from taxing a nonresident unless the nonresident has sufficient connection ("nexus") to the state. Public Law 86-272 was enacted to limit the imposition of state income taxes on out-of-state businesses.

- Most states have adopted the Uniform Division of Income for Tax Purposes Act (UDITPA) or similar provisions to determine how the business and non-business income of multistate (and multinational) business enterprises is allocated and apportioned among the states (and countries) where the enterprise does business. The unitary business principle allows a state to apportion to the state multistate income of separate legal entities if the business activities are related and integrated.

- Most countries have a territorial system of taxation. Countries with a territorial system of taxation tax income from sources within the country but not foreign-source income. The United States and a few other countries (such as Mexico and South Korea) have a worldwide system of taxation. Under the worldwide system of taxation, a country taxes its citizens and residents on all of their income, including income received from both domestic and foreign sources. Nonresidents are taxed on income sourced to the country with a worldwide system of taxation but not on their income from other sources. Taxpayers in countries using the worldwide system of taxation may have their foreign-source income taxed twice—once by their country of residence and a second time by the foreign country. To alleviate double taxation of the same earnings, the United States and other countries using the worldwide system of taxation allow a tax credit for income taxes paid on foreign income. The United

States limits the amount of the foreign tax credit to make sure that foreign-source income is subject to at least the same tax rate as U.S.-source income.

■ Treaties provide special rules for the taxation of nonresidents with income sourced to a party to the treaty. The U.S. Model Income Tax Treaty reflects the basic content of most income tax treaties between the United States and a foreign country.

■ Nonresident alien individuals are subject to U.S. tax on their U.S.-source income. How that income is taxed varies depending on whether or not the income is effectively connected with a U.S. business. Nonresident aliens generally are subject to a 30 percent tax on their U.S.-source gross income. The rate of tax may be reduced by a treaty between the United States and the country where the non-resident alien resides. Income effectively connected with the conduct of a trade or business in the United States is taxed at the same graduated income tax rates that apply to U.S. citizens and residents.

■ Sourcing rules are used to classify income as from a source within the United States, a source without the United States, or a source partly within and partly without the United States. The sourcing rules determine which income of nonresident foreign persons is subject to U.S. taxation. The rules are not as important for U.S. persons because U.S. persons are taxed on their worldwide income. However, the sourcing rules do affect the limit on a person's foreign tax credit.

■ U.S. citizens and residents living abroad may exclude a certain amount of their foreign earned income from their gross income and exclude or take a deduction for a certain amount of their foreign housing expenses.

QUESTIONS

1. List five provisions of the U.S. Constitution that limit a state's power to impose taxes.

2. Define the following type of SALTs: individual income, corporate income, sales, gross receipts, franchise, real property, personal property, unemployment, use, excise, transfer, and severance taxes.

3. Under what circumstances does the Interstate Income Law prohibit a state from taxing income derived within the state by an out-of-state business?

4. Why might a business feel that a gross receipts tax is unfair?

5. What are the steps in the typical state formula used to calculate a corporation's state income tax liability?

6. What is nexus?

7. What is click-through nexus?

8. What is the Uniform Division of Income for Tax Purposes Act?

9. To comply with the Commerce Clause, a state tax must satisfy which requirements?

10. Give five examples of the types of adjustments that states make to a taxpayer's federal tax base.

11. List five in-state activities that the Multistate Tax Commission does not consider either solicitation of orders or ancillary activities.

12. Distinguish between allocation and apportionment.

13. What is the three-factor formula, and how is it calculated?

14. Describe the two tests that are often utilized to determine whether income is business income.

15. Why would a state want to characterize a business as a unitary business?

16. How do you determine whether a business is a unitary business?

17. How are S corporations taxed by states?

18. What are the competing interests of businesses and states with respect to e-commerce?

19. What is a composite income tax return?

20. What are the worldwide and territorial systems of taxation?

21. What is the main drawback of the worldwide system of taxation, and what is done to mitigate that drawback?

22. How can an income tax treaty affect a taxpayer?

23. What is the general rule for sourcing personal services income?

24. How is depreciation treated when sourcing income from personal property?

25. What is the purpose of the sourcing rules? What are the steps involved in sourcing income?

26. How are nonresident alien individuals taxed by the United States?

27. What types of U.S.-source income not connected with a U.S. business are taxed to a nonresident alien individual?

28. What are the general rules for allocating and apportioning deductions?

29. How does the United States tax foreign corporations?

30. What is a controlled foreign corporation, and how are its U.S. shareholders taxed?

31. Describe the foreign earned income exclusion, including the annual limit.

32. What is the housing cost exclusion?

33. Who can take a housing cost deduction?

34. Who is eligible for the foreign tax credit?

35. What is transfer pricing?

36. What limitations are imposed on the amount of the foreign tax credit?

37. What is a corporate inversion, and why is it controversial?

38. What is a tax haven, and what are the tax advantages?

PROBLEMS

39. Welch Manufacturing has $5,000,000 of taxable income. One of the states in which it does business is Kentucky, which uses the three-factor formula with a double-weighted sales factor to apportion income. If Welch Manufacturing's property factor in Kentucky is 0.05, its payroll factor is 0.05, and its sales factor is 0.15, what amount of its taxable income has to be apportioned to Kentucky?

40. Elbert Manufacturing, Inc. does business in two states. Each state uses the single-factor sales formula to apportion income. State 1 imposes a 5% tax on income, and State 2 imposes an 8% tax on income. The company's federal taxable income was $3,000,000. Each state uses federal taxable income as its base for imposing its tax. If the company had $1.5 million in sales in State 1 and $1 million in sales in State 2 and no income allocable to either state, how much does the company owe each state?

41. Holt Industries, Inc. does business in State 1. That state uses federal taxable income as the starting point for calculating state income tax. Interest on state obligations is taxed, but interest on federal obligations is not taxed. Only straight-line depreciation may be deducted. Holt Industries' income and expenses for the year are:

Sales	$200,000
Interest income on federal obligations	$4,000
Interest income on state obligations	$5,000
State taxes	$10,000
MACRS	$15,000
(straight-line depreciation)	$8,000
Cost of sales	$60,000
Other business expenses	$20,000

What is Holt Industries' taxable income for federal and state purposes?

42. Frederick Confectioner does business in multiple states, including one state that uses the UDITPA formula to apportion income. If the company's taxable income is $3,500,000, its property factor in the state is 0.0, its payroll factor is 0.0, and its sales factor is 0.15, what amount of its income has to be apportioned to the state?

43. Darrell Batteries owned property valued at $3,000,000 at the beginning of the year and $3,400,000 at the end of the year. In Florida it owned property valued at $380,000 at the beginning of the year and $420,000 at the end of the year. What is its property factor for Florida?

44. Alvarado Apps, Inc. owned real and tangible personal property valued at $3,000,000 at the beginning of the year and $3,400,000 at the end of the year. It also leased real property for $100,000. In State 1, the company owned real and tangible personal property valued at $400,000 at the beginning of the year and $360,000 at the end of the year. It leased real property In State 1 for $25,000. What Is the company's property factor in State 1?

45. Marcy Industries, Inc. does business in a state that apportions business income using a three-factor formula giving double weight to the sales factor. If the company's business income is $500,000, the property factor is 35%, the payroll factor is 50%, and the sales factor is 45%, how much of its income has to be apportioned to the state?

46. Winifred Luxury Watches operates in Massachusetts and Connecticut. It paid $5,000,000 in compensation to its Massachusetts employees and $3,000,000 in compensation to its Connecticut employees. What is its payroll factor for Connecticut?

47. Carmen Motors, Inc. does business in three states. Its state taxable income is $1,000,000. State 1 uses the UDITPA apportionment formula. State 2 doubles the sales factor. State 3 uses only the sales factor. Given the following information, what is the company's income tax liability in those three states?

Total	State1	State2	State3
Net sales	$2,000,000	$3,000,000	$5,000,000
Property values	$1,000,000	$1,000,000	$3,000,000
Compensation	$300,000	$500,000	$700,000
State income and tax rates	7%	6%	4%

48. Burgess Fabricators, Inc. did business in and is subject to the tax of State 1 and State 2, where it had its commercial domicile. It had the following nonbusiness income for the year:
   - $15,000 in net rental income from real property situated in State 1
   - $10,000 in net rental income from machinery used in State 1
   - $15,000 in capital gains from the sale of real property situated in State 2
   - $8,000 in capital gains from the sale of intangible personal property used in State 1
   - $1,000 in interest paid by a company whose commercial domicile was in State 1
   - $2,000 in dividends paid by a company whose commercial domicile was in State 1

   Under UDITPA, how much of this nonbusiness income should be allocated to State 1, and how much should be allocated to State 2?

49. Cardona Spirits, Inc. operates in two countries, Country A and Country B. It is incorporated in Country A. Its income from sources within Country A is $500,000, and its income from Country B is $200,000. Country A taxes Cardona Spirits' income at 35%, and Country B taxes the company's income at 20%. Compare the amount of taxes that the company will have to pay if (1) Country A has a worldwide system of taxation with a full credit for foreign taxes paid and (2) Country A has a territorial system of taxation.

50. Eloise Caldwell, who resides in the United States, received $60,000 in wages and a $5,000 bonus. During the year, she worked 225 days in the United States and 25 days in France. What is her U.S. and foreign-source income for the year?

51. Owen Lyons, a U.S. citizen who resides in Belgium, received $100 in interest on a U.S. Treasury bond, $200 in interest from a U.S. corporation manufacturing motor vehicles, and $50 in interest from the foreign branch of a U.S. bank. The foreign branch is also engaged in the commercial banking business. What is his U.S. and foreign-source interest income for the year?

52. Russell Manufacturing, Inc. purchased inventory for resale and sold it in the Netherlands for a $25,000 gain. It sold inventory that it had produced in the United States to a German buyer in Germany for a $75,000 gain. It uses the 50/50 method to source income. Its production assets are located solely in the United States. How much of its income is U.S.-source income, and how much is foreign-source income?

53. Underwood Electronics, Inc. sold a patent contingent on its productivity. Use of the patent was by a company doing business in Spain. Underwood Electronics had $55,000 in gain with respect to the patent for the year. Prior to the sale, it had taken $10,000 in depreciation deductions with respect to the property when calculating its U.S. income tax liability. No foreign depreciation deductions were taken. How much of its gain is U.S.-source income, and how much is foreign-source income?

54. Marta Industries, Inc., a U.S. corporation, received $100,000 in rentals from real property located in the United States and $50,000 in rentals from real property located in Germany. It received $75,000 from licenses of patents used in Italy and $35,000 from licenses of patents used in the United States. How much U.S. and foreign-source income did it have for the year?

55. Harig Fabricators, Inc., a U.S. corporation, sold equipment to a company in Switzerland for $500,000. The company purchased the equipment for $350,000 and took $200,000 in depreciation deductions, all allowable in computing the company's taxable income from U.S. sources. Title to the equipment passed in Switzerland. What is the amount of the company's gain, and how much of it is U.S.-source income?

56. Edley Furnishings, Inc., a U.S. corporation, paid dividends to two shareholders with a foreign address and two shareholders who are residents of the United States. One of the shareholders with a foreign address is a U.S. citizen, but neither of the shareholders who are residents is a U.S. citizen. For which shareholders must the company withhold tax?

57. Schiele Soda Machines, Inc. is a German corporation with a branch office in the United States. Its effectively connected profits for the tax year are $800,000. At the beginning of the tax year, it had $1,000,000 in U.S. assets and $450,000 in U.S. liabilities. At the end of the tax year, it had $950,000 in U.S. assets and $350,000 in U.S. liabilities. What amount of branch profits tax does the company owe?

58. Cesar Hayman's employer sent him to Spain. During the tax year, he paid $12,000 for rent, $2,000 to purchase furniture, $1,000 for pay television, $600 for telephone service, and $3,000 for gas and electric charges. How much of these charges are eligible for the housing expense amount?

59. Marcia Hunt is a U.S. citizen. Her employer sent her to Amsterdam for a temporary assignment. She arrived in Amsterdam on May 10, 2017 at 2 p.m. and departed at noon on April 8, 2018. The Netherlands was her tax home during that period of time. She was paid $80,000 for her work in Amsterdam in 2017. How much of that compensation can she exclude from her gross income?

60. Nicholas Ramos is a U.S. citizen. He was able to exclude $60,000 of his foreign earned income. He also had a $30,000 gain from the sale of a capital asset held for more than one year and $20,000 in deductions. How does he calculate his regular income tax liability for the year?

61. Doris McGee, a U.S. citizen, lived in Poland for 270 days in 2017 and qualified for the housing cost exclusion for that year. Her employer provided her with housing that had a fair rental value of $15,000. She also paid $5,000 for utilities (including $1,000 for telephone service), $1,500 for cable TV, and $1,000 for home owners insurance. She did not live in a high cost area. What is her housing cost amount for 2017?

62. Rosa Linens' total taxable income was $2,000,000, and its U.S. tax (before any credit for foreign taxes paid) was $680,000. Its taxable income from foreign sources was $500,000, and it paid $125,000 in foreign taxes on that income. The overall limitation on the amount of the foreign tax credit limits Rosa Linens to what amount?

63. Sims Furnishings, Inc.'s total taxable income was $10 million. Its taxable income from foreign sources was $6 million ($5,000,000 of general category income and $1,000,000 of passive category income). It paid $200,000 on its passive category income and $800,000 on its general category income. What are the company's overall and separate foreign tax credit limitations?

64. Wilkerson Home Goods, Inc. had $2,000,000 in foreign-source income (including $1,500,000 general category income and $500,000 passive activity category income). It had a U.S-source loss of $600,000. How is its U.S.-source loss allocated?

65. Bertha Corporation, a domestic corporation, has $2,000,000 and $1,000,000 of U.S.- and foreign-source income, respectively. The U.S. tax rate is 35% and the foreign rate is 40%. Determine Bertha's excess FTC.

66. Ioren Industries, Inc., a U.S. corporation, had $1,200,000 in U.S.-source taxable income and $800,000 in foreign-source taxable income for the tax year. The company's pre-credit U.S. tax was $680,000. Its foreign-source taxable income included $200,000 in foreign-source dividends, taxed at 5%, and $600,000 in general category income taxed at 15%. What is the company's foreign tax credit for the tax year?

67. Zoila Brewery, Inc., a U.S. corporation, owned 15% of the stock of Zhutan Spirits, Inc., a foreign corporation formed in 2000. During the year, Zhutan Spirits earned $100,000 and paid $20,000 in income taxes on those earnings. The amount of its undistributed earnings prior to making any dividend distributions was $100,000. Zoila Brewery received $9,000 in dividends. What amount of the taxes paid by Zhutan Spirits is creditable to Zoila Brewery?

68. Bernice Wong paid $40,000 in foreign income tax on foreign earned income that she excluded from her U.S. gross income and $20,000 on foreign earned income that she could not exclude from her U.S. gross income. She also paid $10,000 in foreign income tax on dividends that she received and $15,000 on retail purchases. How much of the amount of foreign taxes that she paid is eligible for the foreign tax credit?

69. Ada Fashions, Inc., a domestic corporation, owns 25% of the voting stock of Guadalupe Clothing Manufacturing, Inc., a foreign corporation. During the year, Guadalupe Clothing Manufacturing distributed a $100,000 dividend to Ada Fashions and withheld $15,000 from its payment. As of the close of the tax year, Guadalupe Clothing Manufacturing has $4,000,000 in undistributed post-1986 earnings (not reduced by any dividends during the year). It has paid $800,000 in foreign income taxes on those undistributed earnings. What amount of foreign income tax is Ada Fashions considered to have paid that year?

70. Carr Electronics, Inc., a domestic corporation, owns 5% of the voting stock of Cruz Manufacturing, Inc., a foreign corporation. During the year, Cruz Manufacturing distributed a $20,000 dividend to Carr Electronics and withheld $3,000 from its payment. As of the close of the tax year, Cruz Manufacturing has $2,000,000 in undistributed post-1986 earnings (not reduced by any dividends during the year). It has paid $300,000 in foreign income taxes on those undistributed earnings. What amount of foreign income tax is Carr Electronics considered to have paid that year?

71. Amar Financial Services, Inc. is a cash-basis, calendar-year domestic corporation that has a branch outside the United States. During the year, it paid foreign income taxes amounting to 300,000LC (local currency) each of the first three quarters of the year and estimates that it will owe an additional $250,000 for the year. If the LC exchange rate was $1.80 on March 31, $1.75 on June 30, $1.85 on September 30, and $1.80 on December 31, what amount of foreign income taxes is it considered to have paid for the year?

72. Alexis Computers is a U.S. corporation with a foreign branch in Italy that is a qualified business unit (QBU). The foreign branch had taxable earnings of 500,000 Euros. The average exchange rate for the tax year was 1.35 U.S. dollars for each Euro. What is Alexis Computers' taxable income in U.S. dollars?

73. Topete Appliances, a U.S. corporation that uses the accrual method of accounting and the U.S. dollar as its functional currency, acquired 5,000LC for $7,500 on March 13. On March 15, when the currency exchange rate for 1LC was $1.55, Tope Appliances deposited the 5,000LC in a foreign financial institution. On May 4, when the currency exchange rate for 1LC was $1.60, Topete Appliances withdrew the 5,000LC. On May 5, when the currency exchange rate for 1LC was $1.61, Topete Appliances used the 5,000LC to purchase inventory. What is the amount of Topete Appliances' currency exchange gain or loss?

74. Norton Toys, Inc., a U.S. company, manufactures toys. Foreign sales are made by a wholly owned foreign subsidiary. It costs Norton Toys $5 to manufacture its toys and $1 to market them. It sells the toys for $10. If the foreign tax on sales is 20% and Norton is subject to a U.S. tax of 34%, what transfer price for the toys will maximize Norton Toys' income?

75. Pratt Software, Inc., a foreign corporation, is owned by the following persons:
    - Robyn Taylor, a U.S. citizen, owns 20% of the company's common stock
    - Javier Hoffman, a foreign citizen and Robyn Taylor's spouse, owns 25% of the company's stock
    - Perry Pratt, a Scottish citizen, owns 30% of the company's common stock
    - Ian Malone, an English citizen, owns 5% of the company's common stock
    - Garza Consulting, Inc., a foreign corporation, owns 20% of the company's common stock (Ismael Townsend, a U.S. citizen, owns 50% of Garza Consulting's common stock)

    Is Pratt Software a controlled foreign corporation?

76. **Research Problem.** What formula is used in your state for apportionment of multistate income and what are your corporate income tax rates?

77. **Research Problem.** Which of the following taxes are imposed by your state?

    Corporate income tax, franchise tax, severance tax, individual income tax, real property tax, personal property tax, sales tax, use tax, excise tax, gift tax, estate or death tax.

78. **Tax Return Problem.** Leslie Spurl, a U.S. citizen, was transferred to France by her employer in 2017 and worked in that country for 335 days that year. She had $100,000 of wages but no self-employment income or business/moving expenses and is not claiming any foreign housing exclusion. Leslie is eligible for the foreign earned income exclusion. What form should she use to calculate her foreign earning income exclusion? Fill in that portion of the form.

Appendix

Tax Rate Schedules For 2017

From 1993 through 2000, income has been taxed at the following rates: 15 percent, 28 percent, 31 percent, 36 percent, and 39.6 percent. For 2001 a 10 percent rate was added and the rates above 15 percent were reduced one-half of one percent. The rates above 15 percent were reduced another one-half percent for 2002. For 2004 through 2012, the rates above 15 percent were lowered to 25, 28, 33 and 35 percent. The American Taxpayer Relief Act of 2012 changed the rates again. For 2013 and later, the rates are 15, 25, 28, 33, 35, and 39.6 percent.

The tax rate schedules are subject to an inflation adjustment based on methods prescribed by the Internal Revenue Code. The income ranges and the applicable dollar amounts are adjusted to reflect increases in the Consumer Price Index (CPI). The CPI increase applicable to 2017 is provided by the Bureau of Labor Statistics, and the schedules below and on the following page reflect this adjustment.

Tax Rate Schedule X below is to be used by single individuals or by married persons treated as unmarried that have taxable incomes of $100,000 or more.

Single Individuals—Schedule X

Taxable Income					
Over	But Not Over	Pay	+	% on Excess	of the amount over
$0	$9,325	$0.00		10%	$0
9,325	37,950	932.50		15	9,325
37,950	91,900	5,226.25		25	37,950
91,900	191,650	18,713.75		28	91,900
191,650	416,700	46,643.75		33	191,650
416,700	418,400	120,910.25		35	416,700
418,400	—	121,505.25		39.6	418,400

Tax Rate Schedule Y-1 below is to be used by married taxpayers filing jointly and by surviving spouses that have taxable incomes of $100,000 or more.

Married Individuals, Joint Returns and Surviving Spouses—Schedule Y-1

Taxable Income					
Over	But Not Over	Pay	+	% on Excess	of the amount over
$0	$18,650	$0.00		10%	$0
18,650	75,900	1,865.00		15	18,650
75,900	153,100	10,452.50		25	75,900
153,100	233,350	29,752.50		28	153,100
233,350	416,700	52,222.50		33	233,350
416,700	470,700	112,728.00		35	416,700
470,700	—	131,628.00		39.6	470,700

Tax Rate Schedule Y-2 below is to be used by married taxpayers filing separately and by the bankruptcy estate of an individual debtor that have taxable incomes of $100,000 or more.

Married Individuals, Separate Returns—Schedule Y-2

Taxable Income		Pay	+	% on Excess	of the amount over
Over	But Not Over				
$0	$9,325	$0.00		10%	$0
9,325	37,950	932.50		15	9,325
37,950	76,550	5,226.25		25	37,950
76,550	116,675	14,876.25		28	76,550
116,675	208,350	26,111.25		33	116,675
208,350	235,350	56,364.00		35	208,350
235,350	—	65,814.00		39.6	235,350

Tax Rate Schedule Z below is to be used by individuals who qualify as heads of households that have taxable incomes of $100,000 or more.

Heads of Households—Schedule Z

Taxable Income		Pay	+	% on Excess	of the amount over
Over	But Not Over				
$0	$13,350	$0.00		10%	$0
13,350	50,800	1,335.00		15	13,350
50,800	131,200	6,952.50		25	50,800
131,200	212,500	27,052.50		28	131,200
212,500	416,700	49,816.50		33	212,500
416,700	444,550	117,202.50		35	416,700
444,550	—	126,950.00		39.6	444,550

Tax Rate Schedule for Estates and Trusts. The American Taxpayer Relief Act of 2012 changed the rates again. For 2013 and later, the rates are 15, 25, 28, 33, 35, and 39.6 percent.

Estates and Trusts

Taxable Income		Pay	+	% on Excess	of the amount over
Over	But Not Over				
$0	$2,550	$0.00		15%	$0
2,550	6,000	382.50		25	2,550
6,000	9,150	1,245.00		28	6,000
9,150	12,500	2,127.00		33	9,150
12,500	—	3,232.50		39.6	12,500

Tax Rate Schedule for Corporations. A graduated rate structure is employed in computing the income tax liability of corporate taxpayers. The 5 percent additional tax rate that applies to phase out the benefits of the graduated rates is incorporated in the rate schedule. The phaseout occurs between $100,000 and $335,000 of taxable income by means of an increase in the maximum 34 percent rate to 39 percent.

Corporations

Taxable Income		Pay	+	% on Excess	of the amount over
Over	But Not Over				
$0	$ 50,000	$0		15%	$0
50,000	75,000	7,500		25	50,000
75,000	100,000	13,750		34	75,000
100,000	335,000	22,250		39	100,000
335,000	10,000,000	113,900		34	335,000
10,000,000	15,000,000	3,400,000		35	10,000,000
15,000,000	18,333,333	5,150,000		38	15,000,000
18,333,333	—	0		35	0

Tax Table

2016 Tax Table

See the instructions for line 44 to see if you must use the Tax Table below to figure your tax.

Example. Mr. and Mrs. Brown are filing a joint return. Their taxable income on Form 1040, line 43, is $25,300. First, they find the $25,300-25,350 taxable income line. Next, they find the column for married filing jointly and read down the column. The amount shown where the taxable income line and filing status column meet is $2,871. This is the tax amount they should enter on Form 1040, line 44.

Sample Table

At Least	But Less Than	Single	Married filing jointly*	Married filing separately	Head of a household
			Your tax is—		
25,200	25,250	3,320	2,856	3,320	3,121
25,250	25,300	3,328	2,864	3,328	3,129
25,300	25,350	3,335	(2,871)	3,335	3,136
25,350	25,400	3,343	2,879	3,343	3,144

If line 43 (taxable income) is—		And you are—				If line 43 (taxable income) is—		And you are—				If line 43 (taxable income) is—		And you are—			
At least	But less than	Single	Married filing jointly *	Married filing separately	Head of a household	At least	But less than	Single	Married filing jointly *	Married filing separately	Head of a household	At least	But less than	Single	Married filing jointly *	Married filing separately	Head of a household
		Your tax is—						**Your tax is—**						**Your tax is—**			
0	5	0	0	0	0			**1,000**						**2,000**			
5	15	1	1	1	1												
15	25	2	2	2	2												
25	50	4	4	4	4												
50	75	6	6	6	6	1,000	1,025	101	101	101	101	2,000	2,025	201	201	201	201
						1,025	1,050	104	104	104	104	2,025	2,050	204	204	204	204
75	100	9	9	9	9	1,050	1,075	106	106	106	106	2,050	2,075	206	206	206	206
100	125	11	11	11	11	1,075	1,100	109	109	109	109	2,075	2,100	209	209	209	209
125	150	14	14	14	14	1,100	1,125	111	111	111	111	2,100	2,125	211	211	211	211
150	175	16	16	16	16												
175	200	19	19	19	19	1,125	1,150	114	114	114	114	2,125	2,150	214	214	214	214
						1,150	1,175	116	116	116	116	2,150	2,175	216	216	216	216
200	225	21	21	21	21	1,175	1,200	119	119	119	119	2,175	2,200	219	219	219	219
225	250	24	24	24	24	1,200	1,225	121	121	121	121	2,200	2,225	221	221	221	221
250	275	26	26	26	26	1,225	1,250	124	124	124	124	2,225	2,250	224	224	224	224
275	300	29	29	29	29												
300	325	31	31	31	31	1,250	1,275	126	126	126	126	2,250	2,275	226	226	226	226
						1,275	1,300	129	129	129	129	2,275	2,300	229	229	229	229
325	350	34	34	34	34	1,300	1,325	131	131	131	131	2,300	2,325	231	231	231	231
350	375	36	36	36	36	1,325	1,350	134	134	134	134	2,325	2,350	234	234	234	234
375	400	39	39	39	39	1,350	1,375	136	136	136	136	2,350	2,375	236	236	236	236
400	425	41	41	41	41												
425	450	44	44	44	44	1,375	1,400	139	139	139	139	2,375	2,400	239	239	239	239
						1,400	1,425	141	141	141	141	2,400	2,425	241	241	241	241
450	475	46	46	46	46	1,425	1,450	144	144	144	144	2,425	2,450	244	244	244	244
475	500	49	49	49	49	1,450	1,475	146	146	146	146	2,450	2,475	246	246	246	246
500	525	51	51	51	51	1,475	1,500	149	149	149	149	2,475	2,500	249	249	249	249
525	550	54	54	54	54												
550	575	56	56	56	56	1,500	1,525	151	151	151	151	2,500	2,525	251	251	251	251
						1,525	1,550	154	154	154	154	2,525	2,550	254	254	254	254
575	600	59	59	59	59	1,550	1,575	156	156	156	156	2,550	2,575	256	256	256	256
600	625	61	61	61	61	1,575	1,600	159	159	159	159	2,575	2,600	259	259	259	259
625	650	64	64	64	64	1,600	1,625	161	161	161	161	2,600	2,625	261	261	261	261
650	675	66	66	66	66												
675	700	69	69	69	69	1,625	1,650	164	164	164	164	2,625	2,650	264	264	264	264
						1,650	1,675	166	166	166	166	2,650	2,675	266	266	266	266
700	725	71	71	71	71	1,675	1,700	169	169	169	169	2,675	2,700	269	269	269	269
725	750	74	74	74	74	1,700	1,725	171	171	171	171	2,700	2,725	271	271	271	271
750	775	76	76	76	76	1,725	1,750	174	174	174	174	2,725	2,750	274	274	274	274
775	800	79	79	79	79												
800	825	81	81	81	81	1,750	1,775	176	176	176	176	2,750	2,775	276	276	276	276
						1,775	1,800	179	179	179	179	2,775	2,800	279	279	279	279
825	850	84	84	84	84	1,800	1,825	181	181	181	181	2,800	2,825	281	281	281	281
850	875	86	86	86	86	1,825	1,850	184	184	184	184	2,825	2,850	284	284	284	284
875	900	89	89	89	89	1,850	1,875	186	186	186	186	2,850	2,875	286	286	286	286
900	925	91	91	91	91												
925	950	94	94	94	94	1,875	1,900	189	189	189	189	2,875	2,900	289	289	289	289
						1,900	1,925	191	191	191	191	2,900	2,925	291	291	291	291
						1,925	1,950	194	194	194	194	2,925	2,950	294	294	294	294
950	975	96	96	96	96	1,950	1,975	196	196	196	196	2,950	2,975	296	296	296	296
975	1,000	99	99	99	99	1,975	2,000	199	199	199	199	2,975	3,000	299	299	299	299

(Continued)

3,000

At least	But less than	Single	Married filing jointly *	Married filing separately	Head of a household
			Your tax is—		
3,000	3,050	303	303	303	303
3,050	3,100	308	308	308	308
3,100	3,150	313	313	313	313
3,150	3,200	318	318	318	318
3,200	3,250	323	323	323	323
3,250	3,300	328	328	328	328
3,300	3,350	333	333	333	333
3,350	3,400	338	338	338	338
3,400	3,450	343	343	343	343
3,450	3,500	348	348	348	348
3,500	3,550	353	353	353	353
3,550	3,600	358	358	358	358
3,600	3,650	363	363	363	363
3,650	3,700	368	368	368	368
3,700	3,750	373	373	373	373
3,750	3,800	378	378	378	378
3,800	3,850	383	383	383	383
3,850	3,900	388	388	388	388
3,900	3,950	393	393	393	393
3,950	4,000	398	398	398	398

4,000

At least	But less than	Single	Married filing jointly *	Married filing separately	Head of a household
4,000	4,050	403	403	403	403
4,050	4,100	408	408	408	408
4,100	4,150	413	413	413	413
4,150	4,200	418	418	418	418
4,200	4,250	423	423	423	423
4,250	4,300	428	428	428	428
4,300	4,350	433	433	433	433
4,350	4,400	438	438	438	438
4,400	4,450	443	443	443	443
4,450	4,500	448	448	448	448
4,500	4,550	453	453	453	453
4,550	4,600	458	458	458	458
4,600	4,650	463	463	463	463
4,650	4,700	468	468	468	468
4,700	4,750	473	473	473	473
4,750	4,800	478	478	478	478
4,800	4,850	483	483	483	483
4,850	4,900	488	488	488	488
4,900	4,950	493	493	493	493
4,950	5,000	498	498	498	498

5,000

At least	But less than	Single	Married filing jointly *	Married filing separately	Head of a household
5,000	5,050	503	503	503	503
5,050	5,100	508	508	508	508
5,100	5,150	513	513	513	513
5,150	5,200	518	518	518	518
5,200	5,250	523	523	523	523
5,250	5,300	528	528	528	528
5,300	5,350	533	533	533	533
5,350	5,400	538	538	538	538
5,400	5,450	543	543	543	543
5,450	5,500	548	548	548	548
5,500	5,550	553	553	553	553
5,550	5,600	558	558	558	558
5,600	5,650	563	563	563	563
5,650	5,700	568	568	568	568
5,700	5,750	573	573	573	573
5,750	5,800	578	578	578	578
5,800	5,850	583	583	583	583
5,850	5,900	588	588	588	588
5,900	5,950	593	593	593	593
5,950	6,000	598	598	598	598

6,000

At least	But less than	Single	Married filing jointly *	Married filing separately	Head of a household
6,000	6,050	603	603	603	603
6,050	6,100	608	608	608	608
6,100	6,150	613	613	613	613
6,150	6,200	618	618	618	618
6,200	6,250	623	623	623	623
6,250	6,300	628	628	628	628
6,300	6,350	633	633	633	633
6,350	6,400	638	638	638	638
6,400	6,450	643	643	643	643
6,450	6,500	648	648	648	648
6,500	6,550	653	653	653	653
6,550	6,600	658	658	658	658
6,600	6,650	663	663	663	663
6,650	6,700	668	668	668	668
6,700	6,750	673	673	673	673
6,750	6,800	678	678	678	678
6,800	6,850	683	683	683	683
6,850	6,900	688	688	688	688
6,900	6,950	693	693	693	693
6,950	7,000	698	698	698	698

7,000

At least	But less than	Single	Married filing jointly *	Married filing separately	Head of a household
7,000	7,050	703	703	703	703
7,050	7,100	708	708	708	708
7,100	7,150	713	713	713	713
7,150	7,200	718	718	718	718
7,200	7,250	723	723	723	723
7,250	7,300	728	728	728	728
7,300	7,350	733	733	733	733
7,350	7,400	738	738	738	738
7,400	7,450	743	743	743	743
7,450	7,500	748	748	748	748
7,500	7,550	753	753	753	753
7,550	7,600	758	758	758	758
7,600	7,650	763	763	763	763
7,650	7,700	768	768	768	768
7,700	7,750	773	773	773	773
7,750	7,800	778	778	778	778
7,800	7,850	783	783	783	783
7,850	7,900	788	788	788	788
7,900	7,950	793	793	793	793
7,950	8,000	798	798	798	798

8,000

At least	But less than	Single	Married filing jointly *	Married filing separately	Head of a household
8,000	8,050	803	803	803	803
8,050	8,100	808	808	808	808
8,100	8,150	813	813	813	813
8,150	8,200	818	818	818	818
8,200	8,250	823	823	823	823
8,250	8,300	828	828	828	828
8,300	8,350	833	833	833	833
8,350	8,400	838	838	838	838
8,400	8,450	843	843	843	843
8,450	8,500	848	848	848	848
8,500	8,550	853	853	853	853
8,550	8,600	858	858	858	858
8,600	8,650	863	863	863	863
8,650	8,700	868	868	868	868
8,700	8,750	873	873	873	873
8,750	8,800	878	878	878	878
8,800	8,850	883	883	883	883
8,850	8,900	888	888	888	888
8,900	8,950	893	893	893	893
8,950	9,000	898	898	898	898

9,000

At least	But less than	Single	Married filing jointly *	Married filing separately	Head of a household
9,000	9,050	903	903	903	903
9,050	9,100	908	908	908	908
9,100	9,150	913	913	913	913
9,150	9,200	918	918	918	918
9,200	9,250	923	923	923	923
9,250	9,300	928	928	928	928
9,300	9,350	935	933	935	933
9,350	9,400	943	938	943	938
9,400	9,450	950	943	950	943
9,450	9,500	958	948	958	948
9,500	9,550	965	953	965	953
9,550	9,600	973	958	973	958
9,600	9,650	980	963	980	963
9,650	9,700	988	968	988	968
9,700	9,750	995	973	995	973
9,750	9,800	1,003	978	1,003	978
9,800	9,850	1,010	983	1,010	983
9,850	9,900	1,018	988	1,018	988
9,900	9,950	1,025	993	1,025	993
9,950	10,000	1,033	998	1,033	998

10,000

At least	But less than	Single	Married filing jointly *	Married filing separately	Head of a household
10,000	10,050	1,040	1,003	1,040	1,003
10,050	10,100	1,048	1,008	1,048	1,008
10,100	10,150	1,055	1,013	1,055	1,013
10,150	10,200	1,063	1,018	1,063	1,018
10,200	10,250	1,070	1,023	1,070	1,023
10,250	10,300	1,078	1,028	1,078	1,028
10,300	10,350	1,085	1,033	1,085	1,033
10,350	10,400	1,093	1,038	1,093	1,038
10,400	10,450	1,100	1,043	1,100	1,043
10,450	10,500	1,108	1,048	1,108	1,048
10,500	10,550	1,115	1,053	1,115	1,053
10,550	10,600	1,123	1,058	1,123	1,058
10,600	10,650	1,130	1,063	1,130	1,063
10,650	10,700	1,138	1,068	1,138	1,068
10,700	10,750	1,145	1,073	1,145	1,073
10,750	10,800	1,153	1,078	1,153	1,078
10,800	10,850	1,160	1,083	1,160	1,083
10,850	10,900	1,168	1,088	1,168	1,088
10,900	10,950	1,175	1,093	1,175	1,093
10,950	11,000	1,183	1,098	1,183	1,098

11,000

At least	But less than	Single	Married filing jointly *	Married filing separately	Head of a household
11,000	11,050	1,190	1,103	1,190	1,103
11,050	11,100	1,198	1,108	1,198	1,108
11,100	11,150	1,205	1,113	1,205	1,113
11,150	11,200	1,213	1,118	1,213	1,118
11,200	11,250	1,220	1,123	1,220	1,123
11,250	11,300	1,228	1,128	1,228	1,128
11,300	11,350	1,235	1,133	1,235	1,133
11,350	11,400	1,243	1,138	1,243	1,138
11,400	11,450	1,250	1,143	1,250	1,143
11,450	11,500	1,258	1,148	1,258	1,148
11,500	11,550	1,265	1,153	1,265	1,153
11,550	11,600	1,273	1,158	1,273	1,158
11,600	11,650	1,280	1,163	1,280	1,163
11,650	11,700	1,288	1,168	1,288	1,168
11,700	11,750	1,295	1,173	1,295	1,173
11,750	11,800	1,303	1,178	1,303	1,178
11,800	11,850	1,310	1,183	1,310	1,183
11,850	11,900	1,318	1,188	1,318	1,188
11,900	11,950	1,325	1,193	1,325	1,193
11,950	12,000	1,333	1,198	1,333	1,198

12,000

At least	But less than	Single	Married filing jointly *	Married filing separately	Head of a household
12,000	12,050	1,340	1,203	1,340	1,203
12,050	12,100	1,348	1,208	1,348	1,208
12,100	12,150	1,355	1,213	1,355	1,213
12,150	12,200	1,363	1,218	1,363	1,218
12,200	12,250	1,370	1,223	1,370	1,223
12,250	12,300	1,378	1,228	1,378	1,228
12,300	12,350	1,385	1,233	1,385	1,233
12,350	12,400	1,393	1,238	1,393	1,238
12,400	12,450	1,400	1,243	1,400	1,243
12,450	12,500	1,408	1,248	1,408	1,248
12,500	12,550	1,415	1,253	1,415	1,253
12,550	12,600	1,423	1,258	1,423	1,258
12,600	12,650	1,430	1,263	1,430	1,263
12,650	12,700	1,438	1,268	1,438	1,268
12,700	12,750	1,445	1,273	1,445	1,273
12,750	12,800	1,453	1,278	1,453	1,278
12,800	12,850	1,460	1,283	1,460	1,283
12,850	12,900	1,468	1,288	1,468	1,288
12,900	12,950	1,475	1,293	1,475	1,293
12,950	13,000	1,483	1,298	1,483	1,298

13,000

At least	But less than	Single	Married filing jointly *	Married filing separately	Head of a household
13,000	13,050	1,490	1,303	1,490	1,303
13,050	13,100	1,498	1,308	1,498	1,308
13,100	13,150	1,505	1,313	1,505	1,313
13,150	13,200	1,513	1,318	1,513	1,318
13,200	13,250	1,520	1,323	1,520	1,323
13,250	13,300	1,528	1,328	1,528	1,329
13,300	13,350	1,535	1,333	1,535	1,336
13,350	13,400	1,543	1,338	1,543	1,344
13,400	13,450	1,550	1,343	1,550	1,351
13,450	13,500	1,558	1,348	1,558	1,359
13,500	13,550	1,565	1,353	1,565	1,366
13,550	13,600	1,573	1,358	1,573	1,374
13,600	13,650	1,580	1,363	1,580	1,381
13,650	13,700	1,588	1,368	1,588	1,389
13,700	13,750	1,595	1,373	1,595	1,396
13,750	13,800	1,603	1,378	1,603	1,404
13,800	13,850	1,610	1,383	1,610	1,411
13,850	13,900	1,618	1,388	1,618	1,419
13,900	13,950	1,625	1,393	1,625	1,426
13,950	14,000	1,633	1,398	1,633	1,434

14,000

At least	But less than	Single	Married filing jointly *	Married filing separately	Head of a household
14,000	14,050	1,640	1,403	1,640	1,441
14,050	14,100	1,648	1,408	1,648	1,449
14,100	14,150	1,655	1,413	1,655	1,456
14,150	14,200	1,663	1,418	1,663	1,464
14,200	14,250	1,670	1,423	1,670	1,471
14,250	14,300	1,678	1,428	1,678	1,479
14,300	14,350	1,685	1,433	1,685	1,486
14,350	14,400	1,693	1,438	1,693	1,494
14,400	14,450	1,700	1,443	1,700	1,501
14,450	14,500	1,708	1,448	1,708	1,509
14,500	14,550	1,715	1,453	1,715	1,516
14,550	14,600	1,723	1,458	1,723	1,524
14,600	14,650	1,730	1,463	1,730	1,531
14,650	14,700	1,738	1,468	1,738	1,539
14,700	14,750	1,745	1,473	1,745	1,546
14,750	14,800	1,753	1,478	1,753	1,554
14,800	14,850	1,760	1,483	1,760	1,561
14,850	14,900	1,768	1,488	1,768	1,569
14,900	14,950	1,775	1,493	1,775	1,576
14,950	15,000	1,783	1,498	1,783	1,584

15,000

At least	But less than	Single	Married filing jointly *	Married filing separately	Head of a household
15,000	15,050	1,790	1,503	1,790	1,591
15,050	15,100	1,798	1,508	1,798	1,599
15,100	15,150	1,805	1,513	1,805	1,606
15,150	15,200	1,813	1,518	1,813	1,614
15,200	15,250	1,820	1,523	1,820	1,621
15,250	15,300	1,828	1,528	1,828	1,629
15,300	15,350	1,835	1,533	1,835	1,636
15,350	15,400	1,843	1,538	1,843	1,644
15,400	15,450	1,850	1,543	1,850	1,651
15,450	15,500	1,858	1,548	1,858	1,659
15,500	15,550	1,865	1,553	1,865	1,666
15,550	15,600	1,873	1,558	1,873	1,674
15,600	15,650	1,880	1,563	1,880	1,681
15,650	15,700	1,888	1,568	1,888	1,689
15,700	15,750	1,895	1,573	1,895	1,696
15,750	15,800	1,903	1,578	1,903	1,704
15,800	15,850	1,910	1,583	1,910	1,711
15,850	15,900	1,918	1,588	1,918	1,719
15,900	15,950	1,925	1,593	1,925	1,726
15,950	16,000	1,933	1,598	1,933	1,734

16,000

At least	But less than	Single	Married filing jointly *	Married filing separately	Head of a household
16,000	16,050	1,940	1,603	1,940	1,741
16,050	16,100	1,948	1,608	1,948	1,749
16,100	16,150	1,955	1,613	1,955	1,756
16,150	16,200	1,963	1,618	1,963	1,764
16,200	16,250	1,970	1,623	1,970	1,771
16,250	16,300	1,978	1,628	1,978	1,779
16,300	16,350	1,985	1,633	1,985	1,786
16,350	16,400	1,993	1,638	1,993	1,794
16,400	16,450	2,000	1,643	2,000	1,801
16,450	16,500	2,008	1,648	2,008	1,809
16,500	16,550	2,015	1,653	2,015	1,816
16,550	16,600	2,023	1,658	2,023	1,824
16,600	16,650	2,030	1,663	2,030	1,831
16,650	16,700	2,038	1,668	2,038	1,839
16,700	16,750	2,045	1,673	2,045	1,846
16,750	16,800	2,053	1,678	2,053	1,854
16,800	16,850	2,060	1,683	2,060	1,861
16,850	16,900	2,068	1,688	2,068	1,869
16,900	16,950	2,075	1,693	2,075	1,876
16,950	17,000	2,083	1,698	2,083	1,884

17,000

At least	But less than	Single	Married filing jointly *	Married filing separately	Head of a household
17,000	17,050	2,090	1,703	2,090	1,891
17,050	17,100	2,098	1,708	2,098	1,899
17,100	17,150	2,105	1,713	2,105	1,906
17,150	17,200	2,113	1,718	2,113	1,914
17,200	17,250	2,120	1,723	2,120	1,921
17,250	17,300	2,128	1,728	2,128	1,929
17,300	17,350	2,135	1,733	2,135	1,936
17,350	17,400	2,143	1,738	2,143	1,944
17,400	17,450	2,150	1,743	2,150	1,951
17,450	17,500	2,158	1,748	2,158	1,959
17,500	17,550	2,165	1,753	2,165	1,966
17,550	17,600	2,173	1,758	2,173	1,974
17,600	17,650	2,180	1,763	2,180	1,981
17,650	17,700	2,188	1,768	2,188	1,989
17,700	17,750	2,195	1,773	2,195	1,996
17,750	17,800	2,203	1,778	2,203	2,004
17,800	17,850	2,210	1,783	2,210	2,011
17,850	17,900	2,218	1,788	2,218	2,019
17,900	17,950	2,225	1,793	2,225	2,026
17,950	18,000	2,233	1,798	2,233	2,034

18,000

At least	But less than	Single	Married filing jointly *	Married filing separately	Head of a household
18,000	18,050	2,240	1,803	2,240	2,041
18,050	18,100	2,248	1,808	2,248	2,049
18,100	18,150	2,255	1,813	2,255	2,056
18,150	18,200	2,263	1,818	2,263	2,064
18,200	18,250	2,270	1,823	2,270	2,071
18,250	18,300	2,278	1,828	2,278	2,079
18,300	18,350	2,285	1,833	2,285	2,086
18,350	18,400	2,293	1,838	2,293	2,094
18,400	18,450	2,300	1,843	2,300	2,101
18,450	18,500	2,308	1,848	2,308	2,109
18,500	18,550	2,315	1,853	2,315	2,116
18,550	18,600	2,323	1,859	2,323	2,124
18,600	18,650	2,330	1,866	2,330	2,131
18,650	18,700	2,338	1,874	2,338	2,139
18,700	18,750	2,345	1,881	2,345	2,146
18,750	18,800	2,353	1,889	2,353	2,154
18,800	18,850	2,360	1,896	2,360	2,161
18,850	18,900	2,368	1,904	2,368	2,169
18,900	18,950	2,375	1,911	2,375	2,176
18,950	19,000	2,383	1,919	2,383	2,184

19,000

At least	But less than	Single	Married filing jointly *	Married filing separately	Head of a household
19,000	19,050	2,390	1,926	2,390	2,191
19,050	19,100	2,398	1,934	2,398	2,199
19,100	19,150	2,405	1,941	2,405	2,206
19,150	19,200	2,413	1,949	2,413	2,214
19,200	19,250	2,420	1,956	2,420	2,221
19,250	19,300	2,428	1,964	2,428	2,229
19,300	19,350	2,435	1,971	2,435	2,236
19,350	19,400	2,443	1,979	2,443	2,244
19,400	19,450	2,450	1,986	2,450	2,251
19,450	19,500	2,458	1,994	2,458	2,259
19,500	19,550	2,465	2,001	2,465	2,266
19,550	19,600	2,473	2,009	2,473	2,274
19,600	19,650	2,480	2,016	2,480	2,281
19,650	19,700	2,488	2,024	2,488	2,289
19,700	19,750	2,495	2,031	2,495	2,296
19,750	19,800	2,503	2,039	2,503	2,304
19,800	19,850	2,510	2,046	2,510	2,311
19,850	19,900	2,518	2,054	2,518	2,319
19,900	19,950	2,525	2,061	2,525	2,326
19,950	20,000	2,533	2,069	2,533	2,334

20,000

At least	But less than	Single	Married filing jointly *	Married filing separately	Head of a household
20,000	20,050	2,540	2,076	2,540	2,341
20,050	20,100	2,548	2,084	2,548	2,349
20,100	20,150	2,555	2,091	2,555	2,356
20,150	20,200	2,563	2,099	2,563	2,364
20,200	20,250	2,570	2,106	2,570	2,371
20,250	20,300	2,578	2,114	2,578	2,379
20,300	20,350	2,585	2,121	2,585	2,386
20,350	20,400	2,593	2,129	2,593	2,394
20,400	20,450	2,600	2,136	2,600	2,401
20,450	20,500	2,608	2,144	2,608	2,409
20,500	20,550	2,615	2,151	2,615	2,416
20,550	20,600	2,623	2,159	2,623	2,424
20,600	20,650	2,630	2,166	2,630	2,431
20,650	20,700	2,638	2,174	2,638	2,439
20,700	20,750	2,645	2,181	2,645	2,446
20,750	20,800	2,653	2,189	2,653	2,454
20,800	20,850	2,660	2,196	2,660	2,461
20,850	20,900	2,668	2,204	2,668	2,469
20,900	20,950	2,675	2,211	2,675	2,476
20,950	21,000	2,683	2,219	2,683	2,484

21,000

At least	But less than	Single	Married filing jointly *	Married filing separately	Head of a household
21,000	21,050	2,690	2,226	2,690	2,491
21,050	21,100	2,698	2,234	2,698	2,499
21,100	21,150	2,705	2,241	2,705	2,506
21,150	21,200	2,713	2,249	2,713	2,514
21,200	21,250	2,720	2,256	2,720	2,521
21,250	21,300	2,728	2,264	2,728	2,529
21,300	21,350	2,735	2,271	2,735	2,536
21,350	21,400	2,743	2,279	2,743	2,544
21,400	21,450	2,750	2,286	2,750	2,551
21,450	21,500	2,758	2,294	2,758	2,559
21,500	21,550	2,765	2,301	2,765	2,566
21,550	21,600	2,773	2,309	2,773	2,574
21,600	21,650	2,780	2,316	2,780	2,581
21,650	21,700	2,788	2,324	2,788	2,589
21,700	21,750	2,795	2,331	2,795	2,596
21,750	21,800	2,803	2,339	2,803	2,604
21,800	21,850	2,810	2,346	2,810	2,611
21,850	21,900	2,818	2,354	2,818	2,619
21,900	21,950	2,825	2,361	2,825	2,626
21,950	22,000	2,833	2,369	2,833	2,634

22,000

At least	But less than	Single	Married filing jointly *	Married filing separately	Head of a household
22,000	22,050	2,840	2,376	2,840	2,641
22,050	22,100	2,848	2,384	2,848	2,649
22,100	22,150	2,855	2,391	2,855	2,656
22,150	22,200	2,863	2,399	2,863	2,664
22,200	22,250	2,870	2,406	2,870	2,671
22,250	22,300	2,878	2,414	2,878	2,679
22,300	22,350	2,885	2,421	2,885	2,686
22,350	22,400	2,893	2,429	2,893	2,694
22,400	22,450	2,900	2,436	2,900	2,701
22,450	22,500	2,908	2,444	2,908	2,709
22,500	22,550	2,915	2,451	2,915	2,716
22,550	22,600	2,923	2,459	2,923	2,724
22,600	22,650	2,930	2,466	2,930	2,731
22,650	22,700	2,938	2,474	2,938	2,739
22,700	22,750	2,945	2,481	2,945	2,746
22,750	22,800	2,953	2,489	2,953	2,754
22,800	22,850	2,960	2,496	2,960	2,761
22,850	22,900	2,968	2,504	2,968	2,769
22,900	22,950	2,975	2,511	2,975	2,776
22,950	23,000	2,983	2,519	2,983	2,784

23,000

At least	But less than	Single	Married filing jointly *	Married filing separately	Head of a household
23,000	23,050	2,990	2,526	2,990	2,791
23,050	23,100	2,998	2,534	2,998	2,799
23,100	23,150	3,005	2,541	3,005	2,806
23,150	23,200	3,013	2,549	3,013	2,814
23,200	23,250	3,020	2,556	3,020	2,821
23,250	23,300	3,028	2,564	3,028	2,829
23,300	23,350	3,035	2,571	3,035	2,836
23,350	23,400	3,043	2,579	3,043	2,844
23,400	23,450	3,050	2,586	3,050	2,851
23,450	23,500	3,058	2,594	3,058	2,859
23,500	23,550	3,065	2,601	3,065	2,866
23,550	23,600	3,073	2,609	3,073	2,874
23,600	23,650	3,080	2,616	3,080	2,881
23,650	23,700	3,088	2,624	3,088	2,889
23,700	23,750	3,095	2,631	3,095	2,896
23,750	23,800	3,103	2,639	3,103	2,904
23,800	23,850	3,110	2,646	3,110	2,911
23,850	23,900	3,118	2,654	3,118	2,919
23,900	23,950	3,125	2,661	3,125	2,926
23,950	24,000	3,133	2,669	3,133	2,934

24,000

At least	But less than	Single	Married filing jointly *	Married filing separately	Head of a household
24,000	24,050	3,140	2,676	3,140	2,941
24,050	24,100	3,148	2,684	3,148	2,949
24,100	24,150	3,155	2,691	3,155	2,956
24,150	24,200	3,163	2,699	3,163	2,964
24,200	24,250	3,170	2,706	3,170	2,971
24,250	24,300	3,178	2,714	3,178	2,979
24,300	24,350	3,185	2,721	3,185	2,986
24,350	24,400	3,193	2,729	3,193	2,994
24,400	24,450	3,200	2,736	3,200	3,001
24,450	24,500	3,208	2,744	3,208	3,009
24,500	24,550	3,215	2,751	3,215	3,016
24,550	24,600	3,223	2,759	3,223	3,024
24,600	24,650	3,230	2,766	3,230	3,031
24,650	24,700	3,238	2,774	3,238	3,039
24,700	24,750	3,245	2,781	3,245	3,046
24,750	24,800	3,253	2,789	3,253	3,054
24,800	24,850	3,260	2,796	3,260	3,061
24,850	24,900	3,268	2,804	3,268	3,069
24,900	24,950	3,275	2,811	3,275	3,076
24,950	25,000	3,283	2,819	3,283	3,084

25,000

At least	But less than	Single	Married filing jointly *	Married filing separately	Head of a household
25,000	25,050	3,290	2,826	3,290	3,091
25,050	25,100	3,298	2,834	3,298	3,099
25,100	25,150	3,305	2,841	3,305	3,106
25,150	25,200	3,313	2,849	3,313	3,114
25,200	25,250	3,320	2,856	3,320	3,121
25,250	25,300	3,328	2,864	3,328	3,129
25,300	25,350	3,335	2,871	3,335	3,136
25,350	25,400	3,343	2,879	3,343	3,144
25,400	25,450	3,350	2,886	3,350	3,151
25,450	25,500	3,358	2,894	3,358	3,159
25,500	25,550	3,365	2,901	3,365	3,166
25,550	25,600	3,373	2,909	3,373	3,174
25,600	25,650	3,380	2,916	3,380	3,181
25,650	25,700	3,388	2,924	3,388	3,189
25,700	25,750	3,395	2,931	3,395	3,196
25,750	25,800	3,403	2,939	3,403	3,204
25,800	25,850	3,410	2,946	3,410	3,211
25,850	25,900	3,418	2,954	3,418	3,219
25,900	25,950	3,425	2,961	3,425	3,226
25,950	26,000	3,433	2,969	3,433	3,234

26,000

At least	But less than	Single	Married filing jointly *	Married filing separately	Head of a household
26,000	26,050	3,440	2,976	3,440	3,241
26,050	26,100	3,448	2,984	3,448	3,249
26,100	26,150	3,455	2,991	3,455	3,256
26,150	26,200	3,463	2,999	3,463	3,264
26,200	26,250	3,470	3,006	3,470	3,271
26,250	26,300	3,478	3,014	3,478	3,279
26,300	26,350	3,485	3,021	3,485	3,286
26,350	26,400	3,493	3,029	3,493	3,294
26,400	26,450	3,500	3,036	3,500	3,301
26,450	26,500	3,508	3,044	3,508	3,309
26,500	26,550	3,515	3,051	3,515	3,316
26,550	26,600	3,523	3,059	3,523	3,324
26,600	26,650	3,530	3,066	3,530	3,331
26,650	26,700	3,538	3,074	3,538	3,339
26,700	26,750	3,545	3,081	3,545	3,346
26,750	26,800	3,553	3,089	3,553	3,354
26,800	26,850	3,560	3,096	3,560	3,361
26,850	26,900	3,568	3,104	3,568	3,369
26,900	26,950	3,575	3,111	3,575	3,376
26,950	27,000	3,583	3,119	3,583	3,384

27,000

At least	But less than	Single	Married filing jointly *	Married filing separately	Head of a household
27,000	27,050	3,590	3,126	3,590	3,391
27,050	27,100	3,598	3,134	3,598	3,399
27,100	27,150	3,605	3,141	3,605	3,406
27,150	27,200	3,613	3,149	3,613	3,414
27,200	27,250	3,620	3,156	3,620	3,421
27,250	27,300	3,628	3,164	3,628	3,429
27,300	27,350	3,635	3,171	3,635	3,436
27,350	27,400	3,643	3,179	3,643	3,444
27,400	27,450	3,650	3,186	3,650	3,451
27,450	27,500	3,658	3,194	3,658	3,459
27,500	27,550	3,665	3,201	3,665	3,466
27,550	27,600	3,673	3,209	3,673	3,474
27,600	27,650	3,680	3,216	3,680	3,481
27,650	27,700	3,688	3,224	3,688	3,489
27,700	27,750	3,695	3,231	3,695	3,496
27,750	27,800	3,703	3,239	3,703	3,504
27,800	27,850	3,710	3,246	3,710	3,511
27,850	27,900	3,718	3,254	3,718	3,519
27,900	27,950	3,725	3,261	3,725	3,526
27,950	28,000	3,733	3,269	3,733	3,534

28,000

At least	But less than	Single	Married filing jointly *	Married filing separately	Head of a household
28,000	28,050	3,740	3,276	3,740	3,541
28,050	28,100	3,748	3,284	3,748	3,549
28,100	28,150	3,755	3,291	3,755	3,556
28,150	28,200	3,763	3,299	3,763	3,564
28,200	28,250	3,770	3,306	3,770	3,571
28,250	28,300	3,778	3,314	3,778	3,579
28,300	28,350	3,785	3,321	3,785	3,586
28,350	28,400	3,793	3,329	3,793	3,594
28,400	28,450	3,800	3,336	3,800	3,601
28,450	28,500	3,808	3,344	3,808	3,609
28,500	28,550	3,815	3,351	3,815	3,616
28,550	28,600	3,823	3,359	3,823	3,624
28,600	28,650	3,830	3,366	3,830	3,631
28,650	28,700	3,838	3,374	3,838	3,639
28,700	28,750	3,845	3,381	3,845	3,646
28,750	28,800	3,853	3,389	3,853	3,654
28,800	28,850	3,860	3,396	3,860	3,661
28,850	28,900	3,868	3,404	3,868	3,669
28,900	28,950	3,875	3,411	3,875	3,676
28,950	29,000	3,883	3,419	3,883	3,684

29,000

At least	But less than	Single	Married filing jointly *	Married filing separately	Head of a household
29,000	29,050	3,890	3,426	3,890	3,691
29,050	29,100	3,898	3,434	3,898	3,699
29,100	29,150	3,905	3,441	3,905	3,706
29,150	29,200	3,913	3,449	3,913	3,714
29,200	29,250	3,920	3,456	3,920	3,721
29,250	29,300	3,928	3,464	3,928	3,729
29,300	29,350	3,935	3,471	3,935	3,736
29,350	29,400	3,943	3,479	3,943	3,744
29,400	29,450	3,950	3,486	3,950	3,751
29,450	29,500	3,958	3,494	3,958	3,759
29,500	29,550	3,965	3,501	3,965	3,766
29,550	29,600	3,973	3,509	3,973	3,774
29,600	29,650	3,980	3,516	3,980	3,781
29,650	29,700	3,988	3,524	3,988	3,789
29,700	29,750	3,995	3,531	3,995	3,796
29,750	29,800	4,003	3,539	4,003	3,804
29,800	29,850	4,010	3,546	4,010	3,811
29,850	29,900	4,018	3,554	4,018	3,819
29,900	29,950	4,025	3,561	4,025	3,826
29,950	30,000	4,033	3,569	4,033	3,834

2016 Tax Table — *Continued*

30,000

At least	But less than	Single	Married filing jointly *	Married filing separately	Head of a household
30,000	30,050	4,040	3,576	4,040	3,841
30,050	30,100	4,048	3,584	4,048	3,849
30,100	30,150	4,055	3,591	4,055	3,856
30,150	30,200	4,063	3,599	4,063	3,864
30,200	30,250	4,070	3,606	4,070	3,871
30,250	30,300	4,078	3,614	4,078	3,879
30,300	30,350	4,085	3,621	4,085	3,886
30,350	30,400	4,093	3,629	4,093	3,894
30,400	30,450	4,100	3,636	4,100	3,901
30,450	30,500	4,108	3,644	4,108	3,909
30,500	30,550	4,115	3,651	4,115	3,916
30,550	30,600	4,123	3,659	4,123	3,924
30,600	30,650	4,130	3,666	4,130	3,931
30,650	30,700	4,138	3,674	4,138	3,939
30,700	30,750	4,145	3,681	4,145	3,946
30,750	30,800	4,153	3,689	4,153	3,954
30,800	30,850	4,160	3,696	4,160	3,961
30,850	30,900	4,168	3,704	4,168	3,969
30,900	30,950	4,175	3,711	4,175	3,976
30,950	31,000	4,183	3,719	4,183	3,984

31,000

At least	But less than	Single	Married filing jointly *	Married filing separately	Head of a household
31,000	31,050	4,190	3,726	4,190	3,991
31,050	31,100	4,198	3,734	4,198	3,999
31,100	31,150	4,205	3,741	4,205	4,006
31,150	31,200	4,213	3,749	4,213	4,014
31,200	31,250	4,220	3,756	4,220	4,021
31,250	31,300	4,228	3,764	4,228	4,029
31,300	31,350	4,235	3,771	4,235	4,036
31,350	31,400	4,243	3,779	4,243	4,044
31,400	31,450	4,250	3,786	4,250	4,051
31,450	31,500	4,258	3,794	4,258	4,059
31,500	31,550	4,265	3,801	4,265	4,066
31,550	31,600	4,273	3,809	4,273	4,074
31,600	31,650	4,280	3,816	4,280	4,081
31,650	31,700	4,288	3,824	4,288	4,089
31,700	31,750	4,295	3,831	4,295	4,096
31,750	31,800	4,303	3,839	4,303	4,104
31,800	31,850	4,310	3,846	4,310	4,111
31,850	31,900	4,318	3,854	4,318	4,119
31,900	31,950	4,325	3,861	4,325	4,126
31,950	32,000	4,333	3,869	4,333	4,134

32,000

At least	But less than	Single	Married filing jointly *	Married filing separately	Head of a household
32,000	32,050	4,340	3,876	4,340	4,141
32,050	32,100	4,348	3,884	4,348	4,149
32,100	32,150	4,355	3,891	4,355	4,156
32,150	32,200	4,363	3,899	4,363	4,164
32,200	32,250	4,370	3,906	4,370	4,171
32,250	32,300	4,378	3,914	4,378	4,179
32,300	32,350	4,385	3,921	4,385	4,186
32,350	32,400	4,393	3,929	4,393	4,194
32,400	32,450	4,400	3,936	4,400	4,201
32,450	32,500	4,408	3,944	4,408	4,209
32,500	32,550	4,415	3,951	4,415	4,216
32,550	32,600	4,423	3,959	4,423	4,224
32,600	32,650	4,430	3,966	4,430	4,231
32,650	32,700	4,438	3,974	4,438	4,239
32,700	32,750	4,445	3,981	4,445	4,246
32,750	32,800	4,453	3,989	4,453	4,254
32,800	32,850	4,460	3,996	4,460	4,261
32,850	32,900	4,468	4,004	4,468	4,269
32,900	32,950	4,475	4,011	4,475	4,276
32,950	33,000	4,483	4,019	4,483	4,284

33,000

At least	But less than	Single	Married filing jointly *	Married filing separately	Head of a household
33,000	33,050	4,490	4,026	4,490	4,291
33,050	33,100	4,498	4,034	4,498	4,299
33,100	33,150	4,505	4,041	4,505	4,306
33,150	33,200	4,513	4,049	4,513	4,314
33,200	33,250	4,520	4,056	4,520	4,321
33,250	33,300	4,528	4,064	4,528	4,329
33,300	33,350	4,535	4,071	4,535	4,336
33,350	33,400	4,543	4,079	4,543	4,344
33,400	33,450	4,550	4,086	4,550	4,351
33,450	33,500	4,558	4,094	4,558	4,359
33,500	33,550	4,565	4,101	4,565	4,366
33,550	33,600	4,573	4,109	4,573	4,374
33,600	33,650	4,580	4,116	4,580	4,381
33,650	33,700	4,588	4,124	4,588	4,389
33,700	33,750	4,595	4,131	4,595	4,396
33,750	33,800	4,603	4,139	4,603	4,404
33,800	33,850	4,610	4,146	4,610	4,411
33,850	33,900	4,618	4,154	4,618	4,419
33,900	33,950	4,625	4,161	4,625	4,426
33,950	34,000	4,633	4,169	4,633	4,434

34,000

At least	But less than	Single	Married filing jointly *	Married filing separately	Head of a household
34,000	34,050	4,640	4,176	4,640	4,441
34,050	34,100	4,648	4,184	4,648	4,449
34,100	34,150	4,655	4,191	4,655	4,456
34,150	34,200	4,663	4,199	4,663	4,464
34,200	34,250	4,670	4,206	4,670	4,471
34,250	34,300	4,678	4,214	4,678	4,479
34,300	34,350	4,685	4,221	4,685	4,486
34,350	34,400	4,693	4,229	4,693	4,494
34,400	34,450	4,700	4,236	4,700	4,501
34,450	34,500	4,708	4,244	4,708	4,509
34,500	34,550	4,715	4,251	4,715	4,516
34,550	34,600	4,723	4,259	4,723	4,524
34,600	34,650	4,730	4,266	4,730	4,531
34,650	34,700	4,738	4,274	4,738	4,539
34,700	34,750	4,745	4,281	4,745	4,546
34,750	34,800	4,753	4,289	4,753	4,554
34,800	34,850	4,760	4,296	4,760	4,561
34,850	34,900	4,768	4,304	4,768	4,569
34,900	34,950	4,775	4,311	4,775	4,576
34,950	35,000	4,783	4,319	4,783	4,584

35,000

At least	But less than	Single	Married filing jointly *	Married filing separately	Head of a household
35,000	35,050	4,790	4,326	4,790	4,591
35,050	35,100	4,798	4,334	4,798	4,599
35,100	35,150	4,805	4,341	4,805	4,606
35,150	35,200	4,813	4,349	4,813	4,614
35,200	35,250	4,820	4,356	4,820	4,621
35,250	35,300	4,828	4,364	4,828	4,629
35,300	35,350	4,835	4,371	4,835	4,636
35,350	35,400	4,843	4,379	4,843	4,644
35,400	35,450	4,850	4,386	4,850	4,651
35,450	35,500	4,858	4,394	4,858	4,659
35,500	35,550	4,865	4,401	4,865	4,666
35,550	35,600	4,873	4,409	4,873	4,674
35,600	35,650	4,880	4,416	4,880	4,681
35,650	35,700	4,888	4,424	4,888	4,689
35,700	35,750	4,895	4,431	4,895	4,696
35,750	35,800	4,903	4,439	4,903	4,704
35,800	35,850	4,910	4,446	4,910	4,711
35,850	35,900	4,918	4,454	4,918	4,719
35,900	35,950	4,925	4,461	4,925	4,726
35,950	36,000	4,933	4,469	4,933	4,734

36,000

At least	But less than	Single	Married filing jointly *	Married filing separately	Head of a household
36,000	36,050	4,940	4,476	4,940	4,741
36,050	36,100	4,948	4,484	4,948	4,749
36,100	36,150	4,955	4,491	4,955	4,756
36,150	36,200	4,963	4,499	4,963	4,764
36,200	36,250	4,970	4,506	4,970	4,771
36,250	36,300	4,978	4,514	4,978	4,779
36,300	36,350	4,985	4,521	4,985	4,786
36,350	36,400	4,993	4,529	4,993	4,794
36,400	36,450	5,000	4,536	5,000	4,801
36,450	36,500	5,008	4,544	5,008	4,809
36,500	36,550	5,015	4,551	5,015	4,816
36,550	36,600	5,023	4,559	5,023	4,824
36,600	36,650	5,030	4,566	5,030	4,831
36,650	36,700	5,038	4,574	5,038	4,839
36,700	36,750	5,045	4,581	5,045	4,846
36,750	36,800	5,053	4,589	5,053	4,854
36,800	36,850	5,060	4,596	5,060	4,861
36,850	36,900	5,068	4,604	5,068	4,869
36,900	36,950	5,075	4,611	5,075	4,876
36,950	37,000	5,083	4,619	5,083	4,884

37,000

At least	But less than	Single	Married filing jointly *	Married filing separately	Head of a household
37,000	37,050	5,090	4,626	5,090	4,891
37,050	37,100	5,098	4,634	5,098	4,899
37,100	37,150	5,105	4,641	5,105	4,906
37,150	37,200	5,113	4,649	5,113	4,914
37,200	37,250	5,120	4,656	5,120	4,921
37,250	37,300	5,128	4,664	5,128	4,929
37,300	37,350	5,135	4,671	5,135	4,936
37,350	37,400	5,143	4,679	5,143	4,944
37,400	37,450	5,150	4,686	5,150	4,951
37,450	37,500	5,158	4,694	5,158	4,959
37,500	37,550	5,165	4,701	5,165	4,966
37,550	37,600	5,173	4,709	5,173	4,974
37,600	37,650	5,180	4,716	5,180	4,981
37,650	37,700	5,190	4,724	5,190	4,989
37,700	37,750	5,203	4,731	5,203	4,996
37,750	37,800	5,215	4,739	5,215	5,004
37,800	37,850	5,228	4,746	5,228	5,011
37,850	37,900	5,240	4,754	5,240	5,019
37,900	37,950	5,253	4,761	5,253	5,026
37,950	38,000	5,265	4,769	5,265	5,034

38,000

At least	But less than	Single	Married filing jointly *	Married filing separately	Head of a household
38,000	38,050	5,278	4,776	5,278	5,041
38,050	38,100	5,290	4,784	5,290	5,049
38,100	38,150	5,303	4,791	5,303	5,056
38,150	38,200	5,315	4,799	5,315	5,064
38,200	38,250	5,328	4,806	5,328	5,071
38,250	38,300	5,340	4,814	5,340	5,079
38,300	38,350	5,353	4,821	5,353	5,086
38,350	38,400	5,365	4,829	5,365	5,094
38,400	38,450	5,378	4,836	5,378	5,101
38,450	38,500	5,390	4,844	5,390	5,109
38,500	38,550	5,403	4,851	5,403	5,116
38,550	38,600	5,415	4,859	5,415	5,124
38,600	38,650	5,428	4,866	5,428	5,131
38,650	38,700	5,440	4,874	5,440	5,139
38,700	38,750	5,453	4,881	5,453	5,146
38,750	38,800	5,465	4,889	5,465	5,154
38,800	38,850	5,478	4,896	5,478	5,161
38,850	38,900	5,490	4,904	5,490	5,169
38,900	38,950	5,503	4,911	5,503	5,176
38,950	39,000	5,515	4,919	5,515	5,184

39,000

At least	But less than	Single	Married filing jointly *	Married filing separately	Head of a household
39,000	39,050	5,528	4,926	5,528	5,191
39,050	39,100	5,540	4,934	5,540	5,199
39,100	39,150	5,553	4,941	5,553	5,206
39,150	39,200	5,565	4,949	5,565	5,214
39,200	39,250	5,578	4,956	5,578	5,221
39,250	39,300	5,590	4,964	5,590	5,229
39,300	39,350	5,603	4,971	5,603	5,236
39,350	39,400	5,615	4,979	5,615	5,244
39,400	39,450	5,628	4,986	5,628	5,251
39,450	39,500	5,640	4,994	5,640	5,259
39,500	39,550	5,653	5,001	5,653	5,266
39,550	39,600	5,665	5,009	5,665	5,274
39,600	39,650	5,678	5,016	5,678	5,281
39,650	39,700	5,690	5,024	5,690	5,289
39,700	39,750	5,703	5,031	5,703	5,296
39,750	39,800	5,715	5,039	5,715	5,304
39,800	39,850	5,728	5,046	5,728	5,311
39,850	39,900	5,740	5,054	5,740	5,319
39,900	39,950	5,753	5,061	5,753	5,326
39,950	40,000	5,765	5,069	5,765	5,334

40,000

At least	But less than	Single	Married filing jointly *	Married filing separately	Head of a household
40,000	40,050	5,778	5,076	5,778	5,341
40,050	40,100	5,790	5,084	5,790	5,349
40,100	40,150	5,803	5,091	5,803	5,356
40,150	40,200	5,815	5,099	5,815	5,364
40,200	40,250	5,828	5,106	5,828	5,371
40,250	40,300	5,840	5,114	5,840	5,379
40,300	40,350	5,853	5,121	5,853	5,386
40,350	40,400	5,865	5,129	5,865	5,394
40,400	40,450	5,878	5,136	5,878	5,401
40,450	40,500	5,890	5,144	5,890	5,409
40,500	40,550	5,903	5,151	5,903	5,416
40,550	40,600	5,915	5,159	5,915	5,424
40,600	40,650	5,928	5,166	5,928	5,431
40,650	40,700	5,940	5,174	5,940	5,439
40,700	40,750	5,953	5,181	5,953	5,446
40,750	40,800	5,965	5,189	5,965	5,454
40,800	40,850	5,978	5,196	5,978	5,461
40,850	40,900	5,990	5,204	5,990	5,469
40,900	40,950	6,003	5,211	6,003	5,476
40,950	41,000	6,015	5,219	6,015	5,484

41,000

At least	But less than	Single	Married filing jointly *	Married filing separately	Head of a household
41,000	41,050	6,028	5,226	6,028	5,491
41,050	41,100	6,040	5,234	6,040	5,499
41,100	41,150	6,053	5,241	6,053	5,506
41,150	41,200	6,065	5,249	6,065	5,514
41,200	41,250	6,078	5,256	6,078	5,521
41,250	41,300	6,090	5,264	6,090	5,529
41,300	41,350	6,103	5,271	6,103	5,536
41,350	41,400	6,115	5,279	6,115	5,544
41,400	41,450	6,128	5,286	6,128	5,551
41,450	41,500	6,140	5,294	6,140	5,559
41,500	41,550	6,153	5,301	6,153	5,566
41,550	41,600	6,165	5,309	6,165	5,574
41,600	41,650	6,178	5,316	6,178	5,581
41,650	41,700	6,190	5,324	6,190	5,589
41,700	41,750	6,203	5,331	6,203	5,596
41,750	41,800	6,215	5,339	6,215	5,604
41,800	41,850	6,228	5,346	6,228	5,611
41,850	41,900	6,240	5,354	6,240	5,619
41,900	41,950	6,253	5,361	6,253	5,626
41,950	42,000	6,265	5,369	6,265	5,634

42,000

At least	But less than	Single	Married filing jointly *	Married filing separately	Head of a household
42,000	42,050	6,278	5,376	6,278	5,641
42,050	42,100	6,290	5,384	6,290	5,649
42,100	42,150	6,303	5,391	6,303	5,656
42,150	42,200	6,315	5,399	6,315	5,664
42,200	42,250	6,328	5,406	6,328	5,671
42,250	42,300	6,340	5,414	6,340	5,679
42,300	42,350	6,353	5,421	6,353	5,686
42,350	42,400	6,365	5,429	6,365	5,694
42,400	42,450	6,378	5,436	6,378	5,701
42,450	42,500	6,390	5,444	6,390	5,709
42,500	42,550	6,403	5,451	6,403	5,716
42,550	42,600	6,415	5,459	6,415	5,724
42,600	42,650	6,428	5,466	6,428	5,731
42,650	42,700	6,440	5,474	6,440	5,739
42,700	42,750	6,453	5,481	6,453	5,746
42,750	42,800	6,465	5,489	6,465	5,754
42,800	42,850	6,478	5,496	6,478	5,761
42,850	42,900	6,490	5,504	6,490	5,769
42,900	42,950	6,503	5,511	6,503	5,776
42,950	43,000	6,515	5,519	6,515	5,784

43,000

At least	But less than	Single	Married filing jointly *	Married filing separately	Head of a household
43,000	43,050	6,528	5,526	6,528	5,791
43,050	43,100	6,540	5,534	6,540	5,799
43,100	43,150	6,553	5,541	6,553	5,806
43,150	43,200	6,565	5,549	6,565	5,814
43,200	43,250	6,578	5,556	6,578	5,821
43,250	43,300	6,590	5,564	6,590	5,829
43,300	43,350	6,603	5,571	6,603	5,836
43,350	43,400	6,615	5,579	6,615	5,844
43,400	43,450	6,628	5,586	6,628	5,851
43,450	43,500	6,640	5,594	6,640	5,859
43,500	43,550	6,653	5,601	6,653	5,866
43,550	43,600	6,665	5,609	6,665	5,874
43,600	43,650	6,678	5,616	6,678	5,881
43,650	43,700	6,690	5,624	6,690	5,889
43,700	43,750	6,703	5,631	6,703	5,896
43,750	43,800	6,715	5,639	6,715	5,904
43,800	43,850	6,728	5,646	6,728	5,911
43,850	43,900	6,740	5,654	6,740	5,919
43,900	43,950	6,753	5,661	6,753	5,926
43,950	44,000	6,765	5,669	6,765	5,934

44,000

At least	But less than	Single	Married filing jointly *	Married filing separately	Head of a household
44,000	44,050	6,778	5,676	6,778	5,941
44,050	44,100	6,790	5,684	6,790	5,949
44,100	44,150	6,803	5,691	6,803	5,956
44,150	44,200	6,815	5,699	6,815	5,964
44,200	44,250	6,828	5,706	6,828	5,971
44,250	44,300	6,840	5,714	6,840	5,979
44,300	44,350	6,853	5,721	6,853	5,986
44,350	44,400	6,865	5,729	6,865	5,994
44,400	44,450	6,878	5,736	6,878	6,001
44,450	44,500	6,890	5,744	6,890	6,009
44,500	44,550	6,903	5,751	6,903	6,016
44,550	44,600	6,915	5,759	6,915	6,024
44,600	44,650	6,928	5,766	6,928	6,031
44,650	44,700	6,940	5,774	6,940	6,039
44,700	44,750	6,953	5,781	6,953	6,046
44,750	44,800	6,965	5,789	6,965	6,054
44,800	44,850	6,978	5,796	6,978	6,061
44,850	44,900	6,990	5,804	6,990	6,069
44,900	44,950	7,003	5,811	7,003	6,076
44,950	45,000	7,015	5,819	7,015	6,084

45,000

At least	But less than	Single	Married filing jointly *	Married filing separately	Head of a household
45,000	45,050	7,028	5,826	7,028	6,091
45,050	45,100	7,040	5,834	7,040	6,099
45,100	45,150	7,053	5,841	7,053	6,106
45,150	45,200	7,065	5,849	7,065	6,114
45,200	45,250	7,078	5,856	7,078	6,121
45,250	45,300	7,090	5,864	7,090	6,129
45,300	45,350	7,103	5,871	7,103	6,136
45,350	45,400	7,115	5,879	7,115	6,144
45,400	45,450	7,128	5,886	7,128	6,151
45,450	45,500	7,140	5,894	7,140	6,159
45,500	45,550	7,153	5,901	7,153	6,166
45,550	45,600	7,165	5,909	7,165	6,174
45,600	45,650	7,178	5,916	7,178	6,181
45,650	45,700	7,190	5,924	7,190	6,189
45,700	45,750	7,203	5,931	7,203	6,196
45,750	45,800	7,215	5,939	7,215	6,204
45,800	45,850	7,228	5,946	7,228	6,211
45,850	45,900	7,240	5,954	7,240	6,219
45,900	45,950	7,253	5,961	7,253	6,226
45,950	46,000	7,265	5,969	7,265	6,234

46,000

At least	But less than	Single	Married filing jointly *	Married filing separately	Head of a household
46,000	46,050	7,278	5,976	7,278	6,241
46,050	46,100	7,290	5,984	7,290	6,249
46,100	46,150	7,303	5,991	7,303	6,256
46,150	46,200	7,315	5,999	7,315	6,264
46,200	46,250	7,328	6,006	7,328	6,271
46,250	46,300	7,340	6,014	7,340	6,279
46,300	46,350	7,353	6,021	7,353	6,286
46,350	46,400	7,365	6,029	7,365	6,294
46,400	46,450	7,378	6,036	7,378	6,301
46,450	46,500	7,390	6,044	7,390	6,309
46,500	46,550	7,403	6,051	7,403	6,316
46,550	46,600	7,415	6,059	7,415	6,324
46,600	46,650	7,428	6,066	7,428	6,331
46,650	46,700	7,440	6,074	7,440	6,339
46,700	46,750	7,453	6,081	7,453	6,346
46,750	46,800	7,465	6,089	7,465	6,354
46,800	46,850	7,478	6,096	7,478	6,361
46,850	46,900	7,490	6,104	7,490	6,369
46,900	46,950	7,503	6,111	7,503	6,376
46,950	47,000	7,515	6,119	7,515	6,384

47,000

At least	But less than	Single	Married filing jointly *	Married filing separately	Head of a household
47,000	47,050	7,528	6,126	7,528	6,391
47,050	47,100	7,540	6,134	7,540	6,399
47,100	47,150	7,553	6,141	7,553	6,406
47,150	47,200	7,565	6,149	7,565	6,414
47,200	47,250	7,578	6,156	7,578	6,421
47,250	47,300	7,590	6,164	7,590	6,429
47,300	47,350	7,603	6,171	7,603	6,436
47,350	47,400	7,615	6,179	7,615	6,444
47,400	47,450	7,628	6,186	7,628	6,451
47,450	47,500	7,640	6,194	7,640	6,459
47,500	47,550	7,653	6,201	7,653	6,466
47,550	47,600	7,665	6,209	7,665	6,474
47,600	47,650	7,678	6,216	7,678	6,481
47,650	47,700	7,690	6,224	7,690	6,489
47,700	47,750	7,703	6,231	7,703	6,496
47,750	47,800	7,715	6,239	7,715	6,504
47,800	47,850	7,728	6,246	7,728	6,511
47,850	47,900	7,740	6,254	7,740	6,519
47,900	47,950	7,753	6,261	7,753	6,526
47,950	48,000	7,765	6,269	7,765	6,534

2016 Tax Table — Continued

If line 43 (taxable income) is— At least	But less than	Single	Married filing jointly *	Married filing separately	Head of a household
			Your tax is—		

48,000

At least	But less than	Single	Married filing jointly *	Married filing separately	Head of a household
48,000	48,050	7,778	6,276	7,778	6,541
48,050	48,100	7,790	6,284	7,790	6,549
48,100	48,150	7,803	6,291	7,803	6,556
48,150	48,200	7,815	6,299	7,815	6,564
48,200	48,250	7,828	6,306	7,828	6,571
48,250	48,300	7,840	6,314	7,840	6,579
48,300	48,350	7,853	6,321	7,853	6,586
48,350	48,400	7,865	6,329	7,865	6,594
48,400	48,450	7,878	6,336	7,878	6,601
48,450	48,500	7,890	6,344	7,890	6,609
48,500	48,550	7,903	6,351	7,903	6,616
48,550	48,600	7,915	6,359	7,915	6,624
48,600	48,650	7,928	6,366	7,928	6,631
48,650	48,700	7,940	6,374	7,940	6,639
48,700	48,750	7,953	6,381	7,953	6,646
48,750	48,800	7,965	6,389	7,965	6,654
48,800	48,850	7,978	6,396	7,978	6,661
48,850	48,900	7,990	6,404	7,990	6,669
48,900	48,950	8,003	6,411	8,003	6,676
48,950	49,000	8,015	6,419	8,015	6,684

49,000

At least	But less than	Single	Married filing jointly *	Married filing separately	Head of a household
49,000	49,050	8,028	6,426	8,028	6,691
49,050	49,100	8,040	6,434	8,040	6,699
49,100	49,150	8,053	6,441	8,053	6,706
49,150	49,200	8,065	6,449	8,065	6,714
49,200	49,250	8,078	6,456	8,078	6,721
49,250	49,300	8,090	6,464	8,090	6,729
49,300	49,350	8,103	6,471	8,103	6,736
49,350	49,400	8,115	6,479	8,115	6,744
49,400	49,450	8,128	6,486	8,128	6,751
49,450	49,500	8,140	6,494	8,140	6,759
49,500	49,550	8,153	6,501	8,153	6,766
49,550	49,600	8,165	6,509	8,165	6,774
49,600	49,650	8,178	6,516	8,178	6,781
49,650	49,700	8,190	6,524	8,190	6,789
49,700	49,750	8,203	6,531	8,203	6,796
49,750	49,800	8,215	6,539	8,215	6,804
49,800	49,850	8,228	6,546	8,228	6,811
49,850	49,900	8,240	6,554	8,240	6,819
49,900	49,950	8,253	6,561	8,253	6,826
49,950	50,000	8,265	6,569	8,265	6,834

50,000

At least	But less than	Single	Married filing jointly *	Married filing separately	Head of a household
50,000	50,050	8,278	6,576	8,278	6,841
50,050	50,100	8,290	6,584	8,290	6,849
50,100	50,150	8,303	6,591	8,303	6,856
50,150	50,200	8,315	6,599	8,315	6,864
50,200	50,250	8,328	6,606	8,328	6,871
50,250	50,300	8,340	6,614	8,340	6,879
50,300	50,350	8,353	6,621	8,353	6,886
50,350	50,400	8,365	6,629	8,365	6,894
50,400	50,450	8,378	6,636	8,378	6,904
50,450	50,500	8,390	6,644	8,390	6,916
50,500	50,550	8,403	6,651	8,403	6,929
50,550	50,600	8,415	6,659	8,415	6,941
50,600	50,650	8,428	6,666	8,428	6,954
50,650	50,700	8,440	6,674	8,440	6,966
50,700	50,750	8,453	6,681	8,453	6,979
50,750	50,800	8,465	6,689	8,465	6,991
50,800	50,850	8,478	6,696	8,478	7,004
50,850	50,900	8,490	6,704	8,490	7,016
50,900	50,950	8,503	6,711	8,503	7,029
50,950	51,000	8,515	6,719	8,515	7,041

51,000

At least	But less than	Single	Married filing jointly *	Married filing separately	Head of a household
51,000	51,050	8,528	6,726	8,528	7,054
51,050	51,100	8,540	6,734	8,540	7,066
51,100	51,150	8,553	6,741	8,553	7,079
51,150	51,200	8,565	6,749	8,565	7,091
51,200	51,250	8,578	6,756	8,578	7,104
51,250	51,300	8,590	6,764	8,590	7,116
51,300	51,350	8,603	6,771	8,603	7,129
51,350	51,400	8,615	6,779	8,615	7,141
51,400	51,450	8,628	6,786	8,628	7,154
51,450	51,500	8,640	6,794	8,640	7,166
51,500	51,550	8,653	6,801	8,653	7,179
51,550	51,600	8,665	6,809	8,665	7,191
51,600	51,650	8,678	6,816	8,678	7,204
51,650	51,700	8,690	6,824	8,690	7,216
51,700	51,750	8,703	6,831	8,703	7,229
51,750	51,800	8,715	6,839	8,715	7,241
51,800	51,850	8,728	6,846	8,728	7,254
51,850	51,900	8,740	6,854	8,740	7,266
51,900	51,950	8,753	6,861	8,753	7,279
51,950	52,000	8,765	6,869	8,765	7,291

52,000

At least	But less than	Single	Married filing jointly *	Married filing separately	Head of a household
52,000	52,050	8,778	6,876	8,778	7,304
52,050	52,100	8,790	6,884	8,790	7,316
52,100	52,150	8,803	6,891	8,803	7,329
52,150	52,200	8,815	6,899	8,815	7,341
52,200	52,250	8,828	6,906	8,828	7,354
52,250	52,300	8,840	6,914	8,840	7,366
52,300	52,350	8,853	6,921	8,853	7,379
52,350	52,400	8,865	6,929	8,865	7,391
52,400	52,450	8,878	6,936	8,878	7,404
52,450	52,500	8,890	6,944	8,890	7,416
52,500	52,550	8,903	6,951	8,903	7,429
52,550	52,600	8,915	6,959	8,915	7,441
52,600	52,650	8,928	6,966	8,928	7,454
52,650	52,700	8,940	6,974	8,940	7,466
52,700	52,750	8,953	6,981	8,953	7,479
52,750	52,800	8,965	6,989	8,965	7,491
52,800	52,850	8,978	6,996	8,978	7,504
52,850	52,900	8,990	7,004	8,990	7,516
52,900	52,950	9,003	7,011	9,003	7,529
52,950	53,000	9,015	7,019	9,015	7,541

53,000

At least	But less than	Single	Married filing jointly *	Married filing separately	Head of a household
53,000	53,050	9,028	7,026	9,028	7,554
53,050	53,100	9,040	7,034	9,040	7,566
53,100	53,150	9,053	7,041	9,053	7,579
53,150	53,200	9,065	7,049	9,065	7,591
53,200	53,250	9,078	7,056	9,078	7,604
53,250	53,300	9,090	7,064	9,090	7,616
53,300	53,350	9,103	7,071	9,103	7,629
53,350	53,400	9,115	7,079	9,115	7,641
53,400	53,450	9,128	7,086	9,128	7,654
53,450	53,500	9,140	7,094	9,140	7,666
53,500	53,550	9,153	7,101	9,153	7,679
53,550	53,600	9,165	7,109	9,165	7,691
53,600	53,650	9,178	7,116	9,178	7,704
53,650	53,700	9,190	7,124	9,190	7,716
53,700	53,750	9,203	7,131	9,203	7,729
53,750	53,800	9,215	7,139	9,215	7,741
53,800	53,850	9,228	7,146	9,228	7,754
53,850	53,900	9,240	7,154	9,240	7,766
53,900	53,950	9,253	7,161	9,253	7,779
53,950	54,000	9,265	7,169	9,265	7,791

54,000

At least	But less than	Single	Married filing jointly *	Married filing separately	Head of a household
54,000	54,050	9,278	7,176	9,278	7,804
54,050	54,100	9,290	7,184	9,290	7,816
54,100	54,150	9,303	7,191	9,303	7,829
54,150	54,200	9,315	7,199	9,315	7,841
54,200	54,250	9,328	7,206	9,328	7,854
54,250	54,300	9,340	7,214	9,340	7,866
54,300	54,350	9,353	7,221	9,353	7,879
54,350	54,400	9,365	7,229	9,365	7,891
54,400	54,450	9,378	7,236	9,378	7,904
54,450	54,500	9,390	7,244	9,390	7,916
54,500	54,550	9,403	7,251	9,403	7,929
54,550	54,600	9,415	7,259	9,415	7,941
54,600	54,650	9,428	7,266	9,428	7,954
54,650	54,700	9,440	7,274	9,440	7,966
54,700	54,750	9,453	7,281	9,453	7,979
54,750	54,800	9,465	7,289	9,465	7,991
54,800	54,850	9,478	7,296	9,478	8,004
54,850	54,900	9,490	7,304	9,490	8,016
54,900	54,950	9,503	7,311	9,503	8,029
54,950	55,000	9,515	7,319	9,515	8,041

55,000

At least	But less than	Single	Married filing jointly *	Married filing separately	Head of a household
55,000	55,050	9,528	7,326	9,528	8,054
55,050	55,100	9,540	7,334	9,540	8,066
55,100	55,150	9,553	7,341	9,553	8,079
55,150	55,200	9,565	7,349	9,565	8,091
55,200	55,250	9,578	7,356	9,578	8,104
55,250	55,300	9,590	7,364	9,590	8,116
55,300	55,350	9,603	7,371	9,603	8,129
55,350	55,400	9,615	7,379	9,615	8,141
55,400	55,450	9,628	7,386	9,628	8,154
55,450	55,500	9,640	7,394	9,640	8,166
55,500	55,550	9,653	7,401	9,653	8,179
55,550	55,600	9,665	7,409	9,665	8,191
55,600	55,650	9,678	7,416	9,678	8,204
55,650	55,700	9,690	7,424	9,690	8,216
55,700	55,750	9,703	7,431	9,703	8,229
55,750	55,800	9,715	7,439	9,715	8,241
55,800	55,850	9,728	7,446	9,728	8,254
55,850	55,900	9,740	7,454	9,740	8,266
55,900	55,950	9,753	7,461	9,753	8,279
55,950	56,000	9,765	7,469	9,765	8,291

56,000

At least	But less than	Single	Married filing jointly *	Married filing separately	Head of a household
56,000	56,050	9,778	7,476	9,778	8,304
56,050	56,100	9,790	7,484	9,790	8,316
56,100	56,150	9,803	7,491	9,803	8,329
56,150	56,200	9,815	7,499	9,815	8,341
56,200	56,250	9,828	7,506	9,828	8,354
56,250	56,300	9,840	7,514	9,840	8,366
56,300	56,350	9,853	7,521	9,853	8,379
56,350	56,400	9,865	7,529	9,865	8,391
56,400	56,450	9,878	7,536	9,878	8,404
56,450	56,500	9,890	7,544	9,890	8,416
56,500	56,550	9,903	7,551	9,903	8,429
56,550	56,600	9,915	7,559	9,915	8,441
56,600	56,650	9,928	7,566	9,928	8,454
56,650	56,700	9,940	7,574	9,940	8,466
56,700	56,750	9,953	7,581	9,953	8,479
56,750	56,800	9,965	7,589	9,965	8,491
56,800	56,850	9,978	7,596	9,978	8,504
56,850	56,900	9,990	7,604	9,990	8,516
56,900	56,950	10,003	7,611	10,003	8,529
56,950	57,000	10,015	7,619	10,015	8,541

If line 43 (taxable income) is—		And you are—			
At least	But less than	Single	Married filing jointly *	Married filing separately	Head of a household
		Your tax is—			

57,000

At least	But less than	Single	Married filing jointly *	Married filing separately	Head of a household
57,000	57,050	10,028	7,626	10,028	8,554
57,050	57,100	10,040	7,634	10,040	8,566
57,100	57,150	10,053	7,641	10,053	8,579
57,150	57,200	10,065	7,649	10,065	8,591
57,200	57,250	10,078	7,656	10,078	8,604
57,250	57,300	10,090	7,664	10,090	8,616
57,300	57,350	10,103	7,671	10,103	8,629
57,350	57,400	10,115	7,679	10,115	8,641
57,400	57,450	10,128	7,686	10,128	8,654
57,450	57,500	10,140	7,694	10,140	8,666
57,500	57,550	10,153	7,701	10,153	8,679
57,550	57,600	10,165	7,709	10,165	8,691
57,600	57,650	10,178	7,716	10,178	8,704
57,650	57,700	10,190	7,724	10,190	8,716
57,700	57,750	10,203	7,731	10,203	8,729
57,750	57,800	10,215	7,739	10,215	8,741
57,800	57,850	10,228	7,746	10,228	8,754
57,850	57,900	10,240	7,754	10,240	8,766
57,900	57,950	10,253	7,761	10,253	8,779
57,950	58,000	10,265	7,769	10,265	8,791

58,000

At least	But less than	Single	Married filing jointly *	Married filing separately	Head of a household
58,000	58,050	10,278	7,776	10,278	8,804
58,050	58,100	10,290	7,784	10,290	8,816
58,100	58,150	10,303	7,791	10,303	8,829
58,150	58,200	10,315	7,799	10,315	8,841
58,200	58,250	10,328	7,806	10,328	8,854
58,250	58,300	10,340	7,814	10,340	8,866
58,300	58,350	10,353	7,821	10,353	8,879
58,350	58,400	10,365	7,829	10,365	8,891
58,400	58,450	10,378	7,836	10,378	8,904
58,450	58,500	10,390	7,844	10,390	8,916
58,500	58,550	10,403	7,851	10,403	8,929
58,550	58,600	10,415	7,859	10,415	8,941
58,600	58,650	10,428	7,866	10,428	8,954
58,650	58,700	10,440	7,874	10,440	8,966
58,700	58,750	10,453	7,881	10,453	8,979
58,750	58,800	10,465	7,889	10,465	8,991
58,800	58,850	10,478	7,896	10,478	9,004
58,850	58,900	10,490	7,904	10,490	9,016
58,900	58,950	10,503	7,911	10,503	9,029
58,950	59,000	10,515	7,919	10,515	9,041

59,000

At least	But less than	Single	Married filing jointly *	Married filing separately	Head of a household
59,000	59,050	10,528	7,926	10,528	9,054
59,050	59,100	10,540	7,934	10,540	9,066
59,100	59,150	10,553	7,941	10,553	9,079
59,150	59,200	10,565	7,949	10,565	9,091
59,200	59,250	10,578	7,956	10,578	9,104
59,250	59,300	10,590	7,964	10,590	9,116
59,300	59,350	10,603	7,971	10,603	9,129
59,350	59,400	10,615	7,979	10,615	9,141
59,400	59,450	10,628	7,986	10,628	9,154
59,450	59,500	10,640	7,994	10,640	9,166
59,500	59,550	10,653	8,001	10,653	9,179
59,550	59,600	10,665	8,009	10,665	9,191
59,600	59,650	10,678	8,016	10,678	9,204
59,650	59,700	10,690	8,024	10,690	9,216
59,700	59,750	10,703	8,031	10,703	9,229
59,750	59,800	10,715	8,039	10,715	9,241
59,800	59,850	10,728	8,046	10,728	9,254
59,850	59,900	10,740	8,054	10,740	9,266
59,900	59,950	10,753	8,061	10,753	9,279
59,950	60,000	10,765	8,069	10,765	9,291

60,000

At least	But less than	Single	Married filing jointly *	Married filing separately	Head of a household
60,000	60,050	10,778	8,076	10,778	9,304
60,050	60,100	10,790	8,084	10,790	9,316
60,100	60,150	10,803	8,091	10,803	9,329
60,150	60,200	10,815	8,099	10,815	9,341
60,200	60,250	10,828	8,106	10,828	9,354
60,250	60,300	10,840	8,114	10,840	9,366
60,300	60,350	10,853	8,121	10,853	9,379
60,350	60,400	10,865	8,129	10,865	9,391
60,400	60,450	10,878	8,136	10,878	9,404
60,450	60,500	10,890	8,144	10,890	9,416
60,500	60,550	10,903	8,151	10,903	9,429
60,550	60,600	10,915	8,159	10,915	9,441
60,600	60,650	10,928	8,166	10,928	9,454
60,650	60,700	10,940	8,174	10,940	9,466
60,700	60,750	10,953	8,181	10,953	9,479
60,750	60,800	10,965	8,189	10,965	9,491
60,800	60,850	10,978	8,196	10,978	9,504
60,850	60,900	10,990	8,204	10,990	9,516
60,900	60,950	11,003	8,211	11,003	9,529
60,950	61,000	11,015	8,219	11,015	9,541

61,000

At least	But less than	Single	Married filing jointly *	Married filing separately	Head of a household
61,000	61,050	11,028	8,226	11,028	9,554
61,050	61,100	11,040	8,234	11,040	9,566
61,100	61,150	11,053	8,241	11,053	9,579
61,150	61,200	11,065	8,249	11,065	9,591
61,200	61,250	11,078	8,256	11,078	9,604
61,250	61,300	11,090	8,264	11,090	9,616
61,300	61,350	11,103	8,271	11,103	9,629
61,350	61,400	11,115	8,279	11,115	9,641
61,400	61,450	11,128	8,286	11,128	9,654
61,450	61,500	11,140	8,294	11,140	9,666
61,500	61,550	11,153	8,301	11,153	9,679
61,550	61,600	11,165	8,309	11,165	9,691
61,600	61,650	11,178	8,316	11,178	9,704
61,650	61,700	11,190	8,324	11,190	9,716
61,700	61,750	11,203	8,331	11,203	9,729
61,750	61,800	11,215	8,339	11,215	9,741
61,800	61,850	11,228	8,346	11,228	9,754
61,850	61,900	11,240	8,354	11,240	9,766
61,900	61,950	11,253	8,361	11,253	9,779
61,950	62,000	11,265	8,369	11,265	9,791

62,000

At least	But less than	Single	Married filing jointly *	Married filing separately	Head of a household
62,000	62,050	11,278	8,376	11,278	9,804
62,050	62,100	11,290	8,384	11,290	9,816
62,100	62,150	11,303	8,391	11,303	9,829
62,150	62,200	11,315	8,399	11,315	9,841
62,200	62,250	11,328	8,406	11,328	9,854
62,250	62,300	11,340	8,414	11,340	9,866
62,300	62,350	11,353	8,421	11,353	9,879
62,350	62,400	11,365	8,429	11,365	9,891
62,400	62,450	11,378	8,436	11,378	9,904
62,450	62,500	11,390	8,444	11,390	9,916
62,500	62,550	11,403	8,451	11,403	9,929
62,550	62,600	11,415	8,459	11,415	9,941
62,600	62,650	11,428	8,466	11,428	9,954
62,650	62,700	11,440	8,474	11,440	9,966
62,700	62,750	11,453	8,481	11,453	9,979
62,750	62,800	11,465	8,489	11,465	9,991
62,800	62,850	11,478	8,496	11,478	10,004
62,850	62,900	11,490	8,504	11,490	10,016
62,900	62,950	11,503	8,511	11,503	10,029
62,950	63,000	11,515	8,519	11,515	10,041

63,000

At least	But less than	Single	Married filing jointly *	Married filing separately	Head of a household
63,000	63,050	11,528	8,526	11,528	10,054
63,050	63,100	11,540	8,534	11,540	10,066
63,100	63,150	11,553	8,541	11,553	10,079
63,150	63,200	11,565	8,549	11,565	10,091
63,200	63,250	11,578	8,556	11,578	10,104
63,250	63,300	11,590	8,564	11,590	10,116
63,300	63,350	11,603	8,571	11,603	10,129
63,350	63,400	11,615	8,579	11,615	10,141
63,400	63,450	11,628	8,586	11,628	10,154
63,450	63,500	11,640	8,594	11,640	10,166
63,500	63,550	11,653	8,601	11,653	10,179
63,550	63,600	11,665	8,609	11,665	10,191
63,600	63,650	11,678	8,616	11,678	10,204
63,650	63,700	11,690	8,624	11,690	10,216
63,700	63,750	11,703	8,631	11,703	10,229
63,750	63,800	11,715	8,639	11,715	10,241
63,800	63,850	11,728	8,646	11,728	10,254
63,850	63,900	11,740	8,654	11,740	10,266
63,900	63,950	11,753	8,661	11,753	10,279
63,950	64,000	11,765	8,669	11,765	10,291

64,000

At least	But less than	Single	Married filing jointly *	Married filing separately	Head of a household
64,000	64,050	11,778	8,676	11,778	10,304
64,050	64,100	11,790	8,684	11,790	10,316
64,100	64,150	11,803	8,691	11,803	10,329
64,150	64,200	11,815	8,699	11,815	10,341
64,200	64,250	11,828	8,706	11,828	10,354
64,250	64,300	11,840	8,714	11,840	10,366
64,300	64,350	11,853	8,721	11,853	10,379
64,350	64,400	11,865	8,729	11,865	10,391
64,400	64,450	11,878	8,736	11,878	10,404
64,450	64,500	11,890	8,744	11,890	10,416
64,500	64,550	11,903	8,751	11,903	10,429
64,550	64,600	11,915	8,759	11,915	10,441
64,600	64,650	11,928	8,766	11,928	10,454
64,650	64,700	11,940	8,774	11,940	10,466
64,700	64,750	11,953	8,781	11,953	10,479
64,750	64,800	11,965	8,789	11,965	10,491
64,800	64,850	11,978	8,796	11,978	10,504
64,850	64,900	11,990	8,804	11,990	10,516
64,900	64,950	12,003	8,811	12,003	10,529
64,950	65,000	12,015	8,819	12,015	10,541

65,000

At least	But less than	Single	Married filing jointly *	Married filing separately	Head of a household
65,000	65,050	12,028	8,826	12,028	10,554
65,050	65,100	12,040	8,834	12,040	10,566
65,100	65,150	12,053	8,841	12,053	10,579
65,150	65,200	12,065	8,849	12,065	10,591
65,200	65,250	12,078	8,856	12,078	10,604
65,250	65,300	12,090	8,864	12,090	10,616
65,300	65,350	12,103	8,871	12,103	10,629
65,350	65,400	12,115	8,879	12,115	10,641
65,400	65,450	12,128	8,886	12,128	10,654
65,450	65,500	12,140	8,894	12,140	10,666
65,500	65,550	12,153	8,901	12,153	10,679
65,550	65,600	12,165	8,909	12,165	10,691
65,600	65,650	12,178	8,916	12,178	10,704
65,650	65,700	12,190	8,924	12,190	10,716
65,700	65,750	12,203	8,931	12,203	10,729
65,750	65,800	12,215	8,939	12,215	10,741
65,800	65,850	12,228	8,946	12,228	10,754
65,850	65,900	12,240	8,954	12,240	10,766
65,900	65,950	12,253	8,961	12,253	10,779
65,950	66,000	12,265	8,969	12,265	10,791

2016 Tax Table — *Continued*

If line 43 (taxable income) is—		And you are—			
At least	But less than	Single	Married filing jointly *	Married filing separately	Head of a household
		Your tax is—			

66,000

At least	But less than	Single	MFJ	MFS	HoH
66,000	66,050	12,278	8,976	12,278	10,804
66,050	66,100	12,290	8,984	12,290	10,816
66,100	66,150	12,303	8,991	12,303	10,829
66,150	66,200	12,315	8,999	12,315	10,841
66,200	66,250	12,328	9,006	12,328	10,854
66,250	66,300	12,340	9,014	12,340	10,866
66,300	66,350	12,353	9,021	12,353	10,879
66,350	66,400	12,365	9,029	12,365	10,891
66,400	66,450	12,378	9,036	12,378	10,904
66,450	66,500	12,390	9,044	12,390	10,916
66,500	66,550	12,403	9,051	12,403	10,929
66,550	66,600	12,415	9,059	12,415	10,941
66,600	66,650	12,428	9,066	12,428	10,954
66,650	66,700	12,440	9,074	12,440	10,966
66,700	66,750	12,453	9,081	12,453	10,979
66,750	66,800	12,465	9,089	12,465	10,991
66,800	66,850	12,478	9,096	12,478	11,004
66,850	66,900	12,490	9,104	12,490	11,016
66,900	66,950	12,503	9,111	12,503	11,029
66,950	67,000	12,515	9,119	12,515	11,041

67,000

At least	But less than	Single	MFJ	MFS	HoH
67,000	67,050	12,528	9,126	12,528	11,054
67,050	67,100	12,540	9,134	12,540	11,066
67,100	67,150	12,553	9,141	12,553	11,079
67,150	67,200	12,565	9,149	12,565	11,091
67,200	67,250	12,578	9,156	12,578	11,104
67,250	67,300	12,590	9,164	12,590	11,116
67,300	67,350	12,603	9,171	12,603	11,129
67,350	67,400	12,615	9,179	12,615	11,141
67,400	67,450	12,628	9,186	12,628	11,154
67,450	67,500	12,640	9,194	12,640	11,166
67,500	67,550	12,653	9,201	12,653	11,179
67,550	67,600	12,665	9,209	12,665	11,191
67,600	67,650	12,678	9,216	12,678	11,204
67,650	67,700	12,690	9,224	12,690	11,216
67,700	67,750	12,703	9,231	12,703	11,229
67,750	67,800	12,715	9,239	12,715	11,241
67,800	67,850	12,728	9,246	12,728	11,254
67,850	67,900	12,740	9,254	12,740	11,266
67,900	67,950	12,753	9,261	12,753	11,279
67,950	68,000	12,765	9,269	12,765	11,291

68,000

At least	But less than	Single	MFJ	MFS	HoH
68,000	68,050	12,778	9,276	12,778	11,304
68,050	68,100	12,790	9,284	12,790	11,316
68,100	68,150	12,803	9,291	12,803	11,329
68,150	68,200	12,815	9,299	12,815	11,341
68,200	68,250	12,828	9,306	12,828	11,354
68,250	68,300	12,840	9,314	12,840	11,366
68,300	68,350	12,853	9,321	12,853	11,379
68,350	68,400	12,865	9,329	12,865	11,391
68,400	68,450	12,878	9,336	12,878	11,404
68,450	68,500	12,890	9,344	12,890	11,416
68,500	68,550	12,903	9,351	12,903	11,429
68,550	68,600	12,915	9,359	12,915	11,441
68,600	68,650	12,928	9,366	12,928	11,454
68,650	68,700	12,940	9,374	12,940	11,466
68,700	68,750	12,953	9,381	12,953	11,479
68,750	68,800	12,965	9,389	12,965	11,491
68,800	68,850	12,978	9,396	12,978	11,504
68,850	68,900	12,990	9,404	12,990	11,516
68,900	68,950	13,003	9,411	13,003	11,529
68,950	69,000	13,015	9,419	13,015	11,541

69,000

At least	But less than	Single	MFJ	MFS	HoH
69,000	69,050	13,028	9,426	13,028	11,554
69,050	69,100	13,040	9,434	13,040	11,566
69,100	69,150	13,053	9,441	13,053	11,579
69,150	69,200	13,065	9,449	13,065	11,591
69,200	69,250	13,078	9,456	13,078	11,604
69,250	69,300	13,090	9,464	13,090	11,616
69,300	69,350	13,103	9,471	13,103	11,629
69,350	69,400	13,115	9,479	13,115	11,641
69,400	69,450	13,128	9,486	13,128	11,654
69,450	69,500	13,140	9,494	13,140	11,666
69,500	69,550	13,153	9,501	13,153	11,679
69,550	69,600	13,165	9,509	13,165	11,691
69,600	69,650	13,178	9,516	13,178	11,704
69,650	69,700	13,190	9,524	13,190	11,716
69,700	69,750	13,203	9,531	13,203	11,729
69,750	69,800	13,215	9,539	13,215	11,741
69,800	69,850	13,228	9,546	13,228	11,754
69,850	69,900	13,240	9,554	13,240	11,766
69,900	69,950	13,253	9,561	13,253	11,779
69,950	70,000	13,265	9,569	13,265	11,791

70,000

At least	But less than	Single	MFJ	MFS	HoH
70,000	70,050	13,278	9,576	13,278	11,804
70,050	70,100	13,290	9,584	13,290	11,816
70,100	70,150	13,303	9,591	13,303	11,829
70,150	70,200	13,315	9,599	13,315	11,841
70,200	70,250	13,328	9,606	13,328	11,854
70,250	70,300	13,340	9,614	13,340	11,866
70,300	70,350	13,353	9,621	13,353	11,879
70,350	70,400	13,365	9,629	13,365	11,891
70,400	70,450	13,378	9,636	13,378	11,904
70,450	70,500	13,390	9,644	13,390	11,916
70,500	70,550	13,403	9,651	13,403	11,929
70,550	70,600	13,415	9,659	13,415	11,941
70,600	70,650	13,428	9,666	13,428	11,954
70,650	70,700	13,440	9,674	13,440	11,966
70,700	70,750	13,453	9,681	13,453	11,979
70,750	70,800	13,465	9,689	13,465	11,991
70,800	70,850	13,478	9,696	13,478	12,004
70,850	70,900	13,490	9,704	13,490	12,016
70,900	70,950	13,503	9,711	13,503	12,029
70,950	71,000	13,515	9,719	13,515	12,041

71,000

At least	But less than	Single	MFJ	MFS	HoH
71,000	71,050	13,528	9,726	13,528	12,054
71,050	71,100	13,540	9,734	13,540	12,066
71,100	71,150	13,553	9,741	13,553	12,079
71,150	71,200	13,565	9,749	13,565	12,091
71,200	71,250	13,578	9,756	13,578	12,104
71,250	71,300	13,590	9,764	13,590	12,116
71,300	71,350	13,603	9,771	13,603	12,129
71,350	71,400	13,615	9,779	13,615	12,141
71,400	71,450	13,628	9,786	13,628	12,154
71,450	71,500	13,640	9,794	13,640	12,166
71,500	71,550	13,653	9,801	13,653	12,179
71,550	71,600	13,665	9,809	13,665	12,191
71,600	71,650	13,678	9,816	13,678	12,204
71,650	71,700	13,690	9,824	13,690	12,216
71,700	71,750	13,703	9,831	13,703	12,229
71,750	71,800	13,715	9,839	13,715	12,241
71,800	71,850	13,728	9,846	13,728	12,254
71,850	71,900	13,740	9,854	13,740	12,266
71,900	71,950	13,753	9,861	13,753	12,279
71,950	72,000	13,765	9,869	13,765	12,291

72,000

At least	But less than	Single	MFJ	MFS	HoH
72,000	72,050	13,778	9,876	13,778	12,304
72,050	72,100	13,790	9,884	13,790	12,316
72,100	72,150	13,803	9,891	13,803	12,329
72,150	72,200	13,815	9,899	13,815	12,341
72,200	72,250	13,828	9,906	13,828	12,354
72,250	72,300	13,840	9,914	13,840	12,366
72,300	72,350	13,853	9,921	13,853	12,379
72,350	72,400	13,865	9,929	13,865	12,391
72,400	72,450	13,878	9,936	13,878	12,404
72,450	72,500	13,890	9,944	13,890	12,416
72,500	72,550	13,903	9,951	13,903	12,429
72,550	72,600	13,915	9,959	13,915	12,441
72,600	72,650	13,928	9,966	13,928	12,454
72,650	72,700	13,940	9,974	13,940	12,466
72,700	72,750	13,953	9,981	13,953	12,479
72,750	72,800	13,965	9,989	13,965	12,491
72,800	72,850	13,978	9,996	13,978	12,504
72,850	72,900	13,990	10,004	13,990	12,516
72,900	72,950	14,003	10,011	14,003	12,529
72,950	73,000	14,015	10,019	14,015	12,541

73,000

At least	But less than	Single	MFJ	MFS	HoH
73,000	73,050	14,028	10,026	14,028	12,554
73,050	73,100	14,040	10,034	14,040	12,566
73,100	73,150	14,053	10,041	14,053	12,579
73,150	73,200	14,065	10,049	14,065	12,591
73,200	73,250	14,078	10,056	14,078	12,604
73,250	73,300	14,090	10,064	14,090	12,616
73,300	73,350	14,103	10,071	14,103	12,629
73,350	73,400	14,115	10,079	14,115	12,641
73,400	73,450	14,128	10,086	14,128	12,654
73,450	73,500	14,140	10,094	14,140	12,666
73,500	73,550	14,153	10,101	14,153	12,679
73,550	73,600	14,165	10,109	14,165	12,691
73,600	73,650	14,178	10,116	14,178	12,704
73,650	73,700	14,190	10,124	14,190	12,716
73,700	73,750	14,203	10,131	14,203	12,729
73,750	73,800	14,215	10,139	14,215	12,741
73,800	73,850	14,228	10,146	14,228	12,754
73,850	73,900	14,240	10,154	14,240	12,766
73,900	73,950	14,253	10,161	14,253	12,779
73,950	74,000	14,265	10,169	14,265	12,791

74,000

At least	But less than	Single	MFJ	MFS	HoH
74,000	74,050	14,278	10,176	14,278	12,804
74,050	74,100	14,290	10,184	14,290	12,816
74,100	74,150	14,303	10,191	14,303	12,829
74,150	74,200	14,315	10,199	14,315	12,841
74,200	74,250	14,328	10,206	14,328	12,854
74,250	74,300	14,340	10,214	14,340	12,866
74,300	74,350	14,353	10,221	14,353	12,879
74,350	74,400	14,365	10,229	14,365	12,891
74,400	74,450	14,378	10,236	14,378	12,904
74,450	74,500	14,390	10,244	14,390	12,916
74,500	74,550	14,403	10,251	14,403	12,929
74,550	74,600	14,415	10,259	14,415	12,941
74,600	74,650	14,428	10,266	14,428	12,954
74,650	74,700	14,440	10,274	14,440	12,966
74,700	74,750	14,453	10,281	14,453	12,979
74,750	74,800	14,465	10,289	14,465	12,991
74,800	74,850	14,478	10,296	14,478	13,004
74,850	74,900	14,490	10,304	14,490	13,016
74,900	74,950	14,503	10,311	14,503	13,029
74,950	75,000	14,515	10,319	14,515	13,041

2016 Tax Table — *Continued*

75,000

If line 43 (taxable income) is— At least	But less than	Single	Married filing jointly *	Married filing separately	Head of a household
75,000	75,050	14,528	10,326	14,528	13,054
75,050	75,100	14,540	10,334	14,540	13,066
75,100	75,150	14,553	10,341	14,553	13,079
75,150	75,200	14,565	10,349	14,565	13,091
75,200	75,250	14,578	10,356	14,578	13,104
75,250	75,300	14,590	10,364	14,590	13,116
75,300	75,350	14,603	10,374	14,603	13,129
75,350	75,400	14,615	10,386	14,615	13,141
75,400	75,450	14,628	10,399	14,628	13,154
75,450	75,500	14,640	10,411	14,640	13,166
75,500	75,550	14,653	10,424	14,653	13,179
75,550	75,600	14,665	10,436	14,665	13,191
75,600	75,650	14,678	10,449	14,678	13,204
75,650	75,700	14,690	10,461	14,690	13,216
75,700	75,750	14,703	10,474	14,703	13,229
75,750	75,800	14,715	10,486	14,715	13,241
75,800	75,850	14,728	10,499	14,728	13,254
75,850	75,900	14,740	10,511	14,740	13,266
75,900	75,950	14,753	10,524	14,753	13,279
75,950	76,000	14,765	10,536	14,766	13,291

76,000

At least	But less than	Single	Married filing jointly *	Married filing separately	Head of a household
76,000	76,050	14,778	10,549	14,780	13,304
76,050	76,100	14,790	10,561	14,794	13,316
76,100	76,150	14,803	10,574	14,808	13,329
76,150	76,200	14,815	10,586	14,822	13,341
76,200	76,250	14,828	10,599	14,836	13,354
76,250	76,300	14,840	10,611	14,850	13,366
76,300	76,350	14,853	10,624	14,864	13,379
76,350	76,400	14,865	10,636	14,878	13,391
76,400	76,450	14,878	10,649	14,892	13,404
76,450	76,500	14,890	10,661	14,906	13,416
76,500	76,550	14,903	10,674	14,920	13,429
76,550	76,600	14,915	10,686	14,934	13,441
76,600	76,650	14,928	10,699	14,948	13,454
76,650	76,700	14,940	10,711	14,962	13,466
76,700	76,750	14,953	10,724	14,976	13,479
76,750	76,800	14,965	10,736	14,990	13,491
76,800	76,850	14,978	10,749	15,004	13,504
76,850	76,900	14,990	10,761	15,018	13,516
76,900	76,950	15,003	10,774	15,032	13,529
76,950	77,000	15,015	10,786	15,046	13,541

77,000

At least	But less than	Single	Married filing jointly *	Married filing separately	Head of a household
77,000	77,050	15,028	10,799	15,060	13,554
77,050	77,100	15,040	10,811	15,074	13,566
77,100	77,150	15,053	10,824	15,088	13,579
77,150	77,200	15,065	10,836	15,102	13,591
77,200	77,250	15,078	10,849	15,116	13,604
77,250	77,300	15,090	10,861	15,130	13,616
77,300	77,350	15,103	10,874	15,144	13,629
77,350	77,400	15,115	10,886	15,158	13,641
77,400	77,450	15,128	10,899	15,172	13,654
77,450	77,500	15,140	10,911	15,186	13,666
77,500	77,550	15,153	10,924	15,200	13,679
77,550	77,600	15,165	10,936	15,214	13,691
77,600	77,650	15,178	10,949	15,228	13,704
77,650	77,700	15,190	10,961	15,242	13,716
77,700	77,750	15,203	10,974	15,256	13,729
77,750	77,800	15,215	10,986	15,270	13,741
77,800	77,850	15,228	10,999	15,284	13,754
77,850	77,900	15,240	11,011	15,298	13,766
77,900	77,950	15,253	11,024	15,312	13,779
77,950	78,000	15,265	11,036	15,326	13,791

78,000

At least	But less than	Single	Married filing jointly *	Married filing separately	Head of a household
78,000	78,050	15,278	11,049	15,340	13,804
78,050	78,100	15,290	11,061	15,354	13,816
78,100	78,150	15,303	11,074	15,368	13,829
78,150	78,200	15,315	11,086	15,382	13,841
78,200	78,250	15,328	11,099	15,396	13,854
78,250	78,300	15,340	11,111	15,410	13,866
78,300	78,350	15,353	11,124	15,424	13,879
78,350	78,400	15,365	11,136	15,438	13,891
78,400	78,450	15,378	11,149	15,452	13,904
78,450	78,500	15,390	11,161	15,466	13,916
78,500	78,550	15,403	11,174	15,480	13,929
78,550	78,600	15,415	11,186	15,494	13,941
78,600	78,650	15,428	11,199	15,508	13,954
78,650	78,700	15,440	11,211	15,522	13,966
78,700	78,750	15,453	11,224	15,536	13,979
78,750	78,800	15,465	11,236	15,550	13,991
78,800	78,850	15,478	11,249	15,564	14,004
78,850	78,900	15,490	11,261	15,578	14,016
78,900	78,950	15,503	11,274	15,592	14,029
78,950	79,000	15,515	11,286	15,606	14,041

79,000

At least	But less than	Single	Married filing jointly *	Married filing separately	Head of a household
79,000	79,050	15,528	11,299	15,620	14,054
79,050	79,100	15,540	11,311	15,634	14,066
79,100	79,150	15,553	11,324	15,648	14,079
79,150	79,200	15,565	11,336	15,662	14,091
79,200	79,250	15,578	11,349	15,676	14,104
79,250	79,300	15,590	11,361	15,690	14,116
79,300	79,350	15,603	11,374	15,704	14,129
79,350	79,400	15,615	11,386	15,718	14,141
79,400	79,450	15,628	11,399	15,732	14,154
79,450	79,500	15,640	11,411	15,746	14,166
79,500	79,550	15,653	11,424	15,760	14,179
79,550	79,600	15,665	11,436	15,774	14,191
79,600	79,650	15,678	11,449	15,788	14,204
79,650	79,700	15,690	11,461	15,802	14,216
79,700	79,750	15,703	11,474	15,816	14,229
79,750	79,800	15,715	11,486	15,830	14,241
79,800	79,850	15,728	11,499	15,844	14,254
79,850	79,900	15,740	11,511	15,858	14,266
79,900	79,950	15,753	11,524	15,872	14,279
79,950	80,000	15,765	11,536	15,886	14,291

80,000

At least	But less than	Single	Married filing jointly *	Married filing separately	Head of a household
80,000	80,050	15,778	11,549	15,900	14,304
80,050	80,100	15,790	11,561	15,914	14,316
80,100	80,150	15,803	11,574	15,928	14,329
80,150	80,200	15,815	11,586	15,942	14,341
80,200	80,250	15,828	11,599	15,956	14,354
80,250	80,300	15,840	11,611	15,970	14,366
80,300	80,350	15,853	11,624	15,984	14,379
80,350	80,400	15,865	11,636	15,998	14,391
80,400	80,450	15,878	11,649	16,012	14,404
80,450	80,500	15,890	11,661	16,026	14,416
80,500	80,550	15,903	11,674	16,040	14,429
80,550	80,600	15,915	11,686	16,054	14,441
80,600	80,650	15,928	11,699	16,068	14,454
80,650	80,700	15,940	11,711	16,082	14,466
80,700	80,750	15,953	11,724	16,096	14,479
80,750	80,800	15,965	11,736	16,110	14,491
80,800	80,850	15,978	11,749	16,124	14,504
80,850	80,900	15,990	11,761	16,138	14,516
80,900	80,950	16,003	11,774	16,152	14,529
80,950	81,000	16,015	11,786	16,166	14,541

81,000

At least	But less than	Single	Married filing jointly *	Married filing separately	Head of a household
81,000	81,050	16,028	11,799	16,180	14,554
81,050	81,100	16,040	11,811	16,194	14,566
81,100	81,150	16,053	11,824	16,208	14,579
81,150	81,200	16,065	11,836	16,222	14,591
81,200	81,250	16,078	11,849	16,236	14,604
81,250	81,300	16,090	11,861	16,250	14,616
81,300	81,350	16,103	11,874	16,264	14,629
81,350	81,400	16,115	11,886	16,278	14,641
81,400	81,450	16,128	11,899	16,292	14,654
81,450	81,500	16,140	11,911	16,306	14,666
81,500	81,550	16,153	11,924	16,320	14,679
81,550	81,600	16,165	11,936	16,334	14,691
81,600	81,650	16,178	11,949	16,348	14,704
81,650	81,700	16,190	11,961	16,362	14,716
81,700	81,750	16,203	11,974	16,376	14,729
81,750	81,800	16,215	11,986	16,390	14,741
81,800	81,850	16,228	11,999	16,404	14,754
81,850	81,900	16,240	12,011	16,418	14,766
81,900	81,950	16,253	12,024	16,432	14,779
81,950	82,000	16,265	12,036	16,446	14,791

82,000

At least	But less than	Single	Married filing jointly *	Married filing separately	Head of a household
82,000	82,050	16,278	12,049	16,460	14,804
82,050	82,100	16,290	12,061	16,474	14,816
82,100	82,150	16,303	12,074	16,488	14,829
82,150	82,200	16,315	12,086	16,502	14,841
82,200	82,250	16,328	12,099	16,516	14,854
82,250	82,300	16,340	12,111	16,530	14,866
82,300	82,350	16,353	12,124	16,544	14,879
82,350	82,400	16,365	12,136	16,558	14,891
82,400	82,450	16,378	12,149	16,572	14,904
82,450	82,500	16,390	12,161	16,586	14,916
82,500	82,550	16,403	12,174	16,600	14,929
82,550	82,600	16,415	12,186	16,614	14,941
82,600	82,650	16,428	12,199	16,628	14,954
82,650	82,700	16,440	12,211	16,642	14,966
82,700	82,750	16,453	12,224	16,656	14,979
82,750	82,800	16,465	12,236	16,670	14,991
82,800	82,850	16,478	12,249	16,684	15,004
82,850	82,900	16,490	12,261	16,698	15,016
82,900	82,950	16,503	12,274	16,712	15,029
82,950	83,000	16,515	12,286	16,726	15,041

83,000

At least	But less than	Single	Married filing jointly *	Married filing separately	Head of a household
83,000	83,050	16,528	12,299	16,740	15,054
83,050	83,100	16,540	12,311	16,754	15,066
83,100	83,150	16,553	12,324	16,768	15,079
83,150	83,200	16,565	12,336	16,782	15,091
83,200	83,250	16,578	12,349	16,796	15,104
83,250	83,300	16,590	12,361	16,810	15,116
83,300	83,350	16,603	12,374	16,824	15,129
83,350	83,400	16,615	12,386	16,838	15,141
83,400	83,450	16,628	12,399	16,852	15,154
83,450	83,500	16,640	12,411	16,866	15,166
83,500	83,550	16,653	12,424	16,880	15,179
83,550	83,600	16,665	12,436	16,894	15,191
83,600	83,650	16,678	12,449	16,908	15,204
83,650	83,700	16,690	12,461	16,922	15,216
83,700	83,750	16,703	12,474	16,936	15,229
83,750	83,800	16,715	12,486	16,950	15,241
83,800	83,850	16,728	12,499	16,964	15,254
83,850	83,900	16,740	12,511	16,978	15,266
83,900	83,950	16,753	12,524	16,992	15,279
83,950	84,000	16,765	12,536	17,006	15,291

2016 Tax Table — *Continued*

If line 43 (taxable income) is—		And you are—			
At least	But less than	Single	Married filing jointly *	Married filing separately	Head of a household
		Your tax is—			

84,000

At least	But less than	Single	Married filing jointly	Married filing separately	Head of a household
84,000	84,050	16,778	12,549	17,020	15,304
84,050	84,100	16,790	12,561	17,034	15,316
84,100	84,150	16,803	12,574	17,048	15,329
84,150	84,200	16,815	12,586	17,062	15,341
84,200	84,250	16,828	12,599	17,076	15,354
84,250	84,300	16,840	12,611	17,090	15,366
84,300	84,350	16,853	12,624	17,104	15,379
84,350	84,400	16,865	12,636	17,118	15,391
84,400	84,450	16,878	12,649	17,132	15,404
84,450	84,500	16,890	12,661	17,146	15,416
84,500	84,550	16,903	12,674	17,160	15,429
84,550	84,600	16,915	12,686	17,174	15,441
84,600	84,650	16,928	12,699	17,188	15,454
84,650	84,700	16,940	12,711	17,202	15,466
84,700	84,750	16,953	12,724	17,216	15,479
84,750	84,800	16,965	12,736	17,230	15,491
84,800	84,850	16,978	12,749	17,244	15,504
84,850	84,900	16,990	12,761	17,258	15,516
84,900	84,950	17,003	12,774	17,272	15,529
84,950	85,000	17,015	12,786	17,286	15,541

85,000

At least	But less than	Single	Married filing jointly	Married filing separately	Head of a household
85,000	85,050	17,028	12,799	17,300	15,554
85,050	85,100	17,040	12,811	17,314	15,566
85,100	85,150	17,053	12,824	17,328	15,579
85,150	85,200	17,065	12,836	17,342	15,591
85,200	85,250	17,078	12,849	17,356	15,604
85,250	85,300	17,090	12,861	17,370	15,616
85,300	85,350	17,103	12,874	17,384	15,629
85,350	85,400	17,115	12,886	17,398	15,641
85,400	85,450	17,128	12,899	17,412	15,654
85,450	85,500	17,140	12,911	17,426	15,666
85,500	85,550	17,153	12,924	17,440	15,679
85,550	85,600	17,165	12,936	17,454	15,691
85,600	85,650	17,178	12,949	17,468	15,704
85,650	85,700	17,190	12,961	17,482	15,716
85,700	85,750	17,203	12,974	17,496	15,729
85,750	85,800	17,215	12,986	17,510	15,741
85,800	85,850	17,228	12,999	17,524	15,754
85,850	85,900	17,240	13,011	17,538	15,766
85,900	85,950	17,253	13,024	17,552	15,779
85,950	86,000	17,265	13,036	17,566	15,791

86,000

At least	But less than	Single	Married filing jointly	Married filing separately	Head of a household
86,000	86,050	17,278	13,049	17,580	15,804
86,050	86,100	17,290	13,061	17,594	15,816
86,100	86,150	17,303	13,074	17,608	15,829
86,150	86,200	17,315	13,086	17,622	15,841
86,200	86,250	17,328	13,099	17,636	15,854
86,250	86,300	17,340	13,111	17,650	15,866
86,300	86,350	17,353	13,124	17,664	15,879
86,350	86,400	17,365	13,136	17,678	15,891
86,400	86,450	17,378	13,149	17,692	15,904
86,450	86,500	17,390	13,161	17,706	15,916
86,500	86,550	17,403	13,174	17,720	15,929
86,550	86,600	17,415	13,186	17,734	15,941
86,600	86,650	17,428	13,199	17,748	15,954
86,650	86,700	17,440	13,211	17,762	15,966
86,700	86,750	17,453	13,224	17,776	15,979
86,750	86,800	17,465	13,236	17,790	15,991
86,800	86,850	17,478	13,249	17,804	16,004
86,850	86,900	17,490	13,261	17,818	16,016
86,900	86,950	17,503	13,274	17,832	16,029
86,950	87,000	17,515	13,286	17,846	16,041

87,000

At least	But less than	Single	Married filing jointly	Married filing separately	Head of a household
87,000	87,050	17,528	13,299	17,860	16,054
87,050	87,100	17,540	13,311	17,874	16,066
87,100	87,150	17,553	13,324	17,888	16,079
87,150	87,200	17,565	13,336	17,902	16,091
87,200	87,250	17,578	13,349	17,916	16,104
87,250	87,300	17,590	13,361	17,930	16,116
87,300	87,350	17,603	13,374	17,944	16,129
87,350	87,400	17,615	13,386	17,958	16,141
87,400	87,450	17,628	13,399	17,972	16,154
87,450	87,500	17,640	13,411	17,986	16,166
87,500	87,550	17,653	13,424	18,000	16,179
87,550	87,600	17,665	13,436	18,014	16,191
87,600	87,650	17,678	13,449	18,028	16,204
87,650	87,700	17,690	13,461	18,042	16,216
87,700	87,750	17,703	13,474	18,056	16,229
87,750	87,800	17,715	13,486	18,070	16,241
87,800	87,850	17,728	13,499	18,084	16,254
87,850	87,900	17,740	13,511	18,098	16,266
87,900	87,950	17,753	13,524	18,112	16,279
87,950	88,000	17,765	13,536	18,126	16,291

88,000

At least	But less than	Single	Married filing jointly	Married filing separately	Head of a household
88,000	88,050	17,778	13,549	18,140	16,304
88,050	88,100	17,790	13,561	18,154	16,316
88,100	88,150	17,803	13,574	18,168	16,329
88,150	88,200	17,815	13,586	18,182	16,341
88,200	88,250	17,828	13,599	18,196	16,354
88,250	88,300	17,840	13,611	18,210	16,366
88,300	88,350	17,853	13,624	18,224	16,379
88,350	88,400	17,865	13,636	18,238	16,391
88,400	88,450	17,878	13,649	18,252	16,404
88,450	88,500	17,890	13,661	18,266	16,416
88,500	88,550	17,903	13,674	18,280	16,429
88,550	88,600	17,915	13,686	18,294	16,441
88,600	88,650	17,928	13,699	18,308	16,454
88,650	88,700	17,940	13,711	18,322	16,466
88,700	88,750	17,953	13,724	18,336	16,479
88,750	88,800	17,965	13,736	18,350	16,491
88,800	88,850	17,978	13,749	18,364	16,504
88,850	88,900	17,990	13,761	18,378	16,516
88,900	88,950	18,003	13,774	18,392	16,529
88,950	89,000	18,015	13,786	18,406	16,541

89,000

At least	But less than	Single	Married filing jointly	Married filing separately	Head of a household
89,000	89,050	18,028	13,799	18,420	16,554
89,050	89,100	18,040	13,811	18,434	16,566
89,100	89,150	18,053	13,824	18,448	16,579
89,150	89,200	18,065	13,836	18,462	16,591
89,200	89,250	18,078	13,849	18,476	16,604
89,250	89,300	18,090	13,861	18,490	16,616
89,300	89,350	18,103	13,874	18,504	16,629
89,350	89,400	18,115	13,886	18,518	16,641
89,400	89,450	18,128	13,899	18,532	16,654
89,450	89,500	18,140	13,911	18,546	16,666
89,500	89,550	18,153	13,924	18,560	16,679
89,550	89,600	18,165	13,936	18,574	16,691
89,600	89,650	18,178	13,949	18,588	16,704
89,650	89,700	18,190	13,961	18,602	16,716
89,700	89,750	18,203	13,974	18,616	16,729
89,750	89,800	18,215	13,986	18,630	16,741
89,800	89,850	18,228	13,999	18,644	16,754
89,850	89,900	18,240	14,011	18,658	16,766
89,900	89,950	18,253	14,024	18,672	16,779
89,950	90,000	18,265	14,036	18,686	16,791

90,000

At least	But less than	Single	Married filing jointly	Married filing separately	Head of a household
90,000	90,050	18,278	14,049	18,700	16,804
90,050	90,100	18,290	14,061	18,714	16,816
90,100	90,150	18,303	14,074	18,728	16,829
90,150	90,200	18,315	14,086	18,742	16,841
90,200	90,250	18,328	14,099	18,756	16,854
90,250	90,300	18,340	14,111	18,770	16,866
90,300	90,350	18,353	14,124	18,784	16,879
90,350	90,400	18,365	14,136	18,798	16,891
90,400	90,450	18,378	14,149	18,812	16,904
90,450	90,500	18,390	14,161	18,826	16,916
90,500	90,550	18,403	14,174	18,840	16,929
90,550	90,600	18,415	14,186	18,854	16,941
90,600	90,650	18,428	14,199	18,868	16,954
90,650	90,700	18,440	14,211	18,882	16,966
90,700	90,750	18,453	14,224	18,896	16,979
90,750	90,800	18,465	14,236	18,910	16,991
90,800	90,850	18,478	14,249	18,924	17,004
90,850	90,900	18,490	14,261	18,938	17,016
90,900	90,950	18,503	14,274	18,952	17,029
90,950	91,000	18,515	14,286	18,966	17,041

91,000

At least	But less than	Single	Married filing jointly	Married filing separately	Head of a household
91,000	91,050	18,528	14,299	18,980	17,054
91,050	91,100	18,540	14,311	18,994	17,066
91,100	91,150	18,553	14,324	19,008	17,079
91,150	91,200	18,566	14,336	19,022	17,091
91,200	91,250	18,580	14,349	19,036	17,104
91,250	91,300	18,594	14,361	19,050	17,116
91,300	91,350	18,608	14,374	19,064	17,129
91,350	91,400	18,622	14,386	19,078	17,141
91,400	91,450	18,636	14,399	19,092	17,154
91,450	91,500	18,650	14,411	19,106	17,166
91,500	91,550	18,664	14,424	19,120	17,179
91,550	91,600	18,678	14,436	19,134	17,191
91,600	91,650	18,692	14,449	19,148	17,204
91,650	91,700	18,706	14,461	19,162	17,216
91,700	91,750	18,720	14,474	19,176	17,229
91,750	91,800	18,734	14,486	19,190	17,241
91,800	91,850	18,748	14,499	19,204	17,254
91,850	91,900	18,762	14,511	19,218	17,266
91,900	91,950	18,776	14,524	19,232	17,279
91,950	92,000	18,790	14,536	19,246	17,291

92,000

At least	But less than	Single	Married filing jointly	Married filing separately	Head of a household
92,000	92,050	18,804	14,549	19,260	17,304
92,050	92,100	18,818	14,561	19,274	17,316
92,100	92,150	18,832	14,574	19,288	17,329
92,150	92,200	18,846	14,586	19,302	17,341
92,200	92,250	18,860	14,599	19,316	17,354
92,250	92,300	18,874	14,611	19,330	17,366
92,300	92,350	18,888	14,624	19,344	17,379
92,350	92,400	18,902	14,636	19,358	17,391
92,400	92,450	18,916	14,649	19,372	17,404
92,450	92,500	18,930	14,661	19,386	17,416
92,500	92,550	18,944	14,674	19,400	17,429
92,550	92,600	18,958	14,686	19,414	17,441
92,600	92,650	18,972	14,699	19,428	17,454
92,650	92,700	18,986	14,711	19,442	17,466
92,700	92,750	19,000	14,724	19,456	17,479
92,750	92,800	19,014	14,736	19,470	17,491
92,800	92,850	19,028	14,749	19,484	17,504
92,850	92,900	19,042	14,761	19,498	17,516
92,900	92,950	19,056	14,774	19,512	17,529
92,950	93,000	19,070	14,786	19,526	17,541

2016 Tax Table — *Continued*

If line 43 (taxable income) is—		And you are—				If line 43 (taxable income) is—		And you are—				If line 43 (taxable income) is—		And you are—			
At least	But less than	Single	Married filing jointly *	Married filing separately	Head of a household	At least	But less than	Single	Married filing jointly *	Married filing separately	Head of a household	At least	But less than	Single	Married filing jointly *	Married filing separately	Head of a household
		Your tax is—						Your tax is—						Your tax is—			
93,000						**96,000**						**99,000**					
93,000	93,050	19,084	14,799	19,540	17,554	96,000	96,050	19,924	15,549	20,380	18,304	99,000	99,050	20,764	16,299	21,220	19,054
93,050	93,100	19,098	14,811	19,554	17,566	96,050	96,100	19,938	15,561	20,394	18,316	99,050	99,100	20,778	16,311	21,234	19,066
93,100	93,150	19,112	14,824	19,568	17,579	96,100	96,150	19,952	15,574	20,408	18,329	99,100	99,150	20,792	16,324	21,248	19,079
93,150	93,200	19,126	14,836	19,582	17,591	96,150	96,200	19,966	15,586	20,422	18,341	99,150	99,200	20,806	16,336	21,262	19,091
93,200	93,250	19,140	14,849	19,596	17,604	96,200	96,250	19,980	15,599	20,436	18,354	99,200	99,250	20,820	16,349	21,276	19,104
93,250	93,300	19,154	14,861	19,610	17,616	96,250	96,300	19,994	15,611	20,450	18,366	99,250	99,300	20,834	16,361	21,290	19,116
93,300	93,350	19,168	14,874	19,624	17,629	96,300	96,350	20,008	15,624	20,464	18,379	99,300	99,350	20,848	16,374	21,304	19,129
93,350	93,400	19,182	14,886	19,638	17,641	96,350	96,400	20,022	15,636	20,478	18,391	99,350	99,400	20,862	16,386	21,318	19,141
93,400	93,450	19,196	14,899	19,652	17,654	96,400	96,450	20,036	15,649	20,492	18,404	99,400	99,450	20,876	16,399	21,332	19,154
93,450	93,500	19,210	14,911	19,666	17,666	96,450	96,500	20,050	15,661	20,506	18,416	99,450	99,500	20,890	16,411	21,346	19,166
93,500	93,550	19,224	14,924	19,680	17,679	96,500	96,550	20,064	15,674	20,520	18,429	99,500	99,550	20,904	16,424	21,360	19,179
93,550	93,600	19,238	14,936	19,694	17,691	96,550	96,600	20,078	15,686	20,534	18,441	99,550	99,600	20,918	16,436	21,374	19,191
93,600	93,650	19,252	14,949	19,708	17,704	96,600	96,650	20,092	15,699	20,548	18,454	99,600	99,650	20,932	16,449	21,388	19,204
93,650	93,700	19,266	14,961	19,722	17,716	96,650	96,700	20,106	15,711	20,562	18,466	99,650	99,700	20,946	16,461	21,402	19,216
93,700	93,750	19,280	14,974	19,736	17,729	96,700	96,750	20,120	15,724	20,576	18,479	99,700	99,750	20,960	16,474	21,416	19,229
93,750	93,800	19,294	14,986	19,750	17,741	96,750	96,800	20,134	15,736	20,590	18,491	99,750	99,800	20,974	16,486	21,430	19,241
93,800	93,850	19,308	14,999	19,764	17,754	96,800	96,850	20,148	15,749	20,604	18,504	99,800	99,850	20,988	16,499	21,444	19,254
93,850	93,900	19,322	15,011	19,778	17,766	96,850	96,900	20,162	15,761	20,618	18,516	99,850	99,900	21,002	16,511	21,458	19,266
93,900	93,950	19,336	15,024	19,792	17,779	96,900	96,950	20,176	15,774	20,632	18,529	99,900	99,950	21,016	16,524	21,472	19,279
93,950	94,000	19,350	15,036	19,806	17,791	96,950	97,000	20,190	15,786	20,646	18,541	99,950	100,000	21,030	16,536	21,486	19,291
94,000						**97,000**											
94,000	94,050	19,364	15,049	19,820	17,804	97,000	97,050	20,204	15,799	20,660	18,554						
94,050	94,100	19,378	15,061	19,834	17,816	97,050	97,100	20,218	15,811	20,674	18,566						
94,100	94,150	19,392	15,074	19,848	17,829	97,100	97,150	20,232	15,824	20,688	18,579						
94,150	94,200	19,406	15,086	19,862	17,841	97,150	97,200	20,246	15,836	20,702	18,591						
94,200	94,250	19,420	15,099	19,876	17,854	97,200	97,250	20,260	15,849	20,716	18,604						
94,250	94,300	19,434	15,111	19,890	17,866	97,250	97,300	20,274	15,861	20,730	18,616						
94,300	94,350	19,448	15,124	19,904	17,879	97,300	97,350	20,288	15,874	20,744	18,629						
94,350	94,400	19,462	15,136	19,918	17,891	97,350	97,400	20,302	15,886	20,758	18,641						
94,400	94,450	19,476	15,149	19,932	17,904	97,400	97,450	20,316	15,899	20,772	18,654						
94,450	94,500	19,490	15,161	19,946	17,916	97,450	97,500	20,330	15,911	20,786	18,666						
94,500	94,550	19,504	15,174	19,960	17,929	97,500	97,550	20,344	15,924	20,800	18,679						
94,550	94,600	19,518	15,186	19,974	17,941	97,550	97,600	20,358	15,936	20,814	18,691						
94,600	94,650	19,532	15,199	19,988	17,954	97,600	97,650	20,372	15,949	20,828	18,704						
94,650	94,700	19,546	15,211	20,002	17,966	97,650	97,700	20,386	15,961	20,842	18,716						
94,700	94,750	19,560	15,224	20,016	17,979	97,700	97,750	20,400	15,974	20,856	18,729						
94,750	94,800	19,574	15,236	20,030	17,991	97,750	97,800	20,414	15,986	20,870	18,741						
94,800	94,850	19,588	15,249	20,044	18,004	97,800	97,850	20,428	15,999	20,884	18,754						
94,850	94,900	19,602	15,261	20,058	18,016	97,850	97,900	20,442	16,011	20,898	18,766						
94,900	94,950	19,616	15,274	20,072	18,029	97,900	97,950	20,456	16,024	20,912	18,779						
94,950	95,000	19,630	15,286	20,086	18,041	97,950	98,000	20,470	16,036	20,926	18,791						
95,000						**98,000**											
95,000	95,050	19,644	15,299	20,100	18,054	98,000	98,050	20,484	16,049	20,940	18,804						
95,050	95,100	19,658	15,311	20,114	18,066	98,050	98,100	20,498	16,061	20,954	18,816						
95,100	95,150	19,672	15,324	20,128	18,079	98,100	98,150	20,512	16,074	20,968	18,829						
95,150	95,200	19,686	15,336	20,142	18,091	98,150	98,200	20,526	16,086	20,982	18,841						
95,200	95,250	19,700	15,349	20,156	18,104	98,200	98,250	20,540	16,099	20,996	18,854						
95,250	95,300	19,714	15,361	20,170	18,116	98,250	98,300	20,554	16,111	21,010	18,866						
95,300	95,350	19,728	15,374	20,184	18,129	98,300	98,350	20,568	16,124	21,024	18,879						
95,350	95,400	19,742	15,386	20,198	18,141	98,350	98,400	20,582	16,136	21,038	18,891						
95,400	95,450	19,756	15,399	20,212	18,154	98,400	98,450	20,596	16,149	21,052	18,904						
95,450	95,500	19,770	15,411	20,226	18,166	98,450	98,500	20,610	16,161	21,066	18,916						
95,500	95,550	19,784	15,424	20,240	18,179	98,500	98,550	20,624	16,174	21,080	18,929						
95,550	95,600	19,798	15,436	20,254	18,191	98,550	98,600	20,638	16,186	21,094	18,941						
95,600	95,650	19,812	15,449	20,268	18,204	98,600	98,650	20,652	16,199	21,108	18,954						
95,650	95,700	19,826	15,461	20,282	18,216	98,650	98,700	20,666	16,211	21,122	18,966						
95,700	95,750	19,840	15,474	20,296	18,229	98,700	98,750	20,680	16,224	21,136	18,979						
95,750	95,800	19,854	15,486	20,310	18,241	98,750	98,800	20,694	16,236	21,150	18,991						
95,800	95,850	19,868	15,499	20,324	18,254	98,800	98,850	20,708	16,249	21,164	19,004						
95,850	95,900	19,882	15,511	20,338	18,266	98,850	98,900	20,722	16,261	21,178	19,016						
95,900	95,950	19,896	15,524	20,352	18,279	98,900	98,950	20,736	16,274	21,192	19,029						
95,950	96,000	19,910	15,536	20,366	18,291	98,950	99,000	20,750	16,286	21,206	19,041						

$100,000
or over
use the Tax
Computation
Worksheet

Glossary of Tax Terms

This tax dictionary defines the words and phrases most commonly used in talking about federal taxes. The language of federal taxation is the language of law, accounting, and business. Many of the terms have precise, technical meanings, as compared with their meanings in everyday use. The definitions in this glossary are, of course, only adaptations of the full meanings prescribed by the law, regulations, and rulings, that are discussed in the explanatory text. Refer to this glossary for an introduction to the language of federal taxation.

A

Accelerated Cost Recovery System (ACRS)

This system of recovering the cost of capital expenditures through periodic depreciation deductions (allowances) is mandatory for most depreciable tangible property placed in service after 1980 and before 1987. These costs are recovered over specified recovery periods by means of statutory percentages that do not require the computation of a useful life. An alternative straight-line allowance may be elected over one of several alternate statutory recovery periods.

   Assets placed in service after 1986 must generally be depreciated using a Modified Accelerated Cost Recovery System (MACRS). MACRS generally results in lower depreciation deductions than ACRS because many assets are assigned a longer recovery period. Assets are depreciated using prescribed recovery methods and conventions. The MACRS deduction, however, may be computed by using optional tables, which have ACRS style percentages.

Accounting method

A taxpayer's accounting method is the basis of accounting by which records are kept. Usually, either the *cash* basis or the *accrual* basis is used. Special methods of reporting income, such as the installment basis, are variations of these two methods.

Accounting period

An accounting period is the 12-month period on the basis of which the taxpayer's records are kept. If no books are kept or if no other period is specified, the accounting period is the calendar year. If the books are kept on the basis of a 12-month period ending with a month other than December, the accounting period is a *fiscal* year. A special 52-53-week accounting period is also recognized for income tax purposes.

Accrual basis of accounting

The *accrual* basis is distinguished from the *cash* basis. On the accrual basis, income is accounted for as and when it is earned, whether or not it has been collected. Expenses are deducted when they are incurred, whether or not paid in the same period. In determining when the expenses of an accrual-basis taxpayer are incurred, the all-events test is applied. This test provides that the expenses are deductible in the year in which all of the events have occurred that determine the fact of liability where the amount of the liability can be determined with reasonable accuracy. Generally, all of the events that establish liability for an amount, for the purpose of determining whether such amount has been incurred, are treated as not occurring any earlier than the time that economic performance occurs.

Accumulated adjustments account (AAA)

The accumulated adjustments account consists of post-1982 accumulated gross income less deductible expenses and prior distributions allocable to the account of an S corporation.

Accumulated earnings tax

This additional tax is imposed on a corporation that permits its earnings to accumulate, instead of being distributed, in order to avoid payment of tax on dividends by individual stockholders. Generally, a corporation may accumulate up to $250,000 (only $150,000 for some personal service companies) over the years without risk of incurring this special tax. The applicable amount, plus whatever additional amount is necessary to be retained for the reasonable needs of the business, is allowed as a credit against taxable income. Only the remainder of undistributed income is subject to the accumulated earnings tax.

Adjusted basis

The basis for gain or loss and the basis for depreciation, etc. are explained below under *Basis*. After such a basis is determined, it must be adjusted (a) for capital items that increase it and (b) for deductions that decrease it, such as depreciation, depletion, etc.

Adjusted gross income

Adjusted gross income is gross income reduced by trade or business expenses of individual taxpayers, expenses for property held for production of rents or royalties, and certain loss adjustments. The amount of the adjusted gross income affects the extent to which medical expenses, nonbusiness casualty and theft losses, and charitable contributions may be deducted.

Administrator

Like an executor, the administrator manages the estate of a person who dies intestate or whose named executor fails to act.

Affiliated corporate groups—See Controlled corporate groups

Age 65 and older standard deduction

A taxpayer who has attained the age of 65 before the close of the tax year is allowed an additional standard deduction amount of $1,250 in 2017 if married; $1,550 in 2017 if unmarried.

Alimony

In a legal sense, alimony is support payment made after divorce or legal separation. In some respects, the income tax law definition is broader. It includes payments made under a decree of divorce or separate maintenance, under a decree for support if a wife is separated from her husband, or under a written separation agreement executed by the husband and wife if the wife is separated from her husband and they file separate returns. Alimony payments that meet certain tests are deductible by the payer and are income to the recipient.

All-events test—See Accrual basis of accounting

Alternative minimum tax

Alternative minimum tax rules have been devised to ensure that at least a minimum amount of income tax is paid by corporate and high-income noncorporate taxpayers (including estates and trusts) who reap large tax savings by making use of certain tax deductions and exemptions. A taxpayer's AMT for a tax year is the excess of the tentative minimum tax over the regular tax and must be paid in addition to year-end tax liability. The tentative minimum tax is determined by multiplying the excess of a taxpayer's alternative minimum taxable income over an exemption amount by 26 percent for adjusted gross income up to $187,800 and 28 percent for AGI in excess of $187,800 (20 percent for corporate taxpayers), and then reducing the product by the taxpayer's alternative minimum tax foreign tax credit. AMTI is computed by taking taxable income (including unrelated business taxable income, real estate investment trust taxable income, life insurance company taxable income, or any other income base used to calculate regular tax liability), adding or subtracting special adjustments, and adding tax preference items.

Amortization

The commonly known dictionary meaning of the word *amortization* differs from its income tax application. The principal dictionary meaning is the building up of a fund, through periodic payments, for the purpose of paying off an obligation when it becomes due in thefuture, such as a mortgage. But usually in income tax parlance, amortization means the writing off of an amount over a definite period (such as amortizing a bond premium or discount over the life of the bonds), similar to the depreciation write-off on depreciable property.

Amount realized

The term *amount realized* is given a special meaning in finding gain or loss on a sale or exchange of property. The realized gain or loss is the difference between the amount realized and the *adjusted basis* of the asset. The amount realized is the sum of the money and the fair market value of other property received.

Annualizing

Annualizing is a procedure whereby a taxpayer estimates from the income received during a portion of a year what the income for the entire year will be if income continues to be received at the same rate. This process is used in computing the tax on short-period returns and also for avoiding the penalty for underpayment of estimated taxes.

Annuity

An *annuity* is a periodic payment, whether for a period certain or for one or more lives. Under the general rule for taxing an annuity, the taxpayer's investment in the contract is usually divided by the number of payments expected, and that portion of each payment is nontaxable. The remainder of each payment is taxable as received. The Internal Revenue Service provides tables for computing tax-free portions of annuity receipts.

Assessment of tax

The Commissioner of Internal Revenue places the amount of unpaid tax on a list for collection, in effect a charge against the taxpayer on the books of the government. Before any additional tax may be assessed, the Commissioner must send a notice of deficiency and cannot assess the tax before allowing the taxpayer to file a petition with the Tax Court.

Assignment of income doctrine

The principle that income is taxed to the individual who earned it, even if the right to the income has been transferred to another prior to recognition.

Association

An *association* is a body of persons who unite for some special business or purpose, the body itself being invested with some, but not full, corporate rights and powers. For income tax purposes, an association is taxed in the same manner as a corporation.

B

Bad debt

Whether or not it relates to a business transaction, a bad debt can be deducted in the year in which it becomes uncollectible. If a business debt is partially uncollectible, a portion may be charged off. A nonbusiness bad debt is treated in the same way as a short-term capital loss. A debt that arises from the performance of services or the selling of goods by a cash-basis taxpayer may not be deducted if the income from the services or the profit from the sale has not previously been reported as income. However, a bad debt that arises from the lending of money is deductible, subject to the above-mentioned limitation on a nonbusiness bad debt.

Basis

The term *basis*, for income tax purposes, is used mainly in connection with determining the amount of gain or loss on a sale of property or in computing depreciation. It represents the cost of the property to the taxpayer, actually or constructively, but it has a broader meaning than the term *cost*. The *basis* (adjusted) of property is deducted from the *amount realized* to determine the realized gain or loss on its sale. If the property was acquired by the taxpayer through a purchase, the basis is its cost, except in special circumstances such as in the conversion of the property from personal to rental or other business purposes, in which case the basis for loss and for *depreciation* may be different from the basis for *gain*. If the property was acquired as gift property, inherited property, property received in an exchange, etc., then special rules for finding basis apply.

Bequest

A *bequest* is a gift by will of personal property. The law provides a special basis for finding gain or loss or depreciation in the case of property acquired by bequest. The basis is then the value of the property at the date of the testator's death. If a bequest is of money to be paid at intervals, then to the extent that it is paid out of income from property, it is taxable income to the recipient.

Blind and elderly deduction

An additional standard deduction amount of $1,250 is allowed for an elderly or blind individual who is married or who is a surviving spouse. An additional $1,550 is allowed for a single individual or for a head of household who is elderly or blind. Thus, a married couple, each of whom is both elderly and blind, receives an extra $5,000 ($1,250 × 4) standard deduction.

Boot

Boot is a term that is sometimes used to describe the other property received in an exchange which, but for such other property, would be nontaxable. Partial gain may be recognized from the receipt of such boot, not to exceed the fair market value of the boot. Such boot or other property consists of money or property other than stock or securities (or other than like property in like-kind exchanges) which may be received tax free.

Business purpose

When a transaction occurs it must be grounded in a business purpose other than tax avoidance. Tax avoidance is not a proper motive for being in business. The concept of business purpose was originally set forth in *Gregory v. Helvering*, 35-1 USTC ¶9043, 293 U.S. 465, 55 S.Ct. 266 (1935). In this case, the Supreme Court ruled that a transaction aiming at tax-free status had no business purpose. Further, the Court stated that merely transferring assets from one corporation to another under a plan which can be associated with neither firm was invalid. This was merely a series of legal transactions that when viewed by the Court in its entirety had no business purpose.

C

Cafeteria plan

A *cafeteria plan* is a separate written benefit plan maintained by an employer for the benefit of its employees, under which all participants are employees and each participant has the opportunity to select particular benefits. The participant may choose from among two or more benefits consisting of cash and qualified benefits.

Calendar year

A *calendar year* is a period of 12 months beginning January 1 and ending December 31. It is the most widely used accounting period. It must be used by a taxpayer who does not keep a regular set of books on a different accounting period.

Capital asset

The term *capital asset* in income tax law generally means all business and nonbusiness assets with the following exceptions: inventory, depreciable personal and real property, certain works created through personal efforts, business accounts and notes receivable, and certain U.S. publications.

Capital expenditure

A capital expenditure is one that is made for assets of a more or less permanent nature—those with a useful life of more than one year. Such an expenditure may not be deducted in the year made, even though made in connection with a trade or business. In other words, it is capitalized. But if the assets are wasting assets they may, in proper cases, be the subject of a depreciation deduction. Uniform capitalization rules require capitalization of certain costs and expenditures.

Capital gains

Capital gains are gains from the sale or exchange of a *capital asset* as that term is defined above. The excess of capital gains over capital losses is called capital gain net income. If a capital asset has been held for more than the requisite holding period at the time of sale, the gain is a long-term capital gain. Corporations must treat capital gains as ordinary income.

Capital losses

Capital losses are losses from the sale or exchange of a capital asset. The excess of capital losses over capital gains is called net capital loss. A corporation may deduct a capital loss of any taxable year in that year only to the extent of capital gain. The excess of losses may be carried back three years and carried forward five years, but only as an offset against capital gains of such later years. If there are no such capital gains, the deduction is lost. In the case of an individual, short-term and long-term capital losses are combined for purposes of offsetting up to $3,000 of ordinary income annually. Excess losses may be carried forward indefinitely.

Capitalization—See Capital expenditure

Carryback and carryover

Income tax carrybacks include the net operating loss carryback, the capital loss carryback (for corporations only), the foreign tax credit carryback, and the general business credit carryback. The first two are applied against income and the last two are credits against tax.

Carrying charge

This accounting term denotes an expense for idle or nonproductive property that is incurred for the purpose of *carrying* the property. The income tax law permits a taxpayer to capitalize instead of deducting currently as an expense taxes and interest chargeable to unimproved and unproductive real property. Also, a taxpayer can capitalize otherwise deductible expenses incurred during the period of construction or improvement of real property, and taxes and interest directly related to machinery and equipment purchased, up to the date they are put to productive use. In addition, if the finance or service charge on an installment purchase of personal property is separately stated but the actual interest charge cannot be ascertained, such a charge is referred to as a carrying charge. And a portion of the charge is deductible as interest under a special formula.

Cash basis

The cash basis is one of the two principal recognized methods of accounting. It must be used by all taxpayers who do not keep books. It is elective as to all other taxpayers (except corporations, certain partnerships, and tax-exempt trusts); however, it may not be used if inventories are necessary in order to reflect income. On the cash basis, income is reported only as it is received, in money or other property having a fair market value, and expenses are deductible only in the year they are paid.

Casualty loss

Although deduction for a loss generally is confined to a loss connected with a trade or business or a transaction entered into for profit, the law also allows deduction of a casualty loss for all types of assets, including personal assets such as a home, jewelry, clothing, etc. Theft, although not strictly a casualty, is in the same category for income tax deduction purposes. Personal casualty losses are deductible only to the extent that each such loss exceeds $100 per occurrence in 2017 and that the aggregate excess is greater than 10 percent of adjusted gross income.

Child-care expense—See Dependent care expense

Claim for refund

A claim for refund must be made by a taxpayer entitled to get back part or all of the tax paid. The claim may be made on the tax return or, in the case of individual or corporate income taxes, may be made on Form 1040X or 1120X. In other cases, refund claims should be made on amended returns or Form 843.

Claim of right

The term *claim of right* is used in the Code in connection with money or other property received as income which the recipient holds under a claim of right, but which the recipient is required to restore in whole or in part to the payer in a later year because it develops that the recipient did not have an unrestricted right to such property. If the amount restored exceeds $3,000, Code Sec. 1341 provides some relief, by means of a tax limitation in the year of restoration, from the requirement that the restored amount must be deducted in the year of restoration and may not reduce the income of the prior year. The *right* to the money or other property means a just and legal claim to hold, use, or enjoy it, or to convey or donate it.

Community property

Community property is property owned by husband and wife in community, each sharing equally in the income therefrom. The concept of ownership of property by a husband and wife in community is of Spanish origin, adopted from early Spanish law by nine western and southern states—Alaska, California, Nevada, New Mexico, Arizona, Idaho, Washington, Louisiana, and Texas—as well as Wisconsin.

Complex trust

A complex trust is one which permits accumulation of current income, provides for charitable contributions, or distributes principal during the taxable year. For tax purposes, it is to be distinguished from a *simple trust.*

Conduits

Some entities are not tax paying. They pass through their income (loss) to owners (beneficiaries). A partnership is an example of a conduit. Partnerships do not pay taxes; they merely report the partnership's taxable income or losses. The income (loss) flows directly to the partners. However, partnerships do compute partnership taxable income. Other types of conduits are grantor trusts and S corporations.

Consent dividend

A *consent dividend* is not a dividend actually paid by a corporation. It is merely represented by signed consents by a stockholder to be taxed as if the stockholder has really received the amount of the distribution stated in the consent. It is used in order to avoid the imposition of the accumulated earnings tax and the personal holding company tax in cases where this tax might otherwise be imposed and the company does not wish to make an actual distribution.

Consolidated return

Affiliated corporations may file one consolidated return, eliminating intercompany transactions, instead of filing separate returns.

Constructive ownership of stock

In determining the percentage of stock ownership of a stockholder in a corporation, in order to find whether the stockholder controls the corporation or to make other tests of ownership, the Code in several instances provides that the stockholder will be constructively regarded as the owner of shares of stock held by certain other persons. For example, the rule is applied in disallowing a loss on sales between certain related persons.

Constructive-receipt doctrine

A taxpayer on the cash basis is taxed on income only as it is *received.* However, if the income was unreservedly subject to the taxpayer's demand and the taxpayer could have received it but chose not to do so, it is regarded as having been *constructively received* and is taxable. Interest on a bank deposit is a good example.

Contribution to capital

A contribution to capital denotes the money or other property contributed to a corporation by either a stockholder or a nonstockholder. Where a stockholder advances money to a corporation, the tax question on insolvency of the corporation is whether the money was advanced as a loan or as a capital contribution. If it is a capital contribution, the stockholder may not deduct a nonbusiness bad debt. Where a nonstockholder makes a contribution to a corporation, such as payments by a city to a manufacturer for moving its factory to the city, the contribution is not income to the corporation. The basis of property so contributed (or property purchased with money contributions) is zero. If money is contributed and no property is purchased with it, the basis of the corporation's assets is reduced.

Contributions

Contributions usually means gifts made to charitable organizations. A contribution is deductible by both individuals and corporations, to a limited extent. In some cases, the word *contributions* is used in the Code in a different sense, but in those cases the meaning is apparent from the context. (*Contribution to capital,* above, is a case in point.)

Controlled corporate groups

Controlled groups of corporations basically fall into two classifications: parent-subsidiary controlled groups and brother-sister controlled groups. A parent-subsidiary controlled group is one in which one or more chains of corporations are connected through stock ownership with a common parent corporation. At least 80 percent of the voting power or stock value of each corporation in the group other than the parent is owned by one or more corporations in the group, and the common parent owns at least 80 percent of the voting power or stock value of one of the other corporations in the group. A brother-sister controlled group is a controlled group in which at least 80 percent of the voting power or stock value of two or more corporations is owned by the same five or fewer persons (individuals, estates, or trusts) and these persons own more than 50 percent of the voting power or stock value of each corporation.

A controlled group of corporations should be distinguished from an affiliated group of corporations, a term related to elections to file a consolidated return and to take a 100 percent dividends-received credit. An *affiliated group* is formed when at least 80 percent of the total combined voting power of all classes of stock and at least 80 percent of each class of nonvoting stock of each corporation in the group are owned by one or more other corporations in the group. Thus, a parent-subsidiary group is not an *affiliated* group unless at least 80 percent of the nonvoting stock of each corporation in the group is owned by another corporation in the group. A brother-sister controlled group can never qualify as an *affiliated* group since the voting power of stock value of two or more corporations is owned by a noncorporate entity.

Corporation

For income tax purposes, the word *corporation* has a broader meaning than its customary one. It includes an association, joint stock company, and insurance company. All are taxed as if they were corporations, although insurance companies are subject to special rules and are taxed at special rates.

Cost

Cost is the purchase price paid for property, or the value at which it is taken into income (as in the case of services paid for in property). It is the amount most often applied against the amount realized from the sale of property in determining the profit or loss. It is also the figure most often used in determining the depreciation deduction. However, in special circumstances, where property is not acquired by purchase, there may be a special basis for a finding of gain or loss or depreciation.

Cost depletion—See Depletion

Cost or market, whichever is lower

This phrase is used only in reference to inventory valuations. Most taxpayers prefer to use *cost or market, whichever is lower,* as a basis for valuing their inventories since this method affords an opportunity to take advantage of a drop in the market so that profits can be reduced accordingly before disposition of the goods. If *cost* only is used, a drop in the market cannot affect the income until the merchandise is sold. Either method ((a) cost, or (b) cost or market, whichever is lower) is acceptable, but either one, once adopted, must be followed unless a permission to change is obtained.

Credits against tax

A credit against the tax, or a tax credit, is an amount that is subtracted from the income tax liability of a taxpayer in a given taxable year. The tax credit differs from a deduction in that the credit is subtracted from the tax itself, resulting in a dollar-for-dollar reduction in the tax liability; the deduction is subtracted from either gross income or adjusted gross income, resulting in a reduction in the amount of income subject to tax. A nonrefundable credit is one that cannot be refunded to the extent that it exceeds the income tax of the current year (e.g., the investment credit). A refundable credit can be refunded to the extent that it exceeds tax liability (e.g., the earned income credit).

Credits or refunds

Where tax is overpaid for any year, it ordinarily will be refunded by the IRS if the taxpayer owes no tax for any other year. If the taxpayer does owe a tax, the overpayment is credited against the tax that is due the government, and any balance is refunded. Credits and refunds may be allowed only within specified periods if, within such periods, a claim for refund or credit is filed. See *Claim for refund.*

D

Dealer

A dealer, as referred to in income tax law, is one who sells to customers in the ordinary course of a trade or business. Examples are securities and real estate dealers and other dealers regularly selling on the installment plan.

Death benefit

The Code uses the phrase *death benefit* to exclude from gross income life insurance proceeds payable by reason of death.

Declining-balance method

Declining balance is the name for a method of depreciation under the general rules. An agreed-upon uniform rate is applied, not to the original cost or other basis of an asset but to its depreciating balance. Thus, the amount to which the uniform rate is applied *declines* every year. For this reason, the rate must be higher than the straight-line rate. The Code permits using a rate of up to 200 percent of the straight-line rate.

Deductions from gross income

Deductions from gross income are, as the name indicates, amounts representing expenditures or amounts of such personal exemptions for which deduction is allowed from the amount of gross income reported. They are to be distinguished from *exclusions* from gross income, which are not taken into income at all. Deductions are taken from gross income to arrive at adjusted gross income. See also *Taxable income* and *Adjusted gross income*.

Deficiency

A *deficiency* is the amount by which the actual tax (as it should have been computed) exceeds the amount shown on the return, if any, plus any amounts previously assessed as a deficiency and minus any rebates. See also *Assessment of tax*.

Dependent

A dependent is one of certain specified relatives for whom the taxpayer provides over half of the support for the calendar year. Nonrelatives living as members of the taxpayer's household are also treated as dependents if the support test is met. For each dependent, the taxpayer is allowed a deduction of $4,050 for 2017.

Dependent-care expense

A credit against tax is allowed for employment-related expenses paid by an individual to enable him or her to be gainfully employed. Taxpayers with adjusted gross incomes of $15,000 or less are allowed a credit equal to 35 percent of employment-related expenses. For taxpayers with adjusted gross incomes of over $15,000 through $43,000, the credit is reduced by one percentage point for each $2,000 of adjusted gross income, or fraction thereof, above $15,000. For taxpayers with adjusted gross incomes of over $43,000, the credit is 20 percent of employment-related expenses. The maximum amount of employment-related expenses to which the credit can apply is $3,000 if one child or dependent is involved and $6,000 if two or more are involved.

Depletion

The decrease in natural resources (minerals, coal, timber, etc.) due to their extraction from the source of supply and disposition by sale or otherwise is called depletion. The Code provides allowances for the exhaustion of such assets. There are two methods of computing depletion. One is known as cost depletion, which is the writing off of that part of the cost or other basis of the deposits which the number of units extracted in that year bears to the total estimated number of recoverable units. The other method, called percentage depletion, permits deduction of a specified percentage of the gross income from the property. In each year, the method that results in the greater deduction is to be used.

Depreciation

Depreciation is a decline in value or price. For income tax purposes, it is a deduction to reflect the gradual wasting away of an asset due to the passage of time or the use to which the asset is put, or a combination of both. The Code permits deduction of a reasonable allowance for this exhaustion of property used in a trade or business, including rental property, measured by certain criteria, such as useful life. The Accelerated Cost Recovery System (ACRS) and Modified ACRS (MACRS) are generally referred to as systems of depreciation that provide for recovery of cost over statutory periods that are shorter than the useful life of the property.

Devise

A devise is a gift of real property by will. In the income tax law, the term is used mainly in connection with determining the basis of property so acquired. Basis of property acquired by devise is the value at the date of death of the decedent, or at the alternate valuation date if elected for estate tax purposes. A devise is excluded from gross income for federal income tax purposes.

Disability income exclusion—See Tax credit for the elderly

Dissolution of corporation

The dissolution of a corporation follows its liquidation. It is the technical termination of a corporation's existence by surrender or forfeiture of its charter. A corporation remains liable for the filing of income tax returns as long as it is in existence and until its dissolution, even though it is not doing business.

Distributable net income

To the extent that an estate or trust has distributable net income, every distribution to a beneficiary except lump-sum payments of bequests, devises, or inheritances is taxable income. The distributable net income of an estate or trust is the same as its taxable income, with certain specified modifications.

Distribution by corporation

As used in the income tax law, the term *distribution by corporation* refers to any amounts paid by a corporation to its shareholders, or any property distributed to them, other than for value received in goods or services. It is a broader term than *dividend,* defined below, for a distribution may be a dividend and, therefore, taxable income, or it may be an offset against the stockholder's cost or other basis of the stock.

Dividend

A distribution by corporation, defined above, may be either a dividend or a return of capital invested. If it is a dividend, it is taxed as gross income. A dividend is any distribution by a corporation out of its accumulated earnings and profits or out of earnings and profits of the taxable year as of the close of the year (without diminution by reason of distributions during the year).

Dividends-received deduction

A corporation receives a 70 percent or 80 percent deduction—with limitations—for dividends it receives, unless it is an affiliated corporation which does not, or cannot, file a consolidated return. Such a corporation may elect a 100 percent dividends-received deduction.

Domestic corporation

For tax purposes, a corporation created or organized in the United States or under the laws of the United States or any state.

E

Earned income

Earned income, which is usually defined with reference to the self-employment income rules, generally means wages, salaries, tips, professional fees, and other amounts received as compensation for personal services rendered. This term is often used to distinguish unearned income, which includes interest and dividends. The term is sometimes more specifically defined, e.g., for purposes of the foreign income exclusion and for determining self-employment income. In addition to foreign income and self-employment income, the term is relevant to determining income tax liability of minors, IRA contributions, and credits for low-income and elderly or permanently disabled taxpayers.

Earnings and profits (E&P)

Accumulated earnings and profits, as well as earnings and profits of the current taxable year, measure the amount of a distribution by a corporation to its shareholders which represents a dividend. The earnings and profits of a distributing corporation are not the same as net income or taxable income. They include nontaxable as well as taxable income but do not include realized gains or losses which are not recognized for income tax purposes.

Elderly taxpayers—See Blind and elderly deduction and Tax credit for the elderly

Employee

For income tax purposes, an employee is distinguishable from an independent contractor. This is important, for the withholding of income taxes on wages applies only to an employee. Also, employee status will affect the manner and extent of allowance of some deductions. The regulations state that an employee is one who is subject to the will and control of the employer not only as to what is to be done but as to how it is to be done.

Employee stock option

An employee stock option is an option granted to an employee to purchase the employer's stock. Employee stock options to which special income tax treatment is accorded are known as statutory options. Incentive stock options and employee stock purchase plan options are the only two kinds of statutory options that may still be created and exercised.

Employee Stock Ownership Plan (ESOP)

An ESOP is a qualified stock bonus plan designed to invest primarily in qualifying employer securities.

Entity

Generally, for tax purposes there are four types of entities: individuals, corporations, trusts, and estates. Each entity determines its own tax and files its own tax return. Each tax entity has its specific rules to follow for the determination of taxable income. Basically the concept of "entity" answers the question "Who is the taxpayer?" Note that partnerships were not in the list of entities. For tax purposes partnerships are not tax-paying entities. The income (loss) flows directly to the partners.

Estate

The meaning of this word in the income tax law is much narrower than its general meaning, which, broadly speaking, is an interest in property. For federal tax purposes, it has two specific meanings. The gross estate of a decedent consists of the assets, both probate and nonprobate, of the decedent for estate tax purposes. Taxable estate is the gross estate less deductions and exemptions. In its most widely used sense, for income tax purposes, an estate is a taxpayer. It is the executorship or administration of a decedent's estate, subject to a court having probate jurisdiction by a fiduciary, and is treated as a separate taxpayer. For income tax purposes, although clearly distinguishable, an estate is generally subject to the same Code provisions in determining taxable income as a trust. Each is allowed deductions for distributions to beneficiaries, such deductions representing gross income in the hands of the beneficiaries. Income accumulated that is neither distributed nor distributable during the taxable year is taxable to the estate, after offsetting against it all allowable deductions.

Estimated tax

Individual taxpayers must pay estimated taxes on as many as four payment dates unless estimated tax is not expected to exceed $1,000. A corporation deposits its estimated tax in advance on as many as four payment dates (April 15, June 15, September 15, and December 15 for calendar-year corporations). Trusts and estates must make quarterly estimated tax payments in the same manner as individuals, except that an estate is exempt from making such payments during its first two taxable years.

Excess net passive income—See Passive investment income

Executor

An executor is a person appointed via a will to carry out the testator's directions and to dispose of property according to a will. The executor manages an estate. (Feminine form: executrix.)

Exemption

An exemption is a reduction in net income allowed on account of status or dependency. Thus, in arriving at the tax base, or the figure at which the tax rates are applied, net income is reduced by the amount of personal and dependency exemptions. Individuals, estates and trusts are allowed exemptions. Every estate is allowed an exemption of $600. A trust is allowed an exemption of $100 or $300, depending on the type of trust. Except for dependents, every individual taxpayer is allowed at least one exemption of $4,050 in 2017 (adjusted for inflation). On a joint return, the two (or more) exemptions of both the husband and wife are allowed. One spouse is allowed the exemption (or exemptions) of the other on a separate return if the other has no gross income and is not the dependent of another person. Exemptions also are allowable for dependents of the taxpayer.

Expenses

Expenses, for federal income tax purposes, are divisible into three general classes: (1) trade or business expenses, (2) nonbusiness expenses incurred in connection with the production of income, for management, conservation, or maintenance of property held for production of income, or in connection with the determination, collection, or refund of any tax, and (3) personal, family, or living expenses. Only expenses in the first two categories are deductible.

Expenses in the third category are not deductible, except in a few unusual cases (medical expenses, charitable contributions, etc.) where they are specifically allowed by law.

F

Fair market value

The fair market value of property is that amount which would induce a willing seller to sell and a willing buyer to buy the property. Market quotations are an acceptable measure of value, except where the quantity of property involved is so great that its sale would affect the market quotations before the sale is finished. Unlisted stocks sometimes are valued on the basis of the corporate assets, including goodwill, whether or not they are entered on the books. Real estate is valued on the basis of net earnings, location, etc., and this value is best proved by an expert appraisal.

Fiduciary

This term usually denotes the executor or administrator of the estate of a decedent or the trustee of a trust. Since an estate or trust is a taxpayer, the fiduciary is charged with the responsibility of filing a return for the estate or trust. The term also includes a guardian, conservator, or receiver. See also *Estate*.

Filing of return

Filing a return consists of filling it out and mailing or hand-delivering it, generally, to the appropriate IRS location. The time for filing an income tax return is specifically stated in the law, and penalties may be imposed for late filing.

First-in, first-out rule

This rule is generally applied to otherwise unidentifiable stocks where a number of shares of the same kind of stock have been bought at different times and different prices. If they cannot otherwise be identified, those which were purchased first are regarded as having been sold first in determining the cost price to be applied against the selling price for the purpose of determining any gain or loss on the sale. The term is also applied to inventory items where the LIFO method (see *Last-in, first-out rule,* below) is not used. As so used, the first-in, first-out rule is also referred to as the FIFO method.

Fiscal year

A fiscal year, for income tax purposes, is a period of 12 months, ending on the last day of a month other than December, or the special 52-53-week period. It is thus distinguished from a calendar year, which always ends on December 31. It is a recognized accounting period for income tax purposes.

Foreign corporation

A foreign corporation is one which is not organized under the laws of one of the states or territories or of the United States. Taxation of a foreign corporation depends on whether or not its income is *effectively connected* with a U.S. trade or business. Special rules apply to United States shareholders of certain controlled foreign corporations.

Foreign tax credit or deduction

If a United States citizen or resident or a domestic corporation incurs or pays income taxes to a foreign country, an election may be made to deduct such taxes in determining taxable income or to take them as a credit against United States tax. The election must be made as to all foreign taxes incurred or paid in the taxable year. Generally, the credit will be limited to the percentage of the total tax against which the credit is being taken that the taxable income from foreign countries is of the total taxable income. Special rules apply to a U.S. shareholder of a controlled foreign corporation or a shareholder in a foreign investment company.

G

General business credit

The general business credit consists of the investment tax credit (the sum of the rehabilitation investment credit, the energy investment credit, and the reforestation investment credit), the work opportunity credit, the welfare-to-work credit, the alcohol fuels credit, the research credit, the low-income housing credit, the disabled access credit, the enhanced oil recovery credit, and five other credits.

Gift

A gift has been defined as a valid transfer of property from one to another without consideration or compensation. For income tax purposes, the words *gift* and *contribution* usually have separate meanings, the latter word being used in connection with contributions to charitable, religious, etc. organizations, whereas the word *gift* refers to transfers of money or property to private individuals, needy persons, friends, relatives, etc. The recipient of a gift is not required to include it in gross income. The donor is not entitled to deduct it (except for a business gift to a customer of $25 or less per donee per year).

Grantor trust

A grantor trust is one in which the grantor retains control over the income or principal, or both, to such an extent that the grantor is regarded as being substantially the owner of the trust property and of the income. The grantor is taxable on this trust income. The law contains specific tests to find whether the grantor is the substantial owner of the trust property.

Gross estate

Gross estate is an estate tax term. It means a decedent's entire property which is subject to the estate tax, that is, prior to any deductions.

Gross income

Gross income, for income tax purposes, refers to all income which is taxable. The law enumerates specific items of income which are not to be included in gross income and, therefore, are nontaxable. With these exceptions, all income is includible in gross income.

H

Head of household

Head of household has a specific meaning in the income tax law. By means of a special tax rate table, a head of a household receives a tax advantage over a single individual but less than that afforded a husband and wife who file a joint return. Generally, a head of a household is an unmarried individual who is not a *surviving spouse* and who maintains as a home a household which is the principal place of abode of at least one child or grandchild or any other relative (except a cousin).

Holding period

The holding period of property is the length of time that property has been held by a taxpayer or the length of time the taxpayer is treated for income tax purposes as having held it. The term is most important for income tax purposes as it relates to capital gains transactions. Whether a capital gain or loss is long- or short-term depends on whether the asset sold or exchanged has been held by the taxpayer for more than 12 months.

I

Imputed interest

Taxpayers cannot sell property under a deferred payment contract in which no interest or unrealistically low interest is charged and realize all capital gains or increased capital gains on the sale. Unstated or imputed interest is taxable to the seller as ordinary interest income.

Incentive stock option

The incentive stock option is a statutory employee stock option. No income tax consequences result from the grant or exercise of such an option, and, if holding and other requirements are met, gain on eventual sale of the employer's stock will be long-term capital gain.

Income

Income, in its broad sense, is the gain derived from capital, labor, or both. It is distinguishable from the capital itself. Ordinarily, for income tax purposes, the word *income* is not used alone. It is used in conjunction with such descriptive terms as *gross income, taxable income,* and *adjusted gross income,* all of which are defined herein.

Income effectively connected

All income from U.S. sources which is *effectively connected* with the conduct of a trade or business in the United States is taxed to nonresident aliens and foreign corporations at the same rates as apply to U.S. citizens and domestic corporations. Investment and other fixed or determinable periodical income (interest, dividends, rents, wages, etc.) of a nonresident alien is taxed at a flat 30 percent rate, whether or not the recipient engages in a trade or business in the United States, so long as such income is not effectively connected with a trade or business in the United States. Income is considered effectively connected if it is derived from assets used in, or held for use in, the United States, and if the activities of the U.S. business are a material factor in the realization of the income.

Income-shifting

Income-shifting is the transfer of income from one family member to another who is subject to a lower tax rate or the selection of a form of business that decreases the tax liability for its owners.

Individual Retirement Account (IRA)

Any individual may contribute 100 percent of earned income, up to $5,500 a year, to an IRA ($11,000 on a joint return, i.e. $5,500 per spouse). Taxpayers over age 50 are allowed to contribute an additional $1,000. The contributions are deductible from gross income, except for individuals who participate in a qualified deferred compensation plan with AGI over a certain level ($62,000 in 2017, and for joint filers, $99,000 in 2017. The investment grows tax-deferred, but all withdrawals constitute gross income. A 10 percent penalty on gross income is levied on pre-age 59½ withdrawals, except on account of disability, death, first-time home purchases (up to $10,000), insurance premiums for the unemployed, deductible medical expenses, as well as withdrawals in the shape of annuities. Withdrawals must start with respect to the year the participant reaches age 70½. An IRA may receive tax-deferred rollovers from other qualified plans, including other IRAs. Distributions from IRAs are not subject to withholding.

The Roth IRA began in 1998. Nondeductible contributions to a Roth IRA can be made by individuals with AGI up to $118,000 ($186,000 on a joint return). The income is *never* taxed if the account is more than five years old *and* the participant is deceased, disabled, or over 59½ years old. The overall annual limit is $5,500 ($6,500 for taxpayers over age 50) per individual for *all* contributions to *all* IRAs (except education IRAs), deductible or not in 2017. No age limit exists for establishing, making contributions to, or accumulating funds in a Roth IRA. The 10 percent penalty provisions are the same as for a regular IRA, but the contributions may be withdrawn first, at any time, for any purpose, without tax or penalty consequences.

Inheritance

As distinguished from a bequest or devise, an inheritance is property acquired through laws of descent and distribution from a person who dies without leaving a will. Property so acquired takes as its basis, for gain or loss on later disposition or for depreciation, the fair market value of the property at the date of death of the decedent from whom it is acquired. An inheritance of property does not give rise to taxable income, but the *income* from an inheritance does. And if the inheritance is of income from property, such income is taxable.

Installment method

The installment method of reporting income allows the profit on an installment sale to be taxed over the period that payments are received. The amount taxed in any year is equal to the payments received times the gross profit ratio (the total gross profit divided by the total contract price). However, the entire amount of any gain recaptured under Code Sec. 1245 or 1250 is reported in the year of sale regardless of whether any payment is received in that first year. Use of the installment method is mandatory unless the taxpayer elects not to report on the installment method.

Inter vivos trust

An inter vivos trust is a trust created during the lifetime of the person setting up the trust. A testamentary trust is one set up under the will of the decedent.

Intestate

One not having a will; a person who dies without a will is said to die intestate.

Inventory

An inventory is a detailed list of articles of property. In the true accounting sense, and for income tax purposes, it refers only to a list of articles comprising stock in trade—articles held for sale to customers in the regular course of a trade or business. The cost of goods sold during the year is determined by adding to the inventory at the beginning of the year the purchases made during the year and subtracting from this sum the inventory at the close of the year.

Involuntary conversion

An involuntary conversion of property results when property is destroyed in whole or in part, stolen, seized, requisitioned or condemned (or where there is a threat or imminence of requisition or condemnation) and, as a result, the property is converted into money or other similar property, through insurance proceeds, condemnation awards, etc. The law has special provisions on involuntary conversion only where the conversion results in gain—that is, where the amount recovered exceeds the cost or other basis of the property converted. The law permits the nonrecognition of gain on such an involuntary conversion.

Itemized deductions

Itemized deductions are certain expenses of a personal nature that are specifically allowed as deductions. Included in this group are: moving expenses, medical expenses, state and local income taxes, property taxes, mortgage interest, charitable contributions, personal casualty losses, and miscellaneous employee expenses.

J

Joint return—See Surviving spouse

Joint tenancy

Where property is held in the names of two or more persons with the title passing from the first joint tenant to die to the other joint tenant (or joint tenants) upon death.

Joint venture

A joint venture is an enterprise participated in by associates acting together, there being a community of interests and each associate having a right to participate in its control or management. For income tax purposes, a joint venture is treated in all respects as a partnership, not taxable in its own capacity, but regarded as a taxpayer for the purpose of computing its taxable income, which is distributable among the associates in the proportions agreed upon. Such distributive shares are reported by the associates on their individual income tax returns.

K

Keogh plan—See Self-employed individual's retirement plan

Key employee

Long a term of general application, especially in regard to insurance, *key employee* now has a statutory definition for purposes of the rules that apply to *top-heavy* plans. For these purposes, *key employee* includes an officer of the employer earning more than a specified amount, any one of the 10 employees owning the largest interests in the employer, a 5 percent owner of the employer, or a 1 percent owner who is paid more than $175,000 per year. See also *Top-heavy plan.*

L

Last-in, first-out rule

LIFO is the popular abbreviation for the *last-in, first-out* rule for identifying items in an inventory to determine their cost. By this method, goods remaining on hand at the close of the taxable year are treated as being, first, those included in the opening inventory to the extent thereof, and, second, those acquired during the taxable year.

Legacy

A disposition of personal property by will.

Lien for taxes

The U.S. Treasury Department, as part of its tax collection machinery, has a legal claim to the property of a taxpayer whose taxes are delinquent or overdue. Assessment of tax, demand, and refusal or neglect to pay control the creation and the effective date of the lien. Sometimes the lien will attach to property in the possession of a third-person transferee or fiduciary. Sometimes a creditor or other nontaxpayer, as well as the government, may assert a claim to the same property. The question of priorities must then be settled.

Limitations—See Statute of limitations

Liquidation of corporation

Complete liquidation of a corporation is the winding up of its affairs by the settling of its accounts, the paying of all debts, the collecting of assets and the turning of the remainder over to the shareholders in exchange for their stock. Complete liquidation precedes dissolution of the corporation and is not entirely synonymous with it. See *Dissolution of corporation*. A partial liquidation is a calling in of a part of the stock, with or without cessation of a part of the corporate activities. Special rules apply to the sale by a corporation of its assets as a step in liquidation, and to the treatment of liquidation distributions received by the shareholders.

Long-term capital gain and loss

Long-term capital gains and losses are gains and losses on the sale or exchange of capital assets that have been held for more than 12 months. A net long-term capital gain or loss is the excess of gains over losses, or vice versa. An excess of net long-term capital gains over net short-term capital losses is taxed as ordinary income to corporations.

M

Merger

A statutory merger (that is, one effected under the laws of the state) is a reorganization for income tax purposes, upon which no gain or loss is recognized under the conditions specified in the Code. A merger is the union of two or more corporations into one, the others giving up their existence and transferring all of their properties and liabilities to the one continuing corporation. It is distinguishable from a consolidation, which is the transfer of two or more corporations into a new corporation, the transferring corporations giving up their existence.

Minimum tax—See Alternative minimum tax

Minority interest

Stock ownership of 20 percent or less in a corporation which is at least 80 percent owned by another corporation.

Modified Accelerated Cost Recovery System (MACRS)—
See Accelerated Cost Recovery System (ACRS)

Multiple support agreement

If two or more persons who would otherwise be entitled to an exemption for a dependent together furnish more than one-half of a dependent's support, anyone who furnishes more than 10 percent of the support is entitled to the exemption if all the others who furnish more than 10 percent of the support file written declarations that they will not claim an exemption for the individual supported for that taxable year.

N

Negligence

For income tax purposes, there is a penalty of 5 percent of the underpayment if any part of an underpayment of tax is due to negligence or intentional disregard of rules and Regulations, but without intent to defraud. Negligence is a lack of the reasonable care and caution expected of a prudent person.

Net operating loss (NOL)

A net operating loss is limited substantially to a net loss incurred in the operation of a trade or business, although a casualty loss or a loss from a sale of a business asset is included within its scope. A net operating loss may be carried back two years against the income of those two years to the earliest year first. Any unused portion of such loss may be carried forward past the taxable year for 20 years.

Net passive income—See Passive investment income

Nonrefundable credits

Nonrefundable credits are allowed as an offset against tax liability. Since no payment has been made to the government, the taxpayer cannot receive a refund if the credit exceeds the tax liability.

Nonresident alien

A nonresident alien, for income tax purposes, is an individual who is not a citizen or resident of the United States. Taxation depends on whether U.S. source income is effectively connected with the conduct of a U.S. trade or business. See also *Income effectively connected.*

O

Obsolescence—See Depreciation

Organizational expenses

Organizational expenses are the costs of organizing a corporation before it begins active business. The Code permits amortization of these expenses over a period to be chosen by the taxpayer, but not less than 60 months. Such charging off is elective with the taxpayer. Organizational expenses for this purpose do not include expenses of issuing or selling stock or reorganization expenses unless they are incident to the creation of a *new* corporation.

Overpayment of tax

An overpayment of tax is a payment or a total of payments in excess of the amount determined to be the correct amount of tax for the taxable year. The Code provides that the term includes that part of the amount of the payment of any internal revenue tax which is assessed or collected after the expiration of the limitation period properly applicable to such assessment or collection.

P

Paid-in surplus

Paid-in surplus is an accounting term. It represents amounts paid in to a corporation by its shareholders, not in payment for their stock, but, after their stock has been fully paid for, as additional working capital for the corporation. Such paid-in surplus is not taxable income to the corporation. Nor is it deductible by the shareholder. It becomes an additional cost of the shareholder's stock. If the paid-in surplus consists of property other than money, its basis in the hands of the corporation is the same as it was in the hands of the shareholder.

Parent corporation

A corporation which owns a required percentage of another corporation (subsidiary). Every group of affiliated corporations which files a consolidated return must have a common parent corporation.

Partnership

A partnership does not pay taxes. It is a conduit for nontaxable income, dividend income, partially taxable interest, ordinary income, and the capital gains and losses shares to be taken into the income of the individual partners. For income tax purposes, the term *partnership* is more comprehensive than when taken in its ordinary meaning. It includes a syndicate, group, pool and joint venture, as well as an ordinary partnership, in which two or more persons join their money and/or their skills in carrying on as co-owners a business for profit. If the organization of a limited partnership is more in the nature of an association than a partnership, it is deemed to be an association taxable as a corporation.

Passive activity losses

Losses arising from a passive activity are not deductible, except against income from a passive activity. The unused portion of the loss, however, is not lost but is suspended (i.e., carried over) until offset by passive income in a future tax year or until the entire activity is disposed of in a fully taxable transaction.

Passive investment income

Gross receipts derived from royalties, rents, dividends, interest, annuities, and sales or exchanges of stock or securities of an S corporation.

Net passive investment income. Passive investment income of an S corporation reduced by the allowable deductions directly connected with the production of such income.

Excess net passive income. Portion of net passive investment income for the tax year of an S corporation multiplied by a fraction comprised of (1) the amount by which the total net passive investment income for the tax year exceeds 25 percent of the gross receipts for the tax year, divided by (2) the total gross passive investment income for the tax year.

Pay-as-you-go tax system

The U.S. tax system is often referred to as a pay-as-you-go tax system. Much of the federal government's tax collections come from withholdings and estimated taxes. The various types of taxpayers pay tax throughout the year, not just at year-end. The United States has been on a pay-as-you-go system since 1943.

Penalties

The Code contains two types of additions to the tax—interest and penalties. Interest paid may be deductible; a penalty is not. A penalty usually is distinguishable from interest in that it is imposed at a flat rate without regard to lapse of time.

Pension

A *pension,* if received from a former employer for past services, is taxable; if it is received under Social Security laws, it may be partially taxable. It is exempt to a limited extent when received for injuries or sickness. If it is in the nature of an annuity, it is subject to the rules for annuities.

Pension plan

Pension plan is both a generic term applied to various types of plans designed to provide retirement income and a specific term used to distinguish a particular type of qualified plan from a stock bonus or profit-sharing plan. Qualified plans are accorded a wide range of special tax treatment.

Percentage depletion—See Depletion

Personal exemption—See Exemption

Personal holding company

A personal holding company is a close corporation organized to hold corporate stocks and bonds and other investment assets, including personal service contracts, and employed to retain the income for distribution at such time as is most advantageous to the individual stockholder from a tax viewpoint.

The Code prescribes percentages of certain types of gross income and of stock ownership by five or fewer individuals that will turn an ordinary corporation into a personal holding company. If it falls within this classification, a corporation must pay, in addition to the regular income tax on a corporation, a tax at the rate of 15 percent on its *undistributed* personal holding company income.

Q

Qualified Subchapter S Trust (QSST)

A qualified Subchapter S Trust is a trust with single income beneficiary eligible to be an S corporation shareholder.

R

Real estate investment trust

A qualifying real estate investment trust is one which has at least 100 beneficial owners and which distributes at least 95 percent of its income. The income from the distribution is taxed *only once,* and *only* to the beneficiaries. The trust may not be a personal holding company; it must elect to be treated as a real estate investment trust; and it may not hold property primarily for sale to customers.

Realized v. recognized gain or loss

A gain or loss is realized when a transaction is completed. However, not all realized gains and losses are taxed (recognized). A recognized gain or loss occurs when a taxpayer is obligated to pay tax on a completed transaction.

Recapitalization

A recapitalization is an internal reorganization—that is, a rearrangement of the capital structure of a corporation by changing the kind of stock or the number of shares outstanding or by issuing stock instead of bonds, or vice versa. As distinguished from most other types of reorganization, a recapitalization involves only one corporation and is usually accomplished by the surrender by shareholders or bondholders of their securities for stocks or securities of a different type.

Redemption

Redemption is a buying back, a repurchase. A redemption of stock is its repurchase from the stockholder by the corporation which issued it (whether or not it had originally been issued to the stockholder from whom it is repurchased). A bona fide redemption of stock is treated as a sale or exchange of the stock, and, in the case of a taxpayer other than a dealer in securities, gain or loss on the redemption is a capital gain or loss.

Refund of tax—See Credits or refunds

Regulations

The Commissioner publishes interpretations of the law in the form of Regulations. They do not have the force and effect of law; however, in those cases in which the law on a particular subject calls for rules on that subject to be expounded through Regulations, the courts afford them great weight. Provisions of the Regulations on a particular subject are disapproved by the courts in some rare instances, and in a few cases the weight of authority has resulted in the Commissioner's amending them.

Related taxpayers

The Code does not allow a loss, except in the case of a distribution in liquidation of a corporation, from the sale or exchange of property between related persons. A similar rule bars a deduction for expenses and interest incurred in transactions between related persons when the payer is on the accrual-basis method of accounting and the payee is on the cash-basis method. The following parties are considered related persons for purposes of these rules: (1) members of the same immediate family, except for transfers between spouses or incident to divorce; (2) an individual and a corporation in which the individual owns more than 50 percent of the outstanding stock (directly or indirectly); (3) two members of a controlled corporate group; (4) a trust fiduciary and a corporation of which more than 50 percent of the outstanding stock is owned by the trust or the grantor of the trust; (5) a grantor and fiduciary of any trust; (6) a fiduciary of one trust and a fiduciary of another trust if the same person is the grantor of both trusts; (7) a fiduciary of a trust and any beneficiary of such trust; (8) a fiduciary of a trust and a beneficiary of another trust if the same person is the grantor of the trusts; (9) a person and an exempt charitable organization controlled by that person; (10) a corporation and a partnership if the same person owns more than 50 percent of the outstanding stock in the corporation and more than 50 percent of the interest in the partnership; (11) two S corporations if the same person owns more than 50 percent of the outstanding stock of each corporation; or (12) an S corporation and a C corporation if the same person owns more than 50 percent of the outstanding stock of each corporation.

Reorganization

A *reorganization* occurs when a business undergoes a new capital arrangement, with or without new administration. If only one corporation is involved, it is a *recapitalization.* In income tax law, the term applies only to corporations. The Code contains provisions for nonrecognition of gain or loss on exchanges made in pursuance of a reorganization and the shareholders of the corporations involved exchange their shares or receive distributions without surrender of their shares. The provisions of the Code must be strictly complied with in order for such exchanges or distributions to be nontaxable.

Repairs

Repairs are expenditures made to keep property in good condition, but not basically intended to appreciably prolong the life or increase the value of the property. If the property is business or income-producing property, the amount of ordinary and necessary repairs is deductible.

Replacements

Replacements are expenditures for making good or whole a portion of property which has deteriorated through use or been destroyed through accident. Although deduction for the gradual deterioration or the destruction is allowable, subject to the limitations in the Code, a replacement is a capital expenditure to be distinguished from repairs.

Residual estate

That portion of the estate which remains after the payment of debts, expenses of administration, legacies and devises. It consists of that part of the estate which has not been legally disposed of by the will prior to the carrying out of the residuary clause of said will.

Retirement income credit—See Tax credit for the elderly

S

S corporation

An S corporation, as distinguished from a C corporation (the treatment of whose distributions is governed by Subchapter C), is a small business corporation that meets various requirements and has validly elected not to be taxed at the corporate level. Items of income or loss are passed through to shareholders in much the same manner that such items are passed through to the partner of a partnership.

Section 306 stock

Section 306 is designed to prevent preferred stock *bail-outs* where preferred stock (Section 306 stock) is issued as a dividend and either sold or redeemed in an attempt to realize capital gains. Section 306 accomplishes this by taxing the gain on sale or receipts from redemption as ordinary income to the extent of the corporation's accumulated earnings and profits.

Section 1231 dispositions

If, during the taxable year, the recognized gains on sales or exchanges of property used in the trade or business, plus the recognized gains from the compulsory or involuntary conversion of property used in the trade or business or of capital assets held long-term into other property or money, exceed the recognized losses from such sales, exchanges, and conversions, then such gains and losses are treated as capital gains and losses. If such gains do not exceed such losses, then the gains and losses are treated as ordinary gains and losses. However, to the extent that any Section 1231 gain contains gain from the disposition of Section 1245 or Section 1250 property (see below), such gain will be recaptured as ordinary income to the extent of certain depreciation deductions taken.

Section 1244 stock—See Small business stock

Section 1245 property

Section 1245 property includes depreciable personal property and other depreciable property (other than buildings or their structural components) used in manufacturing, production, or extraction or used in furnishing transportation, communications, electrical energy, gas, water, or sewage disposal services. When Section 1245 property is disposed of, any gain is treated as ordinary income to the extent of depreciation deducted. Thus, although Section 1245 property may also be a Section 1231 asset, Section 1231 gain will be realized on the disposition only to the extent that the gain realized exceeds the post-1961 depreciation. Single-purpose agricultural and horticultural structures and storage facilities used in connection with the distribution of petroleum and its primary products that are placed in service after 1980 are included in the Section 1245 property category. Such property placed in service before 1981 is Section 1250 property. A gain on the sale or disposition of Section 1245 property is taxed as ordinary income to the extent of the depreciation deductions allowed.

Section 1250 property

Section 1250 property is property that is depreciable or recoverable but is not subject to the recapture rule under Code Sec. 1245. This includes all intangible real property (such as leases of land, buildings and their structural components, including elevators and escalators placed in service after 1986) and all other tangible real property except property which is used as an integral part of manufacturing, production or extraction or used in furnishing transportation, communications, electrical energy, gas, water or sewage disposal services, or research or storage facilities used in connection with these activities.

Self-employed individual's retirement plan

Self-employed individual's retirement plans—or, as they are more commonly called, H.R. 10 plans or Keogh plans—are qualified retirement plans that must meet certain special requirements because they benefit owner-employees. The annual limit for a participant in a defined contribution plan for 2017 is the lesser of $54,000 or 100 percent of compensation. With respect to a participant in a defined benefit plan, the maximum benefit is the lesser of $215,000 for 2017 (indexed each year) or average compensation for the participant's three years of highest compensation.

Self-employment income

The Social Security provisions cover self-employed persons so that they are eligible for benefits upon retirement at the same age and in the same manner as wage earners. The combined rate of tax on self-employment income is 15.3 percent for 2017. The rate consists of a 12.4 percent component for old-age, survivors, and disability insurance (OASDI) and a 2.9 percent component for hospital insurance (medicare). For 2017, the maximum self-employment income subject to the OASDI component of the tax rate (12.4 percent) is $127,200; there is no cap on earnings subject to the medicare hospital insurance tax. If net earnings are less than $400, no self-employment tax is payable. Also, self-employed individuals may deduct one-half of the employee's share of the taxes for income tax purposes or, instead of this business expense deduction, they may reduce self-employment income by an amount equal to the product of their net earnings multiplied by one-half of the employer's share for the year. For 2017, this is 7.65 percent of the net earnings from self-employment. The Patient Protection and Affordable Care Act of 2010 imposes several new provisions effective January 1, 2013. The provisions include: 0.9 percent additional medicare tax on wages and self-employment income that exceeds $200,000 for individuals, $250,000 for married couples filing jointly, and $125,000 for married couples filing separate returns.

Short sale

A short sale, as applied to securities, is an agreement to transfer stock that the seller does not own or whose stock certificates are not in the seller's control but must be borrowed to cover the transaction. The borrowed stock must be replaced within a specified time through purchase on the market and transferred to the lender of the borrowed stock. For income tax purposes, there is no gain or loss on the transaction until the short sale is covered by purchase and transfer. Special rules apply for determining whether gain or loss on a short sale is a long-term or short-term capital gain or loss.

Short-term capital gain—See Holding period

Simple trust

A simple trust is one for which the trust instrument requires that all income be distributed currently, with no authority to make charitable contributions. Also, the trust is a simple trust only for a year in which it distributes current income and makes no other distributions to beneficiaries. A simple trust is entitled to a $300 deduction in lieu of a personal exemption. For a year in which the trust does not meet these requirements, it is a *complex trust*.

Small business corporation

A *small business corporation* is defined in the Code for two separate purposes. For the two definitions, see *S corporation* and *Small business stock.*

Small business investment company

A *small business investment company* is a term which, for federal income tax purposes, is restricted to a company operating under the Small Business Investment Act of 1958, that is, a company authorized by that Act to provide equity capital to small business concerns through the purchase of convertible debentures. These companies and their investors are given special income tax advantages, such as a 100 percent dividends-received credit and ordinary loss deductions for the worthlessness of stock or securities held by the investment company or stock issued by the company.

Small business stock

To encourage the flow of new funds into small business, Congress created a stock classification with a special tax treatment. This is Section 1244 stock. Under Code Sec. 1244, an original individual investor can treat a loss on small business corporation stock as an ordinary loss—up to $50,000 on a single return or $100,000 on a joint return. Because the Code Sec. 1244 loss is considered in any net operating loss computation, the carryback and carryover rules apply. To qualify under Code Sec. 1244, the stock must be common stock in a domestic small business corporation.

To encourage investment in small businesses, the PATH Act of 2015 extends permanently 100 percent exclusion of the profit, up to $10 million, made on the sale or exchange of stock of qualified small businesses. The stock must be held for more than five years by a non-corporate investor.

Spin-off

A *spin-off* is a distribution by a corporation of stock or securities in another corporation controlled by it (through at least 80 percent stock ownership) without the surrender of any shares by the shareholders. It is a type of corporate separation. The distribution need not be in reorganization. However, the law contains definite rules requiring that the controlled corporation must have been actively engaged in a trade or business and must continue to be so engaged after the distribution. Furthermore, the trade or business must have been conducted (but not necessarily by the controlled corporation) for at least five years prior to the distribution. The distribution will not be taxable to the shareholders if the distributing corporation distributes at least 80 percent of the outstanding stock of the controlled corporation.

Split-off

A *split-off* is a type of corporate separation, not necessarily in reorganization, whereby a parent corporation distributes to its shareholders stock in a corporation which it controls, under the same conditions as in a *spin-off*, except that the shareholders surrender a part of their stock in the parent corporation for the stock in the controlled corporation. As under the conditions described under *spin-off*, no gain is recognized to the shareholders from the exchange of their shares.

Split-up

A *split-up* occurs where a corporation transfers its assets to two or more corporations in exchange for their stock or securities and then completely liquidates by distributing the stock in the new corporations to its stockholders or security holders in exchange for its own stock. The same nonrecognition treatment applies as in the case of a *spin-off* or a *split-off*.

Standard deduction

Taxpayers receive the benefit of a minimum amount of itemized deductions called the standard deduction. The standard deduction is a fixed amount that is used to simplify the computation of the tax liability.

It is also designed to eliminate lower-income individuals from the tax rolls. All taxpayers subtract from adjusted gross income the larger of their itemized deductions or the standard deduction. The standard deduction is based on the filing status of the taxpayer and is made up of the basic standard deduction plus any additional standard deduction. The standard deduction amounts are adjusted annually for inflation.

An additional standard deduction is allowed aged or blind taxpayers. For 2017, the additional standard deduction is $1,250 for an aged or blind individual who is married or is a surviving spouse; the additional standard deduction is $1,550 for a single individual or for a head of household who is aged or blind. Taxpayers receive an additional standard deduction for being both aged and blind. Thus, a married couple, both aged and blind, receives an additional standard deduction of $5,000 ($1,250 × 4).

Statute of limitations

A statute of limitations sets out the period within which actions may be brought upon claims or within which rights may be enforced. The limitations periods of greatest importance for tax purposes are the three-year period in which a tax deficiency may be assessed (subject to modifications and extensions) and the three-year period in which a taxpayer may claim a refund (also subject to modifications).

Stepped-up basis

A *stepped-up* basis is a higher basis (see *Basis*) than an asset had in the hands of a previous owner. Under present law, this is accomplished through a transfer on which the gain is taxable or through acquisitions (not subject to the carryover basis rules) from a decedent.

Stock bonus plan

A stock bonus plan is established and maintained to provide benefits similar to those of a profit-sharing plan, but the contributions are not necessarily dependent upon profits and the benefits are distributable in the stock of the employer. A stock bonus plan is often referred to as an employee stock ownership plan (ESOP) or an employee stock ownership trust.

Stock option—See Employee stock option

Straight-line depreciation

Straight-line depreciation is the method of writing off the cost or other basis of depreciable assets in equal annual amounts over the estimated useful life of the assets.

Straight-line MACRS election

A taxpayer may elect, under MACRS, to claim straight-line MACRS deductions instead of the regular MACRS allowance. The recovery periods under the straight-line election include the regular recovery period and longer recovery periods. The straight-line MACRS deductions are computed in much the same manner as the deductions under the general rules, except that salvage value is not taken into account.

Subchapter S corporation—See S corporation

Subsidiary—See Parent corporation

Substance v. form

Individuals should arrange their financial transactions in a manner that will minimize their tax liability. If a transaction is all it purports to be and not merely a transaction to avoid taxes, then it is valid. If the transaction is solely to avoid taxes and there is no business purpose to the transaction, then it is invalid. The fact that a taxpayer uses one form of transaction rather than another to minimize taxes does not invalidate the transaction. A good example of when substance v. form is a significant issue is in the area of leases. Payments under a lease are tax deductible. Payments under a purchase agreement are not tax deductible. Therefore, it is of utmost importance to determine the true "substance" of this type of transaction. Questions to be asked might include: Do any equity rights transfer to the lessee at the end of the lease period? May the lessee buy the property at a nominal purchase price? With a lease transaction it is immaterial that the parties refer to the transaction as a lease. The true substance of the transaction controls over the form.

Substituted basis

The basis for gain or loss on sale or for depreciation (see *Basis*) of property may, under certain conditions, be determined by reference to the basis of a prior owner of the property (as in the case of a gift) or by reference to the basis of other property (as in the case of a tax-free exchange). Both are defined in the Code as a substituted basis, although the former is sometimes referred to as a *transferred basis*.

Sum-of-the-years-digits method

The *sum-of-the-years-digits* method of deducting depreciation is a variation of the declining-balance method. Under this method, the successive numbers representing the life of the asset by years (one, two, three, and four, for example, if the asset has a life of four years) are added together (1 + 2 + 3 + 4 = 10), and the first year's depreciation fraction is determined by using as the numerator the number of years of remaining life of the asset and as the denominator the sum of the digits. (Thus, if the life is four years, 4/10 of the cost of the asset would be written off in the first year.) Salvage value reduces the basis under the sum-of-the-years-digits method. Like the declining-balance method, it has the effect of writing off the larger part of the cost in the earlier years when the most depreciation on a new asset is actually sustained.

Surviving spouse

Surviving spouses are entitled to the income-splitting benefits of filing a joint return on the death of one spouse. The joint return is made for the regular tax year of the survivor and the short period of the decedent. Use of joint return rates is also allowed to an unmarried widow or widower who maintains a home as a household for a dependent child. This benefit is limited to the first two tax years following the year in which the decedent spouse died.

T

Tax benefit rule

A recovery is includible in income only to the extent that the deduction reduced tax in any prior year by any amount. Therefore, where a deduction reduced taxable income but did not reduce tax, the recovery amount is excludable from income. This rule applies to both corporate and noncorporate taxpayers.

Tax Court

The United States Tax Court is a legislative court under Article I, Section 8, Clause 9 of the Constitution. Its principal function is to review deficiencies assessed by the Commissioner for income, estate, gift, or certain excise taxes. Hearings are held in principal cities throughout the country.

Tax credit for the elderly

The tax credit for the elderly and the permanently and totally disabled replaced the old retirement income credit. One set of rules for credit purposes applies to individuals who are age 65 or older. Another set of rules applies to federal, state, and local government retirees who are under age 65 and to permanently disabled individuals.

Tax credit stock ownership plan—See Employee Stock Ownership Plan (ESOP)

Tax shelter

Basically, tax shelters are investments that provide investors with the possibility of reducing their current income taxes through methods sanctioned by the tax law, thereby *sheltering* current income from tax. Although tax shelters offer an investor the opportunity to invest in many different kinds of assets and, thus, offer a wide range of potential benefits to their investors, the following basic aims are common to the vast majority of tax shelters: (1) maximizing the tax incentives available to the investors; (2) reducing current income tax liability and deferring taxation on any income or gain from the investment until some future tax year; and (3) permitting investors to use borrowed money to finance their original investments (leveraging). Some tax shelters satisfy all three aims, while others satisfy one or two; some rely heavily on their ability to satisfy only one of the aims.

In recent years, Congress has enacted specific Code provisions aimed at restricting the tax benefits of certain tax shelters that permit high-income taxpayers to reduce or avoid tax. Further, the IRS has been vigilant in its examination of returns of taxpayers that indicate participation in a possibly abusive tax shelter.

Taxable income

Taxable income for a corporation is gross income minus all deductions allowable, including special deductions such as the one for dividends received. Taxable income for individuals who itemize deductions is equal to adjusted gross income minus personal exemptions, minus the greater of the itemized deductions or the standard deduction amount. For nonitemizers, taxable income is adjusted gross income minus personal exemptions minus the standard deduction.

Taxable year

Taxable year means the calendar year or a fiscal year ending during such calendar year upon the basis of which the taxable income is computed. In the case of a return made for a fractional part of a year, *taxable year* is the period for which such return is made.

Tenancy by the entirety

Generally speaking, this is a joint tenancy between husband and wife. A tenancy by the entirety cannot be terminated except by the joint action of the husband and wife during their lives. This is in contrast to a joint tenancy, which either party may terminate merely by conveying the interest to another party.

Tenancy in common

A form of ownership where title is held by two or more persons with each owning a fractional interest in the undivided property. Upon the death of one tenant in common, the interest will not pass to the surviving tenant in common but will become part of the deceased tenant's probate estate and will be distributed according to such tenant's will.

Testamentary trust

A trust which is set up under the will of the decedent. Conversely, an inter vivos trust is one set up during the lifetime of the person setting up the trust.

Testator

One who makes or has made a will; one who dies leaving a will. (Feminine form: testatrix.)

Top-heavy plan

Top-heavy plan refers to a qualified plan that must meet additional requirements because key employees' aggregate accumulated benefits or aggregate accounts exceed 60 percent of all such accumulated benefits or accounts in the plan.

Totten trust

A trust created by the deposit of a person's own money in his or her own name as trustee for another person. This is considered a revocable trust at the will of the trustee until the depositor dies or otherwise completes the gift during his or her lifetime.

Trade or business

A trade or business consists of any activity that occupies the time, attention, and labor of individuals for the purpose of earning a livelihood or making a profit. It includes the rendering of services to others as an employee for compensation, the carrying on of a profession, and every business occupation carried on for subsistence or profit and into which the elements of bargain and sale, barter, exchange, or traffic enter.

Transaction entered into for profit

A broad meaning is accorded the phrase *transaction entered into for profit,* losses from which are deductible. It includes the acquisition of any income-producing property or investment property, as distinguished from property for one's personal use or enjoyment. The acquisition may be by gift or inheritance if the property is investment or income-producing property. In some cases, the term can include a transaction entered into simply to avoid or cut down a loss on another transaction.

Transferee liability

If a taxpayer transfers assets to another at a time when the taxpayer is liable for outstanding income, estate, or gift taxes (whether or not determined) and the remaining assets after the transfer are insufficient to pay such taxes, the person who received the assets is liable for the taxes to the extent of the value of the assets received. If there are two or more transferees, each one is so liable.

Travel expenses

Travel expenses are deductible in determining adjusted gross income in the case of an individual involved in a trade or business or in a transaction entered into for profit. Travel expenses include transportation costs and the amount spent for meals and lodging *while away from home* in the pursuit of a trade or business. However, the 2 percent of adjusted gross income floor applies to unreimbursed travel expenses of employees and the 50 percent limitation applies to meal and entertainment expenses without regard to whether the taxpayer is traveling.

Trust

A fiduciary relationship with respect to property whereby the property is held by one party (the trustee) for the benefit of another party (the beneficiary). A trust is usually set up and governed by a written document.

W

Wash sale

In the language of the stock exchange, a wash sale is the simultaneous or almost simultaneous purchase and sale of the same stock. For income tax purposes, a sale of stock or securities at a loss cannot result in deduction of the loss if substantially identical stocks or securities are purchased within a 61-day period beginning 30 days before the date of the sale and ending 30 days after the sale. The acquisition or reacquisition of such stock or securities has no effect on sales at a gain.

Wherewithal to pay

The concept that the taxpayer should be taxed on a transaction when he or she has the means to pay the tax. For example, a taxpayer owns property that is increasing in value. The IRS does not tax the increased value until the taxpayer sells the property. At the time of sale, the taxpayer has the wherewithal to pay.

Withholding allowance

Since the graduated withholding system could cause taxpayers who have large itemized deductions to be seriously overwithheld, these taxpayers are permitted to claim extra exemptions which are called *withholding allowances*.

Withholding of tax at source

An employer is required to withhold income taxes from the wages of employees. The tax to be withheld is computed under the percentage method or by use of wage-bracket tables. There is also withholding of tax at source in the case of nonresident aliens receiving fixed or determinable annual or periodic income from United States sources.

Finding Lists

References are to paragraph (¶) numbers

Internal Revenue Code Sections, Regulations, Revenue Procedures and Revenue Rulings are to paragraph (¶) numbers.

Internal Revenue Code Sections

Section	¶
1(h)(1)(E)	11,001
11	21,155
11(b)	14,405
21(a)(2)	9015
21(b)(1)	9015
21(b)(2)	9015
21(c)	9015
21(d)(1)	9015
21(d)(2)	9015
21(e)(1)	9015
21(e)(2)	9015
21(e)(4)	9015
21(e)(5)	9015
21(e)(6)	9015
22(a)-(c)	9025
22(c)	9025
22(c)(3)	9025
22(d)(1)	9025
22(e)(1)	9025
22(f)	9025
23	9034
25C	9042
25D	9042
27	14,401
27(a)	9035
31(a)	9105
31(b)	9115
32	9125
33	9135
34	9155; 21,163
38	14,165; 14,401; 21,221
38(c)	9045
39	9045
40	9045
41(a)	9045
41(c)	18,301
42(a)	9045
43	9045
44	9045
45	9045
45A	9045
45C(a)	9045
46(a)	9045
47(a)	9045
47(c)	9045
48(a)	9045
49	9045
49(a)(1)(D)(iv)	7125
50	9045; 15,021
50(a)(1)	14,165
50(c)(3)	9045
51(a)	9045
51(b)	9045
53	9455
55–59	14,415
55(b)	9401
55(d)	9435; 14,415
55(d)(1)(C)(ii)	23,371
56	14,415
56(a)	9401
56(b)	9415
56(b)(1)(E)	9415
56(b)(3)	4615
56(g)(2)	14,415
56(g)(4)(I)	14,415
57	9425
57(a)	14,415
58(a)	9415
59	9445; 14,415
59(c)	23,371
61	13,001; 13,215; 14,301; 22,101
61(a)	4015; 4101; 4655
61(a)(11)	5255
61(a)(12)	4485
62	6115; 6601
62(a)	6560
62(a)(1)	6601
62(a)(4)	6301; 8680; 8701
62(a)(7)	24,625
62(a)(13)	4331
62(c)	8603
66	4215
71–90	4301
71	4451
71(b)(1)(B)	4451
72	24,625
72(a)	5125
72(c)(3)	5125
72(e)(2)(A)	24,325
72(e)(2)(B)	5015; 24,325

References are to paragraph (¶) numbers

References are to paragraph (¶) numbers

References are to paragraph (¶) numbers

References are to paragraph (¶) numbers

References are to paragraph (¶) numbers

References are to paragraph (¶) numbers

References are to paragraph (¶) numbers

References are to paragraph (¶) numbers

References are to paragraph (¶) numbers

References are to paragraph (¶) numbers

References are to paragraph (¶) numbers

References are to paragraph (¶) numbers

2032A(e)(1)	22,195
2032A(e)(2)	22,195
2032A(e)(4)	22,195
2032A(e)(6)	22,195
2032A(e)(7)	22,195
2032A(e)(8)(A)-(E)	22,195
2033	22,101; 22,173; 22,187
2035	22,001; 22,117; 22,141
2035-2038	22,001; 22,165
2035(a)	22,117
2035(a)(2)	22,117; 22,173
2035(b)	22,117
2035(b)(2)	22,117
2035(c)	22,141
2035(c)(3)	22,117
2036	22,117; 22,125; 22,133; 22,141
2037	22,117; 22,133; 22,141
2038	22,117; 22,141; 22,575
2039(a)	22,149
2039(b)	22,149
2040	10,175
2040(a)	22,157
2041(b)(1)	22,165
2041(b)(2)	22,165
2042	22,173
2043	22,175
2044	22,217
2046	22,255
2051	22,001
2053	15,131; 22,001
2053(a)(4)	22,195
2053(c)(1)	22,201
2054	15,131; 22,201
2055	22,001; 22,035; 22,545
2055(a)	22,225
2055(b)	22,225
2055(e)(2)(A)	22,001; 22,225
2055(f)	22,105
2056	22,001; 22,217
2056(b)(1)	22,217
2056(b)(3)	22,217
2056(b)(5)	22,217
2056(b)(6)	22,217
2056(b)(7)	22,217
2056(b)(7)(C)	22,217
2056(c)	22,217
2058	22,001; 22,230
2103(a)	22,101
2106	15,131
2501(a)(1)	22,301; 22,405
2501(a)(5)	22,375
2502(c)	22,301
2503(b)	22,315
2503(e)	22,341; 22,525
2505	22,009
2511(a)	22,405
2513(a)(1)	22,341
2513(a)(2)	22,341
2514	22,165; 22,395
2514(c)(1)	22,395
2514(c)(3)	22,395
2516	22,345
2518	22,255
2519	22,217; 22,375
2522	22,545
2522(b)	22,355
2522(d)	22,355
2523(a)	22,345
2523(c)	22,345
2523(e)	22,345
2523(f)	22,217
2523(i)	22,345
2603	22,565
2604	22,575
2611(b)(1)	22,525
2611(b)(2)	22,525
2612(a)(1)	22,525
2612(b)	22,525
2612(c)(1)	22,525
2612(c)(2)	22,525
2613(a)	22,515
2622(b)	22,575
2631	22,535
2631(c)	22,501
2632	22,535
2641	22,545
2642	22,545
2651(c)(1)	22,515
2651(d)	22,515
2652(c)(1)	22,525
2662	22,565
3121(a)	21,221
3121(a)(6)	3405
3121(v)	24,015; 24,701
3121(v)(1)	24,401; 24,501
3306(r)	24,701
3306(r)(1)	24,401; 24,501
3402	2365
4973	24,801
4974	24,235
4974(a)	24,235; 24,625
4975(c)	24,285
4975(c)(1)	24,601
4975(e)(2)	24,601

References are to paragraph (¶) numbers

References are to paragraph (¶) numbers

6695(f)	2365
6698	19,005
6699	21,185
6701	2365
6724(d)(3)	4451
6903	23,035
7201	1131; 2365
7202	2365
7203	2365; 16,161
7204	2365
7205	2365
7206	2365
7207	2365
7463(a)-(b)	2311
7519	19,280
7520	22,109; 22,149; 22,185; 22,225
7602	2301
7701	14,015
7701(a)(2)	19,001
7701(a)(4)	21,009
7701(a)(9)	25,335
7701(a)(30)	25,315; 25,395
7701(a)(36)	2365
7701(a)(44)	19,025
7801(a)	2211
7802	2211
7805	2225
7805(a)	2035
7872	15,025
7872(c)	4385
7874	25,635

Private Letter Rulings

9015014	6801

Regulations Sections

1.44A-1(c)(1)	9015
1.56(g)-1	14,415
1.61-2(d)(2)(i)	10,135
1.61-2(d)(3)	5185
1.61-3(a)	4355
1.61-6(a)	10,115
1.61-12(a)	4485
1.62-1(g)	6535
1.62-1T(f)	8603
1.71-1(e)	4451
1.72-5(a)(2)(i)	5125
1.72-5(c)	5125
1.72-5(d)	5125
1.72-9	5125
1.83-1(a)	24,735
1.83-1(b)(1)	4601
1.83-1(b)(2)	4601
1.83-3(c)	4601
1.83-7	4655
1.83-7(a)	4655; 24,735
1.106-1	5155
1.118-1	14,201
1.125-1	5195
1.127-2(c)	5201
1.132-2	5101
1.162-2(c)	6545
1.162-3	13,215
1.162-4	6795
1.162-5(a)	8665
1.162-5(b)(3)	8665
1.162-6	8665
1.162-7(a)	14,391
1.162-17(b)	8603
1.162-17(b)(4)	8603
1.162-20(a)(2)	6745
1.162-20(b)	6745
1.162-21(b)	6735
1.162-21(c)	6735
1.165-1(d)(2)(i)	2147; 7301
1.165-1(d)(2)(ii)	2147; 7301
1.165-7(a)(3)(i)	7301
1.165-7(b)(1)	2147
1.165-8(d)	7301
1.165-9(b)(2)	10,215
1.166-1(c)	12,501
1.166-2(b)	6245
1.166-5(a)(2)	12,501
1.166-5(b)	6245
1.167(a)-3	6865
1.167(a)-5	10,115
1.167(g)-1	6855; 10,145; 10,215
1.167(h)-1(b)	23,331
1.167(h)-1(c)	23,331
1.168-1(d)(3)	6835
1.171-1(b)	10,025
1.174-2(a)	6875
1.183-1(b)(1)	7345
1.183-2(b)	7345

References are to paragraph (¶) numbers

References are to paragraph (¶) numbers

References are to paragraph (¶) numbers

References are to paragraph (¶) numbers

References are to paragraph (¶) numbers

Revenue Procedures

Revenue Rulings

References are to paragraph (¶) numbers

Table of Cases

References are to paragraph (¶) numbers

References are to paragraph (¶) numbers

References are to paragraph (¶) numbers

References are to paragraph (¶) numbers

Topical Index

References are to paragraph (¶) numbers

References are to paragraph (¶) numbers

References are to paragraph (¶) numbers

References are to paragraph (¶) numbers

References are to paragraph (¶) numbers

References are to paragraph (¶) numbers

References are to paragraph (¶) numbers

References are to paragraph (¶) numbers

References are to paragraph (¶) numbers

References are to paragraph (¶) numbers

References are to paragraph (¶) numbers

References are to paragraph (¶) numbers

References are to paragraph (¶) numbers

References are to paragraph (¶) numbers

References are to paragraph (¶) numbers

References are to paragraph (¶) numbers

References are to paragraph (¶) numbers

References are to paragraph (¶) numbers

References are to paragraph (¶) numbers

References are to paragraph (¶) numbers

References are to paragraph (¶) numbers

References are to paragraph (¶) numbers

References are to paragraph (¶) numbers

References are to paragraph (¶) numbers

References are to paragraph (¶) numbers

References are to paragraph (¶) numbers

References are to paragraph (¶) numbers